Contemporary Authors

Contemporary Authors

A BIO-BIBLIOGRAPHICAL GUIDE TO
CURRENT AUTHORS AND THEIR WORKS

CYNTHIA R. FADOOL

Editor

volumes 61-64

GALE RESEARCH COMPANY • BOOK TOWER • DETROIT, MICHIGAN 48226

CONTEMPORARY AUTHORS

Published by
Gale Research Company, Book Tower, Detroit, Michigan 48226
Each Year's Volumes Are Cumulated and Revised About Five Years Later

Frederick G. Ruffner, *Publisher*   James M. Ethridge, *Editorial Director*

Cynthia R. Fadool, *Editor*
Jane Bowden, Frances Carol Locher, Frank Michael Soley, *Assistant Editors*
Susan Stefani, *Research Assistant*

Anne Commire, *Consultant*
Eunice Bergin, *Copy Editor*
Laura Bryant, *Operations Supervisor*
Michaeline Nowinski, *Production Manager*

WRITERS

Linda Cairo, Laurelyn Niebuhr, Larry Schoenholtz,
Arlene True, Benjamin True

EDITORIAL ASSISTANTS

Ellen Koral, Norma Sawaya, Shirley Seip

Copyright © 1976
GALE RESEARCH COMPANY

ISBN 0-8103-0028-1

CONTEMPORARY AUTHORS

Indicates that a listing has been compiled from secondary sources believed to be reliable, but has not been personally verified for this edition by the author sketched.

ABEL, Elie 1920-

PERSONAL: Born October 17, 1920, in Montreal, Quebec, Canada; became U.S. citizen in 1952; son of Jacob and Rose (Savetsky) Abel; married Corinne Adelaide Prevost, January 28, 1946; children: Mark, Suzanne. *Education:* McGill University, B.A., 1941; Columbia University, M.S., 1942. *Office:* Office of the Dean, Graduate School of Journalism, Columbia University, New York, N.Y. 10027.

CAREER: Windsor Star, Windsor, Ontario, reporter, 1941; *Montreal Gazette,* Montreal, Quebec, assistant city editor, 1945-46; North American Newspaper Alliance, foreign correspondent in Berlin, Germany, 1946-47; Overseas News Agency, United Nations correspondent, 1947-49; *New York Times,* reporter in Detroit, Washington, Europe, and India, 1949-59; *Detroit News,* Washington, D.C. bureau chief, 1959-61; National Broadcasting Co., New York City, 1961-69, chief of London Bureau, 1956-67, diplomatic correspondent in Washington, 1967-69; Columbia University, New York City, dean of graduate school of journalism, 1969—, Godfrey Lowell Cabot Professor of Journalism, 1969—. Member of board of governors, American Stock Exchange, 1972—; chairman of board of trustees, Greater Washington Educational Television Association. *Military Service:* Royal Canadian Air Force, 1942-45; served as a radar man aboard flying boats based in Scotland, later as a combat correspondent; became acting sergeant.

MEMBER: Sigma Delta Chi, Century Club (New York), Garrick Club (London). *Awards, honors:* George Foster Peabody Award, 1968, for outstanding radio news; Overseas Press Club Award, 1969, for best interpretation of foreign news.

WRITINGS: The Missile Crisis, Lippincott, 1966 (published in England as *The Missiles of October: The Story of the Cuban Missile Crisis, 1962,* MacGibbon & Kee, 1966); (with Marvin Kalb) *Roots of Involvement: The U.S. in Asia, 1784-1971,* Norton, 1971.

SIDELIGHTS: After World War II, Elie Abel covered the Nuremberg war crimes trials for his agency, and also witnessed the first attempts at four-power government in Germany. After he had toured the Soviet Union, he was arrested in Poland by security police. *Avocational interests:* Music and concert-going.

BIOGRAPHICAL/CRITICAL SOURCES: New York Times, December 20, 1969.*

ABEL, Lionel 1910-

PERSONAL: Born November 28, 1910, in New York City; son of Alter and Anna (Schwartz) Abelson; married Sherry Goldman, 1939 (divorced); married Gloria Becker, 1970; children: Merry (deceased). *Education:* Attended St. John's University, 1926-28, and University of North Carolina, 1928-29. *Home:* 429 Richmond Ave., Buffalo, N.Y. 14222. *Office:* English Department, State University of New York, Buffalo, N.Y. 14214.

CAREER: Playwright and drama critic. State University of New York, Buffalo, professor of English, 1967—. Visiting professor of drama, Columbia University, 1961, Rutgers University, 1964; State University of New York at Buffalo, 1965; visiting professor of aesthetics, Pratt Institute, 1962. *Awards, honors:* Obie Award and *Show Business* Award, both 1956, both for "Absalom"; Guggenheim fellowship, 1958-59; Longview Award from Longview Foundation, 1960; National Institute of Arts and Letters award, 1964; Rockefeller Foundation grant, 1966.

WRITINGS—Criticism: *Metatheatre: A New View of Dramatic Form* (collected essays and addresses), Hill & Wang, 1963; (compiler) *Moderns on Tragedy: An Anthology of Modern and Relevant Opinions on the Substance and Meaning of Tragedy,* Fawcett, 1967. Contributor of articles to journals.

Plays: "The Death of Odysseus," first produced in New York at Amato Theatre, 1953; "Absalom," first produced in New York at Artist's Theatre, 1956; "The Pretender," first produced in New York at Cherry Lane Theatre, 1960; "The Wives," first produced in New York, 1965. Plays anthologized in *Playbook: Five Plays for a New Theatre,* edited by James Laughlin, New Directions, 1956; *Artist's Theatre: Four Plays,* edited by Herbert Machiz, Grove, 1960.

Translator: Jean Nicholas Arthur Rimbaud, *Some Poems of Rimbaud,* Exiles Press, 1939; John Rewald, *George Seurat,* Wittenborn, 1943, 2nd revised edition, 1949; Guillaume Apollinaire, *Cubist Painters: Aesthetic Meditations, 1913,* Wittenborn, 1944, 2nd revised edition, 1949; Camille Pissarro, *Letters to His Son Lucien,* Kegan Paul, 1944; Jean Paul Sartre, *Three Plays,* Knopf, 1949; Michel Seuphor, *Piet Mondrian: Life and Work,* Abrams, 1956. Contributor of translations to periodicals.

ABELS, Jules 1913-

PERSONAL: Born June 19, 1913, in Taunton, Mass; son of Bernard and Anna (Sachs) Abels. Education: City College (now City College of the City University of New York), B.A., 1934; Columbia University, LL.B., 1937; Harvard University, M.B.A., 1941. Home: 1650 Harvard Street N.W., Washington, D.C., 20009.

Career: Research Institute of America, New York, N.Y., economic analyst, 1941-51, executive editor, 1948-51; Newsweek (magazine), New York, N.Y., business trends editor, 1951-53; U.S. Government, Small Business Administration, Washington, D.C., chief economist, 1953-60. Member: Phi Beta Kappa.

WRITINGS: The Welfare State: A Mortgage on America's Future, foreword by Raymond Moley, Duell, Sloan & Pearce, 1951; The Truman Scandals, Regnery, 1956; Out of the Jaws of Victory, Holt, 1959; The Rockefeller Billions: The Story of the World's Most Stupendous Fortune, Macmillan, 1965 (published in England as The Rockefeller Millions: The Story of the World's Most Stupendous Fortune, Muller, 1967); The Parnell Tragedy, Macmillan, 1966; The Degeneration of Our Presidential Election: A History and Analysis of an American Institution in Trouble, Macmillan, 1968; In the Time of Silent Cal, Putnam, 1969; Man on Fire: John Brown and the Cause of Liberty, Macmillan, 1971.

WORK IN PROGRESS: A biography of King Charles I of England.

AVOCATIONAL INTERESTS: Chess, music.

*   *   *

ABLEMAN, Paul 1927-

PERSONAL: Born June 13, 1927, in Leeds, Yorkshire, England; married; children: one son. Education: Attended King's College, London. Home: Flat No. 37, Duncan House, Fellows Rd., London N.W.3, England. Agent: Jonathan Clowes, 20 New Cavendish St., London W.1, England.

CAREER: Author and playwright.

WRITINGS—Novels: I Hear Voices, Olympia Press, 1958; As Near As I Can Get, Spearman, 1962; Vac, Gollancz, 1968; The Twilight of the Vilp, Gollancz, 1969; (with others) London Consequences, Greater London Arts Association for the Festivals of London, 1972.

Published plays: Green Julia (produced in Edinburgh, 1965, in New York, 1972), Grove, 1966, new edition, 1973; Tests (playlets), Methuen, 1966; Blue Comedy (includes "Madly in Love" and "Hank's Night"; produced in London, 1968), Methuen, 1968.

Unpublished plays: (With Gertrude Macauley) "Letters to a Lady," produced in London, 1951; "Help!" (revue), produced in London, 1963; "One Hand Clapping" (revue), produced in Edinburgh, 1964; "Dialogues," produced in London, 1965; "Emily and Heathcliff," produced in London, 1967; "The Black General" (adapted from Othello), produced in London, 1969; "Little Hopping Robin," produced in New York, 1973.

Television plays: "Barlowe of the Car Park," 1961; "That Woman is Wrecking Our Marriage," 1969; "Visit from a Stranger," 1970.

Other: Bits (experimental prose written in verse form), Latimer Press, 1969; The Mouth and Oral Sex, Running Man Press, 1969, published as The Sensuous Mouth, Ace Books, 1972. Work represented in anthologies, including Modern Short Comedies from Broadway and London, edited by Stanley Richards, Random House, 1969. Contributor to Transatlantic Review and Men Only.

SIDELIGHTS: Equating theatre with encounter groups, a Time reviewer called Green Julia "a Rorschach-test play and an awfully good one . . . [The kind of play] that leaves the playgoer with the task of figuring out what the play means. In the process each member of the audience reveals himself to himself. . . . It is a play hilariously funny yet shadowed by increasing hysteria." "Ableman's great gift for comic dialogue" is what makes his plays "so delightful, though simple in outline," is Jeremy Kingston's comment. "The texture of the language is rich and marvellously funny," he says. John Hearsum finds the humourous novel Twilight of the Vilp "as spontaneous and colorful as children's painting." F. J. Brown calls the same book "a genuinely satirical novel. . . . a brilliantly imaginative work in which a marvellous gift of language finds expression." Green Julia and "Madly in Love" have both been produced on television.*

*   *   *

ABRAHAMS, William Miller 1919-

PERSONAL: Born January 23, 1919, in Boston, Mass.; son of Louis and Wilhelmina (Miller) Abrahams. Education: Harvard University, B.A., 1941. Home: 375 Pinehill Rd., Hillsborough, Calif. 94010. Office: Atlantic Monthly Press, 8 Arlington St., Boston, Mass. 02116.

CAREER: Atlantic Monthly Press, Boston, Mass., editor, 1955-63, senior editor, 1963—, west coast contributing editor, 1968—. Military service: U.S. Army, 1942-45. Awards, honors: Fellow, Stanford University, 1949-50.

WRITINGS: Interval in Carolina (novel), Simon & Schuster, 1945; By the Beautiful Sea (novel), Dial, 1947; Imperial Waltz (fiction), Dial, 1954; Children of Capricorn, Random House, 1963; (with Peter Stansky) Journey to the Frontier: Two Roads to the Spanish Civil War, Little, Brown, 1966 (published in England as Journey to the Frontier: Julian Bell and John Cornford: Their Lives and the 1930s, Constable, 1966); (editor and author of introduction) Fifty Years of the American Short Story: From the O. Henry Awards, 1919-1970, two volumes, Doubleday, 1970; (with Stansky) The Unknown Orwell, Knopf, 1972. Editor, Prize Stories: The O. Henry Awards, Doubleday, 1967—.

*   *   *

ABRAMS, George J(oseph) 1918-
(George Hipp)

PERSONAL: Born February 14, 1918, in Hoboken, N.J.; son of Leo (a tax consultant) and May (Hipp) Abrams; married Mary Della Sablom, November 15, 1941; children: Adele Lois. Education: Attended Rutgers University, 1936, and Balliol College, Oxford, 1945; New York University, B.S. (magna cum laude), 1947, M.B.A., 1949. Politics: Independent. Religion: Roman Catholic. Home: 22 Dalewood Rd., West Caldwell, N.J. 07006. Agent: Bertha Klausner, 71 Park Ave., New York, N.Y. 10019.

CAREER: Evening Transcript, Orange, N.J., staff writer, 1934-36; National Biscuit Co., New York City, assistant to advertising director, 1936-41; Whitehall Pharmacal Co., New York City, product advertising manager, 1941-46; Eversharp, Inc., New York City, director of marketing research, 1946-47; Block Drug Co., Jersey City, N.J., vice-president of sales and advertising, 1947-55; Revlon, Inc., New York City, vice-president in charge of advertising, 1955-59; president and chief executive officer of cosmetics and toiletries division, Warner-Lambert Pharmaceutical Co., 1959-60; vice-president of corporate development, J. B. Williams Corp., 1960-62; Del Laboratories, Inc., New York City, chairman and president, 1962-65; senior vice-president and marketing executive, William Esty Co., 1965-67; executive vice-president of Reach, McClinton & Co., 1967-69; Cole Fischer Rogow, New York City, president, 1969-71; George J. Abrams & Associates, New York City, president, 1971—. Lecturer in advertising management, New York University Graduate School of Business Administration, 1951-54. Chairman of board, Profit Centers, Inc., 1972—; member of board of governors, United Service Organizations (USO). Trustee, East Orange (N.J.) General Hospital. *Military service:* U.S. Navy, 1941-45; served in European, Atlantic, and Pacific theaters.

MEMBER: Association of National Advertisers, Advertising Club (N.J.; governor, 1955), Beta Gamma Sigma, Alpha Delta Sigma, Alpha Phi Sigma, Pinnacle Club (New York City), Curzon House (London). *Awards, honors:* Award from Association of Advertising Men and Women (N.Y.), 1954; achievement award from Advertising Club of Washington, 1958; Alpha Delta Sigma award, 1958; Free Enterprise Association award, 1964; Brooklyn Philharmonia award, 1970; Association of National Advertisers award, 1970.

WRITINGS: How I Made a Million Dollars with Ideas, Playboy Books, 1973; (under pseudonym George Hipp) *The Guilt of Michael Pagett* (novel), Manor Books, 1974. Contributor to *Writers Digest* and to journals in his field.

WORK IN PROGRESS: Fiction and nonfiction novels; writing television situation series, motion pictures, and television game shows.

*   *   *

ABRAMSON, Paul R(obert)   1937-

PERSONAL: Born November 28, 1937, in St. Louis, Mo.; son of Harry B. J. (a printer and businessman) and Hattie (Lewin) Abramson; married Janet Schwartz, September 11, 1966; children: Lee Jacob, Heather Lyn. *Education:* Washington University, St. Louis, Mo., B.A., 1959; University of California, Berkeley, M.A., 1961, Ph.D., 1967. *Home:* 1331 Lake Lansing Rd., East Lansing, Mich. 48823. *Office:* Department of Political Science, Michigan State University, East Lansing, Mich. 48824.

CAREER: Michigan State University, East Lansing, assistant professor, 1967-71, associate professor of political science, and research associate of Computer Institute for Social Science Research, 1971—. *Military service:* U.S. Army, 1960-62. U.S. Army Reserve, 1962-64; became captain. *Member:* American Political Science Association, American Sociological Association, Phi Beta Kappa. *Awards, honors:* Woodrow Wilson fellow, 1961; Ford Foundation faculty research fellow, 1972-73.

WRITINGS: Generational Change in American Politics, Heath, 1975. Contributor to political science journals.

WORK IN PROGRESS: A book on the political socialization of black Americans; research on political change in America, including interpreting the results of the 1968, 1972, and 1976 elections.

ACE, Goodman   1899-

PERSONAL: Born January 15, 1899, in Kansas City, Mo.; married Jane Sherwood, 1928 (died, 1974); *Education:* Attended Kansas City Junior College. *Home:* Ritz Tower Hotel, 47th St. and Park Ave., New York, N.Y. 10022. *Office: Saturday Review,* 488 Madison Ave., New York, N.Y. 10022.

CAREER: Worked twelve years for *Kansas City Post* (later *Journal-Post*), Kansas City, Mo., as cub reporter, movie and play reviewer, and columnist (columns continued until 1933); began radio career on local station in 1928, while still with the newspaper, with fifteen minute broadcasts which evolved into the "Easy Aces" radio show, with his wife, Jane Goodman; moved their program to Chicago for CBS in 1931, and to NBC in March, 1932; resigned, 1945; chief writer for Danny Kaye radio programs, 1945-46; supervisor of comedy and variety programs for CBS, 1946-47; did "Mr. Ace and Jane" radio show for CBS, 1948-49; appeared as "permanent guest" on "Jane Ace, Disc Jockey" radio show, 1951-52; *Saturday Review,* New York, N.Y. columnist, 1952-55, feature writer ("Top of My Head"), and contributing editor, 1955—. Writer for Tallulah Bankhead program, "Big Show," 1950-52, for Milton Berle show, 1952-55, and for Perry Como show, 1955-59. Writer and producer of variety shows and of five CBS spectaculars; creator of CBS "Open House," 1960. Appeared in short subjects for RKO Films in 1930s. *Member:* Radio Writers Guild (member of council, 1944—).

WRITINGS: Ladies and Gentlemen–Easy Aces, Doubleday, 1970. Also author of "The Trouble with Tracy," a television series, produced in Canada in 1970.*

*   *   *

ACKLEY, Hugh Gardner   1915-

PERSONAL: Born June 30, 1915, in Indianapolis, Ind.; son of Hugh M. (a mathematics professor) and Margaret (a Latin teacher; maiden name, MacKenzie) Ackley; married Bonnie A. Lawry, September 18, 1937; children: David A., Donald G. *Education:* Western State Teachers College (now Western Michigan University), A.B., 1936; University of Michigan, A.M., 1937, Ph.D., 1940. *Home:* 907 Berkshire Rd., Ann Arbor, Mich. 48104. *Office:* Department of Economics, University of Michigan, Ann Arbor, Mich. 48104.

CAREER: Instructor in economics, Ohio State University, Columbus, 1939-40, and University of Michigan, Ann Arbor, 1940-41; Office of Price Administration, Washington, D.C., economist, 1941-43, executive of textile branch, 1944-45, assistant director of Consumer Goods Division, 1945-46; economist in Office of Strategic Services, 1943-44; University of Michigan, assistant professor, 1946-47, associate professor, 1947-51 (on leave, 1951-52), professor of economics, 1952-61 (on leave, 1961-69), Henry Carter Adams University Professor of Political Economy, 1969—. Visiting professor, University of California, Los Angeles, summer, 1950. Economic advisor and assistant director, U.S. Office of Price Stabilization, 1951-52; President's Council of Economic Advisors, member, 1962-68, chairman, 1964-68; U.S. Ambassador to Italy, 1968-69. Director of Social Science Research Council, 1959-62, National Bureau of Economic Research, 1971—, Joint Council on Economic Education, 1971—, and Banco di Roma (Chicago), 1972—. Consultant, National Resources Planning Board, 1940, Economic Stabilization, 1950, Department of the Army, 1961, Baker-Weeks and Co., 1971-75. Member of Democratic Party Council, 1969-72.

MEMBER: American Economic Association (vice-president, 1963), American Academy of Arts and Sciences (fellow), Michigan Academy of Science, Arts, and Letters, American Philosophical Society, Kappa Delta Phi, Tau Kappa Alpha, Sigma Tau Gamma, Phi Kappa Phi. *Awards, honors:* Fulbright Scholar in Italy, 1956-57; Ford Foundation faculty research fellow in Italy, 1961-62; decorated Cavaliere del Gran Croce Ordine del Merito, Italy, 1969; LL.D., Western Michigan University, 1964, and Kalamazoo College, 1967; distinguished alumnus award from Western Michigan University, 1970.

WRITINGS: Macroeconomic Theory, Macmillan, 1961; *Un modello econometrico dello sviluppo italiano nel dopoguerra* (title means "An Econometric Model of Italian Postwar Development"), Giuffre (Rome), 1963; *Stemming World Inflation,* Atlantic Institute, 1971; (with others) *Asia's New Giant: How the Japanese Economy Works,* Brookings Institution, 1976. Columnist, *Dun's Review,* 1971—. Contributor to professional journals. Member of editorial board of *American Economic Review,* 1953-56.

* * *

ADAMS, Francis A(lexandre) 1874-1975

1874—September 17, 1975; American publisher, lecturer, patriotic organization administrator, and writer of political works, biographies, and novels. Obituaries: *New York Times,* September 20, 1975.

* * *

ADAMS, Paul L(ieber) 1924-

PERSONAL: Born January 22, 1924, in Broken Bow, Okla.; son of Moses Robert (a lumber dealer) and Beulah (Lieber) Adams; married Marjorie Pinckney Quackenbos, September, 1946 (divorced, 1952); married Evelia Valdes-Rodriguez, January 31, 1953; children: (first marriage) Christine (Mrs. Daniel Tucker); (second marriage) Gabrielle, Gerald. *Education:* Centre College of Kentucky, A.B. (high honors), 1943; graduate study at Fisk University, 1943, and New York University, 1945-55; Columbia University, M.A., 1948, M.D., 1955; graduate study at Duke University, 1956-60. *Politics:* Libertarian socialist. *Religion:* Society of Friends. *Home:* 1207 Summit Ave., Louisville, Ky. 40204. *Office:* Department of Psychiatry and Behavioral Sciences, Box 1055, University of Louisville, Louisville, Ky. 40201.

CAREER: Bennett College, Greensboro, N.C., instructor in social sciences, 1947-51; Good Samaritan Hospital, Lexington, Ky., internship, 1955-56; Duke University, Durham, N.C., instructor in psychiatry, 1958-60; University of Florida, Gainesville, assistant professor, 1960-65, associate professor, 1965-67, professor of psychiatry and pediatrics, 1967-72, head of Division of Child Psychiatry, 1960-72, director of Children's Mental Health Unit, 1967-72; University of Miami, Miami, Fla., professor of psychiatry, 1972-74, director of psychiatric education, 1972-74; University of Louisville, Louisville, Ky., professor of psychiatry and director of graduate education, 1974—. Diplomate of National Board of Medical Examiners, 1956, American Board of Psychiatry and Neurology, 1963 (general psychiatry), 1964 (child psychiatry), and Pan American Medical Association, 1964. Visiting professor at North Carolina College Graduate School, 1957-60, University of North Carolina College of Dentistry, 1965, 1966, and University of Oslo, 1971; visiting fellow at Hampstead Child Therapy Clinic, London, England, 1966. Director of Cumberland County (N.C.) Guidance Center, 1956-58. Member of Florida Attorney General's Commission on Law Enforcement and the Administration of Justice, 1967-70. Consultant to Veterans Administration, 1961—, South Carolina Department of Mental Health, 1969-71, National Training Laboratories, 1970—, Florida Division of Mental Health, 1973-74, River Region Mental Health Services, juvenile court, public school boards, and rehabilitation centers.

MEMBER: International Association of Social Psychiatry (treasurer of North American section, 1970-74), World Congress of Psychiatry, American College of Psychiatrists (fellow), American Orthopsychiatric Association (fellow; director, 1971-74), American Psychiatric Association (fellow), American Association for Social Psychiatry (vice-president, 1974-76), American Academy of Child Psychiatry (fellow; secretary, 1971-74), Society of Professors of Child Psychiatry, American Association of Psychiatric Clinics for Children (national director, 1969-71), American Federation of Teachers, American Civil Liberties Union, American Association of University Professors (member of executive committee, 1969-70), Academy of Psychosomatic Medicine (fellow), American Association of Psychiatric Services for Children (council member, 1969-72), Northeast Florida Psychiatric Society (president, 1968), Kentucky Psychiatric Society.

WRITINGS: (Editor and contributor) *Psychiatry and Pedodontics,* Florida State Dental Society, 1963; (contributor) John J. Schwab, editor, *Handbook of Psychiatric Consultation,* Appleton, 1968; (editor with Joseph B. Cramer and Henry H. Work, and contributor) *Academic Child Psychiatry,* Society of Professors of Child Psychiatry, 1970; (editor with others, and contributor) *Children's Rights,* Praeger, 1971; (contributor) Jules Masserman and John J. Schwab, editors, *Human Concordance and Discordance,* C. C Thomas, 1972; (editor and contributor), *Humane Social Psychiatry,* Tree of Life Press, 1972; (contributor) I. R. Stuart and L. E. Abt, editors, *Interracial Marriage,* Grossman, 1973; (contributor) Masserman and Schwab, editors, *The Psychiatric Examination,* Grune & Stratton, 1973; *Obsessive Children: A Sociopsychiatric Study,* Brunner, 1973; *Primer of Child Psychotherapy,* Little, Brown, 1974. Contributor to proceedings; contributor of more than fifty articles and book reviews to journals in his field. Member of editorial board, *Journal of Child Psychiatry and Human Development,* 1969—, and *Children's Rights,* 1971-74.

WORK IN PROGRESS: Otto Rank and Child Psychiatry; Fatherless Children; contributing to *Basic Handbook of Child Psychiatry.*

SIDELIGHTS: Adams writes that he grew up in a rural area of central Kentucky, "in depression poverty. Wary of war prosperity and post-war affluence attending war economy. Beginning with pacifism, soon attracted to the socialist and civil liberties causes. First white student at Fisk University since Reconstruction, active in civil rights since 1940, with first Freedom Ride in Kentucky in 1945."

* * *

ADAMS, Robert McCormick 1926-

PERSONAL: Born July 23, 1926, in Chicago, Ill.; son of Robert McCormick and Janet (Lawrence) Adams; married Ruth Salzman Skinner, July 24, 1953; children: Megan. *Education:* University of Chicago, Ph.B., 1947, M.A., 1952, Ph.D., 1956. *Home:* 5201 South Kimbark Ave., Chicago, Ill. 60615. *Office:* Oriental Institute, University of Chicago, 1155 East 58th St., Chicago, Ill. 60637.

CAREER: University of Chicago, Chicago, Ill., instructor, 1955-57, assistant professor, 1957-62, associate professor, 1962-63, professor of anthropology and Near East languages and civilizations, 1963-75, Harold H. Swift Distinguished Service Professor, 1975—, director of Oriental Institute, 1962-68, dean of Division of Behavioral and Social Sciences, 1970-74. Visiting professor at Harvard University, 1962, and University of California, Berkeley, 1963; Lewis Henry Morgan Lecturer at University of Rochester, 1965; American School of Oriental Research (Baghdad), annual professor, 1966-67, resident director, 1968-69. National Research Council's Division of Behavioral Science, member, 1967—, chairman, 1972—. Has conducted field research in Iraq, Iran, Mexico, and Syria. *Military service:* U.S. Naval Reserve, active duty, 1944-46.

MEMBER: American Philosophical Society, National Academy of Sciences, American Association for the Advancement of Science (fellow), American Anthropological Association (fellow), American Academy of Arts and Sciences (fellow), Society for American Archaeology, Middle East Studies Association of North America (fellow), German Archaeological Institute, Sigma Xi.

WRITINGS: *Level and Trend in Early Sumerian Civilization,* Library, University of Chicago, 1956; (editor with C. H. Kraeling) *City Invincible: A Symposium on Urbanization and Cultural Development in the Ancient Near East,* University of Chicago Press, 1960; *Land behind Baghdad: A History of Settlement on the Diyala Plains,* University of Chicago Press, 1965; *The Evolution of Urban Society: Early Mesopotamia and Prehispanic Mexico,* Aldine, 1966; (with Hans J. Nissen) *The Uruk Countryside: The Natural Setting of Urban Societies,* University of Chicago Press, 1972. Contributor of more than eighty articles to professional journals. Advisory editor of archeology for *Encyclopaedia Britannica.*

SIDELIGHTS: Adams' research is an ecologically oriented study of historic patterns of land use settlement and urbanization; he has a comparative interest in other centers of early civilization. *Avocational interests:* Skiing, mountaineering.

* * *

ADDAMS, Charles (Samuel) 1912-

PERSONAL: Born January 7, 1912, in Westfield, N.J.; son of Charles Huey (manager for a piano company) and Grace M. (Spear) Addams; married Barbara Day, May 29, 1943 (divorced October, 1951); married Barbara Barb, December 1, 1954 (divorced, 1956). *Education:* Attended Colgate University, 1929-30, University of Pennsylvania, 1930-31, and Grand Central School of Art, New York, N.Y., 1931-32. *Home:* 25 West 54th St., New York, N.Y., 10020; and Westhampton, N.Y.

CAREER: Worked briefly in New York for a Macfadden publication after submitting first cartoon to the *New Yorker* in 1933; became a free-lance cartoonist, with work appearing regularly in *New Yorker,* 1940—. Work exhibited at Fogg Art Museum, Rhode Island School of Design, Museum of the City of New York, Pennsylvania University Museum, and Metropolitan Museum of Art. *Military service:* U.S. Army, Signal Corps, 1943-46. *Member:* Vintage Car Club of America, Armor and Arms Club, Coffee House. *Awards, honors:* Humor award, Yale University, 1954; special award of the Mystery Writers of America, 1961.

WRITINGS—Cartoons: *Drawn and Quartered* (foreword by Boris Karloff), Random House, 1942, published as *D & Q: The Return of a Classic,* Simon & Schuster, 1962; *Addams and Evil* (with introduction by Wolcott Gibbs), Random House, 1947; *Monster Rally,* Simon & Schuster, 1950; *Homebodies,* Simon & Schuster, 1954; *Nightcrawlers,* Simon & Schuster, 1957; (editor) *Dear Dead Days: A Family Album,* Putnam, 1959; *Black Maria,* Simon & Schuster, 1960; *The Groaning Board,* Simon & Schuster, 1964; (with others) *Think Small,* Golden Press, 1967; *The Charles Addams Mother Goose,* Windmill Books, 1967; *My Crowd,* Simon & Schuster, 1970. Contributor to annual *New Yorker Album.*

Illustrator: John Kobler, *Afternoon in the Attic,* Dodd, 1950.

Contributor of cartoons to *Life, Collier's, Cosmopolitan,* and other periodicals.

SIDELIGHTS: The TV show *The Addams Family* is inspired by Addams' work, and the characters which appear in it are based on those in his cartoons. *Avocational interests:* Vintage sports cars, Civil War history, collecting medieval armor, and archery.

* * *

ADELMAN, Janet (Ann) 1941-

PERSONAL: Born January 28, 1941, in Mount Kisco, N.Y.; daughter of Emanuel (a manufacturer) and Cecile (Greenfeld) Adelman. *Education:* Smith College, B.A. (summa cum laude), 1962; St. Hugh's College, Oxford, graduate study, 1962-63; Yale University, M.A., 1965, M.Phil., 1967, Ph.D., 1969. *Office:* Department of English, University of California, Berkeley, Calif. 94720.

CAREER: University of California, Berkeley, acting assistant professor, 1968-70, assistant professor, 1970-72, associate professor of English literature, 1972—. *Member:* Modern Language Association of America, Shakespeare Association of America. *Awards, honors:* Fulbright fellowship, Oxford University, 1962-63; Woodrow Wilson fellowship, 1964-65.

WRITINGS: *The Common Liar: An Essay on "Antony and Cleopatra",* Yale University Press, 1973; (contributor) Dewey R. Faulkner, editor, *Twentieth Century Interpretations of "The Pardoner's Tale",* Prentice-Hall, 1973.

WORK IN PROGRESS: Editing a collection of criticism on "King Lear"; an essay on "Paradise Lost," for inclusion in a volume to honor Maynard Mack.

* * *

ADELSON, Leone 1908-

PERSONAL: Born June 13, 1908, in New York, N.Y. *Education:* New York University, M.S., 1947. *Politics:* "Reform Democrat." *Residence:* New York, N.Y.

CAREER: Has taught elementary school children, both deaf and hearing; directed a Ford Foundation experiment in closed circuit television; wrote and directed educational television and radio programs for New York, N.Y. Board of Education; served as assistant to school principal; writer. Volunteer guide for Friends of the Zoo (Bronx); member of New York Board of Education's chancellor's hearing committee. *Member:* English Speaking Union, Association of Retired Supervisors.

WRITINGS—Juveniles: *Who Blew That Whistle?,* W. R. Scott, 1946; *The Blowaway Hat,* Reynal-Hitchcock, 1946; *The House with Red Sails,* McKay, 1951; *All Ready for*

Winter, McKay, 1952; (with Lilian Moore) *Old Rosie: The Horse Nobody Understood*, Random House, 1952; (with Moore) *The Terrible Mr. Twitmeyer*, Random House, 1952; *Red Sails on the James*, McKay, 1953; (with Benjamin Gruenberg) *Your Breakfast, and the People who Made It*, Doubleday, 1954; *All Ready for Summer*, McKay, 1956; *All Ready for School*, McKay, 1957; *Please Pass the Grass*, McKay, 1960; *Flyaway at the Air show*, Grosset, 1962; (with Moore) *Mr. Twitmeyer and the Poodle*, Random House, 1963; *Dandelions Don't Bite*, Pantheon, 1972. Author of two children's records for Young People's Records.

SIDELIGHTS: Leone Adelson writes: "Mountains fascinate me and I can well understand how the passion of climbers blinds them to danger. I'll never forget my first trip to Europe and my first sight of the Jungfrau, all pink in the morning sun. I am deeply moved by such people as John Muir and his rugged pioneer mountaineering and deeply grateful for his early efforts to hold back the miners, ranchers and loggers. Alas, I am no mountaineer!'' Her current plans include travel to the Republic of China and to Nepal.

*   *   *

ADLER, Carol   1938-

PERSONAL: Born December 5, 1938, in Rochester, N.Y.; daughter of Leonard A. (an engineer) and Helen (Hurvitz) Stalker; married Samuel Hans Adler (a composer and professor), February 14, 1960; children: Deborah, Naomi. *Education:* Attended Brandeis University, 1956-57; University of Michigan, A.B., 1960. *Religion:* Jewish. *Home:* 54 Railroad Mills Rd., Pittsford, N.Y. 14534.

CAREER: Creative writing instructor at Pittsford-Mendon High School, 1976—. *Member:* International Poetry Society, National Poetry Society, New York Poetry Forum, Texas Poetry Society, Rochester Poetry Society. *Awards, honors: Southwest Review* fiction award, 1963; New York Poetry Forum poetry award, 1974.

WRITINGS: Arioso (poems), Pentagram Press, 1975. Contributor of poems to *Midstream, Reconstructionist, Reform Judaism, European Judaism, Jewish Quarterly, National Law-Arts Review, Facets,* and *Mundus Artium.* Member of editorial board of *Jewish Roots,* 1974—.

WORK IN PROGRESS: Two books of poems; a collection of Jewish poetry, and of secular poetry; a short story collection; with Bogislav Schaeffer, a poetry text for electronic music; with Lou Ouzer, a photo-poetry collection; translations of poetry by Austrian poet, George Trakl, and the Turkish poet, Turgut Uyar.

SIDELIGHTS: Some of Carol Adler's poems have been used as a text for music by composers Warren Benson and Samuel Adler, her husband. In 1971, she composed the text for a choral work by Michael Isaacson. The poem, "We Are the Echoes," is included in the text of *Symphony Number 5* by Samuel Adler. It was premiered by the Fort Worth Symphony on November 9 and 11, 1975, at the Union of American Hebrew Congregations Biennial Convention.

With award-winning photographer, Claire Trotter, she has collaborated on a series of photo-poems. She has translated and published several poems by the Yiddish poet, Israel Emiot, and the Austrian poet, George Trakl. *Avocational interests:* Travel, painting, literature, music, photography, dance.

AERS, David   1946-

PERSONAL: Born October 3, 1946, in Lahore, India; son of Ian and Pamela (Ridgeway) Aers. *Education:* Cambridge University, B.A., 1968, M.A., 1972; University of York, Ph.D., 1971. *Office:* School of English and American Studies, University of East Anglia, Norwich, England.

CAREER: University of East Anglia, Norwich, England, lecturer, 1971—.

WRITINGS: (With Mary Ann Radzinowicz) *Paradise Lost, Books VII-VIII,* Cambridge University Press, 1974; *Piers Plowman and Christian Allegory,* St. Martin's, 1975.

WORK IN PROGRESS: A book with R. I. V. Hodge on literature and ideology; research on the relation of literature, consciousness, and society, especially centered on the later Middle Ages, Langland, and Chaucer.

*   *   *

AHERN, John F(rancis)   1936-

PERSONAL: Born October 14, 1936, in Manchester, N.H.; son of John F. (a colonel in the U.S. Army) and Mary (Devine) Ahern; married Anne O'Brien (a teacher), April 18, 1964. *Education:* Boston College, B.S.B.A., 1958; University of Massachusetts, M.A., 1960, D.Ed., 1969. *Politics:* Democrat. *Religion:* Roman Catholic. *Home:* 30531 East River Rd., Perrysburg, Ohio 43551. *Office:* Department of Elementary and Early Childhood Education, University of Toledo, Toledo, Ohio 43606.

CAREER: Teacher in Chicopee, Mass., 1961-65, and at Wahconah Regional High School, 1965-66; University of Massachusetts, Amherst, instructor in education, 1967-69; University of Toledo, Toledo, Ohio, assistant professor, 1969-72, associate professor, 1972-76, professor of education, 1976—. *Member:* National Council of Social Studies, American Society for Curriculum Development.

WRITINGS: (With Nanci Lucas) *Ideas: Handbook for Teaching Elementary Social Studies,* Harper, 1975.

*   *   *

AHSEN, Akhter   1931-

PERSONAL: Born January 28, 1931, in Lahore, Pakistan; son of Sufi Mohammed (a postmaster) and Zainab Shafi. *Education:* Lahore University, B.A. (honors), 1952, M.A., 1954, Ph.D., 1972. *Office:* Eidetic Analysis Institute, Yonkers, N.Y.

CAREER: Inter-Services Selection Board, Rawalpindi, Pakistan, psychologist, 1955-66; Eidetic Psychotherapy Institute, Philadelphia, Pa., psychologist, 1966-69; Eidetic Analysis Institute, Yonkers, N.Y., director of research and training, 1969—. Chief psychologist for Central Superior Services Commission (Pakistan), 1959-60.

WRITINGS: Eidetic Psychotherapy: A Short Introduction, Brandon House, 1965; *Basic Concepts in Eidetic Psychotherapy,* Brandon House, 1968, 2nd edition, 1973; *Eidetic Parents Test and Analysis: A Practical Guide to Systematic and Comprehensive Analysis,* Brandon House, 1972; *Self-Image Self,* Brandon House, in press; *Psychofeedback* (eidetic workbook-journal), Brandon House, in press; *Half-Brain Images,* Brandon House, in press.

Contributor: Arnold A. Lazarus, *Clinical Behavior Therapy,* Brunner/Mazel, 1972; Violet Franks and Vasanti Burtle, editors, *Women in Therapy,* Brunner/Mazel, 1974. Contributor to professional journals.

SIDELIGHTS: Although influenced by Jaensch and the work of the Marburg school in Germany in the 1920's and 1930's, Ahsen turned away from the study of eidetic disposition and typology to stress it as a universal phenomenon. He describes the basic unit of eidetic therapy as a three-segment experience through the eidetic as an image, as a somatic feeling involving emotional and physiological states, and as meaning of a given experience. Another of his concepts is the consciousness-imagery gap, which he feels is a valuable concept in uncovering discrepancies between a patient's perception and his conscious evaluation of it.

BIOGRAPHICAL/CRITICAL SOURCES: Joseph Wolpc, *The Practice of Behavior Therapy,* Pergamon, 1969; Arnold A. Lazarus, editor, *Behavior Therapy and Beyond,* McGraw, 1971.

* * *

AICHINGER, Peter 1933-

PERSONAL: Born July 13, 1933, in Cloverdale, British Columbia, Canada; son of Constantin Richard and Bridgit Eileen (Woods) von Aichinger; married Sigrid Hagemann (a secretary), November 4, 1972; children: Anne, John, Suzanne, Max. *Education:* Royal Military College, B.A., 1958; University of Toronto, B.A. (honors), 1959; University of Ottawa, M.A., 1963; University of Sussex, D.Phil., 1970. *Home:* 378 Champlain, St. Jean, Quebec, Canada. *Office:* Department of English, College militaire royal, St. Jean, Quebec, Canada.

CAREER: College militaire royal, St. Jean, Quebec, lecturer, 1962-70, assistant professor, 1970-74, associate professor of English, 1974—, chairman of department, 1973—. *Military service:* Canadian Army, Royal Horse Artillery, 1958-62; served in Germany; became lieutenant. *Member:* Association of Canadian University Teachers of English, Canadian Association of University Teachers, Canadian Historical Association, Modern Language Association of America.

WRITINGS: The American Soldier in Fiction: A History of the American War Novel, 1880-1963, Iowa State University Press, 1975. Contributor to learned journals.

WORK IN PROGRESS: Earle Birney, a biography, for Twayne; *The Battle of Fort St. Jean, 1775.*

* * *

AIDENOFF, Abraham 1913-1976

June 14, 1913—January 9, 1976; American statistical economist, United Nations official, consultant to U.S. and foreign governments, and author of books in his field. Obituaries: *New York Times,* January 10, 1976. (See index for previous *CA* sketch)

* * *

AJAYI, J(acob) F(estus) Ade(niyi) 1929-

PERSONAL: Born May 26, 1929, in Ikolc-Ekiti, Nigeria; son of Ezekiel Adeniji (a customary court judge) and Comfort Bolajoko (Omoleye) Ajayi; married Christie Aduke Martins, October 23, 1956; children: Yetunde, Adeniyi, Olufunmilayo, Titilola, Bisola. *Education:* Attended Higher College, Lagos, 1947; University of Ibadan, B.A., 1951; University of Leicester, B.A. (history), 1955; King's College, London, Ph.D., 1958. *Home:* Vice-Chancellor's Lodge, University of Lagos, Lagos, Nigeria. *Office:* Vice-Chancellor's Office, University of Lagos, Lagos, Nigeria.

CAREER: University of Ibadan, Ibadan, Nigeria, lecturer, 1958-62, senior lecturer, 1962-63, professor, 1963-72; University of Lagos, Lagos, Nigeria, vice-chancellor, 1972—. Member, Committee on National Archives, 1961-72, Public Service Commission, Western State, Nigeria, 1966, National Antiquities Commission, 1971-75, and Council of the University of Cape Coast, Ghana; fellow of the Center for Advanced Study in Behavioral Sciences, 1970-71; member of executive board, Association of African Universities, 1974—; chairman of executive committee, International African Institute, 1975—; chairman, United Nations University Council, 1976. *Member:* African Studies Association, Historical Society of Nigeria (president, 1972—), Ghana Historical Association (fellow). *Awards, honors:* LL.D. from University of Leicester, 1975.

WRITINGS: Milestones in Nigerian History, Ibadan University College, 1962; *Western Nigeria: Commission of Inquiry Into the Rise in Fees Charged by Public Secondary Grammar Schools and Teacher Training Colleges,* [Ibadan], 1962; (director of compilation) *Population Census of Nigeria, 1963: Lists of Historical Events for Determination of Individual Ages,* [Ibadan], 1962, 2nd edition (compiled with Adenola A. Igun), 1963; (with Robert Smith) *Yoruba Warfare in the Nineteenth Century,* Cambridge University Press, 1964, 2nd edition, 1971; (editor with Ian Espie) *A Thousand Years of West African History,* Nelson, 1965, revised edition, Ibadan University Press, 1969; *Christian Missions in Nigeria, 1841-1891: The Making of a New Elite,* Northwestern University Press, 1965; (editor with Michael Crowder) *History of West Africa,* two volumes, Longman, 1971, Columbia University Press, 1972; (editor with T. N. Tamuno) *University of Ibadan, 1948-73, A History of the First Twenty-Five Years,* Ibadan University Press, 1973.

WORK IN PROGRESS: Editing Volume VI of the eight volume UNESCO *History of Africa;* editing, with Michael Crowder, a *Historical Atlas of Africa,* in color.

* * *

ALBERT, Burton, Jr. 1936-

PERSONAL: Born September 25, 1936, in Pittsfield, Mass.; son of Burton and Isabel (Deming) Albert; married Lois Bent, June 27, 1963; children: Heather Leigh, Kelley Lynn. *Education:* North Adams State College, B.S. (magna cum laude), 1958; Duke University, M.A., 1962. *Home:* 3 Narrow Brook Rd., Weston, Conn. 06880. *Office: Reader's Digest,* Pleasantville, N.Y. 10570.

CAREER: Elementary school teacher in Greenwich, Conn., 1958-60, 1962-63, high school teacher of English in Greenwich, Conn., 1963-64; Harcourt Brace Jovanovich, Inc., New York, N.Y., assistant editor in language arts, 1964-66; *Reader's Digest,* Educational Division, Pleasantville, N.Y., senior editor and product developer, 1966—. *Member:* International Reading Association, National Council of Teachers of English, Conference on English Education, Conference on College Composition and Communication, California Association of Teachers of English.

WRITINGS: (Contributor) Ronald Noland, Jone Wright, Elizabeth Allen, editors, *An Introduction to Elementary Reading: Selected Materials,* MSS Information, 1971; (with Donald M. Murray) *Write to Communicate: The Language Arts in Process,* Levels 3-6, Reader's Digest Services, Inc., 1973-74; (contributor) Melissa Costello and Reginold Fickett, editors, *Essays in American and English Literature,* MSS Information, in press; *Codes for Kids,*

Albert Whitman, in press; *Puzzle Fun,* Firefly Book Club, in press. Ghostwriter of language arts textbooks. Author of "Reader's Digest Reading Skills Practice Pads," Reader's Digest Services, Inc., 1967. Contributor of articles and poems to education and literature journals, and to children's magazines.

WORK IN PROGRESS: The Cannibal Handed Me Fritos, a book of contemporary riddles and puns; *Jawbreakers: For Riddle Sharks Only!; Let's Play: Brief Learning Games to Play with Your Preschooler; A Witch's Brew of Riddles; Hector: The Tiny Tooth Collector; Crazee Riddle Series; Fun with a Felt-Tip Pen;* general editor for "Reading Skill Builders, Anniversary Edition," publication by Reader's Digest Services, Inc. expected in 1977.

*   *   *

ALBERTI, Robert E(dward)   1938-

PERSONAL: Born May 21, 1938, in Los Angeles, Calif.; son of Samuel Edward (a civil servant) and Carita V. (Schaub) Alberti; married Deborah Anne Millerd (an office manager), September 6, 1958; children: Lawrence Chandler, Melissa Christine. *Education:* California Polytechnic State University, B.S., 1959; California State University, Los Angeles, M.A., 1962; Michigan State University, Ph.D., 1969. *Residence:* San Luis Obispo, Calif. *Agent:* Lachlan P. MacDonald, P.O. Box 1275, San Luis Obispo, Calif, 93406. *Office:* Counseling Center, Califronia Polytechnic State University, San Luis Obispo, Calif. 93407.

CAREER: Arizona State University, Tempe, program director, 1962-63; California State Polytechnic University, Pomona, assistant to vice-president, 1963-65, associate dean of students, 1965-68; California Polytechnic State University, San Luis Obispo, professor and counseling psychologist, 1969—. Impact Publishers, Inc., San Luis Obispo, president, 1970—. Vice-chairman of San Luis Obispo County Coordinating Council on Drug Abuse, 1971-73. *Member:* International Round Table for Advancement of Counseling, American Psychological Association, American Personnel and Guidance Association, Association for the Advancement of Behavior Therapy, American College Personnel Association, Society for Psychological Study of Social Issues, Common Cause, Sierra Club, Phi Delta Kappa.

WRITINGS: (With M. L. Emmons) *Your Perfect Right,* Impact Press, 1970, 2nd edition, 1974; (with Emmons) *Stand Up, Speak Out, Talk Back,* Pocket Books, 1975. Contributor of articles to *Journal of College Student Personnel, New Woman, Self Publishing Writer,* and *Journal of Marriage and Family Counseling.*

WORK IN PROGRESS: Researching positive assertive behavior in children, and faculty development in higher education.

SIDELIGHTS: Robert Alberti writes: "Both *Stand Up, Speak Out, Talk Back* and *Your Perfect Right* resulted from our work with individuals who feel powerless to influence their own lives. Dr. Emmons and I have done much work in this field with students, professionals and the general public. An appalling number of persons are allowing themselves to be manipulated by others. We hope to help many of them through our work and writing." *Avocational interests:* Foreign travel, small boat sailing, amateur radio.

ALBINI, Joseph L(ouis)   1930-

PERSONAL: Born 1930, in Vandergrift, Pa. *Education:* St. Vincent's College, B.A., 1952; Pennsylvania State University, graduate study, 1954; Louisiana State University, M.A., 1956; Ohio State University, Ph.D., 1963. *Office:* Department of Sociology, Wayne State University, Detroit, Mich. 48202.

CAREER: Ohio State University, Columbus, assistant instructor in sociology, 1958-60; Columbus State School, Columbus, Ohio, psychiatric social worker, 1960-63; Institute Treatment Center, Louisville, Ky., director, 1963-64; Bowling Green State University, Bowling Green, Ohio, assistant professor of sociology, 1964-65; Wayne State University, Detroit, Mich., assistant professor, 1965-67, associate professor, 1967-74, professor of sociology, 1974—, instructor at Institute of Labor and Industrial Relations, 1967-70. Instructor at University of Kentucky, Fort Knox Center, 1963-64; University of Windsor, guest lecturer, autumn, 1966, adjunct associate professor, 1968-69; guest lecturer at University of Sierra Leone, winter, 1971; World Campus Afloat, Chapman College, associate professor, autumn, 1971, professor, autumn, 1974; guest lecturer at Cambridge University, University of Aberdeen, University of Sterling, University of Bristol, University of Edinburgh, and University of Wales. Research associate of Kirschner Associates, 1968-69; visiting senior researcher in criminology at University of Glasgow, 1972-73; has testified before U.S. Congress on prisons and prison reform; consultant to Disaster Research Center at Ohio State University.

WRITINGS: (With Benjamin Pasamanick, Frank Scarpitti, Simon Dinitz, and Mark Lefton) *Schizophrenics in the Community,* Appleton, 1966; *The American Mafia: Genesis of a Legend,* Appleton, 1971. Contributor of articles and reviews to professional journals.

WORK IN PROGRESS: Research for a comparison between Great Britain and the United States as to structures and types of organized crime.

*   *   *

ALDEN, John R(ichard)   1908-

PERSONAL: Born January 23, 1908, in Grand Rapids, Mich.; son of Herman and Ida (Jonkmann) Alden; married Pearl B. Wells, December 22, 1934; children: *Anne Maria.* Education: *University of Michigan, A.B., 1929, A.M., 1930, Ph.D., 1939.* Home: *2736 Dogwood Rd., Durham, N.C. 27705.* Office: *408 Perkins Library, Duke University, Durham, N.C. 27706.*

CAREER: University of Michigan, Ann Arbor, Alfred H. Lloyd research fellow, 1939-40; Michigan State Normal College (now Eastern Michigan University), Ypsilanti, Mich., assistant professor of history, 1940-43; Bowling Green State University, Bowling Green, Ohio, assistant professor of history, 1943-45; University of Nebraska, Lincoln, assistant professor, 1945-47, associate professor, 1947-50, professor of history, 1950-55; Duke University, Durham, N.C., professor, 1955-63, James B. Duke Professor of History, 1963—. Visiting professor, University of Chicago, summer, 1949, University of Michigan, summers, 1950, 1954, Columbia University, summer, 1956; Walter Lynwood Fleming Lecturer, Louisiana State University, 1960; Commonwealth Fund Lecturer, University College, London, 1961. *Member:* Organization of American Historians, American Historical Association, Massachusetts Historical Society (corresponding member). *Awards, honors:*

Beveridge Prize from American Historical Association, 1945; Johnson Faculty Research fellow, University of Nebraska, 1948; Guggenheim fellow, 1955-56; Mayflower Society Award, 1969, for *A History of the American Revolution;* American Philosophical Society research grant, 1974.

WRITINGS: John Stuart and the Southern Colonial Frontier: A Study of Indian Relations, War, Trade, and Land Problems in the Southern Wilderness, 1754-1775, University of Michigan Press, 1944; *General Gage in America: Being Principally a History of His Role in the American Revolution,* Louisiana State University Press, 1948; *General Charles Lee: Traitor or Patriot?,* Louisiana State University Press, 1951; (editor) Christopher Ward, *War of the Revolution,* Macmillan, 1952; *The American Revolution, 1775-1783,* Harper, 1954; *The South in the Revolution, 1763-1787,* Louisiana State University Press, 1957; (with Alice Magenis) *A History of the United States,* American Book Co., 1960; *The First South,* Louisiana State University Press, 1961; *Rise of the American Republic,* Harper, 1963; *Pioneer America,* Knopf, 1966; *A History of the American Revolution,* Knopf, 1969 (published in England as *A History of the American Revolution: The British and the Loss of the Thirteen Colonies,* MacDonald, 1969); *Robert Dinwiddie: Servant of the Crown,* University Press of Virginia for Colonial Williamsburg, 1973; (editor) Bernhard Knollenberg, *Growth of the American Revolution,* Free Press, 1974. Contributor of articles on the American Revolution to *World Book Encyclopedia, Encyclopaedia Britannica, Larousse Encyclopedia of Modern History, Encyclopedia Americana,* and other publications.

WORK IN PROGRESS: A lecture series to be delivered during 1976.

* * *

ALDER, Francis A(nthony) 1937-

PERSONAL: Born June 13, 1937, in Pittsburgh, Pa.; son of Stanley A. (a mailer) and Elizabeth (Zak) Alder; married Joanne Fabiano, June 7, 1958; children: Michael, Lori, Julie. *Education:* University of Pittsburgh, B.S., 1958, M.A., 1970. *Religion:* Roman Catholic. *Home:* 85 Thorncrest Dr., McKees Rocks, Pa. 15136.

CAREER: WQED-TV, Pittsburgh, Pa., instructor for educational science series, 1961-63; Keystone Oaks School District, Pittsburgh, Pa., director of elementary education, 1963—. Appeared as "Scientist Alder" on "Mister Rogers Show," a children's television series, 1966-71. Naturalist instructor at Carnegie Museum; consultant to American Institute for Research. *Member:* Association for Supervision and Curriculum Development, South Hills Area School Districts Association.

WRITINGS—For children: *Finding Out About the Sun and the Moon,* Benefic, 1973; *Finding Out About Animals,* Benefic, 1973; *Finding Out About Solids, Liquids, and Gases,* Benefic, 1973. Author of science series television scripts and booklets published by Pennsylvania Department of Education.

WORK IN PROGRESS: Books for young people designed to be part of a single-concept series.

* * *

ALDERMAN, (Barbara) Joy 1931-

PERSONAL: Born October 22, 1931, in Salem, Mass.; daughter of Leon Daniel (a draftsman) and Barbara (Trask) Alderman. *Education:* Children's Hospital School of Nursing, R.N., 1953; Baptist Missionary Training School, B.R.Ed., 1955. *Home:* 11 Otis St., Wakefield, Mass. 01880. *Office:* First Baptist Church, 493 Main St., Malden, Mass. 02148.

CAREER: American Baptist minister; Meshanticut Park Church, Cranston, R.I., director of Christian education, 1957-61; First Baptist Church, Wakefield, Mass., director of Christian education, 1961-63, minister of visitation and social service, 1963—. Secretary of Malden Clergy Association, 1975—.

WRITINGS: Renewed in Strength (devotions), Judson, 1975.

* * *

ALDRIDGE, (Harold Edward) James 1918-

PERSONAL: Born July 10, 1918, in White Hills, Victoria, Australia; son of William Thomas (a newspaper publisher) and Edith (Quayle) Aldridge; married Dina Mitchnik, 1942; children: two sons. *Education:* Attended London School of Economics and Political Science, and Oxford University, 1939. *Home:* 21 Kersley St., London SW11, England. *Agent:* Curtis Brown Ltd., One Craven Hill, London W2 3EW, England.

CAREER: Worked as office boy and file clerk for Melbourne *Sun,* Melbourne, Australia, 1934-37; Melbourne *Herald* and Melbourne *Sun,* Melbourne, Australia, reporter, 1937-38; *Daily Sketch* and *Sunday Dispatch,* London, England, feature writer, 1939; free-lance war correspondent for Australian Newspaper Service and North American Newspaper Alliance in Finland, Norway, Greece, the Middle East and the Soviet Union, 1939-44; *Time* and *Life* correspondent in Teheran, Iran, 1944. Freelance writer, 1944—. *Member:* British Sub-Aqua Club. *Awards, honors:* Rhys Memorial Prize, 1945; World Peace Council Gold Medal; International Organization of Journalists prize, 1967; Lenin Peace Prize, 1972.

WRITINGS—All novels, except as indicated: *Signed With Their Honour,* Little, Brown, 1942, reprinted, White Lion Publications, 1972; *The Sea Eagle,* Little, Brown, 1944, reprinted, White Lion Publications, 1971; *Of Many Men,* Little, Brown, 1946; *The Diplomat,* Bodley Head, 1949, Little, Brown, 1950; *The Hunter,* Little, Brown, 1951; *Heroes of the Empty View,* Knopf, 1954; *Underwater Hunting for the Inexperienced Englishman* (nonfiction), Allen & Unwin, 1955; *I Wish He Would Not Die,* Doubleday, 1958.

Gold and Sand (short stories), Bodley Head, 1960; *The Last Exile,* Doubleday, 1961; *A Captive in the Land,* Hamish Hamilton, 1962, Doubleday, 1963; *The Flying 19* (juvenile), Hamish Hamilton, 1966; *The Statesman's Game,* Doubleday, 1966; *My Brother Tom,* Hamish Hamilton, 1966, published as *My Brother Tom: A Love Story,* Little, Brown, 1967; (with Paul Strand) *Living Egypt* (travel), Horizon Press, 1969; (contributor) *Winter's Tales 15* (anthology), edited by A. D. Maclean, Macmillan, 1969, St. Martin's, 1970; *Cairo: A Biography of a City* (travel), Little, Brown, 1969; *A Sporting Proposition,* Little, Brown, 1973.

Author of play, "The 49th State," produced in London, 1946. Also author of scripts for "Robin Hood" television series. Contributor to *Playboy.*

SIDELIGHTS: Aldridge's experiences as a war correspondent provided him with background material for writing his novels. For this reason, his first novel, *Signed With Their*

Honour was compared to Hemingway's *A Farewell to Arms* and *For Whom the Bell Tolls.*

A later novel, *My Brother Tom,* brought mixed reviews. It was dismissed as "pedestrian" and "moralistic", and praised as being "touching" and "disarmingly written." John Bowen called the book valuable for "its humanity, its gentleness and most of all, to use an old fashioned word, its decency."*

* * *

ALEXANDER, Christine 1893-1975

November 10, 1893—December 24, 1975; American musuem curator, expert on Greek and Roman art, and author of books on art and archaeology. Obituaries: *New York Times,* December 27, 1975; *AB Bookman's Weekly,* January 26, 1976.

* * *

ALEXANDER, Holmes (Moss) 1906-

PERSONAL: Born January 29, 1906, in Parkersburg, W.Va.; son of Charles Butler (an insurance official) and Margaret (Moss) Alexander; married Mary Barksdale (a schoolteacher), June 24, 1933; children: Hunter Holmes, Peter Barksdale, Mary Madge (Mrs. Rene Dufour). *Education:* Princeton University, B.A., 1928; student at Trinity College, Cambridge University, Cambridge, England, 1928-29. *Politics:* Republican. *Religion:* Episcopalian. *Home and office:* 922 25th Street N.W., Washington, D.C. 20037.

CAREER: McDonogh School, McDonogh, Md., English teacher and wrestling coach, 1929-31; Democratic member, Maryland House of Delegates of the Maryland General Assembly, 1931-35; free-lance writer and biographer, 1935-41, 1945—; McNaught Syndicate, New York, N.Y., syndicated political columnist, 1947—. Senior editor, *Kiplinger's Magazine,* Washington, D.C., 1946; regular contributor, *Nation's Business,* 1951; book reviewer and reporter for *Baltimore Sun. Military service:* Maryland National Guard, 1941-42; U.S. Army Air Forces, 1942-45; became major; received Army Air Medal. *Member:* Overseas Writers Association, Sigma Delta Chi, Society of Lees of Virginia, Society of the Cincinnati, 1925 F Street Club, National Press Club, Metropolitan Club (Washington). *Awards, honors:* Litt.D. from Salem College, 1971; Freedom Foundation at Valley Forge honor medal, 1973.

*WRITINGS—*Biography: *The American Talleyrand: The Career and Contemporaries of Martin Van Buren, Eighth President,* Harper, 1935; *Aaron Burr, the Proud Pretender,* Harper, 1937; *The Famous Five* (Henry Clay, Daniel Webster, John Caldwell Calhoun, Robert Marion La Follette, Robert Alphonso Taft), The Bookmailer, 1958; *Washington and Lee: A Study in the Will to Win,* Western Islands, 1966.

Novels: *Twenty of Their Swords,* Dorrance, 1930; *American Nabob,* Harper, 1939; *Dust in the Afternoon,* Harper, 1940; *Selina,* Harper, 1942; *Shall Do No Murder,* Regnery, 1959; *West of Washington,* Fleet Publishing, 1962; *The Spirit of '76,* Arlington House, 1966.

Other: *Tomorrow's Air Age: A Report on the Forseeable Future,* Rinehart, 1953; *How to Read the Federalist,* Western Islands, 1961; *The Equivocal Men: Tales of the Establishment,* Western Islands, 1964; *Between the Stirrup and the Ground: A Book About Horses and People,* National Press, 1967; *Pen and Politics: The Autobiography of a Working Writer,* West Virginia University Library, 1970;

With Friends Possessed: A Personal Story About Man to Man Friendship and Its Place in the History of the Human Heart, Caxton Printers, 1970.

Contributor to *Saturday Evening Post, Harper's, Collier's, Country Life, American Mercury.*

SIDELIGHTS: Holmes Alexander's family came to America from Scotland in the 1630s, founded the city of Alexandria, Virginia, and then followed their kinsman, George Washington, and other members of the family, into the Shenandoah Valley. *Avocational interests:* Reading American history, watching baseball.

* * *

ALEXANDER, Kenneth John Wilson 1922-
(Ken Alexander)

PERSONAL: Born March 14, 1922, in Edinburgh, Scotland; son of William Wilson Alexander; married Angela May Lane, 1949; children: one son, four daughters. *Education:* Attended School of Economics, Dundee; University of London, B.Sc., 1949. *Home:* Ardnacraggan, Callander, Perthshire, Scotland. *Office:* Department of Economics, University of Strathclyde, Glasgow, Scotland.

CAREER: University of Leeds, Leeds, England, research assistant, 1949-51; University of Sheffield, Sheffield, England, lecturer, 1951-56; University of Aberdeen, Aberdeen, Scotland, lecturer, 1957-61; University of Strathclyde, Glasgow, Scotland, professor of economics and head of department, 1961—. Umpire for North Derbyshire District Conciliation Board, 1963; member of the advisory committee for the University of the Air, 1965; governor, Newbattle Abbey College, 1967; economic consultant to the Secretary of State for Scotland, 1968—; member of the executive committee of the Scottish Council (Development and Industry), 1968—; director, Glasgow Chamber of Commerce, 1969—; chairman, Committee on Adult Education in Scotland, 1970; chairman Academic Executive Committee, Scottish Business School, 1972—. Director, Fairfields Ltd. (Glasgow), 1966-68, and Upper Clyde Shipbuilders Ltd., 1968-71; board member, Scott Transport Group, 1968—.

WRITINGS: (Under name Ken Alexander, with John Hughes) *Trade Unions in Opposition,* Fabian Society, 1961; (editor with A. G. Kemp and T. M. Rybozynski) *The Economist in Business,* Augustus M. Kelley, 1967; *Economic Analysis and Forecasting for Business,* Industrial and Commercial Techniques, London, 1969; (with C. L. Jenkins) *Fairfields—A Study of Industrial Change,* Lane, 1970. Also author of *Productivity, Bargaining, and the Reform of Industrial Relations,* 1969. Contributor to professional journals.

AVOCATIONAL INTERESTS: Scottish antiquarianism.*

* * *

ALEXANDER, Shana 1925-

PERSONAL: Born October 6, 1925, in New York, N.Y.; daughter of Milton and Cecelia (Rubenstein) Ager; married Stephen Alexander, 1951 (divorced); children: Katherine. *Education:* Vassar College, B.A., 1945. *Office:* CBS News, 524 West 57th St., New York, N.Y. 10019.

CAREER: With *PM* Magazine, New York City, 1944-47, and *Harper's Bazaar,* New York City, 1946-47; *Flair,* New York City, entertainment editor, 1950; *Life* Magazine, member of staff in New York, 1951-54, on West Coast, 1954-61, staff writer, 1961-64, author of column, "The

Feminine Eye," 1964-69; *McCall's* Magazine, New York, editor, 1969-71; Columbia Broadcasting System, New York City, commentator on radio program, "Spectrum," 1970-72; *Newsweek,* columnist, 1972-75; Columbia Broadcasting System, regular commentator on "Point-Counterpoint" feature of television program, "Sixty Minutes," 1974—. Director of American Film Institute. *Member:* National Women's Political Caucus (founding member). *Awards, honors:* Sigma Delta Chi award and University of Southern California national journalism award, 1965; named Woman of the Year by *Los Angeles Times,* 1967; Golden Pen Award of American Newspaper Women's Club, 1969; achievement award from Women's Division of Albert Einstein College of Medicine, 1976.

WRITINGS: The Feminine Eye, McCall Publishing, 1970; *Shana Alexander's State-by-State Guide to Women's Legal Rights,* Wollstonecraft, 1975; *Talking Women,* Delacorte, 1976.

WORK IN PROGRESS: American Pie, a book on Patricia Hearst and social change in America, publication by Viking Penguin expected in 1977.

* * *

ALEXANDER, Yonah 1931-

PERSONAL: Surname legally changed from Alexandrowitz, 1952; born December 25, 1931, in Grodno, Poland; naturalized U.S. citizen; son of Chaim (a businessman) and Penina (Segalowitz) Alexandrowitz; married Miriam Safrut (a university teacher), December 11, 1956; children: Daphne, Dean. *Education:* Roosevelt University, B.A., 1954; University of Chicago, M.A., 1955; College of Jewish Studies, B.H.L., 1954; Columbia University, Ph.D., 1965. *Religion:* Jewish. *Home:* Glen Drive, Oneonta, N.Y. 13820. *Office:* Department of International and Area Studies, State University of New York College at Oneonta, Oneonta, N.Y. 13820.

CAREER: City University of New York, New York, N.Y., lecturer in general studies at City College and Hunter College, 1961-65, director of Hunter College's study program in Europe and the Middle East, summer, 1961; State University of New York College at Oneonta, assistant professor, 1965, associate professor, 1966-68, professor of international and area studies, 1968—, director of overseas programs in the Middle East, 1967—, member of task force on overseas programs in the Middle East, 1971—. Visiting lecturer at colleges and universities in the United States and Canada. Conducted field research in Asia, Africa, Latin America, and Europe, 1961—. Technical assistance coordinator and liaison officer for Israel's Ministry of Trade and Industry with U.S. Operations Mission in Israel, and the United Nations, 1956.

MEMBER: International Council on Education for Teaching, International Studies Association, Society for International Development, American Society for International Law, Middle East Institute, Royal Geographical Society (fellow). *Awards, honors:* New York State faculty scholar in international studies, 1965-67; research grant from Columbia University's School of Journalism, 1966—, and from Institute for International Order, 1966-73; senior fellowship from American University's Institute for Advanced Studies in Justice, 1971—.

WRITINGS: International Technical Assistance Experts: A Case Study of the U.N. Experience, Praeger, 1966; *Israel: Selected Annotated and Illustrated Bibliography,* Victor Buday, 1968; (editor with Nicholas N. Kittrie) *Cres-*

cent and Star: Arab-Israeli Perspectives on the Middle East Conflict, AMS Press, 1973; *The Role of Communications in the Middle East Conflict: Ideological and Religious Aspects,* Praeger, 1974; (editor) *International Terrorism: National, Regional, and Global Perspectives,* Praeger, 1976. Contributor of articles and reviews to international studies journals.

WORK IN PROGRESS: War and Peace in the Middle East; The Causation and Control of Terrorism, completion expected in 1977.

* * *

ALLEN, Gertrude E(lizabeth) 1888-

PERSONAL: Born July 18, 1888, in Detroit, Mich. *Education:* School of Museum of Fine Arts, Boston, diploma, 1911; Yale University, Mus.B., 1929. *Home:* 59 Sims Rd., Wollaston, Mass. 02170.

CAREER: Professional singer, and teacher of singing privately and in schools, 1915-28; concentrated on art and writing after 1931 when throat operation ended her singing career; began giving chalk talks on nature subjects around New England and the Midwest in 1933, continuing to present programs for schools, libraries, and clubs until 1970. Illustrator for magazines and books; painter of nature tiles. *Member:* American Nature Society, Massachusetts Audubon Society, Audubon Society of New Hampshire, Massachusetts Horticultural Society, Society of Arts and Crafts (Boston; life member and master craftsman).

WRITINGS—Self-illustrated: "Everyday Nature Books for Children" series, published by Houghton: *Everyday Birds,* 1943; *Everyday Animals,* 1961; *Everyday Insects,* 1963; *Everyday Wildflowers,* 1965; *Everyday Trees,* 1968; *Everyday Turtles, Toads and Their Kin,* 1970.

Other: *Tammy Chipmunk and His Friends,* Houghton, 1950. Author of a 75-year history of the Church of Our Saviour in Milton, Mass., privately printed.

WORK IN PROGRESS: Research on fish.

* * *

ALLEN, Gwenfread Elaine 1904-

PERSONAL: Born in 1904, in Denver, Colo.; daughter of John Randolph and Gwenfread (Morgan) Allen. *Education:* University of Hawaii, A.B., 1924. *Home:* 1600 Alamoana Blvd., Apt. 802, Honolulu, Hawaii 96815.

CAREER: Honolulu Star-Bulletin, Honolulu, Hawaii, reporter and department editor, 1922-44; U.S. War Manpower Commission, Honolulu, information specialist, 1944-46; Honolulu Community Chest, Honolulu, public relations director, 1946-47; University of Hawaii, Honolulu, research associate, 1947-49; free-lance writer in public relations, 1949-66; free-lance writer, 1966—. Salvation Army Women's Auxiliary of Honolulu, member, secretary, 1973-76. *Member:* National League of American Pen Women (past president of Honolulu chapter), Zonta International (past president of Honolulu club), Phi Beta Kappa, Theta Sigma Phi (past president of Honolulu chapter). *Awards, honors:* Headliner Award from Theta Sigma Phi, 1953; alumni award from University of Hawaii, 1967.

WRITINGS: Hawaii's War Years, 1941-1945, University of Hawaii Press, 1950; (contributor) Aldyth V. Morris, editor, *Notes and References* (to accompany *Hawaii's War Years*), University of Hawaii Press, 1952; *The Y.M.C.A. in Hawaii, 1869-1969,* Young Men's Christian Association,

1969; *Bridge Builders: The Story of Theodore and Mary Atherton Richards,* Hawaii Conference Foundation, 1970.

Editor of *Hawaii Farm and Home,* 1939-44; advisory editor of *Encyclopedia of Hawaii.*

* * *

ALLEN, Rodney F.   1938-

PERSONAL: Born November 2, 1938, in Wilmington, Del.; married Carol Elizabeth Turner; children: Tracy Elizabeth, Rodney F., Jr., Dianna Carol. *Education:* University of Delaware, B.A., 1961, M.A. (American history), 1967; Carnegie Institute of Technology (now Carnegie-Mellon University), M.A. (comparative history), 1967, Ph.D., 1973; also studied at Wake Forest College, summer, 1964, and American University of Beirut, summer, 1965. *Home:* 1603 Augusta Dr., Holly Hills, Tallahassee, Fla. 32303. *Office:* Department of Social Studies Education, Florida State University, 426 Hull Dr., Tallahassee, Fla. 32306.

CAREER: Junior high school teacher of social studies in New Castle, Del., 1961-63; high school teacher of sociology and American history in Wilmington, Del., 1963-66; Florida State University, Tallahassee, assistant professor, 1968-74, associate professor of social studies education, 1974—. *Awards, honors:* Grants from Danforth Foundation, 1968-71, 1971-73, National Endowment for the Humanities, 1971-73, U.S. Office of Education, 1971-72, Stone Foundation and National Endowment for the Humanities, 1972-75, and Florida Citizens' Committee for the Humanities, 1973.

WRITINGS: The Adams-Jackson Election of 1828: A Teaching Unit, Historical Society of Delaware, 1964; *The War of 1812: A Teaching Unit,* Historical Society of Delaware, 1964; (editor with Peter H. Lyon and John V. Fleckenstein) *Inquiry in the Social Sciences,* National Council for the Social Studies, 1965; (with William J. Kozak and Wayne D. Rodan) *World Population Analysis: A Resource Unit,* Delaware Department of Public Instruction, 1966; (editor with Charles H. Adair) *Violence and Riots in Urban America,* Wadsworth, 1969; (with Robert A. Spivey) *A Guide to "The Bible Reader",* Bruce Books, 1969.

(Contributor) Richard Wisniewski, editor, *Teaching about Life in the City,* National Council for the Social Studies, 1972; (with E. S. Gaustad and R. A. Spivey) *Religious Issues in American Culture,* with teacher's guide, Addison-Wesley, 1972; (with Gaustad and Spivey) *Religious Issues in Western Civilization,* with teacher's guide, Addison-Wesley, 1973; (with Daniel M. Ulrich and Carmelo P. Foti) *The Works of Thy Hands: Scriptures for Reflection in an Age of Environmental Crisis,* St. Mary's College Press, 1973; (with Foti, Ulrich, and Steven Woolard) *Deciding How to Live on Spaceship Earth: The Ethics of Environmental Concern,* Plover Books, 1973; *A Guide to the Plover Series,* Plover Books, 1974; (with Gaustad and Spivey) *Religious Issues in World Cultures,* with teacher's guide, Addison-Wesley, 1976.

Films—All for WFSU-Television: "The Supreme Court Speaks: Learning about Religion in Public Schools," 1971; "Learning about Religion in American History Courses," 1972; "Learning about Religion in World Culture Courses," 1972; "Learning about Religion in Social Issues Courses," 1972. Contributor of articles and reviews to theology, education, and social studies journals.

ALLEN, Walter Ernest   1911-

PERSONAL: Born February 23, 1911, in Birmingham, England; son of Charles Henry and Annie Maria (Thomas) Allen; married Peggy Yorke Joy, 1944; children: two sons, two daughters. *Education:* University of Birmingham, B.A., 1932. *Home:* 6 Canonbury Square, London N.1, England.

CAREER: King Edward's Grammar School, Aston, Birmingham, England, assistant master, 1934; State University of Iowa, Iowa City, visiting lecturer in English, 1935; Cater's News Agency, Birmingham, features editor, 1935-37; Wrought Light Alloys Development Association, Birmingham, assistant technical officer, 1943-45; Coe College, Cedar Rapids, Iowa, Margaret Pilcher Visiting Professor of English, 1955-56; *New Statesman,* London, assistant literary editor, 1959-60, literary editor, 1960-61; Vassar College, Poughkeepsie, New York, visiting professor of English, 1963-64; visiting professor of English at University of Kansas, Lawrence, and University of Washington, Seattle, 1967; New University of Ulster, Londonderry, Northern Ireland, professor of English, 1967-73; Virginia Polytechnic Institute and State University, Blacksburg, C. P. Miles Professor of English, 1974—. Berg Professor of English, New York University, 1970-71; visiting professor of English, Dalhousie University, 1973-74. Broadcaster for the British Broadcasting Corp. on literary subjects. *Member:* Royal Society of Literature (fellow), Society of Authors, Saville Club.

WRITINGS: Innocence is Drowned (novel), M. Joseph, 1938; *Blind Man's Ditch* (novel), M. Joseph, 1939; *Living Space* (novel), M. Joseph, 1940; *Rogue Elephant* (novel), Morrow, 1946; *The Black Country,* P. Elek, 1947; *Arnold Bennett,* Home & Van Thal, 1948, Alan Swallow, 1949, reprint, Folcroft, 1969; (editor) *Writers on Writing,* Phoenix House, 1948, published as *The Writer on His Art,* Whittlesey House, 1949; *Reading a Novel,* Phoenix House, 1949, 4th revised edition, 1965, reprint of 3rd edition, Folcroft, 1970.

Dead Man Over All (novel), M. Joseph, 1950, published as *Square Peg,* Morrow, 1951; (contributor) L.A.G. Strong, editor, *Portraits of People Whose Houses Have Been Preserved by the National Trust,* Naldrett Press, 1951; *Joyce Cary,* Longmans, Green, 1953, revised edition, 1963; *The English Novel: A Short Critical History,* Phoenix House, 1954, Dutton 1955; *The Novel Today,* Longmans, Green, 1955, revised edition, 1960; *Six Great Novelists: Defoe, Fielding, Scott, Dickens, Stevenson, Conrad,* Hamish Hamilton, 1955, Folcroft, 1969; *Threescore and Ten,* Morrow, 1959 (published in England as *All in a Lifetime,* M. Joseph, 1959).

George Eliot, Macmillan, 1964; *Tradition and Dream: The English and American Novel from the Twenties to Our Time,* Phoenix House, 1964, published as *The Modern Novel in Britain and the United States,* Dutton, 1964, published as *Tradition and Dream: A Critical Survey of British and American Fiction from the 1920s to the Present Day,* Penguin, 1965; (author of introduction) *The British Isles in Color,* Viking Press, 1965; *The Urgent West: The American Dream and Modern Man,* Dutton, 1969 (published in England as *The Urgent West: An Introduction to the Idea of the United States,* J. Baker, 1969).

(Contributor) Michael Slater, editor, *Dickens 1970: Centenary Essays,* Stein & Day, 1970; (compiler and author of introduction) *Transatlantic Crossing: American Visitors to Britain and British Visitors to America in the Nineteenth*

Century, Morrow, 1971. Contributor of articles to *New Statesman, Nation, Times Literary Supplement, Daily Telegraph, The Listener,* and *New York Times Book Review.*

* * *

ALLMENDINGER, David F(rederick), Jr. 1938-

PERSONAL: Born May 13, 1938, in Wooster, Ohio; son of David Frederick and Marjorie (Kidder) Allmendinger; married Susan Horsman, December 29, 1965; children: Carolyn Marjorie, Nicholas Eric. *Education:* University of Missouri, B.A., 1961; University of Wisconsin, M.A., 1962, Ph.D., 1968. *Home:* 33 White Clay Dr., Newark, Del. 19711. *Office:* Department of History, University of Delaware, Newark, Del. 19711.

CAREER: Reed College, Portland, Ore., assistant professor of history, 1967-69; Smith College, Northampton, Mass., assistant professor of history, 1969-72; University of Delaware, Newark, associate professor of history and director of American studies, 1974—. Visiting associate professor at University of Michigan, 1973-74. *Member:* American Historical Association, American Studies Association, Organization of American Historians.

WRITINGS: (Editor with wife, Susan Allmendinger) *The American People in the Industrial City,* Pendulum Press, 1973; (editor) *The American People in the Antebellum North,* Pendulum Press, 1973; *Paupers and Scholars: The Transformation of Student Life in Nineteenth-Century New England,* St. Martin's, 1975. Contributor to professional journals. Member of board of editors of *History of Education Quarterly,* 1972—.

WORK IN PROGRESS: Research on poverty in nineteenth-century America, and on the history of higher education for women.

BIOGRAPHICAL/CRITICAL SOURCES: History of Education Quarterly, fall, 1975.

* * *

ALLRED, G. Hugh 1932-

PERSONAL: Born May 22, 1932, in Hill Spring, Alberta, Canada; came to United States in 1948, naturalized citizen, 1956; son of Golden and Josephine (Leavitt) Allred; married Carolyn Crapo, June 27, 1951; children: Steven Hugh, Lynnette (Mrs. Keele Johnson), Sharlene, Gregory Hugh, Jennifer. *Education:* Yale University, student, 1951-52; Brigham Young University, B.A., 1957, M.A., 1960; University of Alberta, graduate study, summers, 1962-63; University of Oregon, Ed.D., 1966. *Politics:* Independent. *Religion:* Church of Jesus Christ of Latter-day Saints (Mormons). *Home address:* P.O. Box 184, Pleasant Grove, Utah 84062. *Office:* Department of Child Development and Family Relationships, Brigham Young University, Provo, Utah 84601.

CAREER: Licensed marriage and family counselor in Utah; Utah State Hospital, Provo, psychiatric aide, 1955-57; high school social studies teacher in Provo, Utah, 1957-60; high school guidance counselor in Lethbridge, Alberta, 1960-64; University of Oregon, Eugene, supervisor of secondary school student teachers, 1964-65; Portland Community Parent Teacher Education Center (family counseling center), Portland, Ore., co-director, 1965; University of Oregon, counseling intern, 1965-66; Eugene Community Parent Teacher Education Center, Eugene, Ore., co-director, 1965-66; Brigham Young University, Provo, Utah, as-

sistant professor of educational psychology, 1966-68, assistant professor, 1968-69, associate professor of child development and family relationships in marriage and family therapy, 1969—. Member of Mormon Tabernacle Choir, 1968—. Director and senior therapist for open forum family counseling programs in several Utah communities, 1968-72; member of examining board for licensing marriage and family counselors in Utah, 1973-76. *Military service:* U.S. Air Force, Chinese linguist, 1952-55; served in Japan and Korea.

MEMBER: American Association of Marriage and Family Counselors (clinical member and approved supervisor), National Council on Family Relationships, American Society of Adlerian Psychology, Utah Parent Teacher Association (life member), Utah Association of Marriage and Family Counselors (president, 1974-76), Phi Delta Kappa.

WRITINGS: Mission for Mother: Guiding the Child, Bookcraft, 1968; *The Challenge to Be One,* Brigham Young University Press, 1974; *On the Level with Self, Family, Society,* Brigham Young University Press, 1974; *How to Strengthen Your Marriage and Family,* Brigham Young University Press, in press. Contributor to counseling and education journals, and to church publications.

WORK IN PROGRESS: Developing interaction analysis instruments for counselors, husbands and wives, and parents and children.

SIDELIGHTS: Allred writes: "The major objectives in my writing have been to help relieve the pain and suffering of people in marriage and families and provide them with alternatives which will increase the possibilities for them to achieve serenity and happiness."

* * *

ALLVINE, Fred C. 1936-

PERSONAL: Born June 17, 1936; married; children: three. *Education:* University of Kansas, B.S., 1958; Harvard University, M.B.A., 1960; Indiana University, D.B.A., 1966. *Home:* 1499 Kingsdown Circle, Dunwoody, Ga. 30338. *Office:* College of Industrial Management, Georgia Institute of Technology, Atlanta, Ga. 30332.

CAREER: University of Kansas, Lawrence, instructor, beginning 1962; Northwestern University, Evanston, Ill., assistant professor beginning 1966; Georgia Institute of Technology, Atlanta, associate professor, 1972-75, professor of industrial management, 1975—. Production supervisor of Kroger (food store chain); owner and operator of retail business. Consultant to government and business. *Member:* American Marketing Association, Beta Gamma Sigma, Omicron Delta Kappa.

WRITINGS: (Contributor) *Minority Economic Development: A Revolution in the Seventies,* Holt, 1971; (editor) *Proceedings of the American Marketing Association: Fall Conference,* American Marketing Association, 1971; (co-author) *Competition Ltd.: The Marketing of Gasoline,* Indiana University Press, 1972; (editor) *Public Policy and Marketing,* American Marketing Association, 1973; (co-author) *Highway Robbery: An Analysis of the Gasoline Crisis,* Indiana University Press, 1974. Contributor to business and marketing journals, to popular magazines, including *Newsday, Business Week,* and *New Republic,* and to newspapers.

WORK IN PROGRESS: Experience in Marketing, a book of experimental readings; *A Faltering Economy,* presenting a non-traditional analysis of the cause of our current economic problems; *Marketing in Action,* an innovative marketing text designed to illustrate marketing theory and concepts through the large numbers of examples based upon case histories of company experiences.

* * *

ALPERT, Mark I(ra) 1942-

PERSONAL: Born November 6, 1942, in Duluth, Minn.; son of Isadore L. (a businessman) and Lillian (Steinberg) Alpert; married Judy Itzkovits, September 3, 1967; children: Nicole Deborah. *Education:* Massachusetts Institute of Technology, S.B., 1964; University of Southern California, M.B.A., 1965, M.S., 1967, D.B.A., 1968. *Politics:* Independent. *Religion:* Jewish. *Home:* 5956 Highland Hills Dr., Austin, Tex. 78731. *Office:* Department of Marketing Administration, University of Texas, B.E.B. 711, Austin, Tex. 78712.

CAREER: California State College, Long Beach, lecturer, 1967-68, assistant professor of marketing, 1968; University of Texas, Austin, assistant professor, 1968-72, associate professor of marketing, 1972—. Principal of Group Seven Associates, 1972—. *Member:* American Marketing Association, American Institute for Decision Sciences, American Psychological Association, Association for Consumer Research, Beta Gamma Sigma.

WRITINGS: (With Frederick D. Sturdivant and others) *Managerial Analysis in Marketing,* Scott, Foresman, 1970; *Pricing Decisions,* Scott, Foresman, 1971; (with Sturdivant and others) *Perspectives in Marketing Management,* Scott, Foresman, 1971. Contributor to professional journals.

WORK IN PROGRESS: Research for a marketing approach to public transportation planning; studying attitudes regarding voting behavior and communication theory.

SIDELIGHTS: Alpert told *CA:* "Much of my current research involves application of marketing techniques to non-traditional problems, such as the marketing of public transportation, and regionalization of emergency medical care. My contention is that these problems need significant consideration of the felt needs of the publics they are supposed to serve in order to more adequately meet society's needs."

* * *

ALTMANN, Alexander 1906-

PERSONAL: Born April 16, 1906, in Kassa, Hungary; became a British subject, 1946; son of Adolf (a rabbi) and Malvine (Weisz) Altmann; married Judith Frank, December 20, 1932; children: Fay Aviva (Mrs. Raphael A. Lunzer), Michael, Eve (Mrs. Yigal Yardeni). *Education:* University of Berlin, Dr.Phil., 1931; Rabbinical Seminary, Berlin, rabbi, 1931. *Home:* 126 Glen Ave., Newton Center, Mass. 02159. *Office:* Brandeis University, Waltham, Mass. 02159.

CAREER: Rabbi in the Jewish community in Berlin, Germany, 1931-38; Rabbinical Seminary, Berlin, professor of Jewish philosophy, 1932-38; communal rabbi in Manchester, England, 1938-59; Institute of Jewish Studies, Manchester, director, 1953-58; Brandeis University, Philip W. Lown Institute, Waltham, Mass., Philip W. Lown Professor of Jewish Philosophy, 1959-76, Philip W. Lown Professor Emeritus, 1976—. Honorary president, Institute of Jewish Studies, University College, London, 1959—. *Member:* American Academy of Arts and Sciences (fellow), American Academy of Jewish Research (fellow; vice-president). *Awards, honors:* M.A., University of Manches-

ter, 1943; D.H.L., Hebrew Union College-Jewish Institute of Religion, 1967; Th.D., University of Munich, 1972.

WRITINGS: Moses Mendelssohn's Fruehschriften zur Metaphysik, Mohr (Tuebingen), 1969; *Studies in Religious Philosophy and Mysticism,* Cornell University Press, 1969; *Moses Mendelssohn: A Biographical Study,* University of Alabama Press, 1973; *Rational and Mystical Theology in Judaism: A Group of Essays,* University of Alabama Press, 1976.

Editor; all published by Harvard University Press, except as noted: *Between East and West: Essays Dedicated to the Memory of Bela Horowitz,* East & West Library, 1958; *Biblical and Other Studies,* 1963; *Studies in Nineteenth-Century Jewish Intellectual History,* 1966; *Biblical Motifs: Origins and Transformations,* 1966; *Jewish Medieval and Renaissance Studies,* 1967.

Translator: (From the Arabic, author of introduction and notes, and abridger) Saadiah ben Joseph, *The Book of Doctrines and Beliefs,* East & West Library, 1946; (and co-author of commentary) *Isaac Israeli: A Neoplatonic Philosopher of the Early Tenth Century,* Oxford University Press, 1958.

General editor, Moses Mendelssohn, *Gesammelte Schriften: Jubilaeumsausgabe,* F. Fromman-G. Holzboog (Stuttgart), 1971—. Editor, *Journal of Jewish Studies,* 1954-59, and *Scripta Judaica,* 1957-65.

* * *

ALVAREZ, Walter C(lement) 1884-1974

PERSONAL: Born July 22, 1884, in San Francisco, Calif.; son of Luis Fernando (a government physician) and Clementina (Schuetze) Alvarez; married Harriet Skidmore Smyth, February 22, 1907; children: Gladys (Mrs. Raymond Archibald), Luis Walter, Robert Smyth, Bernice (Mrs. Bradley Brownson). *Education:* Cooper Medical College (now Stanford University School of Medicine), M.D., 1905; Harvard University, postdoctoral study, 1913. *Politics:* Republican. *Religion:* Congregational. *Home:* Whitehall Hotel, Chicago, Ill. 60611. *Office:* 700 North Michigan Avenue, Chicago, Ill. 60611.

CAREER: Diplomate of American Board of Internal Medicine and American Board of Gastroenterology. Cooper Medical College (now Stanford University School of Medicine), Stanford, Calif., assistant in clinical pathology, 1906-07; in private practice of medicine in Cananea, Mexico, 1907-1910; practicing internist in San Francisco, Calif., 1910-25; Stanford University, Stanford, Calif., assistant in medicine, 1911-12; University of California, San Francisco, assistant in research medicine, 1915-16, instructor, 1916-20, assistant professor, 1920-24, associate professor of medicine, 1924-26; Mayo Clinic, Rochester, Minn., associate in division of internal medicine, 1924-26, senior consultant, 1926-50, consultant emeritus, 1950-74; University of Minnesota, Mayo Foundation, Rochester, associate professor, 1926-34, professor of medicine, 1934-51, professor emeritus, 1951-74; University of Illinois Medical School, Chicago, professorial lecturer in medicine, 1951-52, lecturer emeritus, 1952-74. First Caldwell Lecturer of the American Roentgen Society; trustee, Josiah Macy, Jr. Foundation, 1932-34.

MEMBER: American Medical Association, American Association for the Advancement of Science, American Medical Society (fellow), American College of Physicians (M.S. fellow), Association of American Physicians, American Physiological Society, American Society for Clinical Investigation, Society for Experimental Biology and Medicine, American Gastroenterology Association (president, 1928), American Society of Pharmacology Experimental Therapeutics, American Anthropological Association, American Association of Physical Anthropologists (founding member), Royal Society of Medicine, National Academy of Medicine in Spain, Gastroenterologic Society of Paris, Sigma Xi, Alpha Kappa Kappa, Alpha Omega Alpha, University Club (Chicago). *Awards, honors:* D.Sc. from Hahnemann Medical College of Philadelphia, 1939; Friedenwald Medal from American Gastroenterological Association, 1951; honor award from American Medical Writers' Association, 1952.

WRITINGS: The Mechanics of the Digestive Tract, P. B. Hoeber, 1922, 4th edition published as *An Introduction to Gastro-enterology,* 1948; *Nervous Indigestion,* P. B. Hoeber, 1930; *Nervousness, Indigestion and Pain,* P. B. Hoeber, 1943; *How to Live With Your Nerves,* Wilcox & Follett, 1950; *How to Live With Your Heart Condition,* Wilcox & Follett, 1951; *How to Live With Your Ulcer,* Wilcox & Follett, 1951; *How to Live With Your Allergy,* Wilcox & Follett, 1951; *How to Live With Your Arthritis,* Wilcox & Follett, 1951; *How to Care for the Health of Executives,* Wilcox & Follett, 1951; *How to Live With Your Blood Pressure,* Wilcox & Follett, 1951; *The Neuroses: Diagnosis and Management of Functional Disorders,* Saunders, 1951; *How to Live With Your Migraine (Sick) Headaches,* Wilcox & Follett, 1952; *What a Salesman Should Know About His Health,* Dartnell, 1953; *Danger Signals: Warnings of Serious Disease,* Wilcox & Follett, 1953, 2nd revised edition, Fawcett, 1966.

How to Help Your Doctor Help You, Dell, 1955; (with others) *Medical Writing,* MD Publications, 1956; *Practical Leads to Puzzling Diagnoses: Neuroses That Run Through Families,* Lippincott, 1958; *Live at Peace With Your Nerves,* Prentice-Hall, 1958; *Minds That Came Back,* Lippincott, 1961; *Incurable Physician: An Autobiography,* Prentice-Hall, 1963; *Little Strokes,* Lippincott, 1966; (with Sue March) *Homosexuality and Other Forms of Sexual Deviance* [versus] *Gay Liberation,* the latter by March, Pyramid, 1974; (editor and author of introduction) Ruth C. Adam, *Living With Mysterious Epilepsy,* Exposition Press, 1974; *Nerves in Collision,* Pyramid, 1974.

SIDELIGHTS: During his long career as a physician, Alvarez's accomplishments include being the first physician to perform electrogastrograms on humans, and establishing normal standards of blood pressure. He was also a pioneer in the study of psychosomatic medicine, neuroses, migraines, what he termed "little strokes," and senory epilepsy. *Avocational interests:* Anthropology, mountain climbing, photography, reading, collecting old medical books, and books by physically and mentally handicapped writers.

BIOGRAPHICAL/CRITICAL SOURCES: Newsweek, December 25, 1950; *Harper's,* October, 1955; *Incurable Physician: An Autobiography,* Prentice-Hall, 1963; *Today's Health,* May, 1969.*

(Died, 1974)

* * *

ALVAREZ del VAYO, Julio 1891-1975

February 9, 1891—May 2, 1975; Spanish foreign minister, political activist, ambassador, editor, journalist, and author of autobiography and books on politics. Obituaries: *New York Times,* May 6, 1975.

* * *

AMADON, Dean 1912-

PERSONAL: Born June 6, 1912, in Milwaukee, Wis.; son of Arthur and Mary (Evenson) Amadon; married Octavia Gardella, 1940; children: Susan, Emily. *Education:* Hobart College, B.S., 1934; Cornell University, Ph.D., 1947. *Home:* 25 Kenwood Rd., Tenafly, N.J. 07670. *Office:* American Museum of Natural History, Central Park West at 79th St., New York, N.Y. 10024.

CAREER: Employed with Connecticut Board of Fisheries and Game, 1936-37; American Museum of Natural History, New York, N.Y., 1937—, now chairman of staff and Lamont curator of ornithology. President, board of directors of Slabsides, West Park, N.Y. *Military service:* U.S. Army, 1943-46. *Member:* American Association for the Advancement of Science (fellow), American Ornithologists Society (president), Linnaean Society (president). *Awards, honors:* Sc.D., Hobart College, 1960.

WRITINGS: (With Robert Cushman Murphy) *Land Birds of America,* photographs by Eliot Porter and others, McGraw, 1953; (with Alexander Seidel) *A Child's Book of Wild Birds,* Maxton Publishers, 1955; *Birds Around the World: A Geographical Look at Evolution and Birds,* Natural History Press for American Museum of Natural History, 1966; (author of introduction) John James Audubon, *The Birds of America,* seven volumes, Dover, 1967; (with Leslie Brown) *Eagles, Hawks, and Falcons of the World,* two volumes, McGraw, 1968; (with John E. du Pont) *Notes on Philippine Birds,* Delaware Museum of Natural History, 1970—. Author of numerous papers published by the American Museum of Natural History.*

* * *

AMANN, Peter H. 1927-

PERSONAL: Born May 31, 1927, in Vienna, Austria; son of Paul (a writer and teacher) and Dora (Iranyi) Amann; married Enne Niemi; children: Paula, Sandra, David. *Education:* Oberlin College, B.A., 1947; University of Chicago, M.A. and Ph.D. *Office:* Department of History, University of Michigan–Dearborn, Dearborn, Mich. 48128.

CAREER: Bowdoin College, Brunswick, Me., instructor in history, 1956-59; Oakland University, Rochester, Mich., 1959-65, began as assistant professor, became associate professor of history; State University of New York at Binghamton, associate professor of history, 1965-68; University of Michigan, Dearborn, professor of history, 1968—. *Member:* American Historical Association, American Association of University Professors.

WRITINGS: (Editor and author of introduction) *The Eighteenth Century Revolution: French or Western?,* Heath, 1963; (editor) *Western Society: Institutions and Ideals,* Volume III: *The Modern World, 1650-1850,* McGraw, 1967; *Revolution and Mass Democracy: The Paris Club Movement in 1848,* Princeton University Press, 1975. Contributor to professional journals. Member of editorial board of *French Historical Studies,* 1972-75.

WORK IN PROGRESS: Research on French social history and on the Black Legion.

* * *

AMARY, Issam B(ahjat) 1942-

PERSONAL: Born July 11, 1942, in Jerusalem, Israel;

U.S. citizen; son of Bahjat K. (a merchant) and Essaf (Khaimi) Amary; married Wilma Blinn (a teacher), August 20, 1967; children: Jason Issam, Jarred Jamal. *Education:* Missouri Valley College, B.S., 1968; University of Missouri, Rolla, certificate in hospital management, 1973; Central Missouri State University, M.S., 1974. *Religion:* Christian. *Home:* 711 Plaza Dr., Marshall, Mo. 65340. *Office:* Marshall State School, East Slater, Marshall, Mo. 65340.

CAREER: Marshall State School and Hospital, Marshall, Mo., activity therapist, 1969-71, recreation therapist and coordinator of activity therapy staff, 1971—. Registered master therapeutic recreation specialist; Missouri Special Olympics (for the mentally retarded), assistant state director, 1969-70, executive state director, 1970-72, chairman of board of directors, 1970-73. *Member:* National Recreation and Park Association, National Therapeutic Recreation Society, International Club (Marshall, Mo.), Optimist Club (member of board of directors, 1971-72), Masonic Lodge, Community Theatre, Valley Players, Alpha Psi Omega, Alpha Phi Omega.

WRITINGS: Creative Recreation for the Mentally Retarded, C. C Thomas, 1975; *A Taste of Lebanon: An Exotic Gourmet Experience in Lebanese Foods,* Wallsworth, 1975.

WORK IN PROGRESS: Arts and Crafts: A Therapeutic Treatment Program for the Mentally Retarded; two children's books, *Stories and Legends of Ancient Egypt* and *Ahmed and His Camel.*

SIDELIGHTS: Amary writes: "Through close association with the Special Olympics program I was convinced of the need to provide the mentally retarded with constructive activities that would contribute toward their positive development. I was also convinced that the mentally retarded need guidance and understanding so that they might meet the challenge of life." *Avocational interests:* Travel (United States, Middle East, southern Europe, North Africa), reading, fishing, gourmet cooking.

* * *

AMAYA, Mario (Anthony) 1933-

PERSONAL: Born October 6, 1933, New York, N.Y.; son of Mario A. and Maria Sophia (Mezzatesta) Garofalo. *Education:* Brooklyn College (now of the City University of New York), B.A., 1954; London University Extension at the National Gallery, graduate studies, 1960-62. *Home:* 50 Central Park West, New York, N.Y.

CAREER: Self-employed as author, editor, art critic, and exhibition organizer, London, England, 1956-68; *About the House* (Royal Opera House magazine), London, founding editor, 1962-68; *Art and Artists Magazine,* founding editor, 1966-69; Art Gallery of Ontario, Toronto, Ontario, chief curator, 1969-72; Toronto Dominion Bank, Toronto, responsible for art purchase program, 1970-73; University of Buffalo, Buffalo, N.Y., visiting professor, 1971; New York Cultural Center, New York, N.Y., director, 1972—. *Awards, honors:* William Copley Foundation Award, 1969.

WRITINGS: Pop as Art, Viking, 1965; *Art Nouveau,* Dutton, 1966; *Tiffany Glass,* Walker, 1967.

Catalogs: (Author of introduction) *Pre-Raphaelites: Art Nouveau,* Maas Gallery, London, 1964; *The Obsessive Image, 1960-68: The Opening Exhibition of the Institute of Contemporary Arts at Carlton House Terrace, 10 April–29 May, 1968,* Institute of Contemporary Arts, 1968; (editor) *A Tribute to Samuel J. Zacks from the Sam and Ayala Zacks Collection,* Art Gallery of Toronto, 1971; *John Koch,* New York Cultural Center, 1973.

Member of editorial board, *Art in America,* 1969-72.

WORK IN PROGRESS: Organizing exhibitions, "Bougereau," and "Soft as Art," at New York Cultural Center, and on Vuillard, and French seventeenth and eighteenth century drawings in North American collections, both in Toronto.

* * *

AMERY, (Harold) Julian 1919-

PERSONAL: Born March 27, 1919, in London, England; son of Leopold and Florence Hamer (Greenwood) Amery; married Catherine Macmillan, January 26, 1950; children: one son, three daughters. *Education:* Attended Balliol College, Oxford. *Home:* 112 Eaton Square, London S.W.1, England; and Forest Farm House, Chelwood Gate, Sussex, England. *Agent:* Graham Watson, Curtis Brown Ltd., 1 Craven Hill, London W.2, England.

CAREER: War correspondent in Spanish Civil War for *Daily Telegraph, Daily Express,* and *News Chronicle,* 1938-39; British Legation in Belgrade, attache, also undertaking special missions in Bulgaria, Turkey, Rumania, and the Middle East, 1939-40; liaison officer to Albanian resistance movement, 1944; member of the staff of General Carton de Wiart, Winston Churchill's personal representative with Generalissimo Chiang Kai-shek, 1945; Conservative Party candidate for Preston, Lancashire, 1945; Member of Parliament for Preston North, 1950-66, for Brighton Pavilion, 1969—; Consultative Assembly of the Council of Europe, delegate, 1950-53, 1956; Round Table Conference on Malta, member, 1955; War Office, Parliamentary Under-Secretary of State and Financial Secretary, 1957-58; Colonial Office, Parliamentary Under-Secretary of State, 1958-60; Secretary of State for Air, 1960-62; Minister of Aviation, 1962-64; Minister of Public Building and Works, 1970; Minister for Housing and Construction, 1970-72; Minister of State at Foreign and Commonwealth office, 1972-74. *Military service:* Royal Air Force, sergeant, 1940-41. British Army, active service in Egypt, Palestine, and the Adriatic, 1941-42. *Member:* White's Club, Beefsteak Club, Carlton Club, Buck's Club.

WRITINGS: Sons of the Eagle: A Study in Guerilla War, Macmillan, 1948; *The Life of Joseph Chamberlain, 1901-1903: At the Height of His Power,* St. Martin's Press, 1951; (with others) *What Europe Thinks of America,* John Day, 1953; *Joseph Chamberlain and the Tariff Reform Campaign,* two volumes, Macmillan, 1969; *Approach March* (autobiography), Hutchinson, 1970. Author of pamphlet, *The British Commonwealth and Western Europe,* Longmans, Green, 1952. Contributor to *National Review, Nineteenth Century,* and others.

SIDELIGHTS: A member of a well-known political family, Julian Amery organized the first military mission to the Yugoslav guerilas in World War II, and was dropped by parachute into Albania as a member of the military mission supporting Albanian guerillas against the Axis forces.

Mr. Amery is the son-in-law of former Prime Minister Harold Macmillan. He has travelled extensively in the United States and Canada, as well as in Europe, Africa, and the Middle East. He has also frequently commented on political affairs in the British press and on the British Broadcasting Corporation network.

AVOCATIONAL INTERESTS: Travel, skiing, mountaineering.

AMON, Aline 1928-

PERSONAL: Surname rhymes with "salmon"; born October 15, 1928, in Paris, France; daughter of American citizens, Will Rice (an architect) and Aline (Halstead) Amon; married Laurance Villers Goodrich (an attorney), October 31, 1953; children: Nielsen Halstead, Lauren Aline. *Education:* Wellesley College, B.A., 1950; Art Student's League of New York, further study, 1952, 1953. *Politics:* Democratic. *Religion:* None. *Home:* 295 Henry St., Brooklyn, N.Y. 11201. *Agent:* Curtis Brown Ltd., 60 West 56th St., New York, N.Y. 10022.

CAREER: Appleton-Century-Crofts, Inc., New York, N.Y., secretary in college text department, 1950-51; U.S. Air Force, Paris, France, executive secretary in military liaison office, 1951-52. Director of playground safety program, Brooklyn Heights, 1963-64. *Awards, honors:* New York Public Library listed *Talking Hands* as one of the ten best Christmas gift books, 1968.

WRITINGS—Self-illustrated: Talking Hands: How to Use Indian Sign Language, Doubleday, 1968; *Reading, Writing, Chattering Chimps* (Junior Literary Guild selection), Atheneum, 1975.

WORK IN PROGRESS: Natural science research, particularly in field of animal behavior.

SIDELIGHTS: Aline Amon writes: "My first book was prompted by my son's interest in the Indian sign language. It had been discussed briefly in one of his classes, but he was unable to find any additional material on the subject in our local library. After the two years needed to research, write and illustrate *Talking Hands,* I temporarily retired to become reacquainted with my family and to supervise rather extensive renovations to our antique house [pre-Civil War].

"My new book is again the result of my children's interests. The one thing that most fascinated them among the many articles in natural history magazines that we sometimes discussed at dinner was the thought of 'talking' Chimpanzees. I was very fortunate in having the help and cooperation of the scientists involved in the experiments in human-animal communication. They sent not only their scientific papers and photographs for the book, but also were remarkably patient in answering all my queries and in compiling mini-dictionaries of the signs, symbols and computer designs used with the apes—and also used in my illustrations."

*   *   *

ANDERSON, H. Dewey 1897-1975

January 14, 1897—August 4, 1975; American economist, legislator, civil servant, and author of books on business and health. Obituaries: *Washington Post,* August 10, 1975.

*   *   *

ANDERSON, Howard Peter 1932-

PERSONAL: Born December 10, 1932, in Duluth, Minn.; married, 1959; children: three. *Education:* University of Minnesota, B.B.A., 1955, M.A., 1960, Ph.D., 1964. *Office:* Department of English, Michigan State University, East Lansing, Mich. 48823.

CAREER: Indiana University, Bloomington, lecturer, 1963-64, assistant professor of English, 1964-68; Michigan State University, East Lansing, associate professor, 1968-71, professor of English, 1971—. *Military service:* U.S. Army, 1955-57. *Member:* Modern Language Association of America, American Society for Eighteenth Century Studies, American Association of University Professors.

WRITINGS: (Editor with Philip B. Daghlian and Irvin Ehrenpreis) *The Familiar Letter in the Eighteenth Century,* University of Kansas Press, 1966; (editor and author of introduction with John S. Shea) *Studies in Criticism and Aesthetics, 1660-1800: Essays in Honor of Samuel Holt Monk,* University of Minnesota Press, 1967; (editor) Matthew Gregory Lewis, *The Monk,* Oxford University Press, 1973. Contributor of articles to *Philosophical Quarterly* and *PMLA.**

*   *   *

ANDERSON, P(aul) Howard 1947-

PERSONAL: Born June 6, 1947, in Leicester, England; son of William Howard (a factory transport foreman) and Louise (a hosiery machinist; maiden name, Darlison) Anderson. *Education:* University of Durham, B.Sc., 1968; University of Wales, Aberystwyth, diploma in education, 1970. *Home:* 69, Highbury Rd., Leicester, England.

CAREER: Kineton High School, near Stratford-upon-Avon, Warwickshire, England, teacher of geography and geology, 1970—.

WRITINGS: Forgotten Railways: The East Midlands, David & Charles, 1973.

WORK IN PROGRESS: A railway book concerning selected journeys in the British Isles, including landscapes, places, and characters.

AVOCATIONAL INTERESTS: Travelling to more obscure parts of Britain; fell-walking and mountain-walking in Scotland, the Lake District, and the Pennines; "taking in the atmosphere of a place."

*   *   *

ANDERSON, William Scovil 1927-

PERSONAL: Born September 16, 1927, in Brookline, Mass.; son of Edgar W. (an Episcopal clergyman) and Katrina (a teacher and social worker; maiden name, Brewster) Anderson; married Lorna C. Bassette (a teacher); children: Judith, Blythe, Heather, Meredith, Keith. *Education:* Yale University, B.A., 1950, Ph.D., 1954; studied at Cambridge University, 1952. *Home:* 1424 Lincoln Street, Berkeley, California 94702.

CAREER: Yale University, New Haven, Conn., instructor in classics, 1955-60; University of California, Berkeley, assistant professor, 1960-63, associate professor, 1963-66, professor of classics and comparative literature, 1966—. *Member:* American Philological Association (first vice-president, 1976), Society for Religion in Higher Education, Vergilian Society (trustee, 1967-70).

WRITINGS: Pompey, His Friends, and the Literature of the 1st Century B.C., University of California Press, 1963; *Anger in Juvenal and Seneca,* University of California Press, 1964; *The Art of the Aeneid,* Prentice-Hall, 1966; (editor and author of introduction and commentary) *Ovid's Metamorphoses,* Books 6-10, University of Oklahoma Press, 1972. Contributor to journals in his field. Member of editorial board, *Classical Journal,* 1963-67, *Vergilius,* 1965—, and *Satire Newsletter,* 1965—.

WORK IN PROGRESS: Work on the Teubner text, a critical edition of Ovid's *Metamorphoses,* libri XV.

ANDERTON, Joanne (Marie) Gast 1930-
(Johana Gast Anderton)

PERSONAL: Born March 16, 1930, in Kansas City, Kan.; daughter of Joseph R. and Nellie Catherine Margaret (Blankenship) Gast; married Harold Allison Anderton (a production mechanic), December 18, 1948; children: Joseph Richard II, Rebekka Suzanne. *Education:* Attended Maple Woods College, Kansas City, 1969-73. *Office:* 2016 Clay, North Kansas City, Mo. 64116.

CAREER: Southwestern Bell Telephone Co., Kansas City, Mo., member of directory production layout staff, 1948-49; Rival Manufacturing Co., Kansas City, Mo., credit secretary, 1949-50; Royal-Liverpool Group Insurance, Kansas City, Mo., claims secretary, 1950-51; Ford Motor Co., Claycomo, Mo., member of plant layout staff, 1951-53; Lockheed Aircraft Corp., Kansas City, Kan., secretary, 1954-56; Trans World Airlines, Kansas City, Mo., secretary, 1961; writer, 1962—. Publicity writer for Girl Scouts. Teacher of oil painting and craft classes; craft demonstrator on television. Coordinator and trainer for church nurseries. *Member:* National League of American Pen Women, United Federation of Doll Clubs.

WRITINGS—All under name Johana Gast Anderton: *The Glass Rainbow: The Story of Depression Glass*, Trojan Press, 1969; *Twentieth Century Dolls: From Bisque to Vinyl*, Trojan Press, 1971, revised edition, Athena Publishing, 1974; *Sewing for Twentieth Century Dolls*, Trojan Press, 1970; *More Twentieth Century Dolls*, Athena Publishing, 1974; *Johana's Dolls* (collection of articles and columns), Athena Publishing, 1975.

Editor: Sandra Stout, *The Complete Book of McKee Glass*, Trojan Press, 1972; M. Kelley Ellenberg, *Effanbee: The Dolls with the Golden Hearts*, Trojan Press, 1973; Helen Bullard, *The American Doll Artist*, Volume II, Athena Publishing, 1975; Albina Bailey, *Dressing Dolls in Nineteenth Century Fashion*, Athena Publishing, 1975; Bailey, *First Ladies and Their Rooms*, Athena Publishing, 1976; R. Lane Herron, *Much Ado about Dolls*, Athena Publishing, 1976.

Author of monthly column, "Johana's Dolls," in *Mid-America Reporter*, 1971-73, *Antique Reporter*, 1973-74, and *Doll Castle News*, 1974—. Contributor of articles to *Collectors News, Western Collector*, and other journals.

WORK IN PROGRESS: Volume II of *Sewing for Twentieth Century Dolls*, completion expected in 1979; *The Rag Doll Book*, 1976; *A Doll Atlas of the World*, 1977; *Twentieth Century Toys*, 1977; *Twentieth Century Paper Dolls*, 1978.

*   *   *

ANDRESKI, Stanislav Leonard 1919-

PERSONAL: Name originally Stanislaw Andrzejewski; born May 8, 1919, in Czestochowa, Poland; naturalized British citizen; son of Teofil and Zofia (Karaszewicz) Andrzejewski; married Norma Keith, 1941; married Iris Gillespie, 1959; children: Wanda, Adam, Lucas, Sophia. *Education:* Attended University of Poznan, 1938-39; University of London, B.S., 1943, M.S., 1947, Ph.D., 1952; graduate study at London School of Economics and Political Science, 1943-44. *Office:* Department of Sociology, University of Reading, Whiteknights Park, Reading, England.

CAREER: Rhodes University, Grahamstown, South Africa, lecturer, 1947-53; University of Manchester, Man-

chester, England, senior research fellow, 1954-56; Acton Technical College, London, England, lecturer, 1956-57; Brunel College of Technology, London, lecturer, 1957-60; School of Social Sciences, Santiago, Chile, professor of sociology, 1960-61; Nigerian Institute of Social and Economic Research, Ibadan, senior research fellow, 1962-64; University of Reading, Reading, England, professor and head of sociology department, 1964—. Visiting professor, City College of the City University of New York, 1968-69. *Military service:* Served with the Polish Army in World War II.

WRITINGS: Military Organization and Society, Routledge & Kegan Paul, 1954, 2nd edition, 1968, University of California Press, 1969; *Elements of Comparative Sociology*, Weidenfeld & Nicolson, 1964, published as *The Uses of Comparative Sociology*, University of California Press, 1965; *Parasitism and Subversion: The Case of Latin America*, Random House, 1966; *The African Predicament: A Study in the Pathology of Modernisation*, M. Joseph, 1968, Atherton, 1969; *Social Sciences as Sorcery*, Deutsch, 1972, St. Martin's, 1973; *The Prospects for Revolution in the U.S.A.*, Harper, 1972; *Cultural Pollution*, Deutsch, in press.

Editor: *Herbert Spencer: Principles of Sociology*, Macmillan, 1968, St. Martin's, 1969; (under name Stanislaw L. Andrzejewski) *Uwarstwienie a rozwoj spoleczny: Wybor pism* (title means "Class Structure and Social Development"), Szkola Nauk Politycznych i Spolecznych (London), 1964; *Herbert Spencer: Structure, Function, and Evolution*, M. Joseph, 1971, Barnes & Noble, 1975; *The Essential Comte*, translated by Margaret Clarke, Barnes & Noble, 1974; *Reflections on Inequality*, Croom Helm, 1975; *Max Weber on Capitalism and Bureaucracy*, Allen & Unwin, in press.

Contributor: *Man in Society*, Macdonald & Co., 1964; J. D. Carthy and F. J. Ebling, editors, *The Natural History of Aggression*, Academic Press, 1965; S. Woolf, editor, *European Fascism*, Random House, 1968; S. Woolf, editor, *The Nature of Fascism*, Random House, 1969; R. S. Eisenstadt, editor, *Religion and Capitalism*, Basic Books, 1970; R. Serge Denisoff and others, editors, *Theories and Paradigms in Contemporary Sociology*, F. E. Peacock, 1974.

*   *   *

ANDREWS, (Earl) Frank 1937-

PERSONAL: Born October 31, 1937, in Millville, N.J. *Education:* Attended school in Millville through sixth grade. *Home:* 110 Columbia Ave., Palisades Park, N.J. 07650. *Agent:* Jane Rotrosen, 202 East 48th St., New York, N.Y. 10017. *Office:* Pyramid Publications, 919 3rd St., New York, N.Y. 10022.

CAREER: Pyramid Publications, New York, N.Y., editor, 1975—.

WRITINGS: (Editor with Albert Dickens, and contributor) *Voices from the Big House* (prose anthology), privately printed, 1971, Harlo, 1971; (editor with Dickens, and contributor) *Over the Wall* (prose anthology), Pyramid Publications, 1974; (editor and contributor) *Prose and Cons* (anthology), Pyramid Publications, 1976.

SIDELIGHTS: First jailed at the age of nine for breaking into a candy story, Andrews has spent more than twenty-three of his thirty-seven years behind bars. Until 1975 he had served thirteen years of a fifty-five to sixty-seven year sentence at Rahway State Prison for a series of armed robberies and an escape attempt in which he wounded a sheriff's deputy.

The New Jersey State Parole Board was impressed by his dedication to writing which began before 1967. After 1971 he became a leader in a literary circle behind prison walls. His book caught the attention of the associate publisher at Pyramid, where he was taken on as an editor upon parole. Andrews reports that "the parole board asked me if I might be tempted to go back to crime. I told them I never made more than a hundred bucks in any job I ever pulled; now I can double that by sitting down at a typewriter for a few hours."

BIOGRAPHICAL/CRITICAL SOURCES: New York Times, August 24, 1972; *People,* June 9, 1975; *Publishers Weekly,* June 26, 1975.

* * *

ANGUS, Sylvia 1921-

PERSONAL: Born September 26, 1921, in New York, N.Y.; daughter of Louis (a dentist) and Toni (Rosenberg) Levitt; married Douglas Ross Angus (a professor), June 6, 1941; children: Jameson (daughter), Christopher. *Education:* Attended Cornell University, 1938-40, and George Washington University, 1940-41; St. Lawrence University, B.A., 1952, M.A., 1955. *Politics:* Democrat. *Residence:* Canton, N.Y. *Office:* Department of English, State University of New York at Potsdam, Potsdam, N.Y. 13676.

CAREER: State University of New York at Canton, instructor and director of public relations, 1956-63; St. Lawrence University, Canton, N.Y., instructor, 1960-61; University of Istanbul, Istanbul, Turkey, lecturer in American literature, 1963-64; State University of New York at Potsdam, assistant professor, 1968-73, associate professor of English, 1973—. Canton League of Women Voters, director, 1948-60, president, 1961; president of Grasse River Players (community theater), 1975. *Member:* American Association of University Professors.

WRITINGS: (Editor with husband, Douglas Angus) *Contemporary American Short Stories,* Fawcett, 1967; (editor with D. Angus) *Great Modern European Short Stories,* Fawcett, 1967; *Death of a Hittite* (novel), Macmillan, 1969; (editor with D. Angus) *Love Is the Theme,* Fawcett, 1970; *Arson and Old Lace* (novel), World Publishing, 1972; (editor) *The Trouble Is: Stories of Social Dilemma,* Dickenson, 1973. Contributor of thirty-five articles and short stories to magazines and journals, including *Mademoiselle* and *Saturday Review.*

WORK IN PROGRESS: A suspense novel, *Dead to Rites.*

AVOCATIONAL INTERESTS: Travel, acting, directing.

* * *

ANNAN, Noel Gilroy 1916-

PERSONAL: Born December 25, 1916, in London, England; son of James Gilroy and Fannie (Quinn) Annan; married Gabriele Ullstein, 1950; children: two daughters. *Education:* Kings College, Cambridge, B.A., 1938, M.A. *Home:* 10 Hanover Terrace, Regent's Park, London NW1 4RJ, England. *Office:* University College, Gower Street, London WC1E 6BT, England.

CAREER: Cambridge University, Kings College, Cambridge, England, fellow, 1946, assistant tutor, 1947, lecturer

in politics, 1948-66, provost, 1956-66; University of London, University College, London, England, provost, 1966—. Governor of Stowe School, 1945-66, and of Queen Mary College, London, 1956-60; senior fellow of Eton College, 1956-66; member of Arts Committee of Gulbenkian Foundation, 1957-64; trustee, Churchill College, 1958; chairman, Departmental Committee on the Teaching of Russian in Schools, 1960; chairman, Academic Planning Board, University of East Anglia, 1960, and University of Essex, 1962; director, Royal Opera House, Covent Garden, 1963; fellow of Berkeley College, Yale, 1963; trustee of British Museum, 1963—; member of Academic Advisory Committee of Brunel College, 1964, and Committee on Social Studies, 1964—; Oxford University, Romanes lecturer, 1965; member of Public Schools Commission, 1966-69; chairman, Education Committee, 1971—. *Military Service:* 1940-46; served in British War Office, Staff College, Camberley, and War Cabinet Offices; on Joint Intelligence Staff, and Political Division of British Control Commission.

MEMBER: Royal Historical Society (fellow). *Awards, honors:* Order of the British Empire, 1946; Le Bas Prize, 1948, for essay; James Tait Black Memorial Prize, 1951, for *Leslie Stephen: His Thought and Character in Relation to His Time;* commander, Royal Order of King George I of the Hellenes (Greece), 1962; created Life Peer, 1965; honorary fellow, University College, London, 1968; Diamond Jubilee Medal, Institute of Linguists, 1971; D.Litt., York University; D.Univ., University of Essex.

WRITINGS: Leslie Stephen: His Thought and Character in Relation to His Time, MacGibbon & Kee, 1951, Harvard University Press, 1952; (contributor) J. H. Plumb, editor, *Studies in Social History,* Longmans, Green, 1955; *The Curious Strength of Positivism in English Political Thought,* Oxford University Press, 1959; *Roxburgh of Stowe: The Life of J. F. Roxburgh and His Influence in the Public Schools,* Longmans, 1965, published as *The Headmaster: Roxburgh of Stowe and His Influence in English Education,* Schocken Books, 1966; *The Disintegration of an Old Culture* (Romanes lecture), Clarendon Press, 1966; *What is a University for Anyway* (F. B. Watts Memorial Lecture), University of Toronto, 1971.

* * *

ANSLINGER, Harry Jacob 1892-1975

May 20, 1892—November 14, 1975; American government official, foreign consul, head of narcotics bureau, and author of books in his field. Obituaries: *New York Times,* November 18, 1975. (*CAP*-1; earlier sketch in *CA*-11/12)

* * *

ANTHONY, J(oseph) Garner 1899-

PERSONAL: Born December 19, 1899, in Philadelphia, Pa.; son of Charles Howard and Rachael Edith (Humphreys) Anthony; married Dorothy McClaren, June 29, 1926; children: Patricia Anthony Moses, Garner A. *Education:* Swarthmore College, A.B., 1923; Harvard University, LL.B., 1926. *Politics:* Democrat. *Religion:* Episcopalian. *Home:* 3251 Pacific Heights Rd., Honolulu, Hawaii 96813. *Office address:* Anthony, Hoddick, Reinwald & O'Connor, P.O. Box 3199, Honolulu, Hawaii 96801.

CAREER: Admitted to Hawaii State Bar, 1926, and the U.S. Supreme Court Bar, 1936; Attorney General of Hawaii, 1942-43; in private practice, 1943—. Queen's Medical Center (formerly Queen's Hospital), president, 1945-49, vice-president, 1949-75; delegate to Hawaii State Convention, 1950; regent at University of Hawaii, 1951-58. Member of board of directors of Victoria Ward Ltd. and Olokele Sugar Co. Ltd. *Military service:* Served in U.S. Army during World War I. *Member:* American Bar Association (member of board of governors, 1961-64), American Bar Foundation, American College of Trial Lawyers, Hawaii Bar Association (president, 1937-39), Pacific Club, Oahu Country Club. *Awards, honors:* LL.D., University of Hawaii, 1946.

WRITINGS: Hawaii Under Army Rule, Stanford University Press, 1955, new edition, University Press of Hawaii, 1975. Contributor to law journals.

* * *

APOLINAR, Danny 1934-

PERSONAL: Born March 15, 1934, in Brooklyn, N.Y.; son of Archie and Dorothy (Beckhardt) Apolinar. *Education:* Attended Pratt Institute, 1954. *Home:* 888 Eighth Ave., New York, N.Y., 10023. *Office:* c/o Louis P. Randall, 1501 Broadway, New York, N.Y. 10026.

CAREER: Commercial artist and designer, 1952; pianist, vocalist, dancer, 1959—; composer, author, lyricist, and recording artist. *Military service:* U.S. Army, 1957-59. *Member:* American Federation of Musicians, American Federation of Television and Radio Artists, Actors Equity, American Society of Composers, Authors, and Publishers. *Awards, honors:* Drama Critics Circle award, Outer Circle award, A.S.C.A.P. Pacesetter award, all 1968, for "Your Own Thing."

WRITINGS—Music and lyrics: (With Hal Hester) "Your Own Thing" (book by Donald Driver; produced in New York, 1968), published as *Your Own Thing and Twelfth Night: The Smash-Hit Rock-Musical Together with the Renowned Shakespearean Comedy on Which It Is Based,* Dell, 1970.*

* * *

ARANGO, Jorge Sanin 1916-

PERSONAL: Born November 29, 1916, in Bogota, Colombia; son of Fernando and Maria (Sanin) Arango; married Elizabeth Leighton, 1944; married Judith Brooks Wolpert, December 14, 1951; children: (first marriage) Pedro; (second marriage) Richard, Virginia. *Education:* Attended Universidad Catolica de Chile, 1935-42, and Harvard University, 1942-43. *Home:* 3920 Wood Ave., Miami, Fla. 33133. *Office:* 3141 Commodore Plaza, Miami, Fla. 33133.

CAREER: Arango & Murtra (architects), Bogota, Colombia, head of firm, 1946-59; now practicing architect in Miami, Fla. National University, Bogota, professor of architecture and urban design, 1945-47. Director of public buildings for the Colombian government, 1948-49. Visiting lecturer, University of California, Berkeley, 1956, 1958. *Member:* Colombian Society of Architects (president, 1946-51), Colegio Engineers and Architects of Colombia (president, 1955), American Institute of Architects. *Awards, honors:* Excellence in design awards from Miami and Florida chapters of American Institute of Architects, 1967; design selected by *Architectural Record* as one of best-designed residences in the United States, 1970.

WRITINGS: The Urbanization of the Earth, Beacon Press, 1970. Also author, with C. Martinez, of *Architecture in Colombia,* 1951.

SIDELIGHTS: In 1948, Arango was co-author of the basic plan for the development of Bogota.*

ARBUCKLE, Robert D(ean) 1940-

PERSONAL: Born January 5, 1940, in New Kensington, Pa.; son of Roy A. (with Alcoa Aluminum) and Connie (Santa Maria) Arbuckle; married Lorraine Donati (an elementary school teacher), August 8, 1964; children: Lisa, Robbie. *Education:* Clarion State College, B.S.Ed., 1964; Pennsylvania State University, M.A., 1966, Ph.D., 1972. *Home address:* R.D. 5, Box 226, Apollo, Pa. 15613. *Office:* Pennsylvania State University, 3550 Seventh Street Rd., New Kensington, Pa. 15068.

CAREER: High school teacher of U.S. history in the public schools of Burrell, Pa., 1965-66; University of Pittsburgh, Bradford, Pa., assistant professor of history, 1967-68; Pennsylvania State University, New Kensington, instructor, 1968-72, assistant professor of history, 1972-74, associate director of academic affairs, 1974—. *Member:* American Historical Association, Organization of American Historians, Pennsylvania Historical Association.

WRITINGS: Pennsylvania Speculator and Patriot: The Entrepreneurial John Nicholson, 1757-1800, Pennsylvania State University Press, 1975. Contributor to historical journals.

WORK IN PROGRESS: A book concerning French-American economic ties in the 1790's.

* * *

ARCINIEGAS, German 1900-

PERSONAL: Born December 6, 1900, in Bogota, Colombia; son of Rafael (a farmer) and Aurora (Angueyra) Arciniegas; married Gabriela Vieira, November 19, 1926; children: Aurora, Gabriela Mercedes. *Education:* Universidad Nacional, Bogota, Colombia, LL.D., 1924. *Politics:* Liberal. *Religion:* Roman Catholic. *Home:* Embassy of Colombia, Urbanizacion Campo Alegre, Avenida El Parque, 18 Caracas, Venezuela. *Agent:* American Literary Agency, 11 Riverside Drive, New York, N.Y. 10023.

CAREER: Universidad Nacional, Bogota, Colombia, professor of sociology, 1925-28; *El Tiempo,* Bogota, editor, 1928-30, London correspondent, 1930-33, editor-in-chief, 1933-39, director, 1939. Government of Colombia, vice-consul in London, 1930, charge d'affaires in Buenos Aires, 1939-41, Minister of Education, 1941-42, 1945-46, ambassador to Italy, 1959-62, to Israel, 1960-62, and to Venezuela, 1967—. Member of Colombian Parliament, 1933-34, 1939-40, 1957-58. Visiting professor, Columbia University, 1943, 1948-57, University of Chicago, 1944, Mills College, 1945, University of California at Berkeley, 1945. Director, Cuadernos, Paris, 1963-65; founder, Museo de Arte Colonial, Bogota; director, Ediciones Colombia. *Member:* Academia Colombiana, Academia Colombiana de Historia, Academy of Spain, Academy of Mexico, Academy of Cuba, Academy of Venezuela, National Institute of Arts and Letters (honorary associate), American Committee for Cultural Freedom (former vice-president).

WRITINGS: El estudiante de la mesa redonda, J. Peuyo (Madrid), 1932, 2nd edition, Editorial Minerva, 1933; *La universidad colombiana,* Imprenta Nacional (Bogota), 1932, enlarged edition, 1932; *Memorias de un congresista,* Editorial Cromos, 1933; *Diario de un peaton,* Imprenta Nacional, 1936; *America, tierra firme,* Editiones Ercilla (Santiago), 1937; *Los comuneros,* Editorial ABC, 1938; *Jimenez de Quesada,* Editorial ABC, 1939, translation by Mildred Adams published as *The Knight of El Dorado: The Tale of Don Gonzalo Jimenez de Quesada and His*

Conquest of New Granada, Now Called Colombia, Viking, 1942, reprinted, Greenwood Press, 1968.

Que haremos con la historia, Imprente Lehmann (Costa Rica), 1940; *Los alemanes en la conquista de America,* Editorial Losada (Buenos Aires), 1941, translation by Angel Flores published as *Germans in the Conquest of America: a Sixteenth Century Venture,* Macmillan, 1943, reprinted, Hafner, 1971; (editor) *The Green Continent: A Comprehensive View of Latin America by its Leading Writers,* translated from the Spanish and Portuguese by Harriet de Onis and others, Knopf, 1944, reprinted, 1963; *Biografia del Caribe,* Editorial Sudamericana (Buenos Aires), 1945; *En el pais del rascacielos y las zanahorias,* Libreria Suramerica, 1945; *Este pueblo de America,* Fondo de Cultura Economica (Mexico), 1945; *Caribbean, Sea of the New World,* translated by de Onis, Knopf, 1946; (editor) *El pensamiento vivo de Andres Bello,* Editorial Losada, 1946; *En medio del camino de la vida,* Editorial Sudamericana, 1949.

Entre la Libertad y el miedo, Ediciones Cuadernos Americanos (Mexico), 1952; *The State of Latin America,* translated by de Onis, Knopf, 1952; *Amerigo y el Nuevo Mundo,* Editorial Hermes, 1955, translation by de Onis published as *Amerigo and the New World: The Life and Times of Amerigo Vespucci,* Knopf, 1955; *Italia, guia para vagabundos,* Editorial Sudamericana, 1957; *America magica: Los hombres y los meses,* Editorial Sudamericana, 1959.

America magica II: Las mujeres y las horas, Editorial Sudamericana, 1961; (editor) Ricardo Arenales, *El Terremoto de San Salvador,* 2nd edition, Ministry of Education (San Salvador), 1961; (with others) *Tres ensayos sobre nuestra America,* Biblioteca Cuadernos (Paris), c.1962; *Colombia,* Union Panamericana (Washington), 1962; *El mundo de la bella Simonetta,* Editorial Sudamericana, 1962; *Cosas del pueblo: Cronica de la historia vulgar,* Editorial Hermes (Mexico), 1962; *Entre el Mar Rojo y el Mar Muerto: Guia de Israel,* E.D.H.A.S.A. (Barcelona), 1964; *El continente de siete colores: Historia de la cultura en Americana Latina,* Editorial Sudamericana, 1965, condensation published as *Latinoamerica: El continente de siete colores,* edited by Cecil D. McVicker and Osvaldo N. Soto, Harcourt, 1967, translation of original edition by Joan MacLean published as *Latin America: A Cultural History,* Knopf, 1967; *Temas de Arciniegas: Invitacion a conversar, leer y escribir,* edited by Osvaldo N. Soto and Cecil D. McVicker, Harcourt, 1967; (contributor) Marco Aurelio Alamazan, *Claroscuro,* Ultramar (Mexico), 1967; *Genio y figure de Jorge Isaacs,* Editorial Universitaria de Buenos Aires, 1967; (contributor) Cole Blasier, editor, *Constructive Change in Latin America,* University of Pittsburgh Press, 1968; (compiler) *Colombia: Itinerario y espiritu de la independencia, segun los documentos principales de la revolucion,* Editorial Norma, 1969; *Medio mundo entre un zapato: De Lumumba en el Congo a las brujas en Suecia,* Editorial Sudamericana, 1969; *Nuevo diario de Noe,* Monte Avila (Caracas), 1969.

Nueva imagen del Caribe, Editorial Sudamericana, 1970; *Roma secretissima,* Anaya (Salamanca), 1972.

Contributor to newspapers and magazines including *La Prensa, La Nacion, Cuadernos Americanos.* Editor of *La Revista de la Indias;* co-director, *Revista de America.**

* * *

ARDEN, Jane

PERSONAL: Born in Wales; children: two. *Address:* c/o Calder & Boyars Ltd., 18 Brewer St., London W1R 4AS, England.

CAREER: Playwright and actress; has appeared in British television productions of "Romeo and Juliet," 1947, "The Logic Game," 1965, and in Sartre's "Hui Clos," on stage in own plays, "Dear Liz" and "Conscience and Desire," 1954, and in own film, "The Logic Game," 1965; director of Holocaust Women's Theatre Company, London, England, 1970—; political speaker. Directed film, "The Other Side of the Underneath," 1973.

WRITINGS—Plays: "Conscience and Desire," produced in London, 1954; "Dear Liz," produced in London, 1954; *The Party* (first produced in London at New Theatre, May 28, 1958), Samuel French, 1958; *Vagina Rex and the Gas Oven* (first produced in London at Arts Laboratory, 1969), Calder & Boyars, 1971; "A New Communion: For Freaks, Prophets, and Witches," produced in London and Edinburgh, 1971. Also author of play, "The Other Side of the Underneath," and of screenplays: "The Logic Game," 1966, "Separation," 1968, and "The Other Side of the Underneath," 1973.*

* * *

ARENDT, Hannah 1906-1975

October 14, 1906—December 4, 1975; German-born American political scientist, philosopher, educator, editor, and author. Obituaries: *New York Times,* December 6, 1975, December 9, 1975; *Washington Post,* December 6, 1975; *Publishers Weekly,* December 15, 1975; *Time,* December 15, 1975; *AB Bookman's Weekly,* January 5, 1976; *Current Biography,* February, 1976. (See index for previous *CA* sketch)

* * *

ARENSBERG, Conrad Maynadier 1910-

PERSONAL: Born September 12, 1910, in Pittsburgh, Pa.; son of Charles F. C. and Emily Wright (Maynadier) Arensberg; married Margaret Jacklin Walsh, June 13, 1935; children: Emily Maynadier, Margaret Farrell, Cornelius Wright. *Education:* Harvard University, A.B., 1931, Ph.D., 1934. *Religion:* Episcopalian. *Home:* 445 Riverside Dr., New York, N.Y. 10027. *Office:* Department of Anthropology, Schermerton Hall, Columbia University, New York, N.Y. 10027.

CAREER: Massachusetts Institute of Technology, Cambridge, Mass., assistant professor of social anthropology and member of industrial relations section, 1934-37; U.S. Department of Agriculture, Washington, D.C., consultant, 1938-40; Brooklyn College (now Brooklyn College of the City University of New York), Brooklyn, N.Y., associate professor of social anthropology and chairman of department, 1941-43; Barnard College, New York City, associate professor of sociology and chairman of department, 1946-52; Columbia University, New York City, professor of anthropology, 1952—. Conducted field study in social anthropology, County Clare, Ireland, 1932-34; junior fellow, Harvard University, 1934-37; Lowell lecturer, 1936; member, Social Science Research Council, 1951; research director, UNESCO Institute for Social Sciences, Cologne, 1952. Consultant to Bureau of Indian Affairs, U.S. Department of Interior, 1940-42, and to Socialforschungstelle, Dortmund, Germany, 1950-51. *Military service:* U.S. Army, Military Intelligence, 1943-46; became major.

MEMBER: American Association for the Advancement of

Science, American Anthropological Association, American Sociological Association, Society for Applied Anthropology (founder; president, 1945), Inter-American Society for Anthropology and Geography, Society for Advancement of Management, Harvard Club (New York), St. Botolph Club (Boston).

WRITINGS: The Irish Countryman: An Anthropological Study, Macmillan, 1937, reprinted, Natural History Press, 1968; (with Solon T. Kimball) *Family and Community in Ireland,* Harvard University Press, 1940, 2nd edition, 1968; (editor with others) *Research in Industrial Human Relations: A Critical Appraisal,* Harper, 1957; (with Arthur H. Niehoff) *Technical Cooperation and Cultural Reality,* Agency for International Development, U.S. Department of State, 1963; (with Niehoff) *Introducing Social Change: A Manual for Americans Overseas,* Aldine, 1964; (with Kimball) *Culture and Community,* Harcourt, 1965; *Introducing Social Change: A Manual for Community Development,* 2nd edition, Aldine, 1971. Author, with Eliot D. Chapple, of *Measuring Human Relations,* 1942, and, with Karl Polanyi, of *Trade and Markets in the Early Empires,* 1957. Editor of *American Anthropological Association Manual for Point Four Workers,* 1953. Editor, *Human Organization,* 1946-52, *Journal of Applied Anthropology,* 1947.*

* * *

ARLEN, Michael J. 1930-

PERSONAL: Born December 9, 1930, in London, England; came to United States, 1940; son of Michael (a writer) and Atalanta (Mercati) Arlen; married Ann Warner, March, 1957 (divorced April, 1971); married Alice Albright Hogue, August, 1972; children: (first marriage) Jennifer, Caroline, Elizabeth, Sally; (second marriage) Alicia, James Patrick, Robert (stepchildren). *Education:* Attended Harvard University, 1948-52. *Home:* 60 East Bellevue Pl., Chicago, Ill. 60611. *Office:* c/o The *New Yorker,* 25 West 43rd St., New York, N.Y. 10036; and 33 East Cedar St., Chicago, Ill. 60611.

CAREER: Life magazine, New York City, reporter, 1952-56; *New Yorker* magazine, New York City, staff writer, television critic, 1966—. Juror, Alfred DuPont-Columbia Survey of Broadcast Journalism, 1968-70.

WRITINGS: Living Room War (essays), Viking, 1969; *Exiles,* Farrar, Straus, 1970; *An American Verdict,* Doubleday, 1973; *Passage to Ararat,* Farrar, Straus, 1975. Contributor of articles to *Cosmopolitan, Holiday, Esquire, New York Times Magazine, Harper's, Saturday Review, Atlantic Monthly,* and other periodicals.

SIDELIGHTS: Bob Abel sums up *Living Room War* as "a book that is going to be around a mite longer than anything now on television. [Arlen] is not actually writing about television per se, or a desirable esthetic for it, but about the world as perceived through television. This is the first book, I think, that not only does the medium justice but in all fairness sentences it." Thomas Lask feels that Arlen's pieces, taken from the *New Yorker,* "are not strictly reviews at all," rather, "suitable and sometimes sharp commentary on the American scene."

Exiles, according to Christoper Lehmann-Haupt, "reveals the lives of three extraordinary people and it carries the author toward his soul's interior, there to come to terms, both in his mind and in the reader's, with the essential condition of being an exile." Elizabeth Janeway said of this family memoir and partial autobiography: " . . . [it] is like

looking through a heap of photographs, except that these photographs come alive, for Michael J. Arlen has more than enough of his father's gift to recreate brilliantly this history of exile."

Much of Michael Arlen's work appeared originally in the *New Yorker.**

* * *

ARMAH, Ayi Kwei 1939-

PERSONAL: Born in 1939, in Takoradi, Gold Coast (now Ghana). *Education:* Harvard University, B.A.; attended Achimota College, University of Ghana, and Columbia University. *Address:* c/o Houghton, Mifflin Co., Boston, Mass.

CAREER: Worked in Algiers as translator for the magazine *Revolution Africaine,* as a scriptwriter in Ghana for Ghana Television, and as a teacher of English at a school in Ghana, 1966; *Jeune Afrique* (news magazine), Paris, France, editor and translator, 1967-68. *Awards, honors:* Farfield Foundation grant.

WRITINGS—Novels: The Beautyful Ones Are Not Yet Born, Houghton, 1968; *Fragments,* Houghton, 1970; *Why Are We So Blest,* Doubleday, 1971. Poetry included in anthology, *Messages: Poems from Ghana,* edited by K. Awoonor and G. Adali-Mortty, Heinemann, 1970. Contributor of short stories to *Atlantic* and *Harper's Magazine* and of articles to *New African* and *New York Review of Books.*

BIOGRAPHICAL/CRITICAL SOURCES: Carolyn Riley, editor, *Contemporary Literary Criticism,* Volume V, Gale, 1976.*

* * *

ARMITAGE, Merle 1893-1975

February 12, 1893—March 15, 1975; American stage designer, impressario, editorial art director, and author of books on art, music, cooking, and other topics. Obituaries: *New York Times,* March 18, 1975.

* * *

ARNASON, H(jorvardur) H(arvard) 1909-

PERSONAL: Born April 24, 1909, in Winnipeg, Manitoba, Canada; came to the United States in 1927, naturalized, 1940; son of Sveinbjorn and Maria (Bjarnadottir) Arnason; married Elizabeth Hickox Yard, July 25, 1936; married Elinor Lane Franklin, June 9, 1966; children: (first marriage) Eleanor Atwood, John Yard. *Education:* Attended University of Manitoba, 1925-27; Northwestern University, B.S., 1931, A.M., 1937; Princeton University, M.F.A., 1939; also studied at Institute of Fine Arts, New York University, and Courtauld Institute of Art, University of London. *Home address:* River Road, Roxbury, Conn. 06783.

CAREER: Northwestern University, Evanston, Ill., instructor in art, 1936-38; Frick Collection, New York City, research assistant and lecturer, 1938-42; Hunter College (now of the City University of New York), New York City, lecturer, 1939-42; U.S. Office of War Information, field representative in Iceland, 1942-44, assistant deputy director for Europe with headquarters in Washington, 1944-45; U.S. Department of State, Office of International Information and Cultural Affairs, Washington, D.C., chief of program planning and evaluation unit, 1945-46; U.S. representative on the Preparatory Commission on UNESCO,

London and Paris, 1946; University of Chicago, Chicago, Illinois, visiting professor of art, 1947; University of Minnesota, Minneapolis, professor of art and chairman of department, 1947-61; Solomon R. Guggenheim Foundation, New York City, vice-president for art administration, 1961-69. Director of Walker Art Center, Minneapolis, 1951-61; Carnegie visiting professor at University of Hawaii, 1959; consultant to the Guggenheim Museum, 1969—. Trustee, American Federation of Arts, Solomon R. Guggenheim Foundation, the T. B. Walker Foundation Inc., Joseph H. Hirshhorn Museum, and Jacques Lipchitz Foundation; member of the executive board and chairman of the advisory committee of the International Foundation for Art Research.

MEMBER: College Art Association of America, American Association of Museums, International Council of Museums, United States National Committee for the History of Art, American Association of University Professors, American Society for 18th Century Studies, Societe Francaise d'Etude du 18eme Siecle, Century Club and Princeton Club (New York City). *Awards, honors:* Fulbright fellow in France, 1955-56; Chevalier de l'Ordre des Arts et des Lettres; knight of the Order of St. Olav (Norway); National Endowment for the Humanities senior research fellow, 1971-72.

WRITINGS: Theodore Roszak, Walker Art Center of Minneapolis, in collaboration with the Whitney Museum of American Art, New York, 1956; *Cameron Booth,* American Federation of Arts, 1961; (author of commentary) *Modern Sculpture from the Joseph H. Hirshhorn Foundation Collection,* American Federation of Arts, 1962; *Marca-Relli,* Abrams, 1963; *Ralston Crawford: Oils and Lithographs,* Nordness Gallery, 1963; *Sculpture by Houdon,* Worcester Art Museum, 1964; *Calder,* Van Nostrand, 1966; *History of Modern Art: Painting, Sculpture, Architecture,* Prentice-Hall and Abrams, 1968; *Jacques Lipchitz: Sketches in Bronze,* Praeger, 1969; (with Ugo Mulas) *Alexander Calder,* Viking, 1969; (author of introduction) *Calder,* Viking Press, 1971; (with Jacques Lipchitz) *My Life in Sculpture,* Viking Press, 1972. Author of monographs, catalogs, and articles for encyclopedias and journals.*

* * *

ARNY, Mary (Travis) 1909-

PERSONAL: Born October 13, 1909, in Montclair, N.J.; daughter of Thomas (a clergyman) and Mary (an artist; maiden name, Wilson) Travis; married Robert Allen Arny (an administrator), June 25, 1938; children: Thomas Travis, Mary Katherine (Mrs. Christopher R. Reaske), Nancy Pauline (Mrs. H. Ross Pywell III). *Education:* Douglass College, Rutgers, B.Sc., 1932, Rutgers University, M.Sc., 1936. *Religion:* Congregational. *Home:* 149 Watchung Avenue, Upper Montclair, N.J. 07042.

CAREER: Montclair Public Schools, Montclair, N.J., teacher, 1936-40; lecturer in Biblical literature at Montclair Adult School, Montclair; Montclair State College, Upper Montclair, N.J., began 1955, became associate professor of biology, 1964; now retired. Visiting professor, Upsala College, 1959-60; librarian of Montclair Public Library Heritage Collection, 1954—; trustee, Montclair Nature Center. *Member:* Linnaean Society, Wildlife Conservation Society, Eastern Bird Banding Association, New Jersey Historical Society, New Jersey Audubon Society (member of board of trustees), Federated Naturalists of New Jersey (director,

1946-58), Montclair Historical Society (member of board of trustees), Curie Science Club, Tau Kappa Alpha, Cosmopolitan Club. *Awards, honors:* Coronat Award from St. Edwards University, 1964; New Jersey Association of Teachers of English Award, 1966, for *Red Lion Rampant.*

WRITINGS: First Reach, Madison, 1932; *Birds and Mammals of Montclair,* Pine Tree Press, 1952; *Seasoned With Salt* (autobiography), Westminster, 1954; (with David Alloway) *A Goodly Heritage,* Ray Publishing, 1963; *Commonsense Garden Guide,* Maco, 1964; *Red Lion Rampant,* Ray Publishing, 1964; *Practical Gardening Ideas,* Maco, 1966; (with C. R. Reaske) *Ecology: A Writer's Handbook,* Random House, 1972; *Windows to Wonder: A Laboratory Guide,* Montclair State College Press, 1972. Writer of column for *Montclair Times, Verona Cedar Grove Times* (N.J.), and *Westchester News* (White Plains, N.Y.), 1949—. Contributor of short stories and articles to periodicals.

BIOGRAPHICAL/CRITICAL SOURCES: Mary Travis Arny, *Seasoned With Salt,* Westminster, 1954.

* * *

ARROYO, Stephen J(oseph) 1946-

PERSONAL: Born October 6, 1946, in Kansas City, Mo.; son of Joseph F. (a business executive) and Dolores C. (Eberle) Arroyo; married Kathleen R. Mullins (a businesswoman), October 18, 1971; children: Nathan Daniel. *Education:* Attended Drake University, 1964-65; University of California, Davis, B.A., 1968; California State University, Sacramento, M.A., 1972. *Home:* 1313 Spruce Lane, Davis, Calif. 95616. *Office:* 231 E St., Suite 8, Davis, Calif. 95616.

CAREER: Consulting psychologist (holds California State License in marriage and family counseling) in Davis, Calif., 1972—. Part-time instructor at Sacramento City College, 1973—, and part-time assistant professor at John Fitzgerald Kennedy University, 1973—. *Member:* American Federation of Astrologers, Astrologer's Guild, British Astrological Association. *Awards, honors:* Astrology prize from British Astrological Association, 1973, for writings dealing with astrology and psychology.

WRITINGS: (Editor) *Journal of Charles,* CSA Press, 1971; (contributor) Patrick Harding, editor, *A Study of Relationships,* British Astrological Association, 1973; *Astrology, Psychology, and the Four Elements,* CRCS Publications, 1975. Contributor of over twenty-four articles to *Horoscope, American Astrology, Kosmos, Astrology Now, Aquarian Astrology,* and other magazines.

WORK IN PROGRESS: Two books, *Astrology, Karma, and Transformation,* to be published in late 1976, and *Person to Person Astrology,* 1977.

* * *

ARZT, Max 1897-1975

March 20, 1897—August 31, 1975; Polish-born American rabbi, educator, scholar, seminary administrator, and author of works on theological subjects. Obituaries: *New York Times,* September 1, 1975.

* * *

ASARE, Meshack (Yaw) 1945-

PERSONAL: Surname is pronounced *Ah*-suh-ree; born September 18, 1945, in Nyankumasi; son of Joseph Kwaku (an accountant) and Adjoa (a trader; maiden name, Adoma)

Asare; married Rose Tachie Menson (a bank clerk), 1969 (divorced, 1975); children: Akosua (daughter), Kajo (son). *Education:* Attended University of Science and Technology, Kumasi, Ghana, University of Wisconsin, and School of Journalism and Television, Berkshire, England. *Politics:* "Universalism." *Religion:* Christian. *Home:* Block 424, R9, Sogeco Flats, Tema, Ghana. *Office:* Lincoln Community School, P.O. Box 194, Accra, Ghana.

CAREER: Elementary school teacher in Tema, Ghana, 1966-68; Lincoln Community School, Accra, Ghana, teacher, 1969—. Artist; has made sculptures for the government and for public buildings; illustrator and designer. *Member:* Ghana Association of Artists. *Awards, honors:* First prize in National Schools Art Contest, 1953; British Council scholarship from Arts Council of Ghana, 1962.

WRITINGS: (With others) *Ghana Welcomes You,* Valco, 1968; *Tawia Goes to Sea* (juvenile), Ghana Publishing, 1970, Panther House, 1972; *Seeing the World,* Ghana Publishing, 1975.

Plays: "Ananse and Wisdom" (playlet); "The Outdooring" (playlet); "The Hunter."

Contributor of articles on Ghanian culture to magazines.

WORK IN PROGRESS: Everyone Moves (tentative title); research for *Guiding Creativity* and *Their Own Playthings,* both juvenile books based on culture and classroom observations; a novel.

SIDELIGHTS: Asare writes: "I am simply a very talented individual, easily attaining the heights in whatever I endeavor. I find learning a particularly fascinating experience.... My aim ... is to make young people aware of their world—understand and appreciate it better."

*   *   *

ASHBY, Eric 1904-

PERSONAL: Born August 24, 1904, in London, England; son of Herbert Charles and Helena (Chater) Ashby; married Elizabeth Helen Farries, December 31, 1931; children: Michael, Peter. *Education:* Attended Imperial College of Science, London, 1923-26, and University of Chicago, 1929-31. *Home:* Norman Cottage, Manor Rd., Brandon, Suffolk, England. *Office:* Clare College, Cambridge University, Cambridge, England.

CAREER: University of London, Imperial College of Science, London, England, demonstrator, 1926-29, lecturer, 1931-35; Bristol University, Bristol, England, reader in botany, 1935-37; University of Sydney, Sydney, Australia, professor of botany, 1938-46; University of Manchester, Manchester, England, Harrison Professor of Botany and director of botanical laboratories, 1946-50; Queens University, Belfast, Northern Ireland, president and vice-chancellor, 1950-59, chancellor, 1971—; Cambridge University, Cambridge, England, master of Clare College, 1959-75, vice-chancellor of the University, 1967-69. Visiting lecturer in the United States, 1964, 1970, and 1976. Director of Science Liaison Bureau, 1942-43; counselor and charge d'affaires, Australian Legation, Moscow, 1945-46. Chairman: Australian National Research Council, 1940-42, Adult Education Committee, 1953-54, Department of Scientific and Industrial Research Grants Committee, 1955-60, Commission on Post-Secondary and Higher Education in Nigeria, 1959-61, Committee of Award of Commonwealth Fund, 1963-68, Royal Commission on Environment Pollution, 1970-73, and Working Party on Pollution Control for the United Nations Conference on Environment, 1972.

Trustee: Australian Museum, 1942-46, CIBA Foundation, 1966—, British Museum, 1969-76. Member of Advisory Council on Scientific Policy, 1950-53, Nuffield Provincial Hospitals Trust, 1951-59, Advisory Council on Scientific and Industrial Research, 1954-60, University Grants Committee, 1959-67, Commonwealth Scholarship Commission, 1960-63, Council on the Royal Society, 1964-65, governing body of School of Oriental and African Studies, 1965-70. Vice-chairman, Association of Universities of the British Commonwealth, 1959-61; president, British Association for the Advancement of Science, 1963. Fellow of Imperial College of Science, Royal Society, Royal Institute of Chemistry, Davenport College of Yale University. *Awards, honors:* Knighted, 1956; life peerage, 1973; twenty-two honorary degrees from universities and colleges in several countries; honorary foreign member of American Academy of Arts and Sciences.

WRITINGS: Environment and Plant Development, Edward Arnold, 1931; *German-English Botanical Terminology,* Thomas Murby, 1938; *Challenge to Education,* Angus & Robertson, 1946; *Scientist in Russia,* Penguin, 1947; *Technology and the Academics: An Essay on Universities and the Scientific Revolution,* Macmillan, 1958; *Community of Universities: An Informal Portrait of the Association of Universities of the British Commonwealth, 1913-1963,* Cambridge University Press, 1963; *African Universities and Western Tradition,* Harvard University Press, 1964; (in association with Mary Anderson) *Universities: British, Indian, African: A Study in the Ecology of Higher Education,* Harvard University Press, 1966; (with Anderson) *The Rise of the Student Estate in Britain,* Harvard University Press, 1970; *Masters and Scholars: Reflections on the Rights and Responsibilities of Students,* Oxford University Press, 1970; *Any Person, Any Study: An Essay on Higher Education in the United States,* McGraw, 1971; (with Anderson) *Portrait of Haldane,* Macmillan, 1974.

WORK IN PROGRESS: "The reconciliation of man and nature," a study of social response to environmental hazards.

*   *   *

ASHENFELTER, Orley C(lark) 1942-

PERSONAL: Born October 18, 1942, in San Francisco, Calif.; married, 1965; children: two. *Education:* Claremont Men's College, B.A., 1964; Princeton University, Ph.D., 1970. *Home:* 30 Mercer St., Princeton, N.J. 08540. *Office:* Industrial Relations Section, Princeton University, Princeton, N.J. 08540.

CAREER: Princeton University, Princeton, N.J., lecturer, 1968-70, assistant professor, 1970-71, associate professor, 1971-73, professor of economics, 1973—, director of Industrial Relations Section, 1971-72 and 1973—. Member of National Manpower Policy Task Force Associates, 1968-72; member of advisory board of Institute of Labor-Management Relations at Rutgers University, 1972—; director of Office of Evaluation of U.S. Department of Labor, 1972-73. *Member:* American Economic Association, American Statistical Association, Econometric Society, Industrial Relations Research Association. *Awards, honors:* Woodrow Wilson fellowships, 1964-65 and 1967-68.

WRITINGS: (Contributor) Ronald Wykstra, editor, *Human Capital Formation and Manpower Development,* Free Press, 1971; (editor with Albert Rees, and contributor) *Discrimination in Labor Markets,* Princeton University Press, 1973; (contributor) Glen Cain and Harold Watts, editors, *Income Maintenance and Labor Supply,* Markham, 1973; (contributor) Lloyd Reynolds, Stanley Masters, and Collette Moser, editors, *Readings in Labor Economics and Labor Relations,* Prentice-Hall, 1974; (contributor) T. W. Schultz, editor, *Economics of the Family,* National Bureau of Economic Research, 1974; (contributor) Michael Intriligator and David Kendrick, editors, *Frontiers of Quantitative Economics,* Volume II, North-Holland Publishing, 1974; (contributor) Daniel Hamermesh, editor, *Labor in the Public and Nonprofit Sectors,* Princeton University Press, 1975; (contributor) Phyllis Wallace, editor, *Some New Perspectives on Equal Employment Opportunity: The A.T. & T. Case,* M.I.T. Press, in press; (editor and contributor) *Evaluating the Labor Market Effects of Social Programs,* Princeton University Industrial Relations Section, in press. Contributor of about twenty articles and reviews to economics, labor, and finance journals. Member of board of editors of *Journal of Urban Economics.*

WORK IN PROGRESS: Research on the economic benefits of manpower training.

* * *

ASHER, Robert Eller 1910-

PERSONAL: Born October 18, 1910, in Chicago, Ill.; son of Louis Eller and Alice (Wormser) Asher; married Ethel Stuart Watson, February 2, 1935; children: Robert L., Vicki A. (Mrs. J. D. Lambert). *Education:* Attended Dartmouth College, 1927-30, and University of Berlin, 1930-31; University of Chicago, Ph.B., 1932, M.A., 1934. *Home and office:* 3838 Cathedral Ave., N.W., Washington, D.C. 20016.

CAREER: Researcher for American Public Welfare Association, Chicago, Ill., and Federal Emergency Relief Administration, Washington, D.C., 1934-35; Works Progress Administration (later Work Projects Administration), Washington, researcher, 1935-37, chief of procedures and statistics section in division of professional and service projects, 1937-39; National Youth Administration, Washington, assistant to deputy administrator, 1939-42; War Production Board, Washington, chief of clearance section in office of civilian supply, 1942-43; Lend-Lease Administration, North African Economic Board, Algiers, executive assistant to chief of import division, 1943; Foreign Economic Administration, Washington, deputy chief of planning and control staff for liberated areas, 1944; on civilian staff of displaced persons branch for Supreme Headquarters Allied Expeditionary Forces, and special assistant to chief liaison officer of the United Nations Relief and Rehabilitation Administration, in Europe, 1944-45, director of division of procedural coordination for UNRRA, 1945-46; U.S. Department of State, special assistant to chief of Mission of Economic Affairs, London, England, 1946-47, special assistant to assistant secretary of state for economic affairs, 1951-54; deputy chief of U.S. resident delegation, Economic Commission for Europe, Geneva, Switzerland, 1947-49, chief, 1949-50, advisor to director of European Regional Affairs, 1950-51; Brookings Institution, Washington, senior fellow on foreign policy studies staff, 1954-72; private consultant, 1972—. Vice-president for international affairs, Americans for Democratic Action, 1956-58; vice-president, Center for International Economic Growth, 1961-63; trustee, International Development Conference, 1968—. Consultant to various federal and international agencies.

MEMBER: National Planning Association (member of in-

ternational committee, 1968—), Society for International Development (member of council, 1962-65, and 1975—; vice-president, 1966-68; vice-president (U.S.A.), 1974-75), Council on Foreign Relations, Phi Beta Kappa, Cosmos Club (Washington).

WRITINGS: (With others) *The United Nations and Economic and Social Cooperation,* Brookings Institution, 1957; (with others) *The United Nations and Promotion of the General Welfare,* Brookings Institution, 1957.

Grants, Loans, and Local Currencies: Their Role in Foreign Aid, Brookings Institution, 1961; (with others) *Development of the Emerging Countries: An Agenda for Research,* Brookings Institution, 1962.

Development Assistance in the Seventies: Alternatives for the United States, Brookings Institution, 1970; (with Edward S. Mason) *The World Bank since Bretton Woods,* Brookings Institution, 1973.

Author of pamphlets, and of special reports for the United Nations, the Food and Agriculture Organization, and other agencies. Contributor to professional journals. Member of editorial board, *International Development Review,* 1958-65.

WORK IN PROGRESS: A book tentatively titled *The World Bank and the Poor Countries.*

* * *

ASHLOCK, Patrick (Robert) 1937-

PERSONAL: Born April 13, 1937, in Carrollton, Ill.; son of Robert Lee and Elizabeth (Swires) Ashlock. *Education:* Attended Western Michigan University; Illinois State University, B.S.Ed., 1958; Columbia University, M.A., 1960; University of Texas, Ed.D., 1963; also attended National College of Education. *Office:* Ashlock Learning Center, 820 Ontario, Oak Park, Ill. 60302.

CAREER: Board of Cooperative Educational Services, Valhalla, N.Y., teacher of the physically handicapped, brain-injured, and mentally retarded, 1958-60; teacher of remedial reading in elementary schools, summer, 1960, and teacher of the academically talented, 1960-61, both in Port Huron, Mich.; teacher of adult education reading improvement classes in public schools in Elmwood Park, Ill., 1963-65, high school teacher and director of reading instruction, 1965-67; Rosary College, River Forest, Ill., 1967—. Director and head of elementary day school program at Ashlock Learning Center, 1968—. Lecturer, Bradley University, 1966-67, DePaul University, summer, 1967; Northeastern Illinois State College, lecturer, 1968, assistant professor, 1968—; professor at National College of Education, 1967-68. Private practice in educational and psychological testing in Michigan and Illinois, 1957-67.

MEMBER: International Reading Association, Council for Exceptional Children (life member), National Education Association (life member), Fund for the Perceptually Handicapped, American Montessori Society, American Council on Learning Disabilities, Northwest Suburban Council on Understanding Learning Disabilities, Illinois Council for Exceptional Children, Illinois Montessori Society, Kappa Delta Pi.

WRITINGS: (Contributor) *Reading and Inquiry,* International Reading Association, 1965; (with Alberta Stephen) *Educational Therapy in the Elementary School,* C. C Thomas, 1966; *Teaching Reading to Individuals with Learning Difficulties,* C. C Thomas, in press.

WORK IN PROGRESS: The Ashlock Tests of Visual Perception; Identification of Learning Difficulties, Volume I; *Educational Use of Terminology.*

*   *   *

ASKWITH, Betty Ellen 1909-

PERSONAL: Born June 26, 1909, in London, England; daughter of George Ranken (an industrial conciliator) and Ellen (Peel) Askwith; married Keith Miller Jones, September 2, 1950. *Education:* Attended Lycee Francais, London, 1922-23, North Foreland Lodge, 1923-25. *Home:* 8 Egerton Ter., London S.W.3, England.

CAREER: Novelist, poet, and biographer. *Member:* Royal Society of Literature (fellow).

WRITINGS—Novels: *If This Be Error,* Methuen, 1932; *Green Corn,* Gollancz, 1933; *Erinna,* Gollancz, 1937; *The Admiral's Daughters,* Gollancz, 1947; *A Broken Engagement,* Gollancz, 1950; *The Blossoming Tree,* Gollancz, 1954; *The Tangled Web,* Gollancz, 1960; *A Step Out of Time,* Chatto & Windus, 1966.

Biography: *Keats,* Collins, 1941; *Lady Dilke,* Chatto & Windus, 1969; *Two Victorian Families,* Chatto & Windus, 1971; *The Nytteltons,* Chatto & Windus, 1975.

Poetry: *First Poems,* Martin Secker, 1928; *Poems,* Gollancz, 1933.

With Theodora Benson: *Lobster Quadrille,* Fronto, 1930; *Seven Basketfuls,* Gollancz, 1932; *Foreigners; or, The World in a Nutshell,* Gollancz, 1935; *Muddling Through; or, Britain in a Nutshell,* Gollancz, 1936; *How to Be Famous; or, The Great in a Nutshell,* Gollancz, 1937.

Translator: Noel Devaulx, *The Tailor's Cake* (short stories), Wingate, 1946; Raymond Queneau, *A Hard Winter,* Mcdonald & Co., 1947; Pierre Henri Larthomas, *Meeting,* Gollancz, 1950, published as *Solitaire,* Houghton, 1951.

AVOCATIONAL INTERESTS: Traveling, reading.

*   *   *

ASTON, Michael (Anthony) 1946-

PERSONAL: Born July 1, 1946, in Birmingham, England; son of Harold Henry (a cabinetmaker) and Gladys (Bagnall) Aston; married Linda Jane Wilson (a teacher), July 26, 1974. *Education:* University of Birmingham, B.A., 1967, currently Ph.D. candidate. *Home:* 15 Malvern Ter., Taunton, Somerset, England. *Office:* County Planning Department, County Hall, Taunton, Somerset, England.

CAREER: Tutor at University of Birmingham, 1968-70, and Oxford University, 1970-72; archaeologist at Oxford City and County Museum, Oxford, England, and Somerset County Council Planning Office, Taunton, England, 1972—. Part-time tutor in archaeological techniques, 1972—. *Member:* Royal Archaeological Institute, Society for Medieval Archaeology, Cornwall Archaeological Society, Somerset Natural History and Archaeology Society, Birmingham and Warwickshire Archaeology Society, South Staffordshire Archaeological and Historical Society, Oxford Architectural and Historical Society, Association of County Archaeological Officers.

WRITINGS: (Contributor) R. T. Rowley and M. Davies, editors, *Archaeology and the M40 Motorway,* Oxford University Press, 1973; (with Rowley) *Landscape Archaeology: An Introduction to Fieldwork Techniques on Post-Roman Landscapes,* David & Charles, 1975; *Stonesfield Slate,* Oxford City and County Museum, 1975; *A Survey*

and Interpretation of Earthworks at Bordesley Abbey (monograph), University of Birmingham School of History, in press; (with C. J. Bond) *The Landscape of Towns,* Dent, in press. Contributor of articles to archaeological journals and archaeological society proceedings.

WORK IN PROGRESS: Fieldwork surveys.

*   *   *

ASTOR, Michael Langhorne 1916-

PERSONAL: Born April 10, 1916, in London, England; son of the second viscount and Nancy (Langhorne) Astor; married Barbara Mary Colonsay, 1942 (marriage dissolved, 1961); married Pandora Jones, 1961 (marriage dissolved, 1968); married Judy Innes, 1970; children: (first marriage) two sons, two daughters; (third marriage) one son, one daughter. *Education:* New College, Oxford, diploma degree, 1937. *Home:* Bruern, Churchill, Oxfordshire, England.

CAREER: Conservative Member of Parliament for the Eastern Division of Surrey, 1945-51. Member of London Library, 1967, chairman, 1974—; member of council of the Arts Council of Great Britain, 1968-71. *Military service:* Berkshire Yeomanry and G.H.Q. Liaison Regiment, 1939-45.

WRITINGS: Tribal Feeling (biography), J. Murray, 1963; *Brand* (novel), Weidenfeld & Nicolson, 1967.

WORK IN PROGRESS: Own diaries for the past 15-20 years.

*   *   *

ATCHLEY, Dana W(inslow) 1941-

PERSONAL: Born April 15, 1941, in Boston, Mass.; son of Dana W., Jr. (in electronics) and Barbara (Welch) Atchley; divorced, 1974; children: Megan Welch, Gillian Staton. *Education:* Dartmouth College, B.A. (with distinction), 1963; Yale University, B.F.A., 1964, M.F.A., 1965. *Home and office address:* P.O. Box 183, Crested Butte, Colo. 81224.

CAREER: Marlboro College, Marlboro, Vt., part-time instructor in printmaking and calligraphy, 1963-65; Maryland Institute of Art, Baltimore, instructor in art, 1966-69; University of Victoria, Victoria, British Columbia, assistant professor of visual arts, 1969-71; artist, poet, lecturer, and teacher, conducting visual arts workshops all over the United States, 1971—. Founder and coordinator of SPA-CECO, 1969—. Prints and other art have been included in more than thirty group shows and are represented in permanent collections in the United States, including Museum of Modern Art, and New York Public Library, and abroad, including Vancouver Art Gallery, British Columbia; Stedelijk Museum, Amsterdam; and Museo la Tertulio, Cali, Colombia. Consultant in design and graphic arts.

AWARDS, HONORS: Marcus Heiman Award in the Graphic Arts from Dartmouth College, 1962; New England Bookshow jury award, 1963; award from Moore College, 1968, for exhibition "American Drawing 1968"; University of Victoria research grant, 1970; Canada Arts Council grants, 1970, 1971; National Endowment for the Arts grants, 1972, 1972-74.

WRITINGS: ABC Design, Wittenborn, 1965; *Warm/Cool System: A Portfolio of Sixteen Prints Silk Screened by Dana Atchley,* Stygian Press, 1965; (editor) *Space Atlas* (anthology), Ace Space Co., 1969; (with Jonathan Williams)

Six Rusticated, Wall-Eyed Poems, Maryland Institute Press, 1970; (editor) *Notebook I* (anthology), Ace Space Co., 1971; (contributor) J. G. Bowles and Russell T. Bowles, editors, *This Book Is a Movie,* Delta Books, 1971; (with Williams and Nick Dean) *Blues and Roots/Rue and Bluets: A Garland for the Appalachians,* Grossman, 1971; *Artwork: No Commercial Value,* Grossman, 1971; (contributor) Franklin W. Robinson and Stephen G. Nichols, editors, *The Meaning of Mannerism,* University Press of New England, 1972.

Film: "The Making of a Renaissance Book," American Friends of the Plantin–Moretus Museum, 1967. Contributor to little literary magazines. Has worked as book designer for Doubleday, Grossman, and Aperture. Founding editor and publisher of Stygian Press, 1961-65, and The Press, 1973—.

WORK IN PROGRESS: "During the past three years of travel and work around the U.S. I have compiled a constantly changing audio/image document called 'The Real Life Show' which is shown to audiences wherever I work."

SIDELIGHTS: It has been some two hundred thousand miles since Atchley packed his props and some camouflage into his space van and headed south from British Columbia. Global connections realized through the mails and often extended by various media have become a reality for those who wish to participate. "The Real Life Show" is described as "an electronic magic show with Ace, as The Colorado Spaceman, in the driver's seat presenting real-life stories brought back alive and in living color from a quarter million mile voyage . . . a trip through the borderline spaces and places of the North American Eternal Network. . . ."

Atchley writes: "I've been fixing on different spaces for some time now; exploring this/that and encountering some unbelievably diverse realities—always trying to find a matrix to hold them all together. I am drawn to people who exist at the edge—whose madness gives them access to unimagineable spaces, yet whose sanity enables them to share them with me. As an artist I have drifted from one discipline to another; using whatever concept or technique seemed most suitable for the solution of a particular problem. There have been periods, however, when I built a house or just went fishing. Recently I've thought a lot about becoming a farmer—I mean lettuce is fifty cents a head and where do you go after vegetables?"

BIOGRAPHICAL/CRITICAL SOURCES: Rolling Stone, April 13, 1972.

* * *

ATHEY, Irene J(owett) 1919-

PERSONAL: Born April 4, 1919, in Bradford, Yorkshire, England; naturalized U.S. citizen; married. *Education:* Bingley Training College, teaching credential, 1939; University of London, B.A. (honors), 1950; University of California, Berkeley, M.A.Ed., 1958, Ph.D., 1965. *Home:* 215 Melrose St., Rochester, N.Y. 14619. *Office:* Center for Development, Learning, and Instruction, College of Education, University of Rochester, 518 Lattimore Hall, Rochester, N.Y. 14627.

CAREER: Elementary school teacher in Bradford, England, 1939-41, nursery school teacher, 1941-44; elementary school teacher in London, England, 1944-46; Oxhey Nursery School, Watford, England, director, 1946-50; elementary school teacher in Nachingwea, Tanzania, 1950-52, and Kongwa, Tanzania, 1952-55; Government Primary School, Jesselton, North Borneo (now Sabah), principal, 1955-57; University of California, Berkeley, assistant research psychologist at Institute of Human Development, 1959-62, associate research psychologist, 1962-65, instructor in reading improvement and effective study at Extension Division, Palo Alto, 1960-63; Marymount College, Oakland, Calif., instructor in psychology of reading, summer, 1965; University of Rochester, Rochester, N.Y., associate professor, 1965-70, professor of education, 1970—, professor of psychology, 1972—, chairperson of Center for Development, Learning, and Instruction, 1969—, member of pediatric diagnostic team, 1966-67. Has taught Swahili to adults. Administrator of five-county high school Wide Horizons Program, 1967-68; planner of nine-county Early Childhood Center and its demonstration preschool, 1968-70, member of advisory board, 1968-71. Member of Committee on Inner City Health Services of Health Council of Monroe County, 1967-69; member of advisory board to Monroe Community College, 1968-69, and Mount Hope School, 1974—; member of child health advisory group for Strong Memorial Hospital, 1973—.

MEMBER: International Reading Association, American Psychological Association, American Educational Research Association, National Reading Conference, National Association for the Education of Young Children, Jean Piaget Society, Rochester Association for the Education of Young Children (chairperson of regional conference, 1972-73).

WRITINGS: (Contributor) J. A. Figurel, editor, *Forging Ahead in Reading,* International Reading Association, 1967; *Reading Success and Personality Characteristics in Junior High School Students,* University of California Press, 1969; (with D. O. Rubadeau) *Educational Implications of Piaget's Theory,* Blaisdell, 1970; (contributor) Harry Singer and R. B. Ruddell, editors, *Theoretical Models and Processes in Reading,* International Reading Association, 1970, 2nd edition, in press; (contributor) F. P. Greene, editor, *Reading: The Right to Participate,* National Reading Conference, 1971; (contributor) Greene, editor, *Investigations Relating to Mature Reading,* National Reading Conference, 1972; (contributor) Doris Sponseller, editor, *Play as a Learning Medium,* National Association for the Education of Young Children, 1974; (contributor) S. F. Wanat, Martin Kling, and Harry Singer, editors, *Extracting Meaning from Written Language,* International Reading Association, in press; (contributor) *Highlights of the Preconvention Institutes,* International Reading Association, in press. Contributor of articles and reviews to education and psychology journals. Consulting editor of *Journal of Educational Research,* 1975—.

SIDELIGHTS: Irene Athey speaks French, German, Malay, Spanish, Swahili, and is competent in American Sign Language for the deaf.

* * *

ATKINS, Thomas (Radcliffe) 1939-

PERSONAL: Born April 5, 1939, in Mobile, Ala.; son of Jack R. (an importer) and Sadie B. (Daves) Atkins; married Mary Ellen O'Brien (a lecturer in drama), April 14, 1964; children: Shawn, Mark. *Education:* Duke University, B.A., 1961; Yale University, M.F.A., 1964. *Home:* 6943 Brookview Rd. N.W., Roanoke, Va. 24019. *Office:* Department of Theatre Arts, Hollins College, Box 9602, Hollins College, Va. 24020.

CAREER: Vassar College, Poughkeepsie, N.Y., lecturer

in drama, 1964-65; Hollins College, Hollins College, Va., instructor, 1965-67, assistant professor, 1967-70, associate professor of drama, 1970—, chairman of department of theatre arts, 1971—. Part-time lecturer at City College of the City University of New York, spring, 1971. *Member:* Council of Film Periodical Editors. *Awards, honors:* Woodrow Wilson fellowship, 1961-62.

WRITINGS—Editor: *Sexuality in the Movies,* Indiana University Press, 1975; *Science Fiction Films,* Simon & Schuster, in press; *Graphic Violence on the Screen,* Simon & Schuster, in press; *Frederick Wiseman,* Simon & Schuster, in press; *Ken Russell,* Simon & Schuster, in press; (with John Baxter) *The Fire Came By: The Riddle of the Great Siberian Explosion* (introduction by Isaac Asimov), Doubleday, in press.

Contributor: Frank N. Magill, editor, *Contemporary Literary Scene, 1973,* Salem Press, 1974; Magill, editor, *Literary Annual, 1973,* Salem Press, 1974.

General editor of film series for Simon & Schuster, 1974—. Contributor of plays and articles to film and literary journals, including *Cinefantastique, Sight and Sound, Southern Humanities Review, Mill Mountain Review,* and *Kenyon Review.* Founder, editor, and publisher of *Film Journal,* 1971—.

WORK IN PROGRESS: Research for *The Moviegoing Ritual,* for Indiana University Press; a novel.

AVOCATIONAL INTERESTS: Travel, collecting art and books, photography.

* * *

ATKINSON, (Justin) Brooks 1894-

PERSONAL: Born November 28, 1894, in Melrose, Mass.; son of Jonathan Henry (a journalist) and Garafelia (Taylor) Atkinson; married Oriana MacIlveen (an author), August 18, 1926; children: (stepson) Bruce T. MacIlveen. *Education:* Harvard University, A.B., 1917. *Home:* Durham, N.Y. 12422.

CAREER: Springfield Daily News, Springfield, Mass., reporter, 1917; Dartmouth College, Hanover, N.H., English instructor, 1917-18; *Boston Evening Transcript,* Boston, Mass., reporter and assistant to drama critic, 1918, 1919-22; *Harvard Alumni Bulletin,* Cambridge, Mass., associate editor, 1920-22; *New York Times,* New York, N.Y., book review editor, 1922-25, drama critic, 1925-42, 1946-60, war correspondent in Chungking, China, 1942-44, news correspondent in Moscow, 1945-46, critic-at-large, 1960-65. *Military service:* U.S. Army, 1918. *Member:* New York Drama Critics Circle (first president, 1936), American Academy of Arts and Sciences (fellow), Actors' Equity Association (honorary life member), The Players (New York City). *Awards, honors:* L.H.D. from Williams College, 1941; Pulitzer Prize in journalism, 1947, for series of articles on the Soviet Union; D.H.L. from Adelphi College (now University), 1960; L.L.D. from Pace College (now University), Franklin and Marshall College, Brandeis University, and Clark University, all 1965, from Washington College, 1966, and from Long Island University, 1967; L.D. from Dartmouth College, 1975.

WRITINGS: Skyline Promenades: A Potpourri (nonfiction), Knopf, 1925; *Henry Thoreau: The Cosmic Yankee* (biography), Knopf, 1927; *East of the Hudson* (nonfiction), Knopf, 1931; *The Cingalese Prince* (travel), Doubleday, 1934; *Cleo for Short* (nonfiction), Howell, Soskin, 1940; *Broadway Scrapbook* (collected articles), Theatre Arts,

1947, reprinted, Greenwood Press, 1970; *Once Around the Sun* (essays), Harcourt, 1951; (author of foreword) *New Voices in the American Theatre* (play anthology), Modern Library, 1955; *Tuesdays and Fridays* (collected articles), Random House, 1963; *Brief Chronicles* (collected articles), Coward, 1966; (author of introduction) Marian Spitzer, *The Palace,* Atheneum, 1969; (author of introduction) Norman Nadel, *A Pictorial History of the Theatre Guild,* Crown, 1969; *Broadway* (theatre history), Macmillan, 1970; *This Bright Land: A Personal View,* Natural History Press, 1972; (with Al Hirschfield) *The Lively Years: Reviews and Drawings of the Most Significant Plays since 1920,* Association Press, 1973.

Editor: *College in a Yard: Minutes by Thirty-Nine Harvard Men,* Harvard University Press, 1957; *The Pace Report: Thirty-Five Alumni, Faculty Members, and Administrators Describe a College in Transition,* Pace College, 1966; Henry David Thoreau, *Walden and Other Writings,* Modern Library, 1937; Ralph Waldo Emerson, *Complete Essays and Other Writings,* Modern Library, 1940; *Sean O'Casey Reader: Plays, Autobiographies, Opinions,* St. Martin's, 1968.

SIDELIGHTS: Brooks Atkinson was one of the first elected members of the Theatre Hall of Fame and Museum in 1972. The Mansfield Theater was renamed in his honor in September, 1960. *Avocational interests:* Carpentry and ornithology.

BIOGRAPHICAL/CRITICAL SOURCES: Oriana Atkinson, *Over at Uncle Joe's,* Bobbs-Merrill, 1947; *Newsweek,* December 28, 1959; *New Yorker,* May 14, 1960; *Audubon,* September, 1965; *Saturday Review,* October 8, 1966.

* * *

ATKISSON, Arthur A(lbert, Jr.) 1930-

PERSONAL: Born October 5, 1930, in Omaha, Neb.; son of Arthur Albert (an adhesive products executive) and Doris Irene (Fields) Atkisson; married Evelyn F. Rodtang, August 20, 1948; married second wife, Jean Ann Fuller, April 23, 1971; children: (first marriage) Noel, Christine, Elizabeth, Penelope; (second marriage) Eric. *Education:* Lewis & Clark College, B.S., 1950; University of Oregon, graduate study, 1950-51; University of Southern California, M.P.A., 1968, D.P.A. (with distinction), 1973. *Politics:* Democrat. *Religion:* Protestant. *Home:* 1030 Cornelius, Green Bay, Wis. *Office:* Department of Environmental Administration, University of Wisconsin, Green Bay, Wis. 54302.

CAREER: Bonneville Power Administration, Portland, Ore., administrative analyst, 1951-53; Los Angeles County Chief Administrative Office, Los Angeles, Calif., administrative analyst, 1953-55; Los Angeles County Air Pollution Control District, Los Angeles, Calif., deputy director, 1955-66; University of Southern California, Los Angeles, executive director of Institute of Urban Ecology, 1966-69; University of Texas, Houston, professor of urban health and director of urban health program, 1969-73; Institute of Urban Ecology and Public Affairs, Inc., Houston, Tex., president, 1973-75; University of Wisconsin, Green Bay, professor of environmental administration and chairman of department, 1975—. Member of National Air Pollution Manpower Development and Training Advisory Committee, 1966-71; president of Southeast Texas Environmental Coalition, 1971; president of Texas Environmental Coalition, 1972. Member of adjunct faculty at Rice University, 1972-73. Consultant to U.S. Environmental Protection

Agency, 1968-72. *Military service:* U.S. Army, 1947-48. U.S. Army Reserve, 1951-67; became major.

MEMBER: American Society for Public Administration, American Public Health Association, American Association for the Advancement of Science. *Awards, honors:* Honor medal from Freedoms Foundation, 1951; air conservation award from California Lung Association, 1969.

WRITINGS: (Contributor) *Municipal Public Relations,* International City Managers Association, 1966; (contributor) Harvey S. Perloff, editor, *The Quality of the Urban Environment,* Johns Hopkins Press, 1969; (editor with Richard Gaines) *Development of Air Quality Standards,* C. E. Merrill, 1970; (with W. L. Faith) *Air Pollution,* Wiley, 1972; (contributor) Richard A. Tybout, editor, *Environmental Quality and Society,* Ohio State University Press, 1975. Contributor to professional journals.

WORK IN PROGRESS: Man and Metropolis, with David Martin, examining the impacts of the new metropolitan milieu on human health and well-being, and reviewing U.S. urban policies and programs.

SIDELIGHTS: Atkisson writes: "The erosion of faith in the future, a weakening of our traditional commitment to excellence of performance, and an unfortunately increasing bureaucratization of U.S. society are now threatening the present and future well-being of the U.S. society. Rigorous analysis of the chains of causes leading to unwanted or undesirable social and environmental outcomes is too often neglected by policy makers in favor of politically expedient problem solutions. This view is central to my research and publications."

*   *   *

AUERBACH, Erna   ?-1975

?—June 23, 1975; German-born British painter, educator, art historian, and author of books on art. Obituaries: *AB Bookman's Weekly,* August 25, 1975.

*   *   *

AUSTIN, John   1922-

PERSONAL: Born March 17, 1922, in London, England; son of Guy K. and Joan M. (Walrond) Austin; married Patricia Owens, April 14, 1968 (divorced, 1974); children: Guy II, John Norman. *Education:* Attended University of London. *Politics:* Independent. *Religion:* Episcopal. *Address:* P.O. Box 49957, Los Angeles, Calif. 90049. *Agent:* Arthur Pine Associates, 1780 Broadway, New York, N.Y. 10019.

CAREER: Entertainment journalist since 1945. Motion picture producer in India, 1948-49, and England, 1949-52; West Coast correspondent for Macquarie Broadcasting Service (Sydney, Australia), 1960—. Publisher of *Hollywood Citizen-News,* 1970-71; Hollywood commentator on KHJ-Television, 1970; host of "More Than You Care to Know" and "Teletalk," both on KCRW-Radio, a National Public Radio network station, 1972—. Member of California attorney general's advisory council and Los Angeles County district attorney's advisory council. *Military service:* U.S. Army, Special Services, 1942-45; served in London, England, in France, and in Germany.

WRITINGS: Sex Is Big Business, Tower, 1966; *Hollywood's Unsolved Mysteries,* Ace Books, 1972; *More of Hollywood's Unsolved Mysteries,* Ace Books, 1973; (with George Jessel) *The World I Lived In,* Regnery, 1975; *Sexual Surrogate,* Regnery, in press.

Author of columns distributed by Syndication International. Columnist for *Hollywood Reporter,* 1968-70, *Photoplay,* 1969-71, *Show,* 1970—, and *Entertainment World,* 1970—. West Coast editor and contributor of column, Magazine Management Co., 1965-70; West Coast editor, *Pageant,* 1970—; *Los Angeles Evening Citizen-News,* entertainment editor, 1970-72, contributor of column, 1970—, executive editor and film reviewer, 1972—.

WORK IN PROGRESS: Naked Hollywood, on the early days of Hollywood; *Destruction,* examining the suicides of Pier Angeli, Judy Garland, Gia Scala, and children of famous stars.

SIDELIGHTS: Austin writes: "Having 'grown up' in the entertainment industry as a second generation entertainment journalist [I] feel it necessary to bring out the part of Hollywood never covered in the fan magazines and gossip columns: the behind the scenes look at the stars and the town."

*   *   *

AVICE, Claude   1925-
(Pierre Barbet, David Maine, Olivier Sprigel)

PERSONAL: Born May 16, 1925, in Le Mans, France; son of Leon (a pharmacist) and Renee (Bardet) Avice; married Marianne Brunswick (a pharmacist), July 23, 1952; children: Brigitte Avice Sebag, Patrick, Olivier. *Education:* University of Paris, Docteur en pharmacie, 1954. *Home:* 4 Square de l'Avenue du Bois, Paris 75116, France. *Office:* 151 Boulevard Malesherbes, Paris 75017, France.

CAREER: Pharmacist in Paris, 1952—; director of laboratory for medical analysis, 1955—. Science fiction writer. *Member:* Society of Doctors in Pharmacy, French Society of Astronomy, Science Fiction Writers of America.

WRITINGS—All science fiction—Under pseudonym Pierre Barbet; all published by Presses de la Cite (Paris), except as noted: *Vers un avenir perdu* (title means "Towards a Lost Future"), Gallimard, 1962; *Babel 3,805,* Gallimard, 1963; *Les Limiers de l'infini* (title means "Bloodhounds of the Infinite"), 1966; *Les Cavernicoles de Wolf* (title means "Cave Inhabitants of Wolf"), 1966; *L'Etoile du neant* (title means "The Star of Nought"), 1967; *L'Enigme des quasars* (title means "The Secret of Quasars"), 1967; *Hallali cosmique* (title means "Cosmic Death"), 1967; *La Planete des cristophons* (title means "Planet of Cristophons"), 1968; *Evolution magnetique* (title means "Magnetic Evolution"), 1968; *Vikings de l'espace* (title means "Space Vikings"), 1969; *Les Chimeres de Seginus* (title means "The Chimeras of Seginus"), 1969; *L'Exile du temps* (title means "Exile of Time"), 1969.

Etoiles en perdition (title means "Stars in Distress"), 1970; *Les Maitres des pulsars* (title means "Masters of Pulsars"), 1970; *Les Grognards d'Eridan,* 1970, translation by Hochman published as *Napoleon of Eridan,* DAW Books, 1976; *L'Agonie de la Voie Lactee* (title means "The Agony of the Milky-Way"), 1970; *Les Conquistadores d'Andromede* (title means "The Conquistadors of Andromeda"), 1971; *Le Transmetteur de Ganymede* (title means "Ganymede's Transmitter"), 1971; *Azraec de Virgo* (title means "Azraec of Virgo"), 1971; *A quoi songent les psyborgs,* 1971, translation by Wendane Ackerman published as *Games Psyborgs Play,* DAW Books, 1973; *L'Empire du Baphomet,* 1972, translation by Bernand Kay published as *Baphomet's Meteor,* DAW Books, 1972; *Les Insurges de Laucor* (title means "Insurgents of Launed Planet"), 1972; *La Planete empoisonnee* (title means "P

1972; *Tremplins d'etoiles* (title means "Springboard of the Stars"), 1972; *La Planete enchantee,* 1973, translation by C. J. Richards published as *Enchanted Planet,* DAW Books, 1975; *Iiane de Noldaz* (title means "Iiane of Noldaz"), 1973; *Les Bioniques d'Atria* (title means "Bionics of Atria"), 1973; *Le Batard d'Orion* (title means "The Bastard of Orion"), 1973; *Magiciens galactiques* (title means "Galactic Magicians"), 1974; *L'Univers des Geons* (title means "The Universe of Geons"), 1974; *Croisade stellaire* (title means "Stellar Crusade"), 1974; *Les Mercenaires de Rychna* (title means "The Mercenaries of Rychna"), 1974; *Nymphe de l'espace* (title means "Nymph of Space"), 1975; *Patrouilleur du neant* (title means "Patrol of Nought"), 1976; *Venusine* (title means "Venusian"), in press.

Under pseudonym David Maine: *Les Disparus du club Chronos* (title means "Club Chronos Is Missing"), Albin Michel, 1972; *Guerillero galactique* (title means "Galactic Guerrillas"), Albin Michel, 1976.

Under pseudonym Olivier Sprigel: *Crepuscule du Futur* (title means "Twilight of the Future"), Masque, 1976.

Work represented in anthologies, including *Toxico Futuris,* edited by Michel Demuth, Opta (Paris), 1975; and translation of short story included in *European Anthology,* edited by Donald A. Wollheim, Doubleday, 1976. Contributor of science fiction short stories to French periodicals, including *Policier Mystere Magazine* and *Horizons du Fantastique.*

WORK IN PROGRESS: Ambassade Galactique (Galactic Embassy).

* * *

AXELRAD, Jacob 1899-

PERSONAL: Born May 25, 1899, in Philadelphia, Pa.; son of Abraham (a wheelwright) and Celia (Zion) Axelrad; married Pauline Morse, February 5, 1915 (died, 1952); married Kate Gold (an accountant), November 21, 1953; children: Muriel (Mrs. Joseph Klein). *Education:* New York University, LL.B., 1912, LL.M., 1913. *Home and office:* 55 West 11th St., New York, N.Y. 10011.

CAREER: In private law practice, 1913—. Assistant professor of English, Associated Colleges of New York, 1946-48; lecturer in literature and sociology, Rand School of Social Science, 1948-49. *Member:* American Civil Liberties Union, American Association of University Professors, New York, Massachusetts, and Federal Bar Associations.

WRITINGS: Anatole France: A Life Without Illusions, 1844-1924, Harper, 1944; *Patrick Henry: The Voice of Freedom,* Random House, 1947, reprint, Greenwood Press, 1975; *Philip Freneau: Champion of Democracy,* University of Texas Press, 1967.

WORK IN PROGRESS: A life of Samuel Gridley Howe; a volume of aphorisms; short stories.

* * *

AYERS, Ronald 1948-

PERSONAL: Born January 3, 1948, in Chicago, Ill.; son of Josiea and Mary (a presser; maiden name, McGhee) Ayers; married Adrian Walker, August, 1965 (divorced, 1965; Ronald married Annie Edwards, February 7, 1972; children: Central Staran, Denise Collette. *Education:* Attended Central State None. University, Wilberforce, Ohio, 1965-68. *Politics:* South Vail, ... *Religion:* Roman Catholic. *Home and office:* 14508 ... oor, Ill. 60426.

CAREER: Joseph Ford (auto dealership), Posen, Ill., auto mechanic, 1969-72; Montgomery Ward, Harvey, Ill., auto mechanic, 1972-75; writer.

WRITINGS: Case of the Deadly Triangle (novel), Holloway, 1974. Contributor of short stories to *Mystique.*

WORK IN PROGRESS: A screenplay adaptation of the *Case of the Deadly Triangle;* two mystery novels.

SIDELIGHTS: Ayers told *CA:* "I began reading fiction in high school, and fell in love with it. *A Tale of Two Cities* and *Ivanhoe* stimulated the belief that I wanted to be a writer of novels. Since leaving high school, I have made a study of the novel as an art form, and have collected and read over five hundred. Although I am concentrating on mastering the mystery genre at the moment, I hope to write and publish a mainstream novel one day."

* * *

AYRTON, Michael 1921-1975
(Michael Gould)

February 20, 1921—November 17, 1975; British painter, sculptor, theatre designer, and writer on art and Greek legend. Obituaries: *New York Times,* November 18, 1975; *AB Bookman's Weekly,* December 22-29, 1975. (See index for previous *CA* sketch)

* * *

BABBIDGE, Homer Daniels, Jr. 1925-

PERSONAL: Born May 18, 1925, in West Newton, Mass.; son of Homer and Allalie Lavinia (Adams) Babbidge; married Marcia Joan Adkisson, December 22, 1956; children: Aimee Allison, Sandra Allalie, Alexander Adams. *Education:* Yale University, B.A., 1945, M.A., 1948, Ph.D., 1953. *Home:* 63 Wall St., New Haven, Conn. 06510. *Office:* Timothy Dwight College, Yale University, New Haven, Conn. 06520.

CAREER: Yale University, New Haven, Conn., executive fellow of Pierson College, 1949-57, director of financial aids, lecturer in education, member of board of admissions, 1954-57; special assistant to U.S. Commissioner of Education, Washington, D.C., 1955-56; U.S. Department of Health, Education and Welfare, Washington, D.C., assistant to secretary, 1957-58, director of program for financial assistance to higher education, 1958-59, assistant commissioner and director of division of higher education, 1959-61; American Council on Education, Washington, D.C., vice-president, 1961-62; University of Connecticut, Storrs, president, 1962-72; Yale University, master of Timothy Dwight College and fellow of Institution for Social and Policy Studies, 1972—. Co-founder of American studies at Yale University for foreign students, 1948; trustee of Northeast Utilities, Hazen Foundation, Gannett Foundation, Hartford Hospital, Choate School, Wadsworth Athenaeum; director of Security Corp., Hartford National Bank, Encyclopaedia Britannica, Inc.; chairman, U.S. Advisory Commission on International Educational and Cultural Affairs; chairman, Connecticut Humanities Council; member of the national board of advisors, National Association for Retarded Children.

MEMBER: American Historical Association, American Studies Association, Aurelian Society, Marine Historical Association, Scroll and Key, Elizabethan Club and Fence Club (both Yale), Hartford Twentieth Century Club, Century Club (New York). *Awards, honors:* Named one of 10 Outstanding Young Men of Nation by U.S. Junior

Chamber of Commerce, 1959; Distinguished Service medal from Department of Health, Education and Welfare, 1961; Human Relations award from National Conference of Christians and Jews, 1970; Outstanding Civilian Service medal from the U.S. Department of the Army, 1972. Honorary degrees from Ithaca College, 1960, University of Hartford, 1963, Fairfield University, 1968, Yale University, 1969, Trinity College, 1969, Rosary Hill College, 1969, American International College, 1970, Rollins College, 1971, Rhode Island College, 1972, University of New Haven, 1973.

WRITINGS: Student Financial Aid: A Manual for Colleges and Universities, American College Personnel Association, 1960; (with W. R. Rosenzweig) *The Federal Interest in Higher Education,* McGraw, 1962; (editor and author of introduction) Noah Webster, *On Being American: Selected Writings, 1783-1828,* Praeger, 1967; *Fitted to the Burden* (selected speeches), edited by William T. O'Hara, University of Connecticut Alumni Association, 1972.*

*   *   *

BABBIE, Earl (Robert) 1938-

PERSONAL: Born January 8, 1938, in Detroit, Mich.; son of Herman Octave (an automobile body mechanic) and Marion (Towle) Babbie; married Sheila Trimble (a project assistant for Erhard Seminars Training), May 17, 1965; children: Aaron Robert. *Education:* Harvard University, A.B., 1960; University of California, Berkeley, M.A., 1966, Ph.D., 1969. *Politics:* "Active, reformist, civil libertarian." *Religion:* None. *Home:* 7280 Mokuone St., Honolulu, Hawaii 96825. *Office:* Department of Sociology, University of Hawaii, Honolulu, Hawaii 96822.

CAREER: University of California, Berkeley, research sociologist at Survey Research Center, 1966-68, assistant director of center, 1967-68; University of Hawaii, Honolulu, assistant professor, 1968-70, associate professor, 1970-74, professor of sociology, 1974—, program director for survey research at Social Science Research Institute, 1968-69, director of Institutional Research Office, 1970, director of Survey Research Office, 1970-73, chairman of department of sociology, 1973-74. Partner, Pacific Poll Co. (public opinion polling), 1969-70; visiting scholar at University of California, Berkeley, 1975. Member of Hawaii State Tract Committee, 1969—; president of Save Wawamalu Association, 1971-73; member of Hawaii Visitors Bureau research committee, 1972-74; member of research advisory committee of Hawaii Commission on Children and Youth, 1972-74; member of board of directors of Citizens for Hawaii, 1972-74; vice-president of Hawaii Center for Environmental Education, 1973-74. *Military service:* U.S. Marine Corps, active duty, 1960-63, reserve duty, 1963-66; became first lieutenant.

MEMBER: American Sociological Association, American Association for Public Opinion Research, American Civil Liberties Union, Zero Population Growth, Life of the Land, Pacific Sociological Association. *Awards, honors:* Grant from Haas Community Fund, 1973, for the writing of *The Practice of Social Research;* grant from Erhard Seminars Training of Hawaii, 1975.

WRITINGS: (With Charles Y. Glock and Benjamin B. Ringer) *To Comfort and to Challenge,* University of California Press, 1967; (with William Nicholls) *Oakland in Transition: A Summary of the 701 Household Survey* (monograph), Survey Research Center, University of California,

Berkeley, 1969; *Science and Morality in Medicine,* University of California Press, 1970; *A Profile of the Honolulu Model Neighborhoods: 1969* (monograph), Honolulu Model Cities Project, 1970; *Hubris: Hawaii Uniform Bank and Remote Interactive System* (monograph), Survey Research Office, University of Hawaii, 1971; *The Maximillion Report* (monograph), Citizens for Hawaii, 1972; *Survey Research Methods,* with instructor's manual, Wadsworth, 1973; (contributor) Glock, editor, *Religion in Sociological Perspective,* Wadsworth, 1973; *The Practice of Social Research,* Wadsworth, 1975; (with Robert Huitt) *Practicing Social Research* (manual), Wadsworth, 1975. Contributor to academic journals. Editorial reader for *Sociology of Education,* 1967.

WORK IN PROGRESS: Patterns of American Prejudice, with Charles Glock and Harold Quinley, for Harper; *Society by Agreement,* publication by Wadsworth expected in 1977; *Essays in Metasociology; George Franklin Spinney,* a biography of the journalist involved in the breakup of Tammany Hall; *Social Problems,* Wadsworth, 1979; *Social Anthropology,* Wadsworth, 1981.

SIDELIGHTS: Babbie writes: "I have only recently begun seeing myself as a writer rather than a professor who also writes. As things have turned out, I am able to write textbooks that both instructors and students seem to enjoy and get value from. That's a nice feeling, plus I've discovered you get paid for that." *Avocational interests:* Listening to John Denver's music.

*   *   *

BABCOCK, Dennis Arthur 1948-

PERSONAL: Born June 16, 1948, in Berkeley, Calif.; son of Frederick (an air force career officer) and Dorothy (Vogt) Babcock; married Lorene Kay Evenson (an interior designer), March 7, 1970. *Education:* Iowa State University, B.S., 1970; University of Minnesota, M.A., 1974, currently candidate for Ph.D. *Politics:* Democrat. *Religion:* Lutheran. *Address:* Guthrie Theater, Vineland Pl., Minneapolis, Minn. 55403.

CAREER: High school director of theater in the public schools of Des Moines, Iowa, 1970-72; Guthrie Theater, Minneapolis, Minn., actor/technician, 1974-75, publications director, 1975—. *Member:* Theta Alpha Phi.

WRITINGS: (With Preston Boyd) *Careers in the Theater* (juvenile), Lerner, 1975.

WORK IN PROGRESS: A history of theatre-in-the-round; research on famous actors and actresses.

*   *   *

BABINGTON, Anthony Patrick 1920-

PERSONAL: Born April 4, 1920, in Cork, Ireland; son of Oscar John Gilmore (an engineer) and Anne Honor (Wrixon) Babington; *Education:* Attended Middle Temple, 1946-48. *Home:* 3 Gledhow Gardens, South Kensington, London S.W.1, England.

CAREER: Called to the Bar, London, England, 1948; Central Criminal Court, London Sessions, Middlesex and Kent Bar Messes, South Eastern Circuit, 1948-59; prosecuting counsel to post office, South Eastern Circuit, 1959-64; metropolitan stipendiary magistrate, London, 1964—. *Military Service:* Royal Ulster Rifles and Dorset Regiment, 1940; received Croix de Guerre with Gold Star (France). *Member:* Garrick Club (London) and Kildare (Dublin).

WRITINGS: No Memorial (wartime experiences), Heinemann, 1954; *The Power to Silence: A History of Punishment in Britain,* R. Maxwell, 1968, Pergamon, 1969; *A House in Bow Street: Crime and the Magistracy, London, 1740-1881,* Macdonald & Co., 1969; *The English Bastille: A History of Newgate Goal and Prison Conditions in Britain, 1188-1902,* Macdonald & Co., 1971, St. Martin's, 1972. Also author of *Great Ideas in Law Making.*

*   *   *

BACH, Wilfrid 1936-

PERSONAL: Born February 23, 1936, in Germany; son of Ludwig (a businessman) and Marie (Reuter) Bach; married Anneliese Baumann (a teacher), July 26, 1961; children: Alexander. *Education:* University of Marburg, first state certificate, 1961, second state certificate, 1966; University of Sheffield, Ph.D., 1965. *Home:* Am Berg Fidel 64, 44 Muenster, Germany. *Office:* Department of Geography, University of Muenster, R.-Koch Strasse 26, 44 Muenster, Germany.

CAREER: McGill University, Montreal, Quebec, visiting assistant professor of climatology, 1966-67; University of Cincinnati, Cincinnati, Ohio, assistant professor of environmental health, 1967-70; University of Hawaii, Honolulu, associate professor, 1970-74, professor of air quality control, 1974-75; University of Muenster, Muenster, Germany, professor of applied climatology and environmental studies, and director of Institute of Geography, 1975—.

MEMBER: Air Pollution Control Association, American Association for the Advancement of Science, American Institute of Environmental Sciences, American Meteorological Society, Association of American Geographers, Environmental Action, New York Academy of Sciences. *Awards, honors:* Award from North Atlantic Treaty Organization (NATO), 1962-64; grants from U.S. Department of Health, Education, and Welfare, 1967-68, National Institute of Environmental Health Sciences, 1968-69, National Science Foundation, 1969-72, and from University of Hawaii, Hawaii TBS Respiratory Disease Association, and American Lung Association, 1972-75.

WRITINGS: Atmospheric Pollution, McGraw, 1972; (with Anders Daniels) *Handbook of Air Quality in the United States,* Oriental Publishing, 1975. Contributor of fifty articles to professional journals.

WORK IN PROGRESS: Energy and Environment, publication by Duxbury expected in 1977; research on air quality control, air pollution and climatic change, and assessment of waste heat.

SIDELIGHTS: Bach writes: "My major concern is man's ability of destroying his life-sustaining environment. There are four areas that warrant special attention: 1) The accumulation of heavy metals in the food chain; 2) The proliferation of nuclear power plants and the concomitant problems of theft, sabotage, blackmail, and waste storage; 3) The potential change of the climate through increased emissions of aerosols, carbon dioxide, and waste heat; and 4) The reduction of the stratospheric ozone layer with its implications on health, food production, and climatic change."

*   *   *

̄ERWALD, Sara 1948-

̄*ONAL:* Born January 26, 1948, in New York, N.Y.; ̄ of Herman F. (a stockbroker) and Shirley (Arnoff) ̄ married Edward Lebar (an advertising execu-

tive), December 22, 1974. *Education:* Attended University of Denver, 1965-67; Columbia University, B.A., 1969, M.A., 1970. *Office:* Greenworks, 625 Greenwich St., New York, N.Y. 10014.

CAREER: Public school teacher in New York, N.Y., 1970-71, 1972; Greenworks, New York, N.Y., owner and landscape designer, 1972—. Member of New York Botanical Garden.

WRITINGS: (With Judith Handelsman) *Greenworks: Tender Loving Care for Plants,* Macmillan, 1974. Contributor to *Harper's Bazaar, New York,* and *Wisdom's Child.*

AVOCATIONAL INTERESTS: Spending time on her upstate New York farm.

*   *   *

BAILEY, Pearl (Mae) 1918-

PERSONAL: Born March 29, 1918, in Newport News, Va.; daughter of Joseph James (a minister) and Ella Mae Bailey; married John Randolph Pinkett, Jr., August 31, 1948 (divorced, March, 1952); married Louis Bellson, Jr. (a jazz drummer), November 19, 1952; children: Tony Bellson, DeeDee Bellson (adopted). *Education:* Attended public schools in Philadelphia, Pa. *Address:* Box 52, Northridge, Calif. 91324. *Agent:* William Morris Agency, 1350 Avenue of the Americas, New York, N.Y. 10019.

CAREER: Singer and entertainer, 1933—; vocalist with various popular bands; made Broadway stage debut in "St. Louis Woman," 1946, followed by "Arms in the Girl," 1950, "Bless You All," 1950, "House of Flowers," 1954, "Hello, Dolly," 1967-69; motion pictures include "Variety Girl," 1947, "Isn't It Romantic," 1948, "Carmen Jones," 1954, "That Certain Feeling," 1955, "St. Louis Blues," 1957, "Porgy and Bess," 1959, "All the Fine Young Cannibals," 1960; television work includes the "Pearl Bailey Show," a musical variety program, 1970-71, "Pearl's Kitchen," a cooking show, and guest appearances on several variety programs; night club entertainer in New York, Boston, Hollywood, Las Vegas, Chicago, London; contract recording artist for Coral Records, Decca Records, and Columbia Records.

AWARDS, HONORS: Donaldson award, 1946, for her performance in "St. Louis Woman"; Entertainer of the Year award from *Cue* magazine and special Tony award, both 1967, both for "Hello, Dolly"; March of Dimes Woman of the Year, 1968; U.S.O. Woman of the Year, 1969; citation from Mayor John Lindsay of New York City, 1969.

WRITINGS: The Raw Pearl (autobiography), Harcourt, 1968; *Talking To Myself* (autobiography), Harcourt, 1971; *Pearl's Kitchen: An Extraordinary Cookbook,* Harcourt, 1973.

WORK IN PROGRESS: Duey, a book for children; two other books.

SIDELIGHTS: Pearl Bailey's entertainment career began in 1933 when she won first prize in an amateur night contest at the Pearl Theatre in Philadelphia. She continued in vaudeville, then into cabarets, eventually appearing on the stage, in movies, on television, and as one of the most popular night club performers in the United States and abroad. Irene N. Pompea says: "Although she does not call herself a religious person, other people feel that she is. Her life vividly portrays her concern for humanity and the feeling of love for her fellow-men. When she can no longer sing and dance, then she feels there will be something else in the world for her to do. Her life has run the gamut. She is a mother, a wife, daughter, artist, writer, and friend. 'All I know,' she says, 'is that I am and I live.'" In 1975 President Ford appointed her special advisor to the United Nations. *Avocational interests:* Yoga and cooking.

BIOGRAPHICAL/CRITICAL SOURCES: Time, November 24, 1967; *New York Times,* November 26, 1967; *Newsweek,* December 4, 1967; *Ebony,* January, 1968; *Cue,* January 6, 1968; *Vogue,* April 15, 1968.

* * *

BAILEY, Raymond H(amby) 1938-

PERSONAL: Born January 31, 1938, in Athens, Tex.; son of Raymond G. and Ada Ann (in restaurant business; maiden name, Prince) Bailey; married Patricia Lawson (a teacher), December 21, 1962; children: Ramona Holland, Sarah Elizabeth. *Education:* Baylor University, B.A., 1959; Texas Tech University, M.A., 1964; Northwestern University, further graduate study, summers, 1965-66; Southern Baptist Theological Seminary, M.Div., 1967, Ph.D., 1973. *Home:* 133 Kentucky Dr., Newport, Ky. 41071. *Office:* First Baptist Church, Eighth & York, Newport, Ky. 41071.

CAREER: Ordained Baptist minister, 1958; speech teacher in high school in Orange, Tex., 1960-63; Sul Ross State College (now University), Alpine, Tex., instructor in speech, 1964-65; Hardin-Simmons University, Abilene, Tex., assistant professor of speech and theater, 1965-67; Bellarmine College, Louisville, Ky., associate professor of theology and communications, 1967-73, member of board of trustees, 1971, director of Thomas Merton Study Center, 1973-74; First Baptist Church, Newport, Ky., pastor, 1974—. Member of board of governors of St. Meinrad School of Theology and Seminary, 1972-74. *Member:* Catholic Biblical Society, American Church History Society, Kentucky Humanities Council, Phi Kappa Phi.

WRITINGS: (Contributor) DeWitte Holland, editor, *Preaching in American History,* Abingdon, 1969; (contributor) Holland, editor, *Sermons in American History,* Abingdon, 1971; *Thomas Merton on Mysticism,* Doubleday, 1975. Contributor to religious magazines.

WORK IN PROGRESS: Faith of Our Fathers, Volume VII, a pictorial history of American Christianity; a book on preaching; a biography of Thomas Merton for young readers.

* * *

BAILYN, Bernard 1922-

PERSONAL: Born September 10, 1922, in Hartford, Conn.; son of Charles Manuel and Esther (Schloss) Bailyn; married Lotte Lazarsfeld, June 18, 1952; children: Charles David, John Frederick. *Education:* Williams College, A.B., 1945; Harvard University, M.A., 1947; Ph.D., 1953. *Home:* 170 Clifton St., Belmont, Mass. 02178. *Office:* Department of History, Harvard University, Cambridge, Mass. 02138.

CAREER: Harvard University, Cambridge, Mass., instructor in education, 1953-54, assistant professor, 1954-58, associate professor, 1958-61, professor, 1961-66, Winthrop Professor of History, 1966—. Trevelyan Lecturer at Cambridge University, 1971; trustee of Manhattanville College. *Military service:* U.S. Army, 1943-46. *Member:* American Academy of Arts and Sciences, American Antiquarian Society, National Academy of Education, American Philo-

sophical Society, Royal Historical Society, Massachusetts Historical Society. *Awards, honors:* Harvard Faculty Prize, 1965, for Volume I of *Pamphlets of the American Revolution;* Pulitzer Prize in history and Bancroft Prize, both 1967, both for *The Ideological Origins of the American Revolution;* Robert H. Lord award from Emmanuel College, 1967; National Book award in history, 1975, for *The Ordeal of Thomas Hutchinson.* Honorary degrees from Lawrence University, 1967, Bard College, 1968, Williams College, 1969, and Clark University, 1975.

WRITINGS: The New England Merchants in the Seventeenth Century, Harvard University Press, 1955; (with wife, Lotte Bailyn) *Massachusetts Shipping, 1697-1714: A Statistical Study,* Belknap Press of Harvard University Press, 1959; *Education in the Forming of American Society: Needs and Opportunities for Study,* University of North Carolina Press, 1960; (editor and author of introduction) *Pamphlets of the American Revolution, 1750-1776,* Volume I, Belknap Press of Harvard University Press, 1965; (editor) *The Apologia of Robert Keayne,* Harper, 1965.

The Ideological Origins of the American Revolution, Belknap Press of Harvard University Press, 1967; *The Origins of American Politics,* Knopf, 1968; (editor with Donald Fleming) *The Intellectual Migration: Europe and America, 1930-1960,* Belknap Press of Harvard University Press, 1969; *Religion and Revolution: Three Biographical Studies;* Belknap Press of Harvard University Press, 1970; (editor with Donald Fleming) *Law in American History,* Little, Brown, 1972; *The Ordeal of Thomas Hutchinson,* Belknap Press of Harvard University Press, 1974.

Editor-in-chief, "John Harvard Library," 1962-70; editor with Donald Fleming, "Perspectives in American History," annual of Charles Warren Center for Studies in American History, Harvard University, 1967—. Contributor to symposia, proceedings, and professional journals including *American Historical Review* and *William & Mary Quarterly.*

* * *

BAIRD, Martha (Joanna) 1921-

PERSONAL: Born June 10, 1921, in Dodge City, Kan.; daughter of Harry Charles (a college professor) and Mary Lou (Jones) Baird; married Eli Siegel (founder and teacher of Aesthetic Realism), October 7, 1944. *Education:* Attended Kansas State College, 1939-40; State University of Iowa, B.A., 1943. *Politics:* "I lean towards the Left." *Residence:* New York, N.Y. *Office:* Definition Press, 141 Greene St., New York, N.Y. 10012.

CAREER: WGN (radio station), Chicago, Ill., scriptwriter, 1943; American Guild of Variety Artists (AGVA), New York, N.Y., secretary, 1944-45; Society for Aesthetic Realism, New York, N.Y., secretary, 1946—; Definition Press, New York, N.Y., editor, 1961—.

WRITINGS: Nice Deity (poems), Definition Press, 1955; (with Sheldon Kranz and others) *Personal and Impersonal: Six Aesthetic Realists* (poems), Terrain Gallery, 1959; (editor) Eli Siegel, *James and the Children: A Consideration of Henry James's 'The Turn of the Screw,'* Definition Press, 1968; (with Ellen Reiss) *The Williams-Siegel Documentary,* Definition Press, 1970; (editor) E. Siegel, *Goodbye Profit System,* Definition Press, 1970, adapted, with Tom Shields, as three-act musical play and produced in New York at Terrain Gallery, 1972; *Two Aesthetic Realism Papers,* Definition Press, 1971; (contributor) Vana Earle, *Big Day in Larned,* John Day, 1971.

Composer of "Bilge Concerto" (a music-drama), broadcast on WUWM-FM, Milwaukee, Wis., 1966. Contributor, "Pageant of Literature Series," edited by M. T. Clare, Macmillan, 1965, "Reading Program Series," edited by Marion Gartler, Macmillan, 1965, and "New Basic Readers Series," edited by H. M. Robinson and others, Scott, Foresman, 1970. Poetry anthologized in *Poetry for Pleasure,* Doubleday, 1960. Contributor of poems and articles to periodicals, including *American Dialogue, New York Element,* and *Allegro.* Editor, *Definition: A Journal of Events and Aesthetic Realism,* 1961-67.

WORK IN PROGRESS: Opposites in Music, a book of music criticism based on Aesthetic Realism.

*   *   *

BAIRSTOW, Jeffrey N(oel)   1939-

PERSONAL: Born December 18, 1939, in Bradford, England; son of George and Mabel (Lee Hainsworth) Bairstow; married Susan C. Jones (a biologist), July 14, 1962; children: Anne-Marie, Timothy Michael. *Education:* University of Birmingham, B.Sc., 1960; Fordham University, M.B.A., 1972. *Office: Tennis,* 495 Westport Ave., Norwalk, Conn. 06856.

CAREER: Tennis, Norwalk, Conn., managing editor, 1973—.

WRITINGS: (With Barry Tarshis) *All About Tennis,* Rand McNally, 1975; (with Tarshis) *Tennis,* Signet Books, 1975; (with Pancho Gonzalez) *Tennis Begins at Forty,* Dial, 1976.

*   *   *

BAKER, Herschel Clay   1914-

PERSONAL: Born November 8, 1914, in Cleburne, Tex.; son of Tyler Alexander and Mae (Deffebach) Baker; married Barbara Morris, September 6, 1939; children: Ann, William, Pamela. *Education:* Southern Methodist University, A.B., 1935, Mus.B., 1935; Harvard University, A.M., 1936, Ph.D., 1939. *Home:* 22 Clifton St., Belmont, Mass. 02178. *Office:* Harvard University, 117 Widener Library, Cambridge, Mass. 02138.

CAREER: University of Texas, Austin, instructor, 1939-44, assistant professor of English, 1944-46; Harvard University, Cambridge, Mass., assistant professor, 1946-49, associate professor, 1949-56, professor of English, 1956-67, Higginson Professor of English Literature, 1967—, chairman of department, 1952-56. *Member:* Phi Beta Kappa, Kappa Sigma. *Awards, honors:* Guggenheim fellowships, 1957, 1963; LL.D. from Southern Methodist University, 1966, University of Vermont, 1967.

WRITINGS: John Philip Kemble: The Actor in His Theatre, Harvard University Press, 1942, reprinted, Greenwood Press, 1969; *The Dignity of Man: Studies in the Persistence of an Idea,* Harvard University Press, 1947, published as *The Image of Man: A Study of the Idea of Human Dignity in Classical Antiquity, the Middle Ages, and the Renaissance,* Harper, 1961, reprinted, Peter Smith, c. 1967; *The Wars of Truth: Studies in the Decay of Christian Humanism in the Earlier Seventeenth Century,* Harvard University Press, 1952, reprinted, Peter Smith, 1969; *Hyder Edward Rollins: A Bibliography,* Harvard University Press, 1960; *William Hazlitt,* Belknap Press of Harvard University Press, 1962; *The Race of Time: Three Lectures on Renaissance Historiography,* University of Toronto Press, 1967.

Editor: (With Hyder Edward Rollins) *The Renaissance in England: Non-dramatic Prose and Verse of the Sixteenth Century,* Heath, 1954; William Shakespeare, *Twelfth Night: Or, What You Will,* New American Library, 1965; (with R. M. Lumiansky) *Critical Approaches to Six Major English Works: Beowulf through Paradise Lost,* University of Pennsylvania Press, 1968; *Four Essays on Romance,* Harvard University Press, 1971. Contributor of articles to professional journals. Contributing editor, *The Complete Signet Classic Shakespeare,* 1972.*

*   *   *

BAKER, John W(esley)   1920-

PERSONAL: Born August 6, 1920, in Austin, Tex.; son of William Loyd and Edith (Mosher) Baker; married Mary Ethel Posey (a teacher of deaf students), January 8, 1953; children: Robert Shelton, Frederick Douglas, Brian Lee, John Preston. *Education:* University of Texas, B.A., 1942, graduate study, 1946-47; University of California, Berkeley, Ph.D., 1953; American University, postdoctoral study, 1973—. *Politics:* Democrat. *Religion:* Baptist. *Home:* 6414 Crane Ter., Bethesda, Md. 20034. *Office:* Baptist Joint Committee on Public Affairs, 200 Maryland Ave. N.E., Washington, D.C. 20002.

CAREER: Trinity University, San Antonio, Tex., instructor in political science, 1947-49; University of Florida, Gainesville, assistant professor of political science, 1952-53; Humboldt State College (now University), Humboldt, Calif., assistant professor, 1953-57, associate professor of political science, 1957-58; College of Wooster, Wooster, Ohio, professor of political science and chairman of department, both 1958-69; Baptist Joint Committee on Public Affairs, Washington, D.C., director of research and associate executive director, both 1969—. Associate professor at Trinity University, summer, 1951; visiting professor at University of California, Berkeley, summer, 1966, and at American University, spring, 1968, 1969-73. Research scholar at University of California, Berkeley, 1962-63; guest scholar at Brookings Institution, 1967-68. Member of Democratic Control Committee of Humboldt County, Calif., 1954-58. *Military service:* U.S. Marine Corps Reserve, active duty, 1942-46; became major; received Purple Heart Medal.

MEMBER: International Political Science Association, American Academy of Political and Social Science, American Association for the Advancement of Science, American Political Science Association, Academy of Political Science, American Society for Public Administration, Southern Political Science Association, Pi Sigma Alpha.

WRITINGS: Public Resource Reporting in Florida (monograph), Public Administration Clearing Service, 1953; (with Clem Miller) *Member of the House,* Scribner, 1962; (contributor) *Emerging Patterns of Rights and Responsibilities Affecting Church and State,* Baptist Joint Committee on Public Affairs, 1969; (editor) *Dissent in Church and State,* Baptist Joint Committee on Public Affairs, 1970; (editor and contributor) *Religious Liberty and the Bill of Rights,* Baptist Joint Committee on Public Affairs, 1972. Contributor to *Encyclopedia of Southern Baptists.* Contributor of articles and reviews to professional journals.

WORK IN PROGRESS: Churches as Pressure Groups; Public Aid to Nonpublic Schools; The Right of Privacy.

BALANDIER, Georges (Leon) 1920-

PERSONAL: Born December 21, 1920, in Aillevillers, France; son of Andre and Lucienne (Andre) Balandier; married Claire Tron, September 11, 1947; children: Claude, Ann. *Education:* Lycee Colbert, Paris, Ph.B., 1937; Sorbonne, University of Paris, Ph.D., 1954. *Home:* 13 Square Carpeaux, Paris 18, France. *Office:* 17 rue de la Sorbonne, Paris 5, France.

CAREER: Overseas Office of Scientific and Technological Research, in charge of research in Senegal, Guinea, and the Congo, 1946-52; National Center for Scientific Research, Paris, France, engaged in research, 1952-54; Paris Institute of Political Studies, professor, 1952-62; Sorbonne, University of Paris, France, professor of sociology, 1962—. *Member:* International Association of French Speaking Sociologists (honorary president).

WRITINGS: Tous Comptes Faits, Editions du Pavois, 1948; (with Jean-Claude Pauvert) *Les villages gabonais: Aspects demographiques, economiques, sociologiques, projets de modernisation,* [Brazzaville], 1952; (with Paul Mercier) *Les pecheurs Lebou du Senegal: Particularisme et evolution,* Centre IFAN-Senegal, 1952; *Sociologie actuelle de l'Afrique Noire: Dynamique des changements sociaux en Afrique central,* Presses universitaires de France, 1955, 2nd edition, augmented and updated, published as *Sociologie actuelle de l'Afrique noire: Dynamique sociale en Afrique centrale,* 1963, 3rd edition, 1971, translation by Douglas Garman published as *The Sociology of Black Africa: Social Dynamics in Central Africa,* Praeger, 1970; *Sociologie des Brazzavilles Noires,* A. Colin, 1955; *L'anthropologie appliquee aux problemes des pays sous-developpes,* Cours de droit, 1955; *Le "tiers-monde": Sous-developpement et developpement,* Presses universitaires de France, 1956, new edition (augmented and updated by Alfred Sauvy), 1961; *Afrique ambigue,* Plon, 1957, translation by Helen Weaver published as *Ambiguous Africa: Cultures in Collision,* Pantheon, 1966; *Les pays "sous-developpes": Aspects et perspectives,* Cours de droit, 1959.

(Contributor) *Economic Development and Its Social Implications: Technological Change and Industrialization,* Presses universitaires de France, 1962; *Les pays en voie de developpement: Analyse sociologique et politique,* Cours de droit, 1964; *La vie quotidienne au royaume de Kongo du XVI au XVIII siecle,* Hachette, 1965, translation by Helen Weaver published as *Daily Life in the Kingdom of the Kongo from the Sixteenth to the Eighteenth Century,* Pantheon, 1968; *Anthropologie politique,* Presses universitaires de France, 1967, revised edition, 1969, translation by A. M. Sheridan Smith published as *Political Anthropology,* Pantheon, 1970; (with Jacques Maquet) *Dictionnaire des civilisations africaines,* F. Hazan, 1968; (editor with others) *Perspectives de la sociologie contemporaine: Hommage a Georges Gurvich,* Presses universitaires de France, 1968; (contributor) *Social, Economic and Technological Change: A Theoretical Approach,* Presses universitaires de France, 1968.

Sens et puissance: Les dynamiques sociales, Presses universitaires de France, 1970; *El concepto de "situacion" colonial,* Editorial Jose de Pineda Ibarra (Guatemala), 1970; (editor) *Sociologie des mutations* (proceedings of the seventh meeting of the International Association of French Speaking Sociologists), Anthropos, 1970; *Gurvitch,* Presses universitaires de France, 1972; *Anthropo-logignes,* Presses universitaires de France, 1974. Contributor of articles to professional journals. Director, *Cahiers Internationaux de Sociologie.* Member of editorial board, *La Quinzaine Litteraire.*

SIDELIGHTS: "Balandier has been recognized as a leading sociologist in the study of Third World peoples," believes R. Kent Rasmussen. "[He contributed] a major theoretical statement, setting forth the concept of the 'colonial situation' as a framework for the study of social change among colonized peoples. In the mid-1950's this was a major departure from the traditional 'culture contact' approach, and his ideas have been widely taken up." According to the *Times Literary Supplement,* "Professor Balandier ... writes with an enthusiasm for Africa that at times has lyric qualities. Yet it is an enthusiasm disciplined by wide knowledge and by the scholar's search for objectivity."

* * *

BALDWIN, Clara

PERSONAL: Born in Ironton, Mo.; daughter of John Taylor, Jr. (a lumberman) and Clara Ellen (Delano) Baldwin. *Education:* Attended Northwestern University; received private music instruction. *Residence:* Bethlehem, Pa.

CAREER: Secretary to father in lumber business, Chicago, Ill., 1932-44; lumber broker in Chicago, 1944-47; free-lance writer, 1945—. Has been correspondent around the world for business trade publications, including *Display World,* Chicago correspondent, 1945-47, special correspondent, 1947—, and *Department Store Economist, Eastern Underwriter,* and *New York Journal of Commerce.* Member: Nature Conservancy, State Historical Society of Missouri.

WRITINGS—Juveniles: *Cotton for Jim,* Abingdon, 1954; *Timber from Terry Forks,* Abingdon, 1956; *The Hermit of Crab Island,* Abingdon, 1958; *Little Tuck,* Doubleday, 1959. Work has been anthologized in *Grandma Moses' Storybook,* compiled and illustrated by Anna R. Moses, Random House, 1961. Author of script for film strip "Beginning with God," Lutheran Church in America, 1965. Contributor to children's magazines and trade publications. Executive editor, *Insurance Buyer* and *Insurance Broker,* both 1949-50.

WORK IN PROGRESS: A fictionalized biography for an elementary reader.

SIDELIGHTS: Clara Baldwin writes: "As a child of a lumberman who for many years operated a planing mill in Laurel, Mississippi, and who visited sawmills and stands of timber, often taking the family along for the ride—machines and industrial operations are a part of life ever since I was old enough to remember. I am still fascinated by how the wheels go round—machine wheels, or the mental wheels—what makes things in general tick....Not only was my father and at least one of his brothers lumbermen, but so were their father and uncles, and their father's father. My great grandfather owned timber in southeast Missouri. And the family started there." *Avocational interests:* Art, travel.

* * *

BALDWIN, Hanson W(eightman) 1903-

PERSONAL: Born March 22, 1903, in Baltimore, Md.; son of Oliver Perry (managing editor of Baltimore *Sun*) and Caroline (Sutton) Baldwin; married Helen Bruce, June 8, 1931; children: Barbara, Elizabeth. *Education:* United States Naval Academy, B.S., 1924. *Residence:* Roxbury, Conn.

CAREER: Baltimore *Sun,* Baltimore, Md., police reporter, 1928; *New York Times,* New York, N.Y., reporter, 1929-37, military and naval correspondent, 1937—, covering military activity in such places as the South Pacific, North Africa, Normandy, and Asia, military editor, 1942-68. Life member of board of trustees, George C. Marshall Research Foundation. *Military service:* U.S. Navy, 1920-27, served in Europe and the Caribbean; became lieutenant junioı grade. *Member:* United States Naval Academy Alumni Association (former president). *Awards, honors:* Pulitzer Prize for journalism, 1942; Syracuse University School of Journalism distinguished service medal, 1944; honorary doctorate from Drake University, 1945.

WRITINGS: (Editor with Wayne Francis Palmer) *Men and Ships of Steel,* Morrow, 1935; *The Caissons Roll: A Military Survey of Europe,* Knopf, 1938; (editor with Shepard Stone) *We Saw it Happen: The News Behind the News That's Fit to Print,* Simon & Schuster, 1938; *Admiral Death: Twelve Adventures of Men Against the Sea,* Simon & Schuster, 1939; *United We Stand!: Defense of the Western Hemisphere,* McGraw, 1941 (published in England as *Defense of the Western World,* Hutchinson, 1941); *The American Navy: What We Should Know About It,* Allen & Unwin, 1941, 2nd edition published as *What the Citizen Should Know About the Navy,* Norton, 1942, 3rd edition published as *What You Should Know About the Navy,* Norton, 1943; *Strategy for Victory,* Norton, 1942; (author of commentary) *The Navy at War: Paintings and Drawings by Combat Artists,* Morrow, 1943; *The Price of Power,* Harper for the Council on Foreign Relations, 1948.

Power and Politics: The Price of Security in the Atomic Age, Claremont College, 1950; *Great Mistakes of the War,* Harper, 1950; *Sea Fights and Shipwrecks: True Tales of the Seven Seas,* Hanover House, 1955; *Middle East in Turmoil,* Foreign Policy Association, 1957; *The Great Arms Race: A Comparison of U.S. and Soviet Power Today,* Praeger, 1958; *World War I: An Outline History,* Harper, 1962; *The New Navy,* Dutton, 1964; *Battles Lost and Won: Great Campaigns of World War II,* Harper, 1966; *Strategy for Tomorrow,* Harper, 1970; *The Crucial Years: 1939-1941,* Harper, 1976. Contributor to *Harper's, Reader's Digest, Saturday Evening Post, New York Times Magazine, National Review,* and other periodicals.

WORK IN PROGRESS: Articles for magazines.

BIOGRAPHICAL/CRITICAL SOURCES: National Review, November 28, 1967; *Newsweek,* April 22, 1968.

*   *   *

BALDWIN, Joyce G(ertrude)   1921-

PERSONAL: Born August 8, 1921, in Wembley, Middlesex, England; daughter of Gilbert and Gertrude (Clarke) Baldwin. *Education:* University of Nottingham, B.A. (honors), 1943; University of Cambridge, teaching certificate, 1943; London Bible College, Dip.Th., 1949, B.D., 1958. *Office:* Department of Biblical Studies, Trinity College, Stoke Hill, Bristol BS9 1JP, England.

CAREER: Teacher of modern languages in Liverpool, England, 1945-47, and in Lancashire, England, 1952-56; Dalton House, Bristol, England, lecturer in old testament, 1956-58, vice-principal, 1958-71; Trinity College, Bristol, lecturer in biblical studies, 1971—.

WRITINGS: (Contributor) Donald Guthrie and J. A. Motyer, editors, *New Bible Commentary,* revised edition,

Inter-Varsity Press, 1970; *Haggai Zechariah Malachi,* Tyndale Press, 1972; *Women Likewise* (booklet), Falcon, 1973.

WORK IN PROGRESS: A study of the Book of Daniel.

*   *   *

BALDWIN, Marshall W(hithed)   1903-1975

PERSONAL: Born March 30, 1903, in New Haven, Conn.; son of Charles Sears and Gratia Eaton (Whithed) Baldwin; married Helen Muhlfeld (a history professor), June 18, 1936 (deceased); children: Mary, Margaret (Mrs. Lawrence Glenn). *Education:* Columbia University, B.A., 1924; Princeton University, Ph.D., 1934. *Home:* 82 Ditmars St., Bronx, N.Y. 10464.

CAREER: Briefly held positions as instructor at Yale University, New Haven, Conn., and Rutgers University, New Brunswick, N.J., prior to 1932; New York University, New York, N.Y., instructor, 1932-34, assistant professor, 1935-45, associate professor, 1945-54, professor of history, 1954-72, professor emeritus, 1972-75. Visiting associate professor, University of Notre Dame, 1949-50. *Member:* American Historical Association, American Catholic Historical Association (president, 1941), Mediaeval Academy of America, Phi Beta Kappa. *Awards, honors:* Named Great Teacher of the University, New York University, 1971.

WRITINGS: Raymond III of Tripolis and the Fall of Jerusalem (1140-1187), Princeton University Press, 1936; *The Medieval Papacy in Action,* Macmillan, 1940; (with Carlton J. H. Hayes and Charles Woolsey Cole) *History of Europe,* Macmillan, 1949, revised edition, 1956, reissued in two volumes as *History of Western Civilization,* 1962, 2nd edition, 1967; *The Medieval Church,* Cornell University Press, 1953; (editor) *The First Hundred Years,* University of Pennsylvania Press, 1958, 2nd edition, University of Wisconsin Press, 1969; *Alexander III and the Twelfth Century,* Newman Press, 1968; (editor) *Christianity through the Thirteenth Century,* Harper, 1970. Contributor to *Encyclopaedia Britannica* and *New Catholic Encyclopedia.**

(Died July 3, 1975, in New York, N.Y.)

*   *   *

BALLARD, Allen B(utler, Jr.)   1930-

PERSONAL: Born November 1, 1930, in Philadelphia, Pa.; son of Allen B. and Olive Dorsey (Robinson) Ballard; divorced; children: Alayna, John. *Education:* Kenyon College, B.A. (magna cum laude), 1952; University of Bordeaux, graduate study, 1952-53; Harvard University, M.A., 1957, Ph.D., 1962. *Office:* University Dean for Faculties, City University of New York, 535 East 80th St., New York, N.Y. 10021.

CAREER: Boston University, Junior College, Boston, Mass., instructor in political science, autumn, 1958; Dartmouth College, Hanover, N.H., lecturer in political science, 1960; City College of the City University of New York, New York, N.Y., lecturer, 1961, assistant professor, 1962-67, associate professor of political science, 1967—, assistant dean of college, 1965-67, associate dean, 1967-69, university dean for academic development, 1969-72, university dean for faculties, 1973, 1974—. Visiting professor at Cornell University, summers, 1962, 1964. Member of national screening board for Fulbright scholarships to France, 1964-65, chairman of board, 1965-66; member of board of trustees of Studio Museum in Harlem, chairman of board, 1973-75. *Military service:* U.S. Army, 1953-55; served in France.

MEMBER: American Political Science Association (member of Conference on Communist Studies, 1964-66), American Association for the Advancement of Slavic Studies, Phi Beta Kappa. *Awards, honors:* Fulbright fellowship, France, 1952-53; first award for distinguished service to Black education from Black Alumni Association of Yale University, 1974.

WRITINGS: The Education of Black Folk: The Afro-American Struggle for Knowledge in White America, Harper, 1973. Contributor to political science journals and to *New York Times.*

WORK IN PROGRESS: Research on the Black middle class in Philadelphia, over a period of two centuries; an analysis of the texture of Black life in an urban environment.

* * *

BALLINGER, (Violet) Margaret (Livingstone) 1894-
(Margaret Hodgson)

PERSONAL: Born January 11, 1894, in Glasgow, Scotland; emigrated to South Africa in 1904; daughter of John and Lillias (Burt) Hodgson; married William George Ballinger (a politician), 1934. *Education:* Attended Huguenot College, 1911; Rhodes University College (now Rhodes University), B.A. (honors), 1913; Somerville College, Oxford, M.A., 1917. *Home:* 8 Firdale Rd., Newlands, Cape Province, Republic of South Africa.

CAREER: Rhodes University College (now Rhodes University), Grahamstown, South Africa, lecturer in history and economics, 1918-19; University of the Witwatersrand, Johannesburg, South Africa, senior lecturer in history and economic history, 1920-34; elected to Union Parliament, South Africa, as native representative for Cape Eastern Circle, 1937-60. South African Liberal Party, member, 1953-68, first president, 1953-55, chairman of Cape Division, 1963-68. Dayason Memorial Lecturer, Institute of International Affairs, Australia, 1960; associate fellow, Nuffield College, Oxford, 1961; councillor, University of Cape Town, 1966-72.

MEMBER: Association of University Women, Workers' Educational Association, Association of European and African Women, South African Association of University Women (president, 1932-33). *Awards, honors:* Queen Victoria Scholarship, University of Cape of Good Hope, 1913; medal for dedicated service to Africa from Royal African Society, 1961; LL.D., University of Cape Town, 1962, Rhodes University, 1964.

WRITINGS: (With husband, W. G. Ballinger; under name Margaret Hodgson) *Bechuanaland Protectorate,* Lovedale Press, 1930; (with W. G. Ballinger; under name Margaret Hodgson) *Basutoland,* Lovedale Press, 1931; (contributor) Edward Eyre, *European Civilisation, Its Origin and Development,* Oxford University Press, 1939; *All Union Politics Are Native Affairs,* Society of the Friends of Africa, 1944; *From Union to Apartheid: A Trek to Isolation,* Juta (Cape Town), 1961, Praeger, 1970. Contributor of articles on race and economics to professional journals.

BIOGRAPHICAL/CRITICAL SOURCES: Ronald Segal, *Political Africa: A Who's Who of Personalities and Parties,* Praeger, 1961.

BALME, Maurice (George) 1925-

PERSONAL: Born October 22, 1925, in London, England; son of John Nettleton and Marjorie (Hodgkinson) Balme; married Sarah Naish (an artist), April 4, 1957; children: Oliver, Catherine, Jonathan. *Education:* Trinity College, Oxford, M.A., 1950. *Religion:* Church of England. *Home:* Newlands, Harrow on the Hill, Middlesex HA1 3JD, England.

CAREER: Teacher of classics in schools in Abingdon, England, 1950-51, and Godalming, England, 1951-52; Harrow School, Harrow on the Hill, England, teacher of classics, 1952—, head of department, 1962-72. *Military service:* Royal Marines, 1944-46; became lieutenant. *Member:* Hellenic Society, Classical Association, Joint Association of Classical Teachers (chairman of council, 1969-70), Schools Council Classics Committee.

WRITINGS: (With M. S. Warman) *Aestimanda: Practical Criticism of Latin and Greek Poetry,* Oxford University Press, 1965; (contributor) J. Higginbotham, editor, *Greek and Latin Literature: A Comparative Study,* Methuen, 1969; *Intellegenda: Comprehension Exercises in Latin Prose and Verse,* Oxford University Press, 1970; (with M. C. Greenstock) *Scrutanda: Comprehension Exercises in Latin Prose,* Oxford University Press, 1973; *The Millionaire's Dinner Party* (adapted from "The Satyricon" of Petronius), Oxford University Press, 1973; (with J.H.W. Moorwood) *Cupid and Psyche* (adapted from *The Golden Ass* by Apuleius), Oxford University Press, 1976.

* * *

BALSIGER, David W(ayne) 1945-
(David Wayne)

PERSONAL: Born December 12, 1945, in Monroe, Wis.; son of Leon C. (in real estate) and Dorothy May (a sales clerk; maiden name, Meythaler) Balsiger; married Janie Frances Lewis (an office administrator), September 26, 1969; children: Lisa Atalie, Lori Faith. *Education:* Attended Pepperdine University, 1964-66, Cypress Junior College, 1966, Chapman College's World Campus Afloat, 1967-68, and International College in Copenhagen, 1968; National University, San Diego, Calif., B.B.A., 1976. *Religion:* Neo-Pentecostal. *Home:* 257 Brentwood St., Costa Mesa, Calif. 92627. *Agent:* Barbara Cox, 3810 East Coast Highway, Suite 1, Corona Del Mar, Calif. 92625. *Office:* Donald S. Smith Associates, California Federal Building, Suite 524, Anaheim, Calif. 92801.

CAREER: Bank teller trainee in California, 1964-66; *Anaheim Bulletin,* Anaheim, Calif., chief photographer and feature writer, 1968-69; *Money Doctor* (consumer magazine), Anaheim, Calif., publisher and editor, 1969-70; World Evangelism, San Diego, Calif., media director, 1970-72; Logos International (book publishers), Plainfield, N.J., director of marketing, 1972-73; Master Media (marketing agency), Newport Beach, Calif., president and director, 1973-75; Balsiger Literary Service (religious literary agency), Costa Mesa, Calif., owner and director, 1974—. Vice-president of communications for Donald S. Smith Associates (advertising firm). Associate member of California Republican Central Committee, 1969-70; assistant press agent for Ronald Reagan for Governor, 1966; campaign manager for James E. Johnson's campaign for U.S. Senate, 1974; member of Orange County and San Diego World Affairs Councils, 1969-70. Member of board of directors of Chapman College's World Campus Afloat, 1967, and Chrisma Ministries, 1969-73.

MEMBER: International Platform Association, National Writers Club, Christians for Political Action, National Society of Literature and the Arts, Smithsonian Institution (associate member), California Republican Assembly, University of California Irvine Friends of the Library. *Awards, honors:* Leadership citation from alumni board of Pepperdine University, 1965; named "writer of the month" by *California Writer,* 1967.

WRITINGS: The Satan Seller (life story of former Satanist high priest Mike Warnke), Logos International, 1972; *The Back Side of Satan* (documentary on the seriousness of the occult problem in America), Creation House, 1973; *One More Time* (life story of ex-convict Don Musgraves), Bethany Fellowship, 1974; *Noah's Ark: I Touched It* (story of Fernand Navarra's discovery of wood on Mount Ararat, believed to be from Noah's Ark), Logos International, 1974; *It's Good to Know* (story of Randy Bullock, radical to religious revolutionary), Mott Media, 1975; *Beyond Defeat* (story of black American James E. Johnson, President Ford's commissioner of the Air Quality Control Board), Chosen Books, 1975; *On the Other Side* (story of a man who experienced a death-bed 'out of body spiritual experience"), Logos International, 1976. Foreign feature correspondent for magazines and southern California newspapers, covering forty-five countries abroad. Contributor of articles and photographs to magazines, sometimes under pseudonym David Wayne, including *Christian Bookseller, National Courier, National Star, Your Church, California Farmer,* and *National Tattler.* News editor of *Logos Journal,* 1972-73.

WORK IN PROGRESS: A book, *New Freaks of 1975;* a bi-centennial series, consisting of *Home Life in Colonial Days, Lives of the Signers of the Declaration, History of the United States,* and *The Spiritual Side of George Washington.*

SIDELIGHTS: Politically active, Balsiger, in 1974, spearheaded the investigative efforts preceding a massive Orange County (California) Grand Jury probe into the management of the Tax Assessor's Office, which has produced criminal indictments and convictions against a congressman, local officials, and an officer of a large business conglomerate. *Avocational interests:* Gardening, hiking, camping.

BIOGRAPHICAL/CRITICAL SOURCES: California Writer, November, 1967; *Monroe Evening Times,* May 30, 1975.

*   *   *

BAMBROUGH, (John) Renford 1926-

PERSONAL: Born in 1926; married 1952; children: one son, three daughters. *Education:* Cambridge University, B.A., 1948, M.A., 1952. *Office:* St. John's College, Cambridge, England.

CAREER: Cambridge University, Cambridge, England, fellow of St. John's College, 1950—, tutor, 1952-63, dean, 1964—, supervisor in classics and philosophy, 1950-62, director of studies in philosophy, 1959—, college lecturer in philosophy, 1962—, university assistant lecturer in classics, 1957-62, Stanton Lecturer, 1962-65, university lecturer in classics, 1962-66, university lecturer in philosophy, 1966—. Mahlon Powell Lecturer, Indiana University, 1962; visiting professor, Cornell University, 1962-63, University of California at Berkeley, 1967, University of Oregon, 1967. Cambridge Review, member of management committee, 1951—; member of council and executive committee, 1951-52, chairman, 1971; Cambridge Union Society, steward, 1955-

61, trustee, 1963—; member of council and executive committee, Royal Institute of Philosophy, 1965-72; governor of Sedbergh School, 1961—.

WRITINGS: (Editor and author of introduction and commentary) *The Philosophy of Aristotle: A New Selection,* New American Library, 1963; (editor) G. E. M. Anscombe and others, *New Essays on Plato and Aristotle,* Humanities, 1965; (editor) *Plato, Popper and Politics: Some Contributions to a Modern Controversy,* Barnes & Noble, 1967; *Reason, Truth and God,* Methuen, 1969, Barnes & Noble, 1973; *Wisdom: Twelve Essays,* Rowman & Littlefield, 1974.

Contributor: Peter Laslett, editor, *Philosophy, Politics and Society,* Macmillan, 1956; (with Ronald Hepburn and others) *Religion and Humanism,* BBC Publications, 1964; *New Cambridge Modern History,* Volume XII, 2nd edition, Cambridge University Press, 1968; Robert L. Cunningham, compiler, *Situationism and the New Morality,* Appleton, 1970. Contributor of articles to professional journals, including *American Journal of Jurisprudence, Analysis, Philosophy,* and *Philosophical Quarterly.* Editor, *Philosophy,* 1972—.*

*   *   *

BANFIELD, A(lexander) W(illiam) F(rancis) 1918-

PERSONAL: Born March 12, 1918, in Toronto, Ontario, Canada; son of Alexander Woods (a clergyman) and Ella (Priest) Banfield; married Martha Fern Munro, October 3, 1942; children: Alexander Brian, Candace Ann (Mrs. Leslie Cook), Martha Kim. *Education:* University of Toronto, B.A., 1942, M.A., 1946; University of Michigan, Ph.D., 1951. *Home:* 37 Yates St., St. Catharine's, Ontario, Canada LZR SR3. *Office:* Institute of Urban and Environmental Studies, Brock University, St. Catharine's, Ontario, Canada.

CAREER: National Parks Service, Ottawa, Ontario, mammalogist, 1946-47; Canadian Wildlife Service, Ottawa, chief mammalogist, 1947-57; National Museum of Canada, Ottawa, chief zoologist, 1957-63; National Museum of Natural Sciences, Ottawa, director, 1964-69; Brock University, St. Catharine's, Ontario, professor of ecology, 1969—, director of Institute of Urban and Environmental Studies, 1974—. *Military service:* Canadian Army, 1942-45; became captain. *Member:* Arctic Institute of North America, Canadian Society of Zoologists, Canadian Society of Environmental Biologists, American Association for the Advancement of Science, American Society of Mammalogists, St. Catharine's Symphony Association (director, 1970-75), Sigma Xi, Phi Sigma, Boone and Brockett Club. *Awards, honors:* Canada Centennial Medal from government of Canada, 1967.

WRITINGS: A Revision of the Reindeer/Caribou, Genus Rangifer, National Museum of Canada, 1962; (contributor) V. E. Cahalane, editor, *Alive in the Wild,* Prentice-Hall, 1970; *The Mammals of Canada,* University of Toronto Press, 1974. Contributor of more than one hundred articles to learned journals.

WORK IN PROGRESS: Environmental Impact Assessment in Canada.

*   *   *

BANNISTER, Donald 1928-

PERSONAL: Born May 7, 1928, in Birmingham, England; son of Charles Frederick (a coal miner) and Cissie (Fulford) Bannister; married Roma Scandolo, December 27, 1951; children: Simon Fulford, Shulie Jane, Lucy Ann Francesca, Piers Anthony. *Education:* University of Manchester, B.A., 1956; University of London, diploma in psychology, 1957, Ph.D., 1959. *Politics:* "Anarcho-syndicalist." *Religion:* Atheist. *Office:* Bexley Hospital, Old Bexley Lane, Bexley, Kent, England.

CAREER: Bexley Hospital, Bexley, Kent, England, head of department of psychology, 1959—. Member of external scientific staff of Medical Research Council (London), 1959—; visiting professor at University of Surrey, 1972—. Member of social effects of television advisory group to British Broadcasting Corp. *Member:* British Psychological Society, American Psychological Association.

WRITINGS: (With J.M.M. Mair) *The Evaluation of Personal Constructs,* Academic Press, 1968; (editor) *Perspectives in Personal Construct Theory,* Academic Press, 1970; (with Fay Fransella) *Inquiring Man,* Penguin, 1971; (editor) *Issues and Approaches in the Psychological Therapies,* Wiley, 1975. Contributor of about thirty articles to psychology journals. Also author of *The Open Mind,* a book on science fiction and psychology, as yet unpublished.

WORK IN PROGRESS: A history book, *Mosaic of the American Civil War;* a novel, *Sam Chard;* an article on a study of children's concept of self, to be included in *Continuing Inquiries in Personal Construct Psychology.*

SIDELIGHTS: Bannister writes: "A lazy and discontented and confused psychologist until 1957 when I read 'The Psychology of Personal Constructs' by George Kelly. . . . This showed me that formal psychology could contain the fire, the twisted ingenuity, the personal feel of living. Now I am an energetic, contented, and confused psychologist." *Avocational interests:* "Fanatically concerned about canal sailing, the American Civil War, planning to go back home to Yorkshire."

*   *   *

BARBACH, Lonnie Garfield   1946-

PERSONAL: Born October 6, 1946, in Newark, N.J.; daughter of Marvin M. (a salesman) and Temy (a purchasing coordinator; maiden name, Sokolow) Barbach. *Education:* Simmons College, B.S., 1967; Wright Institute, M.A., 1972, Ph.D., 1974. *Religion:* Jewish. *Residence:* Sausalito, Calif. *Agent:* Rhoda Weyr, 1350 Avenue of the Americas, New York, N.Y. 10019. *Office:* University of California Medical Center, Suite 300, 350 Parnassus, San Francisco, Calif. 94143; and Nexus, 1797 Union St., San Francisco, Calif.

CAREER: University of California Medical Center, Human Sexuality Program, San Francisco, co-director of clinical training, 1973—; Nexus (an institute for relationship training), San Francisco, psychologist, 1975—.

WRITINGS: For Yourself: The Fulfillment of Female Sexuality, Doubleday, 1975. Contributor to journals in her field.

WORK IN PROGRESS: Theory and practice of preorgasmic women's groups: a professional perspective.

SIDELIGHTS: Lonnie Barbach wrote: "My concern is basically to help women assume control over their lives on all levels, professional and personal. Sexual concerns provide one forum for accomplishing this." *Avocational interests:* Travel, different cultures, and sports.

BARBER, D(ulan) F.   1940-
(David Fletcher)

PERSONAL: Born October 11, 1940, in Reading, England; married Patty Kitchen (a writer), March 27, 1968; children: Dan Bowling (step-son). *Education:* Attended Leeds University, 1958-59. *Politics:* Socialist. *Religion:* None. *Agent:* Wallace, Aiken & Sheil, Inc., 118 East 61st St., New York, N.Y. 10021.

CAREER: Worked in publishing houses in London, England; Calder & Boyars Ltd. (publishers), London, editor, 1963-69; full-time author, 1969—. *Member:* Writers Action Group, Writers' Guild of Great Britain, National Council for One Parent Families. *Awards, honors:* Thomas R. Coward Memorial Award in Fiction from Coward-McCann, Inc., for *A Lovable Man.*

WRITINGS: Three Canterbury Tales (retold from Chaucer for children), Blackie & Son, 1966; (editor) J. Stevens Cox, *Concerning Thomas Hardy: A Composite Portrait From Memory,* Skilton, 1968; *Pornography and Society,* Skilton, 1972; *The Horrific World of Monsters* (juvenile), Marshall Cavendish, 1974; *Unmarried Fathers,* Hutchinson, 1975; (editor) *One Parent Families,* Davis-Poynter, 1975; (editor with Giles Gordon) *Members of the Jury,* Wildwood House, 1976.

Under pseudonym David Fletcher: *Miss Primrose,* Hutchinson, 1955; *Angelo Goes to the Carnival,* Hutchinson, 1956; *The Blue Elephants,* Hutchinson, 1957; *Confetti for Cortorelli,* Pantheon, 1957; *The Village of Hidden Wishes,* Pantheon, 1960; *The Children Who Changed,* M. Joseph, 1961; *The King's Goblet,* Pantheon, 1962 (self-illustrated edition published in England under same title, Constable, 1964); *Mother O'Pearl: Three Tales,* Pantheon, 1970; *A Lovable Man,* Macmillan, 1974, Coward, 1975; *A Respectable Woman,* Coward, 1975; (contributor) *Winter's Crimes Seven,* Macmillan, 1975; *Don't Whistle Macbeth,* Macmillan, 1976; *Accomplices,* Macmillan, 1976.

Also author of a television script. Contributor of articles, criticism, and reviews to periodicals.

WORK IN PROGRESS: Research for three books, a study of Victorian homosexuals, a book about death for children, and a critical book about the American musical; continuing research for a study of John Webster and on morality in Charlotte Bronte's life and work.

SIDELIGHTS: Barber told *CA:* "I am a writer because I love the act of writing and have always loved books. I love interpreting and sharing information but best of all I love creating fictional worlds and people. I am now, however, intensely concerned with the working conditions and financial plight of the writer. I want to make the professional lot of the writer a better one, in all directions. I value and strive for professionalism. . . .

"I am a vegetarian, own two cats and want eventually to live in the country with many, many animals. . . . I am a homebody, the world's most untraveled person. This is partly because writers seldom earn enough to permit foreign travel and because there is only one place I've ever wanted to go—America. As far as I can judge I am atypical of most people in my profession because I do really enjoy writing, physically and mentally. I find great difficulty in stopping and get depressed when I am not working." *Avocational interests:* Music (especially opera).

*   *   *

BARBER, William Joseph   1925-

PERSONAL: Born January 13, 1925, in Abilene, Kan; son

of Ward Seymour Henry and Esther (Roop) Barber; married Sheila Mary Marr, April 16, 1955; children: Thomas, John, Charles. *Education:* Harvard University, A.B., 1949, Oxford University, B.A., 1951, M.A., 1955, D. Phil., 1957. *Home:* 306 Pine St., Middletown, Conn. 06457. *Office:* Department of Economics, Wesleyan University, Middletown, Conn. 06457.

CAREER: Kansas State University, Manhattan, assistant professor, 1951-52; Oxford University, Balliol College, Oxford, England, lecturer, 1956; Wesleyan University, Middletown, Conn., 1957—, became professor of economics, 1965, Andrews Professor of Economics, 1972—. American secretary of Rhodes Scholarship Trust, 1970—; member of board of electors of Eastman professorship, Oxford University, 1970—. *Military service:* U.S. Army, 1943-46. *Member:* American Economics Association, Royal Economics Society, African Studies Association, American Association of Rhodes Scholars, Phi Beta Kappa. *Awards, honors:* Rhodes Scholar, 1949-51; Ford Foundation Foreign Area fellow in Africa, 1955-56; M.A., Wesleyan University, 1965.

WRITINGS: The Economy of British Central Africa: A Case Study of Economic Development in a Dualistic Society, Stanford University Press, 1961; *A History of Economic Thought,* Praeger, 1967; (contributor) Gunnar Myrdal, *Asian Drama: An Inquiry into the Poverty of Nations,* Twentieth Century Fund, 1968. Contributor of articles to professional journals.

SIDELIGHTS: A History of Economic Thought has been translated into Swedish, Spanish, Italian, Japanese, and Portuguese.*

* * *

BARBOUR, Roger W(illiam) 1919-

PERSONAL: Born April 5, 1919, in Morehead, Ky.; son of John William (a farmer) and Laura (Hall) Barbour; married Bernice Lewis, December 28, 1938; children: Marsha (Mrs. Edward Carroll Hale, Jr.), Roger W., Jr., James Lewis. *Education:* Morehead State University, B.S., 1938; Cornell University, M.S., 1939, Ph.D., 1949. *Home address:* Route 1, Tates Creek Pike, Lexington, Ky. 40503. *Office:* School of Biology, University of Kentucky, Lexington, Ky. 40506.

CAREER: University of Kentucky, Lexington, instructor, 1950-52, assistant professor, 1952-56, associate professor, 1956-68, professor of zoology, 1968—. Visiting professor at Institut Teknologi di Bandung, 1957-59; field leader for Kentucky Department of Parks. *Military service:* U.S. Army, 1945-46.

MEMBER: American Association for the Advancement of Science, American Society of Mammalogists, American Society of Ichthyologists and Herpetologists, American Ornithologists Union, American Nature Study Society, Wildlife Society (member of task force on rare and endangered wildlife in the southeastern United States), Society for the Study of Amphibians and Reptiles, Kentucky Academy of Science, Kentucky Ornithological Society (past president), Sigma Xi. *Awards, honors:* Award of merit from American Association for Conservation Information, 1967, for contributions to wildlife conservation; award from National Wildlife Federation, 1969, for practicing and promoting conservation of wildlife and natural resources; Wildlife Publication Award from Wildlife Society, 1974, for *Turtles of the United States.*

WRITINGS—All published by University Press of Kentucky: (With Wayne H. Davis) *Bats of America,* 1969; *Amphibians and Reptiles of Kentucky,* 1971; (with Mary E. Wharton) *A Guide to the Wildflowers and Ferns of Kentucky,* 1971; (with Carl H. Ernst) *Turtles of the United States,* 1972; (with Clell T. Peterson, Delbert Rust, Herbert E. Shadowen, and A. L. Whitt, Jr.) *Kentucky Birds: A Finding Guide,* 1973; (with Wharton) *Trees and Shrubs of Kentucky,* 1973; (with Davis) *Mammals of Kentucky,* 1974. General editor of "Kentucky Nature Series," University Press of Kentucky, 1969—. Contributor of about ninety articles to scientific journals. Editor of *Transactions of the Kentucky Academy of Science,* 1959-63.

WORK IN PROGRESS: The American Darters; Mammals of the Eastern United States.

* * *

BARDOLPH, Richard 1915-

PERSONAL: Born February 18, 1915, in Chicago, Ill.; son of Mark and Anna (Veldman) Bardolph; married Dorothy Corlett, July 28, 1945; children: Virginia Ann (Mrs. George Haskett), Mark III, Richard. *Education:* University of Illinois, B.A., 1940, M.A., 1941, Ph.D., 1944. *Religion:* Lutheran. *Home:* 207 Tate St., Greensboro, N.C. 27403. *Office:* Department of History, University of North Carolina, 1000 Spring Garden, Greensboro, N.C. 27412.

CAREER: University of North Carolina, Greensboro, assistant professor, 1944-52, associate professor, 1952-57, professor of history, 1957-70, Jefferson Standard Professor, 1970—, head of department, 1960—. Ford Foundation faculty fellow at Harvard University, 1952-53; Fulbright visiting professor at University of Copenhagen, 1953-54; visiting professor at University of Frankfurt, summer, 1954. Member of regional selection committee of Woodrow Wilson National Fellowship Foundation; member of commission on theology and church relations, Lutheran Church-Missouri Synod; member of executive committee, Lutheran Council in United States.

MEMBER: American Civil Liberties Union, National Association for the Advancement of Colored People, Archaeological Institute of America, American Historical Association, Organization of American Historians, Southern Historical Association, Phi Beta Kappa. *Awards, honors:* Guggenheim fellowship, 1956-57; Mayflower award, 1960, for *Negro Vanguard;* Litt.D., Concordia College, 1968; National Endowment for the Humanities senior fellow, 1971-72.

WRITINGS: Agricultural Literature and the Early Illinois Farmer, University of Illinois Press, 1948; *The Negro Vanguard,* Rinehart, 1959, reprinted, Negro Universities Press, 1972; *The Civil Rights Record: Black Americans and the Law, 1848-1970,* Crowell, 1970. Contributor of articles to encyclopedias and professional journals. Member of board of editors, *Journal of Southern History.**

* * *

BARDOT, Louis 1896-1975
(Pilou)

May 8, 1896—November 5, 1975; French industrialist and writer of poetry under pseudonym Pilou. Obituaries: *Washington Post,* November 9, 1975.

* * *

BARKALOW, Frederick Schenck, Jr. 1914-

PERSONAL: Born February 23, 1914, in Marietta, Ga.

Education: Georgia Institute of Technology, B.S., 1936; University of Michigan, M.S., 1939, Ph.D., 1948. *Politics:* Democrat. *Home:* 1405 Dellwood Dr., Raleigh, N.C. 27607. *Office:* Department of Zoology, North Carolina State University, Box 5577, Raleigh, N.C. 27607.

CAREER: Auburn University, Auburn, Ala., instructor in zoology, 1936-39; Alabama Department of Conservation, Montgomery, chief biologist, 1939-41; North Carolina State College, Raleigh, associate professor, 1947-48, professor of zoology, 1948-63, head of department, 1950-63; North Carolina State University, Raleigh, professor of zoology, 1963—, professor of forestry, 1968—. Principal biologist for North Carolina Wildlife Resources Commission, 1947-50; senior visiting fellow of Organization for European Economic Cooperation, 1960; member of U.S. Department of Agriculture's advisory committee on multiple use of national forests, 1963-68. Delegate to White House Conference on Conservation, 1962. *Military service:* U.S. Army, 1941-46; became lieutenant colonel.

MEMBER: American Association for the Advancement of Science (fellow), American Institute of Biological Sciences, American Ornithologists Union, American Society of Mammalogists (director, 1961-72), Society of Systematic Zoology, Wildlife Society, Society for Technical Communication, Soil Conservation Society of America, Elisha Mitchell Society, Archaeological Society of North Carolina (president, 1959, 1960), North Carolina Academy of Science (vice-president, 1962; president, 1971), North Carolina Wildlife Federation (president, 1966-67, 1974-75; director, 1967—), Biological Society of Washington, Phi Beta Kappa (president of Wake County association, 1954-55), Sigma Xi, Phi Kappa Phi (president of North Carolina state chapter, 1960-61), Xi Sigma Pi, Alpha Zeta. *Awards, honors:* American Motors Conservation Award, 1967; North Carolina governor's award to "conservationist of the year," 1968.

WRITINGS: A Game Inventory of Alabama, Alabama Department of Conservation, 1949; (with Monica Shorten) *The World of the Gray Squirrel,* Lippincott, 1973. Contributor of more than fifty articles to scientific journals.

SIDELIGHTS: Barkalow's present concerns are population dynamics in small mammals, forest game species, and conservation of natural resources.

* * *

BARNABY, Ralph S(tanton) 1893-

PERSONAL: Born January 21, 1893, in Meadville, Pa.; son of Charles Weaver (an engineer) and Jennie (Christy) Barnaby; first wife, Charline Johnson; married Margaret Evans, March 19, 1936. *Education:* Columbia University, M.E., 1915. *Home:* 2107 Chancellor St., Philadelphia, Pa. 19103. *Office:* Franklin Institute, Philadelphia, Pa. 19103.

CAREER: Elco Co., Bayonne, N.J., engineer, 1915-16; Standard Aero Corp., Plainfield, N.J., assistant chief engineer, 1917; U.S. Navy, regular officer, 1917-47, serving as naval constructor and naval aviator and retiring with rank of captain; Franklin Institute, Philadelphia, Pa., engineering executive, 1947-63, consultant, 1963—. Sculptor and painter; bronze busts are in collections of U.S. Naval Academy, Mariners Museum, and David Taylor Model Basin; has done plaques for Wright Brothers Memorial at Kitty Hawk and naval air fields. *Awards, honors*—Military: Legion of Merit, Air Medal. Civilian: Paul Tissandier diploma of Federation Aeronautique nationale; named N.A.A. "Elder Statesman of Aviation"; Warren E. Eaton Soaring Trophy.

WRITINGS—Self-illustrated: *Gliders and Gliding: Design Principles, Structural Features and Operation of Gliders and Soaring Planes,* Ronald, 1930; *How to Make and Fly Paper Airplanes* (juvenile), Four Winds, 1968. Contributor of articles and papers to technical journals.

AVOCATIONAL INTERESTS: Music.

* * *

BARNARD, Christiaan (Neethling) 1922-

PERSONAL: Born November 8, 1922, in Beaufort West, Cape Province, South Africa; son of Adam Hendrik (a Dutch Reformed minister) and Maria Elizabeth (De Swardt) Barnard; married Aletta Gertruida Louw, November 6, 1948 (divorced, 1970); married Barbara Maria Zoellner, 1970; children: (first marriage) Deirdre Jeanne, Andre Hendrick; (second marriage) one son. *Education:* University of Cape Town, M.B., Ch.B., 1946, M.D., 1953, M.Med., 1953; University of Minnesota, M.S., Ph.D., 1958. *Home:* The Moorings, Flamingo Crescent Zeekoevlei, Cape Town, Republic of South Africa. *Office:* Medical School Observatory, University of Cape Town, Cape Town, Republic of South Africa.

CAREER: Groote Schuur Hospital, Cape Town, South Africa, intern, 1947; private practice in Ceres, South Africa, 1948-51; City Fever Hospital, Cape Town, senior resident medical officer, 1951-53; Groote Schuur Hospital, registrar, 1953-55; University of Cape Town, Cape Town, research fellow in surgery, 1953-55; University of Minnesota, Minneapolis, Charles Adams Memorial scholar and Dazian Foundation for Medical Research scholar, 1956-58; University of Cape Town, lecturer and director of surgical research, 1958—, associate professor, 1963—; Groote Schuur Hospital, senior cardiothoracic surgeon, 1958—, head of cardiothoracic surgery unit, 1961—.

MEMBER: South African Medical Association, Society of Thoracic Surgeons, South African Society of Physicians, Surgeons, Gynecologists (founder member). *Awards, honors:* Ernest Oppenheimer Memorial Trust grantee, 1960; Dag Hammarskjold International Prize, Kennedy Foundation Award; Milan International Prize for Science, fellowships in American College of Surgeons, 1963, New York Cardiological Society, 1965, and American College of Cardiology, 1967; numerous honorary degrees, foreign orders and awards, honorary citizenships and freedoms.

WRITINGS: (With Velva Schrire) *The Surgery of Common Congenital Cardiac Malformations,* Harper, 1968; (contributor) *Les greffes du coeur: Interviews du professeur Christiaan Barnard, du Dr. Pierre Grondin et de pluseurs autres,* Editions de l'Homme, Edition Radio-Canada, 1968; (with Curtis Bill Pepper) *Christiaan Barnard: One Life* (autobiography), Macmillan, 1969; *Heart Attack: You Don't Have to Die,* Delacorte Press, 1971 (published in South Africa as *Heart Attack: All You Have to Know about It,* H. Keartland Publishers, 1971). Contributor of numerous articles to medical journals.

SIDELIGHTS: Dr. Christiaan Barnard came to the United States in 1955 to study under Dr. Owen H. Wangensteen at the University of Minnesota Medical School. Initially his research was in the area of gastrointestinal pathology, but he soon focused his attention on heart surgery. His first heart operation was performed in Minneapolis.

After returning to South Africa in 1958, he developed an artificial heart valve, known as the Barnard Valve, for use in open heart surgery, and completed the first successful open heart surgery in South Africa. In 1967 Dr. Barnard performed the world's first successful human heart transplant operation.

AVOCATIONAL INTERESTS: Power boating, water skiing, fishing, playing tennis, and playing the piano.

BIOGRAPHICAL/CRITICAL SOURCES: Peter Hawthorne, *The Transplanted Heart: The Incredible Story of the Epic Heart Transplant Operations by Professor Christiaan Barnard and his Team,* Rand McNally, 1968; L. Edmond Leipold, *Dr. Christiaan N. Barnard: The Man with the Golden Hands,* Denison, 1971.*

*   *   *

BARNES, Jack   1940-

PERSONAL: Born January 30, 1940, in Dayton, Ohio. *Education:* Carleton College, B.A., 1961; graduate study at Northwestern University, 1961-63. *Politics:* Marxist. *Religion:* Atheist. *Office:* Socialist Workers Party, 14 Charles Lane, New York, N.Y. 10014.

CAREER: Young Socialist Alliance, New York, N.Y., national chairman, 1965-66; Socialist Workers Party, New York, N.Y., national organization secretary, 1969-72, national secretary, 1972—. *Member:* Phi Beta Kappa, Pi Delta Epsilon.

WRITINGS: (With George Breitman, Derrick Morrison, Barry Sheppard, and Mary-Alice Waters) *Towards an American Socialist Revolution,* Pathfinder, 1971; (with Joseph Hansen) *A Revolutionary Strategy for the '70's,* Pathfinder, 1972. Contributor to *Militant.*

WORK IN PROGRESS: Political writings on the economy and the political process.

*   *   *

BARON, Herman   1941-

PERSONAL: Born December 23, 1941, in Philadelphia, Pa.; son of Paul and Pearl (Chatis) Baron. *Education:* Drexel University, B.S., 1964, M.S.L.S., 1966. *Home:* 1101 A Passmore St., Philadelphia, Pa. 19111. *Office:* Franklin Mint, Franklin Center, Pa. 19091.

CAREER: U.S. Department of Defense, Philadelphia, Pa., contract auditor, 1965-66; University of Iowa, Iowa City, documents librarian, 1966-67; Institute for Scientific Information, Philadelphia, Pa., manager of journal services, 1967-70; Franklin Mint, Franklin Center, Pa., indexer and cataloger, 1970—. *Member:* American Library Association, American Society of Indexers.

WRITINGS: Concordance to the Poems of Stephen Crane, G. K. Hall, 1975. Also author of *Index to Kirkus Reviews,* Oxford University Press. Editor of *Limited Editions of the Franklin Mint* (annual reference catalog), 1973—.

WORK IN PROGRESS: Index to Esquire Magazine; Index to the Atlantic; Who's Who at the United Nations; The Complete Guide to Nero Wolfe.

AVOCATIONAL INTERESTS: Horticulture, theater, cinema, travel (several trips to the Orient; has climbed Mount Fuji).

*   *   *

BARR, Beverly

PERSONAL: Born in Boston, Mass.; daughter of Oscar (in wholesale fish business) and Marcia (Polimer) Abrams;

married Harold L. Barr (deceased); married Barry C. Shapiro (a podiatrist), May 30, 1966; children: (second marriage) Brenda Allyson. *Education:* Attended Duke University. *Home:* 13 Stratford Rd., Marblehead, Mass. 01945. *Office:* 59 Temple Pl., Boston, Mass. 02111.

CAREER: Owner and operator of a physical fitness salon in Boston, Mass., 1966—. Has made radio and television broadcasts; lecturer. Member of Massachusetts governor's Commission on Physical Fitness and Sports (chairman, 1967-73); appointed by Boston's mayor to organize exercise for the elderly, 1974—. *Awards, honors:* Citation from the governor of Massachusetts, 1964, for work with children, letter of commendation, 1966, for work with adults; award from WBZ-Radio, 1972, for community service in physical fitness.

WRITINGS: I'd Like to See Less of You, Atheneum, 1974.

WORK IN PROGRESS: Family Exercise Book; a book on back problems.

SIDELIGHTS: Beverly Barr writes: "*I'd Like to See Less of You* was actually written years before I ever thought to have it published. . . . In 1974 I walked into a book store to browse. I looked around to find the section that held fitness books. As I looked through them I found that each book gave me a feeling of horror. Most of them were wrong and grossly inadequate. I quickly marched myself back to my salon, forgetting about browsing, pulled out my manuscript, read it over and wrote my pregnancy chapter. After a few days of revisions, it was submitted to the publisher."

BIOGRAPHICAL/CRITICAL SOURCES: Boston Herald-American, May 4, 1971.

*   *   *

BARR, John J(ay)   1942-

PERSONAL: Born August 27, 1942, in Edmonton, Alberta, Canada; son of Victor J. (a retail merchant) and Juanita (a nurse; maiden name, Taylore) Barr; married Norma Jean Picard, June 13, 1964; children: Laura Francine. *Education:* University of Alberta, B.A., 1963, M.A., 1965. *Politics:* Independent. *Religion:* Anglican. *Office:* Syncrude Canada Ltd., Edmonton, Alberta, Canada.

CAREER: Editorialist, *Edmonton Journal,* 1965-68; Alberta Minister of Education, Edmonton, executive assistant, 1969-72; Syncrude Canada Ltd., Edmonton, manager of public affairs, 1972—. *Member:* Canadian Public Relations Society, Alberta Historical Society.

WRITINGS: The Unfinished Revolt: Essays on Western Independence, McClelland & Stewart, 1971; *The Dynasty: The Rise and Fall of Social Credit in Alberta,* McClelland & Stewart, 1974.

*   *   *

BARRIS, Alex   1922-

PERSONAL: Born September 16, 1922, in New York, N.Y.; son of Gus (a waiter) and Katy (a fur finisher; maiden name, Tsakalos) Barbaritis; married Kay Kontozoglus, July 18, 1948; children: Ted, Katy (Mrs. Ted Lonsdale). *Education:* Attended Shipman School of Journalism. *Politics:* Liberal. *Religion:* "Devout Agnostic." *Home and office:* 6639 Birchton Ave., Canoga Park, Calif. 91307.

CAREER: Globe and Mail, Toronto, Ontario, reporter, 1948-50, columnist, 1949-56, re-write man, 1950-51, copy editor, 1951-52, editor of weekly television section, 1955-56;

Telegram, Toronto, author of "The Barris Beat," an entertainment column, 1957-66; free-lance feature writer, 1966—. Host of Canadian Broadcasting Corp. (CBC) television programs "The Barris Beat" (a variety series), 1956-68, "One of a Kind" (panel show), 1958-59, and "Barris & Co." (variety show), 1968, and of "The Barris Beat" (interview show) on CFTO-Television, 1961. Co-producer of own scripts, "Rollin' on the River" series, 1971, and "Rollin' with Kenny Rogers and the First Edition," 1972; associate producer, "Sonny and Cher Nitty Gritty Hour," 1970. *Military service:* U.S. Army, Medical Corps, 1942-45; became staff sergeant; received Bronze Star Medal. *Member:* Writers Guild of America (West section). *Awards, honors:* Television awards from *Liberty* (Canadian magazine), including awards for best new variety series, 1956, and best television series, 1957.

WRITINGS: The Pierce-Arrow Showroom Is Leaking (about Canadian television), Ryerson, 1969; *Hollywood's Other Men* (movie nostalgia; Movie Book Club selection), A. S. Barnes, 1975; *Hollywood's Other Women* (movie nostalgia), A. S. Barnes, 1975; *Stop the Presses!* (about newspapermen in films), A. S. Barnes, in press; *Hollywood According to Hollywood,* A. S. Barnes, in press.

Author of scripts for television series and programs: "Oscar Peterson Jazz Special," 1962; "Bing Crosby Easter Seal Show," 1965; "Al Hirt Tonight, with Shirley Bassey," 1967; "O'Keefe Centre Presents George Burns," 1967; "That Girl," 1969; "Bill Cosby," 1970; "Love American Style," 1973; "Good Times," 1974. Head writer for television series: "The Barbara McNair Show," 1969-71; "The Darin Invasion," 1970; "Rollin' on the River", 1971; "Celebrity Pleasure Hunt," 1974. Co-writer for television programs: "The Doris Day Special," 1970; "The Fifth Dimension Special," 1971; "Rollin' with Kenny Rogers and the First Edition," 1972; "The Wizard of Odds," 1974. Writer for Canadian television programs: "Swing Easy," 1959, 1960; "Joan Fairfax Show," 1959; "Juliette," 1959-63; "Front Page Challenge," 1964-68; "A World of Music," 1966.

Song writer: lyrics for Toronto production of musical comedy "Evelyn," 1964; assorted musical material for "Spring Thaw" and "After Hours," on the Canadian stage. Contributor to magazines and newspapers, including *Toronto Star.*

WORK IN PROGRESS: Two more books about "the movies."

AVOCATIONAL INTERESTS: Music (jazz and show tunes), travel ("my favorite city is Toronto. Still own a country home at Bethany, Ontario.")

* * *

BARRY, Jerome B(enedict) 1894-1975

January 15, 1894—November 1, 1975; American poet and writer of mystery fiction. Obituaries: *New York Times,* November 4, 1975; *AB Bookman's Weekly,* December 1, 1975. (See index for previous *CA* sketch)

* * *

BARTLETT, Vernon 1894-
(Peter Oldfeld, joint pseudonym)

PERSONAL: Born April 30, 1894, in Westbury, Wiltshire, England; son of Thomas Oldfeld and Beatrice (Jecks) Bartlett; married Marguerite van den Bemden, September 25, 1917 (died 1966); married Eleanor Needham Ritchie, 1969; children: (first marriage) Dennis Oldfeld, Maurice Oldfeld. *Education:* Attended Blundell's School, Tiverton, Devon. *Home:* 603 Centoni, 55062, Colle di Compito, Lucca, Italy.

CAREER: Staff member with *London Daily Mail,* London, England, 1916, and Reuters Agency, 1917; *London Times,* special correspondent in Switzerland, Germany, and Poland, 1919-20, correspondent in Rome, 1921-22; League of Nations, London director, 1922-32; British Broadcasting Corp., radio broadcaster on foreign affairs, 1928-34; *News Chronicle,* London, England, member of staff, 1934-54; *Straits Times,* Singapore, political commentator, 1954-61. Independent Progressive member of Parliament for Bridgewater, Somerset, 1938-50; founder, Vox Mundi Books, 1947; member of U.N. Advisory Committee of Experts, 1948. *Military service:* British Army during World War I; invalided home, 1916; served in Flanders and France; became first lieutenant. *Member:* Garrick Club, Beefsteak Club, Special Forces Club. *Awards, honors:* Commander of the British Empire, 1956.

WRITINGS: Leaves in the Wind (poetry), Morland, 1916; *Mud and Khaki: Sketches from Flanders and France,* Simpkin, Marshall, 1917; *Behind the Scenes at the Peace Conference,* Allen & Unwin, 1919; *Songs of the Winds and Seas* (poetry), Elkin Mathews, 1920; *The Brighter Side of European Chaos: A Journalist's Scrapbook,* Heath Cranton, 1925; *Topsy-Turvy* (short stories), Constable, 1927, reprinted, Books for Libraries Press, 1970; (with P. Jacobsson, under joint pseudonym Peter Oldfeld) *The Death of a Diplomat,* Washburn, 1928; *Calf Love,* Lippincott, 1929; (with P. Jacobsson, under joint pseudonym Peter Oldfeld) *The Alchemy Murder,* Washburn, 1929.

The Unknown Soldier, Stokes, 1930; (with Robert C. Sherriff) *Journey's End: A Novel,* Gollancz, 1930, reprinted, 1968; *No Man's Land,* Allen & Unwin, 1930; *The World—Our Neighbour,* Mathews & Marrot, 1931; *Nazi Germany Explained,* Gollancz, 1933; *If I Were Dictator,* Methuen, 1935; *This Is My Life* (autobiography), Chatto & Windus, 1937; *Intermission in Europe: The Life of a Journalist and Broadcaster,* Oxford University Press, 1938; *Tomorrow Always Comes,* Chatto & Windus, 1943, Knopf, 1944; *Go East, Old Man,* Latimer House, 1948; *East of the Iron Curtain,* Latimer House, 1949, M. McBride, 1950.

Struggle for Africa, Praeger, 1953; *Report from Malaya,* Verschoyle, 1954, Criterion Books, 1955; *And Now, Tomorrow,* Chatto & Windus, 1960; *Tuscan Retreat,* Chatto & Windus, 1964, 3rd edition, 1966; *A Book About Elba,* Chatto & Windus, 1965, 3rd edition, 1973; (with John C. Caldwell) *Let's Visit Italy* (juvenile), Burke, 1966, John Day, 1968; *Introduction to Italy,* Chatto & Windus, 1967; *The Past of Pastimes,* Chatto & Windus, 1969; *The Colour of Their Skin,* Chatto & Windus, 1969.

Tuscan Harvest, Chatto & Windus, 1971; *Central Italy,* Hastings House, 1972; *Northern Italy,* Hastings House, 1973; *I Know What I Liked,* Chatto & Windus, 1973. Founder and editor, *World Review,* 1936-40.

WORK IN PROGRESS: A book about Sir Thomas Phillipps, nineteenth century book and manuscript collector, and the Robinson brothers, who purchased the reputed collection in 1946.

AVOCATIONAL INTERESTS: Viticulture and winemaking.

* * *

BARTON, Richard F(leming) 1924-
PERSONAL: Born September 29, 1924, in Oshkosh, Wis.;

son of Dan Wiley and Margaret (Freeman) Barton; married Nancy Ann Schalk, October 25, 1952; children: Ted Steven, Dan Richard, Jean Nancy. *Education:* Northwestern University, B.S. (with highest distinction), 1948; University of California, Berkeley, Ph.D., 1961. *Home:* 5409 Eighth Pl., Lubbock, Tex. 79416. *Office:* College of Business Administration, Texas Tech University, Lubbock, Tex. 79409.

CAREER: Member of advertising staff, Procter & Gamble, 1948-50; member of staff in claims department, Travelers Insurance Co., 1952-58; University of Nebraska, Lincoln, assistant professor of business organization and management, 1961-64; University of Kansas, Lawrence, associate professor of business administration, 1964-67; Texas Tech University, Lubbock, professor of business administration and computer science, 1967—, director of planning and analyses, 1968-71, acting director of computer center, 1970-71. Faculty intern at Ernst & Ernst, 1967; visiting professor at University of Northern Colorado, 1973—; has lectured at Stanford University, Braniff Graduate School of Management, U.S. Naval Postgraduate School, and Systems Development Corp. *Military service:* U.S. Army Air Forces, 1943-45.

MEMBER: Academy of Management, American Institute for Decision Sciences, Institute of Management Sciences, Operations Research Society of America, Association for Business Simulation and Experiential Learning (member of advisory council), Beta Gamma Sigma, Sigma Iota Epsilon. *Awards, honors:* National Science Foundation grant, 1970-71, for computer center support.

WRITINGS: A Primer on Simulation and Gaming, Prentice-Hall, 1970; (contributor) David W. Zuckerman and Robert E. Horn, editors, *The Guide to Simulation Games for Education and Training,* Information Resources, Inc., 1970, 2nd edition, 1972; *The Imaginit Management Game,* with administrator's manual, Active Learning, 1973, 2nd edition, 1974; (contributor) Jean Belch, editor, *Contemporary Games,* Volume I, Gale, 1973; (contributor) John E. Moriarty, editor, *Simulation and Gaming,* National Bureau of Standards, 1974.

Games: "The E&E Management Game," Ernst & Ernst, 1967; "The Caltex Marketing Game," Caltex Petroleum Co., 1969. Contributor to proceedings of the National Gaming Council, and of about forty articles and reviews to professional journals. Member of editorial board of *Simulation and Games,* 1972-75.

SIDELIGHTS: Barton's work has been translated for publication in Japanese and Portuguese.

* * *

BARZUN, Jacques (Martin)   1907-

PERSONAL: Born November 30, 1907, in Creteil, France; son of Henri (a writer) and Anna-Rose (Martin) Barzun; married Marianna Lowell, August, 1936; children: James Lowell, Roger Martin, Isabel. *Education:* Columbia University, A.B., 1927, M.A., 1928, Ph.D., 1932. *Office:* Charles Scribner's Sons, 597 Fifth Ave., New York, N.Y. 10017.

CAREER: Columbia University, New York, N.Y., instructor, 1929-37, assistant professor, 1938-42, associate professor, 1942-45, professor of history, 1945-60, Seth Low Professor of History, 1960-67, University Professor of History, 1967-75, dean of graduate faculties, 1955-58, dean of faculties and provost, 1958-67; Charles Scribner's Sons,

publishers, New York, N.Y., literary advisor, 1975—. Member of board of directors, Macmillan, Inc., 1965-75; trustee, New York Society Library; Extraordinary fellow, Churchill College, Cambridge, 1961—. *Member:* National Institute of Arts and Letters (president, 1972-75), American Academy of Arts and Sciences, Royal Society of Arts (fellow), Council for Basic Education (member of board of directors), American Historical Association, Little Orchestra Society, Inc., Massachusetts Historical Society (corresponding member), Friends of Columbia University Libraries, Phi Beta Kappa, Athenaeum (London), Century Club (New York). *Awards, honors:* American Council of Learned Societies research fellow, 1933-34; Chevalier de la Legion d'Honneur; George Polk Memorial Award, 1967, for *Modern American Usage.*

WRITINGS: The French Race: Theories of Its Origins and their Social and Political Implications Prior to the Revolution, Columbia University Press, 1932, reprinted, Kennikat, 1966; *Race: A Study in Modern Superstition,* Harcourt, 1937, revised edition published as *Race: A Study in Superstition,* Harper, 1956; *Of Human Freedom,* Little, Brown, 1939, revised edition, Lippincott, 1964; *Darwin, Marx, Wagner: Critique of a Heritage,* Little, Brown, 1941, 2nd revised edition, Doubleday, 1958; *Romanticism and the Modern Ego,* Little, Brown, 1943, 2nd revised edition published as *Classic, Romantic, and Modern,* Doubleday, 1961; (with Paul H. Beik, George Crothers, and E. O. Golob) *Introduction to Naval History,* Lippincott, 1944; *The Teacher in America,* Little, Brown, 1945 (published in England as *We Who Teach,* Gollancz, 1946).

Berlioz and the Romantic Century, Little, Brown, 1950, revised edition published as *Berlioz and His Century: An Introduction to the Age of Romanticism,* World Publications, 1962, 3rd edition published under original title in two volumes, Columbia University Press, 1969; (translator) Gustave Flaubert, *Dictionary of Accepted Ideas,* New Directions, 1954; *God's Country and Mine: A Declaration of Love Spiced with a Few Harsh Words,* Little, Brown, 1954, reprinted, Greenwood Press, 1973; *Music in American Life,* Doubleday, 1956; (translator with Ralph H. Bowen) Denis Diderot, *Rameau's Nephew and Other Works,* Doubleday, 1956; *The Energies of Art: Studies of Authors Classic and Modern,* Harper, 1956, reprinted, Greenwood Press, 1975; (translator and author of introduction and notes) Hector Louis Berlioz, *Evenings with the Orchestra,* Knopf, 1956; (with Henry F. Graff) *The Modern Researcher,* Harcourt, 1957, revised edition, 1970; *Lincoln the Literary Genius,* Schori Private Press, 1959; *The House of Intellect,* Harper, 1959.

(Translator with Robert Lowell) Racine and Beaumarchais, *Phaedra and [The Marriage of] Figaro* (the former translated by Lowell, the latter translated by Barzun), Farrar, Straus, 1961; *Science the Glorious Entertainment,* Harper, 1964; *The American University: How It Runs, Where It is Going,* Harper, 1968; *On Writing, Editing, and Publishing: Essays Explicative and Horatory,* University of Chicago Press, 1971; (with Wendell Hertig Taylor) *A Catalogue of Crime,* Harper, 1971; (contributor) Rhodes Boyson, editor, *Education: Threatened Standards–Essays on the Reasons for the Present Decline in Educational Achievement and Suggestions for Its Improvement,* Churchill Press, 1972; *The Use and Abuse of Art,* Princeton University Press, 1974; *Clio and the Doctors: Psycho-History, Quanto-History and History,* University of Chicago Press, 1974; *Simple and Direct: A Rhetoric for Writers,* Harper, 1975.

Editor: *Samplings and Chronicles, Being the Continuation*

of the Philolexian Society History, Columbia University, Philolexian Society, 1927; *Pleasures of Music: A Reader's Choice of Great Writing about Music and Musicians from Cellini to Bernard Shaw,* Viking, 1951 (published in England as *Pleasures of Music: An Anthology of Writing about Music and Musicians from Cellini to Bernard Shaw,* M. Joseph, 1952); George Gordon (Lord) Byron, *Selected Letters,* Farrar, Straus, 1953; (translator, and author of introduction and notes) Hector Louis Berlioz, *New Letters of Berlioz, 1830-1868,* Columbia University Press, 1954; Goethe, *Faust: A Tragedy,* Part 1, Holt, 1955; *History of the Faculty of Philosophy, Columbia University,* Columbia University Press, 1957; John Jay Chapman, *Selected Writings,* Farrar, Straus, 1957; *The Delights of Detection,* Criterion, 1957; (and translator with Albert Bernel) Georges Courteline, *The Plays of Georges Courteline,* Volume I, Theatre Arts, 1961; (and compiler) Wilson Follett, *Modern American Usage: A Guide,* Hill & Wang, 1966; (and author of introduction) *Burke and Hare: The Resurrection Men,* Scarecrow, 1974. Contributor of articles to scholarly periodicals as well as to *Harper's, Atlantic, Vogue, New York Times Magazine, New Republic, Saturday Review,* and others.

BIOGRAPHICAL/CRITICAL SOURCES: Saturday Review of Literature, May 13, 1950; *Time,* December 8, 1958; *Foreign Affairs,* April, 1965; *Newsweek,* November 4, 1968; *American Scholar,* winter, 1972.

*   *   *

BASS, Robert D(uncan) 1904-

PERSONAL: Born September 25, 1904, in Scranton, S.C.; son of Fletcher Graves (a farmer) and Bertha (Matthews) Bass; married Virginia Wauchope (a writer), May 25, 1929; children: Robert Wauchope, George Fletcher. *Education:* Columbia Presbyterian Theological Seminary, student, 1925-27; University of South Carolina, A.B., 1926, M.A., 1927, Ph.D., 1933; postdoctoral study at University of London, 1951, Cambridge University, 1951-52, and Johns Hopkins University, 1952. *Politics:* Independent. *Religion:* Presbyterian. *Home:* 720 Art St., Marion, S.C. 29571.

CAREER: University of South Carolina, Columbia, assistant professor of English literature, 1927-40; U.S. Naval Academy, Annapolis, Md., professor of English literature, 1941-57; Furman University, Greenville, S.C., professor of English literature, 1957-63; Limestone College, Gaffney, S.C., professor of English literature, 1963-65; Erskine College, Due West, S.C., professor of English literature and chairman of department, 1966-70; writer, 1970—. *Military service:* U.S. Navy, 1940-46. U.S. Naval Reserve, 1934-40; became commander.

MEMBER: American Radio Relay League, Phi Beta Kappa. *Awards, honors:* Plaque from the American Revolutionary Round Table, 1959, naming *Swamp Fox: The Life and Campaigns of General Francis Marion* as the best book published about the Revolution in that year; Hum.D., Francis Marion College, 1974.

WRITINGS: The Green Dragoon: The Lives of Banastre Tarleton and Mary Robinson, Holt, 1957; *Swamp Fox: The Life and Campaigns of General Francis Marion,* Holt, 1959; *Gamecock: The Life and Campaigns of General Thomas Sumter,* Holt, 1961; *Ninety Six: The Struggle for the Back Country,* Sandlapper Store, in press. Contributor of poems, sports articles, sketches, and reviews to magazines.

SIDELIGHTS: Bass writes: "Having been reared about a mile from Snow's Island, the hide-out of Francis Marion, I began a study of him and of Banastre Tarleton who nicknamed Marion the Swamp Fox. This led me into the Revolution in South Carolina, which was more of a civil war than a rebellion." *Avocational interests:* Amateur radio (owner and operator of station W4CQG).

*   *   *

BASS, Virginia W(auchope) 1905-

PERSONAL: Born March 5, 1905, in Columbia, S.C.; daughter of George Armstrong (a college professor) and Elizabeth (Bostedo) Wauchope; married Robert Duncan Bass (a college professor), May 25, 1929; children: Robert Wauchope, George Fletcher. *Education:* University of South Carolina, A.B. (magna cum laude), 1927. *Politics:* Independent. *Religion:* Presbyterian. *Home:* 720 Art St., Marion, S.C. 29571.

MEMBER: American Association of University Women, Phi Beta Kappa, Alpha Delta Pi, Annapolis (Md.) Community Orchestra, Marion (S.C.) Historical Society, Palmetto Study Club (Marion; secretary, 1975), Playreaders Club (Columbia, S.C.), Booklovers Club (Annapolis).

WRITINGS—Editor: *Young in Heart,* Coslett, 1967; *Dimensions of Man's Spirit,* Science of Mind, 1975. Contributor to *Home Arts* and *Fate.*

WORK IN PROGRESS: Fairyland Verse, an anthology; *Dreams Can Point the Way,* readings on the spiritual significance of dreams.

*   *   *

BASSETT, James E(lias) 1912-

PERSONAL: Born October 18, 1912, in Glendale, Calif.; son of James Elias and Lucille (Emerton) Bassett; married Wilma Moreland, June 13, 1936; children: Cynthia Ann. *Education:* Bowdoin College, B.A. (cum laude), 1934. *Home:* 15 Malibu Cove Colony, Malibu, Calif. 90265. *Office:* Editorial Department, *Los Angeles Times,* Times Mirror Sq., Los Angeles, Calif. 90053.

CAREER: Los Angeles Times, Los Angeles, Calif., reporter, 1934-37, aviation editor, 1937-41, science editor, 1947-48; *Los Angeles Mirror,* Los Angeles, political editor, 1948-54, city editor, 1954-57, assistant managing editor, 1957-61; *Los Angeles Times,* political analyst and editor, 1961-63, director of editorial pages, 1963-71, associate editor, 1971—. Press secretary for Richard M. Nixon vice-presidential campaign, 1952; public relations director, Republican National Committee, 1954; campaign manager for Vice-President Nixon, 1956; campaign planning activities director for Nixon presidential campaign, 1960. *Military service:* U.S. Naval Reserve, 1941-45; became captain; received Bronze Star medal with combat clasp. *Member:* Authors League of America, Phi Beta Kappa, Psi Upsilon, Kappa Tau Alpha, Los Angeles Press Club.

WRITINGS—War novels: *Harm's Way,* World Publishing, 1962; *The Sky Suspended,* Delacorte, 1968; *Commander Prince, USN: A Novel of the Pacific War,* Simon & Schuster, 1971. Also co-author of *The War Lords,* Weidenfeld & Nicolson.

WORK IN PROGRESS: A history of the *Los Angeles Times* and its relationship to Southern California, completion expected in 1977.

SIDELIGHTS: Harm's Way was filmed by Otto Preminger for Paramount.

BASU, Arindam 1948-

PERSONAL: Born November 12, 1948, in Calcutta, West Bengal, India; son of Pradip (a commercial executive) and Mridula (Mukherjee) Basu; married Minakshi Ghosh (a school teacher), May 29, 1973. *Education:* Attended Indian Institute of Technology, 1965-68; Jadavpur University, B.A. (honors), 1971. *Politics:* "None to speak of." *Religion:* "None to speak of." *Home:* 12/1 Palm Ave., Calcutta 70019, West Bengal, India. *Office:* Ananda Bazar Patrika, 6 Prafulla Sarkar St., Calcutta 700001, West Bengal, India.

CAREER: Ananda Bazar Patrika (publisher of newspapers and magazines), Calcutta, India, advertising manager, 1975—. Novelist.

WRITINGS: Picaro or Me (novel), Writers Workshop (Calcutta), 1972, InterCulture Associates, 1976. Also author of *The Gravedigger,* a novel, as yet unpublished.

WORK IN PROGRESS: Two novels, *Perigreen* and *Zamridamriharidanigubabradabrudeau* (tentative title).

SIDELIGHTS: "My motivation probably comes," Basu wrote to *CA,* "from an irresistible, lyrical, neurotic energy largely promoted by a delinquent adolescence." He also claimed the tentative title of his second novel in progress is not a joke.

*   *   *

BATTY, Linda Schmidt 1940-

PERSONAL: Born April 25, 1940, in San Diego, Calif.; daughter of William Henry (a discount business executive) and Lucille (a restaurant owner; maiden name, Sheldon) Schmidt; married William Batty III (a film and English teacher), December 18, 1965; children: Mary, William IV, John Sheldon. *Education:* University of California, Berkeley, B.A., 1962; Brown University, M.A., 1965; University of Oregon, M.L.S., 1971. *Religion:* Society of Friends (Quakers). *Home address:* P.O. Box 42, Mt. Hermon, Mass. 01354.

CAREER: Schmidt, Etheredge & Chrestman (property investors), San Diego, Calif., partner, 1962—; film bibliographer. Member, Gill (Mass.) Democratic Town Council. *Member:* American Film Institute, War Resisters League, Fellowship of Reconciliation, Planetary Citizenship Register.

WRITINGS: Retrospective Index to Film Periodicals, 1930-1971, Bowker, 1975. Also author of *Film Comment Index, 1962-1972,* and yearly supplements. Reviewer for *American Reference Books Annual.*

WORK IN PROGRESS: Revising *Retrospective Index to Film Periodicals.*

SIDELIGHTS: Linda Batty writes: "World Community and Peace (not defined solely as absence of war) as a way of life are central to my philosophy of life. I became academically involved in film as my awareness of its conscious and unconscious propagandistic influences heightened. The visual nature of film makes it an international language and as such it should be used more for international and humanitarian, rather than national and institutional, reasons."

*   *   *

BAUER, Raymond A(ugustine) 1916-

PERSONAL: Born September 7, 1916, in Chicago, Ill.; son of William Henry and Anna Barbara (Diedrich) Bauer; married Alice Haugh, June 12, 1941 (died, 1965) married Katharine Goldthwaite Dorr Clark, April 30, 1966; children: (first marriage) Linda Carol (Mrs. Donald H. Sibley). *Education:* Illinois Institute of Technology, student, 1936-38; Northwestern University, B.S. (with highest distinction), 1943; Harvard University, M.A., 1948, Ph.D., 1950. *Home:* 16 Highland St., Cambridge, Mass. 02138. *Office:* Harvard University, Graduate School of Business Administration, Boston, Mass. 02163.

CAREER: Crane Co., Chicago, Ill., chemical analyst, 1936-44; Harvard University, Cambridge, Mass., research assistant, 1947-48, Russian Research Center, fellow, 1948-50, lecturer in social psychology, 1950-55, Russian Research Center, research associate, 1950-55; Massachusetts Institute of Technology, Cambridge, Mass., associate professor of social psychology, 1955-57; Harvard University, Graduate School of Business Administration, Ford Foundation visiting professor, 1957-60, professor, 1960—. Research associate, Center for International Studies, 1953-57; fellow, Center for Advanced Studies in Behavioral Sciences, 1955-56; consultant, National Goals Research Staff, White House, 1969-70; member of the steering committee, National Advertising Review Board, 1972-74. *Military service:* U.S. Naval Reserve, 1944-46, Russian language officer, attained rank of lieutenant (j.g.).

MEMBER: American Academy of Arts and Sciences (fellow), American Psychological Association, Eastern Psychological Association, Massachusetts Psychological Association (president, 1964-66), American Sociological Society, American Marketing Association, American Association of Public Opinion Research (president, 1965-66), National Academy of Engineering, Phi Beta Kappa.

WRITINGS: The New Man in Soviet Psychology, Harvard University Press, 1952; (with Edward Wasiolek) *Nine Soviet Portraits,* Wiley, 1955; (with Alex Inkeles and Clyde Kluckhohn) *How the Soviet System Works: Cultural, Psychological, and Social Themes,* Harvard University Press, 1956; (with Inkeles) *The Soviet Citizen: Daily Life in A Totalitarian Society,* Harvard University Press, 1959.

(Editor) *Some Views on Soviet Psychology,* American Psychological Association, 1962, reprinted, Greenwood Press, 1975; (with Ithiel de Sola Pool and Lewis Anthony Dexter) *American Business and Public Policy: The Politics of Foreign Trade,* Atherton, 1963, 2nd edition, 1972; (editor) *Social Indicators,* M.I.T. Press, 1966; (editor with Kenneth J. Gergen) *The Study of Policy Formation,* Free Press, 1968; (with Stephen A. Greyser) *Advertising in America: The Consumer View,* Graduate School of Business Administration, Harvard University, 1968; (with Richard S. Rosenbloom and Laure Sharp) *Second-order Consequences: A Methodological Essay on the Impact of Technology,* M.I.T. Press, 1969.

(With Scott M. Cunningham) *Studies in the Negro Market,* Marketing Science Institute, 1970; (with Dan. K. Fenn Jr.) *The Corporate Social Audit,* Russell Sage Foundation, 1972; *The Obstinate Audience,* Atherton, 1976; (with Robert W. Ackerman) *Corporate Social Responsibility: Text and Cases,* Reston Press, 1976.

Author of technical reports for the Human Resources Research Institute, the Office of Economic Opportunity, and the Harvard Graduate School of Business Administration and Center for International Studies. Contributor to proceedings; also contributor to professional journals, including *Harvard Business Review, Journal of Social Issues,* and *Business and Society Review.*

BEACH, (William) Waldo 1916-

PERSONAL: Born August 2, 1916, in Middletown, Conn.; son of William D. and Edith (Waldo) Beach; married Mary Heckman, January 2, 1943; children: Richard Waldo, Margaret Ann, Elizabeth Ann. Education: Wesleyan University, B.A., 1937; Yale University, B.D., 1940, Ph.D. 1944. Home: 130 Pinecrest Rd., Durham, N.C. 27705. Office: Divinity School, Duke University, Durham, N.C. 27706.

CAREER: Ordained to the Methodist ministry, 1940; Antioch College, Yellow Springs, Ohio, professor of religion and college pastor, 1942-46; Duke University, Divinity School, Durham, N.C., assistant professor, 1946-48, associate professor, 1948-52, professor of Christian Ethics, 1952—, director of graduate studies in religion, 1959-69. Delegate to the North American Conference on Faith and Order of the World Council of Churches, 1956; chairman of Council on Graduate Studies in Religion, 1962-65; trustee of Wesleyan University, 1960-72. Member: American Society of Christian Ethics, Society for Religion in Higher Education, American Theological Society, Phi Beta Kappa.

WRITINGS: (Contributor) Paul Ramsey, editor, Faith and Ethics: The Theology of H. Richard Niebuhr, Harper, 1957, 2nd edition, 1965; Conscience on Campus: An Interpretation of Christian Ethics for College Life, Association Press, 1958; The Christian Life, CLC Press, 1966; The Christian Life: Teacher's Book, CLC Press, 1966; Christian Community and American Society, Westminster Press, 1969; (editor and author of introduction with H. Richard Niebuhr) Christian Ethics: Sources of the Living Tradition, Ronald Press, 1955, 2nd edition, 1973; (editor) Christmas Wonder: An Anthology of Verse and Song, Fortress Press, 1973. Contributor of articles to scholarly books and journals.

* * *

BEATTY, Morgan 1902-1975

September 6, 1902—July 4, 1975; American journalist, news analyst and broadcaster, and writer of guide to Washington, D.C. Obituaries: New York Times, July 7, 1975.

* * *

BEAUCHAMP, Edward R(obert) 1933-

PERSONAL: Surname is pronounced Bo-sham; born December 19, 1933, in New York, N.Y.; son of Edmund Arthur (a steel worker) and Helen (Grimes) Beauchamp; married Nancy Sakomoto (a librarian and translator), October 6, 1966; children: Kevin Kenji. Education: Worcester State College, B.S., 1959, M.Ed., 1961; University of Washington, Seattle, Ph.D., 1973. Politics: Independent. Religion: Christian. Home: 854 Hahaione St., Honolulu, Hawaii 96825. Office: Department of Educational Foundations, University of Hawaii, 1776 University Ave., Honolulu, Hawaii 96822.

CAREER: U.S. Department of Defense, Washington, D.C., teacher of history in schools in Japan, 1961-62, France, 1962-64, and Germany, 1964-66; University of Hawaii, Honolulu, assistant professor, 1969-73, associate professor of history of education, 1973—. Fulbright lecturer at International Christian University, Keio University, and Tokyo University (all Japan), 1975-76. Research assistant to archivists of American Educational Research Association, 1968-69; coordinator of American Samoa Education Contract, for University of Hawaii, 1970-72. Military service: U.S. Marine Corps, 1952-55; served in Korea and Japan.

MEMBER: Comparative and International Education Society, Society for International Development (president of Hawaii chapter, 1973-74), American Historical Association, History of Education Society, Association for Asian Studies.

WRITINGS: An American Teacher in Meiji, Japan, University Press of Hawaii, 1975. Contributor to education and Asian studies journals. Book review editor of Journal of Asian and African Studies, 1971—.

WORK IN PROGRESS: Editing Learning to Be Japanese: Selected Readings on Japanese Education; Educational Dimensions of the American Occupation of Japan: 1945-1952, completion expected in 1977; editing "Education and Development in Asia," a special issue of Asian Profile, publication expected in 1977.

* * *

BECKER, Gary S(tanley) 1930-

PERSONAL: Born December 2, 1930, in Pottsville, Pa.; son of Louis W. and Anna (Siskind) Becker; married Donna Slate, 1955 (deceased); children: Judith Sarah, Catherine Jean. Education: Princeton University, A.B. (summa cum laude), 1951, University of Chicago, A.M., 1953, Ph.D., 1955. Home: 5811 Dorchester Ave., Chicago, Ill. 60637. Office: 1126 East 59th St., Department of Economics, University of Chicago, Ill. 60637.

CAREER: University of Chicago, Chicago, Ill., assistant professor of economics, 1954-57; Columbia University, New York, N.Y., assistant professor, 1957-58, associate professor, 1958-60, professor of economics, 1960-68, Arthur Lehman Professor of Economics, 1968-69; University of Chicago, visiting professor, 1969-70, university professor of economics, 1970—. Member of senior research staff, National Bureau of Economic Research; member of board of publications, University of Chicago Press. Member: National Academy of Sciences, American Economic Association, American Statistical Association, Econometric Society, Phi Beta Kappa. Awards, honors: W. S. Woytinsky award from University of Michigan, 1964, for Human Capital; John Bates Clark medal from American Economic Association, 1967; professional achievement award from University of Chicago Alumni Association, 1968.

WRITINGS: Economics of Discrimination, University of Chicago Press, 1957, 2nd edition, 1971; Human Capital: A Theoretical and Empirical Analysis with Special Reference to Education, Columbia University Press, 1964, 2nd edition, 1975; Human Capital and the Personal Distribution of Income: An Analytical Approach, University of Michigan, 1967; Economic Theory, Knopf, 1971; (editor with William M. Landes) Essays in the Economics of Crime and Punishment, Columbia University Press, 1974; (with Gilbert Ghez) The Allocation of Time and Goods Over the Life Cycle, Columbia University Press, 1975.

WORK IN PROGRESS: A book on the economics of the family.

* * *

BECKHAM, Stephen Dow 1941-

PERSONAL: Born August 31, 1941, in Coos Bay, Ore.; son of Ernest Dow (a teacher, logger, and salesman) and Anna M. (Adamson) Beckham; married Patricia Joan Cox (a music teacher), August, 1967; children: Andrew Dow. Education: University of Oregon, B.A., 1964; University of California at Los Angeles, M.A., 1966, Ph.D., 1969.

Politics: Democrat. *Religion:* Baptist. *Home:* 1749 Birch St., McMinnville, Ore. 97128. *Office:* Department of History, Linfield College, McMinnville, Ore. 97128.

CAREER: Linfield College, McMinnville, Ore., assistant professor, 1969-72, associate professor of history, 1972—. Consultant to Coos, Lower Umpqua, and Sluslaw Indian Tribes, 1972—, Small Tribal Organization of Western Washington, 1973, Oregon Coastal Conservation and Development Commission, 1974-75, Oregon State Parks System, 1974-75, and Oregon State Historic Preservation Program, 1974—. Member of technical advisory task force on estuaries and wetlands of Oregon State Land Conservation and Development Commission, 1975—. Trustee of Neskowin-Coast Foundation, 1974—. *Member:* American Historical Association, Organization of American Historians, Western History Association. *Awards, honors:* Grant from National Endowment for the Humanities, 1972—.

WRITINGS: Requiem for a People: The Rogue Indians and the Frontiersmen, University of Oklahoma Press, 1971; *The Simpsons of Shore Acres,* Arago Books, 1971; *Lonely Outpost: The Army's Fort Umpqua,* Oregon Historical Society, 1971; *Coos Bay: The Pioneer Period, 1851-1890,* Arago Books, 1973; (editor and author of introduction) *Tall Tales from Rogue River: The Yarns of Hathaway Jones,* Indiana University Press, 1974; (contributor) William Sturtevant, editor, *Handbook of the American Indian,* Smithsonian Institution Press, in press; (contributor) William Loy, editor, *Historical Atlas of Oregon,* University of Oregon Press, in press. Contributor to historical journals. Author of television series, "This Land Was Theirs: The Indians of the Oregon Coast," produced by Columbia Broadcasting System and Oregon Educational Broadcasting Co., 1971-72.

WORK IN PROGRESS: Scientist on the Pacific Frontier: George Gibbs, 1815-1873; The Oregon Trail Narratives of Peter Hardeman Burnett.

*   *   *

BECKINGHAM, Charles Fraser 1914-

PERSONAL: Born February 18, 1914, in Houghton, Huntingdonshire, England; son of Arthur and Alice Beckingham; married Margery Ansell, 1946 (died, 1966); married Elizabeth Brine, 1970; children: (first marriage) one daughter. *Education:* Queens College, Cambridge, B.A., 1935, M.A., 1939. *Office:* School of Oriental and African Studies, University of London, Malet St., London WC1E 7HP, England.

CAREER: British Museum, London, temporary assistant cataloguer in department of printed books, 1936-46; served with British Foreign Office, London, England, 1946-51; University of Manchester, Manchester, England, lecturer, 1951-55, senior lecturer, 1955-58, professor of Islamic studies, 1957-65; University of London, School of Oriental and African Studies, London, England, professor of Islamic studies, 1965—. *Military service:* Military and Naval Intelligence, 1942-46. *Member:* Royal Asiatic Society (president, 1967-70), Hakluyt Society (member of council, 1958-62, 1964-69; president, 1969-72, vice-president, 1972—), Royal Society for Asian Affairs (vice-president, 1973).

WRITINGS: (Translator and editor, with George Wynn Brereton Huntingford) Manoel de Almeida, *Some Records of Ethiopia, 1593-1646: Being Extracts from the History of High Ethiopia or Abassia, Together with Bahrey's History of the Galla,* Hakluyt Society, 1954; (author of introduction), *Atlas of the Arab World and the Middle East,* Mac-

millan, 1960; (editor with Huntingford) *Francisco Alvares, The Prester John of the Indies: The Translation of Lord Stanley of Alderley, 1881,* Hakluyt Society, 1961; (editor) James Bruce, *Travels to Discover the Source of the Nile,* Horizon Press, 1967; *The Achievement of Prester John: An Inaugural Lecture Delivered on 17 May, 1966,* Luzac, 1966; (contributor) A. J. Arberry, editor, *Religion in the Middle East,* Cambridge University Press, 1969. Contributor to *Admiralty Handbook of Western Arabia.* Contributor to learned journals. Joint editor of *Journal of Semitic Studies,* 1961-64, editor, 1965.

*   *   *

BECKMANN, David M(ilton) 1948-

PERSONAL: Born February 22, 1948, in Kearney, Neb.; son of Milton W. (a professor) and Leona (a teacher; maiden name, Lange) Beckmann; married Janet Williams (an English teacher), June 17, 1972. *Education:* Yale University, B.A., 1969; Joint Project for Theological Education (Seminex), St. Louis, Mo., M.Div., 1974; London School of Economics and Political Science, University of London, M.Sc., 1975. *Politics:* Democrat. *Home:* 5602 Jones St., Omaha, Neb. 68106.

CAREER: Ordained minister of Lutheran Church, 1974; parochial high school English teacher in Accra, Ghana, 1969; Lincoln Technical College, Lincoln, Neb., director of adult civic education, 1970-71; vicar in Omaha, Neb., 1972-73; Cyrano's Restaurant, St. Louis, Mo., waiter, 1974; assistant pastor in Omaha, Neb., 1974—, on leave to work as assistant director of Ranjpur/Dinajpur Rehabilitation Service of Lutheran World Federation in Dacca, Bangladesh, 1976—. *Member:* Phi Beta Kappa. *Awards, honors:* Woodrow Wilson fellow, 1971; Rockefeller Foundation fellow, 1971.

WRITINGS: Eden Revival: Spiritual Churches in Ghana, Concordia, 1975. Contributor to *Concordia Theological Monthly* and *Afro-American Studies.*

WORK IN PROGRESS: Studies on religious changes associated with economic development including the Afro-Christian indigenous church movements of Africa and Afro-America, the economic impact of Christian missionary activity during the last two centuries, and a Christian theological understanding of economic life.

AVOCATIONAL INTERESTS: Travel.

*   *   *

BEEKMAN, John 1918-

PERSONAL: Born December 2, 1918, in Midland Park, N.J.; son of Thomas (a mason) and Bella (Velzen) Beekman; married Elaine Hummel (a linguist), August 8, 1946; children: Judy, Thomas, Gary. *Education:* Attended Moody Bible Institute, 1943-48, and University of Oklahoma, 1947-48. *Office:* Summer Institute of Linguistics, Dallas, Tex. 75211.

CAREER: American Telephone and Telegraph (A.T. & T.), New York City, assistant manager, 1935-43; Missionary Bible Church, River Grove, Ill., pastor, 1944-46; Wycliffe Bible Translators, Inc., Huntington Beach, Calif., missionary and translator in Mexico, 1947-60; Summer Institute of Linguistics, Dallas, Tex., translation coordinator, 1960—. *Awards, honors:* D.Litt., Biola College, 1974.

WRITINGS: (With John Callow) *Translating the Word of God,* Zondervan, 1974.

BEER, Patricia 1924-

PERSONAL: Born November 4, 1924, in Exmouth, Devonshire, England; married Damien Parsons (an architect). Education: Attended University of Exeter; University of London, B.A. (with honors); St. Hugh's College, Oxford, B.Litt. Home: 1 Lutton Terr., Flask Walk, London N.W.3, England.

CAREER: Lecturer in English at University of Padua, Padua, Italy, 1946-48, British Institute, Rome, Italy, 1948, and Ministero Aeronautica, Rome, 1950; University of London, Goldsmith's College, London, England, senior lecturer, 1962-68; poet; full time writer, 1968—. Member: P.E.N. International, Society of Authors.

WRITINGS—Poems: Loss of the Magyar and Other Poems, Longmans, Green, 1959; The Survivors, Longmans, Green, 1963; Just Like the Resurrection, Dufour, 1967; The Postilion Has Been Struck by Lightening, Macmillan, 1967; The Estuary, Macmillan, 1971; Spanish Balcony, Poem-of-the-Month Club (London), 1973.

Other: (Editor with Ted Hughes and Vernon Scannell) New Poems, 1962: A P.E.N. Anthology of Contemporary Poetry, Transatlantic, 1962; Mrs. Beer's House (autobiography), Macmillan, 1968; An Introduction to the Metaphysical Poets (criticism), Rowman & Littlefield, 1972.

Work represented in anthologies, including: Penguin Book of Contemporary Verse, Penguin, 1962; New Poems, 1965, Hutchinson, 1965; The Borestone Mountain Poetry Awards, Pacific Press, 1966, 1968. Contributor to Listener, New Statesman, Sunday Times, and Time & Tide.

BIOGRAPHICAL/CRITICAL SOURCES: Kenyon Review, Issue 5, 1968; Patricia Beer, Mrs. Beer's House, Macmillan, 1968.

*   *   *

BEER, Samuel Hutchison 1911-

PERSONAL: Born July 28, 1911, in Bucyrus, Ohio; son of William Cameron and Jesse Blanche (Hutchison) Beer; married Roberta Frances Reed, June 22, 1935; children: Katherine, Frances, William. Education: University of Michigan, A.B., 1932; Oxford University, B.A., 1935; Harvard University, Ph.D., 1943. Politics: Democrat. Religion: Presbyterian. Home: 87 Lakeview Ave., Cambridge, Mass. 02138. Office: Department of Government, Harvard University, Cambridge, Mass. 02138.

CAREER: Democratic National Committee, Washington, D.C., staff member, 1935-36; New York Post, New York, N.Y., reporter, 1936-37; Fortune magazine, New York, N.Y., writer and researcher, 1937-38; Harvard University, Cambridge, Mass., instructor, 1938-42, assistant professor, 1946-48, associate professor, 1948-53, professor of government, 1953-71, Eaton Professor of Science of Government, 1971—, chairman of department, 1954-58. Messenger Lecturer, Cornell University, 1969; Americans for Democratic Action, chairman of Massachusetts chapter, 1955-57, national chairman, 1959-62. Military service: U.S. Army, 1942-45, became captain; received Bronze Star. Member: American Political Science Association, Phi Beta Kappa. Awards, honors: Rhodes Scholar, 1932-35; Fulbright fellow and Guggenheim fellow, 1953-54; Woodrow Wilson Foundation Award, 1966, for British Politics in the Collectivist Age.

WRITINGS: The City of Reason, Harvard University Press, 1949, reprinted, Greenwood Press, 1968; (editor) Karl Marx and Friedrich Engels, The Communist Manifesto, AHM Publishing, 1955; Treasury Control: The Co-ordination of Financial and Economic Policy in Great Britain, Clarendon Press, 1956, 2nd edition, 1957; (editor with Adam B. Ulam and author of Part I and Part II) Patterns of Government: The Major Political Systems of Europe, Random House, 1958, 3rd edition, 1973, Part I published as Modern Political Development, Random House, 1974, Part II published as The British Political System, Random House, 1974.

(Contributor) William N. Chambers and Robert H. Salisbury, editors, Democracy in the Mid-Twentieth Century: Problems and Prospects, Washington University Press, 1960, reprinted, Book for Libraries, 1971; Modern British Politics: A Study of Parties and Pressure Groups, Faber, 1965, 2nd edition, 1969; (contributor) Robert A. Goldwin, editor, Liberalism and Conservatism, Public Affairs Conference Center, University of Chicago, 1965; British Politics in the Collectivist Age, Knopf, 1965; (editor with Richard E. Barringer) The State and the Poor, Winthrop Publishers, 1970; (author of foreword) Adam B. Ulam, The Russian Political System (Part V of 3rd edition of Patterns of Government), Random House, 1974; (author of foreword) Suzanne Berger, The French Political System (Part III of 3rd edition of Patterns of Government), Random House, 1974. Contributor to scholarly journals. Associate editor, American Political Science Review.

*   *   *

BEEVERS, John (Leonard) 1911-1975
(John Clayton)

PERSONAL: Born October 18, 1911, in Gildersome, Yorkshire, England; son of John Leonard (a police inspector) and Esther (Schofield) Beevers; married Marjorie Pollard, August 9, 1934 (died, 1962); married Marjorie Singleton Broadbridge, August 19, 1963; children: (first marriage) Susan Jane (Mrs. Kurt Dietl). Education: Queens' College, Cambridge, M.A. (first class honors), 1933. Politics: "To the right of Ghengis Khan." Religion: Roman Catholic. Home: Pebble House, Holt, Norfolk, England.

CAREER: Writer. Daily Dispatch, Manchester, England, reporter, 1933-34; Time and Tide, London, England, literary editor, 1934-35; Sunday Referee, London, England, news editor, 1935-39; Daily Express, London, England, leader writer, 1939-40; Ministry of Information, London, England, journalist, 1940-41; British Broadcasting Corp. (BBC), London, England, senior sub-editor, 1941-47, chief sub-editor, 1947-64, senior duty editor, 1964-69.

WRITINGS: World Without Faith, Harper, 1934; (under pseudonym John Clayton) The Dark Emperor (poems), privately printed, 1947; Storm of Glory: St. Therese of Lisieux (Catholic Family Book Club selection), Sheed, 1949; Joan of Arc, Doubleday, 1951; (translator) Autobiography of St. Therese of Lisieux, Doubleday, 1952; The Sun Her Mantle (study of the appearances of the Virgin Mary), Newman Press, 1953; Shining As Stars (biographies of Leon Dupont and Matt Talbot), Browne & Nolan, 1955, Newman Press, 1956; Our Lady of Fatima, St. Paul Publications, 1956, 1965, Paulist/Newman, 1956, 5th edition, 1958; The Golden Heart: The Story of Beauraing, Browne & Nolan, 1955, Regnery, 1956; Lourdes, Paulist/Newman, 1956; Saint Joan of Arc, Hanover House, 1959; St. Therese of the Child Jesus (biography), Paulist/Newman, 1960; St. Teresa of Avila, Hanover House, 1961; Virgin of the Poor: The Apparitions of Our

Lady at Banneux, Abbey Press, 1972; *A Man for Now: The Life of Damien the Leper,* Doubleday, 1974; (translator) Yves Raguin, *How to Pray Today,* Abbey Press, 1974; (translator) Jean-Pierre de Caussade, *Abandonment to Divine Providence,* Doubleday, 1975.

(Died September 13, 1975)

* * *

BEHRENS, Helen Kindler 1922-

PERSONAL: Born November 2, 1922, in London, England; daughter of Hans (a musician) and Alice (a painter; maiden name, Riddle) Kindler; married Robert H. Behrens (a diplomat and professor), May 5, 1945; children: Christine (Mrs. Bart Grahl), Eric, Yvonne, Diane, Peter. *Education:* Duke University, B.A., 1945. *Home:* 12 Place des Alaouites, Rabat, Morocco.

CAREER: Hilltop (summer theater), Ellicot City, Md., actress, 1939; *Holiday,* Philadelphia, Pa., reader, 1945-46; free-lance writer for magazines, 1945-48; N. W. Ayer (advertising firm), Philadelphia, Pa., production manager, 1946-49; American Embassy, Paris, France, secretary, 1949; volunteer worker abroad. *Member:* Phi Beta Kappa, Chaine des Rotisseurs.

WRITINGS: Diplomatic Dining, Quadrangle, 1974. Columnist for *Foreign Service Journal,* 1966-69. Hostess and author of radio show on Armed Forces Network, Europe, 1957-59.

WORK IN PROGRESS: Researching Moroccan cooking with special emphasis on the Pasha family cooks of Marrakesh; a soup cookbook.

SIDELIGHTS: Helen Behrens is competent in French, German, Spanish, Portuguese, and Italian; she is currently studying Arabic.

* * *

BEHRMAN, Carol H(elen) 1925-

PERSONAL: Born August 24, 1925, in Brooklyn, N.Y.; daughter of Louis (a postman) and Sylvia (Leventhal) Bostwick; married Edward Behrman (an accountant), January 22, 1949; children: Bonnie, Joseph, Linda. *Education:* City College (now City College of the City University of New York), B.S.Ed. (cum laude), 1947; graduate study at Columbia University. *Home:* 325 Howard Ave., Fair Lawn, N.J. 07410. *Office:* Glen Ridge Middle School, Glen Ridge, N.J.

CAREER: Teacher of business education in public schools in New York, N.Y., 1949-54; free-lance writer, 1954-70; teacher of adult secretarial studies in public schools in Fair Lawn, N.J., and River Edge, N.J., both 1970-73; Glen Ridge Middle School, Glen Ridge, N.J., teacher of typing and language arts, 1973—. Has conducted private creative writing workshops. *Member:* Society of Children's Book Writers, New Jersey Education Association, New Jersey Business Education Association.

WRITINGS: There's Only One You (juvenile), Southern Publishing, 1973; *Catch a Dancing Star* (juvenile), Dillon, 1975. Contributor to professional, poetry, and juvenile magazines.

WORK IN PROGRESS: An Indian legend for children in verse, *Little Dreamer,* for Oddo.

SIDELIGHTS: Carol Behrman writes: "I write poetry because it provides an emotional release. A considerable amount of my other writing is directed toward young chil-

dren . . . because communicating with them seems to 'come naturally' to me, and because, while a tremendous responsibility, it is also just plain fun."

* * *

BELL, David S(heffield) 1945-

PERSONAL: Born August 5, 1945; son of Charles C. and Helen (Sheffield) Bell; married Karen Maziarz (a physician), September 1, 1973. *Education:* Attended Harvard University, 1967; Boston University, M.D., 1971. *Agent:* John Hawkins, Paul R. Reynolds, Inc., 599 Fifth Ave., New York, N.Y. 10017.

CAREER: Pediatrician.

WRITINGS: A Time to Be Born, Morrow, 1975.

WORK IN PROGRESS: A biography illustrating the effect of a fatal chronic disease on the development of personality.

* * *

BELL, Jack L. 1904-1975

July 24, 1904—September 15, 1975; American newsman, columnist, political writer, and author of books on politics. Obituaries: *New York Times,* September 16, 1975; *Washington Post,* September 16, 1975; *Time,* September 29, 1975; *Newsweek,* September 29, 1975. (See index for previous *CA* sketch)

* * *

BELL, Norman (Edward) 1899-

PERSONAL: Born July 26, 1899, in Winnemucca, Nev.; son of William John (a mine owner) and Freelie (Choate) Bell; married Ysabel Mary Mannix, September 9, 1939; children: Lucinda Cecile. *Education:* University of Nevada, B.A., 1927. *Home:* 17370 Buena Vista Ave., Sonoma, Calif. 95476.

CAREER: Worked as ranch hand in Nevada, as clerk for Standard Oil Co. in Nevada and California, and as delivery truck driver in San Francisco, Calif., 1920-27; *Reno Evening Gazette,* Reno, Nev., reporter, 1927; *Nevada State Journal,* Reno, reporter, 1928-32; Associated Press, 1932-64, worked as reporter, editor, and feature writer in San Francisco, Fresno, Calif., and Sacramento, Calif., as war correspondent in Pacific theater during World War II, and as correspondent-in-charge of San Diego (Calif.) bureau. *Military service:* U.S. Army, 1917-19.

WRITINGS—Juveniles: Linda's Air Mail Letter, Follett, 1964; *The Weightless Mother,* Follett, 1967. Author of feature stories, including material for children.

WORK IN PROGRESS: Stories for children, including one about a boy who ran himself into a streak of greased lightning, and one about a boy with a tooth in his ear.

SIDELIGHTS: Bell writes that it was the success of his children's feature story on the Russian Sputnik I satellite that "inspired me to try writing for children after retirement from AP." *Avocational interests:* Handyman improvements to his home.

* * *

BELOTE, Julianne 1929-

PERSONAL: Born June 15, 1929, in Alliance, Ohio; daughter of Roy Ellsworth (a machinist) and Lois Ethel (Wilson) Lemon; married Robert G. Belote, Jr. (a publisher), September 2, 1951; children: Robert G. III, Mark, William, Jennifer. *Education:* John Muir Junior College, A.A., 1949; University of California, Berkeley, B.A., 1951; Chicago State College (now University), M.A., 1972. *Politics:* Democrat. *Religion:* "Unencumbered." *Home:* 2145 Donald Dr., Moraga, Calif. 94556.

CAREER: Morgan Park Academy, Chicago, Ill., upper school librarian, 1968-72; writer, 1972—.

WRITINGS: The Compleat American Housewife, 1776, Nitty Gritty Productions, 1974.

WORK IN PROGRESS: A guide book on old inns, restaurants, and sights in the "Mother Lode Country" of California.

SIDELIGHTS: Julianne Belote writes: "When one's husband is a publisher there is very little excuse for not getting into print."

* * *

BENDER, Ross Thomas 1929-

PERSONAL: Born June 25, 1929, in Tavistock, Ontario, Canada; naturalized U.S. citizen, 1965; married Ruth Steinmann, 1950; children: five. *Education:* Attended Toronto Teacher's College, summers, 1947-48, and University of Western Ontario, summers, 1947-53; Goshen College, B.A., 1954, B.D. and M.R.E., both 1956; Yale University, M.A., 1961, Ph.D., 1962; University of Pennsylvania, postdoctoral study, 1970-71. *Home:* 1504 South Eighth St., Goshen, Ind. 46526. *Office:* Associated Mennonite Biblical Seminaries, 3003 Benham Ave., Elkhart, Ind. 46514.

CAREER: Teacher in public schools in Ontario, 1947-53; Rockway Mennonite High School, Kitchener, Ontario, principal, 1956-60; Goshen College Biblical Seminary, Goshen, Ind., assistant professor, 1962-64, associate professor, 1964-66, professor of Christian education, 1966—, dean, 1964—. Ordained Mennonite minister, 1958; associate pastor of churches in Waterloo, Ontario, 1958-60, and Lansdale, Pa., 1970-71; dean of Associated Mennonite Biblical Seminaries, 1964—; Urban Ministries Program for Seminarians, member of administrative board, 1969-75, chairman, 1969-70; executive secretary of Mennonite Board of Congregational Ministries, 1972-74.

MEMBER: Religious Education Association, Association of Professors and Researchers in Religious Education, American Association of Marriage and Family Counselors (clinical member). *Awards, honors:* Lilly Endowment grant, 1967-69, to direct development of a model for theological education in the "Free Church Tradition"; National Institute of Mental Health postdoctoral fellowship, 1970-71; Mennonite Mutual Aid grant, 1974, to direct Project Christian Family Living.

WRITINGS: The People of God: A Mennonite Interpretation of the Free Church Tradition, Herald Press, 1971.

Cassettes, with study guides: "The Christian Family: School of Faith," Word, Inc., 1974; "Old Enough to Get Married?: A Guide to Premarital Counseling," Word, Inc., 1974. Contributor to theology and education journals.

SIDELIGHTS: Bender's theological research has led him to South America, Europe, Asia, and Africa.

* * *

BENDER, Stephen (Joseph) 1942-

PERSONAL: Born July 12, 1942, in Rochester, N.Y.; son of Eugene P. (in management) and Ethel (an executive sec-

retary; maiden name, Rice) Bender; divorced; children: Theresa Ann, Suzanne. *Education:* State University of New York College at Brockport, B.S., 1966; Indiana University, M.S., 1967, H.S.D., 1969. *Home:* 2715 Bayside Walk, San Diego, Calif. 92109. *Office:* Department of Health Science and Safety, San Diego State University, San Diego, Calif. 92182.

CAREER: Rochester Telephone Corp., Rochester, N.Y., draftsman, 1960-61; construction worker in Rochester, N.Y., 1961-62; substitute teacher in elementary schools in Rochester, N.Y., 1965-66; Memphis State University, Memphis, Tenn., assistant professor of health science, 1968-70; San Diego State University, San Diego, Calif., associate professor of health science, 1970—, university ombudsman, 1974—. Member of Memphis Inter-Agency Council on Smoking and Health, 1970; member of board of directors of Memphis Alcohol and Drug Council, 1970. Member of sub-regional training team for California State Drug Education Training Program, 1970; member of Health Professionals Committee of Smoking Research of San Diego, 1971-73; member of California Department of Education Venereal Disease Project, 1972-73.

MEMBER: American School Health Association, American Alliance of Health, Physical Education and Recreation, California School Health Association, California Alliance of Health, Physical Education and Recreation (vice-president, 1973), Phi Delta Kappa, Phi Epsilon Kappa.

WRITINGS: Conceptual Approach to Health: A Guide to Intelligent Self-Direction, W. C. Brown, 1970, revised edition, 1972; *Venereal Disease,* W. C. Brown, 1970, 2nd edition, 1975; *Contraception: By Choice or by Chance?,* W. C. Brown, 1972; *Teaching Elementary Health Science,* Addison-Wesley, 1975; *Health and the Environments of Man,* Addison-Wesley, in press; *Teaching Secondary Health Science,* Wiley, in press. Contributor to health and physical education journals. Member of editorial board of *School Health Review,* 1969-72.

* * *

BENDICK, Robert L(ouis) 1917-

PERSONAL: Born February 8, 1917, in New York, N.Y.; son of Louis G. (a businessman) and Ruth (Feis) Bendick; married Jeanne Garfunkel (a writer and illustrator), November 24, 1940; children: Robert L., Jr., Karen Ann (Mrs. Michael Watson). *Education:* Attended New York University, 1936-37, and C. H. White School of Photography, 1938-39. *Politics:* Democrat. *Religion:* Jewish. *Home and office:* 360 Grace Church St., Rye, N.Y. 10580.

CAREER: Columbia Broadcasting System (CBS) Television, New York, N.Y., cameraman, 1940-42, director of news, special events, and sports, and executive producer or director of several individual programs, 1945-52; Cinerama Corp., New York, N.Y., co-producer and director of "This Is Cinerama" and director of "Cinerama Holiday," 1952-53; National Broadcasting Corp. (NBC) Television, New York, N.Y., producer of "Today Show," 1953-55 and 1958-60, "Wide, Wide World," 1956, "Twenty-Five Years of Life," 1961, "U.S. Steel Opening of the 1964 World's Fair," 1964, "The First Look" (children's series), 1966-67, producer-director of "Bell Telephone Science Trilogy," 1961-62, "Merrily We Roll Along," 1962, "America's Cup Races," 1962, and "The American Sportsman," 1964 and 1969. Producer for C. V. Whitney Productions and Merian C. Cooper, both 1956-57. Producer of All Latin-American Network 1968 Olympics, National Educational Television's

"The Great American Dream Machine" pilot programs, 1970-71 and 1971-72; executive co-producer of Children's Television Workshop's "Feeling Good," 1975. President of Bendick Associates (educational audio-visual company), 1966—. Lecturer at New York University and University of Oklahoma. *Military service:* U.S. Army Air Forces, filmed combat documentaries, 1943-45; served in China-Burma-India theater; received Air Medal with two oak leaf clusters.

MEMBER: National Academy of Television Arts and Sciences (member of board of governors; chairman of New York Emmy Awards Commission), Directors Guild of America, Urban League of Westchester County (member of board of directors). *Awards, honors:* Peabody Award from University of Georgia School of Journalism, 1948, for "United Nations in Action"; Emmy nomination from Academy of Television Arts and Sciences, 1955, for "The American West"; Christopher Award from Christopher Society, 1955, for "This Is Cinerama"; Swiss Government directorial award, 1955, for "Cinerama Holiday"; Albert Lasker Award from Albert and Mary Lasker Foundation, 1958, for "Today Show"; Ohio State Science Award, 1966, for "The First Look"; Emmy awards, 1970-71 and 1971-72, for "The Great American Dream Machine."

WRITINGS—All with wife, Jeanne Bendick: *Television Works Like This* (juvenile), McGraw, 1965; *Filming Works Like This* (juvenile), McGraw, 1970; *The Consumer's Catalog of Economy and Ecology,* McGraw, 1975; *Finding Out About Jobs: Television Reporting,* Parents' Magazine Press, 1976.

Illustrator: Jeanne Bendick, *Exploring an Ocean Tide Pool,* Garrard, 1975.

WORK IN PROGRESS: A book, *Energy from the Wind and Tide,* with Jeanne Bendick, publication by Garrard expected in 1977; a filmstrip, "Monsters and Other Science Mysteries," with Jeanne Bendick.

SIDELIGHTS: Bendick writes that a vital subject to him is "the impact of television on society—the failure of television to understand or respond to its incredible responsibility." He has worked on films in Europe, Asia, Alaska, Southeast Asia, New Zealand, and Australia. *Avocational interests:* Photography, sailing, fishing, oceanography.

*   *   *

BENET, James 1914-

PERSONAL: Born January 7, 1914, in Port Washington, N.Y.; son of William Rose (an author and editor) and Teresa (Thompson) Benet; married Mary Liles, December 13, 1938 (divorced, 1952); married Jane Gugel (a food editor), September 16, 1954; children: Judith (Mrs. Philip Richardson), Mary Kathleen (Mrs. Julian Hale), Peter. *Education:* Stanford University, B.A., 1935. *Politics:* Democrat. *Home:* 181 Edgehill Way, San Francisco, Calif. 94127. *Office:* KQED, 1011 Bryant St., San Francisco, Calif. 94103.

CAREER: Correspondent, *New Republic* (magazine), 1936-39, TASS, New York, N.Y., 1939-46; *San Francisco Chronicle,* San Francisco, Calif., copy editor and reporter, 1948-68; San Francisco State College (now University), San Francisco, associate professor of journalism, 1959-69; KQED (public television), San Francisco, education reporter, 1968—. Research associate, Scientific Analysis Corp., San Francisco. Director, United Cerebral Palsy Association of San Francisco. Served with Spanish Repub-

lican Army, International Brigades, 1937-38. *Member:* Newspaper Guild, National Association of Broadcast Employees and Technicians, National Academy of Television Arts and Sciences (San Francisco chapter). *Awards, honors:* First prize in broadcast division, National Council for Advancement of Education Writing, 1974, for "Sunnyhills."

WRITINGS: A Private Killing, Harper, 1948; *The Knife Behind You,* Harper, 1950; *A Guide to San Francisco and the Bay Area,* Random House, 1963, revised edition, 1967; *SCSD: The Project and the Schools,* Ford Foundation, 1967. Also writer-producer of documentaries for KQED Television: "Hunters Point II," 1972, "Sunnyhills," 1974, "Peninsula School," 1974, "Nueva," 1974, "Oakland Street Academies," 1974, and "The New Teaching," 1975.

WORK IN PROGRESS: On-going research on Bay Area and California schools, with emphasis on the public school system.

AVOCATIONAL INTERESTS: Gardening and skin-diving.

*   *   *

BEN-EZER, Ehud 1936-

PERSONAL: Born April 3, 1936, in Petah Tikva, Israel; son of Binyamin (an agriculturist) and Devora (Lipsky) Ben-Ezer; married Anat Fienberg, August 31, 1969 (divorced, 1972); married Yehudit Tomer (a nurse), September 24, 1974; children: (second marriage) Binyamin. *Education:* Hebrew University of Jerusalem, B.A., 1963. *Religion:* "Jew, Secular." *Address:* 20 Hakalir, P.O. Box 22135, Tel Aviv, Israel.

CAREER: Member of Kibbutz Ein Gedi on shore of Dead Sea, Israel, 1956-58; teacher in night school for adults, near Jerusalem, Israel, 1959-66; free-lance writer in Tel Aviv, Israel, 1966—. *Military service:* Israeli Army, Nahal troops, 1955-56, Israeli Army Reserve, 1967—; served in first aid unit in Six Day War, 1967. *Member:* P.E.N., Hebrew Writers Association. *Awards, honors:* Israeli Prime Minister Prize for creativity, 1975.

WRITINGS: Hamahtzeva (novel; title means "The Quarry"), Am Oved, 1963, adapted by the author as two-act play, first produced in Tel Aviv at Zuta Theatre, April, 1964; *Anshei Sedom* (novel; title means "The People of Sodom"), Am Oved, 1968; *Lo Lagiborim Hamilhama* (novel; title means "Nor the Battle to the Strong"), Levin-Epshtien, 1971; *Laila Beginat Hayerakot Hanirdamim* (juvenile; title means "Night in the Sleeping Vegetable Garden"), Massada, 1971; (editor) *Unease in Zion* (interviews), Quadrangle, 1974. Contributor of weekly column to *Ha'aretz* (daily newspaper), 1970—. Contributor to periodicals.

WORK IN PROGRESS: Research on the image of the Arab in Hebrew literature since the 1880's; a book of poems; a saga about the life of a family in Palestine since the 1830's; a lexicon of articles about more than two hundred Hebrew books; a children's book; memories of the painter, Nahum Gutmann; a book of short stories.

SIDELIGHTS: Ben-Ezer's novel, *The Quarry,* was adapted and broadcast on the Israel National Broadcasting Service, Kol Israel, in 1964, and again in six installments on the "Popular Hebrew" radio program in 1969.

*   *   *

BENNANI, B(en) M(ohammed) 1946-

PERSONAL: Born July 10, 1946, in Lebanon; son of Mohammed Idriss (a Moslem priest) and Mona Bennani; married Karen Ann LaBonte (an artist), September 5, 1970. *Education:* Dartmouth College, B.A., 1968; University of Massachusetts, M.F.A., 1972. *Home:* 111 South Eighth St., Laramie, Wyo. 82070. *Office:* Department of English, University of Wyoming, Box 3353, University Station, Laramie, Wyo. 82071.

CAREER: Berkshire Community College, Pittsfield, Mass., instructor in English, 1970-71; Greenfield Community College, Greenfield, Mass., instructor in English, 1971-72; University of Wyoming, Laramie, instructor in English, 1972—. President, editor-in-chief, and member of board of directors of Ishtar Publications. Special teacher for Monson State Hospital. Academic humanist for Wyoming Council for the Humanities; member of Wyoming poetry-in-the-schools program.

MEMBER: American Association of University Professors, Modern Language Association of America, Associated Writing Programs of America, Coordinating Council of Literary Magazines, Committee of Small Magazine Editors and Publishers, Committee of Small Press Editors, National Society for Literature and the Arts. *Awards, honors:* Fulbright-Hays grant, 1964.

WRITINGS: Zineb: Poems from Morocco, Roger Burt Press, 1968; (editor and translator) *Splinters of Bone: Poems by Mahmoud Darweesh,* Greenfield Review Press, 1974; (editor and translator) *Bread, Hasheesh, & Moon: Three Contemporary Arabic Poets* (Badr Shakir al-Sayyab, Nizar Qabbani, and Adonis) Copper Canyon Press, 1976. Contributor of poems and translations to literary journals, including *Massachusetts Review, Chelsea, Granite, San Francisco Quarterly, Wyoming Review, Contemporary Literature in Translation, Copperhead,* and *Journal of Arabic Literature.* Editor of *Paintbrush: A Journal of Poetry, Translations, and Letters,* 1974—.

WORK IN PROGRESS: The Shoe of Night, a book of poems; a humanistic analysis of the poetry of Mahmoud Darweesh, also called the Poet of the Palestinian Resistance.

SIDELIGHTS: Bennani writes: "I've travelled extensively in the Middle East, Africa, Europe (including Communist countries) and Russia. Travelling is as important to me as writing is."

*   *   *

BENNETT, James D(avid)   1926-

PERSONAL: Born August 2, 1926, in Calhoun, Ky.; son of Louis F. (a judge) and Margaret (Epley) Bennett; married Nina M. Hight (an educator and professional home economist), 1951. *Education:* Centre College of Kentucky, B.A., 1947; Texas Christian College, M.A., 1954; Vanderbilt University, Ph.D., 1968; graduate study, University of Texas, 1955-56. *Religion:* United Methodist. *Office:* Department of History, Western Kentucky University, Bowling Green, Ky. 42101.

CAREER: High school teacher of history in Kentucky, 1947-53; San Antonio College, San Antonio, Tex., instructor, 1954-55, assistant professor of history, 1956-59; Western Kentucky University, Bowling Green, associate professor, 1959-69, professor of history, 1969—. Director of social sciences workshop, Ft. Meyers (Fla.) Public Schools, 1972. *Member:* Organization of American Historians, Southern Historical Association, Western History Association, Filson Club, Phi Alpha Theta, Kiwanis.

WRITINGS: (With Lowell H. Harrison) *A Guide to Historical Research and Writing,* Western Kentucky University, 1970, revised edition, 1974; *Frederick Jackson Turner: American Historian,* Twayne, 1975. Contributor of articles to *Great Plains Journal, The Register of the Kentucky Historical Society, Tennessee Historical Quarterly,* and *Filson Club Historical Quarterly.*

WORK IN PROGRESS: A biography of Joseph Holt; research on Andrew Carnegie's gifts of pipe organs; and the 1876 Centennial Exposition and other U.S. exhibitions and fairs.

*   *   *

BENNETT-ENGLAND, Rodney Charles   1936-

PERSONAL: Born December 16, 1936, in Romford, Essexshire, England; son of Percy Charles and Sylvia (Pickles) England. *Education:* Attended Royal Liberty School, 1948-53. *Politics:* Conservative. *Religion:* Anglican. *Home and office addresses:* 3 Oakley St., Chelsea, London 5W3 5NN, England; and, Dale Cottage, Houghton St. Giles, Walsingham, Norfolk, England.

CAREER: Worked as reporter, columnist, critic, editor, and reviewer for various periodicals, 1953-61; *Sunday Express,* London, England, reporter and columnist, 1961-67; *The Journal,* London, editor, 1965-67; contributing editor to *Lords* and *Penthouse* magazines, 1967-70, and to *Men Only,* 1970-73; RBE Associates Ltd. (public relations and media consultant firm), London, chairman and managing director, 1970—. Writer and lecturer. Member of British Copyright Council, 1965-70; member of Church Assembly, 1967-70; chairman of National Council for the Training of Journalists, 1968-69; member of British Council of Churches, 1968-70; director of Foreign Anglican Church and Educational Association, 1969—; trustee of Albany Trust, 1975—. *Member:* Institute of Journalists (fellow; vice-president, 1968-71), Albany Society (director, 1968—), Royal Society of Arts (fellow), Institute of Directors (fellow), Institute of Public Relations, British Institute of Management, British Society of Authors, Men's Fashion Writers International, Clothing Institute, Pi Delta Epsilon (honorary member), Whitefriars Club, Press Club, Wig and Pen Club. *Awards, honors:* Freeman of City of London, 1967; chosen as first men's fashion writer of the year by Clothing Institute, 1968.

WRITINGS: (Editor) *Inside Journalism,* P. Owen, 1967; (contributor) D. Morgan, editor, *Faith in Fleet Street,* Mowbray, 1967; *Dress Optional: The Revolution in Menswear,* P. Owen, 1967, Dufour, 1968; *As Young as You Look: Male Grooming and Rejuvenation,* P. Owen, 1970. Also author of pamphlets and contributor to over 300 periodicals worldwide.

WORK IN PROGRESS: Fashion and the Artist; Top of the Fops, a book about dandies and their eccentricities; a biography of John Hooper, Bishop of Gloucester and Worcester (c.1485-1555).

AVOCATIONAL INTERESTS: Fashion, food, drink, grooming, antiques.

*   *   *

BENVENISTE, Guy   1927-

PERSONAL: Born February 27, 1927, in Paris, France; son of Raphaël and Lucy de Botton. *Education:* Harvard University, B.S., 1948, M.S., 1950; Stanford University, Ph.D., 1968. *Office:* Department of Education, University of California, Berkeley, Calif. 94720.

CAREER: Stanford Research Institute, Stanford, Calif., research economist, 1954-60; U.S. Department of State, Washington, D.C., special assistant in Office of Education and Cultural Affairs, 1960-61; International Bank for Reconstruction and Development, Washington, D.C., economist in Education Division, 1961-62; UNESCO, Paris, France, senior staff member, 1962-65; University of California, Berkeley, professor of education, 1968—.

WRITINGS: Handbook of African Development, Praeger, 1962; *Agents of Change: Professionals in Developing Countries,* Praeger, 1969; *Bureaucracy and National Planning,* Praeger, 1970; *Politics of Expertise,* Glendessary, 1972.

* * *

BERGER, Elmer 1908-

PERSONAL: Born May 27, 1908, in Cleveland, Ohio; son of Samuel and Selma (Turk) Berger; married Ruth Rosenthal (a lawyer), August 27, 1946. *Education:* University of Cincinnati, A.B., 1929; Hebrew Union College, Rabbi, 1932. *Home:* 1171 Bogey Lane, Sarasota, Fla. 33577. *Office:* 133 East 73rd St., New York, N.Y. 10021.

CAREER: Rabbi in Pontiac, Mich., 1932-36, and Flint, Mich., 1936-43; American Council for Judaism, New York City, executive vice-president, 1943-67; American Jewish Alternatives to Zionism, New York City, president, 1968—.

WRITINGS: The Jewish Dilemma, Devin-Adair, 1945; *Partisan History of Judaism,* Devin-Adair, 1949; *Judaism of Jewish Nationalism,* A. B. Bookman, 1953; *Who Knows Better Must Say So,* Institute for Palestinian Studies (Beirut), 1969; *Peace in the Middle East: How to Achieve It?,* American Enterprise Institute, 1970; (editor) *Letters and Non-Letters,* Institute for Palestinian Studies, 1972. Editor of American Jewish Alternatives to Zionism report.

SIDELIGHTS: A specialist on Zionism and Middle East politics, Berger has traveled extensively in the Arab world. He has a "passable knowledge" of French and German.

* * *

BERGER, Phil 1942-

PERSONAL: Born April 1, 1942, in Brooklyn, N.Y.; son of Jack (a grocer) and Fanny (Finkelstein) Berger. *Education:* Johns Hopkins University, B.A. (cum laude), 1964. *Residence:* New York, N.Y.

CAREER: Greenwich Time (newspaper), Greenwich, Conn., reporter, summers, 1963-64; Associated Press, Atlanta, Ga., newsman, 1964; *Sport* (magazine), associate editor, 1966-67; free-lance writer, 1965-66, 1967—. *Military service:* U.S. Army, 1965-66. U.S. Army Reserve, 1965-71.

WRITINGS: Miracle on Thirty-Third Street: The New York Knickerbockers' Championship Season, Simon & Schuster, 1970; *The Last Laugh: The World of the Standup Comics,* Morrow, 1975. Contributor of more than three hundred stories and articles to popular magazines, including *New York, National Observer, Penthouse, Rogue, Cavalier, Look, Worlds of Tomorrow, Sport, Pageant, Parade,* and *Johns Hopkins,* and to newspapers, including *Village Voice.*

AVOCATIONAL INTERESTS: Reading, backetball, tennis, distance running, New York City.

BIOGRAPHICAL/CRITICAL SOURCES: New York Times, October 22, 1970; *New York Post,* February 8, 1971; *San Francisco Chronicle,* April 9, 1975.

BERGMAN, Arlene Eisen 1942-

PERSONAL: Born November 4, 1942, in New York, N.Y.; daughter of Jack and Sylvia (Warsawer) Eisen. *Education:* Cornell University, B.S., 1965; University of California, Berkeley, M.A., 1966, doctoral candidate, 1966-68. *Politics:* "Revolutionary." *Residence:* San Francisco, Calif. *Office:* New College, San Jose State University, San Jose, Calif. 95192.

CAREER: Movement (newspaper), San Francisco, Calif., editor, 1967-70; Merritt College, Oakland, Calif., instructor in sociology, 1968-69; full-time organizer for anti-war and women's movement, 1970-72; San Francisco State University, San Francisco, lecturer in sociology, 1972-73; San Jose State University, San Jose, Calif., lecturer in politics, sociology and women's studies, 1972—.

WRITINGS: Women of Viet Nam, Peoples Press (San Francisco, Calif.), 1974, revised edition, 1975. Contributor to magazines and newspapers. Editor of *Berkeley Journal of Sociology.*

WORK IN PROGRESS: Research on women's unions in Viet Nam and other countries.

SIDELIGHTS: Arlene Bergman writes: "The book, *Women of Viet Nam,* grew from the questions, needs and encouragement of women active in the women's movement in the United States. I feel stronger, inspired by the experience of women in Viet Nam and want to share this strength and inspiration with as many people as possible. With this book, my teaching and my daily activity, I participate in the struggle for the liberation of women and all oppressed people." *Avocational interests:* Travel (Latin America, including Cuba, Europe, Asia, including Viet Nam, People's Republic of China).

* * *

BERGMANN, Fred L(ouis) 1916-

PERSONAL: Born September 27, 1916, in Tecumseh, Kan.; son of Curt W. and Minna (Herrmann) Bergmann; married Jean B. Marshall, July 6, 1941; children: Juliann (Mrs. Peter Jan Witteveld), John Frederick. *Education:* Washburn University, A.B., 1937; Washington State University, M.A., 1939; George Washington University, Ph.D., 1953. *Politics:* Independent. *Religion:* Episcopalian. *Home:* 205 North Arlington Ave., Greencastle, Ind. 46135. *Office:* Department of English, DePauw University, Greencastle, Ind. 46135.

CAREER: DePauw University, Greencastle, Ind., instructor, 1940-43, assistant professor, 1943-46, associate professor, 1946-54, professor of English, 1954-69, James Whitcomb Riley Professor of English Literature, 1969—, chairman of department, 1956—. *Member:* Societe Francaise d'Etudes du XVIIIth Siecle, Johnson Society, Modern Language Association of America, Society of Professional Journalists, English Speaking Union, American Society for Eighteenth-Century Studies, Great Lakes Colleges Association (English chairman), Indiana College English Association, Benevolent and Protective Order of Elks, Sigma Delta Chi. *Awards, honors:* Folger Shakespeare Library fellow, 1969.

WRITINGS: (With R. W. Pence) *Writing Craftsmanship,* Norton, 1956; *Paragraph Rhetoric,* Allyn & Bacon, 1967; *Sentence Rhetoric,* Allyn & Bacon, 1969; *Essays: Method, Content, Conscience,* William C. Brown, 1970; *Essays,* William C. Brown, 1975. Contributor to professional journals.

WORK IN PROGRESS: Four volumes of *The Dramatic Writings of David Garrick;* a critical edition of *The Clandestine Marriage* by Garrick and Colman.

* * *

BERKEBILE, Don(ald) H(erbert) 1926-

PERSONAL: Born November 21, 1926, in Johnstown, Pa.; son of Arthur William and Edythe Odell (Isenberg) Berkebile. *Education:* Attended Columbia Union College, 1944 and 1948, and University of Pittsburgh, Johnstown Branch, 1949. *Office:* Division of Transportation, Smithsonian Institution, Washington, D.C. 20560.

CAREER: Worked as steelworker and carpenter at various periods, 1947-54; Smithsonian Institution, Division of Transportation, Washington, D.C., exhibits specialist, 1955-60, museum specialist, 1960-73, assistant curator, 1973-74, associate curator, 1974—. *Military service:* U.S. Army, 1945-46. *Member:* Company of Military Historians (fellow; life member), Military Order of Saint Barbara.

WRITINGS: (With Smith Hempstone Oliver) *The Smithsonian Collection of Automobiles and Motorcycles,* Random House, 1968; (with Smith Hempstone Oliver) *Wheels and Wheeling,* Smithsonian Institution Press, 1974; *A Pictorial Album of American Carriages,* Dover, in press; *A Dictionary of Carriage Terms,* Smithsonian Institution Press, in press. Contributor to *Encyclopedia Americana* and *Cowles Comprehensive Encyclopedia.* Contributor to publications of the Smithsonian Institution.

WORK IN PROGRESS: Research on carriage wheel construction, military transport, and blacksmithing; a catalog of the Smithsonian carriage collection.

AVOCATIONAL INTERESTS: Mechanical arts (especially gunsmithing and carriage building; has restored and built replicas for museums).

* * *

BERKMAN, Edward O(scar) 1914-
(Ted Berkman)

PERSONAL: Born January 9, 1914, in Brooklyn, N.Y.; son of Samuel (a dentist) and Bertha (a legal secretary; maiden name, Holtzmann) Berkman; married Annahrae White, July, 1957 (divorced, November, 1958). *Education:* Cornell University, A.B., 1933; also studied at Columbia University, 1934-35, Contemporary School of Music, 1953-54, and University of California, Los Angeles, 1955-56. *Politics:* "Exemplified by Chester Bowles, William O. Douglas." *Religion:* Jewish. *Residence:* New York, N.Y. *Agent:* Owen Laster, William Morris Agency, 1350 Avenue of the Americas, New York, N.Y. 10019.

CAREER: New York Daily Mirror, New York, N.Y., assistant city editor, foreign editor, and re-write man, 1933-36 and 1940-42; screenwriter for various film companies, 1938-40; American Broadcasting Co. and Overseas News Agency, foreign correspondent, 1945-46; United Nations Appeal for Children, worldwide director of information, 1947-48; screenwriter, 1950-60; author and television scriptwriter, 1960—. Lecturer, New School for Social Research, 1968, and Marymount College, 1972-75; former member of board of directors of Trafalgar Hospital; member of board of directors of Center for Creative Learning. *Wartime service:* U.S. Foreign Broadcast Intelligence Service, Balkan-Middle East chief attached to U.S. Army, Psychological Warfare Branch, 1942-46; served in Cairo.

MEMBER: Writers Guild of America, Phi Beta Kappa.

Awards, honors: Best of show gold medals for non-theatrical films from Cleveland Film Festival, 1949, for "All I Need Is a Conference," and from Berlin Film Festival, 1955, for "Strangers in Paradise"; Christopher Award, 1957, for screenplay "Fear Strikes Out"; citation from American Jewish Congress, 1963, for "Cast a Giant Shadow"; fellowship from MacDowell Colony, 1969-70; Oppie award, 1972, naming *To Seize the Passing Dream* as best biographical novel.

WRITINGS—All under name Ted Berkman: *Cast a Giant Shadow* (biography of Colonel David Marcus), Doubleday, 1962, abridged edition, Jewish Publication Society, 1967; *Sabra* (on Israel's six-day war), Harper, 1969; *To Seize the Passing Dream* (biography of James McNeill Whistler), Doubleday, 1972; *The Lady and the Law* (on Fanny Holtzmann), Little, Brown, 1976.

Filmscripts: "The Squeaker," London Films, 1937; "The Green Cockatoo," London Films, 1939; "Bedtime for Bonzo," Universal, 1951; "Fear Strikes Out," Paramount, 1957; "Edge of Fury," United Artists, 1958; "Girl in the Night," Warner Brothers, 1960.

Author of television scripts for "Studio One," "Theater Guild of the Air," "This Proud Land," "Behind Closed Doors," and "Decision" (memoirs of Harry S Truman). Writer of songs and lyrics published by Chappell. Contributor to popular magazines, including *New Republic, American Mercury, Coronet, Diplomat,* and *American Spectator.*

SIDELIGHTS: Beckman gave the first eyewitness account of the King David Hotel explosion from Jerusalem in 1946, later served as informal adviser to Edward R. Murrow on Middle East affairs, and became a lecturer and appeared on national television and radio programs. His political involvement led him to work as campaign aide, speechwriter, and consultant to political figures including Averill Harriman and Chester Bowles.

His life-long involvement with music (his songs were performed at the White House by Hildegarde in 1960) has lately taken him into jazz piano studies. *Avocational interests:* Swimming, table tennis, chess.

BIOGRAPHICAL/CRITICAL SOURCES: New York World-Telegram and Sun, October 9, 1962; *Miami News,* May 5, 1963; *Haaretz,* May 2, 1969; *New York Post,* March 11, 1972.

* * *

BERRIGAN, Edmund Joseph Michael, Jr. 1934-
(Ted Berrigan)

PERSONAL: Born November 15, 1934, in Providence, R.I.; married Sandra Alper; children: Kate, David. *Education:* University of Tulsa, B.A., 1959, M.A., 1962. *Home:* 911 West Diversey Pkwy., Chicago, Ill. 60614.

CAREER: Teacher in poetry workshop in St. Mark's Art Project, New York City, 1966-67; visiting lecturer for Writer's Workshop at University of Iowa, Iowa City, 1968-69; editorial assistant for *Art News;* editor and publisher, "C" Press and "C" Magazine. *Military service:* U.S. Army, 1954-57. *Awards, honors:* Poetry Foundation Award, 1964.

WRITINGS—Poetry: *A Lily for My Love: 13 Poems,* privately printed, 1959; *The Sonnets,* "C" Press, 1964, reprinted, Grove Press, 1967; *Living with Chris,* Boke Press, 1966; *Many Happy Returns to Dick Gallup,* Gabhorn-Hoyem, 1967; *Many Happy Returns: Poems,* Corinth Books, 1969; *Fragment: For Jim Brodey,* Cape Goliard

Press, 1969; (with Anselm Hollo) *Doubletalk*, T. G. Miller, 1969; (with Ron Padgett) *Noh*, privately printed, 1969; (with Tom Clark, Allen Kaplan and Padgett; in German and English) *Guillaume Apollinaire ist tot: Gedichte, Prosa*, Maerz (Frankfurt), 1970; *In the Early Morning Rain*, Cape Goliard Press, 1970, Grossman, 1971; (with Anne Waldman) *Memorial Day*, Poetry Project, 1971; (with Clark and Padgett) *Back in Boston Again*, Telegraph Books, 1972.

Other: *Galileo: Or Finksville* (play), privately printed, 1964; (with Padgett) *Seventeen: Collected Plays*, "C" Press, 1965; (with Padgett and Joe Brainard) *Some Things* (drawings and poems), privately printed, 1965; (with Padgett) *Bean Spasms* (collaborations and solos), Kulchur Press, 1967.

Editor: (With Padgett) Tom Veitch, *Literary Days: Selected Writings*, "C" Press, 1964; Kenward Elmslie, *The Power Plant Poems*, "C" Press, 1965.

Work represented in anthologies, including *Young American Poets*, edited by Paul Carroll, Follett, 1968, *The American Literary Anthology I*, Farrar, Straus, 1968, and *Sparklers*, Random House, 1969. Contributor to *Poetry, Art News, Art and Literature, Angel Hair, Mother*, and *World*.*

* * *

BERRY, Lynn 1948-

PERSONAL: Born September 23, 1948, in Brooklyn, N.Y.; daughter of Richard George (an architect) and Jean (Thurman) Berry. *Education:* Notre Dame College, Cleveland, Ohio, B.A., 1970; Trenton State College, M.Ed., 1975. *Home:* 132 East Cliff St., Somerville, N.J. 08876. *Office:* Hillsborough School, Route 206, Bellemead, N.J. 08876.

CAREER: High school teacher of art in private school in Cleveland, Ohio, 1970-71; Hillsborough School, Bellemead, N.J., middle school teacher of art, 1971—. *Member:* Art Educators of New Jersey.

WRITINGS: (With Max Ellison) *Double Take* (poems), Conway House, 1973.

WORK IN PROGRESS: Writing poems; "various artistic endeavors."

* * *

BESKOW, Bo 1906-

PERSONAL: Born February 13, 1906, in Djursholm; son of Nathanael (a theologian involved in international peace work) and Elsa Beskow; married Greta Berge (a ceramic artist), 1955; children: Maria, Susanna, Peter. *Education:* Studied at Royal Academy of Fine Arts, Stockholm, 1923-26. *Home:* Aasoegatan 203, Stockholm, Sweden; (country home) Mogata, 61400 Soederkoeping, Sweden.

CAREER: Artist. Among his murals are two at United Nations headquarters in New York; has done portraits of Swedish statesmen and other notables, among them John Steinbeck (portraits in 1937, 1946, 1957) and Dag Hammarskjold; his stained glass work is installed in cathedrals at Skara and Vaexjoe; has done stage design for Royal Opera and Royal Dramatic Theatre in Stockholm. *Awards, honors:* Knight of the Northern Cross; Golden Plaque at Bratislava Biennial, 1969, *Figge Builds a Shellhouse*.

WRITINGS: Janne: Rom (title means "Janne in Rome"), Bonniers, 1929; *Flykten till Portugal* (title means "Flight to Portugal"), Wahlstroem & Widstrand, 1937; *Figge*, Geber, 1966; *Figge bygger snaeckhus* (title means "Figge Builds a Shellhouse"), Bonniers, 1967; *Dag Hammarskjoeld: Ett portraet*, Bonniers, 1968, English edition, also by Beskow, published as *Dag Hammarskjoeld: Strictly Personal*, Doubleday, 1969; *Krokodivens middag* (title means "Dinner for a Crocodile"), Bonniers, 1969; *Saang om Sardinien* (title means "Song of Sardinia"), Bonniers, 1971. Contributor to periodicals.

* * *

BETENSON, Lula Parker 1884-

PERSONAL: Born April 5, 1884, in Garfield County, Utah; daughter of Maximillian (a farmer) and Annie (Gillies) Parker; married Joseph A. Betenson, Jr., December 31, 1907 (died July 28, 1948); children: Pauline (Mrs. Lew Applegate), Mark, Scott, John M., Barbara Lou (Mrs. Lee Carlson). *Education:* Educated in public schools in Circleville, Utah. *Politics:* Democrat. *Religion:* Church of Jesus Christ of Latter-day Saints. *Residence:* Circleville, Utah.

CAREER: Writer. Has directed community plays and productions; representative to Utah state legislature (by appointment), 1961.

WRITINGS: Butch Cassidy, My Brother (nonfiction), Brigham Young University Press, 1975.

SIDELIGHTS: Lula Betenson writes: "So many things had been written and told about my brother that I felt it was time for me to set the record straight."

* * *

BEYEA, Basil 1910-
(B. A. Benson)

PERSONAL: Born July 30, 1910, in New York, N.Y.; son of Benjamin N. (a salesman) and Charlotte (Paul) Beyea. *Education:* Princeton University, B.A., 1931; New York School of Social Work (now Columbia School of Social Work), M.S.W., 1935. *Politics:* Democrat. *Religion:* Episcopal. *Home and office address:* 9719 Wintergardens Blvd., Apt. 172, Lakeside, Calif. 92040. *Agent:* Helen Barrett, William Morris Agency, 1350 Avenue of the Americas, New York, N.Y. 10019.

CAREER: Community Service Society, New York City, family case worker, 1932-35; Social Service Bureau, Honolulu, Hawaii, family case worker, 1935-37; public relations director, Boston Family Welfare Society, 1937-40; employed in public relations, Greater New York Fund, 1940-42; chief copy writer in public relations for community chests and councils, New York City, 1946-48; freelance television writer and writer of documentary and educational films, 1948-68; Falkirk Hospital, Central Valley, N.Y., psychiatric social worker, 1968-73. *Military service:* U.S. Army, Signal Corps, 1942-45; became sergeant; received Bronze Star Medal. *Member:* National Association of Social Work, Academy of Certified Social Workers, Authors Guild.

WRITINGS: (Under pseudonym B. A. Benson) *How to Live with a Parakeet*, Messner, 1959; *The Golden Mistress* (historical novel based on early life of Madame Jumel), Simon & Schuster, 1975.

Author of "The Cat Screams" (three-act play), produced on Broadway at Martin Beck Theatre, June, 1942. Under pseudonym B. A. Benson, author of television scripts for series including "Studio One," and "Suspense."

WORK IN PROGRESS: A sequel to *The Golden Mistress,* publication by Simon & Schuster expected in 1977.

AVOCATIONAL INTERESTS: Cats, playing jazz piano.

* * *

BIAL, Morrison David 1917-

PERSONAL: Surname is pronounced "Beal"; born August 29, 1917, in New York, N.Y.; son of Jacob (a diamond setter) and Carrie (Dash) Bial; married Dorothy Berman, November 6, 1954; children: Daniel, Anne Rachel. *Education:* Brooklyn College (now of the City University of New York), B.A., 1941; Jewish Institute of Religion, Rabbi, 1945, M.H.L., 1946. *Home:* 49 Bellevue Ave., Summit, N.J. 07901. *Office:* Temple Sinai, 208 Summit Ave., Summit, N.J. 07901.

CAREER: Rabbi, Temple Emanuel, Lynbrook, N.Y., 1944-46, Beth Shalom Temple, Brooklyn, N.Y., 1946-50, Free Synagogue, Mt. Vernon, N.Y. 1950-52, Temple Sinai, Summit, N.J., 1953—. Instructor at Hebrew Union College, 1956—. *Awards, honors:* D.D. from Jewish Institute of Religion, 1970.

WRITINGS: *The Passover Story,* Behrman, 1951; *The Hanukkah Story* (juvenile), Behrman, 1952; *An Offering of Prayer,* Temple Sinai (Summit, N.J.), 1962; (with Solomon Simon) *The Rabbis' Bible,* Behrman, Volume I, 1966, Volume II, 1969; *Liberal Judaism at Home: The Practices of Modern Judaism,* Temple Sinai, 1967, revised edition, Union of American Hebrew Congregations, 1971; *Questions You Asked,* Behrman, 1972; (editor) Bea Stadtler, *The Holocaust: A History of Courage and Resistance,* Behrman, 1974; *Your Jewish Child,* Union of American Hebrew Congregations, in press.

Poems for cantatas by A. W. Binder; "Israel Reborn," Bloch Publishing, 1949, "Hanukkah of the Maccabees," Transcontinental, 1950; "Passover into Freedom," Transcontinental, 1951. Author of pamphlets. Contributor of articles and reviews to magazines.

* * *

BICKERTON, Derek 1926-

PERSONAL: Born March 25, 1926, in Bebington, England; son of Thomas (an office manager) and Hilda (a teacher; maiden name, Ashall) Bickerton; married Yvonne Harrison (a sex counselor), July 11, 1952; children: James Justin, Ashley Thomas, Julia Regan. *Education:* Cambridge University, B.A., 1949, M.A., 1968, Ph.D., 1975; University of Leeds, diploma, 1967. *Politics:* None. *Religion:* None. *Home:* 1722 Makiki St., Apt. 502, Honolulu, Hawaii 96822. *Office:* Department of Linguistics, University of Hawaii, 1890 East-West Rd., Honolulu, Hawaii 96822.

CAREER: University College of Cape Coast, Cape Coast, Ghana, lecturer in contemporary English, 1964-66; University of Guyana, Georgetown, Guyana, senior lecturer in the English language, 1967-71; University of Lancaster, Lancaster, England, lecturer in linguistics, 1971-72; University of Hawaii, Honolulu, associate professor of linguistics, 1972—. *Member:* Caribbean Linguistics Society (foundation member).

WRITINGS: *Payroll* (thriller), Eyre & Spottiswoode, 1959; *The Gold Run* (thriller), Eyre & Spottiswoode, 1961; *The Murders of Boysie Singh: Robber, Arsonist, Pirate, Mass-Murderer, Vice and Gambling King of Trinidad,* Arthur Barker, 1962; *Tropicana* (biography), Constable,

1963; *Dynamics of a Creole System,* Cambridge University Press, 1975. Contributor to language journals. Advisory editor of *Journal of Creole Studies.*

WORK IN PROGRESS: Research on Hawaiian pidgin and Creole English.

SIDELIGHTS: Bickerton has traveled extensively in southern Europe, West Africa, the Caribbean, and South America. He is interested in all aspects of Hispanic and Black Caribbean culture. He writes of his hope "that the Third World will redress the balance of the other two."

* * *

BICKFORD, Elwood Dale 1927-

PERSONAL: Born August 7, 1927, in Coventry, Vt.; son of Robert L., Sr. (a farmer) and Evangeline (Tyler) Bickford; married Gladys M. Doyle (a correspondent), December 27, 1953; children: Dale Robert, Mary Jane. *Education:* University of Vermont, B.S., 1957, M.S., 1959. *Politics:* Independent. *Religion:* "No formal sect." *Home:* 205 Central St., Topsfield, Mass. 01983. *Office:* 60 Boston St., Salem, Mass. 01970.

CAREER: High school teacher of science in the public schools of Freeport, N.Y., 1959-60; Squibb Division of Olin, New Brunswick, N.J., research scientist, 1960-62; GTE Sylvania Inc., Salem, Mass., photobiologist, 1962—. Chairman, Topsfield Mosquito Control Commission, 1968; member of Town Environmental Commission, 1971, and Topsfield Conservation Commission, 1972. *Military service:* U.S. Army, Signal Corps, 1951-53. *Member:* American Institute of Biological Sciences, American Society for Horticultural Science, American Society for Photobiology, American Society of Plant Physiology, Illuminating Engineering Society. *Awards, honors:* Outstanding service award from National Management Association, 1968; named to U.S. National Committee on Photobiology of the National Research Council of the National Academy of Sciences.

WRITINGS: *Lighting for Plant Growth,* Kent State University Press, 1972. Contributor to journals in his field.

WORK IN PROGRESS: Research on photobiology and photochemotherapy.

AVOCATIONAL INTERESTS: Wood working, painting in different media, gardening, bicycling.

* * *

BIDA, Constantine 1916-

PERSONAL: Born September 24, 1916, in Lvov, Ukrainian S.S.R.; naturalized Canadian citizen; son of Joseph (a civil servant) and Theofila (Delkevych) Bida. *Education:* Attended University of Lvov, 1937-39; University of Vienna, Ph.D., 1943; additional study at University of Bern, 1945-46. *Religion:* Greek Catholic. *Home:* 1364 Wesmar Dr., Ottawa, Ontario, Canada K1H 7T5. *Office:* Department of Slavic Studies, University of Ottawa, Ottawa, Ontario, Canada K1N 6N5.

CAREER: University of Vienna, Vienna, Austria, research assistant at Institute of Slavic Studies, 1943-44; University of Ottawa, Ottawa, Ontario, lecturer, 1952-57, assistant professor, 1957-61, associate professor, 1961-65, professor of Slavic literature, 1965—, chairman of department of Slavic studies, 1957—. Research professor at Ukrainian Catholic University, Rome, Italy.

MEMBER: Modern Language Association, Modern Humanities Research Association, Canadian Linguistic Association, French-Canadian Association for the Advancement of Science, Canadian Association of Comparative Literature (co-founder), American Comparative Literature Association, Canadian Association of Ethnic Studies (founding member), Conference on Ukrainian Studies in Canada (president, 1975-76), American Association for Advancement of Slavic Studies, American Association for the Study of Nationalities in U.S.S.R. and East Europe, Canadian Association of Slavists (president, 1960-61), Ukrainian Shakespearean Society in Canada and Europe (president), Inter-University Committee on Canadian Slavs (president, 1970-71). *Awards, honors:* Canada Council fellowship, 1972-73, research grant, 1974-75.

WRITINGS: Na vershynakh idei i formy, [Toronto], 1958; *Le Premier Kobzar de T. Chevtchenk, 1840,* University of Ottawa, 1961; *Shakespeare and National Traits in Slavic Literatures: The Problems of Interpretation,* Mouton, 1966; *Lesya Ukrainka: Life and Work,* translated by Vera Rich, University of Toronto Press, for Women's Council of the Ukrainian Canadian Committee, 1968; (editor) *Poeziia suchasnogo Kvebeku: Poesie du Quebec contemporain* (anthology), Librairie Deom, 1968; (editor) *Slavs in Canada,* Volume II, Inter-University Committee, 1968; *De Ioannitio Galatovsky eiusque Clavi Cognitionis* [Rome], 1975. Also author of *Soiuz het' mana Ivana Mazepy z Karlom,* 1959. Contributor of articles to journals, including *Canadian Slavonic Papers* and *Slavic and East European Studies.*

WORK IN PROGRESS: Homilies of I. Galatovsky, Volume II, on aspects of style; *Anthology of East-Slavic Literature of the Seventeenth Century;* a ten-volume series of critical text editions of East-Slavic baroque literature.

SIDELIGHTS: Constantine Bida writes: "At the time of the predominant technological trend it is essential to work intensively in the field of the humanities so as to create a healthy and necessary counterbalance."

*   *   *

BIENVENU, Richard (Thomas)   1936-

PERSONAL: Born September 6, 1936, in St. Martinville, La.; son of Wade Thomas and Helen (LaSalle) Bienvenu; married Roberta Kluess (a writer), March 4, 1961; children: David, Micajah. *Education:* University of Southwestern Louisiana, B.A. (summa cum laude), 1958; University of North Carolina, M.A., 1959; Harvard University, Ph.D., 1965. *Address:* R.F.D. 4, Box 167, Columbia, Mo. 65201. *Office:* Department of History, University of Missouri, Columbia, Mo. 65201.

CAREER: Harvard University, Cambridge, Mass., instructor in history, 1964-67; University of Colorado, Boulder, assistant professor of history, 1967-68; University of Missouri, Columbia, assistant professor, 1968-71, associate professor of history, 1971—. *Awards, honors:* Woodrow Wilson fellow, 1958-61; Fels Foundation fellow, 1963-64; Canaday Humanities fellow at Harvard University, summer, 1965; National Endowment for the Humanities summer fellowship, 1968.

WRITINGS: (Also editor and translator of own work from the French) *The Ninth of Thermidor,* Oxford University Press, 1968; (editor and translator from the French with J. Beecher) *The Utopian Vision of Charles Fourier: Selected Texts on Work, Love, and Passionate Attraction,* Beacon Press, 1971; (contributor) Mathe Allain, editor, *France and America: The Revolutionary Experience,* University of

Southwestern Louisiana Press, 1974; (contributor) Glenn Conrad, editor, *Utopians and Utopias,* University of Southwestern Louisiana, 1976. Editor, with John Naylor, of series, "Problems in European History: A Documentary Collection," seven volumes, Oxford University Press, 1968-69. Contributor to *Encyclopedia Americana.*

WORK IN PROGRESS: A general history book on the idea of work in western culture since the Renaissance; a collective biography of the Saint-Simonians which focuses on their experiment in communal living at Menilmontant; a three-hour broadcast commentary, "Operas of Berlioz."

*   *   *

BIERI, Arthur Peter   1931-

PERSONAL: Born June 4, 1931, in Stillwater, Okla.; son of Oscar Charles and Helen C. Bieri; married Alvena N. Brillhart; children: Donna Jean, John Arthur. *Education:* Oklahoma State University, B.S., 1958, M.S., 1964, standard in administration, 1971. *Politics:* Democrat. *Religion:* United Methodist. *Home:* 2023 West 11th, Stillwater, Okla. 74074. *Office:* Stillwater Public Schools, 316 South Stallard, Stillwater, Okla. 74074.

CAREER: Stillwater Public Schools, Stillwater, Okla., physical education teacher and supervisor, 1959—, principal of Lincoln Elementary School, 1965-74; principal of Highland Park Elementary School, 1974—. Has taught swimming for more than twenty-five years, including life saving and water safety, qualified as American Red Cross instructor-trainer in cardio-pulmonary respiration, 1975, and as handicapped instructor-trainer. Inaugurated a fitness and recreation program for Stillwater's mentally retarded children; coordinated workshops on physical education for the mentally retarded. Guest lecturer at colleges and universities, including Oklahoma State University and Oklahoma University. Member of National Intramural Sports Council, 1967; member of Oklahoma White House Conference Committee on Children and Youth, 1971—; executive director of Oklahoma governor's Council on Physical Fitness, 1964; chairman of governor's Council on Youth Groups. Certified aquatic director of national Young Men's Christian Association (YMCA), 1969, aquatic chairman of Stillwater Young Men's Christian Association. Member of board of directors of Payne County Guidance Center, 1970—, Payne County Council for Retarded Children, Stillwater Sheltered Workshop (for the retarded), 1970—, and American Red Cross (Stillwater chapter), 1975. *Military service:* U.S. Air Force, 1951-55; served in Korea; became staff sergeant.

MEMBER: American Association for Health, Physical Education and Recreation (charter member of Aquatic Council, 1968), National Education Association, Oklahoma Association for Health, Physical Education and Recreation, Oklahoma Education Association, Northern Oklahoma Education Association (chairman, 1964-65), Stillwater Education Association. *Awards, honors:* Merit award from American Red Cross, 1961, for life saving, bronze medallion, 1971, for volunteer service in aquatics; Oklahoma gold medallion from State of Oklahoma, 1965, for physical fitness leadership; five-state regional physical fitness leadership award, 1965.

WRITINGS: Action Games, Fearon, 1972. Member of editorial board for *Physical Education Newsletter,* of Oklahoma Association for Health, Physical Education and Recreation, 1965-66; member of editorial committee to develop a swimming program for the handicapped, for national Young Men's Christian Association.

WORK IN PROGRESS: A children's book.

* * *

BILLINGS, Warren M(artin) 1940-

PERSONAL: Born February 4, 1940, in New York, N.Y.; son of H. Warren (an architect) and Rheta M. (Moore) Billings; married Carol Ann Dunlap (a librarian), August 15, 1964; children: Elizabeth Caroline. *Education:* College of William and Mary, A.B., 1962; University of Pittsburgh, A.M., 1964; Northern Illinois University, Ph.D., 1968. *Politics:* Democrat. *Religion:* Episcopalian. *Residence:* New Orleans, La. *Office:* Department of History, University of New Orleans, Lakefront, New Orleans, La. 70122.

CAREER: University of New Orleans, New Orleans, La., assistant professor, 1968-72, associate professor of history, 1972—, acting chairman of department, 1974—. *Member:* American Historical Association, Organization of American Historians, Society for Historical Archaeology, American Association of University Professors (president of local chapter, 1972-73), American Association for State and Local History, Southern Historical Association, Virginia Historical Society. *Awards, honors:* American Philosophical Society grant, 1975.

WRITINGS: The Old Dominion in the Seventeenth Century, University of North Carolina Press, 1975; (contributor) P.E.H. Hair and Nicholas Canny, editors, *The Westward Enterprise: English Activity in Ireland, the Atlantic, and America,* University of Liverpool Press, in press. Contributor to professional magazines and to *Tidewater Review.*

WORK IN PROGRESS: A book on rebellion against authority in seventeenth century Virginia, completion expected about 1977; a book on the development of political and legal institutions in seventeenth century Virginia.

SIDELIGHTS: Billings writes: "My interest in seventeenth century Virginia history stems largely from having grown up in the Tidewater. My family owns a piece of property that was part of one of the first tracts of land patented by Englishmen in our area of Tidewater, Virginia. Our farm has on it the foundation of the original dwelling, and from digging about in it I developed a taste for archaeology and old things." *Avocational interests:* European travel, hunting, fishing, wood working, building ship models, handwork.

* * *

BINDER, Leonard 1927-

PERSONAL: Born August 20, 1927, in Boston, Mass.; son of Morris and Mollie (Winer) Binder; married Yona Shander (a systems analyst), June 29, 1947; children: Naava (Mrs. Sanford Jay Grossman), Guyora (son). *Education:* Harvard University, B.A., 1952, Ph.D., 1956; graduate study at Princeton University, 1952-53, and at Oxford University, 1953-54. *Home:* 5512 South Harper Ave., Chicago, Ill. 60637. *Office:* Department of Political Science, 5828 South University Ave., University of Chicago, Chicago, Ill. 60637.

CAREER: University of California, Los Angeles, instructor, 1956-58, assistant professor of political science, 1958-61; University of Chicago, Chicago, Ill., associate professor, 1961-65, professor of political science, 1965—, director of Center for Middle East Studies, 1973-75. *Member:* Middle East Institute, Middle East Studies Association (founding member, 1967; president, 1973-74), American

Political Science Association (member of council, 1974-75), National Academy of Science, Phi Beta Kappa. *Awards, honors:* Ford Foundation grant, 1954-56; Social Science Research Council grant, 1958-59; Rockefeller Foundation grant in Egypt, 1960-61, and Tunisia, 1965; fellow of Center for Advanced Study of Behavioral Sciences, 1967-68.

WRITINGS: Religion and Politics in Pakistan, University of California Press, 1961; *Iran: Political Development in a Changing Society,* University of California Press, 1962; *The Ideological Revolution in the Middle East,* Wiley, 1964; (editor and contributor) *Politics in Lebanon,* Wiley, 1966; *Factors Influencing Iran's Foreign Policy,* RAND Corp., 1969; (editor with others, and contributor) *Crises and Sequences in Political Development,* Princeton University Press, 1972; (editor and contributor) *The Study of the Middle East: Research and Scholarship in the Humanities and Social Sciences,* Wiley, 1976. Contributor of more than twenty articles to professional journals.

WORK IN PROGRESS: Rural Political Sociology of Egypt: research on Islam and social changes in six countries.

* * *

BINGAMAN, Ron 1936-

PERSONAL: Born March 10, 1936, in Portsmouth, Ohio; son of Wendell Rex (a manager) and Iona Ada (Bailey) Bingaman; married Ann Conner, April 5, 1957 (divorced, January, 1975); children: Jenny, Mandy, Ethan. *Education:* Attended Texas Western College (now University of Texas, El Paso), 1957-58; Ohio State University, B.A., 1960, M.A., 1966. *Politics:* "Independent; lean toward conservative side." *Religion:* "None; formerly Southern Baptist." *Home:* 1270 Bunker Hill Blvd., Columbus, Ohio 43220.

CAREER: United Press International, Columbus, Ohio, reporter, 1960-62; Battelle Memorial Institute, Columbus, Ohio, writer and researcher, 1962-63; Ohio State University, Columbus, director of student publications, 1963-66; Management Horizons, Inc., Columbus, Ohio, vice-president of corporate affairs, 1966-74; free-lance writer in Columbus, Ohio, 1974—. Founder of Graphic Horizons Printing, 1970. *Military service:* U.S. Army, Finance Corps, 1956-58. *Member:* American Marketing Association.

WRITINGS: (Ghost-writer) Robert L. Shook and Herbert Shook, *The Complete Professional Salesman,* Fell, 1974; (with R. L. Shook) *Total Commitment,* Fell, 1975. Contributor to journals.

WORK IN PROGRESS: A sequel to *Total Commitment* concerning twenty famous women; a humorous book on divorce and the resumption of single life in a swinging singles apartment complex, tentatively titled *Divorce Odyssey.*

SIDELIGHTS: Bingaman told *CA:* "The things I consider most important and that I want to spend most of my time on as a writer are: (1) the quality of life, especially family life (why are so many people being divorced, particularly after long marriages?); (2) great figures in American society (what are the ingredients of 'greatness'?); (3) the environment (the preservation of wilderness and wildlife, and the challenges of outdoor life)."

* * *

BIRD, Patricia Amy 1941-

PERSONAL: Born March 15, 1941, in Pittsburgh, Pa.; daughter of Robert Blair (an accountant) and Madeline

(Wehner) Lamison; married Clinton Bird (a computer programmer), October 16, 1965. *Education:* University of Pittsburgh, B.A., 1962. *Home:* 8412 Melba Ave., Canoga Park, Calif. 91304.

CAREER: Westinghouse Electric Corp., Pittsburgh, Pa., computer programmer, 1963-66; Walt Disney Productions, Burbank, Calif., computer programmer, 1969-73; writer. Substitute teacher in French and English.

WRITINGS—Novels: *Island Paradise,* Bouregy, 1974; *Acapulco Passage,* Bouregy, 1975; *Staged for Death,* Bouregy, 1976.

WORK IN PROGRESS: Two novels, *Who Wants Charlie Dead?* and *Bring Back Michael Blainey.*

AVOCATIONAL INTERESTS: Traveling, playing the piano, raising three poodle puppies.

*   *   *

BISHIN, William R(obert) 1939-

PERSONAL: Born September 1, 1939, in New York, N.Y.; son of Arthur and Jean (Dash) Bishin; married Jane Sharlee (divorced); children: Benjamin, Susannah. *Education:* Columbia University, LL.B., 1960; Harvard University, J.D., 1963. *Office:* Law Center, University of Southern California, University Park, Calif. 90007.

CAREER: University of Southern California, University Park, assistant professor, 1963-66, associate professor, 1966-68, professor of law, 1968—. Admitted to New York bar, 1964, and California bar, 1965; visiting scholar at Columbia University, 1968; local juvenile court referee, 1971—. *Member:* California Bar Association, New York Bar Association, Los Angeles County Bar Association. *Awards, honors:* American Council of Learned Societies fellowship, 1968; Justin Dart Award for Curriculum Innovation from University of Southern California, 1969.

WRITINGS: (With C. D. Stone) *Law, Languages, and Ethics,* Foundation Press, 1972. Contributor to law reviews and *Los Angeles Times.* History editor, *Columbia Encyclopedia,* 1960; editor, *Harvard Law Review,* 1961-63.

WORK IN PROGRESS: Psychological and Semantic Presuppositions of Free Expression Protection in the United States; Theory of Linguistic Interpretation for Construing Statutes.

SIDELIGHTS: Bishin is "interested in psychological, epistemological, and semantic assumptions of individuals and of cultures—in how these affect the way in which problems are perceived and resolved in everyday life and in law and government." He considers "most of our social problems due to incoherent and self-defeating psychological and semantic approaches and attitudes."

*   *   *

BISHOP, Michael 1945-

PERSONAL: Born November 12, 1945, in Lincoln, Neb.; son of Lee Otis (in the U.S. Air Force) and Maxine (Mattison) Bishop; married Jeri Whitaker, June 7, 1969; children: Christopher James, Stephanie Nöel. *Education:* University of Georgia, B.A., 1967, M.A., 1968. *Residence:* Pine Mountain, Ga. *Agent:* Virginia Kidd, Box 278, Milford, Pa. 18337.

CAREER: University of Georgia, Athens, instructor in English, 1972-74; freelance writer, 1974—. *Military service:* U.S. Air Force, 1968-72; became captain. *Member:* Science Fiction Writers of America.

WRITINGS: A Funeral for the Eyes of Fire (novel), Ballantine, 1975; *And Strange at Ecbatan the Trees* (novel), Harper, 1976. Short stories anthologized in *Best Science Fiction: 1973,* edited by Harry Harrison and Brian W. Aldiss, Putnam, 1974; *Emphasis,* edited by David Gerrold, Ballantine, 1974; *Annual World's Best Science Fiction,* 1974 and 1975 volumes, edited by Donald A. Wollheim, Daw Books, 1974, 1975. Contributor to science fiction magazines, including *Fantasy and Science Fiction, If, Galaxy, Worlds of Fantasy, Orbit,* and *New Dimensions.*

WORK IN PROGRESS: Two novels, *Stolen Faces,* for Harper, and *A Little Knowledge;* a series of stories, *The Windows in Dante's Hell;* a "children's book for adults," tentatively titled *Rhinoceros Twilight;* a "mainstream" novel.

SIDELIGHTS: Although *A Funeral for the Eyes of Fire* has been called by a reviewer the most impressive first science-fiction novel so far seen in the seventies, Bishop writes: "It is nevertheless a tremendously flawed book. I am in the painful process of learning how to write with more concision, how to structure and plot. My central interest now is becoming the best writer I am capable of being while supporting my family at this task. Without abandoning the s-f and fantasy markets I would also like to devote more time to . . . 'fiction that matters.' Another of my hopes is to bring a certain degree of seriousness and consequentiality to s-f without gutting it of its imaginative vigor or rendering it pretentious."

AVOCATIONAL INTERESTS: Family involvement, reading, remodeling a sixty-year-old house.

*   *   *

BIXLER, R(oy) Russell, Jr. 1927-

PERSONAL: Born April 24, 1927, in Boston, Mass.; son of Roy R. (a machinist) and Bertha (Stiles) Bixler; married Norma Bowman, January 25, 1948; children: four. *Education:* Bridgewater College, B.A., 1947; George Washington University, M.A., 1949; Bethany Theological Seminary, B.D., 1959; graduate study at Duquesne University, 1960-61, and Pittsburgh Theological Seminary, at intervals, 1961-69. *Home:* 4722 Baptist Rd., Pittsburgh, Pa. 15227.

CAREER: Ordained minister of Church of the Brethren, 1958; Pittsburgh Church of the Brethren, Pittsburgh, Pa., pastor, 1959-72, associate minister, 1972—. President and chairman of board of directors of Western Pennsylvania Christian Broadcasting Co., 1970—; member of board of regents of Melodyland School of Theology, Anaheim, Calif., 1974—. *Military service:* U.S. Navy, 1945-46.

WRITINGS: It Can Happen to Anybody!, Whitaker, 1970; (with Michael Gaydos) *Eyes to Behold Him,* Creation House, 1973; (editor) *The Spirit Is a-Movin',* Creation House, 1974; (with Ray Charles Jarman) *Sunrise at Evening,* Whitaker, 1975. Contributor to religious magazines.

*   *   *

BIZARDEL, Yvon 1891-
(Yvon Lapaquellerie)

PERSONAL: Born January 30, 1891, in Barbezieux, France; son of Charles (a lawyer) and Emma (Guedon) Bizardel. *Education:* Attended University of Poitiers, 1910, and University of Bordeaux, 1914. *Religion:* Agnostic. *Home:* 14 rue Charles VII, Nogent-sur-Marne, France 94130.

CAREER: Administrative official in French Government,

Paris, France, serving as curator of Biblioteque Historique, 1933-35, curator of Musee Galliera, 1935-44, and director of fine arts of the City of Paris, 1944-51. Lecturer in United States and Canada by appointment of Alliance Francaise, 1951-52. President of Friends of Musee National de la Cooperation Franco-Americaine, 1974. *Awards, honors:* Officer of Legion of Honor, 1937; named honorary citizen of New Orleans (La.), 1959; Commander of the Polar Star (Sweden).

WRITINGS: American Painters in Paris, translated by Richard Howard, Macmillan, 1960; *Un Americain a la decouverte de l'Auvergne en 1801* (title means "An American Discovering Auvergne in the Year 1801"), Societe des lettres, sciences et arts "La Haute-Auvergne" (Aurillac, France), 1963; *Sous l'occupation: Souvenirs d'un conservateur de musee (1940-1944)* (title means "During German Occupation: Memoirs of a Museum Curator"), Calmann-Levy (Paris), 1964: *Les Americains a Paris pendant la Revolution,* Calmann-Levy, 1972, translation by J. P. Wilson and C. Higginson published as *The First Expatriots: Americans in Paris During the French Revolution,* Holt, 1975.

Under pseudonym Yvon Lapaquellerie: *Amoret* (novel), Calmann-Levy, 1922; *Sept pecheresses, l'hymen et Barbe-Bleue* (novel), Calmann-Levy, 1924; *La princesse Tarakanov* (novel), E. Flammarion (Paris), 1928; *Emile Combes; ou, Le Surprenant roman d'un honnete homme* (biography), E. Flammarion, 1929; *New-York aux sept couleurs* (nonfiction), Valois (Paris), 1930; *Ete indien* (novel), Petite Illustration (Paris), 1932; *Le joli garcon* (novel), E. Flammarion, 1933; *Edouard Daladier* (biography), E. Flammarion, 1940.

Author of introductions to catalogues of art exhibitions. Contributor to *Encyclopedia Americana.*

WORK IN PROGRESS: Research on Franco-American relations.

*   *   *

BLACK, Harry George 1933-

PERSONAL: Born January 31, 1933, in Hammond, Ind.; son of Harry Howard and Therese (Greb) Black; married Marilyn Gaye Gibbons (an accountant), June 21, 1961; children: Gaye Jean, Robin Lynne. *Education:* Attended Indiana University, 1952-53 and 1955-57; Roosevelt University, B.A., 1959, graduate study, 1959-63. *Politics:* Independent. *Religion:* Protestant. *Home:* 7406 Monroe Ave., Hammond, Ind. 46324.

CAREER: Indiana State Employment Service, Hammond, interviewer and counselor, 1959-64; full-time writer in Hammond, Ind., 1964—. Substitute teacher in Hammond Public Schools, 1964-74. *Military service:* U.S. Army, 1953-55. *Member:* Prospector's Club International, National Treasure Hunting Bureau Limited, American Legion, Indiana University Alumni Association, Roosevelt University Alumni Association, Hammond Historical Society.

WRITINGS: The Lost Dutchman Mine: A Short Story of a Tall Tale, Branden Press, 1976. Contributor to *Gold and Western Treasures.*

WORK IN PROGRESS: Research on prehistoric copper miners of the Michigan upper peninsula and Isle Royale, and on the Lost Adams Diggings in New Mexico; a fictionalized book on the Lost Dutchman Mine for grades six through eight, completion expected in 1976.

SIDELIGHTS: Black enjoys looking for lost mines and hidden treasure, and searching out the unusual, such as ghosts and Big Foot. *Avocational interests:* Fishing, hunting, softball, outdoor life.

BIOGRAPHICAL/CRITICAL SOURCES: Hammond Times, December 26, 1969, December 18, 1970, December 21, 1975; *Merrillville Herald,* November 5, 1975.

*   *   *

BLACK, Max 1909-

PERSONAL: Born February 24, 1909, in Baku, Russia; came to the United States in 1940, naturalized in 1948; son of Lionel and Sophia (Divinska) Black; married Michal Landsberg, August 21, 1933; children: Susan Naomi, Jonathan. *Education:* Queens College, Cambridge, B.A., 1930; University of Goettingen, graduate study, 1930-31; University of London, Ph.D., 1939. *Home:* 408 Highland Rd., Ithaca, N.Y. 14850. *Office:* Program on Science, Technology, and Society, 608 Clark Hall, Cornell University, Ithaca, N.Y. 14853.

CAREER: University of London, Institute of Education, London, England, lecturer and tutor, 1936-40; University of Illinois, Champaign, professor of philosophy, 1940-46; Cornell University, Ithaca, N.Y., professor of philosophy, 1946-54, Susan Linn Sage Professor of Philosophy and Humane Letters, 1954—; senior member of Program on Science, Technology, and Society, 1971—. U.S. Department of State Lecturer in India, 1962; Spencer Trask Lecturer, Princeton University, 1963; visiting member, Princeton Institute for Advanced Study, 1970-71; Tarner Lecturer, Cambridge University, 1976. Visiting professor, University of Washington, 1951-52, University of Kyoto, 1957. International Institute of Philosophy (vice-president, 1970), American Philosophical Association (president, 1958), American Academy of Arts and Sciences (fellow), Association of Symbolic Logic, Aristotelian Society. *Awards, honors:* Guggenheim fellow, 1950-51; D.Litt, University of London, 1955; National Science Foundation research grant, 1962-63.

WRITINGS: The Nature of Mathematics: A Critical Survey, Harcourt, 1933; *Critical Thinking: An Introduction to Logic and Scientific Method,* Prentice-Hall, 1946, 2nd edition with notes, 1952; (contributor) *Philosophical Studies: Essays in Memory of L. Susan Stebbing,* Allen & Unwin, 1948; *Language and Philosophy: Studies in Method,* Cornell University Press, 1949, new edition, 1966; *Problems of Analysis: Philosophical Essays,* Cornell University Press, 1954. *Models and Metaphors: Studies in Language and Philosophy,* Cornell University Press, 1962; *A Companion to Wittgenstein's Tractatus,* Cornell University Press, 1964; *The Labyrinth of Language,* Praeger, 1968; *Margins of Precision: Essays in Logic and Language,* Cornell University Press, 1970; (with E. H. Gombrich and Julian Hochberg) *Art, Perception and Reality,* Johns Hopkins Press, 1972; *Caveats and Critiques,* Cornell University Press, 1975. Editor: *Philosophical Analysis: A Collection of Essays,* Cornell University Press, 1950; (with Peter Geach) *Translations from the Philosophical Writings of Gottlob Frege,* Philosophical Library, 1952, 2nd edition, Basil Blackwell, 1960; *The Social Theories of Talcott Parsons: A Critical Examination,* Prentice-Hall, 1961; *The Importance of Language,* Prentice-Hall, 1962, new edition, 1968; William P. Alston and others, *Philosophy in America,* Cornell University Press, 1965; Northrop Frye, Stuart Hampshire, and Conor Cruise O'Brien, *The Morality of Scholarship,*

Cornell University Press, 1967; (with Morton W. Bloomfield) *In Search of Literary Theory,* Cornell University Press, 1972.

Editor of "Contemporary Philosophy" series, Cornell University Press, 1956—. Contributor to symposia, conference proceedings, and to *Encyclopedia of Philosophy.* Contributor of numerous articles to scholarly journals. Co-editor, *Journal of Symbolic Logic,* 1945-51; editor, *Philosophical Review,* 1950—.

* * *

BLACK-MICHAUD, Jacob 1938-

PERSONAL: Born October 24, 1938, in London, England; son of Misha (an industrial designer, architect, and teacher) and Helen (Evans) Black; married Nicole Chouane, May 1, 1963 (divorced, 1967); married Andree Michaud (a rural sociologist), September 19, 1967. *Education:* Attended University of Aix-en-Provence, University of Rome, and University of Freiburg, all 1957-58; Oxford University, B.A. (honors), 1961, M.A., 1964; University of London, M.Phil., 1969, Ph.D., 1976. *Politics:* Marxist. *Religion:* Atheist. *Home address:* c/o Sir Misha Black, 160 Gloucester Rd., London SW7 4QF, England.

CAREER: Thames & Hudson (publishers), London, England, book editor, 1961-62; Editions Robert Laffont (publishers), Paris, France, book editor and picture researcher, 1962-65; UNESCO and Zaire Ministry of Education, Kinshasa, lecturer in English and general studies, 1965-66; Social Science Research Council research fellow in social anthropology in London, England, 1966-72; North Shore Health and Social Service Council, Hauterive, Quebec, head of socio-economic planning and research in rural sociology, 1973-75; Ecole Superieure d'Agronomie Tropical, Nogent-sur-Marne, France, studying tropical agronomy, 1976—. Consultant to Teheran Center for Endogenous Development Studies. *Member:* Royal Anthropological Institute.

WRITINGS: Cohesive Force: Feud in the Mediterranean and the Middle East, St. Martin's, 1975. Contributor to *Man* and to *Middle Eastern Studies.*

WORK IN PROGRESS: Who's Who and Why in Luristan: A Study of Social Stratification and Sedentarization in a Nomadic Tribal Society.

SIDELIGHTS: Black-Michaud writes: "I came late to rural sociology in which I sought, primarily, the adventure of fieldwork in remote regions and, only as an afterthought, a means of heightening my political and social consciousness. From an abstract interest in social structure and academic debate I went on to spend eighteen months doing firsthand sociological research among nomadic tribesmen in the Middle East, growing during this period gradually more aware of the role I could usefully play in helping the inhabitants of underdeveloped rural areas to realize their own potential and develop themselves. I put reflexion into practice on social development projects in the Peruvian Andes and in northeastern Quebec. These experiences taught me that social development is rarely achieved in backward areas by the large-scale intervention of government or international agencies and that to be the least successful it must be paralleled by political education in a strongly anti-capitalist vein. It is my intention in the near future to pursue these ideas at a grass roots level in tropical Africa."

BLADEN, V(incent) W(heeler) 1900-

PERSONAL: Born August 14, 1900, in Stoke on Trent, Staffordshire, England; son of Joseph Clement (a chartered accountant) and Gertrude Easter (Cleverley) Bladen; married Margaret Landon Briggs, June 12, 1929 (deceased); children: Sarah Landon Banbury, Katharine Mary, Norah Landon Ferguson. *Education:* Balliol College, Oxford, B.A., 1921, M.A., 1926. *Religion:* Anglican. *Home:* 400 Walmer Rd., Apt. 1605, Toronto, Ontario, Canada. *Office:* Massey College, University of Toronto, 4 Devonshire Pl., Toronto 5, Canada.

CAREER: University of Toronto, Toronto, Ontario, instructor, 1921, lecturer, 1922-27, assistant professor, 1927-40, associate professor of political economy, 1940-69, professor emeritus, 1969—, chairman of department, 1953-58, director of Institute of Industrial Relations, 1946-50, director of Institute of Business Administration, 1950-53, dean of Faculty of Arts and Science, 1958-67, dean emeritus, 1970—, honorary lecturer at Scarborough College. Royal commissioner on the Canadian automobile industry, 1960; chairman of Commission on the Financing of Higher Education, 1964-65; chairman of Adjustment Assistance Board, 1966-71.

MEMBER: Royal Society of Canada (president of Section Two, 1958-59), Canadian Political Science Association (president, 1948-49), Royal Economic Society, York Club (Toronto). *Awards, honors:* LL.D. from University of Western Ontario, Carleton University, York University, and McGill University; D.Litt. from Acadia University; D.Sc.Soc. from Laval University.

WRITINGS: Introduction to Political Economy, University of Toronto Press, 1940, 3rd edition, 1956; *Financing Higher Education in Canada,* University of Toronto Press, 1965; *The Financing of the Performing Arts,* privately printed, 1971; *From Adam Smith to Maynard Keynes: The Heritage of Political Economy,* University of Toronto Press, 1974. Contributor of over a hundred articles to economic and education journals. Editor of *Canadian Journal of Economics and Political Science,* 1935-47.

* * *

BLADOW, Suzanne Wilson 1937-

PERSONAL: Born October 2, 1937, in Des Moines, Iowa; daughter of Roy R. (a pharmacist) and Dorothy (Inabnet) Wilson; married Terrence Bladow (a pediatrician), June 26, 1960; children: Craig Wilson, Amy Lynn. *Education:* University of Missouri, B.J., 1959. *Home and office address:* Route 5, Box 140-A, Joplin, Mo. 64801.

CAREER: Better Homes and Gardens, Des Moines, Iowa, copywriter in advertising sales promotion, 1959-60; Christian College (now Columbia College), Columbia, Mo., writer for public relations office, 1960-62, editor of *Christian College Alumnae,* 1961-62; University of Missouri, Columbia, writer for publications section of department of alumni activities, 1963-64; free-lance writer, 1971—.

WRITINGS: The Midnight Flight of Moose, Mops, and Marvin (juvenile), McGraw, 1975. Contributor to *Scouting.*

WORK IN PROGRESS: A sequel to *The Midnight Flight of Moose, Mops, and Marvin.*

SIDELIGHTS: Suzanne Bladow writes: "For some time I have suspected a good laugh to be one of the essentials for human survival. Children deserve humor in their books, anywhere from a little to a lot. *Midnight Flight* has its share. It was a story so enjoyable in the writing, the time spent with it seemed a gift to myself.'' *Avocational interests:* Painting.

* * *

BLAINE, Margery Kay 1937-
(Marge Blaine)

PERSONAL: Born December 20, 1937, in New York, N.Y.; daughter of Louis (a pharmacist) and Rosalind (a teacher; maiden name, Klein) Bendis; married Edward Blaine (a high school assistant principal), December 22, 1957; children: Jonathan William, Jennifer Petra. *Education:* Brooklyn College (now of the City University of New York), B.A., 1958; graduate study at University of Colorado, Cornell University, and Brooklyn Museum Art School. *Politics:* Liberal Democrat. *Home and office:* 352 Marlborough Rd., Brooklyn, N.Y. 11226.

CAREER: Kindergarten teacher in Brooklyn, N.Y., 1958-62, 1964-67.

WRITINGS: (Under name Marge Blaine) *The Terrible Thing That Happened at Our House* (juvenile), Parents' Magazine Press, 1975. Contributor to magazines and newspapers, including *Village Voice.*

WORK IN PROGRESS: A series of children's books with contemporary settings and themes.

AVOCATIONAL INTERESTS: Weaving and travel.

* * *

BLAISDELL, Paul H(enry) 1908-

PERSONAL: Born May 9, 1908, in Concord, N.H.; son of Carlyle W. (a musician) and Florence M. (Toof) Blaisdell; married Catharine A. Dunlap, August 19, 1933; children: Peter F., Amy W. *Education:* University of New Hampshire, B.S., 1930, Columbia University, A.M., 1932. *Home:* Cranberry Lane, Moody, Me. 04054.

CAREER: State of New Hampshire, Concord, assistant director of transportation for Public Utilities Commission, 1935-40, director of Travel Division, 1940-42; Office of Price Administration, Washington, D.C., director of mileage program, 1942-45; National Committee for Traffic Safety, Chicago, Ill., executive director, 1945-52; Association of Casualty and Surety Companies, New York, N.Y., director of traffic safety, 1952-60; Insurance Information Institute, New York, N.Y., director of industry relations, 1960-73. President of a Des Plaines, Ill., district board of education, 1949-51; instructor at New York University, 1955-73.

MEMBER: Boy Scouts of America (commissioner of New Jersey's Bergen Council, 1961-70, vice-president, 1970-72; commissioner of Maine's Pine Tree Council, 1974—), Society for the Preservation and Encouragement of Barbershop Quartet Singing in America (secretary of Kennebunk, Me. chapter, 1976—), New York Driver and Safety Educators Association, Masons, DeMolay, Kiwanis Club (president of Concord branch, 1938-40), Tau Kappa Epsilon. *Awards, honors:* Maine Highway Safety Medal from Governor of Maine, 1956-57, for outstanding contribution to highway safety; Boy Scouts of America, Silver Beaver, 1958, Silver Antelope, 1965.

WRITINGS: (Contributor) *Judge and Prosecutor in Traffic Court,* Northwestern University Press, 1951; (contributor) *Driver Education and Traffic Safety,* Prentice-Hall, 1967; *Three Centuries on Winnipesaukee,* New Hampshire Publishing, 1975.

WORK IN PROGRESS: Research for a book on the lake region of New Hampshire.

* * *

BLAKELEY, Phyllis (Ruth) 1922-

PERSONAL: Born August 2, 1922, in Halifax, Nova Scotia, Canada; daughter of Cecil Pearson (a merchant) and Clara (McLearn) Blakeley. *Education:* Dalhousie University, B.A. (cum laude), 1942, B.Ed., 1943, M.A., 1945. *Religion:* Baptist. *Home:* 2160 Connaught Ave., Halifax, Nova Scotia, Canada B3L 2Z3. *Office:* Public Archives of Nova Scotia, Coburg Rd., Halifax, Nova Scotia, Canada B3H 1Z9.

CAREER: Teacher in the elementary schools of Halifax, N.S., 1944-45; Public Archives of Nova Scotia, Halifax, N.S., research assistant, 1945-57, senior research assistant, 1957-59, assistant archivist for Province of Nova Scotia, 1959—. Vice-president of Heritage Trust of Nova Scotia, 1974—. *Member:* Canadian Historical Association, Canadian Authors' Association (president of Nova Scotia Branch, 1959-60, 1964-66; national executive, 1958-60; vice-president of Atlantic Region, 1960-66), Human Rights Federation, Nova Scotia Historical Society (vice-president, 1965-67), Zonta International. *Awards, honors:* Certificate from Federal Department of Indian Affairs and Northern Development, 1969, for contribution to preservation and enrichment of Canada's historical heritage.

WRITINGS: Glimpses of Halifax, 1867-1900, Public Archives of Nova Scotia, 1949; *The Story of Nova Scotia* (juvenile), Dent, 1950; *Nova Scotia: A Brief History* (juvenile textbook), Dent, 1955; (editor) George E. G. MacLaren, *Antique Furniture by Nova Scotian Craftsmen,* Ryerson, 1961; *Ships of the North Shore,* Maritime Museum of Canada, 1963; (with Myra C. Vernon) *The Story of Prince Edward Island* (juvenile textbook), Dent, 1963; (editor) *A Directory of the Members of the Legislative Assembly of Nova Scotia, 1758-1958,* Public Archives of Nova Scotia, 1958; (editor) *Place-Names and Places of Nova Scotia,* Public Archives of Nova Scotia, 1967; *Nova Scotia's Two Remarkable Giants: Anna Swan and Angus MacAskill,* Lancelot Press, 1970; (contributor) *People in States: The Taba Program in Social Science,* Addison-Wesley, 1972; *Atlantic Docupack,* Dent, 1973. Contributor to *Dictionary of Canadian Biography;* contributor to *Canadian Antiques Collector* and journals in her field. Member of editorial board of *Dalhousie Review,* 1975—, and *Nova Scotia Historical Quarterly,* 1971—.

WORK IN PROGRESS: Women in Nova Scotia.

AVOCATIONAL INTERESTS: Gardening.

* * *

BLAZE, Wayne 1951-

PERSONAL: Born July 23, 1951, in Bridgeport, Conn.; son of Charles A. (a mason-contractor) and Evelyn Blaze. *Education:* University of Connecticut, B.A. *Home:* RFD 1, 3 Clint Eldridge Rd., West Willington, Conn. 06279.

CAREER: University of Connecticut, Storrs, co-ordinator of Inner College, 1972-73, director of New Vocations Center, 1973-74; Career Education Project, Providence, R.I., associate director of information unit, 1974-75. Director of External Degree Project, Providence, R.I., 1974.

WRITINGS: A Guide to Alternative Colleges and Universities, Beacon Press, 1974; *External Degree Study: New Route to Careers,* Career Education Project, 1975.

WORK IN PROGRESS: A book tentatively titled *Voices of Men's Liberation.*

* * *

BLETTER, Robert 1933(?)-1976

1933(?)—January 8, 1976; American university administrator, publishing director, and editor of anthologies. Obituaries: *New York Times,* January 10, 1976.

* * *

BLEYTHING, Dennis H(ugh) 1946

PERSONAL: Born October 24, 1946, in Portland, Ore.; son of Stanford H. (a printer) and Antonia I. (a bookkeeper; maiden name, Sampert) Bleything. *Education:* Portland State University, B.S., 1968. *Politics:* "independent (with miniscule 'i')." *Religion:* "pantheistic agnostic." *Residence:* Tigard, Ore. *Office:* The Touchstone Press, Inc., P.O. Box 81, Beaverton, Ore. 97005.

CAREER: Writer. Part-time permanent shipping clerk for Touchstone Press, 1972—. *Member:* Society for Italic Handwriting (Western American branch), Order of the Black Chrysanthemum.

WRITINGS: *Medical Aid in the Wilderness* (booklet), Life Support Technology, 1971; *Poisonous Plants in the Wildermess* (booklet), Life Support Technology, 1971; *Edible Plants in the Wilderness,* two booklets, Life Support Technology, 1972; (with Susan E. Hawkins) *Getting Off on 96 and Other Less Traveled Roads,* Touchstone, 1975; (with Hawkins) *Daytrips from the Valley: Dayhikes and Scenic Drives in the Central Willamette Valley,* Touchstone, in press. Contributor to local outdoor periodicals and of haiku to poetry magazines, including *Dragonfly.*

WORK IN PROGRESS: A speculative fiction novel.

SIDELIGHTS: Bleything writes: "I've always enjoyed 'mixed media' projects, probably because I'm always involved in more than one medium. Even a trailguide is mixed media when it has good, interesting writing, photos and calligraphed maps. Photography, calligraphy, and poetry also mix well. Once I wrote for a fashion show which mixed clothing design, modern dance, poetry, music, and a light show.''

* * *

BLINDERMAN, Abraham 1916-

PERSONAL: Born August 8, 1916, in Brooklyn, N.Y.; son of Samuel (a laundryman) and Fannie (Rochester) Blinderman; married Rita Tublin (a musician), September 29, 1940; children: Mark Elliot, Bonnie. *Education:* Brooklyn College (now of the City University of New York), B.A., 1948; New York University, M.A., 1950, Ph.D., 1963. *Politics:* Independent. *Religion:* Jewish. *Home:* 47 Tanager Lane, Levittown, N.Y. 11756. *Office:* Department of English, State University of New York, Melville Rd., Farmingdale, N.Y. 11735.

CAREER: U.S. Post Office, New York, N.Y., clerk, 1937-48; public school teacher of English in New York, N.Y., 1948-54, Levittown, N.Y., 1954-63, and Syosset, N.Y., 1963-65; State University of New York, Farmingdale, member of faculty in department of English, 1965—. *Military service:* U.S. Navy, 1942-45. *Member:* National Council of English, History of Education Society, New York State United Teachers, Friends of Hofstra University Library. *Awards, honors:* State University of New York

research fellowship, 1971; National Endowment for the Humanities fellowship, 1972-73; Chancellor's Award for excellence in teaching, 1972-73, 1973-74.

WRITINGS: (Contributor) Jack Leedy, editor, *Poetry the Healer,* Lippincott, 1973; (editor) *Critics on Upton Sinclair,* University of Miami Press, 1975; *American Writers on Education before 1865,* Twayne, 1975; *Benjamin Franklin, Benjamin Rush, and Noah Webster,* Stanford University, in press; (contributor) James P. Friel and Peter Deland, editors, *Perspectives in Philosophy,* State University of New York at Farmingdale, in press; *American Writers on Education after 1865,* Twayne, in press. Author of teaching manuals for Prentice-Hall and Glencoe Press. Contributor of articles and reviews to *Newsday, Christian Century,* and more than thirty other periodicals.

WORK IN PROGRESS: Writing a chapter on poetry therapy for a book edited by Jack Leedy.

SIDELIGHTS: Blinderman told *CA:* "A lifelong inferiority complex aggravated by an intense desire for recognition finally triggered me into mediocre authorship. My adolescent messianic flame has dwindled into a barely perceptible flicker, sustained by the heroic life-giving blasts of compassionate editors. My first published article appeared eight years ago when I was fifty. I hope that I'll write one appreciated book before retiring.''

BIOGRAPHICAL/CRITICAL SOURCES: *Newsday,* March 5, 1973.

* * *

BLINN, Walter Craig 1930-

PERSONAL: Born May 16, 1930, in Belleville, Ill.; son of Walter Jacob (a merchant) and Buena Opal (a teacher; maiden name, Craig) Blinn; married Bette Calder, September 21, 1957; children: Mary, David. *Education:* Illinois State University, B.S.Ed., 1951; Oklahoma State University, M.S., 1958; Northwestern University, Ph.D., 1961. *Home:* 2628 Whistler Dr., East Lansing, Mich. 48823. *Office:* Department of Natural Science, Michigan State University, East Lansing, Mich. 48224.

CAREER: Northwestern University, Evanston, Ill., instructor in biology, 1960-61; Michigan State University, East Lansing, instructor, 1961-63, assistant professor, 1963-66, associate professor, 1966-69, professor of natural science, 1969—. *Military service:* U.S. Air Force, 1953-57; became staff sergeant. *Member:* American Association for the Advancement of Science, Sigma Xi. *Awards, honors:* National Science Foundation grant, 1963-65.

WRITINGS: (Editor and contributor) *The Search for Explanation,* Volume III (Blinn was not associated with other volumes), Michigan State University Press, 1968; (editor) *Laboratory Studies in Natural Science,* Volume III (Blinn was not associated with earlier volumes), Michigan State University Press, 1968; (editor and contributor) *Science and Belief,* Michigan State University Press, 1971.

WORK IN PROGRESS: Research on the metaphysical foundations of natural science.

SIDELIGHTS: Blinn believes that "current misunderstanding of science is so pervasive and distortive as to provide a challenge to any science educator or popularizer. My intention is to demonstrate that science, like any human endeavor, is necessarily subjective, growing from underlying systems of belief (world views) which differ from person to person, century to century and one branch of science to another.''

BLOOMFIELD, Masse 1923-

PERSONAL: First name sounds like "macy"; born August 20, 1923, in Franklin, N.H.; son of Harry and Ida (Steinberg) Bloomfield; married Fay Koenigsberg, February 21, 1954; children: Beth, Ellen, Dina. *Education:* University of New Hampshire, B.S., 1948; Carnegie Institute of Technology, M.L.S., 1951. *Politics:* Democrat. *Religion:* Jewish. *Home:* 20733 Stephanie Dr., Canoga Park, Calif. 91306. *Office:* Culver City Library, Hughes Aircraft Co., Culver City, Calif. 90230.

CAREER: U.S. Department of Agriculture, Washington, D.C., librarian, 1951-52; U.S. Naval Ordnance Test Station, China Lake, Calif., librarian, 1952-55; Atomics International, Canoga Park, Calif., librarian, 1955-62, Hughes Aircraft Co., Culver City Library, Culver City, Calif., supervisor, 1962—. President of M. Bloomfield & Co. (trade publishing house), 1975—. Chairman of West Valley Division of United Jewish Welfare Fund, Canoga Park, 1962-64. *Military service:* U.S. Army Air Forces, 1942-45; received Distinguished Flying Cross and Air Medal with four clusters. U.S. Air Force Reserve, 1945-71; retired as lieutenant colonel. *Member:* American Society for Information Science, Special Libraries Association, American Society for Testing Materials, West Valley Folk Dancers.

WRITINGS: How to Use a Library, Mojave Books, 1970; (with Harvey J. Wolf) *Man in Transition,* Mojave Books, 1973. Contributor to library journals. Member of editorial board of *Current Contents-Chemical Sciences,* 1967; book review editor of *Sci-Tech News,* 1970—; book reviewer for *Special Libraries,* 1972—.

*   *   *

BLUMENTHAL, L. Roy 1908-1975

1908—September 30, 1975; American public relations executive and author of text in his field. Obituaries: *New York Times,* October 3, 1975.

*   *   *

BOA, Kenneth 1945-

PERSONAL: Born July 22, 1945, in Kearney, Neb.; son of Kenneth (a bus driver) and Ruthelaine (a driver; maiden name, Kelley) Boa; married Karen Powelson, December 29, 1967; children: Heather Robin. *Education:* Case Institute of Technology (now Case Western Reserve University), B.S., 1967; Dallas Theological Seminary, Th.M., 1972; New York University, doctoral candidate, 1975—. *Religion:* Biblical Christianity. *Home and office:* 133 Eagle Dr., Emerson, N.J. 07630.

CAREER: University of Plano, Plano, Tex., instructor in mathematics, 1969-72; New Life, Inc., Knoxville, Tenn., writer and director of publications and research, 1971—. *Member:* Evangelical Theological Society, Creation Research Society.

WRITINGS: God, I Don't Understand, Victor, 1975. Contributor to *New Life Newsletter.*

WORK IN PROGRESS: A book on religions, cults, and the occult; a book on the "Star of Bethlehem."

SIDELIGHTS: Boa writes: "I am interested in showing that biblical Christianity, more specifically, the claims and credentials of Jesus Christ, has relevance for people and their problems today." *Avocational interests:* Music, art, films.

BOARDMAN, Arthur 1927-

PERSONAL: Born August 18, 1927, in France; son of Arthur Gerry (a singer) and Mary (a librarian; maiden name, Tallman) Boardman; married Patricia O'Brien, March 14, 1948. *Education:* University of Nevada, B.A., 1950, M.A., 1953; University of California, Ph.D., 1965. *Agent:* John Johnson, 12/13 Henrietta St., London WC2E 8LF, England.

CAREER: University of Colorado, Boulder, associate professor of English, 1970—. Fulbright-Hays lecturer at University of Mohammed V, Rabat, Morocco, 1975-77. *Military service:* U.S. Army, 1946-47.

WRITINGS: Captives (novel), Dutton, 1975.

*   *   *

BOCKL, George 1909-

PERSONAL: Born October 20, 1909, in Milwaukee, Wis. *Education:* University of Wisconsin, B.A. *Office:* 2266 North Prospect Ave., Milwaukee, Wis. 53202.

CAREER: Real estate developer in Milwaukee, Wis. Member of board of directors of Mount Sinai Hospital, and Penfield Children's Center. *Member:* National Association of Real Estate Brokers, Council for Wisconsin Writers, Raconteurs, Rotary Club.

WRITINGS: How To Use Leverage to Make Money in Real Estate, Prentice-Hall, 1966; *How Real Estate Fortunes Are Made,* Prentice-Hall, 1972. Contributor to *Milwaukee Journal.*

WORK IN PROGRESS: How To Use the Conduit Technique to Make You Independently Wealthy (tentative title); a novel, *Bend Me But Don't Break Me* (tentative title).

*   *   *

BODDY, Frederick A(rthur) 1914-

PERSONAL: Born May 28, 1914, in Malton, Yorkshire, England; son of Frederick George (a gardener) and Martha (Hurd) Boddy; married Joyce Faulkner, October 14, 1939; children: Christopher David, Dennis Alan. *Education:* Attended University of Nottingham, 1930-31. *Politics:* Independent. *Religion:* Church of England. *Home and office:* The Dell, 72 Dukes Wood Dr., Gerrards Cross, Buckinghamshire, England.

CAREER: Ragdale Hall, Leicestershire, England, improver, 1931-1933; Waddesdon Manor, Aylesbury, Buckinghamshire, England, journeyman, 1933-1936; City of Salford, England, Parks Department, began as assistant propagator, became head gardener, 1936-46; Borough of Sale, Cheshire, England, superintendent of parks, 1946-50; County Borough of Dudley, Worcestershire, England, superintendent of parks, 1950-55; Borough of Ealing, Middlesex, England, superintendent of parks, 1955-65; London Borough of Ealing, Middlesex, England, director of parks, 1965-70; consultant in horticulture, arboriculture, sportsgrounds, and landscape work, 1970—. *Member:* British Institute of Agricultural Consultants, Royal Horticultural Society (associate of honor), Institute of Park Administration (fellow), Arboricultural Association (fellow). *Awards, honors:* National diploma in horticulture from Royal Horticultural Society, 1940; diploma from Institute of Park Administration, 1944.

WRITINGS: Simple Gardening, Hamlyn, 1964; *Highway Trees,* Clarke & Hunter, 1968; *Some Practical Aspects of Parks Design,* Clarke & Hunter, 1970; *Foliage Plants,*

David & Charles, 1973; *Ground Cover and Other Ways to Weed Free Gardens,* David & Charles, 1974. Contributor to journals in his field.

* * *

BODEY, Hugh (Arthur) 1939-

PERSONAL: Born January 15, 1939, in Bristol, England; son of A. E. (a chemist) and C. V. (Taylor) Bodey; married Mary Welch, July 28, 1962; children: Stephen, Andrew, Gillian. *Education:* University of Birmingham, B.A. (honors), 1961; University of Exeter, education certificate, 1962. *Politics:* Liberal. *Religion:* Christian. *Home:* Tracey, Bow, Crediton, Devonshire EX17 6EP, England.

CAREER: Lydney Boys Secondary School, Lydney, Gloucestershire, England, teacher of history and religious studies, 1962-65; Rawthorpe County Secondary School, Huddersfield, Yorkshire, England, teacher, 1965-69; Colne Valley Museum, Golcar, Yorkshire, creator and first director, 1969-73; South Devon Technical College, Torquay, Devonshire, England, lecturer in economic history, 1974—. Visiting lecturer, Huddersfield College of Education (Technical), 1970-74. *Member:* Economic History Society.

WRITINGS: Roads (history), Batsford, 1971; *A Bullet in My Trifle* (humour), privately printed, 1972; *Religion,* Batsford, 1973; *Industrial History in Huddersfield,* Huddersfield Public Library, 1973; *Twenty Centuries of British Industry,* David & Charles, 1975; *Discovering Industrial History and Archaeology,* Shire, 1975; *Teaching Kit: Factories,* Batsford, 1975; *Textiles,* Batsford, 1976; *Mining,* Batsford, in press. Contributor to *Industrial Archaeology.* Author of leaflets for museum visitors.

WORK IN PROGRESS: Industrial Revolution: The British Experience, for Longman, Australia; *Recording Industrial Archaeology,* with Michael R. Hallas, for Shire; a book on starting a museum with no money; continuing research on textile history.

AVOCATIONAL INTERESTS: Gardening, photography, travel, wood turning, lecturing to adults on industrial history.

* * *

BOEHM, William D(ryden) 1946-

PERSONAL: Surname is pronounced "baim"; born November 10, 1946, in Lansing, Mich.; son of Earl William (an industrial engineer) and Deloris (a hospital administrator; maiden name, Charters) Boehm. *Education:* University of Washington, Seattle, B.S., 1968, M.S., 1972. *Religion:* Lutheran. *Home:* 8917 32nd Ave. N.E., Seattle, Wash. 98115.

CAREER: King County Public Health Department, Seattle, Wash., sanitarian, 1975—. U.S. Forest Service, surveying aid, summer, 1965, forestry aid, summer, 1966, biological aid, summer, 1967, forester, summer, 1970; park ranger with National Park Service of U.S. Department of Interior, summer, 1972. *Military service:* U.S. Army, 1968-70. *Member:* Xi Sigma Pi.

WRITINGS: Glacier Bay: Old Ice New Land, Alaska Northwest Publishing, 1975; (contributor) Robert Henning and others, editors, *Alaska Geographic,* volume III, Northwest Publishing, 1975. Contributor to *Pacific Search.*

SIDELIGHTS: Boehm told *CA:* "Glacier Bay was announced by a Lowell Thomas news broadcast in 1974 to be one of the 'Seven Wonders of the World.' Yet, so little is known about it by the public. A summer spent as a park ranger in 1972 inspired me to write about the area in depth, and to photograph as much of its wilderness, moods, and scenic beauty as I could." *Avocational interests:* Mountain climbing, hiking, photography, oil painting, kayaking.

* * *

BOGART, Carlotta 1929-

PERSONAL: Born February 10, 1929, in Waverly, Iowa; daughter of Zera S. and Lucille (McDannell) Fink; divorced in 1963; children: Virginia (Mrs. Terry Lehrling), Kenneth, James. *Education:* Northwestern University, B.S., 1950, M.A.T., 1964. *Home and office:* Media Learning Design, 4849 Shasta Dr., Old Hickory, Tenn. 37138.

CAREER: High school English teacher in Winnetka, Ill., 1964-69; Media Learning Design (in educational materials), Old Hickory, Tenn., partner, 1969—. Teacher of English in public schools in Nashville, Tenn., 1970—. *Member:* International Reading Association, National Education Association, National Council of Teachers of English (life member), Phi Beta Kappa, Pi Lambda Theta.

WRITINGS: (With Annelle S. Houk) *Understanding the Short Story,* Odyssey, 1969; (with Houk) *Media Literacy: Thinking About,* Pflaum/Standard, 1974. Contributor to reading and English journals.

WORK IN PROGRESS: Research on curriculum design in reading.

SIDELIGHTS: Carlotta Bogart writes: "When I resigned from teaching on my fortieth birthday . . . I thought educational reform was just around the corner and possible through print. Now I see reform barely begun, much harder to influence than I had thought, and embedded in popular media like TV and computers whose influences are just beginning to [become] knowable. Educational needs are more complicated, less certain of attention than ever before, and more crucial for the survival of democracy."

* * *

BOLNER, James (Jerome) 1936-

PERSONAL: Born November 2, 1936, in Plancheville, La.; son of Albert (a farmer) and Almeda (Firmin) Bolner; married Myrtle Smith (a teacher), August 9, 1958; children: Anne, James, Jr., Jonathan. *Education:* Louisiana State University, B.S., 1958, M.A., 1960; University of Virginia, Ph.D., 1962. *Politics:* Democrat. *Religion:* Roman Catholic. *Home:* 460 Bancroft Way, Baton Rouge, La. 70808. *Office:* Department of Political Science, Louisiana State University, Baton Rouge, La. 70803.

CAREER: University of Alabama, University, assistant professor of political science, 1962-65; University of Massachusetts, Amherst, assistant professor of political science, 1965-67; Louisiana State University, Baton Rouge, associate professor, 1967-74, professor of political science, 1974—. *Member:* Southern Political Science Association, Louisiana Political Science Association (vice-president, 1974; president, 1975).

WRITINGS: (With Robert A. Shanley) *Busing: The Political and Judicial Process,* Praeger, 1974. Contributor to *Harvard Journal of Legislation, Vanderbilt Law Review,* and *Louisiana Law Review.*

WORK IN PROGRESS: A book on the judicial philosophy underlying school desegregation in the United States from 1954 to the 1970's, completion expected in 1976.

SIDELIGHTS: Bolner told *CA:* "I have been influenced by modern Marxist analyses of American society and by writers such as Teilhard de Chardin and Roger Garaudy."

AVOCATIONAL INTERESTS: Photography, sky-watching, and greenhouse gardening.

* * *

BONAPARTE, Felicia 1937-

PERSONAL: Born October 19, 1937, in Bucharest, Romania; daughter of Simon (a textile designer) and Anna (Weisman) Bonaparte. *Education:* New York University, B.A., 1959, Ph.D., 1970; Yale University, M.A., 1960. *Politics:* "Independent; usually vote Democratic." *Religion:* None. *Home:* 768 Hickory Hill Rd., Wyckoff, N.J. 07481. *Office:* Department of English, City College of the City University of New York, 138th St. and Convent Ave., New York, N.Y. 10031.

CAREER: City College of the City University of New York, New York, N.Y., assistant professor of English, 1970—. *Member:* Modern Language Association of America.

WRITINGS: Will and Destiny: Morality and Tragedy in George Eliot's Novels, New York University Press, 1975.

WORK IN PROGRESS: A book, *The Triptych and the Cross: A Key to George Eliot's Mythologies.*

AVOCATIONAL INTERESTS: Philosophy, music, art.

* * *

BONGIE, Laurence L(ouis) 1929-

PERSONAL: Born December 15, 1929, in Turtleford, Canada; son of Louis Basil and Madalena (Pellizzari) Bongie; married Elizabeth Bryson (a professor of classical literature), July 14, 1958; children: Christopher. *Education:* University of British Columbia, B.A., 1950; University of Paris, D.Phil., 1952. *Residence:* Vancouver, British Columbia, Canada. *Office:* Department of French, University of British Columbia, Vancouver, British Columbia, Canada.

CAREER: University of British Columbia, Vancouver, lecturer, 1953-54, instructor, 1954-56, assistant professor, 1956-62, associate professor, 1962-66, professor of eighteenth century French literature, 1966—, head of department of French, 1966—. Corresponding member of Humanities Research Council of Canada. *Member:* International Association for Eighteenth Century Studies, Canadian Association for Eighteenth Century Studies, American Association for Eighteenth Century Studies, French Association for Eighteenth Century Studies. *Awards, honors:* Medalist of the Government of France, 1950; fellowships from Humanities Research Council of Canada, 1955-56, and Canada Council, 1963-64.

WRITINGS: David Hume: Prophet of the Counter-Revolution, Clarendon Press, 1965. Contributor to language and literature journals.

WORK IN PROGRESS: David Hume and Enlightenment Thought; J. J. Lalande: His Life and Works.

* * *

BONTEMPO, Charles J(oseph) 1931-

PERSONAL: Born July 5, 1931, in New Jersey; son of Emilio J. (a government employee) and Ruth (a businesswoman; maiden name, Verrilli) Bontempo; married Carol J. Snyder, August 25, 1956; children: Elizabeth, Alexandra.

Education: University of Maryland, B.A., 1952, M.A., 1959, further graduate study, 1966-72; attended New York University, 1961-63. *Residence:* Yorktown Heights, N.Y. *Office:* Systems Research Institute, International Business Machines Corp., 219 East 42nd St., New York, N.Y. 10017.

CAREER: International Business Machines Corp. (IBM), computer systems analyst in Gaithersburg, Md., 1964-75, instructor in computer technology and science at Systems Research Institute, New York, N.Y., 1975—. Extension instructor in philosophy, University of Virginia, Falls Church, 1965-73. *Military service:* U.S. Air Force, 1953-55; became second lieutenant. *Member:* Association for Computing Machinery, Phi Kappa Phi.

WRITINGS: (Editor with S. Jack Odell) *The Owl of Minerva* (philosophy), McGraw, 1975. Contributor to technical computer magazines.

* * *

BOOTON, (Catherine) Kage 1919-

PERSONAL: Born April 8, 1919, in Philadelphia, Pa.; daughter of Arthur Vincent (a civil engineer) and Helena (a dietician and teacher; maiden name, Rech) Kage; married John Griffeth Booton (an industrial engineer), January 22, 1944; children: Donna (Mrs. Daniel Carey), Susan (Mrs. Robert Zurburg). *Education:* Attended University of Buffalo and Junior College of Connecticut. *Home:* 11 Baldwin Circle, Route 2, Selinsgrove, Pa. 17870. *Agent:* McIntosh & Otis, Inc., 475 Fifth Ave., New York, N.Y. 10017.

CAREER: Advertising writer in North Tonawanda, N.Y., and personnel worker in Bridgeport, Conn. *Member:* Authors Guild of Authors League of America, Mystery Writers of America.

WRITINGS—All suspense novels: *The Troubled House,* Dodd, 1958; *Place of Shadows,* Dodd, 1959; *Don't Even Whisper,* Cosmopolitan, 1963; *Andrew's Wife,* Doubleday, 1964; *Runaway Home!,* Doubleday, 1967; *Time Running Out,* Doubleday, 1968; *Quite by Accident,* Doubleday, 1972; *The Toy,* Doubleday, 1975. Contributor to popular magazines, including *Ladies' Home Journal, Woman,* and *Elle.*

WORK IN PROGRESS: A book set in the Adirondacks.

AVOCATIONAL INTERESTS: Bridge, golf, travel (taking a houseboat up the Hudson, or across Lake Okeechobee).

* * *

BORNSTEIN, Ruth 1927-

PERSONAL: Born April 28, 1927, in Milwaukee, Wis.; daughter of Adolph and Bertha (Friedman) Lercher; married Harry Bornstein (a designer and builder), January 7, 1951; children: Noa, Jonah, Adam, Jesse. *Education:* University of Wisconsin, Madison, B.S., 1948; graduate study at Art Students League, 1949, and at Cranbrook Academy of Art, 1951. *Home:* 14912 McKendree Ave., Pacific Palisades, Calif. 90272.

MEMBER: Society of Children's Book Writers, Southern California Council on Literature for Children and Young People. *Awards, honors:* Southern California Council on Literature for Children and Young People award for significant contribution to illustration, 1974, for *Son of Thunder.*

WRITINGS—Juvenile fiction; self-illustrated: *Indian Bunny,* Childrens Press, 1973; *Little Gorilla* (Junior Literary Guild selection), Seabury, 1976.

Illustrator: Ethel K. McHale, *Son of Thunder*, Children's Press, 1974.

WORK IN PROGRESS: Writing and illustrating a book, *The Dream of the Little Elephant;* several short stories.

SIDELIGHTS: Ruth Bornstein has had several solo exhibits of her paintings. *Avocational interests:* Singing, dancing, walking, travel, growing vegetables.

* * *

BOSWELL, Jackson Campbell 1934-

PERSONAL: Born October 2, 1934, in Whiteville, N.C.; son of James Franklin (a farmer) and Adele (Callihan) Boswell; married Ann Otway Byrd Castle, 1969. *Education:* University of North Carolina, B.A., 1960, M.A., 1962; attended University of Aix-Marseilles, 1960-61; George Washington University, M.Phil., 1973, Ph.D., 1974. *Home:* 365 North Granada St., Arlington, Va. 22203. *Office:* Department of English, District of Columbia Teachers College, 1100 Harvard St. N.W., Washington, D.C. 20009.

CAREER: College of William and Mary, Williamsburg, Va., instructor in English, 1962-63; Randolph-Macon Woman's College, Lynchburg, Va., instructor in English, 1963-65; District of Columbia Teachers College, Washington, D.C., assistant professor, 1968-74, associate professor of English, 1974—. *Military service:* U.S. Navy, 1954-58. *Member:* Milton Society of America, Modern Language Association of America, American Studies Association, College Language Association, South Atlantic Modern Language Association, Southeastern Renaissance Conference. *Awards, honors:* Ford Foundation travel grant, 1968; Phelps-Stokes Fund research grant, 1972; Folger Shakespeare Library fellow, summer, 1973.

WRITINGS: John Milton's Library: A Catalogue of the Remains of Milton's Library and an Annotated Reconstruction of His Library and Ancillary Reading, Garland Publishing, 1975. Contributor of articles and reviews to professional journals.

WORK IN PROGRESS: Bibliography of Early Americana.

* * *

BOTTNER, Barbara 1943-

PERSONAL: Born May 25, 1943, in New York, N.Y.; daughter of Irving (a business executive) and Elaine (Schiff) Bottner. *Education:* Attended Boston University, 1961-62, and Ecole des Beaux Arts, 1963-64; University of Wisconsin, B.S., 1965; University of California, Santa Barbara, M.A., 1966. *Religion:* Bio-energetics. *Home:* 812 Broadway, New York, N.Y. 10003.

CAREER: Actress, kindergarten teacher, animation producer, writer, and artist; Parsons School of Design, New York, N.Y., instructor, 1973—. *Member:* Graphic Artists Guild, Art Directors Club, Society of Illustrators, Association International of Film Animation, Association of Independent Filmakers and Video. *Awards, honors:* Best Film for Television award from International Animation Festival, Annecy, France, 1973, for "Goat in a Boat."

WRITINGS—Juvenile: What Would You Do with a Giant?, Putnam, 1972; *Fun House,* Prentice-Hall, 1975; *Eek, a Monster,* Macmillan, 1975; *The Box,* Macmillan, 1975; *What Grandma Did on Her Birthday,* Macmillan, 1975; *Doing the Toledo,* Four Winds Press, in press. Au-

thor of film, "Goat in a Boat." Children's book reviewer for *New York Times* Sunday Section. Editorial illustrator for *New York Times, Ms., Viva,* and *Intellectual Digest.* Cartoonist for *Viva* and *Penthouse.*

WORK IN PROGRESS: An adult novel; a two-minute animated film for adults.

AVOCATIONAL INTERESTS: Dancing, cooking.

BIOGRAPHICAL/CRITICAL SOURCES: Rita Xanthoudakis, "All About Time and No Time" (film), New York University, 1974.

* * *

BOWERS, Warner Fremont 1906-
(W. B. Fremont, B. F. Warner)

PERSONAL: Born February 2, 1906, in Jeffersonville, Ind.; son of Merton Aubrey (an Army career officer) and Dorcas (Schutt) Bowers; married Lucile Hinzie (a writer and designer of cross-word puzzles), June 25, 1930; children: Kathryn (Mrs. James R. McLaughlin), Warner Fremont, Jr. *Education:* University of Omaha, A.B., 1929; University of Nebraska, B.Sc., 1930, M.D., 1932; University of Minnesota, M.S., 1936, Ph.D., 1938. *Politics:* "Vote strictly for candidate and not for party." *Religion:* "Protestant (nominal only!)." *Home:* 41 Golf Lane, Huntington, N.Y. 11743.

CAREER: University of Omaha, Omaha, Neb., instructor in comparative anatomy, 1930-31; University of Nebraska, Omaha, intern, 1932-33; University of Minnesota, Minneapolis, resident in surgery, 1933-39; University of Nebraska, instructor in surgery, 1939-40; U.S. Army, career officer, 1940-61, chief of surgery at Winter General Hospital, 1943-45, chief of professional services on hospital ship "Comfort," 1945-46, chief surgical consultant for General MacArthur's headquarters, Far East Command, and chief of surgery in Tokyo, 1946-48, chief surgical consultant and coordinator of consulting activities for Surgeon General, 1948-52, chief of surgical service at Brooke Army Hospital, 1952-56, chief of department of surgery, 1953-56, also chief of clinical surgery at Army Medical Service School, chief of department of surgery at Tripler U.S. Army Hospital, 1956-61, retired as full colonel; New York Medical College, New York, N.Y., professor of clinical surgery, 1962-67, director of Graduate School of Medical Sciences, 1963-67; *Medical World News,* New York, N.Y., medical director, 1967-68; free-lance writer, 1968—. Diplomate of National Board of Medical Examiners, 1935; licensed to practice medicine in Minnesota, 1936, Nebraska, 1939, and New York, 1962; certified by American Board of Surgery, 1941. Special lecturer at Tokyo Imperial University, 1946-48; professor at Baylor University, 1952-56. Member of board of governors of American College of Surgeons, 1948-52.

MEMBER: Pan American Medical Association (fellow; co-chairman of general surgery), Pan Pacific Surgical Association, Society for Surgery of the Alimentary Tract (founding member), Association of Military Surgeons of the United States (life member), National Society for Medical Research (member of national council), Association of American Medical Colleges, Armed Forces Writers League (life member of professional division), American Medical Authors Association (fellow), American Medical Association, Central Surgical Association (founding member), New York State Medical Association, New York County Medical Association, Masons (Scottish Rite), Shriners, Sigma Xi, Alpha Omega Alpha, Phi Rho Sigma. *Awards, honors:* Military: Legion of Merit, nine service medals. Other:

Wellcome Medal from Association of Military Surgeons of the United States, 1955, for his advances in military medicine; Court of honor award from Fiftieth State Exhibition in Hawaii, 1960, for early U.S. issue postage stamp collection.

WRITINGS: (Contributor) Winfield Pugh, editor, *War Medicine,* Philosophical Library, 1942; (editor and contributor) *Surgery of Trauma,* Lippincott, 1952; (contributor) Robert Turell, editor, *Surgical Clinics of North America,* Saunders, 1957; (with Carl W. Hughes) *Surgical Philosophy in Mass Casualty Management,* C. C Thomas, 1960; *Interpersonal Relationships in the Hospital,* C. C Thomas, 1960; *Surgical Gastroenterology,* C. C Thomas, 1960; (contributor) Turell, editor, *Colon and Ano-Rectum,* Saunders, 1960; (with Hughes) *Surgery for Traumatic Lesions of Peripheral Vessels,* C. C Thomas, 1961; (contributor) Lester Williams and Garnet Wynne, editors, *Fundamental Approach to Surgical Problems,* C. C Thomas, 1961; *Surgical Examination Review Book,* Medical Examination Publishing, 1962, 5th edition, 1971; (with T. H. Hewlett and G. J. Thomas) *Manual of Operative Technique,* C. C Thomas, 1963; *Techniques in Medical Communication, Medical Speaking and Writing, Planning and Presenting Medical Meetings,* C. C Thomas, 1963; (contributor) Irving Ariel, editor, *Progress in Breast Cancer,* Grune & Stratton, 1965; *Common Sense Organic Gardening* (Garden Guild Book Club selection), Stackpole, 1974; *Gourmet Cooking with Homemade Wines,* Stackpole, 1975.

Writer of question-and-answer books in surgery and of monographs, mostly for Medical Examination Publishing. Writer of "Homemade Wine in Gourmet Cooking," column in *Purple Thumb,* 1972-74, and "Gourmet Cooking with Homemade Wines," in *Home Beer and Wine Making,* 1974— . Contributor, sometimes under pseudonyms W. B. Fremont and B. F. Warner, of about two hundred articles to American and Japanese medical journals, about a hundred forty articles and stories to popular magazines, and of articles to philatelic journals. Editor of *Journal of International Surgery,* 1965-66.

WORK IN PROGRESS: "At age seventy, have slowed the writing because I have already said much more than I know!"

SIDELIGHTS: A humorist as well as physician, Bowers has written on medicine and medical practice: "Once upon a time, surgeons were interested first in the welfare of their patients; protecting zealously all the patient's bodily secrets; looking with horror at the mere thought of being quoted in the daily press. . . . [Today] only reactionary medical societies wonder where freedom of the press becomes advertising. . . . The urge to tell-all progresses with alarming rapidity as grey beards shake their heads." On population: "When we reach the population level where there is standing room only . . . we might resort to cannibalism. . . . We might revert to class, race and religious wars. . . . We might train people to live underwater. . . . We could send our criminals first . . . we could colonize the moon and other remote bodies. . . . It seems like oversimplification to suggest a good famine, a deliberate increase in auto accidents, a thoroughgoing nuclear war or a return of the Black Death. . . . Doctors continue to fly in the face of Providence by curing more disease, extending life to ever increasing degrees of senility, preserving all sorts of incompetents, treating infertility and in other ways being completely uncooperative. . . . We might close medical schools, forbid doctors to leave big cities, permit practice only one

hour a week, and increase federal grants so that all doctors would go into research instead of private practice."

Bowers worked his way through college and medical school by playing in big dance bands. In 1975, he organized and became director of "The Golden Tones," a senior citizens big dance band in Huntington. The twelve-piece group plays for senior citizen dances, church fairs, and stage productions.

* * *

BOXERMAN, David Samuel 1945-

PERSONAL: Born June 13, 1945, in Florida; son of William I. (a social worker and community organizer) and Florence (an administrative assistant; maiden name, Hornstein) Boxerman; married Yvonne Nina Morris (a librarian and teacher), December 29, 1968; children: Aaron Chaim. *Education:* Attended Los Angeles Valley Junior College and University of Judaism, both 1963-65; San Francisco State College (now University), A.B., 1967; University of Missouri, M.S.W., 1969; San Jose State University, M.A., 1976; further graduate study at University of California, San Francisco. *Religion:* Jewish. *Home:* 476 Oak Court, Menlo Park, Calif. 94025.

CAREER: Camp counselor, youth group leader, and community center worker in Los Angeles and San Francisco, Calif., 1964-67; Jewish Convalescent Hospital, Montreal, Quebec, medical social worker, 1968; Malcolm Bliss Community Mental Health Center, St. Louis, Mo., psychiatric-medical social worker, 1968-69; San Francisco Department of Public Health, Community Mental Health Services, San Francisco, psychiatric social worker in mental retardation program, 1969-70, and at Northeast Community Mental Health Center, 1970-75; in private practice, 1975— . Licensed clinical social worker, and school social worker and guidance counselor by State of California, also has California community college instructor and counselor credentials. Free-lance photographer for United Press International and Associated Press, 1969; free-lance calligrapher and instructor in calligraphy and graphic arts. Member of board of directors of Soviet Jewry Action Group, 1969-70, American Jewish Congress, 1970-74, and Jewish Film Festival, 1972. *Member:* Association for Educational Communications and Technology, California Association for Educational Media and Technology.

WRITINGS: Aleph-Bits Cartoons, Yad Media, 1973; (with Aron Spilken) *Alpha Brain Waves,* Celestial Arts, 1975. Cartoonist for American Jewish Press Association, 1974. Founder and editor of *Exodus* (monthly newspaper "dedicated to the emancipation of Soviet Jewry"); nationally syndicated cartoonist (appearing in over 40 newspapers), 1974— .

WORK IN PROGRESS: Guide to Therapy, a client's psychotherapy handbook for understanding various treatment approaches; *Kirlian Photography for the Layman;* research on indicators of suicide, on current stresses and problems which contribute to formulation of suicidal plans and the carrying out of these intentions.

SIDELIGHTS: Regarding *Alpha Brain Waves,* Boxerman writes: "As a psychiatric social worker I have been regularly involved with people in need of inner calm and tranquility. In recent years I searched for and examined different modes of therapy for alternatives to the more traditional approaches. Biofeedback and alpha brain waves have been found useful and with substantial promise for future developments." In 1970, Boxerman went to the Soviet Union to meet with Soviet Jews and founded his newspaper, "as at that time there was no consistent communication among organizations and groups in the free world who were involved in the plight of the Soviet Jews . . ." *Avocational interests:* Carpentry, woodworking, gardening, sculpting, photography, music.

* * *

BOYD, Shylah 1945-
(Frances Whyatt)

PERSONAL: Born March 8, 1945, in Ohio; daughter of John Hancock Grannis (owner of a yacht basin) and Mary Grosvenor Boyd (a pianist). *Education:* University of Minnesota, B.S., 1968. *Politics:* Feminist and humanist. *Home:* 463 West St., Apt. 116G, New York, N.Y. 10014. *Agent:* Wendy Weil, Julian Bach, Jr., 3 East 48th St., New York, N.Y. 10017.

CAREER: Poet. Poet-in-residence for South Carolina Arts Commission, 1974-76. Has worked as journalist. *Member:* National Organization for Non Parents. *Awards, honors:* MacDowell Colony fellowship, 1973; received Calliope Award, 1974; Triton International Poetry Contest award, 1975.

WRITINGS: American Made (novel), Farrar, Straus, 1975. Poetry anthologized in *Loves, Etc.,* edited by M. Harris, Doubleday, 1973. Contributor sometimes under pseudonym to *Southern Poetry Review, New Republic, Choice, New York Times,* and other publications.

* * *

BOYLAN, Leona Davis 1910-

PERSONAL: Born June 22, 1910, in Geary, Okla.; daughter of James K. Davis and Eva (Deardorff) Davis York; married Eugene Monroe Boylan, August 15, 1933; children: Thomas James, David Eugene, Sheila Marie (Mrs. William Floyd Parsons, Jr.), James Arthur Gillaspy (foster son). *Education:* Hardin College, A.F.A., 1930; attended Otis Art Institute, 1938; University of Arkansas, B.A., 1965; University of New Mexico, M.A., 1966, Ph.D., 1970; studied in Europe, 1967. *Politics:* Republican. *Religion:* Presbyterian. *Home:* 6959 Fords Station Rd., Germantown, Tenn. 38138. *Office:* Department of Art, Memphis State University, Memphis, Tenn. 38152.

CAREER: Commercial artist with several agencies and firms, 1930-50; Arkansas College, Batesville, instructor, 1955-64, assistant professor of art, 1965-68; Memphis State University, Memphis, Tenn., associate professor, 1968-74, professor of art, 1975—, director of inter-disciplinary program in Mexico, 1971-74. *Member:* Southern Art Conference, Mid-South Watercolor Society. *Awards, honors:* Awards for painting in Mid-South and Southwest.

WRITINGS: Spanish Colonial Silver, Museum of New Mexico Press, 1974.

WORK IN PROGRESS: Research on artists of the Mid-South.

* * *

BOYLE, J(ohn) A(ndrew) 1916-

PERSONAL: Born March 10, 1916, in Worcester Park, Surrey, England; son of William Andrew (a bookseller) and Florence May (Roberts) Boyle; married Margaret Elizabeth Dunbar, March 26, 1945; children: Fiona, Louise, Morag. *Education:* Attended University of Goettingen, 1935; Uni-

versity of Birmingham, B.A. (first class honors), 1936; graduate study at University of Berlin, 1936-39; University of London, Ph.D., 1947. *Home:* 266 Rye Rank Rd., Greater Manchester M21 1LY, England. *Office:* Department of Persian Studies, University of Manchester, Manchester, England.

CAREER: Served with Royal Engineers, 1941; seconded to special department of Foreign Office, 1942-50; University of Manchester, Manchester, England, senior lecturer, 1950-59, reader, 1959-66, professor of Persian studies, 1966—. Visiting professor of Persian, University of California, Berkeley, 1959-60. Member of Gibb Memorial Trust, 1970—.

MEMBER: Royal Asiatic Society, British Institute of Persian Studies (member of governing council, 1964—), Iran-Shenasi (Tehran, Iran; member of advisory board, 1969—), British Society for Middle Eastern Studies (member of council, 1973—), Anglo-Mongolian Society (chairman, 1970—), Korosi Csoma Society (Hungary; honorary fellow, 1973), Folklore Society, Society of Authors. *Awards, honors:* Order and Decoration of Sepass, Iran, 1958, for translation of *History of the World-Conqueror;* M.A., University of Manchester, 1970.

WRITINGS: A Practical Dictionary of the Persian Language, Luzac & Co., 1949; (translator) Juvaini, *The History of the World-Conqueror,* Manchester University Press, 1958; *Modern Persian Grammar,* Harrassowitz, 1966; (editor and contributor) *Cambridge History of Iran,* Volume V: *The Saljuq and Mongol Periods,* Cambridge University Press, 1968; (with Karl Jahn) *Rashid al-Din Commemoration Volume, 1318-1968,* Harrassowitz, 1970; (translator) Rashid al-Din, *The Successors of Genghis Khan,* Columbia University Press, 1971. Member of editorial board, "Cambridge History of Iran" series, Cambridge University Press, 1966—.

WORK IN PROGRESS: Translations of *The Ilahi-nama* of Farid al-Din Attar, and *The Il-Khans of Persia* by Rashid al-Din; research on the Alexander Romance, and on Persian history and the history of the Mongol world empire.

SIDELIGHTS: John Boyle has traveled in Turkey, Persia, Afghanistan, Pakistan, India and Mongolia. "Besides the usual European languages" he is conversant in Persian, Arabic, Turkish, and Armenian. *Avocational interests:* Motoring.

* * *

BRACY, William 1915-

PERSONAL: Born March 25, 1915, in Rich Square, N.C.; son of William Arthur (a farmer and merchant) and M. Alida (Dunning) Bracy; married Addie L. Lockridge (a teacher), December, 1962; children: Arthur Craig, William Lee. *Education:* University of North Carolina, A.B., 1936, M.A., 1939, Ph.D., 1949. *Home:* 307 Wyncote Rd., Jenkintown, Pa. 19046. *Office:* Department of English, Beaver College, Glenside, Pa. 19038.

CAREER: University of North Carolina, Chapel Hill, instructor in English, 1948-49; University of Missouri, Columbia, assistant professor of English, 1949-54; *Collier's Encyclopedia,* New York, N.Y., assistant humanities editor, 1955-57; *Encyclopedia Americana,* New York, N.Y., humanities editor, 1958-64; City College of the City University of New York, New York, N.Y., lecturer in English, 1964-65; Beaver College, Glenside, Pa., associate

professor, 1965-69; professor of English, 1969—. Professor
in England with Beaver College London semester, 1970-71.
Military service: U.S. Army, 1942-45; became staff sergeant.

MEMBER: Modern Language Association of America,
Renaissance Society of America, Shakespeare Association
of America. *Awards, honors:* Fellowship from Shakespeare
Institute at Stratford-upon-Avon, England, 1953.

*WRITINGS: The Merry Wives of Windsor: The History
and Transmission of Shakespeare's Text,* University of
Missouri Press, 1952; *Doctor Faustus* (study guide), Study
Master, 1965; (with Charlotte Spivack) *Early English
Drama* (study guide), Study Master, 1966. Contributor to
Encyclopedia Americana and *Collier's Encyclopedia.*

WORK IN PROGRESS: Research on Shakespeare and on
modern drama.

SIDELIGHTS: Bracy has lived in India and England; his
travels include Ireland, France, Italy, Spain, and Central
America.

*   *   *

BRADFORD, Peter Amory 1942-

PERSONAL: Born July 21, 1942, in New York, N.Y.; son
of Amory Howe Bradford and Carol (Rothschild) Noyes;
married Katherine Houston, June 8, 1968; children: Arthur
and Laura (twins). *Education:* Yale University, B.A., 1964,
LL.B., 1968. *Office:* Maine Public Utilities Commission,
Augusta, Me. 04011.

CAREER: State of Maine, Augusta, federal-state coordinator, 1968-71; Maine Public Utilities Commission, Augusta,
commissioner, 1971—, chairman, 1974-75. Member, Ralph
Nader study group on Federal Trade Commission, 1968.

*WRITINGS: Fragile Structures: A Story of Oil Refineries,
National Security, and the Coast of Maine,* Harper Magazine Press, 1975. Contributor to law journals.

*   *   *

BRADLEE, Benjamin C(rowninshield) 1921-

PERSONAL: Born August 26, 1921, in Boston, Mass.; son
of Frederick Josiah (a trustee) and Josephine (deGersdorff)
Bradlee; married Jean Saltonstall, August 8, 1942 (di-
vorced, 1953); married Antoinette Pinchot, July 6, 1956
(divorced November 10, 1975); children: (first marriage)
Benjamin C., Jr.; (second marriage) Dominic, Marina.
Education: Harvard University, A.B., 1943. *Agent:* Ster-
ling Lord, Sterling Lord Agency, 660 Madison Ave., New
York, N.Y. 10021. *Office: Washington Post,* 1150 15th St.
N.W., Washington, D.C. 20073.

CAREER: New Hampshire Sunday News, Manchester,
reporter, 1946-48; *Washington Post,* Washington, D.C.,
reporter, 1948-51; U.S. Foreign Service, press attache in
Paris, France, 1951-53; *Newsweek,* European bureau chief
in Paris, 1953-57, Washington bureau chief, 1957-65; *Washington Post,* managing editor, 1965-68, executive editor,
1968—. *Military service:* U.S. Naval Reserve, 1942-45;
served in Pacific theater; became lieutenant. *Awards,
honors:* Doctor of Letters, Franklin and Marshall College,
1974.

WRITINGS: That Special Grace (eulogy of John F. Kennedy), Lippincott, 1964; *Conversations with Kennedy,*
Norton, 1975.

BRADLEY, Virginia 1912-

PERSONAL: Born December 2, 1912, in Omaha, Neb.;
daughter of Stephen (a lawyer) and Anne (a secretary;
maiden name, Healy) Jonas; married Gerald Bradley (a
business executive), June 8, 1940; children: Stephen, Michael, Betty (Mrs. Alfred Ramsey), Patricia. *Education:*
University of Nebraska, B.F.A., 1933. *Home:* 425 15th St.,
Santa Monica, Calif. 90402.

CAREER: Omaha World Herald, Omaha, Neb., member
of classified advertising staff, 1937-38. Workshop director
of Los Angeles Schools, Adult Division, 1963—, Southern
California Woman's Press Club, 1974—, and Santa Monica
Emeritus College, 1975—. *Member:* Society of Children's
Book Writers, American Film Teachers Association, California Writers Guild, Santa Monica Writers Club (president, 1954-55).

WRITINGS: Is There an Actor in the House? (collection
of dramatic material), Dodd, 1975. Contributor to *Yankee,
Young Miss, McCall's, Girltalk, Southland, Scouting,
Western Family,* and religious journals.

WORK IN PROGRESS: A pre-teen novel tentatively titled, *Six Times Sue;* a collection of original one-act plays
with working title, *Walkup on Christopher and Other
Plays.*

*   *   *

BRADY, Frank 1934-

PERSONAL: Born March 15, 1934, in Brooklyn, N.Y.;
son of James J. (a dispatcher) and Beatrice A. (Mignerey)
Brady; married Roberta Lowe, March 1, 1954 (divorced,
December, 1962); married Maxine Kalfus (an editor),
March 31, 1963; children: (first marriage) Erin, Sean. *Education:* Rutgers University, B.A., 1954; graduate study at
Columbia University, 1974-75. *Politics:* Democrat. *Home:*
175 West 72nd St., New York, N.Y. 10023. *Agent:* Seligmann & Collier, 280 Madison Ave., New York, N.Y.
10016.

CAREER: Association of the Bar of the City of New
York, N.Y., librarian, 1956-58; *Chess Life* (magazine),
Newburgh, N.Y., editor, 1958-61; *Eros* (magazine), New
York, N.Y., associate publisher, 1961-63; *Chessworld*
(magazine), New York, N.Y., editor, 1963-65; *Playboy*
(magazine), Chicago, Ill., associate editor, 1965-69; *Avant-
Garde* (magazine), New York, N.Y., publisher, 1969-70;
writer and radio broadcaster, 1970—. Has broadcast on
Pacific Radio Network, National Public Radio, Metrome-
dia, Public Broadcast Service, and American Broadcasting
Corp. (ABC-TV). *Military service:* New York National
Guard, Field Artillery, 1951-56. *Awards, honors:* Nominated for Luther Mott Award of National Journalism Society, 1975.

WRITINGS: Profile of a Prodigy (biography of chess
player Bobby Fischer), McKay, 1973; *Chess: How to Improve Your Technique,* F. Watts, 1974; *Hefner: An Unauthorized Biography,* Macmillan, 1974; *Soviet Man,* McKay,
in press.

WORK IN PROGRESS: Brady told *CA:* "I am more than
ever dedicated to the art of biography and am currently
researching the lives of several potential subjects, ranging
from a character instrumental in the American Revolution,
to a cinema super-star, to one of the world's richest ty-
coons."

BIOGRAPHICAL/CRITICAL SOURCES: Avant-Garde,
December, 1974; *People,* December 2, 1974; *New York*

Post, December 14, 1974; *Los Angeles Times*, January 16, 1975.

* * *

BRAIMAH, Joseph Adam 1916-

PERSONAL: Born August 31, 1916; son of Sammuel William and Miyama (Yahaya) Braimah; married Bimunka Janaba; children: Joseph Adam, Jr., I. A., Miyama, Asana A. *Education:* Educated in Ghana. *Religion:* Muslim. *Home address:* Kanyase Section, Kpembe, Ghana. *Office:* Eastern Gonja District Council Office, P.O. Box 7, Salaga, Ghana.

CAREER: Gonja Native Administration, secretary of Gonja Native Authority, 1950-51; Gold Coast Legislative Assembly (now parliament of Ghana), member of chieftancy secretariat, 1966-69, regional chief executive of Northern Region, 1969-72. Minister of Ghana's Communication and Works, 1951-54; chairman of Ghana Housing Corp., 1960-63.

WRITINGS: The Two Isanwurfos, Longmans, Green, 1967; *The Ashantis and the Gonja at War*, Ghana Publishing Corp., 1970; *Gonja Drums*, Bureau of Ghana Languages, 1971.

WORK IN PROGRESS: Samory the Black Napoleon, for Ghana Publishing Corp.; *The Founding of the Gonja Empire; Eastern Gonja Customs*.

* * *

BRAMS, Steven J(ohn) 1940-

PERSONAL: Born November 28, 1940, in Concord, N.H.; son of Nathan (a shoe clerk) and Isabelle (Tryman) Brams; married Eva Floderer (a writer), November 12, 1971; children: Julie, Michael. *Education:* Massachusetts Institute of Technology, S.B., 1962; Northwestern University, Ph.D., 1966. *Home:* 4 Washington Square Village, Apt. 2N, New York, N.Y. 10012. *Office:* Department of Politics, New York University, New York, N.Y. 10003.

CAREER: National Institutes of Health, Office of the Director, Bethesda, Md., program analyst, summer, 1962; Office of the Secretary of Defense, Washington, D.C., executive trainee, summer, 1963; Institute for Defense Analyses, Arlington, Va., research associate, 1965-67; Syracuse University, Syracuse, N.Y., assistant professor of political science, 1967-69; New York University, New York, N.Y., associate professor of politics, 1969—. Visiting lecturer at University of Michigan, 1969-70, and University of Pennsylvania, 1972; visiting professor at University of Rochester, 1967, 1968-69, 1971, 1972-73. *Member:* Peace Research Society, American Association for the Advancement of Science, American Political Science Association, International Studies Association, Public Choice Society. *Awards, honors:* National Science Foundation grants, 1968-70, 1970-71, and 1974-75.

WRITINGS: (Contributor) Roderick Bell, David V. Edwards, and R. Harrison Wagner, editors, *Political Power: A Reader in Theory and Research*, Free Press, 1969; (contributor) James N. Rosenau, editor, *International Politics and Foreign Policy: A Reader in Research and Theory*, 2nd revised edition, Free Press, 1969; (contributor) James F. Herndon and Joseph L. Bernd, editors, *Mathematical Applications in Political Science, VI*, University Press of Virginia, 1972; (contributor) Richard G. Niemi and Herbert F. Weisberg, editors, *Probability Models of Collective Decision-Making*, C. E. Merrill, 1972; (contributor) Corne-

lius P. Cotter, editor, *Political Science Annual IV: An International Review*, Bobbs-Merrill, 1973; *Game Theory and Politics*, Free Press, 1975; *Paradoxes in Politics: An Introduction to the Nonobvious in Political Science*, Free Press, 1976. Contributor to journals in his field. Member of editorial board of *Public Choice*, 1973—.

WORK IN PROGRESS: Rules of the Game in American Politics: How They Distribute Power and Why, completion expected in 1977.

* * *

BRAND, Eugene L(ouis) 1931-

PERSONAL: Born November 22, 1931, in Richmond, Ind.; son of Oscar K. and Alice (Nolte) Brand. *Education:* Capital University, A.B., 1953; Lutheran Theological Seminary, B.D., 1957; University of Heidelberg, Dr. Theol., 1959. *Home:* 23 Waverly Place, New York, N.Y. 10003. *Office:* Lutheran Center, 315 Park Avenue South, New York, N.Y. 10010.

CAREER: Ordained minister of Lutheran Church in America, 1960; Lutheran Theological Seminary, Columbus, Ohio, professor of theology and worship, 1960-71; Lutheran Church in America, New York, N.Y., director of commission on worship, 1971-74; Inter-Lutheran Commission on Worship, New York, project director, 1975—. *Member:* National Academy of American Liturgists, American Guild of Organists, Societas Liturgica, Lutheran Society for Worship, Music and Arts, Liturgical Conference.

WRITINGS: The Rite Thing, Augsburg, 1970; *Baptism: A Pastoral Perspective*, Augsburg, 1975.

* * *

BRANDON, Brumsic, Jr. 1927-

PERSONAL: Born April 10, 1927, in Washington, D.C.; son of Brumsic and Pearl (Brooks) Brandon; married Rita Broughton (a teacher), September 30, 1950; children: Linda, Brumsic III, Barbara. *Education:* New York University, student, 1945-46. *Politics:* Independent. *Home:* 210 Rushmore St., Westbury, N.Y. 11590.

CAREER: RAC Service Co., Inc., Alexandria, Va., assistant art director, 1955-57; Bray Studios, Inc. (motion picture producers), New York, N.Y., designer and animator, 1957-69; WPIX-TV, New York, N.Y., television performer, 1969-73; Los Angeles Times Syndicate, Los Angeles, Calif., writer for comic strip, "Luther," 1971—. Member of forum, White House Conference on Children, 1970; member of advisory board, Afro American Bicentennial Corp. *Military service:* U.S. Army, 1950-52; became sergeant. *Member:* American Federation of Television and Radio Artists.

WRITINGS: Luther from Inner City, Eriksson, 1969; *Luther Tells It as It Is*, Eriksson, 1970; *Right On, Luther*, Eriksson, 1971; *Luther Raps*, Eriksson, 1971; *Outta Sight, Luther*, Eriksson, 1972; *Luther's Got Class*, Eriksson, 1975. Publications include comic books for New York State Consumer Protection Board.

Illustrator: Matt Robinson, *The Six Button Dragon*, Random House, 1971.

WORK IN PROGRESS: Luther comic books and short stories; television adaptations of Luther, one to be broadcast by National Broadcasting Co. as "Vegetable Soup"; reading and coloring books.

SIDELIGHTS: Brandon commented: "My objective, in

my comic strip, is to bring to light not only the long ignored 'black perspective,' but the many various philosophical postures found therein.''

* * *

BRANDT, Lucile (Long Strayer) 1900-
(Lucile Long)

PERSONAL: Born July 22, 1900, near Pioneer, Ohio; daughter of Ira E. (a minister) and Della M. (Landis) Long; married J. Clarence Strayer, July 12, 1946 (died August 14, 1953); married Harry A. Brandt, November 6, 1969 (died February 23, 1974). *Education:* Manchester College, B.A., 1924; State University of Iowa, M.A., 1927; summer graduate study at University of Michigan, 1930 and 1936. *Religion:* Church of the Brethren. *Home:* 2736 Third St., La Verne, Calif. 91750.

CAREER: High school teacher of English in Indiana, 1920-26; Mount Morris College, Mount Morris, Ill., assistant professor, 1928-32; Bridgewater College, Bridgewater, Va., assistant professor, became associate professor of English, 1933-34; La Verne College, La Verne, Calif., associate professor, 1954; Manchester College, North Manchester, Ind., exchange associate professor of English, 1954-55; Hillcrest School, Jos, Nigeria, instructor in English, 1965-69.

WRITINGS: (Under name Lucile Long) *Anna Elizabeth,* Brethren Press, 1942; (under name Lucile Long) *Anna Elizabeth, Seventeen,* Brethren Press, 1946; *The Flame Tree* (poems), Brethren Press, 1973. Lesson writer for David C. Cook Publishing Co., 1955-65.

* * *

BRANSCUM, Robbie 1937-

PERSONAL: Born June 17 , 1937, in Arkansas; daughter of Donnie H. (a farmer) and Blanch (Balitine) Tilley; married Duane Branscum (divorced, 1969); married Lesli J. Carrico, July 15, 1975; children: Deborah. *Home:* 19A Sunset Dr., Antioch, Calif. 94509.

WRITINGS—All juvenile: *Me and Jim Luke,* Doubleday, 1971; *Johnny May,* Doubleday, 1975; *Toby, Granny and Gordge,* Doubleday, 1975; *The Three Wars of Billy Joe Treat,* McGraw, 1975.

SIDELIGHTS: Robbie Branscum told *CA* that she gives talks at schools and colleges about how to write with a seventh grade education (her only education was in a one-room school in the hill country of Arkansas).

* * *

BRASHER, Nell 1912-

PERSONAL: Born December 1, 1912; daughter of Monte Zuma (a potter) and Dovie (Stone) Hughey; married Leonard Brasher (a minister), April 19, 1938; children: Freya (Mrs. John Bess), Susan (Mrs. Will Gowers), Robert, Rebecca (Mrs David Mann). *Education:* Attended high school in Perry County, Ala. *Politics:* Republican. *Religion:* Baptist. *Home address:* Route 3, Box 362, Trussville, Ala. 35173.

CAREER: Licensed practical nurse. *Member:* National League of American Pen Women, Quill Club of Birmingham (Ala.).

WRITINGS: (Contributor) James Adair, editor, *Teen With a Future,* Baker Book, 1965; (contributor) Hudson Strode, editor, *Alabama Prize Short Stories 1970,* Strode, 1970; *Angel Tracks in the Cabbage Patch,* William-Fred-erick Press, 1972. Contributor to *Scripture Press, Open Windows, War Cry, Live, Vista,* and *Hampton Roads Reviews.* Author of column "Page from a Diary" in *Birmingham Post-Herald,* 1966-74.

WORK IN PROGRESS: Daddy Poured the Coffee, for Pelican; *Walking in Brightness;* children's stories.

* * *

BRASIER, Virginia 1910-

PERSONAL: Surname is pronounced *Bray*-zee-er; born July 31, 1910, in Toronto, Ontario, Canada; daughter of Harry E. and Lilian Ross (Pringle) Brasier; married Charles D. Perlee (a newspaper editor), October 6, 1932 (died October 3, 1975); children: Charles R., Christopher C., Melinda. *Education:* Studied writing in night school. *Politics:* Democrat. *Religion:* Congregationalist. *Home:* 962 Dolores Dr., Altadena, Calif. 91001.

CAREER: Has free-lanced in public relations; co-columnist, *Pasadena Star-News,* Pasadena, Calif., and *San Bernardino Sun-Telegram,* San Bernardino, Calif., twenty-five years; volunteer social worker; writer. Taught poetry workshop at Pasadena City College, 1955. *Member:* Academy of American Poets, California Writer's Guild, Ina Coolbrith Circle, Another Mother for Peace. *Awards, honors:* Robert Browning Poetry award, University of Redlands, c. 1925; *Yankee Magazine* annual poetry contest award; second prize, Rochester National Festival of Religious Arts.

WRITINGS—Poetry: *The Reflective Rib,* Pasadena Press, 1955; *The Survival of the Unicorn,* Creative Press, 1961; *The Sand Watcher,* Golden Quill, 1974. Poetry anthologized in *College Textbook for Teachers of Children's Literature,* by Miriam Blanton Huber. Contributor of about five thousand poems to national and international magazines and newspapers, including *Los Angeles Times;* contributor of short stories and articles to magazines and newspapers.

WORK IN PROGRESS: A fourth book of poetry; a short play; articles on poetry.

AVOCATIONAL INTERESTS: Gardening (especially bonsai), collecting miniature vases and making arrangements in them, cooking, drinking champagne.

* * *

BRAUND, Harold 1913-
(Hal Braund)

PERSONAL: Born November 26, 1913, in Ceylon; son of Harold James (a tea taster) and Isabella Maud (Jacobs) Braund; married Maxine Velma Strong, September 25, 1946; children: Wendy Ina Katherine, Wilton James. *Education:* Educated in England. *Religion:* Christian. *Home:* 89 Were St., Brighton Beach, Victoria 3186, Australia. *Office:* Haileybury College, Springvale Rd., Keysborough, Victoria 3175, Australia.

CAREER: In oil exploration and drilling and in tin dredging; Steel Brothers & Co., London, England, manager in Burma, 1934-40, and general manager in Pakistan, 1940-65; Norman W. Hutchinson & Sons, Victoria, Australia, general manager, 1966-70; Haileybury College, Keysborough, Victoria, Australia, school accountant, 1970—. Chairman of Norman W. Hutchinson & Sons. *Military service:* Burma Army, 1940-45; became major; received Military Cross. *Member:* Australian Club, Naval and Military Club (Australia), Special Forces Club (London, England), United Kingdom Association of Pakistan (vice-chairman,

1965). *Awards, honors:* Member of Order of the British Empire.

WRITINGS—Books about Asia: *Distinctly I Remember,* Wren Publishing, 1972; *Calling to Mind: Being Some Account of the First Hundred Years (1870-1970) of Steel Brothers & Co. Ltd.,* Pergamon, 1975. Contributor of light verse to magazines, sometimes under name Hal Braund.

*   *   *

BREINES, Paul 1941-

PERSONAL: Surname rhymes with "highness"; April 16, 1941, in New York, N.Y.; son of Simon (an architect) and Nettie (Weisman) Breines; married Winifred Jacoby, March 29, 1964; children: Natasha, Raphael. *Education:* University of Wisconsin, Madison, B.A., 1963, M.A., 1967, Ph.D., 1972; attended Cornell University, 1963-65. *Politics:* "Left pessimist." *Religion:* "Millenarian." *Home:* 102 Trowbridge St., Cambridge, Mass. 02135. *Office:* Department of History, Boston College, Chestnut Hill, Mass. 02167.

CAREER: Boston University, Boston, Mass., assistant professor of social science, 1971-75; Boston College, Chestnut Hill, Mass., assistant professor of history, 1975—.

WRITINGS: (Editor and contributor) *Critical Interruptions,* Herder & Herder, 1970. Contributor of articles to *Telos, Philosophical Forum, Continuum;* contributor of reviews to *Journal of Modern History, European History, American Political Science Review.* Book review editor, *Telos,* 1971—.

WORK IN PROGRESS: (With Andrew Arato) *The Young Lukács; Hope and Despair: Intellectuals and Revolution in 19th and 20th Century Europe.*

*   *   *

BREITMAN, George 1916-

PERSONAL: Born February 18, 1916, in Newark, N.J.; son of Benjamin and Pauline (Trattler) Breitman. *Education:* Attended high school in Newark, N.J. *Politics:* Socialist Workers Party. *Religion:* None. *Office:* c/o Pathfinder Press, 410 West St., New York, N.Y. 10014.

CAREER: Militant, New York, N.Y., editor, 1942-43, 1946-54; *Detroit Free Press,* Detroit, Mich., printer, 1956-57. Writer.

WRITINGS: (Editor) *Malcolm X Speaks,* Pathfinder, 1965; *The Last Year of Malcolm X,* Pathfinder, 1967; (with Jack Barnes, Derrick Morrison, Barry Sheppard, and Mary-Alice Waters) *Towards an American Socialist Revolution,* Pathfinder, 1972; (editor) *Writings of Leon Trotsky,* twelve volumes, Pathfinder, 1969-76.

WORK IN PROGRESS: A book about the assassination of Malcolm X and the distortion of his ideas; a book about Leon Trotsky and the Fourth International.

*   *   *

BREMYER, Jayne Dickey 1924-
(Lee Dickey)

PERSONAL: Born November 12, 1924, in Charleston, W.Va.; daughter of George Henry (an attorney) and Nida (Dickey) Williamson; married John K. Bremyer (an attorney), December 8, 1945; children: John K., Jr., Jeffrey W., Jill. *Education:* Linden Hall Junior College, A.A., 1944; student at Georgetown University, 1945, and University of

Kansas, 1946; McPherson College, B.S., 1965; also took writing courses at Oklahoma University, Houston University and Indiana University. *Politics:* Republican. *Religion:* Methodist. *Home:* 1407 Dover Rd., McPherson, Kan. 67460.

CAREER: Writer. Member of local hospital auxiliary and local cultural arts commission. Hostess of television series "Middle Years." *Member:* Federation of Women's Clubs, Major Poets Society, P.E.O. Sisterhood, Young Writers of the Midwest, American Association of University Women. *Awards, honors:* Prizes from Federation of Women's Clubs writer's contests, 1955-65, for short stories, drama and poetry; from *Writer's Digest,* 1961, for "Mothers Don't Dig"; outstanding poet prize from Writer's Conference at University of Oklahoma, 1972, for "Joy is Loving You."

WRITINGS: (Under pseudonym Lee Dickey) *Journey to a Holy Mountain,* CSA Press, 1973; (editor and contributor) *Dear God: Women in Their Middle Years Talk to God,* Franciscan Herald Press, 1974; *Dear God–Am I Important?,* Word Books, in press; *Journey with Jesus,* Franciscan Herald Press, in press.

Work is anthologized in *Year Book of Modern Poetry,* Young Publications, 1970, and *Lyrics of Love,* Young Publications, 1972. Author and producer of local plays and radio programs. Contributor to popular magazines and literary journals, including *Major Poets Quarterly, American Girl, Homelife, Orion, Outlet, Epic,* and *Era,* and to newspapers.

WORK IN PROGRESS: Wings of Morning Call You Home: How to Die and Live Again; Straight from the Horse's Mouth, a juvenile book on horse shows; *Joy Is Loving You,* an illustrated book of sentiment; *Another Birth,* a novel about love and reincarnation; *Modina's Formula,* a gothic novel; *Golden Feather and Fallen Moon: Indian Love Story on the Trail of Tears.*

SIDELIGHTS: Jayne Bremyer writes: "*Dear God . . .* was written . . . to help me open up my own communication with God—and to find out who I was—in the trying period of depression most women face, when children leave home and their usefulness seems over." *Avocational interests:* Horsemanship and travel.

*   *   *

BRENNER, Summer 1945-

PERSONAL: Born March 17, 1945, in Washington, D.C.; daughter of Edward and Rita (a painter; maiden name, Abelman) Brenner; children: Felix Angel. *Education:* Attended Simmons College, 1963-65, University of Florence, 1965-66, and Sorbonne, University of Paris, 1966-67; Georgia State University, B.A., 1968. *Home:* 552 Alcatraz Ave., Oakland, Calif. 94609.

CAREER: Newsreel (New Left news service), organizer and film distributor in Atlanta, Ga., 1968-69, and Albuquerque, N.M., 1969-70. Proofreader at University of New Mexico, 1969-71.

WRITINGS: Everyone Came Dressed as Water: Poems, 1970-1972, Grasshopper Press, 1973. Work is anthologized in *Rising Tides,* edited by Laura Chester and Sharon Barba, Washington Square Press, 1973. Contributor of poems to magazines including *Stooge, Telephone, Fervent Valley,* and *Best Friends.*

WORK IN PROGRESS: Sweet Intention, prose poem; *From the Heart to the Center: Poems, 1973-1975; The Living Bump,* a juvenile story; a dance-poem, libretto for movement to include "the experience of our own cultural crisis"; a series of poems on industrial products and their origins; a children's story.

SIDELIGHTS: Summer Brenner writes: "I'm particularly interested in the relationship of movement and language. Currently studying several kinds of dance and have performed one poem with movements and a drummer. I have also been involved in puppet theater (1971) and envision the combination of efforts of poetry and performance using movement, masks, music, and sets in a theatrical piece.

"I live in a community of friends. Each of us lends our art to the other and the rotational energy is inspirational. It's most important that I try to touch into our central source and transmit that knowledge and love in my work and life."

* * *

BRETON, Albert 1929-

PERSONAL: Born June 12, 1929, in Montmartre, Saskatchewan, Canada; son of Alberic T. (a general merchant) and Jeanne (Nadeau) Breton; married Margot Fournier (a professor of social work), September 6, 1958; children: Catherine, Natalie, Francoise, Robert. *Education:* St. Boniface College, B.A., 1951; Columbia University, Ph.D., 1962. *Home:* 160 Rosedale Heights Drive, Toronto, Ontario, Canada M4T 1C8. *Office:* Department of Political Economy, University of Toronto, 150 St. George St., Toronto, Ontario, Canada M5S 1A1.

CAREER: University of Montreal, Montreal, Quebec, assistant professor of economics, 1957-65; London School of Economics and Political Science, London, England, lecturer, 1966-67, reader in economics, 1967-69; Harvard University, Cambridge, Mass., visiting professor of Canadian studies, 1969-70; University of Toronto, Toronto, Ontario, professor of economics, 1970—. Director of research, The Social Research Group, 1956-65; guest, Massachusetts Institute of Technology, 1959-60; visiting associate professor, Carleton University, 1964-65; visiting professor, Catholic University of Louvain, 1968-69; member, Committee on Urban Economics, 1972—; member of advisory committee for goals accounting research, National Planning Association, 1974—; member of Canadian economic policy committee, C. D. Howe Research Institute, 1974—. *Awards, honors:* University of Chicago, post-doctoral fellow, 1965-66; Killam Senior Research Scholarship from Canada Council, 1972, 1974.

WRITINGS: (Contributor) M. K. Oliver, editor, *Social Purpose for Canada,* University of Toronto Press, 1961; (contributor) A. Raynauld, editor, *Le Role de L'Etat,* Editions du Jour, 1962; (contributor) G. W. Wilson, H. S. Gordon and S. Judek, editors, *Canada: An Appraisal of Its Needs and Resources,* University of Toronto Press, 1965; *Discriminatory Government Policies in Federal Countries,* Canadian Trade Committee, 1967.

(Contributor) L. H. Officer and L. B. Smith, editors, *Canadian Economic Problems and Policies,* McGraw, 1970; (contributor) S. Tsuru, editor, *A Challenge to Social Scientists,* Asahi Evening News (Tokyo), 1970; (contributor) *Canadian Perspectives in Economics,* Collier-Macmillan, 1972; *A Conceptual Basis for an Industrial Strategy,* Economic Council of Canada, 1974; (contributor) L. H. Officer and L. B. Smith, editors, *Issues in Canadian Economics,* McGraw, 1974; *The Economic Theory of Representative Government,* Aldine, 1974. Contributor of articles to *Journal of Political Economy, Current History, Canadian Journal of Economics and Political Science, Economica,*

American Economic Review, and other professional periodicals.

* * *

BREUER, Bessie 1893-1975

October 19, 1893—September 26, 1975; American editor, novelist, short story writer, and playwright. Obituaries: *New York Times,* September 28, 1975. (*CAP*-2; earlier sketch in *CA*-17/18)

* * *

BREUNIG, LeRoy C(linton) 1915-

PERSONAL: Born March 29, 1915, in Indianapolis, Ind.; son of LeRoy Clinton (a businessman) and Lydia (Latham) Breunig; married Herse Lukia Niskos (an administrator), December 13, 1945; children: Marylly Helle Glankoff (stepdaughter). *Education:* DePauw University, A.B., 1936; Cornell University, M.A., 1938, Ph.D., 1941; also studied at University of Bordeaux, 1936-37. *Home:* 90 Morningside Dr., Apt. 5D, New York, N.Y. 10027. *Office:* Barnard College, Columbia University, New York, N.Y. 10027.

CAREER: Cornell University, Ithaca, N.Y., instructor in Romance languages, 1939-41; Harvard University, Cambridge, Mass., instructor, 1946-48, assistant professor of Romance languages, 1948-53; Columbia University, Barnard College, New York, N.Y., associate professor, 1953-60, professor of French, 1960—, chairman of department, 1953-60, dean of faculty, 1970-75, interim president of college, 1975. *Military service:* U.S. Navy Reserve, active duty, assistant naval attache at U.S. Embassy in Athens, 1941-46; became lieutenant commander.

MEMBER: Modern Language Association of America, American Association of Teachers of French, Phi Beta Kappa, Delta Kappa Epsilon. *Awards, honors:* Named Officier de l'Ordre des Palmes Académiques; Fulbright fellowship to France, 1959-60, and Australia, 1966; Guggenheim fellowship, 1959-60.

WRITINGS: (Editor) Guillaume Apollinaire, *Chroniques d'art* (title means "Chronicles of Art"), Gallimard, 1961; (with Helen Carlson, Renée Geen, and André Mesnard) *Forme et Fond* (title means "Form and Substance"), Macmillan, 1964; (editor with J. C. Chevalier) Apollinaire, *Les Peintres cubistes* (title means "The Cubist Painters"), Hermann, 1965; (contributor) Jean Sareil, editor, *Explication de texte* (title means "Explication of Text"), Prentice-Hall, 1967; *Guillaume Apollinaire,* Columbia University Press, 1969; (editor) Apollinaire, *Apollinaire on Art,* Viking, 1972; (contributor) Mary Ann Caws, editor, *From Dada to Tel Quel,* Wayne State University Press, 1974. Contributor to language and literature journals. Member of editorial board of *Romanic Review.*

WORK IN PROGRESS: Picasso's Poets, an anthology; a French reader containing selections on the nature of language.

* * *

BREW, J(ohn) O(tis) 1906-

PERSONAL: Born March 28, 1906, in Malden, Mass.; son of Michael Parker (a carriage builder) and Edith Ann (Fryer) Brew; married Evelyn Ruth Nimmo, June 11, 1939; children: Alan Parker, Lindsay Edward. *Education:* Dartmouth College, A.B., 1928; Harvard University, Ph.D., 1941. *Home:* 36 Bowdoin St., Cambridge, Mass. 02138.

Office: Peabody Museum, Harvard University, Cambridge, Mass. 02138.

CAREER: Harvard University, Peabody Museum, Cambridge, Mass., assistant to director, 1930-47, director of museum, 1948-67, assistant curator of southwest American archaeology, 1941-45, curator of North American archaeology, 1945-48, director of North American archaeology, 1948-67, university lecturer, 1935-47, Peabody Professor of American Archaeology and Ethnology, 1947-72, Peabody Professor emeritus, 1972—. Distinguished visiting professor, Southern Methodist University, 1972-76. Member and officer of committees for private, public, and government organizations, including UNESCO, National Park Service, and National Survey of Historic Sites and Buildings. Trustee, advisor, and officer of many U.S. museums.

MEMBER: American Anthropological Association (president, 1951), American Academy of Arts and Sciences (fellow), Society for American Archaeology (council member, 1944-46; president, 1949-50), American Antiquarian Society, Prehistoric Society, Association for Preservation Technology, American Association of Museums, Society of Applied Archaeology, Massachusetts Historical Society, Massachusetts Archaeological Society (executive council member, 1941-44, trustee, 1949-52), Colonial Society of Massachusetts, Tree Ring Society, Harvard Faculty Club (president, 1951-55), Cosmos Club (Washington, D.C.). *Awards, honors:* Viking Medal from Wenner-Gren Foundation, 1947; LL.D. from University of Liberia, 1970; named grand commander of Star of Africa.

WRITINGS: The Archaeology of Alkali Ridge, Utah, Peabody Museum, Harvard University, 1946; (with Ross Montgomery and Watson Smith) *Franciscan Awatoui,* Peabody Museum, Harvard University, 1949; (editor) *One Hundred Years of Anthropology,* Harvard University Press, 1968.

WORK IN PROGRESS: Archaeology of the American Southwest; Historic Sites Archaeology.

* * *

BRILOFF, Abraham J(acob) 1917-

PERSONAL: Born July 19, 1917, in New York, N.Y.; son of Benjamin (a butcher) and Anna (Kaplan) Briloff; married Edith Moss, December 22, 1940; children: Leonore, Alice. *Education:* City College of the City University of New York, B.B.A., 1937, M.S.Ed., 1941; New York University, Ph.D., 1965. *Politics:* Democrat. *Religion:* Jewish. *Home:* 99 Grace Ave., Great Neck, N.Y. 11021. *Office:* Department of Accountancy, Bernard M. Baruch College of the City University of New York, New York, N.Y. 10010.

CAREER: New York City Public Schools, N.Y., high school teacher, 1937-44; certified public accountant and consultant in accounting and taxation, 1944—; Bernard M. Baruch College of the City University of New York, New York, N.Y., adjunct lecturer, 1944-65, professor of accounting, 1965—. *Member:* American Accounting Association, American Institute of Certified Public Accountants, New York State Society of Certified Public Accountants. *Awards, honors:* Graham and Dodd Awards from Financial Analysis Federation, 1968 and 1969.

WRITINGS: The Effectiveness of Accounting Communication, Praeger, 1937; *Unaccountable Accounting,* Harper, 1973; *More Debits Than Credits,* Harper, 1976. Contributor to accounting, finance, tax, and law journals.

WORK IN PROGRESS: Continuing research in accounting principles and practices.

SIDELIGHTS: Briloff told *CA:* "My primary objective in writing is to raise the levels of corporate accountability and responsibility generally. As an incident thereto I am seeking to have my profession of accountancy fulfill the responsibilities vested in it by society." *Avocational interests:* Travel, hiking mountain trails.

BIOGRAPHICAL/CRITICAL SOURCES: Institutional Investor, August, 1969; *Dun's Review,* October, 1971.

* * *

BRISCOE, Jill 1935-

PERSONAL: Born June 29, 1935, in Liverpool, England; daughter of William A. (a motor trader) and Peggy (Pont) Ryder; married Stuart Briscoe (a clergyman), July 26, 1958; children: David, Judith, Peter. *Education:* Homerton College, Cambridge, teacher's diploma, 1958. *Religion:* Christian. *Residence:* Brookfield, Wis. *Office:* Elmbrook Church, Brookfield, Wis. 53005.

CAREER: Grade school teacher in Liverpool, England, 1958-60; Capernwray Missionary Fellowship of Torch Bearers, Lancaster, England, missionary with youth mission, 1960-70, superintendent of youth club and nursery school, 1965-70.

WRITINGS: There's a Snake in My Garden (autobiography of work among British teenagers), Zondervan, 1975.

WORK IN PROGRESS: A book of previously taped lectures for women, plays and programs for teenagers in youth ministries, and a new look at a woman's power and place in society.

SIDELIGHTS: Jill Briscoe writes: "After twelve years working full time with European youth . . . my heart is with those who will live in the somewhat frightening but challenging future. I want to challenge them to a philosophy of Christian discipleship I believe is the answer to the world's problems." *Avocational interests:* "Travelling round the world talking to kids and parents wherever they are and wherever I can."

* * *

BRISMAN, Leslie 1944-

PERSONAL: Born May 22, 1944, in New York; married Susan Hawk (an assistant professor of English at Vassar College), March 11, 1973; children: Aviad. *Education:* Columbia University, B.A., 1965; Cornell University, M.A., 1966, Ph.D., 1969. *Home:* 151 College Ave., Poughkeepsie, N.Y. 12603. *Office:* 3135 Yale Station, New Haven, Conn. 06511.

CAREER: Yale University, New Haven, Conn., assistant professor, 1969-74, associate professor of English, 1975—.

WRITINGS: Milton's Poetry of Choice and Its Romantic Heirs, Cornell University Press, 1973.

WORK IN PROGRESS: Romantic Origins; a textbook, *Beginning with Poetry.*

* * *

BROCK, Van(dall) K(line) 1932-

PERSONAL: Born October 31, 1932, in Boston, Ga.; son of William Arthur (a farmer) and Gladys (a teacher; maiden name, Lewis) Brock; married Frances Ragsdale (a writer and editor), August 3, 1961; children: Geoffrey Arthur,

Brantley Ragsdale. *Education:* Student at Florida State University, 1949-50, and Georgia Institute of Technology, 1950-51; Emory University, B.A., 1954, graduate study, summer, 1959; Garrett Theological Seminary, graduate study, 1954-56; University of Iowa, M.A., 1963, M.F.A., 1964, Ph.D., 1970. *Politics:* Democrat. *Religion:* "Unaffiliated." *Home:* 2302 Amelia Cir., Tallahassee, Fla. 32304. *Office:* Department of English, Florida State University, Tallahassee, Fla. 32306.

CAREER: Emerson House (Chicago Commons), Chicago, Ill., group worker, 1954-55; Evanston Children's Home, Evanston, Ill., recreational counselor, 1955-56; Emory University, Atlanta, Ga., librarian, 1958-60; Street & Newsboys Club, Houston, Tex., director, 1960-61; Fulton County Juvenile Court, Atlanta, Ga., intake officer, 1961-62; University of Iowa, Iowa City, instructor in English, 1963-64; Oglethorpe College, Atlanta, Ga., assistant professor of English, 1964-68; University of Iowa, instructor in English, 1968-70; Florida State University, Tallahassee, assistant professor, 1970-75, associate professor of English, 1975—. Recreational counselor for Atlanta's Young Men's Christian Association (YMCA), 1961-62; founder and director of Apalachee Poetry Center, 1973—; coordinator of Tallahassee's poets-in-the-schools program, 1972-74, and poets-in-the-prisons programs (for all Florida), 1974—. *Military service:* Air National Guard, 1957-59. U.S. Air Force Reserve, 1959-63.

MEMBER: College English Association, National Council of Teachers of English, South Atlantic Modern Language Association, Florida College English Association, Florida Council of Teachers of English. *Awards, honors:* First prize from Kansas City Poetry Contest, 1964, for "The Horses"; Borestone Mountain poetry awards, 1965, for "The Seabirds," 1971, 1972, both for "Peter's Complaint"; Georgia Writers Association prizes, all 1967, for "The Daydream," Reeves Lyric Award for "For One Who Is," Maywood Prize for "Complexity of Landscapes," first prize in Best Poems Contest for "Dead Man Creek," and first prize in best article contest for "The Place of the Writer in the Modern World."

WRITINGS: Final Belief (poems), Back Door Press, 1972; (editor) *Lime Tree Prism: Poems by Children,* Apalachee Poetry Center, 1973; (editor) *A Spot of Purple Is Deaf: Children's Poems,* Anhinga Press, 1974; *Illuminated Manuscripts and Other Poems,* New College Press, 1975; (editor) *The Space Behind the Clock: Poems from Florida Prisons,* Anhinga Press, 1975; (editor) *Cafe at St. Marks: The Apalachee Poets,* Anhinga Press, 1975.

Work has been anthologized in *Southern Writing in the Sixties: Poetry,* edited by John Carrington and Miller Williams, Louisiana State University Press, 1969; *New Voices in American Poetry,* edited by David Allan Evans, Winthrop Publishing, 1973; *New Southern Poets,* edited by Guy Owen, University of North Carolina Press, 1975; *New Yorker Book of Poems,* edited by Howard Moss and others.

Reporter for *Wilmington Morning Star,* 1960. Contributor of articles and poems to literary journals, including *New Yorker, Southern Review, Sewanee Review,* and *Yale Review.* Founder and director of Anhinga Press, 1974—. Special editor of Tallahassee poets section of *Apalachee Quarterly,* 1975.

WORK IN PROGRESS: Three poetry collections, *The Evidence and Other Poems, The Nazi Poems,* and *The Land of the Old Fields;* a new sequence of poems, *Roots;* a novel, and short stories, all exploring diversity, difference, and individuality as a way of trying to imagine the basis of a global civilization.

SIDELIGHTS: Brock writes: "I find myself increasingly concerned with the problem of suffering and the need for a joy in and a love of life through which suffering can be transcended and the perception of evil can be endured without evasion and without emotional and intellectual oppression. I firmly believe that we must be able to look without flinching, and without becoming desensitized, at the pervasive existence of evil, injustice, and suffering. But our awareness must not overcome; we must find cause for the celebration of existence, and without complacency." *Avocational interests:* Travel (lived in London; traveled in Europe; vacationed in Mexico).

BIOGRAPHICAL/CRITICAL SOURCES: Florida Flambeau, September 13, 1971; *Tallahassee Democrat,* December 16, 1973.

*   *   *

BRODSKY, Archie   1945-

PERSONAL: Born May 4, 1945, in Philadelphia, Pa.; son of Leon (an accountant) and Rose (Katz) Brodsky. *Education:* University of Pennsylvania, B.A., 1967. *Politics:* Libertarian. *Religion:* None. *Home:* 11 Royce Rd., Apt. 39, Allston, Mass. 02134. *Office address:* Fred's Firm, Inc., P.O. Box 21, Allston, Mass. 02134.

CAREER: Rolling Stone, San Francisco, Calif., rhythm-and-blues record reviewer, 1970; Harvard Business School, Boston, Mass., editorial assistant, 1970-73; Fred's Firm, Inc. (consultants for individuals, small businesses, and non-profit organizations), Allston, Mass., creative director, 1973—; writer. *Military service:* U.S. Air Force Reserve, Medical Corps, 1967-73; became staff sergeant.

WRITINGS: (With Stanton Peele) *Love and Addiction,* Taplinger, 1975; (contributor) Rodney Stark, editor, *Social Problems* (textbook), Random House, 1975; (with Stanley E. Sagov) *The Active Patient's Guide to Better Medical Care,* McKay, in press. Contributor to *Psychology Today, Cosmopolitan,* and *Life and Health.*

WORK IN PROGRESS: The Grand Allusion, a novelette; short stories; co-authoring with Stanton Peele a book on Alfred Hitchcock's films.

SIDELIGHTS: "Up to now," Brodsky wrote, "I have collaborated with psychologists and doctors on writings aimed at freeing people from institutional dependencies, questioning established social arrangements, and helping people be more self-confident and self-sufficient. With the success of the most important of these works, *Love and Addiction,* I hope increasingly to explore my more personal, humanistic, and aesthetic interests in fiction." *Avocational interests:* Songwriting, guitar, jogging, sports, American cinema, the American automobile.

*   *   *

BROH, C(harles) Anthony   1945-

PERSONAL: Born March 7, 1945, in Huntington, W.Va.; son of Charles S. (an insurance salesman) and Shirley (an interior decorator; maiden name, Michelson) Broh. *Education:* Marshall University, A.B., 1967; University of Maryland, graduate study, 1967-68; University of Wisconsin, Madison, M.A., 1969, Ph.D., 1972. *Religion:* Jewish. *Home:* 473 Hamilton St., Apt. 18, Geneva, N.Y. 14456. *Office:* Department of Political Science, Hobart and William Smith Colleges, Geneva, N.Y. 14456.

CAREER: Southern Illinois University, Carbondale, assistant professor of political science, 1972-73; State University of New York College at Geneseo, assistant professor of political science, 1973-75; Hobart and William Smith Colleges, Geneva, N.Y., assistant professor of political science, 1975—.

WRITINGS: Toward a Theory of Issue Voting, Sage Publications, 1973; (with Bruce D. Bowen and Charles Prysby) *Issue Voting: The 1972 Election,* American Political Science Association, 1975. Contributor to social science and political science journals.

WORK IN PROGRESS: Editing *Contemporary Personality Theory and Citizen Participation,* with Kenneth L. Deutsch and Richard P. Farkas, for Sitjoff; *The Study of Elections and Voting Behavior.*

*   *   *

BROKHOFF, John R(udolph)   1913-

PERSONAL: Born December 19, 1913, in Pottsville, Pa.; son of John H. (a businessman) and Gertrude (Heiser) Brokhoff; married Barbara Barnett (a minister), June 9, 1972. *Education:* Muhlenberg College, A.B., 1935, D.D., 1951; University of Pennsylvania, M.A., 1938; Lutheran Theological Seminary, Philadelphia, Pa., B.D., 1938. *Home address:* Route 8, Box 141, Cumming, Ga. 30130. *Office:* Candler School of Theology, Emory University, Atlanta, Ga. 30322.

CAREER: Ordained minister of Lutheran Church in America, 1938; assistant pastor, Richmond, Va., 1938-40; pastor, Marion, Va., 1940-42, Roanoke, Va., 1942-45, Atlanta, Ga., 1945-55, Charlotte, N.C., 1955-62, and Lanadale, Pa., 1962-65; Emory University, Candler School of Theology, Atlanta, professor of homiletics, 1965—. Guest professor, Emory University, 1950-54; lecturer, Gammon Theological Seminary, 1966. Chairman, United Lutheran Radio Committee, 1948-54; moderator of youth program, Radio WSB, Atlanta, 1953-54, Radio WBT, Charlotte, 1955-56, and WSOC-TV, Charlotte, 1957-59; member of answer panel, "Pastors Face Your Questions," WBTV, Charlotte, 1956-62. Member of executive committee, Lutheran Synod of North Carolina, 1959-62; member of executive board, North Carolina Council of Churches, 1962. Member of board of trustees, Lutheran Children's Home of the South, 1951-54; secretary of board of trustees, Protestant Radio Center, Inc., 1959-62. Councillor, National Lutheran Council, 1951-55; member of advisory board, Juvenile Court, Atlanta, 1954; member of consulting committee, United Lutheran Church Department of Architecture, 1956-62. Member, Child Service Association, 1953-54.

MEMBER: Evangelical Ministers Association of Atlanta (president, 1948), Atlanta Christian Council (president, 1950-52), Atlanta Lutheran Pastors' Association (president, 1953), Mecklenburg Christian Ministers' Association (president, 1960), Charlotte Lutheran Pastors' Association (president, 1957-59), Omicron Delta Kappa, Tau Kappa Alpha, Alpha Kappa Alpha. *Awards, honors:* George Washington Medal award from Freedoms Foundation for sermon, "Human Rights or Duties?"

WRITINGS: Read and Live: A Study Dealing with How to Use the Bible, Muhlenberg Press, 1953; *This Is Life,* Revell, 1959; *This Is the Church,* Lutheran Church Press, 1964; *Defending My Faith,* two volumes, Lutheran Church Press, 1966; *Table for Lovers,* CSS Publishing, 1974; (contributor) Charles L. Wallis, compiler, *Eighty-Eight Evangelistic Sermons,* Baker Book, 1974; *If Your Dearest Should Die,* CSS Publishing, 1975; *Wrinkled Wrappings,* CSS Publishing, 1975. Also author of *Youth's World, Christ in the Gospels, Why?,* and *Christian Strategy,* published by Lutheran Church Press. Contributor to *Notable Sermons from Protestant Pulpits* and *Preaching the Nativity.* Contributor of articles to *Christian Century Pulpit, Pulpit Digest,* and *New Pulpit Digest.*

*   *   *

BROMHEAD, Peter (Alexander)   1919-

PERSONAL: Born January 27, 1919, in Madras, India; son of George William (an engineer) and Eva Margaret (McCulloch) Bromhead; married Evelyn Robertson Snodgrass (a justice of the peace), September 16, 1946; children: Marjory-Anne, Alison. *Education:* Exeter College, Oxford, M.A., 1947, D.Phil., 1950. *Home:* Glebe House, Abbots Leigh, Near Bristol, B58 3QU, England. *Office:* Department of Politics, University of Bristol, 40 Berkeley Sq., Bristol BS8 1HY, England.

CAREER: University of Durham, Durham, England, lecturer, 1947-58, senior lecturer, 1958-62, reader in politics, 1962; University of Wales, Swansea, professor of politics, 1963-64; University of Bristol, Bristol, England, professor of politics, 1964—, dean of social sciences, 1970-72. Visiting professor at University of Florida, 1959-60. Chairman of Avon European Movement, 1973—. *Member:* International Political Science Association, National Trust, Political Studies Association of the United Kingdom, Royal Institute of Public Administration, Study of Parliament Group, Avon Conservation Society (chairman, 1974—).

WRITINGS: Private Members' Bills in the British Parliament, Routledge & Kegan Paul, 1956; *The House of Lords in Contemporary Politics,* Routledge & Kegan Paul, 1958, reprinted, Greenwood Press, 1976; *Life in Modern Britain,* Longmans, 1962, 4th edition, 1975; *Life in Modern America,* Longmans, 1970; *The Great White Elephant of Maplin Sands,* Elek, 1973; *Britain's Developing Constitution,* Allen & Unwin, 1974; *Politics in England,* Evans Brothers, in press. Contributor to political science and planning journals.

WORK IN PROGRESS: Research on long-term transport planning in Europe, with particular concern for road, rail, and air infrastructures.

SIDELIGHTS: Bromhead writes: "An interest in communication, both from specialist cultures and non-specialists and across national linguistic boundaries, arises from work lecturing in English or in German, to people for whom English is not the first language, first . . . to groups of German prisoners of war then held in Britain. An interest in the politics of transport . . . recently has been concerned with the selection of modes for development for tasks for which they are best fitted—with effects on the environment and on energy-consumption taken into account. Study of the assumptions on which the supposed need for a new London airport was based led to a series of articles and contributions to press, television, and radio from 1971 to 1974, when the airport scheme was abandoned."

*   *   *

BRONSON, Bertrand Harris   1902-

PERSONAL: Born June 22, 1902, in Lawrenceville, N.J.; son of Thomas Bertrand and Isabel (Harris) Bronson; married Mildred Sumner Kinsley, June 25, 1927. *Education:* University of Michigan, A.B., 1921; Harvard University,

M.A., 1922; Oriel College, Oxford, B.A. (first class honors), 1924, M.A., 1929; Yale University, Ph.D., 1927. *Home:* 927 Oxford St., Berkeley, Calif. 94707.

CAREER: University of Michigan, Ann Arbor, instructor in English, 1925-26; University of California, Berkeley, instructor, 1927-29, assistant professor, 1929-38, associate professor, 1938-45, professor of English, 1945-70, professor-emeritus, 1970—. Visiting professor at Yale University, 1945; Alexander lecturer at University of Toronto, 1948-59; Berg professor at New York University, 1973.

MEMBER: International Folk Music Council, American Academy of Arts and Sciences, Modern Language Association of America, American Musicological Society, American Folklore Society, Society of Ethnomusicology, British Academy (fellow; corresponding member), Philological Association of the Pacific Coast, California Folklore Society, Oxford Society, Faculty Club and Arts Club (both University of California, Berkeley), Phi Beta Kappa, Beta Theta Pi. *Awards, honors:* Guggenheim fellowships, 1943, 1944, 1948; American Council of Learned Societies award, 1959; D.L.H.C. from Laval University, 1961; medal of honor from Rice University, 1962; L.H.D. from University of Chicago, 1968, and University of Michigan, 1970; Wilbur Cross Medal from Yale University, 1970; LL.D. from University of California, 1971.

WRITINGS: Chaucer's House of Fame: Another Hypothesis, University of California Press, 1934; *In Appreciation of Chaucer's Parlement of Foules,* University of California Press, 1935; *Joseph Ritson, Scholar-at-Arms,* University of California Press, 1938; (with J. R. Caldwell, J. M. Cline, G. McKenzie, and J. F. Ross) *Five Studies in Literature,* University of California Press, 1940; (with Caldwell, McKenzie, Ross, W. H. Durham, and B. H. Lehman) *Studies in the Comic,* University of California Press, 1941; (editor) J. J. Gillick, *That Immortal Garland,* [Berkeley], 1941; *Johnson and Boswell: Three Essays,* University of California Press, 1944, published as *Johnson Agonistes and Other Essays,* Cambridge University Press, 1946, University of California Press, 1965; (editor) *Samuel Johnson: Selected Prose and Poetry,* Rinehart, 1952; (with James E. Phillips) *Music and Literature in England in the Seventeenth and Eighteenth Centuries,* University of California, Los Angeles, 1953; (with Lehman, W. M. Hart, L. Bacon, and G. R. Potter) *Five Gayley Lectures, 1947-54,* University of California Press, 1954; (compiler) *Catches and Glees of the Eighteenth Century,* University of California Press, 1955; (contributing editor) G. B. Harrison, general editor, *Major British Writers,* two volumes, Harcourt, 1954, enlarged edition, 1959; (editor) *Samuel Johnson: Rasselas, Poems and Selected Prose,* Rinehart, 1958, 3rd edition, Holt, 1971; *Printing as an Index of Taste in Eighteenth-Century England,* New York Public Library, 1958, revised edition, 1963; (editor) *The Traditional Tunes of the Child Ballads: With Their Texts, According to the Extant Records of Great Britain and America,* Princeton University Press, Volume I, 1959, Volume II, 1962, Volume III, 1966, Volume IV, 1972; *In Search of Chaucer,* University of Toronto Press, 1960; (contributor) James Thorpe, editor, *Relations of Literary Study: Essays on Interdisciplinary Contributions,* Modern Language Association of America, 1967; (contributor) James L. Clifford, editor, *Man Versus Society in Eighteenth-Century Britain: Six Points of View,* Cambridge University Press, 1968; *Facets of the Enlightenment: Studies in English Literature and Its Contexts,* University of California Press, 1968; *The Ballad As Song,* University of California Press, 1969.

BROOKHOUSER, Frank 1912(?)-1975

1912(?)—November 3, 1975; American newsman, columnist, short story writer, and author. Obituaries: *New York Times,* November 4, 1975; *AB Bookman's Weekly,* December 22-29, 1975. (See index for previous *CA* sketch)

* * *

BROOKMAN, Rosina Francesca 1932-
(Rosina Francesca)

PERSONAL: Born March 10, 1932, in Bachszentivan, Hungary; daughter of Johann (a businessman) and Anna (Blechl) Wurtz; married Ronald Brookman (an engineer), October, 1963; children: Michele, Warren. *Education:* California State University, Los Angeles, B.A., M.A. *Politics:* None. *Religion:* None. *Home:* 1942 East Mountain St., Pasadena, Calif. 91104.

CAREER: Former high school teacher of English; now owner of a sewing plant.

WRITINGS: (Under name Rosina Francesca) *How to Marry Somebody Else's Housebroken Husband,* edited by Billie Young, Ashley Books, 1973.

* * *

BROOKS, David H(opkinson) 1929-

PERSONAL: Born April 26, 1929, in Paris, France; son of John (a banker) and Marion (Hopkinson) Brooks; married Jo-An Blanchard (in real estate), June 12, 1952; children: David H., Jr., Gregory Stetson, Laura Blanchard, James. *Education:* Cornell University, B.A., 1952. *Politics:* Republican. *Religion:* Episcopal. *Residence:* Redding, Conn. 06896. *Office: Harper/Atlantic,* New York, N.Y. 10017.

CAREER: Cunningham & Walsh, New York, N.Y., copy writer, 1954-58; Bridgeport Brass Co., Bridgeport, Conn., assistant advertising manager, 1958-60; *Metal Progress* (magazine), Novelty, Ohio, in advertising sales, 1961-63; *Harper/Atlantic,* New York, N.Y., in advertising sales, 1963—. Member of board of directors of Redding Boys Club; manager of Redding Horse Show, 1963; member, Redding Board of Education, 1974—. *Military service:* U.S. Army, Field Artillery, 1952-54; served in Korea; became first lieutenant.

WRITINGS: Gone Away (novel), Harper Magazine Press, 1975.

WORK IN PROGRESS: Another novel.

AVOCATIONAL INTERESTS: Horseback riding, snorkeling, hiking, tennis, squash.

* * *

BROPHY, Elizabeth Bergen 1929-

PERSONAL: Born January 28, 1929, in New York, N.Y.; daughter of James J. (a builder) and Marie (Ahearn) Bergen; married James D. Brophy (a college teacher), March 26, 1951; children: Sheila (Mrs. Steven W. Peiffer), David, Katharine, Elizabeth, James. *Education:* Smith College, B.A., 1959; Sarah Lawrence College, M.A., 1964; Columbia University, Ph.D., 1970. *Home:* 35 Crystal St., Harrison, N.Y. 10523. *Office:* Department of English, College of New Rochelle, New Rochelle, N.Y. 10801.

CAREER: College of New Rochelle, New Rochelle, N.Y., assistant professor of English, 1968—. *Member:* American Society for Eighteenth Century Studies, American Association of University Professors, Modern Language Association of America. *Awards, honors:* Fulbright fellow, University College, London, 1966-67; American Council of Learned Societies fellowship, 1974-75.

WRITINGS: Samuel Richardson: The Triumph of Craft, University of Tennessee Press, 1974.

WORK IN PROGRESS: A study of realism in the characterization of women in eighteenth-century fiction.

*   *   *

BROSMAN, Catharine Savage   1934-
(Catharine Savage)

PERSONAL: Born June 7, 1934, in Denver, Colo.; daughter of Paul Victor and Della Leota (Stanforth) Hill; married Patric Savage, April 7, 1955 (divorced, July, 1964); married Paul W. Brosman, Jr., August 21, 1970; children: (second marriage) Katherine Elliott. *Education:* Rice University, B.A., 1955, M.A., 1957, Ph.D., 1960; University of Grenoble, graduate study, 1957-58. *Home:* 7834 Willow St., New Orleans, La. 70118. *Office:* Department of French and Italian, Tulane University, New Orleans, La. 70118.

CAREER: Rice University, Houston, Tex., instructor in French, 1960-62; Sweet Briar College, Sweet Briar, Va., assistant professor of French, 1962-63; University of Florida, Gainesville, assistant professor of French, 1963-66; Mary Baldwin College, Staunton, Va., associate professor of French, 1966-68; Tulane University, Newcomb College, New Orleans, associate professor, 1968-72, professor of French, 1972—. Visiting associate professor at University of Waterloo, summer, 1970. Member, Modern Language Association of America Commission on the Status of Women in the Professions, 1969-70.

MEMBER: American Association of Teachers of French, Association Amis Andre Gide, Malraux Society, South Central Modern Language Association (vice-president, 1973-74; president, 1974-75), South Atlantic Modern Language Association, Phi Beta Kappa. *Awards, honors:* Fulbright scholarship for University of Grenoble, 1957-58; American Council of Learned Societies grant, 1962; grant from Board of Education of the Presbyterian Church in the United States, 1967; Tulane Research Council grant, 1969.

WRITINGS—Under name Catharine Savage: *Andre Gide: L'evolution de sa pensee religieuse* (title means "Andre Gide: The Evolution of His Religious Thought"), A. G. Nizet, 1962; *Malraux, Sartre, and Aragon as Political Novelists,* University of Florida Press, 1964; *Roger Martin du Gard,* Twayne, 1968.

Under name Catharine Savage Brosman: *Watering* (poems), University of Georgia Press, 1972; (contributor) Guy Owen and Mary C. Williams, editors, *New Southern Poets,* University of North Carolina Press, 1974; (contributor) *Best Poems of 1973,* Pacific Books, 1974. Contributor to language journals and to literary quarterlies. Assistant editor, *French Review,* 1974—.

*   *   *

BROSSARD, Chandler   1922-
(Daniel Harper)

PERSONAL: Born July 18, 1922, in Idaho Falls, Idaho; married, 1948; children: two. *Education:* Self-educated (left school at age 11). *Home:* 251 West 89th St., New York, N.Y. 10024.

CAREER: Washington Post, Washington D.C., reporter,

1940-42; *New Yorker,* New York City, writer and editor, 1942-43; *Time* (magazine), New York City, senior editor, 1944; *American Mercury,* New York City, executive editor, 1950-51; *Look* (magazine), New York City, senior editor, 1956-67; Old Westbury College, Oyster Bay, Long Island, N.Y., associate professor, 1968-70; novelist and playwright. Visiting professor, University of Birmingham, England, 1970. Adjunct professor, Fairleigh Dickinson University, and C. W. Post College.

WRITINGS: Who Walk in Darkness (novel), New Directions, 1952; *The Bold Saboteurs* (novel), Farrar, Straus, 1953; *All Passion Spent* (novel), Popular Library, 1954, published as *Episode with Erika,* Belmont Books, 1963; *The Double View* (novel), Dial, 1960; *The Girls in Rome,* New American Library, 1961; *The Insane World of Adolf Hitler* (nonfiction), Fawcett, 1966; *Love Me, Love Me,* Fawcett, 1966; *The Spanish Scene* (impressions), Viking, 1968; *A Man for All Women,* Sphere Books, 1971; *Wake Up, We're Almost There* (novel), Baron, 1971; *Did Christ Make Love?* (novel), Bobbs-Merrill, 1973.

Under pseudonym Daniel Harper: *The Wrong Turn* (novel), Avon, 1954.

Editor: *The Scene Before You: A New Approach to American Culture,* Rinehart, 1955; *Eighteen Best Stories by Edgar Allan Poe,* Dell, 1965.

Plays: "Harry the Magician," produced in St. Louis, 1961; "Some Dreams Aren't Real," produced in St. Louis, 1962; "The Man with Ideas," produced in St. Louis, 1962.

BIOGRAPHICAL/CRITICAL SOURCES: Max Gartenberg and Gene Feldman, editors, *The Beat Generation and the Angry Young Men,* Citadel, 1958; Seymour Krim, editor, *The Beats,* Fawcett, 1960.*

*   *   *

BROWER, David R(oss)   1912-

PERSONAL: Born July 1, 1912, in Berkeley, Calif.; son of Ross J. (an engineer) and Mary Grace (Barlow) Brower; married Anne Hus (a free-lance editor), May 1, 1943; children: Kenneth David, Robert Irish, Barbara Anne (Mrs. Harper McKee), John Stewart. *Education:* Attended University of California, Berkeley, 1929-31. *Home:* 40 Stevenson, Berkeley, Calif. 94708. *Agent:* Curtis Brown Ltd., 60 East 56th St., New York, N.Y. 10022. *Office:* 529 Commercial St., San Francisco, Calif. 94111.

CAREER: Sierra Club, San Francisco, Calif., editor, 1935-69, director of wilderness outings programs, 1939-56, executive director, 1952-69, honorary vice-president, 1973—; University of California Press, Berkeley, editor, 1941-52; Friends of the Earth Foundation, San Francisco and New York, N.Y., founder, president, and initiator of independent Friends of the Earth organizations in several countries, 1969—. Visiting scholar, Case Western Reserve University, 1974; representative and guest speaker to international and national environmental conferences. Activist in wilderness preservation campaigns, including Saving Dinosaur National Monument, 1952-56, Saving Grand Canyon, 1952-68, Wilderness Act, 1952-64, North Cascades National Park, 1955-68, and Redwood National Park, 1963-68. Founder, Sierra Club Foundation, 1960, and Coleman Watershed Fund; John Muir Institute for Environmental Studies, co-founder, vice-president, 1968-72, director, 1969-71; chairman of academic advisory board and member of environmental sub-committee, International Center for Human Environment, 1975—; member of advisory council of University of California Water Resources Center, and Save-the-Bay Association. *Military service:* U.S. Army, Mountain Troops, 1942-45; became lieutenant. U.S. Army Infantry Reserve, 1945-54; became major; received Combat Infantryman's Badge, Bronze Star.

MEMBER: Natural Resources Council of America (member of executive committee, 1954-59; chairman, 1955-57), Les Amis de la Terre (founder, 1970), Friends of the Earth Ltd. (founder and guarantor, 1971—), Earth Island Ltd. (founder and chairman, 1971—), American Association for the Advancement of Science, American Alpine Club (Western vice-president, 1955-58), National Parks Association (honorary member), Mountaineers (honorary member), Trustees for Conservation (founder, 1954; secretary, 1960-61 and 1964-65; vice-president, 1962-63 and 1966-67; trustee), Rachel Carson Trust for the Living Environment (director, 1966—), League of Conservation Voters (founder and member of steering committee, 1969—), Jordens Vanner (founder, 1971), Oceanic Society (director, 1972-73), Wilderness Society, California Public Conservation Council (member of advisory council, 1958-60), Oregon Cascades Council (director, 1960-63), North Cascades Conservation Council (director, 1957—), Kern Plateau Association (director, 1954—).

AWARDS, HONORS: First class skier award from National Ski Association of America, 1942; conservation merit award from California Conservation Council, 1953; certificate of merit at Nash Conservation awards program, 1953; National Parks Association award, 1956; Leipzig International Book Fair honorary diploma, 1963, for "Exhibit Format" series book *In Wilderness Is the Preservation of the World;* for Sierra Club "Exhibit Format" series: Carey Thomas award for creative publishing, 1964, and awards from American Institute of Graphic Arts, Printing Industries of America, and Western Book Publishers Association; Paul Bartsch award from Audubon Naturalist Society of the Central Atlantic States, 1967; D.Sc., Hobart and William Smith Colleges, 1967; D.H.L., Claremont Men's College Graduate School, 1971, Starr King School for the Ministry, 1971, University of Maryland, College Park, 1973; Doctor of Philosophy, Ecology, University of San Francisco, 1973.

WRITINGS: Remount Blue: The Combat Story of the Third Battalion, Eighty-Sixth Mountain Infantry, University of California Press, 1948; (author of foreword) Robert Wenkam, *Maui: The Last Hawaiian Place,* Friends of the Earth, 1970; (contributor) Harvey Manning, *Cry Crisis: Rehearsal in Alaska,* Friends of the Earth, 1974.

Editor; all published by Sierra Club Books, unless otherwise indicated: *Manual of Ski Mountaineering,* 1942, 4th edition, 1969; *Going Light with Backpack or Burro,* 1951; *The Sierra Club: A Handbook,* 1957.

Eliot Porter, *The Place No One Knew: Glen Canyon on the Colorado,* 1963, revised edition, 1966, abridged edition, 1968; Francois Leydet, *Time and the River Flowing: Grand Canyon,* 1964; John Muir, *Gentle Wilderness: The Sierra Nevada,* 1964, revised edition, 1968; (and contributor) *Wildlands in Our Civilization,* 1964; *Not Man Apart,* 1965; Thomas F. Hornbein, *Everest: The West Ridge,* 1965; Eliot Porter, *Summer Island: Penobscot Country,* 1966, abridged edition, 1968; *The Sierra Club Wilderness Handbook,* Ballantine Books, 1967, 2nd revised edition, 1971; (and author of foreword) Mireille Johnston, *Central Park Country: A Tune Within Us,* 1968; Harvey Manning, *The Wild Cascades: Forgotten Parklands,* Ballantine, 1969; *Wilderness: America's Living Heritage,* 1972.

Editor; all published by Friends of the Earth: (And author of foreword) Max Knight, *Return to the Alps,* 1970; (and author of foreword) Amory Bloch Lovings, *Eryri: The Mountains of Longing,* 1971; (and author of foreword) *Only A Little Planet,* 1972; Susanne Anderson, *Song of the Earth Spirit,* 1973.

Script writer and narrator for several wilderness films, 1940-58. General editor, "Exhibit Format" series, Sierra Club Books, twenty books, beginning 1960. Contributor to national magazines and professional publications. Editor, *Sierra Club Bulletin,* 1946-53, *Sierra Club Annual Magazine,* until 1968.

SIDELIGHTS: In 1939, Brower led the first ascent of Shiprock Mountain in New Mexico, and he has also made several other first ascents in the Sierra Nevada. This ski mountaineering preceded Brower's mountain work with the U.S. Mountain Troops for which he prepared manuals as well as instructed in the Colorado and West Virginia mountain training center. For several years, until his retirement from the Infantry Reserve, Brower acted as director of the Oakland (Calif.) Army Base infantry school.

Between 1939 and 1956, Brower led some four thousand people on prolonged expeditions into remote wilderness areas in connection with his Sierra Club affiliation. He was one of two principal citizen activists responsible for initiating the National Wilderness Preservation system; he originated and promoted the Outdoor Recreation Resources Review, and was involved in several major national park campaigns.

Mountaineer Galen Rowell commented on Brower's achievement: ". . . When the process of evolution becomes subjected to conscious, human guidance—aided and abetted by mass technology—we will have traded the complexity and beauty of the natural world for a macrocosmic iron lung: a mechanical support system dependent on discoveries we have yet to make and a unified global willpower beyond our wildest dreams. Who will regulate our synthetic evolution? Perhaps a United Nations Committee, composed of political appointees? . . . Mountain experiences—intensely personal, subjective memories—are a far cry from the political drawing rooms of world governments. Yet can we think of a single man who has done more to change the face of the future than David Brower? Whether we like or dislike his handling of individual issues, we have to admit his enormous effect on the world."

BIOGRAPHICAL/CRITICAL SOURCES: John McPhee, *Encounters with the Archdruid,* Farrar, Straus, 1971.

* * *

BROWN, Curtis F(ranklin) 1925-

PERSONAL: Born July 15, 1925, in Cambridge, Mass.; son of Thomas Franklin and Mildred Spofford (Curtis) Brown. *Education:* Tufts University, B.A., 1949; Columbia University, M.A., 1952. *Home:* 381 State St., Brooklyn, N.Y. 11217.

CAREER: Tufts University, Medford, Mass., instructor in English, 1951-56; Drexel University, Philadelphia, Pa., instructor in English, 1957-61; Columbia Broadcasting System (CBS) Records, New York, N.Y., popular repertoire literary editor, 1961-68; Praeger Publishers, New York City, chief copywriter, 1968-74; Manhattan Community College of the City University of New York, New York City, assistant to higher education officer, 1974—. *Military service:* U.S. Navy, pharmacist's mate, 1943-46.

WRITINGS: Ingrid Bergman, Pyramid Publications, 1973; *Star-Spangled Kitsch: An Astounding and Tastelessly Illustrated Exploration of the Bawdy, Gaudy, Shoddy Mass-Art Culture in This Grand Land of Ours,* Universe Books, 1975; (contributor) Ted Sennett, editor, *The Movie Buff's Book,* Pyramid Publications, 1975; (contributor) Ted Sennett, editor, *The Book of Old-Time Radio,* Pyramid Publications, 1976.

WORK IN PROGRESS: An essay for inclusion in the sequel to *The Movie Buff's Book,* publication by Pyramid expected about 1977.

SIDELIGHTS: Brown writes that a "lifetime interest in films and the arts in general . . . led to writing *Star-Spangled Kitsch,* an overall view, in pictures and text, of the tastelessly exploitative in American mass culture." *Avocational interests:* Collecting antiques (especially American pressed glass and blue Staffordshire china bearing American scenes).

*   *   *

BROWN, Dennis A(lbert)   1926-

PERSONAL: Born September 29, 1926, in Bettws Newydd, England; son of William Arthur (a horticulturist) and Emily (Lane) Brown; married Rita Gertrude Hook, September 27, 1952; children: Angela Mary, Philip Dennis Spencer. *Education:* Royal Botanical Garden, Kew certificate, 1948; College of British Institute of Park Administration, diploma, 1953. *Home:* 43 Sagamore Rd., Bronxville, N.Y. 10708.

CAREER: Parks foreman in Borough of Hove, Sussex, England, 1950-52, and in County Borough of Derby, England, 1952-55; Borough of Beckenham, Parks Department, Kent, England, technical assistant, 1955-59; Borough of Pudsey, Yorkshire, England, director of parks and cemeteries, 1959-62; Merton and Morden United District Council, Surrey, England, director of parks, 1962-65; London Borough of Haringey, England, director of parks, 1965-67; New York Botanical Garden, New York, N.Y., director of horticulture, 1967-74; City of New York, Parks, Recreation, and Cultural Affairs Department, New York, N.Y., commissioner of horticulture and forestry, 1974—. Horticultural consultant to New York Zoological Society. *Military service:* British Army, 1944-47.

MEMBER: Kew Guild, Institute of Park and Recreation Administration (fellow), American Horticultural Society, Association of Botanical Gardens and Arboreta, Professional Grounds Management Society, Garden Writers of America, National Recreation and Parks Association, American Forestry Association, New York State Recreation and Park Society.

WRITINGS: (Editor) *The Complete Indoor Gardener,* Pan Books, 1974; *The Complete Book of American Houseplants,* Dial, 1976. Contributor of regular column to *Bronxville Review Press,* 1975-76.

WORK IN PROGRESS: Editing American edition of *Gardening for All,* to be published by Octopus Books.

SIDELIGHTS: In his current position with New York City, Brown is responsible for more than two and a half million trees; he and his two brothers are the third generation of professional gardeners in his family. *Avocational interests:* Photography, travel.

*   *   *

BROWN, Doris E.   1910(?)-1975

1910(?)—December 22, 1975; American religious educator,

author of children's books and of pamphlets for Society of Friends. Obituaries: *New York Times,* December 26, 1975.

*   *   *

BROWN, Geoff   1932-

PERSONAL: Born March 5, 1932, in Yorkshire, England; son of Frank and Lily (Spencer) Brown; married Estella Baggley, June 3, 1969. *Education:* Attended Hull College of Art, 1953-57. *Politics:* "Chauvinist." *Religion:* Church of England. *Home:* 180 Cardigan Rd., Bridlington, East Yorkshire, England.

CAREER: Writer. *Military service:* Royal Air Force, 1950-52.

WRITINGS: I Want What I Want (novel), Putnam, 1966; *My Struggle* (novel), St. Martin's, 1975. Contributor to *Lady.*

SIDELIGHTS: "I Want What I Want is about transvestitism," Brown wrote. *"My Struggle* is about paranoid-schizophrenia. It would seem that I write about abnormal psychology. What is it that causes me to concern myself with such murky things when, really, I am so very like Julie Andrews?"

*   *   *

BROWN, Hugh Auchincloss   1879-1975

American engineer and author of book on geophysics. Obituaries: *Time,* November 24, 1975.

*   *   *

BROWN, J(oseph) P(aul) S(ummers)   1930-

PERSONAL: Original name, Joseph Paul Summers; name legally changed, 1945; born August 25, 1930, in Nogales, Ariz.; son of Paul (a cattleman) and Mildred (Sorrells) Summers; married Barbara Jean Barbour, December 21, 1952 (divorced, March, 1956); married Patricia Louise Burr, December 7, 1974; children: (first marriage) William Paul, Paula Ann. *Education:* University of Notre Dame, B.A., 1952. *Politics:* None. *Religion:* Roman Catholic. *Home and office address:* P.O. Box 148, Snowflake, Ariz. 85937.

CAREER: El Paso Herald Post, El Paso, Tex., reporter, 1953-54; professional boxer, 1956-58, 1963-64; self-employed cattleman, 1958—. Mountain climbing instructor for U.S. Forest Service, 1974. *Military service:* U.S. Marine Corps, mountain climbing instructor, 1954-58; became first lieutenant.

WRITINGS—All novels: *Jim Kane,* Dial, 1970, paperback edition published as *Pocket Money,* Award, 1972; *The Outfit,* Dial, 1971; *The Forests of the Night,* Dial, 1974. Contributor to *Arizona Highways.*

WORK IN PROGRESS: A novel, *Log of a Big Hat.*

SIDELIGHTS: Brown writes: "I have been a cattleman all my adult life—born on a ranch of fifth-generation cattle people—also have been pilot in the U.S. and Mexico. I have been a whiskey smuggler and have prospected for gold with diving gear in rivers of Mexico's Sierra Madre. I wrote my first book to see if I could do it, the second because I had to do it and the third because I loved doing it."

BIOGRAPHICAL/CRITICAL SOURCES: Westways, November, 1969.

BROWN, Theo W(atts) 1934-

PERSONAL: Born October 11, 1934, in Melbourne, Australia; son of Albert Henry (a radio technician) and Constance (Chapman) Brown. *Education:* Educated in Australia. *Home:* 21 Woodlands Rd., East Lindfield, New South Wales 2070, Australia. *Office:* Australian Deep Sea Diving and Salvage Service, P.O. Box 125, Roseville, New South Wales 2069, Australia.

CAREER: Australian Deep Sea Diving and Salvage Service, Roseville, New South Wales, founder and director, 1957—; Institute of Medical Research, Papeete, Tahiti, research associate, 1967—; research associate of World Life Institute, 1968—. Research affiliate of School of Biological Sciences, University of Sydney, 1969-73. Has done rescue work for Western Australian Police and Northern Territory Police. Consultant to South Pacific Commission and United Nations. *Military service:* Australian Army, 1954-56; received Silver Medal for Bravery. *Member:* Australian Surf Life Saving Association, Australian Society of Authors.

WRITINGS: Crown of Thorns: The Death of the Great Barrier Reef?, Angus & Robertson, 1972; *Sharks: The Search for a Repellent*, Angus & Robertson, 1973, published in the United States as *Sharks: The Silent Savages*, Little, Brown, 1975. Contributor of about a thousand articles to scientific publications, popular magazines, and newspapers.

WORK IN PROGRESS: Five books; research on sonic shark attractants, on a sonic approach to shark repellents, and on marine pollution.

SIDELIGHTS: Brown lists his major concerns as "protection of human life at sea; assisting man to meet future food requirements; protection, preservation, and conservation of the marine environment." He adds: "Purely to gain funding for research I am writing a number of novels ..."

* * *

BROWN, W(illiam) Norman 1892-1975

PERSONAL: Born June 24, 1892, in Baltimore, Md.; son of George William and Virginia Augusta (Clark) Brown; married Helen Harrison, June 29, 1921; children: Norman, Ursula (Mrs. J. H. Perivier). *Education:* Hiram College, student, 1907-08; Johns Hopkins University, A.B., 1912, Ph.D., 1916, postdoctoral study, 1919-22; University of Pennsylvania, postdoctoral study, 1916-19; studied Sanskrit in Benares, India, 1922-23. *Address:* Moylan, Pa. 19065.

CAREER: Johns Hopkins University, Baltimore, Md., acting head of department of Sanskrit, 1921-22; Prince of Wales College, Jammu, India, professor of English, 1923-24; Johns Hopkins University, associate in Sanskrit, 1925-26; University of Pennsylvania, Philadelphia, professor of Sanskrit, 1926-66, professor emeritus, 1966-75, chairman of oriental studies, 1936-47, chairman of South Asia regional studies, 1947-66, curator of oriental section of university museum, 1942-50. Curator of Indian art at Philadelphia Museum of Art, 1931-54. Organizer and first president of American Institute of Indian Studies, Poona, 1961-71; president, Congress of Orientalists, 1967. Honorary fellow, Deccan College, Poona, Kuppuswauri Research Institute, Madras, and Bhandarkar Oriental Research Institute, Poona; fellow of Indian Council for Cultural Relations, New Delhi. Consultant on South Asian scripts to Mergenthaler Linotype Co., 1932-58. *Military service:* Served with U.S. Naval Aviation Corps and U.S. Naval Intelligence, c. 1918; with U.S. Office of Strategic Services, 1941-45.

MEMBER: American Philosophical Society, American Oriental Society (president, 1941-42), Linguistic Society of America, Association for Asian Studies (president, 1960-61), Royal Asiatic Society (London; fellow), Asiatic Society (Calcutta; honorary fellow), Royal India, Pakistan, and Ceylon Society (London), Philadelphia Oriental Club, Phi Beta Kappa, Delta Upsilon. *Awards, honors:* Guggenheim fellowship, 1928-29; Fulbright research scholar in India, 1954-55; G. V. Watumull Prize from American Historical Association, 1954, for *The United States and India and Pakistan;* honorary degrees include Litt.D. from University of Pennsylvania, 1963, and D.Litt. from University of Madras, 1957, Jnana-Ratna-Kara, West Bengal Government Sanskrit College of University of Calcutta, 1961, University of Michigan, 1965, and Jadavpur University, 1970.

WRITINGS: The Indian and Christian Miracles of Walking on the Water, Open Court, 1928; (editor) Kalikacarya, *The Story of Kalaka*, Lord Baltimore Press, 1933; *A Descriptive and Illustrated Catalogue of Miniature Paintings of the Jaina Kalpasutra as Executed in the Early Western Indian Style*, Lord Baltimore Press, 1934; *Manuscript Illustrations of the Uttaradhyayana Sutra*, American Oriental Society, 1941; (editor and contributor) *India, Pakistan, Ceylon*, Cornell University Press, 1950, revised edition, University of Pennsylvania Press, 1964; *The United States and India and Pakistan*, Harvard University Press, 1953, 2nd revised and enlarged edition published as *The United States and India, Pakistan, and Bangladesh*, 1972; (editor and translator) Sankaracarya, *The Saundaryalahari: or, Flood of Beauty*, Harvard University Press, 1958.

(Editor) *Resources for South Asian Language Studies in the United States*, University of Pennsylvania Press, 1960; *Traditional Culture and Modern Development in India*, South Asia Regional Studies, University of Pennsylvania, 1960; (editor and translator) Vasantavilasa, *The Vasanta Vilasa*, American Oriental Society, 1962; (editor and translator) *The Mahimnastava: or, Praise of Shiva's Greatness*, American Institute of Indian Studies (Poona), 1965; *Man in the Universe: Some Continuities in Indian Thought*, University of California Press, 1966.

Contributor to *Encyclopedia Americana* and to learned and popular journals. Editor of *Journal of the American Oriental Society*, 1926-41.*

(Died April 22, 1975, in West Chester, Pa.)

* * *

BROWNING, Norma Lee 1914-

PERSONAL: Born November 24, 1914, in Spickard, Mo.; daughter of Howard R. and Grace (Kennedy) Browning; married Russell J. Ogg, June 12, 1938. *Education:* University of Missouri, B.J. and A.B. (with distinction), both 1937; Radcliffe College, M.A., 1938. *Home:* 226 Morongo Rd., Palm Springs, Calif. 92262.

CAREER: Chicago Tribune, Chicago, Ill., reporter and feature writer, 1944-66, Hollywood correspondent, 1966-75. News and travel lecturer for Colston Leigh Bureau, 1957-67. Faculty adviser at Interlochen Arts Academy and editorial consultant to National Music Camp (Interlochen, Mich.), 1960-67. *Member:* Mortar Board (president, 1937), Theta Sigma Phi, Kappa Tau Alpha, Alpha Chi Omega. *Awards, honors:* E. S. Beck Award in Reporting from *Chicago Tribune*, 1949, for newspaper series on medical "quacks."

WRITINGS: City Girl in the Country and Other Stories, Regnery, 1955; *Joe Maddy of Interlochen* (foreword by Van Cliburn), Regnery, 1963; (with W. Clement Stone) *The Other Side of the Mind,* Prentice-Hall, 1964; *The Psychic World of Peter Hurkos,* Doubleday, 1970; (with Louella Dirksen) *The Honorable Mr. Marigold: My Life with Everett Dirksen,* Doubleday, 1972; (with Ann Miller) *Miller's High Life,* Doubleday, 1972; *Peter Hurkos: I Have Many Lives,* Doubleday, 1976; *The Borderline World of Sydney Omarr,* Doubleday, 1977. Contributor to national magazines, including *Saturday Evening Post* and *Reader's Digest.*

BIOGRAPHICAL/CRITICAL SOURCES: Editor & Publisher, August 6, 1949; *Time,* December 12, 1949.

*   *   *

BRYAN, J(oseph) III   1904-

PERSONAL: Born April 30, 1904, in Richmond, Va.; son of Joseph St. George and Emily Page (Kemp) Bryan; married second wife, Jacqueline de la Grandiere, 1960; children: St. George II (deceased), Joan (Mrs. Peter Gates), Courtland. *Education:* Princeton University, A.B., 1927. *Religion:* Episcopalian. *Home:* Brook Hill, Richmond, Va.

CAREER: Reporter and editorial writer, *News Leader,* Richmond, Va., and *Chicago Journal,* Chicago, Ill., 1928-31; associate editor, *Parade* Magazine, 1931-32; managing editor, *Town and Country,* 1933-37; associate editor, *Saturday Evening Post,* 1937-40; free-lance writer, 1940—. Trustee and fellow of Virginia Museum of Fine Arts. *Military service:* U.S. Army Reserve, 1927-37; became 1st lieutenant. U.S. Naval Reserve, 1942-53; became lieutenant commander. U.S. Air Force Reserve, 1953-62; became colonel. *Member:* P.E.N., Virginia Historical Society, Society of The Cincinnati, Commonwealth Club (Richmond, Va.), Buck's Club (London), Ivy Club (Princeton), Racquet and Tennis Club (New York City).

WRITINGS: (With Philip Reed) *Mission Beyond Darkness,* Duell, Sloan & Pearce, 1945; (with William F. Halsey) *Admiral Halsey's Story,* Whittlesey House, 1947; *Aircraft Carrier,* Ballantine, 1954; *The World's Greatest Showman: The Life of P. T. Barnum* (juvenile), Random House, 1956; *The Sword over the Mantel,* McGraw, 1960. Contributor of more than a hundred articles to popular magazines, including *Reader's Digest, McCall's,* and *Holiday.*

*   *   *

BRYANT, Cyril E(ric, Jr.)   1917-

PERSONAL: Born August 8, 1917, in Booneville, Ark.; son of Cyril E. and Ruth E. (Best) Bryant; married Flossie Wells, April 29, 1943; children: James Edwin, Mary Elizabeth (Mrs. Leland R. Smith). *Education:* Ouachita College, student, 1934-36; Baylor University, A.B., 1939; Southern Baptist Theological Seminary, graduate study, 1942-43; also attended Boston University. *Politics:* Independent. *Home:* 6609 Brawner St., McLean, Va. 22101. *Office:* Baptist World Alliance, 1628 16th St. N.W., Washington, D.C. 20009.

CAREER: Clergyman of Baptist Church, ordained 1935; Baylor University, Waco, Tex., director of News Bureau, 1939-42; *Arkansas Baptist* (weekly publication), Little Rock, Ark., editor and business manager, 1943-47; Southern Baptist Convention, Nashville, Tenn., director of publicity and press relations, editor of *Baptist Program* and

Baptist Bulletin Service, and founder of Baptist Press News Service, all 1947-49; Baylor University, director of press relations, 1949-52, director of public relations, 1952-57, lecturer in journalism, 1952-57; Baptist World Alliance, Washington, D.C., director of publications, 1957-71, associate secretary, 1971—, also editor of *Baptist World* and director of Baptist World Alliance News Service. *Member:* Associated Church Press, Religious Public Relations Council (president of Washington chapter, 1965-66), Southern Baptist Press Association (president, 1945-46), National Press Club (Washington, D.C.), Sigma Delta Chi.

WRITINGS: (Editor) *Report Book of the Fifth Baptist Youth World Conference, Toronto,* Baptist World Alliance, 1958; (editor with Arnold T. Ohrn) *Report Book of the Tenth Baptist World Congress, Rio de Janeiro,* Broadman, 1960; (editor) *Report Book of the Sixth Baptist Youth World Conference, Beirut,* Baptist World Alliance, 1963; (editor with Josef Nordenhaug) *Report Book of the Eleventh Baptist World Congress, Miami Beach,* Broadman Press, 1965; *Operation Brother's Brother,* Lippincott, 1968; (editor) *Report Book of the Seventh Baptist Youth World Conference, Berne,* Word Books, 1968; (editor) *Report Book of the Twelfth Baptist World Congress, Tokyo,* Judson, 1970; (editor with Debbie Stewart) *Report Book of the Thirteenth Baptist World Congress, Stockholm,* Broadman, 1975; *Who Are the Baptists?,* Baptist Spanish Publishing House, 1976. Contributor to religious and popular magazines, including *Reader's Digest* and *Saturday Review.*

SIDELIGHTS: An ordained Baptist minister, Bryant was convinced early in life that his ministry should be projected to the general reading public rather than to limited church congregations. He has "sought to tell the story of individuals and projects which illustrate Christian (or religious) truth in practical life."

*   *   *

BUBECK, Mark I(rving)   1928-

PERSONAL: Born February 20, 1928, in Clarion, Iowa; son of Floyd I. (a farmer) and Agnes (Howieson) Bubeck; married Anita Harl, September 3, 1949; children: Rhonda (Mrs. Gary Raad), Donna (Mrs. Hans Finzel), Judith. *Education:* Moody Bible Institute, diploma, 1949; Conservative Baptist Seminary, Denver, Colo., diploma in theology, 1953; University of Colorado, student, 1953-55. *Residence:* Oak Park, Ill. *Office:* Judson Baptist Church, 1252 North Austin, Oak Park, Ill. 60302.

CAREER: Ordained Baptist clergyman, 1954; pastor of Baptist churches in Morrison, Colo., 1953-55, and Wheat Ridge, Colo., 1955-68; Judson Baptist Church, Oak Park, Ill., pastor, 1968—. *Member:* Conservative Baptist Association of America (president of Rocky Mountain division, 1962-64), Moody Alumni Association (president, 1970-74).

WRITINGS: The Adversary, Moody, 1975. Contributor to *Moody Monthly.*

WORK IN PROGRESS: The Practical Use of Prayer, completion expected in 1977.

SIDELIGHTS: Bubeck writes: "I saw the need for a practical handbook for Christian believers to know how to overcome their spiritual enemies from a Biblical perspective."

*   *   *

BUCHMAN, Dian Dincin

PERSONAL: Born in New York; daughter of Herman B. (a doctor) and Renee (Meyerovici) Dincin; married

Herman Buchman (a professor, film makeup man, and author), February 20, 1949; children: Cathleen Dincin. *Education:* New York University, B.S., 1943. *Home:* 640 West End Ave., New York, N.Y. 10024. *Agent:* Anita Diamant, 51 East 42nd St., New York, N.Y. 10017.

CAREER: Producer and interviewer for radio show, "Tomorrow's People," WABF-FM, New York, N.Y.; researcher, Louis de Rochemont Films; in public relations for Prentice-Hall and Dick Taplinger associates; currently free-lance journalist. Teaches two preventive health courses at State University of New York College, Purchase. Participant, health conferences, Harvard Medical School and Seoul, Korea, both 1975. Has made television and radio appearances nationally on health topics, particularly natural and herb aspects. *Member:* American Television Society (executive secretary), American Society of Journalists and Authors (member of executive council; co-chairman of nonfiction workshops, three years), Authors League, Association for Humanistic Psychology. *Awards, honors:* Outstanding service award from Society of Magazine Writers, 1972.

WRITINGS: (Co-author) *Trips: New York City Classes,* New York City Board of Education, 1968; *The Sherlock Holmes of Medicine: Doctor Joseph Goldberger,* Messner, 1969; *The Complete Herbal Guide to Natural Health and Beauty,* Doubleday, 1973; *Organic Makeup,* Ace Books, 1975; *Feel Good/Look Great,* Scholastic Book Services, 1976. Narration writer for series of education films. Author of column, "Dian's Herbal Diary," in *Nutritional Update.* Contributor of articles to magazines.

WORK IN PROGRESS: A reference book on natural (non-drug) health field; a book on dream control for young adults.

SIDELIGHTS: Dian Buchman has interviewed over two hundred individuals for "Tomorrow's People" radio program. She enjoys travel and travel comments, and has been throughout Europe and much of the Far East. *Avocational interests:* Films.

* * *

BUCHMAN, Sidney 1902-1975

March 27, 1902—August 23, 1975; American playwright, film producer, and scenarist. Obituaries: *New York Times,* August 25, 1975.

* * *

BUCK, John Lossing 1890-1975

November 27, 1890—September 27, 1975; American religious missionary to China, educator, government advisor on agricultural economics, and writer on topics in his field. Obituaries: *New York Times,* September 29, 1975. (See index for previous *CA* sketch)

* * *

BUCKLEY, James Lane 1923-

PERSONAL: Born March 9, 1923, in New York, N.Y.; son of William Frank, Sr. (in foreign oil exploration) and Aloise (Steiner) Buckley; married Ann Frances Cooley, May 22, 1953; children: Peter Pierce, James Wiggin, Priscilla Langford, William Frank, David Lane, Andrew Thurston. *Education:* Yale University, B.A., 1943, LL.B., 1949. *Religion:* Roman Catholic. *Residence:* New York, N.Y.; and Washington, D.C. *Office:* U.S. Senate, 304 Russell Senate Building, Washington, D.C. 20510.

CAREER: Admitted to Connecticut Bar, 1949; Wiggin & Dana (attorneys), New Haven, Conn., associate, 1949-53; Catawba Corp. (family business), New York, N.Y., vice-president and member of board of directors, 1953-70; U.S. Senate, Washington, D.C., Republican senator from New York, 1971—, member of public works, commerce, and budget committees. *Military service:* U.S. Naval Reserve, active duty, 1943-46; served in the western Pacific; became lieutenant junior grade.

WRITINGS: If Men Were Angels, Putnam, 1975.

AVOCATIONAL INTERESTS: Natural history, classical music.

BIOGRAPHICAL/CRITICAL SOURCES: New York Post, September 18, 1968, November 7, 1970; *New York Times Magazine,* August 9, 1970, August 15, 1971; *New York Times,* November 5, 1970; *Newsweek,* November 16, 1970; *Life,* December 18, 1970.

* * *

BUCKNER, Sally Beaver 1931-

PERSONAL: Born in 1931, in Statesville, N.C.; daughter of Henry George and Foda (Stack) Beaver; married Robert Buckner (a recreation planner, North Carolina Department Natural and Economic Resources); children: Robert, Lynn, Ted. *Education:* University of North Carolina, A.B. (magna cum laude), 1953, Ph.D. candidate, 1976; North Carolina State University, M.A., 1970. *Home:* 3231 Birnamwood Rd., Raleigh, N.C. 27607. *Office:* Department of English, Peace College, Raleigh, N.C. 27607.

CAREER: Writer (assignments and free-lance), Methodist Publishing House, 1959—. Peace College, Raleigh, N.C., teacher of creative writing, 1970—. *Member:* Press Womens' Association, Wake County Mental Health Association, Community Arts Council of Goldsboro, Phi Beta Kappa. *Awards, honors:* Honorable mention from Press Womens' Association, 1968, for feature series; award for poem, "Windhover," 1970.

WRITINGS—Plays: Encounter at the Corner, Westminster Press, 1966; "The Time That's Granted," produced at Peace College, 1972; "Everyperson," produced at Peace College, 1974. Author of commemorative dramas. Author of "Sunday Sketchbook," column in *Goldsboro News-Argus,* 1964-65. Contributor to religious periodicals, to literary magazines, including *Southern Poetry Review,* and to newspapers. Entertainment editor of *Raleigh Times,* 1967-68.

SIDELIGHTS: Sally Buckner is especially interested in working with emotionally disturbed, learning-disabled, or delinquent children and youth. She has taught poetry and playwriting in state and local writers-in-the-schools program, and has conducted poetry workshops at churches.

* * *

BULLARD, Oral 1922-

PERSONAL: Born January 24, 1922, in Vassar, Kan.; son of Elvin Lee and Lois Marcia (Howland) Bullard; married Suzanne Stapleford, February 16, 1946; children: Randall (Mrs. Timothy Sadler), Tracy (Mrs. Michael Tremblay), Eric Lee. *Politics:* Independent. *Religion:* "I believe in God." *Home:* 7375 101st Ave., Beaverton, Ore. 97005 *Office:* Touchstone Press, 10950 Southwest Fifth, Beaverton, Ore. 97005.

CAREER: Arcady Press, Portland, Ore., vice-president,

1956-64, president, 1964-66; Irwin-Hodson Co. (printers), Portland, Ore., vice-president, 1966-70; Touchstone Press, Beaverton, Ore., president and founder, 1965—. Honorary president, Oregon Printing Industry, 1965. *Military service:* 383rd AAA (AW) Bn., 1943-45; served in United States, Australia, New Guinea, Moluccas, and Philippines.

WRITINGS: Crisis on the Columbia, Touchstone, 1968; *Short Trips and Trails: The Columbia Gorge,* Touchstone, 1974. Contributor to magazines and newspapers.

WORK IN PROGRESS: Three novels and a nonfiction book.

AVOCATIONAL INTERESTS: Travel, conservation, the human potential movement.

* * *

BULLER, Herman 1923-

PERSONAL: Born April 30, 1923, in Montreal, Quebec, Canada; son of Joseph and Lily (Fruchter) Buller; married Adele Eve Gottlieb, June 11, 1946. *Education:* Sir George Williams University, B.A., 1943; McGill University, B.C.L., 1946; University of Toronto, B.Ed., 1970. *Religion:* Jewish. *Home:* 9 Kingsbridge Court, #401, Willowdale, Ontario, Canada.

CAREER: Teacher of English literature and creative writing and of economic history, for North York Board of Education and Toronto Board of Education. *Member:* Canadian Authors Association, Ontario Secondary School Teachers Federation. *Awards, honors:* Canadiana Award from Canada National Book Club, 1963, for *One Man Alone.*

WRITINGS: One Man Alone (novel; Canada National Book Club selection), Centennial Press, 1963; *Quebec in Revolt: The Guibord Affair,* Centennial Press, 1965; *The Revolt of the French Canadian Youth,* October Publications, 1966; *Days of Rage* (novel), October Publications, 1974. Contributor of stories to magazines and newspapers.

* * *

BUNTING, Bainbridge 1913-

PERSONAL: Born November 23, 1913, in Kansas City, Mo.; son of William Miller (a merchant) and Ernestine (Bainbridge) Bunting; married Doreien Feise, 1948; children: Emily, Meredith, Findlay. *Education:* University of Illinois, B.S., 1937; Harvard University, Ph.D., 1952. *Home:* 5021 Guadalupe Tr., Albuquerque, N.M. 87107. *Office:* Department of History, University of New Mexico, FAC, Albuquerque, N.M. 87131.

CAREER: University of New Mexico, Albuquerque, assistant professor, 1943-53, associate professor, 1953-60, professor of architectural history, 1960—. Director of survey of Cambridge architecture, Cambridge Historical Commission, Cambridge, Mass., summers, 1964-74; trustee, Museum of Albuquerque, 1969—; member of Old Town Architectural Review Board, Albuquerque, 1965-75. *Member:* Society of Architectural Historians (member of board of directors), Colonial Art Association of America.

WRITINGS: Taos Adobes, Museum of New Mexico, 1962; *Houses of Boston's Back Bay District,* Harvard University Press, 1967; *Historic Architecture in Cambridge: Old Cambridge,* Cambridge Historical Commission, 1973; *Of Earth and Timbers Built,* University of New Mexico Press, 1973.

WORK IN PROGRESS: History of Harvard University Architecture, completion expected in 1978; *History of New Mexican Architecture.*

* * *

BURCHARD, John Ely 1898-1975

December 8, 1898—December 25, 1975; American educator, historian, university administrator, architectural critic, head of wartime military-scientific conservation projects, and author of books on history, architecture, and other topics. Obituaries: *New York Times,* December 27, 1975; *AB Bookman's Weekly,* January 26, 1976; *Current Biography,* March, 1976. (See index for previous *CA* sketch)

* * *

BURDETTE, Franklin 1911-1975

December 7, 1911—August 8, 1975; American educator, political scientist, expert on legislation and local government, editor, and author of articles and books in his field. Obituaries: *Washington Post,* August 12, 1975.

* * *

BURGESS, Mary Wyche 1916-
(Em Burgess)

PERSONAL: Born November 6, 1916, in Greenville, S.C.; daughter of Cyril Granville (an attorney) and Mary (Wheeler) Wyche; married Alfred Franklin Burgess (an attorney), June 25, 1938; children: Mary Wyche (Mrs. Arthur Ervin Lesesne), Caroline (Mrs. Benjamin R. Ansbacher), A. Franklin, Jr., Granville Wyche, Victoria (Mrs. Anthony R. Pitman). *Education:* Randolph-Macon Woman's College, A.B., 1937; Furman University, M.A., 1970. *Politics:* Democrat. *Religion:* Episcopal. *Home:* 308 West Faris Rd., Greenville, S.C. 29605.

CAREER: Greenville Piedmont (daily newspaper), Greenville, S.C., city reporter, 1937-38; *Greenville News,* Greenville, part-time feature writer, 1941-43. *Member:* Phi Beta Kappa, Junior League (Greenville, S.C.), United Way, Girl Scouts of America, Family Service, Symphony Association, Civic Ballet.

WRITINGS: Women in Education, Dillon, 1975. Columnist for *Greer Citizen* (weekly newspaper), 1941-43. Contributor, *Jack and Jill, Sandlapper, South Carolina Magazine,* and religious publications.

WORK IN PROGRESS: Biographical sketches of blacks; a study of heroines of the Revolution; historical articles on South Carolinians; editing letters of a confederate soldier for South Carolina historical magazine; children's stories; short stories.

AVOCATIONAL INTERESTS: Music (violinist with Greenville Symphony for twenty-six years), vegetable gardening, tennis, politics.

* * *

BURK, Bruce 1917-

PERSONAL: Born January 7, 1917, near Juanita, N.D.; son of John L. and Florence A. (Horn) Burk; married Jacqueline M. McClanahan, February 16, 1951; children: Diane, Julie. *Education:* Attended Curtiss-Wright Technical Institute, University of Southern California, and University of California at Los Angeles. *Politics:* Conservative Republican. *Religion:* Lutheran. *Home:* Brewer Rd., Grass Valley, Calif.

CAREER: Hughes Aircraft Co., Culver City, Calif., design engineer, 1937-44, project engineer, 1944-49, director of flight operations, 1949-53; Summa Corporation (formerly Hughes Tool Co.), Culver City, director of flight operations of aircraft division, 1953-72, manager of flight support, 1972-76. Professional realistic bird carver, 1960—; professional bird photographer, 1971—.

WRITINGS: Game Bird Carving, Winchester Publishers, 1972; *Waterfowl Studies,* Winchester Publishers, 1976. Contributor to *Popular Science, Popular Mechanics, Illustrated Mechanix, Workbench, Decoy Collector's Guide,* and *North American Decoys.*

AVOCATIONAL INTERESTS: Painting, photography, woodworking, hunting, aviculture.

* * *

BURNAM, Tom 1913-

PERSONAL: Born October 2, 1913, in Swan Lake, Mont.; son of Clarence Miles and Ora (Bond) Burnam; married Phyllis Anderson (a social worker), March 29, 1940. *Education:* University of Idaho, B.A., 1936, M.A., 1937; University of Washington, Seattle, Ph.D., 1949. *Home:* 2765 South West Park Rd., Lake Oswego, Ore. 97034. *Office:* Department of English, Portland State University, Portland, Ore. 97201.

CAREER: University of Washington, Seattle, instructor in writing and literature, 1949-50; University of Northern Colorado, Greeley, assistant professor, 1950-53, associate professor, 1953-56, professor of English, 1956-63; Portland State University, Portland, Ore., professor of American literature and creative writing, 1963—. Visiting Fulbright professor, University of Helsinki, 1961; U.S. State Department lecturer, American-Scandinavian Seminar, Leangkollen, Norway, 1961. Ground School supervisor, Civil Aeronautics Administration, and instructor, B-29 school, during World War II. *Member:* American Association of University Professors, Modern Language Association of America (president, Rocky Mountain Modern Language Association, 1953-54), Philological Association of the Pacific Coast, Phi Beta Kappa.

WRITINGS: (Contributor) Arthur Mizner, editor, *F. Scott Fitzgerald: A Collection of Critical Essays,* Prentice-Hall, 1963; (contributor) Robert Cecil Pooley, editor, *Perspectives,* Scott, Foresman, 1968; (contributor) William Haney, editor, *Communication and Organizational Behavior,* 3rd edition, Irwin, 1973; *The Dictionary of Misinformation,* Crowell, 1975.

Work represented in anthologies, including: *They Found Adventure,* edited by Charles Carver and others, Prentice-Hall, 1960; *Moments of Decision,* edited by Olson, Scholastic Press, 1961; *Esquire's World of Humor,* Esquire and Harper, 1964; *An Introduction to Literature,* edited by Mary Rohrberger, Random House, 1968. Contributor to *Harper's, Saturday Review, Colorado Quarterly, Georgia Review, Argosy, The Reporter, College English, Empire, American Quarterly, Critic, Western Humanities Review, Esquire, Modern Fiction Studies,* and other periodicals. Member of editorial board, *Harvest* (magazine), 1974—.

WORK IN PROGRESS: A long short story; a scholarly article on Twain and Hemingway; a novel.

SIDELIGHTS: Burnam told *CA:* "I've written for about as long as I can remember; have been lucky enough to see some of it, at least, in print. My current interest in the things we know that just ain't so (to paraphrase Josh Billings) is of long standing, maybe because of my long association with Academe, in which misinformation flourishes as greenly as anywhere else. Maybe more so." *Avocational interests:* "I play golf very badly indeed; own some very expensive cameras and take indifferent pictures with them. . . ."

* * *

BURTON, Anthony 1933-

PERSONAL: Born November 13, 1933, in London, England; son of Arthur J. and Violet R. (Earle) Burton; married Bibiana Rocha, February 23, 1962; children: Jennifer Ann, Emily Francesca, Lawrence Anthony. *Education:* Shoreditch College, University of London, teacher's certificate, 1958; University of Saskatchewan, B.Ed., 1968; University of Alberta, M.Ed., 1970. *Home:* 5 Dubonnet Court, Dartmouth, Nova Scotia, Canada. *Office:* Department of Education, Dalhousie University, Halifax, Nova Scotia, Canada.

CAREER: University of Manitoba, Winnipeg, assistant professor, 1970-75; Dalhousie University, Halifax, Nova Scotia, associate professor of anthropology of education, 1975—. Anthropological consultant in Peru for Canadian International Development Agency, 1974-75. *Military service:* British Army. *Member:* International Studies Association, Canadian Association of University Teachers.

WRITINGS: The Horn and the Beanstalk: Problems and Possibilities in Canadian Education, Holt, 1972; *Options: Reforms and Alternatives for Canadian Education,* Holt, 1973.

WORK IN PROGRESS: A Materialist Anthropology of Education.

SIDELIGHTS: Burton writes: "My interest is . . . in an anthropological approach to educational phenomena, socialization, institutions, children, learning, cognitive development, etc."

* * *

BURTON, Dwight L(owell) 1922-

PERSONAL: Born August 9, 1922, in Stuntz, Minn.; married Edith Stone, March 17, 1949 (divorced, 1967); married Claudia Holland (a teacher), February 15, 1968; children: (first marriage) Barbara Kay, Christine Beryl. *Education:* University of Minnesota, B.S., 1943, M.A., 1947, Ph.D., 1951. *Politics:* Democrat. *Home:* 423 Vinnedge Ride, Tallahassee, Fla. 32303. *Office:* College of Education, Florida State University, 213 Education Building, Tallahassee, Fla. 32306.

CAREER: High school English teacher in Wisconsin, 1946-47; University of Minnesota, Minneapolis, English teacher in university high school, 1947-49, head of department, 1949-52; Florida State University, Tallahassee, assistant professor, 1952-54, associate professor, 1954-57, professor of English education, 1957-62, professor of English, 1965—, head of department of English education, 1962-73, associate dean of College of Education, 1965—. Field reader for U.S. Office of Education's Bureau of Research, 1965—. *Military service:* U.S. Army, 1943-46; became captain; received Purple Heart, Bronze Star, and Croix de Guerre.

MEMBER: National Council of Teachers of English (vice-president, 1966; distinguished lecturer, 1968; chairman of research foundation, 1969-72), Conference on English Education (chairman, 1962-64), National Conference on Research in English. *Awards, honors:* Distinguished service award from National Council of Teachers of English, 1968.

WRITINGS: Literature Study in the High Schools, Holt, 1959, 3rd edition, 1970; (with John S. Simmons) Teaching English in Today's High Schools, Holt, 1965, revised edition, 1970; (with John S. Simmons) Patterns of Literature, four volumes, Singer, 1967; (contributor) Helen Painter, editor, Reaching Children and Young People Through Literature, International Reading Association, 1971; (with Bryant K. Fillion, Kenneth H. Donelson, and Beverly Haley) Teaching English Today, Houghton, 1975. Contributor to English and education journals.

WORK IN PROGRESS: Research on the "response to literature."

SIDELIGHTS: Burton writes: "I am also interested in the sociology and psychology of leisure, and I speak on this topic. I think constructive use of leisure is a major problem of the nation."

*   *   *

BURTON, Robert E(dward) 1927-

PERSONAL: Surname legally changed, 1945; born February 16, 1927, in Detroit, Mich.; son of Edward Marcus and Grace (Burton) Povlitz; married Mary Kathryn Rutten (divorced, 1976); children: Nelson, Marjorie, Denise. Education: University of Michigan, B.S., 1948, A.M.L.S., 1956. Politics: Democrat. Religion: None. Home: 75-D Groton Dr., Williamsville, N.Y. 14221. Office: University Libraries, State University of New York at Buffalo, 304 Lockwood, Buffalo, N.Y. 14214.

CAREER: Statistician for Greater Detroit (Mich.) Hospital Survey Committee, 1948-49; real estate appraiser for City of Detroit, 1949-54; Union Carbide Corp., Linde Division, Speedway, Ind., librarian, 1956-59, Metals Research Laboratories, Niagara Falls, N.Y., librarian, 1959-62; University of Michigan, University Library, Ann Arbor, head of divisional libraries, 1962-75; State University of New York at Buffalo, assistant director for public services at University Libraries, 1975—. Member: Special Libraries Association, Bibliographical Society of America, American Rose Society, Bibliographic Society of the University of Virginia.

WRITINGS: (With Joanne Werger) Roses: A Bibliography, Scarecrow, 1972.

WORK IN PROGRESS: A book on geography and travel, Travels in Oceana, for Gale, completion expected in 1977; a book tentatively titled October Saturdays: Poems, 1964-1976.

*   *   *

BURTT, George 1914-

PERSONAL: Born May 18, 1914, in Vancouver, British Columbia, Canada; son of George Keyes (an accountant) and Josephine (a teacher; maiden name, Woolson) Burtt; married Dorothy Smith, September 23, 1937 (divorced, 1950); married Marian Zametkin (a scientific research worker and teacher), June 3, 1950; children: (first marriage) Gregory, Marcia (Mrs. Richard Challacombe), Jonathan, Portia (Mrs. Robert Jennings); (second marriage) Jennifer Ellen. Education: Attended public schools. Politics: Republican. Home: 7350 Hollywood Blvd., Los Angeles, Calif. 90046. Office: Vector Community Church, 6253 Hollywood Blvd., Los Angeles, Calif. 90028.

CAREER: Worked as ad layout man for newspapers in Washington, D.C., 1935-41; owner of The Ad Shop, Harrisonburg, Va., 1939-41; employed as art director, account executive, creative director at advertising agencies in Philadelphia, Washington, and Baltimore, 1944-48; advertising manager for Western Stove Co., Culver City, Calif., 1948-52; owner of George Burtt Advertising, Hollywood, Calif., 1952-59; creative director of Enyart & Rose Advertising Agency, Los Angeles, 1959-69; Vector Community Church, Hollywood, Calif., pastor, 1967—. Owner, Creative Service Office, 1969—. Member: International Mensa (area vice-chairman, 1966-67), Hollywood Radio and Television Society (honorary life member; managing director, 1952-59).

WRITINGS: Vector Handbook, Adams Press, 1967; Putting Yourself Across with the Art of Graphic Persuasion, Parker & Son, 1972; Psychographics in Personal Growth (monograph), Vector Counseling Institute, 1972; Stop Crying at Your Own Movies, Nelson-Hall, 1975.

WORK IN PROGRESS: The Explicated Tao, in calligraphic manuscript with personal annotations; The Practical Jesus, a commentary on the words of Jesus as applied to daily life; Vector Training Manual, a systematic exposition of how the Vector system of counseling works.

SIDELIGHTS: Burtt is the creator of a "system of viewing human nature which makes it possible by conversation or self-examination to eliminate unwanted behavior patterns. This is a highly effective counseling modality; but more important, as a life-growth adjunct it helps keep from creating new problems the equivalent of the old ones."

*   *   *

BUSCH, Francis X(avier) 1879-1975

May 9, 1879—November 28, 1975; American trial lawyer, corporation counsel, educator, and author of books on famous criminal trials. Obituaries: New York Times, November 29, 1975. (CAP-1; earlier sketch in CA-13/14)

*   *   *

BUSTEED, Marilyn 1937-

PERSONAL: Born July 23, 1937, in Nebraska; daughter of Guy A. (a farmer) and Mertie (Mardis) Roberts; married Richard Busteed (in real estate), August 15, 1956; children: Patrick, Mitchell, Scott. Education: University of Colorado, student, 1968; Colorado State University, B.S., 1975. Home: 4675 Venturi, Fort Collins, Colo. 80521.

CAREER: Writer. Member: Phi Kappa Gamma.

WRITINGS: Phases of the Moon (nonfiction), Shambhala, 1974.

SIDELIGHTS: Marilyn Busteed's current interest are astrological research, and a coordination of this research with psychology.

*   *   *

BUTCHER, Russell Devereux 1938-

PERSONAL: Born February 8, 1938, in Bryn Mawr, Pa.; son of Devereux (an author) and Mary Frances (Taft) Butcher; married Carol Lynne Dunn, February 1, 1958 (divorced March, 1967); married Pamela Richards (a manuscript editor), April 12, 1967; children: (first marriage) Pamela Marie, Neill D.; (second marriage) Wendy Nan. Education: University of Colorado, B.A., 1960; University of Michigan, graduate study of law, 1960, 1961. Home and office address: Seal Harbor, Maine 04675.

CAREER: Sierra Club, San Francisco, Calif., research editor for several exhibit format books, 1961-65; Save-the-

Redwoods League, San Francisco, publicity writer, 1963-65; National Audubon Society, New York, N.Y., conservation specialist and publicity writer, 1965-66; Museum of New Mexico, Santa Fe, chief of public relations and publications, 1967-69; free-lance author, editor, photographer, and public relations representative, 1970—. *Member:* Save-the-Redwoods League (life member), Sierra Club (life member).

WRITINGS: Maine Paradise: Mount Desert Island and Acadia National Park, Viking, 1973; *New Mexico: Gift of the Earth,* Viking, 1975; *The Desert,* Viking, 1976. Contributor to environmental magazines, to *Down East,* and to *New York Times.*

SIDELIGHTS: Butcher writes: "Travel, geography, and natural history are my main interests, with protection of the environment an underlying motivation. All my articles and books at least 'soft-sell' the need to conserve the environment, and many of my articles and editorials focus exclusively on some particular conservation problem. I have traveled throughout the U.S. and to the parks and nature reserves of the Alps region of Europe. Also . . . Canada, the West Indies, and Mexico." Butcher's books are illustrated with his own and others' photographs and drawings. *Avocational interests:* Hiking, canoeing, bird-watching, identification of wildflowers and all forms of plant life.

* * *

BUTLER, Robert Albert 1934-

PERSONAL: Born July 1, 1934, in Thomaston, Ga.; son of Reginald Alton (a textile engineer) and Martha (a musician; maiden name, Smith) Butler; married Alicia Suarez (a Spanish teacher), July 18, 1964; children: Martha Rose, Anthony Alfredo. *Education:* University of North Carolina, Chapel Hill, A.B., 1958, M.A.T., 1966; Duke University, M.A.T., 1961. *Religion:* Methodist. *Home:* 205 Beechwood Drive, Louisburg, N.C. 27549. *Office:* Department of Sociology, Louisburg College, Louisburg, N.C. 27549.

CAREER: Louisburg College, Louisburg, N.C., professor of sociology, 1962—. *Military service:* U.S. Army, 1952-54. *Member:* North Carolina Council for Albert Schweitzer International Prizes, Kappa Delta Pi, Beta Phi Gamma, Alpha Tau Omega.

WRITINGS: Sociology: An Individualized Course, Westinghouse Learning Press, 1971, revised edition, 1975.

SIDELIGHTS: Robert Butler has traveled extensively in Europe and South America. *Avocational Interests:* Classical music, sports, senior citizens, travel.

* * *

BUTTRICK, George Arthur 1892-

PERSONAL: Born March 23, 1892, in Seaham Harbour, Northumberland, England; son of Tom and Jessie (Lambert) Buttrick; married Agnes Gardner, June 27, 1916; children: John Arthur, George Robert, David Gardner. *Education:* Graduate of Lancaster Independent Theological Seminary and Victoria University of Manchester, both 1915. *Home:* 2500 Glenmay Ave., Apt. 304, Louisville, Ky. 40204.

CAREER: Ordained minister of Congregational Church, 1915; pastor in Quincey, Ill., 1915-18, Rutland, Vt., 1919-21, Buffalo, N.Y., 1921-27, and New York City, 1927-54; Harvard University, Cambridge, Mass., preacher and Plummer Professor of Christian Morals, 1954-60, professor

emeritus, 1960—, William Belden Noble lecturer, 1962. Harry Emerson Fosdick visiting professor, Union Theological Seminary (New York City), 1960-61; visiting professor, Garrett Theological Seminary, Northwestern University, 1961-70, Chicago Theological Seminary, 1962, Union Theological Seminary (Richmond, Va.), 1963, Agnes Scott College, 1965, Vanderbilt University Divinity School, 1970-71; James Cook lecturer in various foreign countries, 1951-52; visiting lecturer, Scripps College, 1966, Southern California School of Theology, 1966, Davidson College, 1970, Louisville Presbyterian Theological Seminary, 1972—, and Southern Baptist Theological Seminary, 1972—. President of National Council of Churches of Christ in America, 1939-41. *Member:* American Academy of Arts and Sciences. *Awards, honors:* D.D., Hamilton College, 1927, Middlebury College, 1930, Princeton University, 1940, Harvard University, 1960, Grinnell College, 1963, Bucknell University, 1965; S.T.D., Yale University, 1932, Miami University, 1934, Columbia University, 1944; LL.D., Bethany College, 1940, Davidson College, 1970; Litt.D., Albright College, 1940, Northwestern University, 1963; Guttenberg award, Chicago Bible Society, 1966; L.H.D., College of Wooster, 1967.

WRITINGS: The Parables of Jesus, Doubleday, 1928; *Jesus Came Preaching: Christian Preaching in the New Age,* Scribner, 1931; *The Christian Fact and Modern Doubt: A Preface to a Restatement of Christian Faith,* Scribner, 1934. *Prayer,* Abingdon-Cokesbury Press, 1942; *Christ and Man's Dilemma,* Abingdon-Cokesbury Press, 1946; *So We Believe, So We Pray,* Abingdon-Cokesbury Press, 1951; *Faith and Education,* Abingdon-Cokesbury Press, 1952; *Sermons Preached in a University Church,* Abingdon, 1959. *Biblical Thought and the Secular University,* Louisiana State University Press, 1960; *Christ and History,* Abingdon, 1963; *God, Pain, and Evil,* Abingdon, 1966; *The Beatitudes: A Contemporary Meditation,* Abingdon, 1968; *The Power of Prayer Today,* World Publishing, 1970; (with A. R. Kretzmann and Caryl Micklen) *Prayers for Special Seasons,* Cathedral, 1970.

General editor: (And contributor) *The Interpreter's Bible: The Holy Scriptures in the King James and Revised Standard Versions with General Articles and Introduction, Exegesis, Exposition for Each Book of the Bible,* twelve volumes, Abingdon-Cokesbury Press, 1951-57; *The Interpreter's Dictionary of the Bible: An Illustrated Encyclopedia Identifying and Explaining All Proper Names and Significant Terms and Subjects in the Holy Scriptures, including the Apocrypha, with Attention to Archaeological Discoveries and Researches into the Life and Faith of Ancient Times,* four volumes, Abingdon, 1962.

WORK IN PROGRESS: A book tentatively titled *Preaching Today.*

* * *

BYE, Beryl (Joyce Rayment) 1926-

PERSONAL: Born August 4, 1926, in Maidavale, England; daughter of Leonard and Olive (Stanbridge) Cotterell; married Denis Robert Bye (a civil service executive), August 9, 1945; children: Roger, Susan, Catherine, Andrew. *Education:* Wolsey Hall, Oxford, external study, 1967-68. *Religion:* Church of England. *Home:* 3 Battledown Approach, Cheltenham, Gloucestershire, England.

CAREER: Free-lance writer, 1960—.

WRITINGS: Three's Company, Scripture Union, 1961; *Wharf Street,* Kingfisher Books, 1962; *Prayers at Break-*

fast, Lutterworth, 1964; *A Christian's Guide to Teaching Our Children the Christian Faith*, Hodder & Stoughton, 1965, Moody, 1966; *Please God*, Church Pastoral Aid Society, 1966; *About God*, Church Pastoral Aid Society, 1967; *Nobody's Pony*, Lutterworth, 1967; *Looking into Life*, Lutterworth, 1967; *Jesus Said: Parables and Prayers for Children*, Church Pastoral Aid Society, 1968; *Pony for Sale*, Lutterworth, 1969; *Learning from Life*, Lutterworth, 1969; *Jesus at Work*, Church Pastoral Aid Society, 1969.

Start the Day Well, Lutterworth, 1970; *Beryl Bye's Prayers for All Seasons for Women's Meetings*, Lutterworth, 1971; *People Like Us*, Church Pastoral Aid Society, 1971; *More People Like Us*, Church Pastoral Aid Society, 1972; *To Be Continued*, Church Pastoral Aid Society, 1972; *Belle's Bridle*, Lutterworth, 1973; *Following Jesus*, Church Pastoral Aid Society, 1974; *Family Prayers*, Scripture Union, 1975.

SIDELIGHTS: Beryl Bye told *CA:* "I write from a compulsion to share my views—not always religious ones, and a desire to make people laugh at themselves, and see above and beyond the present materialistic age." *Avocational interests:* Riding, walking, swimming, and conservation.

*   *   *

BYWATER, William G(len), Jr.   1940-

PERSONAL: Born February 15, 1940, in Detroit, Mich.; son of William Glen (a research chemist) and Elma (Miller) Bywater; married Anne Philbin (a professor and artist), June 22, 1966; children: Patrick, Duncan. *Education:* Lehigh University, B.A., 1962; University of Michigan, M.A., 1966, Ph.D., 1966. *Religion:* Unitarian. *Office:* Department of Philosophy, Allegheny College, Meadville, Pa. 16335.

CAREER: Allegheny College, Meadville, Pa., instructor, 1967-70, assistant professor, 1970-74, associate professor of philosophy, 1974—. *Member:* American Society for Aesthetics, American Philosophical Association, Rhetoric Society of America.

WRITINGS: Clive Bell's Eye, Wayne State University Press, 1975. Contributor to journals in his field.

WORK IN PROGRESS: The Commitment to Androgyny.

SIDELIGHTS: William Bywater told *CA:* "As the spouse of a woman who has an active career as an artist, I am caught up in the question of liberation of women and men. My work on androgyny reflects this aspect of my life as well as what I have come to understand as the nature of philosophy."

*   *   *

CAIRD, George Bradford   1917-

PERSONAL: Born July, 9, 1917, in London, England; son of George and Esther Love (Bradford) Caird; married Viola Mary Newport, 1945; children: James Bradford, John Newport, George Overington, Margaret Alison. *Education:* Peterhouse, Cambridge, M.A., 1959; Mansfield College, Oxford, D.Phil., 1944. *Home:* Principal's Lodgings, Mansfield College, Oxford, England.

CAREER: Highgate Congregational Church, London, minister, 1943-46; St. Stephen's College, Edmonton, Alberta, professor of Old Testament language and literature, 1946-50; McGill University, Montreal, Quebec, professor of New Testament language and literature, 1950-59; United Theological College, Montreal, Quebec, principal, 1955-59; Mansfield College, Oxford, senior tutor, 1959-70, principal,

1970-77, Dean Ireland's Professor of Exegesis of Holy Scripture, 1977—, university reader in Biblical studies, 1969. Grinfield Lecturer on the Septuagint at Oxford University, 1961-65. Official observer at Vatican Council, 1962-65; moderator of general assembly of United Reformed Church, 1975-76. *Awards, Honors:* D.D. from St. Stephen's College, Edmonton, 1959, Diocesan College, Montreal, 1959, Mansfield College, Oxford, 1966, University of Aberdeen, 1966; fellow of British Academy, 1973.

WRITINGS: The Truth of the Gospel, Oxford University Press, 1950; (editor with G. W. Briggs and N. Micklem) *The Shorter Oxford Bible*, Oxford University Press, 1951; *The Apostolic Age*, Duckworth, 1955; *Principalities and Powers: A Study in Pauline Theology*, Clarendon Press, 1956; *Making It Visible*, British Council of Churches, 1962; (author of commentary) *The Gospel of St. Luke*, Black, 1963, Penguin, 1964, new edition, Seabury Press, 1968; (with David E. Jenkins) *Jesus and God*, Faith Press, 1965; *Jesus and the Jewish Nation*, Athlone Press, 1965; *A Commentary on the Revelation of St. John the Divine*, Harper, 1966; *Our Dialogue with Rome: The Second Vatican Council and After*, Oxford University Press, 1967; (editor) William H. Cadman, *The Open Heaven: The Revelation of God in the Johannine Sayings of Jesus*, Basil Blackwell, 1969; (with others) *The Christian Hope*, S.P.C.K., 1970; *Paul's Letters from Prison*, Oxford University Press, 1976. Contributor to *Interpreter's Dictionary of the Bible*, 1963, and *Hastings One Volume Dictionary of the Bible*. Contributor of numerous articles to journals, including *Canadian Journal of Theology, Expository Times, Journal of Theological Studies*, and *New Testament Studies*. Member of Apochrypha translation panel for *New English Bible*, 1961-66.

AVOCATIONAL INTERESTS: Bird-watching, chess, music.

*   *   *

CAIRNCROSS, Alexander Kirkland   1911-
(Alec Cairncross)

PERSONAL: Born February 11, 1911, in Lesmahagow, Scotland; son of Alexander Kirkland and Elizabeth Andrew (Wishart) Cairncross; married Mary Frances Glynn, May 29, 1943; children: Frances Anne, Philip Wishart, Alexander Messent, David John, Elizabeth Mary. *Education:* University of Glasgow, M.A., 1933; Trinity College, Cambridge, Ph.D., 1936. *Home:* Master's Lodgings, St. Peter's College, Oxford University, Oxford, England.

CAREER: University of Glasgow, Glasgow, Scotland, lecturer in political economy, 1935-39; West of Scotland Agricultural College, Ayr, lecturer in agricultural economics, 1935-39; War Cabinet Office, London, England, staff member of economic section, 1939-41; administrative assistant of Board of Trade, 1941; Ministry of Aircraft Production, London, staff member of directorate of programs and planning, 1941-45; *Economist*, London, staff member, 1946; economic adviser to Board of Trade, 1946-49; Organization for European Economic Cooperation, Paris, France, director of Economic Division, 1949-50; University of Glasgow, professor of applied economics, and director of department of social and economic research, 1951-61; British Government, London, economic adviser, 1961-64, head of Economic Service, 1964-69; Oxford University, Oxford, England, master of St. Peter's College, 1969—. Director of Economic Development Institute (Washington, D.C.), 1955-56; member of court of governors of London

School of Economics and Political Science (of University of London); chancellor of University of Glasgow, 1972. Advisory committee chairman to Houblon-Norman Trustees; director of Ailsa and Alva Investment Trusts, 1959-61; trustee of Urwick Orr & Partners, 1970; president of Girls' Public Day School Trust, 1972—. Head of economic advisory panel, British Element, Control Commission for Germany, Berlin, 1945-46; member of Wool Working Party, 1946.

MEMBER: Royal Economic Society (president, 1968-70; vice-president, 1970—), National Institute of Social and Economic Research (member of council of management), British Association for the Advancement of Science (section F president, 1969; president, 1970-71), British Academy (fellow), American Academy of Arts and Sciences (foreign honorary member), Scottish Economic Society (president, 1969-73; vice-president, 1973—), United Oxford and Cambridge University Club. *Awards, honors:* Order of St. Michael and St. George, 1950, named knight commander, 1966; honorary degrees include LL.D. from Mount Allison University, 1962, University of Glasgow, 1966, and University of Exeter, 1969; D.Litt. from University of Reading, 1968, and Heriot Watt University, 1969; D.Sc. from University of Wales, 1971, and Queen's University, Belfast, 1972; D.Univ. from Stirling University, 1973.

WRITINGS—All under name Alec Cairncross: *Introduction to Economics,* Butterworth, 1944, 5th edition, 1973; *Home and Foreign Investment, 1870-1913: Studies in Capital Accumulation,* Cambridge University Press, 1953, Kelley, 1974; (editor) *The Scottish Economy: A Statistical Account of Scottish Life by Members of the Staff of Glasgow University,* Cambridge University Press, 1954; *Some Problems of Economic Planning,* Foreign Trade Research Institute, 1957; *The International Bank for Reconstruction and Development,* International Finance Section, Department of Economics and Sociology, Princeton University, 1959.

Monetary Policy in a Mixed Economy, Almqvist & Wiksell, 1960; *Economic Development and the Atlantic Provinces,* Atlantic Provinces Research Board, 1961; *Factors in Economic Development,* Praeger, 1962, Beekman, 1972; *The Short Term and the Long in Economic Planning,* Economic Development Institute (Washington, D.C.), 1966; (editor) *The Managed Economy,* British Association for the Advancement of Science, 1969, Barnes & Noble, 1970.

(Editor) *Papers on Planning and Economic Management,* Manchester University Press, 1970; (editor) *Britain's Economic Prospects Reconsidered,* Allen & Unwin, 1971, State University of New York Press, 1972; *Essays in Economic Management,* Allen & Unwin, 1971, State University of New York Press, 1972; (contributor) G.D.N. Wojswick, editor, *Uses of Economics,* Barnes & Noble, 1972; *Learning to Learn,* University of Glasgow Press, 1972; *Control of Long-Term Investments: A Staff Paper,* Brookings Institution, 1973; *Control Over International Capital Movements,* University of Reading, 1973; (editor with others, and contributor) *Economic Policy for the European Community,* Macmillan, 1974, Holmes & Meier, 1975; *Inflation, Growth, and International Finance,* Allen & Unwin, 1975; (editor with Mohindes Puri) *H. W. Singer: The Strategy of International Development,* Macmillan, 1975; (editor with Puri) *Employment, Income Distribution, and Development Strategy: Essays in Honor of H. W. Singer,* Macmillan, 1976.

Co-author of script for phonotape, "The British Economy," Holt Information Systems, 1972. General editor of "Social and Economic Studies" series, Department of Social and Economic Research, University of Glasgow, 1953-61. Editor, *Scottish Journal of Political Economy,* 1954-61.

AVOCATIONAL INTERESTS: Color photography, travel.

* * *

CAIRNS, David 1904-

PERSONAL: Born June 11, 1904, in Ayton, Berwickshire, Scotland; son of David S. (a minister) and Helen Wilson Cairns; married Rosemary Russell, 1947; children: Elizabeth Mary, John Alexander. *Education:* Balliol College, Oxford, B.A., 1928, M.A., 1938; studied at University of Aberdeen, 1928-31; University of Zurich, 1932-33; University of Montpelier, 1933-34. *Home:* 29 Viewfield Gardens, Aberdeen ABl 7xN, Scotland.

CAREER: Ordained minister of Church of Scotland, 1935. Bridge of Allan, Scotland, minister, 1935-40; Oxford University, Oxford, England, secretary of Student Christian Movement, 1945-47; Christ's College, Aberdeen, Scotland, professor of practical theology, 1948-72, professor emeritus, 1972—. Kerr lecturer, University of Glasgow, 1948; visiting professor, Columbia Seminary, Decatur, Ga., 1961; Cunningham lecturer, University of Edinburgh, 1965; reader in systematic theology, University of Aberdeen, 1965-72. Member of Faith and Order Commission, World Council of Churches, 1958-68. *Military service:* British Army, 1940-45; chaplain. *Awards, honor:* D.D., University of Edinburgh, 1953.

WRITINGS: *The Image of God in Man,* Philosophical Library, 1953 revised and enlarged edition, Fontana Press, 1973; *A Gospel Without Myth? Bultmann's Challenge to the Preacher,* S.C.M. Press, 1960; *In Remembrance of Me: Aspects of the Lord's Supper,* Bles, 1967; *God Up There? A Study in Divine Transcendance,* Westminster Press, 1968; (editor) *Worship Now: A Collection of Services and Prayers for Public Worship,* Saint Andrew Press, 1972.

Translator from the German: Paul Althaus, *The So-Called Kerygma and the Historical Jesus,* Oliver & Boyd, 1959; Joachim Jeremias, *Infant Baptism in the First Four Centuries,* S.C.M. Press, 1960; (with A. W. Loos) Heinrich Emil Brunner, *Truth as Encounter,* S.C.M. Press, 1964; Helmut Gollwitzer, *Rich Christian and Poor Lazarus,* Macmillan, 1970. Also translator of numerous other works, including Emil Brunner's *God and Man in 1436,* and Brunner's *Dogmatics,* Volume III, as well as *The Christian Faith and the Marxist Criticism of Religion.* Contributor of articles to *Scottish Journal of Theology,* and other periodicals.

WORK IN PROGRESS: Studying the relation of faith to history; preparing, possibly for publication, an unpublished work by his father, the late Principal David S. Cairns.

AVOCATIONAL INTERESTS: Painting.

* * *

CALDER-MARSHALL, Arthur 1908-

PERSONAL: Some sources index surname as Marshall; born August 19, 1908, in Wallington, Surrey, England; son of Arthur Grotjan and Alice (Poole) Calder-Marshall; married Violet Nancy Sales, 1934; children: two daughters. *Education:* Hertford College, Oxford, B.A., 1930. *Agent:* Elaine Greene Ltd., 31 Newington Green, London N16 9PW, England.

CAREER: Denstone College, Staffordshire, England, schoolmaster, 1931-33; author, biographer, and critic, 1933—. Scriptwriter for Metro-Goldwyn-Mayer in Hollywood, Calif., 1937. *Wartime service:* British Petroleum Warfare Department, 1941; British Ministry of Information, films division, 1942-45. *Member:* Royal Society of Literature (fellow), Savile Club, National Liberal Club.

WRITINGS—Adult fiction; all novels, except as noted: *About Levy,* J. Cape, 1933, Scribner, 1934; *Two of a Kind,* J. Cape, 1933; *A Crime Against Cania* (short stories), Golden Cockerel Press, 1934; *At Sea,* Scribner, 1934; *Dead Centre,* J. Cape, 1935; *A Pink Doll* (short stories), Grayson Books, 1935; *Pie in the Sky,* Scribner, 1937; *A Date with a Duchess and Other Stories,* J. Cape, 1937; *The Way to Santiago,* Reynal & Hitchcock, 1940; *A Man Reprieved,* J. Cape, 1949; *Occasion of Glory,* J. Cape, 1955; *The Scarlet Boy,* Hart-Davis, 1961, Harper, 1962; *Season of Goodwill* (play based on novel *Every Third Thought,* by Dorothea Malm), French, 1965.

Nonfiction: (With Edward J. H. O'Brien and J. Davenport) *The Guest Book,* Arthur Barker, 1935, Frederick Stokes, 1936; *Challenge to Schools: A Pamphlet on Public School Education,* Hogarth Press, 1935; *The Changing Scene* (essays on English society), Chapman & Hall, 1937; (with others) *Writing in Revolt: Theory and Examples,* Fact, 1937; *The Book Front,* Bodley Head, 1947; (editor and author of introduction) *Tobias Smollet,* Falcon Press, 1950; *The Magic of My Youth* (autobiography), Hart-Davis, 1951; *No Earthly Command* (biography of Alexander Riall Wadham Woods), Hart-Davis, 1957; *Havelock Ellis: A Biography,* Hart-Davis, 1959, published as *The Sage of Sex: A Life of Havelock Ellis,* Putnam, 1960.

The Enthusiast (biography of Joseph Leycester Lyne), Faber, 1962; (editor) *The Bodley Head Jack London,* four volumes, Bodley Head, 1963-66; *The Innocent Eye* (biography of Robert Flaherty), W. H. Allen, 1963, Harcourt, 1966; *Wish You Were Here: The Art of Donald McGill,* Hutchinson, 1966; (editor and author of introduction) *Prepare to Shed Them Now: The Ballads of George R. Sims,* Hutchinson, 1968; (editor and author of introduction) Thomas Paine, *The Rights of Man and Other Writings,* Heron Books, 1970; *Lewd, Blasphemous, and Obscene: Being the Trials and Tribulations of Sundry Founding Fathers of Today's Alternative Societies,* Hutchinson, 1972.

Travel: *Glory Dead* (Trinidad), M. Joseph, 1939; *The Watershed* (Yugoslavia), Contact Publications, 1947.

Children's books: *The Man from Devil's Island,* Hart-Davis, 1958; *The Fair to Middling: A Mystery,* Hart-Davis, 1959; *Lone Wolf: The Story of Jack London,* Methuen, 1961, Duell, Sloan & Pearce, 1962.

Also author of screenplay, "The World Is Rich," 1946, and many documentary filmscripts.*

*　　　*　　　*

CALDWELL, Inga Gilson   1897-

PERSONAL: Born January 11, 1897; daughter of Gilbert C. (a farmer) and Martha (Anderson) Gilson; married Roy Lea Caldwell (a mechanic and farmer), June 25, 1931 (died, 1973); children: Keith. *Education:* Attended Oshkosh State Teacher's College (now University of Wisconsin), 1924-25. *Politics:* Republican. *Religion:* Lutheran. *Address:* R.F.D. 4, Waupaca, Wis. 54981.

CAREER: Elementary school teacher in public schools in

Wisconsin, 1916-63. *Member:* National Federation of State Poetry Societies, Wisconsin Regional Writers (charter member; member of advisory board, 1949-54), Wisconsin Fellowship of Poets (charter member; membership and credentials chairman, 1965-72), Central Wisconsin Circuit (vice-president, 1950-54).

AWARDS, HONORS: Jade ring award from Wisconsin Regional Writers Association, 1950; Wisconsin Fellowship of Poets first place winner, 1965, 1966, 1969, 1974, 1975; Eulalie McCloy Sonnet Award from National Federation of State Poetry Societies, 1969; Nancy Hanks Lincoln Trilogy award, 1970; West Virginia Poetry Society award, 1971; Virginia MacIntyre award, 1972; Kate Heune Memorial Award, 1973; Sarah Curtis Memorial Award, 1974; Poetry Laureate of Louisiana award, 1975.

WRITINGS—All poems: *Still Waters,* Bruce Humphries, 1950; *Giants in My Valley,* Douglas-West, 1972; *Jonquils in December,* Douglas-West, 1974. Contributor of poems to *American Poet, Countryman, Kaleidograph, Creative Wisconsin, Poetry Dial, American Haiku, Haiku West, Haiku Highlights and Other Short Poems, Driftwind, Jeans Journal, Ideals, Prairie Wings, Minneapolis Argus, View,* anthologies, *Northern Springs, Cats Magazine, Wisconsin Harvest, New Poetry Out of Wisconsin,* and *Wisconsin History in Poetry.* Poetry editor of *Creative Wisconsin,* 1954-56.

SIDELIGHTS: Inga Gilson Caldwell told *CA:* "Before my husband died we visited every state west of the Mississippi, and I have traveled in the East as well as to Europe. I still live on the century-old farm which my great-grandfather purchased from the government one hundred fifteen years ago. He chose these one-hundred-eighty acres for nostalgic reasons, surely, because the terrain is so much like his native Norway: beautiful with a high hill, stream, and well-wooded, also with huge rocks to test anyone's skill at farming."

*　　　*　　　*

CALLCOTT, Margaret Law   1929-

PERSONAL: Born August 25, 1929, in Atlanta, Ga.; daughter of Fleming (an insurance executive) and Margaret (Rogers) Law; married George H. Callcott (a professor of history), August 18, 1959; children: W. Hardy, Stephen Law. *Education:* University of North Carolina, A.B., 1950, Ph.D., 1967; Emory University, M.A., 1954. *Home:* 4311 Clagett Rd., Hyattsville, Md. 20782.

CAREER: Writer.

WRITINGS: The Negro in Maryland Politics, Johns Hopkins Press, 1969.

*　　　*　　　*

CALNE, Roy Yorke   1930-

PERSONAL: Born December 30, 1930, in London, England; son of Joseph Robert and Eileen (Gubbay) Calne; married Patricia Doreen Whelan, March 2, 1956; children: Jane, Sarah, Deborah, Suzanne, Russell, Richard. *Education:* Guys Hospital Medical School, London, England, M.B., B.S. (with honors, distinction in medicine), 1953. *Home:* 22 Barrow Road, Cambridge, England. *Office:* Department of Surgery, Cambridge University, Cambridge, England.

CAREER: House appointments at Guys Hospital, London, England, 1953-54; Oxford University, Oxford, England, departmental anatomy demonstrator, 1957-58; Royal

Free Hospital, London, surgical registrar, 1958-60; Peter Bent Brigham Hospital, Harvard Medical School, Cambridge, Mass., Harkness fellow in surgery, 1960-61; St. Mary's Hospital, London, lecturer in surgery, 1961-62; Westminster Hospital, Westminster, England, senior lecturer and consulting surgeon, 1962-65; Cambridge University, Cambridge, England, professor of surgery, 1965—. Trinity Hall, Cambridge University, fellow, 1965—; Addenbrooke's Hospital, Cambridge, England, honorary consulting surgeon, 1965—. Member of Court of Examiners of Royal College of Surgeons, 1970—. *Military service:* Royal Army Medical Corps, 1954-56. *Member:* Royal Society (fellow), Association of Surgeons of Great Britain (fellow), Surgical Research Society. *Awards, honors:* Royal College of Surgeons Hallett prize, 1957; Jacksonian prize, 1961; Cecil Joll prize, 1966; International Society of Surgery prize, 1969; honorary degrees from Cambridge University and University of London.

WRITINGS: Renal Transplantation, Edward Arnold, 1963, new edition, 1967; (with Harold Ellis) *Lecture Notes on General Surgery,* F. A. Davis, 1965, 4th edition, Blackwell Scientific Publications, 1972; *Homo- and Heterotransplantation,* Year Book Medical Publishers, 1966; *A Gift of Life: Observations on Organ Transplantation,* Basic Books, 1970, *Clinical Organ Transplantation,* Blackwell Scientific Publications, 1971; *Organ Grafts,* Edward Arnold, 1975.

AVOCATIONAL INTEREST: Tennis, squash.

*   *   *

CAMARA, Helder Pessoa 1909-
(Dom Helder)

PERSONAL: Born February 7, 1909, in Fortaleza, Ceara, Brazil; son of Joao Eduardo Torres and Adelaide (Rodrigues Pessoa) Camara Filho. *Education:* Educated in Roman Catholic seminaries in Brazil. *Office:* Office of the Archbishop of Recife and Olinda, Avenida Rui Barbosa, Recife, Estado de Pernambuco, Brazil.

CAREER: Ordained Roman Catholic priest, 1931; priest in Fortaleza, Brazil, 1931-36; priest in Rio de Janeiro, Brazil, 1936-52; consecrated bishop, 1952; titular bishop of Salde, Brazil, and auxiliary bishop of Rio de Janeiro, 1952-55; titular archbishop of Salde and auxiliary archbishop of Rio de Janiero, 1955-64; archbishop of Olinda and Recife, Pernambuco, Brazil, 1964—. Organized the Brazilian National Conference of Bishops; co-operated in organization of Council of Bishops of Latin America (CELAM). Member of Conselho Consultivo Internacional da Fundacao do Homen, Scientific Council of Sipri (Stockholm), L'Organisation Internationale Justice et Developpement, and Vienna Institute for Development. *Awards, honors:* Rene Sande Award, 1962; Via International Peace Prize (Italy), 1970; Martin Luther King Memorial Award, 1970; John XXIII Memorial Award from Pax Christi, Spain, 1970; People's Peace Prize, Norway, 1973; Nobel Peace Prize nominee; honorary degrees from colleges and universities, including Harvard University, St. Louis University, University of Louvain, University of Fribourg, University of Paris, and University of Cincinnati.

WRITINGS: (With J. J. Rossi) *Iglesia y desarrola,* Ediciones Busqueda (Buenos Aires), 1966; *Terzo mondo defraudato,* Editrice Missionaria Italiana, 1968, translation from the Italian by William McSweeney published as *The Church and Colonialism: The Betrayal of the Third World,* Dimension Books, 1969; *Revolucao dentro da paz,* Editoria

Sabia, 1968, translation from the Portuguese by Amparo McLean published as *Revolution through Peace,* Harper, 1971; (contributor) *El manifiesto de los obispos del tercer mundo: Una respuesta al clamor de los pobres,* Ediciones Busqueda, 1968; *A universidade e a integracao nacional,* Fundacao Universidade Regional do Nordeste, 1968; *La rebelion de los economistas,* Zero (Spain), 1969.

Spirale de violence, Desclee, DeBrouwer (Paris), 1970, translation from the French by Della Couling published as *Spiral of Violence,* Dimension Books, 1971; *Pobreza, abundancia y solidaridad,* Zero, 1970; *La iglesia en el desarrollo de America Latin,* Zero, 1970; *Une journee avec don Helder Camara,* Desclee, De Brouwer, 1970; *Pour arriver a temps,* Desclee, De Brouwer, 1970, translation from the French by Couling published as *Race against Time,* Sheed, 1971; (author of foreword) Ulrich Stockmann, *Umsturz durch die Gewaltlosen: Eine Initiative,* Patmos (Dusseldorf), 1971; *Le desert est fertile: Feuilles de route pour les minorites abrahamiques,* Desclee, De Brouwer, 1971, translation from the French by Francis McDonagh published as *The Desert Is Fertile,* Orbis Books, 1974. Contributor of articles to journals, including *Commonweal, America, Christian Century.*

SIDELIGHTS: According to *Time:* "A certain grace seems to touch the life of the diminutive (5 ft. 4 in.) Archbishop of Olinda and Recife, Dom Helder Pessoa Camara. Better known to the world simply as 'Dom Helder,' Brazil's famed voice of the poor and preacher of nonviolent revolution is a persistent nettle in the breeches of his country's military regime. At least eight of Dom Helder's associates have been arrested and tortured. He has been castigated as a 'Fidel Castro in cassock' and disdainfully dubbed 'the Red bishop.' Lately he has been so judiciously ignored by Brazil's censored press that some educated people in Rio are surprised to learn that he is still alive. Outside Brazil, though, his name is very much alive—and widely honored."

Archbishop Camara's books have been translated into more than a dozen languages.

BIOGRAPHICAL/CRITICAL SOURCES: The Violence of a Peacemaker, Orbis Books, 1971; Bernhard Moosbrugger and Gladys Weigner, *A Voice of the Third World: Dom Helder Camara,* Paulist/Newman, 1972; Neville Cheetham, *Helder Camara,* S.C.M. Press, 1973; Cyril Davey, *Fifty Lives for God,* Judson, 1973; *Time,* June 24, 1974.

*   *   *

CAMERON, Alan (Douglas Edward) 1938-

PERSONAL: Born March 13, 1938, in Egham, Surrey, England; son of A. D. Cameron; married Averil Sutton, 1962; children: one son, one daughter. *Education:* Oxford University, B.A., 1961, M.A., 1963. *Home:* 81 Harrow View, Harrow, Middlesex, England. *Office:* Department of Latin, University of London, King's College, Strand, London W.C.2, England.

CAREER: Brunswick School, Haywards Heath, England, assistant master, 1956-57; University of Glasgow, Glasgow, Scotland, assistant lecturer, 1961-63, lecturer in humanity, 1963-64; University of London, London, England, lecturer, 1964-71, reader in Latin at Beford College, 1971-72, professor of Latin language and literature at King's College, 1972—. Visiting professor at Columbia University, 1967-68. *Awards, honors:* N. H. Baynes Prize, 1967; John Conington Prize, 1968.

WRITINGS: Claudian: Poetry and Propaganda at the Court of Honorius, Clarendon Press, 1970; (contributor) Arnold H. Jones, J. Morris, and J. R. Martindale, editors, *Prosopography of the Later Roman Empire,* Cambridge University Press, 1971; *Porphyrius the Charioteer,* Clarendon Press, 1973. Contributor to scholarly journals.*

* * *

CAMOIN, Francois Andre   1939-

PERSONAL: Born June 20, 1939, in Nice, France; son of Marcel (a professor) and Andree (Loumeau) Camoin; married Lisa Marlene Kent (an actress), July 7, 1974. *Education:* University of Arizona, B.A., 1964, M.A., 1965; University of Massachusetts, Ph.D., 1967. *Agent:* Nancy Hardin, Ziegler Associates, 9255 Sunset, Beverly Hills, Calif. 90069. *Office address:* P.O. Box 5157, Sherman Oaks, Calif. 91403.

CAREER: Slippery Rock State College, Slippery Rock, Pa., member of faculty, department of English, 1967-68; Denison University, Granville, Ohio, member of faculty, department of English, 1968-71; full-time writer, 1971—. *Member:* American National Theatre Academy.

WRITINGS: Benbow and Paradise, Dutton, 1975.

WORK IN PROGRESS: A novel, *Holy Mother America,* completion expected in 1976; book reviews.

SIDELIGHTS: Camoin cites Zola, Mark Twain, Jack Kerouac, and Saul Bellow as influences on his writing.

* * *

CAMP, Charles L.   1893-1975

March 12, 1893—August 14, 1975; American paleontologist, educator, leader of archaeological expeditions, expert on Western American pioneer life, and author of books for children on fossils and frontier history, and of scholarly works in his field. Obituaries: *New York Times,* August 16, 1975.

* * *

CAMP, Dalton Kingsley   1920-

PERSONAL: Born September 11, 1920, in Woodstock, New Brunswick, Canada; son of Harold Brainard and Rilla (Sanborn) Camp; married Linda Atkins, August 28, 1943; children: David, Gail, Connie, Cheryl Ann, Michael. *Education:* University of New Brunswick, B.A.; Columbia University, M.Sc.; also studied at London School of Economics and Political Science. *Home:* 48 Daneswood Rd., Toronto, Ontario, Canada; and Robertson's Point, Young's Cove Rd., Queen's County, New Brunswick, Canada. *Office:* 43 Eglinton Ave. E., Toronto, Ontario, Canada.

CAREER: J. Walter Thompson Co. Ltd., Toronto, Ontario, copywriter, 1950-52; Locke, Johnson Co. Ltd., Toronto, creative director, 1952-58; Stanfield, Johnson & Hill Ltd., Toronto, vice president, 1958-59; Dalton K. Camp & Associates Ltd., Toronto, president, 1959-69. President, Travel Direction Ltd. National chairman, Progressive Conservative Party Campaign Committee, 1963; president, Progressive Conservative National Association, 1964-69; candidate of Progressive Conservative Party, 1965. *Military service:* Canadian Army during World War II. *Member:* Albany Bayview Country Club, Badminton and Racquet Club, Albany Club.

WRITINGS: Gentlemen, Players and Politicians (memoirs), McClelland & Stewart, 1970.

SIDELIGHTS: Dalton Camp entered Canadian politics as a member of the Liberal Party in the 1940s. He participated in the Liberal Convention of 1948, but the following year became the executive secretary of the New Brunswick Conservatives. During the ensuing fourteen years, he worked for the Tory cause in the Maritime Provinces. According to Des Morton, Camp is "the man who almost singlehandedly bounced the mighty Diefenbaker from the Tory leadership."

* * *

CAMP, William (Newton Alexander)   1926-

PERSONAL: Born May 12, 1926, in Nazareth, Palestine; son of I. N. and Freda Camp; married Patricia Cowan, 1950 (marriage dissolved, 1973); married Juliet Schubart, 1975; children: two sons, one daughter. *Education:* Oriel College, Oxford, M.A., 1954. *Home:* 61 Gloucester Crescent, London N.W.1, England. *Agent:* A. D. Peters & Co. Ltd., 10 Buckingham St., London WC2N 6BU, England.

CAREER: British Travel & Holidays Assoc., London, England, assistant research officer, 1950-54; Consumer Advisory Council, London, assistant secretary, 1954-59; Gas Council, London, assistant secretary, 1960-63, public relations adviser, 1963-67; British Steel Corporation, London, director of information services, 1967-71; in private practice as communications consultant, 1971—. Labour candidate for Solihull, 1950; member of Southwark Borough Council, 1953-56; press adviser to Prime Minister during general election, 1970. Director of Quartet Books. Founder member of Public Enterprise Group.

WRITINGS: Prospects of Love (novel), Longmans, Green, 1957; *Idle on Parade,* MacGibbon & Kee, 1958; *The Ruling Passion,* MacGibbon & Kee, 1959; *The Glittering Prizes: A Biographical Study of F. E. Smith, Earl of Birkenhead,* MacGibbon & Kee, 1960; *A Man's World* (novel), Anthony Blond, 1963; *Two Schools of Thought,* Anthony Blond, 1964; *Flavour of Decay* (novel), Anthony Blond, 1967; *The Father Figures* (novel), Constable, 1970.

* * *

CAMPBELL, Alexander   1912-

PERSONAL: Born October 19, 1912, in Edinburgh, Scotland; son of Alexander Maclean and Elizabeth (Morgan) Campbell; married Jane Young Lowe Shand, June 8, 1937; children: Morgan Brand, Kenneth Maclean, Lesley Ann. *Education:* University of Edinburgh, M.A. (with honours), 1934.

CAREER: Editorial writer for *The Scotsman,* Edinburgh, Scotland, 1935-37, and *East London Daily Dispatch,* East London, South Africa, 1937-42; *The Star,* Johannesburg, South Africa, assistant to the editor, 1942-50; *Time-Life,* New York City, bureau chief in Johannesburg, 1950-54, in New Delhi, India, 1954-56, in Tokyo, Japan, 1956-60, and the Middle East, 1960-61; *The Economist,* London, England, Washington, D.C., correspondent, 1961-63; *New Republic,* Washington, D.C., managing editor, 1964-71; member of editorial board of *Toronto Daily Star,* Toronto, Ontario, beginning, 1971. *Member:* Overseas Writers. *Awards, honors:* Sigma Chi Delta outstanding foreign correspondent award, 1954; Overseas Press Club Award, 1959, for *The Heart of Africa.*

WRITINGS: Smuts and Swastika, Gollancz, 1943; *Empire in Africa,* Gollancz, 1944; *It's Your Empire,* Gollancz, 1945; *South Africa, What Now? An Economic Survey of the Union of South Africa,* Stewart (Cape Town), 1947; (editor and author of epilogue) Hedley A. Chilvers, *Out of the Crucible,* Juta, 1948; *The Heart of Africa,* Knopf, 1954; *The Heart of India,* Knopf, 1958; *The Heart of Japan,* Knopf, 1961; *Unbind Your Sons: The Captivity of America in Asia,* Liveright, 1970; *The Trouble With Americans,* Praeger, 1971.

SIDELIGHTS: In a review of *The Trouble With Americans,* Bill Moyers refers to Campbell as a woodsman who chops through a forest of American myths, and says: "It is probably just as well that . . . Alexander Campbell is now living in Toronto. By the end of his book, he has taken on just about every sacred cow around and a lot of people are going to be looking for him, hand on holster. It is not fashionable in official circles today to say that things are not working well, that America is off course and wandering in a slough.

"Alexander Campbell's journalistic disputation is well worth reading, then, because it is written by a man who sees us as we are and loves us just the same and who believes we are so rich and unusual a people that we have no right to have Troubles. His time contribution is to refute in lively fashion, with pertinent anecdotes and provocative hyperbole, the country-club mentality that prevails in Washington today—'the dangerous delusion that the United States is a place that requires no improvements.'"*

* * *

CAMPBELL, Hope
(Virginia Hughes, G. McDonald Wallis)

PERSONAL: Born in Seattle, Wash.; daughter of Howard Roswell (a business manager) and Genevieve (Talbott) McDonald; married Charles Wallis; children: Christopher, John. *Education:* Attended private schools in Hawaii, China, and California. *Agent:* Malcolm Reiss, Paul R. Reynolds, Inc., 12 East 41 St., New York, N.Y. 10017.

CAREER: Actress, under name Cathy McDonald, in radio soap operas and on television, New York, N.Y., in stock companies in Atlantic City, N.J., Holyoke, Mass., Charleston, W.Va., and Lake George, N.Y., and in hospital shows and with touring companies, the West Coast Company, and United Service Organization (U.S.O.) in European Theater of Operations.

WRITINGS: Liza, Norton, 1965; *Home to Hawaii,* Norton, 1967; *Why Not Join the Giraffes?,* Norton, 1968; *Meanwhile, Back at the Castle,* Grosset, 1970; *No More Trains to Tottenville,* McCall Publishing, 1971; (with Mary Anderson) *There's a Pizza Back in Cleveland,* Four Winds, 1972; *Peter's Angel: A Story About Monsters,* Scholastic Book Services, 1975.

Under name G. McDonald Wallis: *The Light of Lilith,* Ace Books, 1961; *Legend of Lost Earth,* Ace Books, 1963.

Under pseudonym Virginia Hughes: *Peggy Goes Straw Hat,* Grosset, 1963.

* * *

CANAN, James William 1929-

PERSONAL: Born July 9, 1929, in New Castle, Pa.; son of Edwin Earl (a professor) and Frances (Brown) Canan; married Joan Conlin, April 24, 1954; children: Michael, Martha, Ruth, Sara, Timothy. *Education:* Westminster College, New Wilmington, Pa., B.A., 1951; Northwestern University, graduate study, 1954-55. *Politics:* Independent. *Religion:* Roman Catholic. *Home:* 712 South Wakefield

St., Arlington, Va. 22204. *Agent:* Carl Brandt, Brandt & Brandt, 101 Park Ave., New York, N.Y. 10017. *Office:* McGraw-Hill Publications Co., 400 National Press Building, Washington, D.C. 20045.

CAREER: Binghamton Press, Binghamton, N.Y., reporter, 1955-60; Gannett Newspapers, Washington, D.C., correspondent, 1960-66; McGraw-Hill World News, Washington, D.C., correspondent, chiefly writing for *Business Week* Magazine, 1966—. *Military service:* U.S. Army, 1951-54; became lieutenant. *Member:* National Society of Literature and the Arts, National Press Club, Smithsonian Institution, Knights of Columbus. *Awards, honors:* Silver Gavel Award from the American Bar Association and annual press award from New York State Bar Association, both 1965, both for a newspaper series on the Supreme Court and criminal law.

WRITINGS: The Superwarriors, Weybright, 1975. Contributor to *Playboy* and *The Reporter,* and to newspapers.

SIDELIGHTS: Canan writes: "My chief area of interest embraces U.S. defense and foreign policies. I like to think that my first book, *The Superwarriors,* will contribute to public understanding of these policies."

* * *

CANTACUZENE, Julia 1876-1975

June 7, 1876—October 5, 1975; American-born, became Russian princess by marriage; essayist, and author of memoirs and books on Russia. Obituaries: *New York Times,* October 7, 1975.

* * *

CAPRA, Frank 1897-

PERSONAL: Born May 18, 1897, in Palermo, Italy; came to the United States in 1903; son of Salvatore (a fruit grower) and Sarah (Nicolosi) Capra; married Lucille Rayburn Warner, 1932; children: Frank, Jr., Lucille, Tom. *Education:* California Institute of Technology, B.S., 1918. *Address:* P.O. Box 98, La Quinta, Calif. 92253.

CAREER: Began career in motion pictures in the early 1920s, working as a property man, film cutter, assistant director, and writer of film titles and screen plays; in Hollywood, wrote for Hal Roach comedies and Mack Sennett, became a writer for Harry Langdon, and directed for First National before joining Columbia Pictures in 1928; formed Frank Capra Productions in 1941; became president of Liberty Films and, later, became producer and director of Paramount Pictures. Member of board of directors of California Institute of Technology. *Military service:* U.S. Army, engineering instructor, 1918. U.S. Army, Signal Corps, 1941-45; became colonel; awarded Distinguished Service Medal and Legion of Merit for production of army films.

MEMBER: Academy of Motion Picture Arts and Sciences (past president), Screen Directors' Guild (past president). *Awards, honors:* Order of the British Empire; Academy Award for best direction, 1934, for "It Happened One Night," 1936, for "Mr. Deeds Goes to Town," and 1938, for "You Can't Take It with You," for best documentary, 1942, for U.S. Army film, "Prelude to War"; Belgian film award, 1941, for "Arsenic and Old Lace"; New York Film Critics award, 1942, for "Why We Fight," a U.S. Army documentary film.

WRITINGS: Frank Capra: The Name Above the Title (autobiography), Macmillan, 1971.

SIDELIGHTS: Capra is best known as a director of sentimental human comedies. His major films include "That Certain Thing," 1928, "Platinum Blond," 1931, "American Madness," 1931, "The Bitter Tea of General Yen," 1932, "Lady for a Day," 1933, "It Happened One Night," 1934, "Mr. Deeds Goes to Town," 1936, "Lost Horizon," 1937, "You Can't Take It with You," 1938, "Mr. Smith Goes to Washington," 1939, "Meet John Doe," 1941, "It's a Wonderful Life," 1946, "State of the Union," 1948, and "Pocketful of Miracles," 1961.

AVOCATIONAL INTERESTS: Hunting, fishing, music, lecturing at universities.

BIOGRAPHICAL/CRITICAL SOURCES: Richard Griffith, *Frank Capra*, British Film Institute, 1951; Richard Glaetzer and John Raeburn, *Frank Capra, The Man and His Films*, University of Michigan Press, 1975; Leland A. Poague, *The Cinema of Frank Capra: An Approach to Film Comedy*, A. S. Barnes, 1975.

* * *

CARDOZO, Peter 1916-

PERSONAL: Born December 8, 1916, in New York, N.Y.; married Barbara Herron, December 12, 1939 (died, 1963); married Susan Strong (a television actress), April 5, 1964; children: (first marriage) Peter, Jr., Pamela, Christopher; (second marriage) Jonathan. *Education:* Dartmouth College, B.A., 1939. *Home:* 6-C Dickel Rd., Scarsdale, N.Y. 10583. *Office:* Bantam Books, Inc., 666 Fifth Ave., New York, N.Y. 10019.

CAREER: Dartmouth College, Hanover, N.H., instructor of English, 1939-41; scriptwriter, 1941; *Life* Magazine, New York City, film and theatre editor, 1942-45; motion picture scriptwriter for Warner Bros., 1947-49; story editor of "Studio One" television show on CBS-TV, 1950; Fuller & Smith & Ross, Inc. (advertising firm), New York City, vice-president and creative director, 1951-61; Bruns Advertising Agency, New York City, vice-president, creative director, and account supervisor, 1961-69; Electro Optics, Inc., New York City, president, 1969-72, marketing consultant, 1972—; Bantam Books, New York City, director of Premium Marketing Division, 1972—.

WRITINGS—For children: *A Wonderful World for Children*, Bantam, 1956, 4th edition, 1962; (compiler) *The Whole Kids Catalog*, Bantam, 1975. Contributor of articles and stories to popular magazines, including *Cosmopolitan*, *Good Housekeeping*, and *Redbook*.

* * *

CARDUS, Neville 1889-1975

PERSONAL: Born April 2, 1889, in Manchester, England; married Edith Honorine King, 1921 (died, 1968). *Education:* Attended free lectures at University of Manchester, 1904-1912. *Home:* 112 Bickenhall Mansions, Baker Street, London W. 1, England.

CAREER: Shrewsbury School, Manchester, England, assistant cricket coach and secretary to the headmaster, 1912-1916; *Manchester Guardian*, Manchester, reporter, music writer, and cricket correspondent, 1916-27, music critic, 1927-40; *Morning Herald*, Sydney, Australia, music critic and cricket writer, 1941-47; *Sunday Times*, London, England, staff member, 1948-49; *Manchester Guardian*, Manchester, music critic, 1951-75. *Member:* National Liberal Club, Garrick Club. *Awards, honors:* Wagner Medal from City of Bayreuth, 1963; Commander of the British Empire,

1964; Knighted by Queen Elizabeth II, 1967; International Press Club special award, 1970.

WRITINGS: A Cricketer's Book, G. Richards, 1922; *Days in the Sun: A Cricketer's Journal*, G. Richards, 1924, new edition, Hart-Davis, 1948; (editor) Samuel Langford, *Musical Criticisms*, Oxford University Press, 1929; *The Summer Game: A Cricketer's Journal*, Cayme Press, 1929, new edition, Hart-Davis, 1948; *Cricket*, Longmans, Green, 1930, new edition, 1949; *Good Days: A Book of Cricket*, J. Cape, 1934, new edition, Hart-Davis, 1948; (contributor) Thomas Moult, editor, *Bat and Ball*, Arthur Baker, 1935; (author of introduction) Wilhelm Mueller, *Die schonen Muellerin*, Schubert, Die schonen Muellerin Society (London), 1935; *Australian Summer*, J. Cape, 1937, new edition, Hart-Davis, 1949; *Music for Pleasure*, Angus & Robertson, 1942; *Ten Composers*, J. Cape, 1945, enlarged edition published as *A Composers Eleven*, J. Cape, 1958, published as *Composers Eleven*, Braziller, 1959; *English Cricket*, Collins, 1945; *Autobiography*, Collins, 1947, 3rd edition, 1961; *The Essential Neville Cardus*, edited by Rupert Hart-Davis, J. Cape, 1949.

Second Innings (autobiography), Collins, 1950; *Cricket All the Year*, Collins, 1952; (editor and contributor) *Kathleen Ferrier: A Memoir*, Hamish Hamilton, 1954, Putnam, 1955, 3rd edition, Hamish Hamilton, 1969; *Close of a Play*, Collins, 1956; *Talking of Music*, Macmillan, 1957; *Sir Thomas Beecham: A Memoir*, Collins, 1961; *The Playfair Cardus*, Dickens Press, 1963; *Gustav Mahler: His Mind and His Music*, St. Martin's, 1965; *The Delights of Music: A Critic's Choice*, Gollancz, 1966; (compiler with John Arlott) *The Noblest Game: A Book of Fine Cricket Prints*, Harrap, 1969; *Full Score*, Cassell, 1970.

SIDELIGHTS: Sir Neville Cardus was raised in the slums of Manchester by an aunt who he said, "joined the oldest of professions and became an ornament of it." He never knew his parents. Cardus spent his youth working at odd jobs instead of attending school. The *Washington Post* quoted Cardus as having once said: "I am a terribly uneducated man. I took a terrible lot of risks. I suppose now I would have been given a grant and probably would have gone to university and I would probably never have known as much as I know now."*

(Died February 28, 1975, in London, England)

* * *

CARENS, James Francis 1927-

PERSONAL: Born November 13, 1927, in Newbury, Mass.; son of James F. and Kathryn F. (Callahan) Carens; married Marilyn Mumford, June 7, 1961; children: Geoffrey Peter, Timothy Lawrence. *Education:* Harvard University, A.B., 1949; Yale University, M.A., 1951; Columbia University, Ph.D., 1959. *Home:* College Park, Lewisburg, Pa. 17837. *Office:* Department of English, Bucknell University, Lewisburg, Pa. 17837.

CAREER: Bucknell University, Lewisburg, Pa., instructor, 1955-59, assistant professor, 1959-65, associate professor, 1965-70, professor of English, 1970—; director of Bucknell University Press, 1969-72.

WRITINGS: The Satiric Art of Evelyn Waugh, University of Washington Press, 1966; (editor and author of commentary) Oliver St. John Gogarty, *Many Lines to Thee: Letters to G.K.A. Bell from the Martello Tower at Sandycove, Rutland Square, and Trinity College, Dublin, 1904-1907*, Dolmen Press, 1971, Humanities, 1972; (editor and author of introduction) *The Plays of Oliver St. John Gogarty,* Proscenium Press, 1971. Editor, "Irish Writers Series," Bucknell University Press, 1970—. Contributor of articles to professional journals.

BIOGRAPHICAL/CRITICAL SOURCES: Contemporary Literature, Volume 9, number 2, spring, 1968.

* * *

CARINI, Edward 1923-

PERSONAL: Born May 27, 1923, in Glastonbury, Conn.; son of John A. (a realtor) and Rose (Quadiroli) Carini. *Education:* Art Institute of Chicago, B.F.A., 1950. *Home:* 85 Ridgeview Dr., Pleasantville, N.Y. 10570. *Office:* 15 Eward St., Ossining, N.Y. 10562.

CAREER: Self-employed producer of films for children, inventor of toys, artist, and lyric writer, with office in Ossining, N.Y. Had one-man show in New York.

WRITINGS: What Is Big, Holt, 1964; (self-illustrated) *Take Another Look,* Prentice-Hall, 1970. Creator and producer of about forty children's films, including "Tadpole" Films, distributed by Denoyer-Geppert, and of "Kindle" Filmstrips, distributed by Scholastic Magazines. Writer of lyrics for more than one hundred songs.

* * *

CARNICELLI, D(omenick) D. 1931-

PERSONAL: Born October 28, 1931, in Brooklyn, N.Y.; son of Antonio and Julia (Romanelli) Carnicelli; married Joan Valerie Vogel (a teacher), February 23, 1964; children: David, Susan. *Education:* Brooklyn College (now Brooklyn College of the City University of New York), B.A., 1952; Columbia University, M.A., 1959, Ph.D., 1966. *Home:* 50 Wykagyl Terrace, New Rochelle, N.Y. 10804. *Office:* Department of English, Lehman College of the City University of New York, Bronx, New York 10468.

CAREER: High school teacher of English in Brooklyn, N.Y., 1952-53, 1956-60; City University of New York, New York, N.Y., Brooklyn College, lecturer in English, 1960-66, Hunter College, instructor in English, 1966-69, Lehman College, assistant professor, 1969-72, associate professor, 1972-74, professor of English, 1974—. Visiting professor, University of Kent, 1970-71. *Military service:* U.S. Army, 1953-56; served as translator. *Member:* Modern Language Association of America, Renaissance Society of America. *Awards, honors:* City University of New York faculty research grants, 1969-70 and 1970-71.

WRITINGS: Lord Morley's "Tryumphes of Fraunces Petrarcke": The First English Translation of the "Trionfi," Harvard University Press, 1971; (contributor) Harold H. Mosak, editor, *Alfred Adler: His Influence on Psychology Today,* Noyes Press, 1973. Contributor of articles and reviews to *Romance Philology* and *Renaissance Quarterly.*

WORK IN PROGRESS: Editing John Levett's 1599 translation of Machiavelli's *Discorsi,* completion expected in 1976; a critical study of Shakespeare's *Sonnets,* completion expected, 1977-78; a gothic novel set in Canterbury in the late 1960's.

SIDELIGHTS: Carnicelli is competent in Italian, French, German, Latin, and Spanish.

* * *

CARR, Edward Hallet 1892-

PERSONAL: Born June 28, 1892, in England; *Education:* Attended Trinity College, Cambridge. *Home:* Dales Barn, Barton, Cambridgeshire, England. *Office:* Trinity College, Cambridge, England.

CAREER: British Foreign Office, temporary clerk, 1916, attached to delegation to Paris Peace Conference, 1919, temporary secretary at British Embassy, Paris, France, 1920-21, third secretary, 1922-25, second secretary at British Legation, Riga, Lithuania, 1925-29, staff member in London, 1929-30, assistant adviser for League of Nations affairs, 1930-33, first secretary, 1933-36; University College of Wales, Aberystwyth, Wales, Wilson Professor of International Politics, 1936-47; Ministry of Information, director of foreign publicity, 1939-40; *The Times,* London, England, assistant editor, 1941-46; Oxford University, Balliol College, Oxford, England, tutor in politics, 1953-55; Cambridge University, Trinity College, Cambridge, England, fellow, 1955—. *Member:* British Academy (fellow), Oxford Club, Cambridge Club. *Awards, honors:* Commander of the Order of the British Empire, 1920; honorary fellow of Balliol College, Oxford University, 1966; Litt.D., University of Manchester, 1964, Cambridge University, 1967; LL.D., University of Groeningen, 1964.

WRITINGS: Dostoevsky, 1821-1881: A New Biography, Houghton, 1931, reprinted, Barnes & Noble, 1962; *The Romantic Exiles: A Nineteenth-Century Protrait Gallery,* Frederick A. Stokes, 1933; *Karl Marx: A Study in Fanaticism,* Dent, 1934; *International Relations since the Peace Treaties,* Macmillan, 1937, new enlarged edition, 1940, published as *International Relations between the Two World Wars, 1919-1939,* Macmillan, 1947, St. Martin's, 1961; *Michael Bakunin,* Macmillan, 1937; *Britain: A Study of Foreign Policy from the Versailles Treaty to the Outbreak of War,* Longmans, Green, 1939; *Propaganda in International Politics,* Farrar & Rinehart, 1939; *The Twenty Years' Crisis, 1919-1939: An Introduction to the Study of International Relations,* Macmillan (London), 1939, 2nd edition, 1946, St. Martin's, 1956, reprinted, Harper, 1964.

The Future of Nations: Independence or Interdependence?, Kegan Paul & Co., 1941; *Conditions of Peace,* Macmillan, 1942; *Nationalism and After,* Macmillan, 1945; *The Soviet Impact on the Western World,* Macmillan (London), 1946, Macmillan (New York), 1947, reprinted, Fertig, 1973; *The Moral Foundations for World Order,* University of Denver Social Science Foundation, 1948.

A History of Soviet Russia, Macmillan, St. Martin's, Part I: *The Bolshevik Revolution, 1917-1923,* three volumes, 1950-53, Part II: *The Interregnum, 1923-1924,* 1954, Part III: *Socialism in One Country, 1924-1926,* three volumes, 1958-1964, Part IV: (with R. W. Davies) *Foundations of a Planned Economy, 1926-1929,* two volumes, 1969-1971; *Studies in Revolution,* Macmillan, 1950; *The New Society,* Macmillan (London), 1951, St. Martin's, 1957, new edition, Beacon Press, 1957; *German-Soviet Relations between the Two World Wars, 1919-1939,* Johns Hopkins Press, 1951.

What Is History?, St. Martin's, 1961; *The October Revolution: Before and After,* Knopf, 1969 (published in England as *1917: Before and After,* Macmillan, 1969). Also author of published lectures and addresses.

SIDELIGHTS: A. J. P. Taylor described Carr as "an Olympian among historians, a Goethe in range and spirit," and stated that his *History of Soviet Russia* "... stands almost alone as [a] monument of erudition and analysis," and further, "his quality appears just as clearly in the short pieces he has written." A writer for *Virginia Quarterly Review* suggested his essays be considered "a welcome antidote to the offerings of the university and government mystagogues who have filled so many volumes of nonsense about Russia,'' and that "he is a scholar [who] has searched for Truth over a period of nearly eighty years."*

* * *

CARR, Edwin George 1937-

PERSONAL: Born September 25, 1937, in Australia; son of Edwin George and Margery Carr; married Dawn Yvonne Castle, March 18, 1961; children: David Edwin, Evan John, Matthew Trevor. *Education:* Attended Collingwood Technical College and Royal Melbourne Institute of Technology. *Religion:* Reorganized Church of Jesus Christ of Latter-day Saints. *Home:* 78 Banyule Rd., Rosanna, Victoria 3084, Australia. *Office:* Colmax Electric, 18-20 Pickering Rd., Mulgrave, Victoria 2170, Australia.

CAREER: Has worked as electrical mechanic, elevator serviceman, and electrical design draftsman; Colmax Electric, Mulgrave, Victoria, Australia, electrical engineer, 1960—.

WRITINGS: The Future's Advocate (science fiction-religious novel), Herald House, 1975.

WORK IN PROGRESS: Biblical and theological studies.

SIDELIGHTS: Carr writes: "*The Future's Advocate* is written with a view to assist Christian readers in examining their faith and eschatological beliefs and evaluating them in everyday terms. Common Christian concepts such as grace, forgiveness, judgment etc. can become devoid of mundane meaning with frequent use."

* * *

CARR, Lois Green 1922-

PERSONAL: Born March 7, 1922, in Holyoke, Mass.; daughter of Donald Ross (a manufacturer) and Constance (McLaughlin) Green; married Allen Reynolds Clark, May 30, 1946 (divorced, 1963); married Jack Ladd Carr (a city planner), July 28, 1963; children: (first marriage) Andrew Reynolds Clark. *Education:* Swarthmore College, A.B., 1943; Radcliffe College, A.M., 1944; Harvard University, Ph.D., 1968. *Home:* 422 Sixth St., Annapolis, Md. 21453. *Office:* St. Mary's City Commission, Hall of Records, Annapolis, Md. 21401.

CAREER: Cambridge Junior College, Cambridge, Mass., instructor in history, 1946-47; Juilliard School of Music, New York, N.Y., instructor in English, spring semester, 1948; free-lance editor, 1950-51; Alfred A. Knopf, Inc. (publisher), New York, N.Y., assistant editor in college department, 1951-52; free-lance editor, 1952-56; Hall of Records, Annapolis, Md., archivist, 1956-64; historian for St. Mary's City Commission, 1967—. Member of board of directors of Bay Country School, 1966-72.

MEMBER: American Historical Association, Organization of American Historians. *Awards, honors:* National Science Foundation grant, 1972-73.

WRITINGS: (With David W. Jordan) *Maryland's Revolution of Government, 1689-1692,* Cornell University Press, 1974. Contributor to history journals.

* * *

CARR, Virginia Spencer 1929-

PERSONAL: Born July 21, 1929, in West Palm Beach, Fla.; daughter of Louis Perry and Wilma (Bell) Spencer; married Roger Alton Carr, June 14, 1951 (divorced January 2, 1975); children: Karen, Catherine, Kimberly. *Education:* Florida State University, B.A., 1951, Ph.D., 1969; University of North Carolina, Chapel Hill, M.A., 1952. *Religion:* Presbyterian. *Home:* 2909 Cathryn Dr., Columbus, Ga. 31906. *Office:* Department of English, Columbus College, Columbus, Ga. 31907.

CAREER: Palm Beach Junior College, Lake Worth, Fla., instructor in English and journalism, 1960-62; Armstrong State College, Savannah, Ga., assistant professor of English and director of freshman English, 1963-67; Columbus College, Columbus, Ga., associate professor of English, 1969—. Member of board of governors and teacher of creative writing, Musemont Fine Arts Camp. *Member:* Modern Language Association of America, Society for the Study of Southern Literature, American Studies Association, American Association of University Professors, South Atlantic Modern Language Association, Southeastern American Studies Association, Quill and Scroll, Kappa Gamma Delta, Lambda Iota Tau (moderator, Columbus College, 1967-72), Alpha Omicron Pi. *Awards, honors:* Outstanding teacher award, Florida State University, 1968.

WRITINGS: The Lonely Hunter: A Biography of Carson McCullers (introduction by Tennessee Williams), Doubleday, 1975. Contributor of articles and book reviews to *Choice, Haiku Highlights,* and other periodicals.

WORK IN PROGRESS: A critical study titled *Carson McCullers' Search for Meaning,* with Aimee Alexander, publication by David Lewis expected in 1977.

SIDELIGHTS: Virginia Carr told *CA:* "A Ph.D. dissertation on Carson McCullers begun just prior to her death in 1967 was the immediate impetus to the biography that evolved eight years later. In 1969 I moved to Columbus, Mrs. McCullers' hometown, and began depth research. It was in Nyack, N.Y., New York City, Yaddo, Breadloaf, Paris, and other areas out of the South, however, from which the most revealing and multi-faceted portraits of Carson McCullers emerged. The 'McCullers estate' reportedly was opposed to the writing and research of this biography until all principals were dead, but of course, by then I probably would be, too. Anything short of a depth biography of McCullers would have been a travesty, and Carson herself would have led the hooters."

BIOGRAPHICAL/CRITICAL SOURCES: Atlanta Journal-Constitution Magazine, October 5, 1975; *Writers' Digest,* February, 1976.

* * *

CARSON, Ray F(ritziof) 1939-

PERSONAL: Born June 3, 1939, in Chicago, Ill.; son of Raymond Fritziof (an IBM technician) and Daisy (Andrews) Carson. *Education:* Augustana College, Rock Island, Ill., B.S., 1961; University of Illinois, M.S., 1963; Indiana University, Director's Degree, 1969. *Home:* 2106 K St., San Diego, Calif. 92102. *Office address:* P.O. Box 8171, San Diego, Calif. 92102.

CAREER: University of Illinois, Champaign, instructor in physical education, 1963-65; University of Iowa, Iowa City, counselor, 1968-69; San Diego City College, San Diego, Calif., instructor in health and physical education, 1970-72; San Diego Evening College, San Diego, Calif., instructor in judo and karate, 1972-74; Grossmont Union High School District, La Mesa, Calif., teacher of driver education, 1972—. *Member:* National Education Association, United States Wrestling Federation, California

Teachers Association, New York Wrestling Coaches Association, Illinois Wrestling Coaches and Officials Association, California Driver Education Association, Grossmont Education Association.

WRITINGS—All published by A. S. Barnes, except as indicated: (With Buel R. Patterson) *Principles of Championship Wrestling*, 1972; *Systematic Championship Wrestling*, 1973; *Championship Wrestling: Coaching to Win*, 1974; *Encyclopedia of Championship Wrestling Drills*, 1974; (editor) *Championship Wrestling: An Anthology*, privately printed, 1974; *Counter Control for Championship Wrestling*, 1975; *Winning Wrestling Drills of Thirty Successful Coaches*, 1976. Contributor to professional journals.

WORK IN PROGRESS: Stand Up Takedown Style Wrestling, and *Championship Wrestling: Single and Double Leg Takedowns*, completion expected in 1977; *How To Organize and Coach Winning Wrestling*, and *The Winning Edge in Wrestling: An Interdisciplinary Approach*, 1978.

*   *   *

CARTE, Gene E(dward) 1938-

PERSONAL: Born May 9, 1938, in Charleston, W.Va.; son of Henry Lewis and Virginia Ruth (Geene) Carte; married Elaine R. Huddell (a writer), June 21, 1968; children: Carl Adam, Katherine Elaine. *Education:* Florida State University, B.S., 1963; Columbia University, M.A., 1966; University of California, Berkeley, D.Cr., 1972. *Politics:* Independent. *Office:* Department of Criminal Justice, University of Cincinnati, 408 French Hall, Cincinnati, Ohio 45221.

CAREER: Florida State Prison, Raiford, Fla., classification officer, 1963-64; Department of Vocational Rehabilitation, San Francisco, Calif., counselor, 1967-68; Delhi Probation Department, Delhi, India, professional intern, 1968-69; Trenton State College, Trenton, N.J., member of faculty in department of criminal justice, 1971-73; University of Cincinnati, Cincinnati, Ohio, member of faculty in department of criminal justice, 1973—. *Military service:* U.S. Navy, 1956-60. *Member:* American Society of Criminology, American Sociological Association.

WRITINGS: (With wife, Elaine H. Carte) *Police Reform in the United States: The Era of August Vollmer, 1905-1932*, University of California Press, 1975. Contributor to criminology journals.

WORK IN PROGRESS: A book on the history of American policing, including the evolution of ideas about the proper function of the police agency in American cities.

*   *   *

CARTER, J(ohn) Anthony 1943-

PERSONAL: Born September 21, 1943, in Essex, England; son of John (a surgeon) and Hilda (Lee) Carter; married Evelyn Palmer (an interior designer), August 23, 1974. *Education:* Attended South West Essex Technical College and School of Art, 1960-64, and King's College, University of London, 1964-66. *Home:* 3 Ovington Gardens, Flat 10, London S.W.3, England. *Office:* Goldings Lodge, Clays Lane, Loughton, Essex, England.

CAREER: Christie, Manson & Woods, London, England, objets d'art department, auctioneer, 1966-69, representative for Canada in Montreal office, 1969-71; owner of J. Anthony Carter & Co. (dealers in military edged weapons), 1971—. Co-owner of Lyon Press, specializing in books on edged weapons. *Member:* Military Historical Society, Arms and Armour Society, British Field Sports Society, Conservation Society, Imperial German Military Collector's Association (United States), National Federation of the Self-Employed.

WRITINGS: Allied Bayonets of World War Two, Arco, 1969; *The Bayonet, 1850-1970*, Arms & Armour Press, 1974; *German Ersatz Bayonets*, Lyon Press, Volume I: *1914-18*, 1975, Volume II: *Captured, Requisitioned, and Modified Bayonets, 1914-18*, in press. Author of "Bayonets," column in *Guns Review*, 1966—, and "Modern Soviet Bayonets," in *Armies and Weapons*, 1975. Contributor to professional magazines.

SIDELIGHTS: Carter writes that his "...real interest is not in professional armies but in the reactions and behaviour of conscripts and volunteers to warfare especially in the 1914-18 war." *Avocational interests:* Collecting bayonets of the 1914-18 war, English nineteenth-century stone china (especially Masonware), and general antiques; reading, conservation (of wildlife and of worthwhile architecture), current events and politics (Europe, Middle East), travel.

*   *   *

CARTER, Richard 1918-
(Tom Ainslie)

PERSONAL: Born January 24, 1918, in New York, N.Y.; married Gladys Chasins, October 20, 1945; children: Nancy Jane, John Andrew. *Education:* City College (now City College of the City University of New York), B.A., 1938. *Home:* 165 Pinesbridge Rd., Ossining, N.Y. 10562.

CAREER: Billboard magazine, New York, N.Y., music editor, 1940-46; New York Newspaper Guild, New York, N.Y., staff organizer, 1946-47; writer for *New York Daily Mirror*, 1947-49, *New York Daily Compass*, 1949-52, both New York; fulltime author, 1952—. *Military service:* U.S. Army Air Forces, 1942-45; Pacific theater of operations. *Member:* Authors Guild, National Association of Science Writers, National Association for the Advancement of Colored People. *Awards, honors:* George Polk award, 1952.

WRITINGS: (With William J. Keating) *The Man Who Rocked the Boat*, Harper, 1956; *The Doctor Business*, Doubleday, 1958, revised edition, 1961; *The Gentle Legions*, Doubleday, 1961; *Your Food and Your Health*, Harper, 1964; *Breakthrough: The Saga of Jonas Salk*, Trident, 1966; *Superswine*, Trident, 1966; (with Curt Flood) *The Way It Is*, Trident, 1971.

Under pseudonym Tom Ainslie; all published by Simon & Schuster: *The Compleat Horseplayer*, 1966; *Ainslie's Jockey Book*, 1967; *Ainslie's Complete Guide to Thoroughbred Racing*, 1968; *The Handicapper's Handbook*, 1969; *Theory and Practice of Handicapping*, 1969; *Ainslie's Complete Guide to Harness Racing*, 1970; *Ainslie's Compleat Hoyle*, 1975.

*   *   *

CARY, Barbara Knapp 1912(?)-1975

1912(?)—May 4, 1975; American magazine editor, and writer of juvenile biography. Obituaries: *New York Times*, May 6, 1975.

*   *   *

CARY, Otis 1921-

PERSONAL: Born October 20, 1921, in Otaru, Japan; son

of Frank (a missionary) and Rosamond Cozad (a missionary; maiden name, Bates) Cary; married Alice Shepard (a physician), September 12, 1944; children: Beth Deane, Ann Bradford, Frank Bates, Ellen Frederick. *Education:* Amherst College, B.A., 1946; Yale University, M.A., 1951. *Politics:* "Some." *Religion:* Protestant. *Home and office:* Amherst House, Doshisha University, Kyoto 602, Japan.

CAREER: Doshisha University, Kyoto, Japan, assistant professor, 1947-56, professor of American history, 1956—, director of Amherst House, 1947—, trustee, 1968-69, 1972, 1975—, Amherst College, Amherst, Mass., instructor, 1947-50, assistant professor, 1951-64, associate professor of history, 1964—. Councillor, International House of Japan, Inc., 1952—. Trustee of Japan-America Cultural Foundation, Inc., 1955—, chairman of board, 1974—; trustee of Canadian Academy, Kobe, 1962—, chairman, 1962-64, 1968-70. Member, Kyoto-Boston Sister City Committee. *Military service:* U.S. Navy, 1942-46; served in Attu, Kiska, and Saipan campaigns; became lieutenant; received U.S. Strategic Bombing Survey commendation. *Member:* American Historical Association, Association for Asian Studies, Asiatic Society of Japan, Japanese Association for American Studies.

WRITINGS: Nihon no Wakaimono (title means "The Youth of Japan"), Hibiya Shuppan (Tokyo), 1950; *Nihon Kaigen* (title means "Reawakening Japan"), Hosei University Press (Tokyo), 1952; *Jiipu Oku no Hosomichi* (title means "Japan's By-Ways by Jeep"), Hosei University Press, 1953; *Nihon to no Taiwa* (title means "Dialogue with Japan, Over Cultural Borders"), Kodansha, 1968; (author of text) Masamichi Sumiyoshi, *Kyoto* (photo book), *Japan Times* (Tokyo), 1971.

Editor and contributor: *Ajia no Arechi kara,* Kaname Shobo (Tokyo), 1952, translation by author published as *War-Wasted Asia: Letters, 1945-46,* Kodansha, 1975; *Amerika no Shakai to Rekishi* (title means "American Society and History"), Amherst House, 1961; *Adamusuke no Hitobito* (title means "The Adams Family"), Sogensha (Osaka), 1964; *Angro-Amerika kara no Repoota* (title means "Report from Anglo-America"), Amherst House, 1970; *Nihonjin no Saihakken* (title means "The Rediscovery of the Japanese"), Kobunsha (Tokyo), 1972; *Seikatsu no Sutairu to Kachikan* (title means "Style and Value in Living"), Nan-undo (Tokyo), 1973.

Translations: Reinhold Niebuhr, *Amerikashi no Hiniku* (*The Irony of American History*), Shakai Shiso Kenkyukai Shuppanbu (Tokyo), 1954; Reinhold Niebuhr, *Jiga to Rekishi to Taiwa* (*The Self and Dramas of History*), Miraisha (Tokyo), 1964.

WORK IN PROGRESS: A monograph, *Mr. Stimson's "Pet City": The Sparing of Kyoto, 1945.*

SIDELIGHTS: Otis Cary is the third generation of his family in Japan, stretching back to 1879. Though he was born and raised in Japan, his high school and college education took place in the United States. Cary reflects, "I was caught part way through college . . . by Pearl Harbor. I was given the chance to relearn my Japanese. . . . World War II gave me a career and a 'mission' to bind up the wounds of the war."

*   *   *

CASALE, Joan T(herese)   1935-
   (Joan C. Watkins)

PERSONAL: Born October 19, 1935, in Pittsburgh, Pa.; daughter of Jacob T. (a merchant) and Sarah E. (Barr) Casale; married Robert M. Watkins (a technical sales and travel lecturer), November 21, 1959; children: Victoria E. Watkins, Alexandra C. Watkins. *Education:* Seton Hill College, B.A., 1957. *Home:* 5468 Avenida Fiesta, La Jolla, Calif. 92037.

CAREER: Pittsburgh Mercantile Co., Pittsburgh, Pa., advertising copy-writer, 1957; *Chartiers Valley Times,* Pittsburgh, assistant editor, 1957-59; WAMP (now WJAS) radio, Pittsburgh, production assistant, 1958-59; Chatham College, Pittsburgh, assistant public relations director, 1959; KOGO-TV, San Diego, Calif., publicity director, 1959-61; travel lecturer at University of California at San Diego, Irvine, Los Angeles, and Riverside, 1970—, and at San Diego Community Colleges, 1973—. *Member:* Toastmasters International, National Organization for Women (NOW).

WRITINGS: (Under name Joan T. Watkins, with husband, Robert M. Watkins) *The World Travel Planner,* Nash Publishing, 1970; *The Diet Food Finder,* Bowker, 1975.

Contributor; under name Joan C. Watkins, except as indicated: *American Jurisprudence: Proof of Facts,* Bancroft-Whitney, Volume 15, edited by Lawrence H. Davis and Roy Miller, 1964, Volume 22, edited by Edward J. McMahon, 1969, Volume 29, edited by Charles S. Parnell, 1969, Volume I, 2nd edition (under name Joan T. Casale), edited by David A. Winn, 1974.

Contributor to *Travel, Westways, National Review, Venus,* and *Los Angeles Free Press,* sometimes under name Joan C. Watkins. Editor of San Diego County *National Organization for Women Newsletter,* 1973-76.

WORK IN PROGRESS: A politically oriented book on an important feminist issue; a series of food and travel-related books patterned on the format of *The Diet Food Finder.*

SIDELIGHTS: Joan Casale is an "active spokeswoman for women's rights to reproductive freedom in San Diego and national media."

*   *   *

CASEY, Richard Gardiner   1890-

PERSONAL: Born August 29, 1890, in Brisbane, Australia; son of Richard Gardiner and Evelyn Jane (Harris) Casey; married Ethel Marian Sumner Ryan, June 24, 1926; children: Jane Alice Camilla (Mrs. Murray Wynne Macgowan), Richard Charles Donn. *Education:* Attended Melbourne University, 1908-09; Trinity College, Cambridge, B.A., 1913. *Home:* Edrington, Berwick, Victoria 3806, Australia. *Office:* Commonwealth Scientific and Industrial Research Organization, 314 Albert St., East Melbourne, Victoria 3002, Australia.

CAREER: Australian government official. Liaison officer with British Foreign Office, 1924-27 and 1927-31, foreign affairs officer in Canberra, 1927; member of Australian House of Representatives for Corio, 1931-40, serving as assistant federal treasurer, 1933-35, federal treasurer, 1935-39, and minister for supply and development, 1939-40; minister to United States, 1940-42; minister of state resident in the Middle East and member of War Cabinet of United Kingdom, 1942-43; governor of Bengal, 1944-49; federal president of Liberal Party of Australia, 1947-49; member of Australian House of Representatives for Latrobe, 1949-60, serving as minister for works and housing, 1949-51, minister for supply and development, 1949-50, minister for national development, 1950-51, minister in charge of Commonwealth Scientific and Industrial Research Organization, 1950-60, and as minister for external affairs, 1951-60; governor-general of Commonwealth of Australia, 1965-69. Australian government representative at Coronation and Imperial Conference, 1937, and London Conference on Conduct of the War, 1939. *Military service:* British Army, 1914-18; served in Gallipoli and France; became General Staff major; mentioned in dispatches, received Distinguished Service Order and Military Cross.

MEMBER: Australian Institute of Management, Royal Australian College of Surgeons, Royal Australian Chemical Institute, Royal Australian Institute of Architects, and Royal Melbourne Institute of Technology (honorary fellow of all); Institute of Engineers of Australia and Australian Planning Institute (honorary member of both); Athenaeum Club, United Oxford and Cambridge University Club, Melbourne Club (Melbourne), Union Club (Sydney). *Awards, honors:* Privy Councillor, 1939; Companion of Honor, 1944; created baron (life peer), 1961; Knight of the Grand Cross of St. Michael and St. George, 1965; Knight of the Most Noble Order of the Garter, 1969. Honorary degrees from Bates College, 1941, University of Birmingham, 1943, Michigan State University, 1958, Monash University, 1966, University of Tasmania, 1966, University of New South Wales, 1966, University of Papua and New Guinea, 1967, University of Newcastle, 1967, University of Sydney, 1968, Australian National University, 1969.

WRITINGS: An Australian in India, Hollis & Carter, 1947; *Double or Quit: Some Views on Australian Development and Relations,* F. W. Cheshire, 1949; *Friends and Neighbours: Australia and the World,* F. W. Cheshire, 1954, Michigan State College Press, 1955; *Personal Experience, 1939-1946,* Constable, 1962, McKay, 1963; *The Future of the Commonwealth,* Muller, 1963, International Publications, 1964; *Australian Father and Son,* Collins, 1966; *Australian Foreign Minister: The Diaries of R. G. Casey, 1951-1960,* edited by T. B. Millar, Collins, 1972. Also author of government reports and booklets on Australian foreign policy.

WORK IN PROGRESS: Updating and revising past writings.

* * *

CASTRO-KLAREN, Sara 1942-

PERSONAL: Born June 9, 1942, in Arequipa, Peru; daughter of Jose Valdivia Castro (a farmer) and Zoila Rosa Rivas de Castro; married Peter Flindell Klaren (a professor). *Education:* University of California at Los Angeles, B.A., 1962, M.A., 1965, Ph.D., 1968. *Home:* 3 Hilltop, Hanover, N.H. 03755. *Office:* Department of Romance Languages and Literature, Dartmouth College, Hanover, N.H. 03755.

CAREER: California State College (now University), Los Angeles, instructor in Latin American literature, 1968; University of Idaho, Moscow, assistant professor of Latin American literature, 1968-70; Dartmouth College, Hanover, N.H., assistant professor, 1970-75, associate professor of Latin American and comparative literature, 1975—. Language instructor for Peace Corps, summers, 1963, 1964. *Member:* Modern Language Association of America, Instituto Internacional de Literatura Latino Americana. *Awards, honors:* Dartmouth College faculty fellowship, 1973; Mellon Foundation fellowship in the Humanities, 1975-76.

WRITINGS: El mundo magico de Jose Maria Arguedas (title means "The Magical World of Jose Maria Arguedas"), Instituto de Estudios Peruanos, 1973. Contributor of articles to *Modern Language Notes, Latin American Literary Review, Comparative Literature,* and other journals.

WORK IN PROGRESS: The phenomenology of solitude in Latin American literature; a modern history of life in the Andes.

* * *

CATE, Curtis Wolsey 1884-1976

December 5, 1884—January 3, 1976; American educator, headmaster, and author of books on teaching. Obituaries: *New York Times,* January 9, 1976.

* * *

CAVAN, Romilly 1914(?)-1975

British playwright, novelist, and screenwriter. Obituaries: *AB Bookman's Weekly,* December 8, 1975.

* * *

CAVELL, Stanley Louis 1926-

PERSONAL: Born September, 1926, in Atlanta, Ga.; son of Irving H. and Fannie (Segal) Goldstein; married Marcia Schmid, July, 1955 (divorced January, 1963); married Cathleen Cohen, June, 1967; children: (first marriage) Rachel Lee. *Education:* University of California, Berkeley, A.B., 1947; University of California, Los Angeles, graduate study, 1948-51; Harvard University, Ph.D., 1961. *Office:* Emerson Hall, Harvard University, Cambridge, Mass. 02138.

CAREER: Harvard University, Cambridge, Mass., junior fellow of Society of Fellows, 1953-56; University of California, Berkeley, assistant professor of philosophy, 1956-62; Institute for Advanced Studies, Princeton, N.J., fellow, 1962-63; Harvard University, Walter M. Cabot Professor of Aesthetics and General Theory of Value, 1963—.

WRITINGS: Must We Mean What We Say? A Book of Essays, Scribner, 1969; *The World Viewed: Reflections on the Ontology of Film,* Viking, 1971; *The Senses of Walden,* Viking, 1972. Contributor of articles to scholarly journals.*

* * *

CAVIN, Ruth (Brodie) 1918-

PERSONAL: Born October 15, 1918, in Pittsburgh, Pa.; daughter of A. Jacob (a salesman) and Jennie (Soble) Brodie; married Bram Cavin (an editor), November 26, 1946; children: Anthony, Emily, Nora. *Education:* Carnegie Institute of Technology (now Carnegie-Mellon University), B.A., 1941. *Religion:* Atheist. *Home:* 2925 Corydon Rd., Cleveland Heights, Ohio 44118. *Agent:* Robert P. Mills, 156 East 52nd St., New York, N.Y. 10022.

WRITINGS—Adult: Complete Party Dinners for the Novice Cook, Macmillan, 1965. For children: *Timothy the Terror,* Dial, 1973; *One Pinch of Sunshine, One-Half Cup of Rain,* Atheneum, 1973; *The Day It Snowed Colored Snow,* Two Continents, 1974; *Picnic Pickles,* Two Continents, 1974.

AVOCATIONAL INTERESTS: The theater.

* * *

CECIL, (Edward Christian) David (Gascoyne) 1902-

PERSONAL: Born April 9, 1902; son of James Edward

Hubert (a statesman) and Cicely Alice (Gore) Gascoyne-Cecil; married Rachel MacCarthy, 1932; children: Jonathan, Hugh, Laura. *Education:* Christ Church, Oxford, first class in history, 1924. *Home:* Red Lion House, Cranborne, Wimborne, Dorset, England. *Office:* 28 Charlbury Road, Oxford, England.

CAREER: Oxford University, Oxford, England, Wadham College, fellow, 1924-30, New College, fellow, 1939-69, emeritus fellow, 1970—, Goldsmiths' Professor of English Literature, 1948-70. Cambridge University, Leslie Stephen lecturer, 1935, Reed lecturer, 1955; trustee, National Portrait Gallery (England), 1937-51. *Member:* The Poetry Society (president, 1947-48), Jane Austen Society (president, 1965). *Awards, honors:* Companion of Honour, 1949; Litt.D., University of Leeds, 1950, University of London, 1957, University of Glasgow, 1962; LL.D., University of Liverpool, 1951, University of St. Andrews, 1951; Companion of Literature award of Royal Society of Literature, 1972.

WRITINGS: (Co-author with Lady Cynthia M. E. Asquith) *Cans and Can'ts,* Hutchinson, 1927; *The Stricken Deer: Or, the Life of Cowper,* Constable, 1929, Bobbs-Merrill, 1930, new edition, Constable, 1933, reprinted, Collins, 1965; (editor and author of introduction) *Selections from Cowper,* Methuen, 1933; *Sir Walter Scott,* Constable, 1933; *Early Victorian Novelists: Essays in Revaluation,* Constable, 1934, Bobbs-Merrill, 1935, published, with new foreword by the author, as *Victorian Novelists: Essays in Revaluation,* University of Chicago Press, 1958; (editor with Charles W. S. Williams, E. de Selincourt, and E. M. W. Tillyard) *The New Book of English Verse,* Gollancz, 1935; *Jane Austen: The Leslie Stephen Lecture,* Cambridge University Press, 1935, reprinted, Folcroft, 1969; (editor) *An Anthology of Modern Biography,* Nelson, 1936; *The Young Melbourne, and the Story of his Marriage with Caroline Lamb,* Bobbs-Merrill, c. 1939.

(Editor) *The Oxford Book of Christian Verse: Chosen and Edited by Lord David Cecil,* Clarendon Press, 1940, new edition, 1965; *The English Poets* (illustrated), Collins, 1941; (contributor) Sir William Rothenstein, *Men of the R. A. F.,* Oxford University Press, 1942; *Hardy, the Novelist: An Essay in Criticism,* Constable, 1943, Bobbs-Merrill, 1946, new edition, Constable, 1956; *Two Quiet Lives: Dorothy Osborne, Thomas Gray,* Bobbs-Merrill, 1948, new edition, Constable, 1965; *Poets and Storytellers: A Book of Critical Essays,* Macmillan, 1949, new edition, Constable, 1960, Barnes & Noble, 1961; (with the 5th Marquess of Salisbury) *Hatfield House: An Illustrated Survey of the Hertfordshire Home of the Cecil Family,* English Life Publications, 1951; *Lord M.; or, the Later Life of Lord Melbourne,* Constable, 1954; *Melbourne* (containing *The Young Melbourne, and the Story of his Marriage with Caroline Lamb* and *Lord M.; or the Later Life of Lord Melbourne*), Bobbs-Merrill, 1954; *The Fine Art of Reading, and Other Literary Studies,* Bobbs-Merrill, 1957; (author of introduction) Augustus E. John, *Augustus John: Fifty-two Drawings,* New York Graphic Society, 1957; (editor with A. Tate) *Modern Verse in English, 1900-1950,* Macmillan, 1958.

(Author of introduction) Sir William Schwenck Gilbert, *The Savoy Operas,* two volumes, Macmillan, 1962; *Max: A Biography,* Constable, 1964, Houghton, 1965; *Visionary and Dreamer: Two Poetic Painters, Samuel Palmer and Edward Burne-Jones,* Constable, 1969, Princeton University Press, 1970; (compiler and author of introduction) *English Short Stories of My Time,* Oxford University Press, 1970; (editor and author of introduction) *The Bodley Head*

Max Beerbohm, Bodley Head, 1970; (editor) *Max Beerbohm: Selected Prose,* Little, Brown, 1971; (editor) *A Choice of Tennyson's Verse,* Faber, 1971; *The Cecils of Hatfield House: An English Ruling Family,* Houghton, 1973; *Library Looking Glass: A Personal Anthology,* Constable, 1975. Contributor to literary journals.

SIDELIGHTS: Lord Cecil is the younger son of British statesman and Conservative Party leader, James Edward Hubert Gascoyne-Cecil, 4th Marquess of Salisbury, and a grandson of British prime minister Robert Arthur Talbot Gascoyne-Cecil, 3rd Marquess of Salisbury.

*   *   *

CERUTTY, Percy Wells 1895-1975

January 10, 1895—August 14, 1975; Australian athletic trainer, lecturer on physical fitness, and author of books in his field. Obituaries: *New York Times,* August 16, 1975. (See index for earlier *CA* sketch)

*   *   *

CHANDONNET, Ann 1943-

PERSONAL: Surname is pronounced Shan-doe-*nay;* born February 7, 1943, in Lowell, Mass; daughter of Leighton D. (a farmer) and Barbara (Cloutman) Fox; married Fernand Chandonnet (a radio announcer), June 11, 1966; children: Yves, Alexdre Jules. *Education:* Lowell State College, B.S. (magna cum laude), 1964; University of Wisconsin, M.S., 1965; graduate study at Boston University, 1967. *Home address:* P.O. Box A-11, Chugiak, Alaska 99567.

CAREER: Dog-walker, housepainter, secretary; high school English teacher in the public schools of Kodiak, Alaska, 1965-66; Lowell State College, Lowell, Mass., instructor in English, 1966-69; Security National Bank, Oakland, Calif., secretary to manager, 1970-71; First Enterprise Bank, Oakland, Calif., administrative assistant to president, 1971-72; *Anchorage Daily News,* Anchorage, Alaska, food editor, 1975—; free-lance writer. *Member:* National Federation of Press Women, Alaska Press Women, Mayflower Descendants in the State of Alaska. *Awards, honors:* First place from Alaska Press Women, 1975, for a feature article, "Keeping an Ancient Art Alive," a profile of one of the last surviving Aleut basketweavers.

WRITINGS: Incunabula (poems), Quixote Press, 1967; *The Complete Fruit Cookbook,* 101 Productions, 1972; *The Cheese Guide and Cookbook,* Nitty Gritty Productions, 1973. Writer of weekly column, "Eating Alaskan," in *Great Lander,* 1974—. Contributor to *California Girl, Venus, Early American Life, Anchorage Daily News, Great Lander, Women's Circle: Home Cooking, Christian Science Monitor,* and *Alaska Journal.* Food editor of *Diablo Valley Voice,* 1971-72.

WORK IN PROGRESS: The Sow's Ear and the Dreamer, a collection of poems; a series of poems about Alaska; profiles of Alaska pioneers for Bicentennial series.

AVOCATIONAL INTERESTS: Conducting living history interviews, skindiving, backpacking, sewing, gardening.

*   *   *

CHANG, Constance D(an) 1917-

PERSONAL: Born February 2, 1917, in Shanghai, China; daughter of Scott S. L. and San-Tsing (Chong) Dan; married Joseph K. L. Chang (a physician), February 15, 1941;

children: Robert, Philip, Miriam (Mrs. Charles Kao). *Education:* Home Economics Institute, Osaka, Japan, certificate of graduation, 1941; Chinese Art Academy, Hong Kong, certificate of graduation, 1950. *Religion:* Protestant. *Home:* 6-21-3 Seijo, Setagaya-Ku, Tokyo 157, Japan.

CAREER: Tokyo Hotel Co., Tokyo, Japan, advisor, 1959; Chinese Cooking Schools, Tokyo, proprietor, 1960—; Madam Chang's Home Kitchens, Tokyo, proprietor, 1960—. Appeared on cooking programs on NHK-TV, 1959. *Member:* Dinners Club. *Awards, honors:* Food business honors from Japanese government, 1960.

WRITINGS: Practical Chinese Cooking (Chinese language), [Hong Kong], 1960; *Home Style Chinese Cooking* (Japanese language), [Sanwa, Japan], 1961; *Chinese Cookery Cards,* two volumes, Paul Hamlyn, 1965; *Quick and Easy Chinese Cooking,* Chong Import (San Francisco), 1968; *The Chinese Menu Cookbook,* Doubleday, 1971; *The Chinese Party Cookbook,* Doubleday, 1972; *The Japanese Menu Cookbook,* Doubleday, 1976.

AVOCATIONAL INTERESTS: Chinese painting, calligraphy, travel.

* * *

CHANG, Richard T(aiwon) 1933-

PERSONAL: Born September 23, 1933, in Pyongyang, Korea; naturalized U.S. citizen, 1961; son of Chang Duck and Yun Suk (Kim) Chang; married Martha Jean Roby (a social sciences research specialist), August 17, 1957; children: Perry Douglas, Penny Denise. *Education:* Roberts Wesleyan College, B.A., 1958; University of Rochester, M.A., 1960; Yale University, M.A., 1960; University of Michigan, Ph.D., 1964. *Religion:* United Church of Christ. *Home:* 1225 Northwest 36th Terrace, Gainesville, Fla. 32605. *Office:* Department of History, University of Florida, Gainesville, Fla.

CAREER: Kent State University, Kent, Ohio, instructor in history, 1963-64; University of Kansas, Lawrence, visiting assistant professor of history, 1964-65; University of Pittsburgh, Pittsburgh, Pa., visiting assistant professor of history, 1965-66; University of Florida, Gainesville, assistant professor, 1966-70, associate professor, 1970-75, professor of history, 1975—. *Military service:* Republic of Korea Marine Corps, Artillery, 1951-54; became first lieutenant. *Awards, honors:* Fulbright fellowship at Kyoto University, 1962-63; National Endowment for the Humanities fellowship, 1972-73; Japan Foundation research fellowship, 1973-74.

WRITINGS: From Prejudice to Tolerance: A Study of the Japanese Image of the West, 1826-1864 (monograph), Sophia University (Tokyo), 1970; *Historians and Meiji Statesmen: A Quantitative Study* (monograph), University of Florida Press, 1970. Contributor of articles and reviews to Asian studies journals.

WORK IN PROGRESS: Imperial Japan's Quest for Equality with the West: A History of Treaty Revision in Japan, 1868-1899; Historians and Taisho Statesmen; The Justice of the Western Consular Courts in Japan.

* * *

CHANT, Eileen Joyce 1945-
(Joy Chant)

PERSONAL: Surname is pronounced with a long "a"; born January 13, 1945, in London, England; daughter of John Maxwell (a draftsman) and Glenys (Sherwell) Chant.

Education: College of Librarianship, Wales, associate, 1970. *Politics:* Socialist. *Religion:* Christian. *Home:* 280 Haynes Park Ct., Sewins Lane, Hornchurch, Essex, England. *Office:* Central Library, Romford, Essex, England.

CAREER: Librarian in London borough of Havering, England, 1966—. Writer.

WRITINGS—All under name Joy Chant: *Red Moon and Black Mountain* (adult fantasy), Allen & Unwin, 1970; *Fantasy and Allegory in Literature for Children and Young People,* College of Librarianship, Wales (Aberystwyth), 1971. Contributor to education journals.

WORK IN PROGRESS: Drum of Dawn and *Song of the King's Emerald,* both novels.

AVOCATIONAL INTERESTS: Theater (director of young people's group "Hollow Circle Theatre"), political activity, trade union activities.

* * *

CHAO, Buwei Yang 1889-

PERSONAL: Listed in some sources as Pu-wei (Yang) Chao; born November 25, 1889, in Naking, China; daughter of K'uei-Yuan (a government official) and Hsiao Yang; married Yuen Ren Chao (a professor), June 1, 1921; children: Rulan Iris (Mrs. Theodore H. Pian), Xinna Nova (Mrs. Pei-Yung Huang), Lensey (Mrs. Isaac Nemioka), Bella Chao Chiu. *Education:* Attended Tokyo Women's Medical School (now College), 1913-17; Tokyo Imperial University, M.D., 1919. *Politics:* Democrat. *Home:* 1059 Cragmont Ave., Berkeley, Calif. 94708.

CAREER: Ch'ungshih School, Nanking, China, principal, 1912-13; Senjen Hospital, Peking, China, physician and co-owner, 1919-21; writer and translator, 1921—.

WRITINGS: (Translator into Chinese) Margaret Sanger, *Nu-tzu Ying Yu te Chih-shih* (translation of *What Every Woman Should Know*), Commercial Press (Shanghai), 1922; *How to Cook and Eat in Chinese,* John Day, 1945, 3rd revised edition, Random House, 1963; *Autobiography of a Chinese Woman* (translation from Chinese by husband Yuen Ren Chao), John Day, 1947, reprinted, Greenwood Press, 1970; *I-ko nu jen te tzu-chuan* (title means "A Woman's Autobiography"), Biographical Literature (Taipei), 1967; *Tsa chi Chao chia* (title means "Family of Chaos"), Biographical Literature, 1972; *How to Order and Eat in Chinese* (in Chinese and English), Random House, 1974.

WORK IN PROGRESS: A book, *Woman's Place in China.*

* * *

CHAPMAN, Joseph Irvine 1912-

PERSONAL: Born September 4, 1912, in Utica, N.Y.; son of W. Wilfred (a businessman) and Carrie L. (Zapf) Chapman; married Shirley Elain Etter, June 25, 1968; children: Carol, David, Stephen, Rebecca, Rachel, Mary Ruth. *Education:* Eastern Baptist Theological Seminary, B.Th., 1937, M.Div., 1968; Colgate University, B.A., 1939. *Home:* 331 Cedar St., Granville, Ohio 43023. *Office:* Ohio Baptist Convention, 141 East Broadway, Granville, Ohio 43023.

CAREER: Pastor of Baptist churches in Georgetown, N.Y., 1937-41, and Brooklyn, N.Y., 1941-47; Minnesota Convention of American Baptist Churches, Minneapolis, executive minister, 1947-57; pastor of Baptist church in Pontiac, Mich., 1957-60; Ohio Baptist Convention, Granville, executive minister, 1960—. Has served as vice-president of American Baptist Convention, member of National Staff Council, Commission on Relationships, National Ministers Council, Town and Country Commission, Council of Executive Ministers, and Executive Commission of the Fund of the Renewal; member of general board and executive committee of Ohio Council of Churches; member of Midwest Commission on the Ministry. Has served as member of board of directors of Brooklyn Goodwill Industries and vice-president of Protestant Council of New York City (Brooklyn); former member of Pontiac mayor's committee on youth. *Awards, honors:* D.D., Sioux Falls College, 1954; named clergyman of the year by Ohio Council of Churches, 1964; D. Laws, Judson College, 1966.

WRITINGS: First Things First, Judson, 1975. Editor of *Ohio Baptist,* 1960—.

AVOCATIONAL INTERESTS: International travel (eleven trips to forty-nine countries).

*   *   *

CHAPMAN, Marie M(anire)   1917-

PERSONAL: Born December 12, 1917, in Buhl, Idaho; daughter of John Leonard (a newspaper editor) and Emma (Rodman) Manire; married Kenneth Arthur Chapman (a pastor and college teacher), August 6, 1941; children: John Arthur, Fran Chapman Thomas, Ramona, Daniel K. *Education:* Kinman Business University, secretarial diploma, 1935; attended Moody Bible Institute, 1939-41; Lynchburg Baptist College, B.S., 1973. *Religion:* Independent Baptist. *Home address:* Route 1, Box 205B, Amherst, Va. 24521.

CAREER: Oakville Courier, Oakville, Wash., reporter and compositor, 1935-39; Bible Institute Colportage Association (now Moody Press), Chicago, Ill., secretary, 1939-41; *Pacific Builder and Engineer,* Seattle, Wash., circulation manager, 1940; *Daily News Journal,* Murfreesboro, Tenn., feature writer and proofreader, 1952-58; Baptist Sunday School Board, Nashville, Tenn., editorial assistant, 1958-64; Lynchburg Baptist College, Lynchburg, Va., administrative assistant, 1971-73, instructor in Christian education and journalism, 1971—; free-lance editor. Piano teacher.

WRITINGS: Practical Methods for Sunday School Teachers, Zondervan, 1962; *Yelling for Help,* Moody, 1972; *Teaching Aids,* Gospel Promotions, 1973; *Disciples Lessons: Primary,* Gospel Promotions, 1973; *Christian Journalism,* Faithlift Ministries, 1974; *Reachout in Writing,* privately printed, 1974; *Successful Teaching Ideas,* Standard Publishing, 1975.

WORK IN PROGRESS: Resource Book for Children's Choirs; A Dairy and a Lock of Hair, a biography of Narcissa Whitman; *Religious Travelers' Guide; Personifications for Puppets; Young Mother's Story.*

*   *   *

CHARNEY, George   1905(?)-1975

1905(?)—December 13, 1975; Russian-born American attorney, political activist, businessman, and author of political autobiography. Obituaries: *New York Times,* December 14, 1975.

*   *   *

CHASE, Cora G(ingrich)   1898-

PERSONAL: Born May 21, 1898, in Kamilche, Wash.; daughter of Frank George (a printer) and Gazelle (Flynn) Gingrich; married Norbert R. Cormier (a bookkeeper), September 16, 1916 (divorced, 1942); married Wendell Corwin Chase (an artist; maker of woodblock prints), May 27, 1946; children: (first marriage) Ray F., Norbert T., Boyd V. *Education:* Attended University of Washington, Seattle, 1938, 1943-45, and 1971. *Politics:* "Hopeful that the dinosaurs of the military-industrial complex eat themselves to death." *Religion:* ". . . a fellowship that sees all life as one, thus members do not eat fellow creatures and believe that love will overcome evil." *Home address:* Route 1, Box 119, Vaughn, Wash. 98394.

CAREER: Everett Better Business Bureau, Everett, Wash., general office clerk, 1928-29; New York Life Insurance Co., agent in Everett, Wash., 1929; J. C. Penney Co., salesman, 1934-35; Mason County Welfare Department, Shelton, Wash., caseworker, 1936-38; Grant County Welfare Department, Ephrata, Wash., caseworker, 1940-43 and 1947; King County Welfare Department, Seattle, Wash., caseworker, 1943-53; Pierce County Welfare Department, Tacoma, Wash., caseworker, 1959-65.

WRITINGS: Unto the Least (biography), Shorey, 1972. Author of brochures for Family Panel of America, 1962-63. Contributor of articles and reviews to small magazines and newspapers in Washington.

WORK IN PROGRESS: The Oyster Was Our World, an autobiographical account of life on Oyster Bay; a cookbook of wild foods.

SIDELIGHTS: Cora Chase writes that some of her main interests are ". . . keeping up on the skullduggery afoot in the world; hoping the prisons will be emptied of those who are victims of the real criminals who stunt human development for the sake of profit; who are themselves stunted human beings, but sitting in the highest offices of the land, using too much tax money for a military machine designed to police the world, to arrest any who threaten their power, blind to the forces of change evident in such events as the recent peoples' victory in Viet Nam." She is also participating in a movement for an alternative monetary system in which money would not be backed solely by gold or silver or tied to any government, but would be backed by the world's commodities and would have an international and constant value. *Avocational interests:* Gardening, foraging.

*   *   *

CHASE, Ilka   1905(?)-

PERSONAL: Born April 8, 1905(?), in New York, N.Y.; daughter of Francis Dane Chase and Edna (former editor of *Vogue* magazine; maiden name, Allaway) Woolman Chase; married Louis Calhern (an actor), 1926 (divorced); married William B. Murray (a radio executive), July 13, 1935 (divorced); married Norton Sager Brown (a doctor), 1946. *Education:* Attended private schools in New York and France. *Address:* c/o Doubleday and Co., 277 Park Ave., New York, N.Y. 10017.

CAREER: Actress and author. Has appeared in more than twenty Broadway plays, in motion pictures, and on radio and television programs; host of radio interview programs, "Luncheon at the Waldorf" and "Penthouse Party," 1938-45; author of syndicated weekly newspaper column.

WRITINGS—All published by Doubleday, except as indicated—Novels: *In Bed We Cry,* 1943, abridged edition, Avon, 1947; *I Love Miss Tilli Bean,* 1946; *New York 22: That District of the City which Lies Between Fiftieth and*

Sixtieth Streets, Fifth Avenue, and the East River, 1951, reprinted Greenwood Press, 1971; *The Island Players*, 1956; *Three Men on the Left Hand*, 1960; *The Sounds of Home*, 1971; *How Fair the Afternoon*, in press.

Biographical: *Past Imperfect* (autobiography), 1942; *Free Admission* (autobiography), 1948; (with mother, Edna Woolman Chase) *Always in Vogue*, 1954.

Travel: *The Carthaginian Rose*, 1961; *Elephants Arrive at Half-Past Five*, 1963; *Second Spring and Two Potatoes*, 1965; *Fresh from the Laundry*, 1967; *The Varied Airs of Spring*, 1969; *Around the World and Other Places*, 1970; *Worlds Apart*, 1972.

Other: *The Care and Feeding of Friends* (entertaining guide), 1973.

*   *   *

CHASE, Richard 1904-

PERSONAL: Born February 15, 1904, near Huntsville, Ala.; son of Robert Collier and Emma Florence (Chase) Chase. *Education:* Antioch College, B.S., 1929. *Home:* 454 West Bonita, Claremont, Calif. 91711.

CAREER: Writer; lecturer on folklore and teller of tales at schools, colleges, universities, libraries, and clubs throughout the United States; worker in recreational facilities; founder of an Appalachian craft industry; conductor of folk festivals and folk art workshops. *Awards, honors:* Southern California Council on Literature award, 1970, for distinguished contribution to the field of folklore for children and young people; honored by the governor of Virginia, 1972; honored at the Los Angeles Renaissance Pleasure Faire, 1973.

WRITINGS: (Editor) *Old Songs and Singing Games*, University of North Carolina Press, 1938; (editor) *The Jack Tales: Told by R. M. Ward and His Kindred in the Beech Mountain Section of Western North Carolina and by Other Descendants of Council Harmon (1803-1896) Elsewhere in the Southern Mountains: With Three Tales from Wise County, Virginia*, Houghton, 1943; (editor) *Grandfather Tales: American-English Folk Tales*, Houghton, 1948; (compiler) *Hullabaloo, and Other Singing Folk Games*, Houghton, 1949, published as *Singing Games and Play-party Games*, Dover, 1967.

Jack and the Three Sillies, Houghton, 1950; *Wicked John and the Devil*, Houghton, 1951; (editor and author of introduction and notes) *American Folk Tales and Songs, and Other Examples of English-American Tradition as Preserved in the Appalachian Mountains and Elsewhere in the United States*, New American Library, 1956, reprinted, Dover, 1971; (editor and author of introduction) Stephen Crane, *The Red Badge of Courage*, Houghton, 1960; (editor) *Billy Boy* (folk song), Golden Gate Junior Books, 1966.*

*   *   *

CHATHAM, Doug(las) M. 1938-

PERSONAL: Born November 24, 1938, in Monroe, La.; son of Bert and Hazel (May) Chatham; married Jackie Reed, June 5, 1959; children: Teresa, Douglas, Jr. *Education:* Mississippi College, B.S., 1964; New Orleans Baptist Theological Seminary, M.R.E., 1968. *Residence:* Decatur, Ga. *Office:* Our Shepherd's Church, 2650 Young Rd., Stone Mountain, Ga. 30083.

CAREER: Pastor in Greenville, Miss., 1965-67, New Orle-
ans, La., 1968-69, Milton, Fla., 1969-72, and Stone Mountain, Ga., 1972—. Assistant to president of New Orleans Baptist Theological Seminary, 1968-69. Member of archaeological expedition to Beersheba, Israel, 1969. Frequent speaker in charismatic Christian movement. *Member:* Smithsonian Institution.

WRITINGS: Notes on the Rapture, Daniels Publishers, 1973; *The Rapture Book*, Whitaker House, 1974; *The Shepherd's Touch*, Cross Roads Publications, 1975.

WORK IN PROGRESS: Under the Shepherd's Staff; All About Angels.

SIDELIGHTS: Chatham writes that he was saved at age eighteen in jail in New Orleans, and was called to preach at the same moment. He pastored his first church while still on probation in 1958, and was pardoned by the governor in 1959. *Avocational interests:* Archaeology.

*   *   *

CHEKKI, Dan(esh) A(yyappa) 1935-

PERSONAL: Born February 5, 1935, in Haveri, Mysore, India; son of Virappa C. (a pleader) and Chenabasavva Yagati; married Sheela D. Leelavati Metgud, May 8, 1966; children: Mahantesh, Chenaviresh. *Education:* Karnatak University, B.A., 1956, Ph.D., 1966; University of Bombay, M.A., 1958, LL.B., 1959, D.Lib., 1960. *Home:* 38 Fitzgerald Crescent, Winnipeg, Manitoba, Canada R3R 1N8. *Office:* Department of Sociology, University of Winnipeg, 515 Portage Ave., Winnipeg, Manitoba, Canada R3B 2E9.

CAREER: University of Bombay, Government Law College, Bombay, India, lecturer in sociology, 1958-61; Karnatak University, Dharwar, India, lecturer in sociology, 1961-66; University of Winnipeg, Winnipeg, Manitoba, assistant professor, 1968-71, associate professor of sociology, 1971—. Reader at Karnatak University, 1967—. Member of International Committee for Family Research, 1972—. Member of board of directors of Family Bureau of Greater Winnipeg, 1970-74.

MEMBER: International Sociological Association, Canadian Association of South Asian Studies, National Council of Family Relations, Academy of Research (president), American Sociological Association, Indian Sociological Society. *Awards, honors:* Research grant from Karnatak University, 1967-68.

WRITINGS: Social Aspects of Ornaments (originally published in Kannada language), Karnatak University, 1967; (contributor) K. Ishwaran, editor, *Contributions to Asian Studies*, Volume I, E. J. Brill, 1971; *Modernization and Social Change: The Family in India*, Mouton & Co., 1972; *Modernization and Kin Network*, E. J. Brill, 1974; *The Social System and Culture of Modern India*, Garland Publishing, 1975. Contributor to sociology journals. Assistant editor of *International Journal of Comparative Sociology*, 1964; associate editor of *Journal of Comparative Family Studies*, 1970—, and *Contributions to Asian Studies*, 1971-74.

WORK IN PROGRESS: The Sociology of Contemporary India; Sociological Research: International Perspectives, completion expected in 1977; *Mobility Aspirations of Youth*, 1978.

AVOCATIONAL INTERESTS: Photography, art collecting.

CHENEY, Anne 1944-

PERSONAL: Born November 1, 1944, in Birmingham, Ala.; daughter of Alan B. (president of Cheney Lime & Cement) and Billie (Gunter) Cheney. *Education:* Birmingham-Southern College, B.A., 1966; Florida State University, M.A., 1968, Ph.D., 1971. *Home:* G 3 Apartment Heights Dr., Blacksburg, Va. 24060. *Office:* English Department, Virginia Polytechnic Institute and State University, Blacksburg, Va. 24061.

CAREER: Virginia Polytechnic Institute and State University, Blacksburg, instructor, 1968-71, assistant professor of American literature, 1971—. *Member:* Modern Language Association of America, Society for the Study of Southern Literature, Southern Atlantic Modern Language Association.

WRITINGS: Millay in Greenwich Village, University of Alabama Press, 1975. Also author of screenplay, "The Changing Status of Women," released by Virginia Polytechnic Institute and State University, 1974, and two-act play, "A Matter of Principle," as yet neither published nor produced. Contributor of articles to *Context,* and of book reviews to *Roanoke Times.*

WORK IN PROGRESS: A biography, *Lorraine Hansberry,* publication by Twayne expected in 1978; more short stories; a novel.

SIDELIGHTS: Anne Cheney told *CA:* "I am fascinated by people, their backgrounds, their families. I believe that most people are basically good, that they only become evil when they are faced with a question of survival, whether physical, emotional, financial. Unlike Joyce Carol Oates (a masterful writer), I am not interested in dwelling on the violence and evil of people. What I hope to find in my writing is the possibility of human potential. (Forgive me for sounding pretentious.) I am also interested in structures within a society, such as a university administration or even seniority among barmaids.

"I am very concerned," Ms. Cheney continued, "about the equality and independence of women, but I detest the 'rhetoric for rhetoric's sake' of many Women's Lib groups. In my play, 'A Matter of Principle,' the main idea is that women who only intellectualize liberation often ignore emotional liberation; or, that the intellectual should never ignore the emotional. I was attracted to both Edna St. Vincent Millay and Lorraine Hansberry as biographical subjects, for both are first-rate artists, both sought liberation for themselves and others, both surrounded themselves with beauty and sought truth. Marriage and/or men they loved had an important impact on both: marriage nearly destroyed Millay's work; Hansberry's marriage to Robert Nemiroff, I am convinced, served as the catalyst to her finest work."

Ms. Cheney added that she is "presently insecure about creative writing, though that is what I most want to do . . . I wish I had a year off to write. I would become a good housekeeper, play tennis or bowl every day, be easier to live with, and write four hours every day." In describing her interests, Ms. Cheney reflected, "I love to travel, especially to New York, Chicago, and the beach. I hope one day to go to Africa, especially Kenya. I like good Scotch and seafood. I am an avid football fan and enjoy theatre and concerts. In the next life, I plan to be a cocktail waitress."

CHENEY, Theodore Albert 1928- (Ted Cheney)

PERSONAL: Born January 1, 1928, in Milton, Mass.; son of Ralph Albert and Ruth (Rees) Cheney; married Dorothy Catherine Bates, September 3, 1949; children: Glenn Alan, Ralph Hunter, Bonnie Bates, Burke Adams. *Education:* Boston University, A.B., 1951, M.A. (geography), 1952; Fairfield University, M.A. (communication), 1973. *Politics:* "Progressive Conservative." *Religion:* Protestant. *Home:* 399 Round Hill Rd., Fairfield, Conn. 06430. *Office:* Graduate School of Corporate and Political Communication, Fairfield University, Fairfield, Conn. 06430.

CAREER: Photogrammetrist for Park Aerial Surveys, Inc., 1952-54; Cornell University, Ithaca, N.Y., assistant professor of photogrammetry, 1954-58; Geotechnics & Resources, Inc., White Plains, N.Y., vice-president, 1958-64; Dunlap & Associates ("think tank"), Darien, Conn., senior scientist, 1964-69; Fairfield University, Fairfield, Conn., lecturer in communication and administration coordinator, 1969—. *Military service:* U.S. Navy, 1945-47. *Member:* Authors Guild of America, Authors League of America.

WRITINGS: (Editor) *Burma: Landforms, Forestry, Geology,* Cornell University Press, 1956; *Fort Churchill, Manitoba, Canada: An Environmental Analysis,* Cornell University Press, 1957; *Camping by Backpack and Canoe,* Funk, 1970.

Under name Ted Cheney: *Land of the Hibernating Rivers* (juvenile), Harcourt, 1968.

WORK IN PROGRESS: A novel set in Hudson Bay, *Below Harding's Fjord;* editing *Performance Appraisal,* by Howard Smith and Paul Brourer; research for a book about creativity and problem solving, *Soft Logic.*

SIDELIGHTS: Cheney volunteered "to go to Little America, Antarctica at age seventeen while in the U.S. Navy, which led to a life-long interest in polar matters—out of which came my first book. . . . Camping and canoeing as a Boy Scout leader over the years led to the second book."

* * *

CHENNAULT, Anna (Chan) 1925-

PERSONAL: Born June 23, 1925, in Peking, China; came to United States, 1948; naturalized U.S. citizen, 1950; daughter of Ying Wing (a doctor) and Bessie (Jeong) Chan; married Claire Lee Chennault, December 21, 1947 (died July, 1958); children: Claire Anna, Cynthia Louise. *Education:* Ling Nan University, B.A., 1944. *Politics:* Republican. *Religion:* Catholic. *Home:* Watergate East, 2510 Virginia Ave. N.W., Washington, D.C. 20037. *Agent:* (Lectures) W. Colston Leigh, Inc., 1185 Avenue of the Americas, New York, N.Y. 10036. *Office:* Flying Tiger Line, Inc., Investment Bldg., 1511 K St. N.W., Washington, D.C. 20005.

CAREER: Correspondent, Central News Agency, Kunming and Shanghai, China, 1944-48; feature writer, *Hsin Ming Daily News,* Shanghai, 1944-48; Civil Air Transport, Taipei, Taiwan, public relations officer, and editor of *Civil Air Transport Bulletin,* 1946-57; U.S. correspondent, *Hsin Shen Daily News,* Taipei, Taiwan, 1958—; Georgetown University, Washington, D.C., chief of Chinese section of Machine Translation Research Center, 1958-63; Voice of America, Washington, D.C., broadcaster, 1963-66; Central News Agency, Washington, D.C., special correspondent, 1965—; Flying Tiger Line, Washington, D.C., vice-president of international affairs, 1968—. Lecturer in United States and Asia; writer. Founding member and co-chairman, National Heritage Group Council of Republican National Committee; member of Republican National Finance Committee, 1969—. Member of board of directors, District of Columbia National Bank, 1972—. Member of executive committee, American Academy of Achievement. Member of board of trustees, Center for the Study of the Presidency. Advisor, Radio of Free Asia; member in advisory capacity of government and civic organizations, including UNESCO, U.S. Department of Health, Education, and Welfare, President's Advisory Committee on the Arts, American Revolution Bicentennial Advisory Council, National League of Families of American Prisoners and Missing in Southeast Asia, and Chinese-American Citizens Alliance.

MEMBER: International Platform Association, International Club of Washington, Foreign Policy Association, Overseas Press Club of America, National Press Club, American Newspaper Women's Club, National League of American Pen Women, Writers' Association (Free China), National Aeronautic Association, Aerospace Medical Association (honorary fellow), Flying Tigers, Capitol Hill Society, Asian-Pacific Council of American Chambers of Commerce, Army and Navy Club, League of Republican Women of the District of Columbia, U.S. Air Force Wives Club, 1925 F Street Club, Georgetown Club, Century Club, Friends of Chung-ang University, Theta Sigma Phi.

AWARDS, HONORS: Woman of Distinction award, Texas Technological College (now Texas Tech University), 1966; Freedom award, Order of Lafayette, 1966; Freedom Award of Free China Association, 1966; Golden Plate award, American Academy of Achievement, 1967; Litt.S., Chung-ang University, 1967; LL.D., Lincoln University, 1970; H.H.D., Manahath Educational Center, 1970; Chinese-American Citizens Alliance award of honor, 1972; Republican of the Year award, District of Columbia Teachers College, 1974; honorary fellow of Aerospace Medical Association, 1975.

WRITINGS: A Thousand Springs: The Biography of a Marriage, Paul Eriksson, 1962; *Dictionary of New Simplified Chinese Characters,* Machine Translation, Chinese Section, Georgetown University, 1962; *Chennault and the Flying Tigers,* Paul Eriksson, 1963; *Telegraphic Code Chinese-English Dictionary for Machine Translation,* Machine Translation, Chinese Section, Georgetown University, 1963; *Ch'en Hsian-mei shih chien* (radio scripts in Chinese, with English resumes; title means "Chen Hsiang-mei's Time"), Voice of America, 1965. Translator into Chinese of Claire Lee Chennault's book, *Way of a Fighter,* 1955. Author of fifteen books in Chinese, published in Taipei, 1961-67.

WORK IN PROGRESS: The Education of Anna Chennault.

* * *

CHERNAIK, Judith 1934-

PERSONAL: Born October 24, 1934, in New York, N.Y.; daughter of Reuben and Gertrude (Lapidus) Sheffield; married Warren Lewis Chernaik (a lecturer in English), September 2, 1956; children: Laura Rose, David Jacob, Sara Elizabeth. *Education:* Cornell University, B.A., 1955; Yale University, Ph.D., 1964. *Home:* 13 Constantine Rd., London N.W.3, England. *Agent:* Wendy Weil, Julian Bach Literary Agency, 3 East 48th St., New York, N.Y. 10017.

CAREER: Columbia University, New York, N.Y., lecturer in English, 1963-65; Tufts University, Medford, Mass., assistant professor of English, 1965-69; writing and research, 1969-74; University of London, London, England, lecturer in English, 1974-75. *Awards, honors:* Radcliffe Institute fellowship, 1966-68; American Council of Learned Societies fellowship, 1972-73.

WRITINGS: The Lyrics of Shelley, Case Western Reserve University Press, 1972; *Double Fault* (novel), Putnam, 1975. Contributor of articles and reviews to magazines including *Atlantic, Saturday Review,* and *London Magazine* and to newspapers.

WORK IN PROGRESS: A novel based on the life of Eleanor Marx, for Putnam; a study of the major poems of Shelley.

AVOCATIONAL INTERESTS: Music.

* * *

CHETWYND-HAYES, R(onald Henry Glynn) 1919- (Angus Campbell)

PERSONAL: Born May 30, 1919; son of Henry (a movie theatre manager) and Rose May (Cooper) Chetwynd-Hayes. *Education:* Educated in England. *Politics:* Liberal. *Religion:* Church of England. *Home and office:* 42A Church Rd., Richmond, Surrey TW10 6LN, England. *Agent:* London Management, 235/241 Regent St., London W1A 2JT, England.

CAREER: Salesman in London, England, for Harrods Ltd., Army and Navy Stores, and Bourne and Hollingsworth Ltd.; showroom and exhibition manager for Peerless Build-In Furniture Ltd.; writer and editor, 1972—. *Military service:* British Army, 1939-46. *Member:* Society of Authors.

WRITINGS—All fiction: The Man from the Bomb, John Spencer, 1959; *The Dark Man,* Sidgwick & Jackson, 1964; *The Unbidden,* Tandem Books, 1971, Pyramid Press, 1975; *Cold Terror,* Tandem Books, 1973, Pyramid Press, 1975; *The Elemental,* Fontana Books, 1974; *The Night Ghouls,* Fontana Books, 1975; *The Monster Club,* New English Library, 1975; *Terror by Night,* Pyramid Press, 1976; *Tales from the Dark Lands,* Fontana Books, in press.

Editor, all published by Fontana Books, except as noted: *Cornish Tales of Terror,* 1971; (under pseudonym Angus Campbell) *Scottish Tales of Terror,* 1972; *Welsh Tales of Terror,* 1973; *Ninth Fontana Book of Great Ghost Stories,* 1973; *Tenth Fontana Book of Great Ghost Stories,* 1974; *Eleventh Fontana Book of Great Ghost Stories,* 1975; *Terror Tales from Outer Space,* 1975; *First Armada Monster Book* (for children), Armada Books, 1975; *Second Armada Monster Book,* Armada Books, 1976; *Gaslight Tales of Terror,* 1976.

WORK IN PROGRESS: Humorous and factual articles for *Ghoul* (magazine); *Twelfth Fontana Book of Great Ghost Stories; Third Armada Monster Book;* a gothic novel.

SIDELIGHTS: A film "From Beyond the Grave," based on four stories by Chetwynd-Hayes, was made by Amicus Films for Warner Brothers in 1974. "Something in the Woodwork," a television adaptation of Chetwynd-Hayes' story "Household," was shown on "Night Gallery."

* * *

CHEVALIER, Haakon (Maurice) 1902-

PERSONAL: Born September 10, 1902, in Lakewood,

N.J.; son of Emile and Therese (Roggen) Chevalier; married Ruth Bosley, 1922 (divorced, 1931); married Barbara Lansburgh, 1931 (divorced, 1950); married Carol Lansburgh, 1952; children: (first marriage) Jacques Anatole; (second marriage) Suzanne Andree, Haakon Lazarus; (third marriage) Karen Anne. *Education:* Student, Stanford University, 1918-20; University of California, A.B., 1923, A.M., 1925, Ph.D., 1929. *Home:* 19 rue du Mont-Cenis, Paris 18e, France.

CAREER: University of California, Berkeley, Calif., professor of French, 1929-46; French interpreter, United Nations Conference, San Francisco, Calif., 1945, War Criminals Trials, Nuremberg, West Germany, 1945-46, United Nations, Lake Success, N.Y., 1946; full-time translator and author, 1946—. *Member:* P.E.N., Authors League of America, Association Internationale des Interpretes de Conference, Association des Traducteurs Litteraires de France.

WRITINGS: The Ironic Temper: Anatole France and His Time, Oxford University Press, 1932; *For Us the Living,* Knopf, 1949; *The Man Who Would be God,* Putnam, 1959; *Oppenheimer: The Story of a Friendship,* Braziller, 1965; *The Last Voyage of the Schooner Rosamond,* Deutsch, 1970.

Translator: Andre Malraux, *Man's Fate,* Smith & Haas, 1934, reissued, Random House, 1961, 1968; Malraux, *Days of Wrath,* Random House, 1936, McGraw, 1964; Louis Aragon, *The Bells of Basel,* Harcourt, 1936; Aragon, *Residential Quarter,* Harcourt, 1938; Salvador Dali, *The Secret Life of Salvador Dali,* Dial, 1942, 3rd edition, Vision Press, 1968; Vladimir Pozner, *The Edge of the Sword,* Modern Age Books, 1942; Pozner, *First Harvest,* Viking, 1943; Gontran de Poncins, *Home is the Hunter,* Reynal & Hitchcock, 1943; Andre Maurois, *Seven Faces of Love,* Didier, 1944, reissued, Doubleday, 1962; Dali, *Hidden Faces,* Dial, 1944; Joseph Kessel, *Army of Shadows,* Knopf, 1944; Denis de Rougemont, *Devil's Share,* Pantheon, 1944, published as *The Devil's Share: An Essay on the Diabolic in Modern Society,* Meridian Books, 1956; Maurois, *Franklin: The Life of an Optimist,* Didier, 1945; Vercors, *Three Short Novels by Vercors,* Little, Brown, 1947; Simon Gantillon, *Vessel of Wrath,* Putnam, 1947; Dali, *50 Secrets of Magic Craftsmanship,* Dial, 1948.

Dali, *Dali on Modern Art: The Cuckolds of Antiquated Modern Art,* Dial, 1957; (and editor) Stendhal, *A Roman Journal,* Orion Press, 1957; Rene Grousset, *Chinese Art and Culture,* Orion Press, 1959; Michel Seuphor, *The Sculpture of this Century: Dictionary of Modern Sculpture,* Zwemmer, 1959, published as *The Sculpture of This Century,* Braziller, 1960; Louis Aragon, *Holy Week,* Putnam, 1961; Seuphor, *Abstract Painting: Fifty Years of Accomplishment, From Kandinsky to the Present,* Abrams, 1962 (published in England as *Abstract Painting from Kandinsky to the Present,* Prentice-Hall International, 1962); Henri Michaux, *Light Through Darkness,* Orion Press, 1963, published as *Light Through Darkness: Explorations among Drugs,* Bodley Head, 1964; Seuphor, *Abstract Painting in Flanders,* Arcade (Brussels), 1963; Robert Descharnes and Jean-Francois Chabrun, *Auguste Rodin,* Macmillan, 1968; Bob Claessens and Jeanne Rousseau, *Our Breugel,* Fond Mercator (Antwerp), 1969.

Pierre Galante, *Malraux,* Cowles, 1971; Jerzy Szablowski, Sophie Schneebalg-Perelman, and Adelbrecht L. J. van de Walle, *The Flemish Tapestries at Wawel Castle in Cracow: Treasures of King Sigismund Augustus Jagiello,* Fond Mercator (Antwerp), 1972. Contributor to various magazines.

BIOGRAPHICAL/CRITICAL SOURCES: The New York Review of Books, July 2, 1970.

*   *   *

CHILDS, Marquis W(illiam)   1903-

PERSONAL: Born March 17, 1903, in Clinton, Iowa; son of William Henry (a lawyer) and Lilian Malissa (Marquis) Childs; married Lu Prentiss, August 26, 1926 (died June, 1968); married Jane Neylan McBain, August 6, 1969; children: (first marriage) Prentiss, Malissa. *Education:* University of Wisconsin, A.B., 1923; University of Iowa, A.M., 1925. *Home:* 2703 Dumbarton Ave. N.W., Washington, D.C. 20007. *Office:* 1701 Pennsylvania Ave. N.W., Washington, D.C. 20036.

CAREER: United Press International, reporter in Chicago and Midwest, 1923, in New York, 1925-26; *St. Louis Post Dispatch,* St. Louis, Mo., feature writer, 1926-30; freelance writer, 1930-34; *St. Louis Post Dispatch,* special correspondent and member of Washington, D.C. staff, 1934-68. Columnist for United Feature Syndicate, 1944-54. Eric W. Allen Memorial Lecturer at University of Oregon, 1950, and lecturer at Columbia University School of Journalism.

MEMBER: Sigma Delta Chi; Kappa Sigma; Overseas Writers Club (president, 1943-45); Century Club (New York); Gridiron Club (president, 1957); Washington Press Club, Metropolitan Club, and Cosmos Club (all Washington). *Awards, honors:* Order of the North Star (Sweden), Sigma Delta Chi award, 1945, for best Washington correspondent; University of Missouri award for journalism, 1951; Pulitzer Prize for commentary (first time awarded), 1969; LL.D., Upsala College, 1943; Litt.D., University of Wisconsin, 1966, and University of Iowa, 1969.

WRITINGS—Nonfiction: *Sweden: Where Capitalism Is Controlled,* John Day, 1934; *Sweden: The Middle Way,* Yale University Press, 1936, second revised and enlarged edition, 1947; *They Hate Roosevelt!,* Harper, 1936; *Washington Calling!,* Morrow, 1937; *This Is Democracy: Collective Bargaining in Scandinavia,* Yale University Press, 1938; (with William T. Stone) *Toward a Dynamic America: The Challenge of a Changing World,* Foreign Policy Association, 1941; *This is Your War,* Little, Brown, 1942; *I Write from Washington,* Harper, 1942; (author of new evaluation) Brooks Adams, *America's Economic Supremacy,* Harper, 1947, reprinted, Books for Libraries, 1971. *The Farmer Takes a Hand: The Electric Power Revolution in Rural America,* Doubleday, 1952, reprinted, DaCapo Press, 1974; (with Douglass Cater) *Ethics in a Business Society,* Harper, 1954, reprinted, Greenwood Press, 1973; *The Ragged Edge: The Diary of a Crisis,* Doubleday, 1955; *Eisenhower, Captive Hero: A Critical Study of the General and the President,* Harcourt, 1958; (editor with James Reston) *Walter Lippmann and His Times,* Harcourt, 1959, reprinted, Books for Libraries, 1968; *The Peacemakers,* Harcourt, 1961.

Novels: *The Cabin,* Harper, 1944; *Taint of Innocence,* Harper, 1967.

Contributor to *Saturday Evening Post, Life, New Republic, Yale Review, Reader's Digest,* and other periodicals.*

CHILTON, John (James) 1932-

PERSONAL: Born July 16, 1932, in London, England; son of Thomas W. (a singer) and Eileen (Burke) Chilton; married Teresa Macdonald (a bookseller); children: Jennifer, Martin, Barnaby. *Education:* Attended schools in England. *Residence:* London, England. *Office:* Bloomsbury Book Shop, 31-35 Great Ormond St., London W.C.1, England.

CAREER: Has held positions in advertising, and with the *Daily Telegraph,* 1953-57; professional musician, leader of his own band, 1957-59, member of Bruce Turner's Jump Band, 1959-63; public relations work and freelance writing, 1963-67; Bloomsbury Book Shop, London, co-manager, 1967-73; full-time musician, leader of his own band, 1973—; jazz historian and composer. *Military service:* Royal Air Force, 1950-52; became senior aircraftsman. *Member:* National Union of Journalists, Musicians Union, Performing Rights Society.

WRITINGS: (With Max Jones) *Salute to Satchmo,* International Publishing, 1970; (with Jones) *Louis: The Louis Armstrong Story,* Little, Brown, 1971; *Who's Who of Jazz,* Bloomsbury Book Shop, 1970, Chilton, 1971; *Billie's Blues,* Stein & Day, 1975.

SIDELIGHTS: Chilton's band toured the U.S. in 1974 and has recorded for several major American recording companies.

* * *

CHIN, Robert 1918-

PERSONAL: Born March 5, 1918, in New York, N.Y.; son of Chee and Lowe Chin; married Ai-Li Sung (a sociologist), 1943; children: Jeffrey, Carol, Constance. *Education:* Columbia University, B.A., 1939, M.A., 1940, Ph.D., 1943. *Office:* Department of Psychology, Boston University, 755 Commonwealth Ave., Boston, Mass. 02215.

CAREER: Boston University, Boston, Mass., assistant professor, 1947-54, associate professor, 1954-62, professor of psychology, 1962—. Director of Human Relations Center, Boston, 1954-62. *Military service:* U.S. Army, 1942-45; became first leiutenant. *Member:* American Psychological Association (fellow; division president, 1969-70).

WRITINGS: (Editor with W. G. Bennish, K. D. Benne, and K. Corey) *The Planning of Change: A Reader in Applied Behavioral Science,* Holt, 2nd edition (Chin not associated with earlier edition), 1968, 3rd edition, 1976; (with wife, Ai-Li Chin) *Psychological Research in Communist China, 1949-1966,* M.I.T. Press, 1969. General editor, *Journal of Social Issues,* 1959-66.

* * *

CHISHOLM, K. Lomneth 1919-

PERSONAL: Born August 6, 1919, in Detroit, Mich.; daughter of James Kinkaid (a dentist) and Kathryn (Lomneth) Lennox; married R. E. Chisholm (marriage ended, March 17, 1970); children: Rose Marie (Mrs. Charles Cohen), James R., Debra Kennedy, Kathyann, Phyllis Lee. *Education:* Attended Barlow School of Art (Detroit), Wayne State University, and Madison School of Business (Brooklyn, N.Y.). *Politics:* "Conservative—non-committed." *Religion:* "Raised in Christian Science." *Home address:* P.O. Box 224, Scotch Plains, N.J. 07076. *Agent:* Elizabeth R. Otis, McIntosh & Otis, Inc., 475 Fifth Ave., New York, N.Y. 10017. *Office:* Tranquility Studios, P.O. Box 3038 BCS, East Orange, N.J. 07019.

CAREER: Prior to 1950, worked as office manager for Western Union, in personnel for Sperry Gyroscope, held administrative post with Ford Motor Co., and secretarial job with J. C. Penney; instructor at Lane School in Fanwood, N.J., 1954-60; Tranquility Studios, East Orange, N.J., craftswoman, 1960—.

WRITINGS: Candlemaker's Primer, Dutton, 1973. Affiliated with *Packing & Shipping,* 1968-69.

WORK IN PROGRESS: Devil Wind, a novel; *How to Make Flowers,* a craft book; international research on yarns, fibers, and fleeces for a hobby book.

* * *

CHISSELL, Joan Olive

PERSONAL: Born in Cromer, England. *Education:* Royal College of Music, A.R.C.M., G.R.S.M. *Home:* 7d Abbey Rd., St. John's Wood, London N.W.8, England.

CAREER: Lecturer in music for extra-mural departments of Oxford University and University of London, 1943-48; piano teacher in junior department of Royal College of Music, 1943-53; appointed assistant music critic of *Times,* London, 1947; regular broadcaster for British Broadcasting Corp.

WRITINGS: Schumann, Dent, 1948, 2nd edition, 1956, Farrar, Strauss, 1956, revised edition, 1967; *The Concerto: Chamber Music,* Pelican, 1952, revised edition, 1957; (contributor) *Benjamin Britten: A Symposium,* Rockliff, 1953; *Chopin,* Crowell, 1965; *Schumann Piano Music,* University of Washington Press, 1972; *Brahms,* Faber, in press. Contributor to music journals.

AVOCATIONAL INTERESTS: Boating.

* * *

CHITTENDEN, Elizabeth F. 1903-

PERSONAL: Born November 4, 1903, in Brandon, Vt.; daughter of Merritt Darrow (a teacher) and Gertrude (a teacher; maiden name, Cahee) Chittenden. *Education:* Smith College, A.B., 1924; University of Buffalo, M.A., 1936. *Politics:* Independent ("slanted liberal"). *Religion:* Episcopalian. *Home:* 310 Argonne Dr., Kenmore, N.Y. 14217.

CAREER: Teacher of English in Oswego, N.Y., 1924-25; teacher of English in Kenmore, N.Y., 1925-64, chairman of department of English, 1956-64; full-time free-lance writer, 1964—. Director of religious education at Trinity Church, Buffalo, N.Y., 1966-69; volunteer tutor at Episcopal center. *Member:* National League of American Pen Women (recording secretary, Western New York branch, 1974—).

WRITINGS: (Translation editor) Katalin Ertavy-Barath, *Teaspoonful of Freedom,* American-Hungarian Literary Guild, 1968; *Profiles in Black and White: Stories of Men and Women Who Fought Against Slavery* (juvenile), Scribner, 1973. Contributor to *American West, Yankee, Negro History, Vermonter, Church Herald,* and other periodicals.

WORK IN PROGRESS: This Woman Question, a biography of Abigail Scott Duniway, the first woman's rights worker in the Northwest, for junior high readers and up; *We Were a Procession,* a collective biography of little-known women who were early leaders in women's rights.

SIDELIGHTS: Elizabeth Chittenden commented: "[I am] always a Vermonter, who lives in New York State and summers in Maine. Yet, whenever I hear 'America the Beautiful,' I see in my mind's eye Mount Mansfield, Camel's Hump, Lake Champlain, my symbols of Vermont."

CHODES, John 1939-

PERSONAL: Born February 23, 1939, in New York, N.Y.; son of Ralph Jay (an editor) and Henrietta (Jonas) Chodes. *Education:* Hunter College of the City University of New York, B.A., 1963; Germain School of Photography, commercial photography certificate, 1965. *Politics:* "Fluctuating outlook." *Religion:* Jewish. *Home and office:* 411 East 10th St., New York, N.Y. 10009.

CAREER: Full-time writer, 1965-67; *Business Week* (magazine), New York City, sales promotion copywriter, 1967-70; *Forbes* (magazine), New York City, sales promotion copywriter, 1969-71; *Fortune* (magazine), New York City, sales promotion copywriter, 1971-72; *New York Times*, New York City, sales promotion copywriter, 1972-75. *Awards, honors:* Journalistic excellence award from Road Runners Club of America, 1975, for *Corbitt*.

WRITINGS: The Myth of America's Military Power, Branden Press, 1972; *Corbitt*, Tafnews, 1974. Author of "Avenue A Anthology" (series of monologues), first produced in New York at Henry Street Settlement House, 1967.

WORK IN PROGRESS: "An anagorical dream journey following my personal ascent from hell to spiritual revelation," in the form of a novel-length poem.

SIDELIGHTS: Chodes writes: "*The Myth of America's Military Power* was my answer to the peace movement during the Vietnam war. *Corbitt* was the biography of a friend who had a tremendous influence on my life. My new untitled work hopes to reveal, through my growth, the relationship of man to the philosophies that dominate the twentieth century."

*   *   *

CHRISTIE, Agatha (Mary Clarissa) 1890-1976
(Mary Westmacott)

September 15, 1890—January 12, 1976; British mystery novelist, author of stories and romances under pseudonym. Obituaries: *New York Times*, January 13, 1976; *Washington Post*, January 13, 1976; *Detroit Free Press*, January 14, 1976; *Bookseller*, January 17, 1976; *Publishers Weekly*, January 19, 1976; *Time*, January 26, 1976; *Newsweek*, January 26, 1976; *School Library Journal*, February, 1976; *Current Biography*, March, 1976. (See index for previous CA sketch)

*   *   *

CHRISTIE, Lindsay H. 1906(?)-1976

1906(?)—January 13, 1976; American editor and author. Obituaries: *New York Times*, January 16, 1976.

*   *   *

CHURCH, Robert L(eValley) 1938-

PERSONAL: Born August 20, 1938, in St. Louis, Mo.; son of Herbert Frederic (an educator) and Mildred (James) Church; married Olga Maranjian (a nursing educator), June 3, 1965; children: Douglas A. L., Nicholas James. *Education:* Yale University, B.A., 1960; Harvard University, M.A., 1961, Ph.D., 1966. *Home:* 2224 Wesley Ave., Evanston, Ill. 60201. *Office:* School of Education, Northwestern University, 2003 Sheridan Rd., Evanston, Ill. 60201.

CAREER: Harvard University, Cambridge, Mass., instructor in history, 1965-66, assistant professor of educa-

tion, 1966-70; Northwestern University, Evanston, Ill., associate professor, 1970-75, professor of education, 1975—, associate professor of history, 1970-75, associate dean of School of Education, 1975—. *Member:* Organization of American Historians, History of Education Society. *Awards, honors:* Woodrow Wilson fellowship, 1960-61; Shelby Cullom Davis fellowship from Princeton University, 1969-70.

WRITINGS: (With Paul H. Buck, David B. Potts, Arthur Powell, and others) *The Social Sciences at Harvard: From Inculcation to the Open Mind*, Harvard University Press, 1965; (contributor) Lawrence Stone, editor, *The University in Society*, Princeton University Press, 1974; (with Michael Sedlak) *The Educational History of the United States: 1776-1975*, Free Press, in press. Member of editorial board of *History of Education Quarterly*, 1970—; consulting editor for *Encyclopedia of Education*, 1971.

WORK IN PROGRESS: A book on the history of academic psychology in the United States since 1890, with special emphasis on psychology as applied in education, completion expected in 1980.

*   *   *

CIRINO, Robert 1937-

PERSONAL: Born April 22, 1937, in San Fernando, Calif.; son of Mike Louis (an athletic coach) and Frances (Nix) Cirino. *Education:* San Fernando Valley State College (now California State University, Northridge), B.A., 1962; San Francisco State College (now University), graduate study; San Diego State College (now University), teaching credential, 1965; University of Hawaii, M.Ed., 1968. *Politics:* Independent. *Residence:* Hermosa Beach, Calif. *Agent:* Jay Hoffman, 325 East 57th St., New York, N.Y. 10022.

CAREER: Truck driver in San Fernando, Calif., 1957-65; merchant seaman, 1959-61; high school history teacher, football and swimming coach in Huntington Park, Calif., 1965-67; full-time writer, 1967—. Part-time lecturer in English, University of Hawaii. *Military service:* U.S. Army, 1955-57. *Member:* American Federation of Teachers.

WRITINGS: Don't Blame the People: How the News Media Use Bias, Distortion, and Censorship to Manipulate Public Opinion, Random House, 1972; *Power to Persuade: Mass Media and the News*, Bantam, 1974. Contributor to *Los Angeles Free Press*, *Television Quarterly*, and *Los Angeles News Advocate*. Editor, *Grassroots*.

WORK IN PROGRESS: Research on teachers and the media; a book on political bias in entertainment.

SIDELIGHTS: Cirino writes that he is "concerned with bias, distortion, and censorship in New Media" that is designed "to get people to support established priorities and policies."

*   *   *

CISMARU, Alfred 1933-

PERSONAL: Born October 26, 1933, in Paris, France; U.S. citizen; married Pearl Klein (a teacher), 1957; children: Claude, David. *Education:* Fordham University, B.A., 1956; New York University, M.A., 1957, Ph.D., 1960. *Home:* 5307 44th St., Lubbock, Tex. 79414. *Office:* Department of Classical and Romance Languages, Texas Tech University, Box 4649, Lubbock, Tex. 79409.

CAREER: Brooklyn College (now of the City University

of New York), Brooklyn, N.Y., instructor in French and Spanish, 1958-59; St. Michael's College, Winooski, Vt., associate professor, 1959-65, professor of French, 1965-70, chairman of department of languages, 1959-70; Texas Tech University, Lubbock, professor of French, Italian, and Spanish, 1970—. *Member:* Modern Language Association of America, American Association of Teachers of French, American Association of Teachers of Spanish and Portuguese, Texas Association of College Teachers, Vermont Modern Language Association.

WRITINGS: Marguerite Duras, Twayne, 1971; *Boris Vian,* Twayne, 1974; *Moliere and Marivaux: A Comparison,* Texas Tech University Press, 1975. Contributor of about sixty articles to academic journals.

* * *

CIUBA, Edward J(oseph) 1935-

PERSONAL: Born March 20, 1935, in Elizabeth, N.J.; son of Joseph and Anna Ciuba. *Education:* Attended Seton Hall University, 1951-53; Immaculate Conception Seminary, A.B., 1955; Gregorian University, S.T.L., 1959; Pontifical Biblical Institute, S.S.L., 1962; graduate study at Ecole Biblique et Archeologique Francaise, 1962-63. *Office:* Immaculate Conception Seminary, Darlington, Mahwah, N.J. 07430.

CAREER: Roman Catholic priest, ordained, 1959; assistant pastor in Jersey City, N.J., 1960; Immaculate Conception Seminary, Darlington, Mahwah, N.J., professor of Sacred Scripture, 1963—, rector, 1974—. Visiting summer professor at St. Louis University, 1967-68, Notre Dame University, 1969, Fairfield University, 1971-73, and Fordham University, 1974; instructor at Felician College, 1970. Member of Priests' Senate of Archdiocese of Newark, 1966-73, and National Commission for Theological Discussion Between United Methodist Church and Roman Catholic Church, 1971-75.

WRITINGS: Who Do You Say That I Am?, Alba, 1974. Contributor to religious publications.

* * *

CLARK, Colin (Grant) 1905-

PERSONAL: Born November 2, 1905, in England; son of James (a merchant and manufacturer) and Marion Nellie (Jolly) Clark; married Marjorie Tattersall, July 27, 1935; children: Gregory, Nicholas, Christopher, Antony, Bernard, Maurice, Oliver, David, Cecily. *Education:* Oxford University, M.A., 1931; Cambridge University, M.A., 1931. *Office:* Institute of Economic College, Mannix College, Monash University, Clayton, Victoria 3168, Australia.

CAREER: New Survey of London Life and Labour, staff member, 1928-29; Social Survey of Liverpool, Liverpool, England, deputy director, 1929-30; Cabinet Offices, London, England, assistant secretary of Economic Advisory Council, 1930-31; Cambridge University, Cambridge, England, lecturer in statistics, 1931-37; Government of Queensland, Australia, state statistician, 1938-46, Under-Secretary of State for Labour and Industry, 1946-52; financial adviser to state treasury, and director of Bureau of Industry, 1938-52; Oxford University, director of Institute for Research in Agricultural Economics, 1953-69; Econometric Institute of New York, supervisor of research, 1958-61; Monash University, Clayton, Victoria, Australia, research fellow of faculty of economics and politics, 1969—.

Visiting lecturer, University of Sydney, University of Melbourne, and University of Western Australia, 1937-38; visiting professor, University of Chicago, 1952.

MEMBER: Econometric Society (fellow), International Statistical Institute, Royal Statistical Society, Johnsonian Club (Brisbane, Australia). *Awards, honors:* Frances Wood Prizeman of Royal Statistical Society, 1928; Sc.D., University of Milan, 1957; D.Econ., University of Tilburg, 1962; D.Litt., Oxford University, 1971.

WRITINGS: The National Income, 1924-1931, Macmillan, 1932, reprinted, Augustus M. Kelley, 1965; (editor) George T. Jones, *Increasing Return: A Study of the Relation between the Size and Efficiency of Industries, with Special Reference to the History of Selected British and American Industries, 1850-1910,* Cambridge University Press, 1933; *The Control of Investment,* Gollancz, 1933; *Investment in Fixed Capital in Great Britain,* London & Cambridge Economic Service, 1934; *A Socialist Budget,* Gollancz, 1935; (with Arthur C. Pigou) *The Economic Position of Great Britain, 1935,* London & Cambridge Economic Service, 1936; *National Income and Outlay,* Macmillan, 1937, reprinted, Augustus M. Kelley, 1965; (with John G. Crawford) *The National Income of Australia,* Angus & Robertson, 1938; *Australian Economic Progress Against a World Background,* Hassell Press (Adelaide), 1938; *A Critique of Russian Statistics,* Macmillan, 1939. *The Conditions of Economic Progress,* Macmillan, 1940, 3rd edition, St. Martin's, 1957; *The Economics of 1960,* Macmillan, 1942; *The Advance to Social Security,* Melbourne University Press, 1943; *Principles of Public Finance and Taxation,* Federal Institute of Accountants (Brisbane), 1950; *The Have and the Have-Not Countries,* University of Leeds, 1953; *Free Trade: An Immediate Remedy for Britain's Economy,* City Press Newspaper, 1954; *Welfare and Taxation,* Catholic Social Guild (Oxford), 1954; *Population Trends,* Manchester Statistical Society, 1956; *India's Capital Requirements: An Essay,* Eastern Economist (New Delhi), 1956; *The Cost of Living,* Hollis & Carter, 1957; *International Comparison of Rates of Economic Progress,* U.S. Industrial College of the Armed Forces, 1958; *Australian Hopes and Fears,* Hollis & Carter, 1958, Dufour, 1963.

The Economics of Irrigation in Dry Climates, Oxford University, Institute for Research in Agricultural Economics, 1960, 2nd edition, revised and enlarged, Pergamon, 1970; *Growthmanship: A Study in the Mythology of Investment,* Barrie & Rockliff, 1961, 2nd edition, Institute of Economic Affairs (London), 1962; *The Real Productivity of Soviet Russia: A Critical Evaluation,* U.S. Government Printing Office, 1961; (with Henryk Frankel and Lynden Moore) *The Common Market and British Trade,* Praeger, 1962 (published in England as *British Trade in the Common Market: Plain Facts about the Common Market,* Stevens & Sons, 1962); *Taxmanship: Principles and Proposals for the Reform of Taxation,* Institute of Economic Affairs, 1964, 2nd edition, 1970; (with Margaret Haswell) *The Economics of Subsistence Agriculture,* St. Martin's, 1964, 4th edition, 1970; (editor with Geer Stuvel) *Income Redistribution and the Statistical Foundations of Economic Policy,* Bowes, 1964; (editor) *British Wild Life,* Hamlyn, 1966; *Population Growth and Land Use,* St. Martin's, 1967; (editor) *World-Wide Encyclopedia in Colour,* Hamlyn, 1967.

Starvation or Plenty?, Taplinger, 1970; (with Eugene Csocsan de Varallja) *Measurement of Reproduction and Fertility of the Developed Countries,* Oxford University, Institute of Agricultural Economics, 1970; *Why Prices*

Rise, Hawthorn Press, 1971; (with G. T. Jones) *The Demand for Housing,* Centre for Environmental Studies (London), 1971; *The Value of Agricultural Land,* Pergamon, 1973. Author of numerous pamphlets and articles in professional journals. Editor, *Review of Economic Progress* (Australian monthly), 1952—.

WORK IN PROGRESS: Revising, with Ian Carruthers, *Economics of Irrigation.*

SIDELIGHTS: In addition to pursuing his career as an economist, Professor Clark contested seats in the British Parliament as a Labour Party candidate in North Dorset, 1929, Wavertree (Liverpool), 1931, and South Norfolk, 1935. *Avocational interests:* Walking and gardening.

* * *

CLARK, Harry 1917-

PERSONAL: Born December 16, 1917, in San Diego, Calif.; son of Harry (a printer) and Caroline (Smith) Clark; married Margaret Rodwick, July 7, 1957. *Education:* University of California, Berkeley, B.A., 1940, M.L.S., 1956, Ph.D., 1969; University of Southern California, M.S., 1949. *Politics:* Democrat. *Religion:* Unitarian-Universalist. *Home:* 1744 Westbrooke Ter., Norman, Okla. 73069. *Office:* Graduate School of Library Science, University of Oklahoma, Norman, Okla. 73069.

CAREER: Held various positions as a civilian employee of the U.S. Army and Veterans Administration, 1942-47; Alameda County Welfare Association, Oakland, Calif., clerk, 1949-54; Multnomah County Library, Portland, Ore., librarian, 1956-58; Chico State College (now California State University, Chico), Chico, Calif., cataloger and circulation librarian, 1958-63; University of Oklahoma, Norman, assistant professor, 1969-72, associate professor of library science, 1972—. *Military service:* Served with U.S. Armed Forces, 1940-42. *Member:* American Association of Library Schools, American Library Association, American Printing History Association (charter member), Gutenberg Gesellschaft, Western History Association, Oklahoma Library Association, Book Club of California.

WRITINGS: A Venture in History: The Production, Publication, and Sale of the Works of Hubert Howe Bancroft, University of California Press, 1973. Contributor to library and history journals.

WORK IN PROGRESS: Research on the beginnings of printing and the trade in printed books in fifteenth-century Europe.

SIDELIGHTS: Clark writes: "I am interested in the strengths and weaknesses people display in coming to grips with and solving problems in human relations. My research has concerned itself with showing how certain publishers gained public confidence and backing necessary to complete their work." *Avocational interests:* Drama, opera, reading (Western history, printing history, popular works on interpersonal and group relations, mysteries).

* * *

CLARK, John Desmond 1916-

PERSONAL: Born April 10, 1916, in London, England; came to United States in 1961; son of Thomas John Chown and Catherine (Wynne) Clark; married Betty Cable Baume, April 30, 1938; children: Elizabeth Ann (Mrs. David Miall Winterbottom), John Wynne Desmond. *Education:* Cambridge University, B.A. (honors), 1937, M.A., 1942, Ph.D., 1950. *Home:* 1941 Yosemite Rd., Berkeley, Calif.

94707. *Office:* Department of Anthropology, University of California, Berkeley, Calif. 94720.

CAREER: Rhodes-Livingstone Museum, Northern Rhodesia (now Zambia), director, 1938-61; University of California, Berkeley, professor of anthropology, 1961—. Director of excavations in Southern, East, and Equatorial Africa, the Sahara, and Syria, 1938—. Founder member and secretary, Northern Rhodesia National Monuments Commission, 1948-61; member of the Pan-African Congress of Prehistory, 1955; member of the Body Corporate of the Livingstone Museum, Zambia. *Military service:* British Army, 1941-46; served in East Africa, Abyssinia, Somaliland, and Madagascar.

MEMBER: American Academy of Arts and Sciences (fellow), American Association for the Advancement of Science (fellow), Scientific Council for Africa South of the Sahara (corresponding member), British Academy (fellow), Royal Commonwealth Society, Royal Society of South Africa (fellow), Instituto Italiano di Preistoria e Protoistoria, California Academy of Sciences (fellow), Society of Antiquaries of London (fellow), Geographical Institute of Lisbon. *Awards, honors:* Companion, Order of the British Empire, 1960; commander, National Order of Senegal, 1968; Huxley Memorial medal, 1974; Sc.D., Cambridge University, 1975.

WRITINGS: Stone Age Sites in Northern Rhodesia and the Possibilites of Future Research, Rhodes-Livingstone Institute, 1939; *Further Excavations (1939) at the Mumbwa Caves, Northern Rhodesia,* Royal Society of South Africa (Cape Town), 1942; (with others) *The Stone Age Cultures of Northern Rhodesia: With Particular Reference to the Cultural and Climatic Succession in the Upper Zambezi Valley and Its Tributaries,* South African Archaeological Society, 1950, Negro Universities Press, 1970; *The Prehistoric Cultures of the Horn of Africa: An Analysis of the Stone Age Cultural and Climatic Succession in the Somalilands and Eastern Parts of Abyssinia,* Cambridge University Press, 1954, reprinted with a new preface by the author, Octagon, 1972; (editor with Sonia Cole) *Third Pan-African Congress on Prehistory,* Chatto & Windus, 1957; *The Prehistory of Southern Africa,* Penguin, 1959; (contributor) Roger F. H. Summers, editor, *Prehistoric Rock Art of the Federation of Rhodesia & Nyasaland,* National Publications Trust (Salisbury), 1959.

Prehistoric Cultures of Northeast Angola and their Significance in Tropical Africa, Companhia de Diamantes de Angola, 1963; *The Distribution of Prehistoric Culture in Angola,* Companhia de Diamantes de Angola, 1966; (editor with F. Clark Howell) *Recent Studies in Paleoanthropology,* American Anthropological Association, 1966; (editor with Walter W. Bishop) *Background to Evolution in Africa,* University of Chicago Press, 1967; (compiler) *Atlas of African Prehistory,* University of Chicago Press, 1967; *Further Palaeo-Anthropological Studies in Northern Lunda,* Companhia de Diamantes de Angola, 1968; (with others) *Kalambo Falls Prehistoric Site,* Cambridge University Press, Volume I, 1969, Volume II, 1973; *The Prehistory of Africa,* Praeger, 1970. Chief editor, "Robins Series," published by Chatto & Windus, 1960—. Contributor of articles to scholarly journals on prehistoric archaeology.

AVOCATIONAL INTERESTS: Rowing, walking, and photography.

* * *

CLARK, Leroy D.

PERSONAL: Married Christine Philpot (an attorney), July

14, 1964; children: Chad, Kimani. *Education:* City College of City University of New York, B.A., 1956; New York University, graduate study, 1956-58; Columbia University, LL.B., 1961. *Home:* 433 West 162nd St., New York, N.Y. *Office:* School of Law, New York University, New York, N.Y. 10003.

CAREER: State of New York, Attorney General's Office, New York, staff counsel, 1961-62; National Association for the Advancement of Colored People, Legal Defense and Educational Fund, New York, N.Y., assistant counsel and head of civil litigation, 1962-68; New York University, New York, N.Y., professor of law, 1968—. Co-counsel of New York City Special Committee on Racial and Religious Bigotry, 1968; member of board of directors of Commission on Juvenile Justice Standards of Institute for Judicial Administration and American Bar Association. *Member:* American Arbitration Association, National Conference of Black Lawyers, Society of American Law Teachers, Association for Union Democracy (member of board of directors), Phi Beta Kappa.

WRITINGS: (Contributor) Allan C. Ornstein, editor, *Educating the Disadvantaged,* Volume I, AMS Press, 1968; (contributor) *When the Marching Stopped: An Analysis of Black Issues in the '70's,* National Urban League, 1973; (contributor) *Minority Opportunities in Law for Blacks, Puerto Ricans, and Chicanos,* Law Journal Press, 1974; *The Grand Jury: The Use and Abuse of Political Power,* Quadrangle, 1975. Contributor to professional journals. Member of editorial board of *Amsterdam News.*

*   *   *

CLARK, Marden J. 1916-

PERSONAL: Born July 13, 1916, in Morgan, Utah; son of Wallace R. (a farmer-businessman) and Jean (Boyce) Clark; married Bessie Lloyd Soderborg, October 25, 1941; children: Diane (Mrs. Bruce Campbell), Dennis Marden, Sherri Lyn (Mrs. Joseph Heiner), Kevin Wallace, Harlow Soderborg, Krista Jean. *Education:* Brigham Young University, A.B., 1947, M.A., 1949; University of Washington, Ph.D., 1957. *Politics:* Democrat. *Religion:* Church of Jesus Christ of Latter Day Saints. *Home:* 1695 North Oak Lane, Provo, Utah 84601. *Office:* Department of English, Brigham Young University, A240 JKBA, Provo, Utah 84601.

CAREER: Self-employed as a trucker-businessman in Morgan, Utah, 1938-40; Lockheed Aircraft Corp., Burbank, Calif., draftsman-designer, 1941-45; Brigham Young University, Provo, Utah, instructor, 1949-55, assistant professor, 1956-59, associate professor, 1959-64, professor of English, 1964—. Fulbright lecturer, University of Oulu, Finland, 1970-71. *Member:* Modern Language Association of America, American Association of University Professors (local chapter vice-president, 1968-69; president, 1969-70), Rocky Mountain Modern Language Association, Utah Academy of Sciences, Arts, and Letters, Phi Kappa Phi. *Awards, honors:* Brigham Young University research grants, 1962, 1965-68.

WRITINGS: (Editor with Soren Cox and Marshall Craig) *About Language: Contexts for College Writing,* Scribner, 1970, revised edition, 1975; *Modern and Classic: The "Wooing Both Ways,"* C. E. Merrill, 1972. Contributor to *Modern Drama, Studies in the Novel, Brigham Young University Studies,* and *Dialogue: A Journal of Mormon Thought.*

WORK IN PROGRESS: A monograph, *Ulysses and the*

Odyssey; Moods: Of Late, a book of poems, completion expected in 1976; various essays and poems.

SIDELIGHTS: Clark told *CA:* "I enjoy travel, usually by camper. We spent the summer of '71 touring Europe in Volkscamper, and we have traveled extensively in America. I have a large fruit and vegetable garden, run mostly organically. I write poetry that is usually either personal or family oriented. I read French and German and some Finnish."

*   *   *

CLARK, Truman R(oss) 1935-

PERSONAL: Born November 26, 1935, in Wichita, Kan.; son of Harold Truman (a pharmacist) and Lanore (Groves) Clark; married Sally Rogers, August 20, 1964; children: Terry, Susan, Sharon, Timmy, Sandra. *Education:* Abilene Christian College, B.S., 1958; University of Oregon, M.S., 1959; Bryn Mawr College, M.A., 1968, Ph.D., 1970. *Religion:* Church of Christ. *Home:* 1054 West 78th St., Los Angeles, Calif. 90044. *Office:* Department of History, Pepperdine University, 8035 South Vermont, Los Angeles, Calif. 90044.

CAREER: Columbia Christian College, Portland, Ore., instructor in history, 1959-60; Northeastern Christian Junior College, Villanova, Pa., instructor in history, 1965-68; Montgomery County Community College, Conshohocken, Pa., assistant professor of history, 1969-70; Pepperdine University, Los Angeles, Calif., assistant professor, 1970-72, associate professor of history, 1972—, head of department, 1972—. Visiting summer lecturer at University of Pennsylvania, 1969, 1970. *Military service:* U.S. Army, 1960-62. *Member:* American Historical Association, Organization of American Historians, American Association of University Professors.

WRITINGS: Puerto Rico and the United States, 1917-1933, University of Pittsburgh Press, 1975. Contributor to historical journals.

WORK IN PROGRESS: Research on the U.S. overseas empire after 1898, and on Theodore Roosevelt, Jr.

SIDELIGHTS: The first four of Clark's children are adopted, all of varying racial backgrounds. *Avocational interests:* Marathon running (seventy to one hundred miles of training per week, six or more races of twenty-six miles and up per year). Clark has hopes of qualifying for the U.S. Olympic trials, and of being one of the better over-forty distance runners in the country.

*   *   *

CLAY, Marie M(ildred) 1926-

PERSONAL: Born January 3, 1926, in Wellington, New Zealand; daughter of Donald Leolin (a public accountant) and M. Blanche (a musician; maiden name, Godier) Irwin; married Warwick V. Clay (a civil engineer), June 14, 1952; children: Alan V., Jennifer L. *Education:* Victoria University of Wellington, B.A., 1947, M.A., 1949; University of Minnesota, further graduate study, 1951-52; University of Auckland, Ph.D., 1966. *Office:* Department of Education, University of Auckland, Private Bag, Auckland 1, New Zealand.

CAREER: Teacher of backward children in Wellington, New Zealand, 1947-49; school psychologist in Wellington and Auckland, New Zealand, 1949-50, 1956-59; teacher in Wanganui, New Zealand, 1953-54; University of Auckland, Auckland, lecturer and senior lecturer, 1960-74, professor of education and head of department, 1975—. *Member:* International Reading Association, New Zealand Psychological Society, British Psychological Society, International Association for Applied Psychology, Society for Research in Child Development. *Awards, honors:* Fulbright scholarship, University of Minnesota, 1951-52.

WRITINGS: Reading: The Patterning of Complex Behaviour, International Publications Service, 1972; *The Early Detection of Reading Difficulties,* Heinemann Educational Books, 1972. *What Did I Write,* Heinemann Educational Books, 1975.

WORK IN PROGRESS: Record of Oral Language, for school entrants.

SIDELIGHTS: Marie Clay writes: "My field is really the study of how children develop, and the relationships of what we do to children to the kind of citizens we will have in the next generation." *Avocational interests:* Arts and crafts.

* * *

CLAYTON, Paul C(lark) 1932-

PERSONAL: Born November 4, 1932, in West Boylston, Mass.; son of John (a mechanical engineer) and Mildred (Clark) Clayton; married Jacklyn Blake (a teacher of the hearing-impaired), August 5, 1962; children: John Shepherd, Cathryn Hope. *Education:* Middlebury College, A.B., 1955; Andover Newton Theological School, B.D., 1960. *Home:* 26 Sargent St., Needham, Mass. 02192. *Office:* Congregational Church of Needham, 1154 Great Plain Ave., Needham, Mass. 02192.

CAREER: Ordained minister of Congregational Church, 1960; pastor in Orange, Mass., 1959-64, Beverly, Mass., 1965-74, and Needham, Mass., 1974—. Member of board of directors of Massachusetts Conference of United Church of Christ, 1968-72; member of Bass River Day Activity Center for Adult Retarded Persons, 1973-74; member of United Church Board for World Ministries, 1974—.

WRITINGS: Add Salt to Season (non-fiction), Greeno, Hadden, 1973.

* * *

CLINE, C. Terry, Jr. 1935-

PERSONAL: Born July 14, 1935, in Birmingham, Ala.; son of Charles Terry (in the Red Cross) and Mildred (Vann) Cline; married Linda Street (an author), October 23, 1959; children: Cabeth, Blaise Meredith, Charles Terry III, Marc Andrew. *Education:* Attended Florida State University, 1957. *Politics:* "Against." *Home and office:* 66 Hannon Ave., Mobile, Ala. 36604. *Agent:* Jay Garon-Brooke Associates, 415 Central Park West, 17-D, New York, N.Y. 10025.

CAREER: Cline began his career by working a variety of radio and television jobs, including those of announcer, disc-jockey, newsman, and manager in the southeastern United States: House of Chimpions, Thomasville, Ga., owner, 1960-63; Colonial Educational Exhibits, Dothan, Ala., owner, 1964-69; Land Alive Foundation, Mobile, Ala., executive director, 1970-72. *Military service:* U.S. Army, 1960.

WRITINGS: Damon, Putnam, 1975. Cline has also written various articles, a children's play, and a musical.

WORK IN PROGRESS: A novel and a play, both on the psychological-psychosocial aspects of deafness, completion expected in 1976 and 1980, respectively; a novel based on the political history of the United States, 1940-1975, completion expected in 1978.

SIDELIGHTS: Cline commented to *CA:* "I wrote for nothing for a long time. I would do it again. Have confirmed disease that demands it—writeritis. Can't help myself."

* * *

CLINE, Charles (William) 1937-

PERSONAL: Born March 1, 1937, in Waleska, Ga.; son of Paul Ardell (a postmaster) and Montarie (Pittman) Cline; married Sandra Williamsom (an elementary school teacher), June 11, 1966; children: Jeffrey. *Education:* Reinhardt College, A.A., 1957; Cincinnati College-Conservatory of Music, student, 1957-58; George Peabody College for Teachers, B.A., 1960; Vanderbilt University, M.A., 1963. *Home:* 3529 Romence Rd., Kalamazoo, Mich. 49002. *Office:* Department of Literature, Language, and Journalistic Arts, Kellogg Community College, 450 North Ave., Battle Creek, Mich. 49016.

CAREER: Shorter College, Rome, Ga., assistant professor of English, 1963-64; West Georgia College, Carrollton, instructor in English, 1964-68; Kellogg Community College, Battle Creek, Mich., instructor in English and resident poet, 1969—. Manuscript procurement editor for Fiedler Co., Grand Rapids, 1968.

MEMBER: International Belles-Lettres Society, International Platform Association, National Council of Teachers of English, Michigan College English Association, Poetry Society of Michigan (second vice-president, 1975; first vice-president, 1976-77). *Awards, honors:* Poetry prizes from International Belles-Lettres Society (also named to their Poetry Hall of Fame), Poetry Society of Michigan, *Modus Operandi* (also editorial award and writer-of-the-month award), and *Weave Anthology.*

WRITINGS: (Editor) *Forty Salutes to Michigan Poets,* Poetry Society of Michigan, 1975; *Crossing the Ohio* (poems), Golden Quill Press, 1976.

Poems have been included in *Weave Anthology,* edited by Clarence L. Weaver, Bardic Echoes Brochures, 1974; *All-Time Favorite Poetry,* edited by Barbara Fischer, J. Mark Press, 1974; *Webs of Loveliness: Second Weave Anthology,* edited by Weaver, Bardic Echoes Brochures, 1975; *Anthology of World Poets,* edited by Barbara Fischer, J. Mark Press, 1976; *Yearbook of Modern Poetry,* edited by Lincoln B. Young, Young Publications, 1976.

Author of three imagistic poems for "Estampes" by Claude Debussy. Contributor to literary journals, including *North American Mentor, Journal of Contemporary Poets, Modus Operandi,* and *Bardic Echoes.*

WORK IN PROGRESS: A second book of poems.

SIDELIGHTS: Cline writes: "Experiencing the northern winter for the first time was a catalyst for my poetry writing, which started as an occasional pursuit and became serious in 1972. My creative energy still peaks during the winter months." *Avocational interests:* Playing the piano.

BIOGRAPHICAL/CRITICAL SOURCES: Battle Creek Enquirer and News, October 12, 1975.

* * *

CLINE, Rodney 1903-

PERSONAL: Born November 11, 1903, in Lake Charles,

La.; son of William Edward (a lumberman) and Laura (Siling) Cline; married Mildred Elliott, June 15, 1926; children: Kathleen. *Education:* Louisiana Technical University, B.A., 1925; Louisiana State University, M.A., 1932; George Peabody College for Teachers, Ph.D., 1936. *Politics:* Republican. *Religion:* Methodist. *Home:* 250 Clara, Baton Route, La. 70808.

CAREER: High school education and music teacher in Ruston, La., 1929-41, administrative dean, 1940-41; McNeese Junior College, Lake Charles, La., administrative dean, 1941-44; Northeast Louisiana Junior College, Monroe, administrative dean, 1944-50; Louisiana State University, Baton Rouge, professor of history and philosophy of education, 1950-73. Writer, 1945-73. Lecturer at George Peabody College for Teachers, summers, 1947 and 1949, University of California, 1952, and Lehrerkogskallen (Sweden), summer, 1966. *Member:* Southwest Philosophy of Education Society (president, 1964), Louisiana Historical Society, Phi Kappa Phi, Phi Delta Kappa, Kiwanis. *Awards, honors:* General Education Board fellowships, 1932 and 1936; Phi Delta Kappa Award from Louisiana State University, 1972.

WRITINGS: Asbury Wilkinson: Pioneer Preacher, Vantage, 1936; *Builders of Louisiana Education,* Louisiana State University Press, 1967; *Early Institutions and Pioneer Leaders in Louisiana Education,* Claitors, 1969; *Louisiana Education: Its History and Development,* Claitors, 1975. Contributor to education journals.

* * *

CLINTON, Richard Lee   1938-

PERSONAL: Born September 20, 1938, in Cookeville, Tenn.; son of Howard C. (a salesman) and Nelva Dee (Webb) Clinton; married Susan Jeffries, September 17, 1964; children: Lara, Lisa. *Education:* Vanderbilt University, B.A., 1960, M.A. (history) and M.A. (Latin American studies), both 1964; University of North Carolina, Ph.D., 1971. *Politics:* "Democratic (for want of a better alternative)." *Religion:* "Pantheism." *Home:* 114 Meadowbrook Dr., Chapel Hill, N.C. 27514. *Office:* Department of Political Science, University of North Carolina, Chapel Hill, N.C. 27514.

CAREER: First National City Bank of New York, loan officer in overseas division, 1964-68; University of North Carolina, Chapel Hill, assistant professor of political science, research associate of the Carolina Population Center, and member of the curriculum of ecology faculty, all 1971—. Consultant to Agency for International Development and U.S. Department of State. *Military service:* U.S. Marine Corps Reserve, 1958-64. *Member:* International Population Policy Consortium (coordinator; executive secretary, 1972—), American Political Science Association, Latin American Studies Association, Southern Political Science Association, Environmental Defense Fund, American Civil Liberties Union, Common Cause, Public Citizen.

WRITINGS: Problems of Population Policy Formation in Peru, Carolina Population Center, University of North Carolina, 1971; (editor with William S. Flash and R. Kenneth Godwin) *Political Science in Population Studies,* Heath, 1972; (editor with Godwin) *Research in the Politics of Population,* Heath, 1973; (editor) *Population and Politics: New Directions in Political Science Research,* Heath, 1973. Contributor to Inter-American studies and development-oriented journals.

WORK IN PROGRESS: Nobel Laureates Speak as Citizens of the World, with A. V. Martin; research on the concept of eco-development and on political implications of demographic and ecological realities.

SIDELIGHTS: Clinton writes: "My studies have convinced me that the current predicament of mankind is unprecedented and desperate, that the next few generations will quite certainly experience a steady deterioration in their quality of life, and that the survival of civilization and perhaps of our species is becoming increasingly unlikely. Man's technological cleverness has far outrun his wisdom and ability to cope with human and social problems. Present values and institutions—such things as capitalism, materialism, individualism, nationalism, bureaucratic organization, and reliance on continuous growth—must undergo radical alteration if the future is to hold any promise whatever."

* * *

CLOUSER, John William   1932-

PERSONAL: Born March 29, 1932, in Chicago, Ill.; son of LeVerne Hill (a civil engineer) and Lillian Lee (a teacher; maiden name, Jackson) Clouser; married Judith Captain, 1953 (deceased); married Shirley Crawford, 1958 (divorced); married June Moore, 1959 (divorced); married Margaret Lu Covington (a computer operator), July 19, 1975; children: Kurt, Karen, Charlton, Timothy. *Education:* University of Tennessee, student, 1951-53. *Politics:* Liberal. *Religion:* Nichiren Shoshu Buddhism. *Home and office:* 1604 Diamond St., San Francisco, Calif. 94131. *Agent:* Richard Curtis, 156 East 52nd St., New York, N.Y. 10022.

CAREER: Sterchi Furniture Co., assistant office manager in Ashville, N.C., Gadsden, Ala., and Orlando, Fla., 1954-56; Orlando Police Department, Orlando, detective sergeant, 1956-61; incarcerated in Florida Penal System, 1961-64; Marsh Allan Products, Inc., Cleveland, Ohio, machine operator, 1964; living as fugitive in Canada, Mexico, and Southern California, 1964-66; General Cable Corp., Honolulu, Hawaii, cable maker, 1966; American Can Co., San Francisco, Calif., spoilage coordinator, 1967-71; maintenance man for Jewish Community Center, 1972; plant foreman for Transiwrap Plastics, 1973; Goss & Goss Building Materials, San Francisco, Calif., working foreman, 1974. *Military service:* U.S. Naval Reserve, 1949-59; became radarman second class. *Member:* Fraternal Order of Eagles.

WRITINGS: The Most Wanted Man in America (autobiography), Stein & Day, 1975.

WORK IN PROGRESS: Poems of a Fugitive; Death in the Sun (tentative title), an expose of Southern justice, completion expected in 1977; "Southeast to Cuba," a short story about gun running.

SIDELIGHTS: Clouser writes: "Once a career police officer, I was wrongly convicted and sentenced by politically motivated politicians to thirty years in the Florida State Penitentiary. After spending two and a half years writing my own appeal, this wrongful conviction was reversed. In order to avoid retaliation by same politicians for prevailing, I was forced to become a fugitive. Placed on Hoover's Top Ten, I became the only man in America history to defeat him and the F.B.I. by staying a fugitive for ten years, four months, and nineteen days, longer than any Top Tenner, and by outlasting the statute of limitations without getting killed or captured. After experiencing the other side of the fence my concern is now for the exploited peoples of our country."

BIOGRAPHICAL/CRITICAL SOURCES: Argosy, March, 1968; *Inside Detective,* March, 1968, December, 1968; *Life,* April, 1971; *Official Detective,* August, 1972; *True,* September, 1975.

*   *   *

CLYMER, Eleanor 1906-
(Janet Bell, Elizabeth Kinsey)

PERSONAL: Born January 7, 1906, in New York, N.Y.; daughter of Eugene (an engineer) and Rose (Fourman) Lowenton; married Kinsey Clymer (a former newspaperman and social worker), 1933; children: Adam. *Education:* Barnard College, student, 1923-25; University of Wisconsin, B.A., 1928; also studied at Bank Street College of Education and New York University. *Home:* 11 Nightingale Rd., Katonah, N.Y. 10536.

CAREER: During early 1930's, worked in a doctor's office, for a publisher and a social work agency, and taught young children; writer of children's books, 1943—. *Member:* Authors Guild (former chairman of children's book committee), Wilderness Society, Native American Rights Fund. *Awards, honors:* Zyra Lourie Book Award of Woodward School, 1968, for *My Brother Stevie;* Juvenile Literature Award of Border Regional Library Association, Texas, 1971, for *The Spider, the Cave and the Pottery Bowl;* Children's Book Award of Child Study Association of America, 1975, for *Luke Was There.*

WRITINGS: A Yard for John (Junior Literary Guild selection), Dodd, 1943; *Here Comes Pete* (Junior Literary Guild selection), Dodd, 1944; *The Grocery Mouse* (Junior Literary Guild selection), Dodd, 1945; *Little Bear Island,* Dodd, 1945; *The Country Kittens,* Dodd, 1947; *The Trolley Car Family,* McKay, 1947; *The Latch-Key Club,* McKay, 1949.

Treasure at First Base, Dodd, 1950; *Tommy's Wonderful Airplane,* Dodd, 1951; *Thirty-Three Bunn Street,* Dodd, 1952; *Make Way for Water,* Messner, 1953; (with Lilliam Gilbreth) *Management in the Home* (adult book), Dodd, 1954; *Chester,* Dodd, 1955; *Not Too Small After All,* F. Watts, 1955; *Sociable Toby,* F. Watts, 1956; (with Lillian Erlich) *Modern American Career Women,* Dodd, 1959.

Mr. Piper's Bus, Dodd, 1961; *The Case of the Missing Link,* Basic Books, 1962, revised edition, 1968; *Benjamin in the Woods,* Grosset, 1962; *Now That You Are Seven* (part of six-book series), Association Press, in cooperation with Child Study Association of America, 1963; *Search for a Living Fossil: The Story of the Coelacanth,* Holt, 1963 (published in England as *Search for a Fossil,* Lutterworth, 1965); *Harry, the Wild West Horse,* Atheneum, 1963; (with Ralph C. Preston) *Communities at Work* (textbook), Heath, 1964; *The Tiny Little House,* Atheneum, 1964; *Chipmunk in the Forest,* Atheneum, 1965; *The Adventure of Walter,* Atheneum, 1965; *Wheels: A Book to Begin On,* Holt, 1965; *My Brother Stevie,* Holt, 1967; *The Big Pile of Dirt,* Holt, 1968; *Horatio,* Atheneum, 1968; *The Second Greatest Invention: Search for the First Farmers,* Holt, 1969; *Belinda's New Spring Hat* (Junior Literary Guild selection), F. Watts, 1969.

We Lived in the Almont, Dutton, 1970; *The House on the Mountain,* Dutton, 1971; *The Spider, the Cave and the Pottery Bowl,* Atheneum, 1971; *Me and the Eggman,* Dutton, 1972; *How I Went Shopping and What I Got,* Holt,

1972; *Santiago's Silver Mine,* Atheneum, 1973; *Luke Was There,* Holt, 1973; *Leave Horatio Alone,* Atheneum, 1974; *Take Tarts as Tarts Is Passing,* Dutton, 1974; *Engine Number Seven,* Holt, 1975.

Under pseudonym Janet Bell: *Monday-Tuesday-Wednesday Book,* McBride, 1946; *Sunday in the Park,* McBride, 1946.

Under pseudonym Elizabeth Kinsey: *Teddy,* McBride, 1946; *Patch,* McBride, 1946; *Sea View Secret,* F. Watts, 1952; *Donny and Company,* F. Watts, 1953; *This Cat Came to Stay!,* F. Watts, 1955.

WORK IN PROGRESS: Books on Navajo Indians, the Indians of the Northeast, Ireland, Nova Scotia, and autobiographical fiction.

SIDELIGHTS: Mrs. Clymer writes: "At New York University, I studied story writing, but it wasn't till I was married and had a child that I discovered my real interest: children's books. I had worked with children at camps and settlement houses, telling stories and writing about children. Then I went to Bank Street College and studied with Lucy Sprague Mitchell, who was revolutionizing children's literature. She urged her students not to keep repeating time-worn fairy stories but to listen to the children themselves, watch their play, and find out what made sense to them, in other words to be guided by their interests and capacities. Since then I have written realistic fiction for the most part.

"About ten years ago I began to feel I had things I really wanted to say, but I hadn't settled on a way to say them. That was when I wrote *My Brother Stevie.* In that book I tried to write what a real child, living in the inner city, might have said in her own words if she had been telling the unvarnished truth about her life.

"I feel that children's emotions and their problems in dealing with the adult world are very important, and need interpretation, not necessarily in terms of everything turning out happily. At the same time I think that a book for children should not paint a picture that is too threatening or hopeless.

"Since moving from New York to the country village where I live now, I have become much involved with the village library. It is the center of cultural and community activity, and I find it very satisfying to help in various ways."

*   *   *

COCHRAN, Thomas C(hilds) 1902-

PERSONAL: Born April 29, 1902, in New York, N.Y.; son of Thomas (a teacher) and Ethel (Childs) Cochran; married Rosamond Beebe, May 26, 1938. *Education:* New York University, B.S., 1923, M.A., 1925; University of Pennsylvania, Ph.D., 1930. *Politics:* Democrat. *Religion:* Episcopalian. *Home:* 428 Gulph Creek Rd., Box 295, Radnor, Pa. 19087. *Office:* History Department, University of Pennsylvania, Philadelphia, Pa. 19174.

CAREER: New York University, New York, N.Y., instructor, 1927-36, assistant professor, 1936-43, associate professor, 1943-44, professor of history, 1944-50; University of Pennsylvania, Philadelphia, professor of American history, 1950-68, Benjamin Franklin Professor of History, 1968-72, Benjamin Franklin Emeritus Professor of History, 1972—, director of Bicentennial College, 1975-77. Visiting lecturer, Research Center in Entrepreneurial History, Harvard University, 1948-50; visiting professor, Research

Center of Social Sciences, University of Puerto Rico, 1955-56; Walgren Lecturer, University of Chicago, 1957; Pitt Professor, University College, Cambridge University, 1965-66; visiting fellow, St. Antony's College, Oxford University, 1970; Bailey Professor of History, University of North Carolina, 1973-74; visiting professor, University of Delaware, 1973-74; visiting senior scholar, Eleutherian Mills-Hagley Foundation, 1973-75; also visiting professor at Johns Hopkins University and University of California, Los Angeles. Chairman of board, Benjamin Franklin Papers, 1969—. Consultant, National City Bank, 1942-43, American Hawaiian Steamship Co., 1943-44; Bicentennial consultant, St. Regis Paper Co., 1973-74.

MEMBER: American Philosophical Society, American Academy of Arts and Letters, American Historical Association (member of council, 1965-68; president, 1972), Organization of American Historians (member of executive board, 1958-66, member of executive committee and vice-president, 1964-65; president, 1965-66), American Studies Association (member of council, 1968-72), American Association of University Professors, Economic History Association (secretary-treasurer, 1942-46; president, 1958-60), American Civil Liberties Union, National Records Management Council (chairman and president, 1948-50), National Bureau of Economic Research (director, 1949-52), Social Science Research Council (member of board and executive committee, 1962-65), Pennsylvania Historical Association, Historical Society of Pennsylvania (member of council, 1961—), Philadelphia Museum of Art, Philadelphia Art Alliance, Fairmount Park Art Association, Radnor Historical Society. *Awards, honors:* M.A., Cambridge University, 1965; LL.D., University of Pennsylvania, 1972; Thomas Newcomen Award in Business History from Newcomen Society of North America, 1973, for *Business in American Life: A History.*

WRITINGS: New York in the Confederation, University of Pennsylvania Press, 1932; (editor with Jesse D. Clarkson) *War as a Social Institution: The Historian's Perspective,* Columbia University Press, 1941; (with William Miller) *The Age of Enterprise: A Social History of Industrial America,* Macmillan, 1942, revised edition, Harper, 1961; *The Pabst Brewing Company: The History of an American Business,* New York University Press, 1948.

Railroad Leaders: The Business Mind in Action, 1845-1890, Harvard University Press, 1953; *The American Business System: A Historical Perspective 1900-1955,* Harvard University Press, 1957, published as *American Business in the Twentieth Century,* 1972; *The Puerto Rican Businessman: A Study in Cultural Change,* University of Pennsylvania Press, 1959; *A Basic History of American Business,* Van Nostrand, 1959, revised edition, 1969.

(With Thomas E. Brewer) *Views of American Economic Growth,* two volumes, McGraw, 1960; (editor with Wayne Andrews) James Truslow Adams, *Concise Dictionary of American History,* Scribner, 1961, abridged edition, 1962; (with Ruben Reina) *Entrepreneurship in Argentine Culture: Torcuato DiTella and S.I.A.M.,* University of Pennsylvania Press, 1962, published as *Capitalism in Argentine Culture: Torcuato DiTella and S.I.A.M.,* 1971; (editor and author of introduction) *Wealth against Commonwealth,* Prentice-Hall, 1963; *The Inner Revolution: Essays on the Social Sciences and History,* Harper, 1964; (with Arthur Bining) *The Rise of American Economic Life,* 4th edition (Cochran was not associated with earlier editions), Scribner, 1964; *The Great Depression and World War II, 1929-1945,* Scott, Foresman, 1968.

Social Change in America: The Twentieth Century, Harper, 1972 (published in England as *Social Change in Industrial Society,* Allen & Unwin, 1972); *Business in American Life: A History,* McGraw, 1972; *The Uses of History,* Scholarly Resources, 1973; (editor) *Business Enterprise in American Life: Selected Readings,* Houghton, 1974.

Contributor: Allan Nevins and John Krout, editors, *The Greater City: New York, 1898-1948,* Columbia University Press, 1948; *Change and the Entrepreneur,* Harvard University Press, 1949; *An American History,* two volumes, Harper, 1950; Robert E. Spiller and Eric Larrabee, editors, *American Perspectives,* Harvard University Press, 1961; Raymond C. Miller, editor, *Twentieth Century Pessimism and the American Dream,* Wayne State University Press, 1961; (author of foreword) Sidney Goldstein, editor, *The Norristown Study,* University of Pennsylvania Press, 1961; Bruce Mazlish, editor, *The Railroads and Space Progress,* M.I.T. Press, 1965; Carleton C. Qualey, editor, *Thorstein Veblen: The Carleton College Seminar Essays,* Columbia University Press, 1968; (author of introduction) Francis Adams, Jr., editor, *Railroads: Their Origins and Problems,* Harper, 1969; Marvin Meyers, editor, *The Meanings of American History,* Scott, Foresman, 1972.

Editor, "Business History" series, New York University Press, 1945-50, and "The New American State Papers" series, Scholarly Resources, 1972—. Contributor of more than thirty articles to professional journals, including *American Historical Review, Journal of American History, Journal of Economic History, Mississippi Valley Historical Review,* and *American Quarterly. Journal of Economic History,* co-editor, 1945-50, editor, 1950-55; *American Historical Review,* guest editor, 1973-74; advisory editor, 1973—; advisory editor, *Direction,* 1938-43; member of editorial board, *American Year Book* of American Historical Association, 1945-51; consulting editor, Scholarly Resources, 1972—.

WORK IN PROGRESS: America in the World of Business, 1776-1976, completion expected in 1976; *Bicentennial State History Series: Pennsylvania,* 1977.

SIDELIGHTS: A *Choice* reviewer said that *Business in American Life: A History* "provides extraordinary breadth and an admirable fusion of the study of entrepreneurs, and their organizations, with the history of the larger society within which they functioned and which they helped to transform. . . . [Cochran] draws on an astonishing variety of sources and provides the reader with many original insights, a considerable achievement in a book directed at the nonspecialist." A *New York Times Book Review* critic calls it "innovative and important." Elsewhere that same critic observes that "none of Mr. Cochran's themes, or his sources, is absolutely novel, but his cooly detached style, reminiscent of Thorstein Veblen, makes his indictment of business's domination of our society more effective than the preachings of many contemporary 'revisionist' historians."

*   *   *

CODEVILLA, (Maria) Angelo 1943-

PERSONAL: Born May 25, 1943, in Voghera, Italy; son of Angelo (a businessman) and Serena (Almangano) Codevilla; married Ann Blaesser, December 31, 1966; children: David, Peter, Michael. *Education:* Rutgers University, B.A., 1965; Notre Dame University, M.A., 1968; Claremont Graduate School, Ph.D., 1973. *Office:* Hoover Institution, Stanford University, Stanford, Calif.

CAREER: Bendix Corporation, Ann Arbor, Mich., research associate, 1966-67; Grove City College, Grove City, Pa., professor of political science, 1972-74; Stanford University, Hoover Institution, Stanford, Calif., research fellow, 1975—. *Military service:* U.S. Naval Reserve, 1969-71; became lieutenant, junior grade; received joint service commendation medal. *Member:* American Political Science Association. *Awards, honors:* Carnegie European research fellow, 1964; Churchill fellow, 1975.

WRITINGS: *Modern France,* Open Court, 1974. Contributor to *Political Science Reviewer, Intercollegiate Review, Politica.*

WORK IN PROGRESS: *Machiavelli's Prince: A Scholar's Translation; The Political Thought of Charles de Gaulle* and *Italian Politics and the Opening to the Left,* completion of both expected in 1976.

*   *   *

CODY, C(harles) S. 1923-

PERSONAL: Born April 1, 1923, in Chicago, Ill.; son of William (an artist) and Laetitia (Armour) Cody. *Education:* Collegium Augst, B.A., 1944; Trinity College, Dublin, M.A., 1950. *Politics:* None. *Religion:* None.

CAREER: Writer. Secretary-treasurer of L. G. Armour Foundation. *Military service:* Office of Strategic Services, 1944-47.

WRITINGS: *The Witching Night,* World Publishing, 1952; *Armed by Night,* Diana Verlag, 1960; *Dusk into Night,* Munksgaard, 1967; *The Mist of Night,* Diana Verlag, 1971.

WORK IN PROGRESS: A novel.

*   *   *

COFFIN, Lewis A(ugustus) III 1932-

PERSONAL: Born October 1, 1932, in New York, N.Y.; son of Lewis A., Jr. (an architect) and Lois G. (Smith) Coffin; married Angeline Glass, May 21, 1960; children: Tristram Lewis, Andrea W., Jennifer Niles, Jared Starbuck. *Education:* Student at University of Virginia, 1946-48, 1950-52, and New York University, 1948-50; Duke University, M.D., 1956. *Politics:* "Non-aligned conservative." *Religion:* "Universalist." *Office:* 2320 Bath St., Santa Barbara, Calif. 93105.

CAREER: North Carolina Baptist Hospital, Winston-Salem, chief resident in pediatrics, 1959-60; St. Christopher's Hospital for Children, Philadelphia, Pa., resident in pediatrics, 1960-61; physician in private practice, 1962—. Diplomate, American Board of Pediatrics. Member of board of trustees, Child Abuse Listening Mediation. *Military service:* U.S. Naval Reserve, active duty, 1957-59; became lieutenant. U.S. Public Health Service, medical officer in Indian Health Service (Arizona), 1961-62. *Member:* American Medical Association, American Academy of Pediatrics (fellow), Canadian Medical Association, Nutrition Today Society.

WRITINGS: *The Grandmother Conspiracy* (nonfiction book on nutrition), Capra, 1974.

WORK IN PROGRESS: A book on nutrition for all ages, tentatively titled *Nature's Diet.*

SIDELIGHTS: Coffin writes: "I was thrust into nutrition by means of an obese youth and a life-long struggle against obesity in adult life. I was ill-trained to consider nutrition in my practice by my medical training. Stimulated both by parental queries and my observations of malnutrition within my practice, and by an upsurge of research and reports . . . I began to read everything I could find on the subject. As my exposure to this material grew, so did my convictions about diet. Then, truly shocked at what most children eat today, and by the vastness of the advertising media's brainwashing of our youth . . . I wrote *The Grandmother Conspiracy.*"

*   *   *

COFFINET, Julien 1907-

PERSONAL: Born April 18, 1907, in Alfortville, France; son of Louis (a locksmith) and Marie-Louise (Simon) Coffinet; married Aimee Topelberg (a tapestry-weaver), January 3, 1933; children: Emmanuel. *Education:* Drawing courses, 1920-29; apprenticeship in tapestry-weaving, Paris, France, 1921-29; Faculte des Lettres, diplome d'etudes superieurs de philosophie, 1939. *Home:* Begnins (Vaud), Switzerland 1268.

CAREER: La Manufacture des Gobelins, Paris, France, artist, 1921-39; Lycee francais de Montevideo, Montevideo, Uruguay, teacher, 1939-44; Bureau central de l'information francais en America du Sud, secretary general, 1945-47; Ministere de l'information, Paris, editor, 1947; civil servant, 1951-67; weaver of high-warp tapestries, 1967—. Teacher of a course on the technology of tapestry-making, Paris, 1970-71. *Military service:* Member of artillery regiment, 1927-28, 1939. *Member:* Groupe des cartonniers-lissiers romands.

WRITINGS: *El Hombre y la Maquina,* translation from the French by Oberdan Caletti, Ediciones Iman, 1943; *Arachne: ou, L'Art de la tapisserie,* Bibliotheque des Arts, 1971; (with Maurice Pianzola) *La Tapisserie,* Editions de Bonvent, 1971, translation by Julian Snelling and Claude Namy published as *Tapestry,* Editions de Bonvent, 1971, Van Nostrand, 1974. Contributor of articles on tapestry-weaving to *L'Oeil.*

WORK IN PROGRESS: A book on the history and technique of tapestry-weaving, tentatively entitled *Tapisseries d'hier et d'aujourd'hui,* for Editions de la Coulouvreniere.

*   *   *

COHAN, Avery B(erlow) 1914-

PERSONAL: Born July 12, 1914, in Boston, Mass.; son of Max Joseph and Elizabeth (Berlow) Cohan; married Margaret Ann Kelley, January 20, 1948; children: Beth Neal, Judith Kelley, Kevin Berlow, Peter Marshall. *Education:* Cornell University, A.B., 1934; Columbia University, A.M., 1942, Ph.D., 1959; also studied at Harvard University, 1956-57. *Office:* Department of Banking and Finance, University of Georgia, Athens, Ga. 30602.

CAREER: Research assistant with National Bureau of Economic Research, 1942-43; research associate with National Association of Manufacturers, 1944-45; U.S. State Department, Washington, D.C., foreign service attache and economic analyst in Berne, Switzerland, 1945-48, economic analyst in transportation in Washington, D.C., 1948-49, assistant and later full program officer for Economic Cooperation Administration in Stockholm, Sweden, 1949-51; Economic Commission for Europe, Geneva, Switzerland, U.S. resident representative, 1951-53; Top Co., Boston, Mass., salesman, 1953-56; University of North Carolina, Chapel Hill, lecturer, 1957-59, associate professor, 1959-61, professor of finance, 1961-73, chairman of graduate studies in business administration, 1962-67; University of Georgia, Athens, Mills Bee Lane Professor of Finance and Economics, 1973—. Visiting professor at Institut pour l'Etude des Methodes de Direction de l'Enterprise (Lausanne, Switzerland), 1964-65. Member of board of directors of Key Co., 1972—. Chief of insurance branch of United Nations Conference on Trade and Development, 1968-69; member of board of governors of Durham Academy, 1967-69; consultant to National Bureau of Economic Research and to business.

MEMBER: American Economic Association, American Finance Association, Financial Management Association, Southern Economic Association, Southern Finance Association (vice-president, 1974-75), Western Economic Association, Eastern Finance Association, Beta Gamma Sigma.

WRITINGS: (With Thor Holtgren) *Railroad Traffic Expansion and Use of Resources in World War Two,* National Bureau of Economic Research, 1944; *Cartels,* National Association of Manufacturers, 1944; *Cost of Flotation of Long-Term Corporate Debt Since 1935* (monograph), University of North Carolina, 1961; *Private Placements and Public Offerings: Market Shares Since 1935* (monograph), University of North Carolina, 1961; *Yields on Direct Placements since 1951,* Columbia University Press, for National Bureau of Economic Research, 1967; (contributor) J. M. Guttentag, editor, *Essays on Interest Rates,* National Bureau of Economic Research, 1971; *Financial Decision Making: Theory and Practice,* Prentice-Hall, 1972; *Cases in Financial Management,* Prentice-Hall, 1972. Contributor to business, economics, and law journals. Associate editor of *Southern Economic Journal,* 1958-59; book review editor of *Journal of Finance,* 1974—.

WORK IN PROGRESS: The Cost of Capital, a monograph; *The Probability of Default on Corporate Bonds; The Corporate Demand for Total Liquidity;* revising *Financial Decision Making: Theory and Practice;* revising *Cases in Financial Management.*

* * *

COHEN, Matt 1942-

PERSONAL: Born December 30, 1942, in Kingston, Ontario, Canada; son of Morris (a chemist) and Beatrice (Sohn) Cohen. *Education:* University of Toronto, B.A., 1964, M.A., 1965. *Office:* Department of English, University of Alberta, Edmonton, Alberta, Canada.

CAREER: McMaster University, Hamilton, Ontario, lecturer in religion, 1967-68; professional writer, 1968—; University of Alberta, Edmonton, writer-in-residence, 1975—.

WRITINGS: Korsoniloff (novel), Anansi Press, 1969; *Johnny Crackle Sings* (novel), McClelland & Stewart, 1971; *Too Bad Galahad* (story), Coach House Press, 1972, 3rd edition, 1975; *Columbus and the Fat Lady and Other Stories,* Anansi Press, 1972; *The Disinherited* (novel), McClelland & Stewart, 1974; *Wooden Hunters* (novel), McClelland & Stewart, 1975; *Peach Melba* (poetry), Coach House Press, 1975.

WORK IN PROGRESS: A novel; an edition of *The Disinherited,* with a new introduction, for New Canadian Library; a play based on *The Disinherited.*

BIOGRAPHICAL/CRITICAL SOURCES: Graeme Gibson, *Eleven Canadian Novelists,* Anansi Press, 1972.

* * *

COLBERT, Edwin Harris 1905-

PERSONAL: Born September 28, 1905, in Clarinda, Iowa; son of George Harris (a professor of mathematics) and Mary (Adamson) Colbert; married Margaret Mary Matthew (a scientific draftsman of fossils), July 8, 1933; children: George Matthew, David William, Philip Valentine, Daniel Lee, Charles Diller. *Education:* Northwest Missouri State Teachers College (now University), student, 1923-26; University of Nebraska, B.A., 1928; Columbia University, M.A., 1930, Ph.D., 1935. *Politics:* Democrat. *Home address:* Route 4, Box 721, Flagstaff, Ariz. 86001. *Office address:* Museum of Northern Arizona, Route 4, Box 720, Flagstaff, Ariz. 86001.

CAREER: American Museum of Natural History, New York, N.Y., research assistant to paleontologist Henry Fairfield Osborn, 1930-33, assistant curator, 1933-42, acting curator, 1942-43, curator of vertebrate paleontology, 1943, chairman of department of amphibians and reptiles, 1943-45, curator of fossil reptiles and amphibians, 1945-70, curator emeritus, 1970—, chairman of department of geology and paleontology, 1958-60, chairman of department of vertebrate paleontology, 1960-66, created Hall of Early Dinosaurs, 1952, and Hall of Late Dinosaurs, 1956; Museum of Northern Arizona, Flagstaff, curator, 1970—. Columbia University, lecturer, 1938-39, professor, 1945-69, professor emeritus, 1969—; lecturer at University of Pennsylvania, 1938-42, Bryn Mawr College, 1939-42, and University of California, 1945. Academy of Natural Sciences (Philadelphia), associate curator, 1937-48, research associate, 1949—; research associate at Northern Arizona Society of Science and Art, 1949-69; member of New Jersey museum advisory council, 1964-69. Major field work has been conducted in the western and southwestern United States, and in Nebraska, South Dakota, and Florida; he has also worked in Mexico, Brazil, Argentina, Israel, South Africa, Lesotho, India, Australia, New Zealand, Antarctica, England, Switzerland, and Germany.

MEMBER: National Academy of Sciences, American Association for the Advancement of Science (fellow), Geological Society of America (fellow), Paleontological Society (fellow; vice-president, 1962-63), Society of Vertebrate Paleontology (president, 1946-47), American Society of Mammalogists, Society of Ichthyology and Herpetology, Society of Systematic Zoology, Society for the Study of Evolution (president, 1958), Paleontological Society of India (honorary fellow), Academia Nacional de Ciencias (Argentina; corresponding member), New York Zoological Society (fellow), Rochester Museum of Arts and Sciences (fellow), Sigma Xi. *Awards, honors:* Daniel Giraud Elliot Medal from National Academy of Sciences, 1935; medal from American Museum of Natural History, 1970; Sc.D. from University of Nebraska, 1973.

WRITINGS: Siwalik Mammals in the American Museum of Natural History, American Philosophical Society, 1935; *The Origin of the Dog: Wild Dogs and Tame, Past and Present,* American Museum of Natural History, 1939.

Triumph of the Mammals, American Museum of Natural History, 1942; *The Dinosaur Book: The Ruling Reptiles and Their Relatives* (juvenile), American Museum of Natural History, 1945, 2nd edition, McGraw, 1951; *Dinosaurs,* American Museum of Natural History, 1947, 10th edition, 1961; *The Mammal-Like Reptile "Lycaenops,"* American Museum of Natural History, 1948.

(With Charles Craig Mook) *The Ancestral Crocodilian "Protosuchus,"* American Museum of Natural History, 1951; *A Pseudosuchian Reptile from Arizona,* American Museum of Natural History, 1952; (with Dirk Albert

Hooijer) *Pleistocene Mammals from the Limestone Fissures of Szechwan, China*, American Museum of Natural History, 1953; *Evolution of the Vertebrates: A History of the Backboned Animals Through Time*, Wiley, 1955, 2nd edition, 1969; (with John Imbrie) *Triassic Metoposaurid Amphibians*, American Museum of Natural History, 1956; *Millions of Years Ago: Prehistoric Life in North America* (juvenile), Crowell, 1958; (with John H. Ostrom) *Dinosaur Stapes*, American Museum of Natural History, 1958; (with Donald Baird) *Coelurosaur Bone Casts from the Connecticut Valley Triassic*, American Museum of Natural History, 1958.

A New Triassic Procolophonid from Pennsylvania, American Museum of Natural History, 1960; (with William A. Burns) *Digging for Dinosaurs* (juvenile), Children's Press, 1960, new edition, 1967; *Dinosaurs: Their Discovery and Their World*, Dutton, 1961; *The Triassic Reptile "Poposaurus,"* Chicago Natural History Museum, 1961; *The World of Dinosaurs*, Home Library Press, 1961; *The Weights of Dinosaurs*, American Museum of Natural History, 1962; *Fossils of the Connecticut Valley: The Age of Dinosaurs Begins*, Connecticut State Geological and Natural History Survey, 1963, 2nd edition, 1970; *Relationships of the Saurischian Dinosaurs*, American Museum of Natural History, 1964; *The Triassic Dinosaur Genera Podokesaurus and Coelophysis*, American Museum of Natural History, 1964; *A Phytosaur from North Bergen, New Jersey*, American Museum of Natural History, 1965; (with George Marshall Kay) *Stratigraphy and Life History*, Wiley, 1965; *The Age of Reptiles*, Norton, 1965; *New Adaptations of Triassic Reptiles*, Israel Academy of Sciences and Humanities, 1967; *Men and Dinosaurs: The Search in Field and Laboratory*, Dutton, 1968; *A Jurassic Pterosaur from Cuba*, American Museum of Natural History, 1969; (with Dale A. Russell) *The Small Cretaceous Dinosaur Dromaeosaurus*, American Museum of Natural History, 1969.

The Triassic Gliding Reptile Icarosaurus, American Museum of Natural History, 1970; *A Saurischian Dinosaur from the Triassic of Brazil*, American Museum of Natural History, 1970; *Continents and Fossils*, Dutton, 1971; *Wandering Lands and Animals*, Dutton, 1973.

Contributor: George MacGurdy, editor, *Early Man*, Lippincott, 1937; Glenn Jepsen, George Simpson, and Ernst Mayr, editors, *Genetics, Paleontology, and Evolution*, Princeton University Press, 1949; Emil Haury, *Stratigraphy and Archaeology of Ventana Cave Arizona*, University of New Mexico Press, 1950; T. S. Werfoll, editor, *Studies on Fossil Vertebrates*, Athlone Press, 1958; Anne Roe and Simpson, editors, *Behavior and Evolution*, Yale University Press, 1958; L. D. Leet and F. J. Leet, editors, *The World of Geology*, McGraw, 1961; J. J. White, editor, *Study of the Earth: Readings in Geological Science*, Prentice-Hall, 1962; A.E.M. Nairn, editor, *Problems in Palaeoclimatology*, Interscience, 1964; Paul Ehrlich, Richard Holm, and Peter Raven, compilers, *Papers on Evolution*, Little, Brown, 1969; Preston Cloud, editor, *Adventures in Earth History*, W. H. Freeman, 1970; Brainerd Mears, Jr., editor, *The Nature of Geology: Contemporary Readings*, Van Nostrand, 1970; Louis Quan, editor, *Research in the Antarctic*, American Association for the Advancement of Science, 1971; T. Dobzhansky, M. K. Hecht, and W. C. Steere, editors, *Evolutionary Biology*, Volume 6, Appleton, 1971; D. H. Tarling and S. Runcorn, editors, *Implications of Continental Drift to the Earth Sci-*

ences, Academic Press, 1973; Eugenio de Rosa, editor, *La Riscoperta del Terra*, Mondadori (Milan), 1975.

Author of over forty-five scientific papers. Contributor of more than three hundred articles to professional journals. Editor of *Bulletin of the Society of Vertebrate Paleontology*, 1943-45, *Evolution*, 1950-52, and *Curator*, 1958-63.

SIDELIGHTS: Among Colbert's personal discoveries are fifty new species of fossils and ten genera, including a six-foot long dinosaur Coelophysis, and indications that dinosaurs could hear. He regards his vocation as interesting work and has said: "You have to care more about life in the prehistoric ages than fame or wealth. There isn't much money in the study of extinct vertebrates. It's just pure research, without any practical application whatsoever." *Avocational interests:* Reading, nature study, music, history of the American Civil War.

BIOGRAPHICAL/CRITICAL SOURCES: Saturday Evening Post, August 6, 1949; *New Yorker*, August 4, 1956; *New York Times Book Review*, November 24, 1968.

*   *   *

COLBY, Benjamin N(ick)   1931-

PERSONAL: Born September 14, 1931, in Evanston, Ill.; son of Benjamin (in finance) and Sarah (Pulsifer) Colby; married Lore Michael (a linguist), 1956; children: Steven, Alicia. *Education:* Princeton University, A.B. (with high honors), 1953; Harvard University, Ph.D., 1960. *Home:* 221 Morning Canyon Rd., Corona del Mar, Calif. 92625. *Office:* Department of Anthropology, University of California, Irvine, Calif. 92664.

CAREER: Harvard University, Cambridge, Mass., research associate and instructor in social anthropology, 1960-63; Museum of New Mexico, Santa Fe, N.M., curator of laboratory of anthropology, 1964-67; University of North Carolina, Chapel Hill, associate professor of anthropology, 1967-68; University of California, Irvine, associate professor, 1968-71, professor of anthropology, 1971—. Research associate at Cornell University, 1966-67. *Military service:* U.S. Navy, 1953-55; became lieutenant junior grade.

MEMBER: American Anthropological Association (fellow), American Association for the Advancement of Science (fellow), Royal Anthropological Institute of Great Britain and Ireland. *Awards, honors:* Social Science Research Council fellowship, 1959; National Institute of Mental Health grants, Harvard University, 1960-63, Museum of New Mexico Laboratory of Anthropology, 1963-67; National Science Foundation grants, Museum of New Mexico Laboratory of Anthropology, 1966-67, University of North Carolina, Chapel Hill, 1968-69, and University of California, Irvine, 1970-74.

WRITINGS: Ethnic Relations in the Chiapas Highlands, Museum of New Mexico Press, 1966; (with Pierre L. van den Berghe) *Ixil Country: A Plural Society in Highland Guatemala*, University of California Press, 1969. Contributor to anthropology and social science journals.

*   *   *

COLES, William E., Jr.   1932-

PERSONAL: Born January 30, 1932, in Summit, N.J.; children: Rebecca Drake, Jennifer Ann. *Education:* Lehigh University, B.A. (magna cum laude), 1953; University of Connecticut, M.A., 1955; University of Minnesota, Ph.D., 1967. *Home:* 305 Michigan Ave., Swarthmore, Pa. 19081.

Office: Department of Literature and Language, Drexel University, Philadelphia, Pa. 19104.

CAREER: Amherst College, Amherst, Mass., assistant professor of English, 1960-65; Case Western Reserve University, Cleveland, Ohio, assistant professor of English, 1965-70; Drexel University, Philadelphia, Pa., associate professor of English, 1970—. *Member:* National Council of Teachers of English, Phi Beta Kappa, Lambda Alpha Psi.

WRITINGS: The Crucible (study guide), American R.D.M., 1964; *The Light in the Forest* (study guide), American R.D.M., 1965; *Twelfth Night* (study guide), American R.D.M., 1965; *Pygmalion* (study guide), American R.D.M., 1965; *Composing: Writing as a Self-Creating Process,* Hayden, 1974, teachers edition published as *Teaching Composing,* 1974. Contributor to professional journals.

WORK IN PROGRESS: Fantasy: The Language of the Spirit; Thomas Love Peacock: Novelist of Style.

* * *

COLLIS, John Stewart 1900-

PERSONAL: Born February 16, 1900, in Killiney, Ireland; son of W. S. and Edith (Barton) Collis; married Eirene Joy, 1929; married Irene Beddington-Behrens; children: two daughters. *Education:* Balliol College, Oxford, B.A., 1922. *Home:* Park House, Abinger Common, Dorking, Surrey, England.

CAREER: Biographer and writer on natural phenomena. Tutor in literature, 1927-67. *Member:* Royal Society of Literature (fellow). *Awards, honors:* Heinemann Foundation Award for *Down to Earth;* award for services to literature from Queen Elizabeth II, 1970.

WRITINGS: Shaw, Knopf, 1925; *Forward to Nature* (dramatic dialogue), J. Cape, 1927; *Farewell to Argument* (on philosophy, science, and religion), Cassell, 1935; *The Sounding Cataract* (novel), Cassell, 1936; *An Irishman's England,* Cassell, 1937.

While Following the Plough (on agriculture in England), J. Cape, 1946; *Down to Earth* (natural history), J. Cape, 1947; *The Triumph of the Tree* (natural history), J. Cape, 1950, W. Sloane, 1954; *The Moving Waters* (natural history), W. Sloane, 1955; *Havelock Ellis: A Study of His Life and Work,* W. Sloane, 1959 (published in England as *An Artist of Life: A Study of the Life and Work of Havelock Ellis,* Cassell, 1959); *Paths of Light* (essays), Cassell, 1959, published as *The World of Light,* Horizon Press, 1960.

(Contributor) N. Hardy Wallis, editor, *Transactions of the Royal Society of Literature of the United Kingdom,* Royal Society of Literature, 1960; *Marriage and Genius–Strindberg and Tolstoy: Studies in Tragi-Comedy,* Cassell, 1963; *Leo Tolstoy,* Burns & Oates, 1969; *Bound upon a Course* (autobiography), Sidgwick & Jackson, 1971, Dodd, 1973; *The Carlyles: A Biography of Thomas and Jane Carlyle,* Sidgwick & Jackson, 1971, Dodd, 1973; *Christopher Columbus* (biography), Macdonald & Jane's, in press.

Omnibus volumes: *The Vision of Glory: The Extraordinary Nature of the Ordinary* (includes abridgement of *Paths of Light, The Triumph of the Tree,* and *The Moving Waters),* C. Knight, 1972, Braziller, 1973; *The Worm Forgives the Plough* (includes *While Following the Plough* and *Down to Earth),* Braziller, 1973.

AVOCATIONAL INTERESTS: Playing tennis.

COLLOMS, Brenda 1919-

PERSONAL: Born January 1, 1919, in London, England; daughter of Henry James and Jessie (Ward) Stenning; married Albert Lionel Colloms (a lawyer), August 5, 1961; children: Adrian, Martin. *Education:* University of London, B.A. (honors), 1956; University of Liverpool, M.A., 1958. *Home:* 123 Gloucester Ave., London N.W.1, England.

CAREER: Writer; has worked as publisher's reader, translator, story adviser for a film company, and journalist. Lecturer for adult education classes. *Member:* Society of Authors, Working Men's College (honorary librarian).

WRITINGS: Certificate History, four volumes, Dent, 1966-70; *Israel,* Hart-Davis, 1971, John Day, 1972; *Mayflower Pilgrims,* Wayland, 1973; *Charles Kingsley,* Constable, 1975. Contributor to journal of Working Men's College.

WORK IN PROGRESS: A collective biography of Victorian country parsons in England.

* * *

COLMAN, Juliet Benita 1944-

PERSONAL: Born July 24, 1944, in Los Angeles, Calif.; daughter of Ronald (the actor) and Benita (an actress; maiden name, Hume) Colman; married Jim Toland (an artist), March 29, 1974. *Education:* Attended Sorbonne, University of Paris. *Agent:* Betsy Nolan Public Relations, 515 Madison Ave., New York, N.Y. 11022.

CAREER: Secretary and assistant to her stepfather, George Sanders, 1963-65; Young & Rubicam Advertising, London, England, production assistant in television department, 1966-67, employed in television casting department, 1967; writer, 1967—. *Member:* British Film Institute, Friends of Covent Garden.

WRITINGS: Ronald Colman: A Very Private Person, Morrow, 1975.

SIDELIGHTS: Juliet Colman writes that she learned Spanish "while rehabilitating a Moorish fortress (overlooking the Mediterranean)" which she purchased in 1970. She and her husband have divided their time between living there and in London, until recently when they took up residence in Maine. She is considering a book about her recent travels in the United States for the purpose of promoting her first book, explaining that her travels "were both an educational and fascinating experience, especially having lived in Europe for fifteen years and never having travelled around or inside my own country."

* * *

COLVILLE, John Rupert 1915-

PERSONAL: Born January 28, 1915; son of Hon. George and Lady Cynthia Colville; married Lady Margaret Egerton, 1948; children: two sons, one daughter. *Education:* Trinity College, Cambridge, B.A., 1936, M.A., 1941. *Home:* Old Rectory, Stratfield Saye, Reading, Berkshire, England; and 32 Hyde Park Sq., London W.2, England.

CAREER: Page of honor to King George V of England, 1927-31; entered His Majesty's Diplomatic Service, 1937, third secretary at Eastern department of Foreign Office, London, 1937-39; assistant private secretary to Prime Ministers Neville Chamberlain, 1939-40, and Winston Churchill, 1940-41, 1943-45, and Prime Minister Clement Attlee, 1945; first secretary in Southern department of Foreign Office, London, 1945-47; private secretary to Princess Elizabeth (now Queen Elizabeth II), 1947-49; head of chancery, British Embassy, Lisbon, Portugal, 1949-51; counsellor in the Foreign Service, 1951; joint principal private secretary to Prime Minister, 1951-55; Hill Samuel & Co., London, England, director, 1955—. Director of Coutts & Co., Ottoman Bank, Provident Life Association of London, and other companies. *Military service:* Royal Air Force Volunteer Reserve, pilot, 1939-45.

MEMBER: White's Club, Pratt's Club. *Awards, honors:* Officer of the French Legion of Honor, 1947; commander of the Royal Victorian Order, 1949; Companion of the Bath, 1955; honorary fellow of Churchhill College, Cambridge, 1971; Knight Bachelor, 1974.

WRITINGS: Fool's Pleasure: A Leisurely Journey down the Danube, to the Black Sea, the Greek Islands and Dalmatia, Methuen, 1935; (contributor) *Action This Day: Working with Churchill,* Macmillan, 1968; *Man of Valour: The Life of Field-Marshal the Viscount Gort,* Collins, 1972.

*   *   *

COLVIN, Howard Montagu 1919-

PERSONAL: Born October 15, 1919, in Sidcup, Kent, England; son of Montagu and Anne Winifred Colvin; married Christina Edgeworth Butler, 1943; children: two sons. *Education:* University College, London, B.A., 1940; Oxford University, M.A., 1948. *Home:* 50 Plantation Rd., Oxford, England.

CAREER: University of London, University College, London, England, assistant lecturer in history, 1946-48; Oxford University, St. John's College, Oxford, England, fellow and tutor in history, 1948—, librarian, 1950—, reader in architectural history, 1965—. Member of Royal Fine Art Commission, 1962-72, Royal Commission on Historical Monuments, 1963—, and Historic Buildings Council for England, 1970—. *Military service:* Royal Air Force, 1940-46; mentioned in dispatches.

MEMBER: British Academy (fellow), Royal Institute of British Architects (honorary fellow). *Awards, honors:* Sir Banister Fletcher Prize from Society of Authors, 1957, for *A Biographical Dictionary of English Architects;* named commander of Order of the British Empire, 1964.

WRITINGS: The White Canons in England (history of the Premonstratensian Order), Clarendon Press, 1951; *A Biographical Dictionary of English Architects, 1660-1840,* Harvard University Press, 1954; *Ackermann's Oxford,* Penguin, 1954; *A History of Deddington, Oxfordshire,* S.P.C.K., 1963; (with R. Gilyard-Beer) *Shap Abbey, Westmorland,* H.M.S.O., 1963; *The Sheldonian Theatre and the Divinity School,* Sheldonian Theatre, Oxford University, 1964; (editor) *A Catalogue of Architectural Drawings of the Eighteenth and Nineteenth Centuries in the Library of Worcester College, Oxford,* Clarendon Press, 1964; (editor with Maurice James Craig) *Architectural Drawings in the Library of Eton Hall by Sir John Vanbrugh and Sir Edward Lovett Pearce,* Roxburghe Club, 1964; *A Guide to the Sources of English Architectural History,* Pinhorns, 1967; *Royal Buildings,* Country Life Books, 1968; (editor with John Harris) *The Country Seat,* Clarendon Press, 1970; (editor) *Building Accounts of King Henry III,* Clarendon Press, 1971. Editor and contributor, *The History of the King's Works,* H.M.S.O., 1963—. Contributor to architecture and archaeology journals.

COMEAU, Arthur M. 1938-

PERSONAL: Born July 23, 1938, in Haverhill, Mass.; son of Arthur J. (a jazz musician) and Dorothy (Currier) Comeau. *Education:* Attended Bangor Theological Seminary, 1957-59; University of New Hampshire, B.A., 1961; attended Hartford Seminary Foundation, 1963-65. *Home:* 4 Carpenter Close, Ridgefield, Conn. 06877. *Office:* Compton Advertising, 675 Madison Ave., New York, N.Y. 10022.

CAREER: City of New Britain, Conn., minister of education, 1965-68; City of Old Greenwich, Conn., minister of youth, 1968-70; free-lance record producer, 1970-72; Compton Advertising, New York, N.Y., copywriter, 1972—. Film maker, recording artist, and professional musician. Educational consultant to Ridgefield School system. *Member:* American Society of Composers, Authors, and Publishers.

WRITINGS: Busy Day Songbook, Vanguard Press, 1968; *Blueprints for a Gentle Revolution,* United Church Press, 1970; *Fragments from an Unknown Gospel* (poems), United Church Press, 1970; *For the Young Lovers,* United Church Press, 1970; *Doubters and Dreamers,* Upper Room Press, 1972.

Also author of plays, "Romeo and Julie," "The Unmixables," "Hail to Thee," and "New Baby"; of musical comedies, "Hello 'M'," "Genesis," "Some Beautiful Day," "Headlines," and "L.I.F.E., Inc."

WORK IN PROGRESS: Solid Gold, a novel; *The Wine, Sex, and Cheese Diet Book,* a humorous novel; *A Handful of Quietness,* a poetry collection.

SIDELIGHTS: Comeau has released the albums, "Bill Comeau Sings Busy Day," "Gentle Revolution," "Fragments from an Unknown Gospel," "The Great Grizzly Bear Hunt," and "Talking Watergate and Other Follies," all recorded, 1968-75.

*   *   *

COMER, James P(ierpont) 1934-

PERSONAL: Born September 25, 1934, in East Chicago, Ind.; son of Hugh and Maggie (Nichols) Comer; married Shirley Ann Arnold, June 20, 1959; children: Brian Jay, Dawn Renee. *Education:* Indiana University, A.B., 1956; Howard University, M.D., 1960, postdoctoral study, 1961-63; University of Michigan, M.P.H., 1964; Yale University, postdoctoral study, 1964-67. *Home:* 21 Kent Dr., North Haven, Conn. 06473. *Office:* Child Study Center, Yale University, 333 Cedar St., New Haven, Conn. 06510.

CAREER: St. Catharine Hospital, East Chicago, Ind., intern, 1960-61; U.S. Public Health Service, Washington, D.C., lecturer, planner, and clinical psychiatrist in Commission Corps, 1961-68; Children's Hospital of the District of Columbia, Washington, D.C., fellow in child psychiatry at Hillcrest Children's Center, 1967-68; Yale University, New Haven, Conn., assistant professor at Child Study Center, 1968-70, associate professor, 1970-75, professor of psychiatry, 1975—, associate professor in department of psychiatry and Institute of Social Sciences, 1970-75, professor, 1975—, associate dean for student affairs, 1969—, director of Child Study Center School Unit, 1973—, codirector of Baldwin-King School Program, 1968-73, member of board of directors of Afro-American House, 1970-72. Licensed to practice medicine in Maryland, 1960, Indiana, 1961, California and Connecticut, both 1965. Member of psychiatric staff, National Institute of Mental

Health, 1967-68; member of Solomon Fuller Institute, 1973—. Member of advisory boards or committees of Children's Television Workshop, 1970—, Macy Faculty Fellows of the Josiah Macy, Jr. Foundation, 1971-74, and National Board to Abolish Corporal Punishment in the Schools, 1974—; has also served on numerous panels and commissions for government and the private sector, including National Urban League, American Bar Association, and National Institute of Education. Has spoken on radio and television. Consultant to Washington, D.C. Hospitality House, National Congress of Parents and Teachers, and Institute of the Black World. *Military service:* U.S. Public Health Service, surgeon, 1961-68; became lieutenant colonel.

MEMBER: American Medical Association, National Medical Association, American Orthopsychiatric Association, American Psychiatric Association (chairman of Committee of Black Psychiatrists, 1973-75), Society of Health and Human Values, Associates for Renewal in Education, American Academy of Child Psychiatry, National Association of Mental Health (member of professional advisory council, 1971—), National Association for the Advancement of Colored People, Black Coalition of New Haven, Alpha Phi Alpha. *Awards, honors:* Scholarship in academic medicine from John and Mary Markle Foundation, 1969-74; special award from Alpha Phi Alpha, 1972, for outstanding service to mankind; award from Ebony Success Library, 1973; Howard University Distinguished Alumni Award, 1975.

WRITINGS: Beyond Black and White, Quadrangle, 1972; (with Alvin F. Poussaint) *Black Child Care,* Simon & Schuster, 1975.

Contributor to publications, including: Lee Cogan, editor, *Negroes for Medicine,* Johns Hopkins Press, 1968; Ted Gurr and Hugh Graham, editors, *Violence in America: Historical and Comparative Perspectives,* New American Library, 1969; Robert Scott and Wayne Brockriede, editors, *The Rhetoric of Black Power,* Harper, 1969; Charles W. Thomas, editor, *Boys No More: A Black Psychologist's View of Community,* Glencoe Press, 1970; Sidney G. Tickton, editor, *To Improve Learning: An Evaluation of Instructional Technology,* Volume II, Bowker, 1971; Charles V. Willie, Bernard M. Kramer, and Bertram S. Brown, editors, *Racism and Mental Health,* University of Pittsburgh Press, 1973; E. James Anthony and Cyrille Koupernik, editors, *The Child and His Family: Children at Psychiatric Risk,* Volume III, Viley, 1974; Francis A. J. Ianni, editor, *Education and Social Problems,* Scott, Foresman, 1974.

Author of "Developmental Crises in Black Adolescents," Behavioral Sciences Tape Library, 1973. Contributor of more than thirty articles and reviews to proceedings, psychiatric journals, Black studies publications, and popular magazines, including *Redbook* and *Ebony.* Member of editorial board of *American Journal of Orthopsychiatry,* 1969—, *Journal of Youth and Adolescence,* 1971—, and *Journal of Negro Education,* 1973—; member of advisory board of *Renaissance Two: Journal of Afro-American Studies at Yale,* 1971—; editorial consultant to *Journal of the American Medical Association,* 1973—, and *Magazine of the National Association of Mental Hygiene,* 1975—.

BIOGRAPHICAL/CRITICAL SOURCES: New York Times Magazine, April 18, 1971; *Ebony,* September, 1973; *Sepia,* December, 1973, March, 1974; *New York Times,* May 30, 1975.

COMINS, Ethel M(ae)   1901-

PERSONAL: Born May 16, 1901, in Clayton, N.Y.; daughter of Hayes and Alice (Burnham) Comins. *Education:* Attended Plattsburgh State Normal School (now State University of New York College at Plattsburgh), 1919; Syracuse University, B.S., 1930; New York University, M.S., 1936; additional study at Institute de Allende, San Miguel de Allende, Mexico. *Home:* R.F.D. 1, Steele's Point, Clayton, N.Y. 13624.

CAREER: High school teacher in Margaretville, N.Y., 1919-20, Carthage, N.Y., 1920-22, Syracuse, N.Y., 1922-30, and Queens, N.Y., 1930-61; author, artist. Evening school instructor, Queens College (now of the City University of New York), 1955-61. Member of the board, and art director, Thousand Islands Museum. *Member:* National League of American Pen Women (Queens branch president, 1956-58; New York State president, 1960-62; national contest chairman, 1962-64), North Country Artists Guild, Jefferson County Historical Society, Art League of Manatee County, Thousand Islands Museum Artists (president, 1970-72), Delta Kappa Gamma.

AWARDS, HONORS—For writing: Awards from National League of American Pen Women, 1956, 1957, and 1968; Deep South Writers Conference first prizes, 1964, for play, 1967, for feature article, and 1970, for column "Addie Barton Explores Art," and of honorable mention, 1968, for *Cloak of Pride;* award from British Amateur Press Association, 1970, for short story. For artistic work: Awards from Tupper Lake, Jefferson County Fair, and Cranberry Lake, all 1973, Old Forge (N.Y.), 1973 and 1975, and North Country Artists Guild, 1974 and 1975.

WRITINGS—Young adult novels; all published by Bouregy: *The Magic School House,* 1964; *Cloth of Dreams,* 1967; *Island Castle,* 1968; *Beyond the Night,* 1969; *Her Father's Daughter,* 1970; *The Black Jade Filly,* 1971; *Mystery Island,* 1973; *Moon Goddess,* 1974.

Also author of plays, "Disqualified" (one-act) and "A Quiet Evening" (one-act), of column, "Addie Barton Explores Art," and of coloring book. Author of novel, *Cloak of Pride* as yet not published. Contributor of articles to *York State Tradition, Thousand Island Sun,* and *Jefferson County Historical Bulletin.*

SIDELIGHTS: Ethel Comins writes that four of her novels, *Moon Goddess, Mystery Island, Black Jade Filly,* and *Island Castle,* have been sold to *Grit* newspaper serialization. *Avocational interests:* Vacationing by the Saint Lawrence River, international travel, fishing, swimming.

*   *   *

CONLEY, John (Allan)   1912-

PERSONAL: Born January 2, 1912, in Hamilton, Mont.; son of John Martin (a businessman) and Marie (Johnson) Conley; married Erma Faxon, September 20, 1940 (died, 1975). *Education:* University of California, Berkeley, A.B., 1934; Stanford University, Ph.D., 1956. *Religion:* Roman Catholic. *Home:* 1424 South Fairview, Park Ridge, Ill. 60068. *Office:* Department of English, University of Illinois at Chicago Circle, Chicago, Ill. 60680.

CAREER: Stanford University, Stanford, Calif., acting instructor in English, 1943-45; Ohio State University, Columbus, instructor, 1945-47, assistant professor of English, 1947-49; John Carroll University, Cleveland, Ohio, assistant professor, 1950-56, associate professor of English, 1956-61; Queens College of the City University of New

York, Flushing, N.Y., associate professor of English, 1961-68; University of Illinois at Chicago Circle, Chicago, professor of English, 1968—. Visiting associate professor at Brandeis University, 1959-60, and University of California, Riverside, 1964-65.

MEMBER: Modern Language Association of America (chairman of English 2 section, 1973, 1976; member of executive committee, 1974—), Mediaeval Academy of America, Early English Text Society, Scottish Text Society. *Awards, honors:* American Philosophical Society grant, summer, 1971.

WRITINGS: (Editor and contributor) *The Middle English "Pearl": Critical Essays,* University of Notre Dame Press, 1970.

Work has been anthologized in *Great Modern Catholic Short Stories,* edited by Mariella Gable, Sheed, 1942. Contributor to literary and scholarly journals, including *New Mexico Quarterly, Southern Review, Speculum,* and *Studies in Philology.* Member of editorial board of *Medievalia et Humanistica,* 1974—.

WORK IN PROGRESS: Editing *Poetria Nova* by Geoffrey of Vinsauf, for the Chaucer Library; a monograph on *Everyman* and *Elckerlijc.*

SIDELIGHTS: Conley writes: "It is my intention to return to the writing of fiction on my retirement."

* * *

CONSIDINE, Robert (Bernard) 1906-1975
(Bob Considine)

November 4, 1906—September 25, 1975; American journalist, columnist, news broadcaster, author of film scripts and books. Obituaries: *New York Times,* September 26, 1975; *Washington Post,* September 26, 1975; *Time,* October 6, 1975; *Newsweek,* October 6, 1975; *Current Biography,* November, 1975.

* * *

COOPER, Gordon 1932-

PERSONAL: Born March 27, 1932, in Melksham, Wiltshire, England; son of Jack (a trellis dispatcher) and Emma (a cook; maiden name, Hale) Cooper. *Education:* Attended schools in England. *Politics:* None. *Religion:* Anglican. *Home:* 6 Beanacre Rd., Melksham, Wiltshire, England.

CAREER: Clerk for two commercial companies, 1948-67; government service clerk, 1967—.

WRITINGS—All children's novels: *An Hour in the Morning,* Oxford University Press, 1971, Dutton, 1974; *A Time in a City,* Oxford University Press, 1972, Dutton, 1975; *A Second Springtime* (Junior Literary Guild selection in United States), Oxford University Press, 1973, Thomas Nelson, 1975; *Hester's Summer,* Oxford University Press, 1974; *A Certain Courage,* Oxford University Press, 1975.

WORK IN PROGRESS: Research on the effects on the countryside of the dissolution of the monasteries by Henry VIII.

AVOCATIONAL INTERESTS: Theatre, collecting old china.

* * *

CORRIVEAU, Monique 1927-

PERSONAL: Born September 6, 1927, in Quebec, Quebec, Canada; daughter of Francois Xavier (a lawyer) and Bernadette (Rouillard) Chouinard; married Bernard Corriveau (a law notary), September 29, 1951; children: Matthieu, Francois, Bernadette, Marie-Noel, Thomas, Pascal, Vincent, Sophie, Isabelle, Jeanne. *Education:* Attended University of Toronto, 1946-48; Laval University, B.A., 1950, B.Ph., 1950. *Religion:* Catholic. *Home:* 1592 Monseigneur Tache, Quebec 10, Quebec, Canada.

CAREER: Writer. *Member:* Societe des Ecrivains Canadiens. *Awards, honors:* Prix de l'Association Canadien des Educateurs de Langue Francaise, 1958, for *Le Secret de Vanille,* and 1959, for *Les Jardiniers du hibou;* Prix du Concours Litteraire de la Province de Quebec, 1964, and Medaille de l'Association des Bibliothecaires du Canada, 1966, both for *Le Wapiti;* Prix du Concours Litteraire de la Province de Quebec, 1966, for *Le Maitre de Messire;* Prix de la Commission du Centenaire de Canada, 1967, for *Cecile;* Prix Michelle Le Normand from Societe des Ecrivains Canadiens, 1971, for cumulated work.

WRITINGS—All juveniles, except as noted: *Le Secret de Vanille,* Editions du Pelican (Quebec), 1958, revised edition, Editions Jeunesse (Montreal), 1972; *Les Jardiniers du hibou,* Editions Jeunesse, 1963; *Le Wapiti,* Editions Jeunesse, 1964, translation by J. M. L'Heureux published as *The Wapiti,* Macmillan, 1968; *La Maitre de Messire,* Editions Jeunesse, 1965; *Max,* Editions Jeunesse, 1965, school text edition edited by G. A. Klinck, Copp, 1966; *La Petite Fille du printemps,* Editions Jeunesse, 1966; *Max au rallye,* Editions Jeunesse, 1968, school text edition edited by Klinck, Bellhaven House, 1970; *Cecile,* illustrated by daughter, Marie-Noel Corriveau, Editions Jeunesse, 1968; *Le Temoin* (adult novel), Cercle de Livre de France (Montreal), 1969; *Le Garcon au cerf-volant,* Fides, 1974; *Les Saisons de la mer,* Fides, 1975. Also writer of four puppet plays.

WORK IN PROGRESS: Two juveniles, *Max contre Macbeth* and *Max en planeur; Compagnon de soleil,* a science fiction novel; *Les Montcorbier,* historical fiction for adults written in a series of eight or ten "parallel novels" with her sister.

* * *

CORTES, Carlos E(liseo) 1934-

PERSONAL: Born April 6, 1934, in Oakland, Calif.; children: Alana. *Education:* University of California, Berkeley, B.A., 1956; Columbia University, M.S. (journalism), 1957; American Institute for Foreign Trade, B.F.T., 1962; University of New Mexico, M.A. (Portuguese), 1965, Ph.D. (history), 1969. *Office:* Department of History, University of California, Riverside, Calif. 92502.

CAREER: Jensen-Salsbery Chemical Co., Kansas City, Mo., laboratory assistant, summer, 1952; Whitaker Cable Corp., North Kansas City, Mo., cable splicer, summers, 1953-54; *Boxoffice* (magazine), Kansas City, Mo., general assistant, summer, 1956; American Shakespeare Festival, Stratford, Conn., assistant to the director of public relations, 1957; *Phoenix Sunpapers,* Phoenix, Ariz., executive editor, 1959-61; Associated Press, Phoenix, reporter, 1961; American Institute for Foreign Trade, Phoenix, Ariz., assistant to the director of area studies, 1961-62; University of California, Riverside, acting assistant professor, 1968-69, assistant professor, 1969-72, associate professor of history, 1972—, chairman of Latin American studies program, 1969-71, chairman of Chicano studies program, 1972—, assistant to vice-chancellor for academic affairs, 1970-72. Programmer of teaching machines for Learning, Inc., 1961-62.

Member of advisory panels of California State Commission for Teacher Preparation and Licensing, 1974-75. Member of advisory board of Summer Institute for Chicano Studies at California State College (Long Beach), 1970. Consultant to Far West Laboratory for Educational Research and Development, National Endowment for the Humanities, National Institute of Education, U.S. Commission on Civil Rights, Ford Foundation, Educational Testing Service, Council of State Governments. *Military service:* U.S. Army, information specialist, 1957-59.

MEMBER: American Historical Association, American Association of University Professors, Association for Supervision and Curriculum Development, Conference on Latin American History, Historians Film Committee, Latin American Studies Association, National Council for the Social Studies, Social Science Education Consortium, Immigration History Society, Western History Association, Pacific Coast Council on Latin American Studies, Phi Beta Kappa, Phi Kappa Phi, Phi Alpha Theta. *Awards, honors:* Haynes Foundation summer fellowship, 1969; Ford Foundation grant, 1969-70; National Endowment for the Humanities education program grant, 1971-72; Hubert Herring Memorial Award from Pacific Coast Council on Latin American Studies, 1974, for *Gaucho Politics in Brazil: The Politics of Rio Grande do Sul, 1930-1964.*

WRITINGS: (With Richard Kornweibel) *Bibliografia da Historia do Rio Grande do Sul: Periodo Republicano* (title means "Bibliography of the History of Rio Grande do Sul: Republicano Period"), Edicoes da Faculdade de Filosofia, Universidade Federal do Rio Grande do Sul, 1967; (editor with Alfredo Castaneda, Manuel Ramirez III, and Mario Barrera, and contributor) *Mexican Americans and Educational Change,* Mexican-American Studies Program, University of California, Riverside, 1971; (with Pastora Montoro de Lopez-Roman, Leslie S. Offutt, and others) *Research Guide to the Godoi-Diaz Perez Collection in the Library of the University of California, Riverside,* Latin American Studies Program, University of California, Riverside, 1973; (contributor) James A. Banks, editor, *Teaching Ethnic Studies: Concepts and Strategies,* National Council for the Social Studies, 1973; *Gaucho Politics in Brazil: The Politics of Rio Grande do Sul, 1930-1964,* University of New Mexico Press, 1974; *The Mexican American* (reprints), twenty-one volumes, Arno, 1974; (with Leon Campbell and Robert Pinger) *Latin America: A Filmic Approach,* Latin American Studies Program, University of California, Riverside, 1975; (with Arlin Ginsburg, Alan Green, and James Joseph) *The Ethnic Underclass: Blacks, Chicanos, and Native Americans–Three Perspectives on Ethnicity in America,* Putnam, in press; *Understanding You and Them: Tips for Teaching About Ethnicity,* Educational Resources Information Center (ERIC) Clearinghouse for Social Studies and Social Science Education, in press.

Teacher training aids: "A Bicultural Process for Developing Mexican American Heritage Curriculum" (manual), Systems and Evaluation in Education, University of California, Riverside, 1971; "Using Local History: Resources in Social Studies" (two videotapes), Systems and Evaluation in Education, privately printed, 1972; "Concepts and Strategies for Teaching the Mexican-American Experience" (manual with three videotapes), Dissemination Center for Bilingual Bicultural Education, 1974.

Film: (Co-author and co-executive producer) "Northwest from Tumacacori" (documentary), Matrix Media, 1972. Contributor to *Encyclopedia of Latin America.* Contributor of articles and reviews to professional journals. Contributing editor, *Aztlan, International Journal of Chicano Studies Research,* 1969—.

WORK IN PROGRESS: *The Bent Cross: A History of the Mexican American in the San Bernardino Valley,* with the team of the Inland Empire Chicano Cooperative History Project; *A History of Ethnic Music in America,* with Charles Lampkin; *Perspectives on Multicultural Education,* with H. Prentice Baptiste and Judith Palmer; *Struggle for Aztlan: An Interpretive History of the Mexican American; Being American in America,* for Harcourt.

*   *   *

COTTER, Janet M(errill)   1914-

PERSONAL: Born May 15, 1914, in Holyoke, Mass.; daughter of Jason Osborne (a superintendent of schools) and Marjorie (Stevens) Cook; married John G. Cotter (a high school teacher), June 25, 1949; children: John Kevin. *Education:* Smith College, A.B., 1935; Middlebury College, M.A., 1948; University of California, Berkeley, further graduate study, 1961-62. *Home:* 2882 Marineview Dr., San Leandro, Calif. 94577. *Office:* Department of Language Arts, Chabot College, Hesperian Blvd., Hayward, Calif. 94545.

CAREER: High school English teacher in Melrose, Mass., 1937-43; Smith College, Northampton, Mass., assistant to dean of residence, 1946-47; chairman of girls' upper school section of private day school in Rye, N.Y., 1947-49; high school English teacher in San Leandro, Calif., 1954-56, 1958-64; Chabot College, Hayward, Calif., professor of English, 1964—. *Military service:* U.S. Coast Guard, Women's Auxiliary (SPARS), 1943-46; became lieutenant junior grade. *Member:* California Association of Teachers of English, Central California Council of Teachers of English, California Teachers Association, Smith College Club of East Bay.

WRITINGS: *Invitation to Poetry* (textbook), Winthrop Publishing, 1971. Contributor to literature journals.

WORK IN PROGRESS: Research on teaching poetry.

SIDELIGHTS: Janet Cotter spent the spring of 1974 abroad on sabbatical leave, visiting and studying chiefly in Italy in relation to a special Renaissance studies program which she designed and coordinated at Chabot College. *Avocational interests:* Family outings, golfing, foreign travel, concerts, and reading.

*   *   *

COWAN, Ian Borthwick   1932-

PERSONAL: Born April 16, 1932, in Dumfries, Scotland; son of William McAuley (a banker) and Annie (Borthwick) Cowan; married Anna Little Telford, July 16, 1954; children: Gillian Alexandra, Susan Jane, Ingrid Kirsten. *Education:* University of Edinburgh, M.A. (honors), 1954, Ph.D., 1961. *Home:* 119 Balshagray Ave., Glasgow G11 7EG, Scotland. *Office:* Department of Scottish History, University of Glasgow, Glasgow G12 8QH, Scotland.

CAREER: University of Edinburgh, Edinburgh, Scotland, assistant lecturer in Scottish history, 1956-59; Newbattle Abbey College, Dalkeith, Scotland, lecturer in Scottish history, 1959-62; University of Glasgow, Glasgow, Scotland, lecturer, 1962-70, senior lecturer in Scottish history, 1970—. *Military service:* Royal Air Force, 1954-56; became flying officer. *Member:* Historical Association, Scottish History Society, Scottish Church History Society (president, 1971-74).

WRITINGS: Blast and Counterblast: Contemporary Writings on the Scottish Reformation, Satire Society, 1060; *The Parishes of Medieval Scotland,* Scottish Record Society, 1967; (editor with A. I. Dunlop) *Calendar of Scottish Supplications to Rome,* Scottish History Society, 1970; *The Enigma of Mary Stuart,* St. Martin's, 1971; *The Scottish Covenanters: 1660-1689,* Gollancz, 1976; (reviser) D. E. Easson, *Medieval Religious Houses in Scotland* (1st edition, 1957), Longmans, 1976. Contributor to history journals.

WORK IN PROGRESS: Heads of Medieval Religious Houses in Scotland.

SIDELIGHTS: Cowan writes: "I feel it most desirable that the history of Scotland should be given universal prominence. My main interest is in Medieval ecclesiastical history and to this end I have spent at least four weeks each year for the past decade travelling in Italy and studying in the Vatican archives."

* * *

COWLES, Raymond B(ridgeman) 1896-1975

1896—December 7, 1975; South African-born American educator, authority on desert wildlife, ecologist, author of books in his field. Obituaries: *Washington Post,* December 12, 1975.

* * *

COYSH, Victor 1906-

PERSONAL: Born April 24, 1906, in Guernsey, Channel Islands; son of Frederick William and Florence (Guppy) Coysh; married Leila Carey, September 7, 1939. *Education:* Attended Elizabeth College, Guernsey, Channel Islands, 1920-23. *Religion:* Church of England. *Home:* Clos de Saumarez, Delancey, Guernsey, Channel Islands.

CAREER: Secretary, John Mowlen & Co., Ltd., 1923-25; Bournemouth Gas & Water Co., Bournemouth, Hampshire, England, accountant, 1926-45; Guernsey Gas Co., Guernsey, Channel Islands, salesman, 1945-47; *Guernsey Evening Press,* Guernsey, feature writer, 1947—, chief reporter, 1955-71. Parochial officer in Germany, 1975—. Has appeared on British Broadcasting Corp. (BBC) radio and television. *Military service:* British Army, Home Guard, 1940-45. *Member:* Alderney Society (life member), La Societe Guernesiase (past president), Guernsey Society (member of council), Guernsey National Trust (member of council).

WRITINGS: Unknown Guernsey, Guernsey Press, 1934; *Elizabeth College Register,* Volume III, Guernsey Press, 1950; *Guernsey,* Guernsey Press, 1960; *Alderney,* David & Charles, 1974. Editor for La Societe Guernesiase.

WORK IN PROGRESS: Research in Channel Islands history.

AVOCATIONAL INTERESTS: Travel, history, prehistory, Channel Islands.

* * *

CRAGG, Gerald R(obertson) 1906-

PERSONAL: Born October 8, 1906, in Frankford, Ontario, Canada; son of William J. M. and Florence (Jones) Cragg; married Evelyn A. Watson, June 20, 1932; children: Margaret A. (Mrs. R. A. Armstrong), John G., C. Elizabeth. *Education:* University of Toronto, B.A., 1929; Cambridge University, B.A., 1931, M.A., 1935, Litt. D., 1961;

McGill University, Ph.D., 1941. *Home:* 6000 Iona Dr., Vancouver, British Columbia.

CAREER: Minister of United Church of Canada in Ontario, 1932-36; *New Outlook,* Toronto, Ontario, editor, 1936-39; United Theological College of McGill University, Montreal, Quebec, professor of theology, 1939-46; minister of United Church of Canada in Quebec, 1946-58; Andover Newton Theological School, Newton Centre, Mass., professor of church history, 1958-72, Brown Professor of Ecclesiastical History, 1972-75. Dudleian lecturer, Harvard University, 1959; Birks lecturer, McGill University, 1963; Ker lecturer, McMaster University, 1967. *Member:* Royal Society of Canada (fellow), American Society of Church History, Royal Historical Society (England; fellow). *Awards, honors:* Cranmer Prize; D.D., United Theological College, 1948, Victoria University, 1957.

WRITINGS: From Puritanism to the Age of Reason: A Study of Changes in Religious Thought within the Church of England, 1660 to 1700, Cambridge University Press, 1950, revised edition, 1966; *The Interpreter's Bible: Exposition of Romans,* Abingdon, 1953; *Puritanism in the Period of the Great Persecution: 1660-1688,* Cambridge University Press, 1957, Russell & Russell, 1971; *The Church and the Age of Reason: 1648-1789,* Atheneum, 1960; *Reason and Authority in the Eighteenth Century,* Cambridge University Press, 1963; *The Church and the World,* United Church Publishing, 1966; (editor) *The Cambridge Platonists,* Oxford University Press, 1968; (editor) *The Works of John Wesley,* Volume II, Oxford University Press, 1975; *Freedom and Authority,* Westminster, 1975.

WORK IN PROGRESS: The Puritan World of Thought; The Puritan Way of Life.

* * *

CRANE, Donald P(aul) 1933-

PERSONAL: Born March 22, 1933, in New York, N.Y.; son of Paul H. (a motion picture executive) and Janice (Adelsberger) Crane; married Geraldine Alligood, November 7, 1969; children: Ellen Beth, Bonnie Ann. *Education:* Cornell University, B.S., 1955; Georgia State College (now University), M.B.A., 1968, Ph.D., 1970. *Politics:* Republican. *Religion:* Presbyterian. *Home:* 3295 East Wood Valley Rd. N.W., Atlanta, Ga. 30327. *Office:* Department of Management, Georgia State University, University Plaza, Atlanta, Ga. 30303.

CAREER: Kennecott Copper Corp., Hurley, N.M., in industrial relations management, 1957-62; Lockheed-Georgia Co., Marietta, in industrial relations, 1962-63; Xerox Corp., Atlanta, Ga., in sales and marketing, 1964-68; Georgia State University, Atlanta, assistant professor, 1969-72, associate professor of management, 1972—. Certified arbitrator by American Arbitration Association, Federal Mediation and Conciliation Service, and Florida Public Employee Relations Commission. Brehon Burke Somervell distinguished personell management lecturer at U.S. Army War College, 1975. Partner with Phoenix Personnel Consultants, 1968-70. Member of board of directors of Georgia Heart Association, 1970-76; member of Georgia governor's conference on training and development, 1972-73; adviser to Atlanta Manpower Area Training Council, 1973; conducted human relations-team building program for Georgia State Department of Education Food and Nutrition Service, 1974; member of Atlanta Chamber of Commerce Employee Relations Task Force, 1974-75. *Military service:* U.S. Navy, 1955-57; became lieutenant.

MEMBER: Sales and Marketing Executives International, Academy of Management, Industrial Relations Research Association, American Society for Personnel Administration, Society for Professionals in Dispute Resolution, Southern Management Association, Alpha Kappa Psi, Beta Gamma Sigma, Sigma Iota Epsilon. *Awards, honors:* Named "distinguished salesman" by Sales and Marketing Executives International, 1967; grant from U.S. Department of Labor, 1969-70, to study development of Negroes for managerial positions in business; manpower fellow of U.S. Department of Labor, 1970; national research award from American Society for Personnel Administration, 1970; research grant from Urban Observatory, 1971, to study experiences with a four-day forty-hour work week; research grants from Bureau of Business and Economic Research, 1969, 1970, 1971; grants from Urban Life Extension Board, 1973, 1974.

WRITINGS: Personnel Management: A Situational Approach, with teacher's manual, Wadsworth, 1974. Contributor of about twenty articles to business and management journals.

WORK IN PROGRESS: Classics in Public Administration, with William A. Jones, Jr.; *The Public Manager,* with Jones.

SIDELIGHTS: Crane writes: "Because I am concerned about the apparent lack of life direction of many young people today I am actively engaged in research and teaching in the area of career planning."

* * *

CRANWELL, John Philips 1904-

PERSONAL: Born April 1, 1904, in Baltimore, Md.; son of James Harford (a hard wood importer) and Grace (Philips) Cranwell; married Martha McIntyre Taylor, October 29, 1926; children: Thomas George. *Education:* Attended University of Virginia, 1924-26, and Johns Hopkins University, 1926-28. *Politics:* None. *Home and office:* 700 Sixth St. S.E., Washington, D.C. 20003.

CAREER: Stein Brothers & Boyce, Baltimore, Md., stock broker, 1929; Baltimore *Sun,* Baltimore, Md., newspaper reporter and music critic, 1929-30; free-lance writer, 1936-41, 1946—. *Military service:* U.S. Army, 1941-46. *Member:* U.S. Naval Institute, Maryland Historical Society, James Branch Cabell Memorial Library, Conservancy, Cosmos Club (Washington, D.C.).

WRITINGS: (With James P. Cover) *Notes on Figures of Earth,* McBride, 1929; (with William B. Crane) *Men of Marque,* Norton, 1940; *Spoilers of the Sea,* Norton, 1941; *The Destiny of Sea Power,* Norton, 1941; (with Samuel A. Smiley) *U.S. Naval Models and How to Build Them,* Norton, 1947; *Fast and Fancy Cookery,* Doubleday, 1959; *World of Hearty Soups,* Funk, 1969; *Hellfire Cookbook,* Quadrangle, 1975. Food editor of Sentinel Newspapers, 1969-73; book reviewer for *Roanoke World News,* 1925-26, Baltimore *Evening Sun,* 1929-35, and *United States Quarterly Book List* (publication of the Library of Congress), 1947-49; reviewer of classical and popular sound recordings for Baltimore *Sunday American,* 1934-41. Contributor to magazines and newspapers, including *Harper's, U.S. Naval Institute Proceedings, Maryland Historical Magazine, The Townsman,* and other periodicals.

WORK IN PROGRESS: The High Noon Cookbook: Entertaining at Brunch; an historical study of several naval vessels of the same name.

AVOCATIONAL INTERESTS: Photography (especially portraits), building ship models.

* * *

CRAVEN, George M(ilton) 1929-

PERSONAL: Born December 4, 1929, in Philadelphia, Pa.; son of Howard M. and Florence (Karg) Craven; married Rachel E. Juntunen, August 4, 1961; children: Clarence White, Peter. *Education:* Ohio University, Athens, B.F.A., 1953, M.F.A., 1958; graduate study at San Jose State University, 1964; Stanford University, Radio-Television-Film Institute, diploma, 1964. *Residence:* Fremont, Calif. *Office:* Department of Photography, De Anza College, 21250 Stevens Creck Blvd., Cupertino, Calif. 95014.

CAREER: Massachusetts College of Art, Boston, instructor in photography, 1958-60; Everett Community College, Everett, Wash., instructor in photography, 1960-62; Foothill College, Los Altos Hills, Calif., professor of photography, 1962-67; De Anza College, Cupertino, Calif., professor of photography, 1967—. Fulbright-Hayes lecturer at South Devon Technical College, 1969-70. *Military service:* U.S. Air Force, 1954-55; became first lieutenant. *Member:* Society for Photographic Education (United States; director, 1968-69), Society for Photographic Education (United Kingdom; honorary member), International Museum of Photography at George Eastman House, Museum of Modern Art (New York). *Awards, honors:* Fulbright-Hayes Exchange lectureship to England, 1969-70.

WRITINGS: The Group f/64 Controversy, San Francisco Museum of Art, 1963; (contributor) Steven Lewis, James McQuaid, and David Tait, editors, *Photography: Source and Resource,* Light Impressions, 1973; *Object and Image: An Introduction to Photography,* Prentice-Hall, 1975. Contributor to journals in his field. Book reviewer, *Choice,* 1965—.

WORK IN PROGRESS: Research on color photography and photographic history.

SIDELIGHTS: Craven has exhibited his photographs in nine major exhibitions during the last ten years, including one-man shows at the Focus Gallery in San Francisco, University of Oregon Museum of Art, and Moorhead State College.

* * *

CRAVEN, Wesley Frank (Jr.) 1905-

PERSONAL: Born May 19, 1905, in Conway, N.C.; son of Wesley Frank and Elizabeth (Turner) Craven; married Helen G. McDaniel, May 31, 1932; children: Nancy Elizabeth, Betty Morris. *Education:* Duke University, A.B., 1926, M.A., 1927; Cornell University, Ph.D., 1928. *Home:* 36 Scott Lane, Princeton, N.J. 08540. *Office:* Department of History, Princeton University, Princeton, N.J. 08540.

CAREER: New York University, New York, N.Y., instructor, 1928-30, assistant professor, 1930-37, associate professor, 1937-40, professor of history, 1940-50; Princeton University, Princeton, N.J., Edwards Professor of American History, 1950-64, George Henry Davis '86 Professor of American History, 1964-73, professor emeritus, 1973—. *Military service:* U.S. Army Air Forces, 1943-46; became lieutenant colonel; received Legion of Merit. *Member:* American Historical Association, American Antiquarian Society, Organization of American Historians, Colonial Society of Massachusetts, Massachusetts Historical Society, Phi Beta Kappa, Delta Sigma Phi.

WRITINGS: Dissolution of the Virginia Company: The Failure of a Colonial Experiment, Oxford University Press, 1932; An Introduction to the History of Bermuda, [Williamsburg, Va.], 1938; The Southern Colonies in the Seventeenth Century, 1607-1689, Louisiana State University Press, 1949, 2nd edition, 1970; (editor with James L. Cate) The Army Air Forces in World War Two, University of Chicago Press, Volume I: Plans and Early Operations, January, 1939 to August, 1942, 1949, Volume II: Europe: Torch to Pointblank, August, 1942 to December, 1943, 1949, Volume III: Europe: Argument to VE Day, January, 1944 to May, 1945, 1951, Volume IV: The Pacific: Guadalcanal to Saipan, August, 1942 to July, 1944, c. 1952, Volume V: The Pacifico Matterhorn to Nagasaki, June, 1944 to August, 1945, 1953, Volume VI: Men and Planes, 1955, Volume VII: Services Around the World, 1958.

The Legend of the Founding Fathers, New York University Press, 1956; The Virginia Company of London, 1606-1624, Virginia 350th Anniversary Celebration Corp. (Williamsburg), 1957; Why Military History?, U.S. Air Force Academy, 1959; New Jersey and the English Colonization of North America, Van Nostrand, 1964; The Colonies in Transition, 1660-1713, Harper, 1967; White, Red, and Black: The Seventeenth-Century Virginian, University Press of Virginia, 1971.*

*   *   *

CRAWFORD, Charles W(ann) 1931-

PERSONAL: Born October 12, 1931, in Ravenden, Ark.; son of Kermit (a farmer) and Elizabeth (Deyling) Crawford; married Margaret L. Bryant, April 10, 1954; children: Robert L., Charles R. Education: Harding College, B.A., 1953; University of Arkansas, M.A., 1958; University of Mississippi, Ph.D., 1968. Home: 6429 Camberly Court E., Memphis, Tenn. 38138. Office: Oral History Research Office, Memphis State University, Memphis, Tenn. 38152.

CAREER: Lewisville High School, Lewisville, Ark., head of social studies department, 1956-59; Memphis State University, Memphis, Tenn., assistant professor, 1962-70, associate professor of history, 1970—, director of Oral History Research Office, 1962—. Member, Tennessee Historical Commission, 1971-75, and Memphis Bicentennial Commission; chairman, Memphis Heritage Survey, 1974-75. Military service: U.S. Army, 1954-55. Member: Organization of American Historians, Society of American Archivists, Oral History Association (president, 1973-74), Omicron Delta Kappa (national secretary, 1972-75), Phi Alpha Theta. Awards, honors: Omicron Delta Kappa meritorious service certificate, 1972.

WRITINGS: Cal Alley, Memphis State University Press, 1973. Contributor of articles to professional journals.

WORK IN PROGRESS: Research on the history of Memphis.

*   *   *

CRAWLEY, Aidan Merivale 1908-

PERSONAL: Born April 10, 1908, in Kent, England; son of Canon A. S. and Catherine (Gibbs) Crawley; married Virginia Cowles, 1945; children: two sons, one daughter. Education: Oxford University, B.A., 1930, M.A., 1950. Home: 19 Chester Sq., London S.W.1, England.

CAREER: Journalist, 1930-36; educational film producer, 1936-39; Labour candidate for Buckingham division, 1945-48, member of Parliament for Buckingham division, 1945-51, Parliamentary private secretary to Secretaries of State for the Colonies, 1945, 1946-47, delegate to Council of Europe, 1948-49, Parliamentary Under-Secretary of State for Air, 1950-51; documentary film producer and special correspondent for Sunday Times, 1951-55; Independent Television News, founder and editor-in-chief, 1955-56; British Broadcasting Corp. (BBC), London, England, producer of television documentary programs, 1956-60; consultant to Thames Television, 1960-62; Conservative member of British Parliament from West Derbyshire, 1962-67; London Weekend Television, London, England, chairman, 1967-71, president, 1971—. Member of Monckton Commission on the Federation of Rhodesia and Nyasaland, 1959-62. Co-founder and chairman of Haig National Village Cricket Championship, 1971. Military service: Royal Auxiliary Air Force, 1936; Royal Air Force, 1939-45, assistant air attache in Ankara and Belgrade, 1940-41, served in Egypt, 1941, prisoner-of-war, 1941-45.

MEMBER: National Cricket Association (chairman), Marylebone Cricket Club (president, 1973—), White's Club, Queen's Club. Awards, honors: Member of Order of the British Empire.

WRITINGS: Escape from Germany: A History of Royal Air Force Escapes During the War, Simon & Schuster, 1956; DeGaulle: A Biography, Bobbs-Merrill, 1969; The Spoils of War: The Rise of Western Germany Since 1945, Bobbs-Merrill, 1973 (published in England as The Rise of Western Germany, 1945-72, Collins, 1973).

AVOCATIONAL INTERESTS: Cricket.

*   *   *

CREMER, Robert Roger 1947-

PERSONAL: Surname is pronounced "Kramer"; born March 24, 1947, in Chicago, Ill.; son of Robert Roger and Inez (McCollum) Cremer; married Christine Julia Wilson (a university administrative assistant), August 3, 1968. Education: Georgetown University, B.S., 1969; Northeastern Illinois University, M.A., 1971; University of California, Berkeley, M.A., 1976. Home and office: 2360 Woolsey St., Berkeley, Calif. 94705. Agent: Don Shepherd Agency, 1680 Vine St., Suite 1105, Hollywood, Calif. 90028.

CAREER: Fu Jen University, Taipei, Republic of China, instructor in English, 1967-68; Chinese Community Center, Chicago, Ill., instructor in Chinese, 1969-71; elementary school teacher of social studies in public schools in Mt. Prospect, Ill., 1969-71; feature article writer for San Francisco Chronicle and San Francisco Journal, San Francisco, Calif., 1972—. Member: Mongolia Society, Association of Asian Studies.

WRITINGS: Lugosi: The Man Behind the Cape, Regnery, 1976; Lugosi on Screen, Regnery, in press.

WORK IN PROGRESS: A family-authorized biography of character actor, Peter Lorre, tentatively titled, Peter Lorre: An Unforgettable Face on Film, completion expected in 1977; a family-authorized biography of Charles Laughton, with Anthony Laughton, his younger brother, completion expected in spring, 1977.

SIDELIGHTS: Cremer told CA: "I speak Chinese, Japanese, German, French, and Mongolian and have been interested in travel and nonfictional writing for many years. I began writing feature articles on China for a bi-lingual newspaper in San Francisco and from that time on I was infatuated with journalism. I would like to combine my language and area studies and journalistic experience for a career in documentary writing for television and film. I have also found the research skills I acquired during my years in academic pursuits equally beneficial for nonfiction. My research on the family-authorized biography of Bela Lugosi resulted in information never before unearthed about the rather mysterious horror actor. I travelled to Transylvania, where he was born, with his wife of twenty years, Lillian Lugosi Donlevy, and also succeeded in bringing to light the true story behind his drug addiction, through hospital records, interviews with his doctor, chaplain, etc.

"At present, I plan to continue to write in-depth studies of movie actors whose lives reflect the problems and pitfalls of their trade. My main concern in writing Lugosi's biography was to delve into his personal life in order to highlight the fears, anxieties, and uncertainties that drove him to alcoholism, drugs, and self-destruction."

*   *   *

CRIPE, Helen 1932-

PERSONAL: Born March 2, 1932, in Vincennes, Ind.; daughter of Robert Rhodes (a printer) and Helen (Dixon) Petts; married Herbert R. Cripe, Jr., August 10, 1957 (died January 21, 1970). *Education:* Vincennes University Junior College, A.A., 1951; Maryville College, B.A., 1954; University of Notre Dame, M.A., 1968, Ph.D., 1972. *Home:* 38 Whitman Rd., Worcester, Mass. 01609. *Office:* American Antiquarian Society, Worcester, Mass. 01609.

CAREER: Former High school teacher of social studies in public schools in Indiana; American Antiquarian Society, Worcester, Mass., field director of *Index to the Manuscripts of Prominent Americans, 1763-1815,* 1973—. Visiting lecturer at Madison College, Indiana University, University of Virginia, Atlantic Union College, and Southern Illinois University at Carbondale.

WRITINGS: Thomas Jefferson and Music, University Press of Virginia, 1974. Book reviewer for *Worcester Sunday Telegram,* 1974-75.

WORK IN PROGRESS: Further research on Jefferson's music collection, and a social history of Jefferson's family and what happened to them after his death; research on other areas of music history in the United States, particularly the history of the manufacture of musical instruments and individuals connected with their manufacture.

AVOCATIONAL INTERESTS: Listening to records, choral singing, playing the piano and harpsichord, sewing, knitting, doing needlepoint, riding horses, bowling.

*   *   *

CROIZIER, Ralph 1935-

PERSONAL: Born November 8, 1935, in Vancouver, British Columbia, Canada; son of Charles J. and Doris (Price) Croizier; married Marion Heslop (a painter), August 15, 1959; children: Stephen, Janna, Suzanne. *Education:* University of British Columbia, B.A., 1957; University of Washington, Seattle, M.A., 1960; University of California, Berkeley, Ph.D., 1965. *Home:* 58 Landing Rd. N., Rochester, N.Y. 14625. *Office:* Department of History, State University of New York College at Brockport, Brockport, N.Y. 14420.

CAREER: Harvard University, Cambridge, Mass., research fellow on modern China, 1965-66; University of Rochester, Rochester, N.Y., assistant professor, 1966-69, associate professor of history, 1969-75; State University of

New York College at Brockport, professor of history and chairman of department, 1975—. *Member:* Association for Asian Studies. *Awards, honors:* Social Science Research Council grant, 1969-70; Robert Troup Paine Prize from Harvard University Press, 1970; American Council of Learned Societies fellowship, 1973-74.

WRITINGS: Traditional Medicine in Modern China, Harvard University Press, 1968; (editor) *China's Cultural Legacy and Communism,* Praeger, 1970; *Koxinga and Chinese Nationalism,* Harvard University Press, in press. Contributor to history journals.

WORK IN PROGRESS: Research on modern Chinese art and politics.

*   *   *

CROSSMAN, Richard (Howard Stafford) 1907-1974

PERSONAL: Born December 15, 1907, in London, England, son of Stafford (a justice) and Helen (Howard) Crossman; married second wife, Inezita Hilda Baker, 1937; married third wife, Anne Patricia McDougall, June 2, 1954; children: Patrick, Virginia. *Education:* New College, Oxford, B.A.; University of Berlin, graduate study, 1930-31. *Politics:* Labour. *Home:* 9 Vincent Square, London S.W.1, England. *Office:* Department of Health and Social Security, London, England.

CAREER: Oxford University, Oxford, England, fellow of New College and tutor, 1930-37; lecturer, Oxford University Delegacy for Extra Mural Studies and Worker's Educational Association, 1938-40; British Foreign Office, Political Intelligence Department, London, England, director of German section, 1940-43; Allied Forces Headquarters, Algiers, deputy director of psychological warfare, 1943; Supreme Headquarters of the Allied Expeditionary Forces, London, assistant chief of psychological warfare, 1944-45; Labour Member of Parliament from Coventry East, 1945-74, served as Minister of Housing and Local Government, 1964-66, leader of House of Commons and Lord President of the Council, 1966-68; Secretary of State for Social Services in charge of Department of Health and Social Security, 1968-70. Member of Labour Party executive committee, 1952-67. Leader of Labour group on Oxford City Council, 1934-40; member of Malta Round Table Conference, 1945, Anglo-American Palestine Commission, 1946; chairman of working party on National Superannuation, 1956, and working party on science, 1963. *Member:* Athenaeum Club, Farmers' Club, Garrick Club. *Awards, honors:* Order of the British Empire, 1945; Privy Councillor, 1964.

WRITINGS: (Editor) *Oxford and the Groups,* Blackwell, 1934; *Plato To-day,* Allen & Unwin, 1937, Oxford University Press, 1939, revised edition, 1959; *Government and the Governed,* Christopher, 1939, 5th edition, Pica Press, 1969; *How Britain is Governed,* Labour Book Service, 1939; (with Michael Foot) *A Palestine Munich?* (pamphlet), Gollancz, 1946; *Palestine Mission: A Personal Record,* Harper, 1947; (editor and author of introduction) *The God That Failed,* Harper, 1950, reprinted, Books for Libraries, 1972; (editor and contributor) *New Fabian Essays,* Praeger, 1952, reprinted with new introduction by Crossman, Dent, 1970; *Socialism and the New Despotism* (pamphlet), Fabian Society, 1956; *The Charm of Politics and Other Essays in Political Criticism,* Harper, 1958; *Labour in the Affluent Society* (pamphlet), Fabian Society, 1960; *A Nation Reborn: A Personal Report on the Roles Played by Weizmann, Bevin, and Ben-Gurion in the Story of Israel,* Atheneum, 1960 (published in England as *A Nation Re-*

born: The Israel of Weizmann, Bevin, and Ben-Gurion, Hamish Hamilton, 1960).

Planning for Freedom, Hamish Hamilton, 1965; *The Politics of Socialism,* Atheneum, 1965; *Socialism and Planning* (pamphlet), Fabian Society, 1967; (with Lawrence Alloway and Paul Chambers) *Three Studies in Modern Communication,* Panther, 1969; *Paying for the Social Services* (pamphlet), Fabian Society, 1969; *The Myths of Cabinet Government,* Harvard University Press, 1972 (published in England as *Inside View: Three Lectures on Prime Ministerial Government,* J. Cape, 1972); *The Role of the Volunteer in the Modern Social Service* (pamphlet), University of Oxford, 1974.

Contributor: Jacob Peter Mayer, *Political Thought: The European Tradition,* J. M. Dent, 1939, reprinted, Books for Libraries, 1970; Daniel Lerner, *Sykewar: Psychological Warfare against Germany, D-Day to VE-Day,* G. W. Stewart, 1949, reissued, M.I.T. Press, 1971. Contributor of articles and reviews to *New Statesman and Nation, Spectator, New York Times Magazine, New Republic, Observer Review,* and other periodicals. Assistant editor, *New Statesman and Nation,* 1938-55; editor, *New Statesman,* 1970-72.

BIOGRAPHICAL/CRITICAL SOURCES: New York Herald Tribune, November 3, 1946; *Pathfinder,* December 18, 1946; *Palestine Mission: A Personal Record,* Harper, 1947; *Saturday Evening Post,* January 3, 1948; *Spectator,* October 7, 1955; *New Statesman,* July 26, 1968; *Newsweek,* July 6, 1970, June 14, 1971.*

(Died April 5, 1974)

*　　*　　*

CROWLEY, John 1942-

PERSONAL: Born December 1, 1942, in Presque Isle, Me.; son of Joseph B. (a doctor) and Patience (Lyon) Crowley. *Education:* Indiana University, B.A., 1964. *Home:* 71 Lexington Ave., New York, N.Y. 10010.

CAREER: Photographer and commercial artist, 1964-1966; free-lance writer chiefly for films and television, 1966—.

WRITINGS: The Deep (science fiction novel), Doubleday, 1975; *Beasts* (science fiction novel), Doubleday, 1976.

WORK IN PROGRESS: A long novel about fairies, to be called *Little Big; or, the Fairies' Parliament,* completion expected in two or three years.

SIDELIGHTS: Crowley told *CA:* "My life (as that of most writers) is uneventful and sedentary. A distillation of its important occasions will be found (disguised or reinvented) in my two books; and as I am a writer, my opinions on other subjects are (or should be) without interest."

*　　*　　*

CROWTHER, Betty 1939-

PERSONAL: Born November 7, 1939, in Schenectady, N.Y.; daughter of Fred D. (in management) and Mill (Kelly) Crowther; married Edward Miner, 1965 (divorced, 1968). *Education:* Brown University, B.A., 1961; Cornell University, M.A., 1962; University of Wisconsin, Ph.D., 1965. *Home address:* Route 1, Box 109, Glen Carbon, Ill. 62034. *Office:* Department of Sociology, Southern Illinois University, Edwardsville, Ill. 62025.

CAREER: University of Nevada, Reno, assistant professor of sociology, 1965-67; Cooperative Educational Research Laboratory, Northfield, Ill., evaluation director,

1967-68; National Institute of Mental Health, Clinical Research Center, Fort Worth, Tex., research social psychologist, 1968-69; Southern Illinois University, Edwardsville, associate professor, 1969-74, professor of sociology, 1974—, chairman of department, 1970-72. *Member:* American Sociological Association.

WRITINGS: (With E. F. Borgatta) *A Workbook for the Study of Social Interaction Processes: Direct Observation Procedures in the Study of Individual and Group,* Rand McNally, 1965; (contributor) Borgatta, editor, *Social Psychology Readings and Perspective,* Rand McNally, 1967; (with William Bates) *Module: Drugs, Causes, Circumstances, and Effects of Their Use,* General Learning Press, 1973; (with Bates) *Toward a Typology of Opiate Uses,* Schenkman, 1974. Contributor of articles and reviews to psychology, sociology, and education journals. Associate editor of *Heuristica: The Journal of Innovative Sociology,* 1970; consulting editor for *Journal of Educational Research,* 1968—.

WORK IN PROGRESS: Controversial Issues in Statistics; research on the attitudes of physicians, veterinarians, and dentists towards drugs, on student stereotyping of the typical working man, and on marital adjustment of the professional woman.

*　　*　　*

CROXTON, Anthony H(ugh) 1902-

PERSONAL: Born January 9, 1902, in London, England; son of Arthur W. (a journalist and theater manager) and E. Miriam (Garden) Croxton; married M. Winnifred Lloyd-Worth, May 12, 1927; children: Gillian Ann (Mrs. Ian Stewart Gow). *Education:* Educated in London, England. *Religion:* Anglican. *Home:* 6 Mountain View Beach Rd., Fish Hoek, Cape Province, 7975, South Africa.

CAREER: With London North-Western Railway, 1919-23; with London, Midland & Scottish Railway Co., Lancaster, Barrow, and Chester, England, 1923-27; Rhodesia Railways, Bulawayo, in transportation department, 1927-49, district superintendent in Bulawayo and Broken Hill, 1949-51, and Salisbury, 1951-53, railway representative in Northern Rhodesia, 1953-54, deputy chief superintendent of transportation, 1954-56, chief superintendent, 1956-59, principal executive officer of movement, 1959-61, assistant general manager of operations, 1961-62. *Member:* Chartered Institute of Transport (London; fellow), Railway Society of Southern Africa (chairman of Cape section, 1971-73; honorary president and vice-chairman, 1975).

WRITINGS: Railways of Rhodesia, David & Charles, 1973. Contributor to railway magazines and journals on Rhodesia.

WORK IN PROGRESS: Research on railway history and development in Cape Province, South Africa.

SIDELIGHTS: Croxton writes: "To produce such a book . . . involved much correspondence with 'old hands,' the tracing of photographs and documents, a visit to England to consult material in the British Museum and to contact rolling stock builders. My main interest has always been railways . . ." *Avocational interests:* Philately.

*　　*　　*

CUELHO, Art 1943-

PERSONAL: Surname pronounced "quay-low"; born May 20, 1943, in Fresno, Calif.; son of Arthur Joseph (a farmer) and Ida (Laureano) Cuelho; married Linda

Thomas, June 5, 1963 (divorced, 1968); married Suzy Bekes, March 21, 1969; children: Rhonda, Rusty, Eli, Ira. *Education:* Coalinga Junior College, A.A., 1963. *Home:* 20720 South Fruit Ave., Riverdale, Calif. 93656.

CAREER: "Devoted completely to painting, poetry, and fiction." Worked as farmhand, forest fire fighter, and postal employee. Seven Buffaloes Press, Riverdale, Calif., publisher, 1975—. *Member:* Coordinating Council of Literary Magazines.

WRITINGS: Last Foot of Shade (poetry), Holmgangers, 1975; *Some Magic in the Blues* (poetry, drawings, and short prose), Seven Buffaloes Press, 1975. Editor of *Black Jack* (magazine), 1973—.

WORK IN PROGRESS: Ten short novels and several collections of poetry.

SIDELIGHTS: Cuelho told *CA:* "The most vital part of my work is the connection I have with the land; first as native farmboy in the west side of the San Joaquin Valley, and then through adoption as member of an Indian family on the Crow Reservation in Montana. My roots like those of Steinbeck and Faulkner and Wolfe have gone deep into the American earth, and I believe the greatness of our country begins and ends with the common man, since he is the lifeblood of the human drama which literature celebrates as its source. Although I have been able to call a couple of places my home in the West, eight years of my life were spent wandering around America in search of my nation and my relationship with it and its people. A kind of philosophy of youth has come out of my search: 'The desert wind holds all the high cards, but don't ever try to deny the joker in the quicksand.'"

*   *   *

CUISENAIRE, Emile-Georges   1891(?)-1976

1891(?)—January 1, 1976; Belgian educator, inventor, and author of book on teaching methods. Obituaries: *New York Times,* January 3, 1976; *Time,* January 12, 1976.

*   *   *

CUMMING, Patricia (Arens)   1932-

PERSONAL: Born September 7, 1932, in New York, N.Y.; daughter of Egmont (an industrial designer) and Camille Davied (an editor and writer; maiden name, Rose) Arens; married Edward Chandler Cumming, July 7, 1954 (deceased); children: Julie, Susanna. *Education:* Radcliffe College, B.A., 1954; Middlebury College, M.A., 1956. *Home:* 3 Belgravia Pl., Boston, Mass. 02113. *Office:* Writing Program, Massachusetts Institute of Technology, 14E-310D, 77 Massachusetts Ave., Cambridge, Mass. 02139.

CAREER: Theatre Company of Boston, Boston, Mass., co-producer, 1964-65; *Daedalus,* Cambridge, Mass., editorial associate, 1966-69; Massachusetts Institute of Technology, Cambridge, instructor, 1969-72, assistant professor of the humanities, 1972—, co-coordinator of writing program, 1974-75. *Member:* Phi Beta Kappa.

WRITINGS: Afterwards (poetry), Alice James Books, 1974; (with others) *Free Writing: A Group Approach,* Hayden, 1976; *Letter to an Outlying Province,* Alice James Books, in press.

Plays: "The Triangle," first produced in Boston at Image Theatre, 1963; "After Us the Deluge," three-act, first produced in Boston at the Theatre Company of Boston, 1964;

"The Hoax," one-act, first produced in Kingston at University of Rhode Island Summer Theatre Festival, 1973; "Hanging of the Doll," one-act, first produced in Kingston at the University of Rhode Island Summer Theatre Festival, 1973.

Work anthologized in *Best Poems of 1972: Borestone Mountain Poetry Awards of 1973,* edited by Lionel Stevenson and others, Pacific Books, 1973; *The Blacksmith,* edited by Gail Mazor, Blacksmith Press, 1975. Contributor to literary journals including *Kayak, Shenandoah,* and *Hanging Loose.*

*   *   *

CUNLIFFE, John Arthur   1933-

PERSONAL: Born June 16, 1933, in Colne, England; married Sylvia Thompson (a musician); children: Julian Edward. *Education:* North-Western Polytechnic, fellow of Library Association, 1957; Charlotte Mason College, teaching qualification, 1975. *Home:* 32 Greenside, Kendal, Cumbria LA9 4LD, England. *Agent:* A. P. Watt & Son, 26-28 Bedford Row, London WC1R 4HL, England. *Office:* Castle Park School, Kendal, Cumbria LA9 4LD, England.

CAREER: Teacher and librarian at Castle Park School, Kendal, England. *Member:* Society of Authors, National Union of Teachers.

WRITINGS—For children: *Farmer Barnes Buys a Pig,* Deutsch, 1964, Lion Press, 1969; *Farmer Barnes and Bluebell,* Deutsch, 1966; *Farmer Barnes at the County Show,* Deutsch, 1966, published in the United States as *Farmer Barnes at the County Fair,* Lion Press, 1970; *The Adventures of Lord Pip,* Deutsch, 1970; *Farmer Barnes and the Goats,* Deutsch, 1971; *The Giant Who Stole the World,* Deutsch, 1971; *Riddles and Rhymes and Rigmaroles,* Deutsch, 1971; *The Giant Who Swallowed the Wind,* Deutsch, 1972; *Farmer Barnes Goes Fishing,* Deutsch, 1972; *The Story of Giant Kippernose,* Deutsch, 1972; *The Great Dragon Competition,* Deutsch, 1973; *The King's Birthday Cake,* Deutsch, 1973; *Small Monkey Tales,* Deutsch, 1974; *Farmer Barnes and the Snow Picnic,* Deutsch, 1974; *The Farmer, the Rooks, and the Cherry Tree,* Deutsch, 1975; *Giant Brog and the Motorway,* Deutsch, 1975; *Farmer Barnes Fells a Tree,* Deutsch, in press. Contributor to *Children's Book Review.*

SIDELIGHTS: Cunliffe writes: "It's a great privilege to write for children—the most avid, attentive, and enthusiastic audience anywhere in the world. Only the best writing is good enough for them."

*   *   *

CUNNINGHAM, Joseph Sandy   1928-

PERSONAL: Born October 16, 1928, in Sunderland, England; son of Joseph (a teacher) and Esther (Currie) Cunningham; married Jill Orton, January 7, 1953; children: Katharine, Christopher, Simon, Hamish. *Education:* University of Durham, B.A. (first class honors), 1949; Oxford University, B.Litt., 1952. *Home:* 7 Southmeads Close, Oadby, Leicester LE2 2LT, England. *Office:* Department of English, University of Leicester, Leicester LE1 7RH, England.

CAREER: University of Manchester, Manchester, England, lecturer in English, 1954-56; University of Durham, Durham, England, lecturer in English, 1954-63; University of York, York, England, lecturer, 1963-67, reader in English, 1967-75; University of Leicester, Leicester, England, professor of English, 1975—. Visiting professor at University of Toronto, 1966-67. *Military service:* Royal Air Force, 1952-54.

WRITINGS: (Editor) *Collins: Drafts and Fragments,* Oxford University Press, 1956; *Pope: The Rape of the Lock,* Arnold, 1961; (editor) *Pope: The Rape of the Lock,* Oxford University Press, 1966; *The Powers That Be* (poems), Oxford University Press, 1969. Contributor of articles and poems to professional journals.

WORK IN PROGRESS: Editing Marlowe's *Tamburlaine,* for Methuen; a book of poems; a book on Dr. Johnson, for Arnold.

* * *

CURLING, Audrey

PERSONAL: Born in London, England; daughter of Robert Francis (an architect) and Henrietta Frances (Cole) Curling. *Education:* Attended school in London, England. *Home:* 11 Milnthorpe Rd., Chiswick, London, England.

CAREER: Full-time writer in London, England. *Awards, honors:* Best romantic novel of the year award from Romantic Novelists Association, 1972, for *Cry of the Heart,* and 1973, for *A Quarter of the Moon.*

WRITINGS—All novels, except as indicated; all published by Hurst & Blackett, except as indicated: *The Running Tide,* 1963; *Sparrow's Yard,* 1964; *The Young Thackeray* (biography), Roy, 1966; *The Echoing Silence,* 1967, Ace, 1973; *Caste for Comedy,* 1970, Ace, 1973; *The Sapphire and the Pearl,* 1970, Ace, 1973; *Cry of the Heart,* 1971; *A Quarter of the Moon,* 1972; *Shadows on the Grass,* 1973; *Enthusiasts in Love,* 1975. Contributor of articles, short stories, and serials to *Woman's Realm, Woman's Journal, Woman's Own, Woman, Homes and Gardens, Woman and Home, She,* and *Lady.*

WORK IN PROGRESS: Research for a novel on the period 1801-1803, during the Peace of Amiens.

SIDELIGHTS: Audrey Curling told *CA:* "I began by writing plays, took prizes in several competitions, but gave up this form on the advice of a competent critic. Had much more success with stories and articles. Became interested in the problems of housing and the difficulties of obtaining a 'first home' and this, together with a keen interest in boats, boating, and river life launched me into my first novel, *The Running Tide.* After one more contemporary novel, I wrote a biography of the young Thackeray and from then on my efforts have been confined to the historical novel. I have now published seven of these, all based on real people and true to the facts although fictional in style."

* * *

CURRY, Martha Mulroy 1926-

PERSONAL: Born June 30, 1926, in Chicago, Ill.; daughter of Harry Joseph (a stockbroker) and Franc Adele (a teacher; maiden name, Mulroy) Curry. *Education:* Barat College, B.A., 1948; University of Chicago, M.A., 1950; Loyola University, Chicago, Ill., Ph.D., 1972. *Home:* 700 Westleigh Rd., Lake Forest, Ill. 60045. *Office:* Department of English, Barat College, Lake Forest, Ill. 60045.

CAREER: Roman Catholic nun of the Society of the Sacred Heart, 1952—; teacher in Roman Catholic high schools in Chicago, Ill., 1950-51, Lake Forest, Ill., 1955-60, Cincinnati, Ohio, 1960-61, and Omaha, Neb., 1961-65; Duchesne College, Omaha, Neb., instructor in English,

1965-67; Barat College, Lake Forest, Ill., assistant professor, 1969-75, associate professor of English, 1975—, director of Barat's study program at Oxford University, 1971. *Member:* Modern Language Association of America (member of delegate assembly, 1971-74), Society for the Study of Midwestern Literature. *Awards, honors:* National Endowment for the Humanities grant, 1973, for study at University of California, Berkeley.

WRITINGS: (Editor and author of introduction and commentary) *The "Writer's Book" by Sherwood Anderson: A Critical Edition,* Scarecrow, 1975.

* * *

CURTIS, Lynn A(lan) 1943-

PERSONAL: Born May 3, 1943, in Milwaukee, Wis.; son of Raymond Anthony (a postal clerk) and Florence (Mikolajczyk) Curtis; married Carol Edwards, August 27, 1966 (divorced, 1971). *Education:* Harvard University, A.B. (cum laude), 1965; University of London, M.Sc., 1967; University of Pennsylvania, Ph.D., 1972. *Home:* 1313 35th St. N.W., Washington, D.C. 20007. *Office:* Bureau of Social Science Research, 1990 M St. N.W., Washington, D.C. 20007.

CAREER: Boston State Mental Hospital, Boston, Mass., psychiatric social case worker, summers, 1965-66; Harvard University, Regional Science Research Institute, Cambridge, Mass., research analyst, summer, 1967; Institute for Defense Analyses, Arlington, Va., research analyst, summer, 1968; assistant director, National Commission on the Causes and Prevention of Violence, Washington, D.C., 1968-69; Bureau of Social Science Research, Washington, D.C., research associate, 1972—. Research assistant for Arthur D. Little (England), 1965-66.

WRITINGS: (With Alfred Blumenstein) *A National Program of Research, Development, Test, and Evaluation on Law Enforcement and Criminal Justice,* U.S. Government Printing Office, 1969; (with Donald J. Mulvihill and Melvin M. Tumin) *Crimes of Violence: Task Force Report on Individual Acts of Violence,* National Commission on the Causes and Prevention of Violence, U.S. Government Printing Office, three volumes, 1970; *Criminal Violence: National Patterns and Behavior,* Heath, 1974; *Violence, Race, and Culture,* Heath, 1975; (contributor) Stanley Brodsky and Marcia Walker, editors, *Sexual Assault: The Victim and the Rapist,* Heath, 1976. Contributor to journals in the social sciences.

WORK IN PROGRESS: Study of conflict resolution; research on forcible rape and victimization.

SIDELIGHTS: Curtis writes: "I have an interst in action—program direction, political activity, and examination of urban and social problems in publications less clandestine than academic journals. My desire is to apply my knowledge to the articulation and solution of practical and public problems, a task social scientists have too often abandoned because of temperament and training. I am frustrated, like many individuals today, but for the present remain committed to the simultaneous pursuit of research and action within a system which I hope can change and restructure itself to better facilitate progress."

* * *

CURTIS, Thomas Bradford 1911-

PERSONAL: Born May 14, 1911, in St. Louis, Mo.; son of Edward Glion (a lawyer) and Isabel (Wallace) Curtis; married Susan R. Chivvis (an occupational therapist), June 28, 1941; children: Elizabeth Harker, Leland, Allen Glasgow, Charles Miller, Jonathan Bradford. *Education:* Dartmouth College, A.B. (with distinction), 1932; Washington University, St. Louis, Mo., J. D., 1935. *Religion:* Unitarian-Universalist. *Home:* 230 South Brentwood Blvd., Clayton, Mo. 63105; and, Route 1, Fennville, Mich. 49408. *Office:* 135 North Meramec Blvd., Clayton, Mo. 63105; and, 319 North Fourth St., 10th Floor, St. Louis, Mo. 63101.

CAREER: Admitted to Missouri State Bar, 1934, and Federal Bar, 1936; Biggs, Curtis, Casserty & Barnes, St. Louis, Mo., partner and lawyer, 1935—; St. Louis County Board of Election Commissioners, Clayton, Mo., member of board, 1940-42; St. Louis County Republican Committee, Clayton, Mo., member of committee, 1946-50; U.S. House of Representatives, Washington, D.C., Republican representative from Missouri, 12th district, 1951-53, 2nd district, 1953-69, served on House Committee on Expenditures in the Executive Department, 1951-52, Select Committee to Conduct a Study and Investigation of the Problems of Small Business, 1951-52, Ways and Means Committee, 1953-69, Joint Economic Committee, 1953-69, and on Joint Committee on Internal Revenue Taxation, 1964-69, member of Republican Policy Committee, National Republican Congressional Committee, and acting parliamentarian at Republican National Convention, all 1964, ranking Republican member of Joint Committee on Organization of Congress, 1965-69; Republican candidate from Missouri for the U.S. Senate, 1968 and 1974; *Encyclopaedia Britannica,* Chicago, Ill., vice-president and general counsel, 1969-73; Lafayette Federal Savings and Loan, board chairman, 1973—. Writer, 1960—.

Member of Missouri Board of Law Examiners, 1948-50; member of President Nixon's Task Force on International Development and his Commission on All-Volunteer Armed Forces; member of National Commission on Foundations and Private Philanthropy; member of National News Council, 1973-74, and U.S. Advisory Commission on International Educational and Cultural Affairs, 1970-75; chairman of Twentieth Century Fund's task force on financing of Congressional campaigns, 1970; board member and committee chairman of U.S. Chamber of Commerce, 1969-74; member of Commission for Economic Development; chairman of U.S. Rent Advisory Board, 1971-73; chairman of Corp. for Public Broadcasting, 1972-73; chairman of Federal Election Commission, 1975—. Trustee of Dartmouth College, 1951-72, William Woods College, 1962—, Westminster College, 1965—, National College of Education, 1969—, Lincoln Foundation, 1970—, Dartmouth Institute, 1972—, Center for Strategic and International Studies, 1973—, Lincoln Institute, 1975—. *Military service:* U.S. Naval Reserve, active duty, 1942-45; served in the Philippines; became lieutenant commander; received Philippines Freedom Medal.

MEMBER: National Planning Association (trustee, 1969-74), American Bar Association, American Political Science Association, Phi Delta Phi, Phi Sigma Kappa. *Awards, honors:* Honorary degrees include M.A. from Dartmouth College, 1951, LL.D. from Westminster College, 1962, and Washington University, St. Louis, Mo., 1969; Ellis Forshee Award from Missouri Federation for the Blind, 1958; alumni citation from Washington University, 1960; Man of the Year award from *St. Louis Globe-Democrat,* 1960; Perry Award from National Federation for the Blind, 1961; Congressional distinguished service award from American Political Science Association, 1963, 1964; Silver Beaver award, 1964, and Distinguished Eagle award, 1971, both from Boy Scouts of America.

WRITINGS: Eighty-Seven Million Jobs: A Dynamic Program to End Unemployment, Duell, 1962; *Decision Making in the U.S. Congress,* Institute of Government and Public Affairs, University of California, 1969; (with John Robert Vastine, Jr.) *The Kennedy Round and the Future of American Trade,* Praeger, 1971.

WORK IN PROGRESS: The U.S. House of Representatives.

AVOCATIONAL INTERESTS: Tennis, chess.

BIOGRAPHICAL/CRITICAL SOURCES: Newsweek, April 18, 1960, April 17, 1961; *Banking,* May, 1963.

* * *

CUYLER, Susanna (Stevens) 1946-

PERSONAL: Born January 18, 1946, in New York, N.Y.; daughter of Gordon (membership chairman of Bronx Zoo) and Joan (Pratt) Cuyler. *Education:* Attended Villa Mercede, 1965, and Boston University, 1965-68. *Politics:* Radical left. *Home:* 214 Mulberry St., New York, N.Y. 10012. *Agent:* Barthold Fles, 570 Fifth Ave., New York, N.Y. 10017. *Office: Soho Weekly News,* 59 Spring St., New York, N.Y. 10012.

CAREER: Leacock Pennebaker, Inc., New York, N.Y., 16mm film distributor, 1968-70; *Soho Weekly News,* New York, N.Y., administrator/distributor, publicist, and advertising manager, 1974—. Founder and director of Craft Production Center in rural upstate New York, 1972—; manager of B. Rugged (rugmaking/rugteaching company and city store), 1976—. *Awards, honors:* Grant from America the Beautiful Fund, 1972, for foundation of a rural craft center.

WRITINGS: The High Pile Rug Book, Harper, 1974. Author of column, "A Piece of the Cake," for *Soho Weekly News,* 1974—. Contributor to *Margins* and *New York* magazine.

WORK IN PROGRESS: A study of craft centers from historical, psychological, and business points of view; a novel.

AVOCATIONAL INTERESTS: Rural living (Susanna Cuyler lives in a rural area with pond, stream, raft, and dog, and commutes to New York City only once a week for a day).

* * *

CZAPLINSKI, Suzanne 1943-

PERSONAL: Surname is pronounced Cha-*plin*-ski; born January 6, 1943, in Madison, Wis.; daughter of James T. (a lawyer) and Calla (Jepson) Murphy; married Richard Czaplinski (a water resources planner), September 5, 1964; children: Matthew, Anne. *Education:* University of Wisconsin, student, 1961-64, M.A., 1972; Georgetown University, B.A., 1965. *Home:* 12 Pearl St., Montpelier, Vt. 05602.

CAREER: Community College of Vermont, Montpelier, instructor in literature and counselor, both 1974—. Counselor and health care worker for Barre (Vt.) Planned Parenthood, 1974—.

WRITINGS: Sexism in Award Winning Picture Books, Know, Inc., 1972.

SIDELIGHTS: Suzanne Czaplinski writes that her book "began as a very personal exploration into books for my children. Sexism was both rampant and disturbing. Since then I have increased my interest in adult literature, particularly in the area of women's journals.''

* * *

DACE, (Edwin) Wallace 1920-

PERSONAL: Born August 11, 1920, in Rome, N.Y.; married to Beth M.; children: Hal, Teddy. *Education:* Illinois Wesleyan University, A.B., 1943; Yale University, M.F.A., 1948; University of Denver, Ph.D., 1952. *Home:* 2217 Stone Post Rd., Manhattan, Kan. 66502. *Agent:* Ann Elmo Agency, 52 Vanderbilt Ave., New York, N.Y. 10017. *Office:* Department of Speech, Kansas State University, Manhattan, Kan. 66502.

CAREER: Russell Sage College, Troy, N.Y., instructor in theatre, 1952-57; Sweet Briar College, Sweet Briar, Va., assistant professor, 1957-59, associate professor of English, 1959-63; Kansas State University, Manhattan, associate professor, 1963-68, professor of theatre and director of graduate theatre studies, 1968—. Chairman, Tuttle Creek Summer Festival committee, 1964-66; drama advisory panel member, Kansas Cultural Arts Commission, 1966—. Has worked seven seasons in summer theatre; director of over fifty plays, operas, and musical comedies; supervisor of design and construction, Mary Reynolds Babcock Fine Arts Center, 1958-61, Kansas State University Auditorium, 1963-70. *Member:* American Educational Theatre Association, United States Institute for Theatre Technology, Speech Communication Association of America, Phi Kappa Phi, Pi Epsilon Delta, Theta Alpha Phi. *Awards, honors:* First prize in six national playwriting competitions conducted by university, professional, and community theatre organizations, 1960-66; Ford Foundation grant, summer, 1961.

WRITINGS—Nonfiction: *Elements of Dramatic Structure,* AG Press, 1972, *Subsidies for the Theatre: A Study of the Central European System of Financing Drama, Opera, and Ballet,* AG Press, 1972; (with Letitia Dace) *The Theatre Student: Modern Theatre and Drama,* Richards Rosen, 1973. Contributor of articles to *Opera News* and *Educational Theatre Journal.*

Published plays: *Two Plays* (includes "The Sorcerer's Apprentice," as yet unproduced, and "October Festival," first produced at Sweet Briar College, 1961), Whitehall Drama Books (London), 1974. "We Commit This Body," included in anthology, *Best Short Plays of 1959-1960,* edited by Margaret Mayorga, Beacon Press, 1960.

Other plays: "Pamela's Deception," first produced at Russell Sage College, 1954; "The Prophet," first produced in Harper's Ferry, W.Va., 1959; "Flight," first produced at University of Arkansas, 1961; "Journey in July," first produced at Richmond Professional Institute, 1963; (with Letitia Dace) "A Girl Who Said Yes," first produced at Kansas State University, 1969; "The House on Prince Edward Street," first produced at Kansas State University, 1971; "John Brown in Kansas," first produced in Abilene, Kan. at State Historical Theatre, 1971. Also author of "The Flag-Bearer," as yet neither produced nor published.

WORK IN PROGRESS: Three plays: "Commander Stillwagon's Return to His Country" (two acts), "Show Me the Face You Had Before Your Father Was Born" (two acts), "Fate, Fortune and Final Solutions" (one act).

DAGER, Edward Z(icca) 1921-

PERSONAL: Born October 11, 1921, in Warren, Ohio; son of Isaac A. and Nazara (Daghir) Dager; married Esther Currado, September 19, 1953; children: Janet, Michael, Elizabeth. *Education:* Kent State University, B.A., 1950; Ohio State University, M.A., 1951, Ph.D., 1956. *Politics:* Independent. *Home:* 4 Bentana Way, Rockville, Md. 20850. *Office:* Department of Sociology, University of Maryland, College Park, Md. 20742.

CAREER: Ohio State University, Columbus, assistant instructor in sociology, 1953-56; Purdue University, Lafayette, Ind., assistant professor, 1956-60, associate professor, 1960-66, professor of sociology, 1967-68; National Science Foundation, Washington, D.C., staff associate and science manager, 1968-70; University of Maryland, College Park, professor of sociology, 1970—. Visiting professor at Kent State University, summer, 1959; professor at University of Puerto Rico, summer, 1965. Indiana representative to board of National Council on Family Relations, 1958-61, member of Burgess Award committee, 1962, 1967-70, chairman of committee, 1970, member of board of directors, 1968-70; regional vice-president of Indiana Council on Family Relations, 1960-62, president, 1962-64; consultant to National Science Foundation. *Military service:* U.S. Navy, 1942-45.

MEMBER: American Sociological Association, American Association for the Advancement of Science, Southern Sociological Society, District of Columbia Sociological Society. *Awards, honors:* Lilly Endowment grant, 1958-60, for training family life teachers in Indiana; U.S. Office of Education grant, 1967, to study social interactions resulting in school drop-outs; National Science Foundation grant, 1974.

WRITINGS: (Editor) *Socialization,* Markham, 1971.

Contributor: Benjamin Pasamanick, editor, *Epidemiology of Mental Disorders,* American Association for the Advancement of Science, 1959; H. T. Christensen, editor, *Handbook of Marriage and the Family,* Rand McNally, 1964. Contributor of articles and reviews to sociology journals. Book review editor of *Marriage and Family Living,* 1956-59; special review editor of *Sociometry,* 1971, 1973.

WORK IN PROGRESS: Research on the youth culture, on identification, on family integration, on social factors and I.Q., and on the scientist and productivity.

SIDELIGHTS: Dager writes: [My] "research is motivated by the belief that any social system relies on agents of socialization to perpetuate that system. Family and school are the two most important. I am studying the mechanism by which the values of a given society are transmitted from one generation to the next."

* * *

D'ALESSANDRO, Robert (Philip) 1942-

PERSONAL: Born November 29, 1942, in Bronx, N.Y.; son of Frank Philip and Camille D'Alessandro; married Sara Hankinson (an artist), June 19, 1965. *Education:* Pratt Institute, B.F.A., 1965; Brooklyn College of the City University of New York, M.F.A., 1971. *Home:* 176 Clinton Ave., Brooklyn, N.Y. 11205. *Office:* Department of Art, Brooklyn College of the City University of New York, Brooklyn, N.Y. 11210.

CAREER: Photographer. New School for Social Research, New York, N.Y., instructor in photography, 1970-72; Brooklyn College of the City University of New York,

Brooklyn, N.Y., instructor in photography, 1973—. Adjunct instructor at Brooklyn College of the City University of New York, 1970-72; associate adjunct professor at New York University, 1972; visiting photographer at University of New Mexico, spring, 1973. Has taught at photography workshops in the New York area and in San Francisco; has been interviewed on educational television programs; work has been exhibited all over the United States and in London, and is in permanent collections in the United States, Canada, and France.

MEMBER: Society for Photographic Education. *Awards, honors:* Judges' prize from photography exhibit at University of Chicago, 1970, for "City of Man"; first prize at Mount Holyoke College Art Museum exhibition, 1971; grant from New York State Council on the Arts, 1971; grant from National Endowment for the Arts, 1975.

WRITINGS: (Contributor) Nathan Lyons, editor, *Vision and Expression,* Horizon Press, 1968; *Glory* (book of photographs), Elephant Publishing Corp., 1974. Contributor to photography magazines, and to *New York, Pageant, Infinity, National Lampoon,* and *American Journal.*

SIDELIGHTS: D'Alessandro writes that *Glory* consists of photographs of how people used the flag to communicate during "the Nixon years."

BIOGRAPHICAL/CRITICAL SOURCES: Village Voice, October 19, 1972; *Popular Photography,* Bicentennial Annual, 1976.

* * *

DALLAS, Philip 1921-

PERSONAL: Born August 15, 1921, in London, England; became Italian citizen, 1968; son of Ernest Henry and Mabel (Osborne) Dallas; married Maria Cecilia Aymerich di Laconi, June 7, 1963. *Education:* Attended Sandhurst Royal Military Academy, 1940-41. *Religion:* Tridentine Catholic. *Home:* via Dicomano, 9, Rome, Italy. *Agent:* Ray Pierre Corsini, 12 Beekman Pl., New York, N.Y. 10022.

CAREER: J. Walter Thompson Ltd., Bombay, India, founder, and production and script executive of motion picture department, 1946-47; writer, correspondent, and photographic adviser to travel, gourmet, and general periodicals, while residing in Italy, 1948—. Press officer or speaker for various international conferences held in Italy. *Military service:* Served with Indian Cavalry, Royal Indian Navy, and British Royal Navy, 1941-46; held positions including adviser to Indian Department of Information and Broadcasting, 1945, and head of Indian Naval Film Production Office, 1946; became captain. *Member:* International Wine and Food Society (founder and chairman of Rome branch).

WRITINGS: (With Luigi Carnacina) *Italian Home Cooking* (Book-of-the-Month Club cookbook selection), Doubleday, 1972; *The Great Wines of Italy,* Doubleday, 1974 (slightly different edition published in England as *Italian Wines,* Faber, 1974). Author and producer of documentary films for United Nations, Shell Oil Co., CIBA Pharmaceuticals, and other firms. Translator of articles for *Ospitalita* magazine and Italian Foreign Ministry bulletin, and author of monthly page, "News from Rome," 1970; regular correspondent, *Tatler* (London), 1970—. Contributor to publications, including *Atlantic Monthly, Holiday, Venture, Vista, Vintage, Sphere* (Chicago), Washington *Star,* London *Times,* and *Wine and Food* (of International Wine and Food Society).

WORK IN PROGRESS: Three short books: *The Molotov Cocktail Party,* a satire on Roman revolutionaries; a satirical dialogue, *The Revelations of the Devil, as Told to Philip Dallas;* text for a picture book, *Baroque Art of Rome.*

SIDELIGHTS: Dallas commented to *CA:* "We are denying the relation between cause and effect with spurious or 'eutopistic' arguments, to our detriment. Through sophisticated satire, I try to bring back good old pragmatism. As a satirist, I am a humanitarian, of course, but I do not love human beings when they abuse power. We must defend ourselves from usurpers—at home and abroad—with the sword and the pen." *Avocational interests:* "Playing 'bit' parts in movies as a relief from reality, drinking good wine, admiring human beauty, and worrying about the fate of the world!"

* * *

DAL POGGETTO, Newton Francis 1922-

PERSONAL: Born July 13, 1922, in Sonoma, Calif.; son of Newton F. and Marie L. (Murray) Dal Poggetto; married Helene I. Watts, May 14, 1946; children: Lynne Elizabeth, Sandra Hope, Marc Scott. *Education:* Attended University of Colorado, 1940-43, University of New Mexico, 1943-44, and Santa Clara University, 1946-47, 1949-50; University of Denver, B.S., 1948, LL.B., 1949. *Religion:* Roman Catholic. *Home:* 555 Crestway Dr., Sonoma, Calif. 95476. *Office:* 2200 B County Center Dr., Santa Rosa, Calif. 95401; and 164 West Napa St., Sonoma, Calif. 95476.

CAREER: Admitted to California Bar, 1950, and U.S. Supreme Court Bar, 1961; private practice of law in Sonoma, Calif., 1950—. Judge of Sonoma Judicial District, 1951-59; president and chairman of board of directors of Pueblo Investment Co., 1964—, and Dal Poggetto & Jess Professional Corp., 1972—; member of board of governors of Sonoma Valley Boy's Club. Member of California Democratic Committee, 1954-58. *Military service:* U.S. Naval Reserve, active duty, 1943-46; became lieutenant junior grade. *Member:* American Trial Lawyers Association, Veterans of Foreign Wars, American Legion, California Trial Lawyers Association, California State Bar Association, Sonoma County Bar Association (president, 1970-71), Sigma Alpha Epsilon, Commonwealth Club (San Francisco).

WRITINGS: Vintage of a Murder (novel), Forerunner Enterprises, 1974.

WORK IN PROGRESS: A novel, *Lightning in My Fingers.*

* * *

DARROW, Ralph C(arroll) 1918-

PERSONAL: Born July 23, 1918, in Columbus Junction, Iowa; son of C. Sumner (a teacher) and Muzetta (Sheets) Darrow; married Fae Kohls, December 17, 1966; children: Carolyn, Jane and Mary (twins). *Education:* University of Iowa, B.A., 1948, M.A., 1953. *Politics:* Republican. *Religion:* Methodist. *Home:* 1515 South Lincoln St., Kent, Ohio 44240. *Office:* School of Journalism, Kent State University, Kent, Ohio 44242.

CAREER: Daily News, Estherville, Iowa, reporter and photographer, 1948-51; Firestone Corp., Des Moines, Iowa, in public relations and publications, 1953-67; Kent State University, Kent, Ohio, associate professor of public relations, 1967—. *Military service:* U.S. Army Air Forces,

1942-45; B-24 nose gunner; served in Pacific theater; became staff sergeant. U.S. Air Force, 1951; became staff sergeant. *Member:* International Association of Business Communicators (trustee of Akron, Ohio, chapter, 1975-76), Association for Education in Journalism, Public Relations Society of America (member of board of governors of Akron, Ohio, chapter, 1975-76), Sigma Delta Chi (first vice-president of Buckeye chapter).

WRITINGS: House Journal Editing, Interstate, 1974.

* * *

DARROW, Whitney (Jr.) 1909-

PERSONAL: Born August 22, 1909, in Princeton, N.J.; son of Whitney (a publisher) and May Temperance (Barton) Darrow; married Betty Waldo Parish, 1938 (divorced); married Mildred Lois Adkins, October 23, 1942; children: Whitney Barton, Linda Ann. *Education:* Princeton University, A.B., 1931; also attended Art Students League of New York City. *Politics:* Independent. *Home:* 331 Newtown Turnpike, Wilton, Conn. 06897.

CAREER: Free-lance cartoonist, 1931—; *New Yorker* (magazine), New York, N.Y., cartoonist, 1934—. *Member:* Coffee House Club and Dutch Treat Club (New York).

WRITINGS—Cartoons: *You're Sitting on My Eyelashes,* Random House, 1943; *Please Pass the Hostess,* Random House, 1949; *Hold It, Florence,* Dell, 1953; *Stop, Miss!,* Random House, 1957; *Give Up? A New Cartoon Collection,* Simon & Schuster, 1966.

Other: *Animal Etiquette,* Windmill Books, 1969; *I'm Glad I'm a Boy! I'm Glad I'm a Girl!,* Windmill Books, 1970.

Illustrator: Julian Leonard Street, *Need of Change,* Dodd, 1934; George Jean Nathan, *Beware of Parents: A Bachelor's Book for Children,* Farrar, Straus, 1943; Corey Ford, *Office Party,* Doubleday, 1951; Whitney Darrow, Sr., *Princeton University Press: An Informal Account of Its Growing Pains, Casually Put Together at the Point of a Gun for the Intimate Friends of the Press,* Princeton University Press, 1951; Irene Kampen, *Europe Without George,* Norton, 1965; Johnny Carson, *Happiness Is . . . a Dry Martini,* Doubleday, 1965; Johnny Carson, *Misery Is . . . a Blind Date,* Doubleday, 1967; Robert Kraus, *Whitney Darrow' Jr.'s Unidentified Flying Elephant,* Windmill Books, 1968; Samuel Levenson, *Sex and the Single Child,* Simon & Schuster, 1969; Jean Kerr, *Penny Candy,* Doubleday, 1970; Enzo Lunari, *Pierino Viaggia in LSD,* Ferro (Milan), 1970; Marie Winn, *Shiver, Gobble, and Snore,* Simon & Schuster, 1971; Marie Winn, *The Thief-Catcher . . .,* Simon & Schuster, 1972; Marie Winn, editor, *The Fireside Book of Fun and Game Songs,* Simon & Schuster, 1974; Joanna Cole, *Fun on Wheels,* Scholastic Book Services, 1975.

SIDELIGHTS: Darrow studied drawing under George Bridgman, Thomas Benton, and Kimon Nicolaides; his drawing "Bird in Flight" is included in the Roland P. Murdock collection in Wichita, Kansas. His cartoons have appeared in *Judge, Life, Collier's, Ballyhoo, Saturday Review of Literature, College Humor,* and *Saturday Evening Post. Avocational interests:* Golf, bowling.

* * *

DARVAS, Nicholas 1920-

PERSONAL: Born May 23, 1920, in Budapest, Hungary. *Education:* University of Pazmany, Dr. Sociology, 1942. *Agent:* Music Corp. of America, 598 Madison Ave., New York, N.Y.

CAREER: Writer, investor, professional dancer. Former crossword puzzle editor and sports writer.

WRITINGS: How I Made Two Million Dollars in the Stock Market, American Research Council, 1962, revised edition, Lyle Stewart, 1970; *Wall Street: The Other Las Vegas,* Lyle Stuart, 1962; *The Anatomy of Success,* Bobbs-Merrill, 1966. Also author of *The Darvas System for Over the Counter Profits,* Lyle Stuart.

BIOGRAPHICAL/CRITICAL SOURCES: Time, May 25, 1959.

* * *

DAUBENY, Peter (Lauderdale) 1921-1975

PERSONAL: Born April 16, 1921, in Wiesbaden, Germany; son of Cyril (an army officer) and Margaret (Duncan) Daubeny; married Mary Vyvyan Kempster, 1948; children: one son, one daughter. *Education:* Attended Marlborough College; studied at Michel St. Denis School of Acting. *Home:* 26 Chester Sq., London SW1, England.

CAREER: Member of repertory company at Playhouse, Liverpool, England, 1937-39; formed theatrical company, Peter Daubeny Ltd. in 1945, and produced numerous plays; in 1951 began presenting ballet, theater, opera, and individual performers, including Sacha Guitry, Maurice Chevalier, Bertolt Brecht Berliner Ensemble, Indian Ballet, Moscow Arts Theatre, Chinese Classical Theatre, Red Army Choir, Ingmar Bergman's Malmo Theatre, Jerome Robbin's Ballets; founded and produced, in conjunction with the Royal Shakespeare Co., the annual World Theatre Season at the Aldwych Theatre in London, 1964-72, which included performances by Comedie Francaise, Polish Contemporary Theatre, Greek Art Theatre, Czech National Theatre, Polish Popular Theatre, Leningrad Gorki Theatre, and New York Negro Ensemble Co. Consultant director, Royal Shakespeare Co., 1966—. *Military service:* Coldstream Guards, 1939-43; became lieutenant.

MEMBER: Garrick Club. *Awards, honors:* Officer of the Legion of Honor, 1957, chevalier, 1971; Order of the British Empire, 1961, commander, 1967; Gold Cross of the Royal Order of King George I of the Hellenes, 1965; Cavalier of the Order of Merit of the Republic of Italy, 1966; Gold Medal of Czechoslovakia, 1967; Order of Merit of the German Federal Republic, 1971.

WRITINGS—Autobiography: *Stage by Stage,* Murray, 1952; *My World of Theatre,* J. Cape, 1971.

AVOCATIONAL INTERESTS: Theatregoing, collecting first editions, traveling, reading.

OBITUARIES: New York Times, August 7, 1975.

(Died August 6, 1975)

* * *

DAUENHAUER, Richard L(eonard) 1942-

PERSONAL: Born April 10, 1942, in Syracuse, N.Y.; son of Leonard G. (a teacher) and Jane (Grier) Dauenhauer; married Sandra Dudley, 1965 (divorced, 1972); married Nora Marks Florendo, November 28, 1973. Stepchildren: Leonora Florendo, Carmella Tapacio, Lorenzo Florendo, Adela Ransom. *Education:* Syracuse University, B.A., 1964; University of Texas, M.A., 1966; Helsinki University, graduate study, 1966-67; University of Wisconsin, Madison, Ph.D., 1975. *Home and office address:* Alaska Methodist University, P.O. Box 25, Anchorage, Alaska 99504.

CAREER: Alaska Methodist University, Anchorage, assistant professor of comparative literature, 1969-75; Alaska Native Education Board, Anchorage, education specialist, 1975—. Charter member of Tlingit Readers, Inc. Has taught at Sheldon Jackson College, summers, 1972-74, and University of Alaska, summer, 1975. Tlingit researcher for Alaska Native Language Center at Universityof Alaska, 1972-73; language arts specialist for Alaska Bilingual Education Center of Alaska Native Education Board, 1974-75. Has conducted field research in southeast Alaska, the Yukon Territory, and in Eskimo and Athapaskan areas. *Member:* American Folklore Society. *Awards, honors:* Woodrow Wilson fellowship, 1964-65; Fulbright fellowship, 1966-67.

WRITINGS: (Translator with others) Goeran Sonnevi, *On the War: A Bilingual Pamphlet of Poems from the Swedish,* Third Coast Press, 1968; *Tlingit Spelling Book,* Tlingit Readers, Inc., 1974; *Folklore Handbook for Bilingual Classrooms,* Alaska Native Education Board, 1975; *Koyukon Riddles,* Alaska Native Education Board, 1975; (editor with W. Philip Binham, and contributor) *Snow in May: An Anthology of Modern Finnish Writing, 1945-1972,* Associated University Presses, in press; *Phenologies: Poems, 1970-1972,* Thorp Springs Press, in press.

Translations have been anthologized in *Probes: An Introduction to Poetry,* edited by William K. Harlan, Macmillan, 1973. Contributor to *Encyclopedia of World Literature in the Twentieth Century.* Contributor of about eighty poems, translations, and articles to literary journals and little magazines, including *Quixote, Beloit Poetry Journal, Hyperion, Poet Lore, Literary Review,* and *Raven.* Guest editor of *Literary Review,* autumn, 1970.

WORK IN PROGRESS: A cycle of poems about southeast Alaska; translating modern German, Russian, Finnish, and Swedish poems, classical and medieval Greek poems, and Tlingit Indian material.

SIDELIGHTS: Dauenhauer writes: "I am probably best known for my translations. . . . I can speak German, Russian, and Finnish, and I can read over one dozen languages to varying degrees. . . . I disagree with many scholars, but with few poets, in my belief that translation is a discipline of creative writing rather than of scholarship, although scholarship is involved, and although each translation is in a very real sense an act of literary criticism and commentary as well as an act of poetry. . . . It's exciting to find that the dusty poets of antiquity are not so dusty after all. There was nothing dull about their vision. When we translate, we are not revitalizing Rouphinos, Meleagros, Sappho, or any other poet: we are revitalizing ourselves."

AVOCATIONAL INTERESTS: Outdoor activity (hiking, camping, canoeing, fishing, cross country skiing), fencing (sabre and epee), photography, model railroads (N gauge).

* * *

DAVIDSON, Glen W(illiam) 1936-

PERSONAL: Born July 26, 1936, in Wendell, Idaho; son of W. Dean (a rancher and teacher) and Grace (a teacher; maiden name, Barnum) Davidson; married Shirlee Proctor (a registered nurse), November 26, 1971; children: Heather Ann. *Education:* University of the Pacific, A.B. (magna cum laude), 1958; Drew University, B.D., 1961, M.Div. (cum laude), 1961; Claremont Graduate School, Ph.D., 1964; postdoctoral study at University College, Oxford, 1968, and at University of Chicago and Newberry Library, 1967-68. *Religion:* Methodist. *Home:* 807 Randolph Court,

Springfield, Ill. 62702. *Address:* School of Medicine, Southern Illinois University, P.O. Box 3926, Springfield, Ill. 62708.

CAREER: Colgate University, Hamilton, N.Y., instructor, 1964-66, assistant professor of philosophy and religion, 1966-67, assistant chaplain, 1964-67; University of Chicago, Chicago, Ill., assistant professor of church history, 1968-70, associate director and coordinator of professional degrees programs, 1968-70, University of Iowa, Iowa City, research fellow-in-residence, 1970-72; Southern Illinois University, School of Medicine, Springfield, associate professor of psychiatry, and chief of thanatology, 1972—, associate professor of culture and medicine, and chairman of department, 1974—. Lecturer at Mount Saint Vincent University, summer, 1971, and at Chapman College, World Campus Afloat, spring, 1972, Gettysburg College, Wells College, St. John's University, Collegeville, Minn., St. Francis Xavier University, University of Moncton, Columbia University, Universities of Illinois, Iowa, and Texas, Dalhousie University, and at Maryville College. Consultant to Mountain States Tumor Institute, 1972—. Staff member of Memorial Medical Center, Springfield, and St. John's Hospital, Springfield.

MEMBER: Gypsy Lore Society, American Society of Chinese Medicine, American Association of Marriage and Family Counselors (clinical member), Society for Health and Human Values, Institute of Society, Ethics, and the Life Sciences, Society for Values in Higher Education (fellow), Foundation of Thanatology (member of national professional advisory board, 1970—). *Awards, honors:* Research grants from Glide Foundation, 1964-65, Colgate Research Council, 1965-67, Newberry Library, 1967, 1972.

WRITINGS: King Mohammed V of Morocco (monograph), College of the Pacific, 1958; *The Pound Fishers: A Photographic Essay,* privately printed, 1966; (contributor) Sallie TeSelle, editor, *The Rediscovery of Ethnicity: Its Implications for Culture and Politics in America,* Harper, 1973; (author of foreword) Nancy C. Andreasen, *Understanding Mental Illness: A Layman's Guide,* Augsburg, 1974; (author of foreword) David Belgum, *What Can I Do About the Part of Me I Don't Like?,* Augsburg, 1974; *Living With Dying,* Augsburg, 1975; (author of foreword) George Paterson, *Helping Your Handicapped Child,* Augsburg, 1975; (contributor) J. Donald Bane and others, editors, *Death and Ministry: Pastoral Care of the Dying and the Bereaved,* Seabury, 1975; (contributor) Bernard Schoenberg and others, editors, *Bereavement: Its Psychosocial Aspects,* Columbia University Press, 1975; (contributor) Frank Reynolds and Earle H. Waugh, editors, *Encounters with Death: Essays in the History and Anthropology of Religion,* Pennsylvania State University Press, 1976; (editor) *Religion, Culture, and Medicine: An Annotated Bibliography,* Gale, in press. General editor of Augsburg's "Religion and Medicine" series. Author of film, radio, and television scripts. Contributor to professional journals.

WORK IN PROGRESS: The Gypsy's Journey: A Study in North American Culture.

* * *

DAVIES, Evelyn 1924-

PERSONAL: Born April 2, 1924, in Brockenhurst, Hampshire, England; daughter of George William Stanley (a shoemaker) and Ethel Jane (James) Brown; married David John Davies (a publican) (died, 1972); children: Claire Evelyn (Mrs. Jonathan Douglas Blake Tagart), Robert John. *Education:* Attended private and secondary schools in Brockenhurst. *Religion:* Church of England. *Home:* 2 Saxonford Rd., Friars Cliff, Christchurch BH2 34ES, England.

CAREER: Works as a landlady at Haven House Inn, Christchurch, England.

WRITINGS—All for young people: *Little Bear's Feather,* Hamish Hamilton, 1973; *Run for Home,* Hamish Hamilton, 1974; *Joseph's Bear,* Hamish Hamilton, 1975.

SIDELIGHTS: Evelyn Davies commented: "I have always had a great interest in the American Indian and American pioneering days. One of my earliest memories is of standing on a chair to recite 'Hiawatha' as a small child, which is perhaps where my interest first started. And in my stories I like to portray the Indians as having similar feelings of children the world over and to show they were not the 'bad men' films and television would have us believe."

*   *   *

DAVIES, Evelyn A(dele)   1915-

PERSONAL: Born September 14, 1915, in Bangor, Pa.; daughter of Griffith Jones and Annie (Evans) Davies. *Education:* East Stroudsburg State College, B.S., 1936; Columbia University, M.A., 1945, physical therapy certificate, 1948, Ed.D., 1950. *Home:* 905 Meadowbrook, Bloomington, Ind. 47401. *Office:* Health, Physical Education and Recreation Building, Room 112, Indiana University, Bloomington, Ind. 47401.

CAREER: Investigator and visitor for Pennsylvania Department of Public Assistance, 1936-41; Physical education teacher in public schools in Newtown, Pa., 1941-45; supervisor of corrective physical education in public schools in Poughkeepsie, N.Y., 1945-48; Columbia University, Teachers College, New York, N.Y., instructor in physical education, 1948-54; University of California, Los Angeles, assistant professor of adapted physical education, 1950-58; Indiana University, Bloomington, associate professor, 1958-64, professor of adapted physical education, 1964—. Visiting professor at Columbia University, summers, 1952, 1956. Member of advisory board of Monroe County Preschool for Handicapped Children, 1965—; member of advisory committee of Mental Retardation Developmental Training Center, 1970-71; member of executive committee of Indiana Special Olympics. Consultant to Research and Development Center for Handicapped Children and Stonebelt Council for Retarded Children.

MEMBER: American College of Sports Medicine (fellow), American Association for Health, Physical Education and Recreation (member of Research Council), National Association of Physical Education for College Women, American Physical Therapy Association, Midwest Association for Health, Physical Education and Recreation, Midwest Association of Physical Education for College Women, Indiana Association for Health, Physical Education and Recreation, Delta Kappa Gamma, Pi Lambda Theta, Kappa Delta Pi.

WRITINGS: The Elementary Child and His Posture Patterns, Appleton, 1958; (contributor) James F. Magary and John R. Eichorn, editors, *The Exceptional Child: A Book of Readings,* Holt, 1960; (with Ben Bruce) *Golf for Beginners,* Wadsworth, 1962; *Adapted Physical Education,* 2nd edition (with Arthur S. Daniels; Evelyn Davies was not associated with 1st edition), Harper, 1965, 3rd edition (sole author), 1975. Contributor to education and physical educa-

tion journals. Member of editorial board of *Journal of Health, Physical Education and Recreation,* 1960-63.

AVOCATIONAL INTERESTS: Golf, swimming, fishing, music.

*   *   *

DAVIES, Rod   1941-

PERSONAL: Born February 14, 1941, in Luton, England; Canadian citizen; son of Arthur and Doris (Cole) Davies; married Maureen Pearson-Dale (a puzzle maker), August 15, 1969. *Education:* University of Leicester, B.Sc., 1962, Post Graduate Certificate of Education, 1963. *Religion:* "Uncommitted." *Address:* P.O. Box 12, Station "H," Montreal, Quebec, Canada.

CAREER: Beaumont Leys School, Leicester, England, teacher of biology, 1964-66; Wellingborough Technical College, Wellingborough, England, teacher of biology, 1966-67; Berkeley Institute, Hamilton, Bermuda, teacher of biology, 1967-69; writer.

WRITINGS: Your Practical Guide To Fortune-Telling, Zebra Books, 1974. Author of film "Fortune Telling," produced by Canadian Broadcasting Corp., 1973.

WORK IN PROGRESS: A book about Tarot cards; a detective novel.

AVOCATIONAL INTERESTS: Classical guitar, Thomas Hardy, the occult, magic, Bach.

*   *   *

DAVIS, Arthur P(aul)   1904-

PERSONAL: Born November 21, 1904, in Hampton, Va.; son of Andrew (a plasterer) and Frances (Nash) Davis; married Clarice Winn, October 6, 1928; children: Arthur Paul, Jr. *Education:* Columbia University, A.B., 1927, A.M., 1929, Ph.D., 1942. *Politics:* Independent. *Religion:* Episcopalian. *Home:* 3001 Veazey Ter. N.W., Washington, D.C. 20008. *Office:* Graduate School, Howard University, Washington, D.C. 20059.

CAREER: North Carolina College (now North Carolina Central University), Durham, professor of English, 1927-28; Virginia Union University, Richmond, professor of English, 1929-44; Howard University, Washington, D.C., professor of English, 1944-69, university professor, 1969—. Conducted series of talks, "Ebony Harvest," on Radio WAMU-FM, Washington-Baltimore, 1972-73. *Member:* Modern Language Association of America, College Language Association, Phi Beta Kappa. *Awards, honors:* Proudfit fellow, Columbia University, 1937; National Hampton alumni award, 1947; Award from Howard University's Institute for the Arts and Humanities, 1973; award from College Language Association, 1975, for distinguished contribution to literary scholarship.

WRITINGS: (Editor with Sterling A. Brown and Ulysses Lee) *The Negro Caravan,* Dryden, 1941, Arno, 1970; *Isaac Watts: His Life and Works,* Dryden, 1943; (editor with Saunders Redding) *Cavalcade: Negro American Writers from 1760 to the Present,* Houghton, 1971; *From the Dark Tower: Afro-American Writers from 1900 to 1960,* Howard University Press, 1974; (editor with Michael Peplow) *The New Negro Renaissance: An Anthology,* Holt, 1975. Writer of column, "With a Grain of Salt," *Journal and Guide* newspaper, 1933-50.

WORK IN PROGRESS: The Life and Observations of Arthur P. Davis, Middle Class Negro (tentative title).

SIDELIGHTS: Davis writes: "In 1929, I taught my first course in Negro literature. Very, very few Negro and no white schools in those days had a course in this subject. Believing strongly in the importance of the Negro's contribution to American literature, I have devoted practically all of my adult working years to teaching and writing in the field of Negro letters. It has been gratifying to note the subject's growth in popularity since 1929."

* * *

DAVIS, Bette (Ruth Elizabeth) 1908-

PERSONAL: Born April 5, 1908, in Lowell, Mass.; daughter of Harlow Morrell (an attorney) and Ruth (a photographer; maiden name, Favor) Davis; married Harmon Oscar Nelson (a bandleader), August 18, 1932 (divorced); married Arthur Farnsworth (a businessman), December, 1940 (died August, 1943); married William Grant Sherry (an artist), November 30, 1945 (divorced); married Gary Merrill (an actor), August, 1950 (divorced); children: Barbara (Mrs. Jeremy Hyman), Margot Merrill, Michael Merrill. *Education:* Studied at Mariarden School of Dancing and John Murray Anderson Drama School. *Home:* 1 Crooked Mile, Westport, Conn. 06880. *Office address:* c/o Gottlieb Schiff Ticktin Fabricant & Sternklar, 555 Fifth Ave., New York, N.Y. 10017.

CAREER: Actress. Began her acting career with stock companies in Rochester, N.Y. and Dennis, Mass.; gave first performance on Broadway at the Ritz Theatre in "Broken Dishes," 1929. Became screen actress in 1931 and has appeared in more than eighty films, the most notable of which include: "The Man Who Played God," 1932; "Of Human Bondage," 1934; "Bordertown," 1935; "Dangerous," 1935; "Petrified Forest," 1936; "Jezebel," 1938; "Dark Victory," 1939; "Juarez," 1939; "The Old Maid," 1939; "The Private Lives of Elizabeth and Essex," 1939; "The Great Lie," 1941; "The Bride Came C.O.D.," 1941; "All About Eve," 1950; "Payment on Demand," 1951; "Phone Call From a Stranger," 1952; "The Star," 1953; "The Virgin Queen," 1955; "The Catered Affair," 1956; "The Storm Center," 1956; "John Paul Jones," 1959; "Whatever Happened to Baby Jane," 1962; "The Anniversary," 1968; "Connecting Rooms," 1969; "Bunny O'Hare," 1970; "Madam Sin," 1971; "The Game," 1972; "Burnt Offerings," 1975. Founder and first president, Hollywood Canteen, 1942.

MEMBER: Academy of Motion Picture Arts and Sciences (president, 1940). *Awards, honors:* Academy of Motion Picture Arts and Sciences award for best performance by an actress, 1936, for "Dangerous," and 1939, for "Jezebel"; *Picturegoer* Annual Gold Medal, 1940, for performance in "Dark Victory"; New York Film Critics award, 1951, for performance in "All About Eve".

WRITINGS: The Lonely Life (autobiography), Putnam, 1962.

SIDELIGHTS: In an account of a personal appearance made by Bette Davis in Dallas, Harry Bowman wrote: "Bette Davis is as unstuffy a legend as one is likely to encounter ... she accepted questions from the audience. It was here that her honest, forthright character asserted itself and practically bounded across the footlights.

"Bette Davis was everything the crowd had come to see.... When asked how she feels about modern motion pictures as opposed to the more fictional films of the late thirties and early forties, she was honest and unsentimental.

" 'They're different, but then the world is different and motion pictures reflect the world. Trends, morals, viewpoints ... are different today than they were then.... This is a difficult era for women in films and particularly women of my age.'

"She attributes her success to 'drive, work,' and her ability to 'communicate.' 'You must have something within you that comes across the footlights. You must communicate with people.'"

BIOGRAPHICAL/CRITICAL SOURCES: P. Nobel, *Bette Davis: A Biography,* A. Gordon, 1948; *New York Times Magazine,* October 19, 1952; Bette Davis, *The Lonely Life,* Putnam, 1962; *Good Housekeeping,* October, 1968; *New Yorker,* February 17, 1973; *Dallas News,* March 20, 1974; *McCalls,* November, 1974; Whitney Stine, *Mother Goddamn: The Life and Career of Bette Davis,* Hawthorn, 1974.

* * *

DAVIS, I(rene) M(ary) 1926-

PERSONAL: Born July 6, 1926, in Harrow, England; daughter of Hugh Kenneth (a bank clerk) and Patricia (Thom) Davis. *Education:* St. Hilda's College, Oxford, B.A., 1947. *Politics:* "Liberal, small 'l,' save when I contemplate the practical effects of liberalism." *Religion:* "Reared as Presbyterian." *Home:* 34 Parliament Ct., Parliament Hill, London NW3 2TS, England. *Office:* Department of the Environment, 2 Marsham St., London S.W.1, England.

CAREER: Civil servant in British government, serving in Ministry of Works, 1947-59, Ministry of Transport, 1960-67, Ministry of Housing, 1967-71, Countryside Commission, 1971-73, and Department of the Environment, 1973—. *Member:* Historical Association.

WRITINGS: The Black Douglas (biography), Routledge & Kegan Paul, 1974. Contributor to *History Today.*

WORK IN PROGRESS: Research for another biography.

* * *

DAVIS, Jean Reynolds 1927-

PERSONAL: Born November 1, 1927, in Cumberland, Md.; daughter of Foster Ray and Wilhelmina Ferguson (Barrick) Reynolds; married Warren Hirst Davis, Jr. (an Episcopal minister), December 9, 1949 (divorced September 10, 1975); children: Mark Reynolds, Stephen Scott. *Education:* University of Pennsylvania, Mus.B., 1949. *Religion:* Episcopalian. *Home:* Mermont Plaza, Apt. 104, Merion and Montgomery Aves., Bryn Mawr, Pa. 19010. *Agent:* (Lectures) Speaker's Showcase, Philadelphia, Pa.

CAREER: Music Publishers Holding Corp., New York, N.Y., editorial consultant, 1960-65; private teacher of piano; arranger and composer; free-lance writer. *Member:* American Society of Composers, Authors, and Publishers (grantee, 1961). Volunteer worker and teacher at Trenton State Prison. *Awards, honors:* Cultural Olympics award of merit of University of Pennsylvania, for high standard in musical composition, 1953, for chamber opera, "The Mirror."

WRITINGS: Yankee Doodle Doodles, Theodore Presser, 1960; *Slick Tricks,* Witmark, 1962; *Tricks and Treats,* Pro Art Publications, 1963; (with Cameron McGraw) *Doors into Music: A Creative Approach through the Piano,* four volumes, Boston Music Co., 1966; (with McGraw) *Doors into Music Theory: An Activity Book in the Fundamentals of Music,* Boston Music Co., 1966; (with McGraw) *Doors into Technic: Technical Proficiency for the Piano Student,* four volumes, Boston Music Co., 1966; *A Hat on the Hall Table* (autobiography), Harper, 1967; *To God with Love* (devotional literature), Harper, 1968; *Parish Picnic* (novel), Harper, 1970. Also author of *Are These the Wonderful Years?,* published by Abbey Press. Contributor to periodicals, including *Motive,* and *Philadelphia Inquirer.*

Composer of music published by sixteen different music publishers. Unpublished works consist of choral works, a woodwind quintet, two chamber operas, "The Mirror" and "The Elevator," a ballet story, "Shenandoah Holiday" (premiered by the Philadelphia Orchestra, 1961), verse interpretations of Saint-Saens "Carnival of the Animals" and Kabalevsky's "The Comedians" (both performed by the Philadelphia Orchestra), numerous vocal and piano works, and two symphonies.

AVOCATIONAL INTERESTS: Gourmet cooking, art, painting, sewing, interior decoration.

* * *

DAVIS, Morris 1933-

PERSONAL: Born October 9, 1933, in Boston, Mass.; son of Hyman William (an accountant) and Mary (Goldstein) Davis; married Ruth Miller (a job site developer), June 21, 1958; children: Jonathan Miller, Melissa Anne, William Atticus. *Education:* Harvard University, A.B. (cum laude), 1954; Princeton University, A.M. and Ph.D., both 1958. *Politics:* Democrat. *Religion:* Jewish. *Home:* 3 Burnett Circle, Urbana, Ill. 61801. *Office:* Department of Political Science, University of Illinois, 361 Lincoln Hall, Urbana, Ill. 61801.

CAREER: Princeton University, Princeton, N.J., research assistant at Center for International Studies, 1958; University of Wisconsin, Madison, instructor in political science, 1958-59; Dalhousie University, Halifax, Nova Scotia, assistant professor of political science, 1960-62; Tulane University, New Orleans, La., assistant professor, 1962-64, associate professor of political science, 1964-65; University of Illinois, Urbana, associate professor, 1965-68, professor of political science, 1968—. Visiting professor at Dalhousie University, summer, 1971.

MEMBER: Peace Science Society (International), American Political Science Association, Association for Canadian Studies in the United States, Midwest Political Science Association. *Awards, honors:* Social Science Research Council research training fellowship, Iceland, Norway, and England, 1959-60, summer grant, 1963; Canada Council grant, summer, 1961; grants from Atlantic Provinces Studies of Social Science Research Council of Canada, 1962, 1963, 1965; U.S. Public Health Service grant, 1964-67; Guggenheim fellowship, 1967-68; Ford Foundation fellowship, England, Switzerland, and Nigeria, 1969-70; grant from Midwest Universities Consortium for International Activities, summer, 1970; National Science Foundation grant, 1971-74; Isaak Walton Killam senior fellowship from Dalhousie University, 1972-73.

WRITINGS: Iceland Extends Its Fisheries Limits: A Political Analysis, Allen & Unwin, 1963; (with M. G. Weinbaum) *Metropolitan Decision Processes: An Analysis of Case Studies,* Rand McNally, 1969; (with J. F. Krauter) *The Other Canadians: Profiles of Six Minorities,* Methuen, 1971; *Civil Wars and the Politics of International Relief,* Praeger, 1975; *Interpreters for Nigeria,* University of Illinois Press, in press.

Contributor: John Meisel, editor, *Papers on the 1962 Election,* University of Toronto Press, 1964; J. C. Courtney, editor, *Voting in Canada,* Prentice-Hall (Canada), 1967; Richard Rose, editor, *Studies in British Politics,* St. Martin's, 1966; Arend Lijphart, editor, *Politics in Europe,* Prentice-Hall, 1969; J. C. Pierce and R. A. Pride, editors, *Cross-National Micro-Analysis,* Sage Publications, Inc., 1972. Contributor to *World Book Encyclopedia* and to professional journals.

WORK IN PROGRESS: Research on international relief programs for man-made disasters.

* * *

DAVIS, Rocky 1927-

PERSONAL: Born July 24, 1927, in Wilmington, Del.; daughter of Paul D. (a banker) and Katherine (Jaquette) Lovett; married Robert J. Davis, Jr. (a microbiologist), August 9, 1947; children: Robert III, Rodman, Kristy, Jan. *Education:* University of Maryland, B.Sc., 1965, M.Sc., 1966. *Politics:* Independent. *Religion:* Agnostic. *Home and office:* Chotigiri, Route 1, Mead, Okla. 73449. *Agent:* Evelyn Metzger, 1003 Turkey Run Rd., MacLean, Va.

MEMBER: Mark Twain Society, Appalachian Trail Conference, Potomac-Appalachian Trail Club, Oklahoma Trails Association, East African Wildlife Society.

WRITINGS: Sundari (nonfiction; Christian-Herald Family Bookshelf and Farm Journal Book Club selections), Crown, 1975. Contributor to *Grit.*

WORK IN PROGRESS: Malaika, a tale of three orphaned wild animals which the author raised in Uganda during 1971-72.

SIDELIGHTS: Mrs. Davis told *CA* that "life in India—particularly with a leopard—then life in Africa with an infant oribi, baby waterbuck and baby monkey has made me very aware of the horror of guns. Am adamantly opposed to hunting now. Also very concerned about wild animals as pets. Now back to the first love of my life—horses. This time raising Appaloosas, and am now addicted to trail-riding. Speak and write Hindi (Devanagri script). Have traveled extensively in India, Pakistan, Afghanistan, Greece, Spain, United Kingdom, and Ireland."

BIOGRAPHICAL/CRITICAL SOURCES: Durant Daily Democrat, January 9, 1975; *Wilmington News-Journal,* November 7, 1975.

* * *

DAVIS, William C(harles) 1946-

PERSONAL: Born September 28, 1946, in Kansas City, Mo.; son of Eual Edward (a salesman) and Martha (an accountant; maiden name, Noan) Davis; married Pamela S. McIntyre, July 22, 1969; children: M. Jefferson, Rebecca M. *Education:* California State College, Sonoma, A.B., 1968, M.A., 1969. *Politics:* Democrat. *Home:* 204 West Main St., Mechanicsburg, Pa. *Office:* Historical Times, Inc., P.O. Box 1831, Harrisburg, Pa. 17105.

CAREER: Historical Times, Inc., Harrisburg, Pa., magazines editor, 1969—. *Member:* Manuscript Society, Southern Historical Association. *Awards, honors: Breckinridge: Statesman, Soldier, Symbol* received Jules F. Landry Award from Louisiana State University Press, 1973, for the best book on Southern history, literature, and biography, and the Jefferson Davis Award from Museum of the Confederacy and the Confederate Memorial Literary Society, 1974, for the best book on Confederate history.

WRITINGS: (Author of introduction) E. Porter Thompson, *History of the Orphan Brigade,* Morningside Press, 1973; *Breckinridge: Statesman, Soldier, Symbol,* Louisiana State University Press, 1974; *The Battle of New Market,* Doubleday, 1975; *Duel Between the First Ironclads,* Doubleday, 1975. Editor of *American History Illustrated,* 1972—, and *Civil War Times,* 1972—.

WORK IN PROGRESS: A book on the Presidential election of 1860; a book on Abraham Lincoln's assassination.

SIDELIGHTS: Davis writes that his chief interest is in "Civil War era America, particularly Democratic politics of the 1850's, and the military and civil history of the Confederacy. Biography is the essence of history in my opinion, and hence I try to bring a highly personal element of the characters involved to all of my writings."

* * *

DAWN, C(larence) Ernest 1918-

PERSONAL: Born December 6, 1918, in Chattanooga, Tenn.; son of Fred Hartman (a businessman) and Hettie Lou (Gibson) Dawn; married Pansie Mozelle Dooley, July 8, 1944; children: Julia Anne (Mrs. Ronald Kuykendall), Carolyn Louise. *Education:* University of Chattanooga, A.B., 1941; Princeton University, M.A., 1947, Ph.D., 1948. *Home:* 1504 South Grove St., Urbana, Ill. 61801. *Office:* Department of History, University of Illinois, Urbana, Ill. 61801.

CAREER: University of Illinois, Urbana-Champaign, instructor, 1949-52, assistant professor, 1952-55, associate professor, 1955-60, professor of history, 1960—, director of Illinois-Tehran Research Unit in Iran, 1972-74. *Military service:* U.S. Army, 1942-46, 1951-52; became first lieutenant. *Member:* American Historical Association, Middle East Institute, Middle East Studies Association. *Awards, honors:* Social Science Research Council fellowship, 1948-49; fellowship from Joint Institute on Near East studies of Social Science Research Council and American Council of Learned Societies, 1966-67; Fulbright-Hays fellowship, 1966-67.

WRITINGS: (Contributor) Girdhari L. Tikku, editor, *Islam and Its Cultural Divergence,* University of Illinois Press, 1971; (contributor) Abdeen Jabara and Janice Terry, editors, *The Arab World: From Nationalism to Revolution,* Medina University Press, 1971; *From Ottomanism to Arabism: Essays on the Origins of Arab Nationalism,* University of Illinois Press, 1973. Contributor to scholarly journals.

WORK IN PROGRESS: A History of Pan-Arabism; A Modern History of Arab Countries.

SIDELIGHTS: Dawn has traveled and studied in Lebanon, Syria, Jordan, Egypt, and Turkey.

* * *

DEAKINS, Roger Lee 1933-

PERSONAL: Born December 4, 1933, in Decatur, Ill.; son of Byron Floyd (a real estate broker) and Lucille (Conlon) Deakins; married Alice Hanna Simpson (a writer), June 23, 1967; children: Lucy Helyn. *Education:* University of Illinois, B.A., 1956; Harvard University, M.A., 1958, Ph.D., 1965. *Home:* 100 Bleecker St., New York, N.Y. 10012. *Office:* Department of English, New York University, Washington Square, New York, N.Y. 10003.

CAREER: Beloit College, Beloit, Wis., instructor in En-

glish, 1961-65; City College of the City University of New York, New York City, instructor in English, 1965-68; New York University, New York, N.Y., associate professor of English, 1968—. *Member:* Renaissance Society of America, Modern Language Association of America. *Awards, honors:* American Council of Learned Societies fellowship, 1972-73.

WRITINGS: (Editor and translator) *Il Moro: Ellis Heywood's Dialogue in Memory of Sir Thomas More,* Harvard University Press, 1972.

WORK IN PROGRESS: Editing and translating Christoforo Landino's *Disputationes Camaldulenses.*

* * *

DEARDORFF, Robert 1912-

PERSONAL: Born December 11, 1912, in Chambersburg, Pa.; son of William and Susan (Zumbro) Deardorff. *Education:* Columbia University, B.A. (with honors), 1934. *Religion:* Protestant. *Home and office:* Via Marianna Dionigi 57, Rome, Italy.

CAREER: J. M. Mathes, Inc. (advertising firm), New York, N.Y., member of staff, 1940-53; *Travel* (magazine), Floral Park, N.Y., correspondent in Italy, 1956—. *Member:* Society of Magazine Writers, Authors Guild of Authors League of America, Society of American Travel Writers, Stampa Estera.

WRITINGS: Day Outside the City: Trips to Take Out of Paris, London, Venice, Copenhagen, Etc., Holt, 1968. Contributor to popular magazines, including *True, Redbook,* and *Catholic Digest.*

* * *

DEATON, John (Graydon) 1939-

PERSONAL: Born August 19, 1939, in Houston, Tex.; son of Charles F. (an automobile mechanic) and Frances (a beautician; maiden name, Kimberlin) Deaton; married Miriam Ann Garrett (a teacher), August 26, 1960; children: Roger, Stephen, Lara, Jennie. *Education:* Texas A & M University, student, 1957-58; University of Texas, B.A., 1960, M.D., 1963. *Home and office:* 6604 Sumac Dr., Austin, Tex. 78731.

CAREER: Memorial Medical Center, Corpus Christi, Tex., intern, 1963-64; University of Texas, Medical Branch, Galveston, resident in internal medicine, 1964-66, fellow in hematology research, 1966-67; University of Wisconsin, Madison, fellow in immunology, 1969-70; Texas Department of Mental Health and Mental Retardation, Austin, staff physician and medical director at Denton State School and Mexia State School, 1970-71; University of Texas, Austin, visiting lecturer and assistant professor of human physiology, 1972-73; free-lance writer, 1973—. Diplomate of American Board of Internal Medicine. *Military service:* U.S. Air Force, Medical Corps, 1967-69; served as captain. *Member:* Phi Beta Kappa, Alpha Omega Alpha.

WRITINGS: Markets for the Medical Author, Warren Green, 1971; *New Parts for Old: The Age of Organ Transplants,* Franklin Publishing Co., 1974. Contributor of more than thirty articles to medical journals. Contributing editor of *Consultant.*

WORK IN PROGRESS: A self-help book on how people can enjoy better health by eating right, exercising and keeping themselves fit.

SIDELIGHTS: Deaton writes: "My interest in writing

began when I was doing scientific papers; I found that I enjoyed the writing more than the research. Despite having gone all the way through training and receiving Board certification, practicing medicine wasn't what I wanted to do. In 1971 I gave up on it, my wife went back to work teaching school, and I became a house-husband. I work at home, after getting the kids off to school, and part of my day includes washing the clothes, cleaning the house and starting supper. I love writing, and feel that my niche is in translating medical topics into language the non-physician can understand. . . . 'Do you regret going to medical school?' someone asked me. 'No,' I said, 'I think everyone interested in writing should first go to medical school.'" *Avocational interests:* Jogging, listening to "Mississippi John Hurt" record albums, reading.

*   *   *

DECKER, Beatrice 1919-

PERSONAL: Born June 14, 1919, in Pittsburgh, Pa.; daughter of John Charles (a barber) and Beatrice (Levy) Schirm; married Robert Arthur Decker, April 28, 1945 (died July 21, 1961); children: Beatrice (Mrs. Richard F. Vuocolo), Mary Louise (Mrs. Albert D'Ambrosio), Roberta Ann. *Education:* Attended high school in Pittsburgh, Pa. *Religion:* Lutheran. *Residence:* Pittsburgh, Pa. *Office:* Theos Foundation, 11609 Frankstown Rd., Pittsburgh, Pa. 15235.

CAREER: Theos Foundation (organization to assist widows, widowers, and their families), Pittsburgh, Pa. and Lakeview, Ore., founder and executive director, 1962—. *Member:* International Platform Association.

WRITINGS: (With Gladys Kooiman) *After the Flowers Have Gone,* Zondervan, 1973. Contributor to religious publications.

*   *   *

DeFELICE, Louise P(aula) 1945-

PERSONAL: Born February 17, 1945, in Buffalo, N.Y.; daughter of Lewis P. and Stella (Matuszewski) Scheider; married Gary L. DeFelice (a narcotics aftercare officer), 1966; children: David John. *Education:* State University of New York at Buffalo, B.A., 1967; Niagara University, M.A., 1973. *Home:* 6836 Walmore Rd., Niagara Falls, N.Y. 14304.

CAREER: Niagara Falls School System, Niagara Falls, N.Y., English teacher, 1967-71, 1973—. Co-founder of Niagara Education Clinic, 1975.

WRITINGS: Emotional Crisis: How to Cope, How to Recover, Ashley Books, 1975.

*   *   *

De FELITTA, Frank (Paul) 1921-

PERSONAL: Born August 3, 1921, in New York, N.Y.; son of Pat and Genevieve (Sibilio) De Felitta; married Dorothy Gilbert, August 4, 1945; children: Eileen, Raymond. *Education:* Attended University of North Carolina, 1939-40, New School for Social Research, 1947-48. *Home and office:* 3008 Paulcrest Dr., Los Angeles, Calif. 90046. *Agent:* Tim Seldes, Russell & Volkening, Inc., 551 Fifth Ave., New York, N.Y. 10017.

CAREER: Columbia Broadcasting System, New York City, producer, director, writer, 1950-57; National Telefilms Associates, New York City, and Los Angeles, Calif.,

West Coast director of film programming, 1959-61; National Broadcasting Co., New York City, producer, writer, director, 1962—; Universal Studios, Los Angeles, producer, writer, director, 1968-70. *Military service:* U.S. Army Air Forces, 1941-45; served in European theater; became captain; received Distinguished Flying Cross and Air Medal. *Member:* Directors Guild of America, Writers Guild of America.

AWARDS, HONORS: Peabody Awards, 1954, for "Adventure," and 1963, for "American Revolution"; Ohio State University Award, 1957, for "Satan in Salem"; George Polk Award for Journalism, 1957, for "Algeria at Large"; Writers Guild nomination, 1958, for program "They Took a Blue Note"; Thomas Alva Edison Award, 1958, for "Conquest"; Venice Film Festival Award, 1959, for "Waves"; Emmy awards, 1962, for "Emergency Ward," and 1966, for "The Battle of the Bulge"; National Education Association School Bell Award, 1963, for "An Experiment in Excellence"; CINE (Council on International Nontheatrical Events) Gold Eagle Awards, 1964, for "An Experiment in Excellence," 1966, for "The Battle of the Bulge," 1966, for "The World of the Teenager," 1967, for "Pearl Harbor," and 1968, for "The American Image"; Robert J. Flaherty Award, 1966, for film "The World of the Teenager"; Brotherhood Award of National Conference of Christians and Jews, 1967, for film "Mississippi: A Self-Portrait"; George Washington Honor Medal of Freedoms Foundation, 1968, for film "The American Image".

WRITINGS—Novels: *Oktoberfest,* Doubleday, 1973; *Audrey Rose,* Putnam, in press.

Screenplays: "Boy on a Smokestack," 1967; "Success . . . or Something Like It," 1967; (contributor) "Anzio," 1967; "The Buffalo Soldiers," Cherokee Films, 1968; "The First of January," 1970; "The Savage Is Loose," 1971.

Television scripts include: "Adventure," 1953-55; "Music of the South," 1955; "Conquest" series, 1957; "Odyssey" series, 1958; "The Chosen Child," 1962; "Emergency Ward," 1962; "An Experiment in Excellence," 1963; "The Stately Ghosts of England," 1964; "The Battle of the Bulge," 1964; "Mississippi: A Self-Portrait," 1965; "Pearl Harbor," 1966; "The World of the Teenager," 1966; "The American Image," 1967; "Trapped," 1973.

SIDELIGHTS: De Felitta's documentaries "Pearl Harbor," "The Battle of the Bulge," and "Mississippi: A Self-Portrait" are on permanent file with the Library of Congress; "The American Image" is held by the Museum of Modern Art and Whitney Museum.

*   *   *

DE GRAZIA, Ettore 1909-
(Ted De Grazia)

PERSONAL: Born June 14, 1909, in Morenci, Ariz.; son of Domenico (a miner) and Lucia (Gagliarei) De Grazia; married seventh wife, Marion Sheret, 1948; children: twenty-three. *Education:* University of Arizona, B.A., 1944, B.F.A., 1945, M.A., 1945. *Home and office:* 6300 North Swan, Tucson, Ariz. 85705.

CAREER: Artist. Owner and director of Gallery in the Sun and De Grazia Studio Shops in Tucson, Ariz. and of Superstition Mountain Gallery in Apache Junction, Ariz.

WRITINGS—All self-illustrated: *Impressions of Papago and Yaqui Indians,* De Grazia Studios, 1950; *Mission in the Santa Catalinas: A Tale of Apache Indians, Mexicans, and a Mission in Arizona South,* De Grazia Studios, 1951;

The Flute Player: A Fantasy with Dances Inspired by Pottery of Ancient Indians Called Hohokam . . ., De Grazia Studios, 1952; *Padre Nuestro: A Strange Story of Now and Long Ago*, De Grazia Studios, 1953; *The Blue Lady: A Desert Fantasy of Papago Land*, De Grazia Studios, 1957; *Padre Kino: A Portfolio Depicting Memorable Events in the Life and Times of the Heroic and Immortal Priest-Colonizer* (portfolio of twenty prints), Arizona South, 1962; *The Way of the Cross* (fifteen painting reproductions), De Grazia Associates, 1964; *ah ha Toro*, Northland Press, 1967; *The Rose and the Robe: The Travels of Fray Junipero Serra in California*, Best-West Publications, 1968; *De Grazia Paints the Yaqui Easter: Forty Days of Lent in Forty Paintings*, University of Arizona Press, 1968; (with William Neil Smith) *The Seri Indians: A Primitive People of Tibouron Island in the Gulf of California*, Northland Press, 1970; *De Grazia Paints the Signs of the Zodiac* (limited proof edition), Gallery in the Sun, 1971; *De Grazia and His Mountain, The Superstition*, Gallery in the Sun, 1972; *De Grazia Paints Cabeza De Vaca*, Gallery in the Sun, 1973; *De Grazia Moods*, Gallery in the Sun, 1974; *De Grazia Paints the Papago Indian Legends*, Gallery in the Sun, 1975. Contributor of articles to *Arizona Highways*, *Desert*, and *Mountain States Architecture*.

Illustrator: Patricia Benton, *The Young Corn Rises*, Vantage Press, 1953; Patricia Paylore, *Kino, A Commemoration*, Arizona Pioneers' Historical Society, 1961; Alvin Gordon, *Inherit the Earth: Stories from Mexican Ranch Life*, University of Arizona Press, 1963; Gordon, *Brooms of Mexico*, Best-West Publications, 1965; LaVerne Clark, *They Sang for Horses: The Impact of the Horse on Navajo and Apache Folklore*, University of Arizona, 1966; Gordon, *Journeys with Saint Francis of Assisi*, Best-West Publications, 1966; Ray Brandes, editor, *Troopers West: Military and Indian Affairs in the American Frontier*, Frontier Heritage Press, 1970; Mildred Feague, *The Little Indian and the Angel*, Children's Press, 1970; Gordon, *Of Vines and Missions*, Northland Press, 1971.

BIOGRAPHICAL/CRITICAL SOURCES: New Mexico Magazine, January, 1965; *San Diego Magazine*, December, 1968; William Reed, *De Grazia: The Irreverent Angel*, Frontier Heritage Press, 1971.

*   *   *

De JONG, Gerald Francis 1921-

PERSONAL: Surname is pronounced De-young; born November 16, 1921, in Alton, Iowa; son of Otto (a businessman) and Hattie (Douma) De Jong; married Jeannette Masselink, June 5, 1950; children: Owen, Gerald II, Drew, Nanette, Chester, Karl. *Education:* Morningside College, B.A., 1950; graduate study at University of Utrecht, 1953-54; University of Wisconsin, Ph.D., 1956. *Politics:* Independent. *Religion:* Protestant. *Home:* 21 South Pine, Vermillion, S.D. 57069. *Office:* Department of History, University of South Dakota, Vermillion, S.D. 57069.

CAREER: North Dakota State University, Fargo, assistant professor of history, 1956-59; Northwestern College, Orange City, Iowa, academic dean, 1959-65; Midwestern College, Denison, Iowa, professor of history and chairman of department, 1965-69; University of South Dakota, Vermillion, professor of modern European history, 1969—. *Military service:* U.S. Navy, 1942-46. *Member:* American Society of Church History, New York Historical Society, New Jersey Historical Society, Long Island Historical Society, Dutch Immigrant Society. *Awards, honors:* Fulbright scholar to University of Utrecht, 1953-54.

WRITINGS: The Dutch in America, 1609-1974, Twayne, 1975. Contributor to historical journals.

WORK IN PROGRESS: The Dutch Reformed Church in the American Colonies, completion expected in 1977; *The Amoy Mission in China during the Nineteenth Century*, 1978.

*   *   *

de la PORTILLA, Marta (Rosa) 1927-

PERSONAL: Born June 24, 1927, in Havana, Cuba; naturalized U.S. citizen, 1974; daughter of Andres (a businessman) and Angelina (Perez) de la Portilla. *Education:* University of St. Thomas of Villanova, Ph.D. (literature), 1950; University of Havana, Ph.D. (literature), 1950; University of Madrid, Ph.D. (Romanic philology), 1953; also studied at Yale University and Georgetown University. *Religion:* Roman Catholic. *Home:* 345 Main St., Apt. 2N, White Plains, N.Y. 10601. *Office:* Department of Spanish, Manhattanville College, Purchase, N.Y. 10577.

CAREER: University of St. Thomas of Villanova, Havana, Cuba, lecturer in Spanish for foreigners and in history of art, 1951-61, registrar and dean of admissions, 1954-61; Merrimack College, North Andover, Mass., lecturer in Spanish, 1961-62; Salve Regina College, Newport, R.I., assistant professor of Spanish and head of department, 1964-66; Fordham University, Bronx, N.Y., assistant professor of Spanish, 1963-65; Manhattanville College, Purchase, N.Y., assistant professor, 1965-70, associate professor, 1970-75, professor of Spanish, 1975—, head of department, 1974—. Professional adviser to ARHE, Inc., 1971-75.

MEMBER: Asociacion Internacional de Hispanistas, Modern Language Association of America, American Association of Teachers of Spanish and Portuguese, Spanish Institute of America. *Awards, honors:* Fellowship from Institute of Hispanic Culture, 1953-54, to study in Madrid.

WRITINGS: (Editor with others) *Books for Children on Latin America*, UNICEF, 1969; (editor with Thomas Colchie) *Textbooks in Spanish and Portuguese, 1939-1970*, Modern Language Association of America, 1972; (translator from English to Spanish) John J. Kelly, *La Cuba del Padre Spirale*, Ediciones Fe Catolica (Madrid), 1971; (translator from English to Spanish) Robert Hupka, *La Pieta*, Crown, 1975. Author of quotations for Spanish version of UNICEF calendars, 1970-74. Editor of *Noverim* (faculty magazine at University of St. Thomas of Villanova), 1951-61.

WORK IN PROGRESS: Espanol para el Hispanohablante de los Estados Unidos (title means "Spanish for the Spanish speaking in the United States"), for Regents Publishing; research on bilingual students in the United States.

*   *   *

DELIGIORGIS, Stavros (George) 1933-

PERSONAL: Born September 14, 1933, in Romania; son of Alexander and Maria (Calligas) Deligiorgis; married Ioanna S. Palasantzas, December 26, 1960; children: Maria, Katerina. *Education:* Yale University, M.A., 1958; National University of Athens, B.A., 1960; University of California, Berkeley, Ph.D., 1966. *Office:* Department of Comparative Literature, University of Iowa, Iowa City, Iowa 52242.

CAREER: University of Iowa, Iowa City, assistant professor, 1965-68, associate professor, 1968-72, professor of English and comparative literature, 1972—, director of Translation Workshop, 1970-74. Visiting associate professor at University of Illinois, 1969-70; visiting professor at University of Massachusetts, autumn, 1974. Associate of Center for Neohellenic Studies (Austin, Tex.), 1967; fellow of Center for Advanced Studies at University of Illinois, 1968-70. *Member:* Modern Language Association of America, Comparative Literature Association, Mediaeval Academy of America, American Association of University Professors.

WRITINGS: (Translator from English into modern Greek) René Wellek and Austin Warren, *Theoria tes Logotechnias* (title means "Theory of Literature"), Diphros Publishing, 1965; *Narrative Intellection in the Decameron,* Iowa University Press, 1975. Contributor of articles and reviews to comparative literature and foreign studies journals. Guest editor and translator for *Micromegas,* 1971.

SIDELIGHTS: A series of 849 drawings by Deligiorgis has been acquired by the special collection department of the library at University of Iowa.

*   *   *

DE MANIO, Jack   1914-

PERSONAL: Born January 26, 1914, in London, England; son of Jean Batiste and Florence Olga (Sareska) de Manio; married Juliet Gravaeret Kaufmann, 1935 (divorced, 1946); married Loveday Elizabeth Abbott Matthews, 1946; children: (first marriage) one son. *Education:* Attended Aldenham School, 1928-31. *Home:* 105 Cheyne Walk, London S.W.10, England.

CAREER: Broadcaster for the British Broadcasting Corp., Overseas Service, 1946-50, Home Service, 1950-64; freelance broadcaster, 1964—. Host of B.B.C. "Today" program, 1958-71. Director of Neilson McCarthy Ltd. *Military service:* British Army, Royal Sussex Regiment, 1939-46; served with British Expeditionary Force, 1939-40, Middle East Forces, 1940-44, Forces Broadcasting in the Middle East, 1944-46; received Military Cross, 1940. *Member:* Brooks's Club, Marylebone Cricket Club. *Awards, honors:* Radio Personality of the Year award from Variety Club of Great Britain, 1964; Radio Personality of the Year award from British Radio Industries Club, 1971.

WRITINGS: To Auntie with Love (broadcasting anecdotes), Hutchinson, 1967; *Life Begins Too Early: A Sort of Autobiography,* Hutchinson, 1970.

SIDELIGHTS: According to Wilfred De'Ath, "the de Manio persona is not without interest: a curious amalgam of Italian peasant obstinacy which made him cling to his own name ('Just after I joined it was decided that the name de Manio wouldn't do, as it didn't sound English and people might think I was some sort of fake broadcasting from Turin') and sturdy English philistinism of the 'lovable fascist' variety." Arthur Marshall calls de Manio "a genius at the throw-away line, and geniality itself." *Avocational interests:* Fishing.

*   *   *

DE MARCO, Donald   1937-

PERSONAL: Born April 20, 1937, in Fall River, Mass.; married Mary Arendt; children: Jocelyn, Donald, Jr., Paul, Peter. *Education:* Stonehill College, B.S. (general science), 1959, A.B. (philosophy), 1961; graduate study at Bridgewater State Teachers College and at Gregorian University, 1961-62; St. John's University, Jamaica, N.Y., M.A., 1965,

Ph.D. (philosophy), 1969. *Religion:* Roman Catholic. *Home:* 101 Silverspring Cr., Kitchener, Ontario, Canada. *Office:* St. Jerome's College, University of Waterloo, Waterloo, Ontario N2L 3G3, Canada.

CAREER: Stonehill College, North Easton, Mass., lecturer in music aesthetics, 1960-61; junior high school teacher of mathematics in Fall River, Mass., 1962; high school teacher of mathematics and science in Dartmouth, Mass., 1962-63; teacher of mathematics and sciences in private school in Fairhaven, Mass., 1963-64; St. John's University, Jamaica, N.Y., 1965-70, began as instructor, became assistant professor of philosophy; University of Waterloo, St. Jerome's College, Waterloo, Ontario, assistant professor, 1970-75, associate professor of philosophy, 1975—. Piano teacher in Fall River, 1962-64; teacher of medical ethics, St. Joseph's School of Nursing, Guelph, Ontario, 1972, St. Mary's School of Nursing, Kitchener, Ontario, 1972-75. Has directed choirs and given piano recitals. President of board of directors of Birthright of Kitchener-Waterloo, 1971—; member of board of Federated Appeal of Kitchener-Waterloo, 1975—. *Member:* Scientists for Life, Right to Life.

WRITINGS: The Peace Movement without Peer (booklet), Carmelite Nuns of Fort Worth, Tex., 1973; *Abortion in Perspective: The Rose Palace or the Fiery Dragon?,* Hiltz, 1974; (contributor) Mykola Kolankiwsky, editor, *The Passion of Christ,* Niagara Falls Art Gallery and Museum, 1974; (contributor) E. J. Kremer and E. A. Synon, editors, *Death Before Life,* Griffin House, 1974. Author of column "From the Academy" in *Toronto Catholic Register,* 1972. Contributor of more than 150 articles and reviews to more than forty professional journals, magazines, and newspapers. Associate editor of *Child and Family Quarterly.*

*   *   *

DEMARET, Pierre   1943-

PERSONAL: Born October 24, 1943, in Algeria; son of Pierre and Suzette (Gornes) Demaret. *Politics:* Liberal. *Religion:* None. *Home:* 61 Avenue Philippe Auguste, Paris 11, France 75011.

CAREER: Journalist in Paris, 1966-74; free-lance writer, 1974—.

WRITINGS: Guide Solar des Pieds-Noirs, Solar, 1972; (with Jean Mabire) *La Brigade Frankreich,* Fayard, 1973; (with Christian Plume) *Objetif de Gaulle,* Laffont, 1973, translation by Richard Barry published as *Target de Gaulle: The Thirty-One Attempts to Assassinate the General,* Secker & Warburg, 1974, published as *Target de Gaulle: The True Story of the 31 Attempts on the Life of the French President,* Dial, 1975; (compiler) Pierre Rostaing, *Le Prix d'un Serment, 1941-1945: Des Plaines de Russie a l'enfer de Berlin,* Table Ronde, 1975. Also author of television scripts, "Les Dossiers noirs" and "Le Prince Borghese et les hommes Terpilles."

WORK IN PROGRESS: A la recherche de mon pere l'inspecteur Bonny, Edgar Hoover et le FBI, and *Le Prince Borghese,* all for Laffont; *Usiage: Vichy et la Resistance,* for Table Ronde.

*   *   *

DEMING, Louise Macpherson   1916-1976

July 8, 1916—January 26, 1976; American civic worker, educator, editor, and writer on history. Obituaries: *Washington Post,* January 29, 1976.

De MOTT, Donald W(arren) 1928-

PERSONAL: Born November 15, 1928, in Hackensack, N.J.; son of Albert R. (a clergyman) and Alice (Rimback) De Mott; married Shirley Bixby, October 24, 1950; children: Rodney, Laurie, Wendy, Dianne, Sandra. Education: University of Rochester, B.A., 1950, Ph.D., 1957. Politics: "Liberal Party." Religion: Protestant. Home: 4408 East Groveland Rd., Geneseo, N.Y. 14454. Office: Department of Psychology, State University of New York College at Geneseo, Geneseo, N.Y. 14454.

CAREER: University of Rochester, Rochester, N.Y., research associate in psychology, 1958-65, senior research associate, 1965-68; State University of New York College at Geneseo, assistant professor, 1968-70, associate professor of psychology, 1970—. Part-time mentor at Empire State College, 1973—. Military service: U.S. Navy, 1950-53; became lieutenant junior grade. Member: American Association for the Advancement of Science, Sigma Xi. Awards, honors: U.S. Public Health Service research fellowship in psychology, University of Rochester, 1956-58; National Institute of Mental Health grant, 1958—.

WRITINGS: Toposcopic Studies of Learning, C. C Thomas, 1970. Contributor to psychology journals.

WORK IN PROGRESS: Two Sons of Abraham, a religious book.

*   *   *

DEMPSEY, Richard A(llen) 1932-

PERSONAL: Born April 29, 1932, in Detroit, Mich.; son of O. J. and N. J. (Willis) Dempsey; married Marion M. Rankine (a teacher), August 30, 1952; children: Stuart Richard. Education: Eastern Michigan University, B.S., 1954, M.A., 1957; Michigan State University, Ph.D., 1963. Home: 75 Lynwood Rd., Storrs, Conn. 06268. Office: University of Connecticut, Storrs, Conn. 06268.

CAREER: Teacher of English in Michigan schools, 1954-57; principal in Michigan and Ohio schools, 1957-67; assistant superintendent of schools in Darien, Conn., 1967-70; University of Connecticut, professor of educational administration, 1970—. Member: National Association of Secondary School Principals, Association for Supervision and Curriculum Development, American Association of School Administrators, National Association of Elementary School Principals.

WRITINGS: Collective Bargaining in the Public Schools, A. C. Croft, 1971; Differentiated Staffing in the Public Schools, A. C. Croft, 1972; Differentiated Staffing, Prentice-Hall, 1972; School: Pass At Your Own Risk, Prentice-Hall, 1974.

WORK IN PROGRESS: A book on leadership in today's schools.

*   *   *

DEMURA, Fumio 1940-

PERSONAL: Born September 15, 1940, in Yokohama, Japan; son of Shitoshi and Masu (Kawashima) Demura. Education: Attended Nihon University. Home: 901 East 19th St., Santa Ana, Calif. 92706. Office: 1429 North Bristol St., Santa Ana, Calif. 92706.

CAREER: Karate instructor. Awards, honors: Named All Japan Karate Champion, 1961 and 1962; elected to Black Belt Hall of Fame, 1969; Golden Fist award, 1974.

WRITINGS: Shito-Ryu Karate, O'Hara Publications, 1971; Nunchaku: Karate Weapon, O'Hara Publications, 1971; Sai: Karate Weapon, O'Hara Publications, 1974.

WORK IN PROGRESS: Bo: Karate Weapon; Advanced Nunchaku Weapon.

*   *   *

DENHAM, H(enry) M(angles) 1897-

PERSONAL: Born September 9, 1897; son of Henry Mangles and Helen Clare (Lowndes) Denham; married Estelle Margaret Sibbald Currie, 1924; children: one son, two daughters. Education: Attended Royal Naval College, Osborne and Dartmouth, England, and Magdalene College, Cambridge. Home: 8 Carlyle Sq., London S.W.3, England.

CAREER: Royal Navy, retired as captain, 1947; served in the Dardanelles Campaign and in the occupation of the Rhine River in Her Majesty's Rhine Flotilla during World War I; sailed on a round the world cruise with the Prince of Wales in Her Majesty's Ship Renown, 1921; served on the Mediterranean Sea; at Royal Naval Staff College, Greenwich, England, 1936; served as ship commander, 1936-39; naval attache in Denmark, 1940, and in Sweden, 1940-47. Member: Royal Automobile Club, Royal Ocean Racing Club, Royal Cruising Club, Royal Yacht Squadron (Cowes). Awards, honors: Companion of St. Michael and St. George.

WRITINGS—All published by J. Murray, except as indicated: The Aegean: A Sea-guide to Its Coasts and Islands, 1963, 2nd edition, 1970, Scribner, 1971; The Eastern Mediterranean: A Sea-guide to Its Coast and Islands, 1964; The Adriatic: A Sea-guide to Its Coasts and Islands, 1967; The Tyrrhenian Sea: A Sea-guide to Its Coasts and Islands, 1969; Ionian Islands to Rhodes: A Sea-guide, 1972; Southern Turkey, the Levant, and Cyprus: A Sea-guide to the Coasts and Islands, 1973.

WORK IN PROGRESS: Revision of books.

AVOCATIONAL INTERESTS: Yachting.

*   *   *

DENMAN, D(onald) R(obert) 1911-

PERSONAL: Born April 7, 1911, in London, England; son of Robert Martyn and Letitia Kate Denman; married Jessica Hope, 1941; children: two sons. Education: University of London, B.Sc., 1938, M.Sc., 1940, Ph.D., 1945. Home: Pembroke College, Cambridge University, 12 Chaucer Rd., Cambridge, England. Office: Department of Land Economy, Cambridge University, 19 Silver St., Cambridge CB3 9EP, England.

CAREER: Cambridge University, Cambridge, England, university lecturer, 1948-68, professor of land economy, 1968—, head of department, 1962—. Member of the Land Management Committee, Agricultural Improvement Council, 1953-60; fellow of Pembroke College, Cambridge University, 1962—; advisor on development of land economy to the University of Science and Technology, Ghana, and the University of Nigeria, 1963—; member of governing board, Commonwealth Human Ecology Council, 1970—; member of National Commission of UNESCO, 1972—; advisor to the Iranian Government; governor of Canford School. Wartime service: Cumberland War Agricultural Executive Committee, deputy executive officer, 1939-46. Member: Istituto di Diritto Agrario Internazionale e Comparato (Florence; standing committee member, 1960—), Ghana Institution of Surveyors (honorary fellow), Royal Swedish Academy of Forestry and Agriculture (fellow),

Royal Institution of Chartered Surveyors (fellow), Council for National Academic Awards, Conservation Society (vice-president, 1971—), Church Assembly, Carlton Club, Farmer's Club. *Awards, honors:* M.A., Cambridge University, 1948; gold medal, Royal Institution of Chartered Surveyors, 1972; holder of Ivory Horn (Ofo) of Ozo Order of Nobility of Iboland (Nigeria).

WRITINGS: Tenant-Right Valuation in History and Modern Practice, Heffer, 1942; *Tenant-Right Valuation and Current Legislation: Being a Supplement to Tenant-Right Valuation in History and Modern Practice Dealing with the Relevant Provisions of the Agricultural Act, 1947, and the Agricultural Holdings Act, 1948,* Heffer, 1948; *First Footprints* (religious tales), S.P.C.K., 1949.

Estate Capital: The Contribution of Landownership to Agricultural Finance, foreword by the Duke of Northumberland, Verry, 1957; (with O.H.M. Sawyer and J.F.Q. Switzer) *Bibliography of Rural Land Economy and Landownership, 1900-1957: A Full List of Works Relating to the British Isles and Selected Works from the United States and Western Europe,* Department of Estate Management, Cambridge University, 1958; *Origins of Ownership: A Brief History of Land Ownership and Tenure in England from Earliest Times to the Modern Era,* Allen & Unwin, 1958; (with V. F. Stewart) *Farm Rents: A Comparison of Current and Past Farm Rents in England and Wales,* Allen & Unwin, 1959; *Land Ownership and Resources: A Course of Lectures Given at Cambridge in June, 1958,* Bury St. Edmund's Borough Council, c. 1959.

Land in the Market: A Fresh Look at Property, Land, and Prices, Institute of Economic Affairs (London), 1964; (with R. A. Roberts and H.J.F. Smith) *Commons and Village Greens: A Study in Land Use, Conservation, and Management Based on a National Survey of Commons in England and Wales, 1961-66,* Leonard Hill, 1967; (contributor) Norman Macrae, *Homes for the People,* Economic Research Council, 1967; (with Sylvio Prodano) *Land Use: An Introduction to Proprietary Land Use Analysis,* Verry, 1972; *The King's Vista: A Land Reform Which Has Changed the Face of Persia,* Geographical Publications, 1973; *Prospects of Cooperative Planning,* Geographical Publications, 1973; (editor) *Government and the Land,* Volume XIII: *Land Nationalization: A Way Out?,* Institute of Economic Affairs, 1974; *Land Economy: An Education and a Career,* Geographical Publications, 1975.

Author of monographs and research papers. Contributor to conference proceedings and to journals and newspapers in Britain and abroad.

AVOCATIONAL INTERESTS: Travel.

*   *   *

DERENBERG, Walter J(ulius) 1903-1975

December 8, 1903—September 9, 1975; German-born American attorney, expert on trademark and copyright law, author of textbook and articles in his field. Obituaries: *New York Times,* September 10, 1975; *AB Bookman's Weekly,* December 8, 1975.

*   *   *

DESAN, Wilfrid 1908-

PERSONAL: Surname is pronounced De-*sawn;* born March 29, 1908, in Bruges, Belgium; married Elizabeth H. Backus (a reading specialist and teacher), October 23, 1954; children: Paul, Suzanne, Christine. *Education:* Harvard

University, Ph.D., 1951. *Residence:* Washington, D.C. *Office:* Department of Philosophy, Georgetown University, Washington, D.C. 20007.

CAREER: Kenyon College, Gambier, Ohio, assistant professor, 1952-54, associate professor of philosophy, 1954-57; Georgetown University, Washington, D.C., professor of philosophy, 1957—. Visiting professor at Harvard University, 1955-56. *Member:* American Philosophical Association, American Catholic Philosophical Association, Phenomenological Association, Phi Beta Kappa.

WRITINGS: The Tragic Finale: A Study of the Philosophy of Jean-Paul Sartre, Harvard University Press, 1954; *The Planetary Man,* Part I: *A Prelude to a United World,* Georgetown University Press, 1961, reissued as Part I: *A Noetic Prelude to a United World,* Macmillan, 1972, Part II: *An Ethical Prelude to a United World,* Macmillan, 1972; *The Marxism of Jean-Paul Sartre,* Doubleday, 1965.

WORK IN PROGRESS: The Planetary Man, Part III.

SIDELIGHTS: Desan writes: "I have written abundantly on Jean-Paul Sartre . . . because of similarity of background and . . . because of real interest in his work. However, although an admirer and a commentator, I never became a disciple. *The Planetary Man* is . . . to an extent an answer to what I consider to be too subjective and too individualist in Sartre's philosophy." *Avocational interests:* Photography (movie camera man during World War Two).

*   *   *

DESCHENAUX, Jacques 1945-

PERSONAL: Born December 9, 1945, in Fribourg, Switzerland; son of Charles (a manager) and Claire (Deschenaux) Deschenaux; married wife, Claude Michele, April 24, 1976. *Education:* College of St. Maurice, Baccalaureat classique, 1966; University of Fribourg, licencie en droit, 1970. *Religion:* Roman Catholic. *Home:* 126 Route de St. Julien, 1228 Plan-les-Ouates, Geneva, Switzerland. *Office:* Television Suisse Romande, 20 quai E. Ansermet, 1211 Geneva 8, Switzerland.

CAREER: Press manager of Jo Siffert, 1964-71; Television Suisse Romande (Swiss television), Geneva, Switzerland, sports writer, 1973—. Press manager of Grand Prix Swiss Automobile Club, 1975—. *Military service:* Swiss Army, 1968—; now first lieutenant. *Member:* International Racing Press Association, Swiss Press Association, Swiss Association of Sports Journalists, Mylords Club.

WRITINGS: Jo Siffert, William Kimber, 1972. Sports columnist for *La Tribune-Le Matin,* 1969-76.

*   *   *

de SCHWEINITZ, Karl 1887-1975

PERSONAL: Born November 26, 1887, in Northfield, Minn.; son of Paul and Mary Catherine (Daniel) de Schweinitz; married Jessie Logan Dixon, October 4, 1911; married Elizabeth McCord, August 29, 1937; children: (first marriage) Mary (Mrs. Robert W. Wood), Karl, Jr. *Education:* Moravian College, A.B., 1906; University of Pennsylvania, A.B., 1907. *Politics:* Democrat. *Religion:* Moravian. *Residence:* Hightstown, N.J.

CAREER: Newspaper reporter, and later publicity worker, 1907-11; secretary of Pennsylvania Tuberculosis Society, 1911-13; member of executive staff of Charity Organization Society of New York, 1913-18; Family Society of Philadelphia, Philadelphia, Pa., general secretary, 1918-30; Community Council of Philadelphia, Philadelphia, executive secretary, 1930-36; University of Pennsylvania, School of Social Work, Philadelphia, director, 1933-36; executive director of Pennsylvania State Emergency Relief Board, 1936-37; secretary of Pennsylvania State Department of Public Assistance, 1937; University of Pennsylvania, School of Social Work, director, 1938-42; training consultant, Social Security Administration, 1942-44; American Council on Education, Washington, D.C., director of Commission on Education and Social Security, 1944-50; University of California, School of Social Welfare, Los Angeles, visiting professor, 1950, professor of social welfare, 1951-58; author. Chief of social security mission to Egyptian Ministry of Social Affairs, 1951. Secretary of Philadelphia Commission for Unemployment Relief, 1939-42. United Nations consultant, 1952; consultant on social affairs to Middle Eastern and Latin American governments. *Awards, honors:* L.H.D., Moravian College, 1932; Florina Lasker Award in Social Welfare, 1962, for *Interviewing in Social Security.*

WRITINGS: *This Side [of] the Trenches,* with the American Red Cross, D. C. McMurtrie, 1917; *The Art of Helping People Out of Trouble,* Houghton, 1924; *Growing Up: The Story of How We Become Alive, Are Born, and Grow Up,* Macmillan, 1928, 4th edition, 1965 (1st edition published in England as *How a Baby Is Born: What Every Child Should Know,* G. Routledge & Sons, 1932); *England's Road to Social Security: From the Statute of Laborers in 1349 to the Beveridge Report of 1942,* University of Pennsylvania Press, 1943, reprinted, A. S. Barnes, 1961; *People and Process in Social Security,* American Council on Education, 1948; *Social Security for Egypt,* U.S. Government Printing Office, 1952; (with Kenneth W. Thompson and Paul K. Hatt) *Man and Modern Society: Conflict and Choice in the Industrial Era,* Holt, 1953; (with wife, Elizabeth de Schweinitz) *Interviewing in Social Security,* Bureau of Old-Age and Survivors Insurance (Washington, D.C.), 1961, adaptation published as *Interviewing in the Social Services,* National Council of Social Service (London), 1962.

SIDELIGHTS: *Growing Up* was considered a trail blazer in the field of sex education, and was translated into eight languages.

OBITUARIES: *New York Times,* April 21, 1975; *Washington Post,* April 23, 1975.*

(Died April 20, 1975, in Hightstown, N.J.)

*   *   *

DeSHAZO, Edith K(ind)   1920-

PERSONAL: Born February 2, 1920, in Philadelphia, Pa.; daughter of Paul Adolf (an executive) and Edith (an artist; maiden name, Clement) Kind; married Rondal E. DeShazo (an executive), November 17, 1945 (deceased); children: Paula (Mrs. Seth McQuillan), Kathleen (Mrs. John Carnes), John Allen, Patrick George. *Education:* Katherine Gibbs School, certificate, 1939; attended University of Pennsylvania, 1941. *Politics:* "Mugwump." *Religion:* Quaker. *Home and office address:* Box 40, Woodstown, N.J. 08098.

CAREER: Owens Illinois Glass Co., Philadelphia, Pa., secretary, 1939-41; Kind & Knox Gelatin Co., Camden, N.J., secretary and coordinator for government regulatory offices, 1941-46; Ron DeShazo Co., Woodstown, N.J., vice-president, 1953-72, president, 1972—; artist; art critic; free-lance writer. Consultant to New Jersey State Museum,

Delaware Art Museum, and Munson-Williams Proctor Institute, 1968—. *Member:* National Audubon Society, Sierra Club, Artists Equity, New Jersey Audubon Society.

WRITINGS: *Everett Shinn: A Figure in His Time,* C. N. Potter, 1974. Author of column "Sensitive Eye" in *Courier Post,* Camden, N.J., 1964—, and general column in *Today's Sunbeam,* Salem, N.J., 1972—; New Jersey and Delaware art critic, *Philadelphia Inquirer,* 1975—.

WORK IN PROGRESS: Research on Salem County history for a book.

AVOCATIONAL INTERESTS: Painting with watercolors, foreign and domestic travel.

*   *   *

DESMOND, Adrian J(ohn)   1947-

PERSONAL: Born October 6, 1947, in Guildford, Surrey, England; son of William John and Barbara (Dew) Desmond. *Education:* London University, B.Sc. from Chelsea College of Science and Technology, 1969, M.Sc. (history and philosophy of science), 1971, M.Sc. (vertebrate palaeontology) from University College, 1973; Harvard University, further study, 1973—. *Home address:* c/o 48 Collingwood Cres., Boxgrove Park, Guildford, Surrey GU1 2NU, England. *Agent:* Nat Sobel Associates, Inc., 747 Third Ave., New York, N.Y. 10017.

CAREER: Writer, science historian, and paleontologist; occasional broadcaster and journalist. *Member:* British Society for the History of Science, Society of Vertebrate Paleontology.

WRITINGS: *The Hot-Blooded Dinosaurs: A Revolution in Palaeontology,* Dial, 1976. Contributor to scientific journals and to newspapers.

WORK IN PROGRESS: A book on the political, philosophical, and theological motivations and implications in the fossil man controversy, concentrating on the Darwinian era, but continuing the narrative to the present day, publication by Blond & Briggs expected in 1977; a documentary film script on the history of paleontology, for British Broadcasting Corp.

SIDELIGHTS: Desmond writes: "*The Hot-Blooded Dinosaurs* was born out of a desire to show that ideas as much as animals fossilize. The archaic dinosaur image bedevilled paleontology for more than a century. By presenting a radical alternative the onus shifts onto supporters to substantiate the Victorian myth, or bury it.

"History and the ideas that are child to every age bear an intrinsic fascination for me. I hope to present an account of nineteenth century man's begrudging acceptance of his own evolution set against a backdrop of contemporary beliefs—often seemingly remote in nature. Anarchism, Christianity, laissez-faire economics and the clockwork Universe may seem strange bedfellows. Yet this intangible matrix of nineteenth-century thought provides a crucial background for understanding the battle over human evolution. Such apparently disparate disciplines conspired to allow man a history. We became animal."

BIOGRAPHICAL/CRITICAL SOURCES: *Financial Times,* December 11, 1975; *Observer Review,* December 28, 1975.

*   *   *

DESSEL, Norman F(rank)   1932-

PERSONAL: Born July 9, 1932, in Ida Grove, Iowa; son

of Joseph A. and Lelah I. (Bright) Dessel; married Mary-dale Merrill, September 3, 1955; children: Diana E., Dirk N., Jennifer L. *Education:* University of Iowa, A.B., 1957, M.A., 1958, Ph.D., 1961. *Home:* 6443 Lance Ct., San Diego, Calif. 92120. *Office:* Department of Physical Sciences, San Diego State University, San Diego, Calif. 92182.

CAREER: San Diego State University, San Diego, Calif., assistant professor, 1961-64, associate professor, 1964-68, professor of physical sciences, 1968—, head of department, 1968-73. Columbia University/U.S. AID professor at Patna University, 1965. Senior partner, Science Writers, 1967—; vice-president, Consolidated Bioengineering Systems, Inc., San Diego, 1972—. Consultant to U.S. Navy Electronics Laboratory, San Diego, 1962-69; consultant with Ocean Marketing Consultants, San Diego, 1974—. Member of board of directors, San Diego County Council of Boy Scouts of America. *Military service:* U.S. Air Force, pilot, 1953-55; became captain. *Member:* American Association of University Professors, National Science Teachers Association, American Association for the Advancement of Science, American Physical Society, Association for the Education of Teachers in Science, American Optical Society, New York Academy of Sciences, Delta Tau Delta, Sigma Pi Sigma, Phi Mu Alpha, Phi Delta Kappa.

WRITINGS: (With R. B. Nehrich and Voran) *Atomic Light: Lasers,* Sterling, 1968; (with Nehrich and Voran) *Science and Human Destiny,* McGraw, 1973. Contributor to journals in his field.

WORK IN PROGRESS: Research in arctic optical environment; *Joules and Stability of the United States;* a textbook, *Analysis of Major World Systems.*

*   *   *

DETRO, Gene   1935-

PERSONAL: Born November 26, 1935, in Oakland, Calif. *Education:* San Francisco State College (now University), B.A., 1958. *Politics:* None. *Religion:* "Has stopped looking for outward forms from other sources. Takes what comes." *Office:* Northwest Living Department, *Oregon Journal,* Portland, Ore. 97201.

CAREER: United Press International, San Francisco, Calif., began as copyboy, became staff writer, 1954-56; Seaside *News-Sentinel,* Seaside, Calif., editor, 1957-59; Kofman Newspapers, Alameda County, Calif., section editor and writer, 1960-67; Synanon Foundation, Mitchell, Calif., member of research staff and editor of monthly magazine, 1968-70; Desiderata School, Sacramento, Calif., teacher of writing and magazine production, 1971; *Oregon Journal,* Portland, Ore., poetry critic, 1971—; Portland State University, Portland, teacher of poetry workshops, 1975—. Founding director of Portland Poetry Festival, 1973-74; member of board of directors of Portland Poetry Center; consultant to Oregon Arts Commission.

WRITINGS: Extensions (poems), Moon Graphics, 1972; *The Honey Dwarf* (novel), Dustbooks, 1974. Critic for *Small Press Review.*

WORK IN PROGRESS: A Red Hood's for Riding, a novel based on the fairy tale "Red Riding Hood."

BIOGRAPHICAL/CRITICAL SOURCES: Northwest Review, autumn, 1975.

*   *   *

de VILLIERS, Gerard   1929-

PERSONAL: Born December 8, 1929, in Paris, France;

son of Jacques B. de Villiers and Vanentine DuPin (a writer); married Olga Vecchione, August 16, 1956 (divorced, 1961); married Annick Contamine (a screen writer), March 5, 1965; children: (first marriage) Michel; (second marriage) Marion. *Education:* Ecole des Sciences Politiques, degree of political sciences, 1955. *Religion:* Catholic. *Home:* 44 avenue Foch, Paris, France 75016. *Agent:* Georges Borchardt, 145 East 52nd St., New York, N.Y. 10022. *Office:* S.A.S. Productions, rue Servandoni, Paris, France 75006.

CAREER: France-Dimanche (magazine), Paris, France, reporter, 1957-72; writer. *Military service:* French Army Reserve, active duty, 1953-54; became lieutenant. *Member:* French Police Shooting Association, Polo Club of Bagatelle (Paris).

WRITINGS: Le Visage (title means "The Face"), Plon (Paris), 1962; *La Mort aux chats* (title means "Death to the Cats"), Plon, 1969; *Papillon epingle* (title means "Papillion Pinned Up"), Presses de la Cite (Paris), 1970; *Les Bonnes Adresses de S.A.S.: A travers le monde* (title means "The World Guide of S.A.S."), Julliard (Paris), 1971; *La Brigade Mondaine: Dossiers secrets reveles par Maurice Vincent* (title means "Vice Squad: The Secret Files"), Presses de la Cite, 1972, published as *Dossiers roses de la Brigade Mondaine: Reveles par Maurice Vincent* (title means "Vice Squad: The Gay Files"), 1973; *Les Soucis de Si-Sou* (title means "Si-Sou in Trouble"), Presses de la Cite, 1972; *L'Irrisistible Ascension de Mohammad Reza, Shah D'Iran,* Plon, 1975, translation published as *The Rise of Mohammad Reza, Shah of Iran,* Atlantic Monthly Press, 1976.

"Malko" series; original French editions published by Plon, with subsequent translations published as indicated: *S.A.S.: contre C.I.A.,* 1965 (translation by Adrian Shire published in England as *S.A.S. Versus the C.I.A.,* New English Library, 1969), new translation published under same title, Pinnacle Books, 1974; *S.A.S. a Istanbul,* 1966; *Samba pour S.A.S.,* 1966; *S.A.S.: Rendez-vous a San Francisco,* 1966; *S.A.S.: Broie du noir,* 1967; *S.A.S.: Magie noire a New York,* 1967 (translation by Nicholas Leonard published in England as *S.A.S.: Black Magic in New York,* New English Library, 1970), new translation published as *Operation New York,* Pinnacle Books, 1974; *S.A.S. Caraibes,* 1967; *S.A.S.: A l'ouest de Jerusalem,* 1967 (translation by Graham Snell published in England as *S.A.S.: West of Jerusalem,* New English Library, 1969), new translation published under same title, Pinnacle Books, 1973; *S.A.S.: Le Dossier Kennedy,* 1967; *S.A.S.: L'Or de la riviere Kwai,* 1968, translation published as *Malko: Death on the River Kwai,* Pinnacle Books, 1975; *S.A.S.: Les Pendus de Bagdad,* 1968; *S.A.S.: Le bal de la Comtesse Adler,* 1969, translation published as *The Countess and the Spy,* Pinnacle Books, 1974; *S.A.S.: L'Abominable Sirene,* 1969; *S.A.S.: La Panthere d'Hollywood,* 1969; *S.A.S.: Escale a Pago-Pago,* 1969.

S.A.S.: Amok a Bali, 1970; *S.A.S.: Les Trois Veuves de Hong-Kong,* 1970; *S.A.S.: Mission a Saigon,* 1970; *S.A.S.: Operation Apocalypse,* 1970 (translation by Adrian Shire published in England under same title, New English Library, 1970); *S.A.S.: Que viva Guevera,* 1970, translation by Lowel Blair published as *Malko: Que viva Guevara,* Pinnacle Books, 1975; *S.A.S.: Massacre a Amman,* 1971; *S.A.S.: Les Parias de Ceylan,* 1971; *S.A.S.: Requiem pour Tontons Macoutes,* 1971; *S.A.S.: L'Homme de Kabul,* 1971, translation published as *The Man from Kabul,* Pinnacle Books, 1973; *S.A.S.: Cyclone a L'ONU,* 1972;

S.A.S.: L'Heroine de Vientiane, 1972; *S.A.S.* [and] *Safari a La Paz*, 1972; *S.A.S.: L'Ange de Montevideo*, 1973, translation published as *Malko: The Angel of Vengeance*, Pinnacle Books, 1974; *S.A.S.: Murder Inc., Las Vegas*, 1973; *S.A.S.: Mort a Beyrouth*, 1973; *S.A.S.: Kill Kissinger*, 1974, translation published as *Kill Kissinger*, Pinnacle Books, 1974; *S.A.S.: Furie a Belfast*, 1974; *S.A.S.: Rendez-vous a Boris Gleb*, 1974; *S.A.S.: Roulette Cambodgienne*, 1974; *S.A.S.: Guepier en Angola*, 1975; *S.A.S.: Les Otages de Tokyo*, 1975, translation published as *Malko: Hostage in Tokyo*, Pinnacle Books, 1975; *S.A.S.: L'Ordre regne a Santiago*, 1975; *S.A.S.: Les Sorciers du Tage*, 1975.

WORK IN PROGRESS: More in the "Malko" spy series, the next to be set in Manila, and another to be based on a major motion picture; a story of Mrs. Isabel Peron, president of Argentina.

SIDELIGHTS: De Villiers' "Malko" series has been translated into fourteen languages. He told *CA:* "Being basically a journalist, all my books of the "Malko" series, which I call "faction" books are based on contemporary incidents, throughout the world. I have travelled extensively for the last twenty years, covering major stories for my magazine." He is an expert on Iran and the Middle East. De Villiers knows English, Spanish, and "has notions" of German and Persian.

* * *

DEVLIN, L. Patrick 1939-

PERSONAL: Born April 11, 1939, in Paterson, N.J.; married Suzanne Zellers; children: Kathleen, Cristin, Matthew. *Education:* William Paterson College, B.A., 1961; Columbia University, M.A., 1963; Wayne State University, Ph.D., 1968. *Politics:* Democrat. *Home:* 31 Lake St., Wakefield, R.I. 02879. *Office:* Department of Speech, University of Rhode Island, Kingston, R.I. 02881.

CAREER: University of Rhode Island, Kingston, professor of speech, 1967—. Delegate to Democratic National Convention, 1972. *Member:* Speech Communication Association of America, American Association of University Professors, Eastern Communication Association.

WRITINGS: Contemporary Political Speaking, Wadsworth, 1971. Contributor of articles on political communication to professional journals.

WORK IN PROGRESS: A chapter on the impact of the New Hampshire primary election, for inclusion in a book on the 1976 presidential campaign.

* * *

DEVLIN, (Dorothy) Wende 1918-

PERSONAL: Born April 27, 1918, in Buffalo, N.Y.; daughter of Bernhardt Philip (a veterinarian) and Elizabeth (Buffington) Wende; married Harry Devlin (an artist and writer), August 30, 1941; children: Harry Noel, Wende Elizabeth (Mrs. Geoffrey Gates), Jeffrey Anthony, Alexandra Gail (Mrs. James Eldridge), Brion Phillip, Nicholas Kirk, David Matthew. *Education:* Syracuse University, B.F.A., 1940. *Politics:* Independent. *Religion:* Congregationalist. *Home and office:* 443 Hillside Ave., Mountainside, N.J. 07092. *Agent:* Dorothy Markinko, McIntosh & Otis, Inc., 475 Fifth Ave., New York, N.Y. 10017.

CAREER: Free-lance portrait painter and writer. Member of Rutgers University's advisory council on children's literature. *Member:* Authors Guild of Authors League of America, Woman Pays Club. *Awards, honors:* New Jersey Teachers of English award, for *How Fletcher Was Hatched!*; award of excellence from Chicago Book Fair, 1974, for *Old Witch Rescues Halloween.*

WRITINGS—All books for children, with husband, Harry Devlin; all illustrated by Harry Devlin: *Old Black Witch*, Encyclopaedia Britannica Press, 1963; *The Knobby Boys to the Rescue*, Parents' Magazine Press, 1965; *Aunt Agatha, There's a Lion Under the Couch*, Van Nostrand, 1968; *How Fletcher Was Hatched!*, Parents' Magazine Press, 1969; *A Kiss for a Warthog*, Van Nostrand, 1970; *Old Witch and the Polka Dot Ribbon*, Parents' Magazine Press, 1970; *Cranberry Thanksgiving*, Parents' Magazine Press, 1971; *Old Witch Rescues Halloween*, Parents' Magazine Press, 1973.

WORK IN PROGRESS: Cranberry Christmas, with illustrations by husband, Harry Devlin.

SIDELIGHTS: Wende Devlin writes: "My husband and I . . . became children's book oriented when we had seven of our own. We had a built in sounding board for ideas and I can't think of more worthwhile work than pleasing and developing a child's mind and imagination." An adaptation by Gerald Herman of *Old Black Witch* was filmed as "The Winter of the Witch," 1972.

* * *

deVRIES, Egbert 1901-

PERSONAL: Born January 29, 1901, in Grijpskerke, Netherlands; son of Jan (a pastor) and Johanna W. (Luuring) deVries; married Tine Berg, February 18, 1924 (died, 1945); married Alexandrine Duvekot, July 14, 1947; children: (first marriage) Jan Roelof Jacob, Egbert, Johanna R. (Mrs. Maurice Covey), Jacobus Egbert; (second marriage) Alexander, Anna Elise (Mrs. Alfred G. Walton, Jr.), Johan Cornelis. *Education:* State Agricultural University, Wageningen, Netherlands, Agricultural Engineer, 1923, D.Agriculture, 1931. *Religion:* Protestant. *Home:* 39 Deer Lake Park, Chalkhill, Pa. 15421. *Office:* School of Public and International Affairs, University of Pittsburgh, Pittsburgh, Pa. 15260.

CAREER: Government service in Netherlands East Indies, horticultural extension officer, 1924-29, staff member of Bureau of Agricultural Economics, 1929-34, head of Division for General Economic Affairs, 1938-41; University of Batavia, Batavia (now Djakarta), Indonesia, professor of tropical agricultural economics and dean of Agricultural Faculty, both 1941-46; State Agricultural University, Wageningen, Netherlands, professor of tropical agricultural economics and agrarian structures of the Overseas Territories, 1947-50; International Bank for Reconstruction and Development, Washington, D.C., chief of Economic Resources Division, 1950-52, economic adviser to department of technical operations, 1952-53, chief of Agricultural Division, 1953-56; Institute of Social Studies, Hague, Netherlands, rector, 1956-66; University of Pittsburgh, School of Public and International Affairs, Pittsburgh, Pa., professor of international development, 1966-73, professor emeritus, 1973—. Councillor to Netherlands Ministry of Overseas Affairs, 1947-50. Coordinator of agro-economic research for Ford Foundation in Indonesia, 1963-70. Trustee, Interfuture Foundation, 1971—; Obor Foundation, trustee, 1971—, chairman of board, 1975—. Board member, Foundation for Cultural Relations with Surinam and the Netherlands Antilles, 1956-66; vice-chairman of board of directors, Africa Study Center (Leyden), 1958-64; board member,

Mediterranean Social Science Research Council, 1959-65; Council for the Study of Mankind (Santa Monica), board member, 1968—, vice-chairman, 1969-71. Chairman of working committee of Division of Church and Society of the World Council of Churches, 1954-62; chairman of Foundation for Research and Documentation on Social and Developmental Action of the Churches in Developing Countries, 1967—. Consultant to United Nations. Member of advisory board of Delta Foundation, 1955-74; member of Netherlands Advisory Council on Assistance to Developing Countries, 1964-66; adviser to governor of Puerto Rico, 1969.

MEMBER: International Peace Research Society, International Studies Association, Society for International Development (vice-president for Europe, 1963-65), United World Federalists, Academy of Political Science, Academy of Political and Social Science, African Studies Association (fellow), United Nations Association, Netherlands Royal Agricultural Society, Association of Netherlands Agricultural Engineers, Netherlands Economic Institute, National Netherlands Organization for International Assistance (chairman, 1956-61; vice-chairman, 1961-66; distinguished fellow), Netherlands Society for International Affairs (member of board of directors, 1957-64), Eastern Organization for Public Administration (Manila), Institute of Differing Civilizations (Brussels), Rotary International. *Awards, honors:* Knight of the Order of the Netherlands Lion, 1950; commander of the Order of Orange Nassau, 1966; fellowship from Institute of Social Studies in the Hague, Netherlands, 1966.

WRITINGS: Landbouw en Welvaart in Het Regentschap Pasoeroean (title means "Agriculture and Welfare in the Regency Pasuruan"), Veenman, 1931; *De Aarde Betaalt* (title means "The Earth Pays"), Albani, 1949, 2nd edition, 1950; *Man in Rapid Social Change,* Doubleday, 1961; (with Jose Medina Echevarria) *Social Aspects of Economic Development in Latin America,* Volume I, UNESCO, 1962; (editor) *Essays on Unbalanced Growth,* Institute of Social Studies, 1962; (editor with P. G. Casanova) *Social Research and Rural Life in Central America, Mexico, and the Caribbean Region,* UNESCO, 1966; (editor) *Man in Community,* Association Press, 1966; *Essays on the Economic Development of Africa: First Series of Annual Lectures on Development Organized by the Bank of Sudan, Khartoum,* Humanities, 1968; (editor) *Essays on Reciprocity,* Humanities, 1968. Correspondent for *Koninklyke Academic voor Overzeese Wetenshappen.* Corresponding editor of *Development and Change* (of Hague Institute of Social Studies).

WORK IN PROGRESS: Research on social dimensions of development, social aspects of ecological concerns, and coordinated rural development.

SIDELIGHTS: Egbert deVries has traveled all over the world; he speaks French, German, Indonesian, and Spanish. He has been published in Spanish, French, Arabic, Korean, and Mongolian. His first wife died in a Japanese concentration camp in Java, where his second wife had lost a previous husband. *Avocational interests:* Botany, entomology, international travel, collecting stamps.

*   *   *

de WAAL MALEFIJT, Annemarie   1914-

PERSONAL: Born May 23, 1914, in Amsterdam, Holland; came to United States, 1952, naturalized citizen, 1957; daughter of Adrian (a bookseller) and Anne (Asman) de

Waal Malefijt. *Education:* Columbia University, B.A., 1956, Ph.D., 1960. *Home:* 552 Riverside Dr., New York, N.Y. 10027. *Office:* Department of Anthropology, Hunter College of the City University of New York, 695 Park Ave., New York, N.Y. 10021.

CAREER: Hunter College of the City University of New York, New York, N.Y., assistant professor, 1960-63, associate professor, 1963-68, professor of anthropology, 1969—. Consultant to Institute for Study of Man in the Tropics, 1963-65; Human Resources Area Files, 1964-65; and New York Academy of Sciences, 1969—. *Member:* American Anthropological Association (fellow), Royal Anthropological Society of Great Britain (fellow), American Association for the Advancement of Science (fellow), New York Academy of Sciences (fellow), Phi Beta Kappa. *Awards, honors:* Wenner-Gren Foundation grant to Surinam, 1959-60.

WRITINGS: The Javanese of Surinam, Humanities, 1962; *Religion and Culture,* Macmillan, 1968; *Images of Man,* Knopf, 1974. Contributor to professional journals.

WORK IN PROGRESS: Anthropology of Art for Knopf.

*   *   *

DEWHURST, Keith   1931-

PERSONAL: Born December 24, 1931; in Oldham, England; son of J. F. and Lily (Carter) Dewhurst; married Eve Pearce, July 14, 1958; children: Alan, Emma, Faith. *Education:* Peterhouse, Cambridge, B.A. (with honors), 1953. *Home:* 108 Mount View Rd., London N.4, England. *Agent:* William Morris Agency, 147-9 Wardour St., London W.1, England.

CAREER: Lancashire Cotton Corp., Romiley, England, yarn tester, 1953-55; *Manchester Evening Chronicle,* Manchester, England, sports writer, 1955-59; Granada Television Ltd., London, England, presenter of television programs, 1968-69; *The Guardian,* London, England, arts columnist, 1969—. Presenter of British Broadcasting Corp. (BBC) television arts program, "Review," 1972. *Awards, honors:* Japan Prize, 1968, for "Last Bus."

WRITINGS—Plays: "Rafferty's Chant," first produced in London at Mermaid Theatre, June 28, 1967; "Pirates," first produced in London at Royal Court Theatre, December 13, 1970; "Brecht in '26," first produced in London at Theatre Upstairs, 1971; "Corunna!," first produced in London at Theatre Upstairs, 1971; "Kidnapped" (adaptation of novel by Robert Louis Stevenson), first produced in Edinburgh at Royal Lyceum Theatre, 1972; "The Miser" (adaptation from Moliere), first produced in Edinburgh at Royal Lyceum Theatre, May 25, 1973; "The Magic Island," first produced at Birmingham Repertory Theatre, December 19, 1974; "The Bomb in Brewery Street," first produced in Sheffield at Crucible Theatre, May 8, 1975; "One Short," first produced in Sheffield at Crucible Theatre, January 22, 1976.

Television plays: "Think of the Day," 1960; "Local Incident," 1961; "Albert Hope," 1962; "The Chimney Boy," 1964; "The Life and Death of Lovely Karen Gilhooley," 1964; "The Siege of Manchester," 1965; "The Towers of Manhattan," 1966; "Last Bus," 1968; "Men of Iron," 1969; "Why Danny Misses School," 1969; "It Calls for a Great Deal of Love," 1969; "Helen," 1970; "The Sit-In," 1972; "Lloyd George," 1973; "Our Terry," 1975. Also writer of scripts for "Z Cars" series, 1962-67, "Softly, Softly" series, 1967, and other series on English television.

Radio plays: "Drummer Delaney's Sixpence," 1971; "That's Charlie George Over There," 1972.

Plays represented in anthologies, *Plays of the Year 33,* edited by J. C. Trewin, Elek, 1967; *Z Cars: Four Scripts from the Television Series,* edited by Michael Marland, Longman, 1968; *Scene Scripts,* edited by Marland, Longman, 1972.

SIDELIGHTS: Some of Dewhurst's television scripts examine controversial subjects such as segregation and the inadequacy of the British penal system. His more recent stage plays are somewhat experimental in form, utilizing nontraditional staging and direct confrontations between characters and the audience.

* * *

DEYNEKA, Anita 1943-

PERSONAL: Born July 7, 1943, in Seattle, Wash.; daughter of Frank Howard and Ada (McIntosh) Marson; married Peter Deyneka, Jr. (a general director of a mission organization), June 15, 1968. *Education:* Wenatchee Valley College, student, 1961-63; Seattle Pacific College, B.A., 1966. *Religion:* Evangelical Protestant. *Home:* 1200D Bunker Hill Court, Wheaton, Ill. 60187. *Office address:* Slavic Gospel Association, P.O. Box 1122, Wheaton, Ill. 60187.

CAREER: Overseas Radio and Television, Taipei, Taiwan, missionary, spring, 1966; high school English teacher in Wenatchee, Wash., 1966-68; Slavic Gospel Association, Wheaton, Ill., missionary, 1968—. Clerk-typist for U.S. Forest Service, summers, 1963-67. *Member:* Evangelical Press Association, National Religious Broadcasters.

WRITINGS—For children: *Tanya and the Borderguard,* David Cook, 1973; *Fire!,* David Cook, 1974; *Alexi's Secret Mission,* David Cook, 1975.

For adults: (With husband, Peter Deyneka, Jr.) *Christians in the Shadow of the Kremlin,* David Cook, 1974. Contributor to religious periodicals.

WORK IN PROGRESS: A book on the Evangelical Christian-Baptist Church in Siberia.

SIDELIGHTS: Anita Deyneka's travels have taken her to the Far East, South America, Central America, the Soviet Union, and eastern and western Europe.

* * *

DIARA, Schavi M(ali) 1948-

PERSONAL: Name is pronounced Sha-*vee* Ma-*lee* Dee-*are*-ra; born April 30, 1948, in Detroit, Mich.; daughter of William Earl (a mechanical engineer) and Margaret (Walton) Ross; married Agadem Lumumba Diara (a publisher and college counselor), July 25, 1969. *Education:* Wayne State University, B.A., 1970, M.A., 1976. *Politics:* Pan-African Congress. *Religion:* Orthodox Islam. *Residence:* Detroit, Mich. *Office address:* c/o Agascha Productions, P.O. Box 38063, Detroit, Mich. 48238.

CAREER: High school teacher of English and life science in the public schools of Highland Park, Mich., 1970-71; Wayne State University, Detroit, Mich., instructor in English and social studies, 1971-72; Wayne County Community College, Detroit, instructor in English, 1972-73; Roeper City and Country School, Bloomfield Hills, Mich., teacher of English, 1973—. *Member:* Michigan Council of Teachers of English, Michigan Poetry Society, Agascha Speakers Bureau.

WRITINGS: Growing Together (poetry), Agascha Productions, 1972; *Legacy* (anthology of poems, essays, and short stories), Agascha Productions, 1975.

WORK IN PROGRESS: Song for My Father, a novel.

SIDELIGHTS: Schavi Diara wrote: "I feel that it is imperative that Black people recognize their African heritage, take pride in it, relate to it, and begin to move in ways that will cause others to respect us and see us as equals rather than lesser-men." Her long-range goal is to establish a private college-preparatory secondary school which places emphasis on African and African-American studies.

* * *

DICK, Daniel T. 1946-

PERSONAL: Born March 9, 1946, in Lancaster, Pa.; son of Jacob T. (a teacher) and Leona M. (a teacher; maiden name, Stouffer) Dick; married Cathryn J. Dettmann, July 30, 1966; children: Geoffrey T. *Education:* California State University, Fresno, B.A. (with high honors), 1966; Claremont Graduate School, M.A., 1969, Ph.D., 1971. *Residence:* Los Gatos, Calif. 95030. *Office:* Department of Economics, University of Santa Clara, The Alameda, Santa Clara, Calif. 95053.

CAREER: California Institute of Technology, Pasadena, visiting assistant professor of economics, 1970-71; University of Santa Clara, Santa Clara, Calif., assistant professor, 1971—. Summer consultant to State of California Department of Transportation, 1973; president of Strathmore Swim Club, Los Gatos, Calif., 1973. *Member:* American Economic Association, Western Economic Association.

WRITINGS: Pollution, Congestion, and Nuisance: The Economics of Nonmarket Interdependence, Lexington Books, 1974. Contributor to economic journals.

WORK IN PROGRESS: Writing on environmental economics and on the economics of racial discrimination.

AVOCATIONAL INTERESTS: Traveling, enjoying the Sierra, sailing, swimming, water-skiing, snow-skiing.

* * *

DICKINSON, Edward C(live) 1938-

PERSONAL: Born March 6, 1938, in Paget, Bermuda; son of Lionel Gilbert and Eileen (Barlow) Dickinson; married Dorothy Sopper, March 11, 1965; children: Philip, Melanie. *Education:* Westminster School, London, S.C.E.

CAREER: Pronesiam, Inc., Bangkok, Thailand, product manager, 1962-70; Nestle, Switzerland, product manager, 1971-73; Filipro, Manila, Philippines, marketing services manager, 1973-75.

WRITINGS: (With Ben F. King) *A Field Guide to the Birds of Southeast Asia,* Houghton, 1975. Contributor to ornithological journals. Co-editor of *National Historical Bulletin* of Siam Society, 1968-70.

WORK IN PROGRESS: A work on the birds of Thailand, the Philippines, and surrounding countries.

* * *

DIERICKX, C(harles) W(allace) 1921-

PERSONAL: Born August 13, 1921, in Ghent, Minn.; son of Charles (a farmer) and Elizabeth (Buysse) Dierickx; married Dorothy McGovern (a university professor), November 22, 1962; children: Lisa, Ann. *Education:* St. John's University, Collegeville, Minn., B.A., 1941; University of Florida, M.A., 1951; Northwestern University, Ph.D., 1955. *Religion:* Roman Catholic. *Home:* 1136 Sheridan Rd., Wilmette, Ill. 60091. *Office:* Department of Geography, Northeastern Illinois University, 5500 North St. Louis Ave., Chicago, Ill. 60625.

CAREER: Northeastern Illinois University, Chicago, associate professor, 1955-61, professor of geography and environmental studies, 1961—, chairman of department, 1966—.

WRITINGS: (With Jaime Fonseca) *Latin America, Canada, Africa, Australia,* Follett, 1964; *How People Live in Brazil,* Benefic, 1970, 2nd edition, 1973.

SIDELIGHTS: Dierickx recently took a group of students on a tour of Africa. He has also been a tour conductor for travel agencies in Brazil, Southeast Asia, Canada, and the United States.

* * *

DIGGLE, James 1944-

PERSONAL: Born March 29, 1944, in Rochdale, England; son of James and Elizabeth Alice (Buckley) Diggle; married Sedwell Mary Chapman, 1974; children: one son. *Education:* Cambridge University, B.A., 1965, M.A. and Ph.D., 1969. *Office:* Department of Classics, Queens' College, Cambridge University, Cambridge, England.

CAREER: Cambridge University, Cambridge, England, fellow of Queens' College and director of studies in classics, 1966—, librarian, 1969—, praelector, 1971-73, university assistant lecturer, 1970-75, lecturer in classics, 1975—. Governor, Ward-Fremau School, 1973—. *Member:* Cambridge Philological Society (secretary, 1970-74), Society for the Promotion of Hellenic Studies, Housman Society.

WRITINGS: (Editor and author of introductory essay and commentary) *Euripides: Phaethon,* Cambridge University Press, 1970; (editor with F.R.D. Goodyear) Flavius Cresconius Corippus, *Johannidos seu De bellis Libycis libri VIII,* Cambridge University Press, 1970; (compiler and editor with Goodyear) Alfred Edward Housman, *The Classical Papers of A. E. Housman,* Volume I: *1882-1897,* Volume II: *1897-1914,* Volume III: *1915-1936,* Cambridge University Press, 1972. Contributor of articles to journals in his field. Editor, *Proceedings of the Cambridge Philological Society,* 1970—.

* * *

DILKS, David (Neville) 1938-

PERSONAL: Born March 17, 1938, in Coventry, England; son of Neville Ernest and Phyllis (Follows) Dilks; married Jill Medlicott, 1963. *Education:* Oxford University, B.A., 1959. *Home:* Wits End, Long Causeway, Leeds LS16 8EX, England. *Office:* School of History, University of Leeds, Leeds LS2 9JT, England.

CAREER: London School of Economics and Political Science, Aldwych, England, assistant lecturer, 1962-65, lecturer in international history, 1965-69; University of Leeds, Leeds, England, professor of international history, 1969—, chairman of School of History, 1974—, dean of Faculty of Arts, 1975—. Research assistant to Earl of Avon, 1960-62, to Marshal of the Royal Air Force, 1963-65, and to Harold Macmillan, 1964-67. Chairman of Commonwealth Youth Exchange Council, 1968-73. Consultant, Commonwealth Youth Program, 1974-75. *Member:* Royal Commonwealth Society, Royal Historical Society (fellow), Royal Society for the Protection of Birds, Shropshire Ornithological Society, Shropshire Naturalists Trust, Yorkshire Naturalists Trust, Severn Valley Railways Society.

WRITINGS: Sir Winston Churchill, Hamish Hamilton, 1965; *Curzon in India,* Hart-Davis, Volume I: *Achievement,* 1969, Volume II: *Frustration,* 1970, Taplinger, 1970; (editor) *The Diaries of Sir Alexander Cadogan, O.M., 1938-1945,* Cassell, 1971, Putnam, 1972.

WORK IN PROGRESS: An authorized biography of Neville Chamberlain, and a book on British foreign policy, both with Alan Beattie; a contribution to a book on the history of Conservatism.

* * *

DILLON, Martin 1949-

PERSONAL: Born June 2, 1949, in Belfast, Northern Ireland; son of Gerard (a telephone engineer) and Mary Theresa (Clarke) Dillon; married Mildred Smyth (a general administrative officer), August 24, 1973. *Education:* Attended Montfort College, 1961, and Belfast College of Business Studies, 1968-70. *Politics:* "To be revealed." *Office:* British Broadcasting Corp., Ormeau Ave., Belfast, Northern Ireland.

CAREER: Worked as reporter for *Irish News,* 1968-72; and for *Belfast Telegraph,* 1972-73, both in Belfast, Northern Ireland; British Broadcasting Corp., Belfast, regional news assistant, 1973-74, talks producer, 1974—. *Member:* National Union of Journalists.

WRITINGS: (With Denis Lehane) *Political Murder in Northern Ireland,* Penquin, 1973; "The Squad," (play), broadcast by BBC on radio and television, 1976. Also author of plays, "Compound 19" and "On the Way Out," both as yet neither published nor produced.

WORK IN PROGRESS: A play, "The Captives."

AVOCATIONAL INTERESTS: Reading, listening to music, and observing.

* * *

DIMBERG, Ronald G(ilbert) 1938-

PERSONAL: Born April 2, 1938, in California; son of Arvid G. and Lois M. Dimberg; married Arletta Lester (an educator); children: Elliot Lester. *Education:* University of Oregon, B.A., 1960, M.A., 1962; Columbia University, Ph.D., 1970. *Home:* 109 Stewart Circle, Charlottesville, Va. 22903. *Office:* Department of History, University of Virginia, Charlottesville, Va.

CAREER: University of Virginia, Charlottesville, assistant professor, 1970-74, associate professor of history, 1974—, director of East Asian Language and Area Center, 1975—. *Member:* Association for Asian Studies, Society for Asian and Comparative Philosophy.

WRITINGS: The Sage and Society: The Life and Thought of Ho Hsin-Yin, University Press of Hawaii, 1974.

WORK IN PROGRESS: Research on sixteenth century social thought.

SIDELIGHTS: Dimberg's major interests are Chinese and Japanese neo-Confucianism and social thought.

* * *

DINER, Hasia R(ena) 1946-

PERSONAL: Born October 7, 1946, in Milwaukee, Wis.; daughter of Morris (a teacher) and Ita (Eichenbaum) Schwartzman); married Steven Diner (a college professor), July 12, 1970; children: Shira Miriam. *Education:* University of Wisconsin, Madison, B.A., 1968; University of Chicago, M.A.T., 1970; University of Illinois at Chicago Circle, Ph.D., 1975. *Religion:* Jewish. *Home:* 1747 Lanier Pl. N.W., Washington, D.C. 20009. *Office:* Department of History, University of Maryland, College Park, Md. 20742.

CAREER: University of Maryland, College Park, instructor in history, 1975—. Instructor at Federal City College, 1975-76; director of employment discrimination counseling for Women's Legal Defense Fund, 1975—. *Member:* American Historical Association, Organization of American Historians, American Studies Association, National Capitol Labor Historians, Chesapeake Area Women Historians.

WRITINGS: (Contributor) Arthur Schlesinger and Roger Bruns, editors, *Congress Investigates,* Chelsea House, 1975; *In the Almost Promised Land: American Jews and Blacks, 1915-1935,* Greenwood Press, in press.

WORK IN PROGRESS: Women in Urban Society, for Gale's "Information Guide Library."

*   *   *

DITTES, James E(dward) 1926-

PERSONAL: Born December 26, 1926, in Cleveland, Ohio; son of Mercein Edward and Mary (Freeman) Dittes; married Frances Martha Skinner, March 20, 1948; children: Lawrence William (deceased), Nancy Eleanor, Carolyn Ann, Joanne Frances. *Education:* Oberlin College, A.B., 1949; Yale University, B.D., 1954, M.S., 1955, Ph.D., 1958. *Home:* 107 Westminster St., Hamden, Conn. 06518. *Office:* Department of Religious Studies, Yale University, 14 Mansfield St., New Haven, Conn. 06520.

CAREER: American School, Talas, Turkey, instructor in science, 1950-52; ordained minister in United Church of Christ, 1954; Yale University, New Haven, Conn., instructor, 1955-59, assistant professor, 1959-62, associate professor, 1962-67, professor of psychology of religion, 1967—, chairman of department, 1972—, director of graduate studies, 1968-75. Chairman of Council on Graduate Studies in Religion in the United States and Canada, 1970-71. *Military service:* U.S. Naval Reserve, 1945-46. *Member:* American Psychological Association (fellow), Society for the Scientific Study of Religion (executive secretary, 1959-63; president, 1971-73), American Academy of Religion. *Awards, honors:* Guggenheim fellow, 1965-66; Fulbright research fellow in Italy, 1965-66; National Endowment for the Humanities senior fellow, 1972-73.

WRITINGS: Vocational Guidance of Theological Students: A Manual for the Use of the Theological School Inventory, Ministry Studies Board, 1964; (with Robert J. Menges) *Psychological Studies of Clergymen: Abstracts of Research,* Nelson, 1965; *The Church in the Way,* Scribner, 1967; (contributor) Kenneth H. Breimeier, *Relationships between Various Psychological Measures in Use at Various Theological Seminaries,* Ministry Studies Board, 1967; *Minister on the Spot,* Pilgrim Press, 1970; *Bias and the Pious: The Relationship between Prejudice and Religion,* Augsburg, 1973; (contributor) Charles Y. Glock and Phillip E. Hammond, editors, *Beyond the Classics: Essays in the Scientific Study of Religion,* Harper, 1973. Author of research bulletins published by the Ministry Studies Board. Contributor to *The Handbook of Social Psychology,* Addison-Wesley, 1968-70. Editor, *Journal for the Scientific Study of Religion,* 1966-71.

DIXON, Joseph L(awrence) 1896-

PERSONAL: Born January 5, 1896, in Pontotoc County, Miss.; son of J. W. H. (a teacher) and Lida Clay (Horn) Dixon; married Grace Underwood, September 12, 1927 (died, 1953); married Irene Brown, August 23, 1955 (died, 1972); children: (first marriage) Edward, Eugene, Laura. *Education:* "Like Socrates and Charles Dickens, mostly self-educated. Except for mathematics, which was elementary, equal or superior to college graduates." *Religion:* Methodist. *Home:* 1158 North Maxwell Dr., Fayetteville, Ark. 72701.

CAREER: Teacher and construction carpenter, 1919-35; company clerk and subaltern, Civilian Conservation Corps, 1935-41; employed with Welders Supply Co., Little Rock, Ark., 1941-60; poet, author. *Military service:* U.S. Army, 1918-19.

WRITINGS: The Community of the Mind (philosophical essays), Philosophical Library, 1966; *The Analyst and Other Poems,* Crescent, 1974.

*   *   *

DOBKIN De RIOS, Marlene 1939-

PERSONAL: Born April 12, 1939, in New York, N.Y.; daughter of Bernard and Anne (Schwartz) Dobkin; married Yando Rios (an artist), November 7, 1969; children: Gabriela. *Education:* Queens College (now Queens College of the City University of New York), B.A., 1959; New York University, M.A., 1963; University of California, Riverside, Ph.D., 1972. *Home:* 1335 10th Ave., San Francisco, Calif. 94122. *Office:* Medical Anthropology Program, University of California, San Francisco, Calif. 94143.

CAREER: City University of New York, New York, N.Y., part-time lecturer in anthropology at City College and Brooklyn College, 1964-66; University of Massachusetts, Boston, instructor in anthropology, 1966-67; California State University, Los Angeles, assistant professor of anthropology, 1967-68; California State University, Fullerton, assistant professor, 1969-72, associate professor of anthropology, 1972—. Field secretary for Admiralty Islands-New Guinea Expedition of American Museum of Natural History, spring, 1965; research associate at Institute of Social Psychiatry of National University of San Marcos (Lima, Peru), 1968-69; visiting scientist at Smithsonian Institution, summer, 1970; research anthropologist at Metropolitan State Hospital (Norwalk, Calif.), 1970—, psychotherapist at Day Treatment Center and Spanish Language Ward, 1973; consultant to National Commission on Marihuana and Drug Abuse, 1973; associate researcher in anthropology at California College of Medicine at University of California (Irvine), 1974—; post-doctoral researcher and lecturer in Medical Anthropology Program, University of California, San Francisco, 1975-76.

MEMBER: American Anthropological Association (fellow), Royal Anthropological Institute (fellow). *Awards, honors:* U.S. Public Health Service grant, University of California, San Francisco, 1975-76; National Institute on Alcoholism and Alcohol Abuse grant, 1975-76; National Institute of Mental Health research training fellowship, 1975-76.

WRITINGS: (Contributor) Michael J. Harner, editor, *Hallucinogens and Shamanism,* Oxford University Press, 1972; *Visionary Vine: Psychedelic Healing in the Peruvian Amazon,* Chandler Publishing, 1972; (contributor) Ramon de la Fuente and Maxwell Weisman, editors, *Psychiatry:*

Proceedings of the Fifth World Congress of Psychiatry, Volume II, Excerpta Medica, 1973; (contributor) *Drug Use in America: Problems in Perspective,* Volume I, National Commission on Marihuana and Drug Abuse, 1973; (contributor) Thomas Fitzgerald, editor, *Social and Cultural Identity: Problems of Persistence and Change,* University of Georgia Press, 1974.

Contributor to professional journals. Associate editor in ethnopharmacology of *Medical Anthropology Newsletter.*

WORK IN PROGRESS: The Wilderness of Mind: Sacred Plants in Cross-Cultural Perspective.

* * *

DOBRIN, Arthur 1943-

PERSONAL: Born August 22, 1943, in Brooklyn, N.Y.; son of Moe (a truck driver) and Anne (Slavin) Dobrin; married Lyn Fradkin (a writer of children's books, artist, and model), August 30, 1964; children: Eric Simba, Kikora Anana. *Education:* City College of the City University of New York, B.A., 1965; New York University, M.A., 1971; graduate study at Nathan Ackerman Family Institute, 1973-75. *Religion:* Ethical Humanist. *Home:* 613 Dartmouth St., Westbury, N.Y. 11590. *Office:* Ethical Humanist Society, 38 Old Country Rd., Garden City, N.Y. 11530.

CAREER: U.S. Peace Corps, volunteer in Kenya, 1965-67; Ethical Humanist Society of Long Island, Garden City, N.Y., leader, 1968—; poet. Initiator of The Learning Tree (experimental school); summer director of Encampment for Citizenship, Great Falls, Mont., and Tucson, Ariz., 1968, 1969, 1970, 1972; director of Institute for Leadership Development, 1971-72; teacher at Westbury Experimental High School, 1973-74. Board member of Westbury League of Women Voters, 1974-75. *Member:* World Poetry Society, American Association of Marriage and Family Counselors (associate member).

WRITINGS: The Role of Cooperatives in the Development of Rural Kenya (monograph), Rutgers University Press, 1970; (with Kenneth Briggs) *Getting Married the Way You Want,* Prentice-Hall, 1974. Contributor of poems to *Bitterroot, Chelsea, Dark Waters, Street Cries, Compass, Poet, Ocarina, Xanadu,* and *East Africa Journal.*

WORK IN PROGRESS: Sunbird: Poems of East Africa; Canes, poems of Kenya.

BIOGRAPHICAL/CRITICAL SOURCES: Family Circle, June, 1974.

* * *

DOBZHANSKY, Theodosius 1900-1975

January 25, 1900—December 18, 1975; Russian-born American geneticist, educator, expert on evolutionary theory, author of books in his field. Obituaries: *New York Times,* December 19, 1975; *Washington Post,* December 20, 1975; *Time,* December 29, 1975; *AB Bookman's Weekly,* January 26, 1976; *Current Biography,* February, 1976. (*CAP*-1; earlier sketch in *CA*-13/14)

* * *

DODGE, Calvert R(enaul) 1931-

PERSONAL: Born April 15, 1931, in Chicago, Ill.; son of Frank Lawrence and Anna Rose (an artist; maiden name, Manke) Dodge; married Mary R. Melchar, April 2, 1951 (divorced, 1971); children: Lawrence Wesley, Laura Irene

Dodge Schultz, Valerie Le, James Calvert. *Education:* University of Wyoming, B.S., 1949, M.A., 1957; University of Denver, Ph.D., 1971. *Politics:* Democrat. *Religion:* Protestant. *Home:* 4111 Hillbrook Dr., Louisville, Ky. 40220. *Office:* Department of Sociology, University of Kentucky, Box 1036, Louisville, Ky. 40201.

CAREER: Standard Oil Co., Chicago, Ill., director of dealer and employee public relations, youth and educational activities in 17 states, and supervisor of farm and city sales divisions, 1946-55; University of Wyoming, Laramie, instructor in leadership and communications, 1955-58; Western Concrete Products, Laramie, co-founder and president, 1958-63; Boulder County Court, Boulder, Colo., probation counselor and trainer in volunteers program, 1963-64; Colorado Department of Institutions, Division of Youth Services, Denver, director of Training Center, 1964-72; Dodge-Marck Associates (management consulting firm), Denver, Colo. and Louisville, Ky., president, project director and workshop leader, 1972—. Instructor at University of Colorado, 1968-69; instructor in sociology, group dynamics and corrections at University of Kentucky and at Jefferson Community College, 1972—. Certified junior college administrator in California; project director for Kentucky Manpower Development, Inc.; Job Corps management consultant, staff trainer, and camp inspector in California, Virginia, New Mexico, and Nevada, 1968-72; member of national advisory boards of Future Farmers of America, 4-H Club Foundation, and Junior Achievement. *Military service:* U.S. Air Force Reserve, 1961-75, petty officer on a U.S. Navy destroyer, member of North Atlantic Treaty Organization (NATO) inspection team in Paris, 1966, chief training officer for a medical service squadron, 1966-69, leader of Mountain Rescue Team, 1967-70, chief of medical mobilization augmentee program, 1971-72; became major.

MEMBER: Speech Communication Association of America, American Association of University Professors, National Association of Psychiatric Technicians, Association for Humanistic Psychology, General Semantics Association, American Society for Training and Development (president of Rocky Mountain chapter, 1968-69; national vice-president, 1969-70), Alpha Zeta (chancellor, 1949), Omicron Delta Kappa. *Awards, honors:* Outstanding leadership awards from American Society for Training and Development, including Rocky Mountain chapter award, 1969, and national award, 1971; key award from Junior Chamber of Commerce, 1959; Law Enforcement Assistance Administration grants, 1969-70, 1971-72.

WRITINGS: Training Youth Workers: Dialogue and Response, State of Colorado, 1971; *Communication Factors Related to Reduced Recidivism of Paroled Youth in Colorado,* State of Colorado, 1972; *Group Dynamics* (training text), Kentucky Bureau of Corrections, 1975; (editor) *A Nation without Prisons,* Heath, 1975; (editor) *Power and Its Use and Misuse,* International Center for Comparative Criminology, 1975; *Group Dynamics,* National Textbook Co., 1976. Contributor to business, psychiatry, and farming magazines.

WORK IN PROGRESS: Victim-Victim; The Correctional Leader and His Power.

SIDELIGHTS: Dodge has been trained in Gestalt therapy and psychodrama, management, video-tape training and production, and "T-Group training," communication, and transactional analysis. His lectures in these areas are aimed at business and management groups.

DOERINGER, Peter B(rantley) 1941-

PERSONAL: Born February 26, 1941, in Boston, Mass.; son of Frank Atchley and Elizabeth (Musser) Doeringer; married Suzannah J. Fabing, June 19, 1965. *Education:* Harvard University, A.B., 1962, A.M., 1965, Ph.D., 1966. *Home:* 16 Maple Ave., Cambridge, Mass. 02139. *Office:* Department of Economics, Boston University, Boston, Mass. 02215.

CAREER: Harvard University, Cambridge, Mass., instructor, 1966-67, assistant professor of economics, 1967-72, associate professor of political economy, 1972-74; Boston University, Boston, Mass., professor of economics, 1974—. Consultant to Equal Employment Opportunity Commission, 1966-67, to U.S. Department of Labor, 1967—, and to Organization for Economic Cooperation and Development, 1972-73; Boston Area Manpower Planning Council, member, 1970-72, acting chairman, 1971; lecturer at London School of Economics and Political Science, 1971-72. *Member:* American Arbitration Association, American Economic Association, Industrial Relations Research Association.

WRITINGS: (Editor) *Programs to Employ the Disadvantaged,* Prentice-Hall, 1969; (with Michael J. Piore) *Internal Labor Markets and Manpower Analysis,* Heath, 1971. Author of several research reports on problems in economics for the U.S. and Boston city governments. Contributor of articles to professional journals.

* * *

DOLIT, Alan 1934-

PERSONAL: Born July 21, 1934, in New York, N.Y.; son of Morris (a tailor) and Betty (Kurland) Dolitsky; married Catherine Buckles (an art teacher), August 31, 1962; children: Lisa, Carolyn, Linda. *Education:* Hunter College (now Hunter College of the City University of New York), B.A., 1968. *Religion:* "Zen-Unitarian." *Home:* 1387 Scenic Ave., Berkeley, Calif. 94708.

CAREER: Alameda County Department of Social Services, Oakland, Calif., supervisor of social services, 1963—. Founder and "facilitator" of Fat Liberation, 1971—.

WRITINGS: Fat Liberation, Celestial Arts, 1975.

WORK IN PROGRESS: A book on fat, "which will include fat people's feelings, awareness, experiences, fears, desires, dreams, and fantasies as expressed through poetry, drama, art, and photography."

SIDELIGHTS: Dolit writes: "My 'career' in the 'fat' field started when I got tired of (and from) being too fat; and . . . when I realized that although I had been involved in the awareness movement for six-seven years, I was still my fat dumb self; and . . . because I knew that traditional methods . . . had little or no lasting effect for over ninety percent of persons who follow the diets . . . Fat Liberation is the career I am flowing into primarily because it is a synthesis of the best Zen, gestalt, psychodrama, sensory awareness, and meditation have to offer."

BIOGRAPHICAL/CRITICAL SOURCES: Tri-Valley News, October 4, 1974; *San Francisco Examiner,* May 23, 1975.

* * *

DOMAN, Glenn J(oseph) 1919-

PERSONAL: Born August 26, 1919, in Hilltown, Bucks County, Pa.; son of Joseph Jay and Helen Gould (Ricker) Doman; married Hazel Katie Massingham, September 16, 1944; children: Bruce K., Janet J., Douglas Mac. *Education:* Attended Drexel Institute of Technology, 1938; University of Pennsylvania, R.P.T., 1940. *Office:* Institutes for the Achievement of Human Potential, 8801 Stenton Ave., Philadelphia, Pa. 19118.

CAREER: Temple University, Philadelphia, Pa., physical therapist, 1941; Pennsylvania Hospital, Philadelphia, physical therapist, 1945; Norwood Rehabilitation Center, Philadelphia, Pa., director, 1948-55; Institutes for the Achievement of Human Potential, Philadelphia, Pa., founder and director, 1955—. Professor at Avery Postgraduate Institute, 1963—, and at University of Plano, 1965—. Associate director of Centro de Reabilitacao Nossa Senhora da Gloria (Rio de Janeiro), 1959—; associate director of Instituto Para La Organisation Neurologica (Buenos Aires), 1967—. Member of board of trustees, University of Plano; member of board of directors of Maimann Foundation, Pennsylvania Governor's Commission for Human Potential, International Rehabilitation Forum, British Institute for the Achievement of Human Potential, Irish Institute for the Achievement of Human Potential, and Australian Institute for the Achievement of Human Potential. *Military service:* U.S. Army, 1941-45; became first lieutenant; received Distinguished Service Cross, Silver Star, Bronze Star, British Military Cross, and Luxembourg Croix de Guerre. U.S. Army Reserve, 1945-62; became lieutenant colonel.

MEMBER: World Organization for Human Potential (president, 1967-71), American Association for the Advancement of Science, U.S. Army and Navy Legion of Honor (member of board of directors; past national commander), British Officers Club, Early Development Association (Tokyo; member of board of directors), Athenaeum Club (Philadelphia). *Awards, honors:* Roberto Simonsen Medal of Social Service to Brazil, 1959; Gold Medal of Honor of Brazil, 1960; Sc.D. and Trailblazer Award from University of Plano, both 1965; *diploma de honra a. merito,* Piracaba, Brazil, 1965; *diploma de reconhecimento,* Sao Paulo, Brazil, 1965; *diplomo socio-benmento,* Porto Alegre, Brazil, 1965; *diplomo e medalha comemorativa* of Associaco de Paris e Amigos dos Excepcionais, Rio de Janeiro, Brazil, 1965; named Knight of the Order of the Southern Cross (Brazil), 1966; Raymond A. Dart Steel Brain Award, 1971, from United Steelworkers of America.

WRITINGS: Nose Is Not Toes, Jonathan Cape, 1963; *How to Teach Your Baby to Read,* Random House, 1964; *What to Do About Your Brain Injured Child: Or, Your Brain-Damaged, Mentally Retarded, Mentally Deficient, Cerebral Palsied, Spastic, Flaccid, Rigid, Epileptic, Autistic, Athetoid, Hyperactive Child,* Doubleday, 1974; *In a Word,* Doubleday, in press. Author of teacher's manuals. Contributor to physical therapy and education journals and to popular magazines, including *McCall's* and *Ladies' Home Journal.*

* * *

DONALDSON, Frances (Annesley) 1907-

PERSONAL: Born January 13, 1907, in Harrow, England; daughter of Frederick (a playwright) and Leslie (Hoggan) Lonsdale; married John Donaldson (in parliament), February 20, 1935; children: Thomas Hay, Rose Albinia (Mrs. Nicholas Deakin), Catherine Frances (Mrs. Mark Jennings). *Education:* Educated in Bromley, England. *Politics:* Labour. *Religion:* None. *Home:* 1 Chalcot Crescent, London, England.

CAREER: Farmer and writer.

WRITINGS: Freddy Lonsdale, Lippincott, 1958; *The Marconi Scandal,* Harcourt, 1963; *Evelyn Waugh: Portrait of a Country Neighbour,* Chilton, 1968; *Eduard VIII,* Lippincott, 1975.

* * *

DONNER, Stanley T(emple) 1910-

PERSONAL: Born December 1, 1910, in Norfolk, Neb.; son of Herbert T. and Eva (Fountain) Donner; married Joanne E. Emerson, February 19, 1943; children: Victoria, Jan (Mrs. Courtney J. Collins), Megan (Mrs. Richard Heinichen), Mark, Tamsen. *Education:* University of Michigan, B.A., 1932; Northwestern University, M.A., 1940, Ph.D., 1946. *Politics:* Democrat. *Religion:* Methodist. *Home address:* Route 7, Box 528A, Austin, Tex. 78703. *Office:* School of Communication, Department of Radio, Television, and Film, University of Texas, Austin, Tex. 78712.

CAREER: Northwestern University, Evanston, Ill., assistant professor of speech, 1946-48; Stanford University, Stanford, Calif., assistant professor, 1948-51, associate professor, 1951-58, professor of speech and drama, 1958-62, acting head of department, 1961-62, associate head of department of communication, 1962-65; University of Texas, Austin, professor of communication and education, 1965—, chairman of department of radio, television, and film, 1965-71. Fulbright lecturer at University of London, 1963-64; consultant to Westinghouse Broadcasting Corp. *Military service:* U.S. Naval Reserve, active duty, 1942-46; became lieutenant commander.

MEMBER: International Radio and Television Society, National Association of Educational Broadcasters, Speech Association of America, Phi Kappa Phi. *Awards, honors:* Awards for television educational series from Institute for Education by Radio and Television, 1952, for "People, Places, and Politics," from Mental Health Association of California, 1955, for "The Fine Line," and from Institute for Education by Radio and Television, 1962, for "Careers"; senior Fulbright research award, 1955-56, for study in France.

WRITINGS: (Contributor) Wilbur Schramm and others, editors, *Educational Television: The Next Ten Years,* Stanford University Press, 1962; (editor) *The Future of Commercial Television,* Stanford University Press, 1965; (editor) *The Meaning of Commercial Television,* University of Texas Press, 1967; (with Allen Koenig and others) *The Farther Vision: Educational Television,* University of Wisconsin Press, 1968. Also author of *Television Production,* as yet unpublished.

WORK IN PROGRESS: Film as a Kind of Literature, publication expected in 1978.

SIDELIGHTS: Donner writes: "I have lived in England, France, Spain and Mexico. . . . I have found my natural 'home' in Paris. I return there again and again and always with fresh excitement. There I find my creative talent stirred by almost everything I see or do. If my primary interest is in teaching and writing, my secondary interest is in art, and most particularly sculpture. Of the mass media television and film are most inviting to me."

* * *

DONOVAN, Frank (Robert) 1919-1975

November 27, 1919—September 26, 1975; American documentary film producer, editor and author of historical works for adults and children. Obituaries: *New York Times,* September 30, 1975; *Publishers Weekly,* October 20, 1975; *AB Bookman's Weekly,* January 26, 1976. (See index for previous *CA* sketch)

* * *

DOPUCH, Nicholas 1929-

PERSONAL: Born November 15, 1929, in St. Louis, Mo., son of Marco and Mary Rose (Tribulak) Dopuch; married Barbara J. Scholl, March 21, 1954; children: Nicholas Eli, Michael Raymond. *Education:* Indiana State Teacher's College, S.B. (magna cum laude), 1957; University of Illinois, S.M., 1959, Ph.D., 1961. *Home:* 9323 South Hamilton Ave., Chicago, Ill. 60620. *Office:* Graduate School of Business, University of Chicago, 5836 Greenwood Ave., Chicago, Ill. 60637.

CAREER: Anheuser Busch, Inc., St. Louis, Mo., auditor, 1947-48; University of Chicago, Chicago, Ill., professor of accounting, 1961—. Certified public accountant by State of Illinois, 1964. Distinguished Arthur Young Professor of Accounting at University of Illinois, 1970-71. *Member:* American Accounting Association, National Association of Accountants, American Institute of Certified Public Accountants, Illinois Society of Certified Public Accountants (chairman of College of Measurements in Management), Beta Gamma Sigma, Phi Delta Kappa, Phi Kappa Phi, Beta Alpha Psi, Pi Omega Pi. *Awards, honors: Wall Street Journal* award.

WRITINGS: (Contributor) Sidney Davidson, editor, *Handbook of Modern Accounting,* McGraw, 1970; (editor with L. Revsine) *Accounting Research, 1960-1970; A Critical Evaluation,* Center for Continuing Education, University of Illinois, 1973; (with J. Demski and J. Birnberg) *Cost Accounting: Accounting Data for Management's Decisions,* Harcourt, 2nd edition (Dopuch was not associated with 1st edition), 1974. Contributor to accounting journals. Editor, *Journal of Accounting Research.*

* * *

DOSKOCILOVA, Hana 1936-

PERSONAL: Born July 11, 1936, in Jihlava, Czechoslovakia; daughter of Jan (a lawyer) and Maria (Juraskova) Doskocil; married Miroslav Sekyrka (a bookseller), September 21, 1961. *Education:* Attended public schools in Znojmo, Czechoslovakia. *Home:* Praha 10-Vrsovice, Madridska 4/820, Czechoslovakia. *Office:* Albatros, Na Perstyne 1, Prague 1, Czechoslovakia.

CAREER: Clerk in coal store in Jihlava, Czechoslovakia, 1954-56; Academy of Sciences, Prague, clerk, 1956-59; Albatros (publishers for children and young people), Prague, press editor, 1959-61, proofreader, 1961-64, editor in department for small children, 1964—.

WRITINGS—All juvenile: Pohadky pro deti, mamy a taty (title means "Fairy Tales for Children, Mothers, and Fathers"), Statni Nakladatelstvi Detske Knihy (Prague), 1961; *Psanicko pro tebe—O hrackach* (title means "A Letter for You—About Toys"), Statni Nakladatelstvi Detske Knihy, 1964; *Bydlim doma* (title means "I Live at Home"), Statni Nakladatelstvi Detske Knihy, 1966; *Kajetan the Magician* (translated from the German), Artia (Prague), 1967; *Cervena lodicka* (title means "The Little Red Ship"), Mlada fronta (Prague), 1968; *Modern Czech Fairy Tales* (translated from the Czech), Artia, 1969.

Animal Tales (translated from the Czech by Eve Merriam), Doubleday, 1970; *Micka z trafiky a kocour Pivoda* (title means "Pussy Cat from the Tobacconist's and Tomcat Pivoda"), Albatros (Prague), 1971; *Zviratka z celeho sveta* (title means "The Animals from the Whole World"), Albatros, 1971; *Kudy chodi maly lev* (title means "Where the Little Lion Walks"), Albatros, 1972; *Medvedi pohadky* (title means "The Bear Fairy Tales"), Albatros, 1973; *Ukradeny orloj* (title means "Rob of Astronomical Clock"), Materidouska (Prague), 1973; *Basama bernardyn a Vendulka* (title means "St. Bernard Dog Named Basama and a Girl Vendulka"), Orbis (Prague), 1973; *Zviratka z lesa* (title means "The Animals from the Wood"), Albatros, 1974; *Drak Barborak a Ztraceny kral Kulajda* (title means "Dragon Barborak and the Lost King Kulajda"), Albatros, 1974; *Posledniho kousne pes: A dalsich ctyriadvacet prislovi v pohadkach* (title means "The Last Will Be Bitten by the Dog: Proverbial Fairy Tales"), Albatros, 1974.

Writer of juvenile television scripts, 1963-73, animated cartoons, 1969-71, and of a puppet play. Member of editorial council, *Materidouska* (children's monthly), 1966-72.

* * *

DOUGHERTY, Betty 1922-
(Elisabeth Mount)

PERSONAL: Born March 14, 1922, in London, England; daughter of Ernest Frederick (a print manager) and Eleanor (Lynch) Dougherty. *Education:* Attended Ealing School of Art, 1939-42; Hornsey School of Art, art teacher's diploma, 1943. *Home:* Mount Pleasant, Wades Lane, Lower Raydon, Ipswich 1P7 5QW, England. *Office:* Design Council, 28 Haymarket, London SW1Y 4SU, England.

CAREER: Sylvan Press, London, England, art director, 1943-45; free-lance graphic designer, 1945-50; Corinthian Press, London, art director, 1950-52; free-lance graphic designer in London, 1952-56; Design Council, London, art director, 1956—. Teacher of art, craft, and design, 1942-57; adviser to publications panel of Disabled Living Fund. *Member:* Society of Industrial Artists and Designers (fellow).

WRITINGS: Your Leatherwork, Sylvan Press, 1942; *Your Linocraft,* Sylvan Press, 1945; *Green Gardener: Creating a Wild Garden,* David & Charles, 1975. Editor of series "Your Home Crafts," Sylvan Press, 1942-50. Contributor of article, under pseudonym Elisabeth Mount, to *Lady* (magazine).

WORK IN PROGRESS: Grey Gardener: Gardening Gracefully into Old Age.

SIDELIGHTS: Betty Dougherty writes: "*Green Gardener* was entirely a product of 'escapism' from busy city life to calm country living. 'Before and after' photography was extensive and a diary was kept—all source material for this book. Nearly broke my back getting the garden to rights, so *Grey Gardener* is obvious sequel—how *not* to break your back!"

* * *

DOWNES, Randolph C(handler) 1901-1975

July 26, 1901—July 14, 1975; American educator, historian, author of books in his field. Obituaries: *New York Times,* August 1, 1975. (See index for previous *CA* sketch)

DRACHLER, Jacob 1909-

PERSONAL: Born April 4, 1909, in Brooklyn, N.Y.; son of Samuel (a carpenter) and Sarah Drachler; married Rose Kaplowitz (a poet), June 27, 1932; children: Nina (Mrs. Michael Riback). *Education:* New York University, B.S., 1929, M.A., 1934; Brooklyn Museum Art School, further graduate study, 1949-52. *Religion:* Jewish. *Home:* 3814 Maple Ave., Brooklyn, N.Y. 11224.

CAREER: High school English teacher in New York, N.Y., 1931-67; writer and painter, 1947—. *Military service:* U.S. Army Air Forces, 1942-45; became sergeant. *Member:* African Studies Association, West Broadway Gallery (artists cooperative).

WRITINGS: (Editor) *African Heritage,* Macmillan, 1963; (editor with Virginia Terris) *The Many Worlds of Poetry,* Knopf, 1969; (editor) *Black Homeland: Black Diaspora* (anthology), Kennikat, 1975. Contributor to *Midstream.*

WORK IN PROGRESS: Editing *First Person African: Autobiography as a Mirror of Change in Africa.*

SIDELIGHTS: Drachler writes: "During the last twenty years of my teaching career I pursued a concurrent major commitment to painting and sculpture which since 1967 has been virtually my full-time concern." His paintings are shown at the West Broadway Gallery.

* * *

DRACHMAN, Julian M(oses) 1894-
(Ben Adam; Melanie Goodall; Octopus)

PERSONAL: Born February 17, 1894, in New York; son of Bernard (a rabbi) and Sarah (Weil) Drachman; married Emily Deitchman (a teacher), May 1, 1927 (died November 12, 1967); children: Richard J., David A., Daniel B. *Education:* City College (now of the City University of New York), B.S., 1915; Columbia University, M.A., 1916, Ph.D., 1930. *Politics:* Liberal. *Religion:* Jewish. *Home and office:* 225 East 57th St., New York, N.Y. 10022.

CAREER: High school English teacher in New York, N.Y., 1919-20, Bronx, N.Y., 1921-36, and head of department in Brooklyn, N.Y., 1936-62; New School for Social Research, New York, N.Y., lecturer in English, 1961-64; writer, 1964—. Lecturer at City College of the City University of New York, summers, 1959-64; educational curriculum consultant, 1964-67; Camp counselor at Surprise Lake Camp, 1919-20, head counselor at Camp Tabor, 1944, 1945. *Military service:* U.S. Army, Medical Department, 1918-19; became sergeant.

MEMBER: English Graduate Union, Poetry Society of America, Jewish Teachers Association (president, 1945-46), Jewish Teachers Community Chest (member of board of governors, 1945—), New York Association of Chairmen, New York City Association of Chairmen of English (president, 1960-61), Menorah Alumni (president, 1925-30). *Awards, honors:* Award from Montreal Jewish Community Drama Guild, 1955, for short play "The Slave of God's Servant."

WRITINGS: Studies in the Literature of Natural Science, Macmillan, 1930; *Spelling for Secondary Schools* (revised edition; Drachman was not associated with original edition by Harry M. Love), Globe Book Co., 1941; *Making Friends with Words,* Globe Book Co., 1956; *Just Now for Instance* (poems), Stinehour Press, 1969. Contributor of satire and light verse, sometimes under pseudonyms, to periodicals. Editorial writer for *Brooklyn Jewish Examiner,* 1948-49. Editor of *Young Judean,* 1920.

WORK IN PROGRESS: Actual Teaching in the Large Modern High School; Chain Reaction, poems; *Grandpa and the Goat,* a book of essays.

SIDELIGHTS: Drachman writes: "The book on natural science was intended to encourage writers on scientific subjects to try to win readers by striving for literary quality."

*   *   *

DRAKE, Alice Hutchins 1889(?)-1975

1889(?)—February 6, 1975; American researcher, radio lecturer on the arts, and writer of devotional material. Obituaries: *Washington Post,* February 10, 1975.

*   *   *

DRIMMER, Frederick 1916-

PERSONAL: Born August 8, 1916, in Brooklyn, N.Y.; son of John (a restaurant owner) and Mina (Lichtenberg) Drimmer; married Evelyn Laderman (a librarian), August 24, 1940; children: John Andrew, Jean Louisa. *Education:* City College (now of the City University of New York), B.A. (magna cum laude), 1938; Columbia University, M.A., 1940; New School for Social Research, further graduate study, 1947-48. *Home:* 281 Grumman Ave., Norwalk, Conn. 06851.

CAREER: Greenberg (publishing house), New York, N.Y., editor-in-chief, 1940-46; Greystone Press, New York, N.Y., editor-in-chief, 1946-56; Famous Artists School, Inc., Westport, Conn., editor-in-chief, 1956-72; *Funk and Wagnalls Encyclopedia,* New York, N.Y., writer and editor, 1974—. Instructor in English at City College of City University of New York, 1946-47, and at Norwalk Community College, 1966-67. *Military service:* U.S. Naval Reserve, 1943-46; became ensign. *Member:* Phi Beta Kappa.

WRITINGS: (Editor) *The Knapsack Book* (anthology), Greenberg, 1942; (contributor) *Complete Book of Mothercraft,* Greystone, 1952; (editor) *The Animal Kingdom,* three volumes, Greystone, 1953; (editor) *Scalps and Tomahawks* (nonfiction), Coward McCann, 1961; *Very Special People: The Struggles, Loves, and Triumphs of Human Oddities* (nonfiction), Crown, 1973, revised edition, Bantam, 1976; *In Search of Eden* (nonfiction), C. R. Gibson, 1973; *Daughters of Eve* (nonfiction), C. R. Gibson, 1975; (editor) *A Friend Is Someone Special* (anthology), C. R. Gibson, 1975; (contributor) Stephen Rosen, editor, *Future Facts,* Simon & Schuster, 1975. Contributor to *People's Encyclopedia, Reader's Digest Family Health Guide,* and *Reader's Digest "You and the Law."*

WORK IN PROGRESS: Research for a biography of Tom Thumb.

AVOCATIONAL INTERESTS: Travel.

BIOGRAPHICAL/CRITICAL SOURCES: Bridgeport Sunday Post, November 24, 1974.

*   *   *

DRISCOLL, Gertrude 1898(?)-1975

1898(?)—September 11, 1975; American educator, child psychologist, and author of books in her field. Obituaries: *New York Times,* September 12, 1975.

*   *   *

DRUCKER, Peter F(erdinand) 1909-

PERSONAL: Born November 19, 1909, in Vienna, Austria; came to the United States in 1937, naturalized citizen, 1943; son of Adolph Bertram (a lawyer and professor) and Caroline Drucker; married Doris Schmitz, January 15, 1937; children: Kathleen, Vincent, Cecily, Joan. *Education:* Studied at University of Hamburg, 1927-28; University of Frankfurt, LL.D., 1931. *Home:* 636 Wellesley Dr., Claremont, Calif. 91711. *Office:* Claremont Graduate School, Claremont, Calif.

CAREER: General Anzeiger (daily newspaper), Frankfurt, Germany, staff member, 1929-31, foreign and finance editor, 1931-33; economist for international banking house, London, England, 1933-36; American adviser to group of British banks and investment trusts, 1937; American correspondent for several British newspapers, 1939-41; independent private consultant to business and industry, 1940—. Professor of economics at Sarah Lawrence College, 1940-42; professor of philosophy and politics at Bennington College, 1942-49; New York University, professor of management, 1950-72, distinguished university lecturer, 1972-76, professor emeritus, 1976—; Clarke Professor of Social Science and Management at Claremont Graduate School, 1971—.

MEMBER: International Academy of Management (fellow), American Association for the Advancement of Science (fellow; council member, 1967-68), American Academy of Management (fellow), Society for the History of Technology (first vice-president; president, 1965-66). *Awards, honors:* Nine honorary degrees from colleges and universities in Belgium, England, Japan, Switzerland, and the United States; Wallace Clark International Management medal, 1963; Order of the Sacred Treasure, Japan, 1964; Taylor Key from Society for the Advancement of Management, 1967; Presidential citation from New York University, 1969; gold medal from International Management Congress, 1972; other awards from American Marketing Association, American College of Hospital Administration, Italian Management Association, International University for Social Studies (Rome), and Assumption University (Windsor, Ontario).

WRITINGS: Die Rechtfertigung des Voelkerrechts aus dem Staatswillen: Eine logisch-kritische Untersuchung der Selbstverpflichtungs-und Vereinbahrungslehre (title means "The Foundation of International Law in Governmental Commitment"), F. Vahlen (Berlin), 1932; *Friedrich Julius Stahl: Konservative Staatslehre und geschichtliche Entwicklung* (title means "Friedrich Julius Stahl: Conservative Political Theory and Historical Development"), Mohr (Tuebingen), 1933; *The End of Economic Man: A Study of the New Totalitarianism,* John Day, 1939.

The Future of Industrial Man: A Conservative Approach, John Day, 1942, new edition, New American Library, 1965; *Concept of the Corporation,* John Day, 1946, revised edition, 1972.

The New Society: The Anatomy of the Industrial Order, Harper, 1950; *The Practice of Management,* Harper, 1954; *America's Next Twenty Years,* Harper, 1957; *Landmarks of Tomorrow,* Harper, 1959; *Managing for Results: Economic Tasks and Risk-Taking Decisions,* Harper, 1964; *The Effective Executive,* Harper, 1967; *The Age of Discontinuity: Guidelines to Our Changing Society,* Harper, 1969; *Technology, Management, and Society* (essays), Harper, 1970; *Men, Ideas, and Politics* (essays), Harper, 1971; *Management: Tasks, Responsibilities, Practices,* edited by Cass Canfield, Jr., Harper, 1974.

Educational films: "The Effective Executive" and "The Age of Discontinuity," both based on own works.

Contributor to periodicals, including *Harper's, Wall Street Journal, New York Times,* and *Public Interest.*

WORK IN PROGRESS: A book on how pension fund socialism came to America, for Harper.

SIDELIGHTS: Drucker's books have also been published in Portuguese, French, Italian, Japanese, Chinese, German, and fifteen other European and Asiatic languages. *Avocational interests:* Mountaineering, classical Japanese art.

* * *

DUDLEY, Ruth H(ubbell) 1905-

PERSONAL: Born May 14, 1905, in Champlain, N.Y.; daughter of Edward M. and Maude (Hubbell) Dudley. *Education:* Northwestern University, B.S., 1928; Columbia University, graduate study, 1928-29. *Home:* 13560 St. Andrews Dr., #3L, Seal Beach, Calif. 90740.

CAREER: *Oak Park Pictorial News,* Oak Park, Ill., society editor, 1929-30; Sears, Roebuck Co., Chicago, Ill., in sales promotion, 1930-32; Montgomery Ward & Co., Chicago, in sales promotion, 1932-34; Calpro Sales Co., Beverly Hills, Calif., in sales promotion, 1934-38; Perfection Bakery, Santa Monica, Calif., in sales promotion, 1938-40; Douglas Aircraft, Santa Monica, in sales promotion, 1941-45; realtor, 1945-50; free-lance writer and photographer, 1950—.

MEMBER: National Audubon Society, Save the Redwoods League, National Wildlife Federation, Wilderness Society, Save the Children Federation, Sierra Club, National Writers Club, Leisure Whirlers Square Dance Club, Whirler Girls Exhibition Group, Zeta Tau Alpha, Delta Kappa Gamma.

WRITINGS—Juveniles, except as noted: *Hank and the Kitten,* Morrow, 1947; *Sea Shells,* Crowell, 1953; *Good Citizens, Good Neighbors,* Melmont, 1953; *At the Museum,* Melmont, 1956; *My Hobby Is Collecting Seashells and Coral* (young adult), Childrens Press, 1955; *Our American Trees,* Crowell, 1956; *Tip Top Wish,* Crowell, 1958; *Favorite Trees of Desert, Mountain, and Plain* (young adult), Funk, 1963; *Partners in Nature* (young adult), Funk, 1965. Contributor of articles and photographs to popular magazines, including nature and sport magazines, and *Child Life.*

SIDELIGHTS: Ruth Dudley writes: "I was born and raised in the beautiful region of Lake Champlain, N.Y. and the Adirondacks. My mother, especially, was a great nature lover and I guess it rubbed off on me. We spent many summers camping on Lake Champlain, fishing, boating, swimming, and enjoying nature. . . . I hoped, in writing my various books and articles on nature, to inspire a greater understanding and appreciation of nature in our small fry, teen-agers, and young adult—the leaders of tomorrow, so they will conserve and enjoy, not destroy."

AVOCATIONAL INTERESTS: Hiking, bicycling, camping, shelling, ceramics, flora and fauna of desert, mountains and seashore, birds, cats, photography, square dancing, "my neices and nephews," travel (to southern Europe, Alaska, and the Caribbean).

* * *

DUNCAN, Alistair (Charteris) 1927-

PERSONAL: Born October 10, 1927, in Shillong, India; son of Robert Hugh Charteris and Alison Park (Forbes) Duncan; married Mariana Harvey-Kelly, June 16, 1961. *Education:* Attended Marlborough College, 1941-45. *Home and office:* 56A Oakwood Ct., London W.14, England.

CAREER: British Army, officer in Seaforth Highlanders, 1945-48, and Special Air Service Regiment, 1949-58, leaving service as captain; Lloyds Ltd., London, England, insurance broker, 1948-61; Middle East Archive (for written material and photographs emphasizing historic, religious, and educational aspects of the Middle East), London, England, founder and owner, 1961—. Writer and photographer. Administrator of World of Islam Festival, 1975-76. *Member:* Royal Institute for International Affairs, Royal Society for Asian Affairs, British Museum Society, Guild of Travel Writers, Anglo-Arab Association, Council for the Advancement of Arab-British Understanding, Traveller's Club, Special Forces Club.

WRITINGS: *Land of the Rock* (juvenile), Burns & Oates, 1966; *The Noble Sanctuary,* Longmans, 1972; *The Noble Heritage,* Longmans, 1975. Contributor to Middle East journals.

WORK IN PROGRESS: *The Noble Concept.*

SIDELIGHTS: Duncan has traveled extensively through the Arab world. He writes that his continuing objective is "to contribute in some small measure to the furtherance of true understanding and cultural appreciation between East and West."

* * *

DUNN, Halbert Louis 1896-1975

May 17, 1896—November 14, 1975; American statistician, consultant to and head of government agencies, physician, author of books on health. Obituaries: *Washington Post,* November 18, 1975.

* * *

DUNN, Mary Lois 1930-

PERSONAL: Born August 18, 1930, in Uvalde, Tex.; daughter of F. S. (a railroad signal maintainer) and Ruth Alice (Hawkes) Dunn. *Education:* Stephen F. Austin State College (now Stephen F. Austin University), B.A., 1951; Louisiana State University, M.S. in L.S., 1957. *Politics:* "Presently Republican—vote for the man, not the party." *Religion:* Southern Baptist. *Home:* 7555 Katy Freeway, No. 154, Houston, Tex. 77024.

CAREER: Houston Independent School District, Houston, Tex., librarian, 1951—. *Member:* American Library Association, Texas Library Association, Houston Association of School Librarians. *Awards, honors:* Sequoyah Children's Book Award of Oklahoma (determined by vote of children in grades four through nine), 1972, for *The Man in the Box: A Story from Vietnam.*

WRITINGS: *The Man in the Box: A Story from Vietnam,* McGraw, 1968.

WORK IN PROGRESS: A horse story and a book on motorcycles, both for young people.

* * *

DUNTON, Samuel Cady 1910(?)-1975

1910(?)—January 30, 1975; American animal photographer, filmmaker, and author. Obituaries: *New York Times,* February 1, 1976.

DURAND, John Dana   1913-

PERSONAL: Born July 24, 1913, in Washington, D.C.; son of Walter Yale (a teacher and economist) and Sara (Watson) Durand; married Dorothy Martin, February 21, 1942; children: Mark. *Education:* Attended George Washington University, 1929-30, University of North Carolina, 1930-31; Cornell University, A.B., 1933; Princeton University, Ph.D., 1939. *Office:* Population Studies Center, University of Pennsylvania, 3718 Locust Walk, Philadelphia, Pa. 19174.

CAREER: U.S. Bureau of the Census, Washington, D.C., demographer, 1933-36, 1939-47; United Nations, Population Division, New York, N.Y., demographer, 1948-65; University of Pennsylvania, Philadelphia, professor of economics and sociology, 1965—. *Member:* Population Association of America (former president), International Union for Scientific Study of Population, American Statistical Association (fellow; former member of board of directors).

WRITINGS: The Labor Force in the United States, 1890-1960, Social Science Research Council, 1948, reprinted, Gordon and Breach, 1972; *The Labor Force in Economic Development,* Princeton University Press, 1975. Contributor of articles to journals in his field, including *Population Studies, American Journal of Sociology, Proceedings of the American Philosophical Society, Annals of the American Academy of Political and Social Science.*

WORK IN PROGRESS: Research in world demographic history.

* * *

DUTTA, Reginald   1914-
(Rex Dutta)

PERSONAL: Born July 11, 1914, in Lahore, India; son of L. M. (a barrister) and Marguerite (Berghe) Dutta; married Olive Parton-Old, November 8, 1944. *Education:* University of London, B.A. (first class honors), 1937. *Politics:* None. *Religion:* None. *Home:* 49 Blandford St., London W1 3AF, England. *Office:* Fish Tanks Ltd., 49 Blandford St., London W1 H3AF, England.

CAREER: Selfridges Ltd., London, England, manager of tropical aquarium and of aquarium department, 1937-39, merchandise controller, 1940-45; Fish Tanks Ltd. (London's oldest established tropical fish specialists), London, England, managing director, 1945—. Has broadcast on television programs in England, Europe, Canada, the United States, and South Africa. *Military service:* British Army; Territorial Army Reserve, 1938; Army Intelligence, 1939-40; wounded at Dunkirk. *Member:* Zoological Society (fellow), Theosophical Society (member of national executive committee, 1961-70), University of London Union Society (life member).

WRITINGS: The Right Way to Keep Pet Fish, Elliot Books, 1951, 7th edition, 1973, Gramercy, 1974; *Tropical Fish and Fish Tanks,* Collins, 1965; *Encyclopaedia of Tropical Fish,* Pelham Books, 1966; *Manual for Fish Tank Owners,* Pelham Books, 1969; *Beginner's Guide to Tropical Fish and Fish Tanks,* Pelham Books, 1971, revised edition, 1975, Fell, 1975; *Tropical Fish,* Octopus Books, 1972; *Aquascape,* Walter Parish International, in press.

Under nickname Rex Dutta: *Flying Saucer Viewpoint,* Pelham Books, 1970; *Flying Saucer Message,* Pelham Books, 1972; *The Reality of the Occult/Yoga/ Meditation/Flying Saucers,* Pelham Books, 1974. Director of *Flying Saucer Review,* 1955-63, and *Viewpoint Aquarius* (research magazine), 1970—.

WORK IN PROGRESS: Occult Law, to explain how thought power can produce physical results.

SIDELIGHTS: Dutta has conducted research on and has practiced yoga, meditation, and the occult since 1953; he has taught seminars and held lectures internationally. He writes that he is "now seeking to detail the connecting links between the originating thought-impulse and the step by step densification through thought/feelings/etheric until a dense physical result precipitates." He is conducting similar research in the area of psychokinetics, "based on the sevenfold nature of Humanity."

* * *

DUVEEN, Geoffrey   1883-1975

July 4, 1883—November 15, 1975; British barrister, writer on stamps and coins. Obituaries: *AB Bookman's Weekly,* January 5, 1976.

* * *

DUY, Pham   1927-

PERSONAL: Name is pronounced Fam Zooey; born October 5, 1927, in Hanoi, Vietnam; son of Pham Duy Ton (a novelist) and Nguyen Thi Hoa (a poetess); married Pham Thi Thai Hang (a singer), November, 1949; children: Quang, Minh, Hung, Cuong, Thai Hien, Thai Thao, Duc, Thai Hanh. *Education:* Attended School of Art, Hanoi, Vietnam, 1940-41, and Institute of Musicology, Paris, France, 1954-55. *Home:* 400 Nebraska Ave., Fort Walton Beach, Fla. 32548.

CAREER: Conservatory of Music, Saigon, Vietnam, professor of music, 1959-61; Motion Picture Center, Saigon, musician, script writer, movie director, and deputy director, 1963-67; THVN-TV, Saigon, deputy director, 1967-69, program director, 1967-69.

WRITINGS: Musics of Vietnam, edited by Dale R. Whiteside, Southern Illinois University Press, 1975. Author of more than 600 songs in 20 songbooks. Writer, producer and director of more than twenty motion pictures in Vietnam.

WORK IN PROGRESS: An English version of his songs in a "Vietnamerican" songbook.

SIDELIGHTS: Pham Duy came to the United States as a refugee in 1975. He has already given concerts with his wife, and daughter, Thai Hien, all over the United States.

* * *

DVORNIK, Francis   1893-1975

August 4, 1893—November 4, 1975; Czechoslovakian-born American educator, priest, historian and author of books on political and ecclesial history. Obituaries: *New York Times,* November 8, 1975; *Washington Post,* November 10, 1975; *AB Bookman's Weekly,* January 5, 1976. (See index for previous *CA* sketch)

* * *

DYER, Beverly   1921-

PERSONAL: Born April 19, 1921, in Johnstown, Colo.; daughter of Kenneth (a pharmacist) and Priscilla (Eddy) Lloyd; married Louis Dyer (a free-lance movie publicist), August 10, 1941; children: Dion Gary, Dennis Louis, Deidre Ann. *Education:* Attended Colorado State College of Education, 1939-41; Long Beach State College, B.A., 1956; graduate study at University of Southern California and University of California, Los Angeles. *Politics:* Republican. *Religion:* Christian. *Home:* 2838 Onrado St., Torrance, Calif. 90503.

CAREER: Elementary school teacher in Hawthorne, Calif., 1948-53, and in Torrance, Calif., 1954-66. Has worked as piano teacher, church organist, and choir director. Member of Torrance Memorial Hospital Auxiliary. *Member:* Manuscripters, Retired Teachers Association, Amyotrophic Lateral Sclerosis Society, Torrance Education Association. *Member:* American Association of University Women, Republican Women's Club. *Awards, honors:* First prize from Manuscripters, 1972, for short story "No One to Care."

WRITINGS: God Took My Hand, Judson, 1975.

WORK IN PROGRESS: A spy novel; religious history; a gothic novel; five children's mystery books.

SIDELIGHTS: Beverly Dyer writes: ". . . I wanted to be a writer and decided I didn't have a chance. Though I continued to write for my own pleasure I made no attempt to sell during the years that I taught school and raised three children. I broke my neck in an automobile accident in Europe, and spent the next two years in hospitals. During my surgeries . . . I diverted myself with plotting and writing juvenile mystery books. . . . I always wanted to write about the beauty of this world and the things that make life worthwhile. The poetry and philosophical thoughts I wrote for so many years now provide backgrounds for my stories and books. I want to help those who are depressed and discouraged to find the moral goodness that is here on earth. Today in our liberal society I think there is more need for it than ever before." *Avocational interests:* International travel.

* * *

DYROFF, Jan Michael 1942-

PERSONAL: Born August 7, 1942, in Fort Bragg, N.C.; son of John William (a civil servant) and Dorothy Marie (a florist; maiden name, Rutter) Dyroff; married Sharon Dawn Fishbein, May 20, 1973; children: Kerry, Dale. *Education:* Villanova University, A.B., 1964; Boston University, A.M., 1965, Ph.D., 1972. *Residence:* Brighton, Mass.

CAREER: Director of creative writing program at private school in Arlington Heights, Mass., 1968-70; Boston University, Boston, Mass., lecturer in English and associate director of English language program, 1969-70; Lakehead University, Thunder Bay, Ontario, assistant professor of English, 1970-73; Boston University, lecturer in English, 1973-74; William Underwood Co., Westwood, Mass., communications specialist, 1974-75; Boston University, Center for English Language, seminar leader in the language of business, 1975; Massachusetts Occupational Information System, Inc., Wellesly Hills, evaluation specialist, 1976—. *Member:* Authors Guild, Authors League of America.

WRITINGS: The Poems of Rufinos, Books Canada, 1974; *Journies and Shows* (poems), Borealis Press, 1975.

Author of "The Flyting Match" (one-act play), first produced in Philadelphia, Pa. at Wynnewood Theatre, March 8, 1966. Contributor of stories, poems, and articles to literary journals and to *Coin Stamp Antique News.* Poetry editor of *Le Chronic,* 1968.

WORK IN PROGRESS: Research for articles on numismatic history; a new collection of poems.

EAGAR, Frances 1940-

PERSONAL: Born March 26, 1940, in London, England; daughter of Ronald (a surgeon) and Elinor (an archaeologist) Reid; married Michael Eagar (a teacher), September 6, 1963; children: Charlotte Elisabeth, Sophia Helen. *Education:* Studied at New Hall, Convent of the Holy Sepulchre, 1951-59, London College of Secretarial Studies, 1959-60, and Sorbonne, University of Paris, 1961-63. *Politics:* Left wing-liberal. *Religion:* Roman Catholic. *Home:* Ingram's Hall, Shrewsbury School, Shrewsbury, Shropshire, England.

CAREER: Teacher of French at Eton College Choir School, Eton, England, 1963-64, and Faulkner House School, London, England, 1964-65.

*WRITINGS—*All published by Hamish Hamilton: *The Little Sparrow,* 1972; *The Donkey Upstairs,* 1972; *The Tin Mine,* 1973; *The Dolphin of the Two Seas,* 1973; *Midnight Patrol,* 1974; *Cuckoo Clock Island,* 1974; *Timetangle,* in press.

WORK IN PROGRESS: A history of the Incas for Cambridge University Press "Topic" series; a novel set in Cornwall and Devon.

SIDELIGHTS: Mrs. Eagar writes: "I was born during the war, and evacuated to Scotland as Essex was in danger of being invaded. After the war (which I do not recall except the excitement of air raids in the middle of the night), we returned to Essex where I lived with my five brothers and sisters in a rambling old farm house that was mentioned in the *Domesday Book.* It was believed to be haunted, but if this was so the spirits felt very friendly to me. We had ponies, donkies, snakes, dormice, ducks, etc., in the house, and had a very free and independent childhood.

"My twin sister and I attended a convent boarding school where the nuns were great fun, and we thoroughly enjoyed being there. My mother was eccentric; on our holidays she used to take us searching Cornwall or Wales for the Excalibur. We greatly enjoyed these expeditions, regardless of the fruitlessness.

"After school I went to the Sorbonne where I lazed away the time, and on reflection found the hours spent sitting in sidewalk cafes to have been some of the most important times of my life in terms of development of thought. I married when the rain came through the soles of my best shoes, and have been happily married ever since.

"We have two little girls, two dogs, a cat and hamsters. My greatest relaxation is to watch waves, mill streams, waterfalls, or listen to jazz. I enjoy beachcombing, polishing pebbles, and making catamarans for gnomes out of flotsam and jetsam, then watching them sail away out of sight.

"I find childhood a time of particular clarity and enjoy observing things with the innocent eye of a child. Escapism? Nostalgia? In short, I write because I want to write."

* * *

EAKIN, Richard M(arshall) 1910-

PERSONAL: Surname is pronounced *Ay*-kin; born May 5, 1910, in Florence, Colo.; married Mary Mulford, August 8, 1935; children: David Marshall, Dorothy Alice. *Education:* University of Tulsa, student, 1927-29; University of California, Berkeley, A.B., 1931, Ph.D., 1935. *Religion:* Protestant. *Home:* 1627 Spruce, Berkeley, Calif. 94709. *Office:* Department of Zoology, University of California, Berkeley, Calif. 94720.

CAREER: University of California, Berkeley, assistant dean of College of Letters and Science, 1939-42, professor of zoology, 1949—, chairman of department, 1942-48 and 1952-57. Visiting professor at University of Washington, Seattle, summer, 1950; research professor at Miller Institute of University of California, 1961, 1970, chairman of executive committee of institute, 1961-67; lecturer at Smithsonian Institution, 1967. U.S. delegate to Seminar on Retina (Fukuoka, Japan), 1966. *Member:* Institut International d'Embryologie Utrecht (fellow), American Association for the Advancement of Science, American Society of Zoologists (president, 1975), American Society for Cell Biology, Electron Microscope Society of America, Western Society of Naturalists (president, 1949), California Academy of Sciences (fellow), Northern California Society for Electron Microscopy, Phi Beta Kappa, Sigma Xi. *Awards, honors:* National Research Council fellowship, Erlangen and Freiburg, Germany, 1935-36; Guggenheim fellowship, Stanford University, 1953; National Science Foundation senior postdoctoral fellowship, Bern, Switzerland, 1957.

WRITINGS: Vertebrate Embryology (laboratory manual), University of California Press, 1964, 2nd revised edition, 1971; *The Third Eye,* University of California Press, 1973; *Great Scientists Speak Again,* University of California Press, 1975. Contributor to professional journals. Associate editor of *Experimental Zoology,* 1967-70; member of editorial board of *Ultrastructure Research,* 1973—.

SIDELIGHTS: Eakin has made several motion pictures for University of California Media Center, including impersonations of Darwin, Harvey, Beaumont, Mandel, and Pasteur; these films have also been presented on the local educational television network.

*   *   *

ECKEL, Malcolm W(illiam) 1912-

PERSONAL: Born October 11, 1912, in East Orange, N.J.; son of Fred, Jr. (an architect and builder) and Edith (Madison) Eckel; married Mary Constance Winchester, June 3, 1945; children: Malcolm David, Mary Edith (Mrs. Frederick T. La Rochelle), Douglas Winchester, Mark Eugene, Matthew Edward. *Education:* Hobart College, B.A., 1938; Virginia Theological Seminary, B.D., 1941; Oxford University, B.Litt., 1950. *Politics:* Independent. *Home:* 80 Bellevue Ave., Springfield, Mass. 01108.

CAREER: Ordained deacon and priest of Episcopal Church, 1941; assistant rector of church in Stamford, N.Y., 1941; rector of church in Lebanon Springs, N.Y., 1941-43; Darrow School, New Lebanon, N.Y., chaplain, 1941-43, 1946-48, assistant headmaster, 1946-48; assistant vicar, St. Margaret's Church and chaplain, Lady Margaret Hall, Oxford, England, 1948-50; rector of churches in Saratoga Springs, N.Y., 1950-53, and Pittsfield, Mass., 1953-57; Christ Church Cathedral, Springfield, Mass., dean, 1968—. Vice-president of Diocesan Council of Western Massachusetts, and chairman of Board of Examining Chaplains. *Military service:* U.S. Navy, chaplain, 1943-46; became lieutenant.

WRITINGS: The Ethics of Decision Making, Morehouse, 1968.

*   *   *

ECKES, Alfred Edward, Jr. 1942-

PERSONAL: Born July 11, 1942, in North Conway, N.H.;

son of Alfred Edward and Virginia (Marshall) Eckes. *Education:* Washington and Lee University, B.A., 1964; Christ's College, Cambridge, graduate study, 1964-65; Fletcher School of Law and Diplomacy, M.A., 1966; University of Texas, Austin, Ph.D., 1969. *Office:* Department of History, Ohio State University, Columbus, Ohio 43210.

CAREER: Ohio State University, Columbus, assistant professor, 1969-75, associate professor of history, 1975—. Research assistant to U.S. Representative Samuel L. Devine, 1974—. *Member:* Phi Beta Kappa. *Awards, honors:* Fulbright fellowship, 1964-65; Woodrow Wilson fellowship, 1965-66.

WRITINGS: A Search for Solvency: Bretton Woods and the International Monetary System, 1941-1971, University of Texas Press, 1975. Author of news analysis column in *Columbus Dispatch,* 1971-74.

WORK IN PROGRESS: John W. Bricker: An Oral Biography; Competition for Raw Materials in Peace and War: 1915-1975, completion expected in 1978.

*   *   *

EDDISON, John 1916-

PERSONAL: Born September 7, 1916, in Derbyshire, England; son of Frederick William (a clergyman) and Dorothea (Buchanan-Dunlop) Eddison. *Education:* Trinity College, Cambridge, M.A., 1939. *Religion:* Church of England. *Home address:* Durham Lodge, Crowborough, Sussex, England.

CAREER: Curate, St. John's, Tunbridge Wells, England, 1939-43; Scripture Union, London, England, traveling secretary, 1943—. Honorary chaplain to Bishop of Rochester, 1947-59. Member of board of directors of school companies. *Member:* National Club, Marylebone Cricket Club.

WRITINGS—All published by Scripture Union: *Search Party,* 1960; *The Troubled Mind,* 1963, Concordia, 1972; *Christian Answers About Doctrine,* 1966; *Christian Answers to Contemporary Problems,* 1967; *Who Died Why,* 1970; *God's Frontiers,* 1972; *To Tell You the Truth,* 1972; *It's a Great Life,* 1973; *What Makes a Leader,* 1974.

*   *   *

EDDY, John 1932-

PERSONAL: Born January 18, 1932, in Glencoe, Minn.; son of Paul Lewis (a businessman) and Berneice (Greenslit) Eddy; married Elizabeth Ann Hobe, May 17, 1958; children: Mark, Mary, Matthew, Michael. *Education:* University of Minnesota, B.S., 1954; Garrett Theological Seminary, M.Div., 1959; Northwestern University, M.A., 1960; Southern Illinois University, Ph.D., 1968. *Home:* 2419 Simpson St., Evanston, Ill. 60201. *Agent:* Porter, Gould & Dierks, 1236 Sherman Ave., Evanston, Ill. 60202. *Office:* Loyola University of Chicago, 820 North Michigan Ave., Chicago, Ill. 60611.

CAREER: Ordained minister of United Methodist Church, 1960. Central Mindanao Colleges (now University), Musuan, Budkidnon, Philippines, instructor, 1954; worked for United Methodist Church, 1954-68; Johnson State College, Johnson, Vt., assistant professor and dean of students, 1968-69; New Mexico Institute of Mining and Technology, Socorro, professor of psychology and education, 1969-70; Loyola University of Chicago, Chicago, Ill., professor of guidance and counseling, 1970—. Instructor, Scarritt College for Christian Workers, and Mankato State College (now University), both 1961-65; visiting professor at Rust

College, 1963—; adjunct professor of education, University of Albuquerque, 1970. Member of board of trustees of Wesley Foundation, Mankato State College (now University), 1960-65. *Military service:* National Guard, 1964-65.

MEMBER: International Association of Educators for World Peace (world president, 1972-73; North and South American president, 1974-78), World Peace Academy (vice-president, 1974-75), Society for World Service Federation (vice-president, 1975-76), American Personnel and Guidance Association (peace commission chairperson). *Awards, honors:* Television citation from KEYC-TV, Mankato, Minn., 1965; distinguished service award from International Association of Educators for World Peace of Romania, 1974; World Citizen award from Society for World Service Federation, 1975; Peace Scholar award from World Peace Academy, 1975; Bicentennial Counselor award from Bicentennial Crusade for World Peace, 1975; World Peace Center award from Felician College, 1975; Asians for Unity award from Asians for Unity of Chicago, 1975; citation for humanitarian service from Society for World Service Federation, 1975.

WRITINGS: Education and Inquiry, Johnson State College, 1968; *Campus Religious Affairs,* Simon & Schuster, 1969; *Principles of Marketing,* Collier, 1972; *Action and Careers in a New Age,* American Personnel & Guidance Association, 1973; *The Teacher and the Drug Scene,* Phi Delta Kappa, 1973; *A Career Education Primer for Educators,* ERIC Press, 1975; *Peace Education and Human Relations Training,* Stipes, 1976. Contributor to twenty television scripts.

Member of editorial board, *Dialog on Campus,* 1968-70, *Science Activities,* 1969-76, *World Circulation Newsletter* (of International Association of Educators for World Peace), 1973-76, *International Educational Foundations Quarterly,* 1974-76, *Peace Progress,* 1975-78, *Peace Digest,* 1975-76, and *Journal of Peace Education,*

WORK IN PROGRESS: Research on career education in the schools and society, peace education in the schools and society, and drug education that saves people.

AVOCATIONAL INTERESTS: Travel, conservation.

* * *

EDDY, John Percy 1881-1975

May 19, 1881—July 10, 1975; British barrister, judge, lecturer, author. Obituaries: *AB Bookman's Weekly,* August 25, 1975.

* * *

EDELMAN, Lily (Judith) 1915-

PERSONAL: Born September 2, 1915, in San Francisco, Calif.; daughter of Morris and Rachel (Margolis) Podvidz; married Nathan Edelman, May 30, 1936; children: Jean Louise (deceased). *Education:* Hunter College (now Hunter College of the City University of New York), B.A., 1936; Columbia University, M.A., 1938, diploma in adult education from Teachers College, 1954. *Religion:* Jewish. *Home:* 560 Riverside Dr., New York, N.Y. 10027. *Office:* B'nai B'rith, 1640 Rhode Island Ave. N.W., Washington, D.C. 20036.

CAREER: East & West Assoc., New York City, education director, 1945-51; U.S. State Dept., New York City, free-lance writer and editor, 1952-53; National Academy for Adult Jewish Studies, New York City, executive secretary, 1954-57; B'nai B'rith, Washington, D.C., editorial asso-

ciate, 1957-61, director of department of adult education, 1961—. *Member:* B'nai B'rith Women, Adult Education Association, Maryland Association of Adult Education (board member), National Council on Adult Jewish Education, Jewish Book Council, Phi Beta Kappa.

WRITINGS: Mexican Mural Painters and Their Influence in the United States, Service Bureau for Intercultural Education, 1938; *Music in China and Japan: Classroom Material,* Service Bureau for Intercultural Education, 1940; *Japan in Story and Pictures,* Harcourt, 1953; *Hawaii, U.S.A.,* Nelson, 1954; *The Sukkah and the Big Wind* (juvenile), United Synagogue Commission on Jewish Education, 1956; *Israel: New People in An Old Land,* Nelson, 1958, revised edition, 1969, also published as *Modern Israel,* Wilshire, 1969.

(Editor) *Jewish Heritage Reader,* Taplinger, 1965; *Study Guide for Jewish Heritage Reader,* B'nai B'rith Adult Education, 1965; (editor) *Face to Face: A Primer in Dialogue,* B'nai B'rith Adult Education, 1967; (compiler with Goldie Adler) Morris Adler, *May I Have a Word with You?,* Crown, 1967; (translator from the French with author) Elie Wiesel, *A Beggar in Jerusalem,* Random House, 1970; (translator from the French with author) Elie Wiesel, *One Generation After,* Random House, 1970. Editor of "Jewish Heritage Classic Series." Editor, *Jewish Heritage,* 1961—; literary editor, *National Jewish Monthly,* 1970—.

* * *

EDELMAN, Maurice 1911-1975

March 2, 1911—December 14, 1975; British member of Parliament, journalist, author of political novels and nonfiction works. Obituaries: *New York Times,* December 15, 1975; *Time,* December 29, 1975; *AB Bookman's Weekly,* January 5, 1976; *Current Biography,* February, 1976.

* * *

EDELSTEIN, David S(imeon) 1913-

PERSONAL: Born January 19, 1913, in New York, N.Y.; son of William (a grocer) and Clara (Brener) Edelstein; married Frances Fisher (an English teacher), June 4, 1939; children: Helen (Mrs. Henry A. Freedman), Henry, Daniel. *Education:* City College of the City University of New York, B.A., 1932, graduate study, 1939; Columbia University, M.A., 1933, Ph.D., 1949; graduate study at Fordham University, 1936, Hunter College of the City University of New York, 1936, Oxford University, summer, 1937, New York University, 1943 and 1946-1947. *Politics:* Democrat. *Religion:* Jewish. *Home:* 84 Avondale Rd., Yonkers, N.Y. 10710. *Office:* Department of Education, Western Connecticut State College, 181 White St., Danbury, Conn. 06810.

CAREER: High school teacher of social studies in public schools in New York, N.Y., 1934-58, acting chairman of department, 1938-45, chairman of academic subjects, 1945-58; P.S. 13, Bronx, N.Y., junior principal, 1958; Countee Cullen All-Day Neighborhood School, Manhattan, N.Y., principal, 1958-67; Western Connecticut State College, Danbury, associate professor of education, 1967—. Lecturer at City University of New York, City College, 1946-67, and Hunter College, 1964-65, at Yeshiva University, 1960-61, and at University of Colorado, summer, 1961; adjunct professor at Fordham University, 1967-70, and at Lehman College of the City University of New York, 1970-75; in-service instructor for Stamford Board of Education,

1970-71. Social investigator for New York Department of Welfare, summer, 1938; assistant examiner on board of examiners, New York City Board of Education, 1948-76; field supervisor at federally-funded After School Study Centers, 1966-67. Member of school board of Temple Emanuel, 1951-57; chairman of school board of Genesis Hebrew Center, 1961-72, vice-president, 1968-72, president, 1972-74; vice-president of Solomon Schecter Day School, 1961-72; member of executive board of Taxpayers Organization of Northeast Yonkers, 1970—; member of Harlem Neighborhoods Association, 1951-58, and Hutchinson River Council, 1960—.

MEMBER: American Association of School Administrators, American Historical Association, American Printing History Association, American Association of University Professors, National Association of Elementary School Principals, National Council of Local Administrators of Vocational Education, Social Studies Council, Council of Chairmen of Academic Subjects, National Society for the Study of Education, National Urban League, National Association for the Advancement of Colored People, American Association for Ethiopian Jews, Boy Scouts of America, American Red Cross, Connecticut Education Association, New York State Association of Elementary School Principals, New York City Elementary School Principals Association (life member), National Travel Club, Wakefield Fusion Club (chairman of board, 1931-32), Phi Delta Kappa, Phi Alpha Theta.

WRITINGS: Joel Munsell: Printer and Antiquarian, Columbia University Press, 1949, new edition, AMS Press, 1968. Contributor to *Bibliographical Society of America Papers* and to journals.

SIDELIGHTS: Edelstein has travelled extensively in the United States, Canada, Mexico, South America, Europe, the Middle East, the Far East, Africa, and the Southwest Pacific including Australia and New Zealand.

* * *

EDEN, Alvin N(oam) 1926-

PERSONAL: Surname originally Edelstein; legally changed, 1946; born March 21, 1926, in Brooklyn, N.Y.; son of Emmanuel M. (an educator) and Rae (Taran) Edelstein; married Elaine Jaffe (an interior designer), November 20, 1952; children: Robert, Elizabeth. *Education:* Columbia University, B.A., 1948; Boston University, M.D., 1952. *Agent:* Emilie Jackson, Curtis Brown Ltd., 60 East 56th St., New York, N.Y. 10022. *Office:* 107-21 Queens Blvd., Forest Hills, N.Y. 11375.

CAREER: Bellevue Hospital, New York City, intern, 1952-53, resident in pediatrics in University Hospital-Bellevue Medical Center, 1953-55; private practice in pediatrics in Forest Hills, N.Y., 1955—. Diplomate of American Board of Pediatrics; director of department of pediatrics at Wyckoff Heights Hospital, 1958—; New York University Medical Center, instructor, 1955-60, assistant professor, 1960-68, associate professor, 1968—. *Military service:* U.S. Navy, Hospital Corps, 1944-46.

MEMBER: Pan-American Medical Association, American Medical Association, American Academy of Pediatrics (fellow), Leo Taran Foundation (vice-president), New York Pediatric Society, Queens Pediatric Society (past president).

WRITINGS: (With Joan Rattner Heilman) *Growing Up Thin,* McKay, 1975. Author of "Visit with a Pediatrician,"

a monthly column in *American Baby,* 1973—. Contributor to medical journals for professionals and laymen.

WORK IN PROGRESS: A child care book; a book on adolescent obesity.

* * *

EDLIN, Herbert Leeson 1913-

PERSONAL: Born January 29, 1913, in Manchester, England; son of Herbert Ebenezer (a doctor) and Nellie (Leeson) Edlin; married Betty Margaret Pritchard, June 11, 1941; children: two sons. *Education:* University of Edinburgh, B.Sc., 1933; Oxford University, Dip.For., 1934. *Home:* 15 Howard Rd., Coulsdon, Surrey, England.

CAREER: Tropical agriculturist in Malaysia, 1935-40; Forestry Commission of Great Britain, London and Edinburgh, district officer at New Forest, Hampshire, England, 1940-45, publications officer, 1945—. Extra-mural lecturer in conservation at University of London, 1950—.

WRITINGS: British Woodland Trees, Batsford, 1944, 2nd edition, revised, 1945; *Forestry and Woodland Life,* Batsford, 1947; *Woodland Crafts in Britain: An Account of the Traditional Uses of Trees and Timbers in the British Countryside,* Batsford, 1949, 2nd edition, David & Charles, 1973; *British Plants,* Batsford, 1951; *The Changing Wild Life of Britain,* Batsford, 1952; *The Forester's Handbook,* Thames & Hudson, 1953; (with Maurice Nimmo) *Tree Injuries: Their Causes and Their Prevention,* Thames & Hudson, 1956; (with Nimmo) *Treasury of Trees,* Countrygoer Books, 1956; *Trees, Woods and Man,* Collins, 1956, 3rd edition, 1970; *England's Forests: A Survey of the Woodlands Old and New in the English and Welsh Counties,* Faber, 1958; *The Living Forest,* Thames & Hudson, 1958.

Wild Life of Wood and Forest, Hutchinson, 1960; *Wayside and Woodland Trees,* Warne, 1964; *Forestry,* R. Hale, 1966; *Man and Plants,* Aldus Books, 1967, published as *Plants and Man: The Story of our Basic Food,* Natural History Press, 1969; *What Wood Is That? A Manual of Wood Identification,* Viking, 1969; *Collins Guide to Tree Planting and Cultivation,* Collins, 1970; *The Public Park,* Routledge & Kegan Paul, 1971; *Atlas of Plant Life,* John Day, 1973; *Trees and Timbers,* Routledge & Kegan Paul, 1973; (with Nimmo) *The World of Trees,* Orbis, 1974; *The Observer's Book of Trees,* Warne, 1975; *The Natural History of Trees,* Weidenfeld & Nicolson, in press; *The Tree-lover's Key,* Warne, in press.

Author or editor of numerous booklets for the Forestry Commission of Great Britain. Contributor to the *Encyclopaedia Britannica,* and to journals such as *Forestry, Quarterly Journal of Forestry, Scottish Forestry, Commonwealth Forestry Review,* and *The Young Farmer.*

SIDELIGHTS: The Tree-lover's Key is planned as a transatlantic identification book, featuring American trees planted in Europe, and European trees naturalized in America. *Avocational interests:* Mountaineering, wandering in wild places, swimming in rough seas; photographing all these.

* * *

EDWARDS, Anne 1927-

PERSONAL: Born August 20, 1927, in Portchester, N.Y.; daughter of Milton (a salesman) and Marian (Fish) Josephson; married Harvey Wishner (divorced); married Leon Sangamore Becker (divorced); children: Michael

Edwards, Catherine Edwards. *Education:* Attended University of California, Los Angeles, 1943-46, and Southern Methodist University, 1947-48. *Residence:* New York, N.Y. *Agent:* International Creative Management, 40 West 57th St., New York, N.Y. 10019.

CAREER: Author. Lived in Europe for 16 years.

WRITINGS: A Child's Bible, Golden Books, 1967; *The Survivors,* Holt, 1968; *Miklos Alexandrovitch Is Missing,* Coward, 1970; *Shadow of a Lion,* Coward, 1971; *Haunted Summer,* Coward, 1972; *The Hesitant Heart,* Random House, 1973; *Child of Night,* Random House, 1975; *Judy Gurland: A Biography,* Simon & Schuster, 1975; (with Stephen Citron) *The Inn and Us,* Random House, 1976; *Vivian Leigh: A Biography,* Simon & Schuster, 1976; *The Great Houdini,* Putnam, 1976. Writer of scripts for television and of screenplays, "Quantez," released by Universal Pictures, 1957, and "A Question of Adultery," filmed in Britain, 1959; adaptor of screenplays, "The Steps," 1965, and "Funny Girl," with Sidney Buchman, 1967. Contributor of stories and articles to *Harper's, McCalls, Cosmopolitan,* and *Femina.*

WORK IN PROGRESS: Westward: The New World, the story of the Mayflower crossing.

* * *

EDWARDS, Clifford D(uane) 1934-

PERSONAL: Born January 20, 1934, in Atwood, Kan.; son of Murray Frank and Maude (Ray) Edwards; married Neva LouAnn Morgan, August 28, 1954; children: Mark Duane, Marilyn Morgan, Cecily Morgan. *Education:* Ft. Hays Kansas State College, A.B., 1958; University of Michigan, A.M., 1959, Ed.D., 1963. *Home:* 2725 Willow, Hays, Kan. 67601. *Office:* Department of English, Fort Hays Kansas State College, Hays, Kan. 67601.

CAREER: Fort Hays Kansas State College, Hays, Kans., associate professor of English, 1963-69; University of Wisconsin, Platteville, professor of English and chairman of department of English, 1969-74; Fort Hays Kansas State College, professor of English and director of composition, 1974—. *Military service:* U.S. Air Force, 1951-55. *Member:* Modern Language Association of America, Midwest Modern Language Association, National Council of Teachers of English, Phi Kappa Phi. *Awards, honors:* Woodrow Wilson fellow, 1958-59; Danforth associate, 1966—.

WRITINGS: Conrad Richter's Ohio Trilogy: Its Ideas, Themes, and Relationship to Literary Tradition, Mouton & Co., 1970.

* * *

EDWARDS, Elwyn Hartley 1927-
(Edward Leyhart)

PERSONAL: Born April 17, 1927; son of Edward Hartley (an army officer) and May (Kent-Hartley) Edwards; married Mary Purnelle Hodgson; children: Sarah Elizabeth, Louise Mary. *Education:* Attended Indian Military Academy, 1944-45. *Religion:* Church of England. *Home:* Park Stud Cottage, Dedham, Essex, England. *Office: Riding* Magazine, 189 High Holborn, London W.C.1, England.

CAREER: British Army, Brigade of Ghurkas, major, 1945-56; Gibson Saddlery Co., Newmarket, England, director, 1956-64; IPC Magazine Division, London, editor of *Riding,* 1964—. *Member:* Institute of Journalists, British Horse Society, Welsh Pony and Cob Society, British Show

Jumping Association, Arab Horse Society, and other horse societies. *Awards, honors:* Military Cross.

WRITINGS: Saddlery, Country Life, 1963; *Horseman's Guide,* Hamlyn, 1969; *Owning a Pony,* Thomas Nelson, 1970; *From Paddock to Saddle,* Thomas Nelson, 1972; (editor) *Horse and Rider Review,* Ian Allan, 1973; (editor with Candida Geddes) *Complete Book of the Horse,* Ward, Lock, 1973, Arco, 1974; *Go Riding,* Hamlyn, 1975; *Horses and Ponies,* W. H. Allen, 1975. Editor of Thomas Nelson's "Horsemaster Series." Contributor to numerous animal periodicals. Editor of *Encyclopaedia of Riding* and *Problem Horses.*

WORK IN PROGRESS: Horses of the World, publication by Hamlyn expected in 1977, and *Essentials of Riding and Management,* publication by Ward, Lock expected in 1977.

* * *

EGAMI, Tomi 1899-

PERSONAL: Born November 19, 1899, in Japan; daughter of Yaichiro (a landowner) and Egami (Asa) Fujisaki; married Iwao Egami, August 10, 1920; children: Tanekazu. *Education:* Attended Tokyo Culinary College, 1923-26, L'Ecole de Cuisine le Cordon Bleu, Paris, graduate, 1929. *Religion:* Buddhist. *Home and office:* 21 Sanaicho Ichigaya, Shinjuku-ku, Tokyo, Japan.

CAREER: Egami Cooking School, Tokyo, Japan, president, 1930—; Egami Cooking Centre, Tokyo, president, 1967—; Laboratoire Egami, Tokyo, president, 1972—. *Member:* Japanese Cooking School Association (director, 1950-60), East Japan Cooking School Association. *Awards, honors:* Bronze medal from Frankfurt Book Fair, 1968, for *Typical Japanese Cooking.*

WRITINGS: Typical Japanese Cooking, translated by V. A. Mackenzie Skillman, Shibata Publishing (Tokyo), 1959, new edition translated by Noriko Palmer, 1971; *Rice Recipes from Around the World,* Kodansha International (Tokyo), 1966, 2nd edition, 1970; *The Oriental Cookbook,* Kodansha International, 1970 (published in England as *Oriental Cookery,* Ward, Lock, 1970). Also author of *Nihon ryori,* 1962. Regular contributor to periodicals in Japan.

* * *

EHRHART, W(illiam) D(aniel) 1948-

PERSONAL: Born September 30, 1948, in Roaring Spring, Pa.; son of John Harry (a minister) and Evelyn (a teacher; maiden name, Conti) Ehrhart. *Education:* Swarthmore College, B.A., 1973. *Politics:* "Peace and freedom through non-violent action." *Religion:* "Personal—no formal affiliation." *Home:* 114 North Sixth St., Perkasie, Pa. 18944.

CAREER: U.S. Merchant Marine, engineroom wiper, 1973-74; Panelrama, Inc., Havertown, Pa., warehouseman, 1974; Pennsylvania Department of Justice, Special Prosecutor's Office, Philadelphia, Pa., evidence custodian, 1974—. *Military service:* U.S. Marine Corps, 1966-69. *Awards, honors:* Three collegiate awards from Academy of American Poets, 1971, 1972, and 1973.

WRITINGS—Poetry: A Generation of Peace, New Voices Publishing, 1975; (editor with Jan Barry) *Demilitarized Zones,* East River Anthology, in press. Work represented in anthologies, *Winning Hearts and Minds,* First Casualty Press, 1972; *Listen: The War,* U.S. Air Force Academy Association of Graduates, 1974; *Front Lines,* Indochina Curriculum Group, 1975. Contributor of poetry to literary journals, including *New Letters, Small Press*

Review, Samisdat, Spafaswap, and others. Co-editor of *East River Anthology,* 1975—.

SIDELIGHTS: Ehrhart wrote *CA:* "My service in Vietnam became the touchstone to seeing through the myths that official America has come to cloak itself in both at home and abroad. I have become committed to the non-violent re-orientation of American policies, institutions, and attitudes in favor of *real* freedom and true justice for *all* Americans and an end to U.S. economic and military imperialism throughout the world. . . . None of this is to say that America is all bad, but simply that we have a long, long way to go before our Revolution is completed.

"I do not view my writing as a purely political tool; but inevitably, my political and social convictions have exerted a strong influence on my writing. Ideally, one tries to achieve a balance between the functional and the aesthetic."

*   *   *

EHRLICH, Anne Howland   1933-

PERSONAL: Born November 17, 1933, in Des Moines, Iowa; daughter of Winston D. and Virginia (Fitzhugh) Howland; married Paul Ralph Ehrlich (a population biologist), December 18, 1954; children: Lisa Marie. *Education:* Attended University of Kansas, 1952-55. *Home:* Stanford, Calif. 94305. *Office:* Department of Biological Sciences, Stanford University, Stanford, Calif. 94305.

CAREER: Stanford University, Stanford, Calif., research assistant and biological illustrator, 1959—.

WRITINGS: (With husband, Paul R. Ehrlich) *How to Know the Butterflies,* W. C. Brown, 1961; (illustrator) Paul R. Ehrlich and Richard W. Holm, *The Process of Evolution,* McGraw-Hill, 1963; (with P. R. Ehrlich) *Population, Resources, Environment: Issues in Human Ecology,* W. H. Freeman, 1970, 2nd edition, 1972; (with P. R. Ehrlich and John P. Holdren) *Human Ecology: Problems and Solutions,* W. H. Freeman, 1973; (with P. R. Ehrlich) *End of Affluence,* Ballantine, 1974; (with P. R. Ehrlich and Holdren) *World Science,* W. H. Freeman, in press. Contributor to *Compton Yearbook* and *Brittanica Book of the Year,* 1971. Contributor to scientific journals, and to *Saturday Review, American Naturalist, New York Times Magazine, Nature in Focus,* and other periodicals.

*   *   *

EISENBERG, Lee   1946-

PERSONAL: Born July 22, 1946, in Philadelphia, Pa.; son of George M. (a microbiologist) and Eve (Blonsky) Eisenberg. *Education:* University of Pennsylvania, A.B., 1968, M.A., 1970. *Residence:* New York, N.Y. *Office:* Esquire, 488 Madison Ave., New York, N.Y. 10022.

CAREER: Esquire (magazine), New York, N.Y., senior editor, 1974—. Lecturer at New York University, 1974—. *Member:* American Society of Magazine Editors.

WRITINGS: (With Tom Farrell) *Sneaky Feats,* Sheed, 1975. Contributor to popular magazines, including *Rolling Stone, New York Times Book Review,* and *National Review.*

WORK IN PROGRESS: A television special program on the year 1968.

*   *   *

EISENSTEIN, Sam(uel Abraham)   1932-

PERSONAL: Born May 18, 1932, in Bakersfield, Calif.;

married wife, name Bettyrae, 1959; children: David, Channa. *Education:* University of California, Los Angeles, B.A., 1954, M.A., 1959, Ph.D., 1965; Goddard College, M.A. (clinical psychology), 1975. *Home:* 3116 Lake Hollywood Dr., Los Angeles, Calif. 90068.

CAREER: Junior high school English teacher in Los Angeles, Calif., 1955-57; Los Angeles City College, Los Angeles, instructor, 1959-60, 1960-62, assistant professor of English, 1962-69; Pitzer College, Claremont, Calif., associate professor of English and creative writing and chairman of department, 1969-72; Los Angeles City College, professor of English, 1972—. *Awards, honors:* Fulbright fellowship in Japan, 1965-66; grant from University of Minnesota's Office of Advanced Drama Research, 1971; Rockefeller grant, 1975-76.

WRITINGS: (With Harvey Cox) *The Art of Sister Mary Corita Kent,* Pilgrim Publications, 1968; *Boarding the Ship of Death: D. H. Lawrence's Quester Heroes,* Mouton, 1974; *May My Words Feed Others* (fiction), A. S. Barnes, 1974.

Plays: "Masse for the Plague," produced at Company Theatre, 1971; "Father and Son," produced at La Mama Hollywood Theatre, 1975; "The Adolf Hitler Show," produced at Odyssey Theatre, 1975; "A Play on Orphans: A Mime Ballet for Radio," produced on KPFK-FM, 1975.

Work has been anthologized in *American Literary Anthology,* Volume IV, edited by Chaym Zeldis, Harper, 1971. Contributor of stories and poems to magazines and journals, including *Invisible City, Black Box, New York Quarterly, Beyond Baroque, TransPacific,* and *Penthouse.* Drama editor of *Coast* and *Los Angeles News Advocate,* 1969—; editor of *Garuda,* 1973—.

*   *   *

EISLER, Paul (Erich)   1922-

PERSONAL: Born September 3, 1922, in New York, N.Y.; son of Paul Joseph (a music conductor) and Edith (an opera singer; maiden name, Ross) Eisler; married Helga Dorf, November 5, 1940 (divorced April 30, 1961); married Susan Landesman, May 4, 1961 (divorced December 4, 1965); married Edith Nachod (a designer), March 23, 1967; children: Judith Edith, Paul Alfred Vail, Karen Erling, Peter Ross. *Education:* Columbia University, B.S., 1953, M.A., 1955; Boston University, D.M.A., 1965; studied privately with Fritz Reiner, Henry Cowell, and Vladimir Ussachevsky. *Religion:* Episcopalian. *Home:* 84 Siwanoy Blvd., Eastchester, N.Y. 10707. *Office:* Academy of Music and Theatre, 84 Siwanoy Blvd., Eastchester, N.Y. 10707.

CAREER: Bennett College, Millbrook, N.Y., chairman of music department, 1955-60; New England College, Henniker, N.H., dean of arts and sciences, 1960-65; Manhattan School of Music, New York, N.Y., faculty member in department of theory, 1965—; Academy of Music and Theatre, Eastchester, N.Y., director, 1965—. Adjunct associate professor of music, New York University, 1966—; faculty member, Concordia College, Bronxville, N.Y., 1975. Conductor and pianist for opera, operettas, and symphonic works. *Military service:* U.S. Army Air Forces, 1940-45; became captain; received Presidential Citation, Distinguished Flying Cross, and nine Air Medals. *Member:* American Federation of Musicians, Goethe Society of New England, "The Bohemians", Pi Kappa Lambda.

WRITINGS: History of the Metropolitan Opera, 1883-1908, Boston University, 1965; *World Chronology of Music*

History, Oceana, Volume I: 1972, Volume II: 1973, Volume III: 1974.

WORK IN PROGRESS: Approximately nine more volumes in the series, *World Chronology of Music History; Listener's Guide to Symphonic Music,* completion expected in 1976.

SIDELIGHTS: Eisler's father was a pupil of Brahms, Bruckner, and Mahler, and was a conductor with the Metropolitan Opera. His mother was a professional singer in the Metropolitan Opera.

* * *

ELAM, Richard M(ace, Jr.) 1920-

PERSONAL: Born July 16, 1920, in Richmond, Va.; son of Richard Mace (an accountant) and Louise S. Elam. *Education:* Student at Richmond Professional Institute, 1946-47, Phoenix, College, 1947-48, and Arizona State University, 1948-50. *Home:* 1333 Stevens Ridge Dr., Dallas, Tex. 75211. *Office:* Precision Silkscreen, Inc., 2926 Congressman Lane, Dallas, Tex. 75220.

CAREER: Started as bank teller at age seventeen; later show card writer and photographer; secretary-treasurer of Precision Silkscreen, Inc., Dallas, Tex., 1970—. *Military service:* U.S. Army Air Forces, 1942-46; became sergeant.

WRITINGS—All published by Lantern Press: *Teen-Age Science Fiction Stories,* 1952; *Young Visitor to Mars,* 1953; *Young Readers Science Fiction Stories,* 1957; *Teen-Age Super Science Stories,* 1957; *Cave of Living Treasure,* 1958; *Young Stowaways in Space,* 1960; *Young Visitor to the Moon,* 1965. Writer of juvenile stories and articles and creator of puzzles.

SIDELIGHTS: Elam commented: "I started in juveniles originally just to get published, but through the years I have come to believe this field to be more satisfying to me than adult work. In fact, I find juvenile writing easier and with greater freedom of imagination. I haven't published since 1965 but hope to resume shortly, still in the imaginative vein."

Elam's books have been reprinted in the United States, and *Young Visitor to Mars* translated into Dutch and Japanese.

AVOCATIONAL INTERESTS: Music, gardening, psychic research, "reading on unusual subjects."

* * *

ELASHOFF, Janet Dixon 1942-

PERSONAL: Born March 22, 1942, in Princeton, N.J.; daughter of Wilfrid J. (a professor) and Eva (Milne) Dixon; married Robert M. Elashoff (a professor), December 21, 1964; children: Michael Reid, David Alexander. *Education:* Stanford University, B.S., 1962; Harvard University, Ph.D., 1966. *Office:* School of Education, Stanford University, Stanford, Calif. 94305.

CAREER: Stanford University, Stanford, Calif., research associate in anesthesia, 1965-66, assistant professor of education and administrative head of methodology unit at Center for Research and Development in Teaching, 1967-73, assistant professor of education and statistics, 1973-74, statistical adviser at Center for Advanced Study in the Behavioral Sciences, 1974-75; University of California, Los Angeles, associate research statistician in Department of Medicine, 1975—. Visiting professor, Harvard University, 1966. *Member:* Biometric Society, Institute of Mathematical Statistics, American Educational Research Associa-

tion, Psychometric Society, American Statistical Association, Phi Beta Kappa. *Awards, honors:* Palmer O. Johnson Memorial Award, 1971.

WRITINGS: (Contributor) Ralph Bisco, editor, *Computers, Data Bases, and the Social Sciences,* Wiley, 1969; (with R. E. Snow) *A Case Study in Statistical Inference: Reconsideration of the Rosenthal-Jacobson Data on Teacher Expectancy* (technical report), Center for Research and Development in Teaching, Stanford University, 1970; (with husband, R. M. Elashoff) *A Model for Quadratic Outliers in Linear Regression,* Center for Research and Development in Teaching, Stanford University, 1970; (with J. P. Burke) *The Effects of Serial Dependence on Polynomial Regression Models for Individual Growth Data,* Center for Research and Development in Teaching, Stanford University, 1971; (with Snow) *Pygmalion Reconsidered,* Charles A. Jones Publishing, 1971. Contributor of articles and reviews to professional journals. Referee for *Psychometrika, Psychological Reports, Journal of Educational Measurement, Stanford Center for Research and Development Monographs,* and *Review of Educational Research.*

* * *

ELBERT, George A. 1911-

PERSONAL: Born December 23, 1911, in New York, N.Y.; son of August and Blanche Elbert; married Virginie Fowler (a writer and editor); children: Steven, Suzanne. *Education:* Attended Institut Minerva, Zurich, Switzerland, and University of Heidelberg. *Home and office:* 801 West End Ave., New York, N.Y. 10025.

CAREER: Employed with J. B. Neuman (art dealer), 1930-32, Raymond & Raymond (print publishers), 1932-35, Elbert & Co., Inc. (international merchants in vegetable oil and chemicals), 1933-55; free-lance commodity trader, 1950-68; New York Produce Exchange, New York, N.Y., treasurer, 1965-69; writer and photographer, 1968—. *Member:* Indoor Light Gardening Society of America (president, 1972-74), Illuminating Engineering Society.

WRITINGS: (With Edward Hyams) *House Plants,* Funk, 1967; (with wife, Virginie F. Elbert) *Simple Cooking for Sophisticates,* Hearthside, 1968; *The Indoor Light Gardening Book,* Crown, 1973; (with V. F. Elbert) *Fun with Terrarium Gardening,* Crown, 1973; (with V. F. Elbert) *Fun with Growing Herbs Indoors,* Crown, 1974; (with V. F. Elbert) *Plants That Really Bloom Indoors,* Simon & Schuster, 1974; (with V. F. Elbert) *Fun with Growing Odd and Curious House Plants,* Crown, 1975.

Contributor of photographs to McGraw's color slide series "The Wild Flowers of the United States." Contributor to horticultural publications and to *Woman's Day* and *New York Times.* Editor for Ward Locke.

WORK IN PROGRESS: *The Miracle Plant Family,* with wife, Virginie F. Elbert, for Crown; a home decorating book, with V. F. Elbert, for Dutton.

SIDELIGHTS: Elbert told *CA:* "We [my wife and I] look on each of our books as pioneering efforts in a new branch of human activity which will have great importance in the future. Our homes, in our opinion, will be rearranged to accomodate indoor gardens as the need of urban populations for contact with nature becomes more urgent and travel more difficult. We see important applications of indoor gardening to education, rehabilitation therapy, and the improvement of the lot of the chronically ill and aged."

Avocational interests: Music (playing piano); ceramics (potter); belles lettres; comparative history, sociology, economics, and political theory; international travel (especially Italy).

* * *

ELBERT, Virginie Fowler 1912-

PERSONAL: Born February 8, 1912, in Brooklyn, N.Y.; daughter of Fred C. and Anna (Wolsey) Fowler; married George A. Elbert (a writer and editor); children: Steven, Suzanne. *Education:* Attended art school; also studies book design, pottery, and jewelry making privately and with American Institute of Graphic Arts. *Home and office:* 801 West End Ave., New York, N.Y. 10025.

CAREER: Worked in Doubleday Book Shop, New York City, 1939-40; Charles Scribner's Sons, New York City, assistant juvenile editor, 1941-51; Holt, Rinehart & Winston, Inc., New York City, children's book editor and head of department, 1951-57; Alfred A. Knopf, Inc., New York City, children's book editor and head of department, 1958-72; writer, editor, and photographer, 1972—. Has worked as free-lance newspaper and advertising artist; instructor at New York City Community College Institute of Study for Older Adults. *Member:* Children's Book Council (president), American Institute of Graphic Arts, Indoor Light Gardening Society of America (president of metropolitan chapter), American Crafts Council (craftsman member).

WRITINGS: (With Stanley Chin) *Two Lands for Ming* (juvenile novel), Scribner, 1945; (with husband, George A. Elbert) *Simple Cooking for Sophisticates,* Hearthside, 1968; (with G. A. Elbert) *Fun with Terrarium Gardening,* Crown, 1973; (with G. A. Elbert) *Fun with Growing Herbs Indoors,* Crown, 1974; (with G. A. Elbert) *Plants That Really Bloom Indoors,* Crown, 1974; *Potterymaking,* Doubleday, 1974; (with Gloria R. Mosesson) *Jewelry Craft for Beginners,* Bobbs-Merrill, 1975; (with G. A. Elbert) *Fun with Growing Odd and Curious House Plants,* Crown, 1975; *Easy Enameling on Metal,* Lothrop, 1975. Contributor of photographs to slide series "The Wild Flowers of the United States," McGraw, 1966.

WORK IN PROGRESS: The Miracle Plant Family, with husband, George A. Elbert, for Crown; a shellcraft book for Bobbs-Merrill; a home decorating book, with G. A. Elbert, for Dutton; a plant pet book for Doubleday.

SIDELIGHTS: Virginie Elbert commented: "There is a strong need in our mechanized world to return to the use of our hands and eyes to create and make our own personal objects. Without an apprentice system, formal or informal, the beginning skills are lost, and the relearning process can be long and frustrating." *Avocational interests:* International travel (especially Italy and France); photographing wild flowers, buildings, and landscapes; Byzantine and Renaissance art and history; tumbling beach stones gathered in the summer; all crafts.

* * *

ELGIN, (Patricia Anne) Suzette Haden 1936-

PERSONAL: Born November 18, 1936, in Louisiana, Mo.; daughter of Gaylord Lloyd (a lawyer) and Hazel (a teacher; maiden name, Lewis) Wilkins; married Peter Haden, 1955 (deceased); married George Elgin (a sales manager), 1964; children: (first marriage) Michael, Rebecca, Patricia; (second marriage) Benjamin. *Education:* Attended University of Chicago, 1954-56; Chico State College (now Cali-

fornia State University, Chico), B.A., 1967; University of California, San Diego, M.A., 1970, Ph.D., 1973. *Residence:* Cardiff, Calif. *Agent:* James Byron, P.O. Box 2389, Hollywood, Calif. 90028. *Office:* Department of Linguistics, San Diego State University, San Diego, Calif. 92182.

CAREER: ETV (channel 9), Redding, Calif., performer on folk music show and folk guitar instructor show, 1966-68; Chico Conservatory of Music, Chico, Calif., instructor, 1967-68; adult education teacher of French, 1968-69; teacher of guitar and music theory, 1969-70; University of California at San Diego, La Jolla, teacher of basic linguistics for Apache field methods, summer, 1971; San Diego State University, San Diego, Calif., assistant professor of humanities, 1972—. Worked as translator and interpreter for American Bar Association Committee on World Peace through Law. *Member:* Science Fiction Writers of America, Linguistic Society of America, California Linguistic Association. *Awards, honors:* Academy of American Poets Award, University of Chicago, 1955; Eugene Saxon Memorial Trust fellowship in poetry from *Harper's,* 1958.

WRITINGS—Science fiction novels: *The Communipaths,* Ace, 1970; *Furthest,* Ace, 1971; *At the Seventh Level,* Daw Books, 1972. Other: (Contributor) John Kimball, editor, *Syntax and Semantics,* Volumes I and II, Academic Press, 1972; (with John Grinder) *Guide to Transformational Grammar,* Holt, 1973; *What Is Linguistics?,* Prentice-Hall, 1973, workbook published as *Beginning Linguistics Workbook,* 1974; *Pouring Down Words* (English textbook), Prentice-Hall, 1975. Contributor of articles and reviews to linguistic journals and to *Mother Earth News.*

WORK IN PROGRESS: Four novels, *Freeway, Stranger's Crossing, Fair Weather and Foul, Breakdown Tree; Even Grownups Can Learn,* non-fiction; a study of the applicability of pattern recognition techniques as a mechanism for improving basic literacy competencies in English speakers at the postsecondary level; an article on the passive construction in English and Navajo; an article on the mechanisms underlying the Rossian constraints on deletion as a means of preserving constituent structure information, and the relationship of these mechanisms to dialect patterns of perceptual strategies and cognitive procedures for surface structure interpretation of language; a study of the applicability of drama techniques to dialect modification for speakers of Non-Standard English; a case-grammar analysis of Ozark English.

SIDELIGHTS: Suzette Elgin writes: ". . . A great deal of my time, and much of my writing, is devoted to an attempt to destroy the Romantic Love Ethic of our culture, which I see as the major barrier to male/female communication, the major obstacle to women's liberation, and a blasted nuisance generally." Her linguistic specialty is Amerindian languages, especially Navajo, Kumeyaay (a California Indian language), and Hopi. *Avocational interests:* "Theology, particularly seen as a discipline . . . religious language, for example."

* * *

ELIAS, Robert H(enry) 1914-

PERSONAL: Born September 17, 1914, in New York, N.Y.; son of Henry Hart (a broker) and Edna Weil (Bernhard) Elias; married Helen Beatrice Larson (a college teacher and research associate), June 13, 1947; children: Jonathan Hart, Abigail, Sara (Mrs. William Melville Benson), Eben Lars. *Education:* Williams College, A.B., 1936; Columbia University, A.M., 1937; University of Pennsylvania, Ph.D., 1948. *Politics:* Democrat. *Home:* 101 Devon Rd., Ithaca, N.Y. 14850. *Office:* Department of English, Cornell University, Goldwin Smith Hall, Ithaca, N.Y. 14853.

CAREER: University of Pennsylvania, Philadelphia, instructor in English, 1942-45; Cornell University, Ithaca, N.Y., instructor, 1945-49, assistant professor, 1949-51, associate professor, 1951-59, professor of English, 1959-68, Goldwin Smith Professor of English Literature and American Studies, 1968—, Ernest I. White Professor of American Studies, 1959-64, chairman of American studies, 1959-64, 1966-67, 1975—. Fulbright-Hays lecturer at University of Toulouse, 1963-64, and Centre d'Etudes Anglaises et Nord-americaines, 1968. *Member:* Modern Language Association of America, American Studies Association (cofounder of New York State chapter, 1951; past-co-president), American Association of University Professors. *Awards, honors:* Ford Foundation fellowship, 1952-53.

WRITINGS: Theodore Dreiser: Apostle of Nature, Knopf, 1949, revised edition, Cornell University Press, 1970; (editor) Charles Francis Adams, Jr. and Henry Adams, *Chapters of Erie,* Cornell University Press, 1956; (editor) *Letters of Theodore Dreiser,* University of Pennsylvania Press, 1959; *"Entangling Alliances with None": An Essay on the Individual in the American Twenties,* Norton, 1973.

Work is represented in anthologies, including: *The Stature of Theodore Dreiser,* edited by Alfred Kazin and Charles Shapiro, Indiana University Press, 1955; *14 by Emily Dickinson with Selected Criticism,* edited by Thomas M. Davis, Scott-Foresman, 1964; *Evidence for Authorship: Essays on the Problems of Attribution,* edited by David V. Erdman and Ephim G. Fogel, Cornell University Press, 1966; *Sixteen Modern American Authors,* edited by Jackson R. Bryer, Norton, 1973; *Thurber: A Collection of Critical Essays,* edited by Charles S. Holmes, Prentice-Hall, 1974. Contributor to literature and history journals. Associate editor, *Epoch,* 1947-54.

WORK IN PROGRESS: Editing letters of Thomas A. Digges (1742-1821), with Eugene D. Finch.

SIDELIGHTS: Elias writes: "My books are rooted in a concern with the nature of selfhood and the way self-awareness, individual and social, emerges from the encounter with limits; hence, my writing embodies a preoccupation with ideas in literature and their relation to social history, with emphasis on interdisciplinary approaches."

*　　*　　*

ELLIS, Florence Hawley 1906-
(Florence M. Hawley; Florence H. Senter)

PERSONAL: Born September 17, 1906, in Sonora, Mexico; daughter of Fred Graham (a chemist) and Amy (a teacher; maiden name, Roach) Hawley; married Donovan Senter, 1936 (divorced, 1947); married Bruce T. Ellis (a history writer), June 2, 1950; children: (first marriage) Andrea (Mrs. Clint Dodge). *Education:* University of Arizona, A.B., 1927, M.A., 1928; University of Chicago, Ph.D., 1934. *Religion:* Presbyterian. *Home and office:* 1666 Cerro Gordo, Santa Fe, N.M. 87501.

CAREER: Arizona State Museum, Tucson, research assistant, 1928-29; University of Arizona, Tucson, instructor in anthropology, 1929-33; University of New Mexico, Albuquerque, assistant professor, 1934-48, associate professor, 1949-53, professor of anthropology, 1954-71, professor emeritus, 1971—. Part-time associate professor at University of Chicago, 1937, 1938-40; adjunct professor at Eckerd College, 1973—. Member of Museum of New Mexico Foundation Board; teacher and consultant at Ghost Ranch Conference Center; chief curator of Florence Hawley Ellis Museum of Anthropology, Ghost Ranch Museum, Abiquiu, N.M.

MEMBER: Society for American Archaeology, American Society for Ethnohistory (president, 1969), Tree-Ring Society, New Mexico Archaeological Society, Northern Arizona Society for Science and Art, Sigma Xi, Phi Kappa Phi.

WRITINGS—Under name Florence M. Hawley: *The Significance of the Dated Prehistory of Chetro Ketl, Chaco Canyon, New Mexico* (monograph), University of New Mexico, 1934; *Field Manual of Prehistoric Southwestern Pottery Types* (monograph), University of New Mexico, 1936; (with D. D. Brand, F. C. Hibben, and others) *Tseh So: A Small House Ruin, Chaco Canyon, New Mexico* (monograph), University of New Mexico, 1937; *Classification of Black Pottery Pigments and Paint Areas* (monograph), University of New Mexico, 1938; (with Clyde Kluckhohn, Douglas Osborne, and others) *Preliminary Report on the 1937 Excavations, BC 50-51, Chaco Canyon, New Mexico* (monograph), University of New Mexico, 1939; *Tree-Ring Analysis and Dating in the Mississippi Drainage* (monograph), University of Chicago, 1941; *The Indian Problem in New Mexico,* Division of Research, Department of Government, University of New Mexico, 1948.

Under name Florence H. Ellis: *A Reconstruction of the Basic Jemez Pattern of Social Organization, with Comparison to Other Tanoan Social Structures* (monograph), University of New Mexico, 1964; *Where Did the Pueblo People Come From?,* El Palacio, 1967; (contributor) D. E. Walker, Jr., editor, *Systems of North American Witchcraft and Sorcery* (monograph), University of Idaho, 1970; *Anthropological Data Pertaining to the Taos Land Claim,* Clearwater Publishing, 1973; *Anthropology of Laguna Pueblo Land Claims,* Clearwater Publishing, 1973; *Archeologic and Ethnologic Data: Acoma-Laguna Land Claims,* Clearwater Publishing, 1973; *The Hopi: Their History and Use of Lands in New Mexico and Arizona, 1200's to 1900's,* Clearwater Publishing, 1973; *Navajo Indians: Anthropological Study of the Navajo Indians,* Garland Publishing, 1974; *Pueblo Indians: Archaeologic and Ethnologic Data—Acoma-Laguna Land Claims,* Garland Publishing, 1974; *Reconstruction of the Basic Jemez Pattern of Social Organization,* University of New Mexico Press, 1974; *Some Surprising Parallels between Pueblo and Mexican Pantheons and Ceremonies,* University of Arizona Press, in press; *Twelve Thousand Years of Southwestern Indians,* Chandler Publishing, in press.

Contributor of more than a hundred articles to learned journals, under names Florence M. Hawley, Florence Hawley Ellis, and sometimes under name Florence H. Senter.

WORK IN PROGRESS: Several monographs, for Garland Publishing.

SIDELIGHTS: Florence Ellis writes that her interests include "the modern adjustments of the Pueblo Indians, which are more practical, rewarding, and less frenetic than those of many other tribesman." She continues: "I have traveled in Europe, Mexico, and Guatemala . . . I have done a great deal of Southwestern field work in archaeology, directing numerous field schools, and though retired, still do field work as well as write."

ELLIS, Richard E(manuel)   1937-

PERSONAL: Born September 7, 1937, in New York, N.Y.; son of Daniel E. (a worker) and Marion (Gutman) Ellis; married Sharon Jay Waldfogel, February 8, 1959; children: Jonathan Joseph, Daniel Geoffrey, Rebekah Suzanne, Deborah Elizabeth. *Education:* University of Wisconsin, Madison, B.A. (with honors), 1960; University of California, Berkeley, M.A., 1961, Ph.D., 1969. *Politics:* Independent. *Religion:* Jewish. *Home:* 4399 Main St., Snyder, N.Y. 14226. *Office:* Department of History, Ellicott Complex, Amherst Campus, State University of New York at Buffalo, Buffalo, N.Y. 14261.

CAREER: University of Chicago, Chicago, Ill., instructor in history, 1965-68; University of Virginia, Charlottesville, assistant professor, 1968-71, associate professor of history, 1971-74, associate of Center for Advanced Studies, 1972-73; State University of New York at Buffalo, professor of history, 1974—. Instructor at Law and American Society Foundation, summers, 1968-69; Harvard University, fellow of Charles Warren Center for Studies in American History, 1972-73, visiting associate professor, summer, 1973.

MEMBER: American Historical Association, Organization of American Historians, American Society for Legal History, Economic History Association, Agricultural History Association, Southern Historical Society. *Awards, honors:* Woodrow Wilson fellowships, 1960-61 and 1963-64; book prize from National Historical Society, 1972, for *The Jeffersonian Crisis: Courts and Politics in the Young Republic;* Guggenheim fellowship, 1972-73.

WRITINGS: The Jeffersonian Crisis: Courts and Politics in the Young Republic, Oxford University Press, 1971; (contributor) Stanley N. Katz and Stanley I. Kutler, editors, *New Perspectives on the American Past: 1607 to 1877,* 2nd edition (Ellis was not associated with 1st edition), Little, Brown, 1972; (contributor) Armin Rappaport and Richard Traina, editors, *Present in the Past: Source Problems in American History,* Macmillan, 1972; (contributor) Robert H. Ratcliffe, editor, *Law in a New Land* (juvenile text), Houghton, 1972; (contributor) *Annual Editions: Readings in American History,* Dushkin, 1973; (contributor) Lally Weymouth, editor, *Thomas Jefferson: The Man, His World, His Influence,* Putnam, 1973; (contributor) C. Vann Woodward, editor, *Responses of the Presidents to Charges of Misconduct,* Dell, 1974; (contributor) *The Study of American History,* two volumes, Dushkin, 1974. Contributor and member of advisory board, *Encyclopedia of American History.* Contributor of articles and reviews to law and history journals.

WORK IN PROGRESS: Research on the transition from Jeffersonian to Jacksonian democracy; research on the early development of the state's rights argument.

*   *   *

ELSE, Gerald Frank   1908-

PERSONAL: Born July 1, 1908, in Redfield, S.D.; son of Frank Marston and Minnie Marylouise (Beckman) Else; married Martha Post Wight, June 15, 1939 (died, 1961); children: Martha (Mrs. J. S. Wyman, Jr.), Stephen. *Education:* University of Nebraska, student, 1924-27; Harvard University, A.B. (summa cum laude), 1929, M.A., 1932, Ph.D., 1934. *Office:* Center for Coordination of Ancient and Modern Studies, University of Michigan, Ann Arbor, Mich. 48104.

CAREER: Harvard University, Cambridge, Mass., in-

structor in Greek and Latin, 1935-38, faculty instructor, 1938-42; University of Iowa, Iowa City, professor and head of department of classics, 1945-57; University of Michigan, Ann Arbor, professor of Greek and Latin, 1957—, chairman of department of classical studies, 1957-68, director of Center for Coordination of Ancient and Modern Studies, 1969—. Vice-chairman, National Council on the Humanities, 1968-71. *Military service:* U.S. Marine Corps Reserve, 1943-45; became captain.

MEMBER: American Academy of Arts and Sciences (fellow), American Philological Association (president, 1964), Classical Association of the Middle West and South (president, 1955-56), Archaeological Institute of America, Heidelberg Academy of Sciences, Phi Beta Kappa.

WRITINGS: Aristotle's Poetics: The Argument, Harvard University Press, 1957; *The Origin and Early Form of Greek Tragedy,* Harvard University Press, 1965; *Homer and the Homeric Problem,* University of Cincinnati Press, 1965; (translator and editor) Aristotle, *Poetics,* University of Michigan Press, 1967; *The Structure and Date of Book 10 of Plato's Republic,* C. Winter (Heidelberg), 1972; *The Madness of Antigone,* C. Winter, 1976. Contributor of articles and reviews on classical subjects to periodicals.

*   *   *

ELWOOD, Catharyn   1903(?)-1975

1903(?)—September 18, 1975; American nutritionist, lecturer, and writer. Obituaries: *New York Times,* September 22, 1975.

*   *   *

EMRICH, Duncan (Black Macdonald)   1908-
(Blackie Macdonald)

PERSONAL: Born April 11, 1908, in Mardin, Turkey; son of Richard Stanley Merrill (a missionary) and Jeannette (a missionary; maiden name, Wallace) Emrich; married Marion Vallat, February 20, 1940; married Sally Richardson Selden, November 20, 1955. *Education:* Brown University, A.B., 1932; Columbia University, M.A., 1933; University of Madrid, Doctor en Letras, 1934; Harvard University, Ph.D., 1937; additional study at Sorbonne, University of Paris, University of Aix-en-Provence, University of Nancy, University of Cologne, and Escuela de Estudios Arabes. *Home:* 2029 Connecticut Ave. N.W., Washington, D.C. 20008. *Agent:* John Cushman Associates, 25 West 43rd St., New York, N.Y. 10036. *Office:* Department of Literature, American University, Washington, D.C. 20016.

CAREER: Columbia University, New York, N.Y., instructor in English literature, 1937-40; University of Denver, Denver, Colo., assistant professor of English, 1940-42; Library of Congress, Washington, D.C., chief of archives of American folksong, 1945-46, chief of folklore section, 1946-55; U.S. Department of State, cultural attache at American embassy in Athens, Greece, 1955-58, cultural affairs officer and consul at American Consulate General in Calcutta, India, 1959-62, public affairs officer at American embassy in Lome, Togo, West Africa, 1963-66; U.S. Information Agency, Washington, D.C., desk officer for former French West African countries, 1966-69; American University, Washington, D.C., professor of folklore, 1969—. Fulbright lecturer on American civilization at universities of Rome, Naples, Messina, and Palermo, 1948-49. U.S. representative, International Folk Music Council, London, and International Folklore Conference, Paris, both 1948.

Weekly radio broadcaster on folklore, on National Broadcasting Co. program "Weekend," 1953-55. *Military service:* U.S. Army, 1942-45; served with Military Intelligence in Washington, D.C., also served in England, France, and Germany; named American historian to General Eisenhower; became major; received Croix de guerre.

MEMBER: Helenic-American Union (founder), Indo-American Society (founder), Parnassos Society (Athens; honorary member), National Council on Religion in Higher Education, American Folklore Society, Zeta Psi. *Awards, honors:* Hicks Prize in English and Preston Gurney Literary Prize, both from Brown University, 1932; Shattuck Scholar, 1935-36, and Edward Austin fellow, 1936-37, both at Harvard University; Guggenheim fellow, 1949; *The Nonsense Book* was named Children's Book of Library of Congress, 1970, Best Book of the Year by *School Library Journal,* 1970, American Library Association Notable Book, 1970, Top Honor Book of Chicago Book Clinic, 1971, Children's Book of the Year by Child Study Association of America, and received the Lewis Carroll Shelf Award, 1971; *The Hodgepodge Book* was named Outstanding Children's Book by the *New York Times Book Review,* 1972.

WRITINGS—Children's books: *The Cowboy's Own Brand Book,* Crowell, 1954; (compiler) *The Nonsense Book of Riddles, Rhymes, Tongue Twisters, Puzzles and Jokes from American Folklore,* Four Winds Press, 1970; (compiler) *The Book of Wishes and Wishmaking,* American Heritage Press, 1971; (compiler) *The Hodgepodge Book: An Almanac of American Folklore, Containing All Manner of Curious, Interesting, and Out-of-the-Way Information Drawn from American Folklore, and Not to Be Found Anywhere Else in the World; As Well as Jokes, Conundrums, Riddles, Puzzles, and Other Matter Designed to Amuse and Entertain—All of It Most Instructive and Delightful,* Four Winds Press, 1972; *The Whim-Wham Book,* Four Winds Press, 1975.

Adult books; compiler, except as noted: *Casey Jones, and Other Ballads of the Mining West,* W. H. Kistler Stationery Co. (Denver), 1942; *It's an Old Wild West Custom,* Vanguard, 1949; *Comstock Bonanza: Western Americana of J. Ross Browne, Mark Twain, Sam Davis, Bret Harte, James W. Gally, Dan de Quille, Joseph T. Goodman [and] Fred Hart,* Vanguard, 1950; (editor with Charles Clegg) *The Lucius Beebe Reader,* Doubleday, 1967; *The Folklore of Love and Courtship: The Charms and Divinations, Superstitions and Beliefs, Signs and Prospects of Love, Sweet Love,* American Heritage Press, 1970; *The Folklore of Weddings and Marriage: The Traditional Beliefs, Customs, Superstitions, Charms, and Omens of Marriage and Marriage Ceremonies,* American Heritage Press, 1970; (author) *Folklore on the American Land,* Little, Brown, 1972; *American Folk Poetry: An Anthology,* Little, Brown, 1974.

Contributor to folklore journals, and to *Saturday Review, Reader's Digest, Library of Congress Quarterly, Holiday, Moslem World, American Heritage,* and other periodicals; contributor of articles, under pseudonym Blackie Macdonald, to *Police Gazette.*

SIDELIGHTS: Duncan Emrich writes: "I like people, I like folklore, I like to collect, I like to write. The English language is a wonderful thing—from the polished purity of the 18th century to the superb mangling of the present day Bronx. A phrase can make a day: from Montana: 'Well, there goes a ten-dollar Stetson on a five-cent head.' Worth living to read or hear that."

A *Choice* reviewer has called *American Folk Poetry: An Anthology* as close to "pure folk" as one can come to in a printed source and representative of "American poetry at its best, this volume well demonstrates the special aesthetics, as well as the wondrous language those anonymous creators knew so well. . . ."

"Emrich's informal commentary continually prod the reader," notes *Kirkus Reviews,* "towards creative, improvisational application of the material, and the free-wheeling presentation of his scholarly finds . . . makes this encounter with folklore [in *The Hodgepodge Book*] a living, joyous experience." A *Christian Science Monitor* reviewer calls Emrich's *Folklore on the American Land* " a glad and moving book, one which will deeply touch any man or woman who cherishes the wit, the gladness, the imagination, the bravado, the vision, the earthiness, the insight, and the power, which have grown up around and characterize the American land."

BIOGRAPHICAL/CRITICAL SOURCES: Christian Science Monitor, April 27, 1972; *Choice,* December, 1974.

* * *

ENRIGHT, Elizabeth   1909-1968

PERSONAL: Born September 17, 1909, in Oak Park, Ill.; daughter of Walter J. (a political cartoonist) and Maginel (a magazine illustrator; maiden name, Wright) Enright; married Robert Marty Gillham (an advertising man and television executive), April 24, 1930; children: Nicholas Wright, Robert II, Oliver. *Education:* Studied at Edgewood School, Greenwich, Conn., at Art Students League of New York, 1927-28, in Paris, 1928, and at Parsons School of Design. *Residence:* New York, N.Y.

CAREER: Began as magazine illustrator but started writing the stories to accompany her drawings and eventually stopped illustrating; author of books for children and of short stories for adults, appearing in *New Yorker* and other national magazines and published as collections. Lecturer in creative writing at Barnard College, 1960-62, and at writing seminars at Indiana University, University of Connecticut, and University of Utah.

MEMBER: Authors League of America, Pen and Brush Club. *Awards, honors:* John Newbery Medal of American Library Association, 1939, for *Thimble Summer; New York Herald Tribune* Children's Spring Book Festival Award, 1957, for *Gone-Away Lake;* named by American Library Association as U.S. nominee for International Hans Christian Andersen Award, 1963, for outstanding literary quality of complete works; *Tatsinda* was an Honor Book in *New York Herald Tribune* Children's Spring Book Festival, 1963; LL.D., Nasson College, 1966.

WRITINGS—Juvenile fiction; books 1935-51 were self-illustrated: *Kintu: A Congo Adventure,* Farrar, 1935; *Thimble Summer,* Farrar, 1938; *The Sea Is All Around,* Farrar, 1940; *The Saturdays,* Farrar, 1941; *The Four-Story Mistake,* Farrar, 1942; *Then There Were Five,* Farrar, 1944; *The Melendy Family,* three volumes in one (containing *The Saturdays, The Four-Story Mistake,* and *Then There Were Five*), Rinehart, 1947; *A Christmas Tree for Lydia,* Rinehart, 1951; *Spiderweb for Two: A Melendy Maze,* Rinehart, 1951; *Gone-Away Lake,* Harcourt, 1957; *Return to Gone-Away,* Harcourt, 1961; *Tatsinda* (fairy tale), Harcourt, 1963; *Zeee* (fairy tale), Harcourt, 1965.

Adult story collections: *Borrowed Summer and Other Stories,* Rinehart, 1946 (published in England as *The Maple*

Tree and Other Stories, Heinemann, 1947); *The Moment Before the Rain,* Harcourt, 1955; *The Riddle of the Fly and Other Stories,* Harcourt, 1959; *Doublefields: Memories and Stories* (autobiographical sketches, short stories, and one novella), Harcourt, 1966.

Illustrator: Marian King, *Kees,* Harper, 1930; Nellie M. Rowe, *The Crystal Locket,* Albert Whitman, circa 1931; Marian King, *Kees and Kleintje,* Albert Whitman, 1934.

Bulk of her short stories were first published in *New Yorker,* but others appeared in *Ladies' Home Journal, Cosmopolitan, Mademoiselle, Redbook, Yale Review, Harper's, McCall's,* and *Saturday Evening Post.* Her stories were included in *Prize Stories: The O. Henry Awards,* 1946, 1949, 1951, 1955, 1958, 1960, and *Best American Short Stories,* 1950, 1952, 1954. Contributor of reviews of children's books to *New York Times.*

SIDELIGHTS: All but one or two of Elizabeth Enright's children's books still are in print, published now by Holt, Rinehart & Winston and Harcourt Brace Jovanovich, with some paperback editions by Dell. Most of them were published in England by Heinemann, as were the adult story collections. (Obituary entry, *CA-25/28*)

BIOGRAPHICAL/CRITICAL SOURCES: Virginia Haviland, *Children and Literature: Views and Reviews,* Scott, Foresman, 1973.

(Died June 8, 1968)

*   *   *

EPSTEIN, Charlotte   1921-

PERSONAL: Born February 18, 1921, in Brooklyn, N.Y.; daughter of Morris (a house painter) and Pauline (a garment worker; maiden name, Sobel) Epstein. *Education:* Brooklyn College (now of the City University of New York), B.A., 1945; University of Miami, Coral Gables, Fla., M.A., 1953; University of Pennsylvania, Ph.D., 1956; postdoctoral study at San Francisco State College (now University). *Residence:* Philadelphia, Pa. *Office* fiollege of Education, Temple University, Philadelphia, Pa. 19122.

CAREER: High school teacher of English, Latin, French, and social studies in Miami Beach, Fla., 1946-51, assistant principal, 1951-53; National Conference of Christians and Jews, Philadelphia, Pa., assistant director for eastern Pennsylvania and southern New Jersey, 1955-57; University of Pennsylvania, Philadelphia, assistant professor of human relations and staff associate of Greenfield Center for Human Relations, both 1957-61; Philadelphia Police Department, Philadelphia, Pa., social scientist, 1961-66; Temple University, Philadelphia, Pa., associate professor, 1966-69, professor of curriculum and instruction and adjunct professor of nursing, both 1969—. Member of Fellowship Commission's committee on community tensions, 1955—; special examiner for Philadelphia Civil Service Commission to select human relations representative for Center of Human Relations, 1958; research analyst for American Friends Service Committee, 1961; conducted clinic in human relations for police officers at Michigan State University, 1963; member of Philadelphia Board of Education's sub-committee on non-discrimination, 1964. Director of Coppin State College's Intergroup Relations Institute, summers, 1969 and 1970; staff member at Institute for Teacher Corps Leadership, summer, 1969.

WRITINGS: Intergroup Relations for Police Officers, Williams & Wilkins, 1961; (contributor) Alvin Vaughn and Robert A. Shultheis, editors, *Changing Undergraduate Business Teacher Education Programs to Prepare Teachers for Culturally Different Youth,* Center for Vocational and Technical Education, Temple University College of Education, 1968; *Intergroup Relations for the Classroom Teacher,* Houghton, 1968; *Affective Subjects in the Classroom: Exploring Race, Sex, and Drugs,* Intext Publishers Group, 1972; *Effective Interaction in Contemporary Nursing,* Prentice-Hall, 1974; *Nursing the Dying Patient,* Reston, 1975; *Caring for the Aged,* Reston, in press.

WORK IN PROGRESS: A novel, *Murder by Law;* developing materials for patient education by health care professionals.

SIDELIGHTS: Charlotte Epstein writes: "Most of my writing (based on empirical data) deals with relationships between antagonistic groups—primarily racial groups. My aim has been to develop strategies for conflict resolution in productive ways so that people may be free to become all they can be. I write because sometimes I get tired of conflict."

*   *   *

EPSTEIN, William H(enry)   1944-

PERSONAL: Born October 31, 1944, in Easton, Pa.; son of Benjamin M. (a businessman) and Elena (an accountant; maiden name, Freedman) Epstein; married Mildred Rose, June 30, 1968; children: Jessica, Rebecca. *Education:* Dartmouth College, B.A., 1966; Columbia University, M.A., 1967, Ph.D., 1972. *Politics:* Liberal. *Religion:* Jewish. *Home:* 327 West Lutz Ave., West Lafayette, Ind. 47906. *Office:* Department of English, Purdue University, West Lafayette, Ind. 47907.

CAREER: Purdue University, West Lafayette, Ind., instructor, 1970-72, assistant professor, 1972-76, associate professor of English, 1976—. *Member:* Modern Language Association of America, American Society for Eighteenth-Century Studies.

WRITINGS: John Cleland: Images of a Life, Columbia University Press, 1974.

WORK IN PROGRESS: Studies in biographical theory.

SIDELIGHTS: Epstein told *CA:* "I consider lifewriting (biography, autobiography, etc.) the most popular and possibly the most significant literary form of our time. I intend to devote much of my energies in the future to exploring the theory and practice of lifewriting." *Avocational interests:* Eighteenth-century British literature, creative writing, movies, and sports.

*   *   *

ERDMAN, Paul E(mil)   1932-

PERSONAL: Born May 19, 1932, in Stratford, Ontario, Canada; son of Horace H. (a clergyman) and Helen (Bertram) Erdman; married Helly E. Boeglin, September, 1954; children: Constance, Jennifer. *Education:* Concordia College, St. Louis, Mo., B.A., 1954; Georgetown University, B.Sc., 1955; University of Basel, M.A., 1956, Ph.D., 1958. *Religion:* Lutheran. *Residence:* Belvedere, Calif. *Agent:* Ziegler Associates Inc., 9255 Sunset Blvd., Los Angeles, Calif. 90069.

CAREER: European Coal and Steel Community, Luxembourg, economist, 1958-59; Stanford Research Institute, Menlo Park, Calif., and Zurich, Switzerland, economist, 1959-62; Electronics International Capital Ltd., Hamilton, Bermuda, executive vice-president, 1962-65; Salik Bank in

Basel, Basel, Switzerland, vice-chairman, 1965-69; United California Bank in Basel, Basel, vice-chairman, 1969-70; novelist. *Member:* Mystery Writers of America, Authors Guild. *Awards, honors:* "Edgar" from Mystery Writers of America, 1974, for *The Billion Dollar Sure Thing.*

WRITINGS: Swiss-American Economic Relations, J.C.B. Mohr, 1958; *Die Europaeische Wirtschaftsgemeinschaft und die Drittlaender* (title means "The European Economic Community and Third Countries"), J.C.B. Mohr, 1960; *The Billion Dollar Sure Thing* (novel), Scribner, 1973; *The Silver Bears* (novel), Scribner, 1974; *The Crash of '79* (novel), Simon & Schuster, 1967. Contributor to *New York* and *Esquire.*

SIDELIGHTS: Paul Erdman's novels, *The Billion Dollar Sure Thing, The Silver Bears,* and *The Crash of '79,* have been adapted as screenplays. *The Crash of '79* is being filmed by Paramount Pictures.

BIOGRAPHICAL/CRITICAL SOURCES: Adam Smith, *Supermoney,* Random House, 1972; Dana Thomas, *The Money Crowd,* Putnam, 1972; Ray Vicker, *Those Swiss Money Men,* Scribner, 1973.

*   *   *

ERNST, Kathryn (Fitzgerald) 1942-

PERSONAL: Born November 12, 1942, in New York, N.Y.; daughter of Joseph Michael (a physician) and Helen Ann (a social worker; maiden name, Dougherty) Fitzgerald; married John Lyman Ernst, December 11, 1971 (separated, October, 1975). *Education:* Wells College, B.A., 1963; New York University, graduate study, 1963-64. *Residence:* New York, N.Y. *Office:* Franklin Watts, Inc., 730 Fifth Ave., New York, N.Y. 10019.

CAREER: Prentice-Hall, Inc., Englewood Cliffs, N.J., assistant editor of executive letters, 1963-64, associate editor, 1964-65; Small Business Administration, Washington, D.C., confidential assistant for public affairs, 1965-66; Donaldson, Lufkin & Jenrette, New York City, portfolio analyst, 1966-67; Prentice-Hall, Inc., assistant editor in Trade Division, 1968, director of children's books, 1969-74, assistant vice-president in Trade Division, 1972-74; Manuscript Evaluation Service, Inc., Red Hook, N.Y., vice-president and treasurer, 1974-75; Franklin Watts, Inc., New York City, editor-in-chief, 1975-76, vice-president and editorial director, 1976—.

MEMBER: American Library Association, Children's Book Council. *Awards, honors:* Outstanding achievement award from Small Business Administration, 1966; Christopher Award for Editorial Achievement from Christopher Brothers, 1972, for acquiring and publishing anonymously written *Go Ask Alice,* Prentice-Hall, 1971.

WRITINGS: Danny and His Thumb (juvenile), Prentice-Hall, 1973; *Mr. Tamerack's Trees,* Crown, in press.

WORK IN PROGRESS. Charlie's Pets.

*   *   *

ESKENAZI, Gerald 1936-

PERSONAL: Born September 23, 1936, in New York, N.Y.; son of Elias (in garment industry) and Adella (a secretary; maiden name, Schneider) Eskenazi; married Rosalind Gerszkop, August 17, 1963; children: Ellen, Mark, Michael. *Education:* City College of the City University of New York, B.A., 1975. *Politics:* "Pro-good guys." *Religion:* Jewish. *Residence:* Roslyn, N.Y. *Agent:*

Roberta Pryor, International Creative Management, 40 West 57th St., New York, N.Y. 10019. *Office: New York Times,* 229 West 43rd St., New York, N.Y. 10036.

CAREER: New York Times, New York, N.Y., sportswriter, 1959—; St. John's University, Queens, N.Y., adjunct associate professor of journalism, 1974—. *Military service:* U.S. Army, 1960-61. *Member:* Author's Guild, Professional Hockey Writer's Association (president of New York chapter, 1969-70), Baseball Writers's Association of America, Professional Football Writer's Association of America, New York Turf Writers Association. *Awards, honors:* Award for best harness-racing writing, Ohio State School of Journalism, 1967; award for best rodeo-news story from Rodeo Writers Association, 1974; award for best metropolitan writing in New York from Deadline Club, 1975; received ten awards for best stories of the month from *New York Times.*

WRITINGS: Hockey, Rutledge Books, 1969, 2nd revised edition, 1972; *A Year on Ice,* Coward, 1970; *A Thinking Man's Guide to Pro Hockey,* Dutton, 1972, revised edition, 1976; (with Phil Esposito) *Hockey Is My Life,* Dodd, 1972; *Hockey,* Grosset, 1973; *The Derek Sanderson Nobody Knows,* Follett, 1973; *The Fastest Sport,* Follett, 1974; *The Glant Years,* Grosset & Dunlap, in press. Work is represented in annual series, "Best Sports Stories," Dutton, 1974-75, and in "The Way It Was," McGraw, 1974. Contributor to *Encyclopaedia Britannica, Encyclopedia Americana,* and to periodicals, including *New York* and *Sport.*

SIDELIGHTS: Eskenazi commented to *CA* on his sports writing: "Where I can, I prick some balloons; where necessary, I try to reflect the drama and joy of sports. Since I write a story for the *New York Times* practically every day, I enjoy book-writing so much because it doesn't inhibit me in space or time."

*   *   *

ESMAN, Aaron H(irsh) 1924-

PERSONAL: Born December 9, 1924, in Pittsburgh, Pa.; son of Mayer G. (a merchant) and Hermoine (Bernstein) Esman; married Rosa Mencher (an art dealer); children: Susanna (Mrs. Peter Singer), Marjorie, Abigail. *Education:* Cornell University, B.A., 1944, M.D., 1947; attended New York Psychoanalytic Institute, 1954-61. *Home:* 115 East 86th St., New York, N.Y. 10028. *Office:* 120 West 57th St., New York, N.Y. 10019.

CAREER: Psychiatrist in private practice, 1954—. Senior assistant surgeon, New York Public Health Service, 1952-54; psychiatrist-in-charge of children's service, Bellevue Hospital, 1957-59; Jewish Board of Guardians, director of training, 1961-70, chief psychiatrist, 1970—. *Member:* American Psychoanalytic Association, American Psychiatric Association, American Academy of Child Psychiatry, New York Psychoanalytic Society (secretary, 1973-75).

WRITINGS—Editor: *New Frontiers in Child Guidance,* International Universities Press, 1958; (with W. Muensterberger) *Psychoanalytic Study of Society,* Volumes IV-VI, International Universities Press, 1972-74, Volume VII, Yale University Press, 1975 (Esman not associated with earlier volumes); *Psychology of Adolescence,* International Universities Press, 1975. Contributor to professional journals.

WORK IN PROGRESS: Two contributions to journals, one on boredom and the other on juvenile enuresis; research for a work on the psychology of creativity.

AVOCATIONAL INTERESTS: Art, art history, and archaeology.

* * *

ESSLINGER, Dean R(obert)   1942-

PERSONAL: Born June 8, 1942, in Clifton, Kan.; son of Firmin R. (a businessman) and Lucy (Leiszler) Esslinger; married Sandra J. Hanson (a teacher), November 29, 1963; children: Regina, Joel, Carey. *Education:* University of Kansas, B.A., 1964; University of Notre Dame, M.A., 1966, Ph.D., 1972. *Religion:* Roman Catholic. *Home:* 524 Wilton Rd., Towson, Md. 21204. *Office:* Department of History, Towson State College, Baltimore, Md. 21204.

CAREER: Towson State College, Baltimore, Md., instructor, 1968-70, assistant professor, 1970-72, associate professor, 1972-75, professor of history, 1975—. *Member:* American Historical Association (Urban History Group), Organization of American Historians, American Studies Association, Immigration History Society, American Catholic Historical Association, Social Science History Association.

WRITINGS: Immigrants and the City: Ethnicity and Mobility in a Nineteenth-Century Midwestern Community, Kennikat, 1975. Contributor to history journals and Roman Catholic magazines.

WORK IN PROGRESS: Research on the social history of Baltimore, and on immigrants and crime in the nineteenth and twentieth centuries.

* * *

ESTANG, Luc   1911-

PERSONAL: Born November 12, 1911, in Paris, France; son of Lucien (a watchmaker and jeweler) and Marie-Eugenie (Peyroux) Bastard; married Suzanne Bouchereau-Boisgontier, February 18, 1939. *Education:* Attended church schools in Artois, France, and in Belgium. *Home:* 28 rue de l'Universite, Paris 7e, France. *Office:* Editions du Seuil, 27 rue Jacob, Paris 6e, France.

CAREER: La Croix, Paris, France, journalist, 1934-40, chief of literary service, 1940-45, drama critic, 1945-55; Editions du Seuil, Paris, editorial consultant, 1956—; author. Jury member for Theopharste Renaudot Prize, 1944—. *Awards, honors:* Grand Prix de la Societe des Gens de Lettres, 1950, for *Les Stigmates;* Prix de l'Aide a la Pensee Francaise, 1950; Chevalier de la Legion d'honneur, 1961; Grand Prix de litterature de l'Academie Francaise, 1962, for his lifetime achievement in literature; Chevalier des Arts et des Lettres, 1963; Prix Guillaume-Appolinaire de poesie, 1968; Prix des Maisons de la Presse, 1971, for *La Fille a l'oursin.*

WRITINGS—Poetry: Au-dela de moi-meme, Chez l'Aubier, 1938; *Transhumances,* Le Beau Navire, 1939; *Puissance de matin,* P. Seghers (Paris), 1941; *Le Mystere apprivoise,* R. Laffont (Marseille), 1943; *Les Beatitudes,* Gallimard (Paris), 1954; *Le Poeme de la mer,* GLM (Paris), 1950; *Les Quatre Elements; poemes, 1937-1955,* Gallimard, 1956; *D'une nuit noire et blanche,* Gallimard, 1962.

Novels: *Temps d'amour,* R. Laffont, 1947; "Charges d'ames" (trilogy), Editions du Seuil, Volume I: *Les Stigmates,* 1949, Volume II: *Cherchant qui divorer,* 1951, Volume III: *Les Fontaines du grand abime,* 1954; *L'Interrogatoire,* Editions du Seuil, 1957; *L'Horloger du Cherche-Midi,* Editions du Seuil, 1959; *Le Bonheur et le salut,* Editions du Seuil, 1961, translation by Denise Folliot and E.

Mosbacher published as *The Better Song,* Pantheon, 1964; *Que ces mots repondent* (sequel to *Le Bonheur et le salut),* Editions du Seuil, 1964; *L'Apostat,* Editions du Seuil, 1968; *La Fille a l'oursin,* Editions du Seuil, 1971; *Il Etait un Petit Homme,* Volume I: *A La Chasse aux Perdrix,* Volume II: *Boislevent,* Editions du Seuil, 1975.

Essays: *Invitation a la poesie,* R. Laffont, 1943; *Le Passage du Seigneur,* R. Laffont, 1945, 2nd edition, Editions du Seuil, 1969; *Presence de Bernanos,* Plon (Paris), 1947; (with others) *Jean de Boschere, l'admirable,* Au Parchemin d'Anton (Paris), 1952; *Saint-Exupery par lui-meme,* Editions du Seuil, 1956; *Ce que je crois,* B. Grasset (Paris), 1956.

Other: *Olive Tamari,* Sequana (Paris), 1944; *Le Jour de Cain* (play), Editions du Seuil, 1967. Weekly contributor to *Figaro Litteraire.*

AVOCATIONAL INTERESTS: Gardening, swimming, collecting works of art.

* * *

ETS-HOKIN, Judith Diane   1938-

PERSONAL: Born August 8, 1938, in California; daughter of Carl (in import business) and Margaret (Tick) Bregman; divorced; children: Rebecca, Solomon, Gabriel. *Education:* Attended University of San Francisco, 1970-72. *Politics:* "Non-political." *Religion:* Jewish. *Home and office:* 3421 Pacific Ave., San Francisco, Calif. 94118.

CAREER: Judith Ets-Hokin Cooking School, San Francisco, Calif., founder and director, 1973—.

WRITINGS: San Francisco Dinner Party Cookbook, Houghton, 1975. Author of monthly column in *Wine of the Month* (journal), 1974-75.

WORK IN PROGRESS: A cookbook of northern Italian menus.

* * *

ETTLINGER, Gerard H(erman)   1935-

PERSONAL: Born September 30, 1935, in Flushing, N.Y.; son of Hermann J. (an accountant) and Anna (Behringer) Ettlinger. *Education:* Fordham University, A.B., 1959, M.A., 1963; Woodstock College, Ph.L., 1960, S.T.B., 1965, S.T.L., 1967; Oxford University, D.Phil., 1972. *Home:* Jesuit Community, Fordham University, Bronx, N.Y. 10458. *Office:* Department of Theology, Fordham University, Bronx, N.Y. 10458.

CAREER: Entered Society of Jesus (Jesuits), 1953, ordained Roman Catholic priest, 1966; Pontifical Oriental Institute, Rome, Italy, assistant professor of patristic theology, 1972-74; Fordham University, Bronx, N.Y., assistant professor of theology, 1974—. *Member:* Association Internationale d'Etudes Patristiques, North American Patristic Society, Classical Association of the Atlantic States, Catholic Theological Society of America, Mediaeval Academy of America, American Philological Association.

WRITINGS: (Editor and author of introduction) Jean Chrysostome, *A une jeune veuve: Sur le mariage unique* (title means "Consolation for a Young Widow: A Treatise Against Second Marriages"), Les Editions du Cerf, 1968; *Theodoret of Cyrus: Eranistes, Critical Text and Prolegomena,* Clarendon Press, 1975. Contributor to *Oxford Dictionary of the Christian Church.* Contributor of articles and reviews to theology journals.

WORK IN PROGRESS: Editing *De Providentia* (title

means "On Divine Providence"), by Theodoret of Cyrus, and *Commentary on Ecclesiastes* by Gregory of Agrigentum.

* * *

EUNSON, Robert C(harles)   1912-1975

July 23, 1912—May 22, 1975; American newsman, foreign correspondent, broadcast director, author. Obituaries: *New York Times*, May 24, 1975; *Washington Post*, May 24, 1975. (See index for previous *CA* sketch)

* * *

EVANS, Arthur Bruce   1948-

PERSONAL: Born October 24, 1948, in Salem, Mass.; son of Richard Albert (a heavy equipment operator) and M. Kathleen (a laboratory technician; maiden name, Meares) Evans; married Mary Agnes Bertha (a secretary), July 4, 1970. *Education:* Sorbonne, University of Paris, Diplôme d'Etudes, 1969; Tufts University, B.A. (magna cum laude), 1970; Goddard College, M.A., 1973. *Home address:* Hampshire Hill, Worcester, Vt. 05682. *Office:* Montpelier Public Schools, Montpelier, Vt. 05602.

CAREER: Montpelier Public Schools, Montpelier, Vt., high school French teacher, 1970—.

WRITINGS: Jean Cocteau and His Films of Orphic Identity, Associated University Presses, 1975.

SIDELIGHTS: Evans told *CA:* "I live with my wife, Mary, and our small dog, Gus, in a one-roomed red school house (vintage 1840's) which I am slowly renovating. It is located in the mountains of Worcester, Vt." About his work, he wrote: "As a student of French literature and film, I had long been interested in . . . Cocteau. One seemingly overlooked portion of his life and creations, however, concerned Cocteau's complex self-identification with the Greek god Orpheus. My book deals primarily with this omission. In addition, as a prelude to this research it became necessary to clarify Cocteau's use of the film as a poetic medium, and, further, to provide an initiation into the author's remarkable yet wholly esoteric artistic vocabulary." *Avocational interests:* Stained glass work, carpentry, guitar, writing French folk songs, skiing, hunting, fishing, and "simply enjoying the lovely Vermont countryside."

* * *

EVANS, George Ewart   1909-

PERSONAL: Born April 1, 1909, in Abercynon, Glamorganshire, Wales; son of William and Janet (Hitchings) Evans; married Florence Ellen Knappett, April 23, 1938; children: Matthew, Jane, Mary, Susan. *Education:* University of Wales, B.A. (with honors), 1930, Dip. Ed., 1931. *Home:* 19 The Street, Brooke, Norwich NOR 37W, England. *Office:* 3 Queen Sq., London, WC1N 3AU, England.

CAREER: On staff of Sawston, first of Henry Morris's village colleges, 1935-41; author, lecturer, broadcaster, 1948—. University of Essex, Major Burrowes Lecturer, 1972-73, visiting fellow, 1973-76. *Military service:* Royal Air Force, 1941-46. *Member:* Radiowriters' Association (member of executive committee), British Association for the Advancement of Science (president of anthropology section, 1971).

WRITINGS: The Voices of the Children (novel), Penmark Press, 1947; *The Turnpike* (playlet), W. Paxton & Co.,

1950; *The Fitton Four-poster,* Blackie & Son, 1954; *Ask the Fellows Who Cut the Hay,* Faber, 1956, second edition, 1962; (editor) *Welsh Short Stories,* 2nd edition (Evans was not connected with 1st edition), Faber, 1959; *The Horse in the Furrow,* Faber, 1960; *The Pattern under the Plough: Aspects of the Folk-life of East Anglia,* Faber, 1966; *The Farm and the Village,* Faber, 1969; *Where Beards Wag All: The Relevance of the Oral Tradition,* Faber, 1970, published as *Tools of their Trade: An Oral History of Men at Work c. 1900,* Taplinger, 1971; (with David Thomson) *The Leaping Hare,* Faber, 1972; *Acky,* Faber, 1973; *The Days That We Have Seen,* Faber, 1975; *Let Dogs Delight,* Faber, 1975; *From Mouths of Men,* Faber, 1976.

AVOCATIONAL INTERESTS: Walking, gardening, watching Rugby football.

* * *

EVANS, Gwynfor   1912-

PERSONAL: Born September 1, 1912, in Barry, Wales; son of Dan and Catherine Mary (Richard) Evans; married Rhiannon Prys Thomas, 1941; children: four sons, three daughters. *Education:* University of Wales, LL.B., 1934; St. John's College, Oxford, M.A., 1936. *Politics:* Plaid Cymru. *Home:* Talar Wen, Llangadog, Sir Gaerfyrddin, Dyfed, Wales.

CAREER: Qualified as solicitor, 1939; Plaid Cymru (Party of Wales), vice-president, 1943-45, president, 1945—; Member of Parliament for Carmarthen, 1966-70, and 1974—. Honorary secretary of Heddychwyr Cymru (Welsh Pacifist Movement), 1939-45; member of Carmarthen City Council, 1949—; chairman of Union of Welsh Independents, 1954; former member of Welsh Broadcasting Council; member of the Court of Governors and of the Council of the University of Wales and of University College of Wales, Aberystwyth. *Awards, honors:* LL.D., University of Wales, 1973.

WRITINGS: The Radio in Wales, New Wales Union, 1944; *Havoc in Wales: The War Office Demands,* J. E. Jones, 1947; *Plaid Cymru and Wales,* Llyfrau'r Dryw, 1950; *The Labour Party and Welsh Home Rule,* translated by Hywel ap Robert, J. E. Jones, 1954; (with others) *Our Three Nations: Wales, Scotland, England,* Plaid Cymru, 1956; *Rhagom i Ryddid,* Plaid Cymru, 1964; (with Owen Dudley Edwards, Hugh MacDiarmid, Ioan Rhys) *Celtic Nationalism,* Barnes & Noble, 1968; *Aros Mae,* John Penry Press, 1971; *Wales Can Win,* Christopher Davies, 1973; *Nonviolent Nationalism: The Alex Wood Memorial Lecture, 1973,* Fellowship of Reconciliation, 1973. Also author of *Land of My Fathers,* 1974, and *A National Future for Wales,* 1976. Contributor to *Encyclopaedia Britannica.*

* * *

EVANS, Jay   1925-

PERSONAL: Born July 17, 1925, in Concord, N.H.; son of Ira Leon (a printer) and Ruth (Buntin) Evans; married Frances Maxfield, June 4, 1949; children: Eric, Anne. *Education:* Dartmouth College, A.B., 1949; University of New Hampshire, M.A. *Religion:* Episcopal. *Home:* 11 Cottage St., Belchertown, Mass. 01007. *Office:* Robert Crown Center, Hampshire College, Amherst, Mass. 01002.

CAREER: Principal of Conway (N.H.) elementary school, 1950-51; with several private schools, as director, 1952-53, headmaster, 1955-58, as instructor and coach, 1955-62;

Dartmouth College, Hanover, N.H., assistant director of admissions, 1962-74; Hampshire College, Amherst, Mass., director of recreational athletics, 1974—. Coach of U.S. Olympic Kayak Team, Munich, Germany, 1972; advisor to Ledyard Canoe Club, Hanover, N.H., 1962-74; member of U.S. Olympic Kayak Committee, 1969-72. *Military service:* U.S. Army Air Corps, 1943-45; served as lieutenant.

WRITINGS: Fundamentals of Kayaking, Burt, 1964; *Whitewater Coaching Manual,* Dartmouth College Press, 1973; *Kayaking,* Greene, 1975. Contributor to magazines.

* * *

EVANS, Shirlee 1931-

PERSONAL: Born September 4, 1931, in Centralia, Wash.; daughter of Hershal Lee (with the railroad) and Ivy (Bonney) McDowell; married Robert D. Evans (a truck driver), August 19, 1950; children: Daniel, Rodney. *Education:* Attended Clark Junior College, 1961-70, and Moody Bible Institute, 1974. *Politics:* Independent. *Religion:* Conservative Baptist. *Home:* 6100 199th St. N.E., Vancouver, Wash. 98665.

CAREER: Free-lance writer, 1961—. Rural mail carrier, 1961-64; reporter, *Post-Record,* Camas, Wash., 1975—. *Member:* International Rodeo Writers Association, Oregon Association of Christian Writers (corresponding secretary, 1974-75).

WRITINGS: Robin and the Lovable Bronc (teenage novel), Moody, 1974. Contributor to religious magazines. Author of column "The Listening Post," for *Community Post,* 1975—.

WORK IN PROGRESS: Challenge of Faith; Year Without Roses, a novel; another novel.

AVOCATIONAL INTERESTS: Church work, horses, travel.

* * *

EVELING, (Harry) Stanley 1925-

PERSONAL: Born August 4, 1925, in Newcastle-upon-Tyne, England; son of Winifred Amy Louisa Eveling; married Kate Howell (a teacher), 1950; children: Poppy Mair, Benjamin Lawrence David, Sophie Lenore Miriam, Thomas Hugo James. *Education:* Durham University, B.A. (with honours in English), 1950, B.A. (with honors in philosophy), 1953; Lincoln College, Oxford, D. Phil., 1955. *Home:* 30 Comley Bank, Edinburgh EH4 1AS, Scotland. *Agent:* Harvey Unna & Stephen Durbridge Ltd., 14 Beaumont Mews, Marylebone High St., London W.1, England. *Office:* Department of Philosophy, University of Edinburgh, Edinburgh EH8 9YL, Scotland.

CAREER: King's College, University of Aberdeen, Aberdeen, Scotland, assistant lecturer in department of logic and metaphysics, 1956-58; University College of Wales, Aberystwyth, Wales, lecturer in philosophy, 1958-60; University of Edinburgh, Edinburgh, Scotland, senior lecturer in philosophy, 1960—. *Military service:* British Army, 1944-47; served in light infantry. *Member:* Aristotelian Society, Mind Association. *Awards, honors:* Earl Grey fellowship, 1955; Scottish Television Theatre award, 1969, for "The Lunatic, the Secret Sportsman, and the Woman Next Door"; New York Drama Desk award, 1970, for "Dear Janet Rosenberg, Dear Mr. Kooning."

WRITINGS—All plays except as indicated: *H. S. Eveling: Poems,* Fantasy Press, 1956; *The Balachites and the*

Strange Case of Martin Richter ("The Balachites" first produced in Edinburgh, 1963; "The Strange Case of Martin Richter" first produced in Glasgow, 1967, produced in London, 1968), Calder & Boyars, 1970; *The Lunatic, the Secret Sportsman, and the Woman Next Door, and Vibrations* ("The Lunatic, the Secret Sportsman, and the Woman Next Door" first produced in Edinburgh, 1969, produced in London, 1969; "Vibrations" first produced in Edinburgh, 1969, produced in London, 1972), Calder & Boyars, 1970; *Come and Be Killed and Dear Janet Rosenberg, Dear Mr. Kooning* (includes "Jakey Fat Boy"; "Come and Be Killed" first produced in Edinburgh, 1967, produced in London, 1968; "Dear Janet Rosenberg, Dear Mr. Kooning," first produced with "Jakey Fat Boy" in London, 1969, produced in New York, 1970; "Jakey Fat Boy" produced under title "Sweet Alice," Edinburgh, 1971), Calder & Boyars, 1971; *Total Theatre* (criticism), Heriot-Watt University, 1972.

Unpublished plays: "An Unspeakable Crime," first produced in London, 1963; "Mister," first produced in Edinburgh, 1970, produced in London, 1971; "Better Days, Better Knights," first produced in Edinburgh, 1971, produced in London, 1972; "Our Sunday Times," first produced in London, 1971; "Oh, Starlings," first produced in Edinburgh, 1971, "The Laughing Cavalier," first produced in London, 1971; "He Used to Play for Hearts," first produced in Edinburgh, 1971; "Caravaggio Buddy," first produced in Edinburgh, 1972; "Union Jack and Bonzo," first produced in Edinburgh, 1972, produced in London, 1973; "Shivvers," first produced in Edinburgh, 1973, produced in London, 1974; "The Dead of Night," first produced in Edinburgh, 1975.

Television plays: "A Man Like That," 1966; "Ishmael," 1972.

Radio plays: "Dance to Thy Daddy," 1964; "The Timepiece," 1965; "The Queen's Own," 1976.

WORK IN PROGRESS: A play, "Time and Roses"; a study of Schopenhauer, *The Philosophy of Representation.*

* * *

EVINS, Joseph Landon 1910-

PERSONAL: Born October 24, 1910, in DeKalb County, Tenn.; son of James Edgar (a businessman, mayor, and legislator) and Myrtie (Goodson) Evins; married Ann Smartt, June 7, 1935; children: Joanna (Mrs. Malcolm R. Carnahan), Jane (Mrs. Robert J. Leonard), Mary Adelaide. *Education:* Vanderbilt University, A.B., 1933; Cumberland University, LL.B., 1934; George Washington University, further graduate study, 1938-40. *Religion:* Church of Christ. *Home:* 300 Main St., Smithville, Tenn. 37166. *Office:* 2300 Rayburn House Office Building, Washington, D.C. 20515.

CAREER: Admitted to Tennessee bar, 1934; attorney in general practice in Smithville, Tenn., 1934-41; U.S. Congress, Washington, D.C., Democratic member of House of Representatives from Fourth District, has served as chairman of Subcommittees on Public Works Appropriations and Independent Offices Appropriations, on House Small Business Committee, and on Committee on Appropriations, 1947—. Attorney for Federal Trade Commission, 1935-38, assistant secretary, 1938-41; vice-president of First Central Bank (Smithville, Tenn.), 1944-54, president, 1954-63, honorary chairman of board of directors, 1963—. Chairman of DeKalb County Democratic Executive Committee, 1944-45, and Tennessee Democratic Campaign

Committee, 1964; delegate to Democratic National Convention, 1948, 1956, 1960, 1964. *Military service:* U.S. Army, 1942-46; served in European theater; became major.

MEMBER: American Bar Association, American Legion, Veterans of Foreign Wars, Reserve Officers Association, Tennessee Bar Association, Phi Kappa Sigma, Phi Delta Phi, Amvets Forty and Eight, Masons, Shriners, Elks, Lions, Commodore Club, Army-Navy Club. *Awards, honors:* LL.D. from Cumberland University, 1958.

WRITINGS: Understanding Congress, C. N. Potter, 1963.

BIOGRAPHICAL/CRITICAL SOURCES: Susan B. Graves, *Evins of Tennessee,* Popular Library, 1971.

* * *

EWING, Kathryn 1921-
(Kathryn Douglas)

PERSONAL: Born April 12, 1921, in Jenkintown, Pa.; daughter of Richard and Kathryn (Heger) Jockers; married A. Paul Webster, June 13, 1958 (died September 13, 1965); married Douglas H. Ewing (a physicist), May 15, 1969. *Education:* Studied dance privately in Philadelphia and New York City, attended drama school in Philadelphia. *Address:* Box 109, Solebury, Pa. 18963.

CAREER: Heger School, Jenkintown, Pa., teacher of dance, 1937-58; real estate broker in Bucks County, Pa., 1965-69. Member of summer stock productions, 1946-50; teacher of speech and drama at Rosemont College, 1947; writer and actress in television commercials, 1948-50.

WRITINGS: A Private Matter (novel), Harcourt, 1975; (under pseudonym Kathryn Douglas) *Cavendish Square Trilogy* (novel), Ballantine, 1976.

WORK IN PROGRESS: Under pseudonym Kathryn Douglas, *A World of Her Own,* for Ballantine.

* * *

EXMAN, Eugene 1900-1975

July 1, 1900—October 10, 1975; American publishing executive, editor, archivist, author of biographies and historical accounts. Obituaries: *New York Times,* October 12, 1975; *Publishers Weekly,* October 20, 1975. (*CAP*-1; earlier sketch in *CA*-17/18)

* * *

EXTON, Clive (Jack Montague) 1930-

PERSONAL: Born April 11, 1930, in London, England; son of J.E.M. and Marie (Rolfe) Brooks; married Patricia Fletcher Ferguson, 1952 (divorced); married Margaret Josephine Reid, 1957; children: Frances, Sarah, Antigone, Plaxy, Saul. *Education:* Educated in Sussex, England. *Home:* 21 Randolph Crescent, London W.9, England. *Agent:* A. D. Peters & Co., 10 Buckingham St., London W.C.2, England.

CAREER: Worked for advertising firm, 1946-48; also worked as actor, stage manager, and waiter, 1950-59; playwright, 1959—. *Military service:* British Army, 1948-50. *Awards, honors:* Arts Council Bursary grant, 1960.

WRITINGS—Plays: "No Fixed Abode," televised, 1959, published in *Six Granada Plays,* edited by J. O'Toole, Faber, 1960; "Have You Any Dirty Washing, Mother Dear?," first produced in London, 1969, published in *Plays of the Year,* Volume 37, edited by J. C. Trewin, Elek, 1970.

Screenplays: "Night Must Fall," 1963; (with Melvyn Bragg) "Isadora," 1968; "Entertaining Mr. Sloane," 1969; "Ten Rillington Place," 1970; "Doomwatch," 1971; (with David Hemmings) "Running Scared," 1971; (with Terry Nation) "Nightmare Park," 1973; "Hornblower," 1976.

Television plays: "The Silk Purse," 1959; "Kipps" (series), 1960; "Where I Live," 1960; "Some Talk of Alexander," 1960; "Hold My Hand, Soldier," 1960; "I'll Have You to Remember," 1962; "The Big Eat," 1962; "The Trial of Doctor Fancy," 1963; "The Land of My Dreams," 1964; "The Close Prisoner," 1964; "The Boneyard," 1966; "Are You Ready for the Music?," 1966; "The Dream of Timothy Evans," 1970; "Mother and Child," 1970; "Conversation Piece," 1970; "The Rainbirds," 1971; "Legacies" (trilogy), 1973; "Killers" (six plays), 1975; "The Crezz" (series), 1976.

WORK IN PROGRESS: A second stage play; a novel.

BIOGRAPHICAL/CRITICAL SOURCES: John Russell Taylor, *Anger and After,* Metheun, 1962.

* * *

EYRE, Richard M(elvin) 1944-

PERSONAL: Born October 28, 1944, in Baltimore, Md.; son of H. Dean (a businessman) and Ruth (Swenson) Eyre; married Linda Jacobson, July 30, 1969; children: Saren, Shawni, Joshua, Saydria. *Education:* Utah State University, B.S., 1968; Brigham Young University, M.A., 1969; Harvard University, M.B.A., 1971. *Religion:* Mormon. *Home and office:* 1098 Augusta, Salt Lake City, Utah 84108.

CAREER: Bailey, Deardourff & Eyre, Washington, D.C., executive vice-president, 1971-74; R. M. Eyre & Associates, Salt Lake City, Utah, president, 1975—.

WRITINGS: I Challenge You, Bookcraft, 1972; *Relationships,* Bookcraft, 1973; *The Discovery of Joy,* Bookcraft, 1974; *The Birth that We Call Death,* Bookcraft, 1976; *Teaching Children Joy,* Bookcraft, 1976.

WORK IN PROGRESS: Goals, completion expected in 1976; *Who Am I?,* a novel, 1977; *52 Facets of the Personality of Christ,* 1977.

* * *

EZEKIEL, Nissim 1924-

PERSONAL: Born December 16, 1924, in Bombay, India; son of Moses (a biology professor) and Diana (founder and principal of an elementary school) Ezekiel; married Daisy Jacob, 1952; children: Kavita, Kalpana, Elkana. *Education:* University of Bombay, M.A., 1947. *Home:* The Retreat, Bellasis Rd., Bombay 400 032, India. *Office:* Department of English, University of Bombay, Bombay, India.

CAREER: Khalsa College, Bombay, India, lecturer in English, 1947-48; lived in England, 1948-52; writer, 1952—; Mithibai College of Arts, Bombay, professor of English and vice-principal, 1961-72; University of Bombay, Bombay, reader in American literature, 1972—. Visiting professor, University of Leeds, 1964; visiting lecturer, University of Chicago, 1967. Broadcaster on All-India Radio and Bombay Television on literature and art. *Member:* P.E.N. (India). *Awards, honors:* R. K. Lagu Prize from University of Bombay, 1947.

WRITINGS: A Time to Change and Other Poems, Fortune Press, 1952; *Sixty Poems,* Strand Bookshop, 1953; *The Third* (poems), Strand Bookshop, 1958; *The Unfin-*

ished Man: Poems, Writer's Workshop (Calcutta), 1960, reissued as *The Unfinished Man: Poems Written in 1959*, 1965; *The Exact Name: Poems, 1960-1964*, Writer's Workshop, 1965; *Three Plays* (includes "Nalini," "Marriage Poem," and "The Sleepwalker"; all produced in Bombay, 1969), Writer's Workshop, 1969; *The Actor: A Sad and Funny Story for Children of Most Ages*, India Book House, 1974; *Selected Poems, 1965-75*, Oxford University Press, 1976.

Editor: *A New Look at Communism*, Indian Committee for Cultural Freedom, 1963; *Indian Writers in Conference*, All India Writer's Conference (Mysore), 1964; (of Indian section) *Young Commonwealth Poets '65*, Heinemann, 1965; *Writing in India*, P.E.N. All India Center (Mysore), 1965; *An Emerson Reader*, Popular Prakashan (Bombay), 1965; (and author of introduction) *A Martin Luther King Reader*, Popular Prakashan, 1969; Arthur Miller, *All My Sons*, Oxford University Press, 1972.

Work included in anthologies: *An Anthology of Commonwealth Verse*, edited by Margaret J. O'Donnell, Blackie, 1963; *Commonwealth Poems of Today*, edited by Howard Sergeant, John Murray, 1967; *New Voices of the Commonwealth*, edited by Howard Sergeant, Evans Brothers, 1968. Contributor of poems to magazines, including *Encounter, Spectator, Poetry Review*, and *Thought*; contributor of articles to *Z* (magazine). Editor, *Quest*, 1955-57, *Imprint*, 1961-67; editor of poetry page, *Illustrated Weekly of India*; associate editor, *Indian P.E.N.*; *Times of India*, art critic, 1964-67, columnist.

WORK IN PROGRESS: Modern Indian Pointers: A Critical Study; Bounce, a fictional fantasy; "Uncertain Certainties: Reflective Essays," a monthly serial for *Fulcrum*, a Bombay journal; poems and plays; two books for children, for India Book House.

BIOGRAPHICAL/CRITICAL SOURCES: Meena Belliapa and Rajeev Taranath, *The Poetry of Nissim Ezekiel*, Writer's Workshop, 1966; *Quest 74*, January-February, 1972; Chetan Karnani, *Nissim Ezekiel: A Study*, Arnold-Heinemann, 1974; *Journal of South Asian Literature*, fall, 1974; Inder Nath Kher, *Nissim Ezekiel*, Twayne, in press.

* * *

FABER, Richard Stanley 1924-

PERSONAL: Born December 6, 1924, in London, England; son of Sir Geoffrey (a publisher) and Enid (Richards) Faber. *Education:* Christ Church, Oxford, M.A., 1959. *Home:* Flat 3, 81 Gloucester St., London S.W.1, England. *Office:* Foreign and Commonwealth Office, King Charles St., London S.W.1, England.

CAREER: Oxford Union Society, Oxford, England, president, 1949; Her Majesty's Diplomatic Service, 1950—, served in the Foreign Office, and in Baghdad, Paris, Abidjan, and Washington, D.C., head of Rhodesia Political Department in Foreign and Commonwealth Office, 1967-69, counsellor at The Hague, Netherlands, 1969-73, counsellor in Cairo, Egypt, 1973-75, assistant Undersecretary of State, London, England, 1975—. *Military service:* Royal Naval Volunteer Reserve, 1943-46. *Member:* Travellers' Club (London).

WRITINGS: Beaconsfield and Bolingbroke, Faber, 1961; *The Vision and the Need: Late Victorian Imperialist Aims*, Faber, 1966; *Proper Stations: Class in Victorian Fiction*, Faber, 1971; *French and English*, Faber, 1975.

FADIMAN, Clifton (Paul) 1904-

PERSONAL: Born May 15, 1904, in Brooklyn, N.Y.; son of Isidore Michael (a pharmacist) and Grace Elizabeth (a nurse) Fadiman; married Pauline Elizabeth Rush (an editor), 1927 (divorced, 1949); married Annalee Whitmore Jacoby (a writer), 1950; children: Jonathan, Kim, Anne. *Education:* Columbia University, A.B., 1925. *Home:* 4668 Via Roblada, Santa Barbara, Calif. 93110.

CAREER: Ethical Culture (now Fieldston) High School, New York, N.Y., teacher of English, 1925-27; People's Institute, New York, N.Y., lecturer, 1925-33; Simon & Schuster (publishers), New York, N.Y., assistant editor, 1927-29, general editor, 1929-35; *New Yorker* magazine, New York, N.Y., book editor, 1933-43; master of ceremonies or host of radio and television programs, including: "Information, Please!," 1938-48, "Conversation," 1954-57, as well as "Mathematics," "What's in a Word?," "This is Show Business," "Quiz Kids," and "Alumni Fun"; freelance writer and lecturer, 1957—; Encyclopaedia Britannica Educational Corp., consultant in humanities, writer and general editor, "Humanities Film Series," 1963—. Teacher of great books classes in New York, Chicago and San Francisco; Regents Lecturer, University of California at Los Angeles, 1967; instructor, Santa Barbara Writers Conference, 1973, 1974; Woodrow Wilson Foundation Lecturer, Pomona College, 1974; member of board of judges, Book-of-the-Month Club, 1944—, and National Book Award for Children's Books, 1974; member of board of directors, Council for Basic Education; member of advisory board, California Center Films for Children; consultant to Fund for the Advancement of Education, Academy for Educational Development, National Advisory Council for the National Humanities Series, and Center for the Study of Democratic Institutions. *Member:* California Citizens for Better Libraries, Phi Beta Kappa. *Awards, honors:* Saturday *Review of Literature* award for distinguished service to American Literature, 1940, for radio program "Information, Please!"; American Library Association Clarence Day Award, 1969.

WRITINGS: Party of One: The Selected Writings of Clifton Fadiman, World Publishing, 1955; *Any Number Can Play* (essays and criticism), World Publishing, 1957; *The Voyages of Ulysses* (juvenile), Random House, 1959; *The Adventures of Hercules* (juvenile), Random House, 1960; *The Lifetime Reading Plan* (essays and criticism), World Publishing, 1960; *The Story of Young King Arthur* (juvenile), Random House, 1961; *Appreciations: Essays*, Hodder & Stoughton, 1962; *Enter, Conversing* (essays), World Publishing, 1962; *Wally the Word Worm* (juvenile), Macmillan, 1964; *The Literature of Childhood* (lecture), University of Denver Graduate School of Librarianship, 1971; (with Sam Aaron) *The Joys of Wine*, Abrams, 1975.

Translator: Friedrich Nietzsche, *Ecce Homo* [and] *The Birth of Tragedy*, Modern Library, 1926; (with William A. Drake) Franz Werfel, *The Man Who Conquered Death*, Simon & Schuster, 1927; Desider Kostolanyi, *The Bloody Poet: A Novel about Nero*, Macy-Masius, 1927.

Editor: *Living Philosophies*, Simon & Schuster, 1931; *The Voice of the City and Other Stories by O. Henry*, Limited Editions Club, 1935; (and author of introduction and biographical notes) W. H. Auden and others, *I Believe: The Personal Philosophies of Certain Eminent Men and Women of Our Time*, Simon & Schuster, 1939 (published in England as *I Believe—The Personal Philosophies of 23 Eminent Men and Women of Our Time*, Allen & Unwin,

1940, revised edition, 1962); (and author of prologue and commentary) *Reading I've Liked: A Personal Selection from Two Decades of Reading and Reviewing*, Simon & Schuster, 1941; *The Three Readers: An Omnibus of Novels, Stories, Essays and Poems*, Press of the Readers Club, 1943; (and author of introduction) Henry James, *The Short Stories of Henry James*, Random House, 1945; (and author of introduction) Charles Dickens, *The Posthumous Papers of the Pickwick Club*, Simon & Schuster, 1949; (with Charles Van Doren) *The American Treasury, 1945-1955*, Harper, 1955; *Fantasia Mathematica; being a Set of Stories, Together with a Group of Oddments and Diversions, All Drawn from the Universe of Mathematics*, Simon & Schuster, 1958.

Clifton Fadiman's Fireside Reader, Simon & Schuster, 1961; (and author of introduction) *Dionysus: A Case of Vintage Tales about Wine*, McGraw, 1962; *The Mathematical Magpie; being More Stories, Mainly Transcendental, plus Subsets of Essays, Rhymes, Music, Anecdotes, Epigrams, and Other Prime Oddments and Diversions, Rational and Irrational, All Derived from the Infinite Domain of Mathematics*, Simon & Schuster, 1962; (and author of introduction) *Party of Twenty: Informal Essays from Holiday Magazine*, Simon & Schuster, 1963; (with Allan A. Glatthorn and Edmund Fuller) *Five American Adventures*, Harcourt, 1963; (and author of introduction) *Fifty Years; being a Retrospective Collection of Novels, Novellas, Tales, Drama, Poetry, and Reportage, and Essays*, Knopf, 1965; (and compiler with Jean White) *Ecocide—and Thoughts Toward Survival*, Center for the Study of Democratic Institutions, 1971; (with Marianne Carus) *Cricket's Choice*, Open Court, 1974.

Author of introductions to more than thirty books, including works by Edith Wharton, Leo Tolstoy, Herman Melville, Sinclair Lewis, John P. Marquand, Stendhal, Joseph Conrad, and others, 1931—. Regular contributor to *Holiday* magazine, and to *This Week*. Member of board of editors, *Transatlantic*, 1943-45, *Encyclopaedia Britannica*, 1955—, and Open Court Publishing Co.; associate editor, *Gateway to the Great Books;* senior editor, *Cricket: The Magazine for Children*, 1972—.

WORK IN PROGRESS: A large-scale critical history of world children's literature.

AVOCATIONAL INTERESTS: Wine and "the avoidance of exercise."

* * *

FAIRBURN, Eleanor 1928-
(Catherine Carfax)

PERSONAL: Born February 23, 1928, in Ireland; became British subject, 1953; daughter of Michael John and Mary Josephine (Clarke) Lyons; married Brian G. Fairburn (an analytical chemist), 1950; children: Anne Marie (Mrs. Nigel Miller). *Education:* Grafton Academy, Dublin, Ireland, diploma, 1946. *Politics:* None. *Religion:* Roman Catholic. *Home and office:* 199 Oxford Rd., Linthorpe, Middlesbrough, Cleveland TS5 5EG, England. *Agent:* John McLaughlin, Campbell Thomson & McLaughlin Ltd., 31 Newington Green, London N16 9PU, England.

CAREER: Free-lance fashion designer for various magazines, 1954-61; novelist, 1961—.

WRITINGS—Historical novels: *The Green Popinjays*, Hodder & Stoughton, 1962; *The White Seahorse*, Heinemann, 1964; *The Golden Hive*, Heinemann, 1966; *Crowned*

Ermine, R. Hale, 1968; *The Rose in Spring*, R. Hale, 1971, Pinnacle Books, 1973; *Winter Rose, Dark Summer*, R. Hale, 1972; *The Rose at Harvest End*, Reader's Digest Press, 1975; *Winter's Rose*, R. Hale, 1976.

Crime thrillers; under pseudonym Catherine Carfax: *A Silence with Voices*, Macmillan, 1969; *The Semper Inheritance*, R. Hale, 1972; *To Die a Little*, R. Hale, 1972, published as *The Locked Tower*, Fawcett, 1974; *The Sleeping Salamander*, Stein & Day, 1973.

Contributor of short stories and articles to periodicals.

WORK IN PROGRESS: Another historical novel on England in the fifteenth century.

SIDELIGHTS: Eleanor Fairburn told *CA:* "History is my main interest. I think a study of that enriches the present; even my Carfax thrillers have an historical background although set in modern (Victorian onwards) times. I also like to study psychology and languages, crafts, art and science.... I paint, garden, listen to music, admire cats and wild landscapes.... I dislike publicity, crowds and materialism. My Eleventh Commandment, having a stone tablet all to itself, is: Thou shalt not commit cruelty in any form."

BIOGRAPHICAL/CRITICAL SOURCES: G. W. Grubb, *The Grubbs of Tipperary*, Mercier Press, 1972; Bernard Knight, *Lion Rampant*, R. Hale, 1972; Alan Falconer, *The Cleveland Way*, H.M.S.O., 1972; Ian Postlethwaite, *Richard, Third Duke of York*, Richard the Third Society, 1974.

* * *

FALCO, Maria J(osephine) 1932-

PERSONAL: Born July 7, 1932, in Wildwood, N.J.; daughter of John and Mafalda Falco. *Education:* Immaculata College, A.B., 1954; Fordham University, M.A., 1958; Bryn Mawr College, Ph.D., 1963. *Home:* 12 Hobart Ave., Absecon, N.J. 08201. *Office:* Department of Political Science, Stockton State College, Pomona, N.J. 08240.

CAREER: Immaculata College, Immaculata, Pa., instructor, 1957-60, assistant professor of history and political science, 1960-63; Washington College, Chestertown, Md., assistant professor of political science, 1963-64; research assistant for U.S. Senatorial candidate from Pennsylvania, with National Center for Education in Politics faculty fellowship, 1964-65; Le Moyne College, Syracuse, N.Y., assistant professor, 1966-68, associate professor of political science, 1968-73, chairman of department, 1967-73; Stockton State College, Pomona, N.J., professor of political science, 1973—. President of Syracuse chapter of New Democratic Coalition, 1970-71.

MEMBER: American Political Science Association, American Academy of Political and Social Science, American Association of University Professors (vice-president of Le Moyne College chapter, 1971-72), Women's Caucus for Political Science (president-elect, 1975-76), Foundations of Political Theory Group, American Association of University Women, Common Cause, Public Citizen, Northeastern Political Science Association, New York Political Science Association, Pennsylvania Political Science and Public Administration Association. *Awards, honors:* Fulbright fellow at University of Florence, 1954-55; postdoctoral research fellowship at Yale University, 1965-66; National Science Foundation summer grant for Interuniversity Consortium for Political Research at University of Michigan, 1968.

WRITINGS: (Contributor) Rocco Tresolini and John Frost, editors, *Readings in American National Govern-*

ment and Politics, Prentice-Hall, 1966; *Truth and Meaning in Political Science: An Introduction to Political Inquiry,* C. E. Merrill, 1973. Contributor to professional journals.

WORK IN PROGRESS: Bigotry! Ethnic and Machine Politics in a Senatorial Election; a review and critique of empirical theory tentatively titled *Empirical Theory in Political Science: Quo Vadimus?;* editing a collection of papers from the 1975 American Political Science Association convention, *Epistemology and Political Inquiry: A Reader.*

* * *

FANCHER, Ewilda 1928-

PERSONAL: Born August 22, 1928, in Houston, Miss.; daughter of C. Odie (an accountant) and Lizzie Kate (Brown) Trenor; married James Parkes Fancher (a minister), June 11, 1950; children: Robert Trenor, Francis Tilden, James Neil. *Education:* Mississippi College, B.A., 1950; New Orleans Baptist Theological Seminary, Th.M., 1952; Mississippi State College for Women, M.A., 1968. *Religion:* Southern Baptist. *Residence:* Jackson, Miss.

CAREER: Writer of weekly columns, "A Woman's World Reaches Far Beyond the Ironing Board," in *Baptist Record,* 1970—, and "The Last Word—A Woman's Privilege," in *Clarion-Ledger* (Jackson, Miss.), 1972-74; high school teacher of English in Jackson, Miss., 1971—. *Member:* National League of American P.E.N. Women, National Federation of Press Women, Mississippi Press Women. *Awards, honors:* Awards from Mississippi Press Women, 1972, for *The Christian Woman in the Christian Home,* and from National Federation of Press Women, 1972, for her column "Lost Words"; Sesquicentennial Service to Humanity award from Mississippi College, 1975.

WRITINGS: Where is Edwina?, Mississippi Baptist Convention, Women's Missionary Union, 1970; (contributor) William Cannon, editor, *Every Day, Five Minutes With God,* Broadman, 1970; *The Christian Woman in the Christian Home,* Broadman, 1972; (contributor) Evelyn R. Peterson and J. Allan Peterson, editors, *For Women Only,* Tyndale, 1974; *I Have Heard the Rainbow,* Broadman, 1976. Contributor to *Home Life* and *Church Recreation.*

* * *

FANN, K(uang) T(ih) 1937-

PERSONAL: Born February 2, 1937, in Hsin-Chu, Taiwan; married, 1963; children: four. *Education:* University of Illinois, B.A., 1961, M.A., 1963; University of Hawaii, Ph.D., 1966. *Home:* 65 Astley Ave., Toronto, Ontario, Canada M4W 3B5. *Office:* Atkinson College, York University, 4700 Keele St., Downsview, Ontario, Canada M3J 1P3.

CAREER: Cleveland State University, Cleveland, Ohio, assistant professor of philosophy, 1966-68; Florida State University, Tallahassee, assistant professor of philosophy, 1968-70; York University, Downsview, Ontario, associate professor, 1970-72, professor of philosophy, 1972—. *Member:* Canadian Philosophical Society, American Philosophical Society, Society for the Philosophical Study of Marxism (chairman of Western Division, 1970—), Society for Philosophy and Public Policy, Society for Philosophical Journal Editors, Committee of Concerned Asian Scholars. *Awards, honors:* Humanities Council grant, 1970; Social Science Research Council (United States) grant, 1971-72; Canada Council leave fellowship, 1976.

WRITINGS: (Editor) *Wittgenstein: The Man and His Philosophy,* Dell, 1967; (editor) *Symposium on J. L. Austin,* Humanities, 1969; *Wittgenstein's Conception of Philosophy,* University of California Press, 1969, revised edition, 1970; *Peirce's Theory of Abduction,* Nijhoff, 1970; (editor with others) *Readings in U.S. Imperialism,* Sargent, 1971; (editor with others) *From the Other Side of the River: Self-Portrait of China Today,* Anchor Books, 1975. Contributor to academic journals. Founding editor of *Social Theory and Practice,* 1970-72; editor of *Social Praxis: An International and Interdisciplinary Quarterly of Social Thought,* 1973—; member of board of referees of *Philosophical Archives,* 1974—.

* * *

FARLEY, (William) Edward 1929-

PERSONAL: Born June 12, 1929, in Louisville, Ky.; son of Raymond L. (an accountant) and Dora M. (Walker) Farley; married Doris Kimbel (a social worker), August 11, 1951; children: Mark K., Wendy L., Amy C. *Education:* Centre College of Kentucky, B.A. (with honors), 1950; Louisville Presbyterian Seminary, B.D., 1953; Columbia University, Ph.D., 1958. *Politics:* Democrat. *Home:* 415 Grayson Dr., Nashville, Tenn. 37205. *Office:* Divinity School, Vanderbilt University, Nashville, Tenn. 37203.

CAREER: Ordained Presbyterian minister, 1953; DePauw University, Greencastle, Ind., instructor, 1957-59, assistant professor of philosophy, 1959-62; Pittsburgh Theological Seminary, Pittsburgh, Pa., associate professor, 1962-66, professor of theology, 1966-68; Vanderbilt University, Nashville, Tenn., professor of theology, 1968—.

MEMBER: American Association of University Professors, American Philosophical Association, American Academy of Religion, Society for Religion in Higher Education, Society for Phenomenology and Existentialist Philosophy, American Theological Society, New Haven Theological Discussion Group. *Awards, honors:* Kent fellowship from Society for Religion in Higher Education, 1957; Lilly Foundation fellowship in religion, 1962-63; fellowships from American Association of Theology Schools, 1969-70, 1975-76.

WRITINGS: The Transcendence of God: A Study in Contemporary Philosophical Theology, Westminster, 1960; *Requiem for a Lost Piety: The Contemporary Search for the Christian Life,* Westminster, 1966; (contributor) Theodore A. Gill, editor, *To God Be the Glory,* Abingdon, 1973; *Ecclesial Man: A Social Phenomenology of Faith and Reality,* Fortress, 1975. Contributor to theology journals and religious magazines.

WORK IN PROGRESS: Madness and Evil: An Essay on the Human Problem; Ecclesial Reflection (tentative title), a sequel to *Ecclesial Man,* "the two works together amounting to a theological prolegomenon, using methods of phenomenology."

SIDELIGHTS: Farley writes: "I am attempting to do constructive theology, to make some original if modest contribution to the massive complex of problems which Western religious thought now faces due to the intersection of ancient and present (scientific) modes of thought. Most of my work to date has been in the form of constructing an instrument (in this case a mode of reflection) through which to examine the realities, claims, and the like of religious faith. . . . What I have in mind eventually . . . is a rather comprehensive philosophical-theological anthropology. I foresee future work on monographs pertaining to classical theological themes of God, creation and salvation." *Avoca-*

tional interests: Music (singing, jazz trumpet), appearing in local amateur stage productions, travel (has lived in Basel, Switzerland, and visited England and Freiburg, Germany).

* * *

FARMILOE, Dorothy Alicia 1920-

PERSONAL: Born September 8, 1920, in Toronto, Ontario, Canada; daughter of Thomas and Beatrice Daisy (Archer) Roach; married Ray Edwin Farmiloe, September 16, 1939 (died October, 1963); children: Dan, Judith (Mrs. John Long), Linda. *Education:* University of Windsor, B.A., 1967, M.A., 1969. *Home:* 663½ Campbell St., Windsor, Ontario, Canada. *Office:* Department of English, St. Clair College, Windsor, Ontario, Canada.

CAREER: Long Point Lodge, Elk Lake, Ontario, owner and operator, 1955-63; St. Clair College, Windsor, Ontario, teacher of English, 1969—. Member, Windsor Poetry Movement, 1966; organizer of poetry readings in libraries and schools, 1966—; organizer of poster poem exhibit in Windsor, 1971; former publisher, Sesame Press. *Member:* League of Canadian Poets, Writer's Union of Canada, Detroit Women Writers, Windsor Creative Writing Club (founder; director). *Awards, honors:* Metropolitan Society prize, 1975, for poem "Heritage."

WRITINGS: The Lost Island and Other Poems, Gryphon, 1966; (with Len Gaspari and Edward McNamara) *21 X 3* (poems), Gryphon, 1967; *Poems for Apartment Dwellers,* Fiddlehead Press, 1970; (editor and contributor) *Contraverse* (poems), Concorde Press, 1971; *Winter Orange Mood* (poems), Fiddlehead Press, 1973; *Blue Is the Colour of Death* (poems), Fiddlehead Press, 1973; *And Some in Fire* (novel), Alive Press, 1974; *Creative Communication,* Holt, 1974; *Elk Lake Diary Poems,* Highway Book Shop Press, 1976. Also author of play, "What do You Save from a Burning Building?," 1973.

Poems represented in anthologies including: *Temper of the Times,* edited by Ronald Side and Ralph Greenfield, McGraw, 1969, and *Visions 20-20: Fifty Canadians in Search of a Future,* edited by Stephen Clarkson, Hurtig, 1970. Contributor of articles, poems and reviews to professional journals. Former editor, *Mainline.*

WORK IN PROGRESS: A novel; another collection of poetry.

* * *

FARNSWORTH, Dana (Lyda) 1905-

PERSONAL: Born April 7, 1905, in Troy, W.Va.; son of Henry Lyda and Isabell (Waggoner) Farnsworth; married Elma Morris, March 18, 1931. *Education:* West Virginia University, A.B., 1927, B.S., 1931; Harvard University, M.D., 1933. *Home:* 52 Old Concord Rd., Belmont, Mass. 02178. *Office:* 6 Fayette St., Boston, Mass. 02116.

CAREER: Barrackville Public Schools, Barrackville, W.Va., high school teacher of chemistry and physics, 1927-29; Massachusetts General Hospital, Boston, Mass., intern 1933-35; Boston City Hospital, Boston, assistant resident, 1935; Williams College, Williamstown, Mass., assistant director, 1935-41, director of health, 1945-46; Massachusetts General Hospital, Boston, assistant physician, 1946-50, associate physician, 1950-56, physician, 1956-66, member of board of consultation, 1966—. Massachusetts Institute of Technology, Cambridge, professor and medical director, 1946-54, acting dean of students, 1950-51; Harvard University, Cambridge, lecturer in School of Medicine,

1952-54, Henry K. Oliver Professor of Hygiene, member of faculties of arts and sciences and of public health, and director of health services, 1954-71, consultant on psychiatry in School of Public Health, 1971-75, Henry K. Oliver Professor Emeritus, 1971—; Medicine in the Public Interest, Boston, chairman of board of directors, 1973—. Diplomate of American Board of Psychiatry and Neurology. Lowell Institute Lecturer, 1956; Salmon Lecturer, New York Academy of Medicine, 1964; member of board of directors, Douglas A. Thom Clinic for Children, 1947-75, and Joint Commission on Mental Health of Children, 1966-70; consultant to Peter Bent Brigham Hospital, 1954-75; associate physician of adolescent unit, Children's Hospital, 1954-75; trustee, Judge Baker Guidance Clinic, 1971—; vice-chairman, National Commission on Marihuana and Drug Abuse, 1971-73. *Military service:* U.S. Navy Medical Corps, 1941-45; became commander.

MEMBER: American Medical Association, American Academy of Arts and Sciences (fellow), American Psychiatric Association (fellow; chairman of various committees, 1955-69; member of council, 1958-61), American Public Health Association, Group for the Advancement of Psychiatry (president, 1957-59), American Public Health Association, American College Health Association (president, 1953-54), American School Health Association (honorary fellow), British Student Health Association (honorary member), Institutes of Religion and Health (member of board of directors, 1975—). *Awards, honors:* John and Mary R. Markle fellow, 1936-37; Family Life Book Award, 1966, for *Psychiatry, Education, and the Young Adult;* Edward Hitchcock Award from American College Health Association, 1968; William C. Menninger Memorial Award from American College of Physicians, 1970; Distinguished Service award from American Psychiatric Association, 1971; William A. Schonfeld Award from American Society for Adolescent Psychiatry, 1971; Pax Christi Award from St. John's University, 1971; D.Sc. from Salem College, 1959, Williams College, 1961, West Virginia University, 1965, Fairfield University, 1969, and Rockford College, 1972; D.H.L. from Lesley College, 1962, and Roosevelt University, 1970; L.L.D. from University of Notre Dame, 1964, Harvard University, 1971, and Allegheny College, 1973.

WRITINGS: Mental Health in College and University, Harvard University Press, 1957; (with Fred V. Hein) *Living,* 3rd edition (Farnsworth not associated with earlier editions), Scott, Foresman, 1959, 5th edition (with Hein and Charles E. Richardson) published as *Living: Health, Behavior, and Environment,* 1970, 6th edition, 1975; *Perspectives on Living: Readings for College Health Courses,* Scott, Foresman, 1962; (with Jack R. Ewalt) *Textbook of Psychiatry,* McGraw, 1963; (editor) *College Health Administration,* Appleton, 1964; (with L. W. Irwin and others) *Dimensions in Health,* Lyons & Carnahan, 1965, revised edition, 1967; *Psychiatry, Education and the Young Adult,* C. C Thomas, 1966; (editor with Francis J. Braceland) *Psychiatry, the Clergy, and Pastoral Counseling: The St. John's Story,* St. John's University Press, 1969; (editor with Graham B. Blaine Jr.) *Counseling and the College Student,* Little, Brown, 1970. Contributor of over two hundred articles to medical and scholarly journals. Associate editor, *American Journal of Psychiatry,* 1965-73; editorial director, *Medical Insight,* 1969-74, *Psychiatric Annals,* 1969—; member of editorial board, *New England Journal of Medicine,* 1970-73.

FASSLER, Joan (Grace) 1931-

PERSONAL: Born September 23, 1931, in New York, N.Y.; daughter of Jacob V. and Rose (Sandrowitz) Greenberg; married Leonard J. Fassler (an attorney), July 26, 1953; children: David Gary, Ellen Beth. *Education:* College of the City of New York (now City College of the City University of New York), B.B.A., 1953; Columbia University, M.A., 1965, Ph.D., 1969. *Home:* 80 Hickory Hill Dr., Dobbs Ferry, N.Y. 10522. *Office:* Child Study Center, Yale University, 333 Cedar St., New Haven, Conn. 06510.

CAREER: Seventeen-at-School (magazine), New York, N.Y., editorial assistant, 1954-55; *Seventeen* (magazine), New York, N.Y., reader mail editor, 1955-56; Columbia University, Teachers College, New York, N.Y., research assistant at Research and Demonstration Center for Education of Handicapped Children, 1966-67, project associate, 1967-69, research associate, 1969-70, research consultant, 1970-71; Yale University, Child Study Center, New Haven, Conn., research associate in child development and children's literature and member of faculty, 1972—. Visiting lecturer, University of New Hampshire, 1972; moderator of "Conversations with the Very Young," on WNYC-Radio, 1970.

MEMBER: Authors League of America, Association for Childhood Education International, American Orthopsychiatric Association, American Psychological Association, Council for Exceptional Children, National Association for the Education of Young Children, Psi Chi.

WRITINGS—Juveniles: *The Man of the House,* Behavioral Publications, 1969; *All Alone with Daddy,* Behavioral Publications, 1969; *One Little Girl,* Behavioral Publications, 1969; *Don't Worry, Dear,* Behavioral Publications, 1971; *My Grandpa Died Today,* Behavioral Publications, 1971; *The Boy with a Problem,* Behavioral Publications, 1971; (contributor) *Providing the Best for Young Children,* National Association for the Education of Young Children, 1974; (contributor) J. Dissinger and C. Arnold, editors, *Studies in the Psychological Foundations of Exceptionality,* Brooks/Cole, 1975; *Howie Helps Himself,* Whitman, 1975. Contributor to education and psychology journals.

WORK IN PROGRESS: Research on child development and children's literature, especially concerned with the use of books and stories to help children grow.

SIDELIGHTS: Joan Fassler writes: "As a research psychologist working with normal and handicapped children, I saw a great need for more books for young children dealing with selected topics of importance in early child development. For example, as an outgrowth of my work with handicapped children, I wrote *One Little Girl* (the story of a 'slow' child) and *Howie Helps Himself* (the story of a boy confined to a wheelchair). I have attempted to write books for children whenever my own experiences with young children suggest that an important theme merits further storybook portrayal, and whenever my own feelings assure me that there is indeed a story to be told." Mrs. Fassler's first six children's stories were videotaped in 1971 by Videorecord Corp., and were broadcast on WHCT-TV, Hartford, Conn., in 1972.

BIOGRAPHICAL/CRITICAL SOURCES: British Journal of Psychiatry, August, 1972; *Elementary Education,* spring, 1975; *Language Arts,* September, 1975; *Childhood Education,* November, 1975.

FAUST, Naomi F(lowe)

PERSONAL: Born in Salisbury, N.C.; daughter of Christopher Leroy (a minister) and Ada Luella (a teacher; maiden name Graham) Flowe; married Roy M. Faust (a teacher), August 16, 1948. *Education:* Bennett College, Greensboro, N.C., A.B., 1938; University of Michigan, M.A., 1945; New York University, Ph.D., 1963. *Home:* 112-01 175th St., Jamaica, N.Y. 11433. *Agent:* Alex Jackinson, 55 West 42nd St., New York, N.Y. 10036. *Office:* Department of Education, Queens College of the City University of New York, Flushing, N.Y. 11367.

CAREER: Elementary and high school teacher in Gaffney, S.C., and Winston-Salem, N.C., 1938-43; Bennett College, Greensboro, N.C., instructor in English, 1944-45; Southern University, Scotlandville, La., instructor in English, 1945-46; Morgan State College, Baltimore, Md., assistant professor of English, 1946-48; Dudley High School, Greensboro, N.C., teacher of English, 1948-51; New York City Schools, New York, N.Y., teacher of English, 1955-63; Queens College of the City University of New York, N.Y., lecturer, 1964, assistant professor of English education, 1964—.

MEMBER: World Poetry Society Intercontinental, American Association of University Professors, National Education Association, Association of Student Teacher Educators, New York Poetry Forum, Alpha Epsilon, Alpha Kappa Mu. *Awards, honors:* Certificate of Merit from Tulsa Poets, 1970, for poem "A Little Boy's Thoughts As He Sits on His Doorsteps"; third prize from Cooper Hill Writers Conference, 1970, for poem "Goldie."

WRITINGS: Speaking in Verse, Branden Press, 1974; *Discipline and the Classroom Teacher,* Kennikat, in press. Contributor of poetry to magazines.

WORK IN PROGRESS: A second book of verse and poetic prose, tentatively titled, *For 6 to 80.*

SIDELIGHTS: Naomi Faust once said, "I consider my topic to be the essence for poetry, so long as the poem can make the reader re-create worthy images. . . . In short, it is my opinion, that a poem must communicate emotions, observations, thoughts, or experiences with penetrating feelings. . . ."

BIOGRAPHICAL/CRITICAL SOURCES: Afro-American, February 25, 1975.

*   *   *

FAXON, Arba D.   1895(?)-1975

1895(?)—April 6, 1975; American businessman and author. Obituaries: *New York Times,* April 7, 1975.

*   *   *

FEATHER, Leonard G(eoffrey) 1914-

PERSONAL: Born September 13, 1914, in London, England; came to United States in 1935, naturalized citizen, 1948; son of Nathan and Felicia (Zelinski) Feather; married Jane Larrabee, May 18, 1945; children: Lorraine. *Education:* Educated in London, England. *Home:* 3510 Wrightwood Dr., North Hollywood, Calif. 91604.

CAREER: Composer, music critic, and writer, 1933—. Conducted jazz programs for Voice of America, 1950-52, and weekly series, 1967-69; host of music quiz "Platter-Brains" on ABC-Radio, 1953-58; produced music broadcasts for British Broadcasting Corp. (BBC), 1959, and "Jazz Show" for KNBC-Television, 1971. Toured Europe with his own "Jazz Club U.S.A.," 1954; leader of his own band "The Night Blooming Jazzmen" (performing for Mainstream Records), 1972. Has arranged music for orchestras (including Count Basie Band). Lecturer at Marymount College (Los Angeles, Calif.), 1972-74, and University of California, Riverside, 1973-74; national historian of National Association of Jazz Educators, 1976—. Member of advisory board of Newport Jazz Festival.

MEMBER: National Academy of Recording Arts and Sciences (member of governing board, 1968-69), American Society of Composers, Authors, and Publishers, American Federation of Musicians, National Association for the Advancement of Colored People.

WRITINGS: Inside Be-Bop, J. J. Robbins, 1949; *The Encyclopedia of Jazz,* Horizon Press, 1955, yearbook, 1956, revised edition published as *The New Encyclopedia of Jazz,* 1960; *The Book of Jazz: A Guide to the Entire Field,* Horizon Press, 1957, revised edition published as *The Book of Jazz, From Then Till Now: A Guide to the Entire Field,* 1965; *Jazz: An Exciting Story of Jazz Today,* R. E. Petersen, 1958; (with Jack Tracy) *Laughter from the Hip,* Horizon Press, 1963; *The Encyclopedia of Jazz in the Sixties,* Horizon Press, 1966; (with Steve Allen) *Bigger Than a Breadbox,* Doubleday, 1967; (with John Chilton and Max Jones) *Salute to Satchmo,* I.P.C. Specialist and Professional Press, 1970; *From Satchmo to Miles,* Stein & Day, 1972; *The Pleasures of Jazz,* Horizon Press, 1976.

Author of scripts for "Jazz Scene U.S.A.," 1962-63; composer of music or lyrics for instrumental groups and popular singers, including "Evil Gal Blues," "Blowtop Blues," "Salty Papa Blues," "Signing Off," "I Remember Bird," "Twelve Tone Blues," "Mighty Like the Blues," "Whisper Not," "How Blue Can You Get," and "Born on a Friday."

Contributor to *World Book Encyclopedia,* and *World Book Year Book,* 1955, and to magazines, including *London Melody Maker, Esquire, Downbeat, Playboy, International Musician, Show Magazine,* and *Penthouse.*

SIDELIGHTS: Feather composed music for "The Weary Blues," a sound recording of poems by Langston Hughes, for Metro-Goldwyn-Mayer, 1958.

* * *

FELLOWS, Jay 1940-

PERSONAL: Born April 17, 1940, in New York, N.Y.; son of Otis Edward (a professor) and Frances (Young) Fellows. *Education:* Harvard University, B.A. (magna cum laude), 1962; Columbia University, Ph.D., 1969. *Politics:* None. *Religion:* None. *Home:* 560 Riverside Dr., New York, N.Y. 10027. *Office:* Department of English, Herbert H. Lehman College of the City University of New York, Bronx, N.Y. 10468.

CAREER: Fiction writer and free-lance editor, 1969-72; Herbert H. Lehman College of the City University of New York, Bronx, N.Y., adjunct assistant professor of English, 1972—.

WRITINGS: The Failing Distance: The Autobiographical Impulse in John Ruskin, Johns Hopkins Press, 1975.

WORK IN PROGRESS: A book concerning Walter Pater on landscape and time; a book on John Ruskin's *Strange Chords and Lucent Verdure: Centres, Circumferences, and the Maze in John Ruskin.*

AVOCATIONAL INTERESTS: Running with his Borzoi.

FERAZANI, Larry 1938-

PERSONAL: Born October 30, 1938, in Cambridge, Mass.; son of Raymond and Eileen (Coffon) Ferazani; married Beverly Earle, April 30, 1961; children: Lawrence, Stephen. *Education:* Bunker Hill Community College, A.S., 1975. *Religion:* Roman Catholic. *Home:* 34 North Border Rd., Winchester, Mass. 01890. *Office:* Cambridge Fire Department, Cambridge, Mass.

CAREER: Cambridge Fire Department, Cambridge, Mass., firefighter, currently lieutenant. *Military service:* U.S. Army, and U.S. Army Reserve; current rank, major. *Awards, honors:* Citations for *Rescue Squad* from City of Cambridge, and from Massachusetts House of Representatives.

WRITINGS: Rescue Squad (nonfiction), Morrow, 1974.

WORK IN PROGRESS: A book fictionalizing men of the Cambridge Fire Department.

SIDELIGHTS: Ferazani told *CA:* "My writings serve a two-fold purpose: To show the public what the work of firefighters entails and also show the social degradation of our society as seen through a firefighter's eyes."

BIOGRAPHICAL/CRITICAL SOURCES: Harvard Magazine, January, 1975.

* * *

FERGUSON, E(lmer) James 1917-

PERSONAL: Born January 23, 1917, in Provo, Utah; son of Elmer James (a musician) and Rose Marie (Ferguson) Archbold; married Louise Anna Walker, November 12, 1943; children: Bruce W. *Education:* University of Washington, Seattle, B.A., 1939, M.A., 1941; University of Wisconsin, Ph.D., 1951. *Home:* 17 West Terrace Rd., Great Neck, N.Y. 11021. *Office:* "The Papers of Robert Morris," City University of New York, 1411 Broadway, New York, N.Y. 10018.

CAREER: University of Maryland, College Park, 1947-67, began as instructor, became associate professor of history; City University of New York, New York, N.Y., professor of history at Queens College and Graduate Center, 1964-76. Visiting lecturer at University of Illinois, 1951-52; professor at Overseas Extension of University of Maryland, 1953-55, mainly in Germany. *Military service:* U.S. Army, Signal Corps, Alaska Communications System, 1941-45. *Member:* American Historical Association, Organization of American Historians, Columbia University Seminar in Early American History. *Awards, honors:* Dunning Prize from American Historical Association, 1962, for *The Power of the Purse;* Guggenheim fellowship, 1963-64.

WRITINGS: The Power of the Purse: A History of American Public Finance, 1776-1790, University of North Carolina Press, 1961; (editor) *The Selected Writings of Albert Gallatin, 1761-1849,* Bobbs-Merrill, 1967; (editor) *National Unity on Trial, 1781-1786,* Random House, 1970; (editor with John Catanzariti) *The Papers of Robert Morris,* University of Pittsburgh Press, Volume I, 1973, Volume II, 1975; *The American Revolution: A General History, 1763-1790,* Dorsey, 1974; (editor) *Confederation, Constitution, and Early National Period, 1781-1815* (bibliography), AHM Publishing, 1974. Visiting editor of publications at Institute of Early American History and Culture, 1961-62; member of editorial board of "Haym Salomon, Sheftall Family, and Aaron Lopez Papers" of American Jewish Historical Society; member of editorial committee of "Lafayette Papers" of Cornell University.

WORK IN PROGRESS: A History of the Early National Period in the United States, 1789-1815, completion expected in 1977; *Economic Development of the United States, 1750-1815*, 1978.

* * *

FERGUSON, Robert W(illiam) 1940-

PERSONAL: Born January 23, 1940, in Anaconda, Mont.; married November 4, 1964; children: one son, one daughter. *Education:* Fullerton Junior College, A.A., 1961; California State University, Los Angeles, B.S., 1967; graduate study at Orange Coast College, 1968, and University of California, Los Angeles, 1970; California State University, Long Beach, M.S., 1972; U.S. International University, Ph.D. *Home:* 925 Vista Del Gaviota, Orange, Calif.

CAREER: City of Orange, Calif., police patrolman, 1962-64, investigator, 1964-65, alcohol, narcotics, and vice investigator, 1965-68, sergeant, 1968-69; Saddleback College, Mission Viejo, Calif., instructor in administration of justice, 1969-71, director of administration program, 1971—. Instructor at Saddleback College, 1968-69; lecturer at California State University, Los Angeles, Pepperdine University, and Chapman College. Member of California Community College Task Force for Criminal Justice Curriculum Development. *Member:* California Association of Administration of Justice Educators (vice-chairman, 1973), Saddleback College Faculty Association (president).

WRITINGS: Ferguson: Memoirs and Reminiscences of Montana (family biography), Harlow Press, 1973; *The Nature of Vice Control in the Administration of Justice,* West Publishing, 1974; *Readings in Concepts of Criminal Law,* West Publishing, 1975; *Drug Abuse Control,* Holbrook, 1975; *Concepts of Criminal Law,* Holbrook, 1975.

AVOCATIONAL INTERESTS: Sporting activities, youth groups.

* * *

FERRY, W(illiam) Hawkins 1914-

PERSONAL: Born November 18, 1914, in Detroit, Mich.; son of Dexter M., Jr. (a businessman) and Jeannette (Hawkins) Ferry. *Education:* Harvard University, B.A., 1937; additional study, 1937-39. *Home:* 874 Lake Shore Rd., Grosse Pointe Shores, Mich. 48236.

CAREER: D. M. Ferry, Jr. Trustee Corp., Detroit, Mich., treasurer, 1942-59, secretary and treasurer, 1966-72, vice-president and secretary, 1960-65, 1973—; Wayne (now Wayne State) University, Detroit, instructor in art history, 1946-48; art critic and writer. Detroit Institute of Arts, chairman of Metropolitan Art Association, 1947-55, and Friends of Modern Art, 1965—, honorary curator of architecture, 1943—, chairman, Advisory Board for Historic Landmarks and Districts of the City of Detroit, 1969-74; member of Dodge Fountain selection committee, 1971-73; chairman of advisory committee of Wayne State University Press, 1975. *Member:* Friends of Grosse Pointe Library (chairman, historical committee, 1961—), Founders Society of Detroit Institute of Arts (trustee, 1960—), Michigan Society of Architects (honorary member). *Awards, honors:* Award of merit of Historical Society of Michigan, 1968, for *Buildings of Detroit;* D.F.A., Wayne State University, 1972.

WRITINGS: The Buildings of Detroit: A History, Wayne State University Press, 1968; (with Walter B. Sanders) *The Legacy of Albert Kahn,* Detroit Institute of Arts, 1970;

(author of introduction) *Detroit Architecture: ATA Guide,* Wayne State University Press, 1971; (author of introduction) Theodore Parsons Hall and Silas Farmer, *Grosse Pointe on Lake St. Claire,* Gale, 1974. Contributor of articles to *Bulletin of Detroit Institute of Arts, Art Quarterly,* and *Bulletin* (of the Michigan Society of Architects).

WORK IN PROGRESS: Research for possible book on history of Grosse Pointe; preparing catalogue for an exhibition of the work of artist Philip Aziz.

AVOCATIONAL INTERESTS: Collecting modern art, and travel.

* * *

FESHBACH, Norma Deitch 1926-

PERSONAL: Born September 5, 1926, in New York, N.Y.; married Seymour Feshbach (a professor of psychology); children: Jonathan, Laura, Andrew. *Education:* City College (now of the City University of New York), B.S., 1947, M.S., 1949; University of Pennsylvania, Ph.D., 1956. *Residence:* Los Angeles, Calif. *Office:* Department of Education, University of California, 405 Hilgard Ave., Los Angeles, Calif. 90024.

CAREER: Yale University, New Haven, Conn., teacher at Betsy Ross Nursery School, 1947-48, clinical psychologist at Seizure Clinic, 1948; Junior College of Physical Therapy, New Haven, Conn., lecturer in child development, 1948-49; George Washington University, Washington, D.C., research assistant in Human Resources Research Office, 1951-52; Youth Services, Inc., Philadelphia, Pa., clinical and research consultant 1955-61; Stanford University, Stanford, Calif., visiting professor, 1961-62; University of California, Berkeley, lecturer in psychology, 1962-63; University of Colorado, Boulder, research associate at Institute of Behavioral Science, 1963-64; University of California, Los Angeles, associate research psychologist, 1964-65, lecturer at Neuropsychiatric Institute, 1965, assistant professor, 1965-69, associate professor, 1969-74, professor of educational psychology, 1974—, program director at Center for the Study of Evaluation, 1966-69, former head of learning and development program, head of early childhood development program. Psychology intern at Philadelphia General Hospital, 1955-56; research associate at University of Pennsylvania, 1956-57, 1959-61, lecturer, 1956-57; clinical psychologist for California Department of Mental Hygiene, 1965. Certified clinical psychologist in Pennsylvania; licensed clinical and school psychologist in California; diplomate in school psychology, from American Board of Professional Psychology. Member of psychology training review committee for National Institute of Mental Health, 1974—. Adviser on early childhood education to California legislature, 1972-73; trustee of Committee to End Violence Against the Next Generation; member of advisory board of National Committee to Abolish Corporal Punishment in Schools; member of advisory council of Riverside Women's Clinic, 1974—. Consultant to film companies.

MEMBER: International Society for Research on Aggression, International Society for the Study of Behavioral Development, American Association for the Advancement of Science, American Association of University Professors, American Educational Research Association, American Psychology Association (fellow; chairperson of Task Force on Children's Rights, 1975—), National Academy of Professional Psychologists (faculty member), National Association for the Education of Young Children, Society for the Psychological Study of Social Issues (member of council), Society for Research in Child Development, Western Psychological Association, California Association for the Education of Young Children, California Educational Research Association, California Professors of Early Childhood Education, California State Psychological Association, Sigma Xi, Delta Phi Upsilon.

WRITINGS: (With M. Frances Klein, J. M. Novotney, and others) *Guide to the Appraisal of Nursery Schools,* Institute for the Development of Educational Activities, 1970; (with John I. Goodlad and Avima Lombard) *Early Schooling in England and Israel,* McGraw, 1973.

Contributor: B. S. Greenberg and E. B. Parker, editors, *The Kennedy Assassination and the American Public,* Stanford University Press, 1965; W. J. Gnagey, editor, *Readings in the Psychology of Classroom Learning,* Holt, 1969; M. B. Miles and W. W. Charters, Jr., editors, *Learning in the Social Settings,* Allyn & Bacon, 1970; M. L. Silberman, editor, *The Experience of Schooling,* Holt, 1971; W. W. Hartup, editor, *The Young Child,* Volume II, National Association for the Education of Young Children, 1972; Gardner Lindzey, Calvin S. Hall, and Martin Manosevitz, editors, *Theories of Personality: Primary Sources and Research,* 2nd edition, Wiley, 1973; Judy F. Rosenblith, Wesley Allinsmith, and Joanna P. Williams, editors, *Readings in Child Development,* Allyn & Bacon, 1973; Anne E. Pick, editor, *Minnesota Symposia on Child Psychology,* Volume VII, University of Minnesota Press, 1973; Paul H. Mussen and M. R. Rosenzweig, editors, *Concepts in Psychology,* Heath, 1974; P. H. Mussen, John J. Conger, and Jerome Kagan, editors, *Basic and Contemporary Issues in Child Development,* Harper, 1975; Conger, editor, *Contemporary Issues in Adolescent Development,* Harper, 1975; J. DeWit and W. W. Hartup, editors, *Determinants and Origins of Aggressive Behavior,* Mouton & Co., 1975; B. J. Wishart and L. C. Reichman, editors, *Modern Sociological Issues,* Part VII, Macmillan, in press; Vernon Allen, editor, *Inter-age Interaction in Children: Theory and Research on the Helping Relationship,* University of Wisconsin Press, in press; Gerald Koocher, editor, *Children's Rights and the Mental Health Professions,* Wiley, in press.

Contributor to education and psychology journals. Member of editorial board of *Journal of Social Issues;* consulting editor of *Developmental Psychology, Journal of the Psychology of Women, Review of Educational Research.* Consultant to *American Educational Research Journal, Child Development, Merrill-Palmer Quarterly, Journal of Counseling, Journal of Abnormal Psychology,* Allyn & Bacon, and Saunders.

WORK IN PROGRESS: "Studies on Empathic Behavior in Children," to be included in *Progress in Experimental Personality Research,* Volume VIII, edited by B. A. Maher.

*   *   *

FETTERMAN, John   1920-1975

February 25, 1920—June 21, 1975; American journalist, newspaper editor, photographer, and author. Obituaries: *New York Times,* June 23, 1975.

*   *   *

FETZER, John F(rancis)   1931-

PERSONAL: Born April 25, 1931, in New York, N.Y.;

son of John (an attorney) and Mabel (a legal secretary; maiden name, Cramb) Fetzer; married Henriette Lussin (a secondary school teacher), June 24, 1961; children: Darrell, Susan. *Education:* New York University, B.A., 1953; University of Munich, graduate study, 1953-54; Columbia University, M.A., 1956; University of California, Berkeley, Ph.D., 1962. *Religion:* Protestant. *Office:* Department of German and Russian, University of California, Davis, Calif. 95616.

CAREER: Northwestern University, Evanston, Ill., instructor in German, 1962-65; University of California, Davis, assistant professor, 1965-72, associate professor of German, 1972—. *Military service:* U.S. Army, 1956-58. *Member:* American Association of Teachers of German, Phi Beta Kappa. *Awards, honors:* Fulbright grant, 1953-54; American Philosophical Society grant, 1969-70; University of California, Humanities Institute grant, 1969-70, Regents faculty fellowship, 1973.

WRITINGS: Romantic Orpheus: Profiles of Clemens Brentano, University of California Press, 1974. Contributor of articles and reviews to language journals. Member of editorial board of *Die Unterrichtspraxis;* assistant editor of "Romantic Movement Bibliography" for *English Language Notes.*

WORK IN PROGRESS: A monograph on Clemens Brentano, for Twayne; *Melos-Eros-Thanatos: Music, Love, and Death in German Literature from Medieval Times to Thomas Mann,* another monograph.

AVOCATIONAL INTERESTS: Playing piano, tennis.

*   *   *

FFRENCH BLAKE, R(obert) L(ifford) V(alentine)   1913-

PERSONAL: Born March 3, 1913, in Rawalpindi, Pakistan; son of St. John Lucius O'Brien Acheson and Doris Kathleen (Tweedie) ffrench Blake; married Grania Bryde Curran, July 11, 1939; children: Neil St. John, Anthony O'Brien. *Education:* Attended Royal Military College, 1931-33. *Politics:* Conservative. *Religion:* Church of England. *Home and office:* Midgham Park Farm, Woolhampton, Berkshire, England.

CAREER: British Army, 17/21 Lancers, 1933-45; served in North African campaign, 1942-43, and in Italy, 1944-45; left service as lieutenant colonel, 1949. Farmer in Cornwall, 1949-57; self-employed picture restorer, 1967—. Councillor of Newbury Rural District, 1970-73. *Awards, honors*—Military: Distinguished Service Order.

WRITINGS: History of the 17/21 Lancers: 1922-1959, Macmillan, 1962; *Famous Regiments: The 17/21 Lancers,* Leo Cooper, 1968; *The Crimean War,* Leo Cooper, 1971; *Dressage for Beginners,* Seeley Service, 1973; *Elementary Dressage,* Seeley Service, in press.

AVOCATIONAL INTERESTS: Music, gardening, shooting, fishing, riding, skiing, lawn tennis.

*   *   *

FIGUEROA, Pablo   1938-

PERSONAL: Born January 26, 1938, in Santurce, Puerto Rico; son of Sotero and Natividad (Davila) Figueroa. *Education:* City College of the City University of New York, B.A., 1962. *Home and office:* 321 West 22nd St., New York, N.Y. 10011.

CAREER: New York Public Library, New York, N.Y.,

technical assistant, 1965-70; free-lance television producer for National Broadcasting Co., New York, N.Y., 1971—. Photographer and theatrical director.

WRITINGS: Enrique (novel for children), Hill & Wang, 1971. Author of play, "El King Cojo," first produced Off-Off Broadway by INTAR, 1973. Television programs include "Bienvenido Means Welcome," "We, Together," and "The Hispanic Policeman." Writer of filmstrip, "Los Puertorriquenos," and other materials on Puerto Rico.

WORK IN PROGRESS: Cofresi, a short novel for children.

SIDELIGHTS: Figueroa commented: "Believe in no ideology, a few people and all children. Interested in all aspects of the communication arts."

* * *

FILSON, Floyd V(ivian)   1896-

PERSONAL: Born November 15, 1896, in Hamilton, Mo.; son of Thomas Anderson and Sarah Zelma (Adams) Filson; married Wilma H. Nutt, May 1, 1920; children: Lawrence Edwin, Kirby Ann, Don Paul, Abigail Moulton. *Education:* Park College, A.B., 1918, D.D., 1930; McCormick Theological Seminary, B.D., 1922; University of Basel, Th.D., 1930. *Home:* 101 East University Blvd., #19, Tucson, Ariz. 85705.

CAREER: Ordained Presbyterian minister, 1922; McCormick Theological Seminary, Chicago, Ill., instructor in New Testament Greek, 1923-30, professor of New Testament literature and exegesis, 1930-34, professor of New Testament literature and history, 1934-67, professor emeritus, 1967—, dean, 1954-67, acting president, 1956. Moderator of Presbytery of Chicago, 1951-52; member of Standard Bible Committee, 1952—; consultant. *Military service:* U.S. Army, Coast Artillery Corps, 1918-19; became second lieutenant.

MEMBER: Archaeological Institute of America, Society for Biblical Literature and Exegesis (president of Midwest section, 1945-46; national president, 1949), American Academy of Religion (president, 1944), Chicago Society for Biblical Research (president, 1946-47), Alumni Association (Park College; president, 1944-45).

WRITINGS: St. Paul's Conception of Recompense, J. C. Hinrichs, 1931; *Origins of the Gospels,* Abingdon, 1938; (translator with Bertram Lee Woolf) Rudolph Otto, *The Kingdom of God and the Son of Man,* Lutterworth, 1938; *Pioneers of the Primitive Church,* Abingdon, 1940; *One Lord, One Faith,* Westminster, 1943; (with G. Ernest Wright) *The Westminster Historical Atlas to the Bible,* Westminster, 1945, revised edition, 1956; (editor with others) *Westminster Study Bible,* Westminster, 1948; *The New Testament Against Its Environment: The Gospel of Christ the Risen Lord,* Allenson, 1950; (translator) Oscar Cullmann, *Christ and Time,* Westminster, 1950; (editor with Wright) *Westminster Historical Maps of Bible Lands,* Westminster, 1952; *Opening the New Testament* (juvenile), Westminster, 1953; (translator) Cullmann, *Peter: Disciple, Apostle, Martyr,* Westminster, 1953, revised edition, 1962; *Jesus Christ the Risen Lord,* Abingdon, 1956; *Which Books Belong in the Bible: A Study of the Canon,* Westminster, 1957; *A Commentary on the Gospel According to St. Matthew,* Harper, 1960, revised edition, Allenson, 1971; *Three Crucial Decades: Studies in the Book of Acts,* John Knox, 1963; *The Gospel According to John,* John Knox, 1963; *A New Testament History: The Story of the Emerging*

Church, Westminster, 1964; *Yesterday: A Study of Hebrews in the Light of Chapter Thirteen,* Allenson, 1967; *The Gospel for God's People: A Study of the Gospel of Matthew,* with teacher's book, Covenant Life Curriculum Press, 1970. Contributor to theology journals. Editor of *New Testament Book Review,* 1950-56.

* * *

FINK, Edith   1918-

PERSONAL: Born December 28, 1918, in Chicago, Ill.; daughter of Joseph (an inventor) and Ann (Berman) Goldberg; married Robert Fink (a writer), December 28, 1941. *Education:* Attended Art Institute of Chicago, Pierce College, and California State University, Northridge. *Politics:* None. *Home and office:* 18418 Hiawatha St., Northridge, Calif. 91324. *Agent:* Roy Porter, Porter, Gould & Dierks, 1236 Sherman Ave., Evanston, Ill. 60202.

CAREER: Silversmith, lapidary, and teacher of arts and crafts. *Member:* Alpha Mu Gamma.

WRITINGS: Hot Birds and Cold Bottles, Delacorte, 1972; *Household Hints,* Western Publishing Co., 1972. Also translator from Spanish, *The White Rose,* and *The Death Ship,* both by B. Traven. Contributor to *Gourmet, Sunset,* and other magazines.

WORK IN PROGRESS: A novel, *The Hummingbird Express; Neptune's Kitchen,* a shellfish cookbook.

* * *

FINLEY, Lewis M(erren)   1929-

PERSONAL: Born November 29, 1929, in Reubens, Idaho; son of John E. (a logger and blacksmith) and Charlotte (Priest) Finley; married Virginia R. Spousta, February 23, 1957; children: Ellen Annette, Charlotte Louise. *Home:* 3015 Southeast Riviere Dr., Milwaukie, Ore. 97222. *Office:* Family Financial Planners, Inc., 1924 Northeast Broadway, Portland, Ore. 97232.

CAREER: Household Finance Corp., assistant manager in the northwestern states, 1953-56; Doug Gerow Finance, Portland, Ore., manager, 1956-61; Family Financial Planners, Inc., Portland, Ore., president, 1961—. *Military service:* U.S. Army, 1951-53, instructor at Signal School. *Member:* American Association of Credit Counselors, Northwest Association of Credit Counselors.

WRITINGS: The Complete Guide for Getting Yourself Out of Debt, Fell, 1975.

SIDELIGHTS: Finley writes: "I have spent almost my entire life in the study of a jungle and the almost invisible road out of it, some call it credit, I call it the 'debt jungle.' I am motivated toward illuminating the path out of this jungle and in doing so, perhaps fighting the largest, most wealthy group of men that exist anywhere. . . . I hope to be the instrument that completely changes it for the better." *Avocational interests:* Golf, photography, researching his family tree ("I have discovered that my relatives have been in this country since before the 1600's. They were the pioneers who crossed the rivers and deserts of this nation by covered wagon and fought the Indians along the way. They participated in everything from the Salem witch trials and Daniel Boone's discovery of Kentucky to the McIntosh apple.").

* * *

FINNEY, Theodore M(itchell)   1902-

PERSONAL: Born March 14, 1902, in Fayette, Iowa; son

of Ross Lee (a professor and sociologist) and Caroline (Mitchell) Finney; married Myrle Creeley, August 1, 1925. *Education:* University of Minnesota, B.A., 1924; graduate study at Conservatoire Americaine, summer, 1926, and Stern Conservatory, 1927-28; University of Pittsburgh, Litt.M., 1938. *Politics:* Democrat. *Religion:* United Church of Christ. *Home:* 209 Gladstone Rd., Pittsburgh, Pa. 15217.

CAREER: Minneapolis (now Minnesota) Symphony Orchestra, Minneapolis, Minn., violist, 1923-25; music teacher and supervisor in public schools in Council Bluffs, Iowa, 1925; Carleton College, Northfield, Minn., instructor, 1925-27, assistant professor of music, 1927-32; music teacher and supervisor in public schools of Council Bluffs, Iowa, 1933-36; University of Pittsburgh, Pittsburgh, Pa., lecturer, 1936-38, assistant professor, 1938-39, associate professor, 1939-41, professor of music, 1941-68, professor emeritus, 1968—. Member of summer school faculty at Smith College, 1930-38; curator of Warrington Collection in the Library at Pittsburgh Theological Seminary, 1967—.

MEMBER: American Musicological Society, Music Teachers National Association (member of executive committee, 1938-55), Royal Musical Association, Phi Beta Kappa, Phi Delta Kappa, Omicron Delta Kappa, Phi Alpha Theta, Phi Mu Alpha (Sinfonia). *Awards, honors:* First prize from National Composers Congress, 1945, for essay "Musical Nationalism and Patriotism."

WRITINGS: A History of Music, Harcourt, 1935, revised edition, 1947; *Hearing Music,* Harcourt, 1941; *We Have Made Music,* University of Pittsburgh Press, 1955; (contributor) George Swetnam, editor, *Where Else But Pittsburgh!,* Davis & Woode, 1958; (editor) *A Union Catalogue of Music and Books on Music Printed before 1801 in Pittsburgh Libraries,* University of Pittsburgh Press, 1959, revised edition, 1963; (contributor) Arthur Jacobs, editor, *Choral Music,* Penguin, 1963; (contributor) Gustave Reese and Robert J. Snow, editors, *Essays in Musicology,* University of Pittsburgh Press, 1969; (editor) *James Warrington's Psalmody Short Titles,* Pittsburgh Theological Seminary, 1970. Editor for Music Teachers National Association, 1939-50.

WORK IN PROGRESS: "An earlier source for the tune 'Turro.'"

AVOCATIONAL INTERESTS: Gardening, woodworking.

* * *

FIORIO, Franco Emilio 1912-1975

June 12, 1912—May 12, 1975; Italian diplomat, expert on space and aviation, athlete, writer. Obituaries: *Washington Post,* May 16, 1975.

* * *

FISHER, Harold H. 1890-1975

February 15, 1890—November 15, 1975; American historian, educator, administrator, expert on international relations, author of books in his field. Obituaries: *New York Times,* November 17, 1975.

* * *

FISHER, Philip A(rthur) 1907-

PERSONAL: Born September 8, 1907, in San Francisco, Calif.; son of Arthur L. (a physician) and Eugenia (Sam-

uels) Fisher; married Dorothy Whyte, August 14, 1943. *Education:* Stanford University, A.B., 1927, graduate study, 1927-28. *Residence:* San Mateo, Calif. 94402. *Office:* Fisher & Co., 1820 Mills Tower, 220 Bush St., San Francisco, Calif. 94104.

CAREER: Fisher & Co. (investment advisors), San Francisco, Calif., founder and owner, 1931-46, manager, 1946—.

WRITINGS: Common Stocks and Uncommon Profits, Harper, 1958, revised edition, 1960; *Paths to Wealth through Common Stocks,* Prentice-Hall, 1960; *Conservative Investors Sleep Well,* Harper, 1975.

* * *

FISHER, Robert J(ay) 1924-

PERSONAL: Born May 6, 1924, in Chicago, Ill.; son of Ira I. (in produce) and Ida (Fisher) Fisher; married Charlene T. Fisher, June 27, 1948 (divorced, 1975); children: Robin, David. *Education:* Stanford University, B.A., 1947, M.A., 1948, Ed.D., 1952. *Religion:* Jewish. *Home:* 1689 Arlington, Ann Arbor, Mich. 48104. *Office:* Eastern Michigan University, Ypsilanti, Mich. 48197.

CAREER: Elementary school teacher in Redwood City, Calif., 1948-50; curriculum coordinator for San Diego County Schools, 1952-54; Eastern Michigan University, Ypsilanti, Mich., professor of elementary education, 1955—. Exchange professor and researcher in England, 1969-71, and summers, 1972, 1973. *Military service:* U.S. Navy, 1943-46. *Member:* Association for Supervision and Curriculum Development, National Council for the Social Studies, Michigan Council on Social Studies, Michigan Association for Supervision and Curriculum Development, Phi Beta Kappa, Phi Delta Kappa, Kappa Delta Pi.

WRITINGS: Learning How to Learn: The English Primary School and American Education, Harcourt, 1972; (with Wilfred R. Smith) *Schools in an Age of Crisis,* Van Nostrand, 1972.

WORK IN PROGRESS: Research on open education in the United States and England.

* * *

FISHMAN, Lew 1939-

PERSONAL: Born June 20, 1939, in Albany, N.Y.; son of Phillip (a drycleaner and tailor) and Ann (a clerk; maiden name, Bellin) Fishman; married Joanne Alessandroni, November 28, 1964; children: David, Lee. *Education:* Rutgers University, B.A., 1964; University of Suffolk, graduate study in law, 1966-67. *Home:* 76 Highland Ave., Port Washington, N.Y. 11050. *Office:* Long Island Press, Jamaica, N.Y.

CAREER: Sports writer and sports editor for daily newspapers on the East Coast, including *Baltimore Sun, Albany Times-Union,* and *New York Post,* 1962-71; *Long Island Press,* Jamaica, N.Y., sports writer, 1971—. Has worked as public relations representative for Madison Square Garden and as business manager of Peninsula Astro Baseball Club. *Member:* Professional Basketball Writers of America, Professional Football Writers of America, Baseball Writers of America, Golf Writers of America, New York Press Club.

WRITINGS: New York Mets: Miracle at Shea, Prentice-Hall, 1974; *The New York Knicks: Pride of Gotham,* Prentice-Hall, 1974.

FITZSIMONS, Louise 1932-

PERSONAL: Born April 18, 1932, in New Haven, Conn.; daughter of Edmund Francis (a physician) and Mary (Flanery) Fitzsimons. Education: Wellesley College, B.A. (with honors), 1954; Yale University, graduate study, 1954-55; Georgetown University, M.A., 1960; University of Paris, further graduate study, 1959-61. Home: 12 Riveredge, Milford, Conn. 06460. Agent: Collins, Knowlton, Wing, Inc., 60 East 56th St., New York, N.Y. 10022. Office: 1612 20th St. N.W., Washington, D.C. 20009.

CAREER: Egyptian Embassy, Washington, D.C., press aide, 1955-56; U.S. Atomic Energy Commission, Washington, D.C., employed in Division of International Affairs, 1956-59; U.S. Embassy, Paris, France, foreign affairs officer in Office of the Atomic Energy Commission Representative, 1960; Carnegie Endowment for International Peace, New York, N.Y., research editor in department of research and publications, 1962, associate editor, 1962-63; free-lance writer and researcher in Washington, D.C., 1964; U.S. Senate, Washington, D.C., research assistant and speechwriter for Senator Eugene J. McCarthy, 1965-71; free-lance writer and consultant, 1971—.

WRITINGS: The Kennedy Doctrine, Random House, 1972. Author of a national political affairs column in Milford Citizen, 1972—.

WORK IN PROGRESS: A biography of Helen Rogers Reid; research on the roots of modern American political leadership, examined through biographical portraits.

SIDELIGHTS: Louise Fitzsimons writes: "In my current writing, I am trying to apply to the study of political personalities and the political process my years of observation and professional experience in the executive and legislative branches of the U.S. government."

BIOGRAPHICAL/CRITICAL SOURCES: Columbia Journalism Review, January-February, 1973.

*   *   *

FLANERY, E(dward) B(oyd) 1932-

PERSONAL: Born February 10, 1932, in Ecorse, Mich.; son of Edward Boyd (an engineer) and Julia (Beres) Flanery; married JoAnn Wright (an executive secretary), June 7, 1952; children: Frank Boyd, Jolyn (Mrs. M. A. Long), Mark James. Education: Attended Kieo University and Texas A & M University. Politics: Moderate. Religion: Agnostic. Home: 634 Hickory Dr., P.O. Box 254, Cleveland, Okla. 74020. Office: Sun Oil Co., 600 Detroit, Tulsa, Okla. 74102.

CAREER: Sun Oil Co., Tulsa, Okla., began as assistant city ticket and passenger agent, became senior lease operator. Military service: U.S. Army; received Republic of Korea ribbon with spear head.

WRITINGS: The Crack in the Bible, Ashley Books, 1974; Before Genesis: The Many Faces of God, Ashley Books, in press.

WORK IN PROGRESS: Our Chaotic Cosmos, for Ashley Books.

*   *   *

FLEMER, William III 1922-

PERSONAL: Born January 18, 1922, in Princeton, N.J.; son of William, Jr. (a nurseryman) and Emma Louise (Wilkinson) Flemer; married Elizabeth V. S. Sinclair, July 3, 1948; children: Louise W., Harriet D., William IV. Education: Yale University, B.A., 1946, M.S., 1948. Religion: Episcopalian. Address: Princeton Nurseries, P.O. Box 191, Princeton, N.J. 08540.

CAREER: Princeton Nurseries, Princeton, N.J., president, 1948—. Chairman of New Jersey Governor's Rural Advisory Council, 1960-65, of Stony Brook-Millstone Watersheds Association, 1962-65, and of board of directors of U.S. National Arboretum, 1971—. Military service: U.S. Army, 1942-45. Member: International Plant Propagator's Society, Royal Horticultural Society, American Horticultural Society, American Association of Nurserymen (president, 1969-70), Eastern Nurseryman's Association (president, 1963-64), New Jersey Association of Nurserymen (president, 1959-60). Awards, honors: Thomas Roland Medal from Massachusetts Horticultural Society, 1965; American Horticultural Society commercial citation, 1972.

WRITINGS: (Contributor) Henry J. Skinner, editor, Garden Plants in Color, Sweeny, Krist & Dimm, 1958; Shade and Ornamental Trees in Color, Grosset, 1965; Nature's Guide to Successful Landscaping and Gardening, Crowell, 1972.

AVOCATIONAL INTERESTS: Ornithology, ecology.

*   *   *

FLORIOT, Rene 1902-1975

October 20, 1902—December 21, 1975; French trial lawyer, author of books on famous trials and legal subjects. Obituaries: New York Times, December 23, 1975.

*   *   *

FLOWER, Margaret Cameron Coss

PERSONAL: Born in Ashland, Ohio, daughter of John David and Mabel (Beer) Coss; married; children: Nicholas. Education: Bryn Mawr College, B.A., 1928; attended Newnham College, Cambridge. Home: 3 Village Close, London N.W. 3, England.

WRITINGS: (Compiler) Thomas Stanley, 1625-78: A Bibliography of His Writings in Prose and Verse, Cambridge Bibliographical Society, 1950; Victorian Jewellery, Cassell, 1951, revised edition, A. S. Barnes, 1973; (with Oton Grozdic) Essential Yugoslav for Travellers, Cassell, 1958.

*   *   *

FOOTE, Darby Mozelle 1942-

PERSONAL: Born July 30, 1942, in McKinney, Tex.; daughter of Henry and Dessie (Lane) Foster; married Coy Foote (a salesman), July 26, 1960; children: Robert, Fred, Nancy, Ann Marie. Education: McLennan Community College, A.A.S., 1975. Religion: Unity. Home: 5018 Lakemoor Dr., Waco, Tex. 76710. Agent: Paul R. Reynolds, Inc., 12 East 41st St., New York, N.Y. 10017.

CAREER: Has worked for Adult Probation Department, Waco, Tex., Opportunity Center (a home for young probationers), Veterans Administration Day Hospital, and Drying Out Center (a center for recovering alcoholics). Member: Mental Health Associates of Waco, Phi Theta Kappa.

WRITINGS: Baby Love and Casey Blue, Putnam, 1975. Also author of novel, Someday Soon.

AVOCATIONAL INTERESTS: Reading, history, animals, people ("especially children"), clothing design.

FORD, D(ouglas) W(illiam) Cleverley 1914-

PERSONAL: Born March 4, 1914, in Sheringham, England; son of Arthur James (a clerk) and Mildred (Cleverley) Ford; married Olga Mary Gilbart-Smith, June 28, 1939. *Education:* University of London, A.L.C.D. (first class honors), and B.D., 1936, M.Th., 1941. *Home:* Lambeth Palace, London SE1 7JU, England; and Rostrevor, Lingfield, Surrey RH7 6BZ, England.

CAREER: Ordained Anglican priest, 1937; London College of Divinity, London, England, tutor, 1936-39; curate in Bridlington, England, 1939-42; vicar in Hampstead, London, 1942-55, and in Kensington Gore, England, 1955-74; senior chaplain to Archbishop of Canterbury, England, 1975—. Director of College of Preachers, 1960-73; chairman, Queen Alexandra's House Association, 1965-74; governor, Westminster City School, 1965-74; rural dean of Westminster, 1965-73; prebendary of St. Paul's Cathedral, London, 1968; canon of York, 1969; chaplain to Queen Elizabeth II, 1973—. *Member:* Athenaeum Club (London).

WRITINGS: Why Men Believe in Jesus Christ, Lutterworth, 1950.

An Expository Preacher's Notebook, Hodder & Stoughton, 1960, Harper, 1961; *A Theological Preacher's Notebook,* Hodder & Stoughton, 1962; *A Pastoral Preacher's Notebook,* Hodder & Stoughton, 1965; *A Reading of Saint Luke's Gospel,* Lippincott, 1967; *Preaching at the Parish Communion,* Mowbray, Volume I, 1967, Volume II, 1968, Volume III, 1969, Volume VII, 1975; *Preaching Today,* Epworth, 1969.

Preaching through the Christian Year, Mowbray, 1971; *Praying through the Christian Year,* Mowbray, 1973; *Have You Anything to Declare?,* Mowbray, 1973; *Preaching on Opening Occasions,* Mowbray, 1975; *New Preaching From the Old Testament,* Mowbray, 1976. Contributor to *Expository Times.*

AVOCATIONAL INTERESTS: Languages, music, gardening, and maintaining a country cottage.

* * *

FOSTER, F. Blanche 1919-

PERSONAL: Born January 6, 1919, in Centerville, Tenn.; daughter of L. George (a clergyman) and Blanche (a teacher; maiden name, Nunnelly) Foster; married Francis L. Robinson (divorced). *Education:* Tennessee State University, B.S., 1940; Atlanta University, B.L.S., 1947; University of Michigan, A.M.L.S., 1952; further graduate study at Wayne State University, Sophia University, and University of Ghana. *Religion:* Presbyterian. *Home:* 2239 Spruce St., Terre Haute, Ind. 47807. *Office:* South High School Library, 3737 South Seventh St., Terre Haute, Ind. 47802.

CAREER: High school teacher of English in Cookville, Tenn., 1940-43; Camp Breckenridge, Breckenridge, Ky., librarian, 1944-45; U.S. Department of the Navy, Washington, D.C., processor, 1945-46; Huston-Tillotson College, Austin, Tex., librarian, 1947-49; high school librarian in Austin, Tex., 1949-51; librarian for public schools in Detroit, Mich., 1951-71, assistant director of "Focus on Afro-American Culture" program, 1968; University of Ibadan, Ibadan, Nigeria, lecturer in library science, 1971-73; South High School, Terre Haute, Ind., librarian, 1974—. *Member:* Women's International League for Peace and Freedom, American Library Association, American Federation of Teachers, American Association for the Advance-

ment of Colored People, Young Women's Christian Association, Alpha Kappa Alpha. *Awards, honors:* Recognition award from Indiana Black Caucus, 1975.

WRITINGS: Kenya, F. Watts, 1969; *People to Know Better,* Good Reading Communications, 1971; *Dahomey,* F. Watts, 1971; *The West Indies: A Conceptual View,* Carlton, in press. Contributor to *Michigan Challenge.*

SIDELIGHTS: Blanche Foster writes: "The stories my grandmother related greatly influenced my feelings about Africa. She told us of her trip to America on a slave ship with her brothers when she was a very little girl. She told us of the beauties of her land by the waters. And she told us about slavery.... What would I be doing if I had been born a black girl in Africa and where would I be? ... As an adult I have tried to see as many places in the world as I can. Everywhere I go I seem to be attracted to the children who differ in shades of skin color or dress. We get along well together and it is with them and my students that I enjoy some of my best moments of happiness."

AVOCATIONAL INTERESTS: Collecting maps.

* * *

FOX, Dorothea Warren 1914-

PERSONAL: Born January 31, 1914, in Birmingham, Ala.; daughter of William Tilman (an architect) and Dorothea (Orr) Warren; married Charles Fox (an artist), February 15, 1940; children: Charles, Jr., Rebecca Jane (Mrs. James Cottle), Robert, Catlin. *Education:* Attended Birmingham Southern College, 1932-34. *Home address:* Woodcreek Rd., New Fairfield, Conn. 06810.

CAREER: Commercial artist and illustrator. Member of Connecticut artist-in-the-classroom program, 1969-73; member of local Park Board; chairman of board of directors of local library.

WRITINGS—For children: Miss Twiggley's Tree, Parents' Magazine Press, 1966; *Follow Me, the Leader,* Parents' Magazine Press, 1968.

Illustrator: Benjamin Spock, *The Common Sense Book of Baby and Child Care,* Deull, Sloan & Pearce, 1946, 4th edition published as *Baby and Child Care,* 1976; Edward Streeter, *Mr. Hobbs' Vacation* (juvenile), Harper, 1954; Streeter, *Merry Christmas, Mr. Baxter* (juvenile), Harper, 1956. Contributor of illustrations to *Encyclopaedia Britannica.* Contributor to popular magazines, including *Reader's Digest* and to women's magazines.

* * *

FRANCIS, Devon 1901-

PERSONAL: Born April 3, 1901, in South Bend, Ind.; son of Joseph W. (a railroad man) and Grace E. (Cottrell) Francis; married second wife, Rosemary Postle Ball, July 15, 1950; children: (first marriage) Devon Alan; Robert Steward Ball (stepson). *Education:* University of Kansas, A.B., 1924. *Politics:* Republican. *Religion:* Baptist. *Home:* 1600 North Wilmont Rd. #271, Tucson, Ariz. 85712. *Agent:* August Lenninger Literary Agency, 437 Fifth Ave., New York, N.Y. 10016.

CAREER: Associated Press, New York, N.Y., 1925-42, worked as staff writer in Denver, Los Angeles, and Cleveland, as aviation editor in New York City, and as bureau chief in Wichita and Phoenix; *Time* magazine, New York City, staff member, 1942; free-lance writer, 1943-44; *Popular Science* magazine, New York City, assistant to editor,

1944-64, senior editor, 1964-68; free-lance book consultant, 1968—. *Member:* Aviation/Space Writers Association (founding president). *Awards, honors:* First winner, Trans World Airlines, Inc., aviation writing award, 1938; Aviation/Space Writers Association award for best magazine article, 1962.

WRITINGS: Aviation: What Everyone Should Know, Bobbs-Merrill, 1944; *The Story of the Helicopter,* Coward, 1945; *Flak Bait,* Duell, Sloan & Pearce, 1946; *Mr. Piper and His Cubs,* Iowa State University Press, 1973. Contributor of articles to magazines in his field.

* * *

FRANKEL, Bernice

PERSONAL: Born in New York, N.Y.; married Ray Hunold (a photographer). *Home:* 900 Bay St., San Francisco, Calif. 94109.

CAREER: In earlier years was children's book editor and reviewer in New York, N.Y.; was junior author for Macmillan Co. on Harris-Clark readers, writing original stories as well as selecting and adapting material as texts for lower grades; children's book editor for Abelard-Schuman Ltd., and later for Parents' Magazine Press; weekly columnist, "Books for Children," for Saturday Review Newspaper Syndicate, during 1950's. *Awards, honors: Half-as-Big and the Tiger,* illustrated by Leonard Weisgard, was one of fifteen picture books on *New York Times* list of the hundred best children's books of 1961.

WRITINGS—Picture books: *Half-as-Big and the Tiger,* F. Watts, 1961; *Timothy and Alexander the Great,* A. S. Barnes, 1962; *The Seven Monkeys,* A. S. Barnes, 1962; *Tag-Along,* Parents' Magazine Press, 1962; *Two Stories About Rickey,* Whitman Publishing, 1966; *Tom and the Zoo,* Whitman Publishing, 1967; *Grandpa's Policemen Friends,* Whitman Publishing, 1967. Contributor of articles on children's books to *Town and Country, American Home,* and other national magazines.

WORK IN PROGRESS: Travel articles illustrated with her husband's photographs.

SIDELIGHTS: Bernice Frankel wrote: "My husband and I have photographed close to a dozen different deserts, as well as seacoasts from Washington down through Oregon and California to Baja, Mexico. Also woodlands, rain forest in Olympia, most national parks and monuments, rock country such as the Grand Canyon—and most of all our beloved city by adoption, San Francisco. We moved here from New York in 1970 and love it more with each year."

* * *

FRANKEL, Hans H(ermann) 1916-

PERSONAL: Born December 19, 1916, in Berlin, Germany; came to United States, 1935; naturalized U.S. citizen, 1942; son of Hermann Ferdinand (a professor) and Lilli (Fraenkel) Frankel; married Ch'ung-ho Chang (a calligrapher, painter, and poet), November 19, 1948; children: Ian Hermann, Emma Lilli. *Education:* Stanford University, A.B., 1937; University of California, Berkeley, M.A., 1938, Ph.D., 1942, additional study, 1945-47. *Home:* 87 Ridgewood Ave., Hamden, Conn. 06517. *Office:* 309 Hall of Graduate Studies, Yale University, New Haven, Conn. 06520.

CAREER: University of California, Berkeley, lecturer in Spanish, 1945-47; National Peking University, Peking,

China, associate professor of Western languages, 1947-48; University of California, Berkeley, general assistant at East Asiatic Library, 1949-51, lecturer in Oriental languages, 1950-51, research historian at Institute of East Asiatic Studies, 1951-59, lecturer in history, 1957-59; Stanford University, Stanford, Calif., assistant professor of Chinese, 1959-61; Yale University, New Haven, Conn., associate professor, 1961-67, professor of Chinese literature, 1967—. Visiting professor, Universitat Hamburg, 1964, Columbia University, 1966-67, and University of Bonn, 1974. *Wartime service:* Worked for Federal Communications Commission, Office of War Information, and Office of Strategic Services, 1942-45. U.S. Coast Guard Reserve, 1944. *Member:* American Oriental Society, Association for Asian Studies, Chinese Language Teachers Association. *Awards, honors:* Guggenheim fellowship and Yale senior faculty fellowship, 1965-66.

WRITINGS: Catalogue of Translations from the Chinese Dynastic Histories for the Period 220-960, University of California Press, 1957; *The Flowering Plum and the Palace Lady: Interpretations of Chinese Poetry,* Yale University Press, 1976.

Contributor: Arthur F. Wright and Denis Twitchett, editors, *Confucian Personalities,* Stanford University Press, 1962; Golo Mann and August Nitschke, editors, *Propylaen-Weltgeschichte* (title means "World History"), Volume VI, Ullstein, 1964; W. K. Wimsatt, editor, *Versification: Major Language Types,* New York University Press, 1972; Arthur F. Wright and Denis Twitchett, editors, *Perspectives on the T'ang,* Yale University Press, 1973; Cyril Birch, editor, *Studies in Chinese Literary Genres,* University of California Press, 1974. Contributor of articles to journals, including *Comparative Literature, Harvard Journal of Asiatic Studies, Asiatische Studien,* and *Journal of the American Oriental Society.* Associate editor, *Journal of Asian Studies,* during 1950's.

WORK IN PROGRESS: A book on Chinese ballads.

SIDELIGHTS: In addition to being fluent in Chinese, Hans Frankel speaks some French and Spanish, and reads Italian, Portuguese, Latin, and some Japanese. *Avocational interests:* Playing the piano (especially Beethoven), swimming, bicycling, walking, running.

* * *

FRANKLIN, J(ennie) E(lizabeth) 1937-

PERSONAL: Born August 10, 1937, in Houston, Tex.; daughter of Robert (a cook) and Mathie (a maid; maiden name, Randle) Franklin; married Lawrence Siegel, November 12, 1964 (deceased); children: Malika N'zinga. *Education:* University of Texas, B.A., 1964. *Residence:* New York, N.Y.

CAREER: Writer; Freedom School, Carthage, Miss., primary school teacher, summer, 1964; Neighborhood House Association, Buffalo, N.Y., youth director, 1964-65; U.S. Office of Economic Opportunity, analyst in New York, N.Y., 1967-68; Herbert H. Lehman College of the City University of New York, Bronx, N.Y., lecturer in education, 1969-75. *Member:* Author's League of America, Dramatists Guild, Professional Staff Congress. *Awards, honors:* New York Drama Desk Most Promising Playwright Award, 1971, for "Black Girl"; Institute for the Arts and Humanities dramatic arts award, 1974.

WRITINGS: Black Girl: From Genesis to Revelations (non-fiction; includes playscript), Howard University Press, 1976.

Plays: "A First Step to Freedom" (one-act), produced in Harmony, Miss., at Sharon Waite Community Center, 1964; "The Mau Mau Room" (three-act), produced in New York at Negro Ensemble Company, 1969; *Black Girl* (two-act; produced Off-Broadway at Theater de Lys, 1971), Dramatists Play Service, 1972; *The Prodigal Sister* (two-act; produced Off-Broadway at Theatre de Lys, 1976), Samuel French, in press.

Other plays; as yet neither published nor produced: "Cut Out the Lights and Call the Law," three-act; "Four Women," one-act; "The In-Crowd," one-act; "Things Our Way," one-act; "The Enemy," two-act; "MacPilate," one-act; "The Creation," one-act; "Intercession," two-act; "Till the Well Run Dry," three-act. Also author of screenplays, "Black Girl," based on play *Black Girl*, released by Cinerama, 1972, and "If He Has Gun."

WORK IN PROGRESS: Split the Adam: Theological Roots of Ontological Engineering, a research on the effects of meta-biological engineering on the human species, completion expected in 1976; *Artcentric Education: A Unitive Approach to Learning.*

SIDELIGHTS: John Simon observed that in *Black Girl*, Ms. Franklin "has created a striking cast of characters and she can turn out some quite presentable patches of dialogue, as well as produce swift, compelling flare-ups of violence." The play ran for an entire season in New York, and was the only Off-Broadway production of the 1971-72 season to have a film sale. "I feel that plays should not mirror the condition, but be presented in such a way that they leave you with choices," she told Charlayne Hunter. "*Black Girl* is a play about choices. And that's what black theatre and the arts should be about."

"The character of art forms in our culture leaves a strong suggestion of a fundamental theocentric ingredient undergirding American socio-political thought," Ms. Franklin commented to *CA*. "I would like to pursue an insight that the forces and systems which are at work in our culture spring from theological rather than economic ingredients."

BIOGRAPHICAL/CRITICAL SOURCES: New York Times, July 13, 1971; *New York*, August 2, 1971; *Black World*, April, 1972; *Black Creation*, Fall, 1972; *Time*, December 4, 1972.

* * *

FRANZEN, Lavern G(erhardt) 1926-

PERSONAL: Born May 18, 1926, in Leigh, Neb.; son of Frank L. (a bookkeeper) and Addie K. (Korfhage) Franzen; married Mary Ann Karen Langevin (a teacher), August 20, 1948; children: Kathryn (Mrs. Jonathan Miller), Frank, Sheryl, Deborah. *Education:* Concordia Teachers College, Seward, Neb., B.Sc. in Ed., 1948; Concordia Seminary, M.A., 1964. *Politics:* Democrat. *Home:* 512 Hibiscus Dr., Temple Terrace, Fla. 33617. *Office:* Our Redeemer Lutheran Church, 304 Druid Hills Rd., Temple Terrace, Fla. 33617.

CAREER: Ordained minister of Lutheran Church, 1963; parochial high school teacher of New Testament and choral music in Detroit, Mich., 1949-64; pastor in Carrollton, Mich., 1964-69, and Temple Terrace, Fla., 1969—.

WRITINGS: Smile, God Loves You, Augsburg, 1973; *Smile, Jesus Is Lord*, Augsburg, 1975; *He Is Coming*, Lutheran Laymen's League, in press.

WORK IN PROGRESS: Prayers of an Honest Man; Pop Parables; Family Worship to Do; Pop Folk Mass.

FRASER, J(ulius) T(homas) 1923-

PERSONAL: Born May 7, 1923, in Budapest, Hungary; came to U.S. in 1946, naturalized citizen in 1953; son of Francis (an attorney) and Olga (Szigethy) Fraser; married Margaret Cameron (a musician), 1948 (divorced, 1970); married Jane Felsenthal (a school teacher), 1973; children: Thomas C. Fraser, Anne-Marie C. Fraser, Carol Hunsicker, Margaret C. Fraser, Ann Hunsicker. *Education:* Cooper Union School of Engineering, B.E.E., 1951; Technische Universitaet Hannover, Ph.D., 1970. *Politics:* "A Jeffersonian independent." *Religion:* "Christian by private creed." *Office address:* P.O. Box 815, Westport, Conn. 06880.

CAREER: Worked as a machinist, technician, and draftsman in Budapest, Hungary, 1941-44; Allied Control Commission, Rome, Italy, English correspondent, 1945-46; cataloger at Columbia University Libraries, contract inspector for Electrolux Vacuum Cleaners, and laboratory foreman at North American Philips, Inc., 1947-50; Rangertone, Inc., Newark, N.J., design draftsman, 1950-51; Westinghouse Electric Corp., Baltimore, Md., junior engineer, 1951-53; General Precision Laboratory (now Singer-Kearfott, Inc.), Pleasantville, N.Y., staff member, 1955-57, senior staff member, 1957-62, senior scientist in physics department of Research Division, 1962-71; independent researcher in study of time, 1971—. Visiting lecturer at Massachusetts Institute of Technology, 1966-67, and Mt. Holyoke College, 1967-69; visiting professor at University of Maryland, 1969-70; adjunct assistant professor at Fordham University, 1971—.

MEMBER: International Society for the Study of Time (founder and secretary), Institute of Electrical and Electronics Engineers (past senior member).

WRITINGS: Of Time, Passion, and Knowledge: Reflections on the Strategy of Existence, Braziller, 1975.

Editor: (And contributor) *The Voices of Time: A Cooperative Survey of Man's Views of Time as Expressed by the Sciences and the Humanities*, Braziller, 1966; (with F. C. Haber and G. H. Mueller, and contributor) *The Study of Time I*, Springer-Verlag, 1972; (with N. Lawrence, and contributor) *The Study of Time II*, Springer-Verlag, 1975.

Contributor to *Britannica Yearbook of Science and the Future*. Contributor of articles and reviews to scientific journals.

WORK IN PROGRESS: Time as Conflict: Essays on a Comprehensive Philosophy; editing and writing material for *The Study of Time III*, for Springer-Verlag; editing a library of monographs, "Perspectives in the Study of Time" series, publication by Braziller expected in 1977.

SIDELIGHTS: Fraser writes: "As a young child growing up in the Hungarian countryside, I liked to tell people that I shall be 'a blacksmith, explorer, and everyone's friend.' The 'blacksmith' progressed through technician, draftsman, engineer, inventor, physicist, philosopher, and writer to the formulation of a new natural philosophy, that of time as a hierarchy of creative conflicts. The 'explorer' still travels around the world in search for ideas and feelings that hide in various places. The 'friend' remains a profound empathy for people and an unremitting concern with the specialness of being human.

"All three paths are joined in my dedication to the study of time which (by 1976) spans over thirty years. The leitmotivs of my labors trace the chronological development of the theory of time as conflict, as an adolescent in World

War Two watching the clash of cultures and the attendant release of primordial emotions, as a young man, observing America from along the upper Hudson. Because of the absence of ideals inspiring as well as intelligible I see our epoch as essentially uninformed in spite of the spectacular results of man's control of himself and his world. I see my current task as a writer, philosopher, and scientist in recording and understanding the march which is not to the tune of Dies Irae, or even to that of the Communist Internationale, but to something more elemental: it is to the voices of the caged mind which is in revolt against its own, unresolvable conflicts. As an individual I see my responsibility to be part of the motive force behind this march, and pursue it toward its unknown end."

Fraser holds U.S. patents on several technical devices.

*   *   *

FRASER DARLING, Frank   1903-

PERSONAL: Born June 23, 1903, in Scotland; married Marian Fraser, 1925 (divorced, 1948); married Averil Morley, 1948 (died, 1957); married Christina Macinnes Brotchie, 1960; children: (first marriage) one son; (second marriage) two sons, one daughter. *Education:* University of Edinburgh, N.D.A., 1922, Ph.D., 1930, D.Sc., 1939. *Home:* Lochyhill, Forres, Moray, Scotland.

CAREER: Member of agricultural staff, Buckinghamshire (England) County council, 1924-27; University of Edinburgh, Imperial Bureau of Animal Genetics, Edinburgh, Scotland, chief officer, 1930-34; director of development commission of West Highland Survey, 1944-50; University of Edinburgh, senior lecturer in ecology and conservation, 1953-58; Conservation Foundation, Washington, D.C., vice-president, 1959-72; writer, 1972—. Member of Royal Commission on Environmental Pollution, 1970-73. Reith lecturer at British Broadcasting Corp., 1969.

MEMBER: Institute of Biology (fellow), Royal Society of Edinburgh (fellow), Athenaeum Club, New Club (Edinburgh). *Awards, honors:* Leverhulme research fellowship, 1933-36; Carnegie research fellowship, 1936-39; Mungo Park Medal from Royal Scottish Geographical Society, 1947; Rockefeller special research fellowship, 1950; LL.D. from University of Glasgow; D.Sc. from Heriot-Watt University, New University of Ulster, and Williams College; knighted in 1970; centenary medal from U.S. National Park Service, 1972; Order of Golden Ark (the Netherlands), 1973; J. C. Phillips Medal from International Union Conservation of Nature, 1975.

WRITINGS: Animal Breeding in the British Empire: A Survey of Research and Experiment, Oliver & Boyd, 1934; (editor with James H. Ashworth) *A Bibliography of the Works of James Cossar Ewart,* Animal Breeding Abstracts, 1934; *A Herd of Red Deer: A Study in Animal Behaviour,* Oxford University Press, 1937, corrected edition, 1956, Doubleday, 1964; *Bird Flocks and the Breeding Cycle: A Contribution to the Study of Avian Sociology,* Cambridge University Press, 1938; *Wild Country: A Highland Naturalist's Notes and Pictures,* Cambridge University Press, 1938; *The Seasons and the Farmer* (juvenile), Cambridge University Press, 1939; *A Naturalist on Rona: Essays of a Biologist in Isolation,* Clarendon Press, 1939, Kraus Reprint, 1969.

Island Years (on natural history in Scotland), G. Bell, 1940, Pan Books, 1974; *The Seasons and the Fisherman* (juvenile), Cambridge University Press, 1941; *The Story of Scotland,* Collins, 1942; *The Farmyard,* Oxford University

Press, 1943, revised edition published as *Farm Livestock,* 1951; *Wild Life of Britain,* Collins, 1943; *The Care of Farm Animals,* Oxford University Press, 1943, 2nd edition, 1951; *Island Farm* (on natural history and agriculture in Scotland), G. Bell, 1943; *Crofting Agriculture: Its Practice in the West Highlands and Islands,* Oliver & Boyd, 1945; *Natural History in the Highlands and Islands,* Collins, 1947, reissued as *The Highlands and Islands* (with J. Morton Boyd), 1964, 2nd edition, 1969; *Sandy the Red Deer,* Oxford University Press, 1949.

(Author of foreword and introduction) Alasdair Alpin Macgregor, *The Scottish Countryside in Pictures,* Odhams, 1950, Norton, 1960; *The Cattle of St. Mochua: A Paraphrase of the Irish Tale,* Oliver & Boyd, 1950; (with Aldo Starker Leopold) *Wildlife in Alaska: An Ecological Reconnaissance,* Ronald, 1953; (editor) *West Highland Survey: An Essay in Human Ecology,* Oxford University Press, 1955, corrected edition, 1956; *Pelican in the Wilderness: A Naturalist's Odyssey in North America,* Random House, 1956.

An Ecological Reconnaissance of the Mara Plains in Kenya Colony, Wildlife Monographs, 1960; *Wild Life in African Territory: A Study Made for the Game and Tsetse Control Department of Northern Rhodesia,* Oxford University Press, 1960; *Towards a Game Policy for the Republic of Sudan,* Conservation Foundation (New York, N.Y.), 1961; *The Unity of Ecology,* British Association, 1963; *Wild-Life Conservation: The Ethical and Technical Problems,* Conservation Foundation (Edinburgh, Scotland), 1964; (editor with John P. Milton) *Future Environments of North America,* Natural History Press, 1966; (with Noel D. Eichhorn) *Man and Nature in the National Parks: Reflections on Policy,* Conservation Foundation (Washington, D.C.), 1967; *Impacts of Man on the Biosphere,* UNESCO, 1969.

Wilderness and Plenty, Houghton, 1970; *A Conversation on Population, Environment, and Human Well-Being,* Conservation Foundation (Washington, D.C.), 1971; *Environment and Responsibility* (juvenile), National Association of Boys' Clubs, 1973. Also author of *Biology of the Fleece of the Scottish Blackface Breed of Sheep,* 1932, *The Physiological and Genetical Aspects of Sterility in Domesticated Animals,* with William Orr, 1932, and *The Nature of a National Park,* 1968. Contributor to scientific journals.

AVOCATIONAL INTERESTS: Watching animals, English literature.

*   *   *

FREED, Alvyn M.   1913-

PERSONAL: Born June 19, 1913, in Philadelphia, Pa.; son of Jesse (a merchant) and Amy (Jacobs) Freed; married Margaret De Haan (a teacher and writer), May 22, 1947; children: Lawrence Douglas, Jesse Mark. *Education:* Temple University, B.S., 1938, M.A., 1948; University of Texas, Austin, Ph.D., 1955; also studied at University of California, Los Angeles, Miami University, Miami, Fla., and Claremont College. *Home:* 4329 Valmonte Dr., Sacramento, Calif. 95825. *Office:* Jalmar Press, 391 Munroe, Sacramento, Calif. 95825.

CAREER: Physical education teacher in public schools in Philadelphia, Pa., 1940-49; school psychologist in Ventura, Calif., 1949-52; RAND Corp., Santa Monica, Calif., human factors scientist, 1955-57; System Development Corp., Santa Monica, human factors scientist, 1957-61; Aerojet-General Corp., Sacramento, Calif., employed in quality and reliability division, 1961-64; San Juan Unified School District, Sacramento, school psychologist, 1961-64; private practice in Sacramento, 1967—; Jalmar Press, Inc., Sacramento, president and owner, 1973—. Lecturer, University of California, Riverside, 1956-59, Sacramento State College (now California State University, Sacramento), 1961-63. *Military service:* U.S. Army Air Force, 1940-46; became sergeant. *Member:* International Transactional Analysis Association, American Psychological Association, American Society for Clinical Hypnosis, California Psychological Association, Sacramento Psychological Association. *Awards, honors:* Cindy Award from Industrial Film Producers Association, 1963, for film "Power of the Individual."

WRITINGS: T.A. for Kids (and Grown Ups Too), Jalmar Press, 1971; *T.A. for Tots (and Other Prinzes),* Jalmar Press, 1973. Also author of transactional analysis audiovisual package adapted from *T.A. for Tots.* Wrote screenplay for film, "Power of the Individual," produced by Aerojet-General Corp., 1962. Contributor to journals.

WORK IN PROGRESS: T.A. for Teens; T.A. for Tots, Volume II.

SIDELIGHTS: Freed's wife, Margaret, told *CA:* "Three to four thousand schools and churches all over the world" have adopted transactional analysis techniques in their teaching and the California State Department of Education has asked Freed to translate the two books into Spanish. "It's being applied in prisons, hospitals, and seminaries. T.A. says you can change. You don't have to regret all the mistakes of the past. This is one of the really constructive things about it." Freed's publishing company also markets transactional analysis games "Playbouy" and "The OK Game."

* * *

FREEDMAN, Maurice 1920-1975

December 11, 1920—July 14, 1975; British educator, social anthropologist, editor, author of books on Chinese and Jewish cultures. Obituaries: *AB Bookman's Weekly,* September 22-29, 1975. (See index for previous *CA* sketch)

* * *

FREEMAN, Jo 1945-

PERSONAL: Born August 26, 1945, in Atlanta, Ga.; daughter of William Maxwell and Helen Claire (a history teacher; maiden name, Mitchell) Freeman. *Education:* University of California, Berkeley, B.A. (with honors), 1965; University of Chicago, Ph.D., 1973. *Home:* 100 La Salle St., Apt. MB, New York, N.Y. 10027. *Office:* Department of Political Science, State University of New York College at Purchase, Purchase, N.Y. 10577.

CAREER: U.S. Navy Department, Washington, D.C., clerk-typist for Bureau of Ships, 1962; staff member of "Cranston for Senate" campaign in Oakland, Calif., 1964; Southern Christian Leadership Conference, fieldworker and research director in Alabama, Georgia, and Mississippi, 1965-66; *West Side Torch* (community newspaper), Chicago, Ill., co-editor and photographer, 1967; *Modern Hospital,* Chicago, Ill., assistant editor, 1967-68; member of national staff of "McCarthy for President" campaign, 1968; University of Chicago, Chicago, Ill., extension lecturer in political science, autumn, 1971; State University of New York College at Old Westbury, assistant professor of American studies, 1973-74; State University of New York

College at Purchase, assistant professor of political science, 1974—. Civil rights activist, 1963-67; free-lance photographer, 1967-68; lecturer. Member of Twentieth Century Fund's task force on women and employment, 1970; organizer of feminist groups and activities, 1967—; alternate delegate to Democratic National Convention, 1972, and delegate candidate to 1976 convention.

MEMBER: American Political Science Association (member of committee on the status of women), Women's Caucus for Political Science, Caucus for a New Political Science (member of executive committee), Midwest Political Science Association, American Association of University Professors, American Sociological Association, American Civil Liberties Union, Women's Martial Arts Union, Manhattan Women's Political Caucus, National Organization for Women. *Awards, honors:* National finalist in White House fellows competition, 1975; prize for the best scholarly work on women in politics from American Political Science Association, 1975, for *The Politics of Women's Liberation.*

WRITINGS: (Editor) *Women: A Feminist Perspective,* Mayfield, 1975; *The Politics of Women's Liberation: A Case Study of an Emerging Social Movement and Its Relation to the Policy Process,* McKay, 1975.

Contributor: Robin Morgan, editor, *Sisterhood Is Powerful,* Random House, 1970; June Sochen, editor, *The New Feminism in Twentieth Century America,* Heath, 1971; *Discrimination Against Women,* U.S. Government Printing Office, 1971; Anne Koedt and Ellen Levine, editors, *Notes from the Third Year,* privately printed, 1971; Michele Garskof, editor, *Roles Women Play: Readings Toward Women's Liberation,* Brooks/Cole, 1971; Hans Peter Dreitzel, editor, *Recent Sociology Number Four: Family, Marriage, and the Struggle of the Sexes,* Macmillan, 1972; Joan Huber, editor, *Changing Women in a Changing Society,* University of Chicago Press, 1973; Alice Rossi and Ann Calderwood, editors, *Academic Women on the Move,* Russell Sage Foundation, 1973; Jane Jaquette, editor, *Women in Politics,* Wiley, 1974.

Contributor to *Collier's Encyclopedia.* Contributor of nearly thirty articles to academic journals, feminist publications, and popular magazines, including *Nation* and *Ms.* Associate editor, *Journal of Voluntary Research,* 1975—.

WORK IN PROGRESS: Editing an anthology, *Contemporary Social Movements;* research for a book to be called *Affirmative Action;* a book on women hitchhiking alone.

SIDELIGHTS: Jo Freeman has been continuously active in politics since 1952, participating in national and local campaigns. She is also active in the feminist movement and has organized conferences, newsletters, women's centers, and speakers programs. *Avocational interests:* Judo, karate, and aikido.

* * *

FRIEDLANDER, Joanne K(ohn) 1930-

PERSONAL: Born August 22, 1930, in Chicago, Ill.; daughter of Isidore E. (a physician) and Carolyn (Newman) Kohn; married Stanley Friedlander (a business executive), September 10, 1955; children: Mark, Susan. *Education:* University of Colorado, student, 1948-49; Northwestern University, B.A., 1954; Chicago Teachers College, teacher's certificate, 1965. *Politics:* Independent. *Religion:* Jewish. *Home:* 1300 Rosemary Lane, Northbrook, Ill. 60062. *Office:* Kahn Realty, 640 Vernon, Glencoe, Ill. 60022.

CAREER: Former newspaperwoman and teacher; realtor with Kahn Realty, Glencoe, Ill., 1970—. *Member:* League of Women Voters.

WRITINGS: (With Jean Neal) *Stock Market ABC,* Follett, 1969.

SIDELIGHTS: Mrs. Friedlander commented on *Stock Market ABC:* "When my own children received a gift of stock, they asked 'What is the stock market?' Since I could find no simple book to answer their questions and since one million other youngsters own stock, I decided to write my own book."

*   *   *

FRIEDMAN, Lenemaja   1924-

PERSONAL: Given name is pronounced Lain-a-mah-ya; born October 9, 1924, in Nuebrueck, Germany; came to United States, 1927, naturalized citizen, 1938; daughter of Helmuth and Clara (Kennedy) von Heister; married James Francis Sweeney, March 10, 1949 (divorced, 1963); married Daniel Friedman, April 7, 1963 (divorced, 1964); children: (first marriage) Joanne, Linell, Kerry, Sandra. *Education:* Syracuse University, student, 1942-44; University of Washington, Seattle, B.A., 1946; State University of New York at Albany, M.A., 1966; Cornell University, graduate study, summer, 1962; Florida State University, Ph.D., 1969. *Politics:* Democrat. *Religion:* Lutheran. *Home:* 1702 19th St., Columbus, Ga. 31901. *Office:* Department of Language and Humanities, Columbus College, Columbus, Ga. 31907.

CAREER: Fred M. Reast (advertising firm), New York, N.Y., member of staff, 1946-47; Kelly-Kramer (advertising firm), New York, N.Y., production manager, 1947-50; elected tax collector in Roxbury, N.Y., 1958-60; high school librarian in Roxbury, N.Y., 1960-61; high school English teacher in Margaretville, N.Y., 1961-65, and New Paltz, N.Y., 1965-67; Columbus College, Columbus, Ga., assistant professor, 1969-72, associate professor of English literature, 1972—. Member of community theater group "Ninety Miles Off Broadway," 1965-67.

MEMBER: National Council of Teachers of English, American Association of University Professors, South Atlantic Modern Language Association, Lutheran Women's Missionary League (Prince of Peace chapter; president, 1974-76). *Awards, honors:* Best actress of the year award from Francis J. Springer Theater (community theater group), 1975.

WRITINGS: Shirley Jackson (biography), Twayne, 1975.

WORK IN PROGRESS: Research on eighteenth-century theater.

SIDELIGHTS: Lenemaja Friedman writes: "I am very much interested in theater. A pleasurable experience was a trip to London in September of 1974 during which I saw many plays."

*   *   *

FRIEDMAN, Winifred   1923(?)-1975

1923(?)—November 17, 1975; American educator, art historian, and author. Obituaries: *New York Times,* November 18, 1975.

*   *   *

FRIESS, Horace Leland   1900-1975

March 4, 1900—October 12, 1975; American educator, scholar, and author of books on philosophy and religion. Obituaries: *New York Times,* October 13, 1975.

FRIJLING-SCHREUDER, E(lisabeth) C. M.   1908-

PERSONAL: Born August 31, 1908, in Amsterdam, Netherlands; married Albert Rene Frijling (a medical doctor), 1934; children: Albert Rene, Jr., Irene Aliae (Mrs. L. W. Kamphuis). *Education:* University of Amsterdam. *Home:* Soetendaal 17, Amsterdam, Netherlands.

CAREER: Amsterdam Child Guidance Clinic, Amsterdam, Netherlands, medical director, 1949-65; University of Amsterdam, Amsterdam, professor of child psychiatry, 1965-74. *Member:* Dutch Psychoanalytic Society, Dutch Psychiatric Society.

WRITINGS: (With others) *Droom en onthulling, Lezingen gehouden voor het Criminologish Instituut,* Dekker & Van de Vegt (Utrecht), 1948; *Preventie van Neurotische Gedensrelaties,* Van Gorcum (Assen), 1955, 3rd edition, 1970; *Het onvolledige Gezin,* Van Gorcum (Assen), 1959; (with P. J. van der Leeuw) *Hoofdstukken uit de hedendaagse psychoanalyse,* Loghum Slaterus (Arnhem), 1967; *Inleiding tot her Denken van Freud,* Born (Assen), 1970; *Wat zijn dat, Kinderen? Verstandhouding en misverstand,* Wetenschappelijke Uilgeverij, 1971, translation by Katherine Stechmann published as *Children: What Are They?,* International Universities Press, 1974. Also author of over fifty other scientific publications and contributor of chapters to eight books, all in Dutch. Contributor to scientific journals in her field.

WORK IN PROGRESS: A chapter for the *Textbook of Sexology,* to be edited by Musaph and Money.

*   *   *

FRISBIE, Louise K(elley)   1913-

PERSONAL: Legal first name is Mildred; born October 18, 1913, in Jacksonville, Fla.; daughter of Andrew Jackson (a public transportation employee) and Clyde (Williams) Kelley; married Sayer Loyal Frisbie (an editor and publisher), June 30, 1937; children: Sayer Loyal IV. *Education:* Florida Southern College, B.S., 1935. *Politics:* Democrat. *Religion:* Methodist. *Home:* 290 East Hooker St., Bartow, Fla. 33830. *Office: Polk County Democrat,* 190 South Florida Ave., Bartow, Fla. 33830.

CAREER: High school teacher of business law and executive secretary to the school principal in Bartow, Fla., 1935-38; *Polk County Democrat,* Bartow, Fla., reporter, 1944-58, copy editor, 1958—, author of column "Pioneers," 1969—. Has worked as church organist and church youth director. *Member:* Florida Historical Society, Historical Association of Southern Florida, Peace River Valley Historical Society, Polk County Historical Association (member of board of directors), Polk County Historical Commission. *Awards, honors:* Florida Press Association first and second place awards for feature writing, 1954 and 1962 respectively, and special commendation, 1957, for the book, *Here's How: Notes on News Writing;* resolution of appreciation from Florida State Senate, 1975.

WRITINGS: R. H. Williams: Florida Pioneer, privately printed, 1955; *Here's How: Notes on News Writing,* privately printed, 1957; *Peace River Pioneers,* E. A. Seemann, 1974; *Yesterday's Polk County,* E. A. Seemann, in press. The column "Pioneers" also appears in the *Democrat and Leader* (Fort Meade, Fla.). Contributor to newspapers. Editor of quarterly publication of Polk County Historical Association.

AVOCATIONAL INTERESTS: Travel (Caribbean, South America, Central America, Mexico, Great Britain,

Western Europe, Middle East, Asia, Morocco), music (pianist).

*   *   *

FROST, Stanley Brice   1913-

PERSONAL: Born February 17, 1913, in London, England; emigrated to Canada in 1956, naturalized Canadian citizen, 1961; son of Henry George (a missionary) and Rosa (Goodbody) Frost; married Margaret Florence Bradshaw, July 29, 1939; children: David Brice, Valerie Margaret. *Education:* University of London, B.D., 1936, M.Th., 1943; University of Marburg, D.Phil., 1938. *Home:* 5 Granville Rd., Hampstead 254, Montreal, Quebec, Canada H3X 3A9. *Office:* History of McGill Project, McGill University, P.O. Box 6070, Montreal, Quebec, Canada H3C 3G1.

CAREER: Ordained Methodist minister in England, 1939; pastor of Methodist churches in London, England, 1939-42, and in Staffordshire, England, 1942-49; Didsbury College, Bristol, England, held chair of Old Testament languages and literature, 1949-56, special lecturer in Hebrew, 1952-56; McGill University, Montreal, Quebec, professor of Old Testament studies, 1956—, dean of faculty of divinity, 1957-63, dean of faculty of graduate studies and research, 1963-69, vice-principal of university, 1969-74. Minister of United Church of Canada, 1956—. Member of Graduate Record Examinations Board, 1967, 1968-72, Committee on Rationalization of Major Library Holdings, 1969, and Council of Graduate Schools in the United States, 1969; member of executive council of Conference of Rectors and Principals of the Universities of Quebec, 1969-74.

MEMBER: Canadian Biblical Society (president, 1962-63), American Association of Theological Schools (president, 1964-65), Association of Graduate Schools (of Association of American Universities; member of executive committee, 1967-69). *Awards, honors:* D.D. from Victoria University, 1963; D.Litt. from Memorial University, 1967.

WRITINGS: Die Autoritaetslehre in den Werken John Wesleys (title means "The Doctrine of Authority in the Works of John Wesley"), Ernst Reinhardt, 1938; *The Pattern of Methodism,* Methodist Youth Department (London), 1948; *Old Testament Apocalyptic: Its Origin and Growth,* Epworth, 1952; *The Beginning of the Promise: Eight Lectures on the Book of Genesis,* S.P.C.K., 1960; *Patriarchs and Prophets,* McGill-Queen's University Press, 1963; (contributor) J. Philip Hyatt, editor, *The Bible in Modern Scholarship,* Abingdon Press, 1965; (contributor) Jesse H. Ziegler, editor, *Horizons of Theological Education,* American Association of Theological Schools, 1966; *Standing and Understanding: A Reappraisal of the Christian Faith,* McGill-Queen's University Press, 1969; (contributor) Charles M. Laymon, editor, *The Interpreter's One-Volume Commentary,* Abingdon Press, 1971; (contributor) Howard N. Bream, editor, *A Light Unto My Path,* Temple University Press, 1974.

Contributor to *Interpreter's Dictionary of the Bible, The Preacher's Handbook, Hasting's Dictionary of the Bible,* and *Encyclopaedia Britannica.* Contributor of articles and reviews to theology journals. Chairman of educational committee of McGill University Press, 1962-69; chairman of board of directors of McGill-Queen's University Press, 1972-73.

WORK IN PROGRESS: Research for a history of McGill University.

FRUCHTENBAUM, Arnold G(enekovich)   1943-

PERSONAL: Born September 26, 1943, in Tobolsk, Siberia, Russia; son of Henry (a photographer) and Adele (Suppes) Fruchtenbaum; married Mary Ann Morrow, June 29, 1968. *Education:* Attended Shelton College, 1962-65; Cedarville College, B.A., 1966; Hebrew University of Jerusalem, graduate study, 1966-67; Dallas Theological Seminary, Th.M., 1971; New York University, doctoral candidate. *Religion:* "Hebrew-Christian." *Address:* Christian Jew Foundation, P.O. Box 345, San Antonio, Tex.

CAREER: American Board of Missions to the Jews, Dallas, Tex., minister, 1967-71, teacher at Messianic Assembly in Jerusalem, Israel, 1971-73, Englewood Cliffs, N.J., editor, 1973-75; Christian Jew Foundation, San Antonio, Tex., associate director, 1976—.

WRITINGS: Hebrew Christianity: Its Theology, History, and Philosophy, Baker Book, 1974; *Jesus Was a Jew,* Broadman Press, 1975. Editor of *Chosen People,* 1973-75.

WORK IN PROGRESS: With Tim Timmons, *Biblical Love Making,* for Revell; editing *New King James Version* of Old Testament, for Thomas Nelson, completion expected in 1977.

SIDELIGHTS: Fruchtenbaum is anxious to make the position of the Hebrew Chrisitan known in the Jewish community. He ultimately hopes to immigrate to Israel and set up a school of Hebrew Christianity.

*   *   *

FURBEE, Leonard J.   1896(?)-1975

1896(?)—September 17, 1975; American attorney, historian and supervisor at Lincoln Memorial, author of books and articles. Obituaries: *Washington Post,* September 23, 1975.

*   *   *

GABRIEL-ROBINET, Louis   1909-1975

December 17, 1909—June 23, 1975; French attorney, journalist, editor, newspaper executive, and author of books on various topics. Obituaries: *New York Times,* June 25, 1975; *Washington Post,* June 26, 1975.

*   *   *

GADDY, C(urtis) Welton   1941-

PERSONAL: Born October 10, 1941, in Paris, Tenn.; son of George D. (a railroad employee) and Jenola Marie (Rayborn) Gaddy; married Julia Mae Grabiel, August 26, 1962; children: John Paul, James Welton. *Education:* Union University, B.A., 1963; Southern Baptist Theological Seminary, B.D., 1966, Th.M., 1968, Th.D., 1970. *Home:* 6324 St. Henry Dr., Nashville, Tenn. 37205. *Office:* Christian Life Commission of the Southern Baptist Convention, 460 James Robertson Parkway, Nashville, Tenn. 37219.

CAREER: Ordained Southern Baptist minister, 1960; pastor of Baptist churches in Springville, Tenn., 1959-60, Buchanon, Tenn., 1960-62, Paris, Tenn., 1962-64, Paris Crossing, Ind., 1964-70, and Louisville, Ky., 1971-72; Christian Life Commission of the Southern Baptist Convention, Nashville, Tenn., director of Christian citizenship development, 1973—. Instructor at Simmons University, 1968-70, Southern Baptist Theological Seminary, 1969-70, and Bellarmine College, 1970-71. Member of "Moral Side of the News" panel for WHAS-Television and Radio, 1971-72. *Member:* American Society of Christian Ethics.

WRITINGS: Easter Proclamation: Remembrance and

Renewal, Broadman Press, 1974; (contributor of epilogue) Claude A. Frazier, editor, *Politics and Religion Can Mix*, Broadman Press, 1974; (contributor) Charles L. Wallis, editor, *The Ministers Manual*, Harper, 1975; *Profile of a Christian Citizen*, Broadman Press, 1975; *Proclaim Liberty*, Broadman Press, 1975. Author of scripts for "The Christian as Citizen" (series of filmstrips), Broadman Press, in press. Author of church school material. Contributor to church publications, communications magazines, and newspapers.

SIDELIGHTS: Gaddy's two most recent books "have grown out of the conviction that citizenship is an important dimension of Christian discipleship. A moral word is at the heart of the biblical message."

* * *

GADPAILLE, Warren J(oseph) 1924-

PERSONAL: Surname is pronounced *Gad*-pie; born March 12, 1924, in New Orleans, La.; son of Edgar Courtney (in sales) and Viola (Stamm) Gadpaille; married Susan Deeren, November 18, 1967; children: Charles Key, Robert Ewing, Ingrid Maria, Antoine Rudolphe. *Education:* Tulane University, B.A., 1946, M.D., 1952. *Residence:* Conifer, Colo. *Agent:* Alex Sareyan, 419 Park Ave. S., New York, N.Y. 10016. *Office:* 3601 South Clarkson St., Englewood, Colo. 80110.

CAREER: Tulane University, New Orleans, La., instructor in English, 1946-48; Touro Infirmary, New Orleans, intern, 1952-53; Tulane Medical School, Department of Psychiatry, New Orleans, resident and fellow in psychiatry, 1953-56; Tulane University, instructor in psychiatry and neurology, 1955-58; private practice of psychiatry in Englewood, Colo., 1958—. Diplomate of American Board of Psychiatry and Neurology; certified sex educator and sex therapist by American Association of Sex Educators and Counselors. Staff member at Porter Memorial Hospital, 1958—. Adjunct professor at University of Northern Colorado, 1973—. Private practice of psychiatry in New Orleans, La., 1956-58; visiting lecturer at Tulane University, 1958, and University of Denver, 1959; special lecturer at Union College of Nursing (Denver), 1960-65; guest lecturer at Colorado Women's College, 1969-74. Member of board of directors of Denver Lyric Theatre, 1959-66, and Colorado Philharmonic Orchestra, 1969-71. *Military service:* U.S. Army Air Forces, fighter pilot, 1943-45; served in European theater; became first lieutenant; received Bronze Star with seven oak leaf clusters.

MEMBER: American Academy of Psychoanalysis (fellow, 1959—; member of board of trustees, 1973—), Group for the Advancement of Psychiatry (chairman of committee on adolescence, 1975—), American Academy of Child Psychiatry (affiliate member), American Psychiatric Association, American Association of Sex Educators and Counselors (vice-president, 1972-74), American Group Psychotherapy Association, American Society for Adolescent Psychiatry, National Council of Family Relations, Colorado State Medical Society, Louisiana Group Psychotherapy Institute (vice-president, 1956-58), Louisiana Group Psychotherapy Society (president, 1958), Denver Medical Society, Phi Beta Kappa, Alpha Omega Alpha.

WRITINGS: Psychiatric Problems of Delinquency in Louisiana, Louisiana State Department of Institutions, 1957; (with others) *Normal Adolescence: Its Dynamics and Impact*, Scribner, 1968; *The Cycles of Sex: Normal Psychosexual Development*, Scribner, 1975.

Contributor: Alexander Gralnick, editor, *The Collected Award Papers*, Gralnick Foundation, 1966; J. Masserman, editor, *Science and Psychoanalysis*, Grune, Volume XI: *The Ego*, 1967, Volume XV: *Dynamics of Deviant Sexuality*, 1969, Volume XX: *The Dynamics of Power*, 1972; *Sex Education and Counseling*, Sandoz, 1973; Henry Grunebaum and Jacob Christ, editors, *Contemporary Marriage: Structure, Dynamics, and Therapy*, Little, Brown, 1975. Contributor to medical journals. Member of editorial board of *Sexual Behavior*, 1971-73; member of editorial advisory board of *Journal of the American Academy of Psychoanalysis.*

WORK IN PROGRESS: Cross-cultural and cross-species research aimed at refining the theory of the timing and developmental sequence of sexual identity in humans.

SIDELIGHTS: Gadpaille is a professional opera and concert singer, performing in primary baritone and comedy lead roles in opera, operetta, and musical comedy with major American companies; he has also made concert, radio, and television performances with orchestras in the United States and England.

* * *

GALLAGHER, Charles A(ugustus) 1927-

PERSONAL: Born August 18, 1927, in New York, N.Y.; son of Charles A. (a newspaperman and union president) and Therese (Farrell) Gallagher. *Education:* Loyola University, Chicago, Ill., B.A., 1951, P.H.L., 1952; Woodstock College, S.T.L., 1959. *Office:* Marriage Encounter Resource Community, 295 Northern Blvd., Great Neck, N.Y. 11021.

CAREER: Entered Society of Jesus (Jesuits), 1945; teacher of Latin, mathematics, and religion, and basketball coach at Roman Catholic high school in Buffalo, N.Y., 1952-55; ordained Roman Catholic priest, 1958; involved in spiritual training in Port Townsend, Wash., 1959-60; Xavier High School, New York, N.Y., assistant headmaster, 1960-62; Gonzaga Retreat House, Monroe, N.Y., youth retreat master, 1962-67; Marriage Encounter Resource Community, Great Neck, N.Y., executive secretary priest, 1968-74, director, 1974—.

WRITINGS: Marriage Encounter: As I Have Loved You, Doubleday, 1975; (With Joseph McDonald and Judith McDonald) *Marriage Encounter for High School Students*, Sadlier, in press; (with Lyman Coleman) *Evenings for Parents*, Sadlier, in press; (with Coleman) *Evenings for Couples*, Sadlier, in press.

WORK IN PROGRESS: Typical Questions Engaged Couples Ask about Marriage; Formation of Conscience for a Catholic.

SIDELIGHTS: Gallagher's concerns are that "all sorts of lip services [are] being paid to marriage and the family.... But very little positive support is being offered to couples and to parents. The basic problem in the western world is alienation. The answer to that is not fundamentally going to be in the field of economics or education but in relationship. Marriage is the core relationship in human experience. We are a society that is technologically highly developed and personally impoverished. Marriage Encounter, a movement of the Catholic Church ... offers real hope for human progress and development."

* * *

GALLE, F(rederick) C(harles) 1919-

PERSONAL: Surname rhymes with "alley"; born July 10,

1919, in Dayton, Ohio; son of Alfred Max and Lucienne (Rappsiber) Galle; married Elizabeth Nevison (a registered nurse), September 12, 1945; children: Phillip Charles, Peggy Ann. *Education:* Ohio State University, B.S., 1943, M.S., 1947; University of Tennessee, doctoral study, 1947-52. *Religion:* Lutheran. *Home and office address:* Callaway Gardens, Pine Mountain, Ga. 31822.

CAREER: Callaway Gardens, Pine Mountain, Ga., director of horticulture, 1953—, vice-president, 1970—. Member of advisory council for U.S. National Arboretum; member of board of trustees of Cason J. Callaway Memorial Forest. *Military service:* U.S. Army, Armored Field Artillery, 1943-46; served in European theater; became first lieutenant; received Purple Heart with one cluster and Bronze Star Medal.

MEMBER: American Society of Horticultural Science (fellow), American Horticultural Society (president, 1967-70), American Association of Botanic Gardens and Arboreta (past president), American Rhododendron Society (member of board of directors of Mid-Atlantic chapter; vice-president of Eastern section, 1975), Holly Society of America (member of board of trustees), Royal Horticultural Society (England; fellow), Georgia Horticultural Society (charter member). *Awards, honors:* Thomas Roland Medal from Massachusetts Horticultural Society, 1968; professional citation from American Horticultural Society, 1974.

WRITINGS: Native and Some Introduced Azaleas for Southern Gardens, Callaway Gardens, 1969; *Azaleas,* Oxnoor Press, 1974. Author of garden portion of "Rozell Show," on WRBL-Television, 1960—. Contributor to horticultural journals.

* * *

GALLIMARD, Gaston 1881-1975

January 18, 1881—December 25, 1975; French publisher, editor, founder of literary magazine. Obituaries: *Publishers Weekly,* January 19, 1976.

* * *

GALLUCCI, Robert L(ovis) 1946-

PERSONAL: Born February 11, 1946, in Brooklyn, N.Y.; son of Samuel J. and Mae (Hirme) Gallucci; married Adele King (an environmental researcher), September 3, 1967 (divorced, 1975). *Education:* State University of New York at Stony Brook, B.A. (cum laude), 1967; Brandeis University, M.A., 1968, Ph.D., 1974. *Home:* 2811 N St. N.W., Washington, D.C. 20007. *Office:* U.S. Arms Control and Disarmament Agency, Department of State, Washington, D.C. 20451.

CAREER: U.S. Air Force, Office of Research Analysis, Holloman Air Force Base, N.M., consultant, 1967; Lasell Junior College, Auburndale, Mass., instructor in European and American history, 1968-69; Swarthmore College, Swarthmore, Pa., instructor in international relations, American foreign policy, and politics, 1971-73; Johns Hopkins School of Advanced International Studies, Washington, D.C., professorial lecturer in bureaucracy, American foreign policy, arms control and disarmament, 1974, 1975; U.S. Department of State, Arms Control and Disarmament Agency, Washington, D.C., foreign affairs officer for Bureau of Military and Economic Affairs, 1974, foreign affairs officer on non-proliferation staff of Bureau of International Relations, 1975—. Rapporteur for Council on Foreign Relations, 1971-72; research associate of Washington Center

of Foreign Policy Research, 1973-74; consultant to Commission on the Organization of the Government for the Conduct of Foreign Policy, 1974. *Awards, honors:* Woodrow Wilson fellowship, 1967-68; Brookings Institution research fellowship, 1970-71; Rockefeller Foundation post-doctoral fellowship, 1973-74.

WRITINGS: Neither Peace Nor Honor: The Politics of American Military Policy in Viet-Nam, Johns Hopkins Press, 1975. Contributor to *A Dictionary of Politics.*

* * *

GANTRY, Susan Nadler 1947-
(Susan Nadler)

PERSONAL: Born April 1, 1947, in Pittsburgh, Pa.; daughter of Ralph Mark (a business executive) and Anne Belle Nadler; married Christopher Gantry (a musician), March 5, 1976. *Education:* University of Wisconsin, Madison, student, 1965-68; American College in Jerusalem, B.A., 1970. *Residence:* Pittsburgh, Pa.; and Key West, Fla. *Agent:* John Cushman Associates, Inc., 25 West 44th St., New York, N.Y.

CAREER: Key West Popcorn—Spicey Kernel, Key West, Fla., president, 1975—; writer.

WRITINGS—Under name Susan Nadler: *The Butterfly Convention,* Dial, 1976.

WORK IN PROGRESS: A novel, *The Man in the Moon Is a Song and Danceman;* editing a book of her own poems; script for a children's television program; preparing a television program of children's fantasy.

SIDELIGHTS: Susan Nadler's book concerns four months she spent in prison in Mexico after being caught smuggling hashish from Morocco. In her words it "deals with the sixties, and the process of self-discovery, reconciliation between parent and child, and responsibility." She adds: "I am sincerely interested in getting my poetry published, since my poetry makes prose of my life. My second novel . . . is concerned with the love of two friends. I hope to visit Jerusalem soon again as my next novel concerns the Middle East. . . . I hope to travel extensively to South America and Red China."

* * *

GANTZER, Hugh 1931-
(Arvind and Shanta Kale; Shyam Dave, joint pseudonym with wife, Colleen Gantzer)

PERSONAL: Born January 9, 1931, in Patna, Bihar, India; son of Joseph and Maisie (Pereira) Gantzer; married Colleen Adie, November 12, 1960; children: Peter. *Education:* University of Calcutta, B.Commerce, 1953; University of Bombay, LL.B., 1961. *Religion:* Christian. *Home address:* Ockbrook, Mussoorie, Uttar Pradesh, India. *Office:* XXIV/1115 Chakalakil Rd., Perumanoor, Cochin 15, Kerala, India.

CAREER: Mussoorie Times, Mussoorie, India, assistant editor, 1953; Indian Navy, career officer, 1953-70, secretary to commodore commanding southern naval area, 1970, first judge advocate of southern naval area, 1971-73, retiring as commander, 1973; Nilhat Shipping Co., Calcutta, India, first executive, 1973; Standard Tea Exports, Cochin, Kerala, India, manager, 1974; free-lance writer, 1975—. Guest lecturer at Defence Services Staff College.

WRITINGS: The Man-Eater of Nunihat (hunting stories), Hind Pocket Books, 1974.

With wife, Colleen Gantzer, under joint pseudonym Shyam Dave: *The Kumbh Docket* (thriller novel), Jaico Publishing, 1972, InterCulture Associates, 1973; *Ballots for Violence* (thriller novel), Jaico Publishing, 1974; *Operation Overkill* (thriller novel), Orient Paperbacks, 1975; *Kerala* (travel guide), India Tourism Development Corp., in press.

Under pseudonym Arvind and Shanta Kale: *Tantra* (nonfiction), Jaico Publishing, in press. Contributor of stories, articles, and reviews to magazines in India, England, and the United States, including *Christian Science Monitor, Fate,* and *Psychic.*

WORK IN PROGRESS: A novel, *The President's Ransom,* for Orient Paperbacks; a science fiction novel; a brochure for one of India's leading oil industries; a lecture series on India; research on Indian occult practices.

SIDELIGHTS: In spite of his European name, Gantzer is an Indian; his family is of Danish origin, but has lived in India for eight generations.

During his naval career, Gantzer visited a number of countries in Africa and the Mediterranean, as well as Ceylon, Japan, North VietNam, and China, but military restrictions prevented him from writing about his experiences. As a reaction to this, and after a friend's challenge, the Gantzers teamed up to write *The Kumbh Docket,* the first Indian thriller in the "James Bond genre."

Research for their travel book on Kerala showed the Gantzers the wealth of occult lore still kept alive in the tiny backwaters and mountain hamlets of the state, and led to writing *Tantra. Avocational interests:* Photography, folklore, gardening, travel, "the Endangered Art of Conversation."

* * *

GARCIA CASTANEDA, Salvador 1932-

PERSONAL: Born May 25, 1932, in Zamora, Spain; son of Salvador Garcia and Carmen Castaneda; married Sue Paun (a teacher of Romance languages), 1971. *Education:* Universidad de Oviedo, Licenciatura, 1956; University of California, Berkeley, Ph.D., 1967. *Religion:* Roman Catholic. *Home:* 2371 Cambridge Blvd., Columbus, Ohio 43221. *Office:* Department of Romance Languages, Ohio State University, Columbus, Ohio 43210.

CAREER: Spanish Cultural Center, Baghdad, Iraq, director, 1959-62; San Francisco State College (now University), San Francisco, Calif., assistant professor of Romance languages, 1966-68; University of Michigan, Ann Arbor, assistant professor of Romance languages, 1968-71; Ohio State University, Columbus, associate professor of Romance languages, 1972—. *Military service:* Spanish Navy, 1952-54. *Member:* Modern Language Association of America, American Society fo. Eighteenth Century Studies, Asociacion de Orientalistas Espanoles, Centro de Estudios Montanese.

WRITINGS: Las ideas literarias en Espana entre 1840 y 1850 (title means "Literary Ideas in Spain between 1840 and 1850"), University of California Press, 1971; (editor) Juan Eugenio Hartzenbusch, *Los Amantes de Teruel* (title means "The Lovers of Teruel"), Clasicos Castalia, 1971; (editor) Jose Zorrilla, *Don Juan Tenorio,* Editorial Labor, 1975. Contributor of articles and reviews to language journals.

WORK IN PROGRESS: Telesforo de Trueba y Cosio (1799-1835): Life and Works.

SIDELIGHTS: Garcia Castaneda has traveled widely in the Middle East and Europe.

* * *

GARDNER, Robert 1911-

PERSONAL: Born December 27, 1911, in Arlington, Wash.; son of Frank M. (a laborer) and Kate (Hamilton) Gardner; married Kathryn Harris, January 5, 1942; children: Nancy, Patty. *Education:* University of Southern California, A.B., 1933, LL.B., 1935. *Politics:* Republican. *Home:* 320 Evening Canyon Rd., Corona Del Mar, Calif. *Office:* Court of Appeal, State Building, San Bernardino, Calif. 92402.

CAREER: Admitted to the Bar of California, 1936; superior court justice in Orange County, Calif., 1947-70; California Court of Appeal, San Bernardino, presiding justice, 1970—. *Military service:* U.S. Navy, 1944-45; became lieutenant commander; received Bronze Star.

WRITINGS: The Art of Body Surfing, Chilton, 1973.

* * *

GARNET, Eldon 1946-

PERSONAL: Born June 20, 1946, in Toronto, Ontario, Canada; son of Samuel and Sylvia (Goodman) Garnet. *Education:* University of Toronto, B.A., 1969; York University, M.A., 1972. *Home:* 10 St. Patrick St., Toronto, Ontario, Canada. *Agent:* Sydney Coin, 473 Brunswick Ave., Toronto, Ontario, Canada.

CAREER: Editor, poet, 1971—. *Awards, honors:* Grants from Canada Council of Arts and Ontario Arts Council.

WRITINGS: Angel (poems), Press Porcepic, 1971; *Asparagus* (poems), Rumblestill Press, 1973; (editor) *The Book of Process,* Rumblestill Press, 1974; (editor with Brian Trevers) *Plastic Bag,* Rumblestill Press, 1974; *The Last Adventure* (poems), Oberon, 1975; (editor) *The Other Canadian Poetry,* Press Porcepic, 1975. Editor of *Im(pu)lse* magazine.

WORK IN PROGRESS: Book One, poetry and graphics; *The Martyrdom of Jean de Brebeuf,* a long poem.

* * *

GARNETT, Christopher Browne 1906-1975

December 23, 1906—November 21, 1975; American educator, university official, civil servant abroad, author of books and essays on philosophy and related topics. Obituaries: *Washington Post,* November 26, 1975.

* * *

GARRAD, Larch S(ylvia) 1936-

PERSONAL: Born February 12, 1936, in London, England; daughter of Alan Charles and Laurel Helen (Hall) Garrad. *Education:* University of Birmingham, B.A., 1957, Ph.D., 1964; British School at Athens, graduate study, 1957-59. *Residence:* Isle of Man. *Office:* Manx Museum, Douglas, Isle of Man.

CAREER: Manx Museum, Douglas, Isle of Man, assistant keeper, 1964—. *Member:* Royal Geographical Society (fellow), British Trust for Ornithology, Botanical Society of the British Isles, Mammal Society, Conchological Society, Freshwater Biological Association, Museums Association, American Littoral Society.

WRITINGS: (With T. A. Bawden and others) *The In-*

dustrial Archaeology of the Isle of Man, David & Charles, 1972; The Naturalist in the Isle of Man, David & Charles, 1973; A Present from . . . (introduction to souvenirs of resorts in the British Isles since 1800), David & Charles, in press. Contributor to Manx journals.

WORK IN PROGRESS: The Naturalist in the Canary Islands, for David & Charles; Tenerife, publication by David & Charles expected in 1977 or 1978.

SIDELIGHTS: Larch Garrad has traveled in Europe and lived in Greece. One of her current interests is producing small print runs of books for a restricted audience, particularly on Manx subjects such as gardening, souvenirs and other collectable things.

* * *

GARRETT, Howard 1931-

PERSONAL: Born October 13, 1931; son of Edward and Sadie (Ginsberg) Garrett; married Lois Berman, April 16, 1953; children: Harvey, Deborah. Education: Brooklyn College (now of the City University of New York), B.A., 1953. Religion: Jewish. Home: 6 Brookline Dr., Massapequa, N.Y. 11758. Office: Metropolitan Wire Corp., 24-16 Bridge Plaza S., Long Island City, N.Y. 11101.

CAREER: Junior high school teacher in Brooklyn, N.Y., 1955-56; sales manager for Britannica Junior Encyclopaedia, 1956-59; Dexion, Inc. (material handling), New York City, salesman and industrial sales manager, 1959-71; Metropolitan Wire Corp., New York City, salesman and industrial sales manager, 1971—. Performer (lead basso) with Long Island Gilbert and Sullivan Workshop. Member: International Material Management Society (member of board of directors of New York chapter).

WRITINGS: (Editor) Poster Book of Antique Auto Ads, Citadel, 1974.

WORK IN PROGRESS: More art books based on posters and rare periodicals.

AVOCATIONAL INTERESTS: Collecting rare periodicals (owns about thirty thousand pieces of material, especially from the nineteenth and early twentieth centuries, including prints and lithographs).

* * *

GARRISON, James (Dale) 1943-

PERSONAL: Born January 10, 1943, in Bremerton, Wash.; son of Dale Allen (a physician) and Leola Inez (Bass) Garrison; married Susan Howard, June 28, 1969. Education: Princeton University, A.B., 1965; University of California, Berkeley, M.A., 1967, Ph.D., 1972. Home: 3006 Pinecrest Dr., Austin, Tex. 78757. Office: Department of English, University of Texas, Austin, Tex. 78712.

CAREER: Mills College, Oakland, Calif., instructor in English, 1971-73; University of Texas, Austin, assistant professor of English, 1973—. Member: Modern Language Association of America, Augustan Reprint Society. Awards, honors: Woodrow Wilson national fellowship, 1965-66.

WRITINGS: Dryden and the Tradition of Panegyric, University of California Press, 1975.

WORK IN PROGRESS: A monograph on Dryden and His Audience, 1688-1700.

* * *

GATES, William Byram 1917-1975

October 18, 1917—December 22, 1975; American educator, economist, author of book on economic history. Obituaries: New York Times, December 24, 1976; Washington Post, December 26, 1975.

* * *

GATTI, Enzo 1942-

PERSONAL: Born February 21, 1942; son of Giovanni Battista and Maggiorina (Riccabone) Gatti. Education: Gregorianum, M.A. (theology), 1969; Biblicum, M.A. (Biblical literature), 1972. Religion: Roman Catholic. Home: Via San Martino 8, Parma 43100, Italy.

CAREER: Xaverianum, Parma, Italy, professor of Biblical theology. Has worked as translator of scientific works on Biblical literature into Italian from English, German, French, and Spanish.

WRITINGS: Colui che sa il Doloreo dell 'Uomo, Editrice Missionaria Italiana, 1972, translation by Matthew O'Connell published as Rich Church—Poor Church?, Orbis, 1974; Atti degli Apostoli: Il libro della Missione, Editrice Missionara Italiana, 1975.

WORK IN PROGRESS: Research on the intertestamentary period in the hellenistic world.

* * *

GAY-KELLY, Doreen 1952-

PERSONAL: Born May 13, 1952, in New York, N.Y.; daughter of Franklin M. (an artist) and Janice (Meltzer) Gay; married William James Kelly (an actor), July 15, 1972. Education: Attended Pratt Institute, 1970, School of Visual Arts, 1970-73, and Parsons School of Design, 1974. Religion: Jewish. Home and office: 5 Crest Cir., Matawan, N.J. 07747.

CAREER: Pimbi Ltd., Keyport, N.J., designer of jewelry, 1974—; Hallmark Cards, Inc., Kansas City, Mo., designer, 1975—; free-lance writer and illustrator of books and cards.

WRITINGS: (Self-illustrated) Bea's Best Friend (juvenile fiction), Prentice-Hall, 1975.

WORK IN PROGRESS: An illustrated story of a bit of animal life in the jungle, Anjibi's Jungle, completion expected in 1976; a children's cookbook; a wordless picture book.

SIDELIGHTS: Doreen Gay-Kelly told CA: "My main motivation in being a children's book writer and illustrator is my love of the whimsical, enchanting world of childhood and the vivid memories I have of mine. I feel that contemporary artists have a fantastic showcase in children's book art and I want to take advantage of it. My love of the theatre plays an important role in my life: I would like to animate my characters eventually, so that everyone can know them the way I do."

* * *

GAZDA, George M(ichael) 1931-

PERSONAL: Born March 6, 1931, in Thayer, Ill.; son of Thomas A. and Mary (Wargo) Gazda; married Barbara Boyd, July 3, 1954; children: David Andrew. Education: Western Illinois University, B.S., 1952, M.S., 1953; University of Illinois, Ed.D., 1959. Politics: Democrat. Religion: Roman Catholic. Home: 185 Stillwood Ct., Athens, Ga. 30601. Office: Department of Counseling and Student Personnel Services, University of Georgia, Athens, Ga. 30602.

CAREER: University of Illinois, Urbana, assistant professor of counselor education, 1959-62; University of Missouri, Columbia, assistant professor of counselor education, 1962-63; University of Georgia, Athens, associate professor, 1963-67, professor of education, 1967—. Consulting professor of psychiatry, Medical College of Georgia, 1967—. President, Human Relations Consultants, Inc., 1970—. Consultant, U.S. Office of Education, Bureau of Indian Affairs, and Veterans Administration Hospital, Augusta, Ga.

MEMBER: American School Counselor Association, American Psychological Association, American Personnel and Guidance Association (chairperson of ad hoc committee, 1969-71, and committee to revise ethical standards, 1974—; member of board, 1972—; president, 1976-77), American Society of Group Psychotherapy and Psychodrama, Association for Counselor Education and Supervision (president, 1972—), American Group Psychotherapy Association, Association for Specialists in Group Work (president, 1973-74), Student Personnel Association for Teacher Education, National Catholic Guidance Conference, American Rehabilitation Counseling Association, National Vocational Guidance Association, American Catholic Psychological Association, American Educational Research Association, Georgia Psychological Association, Georgia School Counselors. *Awards, honors:* American Personnel and Guidance Association research award, 1968-70.

WRITINGS: (With Jonell H. Folds) *Handbook of Guidance Services,* R. W. Parkinson, 1966; (with Folds) *Group Guidance: A Critical Incidents Approach,* Follett, 1968; *Group Counseling: A Developmental Approach,* Allyn & Bacon, 1971; (with others) *Human Relations Development: A Manual for Educators,* Allyn & Bacon, 1973; *Human Relations Development: A Manual for Health Sciences,* Allyn & Bacon, 1975; (with Catterall) *Strategies for Helping Students,* C. C Thomas, in press.

Editor: (With Robert Clever) *Guidance Readings and Annotated Bibliography,* Superintendent of Public Instruction (Springfield, Ill.), 1961; (and contributor) *Basic Approaches to Group Psychotherapy and Group Counseling,* C. C Thomas, 1968, 2nd edition, 1975; *Innovations to Group Psychotherapy,* C. C Thomas, 1968; *Theories and Methods of Group Counseling in the Schools,* C. C Thomas, 1969, 2nd edition, 1976.

Contributor: M. M. Ohlsen, editor, *Counseling Children in Groups,* Holt, 1973.

Editor, "Group Procedure Sumposium" proceedings, University of Georgia, 1967-73. Contributor of more than one hundred articles and monographs to journals in his field. Editor, *Student Personnel Association for Teacher Education Journal,* 1966-68, and American Personnel and Guidance Association *Newsletter,* 1967-73; member of editorial board, *Together: Journal of the Association for Specialists in Group Work.*

WORK IN PROGRESS: Introduction to the Helping Professions, with Granum, for Allyn & Bacon.

*   *   *

GAZLEY, John G(erow)   1895-

PERSONAL: Born April 6, 1895, in Patterson, N.Y.; son of George Henry (a hotel manager) and Elizabeth R. (Gerow) Gazley; married Lois Cassidy, September 2, 1922 (died January 30, 1957); married Elizabeth Tinsley, October 8, 1959; children: Richard H., Lawrence J. *Education:*

Amherst College, A.B., 1917; Columbia University, A.M., 1918, Ph.D., 1926. *Politics:* Liberal. *Religion:* United Church of Christ. *Home:* 40 School St., Hanover, N.H. 03755.

CAREER: Columbia University, New York, N.Y., instructor in European history and contemporary civilization, 1920-23; Dartmouth College, Hanover, N.H., assistant professor, 1923-26, associate professor, 1926-35, professor of history and international relations, 1935-62, professor emeritus, 1962—. Civilian member of faculty at National War College, 1952; visiting professor at University of Illinois, 1964-65. *Military service:* U.S. Army, 1918-19.

WRITINGS: American Opinion of German Unification, 1848-1871, Columbia University Press, 1926; *Democracy in Great Britain and France Since the World War,* Dartmouth College, 1939; (contributor) Edward Mead Earle, editor, *Nationalism and Internationalism: Essays Inscribed to Carlton J. Hayes,* Columbia University Press, 1950; *The Life of Arthur Young, 1741-1820,* American Philosophical Society, 1973. Contributor to history journals.

SIDELIGHTS: Gazley writes: "My religious outlook has been that of Christian humanism and the social gospel. In public affairs I have inclined toward democratic socialism and pacifism. During World War Two I was very active in various peace planning groups, especially those looking toward a strong international organization."

*   *   *

GEIST, Valerius   1938-

PERSONAL: Born February 2, 1938, in Nikolajew, Russia; moved to Canada, 1953; naturalized Canadian citizen, 1959; son of Alexander Schutor and Olga Geist; married wife, Renate (a scientist), 1961; children: Rosemarie, Karl, Harald. *Education:* University of British Columbia, B.S. (with honors), 1960, Ph.D., 1967. *Office:* Faculty of Environmental Design, University of Calgary, Calgary 44, Alberta, Canada.

CAREER: University of Calgary, Calgary, Alberta, assistant professor and research scientist in Environmental Science Centre, 1968-71, associate professor and director for environmental sciences of faculty of environmental design, 1971—. *Member:* Wildlife Society, Canadian Society of Zoology, Canadian Society of Wildlife and Fishery Biology. *Awards, honors:* National Research Council fellowship at Max Planck Institute for the Physiology of Behavior, 1967-68; publication award from Wildlife Society, 1971, for *Mountain Sheep.*

WRITINGS: Mountain Sheep: A Study in Behavior and Evolution, University of Chicago Press, 1971; (editor with F. Walther) *The Behavior of Ungulates and Its Relation to Management,* International Union for the Conservation of Nature (Morges, Switzerland), 1974; *Mountain Sheep and Man in the Northern Wilds,* Cornell University Press, 1975.

WORK IN PROGRESS: Two books, *Human Adaptations and Environmental Design* and *Deer: A Study in Behavior and Evolution.*

*   *   *

GELB, Joyce   1940-

PERSONAL: Born June 1, 1940, in New York, N.Y.; daughter of I. D. (a teacher) and Rose (Bookbinder) Klein; married Joseph W. Gelb (an attorney), June 26, 1966; children: Andrew, Jonathan. *Education:* City College of the

City University of New York, B.A., 1962; University of Chicago, M.A., 1963; New York University, Ph.D., 1969. *Politics:* Democrat. *Religion:* Jewish. *Home:* 131 Riverside Dr., New York, N.Y. 10024. *Office:* Department of Political Science, City College of the City University of New York, New York, N.Y. 10031.

CAREER: City College of the City University of New York, New York, N.Y., assistant professor of political science, 1964—. *Member:* American Political Science Association.

WRITINGS: (Editor with Marian Palley) *The Politics of Social Change,* Holt, 1971; (with Palley) *Tradition and Change in American Parties,* Crowell, 1975. Contributor to political science and behavioral science journals.

WORK IN PROGRESS: Black-Jewish Relations: The Prospects for Coalition, for American Jewish Committee's Institute on Pluralism and Group Identity.

SIDELIGHTS: Joyce Gelb writes that her interest is "in problems of the powerless in American society, including women and the poor, as well as the continuing role of ethnicity in American politics."

* * *

GELLES, Richard J. 1946-

PERSONAL: Born July 7, 1946, in Newton, Mass.; son of Sidney S. (a neckwear manufacturer) and Clara (Goldberg) Gelles; married Judy S. Isacoff (a research assistant), July 4, 1971; children: Jason Charles. *Education:* Bates College, B.A., 1968; University of Rochester, M.A., 1970; University of New Hampshire, Ph.D., 1973. *Politics:* "Independent pragmatist." *Religion:* Jewish. *Home:* 81 Stonehenge Rd., Kingston, R.I. 02881. *Office:* Department of Sociology, University of Rhode Island, Kingston, R.I. 02881.

CAREER: University of New Hampshire, Durham, instructor in sociology, 1970-73; University of Rhode Island, Kingston, assistant professor of sociology, 1973—. Lecturer at University of Rochester, summer, 1970, 1971. Consultant to Family Development Study of Children's Hospital Medical Center, Emma Pendleton Bradley Hospital, and to Child and Family Services of Newport. Member of Rhode Island Committee on the Battered, Abused, and Neglected Child.

MEMBER: American Association of University Professors, American Sociological Association, National Council on Family Relations, Eastern Sociological Association, New England Social Psychological Association. *Awards, honors:* National Institute of Mental Health grants, 1973-74, 1975-78; U.S. Department of Health, Education and Welfare grant, 1975-77.

WRITINGS: The Violent Home: A Study of Physical Aggression between Husbands and Wives, Sage Publications, 1974.

Contributor: Suzanne K. Steinmetz and Murray A. Straus, editors, *Violence in the Family,* Dodd, 1974; Stella Chess and Alexander Thomas, editors, *Annual Progress in Child Psychology and Child Development,* Brunner, 1974; *Violence Against Children,* Rowohlt Taschenbuch Verlag, 1975; *Nursing Digest 1975 Review of Maternal-Child Health,* Contemporary Publishing, 1975; *Review of Psychiatry and Mental Health and Review of Community Health,* Contemporary Publishing, 1975.

Co-editor of "Teaching Sociology" series, Sage Publica-

tions, 1973—. Contributor to professional journals. Associate editor of *Journal of Applied Communications Research,* 1974—.

WORK IN PROGRESS: Research on a national sample survey of incidence and causes of violence between family members; a study of labeling and classifying child-abuse reports, contributions to *Contemporary Theories about the Family,* edited by Wesley R. Burr, Rueben Hill, F. Ivan Nye, and Ira L. Reiss, and to *The "Eye" of Sociology,* edited by Arthur B. Shostak.

* * *

GERHARDT, Lydia A(nn) 1934-

PERSONAL: Born October 10, 1934, in New Jersey; daughter of Erwin Otto (a banker) and Lydia (a teacher; maiden name, Kaemmerer) Gerhardt. *Education:* Pennsylvania State University, B.S., 1956; University of Wisconsin, M.S., 1958; New York University, Ed.D., 1970. *Home:* 217 Kent St., Apt. 25, Brookline, Mass. 02146. *Office:* Graduate School of Early Childhood, Wheelock College, 200 Riverway, Boston, Mass. 02215.

CAREER: University of Wisconsin, Madison, instructor in child development, 1958-60; Simmons College, Boston, Mass., assistant professor of home economics, 1960-62; Merril-Palmer Institute, Detroit, Mich., member of faculty on early childhood education, 1962-64; Mills College, New York, N.Y., member of education faculty, 1964-70; Wheelock College, Boston, Mass., associate professor of early childhood education, 1971—. Kindergarten teacher in Brookline, Mass., 1974-75. Head counselor and assistant to the director of School of Creative Arts (Vineyard Haven, Mass.), summers, 1948-67. *Member:* Society for Research in Child Development, National Association for the Education of Young Children, American Association of University Professors, Organisation Mondiale pour l'Education Prescolaire, Phi Upsilon Omicron, Omicron Nu, Pi Lambda Theta, Kappa Delta Phi.

WRITINGS: Moving and Knowing: The Young Child Orients Himself in Space, Prentice-Hall, 1973; (contributor) Carol Seefeldt, editor, *Curriculum for the Preschool, Primary Child,* C. E. Merrill, 1976.

WORK IN PROGRESS: Articles on Laban's "Principles of Movement for Teachers of Young Children."

SIDELIGHTS: Lydia Gerhardt writes: "Dancing has been 'my thing' since childhood. I continue to study and in recent years have studied Modern/Jazz/Blues with Consuelo Atlas, Jazz with Bob Gilman, European Folk with Connie Taylor, and Modern with Raye Harrison.... During the summers of 1973 and 1974, I studied at the Dance Notation Bureau in New York City.... My growing understanding of Laban's principles of movement has sparked my concern for 1) the need for movement education in teacher education, 2) the role of movement analysis in early childhood education, and 3) the role of movement in early childhood education.

"During the summer of 1975, I spent eight weeks living with a Tongan family in the 'smallest kingdom of the world.' My initial purpose was primarily 'holiday,' but I got involved in teacher education ... and came back with a lot of pictures of family life in this underdeveloped nation of the South Pacific."

* * *

GERLACH, Vernon S(amuel) 1922-

PERSONAL: Born October 24, 1922, in Michigan; son of

Adolph E. (a teacher) and Adeline (Haney) Gerlach; married Betty Schweppe, July 6, 1946; children: Douglas, David, William, Becky. *Education:* Wayne State University, B.A., 1948; University of Minnesota, M.A., 1955; Arizona State University, Ed.D., 1963. *Religion:* Lutheran. *Home:* 1225 East La Jolla Dr., Tempe, Ariz. 85282. *Office address:* Box F.L.S., Arizona State University, Tempe, Ariz. 85281.

CAREER: Arizona State University, Tempe, research associate, 1962-63, assistant professor, 1963-65; associate professor, 1965-68, professor of education, 1968—. Visiting professor, University of Minnesota, 1973-74. *Member:* American Psychological Association, American Educational Research Association, Association for Educational Communication and Technology, Phi Lambda Theta.

WRITINGS: Teaching and Media, Prentice-Hall, 1971; *Instructional Theory,* University of Nebraska, 1974.

*   *   *

GETTY, Hilda F. 1938-

PERSONAL: Born June 2, 1938, in Buenos Aires, Argentina; daughter of Manuel A. (a professor and mathematician) and Rosalia (Leggiero) Fernandez; married Hugh Getty (divorced, 1974); children: Grace, Leslie, Clyde. *Education:* Received A.S., B.S., and M.F.A. degrees. *Home:* 1912 Mohawk, Fort Collins, Colo. 80521. *Office:* Pitkin Department of Art, Colorado State University, Fort Collins, Colo. 80523.

CAREER: Colorado State University, Fort Collins, 1970—, began as instructor, became associate professor of art, director and creator of "Contemporary Crafts of the Americas Project," 1972-75. Artist involved in metalsmithing, printmaking, and fabric design. *Member:* Society of North American Goldsmiths, American Museum of Natural History, Smithsonian Institution.

WRITINGS: Contemporary Crafts of the Americas, Regnery, 1975.

WORK IN PROGRESS: Crafts: A Light into the Cultural Development.

*   *   *

GETZOFF, Carole 1943-

PERSONAL: Born December 29, 1943, in New York, N.Y.; daughter of Alexander and Frances (Kramer) Getzoff. *Education:* Hunter College of the City University of New York, B.A., 1965. *Politics:* Humanism. *Religion:* Jewish. *Home:* 845 Carroll St., Brooklyn, N.Y. 11215.

CAREER: Pageant (magazine), New York, N.Y., photo editor, 1965-67; natural foods cooking teacher and freelance writer, 1967—. Consultant to New York City Health and Hospitals Corp. and Adelphi National Drug Institute. *Awards, honors:* Tessie K. Scharps essay prize, from Hunter College of the City University of New York, 1965, for "The Friendship of W. B. Yeats and Lady Gregory."

WRITINGS: The Natural Cook's First Book, Dodd, 1974. Columnist, *Village Voice.* Contributor to popular magazines, including *Harper's* and *Ms.*

WORK IN PROGRESS: A novel; a book on the attitudes of women living alone.

SIDELIGHTS: Carole Getzoff writes: ". . . Writing is a form of expression and of poking around inside that can't be duplicated by any other process and I don't believe that any other media will ever take its place. Sometimes I wish it weren't so hard."

BIOGRAPHICAL/CRITICAL SOURCES: San Francisco Chronicle, December 5, 1973; *Yonkers Herald Statesman,* January 2, 1974.

*   *   *

GHADIMI, Hossein 1922-

PERSONAL: Born May 30, 1922, in Meshed, Iran; son of Kutchek (a businessman) and Sedighe Ghadimi; married Ingeborg Hettwer, March 31, 1952; children: Ramin, Roya, Rene, Giselle. *Education:* Teheran University, M.D. (with honors), 1947. *Home and office:* 3612 Bertha Dr., Baldwin Harbor, N.Y. 11510.

CAREER: Teheran Children's Hospital, Teheran, Iran, intern, 1948-50; Southampton Children's Hospital, Southampton, England, junior registrar, 1950-51; University of Shiraz, School of Medicine, Shiraz, Iran, organized department of pediatrics, 1952, associate professor of pediatrics and acting chairman of department, 1952-56, professor of pediatrics and chairman of department, 1956-57; Harvard University, Children's Medical Center, Boston, Mass., research fellow in pediatrics, 1957-59; University of Toronto, Toronto, Ontario, senior research fellow at Research Institute Hospital for Sick Children, 1959-61; State University of New York, Downstate Medical Center, Brooklyn, assistant professor, 1961-67, associate professor, 1967-69, professor of pediatrics, 1969—. Certified by American Board of Pediatrics, 1960; licensed to practice in state of New York, 1963; certification of qualification as laboratory director, from New York State Department of Health. Director of pediatrics at Brooklyn's Methodist Hospital, 1967-74. *Military service:* Iranian Army, 1947-48; served as physician; became first lieutenant.

MEMBER: Society for Pediatric Research (emeritus member), American Pediatric Society, American Academy of Pediatrics, American Society for Clinical Nutrition, American Association for the Advancement of Science, New York Academy of Sciences.

WRITINGS: (Editor and contributor) *Total Parenteral Nutrition: Premises and Promises,* Wiley, 1975.

Contributor: John B. Stanbury, James B. Wyngaarden, and Donald S. Frederickson, editors, *The Metabolic Basis of Inherited Disease,* McGraw, 1960, 3rd edition, 1972; William L. Nyhan, editor, *Amino Acid Metabolism and Genetic Variation,* McGraw, 1967; Moshen Ziai, Charles A. Janeway, and Robert E. Cooke, editors, *Pediatrics,* Little, Brown, 1969; Gordon Farrell, editor, *Mental Retardation,* University of Texas Press, 1969; Robert F. Murray, Jr. and Pearl Lockhart Rosser, editors, *The Genetic, Metabolic, and Developmental Aspects of Mental Retardation,* C. C Thomas, 1972; William L. Nyhan, editor, *Heritable Disorders of Amino Acid Metabolism,* Wiley, 1974. Contributor of about fifty articles to medical journals.

WORK IN PROGRESS: A book on diet, explaining pitfalls and shortcomings of widely used diet-fads and offering scientific information for institution of "tailored diets."

SIDELIGHTS: Ghadimi believes that "protein deprivation is the common denominator in a host of conditions that now exact a high toll in prolonged hospitalization and death, and that parenteral nutrition—nutrients given by vein—using [his] newly developed amino acid preparations can radically change this picture." He makes a convincing plea to physicians to guard against the subtle, imperceptible, but dangerous consequences of protein deprivation in prematures and other troubled infants as well as all severely ill or traumatized patients, adding that in a sense even our best hospitals are "unwitting 'starvation camps' for critically ill or debilitated patients." *Avocational interests:* Water skiing, snow skiing.

* * *

GIALLOMBARDO, Rose (Mary) 1925-

PERSONAL: Born November 12, 1925, in Willimantic, Conn.; daughter of Rosario and Mary (Lidestri) Giallombardo. *Education:* University of Connecticut, B.A. (with honors), 1958; Northwestern University, M.A., 1960, Ph.D., 1965. *Home:* 1451 East 55th St., Chicago, Ill. 60615.

CAREER: Northwestern University, School of Dentistry, Chicago, Ill., lecturer in sociology, 1959-61; New York University, New York, N.Y., instructor, 1964-65, assistant professor of sociology, 1965-66; University of Chicago, Chicago, Ill., assistant professor, 1967-70, associate professor of sociology, 1970-72, senior study director at National Opinion Research Center, 1966-67, research associate at Center for Social Organization Studies, 1967-72. *Member:* American Sociological Association, National Council on Crime and Delinquency, American Academy of Political and Social Science, Society for the Study of Social Problems, American Association of University Professors, Art Institute of Chicago. *Awards, honors:* National Institute of Mental Health research grant, 1968-72.

WRITINGS: Society of Women: A Study of Women's Prisons, Wiley, 1966; (editor) *Juvenile Delinquency: A Book of Readings,* Wiley, 1966, 3rd edition, in press; *Report on the New State Hospital,* Center for Social Organization Studies, University of Chicago, 1968; (contributor) Oscar Grusky and George A. Miller, editors, *The Sociology of Organizations,* Free Press, 1970; (contributor) Anthony L. Guenther, editor, *Criminal Behavior and Social Systems: Contributions of American Sociology,* Rand McNally, 1970; (contributor) Robert R. Bell and Michael Gordon, editors, *The Social Dimension of Human Sexuality,* Little, Brown, 1972; (contributor) Bell, editor, *Studies in Marriage and the Family,* 2nd edition, Crowell, 1973; *The Social World of Imprisoned Girls,* Wiley, 1974; (editor) *Contemporary Social Issues,* Wiley, 1975. Contributor to sociology journals.

WORK IN PROGRESS: Research on contemporary social trends.

* * *

GIBBONS, Barbara (Halloran) 1934-

PERSONAL: Born October 9, 1934, in East Orange, N.J.; daughter of Frank P. and Marion (Whittlesey) Halloran; married Wilbur I. Gibbons (a sales administration manager), December 17, 1960; children: Susan. *Education:* Attended New Jersey State Teachers College (now Montclair State College), 1953-56, and Rutgers University, 1958-60. *Home and office:* 50 West Shore Trail, Lake Mohawk, Sparta, N.J. 07871.

CAREER: Former woman's editor for suburban newspapers; publicity writer for United Fund campaigns; writer of advertising copy for home furnishings field; United Features Syndicate, author of column "The Slim Gourmet," 1971—; *Family Circle* (magazine), author of column "Creative Low-Calorie Cooking," 1971—; *Gourmet Bookshelf,* columnist, 1972—. *Member:* Society of Magazine Writers.

WRITINGS: Creative Low-Calorie Cookbook, Family Circle, 1973; *The Calorie-Watchers' Cookbook,* Consumer Guide, 1975; *Consumer Guide to Diet Cooking,* Consumer Guide, 1975.

WORK IN PROGRESS: The Slim Gourmet Cookbook for Harper.

* * *

GIBBONS, Euell (Theophilus) 1911-1975

September 8, 1911—December 29, 1975; American naturalist, lecturer, author of books on wild foods. Obituaries: *New York Times,* December 30, 1975; *Washington Post,* December 30, 1975; *Detroit Free Press,* December 30, 1975; *Time,* January 12, 1976; *Newsweek,* January 12, 1976; *Publishers Weekly,* January 12, 1976. (*CAP*-2; earlier sketch in *CA*-23/24)

* * *

GIBSON, Elsie (Edith) 1907-

PERSONAL: Born October 3, 1907, in Chicago, Ill.; daughter of Arch Bonnell (a factory foreman) and Violet (Wonders) Fuller; married Royal John Gibson (a minister), May 23, 1934; children: Royal Bricker, David Andre. *Education:* Taylor University, A.B., 1930; Hartford Theological Seminary, B.D., 1933, S.T.M., 1934. *Home and office:* 85 Avery Heights, Hartford, Conn. 06106.

CAREER: Ordained minister of Congregational Church and United Church of Christ, 1935; pastor in Custer, Mont., 1935-36, Binger, Okla., Edmund, Okla., and Glendive, Mont., 1941-42; State Child Welfare, Oklahoma City, Okla., stenographer in the 1950's; Greater Hartford Council of Churches, Hartford, Conn., member of Committee on Church Unity, 1965-75, of Commission on Ecumenical Study and Service, 1969-75, of Faith and Order Department, 1975—.

WRITINGS: When the Minister Is a Woman, Holt, 1970; *Life Is Something Else,* United Church Press, 1974. Contributor to religious publications.

WORK IN PROGRESS: A book.

AVOCATIONAL INTERESTS: Foreign travel, reading biography and autobiography.

* * *

GIESSLER, Phillip Bruce 1938-

PERSONAL: Born May 27, 1938, in Fort Wayne, Ind.; son of Benjamin (a welder) and Loretta (Eicks) Giessler; married Janet Lynne Dienes (a teacher), August 5, 1961; children: David William, Linda Jane. *Education:* Concordia Teachers College, River Forest, Ill., B.S., 1961; Concordia Seminary, M.A.R., 1965; Westminster Theological Seminary, Th.M., 1974; Concordia Theological Seminary, M.Div., 1975. *Residence:* Rocky River, Ohio. *Office:* St. Thomas Lutheran Church, Rocky River, Ohio 44116.

CAREER: Parochial high school teacher of religion in St. Louis, Mo., 1962-63; ordained minister of Lutheran Church, 1967; pastor in Croydon, Pa., 1969-71, and Rocky River, Ohio, 1971—.

WRITINGS: Christian Love: Campus Style, Dillon/Liederbach, 1974, reissued as *Love, Phil,* CSS Publishing, 1975; *To Nathan and Nancy with Luv,* CSS Publishing, 1975; *Christian Nursery School Guidebook for Religion Readiness,* CSS Publishing, 1975.

GILGE, Jeanette 1924-

PERSONAL: Surname is pronounced with two hard "g"'s; born March 31, 1924, in Phillips, Wis.; daughter of Edward and Emma (Meier) Kudrna; married Kenneth Gilge, September 26, 1942; children: Donna (Mrs. Ron Childress), Kent, Karl, Dean; (foster children) Janice (Mrs. Paul Stevko), Dennis. *Education:* Attended Triton College, 1971-74. *Religion:* Christian. *Home:* 1010 North Seventh Ave., Maywood, Ill. 60153.

CAREER: Writer. Lecturer; Christian broadcasting volunteer worker. *Member:* Children's Reading Round Table (Chicago), Off Campus Writers (Winnetka, Ill.), Penhandlers. *Awards, honors:* Triton Summer Writer's Workshop award, 1974; David C. Cook juvenile award, 1975, for *City-Kid Farmer.*

WRITINGS: Never Miss a Sunset (adult), David Cook, 1975; *City-Kid Farmer* (juvenile), David Cook, 1975.

WORK IN PROGRESS: A sequel to *City-Kid Farmer,* tentatively titled *Growing-Up Summer;* a non-fiction book tentatively titled *This New Life,* concerning her commitment to Christ.

SIDELIGHTS: Jeanette Gilge writes: "I believe the battle between good and evil is intensifying and that we will see swift and terrible changes on this earth as God makes a last attempt to warn mankind that growing disregard of Him and of His statutes is intolerable to Him." *Avocational interests:* Nature and the out-of-doors, reading, hiking, bicycle riding.

* * *

GILL, I(nayat) K(hera) 1924-

PERSONAL: Born December 2, 1924, in Sialkot, Pakistan; moved to Germany, 1970, became German citizen, 1975; son of Khera Mall (a farmer) and Mariam Gill; married Andrea Pfeiffer, September 15, 1962; children: Matthias, Stefan, Beate. *Education:* College of Physical Education, Cologne, Germany, diploma, 1959; University of Graz, Ph.D., 1961. *Home:* Luchsweg 67, D 5024 Pulheim, West Germany.

CAREER: Marie Adelaide Leprosy Centre, Karachi, Pakistan, director of rehabilitation, 1962-70; research on rehabilitation of handicapped children through physical education, Cologne, Germany, 1970-72; University of Bielefeld, Bielefeld, Germany, teacher in department of social science, 1972-74; Brauweiler Psychiatric Hospital, Cologne, Germany, director of rehabilitation, 1974—. *Member:* European Leprosy Association, German Association for the Rehabilitation of the Disabled.

WRITINGS: Friends Not Outcasts, Helios, 1972; *Heilpaedagogische Leibeserziehung mit Behinderten* (title means "Curative Physical Education with the Handicapped"), Hans Putty Verlag (Wuppertal, Germany), 1974; *Sport als Mittel der Rehabilitation* (title means "Sport as a Means of Rehabilitation"), G. Schindele Verlag (Karlsruhe, Germany), 1975; *Rehabilitation Research: Possibilities of Sports for Physical Disabled,* G. Schindele Verlag, 1975. Contributor of articles to journals in Pakistan, Germany, United States, and India.

WORK IN PROGRESS: Research for a book on alcoholics and psychiatric patients.

* * *

GILLMOR, Daniel S. 1917(?)-1975

1917(?)—November 20, 1975; American newsman, columnist, foundation executive, editor, and author. Obituaries: *New York Times,* November 21, 1975.

* * *

GIPSON, John (Durwood) 1932-

PERSONAL: Born August 31, 1932, in Turkey, Tex.; son of Felix Claude (a contractor) and Mary Del (Butler) Gipson; married E. Beth Stirman, June 18, 1953; children: Sherri Lynn, Kathy Jo, John David. *Education:* Abilene Christian College, 1949-53. *Home:* 1500 Northwick Ct., Little Rock, Ark. 72207. *Office address:* Box 228, Little Rock, Ark. 72203.

CAREER: Ordained minister of Church of Christ, 1953; worked with churches in Sherman, Odessa, Lamesa, and Fort Worth, all Texas, 1953-67; Sixth and Izard Church of Christ, Little Rock, Ark., minister, 1968—. Lecturer at Abilene Christian College, George Pepperdine University, Lubbock Christian College, Oklahoma Christian College, Fort Worth Christian College, David Lipscomb College, Harding College, and Harding Graduate School; conducts a weekly television program. Member of medical committee of the Arkansas Kidney Foundation; member of board of trustees of Fort Worth Christian College, and Zambia Christian Schools.

WRITINGS: (With Joe R. Barnett) *Happiness Day and Night,* Pathway Publishing, 1968; (with Barnett) *Paths to Peace,* Pathway Publishing, 1969. Staff writer for *20th Century Christian, Power For Today, The World Evangelist,* and *Action.*

WORK IN PROGRESS: Two books, *Some Quiet Place* and *All Things Are Yours.*

* * *

GITIN, Maria (Kathleen) 1946-

PERSONAL: Born April 21, 1946, in Petaluma, Calif.; married David Daniel Gitin (a poet and teacher), March 27, 1969. *Education:* Attended San Francisco State College (now University), 1968, and University of Wisconsin, Madison, 1972-73. *Home:* 2740 Ransford Ave., Apt. 8, Pacific Grove, Calif. 93950.

CAREER: Poet, 1968—; has worked as librarian and as executive secretary; University for Man, Monterey, Calif., teacher of English, 1975—. *Awards, honors:* Writer's award from International P.E.N., 1975, for *Little Movies.*

WRITINGS: Little Movies (poems), Ithaca House, 1975. Contributor to literary magazines, including *Epoch, Greenfield Review,* and *New.*

WORK IN PROGRESS: Another collection of poems.

* * *

GLASER, Daniel 1918-

PERSONAL: Born December 23, 1918, in New York, N.Y.; son of Samuel J. and Lena (Solway) Glaser; married Pearl Bennett, October 11, 1946; children: Lenore Meryl. *Education:* University of Chicago, B.A., 1939, M.A., 1947, Ph.D., 1954. *Home:* 901 South Ogden Dr., Los Angeles, Calif. 90036. *Office:* Department of Sociology, University of Southern California, Los Angeles, Calif. 90007.

CAREER: University of Illinois, Urbana, assistant professor, 1954-58, associate professor, 1958-62, professor of sociology, 1962-68, head of department, 1964-68; Rutgers University, New Brunswick, N.J., professor of sociology, 1968-70; University of Southern California, Los Angeles, professor of sociology, 1970—. Associate commissioner for research of New York State Narcotic Addiction Control Commission, 1968-70. Consultant in criminology. *Military service:* U.S. Army, 1942-46; became warrant officer junior grade; received Bronze Star.

MEMBER: American Sociological Association (chairman of criminology section, 1965), Society for the Study of Social Problems (past member of executive committee), Pacific Sociological Association, Law and Society Association, California Association for Criminal Justice Research (member of executive committee, 1974—), Illinois Academy of Criminology (president, 1965). *Awards, honors:* John Howard Association annual award, 1965, for *The Effectiveness of a Prison and Parole System.*

WRITINGS: The Effectiveness of a Prison and Parole System, Bobbs-Merrill, 1964, abridged and revised edition, 1969; (editor) *Crime in the City,* Harper, 1970; *Social Deviance,* Markham, 1971; *Adult Crime and Social Policy,* Prentice-Hall, 1972; *Routinizing Evaluation,* U.S. Government Printing Office, 1973; (editor) *Handbook of Criminology,* Rand McNally, 1974; *Strategic Criminal Justice Planning,* U.S. Government Printing Office, 1975. Contributor of more than one hundred fifty articles and reviews to scholarly journals. Editor of *Sociology and Social Research,* 1973-76; associate editor of *Social Problems,* 1964-66, *American Journal of Sociology,* 1965-72, *Journal of Research in Crime and Delinquency,* 1967—, *Federal Probation,* 1967—, *Journal of Criminal Law and Criminology,* 1973—, and *Law and Society Review,* 1975—.

WORK IN PROGRESS: A criminology text, for Dryden.

SIDELIGHTS: Glaser's stress in criminology is on the grounding of explanations in social and behavioral science theory and on testing them by rigorous research.

BIOGRAPHICAL/CRITICAL SOURCES: Issues in Criminology, autumn, 1972.

* * *

GLAZER, Tom 1914-

PERSONAL: Born September 3, 1914, in Philadelphia, Pa.; son of Jacob Glazer; married Miriam Reed Eisenberg (a remedial reading teacher), June 25, 1944; children: John Prescott, Peter Reed. *Education:* Studied at City College (now City College of City University of New York), but left in final year, 1941. *Politics:* Independent. *Religion:* Unaffiliated. *Address:* Box 102, Scarborough, N.Y. 10510. *Agent:* Julian Bach, Jr., 3 East 84th St., New York, N.Y. 10017; and other agents.

CAREER: Folksinger, songwriter, and composer. *Member:* American Federation of Musicians, American Guild of Authors and Composers, American Society of Composers, Authors, and Publishers, Screen Actors Guild, Coffee House Club (New York). *Awards, honors:* Silver Medal of U.S. Treasury Department for war bond work during World War II; other awards and prizes for radio, television, and films, and from American Society of Composers, Authors, and Publishers.

WRITINGS—Compiler: *A New Treasury of Folk Songs,* Bantam, 1961; *Tom Glazer's Treasury of Songs for Children* (arranged for piano, with guitar chords), Grosset, 1964; *On Top of Spaghetti* (collection of children's songs with notes on their origin and background; arranged for piano, with guitar chords), Grosset, 1966; *Songs of Peace, Freedom, and Protest,* Fawcett World, 1972; *Eye Winker, Tom Tinker, Chin Chopper: Fifty Musical Fingerplays* (arranged for piano, with guitar chords), Doubleday, 1973.

Recordings sung, or sung and played, include: "Activity and Game Songs," two albums; "Music for 1's and 2's"; "Children's Songs from Latin America" (sung in English and Spanish); "The Musical Heritage of America," two albums; "The Twelve Days of Christmas"; "Do Not Go Gentle..." (song-settings of lyrics of Dylan Thomas, Yeats, Shakespeare, and other poets). Also has written poetry and liner notes for albums.

WORK IN PROGRESS: A large collection of children's songs, tentatively titled *The Complete Book of Children's Songs,* publication by Open Court expected in 1976.

SIDELIGHTS: Glazer told *CA* that one of his prime motivations is "to provide instruction and/or entertainment to as many people as can find my efforts useful. The most vital thing I know of today is to prevent violence while changing the world for the better if possible. All else is secondary, certainly books. Next we must preserve the remaining beauty of the world. I have had a long drawn out love affair with the French language, but the more I study it, the more I realize how few people master their own tongue."

BIOGRAPHICAL/CRITICAL SOURCES: Horn Book, April, 1974.

* * *

GLEASON, Judith 1929-

PERSONAL: Born December 9, 1929, in Pasadena, Calif.; married William Gleason (a lawyer), September 24, 1953; children: Maud, William, Esther, Richard, Helen. *Education:* Radcliffe College, B.A., 1951; Columbia University, M.A., 1954, Ph.D., 1963. *Politics:* "PCI in Italy, usually vote Democratic in U.S." *Religion:* "Santeria." *Home:* Vicolo del Piede 10, Rome, Italy; and 26 East 91st St., New York, N.Y. *Office:* 733 Shimkin Hall, School of Education, New York University, New York, N.Y.

CAREER: Sarah Lawrence College, Bronxville, N.Y., lecturer in literature, 1960-63; author, 1963-70; New York University, New York, N.Y., adjunct associate professor of African arts, 1970—.

WRITINGS: This Africa, Northwestern University Press, 1964; *Agotime,* Grossman, 1970; *Orisha: The Gods of Yorubaland* (juvenile), Atheneum, 1971; *A Recitation of Ifa, Oracle of the Yoruba,* Grossman, 1973; *Santeria, Bronx* (juvenile), Atheneum, 1975.

WORK IN PROGRESS: The Viking Portable Traditional African Reader; a book on the divinities of the Niger River.

AVOCATIONAL INTERESTS: Travel (Brazil and West Africa); ethnic dance, "I have a passionate concern with coordinated physical movement, with drumming (from the dancer's point of view)"; sewing; playing tennis; to "be in the country and be in the city"; gardening; "rivers wherever they may be, preferably hot climates."

* * *

GLEASON, Ralph Joseph 1917-1975

March 1, 1917—June 3, 1975; American jazz critic, journalist, editor, magazine founder, television producer, author. Obituaries: *New York Times,* June 4, 1975; *Washington Post,* June 6, 1975.

* * *

GLENN, Lois (Ruth) 1941-

PERSONAL: Born April 5, 1941, in Beaumont, Tex.;

daughter of Dennie Doom (a general manager of a Texaco distributorship) and Lucile (White) Glenn; married Joe B. Thrash, 1962 (divorced, 1972); married Robert Ewing Campbell (a writer), 1972. *Education:* Lamar University, B.A., 1962; Texas Tech University, M.A., 1966, Ph.D., 1972. *Home:* 3955 Shoal Creek Blvd., 101, Austin, Tex. 78756. *Office:* Bureau of Business Research, University of Texas at Austin, Austin, Tex. 78712.

CAREER: Texas Tech University, Lubbock, instructor in English, 1965-70; University of Southern Mississippi, Hattiesburg, assistant professor of English, 1970-72; Austin Community College, Austin, Tex., instructor in English, 1973-74; University of Texas, Austin, managing editor of *Texas Business Review,* 1975—.

WRITINGS: Charles W. S. Williams: A Checklist, Kent State University Press, 1975. Contributor to scholarly journals.

* * *

GLENN, Morton B(ernard) 1922-

PERSONAL: Born March 21, 1922, in New York, N.Y.; son of Harold and Mimi (Steinberg) Glenn; married Jane Pollack, March 11, 1953 (divorced, 1959); married Justine Manheim, July 21, 1963; children: (first marriage) Wendy Gail, Valerie Beth, John Allan. *Education:* University of Pennsylvania, A.B., 1942, New York University, M.D., 1946. *Home:* 35 East 75th St., New York, N.Y. 10021. *Agent:* Curtis Brown Ltd., 60 East 56th St., New York, N.Y. 10022. *Office:* 121 East 60th St., New York, N.Y. 10022.

CAREER: Bellevue Hospital, New York, N.Y., internship and residency, 1946-47, 1949-52; New York University, New York, N.Y., assistant professor of clinical medicine, 1952—. *Military service:* U.S. Naval Reserve, active duty, 1942-45, 1947-49. *Member:* American Medical Association, American Heart Association, American Diabetes Association, New York Academy of Medicine. *Awards, honors:* Travel award from American Institute of Nutrition, 1963.

WRITINGS: How to Get Thinner Once and for All, Dutton, 1965; *But I Don't Eat That Much: A Diet Specialist Answers His Patients' Questions on Once and for All Reducing,* Dutton, 1974.

* * *

GLICKMAN, Arthur P. 1940-

PERSONAL: Born December 22, 1940, in Pittsburgh, Pa.; son of Joseph E. (a shoe wholesaler) and Sally (a shoe wholesaler; maiden name, Peck) Glickman. *Education:* Duquesne University, B.A., 1964. *Politics:* "Unlabelable." *Religion:* "Self-fulfillment." *Home:* 427 Golden Isles Dr., #11F, Hallandale, Fla. 33009. *Agent:* Carl D. Brandt, Brandt & Brandt, 101 Park Ave., New York, N.Y. 10017.

CAREER: Annapolis Evening Capitol, Annapolis, Md., reporter, 1964-65; reporter, *Maryland Gazette,* 1964-65; *Pittsburgh Press,* Pittsburgh, Pa., reporter, 1965-69; *Wall Street Journal,* New York, N.Y., reporter, 1969-71; now full-time writer in Hallandale, Fla. *Military service:* U.S. Army Reserve, 1963-69. *Awards, honors:* Keystone Press Awards first prize, 1968, for government news series.

WRITINGS: (With Donald Randall) *The Great American Auto Repair Robbery,* Charterhouse, 1972.

WORK IN PROGRESS: A book concerned with insights into the author, the United States, the world, and human nature garnered from traveling around the world with a backpack, tentatively titled, *The World Is My Living Room.*

SIDELIGHTS: Glickman told *CA:* "Curiosity and moral outrage provide the basis for my writing. I originally became a journalist with the idea of developing into a satirist, but slowly evolved more into serious investigative reporting. Newspaper reporting, which I had found stimulating during my twenties, suddenly seemed stifling to me in my early thirties. . . . This led me to quit newspaper work and to turn to books as the best way of expressing myself. The auto repair book was the outgrowth of a feeling that I was constantly being gypped when I got my car repaired and that something should be done about it. Using the royalties from that book, I spent two years off and on traveling to many parts of the world with all my possessions in a small backpack."

* * *

GLIDDEN, Frederick D(illey) 1908-1975
(Luke Short)

1908—August 18, 1975; American writer of Western adventure fiction under pseudonym. Obituaries: *New York Times,* August 19, 1975; *Washington Post,* August 20, 1975; *Newsweek,* September 1, 1975. (*CAP*-2; earlier sketch in *CA*-21/22)

* * *

GODDARD, Gladys Benjamin 1881(?)-1976

1881(?)—January 18, 1976; American writer of poetry, short stories, and a biography. Obituaries: *New York Times,* January 21, 1976.

* * *

GODFREY, Vivian 1921-
(Melita Denning)

PERSONAL: Born November 26, 1921, in London, England; daughter of Ralph (a Criminal Investigation Department—Scotland Yard—inspector) and Florence Sarah (a secretary; maiden name, White) Godfrey; married Leon Roger Barcynski (a writer), June 5, 1970. *Education:* Technical College, Slough, Buckinghamshire, England, intermediate certificate in metallurgy, 1943. *Politics:* "Independent thinker." *Religion:* "Independent thinker." *Office address:* BM-SACRIVERB, London WC1V 6XX, England.

CAREER: Royal Air Force, civilian research and technical worker in England, 1941-44, 1946-48; British Admiralty, Ditton Park, Berkshire, England, civilian research and technical worker, 1944-46; conducted independent research on history, archaeology, and the occult in France, Spain, Italy, Greece, Near East, and Middle East, 1949-52; teacher and researcher in Nicosia, Cyprus, 1952-55; Duckett's Bookshop, London, England, head of foreign book department, 1955-65; Sound Services (in commercial films), London, credit controller, 1966-70; Servotomic (heating and ventilation engineers), London, supervisor of purchase ledger in Industrial Division, 1971-74; free-lance dress and costume designer (under married name, Vivian Barcynska) in London, 1974—. Has been trained in first aid and civil defense.

MEMBER: Order Aurum Solis (collegian member; study director, 1974—), Ghost Club (London), Research into Lost Knowledge Organization. *Awards, honors:* Named dame d'honneur by Sovereign Military Order of the Temple of Jerusalem, 1968, for unpublished work on the Medieval Order.

WRITINGS: (Under pseudonym Melita Denning; with Osborne Phillips—pseudonym of husband, Leon Barcynski) *The Magical Philosophy,* Llewellyn, Volume I: *Robe and Ring: The Philosophy of Magical Art,* 1974, Volume II: *The Apparel of High Magick: Symbolism and the Material Keys,* 1975, Volume III: *The Sword and the Serpent: Qabalah and Magical Art,* 1975, Volume IV: *The Triumph of Light: Psychology and Magick,* in press.

WORK IN PROGRESS: Books based on research into historical problems and mysteries; under pseudonym Melita Denning, a book tentatively titled *Ritual Drama;* under pseudonym Melita Denning, with Osborne Phillips (pseudonym of husband, Leon Barcynski), *The Magical Philosophy,* Volume V: *Mysteria Magica: Rituals, Techniques et Alia,* for Llewellyn, and another similar book for Llewellyn, and several occult novels.

SIDELIGHTS: Vivian Godfrey writes: "The true purpose of every creature is determined by its nature. The true purpose of man in this world is indicated by the structure of the individual (body and psyche together). In the human individual, the rational mind has to direct and to care for the subrational part of the individual: that is, for the emotional, instinctual, and physical organism. This task, however, the rational mind is unlikely to perform aright, and in some ways cannot do so, unless itself becomes receptive to the Intuitive Mind without which human nature is incomplete. Similarly, in the outer world, man has a task of directing and of caring for the whole of subrational nature: not only the young and the backward of humanity, but the whole organic structure of the biosphere. In this great work, however, mankind has in many respects failed; nor can success be expected until the human race, or at least its responsible members, realise their own inner nature and have compassion on it, besides becoming sensitive to those higher powers which normally reach us through developed awareness of the Intuitive Mind." *Avocational interests:* The arts (especially music, poetry, and drama), natural life, wildlife preservation (including marine life).

*   *   *

GOERGEN, Donald 1943-

PERSONAL: Born August 16, 1943, in Remsen, Iowa; son of Julius (a farmer) and Sylvia (Wilhelmi) Goergen. *Education:* Loras College, B.A., 1965; graduate study at Laval University, Kansas Neurological Institute, Mount St. Bernard Seminary, Graduate Theological Union, and Menninger Foundation; Aquinas Institute, M.A., 1968, Ph.D., 1972. *Home and office:* 2570 Asbury, Dubuque, Iowa 52001.

CAREER: Entered the Dominican order, 1970, ordained Roman Catholic priest, 1975; Divine Word College, Epworth, Iowa, instructor in theology, 1968; Kansas Neurological Institute, Topeka, Kan., chaplain, 1969-70; Aquinas Institute, Dubuque, Iowa, assistant professor of theology, 1971—. *Member:* Catholic Theological Society of America, American Academy of Religion, American Teilhard Association.

WRITINGS: The Sexual Celibate, Seabury, 1975. Contributor to academic journals.

WORK IN PROGRESS: Research on Teilhard de Chardin, on Christology, and on homosexuality.

GOITEIN, S(helomo) D(ov)   1900-
(Solomon Dob Fritz Goitein)

PERSONAL: Born April 3, 1900, in Burgkunstadt, Germany; came to United States, 1957; son of Eduard E. (a rabbi) and Frida (Braunschweiger) Goitein; married Theresa Gottlieb (a teacher of eurhythmics), July 16, 1929; children: Ayala (Mrs. Amirav Gordon), Ofra (Mrs. Baruch Rosner), Elon. *Education:* University of Frankfurt on the Main, Ph.D., 1923. *Religion:* Jewish. *Home:* 284 Hamilton Ave., Princeton, N.J. 08540. *Office:* School of History, Institute for Advanced Study, Princeton, N.J. 08540.

CAREER: School teacher in Haifa, Israel, 1923-27; Hebrew University, Jerusalem, Israel, instructor, 1928-32, assistant professor, 1933-46, associate professor, 1947-48, professor of Islamic history, 1949-57, director of School of Oriental Studies, 1949-56; University of Pennsylvania, Philadelphia, professor of Arabic, 1957-71; Institute for Advanced Study, Princeton, N.J., member of staff of School of History, 1971—. Senior education officer of Mandatory Government of Palestine, 1938-48.

MEMBER: American Philosophical Society, Mediaeval Academy of America (fellow), American Academy for Jewish Research (fellow), American Oriental Society (president, 1969-70), Conference on Jewish Social Studies, Middle Eastern Studies Association, Israel Oriental Society (president, 1949-57). *Awards, honors:* Recipient of grants from American Philosophical Society, 1958, 1961, Ulmann Foundations, 1959, Social Science Research Council, 1962, 1968-69, and Guggenheim Memorial Foundation, 1965-66, 1971-73; L.H.D., University of Chicago, 1971, and Gratz College; D.H.L., Jewish Theological Seminary of America, 1973.

WRITINGS: From the Land of Sheba: Tales of the Jews of Yemen, translated by Christopher Fremantle, Schocken, 1947, revised edition, 1973; *Jews and Arabs: Their Contacts through the Ages,* Schocken, 1955, revised edition, 1974; *Studies in Islamic History and Institutions,* Humanities, 1966; *A Mediterranean Society: The Jewish Communities of the Arab World as Portrayed in the Documents of the Cairo Geniza,* University of California Press, Volume I: *Economic Foundations,* 1968, Volume II: *The Community,* 1971; *Letters of Medieval Jewish Traders,* Princeton University Press, 1974.

Under name Solomon Dob Fritz Goitein: *Jemenica: Sprichwoerter und Redensarten aus Zentral-Jemen,* Kommissionsverlag von O. Harrassowitz, 1934; *Baladhuri: Arab Historian,* Hebrew University Press, 1936; *Travels in Yemen,* Hebrew University Press, 1941; *Hora-at ha-ivrit be-Erets Yisrael,* Yavneh Publishing, 1945; *Ha-Islam shel Muhamad,* Library, Hebrew Union College, 1956; (author of introduction) Carl Rathjens, *Jewish Domestic Architecture in San'a, Yemen,* Luzac & Co., 1957; *The Mentality of the Middle Class in Mediaeval Islam,* Centre pour l'Etude des Problems du Monde Musulman Contemporain (Brussels, Belgium), 1961.

Also author of *Hora-at ha-TaNaKH be-vet ha-sefer,* 1942; *Shete masot al sefer Yirmiyah,* 1952; *Umanut ha-sipur ba-Mikra,* 1955, *Iyunim be-Mikra,* 1957; *Ha-Mishpat ha-muslimi be-Medinat Yisrael,* 1957; *Hora-at ha-TaNaKH,* 1957; *The Geniza Collection at the University Museum of the University of Pennsylvania,* 1958; *Sidre himukh,* 1962; *Hora-at ha-Ivrit,* 1967; *Iyunim ba-Mikra,* 1967; and *Al hora-at ha-aravit,* Library, Hebrew Union College. Also editor of *Kitab ansab al-ashraf,* by Ahmad ibn Yahya al-Baladhuri, 1936; and *Ansab al-ashraf,* by Ahmad ibn

Yahya al-Baladhuri, 1964. Also editor and translator of *Masa'ot Habshush,* by Hayyim Habshush, 1939.

WORK IN PROGRESS: A multi-volume series, *Documents on the India Trade during the High Middle Ages; Mediterranean People: Letters and Documents from the Cairo Geniza.*

AVOCATIONAL INTERESTS: Calisthenics, hiking.

*   *   *

GOLD, Don 1931-

PERSONAL: Born March 13, 1931, in Chicago, Ill.; son of Sidney and Bess (Seidler) Gold; married Joan Gallagher Whipple, March 24, 1954 (divorced, 1968); children: Tracy, Paul. *Education:* Northwestern University, B.S.J., 1952, M.S.J., 1953. *Home:* 11 East 88th St., New York, N.Y. 10028. *Agent:* Owen Laster, William Morris Agency, 1350 Avenue of the Americas, New York, N.Y. 10019.

CAREER: Down Beat (magazine), Chicago, Ill., managing editor, 1956-59; *Playboy* (magazine), Chicago, Ill., associate editor, 1959-62; *Saturday Evening Post,* New York, N.Y., associate editor, 1962-64; *Ladies' Home Journal,* New York, N.Y., assistant managing editor, 1964-65; *Holiday* (magazine), New York, N.Y., managing editor, 1965-68; William Morris Agency (literary agency), New York, N.Y., head of literary department, 1968-73; writer, 1973-75; *Travel and Leisure* (magazine), New York, N.Y., managing editor, 1975—. *Military service:* U.S. Army, in Intelligence, 1953-55; became sergeant. *Member:* International P.E.N., Authors Guild of Authors League of America.

WRITINGS: (Editor) *The Human Commitment* (anthology), Chilton, 1967; *Letters to Tracy* (nonfiction), McKay, 1972; *Bellevue* (nonfiction), Harper, 1975. Contributor to popular magazines, including *Harper's, Playboy, Book Digest, Holiday, Ladies' Home Journal, Cosmopolitan, Reader's Digest, Today's Health, Chicago Review,* and *Travel and Leisure.*

WORK IN PROGRESS: A novel, publication by Harper expected in 1977.

SIDELIGHTS: Gold writes: "I set out to discover as much about journalism as I could. . . . In September, 1975, I returned to what I am most fond of, magazine editing. . . . I intend to pursue that as long as I can, as long as magazines survive, while writing books and articles along the way, blending the two elements of my journalistic career that have brought me the greatest satisfaction."

*   *   *

GOLD, Sharlya

PERSONAL: Given name is pronounced to rhyme with "Carla"; born in Los Angeles, Calif.; daughter of Albert (an accountant) and Selma (a pianist and concert singer; maiden name, Mayer) Isenberg; married Leonard Gold (an elementary school principal), 1951; children: Alison, Sheridan, Hilary, Darien. *Education:* San Bernardino Valley College, A.A.; University of California, Berkeley, B.A. *Religion:* Jewish. *Residence:* Capitola, Calif.

CAREER: Former elementary school teacher; reading specialist; instructor of adult classes in writing for children and of children's classes in bookbinding. *Member:* National Writers Club, National League of American Pen Women. *Awards, honors:* First prize in juvenile short story contest conducted by Southern California branch of National League of American Pen Women.

WRITINGS: The Potter's Four Sons, Doubleday, 1969; *Amelia Quackenbush,* Seabury, 1973. Contributor to *The Porcupine Storybook,* Concordia, 1974, and to juvenile magazines, including *Child Playmate, Friend, Working for Boys,* and *Together.*

WORK IN PROGRESS: Two books.

*   *   *

GOLDBERG, Herb 1937-

PERSONAL: Born July 14, 1937, in Berlin, Germany; son of Jacob and Ella (Nagler) Goldberg. *Education:* City College (now City College of the City University of New York), B.A., 1958; Adelphi University, Ph.D., 1963. *Office:* 8899 Beverly Blvd., Los Angeles, Calif. 90048.

CAREER: California State University, Los Angeles, professor of psychology, 1965—; licensed psychologist in private practice of psychotherapy with individuals, couples, and families. *Member:* American Psychological Association, American Academy of Psychotherapists, California State Psychological Association, Phi Beta Kappa.

WRITINGS: (With George R. Bach) *Creative Aggression,* Doubleday, 1974; *The Hazards of Being Male,* Nash Publishing, 1976. Contributor to *American Psychologist, Journal of Abnormal Psychology, Professional Psychology, The Clinical Psychologist, Voices,* and *International Journal of Social Psychiatry.*

*   *   *

GOLDFRANK, Esther S(chiff) 1896-

PERSONAL: Born May 5, 1896, in New York, N.Y.; daughter of Herman J. (a surgeon) and Matilda (Metzger) Schiff; married Walter S. Goldfrank, December 8, 1922 (died September 16, 1935); married Karl August Wittfogel (a professor), March 8, 1940; children: (first marriage) Susan Goldfrank Lennhoff; (stepsons) Max, Alexander, Thomas. *Education:* Barnard College, B.A., 1918; Columbia University, graduate study, 1921-22, 1937. *Politics:* Independent. *Religion:* Jewish. *Home and office:* 420 Riverside Dr., New York, N.Y. 10025.

CAREER: Personal secretary to anthropologist and professor Franz Boas (accompanying him on field trips in New Mexico), 1919-22; University of Washington, Seattle, staff anthropologist for Chinese history project, 1943—. Field research includes study among American Indian pueblos and Blackfoot Indians. *Member:* American Anthropological Association (fellow), Society for American Archaeology, American Ethnological Society (president, 1948), New York Academy of Sciences.

WRITINGS: The Social and Ceremonial Organization of Cochiti, American Anthropological Association, 1927, Kraus Reprint, 1964; *Changing Configurations in the Social Organization of a Blackfoot Tribe During the Reserve Period: The Blood of Alberta, Canada,* J. J. Augustin, 1945, University of Washington Press, 1966; (editor) Elsie Parsons, *Isleta Paintings,* Smithsonian Institution, 1962, revised edition with new foreword, 1970; *The Artist of "Isleta Paintings" in Pueblo Society,* Smithsonian Institution Press, 1967. Contributor to anthropology journals.

WORK IN PROGRESS: Notes on an Undirected Life, her memoirs.

*   *   *

GOLDIN, Milton 1927-

PERSONAL: Born January 8, 1927, in Cleveland, Ohio;

son of Hyman (a musician) and Ida (Felsher) Goldin; married Aranka Nemcek (a musician), June 17, 1950; children: Karen, David. *Education:* New York University, B.A., 1953, M.A., 1955. *Home:* 266 Crest Dr., Tarrytown, N.Y. 10591.

CAREER: New York City Symphony, New York, N.Y., violinist, 1944-45; Denver Symphony Orchestra, Denver, Colo., violinist, 1949-51; American Choral Foundation, New York, N.Y., administrative director, 1955-61; Brookdale Hospital Center, Brooklyn, N.Y., associate director of development, 1963-66; New York University, New York, N.Y., fund raising campaign director for Washington Square College and Graduate School of Arts and Science, 1966-67; Oram Associates, Inc., New York, N.Y., vice-president, 1967-72, executive vice-president, 1972-74; fund raising consultant in New York, N.Y., 1975—. Manager of Amor Artis Chorale and Orchestra, 1961—. *Military service:* U.S. Army, 1945-46.

MEMBER: National Society of Fund Raisers, Organization of American Historians, Phi Beta Kappa, Psi Chi, Mu Sigma. *Awards, honors:* Deems Taylor Award from American Society of Composers, Authors and Publishers, 1970.

WRITINGS: The Music Merchants, Macmillan, 1969. Contributor to music journals and to popular magazines, including *Saturday Review.*

WORK IN PROGRESS: Why They Give: American Jews and Philanthropy, for Macmillan; . . . *And God Bless Standard Oil,* the story of John D. Rockefeller and the beginnings of modern American philanthropy, completion expected in 1977.

SIDELIGHTS: Goldin writes: "Perhaps more than sociologists—but less than psychoanalysts—fund raisers see the greed and the self-sacrifice, the idealism and the ruthlessness, the duplicity and the sincerity that characterize our society. Above all, they see a desperate need for recognition and identity that is often pathological. It is a loss that men in this field capable of addressing profound issues have limited themselves to routine discussions of development techniques."

* * *

GOLDING, Lawrence A(rthur) 1926-

PERSONAL: Born May 8, 1926, in Capetown, South Africa; naturalized U.S. citizen, 1959; son of Reginald G. (a chemist) and Maize (Mitchell) Golding; married Carmen Pollack (a research associate), August 9, 1952; children: Scott Mitchell, Neal Lawrence, Kirk Louis. *Education:* University of Illinois, B.S., 1950, M.S., 1953, Ph.D., 1958. *Home:* 1770 Walnut Rd., Kent, Ohio 44240. *Office:* Applied Physiology Research Laboratory, Kent State University, Kent, Ohio 44242.

CAREER: University of Idaho, Moscow, assistant professor of physical education, 1953-56; Kent State University, Kent, Ohio, assistant professor, 1958-60, associate professor, 1960-66, professor of physical education, 1966—, director of Applied Physiology Research Laboratory, 1958—. Member of national Young Men's Christian Association (YMCA) running program committee, physical education committee, committee on community affairs, and chairman of national physical education assembly; member of board of directors of Ohio-West Virginia area Young Men's Christian Association. Chairman of medical committee of International Federation of Body Builders. Consultant to Cleveland Indians Baseball Club.

MEMBER: American Association for Health, Physical Education and Recreation (fellow), American College of Sports Medicine (fellow), National Research Council, American Association for the Advancement of Science, American Institute of Biological Sciences, National Rehabilitation Association, National Jogging Association, American Association of Corrective Therapy (adviser), Ohio Association for Health, Physical Education and Recreation, Ohio Academy of Science, New York Academy of Science, Sigma Xi, Phi Epsilon Kappa, Omicron Delta Kappa. *Awards, honors:* Grants to study the effect of exercise on coronary risk factors, on cardiovascular efficiency, and on the effect of drugs on athletic performance, from National Institutes of Health, 1959-61, National Science Foundation, 1961-62, American Heart Association, 1962-63, Portage County Heart Association, 1963-75, Akron District Heart Association, 1963-74, East Central Heart Association, 1968-69, and Young Men's Christian Association of Greater New York, 1969-70.

WRITINGS: (With Ronald R. Bos) *Human Anatomy Manual,* Kent State University, 1965; (with Bos) *Scientific Foundations of Physical Fitness Programs,* Burgess, 1967; (contributor) William Morgan, editor, *Ergogenic Aids and Muscular Performance,* Academic Press, 1972; (contributor) Robert L. Morse, editor, *Exercise and the Heart,* C. C Thomas, 1972; (editor with Clayton R. Myers and Wayne E. Sinning) *The Y's Way to Physical Fitness,* Rodale Press, 1973; (with Bos) *Kinesiology,* Burgess, in press. Contributor to academic journals.

WORK IN PROGRESS: Research on altitude acclimatization by hypoxia training, on the effect of continuous and intermittent running on cardiovascular fitness, and on the effect of an anabolic steriod and protein supplement on strength and weight.

* * *

GOLDMAN, Bruce (Eliot) 1942-

PERSONAL: Born April 3, 1942, in Brooklyn, N.Y.; son of Paul S. (a truck driver) and Kate (a teacher; maiden name, Chopnick) Goldman; married Jane Morton (a registered nurse), April 20, 1970 (died April 17, 1973); children: Daniel. *Education:* Columbia University, A.B., 1962. *Religion:* Jewish. *Home and office:* 639 West End Ave., New York, N.Y. 10025.

CAREER: Marschalk Co., New York City, junior copywriter, 1963-65; copywriter in New York City for D.K.G., Inc., 1965-66, Scali, McCabe & Sloves, 1967-70, Young & Rubicam, 1970-72, Needham, Harper & Steers, 1972-73, and Richard K. Manoff, Inc., 1973-74; Promotion Plus, Inc., New York City, copy chief, 1974-75; free-lance copywriter in New York City, 1975—. Instructor at School of Visual Arts, 1965-66; lieutenant in New York City Auxiliary Police, 1966-73; county committeeman for Conservative Party. *Military service:* New York Army National Guard, 1964-70. *Member:* Sports Car Club of America (director of New England region, 1972-73). *Awards, honors:* More than thirty awards, mostly for advertising copywriting.

WRITINGS: Your Check Is in the Mail, Workman Publishing, 1974. Contributor to advertising journals and local magazines.

WORK IN PROGRESS: The Electronic Pickpocket (tentative title), a nonfiction book on electronic funds transfer; a novel whose protagonist perpetrates a monumental credit fraud; research on consumer credit.

SIDELIGHTS: Goldman writes: "After years of giving friends and acquaintances free advice on coping with computer errors, shoddy merchandise, overbilling, gestapo-like tactics of bill collectors, and so on, I sat down and spent more years writing it down, so that people could still fight their battles, but without my being bothered. It didn't work. For one thing, it took more years (and bother) to write it down than it did to talk about. . . . Another reason . . . is that all the people who used to ask me for free advice are now asking for free books, and I'd much rather give away the advice." Goldman added that a major interest in his life is raising his son, who was one month old when his mother died of leukemia. *Avocational interests:* Sports car racing (holds licenses from Sports Car Club of America for national competition, from Federation Internationale de l'Automobile, and from International Motor Sports Association), religious activities.

BIOGRAPHICAL/CRITICAL SOURCES: Atlanta Journal, April 11, 1975; *Newsday,* June 1, 1975.

* * *

GOLDSTEIN, Stephen R(obert)   1938-

PERSONAL: Born July 12, 1938, in Philadelphia, Pa.; married; children: two. *Education:* University of Pennsylvania, A.B. (with highest honors), 1959, LL.B. (summa cum laude), 1962. *Office:* School of Law, University of Pennsylvania, Philadelphia, Pa. 19174.

CAREER: Wolf, Block, Schorr & Solis-Cohen, Philadelphia, Pa., practicing attorney, 1962-64; law clerk to U.S. Supreme Court Justice Goldberg, 1964-65; Wolf, Block, Schorr & Solis-Cohen, practicing attorney, 1965; University of Pennsylvania, Philadelphia, assistant professor, 1966-69, associate professor, 1969-72, professor of law, 1972—. Visiting professor at University of California, Berkeley, 1970-71, and Hebrew University of Jerusalem, 1974-75; member of board of directors of *Philadelphia Jewish Exponent* and Philadelphia chapter of American Jewish Committee; member of Jewish Campus Activities Board; reporter to American Bar Association and Institute of Judicial Administration.

MEMBER: American Association of University Professors (general counsel, 1972-74), American Bar Association, American Law Institute, American Professors for Peace in the Middle East (president of Philadelphia chapter), Phi Beta Kappa, Order of the Coif.

WRITINGS: (With Louis B. Schwartz) *Police Guidance Manuals: A Philadelphia Model,* Office of Law Enforcement Assistance, University of Pennsylvania, 1968; *Materials on School Law,* School of Law, University of Pennsylvania, 1969; (contributor) Earl Phillips, editor, *Proceedings of the National Conference on the Teaching of Anti-Poverty Law,* Association of American Law Schools, 1969; (with Schwartz) *Law Enforcement Handbook for Police,* West Publishing, 1970; *Cases and Materials on Education Law,* School of Law, University of Pennsylvania, 1972, revised edition, 1973; *Law and Public Education,* Bobbs-Merrill, 1974. Contributor to *American Jewish Yearbook, Yearbook of School Law,* and to law journals. Former research editor of *University of Pennsylvania Law Review.*

WORK IN PROGRESS: Juvenile Justice Standards: Schools and Education, with William G. Buss, for Institute of Judicial Administration, American Bar Association; a study of the constitutional right, of lack thereof, of a public school teacher to teach materials over the objection of su-

periors; research on the procedure of impeachment and trial of a president of the United States, focusing on the legal effects of the end of a Congress and the start of a new Congress on a pending impeachment or trial proceeding; research on the meaning of academic freedom and premises based on the American experience.

* * *

GOODRICH, William Lloyd   1910(?)-1975

1910(?)—September 16, 1975; American Episcopalian churchman, author. Obituaries: *Washington Post,* September 19. 1975.

* * *

GOODSELL, Charles T(rue)   1932-

PERSONAL: Born July 23, 1932, in Kalamazoo, Mich.; son of Charles T. (a professor) and Frances (Comee) Goodsell; married Mary Elizabeth MacKintosh, June 13, 1959; children: Holly Delight, Amanda Joy. *Education:* Kalamazoo College, A.B., 1954; Harvard University, M.P.A., 1958, M.A., 1959, Ph.D., 1961. *Politics:* Independent Democrat. *Religion:* Presbyterian. *Home:* 1501 Eddings St., Carbondale, Ill. 62901. *Office:* Department of Political Science, Southern Illinois University, Carbondale, Ill. 62901.

CAREER: U.S. Bureau of the Budget, Washington, D.C., management intern, summers, 1957-59; University of Puerto Rico, Rio Piedras, assistant professor of public administration, 1961-64; Princeton University, Princeton, N.J., research associate at Woodrow Wilson School, 1964-66; Southern Illinois University, Carbondale, associate professor, 1966-72, professor of political science, 1972—. *Military service:* U.S. Army, 1954-56.

MEMBER: American Political Science Association, American Society for Public Administration, Midwest Political Science Association.

WRITINGS: Administration of a Revolution, Harvard University Press, 1965; *American Corporations and Peruvian Politics,* Harvard University Press, 1974. Contributor to professional journals.

SIDELIGHTS: Goodsell writes: "My principal areas of interest are public bureaucracy, politics of the multinational corporation, and Latin American affairs."

* * *

GORDON, (Gilbert) James   1918-

PERSONAL: Born June 1, 1918, in Aberdeen, Scotland; son of James Gilbert (a general secretary of a Young Men's Christian Association) and Anne (Clark) Gordon; married Edith Baxter, December 17, 1940. *Education:* Attended art schools in Liverpool and Halifax, England; Herford School of Art, received art teaching diploma, 1936; Guildhall School of Speech and Drama, licentiate, 1950; Royal College of Speech and Drama, licentiate, 1950; Open University, B.A. (honors), 1974. *Politics:* Conservative. *Religion:* Church of England. *Home:* 7 Rowan Ave., Northampton NN3 1JF, England. *Office:* Department of Education, Northampton House, Northampton NN1 2HX, England.

CAREER: Youth organizer for cities of St. Helens and Liverpool, England, both 1935; teacher of drama and fencing, 1936—. Actor and producer for repertory companies all over England, including that of British Broadcasting Corp., 1940-44; director of Little Theatre groups and art studios in the British Zone of Germany, 1941-51; stage fight arranger for professional and amateur companies; course arranger of youth and adult drama for Northampton Education Department and Youth Department, 1950-74; teacher of drama and fencing, 1974—. Secretary of Hereford Community Council, 1941-50; county drama adviser for Hereford and Northamptonshire, 1950-74; pageant master of Northamptonshire County Show, 1951-72; secretary of Young Men's Christian Association (YMCA) in Halifax and Hereford, England, both 1936-38. *Military service:* British Army, Royal Artillery, 1939-45; served in France and Germany; became captain.

MEMBER: National Association of Drama Advisers (chairman, 1974—), National Union of Teachers, Society of Teachers of Speech and Drama (registrar, 1973—), British Actors Equity Association, Guild of Drama Adjudicators, English-Speaking Board, National Society for Local Government Officers.

WRITINGS: Stage Fights, J. Garnet Miller, 1973; *Three Plays: Mr. Garrick's Young Ladies,* J. Garnet Miller, 1973. Author of critical assessments of plays presented by youth and adult groups in Northamptonshire. Drama critic for *Hereford Times,* 1941-50, and *Worcester Evening News Times,* 1941-50.

WORK IN PROGRESS: Masks and Make-Up, a drama study for schools; *School Drama,* completion expected in 1977; historical research on the steel town of Corby.

SIDELIGHTS: Gordon writes: "I have always had a firm belief that drama was an essential community activity, and that a knowledge of fencing was necessary to mental and body control and stimulation of theatre techniques. Also that the present 'open-ended' approaches to school drama are woolly minded and lacking in motivation." *Avocational interests:* Riding; foil, epee, and sabre fencing; swimming; game fishing.

* * *

GOREN, Judith 1933-

PERSONAL: Born April 5, 1933, in Detroit, Mich.; daughter of Herman (a journalist in public relations) and Evelyn (Apple) Wise; married Robert Goren (an attorney), December 20, 1953; children: Gary, Steven, Nancy. *Education:* Wayne State University, B.A., 1954, M.Ed., 1972. *Home:* 21525 West Thirteen Mile Rd., Birmingham, Mich. 48010. *Office:* The Clinic, 887 East Maple Rd., Birmingham, Mich. 48011.

CAREER: High school teacher of English and journalism in Detroit, Mich., 1954-56; U.S. Air Force, civilian elementary school teacher in Etain, France, 1956-57; Birmingham Community House, Birmingham, Mich., adult education instructor, 1973—; Marygrove College, Detroit, Mich., instructor, 1974-75; The Clinic, Birmingham, Mich., group counselor, 1975—; Wayne State University, College of Lifelong Learning, Detroit, instructor, 1975-76. Consultant to schools for Michigan Council of the Arts, 1975-76. *Member:* International Transactional Analysis Association, Detroit Women Writers.

WRITINGS: Coming Alive (poems), Stone Press, 1975.

Work has been anthologized in *Anthology of Women Poets,* edited by Pamela Vitorine, Dremen Press, 1974; *Ten Michigan Women Poets,* edited by Margaret Kaminski, Glass Bell Press, 1975; *Moving to Antarctica,* edited by Kaminski, Dustbooks, 1975. Contributor of articles to education and religious periodicals, and poems to *Redbook,* and to

literary journals, including *Beloit Poetry Journal, Northeast, Moving Out,* and *North York Poetry Review.* Associate editor of *Humanistic Judaism,* 1968-69.

WORK IN PROGRESS: Poems.

SIDELIGHTS: Judith Goren writes: "Travel with my husband has taken me to Europe, Israel, Mexico, Peru and Central America; to the Mayan ruins of Chichen Itza, Uxmal, Tikal, and Copan, and the ancient Inca ruins at Macchu Picchu, but I'm chiefly concerned with the inner trip, which is how I began writing poetry and how I became involved in the Human Potential movement. I've had professional training and experience in group encounter, transactional analysis, gestalt awareness, bioenergetic bodywork, Silva Mind Control and meditation. I utilize this knowledge for my own personal growth, in my work with others as a group counselor, and in my writing."

* * *

GORHAM, Charles Orson 1911-1975

1911—October 17, 1975; American publishing executive, novelist. Obituaries: *New York Times,* October 19, 1975. (See index for previous *CA* sketch)

* * *

GORSLINE, Douglas (Warner) 1913-

PERSONAL: Born May 24, 1913, in Rochester, N.Y.; son of Henry W. (a real estate broker) and Sarah (Warner) Gorsline; married Elisabeth Evarts Perkins, September 26, 1936 (divorced); married Nel King, April 17, 1959; children: (first marriage) John Warner, Jeremiah Evarts. *Education:* Attended Yale University, 1931-32, and Art Students League, New York City, 1932-35. *Residence:* France. *Agent:* Ted Riley, 252 East 49th St., New York, N.Y. 10017.

CAREER: Artist; work represented in numerous private and public collections, including Butler Institute of American Art, Library of Congress, National Academy of Design, St. Paul Art Gallery, and Houghton Library, Harvard University; has had one-man shows in galleries and institutions nationwide, most recently at Schoelkopf Gallery, New York, Pearl Fox Gallery, Philadelphia, and Memorial Art Gallery, Rochester. Art instructor, Art School of the National Academy, 1960-62; free-lance illustrator. *Member:* National Academy of Design. *Awards, honors:* Purchase awards from American Academy of Arts and Letters, 1962, National Academy of Design, 1963, St. Paul Gallery, and Springfield Museum; Tiffany Foundation grant, 1963; and about a dozen other awards from groups and organizations, including American Watercolor Society, Audubon Artists, and National Arts Club.

WRITINGS—Self-illustrated: Farm Boy, Viking, 1950; *What People Wore: A Visual History of Dress from Ancient Times to Twentieth Century America,* Viking, 1952.

Illustrator: Ferdinand Monjo, *Vicksburg Veteran,* Simon & Schuster, 1971; Ferdinand Monjo, *Me and Willie and Pa: A Story of Abraham Lincoln and His Son Tad,* Simon & Schuster, 1973; Clement Moore, *Night Before Christmas,* Random House, 1975.

SIDELIGHTS: Gorsline enjoys travel in Eurpoe and has made a recent trip to the People's Republic of China.

* * *

GOSHORN, Elizabeth 1953-

PERSONAL: Born April 7, 1953, in Covington, Ky.;

daughter of Richard and Margaret (an English teacher; maiden name, Wright) Morrison. *Education:* Cleveland Institute of Art, B.F.A., 1976. *Address:* % 33 Cliffview, Ft. Thomas, Ky. 41075.

WRITINGS: Shoestrings (juvenile), Carolrhoda, 1975.

WORK IN PROGRESS: Several children's books.

* * *

GOSTELOW, Mary 1943-

PERSONAL: Surname is accented on first syllable; born July 23, 1943, in London, England; daughter of James Macdonald and Lorna Mary (Marlow) Cobban; married Martin F. Gostelow (a photographer), June 20, 1968. *Education:* Educated in England and New York. *Religion:* Anglican. *Home:* 43 Milton Abbas, Blandford Forum, Dorsetshire, England. *Agent:* Julie Fallowfield, McIntosh & Otis, Inc., 18 East 41st St., New York, N.Y. 10017.

CAREER: Book researcher, editorial assistant, journalist, 1964-68; free-lance travel and arts writer, based in Beirut, Lebanon, 1968-72; free-lance writer, journalist, and lecturer on decorative arts, Dorset, England, 1972—. Had lecture tours in the United States, Australia, and South Africa. *Member:* Embroiderers Guild (member of national committee), Costume Society (member of national committee), Museums Association, National Trust, National Association of Decorative and Fine Arts Societies, Costume Society of America, Embroiderers Guild of America, National Standards Council of American Embroiderers.

WRITINGS: A World of Embroidery, Scribner, 1975. Contributor to arts and embroidery magazines in the United States and England. First editor-in-chief of *Caravan,* 1970-72.

WORK IN PROGRESS: Embroidery Design of South Africa, publication expected in 1977; *Embroidery of All Russia; Blackwork; Embroideries of the Middle East.*

AVOCATIONAL INTERESTS: Travel (Africa, the Soviet Union, the Middle East), all art forms.

* * *

GOTTLIEB, Elaine
(Elaine Gottlieb Hemley)

PERSONAL: Born in New York, N.Y.; daughter of Nelson Alfred (a chiropodist) and Ida (a teacher; maiden name, Brauer) Gottlieb; married Cecil Herbert Hemley (a writer), July 3, 1952 (died, 1966); children: Nola (deceased), Jonathan, Robin. *Education:* New York University, B.S.; Ohio University, M.A., 1968. *Home:* 1009 North Niles Ave., South Bend, Ind. 46617. *Agent:* Julie Fallowfield, McIntosh & Otis, 18 East 41st St., New York, N.Y. 10017. *Office:* English Department, Indiana University, 1825 Northside Bvd., South Bend, Ind. 46615.

CAREER: Noonday Press, New York, N.Y., fiction editor, 1951-58; free-lance editor, 1958-68; Slippery Rock State College, Slippery Rock, Pa., assistant professor of English, 1969-70; Stephens College, Columbia, Mo., instructor in English, 1970-72; Indiana University, South Bend, associate professor of English, 1972—, director of Summer Writers Conference, 1973, 1974. Drama judge of South Bend Civic Theatre, 1975—. *Member:* Associated Writing Programs, College English Association, Modern Language Association of America, Midwest Modern Language Association. *Awards, honors:* Fellowship from Yaddo Foundation, 1948, 1950, MacDowell Colony, 1951, 1956, 1970-71,

1974-75, and Indiana University, summer, 1975; O. Henry award, 1972.

WRITINGS: Darkling (novel), Reynal & Hitchcock, 1947; (under name Elaine Gottlieb Hemley) *The Writer's Signature: Idea in Story and Essay,* Scott, Foresman, 1972.

Co-translator from the Yiddish; all by Isaac Bashevis Singer: *Satan in Goray,* Noonday Press, 1955; (with Joseph Singer) *The Magician of Lublin,* Noonday Press, 1960; (with Martha Glicklich and others) *The Spinoza of Market Street,* Farrar, Straus, 1961; *In My Father's Court,* Farrar, Straus, 1966; *The Manor,* Farrar, Straus, 1967; *The Estate,* Farrar, Straus, 1969.

Short story included in *Prize Stories: The O. Henry Awards,* edited by William Abrahams, Doubleday, 1972. Contributor of articles, essays, and short stories to *Southern Review, Southwestern Review, Kenyon, Commentary, Chelsea, Noonday, Lotus,* and other periodicals.

WORK IN PROGRESS: A collection of short stories; a second novel, to be called *Nostalgia.*

AVOCATIONAL INTERESTS: Photography and filmmaking.

* * *

GOTTSCHALK, Paul A. 1939-

PERSONAL: Born April 12, 1939, in Chicago, Ill.; son of Louis (a historian) and Fruma (Kasdan) Gottschalk; married Katherine Kiblinger, August 29, 1964; children: Sarah, Alexander. *Education:* Harvard University, A.B., 1960; University of Chicago, M.A., 1961, Ph.D., 1965. *Office:* Department of English, Cornell University, Ithaca, N.Y. 14853.

CAREER: Chicago Teachers College South, Chicago, Ill., instructor in English, 1963-64; Cornell University, Ithaca, N.Y., instructor, 1965-67, assistant professor, 1967-73, associate professor of English, 1973—. *Member:* Modern Language Association of America, American Association of University Professors. *Awards, honors:* Woodrow Wilson fellow, 1960-62.

WRITINGS: The Meanings of 'Hamlet,' University of New Mexico Press, 1972. Contributor to English journals.

WORK IN PROGRESS: Research on Shakespeare and on the impact of recent philosophy on practical criticism.

* * *

GOUD, Anne 1917-
(Anne-Mariel, Karina)

PERSONAL: Born July 12, 1917, in Soissons, France; daughter of Armely (a bank manager) and Anne (Colas de Lasseux) Goud; married, July 11, 1935; children: Evelyn, Patrick. *Education:* Sorbonne, University of Paris, B.A.; Catholic Institute, B.A. *Politics:* None. *Religion:* Roman Catholic. *Home:* 12 rue Beaujou, Paris 8, France 75008. *Agent:* Jane Browne, 9507 Santa Monica Blvd., Beverly Hills, Calif. 90210.

CAREER: Novelist and writer. *Member:* Societaire de la Ste. des Gens de Lettres de France, Societaire adjoint des Auteurs Dramatiques, Societe des Auteurs, Compositeurs, et Editeurs de Musique. *Awards, honors:* Recipient of romantic novel prize, popular novel prize, Marco Polo Prize, and prize for greatest suspense novel of the year.

WRITINGS—Under pseudonym Anne-Mariel, except as indicated: *La Route sans souvenir,* S.E.P.E. (Paris), 1948; *Les Nuits secretes d'Elisabeth d'Autriche,* S.E.P.E., 1949.

(With Gregoire Leclos) *On joue pour l'honneur*, A. Fayard (Paris), 1954; *Le Caniche mene l'enquete*, Gautier-Languereau (Paris), 1956; *Je me damnerai pour toi* (novel), Tallandier (Paris), 1956; *L'Ombre d'Angela*, A. Fayard, 1956; (under pseudonym Karina) *Le Rubis du Mongol*, Gautier-Languereau, 1956; *La Colombe de la Cane Negra*, A. Fayard, 1956; (under pseudonym Karina) *La Lettre aux cachets rouges*, Gautier-Languereau, 1957; *Lucie, mon doux coeur*, A. Fayard, 1957; *Le Collier de pervenches*, A. Fayard, 1958; *Prelude a l'orange*, Tallandier, 1958; *Le Caniche entre dans la danse*, A. Fayard, 1959; *L'Ombre sur la dune*, Tallandier, 1959.

J'ai choisi mon paradis, Tallandier, 1960; *Pourvu qu'il m'aime*, Tallandier, 1960; *Les Sirenes de l'azur*, Tallandier, 1961; *Le Reve eblouissant*, Tallandier, 1962; *La Prison de bambou*, Editione Karolus, 1962; *Idylle a Vienne*, Tallandier, 1962; *Un Soir, je reviendrai* (novel), Tallandier, 1963, translation published as *One Evening I Shall Return*, Pinnacle Books, 1973; *Via pour New York* (novel), Tallandier, 1963; *Une Minute d'egarement* (novel), Tallandier, 1964; (with Iris Duncan) *Vertige d'un soir* (novel), Tallandier, 1965; *Le Dangereux message*, Tallandier, 1966; *Survint une inconnu* (novel), Castermann, 1966; *Un Amour d'Amerique*, Tallandier, 1967; *Ce soir a Copacabana*, Tallandier, 1968; *Nuit romaine*, Tallandier, 1968; *L'Oiseau du tonnerre* (novel), Castermann, 1968.

Feux rouges a Beverly Hills, Castermann, 1970; *Les Vautours du capitole* (novel), Editions du Dauphin, 1971; *Le Chant du Danube: Les Nuits secretes de Sissi*, Castermann, 1971; *La Vie amoureuse de la marquise de Paieva* (novel), Presses de la Cite (Paris), 1972; *Ce passe qui me haute* (novel), Presses de la Cite, 1972; *Haute surveillance pour Karen*, Tallandier, 1972; *L'Espouse sans alliance: Une Histoire d'amour, un suspense sans precedent*, Presses de la Cite, 1973; *Murder in Venice*, Pinnacle Books, 1974.

With Maurice Dekobra; all published by Presses de la Cite: *L'Amazone de Pretoria*, 1963, translation by Peter J. Sinclair published as *Diamond Queen*, Doubleday, 1965; *Anicia, l'espionne de Moukden*, 1964; *Veronica, qui etes-vous?*, 1965; *Anicia et le sultan rouge*, 1966; *Anicia et le tigre royal*, 1967; *Fascinante Veronica* (novel), 1968; *Rendez-vous chez Maxim's*, 1970.

Contributor to French newspapers.

WORK IN PROGRESS: The Hearst Story.

* * *

GOUGH, Barry Morton 1938-

PERSONAL: Born September 17, 1938, in Victoria, British Columbia, Canada; son of John (an educator and historian) and Dorothy (a pianist; maiden name, Munsey) Gough; married Barbara Louise Kerr, December 21, 1963; children: Melinda, Jason. *Education:* University of British Columbia, B.Ed., 1962; University of Montana, M.A., 1966; Kings College, London, Ph.D., 1969. *Religion:* Anglican Church of Canada. *Home:* 265 Alexandra Ave., Waterloo, Ontario, Canada N2L 1M9. *Office:* Department of History, Wilfrid Laurier University, Waterloo, Ontario, Canada N2L 3C5.

CAREER: Western Washington State College, Bellingham, lecturer, 1968—, assistant professor, 1969-71, associate professor of history, 1972; Wilfrid Laurier University, Waterloo, Ontario, associate professor of history, 1972—. Adjunct professor at University of Waterloo, 1973—; visiting

professor at Duke University, 1974. *Military service:* Royal Canadian Air Force Reserve, 1956. *Member:* Conference on British Studies, Canadian Historical Association, Champlain Society, American Historical Association. *Awards, honors:* Social Science Council-Canada Council publishing award, 1971, for *The Royal Navy and the Northwest Coast;* Leon and Thea Koerner research grant, 1974.

WRITINGS: The Royal Navy and the Northwest Coast of North America, 1810-1914: A Study of British Maritime Ascendancy, University of British Columbia Press, 1971; *To the Pacific and Arctic with Beechey*, Cambridge University Press, 1973; *Canada*, Prentice-Hall, 1975; (editor) *Search for the Visible Past*, Wilfrid Laurier University Press, 1975. Contributor to journals. Corresponding editor of *British Studies Intelligencer*, 1971—. Associate editor of *Albion*, 1968-69, managing editor, 1969-72, editor, 1972—.

WORK IN PROGRESS: Research on British maritime ascendancy on the Northwest Coast of North America before 1810, on the relationship of technology to the British Empire in the nineteenth and twentieth centuries, on Canada in the Commonwealth, and on race relations in the British Empire and Commonwealth.

SIDELIGHTS: Gough has travelled widely in Canada, the United States and Europe. He has lectured in the United States about Canadian-American relations.

* * *

GRACE, Joan C(arroll) 1921-

PERSONAL: Born March 6, 1921, in Brooklyn, N.Y.; daughter of William J. (a United States consul) and Catherine (Hickey) Grace. *Education:* Trinity College, Washington, D.C., B.A., 1943; Columbia University, M.A., 1951, Ph.D., 1969. *Home:* 44 Morningside Dr., New York, N.Y. 10025. *Office:* Humanities Division, Fordham University, Lincoln Center, New York, N.Y. 10023.

CAREER: Appleton-Century-Crofts, New York, N.Y., editor, 1944-48; Seton Hall University, South Orange, N.J., instructor in English, 1948-49; Fordham University, School of Education, New York, N.Y., instructor, 1950-55, assistant professor of English, 1955-68, Liberal Arts College, assistant professor, 1968-75, associate professor of English, 1975—. *Member:* American Association of University Professors, Modern Language Association of America, National Council of Teachers of English, College English Association.

WRITINGS: (With W. J. Grace) *The Art of Communicating Ideas*, Devin-Adair, 1952; *Tragic Theory in the Critical Works of Thomas Rymer, John Dennis, and John Dryden*, Fairleigh Dickinson University Press, 1975. Contributor of reviews to *America*.

WORK IN PROGRESS: A book on Shakespeare's women characters.

SIDELIGHTS: Joan Grace spent her childhood in England. "Perhaps this accounts for a kind of double vision of the United States," she wrote.

* * *

GRAEBNER, Alan 1938-

PERSONAL: Born August 6, 1938, in Pittsburgh, Pa.; son of Oliver E. and Ruth (Niehaus) Graebner; married Margaret Knopp (a physician), December 12, 1958; children: Seth Roberson, Sarah Margaret. *Education:* Valparaiso University, B.A., 1959; Columbia University, M.A., 1961,

Ph.D., 1965. *Home:* 1842 Bohland Ave., St. Paul, Minn. 55116. *Office:* Department of History, College of St. Catherine, St. Paul, Minn. 55105.

CAREER: Concordia College, Moorhead, Minn., assistant professor of American history, 1964-69; College of St. Catherine, St. Paul, Minn., associate professor of American history, 1969—. *Awards, honors:* Woodrow Wilson fellowship, 1959-60; Danforth Foundation fellowship, 1959-64.

WRITINGS: After Eve: The New Feminism, Augsburg, 1972; *Uncertain Saints: The Laity in the Lutheran Church, Missouri Synod 1900-1970,* Greenwood Press, 1975.

WORK IN PROGRESS: A history of women and the family.

* * *

GRAHAM-WHITE, Anthony 1940-

PERSONAL: Born January 8, 1940, in Surrey, England; son of Peter Joseph Dominic (a business executive) and Kathleen Adele (a dog breeder; maiden name, Korts) Graham-White; married Carla Lee Rosen (an assistant professor of dance), June 11, 1965; children: Sean Arden. *Education:* Studied at Rose Bruford Training College of Speech and Drama, Kent, England, 1958-61, and Dartmouth College, 1961-62; Harvard University, A.B. (magna cum laude), 1965; Stanford University, Ph.D., 1969. *Office:* Department of Dramatic Art, University of California, Santa Barbara, Calif. 93106.

CAREER: Southern Methodist University, Dallas, Tex., assistant professor, 1968-73, associate professor of theater, 1973—. Visiting associate professor at University of California, Santa Barbara, 1975-76. Director of American premieres of "Soldier from the Wars Returning" at Dartmouth College, "Eden Beyond Eden" at Southern Methodist University, "Transcending" at Southern Methodist University, and other plays at Harvard University and Stanford University; member of advisory board, Ethnopoetics in the Americas Conference, University of Wisconsin-Milwaukee, 1974. Trustee, McCord-Renshaw Theatre Collection, Dallas, 1971—. *Member:* American Theatre Association (member of research board, 1973—), Modern Language Association of America, African Studies Association, Phi Beta Kappa. *Awards, honors:* Woodrow Wilson fellowship, 1965-66.

WRITINGS: The Drama of Black Africa, Samuel French, 1974. Contributor to *Oxford Companion to the Theatre, Contemporary Dramatists,* and drama journals. *Educational Theatre Journal,* section editor, "Theatre in Review," 1969-71, editor-in-chief, 1972-75; consulting editor, *Journal of African Theatre Arts* (Ibadan), 1973—.

WORK IN PROGRESS: Further research on African drama, modern drama, and traditional performances around the world.

* * *

GRAY, Barry 1916-

PERSONAL: Born July 2, 1916, in Red Lion, N.J.; name legally changed in 1937; son of Manuis Joseph and Dora (Horowitz) Yaroslaw; married Beth Serrao, February 14, 1946 (divorced July 11, 1973); married Judith Margot Morris (a film story editor), September 24, 1973; children: (first marriage) Melodie (Mrs. Richard Kahr), Michael. *Education:* Attended high school in Los Angeles, Calif. *Home:* 425 East 58th St., New York, N.Y. 10022. *Agent:* Seligmann & Collier, 280 Madison Ave., New York, N.Y.

10016. *Office:* WMCA-Radio, 888 Seventh Ave., New York, N.Y. 10019.

CAREER: Worked as staff announcer at radio stations in Southern California, Salt Lake City, Utah, Miami Beach, Fla., and New York, N.Y., 1938-1950; WMCA-Radio, New York, N.Y., commentator and interviewer, 1950—. *Military service:* U.S. Army, 1941-45, 1962-69; became lieutenant colonel. *Member:* American Federation of Television and Radio Artists, Screen Actors Guild. *Awards, honors:* Citation from English Speaking Union, 1958; honor legion from New York Police Department, 1960; commendation from mayor of New York, N.Y., 1973.

WRITINGS: My Night People: 10,001 Nights in Broadcasting (autobiography), Simon & Schuster, 1975. Author of daily column in *New York Post,* 1952-55, and in *Las Vegas Sun,* 1952-55. Contributor of travel articles to *New York Times.*

SIDELIGHTS: Gray, a competent rider, is an auxiliary member of the New York Police Department, mounted section. He has broadcast from Italy (in Italian), and from London, Berlin, Tel Aviv, and Belfast.

* * *

GRAY, Francine du Plessix 1930-

PERSONAL: Born September 25, 1930, in France; came to United States in 1941; daughter of Bertrand (a diplomat) and Tatiana (Iacovleff) du Plessix; married Cleve Gray (a painter), April 23, 1957; children: Thaddeus, Luke. *Education:* Attended Bryn Mawr College, 1948-50, and Black Mountain College, summers, 1951-52; Barnard College, B.A., 1952. *Politics:* Democrat. *Religion:* Roman Catholic. *Residence:* Cornwall Bridge, Conn. 06754. *Agent:* Georges Borchardt, Inc., 145 East 52nd St., New York, N.Y. 10022.

CAREER: United Press International, New York, N.Y., reporter at night desk, 1952-54; *Realities* (magazine), Paris, France, editorial assistant for French edition, 1954-55; freelance writer, 1955—; *Art in America,* New York, N.Y., book editor, 1964-66; *New Yorker,* New York, N.Y., staff writer, 1968—. Distinguished visiting professor at City College of the City University of New York, spring, 1975. Judge of 1974 National Book Award in philosophy and religion.

MEMBER: International P.E.N., Authors Guild of Authors League of America. *Awards, honors:* Putnam Creative Writing Award from Barnard College, 1952; National Catholic Book Award, from Catholic Press Association, 1971, for *Divine Disobedience;* Front Page Award from Newswomen's Club of New York, 1972, for *Hawaii: The Sugar Coated Fortress.*

WRITINGS: Divine Disobedience: Profiles in Catholic Radicalism, Knopf, 1970; *Hawaii: The Sugar Coated Fortress,* Random House, 1972. Contributor of articles, stories, and reviews to popular magazines, including *Vogue, New Yorker, Saturday Review, Ramparts, New York Review of Books, Cosmopolitan,* and *Mademoiselle.*

WORK IN PROGRESS: A novel.

SIDELIGHTS: Francine Gray writes: "My view of writing: It's all a revenge upon reality." *Avocational interests:* Tennis, cooking Provencal food, dancing.

* * *

GRAY, Juanita R(uth) 1918-

PERSONAL: Born February 2, 1918, in Loveland, Okla.;

daughter of John William (a barber) and Betty (Bilyeau) Gray. *Education:* University of Redlands, A.B., 1954; University of Missouri, M.Ed., 1955. *Politics:* Democrat. *Home:* 1421 Walnut Ave., Niagara Falls, N.Y. 14301. *Office:* LaSalle Junior High, Buffalo Ave., Niagara Falls, N.Y. 14301.

CAREER: History teacher in public schools of Tucson, Ariz., 1955-56, Fullerton, Calif., 1956-57, and Niagara Falls, N.Y., 1957-66; guidance counselor in Niagara Falls, 1966—. Counselor for Neighborhood Youth Corps; teacher on educational television.

WRITINGS: (With Louise DeFelice) *Emotional Crises: How to Cope, How to Recover,* Ashley Books, 1975.

WORK IN PROGRESS: Organizing and developing a guidance program for counselors.

SIDELIGHTS: Juanita Gray told *CA* her book resulted from her work with emotionally troubled young people. "Often these young people needed just a little help—help in the form of a friend who would listen to them and interact with them while they tried to find their way and understand what was happening to them."

* * *

GREEN, Constance McLaughlin 1897-1975

August 21, 1897—December 5, 1975; American historian, educator, author of books in her field. Obituaries: *Washington Post,* December 7, 1975; *New York Times,* December 8, 1975; *Time,* December 22, 1975; *AB Bookman's Weekly,* January 5, 1976. (See index for previous *CA* sketch)

* * *

GREEN, Jane 1937-

PERSONAL: Born June 27, 1937, in New York, N.Y.; daughter of Samuel (an attorney) and Mollie (Schmerzler) Oliphant; married Daniel Green, September 20, 1959; children: Matthew, Simon. *Education:* Cornell University, student, 1955-57. *Residence:* Great Neck, N.Y. *Agent:* Marilyn Marlow, Curtis Brown Ltd., 60 East 56th St., New York, N.Y. 10021. *Office:* National Foundation for Sudden Infant Death, Inc., 1501 Broadway, New York, N.Y. 10036.

CAREER: Employed with National Foundation for Sudden Infant Death, New York, N.Y., 1974—.

WRITINGS: (With Virginia Pasley) *You Can Do Anything with Crepes,* Simon & Schuster, 1970; (with Judith Choate) *The Gift-Givers Cookbook,* Simon & Schuster, 1972; (with Choate) *Scrapcraft: 50 Easy-to-Make Handicraft Projects* (juvenile), Doubleday, 1973; (with Choate) *Patchwork* (juvenile), Doubleday, 1975.

WORK IN PROGRESS: A book on beachcraft; research on the canning and preserving of foods.

* * *

GREEN, Jane Nugent 1918-

PERSONAL: Born September 29, 1918, in Detroit, Mich.; daughter of John Ross and Geneva (Stamper) Nugent; married Merlyn Carson Green (an attorney), October 22, 1944; children: Douglas Carson, Robert Scott, Todd Richard, Brian Houston, Andrew Christian. *Education:* State University of Iowa, B.A. (summa cum laude), 1942; University of Minnesota, M.S.W., 1972. *Home:* 1760 Summit Ave., St. Paul, Minn. 55105.

CAREER: Hart Publications Inc., Chicago, Ill., advertising copywriter, 1940-42; International Business Machines Corp., New York, N.Y., systems service executive, 1942-44; Alfred Adler Institute of Minnesota, Minneapolis, member of faculty, 1973—. Metropolitan State Junior College, Minneapolis, Minn., instructor in psychology, 1974. *Member:* St. Paul Junior League (sustaining member), Phi Beta Kappa.

WRITINGS: You and Your Private I: Personality and the Written Self-Image, Llewellyn, 1975. Contributor of poems to literary magazines.

WORK IN PROGRESS: Writing poems.

AVOCATIONAL INTERESTS: Painting, horseback riding, snorkeling, biking, cross-country skiing, travel.

* * *

GREEN, Jonathan (William) 1939-

PERSONAL: Born September 26, 1939, in Troy, N.Y.; son of Alan Singer (a rabbi) and Frances (Katz) Green; married Louise Lockshin (an artist and musician), September 16, 1962; children: Raphael Michael, Benjamin Ethan. *Education:* Attended Massachusetts Institute of Technology, 1958-60, and Hebrew University of Jerusalem, 1960-61; Brandeis University, B.A. (magna cum laude), doctoral study, 1964-67; Harvard University, M.A., 1967. *Home address:* South Great Rd., Lincoln, Mass. 01773. *Office:* Creative Photography Laboratory, Massachusetts Institute of Technology, 120 Massachusetts Ave., Cambridge, Mass. 02139.

CAREER: Free-lance architectural and advertising photographer. Associate photographer for Ezra Stoller Associates, 1967-69; Massachusetts Institute of Technology, Cambridge, Mass., instructor, 1968-69, assistant professor, 1969-73, associate professor of photography, 1973—, director at Visible Language Workshop, 1973—, acting director of Creative Photography Laboratory, 1974—. Proposal reviewer in photography for National Endowment for the Humanities, 1975; consultant to National Endowment for the Arts, 1975. Photographs are included in permanent collections at Boston Museum of Fine Arts, Virginia Museum of Fine Arts, at University of Santa Clara, Massachusetts Institute of Technology, and in Stockholm, Sweden; photographs have been included in over twenty exhibitions; has made photomurals for installation in Boston, Rochester, N.Y., and Chicago. Producer of exhibition panels for American Institute of Architects award exhibitions, 1968—; official exhibition photographer for Alfred Stieglitz Center of the Philadelphia Museum of Art, 1969—. Member of organizational committee and juror for "New England Photo Vision '72," visiting critic at Worcester Museum of Art, 1972; initiated Boston Photography Survey, 1972; member of organizational committee for children's show at Boston Center for the Arts, 1972; advisor and juror for "Photography/Maine 1973."

MEMBER: International Museum of Photography, Society for Photographic Education, Phi Beta Kappa. *Awards, honors:* Danforth Foundation fellow, 1963-67; grants from National Endowment for the Arts and Florence V. Burden Foundation, 1972-73, for *Camera Work: A Critical Anthology;* art publishing award from Art Librarians Society of North America, 1973, for *Camera Work: A Critical Anthology;* award from New York Type Directors Club, 1974, for *The Snapshot.*

*WRITINGS—*All illustrated with photographs: *Camera*

Work: A Critical Anthology, Aperture, 1973; (with Minor White) *Celebrations,* Aperture, 1974; *The Snapshot,* Aperture, 1974. Writer of book jacket copy; writer of advertising copy for Aperture. Contributor of articles and photographs to architecture journals and popular magazines, including *House Beautiful, Popular Photography, American Home, Travel and Leisure, New Yorker,* and *House and Garden.* Editorial consultant to *Aperture,* 1972-73, associate editor, 1974—; associate editor of *Boston Photographic Survey,* 1974—.

WORK IN PROGRESS: General editor of monographs on Lisette Model and Frederick Sommer; research on photography's influence on modern culture and visual perception.

* * *

GREENBERGER, Martin 1931-

PERSONAL: Born November 30, 1931, in Elizabeth, N.J. *Education:* Harvard University, A.B., 1955, A.M., 1956, Ph.D., 1958. *Office:* Department of Mathematical Sciences, Johns Hopkins University, Baltimore, Md. 21218.

CAREER: Harvard University, Cambridge, Mass., member of staff of computation laboratory, 1954-56; International Business Machines (IBM), Cambridge, manager of the applied science Cambridge group, 1956-58; Massachusetts Institute of Technology, Cambridge, assistant professor, 1958-61, associate professor of management, 1961-67; Johns Hopkins University, Baltimore, Md., professor of computer science, 1967-72, professor of mathematical sciences, 1972—, chairman of computer science and director of information processing, both 1967-72. Past chairman of council of Inter-University Communications Council; member of visiting committee at Harvard University, 1975. Consultant to U.S. Congress, Brookings Institution, and National Science Foundation.

MEMBER: Association for Computing Machinery, American Association for the Advancement of Science (fellow), Phi Beta Kappa, Sigma Xi. *Awards, honors:* Guggenheim fellowship, 1965-66.

WRITINGS: (With Guy H. Orcutt, John Korbel, and Alice M. Rivlin) *Microanalysis of Socioeconomic Systems,* Harper, 1961; (editor) *Computers and the World of the Future,* M.I.T. Press, 1964; (editor) *Computers, Communications, and the Public Interest,* Johns Hopkins Press, 1971; (with Julius Aronofsky, James L. McKenny, and William F. Massy) *Networks for Research and Education,* M.I.T. Press, 1974; (with Matthew A. Crenson and Brian L. Crissey) *Models in the Policy Process,* Russell Sage Foundation, 1976. Also co-author of *On-Line Computation and Simulation: The OPS-3 System,* 1967. Reviewer for *Science* and *Computing Surveys.*

WORK IN PROGRESS: A research project to develop new methods in the analysis of energy policy models.

* * *

GREENBIE, Marjorie Barstow 1889(?)-1976

1889(?)—January 28, 1976; American historian, feminist political activist, author of biographies, popular histories, and books on other topics. Obituaries: *New York Times,* January 29, 1976.

* * *

GREENE, Constance C(larke) 1924-

PERSONAL: Born October 27, 1924, in New York, N.Y.; daughter of Richard W. (a newspaper editor) and Mabel (a writer; maiden name, McElliott) Clarke; married Philip M. Greene (a radio station owner), June, 1946; children: Sheppard, Philippa, Stephanie, Matthew, Lucia. *Education:* Attended Skidmore College, 1942-44. *Politics:* Democrat. *Religion:* Roman Catholic. *Address:* R.F.D. #1, Poland Spring, Me. 04274. *Agent:* Marilyn Marlow, Curtis Brown Ltd., 60 East 56th St., New York, N.Y. 10022.

WRITINGS—Juveniles: *A Girl Called Al,* Viking, 1969; *Leo the Lioness,* Viking, 1970; *Good Luck Bogie Hat,* Viking, 1971; *Unmaking of Rabbit,* Viking, 1972; *Isabelle the Itch,* Viking, 1973; *Ears of Louis,* Viking, 1974; *I Know You, Al,* Viking, 1975.

WORK IN PROGRESS: A juvenile book dealing with the death of a sibling; short stories.

* * *

GREENE, Howard R. 1937-

PERSONAL: Born July 26, 1937; son of Charles Bernard and Frieda (Miller) Greene; divorced, 1975; children: Adam Scott, Matthew West. *Education:* Dartmouth College, B.A., 1959; New York University, M.A., 1961; Harvard University, M.Ed., 1964. *Politics:* Independent. *Religion:* Unitarian-Universalist. *Home:* Tall Trees Lane, Wilton, Conn. 06897. *Agent:* Max Gartenberg, 331 Madison Ave., New York, N.Y. 10017. *Office:* Educational Consulting Center, 19 South Compo Rd., Westport, Conn. 06880.

CAREER: Educational Consulting Center, Westport, Conn., director, 1969—. Trustee of Unitarian Church of Westport, Conn., 1971-74. *Military service:* U.S. Army Reserve, 1960-61. *Member:* International Board of Counseling Services, American Personnel and Guidance Association, American Association of Higher Education, New England Association of College Admissions Counselors, Metropolitan Mental Health Association.

WRITINGS: Scaling the Ivy Wall: Admissions to Selective Colleges, Abelard, 1975.

* * *

GREENE, Stephanie 1953-

PERSONAL: Born July 6, 1953, in Brattleboro, Vt.; daughter of Stephen (a publisher) and Janet Churchill (Gould) Greene. *Education:* Attended Middlebury College, and University of California, Berkeley. *Home address:* West Dover, Vt. 05356.

CAREER: Writer.

WRITINGS: (Editor with Russel Hamilton) *What Bothers Us About Grown Ups,* Stephen Greene Press, 1970.

WORK IN PROGRESS: A series of short stories.

AVOCATIONAL INTERESTS: Design, international travel, martial arts.

* * *

GREENWOOD, David Charles 1927-

PERSONAL: Born July 2, 1927, in London, England; son of Reginald (an insurance official) and Anne (Kinghorn) Greenwood. *Education:* University of London, B.A., 1949; University of Nottingham, certificate in education, 1953; further study at Oxford University, 1950-53, and University of California, Los Angeles, 1953-56. *Residence:* Washington, D.C. *Office:* Department of English, University of Maryland, College Park, Md. 20742.

CAREER: Oxford School of Commerce, Oxford, England, lecturer in English, 1950-53; University of California, Los Angeles, associate in Subject A, 1953-61; University of Maryland, College Park, instructor, 1961-69, assistant professor, 1969-72, associate professor of English, 1972—. Consultant to National Science Foundation, 1961-63. *Military service:* Served with Honourable Artillery Company (England), 1945-46. *Member:* American Schools of Oriental Research, Modern Language Association of America, Society of Biblical Literature, Royal Institute of Philosophy.

WRITINGS: (Editor and contributor) *Pictorial History of America,* Year, Inc., 1954; *Essays in Human Relations,* Public Affairs Press, 1956; *Truth and Meaning,* Philosophical Library, 1957; *Solving the Scientist Shortage,* Public Affairs Press, 1958; *History of England,* Littlefield, Adams, 1958; *The Nature of Science, and Other Essays,* Philosophical Library, 1959, reprinted, Kennikat, 1971; *William King: Tory and Jacobite,* Clarendon Press (of Oxford University), 1969. Contributor to *Clergy Review, Russian Orthodox Journal, Shakespeare Quarterly,* and other literary and theological periodicals. Contributing editor, *Caecilia,* 1962-65.

* * *

GREGG, Jess 1926-

PERSONAL: Born March 21, 1926; son of Dean Bradish (an investor) and Edna (Nimocks) Gregg. *Education:* Rollins College, B.A.; graduate study in drama at Yale University. *Home:* 104 Cortland, Winter Park, Fla. 32789. *Agent:* Owen Laster, William Morris Agency, 1350 Avenue of the Americas, New York, N.Y. 10019. *Office:* 86 University Pl., New York, N.Y. 10003.

CAREER: Writer.

WRITINGS: The Other Elizabeth, Rinehart, 1955; *The Glory Circuit,* St. Mark's Press, 1965; *Baby Boy,* Putnam, 1973.

Plays: "The Sea Shell," first performed in England, 1959; "Shout from the Rooftops," first performed in New York, N.Y., 1967.

Author of musical play, "Cowboy," first performed at Goodspeed Opera House. Also author of two screenplays for Twentieth Century-Fox, and of television plays.

WORK IN PROGRESS: A novel, tentatively titled *The Loners.*

* * *

GRIEB, Lyndal 1940-

PERSONAL: Born June 12, 1940, in Doniphan, Mo.; son of Claude Cecil (a vocational agriculture teacher) and Hazel (Brummett) Grieb. *Education:* Southwest Missouri State University, B.S.Ed., 1965; University of Missouri, M.L.S., 1972. *Religion:* Episcopalian. *Home:* 135 North Montgomery, Memphis, Tenn. 38104. *Office:* Memphis and Shelby County Public Library and Information Center, 1850 Peabody, Memphis, Tenn. 38104.

CAREER: High school teacher of English in the public schools of Kansas City, Mo., 1965-68; Kansas City Public Library, Kansas City, acting head of history department, 1970-72; Memphis and Shelby County Public Library and Information Center, Memphis, Tenn., reference librarian in history department, 1972-73, reference librarian for art, music, and theater, 1973—. *Member:* American Library Association, Tennessee Library Association, Metropolitan Opera Guild, Beta Phi Mu.

WRITINGS: The Operas of Gian Carlo Menotti, 1937-1972: A Selective Bibliography, Scarecrow, 1974.

WORK IN PROGRESS: A bibliography on the works of Douglas Moore, American composer; research on Metropolitan Opera literature.

* * *

GRIFFIN, Mary 1916-

PERSONAL: Born December 16, 1916, in Chicago, Ill.; daughter of Michael Anthony (a physician) and Margaret (O'Connor) Griffin. *Education:* Mundelein College, B.Mus.Ed., 1939, A.B., 1942; Catholic University of America, M.A., 1950; Fordham University, Ph.D., 1960. *Politics:* Democrat. *Religion:* Roman Catholic. *Home:* 3500 Lake Shore Dr., Chicago, Ill. 60657. *Agent:* James Brown Associates, Inc., 22 East 60th St., New York, N.Y. 10022. *Office:* Department of English and Communications, Mundelein College, 6363 Sheridan Rd., Chicago, Ill. 60660.

CAREER: Member of religious order, Sisters of Charity of the Blessed Virgin Mary, 1939-73. High school teacher of English, Dubuque, Iowa, 1942-44, Clarke College, Dubuque, instructor in English, 1944-54; Mundelein College, Chicago, Ill., assistant professor, 1954-60, academic dean, 1960-67, professor of English, 1969-70; Alcorn A & M College, Lorman, Miss., visiting professor of English, 1970-73; Mundelein College, professor of English, 1973—. Research fellow, Yale University, 1968-69.

MEMBER: American Association of University Professors, American Association for Higher Education (member of executive committee, 1966-67), American Council on Education, National Commission on Higher Education in Beato Virgo Maria (Blessed Virgin Mary) Colleges (chairman, 1969-71). *Awards, honors:* National Endowment for the Humanities grant, 1972.

WRITINGS: (Editor) *The Trial of Midas II by Charles Burney,* University Microfilm, 1961; (contributor) Louis C. Vaccaro, editor, *Toward New Dimensions of Catholic Higher Education,* Education Research Associates, 1967; *The Courage to Choose,* Little, Brown, 1975. Contributor to *New City.*

WORK IN PROGRESS: The Teaching of Composition by Audio-Visual Methods; V-V-P Visual-Verbal-Print.

SIDELIGHTS: Mary Griffin writes: "In 1963 Pope John XXIII convoked the Vatican Council II and opened up the Catholic Church to a total re-evaluation of itself as an institution. Along with all other Catholics, American nuns began as intensive self examination which led to renewal, reform, and to a virtual revolution within religious life. Before the impetus of the Council had waned, 40,000 nuns had left their orders. My book, *The Courage to Choose,* grew out of the existential anguish and challenge which led to more change than Catholicism had endured since the Protestant Reformation."

* * *

GRIFFITH, William E(dgar) 1920-

PERSONAL: Born February 19, 1920, in Remsen, N.Y.; son of William G. and Sarah (Mitchell) Griffith; married Ingeborg Maria Ehrhardt, 1948; children: Evelyn Elizabeth Griffith Hanson-Lawson, Dorothy Isabelle Griffith Berthold, Oliver William. *Education:* Hamilton College, A.B., 1940; Harvard University, M.A., 1941, Ph.D., 1950. *Politics:* Democrat. *Religion:* Baptist. *Home:* 19 Peacock Farm

Rd., Lexington, Mass. 02173. *Office:* Center for International Studies, Massachusetts Institute of Technology, 30 Wadsworth Street Building, E53-460, Cambridge, Mass. 02139.

CAREER: Chief of de-Nazification branch, U.S. Military Government for Bavaria, 1947-48; Free Europe Committee, New York, N.Y., assistant to president of committee, 1950-51; Radio Free Europe, Munich, Germany, political adviser, 1951-58; Massachusetts Institute of Technology, Cambridge, research associate, 1958-65, professor of political science, 1965-71, Ford Professor of Political Science, 1971—, project director at Center for International Studies. Adjunct professor at Fletcher School of Law and Diplomacy (of Tufts University), 1959—. Consultant to U.S. Department of State and RAND Corp., 1967—. *Military service:* U.S. Army, 1942-45; served in France and Germany; became first lieutenant.

MEMBER: American Political Science Association, American Association for the Advancement of Slavic Studies, Council on Foreign Relations.

WRITINGS: Albania and the Sino-Soviet Rift, M.I.T. Press, 1963; *The Sino-Soviet Rift,* M.I.T. Press, 1964; (editor) *Communism in Europe,* M.I.T. Press, Volume I, 1964, Volume II, 1966; *World Communism Divided* (pamphlet), Foreign Policy Association, 1964; *Sino-Soviet Relations, 1964-1965,* M.I.T. Press, 1967; *Communist Esoteric Communications: Explication de Texte* (monograph), Center for International Studies, Massachusetts Institute of Technology, 1967; *Eastern Europe after the Soviet Invasion of Czechoslovakia,* RAND Corp., 1968; *Moscow, Bonn, and European Security* (monograph), Center for International Studies, Massachusetts Institute of Technology, 1969; *The Middle East Drifts Again Toward War* (monograph), Center for International Studies, Massachusetts Institute of Technology, 1969.

The Soviet-American Confrontation, Center for International Studies, Massachusetts Institute of Technology, 1970, Volume I: *The Global Soviet-American Relationship,* Volume II: *The East-West Confrontation in Europe, 1970: The Soviet-West German Treaty and European Security,* Volume III: *The Great Powers and the Middle East in 1970,* Volume IV: *Sub-Sahara Africa: The Main Trends; The Great Globe Transformed,* Center for International Studies, Massachusetts Institute of Technology, 1971, Volume I: *The Sino-Soviet-American Relationship,* Volume II: *East and Southeast Asia,* Volume III: *The Indo-Pakistani Crisis,* Volume IV: *The Middle East,* Volume V: *Europe; Cold War and Coexistence: Russia, China, and the United States,* Prentice-Hall, 1971; *Latin America* (monograph), Center for International Studies, Massachusetts Institute of Technology, 1972.

Contributor: Leopold Labedz, editor, *Revisionism: Essays on the History of Marxist Ideas,* Allen & Unwin, 1962; Labedz and Walter Laqueur, editors, *Polycentrism,* Praeger, 1962; Kurt London, editor, *New Nations in a Divided World,* Praeger, 1963; Stephen Fischer-Galati, editor, *Eastern Europe in the Sixties,* Praeger, 1963; Zbigniew Brzezinski, editor, *Africa and the Communist World,* Stanford University Press, 1963; *Contemporary Civilization III,* Scott, Foresman, 1964; Adam Bromke, editor, *The Communist States at the Crossroads,* Praeger, 1965; Leopold Labedz, editor, *International Communism after Khrushchev,* M.I.T. Press, 1965; William Zartman, editor, *Intervention and Impact,* New York University Press, 1970; (author of introduction) Daniel Lerner, *Psychological War-*

fare against Nazi Germany, M.I.T. Press, 1971; (author of introduction) William Kintner, *Eastern Europe and European Security,* Dunellen, 1971.

General editor of "Studies in Communism, Revisionism, and Revolution," a series published by M.I.T. Press, and "The World and the Great Power Triangles," series. Contributor of about sixty articles to professional journals, popular magazines, including *New Leader, Atlantic Monthly,* and *New Republic,* and newspapers. Roving editor of *Reader's Digest;* member of editorial board of *Orbis.*

WORK IN PROGRESS: Editing *The Germanies and the East;* research on Iranian foreign policy.

* * *

GRIMES, Lee 1920-
(Fremont Dodge)

PERSONAL: Born February 27, 1920, in Fremont, Neb.; son of George Eichelberger and Eva (Miller) Grimes; married Mary Aileen Cochran, April 29, 1945; children: Robert, Douglas, Diana. *Education:* Yale University, B.A., 1941; graduate study at Columbia University and University of California, Los Angeles. *Home and office:* 426 Prospect St., New Haven, Conn. 06511. *Agent:* Harold Ober Associates, Inc., 40 East 49th St., New York, N.Y. 10017.

CAREER: Oxnard Press-Courier, Oxnard, Calif., managing editor, 1946-63, editor, 1963-67; free-lance writer and journalist, 1967—. Chairman of California Editors' Conference, 1957; foreman of Ventura County Grand Jury, 1959; member of Oxnard library board, 1960-68, and redevelopment agency, 1969-72. *Military service:* U.S. Army, Signal Corps, 1942-46, 1950-52; became captain. *Member:* Peabody Museum Associates (director, 1975—). *Awards, honors:* International Press Institute fellowship, 1958.

WRITINGS: The Eye of Shiva (novel), Warner Paperback, 1974; *The Ax of Atlantis* (novel), Warner Paperback, 1975. Contributor to science fiction magazines, sometimes under pseudonym Fremont Dodge, and to popular magazines, including *McCall's, Reader's Digest,* and *Discovery.*

WORK IN PROGRESS: A novel.

AVOCATIONAL INTERESTS: Travel, photography, reading (especially novels, history, and zoology), stamps.

* * *

GRIMM, Reinhold 1931-

PERSONAL: Born May 21, 1931, in Nuremberg, Germany; came to United States, 1967; son of Eugen (a laborer) and Anna (Kaeser) Grimm; married Anneliese E. Schmidt, September 25, 1954; children: Ruth Sabine. *Education:* Attended University of Colorado, 1952-53; Erlangen University, Ph.D., 1956. *Home:* 3983 Plymouth Circle, Madison, Wis. 53705. *Office:* Department of German, University of Wisconsin, Madison, Wis. 53706.

CAREER: Erlangen University, Erlangen, Germany, assistant professor of German literature, 1957-61; Frankfurt University, Frankfurt, Germany, assistant professor of German literature, 1961-67; University of Wisconsin, Madison, Alexander Hohlfeld Professor of German, 1967—. Visiting professor, New York University and Columbia University, both 1967, and University of Florida, 1973. *Member:* Modern Language Association of America, American Association of Teachers of German (president, 1974-75). *Awards, honors:* Foerderungspreis der Stadt Nuernberg, 1964; Guggenheim fellow, 1969-70.

WRITINGS: Gottfried Benn: Die farbliche Chiffre in der Dichtung (title means "Gottfried Benn: The Color-emblem in Literature"), H. Carl (Nuremberg), 1958, 2nd edition, 1962; *Bertolt Brecht: Die Struktur seines Werkes* (title means "Bertolt Brecht: The Structure of His Work"), H. Carl, 1959, 6th edition, 1972; *Bertolt Brecht,* J. B. Metzler, 1961, 3rd revised edition, 1971; *Bertolt Brecht und die Weltliteratur* (title means "Bertolt Brecht and World Literature"), H. Carl, 1961; (with Heinz Otto Burger) *Evokation und Montage: Drei Beitraege zum Verstaendnis moderner deutscher Lyrik* (title means "Evocation and Montage: Three Contributions towards an Understanding of Modern German Poetry"), Sachse & Pohl, 1961, revised edition, 1967; *Strukturen: Essays zue deutschen Literatur* (title means "Structures: Essays on German Literature"), Sachse & Pohl, 1963; (author of afterword) Denis Diderot, *Das Paradox ueber den Schauspieler* (title means "Denis Diderot: The Paradox of the Comedian"), Insel Verlag, 1964; (with others) *Romanticism Today: Friedrich Schlegel, Novalis, E.T.A. Hoffmann, Ludwig Tieck,* Inter Nationes (Bonn), 1973.

Editor or compiler: (With Wolf-Dieter Marsch) *Die Kunst im Schatten des Gottes: Fuer und wider Gottfried Benn,* Sachse & Pohl, 1962; (with Viktor Zmegac) *Iwan Goll, Methusalem oder Der ewige Buerger: Ein satirisches Drama* (title means "Methusalah and the Eternal Bourgeois: A Satiric Drama"), de Gruyter, 1966; *Episches Theater* (title means "Epic Theater"), Kiepenheuer & Witsch, 1966, 3rd edition, 1972; *Zur Lyrik-Diskussion* (title means "Concerning the Lyric"), Wissenschaftliche Buchgesellschaft, 1966; (and author of introduction) *Deutsche Romantheorien: Beitraege zu einer historischen Poetik des Romans in Deutschland* (title means "German Theories of the Novel: Essays towards a Historical Poetics of the Novel in Germany"), Athenaeum Verlag, 1968; *Bertold Brecht: Leben Eduards des Zweiten von England; Vorlage, Texte und Materialien* (title means "Bertolt Brecht: The Life of Edward II of England; Sources, Texts and Materials"), Suhrkamp, 1968; (with Conrad Wiedemann) *Literatur und Geistesgeschichte: Festgabe fuer Heinz Otto Burger* (title means "Literature and History: A Congratulatory Volume for Heinz Otto Burger"), E. Schmidt, 1968; (with Jost Hermand, and author of introduction) *Deutsche Revolutionsdramen* (title means "German Dramas of Revolution"), Suhrkamp, 1969.

(With Henry J. Schmidt) *Brecht Fibel* (title means "Brecht Primer"), Harper, 1970; (and author of introduction) *Deutsche Dramentheorien: Beitraege zu einer historischen Poetik des Dramas in Deutschland* (title means "German Theories of the Drama: Essays towards a Historical Poetics of the Drama in Germany"), Athenaeum Verlag, 1971; (with Klaus L. Berghahn) *Schiller: Zur Theorie und Praxis der Dramen* (title means "Schiller: Theory and Practice of His Plays"), Wissenschaftliche Buchgesellschaft, 1972; (with Hermand) *Methodenfragen der deutschen Literaturwissenschaft* (title means "Methodological Problems in German Literary Criticism"), Wissenschaftliche Buchgesellschaft, 1973; (with Helene Scher) *Friedrich Duerrenmatt, Die Ehe des Herrn Mississippi: Eine Komoedie* (title means "Friedrich Duerrenmatt, The Marriage of Mr. Mississippi: A Comedy"), Holt, 1973.

Editor, with Jost Hermand, of volumes sponsored by Deutsche Abteilung of Wisconsin University: *Die sogenannten Zwanziger Jahre* (title means "The So-Called Twenties"), Gehlen, 1970; *Die Klassik-Legende* (title means "The Myth of Classicism"), Athenaeum Verlag,

1971; *Exil und innere Emigration* (title means "Exile and Inner Emigration"), Athenaeum Verlag, 1972. Editor or co-editor of yearbooks and journals, mainly on German and comparative literature, including *Monatshefte,* 1967—; *German Studies,* 1969—; and *Brecht-Jahrbuch,* 1971—.

WORK IN PROGRESS: A book on Brecht and Nietzsche; research on the black man in German literature, and on Cuba in German literature.

* * *

GRINDER, Michael 1942-

PERSONAL: Born September 22, 1942, in Detroit, Mich.; son of John Thomas, Sr. (a carpenter) and Eileen (a bookkeeper; maiden name, Marria) Grinder; married Mary Buttemer, July 12, 1967 (divorced, 1976); children: Krista Rene. *Education:* Attended St. Francis Seminary, University of San Diego, and California Western College, all 1961-63; Loyola University, Los Angeles, Calif., B.A., 1965, M.A., 1967, teaching credential, 1967. *Home:* 14322 Jolley Lane, Poway, Calif. 92064.

CAREER: High school teacher of social studies in Poway, Calif., 1967—. Organizes and conducts classes in sensitivity training, transactional analysis, Gestalt and group process skills, re-evaluation counseling, and value clarification. *Member:* American Federation of Labor-Congress of Industrial Organizations (AFL-CIO), California Teachers Association, California Continuation Educators Association, Poway Teachers Association, Pi Gamma Mu.

WRITINGS: One Man's Journey (poems), privately printed, 1971, revised edition, Celestial Arts, 1975; *I Am* (poems), Celestial Arts, 1973. About six posters have been privately printed, 1971-72. Contributor to education journals.

WORK IN PROGRESS: Chairs, a book of collected notes from group classes.

SIDELIGHTS: Grinder spent his early years in a log cabin outside Detroit until his health forced his family to move to California. He studied for the priesthood but finally rejected that way of life. He writes: "I had thought of a priest as being a teacher. That was what I wanted to do most, to teach and to share my thoughts with others. But I discovered that I needed the freedom to have closer relationships with people, to relate to them openly. This kind of freedom isn't always allowed to a priest." Now he teaches at a special high school which enables him to help a student on an individual level, a school which has morning classes and leaves students free for afternoon jobs. *Avocational interests:* Sports (especially basketball), chess, dancing, transcendental meditation, carving and staining wood plaques printed with his own epigrams.

* * *

GROL, Lini Richarda 1913-

PERSONAL: Born October 7, 1913, in Nijmegen, Netherlands; daughter of Johannes and Catharine (Engel) Grol. *Education:* Trained in Netherlands for R.N. and public health nursing; has since taken writing courses at McMaster University, Brock University, and Columbia University. *Politics:* Conservative. *Religion:* Christian. *Home and studio:* Fonthill Studio, 53 South Pelham St., Fonthill, Ontario, Canada LOS 1EO.

CAREER: Nurse in Netherlands before coming to Canada; presently part-time registered nurse on pediatrics ward in Welland County Hospital, Ontario; instructor and lecturer in scissorcraft. Scissor-cutting illustrations in black and white and in color have been shown in Netherlands and at art gallerys and libraries in Ontario. *Member:* Canadian Authors Association, Professional Association of Woman Writers, St. Catharines Arts Council, Hamilton Arts Council, Niagara Falls Arts Association (Ontario), Media Club.

WRITINGS: Repetiuorium (title means "Referendum for the Mental Nursing Student"), De Bussy, 1950; (self-illustrated) *Silent Thoughts and Silhouettes* (poems), privately printed by Trillium Books (Fonthill Studio), 1967; (self-illustrated) *Scissorcraft,* Sterling, 1970; *The Bellfounder's Sons* (juvenile), Bobbs-Merrill, 1971; (self-illustrated) *Lelawala: The Maid of the Mist* (juvenile), Trillium Books, 1972; (self-illustrated) *Tales from the Niagara Peninsula,* Trillium Books, 1973; *De Overjas* (serialized novel in Dutch), Courant, 1973; (self-illustrated) *Three Fables* (juvenile), Trillium Books, 1974; (self-illustrated) *Insiders or Outsiders* (poems), Trillium Books, 1974; (self-illustrated) *Mix and Match* (short stories), Trillium Books, 1975; (self-illustrated) *Magic Gifts* (Christmas stories), Trillium Books, 1975. Stories, articles, poems, and illustrations have been published in magazines in the Netherlands, England, Canada, and the United States.

WORK IN PROGRESS: Two novels, *Out of the Dark* and *The Stepmother.*

SIDELIGHTS: Lini Grol writes: "My viewpoints can be found in my writing, and depend very much on the audience, age or theme I try to convey. I am a Christian and rather conservative in my views. Consideration of the fellowmen is my main theme in life."

Three of Lini Grol's poems were read at the National Arts Centre in Ottawa on May 17, 1970, as part of the program marking the 25th anniversary of the liberation of the Netherlands. The celebration was organized by Canadians from Holland.

*   *   *

GROSS, Sarah Chokla   1906-

PERSONAL: Born October 13, 1906, in New York, N.Y.; daughter of Louis Moses (a civil engineer) and Bassetta (Shore) Chokla; married Benjamin Gross (a manufacturer of house dresses), August 9, 1937 (died August 29, 1974); children: Emily Jane (deceased). *Education:* Southern Methodist University, B.A., 1926, M.A., 1928; further graduate studies at Columbia University, 1934-35, and University of Texas, 1935-37. *Home:* 11 Newkirk Ave., East Rockaway, N.Y. 11518.

CAREER: Instructor in English at Southern Methodist University, Dallas, Tex., 1928-34, University of Texas, Austin, 1935-37, and School of General Studies, Columbia University, New York, N.Y., 1956-57; Franklin Watts, Inc., New York, N.Y., an editor of children's books, 1959-70. Regular reviewer for *Dallas Morning* News, 1930— (associate editor of book page in the 1930's), *Sunday New York Times* Book Section, 1947-62, and *Library Journal,* 1963—; editor of *Broadside* (printed newsletter of Theatre Library Association), 1940-72. *Member:* Women's National Book Association, Theatre Library Association, Long Island Book Collectors.

WRITINGS: (Translator) Claude Cenac, *Four Paws into Adventure,* F. Watts, 1965; (translator) Rene Guillot, *Fonabio and the Lion,* F. Watts, 1966; (translator) Charles Perrault, editor, *Famous Fairy Tales,* F. Watts, 1967; (editor) *Every Child's Book of Verse,* F. Watts, 1968. Editor, *Long Island Book Collector's Journal,* 1972, 1975.

WORK IN PROGRESS: Editing a personal journal, *Green Girl.*

SIDELIGHTS: Mrs. Gross writes: "Miniature books, children's books, books on theatre and costume, [and] fine presses are among my collecting interests—as are antiques, especially glass. I started the Book Fair at Marion Street School in Lynbrook, Long Island—the oldest continuously observed annual school book fair in the U.S. as far as I know (it began in 1949)." Her interest in book fairs brought about a little manual she prepared in 1968 for the Children's Book Council, *Planning a School Book Fair.*

*   *   *

GROVES, Colin Peter   1942-

PERSONAL: Born June 24, 1942, in London, England; son of Harold Victor and Dorothy (Edwards) Groves; married Mary Lynette Douglas, February 10, 1969 (divorced, 1973); married Phyllis Rose Dance (a nurse), January 26, 1974. *Education:* University College, London, B.Sc., 1963; Royal Free Hospital School of Medicine, Ph.D., 1966. *Politics:* Socialist. *Religion:* Agnostic. *Home:* 250 Dryandra St., O'Connor, Australian Capital Territory, Australia 2601. *Office:* Department of Prehistory and Anthropology, Australian National University, Canberra, Australian Capital Territory, Australia 2600.

CAREER: University of California, Berkeley, lecturer in anthropology, 1966-68; Cambridge University, Cambridge, England, demonstrator in anthropology, 1969-73; Australian National University, Canberra, Australian Capital Territory, lecturer in prehistory and anthropology, 1973—. *Member:* International Protection League, Deutsches Gesellschaft fuer Saugetierkunde, Malayan Nature Society, Royal Anthropological Institute, Fauna Preservation Society, Conservation Society, American Society of Mammalogists, East African Natural History Society, Australian Archaeological Association, Australian Society for Social Responsibility in Science.

WRITINGS: Gorillas, Arco, 1970; *Horses, Asses, and Zebras,* David & Charles, 1974. Contributor to encyclopedias and journals.

WORK IN PROGRESS: Research on ecology and taxonomy of primates, rhinoceroses, wild pigs, wild cattle, antelopes, and wombats.

SIDELIGHTS: Groves did research in Tanzania in 1971 and in Celebes in 1975. In 1972 he took part in an expedition to Tana River, Kenya. He speaks French, German, Italian, Indonesian, and Swahili. *Avocational interests:* Music, drama, Greek mythology.

*   *   *

GUILLE, Frances V(ernor)   1908-1975

March 1, 1908—October 22, 1975; American educator, writer and editor. Obituaries: *AB Bookman's Weekly,* December 1, 1975. (See index for previous *CA* sketch)

*   *   *

GUNNARSSON, Gunnar   1889-1975

May 18, 1889—November 21, 1975; Icelandic novelist and playwright. Obituaries: *New York Times,* November 22, 1975; *AB Bookman's Weekly,* December 22-29, 1975.

*   *   *

GYSBERS, Norman C(harles)   1932-

PERSONAL: Born September 29, 1932, in Waupun, Wis.;

married; children: three. *Education:* Hope College, A.B., 1954; University of Michigan, M.A., 1959, Ph.D., 1963. *Office:* College of Education, University of Missouri, Columbia, Mo. 65202.

CAREER: Elementary and junior high school teacher of science in Muskegon Heights, Mich., 1954-56; University of Michigan, Ann Arbor, lecturer in education, 1962-63; University of Missouri, Columbia, assistant professor, 1963-66, associate professor, 1966-70, professor of education, 1970—, director of guidance at Laboratory School, 1963-71. *Military service:* U.S. Army, Artillery, 1956-58.

MEMBER: International Association of Educational and Vocational Guidance, American Personnel and Guidance Association (senator, 1972-75; member of board of directors, 1974—), Association for Counselor Education and Supervision, National Vocational Guidance Association (trustee, 1969-71; president, 1972-73), American School Counselor Association, American Vocational Association, Missouri Guidance Association, Missouri Vocational Association.

WRITINGS: (Editor) *Proceedings: National Seminar on Vocational Guidance,* American Vocational Association and American Personnel and Guidance Association, 1967; (editor with David H. Pritchard) *Career Guidance Counseling and Placement: Proceedings of the National Conference on Guidance, Counseling, and Placement in Career Development and Educational-Occupational Decision Making,* University of Missouri Press, 1969; (editor with W. R. Miller and Earl J. Moore) *Developing Careers in the Elementary School,* C. E. Merrill, 1973; (editor with Moore and Harry Drier) *Career Guidance: Practices and Perspectives,* Charles A. Jones Publishing, 1973; (editor with Moore) *Career Guidance Counseling and Placement—Elements of an Illustrative Program Guide: A Life Career Development Perspective,* University of Missouri, Columbia, 1974.

Contributor: Lawrence Litwach, Russell Getson, and Glenn Saltzman, editors, *Research in Counseling,* F. E. Peacock, 1968; Gordon Law, editor, *Contemporary Concepts in Vocational Education,* American Vocational Association, 1971; John R. Cochran and Herman J. Peters, editors, *Guidance: An Introduction—Selected Readings,* C. E. Merrill, 1972; *Emerging Students . . . and the New Career Thrust in Higher Education,* American College Testing Program, 1972; Gail F. Farwell, Neal R. Gamsky, and Philippa T. Mathiew-Coughlan, editors, *The Counselor's Handbook: Essays on Preparation,* Intext Educational, 1974; C. J. Lucas, editor, *Challenge and Choice in American Education,* Macmillan, in press.

Contributor of over twenty-five articles to professional journals including: *American Vocational Journal, Journal of Counseling and Psychology, Instructor,* and *Journal of Career Education.* Guest editor of "Career Development: Guidance and Education", a special issue of *Personnel and Guidance Journal,* May, 1975. Editor of *Vocational Guidance Quarterly,* 1962-70; chairman of board of editors of American Personnel and Guidance Association, 1967-69.

* * *

HAACK, Susan 1945-

PERSONAL: Born July 23, 1945, in England; daughter of James Oliver (a chemist) and Sybil (a teacher; maiden name, Gardner) Smith; married Robin Haack (a university lecturer), July 8, 1967. *Education:* St. Hilda's College, Oxford, B.A., 1966, B.Phil., 1968; New Hall, Cambridge, Ph.D., 1972. *Home:* 55 Holly Walk, Leamington Spa, Warwickshire, England. *Office:* Department of Philosophy, University of Warwick, Coventry CV4 7AL, England.

CAREER: Cambridge University, New Hall, Cambridge, England, fellow, 1968-71; University of Warwick, Coventry, England, lecturer in philosophy, 1971—. Visiting fellow at Princeton University, 1975-76. *Member:* Aristotelian Society. *Awards, honors:* Harkness Foundation Fellowship, 1975-76.

WRITINGS: Deviant Logic, Cambridge University Press, 1974. Contributor to philosophy journals.

WORK IN PROGRESS: Research on metaphysics (ontology) and philosophy of logic.

* * *

HAAS, James E(dward) 1943-

PERSONAL: Born January 17, 1943, in New York, N.Y.; son of William Joseph (a butcher) and Ellen (Hulser) Haas; married Lynne Flannery (a teacher), March 22, 1969; children: James E., Jr., Daniel Brian. *Education:* St. John's University, Jamaica, N.Y., B.A., 1965; St. Mary's Seminary and University, Baltimore, Md., M.A., 1972. *Religion:* Roman Catholic. *Residence:* Annapolis, Md. *Office:* Time Consultants, P.O. Box 652, Severna Park, Md. 21146.

CAREER: High school English and French teacher in Towson, Md., 1965-67; director of religious education in Roman Catholic church in Baltimore, Md., 1968-74; Twenty-Third Publications, Mystic, Conn., assistant editor, 1974; Time Consultants, Severna Park, Md., religious education consultant, 1974—. Member of faculty at St. Mary's Seminary and University, 1972—; program director of Archdiocese of Baltimore's Congress on Liturgy; program coordinator of East Coast Conference for Religious Education. *Member:* Cedar Ridge Homeowners Association (vice-president).

WRITINGS: Shout Hooray (juvenile), Morehouse, 1972; (with wife, Lynne Haas) *Make a Joyful Noise* (juvenile), Morehouse, 1973; *Praise the Lord* (juvenile), Morehouse, 1974; (author of study and activity guides) Marie McIntyre, *Communion Between Parent and Child,* Twenty-Third Publications, 1974; (with William Freburger) *The Eucharistic Prayers for Children,* Ave Maria Press, 1976.

Author of "Holydays and Holidays," a film strip series, Twenty-Third Publications, 1974—. Contributor to church publications. Associate editor of *Religion Teacher's Journal,* 1974.

WORK IN PROGRESS: A book on liturgy; a book on using audiovisual aids.

SIDELIGHTS: Haas writes: "My books relate to worship for children but are directed toward teachers and ministers on an ecumenical basis." *Avocational interests:* Swimming, tennis, skiing, playing guitar, writing music, international travel.

* * *

HAFFENDEN, Philip Spencer 1926-

PERSONAL: Born January 1, 1926, in Eastbourne, Sussex, England; son of Philemon Spencer (a dairy farmer) and Lily (Carter) Haffenden; married Audrey Elliott (a nurse), March 17, 1948; children: Anne-Michele. *Education:* Attended Oxford University, 1943-44; University of London, B.A., 1952, Ph.D., 1955; Princeton University, postdoctoral study, 1955-56. *Office:* Department of History, University of Southampton, Highfield, Southampton SO9 5NH, England.

CAREER: University of Toronto, Toronto, Ontario, lecturer in history, 1956-57; University of Aberdeen, Aberdeen, Scotland, lecturer in history, 1957-62; University of Southampton, Southampton, England, lecturer, 1962-70, senior lecturer in United States history, 1971—. Visiting professor at University of Michigan, winter, 1967. *Military service:* Royal Navy, 1944-47. *Member:* Royal Historical Society, English Historical Association, British Association for American Studies (treasurer, 1968-73). *Awards, honors:* Walter Frewen Lord Prize from Royal Commonwealth Society, 1955, for essay, "Imperial Centralization, 1675-1688"; Harkness Fund fellowship, 1955; John Carter Brown Library fellowship, 1967; American Council of Learned Societies fellowship, 1973.

WRITINGS: First Poems, Arthur H. Stockwell, 1952; *New England in the English Nation: 1689-1713,* Oxford University Press, 1974. Contributor to *New Cambridge Modern History* and to history journals.

WORK IN PROGRESS: The War of 1812, for Faber; *New England and the Royal Navy in the Eighteenth Century; The American Revolution.*

SIDELIGHTS: Haffenden writes that his "interest in the loss of the American colonies dates from earliest childhood and subsequently broadened to embrace the Anglo-American relationship in its many aspects." *Avocational interests:* Golf, woodcarving, walking.

* * *

HAGEN, John William 1940-

PERSONAL: Born May 11, 1940, in Minneapolis, Minn.; son of Wayne S. (a physician) and Elfie (Erickson) Hagen; children: Darus Gene, Lonny John. *Education:* University of Minnesota, B.A. (magna cum laude), 1962; Stanford University, Ph.D., 1965. *Religion:* Unitarian-Universalist. *Home:* 3421 Burbank Dr., Ann Arbor, Mich. 48105. *Office:* Department of Psychology, University of Michigan, Ann Arbor, Mich. 48104.

CAREER: University of Michigan, Ann Arbor, assistant professor, 1965-69, associate professor, 1969-73, professor of psychology, 1973—, member of departmental executive committee, 1967-71, 1972-74, associate of Institute for the Study of Mental Retardation, 1969-74, chairman of developmental psychology program, 1970—, member of psycholinguistics executive committee, 1971-72, member of policy committee of Center for Early Child Development and Education, 1972—, research scientist at Center for Human Growth and Development, 1974—. Lecturer at University of Minnesota, summer, 1967. Member of Day Care and Child Development Council of America, 1970—. Member of Michigan governor's Commission on the Age of Majority, 1970-71; member of advisory council on testing, evaluation, and research of Michigan Department of Education, 1973-74. Member of joint committee of Plymouth State Home and University of Michigan's Institute of Mental Retardation, 1968-71.

MEMBER: American Psychological Association (fellow), Society for Research in Child Development, American Association of University Professors, Midwestern Psychological Association, Phi Beta Kappa. *Awards, honors:* Woodrow Wilson fellowship, 1962-63; award for undergraduate teaching from Standard Oil Foundation, 1967.

WRITINGS: (With Frank Miltner, S. Martin Taylor, and others) *The Age of Majority,* Office of the Governor (Lansing, Mich.), 1971; (editor with E. M. Hetherington, Reuben Kron, and Aletha Stein) *Review of Research in Child Development,* Volume V (Hagen is not associated with other volumes), University of Chicago Press, in press; (editor with R. V. Kail, Jr.) *Perspectives on the Development of Memory and Cognition,* Lawrence Erlbaum Associates, in press.

Contributor: Willard Hartup, editor, *The Young Child,* Volume II, National Association for the Education of Young Children, 1972; Sylvia Farnham-Diggory, editor, *Information Processing in Children,* Academic Press, 1972; Anne Pick, editor, *Minnesota Symposia on Child Psychology,* Volume VII, University of Minnesota Press, 1973; William Cruickshank and Daniel Hallahan, editors, *Perceptual and Learning Disabilities in Children,* Volume II: *Research and Theory,* Syracuse University Press, 1975; Hayne Reese, editor, *Advances in Child Development and Behavior,* Volume X, Academic Press, 1975; David Peters and David Hultsch, editors, *Infant and Child Development: Theory and Research,* Holbrook, in press. Co-author of about twenty research reports for Department of Psychology, University of Michigan.

Contributor of more than twenty-five articles and reviews to education, psychology, and child development journals. Consulting editor to *Merrill-Palmer Quarterly,* 1968—, *Cognitive Psychology,* 1970—, *Developmental Psychology,* 1970—, *Journal of Experimental Child Psychology,* 1970—, and *Child Development,* 1971—.

WORK IN PROGRESS: "The Development of Selective Attention," for inclusion in *Infant and Child Behavior: A Laboratory Approach,* edited by Lorraine Nadelman, for Harper; research on selective attention in retardates, on the effects of auditory and visual distractions on selective attention, and study of strategies for remembering, applied to children teaching other children.

AVOCATIONAL INTERESTS: Music, travel, skiing.

* * *

HALL, Brian P(atrick) 1935-

PERSONAL: Born December 29, 1935, in London, England; son of Leonard (a clerk) and Elsie (Ross) Hall; married Diane Ellis Jones (a physical therapist and value conference facilitator), May 6, 1961; children: Martin, Christine. *Education:* University of London, certificate in chemistry and mathematics, 1958; University of British Columbia, B.A., 1962; University of Western Ontario, M.Div., 1965; Centro de Investigaciones Culturales, further graduate study, 1966; Clermont Graduate School, Dr.Rel., 1969. *Home:* 5155 Plantation Dr., Indianapolis, Ind. 46250. *Office:* Center for Exploration of Values and Meaning, Suite 213, 6515 East 82nd, Indianapolis, Ind. 46250.

CAREER: Rogers Sugar Refinery, Vancouver, British Columbia, research chemist, 1959-60; part-time chemist, 1960-63; Anglican World Mission, Canadian Mission Board, Overseas Mission, researcher on the possibilities of social services in Venezuela, 1963-66, 1966-68; ordained Episcopal priest, 1966; priest in charge of mission parish in Barrio Cuba, San Jose, Costa Rica, 1966-68; Salvation Army Family Service, Los Angeles, Calif., director of family service, 1968-69; Catholic Family Service, Gary, Ind., director of family and community programs, 1969-71; Center for Exploration of Values and Meaning, Indianapolis, Ind., co-founder and member of board of directors, 1971-73, executive director and president, 1973—, chairman of board of directors, 1973-75. Licensed psychologist in State of Indiana. Adjunct professor at St. Louis University. Fund raiser for Family Institute (Costa Rica); chairman of board of Indianapolis Omega Project, 1975. *Member:* American Association of Pastoral Counselors (fellow), American Association of Family Counselors (clinical member).

WRITINGS: Learning to Live with Change, two volumes, with tape recording, Argus Communications, 1969; *Values: Exploration and Discovery,* with kit, Argus Communications, 1971; *Value Clarification as Learning Process,* Volume I: *A Sourcebook,* Volume II: *A Guidebook,* Volume III (with Maury Smith): *A Handbook for Christian Educators,* Paulist/Newman, 1973; (with Joseph Osburn) *Nog's Vision,* Paulist/Newman, 1973; *The Development of Consciousness: A Confluent Theory of Values,* Paulist/Newman, 1975; *The Chrysalis Child,* Paulist/Newman, 1975; *The Wizard of Maldoone,* Paulist/Newman, 1975. Also author, with Hendrix and Smith, of five volumes in the "Wonder" series for Paulist/Newman, 1974.

Author of tape scripts on teaching. Contributor to church publications. Consultant to Dendron Publishing.

SIDELIGHTS: Hall writes that several years in Latin America helped him to focus interest in the development of consciousness. "Questions such as how do institutions reinforce certain values in individuals, creating or limiting their freedom. The fairy tales in particular look at life styles, values and consciousness raising for alternative futures and life styles of peoples and societies."

AVOCATIONAL INTERESTS: Sailing, fencing with foils, chess, painting, art history, hiking.

BIOGRAPHICAL/CRITICAL SOURCES: U.S. News and World Report, March 17, 1975.

* * *

HALL, Carolyn Vosburg 1927-

PERSONAL: Born July 22, 1927, in Fenton, Mich.; daughter of Guy Melvin (an engineer and inventor) and Doris (a school psychologist; maiden name, Bourns) Vosburg; married Clarence Albert Hall (an engineer), July 26, 1952; children: Randall Ross, Claudia Lee, Garrett Alan. *Education:* Attended Olivet College, 1945-46, and Michigan State University, 1946-47; Cranbrook Academy of Art, B.F.A., 1949, M.F.A., 1951. *Home:* 20730 Kennoway, Birmingham, Mich. 48010.

CAREER: Artist. Instructor in art, North Dakota State College, Fargo, 1949-50; teacher in children's classes at Detroit Institute of Arts, 1967, Flint Institute of Arts, 1969, Pontiac Creative Arts Center, 1970, Texas Creative Stitchers, 1974, and workshop series for Detroit Teachers of Art, 1975—. Founding member of Detroit Council for the Arts, 1961; Bloomfield Art Association, founder, 1958, exhibition director, 1960-65, teacher, 1965—; Cranbrook Academy of Art, founding president of alumni, 1969, member of alumni board, 1969—, director of workshop, 1970; jury member for National Scholastic Arts, 1972. Auctioneer for Channel 56, public television, fund raiser, 1972-74.

MEMBER: Michigan Crafts Council (member of board, 1972—; director of convention, 1974), Michigan State Council for the Arts (founding representative, 1966; member of advisory board, 1974—), Birmingham Sculptors Guild, Birmingham Society of Women Painters,

Birmingham-Bloomfield Art Association. *Awards, honors:* Joy West Memorial Award from Cranbrook Academy of Art, 1951; Michigan Artist-Craftsman Annual award, 1951; Seal Beach (California) National Stitchery Show award, 1963; Michigan Water Color Exhibition award, 1963; Royal Oak Art Association mixed media award, 1964; Michigan Press Association award, 1965, for art column; Birmingham Sculptors Guild award, 1969; Birmingham Society of Women Painters awards, 1969-76; Scarab Club award, 1971.

WRITINGS: Stitched and Stuffed Art, Doubleday, 1974; (self-illustrated) *I Love Popcorn* (juvenile), Doubleday, 1976; (self-illustrated) *I Love Ice Cream* (juvenile), Doubleday, 1976. Also contributor to *Christmas Ideas,* by Rachel Martens, Doubleday. Contributor of weekly column, "Art Critic," to *Birmingham Eccentric,* 1963-73. Contributor to *Midwest Crafts, Working Craftsman* and *Farm Journal.*

SIDELIGHTS: Carolyn Hall told *CA:* "I'm trying to do it all, be a producing artist, writer, wife, parent, person, and it's worth the effort. Doing all this is so much more exciting than not doing it. Like any artist, I create because I have to."

She has had many one person shows in Michigan, Florida, Indiana, Louisiana, and New York. Many of her paintings are in collections throughout Michigan and elsewhere.

* * *

HALL, N(orman) John 1933-

PERSONAL: Born January 1, 1933, in Orange, N.J.; son of Norman C. and Lucille (Hertlein) Hall; married Marianne E. Gsell, October 13, 1968; children: Jonathan. *Education:* Seton Hall University, A.B., 1955, M.A., 1967; Catholic University of America, S.T.B., 1959; New York University, Ph.D., 1970. *Home:* 44 West 10th St., New York, N.Y. 10011. *Office:* Department of English, Bronx Community College of the City University of New York, Bronx, N.Y. 10453.

CAREER: New York University, New York, N.Y., part-time lecturer in English, 1967-70; Bronx Community College of the City University of New York, Bronx, N.Y., assistant professor, 1970-75, associate professor of English, 1975—. Part-time lecturer in English, New School for Social Research, 1970-74. *Member:* Modern Language Association of America, North East Modern Language Association. *Awards, honors:* Research awards from American Council of Learned Societies, 1973, and National Endowment for the Humanities, 1974.

WRITINGS: (Editor) Anthony Trollope, *The New Zealander,* Clarendon Press (Oxford, England), 1972; *Salmagundi: Byron, Allegra, and the Trollope Family,* Beta Phi Mu, 1975. Contributor to literature journals.

WORK IN PROGRESS: Trollope and His Illustrators; a new edition of letters of Anthony Trollope, for Stanford University Press.

* * *

HALL, Ross H(ume) 1926-

PERSONAL: Born November 22, 1926, in Winnipeg, Manitoba, Canada; came to the United States in 1954, naturalized citizen, 1960; son of Reginald Marshall (an agronomist) and Elizabeth (Hume) Hall; married Rachel Gardiner, September 8, 1950; children: Stewart, Donald, Mary Elizabeth. *Education:* University of British Columbia, B.A., 1948; University of Toronto, M.A., 1950; Cambridge University,

Ph.D., 1953. *Agent:* Mrs. Matie Molinar, 44 Douglas Crescent, Toronto, Ontario, Canada. *Office:* Department of Biochemistry, McMaster University, 1200 Main St., Hamilton, Ontario L8S 4J9, Canada.

CAREER: American Cyanamid Co., Lederle Laboratories Division, Prolover, N.Y., research chemist, 1954-58; Roswell Park Memorial Institute, Buffalo, N.Y., cancer research chemist, 1958-67; McMaster University, Health Sciences Centre, Hamilton, Ontario, professor of biochemistry and chairman of department, 1967—. Associate professor of biochemical research, State University of New York, Buffalo, 1964-67. *Member:* American Association for the Advancement of Science, American Association for Cancer Research, American Chemical Society, American Society of Biological Chemists, American Society of Plant Physiologists, Association of Scientific, Engineering, and Technical Societies of Canada, Canadian Biochemical Society (president, 1972-73), Institute of Food Technologists.

WRITINGS: Modified Nucleosides in Nucleic Acids, Columbia University Press, 1971; *Food For Nought: The Decline in Nutrition,* Harper, 1974. Contributor to journals in his field. Associate editor of *Plant Physiology, Nucleic Acids Research,* and *Physiologie Vegetale.*

WORK IN PROGRESS: A book describing a new approach to public health, completion expected in 1976.

SIDELIGHTS: Hall is concerned with the impact of science and technology on society, especially in nutrition, agriculture, and medical technologies.

*   *   *

HALLER, John S(amuel), Jr. 1940-

PERSONAL: Born July 22, 1940, in Pittsburgh, Pa.; son of John S. (an automotive dealer) and Mary Katherine (Nolan) Haller; married Robin Meredith Gillespie (an author), February 3, 1968; children: Peter Nolan. *Education:* Georgetown University, A.B., 1962; John Carroll University, M.A., 1964; University of Maryland, Ph.D., 1968. *Home:* 1127 Ripley St., Gary, Ind. 46403. *Office:* Department of History, Indiana University Northwest, 3400 Broadway, Gary, Ind. 46408.

CAREER: Indiana University Northwest, Gary, assistant professor, 1968-73, associate professor, 1973-76, professor of history, 1976—. *Member:* Association of American Historians, American Institute for the History of Pharmacy, Association for the History of Medicine. *Awards, honors:* Anisfield-Wolf Award in Race Relations, 1971, for *Outcasts From Evolution.*

WRITINGS: Outcasts From Evolution: Scientific Attitudes of Racial Inferiority, 1859-1900, University of Illinois Press, 1971; (with wife, Robin M. Haller) *The Physician and Sexuality in Victorian America,* University of Illinois Press, 1974. Contributor to medical, scientific, and historical journals.

*   *   *

HALSTED, Anna Roosevelt 1906-1975

May 3, 1906—December 1, 1975; American writer, journalist, newspaper editor, broadcaster, presidential aide to father, Franklin D. Roosevelt, and author of books for children. Obituaries: *New York Times,* December 2, 1975; *Washington Post,* December 2, 1975.

HALTER, Jon C(harles) 1941-

PERSONAL: Born November 24, 1941, in Hamilton, Ohio; son of Samuel L. (a purchasing agent) and Helen (an artist; maiden name, Olds) Halter; married Corina Garcia, February 14, 1968; children: Jon Julian, Helen Margaret. *Education:* Syracuse University, B.A., 1964, M.A., 1966. *Religion:* Presbyterian. *Home:* 4 Manor Court, New Brunswick, N.J. 08901. *Office: Boys' Life Magazine,* North Brunswick, N.J. 08902.

CAREER: Peace Corps volunteer in Venezuela, assigned to Venezuelan Scout Association, 1966-68; McGraw-Hill (publishers), New York, N.Y., assistant editor of *National Petroleum News,* 1968-72; *Boys' Life* (magazine), North Brunswick, N.J., associate editor, 1972—. *Member:* Sigma Delta Chi.

WRITINGS—For young readers: *Bill Bradley: One to Remember,* Putnam, 1974; *Reggie Jackson: All Star in Right,* Putnam, 1975.

WORK IN PROGRESS: A nonfiction book on World War II and a historical novel on the Latin American war of independence, both for young readers; a book on Latin American baseball stars.

SIDELIGHTS: Jon Halter told *CA:* "The five major interests of my professional life are journalism, history, sports and athletics, the Scout movement, and Latin America. Growing up in Oxford, Ohio, as the sons of a former high school coach and college athlete, my older brother and I were constantly exposed to sports on all levels. The seasons of our lives were not spring, summer, winter, fall, but rather baseball, football, and basketball. We published our own newspaper on my brother's printing press and I turned out sports columns on my own until I was in high school. By then I knew that I wanted to be (and was suited to be) a journalist more than anything else.

"My Peace Corps assignment led to my interest in Latin America, an area about which I was totally ignorant until then. While in the Peace Corps, I met and married my wife, who is Venezuelan. That event has only helped to perpetuate my interest in the people and history of that area of the world."

*   *   *

HALVERSON, Alton C. O. 1922-

PERSONAL: Born April 23, 1922; son of Alfred E. and Carrie E. (Fadness) Halverson; married Lenore M. Garvue, October 7, 1921; children: Laurel (deceased), Roy, Adrian, Philip, Carol, Dean, Mark. *Education:* Augsburg College, B.A., 1943; Luther Theological Seminary, St. Paul, Minn., B.T., 1945. *Religion:* Lutheran. *Home:* 4925 Arlington Dr., Minnetonka, Minn. 55343. *Office:* Division for World Mission, American Lutheran Church, 422 South Fifth St., Minneapolis, Minn. 55415.

CAREER: Ordained Lutheran minister. Evangelical Lutheran Church, Fort Dauphin, Madagascar, evangelist missionary, 1946-54; Evangelical Lutheran Church, Minneapolis, Minn., field representative and interpreter, 1956-60; American Lutheran Church, Minneapolis, Minn., secretary for interpretation and assistant to director of Division of World Missions, 1960—.

WRITINGS: Madagascar: Footprint at the End of the World, Augsburg, 1973.

SIDELIGHTS: Halverson has visited all areas of his church's overseas ministry shooting films, filmstrips, and gathering resource material. In 1970, he was involved in a filming project in Brazil and Colombia, "seeing and hearing . . . the aspirations of some of the world's 'have-nots' among two hundred seventy five million people in South America."

* * *

HAMBURGER, Robert 1943-

PERSONAL: Born May 30, 1943, in Brooklyn, N.Y.; son of Robert and Mary Jo (Epstein) Hamburger. Education: Cornell University, A.B., 1964; University of Chicago, M.A., 1965, Ph.D., 1969. Office: Department of English, City College of the City University of New York, 132nd St. and Convent Ave., New York, N.Y. 10031.

CAREER: City College of the City University of New York, New York, N.Y., assistant professor of English, 1968—. Member: Oral History Association.

WRITINGS: Our Portion of Hell, Links Books, 1973; The Thirties, Links Books, 1975.

WORK IN PROGRESS: A Stranger in the House: A Study of Maids.

SIDELIGHTS: Hamburger says his books are attempts to make a general reading audience aware of how racial and economic oppression affect the consciousness of minority peoples. An oral history format "gives these ignored people the opportunity to express themselves without the mediating presence of an interpreter."

* * *

HAMBURGH, Max 1922-

PERSONAL: Born February 7, 1922, in Germany; son of Sal and Jenny Hamburgh; married Gertrude Berg; children: Mark, Annette. Education: Fordham University, B.S., 1948; Yale University, M.S., 1949; Columbia University, Ph.D., 1953; University of Pennsylvania, postdoctoral study, 1953-55. Home: 100 Overlook Ter., New York, N.Y. 10040. Office: Department of Biology, City College of the City University of New York, New York, N.Y. 10003.

CAREER: Yale University, New Haven, Conn., instructor in zoology, 1948-49; Columbia University, New York, N.Y., instructor in zoology, 1949-53; Albert Einstein College of Medicine, New York, N.Y., assistant professor of anatomy, 1956-62; City College of the City University of New York, New York, N.Y., assistant professor, 1962-66, associate professor, 1966-70, professor of biology, 1970—. Visiting professor at Albert Einstein College of Medicine, 1962—; chairman of International Symposium on Hormones in Development, 1968. Military service: U.S. Army, Infantry, 1943-45.

MEMBER: American Association of Anatomists, American Teratology Society (charter member), American Society of Zoologists, American Association for the Advancement of Science, American Institute of Biological Sciences, Endocrine Society, Society of Neuroscience, Sigma Xi. Awards, honors: J. J. Newberry Award for Vertebrate Zoology, from Columbia University, 1953.

WRITINGS: Theories of Differentiation, Elsevier, 1971; (editor with E. J. W. Barrington) Hormones in Development, Appleton, 1971; The New Humanism, Philosophical Library, 1975. Contributor of about forty articles to scientific journals.

HAMILTON, Neill Q. 1925-

PERSONAL: Born December 6, 1925, in Pittsburgh, Pa.; son of Alfred Q. (a salesman) and Olive (Allen) Hamilton; married Doris Kissling, March 15, 1952; children: Neill Q. II, Patrick S., Scott A. Education: Duke University, B.S., 1946; Princeton Theological Seminary, B.D., Th.M.; University of Basel, D.Theol., 1956. Politics: Democrat. Religion: Presbyterian. Home: 6 Mansfield Court, Mendham, N.J. 07945. Office: Department of Religion, Drew University, Madison, N.J. 07940.

CAREER: San Francisco Theological Seminary, San Anselmo, Calif., professor of New Testament, 1956-72; Drew University, Madison, N.J., professor of New Testament, 1972—. Military service: U.S. Navy, engineering officer, 1944-48; became lieutenant junior grade. Member: Society of Biblical Literature. Awards, honors: Fulbright study grants, autumn, 1967, to International Christian University, 1969-70, to Tokyo Union Theological Seminary.

WRITINGS: Jesus for a No-God World, Westminster, 1969. Contributor to theology journals.

WORK IN PROGRESS: Research on redaction and critical research in the synoptic Gospels, especially in Mark, and on implications of such research for the life and thought of the present-day church.

SIDELIGHTS: Hamilton writes: "I have an interest in combining Eastern meditation with traditional Christian piety, and that all personal piety must be seen in context of social change and cosmic process." Avocational interests: Cross-country skiing, bicycle touring, raising his own fruits and vegetables.

* * *

HAMILTON, Russell G(eorge) 1934-

PERSONAL: Born August 31, 1934, in New Haven, Conn.; son of Russell G. and Lucinda (Brown) Hamilton; married Cherie VanNockay (a bi-lingual secretary), July 3, 1955; children: Cherie Andrea, Russell Malcolm, Melissa Elena, David Dean. Education: University of Connecticut, B.A., 1956; University of Wisconsin, M.A., 1957; Yale University, Ph.D., 1964. Politics: "Independent: liberal." Home: 126 Melbourne Ave. S.E., Minneapolis, Minn. 55414. Office: Department of Spanish and Portuguese, University of Minnesota, Minneapolis, Minn. 55455.

CAREER: Yale University, New Haven, Conn., instructor in Portuguese, 1962-64; University of Minnesota, Minneapolis, assistant professor, 1964-67, associate professor, 1967-72, professor of Portuguese, 1972—. Translator for Center of Afro-Oriental Studies, University of Bahia, 1960-62; Portuguese language coordinator of Peace Corps project at University of Florida, summer, 1964. Member: American Association of Teachers of Spanish and Portuguese (member of executive council, 1970-73), Modern Language Association of America. Awards, honors: Fulbright grant, Brazil, 1960-62; Fulbright research grant for Portugal, Mozambique, Angola, Cape Verde, 1970-71, to research the book, Voices from an Empire.

WRITINGS: Voices from an Empire: A History of Afro-Portuguese Literature, University of Minnesota Press, 1975. Contributor to scholarly journals.

WORK IN PROGRESS: A book tentatively titled, Lo the Poor Backlander!: Images of the Brazilian in Literature.

SIDELIGHTS: Hamilton has travelled in Brazil, Jamaica, Puerto Rico, Europe, and Portuguese Africa.

HAMMOND, Richard J(ames) 1911-

PERSONAL: Born March 4, 1911, in London, England; son of Edwin James (an office worker) and Helen (Craggs) Hammond; married Kathleen Dobbin, December 30, 1940; children: Clive Montgomery, Stella Margaret. *Education:* London School of Economics, B.A. (first class honors), 1931, M.A., 1934. *Religion:* None. *Home:* 1654 Portola Ave., Palo Alto, Calif. 94306.

CAREER: Instituto Superior de Ciencias Economicas e Financeiras, Lisbon, Portugal, lecturer in English, 1936-38; Keighley Boys' Grammar School, Yorkshire, England, senior history master, 1940-42; Offices of the Cabinet, Historical Section, London, England, official historian, 1942-60; Stanford University, Food Research Institute, Stanford, Calif., professor of economics, 1960-66; Stanford Research Institute, consultant, 1966-68, senior political economist, 1968-75. *Member:* Economic History Society (Great Britain; life member).

WRITINGS: (With Honor Minturn Croome) *The Economy of Britain: A History,* Christophers, 1938, revised edition published as *An Economic History of Britain,* 1947; *Food,* H.M.S.O. and Longmans, Green, Volume I: *The Growth of Policy,* 1951, Volume II: *Studies in Administration and Control,* 1956, Volume III: *Studies in Administration and Control,* 1962; *Food and Agriculture in Britain, 1939-45,* Stanford University Press, 1954; *Benefit-Cost Analysis and Water Pollution Control,* Food Research Institute, Stanford University, 1960; *Portugal's African Problem: Some Economic Facets,* Food Research Institute, Stanford University, 1962; *Portugal and Africa, 1815-1910: A Study in Uneconomic Imperialism,* Stanford University Press, 1966. Contributor of articles to periodicals.

SIDELIGHTS: Hammond writes to *CA:* "I agree with Dr. Samuel Johnson that 'no man but a blockhead ever wrote except for money.' All my books have been commissioned, the largest of them by the British Government as part of the official history of World War II. Most of them have been works of scholarly history, in which my aim has been to tell the truth without fear or favor, and without drawing moral lessons in the manner of the late Lord Acton and others. None of them has enjoyed large sales, nor did I need these to live by; all have received favorable reviews from persons whose opinions I respect. I get a great deal of fun out of manipulating the English language, and the only enemy I have is the American editor, whose equivalent is unknown in England."

*   *   *

HANCOCK, Maxine 1942-

PERSONAL: Born September 2, 1942, in Calgary, Alberta, Canada; daughter of Max E. (a salesman) and Ruth (Woods) Runions; married Campbell Hancock (a farmer), July 7, 1962; children: Geoffrey, Camille, Heather, Mitchell. *Education:* University of Alberta, Ed.B. (with distinction), 1964. *Religion:* Protestant Evangelical. *Residence:* Marwayne, Alberta, Canada.

CAREER: Bonnie Doon Composite High School, Edmonton, Alberta, English teacher, 1964-65; author. *Member:* Canadian Authors' Association.

WRITINGS: Love, Honor and Be Free, Moody, 1975. Author of radio scripts for Alberta School Broadcasts. Contributor of articles to *Moody Monthly, Christian Life, His,* and *Alliance Witness;* contributor of short stories and criticism to various publications.

HAND, (Andrus) Jackson 1913-
(Fred Carpenter)

PERSONAL: Born July 19, 1913, in Ladysmith, Wis.; son of Nathan K. and Essie (a country school teacher; maiden name, Andrus) Hand; married Desire Fitch (a teacher's aide), February 19, 1939; children: Judith Demarest, Andrus Jackson, Jr., Jeffrey Fitch, Jonathan Fitch. *Education:* University of Wisconsin, Madison, B.A., 1937. *Politics:* Conservative Republican. *Religion:* Christian. *Home and office:* 129 Sturges Highway, Westport, Conn. 06880.

CAREER: Furniture Index, Jamestown, N.Y., editor, 1937-40; *National Furniture Review,* Chicago, Ill., editor, 1940-44; Davidson Publishing Co., Chicago, editorial director, 1944-49; *Better Homes & Gardens,* Des Moines, Iowa, handyman editor, 1949-51; *McCall's,* New York, N.Y., home improvement editor, 1951-54; free-lance writer, photographer, editor, and editorial consultant, 1954—. City of Westport, Conn., member of public site and building committee, 1956-72, executive secretary, 1965. *Member:* National Association of Home and Workshop Writers. *Awards, honors:* Honorary degree from University of Wisconsin, School of Journalism, 1974.

WRITINGS: How to Sell More Rugs and Carpets, National Retail Furniture Association, 1942; *Projects You Can Make for Living Outdoors,* Fawcett, 1958; *How to Do Your Own Wood Finishing,* Popular Science Publishing, 1967; *How to Do Your Own Painting and Wallpapering,* Popular Science Publishing, 1968; *Complete Book of Home Repairs and Maintenance,* Popular Science Publishing, 1971; *Modern Woodworking,* Reston, 1975.

Author of home maintenance material for Curtin Publications. Consulting editor, *How Things Work in Your Home and What to Do When They Don't,* Time-Life, 1975. Contributor of articles, sometimes under pseudonym Fred Carpenter, to popular magazines, including *Reader's Digest, Ladies Home Journal,* and *Living Now,* and to house organs for major business firms.

WORK IN PROGRESS: A series of textbooks on home upkeep, woodworking, and other suitable topics for high school shop students, for Reston.

SIDELIGHTS: Hand writes: "My grandfather built barns. My dad was in the logging business. My mother could spell." He started writing at the age of nine, later landed a job as correspondent for the *Milwaukee Journal,* which lasted until his employers discovered he was only fourteen years old. He adds that he is presently living in the third house he "deliberately bought in bad shape to provide fix-it material for articles and photographs. Pretend to take summers off on an island in Georgian Bay where I have two typewriters, a tape recorder, and two pencil sharpeners—but no telephone."

*   *   *

HANDELSMAN, Judith Florence 1948-

PERSONAL: Born January 11, 1948, in New York, N.Y.; daughter of Samuel Milton (a theatrical manager) and Nina (Elman) Handelsman; married Marc Kusnetz (a journalist and producer of NBC-Radio news), July 14, 1974. *Education:* University of Wisconsin, Madison, B.A. (with honors), 1968; Columbia University, M.A.Ed., 1970. *Office:* Greenworks, 625 Greenwich St., New York, N.Y. 10014.

CAREER: WRVR-FM Radio, New York, N.Y., engineer and producer, 1972-73; Greenworks (indoor and outdoor custom plantings and maintenance), New York, N.Y., designer, 1972—. Yoga teacher for Yoga Society of New York.

WRITINGS: (With Sara Baerwald) *Greenworks: Tender Loving Care for Plants,* Macmillan, 1973. Contributor to popular magazines, including *Harper's Bazaar,* and newspapers, including *Wisdom's Child.*

WORK IN PROGRESS: "Mini-documentary" programs for NBC-Radio news, in indoor and outdoor gardening.

* * *

HANDLER, Milton 1903-

PERSONAL: Born October 8, 1903, in New York, N.Y.; son of George and Ray (Friedman) Handler; married Marian W. Kahn, December 21, 1932 (deceased); married Miriam Adler, February 3, 1955; children: Carole Enid (Mrs. Peter Schoenbach). *Education:* Columbia University, A.B., 1924, LL.B., 1926. *Politics:* Democrat. *Religion:* Jewish. *Home:* 625 Park Ave., New York, N.Y. 10021. *Office:* Kaye, Scholer, Fierman, Hays & Handler, 425 Park Ave., New York, N.Y. 10022.

CAREER: Admitted to the bar of the State of New York, 1927. Columbia University, New York, N.Y., 1927—, began as instructor, became professor of law, professor emeritus, 1972—; Kaye, Scholer, Fierman, Hays & Handler, attorneys, New York, N.Y., partner, 1951—. President, New York Majestic Corp., 1937-48; general counsel, National Labor Board, 1933-34; special assistant to general counsel, Department of Treasury, 1938-40; assistant general counsel, Lend Lease Administration, 1942-43; special counsel to Foreign Economic Administration, 1943-44; associate public member, National War Labor Board, 1944; member, Attorney General's National Committee to Study Antitrust Laws, 1954-55; Mitchell Lecturer, University of Buffalo Law School, 1956-57; lecturer, University of Leiden, 1963; deputy chairman of board of governors, Hebrew University.

MEMBER: American Bar Association, American College of Trial Lawyers (fellow), American Bar Foundation (fellow), American Judicature Society, Federal Bar Association, American Friends of Hebrew University (honorary chairman of board of directors), Jewish Academy of Arts and Sciences (member of board of trustees), Conference on Jewish Social Studies (member of board of directors), New York State Bar Association, New York County Lawyers Association (member of board of directors, 1953-56), Association of the Bar of the City of New York, Men's Faculty Club (Columbia University), Lawyer's Club, Harmonie Club. *Awards, honors:* Columbia University bicentennial silver medallion, 1954; Scopus Award from American Friends of the Hebrew University, 1963; LL.D., Hebrew University, 1965.

WRITINGS: Cases and Materials on Law of Vendor and Purchaser, West Publishing, 1933; *Cases and Materials on Trade Regulation,* Foundation Press, 1937, 4th edition, 1967; *A Study of the Construction and Enforcement of the Federal Antitrust Laws,* U.S. Government Printing Office, 1941; *Cases and Materials on Labor Law,* West Publishing, 1944; *Antitrust Perspective,* Columbia University Press, 1957; *Cases and Materials on Business Torts,* Foundation Press, 1972; *Twenty-Five Years of Antitrust,* two volumes, Matthew Bender, 1973. Contributor of articles on antitrust and trademark law to legal journals.

HANIFI, M(ohammed) Jamil 1935-

PERSONAL: Born June 27, 1935, in Kabul, Afghanistan; son of Mohammed Jan and Quraysha (in civil service; maiden name, Ahmadzai) Hanifi; married Sarah Campbell, June, 1958 (divorced, April, 1964); married Marrietta Kassouf (a teacher), May 29, 1964; children: Maryam, Khalid, Sophia, Shah. *Education:* Michigan State University, B.Sc., 1960, M.A., 1962; Southern Illinois University, Carbondale, Ph.D., 1969. *Residence:* DeKalb, Ill. *Office:* Department of Anthropology, Northern Illinois University, DeKalb, Ill. 60115.

CAREER: California State University, Los Angeles, assistant professor of anthropology, 1968-69; Northern Illinois University, DeKalb, associate professor of anthropology, 1969—. *Member:* Association for Asian Studies, Middle Eastern Studies Association, Afghanistan Studies Association (chairman of executive committee), American Anthropological Association (fellow), Society for Applied Anthropology, Royal Anthropological Institute of Great Britain and Ireland, Association of Current Anthropology. *Awards, honors:* Afghanistan Government scholarship, 1957-62.

WRITINGS: Islam and the Transformation of Culture, Asia Publishing House, 1974; *Historical and Cultural Dictionary of Afghanistan,* Scarecrow, 1976. Contributor of articles to journals in his field.

WORK IN PROGRESS: A biography of a peasant Afghan; anthropological research on the Pushtuns of Afghanistan, on urbanization in Central Asia, and on the ethnology of Central Asia.

* * *

HANKINS, Norman E(lijah) 1935-

PERSONAL: Born May 15, 1935, in Greeneville, Tenn.; son of Charles Alexander (a farmer) and Helen Irene Hankins; married Marilyn A. Wampler (a teacher), December 18, 1970. *Education:* Tusculum College, B.S., 1958; East Tennessee State University, M.A., 1962; University of Tennessee, Ed.D., 1964. *Home:* 223 Sequoyah Dr., Johnson City, Tenn. 37601. *Office:* Department of Psychology, East Tennessee State University, Box 2649, Johnson City, Tenn. 37601.

CAREER: Memphis State University, Memphis, Tenn., assistant professor of psychology, 1964-65; East Tennessee State University, Johnson City, assistant professor, 1965-67, associate professor, 1967-73, professor of psychology, 1973—. *Military service:* U.S. Army Reserve, 1958-64. *Member:* American Personnel and Guidance Association, American Rehabilitation Counselors Association, Tennessee Education Association.

WRITINGS: Psychology for Contemporary Education, C. E. Merrill, 1973; *The Devil Can't Make You Do It: A Laymen's Guide to Behavioral Self Control,* Nelson-Hall, in press.

* * *

HANNA, William John 1931-

PERSONAL: Born October 30, 1931, in Cleveland, Ohio; son of William Henry (a businessman) and Anne (a teacher; maiden name, Dobrin) Hanna; married Judith Lynne Selmont (a writer), December 16, 1960; children: Shawn Harrison, Aaron Evan. *Education:* University of California, Los Angeles, B.A., 1957, M.A., 1960, Ph.D., 1962. *Home address:* P.O. Box 1062, Englewood Cliffs, N.J. 07632.

Office: Comparative Urban Studies Center, City University of New York, 33 West 42nd St., New York, N.Y. 10036.

CAREER: Michigan State University, East Lansing, instructor, 1961-62, assistant professor of political science, 1962-65, member of faculty at African Studies Center, 1961-65; American University, Washington, D.C., associate professor, 1965, professor of political science, 1965-68, research scientist, 1965, senior research scientist, 1965-68; City University of New York, New York, N.Y., professor of political science and urban studies at Herbert H. Lehman College and at Graduate School, 1968—, director of Comparative Urban Studies Program, 1972—. Visiting associate of Institute of African Studies at University of Ibadan, 1960, 1963; adjunct professor at New York University, 1970. Senior partner of Hanna and Hanna Associates, 1965—. Consultant to United Nations and U.S. Department of State. *Military service:* U.S. Army, 1952-53.

MEMBER: International Political Science Association, International Sociological Association, International Institute of Differing Civilizations (fellow), American Political Science Association, American Society for Public Administration, American Sociological Association (fellow), Society for Applied Anthropology (fellow). *Awards, honors:* Ford Foundation fellowship for Michigan State University's Overseas Program in Black Africa, 1962-63; U.S. Office of Education international programs grant, 1972-74; Social Science Research Council and American Council of Learned Societies grant, 1973-74; National Science Foundation grant, 1975.

WRITINGS: (With Douglas Steen) *Precision Power Bidding,* Coffin, 1956; (editor and contributor) *Independent Black Africa: The Politics of Freedom,* Rand McNally, 1964; *Politics in Black Africa,* Michigan State University Press, 1964; (with wife, Judith Lynne Hanna) *Polyethnicity and Political Integration in Umuahia and Mbale,* American Society for Public Administration, 1968; *The University Students of Black Africa,* American Institutes of Research, 1970; (with J. L. Hanna) *Urban Dynamics in Black Africa: An Interdisciplinary Approach,* American Institutes for Research, 1969, 2nd edition, Aldine, 1971; *Comparative Urban Politics,* two volumes, Sage Publications, 1972; *University Students and African Politics,* Africana Publishers, 1975. Contributor to professional journals. Editor and publisher of *Comparative Urban Research,* 1972—.

WORK IN PROGRESS: Politics and the Quality of Urban Life.

* * *

HANNAM, Charles 1925-

PERSONAL: Born July 26, 1925, in Essen, Germany. *Education:* Cambridge University, B.A., 1951, M.A., 1961. *Office:* School of Education, University of Bristol, Bristol BS8 1JA, England.

CAREER: Teacher in secondary schools in England, 1951-59; University of Bristol, Bristol, England, member of faculty, 1959—, senior lecturer in education, 1973—. *Military service:* British Army, 1943-47; served in India and Burma.

WRITINGS: (Contributor) M. Ballard, editor, *New Movements in the Study and Teaching of History,* Temple Smith, 1970; (with Pat Smyth and Norman Stephenson) *Young Teachers and Reluctant Learners,* Penguin, 1971; *Parents and Mental Handicap,* Penguin, 1974; (with Smyth and Stephenson) *The First Year of Teaching,* Penguin, 1975. Contributor to journals.

WORK IN PROGRESS: A biographical study of childhood in Germany; working with children who have difficulty in adjusting to schools; small groups, communication, and learning.

* * *

HANNAWAY, Patricia H(inman) 1929-
(Patti Hannaway; pseudonym: L. P. Charnance)

PERSONAL: Born January 25, 1929, in Minneapolis, Minn.; daughter of Ira P. (a seedsman) and Florence E. (Montgomery) Hinman; married Glenn H. Altland, June 12, 1948 (divorced, 1968); married Walter F. Hannaway (a painting contractor), February 7, 1972; children: (first marriage) Glenn H. III (deceased), Stan William (deceased), David Lee, Roger Dean. *Education:* Educated in Minneapolis, Minn. *Religion:* Lutheran. *Home:* 143 Island Way, #3, Clearwater, Fla. 33515. *Office:* Sisters' II Studios, 4236 West Waters Ave., Tampa, Fla. 33614.

CAREER: East Minneapolis Argus, Minneapolis, Minn., free-lance feature writer, 1953-57; advertising copywriter for firms in Minneapolis, 1956-59; free-lance journalist and advertising writer, 1959-62; *Key West Citizen,* Key West, Fla., editor of women's page, 1963-64; Grant Advertising, Miami, Fla., copywriter, 1968-69; Florida Department of Commerce, Tallahassee, information specialist, 1969; advertising copywriter or copy chief for firms in Miami, St. Petersburgh and Clearwater, Fla., 1970-72; currently with Sisters' II Studios, Tampa. Member of Old Island Restoration Foundation, 1966. *Member:* Painting Contractors of America Ladies Auxiliary (member of Florida council), Friends of the Clearwater Public Library (vice-president, 1975-76).

WRITINGS: (Under name Patti Hannaway) *Winslow Homer in the Tropics,* Westover, 1974.

WORK IN PROGRESS: Winslow Homer in the Adirondacks and Canada; Charles E. Burchfield: Master Doodler; Creative Stitchery through the Ages; a novel under pseudonym L. P. Charnance.

AVOCATIONAL INTERESTS: Crewel embroidery, applique, photography, travel.

* * *

HANSON, Michael James 1942-

PERSONAL: Born December 22, 1942, in High Wycombe, England; son of Thomas Frederick (a builder) and Hilda (May) Hanson; married Elisabeth Litvergren, October 30, 1970; children: Silvie, Katja, Rufus. *Education:* University of London, B.Sc., 1964; University of Essex, M.Sc., 1967. *Politics:* Anarchist. *Home and office:* The School House, Sinclairston, Ochiltree, Cumnock, Ayrshire, KA18 2RT, Scotland.

CAREER: Teacher of physics, 1967—.

WRITINGS: The Boomerang Book, Penguin, 1974.

AVOCATIONAL INTERESTS: Boomerangs, kites, windmills, gliding (Hanson told *CA* that he has a "fascination with wind"), rock climbing, woodworking, gardening, wine making, exploring.

* * *

HANSON, Paul D(avid) 1939-

PERSONAL: Born November 17, 1939, in Ashland, Wis.; son of H. Victor (a businessman) and Lydia (Thompson) Hanson; married Cynthia Rosenburger (an organist and pianist), August 20, 1966; children: Amy Elizabeth, Mark Christopher. *Education:* Gustavus Adolphus College, B.A., 1961; Yale University, B.D., 1965; Harvard University, Ph.D., 1970. *Religion:* Lutheran. *Home:* 27 Cushing Ave., Belmont, Mass. 02178. *Office:* Harvard Divinity School, Cambridge, Mass. 02138.

CAREER: Harvard University Divinity School, Cambridge, Mass., assistant professor, 1970-75, professor of Old Testament, 1975—. *Member:* American Schools of Oriental Research, Society of Biblical Literature, Catholic Biblical Association, Society for Religion in Higher Education. *Awards, honors:* Fulbright fellow, 1961-62; Woodrow Wilson fellow, 1965-66; Kent fellow, 1966-70; American Council of Learned Societies fellow, 1973-74.

WRITINGS: (Editor) Hans Walter Wolff, *Hosea,* Fortress, 1974; *The Dawn of Apocalyptic,* Fortress, 1975. Contributor of articles and reviews to journals in his field. Member of editorial board, *Hermeneia,* 1970—.

WORK IN PROGRESS: A commentary on the Book of Zechariah; research on biblical theology and ethics.

SIDELIGHTS: Paul Hanson told *CA* that his main concern was the "discovery of the relevance of ancient Jewish and Christian traditions for responsible and compassionate living in the modern world." He is trained in German, Greek, Hebrew, and other Near Eastern languages; has done archaeological work and scholarly research in Israel in 1969-70, 1973-74.

* * *

HARBERT, Mary Ann 1945-

PERSONAL: Born December 27, 1945, in Arlington, Va.; daughter of Gene W. (a civil engineer) and Polly (Goddard) Harbert. *Education:* Attended Beirut College For Women, Beirut, Lebanon, 1964; University of Utah, B.A., 1968. *Home:* 1045 El Camino, Burlingame, Calif. 94010.

CAREER: Personnel secretary.

WRITINGS: Captivity, Delacorte, 1973.

* * *

HARBINSON, W(illiam) A(llen) 1941-
(John Howarth)

PERSONAL: Born September 9, 1941, in Northern Ireland; son of Alfred (a welder) and Martha (a stitcher; maiden name, Allen) Harbinson; married Ursula Mayer, November 5, 1969; children: Shaun, Tanya. *Education:* Attended Belfast College of Technology, 1956-57, and Liverpool College of Building, 1958-61. *Home:* 6 Albert Mansions, Crouch Hill, London N.8, England. *Agent:* Aaron M. Priest, 15 East 40th St., New York, N.Y. 10016.

CAREER: Apprentice textile engineer, Belfast, Northern Ireland, 1955-57; apprentice gas fitter, Liverpool, England, 1958-61; free-lance writer in London, England, 1967-68; Stonehart Publications, London, subscriptions clerk, 1968-69; *Knave and Fiesta,* London, assistant editor, 1970-71; *Scorpio,* London, assistant editor, 1971-72; chief associate editor in London of *Men Only* and *Club International,* and London office of *Club U.S.A.,* 1972-76; full-time writer in London, 1976—. *Military service:* Royal Australian Air Force, medical clerk, 1961-67. *Member:* International P.E.N., National Union of Journalists, British Film Institute.

WRITINGS—Novels: *Two Gentlemen of Pleasure,* Horwitz, 1967; *The Gentlemen Rogues,* Horwitz, 1967; *The Running Man,* Horwitz, 1967, Award Books, 1970; *Guide for the Single Man,* Horwitz, 1968; *Death of an Idol,* Horwitz, 1969; *Our Girl Friday,* Horwitz, 1969; *Instruments of Death,* Corgi, 1973, published as *None But the Damned,* Pinnacle Books, 1974; *Knock,* Intergroup, 1975; *Meat,* Panther, 1975.

Biographies: *Bronson!,* Pinnacle Books, 1975; *Elvis Presley: An Illustrated Biography,* M. Joseph, 1975, Grosset, 1976; (editor and compiler of photographs) Colin Wilson, *Ken Russell: A Director in Search of a Hero,* Intergroup, 1975.

Author of "Astronaut," a radio play, for BBC, 1972; author of script material for television series "The Explorers," for BBC-TV, 1974. Contributor of stories and articles to men's magazines in the United States, England, and Australia. Film and book reviewer, under pseudonym John Howarth, for *Men Only* and *Club International.*

WORK IN PROGRESS: Novels, *No Limit; The Stopover;* and *The Embattled;* a biography, *George C. Scott.*

SIDELIGHTS: Harbinson writes that he "would not like to be categorized as either an 'intellectual' writer or a 'popular' writer, so keep jumping between both forms of writing to retain a certain amount of freedom." He states he is "not directly interested in politics because I believe that politics does not explain people whereas people do explain politics. More interested in all forms of creativity—professional or amateur—because man's dreams reveal more than man's actions. Finally, never write in the hopes of educating the audience, but simply in the hope that one can briefly remove them from their own lives . . . a modest ambition!"

* * *

HARDY, David A(ndrews) 1936-

PERSONAL: Born April 10, 1936, in Birmingham, England; son of Arthur (a violinist) and Lilian (Andrews) Hardy; married Ruth Margaret Fearn (a music teacher), 1975; children: Karen Dawn. *Education:* Attended private school in England until eleven, and grammar school, 1947-52. *Religion:* Church of England. *Home:* 99 Southam Rd., Hall Green, Birmingham B28 0AB, England. *Office:* Astro Art, 99 Southam Rd., Hall Green, Birmingham B28 0AB, England.

CAREER: Laboratory technician, 1952-54; commercial artist with Cadbury Bros. Ltd., Bournville, England, 1956-65; free-lance artist and writer, 1965—. Has designed and illustrated book jackets. *Military service:* Royal Air Force, 1954-56. *Member:* Royal Astronomical Society (fellow), British Interplanetary Society (associate fellow), British Astronomical Association, Lincoln Astronomical Society (president, 1969-72; vice-president, 1972—).

WRITINGS: (With Patrick A. Moore) *The Challenge of the Stars: A Forecast of the Future Exploration of the Universe,* Rand McNally, 1972; (self-illustrated) *The Solar System,* World's Work, 1975; (self-illustrated) *Rockets and Satellites,* World's Work, in press. Contributor of articles on science and art to various publications.

Illustrator: M. T. Bizony, general editor, *The Space Encyclopedia: A Guide to Astronomy and Space Research,* Dutton, 1957, revised edition, 1960; Patrick Moore, *Astronomy,* Oldbourne, 1961, reissued as *Story of Astronomy,* Macdonald, 1972; George H. Gopsill and Frank Beesley, *Practical Geography,* Macmillan, 1964; Colin Ronan, *The Stars,* Bodley Head, 1965; Ronan, *The Univers,* Oxford

University Press, 1966; W. E. Swinton, *The Earth Tells Its Story,* Bodley Head, 1967; J. Petrie, *The Earth,* Oxford University Press, 1967; Moore, *Space,* Lutterworth, 1968; Moore, *Astronomy for "O" Level,* Duckworth, 1970; Moore, *Mars: The Red World,* World's Work, 1971; Brenda Thompson, editor, *Volcanoes,* Sidgwick & Jackson, 1974; Thompson, editor, *Spaceship Earth,* Sidgwick & Jackson, 1975; John W. Macvey, *Earth Visited?,* Macmillan, 1976. Also illustrator of various children's books, including Methuen's "Outlines," 1957-61, of science fiction published in the United States, Britain, and Germany, and of filmstrips.

SIDELIGHTS: "My chief motivation, since the early 1950's," writes Hardy, "has been to present an *accurate* picture of space and astronomy—in fact any science—especially to children, as so many bad books, cheaply illustrated, have been on sale."

*   *   *

HARDY, Eric

PERSONAL: Born in England; children: two. *Politics:* "Have not voted for over twenty years." *Religion:* "Baptised Church of England." *Home:* 47 Woodsorrel Rd., Liverpool L15 6UB, England.

CAREER: Broadcaster on radio, 1936—, and on television, 1960—, currently broadcasting weekly on "Radio Merseyside," for BBC; university teacher and tutor in natural history. Member of Lancashire and Western Sea Fisheries Committee, 1954-74. *Military service:* British Army, Royal Corps of Signals, 1942-46; became captain. *Member:* National Union of Journalists, Zoological Society of London (fellow, 1934—), Imperial Cancer Research Fund (life governor), Merseyside Aquarist Society (president), Merseyside Naturalists Association (honorary secretary).

WRITINGS: Birds of the Liverpool Area, Arbroath, 1941; *A-Z Pigeon Guide,* Burke, 1951; *The Bird Lover's Week-End Book,* Seeley, 1952; *The Naturalist in Lakeland,* David & Charles, 1974. Also author of *Birds of Palestine,* 1941. Contributor to professional journals. Editor, *Northwestern Bird Report,* 1938—, *Bulletin of the Jerusalem Naturalists Club,* 1944-46, *Wild Birds,* 1947-48, *Nature Lover,* 1948-50.

WORK IN PROGRESS: Research on natural history, including Biblical natural history, birds, botany, fisheries, horticulture.

SIDELIGHTS: Hardy has conducted extensive field studies in the United Kingdom and in the area of the Holy Land; he has been writing on natural history experiences for "well over fifty years."

*   *   *

HARMELINK, Barbara (Mary)

PERSONAL: Born in Ningpo, China; daughter of Albert Allan (a clergyman) and Florence (Searle) Conibear; married Herman Harmelink III (a clergyman and writer), August 11, 1959; children: Herman Alan, Lindsay Alexandra. *Education:* University of Birmingham, B.A. (honors in history), 1952, Certificate of Education, 1953. *Religion:* Reformed Church in America. *Residence:* Poughkeepsie, N.Y.

CAREER: Kingsley School for Girls, Horley, Surrey, England, head of history department, 1953-55; Selhurst Grammar School for Girls, Croydon, Surrey, England, teacher of history, 1955-59. Member of women's commit-

tee, Japanese International Christian University; member of Board of World Missions, Reformed Church in America; director, Reformed Church Weekday Nursery, 1972-75.

WRITINGS: Florence Nightingale: Founder of Modern Nursing (juvenile), F. Watts, 1969.

WORK IN PROGRESS: Research on Queen Victoria and other nineteenth-century material in English history, and on African history, especially the roots of the American Negro and folklore.

Barbara Harmelink spent two years studying at the Guildhall School of Music in London. She plays piano and classical Spanish guitar, and was a member of the Royal Choral Society in London. She has traveled extensively in Western Europe, has visited Peru, Venezuela, Brazil, and Africa. Mrs. Harmelink is competent in French and German and is studying Spanish. *Avocational interests:* Opera, ballet, gardening; visiting art galleries, cathedrals, arboretums, and botanical gardens.

*   *   *

HARNSBERGER, Caroline Thomas   1902-

PERSONAL: Born April 12, 1902, in Columbus, Ohio; daughter of James Oscar (a civil engineer) and Edith (Hiss) Thomas; married Audley E. Harnsberger, May 18, 1926; children: Donald A., Robert T., Ann H. (Mrs. Peter J. Atkinson). *Education:* Attended Juilliard School of Music, 1920-24, Paris Conservatory of Music, 1925-26, Ohio State University, 1929, Chicago College of Music, 1936-45, and Northwestern University, 1954-56. *Politics:* Republican. *Religion:* Congregational. *Home:* 775 Sumac Lane, Winnetka, Ill. 60093. *Office:* Music in Northfield, 446 Central, Northfield, Ill. 60093.

CAREER: Woman's Symphony Orchestra, Chicago, Ill., violinist, 1926-33; Evanston Symphony Orchestra, Evanston, Ill., violinist, 1946—; Music in Northfield (a store), Northfield, Ill., proprietor, 1964—. Faculty member of National College of Education, 1955-57. *Member:* National League of American Pen Women, Women in Communications, Midland Authors, North Shore Musicians Club, Winnetka Music Club.

WRITINGS: Mark Twain at Your Fingertips, Beechhurst, 1948; *The Lincoln Treasury,* Follett, 1950; *A Man of Courage: Robert A. Taft,* Follett, 1952; *Mark Twain, Family Man,* Citadel, 1960; *Mark Twain's Views of Religion,* Schori Press, 1961; *Pilot's Ready Reference,* Aero, 1962, 9th edition, 1975; (editor) *Treasury of Presidential Quotations,* Follett, 1964; *Bernard Shaw: Selections of His Wit and Wisdom,* Follett, 1965; *Everyone's Mark Twain,* A. S. Barnes, 1972.

WORK IN PROGRESS: Gods and Heroes of Greek and Roman Mythology; Ever with Love, a biography of Clara Clemens; compilations on Churchill, Emerson, and Robert Lewis Stevenson; *The Presidents as They Knew Each Other.*

SIDELIGHTS: Caroline Harnsberger became an intimate friend of Mark Twain's second daughter Clara, and was an aide to Hal Holbrook, the actor who portrayed Mark Twain in stage and television productions. *Avocational interests:* Piloting airplanes.

*   *   *

HARPER, Carol Ely
(Ilke Ben, Alfred Goddard)

PERSONAL: Born in Monroe City, Mo.; daughter of Aurelius Wesley (a physician) and Annie Belle (an author; maiden name, Adkisson) Ely; married Maurice Wilson Harper (a tax accountant), March 11, 1925; children: Maurice Ely, Carol-Maura Salisbury (Mrs. Charles A. Kiselyak). *Education:* Attended Whitman College, 1922-25, 1927-28; Whitman Conservatory of Music, teacher's certificate, 1929; University of Washington, B.A., 1952, M.A., 1959; graduate study at University of Birmingham, England, 1954. *Politics:* Republican. *Religion:* Protestant. *Home and office:* 6565 Northeast Windermere Rd., Seattle, Wash. 98105.

CAREER: Oregonian (newspaper), Portland, Ore., correspondent, 1934-36; *Experimenter* (magazine), Walla Walla, Wash., editor, 1944-46; Experiment Press and *Experiment: An International Review of New Poetry,* Seattle, Wash., assistant business manager, 1948, business manager, 1949, managing editor, 1950-57, editor-in-chief of Experiment Press, 1958—. Actress, appearing occasionally with various companies in Pacific-Northwest area; has performed with Cirque Dinner Theatre. Founder of East Oregon Federal Music Project, 1937, Walla Walla Little Theatre, 1944, and Experiment Theatre, 1957. Member of American Security Council. *Member:* International Platform Association, National Federation of Press Women, Daughters of the American Revolution, Pacific Northwest Writers Conference, League of Western Writers, Actors Equity Association, Experiment Group, Washington State Press Women.

WRITING: To a Faulty Lover (poems), Alan Swallow, 1946; *Distichs for a Dancer* (poems), Alan Swallow, 1950; (editor) *Experiment Theatre I* (anthology), Experiment Press, 1960; *Big Bend of Columbia River* (verse novel), Experiment Press, 1976; *Poemes for a Playful New Yorker,* Experiment Press, in press; (editor) *Experiment Theatre II,* Experiment Press, in press. Contributor of fiction and poetry, occasionally under pseudonym Ilke Ben, to periodicals, including *Prairie Schooner, New Mexico Quarterly Review, Commonweal, Massachusetts Review, Canadian Forum,* and *Trails for Juniors.*

WORK IN PROGRESS: The City, a seven-volume multiform epic in "automatic writing"; five novels, for Experiment Press, *There Is No Goodbye, Average Love, Real Ely: Doctor from Missouri* (autobiographical), *The Progress of Mrs. Pope,* and *The Murder of Mata Hari;* three picture-books for children, under pseudonym Alfred Goddard, *Baby Harry's First Seven Words, The Old Woman Who,* and *Butterfly Wings;* editing *Experiment Theatre III* and *IV.*

AVOCATIONAL INTERESTS: Music, painting, iris-hybridizing.

* * *

HARRIS, Delmer (William) 1937-

PERSONAL: Born June 18, 1937, in Orleans, Ind.; son of Elmer W. (a barber) and Wilma (Whitten) Harris; married Joyce A. Crites, June 20, 1958; children: Larry, Alex, Stanley, Carey Ann. *Education:* Milligan College, A.B. (cum laude), 1959; Indiana University, M.A., 1964.

CAREER: Teacher of psychology and history and athletic coach in high schools in Indiana, 1959-65; Earlham College, Richmond, Ind., associate professor, athletic director, and basketball coach, 1965-74; European Pro League, Barcelona, Spain, head coach, 1974-75; Utah Stars (professional basketball team), assistant coach, 1975—. Summer coach for Puerto Rico Pro League, 1969—; member of Pop Warner Football Advisory Board; charter builder of In-

diana Basketball Hall of Fame. *Member:* National Speakers Association, National Association of Basketball Coaches.

WRITINGS: Multiple Defenses for Winning Basketball, Parker Publishing, 1971; *Coaching Basketball's Zone Offenses,* Parker Publishing, in press.

WORK IN PROGRESS: Research for a book set in the 1890's; a juvenile novel, *Playing the Game.*

SIDELIGHTS: Harris gives motivational talks and self-image lectures to school groups, church groups, and civic organizations.

* * *

HARRIS, Helen(a Barbara Mary) 1927-

PERSONAL: Born February 7, 1927, in Buckfastleigh, Devonshire, England; daughter of John Robert Hoare (a surveyor) and Helena Marianne (Coulton) Warren; married Desmond John Harris (agricultural adviser to Ministry of Agriculture), October 18, 1952; children: Christopher John, Jane Helen Mary. *Education:* Studley Agricultural College, National Diploma in Dairying (N.D.D.), 1947. *Religion:* Church of England. *Home:* 34 Ringer's Spinney, Oadby, Leicestershire, England.

CAREER: Ministry of Agriculture, London, England, milk production advisory officer in North Devon, England, and West Devon, England, 1948-56; writer since mid-1960's. Has done occasional broadcasting.

WRITINGS: The Industrial Archaeology of Dartmoor, David & Charles, 1968; *The Industrial Archaeology of the Peak District,* David & Charles, 1971; (with Monica Ellis) *The Bude Canal,* David & Charles, 1972; *The Grand Western Canal,* David & Charles, 1973. Contributor to farming and country life journals.

WORK IN PROGRESS: Continuing research on agriculture and "countryside subjects."

AVOCATIONAL INTERESTS: British countryside, foreign travel, industrial archaeology, canals, local history, English history (especially the eighteenth and nineteenth centuries), photography, ornithology.

* * *

HARRIS, Lloyd J(ohn) 1947-

PERSONAL: Born March 22, 1947, in Los Angeles, Calif.; son of Mervin (a businessman) and Mildred (a matron of the arts; maiden name, Dolkart) Harris. *Education:* Attended University of California, Los Angeles, 1965, and University of California, Berkeley, 1966-69. *Home:* 1043 Cragmont Ave., Berkeley, Calif. 94708. *Office:* Anesthetic Productions/Panjandrum Press, 99 Sanchez, San Francisco, Calif.

CAREER: Cheese Board Collective (cheese store), Berkeley, Calif., member of collective, 1969—. Co-publisher, editor and designer for Panjandrum Press, 1973—; founder of Anesthetic Productions (art productions), 1974—; founder of Lovers of the Stinking Rose (garlic organization), 1975—. Vice-president and member of board of directors of S. Harris Co., Inc.

WRITINGS: The Book of Garlic, Panjandrum Press, 1974. Contributor of poems to *Panjandrum* and articles to *California Living* and *Los Angeles Free Press.*

WORK IN PROGRESS: X-Rocks Art, an anthology of xerox art; *Dear Househusbands,* a novel.

SIDELIGHTS: Harris writes: "The Book of Garlic was written to correct a deficiency in American 'taste.' Also to illustrate certain principles that were overwhelming to me at the time (and still are), one being that complexities are often illustrated by simplicities. I am interested in the concepts of 'play,' 'fantasy,' and 'imagination' and their functions in 'everyday' life."

* * *

HARRIS, Sydney J(ustin) 1917-

PERSONAL: Born September 14, 1917, in London, England; came to United States in 1922; married Grace Miller (divorced, 1951); married Patricia Roche, 1953; children: Carolyn, Michael, Barbara, David, Lindsay. Education: Attended University of Chicago and Central College, Chicago, Ill. Office: Chicago Daily News, 401 North Wabash Ave., Chicago, Ill. 60611.

CAREER: Worked various jobs on Chicago Herald and Examiner and Chicago Daily Times, Chicago, Ill., 1934-36; Beacon (magazine), Chicago, editor, 1937-38; City of Chicago, Chicago, member of staff of public relations department and legal division, 1939-41; Chicago Daily News, Chicago, reporter and feature writer, 1941-44, author of column, "Strictly Personal," now syndicated by Field Newspaper Syndicate to about two hundred newspapers in the United States, Canada, and South America, 1944—, drama critic, 1945—. Instructor, University of Chicago, 1946—; summer faculty member, Aspen Institute for Humanistic Studies; trustee, Francis W. Parker School, Chicago. Member: Associates for the Institute for Psychoanalysis in Chicago (vice-president), Sigma Delta Chi, Arts Club, Headline Club, Press Club. Awards, honors: Ferguson Award, Friends of Literature, 1958; Brotherhood Award, National Conference of Christians and Jews, 1968; LL.D., Villa Maria College; Litt.D., Frances Schimer College.

WRITINGS—All published by Houghton, except as indicated: Strictly Personal, Regnery, 1953; A Majority of One, 1957; To Cry Fear: Desert Fighting at Its Toughest, Brown, Watson, 1960; Last Things First, 1961; On the Contrary, 1964; Leaving the Surface, 1968; For the Time Being, 1972; The Authentic Person: Dealing with Dilemma, Argus Communications, 1972; Winners and Losers, Argus Communications, 1973; The Best of Harris, 1975. Member of usage panel of American Heritage Dictionary.

SIDELIGHTS: Reviewing Leaving the Surface, G. W. Johnson commented that Harris "is enough of a philosopher to distinguish between form and essence, and he is well-enough acquainted with modern thought to realize that many forms of the old moralities are obsolete and actually belie the essence. So he is enough of an image-breaker to give piquancy to observations that are, in fact, truisms. A page of Harris may contain nothing new and yet leave the reader with a pleasing sensation of sharpened perception." Avocational interests: Tennis, chess.

* * *

HARRISON, Carey 1944-

PERSONAL: Born February 19, 1944, in London, England; son of Rex Carey (an actor) and Lilli Maria (an actress; stage name, Lilli Palmer; maiden name, Peiser) Harrison; married Mary Chamberlain (a writer and journalist), October 30, 1971. Education: Cambridge University, B.A., 1965. Politics: Communist.

CAREER: Writer and theatre director in various provincial theatres in England, 1965—; Stables Theatre, Manchester, England, resident writer, 1969-70. Playwright. Member: Writer's Guild of Great Britain.

WRITINGS—Plays: (With others) New Short Plays, Number One (includes one-act play, "Twenty-six Efforts at Pornography"), Methuen, 1968; (with others) New Short Plays, Number Two (includes one-act play, "Lovers"), Methuen, 1969.

Author of nine television plays produced by British Broadcasting Corporation and Granada; also wrote filmscript, "The War Tourist."

WORK IN PROGRESS: Plays, film work, and novels.

* * *

HARRISON, Deloris 1938-

PERSONAL: Born February 4, 1938, in Bedford, Va.; daughter of Ernest and Lucy (a hospital administrator; maiden name, Hall) Harrison; divorced; children: Germaine Auguste Netzband. Education: St. Joseph's College for Women, Brooklyn, N.Y., A.B., 1958; New York University, A.M., 1963. Home address: P.O. Box 698, Hanover, N.H. 03755. Agent: Phyllis Westberg, Harold Ober Associates, Inc., 40 East 49th St., New York, N.Y. 10017. Office: Orford High School, Orford, N.H. 03777.

CAREER: High school teacher of English in New York, N.Y., 1961-68; Dartmouth College, Dartmouth, N.H., assistant professor of English, 1970-72; Windham College, Putney, Vt., assistant professor of creative writing, 1972-74; Orford High School, Orford, N.H., teacher of English, 1974—. Awards, honors: Fulbright exchange teacher in the Netherlands, 1966-67; Bread Loaf Writers' Conference fellowship, 1969.

WRITINGS: (Editor) We Shall Live in Peace: The Teachings of Martin Luther King (juvenile), Hawthorn, 1968; The Bannekers of Bannaky Springs (juvenile), Hawthorn, 1970; Journey All Alone (young adult book), Dial, 1971.

WORK IN PROGRESS: The Notebook of Jason Ellis, a novel told in diary form about a college student who lost both his white mother and black father.

SIDELIGHTS: Deloris Harrison writes: "Although I grew up in New York City's Harlem, I was born on a farm in Virginia in the same house that my mother and all her eight brothers and sisters were born in. As an only child myself, I have always been fascinated by my parents who both came from large families (my father was one of eight children) and by the lives of people who differed from me.

"My first two published books deal with the thinking and lives of two black men who were influential to their times: Banneker to the Revolutionary period and Martin Luther King, Jr., to the period of civil rights struggles in the South. These books were exciting to research, to uncover and develop as it has always been exciting for me to learn about other people's lives.

"But when I think of what I have always loved about writing and what has kept me enthralled with it since the fourth grade, it has been the ability to recall and spin the tales of my own experiences and those of the people I have known and grown up with. That I guess is why writing Journey All Alone was so easy for me because Mildren's life was so close to the life I knew so well."

HARRISON, (Thomas) Ross 1943-

PERSONAL: Born September 26, 1943, in Belfast, Northern Ireland; son of John Geoffrey (a university professor) and Patricia (a psychologist; maiden name, Foster) Harrison; married Gillian Davies, August 17, 1968; children: Sophie. *Education:* Cambridge University, B.A., 1964, Ph.D., 1968; Oxford University, graduate study, 1965-66. *Politics:* Labour. *Religion:* "Nothing orthodox." *Home:* 17 Hardwick St., Cambridge, England. *Office:* Department of Philosophy, King's College, Cambridge University, Cambridge, England.

CAREER: Cambridge University, St. John's College, Cambridge, England, research fellow, 1967-70; University of Bristol, Bristol, England, lecturer in philosophy, 1970-74; Cambridge University, King's College, lecturer in philosophy, 1975—. *Member:* Aristotelian Society.

WRITINGS: On What There Must Be, Oxford University Press, 1974.

WORK IN PROGRESS: Nineteenth Century British Philosophy.

* * *

HARTLEY, Livingston 1900-

PERSONAL: Born December 2, 1900, in Brookline, Mass.; son of Harry (a manufacturer) and Jane Elizabeth (Fletcher) Hartley; married Louise Harris Randolph, March 7, 1931; children: Charles Randolph, Robert Fletcher, Bettina Rathbone Hartley Tierney. *Education:* Harvard University, B.A., 1923, graduate study, 1923-24. *Politics:* Democrat (usually). *Religion:* Episcopalian. *Home:* 3122 O St. N.W., Washington, D.C. 20007. *Office:* Atlantic Council of the United States, 1616 H St. N.W., Washington, D.C. 20006.

CAREER: League of Nations Association, Geneva, Switzerland, member of U.S. delegation, 1925-27; U.S. Foreign Service, Washington, D.C., vice consul in London, England, Pernambuco, Brazil, and Buenos Aires, Argentina, 1928-33; author, 1933-40 and 1945-49; Atlantic Union Committee, member of board of directors, 1949-61; U.S. Citizens Commission on NATO, consultant, 1961-62; Atlantic Council of the United States, Washington, D.C., member of board of directors, 1963—. Member of board of directors of Committee to Defend America by Aiding the Allies, 1940-42. *Military service:* U.S. Navy, 1942-45; became lieutenant commander. *Member:* English-Speaking Union (member of board of directors of Washington, D.C. branch), Metropolitan Club (Washington, D.C.), Harvard Club (Boston and Washington), New Bedford Yacht Club.

WRITINGS: Is America Afraid?, Prentice-Hall, 1937; *Our Maginot Line: Defense of the Americas,* Carrick & Evans, 1939; *Yankee Viking,* Roland Neal Press, 1956; *Atlantic Challenge,* Oceana, 1965; *Looking Forward,* Branden Press, 1975. Contributor to magazines and newspapers.

SIDELIGHTS: Hartley "became interested in international security at Geneva following World War I. Tried to contribute toward it in the Foreign Service and subsequently in articles, books, and organizations. Continued to do so after World War II."

* * *

HARTMAN, Rhondda Evans 1934-

PERSONAL: Born April 6, 1934, in Taber, Alberta, Canada; daughter of Redvers Baden (a farmer) and Frances (a teacher; maiden name, Swennumson) Evans; married Richard Eugene Hartman (an attorney), May 29, 1958; children: Joseph, Claryss Nan, Rienne, Allison, Richard. *Education:* University of Alberta, B.Sc.R.N., 1956. *Religion:* Episcopalian. *Home:* 27 Martin Lane, Englewood, Colo. 80110.

CAREER: Red Deer Health Unit, Lacombe, Alberta, public health nurse, 1956-57; Reddy Memorial Hospital, Montreal, Quebec, nurse, 1957-58; childbirth educator for obstetrician and gynecologist in private practice, Englewood, Colo., 1959—. *Member:* International Childbirth Education Association, La Leche League International, American Academy of Husband Coached Childbirth.

WRITINGS: Exercises for True Natural Childbirth, Harper, 1975.

SIDELIGHTS: Rhondda Hartman has taught workshops for teachers of natural childbirth in California, New Jersey, New Mexico, Colorado, Alberta, and Ontario, and was an observer of Russian obstetrical care in Moscow in 1968. She met and married her husband in Europe. Since then she has travelled in Eastern Europe, Hawaii, Mexico, and Costa Rica.

* * *

HARTZLER, Daniel David 1941-

PERSONAL: Born August 21, 1941, in New Windsor, Md.; son of Byron E. (a mortician) and Thelma (Nusbaum) Hartzler; married Catharine Orr Reese (a mortician), August 11, 1962; children: Jeffrey Stuart, Sandra Lynn. *Education:* Temple University, A.A., 1960. *Politics:* Republican. *Religion:* United Methodist. *Home:* 104 Lambert Ave., New Windsor, Md. 21776. *Office:* D.D. Hartzler & Sons, 310 Church St., New Windsor, Md. 21776.

CAREER: D. D. Hartzler & Sons (funeral homes), New Windsor, Md., mortician, 1963—, president, 1970—. *Member:* National Funeral Director's Association, National Riflemens' Association, Company of Military Historians, Maryland State Funeral Director's Association, Maryland Arms Collectors' Association, Maryland Historical Society, Kentucky Rifle Association, Tri-County Funeral Director's Association (president, 1974-75), Ancient Free and Accepted Masons (master of Plymouth Lodge, 1969, 1971; grand director of ceremonies of Grand Lodge of Maryland, 1972).

WRITINGS: Arms Makers of Maryland, Shumway, 1976. Contributor to periodicals.

WORK IN PROGRESS: Marylanders in the Confederacy, completion expected in 1978.

SIDELIGHTS: Hartzler was an outstanding athlete in baseball, basketball, soccer, and track in college. His parents are excellent hunters, having killed ten bears between them. At an early age he developed an interest in antique weapons. Because weapons manufacturing in Maryland has been overlooked, he has concentrated his research on this state.

* * *

HARVEY, Jonathan 1939-

PERSONAL: Born May 3, 1939, in Sutton Coldfield, England; married Rosaleen Barry; children: Anna, Dominic. *Education:* University of Glasgow, Ph.D., 1964; studied at Princeton University, 1969-70; Cambridge University, M.A., 1971, D.Mus., 1972. *Home:* 25 Leigh Rd., Southampton, England.

CAREER: University of Southampton, Southampton, England, lecturer, 1964-72, senior lecturer in music, 1972—.

WRITINGS: The Music of Stockhausen: An Introduction, University of California Press, 1975. Composer of internationally performed music. Contributor to music journals.

BIOGRAPHICAL/CRITICAL SOURCES: Musical Times, September, 1968, July, 1975; *Music and Musicians,* spring, 1972, March, 1973.

* * *

HAUGH, Robert F(ulton) 1910-

PERSONAL: Born January 9, 1910, in Independence, Kan.; son of Frank A. and Alma (Harlow) Haugh; married Georgia Campbell (a librarian), August 30, 1941. *Education:* University of Kansas, A.B., 1936; University of Oklahoma, graduate study, 1939-40; University of Michigan, Ph.D., 1948. *Home:* 3090 Geddes Ave., Ann Arbor, Mich. 48104. *Office:* Department of English, University of Michigan, Ann Arbor, Mich. 48104.

CAREER: Rodeo performer and carnival worker during his early career; University of Michigan, Ann Arbor, instructor, 1947-48; assistant professor, 1949-56, associate professor, 1956-63, professor of English, 1963—, director of creative writing program, 1966-74. Member of board of governors, Associated Writing Programs, 1970-74. *Military service:* U.S. Navy, 1943-46; became lieutenant; received commendation ribbon and presidential unit citation. *Member:* Modern Language Association of America, Michigan Academy of Arts and Science, Phi Kappa Phi. *Awards, honors:* Jule and Avery Hopwood Award, 1947.

WRITINGS: Joseph Conrad: Discovery in Design, University of Oklahoma Press, 1957; *Nadine Gordimer: The Meticulous Vision,* Twayne, 1974. Contributor of articles to scholarly journals.

WORK IN PROGRESS: A critical study of Nathaniel Hawthorne.

* * *

HAUPT, Zygmunt 1907(?)-1975

1907(?)—May 10, 1975; Polish-born American civil servant, painter, and author of memoirs and stories on Polish life. Obituaries: *Washington Post,* May 16, 1975.

* * *

HAWKINS, John Noel 1944-

PERSONAL: Born May 18, 1944, in Sterling, Ill.; son of Noel James (a salesman) and Kathryn (Dennison) Hawkins; married Judith Ayami Takata (a graphic designer), August 12, 1967; children: Marisa Harumi, Larina Yasuko. *Education:* University of Hawaii, B.A. (with honors), 1967; University of British Columbia, M.A., 1969; George Peabody College for Teachers, Ph.D., 1972. *Home:* 1303 East Third St., Sterling, Ill. 61083. *Office:* Graduate School of Education, University of California at Los Angeles, 405 Hilgarde Ave., Los Angeles, Calif. 90024.

CAREER: Vanderbilt University, Nashville, Tenn., instructor in education and Asian studies, 1969-70; University of California, Los Angeles, professor of comparative education, 1973—. Visiting lecturer at University of Hawaii, 1968-69. *Member:* Comparative and International Education Society (secretary, 1975-77), American Educational Studies Association, Phi Delta Kappa.

WRITINGS: Educational Theory in the People's Republic of China: The Report of Chien Chu-jui, University of Hawaii Press, 1970; *Mao Tse-tung and Education: His Thoughts and Teachings,* Shoe String, 1973.

SIDELIGHTS: Hawkins has travelled to Japan, Hong Kong, and the People's Republic of China. He is competent in Chinese and Japanese.

* * *

HAY, Robert D(ean) 1921-

PERSONAL: Born November 17, 1921, in La Porte, Ind.; married, 1944; children: Sue Ann, Carol Lynn. *Education:* Attended University of Indiana, 1940-42; University of Oklahoma, B.S., 1949, M.B.A., 1950; Ohio State University, Ph.D., 1954; postdoctoral study at Williams College, 1957 and 1962, and at Carnegie Institute of Technology (now Carnegie-Mellon University), 1963. *Home:* 740 Huntsville Rd., Fayetteville, Ark. 72701. *Office:* College of Business Administration, University of Arkansas, Fayetteville, Ark. 72701.

CAREER: University of Arkansas, Fayetteville, instructor, 1949-51, assistant professor, 1951-55, associate professor, 1955-59, professor of management, 1959—, chairman of department, 1955-74. Certified public accountant by American Institute of Accountants, 1949; instructor at Ohio State University, 1952-54. Consultant to business and industry. *Military service:* U.S. Army Air Forces, 1942-47; became captain. U.S. Air Force Reserve, 1947-71; became lieutenant colonel.

MEMBER: International Communications Association, American Business Communications Association (fellow; president, 1967), Society for the Advancement of Management, American Business Communication Association, National Society for Programmed Instruction, Academy of Management, Ozarks Economic Association, Southern Case Research Association, Southwest Management Association, Arkansas College Teachers of Economics and Business, Beta Gamma Sigma, Delta Pi Epsilon (charter member of Sigma chapter), Beta Alpha Psi, Sigma Iota Epsilon, Phi Eta Sigma. *Awards, honors:* Ford Foundation fellowships, 1957, 1962, for study at Williams College; grant from Southern Case Research Association, 1960-61, to study small business; plaque of recognition from American Numismatics Association, 1965.

WRITINGS: (Contributor) J. K. Lasser, editor, *Standard Handbook for Accountants,* McGraw, 1956; (with Raymond V. Lesikar) *Business Report Writing,* Irwin, 1957; *Managerial Staffing and Training Problems of Arkansas Sawmills* (monograph), Industrial Research and Extension Center, University of Arkansas, 1961; (contributor) Merwyn Hargrove, Ike Harrison, and Gene Swearingen, editors, *Business Policy Cases,* Irwin, 1963; (contributor) John Champion and Francis J. Bridges, editors, *Critical Incidents in Management,* Irwin, 1963; *Written Communications for Business Administrators,* Holt, 1965; (contributor) Frank Greenwood, editor, *Casebook for Management and Business Policy: A Systems Approach,* International Textbook Co., 1967; *Introduction to Business,* with instructor's manual, Holt, 1968, programmed instruction workbook, 1969; (contributor) H. N. Groom, editor, *Business Policy and Strategic Action,* Prentice-Hall, 1969; (contributor) Joseph L. Massie and Warren Haynes, editors, *Management: Analysis, Concepts, and Cases,* Prentice-Hall, 1969; (contributor) Preston Le Breton, editor, *New Issues and Directions in Business Administration,*

Southwestern Publishing, 1969; (with Ed Gray and James Gates) *Business and Society: Text and Cases,* Southwestern Publishing, 1976. Contributor of about forty articles to business and economics journals.

AVOCATIONAL INTERESTS: Golf, art collecting (specializing in Indian art in all media).

* * *

HAYDON, A(lbert) Eustace 1880-1975

January 17, 1880—April 1, 1975; Canadian-born minister, educator, and author of books on religion. Obituaries: *New York Times,* April 2, 1975.

* * *

HAYS, Helen Ireland 1903-

PERSONAL: Born February 7, 1903, in Johnstown, N.Y.; daughter of James Stuart (a glove manufacturer) and Anna (Stewart) Ireland; married Douglas Hays, June 23, 1928; children: James Douglas, Helen. *Education:* Wellesley College, B.A., 1925. *Politics:* Republican. *Religion:* Christian. *Home:* 108 South William St., Johnstown, N.Y. 12095; (summers) Canada Lake, N.Y. 12030.

CAREER: English teacher in public schools in Johnstown, N.Y., 1925-27; writer, 1958—. *Member:* Pen and Brush Club (New York, N.Y.), Albany County Poetry Society, League of Women Voters, Red Cross (local chapter).

WRITINGS: The Strawberry Stone (poetry), Golden Quill, 1966; *Roots* (poetry), Golden Quill, 1972.

WORK IN PROGRESS: Yarns Spun in Fulton County, completion expected about 1977; interviews with an artist.

SIDELIGHTS: Helen Hays writes: "I am a strong conservationist. Also much interested in people of other countries who have come here—first and second generation Americans." *Avocational interests:* European travel, painting.

* * *

HEALEY, Robert (Mathieu) 1921-

PERSONAL: Born June 1, 1921, in New York, N.Y.; son of James Christopher (a chaplain to seamen) and Catherine (Mathieu) Healey; married Edith L. Welle (a librarian), June 20, 1953; children: Paul D. *Education:* Princeton University, B.A., 1942; Yale University, M.F.A., 1947, B.D., 1955, M.A., 1956, Ph.D., 1959. *Politics:* Democrat. *Home:* 2005 Simpson St., Dubuque, Iowa 52001. *Office:* Theological Seminary, University of Dubuque, 2570 Asbury Rd., Dubuque, Iowa 52001.

CAREER: Mercerburg Academy, Mercerburg, Pa., instructor in English, 1942-44; Rensselaer Polytechnic Institute, Troy, N.Y., instructor in English, 1948-52; New Haven Council of Churches, New Haven, Conn., director of radio and television, 1954-56; ordained Presbyterian minister, 1956; University of Dubuque, Dubuque, Iowa, associate professor of communications at Theological Seminary, 1956-63, associate professor of church history, 1963-66, professor of church history, 1966—, chairman of Division of Theology and History, 1968-70, interim academic dean, 1970-71. Theologian-in-residence at American Church in Paris, 1965-66; member of advisory board of Dubuque Area Sheltered Workshop, 1972-73; member of advisory committee of America-Holy Land Project, of Hebrew University (Jerusalem) and Jewish Historical Society, 1973-75.

MEMBER: American Academy of Religion, American Society for Church History, Presbyterian Historical Society, Religious Education Association, Society for the Scientific Study of Religion, Ecumenical Theological Research Fraternity (Israel), Association of Faculty and Theological Education Professionals of the Theological Seminary of the University of Dubuque (president, 1972-73, 1975-76). *Awards, honors:* Faculty fellowships from American Association of Theological Schools, 1957-58, for work on *Jefferson on Religion in Public Education,* and 1965-66 for work on *The French Achievement;* resident scholar at Ecumenical Institute for Advanced Theological Studies (Jerusalem), 1973-74, to work on "Concepts of the Jew in the History of American Christian Thought."

WRITINGS: Jefferson on Religion in Public Education, Yale University Press, 1962; *The French Achievement: Private School Aid, A Lesson for America,* Paulist-Newman, 1974.

Author of "Nobody Knows" (one-act play; first produced on WNHC-TV, April, 1954), Baker Plays, 1958. Contributor to theology and church journals. Editorial consultant for *Journal of the Scientific Study of Religion* and the monograph series of the American Academy of Religion; member of editorial board, *Presbyterian Outlook,* 1976.

WORK IN PROGRESS: Research on concepts of the Jew in the history of American Christian thought.

SIDELIGHTS: Healey writes: "A major factor in my intellectual development during the last fifteen years has been the Christian ecumenical movement. Ours is the first (and probably still the only) Protestant theological faculty to move under a Catholic seminary roof, sharing all the facilities of a Dominican school. The consequent intellectual interchange has been stimulating and enlightening and the resulting friendships delightful." *Avocational interests:* Good cuisine (French and Middle Eastern cooking).

* * *

HEALY, Sister Kathleen

PERSONAL: Education: Carlow College, B.A.; University of Pittsburgh, M.A.; University of Wisconsin, Ph.D. *Home and office:* Carlow College, Pittsburgh, Pa. 15213.

CAREER: Roman Catholic religious of Congregation of Sisters of Mercy; former director of Academia Catolica, San Juan, P.R.; Carlow College, Pittsburgh, Pa., professor and chairman of department of English, 1955-76. *Member:* International Poetry Forum (member of board of directors), Modern Language Association of America, National Council of Teachers of English, Theta Sigma Chi, Delta Epsilon Sigma, Lambda Iota Tau.

WRITINGS: (With Adrian van Kaam) *The Demon and the Dove: Personality Growth through Literature,* Duquesne University Press, 1967; *Frances Warde: American Founder of the Sisters of Mercy,* Seabury, 1974. Contributor to *Hispania, Poet Lore, Catholic World, Humanitas,* and other journals.

BIOGRAPHICAL/CRITICAL SOURCES: Commonweal, October 20, 1967; *Christian Century,* March 27, 1968.

* * *

HEATON, Eric William 1920-

PERSONAL: Born October 15, 1920, in England; son of Robert William and Ella Mabel (Brear) Heaton; married Rachel Mary Dodd, 1951; children: Jeremy, Anne, Josephine, Nicholas. *Education:* Christ's College, Cambridge, M.A. *Home:* The Deanery, Durham, England.

CAREER: Ordained priest of Church of England, 1945. Cambridge University, Cambridge, England, Bishop of Derby's chaplain, 1946-53, Gonville and Caius College, chaplain, 1945-46, dean and fellow, 1946-53, tutor, 1951-53; Salisbury Cathedral, Salisbury, England, canon residentiary, 1953-60, chancellor, 1956-60; Oxford University, St. John's College, Oxford, England, fellow, tutor in theology, and chaplain, 1960-74, chairman of council of Headington School, 1968-74, and moderator of general ordination examination, 1971—; Dean of Durham, Durham, England, 1974—. Examining chaplain to Bishop of Portsmouth, 1947-74, Bishop of Salisbury, 1949-64, Archbishop of York, 1951-56, Bishop of Norwich, 1960-71, Bishop of Wakefield, 1961-74, and Bishop of Rochester, 1962-74; select preacher at Cambridge, 1948, 1958, and at Oxford, 1958-59, 1967, 1971.

WRITINGS: His Servants the Prophets, S.C.M. Press, 1949, revised and enlarged edition published as *The Old Testament Prophets,* Pelican, 1958; *The Book of Daniel,* S.C.M. Press, 1965; *Everyday Life in Old Testament Times,* Scribner, 1956; *Commentary on the Sunday Lessons,* Longmans, Green, 1957; *The Hebrew Kingdoms,* Oxford University Press, 1968; *Solomon's New Men: The Emergence of Ancient Israel As a National State,* University Books, 1974. Contributor to theological journals.

* * *

HEATON, Rose Henniker   1884-1975

1884—October, 1975; British poet and author. Obituaries: *AB Bookman's Weekly,* December 22-29, 1975.

* * *

HEDLEY, (Gladys) Olwen   1912-

PERSONAL: Born April 28, 1912, in London, England; daughter of Osborne Janion and Sarah Gladys Patricia (Shelby Jones) Hedley. *Home:* 15 Denny Crescent, London S.E. 11, England. *Agent:* John Johnson, 10 Suffield House, 79 Davies St., London W.1, England.

CAREER: Windsor, Slough and Eton Express (Berkshire County newspaper), Windsor, England, member of editorial staff and editor of women's page, 1932-39; British Red Cross, assistant organizer of hospitals library and V.A.D. nurse in Windsor, during World War II and until 1947; Royal Library, Windsor Castle, Windsor, part-time assistant, 1948-52, librarian, research assistant, and member of Her Majesty's Household, 1952-64. *Member:* Royal Society of Literature (fellow).

WRITINGS: Round and About Windsor and District, Oxley & Son, 1948, revised edition, 1950; *Windsor Castle,* International Publications Service, 1967; *Buckingham Palace,* Pitkin Pictorials, 1968, published as *The Pictorial History of Buckingham Palace,* British Book Centre, 1974; *Fountains Hall,* Pitkin Pictorials, 1968; *City of London,* Pitkin Pictorials, 1969, published as *London in Pictures,* British Book Centre, 1974; *Charles, Twenty-First Prince of Wales,* Pitkin Pictorials, 1969; *"Mayflower" and the Pilgrim Fathers,* Pitkin Pictorials, 1970; *Cambridge: The City and The Colleges,* Pitkin Pictorials, 1971; *Hampton Court Palace,* Pitkin Pictorials, 1971; *Prisoners in the Tower,* Pitkin Pictorials, 1972; *Royal Places,* R. Hale, 1972; *Queen Charlotte,* John Murray, 1975; *The Princes of Wales,* Pitkin Pictorials, 1975; *Kensington Palace,* Pitkin Pictorials, in press; *The Tower of London,* Pitkin Pictorials, in press. Contributor of historical articles to *The Times* (London), *Berkshire Archaeological Journal, Report of the Society of the Friends of St. George's and the Descendants of the Knights of the Garter, Homes and Gardens,* and *History Today.*

WORK IN PROGRESS: The Old Royal Household, for John Murray; *Number 10 Downing Street,* for Pitkin Pictorials.

SIDELIGHTS: Miss Hedley was a resident of Windsor Castle for 16 years, the same castle where 100 years earlier Sir John Owen, one of her Welsh ancestors, was imprisoned with King Charles I during the civil war. She told *CA* that "a collateral ancestor was General Isaac Shelby, who took a prominent part on the American side in the War of Independence, became first governor of Kentucky and was, I believe, honoured by having Shelbyville in Indiana named after him."

* * *

HEFFERN, Richard   1950-

PERSONAL: Born July 24, 1950, in Orange, Calif.; son of Frank S. (a restaurant owner) and Mary Claire (Dominguez) Heffern; married Matilde Lopez (a secondary school teacher), August 21, 1971. *Education:* Attended Fullerton College, 1968-71, and California State University, Fullerton. *Home:* 21147 Esperanza Rd., Anaheim, Calif. 92807.

CAREER: Laboratory technician in Orange, Calif., 1971—; writer. *Member:* Institute for Biological and Botanical Research, Inland Herb Society, Herb Trade Association.

WRITINGS: The Herb Buyer's Guide, Pyramid Publications, 1973; *Secrets of the Mind-Altering Plants of Mexico,* Pyramid Publications, 1974; *The Use of Herbs in Weight Reduction,* Pyramid Publications, 1975; *Ginseng,* Celestial Arts, 1976; (editor) *Advanced Treatise in Herbology,* CSA Press and Trinity Center Press, 1976.

WORK IN PROGRESS: Time Travel: Myth or Reality; research on the uses of herbs in medicine, magic, and ritual by cultures throughout the world.

AVOCATIONAL INTERESTS: Metaphysics, eastern religions.

* * *

HEGEMAN, Elizabeth Blair   1942-

PERSONAL: Born March 28, 1942, in Glen Cove, N.Y.; daughter of George D. (an engineer) and Bonnie (Blair) Hegeman; married Daniel Zwanziger, June 6, 1969 (divorced, November, 1970). *Education:* Radcliffe College, B.A. (magna cum laude), 1963; Columbia University, M.A., 1965; New York University, Ph.D., 1974; W. A. White Institute for Psychoanalysis, Psychotherapy, and Psychology, candidate for certificate. *Home:* 100 Riverside Dr., New York, N.Y. 10024. *Office:* Department of Psychology, John Jay College of Criminal Justice of the City University of New York, 445 West 59th St., New York, N.Y. 10019.

CAREER: Anthropological field work in Colombia, 1962, 1964; Peace Corps, Washington, D.C., lecturer, 1963-64; Manhattan Veteran's Hospital, Manhattan, N.Y., intern, 1965; Children's Hospital, Boston, Mass., research assistant, 1966; John Jay College of the City University of New York, New York, N.Y., assistant professor of counseling and anthropology, 1967—. *Member:* American Psychological Association, Society for Cross-Cultural Research in Psychology, Harry Stack Sullivan Society.

WRITINGS: (With Leonard Kooperman) *Anthropology and Community Action,* Doubleday-Anchor, 1974. Contributor of book reviews to *New York Times.*

WORK IN PROGRESS: A book on the implications of interpersonal psychoanalytic theory for cross-cultural research; articles; research on structuralism and perception.

* * *

HEIFERMAN, Ronald Ian 1941-

PERSONAL: Born August 12, 1941, in New York, N.Y.; son of Benjamin and Sylvia (Perlhof) Heiferman; married Sandra Green, May 26, 1963; children: Brian, Wendy, Kimberly. *Education:* Brooklyn College of the City University of New York, B.A., 1963; Yale University, M.A., 1966; New York University, Ph.D., 1976. *Home:* 21 Meadow Circle Rd., Branford, Conn. 06405. *Office:* Department of History, Quinnipiac College, Hamden, Conn. 06518.

CAREER: Central Connecticut State College, New Britain, visiting assistant professor of Asian studies, 1965-66; Connecticut College, New London, instructor in history, 1966-67; Quinnipiac College, Hamden, Conn., instructor, 1967-68, assistant professor, 1968-71, associate professor of history, 1971—. Fellow at National Library of the Philippines, summer, 1971; visiting scholar at Hoover Institution on War, Revolution and Peace, summer, 1975. *Member:* Association of Asian Studies, Asia Society, Japan Society (New York).

WRITINGS: Air War in China: Chennault and the Flying Tigers, Ballantine, 1971; *World War II,* Octopus, 1973; *Wars of the Twentieth Century,* Octopus, 1975.

Contributor: A.J.P. Taylor, editor, *History of the Twentieth Century,* British Publishing Co., 1970; Basil Liddell-Hart, editor, *History of the First World War,* British Publishing Co., 1973; Sydney L. Mayer, editor, *History of the Second World War,* Phoebus Books, 1974; Warren Lerner, editor, *Essays on Socialism,* Center for International Studies, Duke University, 1976.

* * *

HEIN, Eleanor C(harlotte) 1933-

PERSONAL: Born February 18, 1933, in Racine, Wis.; daughter of Edward (a laborer) and Olga (Kihntopf) Hein. *Education:* Marquette University, B.S., 1954; University of Wisconsin—Milwaukee, graduate study, 1962; University of Colorado, M.S., 1965. *Religion:* Lutheran. *Residence:* San Francisco, Calif. *Office:* School of Nursing, University of San Francisco, Cowell Hall, San Francisco, Calif. 94117.

CAREER: New York Hospital, Payne-Whitney Clinic, New York, N.Y., staff nurse, 1954-56; Mount Zion Hospital, San Francisco, Calif., assistant head nurse, 1956-61; Milwaukee Psychiatric Hospital, Milwaukee, Wis., head nurse, 1961-63; University of Oregon, Portland, instructor in nursing, 1965-67; University of San Francisco, San Francisco, Calif., assistant professor, 1967-73, associate professor of nursing, 1973—. *Member:* American Nurses Association, Health Sciences Communications Association, San Francisco Mental Health Association.

WRITINGS: Communications in Nursing Practice, Little, Brown, 1973.

AVOCATIONAL INTERESTS: Opera, theater, travel, painting, photography, reading.

HEIN, Norvin 1914-

PERSONAL: Born August 19, 1914, in East Canton, Ohio; son of Oscar George (a farmer) and Nova E. (Foltz) Hein; married Mary Jeanne Swaller, June 22, 1951 (died, 1957); married Jeanne Humphreys, June 20, 1959; children: (first marriage) Elisabeth, Christopher; (second marriage) Margaret Jeanne. *Education:* College of Wooster, B.A., 1937; Yale University, B.D., 1946, Ph.D., 1951. *Politics:* Democrat. *Religion:* United Church of Christ. *Home:* 6 Tuttle Rd., Bethany, Conn. 06525. *Office:* 224 Sterling Divinity Quadrangle, Yale University, 409 Prospect St., New Haven, Conn. 06510.

CAREER: Ewing Christian College, Allahabad, India, teacher of English, 1939-42; with Army Young Men's Christian Association of India, 1943-44; Yale University, New Haven, Conn., instructor, 1950-52, assistant professor, 1952-58, associate professor, 1958-75, professor of comparative religion, 1975—. Past member of Hamden (Conn.) City Council. *Military service:* U.S. Merchant Marine, 1944. U.S. Maritime Service, 1944-45. *Member:* American Society for the Study of Religion (president, 1975—), American Oriental Society, Association for Asian Studies, Royal Asiatic Society (London), Connecticut Forest and Park Association (member of board of directors, 1968-72), Phi Beta Kappa. *Awards, honors:* Fulbright grant, 1964-65.

WRITINGS: The Miracle Plays of Mathura, Yale University Press, 1972.

Contributor: Milton Singer, editor, *Traditional India: Structure and Change,* American Folklore Society (Philadelphia), 1959; Charles J. Adams, editor, *A Reader's Guide to the Great Religions,* Free Press, 1965, 2nd revised edition, in press; C. J. Bleeker, G. Widengren, and E. J. Sharpe, editors, *Proceedings of the Twelfth International Congress for the History of Religions,* E. J. Brill, 1975.

WORK IN PROGRESS: Yoga in the Bhagavadgita; The Image of the Greek in Indian Literature; Early Christian Views of Gentile Religions.

SIDELIGHTS: Hein writes: "As a young teacher of English literature in an Indian college I became interested first in my Indian students, then in their Indian religions. I continue to see the study of eastern religions as an aspect of the struggle to understand eastern peoples, and to see our failings in religious understanding as an important part of our limitations in journalism and foreign policy."

* * *

HEINTZ, Ann Christine 1930-

PERSONAL: Born July 25, 1930, in Blue Island, Ill.; daughter of Fred H. (a sales representative and buyer) and Hazel (Hobbs) Heintz. *Education:* Mundelein College, B.A., 1952; Marquette University, M.A., 1962. *Politics:* "Independent; member of 'Network,' national religious women's lobby for social justice." *Home:* 7064 North Damen, Chicago, Ill. 60645. *Office:* St. Mary's Center for Learning, 2044 West Grenshaw, Chicago, Ill. 60612.

CAREER: Roman Catholic nun, entered Sisters of Charity, Beata Virgo Maria (means Blessed Virgin Mary), 1952; high school teacher in parochial schools in Clinton, Iowa, 1955-65, and Cedar Rapids, Iowa, 1966-68; St. Mary's Center for Learning (high school), Chicago, Ill., teacher of journalism and developer of media program, 1968—. Summer instructor at St. Cloud State College, 1968-71, and University of Minnesota, 1972-73. Member of Robert F.

Kennedy Commission of Inquiry into High School Journalism; member of national communication committee of the U.S. Catholic Conference.

MEMBER: Journalism Education Association, UNDA-USA, Women in Communications, Inc., National Association for Media Action, American Film Institute, National Association of Women Religious. *Awards, honors:* Carl Towley Award from Journalism Education Association, 1967, for contributions to journalism education; centennial award from Academy of Our Lady, 1974; named journalism teacher of the year by newspaper fund of *Wall Street Journal,* 1971; Ford Foundation grant, 1974-76, to study the potential role of popular television programs in the learning process; Maxi Award from *Media and Methods,* 1975, for *Mass Media.*

WRITINGS: Persuasion, Loyola University Press, 1970, revised edition, 1974; (with Elizabeth Conley and Lawrence Reuter) *Mass Media,* Loyola University Press, 1972; (contributor) *Captive Voices,* Schocken, 1974; (with Patricia Fitzgerald and Margaret Fieweger) *Independent Learning,* Ginn, 1975; (with Elaine Schuster and Lester Angene) *Experiencing,* Ginn, 1975; (with Schuster and Arlene Larson) *Explaining,* Ginn, 1975; (with Schuster and Isidore Levine) *Analysing,* Ginn, 1975; (with Schuster and Florence Nolte) *Organizing,* Ginn, 1975; (with Schuster and John Ashmead) *Synthesizing,* Ginn, 1975; (with Schuster and Bernard McCabe) *Recognizing,* Ginn, 1975.

Author and producer of television videotapes "What If?" on alternative education, and "To Know Ourselves," for National Council of Teachers of English. Contributor to religious publications and literature journals. Associate editor of *Communication: Journalism Education Today.*

WORK IN PROGRESS: Directing a project to study the potential role of popular television programs in the learning process.

SIDELIGHTS: Ann Heintz writes: "The Kennedy Commission experience could have been demoralizing were it not for the spirit of the members themselves. I knew that the situation in schools around the country would not be good; I knew that censorship and general distrust of students prevailed, but I did not think that I would ever hear as much naivety, insensitivity and cowardice as I did . . . I'd like to think that our work may make a big difference even if I'm not likely to have the pervasive tools to really evaluate the results in school after school across the country.

"I spent my early teaching years in a setting with elementary school teachers where I had an opportunity to observe children in the primary grades. I was appalled at the difference between the six-year-old and the adolescent from the standpoint of creativity, self-direction, and initiative—all of which seemed driven out of the child in ten years. That single realization has shaped my writing, my teaching, and my militancy. . . . It is my hope . . . that high schools are now ready to let students examine the learning process, evaluate their growth and become masters of their own fate."

*   *   *

HEINZ, William Frederick   1899-

PERSONAL: Born August 10, 1899, in Greymouth, New Zealand; son of Emil Philip and Emma Louise Heinz. *Education:* Educated in secondary school in Greymouth, New Zealand. *Home:* 94 Husley St., Flat 4, Christchurch, New Zealand.

CAREER: Plumber in the family firm, 1918-32; sound engineer in Westrex Theatre, 1932-41; New Zealand Radio Corp., Wellington, radio engineer, 1941-43; Ministry of Supply, South Westland, New Zealand, manager of mica mine, 1944-45; theatre engineer in Christchurch, New Zealand, 1946-48; in the electronics business in Christchurch, 1948-52; Christchurch Drainage Board, Christchurch, head of trade waste department, 1952-68; writer, 1968—. Has given broadcast talks. Member of regional committee of Westland Historic Places Trust.

WRITINGS: Prospecting for Gold, Pegasus, 1952, 5th edition, 1975; *The Story of Shantytown,* Pegasus, 1972; (compiler) *Bright Fine Gold: Stories of the New Zealand Gold Fields,* A. H. & A. W. Reed, 1974. Editor of "Men of the West" series for Christchurch Press, 1973—.

WORK IN PROGRESS: New Zealand's Last Goldrush: Kumara; A Gold Digger's Scrap Book, an autobiography, for A. H. & A. W. Reed.

SIDELIGHTS: Heinz writes: "The importance of the Gold Rush in New Zealand from 1861 had a remarkable impact on the settlement of the colony. It is only now that we are beginning to realise the implications of the mixing of the peoples of many European and Asian countries, not forgetting the Australian and Californian gold miners, who as prospector explorers added many Place Names to New Zealand." Heinz has explored most of the geologically interesting parts of New Zealand and, as a mountaineer, has to his credit several first ascents of alpine peaks. He has carried out field research on the West Coast gold drifts, prospecting and advisory work on the antimony lode at Endeavour Inlet, research into the rarer metals, and prospecting for radioactive rocks and gem stones.

BIOGRAPHICAL/CRITICAL SOURCES: Christchurch Press, October 11, 1975.

*   *   *

HEISERMAN, David L(ee)   1940-

PERSONAL: Born July 11, 1940, in Fostoria, Ohio; son of Leland H. (a laborer) and Maudine (Needles) Heiserman; married Judith Hopewell, February 5, 1965; children: Paul. *Education:* Attended Ohio State University, 1961-67; *Politics:* Conservative Republican. *Religion:* "Fundamentalist Christian." *Home:* 1814 Walden Dr., Columbus, Ohio 43229.

CAREER: Franklin University, Columbus, Ohio, instructor in electronics and mathematics, 1969-74; Ohio Institute of Technology, Columbus, associate professor of electronics and mathematics, 1974—. Consulting engineer on technical education systems. *Military service:* U.S. Navy, 1958-61.

WRITINGS: Handbook of Small Appliance Troubleshooting and Repair, Prentice-Hall, 1974; *Radio Astronomy for the Amateur,* TAB Books, 1975; *Major Appliance Troubleshooting and Repair,* Prentice-Hall, in press; *Commercial Radio Systems,* Prentice-Hall, in press; *Robotics for the Amateur,* TAB Books, in press. Contributor of about sixty articles to electronics and science journals.

WORK IN PROGRESS: Computer Systems for the Amateur, for TAB Books.

SIDELIGHTS: Heiserman writes: "I suppose I would be considered a science and technical writer; however I want to do more than simply interpret things of science for the general reading public. . . . My book on radio astronomy . . . not only explains what radio astronomy is and how to build a radio telescope—it also tells the amateur experimenter how he can carry out some sophisticated projects that have a great deal of potential value as far as professional radio astronomy is concerned.

"Every non-fiction book should have an impact upon the reader's life and way of thinking—it is far more important to build positive attitudes and motivate a reader to action than it is to feed him facts."

*   *   *

HELLEN, J(ohn) A(nthony)   1935-

PERSONAL: Born May 12, 1935, in Bodmin, Cornwall, England; son of John Hedley (a company director) and Gladys Irene (Woodward) Hellen; married Ingeborg Friederike, August 8, 1959; children: Christopher, Ulrike, Nicholas, Sigrid, Timothy. *Education:* University of Oxford, B.A., 1959, M.A., 1963; University of Bonn, Dr.Phil., 1964. *Religion:* Anglican. *Home:* Trenance House, Lintzford Rd., Rowlands Gill, Tyne and Wear, England. *Office:* Department of Geography, University of Newcastle upon Tyne, Newcastle upon Tyne, England.

CAREER: British Colonial Service, district officer in Northern Rhodesia, 1959-62; University of Newcastle upon Tyne, Newcastle upon Tyne, England, lecturer in geography, 1964—. *Military service:* Royal Navy, 1953-55; became sub-lieutenant. *Member:* Royal Geographical Society (fellow), Institute of British Geographers, African Studies Association of United Kingdom. *Awards, honors:* Leverhulme European studies fellowship, 1975-76.

WRITINGS: Rural Economic Development in Zambia, 1890-1964, IFO Institute for Economic Research (Munich), 1968; *North Rhine-Westphalia,* Oxford University Press, 1974.

Translator with wife, I. F. Hellen: Helmut Kanter, *Libya: A Geomedical Monograph,* Springer Verlag, 1967; Ludolph Fischer, *Afghanistan: A Geomedical Monograph,* Springer Verlag, 1968; K. F. Schaller and W. Kuls, *Ethiopia: A Geomedical Monograph,* Springer Verlag, 1972; Manfred Domroes, *The Agroclimate of Ceylon,* Franz Steiner Verlag, 1974.

Contributor of articles to journals, including *Agricultural History Review, Erdkunde,* and *International Affairs.* Editor of "Research Series" for Department of Geography, University of Newcastle upon Tyne, 1974. Consulting editor, *Erdkunde,* 1975—.

WORK IN PROGRESS: A book on tropical geography, and a book on German regional planning.

AVOCATIONAL INTERESTS: Classical music making, mountaineering, scouting.

*   *   *

HELLER, Mark   1914-

PERSONAL: Born November 15, 1914, in Wallasey, England; son of Ernest and Phyllis (Ball) Heller; married K. Elaine Rymer (a physician), February 13, 1946; children: Robert, Michael, Jane, David. *Education:* Attended University of Zurich, 1931-34; Cambridge University, M.A. (honors), 1939. *Home:* 26 Prenton Lane, Birkenhead, Merseyside L42 8LB, England. *Agent:* A. P. Watt & Son, 26-28 Bedford Row, London W.C.2, England.

CAREER: Journalist and travel writer. *Military service:* British Army, 1939-46; became major. *Member:* Ski Club of Great Britain, Swiss Alpine Club, Alpine Club.

WRITINGS: (Editor with Malcolm N. H. Milne) *Book of European Skiing,* Holt, 1966; (with Milne) *Teach Yourself Skiing,* Oxford University Press, 1968; *Ski,* Faber, 1969, Transatlantic, 1970; *All About Skiing,* Hamlyn, 1969; *Ski Guide Austria,* Quartet, 1973; *Skiing,* Crowell, 1975. Winter sports correspondent for *Guardian.* Contributor to skiing magazines.

WORK IN PROGRESS: Encyclopaedia of Skiing and the Other Wintersports, publication by Rainbird expected about 1977.

*   *   *

HELMERS, (George) Dow   1906-

PERSONAL: Born March 26, 1906, in Colorado Springs, Colo.; son of Frank and Jessie Helmers; married; children: three daughters. *Education:* Attended Colorado College, two years. *Politics:* Independent. *Religion:* Protestant. *Home:* 3030 Leslie Dr., Colorado Springs, Colo.

CAREER: Retired from business.

WRITINGS: Historic Alpine Tunnel, Sage Books, 1963, 2nd edition, Swallow Press, 1971; *Tragedy at Eden,* Swallow Press, 1971.

WORK IN PROGRESS: Revised editions of booklets originally published by Denver & Rio Grande Railway.

*   *   *

HELMHOLZ, R(ichard) H(enry)   1940-

PERSONAL: Born July 1, 1940, in Pasadena, Calif.; son of Lindsay (a professor) and Alice (Bean) Helmholz. *Education:* Princeton University, A.B., 1962; Harvard University, LL.B., 1965; University of California, Berkeley, Ph.D., 1970. *Religion:* Episcopalian. *Home:* 353 Westgate, St. Louis, Mo. 63130. *Office:* Washington University School of Law, St. Louis, Mo. 63130.

CAREER: Washington University, School of Law, St. Louis, Mo., professor of law and history, 1970—. *Member:* American Society for Legal History, Selden Society, University Club of St. Louis.

WRITINGS: Marriage Litigation in Medieval England, Cambridge University Press, 1974. Contributor to *Law Quarterly Review, American Journal of Legal History,* and other journals in his field.

WORK IN PROGRESS: Cases on Defamation, 1300-1600.

*   *   *

HEMESATH, Caroline   1899-

PERSONAL: Surname is pronounced *Hem*-sat; born July 28, 1899, in Ossian, Iowa; daughter of William Frank (a farmer) and Catherine (Bohr) Hemesath. *Education:* St. Xavier College, Chicago, Ill., B.A., 1937; Catholic University of America, M.A., 1943; further graduate study at University of Iowa. *Home:* Immaculate Conception Convent, 1001 Davis Ave., Dubuque, Iowa 52001. *Office:* Mount St. Francis, Windsor Extension, Dubuque, Iowa 52001.

CAREER: Roman Catholic nun, entered Order of the Sisters of St. Francis of the Holy Family, 1916; teacher of music at parochial schools in Iowa and Ill., 1919-56; Briar Cliff College, Sioux City, Iowa, member of faculty of history and German, 1956-68, professor emeritus, 1967—, manager of college book store, 1956-68; Immaculate Conception Convent, Dubuque, Iowa, teacher of music, 1968-

74; Mount St. Francis, Dubuque, Iowa, translator and assistant archivist, 1974-75; writer, 1975—.

WRITINGS: (Translator from German) Karl Hoermann, *Peace and Modern War in the Judgement of the Church,* Newman, 1966; (translator from German) Theodore Kampmann, *The Year of the Church,* Newman, 1966; *From Slave to Priest,* Franciscan Herald Press, 1973. Contributor to Roman Catholic magazines.

WORK IN PROGRESS: Good Father Gus, a juvenile edition of *From Slave to Priest;* an autobiography; a biography of Father Joseph Eckert; a history of Corpus Christi parish.

SIDELIGHTS: Sister Caroline writes: "I have a very deep interest in the Black people. Negro heroes need to be brought to the fore ... I feel keenly that the Church is so slow in its attention to the needs of the Blacks and was so negligent in the past. I would like to see *From Slave to Priest* filmed as people do not take kindly to reading about this subject."

* * *

HEMMING, Roy 1928-
(Buzz Hamilton)

PERSONAL: Born May 27, 1928, in Hamden, Conn.; son of Benjamin Whitney (in cutlery manufacturing) and Anna (Sexton) Hemming. *Education:* Yale University, B.A., 1949; University of Geneva, graduate study, 1950; Stanford University, M.A., 1951. *Politics:* Independent Republican. *Home:* 1433 Boulevard, New Haven, Conn. 06511. *Office:* Whitney Communications, 150 East 58th St., New York, N.Y. 10022.

CAREER: New Haven Journal-Courier, New Haven, Conn., reporter, 1947; WAVZ-Radio, New Haven, Conn., news editor later program director, 1948-50; Voice of America, New York, N.Y., writer, 1951-52; free-lance writer, 1952-53; National Broadcasting Corp. (NBC), New York, N.Y., researcher in news film library, 1953; Scholastic Magazines, Inc., New York, N.Y., writer, 1954-57, news editor, 1958, music and record columnist, 1959-75, managing editor of *Senior Scholastic,* 1959, editor, 1960-72, editor of *World Week,* 1965-68, executive editor of social studies books and magazines, including *Senior Scholastic, World Week,* and *Junior Scholastic,* 1968-72, editor-at-large and director of publications for Scholastic International, 1972-75; Whitney Communications, New York, N.Y., editor-in-chief of *Retirement Living,* 1975—. Member of pre-selection committee for Montreux International Record Award, 1971—. Member of board of directors of Eastern Music Festival, 1969—. *Military service:* U.S. Naval Reserve, active duty, 1945-46.

MEMBER: Overseas Press Club, Deadline Club, Commonwealth Club of California, Yale Club (New York, N.Y.), Sigma Delta Chi. *Awards, honors:* North Carolina All-America Award from Educational Press Association of America, 1968 and 1969.

WRITINGS: Discovering Music: Where to Start on Records and Tapes, the Great Composers and Their Works, Today's Major Recording Artists (for young people), Four Winds, 1974. Contributor to magazines and newspapers, sometimes under pseudonym Buzz Hamilton. Contributing editor of *Stereo Review,* 1973—.

WORK IN PROGRESS: Revising *Discovering Music,* publication expected about 1978; a special report on the state of concert music broadcasting in the United States.

SIDELIGHTS: Roy Hemming writes that he has "long divided time professionally between writing and editing in international and national affairs with writing in the music field." He has been a special assignments reporter in Viet Nam, 1964, Latin America, 1966, Berlin, 1967, Czechoslovakia, 1968, Russia, 1969, and Ethiopia, 1971.

* * *

HENDERSON, Vivian Wilson 1923-1976

February 10, 1923—January 28, 1976; American labor economist, educator, college president, and author of books in his field. Obituaries: *New York Times,* January 29, 1976; *Washington Post,* January 30, 1976; *Time,* February 9, 1976.

* * *

HENLEY, W(illiam) Ballentine 1905-

PERSONAL: Born September 19, 1905; in Cincinnati, Ohio; married Helen McTaggart, 1942. *Education:* University of Southern California, A.B., 1928, A.M., 1930, J.D., 1933; M.S.P.A., 1935. *Home:* 3251 West Sixth St., Los Angeles, Calif; and Creston Circle Ranch, Paso Robles, Calif.

CAREER: University of Southern California, Los Angeles, director of coordination, 1936-40, acting dean of School of Government, 1936-38, associate professor of public administration and director of in-service governmental training at Civic Center Division, 1938-40; California College of Medicine, Los Angeles, president, 1940-65; University of California, Irvine, provost of College of Medicine, 1965-70; United Church of Religious Science, Los Angeles, Calif., president, 1969—. Owner and operator of Creston Circle Ranch (raises Aberdeen Angus cattle). Member of Los Angeles Board of Water and Power Commissioners, 1944-62, president of board, 1946-47; member of board of governors of Welfare Federation of the Los Angeles area; member of board of directors of Glendale Community Hospital and Southern California Cancer Center; vice-president of Los Angeles Safety Council, 1971—; California member of Western Interstate Commission on Higher Education, 1961-70; member of advisory board of Los Angeles Young Men's Christian Association (YMCA); member of General Motors Corp.'s Speakers Bureau.

MEMBER: International Platform Association (president of Western Division, 1950-51), American Bar Association, American Association of Osteopathic Colleges (past president), American Association for the Advancement of Science, American Management Association, American Association for the History of Medicine, American Academy of Political and Social Science, Defense Orientation Conference Association, American Institute of Management, California Bar Association, Los Angeles County Bar Association, Rotary International (president of Los Angeles club, 1955-56; district governor, 1959-60.) *Awards, honors:* LL.D., Willamette University, 1937; Sc.D., Kansas City College of Osteopathy and Surgery, 1949, Pepperdine College (now University), 1966; L.H.D. from Los Angeles College of Optometry, 1958.

WRITINGS: Man's Great Awakening: Beautiful Mud, Science of Mind, 1974. Also author of *History of the University of Southern California,* 1940.

SIDELIGHTS: Henley recently made a survey trip to Antarctica under the auspices of the U.S. Navy. In September, 1969, he made a survey of North Atlantic Treaty

Organization (NATO) bases, which included those in Germany, Brussels, Greece, the Mediterranean, and Spain.

* * *

HERBST, Robert L(eroy) 1935-

PERSONAL: Born October 5, 1935, in Minneapolis, Minn.; son of Walter P. (a postal supervisor) and Bernice M. (Mikkelson) Herbst; married Evelyn C. Elford, September 22, 1956; children: Eric, Peter, Amy. Education: University of Minnesota, B.S., 1957. Politics: None. Religion: Lutheran. Home: 10444 Fifth Ave. Circle, Bloomington, Minn. 55420. Office: Minnesota Department of Natural Resources, 301 Centennial Office Building, St. Paul, Minn. 55155.

CAREER: Employed by Minnesota Conservation Department, 1957-63; Keep Minnesota Green, Inc., executive secretary, 1963-66; Minnesota Conservation Department, deputy commissioner, 1966-69; Izaak Walton League of America, Minnesota Branch, executive director, 1969-71; Minnesota Department of Natural Resources, St. Paul, commissioner of natural resources, 1971—. Member, State Farm Forestry committee, 1963-66, Water Pollution Control Committee, 1966, State Soil Conservation Commission, 1966; co-chairman, Governor's Conference on Conservation Education, 1965; advisor to Water Resources Review Committee, 1966; governor's representative, Public Land Law Review Commission, 1967. Member: Society of American Foresters (secretary-treasurer, 1965), Izaak Walton League of America, National Camping and Hiking Association, Minnesota Conservation Federation, Alpha Zeta.

WRITINGS: Careers in Environment, Dillon, 1975. Writer of about two thousand forest management plans published by Keep Minnesota Green, Inc., Izaak Walton League of America, and State of Minnesota Department of Natural Resources. Contributor to newspapers and magazines.

* * *

HERD, Dale 1940-

PERSONAL: Born September 7, 1940, in Spokane, Wash.; son of Richard Fay and Ione (Dahlen) Herd. Education: Educated in California, Arizona, Washington, and Utah. Home address: c/o 104 Sunny Dr., Collage Place, Wash. 99324.

CAREER: "Casual laborer."

WRITINGS: Early Morning Wind (short stories), Four Seasons Foundation, 1972; Diamonds (short stories), Mudra, 1975. Poetry represented in Adventures in Poetry. Contributor to Chicago Review.

WORK IN PROGRESS: Hearts and Dreamland Court, both short novels.

* * *

HERNANDEZ, Luis F. 1923-

PERSONAL: Born April 13, 1923, in Los Angeles, Calif.; son of Juan C. (an engineer) and Maria (Pradeau) Hernandez; married Jeanne Altschuler (a teacher), August 20, 1960; children: (stepchildren) Barbara Wolff, Barry Wolff. Education: University of California, Los Angeles, B.A., 1949, M.A., 1974; graduate study at Stanford University, 1951, and University of Southern California, 1952-65; Brigham Young University, doctoral study, 1970. Politics: Democrat. Home: 304 North Bundy Dr., Los Angeles,

Calif. 90049. Office: School of Education, California State University, Northridge, Calif. 91324.

CAREER: High school teacher in Los Angeles, Calif., 1951-66, consultant, 1966-69; California State University, Northridge, assistant professor, 1969-70, associate professor, 1971-75, professor of secondary education, 1975—, associate dean of School of Education, 1973—. Associate director of Hispanic Urban Center; associate member of Danforth Foundation; member of California Council for Teacher Education; member of California Task Force for Integrated Education. Military service: U.S. Navy, 1942-45.

MEMBER: National Council of Teachers of English, Mexican American Educators Association, Teachers of English to Speakers of Other Languages, California Association of Teachers of English, California Bilingual-Bicultural Association, United California Professors, Southern California Social Science Association, Los Angeles Reading Council, Phi Delta Kappa. Awards, honors: Recognized by President Nixon, 1972, for activities as citizen; honored by California Association of Teachers of English, 1973, for writing on Chicanos.

WRITINGS: Standard Oral English: Seventh Grade, Los Angeles City Schools, 1967; Standard Oral English: Tenth Grade, Los Angeles City Schools, 1967; (contributor) Adventures in United States History, Units 3, 6, 7, and 8, Los Angeles City Schools, 1967; (contributor) Voices of Youth, Los Angeles City Schools, 1967; (contributor) Designs for Change: A Strategy for Curriculum Improvement, Parlier Unified School District, 1968; The Story of Western Man, Units 1-5, Los Angeles City Schools, 1969; Mexican American: Readings for Students in Mexican American Studies, Los Angeles City Schools, 1969; A Forgotten American: A Resource Unit on the Mexican American for Teachers, Anti-Defamation League, B'nai Brith, 1969.

(Contributor) Framework in Reading and Literature, California State Department of Education, 1972; The Mexican American in the Schools: An In-Service Program, Hispanic Urban Center (Los Angeles, Calif.), 1972; (contributor) Rudolph Gomez, editor, The Changing Mexican American, University of Texas Press, 1972; (contributor) Dialects and Dialect Learning, National Council of Teachers of English, 1973; The Mexican American in the School: Prototype for In-Service Programs, R. & E. Research Associates, 1975; (contributor) Readings on the Chicano, Chicano Studies Department, California State University, Northridge, in press; Aztlan: The Southwest and Its People, Hayden, in press. Contributor to professional journals.

WORK IN PROGRESS: Maria: A Biography of a Lady Who Went North.

AVOCATIONAL INTERESTS: Art (draws and paints), languages, travel.

* * *

HERNON, Peter 1944-

PERSONAL: Born August 31, 1944, in Kansas City, Mo.; son of Robert M. (a geologist) and Ethel (Grazier) Hernon; married Barbara Elliott, December 27, 1968 (divorced, 1970); married Elinor Griffith (a librarian), December 30, 1972; children: (second marriage) Alison. Education: University of Colorado, B.A., 1966, M.A. (history), 1969; University of Denver, M.A. (library science), 1971; Indiana University, candidate for Ph.D., 1975—. Politics: Liberal independent. Home: 720 College Mall Rd., Apt. I3, Bloomington, Ind. 47401.

CAREER: University of Nebraska, Omaha, reference librarian, 1971-75, instructor, 1971-74, assistant professor of library science, 1974-75; writer, 1975—. *Member:* American Library Association, Nebraska Library Association.

WRITINGS: (With Maureen Pastine and Sara Lou Williams) *Library and Library-Related Publications,* Libraries Unlimited, 1973. Contributor of articles and reviews to library journals.

WORK IN PROGRESS: Perceptions of Full-Time Students toward Academic Librarians: A Research Study, with Maureen Pastine; *University Faculty and Federal Documents: Use Patterns* and *Integration of Library Instruction into the Classroom: Evaluative Methods,* both with Sara Lou Williams.

AVOCATIONAL INTERESTS: Tennis, walking, vegetable gardening, collecting sound recordings.

*   *   *

HERRICK, Robert L(ee)   1930-

PERSONAL: Born September 13, 1930, in Brookfield, Mo.; son of Lowell P. (a clergyman) and Dorothy (Jones) Herrick; married Darlene Lewis (a teacher), August 15, 1954; children: K. Mark, Scott M., Kristina S. *Education:* Westmar College, B.A., 1953; United Theological Seminary, Dayton, Ohio, M.Div., 1956; University of Chicago, M.A., 1958; University of Illinois, Ph.D., 1962. *Politics:* Democrat. *Home:* 1225 Third Ave. S.W., LeMars, Iowa 51031. *Office:* Department of Sociology, Westmar College, LeMars, Iowa 51031.

CAREER: Iglesia Evangelico Unidas, Ponce, P.R., Methodist lay minister, 1956-57; University of Illinois, Urbana, instructor in sociology, 1962; Westmar College, LeMars, Iowa, assistant professor, 1962-64, associate professor, 1964-68, professor of sociology, 1968—. *Member:* American Sociological Association, Association for the Study of Religion, Religious Research Association (director-at-large), American Association of University Professors, Midwest Sociological Society.

WRITINGS: Manual for Discussion Leaders (booklet), Stipes, 1963; *Bible Study Booklet,* Otterbein, 1965; (contributor) Arthur B. Shostak, editor, *Putting Sociology to Work,* McKay, 1974. Contributor of articles, poems, and reviews to church publications, and contributor of reviews to professional periodicals.

WORK IN PROGRESS: Research on formation of concepts and changes in the symbolic meaning of word-concepts in circumstances of social change; studying how individuals use the organizations to which they belong.

*   *   *

HERUM, John (Maurice)   1931-

PERSONAL: Born January 1, 1931, in Bismarck, N. Dak.; son of Maurice (a teacher) and Evelyn (Gorman) Herum; married Jacquelyn Skahill, December 20, 1958; children: Christopher, Susan, Margaret. *Education:* Carroll College, Helena, Mont., B.A., 1951; graduate studies at Fordham University, 1951-52, Catholic University of America, 1957-58, 1960-61, University of Washington, 1958-59, 1960, 1961-62. *Home:* 607 East Capital, Ellensburg, Wash. 98926. *Office:* Department of English, Central Washington State College, Ellensburg, Wash. 98926.

CAREER: Carroll College, Helena, Mont., assistant registrar, 1952-53; National Security Agency, Ft. Meade, Md.,

technical writer and editor, 1955-58; Boeing Corp., Seattle, Wash., funding writer, 1959; Military Manuals, Renton, Wash., technical editor, 1960; Central Washington State College, Ellensburg, Wash., teacher of English, 1962—. Member of the board of trustees, Ellensburg Public Library, 1968-70. *Military service:* U.S. Army, Signal Corps, 1953-55. *Member:* American Association of University Professors, National Council of Teachers of English.

WRITINGS: (With D. W. Cummings) *Writing,* Random House, 1971; (editor with Cummings) *Tempo,* Houghton, 1974. Contributor to *Modern Language Quarterly* and *Language and Style.*

WORK IN PROGRESS: Studies in the sociology of language and the ethnography of literacy; *The Social Origin of Genres,* and *The English Ink Plot,* a book on the spread of international English, completion of both expected about 1980.

SIDELIGHTS: Herum commented to *CA:* "I write because I teach. What I teach is how to read and write English at an adult level. I find that much of our school system seems determined to prevent most students from achieving full literacy—all of the myths, the attitudes, the materials, and the tactics seem designed to exclude as many as possible from a literacy that is fully responsible. I want to change that."

*   *   *

HERWIG, Holger H(einrich)   1941-

PERSONAL: Born September 25, 1941, in Hamburg, Germany; Canadian citizen; son of Henry W. (a forester) and Hella M. (Hahn) Herwig. *Education:* University of Munich, student, 1964; University of British Columbia, B.A. (first class honors), 1965; State University of New York at Stony Brook, M.A., 1967, Ph.D., 1971. *Home:* 7439 Highway 70 S., Apt. 127, Nashville, Tenn. 37221. *Office:* Department of History, Vanderbilt University, Box 6129, Nashville, Tenn. 37235.

CAREER: Indiana University, Bloomington, visiting assistant professor of history, 1971-72; Vanderbilt University, Nashville, Tenn., assistant professor of history, 1972—. *Member:* American Historical Association. *Awards, honors:* Fellow of Alexander von Humboldt Foundation, 1969—; Canada Council fellow at State University of New York, 1970-71.

WRITINGS: (Contributor) Herbert Schottelius and Wilhelm Deist, editors, *Marine und Marinepolitik, 1871-1914* (title means "Navy and Naval Policy"), Droste Verlag, 1972; *The German Naval Officer Corps: A Social and Political History, 1890-1918,* Clarendon Press, 1973; (contributor) Joachim Hutter, Reinhard Meyer and Dietrich Papenfuss, editors, *Tradition und Neubeginn: Internationale Forschungen zur Deutschen Geschichte im 20. Jahrhundert* (title means "Tradition and Newbeginning: International Research in German History in the Twentieth Century"), Carl Heymanns Verlag, 1975; *Politics of Frustration: The United States in German Naval Planning, 1888-1941,* Little, Brown, 1976; *The Navy of Kaiser Wilhelm II,* David & Charles, in press. Contributor to history journals.

*   *   *

HESS, Bartlett L(eonard)   1910-

PERSONAL: Born December 27, 1910, in Spokane, Wash.; son of John Leonard (a clergyman) and Jessie (a clergywoman; maiden name, Bartlett) Hess; married Margaret Johnston (a writer, radio speaker, and Bible teacher), July 31, 1937; children: Daniel Bartlett, Deborah (Mrs. Hans Morsink), John Howard, Janet Elizabeth. *Education:* Park College, B.A., 1931; University of Kansas, M.A., 1932, Ph.D., 1934; McCormick Theological Seminary, M.Div., 1936. *Home:* 16845 Riverside Dr., Livonia, Mich. 48154. *Office:* Ward United Presbyterian Church, 17000 Farmington Rd., Livonia, Mich.

CAREER: Ordained Presbyterian minister, 1936; pastor of Presbyterian churches in Chicago, Ill., 1935-42, Cicero, Ill., 1942-56, and Detroit, Mich., 1956-68; Ward United Presbyterian Church, Livonia, Mich., senior pastor, 1968—. Teacher at Detroit Bible College, 1956-60. Organizer and chairman of Committee for Christian Refugees (Chicago), 1940-42; president of Cicero Ministers' Council, 1950-51; member of committee for Livonia Prayer Breakfast, 1974-76. *Member:* Presbyterians United for Biblical Concerns (member of board of directors, 1975), Phi Beta Kappa, Phi Delta Kappa. *Awards, honors:* Named to Fil-American Team to the Philippines, by the United Presbyterian Church of the U.S.A., 1961.

WRITINGS: (With wife, Margaret Johnston Hess) *How to Have a Giving Church,* Abingdon, 1974.

WORK IN PROGRESS: How to Have a Growing Church, and a book on marriage, both with M. J. Hess.

SIDELIGHTS: Hess writes: "I started Ward United Presbyterian Church, Livonia, Mich., as a branch of Ward Memorial Church, Detroit. I was senior pastor of both churches, 1956-68. When the Livonia church grew to a thousand members it became a separate church with me as senior pastor. It has since grown to more than two thousand two hundred members . . . the great majority under forty years old, a budget over six hundred thousand dollars. Our book . . . and a second book *How to Have a Growing Church* grew out of these experiences." The Hesses have traveled several times around the world, conducted trips to the Bible lands, Mediterranean countries, and to Scandinavia.

*   *   *

HICKOK, Robert (Blair) 1927-

PERSONAL: Born February 2, 1927, in Slaton, Tex.; son of George B. (a civil engineer) and Minnie (Paul) Hickok; married Roanne Newman, June 23, 1953; children: Paul, Laura. *Education:* Yale University, Mus.B., 1949. *Home:* 2301 Glenwood Rd., Brooklyn, N.Y. 11210. *Office:* School of Performing Arts, Brooklyn College of the City University of New York, Brooklyn, N.Y. 11210.

CAREER: Albertus Magnus College, New Haven, Conn., conductor of chorus, 1949-50; U.S. Navy School of Music, Washington, D.C., instructor, 1951-52; Brooklyn College of the City University of New York, assistant professor, 1957-60, associate professor, 1960-64, professor, 1964—, chairman of music department, 1962-69, conductor of chorus and chorale, 1952-73, chairman of commission on the performing arts, 1972-73, now dean of School of Performing Arts. Visiting professor, Union Theological Seminary, summer, 1958, University of New Hampshire, summer, 1968. Conductor, New Haven Chorale, 1951-61, Washington Square Chamber Orchestra, 1963 and 1964, Cantata Singers of New York, 1967-70; associate conductor, New York Pro Musica, 1959-60; head of choral department and conductor of chorus, Manhattan School of Music, 1967-73; founder and conductor, Janus Chorale of New York, 1969—. Guest conductor, lecturer, and officer for

orchestras and choruses in New York. *Military service:* U.S. Army, 1950-52. *Member:* College Music Society.

WRITINGS: Check List of Selected Baroque Choral Works, American Choral Foundation, 1961; *Music Appreciation,* Appleton, 1971, 2nd edition, Addison-Wesley, 1975. General editor of Brooklyn College Choral Series, 1954—; editor of works by composers John Blow, Thomas Tomkins, Jacob Obrecht, and Caspar Othmayr.

*   *   *

HICKS, Raymond L. 1926-

PERSONAL: Born October 26, 1926; son of Fred Lee Reeves and Alma Hicks; married wife, Mary Jayne, June 30, 1950; children: Raymond L., Jr., David. *Education:* Baylor University, B.A., 1950. *Politics:* Democrat. *Religion:* Baptist. *Home:* 3101 Inverness, Waco, Tex. 76701. *Agent:* Safier & Barry, 667 Madison Ave., New York, N.Y. 10021. *Office:* Southwest Advertising, P.O. Box 2117, Waco, Tex. 76703.

CAREER: Advertising executive. *Military service:* U.S. Army Air Forces, pilot, 1943-46. *Member:* Southwest Association of Advertising Agencies (vice-president), Ad Club, Lions, Jaycees, Chamber of Commerce. *Awards, honors:* Named Ad-Man of the Year by Southwest Association of Advertising Agencies, 1956.

WRITINGS: Pitching to Win, A. S. Barnes, 1974; *Brockett,* Davis, 1974. Contributor to sports magazines.

WORK IN PROGRESS: Rape of Lydian Queen, a novel; *The Blue Chip,* a novel.

AVOCATIONAL INTERESTS: Sports, aviation.

*   *   *

HIEBERT, Clarence 1927-

PERSONAL: Born July 12, 1927, in Winnipeg, Manitoba, Canada; son of Cornelius N. and Tina (Harms) Hiebert; married Ferne Kornelsen (a piano instructor), 1950; children: Timothy, Robert, Elizabeth, Susan. *Education:* Tabor College, A.B., 1949; Menninger Foundation School for Psychiatric Aides, diploma, 1950; New York Theological Seminary, B.D., 1954; Phillips University, M.A., 1959; Case Western Reserve University, Ph.D., 1971. *Home:* 305 South Lincoln, Hillsboro, Kan. 67063. *Office:* Department of Religious Studies, Tabor College, Hillsboro, Kan. 67063.

CAREER: Elementary school teacher in Hillsboro, Kan., 1948-49; psychiatric aide in Topeka, Kan., 1949-50; pastor of Mennonite Brethren church in Enid, Okla., 1954-59; Europaeische Mennonitische Bibelschule, Liestal, Switzerland, visiting lecturer in historical and religious studies, 1959-61; Tabor College, Hillsboro, Kan., assistant professor, 1962-67, associate professor, 1967-72; professor of historical and religious studies, 1972—. Part-time instructor at Phillips University, 1956-59; interim pastor of community church in Kabul, Afghanistan, 1974. Vice-chairman of Mennonite Central Committee (Peace Section), 1957-67; member of executive committee of Mennonite Brethren Board of Missions-Services, 1957—; chairman of Enid's Ministerial Alliance, 1957-58. *Member:* Mennonitische Geschichtsverein (Weierhof, Germany).

WRITINGS: The Holdeman People, William Carey, 1973; (contributor) A. J. Klassen, editor, *Church in Mission,* Board of Christian Literature, 1967; (editor) *Brothers in Deed to Brothers in Need: A Scrapbook about Mennonite*

Immigrants from Russia, 1870-1885, Faith & Life, 1974. Contributor to magazines.

WORK IN PROGRESS: A History of the Henderson, Nebraska, Mennonite Brethren Church, completion expected in 1977; *Documents: The Theological Pilgrimage of Mennonite Brethren; The Holdeman People Revisited.*

SIDELIGHTS: Hiebert writes that his special interest is "... the milieu that gives rise to religious movements among people of various cultures and backgrounds—especially North American and Africa, especially Holdemans, Kimbanguists, Anabaptists, and the Jesus Movement." His travels include two years in western Europe, a trip to Rumania with a choir, two trips to the Soviet Union, Mexico, and Israel, as well as a research trip to Zaire.

*   *   *

HIGGS, David (Clive)   1939-

PERSONAL: Born May 14, 1939, in Rugby, England; naturalized Canadian citizen; son of Thomas Leslie (a school teacher) and Phyllis (Stephens) Higgs. *Education:* University of British Columbia, B.A., 1959; Northwestern University, M.A., 1960; University of London, Ph.D., 1964. *Home:* 164 Hillsdale Ave. E., Toronto, Ontario M4S 1T5, Canada. *Office:* Department of History, University of Toronto, 100 St. George St., Toronto, Ontario M5S 1A1, Canada.

CAREER: University of Toronto, Toronto, Ontario, lecturer 1964-65, assistant professor, 1965-71, associate professor of history, 1971—. *Member:* Society for French Historical Studies.

WRITINGS: Ultraroyalism in Toulouse, Johns Hopkins Press, 1973; (contributor) John F. Bosher, editor, *The French Government and Society: 1550-1850,* Athlone Press, 1973. Contributor to history journals.

WORK IN PROGRESS: A History of the Portuguese in Canada, with Grace M. Anderson; *Nobility in French Society: 1800-1870,* completion expected in 1977.

SIDELIGHTS: Higgs writes: "I am interested in marginal groups in society, especially those whose situation is not always seen in that light, like minorities with reactionary ideology or a declining social group. Frequent stays in France over the last fifteen years have been very important to my outlook, particularly for studying the French approach to social thought. As well as French I speak Portuguese and my fascination with Portuguese history and society has steadily increased."

*   *   *

HIGONNET, Margaret Randolph   1941-
(Margaret Hale)

PERSONAL: Born October 2, 1941, in New Orleans, La.; daughter of Guy Adams (a professor) and Margaret (Bullitt) Cardwell; married Mahlon Hale, December 27, 1965 (marriage ended, 1974); married Patrice Louis-Rene Higonnet (a professor), August 14, 1974. *Education:* Bryn Mawr College, B.A., 1963; attended University of Tuebingen, 1963-64, University College, London, 1966-67; Yale University, Ph.D., 1970. *Office:* Department of English, University of Connecticut, Storrs, Conn. 06268.

CAREER: George Washington University, Washington, D.C., instructor in English, 1967-68; University of Connecticut, Storrs, assistant professor of English, 1970—.

Member: Modern Language Association, American Comparitive Literature Association, English Institute. *Awards, honors:* Woodrow Wilson fellow, 1964-65; Fulbright fellow, University of London, 1966-67.

WRITINGS: (Under name Margaret Hale) *Horn of Oberon: Jean Paul Richter's School for Aesthetics,* Wayne State University Press, 1973.

WORK IN PROGRESS: A study of Friedrich Schlegel as literary critic; a book on thematic criticism, completion expected in 1976.

*   *   *

HILKEN, Glen A.   1936-

PERSONAL: Born January 28, 1936, in Batavia, N.Y.; son of Arthur J. and Rubye (Gell) Hilken. *Education:* Hobart College, B.A. (cum laude). *Politics:* None. *Religion:* "Wicca." *Home:* 308 Avenue A, Melbourne Beach, Fla. 32951. *Agent:* Mrs. Carlton Cole, 100 East 50th St., New York, N.Y. 10022. *Office:* P.O. Box 3241, Indialantic, Fla. 32903.

CAREER: J. J. Little & Ives, New York, N.Y., copy editor for *Ready Reference Encyclopedia,* 1961-62; North American Precis Syndicate, New York, N.Y., senior vice-president and editorial director, 1962-67; American Express Travelers Guides, New York, N.Y., editorial director, 1968-69; Charles F. Kettering Foundation, Dayton, Ohio, education writer and multimedia director, 1970-71; writer, editor, and educational director of international chain of astrology schools, 1971—. Consultant to National Commission on the Reform of Secondary Education and Institute for Development of Educational Activities. *Member:* Phi Beta Kappa.

WRITINGS: The Best of Sybil Leek, Popular Library, 1974; *The Legend of Earl Durand,* Manor, 1975; *Inside Bellevue!: A True Story,* Mason/Charter, 1976. Author of "Diary of a Witch," a musical play; "Piney Wood," a feature film script; a television script for the series "The Waltons."

WORK IN PROGRESS: Witchcraft and the Occult, with Sybil Leek; research on Las Vegas gambling and crime for *Las Vegas Blues.*

SIDELIGHTS: Hilken writes: "I have been Sybil Leek's business partner and confidant for the past three and a half years ... [and] Sybil has been the major influence in my life as a writer of my own books. Sybil and I are interested in all matters of the occult and supernatural. ... We both love to travel, and I was sent on a ... tour of the world in 1965."

*   *   *

HILL, Dilys M(ary)   1935-

PERSONAL: Born September 8, 1935, in England. *Education:* University of Leeds, B.A. (honors), 1962, Ph.D., 1964. *Residence:* Southampton, England. *Office:* Department of Politics, University of Southampton, Southampton S09 5NH, England.

CAREER: University of Southampton, Southampton, England, lecturer, 1964-72, senior lecturer in politics, 1973—. Member of General Advisory Council, 1973—, Complaints Review Board of Independent Broadcasting Authority, 1973—, and Public and Social Administration Board of Council for National Academic Awards, 1975—. *Member:* Political Studies Association of United Kingdom (member of executive committee, 1975—), Royal Institute of Public Administration. *Awards, honors:* Ford Foundation research fellowship, 1973-74.

WRITINGS: Participating in Local Affairs, Penguin, 1970; *Democratic Theory and Local Government,* International Publications Service, 1974; *The Planning and Management of Human Settlements with Special Reference to Participation,* International Union of Local Authorities, 1976.

WORK IN PROGRESS: Research on housing policy, on participation and planning, and on local government.

* * *

HILL, Marvin S(idney) 1928-

PERSONAL: Born August 28, 1928, in Washington, D.C.; son of Clarence H. and Emma (Wirthlin) Hill; married Lila Foster, 1953; children: Linda, Leslie, Laura, Jeffery, Steven. *Education:* Brigham Young University, B.A. and M.A., both 1955; University of Chicago, Ph.D., 1968. *Politics:* Independent. *Religion:* Mormon. *Home:* 305 East 4750 North, Provo, Utah 84602. *Office:* Department of History, 339 Maeser Bldg., Brigham Young University, Provo, Utah 84602.

CAREER: Chicago City Junior College, Chicago, Ill., lecturer in history, 1961-62; East Carolina University, Greenville, N.C., assistant professor of history, 1962-65; Brigham Young University, Provo, Utah, associate professor of history, 1966—. Research fellow at Huntington Library, summer, 1971, and at Yale University, 1972-73.

WRITINGS: (Editor with James B. Allen) *Mormonism and American Culture,* Harper, 1972; (with Dallin H. Oaks) *Carthage Conspiracy: The Trial of the Accused Assassins of Joseph Smith,* University of Illinois Press, 1975. Contributor to *Church History.* Member of editorial board, *Journal of Mormon History,* 1975—.

WORK IN PROGRESS: A biography of Joseph Smith.

* * *

HILLES, Frederick W(hiley) 1900-1975

June 1, 1900—December 10, 1975; American scholar, educator, and author or editor of books on eighteenth-century English literature and other topics. Obituaries: *New York Times,* December 12, 1975. (See index for previous *CA* sketch)

* * *

HILLIARD, Sam B(owers) 1930-

PERSONAL: Born December 21, 1930, in Bowersville, Ga.; son of Asa Farris (a farmer and rural mail carrier) and Flora (Bowers) Hilliard; married Joyce Collier (a nurse), June 4, 1955; children: Steven Glen, Anita Joy. *Education:* Attended Emmanuel College, Franklin Springs, Ga., 1950; University of Georgia, A.B., 1960, M.A., 1962; University of Wisconsin, M.S., 1963, Ph.D., 1966. *Home:* 739 North Coventry Dr., Baton Rouge, La. 70808. *Office:* 255 Geology Bldg., Louisiana State University, Baton Rouge, La. 70803.

CAREER: Farmer, 1950, and electrician, 1954-58; University of Wisconsin, Milwaukee, instructor in geography, 1965-67; Southern Illinois University at Carbondale, assistant professor of geography, 1967-71; Louisiana State University, Baton Rouge, associate professor of geography, 1971—, head of department, 1975—. *Military service:* U.S. Navy, 1950-54. *Member:* Association of American Geogra-

phers, Agricultural History Society, Southern Historical Association, American Geographical Society.

WRITINGS: Hog Meat and Hoecake, Southern Illinois University Press, 1972. Contributor to journals in his field.

WORK IN PROGRESS: Southern Food Habits.

* * *

HISKETT, Mervyn 1920-

PERSONAL: Born May 20, 1920, in St. Albans, Hertfordshire, England; son of William Robert (an accountant) and Edith (MacIntyre) Hiskett; married Mary Osborn (a nursing sister, S.R.N., S.C.M.); children: Sarah Elizabeth, Mark William, Simon Philip. *Education:* School of Oriental and African Studies, London, B.A. (honors), 1951, certificate in education, 1960, Ph.D., 1969. *Home:* Cherry Hay, Wrotham Rd., Meopham, Kent DA13 0QQ, England.

CAREER: School for Arabic Studies, Kano, Nigeria, vice-principal, 1952-62; University of London, School of Oriental and African Studies, London, England, lecturer in Hausa studies, 1962—. Visiting professor of Hausa studies at University of Wisconsin, Madison, 1967-70. *Military service:* British Army, Physical Training Corps and Royal Parachute Regiment, 1941-47; became captain. *Member:* African Studies Association of the United Kingdom, Royal Asiatic Society, Royal African Society.

WRITINGS: (With Awad Muhammad Ahmad) *The Story of the Arabs* (Islamic textbook), [London], 1957; (editor and author of commentary and notes) *Tazyin-al-waraqat of Abdullah ibn Muhammad,* Ibadan University Press (Ibadan, Nigeria), 1963; *The Teaching of Arabic,* Longmans, Green, 1963; (translator and author of notes) Alhaji Sir Abubakar Tafawa Balewa, *Shaihu Umar* (novel), Longmans, Green, 1967; (author of introduction) C. L. Temple, *Native Races and Their Rulers,* 2nd edition (Hiskett was not associated with original edition), Cass, 1968; (contributor) James Kritzeck and William H. Lewis, editors, *Islam in Africa,* Van Nostrand, 1969; *The Sword of Truth: The Life and Times of the Shehu Usuman Dan Fodio,* Oxford University Press, 1973; *A History of Hausa Islamic Verse,* School of Oriental and African Studies, University of London, 1975; (editor with Godfrey N. Brown) *Conflict and Harmony in Education in Tropical Africa,* Allen & Unwin, 1975.

Author of programs for African Service of British Broadcasting Corp.: "The Habe Period in Hausa Traditional Verse"; "Three Poets of the Jihad Period: Muhammadu Tukur, Abdullahi dan Muhammadu, and the Shehu Usuman dan Fodio"; "The Coming of the Europeans through the Eyes of the Hausa Poets." Contributor to *Encyclopedia of Islam* and *Cambridge History of Africa.* Contributor of about twenty articles and poems to academic journals, including *Bulletin of the School of Oriental and African Studies, African Language Studies, World Development, Spectrum,* and *Journal of the Royal Asiatic Society.*

AVOCATIONAL INTERESTS: Jogging, skiing, squash, breeding geese, growing vegetables, reading history.

* * *

HITZ, Demi 1942-

PERSONAL: Born September 2, 1942, in Cambridge, Mass.; daughter of William Morris (an architect, actor, and entrepreneur) and Rosamond (an artist; maiden name, Pier) Hunt; married John Rawlins Hitz (a teacher and writer),

December 18, 1965; children: John. *Education:* Attended Instituto Allende and Rhode Island School of Design; Immaculate Heart College, B.A., 1962; University of Baroda, M.S., 1963; further graduate study at China Institute. *Home and office:* 325 Riverside Dr., New York, N.Y. 10025. *Agent:* Pema Browne, 185 East 85th St., New York, N.Y. 10028.

CAREER: Artist; murals, paintings, mosaics, and silk screen prints have been exhibited in museums and galleries in California, New York, N.Y., and Massachusetts, as well as in India. *Member:* China Institute. *Awards, honors:* Fulbright scholarship to India, 1962; awards from *Boston Globe* scholastic competitions, 1961, California State Fair, 1962, Los Angeles County Museum, 1962, California Arts and Science Fair, 1962, and Los Angeles Outdoor Art Festival, 1962.

WRITINGS: The Surangini Tales (juvenile), Harcourt, 1973; *The Classic of Tea,* Little, Brown, 1974; *Feelings* (juvenile), Macmillan, 1975; *The Old China Trade* (juvenile), Coward, in press. Contributor to art, craft, and education journals.

WORK IN PROGRESS: Three children's books; Chinese calligraphy.

SIDELIGHTS: Demi Hitz has painted murals in Mexico, walls for modern homes, and the dome of St. Peter's & Paul's Church in Wilmington, Calif. A filmstrip about her work, "Making Mosaics," was shown in Boston, on CBS-TV, in 1963. *Avocational interests:* Travel (Mexico, Guatemala, Brazil, Chile, England and Japan).

*   *   *

HOCHMAN, Shirley D(ean)   1917-

PERSONAL: Born February 1, 1917, in New York, N.Y.; daughter of John Henry (a hotel manager) and Nellie (Witt) Spaulding. *Education:* Hunter College (now Hunter College of the City University of New York), B.A., 1939; Queens College (now Queens College of the City University of New York), M.A., 1960. *Home and office:* 357 Glen Ave., Sea Cliff, N.Y. 11579.

CAREER: New York City Board of Education, New York, N.Y., supervisor, 1940-71. Nassau Community College, Garden City, N.Y., adjunct instructor, 1973—.

WRITINGS: Identifying Art, Sterling, 1975; *Invitation to Art,* Sterling, 1975.

*   *   *

HODGE, David W(ayne)   1935-

PERSONAL: Born January 15, 1935, in Cedar Rapids, Iowa; son of George A. (in U.S. Postal Service) and Rose Hodge; married Margaret Weingart, August, 1958; children: Catherine Rose. *Education:* State University of Iowa, B.A., 1957, M.A., 1964; University of Georgia, M.F.A., 1967. *Home:* 1027 Wright, Oshkosh, Wis. 54901. *Office:* Department of Art, University of Wisconsin, Oshkosh, Wis. 54901.

CAREER: University of Iowa, Iowa City, instructor in art, 1962-64; University of Wisconsin, Oshkosh, professor of art, 1964—. *Military service:* U.S. Army Reserve, 1953-61.

WRITINGS: Art in Depth, International Textbook, 1970.

*   *   *

HOFFMAN, Willa M(athews)   1914-

PERSONAL: Born January 22, 1914, in Huntington,

W.Va.; married Claude W. Hoffman, 1945; children: Willa Frances. *Education:* Marshall University, A.B., 1935; University of Arizona, M.A., 1941; also studied at University of California, Los Angeles, University of Tampa, and California State University, Northridge. *Home:* 7440 Hesperia Ave., Reseda, Calif. 91335.

CAREER: Junior high school science teacher in West Virginia, eleven years; English teacher and high school counselor in California, twenty-two years. *Military service:* Women's Army Auxiliary Corps (WAAC).

WRITINGS: The Rum Cookbook, Price, Stern, 1972.

WORK IN PROGRESS: A biography of Charles II of England; research on English history.

*   *   *

HOFFMANN, Felix   1911-1975

April 11, 1911—June, 1975; Swiss artist and illustrator of books, including books for children. Obituaries: *Publishers Weekly,* August 18, 1975. (See index for previous *CA* sketch)

*   *   *

HOGAN, Paul   1927-

PERSONAL: Born May 28, 1927, in Philadelphia, Pa.; son of Daniel E. (a builder) and Julia (a teacher; maiden name, Fay) Hogan; married Jo Anne Smith, 1972; children: Paula, Teig, Lisa, Evan, Orin, Michael, Phillip, Erica, Christopher. *Education:* Goddard College, student, 1976—. *Politics:* Radical Democrat. *Home and office:* 26 Buckwalter Rd., Phoenixville, Pa. 19460.

CAREER: Hogan Construction Co., Inc., Phoenixville, Pa., president, 1956-70; Playground Clearing House, Inc., Phoenixville, president, 1973—. Member of Charlestown (Pa.) Planning Commission, 1960-65. Regional director of U.S. Peace Corps in Colombia, 1965-67. *Military service:* U.S. Merchant Marine, 1945-48. U.S. Army, paratrooper, 1950-52. *Member:* International Playground Association (U.S. correspondent). *Awards, honors:* Life saving award from Chester County Volunteer Fire Departments Association, 1964.

WRITINGS: The Train to Bogota, New York Times Co., 1970; *KM 9441: A Trip on the Trans Siberian,* privately printed, 1971; *Hitching in America,* privately printed, 1973; *Playground for Free,* M.I.T. Press, 1974. Contributor to magazines and newspapers.

WORK IN PROGRESS: Research on colonial play in Pennsylvania, especially in Chester County, and on folk art and wall murals as an alternative to graffiti; *Peace Corps, Colombia,* a journal.

AVOCATIONAL INTERESTS: Travel abroad, making movies on people and play.

*   *   *

HOGBEN, Lancelot   1895-1975

December 9, 1895—August 22, 1975; British scholar, biologist and geneticist, historian, linguistician, educator, and author of books on science, mathematics, and other topics. Obituaries: *New York Times,* August 23, 1975; *Washington Post,* August 24, 1975; *Newsweek,* September 1, 1975; *Publishers Weekly,* September 29, 1975.

*   *   *

HOLBROOK, Bill   1921-

PERSONAL: Born August 23, 1921, in Akron, Ohio; son

of Willie Covington (a tirebuilder) and Pansy (Albritton) Holbrook; married Sophie Relich (an office manager), August 22, 1942; children: Karen (Mrs. Frank Guthrie), Billie (Mrs. Bill Teigen), Debbi (Mrs. Alan Pendleton), Lisa. *Education:* Attended University of Akron, 1940. *Religion:* Presbyterian. *Home:* 408 Washington St., Cumberland, Md. 21502. *Office:* Kelly Springfield Tire Co., Cumberland, Md. 21502.

CAREER: Kelly Springfield Tire Co., Cumberland, Md., chief pilot, 1951—, manager of aviation department, 1951—. Glider instructor, 1960—; chairman of Cumberland Municipal Airport Commission, 1968-74; managing partner, Soaring Symposia (publishers), 1969—; consultant to American Management Association, 1974; FAA designated pilot examiner. *Military service:* U.S. Army Air Forces, pilot, 1941-45; served in South Pacific theater; became first lieutenant; received Air Medal with seven oak leaf clusters. *Member:* Soaring Society of America, Experimental Aircraft Society, Lighter Than Air Society, Quiet Birdmen, Imperial Council of the Ancient Arabic Order of the Nobles of the Mystic Shrine for North America. *Awards, honors:* Dapper Dan award, 1974, for world's record flight, and 1975 for winning the 1974 Transcontinental Sailplane Derby; made member of Soaring Hall of Fame, 1975, for flying the world's sailplane "out and return" record of 783 miles and for winning 1974 Transcontinental Sailplane Derby; listed in *Guiness Book of World Records,* 1976.

WRITINGS: Soaring Cross Country, Soaring Symposia, 1974. Contributor to *Soaring.* Editor of *Proceedings of Symposium on Competitive Soaring,* 1969-72.

WORK IN PROGRESS: Corporate Pilot Handbook; Competitive Soaring.

SIDELIGHTS: Holbrook is the current world soaring "out and return" record holder.

* * *

HOLLAND, Marion 1908-

PERSONAL: Born July 7, 1908, in Washington, D.C.; daughter of Maurice Crowther (a zoologist) and Lola (Davis) Hall; married Thomas W. Holland (an economist), 1939; children: Barbara, Nicholas, Judith, Rebecca, Andrew. *Education:* Swarthmore College, A.B., 1929. *Home:* 4100 Rosemary St., Chevy Chase, Md. 20015. *Agent:* McIntosh & Otis, Inc., 18 East 41st St., New York, N.Y. 10017.

CAREER: Author and illustrator of children's books. *Member:* Authors Guild, Children's Book Guild (Washington, D.C.; past president). *Awards, honors:* Boys' Clubs of America Junior Book Award for *Billy's Clubhouse.*

WRITINGS—Self-illustrated, except as noted: *Billy Had a System,* Knopf, 1952; *Billy's Clubhouse,* Knopf, 1955; *No Children, No Pets,* Knopf, 1956; *A Tree for Teddy,* Knopf, 1957; *A Big Ball of String,* Random House, 1958; *Muggsy* (not self-illustrated), Knopf, 1959; *No Room for a Dog,* (not self-illustrated), Random House, 1959; *The Secret Horse,* Little, Brown, 1960; *Teddy's Camp-Out,* Knopf, 1963; *Casey Jones Rides Vanity,* Little, Brown, 1964.

WORK IN PROGRESS: Research on background for a book laid in the 1850's.

SIDELIGHTS: Mrs. Holland comments: "I did a little illustrating for a children's magazine, which requires reading a story in manuscript carefully. (Too often it is possible to conclude that the illustrator did not read the story at all.) Sometimes I thought I could have improved on

a story, which I mentioned to an editor who said, 'If you think it's so easy to write a children's story, why don't you run home and write one?' So I ran home and wrote one, which the editor accepted. As I had a house full of children at the time, it turned out that paper and a typewriter are less vulnerable to accidents than all the paraphernalia an illustrator needs; you can still read a page of type with a little grape jelly on it, but grape jelly on a picture means doing the whole thing over."

* * *

HOLLIS, Helen Rice 1908-

PERSONAL: Born June 4, 1908, in Oklahoma; daughter of George W. and Jeannette (Bradshaw) Rice; divorced; children: Anne Hollis Reese, Richard Avery. *Education:* Oberlin Conservatory of Music, B.Mus., 1930; graduate study at American Conservatory of Music, summers, 1962, 1963; Cleveland Institute of Music, M.Mus., 1964. *Home:* 3725 Reservoir Rd. N.W., Washington, D.C. 20007. *Office:* Division of Musical Instruments, Smithsonian Institution, Washington, D.C. 20007.

CAREER: Smithsonian Institution, Washington, D.C., information specialist, 1964—. Performer of chamber music on piano and harpsichord; lecturer in music.

WRITINGS: Pianos in the Smithsonian Institution, Smithsonian Institution Press, 1973; *The Piano: A Pictorial Account of Its Ancestry and Development,* Hippocrene, 1975. Contributor to *Antiques.*

WORK IN PROGRESS: Musical Instruments in Works of Art at the National Gallery, for National Gallery of Art; research on the history of musical instruments.

SIDELIGHTS: Helen Hollis has traveled in Europe and the Orient, to visit collections of art and musical instruments. In 1949, she inaugurated one of the earliest programs of serious music on television in Cleveland. *Avocational interests:* Far Eastern art.

* * *

HOLMAN, L(loyd) Bruce 1939-

PERSONAL: Born January 30, 1939, in Kansas City, Mo.; son of Myron Auris (an artist) and Marjorie (an artist; maiden name, Little) Holman; married Carol Ann O'Lear (an educator), January 26, 1963. *Education:* University of Missouri at Kansas City, B.A., 1961; Syracuse University, M.A., 1964, Ph.D., 1971. *Office:* The Center for Cinema Animation, Tully, N.Y. 13159.

CAREER: Aircraft Films (motion picture distribution company), Memphis, N.Y., partner, 1964-65; State University of New York, Sperry Learning Resources Center, Cortland, director of graphic and photographic production, 1966-70; *Filmmakers Newsletter,* New York, N.Y., feature editor, 1969—. Owner of Holman Films (film, animation, and graphic art production company), 1962—. Technical supervisor of cinema department at State University of New York at Binghamton, 1972-75; teacher of animation and production technique, 1973-74; director of Center for Cinema Animation, 1975—; teacher of cartoon drawing at Thompkins-Cortland Community College, and puppetry at University College Division of Syracuse University, 1976—; has lectured at Onondaga Community College, Susquehanna School, Syracuse University, and Ithaca College. Designer-director for Computer Image Corp., 1973; member of jury of the first Independent Filmmakers Competition. Paintings have been exhibited in New York state since 1974; cartoons are in permanent collection at House of Humor and Satire (Gabrovo, Bulgaria).

MEMBER: Association Internationale du Film d'Animation, Society of Motion Picture and Television Engineers, University Film Association, Experimental Aircraft Association. *Awards, honors:* U.S. Cine Golden Eagle Award, 1966; diploma from Venice International Festival of Cinemagraphic Art, 1966.

WRITINGS: A Portfolio of Wood-Engravings by Lloyd Bruce Holman, Walnut Press, 1969; *Puppet Animation in the Cinema: History and Technique,* A. S. Barnes, 1974. Contributor to *Anthology of the World Contemporary Cartoon,* published by House of Humor and Satire. Has produced about thirty documentary and educational films, both live-action and animation, as well as short film segments and television commercials. Contributor of more than eighty articles and cartoons to film and media publications.

SIDELIGHTS: Holman designs and builds specialized equipment for use in cinematography, photography, and graphic arts. *Avocational interests:* Fine printing (collects and restores antique letterpress printing equipment for use in fine-art printing), private aviation (holds private pilot's license), antique optical equipment (collects, documents, and restores antique projectors, cameras, and photo-cinema equipment), puppets and puppetry (designs and presents puppet programs).

*   *   *

HOLMES, Charles S(hiveley)   1916-1976

January 13, 1916—January 15, 1976; American educator, and author or editor of books on literature and literary criticism. Obituaries: *New York Times,* January 17, 1976; *Washington Post,* January 17, 1976. (See index for previous *CA* sketch)

*   *   *

HOLST, Lawrence E(berhardt)   1929-

PERSONAL: Born May 1, 1929, in Chicago, Ill.; son of Louis Bakker (an office clerk) and Anida (Jensen) Holst; married Dorothy Carolyn Iverson, August 21, 1955; children: Martha Jean, Steven Thomas, Kristin Louise, Daniel Timothy, David James. *Education:* St. Olaf College, B.A., 1951; Luther Theological Seminary, St. Paul, Minn., B.Th., 1954; Union Theological Seminary, S.T.M., 1959; currently working toward Th.D. at Garrett Theological Seminary. *Home:* 1327 North Elliott, Park Ridge, Ill. 60068. *Office:* Lutheran General Hospital, 1775 Dempster, Park Ridge, Ill. 60068.

CAREER: Ordained minister of Evangelical Lutheran Church, 1954; served at Trinity Lutheran Church, Mason City, Iowa, 1954-58; trainee in clinical pastoral education at St. Luke's Episcopal Hospital, New York, N.Y., 1958, and Lutheran Deaconess Hospital, Chicago, Ill., 1959; Lutheran General Hospital, Park Ridge, Ill., chaplain, 1959—, director of Division of Pastoral Care, 1960—. Accredited by College of Chaplains of American Protestant Hospital Association. *Member:* American Protestant Hospital Association, Association of Clinical Pastoral Education (certified supervisor), Academy for Mental Health and Religion, Park Ridge Kiwanis.

WRITINGS: (Editor with Harold P. Kurtz) *Toward a Creative Chaplaincy,* C. C Thomas, 1973.

SIDELIGHTS: Holst spent fifteen months in Tanzania developing the first known program of clinical pastoral education in Africa, at Kilimanjaro Christian Medical Centre in Moshi.

*   *   *

HOLT, Edgar Crawshaw   1900-1975

November 2, 1900—October 29, 1975; British journalist, and author of novels and historical works. Obituaries: *AB Bookman's Weekly,* December 22-29, 1975. (See index for previous *CA* sketch)

*   *   *

HOLTJE, Herbert F(ranklin)   1931-

PERSONAL: Surname is pronounced *Holt*-jay; born February 24, 1931, in Englewood, N.J.; son of Herbert F. (a marine designer) and Irma Holtje; married Adrienne Ruth Kriebel (a free-lance artist), June 23, 1956; children: James Peter. *Education:* Fairleigh Dickinson University, B.S., 1962, M.A., 1968; graduate study at New School for Social Research, 1969-70. *Home:* 151 Sunset Lane, Tenafly, N.J. 07670. *Office:* Tek-Mark, Inc., 223 Old Hook Rd., Westwood, N.J. 07675.

CAREER: Tek-Mark, Inc. (advertising and public relations), Westwood, N.J.; president, 1960—. Trustee, Tenafly, N. J. Community Chest. *Military service:* U.S. Navy, 1949-53. *Member:* American Psychological Association, American Marketing Association, Public Relations Society of America, Tenafly Swim Club.

WRITINGS: One Hundred Ways to Make Money in Your Spare Time Starting with Less than One Hundred Dollars, Prentice-Hall, 1973; *How To Borrow Everything You Need to Build a Great Personal Fortune,* Prentice-Hall, 1974; *How To Be a Fix-It Genius Using Seven Simple Tools,* McGraw, 1975. Contributor to *Personal Development Newsletter* and scientific journals.

WORK IN PROGRESS: Two handbooks on chemistry and mechanical engineering for McGraw; two books on business and consumer affairs for Prentice-Hall; a photo essay of the construction styles of colonial America.

AVOCATIONAL INTERESTS: Photography, architecture and furnishings of colonial America.

*   *   *

HOLZMAN, Franklyn Dunn   1918-

PERSONAL: Born December 31, 1918, in Brooklyn, N.Y.; son of Abraham (a teacher) and Mollie (a teacher; maiden name, Mandel) Holzman; married Mathilda Sara Wiesman (a professor of psychology), December 14, 1946; children: Thomas Ludwig, David Carl, Miriam Alexandra. *Education:* University of North Carolina, A.B., 1940; Harvard University, M.A., 1948, Ph.D., 1952. *Politics:* Democrat. *Religion:* Jewish. *Home:* 33 Peacock Farm Rd., Lexington, Mass. 02173. *Office:* Department of Economics, Tufts University, Medford, Mass. 02155.

CAREER: U.S. Department of the Treasury, Washington, D.C., economist, 1948-49, consultant, 1949-52; University of Washington, Seattle, assistant professor, 1952-54, associate professor, 1954-58, professor of economics, 1958-61; Tufts University, Medford, Mass., professor of economics, 1961—, Fletcher School of Law and Diplomacy, professor of economics, 1963—. Visiting professor at University of California, Los Angeles, 1956, Stanford University, 1957, Columbia University, 1962, and Massachusetts Institute of Technology, 1963; research associate at Russian Research

Center of Harvard University, 1961—. Consultant to United Nations, U.S. Arms Control and Disarmament Agency, U.S. Congress Joint Economic Committee, U.S. Commission on Trade and Investment Policy, U.S. Department of Commerce, and Brookings Institution. *Military service:* U.S. Army Air Forces, 1942-45; became staff sergeant.

MEMBER: American Economic Association, American Association for the Advancement of Slavic Studies (member of executive committee, 1964-65), American Association for the Study of Soviet-Type Economies (member of executive committee, 1966-67), Econometric Society. *Awards, honors:* Ford Foundation fellowship at Harvard University, 1957-58, 1959-60; Social Science Research Council fellowships at University of Washington, Seattle, 1960, and Tufts University, 1962; American Council of Learned Societies fellowship, 1964; National Science Foundation fellowship at Institute of Applied Economic Research (Paris), 1965-66, and at Tufts University, 1969-72.

WRITINGS: Soviet Taxation: The Fiscal and Monetary Problems of a Planned Economy, Harvard University Press, 1955; (editor) *Readings on Soviet Economy,* Rand McNally, 1962; *Foreign Trade under Central Planning,* Harvard University Press, 1974; *Financial Checks on Soviet Defense Expenditures,* Heath, 1975; *Foreign Trade under Communism: Politics and Economics,* Basic Books, in press. Contributor of about seventy-five articles to economics journals.

WORK IN PROGRESS: A book on economic relations between the United States and the Soviet Union.

*   *   *

HONCE, Charles E. 1895-1975

1895—August 29, 1975; American newsman, bibliophile, and author or editor of books on literary topics. Obituaries: *New York Times,* August 30, 1975; *Washington Post,* August 30, 1975; *Publishers Weekly,* September 15, 1975; *AB Bookman's Weekly,* December 8, 1975.

*   *   *

HOOK, Diana ffarington 1918-

PERSONAL: Born January 25, 1918, in Rio de Janeiro, Brazil; daughter of Adrian ffarington (a manager) and Catherine Margaret (Oldroyd) Bellairs; married Anthony George Berkeley Hook (a bank inspector), December 1, 1951; children: Raymunde Catherine (daughter), John Francis Adrian. *Education:* Attended Regent Street Polytechnic, 1935; London School of Domestic Science, diploma, 1937. *Politics:* "Dislike fanatics and extremists of any sort. Conservative for the most part." *Religion:* "Liberal Catholic Church." *Home:* Mowbray, Asheldon Rd., Wellswood, Torquay, Devonshire TQ1 2QN, England.

CAREER: Cookery adviser to electricity suppliers in London, England, 1937-40; Civil Nursing Reserve, Boscombe Hospital, Bournemouth, England, nursing aide, 1940; Ministry of Supply, London, England, executive officer, 1941-46; Electricity Board, Bristol, England, personnel officer, 1947-49; General Chemical Industries, Johannesburg, South Africa, accountant and statistician, 1949-51; writer, 1965—.

WRITINGS: The I Ching and You, Dutton, 1973; *The I Ching and Mankind,* Routledge & Kegan Paul, 1975.

WORK IN PROGRESS: Books on the occult and on reincarnation.

SIDELIGHTS: Diana Hook writes that her "mother was a world authority on astrology . . . interested in occultism." Her husband is also interested in occultism. When her mother died, Diana Hook found her mother's copy of the *I Ching.* "I decided to give it away as too complicated but it kept coming back. I decided to study it. Hence my books." She adds that she is "interested in occultism, the human mind, and finding out the reason for life here and hereafter." She has lived in South Africa, Brazil and Rhodesia.

*   *   *

HOOTEN, William J(arvis) 1900-

PERSONAL: Born September 5, 1900, in Chocowinity, N.C.; son of William Thomas (a farmer and merchant) and Martha (Jarvis) Hooten; married Grace Bull, June 17, 1922; children: William Pearce, Grace (Mrs. Arthur F. Gates), Charles Carlton. *Education:* Educated in elementary schools of Beaufort and Belhaven, N.C. *Politics:* Independent. *Religion:* Methodist. *Home:* 3611 Clifton Ave., El Paso, Tex. 79903.

CAREER: Associated Press (AP), telegrapher in Arizona and New Mexico, 1918-21, and El Paso, Tex., 1921-27; *El Paso Herald,* El Paso, reporter, 1927-29, city editor, 1929-31; *El Paso Times,* El Paso, city editor, 1931, managing editor, 1931-40, editor, 1940-70, vice-president, 1957-70; writer, 1970—. Member of board of directors of local Red Cross, Yucca Council, Salvation Army, and Boy Scouts of America.

MEMBER: Central Council of Social Agencies (president, 1942-43), El Paso County Historical Society (member of board of directors, 1973-74), El Paso Chamber of Commerce (first vice-president, 1946), Rotary International (vice-president of El Paso club, 1943-44), Masons, Knights Templar, Red Cross of Constantine, Shriners (potentate of El Maida temple, 1948). *Awards, honors:* Best citizen's award from Military Order of World Wars, 1970; Dorrance Roderick distinguished mass communications award from Sigma Delta Chi, 1975.

WRITINGS: Fifty-Two Years a Newsman, Texas Western Press, 1974. Author of column "Everyday Events" in *El Paso Times,* 1940-70.

*   *   *

HOPPER, Vincent Foster 1906-1976

April 19, 1906—January 19, 1976; American educator, administrator, and author, editor, or translator of books on literary topics. Obituaries: *New York Times,* January 21, 1976. (See index for previous *CA* sketch)

*   *   *

HORGAN, John J(oseph) 1910-

PERSONAL: Born July 2, 1910, in Haverhill, Mass.; son of Patrick Sarsfield (a fireman) and Mary Josephine (O'Connor) Horgan; married Margaret Coe, August 22, 1939; children: John Franklin, Richard Allan, Margaret Anne. *Education:* Holy Cross College, Worcester, Mass., Ph.B., 1934; Southeastern University, LL.B., 1939; further graduate study at University of California, Los Angeles, Michigan State University, and University of London. *Politics:* Democrat. *Religion:* Roman Catholic. *Home:* 881 Paseo Ferrelo, Santa Barbara, Calif.

CAREER: Federal Bureau of Investigation (FBI), Washington, D.C., assigned to Communications and Criminal Records Division, 1936-39, special agent, 1939-61; Claremont Colleges, Claremont, Calif., chief of security, 1961; San Bernardino Valley College, San Bernardino, Calif., assistant professor, 1961-69, associate professor of public safety, 1969-73, head of department, 1961-73; writer, 1974—. *Member:* Society of Former Special Agents of the Federal Bureau of Investigation, California State Peace Officers Association, California Association of Administration of Justice Educators.

WRITINGS: Criminal Investigation, McGraw, 1974.

WORK IN PROGRESS: A second edition of *Criminal Investigation.*

SIDELIGHTS: Horgan writes: "Following graduation from college, [I] played three years of professional baseball before joining the FBI in 1936—fulfilling a long ambition to become a 'G' man. My career as a Special Agent ranged through all phases of criminal investigation. [I] participated in FBI sponsored police training programs in various parts of the U.S., and as a counsellor at the FBI National Academy, Washington, D.C."

*   *   *

HORNIK, Edith Lynn   1930-

PERSONAL: Born November 4, 1930, in Zurich, Switzerland; naturalized U.S. citizen; daughter of Simon (a tobacco manufacturer) and Rosa (Bruell) Beer; married Josef Bernard Hornik (a machine tool engineer), February 9, 1958; children: Robert Bernard, Abigail. *Education:* Simmons College, B.S., 1953; University of Lausanne, graduate study, 1954. *Residence:* Scarsdale, N.Y.

CAREER: Free-lance writer. Has lectured on literature and creative writing; has appeared on television and radio programs. *Member:* Authors Guild of Authors League of America.

WRITINGS: You and Your Alcoholic Parent, Association Press, 1974; *The Drinking Woman,* Association Press, in press. Author of "The Young World" in *Scarsdale Inquirer, Riverdale Press,* and *Patent Trader,* all 1964-67. Contributor to magazines and newspapers in the United States and abroad, including *Young Miss, Ingenue, McCall's, Woman's Day, Co-Ed,* and *Living for Young Homemakers.*

SIDELIGHTS: Edith Hornik writes: "I am very much aware of the World War II era and of our silent 1950's student days. Right after World War II due to family circumstances I lived part of each year in Europe and part in the U.S.A. As a woman I came to be aware of the Napoleonic law versus the English law. Living partly in Switzerland before women had the right to vote in that country I became deeply conscious of the subtle differences of the American society's view of women and the European's outlook. I came to see that religion has nothing to do with God but is only a reflection of the society and political atmosphere we live in."

*   *   *

HORRELL, C. William   1918-

PERSONAL: Born October 15, 1918, in Anna, Ill.; son of Clarence W. (a plumber) and Zetta (Hileman) Horrell; married wife Ettelye M. (a teacher), June 5, 1941; children: Bruce W., Jeffrey L. *Education:* Southern Illinois University, B.Ed., 1942; University of Illinois, M.S., 1949; Indiana University, D.Ed., 1955. *Religion:* United Church of Christ. *Home:* 2803 Kent Dr., Carbondale, Ill. 62901. *Office:* Department of Cinema and Photography, Southern Illinois University, Carbondale, Ill. 62901.

CAREER: Horrell Studios, Anna, Ill., owner, 1945-49; Southern Illinois University, Carbondale, professor of cinema and photography, 1949—. *Member:* Professional Photographers of America, National Press Photographers Association, George Eastman House Associates, Sigma Delta Chi, Lions' Club, Elks Club.

WRITINGS: Introductory and Publications Photography, Kenilworth, 1959; *Land Between the Rivers,* Southern Illinois University Press, 1972.

WORK IN PROGRESS: Rocks and Soils of Southern Illinois; Coal: A Portfolio of Photographs.

SIDELIGHTS: Horrell writes that he is very much interested in documentary still photography and ". . . in the approach taken by the F.S.A. photographers of the '30's."

*   *   *

HORWITZ, Sylvia L(aibman)   1911-

PERSONAL: Born September 11, 1911, in Newcastle, Pa.; daughter of Emanuel J. (a stockbroker) and Fanny (Schoenberg) Laibman; married Louis D. Horwitz (a social worker), June 3, 1934; children: Paul. *Education:* Western Reserve University (now Case Western Reserve University), B.A., 1932. *Home:* 14 Ein Rogel, Jerusalem, Israel. *Agent:* Stella Seidenman, 16 Avenue Calas, Geneva, Switzerland.

CAREER: Copywriter in New York, N.Y., 1934-45; Overseas School of Rome, Rome, Italy, founder, 1946, director, 1946-48. Teacher at New School for Social Research, 1964. *Member:* Phi Beta Kappa.

WRITINGS: Toulouse-Lautrec: His World, Harper, 1973; *Francisco Goya: Painter of Kings and Demons,* Harper, 1974. Contributor to *Parents' Magazine, Gourmet,* and *Coronet.*

WORK IN PROGRESS: A biography of Arthur Evans, the excavator of Knossos.

SIDELIGHTS: Sylvia Horwitz has lived abroad for the past thirty years, with stays in Rome, Tunis, Paris, Geneva, and Jerusalem. She has participated in archaeological digs in Carthage and Tiberias.

*   *   *

HOSIER, Helen Kooiman   1928-
(Helen W. Kooiman)

PERSONAL: Surname is pronounced *Hoe*-sher; middle name is pronounced *Koy*-man; born January 26, 1928, in Hull, Iowa; daughter of Henry and Hattie (Brunsting) Westra; married Virgil J. Kooiman, January 26, 1947 (divorced, 1971); married Herman R. Hosier (a school principal), February 14, 1974; children: Barry John, Tonia Kooiman Thompson, Rhonda Kooiman Petrillo, Kraig Peter. *Education:* Attended high school in Sibley, Iowa. *Religion:* Protestant. *Home and office:* 1510 Duran St., Salinas, Calif. 93901.

CAREER: Gospel Book and Gift Shop, Bellflower, Calif., co-owner and manager, 1951-68; Bible Book Store, Buena Park, Calif., co-owner and manager, 1964-70; writer. Director of communications for "Haven of Rest" (radio program), Hollywood, Calif., 1971-72; editorial assistant, Christian Freedom Foundation, Buena Park, Calif., 1970-71.

WRITINGS—Under name Helen W. Kooiman: *Joyfully Expectant: Meditations Before Baby Comes,* Revell, 1966; *Please Pray for the Cabbages: Pint-size Parables for*

Grownups, Revell, 1967; *Cameos: Women Fashioned by God*, Tyndale, 1968; *Small Talk*, Tyndale, 1968; *Living Words of Comfort and Cheer*, Tyndale, 1969; *Transformed: Behind the Scenes with Billy Graham*, Tyndale, 1970; *Silhouettes: Women Behind Great Men*, Word Books, 1972; *Walter Knott: Keeper of the Flame*, Plycon Press, 1973; *Forgiveness in Action*, Hawthorn, 1973; (with Duane Pederson) *Going Sideways: Hope, Love, Life Versus Suicide*, Hawthorn, 1974; (with Pederson) *Day of Miracles*, Hawthorn, 1974.

Under name Helen Kooiman Hosier: *The Other Side of Divorce*, Hawthorn, 1975; *The Caring Jesus: A Woman's View of the Gospel of John*, Hawthorn, 1975; *Profiles: Men and Women Who Are Helping Change the World*, Hawthorn, 1976. Contributor to religious periodicals. Author of radio and television scripts.

* * *

HOUGH, Lindy Downer 1944-

PERSONAL: Surname is pronounced Huff; born July 4, 1944, in Denver, Colo.; daughter of Henry W. (a journalist and publisher of oil and gas publications) and Frances (a consultant and instructor in special education; maiden name, Downer) Hough; married Richard Grossinger (a writer and anthropologist), June 21, 1966; children: Robin (son), Miranda. *Education:* Smith College, B.A., 1966; Goddard College, M.A., 1972. *Home address:* R.F.D. 2, Box 135, Plainfield, Vt. 05667.

CAREER: Teacher of English literature and composition at Eastern Michigan University, 1966-69; assistant to husband, Richard Grossinger, in anthropological research at Mt. Desert Island, Maine, 1969-70; University of Maine, Portland-Gorham, lecturer in English, 1970-71; Goddard College, Plainfield, Vt., visiting artist in literature, 1972-73; poetry reader, free-lance writer, 1973-74; coordinator of Vermont poetry-in-the-schools program of Vermont Council on the Arts, 1974-75. Guest critic, Fourth West Coast Institute for Dance Criticism, 1975. *Awards, honors:* Writer's grant from Vermont Council on the Arts, 1974, for *The Sun in Cancer;* grants from Coordinating Council of Literary Magazines, 1971-75, for editing *Io.*

WRITINGS—Poems: *Changing Woman*, Io Publications, 1971; *Psyche*, North Atlantic Books, 1974; *The Sun in Cancer*, North Atlantic Books, 1975. Contributor of poems to literary journals, including *Truck, Caterpillar,* and *Tree,* and of dance criticism to *Montpelier Times-Argus.* Co-editor and publisher of *Io* (journal of poetry, science and anthropology), 1966—.

WORK IN PROGRESS: A prose work, *Cruel and Imperfect Strangers;* a fourth book of poems; a book of stories about contemporary women.

SIDELIGHTS: Lindy Hough writes: *"The Sun in Cancer* is the most un-abstract, literal writing I have done, probably full of a more mature impatience with societal-sexual forms. I have been a woman writer in a tough poetic tradition: the non-confessional, non-literary tradition of Olson, Duncan, Creeley, Levertov, Kelly. I have learned most from non-literary material (science, anthropology, music, art) and have continually been careful to see myself as a writer working with radical linguistic forms: my own kind of non-fictional prose, poems that speak of relation and place which mirror the complexities life presents."

HOULGATE, Deke 1930-

PERSONAL: Born August 8, 1930, in Los Angeles, Calif.; son of C. E. (a football historian) and Dorothy (Penry) Houlgate; married Olga Katsigeanis (a literary agent), January 29, 1955; children: C. Deke III, John A., David F., Gregory E. *Education:* University of Southern California, B.A., 1954. *Politics:* Republican. *Religion:* Methodist. *Home and office:* 1702 Circle Dr., Redondo Beach, Calif. 90277. *Agent:* Dominick Abel, Room 507, 612 North Michigan Ave., Chicago, Ill. 60611.

CAREER: Los Angeles Times, Los Angeles, Calif., sports deskman, 1952-54; *Las Vegas Sun,* Las Vegas, Nev., reporter, feature writer, and political writer, 1954-56; Los Angeles Times-Mirror Co., Los Angeles, Calif., reporter, 1956-59, management trainee, 1959-60, assistant director of special events, 1960-63; Deke Houlgate Public Relations, Los Angeles, Calif., owner, 1963-67; Deke Houlgate Enterprises (public relations and promotions firm), Redondo Beach, Calif., owner, 1967—. Motor sports writer for *Los Angeles Herald Examiner,* 1969—; auto racing reporter for Associated Press and United Press International, 1969—. Has appeared on Los Angeles area television and radio programs as authority on automotive subjects, automobile racing, and tennis. *Military service:* U.S. Army, 1950-52.

MEMBER: American Auto Racing Writers and Broadcasters Association (general vice-president, 1972—), American Racing Press Association, Sigma Delta Chi, Delta Tau Delta. *Awards, honors:* Nominated for Pulitzer Prize in 1957, for coverage of "Romance of the Skies," an air-sea disaster; awards from American Auto Racing Writers and Broadcasters Association, including news, feature, column, and technical writing awards in 1972, first prize for feature writing, 1973, for a series on "Indianapolis Five Hundred Tragedies," first place for radio writing, 1975, for "A Tribute to Peter Revson."

WRITINGS: The Fastest Men in the World on Wheels, World Publishing, 1971; (with Lyle Kenyon Engel) *The Complete Motorcycle Book,* Scholastic Press, 1974; *Handbook of High Performance Driving,* Arco, in press.

Script writer and producer of "Inside Sports with Sandy Reed," a series on KGFJ-Radio, 1964-65; script writer, producer, and announcer for "Inside Sports: Auto Racing," on KFI-Radio, 1969; script writer and announcer for "Peter Revson: Inside Auto Racing," for KWST-Radio, 1974.

Syndicated motor sports columnist for *Motor Sports Today,* 1968-73. Occasional contributor to *Los Angeles Times, San Francisco Examiner, Chicago Tribune, London Daily Telegraph,* Time-Life, Inc., *Reno Gazette,* and to motoring and racing magazines and sports magazines. Editor and general manager of *North Las Vegas News,* 1955-56; West Coast editor for *Stock Car Racing,* 1971—.

WORK IN PROGRESS: An automobile racing almanac; *Police Reporter,* a novel.

SIDELIGHTS: Houlgate writes that he: "Accepted challenge of Evel Knievel promoter to jump Snake River Canyon in a rocket for one million dollars following publication of critical story in advance of Evel's 'jump'; no money ever appeared, therefore, retired from canyon jumping with perfect record and no injuries." Some of his successful public relations campaigns include the buildup of Carroll Shelby and the Cobra sports car into national prominence, introduction and publicity campaigns under supervision of Bill Dredge of STP turbine race cars, introduction into North America of the Kawasaki line of motorcycles, and promotion of the Virginia Slims Women's Tennis Circuit.

Houlgate writes: "Although most easily recognized as a motor racing and sports writer, I have capabilities in other fields, including automotive, air quality, business, leisure activities, humor, crime, and Hollywood. Strong on research and accomplished in investigative reporting. Long associate with sports began as a child due to my father's involvement as a football writer, historian, statistician, syndicated columnist and after dinner speaker." *Avocational interests:* Tennis, sailing, jogging, bowling, bridge, Mexican history and lore (especially Baja California).

* * *

HOUSEMAN, Barton L(eroy) 1933-

PERSONAL: Born November 12, 1933, in Silver Spring, Md.; son of Melvin R. (an engineer) and Rena (Bouma) Houseman; married Doris VandeRee, August 17, 1955; children: Mark Evan, Jeanne Elaine. *Education:* Calvin College, A.B., 1955; Wayne State University, Ph.D., 1961. *Religion:* Christian. *Home:* 17 Galloway Ave., Cockeysville, Md. 21030. *Office:* Department of Chemistry, Goucher College, Towson, Md. 21204.

CAREER: Goucher College, Towson, Md., assistant professor, 1961-66, associate professor, 1966-72, professor of chemistry, 1972—. Visiting staff member at Los Alamos Scientific Laboratory, 1966—.

WRITINGS: (With Jim Webb) *The You-Don't-Need-A-Man-To-Fix-It Book,* Doubleday, 1973.

WORK IN PROGRESS: Research on high temperature electrochemical batteries which can be used to increase the thermodynamic efficiency of electrical power plants.

* * *

HOWES, Michael 1904-

PERSONAL: Born April 18, 1904, in Scarborough, England; son of Charles A. (a Reuters agent) and Jean Howes; married Dorothy Taylor, April 19, 1925; children: Patricia and Pamela (twins). *Education:* Attended Cambridge University and University of London. *Home and office:* 21 Boscombe Rd., London WI2 9HS, England.

CAREER: Has worked as pharmacist, advertising executive, and sales executive.

WRITINGS: So You Want to Be a Salesman, Colin Venton, 1973; *Amulets,* St. Martin's, 1975. Also author of *The Power Within You, Testimony to Reincarnation,* and *So You Want to Be in Advertising.*

WORK IN PROGRESS: A book that exposes commonplace swindles which beset the public today, *Wooden Nutmegs,* completion expected in 1976.

SIDELIGHTS: Howes has had a life-long interest in Egyptian mythology. He has done extensive archaeological field work in Roman and Bronze-age remains in England. Another area of research is uncovering pre-natal memories by hypnotism.

In his fifty years of writing he has had about two million words published.

* * *

HOZENY, Tony 1946-

PERSONAL: Born August 24, 1946, in Madison, Wis.; son

of Walter J. (a laboratory technician) and Helene (Abel) Hozeny; married Sara J. Daniels, June 21, 1969 (divorced, 1975); children: Jesse. *Education:* University of Wisconsin, Milwaukee, B.A., 1969, graduate study, 1971; Johns Hopkins University, M.A., 1972. *Religion:* None. *Office:* State of Wisconsin Public Service Commission, Madison, Wis.

CAREER: Teaching principal of residential treatment center in Milwaukee, Wis., 1969-71; University of Wisconsin, Milwaukee, lecturer in creative writing, 1971; Rider College, Trenton, N.J., visiting lecturer in English, 1972-73; State of Wisconsin, Public Service Commission, Madison, publications editor, 1974—; instructor in novel writing, University of Wisconsin extension, 1975-76. *Awards, honors:* Leslie Cross Award for best fiction by a Wisconsin author from Council of Wisconsin Writers, 1974, for *Driving Wheel* and *My House Is Dark;* Wisconsin Arts Board fellowship, 1976.

WRITINGS—Novels: *Driving Wheel,* Wisconsin House, 1974; *My House Is Dark,* Wisconsin House, 1974.

WORK IN PROGRESS: Ten-Cent Life, a novel.

SIDELIGHTS: Hozeny writes: "The artist is the person who understands people's dreams and knows how fragile they are." His writing concerns "the dreams and emotions of his characters, who are generally incomplete human beings, taking their identities from people around them instead of from themselves. They are shoe salesmen, waitresses, welfare mothers, garbagemen who have to struggle to keep their precarious lives together. They tend to act impulsively and physically, to feel rather than to intellectualize." Mary Walfoort, in the *Milwaukee Journal,* states that Hozeny's writing is "poetic, honest, deeply felt, and maintains a steady friction against the reader's sensibilities—the nightmare of riding the rails, the chill of the homeless of a winter's day, the loneliness of big cities and the prairies, the wild bouts of passion, the luminous moments of pity and generosity, the cruelties of man to man." *Avocational interests:* Blues, jazz, and country music, good conversation, car travel.

BIOGRAPHICAL/CRITICAL SOURCES: Capital Times, November 19, 1974; *Milwaukee Journal,* April 13, 1975.

* * *

HRUZA, Zdenek 1926-

PERSONAL: Born October 3, 1926, in Prague, Czechoslovakia; son of Antonin and Zdenka Hruza; married Judita Ilkovics (a physician), February 11, 1951; children: Eva, George. *Education:* Charles University, M.D., 1950; Czechoslovak Academy of Sciences, Ph.D., 1956, Sc.D., 1966. *Home:* 28-10 Ditmars Blvd., Long Island City, N.Y. 11105.

CAREER: Charles University, Prague, Czechoslovakia, researcher at School of Medicine, 1950-53; Czechoslovak Academy of Sciences, Prague, medical researcher, 1953-66; New York University, New York, N.Y., research professor of pathology, 1966—. *Member:* American Physiological Society, American Gerontological Society. *Awards, honors:* Research grants from National Institutes of Health and U.S. Public Health Service since 1966.

WRITINGS: Veda o Starnuti (title means "Science about Aging"), Czechoslovak Academy of Sciences, 1966; *Resistance to Trauma,* C. C Thomas, 1971.

WORK IN PROGRESS: Research on aging and atherosclerosis.

HUANG, Ray (Jen-yu) 1918-

PERSONAL: Born June 25, 1918, in Changsha, China; son of Cheng-pai and Chang-shun (Li) Huang; married Gayle Bates, September 20, 1966; children: Jefferson. *Education:* Attended U.S. Command and General Staff College, 1947, University of Michigan, B.A., 1954, M.A., 1957, Ph.D., 1964. *Home:* 10 Bonticouview Dr., New Paltz, N.Y. 12561. *Office:* Department of Asian Studies, State University of New York College at New Paltz, New Paltz, N.Y. 12561.

CAREER: Chinese National Army, served in India, Burma and Manchuria, 1941-50, leaving service as major; Southern Illinois University, Edwardsville, assistant professor of history, 1964-66; Columbia University, New York, N.Y., visiting associate professor of history, 1966; State University of New York College at New Paltz, associate professor, 1967-71, professor of Chinese history, 1971—. Research fellow at Harvard University, 1970-71. *Member:* Association for Asian Studies. *Awards, honors:* American Council of Learned Societies fellowships, 1966, 1972; National Science Foundation grant, 1973; Guggenheim fellowship, 1975-76.

WRITINGS: (Contributor) Charles O. Hucker, editor, *Government in Ming Times: Seven Studies,* Columbia University Press, 1969; (contributor) William Theodore de Bary, editor, *Self and Society in Ming Thought,* Columbia University Press, 1970; *Military Expenditures in Sixteenth Century Ming China,* Oriens Extremus, 1970; *Taxation and Governmental Finance in Sixteenth Century Ming-China,* Cambridge University Press, 1974. Contributor to *Ming Biographical Dictionary.*

WORK IN PROGRESS: This Much We Know About China, a general introduction to Chinese history and culture; collaborating with Joseph Needham on *Science and Civilisation in China,* Volume VII: *Conclusions.*

* * *

HUBERT, Renee Riese 1916-

PERSONAL: Born July 2, 1916, in Wiesbaden, Germany; daughter of Walter (a physician) and Herta (Pataky) Riese; married Judd David Hubert (a college professor), February 14, 1950. *Education:* University of Lyon, B.Ed.L., 1936; Sorbonne, University of Paris, license es lettres, 1939; Columbia University, M.A., 1945, Ph.D., 1951. *Home:* 1106 Cambridge Lane, Newport Beach, Calif. 92660. *Office:* Department of French, University of California, Irvine, Calif. 92660.

CAREER: Sarah Lawrence College, Bronxville, N.Y., instructor, 1951-53; Harvard University, Cambridge, Mass., instructor, 1953-55; Suffolk University, Boston, Mass., assistant professor, 1955-56; San Fernando Valley State College (now California State University, Northridge), assistant professor, 1958-62, associate professor of French and German, and head of department of foreign languages, 1962-65; University of Illinois, Urbana, associate professor, 1965-66; professor of French, 1966-67; University of California, Irvine, professor of French and comparative literature, 1967—. *Member:* International Federation for Modern Languages and Literature, International Association for the Study of French, Modern Language Association of America, American Association of Teachers of French. *Awards, honors:* American Association of University Women fellowship, 1947-48; Guggenheim fellowship, 1964-65; American Council of Learned Societies grant, 1965; fellowship from Creative Arts Institute, University of California, 1968; award from American Philosophical Association.

WRITINGS: La Cite Borgne (poetry; title means "The One-eyed City"), P. Seghers (Paris), 1953; *Asymptotes: Poems* (poetry), Nouvelles Editions Debresse (Paris), 1954; *Le Berceau d'Eve* (title means "Eve's Cradle"), Les Editions de Minuit (Paris), 1957; *Plumes et pinceaux: Dialogue avec la peinture de la veille* (title means "Pens and Brushes: Dialog with Painting of the Recent Past"), Devry-Livres (Paris), 1960; *Chants funebres* (poetry), Subervie (Rodez, France), 1964; (editor) Jules Supervielle and Boris Vian, *Deux pieces sur la fin d'un monde: La belle aux bois* [and] *Les batisseurs d'empire,* Macmillan, 1966; *Apollinaire et Picasso,* Cahiers du Sud, 1966; (contributor) Michel Decaudin, editor, *Guillaume Apollinaire, 1918-1968,* Lettres Modernes (Paris), 1968; *Enchainement* (title means "Charming"), Subervie, 1968; *Natures morte* (title means "Still Lives"), Pierre Oswald (Honfleur, France), 1972. Contributor of numerous articles on contemporary art and literature to journals. Member of editorial boards of professional journals.

WORK IN PROGRESS: A book on surrealism and the interrelation of the arts.

* * *

HUCKLEBERRY, E(vermont) R(obbins) 1894-

PERSONAL: Born June 4, 1894, in Decatur County, Ind.; son of John F. (a Baptist clergyman) and Ella (Robbins) Huckleberry; married Florence Barker, September 3, 1917; children: Robert Neel, Carole (Mrs. Robert Morton). *Education:* Baylor University, student, 1912-14; University of Chicago, S.B., 1917; Rush Medical College, M.D., 1921. *Politics:* Republican. *Religion:* Baptist. *Home and office:* 3594 South 860 E., Apt. 84, Salt Lake City, Utah.

CAREER: Los Angeles County Hospital, Los Angeles, Calif., intern, 1921-22; Oregon State Board of Health, Portland, Ore., engaged in educational work related to venereal disease, 1922-23; country doctor in Tillamook, Ore., 1923-46, McMinnville, Ore., 1946-48, and Umatitta, Ore., 1948-50; industrial physician in Lark, Utah, 1951-63, retired, 1963. Member of general council of American Baptist Convention, 1966-72, member of executive committee of council, 1970-71. *Military service:* U.S. Army, 1917-18; served in Oregon State Guard; became captain. *Member:* American Medical Association, Utah State Medical Society, Masons, Lions.

WRITINGS: The Adventures of Doctor Huckleberry: Tillamook, Oregon, Oregon Historical Society, 1970. Also writer of woodworking handbook.

SIDELIGHTS: Huckleberry writes: "I wanted to leave a record of a good life-style that is no more. It was intended only for family and friends, but an interested friend asked that it be submitted to the Historical Society." *Avocational interests:* Woodcarving and whittling, making jewelry, building play equipment for church schools.

BIOGRAPHICAL/CRITICAL SOURCES: American Baptist, October, 1972; *Skaggs Drug Centers,* January, 1974; *Deseret News,* March 6, 1975.

* * *

HUGHES, Andrew 1937-

PERSONAL: Born August 3, 1937, in London, England; son of Horace (a civil servant) and Nora (Lake) Hughes; married Diane Mary Joan Rycroft, September, 19, 1950;

children: Penelope Anne. *Education:* Worcester College, Oxford, B.A. (with honors), 1960, M.A. and D.Phil., both 1963. *Politics:* "Depends on circumstances." *Home:* 49 Thorncliffe Park Dr., Apt. 120, Toronto M4H 1J6, Ontario, Canada. *Office:* Faculty of Music, University of Toronto, Toronto M5S 1A1, Canada.

CAREER: Queen's University, Belfast, Northern Ireland, assistant lecturer, 1962-64; University of Illinois, Urbana, assistant professor, 1964-67; University of North Carolina, Chapel Hill, associate professor, 1967-69; University of Toronto, Toronto, Ontario, associate professor, 1969-75, professor of music, 1975—. *Member:* International Musicological Society, Royal Musical Association, American Musicological Society, Mediaeval Academy of America. *Awards, honors:* Guggenheim fellowship, 1973-74.

WRITINGS: (Editor) *Fifteenth-Century Liturigcal Music: Antiphons and Music for Holy Week and Easter,* Stainer & Bell, 1968; (editor with Margaret Bent) *The Old Hall Manuscript,* new edition (Hughes and Bent were not associated with earlier edition), American Institute of Musicology, Volumes I and II, 1969, Volume III, 1973; (contributor) Gustave Reese and Robert J. Snow, editors, *Essays in Honor of Dragan Plamenac,* University of Pittsburgh Press, 1969; *Manuscript Accidentals: Ficta in Focus,* American Institute of Musicology, 1972; *Medieval Music: The Sixth Liberal Art,* University of Toronto Press, 1974. Contributor to *Grove's Dictionary* and *Die Musik in Geschichte und Gegenwart;* contributor of articles and reviews to historical and musicological journals.

WORK IN PROGRESS: Two books, *Manuscripts of the Late Medieval Liturgy,* completion expected in 1976, and *A Handbook for Liturgical Studies of the Later Middle Ages;* research for two other possible books, *The Medieval Rhymed Office* and *The Offices of Thomas Becket.*

SIDELIGHTS: Hughes told *CA:* "Although I approach music as a scholarly discipline rather than as a performing art, I nevertheless believe that studies in the history of music are incomplete until realised in sound. To put this belief into practice I like to produce musical dramas and reenactments of musical ceremonies from the Middle Ages. Over the past years I have directed performances, authentically recreated and costumed, of medieval liturgical dramas and of the coronation service of Henry V of England." *Avocational interests:* Travel and photography.

*   *   *

HUGHES, B(asil) P(erronet)   1903-

PERSONAL: Born January 13, 1903, in Heywood, Lancashire, England; son of Edward Basil Armstrong (a priest) and Isabel (Thompson) Hughes; married Joan Marion Worthington, September 6, 1932; children: two sons. *Education:* Royal Military Academy, student, 1921-23. *Politics:* None. *Religion:* Church of England. *Home:* Saint Nicholas Close, Stour Row, near Shaftesbury, Dorsetshire, England. *Agent:* Bolt & Watson Ltd., 8 Storeys Gate, London S.W.1, England. *Office:* Royal Artillery Institution, Woolwich, London S.E.18, England.

CAREER: British Army, 1923-58, retiring as major general. Served in United Kingdom and India, 1923-34, in operations on northwest frontier in 4 (Hazare) Mountain Battalion, 1930, in operations in Mohmand expedition, 1933; served in British Expedition Force France, 1939-40, mentioned in dispatches; served in Anti-Aircraft Command, 1943, in northwest Europe, 1944-45, and in War Office, 1955-58. In charge of regimental collections and libraries,

including Museum of Artillery in the Rotunda at Woolwich. *Member:* Royal Artillery Historical Society. *Awards, honors*—Military: Companion of the Bath, Commander of Order of the British Empire. Other: Lefroy Gold Medal from Royal Artillery Institution, 1975.

WRITINGS: British Smooth-Bore Artillery, Arms & Armour Press, 1969; *The Bengal Horse Artillery,* Arms & Armour Press, 1971; *Firepower: Weapon Effectiveness on the Battlefield, 1630-1815,* Scribner, 1974.

WORK IN PROGRESS: Honour Titles of the Royal Artillery.

*   *   *

HUGHES, Mary Gray   1930-

PERSONAL: Born August 25, 1930, in Brownsville, Tex.; daughter of Hart (a writer) and Mary Gray (Seabury) Stilwell; married J.R.T. Hughes (an economics professor), December 19, 1953; children: Benjamin, Margaret, Charis. *Education:* Attended University of Texas, 1947-48; Columbia University, B.A., 1951; Oxford University, B.Litt., 1953. *Religion:* Episcopal. *Home:* 1016 Ridge Ave., Evanston, Ill. 60202. *Agent:* Pat Myrer, McIntosh and Otis, 475 Fifth Ave., New York, N.Y. 10017.

CAREER: Writer.

WRITINGS: The Thousand Springs, Puckerbrush Press, 1971. Stories have been published in *Best American Short Stories,* edited by Martha Foley, Houghton, 1969, and 1972, and *The Bicentennial Collection of Texas Short Stories,* edited by James P. White, Texas Center for Writers Press, 1974. Contributor of stories to *Atlantic, Esquire, Redbook, Southwest Review, Antioch Review.*

WORK IN PROGRESS: Several stories; a novel.

*   *   *

HUGHES, Patrick   1939-

PERSONAL: Born October 20, 1939, in Birmingham, England; son of Peter (a salesman) and Florence (Watson) Hughes; married former wife, Rennie Paterson; married Molly Parkin (a novelist), March 27, 1971; children: (first marriage) John, James, Solomon. *Education:* James Graham College of Education, Certificate of Education, 1961. *Politics:* Left. *Religion:* Atheist. *Home:* South Cottage, Rosemergy, Pendeen, Penzance, England. *Agent:* A. P. Watt & Son, 26/28 Bedford Row, London W.C.1., England.

CAREER: Leeds College of art, Leeds, England, senior lecturer, 1964-69; artist. *Awards, honors:* First place award from *Transatlantic Review,* 1973, for erotic drawing competition.

WRITINGS: (With George Brecht) *Vicious Circles and Infinity,* Doubleday, 1975.

WORK IN PROGRESS: With Paul Hammond, *Upon the Pun: Double Meaning in Words and Pictures.*

SIDELIGHTS: Hughes wrote that he is particularly interested in paradox, contradiction, absurdity, the imagination, humor, eroticism, and surrealism.

*   *   *

HUGHES, Stephen Ormsby   1924-

PERSONAL: Born January 21, 1924, in Crosby, Lancashire, England; son of George Joseph and Juliet (Ormsby) Hughes; married Reymonde Marie-Antoinette Million (an art dealer), September 1, 1950; children: Gregory, Kathleen. *Education:* Attended schools in England. *Religion:* Roman Catholic. *Home:* 4, Place des Alaouites, Rabat, Morocco. *Agent:* Julian Bach, 3 East 48th St., New York, N.Y. 10017. *Office:* Reuters Ltd., 7, rue de Baghdad, Rabat, Morocco.

CAREER: Journalist in England with *Stroud Journal,* Gloucestershire, 1946-49, *Kent & Sussex Courier,* Tunbridge Wells, 1949-50, in Tripoli, Libya, for Kemsley Newspapers, 1950-51, and in Paris, France, for *Continental Daily Mail,* 1951-52; editor for Reuters Ltd., Paris, 1952-53, and for *Atlantic Courier,* in Casablanca, Morocco, 1953-63; foreign correspondent for Reuters Ltd., in Rabat, Morocco, 1963-75. *Military service:* Royal Air Force, 1941-46; served with Coastal Command; became warrant officer pilot. *Member:* National Union of Journalists (United Kingdom).

WRITINGS: Tight Lines and Dragonflies, Lippincott, 1972; *Vallees Heureuses* (title means "Happy Valleys"), Royal Air Maroc (Morocco), 1972. Also author of radio plays, "Antic Art," 1947, "The Judy's Old Feller," 1948, and "Back to Back," 1949, all produced by British Broadcasting Corp.

WORK IN PROGRESS: Pooty-Bongo, a novel about developing countries, the conflict between the "haves" and "have-nots," based on his experience in Africa and the Arab world.

SIDELIGHTS: Hughes writes: "My major current project concerns the UDC's (under-developed or under-developing countries) or the so-called Third World and the impact at every level of the East-West conflict. The subject demands attention because I believe the UDC's are doomed to disaster; that will have dire consequences also for the developed world, either capitalist or communist, because neither cold war camp is doing anything to help three quarters of the world's population." Hughes contends that the aid that countries of the developed world give "serves their own short-term purposes or helps to lave their consciences."

*   *   *

HUMPHREY, James H(arry) 1911-

PERSONAL: Born February 26, 1911, in Marietta, Ohio; son of Harry and Nellie (Pugh) Humphrey; married Frances Drokopil, March 29, 1945; children: Joy Nell. *Education:* Denison University, B.S., 1933; Western Reserve University (now Case Western Reserve University), M.S., 1946; Boston University, Ph.D., 1951. *Religion:* Protestant. *Home:* 9108 St. Andrews Place, College Park, Md. 20740. *Office:* Department of Physical Education, University of Maryland, College Park, Md. 20740.

CAREER: Bedford (Ohio) Board of Education, director of health and physical education, 1937-49; Michigan State University, East Lansing, assistant professor of health and physical education, 1951-53; University of Maryland, College Park, associate professor, 1953-56, professor of physical education and health, 1956—.*Military service:* U.S. Naval Reserve, 1943-45. *Member:* American Academy of Physical Education, American Alliance for Health, Physical Education, and Recreation, American School Health Association (fellow; past chairman of research council), Society for Research in Child Development (fellow), Association for Anthropological Study of Play. *Awards, honors:* Named distinguished visiting scholar, University of Delaware, 1965; American Alliance for Health, Physical Education, and Recreation National Honor Award, 1972, and R. Tait McKenzie Award, 1976.

WRITINGS: (With Harris F. Beeman) *Intramural Sports: A Text and Study Guide,* William C. Brown, 1954; (with Leslie W. Irwin) *Principles and Techniques of Supervision in Physical Education,* Mosby, 1954, 3rd edition (with Alice M. Love), William C. Brown, 1972; (with Irwin and Warren R. Johnson) *Methods and Materials in School Health Education,* Mosby, 1956; *Elementary School Physical Education, with Emphasis upon Its Integration in Other Curriculum Areas,* Harper, 1958; (editor with Edwina Jones and Martha J. Haverstick) *Readings in Physical Education for the Elementary School,* National Press, 1958, revised edition, 1960.

(With Warren R. Johnson and Virginia D. Moore) *Elementary School Health Education: Curriculum, Methods, Integration,* Harper, 1962; (compiler with Doris E. Terry and Howard S. Slusher) *Readings in Health Education: A Collection of Selected Articles for Use in Personal Health and Health Education Courses,* William C. Brown, 1964; *Child Learning through Elementary School Physical Education,* William C. Brown, 1966, 2nd edition (with daughter, Joy N. Humphrey), 1974; (with Anne Gayle Ingram) *Introduction to Physical Education for College Students,* Holbrook, 1969.

(With Dorothy D. Sullivan) *Teaching Slow Learners through Active Games,* C. C Thomas, 1970; (with Sullivan) *Teaching Reading through Motor Learning,* C. C Thomas, 1973; (with daughter, J. N. Humphrey) *Learning to Listen and Read through Movement,* Kimbo Educational, 1974; *Teaching Elementary School Science Through Motor Learning,* C. C Thomas, 1975; *Education of Children through Motor Activity,* C. C Thomas, 1975.

Author of "Read and Play" series for primary grades, six books, Muller, 1965. Contributor of articles to journals in his field. Research editor, *Journal of School Health,* 1962-65; member of board of associate editors, *Research Quarterly,* 1954-59 and 1960-63.

*   *   *

HUNTER, C. Bruce 1917-

PERSONAL: Born February 24, 1917, in Nova Scotia, Canada; son of Mahlon Johnson and Nema (Dyas) Hunter; married Adele Jordan (a teacher), June 21, 1947; children: Gail. *Education:* Pratt Institute, B.F.A., 1947; Columbia University, M.A., 1948. *Office:* American Museum of Natural History, 79th St. and Central Park W., New York, N.Y. 10024.

CAREER: Dalhousie University, Halifax, Nova Scotia, professor of art, 1947-49; American Museum of Natural History, New York, N.Y., lecturer in archaeology, 1952—, director of Evening School, 1956—, leader of archaeological field study trips to Meso-america and South America, 1956—. Adjunct professor at New York University, 1974-76. *Military service:* U.S. Army, 1941-45, served as cryptographer; became staff sergeant.

WRITINGS: A Guide to Ancient Maya Ruins, Oklahoma University Press, 1974; *A Guide to the Ruins of Ancient Mexico,* Oklahoma University Press, in press. Contributor to journals in his field.

*   *   *

HUNTER, Kim 1922-
(Janet Cole)

PERSONAL: Born November 12, 1922, in Detroit, Mich.; daughter of Donald Cole (an engineer) and Grace (Lind)

Cole Stebbins; married William A. Baldwin, February 11, 1944 (divorced, 1946); married Robert Emmett (a writer), December 20, 1951; children: (first marriage) Kathryn; (second marriage) Sean. *Education:* Attended public schools in Detroit, Mich. and Miami Beach, Fla.; studied acting in Miami Beach, Fla., 1938-40. *Home:* 42 Commerce St., New York, N.Y. 10014. *Agent:* Flora Roberts, 65 East 55th St., New York, N.Y. 10022.

CAREER: Stage, screen, and television actress. Made film debut in "The Seventh Victim," 1943, and has appeared in over twenty films, including "Stairway to Heaven," 1946, "A Streetcar Named Desire," 1951, "Deadline: U.S.A.," 1952, "Planet of the Apes," 1968, and two sequels, 1970 and 1971, "Dark August," 1976. Made Broadway debut in "A Streetcar Named Desire," 1947, and has appeared in over twelve Broadway productions, including "Darkness at Noon," 1951, "The Children's Hour," 1953, and "The Women," 1973; appeared in two national tours, "Two Blind Mice," 1950, "And Miss Reardon Drinks a Little," 1971-72; also has appeared in numerous stock and regional theatres, 1947—, the American Shakespeare Festival, 1961, and at the Library of Congress, 1963 and 1966. Television guest appearances number over 200, the most recent include such shows as "Mission Impossible," "Marcus Welby, M.D.," "Hec Ramsey," "Police Story," "Ironside," and "Ellery Queen." Lecturer on the performing arts, 1954—; actress-in-residence, University of Utah, 1963, Otterbein College, 1965, William Paterson College, 1975; performed one-woman show of selections from Cocteau, O'Neill, and Shakespeare in New Jersey and Indiana, 1965; frequent guest performer on CBS's "Radio Mystery Theatre," 1973—. Recorded two record albums, "From Morning 'Til Night and a Bag Full of Poems," RCA Victor, 1961, and "Come, Woo Me," Unified Audio Classics, 1964.

MEMBER: Academy of Motion Picture Arts and Sciences, National Society of Literature and the Arts, American National Theatre and Academy, Actors Studio, Screen Actors Guild, American Federation of Television and Radio Artists, Actors Equity Association (council member, 1953-59). *Awards, honors:* Donaldson Award and New York Drama Critics Circle Award, both 1948, both for stage performance in "Streetcar Named Desire"; Academy Award, Golden Globe Award, and *Look* Magazine Award, all 1952, all for performance in screen version of "Streetcar Named Desire."

WRITINGS: Kim Hunter: Loose in the Kitchen (autobiographical cookbook), Domina Books, 1975.

WORK IN PROGRESS: "Will I ever write again? I don't know. But now that it's [her book] out, the challenge is intriguing."

SIDELIGHTS: Kim Hunter told *CA:* "The book I've written evolved; it was not the result of a deliberate setting out to 'write a book.' . . . The discipline required to make whatever writing talent I may have work at *all,* was a humbling discovery, and I'm filled with respect—for what I've learned, and what I have yet to learn."

*   *   *

HUPKA, Robert   1919-

PERSONAL: Born August 26, 1919, in Vienna, Austria; son of Josef F. (professor of law and dean at University of Vienna) and Hermine ("an artist with the camera"; maiden name, Brull) Hupka. *Education:* Attended Schottengymnasium, Vienna, 1930-38; University College, London,

1939; St. Joseph's College, Philadelphia, Pa., B.A., 1942; studied music privately in Vienna, London, and Philadelphia. *Religion:* Roman Catholic. *Residence:* New York, N.Y.

CAREER: Radio Corp. of America (RCA) Victor Records, Camden, N.J. (later New York City), librarian and head of special Toscanini project in artists and repertoire department, 1942-49; Camp Acadia, Livingston Manor, N.Y., photography counselor, 1949-50; Columbia Broadcasting System (CBS), New York City, television cameraman, 1950—. Appeared on television and radio programs in the United States and Canada. Producer of sound recordings for Manhattanville College, 1958—; producer of recorded music program for New York World's Fair Vatican Pavilion, 1964-65.

WRITINGS—All with own photographs: (With Samuel Antek) *This Was Toscanini,* Vanguard, 1963; *Michelangelo Pieta,* Crown, 1975. Contributor to religious magazines.

WORK IN PROGRESS: A large-format edition with some life-size photographs of the sculpture "Pieta"; a second book on Toscanini, with bibliography of recordings, broadcasts, and performances; editing *The Spiritual Legacy of Charles Rich;* and *Gregorian Chant: The Forgotten Treasure.*

SIDELIGHTS: Reflecting on his education, Robert Hupka told *CA* that "the venerable, more than 150-year old Schottengymnasium in Vienna . . . one of Austria's most prestigious schools . . . is greatly responsible for many of the higher values of life which I have."

Hupka's grandfather was Ignaz Brull, composer and friend of Brahms. Drawn especially to music—he wanted to be a conductor—Hupka became totally preoccupied with Toscanini from the moment he first heard him at the Salzburg Festivals in 1934 and thereafter by attending for twenty years most of his performances and rehearsals. He writes: "His unique art became the driving force of my life. To me he was synonymous with music . . . a spark from heaven." But the most important person in his life, Hupka writes, has been Charles Rich, "a man of extraordinary spirituality whose life of prayer and learning has deepened my own insights. The publication of his writings, which I intend to edit, would fill a present day need."

Hupka's photographs of Toscanini have been featured on the Italian Toscanini Centennial commemorative stamp, 1967, the Columbia Broadcasting System "Camera Three" and National Broadcasting Corp.'s "Bell Telephone Hour" telecasts, as well as on more than thirty record album covers, in several books, magazines, and other publications.

Hupka's *Michelangelo Pieta* is a book of 150 photographs of the sculpture, a small-size edition measuring 9 inches by 6 inches. He describes it as "a *picture book.* The photographs are really the text and speak the international language of their own. And since this is an international book therefore, which however needs some commentary, I have included commentary in 6 languages—which is also highly unusual since there are not many books in more than 1 or 2 languages, 3 at the most . . . But more important still than the written word are the photographs which, arranged in the form of *a tour* around the Pieta, show the sculpture from every conceivable angle as it has never been seen before. How many books feature a single statue in 150 photographs? 10, 20, maybe 30 . . . yes; but 150?"

BIOGRAPHICAL/CRITICAL SOURCES: Popular Photography, December, 1968.

HUSSEY, John A(dam) 1913-

PERSONAL: Born January 5, 1913, in Oakland, Calif.; son of Wallace Maxwell (a real estate and title company executive) and Ottilia (Gilliland) Hussey; married Virginia Alice Hawkins (an interior decorator), May 16, 1936. Education: University of California, Berkeley, A.B., 1934, M.A., 1935, Ph.D., 1941. Religion: Protestant. Home: 93 Woodland Way, Piedmont, Calif. 94611.

CAREER: General Cable Corp., Emeryville, Calif., supervisor of inspector training, 1941-45; free-lance writer in Oakland, Calif., 1945-47; U.S. National Park Service, historian in San Francisco, Calif., 1947-49, historian in Washington, D.C., 1950-53, regional historian in San Francisco, 1953-69, chief of Western Service Center Division of Historical Studies, 1969-72; free-lance writer, historian, researcher, and consultant in historic preservation and interpretation, 1972—. Consultant for reconstruction of Fort Vancouver in Washington, 1973—, and Fort William in Ontario, 1974. Member of board of directors of Book Club of California, 1956-69. Member: Western History Association, California Historical Society (chairman of historic preservation award committee, 1974—), Roxburghe Club (San Francisco), Phi Beta Kappa, Sigma Alpha Epsilon. Awards, honors: Certificate of merit from Seattle Historical Society, 1958, for History of Fort Vancouver; award of merit from American Association for State and Local History, 1968, for Champoeg; Captain Robert Gray Medal from Washington State Historical Society, 1971.

WRITINGS: Chinook Point and the Story of Fort Columbia (pamphlet), Washington State Parks and Recreation Commission, 1957, revised edition, 1967; The History of Fort Vancouver and Its Physical Structure, Washington State Historical Society, 1957; (editor) The Voyage of the Racoon, Book Club of California, 1958; (with John Shirley Hurst) That the Past Shall Live, National Park Service, 1959; (editor) John A. Swan, A Trip to the Gold Mines of California in 1848, Book Club of California, 1960; (editor) Thomas Starr King, A Vacation Among the Sierras: Yosemite in 1860, Book Club of California, 1962; (with Victor O. Goodwin) Sawtooth Mountain Area Study, Idaho: History, U.S. Forest Service, 1967; Champoeg: Place of Transition, Oregon Historical Society, 1967; (editor) Early Sacramento from the Journals of Prince Paul of Wurttemberg, Sacramento Book Collectors Club, 1973. Contributor to numerous historical journals. Member of publications committee, California Historical Society, 1963-70.

WORK IN PROGRESS: A history of the Bear Flag revolt in California and a popular history of Fort Vancouver, western headquarters of Hudson's Bay Co., 1825-1860.

SIDELIGHTS: Hussey told CA: "Although somewhat disillusioned with the idea that people and nations learn from the lessons of history, I still believe it is worthwhile to seek the truth about the past in the hope that it will illuminate the present and provide guidance for the future. At the very least the historian helps to satisfy a deep human interest in the past and he entertains, on a certain level, as does the novelist, the playwright, or the poet. Thus one of my objectives in historical writing is to be as interesting as possible within the limits of good scholarship."

*   *   *

HUSTON, Mervyn James 1912-

PERSONAL: Born September 4, 1912, in Ashcroft, British Columbia, Canada; son of William Mervyn (a pharmacist) and Irene (Gray) Huston; married Helen Margaret Mc-Bryan, December 18, 1938; children: Bryan Mervyn, Dorna Helen (Mrs. David Thomas Young). Education: University of Alberta, B.Sc., 1934, M.Sc., 1938; University of Washington, Seattle, Ph.D., 1941. Religion: United Church of Canada. Home: 11562 80th Ave., Edmonton, Alberta, Canada. Office: Faculty of Pharmacy, University of Alberta, Edmonton, Alberta, Canada.

CAREER: University of Alberta, Edmonton, assistant professor, 1943-44, professor of pharmacy, 1944—, dean of faculty of pharmacy, 1948—. Member: Canadian Conference on Pharmacy Faculties (chairman, 1948), Canadian Pharmaceutical Association (president, 1969), Canadian Foundation for the Advancement of Pharmacy (president, 1970), Association of Deans of Pharmacy of Canada (president, 1972), Sigma Xi, Phi Sigma, Rho Chi, Phi Delta Theta, Kiwanis Club, Masonic Lodge, Al Azhar Temple, Edmonton Burns Club, Mayfair Golf and Country Club. Awards, honors: Centennial Medal from Government of Canada, 1968; Dr. E. R. Squibb Award from Canadian Pharmaceutical Association, 1971; Alta Achievement Award from Government of Alberta, 1971, all for contribution to the profession.

WRITINGS: Textbook of Pharmaceutical Arithmetic, Canadian Pharmaceutical Association, 1959; Test and Improve Your Scientific Word Power, Canadian Pharmaceutical Association, 1960; The Great Canadian Lover, Musson, 1964; Text and Dictionary of Scientific Words, Canadian Pharmaceutical Association, 1965; Toasts to the Bride, Hurtig, 1969; Canada Eh to Zed, Hurtig, 1974. Contributor to journals in his field. Editor-in-chief of Canadian Journal of Pharmaceutical Sciences, 1965—.

WORK IN PROGRESS: Gophers Don't Pay Taxes.

*   *   *

HUTCHENS, Paul 1902-

PERSONAL: Born April 7, 1902, in Thorntown, Ind.; son of Ira and Eva (Bishop) Hutchens; married Jane Carolyn Freerks, December 24, 1924; children: Pauline (Mrs. Kyle Wilson). Education: Attended Earlham College, 1919-20, and Moody Bible Institute, 1921-23, 1927. Politics: Republican. Home and office: 120 East Winters Dr., Colorado Springs, Colo. 80907.

CAREER: Ordained Baptist minister, 1927. Teacher in rural school, 1920-21; writer.

WRITINGS—All novels except as indicated; all published by Eerdmans, except as indicated: Romance of Fire, 1934; This Way Out, 1935; A Song Forever, 1936; The Last First, 1936; The Voice, 1937; This is Life, 1937; Mastering Marcus, 1938; Yesterday's Rain, 1938; Blaze Star, 1939; Shafted Sunlight, 1939; Windblown, 1939; The Vision, 1940; Cup of Cold Water, 1941; Eclipse, 1942; When God Says "No" (lectures), 1943; Morning Light, 1944; (compiler) How to Meet Your Troubles: True Adventures with Adversity (stories), 1945; Uninterrupted Sky, Van Kampen Press, 1949; The Mystery of the Marsh, Van Kampen Press, 1952; Yours for Four Years, Van Kampen Press, 1954; My Life and I (autobiography), Sugar Creek Press, 1962; East of the Shadows, Moody, 1972.

Juvenile; all published by Eerdmans: The Sugar Creek Gang, 1939; Further Adventures of the Sugar Creek Gang, 1940; We Killed a Bear: A Sugar Creek Gang Story, 1940, published as The Sugar Creek Gang and the Killer Bear, Moody; The Sugar Creek Gang Goes Camping, 1941; The Sugar Creek Gang in Chicago, 1941, published as The

Sugar Creek Gang and the Chicago Adventure, Moody, 1968; *The Sugar Creek Gang in School*, 1942; *Mystery at Sugar Creek*, 1943; *The Sugar Creek Gang Flies to Cuba*, 1944; *A New Sugar Creek Mystery*, 1946; *One Stormy Day at Sugar Creek*, 1946; *Shenanigans at Sugar Creek*, 1947.

All published by Van Kampen Press: *The Sugar Creek Gang Goes North*, 1947; *Adventures in an Indian Cemetery: A Sugar Creek Gang Story*, 1947; *The Sugar Creek Gang Digs for Treasure*, 1948; *North Woods Manhunt: A Sugar Creek Gang Story*, 1948; *The Haunted House at Sugar Creek*, 1949, published as *The Sugar Creek and the Haunted House*, Moody, 1967; *The Sugar Creek Gang on the Mexican Border*, 1950; *Lost in a Sugar Creek Blizzard*, 1950, published as *The Sugar Creek Gang Lost in the Blizzard*, Moody; *The Green Tent Mystery at Sugar Creek*, 1950, published as *The Sugar Creek Gang and the Green Tent Mystery*, Moody; (compiler) *Trails of Yesteryear: Ye Olde Sugar Creek Scrapbook*, 1951; *10,000 Minutes at Sugar Creek*, 1952; *Blue Cow at Sugar Creek*, 1953, published as *Sugar Creek Gang and the Blue Cow*, Moody, 1971; *The Trap Line Thief at Sugar Creek*, 1953, published as *Sugar Creek Gang and the Trapline Thief*, Moody, 1971; *The Watermelon Mystery at Sugar Creek*, 1955, published as *Sugar Creek Gang and the Watermelon Mystery*, Moody, 1971.

All published by Scripture Press: *Sugar Creek Gang at Snow Goose Lodge*, 1957; *Sugar Creek Gang Goes Western*, 1957; *The Old Stranger's Secret*, 1957.

"Sugar Creek Gang" series, published by Moody: *The Sugar Creek Gang and the Timber Wolf*, 1965; *... and the Swamp Robber*, 1966; *... and the Western Adventure*, 1966; *... and the Killer Cat*, 1966; *... and Screams in the Night*, 1967; *... and the Treasure Hunt*, 1967; *... and the Lost Campers*, 1968; *... and the Secret Hideout*, 1968; *... and the Ghost Dog*, 1968; *... and the Palm Tree Manhunt*, 1969; *... and the Treehouse Mystery*, 1972; *... and the Battle of the Bees*, 1972; *... and the Cemetery Vandals*, 1972; *... and the Runaway Rescue*, 1973; *The Sugar Creek Gang: Locked in the Attic*, 1973; Also author of *The Sugar Creek Gang and the Bull Fighter*, *The Sugar Creek Gang and the Mystery Thief*, *Brown Box Mystery*, and *Colorado Kidnapping*, all published by Moody; *The Know-so Christian*, a nonfiction book published in the Kituba language; and author of music and lyrics for hymns.

SIDELIGHTS: One of Hutchens' adult novels has its setting in pre-Castro Cuba. He traveled there to secure background information for the book, *Morning Flight*. Another novel, *The Last First* has been published in Afrikaans, and several of the "Sugar Creek Gang" books have been published in French, German, and Norwegian translations.

BIOGRAPHICAL/CRITICAL SOURCES: Paul Hutchens, *My Life and I*, Sugar Creek Press, 1962.

* * *

HUTCHINS, Maude (Phelps McVeigh)

PERSONAL: Born in New York, N.Y.; daughter of Warren Ratcliffe and Maude (Phelps) McVeigh; married Robert Maynard Hutchins, 1921 (divorced); children: Mary Frances, Joanna Blessing, Clarissa Phelps. *Education:* Yale University, B.F.A., 1926. *Politics:* "No affiliation." *Religion:* Episcopal. *Home:* 1046 Pequot Rd., Southport, Conn. 06490. *Agent:* Harold Ober Associates, Inc., 40 East 49th St., New York, N.Y. 10017.

CAREER: Painter and sculptress. Annual shows at Quest Art Galleries, Chicago, Ill., 1930-39, and Roullier Art Galleries, Chicago, 1942-48; work has been exhibited in one-man shows at Grand Central Art Galleries, Renaissance Society, University of Chicago, St. Louis Museum, Wildenstein Galleries, San Francisco Museum of Art, and Toledo Museum of Art; sculpture has been shown at American Fine Arts Society Galleries third annual national exhibition of American art.

WRITINGS: (With Mortimer Jerome Adler) *Diagrammatics*, Random House, 1932; *Georgiana* (novel), New Directions, 1948; *A Diary of Love* (novel), New Directions, 1950, reprinted, Greenwood, 1971; *Love Is a Pie* (stories and plays), New Directions, 1952; *My Hero*, New Directions, 1953; *The Memoirs of Maisie* (novel), Appleton, 1955; *Victorine* (novel), Alan Swallow, 1959; *The Elevator* (stories), Morrow, 1962; *Honey on the Moon* (novel), Morrow, 1964; *Blood on the Doves* (novel), Morrow, 1965; *The Unbelievers Downstairs* (novel), Morrow, 1967.

Work has been anthologized in *O. Henry Prize Stories*, and *New Directions Annual*. Contributor to periodicals, including *Poetry*, *New Yorker*, *Accent*, *Kenyon Review*, *Foreground*, *Mademoiselle*, *Quarterly Review of Literature*, *Quest*, *Harper's Bazaar*, *Vogue*, and *Ramparts*.

WORK IN PROGRESS: Three novellas, *The Maid of Orleans and the Dolphin*, *Invitation to the Creation*, and *Ye Gods!*

* * *

HUTCHINSON, Eliot Dole 1900-

PERSONAL: Born July 30, 1900, in Cambridge, Mass.; son of Oliver W. (a minister) and Louisa M. (a college professor; maiden name, Dole) Hutchinson; married Hazel Beatrice Blanchard (a librarian), April 3, 1934. *Education:* Harvard University, A.B., 1922, M.A., 1924, Ph.D., 1926. *Politics:* Republican. *Religion:* Protestant. *Home:* 14 Arnold Park, Rochester, N.Y. 14607. *Agent:* A. L. Fierst, 630 Ninth Ave., New York, N.Y. 10036.

CAREER: University of Rochester, Rochester, N.Y., assistant professor of psychology, 1926-43; Sylvania Electric Corp., New York, N.Y., training specialist, 1943-46; University of Rochester, research consultant to School of Medicine and Dentistry, 1950-75. *Member:* American Association for the Advancement of Science, American Association of University Professors, American Psychological Society, Phi Beta Kappa, Sigma Xi. *Awards, honors:* Sheldon fellowship at University of Berlin, 1922-23; Rockefeller Foundation fellowship at Cambridge University, 1927-28.

WRITINGS: How to Think Creatively, Abingdon, 1949; *Rhymes for Our Times*, Windy Row Press, 1971. Contributor to *American Scholar*, *Christian Century*, *Forum*, and *Hygeia*, among others, and to professional journals.

WORK IN PROGRESS: Gadgets: A Fable, and *Adventures in Belief*, "short essays in long verse."

AVOCATIONAL INTERESTS: Remodeling old Colonial houses, painting, writing, antique collecting.

* * *

HUTCHINSON, Peter 1943-

PERSONAL: Born August 24, 1943, in London, England; married Maite Lores; children: Fabian. *Education:* University of Wales, B.Sc., 1965; King's College, University of London, Ph.D., 1970. *Home:* 120 Oxford Rd., Abingdon, Berkshire, England.

CAREER: Elsevier International Projects Ltd., Oxford, England, editor of popular scientific books, 1970—. Part-time researcher in department of zoology, Cambridge University.

WRITINGS: Evolution Explained, David & Charles, 1974. Contributor to scientific journals.

WORK IN PROGRESS: Research on the early evolution of fish.

*   *   *

HUTCHINSON, Ray Coryton   1907-1975

January 23, 1907—1975; British novelist. Obituaries: *AB Bookman's Weekly,* August 25, 1975. (See index for previous *CA* sketch)

*   *   *

HUTTON, Warwick   1939-

PERSONAL: Born July 17, 1939; son of John (an artist) and Helen (Blair) Hutton; married Elizabeth Mills, August 26, 1965; children: Hanno. *Education:* Colchester Art School, N.D.D., 1961. *Politics:* None. *Religion:* None. *Home:* 65 Eden St., Cambridge, England.

CAREER: Illustrator, painter, and glass engraver. Visiting lecturer, Cambridge College of Art and Technology, 1972—, Morley College, 1973-75. *Member:* Cambridge Society of Painters and Sculptors.

WRITINGS: Making Woodcuts, St. Martin's, 1974.

WORK IN PROGRESS: Research for a book on glass engraving.

SIDELIGHTS: Hutton told *CA:* "I am a full time artist. . . . Although I am primarily a painter, the large scale glass engraving technique which my father invented has been passed on to me. When I am not occupied with painting and woodcuts, I carry out commissioned glass engravings for civic buildings, churches, homes, etc."

*   *   *

HUXHOLD, Harry N(orman)   1922-

PERSONAL: Born December 21, 1922, in Oak Park, Ill.; son of Harry Charles (a salesman) and Lillian (Schultz) Huxhold; married Lucille Edythe Koerber, June 11, 1947; children: Pamela Lee, Timothy Joel, Charles Norman, David Mark, James Bartholomew. *Education:* Concordia Seminary, St. Louis, Mo., B.A., 1944, M.Div., 1947; Luther Seminary, St. Paul, Minn., M.Th., 1968; Christian Theological Seminary, Indianapolis, Ind., D.Min. (summa cum laude), 1972; also studied at Concordia Teachers College, River Forest, Ill., 1944-45, Loyola University, Chicago, Ill., 1950-53, and Chicago Theological Seminary, 1957. *Home:* 5153 North Arlington, Indianapolis, Ind. 46226. *Office:* Our Redeemer Lutheran Church, 3421 North Park, Indianapolis, Ind. 46205.

CAREER: Ordained Lutheran clergyman, 1947; Ida B. Wells Lutheran Chapel, Chicago, Ill., teacher, 1944-45; pastor of Lutheran church in Darien, Wis., 1947-49; Lutheran Child Welfare Association, Addison, Ill., assistant executive secretary, 1949-53; pastor of Lutheran church in Palos Park, Ill., 1953-60; University of Minnesota, Minneapolis, campus pastor, 1960-65, president of Council of Religious Advisers, 1963-64; Our Redeemer Lutheran Church, Indianapolis, Ind., pastor, 1965—. Teacher in Lutheran high school in Chicago, Ill., 1955-56; instructor at Valparaiso University, 1958-59, and Christian Theological Seminary, autumn, 1973. Vacancy pastor of Lutheran church in Minneapolis, Minn., 1963-64; pastoral adviser to regional Lutheran Layman's League, 1966-69; third vice-president of English District of the Lutheran Church, 1970-74, second vice-president, 1974—. President of Lutheran Studies, Inc., 1963-65. Member of social service committee of Wheat Ridge Foundation, 1957-65; member of Indianapolis mayor's Youth Commission, 1974—. Recruiter for Purdue University's football staff. Chairperson of special ministries committee of Indianapolis Church Federation, 1975—.

MEMBER: Lutheran Academy of Scholarship, American Academy of Political and Social Science, Academy of Parish Clergy, Academy of Religion and Mental Health, Lutheran Child Welfare Association (president, 1974—). *Awards, honors:* Eddy Hall Award from University of Minnesota, 1965; Hebrew Award for Hebrew scholarship, 1972, and distinguished alumnus award, 1976, both from Christian Theological Seminary.

WRITINGS: Magnificat, Concordia, 1961; *Hear Us, Good Lord* (pamphlet), Lutheran Laymen's League, 1962; *Bless We the Lord,* Concordia, 1963; *Family Altar,* revised edition (Huxhold was not connected with earlier edition), Concordia, 1964; *Vacationing with Christ* (pamphlet), Concordia, 1964; *Responsive Table Prayers,* Concordia, 1964; *One Another's Burdens* (adult Bible study guide and teacher's guide), Concordia, 1964; *The Promise and the Presence,* Concordia, 1965; *Is Justification for Moderns?* (pamphlet), Concordia, 1965; (editor) *Adventures with God,* Concordia, 1966; (with Warren W. Ost) *God in My Leisure* (pamphlet), Concordia, 1967; *Great Prayers,* Concordia, 1968; *What Is the Question?,* Concordia, 1968; (editor) *Christian Education and the Urban Parish,* Lutheran Education Association, 1968.

(Editor with Julius Acker) *Lutheran Book of Prayer,* Concordia, 1970; *The Church in Our House,* Concordia, 1971; *With This Ring,* Concordia, 1971; *Open the Meeting with Prayer,* revised edition, Concordia, 1972; *Power for the Church in the Midst of Chaos,* Concordia, 1972. Contributor to religious magazines. Member of devotional literature committee at Concordia, 1958—.

WORK IN PROGRESS: Unconscious Christians: A Study of the New Piety in America.

*   *   *

HYAMS, Edward (Solomon)   1910-1975

September 30, 1910—November 25, 1975; British journalist, translator, novelist, author of historical and other nonfiction works. Obituaries: *AB Bookman's Weekly,* January 5, 1976. (See index for previous *CA* sketch)

*   *   *

HYDE, Stuart W(allace)   1923-

PERSONAL: Born August 8, 1923, in Fresno, Calif.; son of Henry Jacob (an electrician) and Anna (Stuckert) Hyde; married Allie Bargum (a painter), June 18, 1949; children: Stuart, Jr., John, Allison. *Education:* Attended Fresno State College (now California State University), 1941-43; University of California at Los Angeles, B.A., 1948; Stanford University, M.A., 1950, Ph.D., 1953. *Politics:* Democrat. *Religion:* Presbyterian. *Home:* 586 Chapman Dr., Corte Madera, Calif. 94925. *Office:* Department of Broadcast Communication Arts, San Francisco State University, San Francisco, Calif. 94132.

CAREER: Stanford University, Stanford, Calif., instructor

in radio-television, 1953-55; University of Southern California, Los Angeles, assistant professor of telecommunications, 1955-58; San Francisco State University, San Francisco, Calif., associate professor, 1958-63, professor of broadcast communication arts, 1963—. Member of special committee on parolee employment for San Quentin Prison, 1971—. *Military service:* U.S. Navy, 1943-46; became first lieutenant, junior grade. *Member:* American Council for Better Broadcasts (policy chairman, 1965—), Broadcast Education Association (member of board, 1974-76), Western Educational Society for Telecommunications, Alpha Epsilon Rho. *Awards, honors:* Citation from American Council for Better Broadcasts, 1966, for outstanding contributions on behalf of better radio and television; lifetime honorary membership in Men's Advisory Council (San Quentin inmate group), 1974, for concern and encouragement to the incarcerated men.

WRITINGS: Television and Radio Announcing, Houghton, 1959, revised and enlarged edition, 1972. Contributor of articles to *Encyclopaedia Britannica, Southern Folklore Quarterly, Sponsor, Western Speech, Educational-Instructional Broadcasting, Western Humanities Review.*

WORK IN PROGRESS: Analysis of the Public Arts; Institutional Uses of Electronic Media; third edition of *Television and Radio Announcing.*

SIDELIGHTS: Hyde told *CA:* "Having taught a class in radio and television performance at San Quentin Prison since 1970, my major interest has shifted to non-broadcast uses of video, and to the improvement of communication systems in institutions. Penal and prison reform are essential, but must be related to many changes in our society. My concerns in the field of mass media have to do with the uses of radio and television to help individuals in our society fulfill their human potential.

*   *   *

IFKOVIC, Edward   1943-

PERSONAL: Born June 16, 1943, in North Branford, Conn.; son of Anthony J. (a pattern maker) and Anna (Farkash) Ifkovic. *Education:* Southern Connecticut State College, B.S. (magna cum laude), 1965; University of North Carolina, M.A., 1966; University of Massachusetts, Ph.D., 1972. *Home:* 26 Terryville Ave., Bristol, Conn. 06010. *Office:* Department of English, Tunxis Community College, Farmington, Conn. 06032.

CAREER: High school English teacher in Branford, Conn., 1966-69; University of Massachusetts, Amherst, part-time lecturer in English, 1969-72; Tunxis Community College, Farmington, Conn., assistant professor of English, 1972—, chairman of department, 1974—. Member of World Education Fellowship. *Member:* Modern Language Association of America, Popular Culture Association, Multi-Ethnic Literature in the United States.

WRITINGS: (Editor) *American Letter: Immigrant and Ethnic Writing,* Prentice-Hall, 1975; *The Yugoslavs in America,* Lerner, in press; *For Love of Country: The Development of an American Identity in the Popular Novel, 1893-1913,* Revisionist Press, in press. Contributor to literary magazines, including *America, Review of Comparative Literature, American Notes and Queries, Journal of Popular Culture, Whitman Review, Crescent Review,* and *Winged Purposes.*

WORK IN PROGRESS: Into Other Things, a novel; *Anna Marinkovich,* a novel; a study of Finley Peter Dunne,

literary comedian at the end of the "genteel age" in America.

SIDELIGHTS: Ifkovic writes: "While I was a graduate student I met a girl from Zagreb, Croatia, in Yugoslavia, and she brought me back to my own Croatian roots. Not only did I explore the history of my family in America—dating from grandparents who arrived at Ellis Island around 1907—but I explored the history, literature, and language of the Old Country. In the process I came home to myself as an American with a particular ethnic history. . . . I saw ethnicity not as a divisive chauvinistic force but, instead, a force that leads out of diversity into unity. . . . I have been especially excited by the rise of the 'unmelted' white ethnics—the Polish, the Italian, the Jews, etc.—following after the new Black and Red consciousness."

*   *   *

IINO, (David) Norimoto   1918-

PERSONAL: Born February 11, 1918, in Tokyo, Japan; son of Kichisaburo (a statesman) and Gen (maiden name, Suzuki; a poetess) Iino; married Florence Nagashi (an English teacher), September 24, 1920; children: Yasuko, Noriko, Nakako. *Education:* Auburn Theological Seminary, B.Th., 1936; Boston University, Ph.D., 1941; University of Tokyo, Ph.D., 1948. *Religion:* Methodist. *Home:* 4-22, 3 Chome, Shimoochiai, Shinjuku-ku, Tokyo, Japan 161.

CAREER: Methodist minister in California, 1940-41; Japanese Naval College, Hiroshima Prefecture, Japan, member of faculty, 1941-45; International Christian College, Tokyo, Japan, member of faculty, 1951-75. Fulbright lecturer, University of Iowa, 1964-66, University of Puget Sound, 1972-73, Emory University, 1973, Howard University, 1974, and Monmouth College, 1974-75. *Awards, honors:* Maxwell fellowship; awarded the key to the city of Tacoma, Wash.

WRITINGS: The Culture of the American People (in Japanese), Iwanami, 1946; *Atomic Energy and Peace* (in Japanese), Iwanami, 1946; *Niba,* Nihon Kirisuto Kyodan, 1962; *Henken o koete zen to heiwa,* Meigenshobo, 1963; (with Francis W. Pritchard) *A Seven-Hued Rainbow,* Coe College, 1964; *Zeal for Zen,* Coe College, 1965; *Peace and Good,* Tokyo Publishing House, 1965; *Hints in Haiku: Japan's Pulse-Beat,* Philosophical Library, 1967; *Hope Here: Beyond East and West,* Japan Publications, 1972; (editor) *Haiku,* Rhododendron Press (Tacoma), 1974; (with Murray Moulding) *Thought-Seer,* Monmouth College, 1975. Contributor to *Encyclopaedia Brittanica.*

WORK IN PROGRESS: Three books; *Haiku: The Highway to Happiness, Thought-Seeing in Japan,* and *The Hero of New Japan.*

SIDELIGHTS: Iino told *CA:* "The mating of America and Japan is my hope. New Japan has carried the cruelest cross of the [Second World] war so as to be reborn into a new land with the mission of wound-healing, society-beautifying, hope-radiation, future-brightening. For this I would like to devote myself with utmost zeal, devotion, [and] hope. Sight-seeing is not enough. Thought-seeing is possible through a prayerful rebirth, perpetual penetration beyond the platitudinous, appreciation of the ampersand, East, West, Old, New. We are integrated into future-fore-seers by this regeneration."

*   *   *

INCIARDI, James A(nthony)   1939-

PERSONAL: Born November 28, 1939, in Brooklyn,

N.Y.; son of James A. (a physician) and Marie (Craig) Inciardi; married Carolyn Jo Kincaid, June 20, 1975. *Education:* Fordham University, B.S., 1961; New York University, M.A., 1971, Ph.D., 1973. *Office:* Division of Addiction Sciences, Department of Psychiatry, University of Miami, School of Medicine, Miami, Fla. 33152.

CAREER: New York City Department of Welfare, New York, N.Y., caseworker, 1961-62; New York State Division of Parole, Special Narcotic Project, parole officer, 1962-68; New York State Narcotic Addiction Control Commission, New York, N.Y., research associate, 1968-70, deputy director of research, 1970-71; Metropolitan Dade County Comprehensive Drug Program, Miami, Fla., associate director of research, 1971-73; University of Miami School of Medicine, Miami, Fla., assistant professor, psychiatry department, 1972-73, Division of Addiction Sciences, research associate, 1971-73, adjunct assistant professor, department of epidemiology and public health, 1973-75, assistant professor of psychiatry, 1975; Resource Planning Corp., Miami, Fla., senior associate, 1972-73, vice-president, 1974-75; University of Miami, School of Medicine, Division of Addiction Sciences, project director in National Center for the Study of Acute Drug Reactions, 1975—. Therapist in peer groups, New York City Addiction Services Agency, 1966-67, and Daytop Village, Staten Island, N.Y., 1966-68; supportive counselor, New York State Division of Parole, 1966-68; instructor at City College of the City University of New York, 1969, and New York University, 1969-71; faculty member, U.S. Office of Education Regional Drug Abuse Training Program, Miami, 1972-73, and National Institute of Mental Health Drug Abuse Training Center, Miami, 1972-74, 1975-76. Visiting professor at Ibero Americana University, 1974. Project director of Metropolitan Dade County Manager's Office, 1974-75; technical advisor of Law Enforcement Assistance Administration, St. Petersburg, Fla., 1974-75. Member of National Task Force on Drug Use and Criminal Behavior, U.S. Department of Health, Education and Welfare. Consultant to numerous social service agencies, hospitals, drug addiction, correction, and rehabilitation groups, police departments, and others, national, in several states, and locally. *Member:* American Society of Criminology (member, executive board), American Sociological Association.

WRITINGS: (Contributor) Wolfram Keup, editor, *Drug Abuse: Current Concepts and Research,* C. C Thomas, 1972; (contributor) Carl D. Chambers and Leon Brill, editors, *Methadone: Experiences and Issues,* Behavioral Publications, 1973; (contributor) Daniel Glaser, editor, *Handbook of Criminology,* Rand McNally, 1974; (editor with Chambers, and contributor) *Drugs and the Criminal Justice System,* Sage Publications, 1974; *Careers in Crime,* Rand McNally, 1975; *Chemical Coping,* Spectrum, 1975; (editor with Harvey A. Siegal) *Emerging Social Issues,* Praeger, 1975; (editor with Siegal) *Emerging Criminal Issues,* Praeger, 1976; *The Context of Crime,* Praeger, in press. Contributor to proceedings and journals in his field. Editorial consultant to National Clearinghouse for Drug Abuse Information, 1972, *Drugs: International Journal of Current Therapeutics and Applied Pharmacology Reviews,* 1972, Arbor House Publishers, 1972, and Praeger Publishers, 1974; assistant editor of *Criminology: An Interdisciplinary Journal,* 1973-75; member of editorial board of *Addictive Diseases: An International Journal,* 1973-75; book reviewer for *Sociology: Reviews of New Books,* 1974-75.

INGOLD, Klara (Schmid) 1913-

PERSONAL: Born October 29, 1913, in Bern, Switzerland; came to the U.S. in 1949; daughter of Abundi and Babetta (Lehmann) Schmid; married Bruno N. Ingold (a cabinetmaker), February 12, 1943; children: Beatrix (Mrs. Warren Sorensen), Esther (Mrs. Daniel Hooton), Eva (Mrs. Alan Nelson), Briga (Mrs. Don Westenskow), Monica (Mrs. Allan Cornia). *Education:* Utah State University, B.S., 1961; University of Colorado, M.A., 1965. *Religion:* Church of Jesus Christ of Latter-day Saints (Mormons). *Home:* 674 East Seventh N., Logan, Utah 84321. *Office:* Department of Languages, Utah State University, Logan, Utah 84322.

CAREER: Swiss Government, telegrapher in Bern, Switzerland, 1931-43; Utah State University, Logan, professor of French and German, 1961-75, professor emeritus, 1975—. Church organist, 1932-74.

WRITINGS: (Translator, editor, and contributor) Rudolf Bigler, *Pestalozzi in Burgdorf* (monograph), Utah State University Press, 1972.

WORK IN PROGRESS: Collecting and editing *Sagen, Heldengeschichten und Legenden aus der Schweiz* (title means "Sagas, Heroes' Tales, and Legends from Switzerland").

* * *

INGRAHAM, Mark H(oyt) 1896-

PERSONAL: Born March 19, 1896, in Brooklyn, N.Y.; son of Henry Cruise Murphy (a lawyer) and Winifred (Andrews) Ingraham; married Katherine G. Ely (an etcher), June 26, 1924; children: Winifred (Mrs. Grover Q. Grady), Edward C. *Education:* Cornell University, A.B., 1917; University of Wisconsin, Madison, M.A., 1922; University of Chicago, Ph.D., 1924. *Home:* 602 North Segoe Rd., Madison, Wis. 53705. *Office:* Retirement Consulting Service, University of Wisconsin, 102 Bascom Hall, Madison, Wis. 53706.

CAREER: University of Wisconsin, Madison, instructor, 1919-22, research fellow in mathematics, 1921-22; University of Chicago, Chicago, Ill., research fellow in mathematics, 1922-24; University of Wisconsin, Madison, assistant professor of mathematics, 1924-26; Brown University, Providence, R.I., assistant professor of mathematics, 1926-27; University of Wisconsin, Madison, professor of mathematics, 1927-66, chairman of department, 1932-42, dean of College of Letters and Science, 1942-61, dean and professor emeritus, 1966—, presently operates Retirement Consulting Service. Chairman of divisional committee on scientific personnel and education of National Science Foundation, 1962-67; chairman of American Panel on Education in the Sciences to advise United States-Japan Committee on Scientific Cooperation. Chairman of board of Wisconsin State Teachers Retirement System, 1951-70; trustee of State of Wisconsin Investment Board, 1965-71; member of board of trustees of Ripon College, 1963-69, honorary trustee, 1969—; charter member of board of trustees of College Retirement Equities Fund. *Military service:* U.S. Army, Infantry, 1917-19; became captain.

MEMBER: American Association for the Advancement of Science (fellow; member of board of directors, 1952-56), American Association of University Professors (president, 1938-39), American Mathematical Society (member of board of trustees, 1937-40), Mathematical Association of America, Association of American Colleges, Teachers Insurance and Annuity Association of America (member of board of trustees, 1949-53), Institute of Mathematical Statistics (fellow), Phi Beta Kappa (distinguished lecturer), Sigma Xi, Phi Kappa Phi. *Awards, honors:* Honorary degrees include LL.D. from Lawrence College, 1943, and Ripon College, 1969, Sc.D. from Wesleyan University, 1947, L.H.D. from Edgewood College, 1972, and University of Wisconsin, 1973; grant from U.S. Steel Foundation, 1962-64, to study nationwide faculty benefits other than insurance and annuities; grant from Carnegie Corp. to study retirement systems of Canadian universities; grant from Esso Education Foundation, 1965, to study compensation and conditions of work of college and university administrators.

WRITINGS: (With Frank King) *The Outer Fringe: Faculty Benefits Other than Annuities and Insurance,* University of Wisconsin Press, 1965; (with Samuel Eckles) *Faculty Retirement Systems in Canadian Universities,* University of Toronto Press and Presses de l'universite Laval, 1966; (with King) *The Mirror of Brass: The Compensation and Working Conditions of College and University Administrators,* University of Wisconsin Press, 1968; *Charles Sumner Slichter: The Golden Vector* (biography), University of Wisconsin Press, 1972; (with James Mulanaphy) *My Purpose Holds: Reactions and Experiences in Retirement of TIAA-CREF Annuitants,* Educational Research Division, Teachers Insurance and Annuity Association of America, 1974. Contributor to mathematics and education journals.

WORK IN PROGRESS: An autobiography.

* * *

INGRAM, Collingwood 1880-

PERSONAL: Born October 30, 1880, in London, England; son of William (Baronet) and Mary (Stirling) Ingram; married Florence M. Laing, 1907; children: three sons, one daughter. *Education:* Privately educated. *Home:* The Grange, Benenden, Kent, England.

CAREER: Farmer and one-time wine merchant. *Military service:* Royal Air Force, 1916-18. *Member:* Linnaean Society (fellow), British Ornithologists Union, Japanese Ornithological Society (honorary member). *Awards, honors:* Victoria Medal of Honour, 1952.

WRITINGS: Birds of the Riviera (ornithology), Witherby, 1926; *Isles of the Seven Seas* (travel), Hutchinson, 1936; (self-illustrated) *Ornamental Cherries* (botany), Country Life, 1948; *In Search of Birds* (ornithological travels), Witherby, 1967; *A Garden of Memories* (botanical travels), Witherby, 1970; *Migration of the Swallow* (ornithology), Witherby, 1973. Also author of numerous scientific papers.

WORK IN PROGRESS: Articles for botanical journals.

SIDELIGHTS: Collingwood Ingram is the grandson of Herbert Ingram, the founder of the *Illustrated London News*—the first illustrated newspaper.

* * *

INSALL, Donald W(illiam) 1926-

PERSONAL: Born February 7, 1926, in Clifton, Bristol, England; son of William Robert (a printers manager) and Phyllis Irene (Hill) Insall; married A. Elizabeth Moss, June 13, 1964; children: Robin, Christopher, Hilary. *Education:* Attended University of Bristol, 1942-43, 1947-49, and Royal Academy, London, 1950; School of Planning and Research for Regional Development, diploma (honors),

1951. *Religion:* Church of England. *Home:* 73 Kew Green, Richmond, Surrey TW9 3AH, England. *Office:* Donald W. Insall & Associates, 19 West Eaton Pl., London SW1X 8LT, England.

CAREER: Chartered architect, 1950; member of staff, Claud Phillmore & Aubrey Jenkins, Architects, 1952-53; Donald W. Insall & Associates, London, England, town planning consultant, 1954—. Member of Historic Buildings Council for England, 1972. *Wartime service:* Served in Coldstream Guards, 1944-47.

MEMBER: International Congress of Monuments and Sites (United Kingdom), National Trust (United States), National Trust (United Kingdom), Royal Institute of British Architects (fellow), Royal Society of Arts (fellow), Royal Town Planning Institute (fellow), Royal Photographic Society, Society for the Protection of Ancient Buildings, Association for the Study of Historic Buildings, Association for Preservation Technology (Canada), Georgian Group, Victorian Society, Conference on Training Architects in Conservation (honorary secretary, 1965—), Society of Antiquaries of London (fellow), Rolls Royce Enthusiasts Club. *Awards, honors:* Royal Institute of British Architects, Banister Fletcher essay medal, 1949, Society for the Protection of Ancient Buildings Lethaby scholar, 1949, Neale Bursar medal, 1950; Good Housing Design Medal from Minister of Housing and Local Government, 1962; Civic Trust awards, 1962, 1968, 1971, 1973, 1975; four conservation awards from Royal Institution of Chartered Surveyors, 1972; European Architectural Heritage Year medal, 1975.

WRITINGS: Chester: A Study in Conservation, H.M.S.O., 1969; *The Care of Old Buildings Today,* Architectural Press, 1972, Watson-Guptill, 1974; *Historic Buildings: Action to Maintain the Expertise for Their Care and Repair,* Committee on Monuments and Sites, Council of Europe, 1974; (contributor) Roy Strong and others, *Destruction of the Country House,* Thames & Hudson, 1974. Also author of radio scripts and screenplays.

Contributor to *Encyclopaedia Britannica,* and to technical journals, newspapers, and periodicals.

WORK IN PROGRESS: Care of Old Towns; Lighting of Towns and Buildings.

SIDELIGHTS: Insall has lectured in United States, Canada, Mexico, and Europe. *Avocational interests:* Photography, craftsmanship.

* * *

IORIO, James 1921-

PERSONAL: Born April 7, 1921, in Rende, Italy; son of Frank (a tailor) and Adeline (Verre) Iorio; married Adeline Kocimski (a teacher), June 14, 1947. *Education:* Chicago Teachers College, B.Ed., 1947; University of Chicago, M.A., 1948; DePaul University, M.Ed., 1956. *Residence:* Park Ridge, Ill. *Office:* Thomas A. Edison School, 6220 North Olcott Ave., Chicago, Ill. 60631.

CAREER: Elementary school teacher in Chicago, Ill., 1948-56, assistant principal, 1956-61; Thomas A. Edison School, Chicago, Ill., principal, 1961—. *Military service:* U.S. Army, 1943-46. *Member:* Illinois State Poetry Association.

WRITINGS: The Fifth Season (poems), Golden Quill, 1974; *Silence Interrupted* (poems), Golden Quill, 1976. Contributor of poems to literary magazines, including *Encore, Notable American Poets, Voices International, View,* and *Poetry Today.*

WORK IN PROGRESS: A third collection of poems, *Ring of Fire*.

SIDELIGHTS: Iorio writes: "I believe that poetry is intimate expression to be shared with another human being. It should be unpretentious in form without over-elaborate language and word order standing in the way of communication. I was born in the southern mountains of Italy and grew up in an old Italian neighborhood in Chicago. My bilingual background led to my interest in Italian literature. . . . Undoubtedly the study of Dante and other Italian poets has influenced my own poetry." *Avocational interests:* Travel (Italy, Poland), nature photography, hiking in woods and fields.

*   *   *

IQBAL, Afzal 1919-

PERSONAL: Born August 14, 1919, in Lahore, Pakistan. *Education:* Government College, Lahore, Pakistan, B.A. (honors), 1939; University of the Punjab, M.A., 1941. *Office:* Embassy of Pakistan, Grev Magnigatan 6, Stockholm, Sweden.

CAREER: Ministry of Foreign Affairs, Islamabad, Pakistan, 1950—, served as second secretary at embassies in Iran, 1950, Burma, 1952, first secretary in Spain, 1955-57, England, 1957-58, as deputy secretary for external publicity, 1959-61, served at embassies in Thailand, 1961-63, and Syria, 1963-64, deputy high commissioner at embassy in India, 1964-66, minister in London, England, 1966-69, ambassador to Switzerland and the Holy See, 1969-71, to Bolivia, Colombia, and Paraguay, 1971-73, ambassador to Sweden and Norway, 1973—. Has lectured at Universities of London, Durham, Manchester, Geneva, Berne, Rio de Janeiro, Sao Paulo, Bangkok, Stockholm, Uppsala, Oslo, and Azamgarh, and at Oxford and Cambridge Universities. *Awards, honors:* Decorated by Order of Istihqaq (Syrian Arab Republic), Order of Humayun and Order of Sipas (both Iran), Order of Pius IX (Holy See), and Order of the Grand Cruz do Sul (Brazil); University of the Punjab, Ph.D., 1970.

WRITINGS: (Editor) *My Life: A Fragment* (on the life of Mohamed Ali, leader of the Khilafat Movement of the 1920's), Muhammad Ashraf, 1942, 4th edition, 1966; (editor) *Select Writings and Speeches on Maulana Mohamed Ali,* two volumes, Muhammad Ashraf, 1944, 3rd edition, 1969; *The Life and Work of Maulana Jalaluddin Rumi,* Institute of Islamic Culture (Lahore), 1956, 3rd edition, 1974; *Diplomacy in Islam,* Institute of Islamic Culture, 1961, 2nd edition, 1965; *The Culture of Islam,* Institute of Islamic Culture, 1967, 2nd edition, 1974; *The Life and Times of Maulana Mohamed Ali,* Institute of Islamic Culture, 1974; *The Impact of Maulana Jalaluddin Rumi on Islamic Culture,* Regional Cultural Institute (Tehran), 1975; *The Prophet's Diplomacy,* Claude Stark, Inc., 1975; *Circumstances Leading to the First Afghan War,* Research Society of Pakistan and University of the Punjab, 1975, 2nd edition, 1975; (translator) Albert Camus, *"Ajnabi"* (Urdu translation of "L'Etranger"), Ayeena-i-adab, 1975; *Western Allegations of Obscenity in the Mathnavi: A Refutation,* Premier Publishing, in press. Contributor to magazines and newspapers.

*   *   *

ISAAK, Robert A(llen) 1945-

PERSONAL: Born September 2, 1945, in Akron, Colo.; son of Robert Deets (an electrical engineer) and Margie (a counselor; maiden name, Allen) Isaak; married Gudrun Kamm (a college instructor in German), January 29, 1966. *Education:* Attended American International University, 1962-63, and Pepperdine University (extension in Heidelberg, Germany), 1963-64; Stanford University, B.A., 1966; San Jose State University, M.A., 1967; New York University, Ph.D., 1971. *Office:* Institute on Western Europe, Columbia University, 420 West 118th St., New York, N.Y. 10027.

CAREER: New School for Social Research, New York, N.Y., member of faculty, 1968-69; Fordham University, Bronx, N.Y., instructor, 1969-70, assistant professor of political science, 1970-75; Columbia University, New York, N.Y., visiting scholar and research associate at Institute on Western Europe, 1975—. Adjunct associate professor at Pace University, 1975-76; member of faculty, New School for Social Research, 1976—. "Good-will ambassador" to Switzerland for American Society for Friendship with Switzerland, 1962; faculty sponsor for London School of Economics and Political Science's summer program in comparative government (studying in London, Berlin, Moscow, and Leningrad), 1972. *Member:* American Political Science Association.

WRITINGS: Individuals and World Politics, Duxbury, 1975; (with Ralph Hummel) *Politics for Human Beings,* Duxbury, 1975. Contributor to political science and social science periodicals.

WORK IN PROGRESS: Where Is America Going?, publication by St. Martin's expected in 1977; a novel; a book of poems.

SIDELIGHTS: Isaak writes: "I was always preoccupied with books and wanted to write. These bad habits have plagued me since childhood. Writing, in this sense, is always a search for one's self through a mirror of everyday life that is, at once, both intellectual and aesthetic, detached and dehumanizing. Writing is a way of falling in love or into argument without having to suffer the living consequences. As Nietzsche would say, it is the neurosis that distinguishes my personality."

*   *   *

ISHIGO, Estelle 1899-

PERSONAL: Born July 15, 1899, in Oakland, Calif.; daughter of Bradford (an artist and musician) and Bertha (a concert singer; maiden name, Apffel) Peck; married Arthur Shigeharu Ishigo, August 28, 1929 (died August 18, 1957). *Education:* Attended Otis Art School and Hollywood Art Center; private study of violin and composition. *Home:* 1837 Alexandria Ave., Los Angeles, Calif. 90027.

CAREER: Artist, illustrator, and musician. Illustrator under Vaughn Mechau in Heart Mountain, Wyo., 1942-44; San Pedro Symphony Orchestra, San Pedro, Calif., violinist, 1946-48; Para Venture Associates, illustrator, 1960-64. Private teacher of painting and drawing, 1946—. *Awards, honors:* Plaque from Los Angeles County Board of Supervisors, 1972, for outstanding quality of work in California Historical Society exhibit of World War II internment camps.

WRITINGS: Lone Heart Mountain (story of her internment in a barbed-wire camp for the Japanese during World War II), Ritchie, 1973.

WORK IN PROGRESS: A biography of her husband; an autobiography; research on human relations among Americans of all ancestries, on archaeological and scientific discoveries, and on outer space exploration.

SIDELIGHTS: Estelle Ishigo writes: "Some have wondered why I went to that camp with my husband and also what it was like being married to a Japanese before the war and in the camp. In a time of hostility and danger, if one is in love the greatest desire is to stay close to one's own. . . . When they finally shipped us far out into the freezing windtorn reaches of nowhere, I hoarded and kept every note and sketch I made because I wanted to cry out to all those beyond that desolate horizon, 'Look what you've done! Why? It makes no sense at all!'. . . When it was all over and they allowed us to come back to California, the joy of life that we came into this world with was gone. Los Angeles was grey and dirty and the people in it looked as though they relished and thrived on nothing but hate."

* * *

ISWOLSKY, Helene 1896-1975

July 24, 1896—December 24, 1975; American journalist, educator, social activist, and author of books on political, religious, and social topics. Obituaries: *New York Times,* December 27, 1975. (See index for previous *CA* sketch)

* * *

IVERSON, Lucille K(arin) 1925-

PERSONAL: Born August 3, 1925, in Detroit, Mich.; daughter of Carnot Francis (a teacher) and Esther (Piercey) Iverson; married Pierre R. de Vise, December 21, 1946 (divorced January, 1959); children: Peter Charles. *Education:* Wayne State University, B.A., 1948; University of Chicago, graduate study, 1956 and 1959; New York University, M.A., 1972. *Politics:* Feminist. *Home:* 93 Mercer St., New York, N.Y. 10012. *Agent:* Elaine Markson, 44 Greenwich Ave., New York, N.Y. 10011.

CAREER: Teacher in public high schools in Chicago, Ill., 1954-59, in Brooklyn, N.Y., 1960-65; Bobbs-Merrill Co., New York City, copy editor, 1968-69; film critic on cable television in New York City, 1974 and 1975; Poets-in-the-Schools, New York City, teacher, 1975; *Soho Weekly News,* New York City, columnist, 1975—. Actress, 1955-65; organizer of feminist poetry series at New York University, 1971-73; member of literature committee of International Women's Year, 1975—. *Member:* New York Radical Feminists.

WRITINGS: Outrage (poetry), Know, Inc. (Pittsburgh, Pa.), 1974; (editor with Kathryn Ruby and contributor) *We Become New* (feminist poetry anthology), Bantam, 1975; (editor) *Getting On* (poetry anthology), Sunbury Press, in press. Writer of bi-weekly column on poetry in *Soho Weekly News.* Contributor of poetry to *Nassau Herald, Villager, Libera, Tenth Muse, Washington Square Review,* and *Sunbury* and of articles to *Women and Film.*

WORK IN PROGRESS: A book of poems tentatively titled *A Good Pudding,* publication expected in 1977; research on women in the Victorian era and the novels of Edith Wharton.

SIDELIGHTS: Lucille Iverson told *CA:* "Although I have been writing poetry since my mid-twenties, the women's movement gave me new energy and insight. Prior to 1970, women over 40 who were not already in the professions were 'trashed.' Now, because of increasing job and career opportunities in all fields, it is possible for women with grown families—a large and previously wasted human potential—to have a 'second chance'; to move into the world of work outside the home and acquire power, gain respect, and fulfill themselves as persons."

JACKSON, Archibald Stewart 1922-

PERSONAL: Born January 13, 1922, in Valparaiso, Chile; son of Arthur Stewart (a stockbroker) and Katharine (Robinson) Jackson; married Patricia Cunningham, May 11, 1946; children: Francesca Jackson Garman, Stephanie Jackson Streat. *Education:* Educated in England. *Politics:* Conservative. *Religion:* Church of England. *Home:* Stonycroft, Alvescot, Oxford OX8 2PU, England.

CAREER: Pilot; British Airways, Overseas Division, London Airport, Heathrow, Middlesex, England, airline captain, 1947—. *Military service:* Royal Air Force, 1941-46; became squadron leader. *Member:* British Air Line Pilots Association.

WRITINGS: Civil Aviation: Flight Crews, David & Charles, 1975.

WORK IN PROGRESS: Both Feet in the Air, reminiscences; *Flight to Bermuda,* a novel.

* * *

JACKSON, Geoffrey (Holt Seymour) 1915-

PERSONAL: Born March 4, 1915, in Little Hulton, England; son of Seymour (an engineer) and Marie Cecile Dudley (Ryder) Jackson; married Patricia Mary Evelyn Delany, December 29, 1939; children: Anthony Bernard Seymour. *Education:* Emmanuel College, Cambridge, B.A. (honors), 1936, M.A., 1969. *Religion:* Roman Catholic. *Home:* 63 B Cadogan Sq., London SW1X 0DY, England.

CAREER: British Diplomatic Service, assigned successively to Beirut, Lebanon, Cairo, Egypt, and Baghdad and Basra, Iraq, 1937-56, first secretary in Bogota, Colombia, 1946-50; worked in British Foreign Office, in Latin American Department, 1950-54; British Diplomatic Service, first secretary in Bern, Switzerland, 1954-56, ambassador to Honduras in Tegucigalpa, 1956-60, consul general in Seattle, Wash., 1960-64, senior British trade commissioner in Ontario, 1964-69, ambassador to Uruguay in Montevideo, 1969-71, deputy under-secretary of state in Foreign Commonwealth Office, 1972-73. Attached to United Kingdom delegation to United Nations, 1949, 1953, 1956, 1959, and 1961, and to Economic Commission for Latin America (ECLA) delegation, 1952. *Member:* Society of Authors, Guild of Catholic Writers, Association of Lancastrians (president, 1974-75), Canning Club (London). *Awards, honors:* Commander of the Order of St. Michael and St. George, 1963, Knight Commander, 1971.

WRITINGS: The Oven-Bird (children's stories), Faber, 1972; *People's Prison,* Faber, 1973, published as *Surviving the Long Night: An Autobiographical Account of a Political Kidnapping,* Vanguard, 1974. Contributor to periodicals, including *Observer, Tablet, Listener, Catholic Herald,* and *Daily Telegraph.*

WORK IN PROGRESS: A novel; a political fable, continuation of *The Oven-Bird;* his memoirs of pre-war Levant.

SIDELIGHTS: In January, 1971, while ambassador to Uruguay, Sir Geoffrey Jackson was kidnapped by Tupamaros urban guerrillas, and held prisoner for eight months. Since then, Jackson comments, "I have been a student of terrorism and violence in society—in particular in relation to their impact on education and the young, at primary, secondary, university, state and private levels indiscriminately. I have become a governor of two large schools, a member of the British Broadcasting Corporation's general advisory council, and chairman of its Social Effects of Television Advisory group. My work and writing in 'retirement' are directed against the fragmentation, dissection and depression of the human spirit and towards its reintegration into a more positive, organic and optimistic ethic, based in my case on the Christian tradition, but receptive to others."

BIOGRAPHICAL/CRITICAL SOURCES: Robert Moss, *Urban Guerrillas,* Temple Smith, 1972; Richard Clutterbuck, *Protest and the Urban Guerrilla,* Casseil, 1973; Gerald McKnight, *The Mind of the Terrorist,* M. Joseph, 1974; Clutterbuck, *Living with Terrorism,* Faber, 1975.

* * *

JACKSON, George S(tuyvesant) 1906-1976

February 22, 1906—January 31, 1976; American educator, civil servant, and author of books on historical and literary topics. Obituaries: *New York Times,* February 3, 1976. (*CAP*-1; earlier sketch in *CA*-17/18)

* * *

JACKSON, (William) Keith 1928-

PERSONAL: Born September 5, 1928, in Colchester, Essex, England; son of William James (a businessman) and Beatrice (Hill) Jackson; married Mary Diane Robertson, January 18, 1960; children: Ben, Nigel Guy. *Education:* University of Nottingham, B.A. (first class honors), 1952. *Home:* 19 St. Andrew's Sq., Christchurch, New Zealand. *Office:* Department of Political Science, University of Canterbury, Christchurch, New Zealand.

CAREER: J. & P. Coats, Glasgow, Scotland, trainee, 1954-55; Ministry of Defense, Joint Intelligence Bureau, London, England, researcher, 1955-56; University of Otago, Dunedin, New Zealand, lecturer in political science, 1956-67; University of Canterbury, Christchurch, New Zealand, professor of political science, 1967—. *Military service:* Royal Air Force, 1945-47. *Member:* New Zealand Institute of International Affairs, New Zealand Political Studies Association, New Zealand Institute of Public Administration, New Zealand Historical Association, Australian Political Science Society.

WRITINGS: (With A. V. Mitchell and R. M. Chapman) *New Zealand Politics in Action,* Oxford University Press, 1962; (with J. Harre) *New Zealand,* Walker & Co., 1969; *Fight for Life,* Price Milburn, 1971; *New Zealand Legislative Council,* University of Otago Press, 1972; *New Zealand: Politics of Change,* Reed, 1973. Contributor to professional journals. Author of political commentaries for Radio New Zealand and New Zealand Television. Editorial adviser to *Journal of Commonwealth,* 1972—, *Comparative Studies* (formerly the *Journal of Commonwealth Political Studies*), 1972—, and *Political Science,* 1975—.

WORK IN PROGRESS: Research on various aspects of New Zealand political parties and the New Zealand Parliament.

* * *

JACKSON, Mary 1924-

PERSONAL: Born September 2, 1924, in Durham, N.C.; daughter of Lawrence and Mamie (Hobbs) Ray; married Bradford Cooper, 1952 (deceased); married Stephen H. Jackson, Jr. (employed by General Motors), August 25, 1963; children: (first marriage) Vincent L. *Education:* Educated in public schools of Freemont, N.C. *Politics:* Democrat. *Religion:* Baptist. *Home:* 27 South Logan Ave., Trenton, N.J. 08609.

CAREER: Employed at Unexcell (explosive plant), Cranberry, N.J., 1944, Westinghouse Electric Corp., Trenton, N.J., as coil feeder, 1945-51, General Motors Corp., Trenton, N.J., as punch press operator, 1953-64. Member of board of directors of East Trenton Civic Center, and of Mayor's Advisory Committee; Democratic committee woman. *Awards, honors:* Named "Rookie of the year" by National Association for the Advancement of Colored People (NAACP), 1968; award from Southern Christian Leadership Conference, 1969.

WRITINGS: (With Lil Wishart) *Integrated Cook Book,* Johnson Publishing Co., 1971.

SIDELIGHTS: Mary Jackson was born and raised on a farm. She worked in her father's tobacco fields and, to avoid the cotton fields, she began to cook when she was quite young, for the twenty people on the farm. Some of the recipes in her book date from her childhood.

As an adult she has been involved in political activities, beginning in 1968 with her participation in the "Poor People's March" to Washington, D.C. which ended in "Resurrection City." She was jailed for her work with the Reverend Abernathy, and also worked for Senator Robert Kennedy before his assassination. Since then she has concerned herself with local political and social issues, particularly voter registration programs. *Avocational interests:* Cooking, reading, sewing, making scrap books, crocheting.

* * *

JACOBSEN, Marion Leach 1908-

PERSONAL: Born October 20, 1908, in Prome, Burma; daughter of Harry Clifford (a clergyman) and Amy Ann (Haskin) Leach; married Henry Jacobsen (a writer and editor), February 26, 1949; children: Lorraine Marion. *Education:* Wheaton College, Wheaton, Ill., B.A., 1930; Eastern Baptist Theological Seminary, Philadelphia, Pa., graduate study, 1931-33; Gordon College of Theology, B.D., 1934. *Politics:* Independent. *Religion:* Evangelical Protestant. *Home:* 13652 Silverbell Dr., Sun City, Ariz. 85351.

CAREER: Pastor's assistant, teacher, writer, and editor.

WRITINGS: Good Times for God's People, Zondervan, 1952; *Fun with the Family,* Zondervan, 1954; *The Why and How of a Social Program for Adult Classes,* Scripture Press, 1958; *Popcorn, Kites, and Mistletoe,* Zondervan, 1969; *How to Keep Your Family Together and Still have Fun,* Zondervan, 1972; *Saints and Snobs,* Tyndale, 1972, re-issued as *Crowded Pews and Lonely People,* with discussion guide, 1975.

SIDELIGHTS: Marion Jacobsen writes: "Raised in a rather strict Christian home, our parents nevertheless saw to it that there were plenty of fun and good times in our home. This background led me to write about the importance of family fun in providing good experience and building good relationships in the home." Mrs. Jacobsen says of her latest book that "it deals with the need for personal acceptance, friends, and loving caring in local Christian groups of whatever kind or label . . . the problems that grow out of the failure of many Christians to find (or provide) such friendliness and love. It dares to ask who is responsible for cliquishness and discrimination among God's people—the lonely individual or those who overlook or reject him."

* * *

JACOBSON, Jon 1938-

PERSONAL: Born February 12, 1938, in Oxnard, Calif.;

son of Stanley Joel (a Protestant minister) and Niona (Lindquist) Jacobson; married Sybil Lease Haight (a potter), December 26, 1960; children: Kirsten, Margreta. *Education:* University of California, Berkeley, B.A., 1959, M.A., 1960, Ph.D., 1965. *Home:* 436 Morning Canyon Rd., Corona del Mar, Calif. *Office:* Department of History, University of California, Irvine, Calif. 92664.

CAREER: University of California, Irvine, assistant professor, 1965-71, associate professor of history, 1971—. *Awards, honors:* George Louis Beer Prize from American Historical Association, 1972, for *Locarno Diplomacy.*

WRITINGS: Locarno Diplomacy: Germany and the West, 1925-1929, Princeton University Press, 1972. Contributor to professional journals.

*   *   *

JAGER, Okke   1928-

PERSONAL: Born April 23, 1928, in Delft, Netherlands; son of Johann Coenraad (a surveyor) and Anna Wouterina (Wingerden) Jager; married Antje Lagerwerf, October 1, 1952; children: Ruth, Judith, Job. *Education:* Free University of Amsterdam, D.D., 1962. *Religion:* Reformed Church. *Home:* Jacob Catsstraat 433, Kampen, The Netherlands.

CAREER: Clergyman in the Netherlands, in Vrouwenpolder, 1952-56, Almelo, 1956-60, and Haarlem, 1960-65; broadcaster of religious radio and television, Hilversum, Netherlands, 1965-73; Theological University, Kampen, Netherlands, teacher, 1973—. *Member:* Society of Dutch Literature.

WRITINGS—All published by J. H. Kok (Kampen, Netherlands), except as noted: *Poezie en religie* (title means "Poetry and Religion"), Zomer & Keuning (Wageningen, Netherlands), 1952; *Feest op feest* (title means "Feast After Feast"), Zomer & Keuning, 1956; *Interview met de tijdgeest* (title means "Interview of the Spirit of the Times"), 1956; *Worden als een kind* (title means "To Become Like a Child"), 1956; *Jeugd en evangelie* (title means "Youth and Gospel"), Zomer & Keuning, 1957; *Op de man af* (title means "Straight From the Shoulder"), 1958; *De humor van de Bijbel in het Christelijk leven* (title means "The Humor of the Bible"), 1958; *Uw wil geschiede,* Bosch & Keuning, 1958, translation by M. E. Osterhaven published as *What Does God Want, Anyway?,* Judson, 1972; *Kom haastig! Gedichten over de wederkomst van Jezus* (poetry; title means "The Come-back of Jesus"), 1959; *Zegen u zelf: Tien radio-spreken* (sermons; title means "Bless Yourself"), 1959.

Parade of paradijs (title means "Parade or Paradise"), 1960; *Wij mogen van geluk spreken* (title means "Happiness For Us"), Zomer & Keuning, 1961; *Het eeuwige leven: Met name in verband met de verhouding van tijd en eeuwigheid* (title means "The Everlasting Life: Time and Eternity"), 1962; *Achter een glimlach* (title means "Behind a Smile"), 1964; *Een groene pasen* (title means "Green Easter"), Zomer & Keuning, 1964; *Geloven na kerktijd: Een nieuwe bundel televisie-dagsluitingen* (title means "Belief After Church Hours"), Zomer & Keuning, 1965; *Daglicht: Bijbels dagboek* (title means "Daylight: Exegesis"), 1967; *Eigentijdse verkondiging: Beschouwingen over de vertolking van het Evangelie in het taaleigen van der moderne mens* (title means "Timely Preaching of the Gospel For Modern Man"), 1967; *Een witte kerst* (title means "White Christmas"), Zomer & Keuning, 1968; *Het klagen wordt gezang* (title means "Topics of the Church"), 1969;

Land van Jahwe (title means "Land of Jahwe"), Zomer & Keuning, 1969; *Om razend te worden* (title means "It's Enough to Drive You Mad"), 1969.

Liefde doet wonderen (title means "Love Does Wonders"), Zomer & Keuning, 1970; *Hoedjes met voetjes* (title means "Ironical Stories"), 1970; *Verkondiging en massamedia* (title means "Preaching and Mass Media"), 1971; *Binnenpretjen om buitenbeentjes* (title means "Personalities of Television"), 1971; *Kruisweg* (title means "Via Dolorosa"), Zomer & Keuning, 1972; *Baas boven buis* (title means "Television: Theory and Practice"), 1973; *Bevrijde tijd* (title means "To a Culture of Leisure"), Zomer & Keuning, 1974.

Contributor to journals and periodicals.

*   *   *

JAWORSKYJ, Michael   1921-

PERSONAL: Born April 10, 1921, in Lvov, Ukraine, Russia; became U.S. citizen; son of Andreas and Maria (Kosachevych) Jaworskyj. *Education:* Johns Hopkins University, A.B., 1954, M.A., 1955, Ph.D., 1959. *Home:* 15 East 63rd St., New York, N.Y. 10021. *Office:* Department of Political Science, Hunter College of the City University of New York, 695 Park Ave., New York, N.Y. 10021.

CAREER: Hunter College of the City University of New York, New York, N.Y., instructor, 1959-61, assistant professor, 1961-67, associate professor of political philosophy, 1967—.

WRITINGS: (Editor) *Soviet Political Thought,* Johns Hopkins Press, 1967.

WORK IN PROGRESS: Research on material and socio-psychological preconditions of a communist revolution in the United States.

*   *   *

JENKINS, William A(twell)   1922-

PERSONAL: Born November 18, 1922, in Scranton, Pa.; son of William A. and Thelma Marie (Atwell) Jenkins; married Gloria Hyam, March 3, 1944 (divorced, 1974); married Alice Wyne (a secretary), November 1, 1974; children: (first marriage) William Arthur II, Darcy Ann. *Education:* New York University, B.S., 1948; University of Illinois, M.S., 1949, Ph.D., 1954. *Politics:* Independent. *Religion:* Protestant. *Home:* 8721 Southwest 137th Ave., Miami, Fla. 33183. *Office:* Florida International University, Tamiami Trail, Miami, Fla. 33199.

CAREER: High school teacher in Moline, Ill., 1951-53; Wisconsin State College (now Wisconsin State University), assistant professor of English, 1953-55, associate professor of English and elementary education, 1956; University of Wisconsin, Milwaukee, professor of education, 1958-63, chairman of department of secondary education, 1961-63, associate dean of School of Education, 1963-70; Portland State University, Portland, Ore., professor of education and dean of School of Education, 1970-74; Florida International University, Miami, vice-president for academic affairs, 1974—. Visiting summer professor at University of Hawaii, 1969, and Florida Agricultural and Mechanical University. Consultant to Educational Testing Service, Ford Foundation, and U.S. Office of Education. Chairman of Portland Development Commission (urban renewal), 1973-74. *Military service:* U.S. Army, Corps of Engineers, 1943-46; became first lieutenant. *Member:* National Council of Teachers of English (president, 1968-69), National Conference on Research in English, Wisconsin Council of Teachers of English (president, 1967-68), Phi Delta Kappa, Kappa Delta Pi, Phi Kappa Phi, Pi Lambda Theta.

WRITINGS: (With W. Cabell Greet and Andrew Schiller) *In Other Words: A Beginning Thesaurus,* Lothrop, 1969 published as *My Second Picture Dictionary,* Scott, Foresman, 1971; (with Greet and Schiller) *A Junior Thesaurus: In Other Words,* Lothrop, 1970. Co-author or contributor to about eighty readers published by Scott, Foresman, 1963—. Contributor to professional journals. Editor, *Elementary English* (publication of National Council of Teachers of English), 1961-68.

WORK IN PROGRESS: A chapter on developments in the education of teachers of English in the past quarter century for National Society for the Study of Education yearbook; an evaluation of elementary school language tests.

AVOCATIONAL INTERESTS: Tennis, bicycling, model railroading (HO gauge), and "puttering with a variety of tools."

BIOGRAPHICAL/CRITICAL SOURCES: Education (magazine), April-May, 1962.

* * *

JENNINGS, Elizabeth (Joan) 1926-

PERSONAL: Born July 18, 1926, in Boston, Lincolnshire, England; daughter of Henry Cecil Jennings (a physician). *Education:* St. Annes, College, Oxford, M.A. (honors). *Religion:* Roman Catholic. *Home:* 11 Winchester Rd., Oxford OX2 6NA, England. *Agent:* David Higham Associates Ltd., 5-8 Lower John St., Golden Square, London W1R 4HA, England.

CAREER: Oxford City Library, Oxford, England, assistant, 1950-58; Chatto & Windus, publishers, London, England, reader, 1958-60; poet and free-lance writer, 1961—. Guildersleeve Lecturer, Barnard College, Columbia University, 1974. *Member:* Society of Authors. *Awards, honors:* Arts Council award, 1953, for *Poems;* Somerset Maugham Award, 1965, for *A Way of Looking;* Arts Council bursary, 1965, and 1968; Richard Hillary Memorial Prize, 1966, for *The Mind Has Mountains;* Arts Council grant, 1972.

WRITINGS: Poems, Fantasy Press, 1953; *A Way of Looking: Poems,* Deutsch, 1955, Rinehart, 1956; (editor with Dannie Abse and Stephen Spender) *New Poems 1956: A P.E.N. Anthology,* M. Joseph, 1956; *A Child and the Seashell,* Poems in Folio, 1957; (editor). *The Batsford Book of Children's Verse,* Batsford, 1958; *A Sense of the World: Poems,* Deutsch, 1958, Rinehart, 1959; *Let's Have Some Poetry,* Museum Press, 1960; *Song for a Birth or a Death and Other Poems,* Deutsch, 1961, Dufour, 1962; (editor) *An Anthology of Modern Verse, 1940-60,* Metheun, 1961; *Every Changing Shape* (religion and verse), Deutsch, 1961; *Poetry Today,* Longmans, Green, 1961; (translator) *The Sonnets of Michaelangelo,* Folio Society, 1961, revised edition, Allison & Busby, 1969, Doubleday, 1970; (with Lawrence Durrell and R. S. Thomas) *Penguin Modern Poets I,* Penguin, 1962; *Recoveries: Poems,* Dufour, 1964; *Frost,* Oliver & Boyd, 1964, Barnes & Noble, 1965.

Christian Poetry, Hawthorn, 1965 (published in England as *Christianity and Poetry,* Burns & Oates, 1965); *The Mind Has Mountains,* St. Martin's, 1966; *The Secret Brother and Other Poems for Children,* St. Martin's, 1966; *Collected Poems,* Dufour, 1967; *The Animals' Arrival,* Dufour, 1969; *Lucidities,* Macmillan, 1970; (editor) *A Choice of Christina Rossetti's Verse,* Faber, 1970; *Hurt,* Poem-of-the-Month Club, 1970; (with others) *Folio,* Sceptre Press, 1971; *Relationships,* Macmillan, 1972; *Growing Points,* Carcanet Press, 1975.

Contributor of articles and poems to *New Statesman, New Yorker, The Scotsman, Vogue, Encounter, Spectator* and other periodicals.

WORK IN PROGRESS: More poems and critical writings to be published by Carcanet Press.

SIDELIGHTS: Elizabeth Jennings' manuscripts are in collections of the Oxford City Library, and University of Washington, Seattle. *Avocational interests:* Travel, art, the theatre, conversation.

BIOGRAPHICAL/CRITICAL SOURCES: Michael Schmidt and Grevel Lindop, editors, *British Poetry since 1960,* Carcanet Press, 1972; Carolyn Riley, editor, *Contemporary Literary Criticism,* Volume V, Gale, 1976.

* * *

JENNINGS, Robert E(dward) 1931-

PERSONAL: Born in 1931, in Southampton, N.Y.; son of Robert Rikeman and Mildred (Squires) Jennings; married Audrey L. Atkinson, 1954; children: Nancy Elizabeth, Richard Edward. *Education:* State University of New York at Albany, B.A. (cum laude), 1956, M.A., 1957, Ed.D., 1966. *Politics:* "Yes." *Religion:* "Occasionally." *Home:* 230 Capen Blvd., Buffalo, N.Y. 14226. *Office:* Department of Educational Administration, State University of New York at Buffalo, Buffalo, N.Y. 14214.

CAREER: Reading specialist in public schools in Greene County, N.Y., 1957-61; administrative intern in public school in Chatham, N.Y., 1962-63; State University of New York, assistant to the Provost, 1963-66; U.S. Department of Health, Education, and Welfare, Washington, D.C., Office of Education fellow, 1966-67; State University of New York at Buffalo, assistant professor, 1967-73, associate professor of educational administration, 1973—, assistant dean of faculty of educational studies, 1967-69. Research assistant of Capital Area School Development Association (Albany), 1961-63; instructor for in-service training program for target area school staffs in Buffalo, 1969-70; visiting lecturer at University of Keele, 1973-74. Legislative chairman of Albany District Board of New York State Congress of Parents and Teachers, 1963-64; member of board of directors of Buffalo Community Education Council, 1967-71. *Military service:* U.S. Navy, 1948-52.

MEMBER: American Association of School Administrators, American Association of University Professors, Northeastern Educational Research Association. *Awards, honors:* Grants from Western New York School Development Council, 1968-69, U.S. Office of Education, 1968-70, National Science Foundation, 1969-70.

WRITINGS: Alternative Roles and Inter-Agency Relationships of State Education Agencies in Comprehensive Statewide Planning (monograph), Improving State Leadership in Education Project (Denver, Colo.), 1971; (with Mike M. Milstein) *Educational Policy-Making and the State Legislature: The New York Experience,* Praeger, 1973; (contributor) Milstein and James A. Belasco, editors, *Educational Administration and the Behavioral Sciences: A*

Systems Perspective, Allyn & Bacon, 1973; (with Milstein and James A. Conway) *Understanding Communities*, Prentice-Hall, 1974; *Politics and Policy-Making in Local Education Authorities*, Batsford, 1975. Contributor of articles and reviews to education journals. Editor of *Bulletin of the Politics of Education*, a newsletter of a special interest group in the American Educational Research Association, 1970-71.

WORK IN PROGRESS: Research on the New York governor's program for education.

SIDELIGHTS: Jennings told *CA:* "Much of my writing effort has been directed toward making research findings useful for both professionals and laymen interested in politics and education. My point of view has come to reflect Elliot's statement that education is too important to be left to the educators."

* * *

JENNINGS, Vivien

PERSONAL: Born in Jersey City, N.J. *Education:* Caldwell College, B.A., 1960; Catholic University of America, M.A., 1966; Fordham University, Ph.D., 1972.

CAREER: Roman Catholic nun of Order of Preachers (Dominicans; O.P.) 1952—; teacher in elementary schools and high schools in Newark, N.J., 1954-60; Caldwell College, Caldwell, N.J., assistant professor of English, 1960-69; elected Major Superior of Caldwell Dominican Sisters, 1969, re-elected, 1975—. Chairman of board of trustees of Caldwell College; founder of "Project Link" (a private, non-denominational junior high school); national chairman of Dominican Leadership Conference, 1973-74. *Member:* Leadership Conference of Women Religious (member of national board), Amici Thomae Mori, National Catholic Education Association, Creative Education Association.

WRITINGS: The Valiant Woman at the Heart of Reconciliation, Alba, 1974. Contributor to *Perspectives*. Member of editorial board of *Advocate;* contributing editor, *Nova et Vetera.*

* * *

JENSEN, Lloyd 1936-

PERSONAL: Born August 18, 1936, in Blackfoot, Idaho; son of Willard Hyrum (a carpenter) and Edna (Fackrell) Jensen; married Clara Jane Sayre (a writer), August 31, 1963. *Education:* University of Michigan, A.B., 1958, A.M., 1959, Ph.D., 1963. *Home:* 633 Lombard St., Philadelphia, Pa. 19147. *Office:* Department of Political Science, Temple University, Philadelphia, Pa. 19122.

CAREER: University of Illinois, Urbana, instructor, 1962-63, assistant professor of political science, 1963-65; Northwestern University, Evanston, Ill., assistant professor of political science, 1965-66, associate director of Simulated International Process Project, 1965-66; University of Kentucky, Lexington, associate professor of political science, 1966-71, acting director of Patterson School of Diplomacy, 1968-70; Temple University, Philadelphia, Pa., associate professor of political science, 1971—. *MEMBER:* International Peace Research Society, International Studies Association (member of governing board, 1974-75; vice-president of Greater Philadelphia Area chapter, 1973-74, president, 1974-75), American Political Science Association. *Awards, honors:* National Science Foundation grant, summer, 1964.

WRITINGS: (Contributor) Richard Butwell, editor, *Foreign Policy and the Developing Nations*, University Press of Kentucky, 1969; (contributor) James N. Rosenau, editor, *Linkage Politics*, Free Press, 1969; *Return from the Nuclear Brink*, Heath, 1974. Contributor to political science and international studies journals. Psychology editor of *Background on World Politics*, 1959-61.

WORK IN PROGRESS: A book on comparative foreign policies; research on negotiations for limiting strategic delivery systems.

SIDELIGHTS: Jensen writes: "My major concern has been with the problems of war and peace. Particularly salient is my belief that billions of dollars are wasted on the military establishment with little increase in security."

* * *

JERVELL, Jacob 1925-

PERSONAL: Born May 21, 1925, in Fauske, Norway; son of Sverre (a pastor) and Thora (Mejdell) Jervell; married Kari Lange (a librarian), July 3, 1938; children: Stephen. *Education:* Attended Lund University, 1950; Oslo University, B.D., 1951, D.D., 1959; attended Heidelberg University, 1953, and Goettingen University, 1954-55. *Religion:* Lutheran. *Home:* Silurveien 41 F, Oslo 3, Norway. *Office:* Oslo Universitet, Blindern, Oslo 3, Norway.

CAREER: Oslo University, Oslo, Norway, lecturer, 1955-59, professor of biblical theology, 1960—, dean of faculty of theology, 1975—. Visiting professor, Lund University, 1964, Yale University, 1970, and Aarhus University, 1973. Chairman of Norwegian Christian Student Movement, 1958-65. *Member:* Societe Royale des Lettres de Lund, Norwegian Academy of Science and Letters, Studiorum Novi Testamenti Societas, Norwegian Bible Society (member of board, 1966—).

WRITINGS: Imago Dei (title means "The Image of God"), Vandenhoeck & Ruprecht, 1960; *The Historical Jesus*, Forlaget Land og Kirke, 1962, revised edition, 1969; *Ikke bare ruiner* (title means "Not Only Ruins"), Forlaget Land og Kirke, 1967; *Da fremtiden begynte* (title means "When the Future Began"), Forlaget Land og Kirke, 1967; *Studien zu den Testamenten der 12 Patriarchen* (title means "Studies in the Testaments of the 12 Patriarchs"), A. Toepelmann, 1969.

Luke and the People of God, Augsburg, 1972; *Gud og hans fiender* (title means "God and His Enemies"), Oslo University Press, 1973; *". . . bare all makt"* (title means ". . . Only All Power"), Gyldendal, 1975. Contributor to theological periodicals and other journals.

WORK IN PROGRESS: Social History of Early Christianity, completion expected in 1977.

* * *

JEVONS, Frederic, Raphael 1929-

PERSONAL: Born September 19, 1929, in Vienna, Austria; son of Fritz and Hedwig (Scharf) Bettelheim; married Grete Bradel, December 21, 1956; children: Colin Peter, Norman Thomas. *Education:* Cambridge University, B.A., 1950, M.A., 1953, Ph.D., 1953; postdoctoral study, University of Washington, Seattle, 1953-54. *Office:* Deakin University, P.O. Box 825, Geelong, Victoria 3220, Australia.

CAREER: Cambridge University, Cambridge, England, fellow of King's College, 1953-59, university demonstrator in biochemistry, 1956-59; University of Manchester, Manchester, England, lecturer in biochemistry, 1959-66, professor of liberal studies in science, 1966-75; Deakin University, Geelong, Victoria, Australia, vice-chancellor, 1976—. Interviewer for Civil Service Commission on Final Selection Boards, 1970-75; advisor to Leverhulme project, Strathclyde University, 1972-75; member of joint committee of Science Research Council and Social Science Research Council, 1975; chairman of general studies committee, Schools Council (London), 1974-75. *Awards, honors:* D.Sc., University of Manchester, 1966.

WRITINGS: The Biochemical Approach to Life, Allen & Unwin, 1964, 2nd edition, 1968; *The Teaching of Science: Education, Science and Society,* Allen & Unwin, 1969; (editor with John Knapp and Michael Swanton) *University Perspectives,* University of Manchester Press, 1970; (with John Langrish, Michael Gibbons and W. G. Evans) *Wealth from Knowledge: Studies of Innovation in Industry,* Macmillan, 1972; (editor with H. D. Turner) *What Kinds of Graduates Do We Need?,* Oxford University Press, 1972; *Science Observed: Science as a Social and Intellectual Activity,* Allen & Unwin, 1973. Member of editorial advisory board of *R and D Management* and *Studies in Science Education.*

WORK IN PROGRESS: The relevance of theories of knowledge to the organization of education.

SIDELIGHTS: While at the University of Manchester, Jevons founded the Department of Liberal Studies in Science in order to promote the study of science as a social and intellectual activity. *Avocational interests:* Music, theatre, walking.

*   *   *

JEWELL, Nancy 1940-

PERSONAL: Born August 12, 1940, in Washington, D.C.; daughter of Russell C. (a lawyer) and Ruth (Royes) Jewell. *Education:* Goucher College, B.A., 1962. *Residence:* New York, N.Y. *Office:* Harper & Row Publishers, Inc., 10 East 53rd St., New York, N.Y. 10022.

CAREER: Harper & Row, New York, N.Y., reader, 1966—.

WRITINGS—Juvenile: *The Snuggle Bunny,* Harper, 1972; *Try and Catch Me,* Harper, 1972; *Calf, Goodnight,* Harper, 1973; *Cheer Up, Pig,* Harper, 1975.

WORK IN PROGRESS: Picturebooks.

BIOGRAPHICAL/CRITICAL SOURCES: Villager, May 10, 1973.

*   *   *

JOHN, Helen James 1930-

PERSONAL: Born January 12, 1930, in Brooklyn, N.Y.; daughter of James E. (a government accountant) and Helen (McAlear) John. *Education:* Trinity College, Washington, D.C., A.B., 1951; Catholic University of America, M.A., 1956; University of Louvain, Ph.D., 1963. *Politics:* Democrat. *Home and office address:* Department of Philosophy, Trinity College, Washington, D.C. 20017.

CAREER: Roman Catholic nun of the Sisters of Notre Dame; Trinity College, Washington, D.C., assistant, 1954-55, instructor, 1955-60; assistant professor, 1960-65, associate professor, 1965-68, professor of philosophy, 1968—. *Member:* American Catholic Philosophical Association, Metaphysics Society of America. *Awards, honors:* Ful-

bright study grant, 1958-59; American Endowment for the Humanities grant, 1967-68.

WRITINGS: (Contributor) Daniel Callahan, editor, *Generation of the Third Eye,* Sheed, 1965; (editor with Gerald Kreyche, Jesse Mann and others) *Perspectives on Reality,* Harcourt, 1966; *The Thomist Spectrum,* Fordham University Press, 1966. Contributor to *New Scholasticism, Modern Schoolman, International Philosophical Quarterly, America, Commonweal, Alumnae Journal of Trinity College, The Lamp, Review for Religious,* and *Proceedings of the American Catholic Philosophical Association.*

WORK IN PROGRESS: A book, *Three Dimensions of Commitment.*

*   *   *

JOHNSON, Andrew N(isseu) 1887-

PERSONAL: Born November 10, 1887, in Sparta, Wis.; son of Marcus M. and Susanne (Jensen) Johnson; married Louise C. Weaver, September 13, 1916 (died May 7, 1949); children: Douglas W., Alice J. (Mrs. Richard C. Keller), Gordon A. *Education:* Northwestern University, A.B., 1913, LL.B., 1915. *Office:* Johnson & Sands, 700 First National Bank Building, Minneapolis, Minn. 55402.

CAREER: Admitted to Minnesota State Bar, 1916; lawyer in Minneapolis, Minn., 1916-47; Johnson & Sands, Minneapolis, Minn., partner, 1947—. Dean and trustee of Minneapolis-Minnesota College of Law, 1940-56; William Mitchell College of Law, founder, president, 1956-72, trustee, 1956—. North American Life & Casualty Co., General counsel, 1946-62, director, 1950-54; director of Pure Milk Products Co., 1951-60, and of B. F. Griebenow, 1947-70. Vice-consul of Denmark in Minnesota, 1927-47, consul, 1947-58, consul general, 1958-72.

MEMBER: American Bar Association, Minnesota Bar Association, Hennepin County Bar Association, Minneapolis Business Men's Association (past president), Order of Coif, Alpha Delta Phi, Delta Theta Phi, Minneapolis Club, Minneapolis Athletic Club, Skylight Club, Six O'Clock Club. *Awards, honors:* Named knight of the Order of the Danish Flag, 1939, named knight first class, 1947; King Christian X Medal of Liberation from Government of Denmark, 1945; knight first class of the Order of Vasa (Sweden), 1962; LL.D. from William Mitchell College of Law, 1971; awarded commander cross of the Knighthood of the Danish Flag, 1972.

WRITINGS: Marcus and Susanne the Johnson (sen) Family, Burgess, 1965; *Enforceable World Peace: Thoughts of a Diplomat,* Burgess, 1973.

*   *   *

JOHNSON, Barry L(ee) 1943-

PERSONAL: Born July 28, 1943, in Bloomington, Ill.; son of James R. (in advertising) and Elizabeth (Schultz) Johnson; married Celeste Hoppe, June 10, 1965; children: Tracy Michelle, Dane Christian. *Education:* Wheaton College, Wheaton, Ill., B.A., 1965; Evangelical Theological Seminary, M.Div., 1968. *Home:* 4165 Colemere Court, Dayton, Ohio 45415. *Office:* Shiloh Congregational Church, 5300 Philadelphia Dr., Dayton, Ohio 45415.

CAREER: Ordained United Methodist minister, 1968; pastor of Methodist church in Bensenville, Ill., 1968-70; Euriskon (church renewal organization), West Chicago, Ill., executive director, 1970-75; Shiloh Congregational Church, Dayton, Ohio, senior pastor, 1975—. *Member:* National Association of United Methodist Evangelists.

WRITINGS: *Sometimes There's a Hole in the Ceiling,* Abingdon, 1975; *Euriskon: An Adventure in Discovery for Christians on the Grow!* (with sound tapes), Abingdon, in press. Contributor to religious periodicals.

WORK IN PROGRESS: Research for a book on the will of God in contemporary theology.

SIDELIGHTS: Johnson writes: "My major commitment is to the mainline church. After serving as a local pastor for three years I sensed the widening gap between persons with social concerns and those with an evangelical slant. In response to this I created the Euriskon program. . . . It is a church renewal experience based on preaching, music, and small group work." *Avocational interests:* Basketball, golf, camping.

BIOGRAPHICAL/CRITICAL SOURCES: *Christian Advocate,* April 12, 1973; *Together,* April, 1973.

* * *

JOHNSON, Ben E(ugene) 1940-

PERSONAL: Born August 16, 1940, in Storm Lake, Iowa; son of Jonas Birger (a laborer) and Bernice (Brown) Johnson; married Bonnie McPherson (a teacher), August 24, 1964; children: Steven, Susan, Shelley. *Education:* Detroit Bible College, B.R.E., 1962; Eastern Michigan University, M.A. (history), 1964, M.A. (English), 1967; Washington State University, doctoral study, 1968-69. *Home:* 2245 Heathercliff, Libertyville, Ill. 60048. *Office:* Achieving Greater Proficiency, Inc., 117 West Lake St., Libertyville, Ill. 60048.

CAREER: Pastor of Baptist church in Detroit, Mich., 1961-64; Detroit Bible College, Detroit, Mich., instructor in English and literature, 1964-68; Washington State University, Pullman, university librarian in archives, 1968-69; Trinity College, Deerfield, Ill., assistant professor of English, 1969—, chairman of department, 1969-73. President of Achieving Greater Proficiency Inc. (learning skills firm), 1970—. Founder and president of Quill Associates (literary agency for religious publications). *Member:* International Reading Association, National Council of Teachers of English.

WRITINGS: *Rapid Reading with a Purpose,* Regal Press, 1974; *Learn to Rapid Read,* Sams, 1974; *Learn to Rapid Write,* Sams, 1974. Author of script for "Improving Reading Skills," a videotape. Contributor of about fifty articles and stories to magazines.

WORK IN PROGRESS: *Church Libraries with a Purpose; Rapid Reading Naturally; The Apollo Plot,* a novel.

SIDELIGHTS: Johnson writes: ". . .My AGP courses are the most widely used instructor-taught courses on the college level in the area of rapid reading, memory, and speed writing. A dozen foreign countries also offer the courses. I am now spending two months a year traveling overseas with the Olan Hendrix Management Skills Seminars teaching these skills to non-Americans who are in positions of management in business, education, government, and the church."

* * *

JOHNSON, D(avid) Bruce 1942-

PERSONAL: Born June 19, 1942, in Astoria, Ore.; son of Paul Leon (an oyster farmer) and Louise (Petty) Johnson; married Betty Rose Carpenter, February 14, 1967 (divorced, 1969); married Jeanie Lou Marolf (a dental recep-

tionist), December 26, 1970; children: (first marriage) Kirk; (second marriage) Kimberley. *Education:* Clatsop College, A.A., 1965; University of Oregon, B.S., 1968; Oregon College of Education, graduate study, summers, 1970-72. *Home:* 1182 McCoy, Bay City, Ore. 97107.

CAREER: Tillamook School District #9, Tillamook, Ore., teacher of English and reading, 1969—. Member of drug control staff for Tillamook County Sheriff's Dept., summers, 1973—. *Member:* National Education Association, Oregon Education Association.

WRITINGS: (With John Sauter) *Tillamook Indians of the Oregon Coast,* Binfords, 1974.

AVOCATIONAL INTERESTS: Collecting antiques, sports, science, art.

* * *

JOHNSON, Earl, Jr. 1933-

PERSONAL: Born June 10, 1933, in Watertown, S.D.; son of Earl Jerome (a restaurant owner) and Doris (a schoolteacher; maiden name, Schwartz) Johnson; married second wife, Barbara Yanow (a lawyer), October 11, 1970; children: (first marriage) Kelly Ann, Earl Eric III. *Education:* Northwestern University, B.A. (with honors), 1955, LL.M., 1961; University of Chicago, J.D., 1960. *Politics:* Democrat. *Home:* 204 The Strand, Manhattan Beach, Calif. 90266. *Office:* Law Center, University of Southern California, University Park, Los Angeles, Calif. 90007.

CAREER: Research assistant, American Bar Foundation, 1959-60; U.S. Department of Justice, Washington, D.C., special attorney in Organized Crime Section, working in Washington, D.C., Miami, Fla., and Las Vegas, Nev., 1961-64; Neighborhood Legal Services, Washington, D.C., deputy director, 1964-65; Office of Economic Opportunity, Washington, D.C., deputy director of Legal Services Program, 1965-66, member of national advisory committee, 1965-73, director, 1966-68; University of California, Berkeley, visiting scholar at Center for the Study of Law and Society, 1968-69; University of Southern California, Los Angeles, associate professor, 1969-75, professor of law, 1976—, senior research associate at Social Science Research Institute and director of Dispute Resolution Policy Study, both 1975—. Member of Bar in Illinois, 1960, U.S. Court of Appeals (Ninth Circuit), 1964, District of Columbia, 1965, U.S. Supreme Court, 1966, and California, 1972. Member of executive committee of National Senior Citizens Law Center, 1971-73; president of board of trustees of Western Center on Law and Poverty, 1971-73; vice-president and chairman of executive committee of California Rural Legal Assistance Corp., 1972-74; member of International Legal Center Committee on Legal Services in Developing Countries, 1972-75; secretary of board of directors of Resource Center for Consumers of Legal Services, 1974—. Visiting scholar at University of Florence, 1973, 1975, and co-director of project at its Centro Studi di Diritto Processuale Comparato, 1974—; faculty member of Asian Workshop on Legal Services to the Poor, 1974. U.S. State Department lecturer in Africa, 1975. *Military service:* U.S. Navy, 1955-58; became lieutenant junior grade.

MEMBER: American Bar Association, Association of American Law Schools, National Legal Aid and Defender Association (member of board of directors, 1968—), Law and Society Association, American Academy of Political and Social Science, Delta Sigma Rho, Coif, Deru. *Awards, honors:* Ford Foundation fellowship in criminal law, 1960-61; Dart Award for Academic Innovation, University of Southern California, 1971.

WRITINGS: Justice and Reform: The Formative Years of the O.E.O. Legal Services Program, Russell Sage Foundation, 1974; (with Mauro Cappelletti and James Gordley) *Toward Equal Justice: A Comparative Study of Legal Aid in Modern Societies,* Oceana, 1975; (with Valerie Kantor) *Outside the Courts: A Survey of Diversion Alternatives for Civil Litigation,* National Center for State Courts, in press.

Contributor: F. L. Lindman and D. E. McIntire, editors, *The Mentally Disturbed and the Law,* American Bar Foundation, 1961; F. E. Inbau, C. R. Sowle, and J. R. Thompson, editors, *Cases and Comments on Criminal Justice,* Foundation Press, 1968; D. T. Weckstein, editor, *Education in the Professional Responsibilities of the Lawyer,* University Press of Virginia, 1970; H. M. Hughes, editor, *Delinquents and Criminals: Their Social World,* Allyn & Bacon, 1970; *Selected Readings in Clinical Legal Education,* CLEPR/ILC, 1973; *Clinical Education for the Law Student,* Council on Legal Education in Professional Responsibility, 1973.

Writer of "Director's Column" in *Law and Action,* 1967-68. Contributor to law journals, and to *Centre, New City,* and *Dialogue.* Editor of *University of Chicago Law Review,* 1960.

WORK IN PROGRESS: And Still Love Justice: The Birth and Trauma of the American Legal Services Program; A Theory of Dispute Resolution Alternatives, completion expected in 1977; research on shortcomings in the present legal system, especially its discrimination against the poor and middle classes.

SIDELIGHTS: Johnson writes: "During four years of involvement in legal services for the poor, I was exposed to the netherworld of America's legal system, where the law can only be an enemy and never a friend. I entered that experience a typical white, middle-class lawyer born and raised in a small town in South Dakota who assumed, along with most middle-class Americans, that, for the most part, our laws are equal and our courts just. I came out after four years, simultaneously disillusioned and committed. While I was directing the OEO Legal Services Program, we began, through 'test cases' and legislative advocacy, to chip away at the edifice of oppression our legal system has become. But we still remain a long way from an equitable set of laws or an equal system of justice in the United States. *Toward Equal Justice* describes and appraises legal assistance for the poor throughout the world with special emphasis on the programs existing in the industrialized countries of Europe (East and West) and North America. But even a country as 'backward' and 'barbaric' as Zambia in southern Africa is investing five times more of its national income on equal justice than the 'advanced' and 'civilized' United States."

AVOCATIONAL INTERESTS: Photography, travel (international), tennis, skiing, sketching, reading (detective novels, biographies, history, politics), spectator sports (football and basketball), playing the guitar, watching movies ("good, bad or indifferent").

* * *

JOHNSON, Humphrey Wynne 1925-1976

1925—January 22, 1976; American children's magazine editor, journalist, free-lance writer, and author of a novel for children. Obituaries: *Washington Post,* January 27, 1976.

* * *

JOHNSON, James Turner 1938-

PERSONAL: Born November 2, 1938, in Crockett Mills, Tenn.; son of Walter Turner (a businessman) and Georgie (Swanson) Johnson; married Pamela Jane Bennett, October 19, 1968; children: Christopher Edward Bennett, Ashley Elizabeth Bennett. *Education:* Brown University, A.B., 1960; Vanderbilt University, B.D., 1963; Princeton University, M.A., 1967, Ph.D., 1968. *Home:* 75 West Broad St., Hopewell, N.J. 08525. *Office:* Department of Religion, Douglass College, Rutgers University, New Brunswick, N.J. 08903.

CAREER: Newberry College, Newberry, S.C., instructor in philosophy and religion, 1963-65; Vassar College, Poughkeepsie, N.Y., lecturer in religion, 1968-69; Rutgers University, Douglass College, New Brunswick, N.J., assistant professor of religion, 1969—. *Member:* American Academy of Religion, American Society of Christian Ethics, Council on Religion and International Affairs, Institute of Society, Ethics, and the Life Sciences, Society for Values in Higher Education, American Association of University Professors. *Awards, honors:* Huntington Library fellow, 1970.

WRITINGS: A Society Ordained by God: English Puritan Marriage Doctrine in the First Half of the Seventeenth Century, Abingdon, 1970; (editor with David H. Smith) *Love and Society: Essays in the Ethics of Paul Ramsey,* Scholars' Press, 1974; *Ideology, Reason, and the Limitation of War: Religious and Secular Concepts, 1200-1740,* Princeton University Press, 1975.

WORK IN PROGRESS: A book on the influence of military doctrine on the just war and limited war doctrine since the Middle Ages, completion expected in 1977 or 1978; a book on the uses of history for theological ethics.

SIDELIGHTS: Johnson told *CA:* "Theological ethics is necessarily interdisciplinary, an attempt to relate religion to some secular field or other; I conceive it also to be cross-cultural and historically well-grounded at its best. My books are attempts to probe the historical development of religious and secular ideas and behavior in their influence upon each other."

AVOCATIONAL INTERESTS: Sailing, renovating old houses, photography, travel, and "tinkering with things that don't work."

* * *

JOHNSON, Joan Helen 1931-
(Jo Jeffers)

PERSONAL: Born April 28, 1931, in New Ulm, Minn.; daughter of Norman Lincoln and Geraldine (Scofield) Johnson; married Luis Mario Baeza (a guitarist-singer), April 20, 1975. *Education:* University of Nottingham, certificate in English studies, 1952; Stanford University, B.A., 1954; summer study at University of New Mexico, 1953. *Residence:* Heber, Ariz. *Agent:* Don Shepherd, 1680 Vine St., Hollywood, Calif. 90028.

CAREER: Cattle rancher in Holbrook, Ariz., 1956-64; magazine journalist in Pinetop, Ariz., 1964-72; cattle rancher in Snowflake, Ariz., 1973-74; U.S. Forest Service, Pinedale, Ariz., lookout, 1974—.

WRITINGS: (Under pseudonym Jo Jeffers) *Ranch Wife,* Doubleday, 1963. Also author of *A Ross Santee Sketchbook,* as yet unpublished. Contributor to *Arizona Highways, Arizona, White Mountains Magazine, Persimmon Hill,* and *Writer.*

WORK IN PROGRESS: A series of novels on the people and country of the rural Southwest, the first two volumes tentatively titled *The Bond* and *The Green Leaves of Summer;* movie scripts.

SIDELIGHTS: Joan Johnson told CA: "I have wasted much of my life writing what other people asked me to write, doing what other people wanted me to do. Now I want to spend what time I have left getting to the heart of my subject matter, the land and the people of northern Arizona, the universal and endless struggles between people and within people. Involved are many cultures, many different planes of thought, levels of experience, that can only be expressed through fiction."

* * *

JOHNSON, Robert A. 1921-

PERSONAL: Born May 26, 1921, in Portland, Ore.; son of Alex E. and Gladys (Williamson) Johnson. Education: Attended Oregon State University, Stanford University, C. G. Jung Institute, and Sri Aurobindo Ashram. Religion: Episcopalian. Home address: Box 972, Encinitas, Calif. 92024.

CAREER: Worked as counselor in San Diego, Calif., and as president of St. John's House, Inc., Encinitas, Calif.; currently lecturer at California School of Professional Psychology, San Diego. President of C. G. Jung Group, San Diego, Calif.

WRITINGS: He, Religious Publishing House, 1974.

WORK IN PROGRESS: A book on feminine psychology.

AVOCATIONAL INTERESTS: Harpsichord, clavichord.

* * *

JOHNSON, Robert Sherlaw 1932-

PERSONAL: Born May 21, 1932, in Sunderland, County Durham, England; son of Robert (a marine engineer) and Helen (Smith) Johnson; married Rachael Maria Clarke (a violin teacher), July 28, 1959; children: Rebecca Maria Sherlaw, Cuthbert Sherlaw, Ralph Austin Sherlaw, Griselda Margaret Sherlaw. Education: Royal Conservatory of Music, A.R.C.M., 1951; University of Durham, B.A. (honors), 1953, B.Mus., 1959; Royal Academy of Music, A.R.A.M., 1957; Oxford University, M.A., 1970; University of Leeds, D.Mus., 1971; also studied composition and pianoforte in Paris, 1957-58. Home: Malton Croft, Woodlands Rise, Stonesfield, Oxford OX7 2PP, England. Office: Worcester College, Oxford University, Oxford, England.

CAREER: Composer and pianist. Oxford University, Worcester College, Oxford, England, lecturer and fellow. Member: Composers Guild, Incorporated Society of Musicians, Association of University Teachers. Awards, honors: Radcliffe Award for Composition, 1969.

WRITINGS: Messiaen, University of California Press, 1975. Contributor of articles to magazines.

WORK IN PROGRESS: Musical compositions, including an opera; research on electronic music.

* * *

JOHNSON, William C(lark, Jr.) 1945-

PERSONAL: Born March 5, 1945, in Portland, Ore.; son of William Clark (in business management) and Genevieve L. (Cotterel) Johnson; married Cheryl L. Ashby, August 19, 1967; children: Brendan A. Education: University of Washington, Seattle, student, 1966; Whitworth College, B.A. (cum laude), 1967; State University of New York at Stony Brook, M.A., 1969; University of Denver, Ph.D., 1972. Home: 423 North Florida, DeLand, Fla. 32720. Office: Department of English, Stetson University, Box 1262, DeLand, Fla. 32720.

CAREER: University of Denver, Denver, Colo., instructor in English, 1971-72; Stetson University, DeLand, Fla., assistant professor of English, 1972—. Member: Modern Language Association of America, Mediaeval Academy of America, Society for New Language Study, College English Association, South Atlantic Modern Language Association.

WRITINGS: (Editor with L. C. Gruber, and contributor) New Views on Chaucer: Essays in Generative Criticism, Society for New Language Study, 1973; (with Raymond P. Tripp, Jr.) The Ladder of Language: An Introductory Structural Grammar, Society for New Language Study, 1973, 2nd edition, 1975; (contributor) Tripp and D. Loganbill, editors, Essays on C. S. Lewis, Onny Press, 1975. Contributor of articles and reviews to literature journals.

WORK IN PROGRESS: A book on Chaucer; research on Old English poetry, Beowulf, and Chaucer.

SIDELIGHTS: Johnson writes: "I am interested in comparative religion and epistemology as means of comprehending literary (especially ancient) texts. I would call my 'viewpoint' perennial or in specific terms post-humanistic."

* * *

JONAS, Doris F(rances) 1916-
(Doris F. Klein)

PERSONAL: Born May 21, 1916, in London, England; daughter of L. Edward (a manufacturer) and Gertrude (Froomberg) Warshaw; married Frank Klein, January 14, 1945 (divorced, 1970); married Adolphe David Jonas (a psychiatrist), June 17, 1970; children: (first marriage) Francis Charles, Jill Elise. Education: Attended London School of Economics and Political Science, 1935-37. Politics: Conservative. Home: 24B Wellington Court, London SW1X 7PL, England. Agent: Peter Matson, Harold Matson Co., 22 East 40th St., New York, N.Y. 10016.

CAREER: Editor and ghostwriter, 1937-39; Institute of Theoretical Medicine, New York, N.Y., director of department of anthropology, 1956-72; family psychotherapist in New York, N.Y., 1965-72, and in Wuerzburg, Germany, 1974. Writer. Wartime service: Women's Voluntary Services, Department of Salvage Research, 1939-46. Member: Royal Anthropological Institute (fellow), American Anthropological Association, Current Anthropology (associate). Awards, honors: Pawlowski Peace Prize from Pawlowski Peace Foundation, Wakefield, Mass., 1974, for work on the evolutionary infantilization of man as a factor in violence.

WRITINGS: (Under name Doris Klein, with David Jonas) Man-Child, McGraw, 1970; Young Till We Die, Coward, 1973; (contributor) L. Pawlowski, editor, Paths to Permanent Peace, Volume II, Pawlowski Peace Foundation, 1974; Sex and Status, Stein & Day, 1975; (contributor) Robin Deniston, editor, Man's Concern with Life After Death, Weidenfeld & Nicolson, in press; Other Senses, Other Worlds, Stein & Day, in press. Contributor to professional anthropology and psychiatry journals and medical magazines.

AVOCATIONAL INTERESTS: Art and art history.

* * *

JONAS, Hans 1903-

PERSONAL: Born May 10, 1903, in Moenchengladbach, Germany; came to United States, 1955; naturalized citizen, 1960; son of Gustav and Rosa (Horowitz) Jonas; married

Eleonore Weiner, October 6, 1943; children: Ayalah, Jonathan, Gabrielle. *Education:* Attended University of Freiburg, 1921, 1923-24, University of Berlin, 1921-23, University of Heidelberg, 1926, postdoctoral study, 1929; University of Marburg, Ph.D. (summa cum laude), 1928. *Home:* 9 Meadow Lane, New Rochelle, N.Y. 10805. *Office:* Department of Philosophy, New School for Social Research, 66 West 12th Street, New York, N.Y. 10011.

CAREER: Hebrew University, Jerusalem, Palestine, guest lecturer in philosophy, 1938-39, 1946-48; British Council School of Higher Studies, Jerusalem, lecturer in ancient history, 1946-48; McGill University, Montreal, Quebec, teaching fellow in philosophy, 1949-50; Carleton University, Ottawa, Ontario, visiting professor, 1950-51, associate professor of philosophy, 1951-54; New School for Social Research, New York, N.Y., professor, 1955-66, Alvin Johnson Professor of Philosophy, 1966—, chairman of department, 1956-63 and 1972-75. Visiting professor, Princeton University, 1958, Columbia University, 1961 and 1966-67, Princeton Theological Seminary, 1961-62, Hunter College (now Hunter College of the City University of New York), 1963-64, Union Theological Seminary, 1966-67; Ingersoll Lecturer, Harvard University, 1961; fellow of Center for Advanced Studies, Wesleyan University, 1964-65; member of Committee on Social Thought, University of Chicago, 1968, 1969, and 1970. *Military service:* Royal Artillery, 1940-45; Israeli Army Artillery, 1948-49, became first lieutenant.

MEMBER: American Philosophical Association, American Society for the Study of Religion. *Awards, honors:* Lady Davis Foundation fellow, 1949-50; Rockefeller Foundation fellow, 1959-60; D.H.L. from Hebrew Union College-Jewish Institute of Religion, 1962; National Endowment for the Humanities grant, 1973-74; Rockefeller Foundation grant, 1974-75.

WRITINGS: Augustin und das paulinische Freiheitsproblem: Eine philosophische Studie zum pelagianischen Streit, Vandenhoeck & Ruprecht, 1930, 2nd revised edition, 1965; *Gnosis und spaetantiker Geist,* Vandenhoeck & Ruprecht, Volume I: *Die mythologische Gnosis,* 1934, 3rd revised edition, 1964, Volume II: *Von der Mythologische mystischen Philosophie,* 1934, 3rd revised edition, 1966; *The Gnostic Religion: The Message of the Alien God and the Beginnings of Christianity,* Beacon, 1958, 2nd edition, 1963; *Zwischen Nichts und Ewigkeit: Zur Lehre vom Menschen,* Vandenhoeck-Reihe, 1963; *The Phenomenon of Life: Towards a Philosophical Biology,* Harper, 1966; *Wandel und Bestand: Vom Grunde der Verstehbarkeit des Geschichtlichen* Vittorio-Klostermann, 1970; *Organismus und Freiheit: Ansaetze zu einer philosophischen Biologie,* Vandenhoeck & Ruprecht, 1973; *Philosophical Essays: From Ancient Creed to Technological Man,* Prentice-Hall, 1974.

Contributor: Arthur A. Cohen and Marvin Halverson, editors, *A Handbook of Christian Theology,* Meridian Books, 1958; F. L. Cross, editor, *Texte Untersuchungen zur Geschichte der altch,* Akademie-Verlag, 1962; M. Natanson, editor, *Philosophy of the Social Sciences,* Random House, 1963; J. P. Hyatt, editor, *The Bible in Modern Scholarship,* Abingdon, 1965; Ugo Bianchi, editor, *Le Origini dello Gnosticismo,* E. J. Brill, 1967; A. H. Friedlander, editor, *Out of the Whirlwind,* Union of American Hebrew Congregations, 1968; Francis Oakley and Daniel O'Connor, editors, *Creation: The Impact of an Idea,* Scribner, 1969; R. L. Heilbroner, editor, *Economic Means and Social Ends,* Prentice-Hall, 1969; Paul Freund, editor, *Experimentation*

with Human Subjects, Braziller, 1970; James M. Robinson, editor, *Future of Our Religious Past: Essays in Honor of Rudolph Bultmann,* Harper, 1971. Contributor to *Encyclopedia Hebraica* and *Encyclopedia of Philosophy.* Contributor of articles to *Theologische Zeitschrift, Journal of Philosophy, Review of Metaphysics, Philosophy and Phenomenological Research, Human Biology, Harvard Theological Review, Social Research,* and other publications.

*   *   *

JONES, (Audrey) Christine   1937-

PERSONAL: Born December 25, 1937, in Edgeware, England; came to United States, 1968; daughter of Frederick Albert and Ethel (Morris) Lidster; married A. Barry Jones (a minister), October 17, 1959; children: Glyn, Owen. *Education:* Thronbridge Hall Teacher Training College, teaching diploma, 1958; Ontario Bible College, missionary diploma, 1963. *Religion:* "Born again Christian"; Conservative Congregational Christian Conference. *Home:* 3760 Catalina Dr., Carlsbad, Calif. 92008.

CAREER: Elementary school teacher in Nottingham, England, 1958-59, and Kirkby, England, 1959-60. Faculty member at Forest Home School of Christian Writing, 1974 and 1975, and Hume Lake School of Christian Writing, 1975. *Member:* Minnesota Christian Writers Guild (president, 1972-73).

WRITINGS: Lord, I Want To Tell You Something, Augsburg, 1973; *What Do I Do Now, Lord?* (juvenile), Augsburg, 1976. Contributor to religious magazines.

WORK IN PROGRESS: Mystery of the Carved Seagull (juvenile).

*   *   *

JONES, Elizabeth B(rown)   1907-
(Betty Brown)

PERSONAL: Born September 27, 1907, in Kansas City, Mo.; daughter of James Riley (a paint manufacturer) and Agnes (Gammage) Brown; married Clare Hartley Jones (an attorney and trust officer), June 4, 1929; children: Elizabeth (Mrs. William Taylor), Sara (Mrs. Ray Bowman), David, Phyllis (Mrs. Randy Michael). *Education:* Attended Kansas City University (now University of Missouri, Kansas City), 1947-48. *Religion:* Protestant. *Residence:* Kansas City, Mo. *Office:* Church of the Nazarene, 6401 Paseo, Kansas City, Mo. 64131.

CAREER: Teacher and supervisor of Sunday school classes in Kansas City, Mo., 1940-56; Church of the Nazarene, Kansas City, editorial division of department of church schools, primary editor, 1962—; free-lance writer. Vice-chairperson of primary sub-committee, Aldersgate Publications Association, 1973—; conductor of workshops for local and state church councils; instructor at writers' conferences.

WRITINGS: God's Loving Kindness, Beacon Hill, 1946; *Together With God,* Beacon Hill, 1952; *When You Need a Story,* Beacon Hill, 1953; *Round About Me,* Warner, 1953; *God Loves Me,* Warner, 1954; *God Plans for Happy Families* (preschool), Warner, 1955; *In the Land of the Big Souix* (biography), Beacon Hill, 1955; *When You Need a Missionary Story,* Warner, 1956; *When We Go to Church,* Warner, 1957; *Mirvet of the Mountains,* Nazarene, 1958; *All the Children of the World,* Warner, 1958; *When You Need a Special Story,* Warner, 1959; *Pioneer to the Swazis* (biography), Nazarene, 1959; *When We Share the Bible with Children,* Beacon Hill, 1962; *When You Need a Bible Story,* Beacon Hill, 1966; *Teaching Primaries Today,* Beacon Hill, 1974; *Because God Made Me,* Beacon Hill, 1975; *The Story of God's Love,* Standard, 1976. Also author of curriculum materials for church schools, songs, and scripts for filmstrips. Contributor of articles, stories, puzzles and poems to religious publications. Contributor of devotions and nature stories under pseudonym Betty Brown.

WORK IN PROGRESS: Bible stories about Jesus for beginning readers; Bible stories in poetic form; a collection of nature stories; a book of devotional readings for families.

SIDELIGHTS: Mrs. Jones told *CA:* "As a child, I was surrounded by my loving family, and many good books. I grew up with the desire to share my thoughts and happy experiences with others. . . . My chief motivation has been to help children develop a sense of wonder and a deep abiding faith in a loving heavenly Father."

* * *

JONES, Hortense P. 1918-

PERSONAL: Born January 10, 1918, in Franklin, Va.; daughter of Edgar and Cora Lee (De Loatch) Parker; married Theodore T. Jones, 1940; children: Theodora A. Jones Blackmon, Theodore T., Jr., Lawrence W. *Education:* Hampton Institute, professional diploma, 1936, B.S. in Ed., 1947; New York University, M.A., 1950; further graduate study at New York University, University of Chicago, and University of Puerto Rico. *Home:* 150-23 118th Ave., Jamaica, N.Y. 11434. *Office:* Board of Education, 131 Livingston St., Brooklyn, N.Y. 11201.

CAREER: City Day Care Centers, New York, N.Y., director, 1950-56; New York City Board of Education, New York, N.Y., teacher of early childhood education, 1956-63, assistant director, Bureau of Early Childhood Education, 1963-64, assistant director for more effective schools, Bureau of Early Childhood Education, 1964-69, director for more effective schools, 1969-72, assistant director, Bureau of Early Childhood Education, 1972—. City University of New York, adjunct lecturer at Queens College, 1973-74, Medgar Evers College, 1974-75. Consultant on educational instruction to Peace Corps; consultant to New Jersey State Department of Education.

MEMBER: National Association for Supervision and Curriculum Development, Association for the Study of Afro-American Life and History, National Association of Elementary School Principals, Association for Childhood Education International, International Reading Association, National Association for the Education of Young Children. *Awards, honors:* Sojourner Truth Award of New York State Business and Professional Women's Association, 1968.

WRITINGS—All with Peter Buckley: *Living as Neighbors,* Holt, 1966; *William, Andy and Ramon,* Holt, 1966; *Five Friends at School,* Holt, 1966; *Our Growing City,* Holt, 1968.

* * *

JONES, Jeanne 1937-

PERSONAL: Born May 17, 1937, in Los Angeles, Calif.; daughter of Jesse Ross (a manufacturer) and Kathryn (Jones) Castendyck; married Joseph Bush (a physician), November 4, 1965 (died July 2, 1968); married Robert Letts

Jones, April 15, 1972; children: Thomas Barton Beek, David Benjamin Beek. *Education:* Attended Northwestern University, and University of Southern California. *Religion:* Episcopal. *Agent:* Julian Bach, 3 East 48th St., New York, N.Y. 10017. *Office:* 7730 Herschel, La Jolla, Calif. 92037.

CAREER: Founder of Angelitos del Campo (auxiliary to American Diabetes Association) and president; member of board of directors of San Diego Opera Association. *Member:* National Federation of Press Women, National League of American Pen Women, Authors Guild. *Awards, honors:* First place in adult books from National Federation of Press Women, 1972, for *The Calculating Cook.*

WRITINGS: The Calculating Cook, 101 Productions, 1972; *Diet for a Happy Heart,* 101 Productions, 1975. Food editor of *Forecast.*

WORK IN PROGRESS: Diet Delight Cookbook for Children.

* * *

JONES, Lewis Pinckney 1916-

PERSONAL: Born September 8, 1916, in Laurens, S.C.; son of Barney L. (a school supplier) and Emily (Meng) Jones; married Densmore Faris (a teacher), June 3, 1950; children: Barney, Faris, Meng, Charles. *Education:* Wofford College, A.B., 1938, M.A., 1939; University of North Carolina, Ph.D., 1952. *Religion:* Methodist. *Home:* 325 Rivermont Dr., Spartanburg, S.C. 29302. *Office:* Department of History, Wofford College, Spartanburg, S.C. 29301.

CAREER: Ford High School, Laurens, S.C., English teacher, 1939-42; Wofford College, Spartanburg, S.C., instructor in English, 1946-47, assistant professor of history, 1947-53, associate professor of history, 1953-55, professor of history, 1955-72, Kenan Professor, 1972—, chairman of department, 1962—. Member of state Committee for the Humanities and of local Bicentennial Committee. *Military service:* U.S. Navy, commanding officer of three small ships, 1942-46. *Member:* Southern Historical Association, South Carolina Historical Association (president), South Carolina Historical Society, South Caroliniana Society (vice-president), Phi Beta Kappa.

WRITINGS: Books and Articles on South Carolina: A Guide, University of South Carolina Press, 1970; *South Carolina: A Synoptic History,* Sandlapper Store, 1971; *Stormy Petrel: N. G. Gonzales and His "State",* University of South Carolina Press, 1973; *South Carolina Civil War of 1775,* Sandlapper Store, 1975.

Contributor: Herbert Ravenel Sass, editor, *Outspoken: 150 Years of the News and Courier,* University of South Carolina Press, 1953; Arthur S. Link and Rembert W. Patrick, editors, *Writing Southern History,* Louisiana State University Press, 1965; James B. Meriwether, editor, *South Carolina Journals and Journalists,* University of South Carolina Southern Studies Program, 1975. Contributor to *Encyclopaedia Britannica* and to regional magazines.

WORK IN PROGRESS: A Biography of Martin W. Gray.

* * *

JONES, William M(cKendrey) 1927-

PERSONAL: Born September 19, 1927, in Dothan, Ala.; son of William M. (a salesman) and Margaret (Farmer) Jones; married Ruth Ann Roberts (a piano teacher), August

14, 1952; children: Margaret, Elizabeth, Bronwen. *Education:* University of Alabama, B.A., 1949, M.A., 1950; Northwestern University, Ph.D., 1953. *Religion:* Protestant. *Home:* 209 Russell Blvd., Columbia, Mo. 65201. *Office:* Department of English, University of Missouri, Columbia, Mo. 65201.

CAREER: Wisconsin State College, Eau Claire, assistant professor of English, 1953-55; University of Michigan, Ann Arbor, assistant professor of English, 1955-59; University of Missouri, Columbia, assistant professor, 1959-60, associate professor, 1960-65, professor of English, 1965—. Folger Shakespeare Library research fellow, 1955. *Military service:* U.S. Army, 1945-46. *Member:* Modern Language Association of America, Renaissance Society of America, Shakespeare Association of America, English Renaissance.

WRITINGS: (Editor) *Stages of Composition,* Heath, 1964; (editor) *Fiction: Form and Experience,* Heath, 1969; *A Guide to Living Power,* John Knox, 1975; (with wife, Ruth Ann Jones) *Living in Love,* John Knox, 1976.

* * *

JORALEMON, Ira B(eaman) 1884-1975

1884—August 17, 1975; American consulting mining engineer and geologist, lecturer, and author. Obituaries: *New York Times,* August 23, 1975.

* * *

JORDAN, David K. 1942-

PERSONAL: Born March 11, 1942, in Chicago, Ill. *Education:* University of Chicago, A.B., 1963, Ph.D., 1969; Stanford University, A.M., 1964. *Office:* Department of Anthropology, University of California at San Diego, La Jolla, Calif. 92093.

CAREER: University of California at San Diego, La Jolla, associate professor of anthropology, 1969—. *Member:* American Anthropological Association, Association for Asian Studies, China Society, Royal Anthropological Institute of Great Britain and Ireland, Asiatic Society (Hong Kong), Royal Netherlands Institute of Linguistics, Geography, and Ethnology.

WRITINGS: Guide to the Romanization of Chinese, Mei-Ya Publications, 1971; *Gods, Ghosts, and Ancestors: The Folk Religion of a Taiwanese Village,* University of California Press, 1972; (with Marc J. Swartz) *Anthropology: Perspective on Humanity,* Wiley, 1976.

* * *

JORGENSEN, Joseph G(ilbert) 1934-

PERSONAL: Born April 15, 1934, in Salt Lake City, Utah; son of Joseph Norman and Clela (Bailey) Jorgensen; married Katherine Will (a college lecturer), August 31, 1964; children: Brigham Will, Sarah Katherine. *Education:* University of Utah, B.S., 1956; Indiana University, Ph.D., 1964. *Home:* 1517 Highland Dr., Newport Beach, Calif. 92660. *Office:* Program in Comparative Culture, University of California, Irvine, Calif. 92664.

CAREER: Antioch College, Yellow Springs, Ohio, assistant professor of anthropology, 1964-65; University of Oregon, Eugene, assistant professor of anthropology, 1965-68; University of Michigan, Ann Arbor, associate professor, 1968-71, professor of anthropology, 1971-74, member of interdepartmental linguistics faculty, 1968-74, member of board of directors of American Culture Program, 1970-72;

University of California, Irvine, professor of comparative culture and director of the program, both 1974—. Director of work camp for Northern Ute Tribe, 1960, 1962; member of board of directors of Human Relations Area Files, 1970—, and of Native Struggles Support Group; chairman of local Faculty-Student Committee to Stop the War in Vietnam, 1965-67. Consultant to National Science Foundation.

MEMBER: American Association for the Advancement of Science, Current Anthropology, American Indian Historical Society, Sigma Xi. *Awards, honors:* National Science Foundation fellowship, summers, 1964, 1965, research grant, 1970-73; National Institutes of Health research grant, summer, 1966; American Philosophical Society research grant, summers, 1967 and 1969; Horace H. Rackham senior fellowship, summer, 1972; C. Wright Mills Book Award, from Society for the Study of Social Problems, 1973, for *The Sun Dance Religion;* Guggenheim fellowship, 1974-75.

WRITINGS: Salish Language and Culture: A Statistical Analysis of Internal Relations, History, and Evolution (monograph), Research Center for the Language Sciences, Indiana University, 1969; *The Sun Dance Religion: Power for the Powerless,* University of Chicago Press, 1972; (editor and author of introductions) *Biology and Culture in Modern Perspective: Readings from Scientific American,* W. H. Freeman, 1972; (with Marcello Truzzi) *Anthropology and American Life,* Prentice-Hall, 1974; (editor and contributor) *Comparative Studies by Harold E. Driver and Essays in His Honor,* Human Relations Area Files Press, 1974; (editor and contributor) *Reservation Indian Society Today: Studies in Economics, Politics, Kinship, and Households,* Indian Historian Press, in press; *Western Indians,* Volume I: *Environment, Language, and Culture,* W. H. Freeman, in press.

Contributor: Jack O. Waddell and Michael O. Watson, editors, *The American Indian in Urban Society,* Little, Brown, 1971; Thomas Weaver, editor, *To See Ourselves: Anthropology and Modern Social Issues,* Scott, Foresman, 1973; H. Roy Kaplan, editor, *American Minorities and Economic Opportunities,* F. T. Peacock, in press; William C. Sturtevant, general editor, *Handbook of North American Indians,* Volume IX: *Southwest,* edited by Alfonso Ortiz, and Volume X: *Great Basin,* edited by Warren L. D'Azevedo, Center for the Study of Man, Smithsonian Institution, both in press; John Saxe-Fernandez, editor, *The Crisis of Social Science,* Ciudad Universitaria, in press. Contributor to anthropology journals.

WORK IN PROGRESS: Two more volumes in his series on analysis of the Indians of western North America for W. H. Freeman.

SIDELIGHTS: Jorgensen writes: "My Mormon background made me skeptical of religion, interested in communitarian life, fascinated by philosophy and the philosophy of science, and irritated by institutional racism. My western locus and nexus immersed me in the outdoors, the contradictions in Indian and Mormon life styles, and the disparity between rural and urban areas. I speak Ute and Shoshone."

* * *

JOSEPHSON, Harold 1942-

PERSONAL: Born February 5, 1942, in Brooklyn, N.Y.; son of Eugene and Beatrice (a business manager; maiden name, Blank) Josephson; married Lila Greenblatt (a teacher), August 10, 1963; children: Elissa Ann, Tracy Lynn. *Education:* Brooklyn College of the City University of New York, B.A., 1963; University of Wisconsin, Madison, M.A., 1965, Ph.D., 1968. *Home:* 3809 Rhodes Ave., Charlotte, N.C. 28210. *Office:* Department of History, University of North Carolina, Charlotte, N.C. 28223.

CAREER: Ohio State University, Columbus, instructor in history, 1968-70; University of North Carolina at Charlotte, associate professor, 1970—, co-director of Great Decisions Program, Institute for Urban Studies and Community Service, 1973-76. *Member:* American Historical Association, Organization of American Historians. *Awards, honors:* Carnegie Endowment for International Peace grant, 1967; National Endowment for the Humanities summer grant, 1975.

WRITINGS: James T. Shotwell and the Rise of Internationalism in America, Fairleigh Dickinson University Press, 1975. Contributor of articles and book reviews to journals in his field. Coordinator and co-author of television series of ten programs, "The Making of an American Empire," produced by WTVI, Charlotte, N.C., 1973.

WORK IN PROGRESS: A book, *The Ex-Communist Movement;* journal articles.

* * *

JULTY, Sam 1927-

PERSONAL: Born November 12, 1927, in Bronx, N.Y.; son of Benjamin (a tailor) and Bertha (a nurse; maiden name, Kuvet) Julty; married Elizabeth Kresky (divorced); children: Daniel, Rachel. *Education:* Attended high school in Bronx, N.Y. *Politics:* "Humanity." *Religion:* "Cultural Jewish." *Residence:* Corona, N.Y.; *Office:* 257 Seventh Ave., New York, N.Y. 10001.

CAREER: Has worked as carpenter/electrician/plumber, as an auto mechanic, taxi and truck driver, as automobile shop teacher, technical editor, and free-lance magazine writer. *Member:* International Motor Press Association, Sex Information and Education Council of the United States, Men's Liberation (New York, N.Y.).

WRITINGS: Auto Repairs You Can Do Yourself, Dafran, 1973; *How Your Car Works,* Harper, 1974; *Male Sexual Performance,* Grosset, 1975. Contributor to *Ms., Harper's, Popular Mechanics,* and *New York Times.*

WORK IN PROGRESS: Men's Sexual Fantasies; Dictionary of Sexuality; A History of Medical Care in the United States.

SIDELIGHTS: Julty writes that he enjoys "'translating' technical to everyday English. Foe of mis-information, restraints, sex roles. Want to do more advocacy writing." *Avocational interests:* Sculptor in clay, wood, and stone; active in "Men's Liberation Movement"; counsellor (not therapist) for men and women with problems relating to sex; a "good" cook.

* * *

KABA, Lansine 1941-

PERSONAL: Born January 19, 1941, in Kankan, Guinea; son of Al-Hajj Musa and Haja (Boh Diané) Kaba; married Gail M. Walker. *Education:* Sorbonne, University of Paris, licence, 1966; Northwestern University, Ph.D., 1972. *Home:* 1530 South Sixth St., #C606, Minneapolis, Minn. 55454. *Office:* Department of History, 614 Social Science Bldg., University of Minnesota, Minneapolis, Minn. 55455.

CAREER: High school French teacher in Philadelphia (Pa.) Public School System, 1966-67; French teacher in day

school in Winnetka, Ill., 1967-69; University of Minnesota, Minneapolis, assistant professor, 1970-72, associate professor of history, 1972—. Consultant to Minnesota Art Museum. *Member:* African Studies Association, Association des Historiens Africains. *Awards, honors:* Social Science Research Council award, 1972; Herskovits Award from African Studies Association, 1975, for *The Wahhabiyya: Islamic Reform and Politics in French West Africa.*

WRITINGS: The Wahhabiyya: Islamic Reform and Politics in French West Africa, Northwestern University Press, 1974. Contributor to academic journals. Member of editorial board of *Afrika-Zamani,* the journal of the Association des Historiens Africains, 1972—.

WORK IN PROGRESS: Trade and Politics in the Western Sudan: 1490-1700; The History of Upper Guinea.

SIDELIGHTS: Kaba writes: "I . . . try to write about the history and culture of African peoples in an African perspective that aims at quality and seriousness."

* * *

KACHRU, Braj Behari 1932-

PERSONAL: Born May 15, 1932, in Srinagar, Kashmir, India; came to United States in 1963; son of Shyam Lal (an educator) and Tulsidevi (Tutu) Kachru; married Yamuna Keskar (a professor), January 25, 1965; children: Amita, Shamit. *Education:* Jammu and Kashmir University, B.A. (honors), 1952; Allahabad University, M.A., 1955; University of Edinburgh, Ph.D., 1961. *Religion:* Hindu. *Home:* 2016 Cureton Dr., Urbana, Ill. 61801. *Office:* Department of Linguistics, University of Illinois, Urbana, Ill. 61801.

CAREER: Deccan College Research Institute, Poona, India, fellow in linguistics, 1957-58; Lucknow University, Lucknow, India, assistant professor of English, in charge of linguistics program, 1962-63; University of Illinois, Urbana, research associate in linguistics, 1963-64, assistant professor, 1964-67, associate professor, 1967-70, professor of linguistics, 1970—, head of department, 1969—, associate of Center for Advanced Study, 1971-72. Member of South Asian study committees; co-director of summer program in South Asian study, 1967. Consultant to American Institute of Indian Studies, 1972, Ford Foundation, 1974.

MEMBER: International P.E.N., Linguistic Society of America, American Oriental Society, Linguistic Society of India (life member), Philological Society of Great Britain. *Awards, honors:* Grants from U.S. Office of Health, Education and Welfare's Institute of International Affairs, 1965-72, for *A Reference Grammar of Kashmiri,* and 1970-72, for *An Introduction to Spoken Kashmiri;* faculty research fellow of American Institute of Indian Studies, New Delhi, India, 1967-68 and 1971-72.

WRITINGS: A Reference Grammar of Kashmiri, U.S. Office of Education, 1969; (editor with H. W. Stahlke) *Current Trends in Stylistics,* Linguistic Research, Inc., 1972; (editor with others, and contributor) *Issues in Linguistics: Papers in Honor of Henry and Renée Kahane,* University of Illinois Press, 1973; *An Introduction to Spoken Kashmiri,* two parts, U.S. Office of Education, 1973.

Contributor: C. E. Bazell and other editors, *In Memory of J. R. Firth,* Longmans, 1966; John W. M. Verhaar, editor, *Foundations of Language,* Part III, Volume VIII, D. Reidel (Dordrecht, Holland), 1968; T. Sebeok and others, editors, *Current Trends in Linguistics,* Mouton & Co., 1969; Bh. Krishramurti, editor, *Introduction to Indian Languages,* National Book Trust (New Delhi), in press.

Contributor of articles and reviews to language, education, and Oriental studies journals. Editor of *Studies in Language Learning;* co-editor, *Studies in Hindi Linguistics,* 1970; review editor of *Papers in Linguistics,* 1970—; member of editorial board of *Studies in the Linguistic Sciences,* 1969—, *International Journal of the Sociology of Language* and *International Journal of Stylistics;* has been guest editor of South Asian issues of *International Journal of the Sociology of Language* and *Studies in the Linguistic Sciences;* consultant to *Random House Dictionary of the English Language,* 1965-66.

WORK IN PROGRESS: Continuing research on Indian, English, and Kashmiri language and literature; sociolinguistic research.

* * *

KADISH, Ferne 1940-

PERSONAL: Born May 14, 1940, in Chicago, Ill.; daughter of Louis and Bessie (Mold) Wolner; married Sheldon L. Kadish (a manufacturer), April 16, 1966; children: Ilene, Michael. *Education:* Attended Boston University, 1958-59, and University of Southern California, 1959-60. *Religion:* Jewish. *Agent:* Erica Spellman, International Creative Management, 40 West 57th St., New York, N.Y.

CAREER: Writer. Has worked for City of Hope and Community Outreach program.

WRITINGS—With Kathleen Kurtland: *London on Five Hundred Dollars a Day: Tax and Gratuities Not Included,* Macmillan, 1975; *Los Angeles on Five Hundred Dollars a Day,* Macmillan, in press; *Paris on Five Hundred Dollars a Day,* Macmillan, in press; *New York on Five Hundred Dollars a Day,* Macmillan, in press.

* * *

KAESTNER, Dorothy 1920-

PERSONAL: Born January 1, 1920, in Groton, Conn.; daughter of Frederick Wallace (a carpenter) and Blanche (Burridge) Taylor; married George Kaestner (a store owner), April 22, 1944. *Education:* Studied art, weaving, and design privately. *Religion:* Roman Catholic. *Home:* 101 Maywood Rd., Darien, Conn. 06820. *Office:* Handcraft Shoppe, Darien, Conn. 06820.

CAREER: Durham Enders Razor Co., Mystic, Conn., bookkeeper, 1940-42; Plastic Manufacturing, Stamford, Conn., secretary, 1943-44; Handcraft Shoppe, Darien, Conn., co-owner, 1948—. Weaving and paintings have been exhibited in New England; weaving has also been shown at University of Southwestern Louisiana and in Smithsonian Institution Traveling Exhibition. Has taught weaving, needlepoint, and decoupage; has lectured and conducted workshops.

MEMBER: Handweavers Guild of America, Embroiderers Guild of America (Fairfield County chapter), Handweavers Guild of Connecticut (president, 1954), Society of Connecticut Craftsmen, Silvermine Guild of Artists (artist member). *Awards, honors:* Weaving awards from Handweavers Guild of Connecticut, 1953-63, 1968, Society of Connecticut Craftsmen, 1948, 1955, 1960, 1965, New England Handweavers Seminar, 1957, 1959, 1961, 1963, 1969, and Women's International Exhibit, 1961.

WRITINGS: Four Way Bargello (Needle Arts Society book selection), Scribner, 1972, revised edition, 1974; *Needlepoint/Bargello,* Scribner, 1974.

WORK IN PROGRESS: A book on needlepoint rugs; a book, tentatively titled *Four Way Bargello Method II.*

SIDELIGHTS: Dorothy Kaestner writes: "I have found that many people need to be guided in the use of color. They are afraid of it. Part of my pleasure in life is color." *Avocational interests:* International travel (Ireland, Portugal, Spain, Italy, England.)

* * *

KAFKA, Vincent W(infield) 1924-

PERSONAL: Born February 6, 1924, in Brooklyn, N.Y.; son of Victor (an investment banker) and Tunde (Brajjer) Kafka; married Elizabeth M. Murphy, August 19, 1950; children: Anne, John, Rosemary, Patricia, Sue, Thomas. *Education:* North Carolina State University, B.I.E., 1948; Drexel University, M.B.A., 1956. *Home:* 360 Deerfield Dr., Moraga, Calif. 94556.

CAREER: President of Effective Learning Systems, Moraga, Calif. Member of faculty, University of California, Extension Service, Berkeley, and Diablo Valley College. *Military service:* U.S. Army, 1943-46, 1950-52; became first lieutenant. *Member:* American Society for Training and Development, National Society of Sales Training Executives, National Society for Programmed Instruction, Sales and Marketing Executives Association.

WRITINGS: (With John H. Schaefer) *Open Management,* Peter H. Wyden, 1975. Contributor to journals in his field.

WORK IN PROGRESS: A Practical Guide to the Open Management System; Perceptive Salesmanship.

* * *

KAIKINI, P(rabhakar) R(amrao) 1912-

PERSONAL: Born February 15, 1912, in Bombay, India; son of Ramrao Vithal (a Saraswat Brahmin) and Shantabai (Kaveri) Kaikini; married Sita Ganesh Jeppu (a teacher), October 11, 1952. *Education:* Bombay University, B.A., 1935, M.A., 1941, B.T., 1942. *Politics:* "Follower of Mahatma Gandhi and Jawaharlal Nehru. Would like democracy and freedom for every country in the world; long for One World." *Religion:* Hindu. *Home:* Banarasi Bhaven, 10th Rd., Khar, Bombay 400 052, India.

CAREER: Private tutor of English in Bombay, India, 1936-45; Children's Academy, Bombay, English teacher, 1938-40; All India Weekly, Bombay, editor, 1944; Oriental Publishing Co., Bombay, manager, 1944-45; *Art and Culture,* Calcutta, India, associate editor, 1944-46; *Free Press Journal,* Bombay, sub-editor and reporter, 1945-46; *People's Raj* (Bombay government publication), Bombay, India, editor, 1947-54; *Farmer* (Bombay government publication), Bombay, India, editor, 1954-57; Indian Ministry of Information and Broadcasting, New Delhi, assistant editor and translator of *The Collected Works of Mahatma Gandhi,* 1957-69; National Book Trust, New Delhi, India, editor, 1969-72; *Samyukta Saraswat,* Bombay, executive editor and member of editorial board, 1973—. Indian congressman, 1930—.

WRITINGS—Books of poems: *Flower Offerings,* Bombay Book Depot, 1934; *Songs of a Wanderer,* New Book Co., 1936; *This Civilisation,* New Book Co., 1937; *Shanghai,* New Book Co., 1939; *The Recruit,* New Book Co., 1940; *Snake in the Moon,* New Book Co., 1942; *Look on Undaunted,* New Book Co., 1944; *Selected Poems,* Popular Book Depot, 1946; *Poems of the Passionate East,* New Book Co., 1947; *Some of My Years,* Writers' Workshop (Calcutta, India), 1972, Interculture Associates, 1975.

Poems are anthologized in *The Peacock Lute,* edited by V. N. Bhushan, Padma Publications (Bombay), 1945; *This Strange Adventure,* edited by Fredoon Kabraji, New India Publishing (London), 1947; *Echoes of Experience III,* edited by R. L. Curling and A. Blakeley, Longmans, Green, 1967; *The Treasury of Indo-Anglian Poetry,* Sahitya Akademi (New Delhi), 1970.

WORK IN PROGRESS: A volume of poems, *Death in Dacca.*

SIDELIGHTS: Caught in the turmoil of the struggle for independence when his father worked for the "alien" government and his mother taught spinning, Hindi, and English to women (clandestinely) to promote Gandhi's constructive program and to spread national consciousness, Kaikini spent his youth in a world of contrasts, contradiction, and secrecy. He believes that "... every nation should be allowed to work out its destiny in its own way according to its native genius without external interference of any sort. Only then will man be able to rise to his full spiritual height and realise Wendell Willkie's dream of One World...." *Avocational interests:* Walking, chess, crossword puzzles, reading, television, gardening.

*   *   *

KALBERER, Augustine   1917-

PERSONAL: Born March 8, 1917, in Portland, Ore.; son of August (a farmer) and Helen (Gall) Kalberer. *Education:* Mount Angel Seminary, B.A., 1939, graduate study, 1939-42; University of Toronto, M.A., 1944, Ph.D., 1946; Pontifical Institute of Mediaeval Studies, Toronto, M.S.L., 1945. *Home:* Westminster Abbey, Mission, British Columbia, Canada V2V 4J2. *Office:* Seminary of Christ the King, Mission, British Columbia, Canada V2V 4J2.

CAREER: Entered Ordo Sancti Benedicti (Order of Saint Benedict—Benedictines), 1936, ordained Roman Catholic priest, 1942; Seminary of Christ the King (of Westminster Abbey), Mission, British Columbia, teacher of philosophy, theology, and liturgy, 1946—, director of studies, 1955-69, rector of major seminary, 1969—, rector of minor seminary, 1973—; subprior of Westminster Abbey, 1953—. Member of Theological Commission of Archdiocese of Vancouver.

WRITINGS: Lives of the Saints: Daily Readings, Franciscan Herald, 1975. Author of weekly column on the lives of saints in *British Columbia Catholic, Western Catholic Reporter,* and *Northwest Catholic Progress.* Editor of *Pax Regis* (of Westminster Abbey), 1955-71.

*   *   *

KALIN, Robert   1921-

PERSONAL: Born December 11, 1921, in Everett, Mass.; son of Benjamin (a grocer) and Celia (Kraff) Kalin; married Madelyn Pildish, August 17, 1962; children: Susan Leslie, John Benjamin, Sandra Kim, Richard Dean. *Education:* University of Chicago, B.S., 1947; Harvard University, M.A.T., 1948; Florida State University, Ph.D., 1961. *Home:* 1120 Cherokee Dr., Tallahassee, Fla. 32301. *Office:* Department of Mathematics Education, Florida State University, Tallahassee, Fla. 32306.

CAREER: High school mathematics teacher in Danvers, Mass., 1948-49, and St. Louis, Mo., 1949-52; Naval Air Technical Training Center, Norman, Okla., educational statistician, 1952-53; Educational Testing Service, Princeton, N.J., test specialist and associate in research, 1953-55; College Board's Commission on Mathematics, Princeton,

N.J., executive assistant, 1955-56; Florida State University, Tallahassee, instructor, 1956-61, assistant professor, 1961-63, associate professor, 1963-65, professor of mathematics education, 1965—, chairman of mathematics education program, 1974—. Chairman of Florida State Mathematics Curriculum Guide Committee, 1961-64; chairman of Board of Regents Committee on Educational Television, 1966-68; member of advisory committee to Florida Committee on Mathematics Assessment, 1970—. *Military service:* U.S. Army, 1943-46. *Member:* Mathematical Association of America, National Council of Teachers of Mathematics (Florida representative, 1957-64), Florida Council of Teachers of Mathematics (president, 1960-61), Pi Mu Epsilon.

WRITINGS: (With Henry S. Dyer and Frederick M. Lord) *Problems in Mathematical Education,* Educational Testing Service, 1956.

(With Henry Garland and Eugene Nichols) *Introduction to Sets,* Holt, 1962; *The Arithmetic of Directed Numbers,* Holt, 1962; *Equations and Inequalities,* Holt, 1963; *Introduction to Coordinate Geometry,* Holt, 1963; (with Nichols, Frances Flournoy, and Leonard Simon) *Elementary Mathematics: Patterns and Structure,* eleven volumes, Holt, 1966, revised edition, 1968; (with George Green) *Modern Mathematics for the Elementary School Teacher,* with video tapes, McGraw, 1969.

(With Nichols) *Analytic Geometry,* Holt, 1973; (with Nichols, Flournoy, Simon, Paul A. Anderson, John Schluep, and Leslie A. Dwight) *Holt School Mathematics: Grades K-8,* Holt, 1974.

Author of unpublished educational reports. Contributor to mathematics and education journals. Co-editor, referee, and reviewer of testing for *Mathematics Teacher,* 1957-61; book reviewer for Prentice-Hall.

WORK IN PROGRESS: Creating and evaluating new subject matter and new approaches to the mathematical and pedagogical preparation of elementary school teachers.

*   *   *

KALLESSER, Michael   1886(?)-1975

1886(?)—March 19, 1975; American playwright. Obituaries: *New York Times,* March 21, 1975.

*   *   *

KALNOKY, Ingeborg L(ouise)   1909-

PERSONAL: Born January 27, 1909, in Metz, France; came to the U.S. from Hungary, 1949; daughter of Dietrich and Hertha (Rassmuss) von Breitenbuch; married Count Hugo Kalnoky, June 24, 1934 (deceased); children: Eleonora, Farkas, Anthony, Ingeborg. *Education:* Attended Academy of Fine Arts, Munich, Germany, 1931-33; studied art in Berlin, Germany, 1933-34. *Religion:* Roman Catholic. *Home:* 4654 Nelson Dr., Mobile, Ala. 36608. *Agent:* Bertha Klausner, International Literary Agency, Inc., 71 Park Ave., New York, N.Y. 10016.

CAREER: Olen Co., Mobile, Ala., statistician, 1954-59; Jiffy, Inc., Mobile, head bookkeeper, 1959-67; Alabama Board of Health, Mobile, federal project accountant, 1967-68; doctors' receptionist in Mobile, 1968-70; E. H. Smith & Son (electrical contractors), Mobile, head bookkeeper, 1970—.

WRITINGS: (With Ilona Herisko) *The Guest House* (nonfiction), Bobbs-Merrill, 1974. Author of "Die Zeugen von

Nurnberg" (means "The Witnesses at Nuremberg"), newspaper series in Germany, 1946.

* * *

KALSTONE, Shirlee A(nn) 1932-

PERSONAL: Born September 2, 1932, in Pittsburgh, Pa.; daughter of Daniel C. (an actors' agent) and Irene (Mangold) Comoroda; married Milton C. Staude, December 1, 1953 (divorced, 1959); married Lawrence M. Kalstone (a manufacturer), May 5, 1961; children: (first marriage) Gary M. Education: Attended University of Pittsburgh. Home and office: 250 East 73rd St., New York, N.Y. 10021.

CAREER: Owner of "Poodle Boutique," 1953-60; Kalstone Studios Grooming School, Pittsburgh, Pa., director, 1961-70; Lambert Kay (testing consultants) Pittsburgh, Pa., 1970-72, director of consumer relations in Los Angeles, Calif., 1972-73; VO Toys, Inc., New York, N.Y., consultant to "Ring 5," 1974—. Has lectured on dog grooming in Japan and England; conducted "All About Dogs," on WQED-Television, 1963; volunteer worker for Fund for Animals and American Society for the Prevention of Cruelty to Animals.

MEMBER: Professional Groomers Association (vice-president), National Dog Groomers Association of America (director of public relations). Awards, honors: Award for best technical book from Dog Writers Association of America, 1968, for The Complete Poodle Clipping and Grooming Book; outstanding grooming award from National Dog Groomers Association of America, 1974; founder's award from National Dog Groomer's Association of America, 1975.

WRITINGS: The Complete Poodle Clipping and Grooming Book, Howell Book, 1968; Pet Poodle Grooming Made Easy, Howell Book, 1972; The Kalstone Guide to Grooming Toy Dogs, Howell Book, 1975. Author of consumer booklets on pets; writer of "About Grooming," a column in Pet/Supplies/Marketing (magazine). Contributor to pet magazines. Editor of Professional Groomer, 1970-72.

WORK IN PROGRESS: The Art of Dog Handling, with Frank T. Sabella; a book on grooming hound and terrier dogs.

SIDELIGHTS: Shirlee Kalstone presently breeds and shows poodles and whippets.

* * *

KAMINSKI, Margaret (Joan) 1944-

PERSONAL: Born March 16, 1944, in Detroit, Mich.; daughter of John Joseph (a diemaker) and Gertrude (Malak) Kaminski; married Bruce Charles Bennett, May 30, 1967 (divorced, 1972). Education: Wayne State University, B.F.A., 1966, M.S.L.S., 1969. Politics: Feminist. Religion: None. Home: 242 Ashland, Detroit, Mich. 48215. Office: Public Relations Department, Detroit Public Library, 5201 Woodward Ave., Detroit, Mich. 48202.

CAREER: Detroit Public Library, Detroit, Mich., reference librarian in language, literature, philosophy, and fine arts department, 1969-73, assistant to coordinator of public relations, 1973—. Poet; owner and operator of Glass Bell Press, a poetry press for women. Radio interviewer, writer, and presenter; guest producer of "Dimension," poetry program on WDET-FM.

WRITINGS: (Contributor) Judith McCombs, editor, Free Women (anthology), Red Hanrahan Press (Detroit), 1971; (editor) Moving to Antarctica: An Anthology of Women's Writing, Dustbooks, 1975; (editor and contributor) Ten Michigan Women Poets, Glass Bell Press, 1975; Martinis, White Light Press (Detroit), 1975. Author of monograph, A Short History of the Woman Suffrage Movement in Detroit and Michigan, 1974. Writer of "Dame Philology," monthly column in Margins, 1974—. Contributor of poetry and articles to numerous journals, magazines, and newspapers, including University of Windsor Review, Wayne Literary Review, Detroit Discovery, Detroit News, Mainline, Waves, Off Our Backs, and Library Journal. Editor of Detroit Public Library Staff News Bulletin, 1970-71; co-editor of Moving Out (feminist literary journal), 1971—.

WORK IN PROGRESS: Manuscript of poetry, The Life of the Woman.

SIDELIGHTS: Margaret Kaminski told CA: "I have kept a diary from the age of 12. This diary is my reality; it is almost as if an event has not occurred unless it is recorded in my journals. I then transform the journal into poems, which now amount to over 3,000; but these include all the revisions and rough copies, some of which I never show anyone. My motivation for writing has always come from within, as I do not express myself in speech as often as many people do. I speculate about being a Carmelite, a nun who never speaks.

"In 1971, I became involved in Moving Out . . . [and] learned that other women have been writing all along, and that not only men can have access to journals and readings. I had written for many years before gaining any acceptance at all, and it took the women's movement to do that. For this reason I am deeply committed to Moving Out and to the women who have helped me. I wish to help other women who may think that, because they are creative in other ways than having children, or because they are not encouraged by male teachers and editors, they are odd or inferior in some way."

AVOCATIONAL INTERESTS: Yoga and meditation, travel, photography.

* * *

KANIN, Michael 1910-

PERSONAL: Born February 1, 1910, in Rochester, N.Y.; son of David and Sadie (Levine) Kanin; married Fay Mitchell (a writer), April 7, 1940; children: Josh. Education: Attended Art Students League, 1927, and New York School of Design, 1928. Home and office: 653 Ocean Front, Santa Monica, Calif. 90402.

CAREER: Worked as commercial and scenic artist, musician, and entertainer, 1927-37; now full-time writer. Wrote screenplays for RKO General, Inc., New York, N.Y., 1937-39; produced "A Double Life" for Universal, 1947; co-produced "Goodbye, My Fancy" on Broadway at Morocco Theatre, 1948; directed own screenplay, "When I Grow Up," for Eagle Lion, 1951; produced "Seidman and Son" on Broadway with the Theatre Guild, at Belasco Theatre, 1964. Member: American National Theatre and Academy, Writers Guild of America (member of board, 1943-44; treasurer, 1944-45; also organized Affiliated Committee for Television), American College Theatre Festival, Academy of Motion Picture Arts and Sciences, Dramatists Guild. Awards, honors: Academy Award for best original screenplay, 1942, for "Woman of the Year"; nominations for awards from Academy of Motion Picture Arts and Sciences and Writers Guild of America, 1958, for "Teachers Pet"; American College Theatre Festival bronze medal, 1972, silver medal, 1973.

WRITINGS—Plays; with wife, Fay Kanin: *His and Hers* (three-act; first produced on Broadway at 48th Street Theatre, January 7, 1954), Samuel French, 1954; *Rashomon* (two-act; first produced on Broadway at Music Box Theatre, January 27, 1959), Random House, 1959; "The Gay Life" (two-act), first produced on Broadway at Samuel Shubert Theatre, November 18, 1961; (also with Ben Starr) "M' Lord and Lady" (two-act), first produced in Los Angeles at Camino Theatre, 1974.

Screenplays: "Panama Lady," RKO General, 1939; "They Made Her a Spy," RKO General, 1939; "Anne of Windy Poplars" (based on the novel by L. M. Montgomery), RKO General, 1940; (with Ring Lardner, Jr.) "Woman of the Year," Metro-Goldwyn-Mayer, 1942; (with Lardner) "The Cross of Lorraine," Metro-Goldwyn-Mayer, 1943; "Centennial Summer" (based on the novel by Albert E. Idell), Twentieth Century-Fox, 1946; "Honeymoon" (based on a story by Vicki Baum), RKO General, 1947; "When I Grow Up," Eagle Lion, 1951; "The Outrage" (based on his play with Fay Kanin, "Rashomon"), Metro-Goldwyn-Mayer, 1964; (with Starr) "How to Commit Marriage," Stanley Warner Cinerama, 1969.

Screenplays with Fay Kanin: "Sunday Punch," Metro-Goldwyn-Mayer, 1942; "My Pal Gus," Twentieth Century-Fox, 1952; "Rhapsody" (based on the novel, *Maurice Guest,* by Henry Handel Richardson), Metro-Goldwyn-Mayer, 1954; "The Opposite Sex" (based on the play, "The Women," by Clare Boothe), Metro-Goldwyn-Mayer, 1956; "Teacher's Pet," Paramount Pictures, 1958; "The Right Approach" (based on the play, "The Live Wire," by Garson Kanin), Twentieth Century-Fox, 1961; (and with Alex Coppel) "Swordsman of Sienna" (based on a story by Anthony Marshall), Metro-Goldwyn-Mayer, 1962; "Cabbages and Kings," Talent Associates, 1975. Also wrote "The Source" (based on the novel by James A. Michener), not yet produced.

AVOCATIONAL INTERESTS: Painting, sculpture, music.

* * *

KANTOR, MacKinlay 1904-

PERSONAL: Born February 4, 1904, in Webster City, Iowa; son of John Martin and Effie Rachel (a newspaper editor; maiden name McKinlay) Kantor; married Florence Irene Layne, July 2, 1926; children: Layne Kantor Shroder, Thomas (Tim) MacKinlay. *Education:* Educated at schools in Illinois and Iowa. *Politics:* No party affiliation. *Religion:* No church affiliation. *Residence:* Sarasota, Fla. 33581.

CAREER: Webster City Daily News, Webster City, Iowa, reporter, 1921-25; worked as advertiser and claim correspondent in Chicago, Ill., 1925-26; *Cedar Rapids Republican,* Cedar Rapids, Iowa, reporter and free-lance writer, 1927; *Des Moines Tribune,* Des Moines, Iowa, columnist, 1930-31; worked as scenario writer for Paramount Productions, Metro-Goldwyn-Mayer, 20th Century Fox, and Samuel Goldwyn, all Hollywood, Calif., war correspondent with the Royal Air Force and the U.S. Air Force in Europe, 1943, 1945; New York City Police, New York, N.Y., member of uniformed division, 1948-50; war correspondent with U.S. Air Force in Korea, 1950; technical consultant to U.S. Air Force, 1951—, made study of personnel, equipment, training, and operations of the Italian

and Royal Hellenic Air Forces, 1963. Lincoln College, trustee, 1960-68, honorary trustee, 1968—; member, National Council of the Boy Scouts of America; honorary consultant in American letters to Library of Congress, 1967-73.

MEMBER: Society of American Historians (fellow), American Society for Psychical Research, National Association of Civil War Musicians (honorary member), Sons of Union Veterans of the Civil War, Military Order of the Loyal Legion of the United States (hereditary companion). *Awards, honors:* O. Henry Award, 1935, for "Silent Grow the Guns"; Pulitzer Prize, 1956, for novel *Andersonville;* Medal of Freedom; D.Litt. from Grinnell College, 1957, Drake University, 1958, Lincoln College, 1959, and Ripon College, 1961; LL.D., from Iowa Wesleyan College, 1961.

WRITINGS—All novels except as indicated: *Diversey,* Coward, 1928; *El Goes South,* Coward, 1930; *The Jaybird,* Coward, 1932; *Long Remember,* illustrated by Will Crawford, Coward, 1934; *Turkey in the Straw* (ballads and verse), illustrated by Crawford, Coward, 1935; *The Voice of Bugle Ann,* Coward, 1935, school edition by Frederick Houk Law, Globe Books, 1953; *Arouse and Beware,* Coward, 1936; *The Romance of Rosy Ridge,* illustrated by Crawford, Coward, 1937; *The Boy in the Dark,* International Mark Twain Society, 1937; *The Noise of Their Wings,* Coward, 1938; *Valedictory,* illustrated by Amos Sewell, Coward, 1939.

Cuba Libre: A Story, Coward, 1940; *Angleworms on Toast* (juvenile), illustrated by Kurt Wiese, Coward, 1942; *Gentle Annie,* Coward, 1942; *Happy Land,* Coward, 1943; *Author's Choice* (forty stories and notes), Coward, 1944; *Happy Land and Gentle Annie,* Sun Dial Press, 1944; *Glory for Me* (novel in verse), Coward, 1945; *But Look the Morn* (autobiography), Coward, 1947; *Midnight Lace,* Random House, 1948; *Wicked Water: An American Primitive,* Random House, 1948; *The Good Family,* Coward, 1949.

One Wild Oat, Fawcett, 1950; *Signal Thirty-Two,* Random House, 1950; *Lee and Grant at Appomattox* (juvenile), Random House, 1951; *Don't Touch Me,* Random House, 1951; *Warhoop* (two short novels), Random House, 1952; *Gettysburg* (juvenile), Random House, 1952; *The Daughter of Bugle Ann,* Random House, 1953; *God and My Country,* World Publications, 1954; *Andersonville,* World Publishing, 1955, abridged edition, W. H. Allen, 1956; *Lobo* (reminiscences), illustrated by wife, Irene Layne, World Publishing, 1957; *Silent Grow the Guns, and Other Tales of the American Civil War,* New American Library, 1959; *Frontier: Tales of the American Adventure,* New American Library, 1959; *The Work of St. Francis,* World Publishing, 1959 (published in England as *The Unseen Witness,* W. H. Allen, 1959).

It's About Crime, New American Library, 1960; *If the South Had Won the Civil War* (fiction), Bantam Books, 1961; *Spirit Lake,* World Publishing, 1961; *Three: Happy Land, Lobo, Cuba Libre,* Paperback Library, 1962; *The Gun-Toter and Other Stories of the Missouri Hills,* New American Library, 1963; (with Curtis E. LeMay) *Mission with LeMay: My Story,* Doubleday, 1965; *Story Teller,* Doubleday, 1967; *Beauty Beast,* Putnam, 1968; *The Day I Met a Lion* (nonfiction), Doubleday, 1968; *Missouri Bittersweet* (reminiscences), Doubleday, 1969; (with son, Tim Kantor) *Hamilton County,* Macmillan, 1970; *I Love You, Irene,* Doubleday, 1972; *The Children Sing,* Hawthorn, 1973; *Valley Forge,* M. Evans, 1975. Contributor of stories to *Colophon, Atlantic Monthly, Saturday Evening Post,* and other magazines.

SIDELIGHTS: Kantor once said: "My stories have appeared in an appalling number of magazines, sublime, ridiculous and penny-dreadful. I used to write a great deal of stuff for the pulp detective-and-crime story magazines, in the years when I had to make my living that way, and I don't think that my rather complicated talents were harmed in the least. The severe routine of such endeavor stimulated my sense of plot and construction, which needed such stimulation very badly indeed. I was well aware that the stuff I wrote had little value, except that in most cases it made entertaining narrative."

Kantor also took hobo trips through the Midwest to gather background material for some of his novels. From his experiences with the New York City police force, he produced the novel *Signal Thirty-Two.* A number of his novels have been made into movies, including *The Man From Dakota, Gentle Annie, Glory for Me,* which became "The Best Years of Our Lives," in 1946, and *God and My Country* which became "Follow Me, Boys!," produced by Walt Disney in 1967. *Avocational interests:* Butterfly collecting, mushrooms, the Civil War, golf, exploring caves and battlefields.

BIOGRAPHICAL/CRITICAL SOURCES: Martha E. Ward and D. A. Marquardt, *Authors of Books for Young People,* Scarecrow, 1967.

* * *

KAPLAN, Berton H(arris) 1930-

PERSONAL: Born June 27, 1930, in Winchester, Va.; son of Rueben L. (a merchant) and Jennie (Rosennan) Kaplan; married Ellen Brauer (a computer programmer), June 14, 1959; children: Daniel, Ron. *Education:* Virginia Polytechnic Institute, B.S., 1951; University of North Carolina, M.S., 1952, Ph.D., 1962; graduate study at University of Edinburgh, 1954-55. *Politics:* Democrat. *Religion:* Jewish. *Home:* 66 Oakwood Dr., Chapel Hill, N.C. 27514. *Office:* School of Public Health, University of North Carolina, Chapel Hill, N.C. 27514.

CAREER: University of North Carolina, Chapel Hill, instructor, 1960-62, assistant professor, 1962-67, associate professor of sociology, 1967-72, professor of epidemiology, 1972—. Member of advisory council, American Nurses Foundation, 1970-74. *Military service:* U.S. Air Force, 1952-54. U.S. Air Force Reserve, 1954-58; became first lieutenant. *Member:* American Sociological Association, American Anthropological Association. *Awards, honors:* Social Science Research Council fellow, 1965-66, at Cornell University.

WRITINGS: Blue Ridge: An Appalachian Community in Transition, Center for Appalachian Studies, University of West Virginia, 1971; (editor) *Psychiatric Disorder and the Urban Environment,* Behavioral Publications, 1971; *Explorations in Social Psychiatry,* Basic Books, 1975. Contributor to *Encyclopedia of Social Work,* and to journals in his field.

WORK IN PROGRESS: Research on religion and health.

* * *

KAPLAN, David Gordon 1908-

PERSONAL: Born January 4, 1908, in Chicago, Ill.; son of Joseph (a furrier and trade unionist) and Mary (a fur finisher and cloakmaker; maiden name, Gordon) Kaplan; married Fannie Korman, June, 1931; children: Beth Kaplan Morris, Marlene Kaplan Rotbert. *Education:* City College (now of the City University of New York), B.B.S., 1931; New York State Industrial Teachers Training College, certificate, 1932; New York University, M.A., 1945. *Politics:* Liberal Democrat. *Religion:* Jewish. *Home:* 4801 Northwest 22nd Court, Apt. 214, Lauderhill, Fla. 33313.

CAREER: Fur craftsman and shop steward for fur companies, including a family firm, 1920-36; teacher and department head at New York City High School of Fashion Industries, 1931-70; Tobe-Coburn School, New York, N.Y., lecturer on furs, 1940-67; writer, 1967—. Limited partner of Antonovich Brothers, 1962-68; formed international fur consulting firm, 1960. Founder and president of Metropolitan Labor League, 1936. *Member:* B'nai B'rith, City College of New York Alumni Association, City College of New York Alumni Varsity Association.

WRITINGS: The Fur Book, R. H. Donnelly, 1950; *The World of Furs,* Fairchild, 1970. Contributor of more than a thousand articles on furs and on conservation to magazines and newspapers in the United States, England, and Germany. Founder and editor of Madison Jewish Center *Message,* 1947-61.

WORK IN PROGRESS: A second edition of *The World of Furs;* a semi-fictional family history; articles on growing up in New York City, with publications expected to result.

SIDELIGHTS: Kaplan has behind him seven or more generations of his family in the business of making furs. His parents were revolutionary Mensheviks in Russia at the turn of the century; his mother was jailed and his father exiled to Siberia. The family remained politically active after emigrating from Russia to the United States, helping to form the American Labor Party, from which stem Kaplan's interests in history and economics.

AVOCATIONAL INTERESTS: Basketball, swimming, billiards, philosophy, photography.

* * *

KAPLAN, Howard B(ernard) 1932-

PERSONAL: Born March 17, 1932, in New York, N.Y.; son of Samuel (a businessman) and Esther (Schimmer) Kaplan; married Diane Gray, August 9, 1970; children: Samuel Charles, Rachel Esther. *Education:* New York University, A.B., 1953, M.A., 1954, Ph.D., 1958. *Home:* 2330 Bolsover, Houston, Tex. 77005. *Office:* Baylor College of Medicine, 1200 Moursund, Houston, Tex. 77025.

CAREER: New York University, New York, N.Y., instructor, 1955-57, assistant professor of sociology, 1958; Baylor College of Medicine, Houston, Tex., post-doctoral fellow, 1958-60, assistant professor, 1960-65, associate professor, 1965-70, professor of sociology, 1970—. Visiting assistant professor at University of Houston, 1960-65; visiting associate professor at New York University, 1960, and Rice University, 1967-69. Chairman of Research Bureau's advisory committee and member of board of directors and executive committee of Community Council of Houston and Harris County.

MEMBER: International Society for Research on Aggression, International Sociological Association, American Sociological Association. *Awards, honors:* Russell Sage Foundation postdoctoral fellowship, 1958-60; Milbank faculty fellowship, 1965-72.

WRITINGS: Implementation of Program Change in Community Agencies: Studies of Organizational Innova-

tion, Community Council of Houston and Harris County, 1966; *Program Innovations in Community Agencies,* Hogg Foundation for Mental Health, 1970; *The Sociology of Mental Illness,* College & University Press, 1972; *Self-Attitudes and Deviant Behavior,* Goodyear Publishing, 1975.

Contributor: P. H. Leiderman and David Shapiro, editors, *Psychological Approaches to Social Behavior,* Stanford University Press, 1964; Earl Rubington and M. S. Weinberg, editors, *Deviance: The Interactionist Perspective,* Macmillan, 1968; Erwin O. Smigel, editor, *Handbook on the Study of Social Problems,* Rand McNally, 1971; E. Gartly Jaco, editor, *Patients, Physicians, and Illness,* Free Press, 1972; Paul R. Patterson, Carolyn Denning, and Austin H. Kutscher, editors, *Psychosocial Aspects of Cystic Fibrosis: A Model for Chronic Lung Disease,* Columbia University Press, 1973. Contributor of more than forty articles and reviews to sociology and medical journals.

WORK IN PROGRESS: Research on self-attitudes and deviant behavior, on suicide, and on psychiatric rehospitalization.

* * *

KARON, Bertram Paul 1930-

PERSONAL: Born April 29, 1930, in Taunton, Mass.; son of Harold Banny (a dress pattern maker) and Celia (Silverman) Karon; married Mary Mossop, October 17, 1957; children: Jonathan Alexander. *Education:* Harvard University, A.B., 1952; Princeton University, M.A., 1954, Ph.D., 1957. *Home:* 420 John R, East Lansing, Mich. 48823. *Office:* Psychology Research Building, Michigan State University, East Lansing, Mich. 48824.

CAREER: Educational Testing Service, Princeton, N.J., research fellow in psychometrics, 1952-55; intern in direct psychoanalysis in Gardenville, Pa., 1955-56; Annandale Reformatory, Annandale, N.J., senior clinical psychologist, 1958; Akron Psychological Consulting Service, Akron, Ohio, psychologist and director of research, 1958-59; Philadelphia Psychiatric Hospital, Philadelphia, Pa., research psychologist, 1959, fellow, 1959-61; private practice of psychotherapy in Philadelphia, Pa., 1961-62; Michigan State University, East Lansing, assistant professor, 1962-63, associate professor, 1963-68, professor of clinical psychology, 1968—, director of psychotherapy research project, 1966—. Diplomate of American Board of Professional Psychology, 1965; lecturer at Ypsilanti State Hospital, 1964-65.

MEMBER: American Psychological Association (fellow), Society for Psychotherapy Research, American Statistical Association, Psychologists Interested in the Study of Psychoanalysis, Midwest Psychological Association, Michigan Psychological Association.

WRITINGS: The Negro Personality: A Rigorous Investigation of the Effects of Culture, Springer Publishing, 1958, revised edition published as *Black Scars,* 1975; (editor) Silvan S. Tomkins, *Affects, Imagery, and Consciousness,* Springer Publishing, Volume I, 1962, Volume II, 1963. Contributor of nearly fifty articles to psychology journals. Consulting editor of *Psychotherapy: Theory, Research, and Practice.*

Contributor: Albert I. Rabin, editor, *Projective Techniques in Personality Assessment,* Springer Publishing, 1968; Arthur Nikelly, editor, *Techniques for Behavior Change,* C. C Thomas, 1971; Robert Cancro, editor, *The Schizophrenic Syndrome: An Annual Review,* Brunner, 1971;

Peter Magaro, editor, *The Construction of Madness,* Pergamon, in press.

WORK IN PROGRESS: Research on techniques of psychoanalytic therapy, particularly for schizophrenics, demonstrating that even a small amount of psychoanalytic psychotherapy for schizophrenics leads to more fundamental, more humane, and more lasting recovery than medication.

SIDELIGHTS: Karon writes: "As a child, prejudiced against because I was Jewish, it became clear that someone who was not Jewish could be more effective than I could in reducing that discrimination. So it seemed that I might be more effective in dealing with anti-black discrimination. . . . As a psychologist, I have found that if you do what you consider important, it will eventually be important to the field, even if it does not happen to be fashionable at the time. . . . As a college professor, too, I have learned that what is essential is to share what you consider most important and are fascinated with in your field, including your own work. If you do not, you are cheating the students. . . . If there is nothing that fascinates you in your field, you are in the wrong field."

* * *

KASTL, Lena 1942-

PERSONAL: Born July 28, 1942, in New York, N.Y.; daughter of Joseph and Gussie (Knepper) Hahn; married Albert Kastl, June 6, 1963 (divorced, 1975). *Education:* City College of the City University of New York, B.S., 1963. *Religion:* Jewish. *Home:* 6350 Fredericks Rd., Sebastopol, Calif. 95472. *Office:* Department of Chemistry, Santa Rosa Junior College, Santa Rosa, Calif.

CAREER: Yale Psychiatric Center, New Haven, Conn., high school teacher of science, 1963-64; teacher of English in Saigon, South Vietnam, 1965-66; University of San Francisco, San Francisco, Calif., laboratory technician, 1968-73; Sonoma State Hospital, Brain Research Center, Eldridge, Calif., laboratory technician, 1974-75; Santa Rosa Junior College, Santa Rosa, Calif., laboratory assistant, 1975—. *Member:* American Association for the Advancement of Science.

WRITINGS: (With husband, Albert J. Kastl) *Journey Back: Escaping the Drug Trap,* Nelson-Hall, 1975. Contributor to professional journals.

AVOCATIONAL INTERESTS: Studying language, gardening, making wine, drawing.

* * *

KATCHEN, Carole 1944-

PERSONAL: Born January 30, 1944, in Denver, Colo.; daughter of Samuel (a tavern owner) and Gertrude (Levin) Katchen. *Education:* Attended Ripon College, 1961-62; University of Colorado, B.A. (cum laude), 1965; further study at Hebrew University of Jerusalem, 1965, West Valley College, 1969-70, and Denver Community College, 1973-74. *Home:* 492 South Jasmine St., Denver, Colo. 80222.

CAREER: Has worked as a welfare caseworker, shoe saleswoman, photographer's assistant, preschool teacher, and lecturer; artist whose pastels, paintings, woodblock prints have been exhibited in one-woman shows in Bogota, Columbia, 1974, and in the United States. *Member:* Denver Women's Press Club. *Awards, honors:* Tuttle nonfiction fellow at University of Colorado Writer's Conference, 1966; Bread Loaf Writers' Conference working scholarship, 1971.

WRITINGS—For young people: *I was a Lonely Teen-ager,* Scholastic Book Services, 1965; *The Underground Light Bulb,* Scholastic Book Services, 1969. Contributor to Scholastic Magazines publications and *Denver Post Empire.* Artwork has been represented in *American Artist* magazine. Member of advisory review board, *Colorado Woman Digest.*

SIDELIGHTS: Carole Katchen has hitchhiked across North Africa and from Texas through Mexico and Central America to Peru.

BIOGRAPHICAL/CRITICAL SOURCES: Scope, May 20, 1966; Denver Post *Empire* magazine, December 10, 1972; *Denver Singles Guide,* August, 1975; *American Artist,* September, 1975.

* * *

KATZ, Mort 1925-

PERSONAL: Born May 27, 1925, in Brooklyn, N.Y.; son of Morris (in real estate) and Sophie (Guttman) Katz; married Ellen Loeb (a doctor of medicine), July 18, 1964. *Education:* Sarah Lawrence College, B.A., 1949; Columbia University, M.S.S.W., 1952. *Religion:* Judaism. *Home:* 4318 Briar Creek Lane, Dallas, Tex. 75214. *Office:* Mort Katz—Family Counseling, One North Park East, Suite 320, Dallas, Tex. 75231.

CAREER: Dallas State Mental Health Clinic, Dallas, Tex., social psychotherapist, 1962-69; private practice in social psychotherapy, Dallas, 1969—. Consultant therapist at Center Hospital for Alcoholism, Dallas, 1972-74; trainer at Suicide Prevention Center, Dallas, 1974—. *Military service:* U.S. Army, Medical Corps, 1943-46; served in Pacific theater. *Member:* American Orthopsychiatric Association (fellow), Academy of Certified Social Workers, Family Therapy Association of Texas (president, 1969-70), Texas Society for Social Psychotherapy.

WRITINGS: The Marriage Survival Kit: A Daily Guide to Happier Marriage, Farnsworth Publishing, 1975.

WORK IN PROGRESS: A book on interpersonal relationships.

AVOCATIONAL INTERESTS: Travel, horseback riding, sailing.

BIOGRAPHICAL/CRITICAL SOURCES: Fort Worth Star-Telegram, August 27, 1972.

* * *

KATZENBACH, William E. 1904-1975

August 30, 1904—December 27, 1975; American architect, interior designer, business executive, and author. Obituaries: *New York Times,* December 28, 1975.

* * *

KATZNELSON-SHAZAR, Rachel 1888-1975
(Rachel Shazar)

1888—August 11, 1975; Russian-born Israeli editor, women's labor movement organizer, and author. Obituaries: *Washington Post,* August 12, 1975.

* * *

KAUFMANN, Walter 1933-

PERSONAL: Born August 3, 1933, in Germany; son of Julius and Gerda Kaufmann. *Education:* University of California, Berkeley, A.B., 1956, J.D., 1961; California State

University (now San Francisco State University), M.A., 1975; also studied at University of Wisconsin, Cornell University, and University of California, Los Angeles. *Religion:* Jewish. *Home:* 342 29th Ave., San Francisco, Calif. 94121.

CAREER: Lawyer in private practice in Bakersfield, Calif., 1961-63; Congress of Racial Equility (CORE), attorney, field secretary, legal coordinator for the Fourth Congressional District (Mississippi), and public relations representative and fund raiser, all 1963-65; College of San Mateo, San Mateo, Calif., instructor in psychology and sociology, 1966—, chairman of Social Sciences Division, 1970-73, supervisor of Intern Psychological Services, 1973-74. Instructor at Bakersfield College, 1961-63; private practice in psychotherapy in San Francisco, Calif., 1972—. Clinical intern in psychology at Kaiser Hospital (Santa Clara, Calif.), 1974. Member of the state bars of California and Mississippi and of the Federal Bar; licensed marriage, family, and child therapist. *Awards, honors:* Russell Sage Foundation grant, 1964, to study sociology of law at University of Wisconsin.

WRITINGS: (With Lloyd Saxton) *The American Scene: Social Problems of the Seventies,* Wadsworth, 1971. Contributor to *Behavior Change Annual* and professional journals.

WORK IN PROGRESS: The Growth and Development of Body-Oriented Psychotherapy.

* * *

KEATING, John J. 1918(?)-1975

1918(?)—November 20, 1975; Canadian-born priest, ecumenist, and author of books in the religious field. Obituaries: *New York Times,* November 21, 1975.

* * *

KEDGLEY, Susan (Jane) 1948-

PERSONAL: Born February 1, 1948, in New Zealand. *Education:* Victoria University, B.A., 1968; Otago University, M.A., 1972; Auckland Secondary Teacher's College, graduate teaching diploma, 1972. *Home:* 43 West 93rd St., Apt. 22, New York, N.Y. 10025. *Agent:* Mary Varnham, 43 West 93rd St., Apt. 12, New York, N.Y. 10025. *Office:* United Nations, U.N. Plaza, New York, N.Y. 10017.

CAREER: Current affairs officer for New Zealand Broadcasting Corp., 1969-70; Asia-Pacific Research Unit in Micronesia and Polynesia, research officer, 1970-71; University of Papua New Guinea, Port Moresby, New Guinea, lecturer in political studies, 1971-72; United Nations, New York, N.Y., press officer of twenty-eighth session, 1973, associate human rights officer of Centre for Social Development and Humanitarian Affairs, 1974—. Member of executive committee, New Zealand Equal Pay and Opportunity Council, 1971, National Organization for Non-Parents (United States), 1975, International Women's Year Art Festival, 1975; foundation member and political chairwoman of New Zealand National Organization for Women, 1972; member of women's national executive committee of New Zealand Labour Party, 1972; member steering committee of United Nations Ad Hoc Group for Equal Rights, 1974-75.

WRITINGS: (Co-author) *Sione* (social studies text), Whitcombe & Tombes, 1971; (co-author) *Sexist Society,* Alister Taylor, 1972; (with Wendy James) *Mistresses: The Free Woman—The Unfree Man,* Bobbs-Merrill, 1975. Columnist, New Zealand *Sunday News,* 1972-73. Contributor to *National Business Review, New Zealand Listener, Thursday Magazine* (New Zealand), *Australian National Review, Morning Herald* (Sydney), and *Times* (London).

* * *

KEENAN, Angela Elizabeth 1890-

PERSONAL: Born February 3, 1890, in Leicester, Mass. *Education:* Smith College, A.B., 1911; Catholic University of America, A.M., 1929, Ph.D., 1932. *Home:* Notre Dame Convent, 1220 Main St., Worcester, Mass. *Agent:* Sister Helen Sheehan, Trinity College, Washington, D.C. 20017.

CAREER: Roman Catholic nun of the Sisters of Notre Dame of Namur (S.N.D.). Has served as professor and dean of women at Trinity College, Washington, D.C., Emmanuel College, Boston, Mass., and at Notre Dame Seishin University, Okayama, Japan. *Member:* Phi Beta Kappa.

WRITINGS: Three Against the Wind: The Founding of Trinity College, Washington, D.C., Christian Classics, 1974.

SIDELIGHTS: Sister Angela Elizabeth Keenan writes: "Two aspects of... [writing *Three Against the Wind*] ...were of special interest to me: 1) the opportunity to study from primary sources the unreasonable prejudice against higher education for women in the nineteenth century; and 2) the history of education on many levels in the same era." She has traveled, for research purposes, to Japan, Hong Kong, Thailand, the Holy Land, Greece, Italy, France, and England.

* * *

KEEP, David (John) 1936-

PERSONAL: Born December 4, 1936, in Bedford, England; son of Ralph Henry (a toolmaker) and Mildred (a secretary; maiden name, Ford) Keep; married Carolyn Jean Herbert (a teacher), August 1, 1962; children: Nicholas Herbert, Philippa Ruth. *Education:* New College, Oxford, M.A., 1960; Wesley House, Cambridge, B.A., 1962; University of Zurich, further graduate study, 1962-63; University of Sheffield, Ph.D., 1971. *Home address:* Heatherdene, Woodbury, Exeter EX5 1NR, England.

CAREER: Pastor of Methodist churches in Ibstock, England, 1963-64, and Belper, England, 1964-66; Pilgrim School, Bedford, England, assistant history teacher and head of religious education, 1966-71; Rolle College of Education, Exmouth, England, senior lecturer in religious studies, 1971—. Methodist local preacher, 1956—. Member of Youth Action of Bedford Committee, 1966-71. *Military service:* Royal Air Force, 1955-57. *Member:* Ecclesiastical History Society, Royal British Legion, Youth Hostels Association, National Association of Teachers in Further and Higher Education, Oxford Union, Zwingliverein.

WRITINGS: History through Stamps, David & Charles, 1975. Contributor to ecclesiastical history journals and symposia.

WORK IN PROGRESS: Coordinating British research with the Institut fuer Schweizerische Reformations Geschichte in Zurich; preparing classroom material for helping the religious understanding of children, completion expected in 1977.

SIDELIGHTS: Keep has led study tours to the Soviet Union.

KELLEY, Joseph J(ohn), Jr. 1914-

PERSONAL: Born May 31, 1914, in Philadelphia, Pa.; son of Joseph J. (a real estate broker) and Kathryne Madeleine (Hookey) Kelley; married Eleanor Eileen Dougan, June 11, 1949; children: Roger D., Janet E., Heather Ann (died October 3, 1964). *Education:* La Salle College, B.S., 1937; attended University of Pennsylvania Law School, 1937-39; Temple University, J.D., 1941. *Home:* 15 North 27th St., Camp Hill, Pa. 17011. *Office:* Pennsylvania District Attorneys Association, 2311 Market St., Camp Hill, Pa. 17011.

CAREER: Attorney in private practice in Philadelphia, Pa., 1946-53; Pennsylvania Chamber of Commerce, Harrisburg, legislative counsel, 1953-66; secretary to Governor of Pennsylvania, Harrisburg, 1967; served as Secretary of the Commonwealth of Pennsylvania, Harrisburg, 1968-71; WITF-TV (public broadcasting service), Hershey, Pa., executive director of Division of American History and Culture, 1971-72; Pennsylvania District Attorneys Association, Camp Hill, executive director, 1973—. Lecturer at Valley Forge Military College, 1947-48, and at Drexel University, 1952-53. *Military service:* U.S. Navy, 1941-46; became lieutenant commander. *Member:* Organization of American Historians, American Historical Association, National District Attorneys Association, Historical Foundation of Pennsylvania (director, 1967—). *Awards, honors:* Freedoms Foundation awards, 1953, 1957; honorary citizen of Statesville, N.C., 1967, and of Texas, 1970; Admiral of Great Navy of the State of Nebraska, 1970.

WRITINGS: Life and Times in Colonial Philadelphia, Stackpole, 1973; (with Sol Feinstone) *Courage and Candlelight: Feminine Spirit of '76,* Stackpole, 1974; *Colonial Pennsylvania,* Doubleday, 1976. Author of script, "Ten Days that Changed the World," for WITF-TV, 1971. Contributor to periodicals.

WORK IN PROGRESS: Commentary for a wall chart of Philadelphia in 1776 and a book, *Pennsylvania and the Young Republic,* both for the National Park Service; *The Independent House: The Pennsylvania General Assembly, 1681-1790.*

SIDELIGHTS: "I try to make the past come alive," Kelley wrote, "without superimposing my twentieth-century judgment on men and women who did what they did in the eighteenth century, under given circumstances at a given time. Anything else is fiction."

* * *

KELLIN, Sally Moffet 1932-

PERSONAL: Born April 21, 1932, in New York, N.Y.; daughter of Harold Leroy (an actor) and Sylvia (Field) Moffet; married Robert Dozier, January 21, 1956 (divorced, 1963); married Mike Kellin (an actor), August 3, 1966; children: (first marriage) Harold, Aaron, Brendan; (second marriage) Shauna. *Education:* Studied acting with Sanford Meisner and at Actors Studio. *Home:* 23 Clinton Ave., Nyack, N.Y. 10960. *Agent:* Maximilian Becker, 115 East 82nd St., New York, N.Y. 10028.

CAREER: Actress on stage and television, 1948-58; author.

WRITINGS: A Book of Snails (juvenile), W. R. Scott, 1968.

WORK IN PROGRESS: Man Alive, a novel; research in paternal grandmother's family history for two projected books, a biography or novel about her paternal grandmother titled *Alberta* and a history of the family during the Civil War.

SIDELIGHTS: Sally Kellin writes: "I wrote the snail book because I wanted to find out about snails (they were all over our garden in California and threatened to destroy all vegetation) and had trouble finding information. I decided to fill the gap myself and wrote as I learned—or the other way round."

* * *

KELLUM, D(avid) F(ranklin) 1936-

PERSONAL: Born April 13, 1936, in Babylon, N.Y.; son of Ira William and Ruth (Biglin) Kellum; married Christine Latimer, December 23, 1961 (divorced, 1975); married Elizabeth Ann Creer, July 5, 1975; children: (first marriage) David, Samuel, Zachary. *Education:* Holy Cross College, Worcester, Mass., B.S., 1957; Columbia University, M.A., 1958, Ed.D., 1965. *Office:* Archbishop Jordan High School, Sherwood Park, Alberta, Canada.

CAREER: High school history teacher in Syosset, N.Y., 1958-62; Columbia University, Teacher's College, New York, N.Y., instructor in social studies methods, 1962-64; State University of New York at Oneonta, assistant professor of social science, 1965-67; University of Alberta, Edmonton, associate professor of secondary education, 1967-75; Archbishop Jordan High School, Sherwood Park, Alberta, teacher of English, 1975—. *Awards, honors:* Has received prizes for plays, "The Peephole Confederation," and "Men Under Arms."

WRITINGS: Social Studies: Myths and Realities, Sheed, 1969; *Teaching American History Through Conflicting Interpretations,* Teachers College Press, 1969; *The Falling World of Tristram Pocket* (novel), Tree Frog Press, 1975. Also author of plays, "The Peephole Confederation" and "Men Under Arms."

WORK IN PROGRESS: The Eggshell Cauldron, a novel; "David Descendent," a poem.

SIDELIGHTS: Kellum writes: "After twelve years of university teaching, I have resigned to return to the authenticity of the high school classroom."

* * *

KELLY, Clarence 1941-

PERSONAL: Born November 23, 1941, in Brooklyn, N.Y.; son of Edward (a laborer) and Clair (Bonar) Kelly. *Education:* Catholic University of America, B.A. (magna cum laude), 1969; also studied at Immaculate Conception Seminary, Huntington, N.Y., and International Seminary of St. Pius X, Econe, Switzerland. *Residence:* East Meadow, N.Y. *Office:* St. Pius V Chapel, P.O. Box A1, Wantagh, N.Y. 11793.

CAREER: Roman Catholic priest of Society of Saint Pius X, ordained April 14, 1973; St Pius V Traditional Catholic School, Wantagh, N.Y., founder, rector, and spiritual director. *Military service:* U.S. Air Force, 1959-62.

WRITINGS: Conspiracy against God and Man, Western Islands, 1974.

WORK IN PROGRESS: Research toward a theological refutation of the Reform Movement which is now "in the open" in the Roman Catholic Church.

SIDELIGHTS: Kelly writes that he has "only two concerns at this time—the Roman Catholic Church and the U.S.A. My first book is an attempt to expose the main forces which are seeking their destruction with a special emphasis on the political and historical factor. I am pre-

paring a book now which will deal specifically with the emphasis on the spiritual factor."

* * *

KELLY, Rosalie (Ruth)

PERSONAL: Born in Grand Rapids, Mich.; daughter of Charles (a builder) and Emmeline (Barth) Schley; married Gleason Kelly (in real estate), May 18, 1944; children: Nancy, Meredith (Mrs. Philip Lewis), William. *Education:* Attended Oregon State University, 1939-40. *Home:* 246 Orchard Rd., Orinda, Calif. 94563. *Agent:* Ruth Cantor, 156 Fifth Ave., New York, N.Y. 10010.

CAREER: Has worked as secretary and clerk in private industry, 1930-42, and for U.S. Department of the Interior, 1950-52.

WRITINGS: The Great Toozy Takeover (juvenile), Putnam, 1975. Contributor of short stories to small literary magazines.

WORK IN PROGRESS: Two for the Road, a novel; *Dark Companion,* a suspense novel.

SIDELIGHTS: Rosalie Kelly writes: "Six years ago, when my children were grown . . . I started . . . by enrolling in a creative writing class. Since then I have subordinated all outside interests to my writing. In off hours I read a great deal, from current best sellers to history, philosophy, poetry, and those classics I had never got around to previously."

* * *

KELLY-GADOL, Joan 1928-

PERSONAL: Born March 29, 1928, in Brooklyn, N.Y.; daughter of George V. and Ruth (Jacobsen) Kelly. *Education:* St. John's University College, B.A. (summa cum laude), 1953; Columbia University, M.A., 1954, Ph.D., 1963. *Home:* 150 Claremont Ave., New York, N.Y. 10027. *Office:* Department of History, City College of the City University of New York, New York, N.Y. 10031.

CAREER: City College of the City University of New York, New York, N.Y., lecturer, 1956-63, assistant professor, 1963-68, associate professor, 1968-72, professor of history, 1972—. Visiting assistant professor at Columbia University, 1963-64; professor at Sarah Lawrence College, 1972-74. *Member:* American Historical Association (chairwoman of committee on women historians, 1975), Renaissance Society of America (member of executive board, 1971—), Coordinating Committee for Women in the Historical Profession (co-chairperson for Metropolitan New York region, 1973-74), New York City Renaissance Club. *Awards, honors:* Woodrow Wilson fellowship, 1953-54; Danforth fellowship, 1960-61; National Foundation for the Arts and Humanities, junior fellow, 1967-68.

WRITINGS: (Contributor) Charles H. Carier, editor, *Renaissance to the Counter-Reformation: Essays in Honor of Garrett Mattingly,* Random House, 1965; *Leon Battista Alberti: Universal Man of the Early Renaissance,* University of Chicago Press, 1969; (contributor) Vern Bullough, editor, *The Scientific Revolution,* Holt, 1970; *Bibliography: Women's History,* Sarah Lawrence Publications, 1973; (contributor) Renate Bridenthal and Claudia Koonz, editors, *Becoming Visible,* Houghton, in press; (contributor) Edward Mahoney, Eugene Rice, and other editors, *Philosophy and Humanism: Essays in Honor of P. O. Kristeller,* Columbia University Press, in press. Contributor to *Dictionary of the History of Ideas* and *Encyclopaedia Britannica.*

KENDLE, John Edward 1937-

PERSONAL: Born April 14, 1937, in London, England; son of Arthur (a policeman) and Sybil Violet Mary (Jordan) Kendle; married Judith Ann Halsey (a teacher), August 3, 1963; children: John Stephen, Andrew Bruce, Nancy Elizabeth. *Education:* University of Manitoba, B.A., 1958; University of London, Ph.D., 1965. *Politics:* None. *Religion:* None. *Home:* 149 Glen, Winnipeg, Manitoba, Canada R2M OB5. *Office:* St. John's College, University of Manitoba, Winnipeg, Manitoba, Canada.

CAREER: University of Manitoba, Winnipeg, assistant professor, 1965-70, associate professor, 1970-75, professor of history, 1975—. Visiting research fellow at Research School of Social Sciences at Australian National University, 1967-68, and University of Auckland, 1968. Judge of A. B. Corey Prize in Canadian-American Relations of the Canadian and American Historical Associations, 1974-76. *Member:* Canadian Historical Association, American Committee for Irish Studies.

WRITINGS: The Colonial and Imperial Conferences, 1887-1911: A Study in Imperial Organization, Longmans Canada, 1967; *The British Empire-Commonwealth, 1897-1931,* Warne, 1972; *The Round Table Movement and Imperial Union,* University of Toronto Press, 1975. Contributor to history and political science journals. Member of editorial board of "Canadian Historical Association Papers."

WORK IN PROGRESS: A Biography of John Bracken: Premier of Manitoba, 1922-1943; A Biography of Erskine Childers; Federalism in the United Kingdom.

* * *

KENKEL, William F(rancis) 1925-

PERSONAL: Born February 11, 1925, in East Hyattsville, Md.; son of Anthony B. (an economist) and Anne Marie (Dutweiler) Kenkel; married Marion Scott, March 18, 1947; children: Stephen, Philip, Donald, Kenneth, Kathryn. *Education:* University of Maryland, B.A., 1949, M.A., 1950; Ohio State University, Ph.D., 1952. *Home:* 3421 Westridge Circle, Lexington, Ky. 40502. *Office:* Department of Sociology, University of Kentucky, Lexington, Ky. 40506.

CAREER: Iowa State University, Ames, assistant professor, 1954-57, associate professor, 1957-60, professor of sociology, 1960-67, head of department of sociology and anthropology, 1966-67; University of Kentucky, Lexington, professor of sociology, 1967—, chairman of department, 1970—. Member of executive committee of Iowa Council on Family Relations, 1956-61, president, 1960-61; member of executive committee of National Council on Family Relations, 1959-60, president, 1967-68. *Military service:* U.S. Marine Corps, 1943-44. *Member:* American Sociological Association, Association for the Sociology of Religion, Society for the Study of Social Problems, Midwest Sociological Association, Southern Sociological Association.

WRITINGS: (With John F. Cuber) *Social Stratification in the United States,* Appleton, 1954; (with Cuber and Robert Harper) *Problems of American Society,* Holt, 1956, 4th edition, 1964; *The Family in Perspective: A Fourfold Analysis,* Appleton, 1960, 3rd edition, 1973; (contributor) Nelson Foote, editor, *Consumer Behavior,* Volume IV, New York University Press, 1961; (contributor) E. W. Mueller and Giles C. Ekola, editors, *The Silent Struggle for Mid-America,* Augsburg, 1963; (contributor) Marvin Sussman, editor, *Sourcebook in Marriage and the Family,*

2nd edition, Houghton, 1963; (contributor) *Family Mobility in Our Dynamic Society,* Iowa State University Press, 1963; (contributor) Thomas Lasswell, John Burma, Sidney Aronson, editors, *Life in Society,* revised edition, Scott, Foresman, 1970; (contributor) *Values and Decision Making: Six Historical Papers in Family Economics-Home Management,* American Home Economics Association, 1969; (contributor) William D. deGravelles, Jr. and John H. Kelley, editors, *Injuries Following Rear-End Automobile Collisions,* C. C Thomas, 1969; *Introduction to Sociology,* Canfield Press, 1974.

Contributor to *New Catholic Encyclopedia.* Contributor of about twenty-five articles to sociology journals. Former articles-in-brief editor of *Journal of Marriage and the Family,* presently associate editor; former associate editor of *Sociological Analysis.*

AVOCATIONAL INTERESTS: International travel (Japan, Okinawa, Korea), antique automobiles (owns a Model A Ford), amateur radio operator (holds a general class license).

* * *

KENNA, Peter 1930-

PERSONAL: Surname is pronounced *K*-nar; born March 18, 1930, in Sydney, New South Wales, Australia; son of James O'Connor (a carpenter) and Agnes (Horne) Kenna. *Education:* Educated in Lewisham, New South Wales, Australia. *Politics:* Socialist. *Religion:* Roman Catholic. *Home:* 85 Birchgrove Rd., Balmain, New South Wales 2041, Australia. *Agent:* Howard Nicholson, 17/29B Nelson St., Woollahra, New South Wales 2025, Australia.

CAREER: Entertainer and writer. *Member:* Australian Writers Guild, Actors Equity.

WRITINGS: The Slaughter of St. Teresa's Day (3-act play; first produced in Sidney at Elizabethan Theatre, March 11, 1959), Currency Press, 1972; *A Hard God* (2-act play; first produced at Nimrod Theatre, August 17, 1973), Currency Methuen Drama Press, 1974.

WORK IN PROGRESS: More plays.

SIDELIGHTS: Kenna considers himself "a product of Australian working class Irish-Roman Catholic culture."

* * *

KENNEDY, Andrew (Karpati) 1931-

PERSONAL: Surname legally changed in 1958; born January 9, 1931, in Gyor, Hungary; son of Elemer (a bank manager) and Edith (Szanto) Karpati; married Judith Edmundson Hall, August 23, 1958; children: Veronica, Nicholas. *Education:* University of Bristol, B.A., 1952, Ph.D., 1972. *Politics:* "Radical liberal." *Religion:* Society of Friends (Quakers). *Home:* 5 South Green Rd., Newnham, Cambridge CB3 9JP, England. *Office:* English Institute, University of Bergen, Bergen 5014, Norway.

CAREER: Teacher of English in Clermont-Ferrand, France, 1954-55; Scarborough College, Yorkshire, England, English master, 1955-56; Deacon's School, Peterborough, England, English master, 1956-57; Davies's School, Cambridge, England, tutor in English as a foreign language, 1958-66; University of Bergen, Bergen, Norway, lecturer in English, 1966-72, senior lecturer at English Institute, 1972—. *Member:* Poetry Society (England).

WRITINGS: Six Dramatists in Search of a Language: Studies in Dramatic Language, Cambridge University

Press, 1975. Poetry included in anthology, *New Poetry 1*, edited by Peter Porter and Charles Osborne, Arts Council of Great Britian, 1975. Contributor of poetry to *Outposts*, and articles to *Modern Drama, Plays and Players, Observer*, and other periodicals.

WORK IN PROGRESS: Research on dramatic dialogue, on literature and religion, on critical theory, and on creative writing, especially poetry and plays.

SIDELIGHTS: Kennedy writes: "It is my aim to combine critical and creative writing—especially in drama and poetry. I consider myself a slow developer. I spent my youth recreating for myself a childhood in English (not my mother's tongue). [I am] highly motivated when not depressed."

* * *

KENNEDY, D. James 1930-

PERSONAL: Born November 3, 1930, in Augusta, Ga.; son of George Raymond (a salesman) and Ermine (Roberson) Kennedy; married Anne Lewis, August 25, 1956; children: Jennifer Lynn. *Education:* University of Tampa, B.A., 1958; Columbia Theological Seminary, B.D. (cum laude), 1959; Chicago Graduate School of Theology, M.Th. (summa cum laude), 1969; Trinity Evangelical Divinity School, D.D., 1969; New York University, Ph.D. candidate. *Politics:* Republican. *Home:* 2750 Northeast 58th St., Fort Lauderdale, Fla. 33308. *Office:* Coral Ridge Presbyterian Church, 5555 North Federal Hwy., Fort Lauderdale, Fla. 33308.

CAREER: Ordained minister of Presbyterian Church, 1959; Coral Ridge Presbyterian Church, Fort Lauderdale, Fla., senior minister, 1959—. Faculty member of Billy Graham Schools of Evangelism; president of Evangelism Explosion, Inc.; member of board of directors of National Association of Evangelicals; vice-president of Chicago Graduate School of Theology. *Member:* National Association of Evangelicals. *Awards, honors:* George Washington honor medal award from Freedoms Foundation, 1971, for sermon, "What You Can Do about Communism".

WRITINGS: Evangelism Explosion, Tyndale, 1970; *The God of Great Surprises*, Tyndale, 1973; *This Is the Life: Guidelines for Christian Growth*, Gospel Light, 1973; *Spiritual Renewal*, Gospel Light, 1973; *Truths That Transform*, Revell, 1974. Author of "Like a Mighty Army" (film), produced by Gospel Films, and four lay teaching training films, produced by Gospel Films.

AVOCATIONAL INTERESTS: Music, science, poetry, sports, travel.

BIOGRAPHICAL/CRITICAL SOURCES: Russell Chandler, *Kennedy Explosion*, David Cook, 1971.

* * *

KENNEDY, Don H(enry) 1911-

PERSONAL: Born May 6, 1911, in Quincy, Ill.; son of James L. (in investments) and Mary (Ebbers) Kennedy; married Nina Grodsky, May 11, 1935; children: Joan, Christopher, Mary. *Education:* Attended University of California, Los Angeles. *Religion:* Roman Catholic. *Home:* 1531 Reeves St., Los Angeles, Calif. 90035.

CAREER: Beverly Hills Citizen, Beverly Hills, Calif., author of column, "Beverly Topics," 1932-42, reporter then news editor, 1935-42; North American Aviation, Inc., Los Angeles, Calif., aircraft design engineer, 1942-61; writer, 1961—. *Member:* Society for Nautical Research, Cabrillo Beach Yacht Club.

WRITINGS: History of Beverly Hills, Cawston-Meier, 1935; *Ship Names: Origins and Usages during 45 Centuries*, Mariner's Museum and University Press of Virginia, 1975. Contributor to boating publications.

WORK IN PROGRESS: Research in nautical history; an engineering evaluation of Greek trireme design.

SIDELIGHTS: Kennedy has made about four thousand photographic negatives of commercial vessels for a museum collection. *Avocational interests:* Sailing a twenty-eight foot sloop.

* * *

KENNEDY, Gavin 1940-

PERSONAL: Born February 20, 1940, in Wetherby, Yorkshire, England; son of Robert (a motor mechanic) and Anne (Kennedy) Plenderleith; married Patricia Anne Millar (a college lecturer), July 4, 1973; children: Florence. *Education:* University of Strathclyde, B.A., 1969, M.Sc., 1972; University of Brunel, Ph.D., 1974. *Politics:* "Member of Scottish National Party—I'm a kind of radical democrat." *Religion:* Protestant. *Home:* 4 East Mains Cottage, Gordon, Berwickshire, Scotland. *Agent:* Colin Haycraft, 43 Gloucester Crescent, London N.W.1, England. *Office:* Department of Economics, University of Strathclyde, 173 Cathedral St., Glasgow, Scotland.

CAREER: University of Brunel, Uxbridge, England, lecturer in economics, 1971-73; University of Strathclyde, Glasgow, Scotland, senior lecturer in economics, 1974—. Director of Blair, Kennedy & Associates (management and economic consultants). *Member:* Royal Economic Society, British Institute of Management, Association of Teachers of Management, Writers Guild of Great Britain, Andrew Fletcher Society, Caledonian Club.

WRITINGS: The Military in the Third World, Scribner, 1974; *The Economics of Defence*, Faber, 1975; *The Death of Captain Cook*, Duckworth, in press; *Bligh*, Duckworth, in press; *The Defence Burden in NATO*, A. W. Sijhtoff, in press.

WORK IN PROGRESS: Introducing Political Economy, publication by Duckworth expected in 1977.

SIDELIGHTS: Kennedy writes: "My first two books are extensions of my academic work. In the next two I have written to please myself. The Bligh biography is long . . . and controversial (it defends Bligh and criticizes Fletcher Christian) and I enjoyed the research and the work. . . . The combination of author in economics and historical biography is accidental rather than deliberate . . . I turned to naval history in pursuit of another goal. . . . Idle reading in the field led me to an interest in people like Bligh, Cook, and Nelson. I hope someday to return to my original research interest, feeling that war and economic development is a neglected area." *Avocational interests:* Reading, travel (to Europe to promote "a European federation, with Scotland as an independent member separate from England"), political activities.

* * *

KERN, Robert W(illiam) 1934-

PERSONAL: Born August 8, 1934, in St. Louis, Mo.; son of Russell (a teacher) and Mary (Wilson) Kern; married Elizabeth Wilson, 1960; children: Jonathan, C. Joshua. *Education:* Antioch College, B.A., 1957; University of Chicago, M.A., 1960; University of Chicago, Ph.D., 1966. *Office:* Department of History, University of New Mexico, Albuquerque, N.M. 87106.

CAREER: University of California, Riverside, instructor in history, 1963-66; University of Massachusetts, Amherst, assistant professor of history, 1967-68; University of New Mexico, Albuquerque, assistant professor, 1968-73, associate professor of history, 1974—. Member: American Historical Association, Association of Spanish and Portuguese Historians.

WRITINGS: The Caciques: Oligarchical Politics and the System of Caciquismo in the Luso-Hispanic World, University of New Mexico Press, 1972; Liberals, Reformers, and Caciques in Restoration Spain: 1875-1909, University of New Mexico Press, 1974. Contributor to Massachusetts Review, Iberian Studies, and Journal of Contemporary History.

WORK IN PROGRESS: Red Years/Black Years: Buenaventura Durruti and the Spanish Anarchists: 1911-1937; a history of political and labor forces in modern Spain.

*   *   *

KERR, Alex(ander McBride) 1921-

PERSONAL: Born April 23, 1921, in Perth, Australia; son of William James (an engineer) and Lilian (Weight) Kerr; married Joan Ivy Langridge (a teacher), August 9, 1947; children: Ian, Penelope, Robyn, Andrew, Rosemary. Education: University of London, B.Sc., 1947; University of Western Australia, B.A. (honors), 1948, M.A., 1949, Ph.D., 1957. Religion: Presbyterian. Home: 146 Alderbury St., Floreat Park 6014, Western Australia. Office: School of Social Inquiry, Murdoch University, Murdoch 6153, Western Australia.

CAREER: Worked as Commonwealth statistician and economist, 1950-51; University of Western Australia, Nedlands, lecturer, 1952-53, senior research fellow, 1954-55, senior lecturer, 1956-63, reader, 1964-71, associate professor of economics, 1971-74; Murdoch University, Murdoch, Western Australia, professor of economics, 1975—. Chairman of Consumer Affairs Council of Western Australia. Military service: Citizen Military Forces, 1937-39, 1947-54; Royal Australian Air Force, 1939-45; served as pilot.

MEMBER: Economic Society, Regional Science Association, Australian Institute for Urban Studies, Australia and New Zealand Association for the Advancement of Science, Perth Building Society (director) Perth Chamber of Commerce (member of council). Awards, honors: Fulbright fellowship, 1960; Leverhulme fellowship, 1969.

WRITINGS: Personal Income of Western Australia, Western Australia University Text Books Board, 1951; Northwestern Australia, Western Australia Government Printer, 1962; State and Regional Income Estimation: Theory and Practice, International Scholastic Book Service, 1963; The South West Region of Western Australia, University of Western Australia Press, 1966; Australia's North-West, University of Western Australia Press, 1967, revised edition, International Scholastic Book Service, 1968, 3rd edition, 1976.

*   *   *

KESLER, Jay 1935-

PERSONAL: Born September 15, 1935, in Barnes, Wis.; son of Herbert E. and Elsie (Campbell) Kesler; married Helen Jane Smith, June 7, 1957; children: Laurie, Bruce, Terri. Education: Attended Ball State University, 1953-54; Taylor University, B.A., 1957. Office: Youth for Christ International, North Main St., Wheaton, Ill. 60187.

CAREER: Youth for Christ International, Wheaton, Ill., director of college recruitment, 1962-63, vice-president for personnel, 1963-68, vice-president for field coordination, 1968-73, president, 1973—.

WRITINGS: Let's Succeed with Our Teenagers, David C. Cook, 1973; I Never Promised You a Disneyland, Word, Inc., 1975. Author of "I Never Promised You a Disneyland," column in Campus Life (magazine), 1974-75.

*   *   *

KESSELMAN, Judi R(osenthal) 1934-
(Pauline Turkel)

PERSONAL: Born January 3, 1934, in Bronx, N.Y.; daughter of Samuel S. and Pauline (Turkel) Rosenthal; married Joseph Kesselman, February 27, 1957 (separated September, 1975); children: Joseph Jay, Jeffrey Peter. Education: Brooklyn College (now of the City University of New York), B.A. (cum laude), 1955. Residence: Great Neck, N.Y. Agent: Anita Diamant, 51 East 42nd St., New York, N.Y. 10017.

CAREER: Screen Stories, New York, N.Y. story editor, 1956-58; Sterling Publications, New York City, editor, 1959; Stern Publications, New York City, editor, 1960-61; K.M.R. Publications, New York City, senior editor of Real Story and My Love Secret, 1961-62; free-lance fan magazine writer, 1964-67; Modern Screen, New York City, managing editor, 1965; general article writer, 1970—. Teacher of adult education courses in non-fiction writing, 1974—. Member: Society of Magazine Writers, American Society of Journalists and Authors.

WRITINGS: Stopping Out of College, M. Evans, 1976. Contributor to periodicals and newspapers including New York Times, Chatelaine, Playgirl, Long Island Newsday, Seventeen, and Weight Watchers.

WORK IN PROGRESS: Research for biographies of Joseph Hirshhorn and L. Frank Baum; research for a book on children's learning disabilities.

AVOCATIONAL INTERESTS: Playing piano, hiking, sailing, civic affairs.

*   *   *

KESSLER, Edward 1927-

PERSONAL: Born June 9, 1927, in Oak Hill, W.Va.; son of Oscar Flemington and Blanche (Hawver) Kessler. Education: University of Virginia, A.B., 1949; Rutgers University, M.A., 1964, Ph.D., 1967. Home: 1831 23rd St. N.W., Washington, D.C. 20008. Office: Department of Literature, American University, Washington, D.C. 20016.

CAREER: Union Carbide Corp., New York, N.Y., writer, 1956-58; College of William & Mary, Williamsburg, Va., assistant professor of literature, 1963-65; University of Virginia, Charlottesville, assistant professor of literature, 1965-67; American University, Washington, D.C., assistant professor, 1967-70, associate professor, 1970-75, professor of literature, 1975—. Military service: U.S. Navy, 1952-55; became lieutenant. Member: Modern Language Association of America, Phi Delta Theta. Awards, honors: Images of Wallace Stevens was chosen for "Scholar's Bookshelf" of Modern Language Association of America, 1973.

WRITINGS: Images of Wallace Stevens, Rutgers University Press, 1972; Night Thoughts (poetry with engravings) I.M.P. (Paris), 1973. Contributor of poems to magazines, including American Scholar, Saturday Review, New Yorker, and Virginia Quarterly Review.

WORK IN PROGRESS: A study of Samuel Taylor Coleridge; a book of poems.

*   *   *

KEYISHIAN, Harry   1932-

PERSONAL: Born April 9, 1932, in New York, N.Y.; son of John H. (a rug dealer) and Arax (Artinian) Keyishian; married Marjorie Ann Deiter (a university instructor in English), July 30, 1966; children: Sarah, Elizabeth, Amy, Emily. Education: Queens College (now of the City University of New York), B.A., 1954; New York University, M.A., 1957, Ph.D., 1965. Home: 110 Burnham Parkway, Morristown, N.J. 07960. Office: Department of English, Fairleigh Dickinson University, Madison, N.J. 07940.

CAREER: University of Maryland, College Park, assistant instructor in English for Overseas Program in Newfoundland, 1957-58; City College (now of the City University of New York), New York, N.Y., lecturer in English, 1959-60; City University of New York, Bronx Community College, Bronx, N.Y., lecturer in English, 1961; University of Buffalo, Buffalo, N.Y., instructor in English, 1961-64; Fairleigh Dickinson University, Madison, N.J., assistant professor, 1965-69, associate professor, 1969-73, professor of English, 1973—, chairman of department, 1972-74. Military service: U.S. Naval Reserve, 1950-58; active duty, 1956-58; served in Newfoundland.

MEMBER: Modern Language Association of America, Renaissance Society of America, Popular Culture Association, National Association for Armenian Studies and Research, College English Association, American Society for Theatre Research, Society for Theatre Research (England), Northeast Modern Language Association.

WRITINGS: Michael Arlen, Twayne, 1975.

Poetry has been anthologized in Armenian-North American Poets, edited by Lorne Shiranian, Manna Publishers, 1975. Contributor of articles and reviews to professional journals. Guest editor of Ararat, autumn, 1970.

WORK IN PROGRESS: A study of the revenge theme in literature.

*   *   *

KEYS, Ancel   1904-

PERSONAL: Born January 26, 1904, in Colorado Springs, Colo.; son of Benjamin Pious (a manufacturer) and Caroline (Chaney) Keys; married Margaret Haney; children: Carrie Keys D'Andrea, Henry Michael, Martha Jane. Education: University of California, Berkeley, B.A., 1925, M.A., 1928, Ph.D., 1930; King's College, Cambridge, Ph.D., 1936. Home: 410 Groveland Ave., Minneapolis, Minn. 55403; and Minnelea, 84060 Pioppi, (SA) Italy. Office: Stadium Gate 27, University of Minnesota, Minneapolis, Minn. 55455.

CAREER: National Research Council, Washington, D.C., research fellow in Copenhagen, Denmark, 1930-31; Cambridge University, Cambridge, England, research fellow and demonstrator in physiology, 1931-33; Harvard University, Cambridge, Mass., instructor in biochemical sciences, 1933-36; Mayo Clinic, Rochester, Minn., assistant professor, 1936, associate professor of biochemistry, 1937; University of Minnesota, Minneapolis, associate professor, 1937-39, professor of physiology, 1939-43, professor of physiological hygiene and head of department, both 1943-72, professor emeritus, 1972—. Special assistant to Secretary of War, 1942-44; chairman of Council for Epidemiology Prevention, 1962-66.

MEMBER: International Society for Cardiology, American Heart Association, American Physiological Society, Nutrition Society, American College of Cardiology (fellow), American Society of Biological Chemists, Society for Experimental Biology and Medicine, American Society for Clinical Nutrition, British Nutrition Society, Indian Heart Society (honorary member), Accademia di Medicina (Rome; honorary member), Endocrinology Society of India (honorary member), Accademia di Medicina e Chirurgia (Picento, Italy; honorary member), New York Diabetes Society (honorary member). Awards, honors: Joint Army-Navy award of appreciation, 1948; citation from American Heart Association, 1959; named commander of the Order of the Lion (Finland), 1965; McCollum Award from American Society for Clinical Nutrition, 1967; medal of honor from University of Belgrade, 1967.

WRITINGS: (With others) Human Starvation, two volumes, University of Minnesota Press, 1950; (with wife, Margaret Keys) Eat Well and Stay Well, Doubleday, 1957, revised edition, 1963; (with Margaret Keys) The Benevolent Bean, Doubleday, 1967; How to Eat Well and Stay Well the Mediterranean Way, Doubleday, 1975. Contributor to medical and medical science journals.

WORK IN PROGRESS: Research on the epidemiology of cardiovascular disease and on the relation of diet to health.

SIDELIGHTS: Keys organized and directed the International High Altitude Expedition (studying physiology in the high Andes), 1935; organized and directed the Minnesota Starvation Study, 1942-45, using thirty-six conscientious objectors as volunteer subjects; organized the International Seminar on Epidemiology of Cardiovascular Diseases (sponsored by the International Society of Cardiology yearly since 1968), teaching over two hundred doctors from forty countries; conducted research on the epidemiology of heart disease and diet in Mexico, Hawaii, Japan, Italy, Spain, England, South Africa, Finland, Greece, Yugoslavia, the Netherlands, and Hungary; organized and continues to direct the International Cooperative Study on Epidemiology of Cardiovascular Diseases (in eight countries, sponsored by the U.S. Public Health Service National Heart and Lung Institute, and the American Heart Association). His books have been published in Italian, Finnish, Spanish, German, Portuguese, and Japanese. Avocational interests: Gardening, fruit growing, cooking.

*   *   *

KEYSERLING, Leon H.   1908-

PERSONAL: Born January 22, 1908, in Charleston, S.C.; son of William (a businessman and farmer) and Jennie (Hyman) Keyserling; married Mary Dublin (a consulting economist), October 4, 1940. Education: Columbia University, A.B., 1928, graduate study, 1931-33; Harvard University, LL.B., 1931. Politics: Democrat. Home and office: 2610 Upton St. N.W., Washington, D.C. 20008.

CAREER: Columbia University, New York, N.Y., teacher of economics, 1932-33; Agricultural Adjustment Act, staff attorney, Washington, D.C., 1933; secretary and legislative assistant to U.S. Senator Robert F. Wagner, Washington, D.C., 1933-37, and for U.S. Senate Committee on Banking and Currency, 1935-37; U.S. Housing Authority, Washington, D.C., general counsel, 1937-38, deputy administrator and general counsel, 1938-42, acting administrator, 1941-42; Federal Public Housing Authority, Washington, D.C., acting administrator, 1942; National Housing Agency, Washington, D.C., general counsel,

1942-46; President's Council of Economic Advisors, Washington, D.C., vice-chairman, 1946-49, chairman, 1949-53; practicing attorney and consulting economist to various government agencies, firms, and individuals, Washington, D.C., 1953—. Admitted to bars of New York, Washington, D.C., and the Supreme Court. Founder and president, Congress on Economic Progress, 1953—; member of board of directors, Park Electric Corp, 1956—, and North River Development Co., 1973—; honorary member of faculty, Industrial College of the Armed Forces, 1966—; president, National Committee for Labor Israel, 1970-74. *Member:* American Political Science Association, American Economic Association, American Bar Association. *Awards, honors:* Pabst Post-War Employment Award, 1944, for essay, "The American Economic Goal: A Practical Start Toward Post-War Full Employment."

WRITINGS—All published by Conference on Economic Progress except as indicated: (Editor with Rexford G. Tugwell) *Redirecting Education*, Columbia University Press, Volume I, 1934, Volume II, 1935, reprinted, Books for Libraries Press, 1971; *The Federal Budget and the General Welfare*, 1959; *Inflation: Cause and Cure*, 1959; *Key Policies for Full Employment*, 1960; *The Peace Investment Corporation*, privately printed, 1961; *Poverty and Deprivation in the U.S.*, 1962; *Taxes and the Public Interest*, 1963; *Two Top Priority Programs to Reduce Unemployment*, 1963; *The Prevalent Monetary Policy and Its Consequences*, 1964; *The Toll of Rising Interest Rates*, 1964; *Progress on Poverty: The U.S. at the Crossroads*, 1964.

Agriculture and the Public Interest, 1965; *The Move Toward Railroad Mergers*, Railway Labor Executive's Association, 1965; *The Role of Wages in a Great Society*, 1966; (with others) *A Freedom Budget for All Americans*, 1966; *Goals for Teacher Salaries in Our Public Schools*, 1967; *Achieving Nationwide Educational Excellence*, 1968; *Israel's Economic Progress*, State of Israel Bonds, Development Corporation for Israel, 1968; *Taxation of Whom for What?*, 1969; *More Growth Without Inflation or More Inflation Without Growth?*, 1970; *Wages, Prices and Profits*, 1971; *The Coming Crisis in Housing*, 1972; *The Scarcity School of Economics*, 1973; *Full Employment Without Inflation*, 1975.

WORK IN PROGRESS: Work on full employment legislation, and housing legislation; articles and sketches.

SIDELIGHTS: During his long career as an economist in Washington, D.C., Keyserling has worked as a consultant to various members of the Senate and the House of Representatives. In this capacity, he has been a major participant in studies related to and the actual drafting of legislation. These pieces of legislation include the National Industrial Recovery Act, public works and relief acts, the Social Security Act, the Employment Act of 1946, and the Housing Act of 1949.

* * *

KIERLAND, Joseph Scott 1937-

PERSONAL: Born August 6, 1937, in New York, N.Y.; son of Robert and Dorothy (Nord) Kierland; children: Moira Kathleen. *Education:* University of Connecticut, B.A., 1959; Yale University, M.F.A., 1962. *Home:* 81 Bedford St., New York, N.Y. 10014. *Agent:* Gloria Safier Agency, 667 Madison Ave., New York, N.Y. 10021; and Raines & Raines, 475 Fifth Ave., New York, N.Y. 10017.

CAREER: Cedar Ridge Productions, New York, N.Y.,

executive manager and producer, 1962-64; Lincoln Center for the Performing Arts, New York, N.Y. writer-in-residence, 1965; Mercury Records Inc., Chicago, Ill., executive producer of spoken arts and theatre recordings, 1966; Brandeis University, Waltham, Mass., writer-in-residence, 1967-68; Holiday Inns Inc., New York, N.Y., regional manager of reservation system, 1969—. Member of O'Neill Foundation, 1965—. *Member:* New Dramatists Inc., American Society of Authors, Composers, and Publishers. *Awards, honors:* Playwriting awards from Hunter College of the City University of New York, 1959, Cornell University, 1961, Town Theatre, 1962, University of Chicago, 1965, and New England Theatre Conference, 1973; R.C.A.-N.B.C. fellowship, 1961; Rockefeller Foundation grant, 1968; Dramatists Guild grant, 1971.

WRITINGS—Plays: "Ride the Cock Horse," first produced in New York by New Dramatists, February, 1964; "The Minotaur," first produced in New York by New Dramatists, February, 1965; "The Snow of Southern Summers," first produced in New York, by New Dramatists, September, 1967; "Sunday," first produced at Brandeis University, December, 1967; "Playsongs," first produced at Brandeis University, May, 1969; "Drum-Taps," first produced in New York at Lab Theatre, November, 1974; "Hocus Pocus," first produced in New York by New Dramatists, November, 1975. Also author of "Dance of the Night Foxes," as yet unproduced and unpublished.

WORK IN PROGRESS: Novels, *The Cruellest Month*, and *Blue Dog Blues;* screenplays, "Tato and Teresa," and "The Rape of Molly Jean Bunting."

* * *

KIKER, B(ill) F(razier) 1937-

PERSONAL: Born April 21, 1937, in Elkin, N.C.; son of William J. and Ruby (Jester) Kiker; married Martha J. Parker, August 4, 1962; children: Todd, Brent, Scott. *Education:* Lenoir Rhyne College, A.B. (cum laude), 1961; Tulane University, Ph.D., 1965. *Home:* 637 Woodland Hills W., Columbia, S.C. 29210. *Office:* Department of Economics, University of South Carolina, Columbia, S.C. 29208.

CAREER: University of South Carolina, Columbia, assistant professor, 1965-68, associate professor, 1968-71, professor, 1971-73; Jeff B. Bates Professor of Economics, 1973—, head of department, 1973—, director of Center for Studies in Human Capital, 1972—. Visiting professor at University of Edinburgh, 1973.

WRITINGS: The Concept of Human Capital, University of South Carolina Press, 1966; *A Benefit-Cost Analysis of the South Carolina MDTA Program: Preliminary Report,* Bureau of Business and Economic Research, University of South Carolina, 1968; *Human Capital: In Retrospect,* University of South Carolina Press, 1968; (editor with Robert J. Carlsson, and contributor) *South Carolina Economists: Essays on the Evolution of Antebellum Economic Thought,* Bureau of Business and Economic Research, University of South Carolina, 1969. *An Evaluation of the Economic Effects of the South Carolina MDTA Program,* South Carolina Employment Security Commission, 1971; (editor) *Investment in Human Capital,* University of South Carolina Press, 1971; *A Cost-Effectiveness Analysis of the University of South Carolina MBA-ETV Program,* Alfred P. Sloan Foundation, 1974; (with Earle C. Traynham, Jr.) *The Economic Experience of Return and Non-Return Migrants for the Southeast,* University of South Carolina Press, 1974; *The Concept of Human Capital as an Investment*

Criterion: With Special Reference to Medical Care, Social Security Administration, U.S. Department of Health, Education, and Welfare, 1974; (with James L. Cochrane and Samuel Gubins) *Macroeconomic Analysis and Policy,* Scott, Foresman, 1974. Contributor of about thirty articles and reviews to economic journals.

* * *

KILLEEN, Jacqueline 1931-

PERSONAL: Born November 24, 1931, in San Francisco, Calif.; daughter of John C. (a stock broker) and Rena (Sandow) Traylor. *Education:* University of California, Berkeley, B.A., 1953. *Office:* 101 Productions, 834 Mission St., San Francisco, Calif. 94103.

CAREER: Waikiki Beach Press, Honolulu, Hawaii, advertising manager, 1955-57; Optimist International, St. Louis, Mo., associate editor of *Optimist Magazine,* 1957-61; San Francisco Art Institute, San Francisco, Calif., director of public information, 1962-67; 101 Productions, San Francisco, executive editor, 1968—.

WRITINGS: 101 Nights in California, 101 Productions, 1968 (with annual revisions through 1974); *101 Secrets of California Chefs,* 101 Productions, 1969; *Ecology at Home,* 101 Productions, 1971; *Best Restaurants of San Francisco and Northern California,* 101 Productions, 1975. Writer with Gloria Vollmayer and Charles C. Miller of *California Critic* (a monthly restaurant review).

* * *

KILLION, Ronald G(ene) 1931-

PERSONAL: Born in 1931, in Steger, Ill. *Education:* St. John's College, Winfield, Kan., A.A., 1951; Concordia Seminary, St. Louis, Mo., B.A., 1953, B.D., 1956; Columbia University, M.A., 1964, Ed.D., 1968; also studied at Valparaiso University, 1956, and University of Georgia, 1965. *Home:* 506 South Petty St., Gaffney, S.C. 29340. *Office:* Department of History, Limestone College, Gaffney, S.C. 29340.

CAREER: Concordia Preparatory School, Bronxville, N.Y., teacher of social studies and history, 1956-59; pastor of Lutheran church in Pittsburgh, Pa., 1959-62; Concordia College, Bronxville, N.Y., assistant professor of history, 1963-66; Arkansas State University, State University, assistant professor of European history, 1967-68; Limestone College, Gaffney, S.C., associate professor, 1969-70, professor of history, 1970—, chairman of department, 1969-70, chairman of Division of Social Studies, 1970-76, tennis coach, 1975—. *Military service:* U.S. Army, chaplain, 1961.

MEMBER: American Historical Association, American Political Science Association, Southern Historical Association, Phi Delta Kappa. *Awards, honors:* University of Georgia research fellowship, 1969; nominated "author of the year" by Dixie Writing Council of Georgia, 1972; U.S. Department of Health, Education and Welfare fellowship for study in Pakistan, 1973.

WRITINGS: (With Bobby G. Moss) *The Journal of Michael Gaffney,* Gaffney Ledger, 1971; (with Charles T. Waller) *A Treasury of Georgia Folklore,* Cherokee, 1972; (with Waller) *Slavery Time: When I Was Chillun Down on Marster's Plantation,* Beehive Press, 1973; (with Waller) *Georgia and the Revolution,* Cherokee, 1975. Contributor to *Southern Folklore Quarterly, Sandlapper,* and *Georgia Magazine,* and to newspapers.

WORK IN PROGRESS: The Reform Act of 1867: Selected Documents.

* * *

KINCHELOE, Raymond McFarland 1909-

PERSONAL: Born July 11, 1909, in Sacramento, Ky.; son of Robert McFarland (a school teacher) and Vannie Jane (Reynolds) Kincheloe; married Christina Rebekah Stelling (a teacher and librarian), September 18, 1932; children: Eloise Faith (Mrs. John Bergen), David Wesley, Jonathan Albert, Carol Elaine (Mrs. Jeffrey Adams). *Education:* Nyack Missionary College, Diploma, 1939; Taylor University, B.Re., 1941; Birmingham Southern College, B.A., 1946; Wheaton College, Wheaton, Ill., M.A., 1956; Chicago Graduate School of Theology, M.Div., 1970, M.Th., 1971. *Home and office:* 440 Fourth Ave., Regina, Saskatchewan, Canada S4T 0H8.

CAREER: Clergyman of Christian and Missionary Alliance, ordained 1942; Canadian Bible/Theological College, Regina, Saskatchewan, instructor, 1953-68, assistant professor, 1968-72, associate professor of Greek and prophecy, 1972—, registrar, 1974—. Certified clinic director for Evangelism Explosion, Inc., 1975—. *Member:* Evangelical Theological Society.

WRITINGS: A Personal Adventure in Prophecy: Understanding Revelation, Tyndale, 1974. Contributor to *Alliance Witness.*

SIDELIGHTS: Kincheloe traveled for seven summers with his four children holding musical and missionary services in thirty-seven states and five Canadian provinces.

* * *

KING, Bruce ?-1976
(Zolar)

?—January 15, 1976; American astrologer, publisher, inventor, and author. Obituaries: *New York Times,* January 16, 1976.

* * *

KING, Francis Edward 1931-

PERSONAL: Born November 19, 1931, in San Francisco, Calif.; son of Frank Aloysius and Helene (Johnson) King. *Education:* Gonzaga University, B.A., 1955, M.A., 1956; Alma College, Los Gatos, Calif., S.T.L., 1963; Santa Clara University, S.T.M., 1963; Pontifical Gregorian University, S.T.D., 1971. *Office:* Department of Theology and Religious Studies, University of San Francisco, San Francisco, Calif. 94117.

CAREER: Ordained Roman Catholic priest of Society of Jesus (Jesuit) order, 1962; teacher of French in Roman Catholic high school in San Francisco, Calif., 1956-57; teacher of history, English, and speech at a preparatory college in Fresno, Calif., 1957-59; University of San Francisco, San Francisco, Calif., instructor, 1964-66, assistant professor of theology, 1969—. Assistant professor at Georgetown University, spring, 1966. *Member:* College Theology Society.

WRITINGS: The Institutional Aspects of the Church According to William Law: 1686-1761, Gregorian University Press, 1971. Contributor to *Homiletic and Pastoral Review.*

AVOCATIONAL INTERESTS: Travel (King has visited Western Europe, England and Ireland, Scandinavia,

Greece, Morocco, Israel, Jordan, Egypt, Canada, Alaska, Panama, Venezuela, the Caribbean, Hawaii, Puerto Rico).

* * *

KING, Mark 1945-

PERSONAL: Born May 29, 1945, in Baltimore, Md.; son of Al (a sports film maker) and Bernice (a hospital purchasing agent; maiden name, Housha) King; married Judith Patz (a family therapist), August 19, 1967; children: Shana Leah. *Education:* University of Maryland, B.A., 1967; University of Connecticut, M.A., 1970; Iowa State University, Ph.D., 1973. *Politics:* "Liberal-Radical." *Religion:* None. *Home:* 5712 Beacon St., Pittsburgh, Pa. 15217. *Office:* Department of Child Development, University of Pittsburgh, Pittsburgh, Pa. 15261.

CAREER: Maryland Department of Corrections, Jessup, counselor, 1967-68; Eastern Connecticut State College, Willimantic, instructor in psychology, 1969-70; Iowa State University, Ames, part-time instructor in child development, 1970-72; Duquesne University, Pittsburgh, Pa., assistant professor of psychology, 1972-75; University of Pittsburgh, Pittsburgh, Pa., assistant professor of child development, 1975—. Private practice in psychology. Assistant program manager of Iowa Head Start and Follow-Through supplementary training programs, summer, 1971; former member of Midwest regional planning board of National Council of Family Relations; consultant to National Involvement Institute. *Member:* American Psychological Association, American Association of Clinical Hypnosis, Western Pennsylvania Psychological Association, Pittsburgh Psychological Association.

WRITINGS: For We Are: Toward Understanding Your Personal Potential, Addison-Wesley, 1975; (editor with Ron Valle) *Existential-Phenomenology As an Alternative Approach in Psychology,* Williams & Wilkins, in press. Contributor of articles and reviews to psychology journals.

WORK IN PROGRESS: Toward Understanding the Meaning of Your Life, with Paul Colaizzi; research on parental self-actualization and a child's self-concept.

SIDELIGHTS: King's professional interest is in "personal growth—beyond being normal. I'm particularly interested in the study of consciousness—especially as related to drugs and hypnosis." *Avocational interests:* Gambling, sports.

* * *

KING, Robert R(ay) 1942-

PERSONAL: Born June 8, 1942, in Rock Springs, Wyo.; son of Edward C. and Elinor Marie (Smith) King; married Kay Atkinson (a linguist), December 30, 1969; children: Nathan Atkinson. *Education:* Brigham Young University, B.A., 1966; Fletcher School of Law and Diplomacy, M.A., 1967, M.A.L.D., 1968, Ph.D., 1970. *Home:* Ziehrerstrasse 46, 8025 Unterhaching, West Germany. *Office:* Radio Free Europe, Englischer Garten 1, 8 Munich 22, West Germany.

CAREER: Radio Free Europe, Munich, West Germany, senior analyst for Rumania and Bulgaria, 1970—. Lecturer in international relations at Brigham Young University, Salzburg, Austria, 1971—, and at University of Southern California, Munich, Germany, 1973—. *Member:* American Political Science Association, Association for the Advancement of Slavic Studies.

WRITINGS: (With Stephen E. Palmer, Jr.) *Yugoslav Communism and the Macedonian Question,* Archon

Books, 1971; *Minorities under Communism: Nationalities as a Source of Tension among Balkan Communist States,* Harvard University Press, 1973; (editor with Robert W. Dean) *East European Perspectives on European Security and Cooperation,* Praeger, 1974. Editor and contributor to "Radio Free Europe Research" series, published by Radio Free Europe. Contributor to professional journals.

WORK IN PROGRESS: Research on Rumania and Eastern Europe; *History of the Rumanian Communist,* completion expected in 1977.

* * *

KING, Stephen 1947-

PERSONAL: Born September 21, 1947, in Portland, Me.; son of Donald (a sailor) and Ruth (Pillsbury) King; married Tabitha Spruce (a poet), January 2, 1971; children: Naomi, Joseph Hill. *Education:* University of Maine, B.Sc., 1970. *Politics:* Populist. *Home:* R.F.D. #2, Kansas Road, Bridgton, Me. 04009.

CAREER: Formerly employed as janitor, in mill, and as laundry worker; high school teacher of English in Hampden, Me., two years. *Member:* Authors Guild.

WRITINGS: Carrie (novel), Doubleday, 1974; *Jerusalem's Lot* (novel), Doubleday, 1975. Also author of short stories.

WORK IN PROGRESS: The Shine, a novel about a small boy isolated with his parents in an ominous and snowbound Colorado resort hotel.

AVOCATIONAL INTERESTS: Reading (mostly fiction), jigsaw puzzles, playing the guitar ("I'm terrible and so try to bore no one but myself"), movies.

* * *

KING, Stephen W(illiam) 1947-

PERSONAL: Born January 31, 1947, in San Francisco, Calif.; son of Louis W. (a physician) and Betty Louise (in real estate; maiden name, Pehrson) King; married Leatha-Ann Kleid, June 24, 1967; children: Scott W. *Education:* University of Washington, Seattle, B.A., 1968, M.A., 1969; University of Southern California, Ph.D., 1971. *Office:* Department of Speech Communication, San Diego State University, San Diego, Calif. 92182.

CAREER: San Diego State University, San Diego, Calif., assistant professor, 1971-74, associate professor of speech communication, 1974—. *Member:* Speech Communication Association, Western Speech Communication Association.

WRITINGS: Communication and Social Influence, Addison-Wesley, 1975; (with Larry Samovar and Jack Mills) *Understanding Human Communication,* McGraw, 1976. Consulting editor, *Western Speech Communication,* 1976—.

* * *

KIPPLEY, Sheila K. 1939-

PERSONAL: Born November 8, 1939, in Alma, Mich.; daughter of Fred C. (an accountant) and Rosemary (Grohman) Matgen; married John Francis Kippley (a teacher-director), April 27, 1963; children: Jennifer, Mary, Margaret, Karen. *Education:* University of California, San Francisco Medical School, B.S., 1962. *Religion:* Roman Catholic. *Office:* Couple to Couple League, P.O. Box 11084, Cincinnati, Ohio 45211.

CAREER: Founder with husband, of Couple to Couple League.

WRITINGS: Breastfeeding and Natural Child Spacing, privately printed, 1969; *Breastfeeding and Natural Child Spacing: The Ecology of Natural Mothering*, Harper, 1974; *The Art of Natural Family Planning*, Couple to Couple League, 1975.

SIDELIGHTS: Sheila Kippley told *CA:* "Research led me to understand that only a particular type of mothering associated with breastfeeding would give mothers infertility for a long time after childbirth. Interests in child care with further reading also showed me that this natural form of mothering was truly best for baby."

* * *

KIRALY, Bela (Kalman) 1912-

PERSONAL: Born April 14, 1912, in Kaposvar, Hungary; divorced. *Education:* Ludovika Military Academy, B.A., 1935; General Staff Academy, Budapest, Hungary, M.A., 1942; Columbia University, M.A., 1959, Ph.D., 1966. *Home address:* R.R. 1, Box 550A, Highland Lakes, N.J. 07422. *Office:* Department of History, Brooklyn College of the City University of New York, Brooklyn, N.Y. 11210.

CAREER: General Staff Academy, Budapest, Hungary, professor of military history and superintendent of academy, 1950-51; Brooklyn College of the City University of New York, Brooklyn, N.Y., instructor, 1965-66, assistant professor, 1966-70, associate professor, 1970-71, professor of history, 1971—, professor of history, City University of New York Graduate School, and chairman of East European Section of Center for European Studies, 1969—. Adjunct associate professor, St. John's University, 1969-71; visiting professor, Columbia University, 1971-72, 1975-76, visiting scholar, 1972-73. Member of White House Conference on International Cooperation, 1964. *Military service:* Hungarian Army, commander-in-chief of Infantry, and chief of department of education, training, and sports of Ministry of Defense, 1947-50; became major-general.

MEMBER: American Historical Association, American Association for the Advancement of Slavic Studies. *Awards, honors:* Named honorary member of staff and faculty of U.S. Army Command and General Staff College, 1959; named Teacher of the Year, Brooklyn College of the City University of New York, 1968; American Philosophical Society research grant for research in Vienna and London, 1968.

WRITINGS: The Hungarian Army Under the Soviets (in Japanese), Japan Institute of Foreign Affairs, 1950; *Hungary in the Late Eighteenth Century: The Decline of Enlightened Despotism*, Columbia University Press, 1969; (contributor) Joseph Held and others, editors, *Intellectual History of the Hapsburg Monarchy: 1806-1914*, Columbia University Press, 1975; *Ferenc Deak*, Twayne, 1975; (editor) *Tolerance and Movements of Religious Dissent in East Central Europe*, East European Quarterly and Columbia University Press, 1975; (contributor) Paul Teleki, editor, *Evolution of Hungary and Its Place in European History*, new edition, Academic International, 1975. Contributor to history journals in the United States and abroad.

SIDELIGHTS: In 1951, Kiraly was arrested, sentenced to death, and imprisoned in Budapest. He was paroled in 1956, and became the commander-in-chief of the National Guard of Hungary. He spent the years from 1957 to 1968 lecturing in European, Asian, and American colleges, universities, military academies, and war colleges on the subjects of the Hungarian Revolution, organization, training, and system of Soviet control of the People's Armies of East Central Europe.

KIRCHWEY, Freda 1893-1976

September 26, 1893—January 3, 1976; American magazine editor and publisher, political activist and reformer, and editor of a book on social issues. Obituaries: *New York Times*, January 4, 1976; *Current Biography*, February, 1976.

* * *

KIRK-GREENE, Anthony (Hamilton Millard) 1925- (Nicholas Caverhill)

PERSONAL: Born May 16, 1925, in Tunbridge Wells, England; son of Leslie (a civil engineer) and Helen (Millard) Kirk-Greene; married Helen Margaret Sellar, April 22, 1967. *Education:* Clare College, Cambridge, B.A. (first class honors), 1949; graduate study at Cambridge University, 1955-56, Northwestern University and University of California, Los Angeles, 1958-59, and Edinburgh University, 1965-66. *Home:* 34 Davenant Rd., Oxford, England. *Office:* St. Antony's College, Oxford University, Oxford, England.

CAREER: British Colonial Administrative Service, Northern Nigeria, district officer, 1950-57; Institute of Administration, Zaria, Nigeria, senior lecturer in government, 1957-60; Ahmadu Bello University, Zaria, associate professor of government and head of department, 1961-66; Oxford University, Oxford, England, senior research fellow in African studies, 1967—. Visiting professor, Syracuse University, 1961, University of California, Los Angeles, 1962, 1963, 1967, and 1968, University of Paris, 1971, 1973, and 1975, Scandinavian Institute of African Studies, 1974; Hans Wolff Memorial Lecturer, University of Indiana, 1973; visiting fellow, Clare College, Cambridge, 1967, and Hoover Institution on War, Revolution, and Peace, 1975; scholar-in-residence, Trent University, 1975. Consultant to Kenya Government, 1961, East African Staff College, 1969 and 1970, East African Community, 1972, and African Association for Public Administration and Management, 1975. *Military service:* Royal Warwickshire Regiment, 1943-44. Indian Army, 8th Punjab Regiment, 1944-47; became captain. *Member:* International African Institute, African Studies Association (council member, 1966-69), Royal African Society, Hawks Club, Oxford and Cambridge United University Club. *Awards, honors:* M.A., Cambridge University, 1954, Oxford University, 1967; Harkness fellowship, 1958-59; member of Order of the British Empire, 1963; Canada Council fellowship, 1975.

WRITINGS: This is Northern Nigeria: Background to an Invitation, Government Printer of Northern Nigeria (Kaduna), 1956; *Maiduguri and the Capitals of Bornu*, bilingual edition, Northern Regional Literature Agency (Zaria, Nigeria), 1958; *Adamawa, Past and Present: An Historical Approach to the Development of a Northern Cameroons Province*, Oxford University Press for the International African Institute, 1958, new edition, Humanities, 1969; (with Caroline Sassoon) *The Cattle People of Nigeria*, Oxford University Press, 1959; (with Sassoon) *The Niger*, Oxford University Press, 1961; *Barth's Travels in Nigeria*, Oxford University Press, 1962; *The Principles of Native Administration in Nigeria: Selected Documents, 1900-1947*, Oxford University Press, 1965; (with Sidney Hogben) *The Emirates of Northern Nigeria*, Oxford University Press, 1966; (compiler and translator) *Hausa ba dabo ba ne: A Collection of 500 Proverbs*, Oxford University Press, 1966; (with Yahaya Aliyu) *A Modern Hausa Reader*, McKay, 1967; *Lugard and the Amalgamation of Nigeria: A Docu-*

mentary Record, Frank Cass, 1968; (translator with Paul Newman) *West African Travels and Adventures: Two Autobiographical Narratives from Northern Nigeria*, Yale University Press, 1971; *Crisis and Conflict in Nigeria: A Documentary Sourcebook*, two volumes, Oxford University Press, 1971; (editor) *Gazetteers of the Northern Provinces of Nigeria*, Volume I: *The Hausa Emirates*, Volume II: *The Eastern Kingdoms*, Volume III: *The Central Kingdoms*, Volume IV: *The Highland Chieftaincies*, Frank Cass, 1972; (with Charles Kraft) *Teach Yourself Hausa*, University of London Press, 1973; *Mutumin Kirkii: The Concept of the Good Man in Hausa* (monograph), University of Indiana, 1974; *The Genesis of the Nigerian Civil War* (monograph), University of Uppsala, 1975; (with Pauline Ryan) *Faces North*, Pitkin Publications, 1975; *The Colonial Governor in Africa*, Hoover Institution, 1976.

Contributor: Donald C. Stone, editor, *Education and Public Administration*, International Institute of Administrative Sciences, 1963; James S. Coleman, editor, *Education and Political Development*, Princeton University Press, 1965; L. Franklin Blitz, editor, *The Politics and Administration of Nigeria*, Praeger, 1966; H. Schiffers, editor, *Heinrich Barth Festschrift*, Steiner (Hamburg), 1967; Arnold Rivkin, editor, *Nations by Design*, Doubleday, 1968; John Spencer, editor, *The English Language in West Africa*, Longman, 1968; Robert Rotberg, editor, *African Explorers and Exploration*, Harvard University Press, 1971; C. Fyfe and G. Shepperson, editors, *The Exploration of Africa in the Eighteenth and Nineteenth Centuries*, Edinburgh University, 1972; K. Ingham, editor, *Foreign Relations of African States*, Butterworth & Co., 1974; A. Adedeji and C. Baker, editors, *Education and Research in Public Administration in Africa*, Hutchinson, 1974; Adedeji and G. Hyden, editors, *Developing Research on African Administration*, [Nairobi], 1975; C. Fyfe, editor, *African Studies since 1945*, Longman, 1976.

Author of introduction: C. J. Orr, *The Making of Northern Nigeria*, 2nd edition, Frank Cass, 1965; Heinrich Barth, *Travels and Discoveries in North and Central Africa*, centenary edition, Barnes & Noble, 1965; Sonia Graham, *Government and Mission Education in Northern Nigeria*, Ibadan University Press, 1966; P. A. Benton, *The Languages and People of Bornu*, Frank Cass, 1968; Heinrich Barth, *The Vocabularies of Central African Languages*, Frank Cass, 1970; Frederick Lugard, *Political Memoranda*, Frank Cass, 1971; J. A. Burdon, *History of the Emirates of Northern Nigeria*, Gregg, 1973.

Also author of pamphlets and research papers on African languages, history, and governmental institutions. General editor of Methuen's "Studies in African History" series, 1971—; co-editor of Hoover Institution's "Colonial History Series," 1975—. Contributor of articles and reviews to African and historical journals. Editorial advisor, *Journal of African Administration*, 1957-67, *African Affairs*, 1975—.

WORK IN PROGRESS: A multi-disciplinary study of political leadership in Hausaland; a history of the British Colonial Administrative Service in Africa.

*   *   *

KISSAM, Edward   1943-

PERSONAL: Born May 29, 1943, in Orlando, Fla.; son of Edward M. and Jacqueline Kissam; married Nancy Blecker (a botanist); children: Kyra, Cassady. *Education:* Princeton University, B.A.; graduate study at Magdalen College, Oxford, 1966-67; State University of New York at Buffalo,

Ph.D. candidate. *Politics:* Radical. *Home:* 6379 West Dry Creek, Healdsburg, Calif. 95448. *Office:* 930 Piner Rd., Santa Rosa, Calif. 95401.

CAREER: High school teacher of English in Choueifat, Lebanon, 1967; San Francisco State College (now University), San Francisco, Calif., lecturer in English and linguistics, 1969-70; Sonoma State College, Rohnert Park, Calif., assistant professor of English, 1970-71; worked as a woodcutter, 1973; Alianza Farmworkers' Clinic, Healdsberg, Calif., project coordinator, 1974; Sonoma County People for Economic Opportunity, Sonoma County, Calif., videotape cameraman, 1974, consultant for greenhouse project, 1974, teacher for Manpower project, 1975.

WRITINGS: (Translator from the Aztec) *House of Song* (poems), privately printed, 1964; *The Sham Flyers* (poems), Anvil Press, 1969; *Jerusalem and the People,* Anvil Press, 1972; *The Arabs,* Institute of Further Studies, 1972; (translator with Michael Schmidt from the Aztec) *Flower and Song* (poems), Routledge & Kegan Paul, in press. Contributor of reviews to *Clear Creek,* 1971. Editor of *Burning Water,* 1963-66, and *Audit/Poetry,* 1968. Co-author of "The Newly Poor" (videotape), produced by Sonoma County People for Economic Opportunity, 1974.

WORK IN PROGRESS: A book of peoms, *Serpentine;* research in Mexican ethnobotany, and on medical, legal, and sociological problems of organophosphate use in California.

*   *   *

KISTE, Robert Carl   1936-

PERSONAL: Born August 26, 1936, in Spencer, Ind.; son of Edgar Franklin (a factory worker) and Hazel (a bond underwriter; maiden name, Burch) Kiste; married Valerie Mary Mattea (a jewelry maker), August 29, 1961; children: Vincent Matthew. *Education:* Indiana University, B.A., 1961; University of Oregon, Ph.D., 1967. *Home:* 110157 Stanford Circle, Chaska, Minn. 55318. *Office:* Department of Anthropology, University of Minnesota, Minneapolis, Minn. 55455.

CAREER: University of Utah, Salt Lake City, research assistant on Glen Canyon Archaeological Project, summer, 1959; Indiana University, Bloomington, instructor in anthropology at Archaeological Field School, summer, 1960; Indiana Historical Society, Indianapolis, Indiana, archaeologist, summer, 1961; University of Minnesota, Minneapolis, assistant professor, 1967-70, associate professor of anthropology, 1970—, director of graduate studies, 1969-71. Visiting associate professor at University of Hawaii, spring, 1973. Conducted ethnological field research on Crow Indian Reservation in Montana, summer, 1962, and in the Marshall Islands, 1963-64, 1969, 1973. Consultant to National Science Foundation, Micronesian Legal Services Corp., and to program for the resettlement of the Bikini and Eniwetok communities of the U.S. Trust Territory of the Pacific Islands. *Military service:* U.S. Army, 1954-57.

MEMBER: American Anthropological Association (fellow), Society for Applied Anthropology (fellow), Association for Social Anthropology in Oceania (fellow; member of board of directors), American Ethnological Society, Council for Anthropology and Education, Phi Beta Kappa, Sigma Xi. *Awards, honors:* Woodrow Wilson fellowships, 1961-62, 1965.

WRITINGS: Kili Island: A Study of the Relocation of the Ex-Bikini Marshallese (monograph), Department of Anthropology, University of Oregon, 1968; (contributor) H. Russell Bernard and Pertti Pelto, editors, *Technology and Social Change*, Macmillan, 1972; (contributor) *Eniwetok Atoll Master Plan*, Volume II, Holmes & Narver, 1973; (contributor) *The Diversity of Religious Expression*, World Religions Curriculum Development Center (St. Louis Park, Minn.), 1974; *The Bikinians: A Study in Forced Migration*, Cummings, 1974; (contributor) Michael Lieber, editor, *Exiles and Immigrants in Oceania*, University of Hawaii Press, in press; (contributor) Vern Carroll, editor, *Incest Prohibitions in Polynesia and Micronesia*, University of Hawaii Press, in press.

Co-editor of "The Kiste-Ogan Social Change Series in Anthropology," Cummings, 1972—. Contributor to anthropology journals. Editor of newsletter of Association for Social Anthropology in Oceania, 1970-72; associate editor of *Human Organization*, 1972—.

WORK IN PROGRESS: A book on the forced resettlement of the population of Eniwetok Atoll in the Marshall Islands of Micronesia.

* * *

KISTNER, Robert William 1917-

PERSONAL: Born August 23, 1917, in Cincinnati, Ohio; son of Alfred Charles and Gertrude (Thienes) Kistner; married Georgia Golde Walker, August 26, 1943; children: Dana Anne, Robert William, Stephen Barrett, Peter Allen. *Education:* University of Cincinnati, B.A., 1938, M.D., 1942. *Home:* 454 Grove St., Needham, Mass. 02192. *Office:* 32 Cumberland Ave., Brookline, Mass. 02146.

CAREER: Cincinnati General Hospital, Cincinnati, Ohio, intern, 1942-43, assistant resident in obstetrics, 1946-48, resident, 1948-49; Johns Hopkins Hospital, Baltimore, Md., post-graduate fellow in obstetrical medicine, 1949; Free Hospital for Women, Brookline, Mass., assistant resident in pathology, 1950; Boston Lying-In Hospital, Boston, Mass., assistant resident in pathology, 1951; Kings County Hospital, Brooklyn, N.Y., resident in gynecology, 1951-52; Free Hospital for Women, Brookline, assistant resident in gynecology, 1952, resident, 1953; physician in private practice in Brookline, 1953-75; Harvard University, Cambridge, Mass., instructor in gynecology, 1956-58, associate in obstetrics and gynecology, 1959, assistant professor of obstetrics and gynecology, 1960-75; Boston Lying-In Hospital, Boston, senior obstetrician and gynecologist, 1965-68; Boston Hospital for Women, Boston, senior obstetrician and gynecologist, 1968-73, associate chief of staff, 1974—. Diplomate of American Board of Obstetrics and Gynecology. Instructor at University of Cincinnati, 1946-50, and New York State Medical School, 1951-52. Consultant to U.S. Surgeon General, 1962-70. *Military service:* U.S. Army Air Forces, flight surgeon in Medical Corps, 1943-46; chief of Pacific Division of Air Transport Command, 1946; became major; received Air Medal.

MEMBER: Pan American Cancer Cytology Society (honorary member), American College of Surgeons (fellow), American College of Obstetrics and Gynecology (fellow), American Medical Association, Society for Gynecologic Investigation, American Federation for Clinical Research, American Fertility Society, Endocrine Society, Continental Gynecologic Society, La Sociedad Chilena de Obstetricia y Ginecologia (honorary member), Sociedad Panamena de Obstetricia y Ginecologia (honorary member), Central Association of Obstetricians and Gynecologists (honorary member), Pacific Northwest Gynecological and Obstetrical Society (honorary member), Pacific Coast Fertility Society (honorary member), New England Obstetrical Society, Massachusetts Medical Association, Obstetrical and Gynecologic Society of New Mexico (honorary member), Boston Obstetrical Society, Kansas City Gynecology Society (honorary member), Long Beach Obstetrical and Gynecologic Society (honorary member), Kiamath Academy of Medicine and Science (honorary member), Aesculapian Club, Harvard Club of Boston, Dedham Country and Polo Club (Massachusetts), Longwood Cricket Club (Chestnut Hill, Mass.), Wianno Club (Wianno, Mass.).

WRITINGS: Principles and Practice of Gynecology, Year Book Medical Publishers, 1964, 2nd edition, 1971; *Progress in Infertility*, Little, Brown, 1969, 2nd edition (with S. J. Berkman), 1975; *The Pill: Fact and Fallacy*, Delacorte, 1969; *The Use of Progestins in Obstetrics and Gynecology*, Year Book Medical Publishers, 1969; (with Grant W. Patton) *Atlas of Infertility Surgery*, Little, Brown, 1975. Contributor of more than a hundred fifty articles to medical journals.

SIDELIGHTS: The Pill has been published in six languages, including German.

* * *

KITCHEN, Martin 1936-

PERSONAL: Born December 21, 1936, in Nottingham, England; son of John Sutherland (an insurance manager) and Margaret (Pearson) Kitchen; married Brigitte Meyer (a social worker), March 13, 1960; children: Corinna, Susan. *Education:* Attended Magdalen College, Oxford, 1957-59; University of London, B.A. (honors), 1963, Ph.D., 1966. *Politics:* Socialist. *Religion:* None. *Home:* 1483 29th St., West Vancouver, British Columbia, Canada. *Office:* Department of History, Simon Fraser University, Burnaby, British Columbia 2, Canada.

CAREER: Simon Fraser University, Burnaby, B.C., assistant professor, 1966-69, associate professor of history, 1969—. *Military service:* British Army, 1955-57; became lieutenant.

WRITINGS: The German Officer Corps, 1890-1914, Clarendon Press, 1968; *A Military History of Germany*, Weidenfeld & Nicolson, 1975; *Fascism*, Macmillan, in press; *The Silent Dictatorship: The Politics of the German High Command under Hindenburg and Ludendorff*, Croom Helm, in press. Contributor to professional journals.

WORK IN PROGRESS: Fascism and National Socialism: A Comparative Study.

SIDELIGHTS: Kitchen writes that his work "concentrates on militarism which he examines in terms of the relationships between the army and society, and of the social origins of extreme right wing movements."

* * *

KLAMKIN, Charles 1923-

PERSONAL: Born November 2, 1923, in Brooklyn, N.Y.; son of Harry (a merchant) and Ethel (Heller) Klamkin; married Marian Spungin (a writer), August 22, 1948; children: Joan Klamkin Rainer, Lynn, Peter. *Education:* Clark University, Worcester, Mass., A.B., 1948. *Home and office:* 141 Colonial Rd., Watertown, Conn. 06795. *Agent:* James Oliver Brown, James Brown Associates, Inc., 22 East 60th St., New York, N.Y. 10022.

CAREER: Engaged in retail appliance business as buyer, manager, and owner of stores, 1948-71; writer and photographer, 1971—. Has taught photography at private and public schools, 1973-74. *Military service:* U.S. Army, chief photographer, 1943-45. *Member:* Authors Guild of Authors League of America.

WRITINGS: *If It Doesn't Work, Read the Instructions,* Stein & Day, 1970; *Barns: Their History, Preservation, and Restoration,* Hawthorn, 1973; *How to Buy Major Appliances,* Regnery, 1973; *Weather Vanes,* Hawthorn, 1973; (with wife, Marian Klamkin) *Wood Carvings: North American Folk Sculpture,* Hawthorn, 1974; (with Marian Klamkin) *Investing in Antiques and Popular Collectibles for Pleasure and Profit,* Funk, 1975; (with Elsie Fetterman) *Consumer Education in Practice,* Wiley, in press; *Railroadiana: The Collectibles of Railroading,* Crowell, in press; *Collectibles of the Occult,* Crowell, in press. Contributor to *Nation.*

SIDELIGHTS: Klamkin writes: [I] "spent twenty-two years in retail appliance business until my first book, an expose of that business, made a further career in that area untenable. First book was successful enough to encourage furthering my writing pursuits. Have furnished up to four hundred black and white and color photographs for twenty books on the decorative arts written by my wife, Marian Klamkin."

* * *

KLAPPHOLZ, Kurt 1913-1975

July 5, 1913—March 20, 1975; German-born American rabbi and author of books on religion. Obituaries: *New York Times,* March 26, 1975.

* * *

KLASSEN, Randolph Jacob 1933-

PERSONAL: Born April 21, 1933, in Winnipeg, Manitoba, Canada; son of Jacob Frank (an artist) and Ellie Sophia (Peters) Klassen; married Corinne Peterson, July 11, 1959; children: Timothy, Stephen, Jonathan. *Education:* University of Manitoba, B.A., 1954; Fuller Theological Seminary, graduate study, 1956-58; North Park Theological Seminary, M.Div., 1959. *Home:* 5421 West 87th St., Prairie Village, Kan. 66207. *Office:* 8801 Nall Ave., Prairie Village, Kan. 66207.

CAREER: Ordained minister of Evangelical Covenant Church, 1961; pastor of churches in Winnipeg, Manitoba, 1959-65; in Davis, Calif., 1965-70; and Prairie Village, Kan., 1970—. Member of board of directors of North Park College, 1971—, and Temporary Lodging for Children, 1972—. *Member:* Kiwanis. *Awards, honors:* Art awards for paintings in Winnipeg and Sacramento.

WRITINGS: *Meditations for Lovers: From the Song of Solomon,* Covenant Press, 1974. Contributor to religious periodicals. Member of editorial committee of Covenant Churchmen's Book Club, 1975—.

WORK IN PROGRESS: *Humor in the Bible; Art in the Bible.*

SIDELIGHTS: Klassen has exhibited water color paintings in one-man shows and jury shows. He has designed and built more than fifty art glass windows for churches.

* * *

KLAUSNER, Margot 1905-1976(?)

November 2, 1905—1976(?); German-born Israeli literary agent, publisher, playwright, novelist, short story writer, and author of biographical and other nonfiction works. Obituaries: *AB Bookman's Weekly,* January 26, 1976.

* * *

KLEEBERG, Irene (Flitner) Cumming 1932-

PERSONAL: Born April 21, 1932, in Chicago, Ill.; daughter of James Coale (an advertising executive) and Elsie (a professional volunteer; maiden name, Battin) Cumming; married Fred Martin Kleeberg (a printing consultant), October 20, 1957; children: John Martin, Margaret Anne. *Education:* Wellesley College, B.A., 1954. *Politics:* "Registered Democrat, Socialist at heart." *Religion:* Humanist. *Home and office:* 232 East 58th St., New York, N.Y. 10022.

CAREER: Thames Advertising Service Ltd., London, England, copywriter, 1954-55; L. Bamberger & Co., Newark, N.J., buyer, 1955-56; *Women's Wear Daily,* New York, N.Y., editor, 1956-58; American correspondent for several British trade publications, 1958—; *Homesewing Trade News,* New York, N.Y., fashion and education editor, 1971—. Volunteer, New York City Commission for the United Nations and Consular Corps, 1966—; chairman, 17th Precinct Community Council (police department), 1966-68; member of board of directors, International Community Center, New York, N.Y., 1973—; member of acquaintanceship committee, New York Wellesley Club, 1973—. *Member:* Authors Guild, Women's Fashion Fabrics Association (vice-president), Embroiderer's Guild of Great Britain, Danish Handicraft Guild. *Awards, honors:* Certificate of Merit from the police department, City of New York; Certificate of Appreciation from the City of New York.

WRITINGS: *Make Your Own Pants and Skirts,* Bantam, 1971, revised edition, 1972; *Making School Clothes for Boys and Girls,* Bantam, 1971; *The Blue Jeans Book,* Bantam, 1972; (translator) Rob Herwig, *128 House Plants You Can Grow,* Macmillan, 1972; *Fashion Tops,* Drake, 1973; *Concise Guide to Bicycle Repair,* F. Watts, 1973; *Sewing for Bazaars,* Bantam, 1974; *Butterick Fabric Handbook,* Butterick, 1975; *Bicycle Touring,* F. Watts, 1975. Contributor of articles to *Women's Wear Daily, Baby Talk, Stores Magazine,* and numerous other trade publications.

WORK IN PROGRESS: A book on Christianity for young people; translation, from the Dutch, of a book on dominoes; and research on college admissions procedures.

SIDELIGHTS: Mrs. Kleeberg is very involved in the United Nations. She helps newly arrived foreign diplomats and their families with their adjustment to the city of New York. She is competent in French and Dutch, and knows some Italian and Spanish.

* * *

KLEIN, Daniel Martin 1939-

PERSONAL: Born April 20, 1939, in Wilmington, Del.; son of David Xavier (a chemist) and Sophia (a teacher; maiden name, Posner) Klein; married Beverly Anne Cohen, August 31, 1963 (divorced, 1968). *Education:* Harvard University, A.B., 1961. *Religion:* Jewish. *Home address:* P.O. Box 63, Southfield, Mass. 01259. *Agent:* Paul R. Reynolds, Inc., 12 East 41st St., New York, N.Y. 10017.

CAREER: Social worker and welfare worker in New York, N.Y.; 1962-63; elementary school teacher in Boiceville,

N.Y., 1963-64; television writer in New York, N.Y., 1963-65 (wrote material for television personalities, including Merv Griffin); free-lance writer, 1965—.

WRITINGS: Everything You Wanted to Know about Marijuana, Tower, 1972; *Seven Perfect Marriages That Failed,* Stein & Day, 1975. Author of "We've Come Back for a Little Look Around," a play for National Park Service, 1975 (first produced in Boston, Mass., June, 1975). Contributor of articles and stories to magazines, including *Realist, Saturday Evening Post, McCall's, Eye,* and *Cavalier,* and to newspapers.

WORK IN PROGRESS: A historical play; short stories.

SIDELIGHTS: Klein writes: "My major interest is short stories. I like writing, but now wish I had become a doctor." In 1969, he was one of the inventors of "The Group Therapy Box Game."

*　　*　　*

KLEIN, Maxine 1934-

PERSONAL: Born March 25, 1934, in Blue Earth, Minn.; daughter of Howard Russel (a merchant) and Billie (a merchant; maiden name, Odden) Manther; married Joseph Gallisen (divorced); married Robert Klein (divorced). *Education:* Texas Western College, B.A., 1956; University of Connecticut, M.A., 1958; Cornell University, Ph.D., 1960. *Religion:* None. *Home:* 22 Sunset St., Roxbury, Mass. 02120. *Agent:* Helen Harvey Associates, Inc., 1697 Broadway, New York, N.Y. 10019. *Office:* School for the Arts, Boston University, 855 Commonwealth Ave., Boston, Mass. 02215.

CAREER: Keuka College, Keuka Park, N.Y., instructor in theater arts and director of theater, 1960-62; University of Minnesota, Minneapolis, instructor, 1963-65, assistant professor, 1965-67, associate professor of theater arts, 1967-69; Boston University, Boston, Mass., professor of theater arts, 1969—, director of theater. Has directed plays for theaters in the United States and Canada.

MEMBER: American Educational Theatre Association, American Federation of Musicians, Society of Stage Directors and Choreographers, Actors' Equity Association. *Awards, honors: Village Voice,* Obie Award, 1970, for outstanding direction of play "Approaching Simone"; citation from *Saturday Review,* 1970, for most creative director of the New York season; regional award from NETC, 1973, as outstanding director and teacher.

WRITINGS: Time, Space and Design for Actors, Houghton, 1975.

Plays: "Touch Kiss," first performed at Martinique Theatre, 1973; "Savage," first performed at Berkshire Theatre Festival; "Brain Child," first performed in Philadelphia, 1974; "Tania," first performed in Cambridge, Mass., 1975. Contributor to drama and theater journals.

WORK IN PROGRESS: Theatre for the Ninety-Eight PerCent.

*　　*　　*

KLEIN, Thomas D(icker) 1941-

PERSONAL: Born October 25, 1941, in Chicago, Ill.; son of Milton P. (a publisher) and Ruth (Dicker) Klein; married Erica Karp, June 8, 1969 (divorced, 1975). *Education:* Tufts University, B.A., 1963; Harvard University, M.A.T., 1964; Northwestern University, Ph.D., 1971. *Politics:* Liberal. *Religion:* Jewish. *Home:* 145 Troup St., Bowling Green, Ohio 43402. *Office:* Department of English, Bowling Green State University, Bowling Green, Ohio 43403.

CAREER: High school teacher of English in the public schools of Evanston Township, Ill., 1964-69; Bowling Green State University, Bowling Green, Ohio, assistant professor of English, 1971—. Consultant to Educational Coordinates, Inc., 1967-68; member of Chicago Committee on Urban Opportunity, summer, 1968. *Member:* American Association of University Professors, National Council of Teachers of English, English Association of Ohio, English Association of Northwest Ohio.

WRITINGS: (With Betsy Arons and Howard Millman) *Spinach Is Good for You: A Call for Change in the American Schools,* Popular Press, 1973; *Writing Naturally: A Primer on Lengthening and Shortening,* Lyceum, 1976. Contributor to English journals. Editor of *Journal of the English Association of Northwest Ohio,* 1972—.

WORK IN PROGRESS: A study of the use of student evaluation of teachers, and police-community relations on a university campus.

*　　*　　*

KLEMM, Roberta K(ohnhorst) 1884-

PERSONAL: Born November 29, 1884, in Louisville, Ky.; daughter of Louis (a banker) and Johanna (Poetker) Kohnhorst; married Edward G. Klemm, 1909 (deceased); children: Edward G., Jr. *Education:* Attended University of Chicago, 1903. *Home:* 2034 Eastern Parkway, Louisville, Ky. 40204.

CAREER: Elementary school teacher in Louisville, Ky., 1904-08; poet, 1974—. *Member:* National Association of American Composers and Conductors (life member), American Society of Composers, Authors, and Publishers, Woman's Club (Louisville), Filson Club (Louisville; life member).

WRITINGS: Quest and Other Poems, Echo Publishers, 1974. Music: (With son, Edward G. Klemm, Jr.) *Holiday in Napoli,* Whitney Blake, 1945; (with Klemm) *Shadows,* Whitney Blake, 1945; (with Klemm) *They Never Told Me,* Edition Bristol, 1945; *Souvenir,* Composers Press, 1963. Contributor to magazines and newspapers.

*　　*　　*

KLINK, Johanna L. 1918-

PERSONAL: Born March 6, 1918, in Roermond, Holland; daughter of D. J. (an engineer) and C.J.W.F. (Davyt) Klink. *Education:* University of Leiden, Dr. Theology, 1947. *Home and office:* Bakenessergracht 107, Haarlem, Holland.

CAREER: Ordained minister of Remonstrant (Armenian) Church, 1948; served as minister in various parishes, 1948-68; freelance worker for religious education, lecturer, and writer, 1968—. *Member:* World Council of Churches.

WRITINGS: De Bijbel vandaag (title means "The Bible Today"), De Tijstroom, 1951; *Het is als met* (parables), De Tijstroom, 1952; *Bijbel voor de kindren O.T.* (title means "Bible for Children: Old Testament), Het Wereldvenster, 1958, translation by Patricia Compton published as *Bible for Children,* Volume I, Westminster, 1967; *Bijbel voor de kindren N.T.* (title means "Bible for Children: New Testament) Het Wereldvenster, 1961, translation published as *Bible for Children,* Volume II, Westminster, 1969; *Ter meerdere ere; een gesprek met kerkgangers* (a liturgy for children), Het Wereldvenster, 1965; *Die Theology van de kindren* (title means "The Theology of Children"), Amboboeken, Volume I: *Kind en geloof,* 1970, translation by R. A. Wilson published as *Your Child and Religion,* S.C.M. Press, 1972, Volume II: *Kind en leven,* 1971, Volume III: *Kind op aarde,* 1972.

WORK IN PROGRESS: A book about the Bible for children, *Kleine men en het frote boek;* two books of Bible stories for children, *Words, Images and Stories from the Bible,* and *The Little Man and the Great Book;* articles; lectures.

SIDELIGHTS: Johanna Klink speaks French, German and English. *Avocational interests:* Painting.

* * *

KLUGE, Eike-Henner W. 1942-

PERSONAL: Born August 28, 1942, in West Germany; became Canadian citizen; son of F. F. (a professor) and A. B. Kluge; married Elke B. Freyer (a lecturer), April 15, 1968; children: Andrea, Nicholas. *Education:* University of Calgary, B.A. (honors), 1965; University of Michigan, A.M., 1967, Ph.D., 1968. *Office:* Department of Philosophy, University of Victoria, Victoria, British Columbia, Canada.

CAREER: University of California, Irvine, assistant professor of philosophy, 1968-71; University of Victoria, Victoria, British Columbia, assistant professor, 1971-73, associate professor of philosophy, 1973—. Co-chairman of Citizens' Committee on Corporal Punishment in Schools, Victoria, British Columbia, 1972-73. *Member:* Canadian Philosophical Association, Medieval Association of the Pacific. *Awards, honors:* Woodrow Wilson fellowship, 1967-68.

WRITINGS: (Editor, translator, and author of introduction) *Gottlob Frege on the Foundations of Geometry and Formal Theories of Arithmetic,* Yale University Press, 1971; (translator) William of Ockham's *Commentary on Porphyry,* Franciscan Institute, 1973-74; *The Practice of Death,* Yale University Press, 1975. Referee for *Philosophical Archives,* and *Dialogue.*

WORK IN PROGRESS: Functions and Things; Perception and Awareness; Philosophy and Science Fiction.

* * *

KNIGHT, Roderic C(opley) 1942-

PERSONAL: Born July 25, 1942, in Pasadena, Calif.; son of John Maynard (a real estate salesman) and Gertrude (a dance teacher; maiden name, Copley) Knight; married Gisela Susanne Hauck (a primate research technologist), August 30, 1964; children: Jennifer Kirsten. *Education:* University of California, Santa Barbara, B.A. (cum laude), 1964; University of California, Los Angeles, M.A. (with distinction), 1968, Ph.D. (with distinction), 1973. *Office:* Department of Music, University of Ottawa, Ottawa, Ontario, Canada.

CAREER: Santa Barbara Symphony, Santa Barbara, Calif., second and bass clarinetist, 1963-64; U.S. Peace Corps, Washington, D.C., high school music teacher and band director in Sierra Leone, 1964-66; University of Washington, Seattle, acting assistant professor of music, 1971-74; University of Georgia, Athens, visiting assistant professor of music, summer, 1974; University of Washington, Seattle, supervisor of Media Center, 1974-75; Univer-

sity of Ottawa, Ottawa, Ontario, visiting assistant professor of music, 1975—. Has broadcast on British Broadcasting Corp. radio programs. *Member:* Society for Ethnomusicology, African Music Society, African Studies Association, Pi Kappa Lambda. *Awards, honors:* Fulbright-Hays research grant, 1970.

WRITINGS: Kora Manding: Mandinka Music of The Gambia (song texts and translations with LP record), Ethnodisc, 1972; "Gambie: Mandinka Kora par Jali Nyama Suso" (sound recordings with notes), Disques Ocora, 1972; *Mandinka Jaliya: Professional Music of The Gambia,* University Microfilms, 1973. Contributor to *Grove's Dictionary of Music and Musicians.* Contributor of articles and reviews to professional journals.

WORK IN PROGRESS: Articles on professional musicians in nineteenth-century West Africa, and on the history of the bridge harp from Gingiru to Kora; sound recordings "Santu Suso: Kora Virtuoso" and "The Hunter, the Drummer, and the Blacksmith: Music of the Gambian Mandinka."

* * *

KNOWLES, Henry P(aine) 1912-

PERSONAL: Born December 30, 1912, in Norfolk, Va.; son of Henry Paine and Iola (Bell) Knowles; married Claudia Stanley, June 7, 1937; children: Anne Paine (Mrs. Michael Clocksin), Peter Stanley (deceased). *Education:* U.S. Naval Academy, B.S., 1935; Harvard University, M.B.A., 1947; Stanford University, Ph.D., 1961. *Home:* 16541 41st St., Seattle, Wash. 98155. *Office:* Graduate School of Business Administration, University of Washington, Seattle, Wash. 98105.

CAREER: U.S. Navy, 1937-51, retiring as commander; University of Washington, Seattle, professor of organic behavior, 1957—. *Member:* Academy of Management, Society for Applied Anthropology. *Awards, honors:* Eliot Jones Award from Western Economic Association, 1961.

WRITINGS: Personality and Leadership Behavior, Addison-Wesley, 1971; *Management, Systems, and Society,* Goodyear Publishing, 1976. Contributor to journals.

WORK IN PROGRESS: Research in interpersonal behavior in organizations.

* * *

KNUDSON, Danny (Alan) 1940-

PERSONAL: Born September 28, 1940, in Dunedin, New Zealand; son of George Allan (an electrical engineer) and Jean (McAra) Knudson; married Julie Ellen Smellie, May 11, 1963; children: Deborah Julie, Carol Jean, Claire Ellen. *Education:* University of Otago, B.A., 1966, diploma in education, 1967, M.A., 1974, advanced diploma of teaching, 1974. *Home:* 36 Mayfield Ave., Wakari, Dunedin, New Zealand. *Office:* Green Island School, Howden St., Green Island, Dunedin, New Zealand.

CAREER: Teacher in elementary school in Dunedin, New Zealand, 1962-65; organizing teacher for gifted children in Otago, New Zealand, 1966; area organizer of special classes in schools in Otago and Southland, New Zealand, 1967; Green Island School, Dunedin, New Zealand, deputy principal, 1973—. Lecturer at Dunedin Teacher's College, 1974. Member of New Zealand Educational Institute's yearbook committee; New Zealand gymnastic awards examiner, 1972—.

MEMBER: Intercontinental Biographical Association (fellow), New Zealand Educational Institute (associate; Otago president, 1975), New Zealand Council for Educational Research Electoral College, Otago Institute for Educational Research (member of executive committee, 1973—), Otago School Sports Association (member of executive committee, 1974), Otago Early Settlers' Association.

WRITINGS: The Story of Wakatipu, Whitcombe & Tombs, 1968; The Road to Skippers, A. H. & A. W. Reed, 1974, distributed in the United States as Goldfields Wonderland: The Road to Skippers, Tuttle, 1975; Goldtown School, New Zealand Educational Institute, 1975. Contributor to educational journals.

WORK IN PROGRESS: Editing The Creative Arts, yearbook of New Zealand Educational Institute; Homework? Homework!; developing aspects of language teaching in the primary schools; using his own programmed instruction material and scrambled textbooks in his teaching.

SIDELIGHTS: Knudson writes: "New Zealand is a young country, having been settled by white colonists only a hundred twenty-five years ago, but it can be justly proud of its limited history which is crowded with colourful and exciting developments. Books which record aspects of our past way of life make a fitting contribution to an understanding of the nation's heritage. At the most specific level, a physical feature such as a hillside hut, is all the more significant and memorable when it is known to have unusual associations with past events."

AVOCATIONAL INTERESTS: Coaching children's sports (especially athletics and gymnastics), horse racing.

*   *   *

KO, Won 1925-

PERSONAL: Born December 8, 1925, in Korea; came to United States, 1964; son of Myongchol and Oinye (Kwon) Ko; married Hesun Kim (divorced, 1972); married Young-Ah Lee (a journalist), June 22, 1974; children: Yubong, Yujin, Walter Hyongjin (sons). Education: Attended University of London, 1956-57; Dongguk University, B.A., 1958; University of Iowa, M.F.A., 1965; New York University, Ph.D., 1974. Home: 723 East 27th St., Brooklyn, N.Y. 11210. Office: Brooklyn College of the City University of New York, Bedford Ave., Brooklyn, N.Y. 11210.

CAREER: Soodo Woman's Teachers College, Seoul, Korea, assistant professor of literature, 1960-63; Library of Congress, Washington, D.C., library assistant, 1966-67, reference assistant, 1967-68, reference librarian in Orientalia Division, 1968; Brooklyn College of the City University of New York, Brooklyn, N.Y., instructor, 1970-73, assistant professor, 1974-75, associate professor, 1976—. Instructor, Kon-guk University, Seoul, 1960-64. Coordinator of Friends of Kim China in the U.S.A., 1975. Member: P.E.N. International, American Comparative Literature Association, Association for the Study of Dada and Surrealism, American Oriental Society, Modern Language Association of America. Awards, honors: Poetry award from Kansas City Star, 1966, for "You Are a Metaphor."

WRITINGS—All under name Ko Won; poetry: Yiyurui hangbyon (title means "Antinomic Contradiction"), Sijaska, 1954; T'aeyang ui yon'ga (title means "The Love Song of the Sun"), Yimundang, 1956; Nunuro yaksokhan sigane (title means "At the Time Appointed with Eyes"), Chongsinsa, 1960; Onurun molgo (title means "Far Is To-

day"), Tongmin Munhwasa, 1963; Soksaginun purui kkot (title means "The Whispering Fire's Flower"), Sinhung Ch'ulp'ansa, 1964; The Turn of Zero, Cross-Cultural Communications, 1974. Also author of Buddhist Elements in Dada: A Comparison of Takahashi Shinkichi and Tristan Tzara and The Third Eye Visions (poetry), both as yet unpublished.

Compiler and translator: Contemporary Korean Poetry, University of Iowa Press, 1970.

Contributor of articles in his field to Shantih, Comparative Literature Studies, and Dada/Surrealism. Advisory editor for modern Asian literature issue of TriQuarterly, 1974.

WORK IN PROGRESS: Western Trends in Asian Poetry, a study of the influence of symbolism, dada, and surrealism on Asian poetry.

*   *   *

KOBAL, John 1943-

PERSONAL: Born May 30, 1943, in Ottawa, Ontario, Canada; son of John and Paula Kobal. Education: Attended high schools in Canada and Germany. Home and office: 38 Drayton Ct., London SW10 9RH, England.

CAREER: Actor, 1959-64; British Broadcasting Corp., London, England, broadcaster, 1964-68. Lecturer on films, and free-lance writer.

WRITINGS: (With Raymond Durgnat) Garbo, Studio Vista, 1966; Dietrich, Studio Vista, 1967; (editor) A Pictorial History of the Talkies, Hamlyn, 1968, revised edition published as A New Pictorial History of the Talkies, 1974; Gotta Sing! Gotta Dance!, Hamlyn, 1969; Romance and the Movies: Gods and Goddesses, Studio Vista, 1973; (editor and compiler) Fifty Years of Movie Posters, Hamlyn, 1973; Marilyn Monroe: A Life on Film, Hamlyn, 1974; Through a Lens Softly, Dover, 1976; The Time, the Place, and the Woman: A Biography of Rita Hayworth, McKay, in press; (editor, compiler and author of notes) The Day Before Hollywood, Hamlyn, in press. Contributor to Vogue, Paris Match, Sunday Times, Esquire, and Interview.

*   *   *

KOCH, Thomas J(ohn) 1947-

PERSONAL: Born March 19, 1947, in Grand Forks, N.D.; son of Roland O. (a Lutheran clergyman) and Jean Koch; married Laura Coffin, August 10, 1974. Education: Gustavus Adolphus College, B.A., 1969. Religion: Lutheran. Home: 6212 Golden Valley Rd., Minneapolis, Minn. 55422. Agent: Heidi Lange, Sanford J. Greenburger Associates, 757 Third Ave., New York, N.Y. 10017.

CAREER: U.S. Peace Corps, Washington, D.C., volunteer worker in Kalibo, Aklan, Philippines, 1970-72; writer, 1972—.

WRITINGS: The Year of the Polar Bear, Bobbs-Merrill, 1975.

SIDELIGHTS: Koch writes: "The Year of the Polar Bear is an account of one year in the life of a polar bear cub and his family. 'Little Cub' is a fictional representative of the average polar bear cub as he exists through the first year of life. Based on the journals of explorers, the tales of hunters, and the legends of Polar inhabitants, this book combines Arctic lore with scientific information. Most important, The Year of the Polar Bear is a plea for the survival of the polar bear, an endangered species."

KOLINSKY, Martin 1936-

PERSONAL: Born June 24, 1936, in Winnipeg, Manitoba, Canada; son of Harry (a businessman) and Esther (Promislow) Kolinsky; married Eva Heckel (a University teacher), November 1, 1969; children: Harry, Daniel. Education: University of Saskatchewan, B.A. (cum laude), 1960; London School of Economics and Political Science, Ph.D., 1966. Politics: Moderate. Religion: Jewish. Home: 12 Selly Wick Dr., Birmingham 29, England. Office: Department of Political Science, University of Birmingham, Birmingham B15 2TT, England.

CAREER: University of Birmingham, Birmingham, England, lecturer in sociology, 1966-70, lecturer in political science, 1972—; Hebrew University of Jerusalem, Jerusalem, Israel, lecturer in political science, 1970-72.

WRITINGS: Continuity and Change in European Society, St. Martin's, 1974; (editor with William E. Paterson) Social and Political Movement in Western Europe, Croom Helm, 1976. Contributor to professional journals in England, France, and Israel.

*   *   *

KOLLER, Charles W.

PERSONAL: Born in Texas. Education: Baylor University, A.B., Southwestern Baptist Theological Seminary, Th.M., Th.D. Home: 5317 North Christiana Ave., Chicago, Ill. 60625.

CAREER: Worked as private secretary, accountant, and real estate administrator; student pastor, 1921-27, of Baptist churches in Wellborn, Tex., Riesel, Tex., Hallsburg, Tex., and Morgan, Tex.; pastor of Baptist church in Newark, N.J., 1927-38; Northern Baptist Theological Seminary, Oak Brook, Ill., president, 1938-62, president-emeritus, 1962—. Former member of general council and member of Commission on the Ministry of the Northern (now American) Baptist Convention; former member of state board of New Jersey Baptist Convention; served on boards of Chicago Church Foundation and Midwest Community Council. Military service: U.S. Aviation Service, member of ground forces.

MEMBER: American Baptist Foreign Mission Society (past member of board of directors), Chicago Baptist Association (past member of board of directors), Chicago Bible Society (past member of board of directors). Awards, honors: D.D. from Eastern Baptist Theological Seminary, 1944, and Northern Baptist Theological Seminary, 1962; LL.D. from Baylor University, 1955.

WRITINGS: Tents toward the Sunrise, Judson Press, 1953; Expository Preaching without Notes Plus Sermons Preached without Notes, Baker Book, 1962, Sermons Preached without Notes issued separately by Baker Book, 1964; Sermon Starters, Baker Book, 1973; Pointers for Pastors, Crescendo Book, 1974. Contributor to religious periodicals.

WORK IN PROGRESS: Altars in the Wilderness.

*   *   *

KOLODNY, Annette 1941-

PERSONAL: Born August 21, 1941, in New York, N.Y.; daughter of David (a dentist) and Esther (a teacher; maiden name, Rifkind) Kolodny; married Daniel James Peters (a novelist), June 14, 1970. Education: Brooklyn College of the City University of New York, B.A. (magna cum laude), 1962; University of California, Berkeley, M.A., 1965, Ph.D., 1969; also studied at University of Oslo, summer, 1961. Politics: "Radical Feminist." Home address: R.F.D. 1, Lee Hook Rd., Newmarket, N.H. 03857. Office: Department of English, University of New Hampshire, Durham, N.H. 03824.

CAREER: Newsweek, New York, N.Y., associate to the editor of international editions, 1962-63; Yale University, New Haven, Conn., assistant professor of English and Ezra Stiles fellow, 1969-70; University of British Columbia, Vancouver, assistant professor of English, 1970-74; University of New Hampshire, Durham, assistant professor of English, 1974—. Consultant to Canada Council and RAND Corp.

MEMBER: Modern Language Association of America, American Studies Association, American Society for Eighteenth Century Studies, Canadian Association for American Studies. Awards, honors: Canada Council senior research grant, 1973-74; younger humanist fellowship from National Endowment for the Humanities, 1974-75; Ford Foundation fellowship, 1975-76.

WRITINGS: The Lay of the Land: Metaphor as Experience and History in American Life and Letters, University of North Carolina Press, 1975.

Work is anthologized in I, That Am Ever Stranger: Poems on Woman's Experience, edited by Nancy Esther James, Globe Printing, 1974. Contributor of articles and reviews to literary and women's studies journals, including South Atlantic Quarterly, Critical Inquiry, and Southern Literary Journal. Member of board of editors of American Literature, 1975-78.

WORK IN PROGRESS: Women on the New World Landscape (tentative title), a sequel to The Lay of the Land; Severing the Head from the Body: Form and Dysfunction in Contemporary Literature by Women (tentative title).

SIDELIGHTS: Annette Kolodny writes: "I fear that the human species is hell-bent on self-annihilation, with the United States rather blindly leading the way. We pollute our minds with trivia and our environment with carcinogens. The political and moral awakenings of the nineteen-sixties are now being dismissed—to our peril; and the current women's movement may run out of energy before it achieves the changes it envisions. The nation as a whole is in the hands of the blind, the selfish, and the mediocre."

*   *   *

KORINETZ, Yuri (Iosifovich) 1923-

PERSONAL: Name also appears as Iurii Iosifovich Korinets; born January 14, 1923, in Moscow, Union of Soviet Socialist Republics; son of Josef (a diplomat) and Elly (Nagel) Korientz; married Natalia Burlova (a translator from the English), 1964; children: Ekaterina, Yuri. Education: Student at Art School, Samarkand, Soviet Central Asia, 1948-51, and A. M. Gorky Institute of Literature, Moscow, 1953-57. Home: 125319 Krasnoarmeyskaya 21 kw. 108, Moscow, Union of Soviet Socialist Republics. Agent: VAAP-Bolshaya Bronnaya G-A 103104, Moscow, Union of Soviet Socialist Republics.

CAREER: Full-time writer. Member: Union of U.S.S.R. Writers, Union of the Soviet Societies of Friendship and Cultural Relations with Foreign Countries. Awards, honors: First prize in U.S.S.R. Children's Book Competition dedicated to Lenin's Centenary, 1968, for Tam, Vdali, *za Rekoi (There, Far Beyond the River); Dort weit hinter dem Fluss,* the German translation of *Tam, Vdali, za Rekoi* was runner-up for the German prize for best youth book, 1973, and the Italian edition was named one of the best youth books of 1973 in Italy; his books were selected among the best of the year for inclusion in UNESCO International Youth Library, 1972, 1973, 1974.

WRITINGS: Cybota Subbota v Ponedelnik (title means "Saturday in Monday"; selected verses and poems), Detskaya Literatura, 1966; *Tam, Vdali ze Rekoi* (youth novel), Detskaya Literatura, 1967, translation by Anthea Bell based on German edition published as *There, Far Beyond the River,* J. Philip O'Hara, 1973; (translator into Russian) James Kruess, *Govoriashchaia mashina (Die Sprechmaschine),* Detskaya Literatura, 1969; *Chetyre Sestry* (title means "Four Sisters; selected verses and poems), Detskaya Literatura, 1970; *Privet ot Vernera* (title means "Greeting from Verner"; youth novel), Detskaya Literatura, 1972; *Volodiny Bratya* (title means "Volodya's Brothers"; youth novel), Detskaya Literatura, 1975. Writer of radio plays for children and contributor to Soviet children's magazines.

WORK IN PROGRESS: A new book for children with proposed title of *The Cleverest Horse;* a novel, *Through Fire, Water and Copper Pipes.*

SIDELIGHTS: Korinetz writes: "Being 15 years old I wrote my first story. From that time my dream was to be a writer, or a painter (I [had] visited Moscow art school at that time). My present interests besides writings are hi-fi stereophonic, fishing, travelling, water-colour painting."

There, Far Beyond the River also has been published in England and translated into a total of ten languages, including Norwegian, Czech, Swedish, Italian, French, and Dutch. *Greetings from Verner* and *Volodya's Brothers* have had German editions.

* * *

KOSSOFF, David 1919-

PERSONAL: Born November 24, 1919, in London, England; son of Louis (a tailor) and Annie Kossoff; married Jennie Jenkins, 1946; children: Simon, Paul. *Education:* Attended Northern Polytechnic, 1933-36. *Politics:* None. *Religion:* Jewish. *Home and office:* 45 Roe Green Close, Hatfield, Hertfordshire AL10 9PD, England.

CAREER: Furniture designer, 1936-39; DeHaviland Aircraft Co., draftsman, 1939-45; radio actor for British Broadcasting Corp., 1945-51, writer, 1961—. Illustrator. *Member:* Society of Industrial Arts, Royal Society of Arts (fellow). *Awards, honors:* British Film Academy Award, 1954, for "The Young Lovers."

WRITINGS: Bible Stories Retold, Collins, 1968; *The Book of Witnesses,* Collins, 1971, St. Martin's, 1972, juvenile edition, Paperback Library, 1973; *The Three Donkeys,* Collins, 1972; *Bible Stories* (juvenile), Paperback Library, 1973; *The Voices of Masuda,* St. Martin's, 1973; *The Little Book of Sylvanus,* Collins, 1975. Author of play "On Such a Night," first produced at Oldham Coliseum, September 10, 1968; Bible stories recorded on long playing records, fifteen albums, 1963—.

WORK IN PROGRESS: You Have a Minute, Lord, a book of prayers for bothered men, completion expected in 1976; *Bible Stories* Volume II, 1977.

SIDELIGHTS: Kossoff has presented his Bible stories on radio and television; scripts from these presentations have been performed on record albums. Now he tells his stories in solo performances. He has programs for adults and for children.

* * *

KOVACH, Francis J(oseph) 1918-

PERSONAL: Born July 19, 1918, in Budapest, Hungary; son of Joseph and Anna (Roch) Kovach; married Elizabeth W. Thokoly, July 19, 1942; children: Elizabeth (Mrs. James Cowan), Akos, Leslie, Agnes, Thomas. *Education:* University of Budapest, Absolutorium, 1943; University of Cologne, Ph.D. (summa cum laude), 1959. *Home:* 1426 Beverly Hills, Norman, Okla. 73069. *Office:* Department of Philosophy, University of Oklahoma, Norman, Okla. 73069.

CAREER: High school instructor in Budapest, Hungary, 1943-44; high school teacher and principal in Niederaudorf, Germany, 1947-49, and Luttensee, Germany, 1949-51; College of St. Scholastica, Duluth, Minn., instructor, 1954-55, assistant professor of philosophy, 1955-59; St. Benedict's College, Atchison, Kan., assistant professor of philosophy, 1959-62; Mount St. Scholastica College, Atchison, Kan., assistant professor of philosophy, 1959-62; Villanova University, Villanova, Pa., assistant professor of philosophy, 1962-64; University of Oklahoma, Norman, Skogsberg Associate Professor of Philosophy, 1964-69, professor of philosophy, 1969—.

MEMBER: Societe Internationale pour l'etude de la philosophie medievale, International Scotistic Society, American Catholic Philosophical Association (president of North Central chapter, 1958), American Society for Aesthetics, British Society for Aesthetics, Southwestern Philosophical Society.

WRITINGS: Die Aesthetik des Thomas von Aquin: Eine Genetische und Systematische Analyse (title means "The Aesthetics of Thomas Aquinas: A Genetic and Systematic Analysis"), de Gruyter, 1961; *Philosophy of Beauty,* University of Oklahoma Press, 1974; (contributor) W. Horosz and T. Clements, editors, *Religion and Human Purpose,* Warren Green, in press. Contributor to *New Catholic Encyclopedia.* Contributor of articles and reviews to American and foreign professional journals. Guest editor of *Southwestern Journal of Philosophy,* July, 1974.

WORK IN PROGRESS: Causal Contiguity: An Historico-Critical Analysis; Essays on Causality; research on philosophy of art and on a theory of ethics.

SIDELIGHTS: Kovach writes: "I wrote my *Philosophy of Beauty* and have taught aesthetics for some eighteen years to fight the present trend of viewing beauty merely as being 'in the eye of the beholder,' rather than a quality of natural things and artworks, which, when intuited, delights us and enriches our lives immensely."

* * *

KOWNSLAR, Allan O(wen) 1935-

PERSONAL: Born September 5, 1935, in Wichita Falls, Tex.; son of Dorsey Taylor and Ruth Lorene (Jackson) Kownslar; married Marguerite Louise Hanicak (a teacher), August 19, 1961; children: Donald Taylor, Edward Jonathan. *Education:* Trinity University, San Antonio, Tex., B.A., 1957, M.A., 1960; University of Massachusetts, further graduate study, 1961-63; Carnegie-Mellon University, Ph.D., 1969. *Home:* 7922 Thornhill, San Antonio, Tex. 78209. *Office:* Department of History, Trinity University, San Antonio, Tex. 78284.

CAREER: Teacher in public schools in San Antonio, Tex., 1957-60; San Antonio College, San Antonio, Tex., instructor in history, 1960-61; teacher in public schools in Amherst, Mass., 1961-67; Carnegie-Mellon University, Pittsburgh, Pa., co-director of basic learning project in American history at Curriculum Development Center, 1967-69, research historian and associate professor of history, 1969-70; Trinity University, San Antonio, Tex., associate professor of history, 1970—.

MEMBER: American Historical Association, National Council for the Social Studies, Texas State Historical Association, Texas Council for the Social Studies, Social Science Education Consortium (Boulder, Colo.), Bexar County Council for the Social Studies, Bexar County Social Studies Supervisor's Association, Region XX Social Study Council.

WRITINGS: (Contributor) New Approaches to the Teaching of Social Studies, Yale University Press, 1966; (with Donald B. Frizzle) Discovering American History (for high school students), with activity workbook, testing program, teacher's manuals, and audio-visual kits, Holt, 1967, new edition, 1974; (with Frizzle) Discovering American History: A Rationale, Holt, 1967; Manifest Destiny and Expansionism in the 1840's, Heath, 1967; (editor and contributor) The Americans: A New History of the United States (for junior high school students), with workbook, teacher's manual, testing program, and audio-visual kit, American Heritage Publishing, 1970, 2nd edition, 1974; (with others) The New Social Studies for the Slow Learner: A Rationale for a Junior High School American History Course, American Heritage Publishing, 1970; The Progressive Era: Tradition in a Changing Society, 1900-1917, Heath, 1970; The Texans: Their Land and History (for junior high school students), with teacher's manual and testing program, American Heritage Publishing, 1972; (with William R. Fiedler) Inquiring about American History (for elementary school students), with teacher's manual, testing program, and audio-visual kit, Holt, 1972; (editor and contributor) Teaching American History: The Quest for Relevancy (yearbook of the National Council for the Social Studies), National Council for the Social Studies, 1974; Tips for Teaching about the Bicentennial, Social Science Education Consortium, 1975; (with Terry L. Smart) A New World History (for high school students), with teacher's manual and testing program, Holt, in press. Contributor to professional journals.

SIDELIGHTS: Kownslar appears as the teacher in "Teaching History to Basic Learners" (demonstration films), Holt, 1969.

*   *   *

KOZOL, Jonathan 1936-

PERSONAL: Born September 5, 1936, in Boston, Mass.; son of Harry (a physician) and Ruth (Massell) Kozol. Education: Harvard University, B.A., 1958; graduate study, Magdalen College, Oxford, 1958-59. Politics: Independent. Religion: Jewish. Residence: Boston, Mass. Agent: Brandt & Brandt, 101 Park Ave., New York, N.Y. 10017.

CAREER: Elementary School teacher in Boston, Mass., 1964-65, and in Newton, Mass., 1966-68; Storefront Learning Center, Boston, educational director, 1968-71. Trustee, New School for Children, Roxbury, Mass.; visiting lecturer, Yale University, 1969 and at over 16 U.S. universities, 1971-75; instructor at Center for Intercultural Documentation, Cuernavaca, Mexico, 1969, 1970, and 1974; consultant to U.S. Office of Education, 1965 and 1966. Member: Authors Guild, American P.E.N. Center, Congress on Racial Equality. Awards, honors: Rhodes Scholar, 1958-59; Olympia Award, 1962; Saxton fellowship in creative writing from Harper & Row, 1962; National Book Award, 1968, for Death at an Early Age; Guggenheim fellowship, 1970; Field Foundation fellowship, 1972; Ford Foundation fellowship, 1974.

WRITINGS: Death at an Early Age: The Destruction of the Hearts and Minds of Negro Children in the Boston Public Schools, Houghton, 1967; Free Schools, Houghton, 1972; The Night is Dark and I Am Far From Home, Houghton, 1975. Also author of The Fume of the Poppies (novel). Contributor to Atlantic Monthly, Life, Look, New Republic, Saturday Review, and Harvard Educational Review.

WORK IN PROGRESS: A handbook for public school students about the distortions in standard textbooks, as yet untitled.

*   *   *

KRAMMER, Arnold Paul 1941-

PERSONAL: Born August 15, 1941, in Chicago, Ill.; son of David and Eva (Vas) Krammer; married Rhoda Miriam Nudelman (an artist and potter), June 19, 1968; children: Adam. Education: University of Wisconsin, Madison, B.S., 1963, M.S., 1965, Ph.D., 1970; University of Vienna, diploma, 1964. Religion: Jewish. Home: 1809 Southwood Dr., College Station, Tex. 77840. Agent: Shirley Burke, 370 East 76th St., New York, N.Y. 10021. Office: Department of History, Texas A & M University, College Station, Tex. 77843.

CAREER: Parsons College, Fairfield, Iowa, instructor in history, 1965-67; Rockford College, Rockford, Ill., assistant professor of history, 1970-74; Texas A & M University, College Station, associate professor of history, 1974—. Has presented radio and television lectures throughout the Midwest. Member: Society for Historians of American Foreign Relations, American Historical Association, American Committee of Historians of the Second World War, Slavic Honor Society, Phi Alpha Theta. Awards, honors: American Council of Learned Societies grant, 1972; American Philosophical Society grant, 1973; National Endowment for the Humanities research grant, 1975; The Forgotten Friendship was named "book of the year" by Jewish Book Council of the Jewish Welfare Board in 1975.

WRITINGS: (Contributor) Walid Khalidi, editor, From Haven to Conquest, Institute for Palestine Studies, 1971; The Forgotten Friendship: Israel and the Soviet Bloc, 1947-1953, University of Illinois Press, 1974. Contributor to more than twenty history and political science journals.

WORK IN PROGRESS: The Captive Enemy: German Prisoners of War in the United States During World War Two; Prisoners of War in Russia, 1917-1924; The History of the Palestine Police, 1920-1948; editing The Great Powers in the Modern Middle East, an anthology of readings.

SIDELIGHTS: Krammer writes that he was "born and raised in a Hungarian household where European history and its languages and customs were as vivid as Chicago's North Side beyond the window. Surviving the rigors of Chicago's public school system, I pursued the study of history first as a student, and now as a teacher, and try to present history with a storyteller's verve and a scholar's care. My research has taken me across Europe a number of times, through Eastern Europe and the Soviet Union, as well as the Middle East, and from the Arab-Israeli War of 1967, to the Russian invasion of Czechoslovakia in August of 1968.''

* * *

KRASILOVSKY, M(arvin) William 1926-

PERSONAL: Born June 16, 1926, in New York, N.Y.; son of Michael and Harriet (Wollner) Krasilovsky; married Phyllis Louise Manning (an author), September 14, 1947; children: Alexis, Jessica, Margaret, Peter. *Education:* Cornell University, B.A., 1947, LL.B., 1949. *Politics:* Democrat. *Religion:* Jewish. *Home:* 1177 Hardscrabble Rd., Chappaqua, N.Y. 10514. *Office:* Feinman & Krasilovsky, 424 Madison Ave., New York, N.Y. 10017.

CAREER: Admitted to Bar of New York State, 1952; U.S. Federal District Court in Alaska, law clerk, 1949-52; American Guild of Authors and Composers, New York, N.Y., associate attorney, 1953-61; Warner Brothers Pictures, New York, attorney, 1961-69; Feinman & Krasilovsky (law firm), New York, partner, 1969—. Guest lecturer at University of Pennsylvania, Yale University, Cornell University, Brigham Young University, and University of Miami; attorney for composers and recording artists. *Military service:* U.S. Navy, 1944-46. *Member:* American Bar Association, Copyright Society (trustee). *Awards, honors:* Deems Taylor Award of American Society of Composers, Authors and Publishers, 1967, for *More About This Business of Music.*

WRITINGS: (With Sidney Shemel) *This Business of Music,* Billboard Publications, 1964, revised and enlarged edition, Watson, 1971; (with Shemel) *More About This Business of Music,* Watson, 1967, revised edition, 1974. Also author of *Art and the Law,* for Volunteer Lawyers for the Arts. Contributor to law and copyright journals, and to *Columbia Teachers College Journal* and *Performing Arts Review.*

* * *

KRAUSS, Ellis S(aunders) 1944-

PERSONAL: Born January 8, 1944, in Memphis, Tenn.; son of Irving and Pearl (Kivel) Krauss; married Carol Draper (a college teacher), March 28, 1969; children: Jennifer Rachel. *Education:* Brooklyn College of the City University of New York, B.A. (cum laude), 1964; Stanford University, M.A., 1965, Ph.D., 1973. *Office:* Department of Political Science, Western Washington State College, Bellingham, Wash. 98225.

CAREER: Western Washington State College, Bellingham, lecturer, 1970-71, assistant professor, 1971-74, associate professor of political science, 1974—. Conducted research at Inter-University Center for the Study of the Japanese Language (Tokyo), 1968-69; visiting scholar at Institute of International Relations, of Sophia University, 1969-70. Assistant coordinator of conference on local oppositions in contemporary Japan and of workshop on conflict in contemporary Japan, both for Social Science Research Council.

MEMBER: American Political Science Association, Association for Asian Studies, Center for Japanese Social and Political Studies. *Awards, honors:* Grants from American Council of Learned Societies-Social Science Research Council, and Japan Foundation, all for research in Japan, 1974-75.

WRITINGS: Japanese Radicals Revisited: Student Protest in Postwar Japan, University of California Press, 1974. Contributor of articles and reviews to political science and Asian studies journals.

SIDELIGHTS: Krauss writes: "I would hope that I can make some contribution to bringing the study of Japan into the mainstream of modern social science. This means both applying the concerns and methods of social science to the Japanese experience and using the Japanese experience to criticize and modify the ethnocentric and culturally limited assumptions of much of social science theory and methodology. I have tried in my own work to avoid being dominated either by the methodologically sophisticated but often intellectually sterile approaches of contemporary political science or by the unsystematic dilettantism of the old-fashioned area specialist.''

* * *

KRAWITZ, Herman E(verett) 1925-

PERSONAL: Born June 5, 1925, in New York, N.Y.; son of Harry Aaron (a merchant) and Sarah (Epstein) Krawitz; married Rhoda Nayor (a clinical psychologist), February 17, 1952; children: David, Joshua. *Education:* City College (now City College of the City University of New York), B.S., 1949. *Religion:* Jewish. *Home:* 27 East 95th St., New York, N.Y. 10028. *Office:* New World Records, 3 East 54th St., New York, N.Y. 10022.

CAREER: Founded University Playhouse on Cape Cod, Mass., 1946; founder and general manager of Falmouth Playhouse, Falmouth, Mass., 1950—, Hyannis Music Circus, Hyannis, Mass., 1951—, and South Shore Music Circus, Cohasset, Mass., 1951—; managing director and producer for theatre companies, 1951-53, including Hasty Pudding of Harvard University, 1951-53, and Brattle Theatre, Cambridge, Mass., 1952-53; Metropolitan Opera, New York, N.Y., production analyst and consultant, 1953-54, administrator of stage departments, 1954-58, business and technical administrator, 1958-63, assistant manager, 1963-72; City College of the City University of New York, New York, N.Y., artist-in-residence and consultant, 1972-75; New World Records, New York, N.Y., founder and president, 1975—. Chairman of administration section of Yale University's School of Drama, 1966—; president, Jodav Productions, 1973—, and executive producer of Columbia Broadcasting System's (CBS) television program "Ailey Celebrates Ellington," 1974, "A Child's Christmas in Wales," with the National Theater of the Deaf, 1974, and "Gianni Schicchi," 1975. Consultant to Rockefeller Foundation, 1973—, and Bernard M. Baruch College of the City University of New York, 1974—. *Military service:* U.S. Army, Signal Corps, 1943-46; became sergeant.

WRITINGS: An Introduction to the Metropolitan Opera House (guide book), Saturday Review Press, 1967; *Chagall at the Met,* Tudor Press, 1971; (with Howard Klein) *Royal American Symphonic Theater,* Macmillan, 1975.

* * *

KREISEL, Henry 1922-

PERSONAL: Born June 5, 1922, in Vienna, Austria; naturalized Canadian citizen; son of David Leo (a salesman) and Helen (Schreier) Kreisel; married Esther Lazerson (an archivist), June 22, 1947; children: Philip. *Education:* University of Toronto, B.A., 1946, M.A., 1947; University of London, Ph.D., 1954. *Religion:* Jewish. *Home:* 12516 66th Ave., Edmonton, Alberta, Canada, T6H 1Y5. *Office:*

Department of English, University of Alberta, Edmonton, Alberta, Canada.

CAREER: University of Alberta, Edmonton, lecturer, 1947-50, assistant professor, 1950-55, associate professor, 1955-59, professor of English, 1959—, head of department, 1961-67, acting dean of graduate studies, 1969-70, academic vice-president, 1970—, member of board of governors, 1966-69. Visiting fellow, Wolfson College, Cambridge, 1975; vice-president of Edmonton Art Gallery, 1969-70; member of Fine Arts Committee of Canadian Government, 1959; member of awards jury of Governor-General's Prizes in Literature, 1966-68; chairman of scholarship committee of Canada Council, 1963-66.

MEMBER: Association of Canadian University Teachers of English (president, 1962-63), Royal Society of Arts (fellow), Association of Academic Staff of University of Alberta (president, 1960-61). *Awards, honors:* President's medal for short story writing from University of Western Ontario, 1960, for "The Travelling Nude."

WRITINGS: The Rich Man (novel), McClelland & Stewart, 1948; (editor and author of introduction) John Heath, *Aphrodite and Other Poems,* Ryerson, 1959; *The Betrayal* (novel), McClelland & Stewart, 1964.

Work has been anthologized in *Modern Canadian Stories,* edited by Roberto Ruberto and Glose Rimanelli, Ryerson, 1962; *The Best American Short Stories,* edited by Martha Foley and David Burnett, Houghton, 1966; *A Book of Canadian Stories,* edited by Desmond Pacey, Ryerson, 1966; *Stories from Western Canada,* edited by Ruby Weibe, Macmillan, 1972.

Author of radio and television plays for Canadian Broadcasting Corp. in the 1950's, for programs including "Anthology," "Stage," and "Wednesday Night." Author of "The Betrayal," adaptation of the novel, performed on "Bob Hope Theatre," 1965. Contributor of articles and stories to literary journals, including *Literary Review, Canadian Forum, Canadian Literature, Tamarack Review, Queen's Quarterly, University of Toronto Quarterly,* and *Prism.*

WORK IN PROGRESS: Fiction; a play; research on the relationship between literature and the other arts in the twentieth century.

SIDELIGHTS: The hero of Kreisel's first novel is a poor Galician Jew who, having fled to Canada in 1915, returns to his birthplace twenty years later in an effort to discover his identity. In *The Betrayal* Kreisel deals with the problem of a Jew who, all but destroyed by the Nazis, succeeds in staying alive with the aim of revenging himself upon the man who once betrayed him. Of himself, Kreisel writes: "I came to this country from Austria, via England, having escaped the Nazis in 1938. In my writings I have used the European as well as the Canadian experience. This double experience, and its reflection in novels and stories, has been my major contribution to the literature of this country." Kreisel's works have been translated into German, Italian, and Swedish.

*   *   *

KRESS, Robert (Lee) 1932-

PERSONAL: Born September 22, 1932, in Jasper, Ind.; son of Oscar Michael (a cabinetmaker) and Stella (Schutz) Kress. *Education:* St. Meinrad's College, B.A., 1954; University of Innsbruck, S.T.B., 1956, S.T.L., 1958, currently a candidate for Ph.D.; University of Notre Dame, M.A.,

1964; Pontifical Gregorian University, graduate study, 1965-67; Pontifical University of St. Thomas Aquinas, S.T.D., 1968. *Politics:* Independent. *Home:* 1712 East Mulberry, Evansville, Ind. 47714. *Office address:* P.O. Box 329, University of Evansville, Evansville, Ind. 47702.

CAREER: Ordained Roman Catholic priest, 1958; assistant pastor for Diocese of Evansville, Ind., 1958-64; Washington Catholic High School, Washington, Ind., superintendent, 1959-64; University of Vincennes, Vincennes, Ind., lecturer in religion, 1964; University of Evansville, Evansville, lecturer in philosophy and religion, 1967-70; St. Meinrad College, St. Meinrad, Ind., lecturer in philosophy and theology, 1967-68; Princeton Theological Seminary, Princeton, N.J., visiting fellow, 1970-71; St. Louis University, School of Divinity, St. Louis, Mo., assistant professor, 1971-73; University of Evansville, associate professor of philosophy and religion, 1973—; Indiana University, School of Medicine, Bloomington, visiting lecturer in biomedical ethics, 1973—. Auxiliary chaplain for U.S. Armed Forces in Europe, 1964-66; chaplain of Newman Center and University Christian Movement, 1967-70; director of Newman Foundation, 1967-70; producer and director of television program, "Moral View," WTVW, 1969; consultant and lecturer. *Member:* Catholic Campus Ministry Association, College Theology Society, Catholic Theological Society of America, Religious Educators Association, Evansville Clergy Ecumenical Association, St. Louis Theological Consortium Inter-faculty Dialogue.

WRITINGS: The Sinful Member of the Holy Church, Angelicum University Press (Rome), 1968; *Whither Womankind?,* Abbey Press, 1975; *Come, Pilgrim: Reconciliation Themes for the Holy Year,* Office of Religious Education, 1975; *How Near the End? The Apocalypse and Modern Man,* Abbey Press, 1976; *Mary, Woman for Today,* Alba House, 1976; *Holy Church, Sinful Church,* Abbey Press, 1976. Contributor of articles and reviews to religious journals.

Translator: Hugo Rahner, editor, *The Parish,* Newman, 1957; A. Laepple, *Key Problems of Genesis,* Paulist Press, 1964. Also translator of articles for journals.

Consulting editor of *Theology Digest,* 1971-75.

WORK IN PROGRESS: Three books; a commentary on the book of relevation, a book on Roman Catholicism as the counter-culture in the United States, and an introduction to Christian tradition for college undergraduates.

SIDELIGHTS: Kress has knowledge of Greek, Latin, German, French, Italian, Spanish, and Dutch. He told *CA:* "I strive to help my students and readers critically examine their heritage and tradition and so to relate to it, whether negatively or positively. I urge them to operate on the basis of the classic question, 'What's it all about?'"

*   *   *

KRESSY, Michael 1936-

PERSONAL: Born December 25, 1936, in New York, N.Y.; son of Edmund F. (an artist) and Maryland (a writer-journalist; maiden name Newcomb) Kressy; married Jean Gleichenhaus (an instructor in nursing), October 1, 1964; children: Peter, Sarah. *Education:* Boston University, B.A., 1959; University of Massachusetts, M.F.A., 1969. *Home address:* Lane Village, Ashburnham, Mass. 01430.

CAREER: White Plains Reporter-Dispatch, White Plains, N.Y., general reporter and feature writer, 1962-63; *New York Daily News,* New York, N.Y., assistant editor of employee magazine, 1963-65; Mount Wachusett Community College, Gardner, Mass., instructor in English, 1969-74; *North Country Pilot*, founder and editor, and *Leominster Tribune*, co-founder, 1975—. Has given poetry readings in New England colleges. *Military service:* U.S. Army, translator, 1959-62; served in Germany. *Member:* American Horticultural Society. *Awards, honors:* University of Massachusetts creative writing fellowship, 1966-69; Grant from Corporation for Public Broadcasting, 1968, for experimental sight-sound play "Earth-Toil and Sesame."

WRITINGS: How to Grow Your Own Vegetables, Meredith Corp., 1973, abridged edition, 1975; (contributor) Nora Barraford, Kenneth Gibbs and Stan Rubin, editors, *Working from Silence* (poems), Kendall-Hunt, 1971.

Author of "Race" (one-act play), first performed in New York, N.Y., at New York Theatre Ensemble, November, 1968; and "Earth-Toil and Sesame," a radio play, Corporation for Public Broadcasting, 1969. Contributor to *College English* and *Agora*. Consultant to Houghton, 1972.

WORK IN PROGRESS: Petal Tones, poems, with drawings by his twin brother, Christopher Kressy; *Emil and the Chocolate Chip Cookie* and *Emil and the Rainbow Balloon*, both for children.

SIDELIGHTS: Kressy writes that since college he has been ". . . haunted by question of man's relation to his environment—whether blight or blessing—and the purity of individual man versus obvious failure of collective man. As inveterate taker to the woods, I believe there are subtle clues communicable only by the poet who has few ulterior motives. Purpose in writing is to encourage real and unreal connections first for myself and by happy accident others."

* * *

KRISHNAMURTI, Jiddu 1895-
(Alcyone)

PERSONAL: Born May 22, 1895, in Madanapalle, India; adopted son of Annie Besant (president of the Theosophical Society). *Education:* Educated privately in England. *Office address:* Krishnamurti Foundation of America, P.O. Box 219, Ojai, Calif. 93023; and Krishnamurti Foundation Trust Ltd., 24 Southend Rd., Beckenham, Kent BR3 1SD, England.

CAREER: Founder and head of Order of the Star in the East, 1911-29; lecturer and writer, 1929—; Krishnamurti Foundation of America, Ojai, Calif., and Krishnamurti Foundation Trust Ltd., Kent, England, president of board of directors, 1969—. Summer lecturer at Ommen, Holland, 1924-39, Saanen, Switzerland, 1961—, and Brockwood Park, Hampshire, England, 1969—.

WRITINGS: (Under pseudonym Alcyone) *At the Feet of the Master*, Rajput Press, 1911; (under pseudonym Alcyone) *Education as Service*, Rajput Press, 1912; *Self-Preparation*, Order of the Star in the East, 1926; *The Kingdom of Happiness*, Boni & Liveright, 1927; *Life in Freedom*, Liveright, 1928; *The Pool of Wisdom, Who Brings the Truth, By What Authority, and Three Poems*, The Star Publishing Trust, 1928; *The Immortal Friend*, Boni & Liveright, 1928; *The Song of Life*, Liveright, 1931; *The Cloth of Gold: A Dance-Drama in Verse with a Dream-Epilogue*, Tuttle, 1951; *Education and the Significance of Life*, Harper, 1953; *The First and Last Freedom*, foreword by Aldous Huxley, Harper, 1954; *Commentaries on Living*, edited by D. Rajagopal, Harper, Volume I, 1956, Volume II, 1958, Volume III, 1960.

Life Ahead, edited by Rajagopal, Harper, 1963; *Think on These Things*, edited by Rajagopal, Harper, 1964; *Talks and Dialogues*, Avon, 1968; *Meditations*, 1969, Krishnamurti Foundation, 1969; *Freedom From the Known*, Harper, 1969; *The Only Revolution*, edited by Mary Lutyens, Harper, 1970; *The Penguin Krishnamurti Reader*, compiled by Lutyens, Harper, 1970; *The Flight of the Eagle*, Servire Publishers, 1971; *The Urgency of Change*, edited by Lutyens, Harper, 1971; *The Impossible Question*, Gollancz, 1972, Harper, 1973; *You are the World*, Harper, 1972; *Tradition and Revolution*, edited by Pupul Jayakar and Sunandra Patwardhan, Fernhill, 1973; *Beyond Violence*, Harper, 1973; *The Awakening of Intelligence*, Harper, 1974; *Early Writings of J. Krishnamurti*, Krishna Press, 1974; *Beginnings of Learning*, Harper, 1975. Talks and discussions have been published by The Star Publishing Trust, and by Krishnamurti Writings.

BIOGRAPHICAL/CRITICAL SOURCES: Emily Luytens, *Candles in the Sun*, Lippincott, 1954; Mary Luytens, *To Be Young: Some Chapters of Autobiography*, Hart-Davis, 1956; Chaman Lal Nahal, *A Conversation With J. Krishnamurti*, Arya Book Depot (New Delhi), 1965; John E. Coleman, *The Quiet Mind*, Harper, 1971; *Time*, June 7, 1971; James Webb, *The Occult Underground*, Library Press, 1974.*

* * *

KRISTOF, Ladis K(ris) D(onabed) 1918-

PERSONAL: Born November 26, 1918, in Cernauti, Romania; came to the United States, 1952, naturalized citizen, 1957; son of Witold (a farmer) and Mary (Zawadzki) Krzystofowicz; married Jane McWilliams (a lecturer and writer), December 29, 1956; children: Nicholas. *Education:* Attended University of Poznan, 1937-39; Reed College, B.A., 1955; University of Chicago, M.A., 1956, Ph.D., 1969. *Religion:* Armenian Catholic. *Home address:* Route 2, Box 430, Gaston, Ore. 97119. *Office:* Department of Political Science, Portland State University, Portland, Ore. 97207.

CAREER: Sovromlemm (Soviet-Romanian Lumber Co.), Piatra Neamt, Romania, regional executive director, 1948; Centre du Livre Suisse, Paris, France, manager, 1951-52; University of Chicago, Chicago, Ill., lecturer in political science, 1958-59; Inter-University Project on the History of the Menshevik Movement, New York, N.Y., associate director, 1959-62; Temple University, Philadelphia, Pa., instructor in political science, 1962-64; Stanford University, Stanford, Calif., research fellow at Hoover Institution, 1964-67; University of Santa Clara, Santa Clara, Calif., assistant professor of political science, 1967-68; Stanford University, associate of Studies of the Communist System, 1968-69; University of Waterloo, Waterloo, Ontario, associate professor of political science, 1969-71; Portland State University, Portland, Ore., associate professor, 1971-75, professor of political science, 1975—. Lecturer at Hunter College of the City University of New York, 1960-61. Member of International Young Men's Christian Association (YMCA) Center (Paris), 1950-52. Member of Yamhill County (Ore.) Democratic Central Committee, 1972—. *Military service:* Romanian Army, Corps of Engineers, 1941-44.

MEMBER: International Political Science Association, American Political Science Association, Association of American Geographers, American Association for the Advancement of Science, American Association for the Advancement of Slavic Studies, American Geographical

Society. *Awards, honors:* Canada Council grant for research at University of Waterloo, 1970-71; Fulbright exchange scholarship, University of Bucharest, 1971.

WRITINGS: (Editor with Alexander Rabinowitch and Janet Rabinowitch, and contributor) *Revolution and Politics in Russia*, Indiana University Press, 1972.

Contributor: Peter A. Toma and Andrew Gyorgy, compilers, *Basic Issues in International Relations*, Allyn & Bacon, 1967; C. A. Fisher, editor, *Essays in Political Geography*, Metheun, 1968; S. P. Chatterjee and S. P. Gupta, editors, *Settlement Geography and Historical and Political Geography*, K. P. Bagchi (Calcutta), Volume III and Volume X, both 1972; G. L. Ulmen, editor, *Festschrift in Honor of K. A. Wittfogel*, Mouton, in press. Contributor of articles, stories and reviews to *New Leader, Slavic Review, Studies in Comparative Communism, Canadian Historical Review, American Political Science Review*, and other international publications.

WORK IN PROGRESS: A Biographical Dictionary of Menshevism; The Geopolitics of Russia.

SIDELIGHTS: Kristof writes: "Among my major interests . . . are the philosophical foundations of the man-nature relationship concepts (especially among the Marxists), Marxist-Christian dialogue (with special reference to Teilhard de Chardin), the nature of charisma."

* * *

KRIZAY, John 1926-

PERSONAL: Born June 14, 1926, in Washington, Pa.; son of Stephen J. and Theresa (Gruden) Krizay; married Jane Garland Isaacs (an administrative assistant), August 18, 1950; children: Claudia Anne. *Education:* Attended Buena Vista College, 1947-48, and University of Alabama, 1948-49; George Washington University, B.A., 1951; Yale University, M.A., 1960. *Home:* 65 Observatory Circle N.W., Washington, D.C. 20008. *Office:* U.S. Department of State, 21st and Virginia Aves. N.W., Washington, D.C. 21025.

CAREER: U.S. Department of State, Washington, D.C., member of staff, 1954-55, served in office of German affairs, 1955-57, second secretary of embassies in Bonn, Germany, 1957-59, and Rio de Janeiro, Brazil, 1960-64, first secretary in Rio de Janeiro, 1964, and Leopoldville, the Congo, 1964-66, deputy director of Office of Regional Economic Policy of the Bureau of American Republics Affairs, 1966-69, director of Office of Regional Economic Policy, 1969-70, research director of Twentieth Century Fund study on financing medical costs in the United States, 1970-71, director of Office of Monetary Affairs of the Bureau of Economics and Business Affairs, 1972—. *Military service:* U.S. Army, 1946-47; became staff sergeant.

MEMBER: American Foreign Service Association, Phi Beta Kappa. *Awards, honors:* Norman B. Welch, M.D. Award for meritorious contribution to the literature of medical economics from National Association of Blue Shield Plans, 1974, for *The Patient As Consumer.*

WRITINGS: The Patient As Consumer, Heath, 1974. Contributor to magazines and newspapers.

WORK IN PROGRESS: Is the State Department Obsolete?, a study of structural defects in the State Department which make it a mistrusted organization in the executive branch in the foreign affairs field.

SIDELIGHTS: Krizay writes: "Advancement in the foreign service turned out to be a road to Dullsville. Rank meant pre-occupation with jurisdictional disputes and boring ceremonial responsibilities. I decided to apply my training in economics and discipline in objective observation to the study of some domestic problems; medical costs seemed interesting and, as I was to learn, complex. . . . People, generally, are not turned on by reasonableness but by fault-finding. Nonetheless, I still have hopes of winning attention for reasonableness and analysis as an effective way of writing about current social problems, not only in medicine but other fields as well. I strongly believe that until people learn to accept the notion that diverse groups responding to legitimate motivational forces can lead to a less than optimal solution without there being a villain somewhere in the piece, solutions to problems will be based on emotion, creating more new problems than they solve."

* * *

KRODEL, Gerhard 1926-

PERSONAL: Born February 7, 1926, in Lichtenstein; naturalized U.S. citizen; son of Karl (a pastor) and Kaethe (Biegel) Krodel; married Joan Krtzmann (an editor), September 6, 1952; children: Elizabeth, Katharine, Karla. *Education:* University of Erlangen, Ph.D., 1950; postdoctoral study at University of Tuebingen, 1962. *Home:* 7314 Boyer St., Philadelphia, Pa. 19119.

CAREER: Ordained minister of Lutheran Church in America; pastor, 1951-55; Capital University, Columbus, Ohio, assistant professor of classical languages, 1953-55; Wartburg Theological Seminary, Dubuque, Iowa, associate professor, 1958-61, professor of New Testament, 1961-64; Lutheran Theological Seminary, Philadelphia, Pa., professor of New Testament, 1964—, dean of faculty, 1973—. Visiting professor at State University of Iowa, 1963, Drew University, 1968, and Crozer Theological Seminary, 1969. President of American board for Syrian Orphanage, Khinbet Kanafar, Lebanon. *Member:* Society of Biblical Literature, Studiorum Novi Testamenti Societas, Institute for Antiquity and Christianity, Institute for Textual Research of the New Testament. *Awards, honors:* Order of Merit from Federal Republic of Germany, 1969; D.D., Susquehanna University, 1969.

WRITINGS: (Translator) E. Kaesemann, *The Testament of Jesus*, Fortress, 1968; (editor with R. Kraft) W. Bauer, *Orthodoxy and Heresy in Earliest Christianity*, Fortress, 1971; (with D. B. Watermulder) *Proclamation: Aids for Interpreting the Lessons of the Church Year, Advent-Christmas*, Fortress, 1973. Contributor to theological journals.

WORK IN PROGRESS: Series editor of "The Witnesses of the New Testament" for Fortress.

AVOCATIONAL INTERESTS: Research on Greek manuscripts of the New Testament (visits to monasteries and libraries in Turkey, Cyprus, and Greece in 1969-70 led to the microfilming of fifty manuscripts which had previously been unknown).

* * *

KRUUK, Hans 1937-

PERSONAL: Born November 10, 1937, in Weesp, Netherlands; son of H. A. and M. F. Kruuk; married Jane Sheila Rollo, April 25, 1964; children: Loeske, Johnny. *Education:* University of Utrecht, Ph.D., 1964. *Politics:* Liberal. *Home:* Riverston, Bridgeview Rd., Aboyne, Aberdeenshire, Scotland. *Office:* Institute of Terrestrial Ecology, Banchory, Scotland.

CAREER: Institute of Terrestrial Ecology, Banchory, Scotland, currently research scientist. *Member:* Association for the Study of Animal Behaviour, British Mammal Society, British Ecological Society. *Awards, honors:* Science Medal from Zoological Society of London, 1974.

WRITINGS: (Translator) *Mammals of Europe,* Collins, 1968; *The Spotted Hyena,* University of Chicago Press, 1972; *Hyaena,* Oxford University Press, 1975.

WORK IN PROGRESS: Behaviour and Ecology of European Badgers; Evolution of Social Behaviour in Carnivores.

AVOCATIONAL INTERESTS: Africa (speaks Ki-Swahili).

* * *

KUBIAK, T(imothy) J(ames) 1942-

PERSONAL: Born November 22, 1942, in Toledo, Ohio; son of Benedict J. (a factory worker) and Alice (Hintz) Kubiak; married Sandra Sue Schlosser (a secretary), June 6, 1964 (divorced November 7, 1975); children: Alex, Sarah. *Education:* University of Toledo, B.A., 1965; Michigan State University, M.A., 1967, Ph.D., 1973. *Religion:* Roman Catholic. *Home:* 929 Vicker's Village, Richmond, Ky. 40475. *Office address:* Box 855, Eastern Kentucky University, Richmond, Ky. 40475.

CAREER: State of Michigan, Highways and Transportation Department, Lansing, planner, 1965-67; Wright State University, Dayton, Ohio, instructor in geography, 1967-71; U.S. Department of Agriculture, Economic Research Service, East Lansing, Mich., research assistant, 1971-73; Eastern Kentucky University, Richmond, assistant professor of geography and planning, 1973—. *Member:* American Institute of Planners, Association of American Geographers, Community Development Society, Gamma Theta Upsilon. *Awards, honors:* National Aeronautics and Space Administration, American Society for Engineering Education summer faculty fellow, 1975.

WRITINGS: The Soup Line, A. S. Barnes, 1973. Contributor of several articles to journals in his field.

WORK IN PROGRESS: A book, *Strip Mining in Kentucky;* an article, "General Aviation Development"; pier fishing techniques.

AVOCATIONAL INTERESTS: Salt-water fishing, oil painting, Bonsai, collecting "collectables," beach-combing.

* * *

KUNHI KRISHNAN, T(aramal) V(anmeri) 1919-

PERSONAL: Born March 13, 1919, in Badagara, Kerala, India; son of Kurup V. (a village magistrate) and Lakshmi (Amma) Kunhambu; married Susheela G., June 1, 1947 (divorced); married Prem Singh (a teacher), September 18, 1968; children: (first marriage) Nandita, Indudharan; (second marriage) Satyajit. *Education:* Madras University, student, 1938-43. *Home:* C151 Greater Kailash, New Delhi 48, India. *Office:* Somaiya Publications, F6 Bank of Baroda Building, Parliament St., New Delhi-1, India.

CAREER: Political activist while in prision, 1943, freelance journalist, 1943-49; *Focus* (news magazine), Madras, India, editor, 1949-50; employed with book translation program, 1950-53; *Mathrubhumi* (daily newspaper), Calicut, India, author of column "Foreign Affairs," 1953-60; Book

Industry Council of South India, and Southern Languages Book Trust, Madras, India, general manager, 1960-67; Hind Pocket Books, New Delhi, India, executive director, 1968; with Somaiya Publications, New Delhi, 1968—. *Member:* Indian Council of World Affairs, Press Club of India.

WRITINGS: Chavan and the Troubled Decade, Somaiya Publications, 1971; *The Unfriendly Friends: India and America,* Indian Book Co., 1974. Contributor to *Atlantic Monthly.* Editor of *Anveshanam* (a literary monthly magazine).

SIDELIGHTS: Kunhi Krishnan writes that his "particular interest is politics, which perhaps is an offshoot of political activity, and imprisonment for political offence during the British rule in India."

* * *

KUO, Ting-yee 1904(?)-1975

1904(?)—September 14, 1975; Chinese-born historian, educator, and author of books in his field. Obituaries: *New York Times,* September 16, 1975.

* * *

KURLAND, Michael 1938-
(Jennifer Plum)

PERSONAL: Born March 1, 1938, in New York, N.Y.; son of Jack (a manufacturer) and Stephanie (a dress designer; maiden name, Yacht) Kurland. *Education:* Attended Hiram College, 1955-56, University of Maryland, foreign study in Germany, 1960-61, and Columbia University, 1962-64. *Politics:* Whig. *Religion:* Humanist. *Residence:* Kensington, Calif. *Agent:* Richard Curtis, 156 East 52nd St., New York, N.Y. 10022.

CAREER: Full-time writer, 1963—. High school English teacher in Ojai, Calif., 1968; managing editor, *Crawdaddy Magazine,* 1969. Occasional director of plays for Squirrel Hill Theatre, 1972—. *Military service:* U.S. Army Intelligence, 1958-62. *Member:* Authors Guild, Mystery Writers of America, Science Fiction Writers of America, Institute for Twenty-First Century Studies, Baker Street Irregulars. *Awards, honors:* Edgar scroll from Mystery Writers of America, 1971, for *A Plague of Spies.*

WRITINGS—All fiction: *Mission: Third Force,* Pyramid Publications, 1967; *Mission: Tank War,* Pyramid Publications, 1968; *A Plague of Spies,* Pyramid Publications, 1969; *The Unicorn Girl,* Pyramid Publications, 1969; *Transmission Error,* Pyramid Publications, 1971; (under pseudonym Jennifer Plum) *The Secret of Benjamin Square,* Lancer Books, 1972; *The Whenabouts of Burr,* Daw Books, 1975; *Pluribus,* Doubleday, 1975. Writer of "Impropa-Ganda," column in *Berkeley Barb,* 1967.

WORK IN PROGRESS: A Victorian suspense-detective novel, tentatively titled *The Infernal Device.*

* * *

KUSHNER, Rose 1929-

PERSONAL: Born June 22, 1929, in Baltimore, Md.; daughter of Israel (a tailor) and Fannie (Gravitz) Rehert; married Harvey David Kushner (a systems analyst); children: Gantt Alexander, Todd Roger, Lesley Kim. *Education:* Attended Johns Hopkins University, 1946-47, Baltimore Junior College, 1950-51, and Montgomery Community College, Rockville, Md., 1963-65; University of Maryland, B.S. (summa cum laude), 1972. *Politics:* "Democratic/liberal—leftish." *Religion:* Jewish. *Home:* 9607 Kingston Rd., Kensington, Md. 20795. *Agent:* Elaine Markson, 44 Greenwich Ave., New York, N.Y. 10011. *Office:* Breast Cancer Advisory Center, P.O. Box 422, Kensington, Md. 20795.

CAREER: Free-lance writer (specializing in medical matters, Jewish/Israeli issues, and political topics), 1960—. Vice-president of Breast Cancer Advisory Center. *Member:* Pavlovian Society of North America, American Medical Writers Association, Congressional Periodicals Press Gallery, White House Correspondents Association, Sigma Delta Chi, Kappa Tau Alpha, Phi Kappa Phi. *Awards, honors:* National Media Award from American Psychological Association, 1974, for newspaper publications.

WRITINGS: Breast Cancer: A Personal History and an Investigative Report, Harcourt, 1975. Contributor to magazines and newspapers.

WORK IN PROGRESS: Continuing research on the epidemiology, etiology, and detection and treatment of breast cancer in women in the United States and abroad.

SIDELIGHTS: Rose Kushner writes: "I have rarely been involved in community political or charitable activities except as a writer, and this also applies to broader issues. Everyone has a different way to help a cause; mine has been to write articles for or against, on a voluntary basis. To sum up, much of my writing can be considered 'journalistic social work,' my way of stuffing envelopes or licking stamps."

* * *

LAAS, William M. 1910(?)-1975

1910(?)—October 6, 1975; American editor, newspaperman, and author of books on a variety of topics. Obituaries: *New York Times,* October 8, 1975; *Publishers Weekly,* October 27, 1975.

* * *

LACY, Norris J(oiner) 1940-

PERSONAL: Born March 8, 1940, in Hopkinsville, Ky.; son of Edwin Vemont (a cook) and Lillian (Joiner) Lacy; married Faye Tison (a college teacher), December 21, 1962. *Education:* Murray State University, A.B., 1962; Middlebury College, graduate study, summer, 1962; Indiana University, M.A., 1963, Ph.D., 1967. *Home:* 1904 Countryside Lane, Lawrence, Kan. 66044. *Office:* Department of French, University of Kansas, Lawrence, Kan. 66045.

CAREER: Indiana University, Bloomington, lecturer in French, 1965-66; University of Kansas, Lawrence, assistant professor, 1966-70, associate professor, 1970-75, professor of French language and literature, 1975—, assistant chairman of French and Italian, 1969-72. Visiting professor at University of California, Los Angeles, 1975-76. Has worked as jazz musician and music teacher. *Member:* International Arthurian Society, Mediaeval Academy of America, Modern Language Association of America, American Association of Teachers of French, Societe Rencesvals. *Awards, honors:* Woodrow Wilson fellowship, 1962-63; grants from American Philosophical Society, 1969, American Council of Learned Societies, 1973, and National Endowment for the Humanities, 1975.

WRITINGS: (Editor and contributor) *A Medieval French*

Miscellany, Humanistic Series, University of Kansas, 1972; (editor and author of introduction) J. N. Carman, translator, *From Camelot to Joyous Guard: The Old French "La Mort le Roi Artu",* University Press of Kansas, 1974; (editor) *26 Chansons d'amour de la Renaissance* (title means "26 Renaissance Love Songs"), University Press of Kansas, 1975. Contributor to language and literature journals.

WORK IN PROGRESS: The Craft of Medieval Romance: Narrative Technique in Chretien de Troyes.

AVOCATIONAL INTERESTS: Photography, music.

* * *

LAIRD, Carobeth 1895-

PERSONAL: Born July 20, 1895, in Coleman, Tex.; daughter of James Harvey (an editor) and Emma Cora (Chaddock) Tucker; married John Peabody Harrington, 1916 (divorced, 1923); married George Laird, August 23, 1923 (died April 13, 1940); children: Elizabeth Dresser, Awona, Frances Georgia Culp, Rosaleen Ragsdale, Oliver, Margaret Schweickert, George Theodore. *Education:* Very little formal education. *Politics:* "Liberal, present affiliation, democrat." *Religion:* "Vital to my existence yet impossible to categorize; continually evolving; based largely on the Beatitudes, yet not altogether Christian at its roots." *Home and office:* 13761 Tobiasson Rd., Poway, Calif. 92064.

CAREER: Christian Science practitioner, 1933-63.

WRITINGS: Encounter with an Angry God, Malki Museum Press (Banning, Calif.), 1975; *The Chemehuevis,* Malki Museum Press, 1976. Author of pamphlets. Contributor of poems and articles to *Christian Science Journal* and *Christian Science Sentinel.* Contributing editor, *Journal of California Anthropology,* 1974—.

WORK IN PROGRESS: A book from personal experience on nursing care for the aged; preliminary work for a book of Chemehuevi Indian myths.

SIDELIGHTS: Carobeth Laird told *CA:* "Although my first book has just been published, I am by no means a beginning author. I can never remember a time when I was not interested in writing and trying to teach myself the art of writing. My life appears to have been divided by abrupt dislocations into more or less unrelated segments; yet there is an inner continuity, and every phase has contributed to my development. I would not blot out any of it. I am glad to have traveled over most of the United States by car at a time when towns were less homogenized than they now are and rural areas comparatively untouched. In my adolescence I traveled with my parents in Mexico for several months each year, and learned a little something of the country and the language. It was in Mexico that I first heard English spoken without Southern accent or flat Texas drawl, and began my long love affair with the spoken as well as the written language."

* * *

LAMONT, Helen Lamb 1906(?)-1975
(Helen B. Lamb)

1906(?)—July 21, 1975; American economist, educator, anti-war activist, and author of books on history and related topics. Obituaries: *AB Bookman's Weekly,* August 25, 1975; *New York Times,* September 9, 1975.

LANDSVERK, O(le) G(odfred) 1901-

PERSONAL: Born November 19, 1901, in Whalen, Minn.; son of Tarkjil (a farmer, painter, and poet) and Helga (Oian) Landsverk; married Nordis Valborg Rothnem, December 22, 1940; children: Sonia (Mrs. Gerry Genett), David, Kirsten (Mrs. Warren Netz). *Education:* Luther College, B.A., 1924; University of Minnesota, M.A., 1930; University of Chicago, Ph.D., 1939. *Home and office:* Rushford Ave. at Burr Oak, Rushford, Minn. 55971.

CAREER: High school principal in Goodell, Iowa, 1924-25, Lane, S.D., 1925-27, superintendent of schools, 1927-29; Maquoketa Junior College, Maquoketa, Iowa, instructor in physics and mathematics, 1930-37; Virginia Junior College, Virginia, Minn., instructor in physics and mathematics, 1939-43; University of Chicago Metallurgical Laboratory, Chicago, Ill., research physicist, 1943-46; Argonne National Labortory, Chicago, member of Army-Navy Task Force on atomic weapons, 1946-47; Landsverk Electrometer Co., Chicago and Glendale, Calif., president and chairman of board of directors, 1947-68; lecturer and writer on Norse exploration of North America, 1968—. Teacher of civilian pilot training and civil air regulations, Hibbing State Junior College (now Mesabi State Junior College) Virginia Junior College, 1940-42; instructor, University of Chicago, summer, 1943. Member of executive board, Norwegian-American Museum, 1965—; director, Landsverk Foundation, 1968—. *Member:* World League of Norsemen (president, Los Angeles chapter, 1964-67), Norwegian-American Historical Association (life member), American-Scandinavian Foundation, New England Antiquities Association, Leif Erikson Association of Los Angeles (director of research). *Awards, honors:* Distinguished Service award from Luther College, 1968, for research on Norse presence in the U.S. before Columbus.

WRITINGS: The Kensington Stone: A Reappraisal, Church Press, 1962; (with Alf Monge) *Norse Medieval Cryptology in Runic Carvings,* Norseman Press, 1967; *Ancient Norse Messages on American Stones,* Norseman Press, 1969; *Runic Records of Norsemen in America,* Twayne, 1974. Contributor of articles to archaeological and technical journals, including *Anthropological Journal of Canada* and *Man in the Northwest.*

WORK IN PROGRESS: Continued research and writing on runic inscriptions found in North America.

SIDELIGHTS: Landsverk told *CA:* "As an American of Norwegian descent, I have had a continuing interest in the history of the Norwegian people, particularly the centuries of its greatest expansion and world influence, during the so-called Viking period." As part of his interest in Norwegian exploration, Landsverk spearheaded a campaign to request Congress to establish October 9th as Leif Erikson Day. The resolution was signed into effect in 1964. Landsverk was one of the scientists involved in the atomic bomb tests at Bikini Atoll in 1946.

*   *   *

LANE, Mark 1927-

PERSONAL: Born February 24, 1927, in New York, N.Y.; son of Harry A. (a certified public accountant) and Elizabeth (Brown) Lane. *Education:* Attended Long Island University; Brooklyn Law School, L.L.D., 1951. *Politics:* Democrat. *Home and office:* 105 Second Ave. N.E., Washington, D.C. 20002.

CAREER: Admitted to New York State Bar, 1951; private practice in New York City, 1951-60; New York State Democratic Assemblyman from East Harlem and Yorkville, 1960-62; Catholic University of America, Washington, D.C., professor of law, 1975—. Organizer of The Covered Wagon, Mountain Home, Idaho, 1971; founder and lawyer, Wounded Knee Legal Defense/Offense Committee, 1973—; director, Citizens Commission for Inquiry (CCI), 1975—. Author, filmmaker and lecturer. *Military service:* U.S. Army, 1945-47.

WRITINGS: Rush to Judgment, Holt, 1966; *A Citizen's Dissent,* Holt, 1968; *Chicago Eyewitness,* Astor-Honor, 1968; *Arcadia,* Holt, 1970; *Conversations with Americans,* Simon & Schuster, 1970; (with Donald Freed) *Executive Action,* Dell, 1973. Producer and interviewer in film, "Rush to Judgment," shown by British Broadcasting Corp., January, 1967; scriptwriter with Donald Freed of film, "Executive Action," 1973. Editor of *Helping Hand* (a G.I. newspaper), 1971-73; and *Citizen's Quarterly* (publication of Citizens Commission for Inquiry), 1975—.

WORK IN PROGRESS: A film about the 1973 occupation of Wounded Knee, S.D.; a book about the intelligence community and the assassination of President Kennedy.

SIDELIGHTS: Lane represented Lee Harvey Oswald's interests on behalf of his family at the Warren Commission's inquiry into the assassination of John F. Kennedy. Since the publication of his first book, a rebuke of the commission's conduct and conclusions, he has been actively working for a reexamination of the tragedy. In 1975, Lane was appointed director of the Citizens Commission of Inquiry. This private organization is attempting to "make the American people, the media and Congress aware of the obfuscation by CIA, FBI and other federal police organizations of the facts surrounding the assassination of President John F. Kennedy, the focal point of its efforts hopefully to culminate in a Congressional investigation into the cover-up of these facts and the assassination itself."

Also active in the civil rights movement, Lane was the first legislator arrested on a Freedom Ride (1961), and was the write-in vice-presidential candidate in Dick Gregory's campaign for the presidency in 1968. Lane told *CA:* "I am interested in organizing and working together with people so that we may, collectively, control our destiny."

BIOGRAPHICAL/CRITICAL SOURCES: Village Voice, June 16, 1966; *Playboy,* February, 1967.

*   *   *

LANGGUTH, A(rthur) J(ohn) 1933-

PERSONAL: Born July 11, 1933, in Minneapolis, Minn.; son of Arthur J. and Doris (Turnquist) Langguth. *Education:* Harvard University, A.B., 1955. *Home:* c/o 11935 Kling St., North Hollywood, Calif. 91607. *Agent:* Lynn Nesbit, International Creative Management, 40 West 57th St., New York, N.Y. 10019.

CAREER: Look Magazine, reporter in Washington, D.C., 1959; *Valley Times,* North Hollywood, Calif., reporter, 1960-63; *New York Times,* New York, N.Y., reporter, 1963-65; author. *Military service:* U.S. Army, 1956-58.

WRITINGS: Jesus Christs (novel), Harper, 1968; *Wedlock* (novel), Knopf, 1972; *Marksman* (novel), Harper, 1974; *Macumba: White and Black Magic in Brazil,* Harper, 1975.

*   *   *

LANSING, Alfred 1921-1975

July 21, 1921—August 27, 1975; American editor, and author of historical accounts and other works. Obituaries: *New York Times,* September 4, 1975. (See index for previous *CA* sketch)

* * *

LA PIETRA, Mary 1929-
(Maria Patanne)

PERSONAL: Born November 24, 1929, in Chicago, Ill.; daughter of John Marshall (an accountant) and Margaret (Kloss) Regan; married Vincent LaPietra (a pricing coordinator), January 28, 1956; children: James, Jeanne, Joseph, Mary. *Education:* Attended Triton Junior College. *Politics:* "Avoid them like the plague." *Religion:* Roman Catholic. *Home:* 33 MacArthur Dr., Northlake, Ill. 60164.

CAREER: Held various clerical positions, 1948-52; *Oakleaves* Newspaper, Oak Park, Ill., re-writer, 1952-54; National Association of Retail Grocers, Chicago, Ill., re-writer for magazine *Nargus Bulletin,* 1960-64; City of Northlake, Ill., in public relations, 1971-75; Northlake Public Library, Northlake, Ill., in public relations, 1975—. Co-founder of Northlake Community Theatre.

MEMBER: Children's Reading Round Table, New World Poets Club, Penhandlers, Off-Campus Writers Workshop. *Awards, honors:* Wilmette Children's Theatre awards for plays, 1964, for "A Tomahawk for Christmas," 1973, for "Paddy's Moon," and honorable mention, 1974, for "Gypsy Magic."

WRITINGS—For children: *Paddy's Moon,* Erle Press, 1951; *The King's Donkey,* Van Kampen Press, 1954; *The Mystery in Santa's Workshop,* Westward Ho Press, 1974; *Innkeeper for a King,* David Cook, 1974; *Aram Finds the Master,* David Cook, 1974; *Three Dreams in Bethlehem,* David Cook, 1975; *The Shawl of Waiting* (novel), David Cook, 1976; *A Tomahawk for Christmas* (novel), David Cook, 1976; *Wine for Cana,* David Cook, in press; *Journey to Jerusalem,* David Cook, in press.

Musical plays for children; all three-act: "A Tomahawk for Christmas," 1964; "Paddy's Moon," first performed in Wilmette, Ill., at Wilmette Children's Theatre, October, 1973; "Gypsy Magic," 1974. Contributor of poetry, under pseudonym Maria Patanne, to *New World.*

WORK IN PROGRESS: Two additional sequels to *The Shawl of Waiting;* a musical play for children; a novel for pre-teenagers.

SIDELIGHTS: Mary LaPietra writes: "I have been writing since I knew which end of a pencil you wrote with and which you chewed on (and I still do a good bit of the latter). I am an incurable romantic. I write mainly to entertain, and if there always seems to be a 'moral to the story,' that is probably because of my strict Catholic upbringing. I am definitely NOT a women's libber, having found my own liberation in the pursuit of my career. I deplore the fact that even in children's books today an author has little chance of publishing if there are any 'forbidden' stereotyped characters. For shame! You have shown mother in an apron and father going off to the office! I have written many of these old-fashioned type stories—and they are sitting in my file because the publishers are afraid to touch them." She adds that she is one of eleven children, a "depression baby," and that when she hears the wolf at the door she hires herself out as a temporary typist.

* * *

LARIMORE, Bertha B(urnham) 1915-

PERSONAL: Born November 21, 1915, in Blanding, Utah;

daughter of Wallace A. (a cattleman) and Emma (Rogers) Burnham; married Earl A. Larimore, October 22, 1939 (died July 31, 1967); children: Virginia, Wallace E., Stuart B. *Education:* Attended Ross Business College and Weber State College. *Religion:* Church of Jesus Christ of Latter-day Saints. *Home:* 5130 South 2175 W., Roy, Utah 84067. *Office:* Hill Air Force Base, Utah 84406.

CAREER: U.S. Department of Agriculture, Farm Security Administration, Cortez, Colo., clerk-typist, 1938-39; Douglas Aircraft Co., El Segundo, Calif., key punch operator, 1953-54; Hill Air Force Base, Utah, procurement clerk, 1955-59, editor for technical publications, 1959-61, education counselor for the military, 1961—; lecturer, 1972—. *Member:* Utah State Poetry Society, League of Utah Writers, Aprender Guild (Roy, Utah; vice-president, 1971-73; president, 1973-75).

WRITINGS: Kids Tell It Like It Is!, Horizon, 1972; *Sprouting for All Seasons,* Horizon, 1975. Writer for comedienne Phyllis Diller. Contributor of stories, poems, and articles to literary journals and to popular magazines, including *In, Parents' Magazine, Fate, Better Camping, Humorama, Family Weekly,* and *Utah Sings.*

WORK IN PROGRESS: At the Foot of the Hill, a novel; *Operation Madhouse,* humor; a food and recipe book; research for a humorous travel book.

SIDELIGHTS: Bertha Larimore writes: "I enjoy all types of writing, but particularly humorous material. Also, I prefer to write fiction and not be bound by specific facts." *Avocational interests:* Oil painting, gardening, knitting, dancing, sewing, cooking, playing piano, travel (especially Bolivia and Peru).

* * *

LAROM, Henry V. 1903(?)-1975

1903(?)—December 7, 1975; American college dean, educator, and author of books for children. Obituaries: *New York Times,* December 9, 1975; *AB Bookman's Weekly,* January 26, 1976.

* * *

LARSON, Simeon 1925-

PERSONAL: Born January 21, 1925, in Union City, N.J.; son of Jeronim and Cecelia (Milenkia) Larson; married Angelina T. Puglisi (a teacher), September 3, 1967; children: Lori Ann. *Education:* New York University, B.A., 1952; City College of the City University of New York, M.A., 1963; New School for Social Research, Ph.D., 1971. *Home:* 15 Noel Lane, East Brunswick, N.J. 08816. *Office:* Department of Labor Studies, Rutgers University, 14 College Ave., New Brunswick, N.J. 08903.

CAREER: Worker in the garment industry; organizer, 1956-58, then business agent, 1958-65, for International Ladies' Garment Workers' Union, in the New Jersey area; Rutgers University, New Brunswick, N.J., professor of labor studies, 1970—. Consultant to Thomas A. Edison College. *Military service:* U.S. Navy, 1944-46. *Member:* American Federation of Teachers, University College Labor Education Association.

WRITINGS: Labor and Foreign Policy: Gompers, the American Federation of Labor, and the First World War, Fairleigh Dickinson University Press, 1975. Contributor to *Historian.*

WORK IN PROGRESS: Research for a book on American labor, foreign policy, and national defense from 1920 to the present.

SIDELIGHTS: Larson was active in organizing the first union for shipping clerks in the dress industry in which the membership was predominantly black and Spanish-speaking.

* * *

LARY, N(ikita) M(ichael) 1940-

PERSONAL: Born July 6, 1940, in Washington, D.C.; son of Hal Buckner (an economist) and Nathalie (Boborykine) Lary; married Diana Cecilia Margaret Lainson (a sinologist), September 1, 1965; children: Tatiana Marie, Anna Nathalie. Education: Haverford College, B.A., 1960; King's College, Cambridge, B.A., 1963, M.A., 1967; University of Sussex, D.Phil., 1969. Religion: Russian Orthodox. Home address: P.O. Box 114, King City, Ontario, Canada L0G 1K0. Agent: A. D. Peters, 11 Buckingham St., London W.C.2, England. Office: Division of Humanities (Arts), York University, Toronto, Ontario, Canada M3J 1P3.

CAREER: Library of Congress, Washington, D.C., editor, 1960-61; York University, Toronto, Ontario, assistant professor, 1969-74, associate professor of humanities and English, 1974—.

WRITINGS: (Translator) Bertrand de Jouvenel, The Art of Conjecture, Basic Books, 1967; Dostoevsky and Dickens: A Study of Literary Influence, Routledge & Kegan Paul, 1973.

WORK IN PROGRESS: Russian Film-Adaptations of Dostoevsky's Works; Russian Notions of Liberalism, completion expected in 1978.

SIDELIGHTS: Lary writes: "My origins are American and Russian: the countries I have lived in and know are the United States, Switzerland, England, and Canada; in addition to English, the languages I am more or less at home in are French and Russian. With my background I felt from the start that literature had to be understood in its social, historical and ideological context. Later I was led to consider what a literary work means when it is transported into a different cultural and historical context (and of course what the work means to me in my particular situation)."

* * *

LATHROP, JoAnna 1931-

PERSONAL: Born December 6, 1931, in Lamar, Colo.; daughter of Leonard Ellis (an owner and operator of a retail bakery) and Mabel (Moss) Lathrop. Education: University of Colorado, B.A., 1953; San Fernando Valley State University (now California State University, Northridge), M.A., 1967; University of Nebraska, Ph.D., 1976. Home: 626 Colorado Ave., Ordway, Colo. 81063. Office: Willa Cather Memorial and Educational Foundation, Red Cloud, Neb. 68970.

CAREER: High school English teacher in Colorado, 1953-68; University of Nebraska, Lincoln, instructor in English, 1969-75; Willa Cather Memorial and Educational Foundation, Red Cloud, Neb., director of research, summer, 1975, director of foundation, 1975—. Member: National Education Association, National Council of Teachers of English, Nebraska State Education Association.

WRITINGS: Willa Cather: A Checklist of Her Published Writing, University of Nebraska Press, 1975. Contributor to Prairie Schooner.

WORK IN PROGRESS: Research on framing devices in Willa Cather and Joseph Conrad; research on the possessive individual in Willa Cather.

* * *

LAUBENTHAL, Sanders Anne 1943-

PERSONAL: Born December 25, 1943, in Mobile, Ala.; daughter of Wilbert J. (an accountant) and Mabel (a nurse; maiden name, Sanders) Laubenthal. Education: Spring Hill College, B.A. (summa cum laude), 1965; University of Alabama, M.A., 1967, Ph.D., 1970. Politics: "Basically independent." Religion: Roman Catholic. Office address: HQ 13th Air Force, History Office, Bldg. 2129, Clark Air Base, Philippines.

CAREER: Head Start Project, Mobile, Ala., medical coordinator, 1965; Latin teacher in Mobile, Ala., 1965-66; Troy State University, Troy, Ala., assistant professor of English, 1969-72; U.S. Air Force, Maxwell Air Force Base, Ala., education and training officer, 1973-76, Clark Air Base, Philippines, deputy historian, 1976—, current rank, first lieutenant. Member: Modern Language Association of America, Air Force Association, Historic Mobile Preservation Society, Landmarks Foundation (Montgomery, Ala.), Maxwell AFB Junior Officer Council (vice-president, 1975-76). Awards, honors: Catholic Poetry Association of America award, 1964; National Defense Education Act fellow, 1966-70; Alabama State Poetry Day award, 1969.

WRITINGS: Songs of Mobile (poems), Spring Hill College Press, 1962; The Gates of Wonder (poems), Belmary, 1966; The Last Confederate (novel), Belmary, 1967; Interlude and Other Poems, Belmary, 1969; Excalibur (novel), Ballantine, 1973. Author of four textbooks for Air Force correspondence courses.

WORK IN PROGRESS: A book of connected stories about an imaginary civilization, Terelinderi; a novel set in the twelfth century, Caer Mair; two monographs on Air Force history.

SIDELIGHTS: Laubenthal told CA: "When I was twelve, I decided to be a writer—and I have been at it ever since. I owe a lot to the C. S. Lewis—Charles Williams—J.R.R. Tolkien group. I love to travel—have been to Mexico, Europe, and the Middle East, sometimes on less than $5 a day. This spring I expect to go to the Far East as a military historian."

* * *

LAUGHLIN, Henry Prather 1916-

PERSONAL: Born June 25, 1916, in Hagerstown, Md.; son of John Royer and Myrtle Frances (Binkley) Laughlin; married Marion Page Durkee, June 2, 1941; children: Constance Ann Laughlin Kuhn, John Royer, Robert Scott, Barbara Hilton Laughlin Thornton, Deborah Page. Education: Attended Johns Hopkins University, 1936, 1938; Ursinus College, B.S., 1938; Temple University, M.D., 1941; Washington-Baltimore Psychoanalytic Institute, psychoanalytic training, 1947-52. Home: Seven Springs Farm, Talbot Run Rd., Route 4, Box 292, Mount Airy, Md. 21771. Office: Montgomery House, Suite 207, 4401 East West Highway, Bethesda, Md. 20014; and Parkview Medical Center, 516 Trail Ave., Frederick, Md. 21701.

CAREER: Intern at U.S. Navy Hospital, Washington, D.C., George Washington University Hospital, Washington, and U.S. Navy Hospital, National Naval Medical

Center, Bethesda, Md., 1941-42; resident in psychiatry, at U.S. Navy Hospital, Bethesda, 1942, and Saint Elizabeth Hospital, Washington, 1943; U.S. Public Health Service, Washington, D.C., director of Federal Employee Mental Health Clinic, 1947-49; private practice in psychotherapy and analysis in Bethesda, Md., 1949—. Certified by National Board of Medical Examiners, 1942; diplomate of American Board of Psychiatry and Neurology, 1948; licensed to practice medicine in Pennsylvania, Maryland, and District of Columbia.

Associate clinical professor at George Washington University, 1946—; lecturer at Saint Elizabeth's Hospital, 1956, and U.S. Navy Hospital, Bethesda, 1972—; distinguished visiting professor at University of Louisville, 1974—; visiting professor at University of Cincinnati, Keio University, National University College of Medicine (Seoul), University of Taiwan, Royal Faculty of Medicine (Baghdad), American University (Beirut), University of Istanbul, Institute of Living, University of Michigan, University of Athens, Crownsville Hospital, Springfield Hospital, Walter Reed Army Medical Center, Puerto Rico Psychiatric Institute, and Royal Hospital of Saint Bartholomew (London); Beling-Englander Memorial Lecturer of New Jersey Neuropsychiatric Association and American Psychiatric Association, 1961. Member of attending staff of District of Columbia General Hospital, 1947-53, Walter Reed Hospital, 1949-58, George Washington University Hospital, 1947-62, Suburban Hospital (Bethesda), 1954-64, 1970-71 (chief of psychiatry and neurology, 1954-64, consultant in psychiatry, 1970—). Member of Washington Area Council on Rehabilitation, 1957-59; member of Montgomery County Medical Care Commission, 1951-61, chairman, 1955-60; member of board of directors of Foundation for Community Health, 1966-69. Member of board of trustees of Bethesda Community School, 1951-53; member of future planning committee of Landon School, 1960-62, chairman, 1961-62; member of board of directors of Ursinus College, 1966-67, 1967—. Co-organizer of Alaska-North America Investment Corp., 1956-58, vice-president and member of board of directors, 1958-62; member of board of directors of Capitol Investment Corp., 1959-62, Information Services Corp., 1971-73 (vice-president, 1973—), and Digital Systems Corp., 1974—. *Military service:* U.S. Navy, 1942-47, chief of psychiatry at Special Augmented Hospital, 1944-45, professor in naval hospitals, 1942-47; served in African-European theater and Asiatic-Pacific theater; became lieutenant commander; received three combat stars.

MEMBER: American Medical Association, American Psychiatric Association (fellow; founder of Metropolitan Washington branch, president, 1953-55; chairman of board of trustees of retirement trust, 1964-68), American Society of Psychoanalytic Physicians (fellow), American College of Psychiatrists (fellow; founder, 1952-63; president, 1963-65), American College of Psychoanalysts (fellow; founder, 1950-69; president, 1969-72, 1976-77), American Association for Social Psychiatry (fellow), Modern Founders of the American Psychiatric Association (organizer, 1957-59; chairman, 1959-61), National Psychiatric Endowment Fund (founder, 1958-60; president, 1960—), American Academy of Psychoanalysis (initiator), Foundation of the American College of Psychiatrists (co-founder, 1965-68; member of board of trustees, 1968—), Royal College of Psychiatrists (fellow), Royal Society of Medicine (fellow), Royal Medical-Psychological Association of Great Britain (honorary corresponding member), Southern Psychiatric Association (fellow; member of executive committee, 1972-75),

Eastern Psychoanalytic Association (fellow; founder, 1954-62; president, 1962-65), Montgomery County Medical Society (member of executive board, 1952-73; president, 1959), Washington Medical and Surgical Society (fellow; life member), Washington Psychiatric Society (co-founder, 1947-49; president, 1953-54; president of Maryland chapter, 1968-70), Medical Council of the Washington Metropolitan Area (president, 1959-61), Medical Arts Society of Greater Washington (president, 1964-65; emeritus member, 1969—), Medical and Chirurgical Faculty of Maryland (member of council, 1962-73; vice-president, 1964-65), Tau Kappa Alpha, Phi Chi.

AWARDS, HONORS: American College of Psychiatrists, Bowis citation, 1965, Bowis gold medal, 1976; citation from American Board of Psychiatry and Neurology, 1966; certificate of commendation from American Psychological Association, 1968; physicians' recognition award from American Medical Association, 1969, 1972; distinguished service award from Eastern Psychoanalytic Association, 1972; certificates of commendation from American College of Psychoanalysts, 1974, 1975; life fellowship medal from American Psychiatric Association, 1975.

WRITINGS: (Editor) *Directory of Psychiatrists and Clinical Psychiatric Facilities in the Washington Area,* Washington Psychiatric Society, 1948, 5th edition, 1957, supplement, 1958; (with M. de G. Ruffin) *An Outline of Dynamic Psychiatry,* School of Medicine, George Washington University, 1949, 4th edition, 1954; *A Psychiatric Glossary,* American Psychiatric Association, 1952; *A Psychiatric Contribution to the Development of Executives: The Development of a Psychoanalytically Oriented Approach to Training in Human Relations,* National Institutes of Health, 1953; *The Neuroses in Clinical Practice,* Saunders, 1956; (editor with Alex Castro) *Handbook,* Washington Medical and Surgical Society, 1962, 3rd edition, 1967; (contributor) Paul Cantor, editor, *Traumatic Medicine and Surgery for the Attorney,* Volume VI, Butterworth, 1962; *Mental Mechanisms,* Butterworth, 1963; *The Emotional Reactions to Trauma,* Butterworth, 1967; *The Neuroses,* Butterworth, 1967; *The Ego and Its Defenses,* Appleton, 1970; (contributor) L. M. Caswell, editor, *Attorney's Textbook of Medicine,* Matthew Bender, 1972.

Contributor to *Encyclopaedia Britannica* and *Dorland's Pocket Medical Dictionary.* Contributor of about ninety articles and reviews to medical journals. Member of editorial board of *Maryland State Medical Journal,* 1960-66; editor of *American College of Psychoanalysts Newsletter,* 1969—, and *American College of Psychoanalysts Archives,* 1971—. Manuscript reviewer for *American Journal of Psychiatry,* 1966-67.

WORK IN PROGRESS: Contemporary Dictionary of Psychiatric Terms and Concepts.

*   *   *

LAUX, Dorothy 1920-

PERSONAL: Born August 25, 1920, in Texas; daughter of Tommy G. and Jewel (Buice) McWilliams; married Edward E. Laux (a clergyman), May 23, 1943. *Education:* Baylor University, A.B., 1941. *Religion:* Baptist. *Home:* 6247 Annapolis, Dallas, Tex. 75214.

CAREER: Writer, 1960—.

WRITINGS: Did I Do That (fiction), Broadman Press, 1970. Curriculum writer of church training material for Baptist Sunday School Board, 1960—.

AVOCATIONAL INTERESTS: Bird watching, international travel (has visited thirty-one countries, sometimes as tour conductor).

* * *

LAWLESS, Bettyclare Hamilton 1915-
(Clare Hamilton)

PERSONAL: Born November 22, 1915, in New York, N.Y.; daughter of William F. (a promoter and artist) and Elizabeth (a musician; maiden name, McNally) Hamilton; married Paul Farrar Lawless (a writer), May 20, 1945 (divorced March 2, 1972); children: Kerry Hamilton. *Education:* Attended University of California, Berkeley, 1932-33, and art and fashion art schools. *Politics:* "Middle-of-the-road Republican." *Religion:* Methodist. *Home:* 13804 Bancroft Ave., San Leandro, Calif. 94578. *Office:* San Francisco Convention and Visitors Bureau, 1390 Market St., San Francisco, Calif. 94102.

CAREER: Employed in miscellaneous free-lance commercial and fashion art work in conjunction with teaching of crafts and sketching in San Francisco Bay area, 1936-41; San Francisco Convention and Visitors Bureau, San Francisco, Calif., contracts secretary, 1959—.

WRITINGS—Under name Clare Hamilton: *Twilight Forest* (gothic novel), Pyramid Publications, 1973.

WORK IN PROGRESS: Revising *Green Gold,* a historical romance of the California Gold Rush days; *To See the Elephant,* a mystery novel set in the Gold Rush period; *Seadrift House,* a gothic novel set in the California of the 1860's.

SIDELIGHTS: Bettyclare Lawless writes: "Writing, to start with, was not the primary love of my life. In my youth I was far more involved with both art and music . . . But I did . . . write verse for my own amusement and probable therapy . . . I . . . had no thought of trying to write seriously . . . but my husband dragged me along to a writing class conducted by the late Anthony Boucher in Berkeley, and the seed was probably planted at that time . . . Some fourteen years after *Green Gold* was first discussed, I started to write it. I have never stopped writing since, and my interest in the California setting and California's past continues to enlarge . . . My deeply held conviction that we, as a people, must be aware of our history in order to cope with our present problems, and my concern for better ecological understanding, can both be utilized in such a background as continuing premises in fiction."

* * *

LEACH, Aroline Beecher 1899-

PERSONAL: Born July 3, 1899, in New Haven, Conn.; daughter of Charles Emerson (a paleontologist) and Mary (Galligan) Beecher; married Richard Leach (a foreign service officer), September 12, 1925; children: Mary L. Leach Maltby, Richard M. (deceased). *Education:* Vassar College, B.A., 1921. *Politics:* Independent. *Religion:* Episcopalian. *Residence:* Norfolk, Conn.

CAREER: Secretary, 1921-25; writer. Worker on local community projects. *Member:* Phi Beta Kappa.

WRITINGS—Juveniles: *Mr. Bradley's Car,* F. A. Stokes, 1937; *Miracle of the Mountain* (adaptation of a Rudyard Kipling story), Addison-Wesley, 1969.

SIDELIGHTS: Aroline Leach writes: "As my husband was in the Foreign Service we lived abroad several years.

Our stay in India made me appreciate Kipling's descriptions of the country in his stories."

* * *

LEADER, (Evelyn) Barbara (Blackburn) 1898-
(Barbara Blackburn; pseudonyms: Frances Castle, Jane Grant)

PERSONAL: Born in July, 1898, in Brampton Brien, Hereford, England; daughter of Ernest Murray and Frances Julia (Reid) Blackburn; married Claude Leader, 1927; children: Bernard, David, Caroline. *Education:* Privately educated. *Home:* Anchor Cottage, Latchingdon, Chelmsford, Essex, England. *Agent:* Bolt & Watson, 8 Storey's Gate, London, S.W.1, England.

CAREER: Writer. Worked as secretary at British Air Ministry during World War I.

WRITINGS: Spinners Hall, R. Hale, 1957.

Under name Barbara Blackburn: all novels, except as indicated: *Return to Bondage,* Dial, 1926; *The Season Made for Joy,* M. Secker, 1927; *Sober Feast,* Little, Brown, 1929; *Courage for Martha,* M. Secker, 1930; *Marriage and Money,* M. Secker, 1931; *The Club,* M. Secker, 1932; *The Long Journey,* Cassell, 1933; *Lover, Be Wise,* Cassell, 1934; *Good Times,* Cassell, 1935; "Poor Man's Castle" (play), produced at Arts Theatre, London, 1936.

Abbot's Bank, Hodder & Stoughton, 1948; *Noble Lord: The Life of the Seventh Earl of Shaftesbury,* Home & Van Thal, 1949; *Georgina Goes Home,* Hodder & Stoughton, 1951; *Star Spangled Heavens,* Hodder & Stoughton, 1953; *Summer and Sorrelhurst,* Hodder & Stoughton, 1954; *The Briary Bush,* Hodder & Stoughton, 1954; *The Buds of May,* Hodder & Stoughton, 1955; *The Blackbird's Tune,* Hodder & Stoughton, 1957; *Green for Lovers,* Hodder & Stoughton, 1958.

The Little Cousin, R. Hale, 1960; *The Story of Alix,* R. Hale, 1960; *The Love Story of Mary Britten, M.D.,* R. Hale, 1961; *Doctor and Debutante,* R. Hale, 1961; *Learn Her by Heart,* R. Hale, 1962; *Lovers' Meeting,* R. Hale, 1962; *City of Forever,* R. Hale, 1963; *Come Back, My Love,* R. Hale, 1963.

With daughter, Caroline Leader Holmes, under joint pseudonym Jane Grant: *Come Hither, Nurse,* R. Hale, 1957; *Come Again, Nurse,* R. Hale, 1960; *Sisters under the Skin,* R. Hale, 1965; *Round-the-Clock Nurse,* R. Hale, 1968.

Under pseudonym Frances Castle: (With Peggy Mundy Castle) *The Sisters' Tale,* Little, Brown, 1969; *Tara's Daughter,* Macmillan, 1970; *The Thread of Gold,* Macmillan, 1971.

* * *

LEAVER, Robin Alan 1939-

PERSONAL: Born May 12, 1939, in Aldershot, Hampshire, England; son of Robert James and Violet Hester (Hack) Leaver; married Patricia Joyce Gooding (a nurse), June 30, 1962; children: Martin, Joanna, Kathryn. *Education:* Attended Royal Aircraft Establishment Technical College and Farnborough Technical College, 1954-60, Brasted Place College, Kent, 1960-62, and Clifton Theological (now Trinity) College, Bristol, 1962-64. *Address:* 151 St. Saviours Rd., Reading, Berkshire RG1 6EP, England.

CAREER: Royal Aircraft Establishment, Farnborough, Hampshire, England, apprentice, 1954-60; ordained into the ministry of the Church of England, deacon, 1964, priest,

1965; curate of church in London, England, 1964-67; curate in charge at church in Essex, England, 1967-71; incumbent of St. Mary's Church, Castle Street, Reading, England, 1971—. Honorary member, Riemenschneider Bach Institute, Berea, Ohio, 1973—; chaplain of Luckley-Oakfield School, 1973-75; director, Church Book Room Press, 1975—. *Member:* International Heinrich Schutz Society, The Hymn Society of Great Britain and Ireland, Internationale Arbeitsgemeinschaft fuer Hymnologie. *Awards, honors:* Winston Churchill fellowship for research on J. S. Bach, 1971.

WRITINGS: Luther on Justification, Concordia, 1975; *A Thematic Guide to the Anglican Hymn Book,* Church Book Room Press, 1975; (editor) *John Marbeck,* Sutton Courtenay Press, 1976. Contributor to *Grove's Dictionary of Music and Musicians,* revised edition, Macmillan, in press. Contributor of articles to theological journals, *BACH* (quarterly journal of the Riemenschneider Bach Institute), *Bach-Jahrbuch,* and other publications.

WORK IN PROGRESS: Research on the theological background in Johann Sebastian Bach's life and music; a historical study of the place of the hymn in Church of England worship, tentatively titled *Music and the Liturgy;* a study of the celebration of Reformation anniversaries and festivals in Germany c.1530-1750, with special emphasis on Bach; a study of Miles Coverdale.

* * *

LeBARON, Charles W.   1943-

PERSONAL: Born November 4, 1943, in New York, N.Y.; son of James Wade (in advertising) and Doris (Davison) LeBaron. *Education:* Princeton University, A.B., 1965; Harvard University, M.A.T., 1966. *Home:* 340 East 53rd St., New York, N.Y. 10022. *Agent:* Roslyn Targ, 250 West 57th St., New York, N.Y. 10022. *Office:* Manhattan Developmental Services, 75 Morton St., New York, N.Y. 10014.

CAREER: San Francisco General Hospital, San Francisco, Calif., social worker (alternate service as conscientious objector), 1969-73; Manhattan Developmental Services, New York, N.Y., social worker, 1974—. *Member:* Appalachian Mountain Club, Adirondack Mountain Club, Sierra Club, Kayak and Canoe Club of New York, Met Grotto.

WRITINGS: The Diamond Sky, Dial, 1975.

* * *

LEBER, George L.   1917(?)-1976

1917(?)—January 20, 1976; American association executive, editor, and author. Obituaries: *Washington Post,* January 23, 1976.

* * *

LEDERMAN, Leonard L(awrence)   1931-

PERSONAL: Born November 23, 1931, in New York, N.Y.; son of Hyman G. and Yetta (Dreyfus) Lederman; married Florence Krinsky (a teacher), May 19, 1956; children: Hugh Daniel, Steven Mark, Michael Jay. *Education:* City College (now City College of the City University of New York), B.A., 1953; New York University, M.A., 1957; further graduate study at Columbia University and Princeton University. *Home:* 5602 Ridgefield Rd., Bethesda, Md. 20016. *Office:* National Science Foundation, 1800 G St. N.W., Washington, D.C. 20550.

CAREER: Barnard Research, Inc., New York, N.Y., statistician, 1953-54; Maidenform, Inc., Bayone, N.J., research analyst, 1954-58; Douglas College, Rutgers University, New Brunswick, N.J., instructor in economics, 1956-57; Battelle Memorial Institute (research and development firm), Washington, D.C., fellow and senior research adviser for federal budget and economic studies, 1963-70; National Science Foundation, Washington, D.C., deputy head of Office of Economic and Manpower Studies, 1970-71, acting director, Exploratory Research and Problem Assessment, 1971; Executive Office of the President, Washington, D.C., program manager for productivity assessment for New Technological Opportunities Task Force, 1971-72; National Science Foundation, director of Office of National Research and Development Assessment, 1972—. Coordinator of President's Task Force on Highway Safety; executive secretary of Ad Hoc National Academy of Engineering Committee on Public Engineering Policy's Task Force and Committee on Commercial Uses of Atomic Energy; assistant manager of department of manufacture of U.S. Chamber of Commerce.

MEMBER: American Association for the Advancement of Science, American Economic Association. *Awards, honors:* National Science Foundation awards include certificates of commendation, 1972, 1974, special achievement award, 1972, outstanding performance rating, 1974.

WRITINGS: Federal Funding and National Priorities: An Analysis of Programs, Expenditures, and Research and Development, Praeger, 1971; (contributor) *A Review of the Relationship Between Research and Development and Economic Growth-Productivity,* U.S. Government Printing Office, 1971; (contributor) *Technology: A Key to Economic Growth;* Boston College, 1972.

WORK IN PROGRESS: Research on the economics of technological change, the impacts of federal policy on technological innovation, and the supply of objective information to public policy decision makers.

* * *

LEE, James F.   1905(?)-1975

1905(?)—December 22, 1975; American journalist and author. Obituaries: *Washington Post,* December 23, 1975.

* * *

LEE, Maria Berl   1924-
(Maria Berl-Lee)

PERSONAL: Born July 30, 1924, in Vienna, Austria; came to United States, 1941, naturalized citizen, 1948; daughter of Arthur C. (a judge and lawyer) and Gunda (a teacher; maiden name, Weisel) Berl; married Ray E. Lee, Jr. (a financial analyst and writer), October 13, 1951. *Education:* Nazareth College, B.A. (magna cum laude), 1946; Fordham University, M.A., 1949. *Home:* 68-46 Ingram St., Forest Hills, N.Y. 11375. *Agent:* Ruth Cantor, 156 Fifth Ave., Suite 1005, New York, N.Y. 10010. *Office:* International Institute of Rural Reconstruction, 1775 Broadway, New York, N.Y. 10019.

CAREER: Eastman Kodak, Rochester, N.Y., bilingual secretary, 1946-48; U.S. Embassy, Vienna, Austria, translator and interpreter for Uniformed Services Contingency Option Act, 1949-51; Georgetown University, Washington, D.C., assistant placement director, 1951-53; John F. Fleming (rare book seller), New York City, assistant, 1953-59; Jacobus F. Frank & Co. (importer), New York City, assistant head of Indonesian imports, 1965-69; International Institute of Rural Reconstruction, New York City, assistant to director of public affairs and to U.S. resident director, 1969—. Bilingual free-lance writer, 1942—. *Member:* Austrian Forum, Society of German-American Studies, Verband deutsch-amerikanische Autoren in Amerika, Kappa Gamma Pi, National Writers Club, Nazareth Alumni. *Awards, honors:* Many short story and poetry prizes from organizations and publications, including National Writers Club, *Poetry Parade,* and *Writer's Digest,* 1968-71; citation of merit from Society of German-American Studies, 1973; first prize from Society of German-American Authors, 1975, for novella, "Postskript fuer Lydia."

WRITINGS: Don't Rock the Waterbed (play; produced in United States, 1975), Performance Publishing, 1975. Also author of three novels as yet unpublished, "Late Days in March," "A Force in Motion," and "The Town That Would Allow No Crime." Short story included in anthology, *Beginnings,* Sheed, 1956. Author of literary criticism column, "Literary Accolade," in *Spafaswap* magazine, 1974—. Collaborator for Department of Interior's "Immigrants on Tape" program, 1973. Contributor of articles, short stories, and poetry to popular and literary magazines, including *North American Mentor, Expecting, Bitterroot,* and *Second Coming.*

Under name Maria Berl-Lee: *Ein Tag der Ueberaschungen* (play; produced in Bavaria, 1967), W. Koehler Verlag (Munich), 1966; *Bombe im Tor* (play; produced in Bavaria, 1970), W. Koehler Verlag, 1970; (contributor) Mimi Grossberg, editor, *Oesterreichisches aus Amerika,* Bergland Verlag (Vienna), 1973; *Schaumwein aus meinem Krug* (collection of short stories, poetry, and drama), Bergland Verlag, 1974. Contributor of short stories and poetry to German language periodicals in Germany, Austria, and United States, including *Lyrik und Prosa, Literatur und Kritik,* and *Aufbau.*

WORK IN PROGRESS: Translating *Adventures and Travels of the Baron of Muenchhausen,* for Westburg Associates; a trilogy on ancient Persia, Greece, and Egypt, of which the first two volumes are completed.

SIDELIGHTS: Maria Lee began creating stories in cartoon style before she could write. She told *CA:* "My studies in three languages—first in German, then in French, finally in English, with Spanish, Latin and smatterings of other languages thrown in—has given me an abiding love of words and how they are used, and a deep interest in experimenting with different languages and the connections between them." *Avocational interests:* Travel, music, theatre, hiking, swimming.

* * *

LEE, Walt(er William, Jr.) 1931-

PERSONAL: Born August 16, 1931, in Eugene, Ore.; son of Walter William (a musician) and Okria (Mooney) Lee; married Eve Olveda, May 9, 1959; children: Cindy, Steven Marco. *Education:* California Institute of Technology, B.S. (with honors), 1954; University of California, Berkeley, graduate study, 1954-55. *Religion:* Agnostic. *Office address:* P.O. Box 66273, Los Angeles, Calif. 90066.

CAREER: Hughes Aircraft Co., Los Angeles, Calif., member of technical staff, 1955-59; Technical Communications, Inc., Los Angeles, Calif., vice-president, 1959-62; Hughes Aircraft Co., member of technical staff, 1962—. Consultant to Los Angeles Film Exposition Science Fiction

Marathon, 1975. *Member:* American Film Institute, International Association du Film d'Animation (ASIFA), Los Angeles Film Exposition. *Awards, honors:* Received committee award from World Science Fiction Convention, 1975.

WRITINGS: Reference Guide to Fantastic Films: Science Fiction, Fantasy, and Horror, Chelsea-Lee Books, Volume I: *A-F,* 1972, Volume II: *G-O,* 1973, Volume III: *P-Z,* 1974. Contributor to film journals and to newspapers.

WORK IN PROGRESS: Technological Tyranny in Film; Witchcraft in the Cinema.

BIOGRAPHICAL/CRITICAL SOURCES: Engineering and Science, February-March, 1975.

* * *

LEENHOUTS, Keith J(ames) 1925-

PERSONAL: Born October 17, 1925, in Grand Rapids, Mich.; son of William James (a banker) and Dorothy (Champion) Leenhouts; married Audrey Doris Saari, June 27, 1953; children: William James, David John, Daniel S. (deceased), James Edward. *Education:* Albion College, B.A., 1949; Wayne State University, LL.B., 1952. *Politics:* Independent. *Religion:* Methodist. *Home:* 830 Normandy, Royal Oak, Mich. 48073. *Office:* Volunteers in Probation, National Council on Crime and Delinquency, 200 Washington Square Building, Royal Oak, Mich. 48067.

CAREER: Admitted to state bar of Michigan, 1952; Dell, Heber & Leenhouts, Royal Oak, Mich., attorney, 1953-59; City of Royal Oak, Mich., municipal court judge, 1959-69, district court judge, 1969; Volunteers in Probation of National Council on Crime and Delinquency (formerly Project Misdemeanant Foundation, Inc.), Royal Oak, Mich., president, 1969-71, executive director, 1972—. Lecturer at National College of State Trial Judges, 1967, and National College of State Judiciary, 1972. Member of board of directors of South Oakland County Young Men's Christian Association (YMCA). Consultant to Law Enforcement Assistance Administration. *Military service:* U.S. Army Air Forces, 1944-46.

MEMBER: North American Judges Association (vice-president, 1962-64), American Bar Association, American Correctional Association, Judicial Research Foundation (president, 1966-67), American Judicature Society (member of board of directors, 1969), Veterans of Foreign Wars, American Legion, Michigan Bar Association, Michigan Corrections Association, Royal Oak Lions Club, Tau Kappa Epsilon. *Awards, honors:* Lane Bryant citations, 1963-68; judicial leadership award from North American Judges Association, 1963, 1964; All American City Award, 1968, for work with Volunteers in Probation; annual award from John Howard Association, 1970; Halpern Award, from National Council on Crime and Delinquency.

WRITINGS: (Editor) Joe Alex Morris, *First Offender,* Funk, 1970; *A Father . . . Son . . . and Three Mile Run,* Zondervan, 1975. Contributor to law journals and popular magazines.

BIOGRAPHICAL/CRITICAL SOURCES: Reader's Digest, October, 1965, April, 1968.

* * *

LEES, Ray 1931-

PERSONAL: Born November 28, 1931, in England; son of Herbert (a bus driver) and Ivy (Gilks) Lees; married Sue

Mullock (a lecturer), August 9, 1970; children: Sean, Daniel, Josie. *Education:* University of London, B.Sc. (honors), 1969. *Home:* 9 Northolme Rd., London N. 5, England. *Office:* Department of Social Sciences, Polytechnic of Central London, Regent St., London, England.

CAREER: Recreation organizer at Leybourne Grange Hospital, 1956-61; probation officer, London Probation Service, 1961-65; lecturer at Ipswich Civic College, 1966-67, and at Polytechnic of Central London, 1969-72; University of York, Heslington, England, research fellow in sociology, 1972-75; Polytechnic of Central London, London, England, professor of applied social studies, 1975—, head of department, 1975—. *Member:* Association of Teachers of Social Administration, British Association of Social Workers, British Sociological Association.

WRITINGS: Politics and Social Work, Routledge & Kegan Paul, 1972; *Research Strategies for Social Welfare,* Routledge & Kegan Paul, 1975; (editor with George Smith) *Action Research in Community Development,* Routledge & Kegan Paul, 1975. Contributor to social work journals.

WORK IN PROGRESS: Research on the role of politics and ideology in the formulation of social policy.

* * *

LEGER, (Marie-Rene) Alexis Saint-Leger   1887-1975 (Saintleger Leger, Saint-John Perse)

May 31, 1887—September 20, 1975; French diplomat and poet. Obituaries: *New York Times,* September 22, 1975; *Washington Post,* September 24, 1975; *Newsweek,* October 6, 1975; *Time,* October 6, 1975; *Current Biography,* November, 1975. (See index for previous *CA* sketch)

* * *

LEHRER, Robert N(athaniel)   1922-

PERSONAL: Born January 17, 1922, in Sandusky, Ohio; son of Henry William (a physician) and Margaret (Boyd) Lehrer; married Patricia Lee Martin, July 7, 1945; children: Joan Elizabeth (Mrs. Hunter M. Hess). *Education:* Purdue University, B.S.M.E. (with distinction), 1945, M.S.I.E., 1946, Ph.D., 1949. *Religion:* Episcopalian. *Home:* 1506 Hanover West Dr. N.W., Atlanta, Ga. 30327. *Office:* School of Industrial and Systems Engineering, Georgia Institute of Technology, Atlanta, Ga. 30332.

CAREER: Registered professional engineer; Purdue University, Lafayette, Ind., instructor in engineering, 1946-49; Oregon State College (now University), Corvallis, assistant professor, 1949-50; Georgia Institute of Technology, Atlanta, associate professor, 1950-54, professor of industrial engineering, 1954-58, research associate, 1950-58; Northwestern University, Evanston, Ill., professor of industrial engineering and chairman of department at Technological Institute, 1958-63; Georgia Institute of Technology, professor of industrial engineering, 1963—, associate director of School of Industrial Engineering, 1963-66, director of School of Industrial and Systems Engineering, 1966—. UNESCO expert at Universidad de Guadalajara and Universidad de Guanajuato, 1962-63; industrial engineering adviser to Eindhoven University and to Dutch Ministry of Education, 1962; member of inspection team of Engineers Council for Professional Development; member of National Research Council of American Academy of Sciences, 1965-68; member of industrial research and development panel of National Academy of Sciences and Indonesian Institute of Sciences, 1971. *Military service:* U.S. Naval Reserve, active duty, 1943-46.

MEMBER: American Institute of Industrial Engineers (fellow; vice-president of publications, 1960-62), American Association for the Advancement of Science, Institute of Management Sciences, Operations Research Society of America, American Society for Engineering Education, Sigma Xi, Tau Beta Pi, Phi Kappa Phi, Alpha Pi Mu, Pi Tau Sigma, Phi Delta Theta. *Awards, honors:* Outstanding industrial engineering award from American Institute of Industrial Engineers, 1957, service award, 1960; Distinguished Alumnus award from Purdue University, 1964.

WRITINGS: Work Simplification: Creative Thinking About Work Problems, Prentice-Hall, 1957; *The Management of Improvement: Concepts, Organization, and Strategy,* Reinhold, 1965. Contributor to scientific journals. Associate editor of *Journal of Industrial Engineering,* 1952-53, editor-in-chief, 1953-61, executive editor, 1961-62; consulting editor of "Industrial Engineering and Management Science," a series, Reinhold, 1960-66.

SIDELIGHTS: Lehrer has traveled to Japan, Hong Kong, Thailand, India, Egypt, Greece, Italy, Austria, France, England, the Netherlands, Belgium, Mexico, Venezuela, and Colombia.

* * *

LEINBACH, Esther V(ashti)   1924-

PERSONAL: Born February 29, 1924, in Sherwood, Ore.; daughter of Arthur Ernest (a barber) and Buena Vesta (Jackson) Evans; married Albert Douglas Leinbach (a teacher), August 31, 1947; children: Cathryn Marie, Kevin Arthur. *Education:* Lewis & Clark College, B.S., 1954. *Politics:* Democrat. *Religion:* Religious Society of Friends (Quakers). *Home and office:* 1950 Orchard St., Eugene, Ore. 97403.

CAREER: Public welfare caseworker in Oregon, 1954-58; astrologer, 1961—. Lane Community College, Eugene, Ore., lecturer on astrology in adult education program, 1969—. Has appeared on television and radio programs; lecturer on astrology to public schools and private groups. Member of American Friends Service Committee. *Military service:* U.S. Navy, Women Accepted for Volunteer Emergency Service (WAVES), 1943-44. *Member:* International Society of Astrological Research (member of board of directors), National Astrological Association, Oregon Astrological Association.

WRITINGS: Degrees of the Zodiac, Macoy Publishing, 1972; *Sun Ascendant Rulerships,* Vulcan Books, 1972; *Planets and Asteroids,* Vulcan Books, 1973; *Numerology Multiple Digits and Decanates,* privately printed, 1975.

WORK IN PROGRESS: Research on quincunx influence; chart interpretation.

SIDELIGHTS: Esther Leinbach writes: "Each individual is primarily responsible for his own individual actions. There is no way to avoid this responsibility. It behooves individuals to be aware of their own needs, strengths, and weaknesses and consciously accept and deal with this responsibility. Beyond that we are also units in the body of humanity as a whole. We are affected by what happens to those both near and far. Our responsibility to others rests on our responsibility for ourselves.... From Gandhi 'There is hope for the slave of the brute, none for the slave of love.' Freedom and the ability to resist such pressures is the primary purpose in life. Freedom demands responsibility. Most people give up their freedom in order to avoid responsibility. I believe this is changing. Humanity is growing up and assuming more responsibility on an individual level. That is my hope for the world.''

* * *

LEITCH, Patricia 1933-

PERSONAL: Born July 13, 1933, in Paisley, Renfrewshire, Scotland; daughter of James Ritchie (an engineer) and Anna (Mitchell) Leitch. *Education:* Craigie College of Education, primary teacher's diploma, 1967. *Home:* 11 Argyll Ter., Dunoon, Argyll, Scotland. *Agent:* A.M. Heath & Co. Ltd., 40-42 William IV St., London WE2N 4DD, England.

CAREER: Library assistant in Glasgow Corporation libraries and Renfrewshire County Library, 1954-59; worked at riding school, 1960-61; shop assistant in various bookshops, 1962-63; primary school teacher at Troon Primary School, Ayrshire, 1968-70; typist for various employers, 1971-73; writer, 1974—.

WRITINGS—Juveniles: A Pony of Our Own, Blackie & Son, 1960; *To Save a Pony,* Hutchinson, 1960; *Rosette for Royal,* Blackie & Son, 1963; *Janet Young Rider,* Constable, 1963, published as *Last Summer to Ride,* Funk, 1965; *The Black Loch,* Collins, 1963, Funk, 1968; *Highland Pony Trek,* Collins, 1964; *Riding Course Summer,* Collins, 1965; *Cross Country Pony,* Blackie & Son, 1965; *Treasure to the East,* Gollancz, 1966; *Jacky Jumps to the Top,* Collins, 1973; *First Pony,* Collins, 1973; *Afraid to Ride,* Collins, 1973; *Rebel Pony,* Collins, 1973; *Pony Surprise,* Collins, 1974; *Dream of Fair Horses,* Collins, 1975.

WORK IN PROGRESS: A series for Collins, for children; *The Lordly Ones,* a juvenile novel.

SIDELIGHTS: Patricia Leitch writes: "I have always had a vivid imagination being typical of the Jungian category of introverted intuitive. . . . I have neither a visual nor an aural imagination. It is something else. Most of my books are 'pony books,' some are fantasies but really they all say the same thing—'Sin is Behovely, but all shall be well, and all manner of thing shall be well'. . . . I am a vegetarian and am enthused by the growing synthesis of Eastern and Western cultures.''

* * *

LeMOND, Alan 1938-
(David Tahlaquah)

PERSONAL: Born February 27, 1938, in Evansville, Ind.; son of Jesse Roy and Dorothy E. (Taylor) LeMond; married Mary Anne Hirsch, July 19, 1969; children: Lisa Anne, Nicole Christina. *Education:* Oakland City College, B.A., 1965. *Home:* 40 West 84th St., New York, N.Y. 10024. *Agent:* Owen Laster, William Morris Agency, 1350 Avenue of the Americas, New York, N.Y. 10019.

CAREER: Esquire (magazine), New York City, copywriter, 1965-67; *Cavalier* (magazine), New York City, associate editor, 1967-68, editor, 1968-70; New Earth, Inc. (editorial consulting and packaging firm), New York City, president, 1970—. *Military service:* U.S. Army, 1961-63.

WRITINGS: (With Jay Acton and Parker Hodges) *Mug Shots: Who's Who in the New Earth,* New American Library, 1972; (with Acton) *Ralph Nader: A Man and a Movement,* Paperback Library, 1972; (with Ron Fry) *No Place to Hide: Bugs, Computers, Informers, and Dossiers and What to Do about Them,* St. Martin's, 1975; (with Mark Spitz) *The Mark Spitz Complete Book of Swimming,* Crowell, in press. Contributor of articles and fiction, under pseudonym David Tahlaquah, to *Cavalier, Nugget, Celebrity,* and to movie fan books. Co-founder and editor of *Your Land,* 1972.

* * *

LEONARD, Jonathan N(orton) 1903-1975

PERSONAL: Born May 25, 1903, in Somerville, Mass.; son of Jonathan and Melanie Elisabeth (Norton) Leonard; married Maria Alzamora, December 30, 1933; children: Jonathan. *Education:* Harvard University, A.B., 1925. *Religion:* Unitarian-Universalist. *Residence:* Hastings-on-Hudson, N.Y.

CAREER: Free-lance writer, 1925-43; *Time* (magazine), New York, N.Y., Latin American editor, 1943-45, science editor, 1945-65; Time-Life Books, New York City, staff writer, 1965-68; free-lance writer, 1968-75.

WRITINGS: Ask Me, Too! The Junior Question Book (juvenile), Viking, 1927; *Loki: The Life of Charles Proteus Steinmetz,* Doubleday, 1929; *Crusaders of Chemistry: Six Makers of the Modern World,* Doubleday, 1930, Books for Libraries, 1972; *The Tragedy of Henry Ford,* Putnam, 1932; *Ask Me Again! The Third Question Book,* Viking, 1932; *Men of Maracaibo,* Putnam, 1933; *Tools of Tomorrow,* Viking, 1935; (editor) *Ask Me Again! The Second Omnibus Question Book,* revised edition (sources do not indicate original date of publication), Blue Ribbon Books, 1938; *Three Years Down* (on the "Great Depression"), Carrick & Evans, 1939; *Enjoyment of Science,* Doubleday, 1942; *Flight into Space: The Facts, Fancies, and Philosophy,* Random House, 1953, revised edition, 1958; (editor) *The Time Book of Science,* Random House, 1955; *Exploring Science,* World Publishing, 1959; *The Shards of History,* Nelson-Glueck, 1963.

All with editors of Time-Life; all published by Time-Life Books: (And with Carl Sagan) *Planets,* 1966; *Ancient America,* 1967; *Early Japan,* 1968; *Latin American Cooking,* 1968; *The World of Gainsborough, 1727-1788,* 1969; *American Cooking: New England,* 1970; *American Cooking: The Great West,* 1971; *Atlantic Beaches,* 1972; *The First Farmers,* 1973. Contributor of fiction, articles, and reviews to magazines, including *Saturday Evening Post* and *New York Times Book Review.*

AVOCATIONAL INTERESTS: Cranberry farming.*

(Died May 15, 1975, in New York, N.Y.)

* * *

LESCOE, Francis J(oseph) 1916-

PERSONAL: Born May 17, 1916, in Middletown, Conn.; son of Steven Francis (an electrical engineer) and Mary Emily (Zultanski) Lescoe. *Education:* St. Thomas Seminary, student, 1934-36; St. Mary's University, Baltimore, Md., B.A., 1938, S.T.B., 1940, S.T.L., 1942; University of Toronto, M.A., 1947, Ph.D., 1949. *Home:* 243 Steele Rd., West Hartford, Conn. 06117. *Office:* McAuley Institute of Religious Studies, St. Joseph College, Asylum Ave., West Hartford, Conn. 06117.

CAREER: Ordained Roman Catholic priest, 1942. Assistant pastor in West Hartford, Conn., 1942-46; St. Joseph College, West Hartford, Conn., instructor in religion, 1945-46, assistant professor of philosophy, 1949-50, associate professor, 1950-54, professor, 1954—, chairman of department of philosophy, 1954-69, 1975, professor of palaeography at McAuley Institute of Religious Studies, 1969—, chairman of Institute, 1970—, chairman of Gabriel Marcel

Existentialist Drama Festival Committee. Trustee of Monsignor Edward Reardon Foundation; panelist at World Congress of Theology, 1966. *Member:* North American Patristic Society, American Catholic Philosophical Association, American Association of University Professors, Mediaeval Academy of America.

WRITINGS: (Editor) *The McAuley Lecture Series,* fifteen volumes, St. Joseph College, 1953—; *Sancti Thomae Aquinatis Tractatus de Substantiis Separatis,* St. Joseph College, 1962, translation published as *St. Thomas Aquinas: Treatise on Separate Substances,* St. Joseph College, 1963; *Existentialism: With Or Without God,* Alba, 1973; (editor) *Existentialist Drama of Gabriel Marcel: The Broken World and the Rebellious Heart,* St. Joseph College, 1974; (contributor) Armand Maurer, editor, *St. Thomas Commemorative Studies, 1274-1974,* Pontifical Institute of Mediaeval Studies, University of Toronto, 1974.

WORK IN PROGRESS: Three more volumes of Gabriel Marcel's Existentialist plays; *The Theory of the First Principle in the Summa de Bono of Ulrich of Strasbourg: Critical Text and Study;* general editor of *A Critical Edition of Liber III of the Summa de Bono of Ulrich of Strasbourg,* transcribed from medieval manuscripts.

SIDELIGHTS: Lescoe writes: "Most Americans know existentialism only in terms of the atheism of Jean Paul Sartre and Albert Camus. Few are aware of the fact that existentialism began as a theistic posture in the writings of Soeren Kierkegaard ... a devout Lutheran.... Marcel repeatedly insisted that, in order to appreciate the full dimensions of his existentialist and personalist stance, it was absolutely necessary to read and know all his plays.... In spite of these repeated avowals, the English reading public has had access to only three of his plays in printed form."

Marcel was so pleased with Lescoe's English translations that he granted permission for their publication, and wrote a special introduction, describing their themes and backgrounds. He also gave permission to stage world premieres of his works in English at St. Joseph College, and the drama festival committee, which Lescoe heads, was formed.

Lescoe adds: "By making the thought of this highly originative and insightful author better known, it is hoped that existentialism's stigma of estrangement, absurdity, alienation, and nausea will be, at least, partially removed. Gabriel Marcel is a Christian optimist. His world is one of love, fidelity, fraternity, hope ..."

* * *

LESKO, Leonard Henry 1938-

PERSONAL: Born August 14, 1938, in Chicago, Ill.; son of Matthew E. (a pharmacist) and Josephine Lesko; married Barbara Switalski (an Egyptologist and bibliographer), December 29, 1966. *Education:* Loyola University, Chicago, Ill., B.A., 1961, M.A., 1964; University of Chicago, Ph.D., 1969. *Office:* Department of Near Eastern Studies, University of California, Berkeley, Calif. 94720.

CAREER: Teacher of Latin and Greek at a preparatory seminary in Chicago, Ill., 1961-64; University of Chicago, Epigraphic Survey of Oriental Institute, Luxor, Egypt, Egyptologist epigrapher, 1964-65; University of California, Berkeley, acting instructor, 1966-67, acting assistant professor, 1967-68, assistant professor, 1968-72, associate professor of Egyptology, 1972—, director of Center for Near

Eastern Studies, 1973-75, chairman of department of Near Eastern studies, 1975—.

MEMBER: American Research Center in Egypt (member of board of governors), American Oriental Society, American Philological Association, Egypt Exploration Society, Fondation Egyptologique Reine Elisabeth, Napa Valley Wine Library Association. *Awards, honors:* Younger Humanist fellowship from National Endowment for the Humanities, 1970-71, grant for a late Egyptian dictionary, 1975-76; American Council of Learned Societies grant, 1973-74, for computer-oriented research in the humanities.

WRITINGS: (Contributor with Charles F. Nims, George R. Hughes and others) *Medinet Habu VIII: The Eastern High Gate,* University of Chicago Press, 1970; *The Ancient Egyptian Book of Two Ways,* University of California Press, 1972; *Glossary of the Late Ramesside Letters,* privately printed, 1975. Contributor to *Encyclopedia Americana.* Contributor to professional journals.

WORK IN PROGRESS: Editing *An Introduction to the Egyptian Coffin Texts* for Oriental Institute of University of Chicago; *The Berkeley Late Egyptian Dictionary,* with computer assistance.

SIDELIGHTS: Lesko writes: "My main interest is in ancient Egyptian religious literature. To some extent this means that I must translate and try to explain what the religious texts actually have to say, but I am particularly interested in trying to discover how and why these texts developed into the set forms in which we find them."

* * *

LESSA, William A(rmand) 1908-

PERSONAL: Born March 3, 1908, in Newark, N.J.; son of Luigi and Santina (Menichella) Lessa. *Education:* Harvard University, A.B., 1928; University of Chicago, M.A., 1941, Ph.D., 1947. *Home:* 3429 Woodcliff Rd., Sherman Oaks, Calif. 91403. *Office:* Department of Anthropology, University of California at Los Angeles, Los Angeles, Calif. 90024.

CAREER: Presbyterian-Columbia Medical Center, New York, N.Y., research associate, 1929-30; University of Hawaii, Honolulu, research associate, 1930-33; Brooklyn College (now Brooklyn College of the City University of New York), Brooklyn, N.Y., instructor in anthropology, 1941-42; University of California at Los Angeles, instructor, 1947-49, assistant professor, 1949-55, associate professor, 1955-61, professor of anthropology, 1961-71, professor emeritus, 1971—. Visiting summer professor at Stanford University, 1953, University of Hawaii, 1962, Harvard University, 1963, and Occidental College, 1971; lecturer for Peace Corps Training Program, 1962-66. Has done field work in Hawaii, mainland China, Illinois, and Micronesia. Technical advisor to Twentieth-Century Fox, 1951-52. *Military service:* U.S. Army, 1942-45; became captain; received Bronze Star Medal and five battle stars.

MEMBER: American Anthropological Association (fellow; secretary, 1950-51), American Association for the Advancement of Science (fellow), American Association of Physical Anthropologists, American Folklore Society (vice-president, 1960), Polynesian Society (fellow), Societe des Oceanistes, Society for the History of Discoveries, Royal Anthropological Institute of Great Britain and Ireland (fellow).

WRITINGS: Landmarks in the Science of Human Types, Brooklyn College Press, 1942; *An Appraisal of Constitu-*

tional Typologies, American Anthropological Association, 1942; *Ulithian Personality,* University of California Press, 1954; (editor with Evon Z. Vogt) *Reader in Comparative Religion,* Row, Peterson, 1958, 3rd edition, Harper, 1972; *Tales from Ulithi Atoll,* University of California Press, 1961; *Ulithi: A Micronesian Design for Living,* Holt, 1966; *Chinese Body Divination,* United World, Academy and Fellowship, 1968; *Drake's Island of Thieves: Ethnological Sleuthing,* University Press of Hawaii, 1975. Contributor of more than forty articles to anthropological journals. Editor of *Culture and Society,* 1954-62; associate editor of *American Anthropologist,* 1956-59.

WORK IN PROGRESS: Writing on anthropological subjects.

* * *

LEVENTHAL, Albert Rice 1907-1976
(Albert Rice)

October 30, 1907—January 6, 1976; American publisher, editor, and author of books on publishing, history, and other topics. Obituaries: *New York Times,* January 8, 1976; *Publishers Weekly,* January 19, 1976.

* * *

LEVER, J(ulius) W(alter) 1913-1975
(Walter Lever)

July 24, 1913—November 11, 1975; British educator, playwright, translator, editor and author. Obituaries: *New York Times,* November 15, 1975; *AB Bookman's Weekly,* January 26, 1976. (See index for previous *CA* sketch)

* * *

LEVIN, Molly Apple

PERSONAL: Born in St. Paul, Minn.; daughter of Phillip (a garment worker) and Fanny (in needle trade; maiden name, Waldman) Apple; married Joseph H. Levin (a mathematician), August 31, 1947; children: Theodore C., Andrew E., Charles G. *Education:* University of Minnesota, B.A. (magna cum laude), 1945. *Home:* 4 Pond Brook Circle, Weston, Mass. 02193.

CAREER: Free-lance writer. Script writer and broadcaster for daily "Woman's Show" on Station WASA, Havre de Grace, Md.; research associate, Brandeis University, 1968-73; currently economic analyst, Max O. Urbahn Associates, Lexington, Mass. Member of local school committee, library study committee, junior high school building committee, and special school plant study committee. *Member:* Weston League of Women Voters (member of board of directors).

WRITINGS: (Editor with Ralph W. Conant) *Problems in Research on Community Violence,* Praeger, 1969; (contributor) A. M. Freedman and others, editors, *Comprehensive Textbook of Psychiatry,* 2nd edition, Williams & Wilkins, 1975; *Violence in Society,* Houghton, 1975. Also author of a booklet, *I'll Tell the World,* published by U.S. Department of Defense.

Ghostwriter and author of public information articles for members of U.S. Congress and U.S. Department of State. Contributor to *Encyclopaedic Handbook of Medical Psychology.* Contributor to magazines and newspapers. Editor of *Confrontation,* 1969-71.

WORK IN PROGRESS: "Point and Counterpoint: A Review of the Literature on Student Unrest," to be included in *Student Unrest,* edited by Donald Light.

SIDELIGHTS: Molly Levin writes: "Since I believe that people need not abandon themselves to a destiny either accidental or imposed, I give in occasionally to a nagging Jewish mother complex to scold, shame, or shock the young or the resigned into taking an oar and steering the boat in the desired direction." *Avocational interests:* International travel, cooking, reading.

* * *

LEVINE, Gary 1938-

PERSONAL: Born February 3, 1938, in Kingston, N.Y.; son of Morris (a businessman) and Rose (a businesswoman; maiden name, Scheid) Levine. *Education:* Orange County Community College, A.A., 1957; Hartwick College, B.A., 1959; State University of New York College at Albany, M.A., 1962; Syracuse University, M.A., 1963; St. John's University, Jamaica, N.Y., Ph.D., 1971. *Religion:* Jewish. *Address:* C.P.O. Box 485, Kingston, N.Y. 12401.

CAREER: Manager of scrap metal company in Kingston, N.Y., 1962-69; St. John's University, Jamaica, N.Y., lecturer in history, 1968-70; State University of New York College at New Paltz, instructor in history, summer, 1970; Columbia Greene Community College, Athens, N.Y., associate professor, 1970, professor of history, 1973—. *Member:* American Historical Association, Society for the History of Technology, Society of Automotive Historians, Mutual U.F.O. Network, Greene County Historical Society.

WRITINGS: The Car Solution: The Steam Engine Comes of Age, Horizon Press, 1974. Contributor to *Catskill Quarterly, Barrytown Explorer,* and *Jewish Advocate.*

WORK IN PROGRESS: A non-fiction book about Prohibition-era gangsters.

SIDELIGHTS: Levine writes that he "felt that a thorough history of steam automobiles was needed, especially at a time when air and noise pollution and fuel shortages were widespread. I have also done considerable research on the U.F.O. phenomena and the Prohibition-era gangsters and spend considerable time lecturing on these topics . . .''

* * *

LEVINE, Joan Goldman

PERSONAL: Born in New York, N.Y.; daughter of Edward and Ethel (Schwartz) Goldman; married James A. Levine; children: Jessica, Joshua. *Education:* Attended University of Wisconsin; New York University, B.A.; University of California, Berkeley, secondary teaching credential. *Residence:* Wellesley, Mass.

CAREER: Has taught English, film, and drama in high schools in California and Massachusetts; Wellesley High School, Wellesley, Mass., currently teacher of English, film, and drama. *Member:* Public Action Coalition for Toys, Action for Children's Television, New England Association of Authors and Illustrators, Wellesley League of Women Voters.

WRITINGS: A Bedtime Story (juvenile), Dutton, 1975; *The Santa Claus Mystery* (juvenile), Dutton, 1975. Reviewer for *Voice for Children* and *New York Times.*

SIDELIGHTS: Joan Levine writes: "As a child books always were a great source of pleasure and comfort for me. I can remember crouching under my covers with a flashlight at night, trying to read when I was supposed to be sleeping. When my daughter, Jessica, was born I revisited the world of children's literature and experienced that delight again. I think my writing springs from these two sources: my own childish love of books and my daughter's newly awakened interest.''

BIOGRAPHICAL/CRITICAL SOURCES: Woman's Day, December, 1975.

*   *   *

LEVITT, Morton 1920-

PERSONAL: Born April 26, 1920, in Detroit, Mich.; son of Max and Gussie (Speigelglass) Levitt; married Lucille Shirley Keller, November 1, 1942; children: Susan Eileen, Michael Lee, David Max, Richard Alan. *Education:* Wayne State University, B.S., 1942, M.Ed., 1948; University of Michigan, Ph.D., 1955. *Home:* 540 Rutgers Dr., Davis, Calif. 95616. *Agent:* Al Hart, Fox Chase Agency, 419 East 57th St., New York, N.Y. 10022. *Office:* School of Medicine, University of California, Davis, Calif. 95616.

CAREER: Detroit Board of Education, Psychological Clinic, Visiting Teacher Service, Detroit, Mich., psychologist, 1948-51; Wayne State University, Detroit, Mich., instructor in clinical psychology, 1948-51, instructor in psychiatry, 1951-55, assistant professor, 1955-57, associate professor, 1957-61, professor of psychiatry, 1961-70, assistant dean of admissions and student affairs, 1957-63, associate dean of academic affairs, 1963-70; University of California, Davis, professor of psychology in psychiatry and associate dean of academic affairs, 1970—. Chief consulting psychologist at Children's Hospital of Michigan, 1951-53; associate attending psychologist at Detroit General Hospital, 1952-70; chief psychologist for Rochester (Mich.) Community Schools, 1950-55, director of Mental Hygiene Clinic, 1955-59; director of Highland Park Child Development Clinic, 1956-59. U.S. Peace Corps field selection officer, 1965-70. Visiting professor at University of Edinburgh, 1968, and University of Leyden, 1972; lecturer at Oxford University, 1970. *Military service:* U.S. Army Air Forces, 1941-46.

MEMBER: American Psychological Association, American Orthopsychiatric Association, American Association for the Advancement of Science, Association of American Medical Colleges, New York Academy of Science, Central California Psychiatric Society, San Francisco Psychoanalytic Society.

WRITINGS: (Editor) *Readings in Psychoanalytic Psychology,* Appleton, 1959; *Freud and Dewey on the Nature of Man,* Philosophical Library, 1960, revised edition, Greenwood Press, 1972; (with Reuben Meyer, Mordecai L. Falick, and Ben O. Rubenstein) *Essentials of Pediatric Psychiatry,* Appleton, 1962; (editor with Rubenstein) *Orthopsychiatry and the Law,* Wayne State University Press, 1968; (editor with Rubenstein) *The Mental Health Field: A Critical Appraisal,* Wayne State University Press, 1971; (editor with Rubenstein) *Youth and Social Change,* Wayne State University Press, 1972; (editor with Rubenstein) *On the Urban Scene,* Wayne State University Press, 1972. Contributor of more than sixty articles to psychology, psychiatry, medical, and other scholarly journals. Member of editorial board of *American Journal of Orthopsychiatry,* 1965-72.

WORK IN PROGRESS: A Pious Man at Home: The Strange Story of Richard Nixon and Alger Hiss; Vermont Voices; research on attitudes toward the team approach in health care delivery systems.

LEVY, Bernard 1907-

PERSONAL: Born August 20, 1907, in New York, N.Y.; son of William M. (a physician) and Fannie (Brody) Levy; married Ruth Frances Kruger, August 9, 1946; children: Constance. *Education:* City College (now of the City University of New York), A.B., 1925; Columbia University, M.A., 1926, Ph.D., 1930. *Home:* 200 East 71st St., New York, N.Y. 10021. *Office:* Department of Romance Languages, City College of the City University of New York, 135th St. & Convent Ave., New York, N.Y. 10031.

CAREER: City College of the City University of New York, New York, N.Y., instructor, 1930-37, assistant professor, 1937-48, associate professor, 1948-51, professor of Romance languages, 1951—, supervisor of adult education program, 1945-47, director of School of General Studies, 1948-66. Member of advisory group to New York State Commissioner of Education and State Department of Education, 1959. *Member:* American Association of University Professors, American Association of Teachers of Spanish and Portuguese.

WRITINGS: The Unpublished Plays of Carolet: A New Chapter on the History of the Theatre de la Foire, Institute of French Studies, Columbia University, 1931; (editor with William E. Knickerbocker) *Modern Spanish Prose Readings, 1830-1930,* Appleton-Century Co., 1936; (editor) *Quince Cuentos Populares* (title means ''Fifteen Popular Stories''), Holt, 1939; *A History of Spanish Synonymy,* University of Pennsylvania Press, 1940; *Present-Day Spanish,* Holt, 1940, 3rd edition, 1970; (editor and contributor) *A Grammar of Everyday Spanish,* Dryden, 1950, 2nd edition, 1951. Contributor to language journals.

*   *   *

LEVY, Jonathan 1935-

PERSONAL: Born February 20, 1935, in New York, N.Y.; son of Milton Jerome (a lawyer) and Sylvia (a teacher; maiden name, Narins) Levy; married Geraldine Carro (a journalist), November 24, 1968; children: Catherine Sylvia. *Education:* Harvard University, A.B., 1956; graduate study, University of Rome, Rome, Italy, 1956-57; Columbia University, M.A., 1959, Ph.D., 1966. *Home:* 1165 Fifth Ave., New York, N.Y. 10029.

CAREER: Julliard School of Music, New York, N.Y., instructor in humanities department, 1960-61; Columbia University, New York, N.Y., lecturer, 1960-62; University of California, Berkeley, lecturer in speech, 1964-65; Columbia University, associate professor of English, 1966-69, 1972-73; Manhattan Theatre Club, New York, N.Y., playwright-in-residence, 1973—. *Member:* New Theatre Playwrights Unit, 1966-67, and Playwrights Unit, 1970; cofounder and president, Playwrights for Children's Theatre, 1971-75; senior fellow, Lincoln Center Institute, 1975—. *Member:* American Society of Composers, Authors, and Publishers, Dramatists Guild. *Awards, honors:* Fulbright research grant, 1963-64, New York State Council for the Arts grant, 1973; Creative Arts Public Service grant in playwrighting, 1975.

WRITINGS—Plays: ''Sabbatai Zevi,'' first produced in Boston, Mass., February, 1966; (adaptor from the Italian) Carlo Gozzi, ''Turandot'' (first produced in New Paltz, N.Y., March, 1967), included in *The Genius of the Italian Theatre,* edited by Eric Bentley, New American Library, 1964; ''The Play of Innocence and Change,'' first produced in New York at 92nd St. Young Men's Hebrew Association, June, 1967; ''An Exploratory Operation,'' first produced in New York at The New Jewish Theatre Workshop, March, 1968; "Jack N's Awful Demands," first produced in New York at the Playbox Theatre, June, 1968; (adaptor from the Italian) Carlo Gozzi, "The Little Green Bird," first produced in Southhampton, N.Y., August, 1968; "Ziskin's Revels," first produced in New York at The New Theatre Workshop, October, 1968.

"The Master of the Blue Mineral Mines," first produced in New York at The Barr-Albee Playwrights Unit, December, 1970; "The Shrinking Bride," first produced in New York at the Mercury Theatre, January, 1971; "The Marvellous Adventures of Tyl" (first produced in New York at the Triangle Theatre, June, 1971), included in *Contemporary Children's Theatre*, edited by B. J. Lifton, Avon, 1974; "Master Class," first produced in New York at Manhattan Theatre Club, February, 1972; *Boswell's Journal* (first produced in New York at Alice Tully Hall, Lincoln Center, March, 1972), Ricordi (Milan), 1973; "Charlie the Chicken," first produced in Stratford, Conn., at the American Shakespeare Festival, August, 1972; "Monkey Play," first produced in New York at Clark Center for the Performing Arts, September, 1972; "Marco Polo: A Fantasy for Children," first produced in New York at Manhattan Theatre Club, June, 1973; "Theatre Games," first produced in Calgary, Alberta, Canada at Theatre Calgary, October, 1973; "The Pornographer's Daughter," first produced in New York at Manhattan Theatre Club, February, 1975.

(Contributor) Stanley Burnshaw, editor, *The Poem Itself*, Holt, 1962. Contributor of fiction, poems, and reviews to *Village Voice, Harper's Bookletter, Cricket*, and other publications.

WORK IN PROGRESS: A full-length play and two one-acts for adults; a play with songs for children; a libretto for a one-act opera.

* * *

LEVY, Lester S(tern)   1896-

PERSONAL: Born October 22, 1896, in Philadelphia, Pa.; son of William (a hat manufacturer) and Beatrice (Stern) Levy; married Eleanor Kohn (a potter), October 18, 1922; children: Susan (Mrs. Simon Bodenheimer), Ellen (Mrs. Arnall Patz), Ruth (Mrs. David S. Gottesman). *Education:* Johns Hopkins University, A.B., 1918. *Religion:* Jewish. *Home:* 2 Slade Ave., Pikesville, Md. 21208. *Office:* 600 Reisterstown Rd., Pikesville, Md. 21208.

CAREER: Employed in manufacture of men's hats, with M. S. Levy & Sons, Baltimore, Md., 1919-39, and Men's Hats, Inc., Baltimore, 1939-59; writer, 1959—. President of Associated Jewish Charities of Baltimore, 1943-45; member of board of directors of Maryland Department of Social Services, 1965-75; chairman of board of directors of Baltimore Hebrew College, 1969-70; trustee of University of Baltimore, 1970-73. Member of board of directors of Baltimore Symphony Orchestra, 1968-75. *Military service:* U.S. Army, 1918-19; became sergeant. *Member:* Maryland Historical Society (member of council, 1971-75), Baltimore Bibliophiles (president, 1967-68), Phi Beta Kappa.

WRITINGS: Grace Notes in American History, University of Oklahoma Press, 1967; *Flashes of Merriment,* University of Oklahoma Press, 1971; *Give Me Yesterday,* University of Oklahoma Press, 1975; (author of introduction) *Sousa's Great Marches,* Dover, 1975. Contributor to *Americana* magazine.

WORK IN PROGRESS: Picture the Song, for Johns Hopkins University Press.

SIDELIGHTS: Levy writes that all his studies, interests, and writings have been directed to the relationship of American popular music to American history.

* * *

LEWBIN, Hyman J(oseph)   1894-

PERSONAL: Surname originally Lewbomirski; legally changed, 1915; born August 12, 1894, in Russia; son of Joseph and Brocha (Levitas) Lewbomirski; married Fannie Polonsy, 1918 (died September 4, 1964); married Fay Plishtin-Rossin; children: (first marriage) Beatrice (Mrs. Michael Becker). *Education:* University of Illinois, D.D.S., 1921. *Politics:* "Democrat mostly." *Home:* 8011 Romaine St., Los Angeles, Calif. 90046.

CAREER: Dentist, beginning 1921; writer, 1935—. *Military service:* U.S. Army, Infantry, 1919. *Member:* American Civil Liberties Union, Common Cause, American-Jewish Congress, Los Angeles Yiddish Writers Group.

WRITINGS: Resistance in Minsk (translated from Yiddish by Hersh Smaliar), Judah Magnes Memorial Museum, 1966; *Rebirth of Jewish Art: The Unfolding of Jewish Art in the Nineteenth Century,* Shengold, 1974. Contributor of about a hundred articles to English and Yiddish magazines.

SIDELIGHTS: Over the years Dr. Lewbin has collected more than a thousand books on Jewish art and on Jews in the arts. This collection has been promised to the Frances-Henry Library at California School of Hebrew Union College. He has also collected catalogues, brochures, magazine articles, and newspaper clippings on these topics and on Jewish patrons of the arts and critics. He writes: "My view is in line of human artistic endeavor through the human history and participation in it of Jewish artists. Whether it is the great Greek achievements, the Renaissance artist or the art of today it is all an expression of life at its time and circumstances."

* * *

LEWIN, Esther   1922-

PERSONAL: Born January 27, 1922, in Vancouver, British Columbia, Canada; daughter of Mourell (a watchmaker) and Pauline (Solomovich) Schaffer; married Albert E. Lewin (a screenwriter), June 30, 1946; children: Charles, Elizabeth. *Education:* University of California, Los Angeles, B.A., 1942. *Residence:* Sherman Oaks, Calif.

CAREER: May Co., Los Angeles, Calif., advertising copywriter, 1942-44; Hillman-Shane Breyer, Los Angeles, copywriter and account executive, 1944-51; Rogers and Cowan, Beverley Hills, Calif., public relations and account executive, 1973-75. Founding member of Committee for a Sane Nuclear Policy, 1958, and Women Strike for Peace, 1961; founding board member of Oakwood Secondary School, 1964; member of Los Angeles County Grand Jury, 1971; vice-president of Comprehensive Health-Los Angeles Environmental Committee, 1972-73; Los Angeles City Commissioner on Environmental Quality Board, 1973—.

WRITINGS—All with cousin, Birdina Lewin: *Stewed to the Gills: A Fish and Wine Cookery,* Nash Publishing, 1971; *Rice 'N Easy,* Nash Publishing, 1973; *Women's Lib Cookbook or Whose Place Is in the Kitchen?,* Ritchie, 1973; *Men's Lib Cookbook or Feel Free,* Ritchie, 1973; *Growing Food, Growing Up: A Child's Natural Food Book,* Ritchie, 1973, 2nd edition, 1975; *The Egg and the*

Eye, Ritchie, 1973; *The Absolutely No Calorie Dessert Cookbook,* Anderson, Simon & Ritchie, 1974.

SIDELIGHTS: Esther Lewin told *CA:* "I have always been deeply involved in politics and issues that affect people . . . many of them long before they became popular. I was an early advocate of a ban on nuclear testing and was one of the founders in Los Angeles of Norman Cousin's Committee For A Sane Nuclear Policy and Women Strike for Peace. While trying to save the world (which stubbornly refused to be saved!), Birdina Lewin and I decided to turn some rather considerable culinary talents on the world. Happily, these efforts were more successful. We both love cooking and writing about cooking. One of the drawbacks of being a cookbook author is that suddenly, your friends are afraid to ask you to dinner."

* * *

LEZRA, Grizzella Paull 1934-

PERSONAL: Born September 14, 1934, in Wheeling, W.Va.; daughter of Archibald Woods (a businessman) and Margaret (Kinder) Paull; married Moises Lezra (a banker), July 25, 1957; children: Jack, Anita, Esther. *Education:* Vassar College, A.B., 1956. *Politics:* Democrat. *Religion:* Jewish. *Home:* Qta. Camoruco, II Avda., Altamina entre 9 y 10, Caracas, Venezuela.

CAREER: Elementary school teacher in Tangier, Morocco, 1956-57; high school teacher of English in Madrid, Spain, 1961-62; Instituto Internacional, Madrid, Spain, teacher of English, 1971.

WRITINGS: *The Cat, the Horse and the Miracle,* Atheneum, 1967; *Mechido, Aziza, and Ahmed,* Atheneum, 1969.

SIDELIGHTS: Grizzella Lezra wrote: "The first book came about under doctor's prescription; recovering from hepatitis, I was told to sit still for three months. The only way was to write a book. Other books have been written since, but the motivation was not urgent—and most are not published!"

* * *

LIBERMAN, Robert Paul 1937-

PERSONAL: Born August 16, 1937, in Newark, N.J.; married, 1961 (divorced); married second wife, Janet Brown, 1973; children: (first marriage) two. *Education:* Dartmouth College, A.B. (summa cum laude), 1959, diploma in medicine (with honors), 1960; University of California, San Francisco, M.S., 1961; Johns Hopkins University, M.D., 1963; Harvard University, postdoctoral study, 1966-68. *Home:* 528 East Potrero Rd., Thousand Oaks, Calif. 91360. *Office:* Research Program, Camarillo-Neuropsychiatric Institute, Box A, Camarillo, Calif. 93010.

CAREER: Bronx Municipal Hospital, Bronx, N.Y., intern, 1963-64; Yeshiva University, Albert Einstein College of Medicine, New York, N.Y., intern, 1963-64; Massachusetts Mental Health Center, Boston, resident in psychiatry, 1964-68; Washington School of Psychiatry, Washington, D.C., faculty member of group psychotherapy training program, 1968-70; University of California, Los Angeles, assistant clinical professor, 1970-72, associate clinical professor of psychiatry, 1972-73, associate research psychiatrist and director of clinical research program at Camarillo-Neuropsychiatric Institute, 1973—. Adjunct lecturer at Antioch College West-University Without Walls, 1971—; lecturer at University of California, Santa Barbara, 1971—, and California Lutheran College, 1973—. Senior

psychiatrist at Boston State Hospital Drug Addiction Center, 1965-66; psychiatrist at Faulkner Hospital (Boston), 1966-67, Fairfax Hospital (Falls Church, Va.), 1968-70, Ventura County General Hospital, 1970—, and University of California, Los Angeles Hospital, 1971—; private practice of psychiatry in Reston, Va., 1968-70; director of Oxnard Regional Community Mental Health Center, 1973-74. Psychiatrist for National Institute of Mental Health career development program, 1964-70; surgeon for U.S. Public Health Service, 1964-68; medical officer for U.S. Department of Health, Education & Welfare, 1968-70; research psychiatrist at Saint Elizabeth's Hospital (Washington, D.C.), 1968-70; director of Laboratory of Behavior Modification and Clinical Research Unit at Camarillo State Hospital, 1970-73. Diplomate of National Board of Medical Examiners, 1964; licensed to practice medicine in Massachusetts, Virginia, District of Columbia, and California; diplomate in psychiatry of American Board of Psychiatry and Neurology, 1969; community college instructor credential from California Community Colleges, 1973. Member of junior staff advisory committee to director of National Institute of Mental Health, 1966-70; member of California Conference of Local Mental Health Program Directors' research and evaluation sub-committee, 1971—; member of Ventura Subregion Criminal Justice Planning Board's training and education sub-committee, 1972-74.

MEMBER: American Medical Association, American Association for the Advancement of Science, American Psychiatric Association, Association for the Advancement of Behavior Therapy (member of executive committee, 1970-72; member of board of directors, 1973-77), Physicians for Social Responsibility (member of executive committee), Phi Beta Kappa. *Awards, honors:* Harry Solomon Award from Massachusetts Mental Health Center, 1966; National Institute of Mental Health grants, 1967-68, 1972-75, 1973-75, 1975-78; California Department of Health grant, 1972-75; California Council on Criminal Justice grant, 1972-73; physicians' recognition award in continuing medical education from American Medical Association, 1973-76; National Institute on Drug Abuse research grants, 1974-77, 1975-77; U.S. Department of Health, Education & Welfare grant from Bureau of Handicapped Children, 1975-78.

WRITINGS: *A Guide to Behavioral Analysis and Therapy,* Pergamon, 1972; (with L. W. King, W. J. DeRisi, and M. J. McCann) *Personal Effectiveness: Guiding People to Assert Their Feelings and Improve Their Social Skills,* Research Press, 1975.

Contributor: Thomas Kiresuk, editor, *Program Evaluation Forum,* Minnesota Program Evaluation Project, 1971; G. D. Erickson and T. P. Hogan, editors, *Family Therapy: Theory and Technique,* Brooks-Cole, 1972; C. J. Sager and H. S. Kaplan, editors, *Progress in Group and Family Therapy,* Brunner, 1972; Harvey Tilker, editor, *Abnormal Psychology,* CRM Books, 1972; Peter Houts and Michael Serber, editors, *After the Turn-On, What?,* Research Press, 1972; Richard Rubin, Cyril Franks, Herbert Fensterheim, and Leonard Ullmann, editors, *Advances in Behavior Therapy,* Volume III, Academic Press, 1972; B. M. Deneer and R. D. Price, editors, *Social Action and Reaction,* Holt, 1973; Joel Fischer, editor, *Interpersonal Helping,* C. C Thomas, 1973; Kenneth O. Doyle, editor, *Interaction: Readings in Human Psychology,* Heath, 1973; R. S. Lawrence and R. V. Nelson, editors, *Readings in Abnormal Psychology,* MSS Information Corp., 1973; J. K. Larsen and B. A. Sanderson, editors, *Source Book of Programs: Community Mental Health Centers,* American Institutes for Research, 1973; W. K. DiScipio, editor, *The Behavioral Treatment of Psychotic Illness*, Behavioral Publications, 1974; P. D. Davidson, F. J. Clark, and L. Hamerlynck, editors, *Evaluating Behavioral Programs in Community, Residential, and Educational Settings*, Research Press, 1974; K. S. Calhoun, H. E. Adams, and E. M. Mitchell, editors, *Innovative Treatment Methods in Psychopathology*, Wiley, 1974; L. S. Gorlow and W. F. Katkovsky, editors, *Readings in the Psychology of Adjustment*, 3rd edition (Liberman was not included in earlier editions), McGraw, 1975; H. B. Robach and S. I. Abramowitz, editors, *Group Psychotherapy Research: Commentaries and Readings*, Temple University Press, 1975; William T. Reynolds, editor, *Behavior Therapy in Review*, Jason Aronson, 1975; H. H. Eysenck, editor, *Case Histories in Behavior Therapy*, Routledge & Kegan Paul, 1975; H.L.P. Resnik and H. J. Parad, editors, *Innovations in Emergency Mental Health Services*, Prentice-Hall, 1975; Harold Leitenberg, editor, *Handbook of Behavior Therapy and Modification*, Appleton, 1975; Michel Hersen, Richard Eisler, and P. M. Miller, editors, *Progress in Behavior Modification*, Academic Press, 1975; Jack Zusman and Elmer Bertsche, editors, *The Future Role of the State Hospital*, Health, 1975; L. J. West and Don Flinn, editors, *Treatment of Schizophrenia*, Grune, 1975.

Also author of films, "Reinforcing Social Interaction in a Group of Chronic Schizophrenics," 1970, "Reinforcement Therapy in a Day Hospital," 1971, "Assertive Training," 1972, "Contingency Contracting in Families," 1972, "Personal Effectiveness: Training Skills in a Group," 1974, and "Kids Are People Too: How to Use Social Reinforcement with Children," 1974.

Contributor to *International Encyclopedia of Neurology, Psychiatry, Psychology, and Psychoanalysis*. Contributor of about fifty articles and reviews to medical journals. Member of editorial board of *Journal of Applied Behavior Analysis*, 1972—, *Journal of Marriage and Family Counseling*, 1974—, and *Journal of Behavior Therapy and Experimental Psychiatry*, 1976—.

WORK IN PROGRESS: Conducting research at Institute of Psychiatry and Maudsley Hospital, in London, England.

* * *

LIEBMAN, Charles S(eymour)   1934-

PERSONAL: Born October 20, 1934, in New York, N.Y.; son of Seymour B. (a lawyer) and Libbie (Sussman) Liebman; married Carol Stickler (a university lecturer), January 23, 1959; children: Rivkah, Aaron, Abigail. *Education:* University of Miami, B.B.A., 1956; Johns Hopkins University, graduate study, 1956-57; University of Illinois, M.A., 1958, Ph.D., 1960. *Politics:* Liberal. *Religion:* Jewish. *Home:* 9 Anna Frank St., Petach Tikva, Israel. *Office:* Bar-Ilan University, Ramat-Gan, Israel.

CAREER: University lecturer. *Member:* American Political Science Association, Society for the Scientific Study of Religion. *Awards, honors:* Zvi Luria Prize from World Zionist Organization, 1974, for *The Ambivalent American Jew;* Ford Foundation grant, 1975.

WRITINGS: Suburban Differences and Metropolitan Policies, University of Pennsylvania Press, 1965; *The Ambivalent American Jew*, Jewish Publication Society, 1973; *Aspects of the Religious Behaviour of American Jews*, Ktav, 1974; *Pressure Without Sanctions*, Fairleigh Dickinson University Press, in press. Contributor to journals in his field.

WORK IN PROGRESS: A study of religion and politics in Israel, under a grant from the Ford Foundation.

* * *

LIENTZ, Bennet Price   1942-

PERSONAL: Born October 24, 1942, in Hollywood, Calif.; son of Beverly Price and Josephine (Palen) Lientz; married Martha Benson, August 29, 1964; children: Bennet P., Jr., Andrew Noll, Charles Sumner. *Education:* Claremont Men's College, B.A., 1964; University of Washington, Seattle, M.S., 1966, Ph.D., 1968. *Religion:* Presbyterian. *Home:* 229 21st Pl., Santa Monica, Calif. 90402. *Office:* Graduate School of Management, University of California at Los Angeles, Los Angeles, Calif. 90024.

CAREER: System Development Corp., Santa Monica, Calif., department head and senior research scientist, 1968-70; University of Southern California, Los Angeles, assistant professor, 1970-73, associate professor of engineering, 1973-74; University of California at Los Angeles, associate professor of management, 1974—. Consultant to Atlantic Richfield, 1974—, California Federal Savings, 1974, and County of Los Angeles, 1974—. *Member:* Institute of Management Science, Operations Research Society of America, American Statistical Association, Institute of Mathematical Statistics. *Awards, honors:* National Science Foundation research travel grant, 1972.

WRITINGS: Computer Applications in Operations Analysis, Prentice-Hall, 1975. Contributor to journals in his field.

WORK IN PROGRESS: A study of computer networks, experiments, and economic trade-offs; research in computer security and system development procedures.

* * *

LIGHT, Patricia Kahn   1939-

PERSONAL: Born March 29, 1939, in Elizabeth, N.J.; daughter of Perry and Thelma (Kurtz) Kahn; married Richard J. Light (a professor of statistics and educational policy), June 25, 1965; children: Jennifer, Sarah. *Education:* Bennington College, A.B., 1960; Harvard University, Ed.M., 1966, Ed.D., 1973. *Home:* 47 Audrey Rd., Belmont, Mass. 02178. *Office:* Office of Counseling and Career Development, Harvard University, Graduate School of Business Administration, Cambridge, Mass.

CAREER: High school mathematics teacher in Elizabeth, N.J., 1961-65, chairman of department, 1964-65; psychology intern in public schools of Newton, Mass., 1966-67, high school counselor in Newton, 1967-68; Massachusetts General Hospital, Boston, clinical fellow in psychology, 1968-69; Powell Associates, Inc., Cambridge, Mass., staff psychologist, 1969-74; Harvard University, Cambridge, Mass., psychologist in Office of Counseling and Career Development, 1974—. Licensed psychologist in Massachusetts; private practice in psychology. Counseling intern in public high school in Brookline, Mass., spring, 1967; consulting school psychologist, South Hamilton, Mass., 1972—. *Member:* American Psychological Association (associate member), Eastern Psychological Association, Massachusetts Psychological Association, Pi Lambda Theta.

WRITINGS: Let the Children Speak: A Psychological Study of Young Teenagers and Drugs, Lexington Books, 1975.

WORK IN PROGRESS: Research on two-career families, with a book expected to result.

LILLARD, Charles (Marion) 1944-

PERSONAL: Born February 26, 1944, in Long Beach, Calif.; son of Donald George and Viola Katherine (Brooks) Lillard. *Education:* University of British Columbia, B.A., 1969, M.F.A., 1973. *Home address:* Box 708, Sooke, British Columbia, Canada V0S 1N0. *Office:* Department of Creative Writing, University of Victoria, Box 1700, Victoria, British Columbia, Canada V8W 2Y2.

CAREER: Has worked as a boom man in Alaska, and as a faller, machine operator, and crewboss for Environment Canada, 1960-72; University of British Columbia, Center for Continuing Education, Vancouver, lecturer in poetry and writing, 1971-74; University of Victoria, Victoria, British Columbia, instructor in creative writing, 1974—. Research assistant, National Film Board of Canada, 1973-74; lecturer, Matsqui Institution, 1973-74. *Member:* League of Canadian Poets, Victoria Archaeology Society (founder; president, 1974—). *Awards, honors:* Huntington Poetry Award, 1968; Book Promotion and Editorial Club award, 1972, for *Volvox;* Canada Council grant, summer, 1973; Multi-Cultural Programme grant, 1974; Canada Council Explorations Programme grant, 1975; L.I.P. grant, 1975.

WRITINGS—Poetry: *Cultus Coulee,* Sono Nis Press, 1971; (editor with J. Michael Yates) *Volvox: Poetry from the Unofficial Languages of Canada,* Sono Nis Press, 1971; *Drunk on Wood,* Sono Nis Press, 1973; (contributor) *A Guide to South East Alaska Trails,* Mountaineer Press, 1975; *Jabble,* Kanchenjunga, 1975; (editor with George McWhirter) *Words from the Inside,* Morriss, 1975; *Ana,* Oolichan Books, 1976.

Also author of play, "The Crossing," first produced in Vancouver, British Columbia, November, 1972. Poems represented in anthologies, including *Contemporary Poetry of British Columbia,* edited by J. Michael Yates, Sono Nis Press, 1970, and *Skookum Wawa,* edited by Gary Geddes, Oxford University Press, 1975. Contributor of articles, reviews, fiction, translations, and poems to *Vancouver Magazine, Canadian Literature, Malahat Review, Canadian Fiction Magazine, Quixote, Prism International, Contemporary Literature in Translation, Penumbra, Fiddlehead, West Coast Review,* and other periodicals. Editor, *Newsletter* of the Victoria Archaeology Society, 1975—; associate editor, *Malahat Review,* 1975—; guest editor, *Canadian Fiction Magazine,* summer, 1975.

WORK IN PROGRESS: With Sys Richards, notes and translations from the Danish poems of J. P. Jacobsen.

AVOCATIONAL INTERESTS: The west coast, North Pacific Americana and literature, book collecting.

*   *   *

LIMAN, Ellen (Susan) 1936-

PERSONAL: Born January 4, 1936, in New York, N.Y.; married Arthur Liman (an attorney), September 20, 1969; children: Lewis, Emily, Douglas. *Education:* Barnard College, B.A., 1957. *Home:* 135 Central Park W., New York, N.Y. 10023. *Agent:* Julian Bach, Jr., 3 East 48th St., New York, N.Y. 10017.

CAREER: Writer. Member of board of governors of International Center of Photography, Lincoln Square Neighborhood Center, and Jewish Museum.

WRITINGS: The Money Saver's Guide to Decorating, Macmillan, 1971; *Decorating Your Country Place,* Coward, 1973; (with Carol Panter) *Decorating Your Room: A Do It Yourself Guide,* F. Watts, 1974.

WORK IN PROGRESS: A book for Viking.

*   *   *

LIN, Florence (Shen)

PERSONAL: Married K. Y. Lin (in investments); children: Flora, Kay. *Education:* Attended University of Nanking. *Home:* 4525 Henry Hudson Parkway, Bronx, N.Y. 10471.

CAREER: Cooking teacher and writer, specializing in Chinese food and nutrition. Teacher at China Institute in America, 1960—. Has conducted more than a hundred cooking demonstrations. Consultant to metropolitan restaurants and major food processors.

WRITINGS: Florence Lin's Chinese Regional Cookbook, Hawthorn, 1975.

SIDELIGHTS: As a young woman Florence Lin traveled extensively with her father, visiting all the important cities of China. Her participation in this travel, as well as the dinners that always accompanied each visit, gave her a critical sense of taste. She had opportunities to sample the more unusual delicacies, as well as the finer preparations of the more common. In 1965 and 1969, she returned to the Far East and Southeast Asia, to survey and study the markets, food businesses, and the cooking. Now, her students can prepare Chinese foods, properly order a meal in a Chinese restaurant, and comfortably find their way among the myriad grocery shops in lower Manhattan's Chinatown. She offers beginner's courses, and an advanced course in banquet dishes, Chinese hors d'oeuvres, and a variety of Dim Sum.

*   *   *

LIND, Alan R(obert) 1940-

PERSONAL: Born January 21, 1940, in Chicago, Ill.; son of Albin Matthias (an auditor) and Minnette (Swanson) Lind. *Education:* University of Chicago, B.A. (liberal arts) and B.A. (business administration), 1962; graduate study at Northwestern University, 1964-67. *Politics:* Democratic. *Religion:* Evangelical Covenant. *Home:* 141 Hemlock, Park Forest, Ill. 60466.

CAREER: Illinois Central Magazine, Chicago, Ill., editorial assistant, 1964-66, assistant editor, 1966-71; *Illinois Central Gulf News,* Chicago, editor, 1971-75; Burson-Marsteller (public relations), Chicago, technical writer, 1975— Co-founder, publisher and general editor of Prototype Publications, Park Forest, Ill., 1972—; founder of Transport History Press; lecturer at American Managment Association Seminars, 1973. *Military service:* U.S. Army Reserve, 1963-69. *Member:* International Association of Business Communicators, International Platform Association, American Judicature Society, Association of Railroad Editors, Professional Photographers of America, National Museum of Transport, Chicago Press Club, Chicago Historical Society, Industrial Editors Association of Chicago, Chicago Association of Business Communicators, Chicago Gallery of Photography (exhibiting member, 1970-71), Park Forest Racquet Club.

WRITINGS: (Editor with W. D. Randall) *From Zephyr to Amtrak,* Prototype Publications, 1972; (editor with Randall) *Monarchs of Mid-America,* Prototype Publications, 1973; *Chicago Surface Lines: An Illustrated History,* Transport History Press, 1974, 2nd revised edition, 1974. Publications director of Central Electric Railfans' Association, Chicago, Ill., 1974.

WORK IN PROGRESS: Three books dealing with urban transportation in Minneapolis-St. Paul, St. Louis, and Chicago; a book on the Illinois Central Railroad's motive power.

SIDELIGHTS: "Passenger transportation is my field," Lind wrote, "particularly travel by main line railroad train, and urban transportation by streetcar, motor bus, trolley bus, subway, and elevated. Concern about pollution, the gas shortage, and a re-ordering of national priorities have made both main line train travel and urban public transportation increasingly important in the mid-1970s. In searching for material on transportation, I have visited every continental state and seen much of Canada. My camera is always with me on these trips."

*   *   *

LINDEMANN, Constance 1923-

PERSONAL: Born April 17, 1923, in Ossining, N.Y.; daughter of Harry and Anna (Blau) Spatz; married; children: Lucy Lindemann Newton, Eric. *Education:* California State University, Long Beach, B.A., 1967; University of California at Los Angeles, M.P.H., 1968, Dr. P.H., 1974. *Office:* Department of Social Work, University of Oklahoma, 1005 Jenkins, Norman, Okla. 73069.

CAREER: Arizona State University, Tempe, assistant professor of community health, 1973-75; University of Oklahoma, Norman, assistant professor of social work, 1975—. *Member:* American Public Health Association, American Sociological Association, Delta Omega.

WRITINGS: Birth Control and Unmarried Young Women, Springer Publishing, 1974.

WORK IN PROGRESS: Pregnancy and Unmarried Young Women.

*   *   *

LINDOP, Grevel 1948-

PERSONAL: Born October 6, 1948, in Liverpool, England; son of John Neale (a solicitor) and Winifred (Garrett) Lindop. *Education:* Wadham College, Oxford, B.A., 1970; also studied at Wolfson College, Oxford, 1970-71. *Politics:* Marxist. *Religion:* Theravada Buddhist. *Office:* Department of English, University of Manchester, Manchester M13 9PL, England.

CAREER: University of Manchester, Manchester, England, lecturer in English, 1971—.

WRITINGS: Against the Sea (poems), Carcanet, 1970; (editor with Michael Schmidt, and contributor) *British Poetry Since 1960,* Carcanet, 1972, Dufour, 1973; (editor) *Thomas Chatterton: Selected Poems,* Carcanet, 1972, Dufour, 1973. Contributor to literary magazines, including *Poetry Nation* and *Critical Quarterly.*

WORK IN PROGRESS: A biography of Thomas DeQuincey; research on London life and popular political movements in the age of William Blake.

SIDELIGHTS: Lindop writes: "As a critic I'm concerned with the relationship between individual vision and the social experience of living at a particular moment in history. I see Walter Benjamin as the finest exponent of a criticism which relates and unifies these 'subjective' and 'objective' aspects of experience and their expression in literature. Poetry, criticism, and politics are related for me as means of communication and social action, and therefore also as means of personal growth. In a society which works against human values, only a continual and creative fight back can open the possibility of freedom."

*   *   *

LINDSLEY, Mary F(lora)
(Mary L. Jaffee)

PERSONAL: Born in New York, N.Y.; daughter of Guy Robert (an actor) and Florence (Everett) Lindsley; married Irving Lincoln Jaffee (a writer), January 26, 1963. *Education:* Hunter College (now of the City University of New York), A.B., 1929; Columbia University, M.A., 1932. *Politics:* Independent. *Religion:* Roman Catholic. *Home:* 13361 El Dorado, Apt. 201H, Seal Beach, Calif. 90740.

CAREER: Hunter College (now of the City University of New York), New York, N.Y., instructor, 1930-55, assistant professor, 1955-68, associate professor of English literature and creative writing, 1968-71; writer, 1971—. *Member:* International Biographical Society (fellow), International Institute of Community Service (fellow), United Poets Laureate International, World Poetry Society, Poetry Society of America, American Association of University Women, Accademia Leonardo da Vinci (honorary representative), Australian Society, Dickens Fellowship, New York Poetry Forum (California representative), California Federation of Chaparral Poets (president of Orpheus chapter, 1974-76), Praed Street Irregulars, Sherlock Holmes Society of Los Angeles. *Awards, honors:* Bronze medal from Accademia Leonardo da Vinci, 1965, silver medal, 1966; President Marcos Medal from the Philippines, 1968; golden laurel crown from United Poets Laureate International, 1968, 1969, 1973, 1975; D.H.L. from Free University of Asia, 1969; trophy from California Olympiad of the Arts, 1972; medal from Chinese Poetry Society, 1973; Order of Merit of Eight Chinese Virtues from World University, Hong Kong, 1973; Order of Merit of Six Chinese Arts, 1974; D.L.A. from Great China Arts College of World University, 1973.

WRITINGS: The Uncensored Letter and Other Poems, Island Press Cooperative, 1949; *Grand Tour and Other Poems,* Philosophical Library, 1952; *Promenade* (poems), Accademia Leonardo da Vinci, 1965; *Pomp and Circumstance* (poems), Accademia Leonardo da Vinci, 1966; *Pax Romana* (poems), Accademia Leonardo da Vinci, 1967; *Selected Poems,* Gaus, 1967; *Atma* (poems), Accademia Leonardo da Vinci, 1968; *Rosaria* (poems), Accademia Leonardo da Vinci, 1969; *Work Day of Pierre Toussaint* (poems), Accademia Leonardo da Vinci, 1970; *Circe and the Unicorn* (poems), Accademia Leonardo da Vinci, 1971; *The Masquers* (poems), Accademia Leonardo da Vinci, 1972; *One Life* (poems), Accademia Leonardo da Vinci, 1974; (under name Mary L. Jaffe; with husband, Irving Lincoln Jaffee) *Beyond Baker Street* (short stories), Pontine, 1973; *Anarch's Hand* (poems), Accademia Leonardo da Vinci, 1974; *Night on the Saxon Shore* (poems), Accademia Leonardo da Vinci, 1975; *American Cavalcade* (poems), Dorrance, 1975.

Author of "The Flimflammers" (three-act comedy), with Christine Solomon, produced in Seal Beach, Calif., 1974.

WORK IN PROGRESS: Centennial Child, a novel about life on the stage in the late 1800's and early 1900's.

SIDELIGHTS: Mary Lindsley writes: "I believe that an author has under all his humor the obligation to present the truth as he sees it; to ridicule and oppose what is evil, and to inspire his readers to ideals, constructive action, compassion, and, above all, hope." *Avocational interests:* Play production, photography, cartooning, travel (Europe and Asia).

* * *

LINZEY, Donald Wayne 1939-

PERSONAL: Born September 4, 1939, in Baltimore, Md.; son of Charles Herbert (in U.S. Postal Service) and Dorothy Katherine (Billingsley) Linzey; married Alicia Vogt (a writer, illustrator, and research associate in zoology), June 2, 1963; children: David Wayne, Thomas Alan. *Education:* Western Maryland College, A.B., 1961; Cornell University, M.S., 1963, Ph.D., 1966. *Religion:* Methodist. *Home:* 6312 St. Moritz Dr., Mobile, Ala. 36608. *Office:* Department of Biological Sciences, University of South Alabama, Mobile, Ala. 36688.

CAREER: U.S. Department of Agriculture, Agricultural Research Service, Plant Pest Control Division, Elkridge, Md., inspector, summers, 1957-61; Great Smoky Mountains National Park, Gatlinburg, Tenn., park ranger-naturalist, summers, 1963-65; Cornell University, Ithaca, N.Y., instructor in biology, 1966-67; University of South Alabama, Mobile, assistant professor, 1967-71, associate professor of biological sciences, 1971—, curator of zoology for natural history collections, 1970—. Researcher for National Park Service, 1963-70. Conducts "The Outdoors," a weekly radio program on wildlife and the environment, on WKRG-Radio, 1968—. Member of advisory committee to the Alabama Commissioner of Conservation and Natural Resources, 1971.

MEMBER: American Society of Mammalogists, Wildlife Society, Alabama Academy of Science, Society for the Study of Amphibians and Reptiles, Environmental Defense Fund, National Audubon Society, American Institute of Biological Sciences, Mobile County Wildlife and Conservation Association (member of board of directors, 1974—), Mobile Bay Audubon Society (past president; past chairman of board of directors), Sigma Xi, Beta Beta Beta.

WRITINGS: (With wife, Alicia V. Linzey) *Mammals of Great Smoky Mountains National Park* (for laymen), University of Tennessee Press, 1971; (with A. V. Linzey) *Alabama Wildlife*, privately printed, Volume I, 1972, Volume II, 1973; (contributor) J. N. Layne, editor, *Rare and Endangered Plants and Animals of Florida*, Florida Game and Freshwater Fish Commission, in press; (contributor) J. L. Wolfe, editor, *Rare and Endangered Vertebrates of the Southeastern United States*, Southeastern Chapter, Wildlife Society, in press; (with A. V. Linzey) *Mammals of Alabama*, University of Alabama Press, in press; (contributor) S. Anderson, editor, *Mammalian Species*, American Society of Mammalogists, in press; *Snakes of Alabama*, Strode, in press.

Author of "Alabama Wildlife," a weekly column in *Mobile Press-Register*, 1971—. Contributor of over twenty-five articles to scientific periodicals.

* * *

LIPPINCOTT, David (McCord) 1925-

PERSONAL: Born June 17, 1925, in New York, N.Y.; son of William Jackson (a banker) and Dorothy (McCord) Lippincott; married Joan Bentley, October 16, 1959; children: Christopher Bentley. *Education:* Yale University, B.A., 1949. *Politics:* Independent. *Religion:* Episcopalian. *Home and office:* Birch Mill Rd., Old Lyme, Conn. 06371. *Agent:* Wallace, Aitken & Sheil, 118 East 61st St., New York, N.Y. 10021.

CAREER: McCann-Erickson, Inc. (advertising firm), New York City, copywriter, 1950-53, television head, 1953-58, vice-president and associate creative director, 1958-63, senior vice-president, 1963-69 and 1969-70, executive director of McCann-Erickson Ltd. in England, 1965-66; Erwin-Wasey, Ruthrauf & Ryan (advertising firm), Los Angeles, Calif., vice-chairman of the board of directors, 1967-68; novelist, composer-lyricist, and television writer, 1950—. Managing director of Center of Advanced Practices, Interpublic Group of Companies, 1963-66. *Military service:* U.S. Army Intelligence, 1943-45; received Bronze Star. *Member:* American Society of Composers, Authors, and Publishers, American Guild of Authors and Composers, The Players (New York City).

WRITINGS: E Pluribus Bang!, Viking, 1971; *Voice of Armageddon,* Putnam, 1974; *Tremor Violet,* Putnam, 1975; *Eye of the Camel,* New American Library, 1976. Author of television plays, "Peter Who Wished" and "The Dog" and of scripts for "Studio One," "Captain Kangaroo," and other television shows. Composer-lyricist of 28 published songs, of the record album, "The Body in the Seine," and of three songs in the Broadway revue, "Pleasure Dome."

WORK IN PROGRESS: The Cistern, both as a novel and as a screenplay.

* * *

LIPSKY, Michael 1940-

PERSONAL: Born April 13, 1940, in New York, N.Y.; married; children: two. *Education:* Oberlin College, B.A., 1961; Princeton University, M.P.A. and M.A., both 1964, Ph.D., 1967. *Home:* 42 Brington Rd., Brookline, Mass. 02146. *Office:* Department of Political Science, Massachusetts Institute of Technology, Cambridge, Mass. 02139.

CAREER: University of Wisconsin, Madison, assistant professor of political science and staff associate of Institute for Research on Poverty, both 1966-69; Massachusetts Institute of Technology, Cambridge, associate professor, 1969-75, professor of political science, 1975—.

WRITINGS: Protest in City Politics: Rent Strikes, Housing, and the Power of the Poor, Rand McNally, 1970; (contributor) Harlon Hahn, editor, *People and Politics in Urban Society: Urban Affairs Annual Reviews,* Volume VI, Sage Publications, 1972; (contributor) H. George Frederickson, editor, *Politics, Public Administration, and Neighborhood Control,* Chandler, 1972; (contributor) David Perry and Herbert Hirsch, editors, *Violence as Politics,* Harper, 1973; (editor and author of introduction) *Law and Order: Police Encounters,* Transaction Books, 1970, 2nd edition, 1973; (contributor and senior advisor) *American Government Today,* Del-Mar Co., 1974; (editor with Willis Hawley, and contributor) *Theoretical Perspectives in Urban Politics,* Prentice-Hall, 1976; (with David J. Olson) *Riot Commission Politics: The "Processing" of Racial Crisis in America,* Transaction Books, 1976. Contributor to political science and law journals.

* * *

LIPSON, Harry A(aron, Jr.) 1919-

PERSONAL: Born March 10, 1919, in Wilkes-Barre, Pa.; son of Harry Aaron (a business executive) and Irma (Lowenstein) Lipson; married Miriam Lipson, July 5, 1948 (died October, 1971); married Adele Bloch Bear, August 27, 1972; children: (first marriage) Harry Aaron III, Carolyn Miriam; (second marriage) Jeanne Adele Bear, Martha

Bloch Bear. *Education:* University of Alabama, B.A., 1939; Northwestern University, M.B.A., 1941; University of Pennsylvania, Ph.D., 1955; University of California, Berkeley, postdoctoral study, summer, 1960. *Religion:* Jewish. *Home:* 2825 Montclair Rd., Tuscaloosa, Ala. 35401. *Office:* Department of Marketing, University of Alabama, Box 5021, University, Ala. 35486.

CAREER: Mandel Brothers (department store), Chicago, Ill., research assistant to merchandising manager, 1939-40; Sally Frocks, Chicago, Ill., research assistant to merchandising manager, 1940-41; University of Alabama, University, instructor in economics, 1941-43; assistant professor, 1948-53, associate professor, 1953-57, professor of marketing, 1957—, Board of Visitors research professor, 1973—, head of department, 1960-69, faculty research associate, spring, 1971, 1972. Instructor, Pennsylvania Area College, 1946-48; visiting professor, Ashridge Management College, autumn, 1972; visiting scholar at Virginia Polytechnic Institute and State University, 1974, and Western Carolina University, 1974; research associate, Alabama Highway Research Projects, 1963-66; senior consultant, Harry A. Lipson & Associates; consultant to U.S. Department of Justice and Federal Reserve Bank. Past president of Tuscaloosa Federated Charities; past member of board of directors of Tuscaloosa Junior Chamber of Commerce. *Military service:* U.S. Army Air Forces, 1943-46.

MEMBER: American Marketing Association, Southern Marketing Association (president, 1969-70), Southern Economic Association, Beta Gamma Sigma, Alpha Kappa Psi, Chi Alpha Phi, Pi Sigma Epsilon. *Awards, honors:* Ford Foundation fellowship, summer, 1960; Morris L. Mayer outstanding teacher award, from University of Alabama, 1970.

WRITINGS: A Selected and Annotated Bibliography of Accounting Materials for Retail Concerns, Bureau of Business Research, University of Alabama, 1951; *Profitable Buying for Small Retailers* (monograph), Small Business Administration, 1957; *Ten Alabama Small Retail Cases* (monograph), Bureau of Business Research, University of Alabama, 1961; *Selected Cases of Alabama Small Retail Stores* (monograph), Bureau of Business Research, University of Alabama, 1963; (with Charles Thomas Moore, Morris L. Mayer, J. Barry Mason, and others) *A Study of the Expected Economic and Social Impact of Interstate Highways in the Industrial and Commercial Trading Area of Birmingham, Alabama* (monograph), School of Commerce and Business Administration, University of Alabama, *First Phase,* 1964, *Final Report,* 1965; (with John R. Darling) *Cases in Marketing: An Administrative Approach,* Wiley, 1971; (with Darling) *Introduction to Marketing: An Administrative Approach,* Wiley, 1971, with study guide published as *Decision Exercises in Marketing,* 1971; (with Darling) *Marketing Fundamentals: Text and Cases,* with instructor's manual and examination manual, Wiley, 1974.

Contributor: Philip D. Grub and Mika Kaskimies, editors, *International Marketing in Perspective,* Sininen Kirja Oy, 1971; Louis E. Boone, editor, *Management Perspectives in Marketing,* Dickenson, 1972; Norman A. P. Govoni, editor, *Contemporary Marketing Research,* General Learning Press, 1972; George P. Morris and Robert W. Frye, editors, *Current Marketing Views,* Canfield Press, 1973; William Lazer and Eugene J. Kelley, editors, *Managerial Marketing,* Irwin, 1973; Hans B. Thorelli, editor, *International Marketing Strategy,* Penguin, 1973; Lazer and Kelley, editors, *Social Marketing,* Irwin, 1973; Eugene M. Johnson, Ray S. House, and Carl D. McDaniel, Jr., editors, *Contemporary Marketing,* Dryden, 1974; George Fisk, editor, *Marketing and Social Priorities,* American Marketing Association, 1974. Contributor to business journals, Member of board of reviewers of *Journal of Marketing,* 1960—.

WORK IN PROGRESS: Research on comprehensive corporate planning processes and management models being developed by large national and multinational organizations, on organization structures and operating procedures of private, state-owned, and quasi-public international trading companies, on mainstream retail management strategies and retail structures in developed and developing countries, on the impact of double-digit inflation on the modernization of retail structures in developed and developing countries, and on corporate business and social performance measurement.

* * *

LITHWICK, Norman Harvey 1938-

PERSONAL: Born October 10, 1938, in Ottawa, Ontario, Canada; son of Arnold and Rose Lillian (Esar) Lithwick; married Yvonne Kate Baher, March 12, 1964; children: Alexander, Dahlia, Hillel. *Education:* University of Western Ontario, B.A. (honors), 1960; Harvard University, A.M., 1962, Ph.D., 1963. *Religion:* Jewish. *Residence:* Ottawa, Ontario, Canada. *Office:* Department of Economics, Carleton University, Ottawa, Ontario, Canada K1S 5B6.

CAREER: Carleton University, Ottawa, Ontario, assistant professor, 1963-67, associate professor, 1967-71, professor of economics, 1971—. Assistant secretary to Ministry of Urban Affairs, 1970-71; director of Institute of Canadian Studies, 1972-73; consultant to Royal Commission on Taxation, 1963-65, and to Science Council of Canada, 1967-68. *Member:* Canadian Economic Association, American Economic Association. *Awards, honors:* C. D. Howe fellow at Hebrew University of Jerusalem, 1969-70.

WRITINGS: Economic Growth in Canada: A Quantitative Analysis, University of Toronto Press, 1967, 2nd edition, 1970; (contributor) M. Brown, editor, *The Theory and Empirical Analysis of Production,* National Bureau of Economic Research, 1967; *Prices, Productivity, and Canada's Competitive Position,* Private Planning Association of Canada, 1967; (with Thomas Allen Wilson) *The Sources of Economic Growth: An Empirical Analysis of the Canadian Experience,* Queen's Printer, 1968; (editor with Gilles Paquet) *Urban Studies: A Canadian Perspective,* Methuen, 1968; *Canada's Science Policy and the Economy,* Methuen, 1969; *Urban Canada, Problems and Prospects: A Report,* Central Mortgage & Housing Corp., 1970. Contributor to economic journals.

WORK IN PROGRESS: Research in urban and regional studies and economic policy.

* * *

LITTLEJOHN, (Cameron) Bruce 1913-

PERSONAL: Born July 22, 1913, in Pacolet, S.C.; son of Cameron and Lady Sara (Warmoth) Littlejohn; married Inell Smith, February 7, 1942 (died July 16, 1962); children: Inell (Mrs. Dan L. Allen III), Cameron Bruce, Jr. *Education:* Wofford College, A.B., 1935; University of South Carolina, LL.B., 1936, J.D., 1970. *Religion:* Baptist. *Home:* 450 Connecticut Ave., Spartanburg, S.C. 29302. *Office:* Supreme Court of South Carolina, Magnolia St., Spartanburg, S.C. 29302.

CAREER: Attorney in Spartanburg, S.C., 1936-43, 1946-49; circuit trial court judge of Seventh District, covering Spartanburg, Cherokee, and Union counties (all S.C.), 1949-67; Supreme Court of South Carolina, Spartanburg, associate justice, 1967—. Democratic member of South Carolina House of Representatives, 1937-43, speaker of House, 1947-49; has served as delegate to county, state, and national Democratic conventions, and as a delegate to National Conference of State Trial Judges and National Appellate Judges Conference; member of state Judicial Council and chairman of Commission on Judicial Procedure and Congested Dockets, 1957-67; permanent member of Fourth U.S. Court of Appeals Judicial Conference. President of Pine Street Motel Co. Member of board of trustees of North Greenville Junior College, 1962-67; member of Wofford College Alumni Board, 1966-68; member of national and schools awards jury of Freedoms Foundation, 1968. Military service: U.S. Army, prosecutor of Japanese war criminals in the Philippines, 1943-46; became first lieutenant.

MEMBER: American Bar Association, South Carolina Bar Association, Spartanburg County Bar Association, American Legion, Veterans of Foreign Wars, Blue Key, Civitan. Awards, honors: LL.D. from Wofford College, 1968.

WRITINGS: Laugh with the Judge, Sandlapper Store, 1974. Contributor to law journals.

*   *   *

LIU, Alan P(ing-) L(in)   1937-

PERSONAL: Born January 14, 1937, in Suchow, China; son of Tsun-liang (in civil service) and Chiang-ching (Li) Liu; married Lillian Li-jung Ma (a computer operator), August, 1961; children: Alice, Amy, Andrew. Education: Tunghai University, B.A., 1959; University of Washington, Seattle, M.A., 1963; Massachusetts Institute of Technology, Ph.D., 1968. Home: 5040 San Julio Ave., Santa Barbara, Calif. 93111. Office: Department of Political Science, University of California, Santa Barbara, Calif. 93106.

CAREER: China Post, Taipei, Taiwan, reporter, 1961; Massachusetts Institute of Technology, Cambridge, research assistant in political communication at Center for International Studies, 1963-67; University of Michigan, Ann Arbor, research associate in political science at Center for Chinese Studies, 1967-69; University of California, Santa Barbara, assistant professor, 1969-74, associate professor of political science, 1974—.

WRITINGS: (Contributor) John A. Lent, editor, The Asian Newspapers' Reluctant Revolution, Iowa University Press, 1971; Communications and National Integration in Communist China, University of California Press, 1971; (contributor) Lent, editor, Newspapers in Asia, Heinemann, 1974; Political Culture and Group Conflict in Communist China, American Bibliography Center, Clio Press, in press.

Monographs—all published by Center for International Studies, Massachusetts Institute of Technology: Radio Broadcasting in Communist China, 1964; Book Publishing in Communist China, 1965; The Use of Traditional Media for Modernization in Communist China, 1965; The Film Industry in Communist China, 1965; The Press and Journals in Communist China, 1966. Contributor to journalism and political science magazines.

WORK IN PROGRESS: Political Leadership in Communist China; Political Idealogy of the Youth in Communist China.

LLOYD, Craig   1940-

PERSONAL: Born February 13, 1940, in Port Chester, N.Y.; son of John William (a college professor) and Ruth (Craig) Lloyd; married Caryl Ann Lefstad (a college teacher), April 2, 1966; children: John Craig. Education: Middlebury College, B.A. (cum laude), 1963; University of Iowa, M.A., 1964, Ph.D., 1970; also studied at London School of Economics and Political Science, 1960-61. Home: 1313 17th Ave., Columbus, Ga. 31901. Office: Department of History, Columbus College, Columbus, Ga. 31907.

CAREER: Columbus College, Columbus, Ga., assistant professor of American History, 1971—. Assistant professor of history, University of Iowa, summers, 1971, 1974. Member: Organization of American Historians.

WRITINGS: Aggressive Introvert: Herbert Hoover and Public Relations Management, 1912-1932, Ohio State University Press, 1973.

WORK IN PROGRESS: Research on author David Henshaw.

SIDELIGHTS: Lloyd writes: "The most important American historians influencing my general views on American history have been dissenters from the traditional 'Whig history' approach to historical issues—men as diverse as William A. Williams, Richard Hofstadter, and Christopher Lasch."

*   *   *

LLOYD, Cynthia B(rown)   1943-

PERSONAL: Born March 24, 1943, in New York, N.Y.; married; children: one. Education: Bryn Mawr College, B.A. (cum laude), 1964; Columbia University, M.A., 1967, Ph.D. (with distinction), 1972. Home: 285 Riverside Dr., New York, N.Y. 10025. Office: Department of Economics, Barnard College, New York, N.Y. 10027.

CAREER: Federal Reserve Bank, New York, N.Y., research assistant in foreign research department, 1964-65; United Nations, New York, N.Y., associate social affairs officer in Population Division, summers, 1968-69; Barnard College, New York, N.Y., instructor, 1970-72, assistant professor of economics, 1972—. Member: American Economic Association, Population Association of America, American Association of University Professors, Eastern Economic Association.

WRITINGS: (Editor and contributor) Sex, Discrimination, and the Division of Labor, Columbia University Press, 1975. Contributor to academic journals.

WORK IN PROGRESS: The Economics of Sex Differentials, with Beth Niemi, for Columbia University Press; a study of sex differentials in labor supply elasticity.

*   *   *

LOESCHER, Ann Dull   1942-

PERSONAL: Born November 11, 1942, in New Jersey; daughter of Floyd N. (an insurance agent) and Ann (a craft teacher; maiden name, Spence) Dull; married Gilburt Damian Loescher (a professor of international relations), September 25, 1971. Education: Colby-Sawyer College, A.A., 1962; University of Connecticut, B.A., 1965; Southern Connecticut State College, M.A., 1968. Residence: London, England. Agent: Marilyn Marlow, Curtis Brown Ltd., 60 East 56th St., New York, N.Y. Office: American Community School, 5 Netherhall Gardens, London N.W.3, England.

CAREER: Elementary school teacher in Niantic, Conn., 1965-68; American Community School, London, England, elementary school teacher, 1968—, assistant principal, 1973-75.

WRITINGS: (With husband, Gilburt Damian Loescher) *The Chinese Way,* Harcourt, 1974.

WORK IN PROGRESS: Two books, *Human Rights and Political Prisoners* and *Food, Population, and Resources,* both with husband, Gilburt Damian Loescher.

SIDELIGHTS: Ann Loescher has traveled in western Europe, Rumania, Hungary, Yugoslavia, the Soviet Union, Mongolia, and the People's Republic of China. *Avocational interests:* Photography (especially black and white), hiking, reading, cooking.

* * *

LOESCHER, Gil(burt Damian) 1945-

PERSONAL: Born March 7, 1945, in San Francisco, Calif.; son of Burt G. (a rancher) and Helene (Aachen) Loescher; married Ann Dull (a teacher), September 25, 1971. *Education:* St. Mary's College of California, B.A., 1967; Monterey Institute of Foreign Studies, M.A., 1969; London School of Economics and Political Science, Ph.D., 1975. *Religion:* Roman Catholic. *Home:* 23 South Hill Park Gardens, London NW3 2TD, England. *Agent:* Marilyn Marlow, Curtis Brown Ltd., 60 East 56th St., New York, N.Y. 10022. *Office:* Department of Government, University of Notre Dame, Notre Dame, Ind. 46556.

CAREER: American Community School, London, England, principal, 1969-71; University of Notre Dame, Notre Dame, Ind., visiting assistant professor of international relations and Asian affairs, 1975—. *Member:* Amnesty International (London), Association for Asian Studies, American Political Science Association.

WRITINGS: (With wife, Ann Dull Loescher) *The Chinese Way,* Harcourt, 1974.

WORK IN PROGRESS: Two books, *Human Rights and Political Prisoners* and *Food, Population, and Resources,* both with wife, Ann Dull Loescher.

SIDELIGHTS: Loescher feels that "young Americans are culture-bound" and his aim is to acquaint them with international issues. He has traveled in western and eastern Europe, and Soviet Union, North Africa, and the People's Republic of China. *Avocational interests:* Reading, writing, hiking, theatre, most sports.

* * *

LOEWENTHAL, L(eonard) J(oseph) A(lfonso) (Alfonso Lowe)

PERSONAL: Born June 3, 1903, in Liverpool, England; son of Max (a physician) and Amanda (Kehr) Loewenthal; married Stella Regina, June 26, 1950. *Education:* University of Liverpool, M.B., Ch.B. (honors), 1925, D.T.M., 1930, D.T.H., 1931; F.R.C.P. *Home:* Apartado de Correos 79, Sitges, Barcelona, Spain. *Agent:* Richard Scott Simon, 36 Wellington St., London WC2E 7BD, England.

CAREER: Liverpool Royal Infirmary, Liverpool, England, medical registrar, 1925, clinical assistant, 1927-30; Liverpool Hospital for Cancer and Skin Diseases, Liverpool, hon. assistant physician, 1928-31; medical officer in the Uganda, Africa, Medical Service, 1931-41, serving in Kampala at the Mulago Hospital; consultant dermatologist in Johannesburg, South Africa, 1946-70. Consultant to South African Institute for Medical Research, 1958-70. *Military service:* South African Army, 1940-45; became lieutenant colonel.

MEMBER: Royal College of Physicans (fellow), American Dermatological Association, American Academy of Dermatology, South African Dermatological Association (past president), Royal Academy of Cordoba (corresponding fellow).

WRITINGS: (Editor and contributor) *The Exzemas,* Livingston, 1954.

Under pseudonym Alfonso Lowe: (Self-illustrated) *The Barrier and the Bridge: Historic Sicily,* Norton, 1972; *The Catalan Vengeance,* Routledge & Kegan Paul, 1972; *The Companion Guide to the South of Spain,* Collins, 1973; *La Serenissima: The Last Flowering of the Venetian Republic,* Cassell, 1974.

WORK IN PROGRESS: The Roman Roads of Spain; The Spanish, for Gordon-Cremonesi (London).

SIDELIGHTS: Loewenthal lived in Uganda for ten years; he has also traveled in Europe, the Near East, and Iran. A classical scholar, he has studied Latin and Greek, and speaks French, Spanish, Italian, German, and several African languages.

* * *

LOFLAND, Lyn (Hebert) 1937-

PERSONAL: Born December 2, 1937, in Everett, Wash.; daughter of Lisle F. (a merchant) and Estelle (Hogan) Herbert; married John Lofland (a professor of sociology), January 2, 1965. *Education:* Stanford University, student, 1955-56; Antioch College, B.A., 1960; University of Michigan, M.A., 1966; University of California, San Francisco, Ph.D., 1971. *Home:* 523 E St., Davis, Calif. 95616. *Office:* Department of Sociology, University of California, 102P Young Hall, Davis, Calif. 95616.

CAREER: Peter Kiewit & Sons, Inc., Omaha, Neb., administrative assistant, 1960-61; Douglas County Alcoholic Treatment Center, Omaha, Neb., social worker, 1961-64; Eastern Michigan University, Ypsilanti, instructor in sociology, spring, 1968; University of California, Berkeley, acting assistant professor of sociology, 1970-71; University of California, Davis, assistant professor of sociology, 1971—. Founding member of Chicago School Irregulars, 1968-70; co-organizer of Northern California Sociologists Against the War, 1970.

MEMBER: American Sociological Association, Society for the Study of Social Problems, Sociologists for Women in Society, Society for the Study of Symbolic Interaction (charter member), Common Cause, American Civil Liberties Union, Consumers Union, Pacific Sociological Association, California Historical Society.

WRITINGS: (With husband, John Lofland) *Deviance and Identity,* Prentice-Hall, 1969; *A Word of Strangers: Order and Action in Urban Public Space,* Basic Books, 1973; (contributor) Rosabeth Kanter and Marcia Millman, editors, *Another Voice: Feminist Perspectives on Social Life and Social Science,* Doubleday Anchor, 1975. Contributor to sociology journals. Vice-editor of *Urban Life and Culture,* 1973-75, consulting editor, 1972-73, 1975—; associate editor of *Contemporary Sociology,* 1974—; referee for *Social Problems, Sociological Inquiry, Social Forces, American Sociologist,* Wadsworth, and Prentice-Hall.

WORK IN PROGRESS: Four books, tentatively titled

Countering Student Passivity: Two Suggestions for Organizing a Large Course in Urban Sociology, The Happy Death People: Notes on a Growing Social Movement, The Social Construction of Grief in the Mass Media, and *Daily Death: Coping Strategies among Death Workers;* continuing research on human loss and human connection.

* * *

LOGAN, Elizabeth D(ulaney) 1914-

PERSONAL: Born October 26, 1914, in Bowling Green, Ky.; daughter of Emmett G. and Effie W. Logan; married Lloyd Collins (a writer), April 18, 1941 (deceased). *Education:* Attended Antioch College; studied painting with Carl Holty and Hans Hofman. *Home and office:* 65 West 95th St., New York, N.Y. 10025. *Agent:* George Borchardt, Inc., 145 East 52nd St., New York, N.Y. 10022.

CAREER: Commercial artist of decorative illustrations, 1940—; designer of crafts for women's publications, 1954—. Has had exhibits of drawings and water colors in Louisville, Ky. and New York, N.Y.

WRITINGS: Scrap Craft Ideas for Holidays and Parties, Scribner, 1973; *Shell Crafts,* Scribner, 1974. Author of children's Christmas stories for Fawcett.

WORK IN PROGRESS: A book on kitchen crafts, for Viking.

* * *

LOMAX, John A(lbert) 1930-

PERSONAL: Born July 31, 1930, in Philadelphia, Pa.; son of Vernal R. (a postal worker and writer) and Julia (a domestic worker; maiden name, Page) Lomax; married Helen Louise Taylor, April 26, 1956; children: John, Rodney, Dowel, Channing. *Education:* Attended Pennsylvania State University, 1950, and Temple University, 1961; Philadelphia Wireless Technological Institute, diploma, 1958. *Politics:* Deductive reasoning. *Religion:* Philosophy. *Home:* 410 East Jefferson St., Media, Pa. 19063.

CAREER: Computer engineer with Burroughs, 1957-58, Univac, 1958-61, General Electric, 1961-71, Burroughs, 1974—. *Military service:* U.S. Air Force, 1950-54; became staff sergeant.

WRITINGS: Sezz Who (fiction), Ashley Books, 1974.

WORK IN PROGRESS: Charlie's Store, completion expected in 1977; *Roaring Fifties; Sign of the Beast.*

SIDELIGHTS: "I am black, but first I am a writer," Lomax told *CA,* "a writer of that which exists. The truth. Therefore, I don't want my writings to be black or white; just good structured prose. First I inform, then as a by-product I entertain."

* * *

LOMBARDI, Mary 1940-

PERSONAL: Born June 21, 1940, in Los Angeles, Calif.; daughter of John (an educator) and Mary Ellen (an educator; maiden name, Maher) Lombardi. *Education:* Occidental College, B.A., 1961; University of California, Los Angeles, M.L.S., 1965, doctoral candidate, 1972—; Indiana University, M.A., 1971. *Home:* 1508 Spruce Lane, Davis, Calif. 95616.

CAREER: University of California, Los Angeles, reference librarian intern at research library, 1964-65; New York Public Library, New York, N.Y., reference librarian in reference department and music department, 1965-66; Juilliard School, New York, N.Y., cataloger in library, 1966-67; H. W. Wilson Co., Bronx, N.Y., indexer of library literature, 1967-69; Indiana University, Bloomington, assistant to Latin American bibliographer, 1969-70; Instituto Brasileiro de Bibliografia e Documentação, Rio de Janeiro, Brazil, member of visiting faculty, 1971; University of California, Los Angeles, translator and abstractor of periodical articles in Spanish and Portuguese, 1972; free-lance indexer in editorial departments of publishing firms, 1972—, including Brooks/Cole Publishers, Canfield Press, Glencoe Press, Indiana University Press, and Stanford University Press. Reference librarian at West Los Angeles College, and at Glendale College (also cataloger), and cataloger at Los Angeles City College, all 1972-73; member of visiting faculty at University of Southern California, summers, 1973-75.

MEMBER: American Association of University Professors, American Historical Association, American Library Association, American Society of Indexers, Latin American Studies Association, Pacific Coast Council on Latin American Studies, West Coast Association of Women Historians, Sierra Club. *Awards, honors:* Foreign Area fellowship for Latin American study, 1970-72.

WRITINGS: Brazilian Serial Documents: A Selective and Annotated Guide, Indiana University Press, 1974. Contributor to history journals.

WORK IN PROGRESS: Research on women in Brazil, especially women artists, writers, musicians, and other professionals; a faceted classification for women's studies.

* * *

LONG, David F(oster) 1917-

PERSONAL: Born December 8, 1917, in Cleveland, Ohio; son of Roger and Christine (Foster) Long; married third wife, Susan Robinson (a teacher), June 6, 1969; children: Elisabeth B., Roger D., Craig R. *Education:* Dartmouth College, A.B., 1939; Columbia University, A.M., 1948, Ph.D., 1950; University of Waikato, postdoctoral fellow, 1974. *Politics:* Democrat. *Home address:* Route 2, Box 125, Dover, N.H. 03820. *Office:* Department of History, University of New Hampshire, Durham, N.H. 03824.

CAREER: High school history teacher in New Hampshire and New York, 1939-48; University of New Hampshire, Durham, assistant professor, 1948-50, associate professor, 1950-59, professor of history, 1959—. Fulbright lecturer at University of Ceylon, 1956-57, 1958-59, and Makerere University, 1965-66; U.S. State Department lecturer at University of Sierra Leone, 1966; U.S. Information Service lecturer in Africa, 1966, and in East Asia, Southeast Asia, and the South Pacific, all 1974.

MEMBER: American Association of University Professors, American Historical Association, Organization of American Historians, Society for the Historians of American Foreign Relations, Authors Guild of Authors League of America. *Awards, honors:* Rockefeller Foundation grant, 1958-59; Ford Foundation grant, 1960-61; U.S. State Department grant, 1966; Fulbright research grant, East Asia, 1974; honorary fellow of Australian National University, 1974.

WRITINGS: (With Robert E. Riegel) *The American Story,* two volumes, McGraw, 1955; *The Outward View: An Illustrated History of U.S. Foreign Relations,* Rand McNally, 1964; *Nothing Too Daring: A Biography of Commodore David Porter, 1780-1843,* U.S. Naval Institute, 1970. Contributor to history journals.

WORK IN PROGRESS: Martial Thunder: Official American Armed Interventions in Asia during the Nineteenth Century; a chapter on the U.S. Navy, 1815-1842, for inclusion in a bicentennial history of the U.S. Navy.

AVOCATIONAL INTERESTS: Foreign travel (more than eighty countries).

* * *

LOPEZ, Vincent (Joseph) 1895-1975

December 30, 1895—September 20, 1975; American bandleader and pianist, numerologist, and author of books on numerology and astrology and an autobiography. Obituaries: *New York Times,* September 21, 1975.

* * *

LORD, Robert (Needham) 1945-

PERSONAL: Born July 18, 1945, in Rotorua, New Zealand; came to United States, 1974; son of Richard Henry (a banker) and Bebe (Cooke) Lord. *Education:* Victoria University of Wellington, B.A., 1969; Wellington Teachers College, teaching diploma, 1970. *Home:* Apt. 12, 43 West 93rd St., New York, N.Y. 10025. *Agent:* Gilbert Parker, Curtis Brown Ltd., 60 East 56th St., New York, N.Y. 10025.

CAREER: Worked as an oil rigger, cosmetics salesman, and refrigeration worker; AMP Insurance, Invercargill, New Zealand, clerk, 1963-64; *Dominion* (daily newspaper), Wellington, New Zealand, journalist, 1964-65; teacher in Wellington, 1970-71; Downstage Theatre, Wellington, publicity agent and stage manager, 1972-74; playwright in New York, N.Y., 1974—. *Member:* P.E.N. (New Zealand), Actors Equity (New Zealand). *Awards, honors:* Katherine Mansfield Young Writers Award, 1969, for short stories; Queen Elizabeth Arts Council of New Zealand grants, 1970, 1972, 1973, and 1974.

WRITINGS—Plays: "It Isn't Cricket" (two-act), first produced in Wellington, New Zealand, at Downstage Theatre, 1971; "Meeting Place" (two-act), first produced in Wellington at Downstage Theatre, 1972; *Balance of Payments* (one-act; first produced in Wellington at Unity Theatre, 1972), University of Queensland Press (St. Lucia, Australia), 1976; "Nativity" (one-act), first produced in Auckland, New Zealand, at Theatre Co-Op, 1973; "Friendship Centre" (one-act), first broadcast on television in New Zealand, 1973, produced in Christchurch, New Zealand, by Pegasus Players, 1975; "Heroes and Butterflies" (three-act), first produced in Auckland at Mercury Theatre, 1974; "Well Hung" (two-act), first produced in Wellington at Downstage Theatre, 1974, produced in Providence, R.I., by Trinity Square Repertory Co., 1974; "Dead and Never Called Me Mother" (three-act), first produced in New London, Conn., at Eugene O'Neill Memorial Theatre Center, 1975. Also author of "Glitter and Spit," 1974, and "I'll Scream If I Want To," 1975, both as yet neither published nor produced.

Radio plays: "Moody Tuesday," first broadcast by New Zealand Broadcasting Corp., 1972; "The Body in the Park," first broadcast by NZBC, 1973, rewritten version broadcast by British Broadcasting Corp., 1976; "Blood on My Sprigs," first broadcast by NZBC, 1973.

Scriptwriter of short films, including "The Day We Landed on the Most Perfect Planet in the Universe," produced by Pacific Films, New Zealand, 1973. Short plays contributed to *Act* magazine.

WORK IN PROGRESS: A novel, *My Nervous Breakdown and Other Adventures,* completion expected in 1977; two plays, "Kate" and "Failures and Victories."

SIDELIGHTS: Lord told *CA:* "In my native New Zealand I wrote a number of short stories and entertained an interest in theater. On the suggestion of a friend I wrote a play early in 1971, and suddenly seemed to have found a vocation which I have pursued ever since. In a small country containing few theaters, I did not imagine that a career as a playwright would last long and had no plans to move abroad until I was invited to Australia in 1973. On this visit I met some enchanting Americans who suggested I should visit the States which, in 1974, I did. A short holiday expanded, some plays produced, the way of life and the challenges enjoyed and this is now my home."

* * *

LORENZ, Konrad Zacharias 1903-

PERSONAL: Born November 7, 1903, in Vienna, Austria; son of Adolf (an orthopedic surgeon) and Emma (Lecher) Lorenz; married Margarethe Gebhardt (a gynecologist), June, 1927; children: Thomas, Agnes, Dagmar. *Education:* Attended Columbia University, 1922; University of Vienna, M.D., 1928, Ph.D. (zoology), 1933. *Home:* A-3422 Altenberg, Adolf-Lorenzgasse 2, Austria. *Office:* Institut fuer Vergleichende Verhaltensforschung, Abt. 4 Tiersoziologie, A-3422 Altenberg, Adolf-Lorenzgasse 2, Austria.

CAREER: University of Vienna, Vienna, Austria, lecturer in comparative anatomy and animal psychology, 1937-40, university lecturer, 1940; University of Koenigsberg, Koenigsberg, Germany, professor and head of the department of general psychology, 1940-42; Institute of Comparative Ethology, Altenberg, Austria, director, 1949-51; Max Planck Society for the Advancement of Science, Institute for Marine Biology, head of research station for physiology of behavior in Buldern, Germany, 1951-58, Institute for Behavior Physiology, Seewiesen, Germany, co-founder, 1958, co-director, 1958-61, director, 1961-73; Austrian Academy of Science, Institute of Comparative Ethology, Vienna, director of department of animal sociology, 1973—. Honorary professor at University of Muenster, 1953, University of Munich, 1957, University of Vienna, 1974—, and University of Salzburg, 1974—. Lecturer at numerous educational institutions worldwide. *Military service:* German Army, physician, 1942-44; captured in Russia and returned to Austria, 1948. *Member:* Pour le Merite for Arts and Science, Austrian Academy of Sciences, Bavarian Academy of Sciences, American Philosophical Society, Association for the Study of Animal Behaviour, American Ornithology Union, Deutsche Akademie der Naturforscher Leopoldina, Royal Society (foreign member), National Academy of Sciences (foreign associate). *Awards, honors:* Gold Medal from Zoological Society of New York, 1955; City of Vienna Prize, 1959; Gold Boelsche Medal, 1962; Austrian Distinction for Science and Art, 1964; Prix Mondial, Cino de Duca, 1969; Kalinga Prize from UNESCO, 1970; Nobel Prize for Physiology or Medicine, 1973. Honorary degrees from University of Leeds, 1962, University of Basel, 1966, Yale University, 1967, Oxford University, 1968, University of Chicago, 1970; University of Durham, 1972; University of Birmingham, 1974; Grosses Verdienstkreuz der Bundesrepublik Deutschland, 1974; Bayerischer Verdienstorden, 1974.

WRITINGS: Er redete mit dem Vieh, den Voegeln, und den Fischen, Borotha-Schoeler (Vienna), 1949, 17th edition, 1958, U.S. edition, edited bv Eva Schiffer, Scott, Foresman, 1968, translation by Marjorie Kerr Wilson, with illustrations by the author and foreword by Sir Julian Huxley, published as *King Solomon's Ring: New Light on Animal Ways,* Crowell, 1952; *So kam der Mensch auf den Hund,* Borotha-Schoeler, 1950, translation by Marjorie Kerr Wilson, with illustrations by the author and Annie Eisenmenger, published as *Man Meets Dog,* Methuen, 1954, Houghton, 1955; (contributor) Claire H. Schiller, editor and translator, *Instinctive Behavior: The Development of a Modern Concept,* International Universities Press, 1957.

Das sogenannte Boese: Zur Naturgeschichte der Aggression, Borotha-Schoeler, 1963, translation by Marjorie Latzke, with foreword by Sir Julian Huxley, published as *On Aggression,* Methuen, 1966, translation by Marjorie Kerr Wilson published under same title, Harcourt, 1966; *Gestaltwahrnehmung als Quelle wissenschaftlicher Erkenntnis* (title means "Gestalt Perception as a Source of Scientific Knowledge"), Wissenschaftlicher Buchgesellschaft (Darmstadt), 1964; *Darwin hat recht gesehen* (title means "Darwin Saw the Truth"), Neske (Pfullingen), 1965; *Ueber tieresches und menschliches Verhalten,* R. Piper (Munich), 1965, selections published as *Vom Weltbild des Verhaltensforschers,* Deutscher Taschenbuch-Verlag (Munich), 1968, translation of unabridged edition by Robert Martin published as *Studies in Animal and Human Behavior,* two volumes, Harvard University Press, 1970-71; *Evolution and Modification of Behavior,* University of Chicago Press, 1965; *Der Vogelflug* (title means "Bird Flight"), Neske, 1965; (with Paul Leyhausen) *Antriebe tierischen und menschlichen Verhaltens,* R. Piper, 1968, translation by B. A. Tonkin published as *Motivation of Human and Animal Behavior: An Ethological View,* Van Nostrand, 1973.

Die acht Todsuendender der zivilisierten Menschheit, R. Piper, 1973, translation by Marjorie Kerr Wilson published as *Civilized Man's Eight Deadly Sins,* Harcourt, 1974; *Die Rueckseite des Spiegels: Versuch einer Naturgeschichte menschlichen Erkennens* (title means "The Other Side of the Mirror"), R. Piper, 1973.

Also author of *Principles of Ethology,* translated by Erich Klinghammer, 1961. Contributor of articles to numerous journals in his field. Co-editor of *Zeitschrift fuer Tierpsychologie* (occasional periodical of Deutsche Gesellschaft fuer Tierpsychologie), 1937—.

WORK IN PROGRESS: A continuation of *Die Rueckseite des Spiegels;* a book on basic ethology.

SIDELIGHTS: The acknowledged father of modern ethology, Lorenz has contributed toward a greater understanding of human behavioral patterns through the study of animals in their natural environment. Working with Oskar Heinroth, he identified the early biological learning process of imprinting, which, although the cybernetics are not understood, has been successfully applied in psychoanalysis and psychiatry.

Of his work, Maxine Kingston wrote: "Lorenz integrates poetry and science by describing animal behavior with accuracy and beauty. A zoologist who sometimes seems to take flight with his jackdaws, ravens, and greylag geese, Lorenz, perhaps believing his own delightful use of language merely 'scientific,' often uses the classical English poets and Goethe . . . to help him introduce chapters and to culminate both scientific and philosophical speculations."

The books are more controversial in the scientific commu-

nity. In answer to the criticism that his work is speculative and anthropomorphic, Lorenz once said: "If in an octopus or a squid I find an eye, with lens, an iris, a nerve—I need not even observe the animal—I need only to state these formal analogies to know it is an eye, which has evolved to see with. It has the same formation as my eye, my vertebrate eye, which has evolved independently of the octopus eye, but a detailed similarity informs me it has the same function, and nobody balks at calling it an eye. . . . Construct a computer model of an animal being jealous—one system having a social relationship with another, resenting a third one doing the same, and interacting with both and trying to break up their relationship. This function would presuppose an enormous complication, much more so than the functioning of an eye. You can speak of jealousy with respect to dogs and ganders, certainly. Assertions that these are false analogies or anthropomorphizations betray a lack of understanding of functional conceptions. To call the animal jealous is just as legitimate as to call an octopus' eye an eye or a lobster's leg a leg."

BIOGRAPHICAL/CRITICAL SOURCES: Zeitschrift fuer Tierpsychologie, 1963; *Harper's,* May, 1968; *New Yorker,* March 8, 1969; *English Journal,* January, 1973; *Newsweek,* August 6, 1973, October 22, 1973; *Time,* October 22, 1973; *Science,* November 2, 1973; *Psychology Today,* November, 1974.

*   *   *

LOUGHHEAD, LaRue A(lvin) 1927-

PERSONAL: Born June 13, 1927, in Madison, N.Y.; son of Harold C. (a minister) and Leda (McClelland) Loughhead; married Elizabeth Claibourne Johnson, June 15, 1947; children: David, Stephen, Beth. *Education:* Attended Bucknell University, 1944-45; Knox College, B.A., 1947; Colgate Rochester Divinity School, B.D., 1950; Eden Theological Seminary, further study, 1973—. *Home:* 3393 South Dallas Court, Denver, Colo. 80231. *Office:* Calvary Baptist Church, 6500 East Girard, Denver, Colo. 80222.

CAREER: Ordained minister of American Baptist Church, 1950; pastor of churches in Hudson Falls, N.Y., 1950-59, and St. Louis, Mo., 1959-69; Calvary Baptist Church, Denver, Colo., pastor, 1969—. *Awards, honors:* Edward H. Rhoades Award for Outstanding Ministry through the Urban Church, granted by the Home Mission Society of the American Baptist Churches, 1972.

WRITINGS: Eyewitnesses at the Cross, Judson Press, 1974.

*   *   *

LOUIS, Paul P(anickavede) 1918-

PERSONAL: Born September 26, 1918, in Pallithode, India; son of Louis Paulose (a farmer) and Achamma (Therath) Panickavede. *Education:* St. Joseph Pontifical Seminary, Ph.L., 1944, S.T.L., 1947; University of San Francisco, B.S., 1955; University of Detroit, M.B.A., 1956; Michigan State University, D.Ed., 1960. *Politics:* None. *Home:* 201 West Spring Valley, Centerville, Ohio 45459. *Office:* Department of Economics, University of Dayton, Dayton, Ohio 45409.

CAREER: Ordained diocesan Roman Catholic priest, 1947. St. John Bosco Manufacturing Co., Kerala, India, president, 1949-53; Aquinas College, Grand Rapids, Mich., instructor, 1957-58; Nazareth College, Kalamazoo, Mich., instructor, 1958-59; University of San Diego, San Diego,

Calif., assistant professor of business and economics, 1959-63; University of Dayton, Dayton, Ohio, associate professor, 1964-72, professor of economics, 1972—. Associate pastor of Roman Catholic church in Miamisburg, Ohio, 1970. Founder of St. Rita's Poor Home; director of Catholic Charities, 1949-53. Chairman, Beekman Motors, Inc., 1975. Founder and director of India Cultural Center; president of Farmer's Cooperative, 1948-52; founder of Milk for Babies Club, 1966-72.

MEMBER: American Economic Association, American Education Association, Society for Advancement of Management, Alpha Kappa Psi. *Awards, honors:* Papal Chamberlain Award from Pope Paul VI, 1965.

WRITINGS: Exotic Recipes of India: A Cookbook, Colonial Printers, 1960; *Readings in the History of Economic Thought,* McCutchan, 1971; *Economic Geography: Economic Growth and Development,* University of Dayton Press, in press. Author of fourteen books in Malayalam language, 1947-52. Editor of *Labour,* 1949-53.

WORK IN PROGRESS: Makers of American Business.

* * *

LOVELL, Mark 1934-
(Peter Rowlands)

PERSONAL: Born September 3, 1934, in London, England; son of Maurice Henry (a journalist) and Hilda (a teacher; maiden name, Rowland) Lovell; married Ann Scott-Buccleuch, August 8, 1959 (divorced, 1975); married Susi Hock, November 29, 1975; children: (first marriage) Frank, Sara, Simon, Stephen. *Education:* Jesus College, Cambridge, B.A. (honors), 1959. *Politics:* None. *Address:* c/o P. Hock, Wittenham, Woolton Hill, Newbury, Berkshire, England. *Office:* Lovell & Oakes, 15 Lower Regent St., London S.W.1, England; and, Creative Research Group, 161 Eglinton Ave. E., Toronto, Ontario, Canada M5A 3W7.

CAREER: British Market Research Bureau, London, England, head of group, 1959-63; Marplan Ltd., London, England, director, 1963-66; Leo Burnett Ltd., London, England, director, 1966-75; Lovell & Oakes, London, England, partner, 1975—; Creative Research Group, Toronto, Ontario, vice-president, 1976—. Chairman of London Regional Society for Autistic Children, 1968-75. *Military service:* Royal Navy, 1953-55; became sub-lieutenant. *Awards, honors:* Thomson silver medal, 1967, gold medals, 1968 and 1969, all for advertising and media research.

WRITINGS—All nonfiction: (Under name Peter Rowlands) *The Fugitive Mind,* Dent & Sons, 1972; (under name Peter Rowlands) *Children Apart,* Dent & Sons, 1973; (under name Peter Rowlands) *Gifted Children,* Dent & Sons, 1974; *How Children Grow,* two volumes, Routledge & Kegan Paul, 1975-76; (with Jack Potter) *Assessing the Effectiveness of Advertising,* Business Books, 1976; *Passing Examinations,* Faber & Faber, 1976. Contributor to advertising and business journals. Contributor of regular column to *Esomar.*

* * *

LOVETT, Margaret (Rose) 1915-

PERSONAL: Born August 30, 1915, in Buenos Aires, Argentina; daughter of William (a businessman) and Effie (Evans) Lovett. *Education:* St. Hugh's College, Oxford, B.A. (second class honors), 1936. *Politics:* "liberal (small

'l')." *Religion:* Church of England. *Home:* 61 Wootton, Boar's Hill, Oxford, England.

CAREER: Teacher of history in a preparatory school in Hampton, England, 1956-66; Hephaistos School (for physically handicapped boys), Reading, England, teacher of history, 1966—.

WRITINGS—All for children: *Adventure for Fivepence,* Faber, 1945; *Family Pie,* Faber, 1947; *No Other Children,* Faber, 1949; *Sir Halmanac and the Crimson Star,* Faber, 1965; *The Great and Terrible Quest,* Holt, 1967; *Jonathan,* Dutton, 1972.

WORK IN PROGRESS: A history of the Hephaistos School, with its founder, Dorothy Woolley.

SIDELIGHTS: Margaret Lovett writes: "I write for children partly because I think children very important, and partly because a real plot and regard for moral values are more acceptable these days in children's books than in those for adults."

* * *

LOVOLL, Odd Sverre 1934-

PERSONAL: Born October 10, 1934, in Sande in Sunnmoere, Norway; naturalized U.S. citizen; son of Alf (a commercial fisherman) and Astrid (Aase) Lovoll; married Else Navekvien (a cook), March 30, 1958; children: Audrey, Ronald. *Education:* Attended Oslo Teachers' Training College, 1956-58, University of Oslo, and University of Bergen, 1960-67; University of North Dakota, M.A., 1969; University of Minnesota, Ph.D., 1973. *Religion:* Lutheran. *Home:* 305 South Linden Pl., Northfield, Minn. 55057. *Office:* Department of Norwegian, St. Olaf College, Northfield, Minn. 55057.

CAREER: High school teacher of English, history, and Norwegian in Norway, 1958-67; University of North Dakota, Grand Forks, instructor in Norwegian, 1967-70; St. Olaf College, Northfield, Minn., assistant professor of Norwegian, 1971—. *Member:* Society for the Advancement of Scandinavian Studies, Norwegian-American Historical Association.

WRITINGS: A Folk Epic: The Bygdelag in America, Norwegian-American Historical Association, 1975; (with Kenneth O. Bjork) *The Norwegian-American Historical Association, 1925-1975,* Norwegian-American Historical Association, 1975. Contributor to Norwegian-American studies journals. Member of editorial board of Norwegian-American Historical Association.

WORK IN PROGRESS: A study of the Norwegian immigrant press in America.

SIDELIGHTS: Lovoll writes: "I spent a large part of my childhood and youth in Seattle, Washington, and returned to my native Norway at the age of seventeen. In 1967 I again moved to the United States. . . . My own experience has developed in me a strong interest in and a strong desire to know the immigrant experience in general."

* * *

LOW, Alice 1926-

PERSONAL: Born June 5, 1926, in New York, N.Y.; daughter of Harold (in textiles) and Anna (a writer of children's books; maiden name, Epstein) Bernstein; married Martin Low (owner of a film studio), March 25, 1949; children: Andrew, Katherine, David. *Education:* Smith College, B.A., 1947; also attended Columbia University. *Resi-*

dence: Briarcliff Manor, N.Y. *Agent:* Russell & Volkening, Inc., 551 Fifth Ave., New York, N.Y. 10017.

CAREER: Warren Schloat Productions, Tarrytown, N.Y., writer and producer of educational filmstrips, 1968-72; Birch Wathen School, New York, N.Y., teacher of creative writing, 1972-73; Random House, New York, N.Y., free-lance editor, 1975—. Guide to the Museum of the City of New York. *Member:* Authors Guild of Authors League of America, American Society of Composers, Authors, and Publishers.

WRITINGS—Juveniles: *Open My Suitcase,* Simon & Schuster, 1954; *Out of My Window,* Random House, 1962; *Grandmas and Grandpas,* Random House, 1962; *Summer,* Random House, 1963; *Taro and the Bamboo Shoot* (adaptation of a folk tale), Pantheon, 1964; *A Day of Your Own, Your Birthday,* Random House, 1964; *What's in Mommy's Pocketbook?,* Golden Press, 1965; *Kallie's Corner,* Pantheon, 1966; *At Jasper's House and Other Stories,* Pantheon, 1968; *Witches' Holiday,* Pantheon, 1971; *Herbert's Treasure,* Putnam, 1971; *David's Windows,* Putnam, 1974.

Work has been anthologized in *Captain Kangaroo's Read Aloud Book,* Random House, 1962; *Captain Kangaroo's Sleepytime Book,* Random House, 1963.

Filmstrips—author of scripts for "Folk Songs and the American Flag," "Folk Songs and the Declaration of Independence," "Folk Songs and Abraham Lincoln," and "Folk Songs and Frederick Douglas," all for Warren Schloat Productions, 1968-70; "First Things, Social Reasoning" (series of eight filmstrips), Guidance Associates, 1973-74; "You Can Be Anything," Teaching Resource Films, 1975; "Bringing Home the Beach," Guidance Associates, 1975. Author of scripts and producer of "Folk Songs and the Railroad," "Cowboys," and "Whaling," all for Warren Schloat Productions, 1970-72; "History of the City," Warren Schloat Productions, 1972.

Author of operetta for elementary school children and of material for UNICEF. Contributor of stories to young adult magazines, including *Ingenue* and *Seventeen.*

WORK IN PROGRESS: A children's book; short stories.

SIDELIGHTS: Alice Low writes: "My mother wrote children's books and . . . many of her friends were in the arts and publishing. Birch Wathen School also encouraged creativity . . . we made books, puppets, gave plays, painted, sang, etc. under the guidance of people in the arts." *Avocational interests:* "Painting and ceramics were my first interests, and I still make ceramics in between books, and sing in a local chorus. Travel stimulates, and many a line has come to me on a tennis court or a walk."

*   *   *

LOWE, Roberta (Justine) 1940-

PERSONAL: Born June 2, 1940, in Portland, Ore.; daughter of Robert Stuart and Noni (Ellingson) Long; married Donald Clark Lowe (a photographer), December 2, 1966. *Education:* Attended Reed College, 1958-60; Portland State University, B.A., 1969. *Home and office address:* P.O. Box 217, Sandy, Ore. 97055.

CAREER: Professional dancer, 1961-63. Full-time writer.

WRITINGS—All with photographs by husband, Donald Lowe: *One Hundred Oregon Hiking Trails,* Touchstone, 1969; *One Hundred Northern California Hiking Trails,* Touchstone, 1970; *One Hundred Southern California Hiking Trails,* Touchstone, 1972; *Eighty Northern Colo-*

rado Hiking Trails, Touchstone, 1973; *Seventy Hiking Trails: Northern Oregon Cascades,* Touchstone, 1974; *Mount Hood,* Caxton, 1975. Monthly columnist on outdoors for *Oregon Times,* 1975—.

WORK IN PROGRESS: A trail book of the Oregon coast; more hiking guides for Oregon, California, and Colorado.

AVOCATIONAL INTERESTS: Ballet, piano, and music in general.

*   *   *

LOWENFELD, Andreas F(rank) 1930-

PERSONAL: Born May 30, 1930, in Berlin, Germany; son of Henry (a physician) and Yela (a physician; maiden name, Herschkowitsch) Lowenfeld; married Elena Machado, August 11, 1962; children: Julian, Marianna. *Education:* Harvard University, A.B., 1951, LL.B., 1955. *Office:* School of Law, New York University, New York, N.Y. 10003.

CAREER: Hyde & deVries, New York, N.Y., attorney, 1958-61; U.S. Department of State, Office of Legal Adviser, special assistant to the legal adviser, 1961-63, assistant legal adviser for economic affairs, 1963-65, deputy legal adviser, 1965-66; Harvard University, Cambridge, Mass., fellow of John F. Kennedy Institute of Politics, 1966-67; New York University, New York, N.Y., professor of law, 1967—. *Military service:* U.S. Army, 1955-57. *Member:* American Society for International Law, American Bar Association, American Arbitration Association, Council on Foreign Relations, Association of the Bar of the City of New York.

WRITINGS: (With Abram Chayes and Thomas Ehrlich) *International Legal Process,* Little, Brown, Volume I, 1968, Volume II, 1969; (editor) *Expropriations in the Americas,* Dunellen, 1971; *Aviation Law,* Matthew Bender, 1972, supplement, 1974; *International Private Trade,* Matthew Bender, 1975. Contributor to law and foreign affairs journals.

WORK IN PROGRESS: "International Economic Law," a series of books on the legal aspects of international economic activity.

*   *   *

LOWNDES, Betty 1929-

PERSONAL: Born August 17, 1929; daughter of Ernest and Elsie (Sladen) Bowker; married Thomas Douglas Lowndes (head of education department of British Film Institute), March 25, 1954; children: Paul Douglas. *Education:* Carlisle College of Art, certificate in arts and crafts, 1953; attended Sidney Webb College, 1964-65; University of London, received art teaching certificate for infants and juniors. *Religion:* Church of England. *Home:* 6 Kenmore Gardens, London N13 5DN, England.

CAREER: Worked as art teacher at convent in Carlisle, England; Wilbury Way Infant School, London, England, teacher of English and head of department, with special responsibility for drama, 1966—.

WRITINGS: Movement and Drama in the Primary School, Batsford, 1970, published as *Movement and Creative Drama for Children,* Plays, 1971.

WORK IN PROGRESS: Equal Chance (tentative title), a book on pre-school education.

SIDELIGHTS: Betty Lowndes writes: "When working in the convent discovered many kids were afraid of art. . . .

This was obviously conditioned by previous adult teaching or home experience." Then she "discovered . . . kids did not talk much—therefore used art . . . to initiate dramatic play lessons. . . ." She has lived in Germany, and visited Spain and France. Her book has been published in Danish. *Avocational interests:* Photography.

* * *

LOWRY, Robert (James Collas) 1919-
(James Caldwell)

PERSONAL: Born March 28, 1919, in Cincinnati, Ohio; son of Beirne Clem (a railroad yardmaster) and Alma (a telephone operator; maiden name, Collas) Lowry; married Antoinette LoBianco, May, 1958 (divorced, 1965); children: David Beirne, Beirne Clem, Giacomo LoBianco. *Education:* Attended University of Cincinnati, 1937-38. *Home and office:* 3747 Hutton St., Cincinnati, Ohio 45226.

CAREER: The Little Man Press, Cincinnati, Ohio, editor and publisher, 1938-42; New Directions Publishing Corp., New York, N.Y., editor, writer, book designer, and production manager, 1945-46; *Time* magazine, New York, staff writer, 1949-50; Popular Library, Inc., New York, reader, editor, and copy writer, 1951-56; National Genius Books, Cincinnati, editor, 1959; *Cincinnati Enquirer*, Cincinnati, copy writer, 1963; writer. *Military service:* U.S. Army Air Forces, 1942-45; served in Africa and Europe; received six battle stars. *Member:* Disabled American Veterans. *Awards, honors:* O. Henry Award, 1950, for story "Be Nice to Mr. Campbell."

WRITINGS—Novels, except as indicated: (Author of interludes) *The State of the Nation: Eleven Interpretations by Saroyan and Others,* Little Man Press, 1940; *The Blaze beyond the Town* [and] *The Toy Balloon* [and] *Phisterus* (short stories), Piccolo Uomo (Bari, Italy), 1945; *The Journey Out: Three Stories,* Piccolo Uomo, 1945; *Casualty,* New Directions, 1946, reprinted, Greenwood Press, 1971; *Find Me in Fire,* Doubleday, 1948; *The Wolf That Fed Us* (short stories), Doubleday, 1949, reprinted, Greenwood Press, 1970; *The Big Cage,* Doubleday, 1949.

The Violent Wedding, Doubleday, 1953, reprinted, Greenwood Press, 1970; *Happy New Year, Kamerades!: Eleven Stories,* Doubleday, 1954; *What's Left of April,* Doubleday, 1956; *New York Call Girl* (short stories), Doubleday, 1958; *The Prince of Pride Starring,* L. H. Haines, 1959; *That Kind of Woman* (from the original screenplay by Walter Bernstein, based on a story by Lowry), Pyramid Books, 1959.

Party of Dreamers (short stories), Fleet Publishing, 1962; *The Last Party: A Memorable Collection of Short Stories,* Popular Library, 1965.

Under pseudonym James Caldwell: *Defense in University City,* Little Man Press, 1939.

Author of several limited editions of poetry, privately printed. Short stories have been included in anthologies. Contributor of book reviews to *Saturday Review* and *New York Times Book Review,* 1951-56. Contributor of short stories, book reviews, and articles to periodicals in the United States and abroad.

WORK IN PROGRESS: Several volumes of poetry.

SIDELIGHTS: Lowry told *CA:* "The war was of paramount importance in giving a world-canvas to my ability to portray human beings under conditions of major stress. After the war, major careers (artist, prize fighter, motion picture star) were seen under the stress of American life and mores."

Robert Lowry collections have been established at Boston University, University of Southern California, and Kent State University.

* * *

LUCE, Celia (Geneva Larsen) 1914-

PERSONAL: Born December 3, 1914, in Provo, Utah; daughter of B. F. and Geneva (Day) Larsen; married Willard Luce (a writer and photographer), June 3, 1940; children: Willard Ray III, Loretta. *Education:* Brigham Young University, B.S., 1938. *Religion:* Church of Jesus Christ of Latter-Day Saints (Mormons). *Home:* 710 North 600th W., Provo, Utah 84601. *Office:* Hillcrest School, Orem, Utah 84057.

CAREER: Elementary teacher in Utah public schools: Bear River City, 1936-37, Spring Lake, 1938-40, Orem, 1944—. *Member:* League of Utah Writers.

WRITINGS—Juveniles; all with husband, Willard Luce: *Utah Past and Present,* Utah Color, 1958; *Timmy and the Golden Spike,* Garrard, 1963; *Jim Bridger: Man of the Mountains,* Garrard, 1966; *Sutter's Fort: Empire on the Sacramento,* Garrard, 1969; *Lou Gehrig: Iron Man of Baseball,* Garrard, 1970; *Utah!,* Peregrine Smith, 1975.

Work has been anthologized in *Heroes of the Home Run,* edited by Bennett Wayne, Garrard, 1973; *Adventures in Buckskin,* edited by Wayne, Garrard, 1973. Contributor to magazines and newspapers, including *Relief Society Magazine.*

AVOCATIONAL INTERESTS: Photography.

* * *

LUCE, J(ohn) V(ictor) 1920-

PERSONAL: Born May 21, 1920, in Dublin, Ireland; son of Arthur Aston (a professor) and Lillian Mary (Thompson) Luce; married Marjorie Lyndall Miles, June 21, 1948; children: Christina, Jane, Alice. *Education:* Trinity College, Dublin, B.A., 1942, M.A., 1945; Oxford University, M.A., 1946. *Religion:* Church of Ireland. *Home:* 13 Bushy Park Rd., Dublin 6, Ireland. *Office:* Department of Classics, 40 Trinity College, University of Dublin, Dublin 2, Ireland.

CAREER: University of Glasgow, Glasgow, Scotland, lecturer in Greek, 1946-48; University of Dublin, Trinity College, Dublin, Ireland, fellow, 1948—, reader, 1963-71, associate professor of classics, 1971—, public orator for university, 1971—. Visiting professor at Trinity College, Hartford, Conn., 1961-62, University of Michigan, 1969, and Indiana University, 1975. Governor of Erasmus Smith Schools, 1970—. *Member:* Royal Irish Academy, Society for Hellenic Studies.

WRITINGS: Lost Atlantis, McGraw, 1969 (published in England as *The End of Atlantis,* Thames & Hudson, 1969); (with W. B. Stanford) *The Quest for Ulysses,* Praeger, 1975; *Homer and the Heroic Age,* Harper, 1975.

WORK IN PROGRESS: The Evolution of Greek Culture; research on the effects of the Thera eruption on Minoan Crete.

SIDELIGHTS: Luce writes: "My first research interests were in Greek philosophy. . . . Interest in Aegean archaeology was stimulated by travel in the Eastern Mediterranean. Since 1964 I have been a lecturer on seventeen Hellenic Cruises arranged by Swan Hellenic Ltd. I have also travelled extensively on my own in Greece."

LUCE, Willard (Ray) 1914-

PERSONAL: Born September 18, 1914, in Price, Utah; son of Willard Ray (a salesman) and Rachel (Olsen) Luce; married Celia Larsen (a teacher and writer), June 3, 1940; children: Willard Ray III, Loretta. *Education:* Brigham Young University, B.S., 1947. *Religion:* Church of Jesus Christ of Latter-Day Saints (Mormons). *Home:* 710 North 600th W., Provo, Utah 84601.

CAREER: Teacher in public elementary schools in Utah: East Summit, 1938-39, Blanding, 1939-43, Orem, 1944-45; physical education teacher in high school in Blanding, 1943-44; Brigham Young University, Provo, Utah, instructor in journalism, 1946-47; teacher in elementary schools of Orem, 1947-54; free-lance writer and photographer and owner of post card company, 1954-56; elementary school teacher in Orem, 1956-73; free-lance writer and photographer, 1973—. *Wartime service:* Served in Merchant Marine, 1945-46. *Member:* National Education Association, Utah Education Association, League of Utah Writers (past president).

WRITINGS—For children: (With wife, Celia Luce) *Utah, Past and Present*, Utah Color, 1958; *The Red Stallion*, Deseret, 1961; (with C. Luce) *Timmy and the Golden Spike*, Deseret, 1963; (with C. Luce) *Jim Bridger: Man of the Mountains*, Garrard, 1966; (with C. Luce) *Sutter's Fort: Empire on the Sacramento*, Garrard, 1969; (with C. Luce) *Lou Gehrig: Iron Man of Baseball*, Garrard, 1970; *Birds That Hunt*, Follett, 1970; (with C. Luce) *Utah!*, Peregrine Smith, 1975.

Work has been anthologized in *Heroes of the Home Run*, edited by Bennett Wayne, Garrard, 1973; *Adventures in Buckskin*, edited by Wayne, Garrard, 1973. Photographs have been included in *Around the U.S.A. in a Thousand Pictures*, edited by A. Milton Runyon and Vilma F. Bergane, Doubleday, 1955, 2nd edition, 1965, and in *Jerry Lindsey: Explorer to the San Juan*, Deseret, 1958. Author of scripts and photographs for ten sound filmstrips for Creative Visuals, 1974; and three for Outdoor Pictures, 1975. Contributor of travel articles and photographs to magazines and newspapers, including *Natural History, Popular Photography, Ranger Rick's Nature Magazine, Ford Times, Dodge News,* and *Denver Post.*

WORK IN PROGRESS: Text and photographs for *The Gigantic Pygmy Forests.*

SIDELIGHTS: Utah Past and Present and *Utah!* are used as textbooks in the Utah elementary schools.

*   *   *

LUCIANI, Vincent 1906-

PERSONAL: Born August 31, 1906, in Hoboken, N.J.; son of Michele (a merchant) and Agnese (Perna) Luciani; married Margie Montenegro, February 2, 1938; children: Norma Francesca. *Education:* City College (now of the City University of New York), A.B. (magna cum laude), 1926; Columbia University, A.M., 1930, Ph.D., 1936. *Politics:* Independent. *Religion:* Agnostic. *Home:* 25 Cooper St., New York, N.Y. 10034.

CAREER: City College (now of the City University of New York), New York, N.Y., tutor, 1927-35, instructor, 1935-44, assistant professor, 1944-49, associate professor, 1949-60, professor of Romance languages, 1960-63, professor emeritus, 1963—. Instructor at Columbia University, summers, 1929-30; associate professor at University of California, Berkeley, summer, 1950. *Member:* Modern Language Association of America, American Association of Teachers of Italian (president, 1953), Phi Beta Kappa.

WRITINGS: Francesco Guicciardini and His European Revolution, K. Otto, 1936; *Modern Italian Fiction in America, 1929-1954: An Annotated Bibliography of Translations*, New York Public Library, 1956; *A Concise History of the Italian Theatre*, S. F. Vanni, 1961; (editor and author of notes) M. Betti, *Corruzione al Palazzo di Giustizia*, S. F. Vanni, 1961; (editor and author of notes) G. Giacosa, *Come le Foglie*, S. F. Vanni, 1961; (editor and author of notes) Carlo Goldoni, *Le Suraine per la Villeggiatura*, S. F. Vanni, 1961; (editor and author of notes) R. Bracco, *Il Piccolo Santo*, S. F. Vanni, 1961; *Italian Idioms with Proverbs*, S. F. Vanni, 1964; (translator and author of introduction) Pierre Beaumarchais, *Le Barbier de Seville* [and] *Le Mariage de Figaro* (title means "The Barber of Seville" and "The Marriage of Figaro"), published in one volume, Barron's, 1964; (editor) Niccolo Machiavelli, *La Mandragola*, S. F. Vanni, 1965; (editor) Goldoni, *La Locandiera*, S. F. Vanni, 1965; *Two Hundred One Italian Verbs Fully Conjugated in All the Tenses, Alphabetically Arranged*, Barron's, 1966; *A Brief History of Italian Literature*, S. F. Vanni, 1967. Contributor of articles and reviews to language journals.

*   *   *

LUHRMANN, Winifred B(ruce) 1934-

PERSONAL: Born November 19, 1934, in Greenfield, Mass.; daughter of Frederick R. (a clergyman) and Mildred (a minister; maiden name, Blair) Bruce; married George W. Luhrmann (a psychiatrist), June 16, 1956; children: Tanya, Anna, Alice. *Education:* Boston University, B.A., 1956. *Home and office:* 157 Winthrop Pl., Englewood, N.J. 07631.

CAREER: Free-lance writer, 1956-62; Pitman Publishing Co., New York City, assistant editor, 1962; American Book Co., New York City, assistant editor, 1963; Grolier, Inc., New York City, editorial re-writer for *The Book of Knowledge,* 1964-65; free-lance writer, 1965—. *Member:* American Association of University Women.

WRITINGS: The First Book of Gold, F. Watts, 1968. Also author of short stories. Contributor to *Baby and Child Care Encyclopedia.*

WORK IN PROGRESS: A children's book; a gothic novel of the American pre-revolutionary period; a biography of Anne Hutchinson; research on early American history.

SIDELIGHTS: Winifred Luhrmann writes: "Am fascinated by early development of America—especially the New England area—the integration with and death of the Indians and the early concepts of discipline and sin. I am myself descended from early Americans and am part Indian. Have also inherited a fascination for theology which extends my sympathies."

*   *   *

LUIS, Earlene W. 1929-

PERSONAL: Born October 21, 1929, in Alabama; daughter of Paul A. (a farmer) and Millie O. (Robinson) Woods; married Reinaldo Luis, June 24, 1950 (divorced, 1969); children: Paul, Rebecca (Mrs. Phillip Mydelski), Kathleen, John. *Education:* Attended King College, Bristol, Tenn., 1948-50; University of Alabama, B.S.Ed., 1952. *Home:* 23 Treasure Dr., Tampa, Fla. 33609. *Office:* Department of English, Hillsborough High School, Tampa, Fla.

CAREER: Sunland Training Center, Gainesville, Fla., teacher, 1955-58; elementary school teacher, 1960-69; Hillsborough High School, Tampa, Fla., teacher of English, 1969—. Social worker in Hillsborough County, Fla., 1960. *Member:* Bonsai Clubs International, Bonsai Societies of Florida. *Awards, honors:* Edith Busby Award from Dodd, Mead, 1966, for *Wheels for Ginny's Chariot.*

WRITINGS—Juveniles: (With Barbara Miller) *Wheels for Ginny's Chariot,* Dodd, 1966; (with Miller) *Listen, Lissa!,* Dodd, 1969. Contributor to English and education journals, and to *Florida Bonsai.*

WORK IN PROGRESS: No Visa for Roberto, with Barbara Miller, a book about a Cuban refugee youth; another book with Miller about a Vietnamese refugee child.

SIDELIGHTS: Earlene Luis writes: "The first two books are concerned with handicapped persons—we felt these young people have few fictional characters with whom they can identify.... I speak Spanish fluently, and have been very much interested in the problems of people who must adapt to a new culture...." *Avocational interests:* Growing Bonsai trees, gardening.

* * *

LUKA, Ronald 1937-

PERSONAL: Born April 26, 1937, in Chicago, Ill.; son of John J. and Emily (Natzke) Luka. *Education:* Catholic University of America, S.T.L., 1963, M.A., 1965. *Home and office:* Louisiana State University, Box CC, Baton Rouge, La. 70803.

CAREER: Ordained Roman Catholic priest of Congregatio Missionariorum Filiorum Immaculati Cordis Beatae Maria Virginia (Congregation of Missionary Sons of the Immaculate Heart of the Blessed Virgin Mary; Claretian Fathers; C.M.F.) 1963; Southwest Texas State College, San Marcos, chaplain and instructor in religious studies, 1965-66; Long Island University, C.W. Post College, Brookville, N.Y., chaplain and adjunct associate professor of religious studies, 1966-75; Louisiana State University, Baton Rouge, chaplain, 1975—. Chaplain at State University of New York Junior College at Farmingdale and at New York Institute of Technology, both 1966-75. Active in Marriage Encounter and in Charismatic Renewal movements. *Member:* Catholic Campus Ministry Association.

WRITINGS: The Way of the Cross Today, Ave Maria Press, 1967; *The Challenge of the Secular Campus,* Ave Maria Press, 1968; *Hangups in Religion,* Claretian Publishing, 1970; *When a Christian and a Jew Marry,* Paulist/Newman, 1973. Contributor to religious publications.

WORK IN PROGRESS: Manuscripts on the interfaith person, the education of children in interfaith marriages, the relationship between American values and Christian values, and a religious perspective of open marriage; research on the university chaplain and family life.

* * *

LUKER, Kristin Carol 1946-

PERSONAL: Born August 5, 1946, in San Francisco, Calif.; daughter of James Wester (a colonel in the U.S. Air Force) and Bess (a herbalist; maiden name, Littlefield) Luker. *Education:* Attended University of California, Berkeley, 1964-66, A.B. (with high honors), 1968, postdoctoral study, 1973-74; University of Madrid, student, 1966-67; Yale University, M.Phil., 1970, Ph.D., 1973. *Home:* 2612 Dana St., Berkeley, Calif. 94704. *Office:* Department of Sociology, University of California at San Diego, La Jolla, Calif. 92037.

CAREER: Quinnipiac College, Cheshire, Conn., acting assistant professor of sociology, 1971; University of California, Berkeley, lecturer in sociology, summer, 1974; California State University, San Francisco, lecturer in sociology, 1974-75; University of California at San Diego, La Jolla, assistant professor of sociology, 1975—. Visiting assistant professor at Mills College, 1974-75. *Member:* American Sociological Association, Sociologists for Women in Society, Population Association of America, National Organization for Women, League of Associated Women (University of California, Berkeley).

WRITINGS: Abortion in the San Francisco Bay Area (monograph), Planned Parenthood/World Population, 1972; *Abortion Histories of Five Hundred Women* (monograph), Planned Parenthood/World Population, 1972; *Taking Chances: Abortion and the Decision Not to Contracept,* University of California Press, 1975.

WORK IN PROGRESS: Research on men, specifically on the experiences of men whose partners have abortions, and on the social history of fatherhood.

SIDELIGHTS: According to Kristin Luker, hers is a "feminist book looking at the situation from a woman's point of view and sympathetic to women who find themselves pregnant." She has done extensive research in the areas of abortion, contraception, and population control. In addition to social demography, her areas of expertise include medical sociology, methodology, sociology of the family, and sociology of mental illness. An active participant in the "women's movement," she has worked as a consultant to women's groups and women's projects.

* * *

LUNDBERG, Margaret (Jessie) 1919-

PERSONAL: Born September 16, 1919, in Lebanon, N.H.; daughter of Pedro Mackay (a consul) and Sarah Ellen (Wood) de Almeida; married Craig Elliott Lundberg (a corporation president), February 22, 1941; children: Christopher Paul, Jean Ellen. *Education:* Wellesley College, B.A., 1940; Tufts University, M.A., 1961, Ph.D., 1967. *Home:* 16 Orchard Lane, Wayland, Mass. 01778.

CAREER: Boston University, Boston, Mass., assistant professor of social sciences, 1966—. Researcher at Harvard University Graduate School of Education, 1960-61, and Tufts University Medical School, 1961-62. *Member:* American Sociological Association, Society for Research in Child Development, Massachusetts Sociological Association, Delta Kappa Gamma.

WRITINGS: The Incomplete Adult: Social Class Constraints on Personality Development, Greenwood Press, 1974.

WORK IN PROGRESS: A book applying the findings of developmental psychology to the evolution of society, completion expected in 1977-78.

* * *

LUNENFELD, Marvin C. 1934-

PERSONAL: Born September 10, 1934, in New York, N.Y.; married Katharine A. Daly (an editor and writer), 1960; children: Peter Benjamine. *Education:* City College (now of the City University of New York), B.B.A., 1957; New York University, M.A., 1963, Ph.D., 1968. *Office:*

Department of History, State University of New York, College at Fredonia, Fredonia, N.Y. 14063.

CAREER: University of Maryland, Overseas Program in Spain, lecturer in history, 1964; City College of the City University of New York, instructor in history, 1967-68; Rutgers University, New Brunswick, N.J., instructor in history, 1968-70; State University of New York, College at Fredonia, associate professor of history, 1970—. New School For Social Research, New York, N.Y., lecturer in history, 1967—. *Military service:* U.S. Army, 1958. U.S. Army Reserve, 1958-64. *Member:* Society for Spanish and Portuguese Historical Studies, Renaissance Society, American Historical Association.

WRITINGS: The Council of the "Santa Hermandad": A Study in the Pacification Forces of Ferdinand and Isabella, University of Miami Press, 1970. Contributor of reviews to various journals.

WORK IN PROGRESS: Mainly on the Plain: Spain and Its Cities, a history of the cities of Spain from Roman times to the present; *Speaking of Spain: An Anthology.*

*　　*　　*

LURIA, S(alvador) E(dward)　1912-

PERSONAL: Born August 13, 1912, in Turin, Italy; came to United States, 1940, naturalized citizen, 1947; son of David and Ester (Sacerdote) Luria; married Zella Hurwitz (a psychologist), April 24, 1945; children: Daniel David. *Education:* University of Turin, M.D., 1935. *Politics:* Independent Socialist. *Home:* 48 Peacock Farm Rd., Lexington, Mass. 02173. *Office:* Department of Biology, Massachusetts Institute of Technology, Cambridge, Mass. 02139.

CAREER: Curie Laboratory, Institute of Radium, Paris, France, research fellow, 1938-40; Columbia University, New York, N.Y., research assistant in surgical bacteriology, 1940-42; Indiana University, Bloomington, instructor, 1943-45, assistant professor, 1945-47, associate professor of bacteriology, 1947-50; University of Illinois, Urbana, professor of bacteriology, 1950-59; Massachusetts Institute of Technology, Cambridge, professor of microbiology, 1959-64, Sedgwick Professor of Biology, 1964—, Institute Professor, 1970—, director of Center for Cancer Research, 1972—. Investigator, Office of Scientific Research and Development, Carnegie Institute of Technology (now Carnegie-Mellon University), 1945-46; non-resident fellow, Salk Institute for Biological Studies, 1965—, trustee, 1972-75. Jesup lecturer at Columbia University, 1950; lecturer at University of Colorado, 1950; Nieuwland lecturer at University of Notre Dame, 1959; Dyer lecturer at National Institutes of Health, 1963.

MEMBER: National Academy of Sciences, American Academy of Arts and Sciences, American Philosophical Society, American Association for the Advancement of Science, American Society for Microbiology (president, 1967-68), Genetics Society of America, Federation of American Scientists.

AWARDS, HONORS: Guggenheim fellow at Vanderbilt University and Princeton University, 1942-43, and Pasteur Institute, Paris, 1963-64; recipient with two other biologists of Nobel Prize in medicine, 1969, for discoveries relating to the replication mechanism and the genetic structure of viruses; D.Sc. from University of Chicago, 1967, Rutgers University, 1970, Indiana University, 1970, Brown University, and University of Palmero.

WRITINGS: General Virology, Wiley, 1953, 2nd edition (with James E. Darnell), 1967; *Life: The Unfinished Experiment,* Scribner, 1973; *36 Lectures in Biology,* M.I.T. Press, 1975. Contributor to scientific journals and to *Prism, New York Review of Books,* and *Boston Globe.* Editor, *Virology,* 1955—; section editor, *Biological Abstracts,* 1958—; member of editorial board, *Daedalus,* 1972—.

WORK IN PROGRESS: A new edition of *General Virology;* a novel, tentatively titled *Random Walk,* completion expected in 1977.

SIDELIGHTS: Luria started writing on general topics "in opposition to the Vietnam war and other issues." His *General Virology* has been translated into Italian, Rumanian, Polish, and Japanese. *Life: The Unfinished Experiment* has appeared in Italian, French, German, and Japanese editions.

BIOGRAPHICAL/CRITICAL SOURCES: New York Times, October 17, 1969; *Time,* October 24, 1969.

*　　*　　*

LUTZ, Paul E(ugene)　1934-

PERSONAL: Born June 25, 1934, in Hickory, N.C.; son of Cy Emmett (a clergyman) and Ruth (Karriker) Lutz; married Alice Patterson (a secretary), June 8, 1957; children: Carol. *Education:* Lenoir Rhyne College, A.B., 1956; University of Miami, Coral Gables, Fla., M.S., 1958; University of North Carolina, Ph.D., 1962. *Religion:* Lutheran. *Home:* 4001 Cascade Dr., Greensboro, N.C. 27410. *Office:* Department of Biology, University of North Carolina, Greensboro, N.C. 27412.

CAREER: University of North Carolina, Greensboro, instructor, 1961-62, assistant professor, 1962-66, associate professor, 1966-70, professor of biology, 1970—. Member of board of trustees of Lenoir Rhyne College, 1963—. Chairman of Guilford County Advisory Board for Environmental Quality, 1974-75; member of advisory committee on environment of Piedmont Triad Council of Governments, 1975—. Member of board of social ministry of Lutheran Church in America, 1970-72, member of management committee of Division for Mission in North America, 1972—.

MEMBER: American Association for the Advancement of Science, Ecological Society of America, American Society of Zoologists, American Institute of Biological Sciences, Association of Southeastern Biologists, North Carolina Academy of Science, Sigma Xi. *Awards, honors:* Distinguished service award from Lenoir Rhyne College, 1971.

WRITINGS: (With H. Paul Santmire) *Ecological Renewal,* Fortress, 1972. Contributor of about fifty articles to scientific publications.

*　　*　　*

LUZI, Mario　1914-

PERSONAL: Born October 20, 1914, in Florence, Italy, son of Marglenita (Paxim) Luzi; married Elena Monali (a teacher), June 20, 1942; children: Gianni. *Education:* University of Florence, D.Ph., 1936. *Religion:* Catholic. *Home:* Belbariva 20, Florence, Italy 50136.

CAREER: University of Florence, Florence, Italy, professor of French literature, 1938—. Poet. *Awards, honors:* Premio Marzotto Narrative o Poesia, 1957, for *Onore del vero;* Premio Taormina, 1964, for *Nel magma.*

WRITINGS: Un'illusione platonica e altri saggi (essays), Edizioni di rivoluzione (Florence), 1941, enlarged edition,

M. Boni (Bologna), 1972; *Biografia a Ebe,* Vallecehi (Florence), 1942; *Un brindisi* (poetry), G. C. Sansoni (Florence), 1946; *L'inferno e il limbo* (essays; title means "Hell and Limbo"), Marzocco (Florence), 1949, enlarged edition, Casa editrice Il Saggiatore (Milan), 1964.

Primizie del deserto (poetry; title means "First Fruits of the Desert"), Schwarz (Milan), 1952; *Studio su Mallarme,* G. C. Sansoni, 1952; *Aspetti della generazione napoleonica: Ed altri soggi di letteratura francese* (essays), Guanda (Parma), 1956; *Onore del vero* (poetry; title means "Honor of Truth"), N. Pozza (Venice), 1957; (editor) *L'idea simbolista,* Garzanti (Milan), 1959.

Il qiusto dell vita (poetry; title means "What is Right in Life"), Garzanti, 1960, 2nd edition, 1971; *Lo stile di Constant,* Il Saggiatore, 1962; *Nel Magma* (poetry; title means "In the Magma"), Garzanti, 1963, 2nd edition, All'Insegna del Pesce d'Oro (Milan), 1964, enlarged edition, Garzanti, 1966; *Dal fondo delle campagne* (poetry; title means "From the Bottom of the Field), Einaudi (Torino), 1965; *Tutto in questione* (essays), Vallecchi, 1965; (editor) *Faraoni* (memoirs of Enzo Faraoni), Galleria Pananti (Florence), 1969.

(Author of text with Mario de Micheli) *Cento opere di Carlo Carra,* Galleria d'arte moderna Fratelle Falsetti (Prato), 1971; *Su fondamenti invisibili* (poetry), Rizzoli (Milan), 1971; (with Carlo Cassoea) *Poesia e Romanzo* (poetry), Rizzoli, 1973; *Ipazia* (one-act play), Scheiwiller, 1973; *Vicissitudine e forma* (essay), Rizzoli, 1974; *In the Dark Body of Metamorphosis and Other Poems,* translated by Isidore Lawrence Salomon, Norton, 1975.

Contributor to *Corriere della Sera* and *Il Giornale Nuovo.*

* * *

LYLE, Guy R(edvers)   1907-

PERSONAL: Born October 31, 1907, in Canada; son of John Percival and Marie Dolores B. Lyle; married Margaret White; children: John Donald, Jennifer Ann, Christopher, Ellen. *Education:* University of Alberta, A.B., 1927; Columbia University, B.S., 1929, M.S., 1932. *Home:* 2229 Tanglewood Rd., Decatur, Ga. 30033.

CAREER: Antioch College, Yellow Springs, Ohio, librarian, 1929-35; Woman's College of the University of North Carolina (now University of North Carolina), Greensboro, librarian and professor, 1936-44; Louisiana State University, Baton Rouge, director of libraries, 1944-54; Emory University, Atlanta, Ga., professor of library science and director of libraries, 1954-72. Visiting professor at University of Illinois, 1935-36, 1942-43, and summer, 1949, University of North Carolina, 1938, 1953, Columbia University, 1946, 1947, and University of California, 1968; visiting professor of library science, University of Puerto Rico, spring, 1973, University of Southern California, Los Angeles, spring, 1974; visiting lecturer at Keio University, 1957. *Awards, honors:* LL.D., University of Alberta, 1964; J. B. Lippincott Award from American Library Association, 1972.

WRITINGS: Administration of the College Library, H. W. Wilson, 1944, 4th edition, 1974; *Bibliography of Christopher Morley,* Scarecrow, 1952; (with Kevin Guinagh) *I Am Happy To Present,* H. W. Wilson, 1953, 2nd edition, 1968; *The President, the Professor, and the College Library,* H. W. Wilson, 1963; *The Librarian Speaking,* University of Georgia Press, 1970.

BIOGRAPHICAL/CRITICAL SOURCES: E. I. Farber and Ruth Walling, *The Academic Library: Essays in Honor of Guy R. Lyle,* Scarecrow, 1974.

* * *

LYNN, Naomi B.   1933-

PERSONAL: Born April 16, 1933, in New York, N.Y.; daughter of Car (in Department of Immigration) and Maria (Lebron) Burgos; married Robert Athan Lynn (dean of College of Business at Kansas State University), August 28, 1954; children: Mary Lou, Nancy Ruth, Judith May, Joan Ellen. *Education:* Maryville College, Maryville, Tenn., B.A. (cum laude), 1954; University of Illinois, M.A., 1958; University of Kansas, Ph.D., 1970. *Religion:* Presbyterian. *Home:* 1324 North Eighth, Manhattan, Kan. 66502. *Office:* Department of Political Science, Kedzie Hall, Kansas State University, Manhattan, Kan. 66506.

CAREER: Central Missouri State University, Warrensburg, instructor in political science, 1966-68; Kansas State University, Manhattan, assistant professor, 1970-75, associate professor of political science, 1975—, overseer of University Without Walls, 1974-77.

MEMBER: International Studies Association, American Political Science Association (delegate of Tribunal to International Women's Year, 1975), American Society for Public Administration (director of Kansas City chapter, 1971-72, 1974-76), Women's Caucus for Political Science (member of executive committee, 1971-74; vice-president, 1974-75; president, 1975-76), Midwest Political Science Association, Southern Political Science Association, Western Political Science Association, Southwest Political Science Association, Midwest Women's Political Science Caucus (chairperson, 1972-74), Kansas League of Women Voters (member of board of directors, 1969-70, Phi Sigma Alpha.

WRITINGS: (With Arthur McClure) *The Fulbright Premise: Senator J. William Fulbright and Presidential Power in Foreign Policy,* Bucknell University Press, 1973; (contributor) Jane S. Jaquette, editor, *Women in Politics,* Wiley, 1974; (with Ann B. Matasar and Marie Rosenberg) *Undergraduate Research Guide to Women's Studies,* General Learning Corp., 1974; (with Richard Vaden) *A Bridge to the East Destroyed,* with teaching notes, Inter-Collegiate Case Clearing House, Harvard University, 1974; (contributor) Jo Freeman, editor, *Women: A Feminist Perspective,* Mayfield, 1975.

Contributor of articles and reviews to personnel and political science journals. Abstractor for *Women's Studies Abstracts,* 1973-75; reader for *Journal of Military and Political Sociology;* reviewer for Houghton.

* * *

MacEWAN, Paul W.   1943-

PERSONAL: Born April 8, 1943; son of Horace F. (a clergyman) and Alyce D. (a teacher) MacEwan; married Carol Elizabeth Osborne, September 1, 1962; children: Deborah J., Kimberly D., Paul R., P. Edward. *Education:* Nova Scotia Teachers College, received diploma, 1963; College of Cape Breton, graduate study, 1963-69. *Politics:* New Democratic Party. *Religion:* Christian. *Home:* 1049 Victoria Rd., Sydney, Nova Scotia, Canada. *Office:* 700 Victoria Rd., Sydney, Nova Scotia, Canada.

CAREER: Public school teacher in Sydney, Nova Scotia, 1963-70; Legislative Assembly of Nova Scotia, Halifax, member of legislature, 1970—. *Awards, honors:* Canada Council grant for writing, 1972.

WRITINGS: Miners and Steelworkers: Labor in Cape Breton, A. M. Hakkert, 1975. Columnist, "Labor and Politics in Cape Breton" in *Cape Breton Highlander*, 1965-70. Contributor to newspapers.

WORK IN PROGRESS: Confederation and the Maritimes.

SIDELIGHTS: MacEwan comments that *Miners and Steelworkers* "is the history of my own people and the political movement I adhere to, from its origins up to the present."

* * *

MACK, Max Noble 1916-

PERSONAL: Born December 4, 1916, in Newton, Kans.; son of George August and Mary Ann (Ulam) Mack; married Rita Judd, August 11, 1950 (divorced January, 1960); children: Josephine, Paula. *Education:* University of California, Berkeley, A.B., 1938, further study, 1939-40; California State University, Northridge, M.A., 1968. *Politics and religion:* "Resigned from American Communist Party in 1957. Presently not affiliated to any party or church." *Address:* P.O. Box 928, Topanga, Calif. 90290.

CAREER: Teacher in public and private schools in Lincoln, Calif., 1957-58, Redding, Calif., 1958-59, and Van Nuys, Calif., 1963-68; West Valley Center for Educational Therapy, Canoga Park, Calif., educational therapist, 1968-74. *Military service:* U.S. Army Air Forces, 1941-45; served as aerial navigator in Mediterranean theatre; became first lieutenant.

WRITINGS: Is It Legal to Barbecue an Eagle?, Noble Prentiss, 1974.

WORK IN PROGRESS: Dialogues on Literature, Magic, Art, and Life, with daughter, Paula Mack.

SIDELIGHTS: Mack spent thirteen months in a German prison camp during World War II. He states that he wrote his book, which was illustrated by his daughter, in order to set down the truth about his life—especially its revolutionary aspects.

* * *

MacKAYE, Benton 1879-1975

1879—December 11, 1975; American forester, association executive, and author of books on geography and regional planning. Obituaries: *New York Times*, December 13, 1975.

* * *

MacKINNON, Edward Michael 1928-

PERSONAL: Born June 30, 1928, in Boston, Mass.; son of Michael Andrew (a realtor) and Anna (MacIsaac) MacKinnon; married Barbara A. Bacon (a philosophy professor), March 4, 1972; children: Jennifer Ann. *Education:* Boston College, B.A., 1949, M.A. (philosophy), 1954; Harvard University, M.A. (physics), 1955; St. Louis University, Ph.D., 1958; Weston College, S.T.L., 1962. *Politics:* Democrat. *Home:* 6120 Hill Rd., Oakland, Calif. 94618. *Office:* Department of Philosophy, California State University, Hayward, Calif. 94542.

CAREER: Boston College, Chestnut Hill, Mass., assistant professor, 1965-67, associate professor, 1967-69, professor of philosophy, 1969-71; California State University, Hayward, professor of philosophy, 1971—. *Member:* American Philosophical Association, American Physical Society, Phi-

losophy of Science Association, American Association for the Advancement of Science, American Association of University Professors, Sigma Xi.

WRITINGS: Truth and Expression: The 1968 Hecker Lectures, Newman Press, 1971; *The Problem of Scientific Realism*, Appleton, 1971. Contributor to journals in his field. Associate editor, *Continuum*, 1967-70, *Philosophy Forum*, 1968—.

* * *

MacLEOD, Duncan J(ohn) 1939-

PERSONAL: Born October 7, 1939, in Belgaum, India; son of Douglas (a youth officer) and Edith (Burgess) MacLeod; married Rosalind Mary Smith, January 22, 1966; children: Joanna Louise, Damian Richard. *Education:* London School of Economics and Political Science, University of London, B.A., 1963; Churchill College, Cambridge, Ph.D., 1969. *Politics:* "Humane." *Home:* 17 Littleworth Rd., Wheatley, Oxfordshire, England. *Office:* St. Catherine's College, Oxford University, Oxford, England.

CAREER: Teacher of history in grammar school in Oxford, England, 1963-64; University of London, London, England, lecturer in American history, 1968-72; Oxford University, Oxford, England, member of faculty of modern history and fellow of St. Catherine's College, 1972—. *Member:* British Association for American Studies, American Historical Association, Organization of American Historians. *Awards, honors:* International fellow of American Council of Learned Societies, 1965-67.

WRITINGS: Slavery, Race, and the American Revolution, Cambridge University Press, 1975.

WORK IN PROGRESS: Research on black and white history in the American South.

SIDELIGHTS: "I see my greatest challenge as one of seeing American history whole," MacLeod wrote. "In particular, the history of the South is the history of both blacks and whites, but it is the history of blacks and whites together, not apart."

* * *

MACLURE, (John) Stuart 1926-

PERSONAL: Born August 8, 1926, in London, England; son of Hugh Seton (a stockbroker) and Bertha (Hodge) Maclure; married Constance Mary Butler, August 9, 1951: children: Michael Stuart, Susan Mary, Clare Elizabeth. *Education:* Christ's College, Cambridge, B.A. (first class honors), 1949, M.A., 1950. *Religion:* Methodist. *Home:* 109 College Rd., Dulwich, London SE21 7HN, England. *Office: Times Educational Supplement*, New Printing House Sq., Gray's Inn Rd., London WC1X 8FZ, England.

CAREER: Times, London, England, editorial probationer, 1950-51, reporter for *Times Educational Supplement*, 1951-54, editor of *Education*, 1954-69, editor of *Times Educational Supplement*, 1969—. *Military service:* Royal Naval Volunteer Reserve, 1945-47; became sub-lieutenant. *Member:* Royal Society of Arts (fellow).

WRITINGS: (Editor with T. E. Utley) *Documents on Modern Political Thought*, Cambridge University Press, 1956; (editor) *English Educational Documents: 1816 to the Present Day*, Methuen, 1965; *Curriculum Development in Practice*, H.M.S.O., 1968; *A Hundred Years of London Education*, Allen Lane, 1970; *Innovation in Education in Sweden*, Centre for Educational Research and Innovation

(Paris, France), 1970; *Styles of Curriculum Development,* Centre for Educational Research and Innovation (Paris, France), 1973. Contributor to magazines and newspapers.

AVOCATIONAL INTERESTS: Cricket, ornithology.

* * *

MACOMBER, William (Butts, Jr.) 1921-

PERSONAL: Born March 28, 1921, in Rochester, N.Y.; son of William Butts and Elizabeth Currie (Ranlet) Macomber; married Phyllis Dorothy Bernau, December 28, 1963. *Education:* Yale University, A.B., 1943, M.A., 1946; Harvard University, LL.B., 1949; University of Chicago, M.A., 1951. *Office:* American Embassy, Ankara, Turkey.

CAREER: Boston University, Boston, Mass., lecturer in government, 1947-49; Central Intelligence Agency (CIA), Washington, D.C., member of staff, 1951-53; U.S. State Department, Washington, D.C., special assistant in intelligence, 1953-54; administrative assistant to U.S. Senator John Sherman Cooper, Washington, D.C., 1954; special assistant to Under-Secretary of State Herbert Hoover, Jr., Washington, D.C., 1955, and to Secretary of State John Foster Dulles, Washington, D.C., 1955-57; assistant Secretary of State for Congressional Relations, Washington, D.C., 1957-62; U.S. Ambassador to Jordan, 1961-64; U.S. Agency for International Development, Washington, D.C., assistant administrator, 1964-67; U.S. State Department, assistant secretary for Congressional Relations, 1967-69, deputy Under-Secretary of State for Administration, 1969-73; U.S. ambassador to Turkey, in Ankara, 1973—. Alumni trustee of Phillips Andover Academy, 1957-60. *Military service:* U.S. Marine Corps, 1943-46; became lieutenant. *Member:* Genesee Club.

WRITINGS: The Angels Game: A Handbook of Modern Diplomacy, Stein & Day, 1975.

* * *

MADIAN, Jon 1941-

PERSONAL: First syllable of surname rhymes with "fade"; born May 10, 1941, in New York, N.Y.; son of Sydney (an administrator) and Anna (a teacher; maiden name, Leiber) Madian; married Gisele Marosi, July 14, 1960 (divorced, 1974); children: Lorraine, Andrea. *Education:* Attended University of California, Riverside and Dartmouth College; University of California, Los Angeles, further study, 1962-67. *Politics:* Democratic free enterprise socialism. *Home and office:* 27 Voyage St., Venice, Calif. 90291.

CAREER: Southern California Counseling Center, Los Angeles, supervisor, 1974—. Private practice as marriage, family, and child counselor.

WRITINGS—Juvenile: *Beautiful Junk: The Story of the Watts Towers,* Little, Brown, 1968; *Two Is a Line,* Platt, 1971; *Lines Make Me Lonely,* Ginn, 1972.

WORK IN PROGRESS: A children's science fiction adventure.

SIDELIGHTS: Madian commented: "I find that literature and psychotherapy are like two sides of a coin, i.e. personal images and history on one side, cultural images on the other. The writer creates images. The therapist, like the critic or historian, analyses and catalyzes them."

BIOGRAPHICAL/CRITICAL SOURCES: Commonweal, November 22, 1968; *National Review,* December 17, 1968.

MAEROFF, Gene I(rving) 1939-

PERSONAL: Born January 8, 1939, in Cleveland, Ohio; son of Harry and Charlotte (Szabo) Maeroff; married Marilyn Eve Horowitz, August 26, 1961; children: Janine Amanda, Adam Jonathan, Rachel Judith. *Education:* Ohio University, B.S., 1961; Boston University, M.S., 1962. *Residence:* Great Neck, N.Y. *Office:* New York Times, 229 West 43rd St., New York, N.Y. 10036.

CAREER: Rhode Island College, Providence, news bureau director, 1962-64; *Akron Beacon Journal,* Akron, Ohio, religious editor, 1964-65; *Cleveland Plain Dealer,* Cleveland, Ohio, member of staff, 1965-69, associate editor, 1969-71; *New York Times,* New York, N.Y., education writer, 1971—. Trustee, Jewish Family Service Association, and Ed Bang Journalism Scholarship Foundation. *Member:* Omicron Delta Kappa, Kappa Tau Alpha, Phi Sigma Delta. *Awards, honors:* Recipient of awards from Education Writers Association, International Reading Association, Press Club of Cleveland, and Associated Press of Ohio.

WRITINGS: The New York Times Guide to Suburban Public Schools, Quadrangle, 1975. Contributor to *New York Times Magazine, New York, Nation, New Republic, Coronet, Saturday Review,* and *Parade.*

* * *

MAESTRO, Betsy 1944-

PERSONAL: Born January 5, 1944, in New York, N.Y.; daughter of Harlan R. (a design consultant) and Norma (in education; maiden name, Sherman) Crippen; married second husband, Giulio Maestro (an illustrator), December 16, 1972; children: (second marriage) Daniela Marisa. *Education:* Southern Connecticut State College, B.S., 1964, M.S., 1970. *Politics:* Democrat. *Home:* 702 Summer Hill Rd., Madison, Conn. 06443. *Office:* Deer Run School, Route 80, East Haven, Conn. 06512.

CAREER: Deer Run School, East Haven, Conn., kindergarten teacher, 1964—. *Member:* National Education Association, Connecticut Education Association, East Haven Education Association.

WRITINGS: (With husband, Giulio Maestro) *A Wise Monkey Tale,* Crown, 1975; *Where Is My Friend?,* Crown, 1976; *Fat Polkadot Cat and Other Haiku,* Dutton, 1976; *In My Beat,* Crowell, in press.

WORK IN PROGRESS: Harriet Goes to the Circus, publication by Crown expected in 1977; word and number concept books for very young children.

AVOCATIONAL INTERESTS: Reading, cooking, gardening, photography, travel.

* * *

MAGARY, Alan 1944-

PERSONAL: Surname is pronounced Muh-*geh*-ree; born December 30, 1944, in San Francisco, Calif.; son of Frank A. (a foreign service officer) and Laura (a secretary; maiden name, Forsberg) Magary; married Kerstin Fraser (a writer and editor), April 8, 1972. *Education:* Middlebury College, B.A., 1966. *Home:* 46 Alvarado St., San Francisco, Calif. 94110. *Agent:* Max Gartenberg, 331 Madison Ave., New York, N.Y. 10022.

CAREER: Middletown Press, Middletown, Conn., reporter, 1964-71 (part time); freelance writer, 1971-74; California Coastal Zone Conservation Commission, San Francisco, Calif., editor of coastal plan, 1974—. *Military service:* U.S. Army, 1967-70; received Bronze Star. *Member:* Sierra Club, East African Wildlife Society, Heritage, Victorian Alliance, SPUR, San Francisco Zoological Society.

WRITINGS: (Editor with wife, Kerstin Fraser, and John Hirsch) *Fodor's Europe on a Budget,* Fodor/McKay, 1972, 4th revised edition, 1975; (with K. Fraser) *East Africa: A Travel Guide,* Harper, 1975.

WORK IN PROGRESS: California: A Guide, for Harper; researching the CIA, modern-day dandies, and manhole covers, "nowhere and San Francisco, in an idle sort of way."

SIDELIGHTS: Magary wrote: "My major writing achievement (and my wife's) is *East Africa: A Travel Guide,* a mammoth, comprehensive, and unique . . . book written in an octagonal garden cottage outside Nairobi in spurts during sixteen months of travels around Eastern Africa, mainly in a Land Cruiser. . . . The expedition took about two years to get underway. Incidentally, my wife was originally an expedition partner signed up through a classified ad; we got married the day before leaving for Africa!"

*   *   *

MAGARY, Kerstin Fraser   1947-

PERSONAL: Born March 20, 1947, in Oakland Calif.; daughter of Peter E. (a printing salesman) and Frances Euphrosyne (a teacher; maiden name, Olsson) Fraser; married Alan Magary (a writer and editor), April 8, 1972. *Education:* Attended University of California, Berkeley, 1965; Mills College, Oakland, Calif., B.A., 1969. *Home:* 46 Alvarado St., San Francisco, Calif. 94110. *Agent:* Max Gartenberg, 331 Madison Ave., New York, N.Y. 10022.

CAREER: World Airways, Oakland, Calif., flight attendant, 1969; Bank of America International, San Francisco, Calif., researcher and writer, 1969-71; free-lance writer and photographer in Eastern Africa, New York, and California, 1971-75; Wilton, Coombs & Colnett Advertising, San Francisco, advertising account executive, 1974-75; Gensler & Assoc. (architects), San Francisco, editor, 1975—. *Member:* Sierra Club, National Organization for Women, East African Wildlife Society, San Francisco Women in Advertising, Victorian Alliance, Heritage, SPUR, San Francisco Zoological Society.

WRITINGS: (Editor with husband, Alan Magary, and John Hirsch) *Fodor's Europe on A Budget,* Fodor/McKay, 1972, 4th revised edition, 1975; (with A. Magary) *East Africa: A Travel Guide,* Harper, 1975.

WORK IN PROGRESS: California: A Guide, for Harper.

*   *   *

MAHON, Julia C(unha)   1916-

PERSONAL; Born February 20, 1916, in Phenix City, Ala.; daughter of Francis Cornelius (a textiles worker) and Ferol (Smith) Cunha; married Edmund Mahon (a machine repairman), November 14, 1936; children: John, Paul, Rosemary (Mrs. John Adamec), Thomas, Elizabeth Ann (deceased). *Education:* Attended Willimantic State College, 1960-62, Harvard University, 1963, and University of Rhode Island, 1972-73. *Politics:* Independent. *Religion:* Roman Catholic. *Home address:* Route 193, Thompson, Conn. 06277. *Office:* Tourtellotte Memorial High School, North Grosvenordale, Conn. 06255.

CAREER: Tourtellotte Memorial High School, North

Grosvenordale, Conn., librarian, 1960—. Conducted creative writing workshops in student leadership conferences at University of New Hampshire and at Rhode Island College. *Member:* New England Educational Media Association, Northeastern Connecticut Librarians' Swap Group.

WRITINGS—Juvenile: His Name Is Jesus, Grail, 1953; *Mystery at Old Sturbridge Village,* Albert Whitman, 1966; *The First Book of Creative Writing,* F. Watts, 1968. Contributor of articles, stories, and poems to religious and popular magazines, including *Time.*

WORK IN PROGRESS: A collection of famous American trials, *Principals and Principles;* the story of a runaway slave girl during the American Revolution, *Mystery at the Vernon Stiles Inn.*

SIDELIGHTS: Julia Mahon writes: "As the second oldest of ten children, I had ample opportunity through the years to exercise my talents as a story-teller for the younger children. One was a series of humorous tales concerning the misadventures of a bumbling character named Itty Artic, which the little ones found vastly entertaining. . . . It was 1953 when my first children's book was published. By one of those strange ironies of life, it appeared about the time our baby, Betty, died of leukemia. . . . I now find myself looking forward to retirement when I can devote more time to the writing which has been such a vital part of my being virtually all of my life. And, as long as I am wanted, I shall continue to teach in the Confraternity of Christian Doctrine, which I think represents one of the greatest needs of our children today."

*   *   *

MAHONEY, Irene   1921-

PERSONAL: Born May 5, 1921, in Brooklyn, N.Y.; daughter of Florence (a New York police officer) and Mary (O'Rourke) Mahoney. *Education:* College of New Rochelle, B.A., 1941; Fordham University, M.A., 1948; Catholic University of America, Ph.D., 1958. *Home:* 173 Woodland Ave., New Rochelle, N.Y. 10801. *Agent:* Claire Smith, Harold Ober Associates, 40 East 49th St., New York, N.Y. 10017. *Office:* Department of English, College of New Rochelle, New Rochelle, N.Y. 10801.

CAREER: Roman Catholic nun of Order of St. Ursula (O.S.U.), 1945—; College of New Rochelle, New Rochelle, N.Y., associate professor, 1962-69, professor of American literature, 1969—, writer-in-residence, 1970—. *Awards, honors:* Franco-American Cultural Service and Educational Aid grant, France, summer, 1967.

WRITINGS: Marie of the Incarnation: Mystic and Missionary, Doubleday, 1964; *Royal Cousin: The Life of Henri IV of France,* Doubleday, 1970; *Madame Catherine: The Life of Catherine de Medici,* Coward, 1975.

WORK IN PROGRESS: A gothic novel.

SIDELIGHTS: Irene Mahoney writes: "I must have wanted desperately to be a writer, because I worked so hard to get there. As a Roman Catholic nun, the 'system' did not provide very well for the creative person. There was work to be done and not much time for 'day dreaming.' At some point, however, I realized that I could not live at all if life did not include writing. The fight has been worth it. Twenty years later I have managed to integrate my teaching, my writing, and the dimension of my religious life."

MAHONEY, J. Daniel 1931-

PERSONAL: Born September 7, 1931, in Orange, N.J.; son of Daniel Vincent (an attorney) and Louisa (Dunbar) Mahoney; married Kathleen Mary O'Doherty, October 22, 1955; children: Daniel, Kieran, Francis, Mary, Eileen. Education: St. Bonaventure University, B.A. (magna cum laude), 1952; Columbia University, LL.B., 1955. Politics: Conservative. Religion: Roman Catholic. Home: 82 Brookfield Rd., Mount Vernon, N.Y. 10552. Office: Wormser, Kiely, Alessandroni, Mahoney, & McCann, 100 Park Ave., New York, N.Y. 10017.

CAREER: Admitted to the Bar of New York, 1958; Simpson, Thacher & Bartlett (law firm), New York, N.Y., associate, 1958-62; chairman of the Conservative Party of New York State and New York City, 1962—; Wormser, Kiely, Alessandroni, Mahoney, & McCann (law firm), New York, N.Y., partner, 1965—. Military service: U.S. Coast Guard Reserve, 1955-58; became lieutenant. Member: American Bar Association, New York State Bar Association, Phi Alpha Delta.

WRITINGS: Actions Speak Louder: The Story of the New York Conservative Party, Arlington House, 1968. Contributor of articles and book reviews to American Bar Association Journal, Columbia Law Review, National Review, and Modern Age.

*　　*　　*

MAISKY, Ivan (Mikhailovich) 1884-1975

January 19, 1884—1975; Soviet diplomat, historian, and author of memoirs, a novel, and historical works. Obituaries: Washington Post, September 5, 1975.

*　　*　　*

MAKERNEY, Edna Smith 1921-

PERSONAL: Born June 4, 1921, in Belton, Tex.; daughter of Aubrey Crestal (a building contractor) and Vera (Tanner) Smith; married Buck Wayne Makerney (a rancher), September 9, 1939; children: Aubrey Wayne, Mary Althea (Mrs. Michael Eugene Galipp). Education: Henderson County Junior College, A.S., 1957; East Texas State University, B.S., 1963, M.S.L.S., 1967; George Peabody College for Teachers, further graduate study, 1969. Politics: Independent. Religion: Baptist. Home: 203 Southwest 11th, Seminole, Tex. 79360. Office: Seminole Public School District, 508 Ave. C S.W., Seminole, Tex. 79360.

CAREER: Texas State Department of Public Welfare, field worker in Dallas, 1959-62, and Athens, 1962-63; librarian in junior high school in Dallas, Tex., 1963-65; Henderson County Junior College, Athens, Tex., assistant librarian, 1965-72; Seminole Public School District, Seminole, Tex., junior high school librarian, 1972—. Member: National Education Association, Texas State Teachers Association, Texas Association of School Librarians, Seminole Education Association, Classroom Teachers of Seminole, Alpha Chi.

WRITINGS: Cissy's Texas Pride (juvenile), Abingdon, 1975.

WORK IN PROGRESS: The Three of Us—And You (tentative title), for young teen-aged girls.

SIDELIGHTS: Edna Makerney writes: "I had planned to begin my writing career when I retired as school librarian but I became so infuriated and disappointed with some of the books now being published for children that I plunged into it five years early because I thought I could do a better job. I'm still amazed that my first attempt was successful." Avocational interests: "I love Texas, farm life, fishing, and football. The Dallas Cowboys is my favorite team. I also like gardening and needlework."

*　　*　　*

MALMO, Robert Beverley 1912-

PERSONAL: Born October 24, 1912, in Canal Zone, Panama; son of Robert H. and Mary Welby (Beverley) Malmo; married second wife, Mary Rose Helen Pitts, August 12, 1966; children: (first marriage) Marjorie L. (Mrs. Peter Ensminger). Education: University of Missouri, B.A. (with distinction), 1935, M.A., 1937; Yale University, Ph.D., 1940. Office: Allan Memorial Institute, McGill University, 1033 Pine Ave. W., Montreal, Quebec, Canada.

CAREER: Norwich State Hospital, Norwich, Conn., intern, 1941-42; National Institute of Health (now National Institutes of Health), Bethesda, Md., psychophysiologist, 1942-44, public health officer, 1944-45; McGill University, Montreal, Quebec, 1945—, became professor of psychology, and member of staff of neuropsychology laboratory at Allan Memorial Institute. Member of associate committee on experimental psychology of National Research Council; member of experimental psychology section of National Institutes of Health; member of scientific advisory council of Discus.

MEMBER: Canadian Psychological Association (fellow; past president), American Psychological Association, Experimental Psychology Study Society, Psychological Association of Quebec (past president), Phi Beta Kappa, Sigma Xi, Lambda Chi Alpha, Phi Eta Sigma. Awards, honors: Canadian centennial medal, 1967; citation of merit from University of Missouri, 1969; LL.D. from University of Manitoba, 1970.

WRITINGS: On Emotions, Needs, and Our Archaic Brain, Holt, 1975.

SIDELIGHTS: Of his book, Malmo writes: "While this serves to bring together certain experimental findings from our laboratory, its purposes are much broader than this. The book is designed to teach undergraduates something about psychophysiology and neuropsychology. Technical jargon is avoided and essential technical terms are defined throughout the book. A considerable amount of relevant research from other laboratories is presented.

"Working with problems such as chronic anxiety, tension headaches, and cardiovascular distress made us aware of some apparent limitations inherent in the ways our brains function. Archaic brain in the title refers to these and other limitations, some of which are discussed at length in the book."

*　　*　　*

MALZBERG, Barry N. 1939-
(K. M. O'Donnell)

PERSONAL: Born July 24, 1939, in New York, N.Y.; son of Michael and Celia (Feinberg) Malzberg; married Joyce Nadine Zelnick, May 31, 1964; children: Stephanie Jill, Erika Cornell. Education: Syracuse University, A.B., 1960, graduate study, 1964-65. Residence: Teaneck, N.J.

CAREER: Novelist. Awards, honors: John W. Campbell Memorial Award, 1972, for Beyond Apollo; Schubert Foundation playwriting fellow; Cornelia Ward creative writing fellow.

WRITINGS: Oracle of the Thousand Hands, Olympia, 1969; Screen, Olympia, 1969; Final War and Other Fantasies (stories; also see below), Ace Books, 1969; The Confessions of Westchester County, Olympia, 1971; The Falling Astronauts, Ace Books, 1971; Beyond Apollo, Random House, 1972; The Spread, Belmont Books, 1972; The Masochist, Belmont Books, 1972; The Case for Elizabeth Moore, Belmont Books, 1972; Revelations, Paperback Library, 1972; Overlay, Lancer, 1972; The Men Inside, Lancer, 1972; Phase IV, Pocket Books, 1973; In the Enclosure, Avon, 1973; Herovit's World, Random House, 1973; The Day of the Burning, Ace Books, 1974; (compiler with Edward L. Ferman) Final Stage, McKay, 1974; Out from Ganymede and Other Stories, Paperback Library, 1974; The Destruction of the Temple, Pocket Books, 1974; On a Planet Alien, Pocket Books, 1974; The Sodom and Gomorrah Business, Pocket Books, 1974; The Tactics of Conquest, Pyramid, 1974; Underlay, Avon, 1974; Guernica Night, Bobbs-Merrill, 1975; The Many Worlds of Barry Malzberg (stories), Popular Library, 1975; Conversations, Bobbs-Merrill, 1975; The Gamesman, Pocket Books, 1975, Galaxies, Pyramid, 1975; (compiler with Ferman) Arena, Doubleday, 1976; Scop, Pyramid, 1976; The Best of Barry N. Malzberg (stories), Pocket Books, 1976; (with Bill Pronzini) The Running of Beasts, Putnam, 1976.

Under pseudonym K. M. O'Donnell: The Empty People, Lancer, 1969; Final War (published with Treasure of Tau Ceti by John Rackham), Ace Books, 1969; Dwellers of the Deep, Ace Books, 1970; Universe Day, Avon, 1971; Gather in the Hall of the Planets, Ace Books, 1971; In the Pocket and Other Science Fiction Stories, Ace Books, 1971. Contributor of more than one hundred fifty short stories to science fiction periodicals, Ellery Queen's Mystery Magazine, Mike Shane, and men's magazines.

WORK IN PROGRESS: With Bill Pronzini, Justice, publication by Putnam expected in 1977.

*   *   *

MANCHESTER, Paul T(homas) 1893-

PERSONAL: Born September 27, 1893, in Barkeyville, Pa.; son of Charles (a professor and college president) and Lovana (Thomas) Manchester; married Emeline Speier, February 14, 1921; children: Paul Thomas, Jr., Emily (Mrs. Alex S. Townes). Education: Park College, B.A., 1914; Vanderbilt University, M.A., 1921; George Peabody College for Teachers, Ph.D., 1927. Politics: Republican. Religion: Presbyterian. Home: 805 Timber Lane, Nashville, Tenn. 37215.

CAREER: Instituto Ingles, Santiago, Chile, professor of English, 1914-17; Ogden College, Bowling Green, Ohio, professor of modern languages, 1918-19; Vanderbilt University, Nashville, Tenn., assistant professor of Romance languages, 1919-27; Colorado State Teachers College (now University of Northern Colorado), Greeley, professor of Romance languages, 1927-28; Vanderbilt University, assistant professor, 1928-42, associate professor, 1942-45, professor of Romance languages, 1945-63, professor emeritus, 1963—, head of department, 1952-63. Visiting professor at University of Florida, 1921, University of Alabama, 1928, Texas Technological College (now Texas Tech University), 1935-36, Stephen F. Austin State Teachers College (now Stephen F. Austin State University), 1938, Jacksonville University, 1963-65, and Montgomery Bell Academy, Nashville, Tenn., 1965-72. Military service: U.S. Army, Chemical Warfare, 1918-19.

MEMBER: Modern Language Association of America, American Association of Teachers of Spanish and Portuguese, American Association of Teachers of French, South Atlantic Modern Language Association (president, 1951-52), Phi Beta Kappa, Phi Sigma Iota, Kappa Delta Pi. Awards, honors: Decorated by Government of Chile with Orden al Merito Bernardo O'Higgins, 1952, for translations of epic poems Arauco Domado and La Araucana.

WRITINGS: Language Exercises for Learning Spanish, Scott, Foresman, 1926; A Bibliography and Critique of the Spanish Translations from the Poetry of the United States, Peabody Press, 1927; Le Tour du Monde of Jules Verne, Allyn & Bacon, 1928; El Final de Norma of Alarcon, Appleton, 1932; La Barraca of Blasco Ibanez, Macmillan, 1933; La Malquerida of Benavente, Crofts, 1935.

Les Affaires sont les Affaires of Mirbeau, Appleton, 1940; A French Verb Book, Crofts, 1941; (translator with C. M. Lancaster) La Araucana, Vanderbilt University Press, 1945; (translator with Lancaster) Arauco Domado (title means "Arauco Tamed"), University of New Mexico Press, 1948; (translator) Joyas Poeticas (title means "Poetic Gems"), Ungar, 1951; (translator and editor) Miguel Cervantes, Don Quixote of la Mancha, Fawcett, 1973.

Contributor of chapters to books, including South Atlantic Studies for Sturgis Leavitt, Scarecrow Press, 1953. Contributor of book reviews and articles to Poet Lore, Modern Language Journal, World Affairs, and other journals.

SIDELIGHTS: Manchester has conducted studies in Chile, Spain, and France.

*   *   *

MANDELL, Betty Reid 1924-

PERSONAL: Born November 4, 1924, in Denver, Colo.; daughter of Aubrey W. (a farmer) and Ruth (Flint) Reid; married Marvin L. Mandell (a professor), 1954; children: Christine, Charlotte. Education: Colorado State University, B.S., 1945; Union Theological Seminary, M.A., 1947; Columbia University, M.S.W., 1952. Politics: Democratic socialist. Religion: None. Home: 102 Anawan Ave., West Roxbury, Mass. 02132. Office: Department of Sociology and Anthropology, Boston State College, 625 Huntington Ave., Boston, Mass. 02115.

CAREER: University of Iowa, Iowa City, assistant professor of social work, 1964-67; Child and Family Services, Inc., Hartford, Conn., social worker, 1967-69; Northeastern University, Boston, Mass., assistant professor of social welfare, 1969-72; Boston State College, Boston, Mass., assistant professor of social welfare, 1972—. Member: Massachusetts Association of Social Workers (member of executive board, 1975—), Copley Square High School Parents' Association.

WRITINGS: Where Are the Children? A Class Analysis of Foster Care and Adoption, Heath, 1973; (editor) Welfare in America: Controlling the 'Dangerous Classes,' Prentice-Hall, 1975. Contributor to journals in her field. Member of editorial board, Social Work, 1967-72.

WORK IN PROGRESS: A book on female sexuality.

*   *   *

MANDER, Anica Vesel 1934-

PERSONAL: Given name is pronounced An-itsa; born October 21, 1934, in Sarajevo, Yugoslavia; daughter of Joseph (a lawyer) and Mela (Hofbauer) Vesel; married Jerry

Mander (a writer), November 27, 1965; children: Yari Vesel, Kai Vesel. *Education:* University of California, Berkeley, B.A. (with honors), 1952, M.A., 1960. *Politics:* "Feminist." *Home:* 1166 Filbert St., San Francisco, Calif. 94109. *Office:* Alyssum, 1719 Union St., San Francisco, Calif. 94123.

CAREER: Assistant to U.S. correspondent in Paris, 1960-62; Boston University, Boston, Mass., lecturer in French, 1962-65; San Francisco State College, San Francisco, Calif., assistant professor of French, 1965-71; Alyssum, San Francisco, Calif., organizer and facilitator of women's studies program, 1972—. Lecturer in Italian at Harvard University, 1962-63; coordinator of women's studies at Esalen Institute.

WRITINGS: (Contributor) Anne Kent Rush, editor, *Getting Clear: Bodywork for Women,* Bookworks and Random House, 1973; (with Rush) *Feminism as Therapy,* Bookworks and Random House, 1974; (contributor) D. K. Carter and E. Rawlings, editors, *Psychotherapy for Women: Treatment toward Equality,* C. C Thomas, 1975. Editor and co-publisher of Moon Books.

WORK IN PROGRESS: Homecoming, an autobiographical novel of three generations of women in the same family, on female consciousness.

SIDELIGHTS: Anica Mander writes: "I am a writer and a historian. I am working collectively with other women and reexamining past misinformation which has been imposed on us by a white male dominated society. I am interested in healing myself and society of hierarchical, imperialist ego-motivated power structures. With other women I am learning to build a base of unity through collectivity and correct my identity from male identified to female identified." She speaks Italian and French in addition to English and her native Serbo-Croation. She has lived in Yugoslavia, Italy, France.

* * *

MANN, Bob 1948-

PERSONAL: Born July 30, 1948, in Philadelphia, Pa.; son of Stanley W. (a businessman) and Bernice (Sherman) Mann. *Education:* Harvard University, B.A., 1970; Northeastern University, M.B.A., 1973; Southwestern University, J.D. candidate, 1974—. *Home:* 726 Williamson Rd., Bryn Mawr, Pa. 19010.

CAREER: Olin Ski Demonstration Team, Aspen, Colo., captain, 1971-74; Salomon/North America, Peabody, Mass., skiing consultant, 1973-74, director of summer freestyle ski camp, Squaw Valley, Calif., summer, 1974; Community Legal Assistance Center, Los Angeles, Calif., student director, 1974—.

WRITINGS: Hot Dog Skiing, Norton, 1974.

WORK IN PROGRESS: A film script, "Taking Care of Business," about two Harvard graduates who give up an aristocratic life style to compete as skiers.

SIDELIGHTS: Mann writes: "Although heavily involved in skiing for most of each year . . . I feel one needs the total development—mental as well as physical. It was for that reason as well as to become a more aware and self-sufficient individual that during the off-seasons I returned to school each year until I obtained a Masters Degree in Business and at present am in the process of obtaining my law degree. These can be as vital in sports as the talent itself."

MANN, Dale 1938-

PERSONAL: Born April 22, 1938, in Alhambra, Calif.; married Sandra Rodman (a director of a day care center). *Education:* University of California, Berkeley, A.B., 1963; Columbia University, Ph.D., 1971. *Office:* Teachers College, Columbia University, New York, N.Y. 10027.

CAREER: U.S. Forest Service, San Bernardino, Calif., management analyst, 1963; U.S. Office of Education, Washington, D.C., program planning associate for Bureau of Research, 1964-66; Executive Office of the President, Washington, D.C., special analyst of education for Bureau of the Budget, beginning 1966; Columbia University, Teachers College, New York, N.Y., associate professor of educational administration, 1973—. *Military service:* U.S. Army, 1957-59. *Member:* American Political Science Association, American Society for Public Administration, American Educational Research Society. *Awards, honors:* Alternate fellow of Spencer Foundation, 1974.

WRITINGS: Administrator-Community-School Relationships in New York State, New York State Commission on the Quality, Cost and Financing of Education, 1971; *Shared Control in Urban Neighborhood Schools: An Interpretive Essay and Bibliography,* National Committee for an Effective Congress/National Institute of Education, 1973; *A Principal's Handbook for Shared Control in Urban Neighborhood Schools,* National Committee for an Effective Congress/National Institute of Education, 1973; (with P. W. Greenwood and M. W. McLaughlin) *The Process of Change: Innovations in Classroom Organization and Staff Development,* RAND Corp., 1975; *Policy Decision Making in Education: An Introduction to Calculation and Control,* Teachers College Press, 1975; *The Politics of Administrative Representation: School Administrators and Local Democracy,* Heath, 1976. Contributor to education journals. Editor of *Teachers College Record,* February, 1976.

* * *

MAQUET, Jacques Jerome Pierre 1919-

PERSONAL: Surname sounds like "McKay"; born August 4, 1919, in Brussels, Belgium; came to United States, 1967, naturalized, 1974; son of Jerome (a state administrator) and Jeanne (Lemoine) Maquet; married Emma de Longree, June 17, 1947 (divorced, 1969); married Gisele Cambresier, November 13, 1970; children: (first marriage) Bernard, Denis. *Education:* University of Louvain, LL.D., 1946, D.Phil., 1948; University of London, Ph.D., 1952; University of Paris, D.Litt., 1973. *Home:* 2081 Linda Flora Dr., Los Angeles, Calif. 90024. *Office:* Department of Anthropology, University of California, Los Angeles, Calif. 90024.

CAREER: Institute for Scientific Research in Central Africa, Astrida, Ruanda-Urundi (now Butare, Rwanda), field anthropologist, 1949-51, research director of Social Sciences Center, 1951-57; State University of Congo, Elisabethville, Congo (now Lubumbushi, Zaire), professor of anthropology, 1957-60; University of Paris, Ecole Pratique des Hautes Etudes, Paris, France, research director of anthropology, 1961-68; Case Western Reserve University, Cleveland, Ohio, professor of anthropology, 1968-70; University of California, Los Angeles, professor of anthropology, 1971—. Visiting professor, Northwestern University, 1956, University of Brussels, 1963-68, Harvard University, 1964, University of Montreal, 1965, University of Pittsburgh, 1967, Stanford University, 1976. Secretary, Inter-

African Committee for the Social Sciences, 1953-56; consultant in Museology, UNESCO, 1964-65. *Member:* International Institute of Differing Civilizations, Association internationale des sociologues de langue francaise, Societe des Gens de lettres de France, Association for Asian Studies, International African Institute, Current Anthropology (associate), American Anthropological Association (fellow). *Awards, honors:* Emile Waxweiler award from Royal Academy of Belgium, 1961, for *Premise of Inequality in Ruanda;* Wenner-Gren Foundation grants, 1965 and 1973; best French book on African art award, 1966, for *Afrique: Les Civilisations noires.*

WRITINGS: Sociologie de la connaissance, sa structure et ses rapports avec la philosophie de la connaissance: Etude critique des systemes de Karl Mannheim et de Pitirim A. Sorokin, Institut de recherches economiques et sociales (Louvain, Belgium), 1949, 2nd edition, Institut de sociologie de l'universite libre de Bruxelles (Brussels), 1969, translation by John F. Locke published as *The Sociology of Knowledge, Its Structure and Its Relation to the Philosophy of Knowledge: A Critical Analysis of the Systems of Karl Mannheim and Pitirim A. Sorokin,* Beacon Press, 1951, reprinted, Greenwood Press, 1973; *Le Systeme des relations sociales dans le Ruanda ancien,* Musee royal d'Afrique centrale (Tervuren, Belgium), 1954, translation by the author published as *The Premise of Inequality in Ruanda: A Study of Political Relations in a Central African Kingdom,* Oxford University Press for the International African Institute, 1961; *Aide-memoire d'ethnologie africaine* (title means "Manual of African Ethnology"), Academie royale des sciences d'outremer (Brussels), 1954; *Ruanda: Essai photographique sur une societe africaine en transition* (title means "Photographic Essay on an African Society in Transition"), Elsevier (Brussels), 1957; (with Marcel d'Hertefelt) *Elections en societe feodale: Une Etude sur l'introduction du vote populaire au Ruanda-Urundi* (title means "Elections in a Feudal Society: A Study of the Introduction of Popular Vote in Ruanda-Urundi"), Academie royale des sciences d'outremer, 1959; *Afrique: Les Civilisations noires,* Horizons de France (Paris), 1962, 2nd edition, 1968, published as *Les Civilisations noires: Histoire, techniques, arts, [et] societes,* Gerard (Verviers, Belgium), 1966, translation by Joan Rayfield published as *Civilizations of Black Africa,* Oxford University Press, 1972; *Africanite: Traditionnelle et moderne,* Presence africaine (Paris), 1967, translation by Joan Rayfield published as *Africanity: The Cultural Unity of Black Africa,* Oxford University Press, 1972; (editor with Georges Balandier) *Dictionnaire des civilisations africaines,* Hazan (Paris), 1968, translation by Mariska Caroline Peck, Beltina Wadia, and Peninah Heimark published as *Dictionary of Black African Civilization,* Leon Amiel, 1974; *Pouvoir et societe en Afrique,* Hachette (Paris), 1971, translation by Jeanette Kupfermann published as *Power and Society in Africa,* McGraw, 1971.

Contributor: Daryll Forde, editor, *African Worlds,* Oxford University Press, for the International African Institute, 1954; F. S. C. Northrop and Helen Livingston, editors, *Cross-Cultural Understanding: Epistemology in Anthropology,* Harper, 1964; Paul Alexandre, editor, *L'Heritage de l'homme,* Editions de la Grange-Bateliere (Geneva, Switzerland), 1967; Mary Douglas and Phyllis M. Kaberry, editors, *Man in Africa,* Tavistock Publications, 1969; Philip K. Bock, editor, *Cultural Shock: A Reader in Modern Cultural Anthropology,* Knopf, 1970; Ronald Cohen and John Middleton, editors, *From Tribe to Nation in Africa,* Chandler Publishing, 1970; Arthur Tuden and Leonard Plotnicov, editors, *Social Stratification in Africa,* Free Press, 1970; James A. Clifton, editor, *Applied Anthropology: Readings in the Use of the Science of Man,* Houghton, 1970; Hubert Deschamps, editor, *Histoire generale de l'Afrique noire,* Presses Universitaires de France (Paris), 1970.

Wrote screenplay for motion picture, "Ruanda: Tableaux d'une feodalite pastorale," filmed in 1956. Contributor to *International Encyclopedia of the Social Sciences, Encyclopaedia Universalis* and of over 200 articles and reviews to scholarly journals. Editor of *Jeune Afrique,* 1958-60.

WORK IN PROGRESS: Research for books and journal articles on intentional communities, on comparative symbolism, and on meditation.

* * *

MARCH, Robert H(erbert) 1934-

PERSONAL: Born February 28, 1934, in Chicago, Ill.; son of Herbert (a trade unionist) and Jane (Grbac) March; married Georgianna Pugh, January 5, 1953 (divorced, 1970); children: Thomas. *Education:* University of Chicago, A.B., 1952, M.S., 1955, Ph.D., 1960. *Home:* 122 East Gilman St., Madison, Wis. 53703. *Office:* Department of Physics, University of Wisconsin, Madison, Wis. 53706.

CAREER: University of Wisconsin, Madison, instructor, 1961-62, assistant professor, 1962-65, associate professor, 1965-71, professor of physics, 1971—. Visiting scientist at Lawrence Berkeley Laboratory, 1963-66, Conseil Europeen pour la Recherche Nucleaire (now Organisation Europeene pour la Recherche Nucleaire), 1965-68, and Fermilab, 1970—. *Member:* American Physical Society, American Association of University Professors, Federation of American Scientists. *Awards, honors:* American Institute of Physics-U.S. Steel Foundation Science Writing Awards, 1971, 1975.

WRITINGS: Physics for Poets, McGraw, 1970. Contributor to encyclopedias and to popular magazines and scientific journals.

WORK IN PROGRESS: A historical and biographical popular introduction to subnuclear physics.

SIDELIGHTS: March writes " ... from a strong conviction that science is one of the humanities if properly viewed and presented." His book has been published in Polish and Japanese.

* * *

MARCKWARDT, Albert H(enry) 1903-1975

December 1, 1903—August 20, 1975; American educator, linguist, and author or editor of books in his field. Obituaries: *New York Times,* August 22, 1975; *AB Bookman's Weekly,* September 22-29, 1975. (See index for previous *CA* sketch)

* * *

MARDEN, William (Edward) 1947-

PERSONAL: Born March 24, 1947, in Palatka, Fla.; son of Roy Foster (a prison counselor) and Elena (Polverino) Marden. *Education:* St. Johns River Junior College, A.A., 1967; University of Florida, B.S.Journalism, 1969. *Politics:* Republican. *Religion:* Roman Catholic. *Home:* 4125 B Baltic St., Jacksonville, Fla. 32210. *Office:* Florida Publishing Co., 1 Riverside Ave., Jacksonville, Fla. 32202.

CAREER: *Sarasota Herald Tribune,* Sarasota, Fla., reporter, 1969-70; *St. Petersburg Independent,* St. Petersburg, Fla., reporter, 1971-72; *Florida Times Union,* Jacksonville, reporter, 1972—. *Member:* Authors Guild of Authors League of America, Sigma Delta Chi.

WRITINGS: The Exile of Ellendon (science-fiction), Doubleday, 1974. Contributor of true crime stories to detective magazines.

WORK IN PROGRESS: A suspense-science fiction novel of an alternate earth, *Hunter's Prey.*

SIDELIGHTS: Marden writes: "I've been a writer since I learned in the fourth grade that the way to make friends and influence people was to write stories featuring those self same people, but I didn't get into it in an organized way until a bout of boredom past midnight at the *Sarasota Herald Tribune* led to the birth of Hank Dell, hero of *The Exile of Ellendon.* The experience of actually being paid money to spin dreams is a better high than anything which can be smoked, drunk, inhaled, or injected, and I'd like to repeat the experience."

*   *   *

MARGULIES, Leo   1900-1975

1900—December 26, 1975; American magazine editor and publisher, book publisher, and anthologist of mystery and science fiction. Obituaries: *New York Times,* December 29, 1975.

*   *   *

MARGULIES, Newton   1932-

PERSONAL: Born February 19, 1932, in New York, N.Y.; son of Robert and Pauline (Daduk) Margulies; married Dorothy Jean Clevenger, 1959; children: Gordon, Steven, Jeffrey. *Education:* Brooklyn Polytechnic Institute, B.S.E., 1958; Massachusetts Institute of Technology, M.S.I.M., 1960; University of California, Los Angeles, Ph.D., 1965. *Office:* Graduate School of Administration, University of California, Irvine, Calif. 92664.

CAREER: San Fernando Valley State College (now California State University, Northridge), Northridge, Calif., assistant professor of management, 1962-64; Case Institute of Technology (now Case Western Reserve University), Cleveland, Ohio, assistant professor of organizational behavior, 1964-66; University of Miami, Coral Gables, Fla., associate professor of management, 1966-68; TRW Systems Group, Redondo Beach, Calif., member of consulting staff, 1968-69; University of California, Irvine, lecturer, 1969-72, associate professor of administration and associate dean of Graduate School of Administration, 1972—. *Military service:* U.S. Army, Signal Corps, 1954-55.

WRITINGS: (With A. P. Raia) *Organizational Development: Values, Process, and Technology,* McGraw, 1972; (with John Wallace) *Organizational Change: Techniques and Applications,* Scott, Foresman, 1973. Contributor to business administration journals.

WORK IN PROGRESS: Organizational Development: An Integrated View of Theory and Practice, for McGraw.

*   *   *

MARHOEFER, Barbara (McGeary)   1936-

PERSONAL: Born July 18, 1936, in Jersey City, N.J.; married Laurence Joseph Marhoefer (an attorney), December 26, 1960; children: John, Mary Beth, Melinda.

Education: Trinity College, Washington, D.C., B.A., 1958; Columbia University, M.S., 1960. *Agent:* Lurton Blassingame, 60 East 42nd St., New York, N.Y. 10017.

CAREER: Elizabeth Daily Journal, Elizabeth, N.J., general assignment reporter, 1958-60; *Suffolk Sun,* Long Island, N.Y., feature writer, 1967-69; *New York Times,* New York, N.Y., part-time reporter (stringer), 1970—. Instructor in journalism at Temple University, 1974—. *Member:* Historical Society of Pennsylvania, Sigma Delta Chi.

WRITINGS: Witches, Whales, Petticoats, and Sails, Kennikat, 1971, 2nd edition, 1974. Contributor to history journals and to *Long Island Forum.*

WORK IN PROGRESS: A bicentennial series on Long Island and the American Revolution, for Long Island Lighting Co.; a book of eyewitness accounts of the American Revolution.

*   *   *

MARION, Frieda   1912-
(Arden Kent, Friedl von Castelhun)

PERSONAL: Born October 17, 1912, in Rowley, Mass.; daughter of Fredric Karl (an electrical engineer) and Bertha (Burke) Castelhun; married Donald J. Marion (a sonar technican), October 17, 1934; children: Donna Marise Titus, Donald Theodor. *Education:* Studied art in Boston, Mass., two years, and in Rockport, Mass. *Religion:* Unitarian. *Address:* 14 Zabriskie Dr., Newburyport, Mass. 01950.

CAREER: Former teacher of art at private schools in Newburyport and Malden, Mass.; *Newburyport Daily News,* Newburyport, special feature writer and columnist, 1941-66; freelance writer. Public information chairperson, Haverhill Area Mental Health and Retardation Board, 1971-73. *Member:* Doll Collectors of America, United Federation of Doll Clubs, First Religious Society, Study Club (Newburyport, Mass.).

WRITINGS: (Contributor) *Guideposts Christmas Treasury,* Guideposts Associates, 1972; (self-illustrated) *China Half-Figures Called Pincushion Dolls,* J. Palmer, 1974; (contributor) A. Christian Revi, editor, *Spinning Wheel's Complete Book of Dolls,* Hanover Press, 1975. Poetry, sometimes under pseudonym Friedl von Castelhun, represented in anthologies: *Book of American Verse,* edited by Harry Bristol Williams, American Publishing, 1930; *The Spring Anthology,* Mitre Press, 1930; *Principal Poets of the World,* Mitre Press, 1932; *The Muse of 1942,* edited by Ann A. Kurdt, Horizon House, 1942.

Writer of newspaper column, "The Clinic," under pseudonym Arden Kent, 1941-42; and of "Salt and Pepper," 1949-52. Contributor of articles and poems, sometimes under pseudonym to *Pacific Weekly, The Poet, Author and Journalist, Woman's Day, New Hampshire Profiles, Ebony, Christian Science Monitor, Antiques Journal, Spinning Wheel, Boston Globe,* and other periodicals.

WORK IN PROGRESS: Continued research on porcelain figures for an article; a children's book to be self-illustrated; preparing a lecture series.

SIDELIGHTS: Freida Marion writes: "I am in the position of having had close personal association with two generations which came before me, as well as being close to the two generations which have followed my own, and this expanded viewpoint covering the lives of five generations I consider to be one of the benefits of growing older." She has traveled in England, France, Germany, Turkey, and Spain, where she lived for about one year.

BIOGRAPHICAL/CRITICAL SOURCES: Lawrence Daily Eagle, August 1, 1957.

* * *

MARK, Yudel 1897-1975

1897—August 1, 1975; Lithuanian-born American lexicographer, educator, and author. Obituaries: *New York Times,* August 5, 1975.

* * *

MARKER, Lise-Lone (Christensen) 1934-

PERSONAL: Born September 23, 1934, in Aalborg, Denmark; daughter of Henry M. (a medical doctor) and Gudrun (Haugen Johansen) Christensen; married Frederick J. Marker (a university professor), November 27, 1959. *Education:* Attended Vassar College, 1953-54; University of Copenhagen, Magister artium, 1961; Yale University, Ph.D., 1968. *Home:* 144 Banbury Rd., Don Mills, Ontario M3B 2L3, Canada. *Office:* Graduate Centre for Study of Drama, University of Toronto, Toronto M5S 2E1, Canada.

CAREER: Danish Royal Theatre, Copenhagen, Denmark, librarian of theater collection, 1955-65; Teaterdirektoerforeningens Skuespillerskole (acting academy), Copenhagen, Denmark, lecturer in theatre history, 1957-65; Folkeuniversitetet, Copenhagen, Denmark, lecturer in theater history, 1958-60; University of Copenhagen, Copenhagen, Denmark, assistant professor of theater history, 1961-65, research fellow, 1962-65; University of Toronto, Graduate Drama Centre, Toronto, Ontario, assistant professor, 1968-71, associate professor of theatrical history, 1971—. Archives committee consultant, Stratford Shakespeare Festival, 1971-73.

MEMBER: International Federation for Theatre Research, American Society for Theatre Research, Canadian Association of University Teachers. *Awards, honors:* American-Scandinavian Foundation scholar at Vassar College, 1953-54; University of Copenhagen fellow, 1962-65; Yale University fellow, 1965-67; Canada Council research and publication grants, 1971, 1972, 1973; Nordisk Kulturfond grant, 1974; Canada Council leave fellowship, 1974-75.

WRITINGS: David Belasco: Naturalism in the American Theatre, Princeton University Press, 1975; (with husband, Frederick J. Marker, Michael Booth, and Robertson Davies) *Revels History of Drama in English, Volume VI, 1750-1880,* Barnes & Noble, 1975; (with Frederick J. Marker) *The Scandinavian Theatre: A Short History,* Rowman & Littlefield, 1975.

Contributor: David Galloway, editor, *The Elizabethan Theatre,* Volume II, Macmillan of Canada, 1970; Daniel Haakonsen, editor, *Contemporary Approaches to Ibsen,* Volume II, Oslo University Press, 1971; Margret Dietrich, editor, *Regie in Dokumentation, Forschung, und Lehre,* Otto Mueller Verlag, 1975. Contributor of drama criticism and reviews to *Roskilde Dagblad,* 1955-61, and *Roskilde Tidende,* 1961-65; more recently contributor to *Theatre Survey, Theatre Research, Quarterly Journal of Speech,* and other journals. Associate editor, *Modern Drama,* 1972—, and *Scandinavian Studies,* 1973—.

WORK IN PROGRESS: Research in methodology of promptbook research, in theater audiences, and in Aaron Hill's theory of acting.

MARKLEY, Kenneth A(lan) 1933-

PERSONAL: Born September 30, 1933, in Harrisburg, Pa.; son of Charles Donald (a government employee) and Gladys E. (Wallis) Markley; married Susan Watson (a registered nurse), September 14, 1957; children: Jennifer E., Christopher D. *Education:* Dickinson College, B.A., 1955; Syracuse University, graduate study, 1955-57; New York University, M.A., 1959; Reformed Episcopal Seminary, further graduate study, 1964-66. *Politics:* Conservative. *Religion:* Protestant-Christian and Missionary Alliance. *Home and office:* 104 North 26th St., Camp Hill, Pa. 17011.

CAREER: High school biology teacher in Hershey, Pa., 1958-59; United Cerebral Palsy, Camp Hill, Pa., executive director, 1959-64; Dickinson College, Carlisle, Pa., instructor in psychology, 1963—. Eastern director of Narramore Christian Foundation and Rosemead Graduate School of Psychology. Leader of seminars on marriage and family. *Military service:* U.S. Army, military psychologist in Adjutant General's Corps, 1955-57; became first lieutenant. *Member:* American Psychological Association, Christian Association for Psychological Studies, American Academy of Human Services, International Order of St. Luke the Physician, International Platform Association.

WRITINGS: Our Speaker This Evening, Zondervan, 1974. Contributor to psychology journals and religious publications.

WORK IN PROGRESS: A book, *Why a Psychologist Believes the Bible;* research on the relationship between spiritual and psychological problems, and on interpersonal relationships between family members and Biblical theology.

SIDELIGHTS: Markley writes: "My overall motivation in life is to glorify God and work under His guidance to bring help and insight to persons and families from Scriptural research. Every evidence available points to the necessity of persons being tied back together with God through a personal submission to His Son Jesus Christ."

* * *

MARKS, Claude (Mordecai) 1915-

PERSONAL: Born November 13, 1915, in London, England; came to the United States in 1938, naturalized citizen, 1942; son of Joseph Morris (a furrier) and Hylda Rose (Davis) Marks; married Sue Blagden, September 8, 1942; children: David. *Education:* Trinity College, Cambridge, M.A. (honors), 1936; State University of Iowa, M.F.A., 1948. *Politics:* Democrat. *Home:* 315 Central Park W., New York, N.Y. 10025. *Agent:* Russell & Volkening, Inc., 551 Fifth Ave., New York, N.Y. 10017.

CAREER: State University of Iowa, Iowa City, assistant professor of art, 1948-50; painter and scenic designer in England, 1950-56, and New York, N.Y., 1956-59; Metropolitan Museum of Art, New York, N.Y., guest lecturer, 1959—. Member of faculty at Parsons School of Design, New School for Social Research, Juilliard School of Music, and School of Visual Arts. Has had painting exhibits in one-man shows in New York, including Lincoln Center, and in England. *Military service:* U.S. Army Air Forces, 1941-45; became sergeant. *Member:* College Art Association of America, United Scenic Artists Union of America.

WRITINGS: From the Sketchbooks of the Greek Artists, Crowell, 1972; *Pilgrims, Heretics, and Lovers: A Medieval Journey,* Macmillan, 1975. Contributor to theater arts journals.

SIDELIGHTS: Marks paints theater drawings and portraits, combining interests in art and the theater. He has also worked as a stage designer. Avocational interests: History, literature, languages (especially French, Italian, German, and Spanish), international travel (especially Europe and Turkey).

BIOGRAPHICAL/CRITICAL SOURCES: Theatre Arts, November, 1961; Playbill, May, 1972.

* * *

MARKS, J(ames) M(acdonald) 1921-

PERSONAL: Born October 6, 1921, in Shanghai, China; son of Samuel (a transport adviser) and Catherine (Kilpatrick) Marks; married Jean Lawrie Murrell, October 25, 1954; children: Catherine, Alan. Education: Attended University of Glasgow, 1939-40. Politics: Conservative. Religion: Church of England. Residence: Reading, England.

CAREER: British Army, 1941-59, served as platoon leader and company commander in Burma, 1942-44, and Java, 1945-46, served with 10th Gurkha Rifles in Malaya, 1949-59, leaving service as major; planter in North Borneo (Sabah) highlands, 1959-60; assistant accountant in Sydney, Australia, 1960-61; with British Broadcasting Corp., 1961—. Awards, honors—Military: Mentioned in dispatches.

WRITINGS:—All fiction for young people: Ayo Gurkha!, Oxford University Press, 1971; Snow-Lion, Oxford University Press, 1972; Jason, Oxford University Press, 1973, published as Hijacked (Junior Literary Guild selection), Thomas Nelson, 1975; The Triangle, Oxford University Press, 1974.

AVOCATIONAL INTERESTS: Travel (India, Nepal).

* * *

MARLOWE, Don

PERSONAL: Born in Duluth, Minn. Education: Harvard University, B.A., 1948. Home address: P.O. Box 1621, Hollywood, Calif. 90028.

CAREER: Stage and film actor, screenwriter, and night club performer. Member: Screen Actors Guild, American Federation of Television and Radio Actors. Awards, honors: Award for best comedy performance by an actor from TV Mirror, 1958, for "The Nineteenth Hole."

WRITINGS: The Hollywood That Was, Branch-Smith, 1968. Author of television scripts for "Dragnet" and "Gunsmoke."

SIDELIGHTS: Marlowe made his first stage appearance at the age of three in a Los Angeles production of "Babes in Toyland." His first film role was in a Laurel and Hardy movie, which was followed by 283 appearances as Porky in the "Our Gang" series. A part in "The Whispering Shadow" with Bela Lugosi began a friendship that ended only with Lugosi's death. Marlowe has continued to perform in films, in stage productions, including nation-wide tours, and on television, on "The Bob Cummings Show," "Dragnet," and other programs.

* * *

MARSH, Spencer 1931-

PERSONAL: Born January 25, 1931, in Colorado; son of Spencer W. and Neomia (Sullivan) Marsh; married Doris Burke (a children's work coordinator), June 10, 1955; children: Wendy, Sharee, Julie. Education: Whitworth College, B.A., 1957; Princeton Theological Seminary, M.Div., 1961. Politics: Liberal. Home: 407 14th St., Santa Monica, Calif. 90403. Agent: Toni Mendez, Inc., 140 East 56th St., New York, N.Y. 10022. Office: Brentwood Presbyterian Church, 12000 San Vicente Blvd., Los Angeles, Calif. 90049.

CAREER: Ordained Presbyterian minister, 1961; pastor of Presbyterian churches in Colorado Springs, Colo., 1961-64, Bethlehem, Pa., 1964-66, Kansas City, Mo., 1966-68, and Portland, Ore., 1968-71; Brentwood Presbyterian Church, Los Angeles, Calif., senior pastor, 1971—. Retreat and conference leader. Member of local Council on Alcoholism; vice-president of Brentwood-San Vicente Association, 1975-76. Military service: U.S. Army, 1951-53.

WRITINGS: God, Man, and Archie Bunker, Harper, 1975. Contributor to religious periodicals.

WORK IN PROGRESS: The Totally Fascinating Edith Bunker, using scripts from television series "All in the Family," for Tandem Productions.

* * *

MARTH, Del 1925-

PERSONAL: Born September 9, 1925, in Wausau, Wis.; son of Herman A. and Laura (Tanck) Marth; married Martha J. Campbell (a writer); children: Jamey, Paul, Nancy. Education: Attended Northwestern University, 1947; University of Wisconsin, B.S., 1951. Residence: St. Petersburg, Fla. Address: P.O. Box 981, St. Petersburg, Fla. 33731.

CAREER: St. Petersburg Times, St. Petersburg, Fla., editor, 1956-72; Willow Creek (publishers), St. Petersburg, president, 1970—; West Coast Productions, Inc. (publishers), St. Petersburg, president, 1975—. Military service: U.S. Army, 1943-46; became sergeant.

WRITINGS: St. Petersburg in Maps, Marco Polo Press, 1972; (with wife, Martha Marth) Florida Almanac, West Coast Productions, 1972, 2nd edition, 1975; Yesterday's Sarasota, E. A. Seemann, 1973; Yachting Guide to Florida's West Coast, West Coast Productions, in press.

WORK IN PROGRESS: Two books, Letters to a Married Priest, and Fort Apache's Thin Blue Line, with John Ferrara.

* * *

MARTIN, Frances M(cEntee) 1906-

PERSONAL: Born October 23, 1906, in Montclair, N.J.; daughter of Thomas Lockley and Frances (Layng) McEntee; married Frederick Ellis Martin (a lawyer), April 25, 1925; children: Jane Lockley (Mrs. Joseph Douglas Deal, Jr.), Frederick E., Jr., Thomas Lockley (deceased). Education: Attended Barnard College, 1923-24; Old Dominion University, B.A. (with honors), 1962, M.A., 1967. Politics: Democrat. Religion: Episcopal. Home: 1544 Cloncurry Rd., Norfolk, Va. 23505.

CAREER: Irene Leache Memorial, Norfolk, Va., member of executive board and literary chairman, 1970—. Awards, honors: Received awards for poetry and prose from Irene Leache Memorial, 1940-65; horticultural award from Garden Club of America, 1970, for What to Do When.

WRITINGS—All juvenile novels; all published by Harper: Knuckles Down, 1942; No School Friday, 1945; Sea Room, 1947; Nine Tales of Coyote, 1950; Nine Tales of Raven, 1951, published with new introduction as Raven Who Sets

Things Right, 1975; *Pirate Island,* 1955. Author of children's plays, 1940-60, including "Doodle's Dilemma," "Snow White," and "Sleeping Beauty." Also author of *What to Do When,* for Garden Club of Norfolk. Children's book editor of *Norfolk Virginian Pilot,* 1950-57.

AVOCATIONAL INTERESTS: American Indians, environmental concerns.

* * *

MARTIN, Harold Harber   1910-

PERSONAL: Born September 17, 1910, in Commerce, Ga.; son of Gabriel Pierce (a lawyer and judge) and Mary Edna (Harber) Martin; married Boyce Lokey, April 23, 1935; children: Marian (Mrs. Thorpe Mealing), Harold, Jr., John, Nancy (Mrs. David Sparks). *Education:* University of Georgia, A.B., 1933. *Politics:* Democratic. *Religion:* Episcopalian. *Home and office:* 2895 Normandy Dr. N.W., Atlanta, Ga. 30305. *Agent:* George Scheer, P.O. Box 807, Chapel Hill, N.C. 27514.

CAREER: Atlanta Georgian, Atlanta, Ga., sports writer, 1933-34, feature writer, 1934-39; *Atlanta Constitution,* Atlanta, columnist, 1939-74; *Saturday Evening Post,* associate editor, 1951-53, contributing editor, 1958-63, editor at large, 1964-69. Lecturer in journalism, Georgia State University, 1972—. Trustee, Warm Springs Foundation; member of board of directors, St. Jude's House; president, Georgia Cooperative Services for the Blind. *Military service:* U.S. Marine Corps, 1944-45; became 1st lieutenant; received Bronze Star. *Member:* Marine Corps Correspondents Association, Authors Guild, National Trust for Historic Preservation, Washington Press Club, Atlanta Press Club, Sigma Delta Chi, Pi Delta Epsilon. *Awards, honors:* Lillian Smith Award from Southern Regional Council for *Ralph McGill, Reporter.*

WRITINGS: (With Matthew Ridgway) *Soldier: The Memoirs of Matthew B. Ridgway,* Harper, 1956; *Fathers Day Comes Once a Year—And Then it Always Rains,* Putnam, 1960; *Starlifter: Lockheed's Flying Truck,* Stephen Greene, 1972; *Ralph McGill, Reporter,* Little, Brown, 1973; *Three Strong Pillars* (history of Trust Co. of Georgia), Trust Co. of Georgia, 1974. Also author of biography, *Robert W. Woodruff, A Restless Face,* as yet unpublished.

WORK IN PROGRESS: A history of Georgia for the Georgia Association of State and Local History, completion expected in 1976; a biography of William B. Hartsfield, former mayor of Atlanta, for Atlanta Historical Society, completion expected in 1977.

SIDELIGHTS: On self-dictated orders, Martin roamed the Pacific theatre during World War II. For the resulting stories and magazine articles he received the Bronze Star.

* * *

MARTIN, Jose L(uis)   1921-
   (Ramar Yunkel)

PERSONAL: Born July 11, 1921, in Vega Baja, P.R.; son of Isidoro (an accountant) and Carmen (Montes) Martin; married Blanca Rodriguez (a teacher); children: five. *Education:* University of Puerto Rico, B.A. 1942, M.A., 1953; Columbia University, Ph.D., 1965. *Residence:* New York, N.Y. *Office:* Department of Puerto Rican Studies, City College of the City University of New York, New York, N.Y. 10031.

CAREER: University of Puerto Rico, Rio Piedras, instructor in Spanish, 1954-58; Columbia University, New York, N.Y., lecturer in Spanish, 1959-62; Queens College of the City University of New York, Flushing, N.Y., instructor in Spanish, 1963-65; Inter-American University, San Juan, P.R., associate professor of Spanish, 1966-68; Illinois State University, Normal, associate professor of Spanish-American literature, 1968-72; City College of the City University of New York, New York, N.Y., associate professor of Puerto Rican literature and stylistics, 1972—. Visiting professor, New York University, summer, 1960; associate professor, Hofstra University, summer, 1964; member of board of directors, Institute of Puerto Rico, 1972—. *Military service:* U.S. Army, 1943-46; became staff sergeant. *Member:* Modern Language Association of America, Association of Teachers of Spanish and Portuguese, Instituto Internacional de Literatura Iberoamericana, Instituto de Literatura Puertorriquena, Asociacion de Escritores de Puerto Rico, Sigma Delta Pi (honorary member) *Awards, honors:* Diploma from Nueva Narrativa Hispanoamericana, 1971; Order of Don Quixote, from Sigma Delta Pi, 1973; Institute of Puerto Rico in New York literature award, 1975.

WRITINGS: La poetica de Oppenheimer (title means "The Poetry of Oppenheimer"), Editorial Asomante, 1952; *Agonia del Silencio* (poetry; title means "Agony of Silence"), Editorial Orfeo, 1953; *Analisis Estilistico de Tapia* (title means "Stylistic Analysis of Tapia"), Institute of Puerto Rican Culture, 1958; *Meditaciones Puertorriquenas* (title means "Puerto Rican Meditations"), Departamento de Instruccion Publica, 1959; *Arco y Flecha* (title means "Bow and Arrow"), Editorial Club de la Prensa, 1961; *La Poesia de Jose Eusebio Caro* (title means "The Poetry of Jose Eusebio Caro"), Instituto Caro y Cuervo (Bogota), 1966; *Romancero del Cibuco* (title means "Ballads from the Cibuco"), Editorial Orion, 1970; (under pseudonym Ramar Yunkel) *El Retorno* (title means "The Return"), Editorial Latino-Americana, 1971; *Critica Estilistica* (title means "Stylistic Criticism"), Editorial Gredos, 1972; *El Teatro de Rene Marques* (title means "The Theatre of Rene Marques"), Instituto de Cultura Puertorriquena, in press.

Contributor to *La Torre, Asomante, Revista del Instituto de Cultura Puertorriquena, Artes y Letras, Revista de Letras, Prensa Literaria, Revista Hispanica Moderna, Cuadernos Hispanoamericanos, Nueva Narrativa Hispanoamericana, Sin Nombre,* and other periodicals. Founder and former editor, *Ateneo, Olimpo* and *Aulas;* former co-editor, *Pegaso* and *Orfeo.*

WORK IN PROGRESS: A novel, *Bridge to Eternity,* under pseudonym Ramar Yunkel; research on Antillean literature for a book; *Historia de la Literatura Puertorriquena* (title means "A History of Puerto Rican Literature").

SIDELIGHTS: Martin has traveled extensively in the United States, Latin America and Europe. He paints in oils and has shown his work at exhibitions in San Juan and New York.

* * *

MARTIN, Philip (John Talbot)   1931-

PERSONAL: Born March 28, 1931, in Melbourne, Victoria, Australia; son of Henry Martin (a public servant) and Lorna (Talbot) Martin. *Education:* Attended Xavier College, Melbourne, Australia, and University of Melbourne. *Religion:* Roman Catholic. *Office:* Department of English, Monash University, Clayton, Victoria 3168, Australia.

CAREER: University of Melbourne, Melbourne, Victoria, Australia, publications officer, 1956-60, tutor in English,

1960-62; Australian National University, Canberra, Australian Capital Territory, lecturer in English, 1963; Monash University, Clayton, Victoria, Australia, lecturer, 1964-70, senior lecturer in English, 1971—. Visiting lecturer at University of Amsterdam, 1967. Broadcaster for Australian Broadcasting Commission.

WRITINGS: Voice Unaccompanied (poems), Australian National University Press, 1970; *Shakespeare's Sonnets: Self, Love, and Art* (criticism), Cambridge University Press, 1972; *A Bone Flute* (poems), Australian National University Press, 1974; (contributor) Bernard Hickey, editor, *Antologia della poesia australiana contemporanea,* Nuova Accademia (Milan), 1976. Writer of television scripts. Contributor of poems, articles, and reviews to Australian and British journals.

WORK IN PROGRESS: A volume of poems; a play for radio, *The Dune-Ship;* translations of Swedish and Hungarian poems.

SIDELIGHTS: Martin finds no conflict between the roles of poet and university professor. His criticism is closely related to his teaching, and he regards broadcasting as an extension of his other pursuits. He writes that his poetry is "modern-traditional rather than avant-garde, and is concerned with love and death, with relationships between people and with the continuity of past and present." An interview with him has been taped by the oral history section of the National Library of Australia, Canberra.

*   *   *

MARTINDALE, Colin (Eugene) 1943-

PERSONAL: Born March 21, 1943, in Fort Morgan, Colo.; son of Roy Woodrow and Martha (Dill) Martindale; married Judith Calhoun Kopecky, August 21, 1964 (divorced, 1973). *Education:* University of Colorado, B.A. (summa cum laude), 1964; Harvard University, Ph.D., 1970. *Home:* 89 Third St., Bangor, Maine 04401. *Office:* Department of Psychology, University of Maine, Orono, Maine 04473.

CAREER: Kennedy Memorial Hospital, Boston, Mass., part-time staff psychologist, 1968-69; Veterans Administration Hospital, Palo Alto, Calif., intern, 1969-70; University of Maine, Orono, assistant professor, 1970-73, associate professor of psychology, 1973—.

MEMBER: International Association for Semiotic Studies, International Association for Empirical Aesthetics, International Neuropsychology Association, International Society for the Comparative Study of Civilizations, American Association for the Advancement of Science, American Psychological Association, American Society for Aesthetics, Association for Computational Linguistics, Association for Literary and Linguistic Computing, Dante Society of America, Modern Language Association of America, Poe Studies Association, Society for General Systems Research, Eastern Psychological Association, Phi Beta Kappa, Psi Chi. *Awards, honors:* First prize from Ninth Annual Creative Talent Awards Program of the American Institutes for Research, 1970.

WRITINGS: Romantic Progression: The Psychology of Literary History, Hemisphere, 1975; (contributor) Donald Spence, editor, *Psychoanalysis and Contemporary Science,* Volume IV, Macmillan, 1975. Contributor of about thirty articles to scientific journals. Member of board of editors of *Scientific Aesthetics,* 1975—; member of board of advisory editors of *Poetics,* 1975—.

WORK IN PROGRESS: Cognition and Consciousness; a contribution to be included in *Artists and Their Symbols,* edited by Frank Barron and William McCormack, for University of California Press; research on interaction and attraction on two state hospital wards, on lexical differences between working and resistance sessions in psychoanalysis, and on correlates of schizophrenic interaction.

*   *   *

MARTINETZ, V(ivian) L. 1927-
(Vivian L. Broussard)

PERSONAL: Born February 6, 1927, in New York; daughter of Harry (in import-export business) and Rosa (Krengel) Kringle; married Elmer James Broussard, 1945 (divorced); married David F. Martinetz (in airline business), February 22, 1960; children: Dorron Leigh, Sybil Denise. *Education:* Hunter College (now of the City University of New York), B.A., 1952; Columbia University, M.S., 1953. *Residence:* El Paso, Tex.

CAREER: Blumencranz & Co., Inc. (insurance company), New York, N.Y., in special accounts, 1958-68; Bookstaver Co. (insurance company), New York, N.Y., office manager, 1968-69; Stokes Insurance Service, El Paso, Tex., part-time member of office staff, 1971—. *Member:* National Federation of Press Women, Armed Forces Writers League, Manuscript Club (El Paso).

WRITINGS: The Last Walk Is Alone, Tarnhelm Press, 1973. Also author, under name Vivian L. Broussard, of a book of poems, *Song of the Shell,* c. 1945.

WORK IN PROGRESS: A science fiction novel of metaphysics, tentatively titled *The Lost Chapter; Hard, Thin Lips,* a novel.

SIDELIGHTS: Vivian Martinetz specifies that her interest is in metaphysics, not occultism. *Avocational interests:* International travel (Brazil, Germany, Israel, Italy, Portugal, Peru, Greece, Mexico, Austria, Fiji, New Zealand).

*   *   *

MARTINEZ, Raymond J(oseph) 1889-

PERSONAL: Born October 17, 1889, in West Baton Rouge, La.; son of Albert J. (a sugar planter) and Olivia (Marionneaux) Martinez; married Lavinia Barton Sims, 1914 (died, 1935); married Phyllis Ward McPhillimy, May 15, 1943; children: (first marriage) William Barton. *Education:* Attended Louisiana State University, 1907. *Politics:* Republican. *Religion:* Episcopalian. *Home and office:* 436 Central Ave., Jefferson, La. 70121.

CAREER: Hamilton Rubber Co., Trenton, N.J., southern agent, 1910-20; *New Orleans States,* New Orleans, La., editor of commercial and industrial pages, 1920-24; *Rice Journal,* New Orleans, editor, 1924-41; Louisiana Sugar and Rice Exchange, New Orleans, secretary and manager, 1935-45; free-lance writer, 1945—. *Wartime service:* U.S. Maritime Commission, chief of public relations and co-organizer of American Merchant Marine Educational Fund, 1943-47. *Member:* Louisiana Genealogical and Historical Society, Louisiana Landmarks Society, Louisiana Folklore Society, Genealogical Research Society of New Orleans.

WRITINGS—All published by Hope Publications, except as noted: *The American Intercedes and Southern Methods* (two plays), L. Graham Co., 1916; *In the Parish of St. John* (novel), G. A. Martin & Co., 1925; *The Miser's Cup* (play), 1935; *Story of the Riverfront at New Orleans,* 1948;

Louisiana Cookery: Featuring the Products of Louisiana, 1950; *Mysterious Marie Laveau, Voodoo Queen, and Folk Tales Along the Mississippi,* Harmanson, 1956; *The Immortal Margaret Haughery,* Industries Publishing Agency, 1957; *Steamboat Days on the Mississippi,* 1957; (with Helen Henriques Hardy) *Louisiana Fabulous Foods and How to Cook Them,* 1957; *The Story of Spanish Moss and Its Relatives: What It Is and How It Grows,* 1959, revised edition published in *The Story of Spanish Moss: What It Is and How It Grows and The Wax Tree: Louisiana's Forgotten Product* (the latter by Jack D. L. Holmes), 1968; *Pierre George Rousseau: Commanding General of the Galleys of Mississippi . . . ,* 1965, revised edition published as *Rousseau: The Last Days of Spanish Louisiana,* 1975; (with Jack D. L. Holmes) *New Orleans: Facts and Legends,* 1969; *Portraits of New Orleans Jazz: Its People and Places,* 1971, revised edition, 1974. Contributor to *Dixie Roto* (magazine).

AVOCATIONAL INTERESTS: Genealogy and English history of the Tudor and Stuart periods.

*   *   *

MARTINO, Joseph P(aul) 1931-

PERSONAL: Born July 16, 1931, in Warren, Ohio; son of Joseph (a barber) and Anna (Kubina) Martino; married Mary L. Bouquot, May 18, 1957; children: Theresa, Anthony, Michael. *Education:* Miami University, Oxford, Ohio, A.B., 1953; Purdue University, M.S., 1955; Ohio State University, Ph.D., 1961. *Politics:* "Free-enterprise libertarian." *Religion:* Roman Catholic. *Home:* 819 North Maple Ave., Fairborn, Ohio 45324. *Office:* University of Dayton Research Institute, Dayton, Ohio 45469.

CAREER: U.S. Air Force, career officer, 1953-75, holding positions in operations analysis, engineering, and related fields, retiring as colonel; University of Dayton Research Institute, Dayton, Ohio, research scientist, 1975—. *Member:* Institute of Electrical and Electronics Engineers, American Institute of Aeronautics and Astronautics, Operations Research Society of America, Institute of Management Sciences. *Awards, honors*—Military: Commendation Medal with two Oak Leaf Clusters.

WRITINGS: Technological Forecasting for Decisionmaking, American Elsevier, 1972; (editor) *Introduction to Technological Forecasting,* Gordon & Breach, 1972. Contributor of science fiction to *Analog, Galaxy,* and *If.* Associate editor of *Technological Forecasting and Social Change,* 1971—; technical forecasting editor of *Futurist,* 1968—.

WORK IN PROGRESS: Science fiction stories dealing with the impact of technology on society.

*   *   *

MARZANI, Carl (Aldo) 1912-

PERSONAL: Born March 4, 1912, in Rome, Italy; son of Gabriel (a miner) and Enrica (Gorga) Marzani; married first wife, Edith Eisner (an actress), 1937 (deceased); married Charlotte Pomerantz (a writer of children's books), November 12, 1966; children: (first marriage) Judith Enrica (Mrs. Alan Spector), Anthony H.; (second marriage) Gabrielle Rose, Daniel Avram. *Education:* Williams College, B.A., 1935; Oxford University, B.A., 1938. *Politics:* Independent socialist. *Religion:* None. *Home:* 260 West 21st St., New York, N.Y. 10011.

CAREER: Volunteer in Spanish Civil War, 1936-37; New

York University, New York, N.Y., instructor in economics, 1939-41; U.S. Office of Strategic Services, Washington, D.C., member of staff, 1942-45; U.S. Department of State, Washington, D.C., deputy division chief, 1945-46; independent film producer, New York, N.Y., 1946-49; convicted in federal court of hiding Communist affiliation during a loyalty test while with Department of State, he spent 1949-51 as prisoner in Lewisburg Penitentiary, Lewisburg, Pa.; United Electrical, Radio and Machine Workers of America, New York, N.Y., co-director of education, 1951-54; Marzani & Munsell (publishers), New York, N.Y., president, 1954-67; engaged in real estate operations as owner and builder, New York, N.Y., 1967-70. *Military service:* U.S. Army, Office of Strategic Services, 1943-45; became master sergeant. *Member:* Veterans of the Abraham Lincoln Brigade.

WRITINGS: We Can Be Friends (on relations with Russia), foreword by W. E. B. DuBois, Topical Books, 1952, reprinted with new introduction by Barton J. Bernstein, Garland Publishing, 1972; *The Open Marxism of Antonio Gramsci,* Cameron Associates, 1957; *The Survivor* (novel), Cameron Associates, 1958; (with Victor Perlo) *Dollars and Sense of Disarmament,* Marzani & Munsell, 1960; (translator) Giuseppe Boffa, *Inside the Khrushchev Era,* Marzani & Munsell, 1960; (with Robert E. Light) *Cuba versus CIA,* Marzani & Munsell, 1961; (editor and contributor) *The Shelter Hoax,* Marzani & Munsell, 1962; *The Wounded Earth: An Environmental Survey,* Young Scott Books, 1972. Writer of film scripts for "War Department Report," 1944, and "Deadline for Action," 1946.

WORK IN PROGRESS: Studies on George Orwell and on U.S. foreign policy.

SIDELIGHTS: Dollars and Sense of Disarmament was published in Moscow, 1961. Marzani says that he has visited "most socialist countries, including Cuba," traveled all over Europe, and in the Near and Far East. *Avocational interests:* Reading, fishing.

*   *   *

MASSEY, Erika 1900-
(Erika Zastrow)

PERSONAL: Born September, 1900, in Baltimore, Md.; daughter of Benno and Anna Marie (Todt) von Zastrow; married Howard F. Massey, January 12, 1918 (died, 1957); children: G. E. Massey. *Education:* Attended Columbia University, 1916, and Hunter College of the City University of New York, 1917. *Residence:* Long Beach, Calif.

CAREER: Secretary in New Rochelle, N.Y., 1920-21, in Germany, 1922-23, in Mt. Vernon, N.Y., 1924-56, and in Long Beach, Calif., 1957-74. Church organist and choir director in Mt. Vernon, 1952-56; organist in Long Beach, 1964-68.

WRITINGS—Juvenile novels: *A Career for Carol,* Bouregy, 1967; *A Penney for the Wishing Well,* Bouregy, 1968; *My Love to Give,* Bouregy, 1970.

Under name Erika Zastrow: *Broken Arcs,* Holt, 1932; *The Possessed,* Holt, 1933 (published in England as *Subjection,* Hurst, 1933); *Fair Flowering,* Gramercy, 1938.

Contributor of short stories and serialized novellas to *Woman's Home Companion, Cosmopolitan,* and *McCalls.*

WORK IN PROGRESS: A novel, as yet untitled.

MATHES, W(illiam) Michael 1936-

PERSONAL: Born April 15, 1936, in Los Angeles, Calif.; son of William C. (a U.S. district judge) and Rilla (Moore) Mathes. *Education:* Loyola University, Los Angeles, Calif., B.S., 1957; University of Southern California, M.A., 1962; University of New Mexico, Ph.D., 1966. *Religion:* Roman Catholic. *Home address:* P.O. Box 1227, Sonoma, Calif. 95476. *Office:* Department of History, University of San Francisco, San Francisco, Calif. 94117.

CAREER: University of New Mexico, Albuquerque, special collections librarian in Coronado Room, 1963-65; University of San Francisco, San Francisco, Calif., assistant professor, 1966-71, associate professor, 1971-75, professor of history, 1975—. Agente de Canje at National Archives of Mexico, 1960—; director, Archivo Historico, La Paz, B.C.S., 1974—. Consultant, Oakland Museum, 1967-69. *Member:* American Historical Association, Catholic Historical Association, Western Historical Association, California Historical Society, San Diego Historical Society, Phi Alpha Theta. *Awards, honors:* Fulbright grant to Spain, 1962-63; Del Amo fellow in Spain, 1965-66.

WRITINGS: (Editor) *Californiana* (in Spanish), seven volumes, J. Porrua Turanzas, 1965-72; (editor) *Documentos para la historia de la demarcacion comercial de California, 1583-1632* (title means "Documents for the History of the Commercial Charting of California"), J. Porrua Turanzas, 1965; (transcriber, translator, and author of annotations), Juan Cavallero Carranco, *The Pearl Hunters in the Gulf of California, 1668,* Dawson's Book Shop, 1966; *Vizcaino and Spanish Expansion in the Pacific Ocean, 1580-1630,* California Historical Society, 1968; (editor) *Documentos para la historia de la explotacion comercial de California, 1611-1679* (title means "Documents for the History of the Commercial Exploitation of California"), J. Porrua Turanzas, 1968; (editor) Eusebio Francisco Kino, *First from the Gulf to the Pacific,* Dawson's Book Shop, 1969; (transcriber, translator, and author of annotations) *The Capture of the "Santa Ana," Cabo San Lucas, November, 1587: The Accounts of Francis Pretty, Antonio de Sierra, and Tomas de Alzola,* Dawson's Book Shop, 1969; *Reparo a errores de la navegacion Espanola* (title means "Correction of Errors in Spanish Navigation"), J. Porrua Turanzas, 1970; *To Save a City: The Desague,* Americas, 1970; *The Conquistador in California: The Voyage of Fernando Cortes to Baja California in Chronicles and Documents, 1535,* Dawson's Book Shop, 1973. Contributor to Spanish studies and California studies journals. Associate editor, California Historical Society, 1967-69; advisory editor, San Diego Historical Society, 1970—.

WORK IN PROGRESS: Research on the history of California in the seventeenth century, on the history of drainage of the lakes of Mexico, and on the history of convalescent hospitals in Mexico.

SIDELIGHTS: Mathes has lived in Spain and Mexico.

* * *

MATHIAS, Frank Furlong 1925-

PERSONAL: Born May 23, 1925, in Maysville, Ky.; son of Charles Lindsay (a salesman) and Nancy (Furlong) Mathias; married Florence Duffy, August 23, 1958; children: Nancy Browning, Frank Furlong, Susan Elizabeth. *Education:* University of Kentucky, B.A., 1950, M.A., 1961, Ph.D., 1966; graduate study at Mexico City College, 1950-51. *Politics:* Democrat. *Religion:* Roman Catholic. *Home:* 2728 Corlington Dr., Dayton, Ohio 45440. *Office:* Department of History, Box 155, University of Dayton, Dayton, Ohio 45409.

CAREER: Dance band musician in Ohio Valley area, 1940-55; National Airlines, Miami, Fla., ticket agent, 1951; U.S. Steel, Beaumont, Tex., messenger, 1951; high school teacher of Spanish and English in the public schools of Cincinnati, Ohio, 1951-52; in sales promotion for Lorillard Tobacco Co. in eastern Kentucky, 1953-57; West Virginia Institute of Technology, Montgomery, member of staff of history department, 1962-63; University of Dayton, Dayton, Ohio, 1963—, became professor of history. *Military service:* U.S. Army, Infantry, 1943-46; served in South Pacific theater; became sergeant; received Luzon Invasion Bronze Arrow. *Member:* Organization of American Historians, American Catholic Historical Association, Southern Historical Association, Kentucky Historical Association, Ohio Academy of History.

WRITINGS: (Editor) *Incidents and Experiences in the Life of Thomas W. Parsons,* University Press of Kentucky, 1975; *Albert D. Kirwan: A Man for All Seasons,* University Press of Kentucky, 1975. Contributor of articles and book reviews to religion and history journals.

WORK IN PROGRESS: Contributing to *A History of Nicholas County, Kentucky;* an article for *Encyclopedia of Southern History; The Foundations of Kentucky Politics;* a contribution to a festschrift for the University of Vienna, celebrating the twentieth anniversary of the Fulbright program there.

* * *

MATRAT, Jean 1915-

PERSONAL: Born April 14, 1915; son of Jean and Marcelle (Puyo) Matrat. *Education:* Sorbonne, University of Paris, diplome d'etudes superieures, 1934. *Politics:* None. *Religion:* None. *Home:* 44 rue des Sablous, 95220 Herblay, France.

CAREER: Ecole secondaire Montaigne, Herblay, France, teacher of French and English, 1939-65; writer.

WRITINGS: *Camille Desmoulins,* Editions des Jeunes Auteurs Reunis (Paris), 1956; *Le Cardinal de Retz, de la guerre civile consideree comme un des beaux arts,* Structures nouvelles (Paris), 1969; *Mussolini,* Structures nouvelles, 1969; *Oliver Cromwell,* Hachette (Paris), 1970; *Robespierre; ou, la tyrannie de la majorite,* Hachette, 1971, translation by Alan Kendall and Felix Brenner published as *Robespierre: The Tyranny of the Majority,* Scribner, 1975; *Henry VIII,* Nouvelles Editions Debresse (Paris), 1972; *Winston Churchill,* Nouvelles Editions Debresse, 1973. Also author of French language readers published by University of London Press.

WORK IN PROGRESS: A biography of Joseph Fouche; research in English history and on the French revolution.

* * *

MATTHEWS, William (Richard) 1905-1975

PERSONAL: Born June 25, 1905, in London, England; came to United States, 1938, naturalized citizen; son of William Eldridge and Anne Louise (Rodwell) Matthews; married Lois Nicholson Emery, December 18, 1948. *Education:* Birkbeck College, London, B.A. (with honours), 1929, M.A. (with distinction), 1931, Ph.D., 1934. *Home:* 189 Greenfield Ave., Los Angeles, Calif. 90049. *Office:* Department of English, University of California, Los Angeles, Calif. 90024.

CAREER: Diplomatic and Indian Civil Service, London, England, tutor, 1934-37; University of London, London, lecturer in English at Westfield College, 1936, at Birkbeck College, 1937; University of Wisconsin, Madison, instructor in English, 1938-39; University of California, Los Angeles, assistant professor, 1939-41, associate professor, 1941-48, professor of English, 1948-72, professor emeritus, 1972-75, director of Center for Medieval and Renaissance Studies, 1970-72. Visiting professor at University of Manchester, 1951, and King's College, London, 1955; University of Pittsburgh, Mellon Distinguished Professor, 1966-67, visiting professor, 1972-c.1974; honorary fellow, Merton College, Oxford.

MEMBER: International Association of University Professors of English (president, 1971-74), American Academy of Arts and Sciences (fellow), Modern Language Association of America (member of council, 1966), Linguistic Society of America, American Dialect Society, Mediaeval Academy of America, Philological Association of the Pacific Coast (president, 1964-66). *Awards, honors:* Guggenheim fellow, 1946, 1958; Distinguished teaching award from University of California, Los Angeles, 1967; D.Lett., Claremont Graduate School, 1967.

WRITINGS: Cockney Past and Present: A Short History of the Dialect of London, Routledge, 1938, reprinted, Gale, 1970; *English Pronunciation and Shorthand in the Early Modern Period,* University of California Press, 1943; (with Dixon Wecter) *Our Soldiers Speak, 1775-1918,* Little, Brown, 1943; (compiler with Roy Harvey Pearce) *American Diaries: An Annotated Bibliography of American Diaries Written prior to the Year 1861,* University of California Press, 1945; (compiler) *British Diaries: An Annotated Bibliography of British Diaries Written between 1442 and 1942,* University of California Press, 1950; *Canadian Diaries and Autobiographies,* University of California Press, 1950; (compiler) *British Autobiographies: An Annotated Bibliography of British Autobiographies Published or Written before 1951,* University of California Press, 1955.

The Tragedy of Arthur: A Study of the Alliterative "Morte Arthure," University of California Press, 1960; (editor) *Later Medieval English Prose,* Owen, 1962, Appleton, 1963; (editor and contributor) *Medieval Secular Literature: Four Essays,* University of California Press, 1965; *The Ill Famed Knight: A Skeptical Inquiry into the Identity of Sir Thomas Mallory,* University of California Press, 1966; (editor) Samuel Pepys, compiler, *Charles II's Escape from Worcester: A Collection of Narratives,* University of California Press, 1966; (compiler) *Old and Middle English Literature,* Appleton, 1968; (editor with Robert Latham) Samuel Pepys, *The Diary of Samuel Pepys: A New and Complete Transcription,* eight volumes, University of California Press, 1970-74; (compiler) *American Diaries in Manuscript: A Descriptive Bibliography,* University of Georgia Press, 1974. Contributor to scholarly journals in his field.*

(Died June 10, 1975, in Los Angeles, Calif.)

* * *

MATTISON, Judith 1939-

PERSONAL: Born December 9, 1939, in Milwaukee, Wis.; daughter of Arthur D. (a salesman) and Junice (Magnuson) Nelson; married John K. Mattison (a minister), August 25, 1962; children: Theodore John, Michael Andrew. *Education:* University of Minnesota, B.S., 1961. *Home:* 5029 Oakland Ave. S., Minneapolis, Minn. 55417. *Office:* Minneapolis Public Schools, Minneapolis, Minn.

CAREER: Elementary school teacher in public schools in Hopkins, Minn., 1961-62, 1963-65, and in East Hartford, Conn., 1962-63; Minneapolis Public Schools, Minneapolis, Minn., volunteer, 1968-73, radio writer and producer, 1974—. Volunteer at Cambridge State Hospital, 1968-72. Member of Minneapolis Aquatennial, 1960-61, and Minnesota Chorale, 1975—. Member of Centennial District school board, 1971-75. *Member:* Alpha Gamma Delta.

WRITINGS: From a Woman's Heart, Augsburg, 1969; *Prayers from a Woman's Heart,* Augsburg, 1972; *Prayers from a Mother's Heart,* Augsburg, 1975. Contributor to *Lutheran, Lutheran Standard, Lutheran Women,* and *Scope.*

WORK IN PROGRESS: A book of poetry for people who are related to chemically dependent persons, *Early Mourning;* two books of poems, *Love Affair,* and an untitled volume; a book about a teenager's searching and problems, for Augsburg.

SIDELIGHTS: Judith Mattison told *CA:* "I write about feelings. I think human beings may have vastly different experiences and backgrounds, but we understand one another when we begin to identify with another's feelings. We understand grief and confusion, despair and frustration, decency and love. In that way, I may choose to write about hungry children, because I understand something of what it might be to be the mother of a hungry child agonizing over her child's need and want. I write because I care about people."

* * *

MAURY, Inez 1909-

PERSONAL: Born November 12, 1909, in Anaconda, Mont.; daughter of Patrick Martin (a railroad official) and Elle (LaBelle) Halloran; married Lowndes Maury (a composer and piano teacher), June 1, 1940; children: Elizabeth Fontaine (Mrs. David Fox). *Education:* Cincinnati Conservatory of Music, Certificate in Voice and Diploma in Piano, 1931; Los Angeles City College, B.A., 1953. *Politics:* Democrat. *Religion:* Unitarian Universalist. *Home:* 4279 Farmdale Ave., North Hollywood, Calif. 91604.

CAREER: Music teacher in the Los Angeles, Calif., County Schools, 1939-40; private home studio for piano, North Hollywood, Calif., 1943-62; Lou Maury Piano School, North Hollywood, teacher, 1962—. Consultant to Correlation Music Industries, 1971—; singer for radio, recordings, and motion picture studios. *Member:* National Woman's Party, People's Lobby, Cancer Control Society, Another Mother for Peace, Los Angeles Sierra Club, Dominant Club of Los Angeles.

WRITINGS: (With husband, Lowndes Maury) *Magic Lines and Spaces,* Correlation Music Industries, 1973, Instruction Books I and II and Repertoire Books I and II, 1973, Instruction Book III and Repertoire Book III, 1975; *My Mother the Mail Carrier* (juvenile), Feminist Press, 1975.

WORK IN PROGRESS: My Mother the Gardener (juvenile); *The Joy of Not Cooking* (tentative title).

* * *

MAUTNER, Franz H(einrich) 1902-

PERSONAL: Born June 8, 1902, in Vienna, Austria; came to United States in 1938; son of Adolf Albert and Gabriele Mautner; married Hedwig Herrmann (a teacher), December 24, 1928; children: Johanna Elizabeth (Mrs.

Thomas Plaut), Mary Helen. *Education:* University of Heidelberg, student, 1921; University of Vienna, Dr.Phil., 1926. *Home:* 408 Walnut Lane, Swarthmore, Pa. 19081.

CAREER: Classical grammar school teacher of German and French in Vienna, Austria, 1927-29; University of Besancon, Besancon, France, lecturer in German, 1929-30; classical grammar school in Vienna, teacher, 1930-32, professor of German and French, 1933-38; Indiana University, Bloomington, assistant professor of German, 1939-40; Hobart College, Geneva, N.Y., assistant professor of German, 1941-44; Ohio Wesleyan University, Delaware, assistant professor of language and literature, 1944; U.S. Department of State, Washington, D.C., professional writer in German, 1945; Ohio Wesleyan University, assistant professor of language and literature, 1946-48; Kenyon College, Gambier, Ohio, associate professor of German and comparative literature, 1948-52; Sarah Lawrence College, Bronxville, N.Y., lecturer in German, 1953-55; Swarthmore College, Swarthmore, Pa., associate professor, 1955-58, professor of German, 1958-72, professor emeritus, 1972—. Docent at People's University (Vienna), 1936-38; lecturer at Johns Hopkins University, 1939, and Queens College (now of the City University of New York), 1953-55; visiting professor at Princeton University, 1962, University of Pennsylvania, 1964, Bryn Mawr College, 1971, and Cornell University, 1975.

MEMBER: International Arthur Schnitzler Research Association, Internationale Vereinigung fuer germanische Sprach- und Literatur wissenschaft, International Nestroy Society, International Comparative Literature Association, International Association for Studies in German Language and Literature, Modern Language Association of America, Modern Humanities Research Association, American Association of Teachers of German, American Comparative Literature Association, American Council for the Study of Austrian Literature (vice-president, 1969-72), American Association of University Professors, Thomas Mann Society, Phi Beta Kappa. *Awards, honors:* American Council of Learned Societies scholarship, 1954; Guggenheim fellowships, 1964-65, 1968-69; Austrian Cross of Honor (first class) for Arts and Letters, 1969.

WRITINGS: Johann Nestroy und seine Kunst (title means "Johann Nestroy and His Art"), O. Lorenz, 1937; *Moerikes "Mozart auf der Reise nach Prag"* (title means "Moerike's 'Mozart on His Journey to Prague'"), Scherpe-Verlag, 1957; *Lichtenberg: Geschichte seines Geistes* (title means "Lichtenberg: A History of His Mind"), de Gruyter, 1968; *Nestroy,* Stiehm, 1974.

Editor: Nestroy, *Der Talisman* (title means "The Talisman"), Scho, 1935, revised edition, 1958; Nestroy, *Ausgewaehlte Werke* (title means "Selected Writings"), O. Lorenz, 1938; (translator and editor with Henry Hatfield) *The Lichtenberg Reader: Selected Writings of Georg Christoph Lichtenberg,* Beacon Press, 1959; Lichtenberg, *Gedankenbuecher* (title means "Books of Thoughts"), Fischer Buecherei, 1963, revised edition, Stiehm, 1967; Nestroy, *Das Maedl aus der Vorstadt* (title means "The Girl from the Suburb"), Reclam, 1968; (with Hatfield) Lichtenberg, *Lichtenberg: Aphorisms and Letters,* Cape Editions, 1969; Nestroy, *Komoedien* (title means "Comedies"), three volumes, Insel-Verlag, 1970; Nestroy, *Wort und Wesen* (title means "Words and Substance"), Insel-Verlag, 1974.

Contributor: *Das Deutsche Drama* (title means "The German Drama"), August Beigel, 1958; *Georg Buechner,* Wissenschaftliche Buchgesellschaft, 1965; *Adalbert Stifter: Studien und Interpretationen* (title means "Adalbert Stifter: Studies and Interpretation"), Stiehm, 1968; *Wie, warum, und zu welchem Ende wurde ich Literaturhistoriker?* (title means "How, Why, and to What End Did I Become a Literary Historian?"), Suhrkamp, 1972. Contributor to *Columbia Dictionary of Modern European Literature, Fischer-Lexikon: Literatur,* and *Handbook of Austrian Literature.* Contributor to academic journals and festschriften.

WORK IN PROGRESS: Research on comedy and language and on methods of literary history and criticism.

AVOCATIONAL INTERESTS: Mountain climbing, swimming.

*   *   *

MAXWELL, W(illiam) David   1926-

PERSONAL: Born October 13, 1926, in Fayetteville, N.C.; son of Thomas Marion and Lois (Purdue) Maxwell; married Ruth Bryant, July 29, 1949; children: Susan, Marian. *Education:* University of North Carolina, A.B., 1949, M.A., 1954; Johns Hopkins University, Ph.D., 1958. *Home:* 1802 Shadowwood Dr., College Station, Tex. 77840. *Office:* College of Liberal Arts, Texas A & M University, College Station, Tex. 77843.

CAREER: University of North Carolina, Chapel Hill, part-time instructor in economics, 1952-54; Johns Hopkins University, McCoy College, Baltimore, Md., instructor in economics, 1954-56; University of South Carolina, Columbia, assistant professor of economics, 1956-57; Tulane University, New Orleans, La., assistant professor, 1958-60, associate professor of economics, 1960-65, chairman of department, 1960-63; Thammasat University, Bangkok, Thailand, visiting scholar, 1965-66; Indiana University, Bloomington, professor of business economics and public policy, 1966-70; Texas A & M University, College Station, professor of economics and dean of liberal arts, both 1970—. Coordinator of Southern Bell Seminar, 1963; member of Woodrow Wilson fellowship regional selection committee, 1964-65; co-leader of U.S. Agency for International Development (USAID) and government of Thailand evaluation project on agricultural sector analysis, 1974-75; member of board of directors of Arts Council of Brazos; consultant to Rockefeller Foundation. *Military service:* U.S. Navy, 1944-47, 1950-52; became lieutenant junior grade.

MEMBER: American Economic Association, Econometric Society, Asia Society, Southern Economic Association, Phi Beta Kappa, Sigma Pi Alpha, Beta Gamma Sigma, Delta Sigma Pi, Phi Kappa Phi.

WRITINGS: The Jefferson Parish School Board: A Study of School Administration at the Local Level (monograph), Jefferson Committee for Better Schools, 1963; *A College Reader for Instruction,* Genesee Community College, 1968; (contributor) Sydney M. Blummer, editor, *Readings in Micro Econimics,* International Textbook, 1969; (contributor) Richard E. Neel, editor, *Reading in Microeconomics,* South-Western Publishing, 1969; *Price Theory and Applications in Business Administration,* Goodyear Publishing, 1970; (editor with W. Lee Baldwin) *The Role of Foreign Investment and Assistance in Thailand's Economic and Social Development,* Heath, 1975. Contributor to economics and education journals.

MAYERS, Lewis 1890-1975

June 20, 1890—December 31, 1975; American attorney, educator, and author of books on American law. Obituaries: *New York Times*, January 4, 1976.

* * *

McCANDLISH, George E(dward) 1914(?)-1975

1914(?)—May 19, 1975; American educator, and author or editor of books on American literature. Obituaries: *Washington Post*, May 21, 1975.

* * *

McCARTHY, Cavan 1943-

PERSONAL: Born April 1, 1943, in Bristol, England; son of Patrick Michael and Louise Frances (Simpkins) McCarthy; married Maryvonne Judith Fear; children: Merida. *Education:* University of Leeds, B.A., 1965; Leeds Polytechnic, associate of Library Association, 1966; State University of New York, Albany, M.L.S., 1976. *Home:* 35 Walsh Ave., Bristol BS14 9SL, England.

CAREER: College of Technology and Design, Blackburn, England, assistant librarian, 1967; University of Leeds, Leeds, England, assistant librarian at Brotherton Library, 1967-73; Ahmadu Bello University, Zaria, Nigeria, lecturer in library science, 1973-74; State University of New York at Albany, teaching assistant in library science, 1975—. Librarian in Sao Paulo, Brazil, 1971-72.

WRITINGS: Developing Libraries in Brazil, Scarecrow, 1975.

Work is anthologized in *An Anthology of Concrete Poetry,* edited by Emmett Williams, Something Else Press, 1967; *Once Again,* edited by Jean-Francois Bory, New Directions, 1968. Contributor of articles and poems to library journals and little magazines, including *Small Press Review.* European editor and compiler of *Directory of Little Magazines* in the late 1960's. Editor and publisher of *Tlaloc,* 1964-71.

SIDELIGHTS: McCarthy writes: "In 1971-72 I worked in and travelled all over Brazil, visiting libraries. My main concern now is for librarianship in underdeveloped countries and I expect to be back in the Third World shortly." *Avocational interests:* Small press printing and publishing.

* * *

McCAULEY, Michael F(rederick) 1947-

PERSONAL: Born April 12, 1947, in Chicago, Ill.; son of George Lawrence (a stationary engineer) and Virginia (Johnson) McCauley; married Gabrielle Goder, May 29, 1971; children: Megan Colleen. *Education:* Loyola University, Chicago, Ill., A.B., 1969. *Office:* Thomas More Association, 180 North Wabash Ave., Chicago, Ill. 60601.

CAREER: Taught high school English at Woodlands Academy, Lake Forest, Ill., briefly, beginning c. 1969; Thomas More Association, Chicago, Ill., editor, now executive editor of newsletters, including *Overview, Markings, You,* and *Stress.*

WRITINGS: (Editor) *On the Run: Spirituality for the Seventies,* Thomas More Press, 1974; *A Contemporary Meditation on Doubting,* Thomas More Press, in press. Contributor of book reviews to *Critic* and *Commonweal.*

* * *

McCLARY, Andrew 1927-

PERSONAL: Born April 15, 1927, in Chicago, Ill.; son of George Brewer (an engineer) and Adelaide (Caldwell) McClary; married Jane Beaver (a librarian), September 7, 1954; children: Ann Louise, Susan Elisabeth. *Education:* Dartmouth College, A.B., 1950; University of Michigan, M.A. and M.S., both 1954, Ph.D., 1959. *Office:* Department of Natural Science, Michigan State University, East Lansing, Mich. 48823.

CAREER: University of Wisconsin, Milwaukee, assistant professor, 1959-64, associate professor of zoology, 1964; Michigan State University, East Lansing, assistant professor, 1964-66, associate professor, 1966-70, professor of natural science, 1970—. *Member:* American Association for the Advancement of Science, Sigma Xi. *Military service:* U.S. Navy, 1945-46.

WRITINGS: Biology and Society: The Evolution of Man and His Technology, Macmillan, 1975.

WORK IN PROGRESS: Research on evolutionary changes in health of peoples of the Western world, on perceptions of health, and on what it means to be healthy.

SIDELIGHTS: McClary writes that his "major interests, which stem from training in sociology, anthropology, and zoology, relate to trying to interpret [the] impact of modern technology on Western man utilizing the combined viewpoints, methodologies of these three fields."

* * *

McCLUNG, Floyd, Jr. 1945-

PERSONAL: Born August 3, 1945, in Long Beach, Calif.; son of Floyd L. (a minister) and Enetha (Holman) McClung; married Sally Claiborn, June 2, 1967; children: Misha (daughter), Matthew. *Education:* Southern California College, B.A., 1967. *Religion:* Christian. *Residence:* The Netherlands.

CAREER: World traveler and religious lecturer.

WRITINGS: To Be Or Not To Be, Truth Press, 1974; *Dead Men Don't Think,* Truth Press, 1974; *Just Off Chicken Streen,* Revell, 1975.

WORK IN PROGRESS: Welcome to the Family, for Bethany Fellowship; research on creativity and its role in expressing the Christian view of reality.

SIDELIGHTS: "The source of my motivation is the God who is there," McClung wrote. "He is the only adequate explanation I have found for man, the world, and all that is. He is the only presupposition I have big enough to give unity in the midst of life's diversity without swallowing it up." McClung's major interests are in the area of understanding young people, especially alienated young people.

* * *

McCRACKEN, Mary Lou 1943-

PERSONAL: Born April 26, 1943, in Louisville, Miss.; daughter of James D. (a teacher) and Catherine (Hughes) Oswalt; married Laurin McCracken (an architect), August 13, 1965; children: Leslie. *Education:* Mississippi University for Women, B.F.A., 1965; graduate study at Kean College of New Jersey, 1974. *Religion:* Protestant. *Residence:* East Windsor, N.J. *Office:* Princeton Montessori School, Princeton, N.J. 08540.

CAREER: Teacher of art and department chairman in secondary schools of Houston, Tex., 1965-67; Overseas Education Association, Kitzingen, West Germany, teacher, 1968-69; Army Adult Education, Kitzingen, West Germany, teacher of English, 1968; Princeton Montessori

School, Princeton, N.J., art teacher and consultant, 1973—. *Member:* National Art Education Association.

WRITINGS: The Deep South Natural Foods Cookbook, Stackpole, 1975.

WORK IN PROGRESS: Developing a Montessori art program for the pre-primary child.

AVOCATIONAL INTERESTS: Travel, gardening.

* * *

McELROY, Bernard (Patrick, Jr.) 1938-

PERSONAL: Born September 25, 1938, in Newark, N.J.; son of Bernard Patrick (a lawyer) and Agnes (Donelly) McElroy. *Education:* University of Notre Dame, B.A., 1960; Cornell University, M.A., 1968, Ph.D., 1971. *Home:* 1355 North Sandburg Ter., Chicago, Ill. 60610. *Office:* Department of English, Loyola University of Chicago, Chicago, Ill. 60626.

CAREER: Basford, Inc. (advertising agency), New York, N.Y., research associate, 1964-66; Loyola University of Chicago, Chicago, Ill., instructor, 1970-71, assistant professor, 1971-75, associate professor of English, 1975—, member of faculty of Rome Center of Liberal Arts, 1973-74. Member of junior governing board of Chicago Symphony Orchestra. *Military service:* U.S. Army, Signal Corps, 1960-64; served in Germany; became first lieutenant. *Member:* Modern Language Association of America, American Shakespeare Association, University of Chicago Renaissance Seminar. *Awards, honors:* Younger humanist fellowship from National Endowment for the Humanities, 1974.

WRITINGS: Shakespeare's Mature Tragedies, Princeton University Press, 1973.

WORK IN PROGRESS: The Modern Grotesque: Study of a Phenomenon in Twentieth Century Fiction.

AVOCATIONAL INTERESTS: Opera, music, gourmet cooking.

* * *

McEWAN, Ian 1948-

PERSONAL: Born June 21, 1948, in Aldershot, England; son of David (a soldier) and Rose (Moore) McEwan. *Education:* University of Sussex, B.A. (honors), 1970; University of East Anglia, M.A., 1971. *Home:* 305F Clapham Rd., London S.W.9, England. *Agent:* A. P. Watt & Son, 26-28 Bedford St., London, W.1, England.

CAREER: Writer.

WRITINGS: First Love, Last Rites (short stories), Random House, 1975. Also author of "Jack Flea's Birthday Celebration," a television play, for British Broadcasting Corp., 1975, and "Conversation with a Cupboard-man," a radio play, for British Broadcasting Corp., 1975. Contributor to *Radio Times* and literary journals in Europe and the United States, including *Transatlantic Review, American Review, New American Review, Tri-Quarterly, Amazing Stories,* and *New Review.*

WORK IN PROGRESS: Short stories; a novel.

* * *

McFARLAND, Kenton D(ean) 1920-

PERSONAL: Born October 11, 1920, in Branson, Mo.; son of Ira C. (a blacksmith) and Mamie (Cox) McFarland; married Sadako Aoki, April 9, 1958; children: Amy, Betsy. *Education:* Sacramento Junior College, A.A., 1940; San Jose State College (now University), student, 1940-41; Syracuse University, B.A., 1961. *Politics:* Independent. *Reli-*

gion: Church of Religious Science. *Home:* 28315 South Ella Rd., Rancho Palos Verdes, Calif. 90274. *Office:* Ralph M. Parsons Co., 100 West Walnut St., Pasadena, Calif. 91124.

CAREER: U.S. Air Force, career officer, 1942-64, retiring as colonel; served as pilot, 1962-64, information officer, 1954-64, served in Europe and the Caribbean; Ralph M. Parsons Co., Pasadena, Calif., public relations manager, 1964—. Writer for United Press International (UPI), 1946-48. *Member:* Quiet Birdmen. *Awards, honors*—Military: Distinguished Service Cross, Distinguished Flying Cross, Air Medal with four oak leaf clusters, eleven medals.

WRITINGS—Juveniles: (With James C. Sparks) *Midget Motoring and Karting,* Dutton, 1961; *Airplanes: How They Work,* Putnam, 1966. Has worked as ghost writer.

SIDELIGHTS: McFarland writes: "During my growing up years, being a writer was the last thing in the world I ever thought about doing—I wanted to fly an airplane. As it happened, my senior year in college was interrupted by World War Two and within one month I found myself taking my first airplane ride. ... Later, after the war was over and I returned to civilian life, I was practically thrust into the news business almost as abruptly as my entrance into the flying business. ... It was during my assignment in New York City starting in 1958 that I started to take a serious look at doing something besides writing news releases for the Air Force, and as often has been the case in my life, again I rather inadvertently got involved in writing the book about midget motoring."

* * *

McGEACHY, D(aniel) P(atrick) III 1929-

PERSONAL: Born November 19, 1929, in Atlanta, Ga.; son of Daniel Patrick, Jr. (a clergyman) and Beth (McClure) McGeachy; married Alice Neely (a teacher-counselor), August 28, 1952; children: Daniel, Elizabeth, Martin. *Education:* Davidson College, A.B., 1951; Union Theological Seminary in Virginia, B.D. (cum laude), 1954, Th.M., 1955; San Francisco Theological Seminary, S.T.M., 1975. *Politics:* Democrat. *Home:* 621 Brook Hollow Rd., Nashville, Tenn. 37205.

CAREER: Ordained Presbyterian minister, 1954; pastor of churches in Sylva, N.C., 1955-59, Gainesville, Ga., 1959-66, and Nashville, Tenn., 1966-72; A New Song (consultants in liturgical renewal), Nashville, director, 1973—; Rockvale Cumberland Presbyterian Church, Rockvale, Tenn., pastor, 1975—.

WRITINGS: A Matter of Life and Death, John Knox, 1966; *Common Sense and the Gospel,* John Knox, 1969; *Beyond the Facts, Acts,* Friendship, 1973; *The Gospel According to Andy Capp,* John Knox, 1973; *A New Song,* A New Song, 1973; *Traveling Light,* Abingdon, 1975.

WORK IN PROGRESS: A book on prayer; a secular adventure novel.

* * *

McGINN, Maureen Ann
See SAUTEL, Maureen Ann

* * *

McGRATH, Francis E. 1903(?)-1976

1903(?)—January 24, 1976; American teacher and playwright. Obituaries: *New York Times,* January 26, 1976; *Washington Post,* January 27, 1976.

* * *

McGRATH, Sylvia Wallace 1937-

PERSONAL: Born February 27, 1937, in Montpelier, Vt.;

daughter of George John (an ornithologist) and Martha (a mathematics instructor; maiden name, Cooper) Wallace; married W. Thomas McGrath (a forestry professor), June 11, 1966; children: Sandra Jean, Charles George. *Education:* Michigan State University, B.A., 1959; Radcliffe College, M.A., 1960; University of Wisconsin, Madison, Ph.D., 1966. *Religion:* Protestant. *Home:* 1112 Murry St., Nacogdoches, Tex. 75961. *Office:* Box 3013, Stephen F. Austin State University, Nacogdoches, Tex. 75961.

CAREER: Elementary school teacher in Falmouth, Mass., 1960-61, Corte Madera, Calif., 1961-62; Stephen F. Austin State University, Nacogdoches, Tex., assistant professor, 1968-73, associate professor of history, 1973—. Ordained elder of Presbyterian Church. *Member:* Organization of American Historians, Southern Historical Association, State Historical Society of Wisconsin, Alpha Lambda Delta, Phi Alpha Theta.

WRITINGS: Charles Kenneth Leith, Scientific Adviser, University of Wisconsin Press, 1971.

WORK IN PROGRESS: Research in the history of American science, and in women in history.

AVOCATIONAL INTERESTS: Camping, canoeing, travel.

* * *

McGUIRE, Robert G. (III) 1938(?)-1975

1938(?)—August 16, 1975; American educator, and author of books on black studies. Obituaries: *Washington Post,* August 19, 1975.

* * *

McHALE, John

PERSONAL: Born in Scotland. *Education:* Educated in United Kingdom and United States; earned Ph.D. *Office:* Center for Integrative Studies, State University of New York at Binghamton, Binghamton, N.Y. 13901.

CAREER: Southern Illinois University, Carbondale, executive director of World Resources Inventory, 1962-68; State University of New York at Binghamton, director of Center for Integrative Studies, 1968—. Artist and designer; has exhibited work in Europe, 1950—. *Member:* World Academy of Art and Science (fellow), World University Council, Continuing Committee of the World Future Research Congress, World Future Society, Royal Society of Arts (fellow), American Sociological Association, Institute of Ecology, Society for Advancement of General Systems Theory, Society for the History of Technology, American Geographical Society (fellow), New York Academy of Sciences (fellow). *Awards, honors:* Medaille d'Honneur en Vermeil from Societe d'Encouragement au Progres, 1966.

WRITINGS: R. Buckminster Fuller, Braziller, 1962; (with R. Buckminster Fuller and others) *World Design Decade, 1965-74,* Southern Illinois University, 1963-67; (editor) R. Buckminster Fuller, *Comprehensive Thinking,* Southern Illinois University, 1965; *The Future of the Future,* Braziller, 1969; (contributor) Gillo Dorfles, *Kitsch: The World of Bad Taste,* Universe Books, 1969; *The Ecological Context,* Braziller, 1970; *World Facts and Trends,* P. F. Collier, 1972.

* * *

McHENRY, Paul G(raham), Jr. 1924-

PERSONAL: Born January 23, 1924, in Chicago, Ill.; son of Paul G. and Agnes (King) McHenry; married Carol McCown, November 6, 1948; children: Lynn, James, Bruce. *Education:* University of New Mexico, B.B.A., 1948, M.Arch., 1974. *Politics:* Republican. *Religion:* Lutheran. *Home and office address:* Box 462, Corrales, N.M. 87048.

CAREER: Self-employed architectural designer and builder. Visiting lecturer at University of New Mexico, and other schools. Member of board of directors of Museum of Albuquerque, 1967—. *Military service:* U.S. Air Force, served during World War II, recalled during Korean War; became captain. *Member:* International Council of Monuments and Sites, Sigma Chi. *Awards, honors:* National Endowment for the Arts grant for investigation and documentation of prehistoric building methods.

WRITINGS: Adobe: Build it Yourself, University of Arizona Press, 1972.

WORK IN PROGRESS: Books on adobe house plans, prehistoric building methods, and owner built homes.

* * *

McKELVEY, John J(ay), Jr. 1917-

PERSONAL: Born July 16, 1917, in Albany, N.Y.; son of John Jay (a lawyer) and Louise (Brunning) McKelvey; married Josephine Faulkner (a librarian), June 28, 1941; children: John Jay III, Richard Drummond, Edward Faulkner, Laurence Brunning. *Education:* Oberlin College, A.B., 1939; Virginia Polytechnic Institute and State University, M.S., 1941; Cornell University, Ph.D., 1945. *Politics:* "Unimportant." *Religion:* "Unimportant." *Home:* 12 Barnes Ter., Chappaqua, N.Y. 10514. *Office:* Rockefeller Foundation, 1133 Avenue of the Americas, New York, N.Y.

CAREER: Investigator for New York State Agricultural Experiment Station, 1942-45; Rockefeller Foundation, New York, N.Y., associate deputy director, 1945-66, deputy director of agricultural sciences, 1966-68, Latin American fellowship grant and fellowship officer, 1952-59, African grants and fellowships officer, 1959—. Trustee, International Institute for Tropical Agriculture, Ibadan, Nigeria, 1971—; member of board of governors, Institute for Agricultural Research, Ahmadu Bello University, Zaria, Nigeria, 1971—. Town and community chairman, United Way. *Member:* American Association for the Advancement of Science, Entomological Society of America, American Phytopathological Society, Association for the Advancement of Agricultural Sciences in Africa.

WRITINGS: Man Against Tsetse: Struggle for Africa, Cornell University Press, 1973; (with R. L. Metcalf) *Insecticides for the Future: Needs and Prospects,* Wiley Interscience, in press; (with H. Shorey) *Controlling Insect Behavior,* Wiley Inter-science, in press.

WORK IN PROGRESS: Research in river blindness.

AVOCATIONAL INTERESTS: Beekeeping, photography, farming, building.

* * *

McKENDRY, John (Joseph) 1933-1975

January 5, 1933—June 23, 1975; Canadian-born museum curator and author of books on art and related topics. Obituaries: *New York Times,* June 25, 1975; *AB Bookman's Weekly,* August 25, 1975.

McKENNEY, Mary 1946-

PERSONAL: Born October 30, 1946, in Menominee, Mich.; daughter of William Henry (a foundry worker) and Louise (a practical nurse; maiden name, Larsen) McKenney. Education: Michigan State University, B.A. (with honors), 1969; University of Michigan, M.A.L.S., 1970. Politics: "Working class Lesbian-Feminist." Residence: San Francisco, Calif.

CAREER: Radical Research Center, Northfield, Minn., co-editor of Alternative Press Index, 1970-71; St. Mary's College of Maryland, St. Mary's City, periodicals librarian, 1971-72; Commerce Clearinghouse, San Rafael, Calif., head of proofreading department, 1973; American Review of Respiratory Disease, San Francisco, Calif., copy editor, 1974—. Member: Women Library Workers, Southern Poverty Law Center.

WRITINGS: Divorce: A Selected Annotated Bibliography, Scarecrow, 1975. Contributor to library journals.

WORK IN PROGRESS: Research on the "myth of professionalism."

* * *

McKILLOP, Susan Regan 1929-

PERSONAL: Born April 20, 1929, in Woodland, Calif.; daughter of William Michael (a professor) and Susan (a university administrator; maiden name, Cobb) Regan; married Allan A. McKillop (a professor), June 30, 1954; children: Mary Alexis, Allan Michael. Education: University of Missouri, A.B. (with honors) and B.Journalism, both 1951; University of California, Berkeley, M.A., 1953; Harvard University, Ph.D., 1966. Home: 535 Miller Dr., Davis, Calif. 95616. Office: Department of Art, California State University, 6000 J St., Sacramento, Calif. 95819.

CAREER: University of California, Davis, assistant professor of art history, 1964-71, assistant dean of College of Letters and Science, 1966-67; California State University, Sacramento, lecturer in art history, 1971—. Lecturer at California State College, Sonoma, 1975—. Member of board of directors of Crocker Art Gallery Association, E. B. Crocker Art Gallery, Sacramento, 1972—. Member: College Art Association.

WRITINGS: Robert Bechtle, E. B. Crocker Art Gallery, 1973; Franciabigio, University of California Press, 1974.

WORK IN PROGRESS: Editing Jerald Silva (tentative title); research on Medici symbolism and the political aspects of Medici visual commissions.

* * *

McKINNELL, James 1933-

PERSONAL: Born March 22, 1933, in Linn Township, Walworth County, Wis.; son of James Charles (a farmer) and Margaret (Wiedenhoft) McKinnell; married Letha Miriam Miller (a teacher), March 22, 1959; children: James, Andrew. Education: Grinnell College, B.A., 1957; Eden Theological Seminary, graduate study, 1957-58; Bethany Theological Seminary, B.D., 1961. Home: 6909 Auburn Rd., Rockford, Ill. 61103. Office: First Church of the Brethren, 6909 Auburn Rd., Rockford, Ill. 61103.

CAREER: Farmer in Walworth, Wis., 1950-53; pastor of Churches of the Brethren in Grinnell, Iowa, 1955-57, Hagerstown, Md., 1959-60, Worthington, Minn., 1961-67, and New Paris, Ind., 1967-74; First Church of the Brethren, Rockford, Ill., pastor, 1974—. Chairman of Migrant Ser-

vice Committee of Elkhart and Kosciusko counties, Indiana, 1968-69. Member: Rockford Clergy Association, Phi Beta Kappa.

WRITINGS: Now About Peace, Brethren Press, 1971. Contributor to church publications.

WORK IN PROGRESS: A book, Dactylic Theology: Faith on Five Fingers; "In Your Hand," a filing system for pastors and other religious leaders; a sail-equipped vertical-axle electrical generation system.

SIDELIGHTS: McKinnell writes: "I was raised on a dairy farm in southern Wisconsin, the eldest son of a Scotch-Irish father and German mother. I attended country-school and a small high school in Walworth, Wisconsin. I intended to make farming my career, when an encounter with Jesus Christ . . . led me to begin training for the ministry at Grinnell College. One of the unexpected curriculum requirements at Grinnell in the middle 1950's was military science. . . . After completing college, I began to search for a theological school that was affiliated with a Christian denomination that had an active pacifist program. I chose the Church of the Brethren." Avocational interests: Camping, mechanics and inventing, research on his family tree.

* * *

McKITTRICK, David 1938-

PERSONAL: Born April 13, 1938, in Belfast, Northern Ireland; son of David and Louisa (Linton) McKittrick; married Evelyn Ferguson, July 13, 1959; children: Amanda, Christopher. Education: Stranmillis College of Education, Belfast, teacher's certificate, 1958; Sigurd Leeder School of Dance, diploma, 1963; attended University of London, 1971-73. Home: Mount Villa, Portland Place, Helsby, Cheshire, England. Office: I. M. Marsh College of Physical Education, Liverpool, England.

CAREER: Strandtown Primary School, Belfast, Northern Ireland, artmaster, 1955-58; Eastham Education Authority, London, England, dance teacher, 1963-65; Worcester College of Education, Worcester, England, lecturer in dance, 1966-69; University of Alberta, Edmonton, lecturer in dance, 1970; University of London, Goldsmith's College, London, England, senior lecturer, 1971-74; I. M. Marsh College of Physical Education, Liverpool, England, principal lecturer, 1975—.

WRITINGS: Dance: In the Middle Years of Schooling, Macmillan, 1972.

WORK IN PROGRESS: A book on imagination in the arts.

* * *

McLAUGHLIN, Charles Bernard 1937-

PERSONAL: Born May 20, 1937, in Waltham, Mass. Education: Boston State College, B.S., 1959; Boston College, M.Ed., 1961; Calvin Coolidge College, certificate of specialization, 1962; Brantridge Forest College, Ps.D., 1968; Avon University, Ph.D., 1969; also studied at Boston University and Framingham State College. Religion: Roman Catholic. Home: 40 Fairmont Ave., Waltham, Mass. 02154.

CAREER: Marlboro, Mass., Public School System, junior high school teacher of English, guidance counselor, and school psychologist, 1960-76. Registered sports official for sandlot, high school, and college baseball, basketball, and soccer; semi-professional baseball player for Massachusetts

Pioneer League, 1953-54; player-manager for Waltham Chlorophylls, 1955-62; general manager, Waltham City Club, 1963-64. Member of Waltham School Committee Athletic Advisory Board, 1973-76. Professor of psychology at Avon University, 1967-69, continuing fellow; graduate lecturer at East Coast University, 1969-76. Recreation leader, Boston Metropolitan Commission, 1961-74. *Member:* Massachusetts Baseball Conference Association (founder and first president), Massachusetts Conference Umpiring Association (past commissioner).

WRITINGS: Second Row Third Seat (comparison of homogeneous and heterogeneous grouping in public schools), Pine Hill Press, 1969; *Donna's Hell* (hardships of youth living in big cities), Pine Hill Press, 1971; *Ouch It Hurts* (guidance journal for teenagers), Dnomro, 1972; *The Elm Is Green* (non-fiction story of elderly immigrants), Dnomro, 1974. Author of column, "Teacher Says," appearing in several newspapers, 1964-66. Sports writer for Watham *News Tribune,* 1956-66.

WORK IN PROGRESS: Anatomy of a Schoolteacher, publication expected in 1977.

SIDELIGHTS: McLaughlin writes: "Today's public secondary schools are providing a setting of homogeneous cohesiveness while training young Americans for a world of heterogeneity.... Children are innocently thrown into homogeneous classrooms where they are matched and statistically paired with their own likenesses. Those on the lowest step of the ladder are losers before they start, while those of the top group must be constant winners at any cost.... Those somewhere between are relegated to the masses of the school's overlooked. Such school grouping principles ... result in a drawing together of the desirables and a withdrawing of the undesirables. The effect is one of educational segregation, publicly accepted by many who openly fight the evils of other segregations in public classrooms." *Avocational interests:* Real estate (maintains a vacation home on one of the sea islands off the coast of Beaufort, S.C., and owns other property in the Bahamas, Florida, New Mexico, New Hampshire, and Canada).

* * *

McLIN, Ruth (Arlene) 1924-

PERSONAL: Born March 9, 1924, in Loma Linda, Calif.; daughter of Seth Floyd (a registered nurse) and Lydia (Leer) Harris; married Glen C. McLin (a medical technologist), September 20, 1944; children: James, Glenys, Ralph. *Education:* Pacific Union College, B.A., 1968. *Religion:* Seventh-day Adventist. *Home address:* P.O. Box 163, Deer Park, Calif. 94576.

CAREER: Has worked as secretary, public relations director, teacher, and magazine editor; now full-time writer. Part-time high school teacher of religion. *Member:* Angwin Christian Writers.

WRITINGS: (With Jeanne Larson) *Fifty-Two Sabbath Menus,* Southern Publishing, 1969; (with Larson) *Creative Ideas for Child Training,* Review & Herald, 1973; (with Larson) *The Vegetable Protein and Vegetarian Cookbook,* Arco, 1974; *The Family That Had Everything But Money* (for young people), Review & Herald, 1975. Contributor to magazines and newspapers, including *Review and Herald, Little Friend, Primary Treasure, Youth's Instructor, All-Pets, Camping Guide, Outdoor World, Cleveland Plain Dealer,* and *Alaska.*

SIDELIGHTS: Ruth McLin writes: "In *The Family That*

Had Everything But Money, I view the Depression years through my own eyes as a child with the hope that children who read may recognize fundamental values of life." *Avocational interests:* Nature study, travel, hiking, camping, canoeing, photography, flowers, raising bonsai.

* * *

McMULLIN, Ruth R(oney) 1942-
(Ruth Anne Roney)

PERSONAL: Born February 9, 1942, in New York, N.Y.; daughter of Richard Thomas (in publishing) and Virginia (Goodwin) Roney; married Thomas Ryan McMullin (group counsel for Xerox), April 27, 1968; children: David Patrick. *Education:* Connecticut College, B.A., 1963. *Home and office:* 17 Woodside Lane, Westport, Conn. 06880.

CAREER: McGraw-Hill, Inc., New York, N.Y., market researcher for *Aviation Week,* 1962-64; Doubleday & Co., New York, associate editor of "Books for Young Readers," 1964-67, manager of Natural History Press, 1967-70; Weston Woods, Inc., Weston, Conn., manager, 1970, vice-president and treasurer, 1970-71. Member of board of directors of Saugatuck Valley Audubon Society, 1971-72.

WRITINGS: (With Alan Meckler) *Directory of Oral History Collections,* Bowker, 1975.

Under name Ruth Ann Roney: *Doubleday Guide to Federal Aid Programs: 1966-1967,* Doubleday, 1966; *Doubleday Guide to Federal Aid Programs: 1967-1968,* Doubleday, 1968; (editor) *Expeditions: Science Adventures,* Doubleday, 1970.

WORK IN PROGRESS: A cookbook.

* * *

McNUTT, Dan James 1938-

PERSONAL: Born April 5, 1938, in Glace Bay, Nova Scotia, Canada; son of Howard Fulton (a teacher) and Isabel (MacDonald) McNutt; married Elaine Van Dyke, April 25, 1968; children: Robert, Dan. *Education:* Mount Allison University, B.A., 1967; University of Texas, El Paso, M.A., 1969; University of Kentucky, further graduate study, 1969-70; Dalhousie University, Ph.D., 1974. *Religion:* United Church of Canada. *Home:* 790 Springland Dr., Apt. 133, Ottawa, Ontario K1V 6L7, Canada.

CAREER: Toronto General Trust Corp., Toronto, Ontario, trust accountant, 1958-59; Algoma Ore Properties, Jamestown, Ontario, miner, 1959-60; Pioneer Drilling Co., Hobbs, N.M., oil well serviceman, 1961; Canadian National Railroad, Toronto, Ontario, carman, 1963-64, 1965; Anaconda American Brass Corp., Toronto, Ontario, mill hand, 1966; Canadian Government, Ottawa, Ontario, writer, 1974—. *Military service:* U.S. Army, Infantry, military police, 1961-63; served in Germany.

WRITINGS: The Eighteenth-Century Gothic Novel: An Annotated Bibliography of Criticism and Selected Texts, Garland Publishing, 1975; (editor) George Wilcox, *History of Rural Mail in Canada,* Public Affairs Branch, Canada Post, 1975.

WORK IN PROGRESS: Annotated bibliographies of the nineteenth-century gothic novel, of Edgar Allan Poe, and of Sterne.

* * *

McSWEENY, Maxine 1905-

PERSONAL: Born June 11, 1905, in Broken Bow, Neb.;

daughter of John Sumner (a rancher) and Nell (McComas) Squires; married Daniel McSweeny, October 3, 1929 (died, 1936); married George Hjelte (a recreation consultant and writer), November 3, 1973; children: (first marriage) Frances (Mrs. Joseph Anthony Burgard). *Education:* Cumnock School, Diploma, 1926; attended University of California at Los Angeles, 1923, New York University, 1941, and Columbia University, 1941. *Religion:* Roman Catholic. *Home:* 1075 East Ocean Blvd., Long Beach, Calif. 90802.

CAREER: May Company Stores, Los Angeles, Calif., storyteller, 1925; Santa Monica Public Library, Santa Monica, Calif., storyteller, 1926; *Long Beach Sun,* Long Beach, Calif., drama critic, 1927; Walburg Studio, Fullerton, Calif., teacher, 1927; Los Angeles City Recreation and Park Department, Los Angeles, Calif., children's drama specialist, 1927-65. *Member:* American Association for Health, Physical Education and Recreation, American Educational Theater Association, California Park and Recreation Society, Chi Kappa Rho, P.E.O. Sisterhood.

WRITINGS: (Contributor) Charles Brightbill, editor, *The Recreation Program,* Athletic Institute, 1954; *Creative Children's Theatre for Home, School, Church, and Playground,* A. S. Barnes, 1974; *Christmas Plays for Young Players,* A. S. Barnes, in press. Contributor to *Recreation.* Editor of *American Recreation Society Bulletin,* 1953-54.

WORK IN PROGRESS: A book, *The Modern Recreator,* with husband George Hjelte.

* * *

McVEIGH, Malcolm J(ames) 1931-

PERSONAL: Born February 11, 1931, in Painesville, Ohio; son of Charles J. D. (a physician) and Helen (Brandt) McVeigh; married Marion Boyd (a dietician and missionary), November 25, 1957; children: Patricia Helen, Deborah Florence, Rebecca Lynn. *Education:* Rutgers University, B.S., 1952; Drew Theological Seminary, B.D., 1956; language study in Portugal, 1957-58; Union Theological Seminary, New York, N.Y., S.T.M., 1963; Boston University, Ph.D., 1971. *Home address:* P.O. Box 21198, Nairobi, Kenya.

CAREER: Ordained minister and missionary of United Methodist Church, 1957—; missionary service with Methodist Church in Angola, 1958-61; Congo Protestant Relief Agency, Kinshasa, Zaire, director of material aid, 1965-68; University of Nairobi, Nairobi, Kenya, visiting lecturer in philosophy and religious studies, 1971—. *Member:* American Society of Missiology.

WRITINGS: (Editor with others) *Kenya Churches Handbook: The Development of Kenyan Christianity, 1498-1973,* Evangel Publishing House, 1973; *God in Africa,* Claude Stark, 1974; (editor with others) *World Christian Handbook,* Macmillan, new edition (McVeigh was not associated with earlier editions), 1976.

SIDELIGHTS: McVeigh is competent in German, Portuguese, French, Kimbundu, and Kiswahili.

* * *

McWHIRTER, A(lan) Ross 1925-1975

August 12, 1925—November 27, 1975; British journalist, publisher, and joint compiler of *Guinness Book of World Records.* Obituaries: *Washington Post,* November 28, November 29, 1975; *Time,* December 8, 1975; *Publishers Weekly,* December 8, 1975; *AB Bookman's Weekly,* December 22-29, 1975; *Bookseller,* January 17, 1976. (See index for previous *CA* sketch)

* * *

MEGGS, Brown (Moore) 1930-

PERSONAL: Born October 20, 1930, in Los Angeles, Calif.; son of Charles Winfield and Margarette (Brown) Meggs; married Nancy Bates Meachen, June 16, 1954; children: Brook Meachen (son). *Education:* Attended California Institute of Technology, 1948-49, Harvard University, 1949-51. *Home:* 1450 El Mirador Dr., Pasadena, Calif. 91103. *Office:* 1750 North Vine St., Hollywood, Calif. 90028.

CAREER: Warner Brothers Pictures Corp., Burbank, Calif., story analyst, 1951; Jam Handy Organization, Detroit, Mich., writer of industrial films, 1955-57; Capitol Records, Inc., Hollywood, Calif., merchandising project manager, 1958-59, director of public relations, 1959-62, director of eastern operations in New York City, 1962-64, vice-president of merchandising and advertising, 1964-67, vice-president of classics and international, 1967-70, vice-president and assistant to the president, 1970-71, vice-president of marketing, 1971-73, executive vice-president, 1973—, chief operating officer, 1974-76; Capitol Industries-EMI, Inc., Hollywood, vice-president and assistant to president, 1976—. *Military service:* U.S. Army, Counter Intelligence Corps, 1953-54. *Member:* Authors Guild, Mystery Writers of America. *Awards, honors:* Western heritage award from Cowboy Hall of Fame and Western Heritage Center, 1962; Edgar Allan Poe special award from Mystery Writers of America, 1974, for *Saturday Games.*

WRITINGS: Saturday Games (novel), Random House, 1974; *The Matter of Paradise* (novel), Random House, 1975. Contributor of stories and articles to *True, Esquire, McCall's, Western Horseman, Caper, Sports Car Illustrated,* and other popular magazines.

WORK IN PROGRESS: Two novels, *Aria* and *The War Train,* completion of both expected in 1976.

* * *

MEIER, Heinz K(arl) 1929-

PERSONAL: Born October 13, 1929, in Zurich, Switzerland; married Regula A. Schlatter (a professor), April 12, 1955; children: Barbara A., Christine E., Markus H., Peter E. *Education:* Evangelisches Lehrerseminar, Zurich, Switzerland, B.A., 1949; University of Zurich, M.A., 1953; Emory University, Ph.D., 1959. *Home:* 216 East 39th St., Norfolk, Va. 23504. *Office:* School of Arts & Letters, Old Dominion University, Norfolk, Va. 23508.

CAREER: Teacher in public schools in Switzerland, 1950-55; Emory University, Atlanta, Ga., instructor in French, 1955-56, German, 1956-58, and history, summer, 1958; Athenaeum, Zurich, Switzerland, instructor in English and history, 1959-60; Old Dominion University, Norfolk, Va., assistant professor, 1960-63, associate professor, 1963-66, professor, 1966-68, Louis I. Jaffe Professor of History, 1968-75, dean of School of Arts and Letters, 1975—, chairman of department, 1973-75, director of graduate studies, 1967-73. Visiting professor at University of the West Indies, 1966-67.

MEMBER: American Historical Association, Swiss American Historical Society (president, 1964-66, 1968-74), Society for the History of American Foreign Relations, American Association of University Professors, Phi Alpha

Theta. *Awards, honors:* Summer grant from Swiss National Foundation, 1966.

WRITINGS: The United States and Switzerland in the Nineteenth Century, Humanities, 1963; *Friendship under Stress: U.S.-Swiss Relations, 1900-1950,* Herbert Lang & Co., 1970; (editor) *Memoirs of a Swiss Officer in the American Civil War,* Herbert Lang & Co., 1972.

WORK IN PROGRESS: Switzerland during the Nazi Era.

* * *

MEIN, Margaret

PERSONAL: Born in Preston, England. *Education:* Oxford University, B.A. (honors), 1945, diploma in education, 1946; University of London, B.A. (honors), 1950, Ph.D., 1953. *Office:* Westfield College, University of London, Kidderpore Ave., Hampstead, London NW3 7ST, England.

CAREER: High school teacher of French, 1946-50 and 1953-61; Oxford University, Oxford, England, tutor at St. Hilda's College, 1961-66, lecturer in French, 1961-66; University of London, London, England, lecturer in French at Westfield College, 1966—.

WRITINGS: Proust's Challenge to Time, Manchester University Press, 1962; *A Foretaste of Proust: A Study of Proust and His Precursors,* Heath, 1974. Contributor to French and English language and literature journals.

WORK IN PROGRESS: Continuing research on Proust.

AVOCATIONAL INTERESTS: Music.

* * *

MEISS, Millard (Lazare) 1904-1975

PERSONAL: Born March 25, 1904, in Cincinnati, Ohio; son of Leon (a businessman) and Clara (Loewenstein) Meiss; married Margaret Louchheim, March 15, 1928; children: Elinor Siner; one son (deceased). *Education:* Princeton University, A.B., 1926; graduate study, Harvard University, 1928; New York University, M.A., 1931, Ph.D., 1933. *Office:* Institute for Advanced Study, Princeton, N.J. 08540.

CAREER: Shroder & Koppel, New York, N.Y., assistant superintendent of building construction, 1926-28; New York University, New York City, lecturer in art history, 1931-33; Columbia University, New York City, 1934-53, began as lecturer, became professor of fine arts and archaeology; Harvard University, Cambridge, Mass., professor of fine arts and curator of paintings at Fogg Museum, 1954-58; Institute for Advanced Study, Princeton, N.J., professor of history of art, 1958-74, professor emeritus, 1974-75. Guest director and visiting scholar, I Tatti, Florence, Italy; chairman, American Committee for the Restoration of Italian Monuments, Inc., 1946-51; honorary trustee, Metropolitan Museum of Art, 1968; honorary fellow, Pierpont Morgan Library.

MEMBER: American Academy of Arts and Sciences (fellow), American Philosophical Society, Mediaeval Academy of America (fellow), College Art Association of America (former director; member of executive committee, 1940-47, 1952-57; secretary, 1943; vice-president, 1954-56), British Academy (corresponding member), Accademia Senese degli Intronati (corresponding member), Societe des antiquaries de France (corresponding member), La Colombaria Tuscan Academy of Science and Letters, Academia Clementina (Bologna; corresponding member), Accademia delle Arti del Disegno (Florence; corresponding member), Phi Beta Kappa. *Awards, honors:* John Wanamaker English Prize from Princeton University, 1925; decorated Stella della Solidarieta, 1949, decorated grande ufficiale, 1968; Haskins Medal from Mediaeval Academy of America, 1953; Lewis Prize from American Philosophical Society; Morey Award from College Art Association, 1969; Litt.D., from University of Florence, 1968, Princeton University, 1973, and Columbia University, 1975.

WRITINGS: Painting in Florence and Siena after the Black Death, Princeton University Press, 1951; *Andrea Mantegna as Illuminator: An Episode in Renaissance Art, Humanism, and Diplomacy,* Columbia University Press, 1957.

Giotto and Assisi, New York University Press, 1960; (editor) *De Artibus Opuscula XL: Essays in Honor of Erwin Panofsky,* two volumes, Buehler Buchdruck (Zurich), 1960, New York University Press, 1961; (with Leonetto Tintori) *The Painting of the Life of St. Francis in Assisi; with Notes on the Arena Chapel,* New York University Press, 1962; (editor) *Studies in Western Art: Acts of the International Congress of the History of Art,* Volume I: *Romanesque and Gothic Art,* Volume II: *The Renaissance and Mannerism,* Volume III: *Latin American Art and the Baroque Period in Europe,* Volume IV: *Problems of the Nineteenth and Twentieth Centuries,* Princeton University Press, 1963; *Giovanni Bellini's St. Francis in the Frick Collection,* Princeton University Press, for the Frick Collection, 1964; *French Painting in the Time of Jean de Berry,* Volume I: *The Late XIV Century and the Patronage of the Duke,* two books, Phaidon, 1967, Volume II: *The Boucicaut Master,* Phaidon, 1968, Volume III: *The Limbourgs and Their Contemporaries,* two books, Braziller, 1973; (with Peter Brieger and Charles Singleton) *Illuminated Manuscripts of the Divine Comedy,* Princeton University Press, 1969; (with Joan Longnon and R. Cazelles) *The "Tres Riches Heures" of Jean, Duke of Berry,* Braziller, 1969.

The Great Age of Fresco: Discoveries, Recoveries, and Survivals, Braziller, 1970; *The Master of the Breviary of Jean Sans Peur and the Limbourgs,* Oxford University Press, 1971; (author of introduction and commentary with Edith W. Kirsch) *Giovannino de'Grassi, The Visconti Hours,* Braziller, 1972; (author of introduction) *The Rohan Master,* Braziller, 1972; (author of commentary with Elizabeth Beatson) *The Belles Heures of Jean, Duke of Berry,* Braziller, 1974; *The Painter's Choice: Problems in the Interpretation of Renaissance Art,* Harper, 1976.

Contributor of articles to journals in his field, published in the United States and abroad. *Art Bulletin,* editor-in-chief, 1940-42, member of editorial board, 1943-75; member of editorial board, *Magazine of Art,* 1948-52.*

(Died June 12, 1975, in Princeton, N.J.)

* * *

MELESKI, Patricia F(erguson) 1935-

PERSONAL: Born December 30, 1935, in Poteau, Okla.; daughter of Thomas Harold (a postal employee) and Wanda (maiden name, Wolf; a secretary) Ferguson; married Richard P. Meleski (a photographer), August 1, 1962; children: Richard, Corin, Michael, Steven, Nicholas, Melanie. *Education:* New Mexico State University, B.A., 1959; graduate study at University of New Mexico, 1964-75, University of Albuquerque, 1974. *Home and office:* 4821 Sunningdale Court N.E., Albuquerque, N.M. 87110.

CAREER: Las Cruces Public Schools, Las Cruces, N.M., teacher, 1959-62; Albuquerque Public Schools, Albuquerque, N.M., head of English department, 1962-75.

WRITINGS: Echoes of the Past: New Mexico's Ghost Towns, University of New Mexico Press, 1972. Contributor to *True West, Frontier Times,* and other periodicals.

WORK IN PROGRESS: Further research on the 2,000 ghost towns in New Mexico, with emphasis on Bernalillo County's ninety or more examples.

*   *   *

MELLERT, Robert B(oros) 1937-

PERSONAL: Born February 23, 1937, in Cleveland, Ohio; son of Herbert George and Gizella Marie (Boros) Mellert; married Ellen Simonetti (an educator), November 29, 1975. *Education:* John Carroll University, A.B. (summa cum laude), 1958; Universite de Fribourg, S.T.L. (magna cum laude), 1968; Fordham University, Ph.D., 1972. *Religion:* Roman Catholic. *Home:* 91 Center Ave., Keansburg, N.J. 07734. *Office:* Brookdale Community College, Lincroft, N.J. 07738.

CAREER: High school teacher, 1960-64; University of Dayton, Dayton, Ohio, assistant professor of religious studies, 1971-74; Brookdale Community College, Lincroft, N.J., assistant professor of philosophy, 1975—. Member of faculty at New York Institute of Credit, 1975—. Member of Yale University School of Medicine's task force on genetics and reproduction, 1974-75. *Member:* World Future Society, American Philosophical Association, American Society of Christian Ethics.

WRITINGS: What Is Process Theology?, Paulist/Newman, 1975. Contributor to *Process Studies.*

WORK IN PROGRESS: A book on the application of process philosophy to current environmental problems.

SIDELIGHTS: Mellert writes: "My introduction to process philosophy was not without difficulty. After my first graduate course in Whiteheadian thought I realized I still knew hardly even the terminology. But I continued to pursue the subject, because I felt that there was something important in what he seemed to be saying about reality. I am thankful now that I undertook the effort; it has given me a new understanding of the world and my place in it."

*   *   *

MELLOR, William Bancroft 1906-

PERSONAL: Born March 31, 1906, in Philadelphia, Pa.; son of W. Bancroft (an investment banker) and Elizabeth (Hanson) Mellor; married Helen Throckmorton, 1933 (divorced, 1940); married Edith Evoy, 1940 (divorced, 1947); married Mary Lee Latrobe Bateman, 1952 (divorced, 1957); children: Wendy (Mrs. G. E. Abbott), Elizabeth. *Education:* Attended University of Pennsylvania, University of Southern California, and University of California, Los Angeles. *Politics:* Conservative Republican. *Religion:* Episcopal. *Residence:* New York, N.Y. *Agent:* Oliver G. Swan, Julian Bach, Jr., 18 East 48th St., New York, N.Y. 10017.

CAREER: Reporter, feature writer, and editor for newspapers in New York, San Francisco, Sacramento, Philadelphia, Trenton (N.J.), and Washington, D.C., 1925-45; editorial, motion picture, and exhibit consultant to government agencies, 1953-68; contract writer for U.S. Information Agency and U.S. Department of Defense. Staff member of delegations to United Nations International Conferences on Peaceful Uses of Atomic Energy, 1958, 1964. *Awards, honors:* Mercantile Library Award, 1942, for newspaper articles.

WRITINGS: Sank Same, Howell-Soskin, 1944; *Patton: Fighting Man,* Putnam, 1946; *The Last Cavalier,* Putnam, 1971. Author of scripts for documentary and training films. Author of anonymous books for National Society of Professional Engineers and classified books for the U.S. Government. Contributor to magazines.

WORK IN PROGRESS: A book on the present state of the U.S. defense posture.

SIDELIGHTS: Mellor's award winning newspaper articles were written following a four-hour walk through the streets of Philadelphia dressed in a Nazi U-Boat commander's uniform—two months after the start of World War II—without a challenge.

*   *   *

MELWANI, Murli Das 1939-

PERSONAL: Born August, 1939, in Sind, Pakistan; son of Herkishendas S. (a businessman) and Putli (Samtani) Melwani; married Mona Tirathdas (a journalist), February 21, 1966; children: Arvind (son), Arpan (daughter). *Education:* St. Edmund's College, Shillong, India, B.A. (honors), 1958; Gauhati University, M.A., 1966. *Politics:* None. *Religion:* Hindu and Sikh. *Home:* 8 Ferndale, Shillong-1, Meghalaya 793001, India.

CAREER: Lalchand (retail textile store), Shillong, India, manager, 1959-69; Coca Cola Co., Shillong, distributor, 1969-71; Sankardev College, Shillong, lecturer in English, 1971—.

WRITINGS: Stories of a Salesman (short stories), Writer's Workshop (Calcutta), 1967; *Deep Roots* (three-act play), Writer's Workshop (Calcutta), 1970; *Critical Essays on Indo-Anglian Themes,* Writer's Workshop (Calcutta), 1971, 2nd edition, M/s Prakash Book Depot, in press. Contributor to Indian magazines and newspapers. Member of reviewing staff of *Books Abroad;* joint editor, *Forward,* 1960-61.

WORK IN PROGRESS: A novel, tracing the declining fortunes of a man who pins an almost gambler's faith on a local sport, archery; a collection of short stories, dealing with the paradox of violence in a professedly non-violent Gandhian country, and the prevalence of superstition (and even human sacrifice) in a nuclear-age India; research on the Indian short story in English, with publication expected to result.

SIDELIGHTS: Melwani writes of his work: "The stories in my first collection show the way in which some people live. Although set against the background of a small town, the stories focus on the universal aspects of human behaviour." About *Deep Roots* he says: "The theme of the play . . . is alienation. It portrays the dilemma of a young man who belongs neither to tradition nor to Western culture."

Of himself, he writes: "I'm of course the joker in the Sindhi pack. I've neither made tons of money nor written much . . . A fire in 1966 destroyed my shop and house. Biggest personal loss a small library (built up by books begged, borrowed, and stolen). Have started a new shop; doing well. Net result: materially, losses covered; spiritually poorer. Haven't written much after the fire. Can do it still—like a chore—but the old urge missing. . . ." Melwani has acted in and directed college drama festival plays. He received an acting award from St. Edmund's College in 1958.

*   *   *

MERRIAM, Harold G(uy)   1883-

PERSONAL: Born September 6, 1883, in Westminster, Mass.; son of Joel Harvey (a bookkeeper) and Anna P. (Mansfield) Merriam; married Doris Foote, August 3, 1915 (died March 23, 1970); children: Alison W. (Mrs. Philip W. Payne), Alan Parkhurst. *Education:* University of Wyoming, B.A., 1905; Oxford University, B.A., 1907, M.A., 1912; Harvard University, further graduate study, 1910; Columbia University, Ph.D., 1939. *Home:* 304 Westview Dr., Missoula, Mont.

CAREER: Whitman College, Walla Walla, Wash., instructor in English, 1908-10; Beloit College, Beloit, Wis., instructor in English, 1911-13; Reed College, Portland, Ore., assistant professor of English, 1913-19; Montana State University (now University of Montana), Missoula, professor of English, 1919-54, professor emeritus, 1954—, adjunct lecturer, 1954—, chairman of department, 1918-54, chairman of Division of Humanities, 1933-52. Visiting professor, University of Oregon, 1939-40, and visiting summer professor at University of Colorado, and San Diego State University; founder and first president of Montana Institute of the Arts, 1948-50; state director of writer's project for Works Progress Administration, 1937; former member of Missoula City Zoning Commission and Missoula County Library Board. *Wartime service:* Young Men's Christian Association volunteer in France, 1917-18.

MEMBER: American Association of University Professors. *Awards, honors:* Rhodes scholar at Oxford University, 1904-07; LL.D. from University of Wyoming, 1962; D.Litt. from University of Montana, 1963; Montana Arts Council Award, 1975; Montana Governor's Citation, 1975.

WRITINGS: (Editor) *Northwest Verse: An Anthology,* Caxton, 1931; *Edward Moxon: Publisher of Poets,* Columbia University Press, 1939; (editor with John E. Moore and Baxter Hathaway) *Readings for an Air Age: Training in Oral and Written Thought,* Macmillan, 1943; (editor) *Recollections of Charley Russell,* University of Oklahoma Press, 1963; *"The Frontier"* and *"The Frontier and Midland,"* privately printed, 1964; *Seed in the Soil,* Mountain Press, 1967; (editor) *Montana Adventure: Recollections of Frank Bird Linderman,* University of Nebraska Press, 1968; (editor) *Way Out West: Recollections and Tales,* University of Oklahoma Press, 1969; *The University of Montana: A History,* University of Montana Press, 1970; *Frontier Woman: The Story of Mary Ronan,* University of Montana Press, 1973. Editor and publisher of *Frontier,* 1920-33, and *Frontier and Midland,* 1933-39.

WORK IN PROGRESS: Editing Western manuscripts; compiling a book to be titled *Art in Montana.*

SIDELIGHTS: Merriam has traveled in Europe, Central and South America (especially Argentina), and the Caribbean.

*   *   *

MERRILL, Dean   1943-

PERSONAL: Born December 17, 1943, in Los Angeles, Calif.; son of D. Raymond (a minister) and Mary Lucille (Frantz) Merrill; married Grace LaVonne Danielson, June 25, 1966; children: Nathan, Rhonda, Tricia. *Education:* Chicago Bible College, Th.B., 1964; Syracuse University,

M.A., 1970. *Religion:* Christian. *Office:* David C. Cook Publishing Co., 850 North Grove Ave., Elgin, Ill. 60120.

CAREER: Campus Life (magazine), Carol Stream, Ill., various editorial positions, 1965-69 and 1971-73; Oral Roberts University, Tulsa, Okla., director of university information, 1970-71; Creation House, Inc. (publishers), Carol Stream, Ill., executive editor, 1973-74; David C. Cook Publishing Co., Elgin, Ill., manager of editorial research, and development, 1974—. *Member:* Evangelical Press Association, Associated Church Press.

WRITINGS: (With Ken Taylor) *The Jesus Book,* Tyndale, 1971; (with Taylor) *The Way,* Tyndale, 1972; (with Harold Myra) *Rock, Bach, and Superschlock,* A. J. Holman, 1972; (with Janet Lynn) *Peace and Love,* Creation House, 1973; (editor with Clayton Baumann) *Crowdbreakers,* Regal Books, 1974. Contributor to religious periodicals.

*   *   *

MERSMANN, James Frederick   1938-

PERSONAL: Born December 25, 1938, in Richmond, Kan.; son of Fred and Regina (Lickteig) Mersmann; married Karolyn Decker (a secretary), September 29, 1959; children: Dianne, Tim, Jeff, Susan. *Education:* University of Missouri at Kansas City, B.A., 1965; University of Kansas, M.A., 1967, Ph.D., 1972. *Home:* 929 Shades Glen Dr., Birmingham, Ala. 35226. *Office:* Department of English, University of Alabama, Birmingham, Ala. 35294.

CAREER: Mt. St. Scholastica College, Atchison, Kan., instructor in English, 1969-71; Benedictine College, Atchison, assistant professor of English, 1971-73; University of Alabama, Birmingham, assistant professor, 1973-75, associate professor of English, 1975—. *Military service:* U.S. Marine Corps, 1956-58. *Member:* Modern Language Association of America, American Association of University Professors, Southern Atlantic Modern Language Association. *Awards, honors:* Woodrow Wilson fellow at University of Kansas, 1965-66; National Endowment for the Humanities, summer seminar, 1973.

WRITINGS: Out of the Vietnam Vortex: A Study of Poets and Poetry Against the War, University Press of Kansas, 1974.

*   *   *

METZ, Robert (Henry)   1928-

PERSONAL: Born December 5, 1928, in Kingston, Pa.; son of Carl Adam (a minister) and Lucille Allen (Cobb) Metz; married Claire Delage, June, 1956 (divorced, June, 1975); married Elizabeth Ann Brady (a psychiatric nurse), July 5, 1975; children: (first marriage) Paul Charles, Melissa Ann, Andrew Michael. *Education:* Denison University, B.A., 1951; Case Western Reserve University, LL.B., 1955. *Residence:* New York, N.Y. *Office: New York Times,* 229 West 43rd St., New York, N.Y. 10036.

CAREER: New York Times, New York, N.Y., financial columnist, 1966—. *Military service:* U.S. Marine Corps, 1946-47. *Awards, honors:* Neiman fellow at Harvard University, 1965-66; Gerald Loeb Award for financial journalism, 1971.

WRITINGS: How to Shake the Money Tree, Putnam, 1966; *Franchising: How to Select a Business of Your Own,* Hawthorn, 1969; *CBS: Reflections in a Bloodshot Eye,* Playboy Press, 1975.

WORK IN PROGRESS: A book on NBC's "Today

Show," tentatively titled *Today Is Forever,* for Playboy Press; a self-help book on finance, *Jackpot!: All You Need to Know about Smart Money Investing in the New Wall Street,* for Simon & Schuster; a novel about mental hospitals, *Calamity in Cracker Land.*

AVOCATIONAL INTERESTS: Amateur theatrics.

* * *

METZGER, Walter P. 1922-

PERSONAL: Born May 15, 1922; son of Herman and Rae (Zuckerbrod) Metzger; married Loya Ferguson (a sociologist), June 23, 1961; children: Hilary, Gillian. *Education:* City College (now of the City University of New York), B.S.S., 1942; Columbia University, M.A., 1945; State University of Iowa, Ph.D., 1950. *Home:* 460 Riverside Dr., New York, N.Y. 10027. *Office:* Department of History, Columbia University, New York, N.Y. 10027.

CAREER: State University of Iowa, Iowa City, instructor in history, 1947-50; Columbia University, New York, N.Y., 1950—, began as instructor, professor of history, 1957—. Lecturer at Salzburg Seminar, summer, 1956; member of faculty of Danforth Foundation workshops, summers, 1968-70, 1974. Fellow of Center for Advanced Study in the Behavioral Sciences, 1956-57; member of board of scholars of Higher Education Research Institute (at University of California, Los Angeles), 1974—. Co-chairman of Council on Teaching and Learning of Myerson Commission (Ford Foundation), 1969-71; member of panel on benefits of higher education of National Academy of Sciences, 1972-75; member of panel on human resources of National Research Council, 1975—; member of advisory panel to Public Broadcasting System, 1974—.

MEMBER: American Association of University Professors, American Academy of Arts and Sciences (fellow), Phi Beta Kappa. *Awards, honors:* Grants from Louis Rabinowitz Foundation, 1952-53, Social Science Research Council, 1963, and Carnegie Corp., 1960, 1970.

WRITINGS: (With George L. Mosse) *Outline and Sources: History of Western Civilization,* W. C. Brown, 1948; (with May Brodbeck and James Grey) *American Non-Fiction, 1900-1950* (interpretive essays), Regnery, 1952; (with Richard Hofstadter) *Development of Academic Freedom in the United States,* Part II published as *Academic Freedom in the Age of the University,* both Columbia University Press, 1955; (with Paul Goodman and John R. Searle) *Freedom and Order in the University,* Western Reserve Press, 1967; (with Fritz Machlup) *Neutrality or Partisanship: A Dilemma of Academic Institutions,* Carnegie Foundation for the Advancement of Teaching, 1971.

Contributor: R. M. MacIver, editor, *Dilemmas of Youth,* Harper, 1961; Louis Gottschalk, editor, *Generalizations in the Writing of History,* University of Chicago Press, 1963; Owen A. Knorr and W. John Miner, editors, *Order and Freedom on the Campus,* Western Interstate Commission for Higher Education, 1965; John McCord, editor, *Dimensions of Academic Freedom,* University of Illinois Press, 1969; Immanuel Wallerstein and Paul Starr, editors, *University Crisis Reader II,* Vintage, 1971; Robert A. Altman and Carolyn M. Nyerly, editors, *The Public Challenge and the Campus Response,* Western Interstate Commission for Higher Education, 1971; William Keast, editor, *Faculty Tenure,* Jossey-Bass, 1973. Contributor of articles and reviews to academic journals.

MEYER, Mabel H. 1890(?)-1976

1890(?)—January 16, 1976; American welfare administrator, and author of books on religion for children. Obituaries: *New York Times,* January 18, 1976.

* * *

MEYERSON, Edward L(eon) 1904-

PERSONAL: Born September 14, 1904, in New York, N.Y.; son of Meyer and Celia (Reisman) Meyerson; married Alice Tannenbaum (a dramatic reader), June 29, 1930; children: Philip. *Education:* Attended Crane Junior College, 1921-23; Northwestern University, Diploma in Commerce, 1925; graduate study at Loyola University, Chicago, Ill., 1926-27, and New School for Social Research, 1953-57. *Home and office:* 1414 San Carlos Ave., Apt. 106, San Carlos, Calif. 94070.

CAREER: Licensed public accountant in New York, N.Y., 1928-66; Credit Exchange, New York, N.Y., credit consultant, 1966-71; Wadsworth Publishing Co., Belmont, Calif., editor and accounting and credit manager, 1971-74; writer, 1974—. Lecturer at City College (now City College of the City University of New York) and at Henry George School of Social Science, both during 1950's. Director of poetry workshops in San Carlos and Redwood City, Calif. Has given poetry readings in California and on radio programs. *Member:* World Poetry Society, Poetry Society of America, Academy of American Poets, New York Poetry Forum. *Awards, honors:* First prize from *Voices International,* 1968, for poem "Hurry, Feet, Hurry"; poetry prize from South and West literary festival, 1969, for "Haight-Ashbury"; second poetry prize from *South and West,* 1972, for "Liturgy for the Living"; first prize from *South and West,* 1974, for short story "Blood of Christ."

WRITINGS—Poetry: *Parcae,* Poets Press, 1934; *Flying Dust,* Poetry Publications, 1937; *The Seed Is Man,* William-Frederick, 1967; *Chameleon,* Branden Press, 1971; (editor) *San Carlos Poetry Workshop Anthology,* San Carlos Fine Arts Commission, Issue I, 1974, Issue II, 1975. Contributor to magazines and newspapers. Assistant book editor for *South and West.*

WORK IN PROGRESS: Liturgy for the Living: Selected Poems, 1960-1975.

* * *

MICHAELS, Leonard 1933-

PERSONAL: Born January 2, 1933, in New York, N.Y.; son of Leon (a barber) and Anna (Czeskies) Michaels; married Priscilla Older, June 30, 1966; children: Ethan, Jesse. *Education:* Attended New York University, 1949-53; University of Michigan, M.A., 1956, Ph.D., 1966. *Agent:* Lynn Nesbit, 1301 Avenue of the Americas, New York, N.Y. 10019. *Office:* Department of English, University of California, Berkeley, Calif. 94720.

CAREER: University of California, Davis, professor of English, 1966-68; University of California, Berkeley, professor of English, 1968—. *Awards, honors:* Guggenheim fellow, 1969; National Endowment for the Humanities fellow, 1970.

WRITINGS: Going Places, Farrar, Straus, 1969; *I Would Have Saved Them If I Could,* Farrar, Straus, 1975.

* * *

MIDTLYNG, Joanna 1927-

PERSONAL: Born October 5, 1927, in Deer Lodge,

Mont.; daughter of Robert and Lottie Nettle (Jones) Midtlyng. *Education:* University of Montana, B.A., 1950; University of Washington, Seattle, M.S., 1959; Indiana University, P.E.D., 1971; summer study at University of California, Berkeley, 1952, Springfield College, Springfield, Mass., 1961, University of Colorado, 1962, University of Illinois, 1963, University of Oregon, 1964. *Office:* Department of Women's Physical Education, Ball State University, Muncie, Ind. 47306.

CAREER: Custer County Junior College and High School, Miles City, Mont., physical educator, 1950-52; Deer Lodge City Schools, Deer Lodge, Mont., supervisor of physical education, 1952-57; Illinois State University, Normal, assistant professor of physical education, 1958-66; Indiana University, Bloomington, associate instructor in physical education, 1967-71; Ball State University, Muncie, Ind., associate professor of physical education, 1971—, associate director of aquatics, 1971—. Conference director of First National Conference on Professional Standards in Aquatics, American Association for Health, Physical Education and Recreation, 1970; director of National Aquatic Symposium, 1975.

MEMBER: American Association of University Professors; American Alliance of Health, Physical Education and Recreation; National Association for Physical Education of College Women; National Foundation of Health, Physical Education and Recreation; Midwest Association for Physical Education of College Women. *Awards, honors:* Dolphin Award from University of Oregon, 1970, and honor award, 1970, and service award, 1971, both from American Association for Health, Physical Education and Recreation, all for contributions to aquatics; service award from Association for Research, Administration, Professional Councils, and Societies, 1975.

WRITINGS: Swimming, Saunders, 1974. Editor of *Aquatic Guide,* 1973-75.

WORK IN PROGRESS: Another book on swimming, completion expected in 1977.

AVOCATIONAL INTERESTS: Snow skiing, equitation.

*   *   *

MIERS, Suzanne (Doyle)   1922-

PERSONAL: Born December 29, 1922, in Luebo, Zaire; U.S. citizen; daughter of Donald Bryce (a mining engineer) and Joyce (Kenedy) Doyle; married Richard C. H. Miers (a brigadier general in the British Army), November 26, 1949 (died, 1962); children: Caroline, Charles. *Education:* University of London, B.A. (honors), 1944, M.A., 1949, Ph.D., 1969. *Religion:* Episcopalian. *Home:* 3 Longmeadow Court, Route 1, Athens, Ohio 45701. *Office:* Department of History, Ohio University, Athens, Ohio 45701.

CAREER: University of London, Bedford College, London, England, assistant lecturer in history, 1946-48; University of Singapore, Singapore, lecturer in history, 1955-58; University of Wisconsin, Madison, visiting lecturer in African history, 1967-70; Ohio University, Athens, assistant professor, 1970-71, associate professor of African history, 1971—, director of African studies program, 1975—. Lecturer in history at University of Malaya, 1955-58.

MEMBER: American Historical Association, African Studies Association, Historical Association of Kenya. *Awards, honors:* Baker Award from Ohio University, 1972, for collection of oral traditions on the suppression of slavery and the slave trade; Social Science Research Council grant, 1972-73.

WRITINGS: (Contributor) Prosser Gifford and William Roger Louis, editors, *Britain and Germany in Africa: Imperial Rivalry and Colonial Rule,* Volume I, Yale University Press, 1967; *Britain and the Ending of the Slave Trade,* Longman, 1975. Contributor of articles and reviews to African studies journals.

WORK IN PROGRESS: Editing *Slavery in Africa,* with Igor Kopytoff; research for a book on the European powers and the ending of the slave trade and slavery in the twentieth century.

*   *   *

MIKOLAYCAK, Charles   1937-

PERSONAL: Born January 26, 1937, in Scranton, Pa.; son of John Anthony and Helen (Gruscelak) Mikolaycak; married Carole Kismaric (a picture editor and author), October 1, 1970. *Education:* Pratt Institute, B.F.A., 1958; New York University, further study, 1958-59. *Home:* 115 East 90th St., Apt. 1-E, New York, N.Y. 10028.

CAREER: Du Crot Studios, Hamburg, Germany, illustrator and designer, 1959; free-lance illustrator and designer, 1962—; Time-Life Books, New York, N.Y., designer, 1963—. Illustrations for three children's books are in Kerlan Collection at University of Minnesota; other illustrations are in permanent collection of International Youth Library, Munich, Germany. *Military service:* U.S. Army, 1960-62; became sergeant.

MEMBER: American Institute of Graphic Arts. *Awards, honors:* Books he designed or illustrated were included among the fifty best books of the year in American Institute of Graphic Arts Shows, 1967, 1968, 1970, 1973, 1974, and in Chicago Book Clinic Best of the Year Show, 1967, 1971, 1972; Printing Industries of America Graphic Design Awards for *Great Wolf and the Good Woodsman,* 1967, *Mourka, the Mighty Cat,* 1970, *Fabulous Century 1960-1970,* 1971, *Grand Canyon,* 1972, and *Great Divide,* 1973; Society of Illustrators Gold Medal for book art direction, 1970; *How the Hare Told the Truth About His Horse* was among the twenty-one books from which American Institute of Graphic Arts selected illustrations to enter in Biennial of Illustrations, Bratislava, 1973, and also was nominated for Caldecott Medal of American Library Association, 1973; *Shipwreck* and *The Feast Day* were included in American Institute of Graphic Arts Children's Book Show for 1973-74; *Shipwreck* was among twenty-seven books selected for Children's Book Showcase of Children's Book Council, 1975.

WRITINGS: (Adapter with wife, Carole Kismaric, from Norwegian folktale, and illustrator) *The Boy Who Tried to Cheat Death* (juvenile), Doubleday, 1971.

Illustrator—Adult books, published in Japanese: Feodor Dostoevski, *Crime and Punishment,* Kawade Shobo (Tokyo), 1966; Feodor Dostoevski, *The Brothers Karamazov,* Kawade Shobo, 1967.

Illustrator and designer—Children's books: Helen Hoover, *Great Wolf and the Good Woodsman,* Parents' Magazine Press, 1967; Brothers Grimm, *Little Red Riding Hood,* C. R. Gibson, 1968; Brothers Grimm, *Grimm's Golden Goose,* Random House, 1969; Jane Lee Hyndman under pseudonym Lee Wyndham, *Mourka, the Mighty Cat,* Parents' Magazine Press, 1969; Jane Lee Hyndman under pseudonym Lee Wyndham, *Russian Tales of Fabulous Beasts and Marvels,* Parents' Magazine Press, 1969.

Cynthia King, *In the Morning of Time,* Four Winds, 1970;

Barbara Rinkoff, *The Pretzel Hero*, Parents' Magazine Press, 1970; Eric Sundell, *The Feral Child*, Abelard-Schuman, 1971; Margaret Hodges, reteller, *The Gorgon's Head*, Little, Brown, 1972; Barbara K. Walker, *How the Hare Told the Truth About His Horse*, Parents' Magazine Press, 1972; Edwin Fadiman, Jr., *The Feast Day*, Little, Brown, 1973; Vera Cumberlege, *Shipwreck*, Follett, 1974; Mirra Ginsburg, translator, *How Wilka Went to Sea and Other Tales from West of the Urals*, Crown, 1975; Marion L. Starkey, *The Tall Man From Boston*, Crown, 1975.

Editor and designer: Ken Dallison, *When Zeppelins Flew*, Time-Life, 1969; Fred Freeman, *Duel of the Ironclads*, Time-Life, 1969; Paul Williams, *The Warrior Knights*, Time-Life, 1969.

WORK IN PROGRESS: Writing and illustrating two books, *The Rumor of Pavel and Paali* and *And So He Kissed Her*.

SIDELIGHTS: Mikolaycak writes: "I am an illustrator because I must illustrate, and I am a book designer because I love books. Obviously the field in which the two meet is the one which makes me most happy—children's books. I can usually find something in most stories which makes me excited; be it a locale or period of time requiring great research, or a sense of fantasy which permits me to exercise my own fantasies pictorially, or great writing which forces me to try to match it in visual images.

"I am particularly fond of epics and folk tales. I care not how many times they have been illustrated before; the challenge is to find the truth for myself and depict it. When I illustrate I am aware of many things; storytelling, graphic design, sequence of images and my own interests in which I can indulge. I never 'draw-down' to a projected audience. I feel children are most surprisingly capable of meeting a challenge and instinctively understand a drawing. Perhaps it will lead them to ask a question or wonder in silence—either will help them to learn or to extend themselves. I have experienced that if I am satisfied with one of my books, both children and adults will often get from it more than I ever realized I was putting into it.

AVOCATIONAL INTERESTS: Reading, theatre, films, travel.

BIOGRAPHICAL/CRITICAL SOURCES: Sam L. Sebesta and William Iverson, *Literature for Thursday's Child*, Science Research Associates, 1975.

* * *

MIKUS, Joseph A(ugust) 1909-

PERSONAL: Born July 3, 1909, in Kriva, Czechoslovakia; naturalized U.S. citizen, 1946; son of Joseph (a farmer) and Christina Mikus; married Renee Perreal (a professor), September 2, 1946; children: Isabelle. *Education:* Gymnasium Levoca, B.A., 1929; Bratislava University, J.D., 1934; George Washington University, M.Comparative Law, 1966. *Religion:* Roman Catholic. *Home:* 3619 Alton Pl. N.W., Washington, D.C. 20008. *Office:* Georgian Court College, Lakewood, N.J. 08701.

CAREER: Staff member in diplomatic and civil service in Czechoslovakia, 1935-48; free-lance writer and researcher in Paris, France, 1948-52; guide and interpreter for U.S. Department of State, and translator in Washington, D.C., 1952-59; St. John's University, Jamaica, N.Y., assistant professor of history and international relations, 1959-61; law librarian, guide, and interpreter in Washington, D.C., 1961-68; Georgian Court College, Lakewood, N.J., pro-

fessor of history, 1968—. *Member:* American Political Science Association, American Society of International Law, American Historical Association.

WRITINGS: (Editor) *Conference d'information du mouvement federal de l'Europe centrale*, [Paris], 1950, *La Slovaquie: Individualite politique de l'Europe centrale*, Centre de documentation internationale, 1952; *The Three Slovak Bishops; Their Struggle for God and Slovakia Until Their Condemnation by the Communists in 1951*, translated by Daniel Drab, Slovak Catholic Federation of America, 1953; *La Slovaquie dans le drame de l'Europe: Histoire politique de 1918 a 1950*, Les Iles d'or, 1955; *Slovakia: A Political History, 1918-1950*, translated from French by Mikus and Kathryn Day Wyatt, Marquette University Press, 1963; *V Krazoch Dediny* (short stories), Jednota, 1968; (with J. A. Kirschbaum) *Slovakia: Historical and Cultural Background*, Slovak World Congress, 1971; *Pride in Slovak Origin*, Jednota, 1973.

WORK IN PROGRESS: Slovakia: A Political Reality in Central Europe; International Law: Between Power Politics and World Law; Foreign Policy and Diplomacy; Russian Mentality.

* * *

MILES, Bebe (Louise) 1924-

PERSONAL: Born March 18, 1924, in New York, N.Y.; daughter of Philip J. (an insurance executive) and Louise (a nurse; maiden name, Stephan) Priore; married Robert T. Miles (a safety engineer), August 29, 1946; children: Diane, Victoria (Mrs. Richard Smith), Robin. *Education:* Syracuse University, B.A. (magna cum laude), 1945. *Politics:* Republican. *Religion:* Christian. *Home address:* Philip Circle, R.D. 4, Doylestown, Pa. 18901.

CAREER: Binghamton Sun, Binghamton, N.Y., reporter, 1945-46; Syracuse University, Syracuse, N.Y., editor of alumni magazine, 1946-47; free-lance writer, 1947-65; Bryn Mawr Hospital, Bryn Mawr, Pa., in public relations, 1965-66; Bucks County Bar Association, Doylestown, Pa., in public relations, 1966—. Employed in public relations by W. Atlee Burpee, 1972-73; member of staff of Bowman's Hill State Wildflower Preserve.

MEMBER: Garden Writers Association of America (member of executive board, 1974-76), Pennsylvania Horticultural Society, Bucks County Audubon Society, Bucks County Historical Society, Doylestown Nature Club (member of executive board), Bowman's Hill State Wildflower Preserve (member, executive committee), Phi Beta Kappa, Alpha Chi Omega, Syracuse University Alumnae Association. *Awards, honors:* Award from Garden Federation of Pennsylvania, 1971, for *Bluebells and Bittersweet*.

WRITINGS: The Wonderful World of Bulbs, Van Nostrand, 1963; *Bluebells and Bittersweet*, Van Nostrand, 1970; *Designing with Natural Materials*, Van Nostrand, 1975. Contributor to gardening magazines and to *Ranger Rick* (children's nature magazine).

WORK IN PROGRESS: Bulb Guide, for Vineyard Books (New York); *Wildflowers*, for Hawthorn.

* * *

MILES, Dorien K(lein) 1915-
(Svlva Miles)

PERSONAL: Born September 17, 1915, in Kimball, Neb.; daughter of Ben (a petroleum distributor) and Frances (a teacher; maiden name, Houston) Klein; married Delbert L.

Miles (chief clerk of post office), August 20, 1937; children: Rosalee (Mrs. James Hughes), William, Janis (Mrs. Douglas Worrell), Karen (Mrs. Edward Berney, Jr.), Kathleen (Mrs. Artur Hohl), Robert. *Education:* Attended Kearney State College, 1933-34, and Olympic Community College, 1955-56. *Politics:* "Democrat, not always following party line." *Religion:* Baptist. *Home:* 1623 Jacobsen Blvd., Bremerton, Wash. 98310.

CAREER: Manette Community Church, Bremerton, Wash., secretary, 1965-74; clerk at Manette Post Office, 1974—. *Member:* Pacific Northwest Writers Conference, Washington Poets Association, Seattle Free Lances, Kitsap Writers Club (president, 1973-74). *Awards, honors:* Second place in novel competition from Pacific Northwest Writers Conference, 1970, for *Shadow over Beauclaire;* honorable mention in free verse from National League of American Pen Women, 1974, in children's poetry, 1975.

WRITINGS: (Under pseudonym Sylva Miles; with Sylva Mularchyk) *Shadow Over Beauclaire* (novel), Bouregy, 1975. Contributor of more than twenty poems, short stories, and articles to *Parents Magazine* and other periodicals.

WORK IN PROGRESS: A collection of light and serious verse, *Changing Seasons;* a mystery novel, *Heartbreak House,* completion expected in 1976; a historical novel tentatively titled *Jonathan Houston.*

* * *

MILES, George C(arpenter) 1904-1975

September 30, 1904—November, 1975; American numismatist, epigraphist, educator, and author of books in his field. Obituaries: *AB Bookman's Weekly,* January 26, 1976.

* * *

MILLER, Beulah Montgomery 1917-

PERSONAL: Born September 27, 1917, in Kansas City, Mo.; daughter of William T. (in railroading) and Martha (Calhoun) Montgomery; married George Byron Miller (a pharmacist), January 13, 1937 (deceased); children: Mary Belle (Mrs. Steven Varen). *Education:* Part-time student at University of California at Los Angeles, 1940-65. *Politics:* Republican. *Religion:* Protestant. *Home:* 107 Blue Skies Village, Rancho Mirage, Calif. 92270. *Agent:* Faustina Orner Associates, Inc., 7046 Hollywood Blvd., Los Angeles, Calif. 90028.

CAREER: Worked with pharmacist husband in store he owned (Miller Drugs, Santa Monica, Calif.), as bookkeeper, purchasing agent, and saleswoman, from 1938 until his death; novelist.

WRITINGS: The Fires of Heaven (novel), Douglas-West, 1974. Contributor of short stories to *Liberty* and other national magazines.

WORK IN PROGRESS: A nonfiction book, *Young Land,* about homesteading in Colorado in 1925; two novels, *The Savage Nest,* focusing on the population explosion when the impact was at its peak in the 1960's, and *Witches Hair,* about a dustbowl family in California in the early days of World War II.

* * *

MILLER, Hugh 1937-

PERSONAL: Born April 27, 1937, in Wishaw, Lanarkshire, Scotland; son of James Weir (an engineer) and Alice (Waddell) Miller; married Anne McNeil, 1958 (divorced, 1966); married Margaret Elizabeth Jenson, January 25, 1967; children: (first marriage) Lesley (daughter); (second marriage) James, Rachel. *Education:* Attended University of Glasgow, Stow College, and London Polytechnic. *Home:* 40 St. John's Court, Warwick, Warwickshire, England. *Office:* 4 Bertic Ter., Leamington Spa, Warwickshire, England.

CAREER: Scottish Independent Television, Glasgow, editorial assistant, 1958-60; technical and photographic assistant to a forensic pathologist at University of Glasgow, 1960-62; Unique Studios, London, England, manager, 1963-64, co-owner, 1965-70; writer, 1972—. Former trustee of Jude Trust.

*WRITINGS—*Novels: *The Open City,* New English Library, 1973; *Drop Out,* New English Library, 1973; *Short Circuit,* New English Library, 1973; *Kingpin,* New English Library, 1974; *Double Deal,* New English Library, 1974; *Feedback,* New English Library, 1974; *Ambulance,* St. Martin's 1975; *The Dissector,* New English Library, in press.

Books for sleight-of-hand and paranormalist entertainers: *A Pocketful of Miracles,* Unique Books, 1969; *Secrets of Gambling,* Unique Books, 1970; *Professional Presentations,* Tannen, 1971; *Koran's Legacy,* Repro 72, 1973.

Author of scripts for instructional films: "Basic Post Mortem Technique," Advent Productions (London), 1962; "Close-Up with Cards," Davis Films (Chicago), 1971. Also author of documentary filmscript, "Levels," 1973.

Editor, *Bulletin,* 1967-69, *Gen,* 1968-71.

WORK IN PROGRESS: The Saviour, an allegory concerning the rise of a pop-philosophy cult figure, publication by New English Library expected in 1977.

SIDELIGHTS: Miller writes: "The drive central to all my fiction is an impulse towards presenting the reader with a balanced amalgam of entertainment, enlightenment, and concern. The colorations and distortions of professional and emotional commitments, produced in ordinary people, provide a foundation for viable fiction; the same stresses, working on extraordinary people, can make a fascinating additive to the structure. . . . I make it my personal concern to ensure—as best I can—that the quality of escape in my work is such that readers are not merely anaesthetised for a time, but emerge with some change of outlook applicable to everyday existence." *Avocational interests:* Photography, hi-fi.

BIOGRAPHICAL/CRITICAL SOURCES: Coventry Telegraph, August 28, 1974.

* * *

MILLER, Lanora 1932-
(Lanora F. Welzenbach)

PERSONAL: Born November 8, 1932, in Albia, Iowa; daughter of Blaine Edmund (a farmer) and Velma (Wilkin) Miller; married Donald E. Welzenbach (an editor), December 9, 1953; children: Michael, Christopher, Karl, Erica, Johanna. *Education:* Attended Park College, University of Iowa, George Washington University, and University of Virginia. *Politics:* Democrat. *Home:* 3405 North 15th St., Arlington, Va. 22201. *Agent:* Marian McNamara, A. Watkins, Inc., 77 Park AVe., New York, N.Y. 10016. *Office:* National Association of College and University Business Officers, Washington, D.C.

CAREER: Democrat, Davenport, Iowa, society reporter and feature writer, 1952-53; National Association of College and University Business Officers, Washington, D.C., editor, 1973—. Member: Mystery Writers of America, Authors Guild of Authors League of America, Common Cause. Awards, honors: Second prize in national contest sponsored by Writer's Digest and Lancer Books, 1971, for Quickthorn.

WRITINGS—Gothic novels: Quickthorn, Ace, 1975; The Devil's Due, Ace, 1975. Contributor of articles and short stories for adults and children to magazines, under pseudonyms.

WORK IN PROGRESS: Two more Gothic novels, one of them for Ace.

AVOCATIONAL INTERESTS: Travel (has lived in the Far East and England), reading, writing, studying, swimming, listening to music.

* * *

MILLER, Mary Beth 1942-
(Mary Beth)

PERSONAL: Born December 18, 1942, in Louisville, Ky.; daughter of Chester F. (a printer) and Nellie (Logston) Miller. Education: Kentucky School for the Deaf, Diploma, 1961; Gallaudet College, B.A., 1967; Connecticut College, M.A., 1974. Residence: New York, N.Y. Office: Deafness Research and Training Center, New York University, 80 Washington Sq. E., New York, N.Y. 10003.

CAREER: Actress with National Theatre of the Deaf and Little Theatre of the Deaf, Waterford, Ct., 1967-74; New York University, New York, N.Y., associate research scientist at Deafness Research and Training Center, 1974—. Awards, honors: Member of National Theatre of the Deaf troupe which received Mademoiselle Special Recognition Award.

WRITINGS: (Under name Mary Beth; with Remy Charlip and others) Handtalk: An ABC of Finger Spelling and Sign Language (juvenile), Parents' Magazine Press, 1974.

WORK IN PROGRESS: More books on sign language for young people.

SIDELIGHTS: Mary Beth Miller wrote: "My life was never dull or lonely. Coming from deaf parents, our lives were filled with memories of storytelling in Sign Language, Christmas carols and the togetherness of a family. My world may be silenced by sickness but there's music inside me playing all day and I enjoy life tremendously."

* * *

MILLETT, Fred B(enjamin) 1890-1976

1890—January 1, 1976; American educator, literary critic, and author or compiler of books on education and other topics. Obituaries: New York Times, January 2, 1976.

* * *

MILLSTEIN, Rose Silverman 1903(?)-1975
(Rose Silverman)

1903(?)—November 10, 1975; Russian-born American journalist, columnist, playwright, and biographer. Obituaries: Washington Post, November 15, 1975.

* * *

MILNE, Christopher 1920-

PERSONAL: Born August 21, 1920, in London, England; son of A(lan) A. (author of "Winnie the Pooh" series) and Dorothy (de Selincourt) Milne; married Lesley de Selincourt (a bookseller), July 24, 1948; children: Clare. Education: Trinity College, Cambridge, B.A. (honours), 1947. Home: Embridge Forge, Dartmouth, Devonshire, England. Agent: Curtis Brown Ltd., 60 East 56th St., New York, N.Y. 10022.

CAREER: Harbour Bookshop, Dartmouth, England, owner, 1951—. Military service: British Army, Royal Engineers, 1941-46; served in the Middle East and Italy; became lieutenant.

WRITINGS: The Enchanted Places (autobiography), Methuen, 1974, Dutton, 1975.

SIDELIGHTS: Milne is the original Christopher Robin of his father's much-loved writings on "Winnie the Pooh."

* * *

MILNER, Lucille Bernheimer 1888(?)-1975

1888(?)—August 14, 1975; American civil liberties union founder and executive, and author of autobiographical account. Obituaries: New York Times, August 18, 1975.

* * *

MISHRA, Vishwa Mohan 1937-

PERSONAL: Born November 12, 1937, in India; U.S. citizen; son of Sheoneth Mishra; married Ruth Hutchins, 1960 (died, 1974); children: Aneil Kumar, Allan Kumar, Anand Kumar. Education: Patna University, B.A. (honors), 1954, M.A. (psychology), 1956; University of Georgia, M.A. (journalism), 1958; University of Minnesota, Ph.D., 1969. Home: 2176 Donovan Pl., Okemos, Mich. 48864. Office: School of Journalism, Michigan State University, East Lansing, Mich. 48824.

CAREER: Hindusthan Samachar Ltd. (wire service), India, staff reporter, 1950-56; Communique, Los Angeles, Calif., associate editor, 1958-59; KTIS (radio station), Minneapolis, Minn., program moderator, 1959-60; India for Christ, Inc., Minneapolis, Minn., president, executive director, minister, and trustee, 1960-65; University of Oklahoma, Norman, assistant professor of journalism, 1968-69; Michigan State University, East Lansing, assistant professor, 1969-72, associate professor of journalism, 1972—, associate director of International Communication Summer Seminar in Yugoslavia, 1972, director of America for Effective Law Enforcement Media Project, 1972-73, acting director of College of Communication Arts Research Center, spring, 1973. Visiting scholar at Institute of Social Research, University of Michigan, 1971. President of Communication Consultants International, Inc., 1975—. Director of market research, Panax Corp., 1975.

MEMBER: International Communication Association, American Association of University Professors, Society for International Development, Radio-Television News Directors Association, Kappa Tau Alpha, Sigma Delta Chi, East Lansing Rotary Club. Awards, honors: National Science Foundation fellow in political communications, 1969; Ford Foundation research grant, 1971-72, 1973.

WRITINGS: Communication and Modernization in Urban Slums, Asia Publishing House, 1972; The Basic News Media and Techniques, Asia Publishing House, 1972; Mass Media and Modernization in South Asia: A Selected Bibliography, Asian Studies Center, Michigan State University, 1973. Contributor to journals in his field.

WORK IN PROGRESS: Co-authoring *Mass Communication Systems: An Interaction Analysis;* writing on communication and television network news and law enforcement.

SIDELIGHTS: Mishra is competent in French, Spanish, Sanskrit, Urdu, and German.

* * *

MITCHNER, Stuart 1938-

PERSONAL: Born October 27, 1938, in Hutchinson, Kan.; son of Robert W. (a professor of English) and Ann (Patterson) Mitchner; married Leslie Strock (a free-lance editor), October 8, 1966. *Education:* Indiana University, A.B., 1960; Rutgers University, graduate study, 1968—. *Home and office:* 69 Patton Ave., Princeton, N.J. 08540. *Agent:* James Brown Associates, 22 East 60th St., New York, N.Y. 10022.

CAREER: Eighth Street Bookshop, New York, N.Y., clerk, 1961; Paper Editions Corp. (paperback wholesaler), San Francisco, Calif., warehouse foreman, 1961-62; W. W. Norton & Co., New York, N.Y., college traveler, 1964-65; writer. Teacher of course in composition at Rutgers University, 1976. *Member:* American Film Institute, Modern Language Association of America.

WRITINGS: Let Me Be Awake, (novel), Crowell, 1959; *Indian Action* (travel memoir), Little, Brown, 1976. Contributor to *Folio* and *Partisan Review.*

WORK IN PROGRESS: An "unconventional study" of American movies in the twenties, thirties, and forties; a sequel to *Indian Action,* Covering adventures in the Middle East, North Africa, India, and the United States; a dissertation on plays by Marlowe and Shakespeare.

* * *

MITRANY, David 1888-1975

January 1, 1888—1975; Hungarian-born British political scientist, economist, educator, and author of books in his field. Obituaries: *AB Bookman's Weekly,* September 22-29, 1975.

* * *

MOHAN, Peter John 1930-

PERSONAL: Surname is pronounced *Mo*-en; born April 26, 1930, in Reading, England; son of John Leslie (a teacher) and Dorothy (a teacher; maiden name, Angel) Mohan; married Christine Bakel (a teacher); children: Paul. *Education:* Bognor Regis College of Education, teacher's certificate, 1954. *Politics:* None. *Religion:* None. *Home and office:* Newhaven, Marsh Lane, Easton-in-Gordano, Bristol BS20 0NH, England.

CAREER: Spent four years as a market gardener, 1946-49; primary school teacher in Faringdon, Berkshire, England, 1954-61, and in Chagford, Devon, England, 1961-62; British School, Montevideo, Uruguay, teacher of general subjects, 1963-64, deputy headmaster of junior school, 1964-65, headmaster of junior school, 1965-66; St. Anne's Park Junior School, Bristol, England, teacher of general subjects, 1967-69; Knowle Junior School, Bristol, deputy headmaster, 1969-70. *Military service:* Royal Air Force, 1949-51. *Member:* National Anglers' Council, British Carp Study Group (founder, 1969; secretary, 1969—), Carp Anglers' Association (founder, 1975; secretary, 1975—).

WRITINGS: All About Carp Fishing, IPC, 1970; *Carp for Everyone,* David & Charles, 1972; *Cypry: The Story of a Carp* (fictionalized natural history), Pelham Books, 1973; *Table Tennis for All,* David & Charles, in press; *Carp,* Allan, in press. Contributor to *Angling Times, Anglers Mail, Angling, Fisherman,* and *Sheffield Angling Telegraph.* Contributor of regular column to *Coarse Fisherman,* 1975—. Editor of *Carp,* 1969—, and *Carp Anglers Association News,* 1975—.

WORK IN PROGRESS: A fishing book, *The Redmire Story;* a natural history book.

SIDELIGHTS: Mohan lived in Uruguay four years and represented that country in the World Table Tennis Championships in Stockholm, Sweden, in 1967. He has won more than forty trophies for table tennis. He has visited more than twenty-three countries and drives at least thirty thousand miles a year. *Avocational interests:* Fishing, table tennis, tennis, bridge, chess, rapid reading, travel.

* * *

MOLDAFSKY, Annie 1930-

PERSONAL: Born September 4, 1930, in Hartford, Conn.; daughter of Jacob (in real estate) and Esther (Folander) Siegelbaum; married Robert Moldafsky (an industrial designer), March 29, 1952; children: Jon, Jamie (daughter). *Education:* Stephens College, A.A., 1950; also attended Connecticut State Teachers College, Washington University, St. Louis, Mo., and Northwestern University. *Residence:* Glencoe, Ill. *Agent:* Toni Mendez, Inc., 140 East 56th St., New York, N.Y. 10022.

CAREER: Writer. Course coordinator for Loop College, 1974-75. Member of board of trustees of Chicago International Program, 1969-74, Council of International Programs (Cleveland), 1973-74, and Glencoe Public Library, 1975-81; member of Children's Reading Roundtable, Institute of International Education, Chicago Council on Foreign Relations, and Friends of the Chicago Public Library. *Member:* American Society of Journalists and Authors, Chicago Women in Publishing.

WRITINGS: The Good Buy Book, Swallow Press, 1974. Work has been anthologized in children's books, including *The Purple Turtle,* edited by Justin Fishbein, Science Research Associates, 1966; *Cracking the Code,* edited by Glen H. Phillips, Science Research Associates, 1968. Contributor to popular magazines, including *House Beautiful,* and to newspapers. Contributing editor of *Working Craftsman.*

WORK IN PROGRESS: The Put It All Together Book.

* * *

MOLEY, Raymond (Charles) 1886-1975

PERSONAL: Born September 27, 1886, in Berea, Ohio; son of Felix James and Agnes (Fairchild) Moley; married Eva Dall, August 14, 1916 (divorced); married Frances S. Hebard, January 15, 1949; children: (first marriage) Malcolm and Raymond (twins); (second marriage) Nell. *Education:* Baldwin-Wallace College, Ph.B., 1906; Oberlin College, A.M., 1913; Columbia University, Ph.D., 1918. *Politics:* Democrat until 1936; Republican thereafter. *Residence:* Phoenix, Ariz.

CAREER: Superintendent of public schools in Olmsted Falls, Ohio, 1907-10; lived in New Mexico and Colorado, 1910-12; high school history teacher in Cleveland, Ohio, 1912-14; Western Reserve University (now Case Western Reserve University), Cleveland, Ohio, instructor, 1916-18, assistant professor of politics, 1918-19; Cleveland Foundation, Cleveland, Ohio, director, 1919-23; Columbia University, New York, N.Y., associate professor of government, 1923-28, professor of public law, 1928-54; writer. Involved in Franklin Delano Roosevelt's election to governership of New York, 1928, and campaign speech writer and adviser for his presidential campaign; appointed assistant U.S. Secretary of State, 1933; left Roosevelt administration in 1933. Director of Americanization activities for Ohio State Council of Defense, 1918-19; research director of New York State Crime Commission, 1926-27, and New York State Commission on the Administration of Justice, 1931-33. Radio commentator for American Broadcasting Co. (ABC), 1945. Adviser to Lincoln Foundation; trustee, Claremont Men's College, Baldwin-Wallace College, and Vermont College.

AWARDS, HONORS: LL.D. from Baldwin-Wallace College and Washington and Jefferson College, both 1933, Claremont Men's College, 1966, and University of Hartford, 1970; Litt.D. from Miami University, Oxford, Ohio; D.C.L. from Whitman College, 1950.

WRITINGS: Lessons in American Citizenship for Men and Women Preparing for Naturalization, Cleveland Citizens Bureau, 1919, 10th edition, 1930; (with Huldah Florence Cook) *Lessons in Democracy: For Use in Adult Immigrant Classes,* Macmillan, 1919; *Parties, Politics, and People: Four Lectures to the League of Women Voters of Cleveland,* League of Women Voters of Cleveland, 1921, revised edition, National League of Women Voters, 1923; (with Helen M. Rocca) *The Outline of Government in the United States,* National League of Women Voters, 1922, revised edition, 1925; *Politics and Criminal Prosecution,* Minton, Balch & Co., 1929, reprinted, Arno, 1974.

Our Criminal Courts, Minton, Balch & Co., 1930, Arno, 1974; *Tribunes of the People: The Past and Future of the New York Magistrates' Courts,* Yale University Press, 1932; *Are We Movie-Made?,* Macy-Masius, 1938; *After Seven Years: A Political Analysis of the New Deal,* Harper, 1939, reprinted, Da Capo Press, 1972; *The Hays Office,* Bobbs-Merrill, 1945, reprinted, Jerome S. Ozer, 1971; *Twenty-Seven Masters of Politics: In a Personal Perspective,* Funk, 1949, reprinted, Greenwood Press, 1972.

How to Keep Our Liberty: A Program for Political Action, Knopf, 1952; *The American Century of John C. Lincoln,* Duell, Sloan & Pearce, 1962; *The Republican Opportunity,* Duell, Sloan & Pearce, 1962; *The Republican Opportunity in 1964,* Duell, Sloan & Pearce, 1964; (with Elliott A. Rosen) *The First New Deal,* Harcourt, 1966; *The American Legion Story,* foreword by J. Edgar Hoover, Duell, Sloan & Pearce, 1966, reprinted, Greenwood Press, 1975; *Daniel O'Connell: Nationalism Without Violence,* Fordham Publishing, 1974.

Author of reports published by Cleveland Foundation, National Crime Commission, Missouri Association for Criminal Justice, American Enterprise Association, and others. Weeky comment columns distributed by McNaught Newspaper Syndicate, 1933-41, and Associated Newspapers beginning in 1941. Contributor to magazines and newspapers. Founder and editor of national weekly magazine, *Today,* 1933-37; upon merger with, and adoption of title of *Newsweek* in 1937, became associate editor, and author of weekly column "Perspective," 1937-68.

WORK IN PROGRESS: Memoirs, from period encompassing McKinley's Presidency.

SIDELIGHTS: Moley became prominent in politics when he was chosen by Presidential hopeful Franklin D. Roosevelt to head the group of political and economic advisers that soon became known as the "Brain Trust." Moley is credited with having coined the term "New Deal."

OBITUARIES: New York Times, February 19, 1975; *Newsweek,* March 3, 1975; *Time,* March 3, 1975; *AB Bookman's Weekly,* March 17, 1975; *Current Biography,* April, 1975.*

(Died February 18, 1975, in Phoenix, Ariz.)

* * *

MONDAY, James 1951-

PERSONAL: Born January 24, 1951, in San Francisco, Calif.; son of Walter Johnston (an engineer) and Ruth (Atkins) Monday. *Education:* Antioch College, B.A., 1972. *Office:* St. Heironymous Press, P.O. Box 9431, Berkeley, Calif. 94709.

CAREER: Printer for St. Heironymous Press, Berkeley, Calif.

WRITINGS: (With Jeffery Monday) *Blue Prints* (poems), St. Heironymous Press, 1972; *Tesseract* (poems), St. Heironymous Press, 1974.

WORK IN PROGRESS: A screenplay "The Enormous Room," adapted from Cummings' novel; a third book of poems, *Colour by Way of Spontaneous Combustion.*

* * *

MONKKONEN, Eric H(enry) 1942-

PERSONAL: Surname is pronounced *Monk*-ko-nen; born August 17, 1942, in Kansas City, Kan.; son of Hugo W. (a union official) and Kathrine (a secretary; maiden name, Hazen) Monkkonen; married Judith Willmmson (a librarian), 1964; children: Pentti. *Education:* University of Minnesota, B.A., 1964, M.A., 1968, Ph.D., 1973. *Politics:* Liberal. *Religion:* None. *Office:* Department of History, University of California, Los Angeles, Calif. 90024.

CAREER: University of North Carolina at Charlotte, assistant professor of urban history, beginning 1973; now member of staff of department of history, University of California, Los Angeles. *Member:* American Historical Association, Organization of American Historians, Social Science History Association.

WRITINGS: The Dangerous Class: Crime and Poverty in Columbus, Ohio, 1865-1885, Harvard University Press, 1975. Contributor to professional journals.

WORK IN PROGRESS: The Police and the Dangerous Class: Their Growth and Change, 1860-1920, completion expected in 1977.

* * *

MOODY, Ernest A(ddison) 1903-1975

September 27, 1903—December 21, 1975; American educator and author, editor, or translator of books on medieval philosophy and other topics. Obituaries: *New York Times,* December 23, 1975. (See index for previous *CA* sketch)

* * *

MOONEY, Elizabeth C(omstock) 1918-

PERSONAL: Born February 8, 1918, in Rome, N.Y.; daughter of Edward Hulett and Elizabeth (Baker) Comstock; married Booth Mooney (a writer), March 9, 1946; children: Edward, Joan. *Education:* Smith College, B.A., 1939. *Politics:* Democrat. *Religion:* Episcopal. *Home:* 5709

Overlea Rd., Washington, D.C. 20016. *Agent:* Paul R. Reynolds, Inc., 12 East 41st St., New York, N.Y. 10017.

CAREER: Employed in war-related secretarial positions, 1939-43; *Utica Press and Observer-Dispatch,* Utica, N.Y., reporter, 1943-45, bureau chief, 1945-46; free-lance writer, 1946—. *Member:* English Speaking Union, Kenwood Golf Club (Washington, D.C.).

WRITINGS—All for young people: *Jane Addams,* Follett, 1968; *The Mystery of the Narrow Land,* Follett, 1969; *The Sandy Shoes Mystery,* Lippincott, 1970. Author of "The Land and People of Asia," a film strip, National Geographic Society, and "Rats in the Suburbs," a television script adapted from one of her own published stories, Multimedia, 1974. Contributor to magazines, including *Smithsonian, Ladies' Home Journal, Yankee, Washingtonian,* and *Maryland.*

WORK IN PROGRESS: A juvenile book, tentatively titled *The Biggest Toy in the World;* a book on ballooning; a novel on a kidnapping; a book on the National Zoo; a book on insomnia, with Richard Wyatt.

SIDELIGHTS: Elizabeth Mooney writes: "I went into writing quite naturally from newspaper reporting. When I married and the children were young I wrote children's books because I understood young people. When they grew up and started making their telephone calls upstairs, I went back to freelance journalism which took me out into the world again and kept me in contact with people."

* * *

MOORE, Bob 1948-

PERSONAL: Born January 28, 1948, in Staten Island, N.Y.; son of Barnett M., Sr. and Lillian (Nelson) Moore; married Carol Peckio (a teacher), June 5, 1971. *Education:* Brooklyn College of the City University of New York, B.A., 1970; Brooklyn Law School, J.D., 1974. *Home:* 2235 East 57th Pl., Brooklyn, N.Y. 11234.

CAREER: Public school teacher in Brooklyn, N.Y., 1970-75; attorney in Brooklyn, N.Y., 1975—.

WRITINGS: Welcome to #57: Four Years of Teaching and Learning in Bedford-Stuyvesant, Putnam, 1975.

WORK IN PROGRESS: An authorized biography of Albert Shanker, president of American Federation of Teachers and United Federation of Teachers, and a vice-president of the American Federation of Labor-Congress of Industrial Organizations (AFL-CIO).

* * *

MOORE, Carman L(eroy) 1936-

PERSONAL: Born October 8, 1936, in Lorain, Ohio; son of Claude Leroy (a laborer) and Jessie (Franklin) Moore; married Susan Stern (a social worker), November 22, 1963; children: Martin Douglass, Justin Charles. *Education:* Ohio State University, B.Sc., 1958; Juilliard School of Music, M.Sc., 1966. *Home:* 65 West 90th St., New York, N.Y. 10024.

CAREER: Composer. Member of information staff, New York (City) Public Library, 1958-63; columnist and critic for *Village Voice,* 1965—. Member of staff, Manhattanville College, 1968-71; assistant professor of music history, Yale University, 1969-71, Queen's College of the City University of New York, 1971-74, and Brooklyn College of the City University of New York, 1971-74. *Member:* American Society of Composers, Authors and Publishers, Society of Black Composers, American Music Center.

WRITINGS: Somebody's Angel Child: The Story of Bessie Smith, Crowell, 1970; *Black Music History,* Doubleday, 1976. Contributor to *New York Times, Saturday Review, Eye Magazine,* and *Vogue.*

AVOCATIONAL INTERESTS: Tennis, travel.

BIOGRAPHICAL/CRITICAL SOURCES: New York Sunday Times, January 21, 1975.

* * *

MOORE, Marcia 1928-

PERSONAL: Born May 22, 1928, in Cambridge, Mass.; daughter of Robert Lowell (a businessman) and Eleanor (Turner) Moore; married Mark Douglas (a writer), January 11, 1966 (separated, 1972); children: Louisa Roof, Christopher Roof, Jonathan Roof. *Education:* Radcliffe College, B.A., 1960. *Home:* 2121 Villa Heights Rd., Pasadena, Calif. 91107. *Agent:* Robin Moore, 279 Sturgis Highway, Westport, Conn. 06880.

CAREER: Writer. Lecturer and teacher of yoga, astrology, parapsychology, and metaphysics. Has appeared on national television programs, including "The Virginia Graham Show," "The Mike Douglas Show," and "The David Susskind Show." *Member:* Phi Beta Kappa.

WRITINGS: (With Mark Douglas) *Diet, Sex, and Yoga,* Arcane, 1966; (with Douglas) *Yoga: Science of the Self,* Arcane, 1967; (with Douglas) *Reincarnation: Key to Immortality,* Arcane, 1968; (with Douglas) *Astrology in Action,* Arcane, 1970; (with Douglas) *Astrology: The Divine Science,* Arcane, 1971; *Hypersentience: How You Can Revisit Your Former Lifetimes in Order to Understand This One Better,* Crown, in press. Contributor to magazines, including *Life, Cosmopolitan,* and *Woman's Day.* Editor of *Hypersentience Bulletin.*

WORK IN PROGRESS: The Astrological Experience and *The Astrological Tradition,* both for Para-Research, completion expected in 1977; several books on hypersentience.

SIDELIGHTS: Marcia Moore, sister of popular novelist Robin Moore, writes: "I do not have a specific place of residence; rather my function is that of a cell in the bloodstream of humanity which remains continually in motion. At this time my residence is a motor home which is parked in an oak grove. . . . I consider myself to be a member of the Holy Order of Wanderers (HOW), an ancient and honorable, but non-organized, group of servers who move freely throughout the body of humanity." Her main activity at present is conducting workshops to demonstrate and instruct people in "hypersentience," a technique which "enables people to recollect and re-experience their former lifetimes." She has studied yoga and Oriental philosophy in India. *Avocational interests:* Yoga, hiking in the California mountains.

BIOGRAPHICAL/CRITICAL SOURCES: Jess Stearn, *Yoga, Youth, and Reincarnation,* Doubleday, 1965.

* * *

MOORE, Robert Etheridge 1919-

PERSONAL: Born December 31, 1919, in Macon, Ga.; son of Robert Archer and Nell (Etheridge) Moore. *Education:* Washington College, Chestertown, Md., B.A., 1940; Yale University, Ph.D., 1943. *Politics:* None. *Religion:* Episcopalian. *Home:* 1932 East River Ter., Minneapolis, Minn. 55414. *Office:* Department of English, University of Minnesota, Minneapolis, Minn. 55455.

CAREER: Yale University, New Haven, Conn., instructor in English, 1943-45; University of Minnesota, Minneapolis, assistant professor, 1945-52, associate professor, 1952-60, professor of English, 1961—, chairman of department, 1969-71, director of graduate study, 1967-69. Member of board of directors of Guthrie Theatre, 1972—. *Member:* Modern Language Association of America, National Council of Teachers of English, American Association of University Professors.

WRITINGS: Hogarth's Literary Relationships, University of Minnesota Press, 1948; *Henry Purcell and the Restoration Theatre,* Harvard University Press, 1961; (contributor) Howard Anderson and John S. Shea, editors, *Studies in Criticism and Aesthetics: 1660-1800,* University of Minnesota Press, 1967; (with Jean H. Hagstrum) *Changing Taste in Eighteenth-Century Art and Literature,* University of California, Los Angeles, 1972. Contributor of articles and reviews to professional journals.

WORK IN PROGRESS: Research on the relationship between literature and the other arts.

SIDELIGHTS: Moore writes: "I was one of the pioneers in educational television (KTCA-TV) in Minnesota, giving a six-month's series on Shakespeare twice weekly in 1958 and another Shakespearean series in 1962." He has lived in England.

* * *

MORDOCK, John B. 1938-

PERSONAL: Born August 2, 1938, in Cumberland, Md.; son of John B. (a buyer) and Nancy (James) Mordock; married Judith Hutchison (a nurse), December 29, 1963; children: Kalay Denise, Kaylin Jaie. *Education:* Springfield College, B.S., 1960; University of Illinois, M.A., 1961; University of Hawaii, Ph.D., 1967; Devereux Foundation, postdoctoral study, 1966-67. *Politics:* Liberal Republican. *Religion:* Protestant. *Home:* 15 Sparkling Ridge Rd., New Paltz, N.Y. 12561. *Office:* Astor Home for Children, Rhinebeck, N.Y. 12572.

CAREER: Psychology trainee at Diamond Head Mental Health Clinic, Honolulu, Hawaii, 1965-66, and at Little Flower Children's Services, Long Island, N.Y., 1966; Devereux Foundation, Devon, Pa., coordinator of research at Institute for Research and Training, 1967-69; Astor Home and Child Guidance Centers, Rhinebeck, N.Y., coordinator of Beacon Center, 1969-70, senior psychologist, 1969-73, acting chief psychologist at Bronx, N.Y. center, 1973-74, chief psychologist for residential service, 1973-75, director of Astor Day Treatment Center, 1975—. Diplomate in school psychology of American Board of Professional Psychology; New York State licensed psychologist and certified school psychologist. Supervisor of school psychological services for various local schools, 1969-74; project consultant, Beckman Learning Center, 1971—. Lecturer at University of Hawaii, 1963-65, Pennsylvania State University, 1966-69, and State University of New York College at New Paltz, 1972-73; distinguished visiting professor at University of Wisconsin, Green Bay, summer, 1975. Group psychotherapist for Group of Devon, 1968-69; member of curriculum advisory committee for Dutchess Community College, 1970-73; member of child development committee of Dutchess County legislature.

MEMBER: American Psychological Association, American Association on Mental Deficiency, Council for Exceptional Children, Society for Research in Child Development, New York Association of School Psychologists

(delegate, 1971-72), Mid-Hudson Psychological Association, Federation of Fly Fishermen. *Awards, honors:* National Science Foundation summer research fellow, 1964; National Institute of Mental Health postdoctoral fellowship, 1966-67.

WRITINGS: (With H. Platt) *The Houseparent's Attitude Scale,* Institute for Research and Training, Devereux Foundation, 1968; (with Platt) *The Inventory of Family Life and Attitudes: Child Care Worker Edition,* Institute for Research and Training, Devereux Foundation, 1968; (contributor) R. F. Blanco, editor, *Prescriptions for Children with Learning and Emotional Problems,* C. C Thomas, 1972; *The Other Children: An Introduction to Exceptionality,* Harper, 1975. Contributor of about fifty articles to psychology, psychiatry, and education journals. *School Psychologist,* contributing editor, 1969-71, associate editor, 1971-73.

WORK IN PROGRESS: Fantasy, Play, and Play Therapy; Children and Families in Residential Treatment; articles on exceptional children, disciplinary practices, and child rearing, for non-professional audience; articles on sport fishing.

SIDELIGHTS: Dr. Mordock writes: "As a scientist-practitioner I became concerned with the gap between research findings and utilization of these findings by the general public. Consequently, I decided to try and present these findings to the public, both lay and informed, in a manner that would lead to their acceptance and utilization."

* * *

MORGAN, Arthur Ernest 1878-1975

June 20, 1878—November 16, 1975; American civil engineer, educator, college administrator, and author. Obituaries: *New York Times,* November 17, 1975; *Current Biography,* January, 1976. (See index for previous *CA* sketch)

* * *

MORGAN, Fred Bruce, Jr. 1919-1975

March 12, 1919—October 2, 1975; American minister, educator, and author of books on religious topics. Obituaries: *New York Times,* October 4, 1975.

* * *

MORGAN, Paul 1928-

PERSONAL: Born February 6, 1928, in Hereford, Tex.; son of Thurman (a clergyman) and Sarah (Williams) Morgan; married Ruth Kraushaar, June 29, 1967; children: Margaret Vashti. *Education:* Texas Christian University, B.M., 1949; University of Chicago, M.A., 1951; University of York, Ph.D., 1969. *Home and office:* 2508 Shirley Ave., Fort Worth, Tex. 76109.

CAREER: High school teacher of music at American schools in Japan and Germany, 1951-57; Tea Cart (restaurant), Fort Worth, Tex., manager, 1957-60; Sam Houston State University, Huntsville, Tex., instructor in English, 1960-64; William Woods College, Fulton, Mo., professor of English and chairman of department, 1967-71; Texas Wesleyan College, Fort Worth, visiting professor of English, 1971-72; Trinity Valley School, Fort Worth, Tex., English teacher, 1972—. Teacher at Texas Christian University, Special Division, 1973—. *Member:* South Central Modern Language Association.

WRITINGS: Sacrapant: The Sorcerer (children's opera),

Novello, 1967; (with sister, Sue Scott) *The D.C. Dialect: How to Master the New Language of Washington in Ten Easy Lessons,* New York University Press, 1975.

Plays: "The Algolagnia Game" (two-act), first performed in Fulton, Mo., at Westminster-William Woods Theatre, December, 1970; (with S. Scott) "The Pride of Noble Watkins" (two-act), first performed in Hermosa Beach, Calif., at Neal Reck Theatre, February, 1975. Contributor to literature journals.

WORK IN PROGRESS: The Great Language Rip-Off: How Educators Con the Public, with sister, Sue Scott.

* * *

MORGAN, Sharon A(ntonia) 1951-
(Karama Fufuka)

PERSONAL: Born January 30, 1951, in Chicago, Ill.; daughter of Arthur (a cabdriver) and Delores (Nicholson) Leslie; married Vincent Morgan, July 12, 1969 (separated, 1974); children: Vincent Scott. *Education:* Attended University of Illinois, 1968, and Loop City College, 1970-71. *Home:* 4840 South King Dr., Chicago, Ill. 60615. *Office:* Provident Hospital, 426 East 51st St., Chicago, Ill. 60615.

CAREER: Mandabach & Simms, Inc., Chicago, Ill., secretary to president, 1968-69; Morgan Services, Inc., Chicago, Ill., secretary-receptionist, 1969-71; American Bar Foundation, Chicago, Ill., secretary, 1971-72; Learning House, Inc., Atlanta, Ga., administrative assistant, 1972-73; Battelle Regional Centers Program, Atlanta, Ga., secretary-receptionist, 1973-74; Woodlawn Organization/Woodlawn Community Development Corp., Chicago, Ill., administrative assistant, 1974-75; Provident Hospital, Chicago, Ill., executive assistant, 1975—. Associate director, Provident Community Development Corp., Chicago. *Member:* League of Black Women, Children's Reading Round Table.

WRITINGS—Under pseudonym Karama Fufuka: *Nguzo Saba: The Seven Principles of Nationbuilding,* privately printed, 1972; *My Daddy Is a Cool Dude* (juvenile), Dial, 1975. Contributor to *Ebony, Jr.,* and *Essence.* Lifestyles editor of Woodlawn Community *Observer,* 1975—.

WORK IN PROGRESS: Lisa Finds a Friend (juvenile); a book of character sketches; essays; children's literature.

AVOCATIONAL INTERESTS: Sewing, painting, reading, crocheting, interior decorating.

* * *

MORIARTY, Tim 1923-

PERSONAL: Born May 22, 1923, in Southbridge, Mass.; son of Timothy J. and Beatrice (Tully) Moriarty; married Lauretta Cardinal, October 26, 1946; children: Maureen (Mrs. William Schab), T. Kevin, Brian. *Education:* Attended Roman Catholic high school in Southbridge, Mass. *Religion:* Roman Catholic. *Home:* 46 Princeton St., Rockville Centre, N.Y. 11570. *Office: Newsday,* 550 Stewart Ave., Garden City, N.Y.

CAREER: United Press International (UPI), New York, N.Y., sports writer, 1946-66; *Newsday,* Garden City, N.Y., sports writer, 1966—. *Military service:* U.S. Navy, radio operator, 1942-45. *Member:* Professional Hockey Writers' Association (past president of New York chapter), Baseball Writers Association.

WRITINGS: The Brothers Esposito, Hawthorn, 1971; (with Emile Francis) *Secrets of Winning Hockey,* Doubleday, 1972; (with Vic Hadfield) *Vic Hadfield's Diary,* Double-

day, 1973; *Hockey's Hall of Fame,* Avon, 1974; (with Gump Worsley) *They Call Me Gump,* Dodd, 1975; *The Incredible Islanders,* Sorkin-Levine, 1976.

* * *

MORKEN, Lucinda Oakland 1906-

PERSONAL: Born October 7, 1906, in Wisconsin; daughter of Odell and Josephine (Thompson) Oakland; married Hans R. Morken (a farmer), June 17, 1939; children: Solveig (Mrs. Larry Blegen), Harald Odell, Margaret (Mrs. David Van Dorn), Betsy (Mrs. Paul H. Olson). *Education:* St. Olaf College, B.A., 1928; also studied at University of Minnesota and University of Wisconsin, Madison. *Religion:* Lutheran. *Home address:* Eltrick, Wis. 54627.

CAREER: Gale College, Galesville, Wis., librarian and teacher of English, 1929-33; high school English teacher in Wausau, Wis., 1934-39, Taylor, Wis., 1938-39, Fort Thomas, Ariz., 1955-58, and Blair, Wis., 1958-71. *Member:* Wisconsin Fellowship of Poets.

WRITINGS: Lines Across My Sky (poems), Windy Row Press, 1973. Poems are included in *Poetry Out of Wisconsin,* edited by August Derleth and R. E. Larsson, H. Harrison, 1937, and *New Poetry Out of Wisconsin,* edited by Derleth, Stanton & Lee, 1969, as well as in several other anthologies. Contributor to literary magazines, including *Wisconsin History Through Poetry, Encounters, Pen and Plow, Creative Wisconsin,* and *Country Poet,* and to local newspapers.

WORK IN PROGRESS: Translating old church records from Norwegian into English.

SIDELIGHTS: Lucinda Morken now lives on a one hundred-ninety acre farm in Wisconsin that has been in her family since 1857.

* * *

MORMAN, Jean Mary 1925-

PERSONAL: Born January 26, 1925, in Chicago, Ill.; daughter of Frank J. (a hardware wholesaler) and Marie (Mauch) Morman; married R. Timothy Unsworth (in public relations), June 21, 1970. *Education:* St. Xavier College, B.A., 1955; University of Notre Dame, M.F.A., 1963; also studied at University of Georgia, Art Institute of Chicago, and in Europe. *Home:* 505 North Lake Shore Dr., Chicago, Ill. 60611. *Office:* Department of Fine Arts, Loyola University, 820 North Michigan, Chicago, Ill. 60611.

CAREER: Elementary teacher in parochial schools in Chicago, Ill., 1946-47, Oak Park, Ill., 1947-49, Milwaukee, Wis., 1949-52, Chicago, 1952-55; Mother McAuley High School, Chicago, art teacher and chairman of department, 1956-67; St. Xavier College, Chicago, Ill., assistant professor of art and chairman of department, 1967-69; Loyola University, Chicago, Ill., assistant professor, 1970, associate professor of fine arts, 1971—. Adjunct professor at Art Institute of Chicago; visiting professor at Portland State University and St. Mary's College, Winona, Minn.; artist-in-residence at Indianapolis Museum of Art. Has appeared on television programs, including "Today Show." Has had exhibits of her work, including sculpture, sand cast wall murals, graphics, and banners. *Member:* National Art Education Association, Educational Arts Association, Illinois Art Education Association (past president).

WRITINGS: Art: Of Wonder and a World (textbook), Art

Education, 1967; *Art: Tempo of Today* (textbook), Art Education, 1969; *Wonder Under Your Feet* (handbook of arts for the layman), Harper, 1973. Contributor to art and education journals.

WORK IN PROGRESS: Research on the role of the arts in the total education process, the development of a program and a teacher-training plan for an interdisciplinary approach to the arts in education.

SIDELIGHTS: In her third book, Jean Morman writes:
"Art is as broad as time,
as shallow-deep
as the
creek-to-ocean many-ness of water,
as down-to-earth as gravel,
and as soaring high
as a moon flight.
Art is as individual as one person,
and as varied as all mankind.

"You may probe aesthetic theories
and diagram dynamics of composition.
But until you learn to look under your feet—
and up close and wide-angle—
    until you break the dark glass of
    IDENTIFY
    and start really
    SEEING—
art will remain for you
skillful things
that other people do."

*   *   *

MORRISON, Dorothy Nafus

PERSONAL: Born in Nashua, Iowa; daughter of Roy A. (a merchant) and Edwinna (a teacher of Latin and German; maiden name, Bolton) Nafus; married Carl V. Morrison (a psychiatrist); children: James, Anne (Mrs. John Feighner), David, John. *Education:* State University of Iowa, B.A. *Residence:* Beaverton, Ore. *Agent:* Ruth Cantor, 156 Fifth Ave., New York, N.Y. 10010.

CAREER: Teacher of stringed instruments in public schools in Beaverton, Ore., 1954-66; writer, 1965—.

WRITINGS—For children: *The Mystery of the Last Concert*, Westminster, 1971; (with husband, Carl V. Morrison) *Can I Help How I Feel?* (nonfiction), Atheneum, in press.

WORK IN PROGRESS: A biography of Dr. John Mc-Loughlin.

SIDELIGHTS: Dorothy Morrison writes: "*The Mystery of the Last Concert* arose from my lifelong interest in orchestral music, and its background is similar to the Portland Junior Symphony. I hoped that its readers would derive some awareness of how it feels to play in a large orchestra, and the obligations it entails." Of her teaching, she writes: "My finest hours were carrying a string bass in my Volkswagen, in good weather only, as the fingerboard and scroll had to go through the open sun roof."

*   *   *

MORRISON, Marsh 1902-
(Analyticus Marsh)

PERSONAL: Born October 29, 1902, in Baltimore, Md.; son of Harry (a merchant) and Frances Morrison; married Vera Young, April, 1954 (divorced, 1962); married Hana Heller (a psychologist), January 31, 1971; children: (first marriage) Gera (Mrs. Ted Curry). *Education:* Palmer College of Chiropractic, D.C. and Ph.C., 1927; Lincoln College of Chiropractic, F.I.C.C., 1939; also studied at National Chiropractic College and International College of Chiropractic. *Religion:* Presbyterian. *Home and office:* 55 Central Park W., New York, N.Y.; and Cuernavaca, Mexico. *Agent:* Eugene M. Schwartz, 200 Madison Ave., New York, N.Y. 10016.

CAREER: Worked on *New York Journal*, New York City, 1920-23; chiropractor in private practice, 1927-62; writer and lecturer, 1962-69; Healing Arts Skills, Inc., New York City, president, 1969—. Director of International Marsh Morrison Seminars of Neurological Techniques, 1962—; visiting professor at Columbia Institute of Chiropractic. *Member:* Authors League of America, Center for Creative Arts (Cuernavaca), Ethical Culture Society (New York), Masons. *Awards, honors:* Named "chiropractor of the year," 1974, by Living Principles Doctors of Chiropractic Association.

WRITINGS: They Called Him Doctor (novel), Fell, 1956; *The Climate of Passion* (novel), Fell, 1959; *Doctor Morrison's Miracle Body Tune-Up for Rejuvenated Health*, Prentice-Hall, 1973; *Foods for Longevity*, Mega-Man Books, 1974; *Bleeding Hemorrhoids and Constipation*, Improvement Books Co., 1975; *The Restoration of Nervous and Emotional Health*, Improvement Books Co., 1975; *Natural Aids for the Prostate Gland*, Improvement Books Co., 1975; *Foods as Medicines* (booklet), Greenland Division, Downe Communications, 1975.

(Under pseudonym Analyticus Marsh) *Fugitives from a Brain Gang*, Harbinger House, 1934. Editor of *Marsh Morrison International Report*, 1969-75, and *Marsh Morrison Health-Simplifier Newsletter*, 1973—.

WORK IN PROGRESS: Adventures in Research: How to Gain and Maintain Health by Avoiding the Medical Doctor (tentative title).

SIDELIGHTS: Morrison writes that his "major interest is in proving (and documenting) that what is denominated 'medical science' is not a science but only an art, and a third-grade art rather than a first-grade one like music or cabinet-making—and that the hope of the sick world lies not in drugs (the body makes its own cortisone, pepsin, adrenalin, etc.) but in returning the body to its inherent built-in self-healing capacities."

*   *   *

MORROW, Mary Lou 1926-

PERSONAL: Born June 3, 1926, in Lewiston, Mont.; daughter of Stanford (a high school superintendent) and Bernice (Flook) Hannah; married John M. Morrow (a forest ranger), February 2, 1947; children: Linda Morrow Cuddy, David Michael, John K., Karen Lee Morrow Walsh. *Education:* University of California, Berkeley, A.A., 1946; attended San Jose State College (now University), 1946-47. *Religion:* Protestant. *Home:* 10951 Nicosia Place, Lakeside, Calif. 92040.

CAREER: Substitute elementary school teacher in Ukiah, and Placerville, Calif., 1960-72; currently home tutor, artist and writer. *Member:* Dilly-Dauber Art Association.

WRITINGS—Self-illustrated: *HELP! For Elementary School Substitutes and Beginning Teachers*, Westminster, 1974; *124 Easy-to-do Art Ideas*, Morgan, in press. Contributor to *Church Teacher*.

WORK IN PROGRESS: A book on drawing for children's

use, completion expected in 1976; stories for children using phonetic vocabulary.

SIDELIGHTS: Mary Lou Morrow told *CA* that during her years as a substitute teacher she "accumulated a notebook full of ideas a substitute could use in the class-room on short notice—ones that didn't require special materials." She organized and illustrated the notebook to produce her first book.

* * *

MORROW, Patrick David 1940-

PERSONAL: Born October 1, 1940, in Inglewood, Calif.; son of Patrick Francis (an appraiser and writer) and Marilyn (a writer and teacher; maiden name, Keefe) Morrow; married Judith R. Spenceley, June 28, 1964 (divorced April 9, 1975); married Mary Elizabeth Vehrs (a special education teacher), August 19, 1975; children: (first marriage) Milan Elizabeth, Christopher Patrick. *Education:* Attended Sacramento State College, 1958-61; University of Southern California, B.A., 1963; University of Washington, Seattle, M.A., 1965, Ph.D., 1969; also attended University of California, Berkeley, and Free University of Seattle. *Politics:* Democrat. *Religion:* Roman Catholic. *Home:* 322 Shelton Rd., Auburn, Ala. 36830. *Office:* Department of English, Auburn University, Auburn, Ala. 36830.

CAREER: Professional musician, 1957-62; U.S. Veterans Administration, Property Management Division, Sacramento, Calif., technical writer, 1963; University of Washington, Seattle, instructor in English, 1968-69; University of Southern California, Los Angeles, assistant professor of English and American studies, 1969-75; Auburn University, Auburn, Ala., associate professor of English, 1975—. Visiting associate professor at University of New Mexico, summer, 1972; visiting lecturer at Idaho State University, summer, 1974. French interpreter for Eighth Winter Olympic Games (Squaw Valley, Calif.), 1960. Volunteer worker with retarded and handicapped children.

MEMBER: Modern Language Association of America, American Studies Association, Popular Culture Association, Western American Literature Association (member of executive council, 1972—), South Atlantic Modern Language Association. *Awards, honors:* National Endowment for the Humanities grant, 1974-75, for curriculum development and publication; Egan Foundation fellowships, 1971, 1974; Leo S. Bing fellowship, from University of Southern California, 1971.

WRITINGS: (Translator, editor, and author of introduction) *Porcelain Butterfly: Five French Symbolist Poets in Translation* (bi-lingual text), Red Hill Press, 1971; *Bret Harte* (pamphlet), Boise State University, 1972; (contributor) Edward F. Heenan, editor, *Mystery, Magic, and Miracle: Religion in a Post-Aquarian Age,* Prentice-Hall, 1973; *Radical Vistas: Eight Essays on American Literature,* Fault Press, 1974; (editor) *Perspectives on Bob Dylan,* Popular Press, in press. Contributor to academic journals. Member of editorial board of *Western American Literature, Journal of Popular Culture,* and *Popular Music and Society.*

WORK IN PROGRESS: Tales, Letters, and Legends from Old Dakota; Bret Harte: Literary Critic; Melodrama and Naturalism in American Literature.

SIDELIGHTS: Morrow writes: "I consider myself ... primarily a critic—of life, culture, human relationships, and art. To me the primary function of criticism ... is explica-

tion and not attack. My ideal critic strives to make clear what is obscure, not to pass moral judgments from on high. I strive for the personal voice and vision that the shared experience of reader and writer under these terms makes all concerned better able to understand life and cope with it." Morrow made a tape recording, "Bret Harte," for Everett/Edwards, 1974.

* * *

MOSS, Frank Edward 1911-

PERSONAL: Born September 23, 1911, in Salt Lake City, Utah; son of James Edward (an educator) and Maud (Nixon) Moss; married Phyllis Hart, June 20, 1934; children: Marilyn Moss Armstrong, Edward, Brian, Gordon. *Education:* University of Utah, B.A. (magna cum laude), 1933; George Washington University, J.D. (cum laude), 1937. *Politics:* Democrat. *Religion:* Mormon. *Office:* New Senate Office Building, Washington, D.C. 20510.

CAREER: Admitted to the Bar of Utah, 1938; Securities and Exchange Commission, Washington, D.C., staff member, 1937-39; judge of the City Court of Salt Lake City, Utah, 1940-50; county attorney of Salt Lake County, Utah, 1951-58; Moss & Hyde, Salt Lake City, Utah, partner, 1951-55; Moss & Cowley, Salt Lake City, Utah, partner, 1955-59; member of the U.S. Senate from Utah, 1958—. *Military service:* U.S. Army Air Forces, 1942-46; U.S. Air Force Reserve, 1946-71, became colonel. *Member:* American Bar Association, Judge Advocates Association of the United States, National Association of County and Prosecuting Attorneys (president, 1956-58), Utah Bar Association, Utah Association of County Officials (president, 1955-56), Air Reserve Association (national vice-president), American Legion, Veterans of Foreign Wars, Reserve Officers Association, Phi Kappa Phi, Phi Delta Phi, Pi Kappa Alpha.

WRITINGS: Water Crisis, Praeger, 1967.

* * *

MOUSSARD, Jacqueline 1924-
(Jacqueline Cervon)

PERSONAL: Born July 6, 1924, in Cervon, Nievre, France; daughter of Lucien (a cabinet maker) and Audree Sene; married Serje Moussard (in electronics), December 31, 1945; children: Catherine Moussard Berthet, Jean-Marc, Guillaumette Moussard Alami. *Education:* Lycee Paul Bert, Paris, licence d'enseignement es lettres classiques, 1944; also attended Sorbonne, University of Paris. *Home:* Cervon, 58800 Corbigny, France.

CAREER: Journalist, 1946-47, teacher, 1948-52, and secretarial director, 1953-54, all in Djibouti, East Africa; writer. *Awards, honors:* Prix de l'Academie Francaise, 1965, for *Ali, Jean-Luc et la gazelle;* Prix des parents d'eleves, 1967, for *Le Tresor de Nikos;* Prix Jeunesse, 1968, for *L'Aiglon d'ouazazate;* Prix la joie par le livre, and Mention du prix europeen de la ville de Caorle (Italy), both 1968, for *Le Naufrage de Rhodes;* Prix Fantasia, 1970, for *Joao de Tintubal;* Prix la joie par le livre, 1971, for *Malik le garcon sauvage;* diplome meilleur livre loisirs jeune, 1972, for *Le Nain et le Baobab,* and 1974, for *Coumba du pays oublie des pluies;* Prix de la jeunesse de la CRPFL (associated French, Swiss, and Belgian radio), 1973, for *Le Chasseur au lasso;* Selection 1000 jeunes lecteurs, 1973, for *Le Tambour des sables.*

WRITINGS—All under pseudonym Jacqueline Cervon: *Benoit, l'arbre et la lune,* Editions G.P., 1969.

Children's books; all published by Editions G.P., except as noted: *Ali, Jean-Luc et la gazelle,* 1963; *Quand la terre trembla a Skoplje,* 1965, translation by John Buchanan-Brown published as *The Day the Earth Shook,* Bodley Head, 1967, Coward, 1969; *Le coquillage rose de Catissou,* Magnard, 1965; *Le Tresor de Nikos,* Magnard, 1966; *Selim, le petit marchand de bonheur,* 1967; *Belle agao,* Magnard, 1967; *Le Naufrage de Rhodes,* 1968, translation by Thelma Niklaus published as *Castaway from Rhodes,* Watts, 1973; *L'Aiglon d'ouazazate,* Editions de l'Amitie, 1968; *Les Pigeons d'Urgup,* Presses de la Cite (Paris), 1968; *Joao de Tintubal,* Magnard, 1969.

Le Defi au soleil, 1970; *Malik, le garcon sauvage,* Magnard, 1970; *Le fouet et la cithare,* 1971; *Les Moissons du desert,* 1971; *Le Tambour des Sables,* 1972; *Le Nain et la Baobab,* 1972; *Djinn la malice,* 1972; *Le Chasseur au lasso,* 1973; *Dianfo de l'ile verte,* 1973; *Coumba du pays oublie des pluies,* 1974.

Also author of *Les Chevaliers du Stromboli,* Editions G.P., *Francesco,* Editions G.P., and *Prince des Neiges,* Editions G.P.

WORK IN PROGRESS: La Jarre percee, a story set in Dahomey in the eighteenth century, for Editions G.P.

BIOGRAPHICAL/CRITICAL SOURCES: Marc Soriano, *Guide de Litterature pour la jeunesse,* Flammarion, 1975.

* * *

MOYERS, Bill 1934-

PERSONAL: Given name legally changed from Billy Don; born June 5, 1934, in Hugo, Okla.; son of John Henry (a laborer) and Ruby (Johnson) Moyers; married Judith Suzanne Davidson, December 18, 1954; children: William Cope, Alice Suzanne, John Davidson. *Education:* Attended North Texas State University, 1952-54, and University of Edinburgh, 1956-57; University of Texas, Austin, B.J. (honors), 1956; Southwestern Baptist Theological Seminary, B.D., 1959. *Address:* 304 West 58th St., New York, N.Y. 10019.

CAREER: News Messenger, Marshall, Tex., reporter and sports editor, 1949-54; KTBC Radio and Television, Austin, Tex., assistant news editor, 1954-56; served as student minister at two churches in Austin, 1954-56, and at a rural Oklahoma church, 1957-59; special assistant to Senator Lyndon B. Johnson, 1959-60, executive assistant during vice-presidential campaign, 1960, and early 1961; associate director in charge of public affairs for the Peace Corps, 1961, deputy director, 1962-63; special assistant to President Lyndon B. Johnson, 1963-65, press secretary to the President, 1965-67; *Newsday,* Garden City, N.Y., publisher, 1967-70; host of "This Week" (public affairs broadcast) for National Educational Television, 1970; Educational Broadcasting Corp., New York, N.Y., editor-in-chief of "Bill Moyers' Journal," 1971—. Director, Harte-Hanks Newspapers, Inc., and Mitchell, Hutchins, Inc. Trustee of Rockefeller Foundation, Benedict College, and Institute of International Social Research; member of board of visitors, John F. Kennedy School of Government, Harvard University; member of board of directors, Center for the Study of Television and Politics; former director of Council on Foreign Affairs. *Awards, honors:* Rotary International Fellowship, 1956; three Emmy Awards from National Academy of Television Arts and Sciences, including outstanding broadcaster of 1974.

WRITINGS: Listening to America: A Traveler Rediscovers His Country, Harper Magazine Press, 1971.

SIDELIGHTS: Moyers' book, the result of a 13,000 mile trip throughout the United States, by bus, car, and plane, is, according to Haynes Johnson, "eloquent and wise, full of insights and touches that illuminate the real America—not the mythical Middle America of the cheap political slogans, nor the hostile, rapacious, corrupt America of the radical folklore. Bill Moyers is a superb journalist, a rare blend of a painstaking, perceptive reporter and a sensitive, moving writer. He has written a great book. Let the adjectives run. His America is confused, troubled, uncertain, but not wallowing in despair. And it is an America in the midst of great change, much of it for the better.''

* * *

MUELLER, John E(rnest) 1937-

PERSONAL: Born June 21, 1937, in St. Paul, Minn.; son of Ernst A. (a manufacturer) and Elsie (Schleh) Mueller; married Judith A. Reader, September 6, 1960; children: Karl, Karen, Susan. *Education:* University of Chicago, A.B., 1960; University of California, Los Angeles, Ph.D., 1965. *Home:* 246 Roslyn St., Rochester, N.Y. 14619. *Office:* Department of Political Science, University of Rochester, Rochester, N.Y. 14627.

CAREER: University of Rochester, Rochester, N.Y., assistant professor, 1965-69, associate professor, 1969-72, professor of political science, 1972—.

WRITINGS: (Editor) *Approaches to Measurement in International Relations,* Appleton, 1969; *War, Presidents, and Public Opinion,* Wiley, 1973; *Films on Ballet and Modern Dance,* American Dance Guild, 1974. Author of "Film," a column in *Dance Magazine,* 1974—. Contributor to political science journals.

WORK IN PROGRESS: Research on the use of films in dance and in foreign policy courses.

* * *

MUHLHAUSEN, John Prague 1940-

PERSONAL: Born January 29, 1940, in Westport, Conn.; son of Edward C. (a banker) and Alice (a magazine editor; maiden name, Scofield) Muhlhausen; married Kitza T. Them, April 13, 1968; children: David Prague. *Education:* College of William and Mary, student, 1958-60; Rhode Island School of Design, B.F.A., 1963; School of Visual Arts, New York, N.Y., further study, 1964. *Politics:* Independent. *Religion:* Protestant. *Home:* 6851 Roswell Rd. N.E., Atlanta, Ga. 30328. *Office:* John Muhlhausen Design, Inc., Atlanta, Ga. 30328.

CAREER: Cambridge Seven Associates, Cambridge, Mass., designer, 1964-66; Visuel Kommunications, Copenhagen, Denmark, designer, 1966-67; Hauser Associates, Atlanta, Ga., graphic designer, 1967-72; Jova, Daniels, Busby, Atlanta, Ga., graphic designer, 1972-74; John Muhlhausen Design, Inc., Atlanta, Ga., president, 1974—. *Member:* American Institute of Graphic Arts. *Awards, honors: Industrial Design Review,* 1969 and 1971; *Graphis Annual,* 1970 and 1972; Midwest Book Competition, 1971; Chicago Book Clinic, 1971; gold medal at Industrial Graphics International, 1972, for best in show; *Wind and Sail* named one of fifty best books of the year, 1972, by American Institute of Graphic Arts (AIGA).

WRITINGS—Self-illustrated: Wind and Sail, Quadrangle, 1971.

SIDELIGHTS: Muhlhausen's goal is "to transcend language barriers through the use of graphic symbols; i.e., visual communications." He presently organizes and teaches junior sailing programs. *Avocational interests:* Travel (Europe, Africa, Asia, North and South America).

* * *

MUILENBURG, Grace (Evelyn) 1913-

PERSONAL: Surname is pronounced *Mile*-n-burg; born September 19, 1913, in Dexter, Kan.; daughter of Guy Emmit (a manager of a feed department) and Lucy Myrtle (Sinclair) Metcalf; married Virgil Carl Muilenburg, December 28, 1936 (died September 29, 1939); children: George Neal. *Education:* Southwestern College, Winfield, Kan., teaching certificate, 1933; Kansas State College, further study, 1940; University of Kansas, B.S., 1947; University of Missouri, M.A., 1969. *Politics:* "Disenchanted democrat." *Religion:* "?" *Home:* 2075 College View Rd., Manhattan, Kan. 66502. *Office:* Office of the Vice-President for Agriculture, Kansas State University, Manhattan, Kan. 66506.

CAREER: Elementary school teacher in rural schools in Kansas, 1933-37, 1939-42; North American Aviation, Kansas City, Mo., engineering draftsman, 1943-45; Kansas Geological Survey, Lawrence, Kansas, writer and editor, 1946-66, supervisor of drafting, 1946-55, director of public information and education, 1955-66; University of Missouri, Columbia, editor and technical writer for vice-president for university-wide research, 1966-69; Kansas State University, Manhattan, assistant professor, 1969-74, associate professor of agriculture, 1974—, assistant editor at Agricultural Experiment Station, 1969-74, associate editor, 1974—.

MEMBER: American Association of Agricultural College Editors, Geological Society of America, Women in Communications (president of Manhattan chapter, 1970-71), Kansas Press Women of National Federation of Press Women (historian, 1972-74), Kansas State Historical Society, Gamma Sigma Delta.

WRITINGS: The Kansas Scene, Kansas Geological Survey, 1953; *Featuring the Kansas Landscape* (pamphlet), Kansas Geological Survey, 1961; (with W. W. Hambleton, E. D. Geobel, A. L. Hornbaker, and R. L. Smith) *Economic Development for Kansas: A Sector Report on Its Mineral and Water Resources,* Center for Research in Business, University of Kansas, 1962; (with Ada Swineford) *Land of the Post Rock: Its Origins, History, and People,* University Press of Kansas, 1975. Contributor to academic journals.

WORK IN PROGRESS: Research on the Flint Hills of Kansas, with Ada Swineford, with a book expected to result; collecting historical and natural information on other Kansas regions.

SIDELIGHTS: Grace Muilenburg writes: "From the time I climbed my first tree, I have been interested in the world about me and what motivates people and other living things in it. My long association with geologists has intensified my appreciation for the natural scene and how the use of the land and other natural resources influences or is influenced by 'people' activities. For several decades I have been observing and collecting information on a specific geographic area: my native Kansas, which has as exciting a history and as varied scenery and resources as any state. I am now committed (by an inner driving force) to telling the story of 'my' prairie state by attempting to put into perspec-tive its historical and physical facets ... Once we begin to understand and appreciate our total environment through interrelations, we enrich our living, sharpen our abilities to communicate, and come closer to achieving a unified goal—where the destiny of each is perceived as the destiny of all."

* * *

MULHOLLAND, Jim 1949-

PERSONAL: Born October 27, 1949, in New York, N.Y.; son of Edward Charles and Dolores Mulholland. *Education:* Rutgers University, B.A., 1971. *Home and office:* 155 East 50th St., New York, N.Y. 10022.

CAREER: National Broadcasting Co. (NBC), New York, N.Y., writer for television program "The Tonight Show," 1970-73; American Broadcasting Co. (ABC), New York City, writer for television programs "The Dick Cavett Show," 1973, and "The Jack Paar Show," 1974; free-lance writer, 1974—. Television writing also includes material for comedy programs "Mary Tyler Moore" and "All in the Family."

WRITINGS: The Abbott and Costello Book, Popular Library, 1975.

WORK IN PROGRESS: The Films of Bob Hope; The Great Television Comedians; a comic novel; a screenplay and a play (both comedies).

* * *

MULLEN, Cyril J. 1908-
(C.J.J. Mullen)

PERSONAL: Born April 25, 1908, in Chicago, Ill.; son of John H. (an executive and manager) and Margaret Ida (Riordan) Mullen; married to second wife, Katherine Rebecca Buchanan (a newspaperwoman and advertising copywriter); children: (first marriage) John Leo, James (deceased). *Education:* University of Notre Dame, A.B., 1930; Chicago Academy of Art, graduate, 1932; also attended classes at Northwestern University. *Home and office:* 513 Golden Meadows Rd., N.W., Albuquerque, N.M. 87114.

CAREER: Sears, Roebuck & Co., Chicago, Ill., editor of monthly magazine, 1933-37; Pedlar & Ryan (advertising agency), New York, N.Y., writer, then radio copy chief, 1937-47; Needham, Louis & Brorby (advertising agency), Chicago, director of writing, 1947-52; Tatham-Laird (advertising agency), Chicago, group creative director, 1952-59; Lake-Spiro-Shurman (advertising agency), Memphis, Tenn., associate copy chief, 1959-66.

*WRITINGS—*Under name C.J.J. Mullen: *Life on a Slightly Used Horse,* A. S. Barnes, 1975. Contributor to *Chronicle of the Horse.*

SIDELIGHTS: Mullen, whose office now "is a functional room at the back of my house," told *CA* his early hobby of drawing was gradually supplanted by an interest in writing. "My grandmother," he said, "wrote a novel.... My father, who appeared to some a hard-nosed businessman, wrote verse.... Started out (college) as a writer: now, semi-retired, am ending up the same way. I suppose reading the classics, especially Plato, Montaigne, Swift, Pascal, Kant, and Schopenhauer, could be called a minor passion. Horses, riding and fox-hunting were my major athletic interests after college days."

BIOGRAPHICAL/CRITICAL SOURCES: Chronicle of

the Horse, May 8, 1975; *Western Horseman,* June, 1975; *Buffalo Courier Express,* October 5, 1975.

* * *

MULLER, Priscilla E(lkow)   1930-

PERSONAL: Born February 15, 1930, in New York, N.Y.; daughter of John and Katherine (Bulka) Elkow; married C. Robert Muller (self-employed), May 6, 1950. *Education:* Brooklyn College (now Brooklyn College of the City University of New York), B.A., 1951; New York University, M.A., 1959, Ph.D., 1963. *Politics:* Independent. *Residence:* Brooklyn, N.Y. *Office:* Hispanic Society of America, 613 West 155th St., New York, N.Y. 10032.

CAREER: Brooklyn College (now of the City University of New York), Brooklyn, N.Y., administrative assistant, 1951-58; Hispanic Society of America, New York, N.Y., curator of metalwork, 1964-67, curator of paintings, 1967-73, curator of the museum, 1973—. Visiting lecturer at Brooklyn College, 1966; consultant to Time-Life Books, 1968, 1969. *Member:* International Council of Museums, College Art Association, Renaissance Society of America, Hispanic Society of America, Society for Hispanic Art Historical Studies, Real Academia de Ciencias, Bellas Letras y Mobles Artes de Cordoba (corresponding member).

WRITINGS: Jewels in Spain: 1500-1800, Hispanic Society of America, 1972; *Francisco Goya: Portraits in Paintings, Prints, and Drawings,* Virginia Museum of Fine Arts, 1972. Contributor to *Encyclopedia Americana* and to art and library journals.

WORK IN PROGRESS: Researching Spanish art from the Renaissance to the present.

SIDELIGHTS: Priscilla Muller is competent in French, Spanish, German, Italian, Portuguese, Catalan, and Russian.

* * *

MULLINS, Vera (Annie) Cooper   1903-

PERSONAL: Born July 3, 1903, in Leakey, Tex.; daughter of Marion Authur (a physician) and Sarah Elizabeth (Smith) Cooper; married Roy Curtis Mullins, June 27, 1925; children: Roy Curtis, Jr., Douglas Dale. *Education:* Attended Abilene Christian College, West Texas State Teachers College, and Hardin Junior College. *Politics:* Independent "but usually vote Democrat." *Religion:* Church of Christ. *Residence:* Wichita Falls, Tex.

CAREER: Free-lance writer. Elementary school teacher in country schools in Childress County, Tex., 1922-25, and in public schools in Childress City, Tex., 1925-29; substitute teacher in public schools in Wichita Falls, Tex., 1944-45.

WRITINGS—For children: *Kala and the Sea Bird,* Golden Gate Junior Books, 1966; *Kalo and the Treasure Paper,* Moody, 1974; *Ronnie and the Texas Camel,* Moody, in press. Contributor to children's magazines, church school publications, and newspapers.

WORK IN PROGRESS: Research on family history and genealogy.

SIDELIGHTS: Vera Mullins didn't begin to write until she was forty-one years old. Her main interest at present is teaching Christianity to young children and encouraging them to study the Bible.

MURCH, Edward (William Lionel)   1920-

PERSONAL: Born April 20, 1920, in Plymouth, Devonshire, England; son of Theodore Edward (a naval officer) and Jane Elizabeth (Roberts) Murch; married Betty Doreen Wakefield, October 26, 1946. *Education:* Educated in England. *Religion:* Quaker (Attender). *Home:* Heatherdene Dousland, Yelverton, Devonshire PL20 6LV, England. *Office:* Department of Health and Social Security, Plymouth, Devonshire, England.

CAREER: Department of Health and Social Security, Plymouth, Devonshire, England, higher executive officer, 1949—; writer and playwright, 1949—. *Military service:* Royal Navy Volunteer Reserve, 1940-46; became lieutenant. *Member:* International Society of Arts and Letters (fellow), Royal Society of Arts (fellow), Society of Authors, Quaker Fellowship of the Arts.

WRITINGS—All plays: *The Poet of Goosey Fair,* Metheun, 1949; *Things That Go Bump,* Deane, 1951; *Morning Noon and Night,* Deane, 1953; *The Thin Red Line,* Deane, 1954; *Spring Flowers for Marguerite,* Deane, 1954; *The Parting Shot,* Deane, 1956; *The Journey of the Star: A Nativity Play for Seven Women,* Deane, 1962; *Tell it to the Wind,* Yennandon Plays, 1964; *The Dipper,* Yennandon Plays, 1964; *Five Minutes from the Sea,* Deane, 1965; *The Beggars of Bordeaux,* Yennandon Plays, 1966, *No Name in the Street,* Yennandon Plays, 1966; *Caroline,* Deane, 1966; *On the Hill,* Deane, 1967; *Saint Germaine,* Yennandon Plays, 1967; *The Trials of Captain Savage,* Deane, 1967; *Wits' End,* Yennandon Plays, 1968; *The Last Blue Mountain,* Yennandon Plays, 1972. Contributor to *Reynard* (Journal of the Quaker Fellowship of the Arts).

WORK IN PROGRESS: Christmas Voices: Some Variations on a Theme, a play, completion expected, 1976.

SIDELIGHTS: Murch told *CA,* "My plays are performed in little theatres, village halls, etc. The majority of them have been festival (tournament) winners. *No Name in the Street,* my most successful play was written one wet June morning: It was the best day's work I ever did." *No Name in the Street* has been broadcast on television in the United States and performed all over the world.

* * *

MURDOCK, Kenneth Ballard   1895-1975

June 22, 1895—November 14, 1975; American educator, and author or editor of literary and historical works. Obituaries: *Publishers Weekly,* December 1, 1975; *AB Bookman's Weekly,* December 8, 1975.

* * *

MURPHET, Howard   1906-

PERSONAL: Born November 4, 1906, in Australia; son of Edward (a farmer) and Caroline (Presnell) Murphet; married Iris Godfrey (a nursing sister), May 16, 1959; children: Richard, David. *Education:* Attended University of Tasmania. *Agent:* Alec Harrison & Associates, 118 Fleet St., London E.C.4, England.

CAREER: Teacher in Tasmania, 1930-34; *Lintas,* Sydney, Australia, in advertising and publicity, 1936-39; public relations officer for western Europe of Navy, Army and Air Force Institutes, 1946-51; CSR Chemicals, Sydney, Australia, public relations and advertising manager, 1952-60; free-lance writer, 1960—. *Military service:* British Army, in charge of British press section of Nuremburg trials, 1941-46; served in Sicily, Italy, Normandy, and Paris; became major. *Member:* Returned Services League (Australia).

WRITINGS: Yoga for Busy People, Oldbourne, 1965; *Sai Baba: Man of Miracles*, International Publications Service, 1971; *Hammer on the Mountain*, Theosophical Publishing, 1972; *When Day Light Comes*, Theosophical Publishing, 1975. Contributor to magazines in England and abroad.

WORK IN PROGRESS: Another book on Sai Baba of India; a book of short stories; autobiographical essays.

SIDELIGHTS: Murphet writes: "My main motivation in writing is to express my view of the deepest truths of life; these are essentially spiritual truths. My interests in the search for such truths have led me to yoga, Indian philosophy, parapsychology, and areas of occultism. In India, where I spent years after travelling the world, I found some great teachers of truth, the greatest being Satya Sai Baba who teaches how to live and how to die, establishing colleges for this new education."

*   *   *

MURPHY, Frank Hughes   1940-

PERSONAL: Born August 26, 1940, in Hamlet, N.C.; son of John J. and Annabel (Hughes) Murphy; married Catherine Little (an education consultant), May 11, 1963; children: Margaret, Con, Gillian. *Education:* University of North Carolina, A.B. (with honors), 1961, Ph.D., 1971; University of Florida, M.A., 1963. *Residence:* New Orleans, La. *Office:* Department of English, University of New Orleans, Lake Front, New Orleans, La. 70122.

CAREER: University of Maryland Overseas Division (France), instructor in English, 1964-66; part-time instructor in English at North Carolina State University at Raleigh, and at Fort Bragg, 1967-69; University of New Orleans, New Orleans, La., assistant professor of English, 1970—. *Military service:* U.S. Air Force, 1963-67; became captain. *Member:* Phi Beta Kappa.

WRITINGS: Yeats's Early Poetry, Louisiana State University Press, 1975.

WORK IN PROGRESS: A student's guide to the study of poetry.

*   *   *

MURPHY, James F(redrick)   1943-

PERSONAL: Born August 31, 1943, in Oakland, Calif.; son of Fredrick and Ruth (a nurse; maiden name, Thompson) Murphy; married Elizabeth Ann Dealey, June 11, 1966 (divorced); children: Erin. *Education:* San Francisco State College (now University), B.A., 1966; Indiana University, M.S. (with honors), 1967; Oregon State University, Ph.D., 1972. *Politics:* Democrat. *Home:* 5005 Alan Ave., San Jose, Calif. 95124. *Office:* Department of Recreation and Leisure Activities, San Jose State University, San Jose, Calif. 95192.

CAREER: Community College of Baltimore, Baltimore, Md., instructor in recreation leadership, 1967-68; San Jose State University, San Jose, Calif., assistant professor, 1968-70, 1972-74, associate professor of recreation and leisure studies, 1974—. Instructor at Oregon State University, summers, 1970-71; visiting associate professor at University of Illinois, summer, 1975, and University of North Carolina, summer, 1976. Administrative assistant at Camp Trinity (Hayfork, Calif.), summers, 1963-65; playground director of Oakland (Calif.) Recreation and Park Department, 1965; recreation intern and coordinator of personnel and recruitment for Baltimore Bureau of Recreation, 1967-68; supervisor of Sunnyvale (Calif.) Parks and Recreation

Department, summers, 1968-69. Member of board of directors of recreation advisory committee at Ohlone College, 1972—, and Monterey Peninsula College, 1972-75; member of advisory board of New Games Foundation.

MEMBER: National Recreation and Park Association, Society of Park and Recreation Educators (member of board of directors, 1974-77), American Alliance for Leisure and Recreation, European Centre for Leisure and Education (Prague), Recreation and Park Educators of California. *Awards, honors:* Recreation literature special award of merit from Pi Sigma Epsilon, 1970; Professional Merit award for literary contributions from National Student Recreation and Park Society, National Recreation and Park Association, 1975.

WRITINGS: (Editor with John A. Nesbitt and Paul D. Brown, and contributor) *Recreation and Leisure Service for the Disadvantaged: Guidelines to Program Development and Related Readings*, Lea & Febiger, 1970; (contributor) Larry Neal, editor, *Leisure and the Schools*, Center for Leisure Studies (Eugene, Ore.), 1972; (contributor) Thomas A. Stein and H. Douglas Sessoms, editors, *Recreation and Special Populations*, Holbrook, 1973, 2nd edition, in press; (contributor) Joseph J. Bannon, editor, *Outreach: Extending Community Service in Urban Areas*, C. C Thomas, 1973; (with Brown, William Niepoth, and John Williams) *Leisure Service Delivery System: A Modern Perspective*, Lea & Febiger, 1973; *Concepts of Leisure: Philosophical Implications*, Prentice-Hall, 1974; *Recreation and Leisure Service: A Humanistic Perspective*, W. C. Brown, 1975; (with Dennis Howard) *Contemporary Community Recreation: The Dynamics of Leisure Service Delivery*, Lea & Febiger, in press; (contributor) Lu Charlotte, editor, *A Leisure Perspective of Aging*, Lea & Febiger, in press.

Contributor of articles and reviews to professional journals. Member of editorial board of *San Jose Studies*, 1974—; member of advisory board of *Leisure Today*, 1973—; member of *Forum Newsletter* committee of Society of Park and Recreation Educators, 1969-70, 1971-72, member of research and scholarly publications committee, 1972-73; associate editor, *Journal of Leisure Research*, 1975-77.

SIDELIGHTS: Murphy sees a "... need for people to work closely together in a non-threatening manner and assume more control over our own lives."

*   *   *

MURTAGH, John M(artin)   1911-1976

February 26, 1911—January 13, 1976; American judge and author. Obituaries: *Time*, January 26, 1976. (See index for previous *CA* sketch)

*   *   *

MUTHESIUS, Stefan   1939-

PERSONAL: Born July 30, 1939, in Berlin, Germany; son of Karl Volkmar (a journalist) and Helene (Rossbach) Muthesius; married Anna Maria Butterworth, 1971; children: Bianca Helena. *Education:* University of Marburg and University der Lahn, Dr.Phil., 1969; also studied at University of Munich and Courtauld Institute of Art, University of London. *Home:* 72 Helena Rd., Norwich NR2 3BZ, England. *Office:* School of Fine Arts, University of East Anglia, Norwich NR4 7TJ, England.

CAREER: University of East Anglia, Norwich, England, lecturer in fine arts, 1968—. Member of faculty at Johns

Hopkins University, spring, 1972. *Member:* Society of Architectural Historians, Verband Deutscher Kunsthistoriker, Norwich Society (member of committee).

WRITINGS: The High Victorian Movement in Architecture, 1850-1870, Routledge & Kegan Paul, 1972; *Das englische Vorbild: Eine Studie zu den deutschen Reformbewegungen in Architektur, Wohnbau und Kunstgewerbe im spaeteren 19, Jahrhundert* (title means "England as a Model: A Study of German Reform Movements in Architecture, Domestic Architecture and Applied Arts in the Later 19th Century"), Prestel Verlag Muenchen, 1974; (with Bridget Wilkins) *Europe, 1900-1914,* Milton Keynes, 1975. Contributor to English and German language art history journals.

WORK IN PROGRESS: Research on nineteenth-century domestic architecture in England and Europe.

* * *

MYERS, Andrew Breen 1920-

PERSONAL: Born September 28, 1920, in New York, N.Y.; son of Andrew J. (an engineer) and Margaret (a registered nurse; maiden name, Breen) Myers; married Margaret Lohrmann (a physician), July 4, 1949; children: Cathleen, Christopher, Andrew. *Education:* Fordham University, A.B., 1940; attended Biarritz American University, 1945-46; Columbia University, M.A., 1947, Ph.D., 1964. *Religion:* Roman Catholic. *Home:* 144-89 38th Ave., Flushing, N.Y. 11354. *Office:* Department of English, Dealy Hall, Fordham University, New York, N.Y. 10458.

CAREER: High school teacher of geometry in New York, N.Y., 1942-43; Fordham University, New York, N.Y., instructor, 1946-51, assistant professor, 1951-67, associate professor, 1967-75, professor of American literature, 1975—, associate director of development, 1964-66. Lecturer at Columbia University, 1955-56, and Queens College of the City University of New York, 1963-64; instructor at College of Mount St. Vincent, 1960-62, assistant professor, 1962-64. *Military service:* U.S. Army, 1943-46.

MEMBER: American Association of University Professors, Modern Language Association of America, American Studies Association, Bibliographical Society of America (member of council and treasurer, 1974—), Manuscript Society, Melville Society, New-York Historical Society (Pintard fellow; member of Pintard council, 1970-74), Pierpont Morgan Library (fellow), Grolier Club (member of council, 1974—), Lotos Club. *Awards, honors:* Achievement Award in Education, Fordham College Alumni Association, 1970.

WRITINGS: (Editor) *Washington Irving: A Tribute,* Sleepy Hollow Restorations, 1972; (editor) *The Knickerbocker Tradition,* Sleepy Hollow Restorations, 1974; (editor) *The Worlds of Washington Irving,* Sleepy Hollow Restorations and New York Public Library, 1974. Contributor of articles and reviews to literature and library journals. Member of editorial advisory board of Fordham University Press; research consultant to Sleepy Hollow Restorations.

WORK IN PROGRESS: Washington Irving, a biography, for Twayne; editing *A Century of Criticism of Washington Irving,* Sleepy Hollow Restorations; editing with others, *The Complete Works of Washington Irving.*

AVOCATIONAL INTERESTS: Travel, collecting books and manuscripts in American literature (especially of Irving, Cooper, and Bryant), singing (former baritone in choirs), fishing.

BIOGRAPHICAL/CRITICAL SOURCES: New York Times, June 10, 1974; *Fordham,* autumn, 1974.

* * *

MYERS, Bernice

PERSONAL: Born in Bronx, N.Y.; daughter of Leonard (a jewelry designer) and Anna (a dressmaker; maiden name, Marer) Kaufman; married Lou Myers (a cartoonist and writer), June 5, 1947; children: Marc Lee, Danny Alan. *Education:* Brooklyn College (now of the City University of New York), student in degree program sponsored by Ford Foundation for adults, 1966. *Home:* 58 Lakeview Ave. W., Peekskill, N.Y. 10566.

CAREER: After high school worked at various jobs in garment industry, including model, designer assistant, and sketcher, 1943-45; Columbia Pictures, New York, N.Y., employee in photostat department and illustrator of spots for movie ads, 1945-47; author and illustrator of children's books. Occasional advertising illustrator. *Member:* Authors Guild.

WRITINGS—Self-illustrated juveniles: Olivier, l'ours savant, Hachette, 1956; *Voila le facteur,* Hachette, 1957; *Les Quatre Musiciens,* Hachette, 1957; *Not This Bear!,* Four Winds, 1968; *My Mother Is Lost,* Scholastic Book Services, 1971; *Come Out Shadow, Wherever You Are,* Scholastic Book Services, 1971; *The Apple War,* Parents' Magazine Press, 1973; *Shhhh! It's a Secret,* Holt, 1973; *Chicken Feathers,* Holt, 1973; *The Safest Place,* Holt, 1973; *Nobody Knows Me,* Macmillan, 1974; *Where's a Dog?,* Holt, 1974; *A Lost Horse,* Doubleday, 1975; *Herman and the Bears Again,* Scholastic Book Services, 1976. Writer of stories for readers published by Holt, 1972, and Macmillan, 1973.

Illustrator: Mary Elting under pseudonym Benjamin Brewster, *It's a Secret,* Grosset, 1950; Inez McClintock, *Billy and His Steam Roller,* Grosset, 1951; Burl Ives, *Sailing on a Very Fine Day,* Rand McNally, 1954; (with husband, Lou Myers) adapted from Charles Perrault, *Puss-in-Boots,* Rand McNally, 1955; Samuel Epstein and Beryl Williams, *First Book of Mexico,* F. Watts, 1955; Caroline Horowitz under pseudonym Jane K. Lansing, *Being Nice Is Lots of Fun,* Hart, 1955; Rose Wyler, *First Book of Weather,* F. Watts, 1956; Rose Wyler and Gerald Ames, *What Makes It Go?,* McGraw, 1958; Margaret O. Hyde, *Off into Space! Science for Young Space Travelers,* McGraw, 1959, 3rd edition, 1969; Irving A. Leitner, *Pear Shaped Hill,* Golden Press, 1960; John Lawrence Peterson, *How to Write Codes and Send Secret Messages,* Four Winds, 1970.

Also illustrator of science series by Tillie S. Pine and Joseph Levine; published by McGraw, except as noted: *Sounds All Around,* 1958; *Water All Around,* 1959; *Air All Around,* 1960; *Friction All Around,* 1960; *Light All Around,* 1961; *Electricity All Around,* 1962; *Gravity All Around,* 1963; *Heat All Around,* 1963; *Simple Machines and How We Use Them,* Whittlesey House, 1965; *Weather All Around,* 1966; *Rocks and How We Use Them,* Whittlesey House, 1965; *Weather All Around,* 1966; *Rocks and How We Use Them,* Whittlesey House, 1967; *Trees and How We Use Them,* 1969.

SIDELIGHTS: Bernice Myers said: "I rarely write with a theme in mind. I begin with a sentence, any sentence which should lead to a second and then a third and so forth finally culminating in a children's story. There are times I can manage a sentence, sometimes five, even ten and then come to a dead end. I have drawers full of sentences, running from one to dozens. If a last sentence *is* finally written, I then begin the process of honing and grooming those sentences, rearranging them within the context of the story, adding words, and eliminating others . . . all this done with the idea of the pictures in mind. In this way I have eliminated many ideas in writing which will be explained by the pictures themselves and so instead of the drawings illustrating the story, I somehow hope that the drawings juxtapose the story and contribute an added dimension.'' *Avocational interests:* Tennis.

* * *

MYERS, Norma 1929-

PERSONAL: Born May 25, 1929, in Boston, Mass.; daughter of Louis (a broker) and Ruth T. (Scheffreen) Fishel; married Lewis Myers (president of Omega Wire), January 18, 1953; children: Susan, Wendy, Sarah. *Education:* Attended University of Michigan and Tobe Coburu School. *Home:* 7 Lenox Pl., Scarsdale, N.Y. 10583. *Agent:* John Cushman Associates, Inc., 24 West 43rd St., New York, N.Y. 10036.

CAREER: Filene's, Boston, Mass., assistant buyer, 1951-53; Gilchrist's, Boston, coordinator of ready-to-wear clothing for branch stores, 1953-55; now teacher and writer. *Member:* League of Women Voters of Scarsdale (member of board of directors).

WRITINGS: (With Joan Scobey) *Gifts from the Kitchen,* Doubleday, 1973; (with Scobey) *Gifts from Your Garden,* Bobbs-Merrill, 1975.

* * *

MYRA, Harold L(awrence) 1939-

PERSONAL: Born July 19, 1939, in Camden, N.J.; son of John S. and Esther (Christensen) Myra; married Jeanette Austin (a registered nurse), May 7, 1966; children: Michelle, Todd, Gregory. *Education:* East Stroudsburg State College, B.S., 1961. *Home:* 8221 Kay Court, Annandale, Va. 22003. *Office: Christianity Today,* Washington Building, Washington, D.C.

CAREER: Campus Life, Wheaton, Ill., publisher, 1961-75; *Christianity Today,* Washington, D.C., president and publisher, 1975—. *Military service:* U.S. Marine Corps Reserve, active duty, 1957-62.

WRITINGS: No Man in Eden, Word, Inc., 1969; *Michelle, You Scallawag, I Love You,* John J. Benson, 1972; *The New You,* Zondervan, 1972; *Is There a Place I Can Scream?,* Doubleday, 1975; *Elsbeth,* Revell, 1976.

* * *

NAM, Koon Woo 1928-

PERSONAL: Born May 1, 1928, in Korea; naturalized U.S. citizen; son of Sang-pil and Soon-rok (Lee) Nam; married Jane MacDonald, 1967; children: Ellen R. *Education:* Kyunghee University, B.A., 1958; University of Rhode Island, M.A. (English), 1963; University of Massachusetts, M.A. (political science), 1965, Ph.D., 1970. *Home address:* Keene St., Box 21, Bourne, Mass. 02532.

CAREER: University of Connecticut, Storrs, instructor in Far Eastern politics, 1969-70; Mark Hopkins College, Brattleboro, Vt., adjunct senior fellow in political science, 1970-71; Marist College, Poughkeepsie, N.Y., assistant professor of the history of East Asia, 1971-72; Rosary Hill College, Buffalo, N.Y., assistant professor of political sci-

ence, 1972-74; Massachusetts Maritime Academy, Buzzards Bay, associate professor of American government and international relations, 1974—. Translator for U.S. Joint Publications and Research Service, 1972-75.

WRITINGS: The North Korean Communist Leadership, 1945-65, University of Alabama Press, 1974. Contributor to Asian studies and Pacific studies journals.

WORK IN PROGRESS: Research on the evolution of North Korean Communist thought.

* * *

NAMIER, Julia 1893-
(Julia Mikhailovna de Beausobre)

PERSONAL: Born October 26, 1893, in St. Petersburg, Russia; daughter of Michael (a landowner) and Julia (Riaboushynski) Kazarin; married Nicholas Vladimir de Beausobre, February 3, 1917 (died, 1933); married Lewis Bernstein Namier, June 4, 1948 (died, 1960); children: two (deceased). *Education:* Educated privately. *Religion:* Russian Orthodox. *Home:* Woodcote Grove House, Coulsdon, Surrey, London, CR3 2XL, England. *Awards, honors:* James Tait Black Memorial Prize, 1972, for *Lewis Namier.*

WRITINGS—Under name Julia de Beausobre: *The Woman Who Could Not Die* (autobiographical account of imprisonment in Russia), Viking, 1938, issued with a preface by Rebecca West, Gollancz, 1948; *Creative Suffering,* Dacre Press, 1940; (compiler, translator, author of foreword) Macarius, Starets of Optina, *Russian Letters of Direction, 1834-60,* Dacre Press, 1944; *Flame in the Snow: A Russian Legend,* Constable, 1945, Seabury, 1975.

Under name Julia Namier: *Lewis Namier: A Biography,* Oxford University Press, 1971.

Contributor of articles and book reviews to periodicals, including *Times Literary Supplement,* 1940-48, and *Time and Tide;* contributor to *Theoria to Theory,* 1971—.

WORK IN PROGRESS: Aliosha's Way, an account of contemplative prayer in the U.S.S.R. since 1930; *Judas, Apostle to the Russians,* on the legend begun in the Kievan period of the tenth to thirteenth centuries and brought up to date.

* * *

NASAW, Jonathan Lewis 1947-

PERSONAL: Born August 26, 1947; son of Joshua J. (a lawyer) and Beatrice (a teacher; maiden name, Kaplan) Nasaw; married Soo Stone, June 22, 1969 (divorced January, 1973). *Education:* Attended University of Wisconsin, 1965-66; State University of New York at Stony Brook, B.A. *Politics:* "Not much". *Religion:* Arica. *Residence:* Troy, Mich. *Agent:* Steve Sheppard, Paul R. Reynolds Agency, Inc., 12 East 41st St., New York, N.Y. 10017.

CAREER: Teacher in Williamsport, Pa., 1971-72; Wave (trio), St. Croix, Virgin Islands, bassman, 1973; Sundance (musical group), St. Croix, Virgin Islands, bassman and backup vocals, 1973; teacher of meditation at Arica Institute, 1973—.

WRITINGS: Easy Walking, Lippincott, 1975.

WORK IN PROGRESS: A novel, *Clear Light.*

SIDELIGHTS: Nasaw wrote: "I think it's important to get straight for the record—this is a scoop, *CA*—that *Easy Walking* is a 'non-fiction novel' and is as much fiction as biography. The PR people say it's all true. Nonsense! . . . I wanted to be a writer or a musician since I was knee-high. ... Now that I've been both I decided to share my writing and keep my music for myself. I teach meditation ... as my principal avocation, and that helps me keep tabs on what's really important to me about writing (creation and communication) and what's not (interviews and ego strokes).''

* * *

NASH, Ralph (Lee) 1925-

PERSONAL: Born February 22, 1925, in Sullivan, Ind.; son of Cecil E. and Flossie (Raines) Nash; married Berta Sturman, December 17, 1949; children: Thomas, Richard. *Education:* Duke University, A.B., 1945, M.A., 1946; Harvard University, Ph.D., 1951. *Home:* 10155 Talbot, Huntington Woods, Mich. 48070. *Office:* Department of English, Wayne State University, Detroit, Mich. 48202.

CAREER: University of Louisville, Louisville, Ky., instructor in English, 1948-50; Washington University, St. Louis, Mo., instructor in English, 1950-54; Wayne State University, Detroit, Mich., instructor, 1955-58, assistant professor, 1958-61, associate professor, 1961-64, professor of English, 1955—, chairman of department, 1968-72. *Member:* American Association of Teachers of Italian, Renaissance Society of America.

WRITINGS: (Editor and translator) Jacopo Sannazaro, *Arcadia and Piscatorial Ecologues,* Wayne State University Press, 1966. Contributor of about twenty articles and some poems to academic journals.

* * *

NATHAN, Joan 1943-

PERSONAL: Born January 26, 1943, in Providence, R.I.; daughter of Ernest (chairman of the board of directors of Elmwood Sensors) and Pearl (Gluck) Nathan; married Allan Gerson (a lawyer), October 20, 1974. *Education:* Attended University of Grenoble, 1960, and Sorbonne, University of Paris, 1963-64; University of Michigan, B.A. (with high honors), 1965, M.A., 1966. *Politics:* Democrat. *Religion:* Jewish. *Home and office:* 33 Concord Ave., Apt. 18, Cambridge, Mass. 02138.

CAREER: Permanent Mission of Madascagar to the United Nations, New York, N.Y., administrative assistant to the ambassador, 1967-68; Institute of International Education, New York, N.Y., public information specialist, 1968-69; Municipality of Jerusalem, Israel, foreign press officer to mayor, 1970-72, Guggenheim Productions, Washington D.C., assistant producer of film documentary "Jerusalem Lives," 1973; Office of the Mayor, New York, N.Y., director of public information for office of midtown planning and development, 1973-74, coordinator of mayor's "Walk 'n' Talk" program for department of public events, 1974—; writer, 1970—. Member of board of directors of Window Shop Scholarships, 1974—; member of executive committee of International Medical and Research Foundation, 1973-74. Teacher of English as a foreign language for United Nations Secretariat, 1967-68, and American Council of Emigres in Professions, 1968. *Member:* National Association for the Advancement of Colored People (member of Mid-Manhattan executive board, 1968-70), University Club.

WRITINGS: Tips for Vips: A United Jewish Appeal Guide to Israel, United Jewish Appeal, 1973; (with Judy Stacey Goldman) *The Flavor of Jerusalem,* Little, Brown,

1975. Contributor to *Present Tense, Providence Journal, Boston Globe,* and *Jerusalem Post.*

AVOCATIONAL INTERESTS: Skiing, tennis, cooking.

* * *

NAVA, Julian 1927-

PERSONAL: Born June 19, 1927, in Los Angeles, Calif.; son of Julian and Refugio (Flores) Nava; married Patricia Lucas, June 30, 1962; children: Catherine and Carmen (twin daughters), Paul. *Education:* East Los Angeles Junior College, A.A., 1949; Pomona College, A.B., 1951; Harvard University, A.M., 1952, Ph.D., 1955. *Politics:* Democrat. *Home:* 18308 Septo, Northridge, Calif. 91234. *Office:* Board of Education, 450 North Grand Ave., Los Angeles, Calif. 90012.

CAREER: U.S. Cultural Center, Caracas, Venezuela, instructor in English and U.S. history, 1953-54; University of Puerto Rico, Rio Piedras, lecturer in humanities, 1955-57; California State University, Northridge, assistant professor, 1957-61, associate professor, 1961-65, professor of history, 1965—. Fulbright lecturer at Universidad de Valladolid, 1962-63; founding director of Centro de Estudio Universitarios Colombo-Americano, 1964-65. Member of Los Angeles board of education. Chairman of founding committee to preserve the history of Los Angeles, 1961-62; founding director of Great Lakes Colleges Association Center in Bogota, 1964-65; member of governing board of California State Colleges' Inter-America Institute, 1966; member of board of directors of Los Angeles World Affairs Council, 1970, Plaza de la Raza, 1970—, Hispanic Urban Center, 1971—, and National Hispanic Scholarship Foundation, 1975—; member of advisory committee of Mexican American Legal Defense and Education Fund, National Urban Coalition, Bilingual Children's Television, La Raza Television, Educational Testing Service; member of Mexican advisory committee to California superintendent of public instruction. *Military service:* U.S. Navy, Air Force, 1945-46. *Member:* American Historical Association.

WRITINGS: Mexican Americans: Past, Present and Future (high school text), American Book Co., 1969; *Mexican Americans: A Brief Look at Their History,* Anti-Defamation League of B'nai B'rith, 1970; (author of foreword) Nathaniel Wagner and Maesha Haug, *Chicanos: Social and Psychological Perspectives,* Mosby, 1971; (editor) *The Mexican American in American History* (high school text), American Book Co., 1973; (editor) *Viva la Raza!: Readings on Mexican Americans,* Van Nostrand, 1973; *Mexican Americans Today: In Search of Opportunity* (booklet), Xerox Educational Publishing, 1973; (author of preface) Abraham Hoffman, *Unwanted Mexican Americans in the Great Depression,* University of Arizona Press, 1974; *Our Hispanic American Heritage* (booklet), Xerox Educational Publishing, 1974; (contributor) Gus Tyler, editor, *Mexican-Americans Tomorrow,* University of New Mexico Press, 1975; (with Robert Barger) *A General History of California* (college text), Benziger, 1976.

"Bilingual Stories for Today," a series published by Aardvark Media; all 1974: *Myself/Yo* (Grade One); *My Friends/Mis Amigos* (Grade Two); *My Family/Mi Familia* (Grade Three); *Happy Days/Dias Felices* (Grade Four); *Names and Places/Nombres y Lugares* (Grade Five); *Customs Across the Border/Costumbres del Otro Lado de la Frontera* (Grade Six); *A Traditional Voice in the Barrio/Una Voz Tradicional del Barrio* (Grade Seven); *Mexican American Profiles/Perfiles Mexicoamericanos* (Grade Eight).

Contributor to *Reader's Encyclopedia* and to professional journals.

WORK IN PROGRESS: A History of Mexico.

* * *

NAVROZOV, Lev 1928-

PERSONAL: Born November 26, 1928, in Moscow, Russia; came to United States, 1972; son of Andrey (a writer) and Dina (a medical doctor; maiden name, Mintz) Navrozov; married Muza Levit (an editor), 1955; children: Andrey. *Education:* "Self-educated—in Russia there is no education in the humanist sense." *Home:* 3419 Irwin Ave., New York, N.Y. 10463.

CAREER: Writer. Free-lance translator of Russian literature into English as cover profession for writing in Russian underground, 1950-71.

WRITINGS: The Education of Lev Navrozov, Harper, 1974. Contributor of essays to *Commentary.*

WORK IN PROGRESS: Second and subsequent books of seven-book cycle, of which *The Education of Lev Navrozov* is the first; a one-actor play, "Welcome to Soviet America!"

SIDELIGHTS: After waiting three months for a visa, Navrozov left the Soviet Union in 1972, smuggling out a cycle of writings that he had worked on for almost twenty years. *The Education of Lev Navrozov* is the first publication of those secret writings that the author, because of his status as one of Russia's most highly valued translators and his outward behavior as an exemplary Soviet citizen, was able to write and research with relative freedom.

Navrozov told Irina Kirk that the single most important idea that Americans should know about Russia is "that the people of Russia are human. Like Americans are. Except that the people of Russia are in a bad historic predicament, while the historic luck of Americans is in. Yet the survival of the lucky Americans depends on those who are now in a bad historic predicament."

Robert Massie said of *The Education of Lev Navrozov,* "As if Proust had somehow blended with Orwell . . ., this work is destined to become a twentieth-century classic. . . . It places Navrozov immediately among the few important writers of this century."

BIOGRAPHICAL/CRITICAL SOURCES: Irina Kirk, *Profiles in Russian Resistance,* Quadrangle, 1975.

* * *

NEAL, Patsy 1938-

PERSONAL: Born April 19, 1938, in Elberton, Ga.; daughter of George Milton and Margaret (Eavenson) Neal. *Education:* Wayland College, B.S. (cum laude), 1960; University of Utah, M.S., 1963. *Home address:* Box 261, Etowah, N.C. 28729. *Office:* Department of Physical Education, Brevard College, Brevard, N.C. 28712.

CAREER: University of Utah, Salt Lake City, instructor, 1963-66; Brevard College, Brevard, N.C., instructor, 1966-68, assistant professor, 1968-72, associate professor of physical education, 1972—. Instructor at Fourth National Institute on Girls and Women's Sports, 1964. Member of Amateur Athletic Union and Division for Girls' and Women's Sports basketball rules committee, 1964-66, 1973-75; member of basketball sub-committee of United States Collegiate Sports Council, 1968-70. *Awards, honors:* National free-throw champion, 1957; Amateur Athletic Union All-

American in basketball, 1959, 1960, 1965; Freedoms Foundation awards, 1961, 1963, 1966, and 1972, for essays.

WRITINGS: Basketball Techniques for Women, Ronald, 1966; *Coaching Methods for Women,* Addison-Wesley, 1969; *Sport and Identity,* Dorrance, 1972; *So Run Your Race* (poetry), Zondervan, 1974; (with Thomas Tutko) *Coaching Girls and Women: Psychological Perspectives,* Allyn & Bacon, 1975. Contributor to physical education journals; contributor of poetry and short stories to literary magazines.

SIDELIGHTS: Patsy Neal was a member of the U.S. basketball team in the 1959 Pan-American games and against the Russian all-star team touring the United States in 1959-60. She was captain of the U.S. team in the World Basketball Tournament in Peru in 1964, and toured with the U.S. team in Russia, France, and Germany in 1965. Her championship score in national free-throw competition in 1957 was 48 of 50.

BIOGRAPHICAL/CRITICAL SOURCES: Sportswoman, November-December, 1974.

* * *

NEALE, John E(rnest) 1890-1975

December 7, 1890—September 2, 1975; British educator, historian, and author of biographical and historical works. Obituaries: *New York Times,* September 4, 1975; *Washington Post,* September 6, 1975; *Publishers Weekly,* September 15, 1975.

* * *

NEAMAN, Judith S(ilverman) 1936-

PERSONAL: Born September 20, 1936, in Syracuse, N.Y.; daughter of Jesse (an engineer) and Beatrice (a teacher; maiden name, Rosenbloom) Silverman; married Peter Gordon Neaman (a medical-pharmaceutical administrator), February 16, 1964; children: Adam Piers. *Education:* University of Michigan, B.A. (cum laude), 1959; Columbia University, M.A. (with honors), 1960, Ph.D., 1968. *Residence:* New York, N.Y.

CAREER: High school teacher of English in private school in New York, N.Y., 1960-62; Herbert H. Lehman College (now Lehman College of the City University of New York), Bronx, N.Y., lecturer in English, 1963-68; Hofstra University, Hempstead, N.Y., assistant professor of medieval and American literature, 1968-74; Creative Teaching Workshop, New York, N.Y., educational consultant and adviser, 1975—. Lecturer at Columbia University, summers, 1970—; adjunct professor at Hunter College of the City University of New York, 1974-75, Member of board of Bridge (mental health organization), 1963-65. *Member:* International Courtly Literature Society, American Association of University Professors, Mediaeval Academy of America, Modern Language Association of America. *Awards, honors:* National Endowment for the Humanities summer fellowship, 1973.

WRITINGS: (With Rhoda B. Nathan) *The American Vision: The Individual and Collective Modes,* Scott, Foresman, 1973; *Suggestion of the Devil: The Origins of Madness,* Doubleday Anchor, 1975. Contributor to journals, including *Philological Quarterly.* Editor of American Association of University Professors chapter newsletter, 1972-73.

WORK IN PROGRESS: Research on medieval optics; journal articles on literary topics.

SIDELIGHTS: Judith Neaman is a painter and has had two one-woman watercolor shows in New York City. She is "happiest when making things, such as books, intellectual constructs, or paintings."

*   *   *

NEELY, Martina 1939-

PERSONAL: Born February 1, 1939, in Akron, Ohio; daughter of Lester Adam and Elizabeth (Molnar) Winemiller; married William Jewell Neely (a writer), November 27, 1965; children: Anna, Susan, Walter III. *Politics:* Republican. *Religion:* Methodist. *Home and office address:* P.O. Box 500, Jane-Lew, W.Va. 26378.

CAREER: Writer.

WRITINGS: (With Hermann G. Rusch) *Greenbrier Cookbook,* Regnery, 1975.

AVOCATIONAL INTERESTS: Painting (watercolors), gardening, cooking.

*   *   *

NEIBURG, Gladys Eudas 1898-

PERSONAL: Surname is pronounced Nee-burg; born July 29, 1898, in St. Albans, Vt.; daughter of Louis Mendel (a junk dealer) and Lena (a grocery store operator; maiden name, Press) Neiburg. *Education:* University of Vermont, B.A., 1949. *Politics:* "Republican who very often votes for the person—not party." *Religion:* Jewish. *Home and office:* 39 Federal St., St. Albans, Vt. 05478.

CAREER: Clerk-stenographer in St. Albans, Vt., 1916-38; merchant, 1936—. President of local writers workshop, 1949-70; chairman of St. Albans Bi-Centennial Art Exhibit. *Member:* Jewish National Fund, United Jewish Appeal, Hebrew Immigrant Aid Society, Hadassah, League of Vermont Writers, Poetry Society of Vermont, Vermont Folklore Society, Franklin County Humane Society (past president). *Awards, honors:* Award from Jewish National Fund, 1970, for her campaign to plant trees in Israel; Masada Award from Jewish National Fund, 1975, for campaign to sell Israeli bonds; Golden Book Award from Jewish National Fund, 1975; award from Ner Israel Rabbinical College, 1975; merit award from Federated Garden Clubs of Vermont, 1975, for raising funds to plant more than nine thousand trees in Israel.

WRITINGS: Whispering Pines (poems), Windy Row Press, 1974. Writer of columns, "Sense and Nonsense" in *St. Alban's Messenger,* 1965, and "Pondering Out Loud" in *St. Alban's Messenger,* 1968.

SIDELIGHTS: Gladys Neiburg has visited Israel three times since 1961. *Avocational interests:* Creative writing, painting, cats, lecturing on Judaism and Israel.

BIOGRAPHICAL/CRITICAL SOURCES: Jewish Post, June 20, 1975.

*   *   *

NEIGHBOURS, Kenneth Franklin 1915-

PERSONAL: Born September 21, 1915, in Fannin County, Tex.; son of Daniel Eben (a farmer) and Edna (Bruton) Neighbours. *Education:* Southern Methodist University, B.A., 1948, M.A., 1949; University of Texas, Ph.D., 1955. *Politics:* "Independent—usually Democrat." *Religion:* Methodist Episcopal Church, South. *Home:* 207 East Church St., Olney, Tex. *Office:* Midwestern University, 3400 Taft, Wichita Falls, Tex. 76308.

CAREER: Allen Military Academy, Bryan, Tex., instructor in history, 1952-55; Midwestern University, Wichita Falls, Tex., professor of American history, 1955—. Consultant, U.S. Department of Justice, 1968-69; president of Fort Belknap Archives, 1961-73. *Military service:* U.S. Army, 1942-45. *Member:* American Historical Association, Organization of American Historians, Southern Historical Association, Western Historical Association, West Texas Historical Association.

WRITINGS: Fort Belknap: Outpost on the Texas Frontier, Fort Belknap Society, 1961; (co-author) *Frontier Forts of Texas,* Texian Press, 1966; (co-author) *Apache Ethnohistory,* Garland Publishing, 1973; *Indian Exodus: Texas Indian Affairs, 1835-1859,* Nortex, 1973; *Robert S. Neighbours and the Texas Frontier,* Texian Press, 1975. Contributor to scholarly journals.

WORK IN PROGRESS: History of the Tonkawa Indians; History of the Aipan Apache.

*   *   *

NELSON, Eugene 1929-

PERSONAL: Born September 10, 1929, in Modesto, Calif.; son of Eugene (a grower) and Marjorie (Scott) Nelson; children: Tamar, Shelley. *Education:* Studied at Handy Writers Colony, 1953, 1956, 1957. *Politics:* "Industrial Workers of the World." *Religion:* "Industrial Workers of the World." *Home address:* P.O. Box 7037, Santa Rosa, Calif. 95401. *Agent:* Jed Mattes, 40 West 57th St., New York, N.Y.

CAREER: Farm worker, reporter, labor organizer. *Member:* Industrial Workers of the World.

WRITINGS: Huelga: The First One-Hundred Days of the Delano Grape Strike, Farm Worker Press, 1966; *Bracero* (novel), Peace Press, 1975; (editor and compiler) *Pablo Cruz and the American Dream,* Peregrine Smith, 1975.

WORK IN PROGRESS: Tales of Crapitalism (short stories); *Fantasia of a Revolutionary,* for City Lights; a novel on the Delano strike; a book on farm labor in Texas; poems; case histories of undocumented immigrants from Mexico.

AVOCATIONAL INTERESTS: Man-woman relationships.

*   *   *

NELSON, Lois (Ney) 1930-

PERSONAL: Born March 23, 1930, in Washington, D.C.; daughter of Rudolph N. (an attorney and businessman) and Gertrude (Owlick) Miller; married Marton Nelson (a physician, professor, and county health officer), December 29, 1950; children: Steven David. *Education:* University of California, Los Angeles, B.A., 1953, M.Ed., 1957, Ed.D., 1964. *Home:* 7 Lakeview Dr., Daly City, Calif. 94015. *Office:* Department of Elementary Education, San Francisco State University, San Francisco, Calif. 94132.

CAREER: Elementary school teacher in Los Angeles, Calif., 1953-59, curriculum consultant, 1959-60; University of California, Los Angeles, instructor in Education Extension, 1959-63, supervisor and demonstration teacher at university elementary school, 1960-63; San Francisco State University, San Francisco, Calif., assistant professor, 1965-68, associate professor, 1968-73, professor of education, 1973—. Lecturer and assistant professor at University of California, Los Angeles, summers, 1959, 1960, 1963,

1964; research associate at Research and Development Center of Stanford University, 1966-67.

MEMBER: Association for Childhood Education International (member of national research committee, 1967-70); American Society for Childhood Development; American Association of University Women; American Educational Research Association; Association of California School Administrations, California Educational Research Association; University of California, Los Angeles Bay Area Alumni Association; University of California, Los Angeles, Doctors of Education Association; Phi Delta Kappa; Pi Lambda Theta; Delta Phi Epsilon. *Awards, honors:* Ella Victoria Dobbs award, 1975.

WRITINGS: Fostering Creativity, Academic Reading, 1967; *The Nature of Teaching: A Collection of Readings,* Blaisdell, 1969. Contributor to education journals. Writer, with others, of column in *Today's Education,* 1975-76. Member of reviewing committee of *Planning and Organization for Teaching* (of the National Education Association), 1963; consulting editor for *Journal of Educational Research,* 1972—.

WORK IN PROGRESS: "The Development of Conservation Concepts in Children from Low Income Families."

BIOGRAPHICAL/CRITICAL SOURCES: Elementary English, March, 1966; *Review of Educational Research,* April, 1967.

* * *

NELSON, Peter 1940-

PERSONAL: Born July 30, 1940, in St. Louis, Mo.; son of Ralph Arnold and Catherine (English) Nelson. *Education:* Occidental College, B.A., 1964; California State University, Los Angeles, graduate study, 1965; University of California, Irvine, M.F.A., 1969. *Religion:* Christian. *Home:* 256 East Mendocino, Altadena, Calif. 91001. *Office:* Department of English, University of Hawaii, Honolulu, Hawaii 96822.

CAREER: County of Los Angeles, Los Angeles, Calif., with public information office, 1963-64; M.S.E.I. (public relations firm), Palm Springs, Calif., publicist, 1965-66; Fawcett-McDermott Associates (advertising firm), Honolulu, Hawaii, staff associate, 1966; Pasadena Art Museum, Pasadena, Calif., editorial consultant, 1967-70, media director, 1969-70; University of Hawaii, Honolulu, instructor, 1968-69, 1970-73, assistant professor of English, 1973—. Teacher of Transcendental Meditation, 1974—; associate professor of literature, Maharishi International University, Fairfield, Iowa, 1975-76. Member of Hawaii Literary Arts Council, 1974—. *Awards, honors:* Occidental Faculty Writing Award; Francis Moffit Hope Prize for poetry.

WRITINGS: Between Lives (poems), Ironwood Press, 1974. Also editor of several catalogue essays and books on modern and contemporary art, 1967-71. Advisory editor, *Hawaii Review,* 1972-74.

WORK IN PROGRESS: A collection of poems; an anthology of twenty-five young Hawaiian poets, completion expected in 1976.

SIDELIGHTS: Nelson has traveled and lived in the Pacific, Asia, and Europe.

* * *

NEMSER, Cindy 1937-

PERSONAL: Born March 26, 1937, in Brooklyn, N.Y.; daughter of William (a businessman) and Helen (Nelson) Heller; married Charles Nemser (a salesman), December 16, 1956; children: Cathy. *Education:* Brooklyn College (now of the City University of New York), B.A., 1958, M.A. (English), 1963; New York University, M.A. (art history), 1966. *Religion:* Jewish. *Home and office:* 41 Montgomery Pl., Brooklyn, N.Y. 11215.

CAREER: Teacher of elementary grades in the public schools of New York City, 1958-64; Museum of Modern Art, New York City, curatorial interne, 1965; *Feminist Art Journal,* New York City, editor, 1972—; *Arts Magazine,* New York City, contributing editor, 1973—. Visiting lecturer at New York University, University of Wisconsin, Pratt Institute, and University of Rhode Island. *Member:* Women in the Arts (founding member), Women's Caucus for Art (member of board of directors, 1975), College Art Association.

WRITINGS: Art Talk: Conversations with Twelve Women Artists, Scribner, 1975. Contributor to art journals, and to *Women: A Journal of Liberation, Ms., Soho Weekly News,* and *Village Voice.* Art critic for *Changes,* 1972.

WORK IN PROGRESS: Research on women in the arts, and the history of women artists; a monograph on Alice Neel; autobiographical fiction.

* * *

NESBITT, Ralph Beryl 1891(?)-1975

1891(?)—November 14, 1975; American minister, missionary, and author. Obituaries: *Washington Post,* November 20, 1975.

* * *

NETANYAHU, Benzion 1910-

PERSONAL: Born March 25, 1910; son of Nathan (a rabbi) and Sarah (Lurie) Mileikowsky; married Cela Segal, September 7, 1944; children: Jonathan, Benjamin, Iddo. *Education:* Hebrew Teachers Seminary, Jerusalem, Israel, teacher's diploma, 1929; Hebrew University of Jerusalem, M.A., 1933; Dropsie College, Ph.D., 1947. *Home:* 30 Uptown Village, Ithaca, N.Y. 14850. *Office:* Department of Semitic Languages and Literatures, Cornell University, 166 Rockefeller Hall, Ithaca, N.Y. 14853.

CAREER: Co-editor of *Betar* (Hebrew monthly), 1933-34; *Hayarden* (daily newspaper), Jerusalem, Israel, editor, 1934-35; Zionist Political Library, Jerusalem and Tel-Aviv, Israel, editor, 1935-40; New Zionist Organization of America, New York, N.Y., executive director, 1940-48; *Encyclopedia Hebraica,* Jerusalem, editor-in-chief, 1948-62; Dropsie College, Philadelphia, Pa., professor of Hebrew language and literature, and chairman of department, 1957-66, professor of medieval Jewish history and Hebrew literature, 1966-68; University of Denver, Denver, Colo., professor of Hebraic studies, 1968-71; Cornell University, Ithaca, N.Y., professor of Judaic studies, 1971—, chairman of department of Semitic languages and literatures, 1971-75. Member of American Zionist Emergency Council, 1945-48. *Member:* American Academy for Jewish Research (fellow; executive member, 1967—), Institute for Advanced Religious Studies (member of advisory council, 1967—).

WRITINGS: (Contributor) Max Nordau, editor, *Political Writings* (in Hebrew), two volumes, Hozaah Medinit (Tel-Aviv), 1936-37, 2nd edition, 1946; (editor and contributor) Theodore Herzl, *Letters, 1896-1904* (in Hebrew), Hozaah Medinit, 1937, 2nd edition, 1949; (editor) Israel Zangwill,

Road to Independence: Collected Works on the Jewish Question (in Hebrew), Hozaah Medinit, 1938; (contributor) Zangwill, editor, *Collection of Essays,* Hozaah Medinit, 1939; (editor and contributor) *Max Nordau to His People,* Scopus Publishing, 1941; (editor and contributor) Leo Pinsker, *Road to Freedom,* Scopus Publishing, 1944; *Don Isaac Abravanel: Statesman and Philosopher,* Jewish Publication Society, 1953, 3rd edition, 1972; (editor and contributor) Nordau, *Collected Works* (in Hebrew), four volumes, World Zionist Organization Publications, 1954-62; *The Marranos of Spain,* American Academy for Jewish Research, 1966, 2nd edition, 1973.

General editor of *The World History of the Jewish People,* Volume I, Rutgers University Press, 1964. Contributor to *Proceedings* of American Academy for Jewish Research, and to *Encyclopedia Hebraica.* Co-editor of *Jewish Quarterly Review,* 1959-60; editor of *Zionews* (of New Zionist Organization of America), 1942-44.

WORK IN PROGRESS: The Marranos of Spain According to the Spanish and Latin Sources of the Fifteenth Century; Spanish and Non-Spanish Historiography on the Marranos and the Inquisition.

* * *

NETTING, Robert M(cCorkle) 1934-

PERSONAL: Born October 14, 1934, in Racine, Wis.; son of Robert J. (a minister) and Martha (McCorkle) Netting; married Jacqueline Frazier, 1963; children: Robert F., Jessa F., Laurel M. *Education:* Yale University, B.A., 1957; University of Chicago, M.A., 1959, Ph.D., 1963. *Office:* Department of Anthropology, University of Arizona, Tucson, Ariz. 85721.

CAREER: University of Chicago, Chicago, Ill., lecturer in social science, 1962-63; University of Pennsylvania, Philadelphia, assistant professor, 1963-68, associate professor of anthropology, 1968-72; University of Arizona, Tucson, professor of anthropology, 1972—. *Member:* American Anthropological Association, American Ethnological Society. *Awards, honors:* Social Science Research Council grant for work in Nigeria, 1966-67; Guggenheim fellowship, 1970-71.

WRITINGS: (Editor with F. Gearing and L. Peattie) *Documentary History of the Fox Project,* Department of Anthropology, University of Chicago, 1960; *Hill Farmers of Nigeria,* University of Washington Press, 1968.

WORK IN PROGRESS: A study of the cultural ecology and historical demography of a Swiss Alpine community, researched on Guggenheim fellowship.

* * *

NEUFFER, Irene LaBorde 1919-
(Rene LaBorde)

PERSONAL: Surname is pronounced *Knife*-er; born December 16, 1919, in Columbia, S.C.; daughter of Pierre Fabian (an attorney) and Irene (Thomas) LaBorde; married Claude Henry Neuffer (a professor of English), March 1, 1953; children: Rene LaBorde (daughter), Francis Henry, Pierre LaBorde. *Education:* University of South Carolina, A.B. (magna cum laude), 1941, M.A., 1948; Duke University, further graduate study, 1948-50. *Politics:* Democrat. *Religion:* Episcopalian. *Home and office:* 4532 Meadowood Rd., Columbia, S.C. 29206.

CAREER: High school English teacher and basketball coach in York, S.C., 1941-42; University of South Carolina, Columbia, assistant professor of English, 1946-53;

free-lance writer, 1954—. Substitute teacher in public and parochial schools; teacher of adult evening classes in public schools. Co-chairman of Stop ERA (the Equal Rights Amendment) program in South Carolina. Publicist for local organizations. *Military service:* U.S. Army Air Forces, squadron commander, 1942-46; became captain. *Member:* South Carolina Historical Society, South Caroliniana Society, South Carolina Genealogical Society, Richland County Historical Society, Historic Columbia Foundation, Phi Beta Kappa.

WRITINGS: (Under maiden name, Irene LaBorde) *Petticoat Eagles* (history of Women's Army Corps Air Corps Squadron at Hendricks Field, Fla.), privately printed, 1944; (with husband, Claude Henry Neuffer) *The Name Game: From Oyster Point to Keowee,* Sandlapper Store, 1972; (editor and author of introduction, under name Rene LaBorde, with C. H. Neuffer) J. Gordon Coogler, *Purely Original Verse, 1897,* Vogue Press, 1974. Contributor of about three hundred articles to literary journals, including *Sandlapper* and *Georgia Review,* and to newspapers. Member of editorial staff of *Names in South Carolina.*

WORK IN PROGRESS: Feature articles and personal essays for newspapers and magazines.

SIDELIGHTS: Irene Neuffer writes: "In my youth I aimed to be the first woman editor of the *New York Times;* but several years ago when I finally got that far north with Claude ... I dropped by the *Times* office to tell them I wasn't interested anymore. It's much more rewarding to write with my favorite professor for the first state place-name journal in the United States and to search out the origins of such gems as Frog Level, Nine Times, and Satchel Ford Road." She adds: "I won Democratic nomination for school board (1972) in a hot and violent race, was trounced by Republicans in general election—I was muddy but unbowed, and decided my skin wasn't thick enough."

* * *

NEUMANN, Gareth William 1930-

PERSONAL: Born August 30, 1930, in New York, N.Y.; son of Aaron (a business executive) and Lillian (Nagel) Neumann; married Florence Bassi, December 4, 1953; children: Gareth W., Jr., Aaron W., Jeffrey S. *Education:* Attended high school in Scarsdale, N.Y. *Religion:* Christian Science. *Home:* 1660 Sheridan Rd., Glendale, Calif. 91206. *Office:* 3223 North Verdugo Rd., Glendale, Calif. 91208.

CAREER: Petersen Publishing Co., Los Angeles, Calif., editor, 1961-66; L. M. Cox Manufacturing Co., Santa Ana, Calif., director of advertising and public relations, 1966-67; Bill Neumann & Associates, Glendale, Calif., president, 1967—; Automotive Performance Systems, Glendale, Calif., president, 1971—. *Member:* American Auto Racing Writers and Broadcasters Association.

WRITINGS: (With Henry G. Felsen, Mickey Thompson, Ed Roth, Tom MacPherson) *Here Is Your Hobby ... Car Customizing,* Putnam, 1965; (with Bob Braverman) *Here Is Your Hobby ... Slot Car Racing,* Putnam, 1966, revised edition, 1969; *Here Is Your Hobby ... Model Car Building,* Putnam, 1971. Contributor to *Hot Rod, Popular Hot Rodding,* and *Road Test.*

* * *

NEUTRELLE, Dale 1937-

PERSONAL: Born September 29, 1937, in Norfolk, Va.;

daughter of Edward Wadsworth and Gladys V. (Edwards) Dashiell; married Robert E. Neutrelle (a publisher), July 5, 1957; children: Eva Danielle, Jennifer Renee. *Politics:* "A dirty business." *Religion:* None. *Home address:* P.O. Box 612, Ramona, Calif. 92065. *Office:* Acoma Books, P.O. Box 4, Ramona, Calif. 92065.

CAREER: North County Health Project, Ramona, Calif., medical receptionist, 1973—; Acoma Books, Ramona, bookseller, 1973—. Member of board of directors of North County Health Project.

WRITINGS: Wild Things to Cook, Acoma Books, 1974. Co-author of "Acoma Books: Americana," a monthly catalog of books on anthropology, archaeology, ethnology, native Americans, and the Southwest, 1973—.

WORK IN PROGRESS: Another cookbook.

SIDELIGHTS: Dale Neutrelle writes that her "cookbook was written to preserve for my daughters recipes from another time and place. Few young girls know how to cook game today, they may need that knowledge someday." She is particularly interested in a "quality of life based on mutual respect, education of individuals not cattle, freedom of the mind, privacy of individual." *Avocational interests:* Chess, music, theater, ballet.

* * *

NEVO, Ruth 1924-

PERSONAL: Born August 7, 1924, in Johannesburg, South Africa; daughter of Benjamin (a physician) and Henrietta (Goldsmith) Weinbren; married Natan Nevo (a journalist), December 25, 1952; children: Yiztchak, Gideon, Amos. *Education:* University of Witwatersrand, B.A., 1946, M.A., 1950; Hebrew University of Jerusalem, Ph.D., 1960. *Politics:* "No party card." *Religion:* "Jewish, if at all." *Home:* 22 Hehalutz, Jerusalem, Israel. *Office:* Department of English, Hebrew University of Jerusalem, Jerusalem, Israel.

CAREER: Hebrew University of Jerusalem, Jerusalem, Israel, instructor, 1951-61, lecturer, 1961-64, senior lecturer, 1965-68, associate professor, 1969-73, professor of English, 1973—. *Member:* International Association of University Professors of English, University Teachers of English Association, Shakespeare Association.

WRITINGS: The Dial of Virtue (non-fiction), Princeton University Press, 1963; *Tragic Form in Shakespeare,* Princeton University Press, 1972; (translator from the Hebrew of poems of Jehuda Amichai) Daniel Weisbott and Robert Friend, editors, *Modern Poetry in Translation,* Compton Press, 1974; (translator from the Hebrew of poems of Jehuda Amichai) Barry Callaghan, editor, *Exile,* University of Toronto Press, 1975. Contributor to Northwestern University *Tri-Quarterly.*

WORK IN PROGRESS: A book on comic form; research on modern poetry and poetics, and on Judaic sources and comparisons in the poetry of Protestantism in the seventeenth century.

AVOCATIONAL INTERESTS: Painting, drawing, horseback riding.

* * *

NEWBILL, James Guy 1931-

PERSONAL: Born September 30, 1931, in Yakima, Wash.; son of Guy N. and Loraine (Wilson) Newbill; married Janice Koenekamp (a secretary), September 17, 1951; chil-

dren: Catherine Mae, Barbara Loraine, Mary Elizabeth. *Education:* Yakima Valley Junior College, A.A., 1951; University of Washington, Seattle, B.A., 1953, M.A., 1960. *Politics:* Republican. *Religion:* Presbyterian. *Home:* 7704 Tieton Dr., Yakima, Wash. 98902. *Office:* Department of History, Yakima Valley College, Yakima, Wash. 98902.

CAREER: Yakima Valley College, Yakima, Wash., instructor in history, 1960—. *Member:* American Historical Association, National Education Association, American Association for Higher Education (member of state board, 1969-72), Pacific Northwest Labor History Association, Washington Education Association. *Awards, honors:* Fulbright scholarships to Italy, 1958, and Greece, 1964; William Robertson Coe fellowship, Stanford University, 1962.

WRITINGS: (Editor with Roger Van Winkle and Robert Gedosch) *The American Spectrum,* Wadsworth, 1972. Member of editorial board of *Community College Social Science Quarterly.*

WORK IN PROGRESS: Research on the Industrial Workers of the World (IWW) in the Yakima Valley between 1910 and 1936.

* * *

NEWMAN, E. J. 1943-

PERSONAL: Born August 16, 1943, in Paterson, N.J.; son of Samuel J. (a businessman) and Myra (a secretary; maiden name, Lichtman) Newman. *Education:* Rutgers University, B.A., 1965; University of California, Berkeley, M.A., 1966; University of Wisconsin, Madison, Ph.D., 1971. *Office:* Department of History, University of Sydney, Sydney NSW2006, Australia.

CAREER: University of Sydney, Sydney, Australia, lecturer in Central European history, 1971—. *Member:* Australasian Society for European History (secretary, 1976—), Leo Baeck Institute, Australian Historical Association.

WRITINGS: Restoration Radical: Robert Blum and the Challenge of German Democracy, 1807-1848, Branden Press, 1974; *The Old Order in Europe, 1648-1788,* Pergamon, 1976. Also editor of European history series for high school students.

WORK IN PROGRESS: German-Turkish Diplomatic and Financial Relations, 1897-1914.

* * *

NEWMAN, Randolph H. 1904-1975

July 3, 1904—October 9, 1975; German-born American attorney, and author of books in his field. Obituaries: *New York Times,* October 11, 1975.

* * *

NICOL, Davidson (Sylvester Hector Willoughby) 1924-
(Abioseh Nicol)

PERSONAL: Born September 14, 1924, in Freetown, Sierra Leone; married Marjorie Esme Johnston (a physician), August 12, 1950; children: Aina, Charles, Olukayode (son). *Education:* Christ's College, Cambridge, B.A., 1946, M.A., M.D., Ph.D. *Religion:* Christian. *Home:* 333 East 46th St., Apt. 10B, New York, N.Y. 10017. *Agent:* David Higham Associates Ltd., 5-8 Lower John St., Golden Square, London W1R 4HA, England. *Office:* United Nations Institute for Training and Research (UNITAR), 801 United Nations Plaza, New York, N.Y. 10017.

CAREER: University of London, London Hospital Medical College, London, England, house physician and research assistant, 1950-52; The Medical School, Ibadan, Nigeria, university lecturer, 1952-54; Cambridge University, Cambridge, England, Beit Memorial Fellow, 1954, fellow and supervisor in natural sciences and medicine at Christ's College, 1957-59; Sierra Leone Government, senior pathologist, 1958-60; Fourah Bay College, Freetown, Sierra Leone, principal, 1960-67; University of Sierra Leone, Freetown, vice-chancellor, 1966-68; ambassador from Sierra Leone to United Nations, 1968-71; high commissioner of the Republic of Sierra Leone to United Kingdom, and ambassador to Denmark, Norway, Sweden, and Finland, 1971-72; under-secretary of United Nations and executive director of United Nations Institute for Training and Research (UNITAR), 1973—. Delegate to World Health Organization Assembly, 1959-60; chairman of Sierra Leone National Library Board, 1959-65; member of West African Council for Medical Research, 1959-62; president, Sierra Leone Red Cross Society, 1962-66. Director, Central Bank of Sierra Leone. Honorary member, Ghana Academy of Sciences. *Awards, honors:* Margaret Wrong Prize, 1951; Independence Medal, Government of Sierra Leone, 1961; D.Sc. from University of Newcastle upon Tyne, and Kalamazoo College, both 1964; named Companion of the Order of St. Michael and St. George, 1964; LL.D., University of Leeds, 1968; D.Litt., Davis-Elkins College, 1971.

WRITINGS: Alienation: An Essay, MacGibbon & Kee, 1960; *Africa: A Subjective View,* Longmans, Green, 1964; *The Truly Married Woman and Other Stories,* Oxford University Press, 1965; *Two African Tales,* Cambridge University Press, 1965; *Africanus Horton: The Dawn of Nationalism in Modern Africa,* Longmans, Green, 1969, published as *Black Nationalism in Africa, 1867,* Africana Publishing, 1969.

Contributor of chapters to medical publications, and articles to medical journals. Verse is included in: *Poems from Black Africa,* edited by Langston Hughes, Indiana University Press, 1963; *West African Verse,* edited by D. I. Nwoga, Longmans, Green, 1967; and others. Contributor of verse to periodicals, including *Encounter, Blackwood's Magazine,* and *Twentieth Century,* and articles to *London Times, Guardian, Economist,* and others.

SIDELIGHTS: Nicol's poetry has been broadcast by the British Broadcasting Corp. in Nigeria and elsewhere in Western Africa. *Avocational interests:* Antiques, especially old maps and coins.

BIOGRAPHICAL/CRITICAL SOURCES: Ezekiel Mphahlele, The African Image, *Faber, 1962; Anne Tibble,* African-English Literature, *P. Owen, 1965; G. J. Williams, editor,* A Bibliography of Sierra Leone, 1925-1969, *Africana Publishing, 1970; Adrian A. Roscoe,* Mother in Gold: A Study in West African Literature, *Cambridge University Press, 1971.*

*   *   *

NIERENBERG, Gerard I(rwin)   1923-

PERSONAL: Born July 27, 1923, in New York, N.Y.; son of George T. and Sally (Siegel) Nierenberg; married Juliet V. Low, October 9, 1943; children: Roy, Roger, George. *Education:* Attended New York University, 1939, and Brooklyn Law School, 1941-45; St. Lawrence University, LL.B., 1945. *Home:* 24 Snapdragon Lane, Roslyn Heights, N.Y. 11577. *Agent:* Julian Bach, 3 East 48th St., New York, N.Y. 10017. *Office:* Nierenberg, Zeif & Weinstein, 230 Park Ave., Suite 460, New York, N.Y. 10017.

CAREER: Admitted to the Bar of New York State, 1946; Nierenberg, Zeif & Weinstein, New York, N.Y., senior law partner, 1946—. President of Institute of General Semantics, 1970-73. *Military service:* U.S. Army Air Forces, 1942-44. *Member:* American Bar Association, Association of the Bar of City of New York. *Awards, honors:* New York Society for General Semantics award, 1969; Interfaith Movement, Inc. award; La Academia Mexicana de Derecho Internacional award.

WRITINGS: The Art of Negotiating, Hawthorn, 1968; *Creative Business Negotiating,* Hawthorn, 1971; (with Henry Calero) *How to Read a Person Like a Book,* Hawthorn, 1971; *Fundamentals of Negotiating,* Hawthorn, 1973; (with Calero) *Meta-Talk: A Guide to the Hidden Meaning of Conversation,* Simon & Schuster, 1973; *How to Give and Receive Advice,* Simon & Schuster, 1975. Contributor to *Pageant, This Week, Franchising Around the World, Vogue, New Woman, Coronet, Retail Overview, Labor Law Journal,* and newspapers.

WORK IN PROGRESS: Creativity Is a Skill and Can Be Learned.

SIDELIGHTS: Nierenberg's books have been used as the basis for seminars for business executives and government officials throughout the world.

*   *   *

NITTLER, Alan Hopkins   1918-

PERSONAL: Born July 14, 1918, in Santa Cruz, Calif.; son of Adolph Nicholas (a physician) and Irma (Hopkins) Nittler; married Dorothy Lang, February 9, 1945; children: Karen (Mrs. William Parodi), Ellyn (Mrs. Kenneth Cowell), Lane (Mrs. Rodney Barney). *Education:* University of California, Berkeley, A.B., 1940; University of Cincinnati, M.D., 1943. *Religion:* Christian. *Home:* 3 Lahai Roi Lane, Aptos, Calif. 95003. *Office:* 1830 Commercial Way, Santa Cruz, Calif. 95065.

CAREER: Private practice of metabolic nutrition in Santa Cruz, Calif., 1946—. *Military service:* U.S. Army, Medical Corps, 1944-46; became captain. *Member:* International Academy of Metabology, International Academy of Preventive Medicine, International College of Applied Nutrition.

WRITINGS: New Breed of Doctor, Pyramid, 1972; *Questions and Answers from Let's Live,* Pyramid, 1976; *New Breed of Patient,* Pyramid, 1976. Columnist for *Let's Live,* 1968-75, *When* (World Health and Ecology news), 1976—, and for *Total You,* 1976—.

*   *   *

NOBLE, Joseph Veach   1920-

PERSONAL: Born April 3, 1920, in Philadelphia, Pa.; son of Joseph Hadermann and Helen Elizabeth (Veach) Noble; married Olive A. M. Mooney, June, 1941; children: Josette, Ashley, Laurence. *Education:* Attended University of Pennsylvania, 1942. *Home:* 107 Durand Rd., Maplewood, N.J. 07040. *Office:* Museum of the City of New York, Fifth Ave., 103rd to 104th St., New York, N.Y. 10029.

CAREER: Filmmaker, museum executive, and ceramic archaeologist. DeFrenes & Co. Studios, Philadelphia, Pa., cameraman and film director, 1939-41; Station WPTZ-TV, Philadelphia, studio manager, 1941-42; DeFrenes & Co.

Studios, studio manager, 1946-49; Murphy-Lillis Productions, New York, N.Y., general manager, 1949-50; Film Counselors, Inc., New York, N.Y., executive vice-president, 1950-56, director, 1950—. Metropolitan Museum of Art, New York, N.Y., operating administrator, 1956-67, vice-director for administration, 1956-70; Museum of the City of New York, New York, N.Y., director, 1970—. Lecturer, City College (now of the City University of New York), 1949-50. Former chairman and trustee, New York State Historic Trust, former chairman of Museums Council of New York City; trustee of Corning Museum of Glass; trustee and vice-president of Brookgreen Gardens (South Carolina). *Military service:* U.S. Army, Signal Corps, assistant chief of camera branch of Photographic Center, 1942-46.

MEMBER: International Institute for Conservation of Historic and Artistic Works, Archaeological Institute of America (trustee; honorary life fellow), American Association of Museums, American Ceramic Circle, Cultural Institutions Group, National Academy of Design (honorary life fellow), National Sculpture Society (professional member), National Trust for Historic Preservation, Society of Architectural Historians, Society for the Promotion of Hellenic Studies (life member), America-Italy Society (trustee), Save Venice, Inc. (co-chairman), Vereinigung der Freunde Antiker Kunst (Switzerland), New York State Association of Museums (past president), Brooklyn Institute of Arts and Sciences, Metropolitan Museum of Art (life fellow), Queens College Art Association (life member), Century Association (New York, N.Y.), Explorers Club, Maplewood Country Club (New Jersey). *Awards, honors:* Scientific documentary medal from Venice Film Festival, 1948, for "Photography in Science."

WRITINGS: The Technique of Attic Vase-Painting, Metropolitan Museum of Art, 1960; *The Historical Murals of Maplewood,* [Maplewood, N.J.], 1961; (with Dietrich Von Bothmer) *An Inquiry into the Forgery of the Etruscan Terracotta Warriors in the Metropolitan Museum of Art,* Metropolitan Museum of Art, 1961; *The Techniques of Painted Attic Pottery,* Watson-Guptill, 1965. Contributor to *Encyclopaedia Britannica* and to archaeology and philosophy journals.

SIDELIGHTS: Noble has an extensive collection of Greek and Roman antiquities; he owns the largest American private collection of ancient Athenian vases. He maintains a ceramic workshop and laboratory in his home. Among his most notable achievements are technical analyses that proved the forgeries of the three Etruscan terracotta warriors at the Metropolitan Museum of Art, the largest art forgery ever discovered. In 1971, Noble created "Drug Scene," the first museum presentation of such a provocative nature, and in 1972 he staged "Cityrama," a multi-media exhibition including three-dimensional historical objects.

* * *

NOLTE, Elleta 1919-

PERSONAL: Born March 18, 1919, in Waurika, Okla.; daughter of Jacob Asbury (a farmer) and Ethel (Burns) Bullard; married Quenton Nolte (a self-employed public accountant), January 27, 1944; children: Quenton, Jr., Dale, David, Alan, Marsha (Mrs. Ron Luke), Dwaine, Patricia, Gary, Leigh Ann. *Education:* Attended public schools in Oklahoma. *Politics:* Independent. *Religion:* Catholic. *Home:* 2004 Williston, Pampa, Tex. 79065. *Office:* Cabot Corp., Box 1101, Pampa, Tex. 79065.

CAREER: Designer, writer, and editor of Scrapbook, Unique! Co. (scrapbook manufacturer).

WRITINGS: Westward Ha!, Pelican, 1974.

* * *

NORDIN, D(ennis) Sven 1942-

PERSONAL: Surname rhymes with "sardine"; born September 2, 1942, in Chicago, Ill.; son of Sven Verner (a carpenter) and Maj (Persson) Nordin; married Gun Hellstadius (an order clerk), August 9, 1974; children: Lars Aake, Sven Peter. *Education:* Lincoln Memorial University, A.B., 1964; Mississippi State University, M.A., 1965, Ph.D., 1969. *Politics:* Social Democrat. *Religion:* Lutheran. *Home:* Froegatan 2, 52400 Herrljunga, Sweden.

CAREER: Georgia Southwestern College, Americus, assistant professor of history, 1967-68; Chicago State University, Chicago, Ill., assistant professor of history, 1968-71; Bryant College, Smithfield, R.I., assistant professor of history, 1971-75; sales promoter for Howmedica, Belgium, 1976—. *Member:* American Historical Association, Organization of American Historians, Economic History Association, Agricultural History Society, Southern Historical Association, Phi Alpha Theta, Phi Kappa Phi. *Awards, honors:* Hammond Award from Phi Alpha Theta, 1970.

WRITINGS: Rich Harvest: A History of the Grange, 1867-1900, University Press of Mississippi, 1974.

WORK IN PROGRESS: A biography of Arthur W. Mitchell.

* * *

NORLING, Rita

PERSONAL: Daughter of Alexander and Anna (Vassilieva) Kondratieff; married Marvin M. Norling, January 20, 1954 (divorced February, 1965); children: Robert, Marvin, Jr., Kenneth. *Education:* Attended Municipal College, Shanghai. *Politics:* None. *Residence:* Oceanside, Calif.

CAREER: New York model. Owner and founder of Cosmic Medium Teachings and of an occult mail-order supply firm.

WRITINGS: Rituals and Magic for Perfect Living, Parker Publishing, 1974.

WORK IN PROGRESS: The Galloping Dumb Fisherman (tentative title); *The Cyclone-Miracle Diet; White Star* (juvenile).

AVOCATIONAL INTERESTS: Fishing; camping; traveling; visiting quaint, unusual towns with cobbled streets.

BIOGRAPHICAL/CRITICAL SOURCES: Los Angeles Herald-Examiner, February 9, 1969; *San Fernando Valley News,* March 29, 1969; *Los Angeles Times,* April 13, 1969; *San Fernando Valley Daily News,* July 9, 1969; *Los Angeles Times San Gabriel Valley,* October 30, 1969; *National Examiner,* March 9, 1975.

* * *

NORMAN, Bruce 1936-

PERSONAL: Born February 11, 1936, in England; married Psyche Patricia Catling; children: Rebecca, Caspar. *Education:* University of Nottingham, B.A. (honors), 1959; University of Manchester, certificate of education, 1960. *Home:* 14 The Ryde, Hatfield, Hertfordshire, England. *Agent:* Thomson, Campbell & McLaughlin, 31 Newington Green, London N16 9PU, England. *Office:* British Broadcasting Corp., Kensington House, Richmond Way, London W14 0AX, England.

CAREER: Teacher of English in England, 1960-64, and Vallejo, Calif., 1964-65; Granada Television Ltd., Manchester, England, writer, 1966-69; Thames Television Ltd., London, England, theatre critic, 1969-70; British Broadcasting Corp., London, England, television writer, director, and producer, 1970—. *Member:* Writers Guild of Great Britain, National Union of Journalists, Association of Cinematography and Television Technicians, British Academy of Film and Television Arts. *Awards, honors:* Award from British Academy of Film and Television Arts, 1975, naming "Horizon" the best television documentary series; award from Writers Guild of Great Britain, 1975, naming "Microbes and Men" best television documentary script.

WRITINGS: Secret Warfare: The Battle of Codes and Ciphers, Acropolis Books, 1973; *The Inventing of America,* BBC Publications, 1975. Contributor to *Sunday Times* (London).

Author of television plays, "Lancashire Night Out," "The Appointment," "The Recluse," and "Coronation Street," all for Granada-TV, 1966-69; wrote scripts for "Microbes and Men" series, BBC-TV, 1973, and "Marie Curie" series, BBC-TV, 1976.

Writer of television documentary films, "Cities at War: London, Berlin, Leningrad," for Granada-TV, 1969; also producer and director, "Where Are You Going To My Pretty Maid?" for BBC-TV, 1969; "Charles Dickens," for Thames-TV, 1970; "The Codebreakers," "The Case of the Midwife Toad," "The Rat Man," "Fire!," "The Inventing of America" (as writer only; also broadcast on NBC-TV in the United States), and "The Inventing of Television," all for BBC-TV, 1971—. Editor of "Horizon" science-documentary series for BBC-TV, broadcast on WGBH-TV in the United States, 1973-75.

Wrote feature film script, "Carlotta," 1974-75, and radio scripts on D. H. Lawrence and John Lennon for KPFA-Radio, San Francisco, Calif., 1964-65, and on Thomas Chatterton for BBC-Radio, 1970.

WORK IN PROGRESS: A biography of film director Fred Zinnemann; a history of the development of television.

*   *   *

NORTH, Christopher R(ichard)   1888-1975

1888—July 29, 1975; British minister, missionary, educator, and author of works on Old Testament theology. Obituaries: *AB Bookman's Weekly,* September 8, 1975.

*   *   *

NORTON, Frank R. B(rowning)   1909-
(Browning Norton)

PERSONAL: Born March 5, 1909, in Parkman, Ohio; son of Melvin H. (a school superintendent) and Ruby (Browning) Norton; married Agnes Cluse (a psychologist), April 26, 1941; children: John Melvin, Mary Browning (Mrs. David C. White). *Education:* Ohio Wesleyan University, B.A., 1930; Westminster College, New Wilmington, Pa., M.S.Ed., 1950. *Politics:* "Disgusted Citizens of America." *Home and office:* 2853 Northwest Blvd., Columbus, Ohio 43221.

CAREER: Worked as high school teacher, basketball coach, circus press agent, advertising and insurance sales-

man, 1930-36; employed by Hull Resurfacing Co., Butler, Pa., 1936-41; *Painesville Telegraph,* Painesville, Ohio, reporter and sports editor, 1941-43; *Youngstown Vindicator,* Youngstown, Ohio, editor, 1943-59; Ohio State University, Columbus, professor of journalism, 1959-71; writer, 1971—. *Member:* Mystery Writers of America.

WRITINGS: (With J. Eugene Haas) *Human Response in Selected Communities,* National Academy of Sciences, 1970. Also editor-in-chief of *Understanding the Construction Industry* (textbook), published by Instruction Systems, Inc.

Under name Browning Norton: (With Charles Landolf) *I Prefer Murder,* Graphic Books, 1956; *Tidal Wave,* Ace, 1960; *Johnny/Bingo,* Coward, 1971; *Help Me, Charley Buoy,* Coward, 1971.

Stories have been anthologized in *The Queen's Awards,* edited by Ellery Queen, Little Brown, 1953; *The Permanent Playboy,* Crown, 1959; *With Malice Toward All,* Putnam, 1968. Contributor to mystery magazines and popular periodicals, including *McCall's, Playboy, Adventure,* and *Redbook.*

WORK IN PROGRESS: A third juvenile book.

SIDELIGHTS: In 1965, Norton worked as investigator for the Disaster Research Center at Ohio State University, studying several communities and native villages located near the Alaskan earthquake of 1964. His work has been published in England and Sweden. *Avocational interests:* Travel, golf, reading, convivial friends.

*   *   *

NORTON, Frederick H.   1896-

PERSONAL: Born October 23, 1896, in Manchester, Mass.; son of Charles L. (an educator) and Frances (Torrey) Norton; married Ann Harris, May 15, 1923; children: Frederick H., Jr., Jane, Nancy. *Education:* Massachusetts Institute of Technology, B.S., 1918. *Home and office:* 90 Revere St., Gloucester, Mass. 01930.

CAREER: National Advisory Committee for Aeronautics, Langley Field, Va., assistant physicist, 1918-20, physicist, 1920-21, chief physicist, 1921-23; director of refractories at Babcock, Wiler & Co., 1923-27; Massachusetts Institute of Technology, Cambridge, assistant professor, 1927, associate professor, 1927-35, professor of ceramics, 1935-61. Writer. Chairman of Gloucester Conservation Commission; trustee of Addison Gilbert Hospital. *Member:* American Ceramic Society (honorary member), British Ceramic Society (honorary member). *Awards, honors:* Awards from American Ceramic Society, 1961, 1968, and 1974; D.Sc. from Alfred University, 1949, and University of Toledo, 1954; award from University of Florida, 1975, for contributions to ceramic processing science.

WRITINGS: Refractories, McGraw, 1921, 4th edition, 1968; *Creep of Steel,* McGraw, 1929; *Elements of Ceramics,* Addison-Wesley, 1952, 2nd edition, 1974; *Fine Ceramics,* McGraw, 1956; *Ceramics for the Artist Potter,* Addison-Wesley, 1956.

SIDELIGHTS: Norton has lectured in England and Egypt, at schools and for industries.

*   *   *

NORTON, Thomas Elliot   1942-

PERSONAL: Born November 14, 1942, in Oak Bluffs, Mass.; son of B. Elliot and Evelyn (Devine) Norton; married Jacqueline Loney, June 7, 1965. *Education:* Massachusetts State College at Bridgewater, B.S., 1964; University of Massachusetts, M.A., 1966; University of Tennessee, Ph.D., 1972. *Address:* P.O. Box 827, Edgartown, Mass. 02539. *Office:* Dukes County Historical Society, Edgartown, Mass.

CAREER: Teacher of special education in public schools in Orange, Mass., 1965-66; Western Kentucky University, Bowling Green, instructor in history, 1971-72; Dukes County Historical Society, Edgartown, Mass., director, 1972—. *Awards, honors:* Ford Foundation grant, 1970-71; National Endowment for the Humanities grant, 1974; Society of Colonial Wars citation of honor, 1975, for *Fur Trade in Colonial New York.*

WRITINGS: The Fur Trade in Colonial New York, 1686-1776, University of Wisconsin Press, 1973.

* * *

NOVIK, Mary 1945-

PERSONAL: Born January 15, 1945, in Victoria, British Columbia, Canada; daughter of Gerald (a land surveyor) and Lillian (a teacher; maiden name, Young) Emerson; married Orest Novik (a corporate planner), July 1, 1965; children: Keir. *Education:* University of British Columbia, B.A. (honors), 1966, Ph.D., 1973. *Home:* 2106 Mountain Highway, North Vancouver, British Columbia, Canada. *Office:* Department of English, Vancouver Community College, Langara, 100 West 49th, Vancouver, British Columbia, Canada.

CAREER: Vancouver Community College, Vancouver, British Columbia, instructor in English, 1974—. *Awards, honors:* Publication grant from Humanities Research Council of Canada, 1973, for *Robert Creeley: An Inventory, 1945-1970.*

WRITINGS: Robert Creeley: An Inventory, 1945-1970, Kent State University Press, 1973. Contributor to *West Coast Review* and *Athanor.* Poetry reviewer for *Vancouver Sun.*

WORK IN PROGRESS: Research on contemporary Canadian poetry.

SIDELIGHTS: Mary Novik writes: "I am of the opinion that Canadian poetry has undergone a renaissance since 1962 equal to the remarkable Black Mountain-San Francisco poetry renaissance which took place in the U.S. a decade earlier."

* * *

NOZICK, Robert 1938-

PERSONAL: Born November 16, 1938, in Brooklyn, N.Y.; son of Max (a manufacturer) and Sophie (Cohen) Nozick; married Barbara Claire Fiere (a teacher), August 15, 1959; children: Emily Sarah, David Joshua. *Education:* Columbia University, A.B., 1959; Princeton University, A.M., 1961, Ph.D., 1963. *Politics:* Libertarian. *Religion:* Jewish. *Residence:* Belmont, Mass. *Office:* Emerson Hall, Harvard University, Cambridge, Mass. 02138.

CAREER: Princeton University, Princeton, N.J., assistant professor of philosophy, 1962-63, 1964-65; Harvard University, Cambridge, Mass., assistant professor of philosophy, 1965-67; Rockefeller University, New York, N.Y., associate professor of philosophy, 1967-69; Harvard University, professor of philosophy, 1969—. Fellow, Center for Advanced Study in the Behavioral Sciences, 1971-72.

Member: American Association of University Professors, American Civil Liberties Union, American Philosophical Association, Society for Ethical and Legal Philosophy, Jewish Vegetarian Society, Phi Beta Kappa. *Awards, honors:* National Book Award, 1975, for *Anarchy, State, and Utopia.*

WRITINGS: Anarchy, State, and Utopia, Basic Books, 1974. Contributor to professional journals. Member of editorial board, *Philosophy and Public Affairs,* 1971—.

WORK IN PROGRESS: A philosophical work; a series of philosophical fables and stories.

* * *

NUELLE, Helen S(hearman) 1923-

PERSONAL: Born August 1, 1923, in St. Louis, Mo.; daughter of George S. and Winafred (Burns) Shearman; married Raymond Nuelle (a cost accountant), June 4, 1949; children: Adrienne (Mrs. Lawrence W. Laughlin). *Education:* Attended high school in St. Louis, Mo. *Politics:* Independent. *Religion:* Roman Catholic. *Home:* 2525 Yorkshire Dr., Florissant, Mo. 63033. *Agent:* Donald MacCampbell, 12 East 41st St., New York, N.Y. 10017.

CAREER: Office worker; writer. *Member:* Missouri Historical Society.

WRITINGS—All gothic novels: *Evil Lives Here,* Avalon, 1973; *The Shadows of Amanda,* Dell, in press; *Curse All Who Come After,* Manor, in press.

WORK IN PROGRESS: A gothic mystery, *The Pictures at Peacock Hill;* a gothic novel, *Sins of the Past;* a murder mystery, *Land Where Our Fathers Died.*

* * *

NUGENT, Robert 1920-

PERSONAL: Born September 12, 1920, in Tacoma, Wash. *Education:* University of California, Los Angeles, B.A., 1942; Yale University, Ph.D., 1950; University of California, Berkeley, B.L.S., 1954; also studies at University of Paris, 1949. *Politics:* Republican. *Religion:* Anglican. *Office:* Library, Lake Erie College, Painesville, Ohio 44077.

CAREER: University of California, Santa Barbara, instructor in French, 1950-53; Claremont College, Claremont, Calif., reference librarian, 1954-56; Lake Erie College, Painesville, Ohio, professor of modern languages and college librarian, 1956—. *Military service:* U.S. Marine Corps Reserve, active duty, 1942-46; became first lieutenant. *Member:* American Association of Teachers of French, American Association of Teachers of Italian, American Association of Teachers of Spanish and Portuguese.

WRITINGS: (Translator) *Jean de Sponde: Sonnets on Love and Death,* Lake Erie College, 1962; *The Silent Voice* (poems), Black Knight Press, 1964; *Paul Eluard* (biography), Twayne, 1974. Contributor to literature journals.

WORK IN PROGRESS: Baudelaire and Romantic Myth; translating Japanese poems.

* * *

NUQUIST, Andrew E(dgerton) 1905-1975

December 3, 1905—September 4, 1975; American educator, missionary teacher, columnist, and author or editor of books on state and local government. Obituaries: *New York Times,* September 6, 1975.

NYABONGO, Akiki K. 1905-1975

1905—October 2, 1975; Ugandan-born prince, and author of a novel and collections of stories. Obituaries: *New York Times,* October 17, 1975.

*   *   *

O'BRIEN, Esse Forrester 1895(?)-1975

1895(?)—May 21, 1975; American poet and author of non-fiction for children and adults. Obituaries: *AB Bookman's Weekly,* August 25, 1975.

*   *   *

O'BRIEN, Lee 1948-

PERSONAL: Born April 17, 1948, in Littleton, N.H. *Education:* Attended College of New Rochelle, 1966-68; University of Iowa, B.A., 1973; University of Massachusetts, M.F.A., 1976. *Residence:* Amherst, Mass. 01002. *Agent:* L. David Otte, Otte Co., 9 Park St., Boston, Mass. 02108.

CAREER: Writer and actress.

WRITINGS—Mystery novels: *Sweet William Is Dead,* Popular Library, 1975; *When She Wakes,* Popular Library, 1975. Also author of "Murder in the Home" (teleplay based on *Sweet William Is Dead*).

WORK IN PROGRESS: A feature length film script.

AVOCATIONAL INTERESTS: Reading mystery novels.

*   *   *

O'BROIN, Leon 1902-

PERSONAL: Surname is pronounced "O'Brin"; born November 10, 1902, in Dublin, Ireland; son of J. P. and Mary (Killeen) Byrne; married Cait O'Reilly, August 19, 1925; children: Eimear, Coilin, Eithne O'Broin Winder, Noirin, Blanaid O'Broin MacGinty. *Education:* Attended University College, Dublin, 1922-23; and King's Inns, 1923-24. *Home:* St. Raphael, 128 Stillorgan Rd., Dublin 4, Ireland.

CAREER: Called to the Bar, Dublin, Ireland, 1924; worked as an attorney-at-law, 1924-47; Government of Irish Republic, Department of Posts and Telegraphs, Dublin, secretary general, 1947-67. *Member:* Royal Irish Academy (senior vice-president, 1976), Irish Historical Society (president, 1974-76), Military History Society of Ireland (member of council, 1974). *Awards, honors:* J.D. from National University of Ireland, 1966.

WRITINGS: The Unfortunate Mr. Robert Emmet, Clonmore & Reynolds, 1958; *Dublin Castle and the 1916 Rising,* Helicon, 1966, revised edition, Sidgwick & Jackson, 1971, New York University Press, 1971; *Chief Secretary: Augustine Birrell in Ireland,* Chatto & Windus, 1969, Shoe String, 1970; *Fenian Fever: An Anglo-American Dilemma,* New York University Press, 1971; *Revolutionary Underground: The Story of the Irish Republican Brotherhood,* Macmillan, 1976; *The Prime Informer: A Suppressed Scandal,* Sidgwick & Jackson, in press.

WORK IN PROGRESS: The Phoenix Conspiracy.

*   *   *

O'CONNOR, Richard 1915-1975
(Frank Archer, John Burke, Patrick Wayland)

PERSONAL: Born March 10, 1915, in LaPorte, Ind.; son of Richard Edward and Hilda (Waldschmidt) O'Connor; married Olga Derby, December 28, 1939. *Education:* Attended schools in Milwaukee, Wis. *Address:* RFD 1, Box 159, Ellsworth, Me. 04605.

CAREER: Worked briefly as an actor, appearing on Broadway in two plays; newspaperman in Chicago, Detroit, New Orleans, Boston, Washington, Los Angeles, and New York, 1936-57; biographer and novelist, 1957-75.

WRITINGS—Biography: *Thomas: Rock of Chickamunga,* Prentice-Hall, 1948; *Hood: Cavalier General,* Prentice-Hall, 1949; *Sheridan: The Inevitable,* Bobbs-Merrill, 1953; *Bat Masterson,* Doubleday, 1957; *Wild Bill Hickok,* Doubleday, 1959; *Patt Garrett: A Biography of the Famous Marshall and the Killer of Billy the Kid,* Doubleday, 1960; *Black Jack Pershing,* Doubleday, 1961; *Gould's Millions,* Doubleday, 1962; *The Scandalous Mr. Bennett,* Doubleday, 1962; *Courtroom Warrior: The Combative Career of William Travers Jerome,* Little, Brown, 1963; *Jack London: A Biography,* Little, Brown, 1964; *Bret Harte: A Biography,* Little, Brown, 1966; *Ambrose Bierce: A Biography,* Little, Brown, 1967; (with Dale L. Walker) *The Lost Revolutionary: A Biography of John Reed,* Harcourt, 1967; *John Lloyd Stephens: Explorer of Lost Worlds,* McGraw, 1968; *The First Hurrah: A Biography of Alfred E. Smith,* Putnam, 1970; *O. Henry: The Legendary Life of William S. Porter,* Doubleday, 1970; *The Cactus Throne: The Tragedy of Maximillian and Carlotta,* Putnam, 1971; *Heywood Broun: A Biography,* Putnam, 1975.

Histories: *High Jinks on the Klondike,* Bobbs-Merrill, 1954 (published in England as *Gold, Dice, and Women,* Redman, 1956); *Guns of Chickamunga,* Doubleday, 1955; *Down to Eternity: How the Poor Edwardian and His World Died with the Titanic,* Fawcett, 1956; *Company Q,* Doubleday, 1957; *Johnstown the Day the Dam Broke,* Lippincott, 1957; *Hell's Kitchen: The Roaring Days of New York's Wild West Side,* Lippincott, 1958; *Officers and Ladies,* Doubleday, 1958; *The Vandal* (historical fiction), Doubleday, 1960; *The German Americans: An Informal History,* Little, Brown, 1968; *Pacific Destiny: An Informal History of the U.S. in the Far East, 1776-1968,* Little, Brown, 1969; *The Irish: A Portrait of a People,* Putnam, 1971; *The Oil Barons: Men of Greed and Grandeur,* Little, Brown, 1971; *Iron Wheels and Broken Men: The Railroad Barons and the Plunder of the West,* Putnam, 1973; *The Spirit Soldiers: A Historical Narrative of the Boxer Rebellion,* Putnam, 1973; *The Golden Summers: An Antic History of Newport,* Putnam, 1974.

Juvenile biography—All published by McGraw: *Young Bat Masterson,* 1967; *Sitting Bull: War Chief of the Sioux,* 1968; *Gentleman Johnny Burgoyne,* 1969; *The Common Sense of Tom Paine,* 1969; *John Steinbeck,* 1970; *Ernest Hemingway,* 1971; *Sinclair Lewis,* 1971.

Mysteries under pseudonym Frank Archer: *The Malabang Pearl,* Doubleday, 1964; *Out of the Blue,* Doubleday, 1964; *The Widow Watchers,* Doubleday, 1965.

Under pseudonym John Burke: *Winged Legend: The Story of Amelia Earhart,* Putnam, 1970; *Buffalo Bill: The Noblest Whiteskin,* Putnam, 1972; *Duet in Drinks: The Flamboyant Saga of Lillian Russell and Diamond Jim Brady in America's Guilded Age,* Putnam, 1972.

Mysteries under pseudonym Patrick Wayland: *Counterstroke,* Doubleday, 1964; *Double Defector,* Doubleday, 1964; *The Waiting Game,* Doubleday, 1965.

SIDELIGHTS: O'Connor's biography, *Bat Masterson,* was the basis for a television series of the same name. His manuscripts are collected in the University of Maine Library.

(Died February 15, 1975)

OCVIRK, Otto G(eorge) 1922-

PERSONAL: Born November 13, 1922, in Detroit, Mich.; son of Joseph (a tailor) and Louise (Eckle) Ocvirk; married Betty Lebie, June 11, 1949; children: Robert Joseph, Thomas Frederick, Carol Louise. *Education:* State University of Iowa, B.F.A., 1949, M.F.A., 1950. *Home:* 231 Haskins St., Bowling Green, Ohio 43402. *Office:* School of Art, Bowling Green State University, Bowling Green, Ohio 43402.

CAREER: Bowling Green State University, Bowling Green, Ohio, instructor, 1950-55, assistant professor, 1955-60, associate professor, 1960-64, professor of art, 1965—. Scoutmaster, assistant scoutmaster, and committeeman of Boy Scouts of America, 1959-75. *Military service:* U.S. Army, 1943-46. *Member:* National College Art Association of America, Mid-America College Art Association, Michigan Printmaker's Society (board member, 1953-55), Ohio Printmaker's Society (board member, 1955-57), Delta Phi Delta. *Awards, honors:* Twenty-four awards for prints, painting, and sculpture throughout the United States, 1948-58; Broadcast media award from Broadcasting Industry Conference, 1969, for course direction.

WRITINGS: (With Robert Bone, Robert Stinson, and Philip Wigg) *Art Fundamentals: Theory and Practice,* W. C. Brown, 1960, 3rd edition (with Bone and Stinson), 1975.

* * *

ODEGARD, Holtan Peter 1923-

PERSONAL: Born April 21, 1923, in Madison, Wis.; son of Sigurd Louis and Helena (Martinson) Odegard; married Margaret Lee Bond; children: Wendy Ellen, David Sigurd, Nils Peter, Duncan Jack, Adam. *Education:* Harvard University, A.B., 1947; University of Wisconsin, M.A., 1950, Ph.D., 1959. *Home:* Route 3, Cove Rd., Hudson, Wis. 54016.

CAREER: University of Wisconsin, Madison, teaching assistant, 1952-54; City-County Planning Commission, Rockford, Ill., associate planner, 1954-61; City of Bloomington, Minn., Planning Department, planning director, 1961-66; Minnesota-Wisconsin Boundary Area Commission, Hudson, Wis., executive director, 1966-68; Souris-Red-Rainy River Basins Commission, Moorhead, Minn., planning director and program coordinator, 1968-70; private governmental planning and environmental consultant, 1970—; State of Wisconsin, Madison, Executive Assessment Program, executive assessor, 1974—. Visiting professor, University of Minnesota, 1973—, University of Wisconsin, River Falls, 1975—. *Military service:* U.S. Army. *Member:* American Institute of Planners, American Society for Public Administration. *Awards, honors:* Office of Water Resources Research grant, 1971-73.

WRITINGS: Sin and Science, Antioch Press, 1956, reprinted, Greenwood, 1973; *Politics of Truth: Toward Reconstruction in Democracy,* University of Alabama Press, 1971; *The Planning Audit: A Framework with Particular References to River Basin Planning,* Advance Planning Publications, 1974.

WORK IN PROGRESS: The Ungovernability of Man—And How Direct Democracy Can Be Organized Under the Constitution To Do Something About It.

O'DELL, Scott 1903-

PERSONAL: Born May 23, 1903, in Los Angeles, Calif.; son of Bennett Mason and May Elizabeth (Gabriel) O'Dell. *Education:* Attended Occidental College, 1919, University of Wisconsin, 1920, Stanford University, 1920-21, and University of Rome, 1925.

CAREER: Formerly a cameraman and a book editor for Los Angeles newspaper; full-time writer, 1934—. *Military service:* U.S. Air Force. *Awards, honors:* Rupert Hughes award, 1960, John Newbery medal, 1961, Southern California Council on Literature for Children and Young People notable book award, 1961, Hans Christian Andersen award of merit, 1962, William Allen White award, 1963, German Juvenile International Award, 1963, and Nene award, 1964, all for *Island of the Blue Dolphins;* Newbery honor award, 1967, and German Juvenile International Award, 1968, both for *The King's Fifth;* Newbery honor awards, 1968, for *The Black Pearl,* and 1971, for *Sing Down the Moon;* Hans Christian Andersen medal, 1972; University of Southern Mississippi medallion, 1976.

WRITINGS: Representative Photoplays Analyzed: Modern Authorship, Palmer Institute of Authorship, 1924; *Woman of Spain: A Story of Old California* (novel), Houghton, 1934; *Hill of the Hawk* (novel), Bobbs-Merrill, 1953; (with William Doyle) *Man Alone,* Bobbs-Merrill, 1953; *Country of the Sun: Southern California, an Informal History and Guide,* Crowell, 1957; *The Sea Is Red: A Novel,* Holt, 1958; (with Rhoda Kellogg) *The Psychology of Children's Art,* Communications Research Machines, 1967.

Juvenile literature—All published by Houghton: *Island of the Blue Dolphins,* 1960; *The King's Fifth,* 1966; *The Black Pearl,* 1967; *The Dark Canoe,* 1968; *Journey to Jericho,* 1969; *Sing Down the Moon,* 1970; *The Treasure of Topo-el-Bampo,* 1972; *The Cruise of the Arctic Star,* 1973; *Child of Fire,* 1974; *The Hawk That Dare Not Hunt by Day,* 1975; *Zia,* 1976.

WORK IN PROGRESS: 290, publication expected late 1976.

SIDELIGHTS: The Island of Blue Dolphins was filmed by Universal in 1963 and *The Black Pearl* in 1976.

* * *

OENSLAGER, Donald (Mitchell) 1902-1975

PERSONAL: Born March 7, 1902, in Harrisburg, Pa.; son of John (a physician) and Jane (Connely) Oenslager; married Mary Osborne Polak, March, 1937. *Education:* Harvard University, A.B., 1923. *Religion:* Episcopalian. *Home:* 825 Fifth Ave., New York, N.Y. 10021. *Office:* 1501 Broadway, Suite 1915, New York, N.Y. 10036.

CAREER: Middlebury College, Middlebury, Vt., instructor in scenic design, 1925; Yale University, New Haven, Conn., 1925-71, began as instructor, became professor of drama, professor emeritus, 1971-75; City University of New York, Graduate Center, New York, N.Y., professor of theatre, 1971-72. Instructor at American Academy of Dramatic Arts, 1926; artist-in-residence, American Academy in Rome, 1953. Theatrical designer in New York, N.Y., and New Haven, Conn., 1925-1975, designing sets for more than two-hundred fifty plays, musicals, ballets, and operas. Dramas and musicals include "The Emperor Jones," Yale University Theatre, New Haven, Conn., 1931; "Anything Goes," Alvin Theatre, New York City, 1934; "Of Mice and

Men," Music Box Theatre, New York City, 1936; "I'd Rather Be Right," Alvin Theatre, 1937; "Born Yesterday," Lyceum Theatre, New York City, 1946; "The Father," Cort Theatre, New York City, 1949; "J.B.," Yale University Theatre, 1958; "A Majority of One," Schubert Theatre, New York City, 1959; and "A Case of Libel," Longacre Theatre, New York City, 1963. Operas include "Otello," Metropolitan Opera House, New York City, 1937; "La Traviata," Central City Opera Association, New York City, 1946; "La Boheme," Central City Opera Association, 1952; "Madame Butterfly," Central City Opera Association, 1964; and "La Tosca," 1966.

Member of Mayor La Guardia's Art Committee of One Hundred, 1934, President's Advisory Committee on the Arts, 1960-62, U.S. National Commission for UNESCO, 1963-68, and Art Commission of New York, 1965-75; member of board or advisory council, Neighborhood Playhouse School of the Theatre, 1930-63, Cooper Union Art School, 1946, Chicago Institute of Design, 1952-75, Metropolitan Vocational School, 1953-75, Parsons School of Design, c.1952-75, and American Theatre Wing, 1957-75; member of board of trustees, Pratt Institute, 1948-75, Brooklyn Institute of Arts and Sciences, 1957-75, MacDowell Colony, 1961-68, American Academy of Dramatic Arts, c.1964-75, and Museum of the City of New York. Consultant on theatre architecture and design for American Pavillion Theatre at Brussels World Fair, 1958, Montreal Cultural Center, 1961, Philharmonic Hall of Lincoln Center, 1962, 1969, John F. Kennedy Center for the Performing Arts, 1968, and others. *Military service:* U.S. Army Air Forces, 1942-45; became major; received Bronze Star.

MEMBER: American National Theatre and Academy (first vice-president, 1962-69; member of board of directors, 1964-68), American Federation of Arts (member of board of trustees, 1966-75), Royal Society of Arts (Benjamin Franklin fellow), Association Internationale de Bibliophile, Master Drawing Association (former vice-president), Master Drawing Society (member of national committee), Municipal Art Society (member of board of directors, 1954-68), Phi Beta Kappa. Salmagundi Club, Century Association, Harvard Club, Grolier Club, Coffee House Club. *Awards, honors:* Sachs travel grant for study in Europe, 1923-24; American School of Design Scroll of Honor, 1939; U.S. State Department grants for travel to Latin America, 1950, Yugoslavia, 1953, Iceland, Ireland and Finland, 1955; Pennsylvania Ambassador award, 1950; D.F.A. from Colorado College, 1953; Antionette Perry (Tony) Award for set design, 1959, for "A Majority of One"; Ford Foundation Grant, 1960; U.S. Specialist grant for travel to Tokyo, 1963.

WRITINGS: Scenery Then and Now, Norton, 1936, reprinted, Russell & Russell, 1966; *Theatre of Bali* (booklet), privately printed, 1940; *Four Centuries of Theatre Design: Drawings from the Donald Oenslager Collection,* Yale University Art Gallery, 1964; (author of introduction) Robert Edmond Jones, *Drawings for the Theatre,* 2nd edition, Theatre Arts Books, 1970; (contributor) *Artist of the Theatre: Alexandra Exter,* New York Public Library, 1974; (editor) *Four Centuries of Scenic Invention: Drawings from the Collection of Donald Oenslager,* Pierpont Morgan, 1974; *Theatre Design: Four Centuries of Scenic Invention,* Viking, 1975. Also editor of *Notes on Scene Painting.* Contributor to *Encyclopaedia Britannica.* Also contributor of articles to *New York Times, Saturday Review,* and to periodicals in his field.

SIDELIGHTS: Donald Oenslager's designs have been exhibited in one-man shows in New York, New Haven, Detroit, and with the American Federation of Arts traveling exhibit. His work is included in the collections of the Metropolitan Museum of Art, Museum of Modern Art, Boston Museum of Fine Arts, Detroit Institute of Arts, and the Museum of the City of New York.*

(Died June 21, 1975, in Bedford, N.Y.)

* * *

O'FAOLAIN, Sean 1900-

PERSONAL: Name originally John Whelan, changed to Gaelic variant, 1916; born February 22, 1900, in Cork, Ireland; son of Denis and Bridget (Murphy) Whelan; married Elleen Gould, 1928; children: Julie, Stephen. *Education:* University College at Cork of National University of Ireland, M.A., 1925; Harvard University, M.A., 1929. *Home:* 17 Rosmeen Park, Dunaoire, County Dublin, Ireland. *Agent:* A. P. Watt, 26/28 Bedford Row, London W.C.1, England.

CAREER: Fought in Irish Revolution, 1918-21; Irish Republican Army, director of publicity, 1923; Harvard University, Cambridge, Mass., and Boston College, Boston, Mass., lecturer in English, both 1929; St. Mary's College, Strawberry Hill, England, lecturer in English, 1929-33; full-time author, 1932—. *Member:* Arts Council of Ireland (director, 1957-59), Irish Academy of Letters. *Awards, honors:* John Harvard fellowship, 1928-29; Femina Prize nomination, 1932, for *Midsummer Night Madness and Other Stories;* D.Litt., Trinity College, Dublin, 1957.

WRITINGS—Short stories: *Midsummer Night Madness and Other Stories,* Viking, 1932; *There's a Birdie in the Cage,* Grayson, 1935; *The Born Genius: A Short Story,* Schuman's, 1936; *A Purse of Coppers: Short Stories,* J. Cape, 1937, Viking, 1938; *Teresa and Other Stories,* J. Cape, 1947, published as *The Man Who Invented Sin and Other Stories,* Devin-Adair, 1948; *The Finest Stories of Sean O'Faolain,* Little, Brown, 1957 (published in England as *The Stories of Sean O'Faolain,* Hart-Davis, 1958); *I Remember! I Remember! Stories,* Little, Brown, 1962; *The Heat of the Sun: Stories and Tales,* Little, Brown, 1966; *The Talking Trees and Other Stories,* Little, Brown, 1970; *Foreign Affairs and Other Stories,* Little, Brown, 1976.

Novels: *A Nest of Simple Folk,* J. Cape, 1933, Viking, 1934; *Bird Alone,* Viking, 1936; *Come Back to Erin,* Viking, 1940, reprinted, Greenwood Press, 1972.

Biographies: *De Valera,* Penguin, 1939; *Constance Markievicz; or, The Average Revolutionary,* J. Cape, 1934, revised edition published as *Constance Markievicz,* Sphere Books, 1968; *King of the Beggars: A Life of Daniel O'Connell, the Irish Liberator, in a Study of the Rise of the Modern Irish Democracy, 1775-1847,* Viking, 1938, abridged edition, Parkside Press (Dublin), 1945, reprinted, Allen Figgus (Dublin), 1970; *The Great O'Neill: A Biography of Hugh O'Neill, Earl of Tyrone, 1550-1616,* Duell, Sloan & Pearce, 1942, reprinted, Mercier Press, 1970; *Newman's Way: The Odyssey of John Henry Newman,* Devin-Adair, 1952 (published in England as *Newman's Way,* Longmans, Green, 1952); *Vive Moi!* (autobiography), Little, Brown, 1964 (published in England as *Vive Moi! An Autobiography,* Hart-Davis, 1965).

Travel: *An Irish Journey,* Longmans, Green, 1940; *A Summer in Italy,* Eyre & Spottiswooke, 1949, Devin-Adair, 1950; *An Autumn in Italy,* Devin-Adair, 1953 (published in England as *South to Sicily,* Collins, 1953).

Other: (Editor) *Lyrics and Satires from Tom Moore,* Cuala Press (Dublin), 1929; (editor) *The Autobiography of Theobald Wolfe Tone,* Thomas Nelson, 1937; *She Had to Do Something: A Comedy in Three Acts* (first produced in Dublin, 1937), J. Cape, 1938; (compiler) *The Silver Branch: A Collection of the Best Old Irish Lyrics, Variously Translated,* Viking, 1938, reprinted, Books for Libraries, 1968; *The Story of Ireland* (history), Collins, 1943; (editor and author of foreword) Samuel Lover, *Adventures of Handy Andy,* Parkside Press, 1945; (author of preface) D 83222, *I Did Penal Servitude,* Metropolitan Publishing (Dublin), 1945; *The Irish,* Penguin, 1947, published as *The Irish: A Character Study,* Devin-Adair, 1949, revised and updated edition, Penguin, 1969; *The Short Story* (criticism and stories), Collins, 1948, Devin-Adair, 1951; *The Vanishing Hero: Studies in Novelists of the Twenties,* Eyre & Spottiswoode, 1956, Little, Brown, 1957, published as *The Vanishing Hero: Studies of the Hero in the Modern Novel,* Grosset, 1957; (editor) *Short Stories: A Study in Pleasure,* Little, Brown, 1961.

Contributor of short stories and articles to numerous magazines, journals, and other periodicals. Editor, *Bell* (Irish periodical), 1940-45.

SIDELIGHTS: "Irish writing of the last fifty years," wrote Grattan Freyer, "has been preoccupied with three or four major themes which mark off its subject matter from that of British or American writers. Each of these themes is well represented in O'Faolain's work. There is the Irish countryside, so curiously distinctive, its bogs, mountains and watery light casting a melancholy charm both on those who live there and on outsiders who visit them. There is the period of the Irish 'troubles,' now often referred to grandiloquently as the War of Independence against Britain. Then there is the religious question: for good or ill, Irish Catholicism is a brand of its own. Finally, there is the theme of exile.... O'Faolain's work has been profoundly affected by spells of study and teaching in America and by two quite lengthy stays in Italy."

In 1968, O'Faolain amplified Freyer's observations in an article in the *New York Times Book Review:* "I like to think of all writers as colored—to many men and women, irrespective of what or where they write, dyed Irish, English, French, German, Argentinian, Greek, Indian, American....

"To be a writer dyed in Ireland means first and last to be steeped in a special kind of ancestral memory. Everything else that is 'Irish' stems from this. It involves, especially, some of our most valuable and most tiresome inner conflicts, without which we could not get going at all....

"But supposing a man is a writer—a man whose whole-day, lifelong profession depends on applying his *controlled* imagination to topical reality? You can see how easily an over-importunate time sense could refract or shadow, diminish or magnify all topical reality in the mind of any man whose mistress is his imagination.... I maintain that, from the very start, almost every Irish writer has descended to the earth of everyday life with difficulty and that his grip on it is always tenuous....

"I know that it was not until I felt myself, as a youth, thoroughly insecure, schizoid and alienated from my home and from country that I wanted to write about both. I owe it all to the policeman father whom I so revered and admired that he taught me to love the British Empire until I learned that I could not live until I hated it.... What re-

leased me from all that was a single night at an Abbey Theater play, seen in Cork when I was 15. For years I had seen only plays straight from the West End of London. Here was a most moving play about Irish peasants, shopkeeping and farming folk, men and women who could have been any one of my uncles and aunts down the country. It brought me strange and wonderful news—that writers could also write books and plays about the common everyday reality of Irish life."

Although O'Faolain has mostly written about his home and people, P. A. Doyle has observed: "If ... we esteem what we recognize as true in literature, then his novels must be granted much praise because the truth and depth of his portrayals of life and his characterizations have a validity that while on occasion peculiar to the Irish scene generally transcends the limits of one locale and reaches a universality which cannot only be recognized in the mind but also cherished in the heart."

Two play adaptations of O'Faolain's short stories, "Mother Mathilda's Book" and "The Man Who Invented Sin," were broadcast by Granada Television Ltd. in England, August 19, 1970.

AVOCATIONAL INTERESTS: Travel and gardening.

BIOGRAPHICAL/CRITICAL SOURCES: Donat O'Donnell, *Maria Cross: Imaginative Patterns in a Group of Modern Irish Catholic Writers,* Oxford University Press, 1952; Maurice Harmon, *Sean O'Faolain: A Critical Introduction,* University of Notre Dame Press, 1966; *New Republic,* February 25, 1967; *South Atlantic Quarterly,* autumn, 1967; *New York Times Book Review,* May 12, 1968; Paul A. Doyle, *Sean O'Faolain,* Twayne, 1969; Carolyn Riley, editor, *Contemporary Literary Criticism,* Volume I, Gale, 1973.

* * *

OGILVIE, Gordon (Bryant) 1934-

PERSONAL: Born May 8, 1934, in Christchurch, New Zealand; son of Maxwell Gordon (an orchardist) and Margaret (a nurse; maiden name, Bryant) Ogilvie; married Elisabeth Hanna (a librarian and writer), August 27, 1960; children: Frances Anne, Margaret Lynley, Susan Jennifer. *Education:* University of Canterbury, B.A., 1955; Victoria University of Wellington, M.A., 1956; Post Primary Teachers College, teaching certificate, 1957. *Religion:* Church of England. *Home:* 5 Centaurus Rd., Christchurch, Canterbury, New Zealand. *Office:* Staff Room, St. Andrew's College, Christchurch, Canterbury, New Zealand.

CAREER: Lived in Great Britain and Europe, 1958-59, working as a supply teacher in London at times; high school teacher in Christchurch, New Zealand, 1960-68; St. Andrew's College, Christchurch, teacher of English, 1969—, head of department, 1970—. *Member:* English Teachers Association, Post Primary Teachers Association, Historic Places Trust, Aviation Historical Society, Museum of Transport and Technology, Highland Pipers Association.

WRITINGS: St. Mary's Heathcote Centennial History, Willis & Aiken, 1960; *Moonshine Country,* Caxton Press (Christchurch), 1971; *The Riddle of Richard Pearse,* Tuttle, 1974, revised edition, 1975. Contributor to education, literary, historical, and aviation journals, and to newspapers.

WORK IN PROGRESS: A history of the Christchurch Port Hills; a history of Banks Peninsula, Canterbury; a biography of an early Canterbury pioneer; a children's novel based on life in pioneer times in Christchurch.

SIDELIGHTS: Ogilvie writes: "New Zealand is a relatively young and raw country, with barely a hundred fifty years of European settlement. She has a vivid history and has produced many colourful and resourceful inhabitants. There is plenty to write about, especially in the nonfiction field. Every so often you can strike genuine gold, as with Richard Pearse, a completely obscure backblocks farmer who built an aeroplane at the turn of the century and attempted to fly it at the time the Wright brothers were conducting their first powered flight experiments. He later designed, constructed, and patented between 1933-51 a vertical take-off aircraft which was not discovered until after Pearse's death in a mental hospital in 1953."

* * *

O'GORMAN, Frank 1940-

PERSONAL: Born December 9, 1940, in Manchester, England; son of Ernest (a laborer) and Maud O'Gorman; married Else Buch Kristensen (a teacher), July 8, 1965; children: Annelise, Adam Christian. *Education:* University of Leeds, B.A., 1962, Corpus Christi College, Cambridge, Ph.D., 1965. *Home:* 17 Oughtrington Ln., Lymm, Cheshire, England. *Agent:* A. D. Peters, 10 Buckingham St., Adelphi, London W.C.2, England. *Office:* Department of History, University of Manchester, Oxford Rd., Manchester M13 9PL, England.

CAREER: University of Manchester, Manchester, England, lecturer in modern history, 1965—. *Member:* Historical Association, Royal Historical Society (fellow).

WRITINGS: The Whig Party and the French Revolution, Macmillan, 1967; Edmund Burke: His Political Philosophy, Indiana University Press, 1973; The Rise of Party in England, Allen & Unwin, 1975. Contributor to historical journals.

WORK IN PROGRESS: Parties and Elections in Eighteenth and Nineteenth Century England: A Psephological Appraisal; Historical Thought since the Renaissance; After Namier: The Current State of Eighteenth Century Scholarship.

SIDELIGHTS: O'Gorman writes that he deplores "the deepening specialisation of academic history and the erection of artificial barriers between its subsections. [He is] horrified by the terrible continuation of purposeless 'neutral' or 'chronological' history, [preferring] either a thematic approach or one which recaptures the totality of a society in past times."

* * *

O'HAIR, Madalyn 1919-

PERSONAL: Born April 13, 1919, in Pittsburgh, Pa; daughter of John Irvin (a civil engineer) and Lena (Scholle) Mays; married second husband, Richard Franklin O'Hair (an intelligence agent), October 18, 1965 (divorced, 1976); children: William J. Murray III, Jon Garth Murray, Robin Murray O'Hair. *Education:* Attended University of Toledo, 1936-37, University of Pittsburgh, 1938-39; Ashland College, B.A., 1948; graduate study, Western Reserve University (now Case Western Reserve University), 1948-49, Ohio Northern University, 1949-51; South West Texas College of Law, LL.B., 1953, converted to J.D., 1975; Howard University, M.P.S.W., 1954; Minnesota Institute of Philosophy, Ph.D., 1971. *Politics:* "Individual An-

archist." *Religion:* American Atheist. *Home:* 4203 Shoal Creek Blvd., Austin, Tex. 78756. *Office:* American Atheists, Inc., 4408 Medical Pkwy., Austin, Tex. 78756.

CAREER: Supervisor of psychiatric social workers at state welfare, probation, and family and children's agencies in Houston, Tex., 1952-56, and Baltimore, Md., 1959-63; U.S. Department of Health, Education and Welfare, Washington, D.C., staff attorney, 1956-59; American Atheists, Inc., Austin Tex., founder, 1965; American Atheist Center, Austin, president, 1965-76. Director, American Atheist Radio series (broadcast on twenty-one stations), 1968-76; founder, Charles E. Stevens American Atheist Library and Archives, Inc., 1970. *Military service:* Women's Army Corps, 1943-46; became second lieutenant. *Member:* Society of Separationists (founder; secretary, 1965-75, president, 1975—).

WRITINGS—All published by American Atheist Press, except as indicated: Why I Am an Atheist, 1965; What on Earth Is an Atheist!, 1966; The American Atheist, 1967; An Aetheist Epic, 1968; The Atheist World, 1969; An Atheist Speaks, 1970; Let Us Prey: An Atheist Looks at Church Wealth, 1970; Understanding Atheism, 1971; An Atheist Believes, 1971; (author of introduction) Atheist Magazines: A Sampling, 1927-70, Arno, 1972; Atheism: Its Viewpoint, 1972; Letters from Atheists, 1972; Letters from Christians, 1973; Freedom Under Seige: The Impact of Organized Religion on Your Liberty and Your Pocketbook, J. P. Tarcher, 1974; Religious Factors in the War in Vietnam, 1975.

Feature writer for *American Atheist Magazine,* and for American Atheist Radio series. Advisory editor on atheism to *New York Times,* Arno Press, and for *The Atheist Viewpoint,* twenty-seven volumes, 1972.

WORK IN PROGRESS: Further research in respect to religion, "its origin, its evolution, its political interventions in diverse nations, its wealth, its insanity."

SIDELIGHTS: Mrs. O'Hair once said that she has been an atheist since the age of twelve when she "read the Bible one weekend and realized it was a perfectly bizarre book." In 1959, she and her eldest son sued the Baltimore Public Schools in protest against bible reading and prayer recitation in classes. She challenged the constitutionality of those practices and won her case in the Supreme Court in 1963.

As a result of her beliefs and activities, her home and family members have been assaulted. She said, "our house was attacked scores of times. Our car was destroyed; my eldest son was attacked physically hundreds of times; I was severely beaten; my mother was knocked unconscious by policemen; and my father suffered a fatal heart attack during an assault on our home."

In spite of the heated controversy surrounding Mrs. O'Hair and her work, the American Atheist movement continues to grow. Mrs. O'Hair maintains "with 23% of the population now Atheist or Agnostic, it becomes increasingly important to evaluate, honestly, the impact of religion in our culture and the residual lag of that influence on our institutions. It is also necessary to sort out fact from religious propaganda and to analyze cause and protect result of a thoroughly rational approach to living and to a culture predicated thereon."

* * *

O'HANLON, Daniel John 1919-

PERSONAL: Born May 10, 1919, in Wallsend-on-Tyne, England; came to the United States in 1920; son of Dan (in insurance and real estate) and Margaret Alice (Cottam) O'Hanlon. *Education:* Loyola University, Los Angeles, Calif., B.A. (summa cum laude), 1939; Gonzaga University, M.A., 1946; Milltown Park, Dublin, Ireland, S.T.L., 1953; Gregorian University, S.T.D., 1958; also studied at Universities of Fribourg and Tuebingen, and at Harvard University and Syracuse University. *Home:* 1756 Le Roy, Berkeley, Calif. 94709. *Office:* Jesuit School of Theology, Graduate Theological Union, 1735 Le Roy, Berkeley, Calif. 94709.

CAREER: Entered Society of Jesus (Jesuits), 1939; Loyola University, Los Angeles, Calif., instructor in philosophy, 1946-49; ordained Roman Catholic priest, 1952, completed Jesuit training in Port Townsend, Wash., 1953-54; Alma College, Los Gatos, Calif., associate professor, 1959-64, professor of fundamental theology, 1964-65; Graduate Theological Union, Berkeley, Calif., professor of systematic theology at Jesuit School of Theology, 1965—. Staff member and interpreter for Vatican Secretariat for Christian Unity, 1964-65; visiting professor at Stanford University, 1965, and University of California, Santa Barbara, winter, 1969; member of U.S. Bishops Committee on Education for Ecumenism, 1965—; member of board of directors of North American Liturgical Conference, 1966-69, Institute for Ecumenical and Cultural Research, 1967-71, and Divinity School of St. Louis University, 1969—.

MEMBER: Catholic Theological Society of America, Society for Religion in Higher Education, Pacific Coast Theological Society, Catholic Biblical Association.

WRITINGS: (Editor with Daniel J. Callahan and Heiko Oberman) *Christianity Divided,* Sheed, 1961; (editor with Hans Kueng and Yves Congar) *Council Speeches of Vatican II,* Paulist/Newman, 1965; *What's Happening to the Church,* St. Anthony Messenger Press, 1974. Correspondent for *America,* summer, 1963. Contributor to scholarly theological journals and to popular magazines, including *America, Commonweal,* and *Saturday Review.*

WORK IN PROGRESS: A book about his year of exploration of Eastern religious experience in India and the Buddhist countries.

SIDELIGHTS: O'Hanlon writes: "I spent many years working in the Protestant-Catholic ecumenical movement, and now I have begun to enlarge my horizons and see how bridges can be built between East and West, especially between Christianity and Hinduism and Buddhism. But that puts it too abstractly. What I want to do first of all, while remaining a Christian, is bring these elements to a living unity in my own life, and in doing that, help others to do the same." O'Hanlon studied Hinduism and Buddhism in India, Sri Lanka, Thailand, Burma, and Japan, 1973-74. His books have been published in Dutch, Spanish, French, and German. *Avocational interests:* Sailing.

BIOGRAPHICAL/CRITICAL SOURCES: National Catholic Reporter, July 18-September 19, 1975.

* * *

O'HANLON, Thomas J(oseph) 1933-

PERSONAL: Born September 1, 1933, in Wexford, Ireland; came to United States, 1957; son of Thomas J. (a farmer) and Ann (O'Reilly) O'Hanlon; married Grainne Plunkett (a news correspondent), October 17, 1955; children: Isolde. *Education:* Attended St. Mary's College, Dublin, Ireland, 1950-53. *Politics:* Independent. *Home:* 430 Beach 143 St., Neponsit, N.Y. 11694. *Agent:* John

Cushman Associates, Inc., 25 West 43rd St., New York, N.Y. 10036.

CAREER: Newspaperman in Dublin, Ireland, 1953-57; Transport Workers Union, New York, N.Y., speechwriter, 1957-60; free-lance writer, 1960-62; *Dun's Review,* New York, N.Y., senior editor, 1962-65; *Fortune* (magazine), New York, N.Y., associate editor, 1965-70, member of board of editors, 1970-73; free-lance writer, 1973—.

WRITINGS: The Irish (nonfiction), Harper, 1975.

WORK IN PROGRESS: The American Corporation; research on the world's wealthiest families.

SIDELIGHTS: O'Hanlon came to the United States and "... wrote extensively on topics relating to American business, from Howard Hughes to General Motors. I returned to Ireland in 1973 where I spent a year researching a book, *The Irish,* which describes how the Hibernians really are, not how they want others to perceive them."

BIOGRAPHICAL/CRITICAL SOURCES: Fortune, March, 1968.

* * *

OKUN, Arthur M. 1928-

PERSONAL: Born November 28, 1928, in Jersey City, N.J.; son of Louis and Rose (Cantor) Okun; married Suzanne Grossman, July 1, 1951; children: Lewis Edward, Matthew James, Steven John. *Education:* Columbia University, A.B., 1949, Ph.D., 1956. *Home:* 2809 Ellicott St. N.W., Washington, D.C. 20008. *Office:* Brookings Institution, 1775 Massachusetts Ave., Washington, D.C. 20036.

CAREER: Yale University, New Haven, Conn., instructor, 1952-56, assistant professor, 1956-60, associate professor, 1960-63, professor of economics, 1963-67, staff member of Cowles Foundation for Research in Economics, 1956-57; Council of Economic Advisers, Washington, D.C., staff economist, 1961-62, member of council, 1964-68, chairman, 1968-69; Brookings Institution, Washington, D.C., senior fellow, 1969—. Consultant, Donaldson, Lufkin & Jenrette, 1969—, American Security & Trust Company, 1970—. *Member:* American Statistical Association (fellow), American Academy of Arts and Sciences (fellow), Econometric Society (fellow), American Economic Association (vice-president, 1972), Phi Beta Kappa. *Awards, honors:* M.A., Yale University, 1963; Medal for Excellence, Columbia University, 1968; McKinsey Foundation Book Award, 1970, for *The Political Economy of Prosperity.*

WRITINGS: (Editor and author of introduction) *The Battle Against Unemployment: An Introduction to a Current Issue of Public Policy,* Norton, 1965, 2nd edition, 1972; (with Henry M. Fowler and Milton Gilbert) *Inflation: The Problems It Creates and the Policies It Requires,* New York University Press, 1970; *The Political Economy of Prosperity,* Brookings Institution, 1970; *Equality and Efficiency: The Big Tradeoff,* Brookings Institution, 1975. Editor, *Yale Economic Essays,* 1963-64; co-editor, *Brookings Papers on Economic Activity,* 1970—. Contributor to professional journals.

* * *

OLCHESKI, Bill 1925-

PERSONAL: Born July 20, 1925, in Pennsylvania; son of Stanley (an electrician) and Julia (Gruzeski) Olcheski; married Rosemary Breslin, September 5, 1953; children: Julie (Mrs. James Stirling), Bill, Jr., Cathy A., Susan, James.

Education: University of Missouri, B.J., 1950. *Politics:* Independent. *Religion:* Roman Catholic. *Home:* 6711 Moly Dr., Falls Church, Va. 22046. *Agent:* Wenk Organization, 117 East 18th St., New York, N.Y. 10003. *Office:* Olcheski Enterprises, 450 West Broad St., Falls Church, Va. 22046.

CAREER: Elmira Star Gazette, Elmira, N.Y., feature writer, 1951; *Air Force Times,* Washington, D.C., associate editor, 1953-65; *Federal Times,* Washington, D.C., editor, 1965-72; Olcheski Enterprises (public relations firm), Falls Church, Va., president, 1972—. Owner of B & W Stamp Co. (mail order company), 1956—. Teacher of local adult education courses in public relations, 1975—. First vice-president of Falls Church (Va.) Chamber of Commerce, 1976—. *Military service:* U.S. Army, Infantry, 1943-46; served in the Philippines and Okinawa. U.S. Air Force, information officer, 1951-53. *Member:* National Press Club, American Society of Training Directors, Edward Douglass White Toastmaster Club (past president), Sigma Delta Chi.

WRITINGS: (Editor) Bernard Haldane, *Career Satisfaction and Success,* American Management Association, 1974; *Beginning Stamp Collecting,* McKay, in press. Stamp editor of Army Times Publications, 1953-72; Washington editor of *Postal and Federal Employees News Digest,* 1975—; editor and publisher of *NCOA News* (of Noncommissioned Officers Association), 1974—, and *Stamps and Coins,* 1974—; editorial consultant to *Federal Employees News Digest,* Bernard Haldane Associates, Guild of Prescription Opticians of Metropolitan Washington, and Amtrak. Contributor to philately journals.

WORK IN PROGRESS: Teaching a course in "writing for fun and money."

SIDELIGHTS: Olcheski began collecting stamps in a military hospital in 1952. Then he introduced the hobby to his family; now everyone, including his father in Pennsylvania, helps out with his mail order business, the newsletter, and the youth clubs through which he promotes stamp collecting as a family hobby.

*   *   *

OLIVIER, Charles P(ollard)   1884-1975

April 10, 1884—August 14, 1975; American astronomer, educator, and author of books in his field. Obituaries: *New York Times,* August 18, 1975; *Washington Post,* August 20, 1975.

*   *   *

OLLIER, Cliff(ord) David   1931-

PERSONAL: Born October 26, 1931, in Salford, England; son of Frank (a shopkeeper) and Dora (West) Ollier; married Joanna Maria Rulikowska, May 19, 1962; children: Katy, Christopher. *Education:* University of Bristol, B.Sc., 1953, M.Sc., 1955, D.Sc., 1975. *Home:* 149 Springvale Dr., Canberra, Australia. *Office:* Research School of Pacific Studies, Australian National University, P.O. Box 4, Canberra, Australia 2600.

CAREER: Department of Agriculture, Entebbe, Uganda, geologist, 1956-58; University of Melbourne, Melbourne, Australia, senior lecturer in geology, 1959-66; University of Papua New Guinea, Boroko, head of geology department, 1967-69; Canberra College of Advanced Education, Canberra, Australia, head of geology department, 1969-75; Australian National University, Canberra, research fellow at Research School of Pacific Studies, 1975—. *Member:*

Geological Society of Australia (past chairman), Royal Geographical Society (fellow), Geological Society of London (fellow).

*WRITINGS—*Non-fiction: *Weathering,* American Elsevier, 1969; *Volcanoes,* M.I.T. Press, 1970; *Earth History in Maps and Diagrams,* Longman, 1973; *Weathering and Landforms,* Macmillan, 1974; *Ayers Rock and the Olgas in Colour,* Rigby, in press. Contributor to *Encyclopaedia Britannica,* Reinhold *Encyclopedia of Geomorphology,* Melbourne University Press *Encyclopedia of Papua and New Guinea,* and other publications. Contributor of more than a hundred articles to science and education journals.

WORK IN PROGRESS: Research for a book on the major features of the earth's scenery, and its relationship to continental drift, mountain building, and other earth movements.

SIDELIGHTS: Ollier writes: "I found a good way to extensive travel to interesting places was to be an academic geologist. To maintain such a job it is necessary to write, and eventually I was asked to write books. I like writing, but as it comes to me easily I shall probably never be an artistic writer."

*   *   *

OLSON, Alan M(elvin)   1939-

PERSONAL: Born January 7, 1939, in Minneapolis, Minn.; son of Melvin Olaf (a farmer and painter) and Luella (Randall) Olson; married Janet Pederson (a teacher and artist), July 1, 1961; children: Maren Kirsten, Sonja Astrid. *Education:* St. Olaf College, B.A., 1961; Luther Theological Seminary, M.Div., 1965; Nashotah House Episcopal Theological Seminary, further graduate study, 1966-67; Boston University, Ph.D., 1973. *Politics:* Independent. *Home:* 20 Benjamin Rd., Belmont, Mass. 02178. *Office:* Department of Religion, Boston University, 232 Bay State Rd., Boston, Mass. 02215.

CAREER: Ordained Lutheran minister, 1965; vicar of Lutheran church in Garden Grove, Calif., 1963-64; assistant pastor of church in Oconomowoc, Wis., 1965-69; Boston University, Boston, Mass., assistant professor of philosophy and theology, 1969-71; lecturer in theology, 1972-73; assistant professor of philosophy and religion, 1973—, executive assistant to the dean of School of Theology, 1972-73, member of board of directors of Institute of Philosophy of Religion and Philosophy of Theology, 1973—, associate chairman of department of religion, 1975—. Lecturer at Emmanuel College (Boston, Mass.), 1970-72. *Member:* American Philosophical Association, American Academy of Religion, Boston Theological Society.

WRITINGS: (Editor and contributor) *Disguises of the Demonic: Contemporary Perspectives on the Power of Evil,* Association Press, 1975. Contributor to theology journals.

WORK IN PROGRESS: Transcendence and the Spirit, on the philosophy of Karl Jaspers; *Forms of the Spirit in Contemporary Culture;* editing *Philosophy and Religion in America: Retrospective and Prospective.*

SIDELIGHTS: Olson writes: "Particularly gratifying to me as a philosopher of religion and teacher is the current revival of interest on the part of many students in the religious traditions, symbols, and myths of the past. This quest for a retrieval of meaning through a fresh encounter with antiquity provides a context of discovery far more productive and constructive than one confined to the exigencies of momentary social and political relevance."

OLSON, Bernhard Emanuel   1910-1975

February 27, 1910—September 22, 1975; American minister, educator, and author of books in his field. Obituaries: *New York Times*, September 23, 1975; *Washington Post*, September 24, 1975. (See index for previous *CA* sketch)

* * *

OLSON, (Carl Bernard) David   1904-

PERSONAL: Born September 27, 1904, in Foster City, Mich.; son of John Olaf and Anna (Johnson) Olson; married Grace E. Gehrs, September 7, 1935. *Education:* Educated in public schools in Bark River Township, Mich. *Politics:* "Best candidate, Republican or Democrat." *Religion:* Protestant. *Home:* 8107 North Octavia Ave., Niles, Ill. 60648.

CAREER: Farmer, 1910-22; lumberjack, 1922-23; automobile mechanic, 1923-28, 1929-46; auto service manager, 1928-29; owner and operator of an auto repair service, 1946-71; writer, 1971—. In 1934, started Local 701 (automobile mechanics union); former member of board of directors of Lincolnwood (Ill.) Chamber of Commerce.

WRITINGS: Life on the Upper Michigan Frontier, Branden Press, 1974.

WORK IN PROGRESS: A book covering his years in Chicago since 1923.

SIDELIGHTS: Olson writes: "The book was written entirely from the recollections of the period, based on what I experienced, what I heard and what I saw. The logging industry pioneer atmosphere was a melting pot because of heavy emigration. The span of time in the book sees logging pass its zenith and agriculture taking over. It evolved into both a unique class of people as well as a unique environment. It was a period of high individual integrity and a time when the character of each person's individuality stood out more strongly."

* * *

OLSON, Harry E(dwin), Jr.   1932-

PERSONAL: Born July 24, 1932, in Minneapolis, Minn.; son of Harry E. and Minnie (Anderson) Olson; married Evangeline Ann Farness, June 5, 1954; children: Gregg, Brent, Dana. *Education:* University of Minnesota, student, 1950; Augsburg College, B.A., 1953; Luther Seminary, St. Paul, Minn., graduate study, 1953-54; Lutheran School of Theology, Chicago, Ill., M.Div., 1957; North Dakota State University, M.S., 1972; University of Sarasota, Ph.D., 1973. *Home address:* R.R.7, Box 731, Mound, Minn. 55364. *Office:* Marketplace Ministries, 1415 East Wayzata Blvd., Wayzata, Minn. 55391.

CAREER: Aluminum Company of America, Wear Ever Division, Minneapolis, Minn., salesman, 1951-53, college general agent, 1952-53; ordained Lutheran clergyman, 1957; parish intern in Lutheran church in Worcester, Mass., 1955-56, senior pastor in Naperville, Ill., 1957-61; Messiah Lutheran Church, Fargo, N.D., senior pastor, 1961-75; writer and lecturer, 1975—. Member of Executive Program Center of Marketplace Ministries, 1970-76, chairman, 1975, host of their syndicated radio program "Sober Up!" 1976. Founder and executive director of Messiah Foundation for Christian Communications, 1966; guest chaplain for U.S. Congress, 1962. Member of board of directors of local Vocational Training Center; director of Community Homes, Inc.; member of board of trustees of local United Fund; member of local Drug Abuse Fund and mayor's

Committee on the Aging; member of Lutheran Committee on Stewardship and Committee on Youth and Camping; chairman of Synodical Committee on American Missions.

MEMBER: Ministerium of the Lutheran Church in America, American Advertising Federation, Academy of Management, Sales, and Marketing Executives Club International, National Management Association, National Speakers Association, American Society of Association Executives, National Farm and Power Equipment Dealers Association, Lions, Young Men's Christian Association (YMCA). *Awards, honors:* Outstanding service award from Distributive Education Clubs of America, 1972; Motivational Spark Plug Award from Automotive Wholesalers Association, 1974; named "ambassador of sales" by Sales and Marketing Executives Club International, 1974.

WRITINGS: (Contributor) *Augsburg Sermons,* Augsburg, 1973; *Monday Morning Christianity,* Augsburg, 1975. Contributor to magazines.

WORK IN PROGRESS: Somebody's Got to Trust Somebody (tentative title); *Help Yourself Become Your Best* (tentative title); research on the problem drinker within the work culture.

SIDELIGHTS: Olson, as a former salesman, maintains a keen interest in the function of the individual in relation to his work. He identifies himself with the salesperson's role in life and has sought to understand their personalities, problems, and unlimited objectives. He writes: "I have recently concluded seventeen years as a parish minister ... to devote full time in writing and lecturing. The prime area of communication is in the business community. It is my feeling that the job environment is a most dominant influence in the development of and life style of individuals during their adult life.... The work environment provides opportunity for the expression and creativity of one of God-given potential. It is in this situation that we have the ability to test the results of our efforts as well as an awareness, or have to be smothered by or within organizations. The organization exists as a laboratory of personal growth and effectiveness for the expression of individual traits and the satisfaction of personal goals." Olson's sound recordings include "Reach Beyond Your Grasp," 1970; "Slice Through the Conversation and Get the Job Done," 1973; "There's No Magic Wand," 1973; "Break Through the Impossible Barrier," 1974.

BIOGRAPHICAL/CRITICAL SOURCES: Chicago Daily News, May 26, 1973; *Nation's Business,* May, 1973.

* * *

OLSON, Richard Paul   1934-

PERSONAL: Born July 19, 1934, in Rapid City, S.D.; son of Ole (a minister) and Hazel (a county auditor; maiden name, Doty) Olson; married Mary Ann Edland, June 3, 1957; children: Julie, Lisa, Laurie. *Education:* Sioux Falls College, B.A. (with honors), 1956; Andover Newton Theological School, B.D., 1959, S.T.M. (with honors), 1960; Boston University, Ph.D., 1972. *Residence:* Racine, Wis. *Office:* First Baptist Church, 801 Wisconsin Ave., Racine, Wis. 53403.

CAREER: Ordained American Baptist minister in 1959; minister in Parker, S.D., 1960-63, and in Beaver Dam, Wis., 1963-67; associate minister in Lexington, Mass., 1967-71; First Baptist Church, Racine, Wis., senior pastor, 1971—. Professor at Sioux Falls College, 1961-62; teacher at Beaver Dam Vocational Technical School, 1965-67; field education supervisor at Harvard Divinity School, 1970-71; lecturer at College of Racine, 1972-74, and Holy Redeemer college, 1973-74; counselor at Addiction Center of Racine, 1973—. Member of advisory committee on desegregation of Racine Unified School District, 1974-76, and of Funeral and Memorial Society of Racine and Kenosha, 1974-76; president of Common Downtown Cooperative Parish of Racine, 1974. *Member:* American Society of Christian Ethics, Ministers Council of American Baptist Churches.

WRITINGS: A Job or a Vocation, Thomas Nelson, 1973. Contributor to *Directions 80, Christian Home, Baptist Leader, Adult Class, High Call,* and *Foundations.*

WORK IN PROGRESS: A book on pastoral sociology; a book on Christian vocation for the middle aged.

* * *

OLTHUIS, James H(erman) 1938-

PERSONAL: Surname is pronounced *Ol*-thi-us; born November 1, 1938, in Edmonton, Alberta, Canada; son of John (a bakery executive) and Jennie (Wierenga) Olthuis; married Jean Tuininga (a curriculum researcher and writer), August 26, 1959; children: Douglas John, Christine Janet. *Education:* Calvin College, B.A., 1960, B.D., 1963; Free University of Amsterdam, Ph.D., 1968. *Politics:* "Interested in a new third 'Christian' party." *Religion:* Christian Reformed. *Home:* 54 Tidworth Sq., Agincourt, Ontario, Canada M1S 2V3. *Office:* Department of Theology, Institute for Christian Studies, 229 College St., Toronto, Ontario, Canada.

CAREER: Institute for Christian Studies, Toronto, Ontario, professor of theology and ethics, 1968—. *Member:* Association for the Advancement of Christian Scholarship, Canadian Theological Society.

WRITINGS: Facts, Values, and Ethics, Humanities, 1968; (contributor) *Out of Concern for the Church,* Wedge, 1970; (contributor) Robert Lee Carrill, editor, *Will All the King's Men . . .,* Wedge, 1972; (contributor) Carvill, editor, *To Prod the Slumbering Giant,* Wedge, 1972; *I Pledge You My Troth: A Christian View of Marriage, Family, Friendship,* Harper, 1975.

WORK IN PROGRESS: Beyond the Old and New Moralities: A Third Alternative; a volume on theological hermeneutics; co-authoring "Models of Men," for *Theology and Psychology.*

BIOGRAPHICAL/CRITICAL SOURCES: Toronto Star, September 8, 1972.

* * *

O'NEIL, Terry 1949-

PERSONAL: Born July 8, 1949, in Natrona Heights, Pa.; son of Joseph Emmett and Louise Mary (an insurance agent; maiden name, Quinn) O'Neil. *Education:* University of Notre Dame, A.B., 1971; Columbia University, M.S., 1974. *Politics:* Democrat. *Religion:* Roman Catholic. *Home:* Apt. 2504, 300 East 59th St., New York, N.Y. 10022. *Agent:* Jacques De Spoelberch, Norwalk, Conn. *Office:* ABC Sports, 1330 Ave. of the Americas, New York, N.Y. 10019.

CAREER: American Broadcasting Companies, Inc., ABC-TV Sports, New York, N.Y., researcher, 1971-72, statistician, 1972-75, associate producer, 1975—. Newscaster and sportscaster, WCEX-TV, Richmond, Va., 1974. *Member:* Writers Guild of America. *Awards, honors:* Emmy Award,

1972, for research on ABC-TV telecasts of Olympic Games in Munich, 1972.

WRITINGS: (Editor with Mickey Herskowitz and Howard Cosell) *Cosell,* Playboy Press, 1973; (with Rocky Bleier) *Fighting Back,* Stein & Day, 1975. Also editor of quiz book and record book, *ABC's Wide World of Sports,* 1973. Writer of ten programs for ABC-TV. Contributor of more than one hundred articles to periodicals.

WORK IN PROGRESS: Writing three two-hour Olympic specials for ABC-TV.

* * *

OPDAHL, Keith Michael 1934-

PERSONAL: Born November 4, 1934, in Chicago, Ill.; son of Olaf Solomon (a dentist) and Florence (Holmquist) Opdahl; married Martha Donovan, June 5, 1965; children: Michael, Cristina. *Education:* Denison University, B.A., 1956; University of Illinois, M.A., 1957, Ph.D., 1961. *Residence:* Greencastle, Ind. *Office:* Department of English, DePauw University, Asbury Hall, Greencastle, Ind. 46135.

CAREER: University of Wisconsin, Madison, instructor, 1961-63, assistant professor of English, 1963-67; DePauw University, Greencastle, Ind., assistant professor, 1967-68, associate professor of English, 1968—. *Member:* Modern Language Association of America. *Awards, honors:* Fulbright fellow, 1971-72.

WRITINGS: The Novels of Saul Bellow, Pennsylvania State University Press, 1967.

WORK IN PROGRESS: Research on Hemingway and Fitzgerald; a novel; a book on the "new realism".

* * *

OPIE, Iona 1923-

PERSONAL: Born October 13, 1923, in Colchester, England; daughter of Sir Robert George (a pathologist) and Olive (Cant) Archibald; married Peter Opie (an author and folklorist), September 2, 1943; children: James, Robert, Letitia. *Education:* Attended schools in England. *Home:* Westerfield House, West Liss, Hampshire, England.

CAREER: Author. *Military service:* Women's Auxiliary Air Force, meteorological section, 1941-43; became sergeant. *Awards, honors:* Coote Lake Research Medal, 1960, jointly with husband, Peter Opie; M.A., Oxford University, 1962; joint winner of European Prize of City of Caorle (Italy), 1964; Chicago Folklore Prize, 1970, jointly with husband.

WRITINGS—All with husband, Peter Opie, except as noted: (Compiler) *I Saw Esau,* Williams & Norgate, 1947; (editor) *The Oxford Dictionary of Nursery Rhymes,* Oxford University Press, 1951, reprinted, 1962; (sole editor) *Ditties for the Nursery,* Oxford University Press, 1954; (compiler) *The Oxford Nursery Rhyme Book,* Oxford University Press, 1955; *Christmas Party Games,* Oxford University Press, 1957; *The Lore and Language of Schoolchildren,* Oxford University Press, 1959; (compiler) *The Puffin Book of Nursery Rhymes,* Penguin, 1963; (compiler) *A Family Book of Nursery Rhymes,* Oxford University Press, 1964; *Children's Games in Street and Playground,* Oxford University Press, 1969; *Children's Games,* Oxford University Press, 1969; (editor) *Three Centuries of Nursery Rhymes and Poetry for Children,* Oxford University press, 1973; (editor) *The Oxford Book of Children's Verse,* Oxford University Press, 1973.

Contributor to *Encyclopaedia Britannica, New Cambridge Bibliography of English Literature,* and other reference works. Did series of broadcasts on "The Lore and Language of Schoolchildren," British Broadcasting Corp., 1960.

SIDELIGHTS: Iona Opie and her husband have collaborated for more than a quarter of a century in their study of children's lore and literature, and in the process have assembled a library of early children's books, as well as collections of comics, toys, games, and educational aids. Their sources of research vary from tracing the history of a medieval song at the British Museum, to visiting a back street to talk to a group of children about the games they play; they also receive assistance from interested persons in various parts of the world.

AVOCATIONAL INTERESTS: Gardening, travel.

* * *

ORDISH, George 1908-

PERSONAL: Born March 25, 1908, in London, England; son of Francis Prior and Lilian (Edmonds) Ordish; married Olive Harvey-James (a writer), children: Caron Jennifer, Roger, Pamela Meliora. *Education:* University of London, Dip.Hort., 1937, B.Sc. (Econ.), 1945. *Agent:* Mrs. D. Owen, 78 Narrow Street, London E14 8BP, England.

CAREER: Imperial Chemicals Industries Ltd., London, England, pest control expert, 1938-59; Foreign and Commonwealth Office, Ministry of Overseas Development, London, pest control expert, 1956-62; *Tropical Science* (magazine), London, England, editor, 1966-72. Pest control expert for United Nations in New York and Mexico, and for Food and Agriculture Organization in Rome, Italy, 1957-60. *Member:* International Organization for Biological Control, Association of Applied Biologists, Guild of Agricultural Journalists, Circle of Wine Writers (honorary treasurer), Baconian Club, English Vineyards Association. *Awards, honors:* New York Secondary Education Board Book Award, 1961, for *The Living House.*

WRITINGS: Untaken Harvest, Constable, 1952; *Wine Growing in England,* Hart Davis, 1953; *Garden Pests,* Hart Davis, 1956; *The Living House,* Lippincott, 1959; (with Ed Hyams) *The Last of the Incas,* Simon & Schuster, 1964; *Man, Crops, and Pests in Central America,* Pergamon, 1964; (with Pearl Binder) *Pigeons and People,* Dobson, 1967; *Biological Methods of Pest Control,* Constable, 1967; (with Pearl Binder) *Ladies Only* (novel), Dobson, 1972; *The Great Wine Light,* Scribners, 1972; *John Curtis: Pioneer of Pest Control,* Osprey, 1974; *The Year of the Butterfly,* Scribners, 1975; *The Constant Pest,* Scribner, in press.

Translator: Jose Maria Tey, *Hong Kong to Barcelona in the Junk 'Rubia',* Harrap, 1962; Roger Callois, *The Mask of Medusa,* Gollancz, 1964; Remy Chauvin, *Animal Societies,* Gollancz, 1968; Alfred Metraux, *The History of the Incas,* Pantheon, 1968; Remy Chauvin, *The World of Ants,* Gollancz, 1970; (with Caron Shipton) Richard Armand, Robert Iattes, and Jacques Lesbourne, *The Management Revolution,* Macdonald, 1970. Editor, *PANS* (Pest Articles and News Summary), 1960-66.

WORK IN PROGRESS: Work on the English vineyards and ants.

* * *

ORGILL, Michael (Thomas) 1946-

PERSONAL: Born November 7, 1946, in New York, N.Y.; son of William Austin (an artist) and Minnie Mae (McInnis) Orgill; married Helen Kowalski (an insurance claims supervisor), February 8, 1969. *Education:* Attended State University of New York at Binghamton, 1964-68. *Home and office address:* P.O. Box 64, Glen Cove, N.Y. 11542.

CAREER: G/A/F Corp., Binghamton, N.Y., film processor, 1966; Ehrenreich Photo-Optical, Garden City, N.Y., in customer relations, 1969; Key Color Corp., Mineola, N.Y., film processer, 1971—. *Member:* Science Fiction Writers of America.

WRITINGS: Anchored in Love: The Carter Family Story, Revell, 1975; (with others) *A Planet Named Cleopatra,* Pyramid, in press.

Short stories have been anthologized in *The Tunnel and Other Stories,* edited by Roger Elwood, Lerner, 1974; *The Mind Angel and Other Stories,* edited by Elwood, Lerner, 1974; *Of Times Beyond,* edited by Sandra Ley, Pocket Books, in press.

Author of "The Tower" (radio play on a sound recording), Other World Records, 1973. Staff writer for bulletin of Science Fiction Writers of America.

WORK IN PROGRESS: A science fiction novel series, in three volumes, dealing with the complete transfiguration of life on Earth; research on the philosophical implications of death and the idea of immortality; short stories; novellas.

* * *

ORKIN, Harvey 1918(?)-1975

1918(?)—November 3, 1975; American motion picture executive, talent agent, television writer, and novelist. Obituaries: *New York Times,* November 5, 1975; *AB Bookman's Weekly,* January 5, 1976.

* * *

OSBORNE, John (Franklin) 1907-

PERSONAL: Born March 15, 1907, in Corinth, Miss.; son of John F. and Norma (Curry) Osborne; married Gertrude McCullough, May 9, 1942; children: John F. *Education:* Attended Southwestern University, 1925-26, and University of Colorado, 1926-27. *Home:* 2917 O St. N.W., Washington, D.C. 20007. *Office:* 1220 19th St. N.W., Washington, D.C. 20036.

CAREER: Memphis Commercial Appeal, Memphis, Tenn., reporter, 1927-28; Associated Press, reporter, 1928-31; Tennessee Valley Authority (TVA) and National Recovery Act (NRA), public relations officer, 1933-35; *Newsweek,* New York, N.Y., staff member, 1936-38; Time, Inc., writer, editor, and foreign correspondent, 1938-61; free-lance writer, 1961-68; *New Republic,* Washington, D.C., associate and senior editor, 1968—. *Member:* Federal City Club and Cosmos Club (both Washington, D.C.).

WRITINGS: (With the editors of *Life*) *Britain,* Time, Inc., 1961, revised English edition, Sunday Times, 1962, published as *Britain: The Land, the People, the Spirit,* Time, Inc., 1967; (with the editors of Time/Life Books) *The Old South: Alabama, Florida, Georgia, Mississippi, South Carolina,* Time/Life, 1968; *The Nixon Watch* (illustrated by Robert Osborn), Liveright, 1970; *The Second Year of the Nixon Watch* (illustrated by Bill Mauldin), Liveright, 1971; *The First Two Years of the Nixon Watch* (contains *The Nixon Watch* and *The Second Year of the Nixon Watch*) Liveright, 1971; *The Third Year of the Nixon*

Watch (illustrated by Pat Oliphant), Liveright, 1972; *The Fourth Year of the Nixon Watch* (illustrated by Paul Conrad), Liveright, 1973; *The Last Nixon Watch* (illustrated by Paul Szep), New Republic, 1975.

BIOGRAPHICAL/CRITICAL SOURCES: Newsweek, June 22, 1970.

*   *   *

OSBORNE, Juanita Tyree 1916-

PERSONAL: Born August 31, 1916, in Irvine, Ky.; daughter of Charles G. (in railroad business) and Sally (Turpin) Tyree; married Harry C. Osborne (in insurance business), February 6, 1938; children: Jerry, Robert, Charles, Linda. *Education:* Attended Modesto Junior College. *Religion:* Presbyterian. *Home and office:* 1310 Stage Ave., Memphis, Tenn. 38127.

CAREER: Writer.

WRITINGS—Gothic novels: *Tornado,* Ace, 1954; *The Shrinking Pond,* Bouregy, 1974; *The Wind-Bells of Lovingwood,* Bouregy, 1974; *Rendezvous at the Hallows,* Bouregy, 1975; *The Cottage at Barron Ridge,* Bourgey, 1975. Editor of *Scribblings* (literary magazine), at Modesto Junior College, 1934-36.

WORK IN PROGRESS: Another gothic novel.

*   *   *

OSBORNE, William A(udley) 1919-

PERSONAL: Born July 22, 1919, in Brooklyn, N.Y.; son of Audley and Sarah (Kinavy) Osborne; married Margaret C. O'Rourke, August 5, 1946; children: seven. *Education:* St. John's University, Jamaica, N.Y., B.A., 1941, graduate study, summer, 1948; Niagara University, M.A., 1942; summer graduate study, Johns Hopkins University, 1948; Columbia University, Ph.D., 1954. *Home:* 22 Tamarac Ave., New City, N.Y. 10956. *Office:* Department of Sociology, St. John's University, Jamaica, N.Y. 11439.

CAREER: Mount St. Mary's College, Emmitsburg, Md., instructor in history and political science, 1946-49; Columbia University, Teachers College, New York, N.Y., instructor in social science, 1950-52; St. Joseph College, Emmitsburg, chairman of department of social science, 1953-58; Gonzaga University, Spokane, Wash., acting dean of School of Education, 1958-60; St. John's University, Jamaica, N.Y., professor of sociology, 1960—, assistant to president of university, 1960-62. Lecturer, CBS-Television, summer, 1972. Senior associate, Foy, Falcier Associates (consulting firm), 1971—. *Military service:* U.S. Air Force, 1942-46. U.S. Air Force Reserve, 1946-51. *Member:* American Sociological Association, Society for the Scientific Study of Religion, Eastern Sociological Association.

WRITINGS: The Segregated Covenant, Herder & Herder, 1967; (contributor) Philip Gleason, editor, *Contemporary Catholicism in the United States,* University of Notre Dame Press, 1969; (contributor) F. J. Coppa and P. C. Dolce, editors, *Cities in Transition,* Nelson-Hall, 1972. Author of monographs for Center for the Study of Democratic Institutions. Contributor to *Cross Currents, Commonweal, American Sociological Review,* and *Journal for the Scientific Study of Religion.*

WORK IN PROGRESS: Research on sources of spiritual development in contemporary Christian churches; study of the diffusion of acupuncture in the United States.

OSGOOD, Don 1930-

PERSONAL: Born November 15, 1930, in Brookdale, N.Y.; son of Dennis Wright (a minister) and Clara (Parker) Osgood; married Joan Timpson (a musician), June 10, 1952; children: Kevin, Jeff, Drew, Trevor. *Education:* Attended Houghton College, Centenary College, University of Maryland, Long Island University, and C. W. Post College. *Religion:* Christian. *Home:* Buck Hill Lane, Pound Ridge, N.Y. 10576. *Office:* IBM Corp., 1000 Westchester Ave., White Plains, N.Y. 10604.

CAREER: Linotype setter, 1949-50; International Business Machines (IBM), Kingston, N.Y., in personnel, 1956-60, manager of Personnel Board and Benefits Administration, Bethesda, Md., 1961-62, personnel representative of Federal Systems Center, Bethesda, Md., 1963-64, manager for management development, Federal Systems Center, Washington, D.C., 1965-67; IBM Southeast Management School, Warrenton, Va., program manager-director, 1967-68; IBM Management School, program manager in Glen Cove, N.Y., and Sands Point, N.Y., 1969-72; IBM Data Processing Division, Kansas City, Kan., district personnel programs manager, 1972; IBM World Trade Corp., New York, N.Y., program manager of personnel planning, 1973; IBM Corp., Systems Development Division, White Plains, N.Y., program manager of education, 1974—. Adjunct instructor at Marymount College; director of Career Performance Group (consulting partnership); co-founder of Aspen Hill Wesleyan Church, Rockville, Md.; president of Onteora Council for Released Time Christian Education. *Military service:* U.S. Air Force, 1951-55. *Member:* National Society for the Study of Communication, American Society for Training and Development. *Awards, honors:* IBM outstanding contribution award, 1970, for conduct of programs for management education.

WRITINGS: The Family and the Corporation Man, Harper, 1975. Contributor to *Personnel.*

WORK IN PROGRESS: Family Parables; The Slaying of Don and His Neighbors and How They Grew; Find a Spiritual Strategy to Handle Your Career and Life Crises, completion expected in 1978.

AVOCATIONAL INTERESTS: Sailing, swimming, camping, jogging, reading.

*   *   *

OSMAN, Jack D(ouglas) 1943-

PERSONAL: Born January 26, 1943, in Philadelphia, Pa.; son of William Henry and Eva Mae (Given) Osman; married Joan Grace Cooper (a sewing instructor), January 29, 1966; children: Scott Allen, Brooks Douglas. *Education:* West Chester State College, B.S., 1965; University of Maryland, M.A., 1967; Ohio State University, Ph.D., 1971. *Home:* 512 Talbott Ave., Lutherville, Md. 21093. *Office:* Department of Health Science, Towson State College, Baltimore, Md. 21204.

CAREER: High school teacher of health education in Washington, D.C., 1967-69; Ohio State University, Columbus, instructor in health education, 1969-71; Towson State College, Baltimore, Md., associate professor of health science, 1971—. Associate of Sex Information and Education Council of the United States; member of Towson State Presidential Task Force on Economics, 1973—; consultant to National Dairy Council. *Member:* Association for the Advancement of Health Education, American School Health Association (fellow; state chairman, 1973—), American Association of Sex Educators and Counselors, Nutrition Today Society, Society for Nutrition Education, Maryland Association for Higher Education.

WRITINGS: (Contributor) Howard Kirschenbaum and Sidney B. Simon, editors, *Readings in Values Clarification,* Winston Press, 1973; (with Clint E. Bruess) *Nutrition Teaching Manual for Allied Health Workers in India,* Johns Hopkins University, 1973; *Thin from Within,* Hart Publishing, 1976. Contributor of about twenty-five articles and reviews to education and health journals. Chairman of editorial committee for "Family Life and Sex Education," for District of Columbia schools, 1968.

WORK IN PROGRESS: A college level health textbook, with Neil Gallagher, Ken Ainley, Norm Sheets and Clint E. Bruess; *Sexual Education with a Focus on Values* (tentative title); *Humanizing Nutrition Education* (tentative title), completion expected in 1977.

SIDELIGHTS: Osman writes: "After spending four-and-a-half years in ... high school ... (during which time I flunked English three times), I realized that I didn't enjoy learning and desired to join the teaching force and do my part to change education from within ... I believe that an effective educator entertains through subject matter, enabling learning to 'sneak' into one's head." *Avocational interests:* Photography, developing multi-media presentations, fitness (jogging, cycling, walking), camping, "learning and living life to its fullest."

* * *

OTTO, Margaret Glover   ?-1976

?—January 6, 1976; American literary agent, editor, and author of books for children. Obituaries: *Publishers Weekly,* February 9, 1976.

* * *

OWENS, Richard Meredith   1944-

PERSONAL: Born January 11, 1944; son of Gilbert Meredith and Charlotte (Vainder) Owens. *Education:* Attended Johns Hopkins University. *Home:* 150 Green St., San Francisco, Calif. 94111.

CAREER: Works in advertising, marketing and design. *Awards, honors:* Best promotion of year award from *Advertising Age,* 1974, for Levi's Denim Art Contest.

WRITINGS: American Denim, Abrams, 1975; *How To Decorate Your Levi's,* Simon & Schuster, in press. Contributor to *Media Scope.*

WORK IN PROGRESS: The Art of Batik ... Jerome Wallace: The Batik Man of Kauai.

* * *

OWINGS, Nathaniel Alexander   1903-

PERSONAL: Born February 5, 1903, in Indianapolis, Ind.; son of Nathanial Fleming (an importer and merchant of fine woods) and Cora Nima (Alexander) Owings; married Emily Huntington Otis, September 5, 1931 (divorced, 1953); married Margaret Wentworth (an artist, writer, and conservationist), December 30, 1953; children: (first marriage) Emily, Natalie, Jennifer, Nathaniel. *Education:* University of Illinois, student, 1921-22; Cornell University, B.S., 1927. *Home:* Big Sur, Calif. 93920; Festina Lente, Route 1, Box 231, Santa Fe, N.M. 87501.

CAREER: Architect and planner. York & Sawyer (architectural firm), New York, N.Y., draftsman, 1927-28; 1933

Century of Progress Exposition, Chicago, Ill., member of architectural commission and development supervisor, 1930-35; Skidmore, Owings & Merrill (architectural firm), Chicago, Ill., founding partner, 1936—. Chairman, Chicago Planning Commission, 1948-51; chairman of President's Council on Design of Pennsylvania Avenue, 1962-64, chairman of Temporary Commission on Pennsylvania Avenue, 1964-73, member of Permanent Commission on Pennsylvania Avenue, 1973—; vice chairman, California Highway Scenic Roads Commission, 1964-67; chairman of the board of control, Urban Design Concept Team, 1967—; Secretary of Interior Advisory Board on National Parks, Historic Sites, Buildings and Monuments, member, 1966-70, chairman, 1970-72; member of visiting committee, Joint Center for Urban Studies, Massachusetts Institute of Technology-Harvard University, 1965-70; trustee, American Academy of Rome, 1968—.

MEMBER: American Institute of Architects (fellow; co-chairman, executive committee of Human Resources Council, 1970—), National Academy of Design (academician), National Academy of Art, Sierra Club (honorary life member), Century Association (New York), Commercial Club, Wayfarers Club (Chicago). *Awards, honors:* Conservation Service award of U.S. Interior Department, 1968; LL.D., Ball State University, 1970; L.H.D., Indiana University, 1974.

WRITINGS: The American Aesthetic, Harper, 1968; *The Spaces In Between: An Architect's Journey* (autobiography), Houghton, 1973.

WORK IN PROGRESS: A book on the land use ethic and the conservation of open space.

SIDELIGHTS: Mr. Owings is a registered professional architect in twenty-five states of the United States. Private commissions include the reflecting basin before the U.S. Capitol Building in Washington, D.C., Lever House, the Chase Manhattan Bank, and the Union Carbide Building in New York, the John Hancock Center in Chicago, the Crown Zellerbach and Alcoa buildings in San Francisco, the Oakland Coliseum in Oakland, Calif., the Qantas Hotel in Sydney, Australia, and the Mauna Kea Hotel on Maui, Hawaii. Mr. Owings produced a one-man showing of architectural drawings at the Museum of Modern Art, New York, in 1950.

AVOCATIONAL INTERESTS: Horseback riding, travel, hiking.

* * *

PACKARD, Sidney R(aymond)   1893-

PERSONAL: Born September 7, 1893, in Brockton, Mass.; son of Fred L. and Jennie E. (Lord) Packard; married Mildred E. Rackliffe, June 8, 1921; children: Elizabeth P. (Mrs. James B. Sprague). *Education:* Amherst College, B.A. (summa cum laude), 1915; Harvard University, A.M., 1916, Ph.D., 1921. *Home:* 126 Vernon St., Northampton, Mass. 01060.

CAREER: Smith College, Northampton, Mass., assistant professor, 1921-23, associate professor, 1924-30, professor of medieval history, 1930-63, Sydenham Clark Parsons Professor of History, 1952-61, professor emeritus, 1963—. Visiting professor at Amherst College, 1924, and Harvard University, 1945. Member of founding committee, Hampshire College. *Military service:* U.S. Naval Reserve, active duty, 1917-18. *Member:* Mediaeval Academy of America (member of executive committee, 1930-45; member of council, 1936-40), Royal Historical Society (fellow). *Awards, honors:* Guggenheim fellowship, 1929-30; D.J.U. from University of Caen, 1957; D.H.L. from Amherst College and University of Massachusetts, both 1960.

WRITINGS: *The Judicial Organization of Normandy, 1189-1204*, Stevens & Sons, 1924; (editor) *Miscellaneous Records of the Norman Exchequer, 1190-1204*, Smith College Studies in History, 1927; *Europe and the Church under Innocent III*, Holt, 1927, revised edition, Russell & Russell, 1968; *The Norman Communes under Richard and John, 1189-1204*, Houghton, 1929; *England and the Church under Innocent III*, G. Bell, 1930; *The Process of Historical Revision: New Viewpoints in Medieval European History*, Smith College, 1962; *Twelfth-Century Europe: An Interpretive Essay*, University of Massachusetts Press, 1973. Co-editor of forty-volume series, "Berkshire Studies in European History," 1927-63. Contributor to publications in his field.

SIDELIGHTS: Packard has traveled and studied in England, France, and other parts of western Europe.

*   *   *

PADDOCK, Paul (Ezekiel, Jr.) 1907-1975

October 31, 1907—August 29, 1975; American foreign service officer, businessman, and author. Obituaries: *New York Times*, August 30, 1975; *Washington Post*, September 1, 1975; *Publishers Weekly*, September 15, 1975. (*CAP*-2; earlier sketch in *CA*-21/22)

*   *   *

PADGETT, Dora 1893(?)-1976

1893(?)—January 24, 1976; American editor and author. Obituaries: *Washington Post*, February 1, 1976.

*   *   *

PAGE, Norman 1930-

PERSONAL: Born May 8, 1930, in Kettering, England; son of Frederick Arthur and Theresa Ann (Price) Page; married Jean Hampton, March 29, 1958; children: Camilla, Benjamin, Barnaby, Matthew. *Education:* Emmanuel College, Cambridge, B.A., 1951, M.A., 1955; University of Leeds, Ph.D., 1968. *Home:* 11528 80th Ave., Edmonton, Alberta, Canada. *Office:* Department of English, University of Alberta, Edmonton, Alberta, Canada T6G 2E1.

CAREER: High school teacher of English in England, 1951-60; Ripon College of Education, Yorkshire, England, principal lecturer in English and head of department, 1960-69; University of Alberta, Edmonton, assistant professor, 1969-70, associate professor, 1970-75, professor of English, 1975—. *Awards, honors:* Canada Council research grants, 1971, 1973, and 1975.

WRITINGS: (Editor) Charles Dickens, *Bleak House*, Penguin Books, 1971; *The Language of Jane Austen*, Blackwell, 1972; *Speech in the English Novel*, Longmans, 1973; (editor) *Wilkie Collins: The Critical Heritage*, Routledge & Kegan Paul, 1974; *Thomas Hardy*, Routledge & Kegan Paul, in press. Contributor of articles and book reviews to professional and scholarly journals.

WORK IN PROGRESS: *Dickens and the Language of Comedy;* editing Thomas Hardy's *Jude the Obscure*, for Norton.

PAISLEY, Tom 1932-
(T. Ernesto Bethancourt)

PERSONAL: Name originally Thomas E. Passailaigue; born October 2, 1932, in Brooklyn, N.Y.; son of Aubrey Ernesto (a truck driver) and Dorothy (Charest) Passailaigue; married Nancy Yasue Soyeshima (a ceramics designer), May 9, 1970; children: Kimi, Thea. *Education:* Studied pre-law evenings at City College of the City University of New York. *Politics:* Registered Democrat. *Religion:* Roman Catholic. *Home:* 141 Norfolk St., Brooklyn, N.Y. 11235.

CAREER: Singer, guitarist, composer, full-time, 1958-72; writer of RCA Record Club magazine, *Medley*, 1972; resumed full-time performing and writing, 1973—. Has held numerous odd jobs including a time during the 1950's as an undercover claims investigator for Lloyd's of London in New York. *Military service:* U.S. Navy, 1950-53. *Member:* American Federation of Musicians, American Society of Composers, Authors, and Publishers. *Awards, honors:* Popular Division Awards from American Society of Composers, Authors, and Publishers, 1969-70.

WRITINGS—Juvenile novels: (Under pseudonym T. Ernesto Bethancourt) *New York City Too Far from Tampa Blues*, Holiday House, 1975; *Mutt!* (fantasy), Holiday House, 1976.

Began writing his own songs, as well as comedy material for others, during mid-1960's; wrote social satire in music, "I Want to Be the Token Negro at the Party," performed in New York, N.Y., at Upstairs at the Downstairs, 1967, and additional material performed there, 1967-71; staff lyricist with Cy Coleman, 1970-71, writing libretto and lyrics for "Cities," as yet unproduced, and other works; four songs have been published in Silver Burdett's textbook series, "Music," 1973, 1974, 1975. Also author of two unproduced television pilot programs. Contributing editor, *High Fidelity*, 1967-68.

WORK IN PROGRESS: A novel.

SIDELIGHTS: Tom Paisley writes of his early career: "While investigating a claim [for Lloyd's of London] in Mt. Vernon, N.Y., which is close by a race track, I found a place that would pay me more money to play and sing than I could make in the claims business. I never looked back. Had more fun playing and singing for horsey types than filing reports. Ended up in Greenwich Village during the folk music boom of the early 60's, playing in coffee houses with such now well known people as Bill Cosby, Bob Dylan, Peter, Paul and Mary, et al.

"When folk music became a national craze, I toured the country playing colleges, auditoriums, and night clubs. Appeared on national TV at the time on a show called 'Hootenanny'. For a brief time I had the good fortune to know the late Josh White. . . . I had a chance to learn such blues guitar as I play from Josh, who was a profound influence on my work.

"When the Beatles hit and folk music sank below the waters of the Mersey, I went into a number of small clubs and lounges. It was at this time that I began to write for acts other than myself." Paisley continues to say that his effort "to go straight" by writing for *Medley* magazine in 1972 was "the most stultifying twelve months in my life." While in the process of re-establishing himself as a performer, Paisley was encouraged to finish the four chapters of a novel he had begun earlier "and abandoned in the interest of making a living." The book was published as *New York City Too Far from Tampa Blues.*

Paisley told *CA:* "I've never written for any purpose but to entertain. I attach no social or political significance to anything I've written. If any socio-political comment can be inferred, it's only because I'm reporting what I've seen and heard." Paisley speaks Spanish and French, and lived in France, 1959-60.

AVOCATIONAL INTERESTS: Paisley notes that he is "a classic car nut and movie buff."

* * *

PALFREY, Thomas R(ossman) 1895-

PERSONAL: Born October 22, 1895, in Vincennes, Ind.; son of Thomas Fairbanks (a wholesale merchant) and Mary (Lyon) Palfrey; married Magdalen Fettig; children: Thomas Rossman, Jr. *Education:* University of Toulouse, Diplome d'Etudes, 1919; Indiana University, B.A., 1920, M.A., 1922; University of Paris, Doctorat de l'Universite, 1927. *Politics:* Democrat. *Religion:* Episcopalian. *Home:* 237 East Concordia Dr., Tempe, Ariz. 85282.

CAREER: Indiana University, Bloomington, instructor in Romance languages, 1920-23; University of Illinois, Urbana, 1925-30, began as instructor, became assistant professor of Romance languages; Northwestern University, Evanston, Ill., associate professor, 1930-36, professor of Romance languages, 1936-62, professor emeritus, 1962—; Arizona State University, Tempe, professor of Romance languages, 1962-66. Visiting professor, New Mexico Highlands University, 1936, and University of California, Los Angeles, 1947; member of faculty, Army Command and General Staff College, 1948, 1949, 1951; Army Reserve School, assistant commandant, 1950, commandant, 1951-53. *Military service:* U.S. Army, 1916-55, served on Mexican border, 1916-17, and with American Expeditionary Forces in France, 1917-19, served in Europe, 1942-46; retired as colonel; received Bronze Star, Officer, Ordre de la Couronne, Chevalier, Legion d'Honneur, and Croix de Guerre avec Palme. *Member:* Modern Language Association of America, American Association of University Professors, Phi Beta Kappa, Pi Delta Phi. *Awards, honors:* American Field Service fellow, 1923-25.

WRITINGS: L'Europe litteraire (1833-34): Un essai de periodique cosmopolite, Champoin (Paris), 1927; (editor with William Holbrook) *Medieval French Literature: Representative Selections in Modernized Versions,* Appleton, 1934; (editor with Samuel Frederick Will) *Petite anthologie: Poesies francaises,* Crofts, 1936; (compiler with Henry E. Coleman, Jr.) *Guide to Bibliographies of Theses: United States and Canada,* American Library Association, 1936, 2nd edition, 1940; (compiler with Holbrook and Joseph Guerin Fucilla) *A Bibliographical Guide to the Romance Languages and Literatures,* Chandler, 1939, 8th edition, 1971. Also editor of text editions of works by Claude Farrere, Louis Charles Alfred de Musset, Benoite de Sainte Marie and others, 1930-1939.

* * *

PALLEY, Marian Lief 1939-

PERSONAL: Born June 28, 1939, in New York, N.Y.; daughter of Samuel (a teacher) and Frances (a teacher; maiden name, Levy) Lief; married Howard Palley (a professor), April 21, 1961; children: Stephen, Elizabeth. *Education:* Syracuse University, B.A., 1960, M.A., 1963; New York University, Ph.D., 1966. *Home:* 11 North Townview, Newark, Del. 19711. *Office:* Department of Political Science, University of Delaware, Newark, Del. 19711.

CAREER: High school social studies teacher in New York, N.Y., 1961-62, and Wayne, N.J., 1962-63; University of Wisconsin, Milwaukee, acting instructor in political science, spring, 1966; Rutgers University, New Brunswick, N.J., assistant professor of political science at Newark College of Arts and Sciences, 1967-70, assistant professor of political science at New Brunswick campus, 1969-70; University of Delaware, Newark, assistant professor, 1970-73, associate professor of political science, 1973—. Visiting fellow at University of Pennsylvania, 1974-75.

MEMBER: American Political Science Association, Policy Studies Association, Pi Sigma Alpha. *Awards, honors:* Fellow in academic administration from American Council on Education, 1974-75.

WRITINGS: (Editor with Joyce Gelb) *Political Parties and Social Change,* Associated Educational Services Corp., 1969; (editor with Gelb) *The Politics of Social Change: A Reader for the Seventies,* Holt, 1971; (with Gelb) *Tradition and Change in American Party Politics,* Crowell, 1975; (contributor) Dorothy James, editor, *Analyzing Poverty Policy,* Heath, 1975. Contributor to political science and behavioral science journals. *American Behavioral Scientist,* co-editor, May, 1972, editor, March-April, 1974.

WORK IN PROGRESS: Urban Public Policies: A Study of Linkages, publication by Heath expected in 1977.

* * *

PALLIS, Alexander (Anastasius) 1883-1975

1883—June 27, 1975; Greek diplomat and author of books about Greece. Obituaries: *AB Bookman's Weekly,* August 25, 1975.

* * *

PALMER, (Ruth) Candida 1926-

PERSONAL: Born June 19, 1926, in Germany; came to United States, became U.S. citizen; daughter of Volker (a doctor of law and ceramics researcher) and Maria (Carstens) Heine; married Vail Palmer (a college professor), December 6, 1952; children: Logan, Crystal. *Education:* New Zealand College of Pharmacy, M.P.S. Ph.C., 1947; attended Woodbrooke College, 1952 and 1975, Kentucky Wesleyan College, 1968, Ohio University, 1973, Rio Grande College, 1975. *Politics:* Independent. *Religion:* Society of Friends (Quaker). *Home address:* P.O. Box 176, Rio Grande, Ohio 45674. *Agent:* Ruth Cantor, 156 Fifth Ave., New York, N.Y. 10010. *Office:* National Wildlife Federation, 1412 16th St. N.W., Washington, D.C. 20009.

CAREER: Pharmacist in New Zealand, 1944-52; free-lance writer and publisher, 1962-74; *Small World* (magazine of U.S. committee for UNICEF), Philadelphia, Pa., associate editor, 1974; *Ranger Rick's Nature Magazine* (children's publication of National Wildlife Federation), Washington, D.C., associate editor for production, 1975—. Delegate from New Zealand to Friends World Conference in England, 1952. *Member:* Authors Guild, Authors League of America, Women's International League for Peace and Freedom, Faculty Women's Club (Rio Grande College).

WRITINGS—All juveniles: Snow Storm Before Christmas, Lippincott, 1965; *A Ride on High,* Lippincott, 1966; (with others) *All Sorts of Things* (reading text), Ginn, 1969; (with T. Clymer and others) *On the Edge* (reading text), Ginn, 1970; (with W. K. Durr and others) *Fiesta* (reading text), Houghton, 1971; *Kim and the Yellow Machine,*

Ginn, 1972; *The Soapsuds Fairy*, Ginn, 1972; (self-illustrated) *Sidings* (poetry), privately printed, 1972; (self-illustrated) *Extra Cranks Free*, privately printed, 1973. Wrote weekly column, "Life Is Full of Surprises," for *Owensboro Star* (Ky.), 1968. Regular contributor to *Friends Journal* and *Quaker Life;* contributor of poems, stories, and articles to periodicals, including *Green River Review, Highlights for Children, Home Life,* and *Ranger Rick's Nature Magazine.*

WORK IN PROGRESS: Poetry for children and adults; *Sidings II,* another anthology of poems, completion expected in 1976; two stories for children.

SIDELIGHTS: "As a young person I had a strong urge to write and had some work published in pharmaceutical magazines, some religious newsletters, etc. Not till my own children started in school did I seriously take up writing for publication. Our children started school in the large city schools in Chicago and Philadelphia among black youngsters who had rarely been outside the ghetto and had no reading materials which depicted the city or them. It seemed an impossible expectation of both teachers and students to teach reading to these youngsters from white, suburban, middle-class oriented materials, such as the 'Dick and Jane' series. In the early 1960's there was little editorial sympathy or daring in this area; when my first book came out depicting the inner city minority-group children the first mildly integrated readers were coming on the market also. The first review of my *Snow Storm Before Christmas* could have been written by a hate group instead of by a recognized reviewing medium, so negative was the reception. However, it wasn't long before educational reviews and library reviews, as well as the *New York Times,* credited the positive contribution this necessary reading material for non-white children represented."

*　　*　　*

PALMER, Roy (Ernest) 1932-

PERSONAL: Born February 10, 1932, in Leicestershire, England; son of George Herbert (a truck driver) and Gwendoline (Cooper) Palmer; married Patricia Madin (a teacher), August 1, 1953; children: Simon James, Adam George, Thomas Eric. *Education:* University of Manchester, B.A., 1953, M.A., 1955. *Politics:* None. *Religion:* None. *Home:* 4 Victoria Rd., Birmingham B17 0AN, England.

CAREER: High school teacher, 1958-61, and grammar school teacher, 1961-63, both in Yorkshire, England; Shenley Court Comprehensive School, Birmingham, England, head of modern languages department, 1963-69, deputy headmaster, 1969-72; Dame Elizabeth Cadbury School, Birmingham, headmaster, 1972—. *Military service:* British Army, 1955-57. *Member:* English Folk Dance and Song Society, Society for Oral History.

WRITINGS: (Editor) *French Travellers in England,* Hutchinson, 1960; (editor) *Room for Company,* Cambridge University Press, 1971; (editor) *The Painful Plough,* Cambridge University Press, 1972; (editor) *Songs of the Midlands,* Norwood, 1972; (editor) *The Valiant Sailor,* Cambridge University Press, 1973; (contributor) *Folklore: Myths and Legends of Britain,* Reader's Digest Association, 1973; (editor) *Love Is Pleasing,* Cambridge University Press, 1974; (editor) *Poverty Knock,* Cambridge University Press, 1974; (editor) *A Touch on the Times,* Penguin, 1974; (editor with Jon Raven) *The Rigs of the Fair,* Cambridge University Press, 1976; *Warwickshire Folklore,* Batsford, 1976. Contributor of articles and reviews to magazines.

WORK IN PROGRESS: Editing *The Rambling Soldier,* publication by Penguin expected in 1977; editing, with A. Adams and R. Leach, a four-volume series, "Feasts and Seasons," for Blackie & Son; editing, with Leach, a symposium on folk music in education for Cambridge University Press; continued research on the folksong as social history, on broadside ballads, and on folklore and custom.

SIDELIGHTS: Palmer has produced, and performed for, Topic Records albums, "The Wide Midlands," 1971, "The Painful Plough," 1972, and "Room for Company," 1972; he produced "George Dunn," 1974, and "Cecilia Costello," 1975, both for Leader Records. Palmer was musical director and performer for "The Wellesbourne Tree" (a documentary drama), first produced in Birmingham, England at Cannon Hill Arts Centre, March, 1972; he has also acted as advisor to theatres, including the Traverse in Edinburgh, and the Duke of York's Theatre in Lancaster.

*　　*　　*

PALMER, Spencer J(ohn) 1927-

PERSONAL: Born October 4, 1927, in Eden, Ariz.; son of John LeRoy (a farmer) and Eliza Elizabeth (Motes) Palmer; married Shirley Ann Hadley (a nurse), May 8, 1956; children: Dwight, Jennette, James. *Education:* Eastern Arizona College, B.A., 1947; Brigham Young University, M.A., 1952; University of California, Berkeley, Ph.D., 1964. *Religion:* Church of Jesus Christ of Latter-day Saints (Mormons). *Home:* 1159 East Mountain Ridge Rd., Provo, Utah 84601. *Office:* Department of Asian Studies, Brigham Young University, 121 FOB, Provo, Utah 84602.

CAREER: Brigham Young University, Provo, Utah, assistant professor, 1962-64, associate professor, 1964-69, professor of history and religion, 1969—, director of Asian Research Institute. President of Korean Mission of the Church of Jesus Christ of Latter-day Saints, 1965-68. *Military service:* U.S. Army, chaplain, 1952-53; became lieutenant. *Member:* Royal Asiatic Society (member of board of directors of Korea branch 1966-68), Phi Theta. *Awards, honors:* Grants from Institute of East Asiatic Studies at University of California, Berkeley.

WRITINGS: Erastus and Fanny Hancock: An Informal Family History, Weurth, 1957; *Korean-American Relations: The Period of Growing Influence, 1887-1895,* University of California Press, 1963; *Mormonism: A Message for All Nations,* Brigham Young University Press, 1965; (contributor) *The Feel of Korea: A Symposium of American Comment,* Hollym (Seoul), 1966; *Korea and Christianity: The Problem of Identification with Tradition* (monograph), Royal Asiatic Society, 1967; (editor) *The New Religions of Korea,* Royal Asiatic Society, 1967; *Historical Churches and Indigenous Movements in Northeast Asia,* Burgamo Mission Conference, 1969.

The Church Encounters Asia, Deseret, 1970; (contributor) *Korea's Response to the West* (monograph), Korea Research & Publications, 1971; *Educational Needs of the Church of Jesus Christ of Latter-day Saints in Asia,* Brigham Young University Press, 1972; *Education in Korea,* Brigham Young University Press, 1972; *Studies in Asian Genealogy,* Brigham Young University Press, 1972; *Asian Educational Resources Project Reports: Educational Needs in Asia,* Brigham Young University Press, 1973; *Education in Korea,* Brigham Young University Press, 1973.

Author of Aaronic and Melchizedek Priesthood lesson manuals for the Church of Jesus Christ of Latter-day

Saints. Contributor to *Jefferson Encyclopedia.* Contributor to professional journals.

WORK IN PROGRESS: The Universality of the Gospel, for Deseret; *The Cult of Confucius.*

SIDELIGHTS: Palmer studied Confucian rituals in Japan, Korea, and Taiwan in 1969, and again in 1974 in these places and in Hong Kong. In 1972, he directed a study of educational trends and needs in Japan, Korea, Hong Kong, Taiwan, and the Philippines, for the Mormon Commissioner of Education.

* * *

PALOMO, G(aspar) J(esus) 1952-

PERSONAL: Born April 11, 1952, in Havana, Cuba; son of Gasper (a waiter) and Elena (Noriega) Palomo. *Education:* Attended school in Flushing, N.Y. *Religion:* Spiritualist. *Home:* 410 McKinley St., Fairview, N.J. 07022; and 42 West 13th St., New York, N.Y. 10011.

CAREER: Yale Club, New York, N.Y., waiter, 1968-70; Waldorf-Astoria Hotel, New York, waiter, 1972-73; author. *Military service:* U.S. Army, 1971.

WRITINGS: The Mask of Fools (poems), Franklin Publishing, 1974.

WORK IN PROGRESS: A second collection of poetry; a collection of short stories and one of astrological biographies.

AVOCATIONAL INTERESTS: The occult, sky diving, travel, filmmaking.

* * *

PANNOR, Reuben 1922-

PERSONAL: Born July 4, 1922, in Kovna, Lithuania; son of Isadore (a clothing operator) and Rose (Moscovitch) Pannor; married Sydell Albers (a sociologist), June 19, 1950; children: Suzanne, Geraldine, Jonathan. *Education:* Cornell University, B.S., 1949; Columbia University, M.S., 1951. *Home:* 14607 Bestor Blvd., Pacific Palisades, Calif. 90272.

CAREER: Lehigh Valley Child Guidance Clinic, Bethlehem, Pa., psychiatric social worker, 1951-53; Vista Del Mar Child-Care Service, Los Angeles, Calif., caseworker, 1953-55, supervisor of students, 1954-66, casework supervisor, 1955-68, district director, 1958-67, director of social work and research, and acting unit supervisor, 1970-73, assistant director, 1973—. Co-director of research project for U.S. Children's Bureau, 1963-67. Member of board of directors, Los Angeles Council for Sex Information and Education. Member of California governor's Conference on Teenage Parents, 1964, and of task force committee to study services to unmarried parents, 1968-69. Member of advisory committee of Welfare Planning Council. *Military service:* U.S. Army Air Forces, 1945-47. U.S. Air Force, 1947-49. *Member:* National Association of Social Workers, Academy of Certified Social Workers, National Alliance Concerned with School-Age Pregnancy (member of board of directors). *Awards, honors:* U.S. Department of Health, Education and Welfare research grant, 1963-67.

WRITINGS: (Contributor) *Illegitimacy: Data and Findings for Prevention, Treatment and Policy Formulation,* National Council on Illegitimacy, 1965; (with Byron W. Evans and Fred Massarik) *The Unmarried Father: Findings and Implications for Practice,* National Council on Illegitimacy, 1968; *The Unmarried Father; New Ap-*

proaches for Helping Unmarried Young Parents, Springer Publishing, 1971; (contributor) *Clinical Obstetrics and Gynecology on Human Reproduction Problems of the Adolescent,* Harper, 1971. Contributor to professional journals and to magazines.

SIDELIGHTS: Pannor first focused attention on the needs of the unmarried father and subsequently pioneered work in developing techniques and approaches to working with him. His institutes, publications, workshops, and public appearances have resulted in programs for unwed fathers in agencies in the United States, Canada, and England. His focus on the unmarried father has broadened to a need to provide services and assistance to young fathers, whether married or not, so that they might be better prepared for their role as fathers and husbands.

BIOGRAPHICAL/CRITICAL SOURCES: Cosmopolitan, May, 1963; Joan Beck, *Halfway to Heartbreak: Our Unwed Teen Fathers,* Florence Crittenton Association, 1964; *Today's Health,* February, 1965; *SK & F Psychiatric Reporter,* March-April, 1968; *Coronet,* June, 1970; *Glasgow Herald,* July 22, 1971; *Detroit News,* November 14, 1971.

* * *

PAPPAS, Lou Seibert 1930-

PERSONAL: Born August 1, 1930, in Corvallis, Ore.; daughter of Emil E. (a wholesale grocer) and Norma (Helgesson) Seibert; married Nicholas Pappas (a consultant), November 21, 1956; children: Derek, Alexis, Christian, Niko. *Education:* Oregon State University, B.S., 1952. *Home and office:* 290 Golden Hills Dr., Portola Valley, Calif. 94025.

CAREER: Sunset (magazine), Menlo Park, Calif., staff home economist, 1952-58, 1964-71; De Anza College, Cupertin, Calif., instructor in home economics, 1972—. Consultant to Western food firms, and to Ortho Books. *Member:* Home Economists in Business. *Awards, honors:* Hope Chamberlain Award, from Oregon State University, 1975.

WRITINGS: Crossroads of Cooking, Ritchie, 1973; *Greek Cooking,* Harper, 1973; *Party Menus,* Harper, 1974; *Bread Baking,* Nitty Gritty Productions, 1975; *Crockery Pot Cookbook,* Nitty Gritty Productions, 1975.

AVOCATIONAL INTERESTS: Travel (Europe, Mexico).

* * *

PARK, Chung Hee 1917-

PERSONAL: Born September 30, 1917, in Kyongsang Pukto, Korea; son of Sung Bin (a farmer) and Nam Ee (Paik) Pak; married third wife, Yook Young Soo, December, 1950 (died, August 15, 1974); children: (previous marriage) daughter; (third marriage) Keun Hae, Keun Yong (daughters), Chi Man (son). *Education:* Taegu Normal School, elementary teacher's certificate, 1937. *Home and office:* Chong Wa Dae, Seoul, Korea.

CAREER: Mun'gyong Primary School, Mun'gyong, Korea, teacher, 1937-40; Japanese Army, attended military academies and fought in Manchuria, 1940-45; entered Korean Army and attended Korean Military Academy, 1946; fought in Korean War; became brigadier general, 1953; served as commandant of artillery school, 1954, 5th Infantry Division, 1955-57, 7th Infantry Division, 1957-58; chief of staff of 1st Army, 1958-59; commanding general of 6th Military District, 1959-60, and of 2nd Army, 1960-61;

led military junta in revolution against government in 1961; Supreme Council for National Reconstruction (intermediate governmental body of Korea), vice-chairman, 1961, chairman, 1961-62; assumed office of acting president of Republic of Korea, 1962, concurrently premier, June-July, 1962; left military with rank of full general in 1963 to run as presidential candidate of Democratic Republican party; president of Republic of Korea, 1963—. Honorary president of Boy Scouts of Korea and Korean Red Cross; honorary advisor to Asian Peoples Anti-Communist League. *Awards, honors:* Bao-Quoc-Huan-Chuong and Kim Khanh special grade from Republic of Viet Nam; Order of Propitious Clouds special cordon, Republic of China; Order of Merit grand cross, Germany; Grand Croix de Lordre, Niger; and other decorations.

WRITINGS: Our Nation's Path, Hollym (Seoul), 1962; *The Country, the Revolution and I,* Hollym, 1963. Also author of *Leadership in the Midst of the Revolutionary Process,* 1961; *People's Path to the Fulfilment of Revolutionary Task: Direction of National Movement,* 1961; *To Build a Nation,* 1972.

SIDELIGHTS: A strong anti-communist and militarist, Park has often been the target of assassination plots. In a tragic attempt on his life in Japan in 1974, Mrs. Park and a presidential aide were killed.

* * *

PARKS, Pat 1918-

PERSONAL: Born March 17, 1918, in Minnesota; daughter of Edward William (a building contractor) and Gertrude (a writer; maiden name, Stoddard) Dennstedt; married Boyce Parks (a photographer), July 12, 1939; children: Toni (Mrs. David Chambers). *Education:* Studied at Los Angeles Art Center. *Home and office address:* P.O. Box 29, Summerland Key, Fla. 33042.

CAREER: San Diego Sun, San Diego, Calif., author of column, 1937-39; *Progress Journal,* San Diego, editor, 1941-43; KFMB-Television, San Diego, programmer, 1952-53; *Key West Citizen,* Key West, Fla., author of column "Visiting Along the Lower Keys," 1960—.

WRITINGS: The Railroad That Died at Sea, Stephen Greene Press, 1968. Also author of column in *Natural Foods,* 1974—; and of "Floridiana," in *Purple Martin News,* 1974—.

WORK IN PROGRESS: Compiling eighteen years of research on the history, folklore, and meaning of life in the Florida Keys.

SIDELIGHTS: Pat Parks writes that an "excellent teacher of high school journalism motivated me towards the press. Pulitzer Prize winning editor of the *Sun* convinced me college would ruin my writing so I went to work at age eighteen despite one scholarship and promise of another. Marriage and subsequent travels led us to Haiti, Mexico, and Peru as a photojournalistic team. Intense interest in all facets of life in the Florida Keys has kept me writing and researching to this day without thought of retirement."

* * *

PASOLINI, Pier Paolo 1922-1975

March 5, 1922—November 2, 1975; Italian film director, poet, critic, novelist. Obituaries: *New York Times,* November 3, 1975; *Time,* November 17, 1975; *Current Biography,* January, 1976.

PASTAN, Linda 1932-

PERSONAL: Born May 27, 1932, in New York, N.Y.; daughter of Jacob L. (a physician) and Bess (Schwartz) Olenik; married Ira Pastan (a molecular biologist), June 14, 1953; children: Stephen, Peter, Rachel. *Education:* Radcliffe College, B.A., 1954; Simmons College, M.L.S., 1955; Brandeis University, M.A., 1957. *Religion:* Jewish. *Home:* 11710 Beall Mountain Rd., Potomoc, Md. 20854.

CAREER: Writer.

WRITINGS: A Perfect Circle of Sun (poetry), Swallow Press, 1971; *On the Way to the Zoo* (poetry), Dryad, 1975; *Aspects of Eve* (poetry), Liveright, 1975.

* * *

PATE, Billie 1932-

PERSONAL: Born June 1, 1932, in Blaine, Tenn.; daughter of Roy T. and Hattie Mae (Norton) Pate. *Education:* Carson-Newman College, B.A. (magna cum laude), 1954; Southern Baptist Theological Seminary, M.R.E., 1957; special study with Margolis Consultants, Washington, D.C., 1972; University of Louisville, M.S.S.W., 1974. *Home:* Alamo Rd., Route 7, Brentwood, Tenn. 37027.

CAREER: High school teacher of English in Kingsport, Tenn., 1954-55; Southern Baptist Convention, National Woman's Missionary Union, Birmingham, Ala., promotion associate, 1957-65, director of Field Services department, 1965-69; Southern Baptist Convention, Baptist Sunday School Board, Nashville, Tenn., editor of youth materials, 1969-71, coordinator of Church Study Course, 1971-72, supervisor of Youth Section, Church Training Department, 1974—. *Member:* National Association of Social Workers, Southern Baptist Religious Education Association.

WRITINGS: Young Woman's Auxiliary Manual, Woman's Missionary Union, Southern Baptist Convention, 1960; *Bonanza South,* Home Mission Board, Southern Baptist Convention, 1964; *Woman's Missionary Union Manual,* Woman's Missionary Union, Southern Baptist Convention, revised edition, 1970; *Youth and Celebrative Worship* (booklet), Sunday School Board, Southern Baptist Convention, 1972; *Rags, Tags, and Gentle Tears* (poems and epigrams), Broadman, 1973; *Touch Life* (poems), Broadman, 1974. Creator of six contemporary posters published by Broadman, 1971.

AVOCATIONAL INTERESTS: Travel, photography.

* * *

PATENT, Dorothy Hinshaw 1940-

PERSONAL: Born April 30, 1940, in Rochester, Minn.; daughter of Horton Corwin (a physician) and Dorothy (Youmans) Hinshaw; married Gregory Joseph Patent (a professor of zoology), March 21, 1964; children: David Gregory, Jason Daniel. *Education:* Stanford University, B.A., 1962; University of California, Berkeley, M.A., 1965, Ph.D., 1968; also studied at University of Washington, Friday Harbor, 1965-67. *Home:* 2316 42nd St., Missoula, Mont. 59801.

CAREER: Sinai Hospital, Detroit, Mich., post-doctoral fellow, 1968-69; Stazione Zoologica, Naples, Italy, post-doctoral researcher, 1970-71; University of Montana, Missoula, faculty affiliate in department of zoology, 1975—. Member of board of directors of Missoula Farmers' Market. *Member:* Association of Women in Science, Society of Children's Book Writers. *Awards, honors:* National Science Teachers Association named *Weasels, Otters, Skunks and Their Family* as outstanding science trade book in 1973.

WRITINGS—For children: *Weasels, Otters, Skunks and Their Family*, Holiday House, 1973; *Microscopic Animals and Plants*, Holiday House, 1974; *Frogs, Toads, Salamanders and How They Reproduce*, Holiday House, 1975; *How Insects Communicate*, Holiday House, 1975. Contributor to gardening and farming magazines and to scientific journals.

WORK IN PROGRESS: A book on insect-plant relationships, for Holiday House; a book on the life history of fishes and their methods of reproduction, Holiday House; an adult book on communication by chemical means.

AVOCATIONAL INTERESTS: Gardening, international folk dancing, travel (Europe, especially Yugoslavia, Greece, and Italy).

BIOGRAPHICAL/CRITICAL SOURCES: San Rafael Independent-Journal, January 26, 1974.

*   *   *

PATERSON, William E(dgar)   1941-

PERSONAL: Born September 26, 1941, in Blairatholl, Scotland; son of William Edgar (a surveyor) and Williamina (McIntyre) Paterson; married Jacqueline Cramb, August 3, 1964 (died June 25, 1974); children: William, John. *Education:* University of St. Andrews, M.A., 1964; London School of Economics and Political Science, M.Sc., 1965, Ph.D., 1972. *Politics:* "Disillusioned Labour." *Home:* 10 Pebble Mill Rd., Birmingham B5 7SA, England. *Office:* Department of Politics, University of Warwick, Coventry CV4 7AL, England.

CAREER: University of Aberdeen, Aberdeen, Scotland, lecturer in international politics, 1967-70; University of Warwick, Coventry, England, Volkswagen Lecturer in German Politics, 1970—. *Member:* Royal Institute of International Affairs, Association for the Study of German Politics (chairman).

WRITINGS: (With I. R. Campbell) *Social Democracy in Post-War Europe*, St. Martin's, 1974; *The S.P.D. and European Integration*, Heath, 1974.

WORK IN PROGRESS: Social and Political Movements in Western Europe.

AVOCATIONAL INTERESTS: Travel in Scotland and Germany.

*   *   *

PATTEN, Bebe H(arrison)   1913-

PERSONAL: Born September 3, 1913, in Waverly, Tenn.; daughter of Newton Felix and Mattie (Whitson) Harrison; married Carl Thomas Patten, October 26, 1935 (died, 1959); children: Rebecca and Priscilla (twins), Carl Thomas, Jr. *Education:* McKinley Roosevelt Graduate College, D.D., 1941. *Politics:* Democrat. *Religion:* Christian Evangelical Church of America. *Home:* 190 Alderwood Rd., Walnut Creek, Calif. 94596. *Office:* Christian Evangelical Churches of America, Inc., 2433 Coolidge Ave., Oakland, Calif. 94601.

CAREER: Evangelist, speaking all over the United States, 1933-44; Patten Bible College, Oakland, Calif., founder and president, 1944—. Founder and president of Christian Evangelical Churches of America, 1944—; founding director of Patten Academy of Christian Education,

1945—. Conducted "The Shepherd Hour," on KFAX-Radio, 1960-75. *Awards, honors:* D.Litt. from Temple Hall College and Seminary, 1945.

WRITINGS: Give Me Back My Soul, Revell, 1973. Editor of *Trumpet Call*, 1954—.

SIDELIGHTS: Bebe Patten has led nine pilgrimages to Israel. Her book has been published in Spanish and Japanese. *Avocational interests:* Swimming, tennis, cats.

*   *   *

PATTERSON, Samuel White   1883-1975

December 25, 1883—November 20, 1975; American educator, author of biographies and other works. Obituaries: *New York Times*, November 22, 1975; *AB Bookman's Weekly*, January 5, 1976. (*CAP*-2; earlier sketch in *CA*-17/18)

*   *   *

PATTERSON, Sylvia W(iese)   1940-

PERSONAL: Born June 27, 1940, in Boston, Mass.; daughter of Herbert Edward (an industrial contractor) and Mary (Cavin) Wiese; married William Henry Patterson, Jr. (a mathematics professor), June 2, 1962; children: Deborah Ann. *Education:* Louisiana State University, B.S., 1961; University of Southwestern Louisiana, M.A., 1965; Florida State University, Ph.D., 1969. *Home:* 220 Orangewood, Lafayette, La. 70501. *Office:* Department of English, University of Southwestern Louisiana, Lafayette, La. 70501.

CAREER: Louisiana Department of Welfare, Baton Rouge, computer programmer, 1961-63; University of Houston, Houston, Tex., lecturer in English, 1965-66; University of Southwestern Louisiana, Lafayette, assistant professor, 1969-73, associate professor of English, 1973—. Member of Mayor's Environmental Services Committee, Lafayette, La., 1973—. President, Lafayette Greenbelt Inc., 1975—. *Member:* Modern Language Association of America, American Society for Eighteenth-Century Studies, College English Association, American Association of University Women. *Awards, honors:* Grant from American Association of University Women, 1975.

WRITINGS: Rousseau's Emile and Early Children's Literature, Scarecrow, 1971. Contributor to English journals.

WORK IN PROGRESS: Writing on the medieval play, *Everyman.*

AVOCATIONAL INTERESTS: Travel, especially in England (Sylvia Patterson attempted to retrace Johnson and Boswell's walking tour of the Hebrides in 1972).

*   *   *

PAUL, Florrie   1928-

PERSONAL: Born November 23, 1928, in Brooklyn, N.Y.; daughter of Samuel (a policeman) and Sophie (Meltzer) Levy; married Norman J. Paul (a purchasing coordinator), November 22, 1951; children: Diane, Steven, Douglas. *Education:* Attended high school in Brooklyn, N.Y. *Home and office:* 21 Almroth Dr., Wayne, N.J. 07470.

CAREER: Marine Park Co-operative Nursery School, Marine Park, Brooklyn, N.Y., founder and president, 1957-61; dental assistant and office manager in Staten Island, N.Y., 1962-68; pediatrician's receptionist in Wayne, New Jersey, 1969-72; lecturer and demonstrator of creative food presentation, "Incredible Edibles," 1972—. Visiting lecturer at Montclair State College, Rutgers University, and Brandeis University National Women's Committee; conductor of private workshops in culinary arts.

WRITINGS: How To Create Incredible Edibles: An Illustrated Guide to Imaginative Food Preparation, Fell, 1975. Contributor to *Creative Crafts, Mail Box News,* and *Today's Health.*

BIOGRAPHICAL/CRITICAL SOURCES: Bergen Record, November 11, 1973; *New York Times,* November 25, 1973; *New York Times Cooking School Round-Up,* 1973, 1974; Roberta Roesch, *There's Aways a Right Job for Every Woman,* Putnam, in press.

* * *

PAUL, Norman L(eo) 1926-

PERSONAL: Born July 5, 1926, in Buffalo, N.Y.; son of Samuel Joseph (a retailer) and Tannie (Goncharsky) Paul; married Betty Byfield (a social worker), June 8, 1951; children: Marilyn Byfield, David Alexander. *Education:* University of Buffalo, M.D., 1948; University of Cincinnati, post-doctoral study, 1949-50. *Home:* 26 Barberry Rd., Lexington, Mass. 02173. *Office:* Doctors' Building, Suite 404, 720 Harrison Ave., Boston, Mass. 02118.

CAREER: Massachusetts Mental Health Center, Boston, resident, 1952-55, research fellow in psychiatry, 1955-56, assistant physician, 1957; fellow in child psychiatry, James Jackson Putnam Children's Center, Boston, Mass., 1957-58, 1959-60, Massachusetts General Hospital, Boston, 1958-59; Massachusetts Mental Health Center, chief psychiatrist at Day Hospital, 1960-64; Tufts University, Medical School, Boston, Mass., assistant clinical professor of psychiatry, 1964-70; Boston University, Boston, Mass., research assistant professor, 1970-71, lecturer, 1971—. Fellow at Harvard University, 1952-55, instructor, 1961-64, assistant clinical professor, 1971-74; visiting lecturer at Lafayette Clinic, Detroit, Mich., 1970. Director of conjoint family therapy and coordinator of group psychotherapy at Boston State Hospital, 1964-65; associate attending physician in psychiatry at Boston City Hospital, 1971-74. Media presentations include "Separation Anxiety, Separation, Growth, and the Human Life Cycle," on WGBH-FM Radio, 1963; "Trouble in the Family," for National Educational Television (NET), 1965; "It Began on Saturday Morning," on WGBH-FM Radio, 1965; "A Chance to Grow," on WGNH-FM Radio, 1967; "Divorce and Family Therapy," on WBZ-Television, 1970; "Families: On the Road to Somewhere," on WRC-Television, 1973. Chairman of family therapy workshops. Consultant to Arthur D. Little. *Military service:* U.S. Air Force, Medical Corps, 1950-52; served as captain.

MEMBER: American Association for the Advancement of Science, Association for Research in Nervous and Mental Disorders, American Medical Association, American Orthopsychiatric Association (fellow), Group for the Advancement of Psychiatry, Society for Family Therapy and Research, American Psychiatric Association (fellow), Royal Society of Medicine (fellow), Massachusetts Medical Society (fellow), Massachusetts Council on Family Life, Massachusetts Organization to Repeal Abortion Laws (MORAL). *Awards, honors:* Peabody Broadcasting Award from Academy of Television Arts and Sciences, 1965, for television program "Trouble in the Family;" nominated for Emmy Award by Academy of Television Arts and Sciences, 1966, for "Trouble in the Family;" named "young psychiatrist of the year" by the Institute of the Pennsyl-

vania Hospital, 1966; certificate of commendation from Massachusetts Association for Mental Health, 1967, for "A Chance to Grow;" certificate of merit from Massachusetts Council on Family Life, 1967.

WRITINGS: A Chance to Grow (from the radio series), WGBH Educational Foundation, 1967; *Action for Children's Television,* Avon, 1971; (with wife, Betty Byfield Paul) *A Marital Puzzle,* Norton, 1975. Member of editorial board of *Family Process* and *Archives of the Foundation of Thanatology.*

WORK IN PROGRESS: Research on specific emotional triggers and ictal amnesia in psychomotor epilepsy; directing "Family in Crisis," a television pilot program, for Harvard University's Graduate School of Education.

SIDELIGHTS: Paul writes: "I believe that the layman is desperately in need of understandable information via books and other media about the natural processes of life, especially how to cope with change-points in the life cycle. In my research on epilepsy and other psychosomatic disorders, I am interested in finding out new possibilities for more effective coping of these psychosomatic entities and finding out how such information can neutralize the toll taken on the individual." His special interest is "using the total family unit as the instrument for preventive services."

A sound recording has been made from Paul's radio series, "A Chance to Grow," for use in school systems in the United States and abroad.

* * *

PAULSSON, Bjoern 1932-

PERSONAL: Born January 31, 1932, in Bergen, Norway; son of Gustaf and Anna (Konow) Paulsson; married Sigrid Nyhus, October 15, 1957; children: Gry-Anne, Siss-Tone, Sigbjoern. *Education:* Attended Norwegian Air Force schools, 1955-57, 1959, 1965. *Politics:* "Not very interested." *Religion:* Protestant. *Home:* Tonetun, 1560 Larkollen, Rygge, Norway. *Office:* Royal Norwegian Air Force, Rygge Air Base, Rygge, Norway.

CAREER: Royal Norwegian Air Force, career officer, 1957—, jet pilot, 1957-60, radar controller, 1960—; present rank, captain.

WRITINGS: Blind Landing (juvenile), Aschehoug & Co., 1968, English translation by Constance F. Toverud published as *Blindlanding,* Harcourt, 1970; *Noedrop fra Ishavet* (title means "S.O.S. from the Arctic"), Aschehoug & Co., 1970; *Paa vei mot Vingen* (title means "The Way to the Wing"), 1973.

SIDELIGHTS: Paulsson writes: "I am trying in my books to give the younger and the older generation a little natural look inside professional work such as the piloting of aircraft, and the problems that can arise."

* * *

PAYER, Cheryl Ann 1940-

PERSONAL: Born August 16, 1940, in Atchison, Kan.; daughter of V. Eugene and Frances (Loomis) Payer; married Robert L. Goodman, August 28, 1966 (divorced, 1968). *Education:* University of Kansas, B.A., 1961; University of California, Berkeley, M.A., 1964; Harvard University, Ph.D., 1971. *Politics:* "*Monthly Review* socialism; anti-imperialist." *Agent:* Deborah Rogers, 29 Goodge St., London W1P 1FD, England. *Office:* Pacific Studies Center, 1963 University Ave., Palo Alto, Calif. 94303.

CAREER: Spelman College, Atlanta, Ga., instructor in Asian history, 1966-68; free-lance journalist in Southeast Asia (including the Philippines, Indonesia, and Sri Lanka), 1971-72; Voluntary Committee on Overseas Aid and Development, London, England, research officer, 1973-74; Pacific Studies Center, Palo Alto, Calif., associate, 1975—. *Member:* American Political Science Association, Committee of Concerned Asian Scholars, Society of Authors (England).

WRITINGS: *The Debt Trap: The I.M.F. and the Third World,* Penguin, 1974, Monthly Review Press, 1975; (editor and contributor) *Commodity Trade of the Third World,* Halsted, in press. Contributor to political science and international studies journals. Book review editor of *Bulletin of the Concerned Asian Scholars,* 1975—.

WORK IN PROGRESS: Research on foreign influence on the political and economic development of Indonesia, 1945—.

SIDELIGHTS: Cheryl Payer writes that she "was trained as a China specialist, became interested in international economic relations," and now "aspires to study the real world without regard for artificial boundaries of academic disciplines and to communicate in clear, non-technical language accessible to the general reader."

* * *

PEARCE, Janice 1931-

PERSONAL: Born August 8, 1931, in Salt Lake City, Utah; daughter of Kelly Bradford (a railroad ticket clerk) and Thyra (Morgan) Pearce. *Education:* University of Utah, B.S., 1952, Ph.D., 1974; Washington State University, M.S., 1960; Stanford University, graduate study, 1966-67. *Religion:* Church of Jesus Christ of Latter-day Saints (Mormon). *Home:* 282 North Fourth E., Hyde Park, Utah 84318. *Office:* Department of Health, Physical Education and Recreation, Utah State University, Logan, Utah 84322.

CAREER: Junior high school teacher of physical education and English in San Bernardino, Calif., 1952-53; high school teacher of health education, physical education, and physiology in Salt Lake City, Utah, 1953-56; teaching assistant in physical education, Washington State University, Pullman, 1956-57; Utah State University, Logan, instructor, 1957-64, assistant professor and chairman of health science program, 1964-73, associate professor of health education, 1974—. Chairman of Bear River Advisory Council on Alcoholism and Other Drug Dependencies.

MEMBER: American School Health Association (member of governing council), Association for the Advancement of Health Education, American Association for Health, Physical Education and Recreation, National Association of Parliamentarians, National Federation of Business and Professional Women, Western Society for the Education of College Women, Consortium of Utah Women in Higher Education, Utah Federation of Business and Professional Women, Mortar Board, Alpha Lambda Delta.

WRITINGS: (Contributor) Brent Hafen, editor, *Health for the Secondary Teacher,* W. C. Brown, 1971; (with brother, Wayne Pearce) *Tennis,* Prentice-Hall, 1971. Contributor to health and physical education journals. Member of editorial board of American School Health Association.

WORK IN PROGRESS: A book on mental-emotional health, for use in junior and senior high school health classes; research on values in health teaching and on fitness activities for women.

AVOCATIONAL INTERESTS: Tennis, skiing, fishing.

* * *

PEARL, Hal 1914(?)-1975

1914(?)—December 17, 1975; American newsman, editor, and author of juvenile fiction. Obituaries: *New York Times,* December 19, 1975.

* * *

PEARL, Virginia L(ou) 1930-

PERSONAL: Born June 24, 1930, in St. Mary's Kan.; daughter of Thomas Michael (an agriculturalist-rancher) and Florence (Doyle) Pearl. *Education:* Marymount College, B.A., 1954; Catholic University of America, graduate study, 1962-63; Loyola University, Chicago, Ill., M.Re., 1969. *Politics:* Democrat. *Home:* Sisters of St. Joseph of Concordia, Nazareth Motherhouse, Concordia, Kan. 66901. *Office:* 1622 Blake Ave., Glenwood Springs, Colo. 81601.

CAREER: Public school teacher in Topeka, Kan., 1954-58; entered Roman Catholic order of Sisters of St. Joseph (C.S.J.), 1958, pastoral commission, 1968; pastoral minister in Clyde, Kan., 1967-70; Cure of Ars Parish, Leawood, Kan., pastoral minister and director of religious education, 1970-75; St. Stephen's Parish, Glenwood Springs, Colo., pastoral minister and director of family religious education, 1975—. Member of board of trustees of Johnson County Community College, 1974—; member of board of directors of Diocesan Pastoral Ministry, 1975. *Member:* League of Women Voters, National Directors of Religious Education, Coordinators of Religious Education Directors, National Catholic Education Association, Kansas Psychological Association.

WRITINGS: *Structuring Parish Religious Education Programs,* Paulist/Newman, 1975; *A Bunch of Daisies: Model for a Family Program,* Sheed, 1975; *Take Time: Pastoral Ministry and Family Programs,* Sisters of St. Joseph, 1975. Contributor to *Religion Teachers Journal.* Consultant to Paulist/Newman Press, 1966—.

WORK IN PROGRESS: Monthly packets to accompany *A Bunch of Daisies: Model for a Family Program,* to help congregational leaders to implement the program; writing a program, "Let us Celebrate the Eucharist," for Silver Burdett.

SIDELIGHTS: Virginia Pearl told *CA:* "A trip through the Yukon and Alaska opened avenues of experience and thought for me about the Teilhard thrust toward Omega point to which all creation is directed. Many back-pack trips into the wilderness areas of Colorado and Canada have influenced me, especially in the areas of the need for contemplation within family life, and the idea that family growth takes place in the ordinary."

* * *

PEARLMAN, Daniel (David) 1935-

PERSONAL: Born July 22, 1935, in New York. *Education:* Brooklyn College (now of the City University of New York), B.A., 1957; Columbia University, M.A., 1958, Ph.D., 1968. *Home:* 1972 Rockaway Parkway, Brooklyn, N.Y. 11236. *Agent:* Alex Jackinson, 55 West 42nd St., New York, N.Y. 10036.

CAREER: Brooklyn College (now of the City University of New York), Brooklyn, N.Y., instructor in English, 1958-

60; University of Arizona, Tucson, instructor in English, 1960-62; Brooklyn College of the City University of New York, instructor in English, 1962-67; Monmouth College, West Long Branch, N.J., assistant professor of English, 1967-69; Mercer Community College, Trenton, N.J., professor of English and chairman of department, 1969-71; Columbus International College, Seville, Spain, director of academic affairs, 1972-73; Universidad de Sevilla, Seville, Spain, visiting professor of English, 1973-74; Herbert H. Lehman College of the City University of New York, Bronx, N.Y., assistant professor of academic skills, 1974-76; self-employed writer, 1976—. *Member:* Modern Language Association of America. *Awards, honors:* American Philosophical Society research grants, 1968, 1971; American Council of Learned Societies research fellowship, 1971-72, for literary research abroad.

WRITINGS: Guide to Rapid Revision, Odyssey, 1965, 2nd edition, Bobbs-Merrill, 1974; *The Barb of Time: On the Unity of Ezra Pound's Cantos,* Oxford University Press, 1969. Also author of two as yet unpublished novels, *Astrobal* and *The Interview.* Contributor of articles and reviews to literature journals. Associate editor of *Paideuma* (journal of Ezra Pound scholarship).

WORK IN PROGRESS: A novel, *Laputa;* and a textbook, *ESL Guide to English Composition.*

SIDELIGHTS: Pearlman has lived in Spain for three years, where he lectured on English literature at the University of Seville in Spanish, and in Italy; he also speaks French, Portuguese, Italian, Hebrew, and German; he has traveled in Mexico and Europe.

* * *

PEARSON, Norman Holmes 1909-1975

April 13, 1909—November 6, 1975; American educator, scholar, and author or editor of books on English and American literature. Obituaries: *New York Times,* November 7, 1975; *Washington Post,* November 9, 1975. (*CAP*-1; earlier sketch in *CA*-15/16)

* * *

PEATTIE, Mark R(obert) 1930-

PERSONAL: Born May 3, 1930, in Nice, France; son of Donald Culross (an author) and Louise (an author; maiden name, Redfield) Peattie; married Alice Richmond, June 21, 1955; children: Victoria, Caroline, David. *Education:* Pomona College, B.A., 1951; Stanford University, M.A., 1952; Princeton University, Ph.D., 1972. *Politics:* Democrat. *Religion:* Protestant. *Home:* 829 North Thomas, State College, Pa. 16801. *Office:* 704 Liberal Arts Tower, Pennsylvania State University, University Park, Pa. 16802.

CAREER: U.S. Information Agency, Washington, D.C., assistant cultural affairs officer at American Embassy in Phnom Penh, Cambodia, 1955-57; American Cultural Center, Sendai, Japan, director, 1958-60; American Embassy Japanese Language School, Tokyo, language officer, 1960-62; American Cultural Center, Kyoto, Japan, director, 1962-67; U.S. Information Agency, Washington, D.C., Japan-Korea desk officer, 1967-68; Pennsylvania State University, University Park, assistant professor of Japanese history, 1972—. *Military service:* U.S. Army, Counter Intelligence Corps, 1952-54. *Member:* Association for Asian Studies.

WRITINGS: Ishiwara Kanji and Japan's Confrontation with the West, Princeton University Press, 1975.

WORK IN PROGRESS: A History of Japanese Colonialism, 1895-1945.

SIDELIGHTS: Peattie writes: "Ever since my father (the writer and naturalist, Donald Culross Peattie) introduced me to the wonders of history as a boy, it has been the intellectual passion of my life, reading it as a youngster and college student, seeing some of it made during my years as a representative of my country in the Far East, and now in my academic career, writing it. . . . I am absorbed in the modern history of Japan, particularly the problem of how a country so isolated and with relatively few resources and a feudal tradition should have risen within a span of a mere fifty years to have become a major world power. In many ways, of course, the costs to Japan of this forced-draft modernization have been heavy. Ultimately they led directly to the tragedy of the Pacific War and Japan's collision with America . . . so much of the American writing on Japan's military modernization has been simplistic and polemical. My purpose . . . has been neither to praise nor condemn, but merely to understand this dilemma of Japan's modernization."

AVOCATIONAL INTERESTS: Travel, classical music, military and naval history of all ages and places, history of exploration.

* * *

PEIL, Margaret 1929-

PERSONAL: Born 1929, in Racine, Wis. *Education:* Milwaukee-Downer College, B.S., 1951; Fordham University, M.A., 1961; University of Chicago, Ph.D., 1963. *Office:* Centre of West African Studies, University of Birmingham, Birmingham 15, England.

CAREER: University of Ghana, Legon, lecturer in sociology, 1963-68; University of Birmingham, Birmingham, England, lecturer, 1968-71, senior lecturer in sociology, 1972—. Senior lecturer at University of Lagos, 1971-72. *Member:* International Sociological Association, International African Institute.

WRITINGS: The Ghanaian Factory Worker, Cambridge University Press, 1972; (with David Lucas) *Survey Research Methods for West Africa,* Human Resources Research Unit, University of Lagos, 1972; *Nigerian Politics: The People's View,* Cassell, 1976. Contributor to journals. Editor of *Ghana Journal of Sociology,* 1966-68.

WORK IN RPOGRESS: An Introduction to African Societies, an introductory sociology text for African universities, to be published by Longman.

* * *

PELLING, Henry Mathison 1920-

PERSONAL: Born August 27, 1920, in Cheshire, England; son of Douglas Langley and Maud Mary (Mathison) Pelling. *Education:* St. John's College, Cambridge University, Classics Tripos Part I, 1941, History Tripos Part II, 1947, Ph.D., 1950. *Home and office:* St. John's College, Cambridge CB2 1TP, England.

CAREER: Oxford University, Queen's College, Oxford, England, fellow, 1949-65, tutor, 1950-65, dean, 1963-64; Cambridge University, Faculty of History, Cambridge, England, assistant director of research, 1966—, fellow of St. John's College, 1966—. Smith Mundt Scholar at University of Wisconsin, 1953-54; Rockefeller Scholar, 1959. *Military service:* British Army, 1941-45; served in northwestern European campaign, 1944-45; became officer in

Royal Engineers. *Member:* National Liberal Club, Royal Commonwealth Society.

WRITINGS: (Editor) *The Challenge of Socialism,* A. & C. Black, 1954, 2nd edition, 1968; *The Origins of the Labour Party, 1880-1900,* St. Martin's, 1954, 2nd edition, Clarendon Press, 1965; *America and the British Left from Bright to Bevan,* A. & C. Black, 1956, New York University Press, 1957; *The British Communist Party: A Historical Profile,* A. & C. Black, 1958, 2nd edition, 1975; (with Frank W. Bealey) *Labour and Politics, 1900-1906: A History of the Labour Representation Committee,* St. Martin's, 1958; *American Labour,* University of Chicago Press, 1960; *Modern Britain, 1885-1955,* Thomas Nelson, 1960, Norton, 1966; *A Short History of the Labour Party,* St. Martin's, 1961, 5th edition, 1976; *A History of British Trade Unionism,* St. Martin's, 1963, 2nd edition, 1972; *Social Geography of British Elections, 1885-1910,* St. Martin's, 1967; *Popular Politics and Society in Late Victorian Britain: Essays,* St. Martin's, 1968; *Britain and the Second World War,* Collins, 1970; *Winston Churchill,* Dutton, 1974. Contributor to numerous periodicals and journals.

WORK IN PROGRESS: A study of the Attlee government, 1945-51.

AVOCATIONAL INTERESTS: Films and observing elections.

* * *

PELTON, Barry C(lifton) 1935-

PERSONAL: Born March 3, 1935, in Rockwall, Tex.; son of Barry Clifton and Rose (Willeford) Pelton. *Education:* East Texas State University, B.S., 1957, M.Ed., 1959; University of Southern California, Ed.D., 1966. *Home:* 2340 Goldsmith, Houston, Tex. 77025. *Office:* Department of Health and Physical Education, University of Houston, Cullen Blvd., Houston, Tex. 77004.

CAREER: City of Garland, Garland, Tex., summer recreation director, 1955, 1956; high school teacher of physical education at public schools in Dallas, Tex., 1957-60, and Culver City, Calif., 1960-63; Louisiana State University, Baton Rouge, instructor in physical education and director of basic instruction program of physical education for men, 1967-68; University of Houston, Houston, Tex., associate professor of education, 1968—, acting associate graduate dean, College of Education, 1971. Recreation leader and consultant, city of Culver City, Calif., 1962-64. U.S. delegate to International Conference on Sport and Physical Education, London, England, and Madrid, Spain, 1966, and International Council for Health, Physical Education, and Recreation, 1971, 1975.

MEMBER: International Council for Health, Physical Education and Recreation, American Association of University Professors, American Association for Health, Physical Education and Recreation (member of executive committee, 1973-75), National College Physical Education Association for Men, National Education Association, Association for Research Administration and Professional Societies Councils (member of executive committee, 1972-74), Southern District of Health, Physical Education and Recreation, Texas Association for Health, Physical Education and Recreation, Texas Association of College Teachers, Texas State Teachers Association, Phi Delta Kappa.

WRITINGS: Tennis, Goodyear Publishing, 1969; *New Curriculum Perspectives for Collegiate Physical Education,* W. C. Brown, 1970; *Badminton,* Prentice-Hall, 1971;

(contributor) Johnson, Perry and others, editors, *Teacher's Manual,* Prentice-Hall, 1971; (contributor) J. Tillman Hall, editor, *Teacher's Manual,* Goodyear Publishing, 1973; (contributor) Robert N. Singer, editor, *Physical Education: Foundations and Concepts,* Holt, 1976. Contributor to proceedings and physical education journals.

WORK IN PROGRESS: Physical Education in Transition (text for teacher education).

* * *

PEMBROOK, Linda 1942-

PERSONAL: Born September 29, 1942, in Chelsea, Mass.; daughter of Harold Ernest (a business executive) and Georgianna (Harris) Pembrook; children: Johanna Gail. *Education:* Attended Middlebury College, 1959-61; University of Washington, Seattle, B.A., 1963; Hunter College of the City University of New York, graduate study. *Religion:* Protestant. *Home and office:* 400 West End Ave., New York, N.Y. 10024.

CAREER: Secretary in Seattle, Wash., 1964, and New York, N.Y., 1964-65; Science & Medicine Publishing, New York, N.Y., editorial assistant, 1966-67; Harcourt, Brace & World (publishers), New York, N.Y., copy editor in school department, 1967-68; Macmillan Publishing Co., New York, N.Y., editor in Textbook Division, 1968-70; free-lance writer, 1974—. Member of Collegiate Chorale. *Member: National Association of Science Writers.*

WRITINGS: How to Beat Fatigue, Doubleday, 1975. Contributor to medical journals and to popular magazines, including *New York* and *Parents' Magazine,* and to newspapers.

WORK IN PROGRESS: A book for the Planned Parenthood Association.

SIDELIGHTS: Linda Pembrook writes that she is "motivated by a love of adventure, strange situations, foreign countries...." She has traveled in eastern and western Europe.

* * *

PERIGOE, J. Rae 1910-

PERSONAL: Born October 17, 1910, in Echo Bay, Ontario, Canada; son of Thomas Byron (a merchant) and Mary-Jane (Speirs) Perigoe; married Elsie Jean Alton, October 3, 1936; children: John Thomas, Mary Elizabeth Perigoe Malcolm, Ross Alton. *Education:* McMaster University, B.A., 1932; University of Toronto, M.A., 1933. *Home:* 60 Glen Watford Dr., Agincourt, Ontario, Canada M1S 2C5. *Office:* Presentation of Canada Ltd., 602 2221 Yonge St., Toronto, Ontario, Canada M4S 2B4.

CAREER: McLean Hunter Publishing Co., Toronto, Ontario, editor, bookseller, and stationer, 1938-41; Somerville Ltd., London, Ontario, personnel and industrial relations manager, 1941-51; Presentation of Canada Ltd., Toronto, Ontario, vice-president, 1951—. Director of paper and container conservation for Wartime Prices and Trade Board, 1943-45.

WRITINGS: Getting Your Point Across, Federation of Canadian Personnel Associations, 1967; *The Best of the Canadian Personnel and Industrial Relations Journal,* Federation of Canadian Personnel Associations, 1971; *Message and Meaning,* Prentice-Hall (Canada), 1974. Editor-in-chief of publications of Industrial Supervisory Institute; editor of *Canadian Personnel and Industrial Relations Journal.*

PERLMAN, Janice E(laine) 1943-

PERSONAL: Born July 12, 1943, in New York, N.Y.; daughter of Ely (a physician) and Norma (Rackow) Perlman. *Education:* Cornell University, B.A., 1965; Massachusetts Institute of Technology, Ph.D., 1971. *Home:* 1508 La Loma, Berkeley, Calif. 94708. *Office:* Department of City and Regional Planning, University of California, Berkeley, Calif. 94720.

CAREER: University of California, Santa Cruz, assistant professor of politics and community studies, 1971-73; University of California, Berkeley, assistant professor of city and regional planning, 1973—. Has lectured at Federal Universities of Minas Gerais and Brasilia, at Brazilian Institute for Municipal Administration, and at Stanford University; a speaker for Institute for World Order. Member of board of trustees of Common College. Member of national screening committee of Social Science Research Council. Has conducted field research in the United States and abroad, including Central and South America (especially Brazil), People's Republic of China, Paris, and southern Europe. Consultant to the United National and the International Bank for Reconstruction and Development.

MEMBER: International Sociological Association, American Association for the Advancement of Science, American Political Science Association, American Sociological Association, Latin American Studies Association, Women's Coalition on Latin America, Organization of Women Architects, American Institute of Planners, Phi Beta Kappa, Phi Kappa Phi, Alpha Kappa Delta, Alpha Lambda Delta. *Awards, honors:* Woodrow Wilson fellowship, 1965-66; National Institute of Mental Health fellowship, 1966-71; National Science Foundation grant, 1968-69; grants from Institute of International Studies, Institute of Urban and Regional Development, and Center for Community Change, all 1974-75; Ford Foundation travel grant, 1975; award from social science program of the French Government, 1976.

WRITINGS: Methodological Notes on Complex Survey Research Involving Life History Data (monograph), Institute of Urban and Regional Development, University of California, Berkeley, 1974; *Government Policy toward Brazilian Favela Dwellers* (monograph), Institute of Urban and Regional Development, University of California, Berkeley, 1974; *The Power and Persistence of Poverty Paradigms: Comparative Ideologies on Poverty in the United States and Latin America* (monograph), School of Architecture and Urban Planning, University of California, Los Angeles, 1975; *The Myth of Marginality: Urban Poverty and Politics in Rio de Janeiro,* University of California Press, 1976; *Portrait of the People: Migrants to Rio de Janeiro* (monograph), Center for International Studies, Massachusetts Institute of Technology, in press. Contributor to political science and social science journals.

WORK IN PROGRESS: Urban Social Movements in the Contemporary U.S.A., completion expected in 1977.

* * *

PERRELLA, Robert 1917-

PERSONAL: Born July 1, 1917, in New York; son of Dominick (a carpenter) and Rosina (DelRe) Perrella. *Education:* Attended Fordham University, Catholic University of America, St. Francis Seraphic Seminary, West Andover, Mass., and St. Anthony's Seminary, Catskill, N.Y. *Agent:* Dan Leeds, 45 West 45th St., New York, N.Y.

CAREER: Ordained Roman Catholic priest; serves as permanent national chaplain of Actor's Youth Fund. *Member:* American Guild of Variety Artists (chaplain).

WRITINGS: They Call Me the Showbiz Priest, Simon & Schuster, 1973.

SIDELIGHTS: Perrella writes: "My relationship to showbiz was strictly accidental. I met accidentally a young and up-coming vocalist and associated with him for many years. His name is Perry Como. Hence, my entre into showbiz. For the past thirty years, I have married, baptized, buried, counseled many personalities, the known and unknown of the showbusiness world."

* * *

PETRAS, James Frank 1937-

PERSONAL: Born January 17, 1937, in Lynn, Mass.; married Elizabeth L. McLean, 1959; children: two. *Education:* Boston University, B.A. (cum laude), 1958; University of California, Berkeley, M.A., 1963, Ph.D., 1967. *Home:* 3133 Cortland Dr., Vestal, N.Y. *Office:* Department of Sociology, State University of New York at Binghamton, Binghamton, N.Y. 13901.

CAREER: Pennsylvania State University, University Park, research associate at Institute of Public Administration, 1967-72, assistant professor, 1967-69, associate professor of political science, 1969-72, also project director of public administration and agrarian reform program in Chile and Peru; State University of New York at Binghamton, professor of sociology, 1973—. Resident scholar at Center for the Study of Democratic Institutions, 1967; visiting lecturer at Torcuato Di Tella Institute, Center of Development Studies (Caracas), Universidad Nacional (Montevideo), and Universidad San Andres; lecturer at colleges and universities in the United States and Europe.

MEMBER: American Sociological Association, American Political Science Association, Latin American Studies Association (member of executive council, 1971-72). *Awards, honors:* Latin American studies research fellowship from Doherty Foundation, 1965-66, for field research in Chile; Social Science Research Council grant, summer, 1970, 1975; Ford Foundation faculty fellowship, 1970-71.

WRITINGS: Chilean Christian Democracy (monograph), Institute of International Studies, University of California, Berkeley, 1967; (editor with Maurice Zeitlin) *Latin America: Reform or Revolution?,* Fawcett, 1968; *Political and Social Forces in Chilean Development,* University of California Press, 1969; (editor with Martin Kenner) *Fidel Castro Speaks,* Grove, 1969; (with Zeitlin) *El Radicalismo Politico de la Clase Trabajadora Chilena* (title means "Chilean Working Class Radicalism"), Centro Editor de America Latina, 1970; *Politics and Structure in Latin America,* Monthly Review Press, 1970; (with Robert La-Porte) *Cultivating Revolution: The United States and Agrarian Reform in Latin America,* Random House, 1971; *Los Militares Peruanos: Modernizadores o Revolucionarios?* (title means "Peruvian Military: Modernizers or Revolutionaries?"), Amorotu, 1971; *America Latina: Politica y Economia* (title means "Latin America: Politics and Economy"), Editorial Periferia, 1972; (with Hugo Zemelman) *Peasants in Revolt,* University of Texas Press, 1973; *Latin America: Dependence or Revolution,* Wiley, 1973; *Puerto Rico and the Puerto Rican Experience,* Schenkman, 1974; (editor with Adalberto Lopez) *The United States and Chile* (Macmillan Book-of-the-Month selection), Monthly Review Press, 1975; (with Morris Morley) *U.S. Imperialism and the Overthrow of Allende,* Monthly Review Press, 1975.

Contributor: John Playford and Charles A. McCoy, editors, *Apolitical Politics,* Crowell, 1967; Marvin Gettleman, editor, *The Great Society Reader,* Random House, 1967; Rodolfo Stavenhagen, editor, *Agrarian Problems and Peasant Movements in Latin America,* Doubleday, 1970; Edward O. Lauman and other editors, *The Logic of Social Hierarchies,* Markham, 1970; David Mermelstein and Robert Lekachman, editors, *Economics: Mainstream Readings and Radical Critiques,* Random House, 1970; James Colonesse, editor, *Conscientization for Liberation,* U.S. Catholic Conference, 1970; Marvin Surkin, editor, *Essays in the New Political Science,* Basic Books, 1970; Michael Parenti, editor, *Trends and Tragedies in American Foreign Policy,* Little, Brown, 1971; J. David Colfax and Jack L. Roach, editors, *Radical Sociology,* Basic Books, 1971; Louis Wolf Goodman, editor, *Workers and Managers in Latin America,* Heath, 1972; Lawrence Graham, editor, *Administering Change in Latin America,* Duke University Press, 1973; Ronald Chilcote, editor, *Latin America,* Schenkman, 1974; Paul Sweezy, editor, *Revolution and Counter-Revolution in Chile,* Monthly Review Press, 1974; Ronald Radosh, editor, *The New Cuba: An Anthology of Critical Evaluation,* Crowell, 1975. Contributor of about eighty articles and reviews to scholarly journals.

* * *

PETRICH, Patricia Barrett 1942-

PERSONAL: Born August 18, 1942, in San Francisco, Calif.; daughter of Edward John (an engineer for Pacific Telephone Co.) and Grace (Lynch) Barrett; married Donald Allen Petrich (a packaging salesman and designer), December 19, 1970. *Education:* San Francisco State College (now University), B.A., 1965, graduate study, 1965-66; also attended California State University, Hayward, University of California, Berkeley, and San Jose State University. *Home:* 140 Bridgeport Dr., El Granada, Calif. 94018. *Office:* Martin School, South San Francisco Unified School District, 398 B St., South San Francisco, Calif.

CAREER: Elementary school teacher in South San Francisco, Calif., 1966-67, and Stoneham, Mass., 1967-68; South San Francisco Unified School District, South San Francisco, Calif., teacher at Martin School, 1968—.

WRITINGS—All with Rosemary Dalton; all self-illustrated: *The Kid's Cookbook,* Nitty Gritty Productions, 1973; *The Kid's Garden Book,* Nitty Gritty Productions, 1974; *The Kid's Arts and Crafts Book,* Nitty Gritty Productions, 1975.

WORK IN PROGRESS: A pet care book for children; children's story books.

SIDELIGHTS: Patricia Petrich writes: "I have wanted, for as long as I can remember, to write and illustrate a really good children's book—one meaningful to children in a special way. I think that books I knew and loved early in my life influenced me in this way. They colored my life and are with me still." Her published books include pictures drawn by school children. *Avocational interests:* Drawing, arts and crafts (takes classes each summer), doing grave-rubbings, scrimshaw, Mexican and American Indian art, flying with her pilot husband, international travel.

* * *

PETTY, Roberta 1915-
  (Haris Petie)

PERSONAL: Born June 26, 1915, in Boulder Creek, Calif.;

daughter of William Henry (in lumber business) and Isobel (Harris) Pfafflin; married Robert Petty (deceased); children: Isobel, Virginia. *Education:* Attended Rochester Institute of Technology, 1932-33; and Otis Art Institute, 1934. *Residence:* North Bergen, N.J. *Agent:* Florence Alexander, 50 East 42nd St., New York, N.Y. 10017.

CAREER: Artist and illustrator of children's books.

WRITINGS—Juvenile; self-illustrated and under pseudonym Haris Petie: *Billions of Bugs,* Prentice-Hall, 1975; *The Seed the Squirrel Dropped,* Prentice-Hall, in press. Illustrator of more than fifteen books for children.

SIDELIGHTS: Roberta Petty lived in Paris for four years. One of her current interests is ecology.

* * *

PETZOLD, Paul 1940-

PERSONAL: Born September 12, 1940, in Epsom, Surrey, England; son of Max Leo and Iris (Hopps) Petzold. *Education:* Attended Polytechnic Film School, London, 1958-61. *Home:* 4A Alexandra Mans., West End Lane, London NW6 1LU, England. *Office:* Focal Press, 31 Fitzroy Sq., London W.1, England.

CAREER: Free-lance filmmaker, 1961-62; Focal Press, London, England, book editor, 1962—. Co-director of screenplay, "Background to Ballet," for British Broadcasting Corp. (BBC), 1962.

WRITINGS: All in One Cine Book, Focal Press, 1969, 3rd edition, 1974, published as *All in One Movie Book,* Amphoto, 1969, 3rd edition, 1974; *Light on People in Photography,* Amphoto, 1971; (with Freddie Young) *The Work of the Motion Picture Cameraman,* Hastings House, 1972; *Effects and Experiments in Photography,* Amphoto, 1972; *Photoguide to Moviemaking,* Amphoto, 1975; *Photoguide to Low Light Photography,* Amphoto, 1976.

WORK IN PROGRESS: A book on filming for television; a book on lighting for photography.

* * *

PEZZUTI, Thomas Alexander 1936-

PERSONAL: Born December 29, 1936, in Harrisburg, Pa.; son of Hamil Ralph (a surgeon) and Dorothea (a nurse; maiden name, Graham) Pezzuti. *Education:* University of Notre Dame, B.Arch., 1959. *Home:* 1042 Sixth St., Santa Monica, Calif. 90403. *Office:* Woodford & Bernard, Architects, 410 North LaBrae Ave., Los Angeles, Calif. 90036.

CAREER: Weiss Associates, New York, N.Y., architect, 1961-62; taught at University of Notre Dame, Notre Dame, Ind., 1962-63; Lacy, Atherton & Davis, Harrisburg, Pa., architect, 1963-66; Warner Brothers Inc., Burbank, Calif., set designer in movie studio, 1966-67; Gruen Associates, Los Angeles, Calif., architect, 1968-70; Property Research Corp., Los Angeles, assistant director of architecture, 1970-72; Woodford & Bernard, Los Angeles, director of business development, 1972—. Chairman of local citizen action service. *Military service:* U.S. Army, Corps of Engineers, 1959-60. *Member:* International Mensa Society, American Institute of Architects.

WRITINGS: You Can Fight City Hall and Win, Sherbourne, 1974.

* * *

PHAIR, Judith Turner 1946-

PERSONAL: Surname is pronounced Fair; born October

18, 1946, in Woburn, Mass.; daughter of Robert Alan (a machinist) and Emily (Thorne) Turner; married Robert Donald Phair (a physiologist), August 10, 1968. *Education:* Simmons College, B.A. (with high distinction), 1968; University of Maryland, M.A., 1973. *Home:* 4788 Washtenaw, Ann Arbor, Mich. 48104. *Office:* University of Michigan—Dearborn, 4901 Evergreen, Dearborn, Mich. 48126.

CAREER: Hollister Publications (now Paddock Publications), Wilmette, Ill., reporter, 1968-69; University of Cincinnati, Cincinnati, Ohio, information writer, 1969-71; *Where* (magazine), Washington, D.C., editor, 1971-72; University of Michigan—Dearborn, information officer, 1973—. *Member:* Council for the Advancement and Support of Education, University of Michigan—Dearborn Women's Commission (member of executive board).

WRITINGS: A Bibliography of William Cullen Bryant and His Critics: 1808-1972, Whitston Publishing, 1975. Contributor to *Glamour* and *Washingtonian.*

WORK IN PROGRESS: Research on the role of the press in the American revolutionary period.

SIDELIGHTS: Judith Phair writes: "I'm especially fascinated by the evolution of the American press and the role of the press in society and politics. My interest in Bryant stems from his career as a journalist and his influence in the evolution of the big city American newspaper. I hope to do more work in the future with Bryant and other representative journalists of the late nineteenth and early twentieth centuries."

* * *

PHELPS, Thomas Ross 1929-

PERSONAL: Born January 10, 1929, in Livingston, Mont.; son of Thomas Murray (a railroad conductor) and Minerva (Lynam) Phelps. *Education:* Seattle University, B.S.S., 1951; University of Washington, Seattle, M.S.W. and M.A., both 1959; Florida State University, Ph.D., 1969. *Religion:* Roman Catholic. *Home:* 3150 Notre Dame Dr., Sacramento, Calif. 95826. *Office:* Department of Criminal Justice, California State University, 6000 Jay St., Sacramento, Calif. 95819.

CAREER: California State University, Sacramento, instructor in criminology, 1962-64; Florida State University, Tallahassee, instructor, 1965-69, assistant professor of criminology, 1969-70; California State University, Sacramento, associate professor, 1970-72, professor of criminal justice, 1972—. Lecturer at National College of Juvenile Justice, at University of Nevada, Reno, 1973—. Technical assistant to Youth Development and Delinquency Prevention Administration of U.S. Department of Health, Education and Welfare, 1969-70; member of regional criminal justice advisory committee on manpower development of the U.S. Department of Justice's Law Enforcement Assistance Administration, 1972; member of manpower development advisory committee of California Council on Criminal Justice, 1972—. Member of the governor's committee of Project Safer California. *Military service:* U.S. Army, 1954-55. *Member:* American Sociological Association, National Council on Crime and Delinquency, Society for the Study of Social Problems, American Society of Criminology.

WRITINGS: (Editor with Gary Perlstein) *Alternatives to Prison: Community-Based Corrections,* Goodyear Publishing, 1975; *Juvenile Delinquency: A Contemporary View,*

Goodyear Publishing, in press. Contributor to *Abstracts for Social Workers.*

WORK IN PROGRESS: Introduction to Criminal Justice; Research Methods in Criminal Justice.

SIDELIGHTS: Phelps writes: "I am concerned, as was Beccaria the founder of the classical school of criminology, that we have a society of kind and civilized people. I hope that my interest in criminal justice manpower development will contribute to the achievement of such a goal." *Avocational interests:* Travel, reading (in the arts and humanities).

* * *

PHILLIPS, (Elizabeth Margaret Ann) Barty 1933-

PERSONAL: Born May 4, 1933, in Dorking, England; daughter of Henry Lloyd (a headmaster) and Margaret (Strawn) Brereton; married Pearson Phillips (a journalist), April 16, 1955 (divorced, 1965); children: John, Jane, Charles. *Education:* Educated in Scotland, England, and Germany. *Home:* Cottage, Marden Hill, Hertfordshire, England. *Agent:* Patrick Seale Associates, 4 Motcombe St., London, England. *Office: Observer,* 160 Queen Victoria St., London, England.

CAREER: Editor's secretary, *Nova Magazine;* sub-editor, *Good Housekeeping* (magazine), London, England; *Observer,* London, home editor, 1968—. Conducted occasional household television program, "Pebble Mill at One," for British Broadcasting Corp., 1975.

WRITINGS: How to Decorate Without Going Broke, Doubleday, 1974; (contributor) Beverley Hilton and Maria Kroll, editors, *The House Book,* Mitchell Beazley, 1975; (author of bibliography) Eva Wilson, editor, *The Observer Book of Kitchen Ideas,* Macmillan, in press; (contributor) Theo Hodges, editor, *Household Manual,* Reader's Digest Press, in press.

* * *

PHILLIPS, Cabell (Beverly Hatchett) 1905(?)-1975

1905(?)—November 14, 1975; American political journalist and author or editor of historical works. Obituaries: *New York Times,* November 15, 1975; *Washington Post,* November 16, 1975; *Publishers Weekly,* December 1, 1975; *AB Bookman's Weekly,* December 8, 1975.

* * *

PHILLIPS, Josephine E(lvira Frye) 1896-1975

March 18, 1896—July 29, 1975; American educator, businesswoman, bibliophile, and author. Obituaries: *AB Bookman's Weekly,* October 13, 1975. (See index for previous CA sketch)

* * *

PHILLIPS, Wendell 1921-1975

September 25, 1921—December 4, 1975; American archaeologist, explorer, oilman, and author. Obituaries: *New York Times,* December 5, 1975; *Washington Post,* December 7, 1975; *AB Bookman's Weekly,* January 26, 1976; *Current Biography,* February, 1976. (*CAP*-2; earlier sketch in *CA*-23/24)

* * *

PHILPOTT, Kent 1942-

PERSONAL: Born January 27, 1942, in Portland, Ore.;

son of Vernon Clymer (a salesman) and Zoe (Conn) Philpott; married Roberta Davidson (a switchboard operator), May 9, 1961; children: Dawn Doreen, Grace Marie, Vernon Robert. *Education:* Glendale College, student, 1959-61; Napa College, A.A., 1964; California State University, Sacramento, B.A., 1965; Golden Gate Baptist Seminary, M.Div., 1969. *Religion:* Nondenominational. *Home:* 671 Knocknaboul Way, San Rafael, Calif. 94903. *Office:* 2130 Fourth St., San Rafael, Calif. 94901.

CAREER: "Free-lance street ministry" in Haight-Ashbury area of San Francisco, Calif., 1967-70; House Ministries, Inc., San Francisco, Calif., president, 1970—. Pastor of Baptist church in Byron, Calif., 1966-68, and Church of the Open Door, San Raphael, Calif., 1974—. *Military service:* U.S. Air Force, 1961-65. *Member:* Evangelical Concerns (member of board of directors).

WRITINGS: A Manual of Demonology and the Occult, Zondervan, 1973; *If the Devil Wrote a Bible ...,* Logos International, 1974; *The Third Sex?,* Logos International, 1975; *A Handbook of Theology for New Believers,* Logos International, in press.

*   *   *

PIERCE, Edith Gray   1893-
(Marian Gray)

PERSONAL: Born December 22, 1893, in Columbus Junction, Iowa; daughter of James Edward (a farmer) and Margaret J. (Dawdy) Gray; married Chester Earl Pierce, May 31, 1912 (deceased); children: Alice Elizabeth (Mrs. Harold R. Piercy), James Gray, Robert Edward (deceased). *Education:* Attended University of Iowa. *Politics:* Republican. *Religion:* Methodist. *Home and office:* Evergreen Farm, Columbus Junction, Iowa 52738.

CAREER: County chairman of Rural Women's Farm Bureau, 1922-24, and Girls 4-H Clubs, 1925-30. President of Iowa Council of Republican Women, 1951-52. *Member:* National League of American Pen Women (regional chairman, 1969-70), National Federation of Womens Clubs, National Federation of Music Clubs. *Awards, honors: Des Moines Register* community service award, 1926.

WRITINGS: Horace Mann: Our Nation's First Educator (for young people), Lerner, 1972. Contributor, sometimes under pseudonym Marian Gray, to *Organic Gardening, Flower Grower, Flower and Garden, Popular Gardening, Capper's Farmer, Farmers Wife, Dog World, Lady's Circle, Farm Wife News,* and *Des Moines Register.* Author of pageant for Columbus Junction Centennial Celebration, 1974. Regional editor, *The Pen Woman* (of National League of American Pen Women), 1969-72.

WORK IN PROGRESS: Three Explorers: Marquette, Joliet and La Salle; a book on Ralph J. Bunche for junior high school readers.

SIDELIGHTS: Edith Pierce's ancestors came from England in 1840 to Iowa (then Wisconsin Territory), and settled on the farm where she now lives.

*   *   *

PILKINGTON, William T(homas, Jr.)   1939-

PERSONAL: Born June 29, 1939, in Fort Worth, Tex.; son of William Thomas, Sr. and Alice (Levey) Pilkington; married Betsy Walter (a teacher), January 20, 1968; children: Michael Thomas. *Education:* University of Texas, Arlington, B.A., 1961; Texas Christian University, M.A., 1963, Ph.D., 1968. *Politics:* Independent. *Home address:* Star Route, Box 101, Stephenville, Tex. 76401. *Office:* Department of English, Tarleton State University, Stephenville, Tex. 76402.

CAREER: Southwest Texas State University, San Marcos, instructor in English, 1965-68; Texas Christian University, Fort Worth, instructor in English, 1968-69; Tarleton State University, Stephenville, Tex., assistant professor, 1969-71, associate professor of English, 1971—. *Member:* American Studies Association, Modern Language Association of America, South Central Modern Language Association, Western Literature Association (member of executive council, 1973-76), Texas Folklore Society.

WRITINGS: My Blood's Country: Studies in Southwestern Literature, Texas Christian University Press, 1973; (editor) *Tacey Cromwell,* University of New Mexico Press, 1974; *Harvey Fergusson,* Twayne, 1975; (editor) *Grant of Kingdom,* University of New Mexico Press, 1975. Contributor of articles to *Studies in Short Fiction, Western American Literature, New Mexico Quarterly, South Dakota Review,* and others.

WORK IN PROGRESS: Current research is in the novel of the American West and in the literary history of Texas.

SIDELIGHTS: Pilkington told *CA:* "My main vocational and avocational interest is the literature of the American West and Southwest—primarily fiction. This interest is stimulated by nothing more complicated than a liking for these regions—topographically, culturally, literarily." *Avocational interests:* Reading, playing tennis, listening to country and western music, harvesting mesquite beans, and drinking Lone Star beer ("not necessarily in that order").

*   *   *

PILL, Virginia   1922-

PERSONAL: Born April 29, 1922, in Jamestown, N.Y.; daughter of John V. and Minnie T. (Heglund) Parsons; married John Joseph Pill (a superintendent of schools), May 23, 1942; children: Kathleen B., Jeffrey J. *Education:* Western Washington State College, B.A.Ed., 1962; Washington State University, graduate study, 1966-67. *Politics:* Independent. *Religion:* Lutheran. *Home address:* Route 5, Box 940, Shelton, Wash. 98584. *Office:* Hood Canal School, R.R.5, Box 392, Shelton, Wash. 98584.

CAREER: Lawrence Fuel Co., Hoquiam, Wash., bookkeeper, 1942-45; Western Washington State College Bookstore, Bellingham, clerk, 1947-50; teacher in Shelton, Wash., 1950-54; Hood Canal School, Shelton, Wash., teacher, 1962-66, 1967—. *Member:* National Education Association, Smithsonian Institution, Pacific Northwest Writers, Washington Education Association, Mason County Hospital Guild.

WRITINGS: (With Marjorie Furlong) *Starfish,* Ellison Industries, 1970, 2nd edition, 1970; *Edible?: Incredible!,* Ellis Robinson, 1972; *Wild Edible Fruits and Berries,* Naturegraph, 1974.

WORK IN PROGRESS: A second part to *Wild Edible Fruits and Berries; Edible Seaweed;* tasting and photographing edible plants and animals of fresh water areas, for a book.

SIDELIGHTS: Virginia Pill writes: "After several years in college towns, I am now settled in a home built by a salt water fiord called Hood Canal (which is not a canal) in Western Washington. Even though my front door opens to the salt water beach, our holidays include other salt water areas such as the California and Oregon coasts, the San

Juan Islands of Washington, and the beaches of Hawaii. Each trip is also a learning experience in culinary delights collected from the land and water.

"My philosophy is that the more people understand the environment around them, the more inclined they will be to protect and care for it. I am a self-styled naturalist who enjoys sharing what knowledge I possess with others through my teaching and writing in the hope that others may gain new respect for the plants and animals of our planet Earth." *Avocational interests:* Water skiing, swimming, boating, reading, hiking, golfing.

* * *

PINERO, Miguel (Gomez) 1946-

PERSONAL: Born December 12, 1946, in Puerto Rico; son of Miguel Angel and Adelina (Pinero) Gomez. *Education:* Attended public schools in New York City. *Agent:* Niel Ganchieu, 1370 Avenue of the Americas, New York, N.Y.

CAREER: Actor and writer. *Awards, honors:* New York Drama Critics Circle Award, Obie Award, and Drama Desk Award, all 1974, all for *Short Eyes.*

WRITINGS: Short Eyes (play; first produced in New York at Theatre of Riverside Church, January, 1974, produced Off-Broadway at Public Theatre, March, 1974), Hill & Wang, 1975; (editor) *Nuyorican Poets,* Morrow, 1975.

SIDELIGHTS: Pinero began writing and acting in Clay Stevenson's theatre workshop while an inmate of Sing Sing prison. *Short Eyes* was written in prison and produced after the playwright's parole. In spite of Pinero's claim that the play was only "a slice of life in prison," Jack Kroll believes: "it isn't occupational therapy and it isn't a freak show; it's an authentic, powerful theatrical piece that tells you more about the anti-universie of prison life than any play outside the work of Jean Genet."

BIOGRAPHICAL/CRITICAL SOURCES: New York Times, May 27, 1972; *Newsweek,* April 8, 1974; Carolyn Riley, editor, *Contemporary Literary Criticism,* Volume IV, Gale, 1974.

* * *

PINTO, David 1937-

PERSONAL: Born January 18, 1937, in New York, N.Y.; son of Morris (a printer) and Lillian (a librarian; maiden name, Feingless) Pinto; married Susan Schinitsky (a magazine editor), March 6, 1971. *Education:* Hunter College (now of the City University of New York), B.A., 1959. *Politics:* Democrat. *Religion:* Jewish. *Home:* 307 East 37th St., New York, N.Y. 10016. *Office:* Lebhar-Friedman, Inc., 2 Park Ave., New York, N.Y. 10016.

CAREER: Lebhar-Friedman, Inc., New York, N.Y., magazine editor (editor of monthly publication for drug store retailers), 1966—. *Military service:* U.S. Army, 1959-61.

WRITINGS: How to Make Ecology Work for You, Lebhar-Friedman, 1972.

AVOCATIONAL INTERESTS: International travel.

* * *

PIPER, William Bowman 1927-

PERSONAL: Born December 7, 1927, in Lexington, Ky.; son of Lewis A. (a teacher) and Anna (a teacher; maiden name Zink) Piper; married Katharine Welles, August 22, 1955; children: Henry, Walter, Anthony, Anne. *Education:* Harvard University, B.A. (magna cum laude), 1951; Columbia University, M.A., 1952; University of Wisconsin, Ph.D., 1958. *Home:* 2132 Dryden Rd., Houston, Tex. 77025. *Office:* Department of English, Rice University, Houston, Tex. 77001.

CAREER: Cornell University, Ithaca, N.Y., instructor in English, 1958-61; University of Louisville, Louisville, Ky., assistant professor of English, 1961-64; Western Reserve University (now Case Western Reserve University), Cleveland, Ohio, associate professor of English, 1964-69; Rice University, Houston, Tex., professor of English, 1969—. *Military service:* U.S. Army, 1946-48; became staff sergeant. *Member:* Modern Language Association of America, South Central Modern Language Association. *Awards, honors:* Fulbright scholar, 1957-58.

WRITINGS: Laurence Sterne, Twayne, 1965; *The Heroic Couplet,* Press of Case Western Reserve University, 1969; (editor with Robert A. Greenberg) *The Critical Swift,* Norton, 1972; *The Sense of 'Gulliver's Travels'* (monograph), Rice University Studies, 1975. Contributor of essays, reviews, and poems to literary journals.

WORK IN PROGRESS: The Literature of Common Sense; A Heroic Couplet Anthology; An Essay in Judgment: Shakespeare's Sonnets.

* * *

PIPPING, Ella (Geologica) 1897-

PERSONAL: Born August 19, 1897, in Teisko, Finland; daughter of Johan Axel (a lawyer) and Florence (von Schoultz) Tammelander; married Hugo Edvard Pipping (a professor), July 8, 1922 (died April 13, 1975); children: Jost Joachim (deceased), Helena (Mrs. Carl Fredrik Meinander); Fredrik. *Education:* Attended University of Helsinki, 1916-21. *Politics:* Swedish People's Party. *Religion:* Lutheran. *Home:* Kyosti Kalliosvag 8B, Helsinki 57, Finland. *Agent:* Holger Schildt, Annegatan 16, Helsinki 12, Finland.

CAREER: Lecturer in Sweden and worker for evacuation of Finnish children to Sweden, 1940-44; active in administrating home for the aged in Helsinki, Finland, 1946-72. *Awards, honors:* Medal Pro Benignitate Humanna, 1918; Cross of Liberty, 4th Class, 1939; Medal of Liberty, 1st Class, 1943; Swedish Literary Society of Finland award, 1968, for *En orons legionaer.*

WRITINGS: (Translator from German to Swedish) Clemens Brentano, *Romantiska sagor,* Schildts (Helsinki), 1923; *Yag,* Gtava Kuslannos, 1937, translation into Finnish by the author published as *Jag,* Soderstrom & Co. (Helsinki), 1937; *En orons legionaer: Nils Gustav von Schoultz,* Schildts, 1967, translation from the Swedish by Naomi Walford published as *Soldier of Fortune: The Story of a Nineteenth Century Adventurer,* Gambit, 1971 (published in England as *This Creature of Fancy,* Macdonald, 1972); *Indien bortom haven,* Schildts, 1972. Editor, *Husmodern,* 1945-50.

SIDELIGHTS: Ella Pipping told *CA* that she used the letters and diaries in the family archives for her writing. She tries to keep strictly to her original sources in order to write about her ancestors' life in a past era. She has traveled all over England, France, Germany, Holland, Poland, Scotland, the Scandinavian countries, and parts of Africa. She speaks Swedish, German, English and "a bit of French." *Avocational interests:* Fine books, music and flowers.

PLATT, Frederick 1946-

PERSONAL: Born May 11, 1946, in Rochester, N.Y. *Education:* University of Pennsylvania, A.B., 1968. *Politics:* Republican. *Religion:* Episcopalian. *Home and office:* 2009 North John Russell Cir., Elkins Park, Pa. 19117; Newport, R.I.

CAREER: New Yorker, New York, N.Y., editorial assistant, 1968; Conde Nast Publications, New York, N.Y., assistant librarian, 1971; free-lance writer, 1972—. *Wartime service:* Alternate service as conscientious objector; case worker for New York City Department of Social Services, 1969-71.

WRITINGS: America's Gilded Age: Its Architecture and Decoration, A. S. Barnes, 1975; *Nedeva* (a biography of Mr. and Mrs. Edward T. Stotesbury), A. S. Barnes, 1976; *The Architecture of Horace Trumbauer,* A. S. Barnes, 1976. Contributor to *New York Times* and several magazines.

WORK IN PROGRESS: A series of humorous short stories.

SIDELIGHTS: "Beauty is a word out-of-fashion," Platt wrote, "but to me it is a cardinal word in all the arts, including writing. Why do I need to look at art that reflects ugliness when I can see ugliness aplenty in the real world?... My aim is to create beauty and to point out beauty in the work of others." *Avocational interests:* Electronics, history of science, classical music.

*   *   *

PLATT, Rutherford 1894-1975

August 11, 1894—March 28, 1975; American business executive, photographer, and author of books on nature and related topics. Obituaries: *New York Times,* March 30, 1975.

*   *   *

PLATTS, Beryl 1918-
(Beryl Seaton)

PERSONAL: Born October 30, 1918, in London, England; daughter of Hugh (a landowner) and Elizabeth Mary Glasspoole (Pooley) Seaton; married John Anthony Calvert Platts (an architect), January 26, 1941 (died, May 17, 1959); children: Elizabeth, John. *Education:* Attended private schools in England. *Home:* 9 Crooms Hill, Greenwich, London S.E.10, England.

CAREER: Free-lance writer in London, England, 1938-59; *Country Life,* London, assistant to architectural department, 1962-63, sub-editor, 1963-64, editor of "Collectors' Questions," 1964—. *Member:* Institute of Journalists.

WRITINGS: A History of Greenwich, David & Charles, 1973. Contributor, sometimes under name Beryl Seaton, of articles and short stories to *Cornhill, Punch, Harper's Bazaar, Country Life, Good Housekeeping, Spectator, Time and Tide,* and other periodicals.

WORK IN PROGRESS: An account of the Seton/Seaton family, *Scottish Hazard;* a play, *Waltheof;* poems, *Do Not Speak to the Grieving Woman.*

*   *   *

PLOSCOWE, Morris 1904-1975

January 25, 1904—September 21, 1975; Polish-born American magistrate, attorney, educator, and author or editor of books on legal subjects. Obituaries: *New York Times,* September 22, 1975. (See index for previous *CA* sketch)

*   *   *

POH, Caroline (Anne) 1938-

PERSONAL: Born May 7, 1938, in Green Bay Wis.; daughter of Herbert Siegfried (a consulting engineer) and Ethel (Boehm) Foth; married James Poh (an advertising manager), December 28, 1957; children: Jennifer Anne, James Andrew, Daniel Herbert. *Education:* University of Wisconsin, Madison, student, 1955-57; Boston University, B.S. (summa cum laude), 1958. *Home:* 3536 North Frederick Ave., Shorewood, Wis. 53211. *Office:* Lee Baker Associates, 1028 East Juneau Ave., Milwaukee, Wis. 53202.

CAREER: Hoag & Provandie Advertising, Boston, Mass., copywriter, 1958; *Select Magazine,* Madison, Wis., advertising manager, 1959-60; *Career Magazine,* Milwaukee, Wis., editor, 1960-61; Moynihan Associates, Milwaukee, account executive, 1961-63; United Community Services, Milwaukee, director of publications, 1963-64; free-lance copywriter, 1964-71; Lee Baker Associates (public relations firm), Milwaukee, associate, 1971—.

WRITINGS: (Editor) *The Life of Man,* Country Beautiful Corp., 1973. Editor of *Executive* (monthly publication of Wisconsin Savings & Loan League).

WORK IN PROGRESS: Two mystery novels, *Murder in a Minor Key* and *That's Not Like Daisy.*

SIDELIGHTS: Caroline Poh writes: "In *The Life of Man,* I traced the stages of man's journey through life as it has been chronicled by great authors through the ages, so that the reader can gain new insight into what it means to be young, to be old, or to have reached some point along the way. In the reading of authors from many times, places and cultures, it becomes evident how much is universal in the human experience."

*   *   *

POHL, Frederick 1919-

PERSONAL: Born November 26, 1919, in New York, N.Y.; son of Fred George (a salesman) and Anna Jane (Mason) Pohl; married Doris Baumgardt (divorced, 1944); married Dorothy Louise LesTina (divorced, 1947); married Judith Merril (divorced, 1952); married Carol M. Ulf, September 15, 1952; children: Ann (Mrs. Walter Weary), Karen, Frederick III (deceased), Frederick IV, Kathy. *Education:* Attended public schools in Brooklyn, N.Y., "dropped out in senior year." *Politics:* Democrat. *Religion:* Unitarian. *Home and office:* 386 West Front St., Red Bank, N.J. 07701. *Agent:* Robert P. Mills Ltd., 156 West 52nd St., New York, N.Y. 10022.

CAREER: Popular Publications, New York, N.Y., editor, 1939-43; Popular Science Publishing Co., New York, N.Y., editor in book department and assistant circulation manager, 1946-49; literary agent, 1946-53; free-lance writer, 1953-60; *Galaxie* Magazine, New York, N.Y., editor, 1961-69; Ace Books, New York, N.Y., executive editor, 1971-72; Bantam Books, New York, N.Y., science fiction editor, 1973—. Staff lecturer, American Management Association, 1966-69; cultural exchange lecturer in science fiction for U.S. Department of State in Yugoslavia, Romania, and the Soviet Union, 1974; also lecturer at more than two hundred colleges in the United States, Canada, and abroad; represented United States at international literary conferences in England, Italy, Brazil, Canada, and Japan. Has appeared on more than four hundred radio and television programs in nine countries. County committeeman, Democratic Party, Monmouth City, N.J., 1956-69; member of board of directors, Opera Theatre, N.Y., 1966—; trustee, The Harbour School, Red Bank, N.J., 1972—, and First Unitarian Church of Monmouth City, 1973—. *Military service:* U.S. Army Air Forces, 1943-45; received seven battle stars. *Member:* Science Fiction Writers of America (president, 1974—), British Interplanetary Society, American Astonautical Society, World Future Society, American Civil Liberties Union (trustee, Monmouth City, N.J., 1968-71), New York Academy of Sciences. *Awards, honors:* Edward E. Smith Memorial Award, 1966; International Science Fiction Achievement Awards (Hugo), 1966, 1967, 1968, for best editor, and 1974, for best short story, "The Meeting."

WRITINGS—All science fiction except as indicated; all published by Ballantine, except as noted: (With Lester Del Rey) *Preferred Risk,* Simon & Schuster, 1955; *Alternating Currents* (short stories), 1956; *Edge of the City* (novel based on screenplay by Robert Alan Aurthur), 1957; *Slave Ship,* 1957; *Tomorrow Times Seven: Science Fiction Stories,* 1959; *The Man Who Ate the World,* 1960; *Drunkard's Walk,* 1960; *Turn Left at Thursday: Three Novelettes and Three Stories,* 1961; *The Abominable Earthman,* 1963; *The Case Against Tomorrow: Science Fiction Short Stories,* 1965; *A Plague of Pythons,* 1965; *The Frederik Pohl Omnibus,* Gollancz, 1966; *Digits and Dastards,* 1966; *The Age of the Pussyfoot,* 1969; *Day Million* (short stories), 1970; *Practical Politics, 1972* (non-fiction), 1971; *The Gold at the Starbow's End,* 1972; (with wife, Carol Pohl) *Jupiter,* 1973.

With Cyril M. Kornbluth: *The Space Merchants,* 1953; *Search the Sky,* 1954; *Gladiator-at-Law,* 1955; *A Town is Drowning,* 1955; *Presidential Year,* 1956; *Wolfbane,* 1959; *The Wonder Effect,* 1962.

With Jack Williamson: *Undersea Quest,* Gnome Press, 1954; *Undersea Fleet,* Gnome Press, 1956; *Undersea City,* Gnome Press, 1958; *The Reefs of Space,* 1964; *Starchild,* 1965; *Rogue Star,* Dobson, 1972.

Editor: *Beyond the End of Time,* Permabooks, 1952; *Star Science Fiction Stories,* 1953; *Star Short Novels,* 1954; *Assignment in Tomorrow: An Anthology,* Hanover House, 1954; *Star of Stars,* Doubleday, 1960; *The Expert Dreamers,* Doubleday, 1962; *Time Waits for Winthrop,* Doubleday, 1962; *The Seventh Galaxy Reader,* Doubleday, 1964; *Star Fourteen,* Whiting & Wheaton, 1966; *The If Reader of Science Fiction,* Doubleday, 1966; *The Tenth Galaxy Reader,* Doubleday, 1967; *The Eleventh Galaxy Reader,* Doubleday, 1969; *Nightmare Age,* 1970; *Best Science Fiction for 1972,* Ace Books, 1973; (with Carol Pohl) *Science Fiction: The Great Years,* Ace Books, 1973.

Contributor: Harlan Ellison, editor, *Dangerous Vision,* Doubleday, 1967; Damon Knight, editor, *Orbit 11,* Putnam, 1972. Also contributor to *Galaxy, Worlds of Fantasy, Science Fiction Quarterly, Rogue, Impulse, Astonishing, Imagination, If, Beyond, Playboy, Infinity,* and other science fiction magazines.

*   *   *

POLLOCK, George   1938-

PERSONAL: Born May 2, 1938, in Boston, Mass.; son of George Francis (a laborer) and Ruby (a registered nurse; maiden name, De Rosier) Pollock; married Phyllis Ane (a bookkeeper), June 29, 1963; children: Gregory Francis,

Jonathan Edward. *Education:* Merrimack College, B.A., 1962; University of Massachusetts, M.A., 1966. *Politics:* None. *Religion:* None. *Home:* 4 Yellow Pine Circle, Middletown, Conn. 06457. *Office:* Xerox Education Publications, 247 Long Hill Rd., Middletown, Conn. 06457.

CAREER: School teacher in Kenya, East Africa, 1963-65, and Nigeria, West Africa, 1966; Xerox Education Publications, Middletown, Conn., editor, 1966—. *Awards, honors:* Award from Education Press Association of America, 1972, for excellence in educational journalism.

WRITINGS: (With Don Long) *Weekend Tennis: The Hacker's Handbook,* Tempo Books, 1974; *The American Family,* Xerox Education Publications, 1975.

WORK IN PROGRESS: A novel "that will be the last word on the human condition."

SIDELIGHTS: Pollock writes: "I write mainly to prove to myself that I am not just a corporate flunky, although this is yet to be established. I am also trying to make some money by writing. I hoped to get rich on the tennis book, but so far have raked in six hundred dollars. I am presently looking for an idea for a popular novel that can be sold to the movies. Meanwhile, while waiting for the muse and fame, I am having a fantastic love affair." *Avocational interests:* Photography.

*   *   *

POMADA, Elizabeth   1940-

PERSONAL: Born June 12, 1940, in New York, N.Y.; daughter of Maxim (a businessman) and Rita (a social worker; maiden name, Ross) Pomada. *Education:* Cornell University, B.S., 1962. *Office:* Larsen/Pomada, 1029 Jones St., San Francisco, Calif. 94109.

CAREER: Editorial assistant in New York City, 1962-63; promotion assistant in New York City for National Aeronautics Space Administration Institute for Space Studies, 1963-64, Holt, Rinehart & Winston, 1964-66, and David McKay, 1966-67; Dial Press, New York City, library promotion director, 1967-69; Bernard Kaplan Associates, New York City, account executive, 1969-70; self-employed in San Francisco, Calif., 1970—; writer.

WRITINGS: (Editor with Michael Larsen) *California Publicity Outlets,* Unicorn Systems, 1972; *Places to Go with Children in Northern California,* Chronicle Books, 1973. Book reviewer for *San Francisco Chronicle,* 1974—; art columnist for *San Francisco Magazine,* 1974-75. Contributor of articles to consumer, shelter, and art magazines.

*   *   *

POMERANTZ, Sidney I(rving)   1909-1975

September 4, 1909—June 15, 1975; American historian, educator, and author. Obituaries: *AB Bookman's Weekly,* August 25, 1975.

*   *   *

POMEROY, Kenneth B(rownridge)   1907-1975

May 17, 1907—July 31, 1975; American conservationist, forester, and author. Obituaries: *Washington Post,* August 3, 1975.

*   *   *

PORTER, Fairfield   1907-1975

June 10, 1907—September 18, 1975; American painter, educator, art critic, columnist, and author. Obituaries: *New York Times,* September 20, 1975.

POST, Henry 1948-
(Ryhen Spot)

PERSONAL: Born November 11, 1948, in Long Island, N.Y.; son of Henry A. V. (a designer) and Margaret (an artist; maiden name, Magee) Post. *Education:* Lake Forest College, B.A., 1971; University of Chicago, graduate study, 1972-74. *Religion:* Society of Friends. *Home:* 152 Wooster St., New York, N.Y. 10012. *Agent:* Scott Meredith Literary Agency, Inc., 845 Third Ave., New York, N.Y. 10022. *Office:* 807 Washington St., New York, N.Y. 10014.

CAREER: Prentice-Hall, Inc., Englewood, N.J., advertising copywriter, 1971-72; *Soho Weekly News,* New York City, editor, 1974; full-time writer in New York City, 1975—. Creative consultant for Media Projects, 1971-72. *Member:* Spam Belt Club. *Awards, honors:* North American sunfish champion, 1967.

WRITINGS: Clay Play: Learning Games for Children, Prentice-Hall, 1972. Contributor, sometimes under pseudonym Ryhen Spot, to *Penthouse, Viva, Oui, Playboy, Harper's Magazine, Art in America, Interview, New Dawn, Playgirl,* and *New Times.*

WORK IN PROGRESS: Scripts; a novel, *The Poseur Adventures.*

SIDELIGHTS: During his early career Post was a sailing teacher on Fire Island, a professional bassoonist in New England, director of a children's theater in Illinois, a social worker in England, and an archaeologist in Greece and Turkey.

*   *   *

POST, Joyce A(rnold) 1939-

PERSONAL: Born January 10, 1939, in Harrisburg, Pa.; daughter of Lawrence W. (a sheet-metal worker) and Edna (Stutz) Arnold; married Jeremiah B. Post (a map librarian), April 15, 1967; children: Jonathan. *Education:* Susquehanna University, A.B., 1960; Drexel University, M.S.L.S., 1961. *Home:* 4613 Larchwood Ave., Philadelphia, Pa. 19143.

CAREER: Philadelphia Civic Center, Foreign Trade Library, Philadelphia, Pa., chief librarian, 1963-65; Pennsylvania State Library, Law Library Bureau, Harrisburg, assistant law librarian, 1965-67; Free Library of Philadelphia, Reader Development Program, Philadelphia, technical services librarian, 1967-68; Drexel University, Graduate School of Library Science, Philadelphia, research specialist, 1971—. *Member:* American Library Association, American Society of Indexers, Beta Phi Mu.

WRITINGS: Index to Members' Collecting Interests, Private Libraries Association, 1968; *Let's Drink to That . . .* (nonfiction), Owlswick Press, 1970; (contributor) Guy Garrison, editor, *Total Community Library Service,* American Library Association, 1973; *Consolidated Index to the Hexamer General Surveys,* privately printed, 1974; (with Thomas Childers) *The Information Poor in America,* Scarecrow, 1975.

WORK IN PROGRESS: The Blue Collar Adult's Use of Information, with Thomas Childers, completion expected in 1976; with husband, Jeremiah B. Post, *Travel in the United States: A Guide to Information Sources,* 1979; *Index to The Private Library.*

POTTER, Charles E(dward) 1916-

PERSONAL: Born October 30, 1916, in Lapeer, Mich.; son of Fred and Sarah (Converse) Potter; married Mary Elizabeth Bryant Wimser, May 7, 1960; children: Henry Richard Wimser (deceased), Wendy (Mrs. Chris Cundy). *Education:* Eastern Michigan University, A.B., 1938. *Religion:* Methodist. *Home address:* Wyemoor, Box 171, Queenstown, Md. 21658. *Office:* Potter International, 1140 Connecticut Ave. N.W., Washington, D.C. 20036.

CAREER: Bureau of Social Aid, Cheboygan County, Mich., administrator, 1939-42; Retraining and Reemployment Administration, Washington, vocational rehabilitation advisor, 1946-47; Republican member of U.S. House of Representatives from Cheboygan, Mich., 1947-52; Republican member of U.S. Senate from Michigan, 1952-59; Potter International, Inc., Washington D.C., consultant and president, 1962—. Member of American Battle Monuments Commission, and Washington Real Estate board; trustee of 1972 Campaign Liquidation Trust. *Military service:* U.S. Army, 1942-46; became major; served in European theater; received Silver Star, Bronze Star, Purple Heart with two clusters, and French Croix de Guerre with Silver Star.

MEMBER: National Association of Securities Dealers, National Rehabilitation Association (director), Capitol Hill Club. *Awards, honors:* Named "hero of the month" by Disabled American Veterans, 1951; Veterans of Foreign Wars award, 1951, for distinguished service to veterans; U.S. Junior Chamber of Commerce award, 1952; *Parents' Magazine* award, 1955, and Goodwill Industries of America award, 1957, both for goodwill toward the handicapped.

WRITINGS: Days of Shame, Coward, 1965.

*   *   *

POVENMIRE, (Edward) King(sley) 1904-

PERSONAL: Surname is pronounced *Pah*-ven-mire; born October 5, 1904, in Laurelville, Ohio; son of Samuel Daniel (a pharmacist) and Bertha (a piano teacher; maiden name, Defenbaugh) Povenmire; married Goldie Stewart (a high school nurse), November 29, 1934; children: Harlo Kingsley, Richard Stuart. *Education:* Attended Garrett Biblical Institute, 1927-28; Ohio State University, B.Sc., 1929; Yale University, M.F.A., 1940. *Religion:* United Methodist. *Home:* 8301-368 Mission Gorge Rd., Santee, Calif. 92071.

CAREER: Drama teacher and theater director in high schools in Circleville, Mansfield, Columbus, and Norwood, Ohio, 1933-43, and in San Diego, Calif., 1945-46; San Diego State College (now University), San Diego, Calif., assistant professor, 1946-48, associate professor, 1948-60, professor of theater and verse choir, 1960-71, director, 1946-71. Drama director for Northern Hills Little Theatre, Norwood, Ohio, 1941-43; for Globe Theatre, 1946—, and Starlight Opera, 1947— (both in San Diego). Presently teaching choral speaking and verse choir to teachers-in-service in San Diego; director of verse choir for local churches; communications consultant for General Dynamics Corp. and Sea World, Inc., 1955-65. *Wartime service:* Army-Navy Young Men's Christian Association-United Service Organizations, program secretary in San Diego area, 1943-45. *Member:* American Association of University Professors, California Teachers Association. *Awards, honors:* California State Colleges, Distinguished Teaching award, 1969; Outstanding Faculty award, 1971.

WRITINGS: Choral Speaking and the Verse Choir, A. S. Barnes, 1975.

WORK IN PROGRESS: Revising "Command the Morning," a three-act drama of American farm life in 1896.

SIDELIGHTS: Povenmire writes: "I do believe in the Educational Theatre as a vital means of causing young people to examine and experience values in living. In fact, I left the ministry of the church to enter this field for this purpose. This same motivation led me into the teaching of Creative Dramatics and forty years of Verse Choir directing and teaching. The influence of this 'cluster' of creative fields is further expanded by teaching teachers to implant their benefits in the lives of their pupils."

* * *

POWELL, Geoffrey Stewart 1914-
(Tom Angus)

PERSONAL: Born December 25, 1914, in Scarborough, England; son of Owen Welch and Ada Jean (King) Powell; married Anne Felicity Wadsworth (a teacher), July 7, 1944; children: Rosemary Anderson, John Powell. *Education:* Studied at private schools in England. *Home:* 12 Chester Close, London SW13 OJE, England. *Agent:* A. M. Heath & Co., 44 Charing Cross Rd., London W.C.2, England.

CAREER: British Army, 1939-64; retiring as colonel. *Member:* Royal United Services Institute, Royal Asiatic Society, Institute of Archaeology, Army and Navy Club. *Awards, honors*—Military: Military Cross.

WRITINGS: The Green Howards (history), Hamish Hamilton, 1968; *The Kandyan Wars: The British Army in Ceylon, 1803-1818,* Shoe String Press, 1973; (under pseydonum Tom Angus) *Men at Arnhem,* Seeley Service & Co., 1976. Contributor to *History Today, Army Quarterly, Ceylon Journal of Historical and Social Studies,* and *British History Illustrated.*

WORK IN PROGRESS: With Roy Fullick, *Suez, 1956,* for Hamish Hamilton.

SIDELIGHTS: Powell has traveled extensively in Asia, Africa, and North America.

* * *

POWELL, (Caryll) Nicolas (Peter) 1920-

PERSONAL: Born May 20, 1920, in Johannesburg, South Africa; son of Owen Price (a mining engineer) and Nora (Webb) Powell. *Education:* University of Strasbourg, student, 1937-38; Peterhouse, Cambridge, B.A., 1941, M.A., 1945. *Religion:* Church of England. *Home:* 269 Keizersgracht, Amsterdam, Netherlands. *Agent:* David Higham Associates, 5-8 Lower John St., London W.1, England. *Office:* British Council, 65 Davies St., London W.1, England.

CAREER: With British Council in London, England, 1949-51, as second secretary of embassy in Bonn, West Germany, 1954-59, in Cologne, West Germany, 1959-62, in London, 1962-68, in Vienna, Austria, 1968-75, and in Amsterdam, Netherlands, 1975—. *Military service:* Royal Marines, Commandos, 1940-49, prisoner of war in Italy, 1942-43; received Distinguished Service Order. *Member:* Society of Authors, Royal Society of Literature (fellow), Vienna Secession (honorary corresponding member), Reform Club, Victorian Society. *Awards, honors:* Order of the British Empire, 1975; Josef Hoffmann Ehrung Award from Vienna Secession, 1975.

WRITINGS: The Hills Remain (novel), Bodley Head, 1947; *The Drawings of Henry Fuseli,* Faber, 1951; *From Baroque to Rococo,* Praeger, 1959; *Fuseli: The Night Mare,* Viking, 1973; *The Sacred Spring: The Arts in Vienna, 1898-1918,* New York Graphic Society, 1974.

WORK IN PROGRESS: Secession Posters, for Studio Vista; *Dear Old Trieste,* for Faber.

SIDELIGHTS: Powell writes that his main interests are baroque architecture in Austria and Germany, Viennese *Jugendstil,* Henry Fuseli, and eighteenth- and nineteenth-century English drawings. He has traveled in Italy, Morocco, southern Germany, and Austria, having spent his childhood in France and Belgium.

BIOGRAPHICAL/CRITICAL SOURCES: Hilary St. George Saunders, *The Green Beret,* M. Joseph, 1949.

* * *

POWER, John 1927-

PERSONAL: Born October 28, 1927, in Waterford, Ireland; son of Nicholas (a farmer) and Helena (Tobin) Power. *Education:* University College, Cork, B.A. (honors), 1948; Angelicum University, S.T.L., 1955; Biblical Institute, Rome, L.S.S., 1957; St. Anselmo College, diploma, 1966. *Home:* Missioni Africane, Via Della Nocetta 111, Roma 00164, Italy.

CAREER: Roman Catholic priest of Society of African Missions (S.M.A.), ordained 1953; missionary in Nigeria, 1957-60; African Missions Seminary, Newry, Ireland, professor of scripture, 1960-68; Society of African Missions, Rome, Italy, vicar general, 1968—.

WRITINGS: Set My Exiles Free, Gill & Macmillan, 1967, published as *Salvation History,* Alba, 1968; *Look toward the East,* Gill & Macmillan, 1969; *Mission Theology Today,* Gill & Macmillan, 1971. Contributor to religious publications.

WORK IN PROGRESS: Writing on signs of the times, on the religious motivation of missionary activity, and on reconciliation as a moral imperative.

* * *

POWERS, Jeffrey W(ells) 1950-

PERSONAL: Born October 31, 1950, in Santa Monica, Calif.; son of Keith Grimes (an aerospace engineer) and Kathryn (a psychologist; maiden name, Wells) Powers. *Education:* Pitzer College, student, 1971—. *Politics:* "No stomach for." *Religion:* "No stomach for." *Home and office:* 150 West Ninth St., Claremont, Calif. 91711. *Agent:* Francis Turcotte III, P.O. Box 38363, Hollywood, Calif. 90038.

CAREER: Book House (bookstore), Claremont, Calif., clerk, 1974-75; *Grove: Contemporary Poetry and Translation,* Claremont, editor, 1974-75; *Marilyn: A Magazine of New Poetry,* Claremont, co-founding editor, 1975—.

WRITING: Thrones and Dominions (poetry), Pygmalion Press, 1974; *The Tinsel Town Poets* (anthology), Pygmalion Press, 1974. Author of "The Californians" (eighteen-act play), broadcast over KSPC-FM Radio, Claremont, Calif., 1975. Contributor to *Paris Review, Madrona, Loon,* and *Chowder Review.*

WORK IN PROGRESS: Two poem cycles, *Sister City* and *Blueprint for a Statement of Fact,* completion of both expected in 1976.

SIDELIGHTS: Powers told *CA:* "I have become increasingly interested in exploiting radio as a means of extending poetry into the community, with the end in mind of, finally, increasing its accessibility and attraction to humankind." He has lived in Great Britain and Venezuela. *Avocational interests:* Classical music, cinema.

* * *

PREBLE, Duane 1936-

PERSONAL: Born May 20, 1936, in National City, Calif.; son of Bennett (a chemical engineer) and Mary S. (Williams) Preble; married Sarah Ann Hamilton, March 13, 1961; children: Jeffrey, Malia. *Education:* University of California, Los Angeles, B.A., 1959; University of Hawaii, M.F.A., 1963. *Office:* Department of Art, University of Hawaii, 2560 Campus Rd., Honolulu, Hawaii 96822.

CAREER: University of Hawaii, Honolulu, instructor, 1963-67, assistant professor, 1967-70, associate professor of art, 1970—. Has exhibited paintings, prints, and sculpture in Hawaii. Chairman of Honolulu Commission on Culture and the Arts, 1972-74; trustee of Honolulu Academy of Arts, 1973—, and Hawaii Mission Children's Society Museum, 1974—. *Military service:* U.S. Army, 1959-61. *Member:* Life of the Land (member of board of directors), Sierra Club, Honolulu Painters and Sculptors League.

WRITINGS: Man Creates Art Creates Man, McCutchan, 1972, revised edition published as *We Create Art: Art Creates Us,* Canfield Press, 1976.

* * *

PRESTON, Dickson J(oseph) 1914-

PERSONAL: Born March 22, 1914, in Monticello, Ind.; son of Charles S. (an editor and teacher) and Helen (a teacher; maiden name, Hurst) Preston; married Janet Longley, June 17, 1939; children: Dickson Hurst. *Education:* DePauw University, B.A., 1936; attended University of Iowa, 1938-39. *Address:* R.D. 5, Box 607, Easton, Md. 21601. *Office:* Star Democrat, Easton, Md. 21601.

CAREER: Indianapolis Times, Indianapolis, Ind., reporter and copy editor, 1937-38; Indiana Writers Project, Indianapolis, assistant state director, 1939-42; *Cleveland Press,* Cleveland, Ohio, world news editor, 1943-52; Scripps-Howard Newspapers, Washington, D.C., reporter, 1952-66; *Star Democrat,* Easton, Md., columnist, 1970—. *Member:* National Press Club, Maryland Ornithological Society (vice-president, 1972-74), Talbot County Bird Club (president, 1968-70), Tidewater Camera Club (member of executive board, 1974—), Delta Kappa Epsilon, Sigma Delta Chi. *Awards, honors:* Reporting award of Cleveland Newspaper Guild, 1955; best in show award in Blackwater wildlife photo contest, 1972.

WRITINGS: (Editor) *Indiana: A Guide to the Hoosier State,* Oxford University Press, 1941; *Wye Oak: The History of a Great Tree,* Tidewater, 1972. Editor of *The Waterfowl Festival Book,* 1972-73; contributor to *Baltimore Sun Sunday Magazine, American Forests,* and other periodicals.

WORK IN PROGRESS: La Fayette, We Were Here, an account of La Fayette's triumphal tour of America in 1824-25; *Talbot: A Study in Liberty,* a modern history of Talbot County, Md.

SIDELIGHTS: Preston told *CA:* "I reject both the 'inspirational' and 'bunk' views of history; it seems to me we cannot possibly know where we are going unless we know where we have been. My method is to examine specific events of the past with a reporter's eye for detail and a writer's sense of the significance of seemingly small things.

"My regular column in *The Star Democrat* exemplifies this approach. Called 'The Way It Was,' it chronicles each week the events which made news locally exactly 150 years ago, as revealed in local newspapers of the period, and relates them to the present."

* * *

PRESTON, Frances I(sabella) 1898-

PERSONAL: Born July 18, 1898, in Stratford, New Zealand; daughter of James (a photographer) and Helen Frederica (Coombridge) McAllister; married John Preston, August 11, 1926 (deceased); children: Helen Margaret (Mrs. Geoffrey Gordon Dunckley), Jances (Mrs. William Gordon Hunt), Allister, Flora (Mrs. Russell Nelson Smith). *Education:* University of Otago, M.B.Ch.B., 1922. *Religion:* Church of England. *Home:* 80 London St., Flat C, Dunedin, Otago 12, New Zealand.

CAREER: Medical practitioner in rural districts in New Zealand, 1922, 1925; New Plymouth Hospital, Plymouth, New Zealand, house surgeon, 1923-24; Pleasant Valley Sanatorium, Palmerston, Otago, New Zealand, relieving medical superintendent, 1925. *Member:* Medical Women's Association (International), Pan Pacific and South East Asia Women's Association, Medical Women's Association (New Zealand), Federated Farmers (Women's Division; dominion life member; vice president, 1928-29), Federated University Women, Public Art Gallery Society, Concert Society of New Zealand, Otago Art Society, Otago Pioneer Women's Association.

WRITINGS: Lady Doctor: Vintage Model, A. H. & A. W. Reed (Wellington), 1974.

WORK IN PROGRESS: A history of the Preston family.

SIDELIGHTS: Frances Preston writes that her book was "written with a view to highlighting prejudice suffered by early women doctors with hopes of more rapid recognition of women in this field." *Avocational interests:* Watercolor painting, classical music (once played organ and violin).

* * *

PRICE, E(dgar) Hoffmann 1898-

PERSONAL: Born July 3, 1898, in Fowler, Calif.; son of Murtilah Elijah (a horticulturist) and Maria Theresa (Hoffmann) Price. *Education:* U.S. Military Academy, Sc.B., 1923. *Politics:* Conservative Republican. *Religion:* Taoist-Buddhist.

CAREER: Writer. Has worked as photographer, microfilm technician, astrologer, and superintendent of an acetylene plant. *Military service:* U.S. Army, Cavalry, 1917-19; U.S. Coast Artillery Corps, 1923-24; became lieutenant.

WRITINGS: Strange Gateways (fantasy), Arkham, 1967; *Far Lands, Other Days* (fantasy), Carcosa, in press. Contributor of stories to adventure magazines, including *Argosy, Adventure,* and *Short Stories.*

WORK IN PROGRESS: Trooper of the Fifteenth Horse, memoirs of the Philippines, Japan, and France, and later career; *Foreign Devil in Chinatown,* with own photographs, non-fiction; *Book of the Dead,* about deceased fellow writers.

AVOCATIONAL INTERESTS: Oriental philosophy and culture (with Islamic and Chinese emphasis), motoring, gourmet cooking (especially Chinese, Indian, and Mexican cooking), photography, and collecting Oriental rugs.

PRICE, Nelson Lynn 1931-

PERSONAL: Born August 24, 1931, in Osyka, Miss.; son of Robert S. and Genevieve (Dykes) Price; married Trudy Knight, February 12, 1956; children: Lynn, Sharon. *Education:* Southeastern Louisiana University, B.S., 1953; New Orleans Baptist Theological Seminary, Th.M., 1957. *Home:* 431 Keeler Woods Dr., Marietta, Ga. 30060. *Office:* 774 Roswell St., Marietta, Ga.

CAREER: Pastor in New Orleans, La., 1957-65; Roswell Street Baptist Church, Marietta, Ga., pastor, 1965—. Member of board of trustees of New Orleans Baptist Theological Seminary, 1963—; member of Georgia Board of Human Resources, 1974—. Moderator of WBIE radio program, "Let's Face It . . . ," 1966—. *Awards, honors:* Cobb County Chamber of Commerce public service award, 1968; Liberty Bell Award from Cobb County Bar Association, 1968; Cobb County Citizen of the Year Award from *Marietta Daily Journal*, 1969.

WRITINGS: I've Got to Play on Their Court (nonfiction), Broadman Press, 1976. Also author of *Shadows We Run From*, Broadman Press. Contributor of weekly editorial to *Marietta Daily Journal*, 1966—.

* * *

PRIESTLEY, Mary 1925-

PERSONAL: Born March 4, 1925, in London, England; daughter of J. B. Priestley (an author) and Winifred Mary (an author; maiden name, Holland) Priestley Bannerman; married Sigvald Michelsen (a violinist), January 20, 1949 (divorced, 1957); children: Peter, John Priestley, David Priestley. *Education:* Attended the Royal College of Music, London, 1941-46, and Geneva Conservatoire, Switzerland, 1947-48; Guildhall School of Music & Drama, L.G.S.M., 1969; attended Institute of Group Analysis, 1972-74. *Home:* 0/51 Barkston Gardens, London S.W. 5, England. *Agent:* P. Kavanagh, A. D. Peters, 10 Buckingham St., London, W.C.2, England.

CAREER: Marlborough Day Hospital, London, England, music therapist, 1970-71; Ladbrokegrove Psychiatric Day Centre, London, music therapist, 1970-71; St. Bernard's Hospital, London, music therapist, 1969—; In private practice of music therapy, 1970—. Inner London Probation Service, London, music therapist, 1974-76. *Member:* British Society for Music Therapy (member of executive committee, 1973-75), Incorporated Society of Musicians, European String Teachers Association, Royal Anthropological Society, Institute of Religion and Medicine.

WRITINGS: Going Abroad, Collins, 1965; *Music Therapy in Action*, St. Martin's, 1975. Contributor of articles to *Times* (London), *Guardian, Nursing Times, Marriage Guidance, Daily Mail, New Society* and *New Psychiatry*, and others.

WORK IN PROGRESS: Research into psychic mechanisms of defense for a possible book for the layman.

AVOCATIONAL INTERESTS: Ceramic sculpture, line drawings.

* * *

PRIMACK, Joel (Robert) 1945-

PERSONAL: Born July 14, 1945, in Santa Barbara, Calif.; son of Roy (a businessman) and Loretta (Zabarsky) Primack. *Education:* Princeton University, A.B. (summa cum laude), 1966; Stanford University, Ph.D., 1970. *Politics:* "Jeffersonian." *Religion:* Jewish. *Residence:* Santa Cruz, Calif. *Office:* Department of Physics, University of California, Santa Cruz, Calif. 95064.

CAREER: Stanford Linear Accelerator Center, Stanford, Calif., research associate, 1970; Harvard University, Cambridge, Mass., junior fellow of Society of Fellows, 1970-73; University of California, Santa Cruz, assistant professor of physics, 1973—. Consultant to Ford Foundation Energy Policy Project and McGovern-for-President campaign. *Member:* American Physical Society, American Association for the Advancement of Science, Federation of American Scientists (member of national council, 1970-74), Sierra Club. *Awards, honors:* Woodrow Wilson fellowship, 1966; National Science Foundation fellowship, 1966-70; A. P. Sloan Foundation research fellowship, 1974—.

WRITINGS: (With Frank von Hippel) *The Politics of Technology: Activities and Responsibilities of Scientists in the Direction of Technology*, Stanford Workshops on Political and Social Issues, Stanford University, 1970; (with von Hippel) *Advice and Dissent: Scientists in the Political Arena*, Basic Books, 1974. Contributor to professional journals and popular magazines.

WORK IN PROGRESS: Editing a special report on nuclear reactor safety, an expanded version of an earlier article in *Bulletin of the Atomic Scientists;* continuing research on elementary particle theory.

SIDELIGHTS: Primack writes: "Starting in my last year in graduate school, and continuing as a Harvard Junior Fellow, I have devoted considerable thought and effort toward improving the democratic control of technology in our society. I am particularly proud to have had a hand in creating the Stanford Workshops on Political and Social Issues at Stanford University, the Forum on Physics and Society of the American Physical Society, and the AAAS-APS Congressional Fellowships for Scientists."

* * *

PRISCO, Salvatore III 1943-

PERSONAL: Born October 1, 1943, in Jersey City, N.J.; son of Salvatore (a businessman) and Libra (Deputato) Prisco; married Dorothy DeSteno (a fashion copywriter), July 15, 1967; children: Lisa Natalie. *Education:* St. Peter's College, B.S., 1964; Rutgers University, M.A., 1965, Ph.D., 1969. *Home:* 105 Shippen St., Weehawken, N.J. 07087. *Office:* Department of History, Union College, Cranford, N.J. 07016.

CAREER: University of Alabama, University, assistant professor, 1969-72, associate professor of history, 1972-74; Union College, Cranford, N.J., lecturer in history, 1975—. Member of governing board of Civil Liberties Union, Tuscaloosa, Ala., 1970-71. *Member:* Organization of American Historians, Academy of Political Science, American Historical Association, Society for Historians of American Foreign Relations. *Awards, honors:* Windham Foundation research grant, 1972-73.

WRITINGS: John Barrett: Progressive Era Diplomat, University of Alabama Press, 1973. Contributor to history journals. Abstract editor of *Historical Abstracts*, 1972-75, and *America: History and Life*, 1972-75.

WORK IN PROGRESS: A collective biography of Progressive Era American diplomats, 1890-1920; a study of the interrelationship of sectional and national interests in U.S. foreign relations.

AVOCATIONAL INTERESTS: Travel, tennis.

PRITCHETT, V(ictor S(awdon) 1900-

PERSONAL: Born December 16, 1900, in Ipswich, England; son of Sawdon and Beatrice (Martin) Pritchett; married Dorothy Roberts, October 2, 1936; children: Josephine (Mrs. Brian Murphy), Oliver. *Education:* Educated in Dulwich, England. *Home:* 12 Regents Park Ter., London N.W.1, England. *Office:* c/o *New Statesman,* 10 Great Turnstile, London, W.C.1, England.

CAREER: Novelist and literary critic. Worked in the leather trade and as a commercial traveler and shop assistant; free-lance journalist in France, Ireland, Spain, Morocco, and the United States, 1921-28; *New Statesman,* London, England, literary critic, 1928-65, director, 1951—; *Nation,* director. Christian Gauss Lecturer, Princeton University, 1953; Beckman Professor, University of California, Berkeley, 1960; writer-in-residence, Smith College, 1966; Zisskind Professor, Brandeis University; Clark Lecturer, Cambridge University, 1969; visiting professor, Columbia University, 1970. *Member:* Royal Society of Literature (fellow), English P.E.N. Club (president, 1971), American Academy of Arts and Sciences (honorary foreign member), American Academy of Arts and Letters (honorary foreign member), National Institute of Arts and Letters (honorary foreign member), Garrick Club, Savile Club. *Awards, honors:* Royal Society of Literature Award, 1967, for *A Cab at the Door;* Commander of British Empire, 1968.

WRITINGS—Nonfiction: *Marching Spain,* Benn, 1928; *In My Good Books,* Chatto & Windus, 1942, reprinted, Kennikat, 1970; *The Living Novel,* Chatto & Windus, 1946, Reynal, 1947, revised and expanded edition published as *The Living Novel, And Later Appreciations,* Random House, 1964; (with Elizabeth Bowen and Graham Greene) *Why Do I Write?* Percival Marshall, 1948; *Books In General,* Harcourt, 1953; *The Spanish Temper,* Knopf, 1954; *London Perceived,* Harcourt, 1962, 2nd edition, 1963; *Foreign Faces,* Chatto & Windus, 1964, published as *The Offensive Traveller,* Knopf, 1964; *New York Proclaimed,* Harcourt, 1965; *The Working Novelist,* Chatto & Windus, 1965; *Dublin: A Portrait,* Harper, 1967; *A Cab at the Door: A Memoir,* Random House, 1968 (published in England as *A Cab at the Door: An Autobiography, Early Years,* Chatto & Windus, 1968); *George Meredith and English Comedy,* Random House, 1970; *Midnight Oil* (autobiography), Chatto & Windus, 1971, Random House, 1972; *Balzac,* Random House, 1974.

Novels: *Clare Drummer,* Benn, 1929; *Shirley Sanz,* Gollancz, 1932, published as *Elopement into Exile,* Little, Brown, 1932; *Nothing Like Leather,* Macmillan, 1935; *Dead Man Leading,* Macmillan, 1937; *Mr. Beluncle,* Harcourt, 1951.

Short stories: *The Spanish Virgin and Other Stories,* Benn, 1930; *You Make Your Own Life,* Chatto & Windus, 1938; *It May Never Happen and Other Stories,* Chatto & Windus, 1945, Reynal, 1947; *Collected Stories,* Chatto & Windus, 1956, published as *The Sailor, Sense of Humor, and Other Stories,* Knopf, 1956, and as *The Saint and Other Stories,* Penguin, 1966; *When My Girl Comes Home,* Knopf, 1961; *The Key to My Heart: A Comedy in Three Parts* (contains "The Key to My Heart," "Noisy Flushes the Birds," and "Noisy in the Doghouse"), Chatto & Windus, 1963, Random House, 1964; *Blind Love and Other Stories,* Chatto & Windus, 1969, Random House, 1970; *The Camberwell Beauty,* Random House, 1975.

Editor: Robert Louis Stevenson, *Novels and Stories: Se-* *lected,* Duell, Sloan & Pearce, 1946; Robert Southey, *The Chronicle of the Cid,* J. Enschede en Zonen for Limited Editions Club, 1958.

Writer of weekly column, "Books in General," in the *New Statesman.* Has written for British Broadcasting Corporation programs, "Shakespeare, the Comprehensive Soul," 1965, and "Balzac," 1975. Contributor to *New York Review of Books, New Statesman, Holiday, New York Times Book Review, English Review, New Yorker, Playboy,* and other periodicals.

BIOGRAPHICAL/CRITICAL SOURCES: New York Herald Tribune Book Review, April 25, 1954; *New York Times Book Review,* April 25, 1954; *Newsweek,* April 22, 1968; *Time,* May 17, 1968; Carolyn Riley, editor, *Contemporary Literary Criticism,* Volume V, Gale, 1976.

* * *

PROCTOR, Dorothea Hardy 1910-

PERSONAL: Born July 18, 1910, in Calhan, Colo.; daughter of James Edson (a merchant and gentleman farmer) and Louise (Scheible) Hardy; married Percy Quayle Proctor (president of oil companies and radio); children: Edwin Gover III (deceased). *Education:* Attended University of Tulsa, 1935-37, and Philbrook Museum; private study under master painters and sculptors. *Politics:* "For the man." *Religion:* Methodist Episcopal. *Home:* 1542 East 34th St., Tulsa, Okla. 74105. *Agent:* Clara Laster, 204 East 45th Pl., Tulsa, Okla. 74105.

CAREER: Painter, sculptor, and poet. *Member:* Tulsa Opera Guild, Tulsa Philharmonic Art Council, Philbrook Museum (charter member). *Awards, honors:* Sculpture award; several poetry awards.

WRITINGS: Listening for Absolutes (poetry), South & West, 1968; *The Delight of Being* (poetry and sculpture), Olivant, 1971. Contributor of articles and poetry to *Oklahoma Today, American Artist,* and other national and international magazines.

WORK IN PROGRESS: Poetry and sculpture.

* * *

PROVO, Frank 1913(?)-1975

1913(?)—November 20, 1975; American radio and television writer, educator, and author of a novel and a play. Obituaries: *New York Times,* November 22, 1975.

* * *

PRUTHI, Surinder P(aul) S(ingh) 1934-

PERSONAL: Born February 22, 1934, in Bhadewala, India; son of A. S. (a physician) and Jagjit (Kaur) Pruthi; married Vanita S. P. Chhabra (a consultant), 1964; children: Avantika (daughter), Anurup (son). *Education:* London School of Economics and Political Science, Ph.D., 1961; Harvard University, diploma, 1963. *Home and office:* Dr. Pruthi & Associates, 8A Oyster Apts., Pilot Bunder Rd., Colaba, Bombay 400005, India.

CAREER: Dr. Pruthi & Associates (economic management and corporate consultant), Colaba, Bombay, India, managing director, 1972—. Member of executive council of University of Bombay, 1975—; visiting United Nations professor, 1971, 1973, 1975. Advisor to Health Administration of Government of Maharashtra, 1974-75. *Member:* Family Planning Association of India. *Awards, honors:* Escort Award from Delhi Management Association, 1973, for *Economic and Managerial Environment in India.*

WRITINGS: *Management of Plans,* Ahmed Management Association, 1967; *Business and Government,* Asia Publishing House, 1972; *Economic and Managerial Environment in India,* Progressive Corporation, 1972; *Hospital Administration,* Government of Maharashtra, 1974; *Multinationals in Developing Countries,* Leslie Sawhny, 1975. Also author of *Personnel Administration and Developing Economies.*

* * *

PRYDE, Philip Rust   1938-

PERSONAL: Born January 8, 1938, in Pittsfield, Mass.; son of David R. (a mechanical engineer) and Viola (Rust) Pryde; married Lucy Tripp (a teacher), June 24, 1961. *Education:* Amherst College, A.B., 1959; University of Washington, Seattle, M.A., 1965, Ph.D., 1969. *Religion:* Protestant. *Residence:* San Diego, Calif. *Office:* Department of Geography, San Diego State University, San Diego, Calif. 92182.

CAREER: San Diego State University, San Diego, Calif., assistant professor, 1969-72, associate professor, 1972-75, professor of geography, 1975—. Member of Carlsbad Environmental Pollution Commission, 1970—; co-chairman of San Diego County Regional Goals Program, 1971-73; member of policy advisory committee of Comprehensive Planning Organization of San Diego County, 1972—. *Military service:* U.S. Army, Security Agency, 1960-63. *Member:* Association of American Geographers, American Geographical Society, American Association for the Advancement of Slavic Studies, Sierra Club (vice-chairman of San Diego chapter, 1975-76). *Awards, honors:* Foreign area fellowship from Social Science Research Council and American Council of Learned Societies, 1966-69.

WRITINGS: *Conservation in the Soviet Union,* Cambridge University Press, 1972; *San Diego: An Introduction to the Region,* Kendall/Hunt, 1976. Contributor to *Environment, American Scientist, Sierra Club Bulletin, National Parks Magazine, Geographical Review,* and *Environment Southwest.*

AVOCATIONAL INTERESTS: Photography.

* * *

PUDDEPHA, Derek (Noel)   1930-

PERSONAL: Born December 11, 1930, in Birmingham, England; son of Horace (a government officer) and Edna (Clapshaw) Puddepha; married Angela Long (a lecturer), September 5, 1956; children: Clare, Margot, Bridget. *Education:* Attended school in England. *Religion:* Church of England. *Home:* 15 Quantock Rd., Weston-super-Mare, Avon, England. *Office:* Town Hall, Weston-super-Mare, Avon, England.

CAREER: *Walsall Observer,* Walsall, England, reporter, 1952-54; *Birmingham Post and Mail,* Birmingham, England, reporter, 1954-58; *Express and Echo,* Exeter, England, chief reporter, 1958-74; Woodspring District Council, Weston-super-Mare, Avon, England, press officer, 1974—. *Military service:* Royal Air Force, 1949-51.

WRITINGS: *Fly Fishing Is Easy,* David & Charles, 1968; *Coarse Fishing Is Easy,* David & Charles, 1970. Contributor to angling journals.

* * *

PULIGANDLA, Ramakrishna   1930-

PERSONAL: Born September 8, 1930, in Nellore, Andhra, India; son of Venkataraman (a landlord) and Chaturvedula (Sitamma) Puligandla; married Vathyam Janaki, August 3, 1949; children: Balaram, Sita, Usha, Vijay, Russell. *Education:* Andhra University, B.Sc., 1949, M.Sc., 1951; Purdue University, M.S., 1960; University of South Dakota, A.M., 1962; Rice University, Ph.D., 1966. *Home:* 1812 Kensington, Toledo, Ohio 43607. *Office:* Department of Philosophy, University of Toledo, Toledo, Ohio 43606.

CAREER: Andhra University, V. R. College, Nellore, India, lecturer in physics, 1951-58; Yankton College, Yankton, S.D., associate professor of physics, 1960-63; Texas Southern University, Houston, assistant professor of mathematics, 1964-65; University of Toledo, Toledo, Ohio, associate professor, 1966-70, professor of philosophy, 1970—. Visiting lecturer at Knox College, 1965-66. *Member:* American Philosophical Association, Philosophy of Science Association, Association for Symbolic Logic, Royal Institute of Philosophy, American Association for the Advancement of Science, Society for Asian and Comparative Philosophy, Phi Kappa Phi.

WRITINGS: *Fact and Fiction in B. F. Skinner's Science and Utopia,* Warren H. Green, 1974; *Fundamentals of Indian Philosophy,* Abingdon, 1975; *An Examination of the Copenhagen Interpretation of Quantum Theory,* Motilal Banarsidas, in press. Contributor of about forty papers to journals in his field. Assistant editor of *Philosopher's Index,* 1969—; consultant and reviewer for *Choice,* 1966—.

WORK IN PROGRESS: A novel, *The Two Lives of Amanda; Quest of Transcendence: Toward the Unity of Knowledge and Being.*

AVOCATIONAL INTERESTS: Tennis, classical music, camping, travel.

* * *

PULKINGHAM, Betty (Jane)   1928-

PERSONAL: Born August 25, 1928, in Burlington, N.C.; daughter of Leo (a lawyer and judge) and Betty (Knott) Carr; married William Graham Pulkingham (an Episcopalian priest), September 1, 1951; children: William Graham III, Mary Graham, Nathan Carr, Elizabeth Jane, Martha Louise, David Earle. *Education:* University of North Carolina, Greensboro, B.S. (magna cum laude), 1949; graduate study at Eastman School of Music. *Religion:* Episcopalian. *Home and office:* Cathedral of the Isles, Millport, Isle of Cumbrae, Cuningham KA28 0HE, Scotland.

CAREER: Music theory instructor at University of Texas, 1949-52; Austin (Tex.) High School, choral music teacher, 1956-57; private piano teacher in Galveston, Tex., 1958-60; Church of the Redeemer, Houston, Tex., choir director, 1964-71. Member of Community of Celebration Christian Trust, currently living in Scotland.

WRITINGS: (Arranger and compiler with Oressa Wise) *Songs of Fellowship,* privately printed, 1972, Net Music Co., 1975; (editor with Jeanne Harper) *Sound of Living Waters,* Eerdmans, Part I, 1974, Part II, in press.

WORK IN PROGRESS: Collecting materials for a book about her family.

* * *

PULLAPILLY, Cyriac K(alapura)   1932-

PERSONAL: Born June 15, 1932, in Kerala, India; naturalized U.S. citizen; son of Joseph and Anna (Mathai) Pullapilly; married Elizabeth Antonnette Phillips, June 17, 1969;

children: Kavita Ann, Anand Joseph. *Education:* St. Thomas College and St. Joseph's Pontifical Seminary, Kerala, India, A.B., 1958; DePaul University, graduate study, 1959-60; University of Chicago, Ph.D., 1968. *Home:* 53310 Peggy Lane, South Bend, Ind. 46635. *Office:* Department of History, St. Mary's College, Notre Dame, Ind. 46556.

CAREER: Ordained Roman Catholic priest of Syro-Malabar Church (an Oriental Rite church in India), 1958; Diocesan Court for the canonization of Sister Alphonsa, Palai, India, secretary, 1958-59; assistant pastor of Roman Catholic churches in Chicago, Ill., 1959-65; Illinois State University, Normal, assistant professor of history, 1965-67; Middlebury College, Middlebury, Vt., assistant professor of religious history, 1967-70; St. Mary's College, Notre Dame, Ind., associate professor of history, 1970—. Chairman of Central Renaissance Conference, 1975. Director of St. Joseph's Youth Institute (Kerala), 1958-59. Co-host of "Window to the World," a series on WSBT-Television, 1975—.

MEMBER: International Platform Association, American Historical Association, American Catholic Historical Association, Church History Society, Renaissance Society of America, Society for Reformation Research, American Society of Church History, American Academy of Religion, Society for the Scientific Study of Religion, Mediaeval Academy of America, Association for Asian Studies, Association of Scholars for the Study of the Religions of South India, American Association of University Professors, Forum for Contemporary History, American Academy of Political and Social Sciences, Association for South Asian Studies (Australia), Kerala History Association, Indiana Academy of Social Sciences. *Awards, honors:* American Council of Learned Societies grant, 1973; from Southeastern Institute of Medieval and Renaissance Studies fellowship, 1974.

WRITINGS: Communist United Fronts (in Malayalam), Sacred Heart League, 1953; *Whither the Youth of India* (in Malayalam), Mar Thoma Sleeha Press, 1956; *Within the Cloisters* (in Malayalam), St. Joseph's Press, 1958; *For God and Country* (in Malayalam), Sacred Heart League, 1958; *Caesar Baronius: Counter Reformation Historian,* University of Notre Dame Press, 1975.

Contributor to *Encyclopaedia Britannica.* Contributor of articles and reviews to scholarly journals. Associate editor of *Homefield,* 1953-58; founder and editor of *Vidyalokam,* an education journal, 1955-56; special editor of *Journal of South Asian Literature,* spring, 1975.

WORK IN PROGRESS: Counter Reformation: An Intellectual History, for University of Notre Dame Press; *India Since Independence, 1947: A Historical Survey;* translating into English *Philippus Sive de Christiana Laetitia Dialogus* (title means "Philip or the Dialogue on Christian Felicity"), by a disciple of St. Philip Neri, very probably by Cardinal Agostino Valier; *The St. Thomas Christians of India;* research on counter-Reformation historiography, with respect to Cardinal Baronius; a case study of Muhammed Bashir and politicization of Malayalam literature; studying the Izhavas of Kerala and their historic struggle for social acceptance.

SIDELIGHTS: Pullapilly writes: "Having written many works of a specialized nature, useful and appealing only to a limited audience, I am now thinking in terms of broadening the scope of my literary works to reach the general audience. I am toying with the idea of writing novels or popular historical works that may help enliven the fundamental noble goals for which this nation was founded and which were by and large forgotten in the last few decades." Pullapilly speaks French, Italian, Spanish, Portuguese, Hindi, Malayalam, and Tamil, and is competent in Latin, Sanskrit, and Aramaic.

* * *

PURNELL, Idella 1901-
(Idella Purnell Stone, Ikey Stone)

PERSONAL: Born April 1, 1901, in Guadalajara, Mexico; daughter of George Edward (a dentist) and Idella (Bragg) Purnell; married Remington Stone, September 10, 1932 (deceased); children: Maryjane (Mrs. Robert Osborn), Remington P.S., Carrie (Mrs. Johnnie Ceniceros). *Education:* University of California, Berkeley, B.A., 1922; Dianetic Research Centers, H.D.A., 1950, D.Scn., 1954. *Politics:* "Middle of the road Democrat." *Religion:* Huna, Scientology, Christian. *Home and office:* 321 East Grandview, Sierra Madre, Calif. 91024.

CAREER: Primary school teacher in Guadalajara, Mexico, 1915; U.S. Foreign Service, secretary in American Consulate in Guadalajara, 1922-24; founder, publisher, and editor, *Palms* poetry magazine, 1923-30; Los Angeles Public Library, Los Angeles, Calif., head of foreign book department, summer, 1925; University of Guadalajara, Guadalajara, organizer and dean of first summer session, 1932; opened and operated gold mine in Ameca, Mexico, 1935-37; taught creative writing in Los Angeles, 1938-39; riveter for Douglas Aviation and for Fletcher Aviation during World War II; Dianetic Center for Dianetics and Scientology, Pasadena, Calif., director, 1951-57, practitioner, 1957-66; free-lance writer. *Member:* Inter-America Society, Poetry Society of America, Science Fiction Writers Association, Mexican Congress of Fine Arts and Humanities (permanent member). *Awards, honors: The Merry Frogs* named Julia Ellsworth Ford Foundation Book, 1936; diploma from Second Mexican Congress for the Fine Arts and Humanities, 1967; *Saturday Review* poetry award.

WRITINGS—Juveniles, except as noted; all published by Macmillan, except as noted: *The Talking Bird: An Aztec Story Book; Tales Told to Little Paco by His Grandfather,* 1930; *Why the Bee Is Busy, and Other Rumanian Fairy Tales: Told to Little Marcu by Baba Maritza,* 1930; *The Wishing Owl: A Maya Storybook,* 1931; *Little Yusuf: The Story of a Syrian Boy,* 1931; *The Lost Princess of Yucatan,* Holt, 1931; *The Forbidden City,* 1932; (contributor) Emma Lindsay-Squier, *Gringa* (adult nonfiction), Houghton, 1934; *Pedro the Potter,* Thomas Nelson, 1935; *The Merry Frogs,* Suttonhouse, 1936.

(Adapter) Felix Salton, *Walt Disney's Bambi,* Heath, 1944; (contributor) Witter Bynner, *Journey with Genius: Recollections and Reflections Concerning D. H. Lawrence* (adult nonfiction), John Day, 1951; *Luther Burbank: El Mago de las Plantas* (title means "Luther Burbank: The Magician of the Plants"), Espasa Calpe (Argentina), 1955; (contributor) Edward H. Nehls, editor, *D. H. Lawrence: A Composite Biography* (adult nonfiction), three volumes, University of Wisconsin Press, 1957-59.

Under name Idella Purnell Stone: (Compiler and author of introduction) *Fourteen Great Tales of ESP* (science fiction), Gold Medal Books, 1969; (compiler and author of introduction) *Never in This World* (science fiction), Fawcett, 1971; *Thirty Mexican Menus in Spanish and English* (cookbook), Ritchie, 1971.

Stories and poems represented in children's and adult anthologies. Contributor of poetry, book reviews, short stories, and articles to literary and popular magazines for children and adults, including *Saturday Review, Saturday Evening Post, New York Post, Chatelaine, Christian Science Monitor, Child Life,* and *Torchbearer,* and to newspapers, including *New York Herald Tribune, Los Angeles Times,* and *Sierra Madre View.*

WORK IN PROGRESS: My Life as a Liberated Woman, an autobiography; *Return Through Time,* a book on dianetic practice; two novels; science fiction stories, under name Ikey Stone; translations, *Mexican Herbal Wisdom,* and *Myths and Legends of Mexico,* from the Spanish.

* * *

PUTNAM, Hilary 1926-

PERSONAL: Born July 31, 1926, in Chicago, Ill.; son of Samuel (a writer) and Riva (Sampson) Putnam; married Erna Diesendruck, November 1, 1948 (divorced, 1962); married Ruth Anna Hall (an associate professor of philosophy), August 11, 1962; children: Erika, Samuel, Joshua, Polly. *Education:* University of Pennsylvania, B.A., 1948; University of California at Los Angeles, Ph.D., 1951. *Office:* Department of Philosophy, Harvard University, Cambridge, Mass. 02138.

CAREER: Northwestern University, Evanston, Ill., instructor in philosophy, 1952-53; Princeton University, Princeton, N.J., assistant professor, 1953-60, associate professor of philosophy, 1960-61; Massachusetts Institute of Technology, Cambridge, professor of philosophy, 1961-65; Harvard University, Cambridge, Mass., professor of philosophy, 1965—. Visiting research professor at Minnesota Center for Philosophy of Science, 1957. *Member:* American Mathematical Society, American Philosophical Association (vice-president of Eastern Division, 1975-76, president, 1976-77), Association for Symbolic Logic, Philosophy of Science Association. *Awards, honors:* Rockefeller Foundation research fellow, 1951-52; Guggenheim Foundation fellow, 1960-61.

WRITINGS: (Contributor) Sidney Hook, editor, *Dimensions of Mind,* New York University Press, 1960; (contributor) Herbert Feigl and Grover Maxwell, editors, *Minnesota Studies in the Philosophy of Science,* Volume III, University of Minnesota Press, 1960; (editor with Paul Benacerraf) *Philosophy of Mathematics* (anthology), Prentice-Hall, 1964; *Philosophy of Logic,* Harper, 1971; *Mathematics: Matter and Method,* Cambridge University Press, 1975; *Language, Mind, and Reality,* Cambridge University Press, 1975. Contributor of about seventy articles to professional journals.

WORK IN PROGRESS: Meaning and Knowledge for Routledge & Kegan Paul, John Locke lectures given at Oxford University, 1976.

SIDELIGHTS: Putnam wrote that he is interested in trying to reunify philosophy of science and moral philosophy. *Avocational interests:* Camping, hiking.

* * *

QUAIN, Edwin A. 1906(?)-1975

1906(?)—December 23, 1975; American priest, educator, college administrator, publishing director, and editor. Obituaries: *New York Times,* December 24, 1975; *Publishers Weekly,* February 2, 1975.

QUINLEY, Harold E(arl) 1942-

PERSONAL: Born September 26, 1942, in Oak Park, Ill.; son of Marvin H. (an insurance agent) and Dorothy (Felio) Quinley; married Margarita Santander, September 2, 1967 (divorced, 1972); married Ruth Ann Becker (a university teacher), August 26, 1975; children: Lawrence. *Education:* Lawrence University, B.A., 1964; Stanford University, M.A., 1965, Ph.D., 1970. *Home:* P.O. Box 930, Manhattanville College, Purchase, N.Y. 10577.

CAREER: Brown University, Providence, R.I., assistant professor of political science, 1970-73; Stanford University, Institute of Political Studies, Stanford, Calif., research associate and visiting scholar, 1973-75; Manhattanville College, Purchase, N.Y., assistant professor of political science, 1975—. *Member:* American Political Science Association. *Awards, honors:* Social Science Research Council fellow, 1969-70; National Endowment for the Humanities fellow, 1973-74.

WRITINGS: (With Heinz Eulau) *State Officials and Higher Education,* McGraw, 1970; (with Rodney Stark, Bruce Foster, and Charles Glock) *Wayward Shepherds: Prejudice and the Protestant Clergy,* Harper, 1971; (editor) *Toward a New Public Policy,* James Freel, 1971; *The Prophetic Clergy: Social Activism Among Protestant Ministers,* Wiley-Interscience, 1974.

WORK IN PROGRESS: A book with Charles Glock, *Patterns of American Prejudice,* for Harper.

* * *

RABALAIS, Maria 1921-

PERSONAL: Surname is pronounced *Rob*-lay; born June 21, 1921, in Louisiana; daughter of Henry Joseph (a librarian) and Blanche Marie (Guilbeau) Rabalais. *Education:* Loyola University of the South, New Orleans, La., B.S., 1963; Catechetical and Pastoral Institute of Notre Dame, M.R.E., 1973. *Home:* 3080 Kleinert Ave., Baton Rouge, La. 70806. *Office:* Committee on Children's (Worship) Liturgy, Box 2028, Baton Rouge, La. 70821.

CAREER: Roman Catholic nun of the Congregation of St. Joseph (C.S.J.); teacher in parochial schools of New Orleans and Baton Rouge, La., 1945-74; Baton Rouge Diocesan Committee on Children's Liturgy, Baton Rouge, La., initial organizer and chairperson, 1967—; faculty member of Catechetical and Pastoral Institute, Loyola University of the South, 1975—. Coordinator of liturgy and religious education, St. Patrick Parish, Baton Rouge, La.

WRITINGS—With Howard Hall: *Children, Celebrate!,* Paulist-Newman, 1974; *Come, Be Reconciled,* Paulist-Newman, 1975. Contributor to *Children's Liturgy.* Author of "Creative Children's Worship," a 16-mm film, 1969.

WORK IN PROGRESS: Co-authoring "The How and Why of Children's Worship," a slide-cassette lecture, and "Ministry of Reconciliation in Life and Prayer," an Advent program.

* * *

RABAN, Jonathan 1942-

PERSONAL: Born June 14, 1942, in Fakenham, Norfolk, England; son of Peter (an Anglican clergyman) and Monica (Sandison) Raban. *Education:* University of Hull, B.A., 1963, additional study, 1963-65. *Politics:* "Reluctantly Socialist." *Religion:* None. *Home:* 80 Redcliffe Sq., London S.W.10, England. *Agent:* Anthony Sheil Associates, 52 Floral St., London W.C.2, England.

CAREER: University College of Wales, Aberystwyth, lecturer in English literature, 1966-67; University of East Anglia, Norwich, England, lecturer in English literature, 1967-69; free-lance writer and journalist, 1969—. Visiting lecturer, Smith College, 1972. *Member:* Royal Society of Literature (fellow), Society of Authors, Savile Club.

WRITINGS: The Technique of Modern Fiction: Essays in Practical Criticism, Edward Arnold, 1968, University of Notre Dame Press, 1969; *Mark Twain: Huckleberry Finn,* Barron's, 1968; *The Society of the Poem,* Harrap, 1971; *Soft City,* Dutton, 1974; (editor) *Robert Lowell's Poems: A Selection,* Faber, 1974.

Television plays: "Square," Granada, 1971; "Snooker," 1975, "The Water Baby," 1975, and "Mother," in production, all for BBC-TV. Radio plays: "A Game of Tombola," 1972, "At the Gate," 1973, "The Anomaly," 1974, and "The Daytrip," 1976, all for BBC Radio 3. Contributor to periodicals, including *New Statesman, New Review, Encounter, London Magazine,* and *Sunday Times.*

WORK IN PROGRESS: Temporary People, publication by Fontana expected in 1977.

SIDELIGHTS: Raban writes that "Both *Soft City* and my book-in-progress, *Temporary People,* grow out of my interest, which is close to obsessional, in the social life of large cities, and in London in particular. I am myself an urban immigrant; I came to live in London when I was 27 and I am still trying to puzzle out the odd, neurotic love affair which a citizen may have with his city. I feel a particular closeness to those Victorian writers like Mayhew, Thackeray, and Kingsley, who took London as their single greatest inspiration."

* * *

RABINOVICH, Abraham 1933-

PERSONAL: Born December 6, 1933, in New York, N.Y.; son of David (a businessman) and Eva (Flohr) Rabinovich; married Rachel Kaplan (a teacher), August 24, 1969; children: Michal, Dana. *Education:* Brooklyn College (now of the City University of New York), B.A., 1956. *Religion:* Jewish. *Home:* Mishmar Hagvul 2, Jerusalem, Israel. *Office: Jerusalem Post,* Jerusalem, Israel.

CAREER: Perth Amboy Evening News, Perth Amboy, N.J., reporter, 1959-61; *Newsday,* Long Island, N.Y., reporter, 1962-66; *Suffolk Sun,* Long Island, N.Y., reporter, 1966-67; interviewed 300 persons and wrote *The Battle for Jerusalem,* 1967-69; *Jerusalem Post,* Jerusalem, Israel, reporter, 1969—. Special correspondent for *Newsday,* 1973—. *Military service:* U.S. Army, 1957-58.

WRITINGS: The Battle for Jerusalem, Jewish Publication Society, 1972.

WORK IN PROGRESS: A book on post-1967 Jerusalem.

* * *

RABINOW, Paul 1944-

PERSONAL: Born June 21, 1944, in Tampa, Fla.; son of Irving (a social worker) and Mildred (a social worker; maiden name, Futterman) Rabinow. *Education:* University of Chicago, B.A., 1965, M.A., 1968, Ph.D., 1970. *Home:* 215 East 12th St., New York, N.Y. 10003. *Office:* Richmond College of the City University of New York, Staten Island, N.Y. 10301.

CAREER: Richmond College of the City University of New York, Staten Island, N.Y., assistant professor, 1970-72, associate professor of anthropology, 1973—.

WRITINGS: Symbolic Domination: Cultural Form and Historical Change in Morocco, University of Chicago Press, 1975.

WORK IN PROGRESS: Reflections on Fieldwork, completion expected in 1976.

* * *

RADER, Dotson 1942-

PERSONAL: Born July 25, 1942, in Minnesota; son of Paul Carlyle (a preacher) and Lois (an organist; maiden name, Schacht) Rader. *Education:* Attended Columbia University, 1963-68. *Politics:* Democratic Socialist. *Home:* 1 West 72nd St., New York, N.Y. 10023. *Agent:* Betty Anne Clarke, International Creative Management, 40 West 57th St., New York, N.Y. *Office: Esquire* Magazine, 488 Madison Ave., New York, N.Y. 10022.

CAREER: Writer. Editor of *Defiance* magazine, 1969-71; *Evergreen Review,* New York City, contributing editor, 1969-71; *New Politics,* New York City, editorial consultant, 1971—; *Esquire* magazine, New York City, contributing editor, 1972—. Co-chairman, Peoples Coalition for Peace and Justice; chairman, Humanitas; traveler, Students for a Democratic Society. *Member:* P.E.N., Authors League, War Resisters League.

WRITINGS: I Ain't Marchin' Anymore! (memoir), McKay, 1969; *Government Inspected Meat* (novel), McKay, 1970; *Blood Dues* (memoir), Knopf, 1973; *The Dream's on Me* (novel), Putnam, 1975. Also writer of screenplay, "The Bronze Lily," 1975.

WORK IN PROGRESS: A novel, completion expected in 1977; a television script, "The Great American Trial."

* * *

RAE, Milford Andersen 1946-
(Rusty Rae)

PERSONAL: Born October 5, 1946, in Sheridan Wyo.; son of Joseph (a photographer) and Ruth (a receptionist; maiden name, Stutsman) Rae; married Claudia Jane Neubauer (a home economics teacher), May 23, 1970. *Education:* Attended Tacoma Community College, 1966-67, and University of Washington, Seattle, summer, 1969; Linfield College, B.A., 1970. *Politics:* Independent. *Religion:* 'Yes.'' *Home:* 1513 Center Blvd., Springfield, Ohio 45506. *Office:* American Motorcycle Association, P.O. Box 141, Westerville, Ohio 43081.

CAREER: Port Orchard Independent, Port Orchard, Wash., news editor, 1970; *McMinnville News Register,* McMinnville, Ore., sports editor, 1970-73; American Motorcycle Association, Westerville, Ohio, photography editor, 1973—. Sports information director at Linfield College, 1970-73. *Member:* National Press Photographers Association, American Power Boat Association. *Awards, honors:* First prize in National Association of Intercollegiate Athletics photography contest, 1972, and Federation Internationale Motorcycliste photography contest, 1974.

WRITINGS—Under name Rusty Rae: *Speed and Spray: The Story of Stock Outboard Power Boat Racing* (with own photographs), Stackpole, 1975. Has written material for Associated Press. Contributor to magazines and newspapers.

WORK IN PROGRESS: Books on the Daytona 200, on automotive maintenance for the housewife, and on photography; racing books for children; a television script for the series "MASH."

SIDELIGHTS: A reply to a fan letter from racing driver Bill Muncey led Rae to stock outboard racing. He worked for several Unlimited crews taking pictures when these boats visited Seattle. More recently, between picture-taking duties at the Dayton Nationals, he found time to compete in two hydroplane races. *Avocational interests:* All sports (especially playing handball), reading, travel.

* * *

RAEFF, Marc 1923-

PERSONAL: Born July 28, 1923, in Moscow, Russia; came to United States, 1941; naturalized U.S. citizen, 1943. *Education:* Attended City College (now City College of the City University of New York), 1942-43; Harvard University, M.A., 1947, Ph.D., 1950. *Office:* Department of History, Columbia University, New York, N.Y. 10027.

CAREER: Clark University, Worcester, Mass., 1949-61, began as instructor, became associate professor of history; Columbia University, New York, N.Y., associate professor, 1961-65, professor of Russian history, 1965-73, Bakhmeteff Professor of Russian Studies, 1973—. Visiting scholar at University of Washington, 1952-53; Fulbright professor at Sorbonne, University of Paris, 1960-61; exchange scholar at Institute of History, Academy of Sciences of the U.S.S.R., 1965, 1968, 1972; visiting professor at Free University of Berlin, 1966, University of Colorado, 1969, and University of Cologne, 1970; guest member of Max Planck Institute of History in Goettingen, 1972; member of U.S. delegation to Soviet-American Historical Colloquium, 1972, and to Polish-American Historical Colloquium, 1974. *Military service:* U.S. Army, 1943-46; interpreter and interrogator; became sergeant. *Member:* Institut d'Etudes Slaves (Paris), Phi Beta Kappa. *Awards, honors:* Guggenheim fellow, 1957; Social Science Research Council fellow, 1958-60; American Philosophical Society grants, 1961, 1966, 1970; National Foundation on Arts and Humanities senior fellow, 1968; Robert H. Lord award from Emmanuel College, 1971; American Council of Learned Societies grant, 1972; National Endowment for the Humanities independent research grant, 1975-76.

WRITINGS: Siberia and the Reforms of 1822, University of Washington Press, 1956; *M. M. Speransky: Statesman of Imperial Russia*, Nijhoff, 1957, revised edition, 1969; (contributor) Hugh McClean, George Fischer, and Malia, editors, *Russian Thought and Politics*, Harvard Slavic Studies, Harvard University Press, 1957; (editor) *Peter the Great: Reformer or Revolutionary?*, Heath, 1963, revised edition published as *Peter the Great Changes Russia*, 1972; *Origins of the Russian Intelligentsia: The Eighteenth Century Nobility*, Harcourt, 1966; (editor) *The Decembrist Movement*, Prentice-Hall, 1966; (editor) *Plans for Political Reform in Imperial Russia: 1730-1905*, Prentice-Hall, 1966; (editor) *Russian Intellectual History: An Anthology*, Harcourt, 1966; (contributor) Gerald N. Grob, editor, *Statesmen and Statecraft of the Modern West*, Barre, 1967; *Imperial Russia: The Coming of Age of Modern Russia*, Random House, 1970; (contributor) Robert Forster and J. P. Greene, editors, *Preconditions of Revolution in Early Modern Europe*, Johns Hopkins Press, 1970; (contributor) Edward Allworth, editor, *Soviet Nationality Problems*, Columbia University Press, 1971; (editor) *Catherine II: A Profile*, Hill & Wang, 1972; (contributor) J. G. Garrard, editor, *The Eighteenth Century in Russia*, Oxford University Press, 1973; (contributor) Robert Auty and Dmitri Obolensky, editors, *Companion to Russian Studies*, Cambridge University Press, 1975. Contributor of articles to *Encyclopaedia Britannica*, 1974, and to journals in his field, including *Oxford Slavonic Papers, Slavic Review,* and *Slavonic and East European Review*.

* * *

RAGAWAY, Martin A(rnold) 1928-

PERSONAL: Born January 29, 1928, in Brooklyn, N.Y.; son of Philip (a pharmacist) and Evelyn (Mandelbaum) Ragaway; married Donna Jo Whitman, 1952 (divorced, 1959); married Connie Hunter Webber, 1969 (divorced, 1972); children: (first marriage) Jill; (second marriage) Philip. *Education:* New York University, B.S., 1945. *Home:* 1172 Casa Verde Way, Palm Springs, Calif. *Agent:* Shapiro Lichtman, 9100 Sunset Blvd., Beverly Hills, Calif. 90210. *Office: Funny Funny World,* 407 North Maple Dr., Beverly Hills, Calif. 90210.

CAREER: New York Mirror, New York, N.Y., assistant Brooklyn editor; became writer for television films and radio; currently editor and publisher of *Funny Funny World,* Beverly Hills, Calif. *Member:* Alpha Phi Sigma. *Awards, honors:* Emmy Awards from Academy of Television Arts and Sciences for material written for Dick Van Dyke, and for material written for Red Skelton; awards from Writer's Guild, for material written for Dick Van Dyke, and for writing Alan King's "Wonderful World of Aggravation"; received National Scholastic Award for material written for Bill Cosby.

WRITINGS: (With Milton Berle) *Out of My Trunk,* Blue Ribbon Books, 1945; *Good News/Bad News Book,* Price, Stern, 1972; *The World's Worst Golf Jokes,* Price, Stern, 1972; *The World's Worst Doctor Jokes,* Price, Stern, 1972; *The World's Worst Lawyer Jokes,* Price, Stern, 1972; *The World's Worst Psychiatrist Jokes,* Price, Stern, 1974.

Films: "The Milkman," Universal, 1950; "Abbot and Costello in the Foreign Legion," Universal, 1950; "Ma and Pa Kettle Go to Town," Universal, 1950; "Lost in Alaska," Universal, 1952, "Ma and Pa Kettle Go to the Fair," Universal, 1952. Has written television and radio material for performers including Milton Berle, Dinah Shore, Bob Hope, Red Skelton, Jackie Gleason, and Lucille Ball. Contributor to magazines and newspapers.

SIDELIGHTS: Ragaway writes: "*Funny Funny World* has twenty correspondents around the world and possibly the most elite circulation list including heads of state, congressmen, senators, college presidents, etc. I take humor very seriously. Life is a strait jacket if you insist on adhering to it humorlessly. I probably know more about the funny, odd, strange wacky things happening around the world than any other human being alive. My daily goal: To contribute to the sum total of human laughter."

* * *

RAIA, Anthony P(aul) 1928-

PERSONAL: Surname is pronounced *Ray-ah;* born May 24, 1928, in Clifton, N.J.; son of Dominick and Louise (Costello) Raia; married Beverlee Joan Otto, May 26, 1962; children: Lynda Louise, Mark Anthony. *Education:* Columbia University, B.S., 1956; University of California, Los Angeles, M.B.A., 1960, Ph.D., 1963. *Home:* 313 18th St., Manhattan Beach, Calif. 90266. *Office:* Graduate School of Management, University of California, Los Angeles, Calif. 90024.

CAREER: Progressive Electronics Co., Inc., Passaic, N.J., plant supervisor, 1945-49; Prescott Appliance Centers, Woodridge and Fairlawn, N.J., owner and operator, 1949-51; Progressive Electronics Co., Inc., co-owner and vice-president, 1956-58; San Fernando Valley State College (now California State University), Northridge, assistant professor of management, 1962-63; University of Maryland, College Park, assistant professor of business administration, 1963-65; University of Miami, Coral Gables, Fla., associate professor of management, 1965-68; TRW Systems Group, Redondo Beach, Calif., internal consultant, 1968-69; University of California, Los Angeles, professor of management and assistant dean for executive education, 1969—. Has developed management training and organizational development programs for major businesses, schools, and research and development firms; consultant to National Bureau of Standards, Pacific Missile Range, Stanford Research Institute, Systems Development Corp., and Rockwell International. *Military service:* U.S. Air Force, radar maintenance supervisor, 1951-53. Air National Guard, communications and electronics officer, 1948—.

MEMBER: International Association of Applied Social Scientists, Academy of Management, American Association for Humanistic Psychology, Beta Gamma Sigma.

WRITINGS: (With Robert E. Schellenberger) *MANSYM: A Dynamic Management Stimulator,* Brown Book, 1965; (with Jay Craven) *COMPUMAN: Dynamic Management Decision-Making,* Office of Publications, University of Miami (Coral Gables, Fla.), 1967; (with Newton Margulies) *Organizational Development: Values, Process, and Technology,* McGraw, 1972; *Managing by Objectives,* Scott, Foresman, 1974; *The Theory and Practice of Organizational Development,* McGraw, in press. Contributor to business journals.

* * *

RAIFF, Stan 1930-

PERSONAL: Born July 28, 1930, in New York, N.Y.; son of Samuel J. (a lawyer and certified public accountant) and Betty (an artist) Raiff. *Education:* Syracuse University, M.A., 1952. *Politics:* "Equal rights for all." *Home:* 438 West 20th St., New York, N.Y. 10011. *Office:* Youth Education, 10 East 40th St., New York, N.Y. 10016.

CAREER: Arlington County (Va.) School System, special teacher, writing, producing, and directing television and radio programs, 1952-55; Western Pacific Railroad, San Francisco, Calif., writer in community relations department, 1955-57; National Association for Broadcasters, Washington, D.C., youth director, 1957-60; European Travel Commission, New York City, vice-president of travel promotions, 1960-68; Inter-Public Group of Companies, New York City, marketing specialist, 1968-69; Youth Education (multi-media education company), New York City, president and owner, 1970—. Vice-president of Industry Education Corp.

WRITINGS: Get Ready! Get Set! Go!: A European Travel Guide for Young People, Doubleday, 1970. Author of more than a hundred television scripts for young people and of scripts for two sound recordings.

SIDELIGHTS: Raiff writes: "All of my professional time is spent helping young people explore with their teachers and parents how they can find out all the potential they may have. These explorations are done in a simple yet sophisticated manner. There is never any condescension in terms of being directed toward young people." His firm creates, produces, and distributes multi-media programs to schools, homes, and communities. "The programs are open-ended

allowing people to examine their options, trade-offs, and risks and then make their own personal choices." Raiff has directed and produced children's theater productions.

* * *

RAMAGE, James A(lfred) 1940-

PERSONAL: Born May 6, 1940, in Paducah, Ky.; son of Newman (a farmer) and Helen (Culp) Ramage; married Ann Winstead (an accountant), June 6, 1964; children: Andrea Suzanne. *Education:* Murray State University, B.S., 1965, M.A., 1968; University of Kentucky, Ph.D., 1972. *Politics:* Democrat. *Religion:* Baptist. *Home:* 369 Knollwood Dr., Highland Heights, Ky. 41076. *Office:* Department of History, Northern Kentucky State College, Highland Heights, Ky. 41076.

CAREER: High school teacher of history in the county schools of St. Louis, Mo., 1965-67; Northern Kentucky State College, Highland Heights, assistant professor, 1972-75, associate professor of history, 1975—, assistant to the president, 1972—. Chairman of Citizens Task Force for Planning, City of Highland Heights, Ky., 1974-75, and Recreation Commission for Highland Heights, 1975—. *Military service:* U.S. Air Force, 1958-62. *Member:* Southern Historical Association, Kentucky Historical Society, Red River Valley Historical Association, Filson Club, Phi Alpha Theta.

WRITINGS: John Wesley Hunt: Pioneer Merchant, Manufacturer, and Financier, University Press of Kentucky, 1974; *Holman Hamilton: A Biographical Sketch,* University Press of Kentucky, 1975.

* * *

RANDAL, Beatrice [a pseudonym] 1916-

PERSONAL: Born March 9, 1916, in southern Minnesota; married, November 6, 1943 (husband is retired employee of U.S. Department of Justice); children: two sons. *Education:* Attended University of Minnesota, 1934-37. *Politics:* Republican. *Religion:* Lutheran. *Residence:* A suburb of Los Angeles, Calif.

CAREER: Secretary, bookkeeper, and writer. *Member:* Municipal Art Association, Southern California Designer-Craftsmen Guild. *Awards, honors:* Art awards for enamel paintings.

WRITINGS: A New World in the Making: The Second Coming of Christ, Crescent, 1974.

WORK IN PROGRESS: Continuing study of the "holy Scripture and the word of God as it is revealed to me."

SIDELIGHTS: Beatrice Randal told *CA* that the book "on the second coming of Christ is autobiographical and details the religious conversion of the author. A practical business woman I worked as a secretary-bookkeeper for many years.... On a memorable day in August, 1967, the Holy Trinity revealed Himself to me and ... explained I was to act as scribe and historian in bringing the very word of God to people everywhere ...." *Avocational interests:* Enamel paintings, oils, and watercolors (her paintings have been shown in museums).

* * *

RANDALL, Donald A. 1933-

PERSONAL: Born August 31, 1933, in Lyons, Ga.; son of Foy Clifford (a veterinarian) and Annie M. (Autrey) Randall; married Mary Carey Overton (business manager of

Smithsonian), December 30, 1966; children: Richard Malone. *Education:* Mercer University, LL.B., J.D., both 1954. *Religion:* Baptist. *Home:* 5131 North 15th St., Arlington, Va. 22205. *Agent:* Brandt & Brandt, 101 Park Ave., New York, N.Y. 10017. *Office:* 1000 Connecticut Ave. N.W., Washington, D.C. 20036.

CAREER: Federal Trade Commission, New Orleans, La., attorney, 1961-67; U.S. Senate Judiciary Committee, Washington, D.C., counsel to subcommittee on antitrust and monopoly, 1967-73; Wynne, Jaffe & Tinsley, Washington, D.C., partner, 1973-74; in private practice, 1974—. *Military service:* U.S. Army, 1955-61. *Member:* U.S. Supreme Court Bar Association, Federal Bar Association, Georgia Bar Association, District of Columbia Bar Association.

WRITINGS: (With Arthur Glickman) *The Great American Auto Repair Robbery,* Charterhouse, 1972. Author of a monthly column in *Automotive Body Repair News.* Contributor to motor magazines.

SIDELIGHTS: Randall writes: "As counsel to the U.S. Senate investigation of automotive repair industry I gained a special appreciation for the problems faced by the American motorists. My book was an effort to promote voluntary changes in the industry and legislative changes where voluntary changes failed to appear."

* * *

RANKIN, Ruth (DeLone) I(rvine) 1924-
(Ruth DeLone)

PERSONAL: Born April 11, 1924, in Hapeville, Ga.; daughter of William Stafford (in real estate) and Ruth (Bankston) Irvine; married Robert Rankin (a railway clerk), January 18, 1942; children: Mrs. Robert T. Jackson, Jr., Robert Irvine, Gerald Eugene. *Education:* Attended high school in Macon, Ga. *Politics:* "Mugwump." *Religion:* Methodist. *Home and office:* 2275 Wildwood Dr., Macon, Ga. 31204.

CAREER: Substitute teacher in the public schools of Macon, Ga., 1950-70.

WRITINGS: (Under name Ruth DeLone) *Don't Walk on Your Feet,* Branden Press, 1975.

WORK IN PROGRESS: Listen (children's poetry); *A Working Faith with God.*

SIDELIGHTS: Ruth Rankin told *CA,* "Almost everyone wants to know himself/herself better. Self-analysis through writing is a private, practical, inexpensive way. It is, also, amazingly simple. For me, it was making a conscious effort to remember as much as possible about my life. It was written as it came, regardless of how disconnected, unrelated, or foolish it seemed. No effort was made to sort it.... Perhaps my deepest motivation is an unvarnished delight with each new day. When I realize that *this day* is unique in history; never 'having been,' never 'to be' again—my obligation to live it fully is a prerequisite to breathing!" *Avocational interests:* Sewing, gardening, sketching, walking.

* * *

RAO, B. Shiva 1900(?)-1975

1900(?)—December 15, 1975; Indian political figure, newspaperman, and author. Obituaries: *New York Times,* December 21, 1975.

RAPER, Arthur F(ranklin) 1899-

PERSONAL: Born November 8, 1899, near Lexington, N.C.; son of William F. (a farmer) and Julia (Crouse) Raper; married Martha Elizabeth Jarrell, June 12, 1930; children: Charles, Harrison, Jarrell, Margaret Raper Hammun. *Education:* University of North Carolina, A.B., 1924, Ph.D., 1931; Vanderbilt University, M.A., 1925. *Politics:* "Usually a Democrat." *Religion:* "At first Moravian, then Methodist by marriage." *Home:* 10801 Miller Rd., Oakton, Va. 22124.

CAREER: Commission on Interracial Cooperation, Atlanta, Ga., research secretary, 1926-39; Carnegie-Myrdal Study of the American Negro, New York, N.Y., research associate, 1939-40; U.S. Department of Agriculture, Bureau of Agricultural Economics, Greene County, Ga., social science analyst, 1940-42, social science analyst and principal social scientist in Washington, D.C., 1942-52; Mutual Security Agency, Far East Division, Washington, D.C., consultant, working with Philippines Council on field study of local rural life, 1952; U.S. Agency for International Development, Washington, D.C., project evaluation adviser in Taiwan, 1952-54, consultant to Community Development Division on Middle East and South Asia, 1954-55, regional community development adviser for International Cooperation Administration in the Middle East and North Africa, 1955-58, member of training development staff and Career Development Division, 1958, assistant chief of orientation and counseling branch, 1958-61, acting chief, 1961-62; Michigan State University, East Lansing, senior adviser to Pakistan Academy for Rural Development in Comilla, East Pakistan, 1962-64, member of Pakistan Project, 1964-65, member of sociology staff, 1964-67, visiting professor of Asian studies, 1966-67. *Member:* American Sociological Association, Rural Sociological Society, Society for International Development, Southern Sociological Association.

WRITINGS: The Tragedy of Lynching, University of North Carolina Press, 1933; *Preface to Peasantry,* University of North Carolina Press, 1936; *The South's Landless Farmers* (pamphlet), Commission on Interracial Cooperation, 1937. (With Ira deA. Reid) *Sharecroppers All,* University of North Carolina Press, 1941; *Tenants of the Almighty,* Macmillan, 1943; *Machines in the Cotton Fields* (pamphlet), Southern Regional Council, 1946.

(With Carl C. Taylor, Douglas Ensminger, and others) *Rural Life in the United States,* Knopf, 1950; (with Herbert Passin and others) *The Japanese Village in Transition,* Supreme Commander for Allied Powers (Tokyo), 1950; (contributor) Louis W. Jones, editor, *The Changing Status of the Negro in Southern Agriculture,* Tuskegee Institute, 1950; (with wife, Martha J. Raper) *Guide to Agriculture, U.S.A.,* U.S. Government Printing Office, 1951; (contributor) L. A. Potts, editor, *Land Tenure in the Southern Region,* Tuskegee Institute, 1951; *Rural Trends: A Graphic Presentation* (pamphlet), Cooperative Extension Service and Bureau of Agricultural Economics, U.S. Department of Agriculture, 1952; *Rural Taiwan: Problem and Promise,* Joint Commission on Rural Reconstruction, U.S. Operations Mission, 1953; *Rural Taiwan Today* (pamphlet), U.S. Aid Mission to Formosa, 1953; (with Harold Pedersen) *The Plantation in Transition* (pamphlet), Mississippi Agriculture Experiment Station, Mississippi State College, 1954; *Cultural Briefing for Taiwan* (pamphlet), U.S. Aid Mission to Taiwan, 1954.

(With Harry L. Case and others) *Rural Development in*

Action: The Comprehensive Experiment at Comilla, East Pakistan, Cornell University Press, 1970; (contributor) Carle C. Zimmerman and Richard E. Dewors, editors, *Sociology of Underdevelopment,* Copp, 1970. Contributor of about thirty-five articles to professional journals.

WORK IN PROGRESS: Research on current social and economic conditions; preparing personal papers for submission to the Southern Historical Collection at University of North Carolina Library.

SIDELIGHTS: Between 1947-50 Raper made three trips to Japan as consultant to Allied Occupation Command on agrarian reforms; in 1950, he prepared an orientation manual on rural life in the United States for foreign visitors; in 1951, organized a study on appropriate rural audio-visual materials for eleven Asian countries, for International Motion Picture Division of the U.S. Department of State; and in late 1951 made a trip to southeast Asia to discuss with Missions Directors means of increasing aid to villagers. *Avocational interests:* Growing organic beef, fruits, and vegetables; participating in civic and church activities.

* * *

RAPHAEL, Dana

PERSONAL: Married Howard Jacobson; children: Brett, Seth, Jessa. *Education:* Columbia University, B.A., 1956, Ph.D., 1966. *Religion:* Society of Friends (Quakers). *Home and office:* 666 Sturges Highway, Westport, Conn. 06880.

CAREER: Columbia University, New York, N.Y., consultant to International Institute for the Study of Human Reproduction, 1973-74; Human Lactation Center, Westport, Conn., director of breastfeeding research and director of center, 1974—. *Member:* American Association for the Advancement of Science, American Anthropological Association, New York Academy of Sciences.

WRITINGS: The Tender Gift, Prentice-Hall, 1973; (editor) *Being Female,* Mouton & Co., 1975.

WORK IN PROGRESS: The Anthropology of Human Reproduction.

* * *

RAPOPORT, Rhona (Ross) 1927-

PERSONAL: Born January 29, 1927, in South Africa; daughter of Ely (a businessman) and Cecilia Ross; married Robert N. Rapoport (a sociologist), February 14, 1957; children: Lorna, Alin. *Education:* University of Capetown, B.Soc.Sci., 1946; London School of Economics and Political Science, Ph.D., 1951. *Home:* 7 Kidderpore Ave., London NW3 7SX, England.

CAREER: Sociologist, East African Institute of Social Research, University College of East Africa, 1951-52; assistant psychologist, Tavistock Clinic, 1952-53; engaged in various research programs, 1953-59, including work as research associate for Joint Commission for the Study of Mental Illness and Health in the United States, 1957-59; lecturer on mental health at Harvard University School of Public Health and Medical School, and director of family research for the university's Community Health Program, 1959-66; consulting sociologist, 1967-71; senior social scientist, Tavistock Institute of Human Relations, 1969-73; Institute of Family and Environmental Research, London, England, co-director, 1973—. Member of executive boards, International Scientific Commission on the Family and Human Resources Center of the Tavistock Institute, both

1970—. *Member:* International Sociological Association, International Psychoanalytic Society, British Sociological Association, British Psychoanalytic Society, American Sociological Association.

WRITINGS: (With Michael Fogarty) *Sex, Career, and Family,* Sage Publications, 1971; *Dual Career Families,* Penguin, 1971, 2nd edition, in press; *Leisure and the Family Life Cycle,* Routledge & Kegan Paul, 1975. Advisory editor of *Family Process,* 1966—.

WORK IN PROGRESS: Parents' Needs, with husband, Robert Rapoport, and others.

* * *

RATCLIFF, Carter 1941-

PERSONAL: Born August 20, 1941, in Seattle, Wash.; son of Francis Kenneth (a corporation executive) and Marian Elizabeth (Carter) Ratcliff; married Phyllis Derfner (a writer), January 28, 1974. *Education:* University of Chicago, B.A., 1963. *Home:* 67 East 11th St., New York, N.Y. 10003.

CAREER: St. Mark's Church, New York, N.Y., director of poetry workshop, 1969-70; School of Visual Arts, New York, N.Y., lecturer, 1971-75; Philadelphia College of Art, Philadelphia, Pa., lecturer, 1973; New York University, School of Continuing Education, New York, N.Y., lecturer, 1973-75. *Military service:* U.S. Army, 1964-65. *Member:* International Association of Art Critics. *Awards, honors:* Poets Foundation grant, 1969; Art Critics' fellowship from National Endowment for the Arts, 1972.

WRITINGS: Fever Coast (poems), Kulchur Press, 1973. Poems anthologized in *The World,* edited by Anne Waldman, Bobbs-Merrill, 1969; *Another World,* edited by Waldman, Bobbs-Merrill, 1971. Contributor to *Britannica Encyclopedia of American Art* and to poetry journals and art exhibition catalogues. Editorial associate of *Artnews,* 1969-72; advisory editor of *Art International,* 1970-75; staff correspondent for *Art Spectrum,* 1975.

WORK IN PROGRESS: Research on American art criticism for a six-part series of articles; a book of poems.

* * *

RATLIFFE, Sharon A(nn) 1939-

PERSONAL: Born September 23, 1939, in Dearborn, Mich.; daughter of Harold LaVern and Evalyn (a bookkeeper; maiden name, Ahrens) Ratliffe. *Education:* Western Michigan University, B.A. (cum laude), 1963; Wayne State University, M.A., 1965, Ph.D., 1972. *Office:* Department of Speech Communication, Ambassador College, Pasadena, Calif. 91123.

CAREER: Part-time teacher and creative dramatics specialist in elementary schools in Evanston, Ill., autumn, 1963, and in elementary and high schools in Dearborn, Mich., 1964-65; Western Michigan University, Kalamazoo, instructor, 1965-72, assistant professor, 1972-74, associate professor of communication arts and sciences, 1974-76, assistant director of Children's Experimental Theatre, 1974, associate director of theater, 1975-76; Ambassador College, Pasadena, Calif., associate professor of speech communication, 1976—. Instructor at Kalamazoo College, autumn, 1968.

MEMBER: Speech Communication Association of America, American Association of University Professors, American Association of University Women, National Council of Teachers of English, Language Arts Task Force, Central States Speech Association (member of executive committee, 1973—; first vice-president, 1975-76), Michigan Speech Association (chairman of research committee, 1967-68; member of executive council, 1967-68, 1969-77; executive secretary, 1969-72; president, 1975-76), Michigan Council of Teachers of English, Kappa Delta Pi, Theta Alpha Phi. *Awards, honors:* Outstanding young teacher award from Central States Speech Association, 1970.

WRITINGS: (Contributor) Kenneth Hance, editor, *Discussion and Argumentation-Debate in the Secondary School,* National Textbook Co., 1968; (contributor) Hance, editor, *Dramatic Arts in the Secondary School,* National Textbook Co., 1968; (contributor) Hance, editor, *Speech in the Junior High School,* National Textbook Co., 1968; (with Deldee M. Herman) *Adventures in the Looking-Glass: Experiencing Communication with Your-Self and Others,* National Textbook Co., 1972, revised edition, 1974; (contributor) R. R. Allen and P. Judson Newcombe, editors, *New Horizons for Teacher Education in Speech Communication: Report of the Memphis Conference of Teacher Educators,* National Textbook Co., 1974; (with Ernest Stech) *Working in Groups,* National Textbook Co., 1976.

Author of booklets for school drama and media programs. Co-editor of "Michigan Speech Association Curriculum Guide Series," 1972; editor of "Reviews of Teaching/Learning Resources," in *Communication Education,* 1976-78. Contributor to communication and education journals. Editor of *Speech in the Secondary Schools Newsletter* (of Speech Communication Association of America), 1969-71, and *Newsletter of the Central States Speech Association Advisory Committee,* 1973-76. Consultant to National Textbook Co.

WORK IN PROGRESS: Research on language use, interpersonal communication, and the adolescent self-concept, and on the status of speech teachers and/or teachers academically prepared to teach speech in Michigan high schools.

*   *   *

RAU, Margaret 1913-

PERSONAL: Surname rhymes with "now"; born December 23, 1913, in Swatow, China; daughter of George Wright (a missionary) and Mary Victoria (a missionary; maiden name, Wolfe) Lewis; married Neil Rau (a writer), 1935 (died, 1971); children: Robert, Peter, Peggy, Frank, Thomas. *Education:* Studied under private tutor in China; attended University of Chicago, 1931, Columbia University, 1932, and University of Redlands, 1933-34; Riverside Library College (Calif.), degree, 1934. *Home:* 823 South Plymouth Blvd., Apt. 12, Los Angeles, Calif. 90005.

CAREER: Writer. *Member:* Photographic Society of America, United States-China People's Friendship Association, National Writers Guild.

WRITINGS—Juvenile books: *Band of the Red Hand,* Knopf, 1938; *Dawn from the West,* Hawthorn, 1964; *The Penguin Book,* Hawthorn, 1968; *The Yellow River,* Messner, 1969; *The Yangtze River,* Messner, 1970; (self-illustrated with photographs) *Jimmy of Cherry Valley,* Messner, 1973; *Our World: The People's Republic of China,* Messner, 1974.

Adult books with husband, Neil Rau: *My Father, Charlie Chaplin,* Random House, 1960; *Act Your Way to Suc-*

cessful Living, Prentice-Hall, 1966; *My Dear Ones,* Prentice-Hall, 1971.

Collaborator with husband on material used by Norman Lear for film, "Cold Turkey." Writer of pamphlets on China. Contributor to *Parents' Magazine* and *Cricket.*

WORK IN PROGRESS: A book on the panda in the wild, for Knopf; a nature book on the albatross; a book on the musk ox, for Crowell; a picture-text book about modern China based on her own observations and illustrated with her own photographs.

SIDELIGHTS: Margaret Rau writes: "I grew up in China where I spoke Chinese for four years before learning English. I have always felt a deep and abiding love for the countryside in which I grew up and for the people among whom I found myself. Now with China taking a new and ever-growing role in the modern world I feel it imperative that our young people know something about this great country and the Chinese—their aims, dreams and hopes. In 1974 I paid a visit to the People's Republic of China and hope it will be the first of many...." Mrs. Rau has also traveled in Europe and the Soviet Union.

*   *   *

RAWICK, George P(hilip) 1929-

PERSONAL: Born December 8, 1929, in Brooklyn, N.Y.; son of Julius L. and Miriam (Shapiro) Rawick; divorced; children: Jules D., Che Calle. *Education:* Oberlin College, A.B., 1951; University of Wisconsin, M.S., 1953, Ph.D., 1957; additional study at Western Reserve University (now Case Western Reserve University), and Harvard University. *Politics:* "Libertarian socialist."

CAREER: Fund for the Republic, Inc., New York, N.Y., research associate, 1954-57; University of Chicago, Chicago, Ill., instructor in social science, history, and labor education, 1958-60; Wayne State University, Monteith College, Detroit, Mich., assistant professor of sociology, 1960-63; writer, and lecturer to university groups and trade union groups in Europe, primarily England, 1963-64; Oakland University, Rochester, Mich., lecturer, 1964-65, associate professor of sociology, 1965-70; Washington University, St. Louis, Mo., visiting associate professor, 1969-70, associate professor of sociology, 1970-72; Empire State College of the State University of New York, Saratoga Springs, professor of sociology in Learning Resources Development Faculty, 1972-76; University of Missouri, St. Louis, visiting professor in department of history, 1976. Lecturer, Brooklyn College of the City University of New York, 1955-56, summer, 1962, Henry Ford Community College, 1964-65, member of faculty, University of Alberta, summer, 1968; has lectured at universities in United States, Canada, England, West Germany, and Italy. Co-director, Kansas Federation of Labor summer workshop, University of Kansas, 1959, and American Indian affairs workshop, University of Colorado, summer, 1963, 1965, 1968. *Awards, honors:* Social Science Research Council fellow at Cornell University and Columbia University, 1957-58.

WRITINGS: (With Ed Clark) *U.S.A.: Dalle Strade Alle Fabbriche* (title means "From the Street to the Factory"), Feltrinelli, 1968; *From Sundown to Sunup: The Making of the Black Community* (Volume I in the series, *The American Slave* [also see below]), Greenwood Press, 1972; (editor) *The American Slave: A Composite Autobiography,* Greenwood Press, Volumes 1-19, 1972-73, Volumes 20-29 (with co-editors Ken Lawrence and Jan Hillegas), and with new introduction, in press; (with others) *Operai e stato:*

Lotte operaie e riforma della stato capitalitico tra revioluzione d'Ottobre e New Deal (title means "Workers and the State: The Workers' Struggle and the Reform of the Capitalist State from the October Revolution to the New Deal"), Feltrinelli, 1972.

Contributor: Howard Quint, Dean Albertson, and Milton Cantor, editors, *Main Problems of American History,* two volumes, Dorsey, 1964; Thomas T. Hammond, editor, *Soviet Foreign Relations and World Communism: A Selected Annotated Bibliography of 7,000 Books in 30 Languages,* Princeton University Press, 1965; Joseph R. Conlin, editor, *The American Radical Press, 1880-1960,* two volumes, Greenwood Press, 1974.

Contributor to Monteith College Social Science *Readings,* and *Proceedings* of American Ethnological Society; contributor of articles and reviews to periodicals, including *South Atlantic Quarterly, New University Thought,* and *International Socialism.* Editor, *Anvil and Student Partisan,* 1955-58; co-editor, *New Politics,* 1960-62; member of editorial board, *American Studies,* 1970-74.

WORK IN PROGRESS: The Social History of the American People: Race, Class, Sex, and Ethnicity in American Life; two textbooks on American racism.

SIDELIGHTS: George Rawick told *CA:* "I have been a socialist since the age of twelve. American socialism since the death of Eugene Debs has not Americanized itself. It has been Russian, Chinese, Cuban, etc., but never rooted in the American experience. Thus, for example, there is no real socialist history of the American people; just structuralist tirades that prove that America is a terrible place and Americans terrible people. Being proudly an American patriot I want to write a socialist history of the American people."

* * *

RAY, JoAnne 1935-

PERSONAL: Born June 19, 1935, in Duluth, Minn.; daughter of Robert Earl (a railroad inspector) and Trudie (Burford) Green; married Glenn H. Ray (administrator in a state agency), May 25, 1957; children: Christian, Anne, Andrew. *Education:* University of Minnesota, B.A., 1957, M.A., 1966. *Home:* 14624 Woodhill Ter., Minnetonka, Minn. 55343.

CAREER: University of Minnesota, Minneapolis, an editor, 1958-62; Minnesota Association for Retarded Children, Minneapolis, public information director, 1962-64; National University Extension Association, Minneapolis, Minn., editor, 1964-71; Minnesota State Horticultural Society, St. Paul, editor, 1974—.

WRITINGS—Juvenile books; all published by Lerner: *American Assassins,* 1974; *Careers With a Television Station,* 1974; *Careers in Football,* 1974; *Careers in Hockey,* 1974; *Careers in Computers,* 1974; *Careers With a Police Department,* 1974.

WORK IN PROGRESS: Biography of Maud Hart Lovelace, author of children's books, for a volume on women in Minnesota history.

* * *

RAY, John B(ernard) 1930-

PERSONAL: Born January 9, 1930, in Indiana, Pa.; son of Harry Wilson (a farmer) and Florence (Moore) Ray; married Katherine Amelia Theiss (a teacher), March 20, 1959;

children: David, Barbara. *Education:* Indiana University, B.S., 1951, Ph.D., 1968; University of Pittsburgh, M.Litt., 1956. *Home:* 1203 Scottland Dr., Murfreesboro, Tenn. 37130. *Office:* Department of Geography and Earth Science, Middle Tennessee State University, Murfreesboro, Tenn. 37130.

CAREER: University of Wisconsin—Whitewater, associate professor of geography, 1968—. Professor at Kent State University, 1968-69, and Middle Tennessee State University, 1975—. *Member:* International Oceanographic Society, World Federalists, Association of American Geographers, National Council for Geographic Education, Wisconsin Council for Geographic Education, Alpha Omega Gamma, Gamma Theta Upsilon, Kiwanis International. *Awards, honors:* National Science Foundation college science faculty fellowship, 1966-67; Frick Foundation fellowship, Pennsylvania State University, summer, 1961.

WRITINGS: Christmas Holidays around the World, Comet Press, 1959; *Materials of Geography for Educational Use,* Burgess, 1964; (with Douglas A. James) *Physical Geography and Earth Science,* National Press, 1970; *The Oceans and Man,* Kendall/Hunt, 1975.

Contributor: *Neighbors Across the Seas* (junior high school textbook), Holt, 1964; *Neighbors in the Americas* (junior high school textbook), Holt, 1964; H. F. Raup and Clyde Smith, editors, *A Geography of Ohio,* Kendall/Hunt, 1973. Contributor to geography journals.

WORK IN PROGRESS: Research on man's political jurisdiction over the oceans.

SIDELIGHTS: Ray writes: "I consider myself a political-historical-cultural geographer with a particular interest in man's interaction with the oceans in terms of living resources, hard minerals, energy resources, etc. The relationship between man and the oceans is one of the most significant contemporary issues in international relations."

* * *

READ, R. B. 1916-

PERSONAL: Born April 25, 1916, in Indiana; son of William Ludd and Matilda (Burns) Read; married Ann Wyckoff, July 23, 1943 (divorced, 1964); children: Tess, Timon Wyckoff. *Education:* Reed College, B.A., 1938. *Politics:* Democrat. *Religion:* Agnostic. *Home:* 157 Park Pl., Point Richmond, Calif. 94801.

CAREER: Consultant in urban and regional economics at Center for Regional Economic Studies at University of Pittsburgh, Pittsburgh, Pa., 1962-63, for City of San Francisco, Calif., 1968-69, at Institute for Urban Studies at Washington University, St. Louis, Mo., 1969-75, at Marshall, Kaplan, Gans & Kahn, San Francisco, 1972-73, and at Skidmore, Owings & Merrill, San Francisco, 1973. *Military service:* U.S. Naval Reserve, active duty, 1941-45. *Awards, honors:* Merit award from *Progressive Architecture,* 1974, for *The San Antonio River Corridor.*

WRITINGS: San Francisco Underground Gourmet, Simon & Schuster, 1969, 3rd edition, 1975; (with Charles L. Leven) *A River, A Region, and A Research Problem* (impact of Arkansas River Development Project on its basin), Institute of Water Resources, Army Corps of Engineers, 1971; *Urban Decay in St. Louis,* National Technical Information Service, 1972; *The San Antonio River Corridor,* for the City of San Antonio and Bexar County, 1973; *Gastronomic Tour of Mexico,* Doubleday, 1973; (with Leven, James T. Little, and Hugh O. Nourse) *The Contemporary*

Neighborhood Succession Process: Lessons in the Dynamics of Decay, Washington University Press, 1975, published as *Why Neighborhoods Change: Lessons in the Dynamics of Decay,* Praeger, 1976. Author of "The Underground Gourmet," a column in *San Francisco Examiner* three times a week, 1975—. Editor for the President's Appalachian Regional Commission, for California Coastal Commission, and for San Francisco Charter Revision Committee.

* * *

REARDON, John J(oseph) 1926-

PERSONAL: Born October 16, 1926, in Waterbury, Conn.; son of John L. and Margaret (Malone) Reardon; married Joan Biederstedt (a professor of English), June 6, 1964. *Education:* College of the Holy Cross, B.S., 1947; Trinity College, Hartford, Conn., M.A., 1950; Georgetown University, Ph.D., 1953. *Home:* 140 East Franklin Pl., Lake Forest, Ill. 60045. *Office:* Department of History, Loyola University, 820 North Michigan Ave., Chicago, Ill. 60611.

CAREER: Carroll College, Helena, Mont., assistant professor of history and chairman of department, 1953-54; Loyola University, Chicago, Ill., instructor, 1954-57, assistant professor, 1957-72, associate professor, 1972-74; professor of history, 1974—. *Member:* Institute of Early American History and Culture, American Historical Association, Organization of American Historians, Lake Forest-Lake Bluff Historical Society (charter member). *Awards, honors:* Danforth Foundation associate; Lucius N. Littauer Foundation research grant, 1961-62.

WRITINGS: Edmund Randolph: A Biography, Macmillan, 1975. Contributor to *American People's Encyclopedia* and to history magazines. Editorial adviser to Laidlaw Brothers; editorial consultant to *Historian.*

WORK IN PROGRESS: One Who Presided: A Biography of Peyton Randolph, for Colonial Williamsburg Foundation.

AVOCATIONAL INTERESTS: Hiking, gardening, swimming.

* * *

RECK, W(aldo) Emerson 1903-

PERSONAL: Born December 28, 1903, in Greenville, Ohio; son of Samuel Harvey (a farmer) and Effie D. (Arnett) Reck; married Hazel Winifred January, September 7, 1926; children: Phyllis (Mrs. Louis E. Welch, Jr.), Elizabeth Ann (Mrs. Gabriel J. Lada). *Education:* Wittenberg University, A.B. (cum laude), 1926; University of Iowa, M.A., 1946. *Religion:* Lutheran. *Home:* 61 Hedgely Rd., Springfield, Ohio 45506.

CAREER: Springfield News, Springfield, Ohio, reporter, 1922-26; Midland College, Fremont, Neb., publicity director, 1926-28, director of public relations and assistant professor of journalism, 1928-40; Colgate University, Hamilton, N.Y., director of public relations, 1940-48; Wittenberg University, Springfield, Ohio, vice-president, 1948-70, vice-president emeritus, 1970—; Cumerford Corp., Fort Lauderdale, Fla., public relations specialist, 1970—. Managing editor of *Fremont Morning Guide,* 1939; visiting lecturer at State University of Iowa, summers, 1941-42, and University of Wyoming, summer, 1948; co-director of Seminar on Public Relations for Higher Education at Syracuse University, summers, 1944-46. Member of national Lutheran Edu-

cational Conference; member of Commission on Church Papers of United Lutheran Church, 1951-62, committee member of department of press, radio, and television, 1955-60; member of board of publication of Lutheran Church in America, 1962-72, committee member of Office of Communication, 1972—; chairman of public relations committee of Council of Protestant Colleges and Universities, 1961-65. Public relations consultant, 1970—.

MEMBER: American College Public Relations Association (vice-president, 1936-38; president, 1940-41), Lutheran College Public Relations Association (president, 1951-53), Public Relations Society of America (member of national judicial council, 1952), School Public Relations Association, American Association of University Professors, Ohio Public Relations Officers (president, 1954-55), Sigma Delta Chi, Pi Delta Epsilon, Delta Sigma Phi, Blue Key, Elbeetian Legion. *Awards, honors:* Distinguished service award from American College Public Relations Association, 1942, additional awards for his interpretation of higher education, 1944, 1947; LL.D. from Midland College, 1949.

WRITINGS: Public Relations: A Program for Colleges and Universities, Harper, 1966; *College Publicity Manual,* Harper, 1948; (contributor) P. F. Valentine, editor, *American College,* Philosophical Society, 1949; (contributor) Philip Lesly, editor, *Public Relations Handbook,* Prentice-Hall, 1950, 3rd edition, 1976; *American College Public Relations Association's First Fifty Years: 1917-1967,* American College Public Relations Association, 1967; *The Changing World of College Relations,* American College Public Relations Association, 1975. Writer of a column on the American Revolution in *Springfield Sun,* 1974—. Contributor to professional and popular magazines, and to newspapers.

WORK IN PROGRESS: Revising *Public Relations: A Program for Colleges and Universities;* research on the American Revolution, Abraham Lincoln, the Civil War, and other historical subjects.

* * *

REDDICK, L(awrence) D(unbar) 1910-

PERSONAL: Born March 3, 1910, in Jacksonville, Fla.; son of Amos and Fannie (Ethridge) Reddick; married Ella Ruth Thomas, December 25, 1938. *Education:* Fisk University, A.B. (magna cum laude), 1932, M.A., 1933; University of Chicago, Ph.D., 1939. *Home:* 8029 Stenton Ave., Philadelphia, Pa. 19150. *Office:* Department of History, Temple University, Philadelphia, Pa. 19122.

CAREER: Kentucky State College (now University), Frankfort, assistant professor of history, 1933-35; Dillard University, New Orleans, La., associate professor of history, 1935-38; New York Public Library, New York, N.Y., curator of Schomberg Collection, 1939-48; University of Atlanta, Atlanta, Ga., professor of history and chief librarian, Trevor Arnett Library, 1948-55; Alabama State College (now University), Montgomery, professor of history and chairman of department, 1956-60; Coppin State College, Baltimore, Md., professor of history, 1960-69; Opportunities Industrialization Center Institute, Washington, D.C., director, 1966-68, coordinator of national policies and programs, 1968-70; Temple University, Philadelphia, Pa., adjunct professor, 1968-70, professor of Afro-American history, 1970—. Part-time lecturer, City College (now of the City University of New York), 1941-48; and New School for Social Research, 1946-48.

MEMBER: American Historical Association, American

Library Association, Association for the Study of Negro Life and History, American Teachers Association, Southern Historical Association, Phi Beta Sigma. *Awards, honors:* Julius Rosenwald fellow, 1939.

WRITINGS: (With Sherman Savage) *Our Cause Speeds On,* Fuller Press, 1957; *Crusader Without Violence: A Biography of Martin Luther King, Jr.,* Harper, 1959; (with others) *The Southerner as American,* University of North Carolina Press, 1960; (with Agnes McCarthy) *Worth Fighting For: The History of the Negro in the United States During the Civil War and Reconstruction,* Doubleday, 1965; *To Improve Teachers for Inner-City Schools,* Coppin State College, 1967; *The Essence of OIC: Manpower Training for Disadvantaged Adults,* Opportunities Industrialization Center, 1971. Also author of *Library Sources for Negro Studies,* and *Our Colleges and the Industrialization of the South.* Contributor to professional journals and to *Nation* and *New Republic.* Member of editorial board of *Journal of Negro History,* 1937-39, 1952—; special editor of *Journal of Educational Sociology,* 1944-45.

SIDELIGHTS: Reddick has traveled in Europe, Africa, and the West Indies. In 1959, he took a six week tour of India with the subject of his biography, Martin Luther King, Jr.

*   *   *

REDDY, Michael   1933-

PERSONAL: Born June 14, 1933, in England; son of Joseph (a clerical officer) and Ellen (Hardman) Reddy. *Education:* University of Manchester, B.A. (honors), 1954; Heythrop College, Oxford, Lic.Theol., 1966; Ohio State University, Ph.D., 1971. *Home:* 40 Staveley Rd., Dunstable, Bedfordshire, England.

CAREER: Private practice in psychotherapy in Dunstable, England, 1966—. *Member:* British Psychological Society, Psychology and Psychotherapy Association, Institute of Transactional Analysis (chairman, 1975-76), American Psychological Association.

WRITINGS: Stop the Church, Liguorian Press, 1971.

WORK IN PROGRESS: Transactional Analysis, completion expected in 1977.

SIDELIGHTS: Reddy writes that he is "first and foremost a therapist, with a passionate interest in finding out what that means . . . it means being an artisan and a craftsman rather than a master or a guru." He has traveled internationally and "values privacy above all."

*   *   *

REED, Louis S(chultz)   1902-1975

October 17, 1902—December 6, 1975; American medical economist, educator, and author. Obituaries: *Washington Post,* December 8, 1975.

*   *   *

REED, (Fred) Mort(on)   1912-

PERSONAL: Born September 27, 1912, in Chicago, Ill.; son of Fred Earl (a businessman) and Lucy Temple (Morton) Reed; married Betty N. Franks (a nurse), October 15, 1939; children: Safrona Francine. *Education:* Attended Commercial Art Academy, Cincinnati, Ohio. *Politics:* Republican. *Religion:* Protestant. *Home and office:* 1572 Bellevue Dr., Wooster, Ohio 44691. *Agent:* Toni Mendez, Inc., 140 East 56th St., New York, N.Y. 10022.

CAREER: Free-lance designer, 1935-46; U.S. Steel Fabricators, Inc., Wooster, Ohio, designer, 1946-50; Gerstenslager Co., Wooster, Ohio, writer and illustrator, 1950-60; Rubbermaid, Inc., Wooster, Ohio, product planner, 1960-61; *Coin World* (magazine), Sidney, Ohio, illustrator, 1962—. Member of U.S. Assay Commission, 1974-75. *Military service:* U.S. Navy, 1931-35, 1942. *Member:* American Numismatic Association (member of board of governors, 1975-77), Numismatic Literary Guild. *Awards, honors:* Award from Numismatic Literary Guild, 1973, for best column "Coinology."

WRITINGS: Odd and Curious (monies of the world), Fisher Publishing, 1963; *Complete Encyclopedia of U.S. Coins,* Cowles, 1969, revised edition, 1970; *Encyclopedia of U.S. Coins,* Regnery, 1972, revised edition, 1972; *Coins: An Investors and Collectors Guide,* Regnery, 1973. Author of "Money Clips," a coin column for Newspaper Enterprise Association, 1966-75.

WORK IN PROGRESS: Illustrated History of U.S. Coins; Coinology.

SIDELIGHTS: Reed writes: "Counterfeiting coins and currency is a wide spread practice in the world and one that directly affects the coin collecting industry. I have been extremely interested in this form of illegal reproduction and designing new ways of detecting fake and unlawful coins has played a major role in my books as well as my newspaper columns."

*   *   *

REEDY, William A.   1916(?)-1975

1916(?)—December 15, 1975; American journal editor and writer on photography. Obituaries: *New York Times,* December 17, 1975.

*   *   *

REEMS, Harry   1947-

PERSONAL: Name originally Herbert Streicher; born August 27, 1947, in New York, N.Y.; son of Rose (Stienberg) Streicher. *Education:* Attended University of Pittsburgh, 1965-66. *Politics:* "People's Liberation." *Residence:* New York, N.Y. *Agent:* Janice S. Morgan, 250 West 57th St., New York, N.Y. 10019. *Office:* 330 West 45th St., #J, New York, N.Y. 10036.

CAREER: Actor; acting career includes two seasons with National Shakespeare Co., one season, Cafe La Mama, and Off-Broadway shows with New York Theatre Ensemble, and at Cooper Square Arts Theatre; has also acted in night clubs, made television commercials and public appearances. Film maker; has been cameraman, producer, sound engineer, lighting engineer, director, and editor, five years. Lectures on film making and sociology at colleges. *Military service:* U.S. Marine Corps, 1966-68. *Member:* Screen Actors Guild, Actors Equity Association, American Guild of Variety Artists.

WRITINGS: Here Comes Harry Reems, Pinnacle Books, 1975.

WORK IN PROGRESS: A novel.

SIDELIGHTS: Harry Reems says he was the male star in nine of the eleven pornographic films which grossed in excess of a million dollars; he feels he is best known for his roles as the doctor in "Deep Throat" and the devil in "The Devil and Miss Jones." Reems plans to expand the pornographic scene to merge with legitimate major studios. He says he has "gained approval of Screen Actors Guild to sanction films of a pornographic rating."

BIOGRAPHICAL/CRITICAL SOURCES: Screen World, 1972, 1973, 1974, 1975; *Playboy,* August, 1973; *Erotic Cinema,* January, 1974; Steven Zito, *Sinema,* Praeger, 1975; *Viva,* October, 1975.

* * *

REEVES, Earl J(ames, Jr.) 1933-

PERSONAL: Born March 16, 1933, in Muskogee, Okla.; son of Earl James (a clergyman) and Bernice (Jordan) Reeves; married Wilma Gail Reece (a public school employee), August 30, 1959; children: Barbara, Gregory, Carolyn. *Education:* Wichita State University, B.A., 1954, M.A., 1959; University of Kansas, Ph.D., 1962. *Religion:* Presbyterian. *Home:* 5212 South 76th East Ave., Tulsa, Okla. 74145. *Office:* Department of Urban Studies, University of Tulsa, 600 South College, Tulsa, Okla. 74104.

CAREER: University of Kansas, Lawrence, instructor in political science, 1961-62; University of Nebraska, Omaha, assistant professor of political science, 1962-64; University of Missouri, St. Louis, associate professor of political science, 1964-70; University of Tulsa, Tulsa, Okla., associate professor, 1970-72, professor of political science, 1972—, director of urban studies, 1970—. Associate director of Center for Community and Metropolitan Studies, 1965-70. Vice-president of City Council of Berkeley, Mo., 1966-70; consultant to Tulsa area Agency on Aging, 1973—, and to Leadership of Tulsa, 1973—; member of Community Relations Commission of Tulsa, 1971-75, chairperson, 1975. *Military service:* U.S. Air Force, 1954-58. U.S. Air Force Reserve, 1958-72. *Member:* American Political Science Association, American Society for Public Administration, Council of University Institutes of Urban Affairs, Kiwanis International.

WRITINGS: (Contributor) Richard Stauber, editor, *Approaches to the Study of Urbanization,* University Press of Kansas, 1964; (with William Rivers, William Blankenburg, and Kenneth Stark) *Back-Talk: Press Councils in America,* Canfield Press, 1972; (contributor) Robert Clouse, Robert Linder, and Richard Pirard, editors, *The Cross and the Flag,* Creation House, 1972. Contributor to professional journals. Research editor of *Midwest Review of Public Administration.*

WORK IN PROGRESS: With Anthony Filipovitch, *Urban Community,* for Gale Information Guide Library series; conducting research and making videotapes on aging and retirement planning.

* * *

REEVES, Gene (Arthur) 1933-

PERSONAL: Born April 2, 1933, in Franklin, N.H.; son of Eugene Victor and Parmelie (Twombly) Reeves; married Joan D. Shaw, 1957; children: Eva, Anna. *Education:* University of New Hampshire, B.A., 1956; Boston University, S.T.B., 1959; Emory University, Ph.D., 1963. *Home:* 430 Fairfield Pike, Yellow Springs, Ohio 45387. *Office:* Office of Academic Dean, Wilberforce University, Wilberforce, Ohio 45384.

CAREER: Tufts University, Medford, Mass., assistant professor of philosophy and theology, 1962-67; Wilberforce University, Wilberforce, Ohio, professor of philosophy, 1967—, chairman of department, 1967-71, chairman of Division of Humanities, 1971-72, associate academic dean,

1972—. Part-time professor at Antioch College, 1969, 1970; group social worker at Daniel Webster Home for Children, 1956-57; minister at Unitarian-Universalist churches in Atlanta, Georgia, 1961-62, and Dayton, Ohio, 1969—. Served on Massachusetts Council of Churches' department of social responsibility; founder of Somerville Seminar on Social Issues; founder and first president of Somerville Committee for Racial Understanding; helped organize Boston Area Faculty Group on Public Issues. *Military service:* U.S. Army Reserve, Adjutant General's Corps, 1956-65.

MEMBER: American Association for Higher Education, American Philosophical Association, Metaphysical Society of America, Society for the Study of Process Philosophies, Society for Philosophy and Public Policy, American Academy of Religion, Society for the Scientific Study of Religion, American Academy for Political and Social Science, American Association of University Professors, American Civil Liberties Union, National Association for the Advancement of Colored People, National Committee for a Sane Nuclear Policy, United World Federalists, Americans for Democratic Action (chapter vice-chairman), Fellowship of Reconciliation, Zero Population Growth (member of national board; president of local chapter), United Nations Association, Congress on Population and Environment, Ohio Philosophical Association. *Awards, honors:* Tufts University research fellowship, 1967.

WRITINGS: (Editor with Delwin Brown and Ralph E. James, Jr., and contributor) *Process Philosophy and Christian Thought,* Bobbs-Merrill, 1971; (contributor) P. A. Schilpp, editor, *The Philosophy of Gabriel Marcel,* Open Court, in press. Contributor to theology and philosophy journals. Editor of *Crane Review,* 1965-67.

WORK IN PROGRESS: Research on A. N. Whitehead's metaphysics, on science and ethics related to the is/ought question, on relationships between international poverty and development and the population-environment crisis, and on utopian thought.

* * *

REICH, Steve 1936-

PERSONAL: Born October 3, 1936, in New York, N.Y. *Education:* Cornell University, B.A. (with honors), 1957; Juilliard School of Music, graduate study, 1958-61; Mills College, M.A., 1963; further graduate study at University of Ghana, 1970, and American Society for Eastern Arts, summers, 1973-74. *Religion:* Jewish. *Home:* 16 Warren St., New York, N.Y. 10007.

CAREER: Composer and performer in San Francisco, Calif., 1963-65; composer and performer in his own music ensemble in New York, N.Y., 1965—, including Carnegie Hall, Town Hall, and Museum of Modern Art. Collaborated on music and dance concerts throughout Europe and at New York University, 1972-73. *Awards, honors:* National Endowment for the Arts grant, 1974; New York State Council on the Arts grant, 1974.

WRITINGS: Writings about Music (essays), New York University Press, 1974. His recorded compositions include "Come Out," Odyssey, 1967; "It's Gonna Rain" and "Violin Phase," Columbia Records, 1969; "Four Organs," Angel Records, 1973; "Drumming," "Six Pianos," "Music for Mallet Instruments, Voices, and Organ," Deutsche Grammophon, 1974. Other compositions include "Phase Patterns," "Clapping Music," and "Music for Pieces of Wood."

WORK IN PROGRESS: Composing "Music for Eighteen Musicians."

SIDELIGHTS: During the summer of 1970, Reich studied drumming with a master drummer of the Ewe tribe at the Institute for African Studies in Ghana. During the summers of 1973-74 he studied Balinese Gamelan Semar Pegulingan, a specialized tuned percussion music.

BIOGRAPHICAL/CRITICAL SOURCES: Musical Times, March, 1971; Artforum, May, 1972.

*   *   *

REICHARD, Gary Warren 1943-

PERSONAL: Born November 23, 1943, in Philadelphia, Pa.; son of David Carl (a salesman) and Gabrielle (Doane) Reichard; married Marcia Ann King (a research specialist), August 7, 1965; children: Jennifer Doane, James Jeffrey. Education: College of Wooster, B.A., 1965; Vanderbilt University, M.A., 1966; Cornell University, Ph.D., 1971. Home: 188 East Tulane Rd., Columbus, Ohio 43202. Office: Department of History, Ohio State University, Columbus, Ohio 43210.

CAREER: College of Wooster, Wooster, Ohio, instructor in history, 1967-69; Ohio State University, Columbus, assistant professor of history, 1971—. Member: American Historical Association, Organization of American Historians, Southern Historical Association, Phi Beta Kappa. Awards, honors: Danforth associate, 1974.

WRITINGS: The Reaffirmation of Republicanism: Eisenhower and the Eighty-Third Congress, University of Tennessee Press, 1975. Contributor of articles and reviews to history journals.

WORK IN PROGRESS: Executive-Congressional and Partisan Interaction Over Foreign Policy-Making: 1953-1961; a college-level American history textbook, with Joan Gunderson, H. Viscount Nelson, Ronald Satz, and Edmund White.

*   *   *

REICHL, Ruth 1948-

PERSONAL: Born January 16, 1948, in New York, N.Y.; daughter of Ernst (a book designer) and Miriam (a musicologist; maiden name, Brudno) Reichl; married Douglas Hollis (an artist and sculptor), September 5, 1970. Education: University of Michigan, B.A. (with honors), 1968, M.A., 1970. Home and office: 1912 Channing Way, Berkeley, Calif. 94704.

CAREER: Ernst Reichl Associates, New York, N.Y., book designer, 1970-73; Glass Art (magazine), Berkeley, Calif., art director, 1973; free-lance book designer, 1973—. Collective member and owner of Swallow Restaurant, 1974—.

WRITINGS: Mmmmm: A Feastiary (cookbook), Holt, 1972.

WORK IN PROGRESS: Tough Tuffett, a novel about a woman who has everything and can't figure out what to do with it; Liberal Guilt, another novel.

SIDELIGHTS: Ruth Reichl writes: "When I wrote Mmmmm there seemed to be very little straightforward discussion of food. Cookbooks either made a sacred business out of cooking, or treated food as a nasty but necessary human need which should be disposed of as efficiently, and with as little mess, as possible. I thought the subject deserved both passion and honesty. Cooking, like anything else, can be wonderful and still sometimes you don't want to be bothered."

*   *   *

REID, Jan 1945-

PERSONAL: Born March 18, 1945, in Abilene, Tex.; son of Charles Cleon (a refinery worker) and Elsie (Shelton) Reid. Education: Midwestern University, B.A., 1968; University of Texas, M.A., 1972. Politics: "Disgruntled and dismayed." Religion: "Fallen fundamentalist." Home: 232 Dallas, New Braunfels, Tex. 78130.

CAREER: Employers Casualty Co., Dallas, Tex., insurance underwriter, 1968-70; reporter, Mt. Pleasant Tribune, Mt. Pleasant, Tex., and New Braunfels Herald, New Braunfels, Tex., 1972-75; writer, 1972—. Military service: U.S. Marine Corps Reserve, 1964-70.

WRITINGS: The Improbable Rise of Redneck Rock (journalism), Heidelberg Publishers, 1974. Contributing editor of Texas Monthly.

WORK IN PROGRESS: Deerinwater, the first of a trilogy of Texas-based novels, completion expected in 1977.

SIDELIGHTS: Reid writes: "I am most interested in writing fiction, though it is a far more difficult form for me than journalism, which I will continue to pursue on a limited basis. I am intrigued by the forces of history, but not very much by academic historians; I might like to try my hand at biography. I wish I were more proficient in Spanish, for language is the real border between the two American civilizations, not the Rio Grande."

*   *   *

REID, Jim 1929-

PERSONAL: Born July 8, 1929, in St. Louis, Mo.; son of Joseph Edward (a pipefitter) and Grace (McArthur) Reid; married Janice Radford (a teacher), June 3, 1950; children: Jim, Jr., Joseph, Judy, Jean, Janet, Janelle. Education: Attended Hannibal LaGrange College, 1955-56; Grand Canyon College, B.A., 1959; Midwestern Baptist Seminary, M.Div., 1962. Home: 229 West Basic Rd., Henderson, Nev. 89015. Office: Las Vegas Resort Chaplaincy, 120 Flamingo Rd., Las Vegas, Nev. 89114.

CAREER: Auto parts salesman in St. Louis, Mo., 1945-56; ordained minister of Baptist Church, 1962; pastor in Willcox, Ariz., 1962-65, and Henderson, Nev., 1965-70; Las Vegas Resort Chaplaincy, Las Vegas, Nev., chaplain to Las Vegas Strip, 1970—. Military service: U.S. Marine Corps Reserve, active duty, 1950-53; served in Korea; became sergeant.

WRITINGS: Praising God on the Las Vegas Strip, Zondervan, 1975. Contributor to Proclaim.

WORK IN PROGRESS: Opening Acts on the Las Vegas Strip.

BIOGRAPHICAL/CRITICAL SOURCES: Home Mission, February, 1971; New York Times, October 7, 1973; World Mission Journal, February, 1974; Los Angeles Times, March 24, 1974; Wall Street Journal, May 21, 1974; Kansas City Star, September 8, 1974; Las Vegas Review Journal, October 6, 1974; St. Louis Globe Democrat, September 21, 1975; National Enquirer, March 2, 1976; Galaxy (magazine), June, 1976.

*   *   *

REILLY, Judith G(ladding) 1935-

PERSONAL: Born November 28, 1935, in Middletown,

Conn.; daughter of G. Roger (a chemist and engineer) and Emma (Rutty) Gladding; married James A. Reilly (an optical research physicist), September 16, 1958; children: Thomas E. *Education:* Clark University, A.B., 1958, A.M., 1960. *Home:* 40 Loring St., Auburn, Mass. 01501. *Office:* Department of Physical Science, Quinsigamond Community College, 670 West Boylston St., Worcester, Mass. 01606.

CAREER: Reed Plastics, Worcester, Mass., consultant, 1958-59; Assumption Preparatory School, Worcester, Mass., teacher of physics, 1963; Quinsigamond Community College, Worcester, Mass., instructor, 1963-65, assistant professor, 1965-68, associate professor, 1968-72, professor of physical science, 1972—. Instructor at Clark University's Evening College, 1963—. *Member:* Sigma Pi Sigma, Alpha Sigma Lambda. *Awards, honors:* Outstanding teacher of the year awards, 1971, 1975.

WRITINGS: (With Adrian Vander Pyl) *Physical Science: An Interrelated Course,* with study guide, Addison-Wesley, 1970.

SIDELIGHTS: Judith Reilly writes that she is "primarily interested in teaching physics and the other sciences to non-science majors. It is my conviction that everyone must have a rudimentary understanding of the sciences to make rational decisions in the modern world. . . ."

*   *   *

REINER, William B(uck)   1910-1976

May 23, 1910—January 24, 1976; American educator, and author of juveniles and books on education. Obituaries: *New York Times,* January 26, 1976. (See index for previous *CA* sketch)

*   *   *

REISS, Alvin   1932-

PERSONAL: Born October 31, 1932, in Fort Still, Okla.; son of Clarence Gustav Alvin and Mabel (Craig) Reiss; married Audrey Spencer, September 1, 1951 (divorced, 1974); children: Belinda Janette, Karen Mercedes. *Education:* Attended University of Oregon, 1950-51, and Southern Oregon College, 1968-69. *Home:* 435 Holly St. #10, Ashland, Ore. 97520. *Office: Medford Mail Tribune,* 33 North Fir St., Medford, Ore. 97501.

CAREER: Union Pacific Railroad, traffic clerk in Eugene, Ore., 1952-55, office manager in Medford, Ore., 1955-66; KBOY-FM Radio, Medford, announcer and programmer, 1961-66, program director, 1966-69; *Medford Mail Tribune,* Medford, staff writer covering film and drama, 1969—. KYJC Radio, Medford, news director, 1969-73, producer and writer of public affairs program, "Insight," 1971-73; radio broadcast coordinator, Oregon Shakespearean Festival, 1969. *Member:* Society of Professional Journalists, Poetry Society of America, Sigma Delta Chi. *Awards, honors:* Birmingham (Ala.) Festival of the Arts, first award for television drama, 1963, for "Evidence for the Defense," fourth award, 1964, for "Morrison's Ledger"; first prize from Western States Playwriting Competition, 1965, for "The Smallest Giant"; John Masefield Memorial Award from Poetry Society of America, 1970.

WRITINGS: "The Smallest Giant" (three-act play), first produced in Eugene, Ore., at Very Little Theatre, May, 1965.

Screenplays: "Evidence for the Defense," ETV (Birmingham, Ala.), 1963; "Morrison's Ledger," Birmingham, Ala.

Festival, 1964; "Boots Don't Make the Cowboy" (based on a story by Larry Lansburgh and William Anderson), Larry Lansburgh Films, 1972.

Also author of plays, "The Great American Oil Dig" (three-act), and "River Children" (two-act), as yet neither published nor produced. Work represented in *The Diamond Anthology,* edited by Charles Angoff and others, A. S. Barnes for the Poetry Society of America, 1971. Contributor to periodicals, including *Southern Oregon Review, Mississippi Valley Review, Escapade, McCall's,* and *Oregonian* (newspaper).

WORK IN PROGRESS: A novel, *The Passing Joy;* a book of short stories, *How Freddie Krauss Improved His Luck When He Departed by Way of the Chimney, and Other Stories;* a drama, "From the Memoirs of Soldier Stone," and a comedy; "The Vulcan Factor", for television; poems, short stories, and newsfeatures.

AVOCATIONAL INTERESTS: Still photography.

*   *   *

REITMEISTER, Louis Aaron   1903-1975

February 2, 1903—August 20, 1975; American administrator, lecturer, and author of works on philosophy and related topics. Obituaries: *AB Bookman's Weekly,* September 8, 1975. (See index for previous *CA* sketch)

*   *   *

RENDELL, Joan

PERSONAL: Born in Launceston, Cornwall, England; daughter of Gervase (a senior civil servant) and Maud (Culley) Rendell. *Education:* Attended Ealing School of Art. *Religion:* Church of England. *Home:* Tremarsh, Launceston, Cornwall, England. *Agent:* Bolt & Watson, 8 Storey's Gate, London S.W.1, England.

CAREER: Writer, broadcaster, lecturer, and craftswoman. Free-lance contributor to programs produced by British Broadcasting Corp. and Independent Television Authority. Free-lance correspondent for *Western Morning News* and *Cornish and Devon Post.* Television and radio monitor for Tellesc Monitors Ltd., London, England, 1965-75. Chairman of regional community groups committee of National Savings Movement; Launceston Floral Art Group, life member, and chairman, 1965-69, 1975—; member of regional Gas Consumer's Council, 1972-75. *Member:* Werrington Conservative Association (vice-chairman), Launceston Old Cornwall Society, Plymouth Mineral & Mining Club. *Awards, honors:* Member of Order of the British Empire.

WRITINGS: (Contributor) Harold K. Starke, editor, *Young Collector's Book,* Burke, 1953; *Collecting Matchbox Labels,* Arco, 1963; *Flower Arrangement with a Marine Theme,* David & Charles, 1967; *Matchbox Labels,* David & Charles, 1968; *Collecting Natural Objects,* David & Charles, 1972, Castle Books, 1973; *Collecting Out of Doors,* Routledge & Kegan Paul, in press; *Your Book of Corn Dollies,* Faber, in press. Contributor to magazines and regional newspapers in Great Britain. Honorary editor of British Matchbox Label & Booklet Society.

WORK IN PROGRESS: Country Crafts, publication by Routledge & Kegan Paul expected in 1977.

AVOCATIONAL INTERESTS: Collecting sand pictures and commemorative mugs, photography, travel (Europe, United States, Africa, Middle East, Mexico).

RENNERT, Maggie   1922-
(Maggie Rennert Nunley)

PERSONAL: Born February 11, 1922, in New York; widowed; children: two children; three step-children. *Education:* Studied journalism and political science. *Home:* Rehov Hagamal 5/5, Shikun Hay-le-deugma, Beer-Sheva, Israel; c/o Don Preston, 97 Walnut St., Blauvelt, N.Y. 07193.

CAREER: Editor for National Education Association, Van Leer Foundation, Research Analysis Corp., and for various trade magazines; worked as reporter for a Washington news service; novelist, 1968—. Visiting lecturer, Tufts University Experimental College.

WRITINGS: A Moment in Camelot (novel), Geis, 1968; *Circle of Death* (mystery novel), Prentice-Hall, 1974; *Operation Alcestic* (mystery novel), Prentice-Hall, in press. Contributor to poetry to *Saturday Review* and other magazines since 1956; contributor of book reviews to *Saturday Review, Washington Post, Boston Globe,* and other newspapers. Book review columnist for *New York Herald Tribune,* 1964-66.

WORK IN PROGRESS: A journal of personal experiences in Israel; a third mystery novel for Prentice-Hall; a novel; poems.

SIDELIGHTS: Maggie Rennert wrote: "One of my children observed once (rather vexedly) that what I always seem to want to do most is whatever I haven't done before. Fair enough. (Except that I do do a thing over and over until I'm convinced that I've got the hang of it. Hence, the years and years of poems.) I dislike theorizing and hold a low opinion of the academic world. . . . In 1961, a poetry magazine ran a piece about me that called me the 'authentic voice of American poetry.' I couldn't write for six months afterward, and I'm scared even to *think* about it again."

*   *   *

RESNICK, Rose

PERSONAL: Born in New York, N.Y. *Education:* Hunter College (now of the City University of New York), B.A., 1932; University of California, Berkeley, M.A. (secondary education), 1943; San Francisco State College (now University), M.A. (special education), 1960; also studied at Manhattan School of Music, Fountainbleu Conservatory of Music, and San Francisco Conservatory of Music. *Office:* California League for the Handicapped, 1299 Bush St., San Francisco, Calif. 94109.

CAREER: San Francisco Center for the Blind (first local center for the blind), San Francisco, Calif., organizer, 1942, director, 1958; conducted lecture and piano tour in western states, 1943; worked at Enchanted Hills Camp, 1943-47; Enchanted Hills Foundation, founder and executive director, 1947-58; San Francisco Lighthouse for the Blind, San Francisco, Calif., director of rehabilitation program, 1958-60; California League for the Handicapped, San Francisco, founder and executive director, 1961—. Founded the first year-round recreational and camping facility for blind children in Los Angeles, Calif., 1949; teacher of course in understanding blindness for adult education program in San Francisco public schools, 1956.

MEMBER: Pilot International, Bay Area Personnel Women, Pi Lambda Theta, Mu Phi Epsilon, Phi Mu. *Awards, honors:* Presidential citation for meritorious service to the handicapped, 1960; Community service award from Business and Professional Women's Club of San Francisco, 1971; Hannah G. Solomon Award for community service from National Council for Jewish Women, 1973; outstanding achievement award from California Federation of Women's Clubs, 1973; named Professional Woman of the Year by Pilot International, Sears Roebuck and President's Committee on Employment of the Handicapped, 1974.

WRITINGS: Sun and Shadow: The Autobiography of a Woman Who Happens to Be Blind, Atheneum, 1975. Contributor to nursing and education journals.

SIDELIGHTS: Rose Resnick lost her sight at the age of two. Her interest in the field of social welfare began with her founding the first camp in the West for blind children, patterned on those for seeing boys and girls. She was influential in appealing to the California legislature for admission of blind children to the public schools and was successful in introducing physical education for blind children in San Francisco schools.

*   *   *

RESTAK, Richard M(artin)   1942-

PERSONAL: Born February 4, 1942, in Wilmington, Del.; son of Lewis J. (a physician) and Alice (Hynes) Restak; married Carolyn Serbent, October 12, 1968; children: Jennifer, Alison. *Education:* Gettysburg College, A.B., 1962; Georgetown University, M.D., 1966. *Home:* 3113 38th St. N.W., Washington, D.C. 20016. *Agent:* David Obst, P.O. Box 11004, Washington, D.C.

CAREER: St. Vincent's Hospital, New York, N.Y., intern, 1966-67; Mount Sinai Hospital, New York, N.Y., psychiatric resident, 1967-68; Georgetown University Hospital, Washington, D.C., psychiatric resident, 1968-69; George Washington University Hospital, Washington, D.C., resident in neurology, 1970-73; neurologist and neuropsychiatrist in Washington, D.C., 1973—. Clinical instructor at Georgetown University, 1975—; visiting lecturer at Kenyon College, Wright State Medical School, University of Kentucky, and Ohio State University. Consultant to British Council for Science and Society, and Kennedy Institute for the Study of Human Reproduction and Bioethics.

WRITINGS: Premeditated Man: The Bioethics and Control of Future Human Life, Viking, 1975. Contributor of articles and reviews to psychology journals and to newspapers and magazines, including *Saturday Review, New York Times,* and *Washington Post.*

WORK IN PROGRESS: A series of profiles of contemporary scientists, for magazine publication.

SIDELIGHTS: Restak writes: "The issues of science are just too important to be decided by scientists alone but must be democratized so that the general public can decide about them. The first step toward decision must be information. . . . My writing efforts have been dedicated to . . . substituting a clearly written and hopefully interesting prose style for the ponderous pomposity that presently makes up so much of contemporary science writing. . . . My writing ambitions are not all medical (I hope one day to do a biography of W. Somerset Maugham . . .) but at this point I think science, particularly biomedical science, forms the material out of which the eschatology of the latter part of the twentieth century will be constructed." *Avocational interests:* English literature.

REYNOLDS, Alan 1942-

PERSONAL: Born April 11, 1942, in Abilene, Tex.; son of Alan D. (an actor) and Rosine (a teacher; maiden name, McDougall) Reynolds; married Karen Kane, February 28, 1965; children: Melissa, John. *Education:* University of California, Los Angeles, B.A., 1965; graduate study at California State University, Sacramento, 1967-71. *Residence:* Morristown, N.J. *Office:* Argus Research Corp., 140 Broadway, New York, N.Y. 10005.

CAREER: J. C. Penney Co. (department stores), Sacramento, Calif., department manager, 1965-71; *National Review,* New York, N.Y., contributing editor, 1972-75; Argus Research Corp., New York, N.Y., economist, 1975—. *Member:* Mont Pelerin Society.

WRITINGS: The Balancing Act: Black Studies Revisited, Open Court, 1974. Contributor to professional journals and to *New York Times.* Contributing editor of *Reason,* 1973—; associate editor of *Alternative,* 1973—.

WORK IN PROGRESS: Research on welfare and poverty, and on price controls, with books expected to result.

SIDELIGHTS: Reynolds describes himself as a man "roughly associated with the 'Chicago School' of economics, and with a libertarian philosophic outlook tempered by the scientific method."

* * *

REZNIKOFF, Charles 1894-1976

August 31, 1894—January 22, 1976; American poet, editor, and author. Obituaries: *New York Times,* January 23, 1976. (See index for previous *CA* sketch)

* * *

RHODEHAMEL, Josephine DeWitt 1901-

PERSONAL: Born September 24, 1901, in Soda Springs, Idaho; daughter of Charles Curtis (a teacher) and Josephine (a teacher; maiden name, Condon) DeWitt; married Harry Ernest Rhodehamel (an accountant), July 5, 1941; children: Michele (Mrs. Thomas Russell Driscoll). *Education:* University of California, Berkeley, A.B., 1926, certificate of librarianship, 1931, M.A., 1939. *Politics:* Democrat. *Home:* 74 Granite St., Ashland, Ore. 97520.

CAREER: Mills College, Oakland, Calif., library assistant, 1921; Oakland Public Library, Oakland, Calif., substitute librarian, 1922-26, library assistant, 1926-28, bibliographical assistant, 1928-34, assistant reference librarian, 1934-50, head of history division and California Room, 1950-53; Tulare County Library, Visalia, Calif., reference librarian, 1953-63; writer, 1963—. *Member:* National Organization for Women, Oregon Shakespearean Festival Association, Tulare County Historical Society, Tudor Guild (Ashland, Ore.).

WRITINGS: The Black Man's Point of View, Oakland Acorn Club, 1930; *An Oakland Chronology,* Oakland Public Library, 1952; (with Raymund Francis Wood) *Ina Coolbrith: Librarian and Laureate of California,* Brigham Young University Press, 1973. Contributor to professional journals.

WORK IN PROGRESS: Two books for children, *Frontier Stories from Indiana to Idaho* and *Travels with Demmy the Trailer Cat.*

SIDELIGHTS: Josephine Rhodehamel was born in a little Mormon town on the old California and Oregon trails. Her parents were pioneer school teachers there. Early in her career, she met Ina Coolbrith, who was then in the last year of her life.

* * *

RIBAL, Joseph E(dward) 1931-

PERSONAL: Born September 28, 1931, in Oak Park, Ill.; son of Joseph Edward and Blanche (Vleek) Ribal; married Louise S. Bohman; children: Laura, David. *Education:* Received degrees from Northern Illinois University, 1952; University of Chicago, 1953; University of Southern California, 1962. *Office:* Division of Behavioral Sciences, El Camino College, El Camino, Calif. 90506.

CAREER: El Camino College, El Camino, Calif., professor of psychology, 1958—; private practice of psychology in Huntington Beach, Calif., 1963—. Consultant to Random House, Holt Rinehart & Winston, Glencoe Press, and other publishers. *Member:* American Psychological Association, American Sociological Association.

WRITINGS: Learning Sex Roles: American and Scandinavian Contrasts, Harper, 1973.

WORK IN PROGRESS: Research on sex; developing audio-visual materials.

* * *

RICCARDS, Michael P(atrick) 1944-

PERSONAL: Born October 2, 1944, in Elizabeth, N.J.; son of Patrick P. (an accountant) and Margaret (Finelli) Riccards; married Barbara Dunlop, June 6, 1970; children: Patrick Richard. *Education:* Rutgers University, B.A., 1966, M.A., 1967, M.Phil., 1969, Ph.D., 1970. *Office:* Department of Political Science, State University of New York College at Buffalo, 1300 Elmwood Ave., Buffalo, N.Y. 14222.

CAREER: Special assistant to chancellor of higher education in New Jersey, 1969-70; State University of New York College at Buffalo, assistant professor, 1970-73, associate professor of political science, 1973—, chairman of department, 1974—. *Military service:* U.S. Army National Guard, 1967-73. *Awards, honors:* Fulbright fellowship, Japan, 1973; research fellowship from Henry L. Huntington Library, 1974.

WRITINGS: The Making of the American Citizenry: An Introduction to Political Socialization, Crowell, 1973; (editor with Philip Abbott) *Reflections on American Political Thought: From Past to Present,* Crowell, 1973. Also author of play, "Lincoln," as yet neither published nor produced.

WORK IN PROGRESS: A History of the American Presidency.

* * *

RICE, James 1934-

PERSONAL: Born February 10, 1934, in Coleman, Tex.; son of James W. (a railroad worker) and Mary (Jennings) Rice; married Martha Oustad (a secretary/editor), June 4, 1954; children: Zel, Maria, Lyn, Patti, Jason. *Education:* University of Texas, B.F.A., 1959; Howard Payne College, M.Ed., 1960. *Address:* P.O. Box 630, Loranger, La. 70446. *Agent:* Toni Mendez, 140 East 56th St., New York, N.Y. 10022.

CAREER: Teacher of art and music in public schools of Kingsville, Tex., Hampton, Va., and the Canal Zone, 1959-64; Southeastern Louisiana University, Hammond, assistant professor of art, 1964-66; Louisiana State University, Baton Rouge, assistant professor of art, 1967-68; Southeastern Louisiana University, assistant professor of art, 1969-75; author and illustrator, 1973—. *Military service:* U.S. Army, 1955-56.

WRITINGS—Self-illustrated books for children: *Gaston the Green-Nosed Alligator*, Pelican, 1974; *Lyn and the Fuzzy*, Pelican, 1975; *Cajun Alphabet*, Pelican, in press; *Gaston Goes to the Mardi Gras*, Pelican, in press.

Illustrator: J. B. Kling, *Cajun Night before Christmas*, Pelican, 1973; Alice Durio, *Cajun Columbus*, Pelican, 1975.

WORK IN PROGRESS: An adult novel, *Nashville 98; Cajun Folk Tales*, with Howard Jacobs; three children's books, *Ghost of Pont Diable*, *Raymond*, and *P & J Meet the Swamp Woman*.

AVOCATIONAL INTERESTS: Reading, chess, playing piano and woodwinds, motorcycling, painting and sculpture.

*   *   *

RICHARDS, Guy   1905-

PERSONAL: Born May 18, 1905, in New York, N.Y.; son of Guy (a banker) and Alice Lydia (Reese) Richards; married first wife, June 21, 1932 (divorced July 8, 1938); married Mary Spence Francis, August 26, 1940; children: Antonia (Mrs. Graham Judson), Pamela (Mrs. J. G. Smit). *Education:* Yale University, Ph.B., 1927. *Politics:* Republican. *Religion:* Episcopalian. *Home and office:* 340 East 57th St., New York, N.Y. 10022.

CAREER: Member of Whitney South Sea Expedition to New Guinea and Solomon Islands for American Museum of Natural History, 1927; worked as reporter for *New York Sun*, Newhouse Newspapers, and *New York Daily News*, all New York, N.Y.; *New York Journal-American*, New York, N.Y., began as reporter and feature writer, became city editor. Member of board of trustees, Graham Home for Children. *Military service:* U.S. Marine Corps, 1942-44; became major; served in Pacific Theatre. U.S. Marine Corps Reserve; current rank, lieutenant colonel. *Member:* American Museum of Natural History (associate member), First Marine Division, U.S. Naval Institute (associate member), Sheffield Historical Society, Century Club. *Awards, honors:* Received two Page One Awards from New York Newspaper Guild; Order of Silurians prize; Correction Officers' Benevolent Association special award; and Free Assembly of Captive European Nations award.

WRITINGS: Two Rubles to Times Square (novel), Duell, Sloan & Pearce, 1956 (published in England as *Brother Bear*, M. Joseph, 1957); *Imperial Agent* (nonfiction), Devin-Adair, 1966; *The Hunt for the Czar*, Doubleday, 1970; *The Rescue of the Romanovs*, Devin-Adair, 1975. Contributor of more than one hundred fifty articles to *Life*, *Liberty*, *Marine Corps Gazette*, *Leatherneck*, *Adventure*, and other periodicals.

WORK IN PROGRESS: A history of the Polish underground as a source of intelligence help to the West.

*   *   *

RICHARDS, Martin P(aul) M(eredith)   1940-

PERSONAL: Born January 26, 1940, in Cambridge, England; son of Paul Westmacott (a botanist) and Anne (a botanist; maiden name, Hotham) Richards. *Education:* Trinity College, Cambridge, B.A., 1962, M.A. and Ph.D.,

both 1965. *Home:* 57 Selwyn Rd., Cambridge, England. *Agent:* John Wolfers, 2 Regents Sq., London W.C.1, England. *Office:* Medical Psychology Unit, Cambridge University, Cambridge, England.

CAREER: Princeton University, Princeton, N.J., visiting fellow in biology, 1966-67; Harvard University, Cambridge, Mass., visiting fellow at Center for Cognitive Studies, 1967; Cambridge University, Cambridge, England, research worker in medical psychology unit, 1967—, lecturer in social psychology, 1970—. Adviser to National Childbirth Trust.

MEMBER: Zoological Society, British Society for Social Responsibility in Science, Society for the Study of Animal Behaviour, Society for Research in Child Development, Society for the Study of Fertility. *Awards, honors:* Postdoctoral fellowships from Science Research Council, 1965-67, Trinity College, Cambridge, 1965-69, and Mental Health Research Fund, 1969-70.

WRITINGS: (Editor with Kenneth Richardson and David Spears) *Race, Culture and Intelligence*, Penguin, 1972; (editor) *The Integration of a Child into a Social World*, Cambridge University Press, 1974. Contributor to scientific and popular journals. Member of editorial board of *Journal of Biosocial Science* and *Cognition*. Adviser to Penguin Books, Inc.

WORK IN PROGRESS: A book on the organization and effectiveness of medical care; a book on the development of children, for Doubleday.

SIDELIGHTS: Richards writes: "I have longstanding doubts about the effectiveness of scientific research for producing beneficial change. Through writing, teaching, and other activities I have attempted to both expose the weaknesses and dangers in current scientific work and to strive to find better methods and strategies through my own scientific research."

*   *   *

RICHARDSON, Henry V(okes)-M(ackey)   1923-

PERSONAL: Born February 3, 1923, in Baltimore, Md.; son of William Augustus (a commodore in U.S. Navy) and Eileen (du Bruyeres) Richardson; married Patricia Stuart Hagel, May 7, 1966. *Education:* Attended University of Edinburgh, 1938-39; United States Naval Academy, B.S., 1943; University of Washington, Seattle, M.A., 1963. *Residence:* Walla Walla, Wash. *Agent:* Joan Raines, Raines & Raines, 244 Madison Ave., New York, N.Y. 10016.

CAREER: Northwest Steel Rolling Mills, Seattle, Wash., executive, 1952-60; vice-president, 1960-62; Eastern Washington State College, Cheney, assistant professor, 1965-66, associate professor, 1966-67, professor of literature, 1967-68; Walla Walla Valley College, Walla Walla, Wash., professor of philosophy, 1968—. Lecturer at University of Washington, Seattle, 1959-64. *Military service:* U.S. Navy, 1940-51; fighter and divebomber pilot; became lieutenant commander; received three Purple Hearts and Distinguished Flying Cross. *Member:* Society of Canadian Loyalists, Sons of the American Revolution.

WRITINGS: Not All Our Pride, Braziller, 1965; *Skarra* (novel), T. Y. Crowell, 1975. Contributor to *Appalachian Journal*.

WORK IN PROGRESS: Writings on Americana, for use in the American Studies Series, American Heritage, and American Society of Arts and Sciences; a compilation of journal articles for book.

RICHARDSON, Justin 1900(?)-1975

1900(?)—August 28, 1975; British poet. Obituaries: *AB Bookman's Weekly,* December 1, 1975.

* * *

RICHARDSON, Stephen A. 1920-

PERSONAL: Born June 24, 1920, in England; U.S. citizen; married, 1945; children: four. *Education:* Harvard University, B.S. (magna cum laude), 1949; Cornell University, M.S., 1951, Ph.D., 1954. *Office:* Department of Pediatrics and Community Medicine, Albert Einstein College of Medicine, 1300 Morris Park Ave., New York, N.Y. 10461.

CAREER: Cornell University, Ithaca, N.Y., research associate at Social Science Research Center, 1951-56; Association for the Aid of Crippled Children, New York, N.Y., assistant director, 1956-61, acting executive director, 1961-62, assistant director, 1962-64, director of research, 1964-68; University of London, London, England, visiting scholar, 1968-69; Albert Einstein College of Medicine, New York, N.Y., professor of pediatrics and community health, 1969—, director of social ecology research unit, 1970—. Fellow of Center for Advanced Study in the Behavioral Sciences, 1954-55; trustee of Easter Seal Foundation, 1971-74; member of research advisory committee of the American Foundation for the Blind and for Planned Parenthood; member of advisory committee of Quaker United Nations Program.

MEMBER: International Organization for the Study of Human Development, American Sociological Association (fellow), American Psychological Association, Society for Research in Child Development, American Academy of Cerebral Palsy (associate member), Phi Beta Kappa, Phi Kappa Phi.

WRITINGS: (Contributor) Renato Tagiuri and Luigi Petrullo, editors, *Person Perception and Interpersonal Behavior,* Stanford University Press, 1958; (contributor) James D. Thompson and other editors, *Comparative Studies in Administration,* University of Pittsburgh Press, 1959; (contributor) Herbert G. Birch, editor, *Brain Damage in Children: The Biological and Social Aspects,* Williams & Wilkins, 1965; (with B. S. Dohrenwend and D. Klein) *Interviewing: Its Forms and Functions,* Basic Books, 1965; (editor with Alan F. Guttmacher) *Childbearing: Its Social and Psychological Factors,* Williams & Wilkins, 1967; (with Herbert G. Birch and others) *Mental Subnormality in the Community: A Clinical and Epidemiological Study,* Williams & Wilkins, 1970; (editor with N. Begab) *The Mentally Retarded and Society,* University Park Press, 1975. Contributor to academic and medical journals.

* * *

RICHMOND, Dick 1933-

PERSONAL: Born May 16, 1933, in Parma, Ohio; son of Arthur James (a salesman) and Frances (Visosky) Richmond; married Charlotte Jean Schwoebel (a secretary for Juvenile Probation), December 18, 1954; children: Kris Elaine, Leigh Allison, Paul Evan. *Education:* Washington University, St. Louis, Mo., A.B., 1961. *Residence:* Belleville, Ill. *Agent:* James Brown, 22 East 60th St., New York, N.Y. 10022. *Office:* St. Louis Post-Dispatch, 900 North 12th Blvd., St. Louis, Mo. 63101.

CAREER: Farm Fresh Markets, Phoenix, Ariz., clerk and cashier, 1948-52; National Tool, Cleveland, Ohio, precision tool inspector, 1952-53; United Press International News-

pictures, St. Louis, Mo., photographer, 1957-62, bureau manager, 1961-62; *St. Louis Post-Dispatch,* St. Louis, Mo., editor, 1962—, columnist, 1972—. *Military service:* U.S. Air Force, 1953-57; became staff sergeant.

WRITINGS: (With Roy Volker) *Treasure Under Your Feet: Adventurers' Handbook of Metal Detecting,* Regnery, 1974.

WORK IN PROGRESS: A novel, *The Evil That Men Do;* with Roy Volker, *In the Wake of the Golden Galleons,* an autobiography.

SIDELIGHTS: Richmond has been involved in expeditions in search of sunken Spanish treasure ships. He wrote, "This closeness with the sea has enlightened [me] as to all that must be done to preserve this last great frontier on earth while exploiting it as intelligently as possible."

* * *

RICHMOND, Velma E. B(ourgeois) 1931-

PERSONAL: Born March 12, 1931, in New Orleans, La.; daughter of Harold Septime (an engineer) and Merle Mary (Mandart) Bourgeois; married Hugh MacRae Richmond (a professor of English), August 9, 1958; children: Elizabeth Merle, Claire Isabel. *Education:* Louisiana State University, B.A., 1951, M.A., 1952; Johns Hopkins University, graduate study, 1952-53; Oxford University, B.Litt., 1957; University of North Carolina, Ph.D., 1959. *Religion:* Roman Catholic. *Home:* 1280 Grizzly Peak Blvd., Berkeley, Calif. 94708. *Office:* Department of English, Holy Names College, Oakland, Calif. 94619.

CAREER: Louisiana State University, Baton Rouge, instructor in English, 1957-58; Holy Names College, Oakland, Calif., instructor, 1958-60, assistant professor, 1960-64, associate professor, 1964-68, professor of English, 1968—, head of department, 1970—. *Member:* Modern Language Association of America, Modern Humanities Research Association, Mediaeval Academy of America, Early English Text Society, Renaissance Society of America, College English Association, American Comparative Literature Association, Medieval Association of the Pacific, International Federation for Modern Languages and Literatures. *Awards, honors:* Fulbright scholar at Oxford University, 1957.

WRITINGS: Laments for the Dead in Medieval Narrative, Duquesne University Press, 1966. Regular reviewer for *Voice,* 1964-71.

WORK IN PROGRESS: The Popularity of Middle English Romance, a study of Muriel Spark.

* * *

RICOEUR, Paul 1913-

PERSONAL: Born February 27, 1913, in Valence, France; son of Jules (a professor) and Florentine (Favre) Ricoeur; married Simone Lejas, August 14, 1935; children: Jean-Paul, Marc, Noelle Paccard, Olivier, Etienne. *Education:* Attended University of Rennes; University of Paris, agregation de philosophie, 1935, D. es lettres, 1950. *Home:* 19 rue d'Antony, 92290 Chatenay-Malabry, France. *Office:* Department of Philosophy, University of Paris, Nanterre, France.

CAREER: University of Strasbourg, Strasbourg, France, professor of philosophy, 1948-57; University of Paris, Paris, France, professor of philosophy, 1957—. Visiting professor, Yale University, 1964, University of Montreal,

1965, University of Louvain, 1970; John Nuveen Professor of History of Philosophy, University of Chicago, 1971. *Member:* Institut International de Philosophie. *Awards, honors:* Honorary degrees from University of Basel, 1964, University of Montreal, 1968, University of Chicago, 1969, University of Nijmegen, 1970, Ohio State University, 1970, DePaul University, 1973, University of Zurich, 1973, and Boston College, 1975.

WRITINGS: (With Mikel Dufrenne) *Karl Jaspers et la philosophie de l'existence,* Editions de Seuil, 1947; *Gabriel Marcel et Karl Jaspers: Philosophie du mystere et philosophie du paradoxe,* Editions de Seuil, 1948; *Philosophie de la Volonte,* Aubier, 1950-60, Part I: *Le Volontaire et l'involontaire,* translation by Erazim V. Kohak published as *Freedom and Nature: The Voluntary and the Involuntary,* Northwestern University Press, 1966, Part II: *Finitude et culpabilite,* Book 1: *L'Homme faillible,* translation by Charles Kelbley published as *Fallible Man,* Regnery, 1965, Book 2: *La Symbolique du mal,* translation by Emerson Buchanan published as *The Symbolism of Evil,* Harper, 1967; (editor) Emile Brehier, *Histoire de la philosophie allemande,* 3rd edition (Ricoeur was not associated with earlier editions), J. Vrin, 1954; *Histoire et verite,* Editions de Seuil, 1955, 2nd edition, 1964, 3rd edition, 1966, translation of 2nd edition by Kelbley published as *History and Truth,* Northwestern University Press, 1965; (editor) Pierre Thevenaz, *L'Homme et sa raison,* two volumes, Editions de la Baconniere, 1956.

Etre: Essence et substance chez Platon et Aristote, Centre de Documentation Universitaire (Paris), 1960; *Husserl: An Analysis of His Phenomenology,* translated from the French by Edward G. Ballard and Lester E. Embree, Northwestern University Press, 1967; *De l'Interpretation: Essai sur Freud,* Editions de Seuil, 1967, translation by Denis Savage published as *Freud and Philosophy: An Essay on Interpretation,* Yale University Press, 1970; (with others) *Pourquoi la philosophie?,* Editions de Sainte-Marie (Montreal), 1968, 2nd edition, Les Presses de l'Universite de Quebec, 1970; *Entreriens Paul Ricoeur, Gabriel Marcel,* Aubier-Montaigne, 1968, translation by Stephen Jolin and Peter McCormick included in *Tragic Wisdom and Beyond,* Northwestern University Press, 1973; *Le Conflit des interpretations: Essais d'hermeneutique,* Editions de Seuil, 1969, translation edited by Don Inde published as *The Conflict of Interpretations: Essays in Hermeneutics,* Northwestern University Press, 1974; (with Alasdair C. MacIntyre) *The Religious Significance of Atheism,* Columbia University Press, 1969; (with Leon Dion and Edward F. Sheffield) *L'Enseignement superieur: Bilans et prospective,* Presses del'Universite de Montreal, 1971; *Political and Social Essays,* edited by David Stewart and Joseph Bien, Ohio University Press, 1974; *La Metaphore vive,* Editions du Seuil, 1975, English translation, University of Toronto Press, in press. Director, *Revue de Metaphysique et de Morale.*

*   *   *

RICOU, Laurence (Rodger) 1944-

PERSONAL: Born October 17, 1944, in Brandon, Manitoba, Canada; son of Reginald Thomas (an advertising agent) and Gladys (Hawke) Ricou; married Treva Carolyn Clendenning (a librarian), June 21, 1966; children: Marc Laurence, Liane Adele. *Education:* Brandon College, University of Manitoba, B.A., 1965; University of Toronto, M.A., 1967, Ph.D., 1971. *Home:* 619 12th St. S., Lethbridge, Alberta, Canada T1J 2S1. *Office:* Department of

English, University of Lethbridge, Lethbridge, Alberta, Canada T1K 3M4.

CAREER: University of Lethbridge, Lethbridge, Alberta, assistant professor, 1970-75, associate professor of English, 1975—, chairman of department, 1973—. Chairman of Lethbridge pre-school services project, 1975-76. *Member:* Association of Canadian University Teachers of English, Canadian Association for Commonwealth Language and Literary Studies, Humanities Association of Canada, Association for Canadian and Quebec Literatures, Modern Language Association of America. *Awards, honors:* Humanities Research Council of Canada grant, 1973, for *Vertical Man/Horizontal World: Man and Landscape in Canadian Prairie Fiction;* Ontario Arts Council grant, 1976; Canada Council leave fellowship, 1976-77.

WRITINGS: Vertical Man/Horizontal World: Man and Landscape in Canadian Prairie Fiction, University of British Columbia Press, 1973; (author of introduction) Patricia Blondal, *A Candle to Light the Sun,* McClelland & Stewart, 1976; (editor and author of introduction) *Twelve Prairie Poets* (anthology), Oberon Press, 1976. Contributor of articles and reviews to literary journals.

WORK IN PROGRESS: Patricia Blondal, a biographical and critical study; a book on images of childhood in Canadian literature.

*   *   *

RIEFE, Alan 1925-
(Barbara Riefe)

PERSONAL: Born May 18, 1925, in Waterbury, Conn.; son of B.H.C. (a businessman) and Beatrice (Wise) Riefe; married Martha Daggett, June 10, 1948 (died May 16, 1949); married Barbara Dube, February 9, 1955; children: Martha, Leslie, Sidney, Jordan. *Education:* Colby College, B.A., 1950. *Residence:* Greenwich, Conn. *Agent:* Knox Burger Associates Ltd., 39½ Washington Sq. S., New York, N.Y. 10012.

CAREER: Free-lance writer. Wrote twenty-seven network television programs, 1951-65, including "Pulitzer Prize Playhouse," for American Broadcasting Co., "Studio One," for Columbia Broadcasting System, eight years as sole writer of "Masquerade Party," and over two years as chief writer of "Keep Talking." *Military service:* U.S. Army, World War II; served in European theater of operations; received three battle stars.

WRITINGS: Tales of Horror, Pocket Books, 1965; *Manual for Woman Drivers,* Fawcett, 1966; *I Am Your President* (satire), Curtis Books, 1972; (editor with Dick Harrington) *Sanford and Son,* Curtis Books, 1973.

"Cage" series, published by Popular Library, 1975: *The Lady Killers; The Conspirators; The Black Widower; The Silver Puma; The Bullet-Proof Man; The Killer with the Golden Touch.*

"Tyger" series, published by Popular Library, 1976: *Tyger at Bay; Tyger by the Tail; The Smile on the Face of the Tyger; Tyger and the Lady; Hold That Tyger; Tyger, Tyger, Burning Out.*

Gothic novels, under pseudonym Barbara Riefe; all published by Popular Library, 1976: *Barringer House; Rowleston; Auldearn House.*

Contributor of satirical pieces to *True,* and science fiction stories to *Boys' Life.*

WORK IN PROGRESS: Two American frontier novels, *A*

Fire on the Wind and *The Bravo Line,* both for Popular Library; a cowboy novel for Playboy Press; writing and producing "Jazz Milestones," a six-film history, for New York Times Teaching Resource Films.

AVOCATIONAL INTERESTS: Travel (has visited Europe, Mexico, and the Caribbean).

* * *

RIEGLE, Donald W(ayne), Jr. 1938-

PERSONAL: Born February 4, 1938, in Flint, Mich.; son of Donald Wayne and Dorothy (Fitchett) Riegle; married Meredith Ann White, January, 1972. *Education:* Attended Flint Junior College, 1956-57, and Western Michigan University, 1957-58; University of Michigan, B.A., 1960; Michigan State University, M.B.A., 1961; Harvard University, further graduate study, 1964-66. *Office:* 300 Metropolitan Building, 432 North Saginaw St., Flint, Mich. 48502; and 438 Cannon House Office Building, Washington, D.C. 20515.

CAREER: International Business Machines Corp. (IBM), senior pricing analyst, 1961-64; Harvard University, Cambridge, Mass., member of faculty, 1965-66; Republican member of U.S. House of Representatives from the Seventh District (Michigan), Washington, D.C., 1966-73, Democratic member, 1973—, member of appropriations committee, 1967-73, currently member of foreign affairs committee. Member of faculty at Michigan State University, 1962; and at Boston University, 1965. *Awards, honors:* LL.D. from St. Benedict's College, and Defiance College; named one of America's ten outstanding young men by U.S. Junior Chamber of Commerce, 1967, and one of two best Congressmen of the year by *Nation,* 1967.

WRITINGS: (With Trevor Armbrister) *O Congress,* Doubleday, 1972.

* * *

RIFE, J(ohn) Merle 1895-

PERSONAL: Born October 26, 1895, near Clifton, Ohio; son of John Brough (a farmer) and Estella (Stewart) Rife; married Ruth Ramsey, June 24, 1921 (died February 12, 1965); married Marie Henke, March 1, 1969; children: Edith Cecilia (Mrs. Jack R. Shegog), John Merle, Margaret E. Blackburn, Helen Ramsey (Mrs. Edward Andrew Graban). *Education:* Cedarville College, A.B., 1916; Xenia Theological Seminary, graduate study, 1919-21; Indiana University, M.A., 1927; University of Chicago, Ph.D., 1931. *Politics:* Democrat. *Home:* 160 Mount Holly Rd., Amelia, Ohio 45102.

CAREER: High school principal in Amelia, Ohio, and Green County Ohio, 1916-1918; American Rolling Mill Co., Middletown, Ohio, chemist, 1918-19; ordained United Presbyterian minister, 1921; pastor of United Presbyterian churches in Fair Haven, Ohio, 1921-23, and Bloomington, Ind., 1924-27; Tarkio College, Tarkio, Mo., professor of classical languages, 1927-32; Earlham College, Richmond, Ind., professor of classical languages and religion, 1932-36; Muskingum College, New Concord, Ohio, professor of Greek and Bible, 1936-64; Southwestern at Memphis, Memphis, Tenn., professor of Greek, 1965-66; Claflin College, Orangeburg, S.C., professor of Bible, 1967-68; writer, 1969—. Fulbright lecturer at National University (Athens), 1952-53. *Member:* Society of Biblical Literature, The Pennsylvania German Society.

WRITINGS: A Beginning Greek Book, Reiff Press, 1941,

revised edition, 1964; *The Nature and Origin of the New Testament,* Philosophical Library, 1975. Contributor of about forty articles to magazines.

AVOCATIONAL INTERESTS: Travel (especially Europe and the Mediterranean, and Israel), research on dextrality, genealogy.

* * *

RIGBY, Andrew 1944-

PERSONAL: Born November 25, 1944, in Lancashire, England; son of Joseph and Sylvia (Clare) Rigby; married Susan Matthews, August 31, 1967; children: Emma Clare. *Education:* University of Birmingham, B.So.Sc., 1967, Ph.D., 1970; University of Essex, M.A., 1968. *Home:* Bogfur, Kemnay, Aberdeenshire, Scotland. *Office:* Aberdeen Peoples Press, 167 King St., Aberdeen, Scotland.

CAREER: University of Aberdeen, Aberdeen, Scotland, lecturer in sociology, 1970-74; Aberdeen Peoples Press, Aberdeen, Scotland, journalist and printer, 1974—.

WRITINGS: Alternative Realities, Routledge & Kegan Paul, 1974; *Communes in Britain,* Routledge and Kegan Paul, 1975.

WORK IN PROGRESS: Research on alternative lifestyles and on the relationship between religion and art.

* * *

RIGGS, William (George) 1938-

PERSONAL: Born May 24, 1938, in Wellsville, N.Y.; son of Richard E. and Elizabeth (Hyde) Riggs; married Jan Fitzer, August 29, 1965; children: Rachel, Paige, Nora. *Education:* University of Rochester, A.B., 1960; University of California, Berkeley, M.A., 1962, Ph.D., 1968. *Home:* 148 Elgin St., Newton, Mass. 02159. *Office:* Department of English, Boston University, 236 Bay State Rd., Boston, Mass. 02215.

CAREER: Boston University, Boston, Mass., instructor, 1967-68, assistant professor, 1968-73, associate professor of English, 1973—. *Member:* Modern Language Association of America, Renaissance Society of America. *Awards, honors:* American Council of Learned Societies study fellowship, 1973-74.

WRITINGS: The Christian Poet in "Paradise Lost," University of California Press, 1972. Contributor to literature journals.

WORK IN PROGRESS: Research on the Renaissance, neo-Platonism, Milton, and Shakespeare.

* * *

RIKHOFF, Jean 1928-

PERSONAL: Born May 28, 1928, in Chicago, Ill.; daughter of Harold Franklin (a businessman) and Blanche (a teacher; maiden name, Bowlus) Rikhoff; divorced; children: Allison, Jeffrey. *Education:* Mount Holyoke College, B.A., 1948; Wesleyan University, M.A., 1949. *Politics:* Democrat. *Home:* R.D.2, Salem, N.Y. 12865. *Agent:* Barthold Fles Literary Agency, 507 Fifth Ave., New York, N.Y. 10017. *Office:* Department of English, Adirondack Community College, Glens Falls, N.Y. 12801.

CAREER: Instructor in English, University of Maryland Overseas Program; editorial assistant, *Gourmet* magazine; Adirondack Community College, Glens Falls, N.Y., assistant professor of English, 1969—. Free-lance writer. Chairman of university awards committee, State University of New York. *Awards, honors:* Eugene Saxton fellowship for creative writing, 1958; National Endowment for the Humanities fellowship, 1972.

WRITINGS: Dear Ones All, Viking, 1961; (editor) *Quixote Anthology,* Grosset, 1962; *Voyage In, Voyage Out,* Viking, 1963; *Rites of Passage,* Viking, 1966; *Buttes Landing,* Dial, 1973; *One of the Raymonds,* Dial, 1974; *The Sweetwater,* Dial, in press.

Juvenile: *Writing About the Frontier: Mark Twain,* Encyclopedia Britannica, 1963; *Robert E. Lee: Soldier of the South,* Putnam, 1968.

Short stories, poems, and articles have appeared in various publications.

*   *   *

RILEY, Lawrence   1897(?)-1975

1897(?)—November 29, 1975; American playwright and screenwriter. Obituaries: *New York Times,* December 3, 1975.

*   *   *

RIMINGTON, Critchell   1907-1976

February 16, 1907—January 30, 1976; American magazine editor and publisher, and author or editor of books on yachting, and other subjects. Obituaries: *New York Times,* February 1, 1976.

*   *   *

RIMLAND, Ingrid   1936-

PERSONAL: Born May 22, 1936, in Halbstadt, Ukraine; daughter of Friedrich and Evelyn (Loetkemann) Brandt; separated; children: Erwin, Rudy. *Education:* Wichita State University, B.A. (magna cum laude), 1971; University of the Pacific, M.A., 1973, Ed.D. candidate. *Home:* 6301 Herndon Pl., Stockton, Calif. 95207. *Office:* 1931 Kiernan Ave., Modesto, Calif. 95350.

CAREER: Teacher of German in a private school in Argentina, 1956-58; Stanislaus Union School District, Modesto, Calif., psychometrist, 1974—. *Member:* California Association of School Psychologists and Psychometrists, Phi Kappa Phi.

WRITINGS: Psyching Out Sex, Westminster Press, 1975.

WORK IN PROGRESS: The Loaded Dice, a historical novel, for Concordia; research on gifted children.

SIDELIGHTS: Ingrid Rimland left Russia with her family during World War II; they emigrated to Paraguay with a group of Mennonite refugees who set out to pioneer the Paraguayan jungle. She emigrated to Canada with her husband and child in 1960, and came to the United States in 1967.

*   *   *

RIMMER, C(harles) Brandon   1918-

PERSONAL: Born February 21, 1918, in Los Angeles, Calif.; son of Harry (a clergyman and writer) and Mignon (Brandon) Rimmer; married Florence Caldwall (a teacher), July 2, 1942; children: David, Paul Douglas, Daniel Harry, Donna. *Education:* University of Southern California, B.A., 1950; Fuller Theological Seminary, M.Div., 1956. *Religion:* Non-denominational. *Office:* 212 North Orange St., Glendale, Calif. 91203.

CAREER: First Presbyterian Church of Hollywood, Hollywood, Calif., in Christian education department; served as pastor of non-denominational church, 1957-64; Baird Aviation, Burbank, Calif., worked as commercial pilot; Electronic Calculating Service, Los Angeles, Calif., began as corporation pilot, became sales manager for scientific computer applications; manager of bookstore in Glendale, Calif., 1971—; writer, 1971—. *Military service:* U.S. Army Air Forces, pilot in "The Devil's Brigade," 1941-47; became captain; received Distinguished Flying Cross.

WRITINGS: Mayhem and Mercy, Creation House, 1972; *Religion in Shreds,* Creation House, 1973; *Harry,* Creation House, 1973; (with Bill Brown) *The Unpredictable Wind,* Thomas Nelson, 1974; *Tell the Rock I'm Alive,* Successful Living, 1975.

WORK IN PROGRESS: A book on Israel.

*   *   *

RIOU, Roger   1909-

PERSONAL: Born August 16, 1909, in Le Havre, France; son of Yves and Rosalie (Guillou) Riou. *Education:* Studied at Montfort Fathers Institute, University of Lille, and University of Strasbourg. *Home and office:* 80 Rue de la Tombe Issoire, Paris 75014, France.

CAREER: Entered religious order of Montfort Fathers, 1931, ordained Roman Catholic priest, 1938; missionary in Haiti, 1938-69; director of Fondation Roger Riou (international service for aid of countries needing help), 1970—. *Military service:* French Army, 1933-34. *Member:* Society of French Language on Sea and Overseas. *Awards, honors:* Wicking Prize from Jours de France, 1975; Prix Verite from Parisien Libere, 1975; Officier de l'Ordre National de la Sante de la Republique d'Haiti; Officier de l'Ordre National "Honneur et Merite" de la Republique d'Haiti.

WRITINGS: A Dieu la Tortue, Robert Laffont, 1974; translation by Martin Sokolinski published as *The Island of My Life,* Delacorte, 1975.

*   *   *

ROBARDS, Sherman M(arshall)   1939-
(Terry Robards)

PERSONAL: Born October 7, 1939, in New York, N.Y.; son of Sidney M. (a business executive) and C. Louise (Sherman) Robards; married Susan Lee Hayes, January 14, 1962; children: John M., Jeffrey S. *Education:* Hamilton College, B.A., 1961. *Office: New York Times,* 229 West 43rd St., New York, N.Y. 10036.

CAREER: New York Herald Tribune, New York, N.Y., assistant financial editor, 1963-66; *Fortune,* New York, N.Y., associate editor, 1966-67; *New York Times,* New York, N.Y., staff writer, 1967-73, 1975—, foreign correspondent, 1973-75. Commentor on "The Topic Is Wine," WQXR Radio, New York, N.Y., 1972—. Lecturer on wine. *Member:* International Wine and Food Society, Confrerie des Chevaliers du Tastevin (commandeur), Commanderie de Bordeaux (governor), Foreign Press Association in London, Wine Society Dining Club (London), Confrerie de la Chaine des Rotisseurs, Deadline Club, Sigma Delta Chi.

WRITINGS: Wine Cellar Journal, Quadrangle, 1974; *The New York Times Book of Wine,* Quadrangle, 1976. Contributor to wine journals.

ROBBINS, June
(Julie, Julie of Colorado Springs)

PERSONAL: Born in Genesee, Pa.; daughter of O. E. Robbins; separated. *Education:* Crawford W. Long School of Nursing, R.N., 1947; University of Colorado, B.A., 1974. *Home:* 105 Everett Dr., Colorado Springs, Colo. 80911.

CAREER: Registered nurse in hospitals in Arkansas, Texas, Pennsylvania, California, and Colorado, 1947-50; nurse in U.S. Army Hospital, Fort Carson, Colo., 1950—. Private duty nurse in several states. *Member:* Centro Studi e Scambi Internazionali (Rome), International Poetry Society (England), World Poetry Society, National Pen Women, Colorado State Poetry Association, Poetry Society of Michigan, Poetry Fellowship of Colorado Springs. *Awards, honors:* American Poetry Fellowship Society award, 1970; Gemstone award from *Voices International,* 1972; *South and West* award, 1973.

WRITINGS: (Under pseudonym, Julie of Colorado Springs) *Poetry and Peanut Butter,* privately printed, 1970; (under pseudonym, Julie of Colorado Springs) *A Love Letter and Other Poems,* Love Street Books, 1975.

Work represented in anthologies, under pseudonyms Julie or Julie of Colorado Springs, including *Moon Age Poets Anthology,* edited by Jaye Giammarino, Prairie Press Books, 1970; and *Outstanding Contemporary Poetry,* edited by Dale and Arthur Moore, Pied Piper Press, 1972. Contributor of poems, sometimes under pseudonym Julie of Colorado Springs, to *Voices International, Tempo, Pegasus,* and *Gazette Telegraph.*

WORK IN PROGRESS: An Amethyst Remembrance.

SIDELIGHTS: June Robbins told *CA:* "I write because of 'a poem that comes in the window and grabs me.' Also because of a belief that my writing is a gift from some other consciousness. Therefore, I can claim no credit. All proceeds go to my special charity, Jewish Documentation Center, Vienna, Austria." *Avocational interests:* Music, reading, travel, flying.

BIOGRAPHICAL/CRITICAL SOURCES: Colorado Springs Gazette Telegraph, April 1, 1970.

* * *

ROBERTS, Elizabeth H. 1913-

PERSONAL: Born April 11, 1913, in New York; daughter of Harry and Leah Lilly (Lang) Rosenblum; married Nathan Wasserheit (an attorney), November 22, 1951 (died January 4, 1975); children: Judith N. *Education:* Attended Brooklyn College of the City University of New York; Long Island University, D.P.M., 1943. *Office:* 133 East 58th St., New York, N.Y. 10022.

CAREER: Senior podiatrist at New York Infirmary, 1945—; New York College of Podiatric Medicine, New York, N.Y., director of department of practice administration, 1951-63, professor of podiatric medicine, 1964-74, professor emeritus, 1974—, chairman of department of regional anatomy, 1954-67; writer, 1974 . Member of staff of Midtown Hospital, 1970—; member of New York State Board for Podiatry, 1974—. Has made television and radio broadcasts and public lectures. *Member:* American Medical Writers Association, Academy of Podiatric Medicine (fellow); American Association of Hospital Podiatrists.

WRITINGS: On Your Feet (foot care for the lay reader), Rodale Press, 1975. Contributor and consultant to *Consumer Research.*

AVOCATIONAL INTERESTS: Travel, sculpting.

* * *

ROBERTS, Janet Louise 1925-
(Louisa Bronte; Rebecca Danton; Janette Radcliffe)

PERSONAL: Born January 20, 1925, in New Britain, Conn.; daughter of Walter Nelson (a clergyman) and Marjorie Mae (Miller) Roberts. *Education:* Otterbein College, B.A., 1946; Columbia University, M.S.L.S., 1966. *Politics:* None. *Religion:* United Methodist. *Residence:* Dayton, Ohio. *Agent:* Jay Garon, Jay Garon-Brooke Associates, Inc., 415 Central Park W., #17D, New York, N.Y. 10025.

CAREER: Reference librarian, 1966—. *Member:* American Library Association, Mystery Writers of America, Ohio Library Association.

WRITINGS: Jewels of Terror, Lancer Books, 1970; *The Weeping Lady,* Lancer Books, 1971; *Ravenswood,* Avon, 1971; *Love Song,* Pinnacle Books, 1971; *Dark Rose,* Lancer Books, 1971; *The Devil's Own,* Avon, 1972; *The Curse of Kenton,* Avon, 1972; *Marriage of Inconvenience,* Dell, 1972; *Rivertown,* Avon, 1972; *My Lady Mischief,* Dell, 1973; *The Dancing Doll,* Dell, 1973; *The Dornstein Icon,* Avon, 1973; *The Golden Thistle,* Dell, 1973; *Isle of the Dolphins,* Avon, 1973; *La Casa Dorada,* Dell, 1973; *The Cardross Luck,* Dell, 1974; *The First Waltz,* Dell, 1974; *Castlereagh,* Pocket Books, 1975; *Jade Vendetta,* Pocket Books, in press; *Wilderness Inn,* Pocket Books, in press.

Under pseudonym Rebecca Danton: *Sign of the Golden Goose,* Popular Library, 1972; *Black Horse Tavern,* Popular Library, 1972.

Under pseudonym Louisa Bronte: *Lord Satan,* Avon, 1972; *Her Demon Lover,* Avon, 1973; *Greystone Tavern,* Ballantine, 1975; *Gathering at Greystone,* Ballantine, 1976; *Freedom Trail to Greystone,* Ballantine, in press; *Casino Greystone,* Ballantine, in press; *Greystone Rumrunners,* Ballantine, in press; *Greystone Heritage,* Ballantine, in press.

Under pseudonym Janette Radcliffe: *The Blue-Eyed Gypsy,* Dell, 1974; *The Moonlight Gondola,* Dell, 1975; *Gentleman Pirate,* Dell, 1975; *White Jasmine,* Dell, in press; *Lord Stephen's Lady,* Dell, in press; *Azure Castle,* Dell, in press. Contributor to *Writer's Digest.*

WORK IN PROGRESS: Regency historical novels.

SIDELIGHTS: Janet Roberts writes: "In early years I worked at clerk-typist positions, taking long vacations to live and write in Florence, Rome, and London. After receiving my library degree, I was able to do better historical research as well as work in a public library.... The two careers complement each other beautifully. I now travel on vacations to various places to use as backgrounds for my novels, as Vienna, Athens, Madrid, the Bahamas, Hawaii."

* * *

ROBERTS, (Thomas) Patrick 1920-

PERSONAL: Born August 12, 1920, in London, England; son of Robert Lewis and Muriel (Henderson) Roberts; married Hilary Hope-Sanders, May, 1949 (divorced, 1954); married Judith Henham Carr (a journalist), May 17, 1955; children: Mark Lindsay, Andrew Michael. *Education:* Christ Church, Oxford, B.A., 1943, M.A. (honors), 1946. *Home:* 4 Knoyle Rd., Brighton BN1 6RB, England. *Office:*

Department of English, University College, University of London, Gower St., London WC1E 6BT, England.

CAREER: Oxford University, Oxford, England, staff tutor for extra-mural studies, 1949-60, senior staff tutor, 1960-65; University of London, London, England, lecturer in English, 1965—, departmental tutor, 1971-74. Part-time lecturer at University of Keele, 1950-53; lecturer at summer schools of London University and Colgate College; visiting professor, Dartmouth College, summer, 1975. Military service: British Army, 1940-45; became captain; received Burma Star.

WRITINGS: The Psychology of Tragic Drama, Routledge & Kegan Paul, 1975.

WORK IN PROGRESS: Literature and Psychoanalysis; Comparative Studies in Classical and English Literature; research on Thomas Hardy and on Ibsen.

SIDELIGHTS: Roberts writes: "I believe that psychoanalytical ideas and experience can be brought to bear in an illuminating way on a wide variety of authors, texts, and themes." Avocational interests: Walking, travel (especially mountains and art galleries), attending operas.

*   *   *

ROBERTS, Steven V(ictor) 1943-

PERSONAL: Born February 11, 1943, in Bayonne, N.J.; son of Will R. (a businessman) and Dorothy (Schanbam) Roberts; married Corinne Claiborne Boggs (a television producer and writer), September 10, 1966; children: Lee Harriss, Rebecca Boggs. Education: Harvard University, B.A., 1964. Religion: Jewish. Home: 5 Agias Sophias, Neo Psychico, Athens, Greece. Agent: Lois Wallace, 118 East 61st St., New York, N.Y. 10021. Office: Foreign Desk, New York Times, 229 West 43rd St., New York, N.Y. 10036.

CAREER: New York Times, New York, N.Y., metropolitan reporter, 1965-69, Los Angeles bureau chief, 1969-74, Athens bureau chief, 1974—. Member: American Newspaper Guild, Harvard Alumni Association (member of board of directors).

WRITINGS: Eureka! (essays on California), Quadrangle, 1974. Contributor of more than fifty articles to popular magazines, including Esquire, Playboy, Saturday Review, and Commonweal.

SIDELIGHTS: Roberts writes: "I am primarily a newspaperman, and my book is a collection of pieces written over a five-year assignment in California. I often believed that California was to the rest of America what America was to Europe: a new land, free from the past, open to experimentation, and that's what the book is about."

*   *   *

ROBERTSON, D(urant) W(aite), Jr. 1914-

PERSONAL: Born October 11, 1914, in Washington, D.C.; son of Durant Waite and Emma (Jones) Robertson; married Betty McLean Hansen, July 17, 1937; children: Susanna, Durant Waite III, Douglas. Education: University of North Carolina, Chapel Hill, B.A., 1935, M.A., 1937, Ph.D., 1945. Home: 93 Maclean Cir., Princeton, N.J. 08540. Office: Department of English, Princeton University, Princeton, N.J. 08540.

CAREER: University of Maryland, College Park, instructor in English, 1938-42; University of North Carolina, Chapel Hill, instructor in English, 1942-44; Yale University, New Haven, Conn., instructor in English, 1945-46; Princeton University, Princeton, N.J., instructor, 1946-47, assistant professor, 1947-55, associate professor, 1955-60, professor of English, 1960-71, Murray Professor of English Literature, 1971—. Member: Mediaeval Academy of America, Renaissance Society of America. Awards, honors: American Council of Learned Societies fellow, 1945-46; Guggenheim fellow, 1957; D.Litt. from Villanova University, 1973.

WRITINGS: (With Bernard F. Huppe) Piers Plowman and Scriptural Tradition, Princeton University Press, 1951; (translator) St. Augustine, On Christian Doctrine, Liberal Arts Press, 1958; A Preface to Chaucer: Studies in Medieval Perspectives, Princeton University Press, 1962; (with Huppe) Fruyt and Chaf, Princeton University Press, 1963; Chaucer's London, Wiley, 1968; (editor) The Literature of Medieval England, McGraw, 1970; Abelard and Heloise, Dial, 1972. Contributor of articles and reviews to scholarly journals including Speculum, Comparative Literature, Studies in Philology, and American Benedictine Review.

WORK IN PROGRESS: Research for a book, An Introduction to the Canterbury Tales.

SIDELIGHTS: Robertson writes: "It has always been my contention that studies of earlier literature, including critical evaluations of that literature, should be based firmly on knowledge gained from primary sources. If we cannot understand literary works in terms that would have been understood by their authors we shall not understand them at all."

*   *   *

ROBERTSON, Dougal 1924-

PERSONAL: Born January 29, 1924, in Edinburgh, Scotland; son of John Ireland (a music teacher) and Mary (Clarke) Robertson; married Linda Poyser (a midwife), September 29, 1951; children: Anne Marilyn, Douglas J. P., Neil Stewart Clarke, Alexander Stewart Clarke. Education: Attended Leith Nautical College. Residence: Leek, Staffordshire, England.

CAREER: British Merchant Navy, 1941-53, leaving service as master mariner; has worked as a farmer; author, 1973—.

WRITINGS: Survive the Savage Sea, Praeger, 1973; Sea Survival: A Manual, Praeger, 1975.

WORK IN PROGRESS: The China Coast During the Revolution, 1948-1952.

AVOCATIONAL INTERESTS: Yachting, hillwalking, music, poetry, French, rugby football, travel, adventure.

*   *   *

ROBERTSON, Patrick 1940-

PERSONAL: Born March 21, 1940, in Gloucester, England; son of Roy (a dental surgeon) and Kate (Barford) Robertson; married Karla Ehrlich (a motion picture production assistant), July 3, 1971. Education: Educated in England. Politics: "Traditionalist liberal." Religion: Roman Catholic. Home: 81 Theberton St., London N.1, England. Agent: Campbell Thomson & McLaughlin Ltd., 31 Newington Green, London N.16, England. Office: Department for National Savings, Blythe Rd., London W.44 1SB, England.

CAREER: British Broadcasting Corp., London, England, information officer, 1965-69; Ministry of Transport, London, England, information officer, 1969-73; Department for

National Savings, London, England, chief press officer, 1973—. *Member:* Society of Authors, Ephemera Society (secretary, 1975—), Oriental Club. *Awards, honors:* Commendation by the selection committee for the Library Association's McColvin Medal, 1974.

WRITINGS: The Book of Firsts, C. N. Potter, 1974 (published in England as *The Shell Book of Firsts,* M. Joseph, 1974).

WORK IN PROGRESS: The American Book of Firsts.

AVOCATIONAL INTERESTS: Collecting and preserving early magazines.

BIOGRAPHICAL/CRITICAL SOURCES: Guardian, October 17, 1974.

* * *

ROBINSON, Cervin 1928-

PERSONAL: Born May 18, 1928, in Boston, Mass.; son of Frank J. (an architect) and Mary (Burchill) Robinson; married Lucy Hodgson (an artist), June 20, 1961; children: Samuel Hodgson, Moses Hazard. *Education:* Harvard University, A.B., 1950. *Home:* 251 West 92nd St., New York, N.Y. 10025.

CAREER: Architectural Review, London, England, American representative, 1957—. *Member:* Society of Architectural Historians. *Awards, honors:* Guggenheim fellowship, 1971-72.

WRITINGS: (With Rosemarie Haag Bletter) *Skyscraper Style: Art Deco New York,* Oxford University Press, 1975. Contributor to architecture journals.

* * *

ROBINSON, Jan M. 1933-

PERSONAL: Born October 30, 1933; daughter of Joseph Edward and Janice (Howes) Lanoue; married Peter D. Robinson, Jr. (a salesman and insurance investigator), November 22, 1952; children: Vickie, Peter, David, Gail. *Education:* Attended business college, one year. *Politics:* Independent ("with Republican tendencies"). *Religion:* Protestant. *Home:* Pumpkin Hollow, Conway, Mass. 01341. *Agent:* Curtis Brown Ltd., 60 East 56th St., New York, N.Y. 10022.

CAREER: Copywriter, typist, and kindergarten teacher in earlier years; teacher of arts and crafts in grammar school enrichment program, Conway, Mass., 1970-71. *Member:* National Wildlife Federation, National Audubon Society.

WRITINGS: The December Dog, Lippincott, 1969. Contributor to *Jack and Jill* and local newspaper.

WORK IN PROGRESS: Two books for children, *Pigpen Poet* and *Mystery beyond the Hedge.*

SIDELIGHTS: Jan Robinson writes: "I have four teenage children, a ten-room house to care for, over forty animals to tend to, and that takes care of most of my time. We also take a Fresh Air child each summer. In the leftover moments when I'm not writing I am active in conservation of wildlife, ecology and the out-of-doors in general. . . . I play classical guitar much to the disgust of my children; speak passable French, believe in God and the balance of nature; love living in a rural area and feel close to its growth problems; and am terrified by urban problems. Four of my idols are Thoreau, Jack London, Thornton Burgess, and Paul Newman.

ROBINSON, Lytle W(ebb) 1913-

PERSONAL: Born April 11, 1913, in McMinnville, Tenn.; son of Walter Aubrey (a manufacturer's representative) and Jessie Mae (a piano teacher; maiden name, Webb) Robinson; married Barbara Munson (an editor), October 16, 1948; children: Carolyn, Stephen, David, Tanya. *Education:* Attended Pelman Institute, 1935-36, Mildred I. Reid Writers Colony, 1943. *Politics:* "Liberal-radical Democrat." *Religion:* Protestant. *Home and office:* 8005 Cloud Rd., Tucson, Ariz. 85715. *Agent:* Georges Borchardt, Inc., 145 East 52nd St., New York, N.Y. 10022.

CAREER: Worked in general merchandise lines in the South and Midwest, 1934-59; Corps of Army Engineers, Marion, Ohio, technical writer, 1959-62; owner and director of Tucson School of Writing, 1963; appointed a civil deputy sheriff, Pima County, Ariz., 1965-75. Member of state board of directors of Arizona Consumers Council, 1971-72; treasurer of Arizona Democrats for McCarthy, 1968; treasurer of District Democratic Club, 1970-72; Democratic precinct captain, 1968-74; state convention committeeman, 1968, 1972. *Military service:* U.S. Army, 1943-46; became sergeant. *Member:* American Association of Retired Persons, Society of Southwestern Authors, Association for Research and Enlightenment, Psychical Aid Foundation (treasurer and board member, 1972).

WRITINGS: Edgar Cayce's Story of the Origin and Destiny of Man, Coward, 1972; *Is It True What They Say About Edgar Cayce?,* Neville Spearman, 1976. Contributor of short stories, articles and humorous pieces to *Cosmopolitan, American Mercury,* trade journals, men's, travel, and general interest publications.

WORK IN PROGRESS: Articles and short pieces on current newsworthy subjects.

SIDELIGHTS: Lytle Robinson told *CA:* "Is the subject important? Is it something the public ought to know? Will it help people? Is it new and fresh? I have long been interested in political, social and economic concerns along with psychic phenomena. There is a great and urgent need for solutions to the ills of our society, and the growing consumer's and producer's cooperative movement appears to be the best hope."

AVOCATIONAL INTERESTS: Gardening, traveling (has lived in a dozen states and traveled in sixteen foreign countries).

* * *

ROBINSON, Maudie Millian Oller 1914-

PERSONAL: Born August 4, 1914, in Norris, Okla.; daughter of William Randolph (a farmer and merchant) and Fannie Elizabeth (Kimbrough) Oller; married William Cole Lewis, May 5, 1933 (divorced, 1940); married Charles Hugh Robinson (an educator and administrator of schools in New Mexico), September 6, 1942; children: (first marriage) Betty Carole (Mrs. Donald George Worrall). *Education:* Attended Highlands University, 1950-58. *Politics:* Republican. *Religion:* Presbyterian. *Home and office:* 105 Torreon, Clovis, N.M. 88101. *Agent:* August Lenniger, Lenniger Literary Agency, Inc., 437 Fifth Ave., New York, N.Y. 10016.

CAREER: Worked as bookkeeper and secretary for businesses, Veteran's Administration, and Vaughan Municipal Schools in Vaughan, N.M., and Las Vegas, N.M., 1943-58; free-lance writer, 1958-63; Navajo Lodge, Las Vegas, N.M., manager, 1963-73; free-lance writer, 1973—.

Member of Friends of the Clovis Library. *Member:* New Mexico Book League, Order of the Eastern Star.

WRITINGS: Children of the Sun: The Pueblos, Navajos, and Apaches of New Mexico (juvenile), Messner, 1973. Contributor of articles and stories to popular magazines, including *She, Reader's Digest,* and *Homemaker.*

WORK IN PROGRESS: Two novels, *Unvarnished,* and *Jimson Weed;* a juvenile, *Mystery of the Squash Blossom Necklace;* two books, *The Proverbial Way,* and *A Do-It-Yourself Book on How To Do Nothing.*

SIDELIGHTS: Maudie Robinson writes: "I grew up in a very close-knit family in the eastern hills of Oklahoma.... The small place ... where I was born was originally called Bugscuffle! ... My father was a mixture of English and German and a perfectionist in all his endeavors.... My mother was a delightful mixture of Irish and Cherokee.... We grew up among the Choctaws and Cherokees, and my father was always their friend and champion.

"New Mexico has been my home since 1930, and for me, it is truly a Land of Enchantment. I am vitally interested in Southwest history and the Indians who inhabit the land now and those of long ago. I enjoy tramping through the hills and over the prairies, visiting old ruins, and searching through junk shops and second-hand stores for that rare Old West Book that has long been out of print."

* * *

ROBINSON, Nancy (Lou) M(ayer) 1930-

PERSONAL: Born August 30, 1930, in Houston, Tex.; daughter of Sidney L. (a salesman) and Bertha-Louise (Heyman) Mayer; married Halbert B. Robinson (a professor of psychology), June 24, 1951; children: Christine Louise, Laura Ann, David Merrill, Elizabeth Mayer. *Education:* Stanford University, A.B. (with highest honors), 1951, M.A., 1953, Ph.D., 1958. *Office:* Child Development and Mental Retardation Center, University of Washington, Seattle, Wash. 98195.

CAREER: Veterans Administration Hospital, Palo Alto, Calif., psychiatric intern, 1951-53; Santa Clara County Adult and Child Guidance Center, San Jose, Calif., intern, 1953; Veterans Administration Hospital, Denver, Colo., intern, 1954-55, Mental Hygiene Clinic, intern, 1955; Veterans Administration Hospital, Palo Alto, Calif., psychiatric intern, 1955-56; Santa Clara County Probation Department, San Jose, Calif., intern, 1957; Stanford University, Stanford, Calif., postdoctoral research associate, 1958-59; North Carolina College (now North Carolina Central University), Durham, visiting assistant professor of psychology, 1960-61; University of North Carolina, Chapel Hill, acting assistant professor of psychology and director of psychological services and training at Murdoch Center (for the retarded), 1961-62, research associate, 1962-63, acting assistant professor, 1963-64, lecturer, 1964-66, assistant professor of education, 1966-68; University of Washington, Seattle, research associate, 1967-74, lecturer, 1973-74, associate professor of psychiatry and behavioral sciences, 1974—, head of discipline at Child Development and Mental Retardation Center, 1974—. Psychology intern at Stanford University's Psychological Clinic, 1951-54, 1955-57, and School of Medicine, 1955-56. Visiting assistant professor at San Francisco State College (now University), 1958, and Duke University, 1963. Coordinator of research at Frank Porter Graham Child Development Center at University of North Carolina's Mental Retardation Center, 1966-69; coordinator of International Study Group for Early Child Care, 1968—. *Member:* American Psychological Association, Society for Research in Child Development, American Association for Mental Deficiency, Phi Beta Kappa, Sigma Xi.

WRITINGS: (With husband, Halbert B. Robinson) *The Mentally Retarded Child: A Psychological Approach,* McGraw, 1965, 2nd edition, 1976; (contributor) P. H. Mussen, editor, *Carmichael's Manual of Child Psychology,* Wiley, 1970; (contributor) I. J. Gordon, editor, *Seventy-First Yearbook: National Society for the Study of Education,* University of Chicago Press, 1972; (contributor) *Mental Health from Infancy through Adolescence,* Harper, 1973; (with H. B. Robinson, M. Wolins, U. Bronfenbrenner, and J. B. Richmond) *Early Child Care in the United States* (monograph), Gordon & Breach, 1974.

Co-editor with H. B. Robinson of "International Monograph Series on Early Child Care," Gordon & Breach, 1972—. Contributor to *World Book Encyclopedia* and to psychology and education journals. Member of editorial review board of *Child Development,* 1966-71; associate editor of *American Journal of Mental Deficiency,* 1975—.

WORK IN PROGRESS: Research on progress in early intervention with handicapped infants and follow-up of children given neonatal intensive care.

SIDELIGHTS: "International Monograph Series on Early Child Care" includes monographs on Hungary, Sweden, Switzerland, France, Israel, Yugoslavia, Poland, Russia, Cuba, and India, as well as United States and Great Britain.

* * *

ROBLEY, Grace 1918-

PERSONAL: Born December 21, 1918, in Montana; daughter of Joe and Marie (Huotari) DeVries; married Wendell Robley (a radiologist and priest), September 25, 1942; children: Donald, Carol (Mrs. Ken Shawhan), Dianne (Mrs. Steve Mindt). *Education:* Dakota Wesleyan University, B.S., 1942; Grace College of Discipleship and Theology, M.Counseling and Theology, 1974, D.Counseling and Theology, 1975. *Politics:* Independent. *Home:* 9601 Candy Lane, La Mesa, Calif. 92041. *Agent:* Dave Balsiger, 257 Brentwood St., Costa Mesa, Calif. 92627. *Office:* Grace Ministry, 9601 Candy Lane, La Mesa, Calif. 92041.

CAREER: Wesley Memorial Hospital, Chicago, Ill., in dietetic department, 1942-43; church and community volunteer worker, serving as church school teacher, youth group leader and superintendent, and as hospital volunteer, 1943-68; Grace Ministry, La Mesa, Calif., counselor, 1968—. Professor at Grace College of Discipleship and Theology, 1970—; priest at Grace Ministry Chapels in Orange and La Mesa, Calif., both 1973—. *Member:* Woman's Society of Christian Service (past local and district president), Woman's Auxiliary of San Diego County Medical Society, Grossmont Hospital Auxiliary (life member; past area chairman), Grossmont Concert Association (past president of women's committee).

WRITINGS: (With husband, Wendell Robley) *Spirit-Led Family,* Whitaker House, 1974; (with W. Robley) *Spank Me If You Love Me,* New Leaf Press, 1975.

WORK IN PROGRESS: Healing, Spiritual Sexuality, and *Christian Ethics,* all with husband, Wendell Robley.

AVOCATIONAL INTERESTS: Travel (Japan, Canada, Italy, Greece, Turkey, Lebanon, Egypt, England, Israel).

ROBLEY, Wendell 1916-
(Rob Robley)

PERSONAL: Born June 15, 1916, in South Dakota; son of Jesse (a farmer) and Anna (Tjomsland) Robley; married Grace DeVries (a priest, professor, and counselor), September 25, 1942; children: Donald, Carol (Mrs. Ken Shawhan), Dianne (Mrs. Steve Mindt). *Education:* Dakota Wesleyan University, student, 1942; Northwestern University, B.S. and M.D., both 1944; Grace College of Discipleship and Theology, D. Counseling and Theology, 1974. *Politics:* Independent. *Home:* 9601 Candy Lane, La Mesa, Calif. 92041. *Agent:* Dave Balsiger, 257 Brentwood St., Costa Mesa, Calif. 92627. *Office:* Grace Ministry, 9601 Candy Lane, La Mesa, Calif. 92041; and, 8600 La Mesa Blvd., La Mesa, Calif. 92041.

CAREER: U.S. Navy, career officer, 1942-54; serving as radiologist in navy hospitals; left service as lieutenant commander; radiologist in La Mesa, Calif., 1953—. Grace Ministry, La Mesa, Calif., counselor, 1968—; president and professor at Grace College of Discipleship and Theology, 1970—; priest at Grace Ministry Chapels in Orange and La Mesa, Calif., 1973—. Senior high school youth counselor. *Member:* American Medical Association, Radiological Society of North America, California Medical Association, San Diego County Medical Society, San Diego Radiological Society, California Medical Society, National Medical Veterans Society, Christian Medical Society, Alpha Omega Alpha.

WRITINGS—All under name Rob Robley: (With wife, Grace Robley) *Spirit-Led Family,* Whitaker House, 1974; (with G. Robley) *Spank Me If You Love Me,* New Leaf Press, 1975.

WORK IN PROGRESS: Healing, Spiritual Sexuality, and *Christian Ethics,* all with wife, Grace Robley.

AVOCATIONAL INTERESTS: Travel (Japan, Canada, Italy, Greece, Turkey, Lebanon, Egypt, England, Israel).

* * *

ROCHE, J. Jeffrey 1916(?)-1975

1916(?)—March 10, 1975; American journalist, editor, and author. Obituaries: *New York Times,* March 12, 1975.

* * *

ROCHE, Kennedy Francis 1911-

PERSONAL: Born December 7, 1911, in Ireland; son of Maurice (a photographer) and Frances (Farrell) Roche; married Mary McCarthy, July 17, 1955; children: Maurice, Edward, Kennedy Francis, Jr. *Education:* National University of Ireland, University College, Cork, B.A., 1938, M.A., 1943. *Politics:* "Reasonably liberal-conservative (I should hope)." *Religion:* Roman Catholic. *Home:* Brierley, Waterfall Rd., Bishopstown, Cork, Ireland. *Office:* Department of Modern History, University College, National University of Ireland, Cork, Ireland.

CAREER: Clerk of District Courts in Mallow and Buttevant, Cork, Ireland, 1938-48; National University of Ireland, College in Cork, lecturer in modern history, 1948—. *Member:* Irish Federation of University Teachers, Irish Historical Society, Cork Historical and Archaeological Society.

WRITINGS: (Contributor) Daniel O'Connell, editor, *Nine Centenary Essays,* Browne & Nolan, 1949; (contributor) James Hogan, editor, *Historical Studies III: London,* Bowes & Bowes, 1961; *Rousseau: Stoic and Romantic,* Methuen, 1974; (contributor) J. G. Barry, editor, *Historical Studies IX: Belfast,* Blackstaff Press, 1975.

WORK IN PROGRESS: Research on nominalist elements in the thought of J. J. Rousseau.

SIDELIGHTS: Roche writes: "My motive in writing: to seek to understand, from a relatively conservative point of view, the causes of discontent with historic Western Civilisation on the part of revolutionists and non-conformists, and to think out for myself what the real weaknesses of that civilisation are."

* * *

ROCHE, Orion 1948-

PERSONAL: Born January 1, 1948, in New Orleans, La.; son of Danton deRohan (a physician) and Marie (an artist; maiden name, Beyle) Roche. *Education:* Harvard University, A.B., 1969; University of California, Berkeley, M.A., 1971. *Residence:* Philadelphia, Pa. *Address:* Pulse-Finger Press, Box 16697, Philadelphia, Pa. 19139.

CAREER: Pulse-Finger Press, Philadelphia, Pa., editor, 1969—.

WRITINGS: Arnarclaw (poems), Pulse-Finger Press, 1973.

SIDELIGHTS: Roche told *CA:* "I am very much concerned with making a contribution to the small press movement in the U.S., to offering an alternative for writers, especially poets, to the conglomerated commercial presses. Historically, the independent press movement has nourished American literature; that nourishment is needed now."

* * *

ROCKLIN, Ross Louis 1913-
(H. F. Cente, Ross Rocklynne, Carlton Smith)

PERSONAL: Born February 21, 1913, in Cincinnati, Ohio; son of Francis Joseph (a machinist) and Rose Lena (Vandermullen) Rocklin; married Frances Rosenthal, September 16, 1941 (divorced, 1947); children: Keith Alan, Jeffrey David. *Education:* Educated in Cincinnati, Ohio. *Politics:* "Not particularly." *Religion:* "Have studied many." *Home and office:* 456 South Lake St., Los Angeles, Calif. 90057.

CAREER: Writer. Has worked as a story analyst for Warner Bros. (motion picture studio), in Hollywood, Calif., and for a literary agency; has also worked as a salesman and repairman of sewing machines, taxicab driver and dispatcher, lumberjack, sales clerk in an art shop, and building manager.

WRITINGS—Under pseudonym Ross Rocklynne: (Contributor) Harlan Ellison, editor, *Again, Dangerous Visions,* Doubleday, 1972; *The Men and the Mirror* (stories), Ace Books, 1973; *The Sun Destroyers,* Ace Books, 1973. Also author of a book, *What to Do About Pain,* as yet unpublished. Contributor of over one hundred stories to science fiction magazines, and of one story, under each of two pseudonyms H. F. Cente and Carlton Smith, to *Planet Stories.*

BIOGRAPHICAL/CRITICAL SOURCES: Harlan Ellison, editor, *Again, Dangerous Visions,* Doubleday, 1972.

* * *

ROCKNE, Dick 1939-

PERSONAL: Born August 19, 1939, in Seattle, Wash.; son

of Lars (a carpenter) and Carin (Lundeen) Rockne; married Charlotte Hansen, September 18, 1960; children: Joseph, Andrew, Matthew. *Education:* Central Washington State College, B.A., 1961. *Home:* 8704 Madrona Lane, Edmonds, Wash. 98020. *Office: Seattle Times,* Fairview Ave. N. & John St., Seattle, Wash. 98111.

CAREER: Republic Publishing Co., Yakima, Wash., newspaper reporter, 1961-63; *Seattle Times,* Seattle, Wash., reporter, 1963—. *Military service:* U.S. Army Reserve, 1957-60. *Awards, honors:* State sportswriting awards from Sigma Delta Chi, 1970, 1972.

WRITINGS: Bow Down to Washington (history of football at University of Washington, Seattle), Strode, 1975.

AVOCATIONAL INTERESTS: Camping, vegetable gardening.

*   *   *

RODELL, Marie F(reid)   1912-1975
(Marion Randolph)

1912—November 9, 1975; American literary agent, editor, mystery novelist, and author of a textbook on mystery fiction. Obituaries: *New York Times,* November 10, 1975; *Publishers Weekly,* November 17, 1975.

*   *   *

ROECKER, W(illiam) A.   1942-

PERSONAL: Born January 17, 1942, in Madison, Wis.; son of Alan Wallace (a science librarian) and Maxeen (Spees) Roecker. *Education:* University of Oregon, B.S., 1966, M.F.A., 1967. *Home:* 1640 North Campbell, Tucson, Ariz. 85719. *Office:* Department of English, University of Arizona, Tucson, Ariz. 85721.

CAREER: Lane Community College, Eugene, Ore., part time instructor in English, 1967; University of Arizona, Tucson, instructor, 1968-72, associate professor of English, 1972—. *Awards, honors:* National Endowment for the Arts award, 1973, for writing.

WRITINGS: Williamette (poetry chapbook), Baleen Press, 1970; (editor and author of introduction) *Stories That Count* (anthology), Holt, 1971; *You Know Me* (poems), Sumac Press, 1972. Poems anthologized in *Yearbook of Modern Poetry,* edited by Jeanne Hollyfield, Young Publications, 1971; *Recycle This Poem,* Dragonfly Press, 1971; *The Erotic Anthology,* Signet Books, 1972; *Poetry of the Desert Southwest,* edited by James E. Quick, Baleen Press, 1973. Contributor of poems to *Nation, McCall's,* and *Chicago Tribune Sunday Magazine;* contributor of poems, short stories, and reviews to over forty journals in his field. Assistant editor of *Northwest Review,* 1967.

*   *   *

ROETTER, Charles Frederick   1919-
(Satiricus)

PERSONAL: Born August 27, 1919, in Berlin, Germany; son of Frederick (an attorney) and Ada Roetter; married Barbara Patty Johnson, September 8, 1942; children: Martyn, Christine. *Education:* Attended University of London, 1937-39; Peterhouse College, Cambridge, LL.B., 1941. *Home:* 5 Balmoral Mansions, Clevedon Rd., Twickenham, Middlesex, England. *Agent:* John Farquharson, 15 Red Lion Sq., London WC1R 4QW, England. *Office:* British Broadcasting Corp., Broadcasting House, London W1A 1AA, England.

CAREER: British Foreign Office, London, England, special adviser in political intelligence department, 1941-46; British Broadcasting Corp., London, England, correspondent on international affairs, 1946—, head of special diplomatic unit, 1960-64, editor in charge of "BBC Europe" (English broadcasts to Europe), 1964, and "The World Tonight" (daily program), 1974. *Member:* Travellers' Club (London), Tyrells Wood Golf Club, Bushmen.

WRITINGS: (With Emily Hahn) *Meet the British,* Newman Neame, 1953; (with Geoffrey Willans) *The Wit of Winston Churchill,* Parrish, 1954; *Fire Is Their Enemy,* Angus & Robertson, 1962; *The Diplomatic Art,* Macrae, 1963; *The Art of Psychological Warfare,* Stein & Day, 1974 (published in England as *Psychological Warfare,* Batsford, 1974).

Under pseudonym Satiricus, author of monthly column, "International Panorama" in *Cheshire Life,* 1961—.

Editor and compiler of historical sections of *Junior Pears Encyclopaedia* and *Pears Encyclopaedias.* Contributor to *Reader's Digest Great World Atlas, Reader's Digest Complete Atlas of the British Isles, Purnell's History of the Second World War,* and to magazines in England and the United States, including *Reader's Digest.*

WORK IN PROGRESS: Research for a book analyzing the effect of human foibles and errors in politics, especially international affairs; research to discover whether more rapid and comprehensive means of communication increase or reduce understanding, whether language is a help or a barrier, and whether the world would be better or worse off if everyone spoke the same language.

SIDELIGHTS: Roetter writes: "To me, history is so fascinating because the versions intelligent men and women give of important events, are frequently incompatible. The same is true of the contemporary scene, and the reader, viewer, or listener is left wondering whether the people addressing him, are in fact describing the same event. To illuminate, even briefly, merely a fraction of the methods by which we conduct our affairs, is my great concern, and it affords me immense satisfaction, if I feel I am succeeding in doing so occasionally in my work." *Avocational interests:* Travel, golf, "cutting a split second off my time tobogganing down the Cresta Run."

*   *   *

ROFFMAN, Howard   1953-

PERSONAL: Born April 18, 1953, in Philadelphia, Pa.; son of Daniel (a salesman) and Anita (Golden) Roffman. *Education:* University of Pennsylvania, B.A., 1974; attending Spessard Holland Law Center, 1974—. *Home:* 8829 Blue Grass Rd., Philadelphia, Pa. 19152.

CAREER: Student.

WRITINGS: Presumed Guilty: Lee Harvey Oswald in the Assassination of President Kennedy, Fairleigh Dickinson University Press, 1975; *Understanding the Cold War: A Study of the Cold War in the Interwar Period,* Fairleigh Dickinson University Press, in press. Contributor to law journals.

WORK IN PROGRESS: Legal research and research on open government for governmental responsibility.

*   *   *

ROGERS, A(mos) Robert   1927-

PERSONAL: Born September 9, 1927, in Moncton, New

Brunswick, Canada; son of Amos R. (a farmer) and Ethel (Lutes) Rogers; married Rhoda M. Page, December 18, 1960; children: Mark. *Education:* University of New Brunswick, B.A., 1948; University of Toronto, M.A., 1950; University of London, Academic Post Graduate Diploma in Librarianship, 1953; University of Michigan, Ph.D., 1964. *Politics:* Democrat. *Religion:* United Methodist. *Home:* 1965 Pine View Dr., Kent, Ohio 44240. *Office:* School of Library Science, Kent State University, Kent, Ohio 44242.

CAREER: University of New Brunswick, Fredericton, assistant librarian, 1951-55, executive librarian, 1955-56; Detroit Public Library, Detroit, Mich., adult assistant, 1957-59; Bowling Green State University Library, Bowling Green, Ohio, assistant to director, 1959-61, acting director, 1961-64, director, 1964-69; Kent State University, Kent, Ohio, professor of library science, 1969—. *Member:* American Library Association (council member, 1972—), Canadian Library Association, Library Association of Great Britain, National Education Association, American Association of University Professors, Ohio Library Association. *Awards, honors:* Best article of the year award from Ohio Library Association, 1973, for "Some Impressions of Three Russian Libraries," *Ohio Library Association Bulletin.*

WRITINGS: The White Monument, Ryerson, 1955; *The Humanities: A Selective Guide to Information Sources,* Libraries Unlimited, 1974. Contributor to library journals.

WORK IN PROGRESS: A book on information sources in philosophy; a report for Northeastern Ohio Library Association; a chapter for the American Library Association centennial festschrift on library buildings, 1876-1976.

* * *

ROGERS, Josephine 1925-

PERSONAL: Born May 6, 1925, in Sydney, New South Wales, Australia; daughter of Percy (a compositor) and Dora (Scoular) Rogers. *Education:* University of Sydney, B.S., 1944; Royal Prince Alfred Hospital, certificate of dietetics, 1945. *Home:* Mort St., Randwick, New South Wales 2031, Australia. *Office:* Royal Prince Alfred Hospital, Missenden Rd., Camperdown, New South Wales 2050, Australia.

CAREER: Royal Prince Alfred Hospital, Camperdown, New South Wales, Australia, chief dietitian, 1948—. Lecturer at University of Sydney, 1968—. *Member:* New South Wales Institute of Dietitians (chairman, 1974—).

WRITINGS: (With F. W. Clements) *Food and Diet for Family Health in Australia and New Zealand,* Reed, 1972.

* * *

ROLAND, Albert 1925-

PERSONAL: Born December 9, 1925, in Pinerolo, Italy; son of Carlo and Mary (Bellini) Roland; married Jo Ann Alkire (a teacher), December 20, 1950; children: Ann Claire, Kathryn Lei, Daniel Arnaud, Paul Alkire, Carl Albert. *Education:* Attended University of Rome and University of Turin, 1944-47; Bethel College, Newton, Kan., B.A., 1948; University of Kansas, M.A., 1951. *Religion:* "Grew up in Waldensian family." *Home:* 3717 Underwood St., Chevy Chase, Md. 20015. *Office:* U.S. Information Agency, 1776 Pennsylvania Ave., Washington, D.C. 20547.

CAREER: Capper Publications, Topeka, Kan., editor,

1951-57; U.S. Information Agency, Washington, D.C., magazine editor in Washington, D.C., 1957-64, editorial director in Manila, the Philippines, 1964-69, in charge of publications program in Washington, D.C., 1969—.

WRITINGS: Christian Values in Recent Fiction, University Press of Kansas, 1951; (editor with Richard Wilson and Michael Rahill) *Adlai Stevenson of the United Nations,* Free Asia Press, 1965; *Great Indian Chiefs* (juvenile), Crowell-Collier, 1966, revised edition, 1972; *The Philippines* (juvenile), Macmillan, 1967; (contributor) Hennig Cohen, editor, *The American Culture,* Houghton, 1968; *Profiles from the New Asia* (juvenile), Macmillan, 1970. Contributor to literary journals, including *Antioch Review, Western Humanities Review, American Quarterly,* and *Quill.*

WORK IN PROGRESS: A book of profiles of immigrants.

SIDELIGHTS: Roland writes: "The first magazine I edited was a four-page, poorly mimeographed job some friends and I started publishing in high school—a rather unusual venture in the northern Italian town where I was born. Still a teenager, in Italian magazines, I grappled with semi-philosophical and political issues—and wrote love poems. Later I did quite a bit of travel writing. A lifelong fascination with the American Indians—going back to the summer days in the foothills of the Alps when, decked out in full turkey-feather bonnet, I was 'Powerful Jaguar'—resulted eventually in my first book for Macmillan, *Great Indian Chiefs.* . . .Three of my books are classed as 'juveniles' but there was no conscious effort on my part to single out an audience, except for the deliberate avoidance of useless big words and overly involved sentences."

AVOCATIONAL INTERESTS: Travel, tennis.

* * *

ROLLER, Duane H(enry D(uBose) 1920-

PERSONAL: Born March 14, 1920, in Eagle Pass, Tex.; son of Duane Emerson and Doris Della (DuBose) Roller; married Marjorie Fair Williamson, March 15, 1942; children: Duane Williamson. *Education:* Columbia University, A.B., 1941; Purdue University, M.S., 1949; Harvard University, Ph.D., 1954. *Home:* 648 South Lahoma St., Norman, Okla. 73069. *Office:* History of Science Collections, 401 West Brooks, Room 339, University of Oklahoma, Norman, Okla. 73069.

CAREER: University of Oklahoma, Norman, assistant professor, 1954-58, associate professor, 1958-62, McCasland Professor of History of Science, 1962—, curator of DeGolyer Collection, 1954-58, curator of History of Science Collections, 1958—, assistant director for special collections of the university library, 1971—, university research institute, member of board of directors, 1957-61, vice-president, 1967. Chairman, U.S. Committee on the History and Philosophy of Science, 1964-65. *Military service:* U.S. Naval Reserve, 1941-62; active duty, 1941-46; became lieutenant commander. *Member:* International Academy of History of Sciences (corresponding member), American Association for the Advancement of Science (fellow), History of Science Society, American Association of University Professors, Midwest Junto (president, 1960-61), Oklahoma Academy of Sciences, Phi Beta Kappa, Sigma Xi. *Awards, honors:* National Science Foundation senior postdoctoral fellow, 1961-62.

WRITINGS: (With father, Duane E. Roller) *Development of the Concept of Electrical Charge: Electricity from the*

Greeks to Coulomb, Harvard University Press, 1954; (compiler) *A Checklist of the E. DeGolyer Collection in the History of Science and Technology,* University of Oklahoma Library, 1954; (with Gerald Holton) *Foundations of Modern Physical Science,* Addison-Wesley, 1957; (editor with D. E. Roller and James B. Conant) *Harvard Case Histories in Experimental Science,* two volumes, Harvard University Press, 1957; *The De Magnete of William Gilbert,* International Antiquariaat, 1959; *Perspectives in the History of Science and Technology,* University of Oklahoma Press, 1971; (with Marcia M. Goodman) *A Catalogue of the History of Science Collections of the University of Oklahoma Libraries,* Mansell, 1976. Editor, *Landmarks of Science,* 1967—.

*   *   *

ROONEY, James R(owell)   1927-

PERSONAL: Born December 16, 1927, in Brooklyn, N.Y.; son of James R. and Hellen (Belt) Rooney; married Audrey Heyman (an artist), October 15, 1960; children: Melinda Grace, Alec James. *Education:* Dartmouth College, A.B., 1949; Cornell University, D.V.M., 1952; Virginia Polytechnic Institute and University, M.S., 1957. *Politics:* "Philosophical Anarchist." *Religion:* "Nominal Episcopal." *Home:* 46 West Fourth St., New Castle, Del. 19720. *Office:* New Bolton Center, Kennett Square, Pa. 19348.

CAREER: Virginia Polytechnic Institute and University, Blacksburg, began as assistant professor, became professor of veterinary pathology, 1952-54; U.S. Army Biological Laboratories, Frederick, Md., chief of laboratories, 1958-60; University of Kentucky, Lexington, professor of veterinary pathology, 1961-69; University of Pennsylvania, New Bolton Center, Kennett Square, professor of veterinary pathology, 1969—. *Military service:* U.S. Army, Veterinary Corps, 1952-54; became first lieutenant.

MEMBER: American College of Veterinary Pathologists, American Association of Equine Practitioners, Royal Veterinary College (Sweden; fellow). *Awards, honors:* Model Cities drama award, 1973, for play "You Just Think About That"; M.A. from University of Pennsylvania, 1974; winner of bicentennial play contest, Delaware Theatre Association, 1975, for "Michael Doughtery."

WRITINGS: (With W. O. Sack) *Guide to the Dissection of the Horse,* Edwards Brothers, 1954, 2nd edition (with Sack and R. E. Habel), 1967; *Biomechanics of Lameness in Horses,* Williams & Wilkins, 1969; *Autopsy of the Horse,* Williams & Wilkins, 1970; *Clinical Neurology of the Horse,* Kennett News and Advertiser Press, 1971; *The Lame Horse,* A. S. Barnes, 1974; *The Sick Horse,* A. S. Barnes, in press.

Plays: " ... And Obey" (three-act), first produced in Bryn Mawr, Pa. at Cabrini College, 1972; "This Message Brought to You By ... " (one-act), first produced in Wilmington, Del. by the Immanuel Players, 1973; *The Demon Cat* (one-act), Proscenium, 1974; "To Whom We Tithe" (one-act), first produced in Wilmington by the Immanuel Players, 1974. Also writer of unpublished and as yet unproduced plays, "You Just Think About That" and "Michael Doughtery."

WORK IN PROGRESS: Plays.

SIDELIGHTS: Rooney writes: "My major interest is theatre....The long term study of an animal, the horse, leads me to consideration of the interactions of the most complex animal, man, and thus and so I find myself a playwright." *Avocational interests:* The development of a veterinary association for the creative and performing acts.

*   *   *

ROQUEMORE, Kathleen (Ann)   1941-

PERSONAL: Born July 29, 1941, in Waukegan, Ill.; daughter of Malcolm Stewart and Catherine (Emerick) Main; married Andrew Poulson, 1960 (divorced, 1969); married Thomas Roquemore (operator of mobile home repair service), 1969; children: (first marriage) Patrick, Thomas, Penne; (second marriage) Stacy William, Jaimy Adam, Tobey. *Education:* Attended schools in Illinois and California. *Politics:* "Patriotic American desiring new breed of politicians that will work for our country." *Religion:* "Metaphysics—Truth Study." *Home and office address:* General Delivery, Parks, Ark. 72950.

CAREER: Institute of Scientific Suggestion, Amarillo, Tex., self-hypnosis instructor in sales management, 1972; Meditation Unlimited, Amarillo, Tex., co-founder and instructor, 1972-73; self-employed numerologist, meditation instructor, therapist, counselor, lecturer, and masseuse in Amarillo, Tex., 1973—. Division manager of Liberty Foods & Metals (Amarillo), 1974. *Member:* New Age Foundation (president of New Journey Group, 1974—).

WRITINGS: It's All in Your Numbers: The Secrets of Numerology, Harper, 1975. Writer of "Astro-guide" for *Amarillo Advocate,* 1974; columnist for *Waldron News.*

WORK IN PROGRESS: Meditation: Brand Z, instruction in combined active and passive meditation technique, how and why it works, and extensive exercises; *The Path of the Disciple; Why Are We Here?; The One You Love; An Exploration of Mysteries: Atlantis, Fact or Fantasy ... UFO's ... The Bermuda Triangle Occurrences ... The Future of Earth;* research on Biblical prophecies and revelations, on spiritual or psychic healing techniques, on photochromotherapy, and on progressed numerological charts for determining possible future trends, circumstances, events, and best choices of action and interests.

SIDELIGHTS: Kathleen Roquemore writes: "The main motivation for my writing and activities is a desire to increase my own understanding and aid others to understand more about themselves, their lives, spirituality and God, and the times in which we are living as well as ways in which we can live a richer, fuller, better life. Almost all of my interests are to some degree related to metaphysics, which I define as being scientific spirituality and a deep search for Truths and understanding. All of my writing is inspired and directed by my spirit guides and revelations received. I am a firm believer in the unseen realms, the latent spirit powers of mankind and our divine nature, and it is my hope to aid others' awareness of their reality."

*   *   *

ROSBOTTOM, Ronald C(arlisle)   1942-

PERSONAL: Born July 15, 1942, in New Orleans, La; son of Albert Carlisle (a sales manager) and Marjorie (Chavez) Rosbottom; married Betty Griffin (a museum aide), September 5, 1964; children: Michael Keith. *Education:* Attended Sorbonne, University of Paris, 1962-63; Tulane University, B.A., 1964; Princeton University, M.A., 1966, Ph.D., 1969. *Home:* 1925 Concord Rd., Columbus, Ohio 43212. *Office:* Department of Romance Languages, Ohio State University, 1841 Millikin Rd., Columbus, Ohio 43210.

CAREER: University of Pennsylvania, Philadelphia, instructor, 1967-69, assistant professor of French, 1969-73; Ohio State University, Columbus, associate professor of French literature and criticism, 1973—. Member: Modern Language Association of America, American Society for Eighteenth Century Studies, American Association of Teachers of French, Societe Francaise d'Etude du 18e Siecle. Awards, honors: Woodrow Wilson fellow, 1966-67; grant-in-aid from American Council of Learned Societies, summer, 1972; American Philosophical Society grant, summer, 1973.

WRITINGS: (Contributor) Peter Hughes and David Williams, editors, The Varied Pattern, Hakkert, 1971; Marivaux's Novels: Theme and Function in Early Eighteenth-Century Narrative, Fairleigh-Dickinson University Press, 1974; (editor) Studies in Eighteenth-Century Culture, University of Wisconsin Press, Volume V, 1975, Volume VI, 1976. Contributor to journals. Editorial advisor to Studies in Burke and His Time, 1971—.

WORK IN PROGRESS: Choderlos de Laclos for Twanye; an evaluation of the eighteenth-century novel and the history of ideas.

*   *   *

ROSE, R(obert) B(arrie)   1929-

PERSONAL: Born July 10, 1929, in Bebington, England; son of Charles William (a railway clerk) and Elsie (an office worker; maiden name, Brown) Rose; married, wife's name Madeline Mary, October 16, 1954; children: Alison, Michael James. Education: University of Manchester, B.A. (honors), 1950, M.A., 1953. Office: Department of History, University of Tasmania, Hobart, Tasmania.

CAREER: Pilgrim Trust, London, England, editorial research assistant, 1956-59; University of Sydney, Sydney, Australia, 1960-70, began as lecturer, became senior lecturer, then reader in history; University of Tasmania, Hobart, professor of history, 1971—, dean of arts, 1976—. Member of schools board of Tasmania, 1974—. Military service: British Army, 1953-54; became sergeant. Member: Tasmanian Historical Research Association, Australian Society for European History, French Historical Society, Societe des Etudes Robespierristes, Derwent Sailing Squadron.

WRITINGS: (Contributor) The Victoria History of the County of Warwick, Volume VII, University of London, 1964; (with N. K. Meaney and F. G. Stambrook) Worlds Old and New, F. W. Cheshire, 1964; The Enrages: Socialists of the French Revolution?, Cambridge University Press, 1965; The Russian Revolution of 1917, F. W. Cheshire, 1970; Paradigm for Revolution?: The Paris Commune, 1871-1971, Australian National University Press, 1972; (with Meaney and others) The West and the World, Science Press (Sydney, Australia), 1972; Gracchus Babeuf, 1760-1797: The First Modern Communist, Open Court, 1976. Contributor to history journals.

WORK IN PROGRESS: Democratic Ideas and Organization in Paris, 1789-1792, completion expected in 1978.

SIDELIGHTS: Rose writes: "As an historian I am interested in history from below, the history of the ideas, aspirations and institutions of the mass of ordinary men and women, and especially in the . . . questions of liberty and the exercise and restraint of political power."

ROSE, Stuart   1899(?)-1975

1899(?)—August 11, 1975; American book and magazine editor, literary consultant, and author. Obituaries: New York Times, August 15, 1975; Washington Post, August 17, 1975; AB Bookman's Weekly, September 8, 1975.

*   *   *

ROSEN, Paul L(yon)   1939-

PERSONAL: Born June 16, 1939, in Yonkers, N.Y.; son of David and Shirley (Siskin) Rosen; married Virginia Heather McConnell (a psychiatric clinician), December 20, 1964; children: Heather, Rachael. Education: Lehigh University, B.A. (cum laude), 1961; New School for Social Research, M.A., 1963, Ph.D., 1971. Home: 69 Broadway Ave., Ottawa, Ontario, Canada K1S 2B5. Office: Department of Political Science, Carleton University, Ottawa, Ontario, Canada K1S 5B6.

CAREER: New York University, New York, N.Y., lecturer in sociology, 1963-64; Carleton University, Ottawa, Ontario, lecturer, 1964-65, assistant professor, 1965-69, associate professor of political science, 1969—. Member: American Political Science Association, Phi Alpha Theta. Awards, honors: Canada Council grant, 1975—.

WRITINGS: The Supreme Court and Social Science, University of Illinois Press, 1972.

WORK IN PROGRESS: A Political and Legal Theory of Dissent and Disobedience and the Dilemma of Constitutional Government.

*   *   *

ROSENBERG, Arthur D(onald)   1939-

PERSONAL: Born June 14, 1939, in New York, N.Y.; son of Joseph and Rose (Shagrofsky) Rosenberg. Education: Attended Whittier College, 1957-59, University of California, Los Angeles, 1959-61, and University of Grenoble, 1965-68. Home: 18 Parc Chateau-Banquet, CH-1202, Geneva, Switzerland. Office: International Labour Office, Geneva, Switzerland.

CAREER: International Olympic Committee, Grenoble, France, translator and interpreter, 1965-68; McGraw-Hill Book Co., New York, N.Y., marketing manager, 1968-72; Harcourt Brace Jovanovich, New York, N.Y., assistant manager of international branch, 1972-73; Dun Donnelly Publishing Co., New York, N.Y., business, economics, and mathematics editor, 1973-75; International Labour Office, Geneva, Switzerland, sales promotion officer, 1975—. Teacher of French and English, University of Stockholm, 1962-63, Berlitz School, Paris, 1963-64, McGraw-Hill Book Co., 1970-71; lecturer at Union College, Union, N.J., 1971-72. Member: American Mathematical Society, American Marketing Society, American Economic Society, Academy of Management, United States Chess Federation.

WRITINGS: Chess for Children and the Young at Heart (juvenile and adult), Atheneum, 1976.

WORK IN PROGRESS: A restaurant guide to Geneva, Switzerland; fiction.

SIDELIGHTS: Rosenberg speaks French, Spanish, German, Italian, Hebrew, and Swedish. He began to play chess at ten years of age.

*   *   *

ROSENBERG, William Gordon   1938-

PERSONAL: Born September 29, 1938, in Philadelphia,

Pa.; son of Gordon William (a manufacturer) and Constance (a teacher; maiden name, Fridenberg) Rosenberg; married Elinor Borenstein (a social worker), June 26, 1960; children: Peter, Sarah. *Education:* Amherst College, B.A., 1960; Harvard University, M.A., 1961, Ph.D., 1967. *Residence:* Ann Arbor, Mich. *Office:* Department of History, University of Michigan, Ann Arbor, Mich. 48104.

CAREER: University of Michigan, Ann Arbor, assistant professor, 1967-71, associate professor of Russian history, 1971—. *Military service:* U.S. Army Reserve, 1961-68. *Member:* American Historical Society, American Association for the Advancement of Slavic Studies.

WRITINGS: A. I. Denikin and the Anti-Bolshevik Movement in South Russia, Amherst College Press, 1961; *Liberals in the Russian Revolution,* Princeton University Press, 1974. Contributor to *New Leader, Michigan Quarterly Review,* and professional journals.

WORK IN PROGRESS: Russian Labor History; History of the Russian Revolution.

* * *

ROSENBLUTH, Gideon 1921-

PERSONAL: Born January 23, 1921, in Berlin, Germany; became Canadian citizen; son of Martin and Marie Rosenbluth; married Annemarie Fischl (a social worker), June 6, 1944; children: Vera Ann, David Peter. *Education:* Attended University of London, 1938-40; University of Toronto, B.A., 1943; Columbia University, Ph.D., 1953. *Office:* Department of Economics, University of British Columbia, Vancouver, British Columbia, Canada.

CAREER: Service in Canadian federal government, 1943-48; Princeton University, Princeton, N.J., lecturer in economics, 1949-50; National Bureau of Economic Research, New York, N.Y., research training fellow in economics, 1951-52; Stanford University, Stanford, Calif., assistant professor of economics, 1952-54; Queen's University, Kingston, Ontario, associate professor of economics, 1954-62; University of British Columbia, Vancouver, professor of economics, 1962—. *Member:* Royal Economic Society, Econometric Society, Canadian Economics Association, Canadian Political Science Association, Canadian Association of University Teachers (president, 1966-67), American Economic Society. *Awards, honors:* Skelton-Clark fellow, 1955-56; Canada Council fellowship, 1961-62; Ford Foundation grant, 1967-68.

WRITINGS: (Contributor) O. Morgenstern, editor, *Economic Activity Analysis,* Wiley, 1954; (contributor) G. J. Stigler, editor, *Business Concentration and Price Policy,* Princeton University Press, 1955; *Concentration in Canadian Manufacturing Industries,* Princeton University Press, 1957; (contributor) Michael Oliver, editor, *Social Purpose for Canada,* University of Toronto Press, 1961; (with H. G. Thoubuon) *Canadian Anti-Combines Administration, 1952-60,* University of Toronto Press, 1963; *The Canadian Economy and Disarmament,* Macmillan, 1967. Contributor of articles to journals in his field. Editor of *Canadian Journal of Economics,* 1972—.

WORK IN PROGRESS: Research on business cycles, on the theory of monopolistic competition, and on the theory of economic development.

* * *

ROSI, Eugene J(oseph) 1931-

PERSONAL: Born January 20, 1931, in Hartford, Conn.;

son of Angelo and Iona (Bioncaloni) Rosi; married Pamela Sheffield, April 12, 1958; children: Christina, Ian. *Education:* Syracuse University, B.A., 1952, M.A., 1953; Johns Hopkins University, School of Advanced International Studies, Bologna, Italy, diploma, 1958; Columbia University, Ph.D., 1964. *Politics:* Democrat. *Religion:* Roman Catholic. *Office:* Department of Political Science, Dickinson College, Carlisle, Pa. 17013.

CAREER: Columbia University, New York, N.Y., instructor in government, 1964-65; Dickinson College, Carlisle, Pa., assistant professor of political science, 1965-67; Dickinson Center, Bologna, Italy, associate professor of political science, 1967-69, director, 1967-69; Dickinson College, associate professor of political science, 1969-72; Dickinson College, Center for International Studies, Bologna, Italy, associate professor of political science, 1972-73, director of undergraduate studies, 1972-73; Dickinson College, professor of political science, 1973—, coordinator of Long-Range Planning, 1973—. Consultant to U.S. Army War College, 1973-74. *Military service:* U.S. Navy, 1954-57. U.S. Naval Reserve, 1958-60; became lieutenant senior grade.

MEMBER: American Political Science Association, International Studies Association, American Association of University Professors, Inter-University Seminar on Armed Forces and Society, Society for College and University Planning. *Awards, honors:* American Philosophical Society research grant, 1971.

WRITINGS: (Contributor) Aaron Wildavsky, editor, *The Presidency,* Little, Brown, 1969; (contributor) *The Foreign Affairs Fifty-Year Bibliography,* Council on Foreign Relations, 1972; (editor and contributor) *American Defense and Detente: Readings in National Security Policy,* Dodd, 1973. Contributor to journalism and political science journals.

WORK IN PROGRESS: Research on public opinion and national security policy; army officers' perceptions of international politics; Italian national security policy.

AVOCATIONAL INTERESTS: Foreign travel.

* * *

ROSNER, Lynn 1944-

PERSONAL: Born January 24, 1944, in New York, N.Y.; daughter of Hyman and Joan (Mulhern) Rosner. *Education:* Attended Goddard College, 1961-62; Columbia University, B.A., 1973; University of New Mexico, M.A. candidate. *Home:* 4300 Sunningdale Ave. N.E., Albuquerque, N.M. 87110. *Office:* Vista Sandia Hospital, Albuquerque, N.M. 87114.

CAREER: American Civil Liberties Union, New York, N.Y., administrative assistant, 1966-73; Jewish Community Council, Albuquerque, N.M., assistant director of summer day camp, 1972-73; Technical-Vocational Institute, Albuquerque, N.M., high school teacher of recreation assistants, 1973-75; Vista Sandia Hospital, Albuquerque, N.M., director of occupational and recreational therapy, 1976—. Free-lance typist; professional singer and guitarist. Supervisor, Bronx Model Cities, 1969-73; administrative assistant, Navajo Youth Recreation Project, 1973-75; member of Albuquerque Metropolitan Youth Task Force, 1973-74. *Member:* American Association for Leisure, National Recreation and Park Association, Society for Park and Recreation Educators, Audubon Society, New Mexico Recreation and Park Association, Phi Beta Kappa.

WRITINGS: Let's Go to a Horse Show, Putnam, 1975. Contributor to *Inroads.*

* * *

ROSS, David 1896-1975

July 7, 1896—November 12, 1975; American radio and television broadcaster, poet, and editor of anthologies. Obituaries: *New York Times,* November 14, 1975; *AB Bookman's Weekly,* December 8, 1975.

* * *

ROSS, Ishbel 1897-1975

1897—September 21, 1975; Scottish-born American journalist, and author of novels, biographies, and other nonfiction. Obituaries: *New York Times,* September 23, 1975; *AB Bookman's Weekly,* December 1, 1975.

* * *

ROSS, Leah 1938-
(Mary Haydn Webb)

PERSONAL: Born August 13, 1938, in Cleveland, Ohio; daughter of Hiram Collins (a writer, editor, and teacher) and Rachel (a librarian; maiden name, Norris) Haydn; married S. David Webb, September 1, 1958 (divorced, 1967); children: Alexander Matthew. *Education:* Cornell University, student, 1956-58; University of California, Berkeley, A.B. (with honors), 1960; University of Florida, M.A., 1967. *Politics:* None. *Religion:* None. *Home:* 1613 Addison St., #C, Berkeley, Calif. 94703. *Agent:* Toby Eady, 64 Lexham Gardens, London W.8, England. *Office:* Black Repertory Group, 1719 Alcatraz Ave., Berkeley, Calif. 94703.

CAREER: Santa Fe Junior College, Gainesville, Fla., instructor in liberal arts, 1966-67; Merritt College, Oakland, Calif., instructor in English, 1967-68; reading teacher in public school in Alachua, Fla., 1968-69; Micanopy Group Companies, Alachua, research assistant, 1969-70; Division of Family Services, Gainesville, social worker and community development specialist, 1970-72; Neighborhood Youth Corps, Gainesville, counselor, 1973; University of Florida Press, Gainesville, copy editor, 1973-74; University of Florida, Personalized Learning Center, Gainesville, secretary and supervisor, 1974; Lees' Pre-School Center, Alachua, director, 1974-75; Black Repertory Group, Berkeley, Calif., theater arts technician, 1975—. Governess, summer, 1955; organizer and supervisor of summer vacation trips for underprivileged children, for *New York Herald Tribune* Fresh Air Fund, summers, 1958-59; organizer, teacher, and director for Modern Dance Program of Center Dance Group (Alachua), 1965-67, 1968-72; policy advisory committee representative for the poverty program of Alachua County, 1966-67, 1972; organized Community Loan Fund (for low-income families in Gainesville), 1970-73, and Emergency Loan Fund within the local welfare program, 1970-72; worked with local Emergency Shelter Committee and its Pleasant House, 1972-73. *Member:* Phi Beta Kappa.

WRITINGS: (Under pseudonym Leah Ross) *Dark Roads* (novel), Harcourt, 1975. Contributor of poems to *American Scholar.*

WORK IN PROGRESS: A book of poems; a book of travel journals, concerning her hitch-hiking trip through Europe and Africa with her son, 1972-73.

SIDELIGHTS: Leah Ross writes: "Artists are mediums through whom the wisdom of the universe passes. My ex-perience is a tool by means of which I learn. My art is a tool by means of which I teach. I see us all as being in an era of explosive change. Most of the most advanced thinkers that I am aware of including writers such as Doris Lessing have said that human consciousness is about to change radically. Something is coming and artists, in their different ways, will herald it. My conception of art was influenced by my working with dance groups and a theater production. The notion of art as somehow communal rather than individual became one of my basic ideas on the subject—Katherine Dunham's notion of 'social' rather than 'fine' arts. My conception of art was also influenced by an involvement with visual images so that my attempt is always to write so that my words could be easily translated into film images ... The persistence of hunger, poverty, and racism in a world which is full of ignorance and money defines my life, my goals and the messages I send out. No real change can come until each person humanizes him/ herself. Part of the significance of the Women's Movement lies in this, that in the future, as women become less oppressed, men will be allowed to feel more and learn more (will be less technically and more humanistically oriented), new balances will be achieved ...''

* * *

ROSSITER, Frank R(aymond) 1937-

PERSONAL: Born December 21, 1937, in Abington, Pa.; son of Frank A. (an envelope manufacturer) and Dorothy (Weiss) Rossiter. *Education:* Harvard University, A.B. (magna cum laude), 1959; University of Pennsylvania, M.S.Ed., 1964; Princeton University, Ph.D., 1970. *Home:* 7912 Shining Willow Lane, Dallas, Tex. 75230. *Office:* Department of History, University of Texas at Dallas, Box 688, Richardson, Tex. 75080.

CAREER: High school teacher of social studies in Montgomery County, Pa., 1963-66; University of Michigan, Ann Arbor, assistant professor of history, 1970-75; University of Texas at Dallas, Richardson, associate professor of history and American studies, 1975—. *Military service:* U.S. Navy, 1959-62; became lieutenant. *Member:* American Studies Association, American Historical Association, Organization of American Historians. *Awards, honors:* Woodrow Wilson fellow, 1966-67; Younger Humanist fellowship from National Endowment for the Humanities, 1973-74.

WRITINGS: Charles Ives and His America, Liveright, 1975. Contributor to *Yearbook for Inter-American Musical Research* and *Dictionary of American Biography.*

WORK IN PROGRESS: Research on American culture, particularly the role of music and the other arts.

* * *

ROTENSTREICH, Nathan 1914-

PERSONAL: Born March 31, 1914, in Sambor, Poland; immigrated to Palestine, 1932; son of Ephraim and Mirjam (Eifermann) Rotenstreich; married Binah Metzger, March 3, 1936. *Education:* Hebrew University of Jerusalem, M.A., 1936, Ph.D., 1938; University of Chicago, postdoctoral study, 1949. *Home:* 7 Marcus St., Jerusalem, Israel. *Office:* Department of Philosophy, Hebrew University, Jerusalem, Israel.

CAREER: Youth Aliyah Teachers Training College, Jerusalem, Israel, principal, 1944-51; Hebrew University, Jerusalem, Israel, member of faculty, 1951—, Ephrat Noa Professor of Philosophy, 1955—, dean of humanities, 1957-61, rector of university, 1963-69, head of Institute of Philosophy, 1971-74. Center for the Study of Democratic Institutions, visiting fellow, 1970, associate, 1972; visiting professor, City College of the City University of New York, 1969-70. *Member:* International Institute of Philosophy, Israel National Academy of Sciences and Humanities. *Awards, honors:* Tscernichowski prize, 1955; Israel Prize for Humanities, 1963.

WRITINGS: Between Past and Present: An Essay on History, with foreword by Martin Buber, Yale University Press, 1958; *Spirit and Man: An Essay on Being and Value,* Nijhoff, 1963; *The Recurring Pattern: Studies in Anti-Judaism in Modern Thought,* Weidenfeld & Nicolson, 1963, Horizon Press, 1964; *Humanism in the Contemporary Era,* Mouton & Co., 1963; *Experience and Its Systemization: Studies in Kant,* Nijhoff, 1965, 2nd edition, 1972; *Basic Problems of Marx's Philosophy,* Bobbs-Merrill, 1965; *On the Human Subject: Studies in the Phenomenology of Ethics and Politics,* C. C Thomas, 1966; *Jewish Philosophy in Modern Times: From Mendelsshon to Rosenzweig,* Holt, 1968; *Tradition and Reality,* Random House, 1972; *Philosophy: The Concept and Its Manifestations,* Reidel, 1973; *From Substance and Subject: Studies in Hegel,* Nijhoff, 1974. Also author of some twenty books in Hebrew, on politics, history, and philosophy of Judaism, published in Israel, 1939—.

WORK IN PROGRESS: Power and Its Mold: An Essay in Social and Political Philosophy; Theory and Practice: An Essay on Human Intentionalities.

SIDELIGHTS: Of *Jewish Philosophy in Modern Times,* Arthur A. Cohen writes in the *New Republic:* "It is to the complex rethinking of classic Judaism in the light of the Kantian revolution that Nathan Rotenstreich's brilliant book, *Jewish Philosophy in Modern Times,* is directed. Rotenstreich, a careful and scrupulous scholar, shows how Jewish thinkers, disarmed by Kant's critique of *religious* metaphysics, sought to salvage Judaism by making ethics its quasi-autonomous essence."

*   *   *

ROTH, Herbert (Otto)   1917-

PERSONAL: Born December 7, 1917, in Vienna, Austria; son of Emil (an engineer) and Therese (Heilpern) Roth; married Margaret Frances Hogben, November 29, 1946; children: Martin, Stephen, Janet. *Education:* Victoria University of Wellington, B.A., 1947; New Zealand Library School, diploma, 1947. *Politics:* "Left-wing." *Religion:* None. *Home:* 69 Carlton St., Hillsborough, Auckland 4, New Zealand. *Office:* Library, University of Auckland, Private Bag, Auckland, New Zealand.

CAREER: National Library Service, Wellington, New Zealand, head of cataloging section, 1948-52, head of reference section, 1952-61; University of Auckland, Auckland, New Zealand, deputy librarian, 1962—. *Military service:* Royal New Zealand Air Force, 1944-46. *Member:* New Zealand Library Association (member of council, 1963-67), Association of University Teachers. *Awards, honors:* New Zealand Library Association fellowship, 1964, and John Harris Award, 1965, for *A Bibliography of New Zealand Education.*

WRITINGS: George Hogben, New Zealand Council for Educational Research, 1952; *A Bibliography of New Zealand Education,* New Zealand Council for Educational Research, 1964; *Labour Legislation in New Zealand,* Uni-

versity of Auckland Press, 1964; (with Rona Bailey) *Shanties by the Way,* Whitcombe & Tombs, 1967; *New Zealand Trade Unions: A Bibliography,* University of Auckland Press, 1970; *Trade Unions in New Zealand: Past and Present,* Reed Education, 1973, revised edition, 1974. Contributor of articles and reviews to professional journals.

SIDELIGHTS: Roth writes: "My main interest is New Zealand social history, and particularly the history of the labour movement. Besides writing about it, I have also accumulated what is probably the most comprehensive private collection of books and journals, pamphlets, leaflets, posters, etc. in this subject."

*   *   *

ROTH, Robert Paul   1919-

PERSONAL: Surname rhymes with "boat"; born December 8, 1919, in Milwaukee, Wis.; son of Paul Wagner (a clergyman) and Rose Marie (Schulzke) Roth; married Margaret Beckstrand (a professor of child development), June 17, 1943; children: Erik, Maren (Mrs. Thomas Hood), Maarja (Mrs. Rolf Evenson), John, Sonja. *Education:* Carthage College, B.A., 1941; University of Illinois, M.A., 1942; Northwestern Lutheran Theological Seminary, B.D., 1945; University of Chicago, Ph.D., 1947. *Politics:* Independent. *Home:* 4194 Hillcrest Lane, Wayzata, Minn. 55391. *Office:* Office of Dean, Northwestern Lutheran Seminary, 1501 Fulham St., St. Paul, Minn. 55108.

CAREER: Ordained Lutheran minister, 1945; Luthergiri Seminary, Rajahmundry, India, professor of theology, 1946-48; Augustana College, Rock Island, Ill., associate professor of philosophy, 1948-49; St. Paul's Lutheran Church, Red Wing, Minn., pastor, 1949-53; Lutheran Theological Southern Seminary, Columbia, S.C., professor of New Testament, 1953-61, dean of Graduate School, 1954-61; Northwestern Theological Seminary, St. Paul, Minn., professor of systematic theology, 1961-68, dean, 1968—. Member of Planning Commission of Minnetonka School District, 1961-63; lecturer at Ecumenical Institute, Geneva, Switzerland, summer, 1963. Chairman of Lutheran Church in America Commission on Architecture, 1964-68, and Committee on Worship, 1975—; president of Consortium of Minnesota Seminary Faculties, 1973-75.

MEMBER: Lutheran Professors Association, North American Academy of Ecumenists. *Awards, honors:* D.D., Roanoke College, 1958; American Association of Theological Schools fellow, Switzerland, 1966-67; Aid Association for Lutherans research grant, 1976.

WRITINGS: (Contributor) T. K. Thompson, editor, *Stewardship in Contemporary Theology,* Association Press, 1960; (contributor) Carl F. H. Henry, editor, *The Biblical Expositor,* A. J. Holman, 1960; (contributor) Helmut Lehmann, editor, *Meaning and Practice of the Lord's Supper,* Muhlenberg Press, 1961; (contributor) Henry, editor, *Basic Christian Doctrines,* Holt, 1962; (contributor) Kendig Brubaker Cully, editor, *Westminster Dictionary of Christian Education,* Westminster Press, 1963; (contributor) Henry, editor, *Christian Faith and Modern Theology,* Channel Press, 1964; (contributor) Wilbur G. Volker, editor, *Uniform Lesson Commentary,* Fortress, 1964; (with Gerald B. Strickler) *The Acts of the Apostles,* Board of Parish Education of the Lutheran Church in America, 1967; *Story and Reality,* Eerdmans, 1973. Contributor to *Lutheran Quarterly, Dialog, Christianity Today, Religion in Life, Minnesota Medicine,* and other journals and magazines. Member of general editorial committee of *New International Bible,* 1968-73.

WORK IN PROGRESS: Theologians of the Twentieth Century, for Fortress.

AVOCATIONAL INTERESTS: Painting watercolors, sailing, canoeing, skiing.

*   *   *

ROTHBLATT, Donald N(oah)   1935-

PERSONAL: Born April 28, 1935, in New York, N.Y.; son of Harry and Sophie (Chernofsky) Rothblatt; married Ann Vogel (a teacher), June 16, 1957; children: Joel M., Steven S. *Education:* City University of New York, B.Civil Engineering, 1957; Columbia University, M.S., 1963; Institute of Social Studies, The Hague, diploma in comprehensive planning, 1964; Harvard University, Ph.D., 1969. *Home:* 1957 Sycamore Glen, San Jose, Calif. 95125. *Office:* Department of Urban and Regional Planning, San Jose State University, San Jose, Calif. 95192.

CAREER: New York City Planning Commission, New York, N.Y., planner, 1961-62; New York Housing and Redevelopment Board, New York, N.Y., planner, 1963-66; Harvard University, Cambridge, Mass., research fellow at Center for Environmental Design Studies, 1965-71, assistant professor of city and regional planning, 1969-71; San Jose State University, San Jose, Calif., professor of urban and regional planning, 1971—, chairman of department, 1971—. Member of local citizens' community improvement committee. *Military service:* U.S. Army, Corps of Engineers, 1957-58; became first lieutenant.

MEMBER: American Institute of Planners (member of task force on national urban policy, 1972-76), Association of Collegiate Schools of Planning (president, 1974-76), California Committee on Environmental Design Education (chairman, 1973-75). *Awards, honors:* Traveling fellowship from Dutch Government, 1964; William F. Milton Research Fellow, Harvard University, 1970-71; faculty research grant from National Science Foundation, 1972-76.

WRITINGS: Human Needs and Public Housing, New York City Housing Library, 1964; *Thailand's Northeast,* Center for Environmental Design Studies, Harvard University, 1967; *Regional Planning: The Appalachian Experience,* Heath, 1971; *Allocation of Resources for Regional Planning,* Appalachian Regional Commission, 1972; (editor) *National Policy for Urban and Regional Development,* Heath, 1974. Contributor to planning, urban studies, and regional studies journals.

WORK IN PROGRESS: An Approach to Metropolitan-Wide Conflict Resolution: The Multiple Advocacy Process; Suburbia: The Future of Urban America.

*   *   *

ROTHENBERG, Robert Edward   1908-

PERSONAL: Born September 27, 1908, in New York, N.Y.; son of Simon (a psychiatrist) and Caroline (Baer) Rothenberg; married Lillian Lustig (a hospital administrator), June 8, 1933; children: Robert P., Lynn Barbara (Mrs. Richard L. Kay). *Education:* Cornell University, A.B., 1929, M.D., 1932; graduate study at Royal Infirmary, Edinburgh, 1934-35. *Home:* 35 Sutton Pl., New York, N.Y. 10022. *Office:* 870 Fifth Ave., New York, N.Y. 10021

CAREER: Jewish Hospital and Medical Center of Brooklyn, Brooklyn, N.Y., intern, 1932-34; private practice as a surgeon in New York, N.Y., 1935—; Downstate State University College of Medicine, New York, N.Y., clinical assistant professor of environmental medicine and community health, 1950-60; Jewish Hospital and Medical Center of Brooklyn, attending surgeon, 1954-74; French-Polyclinic Medical School and Health Center, New York, N.Y., attending surgeon, 1962—. Diplomate of American Board of Surgery; president of Medbook Publications, Inc., 1966—, chairman of Medical Group Council, 1947-64; member of medical advisory board of Hotel Association and Hotel Workers Health Plan, 1950-60; member of board of directors of Health Insurance Plan of Greater New York, 1954-64; civilian consultant to U.S. Army Hospital, Ft. Jay, N.Y., 1960-66; consultant to Office and Professional Employees International Union (local 153) Health Plan, 1960—, United Automobile Workers (local 259) Health Plan, 1960—, and Sanitationmens Security Benefit Fund, 1964—; member of advisory board of Hospital Workers Health Plan, 1970—; member of board of trustees, French-Polyclinic Medical School and Health Center, 1972—; director of Surgery International of Ladies Garment Workers Union, 1971—. *Military service:* U.S. Army, Medical Corps, 1942-46; became lieutenant colonel. *Member:* American College of Surgeons, American Medical Association, New York State Medical Society, Kings County Medical Society, New York County Medical Society, Brooklyn Surgical Society.

WRITINGS: Group Medicine and Health Insurance in Action, Crown, 1949, revised edition, 1975; *Understanding Surgery,* Pocket Books, 1955, revised edition, 1976; *The New Illustrated Medical Encyclopedia,* four volumes, Abradale Press, 1959, revised edition, 1975; *The New American Medical Dictionary and Health Manual,* New American Library, 1962, revised edition, 1975; *Health in the Later Years,* New American Library, 1964, revised edition, 1972; *Reoperative Surgery,* McGraw, 1964; *The New Illustrated Child Care Encyclopedia,* twelve volumes, Dell, 1966, revised edition, Fuller & Dees, 1972; *The Doctors' Premarital Medical Adviser,* Grosset, 1969; *The Fast Diet Book,* Grosset, 1971; *The Complete Home Medical Encyclopedia and Guide to Family Health,* twenty volumes, Abradale Press, 1973; *Our Family Medical Record Book,* Abradale Press, 1973; *The Complete Surgical Guide,* Simon & Schuster, 1974; *What Every Patient Wants to Know,* New American Library, 1975; *The Complete Book of Breast Care,* Crown, 1975; *Disney's Children's World of Health,* Grolier, 1976. Contributor to medical journals.

WORK IN PROGRESS: Research on breast disease.

*   *   *

ROTHROCK, George A(bel)   1932-

PERSONAL: Born November 11, 1932, in Wilmington, Del.; son of George A. (a toolmaker) and Marian (Titter) Rothrock; married Elsie Sine Thomsen, November 2, 1956 (divorced, 1966); married Willy Vogelzang, November 10, 1972; children: Ellen Nicole, Marian Michele, Grace Annette. *Education:* University of Delaware, B.A., 1954; graduate study at University of Grenoble, 1954-55; University of Minnesota, M.A., 1956, Ph.D., 1958. *Home:* Suite 1203, 11111 87th Ave., Edmonton, Alberta T6G 0X9, Canada. *Office:* Department of History, University of Alberta, Edmonton T6G 2E1, Canada.

CAREER: University of Omaha (now University of Nebraska at Omaha), Omaha, Neb., instructor, 1958-62, assistant professor of history, 1962-63; University of Saskatchewan, Saskatoon, assistant professor of history, 1963-64; University of Alberta, Edmonton, associate professor, 1964-71, professor of history, 1971—. Instructor, Offutt Air

Force Base, 1959-60, Lincoln Air Force Base for University of Omaha, 1960-61, Detroit Adult Center for University of Michigan, 1962-63, and Camrose Community College, 1965-66; visiting professor, University of Minnesota, 1961, University of Nebraska, Lincoln, 1962, and University of Michigan, 1962-63. *Member:* American Historical Association, Society for French Historical Studies, Royal Historical Society (fellow). *Awards, honors:* Fulbright fellowship to University of Grenoble, 1954-55; American Philosophical Society research grant, 1963; Canada Council research grant, 1968-69.

WRITINGS: (Translator and author of introduction) Sebastien Le Prestre de Vauban, *A Manual of Siegecraft and Fortification,* University of Michigan Press, 1968; *Europe: A Brief History,* Rand McNally, 1971, revised and enlarged edition (with Tom B. Jones), two volumes, 1975. Contributor to history journals.

WORK IN PROGRESS: With F. J. Hebbert, *Sebastien Le Prestre de Vauban: A Biography; Huguenot: The Biography of a Minority* for Nelson-Hall.

*   *   *

ROTHSTEIN, Samuel 1921-

PERSONAL: Born January 12, 1921, in Moscow, Soviet Union; came to Canada, 1922, naturalized Canadian citizen, 1929; son of Louis Israel and Rose (Checov) Rothstein; married Miriam Ruth Teitelbaum, August 26, 1951; children: Linda Rose, Sharon Lee. *Education:* University of British Columbia, B.A., 1939, M.A., 1940; University of California, Berkeley, further graduate study, 1941-42, B.L.S., 1947; University of Washington, Seattle, further graduate study, 1942-43; University of Illinois, Ph.D., 1954. *Religion:* Jewish. *Home:* 1416 West 40th Ave., Vancouver, British Columbia, Canada V6M 1V6. *Office:* School of Librarianship, University of British Columbia, Vancouver 8, British Columbia, Canada.

CAREER: University of California, Berkeley, principal library assistant, 1947; University of British Columbia, Vancouver, librarian, 1947-51, 1954-61, acting university librarian, 1961-62, professor of library science, 1962—, director of School of Librarianship, 1962-70. Visiting professor at University of Hawaii, 1969, University of Toronto, 1970, and Hebrew University of Jerusalem, 1973. Member of Commission for a National Plan for Library Education, 1963—; member of council of British Columbia Medical Library Service, 1961; member of Canadian Advisory Board of Scientific and Technological Information, 1972—. Member of council of International House Association of British Columbia, 1959-60. Member of council of Pacific Division of Canadian Jewish Congress, 1962—; president of board of directors of Jewish Community Centre of Vancouver, 1972—. *Military service:* Canadian Army, 1943-46.

MEMBER: Canadian Association of University Teachers, Canadian Library Association (member of council), Bibliographical Society of Canada (member of council, 1959—), American Library Association (member of council, 1964-68), Association of American Library Schools (president, 1968-69), British Columbia Library Association (president, 1959-60), Institute for Professional Librarians of Ontario, Pacific Northwest Library Association (president, 1963-64). *Awards, honors:* Carnegie Corp. fellowship, 1951; Helen Gordon Stewart Award, 1970, from British Columbia Library Association; D.Litt. from York University, 1971.

WRITINGS: The Development of Reference Services through Academic Traditions, Public Library Practice, and

Special Librarianship (monograph), Association of College and Reference Libraries, 1955; (editor with Marion Gilroy) *As We Remember It,* School of Librarianship, University of British Columbia, 1970; (with R. Blackwell and Archibald MacLeish) *The Library—The University,* Shakespeare Head Press, 1972. Also author with others of *Training Professional Librarians for Western Canada,* 1957. Contributor to professional journals.

WORK IN PROGRESS: A History of Academic Libraries in the United States: 1876-1976; The Development of Libraries in British Columbia.

*   *   *

ROWLEY, Anthony 1939-

PERSONAL: Born July 10, 1939, in Tettenhall, Staffordshire, England; son of Herbert Reade (an engineer) and Alice Mary (Whitehurst) Rowley; married Judith Glover (a writer), December, 1960 (divorced July, 1971); children: Sonja Judith, Isobel Antonia. *Education:* Attended University of Birmingham, 1957-60. *Politics:* Conservative. *Religion:* Church of England. *Home:* 25 Elvaston Pl., London S.W.7, England. *Agent:* Murray Pollinger, Laurence Pollinger Ltd., 11 Long Acre, London, England. *Office: Times,* New Printing House Sq., London, England.

CAREER: Times, London, England, European industrial correspondent, and financial journalist. *Member:* Campden Hill Lawn Tennis Club, Bosham Sailing Club.

WRITINGS: (Editor and contributor) *The Barons of European Industry,* Croom Helm, 1974. Contributor to magazines.

*   *   *

ROY, Michael 1913-
(Mike Roy)

PERSONAL: Born July 18, 1913, in Hanaford, N.D.; son of Louis J. (a barber) and Marie (Bostrum) Brant; married Alison Belyea, February 4, 1948; children: Robin, Dana. *Education:* University of Minnesota, B.A.; University of Chicago, M.A. *Politics:* Republican. *Religion:* Presbyterian. *Home:* 4318 Highgrove, Torrance, Calif. *Office:* CBS-KNX-Radio, 6121 Sunset, Hollywood, Calif. 90028.

CAREER: News editor, sports editor, and writer on WCCO-Radio, Minneapolis, Minn., and radio announcer and master of ceremonies on WMAQ-Radio, Chicago, Ill., 1937-44; master of ceremonies on radio programs, including "Edgar Bergen and Charlie McCarthy" and "The Abbott and Costello Show," in California, and later host of "Secrets of a Gourmet" television show on experimental station W6XAO-TV, Los Angeles, 1944-50; host of "Mike Roy's Kitchen" radio show, 1950-62; KNX-Radio, Hollywood, Calif., host of radio cooking show, "At Your Service," beginning 1962. Chef and writer.

*WRITINGS—*All under name Mike Roy: *Mike Roy Cookbook Number One: Gourmet Recipes,* Ritchie, 1966; *Mike Roy Cookbook Number Two: Everyday Recipes,* Ritchie, 1968; (editor) *Discovering Italian Wines,* Ritchie, 1971; *Mike Roy Cookbook Number Three: Food and Friends,* Ritchie, 1972; *Mike Roy Cookbook Number Four: From the Master Chef,* Ritchie, 1973; *Mike Roy Cookbook Number Five: More Food and Friends,* Ritchie, 1974; *Mike Roy's American Kitchen,* Harper, 1974.*

*   *   *

ROYLANCE, William H(erbert) 1927-

PERSONAL: Born October 18, 1927, in Rexburg, Idaho;

son of Darwin T. (a salesman) and Alta (Remington) Roylance; married Grace Arlene Johnson, August, 1957 (divorced, 1958). *Education:* University of Utah, B.A., 1957. *Politics:* Liberal Democrat. *Religion:* None. *Home:* 1654 Redondo Ave., Salt Lake City, Utah 84105.

CAREER: U.S. Post Office, Salt Lake City, Utah, clerk, 1952—.

WRITINGS: Complete Book of Insults, Boasts, and Riddles, Parker Publishing, 1970; *I Shoulda Said ...: A Treasury of Insults, Put-Downs, Boasts, Praises, Witticisms, Wisecracks, Comebacks, and Ad Libs,* Parker Publishing, 1973. Contributor of jokes and articles to *Playboy* and newspapers.

WORK IN PROGRESS: One Hundred One Ways to Earn Money; The Devil's Dictionary Redone; Insults, Insults; The Book of Johns: A Lighthearted Look at the Toilets and Toilet Habits of the World; How to Use the Law to Ruin Your Husband.

SIDELIGHTS: Roylance has traveled extensively, especially in South America. He took a honeymoon trip around the world on motorscooter and a river-running trip in Mexico which made headlines when the party was supposedly lost.

* * *

ROYLE, Edward 1944-

PERSONAL: Born March 29, 1944, in Huddersfield, Yorkshire, England; son of Fred (a clerk) and Gladys (a millworker and cook; maiden name, Lane) Royle; married Jennifer du Plessis (a teacher), August 2, 1968. *Education:* Christ's College, Cambridge, B.A., 1965, M.A. and Ph.D., 1969. *Politics:* "Liberal Radical." *Religion:* Methodist. *Office:* Department of History, University of York, Heslington, York YO1 5DD, England.

CAREER: Cambridge University, Selwyn College, Cambridge, England, fellow and lecturer in history, 1968-72; University of York, York, England, lecturer in history, 1972—. *Member:* Historical Association, Ecclesiastical Historical Society, Society for Study of Labour History, Cambridge Historical Society.

WRITINGS: Radical Politics, 1790-1900: Religion and Unbelief, Longman, 1971; *Victorian Infidels* (monograph), Manchester University Press, 1974; *Index to the Papers of Charles Bradlaugh,* E. P. Publishing, 1975; *The Infidel Tradition from Paine to Bradlaugh,* Macmillan, 1976. Contributor to *Freethinker* and *Historical Journal.*

WORK IN PROGRESS: Introductions to reprints of lives of Robert Cooper and Charles Southwell, for Pemberton Books; *Brief Study of C. J. Holyoake,* Pemberton Books; *Study of the Owenite Community at Queenwood; Study of Freethought and Radicalism under C. Bradlaugh and G. W. Foote: 1866-1915.*

* * *

ROZEK, Evalyn Robillard 1941-

PERSONAL: Born September 7, 1941, in Kewaunee, Wis.; daughter of Norbert J. and Elaine (Thibodeau) Robillard; married Ronald T. Rozek (a design technician), September 12, 1964; children: Norbert, Kurt. *Education:* Currently attending University of Wisconsin, Green Bay. *Home:* 708 St. Joseph St., Green Bay, Wis. 54301.

CAREER: Secretary of Green Bay Writers' Club, 1973, 1975.

WRITINGS: Tinker's Rescue (juvenile picture story), Carolrhoda Books, 1975. "What Harold Was Afraid Of" (three-act play), first produced in Green Bay, Wis. at Next Door Theatre, November, 1973. Contributor of humorous column, "Faces of Evie," to *Green Bay Daily News.*

WORK IN PROGRESS: "Happy Birthday, Yankee Doodle"; a three-act bicentennial play for children to be produced in 1976 at the Next Door Theatre.

* * *

RUBINSTEIN, Paul (Arthur)

PERSONAL: Born January 29, 1935, in Warsaw, Poland; son of Arthur (a concert pianist) and Aniela (Mlynarska) Rubinstein; married Brenda Stern, October, 1959 (divorced, 1962); married Leslie Nussbaum, April 4, 1963 (divorced, 1969); married Joy Kahn, May 11, 1971; children: Jason Arthur. *Education:* Attended Yale University, 1951-53; University of Pennsylvania, B.S., 1956; graduate study at Fordham University, 1961-62. *Politics:* Republican. *Religion:* None. *Home:* 136 East 64th St., New York, N.Y. 10021. *Agent:* Theron Raines, Raines & Raines, 244 Madison Ave., New York, N.Y. 10016. *Office:* Becker Securities Corp., 55 Water St., New York, N.Y. 10041.

CAREER: RCA Red Seal Records, New York, N.Y., advertising manager, 1959-68; Becker Securities Corp., New York, N.Y., stockbroker, assistant vice-president, 1968—. *Military service:* U.S. Army, 1958-59. U.S. Army Reserve, 1959-66; became first lieutenant. *Awards, honors:* Tastemakers Award from R. T. French Co., 1973, for *Feasts For Two.*

WRITINGS: (With wife, Leslie Rubinstein) *The Night before Cookbook,* Macmillan, 1967; *Feasts for Two,* Macmillan, 1973; *Feasts for Twelve,* Macmillan, 1975; (with Peter Tanous) *The Petrodollar Takeover* (novel), Putnam, 1975. Contributor to *Cavalier, Family Circle, Harper's Bazaar,* and *Parent's.*

WORK IN PROGRESS: A novel tentatively entitled *The Counterfeiters; Just Good Food* (proposed title), a cookbook for Scribner.

BIOGRAPHICAL/CRITICAL SOURCES: New York Herald Tribune, June 13, 1965; *New York Times,* February 10, 1966; *Los Angeles Times,* November 2, 1967; *Christian Science Monitor,* May 21, 1970; *Woman's Day,* June, 1973; *Bride's Magazine,* February 3, 1974; *Atlanta Constitution,* May 16, 1974; *Yale Alumni Magazine,* October, 1974; *Oregon Journal,* February 17, 1975.

* * *

RUDHART, Alexander 1930-

PERSONAL: Born May 24, 1930, in Vienna, Austria; naturalized U.S. citizen; son of Hugo Alexander (a teacher) and Leopoldine (Gruener) Rudhart; married, 1963; children: one. *Education:* University of Vienna, Doctor Juris Utriusque, 1952, Ph.D., 1962; Columbia University, Ph.D., 1962. *Religion:* Roman Catholic. *Home:* 189 Gypsy Rd., King of Prussia, Pa. 19406. *Office:* Department of History, Villanova University, Villanova, Pa. 19085.

CAREER: Villanova University, Villanova, Pa., instructor, 1954-55, assistant professor, 1955-61, associate professor, 1962-69, professor of modern European history, 1969—. *Member:* American Historical Association, American Association of University Professors.

WRITINGS: Twentieth Century Europe, Lippincott, 1975.

WORK IN PROGRESS: Europe from the Cold War to Detente; Germany East and West: A Contrast in Social and Political Development.

AVOCATIONAL INTERESTS: Travel (Europe, Latin America), target shooting, boating, painting, sculpture, carpentry, music.

* * *

RUDOLF, Anthony 1942-

PERSONAL: Born September 6, 1942, in London, England; son of Henry Cyril (a certified public accountant) and Esther (Rosenberg) Rudolf; married Brenda Marshall (a book designer), March 15, 1970; children: Nathaniel. *Education:* British Institute, Paris, France, certificate (with distinction), 1961; Trinity College, Cambridge, B.A., 1964. *Politics:* "Radical Progressive." *Religion:* Jewish. *Home:* 23 Fitzwarren Gardens, London N.19, England.

CAREER: Junior executive with British Travel Association, London, England, and Chicago, Ill., 1964-66; teacher of English and French in London School Service, and private teacher of English as a foreign language, 1967-68; worked in London bookshops including a period as co-proprieter of own business, 1969-71; *European Judaism,* London, literary editor, 1970-72, managing editor, 1972-75. Has broadcast for British Broadcasting Corp.-Radio, British Broadcasting Corp. World Service, and French radio, and given poetry readings in Great Britain and Macedonia. *Member:* National Poetry Centre (member of general council).

WRITINGS: (Translator) *Selected Poems of Yves Bonnefoy,* J. Cape, 1968, Grossman, 1969; (translator) Ana Novac, *The Soup Complex* (play), Stand, 1972; (editor with Richard Burns) *An Octave for Paz,* Menard, 1972; (translator) *Tyorkin and the Stovemakers: Selected Verse and Prose of Alexander Tvardovsky,* Carcanet, 1974; (compiler) *Edmund Jabés Bibliography,* Menard, 1974; (translator with D. Weisshort) *Selected Verse of Evgeni Vinokurov,* Carcanet, 1975; (translator with Petru Popescu) *Poems of Petru Popescu,* Omphalos, 1975; (editor) *Poems for Shakespeare IV,* Globe Playhouse Trust Publications, 1975. Contributor of poems, articles, and reviews to literary journals, including *Tree, Holy Beggars Gazette, Roy Rogers, Nation,* and *Contemporary Literature in Translation.* London editor of *Stand.* Founder and co-editor of *Journals of Pierre Menard.* Advisory editor of *Modern Poetry in Translation* and *Heimler Foundation Newsletter.* Guest editor of *Cambridge Opinion/Circuit,* 1968, *Workshop,* 1971, *Poetry Review,* 1971, *Modern Poetry in Translation,* 1973, *New Linguist,* 1973, *Books,* 1974, and *Roy Rogers,* 1974.

WORK IN PROGRESS: Translating *Selected Poems of Edmond Jabes,* for Tree Books; *The Same River Twice,* poems, Carcanet.

SIDELIGHTS: Rudolf writes that his major interests are "politics—tradition of democratic socialism; Judaism—European cultural tradition; literature—poetry of Europe and the U.S.A. The impossible ideal is an epic poem that would fuse all three."

* * *

RUEBSAAT, Helmut J(ohannes) 1920-

PERSONAL: Born April 14, 1920, in Krefeld, Germany; son of Hubert (an agricultural counselor) and Maria (Lamberty) Ruebsaat; married Bernice Lacourse, August 10, 1968; children: Norbert, Ulrike, Suzanne, Gisela, Stephen. *Education:* Attended University of Koenigsberg, 1940, and University of Prague, 1941-43; University of Munich, 1944-45; University of Bonn, M.D., 1946. *Religion:* Anglican. *Home:* 5479 Elizabeth St., Vancouver, British Columbia, Canada V5Y 3J7. *Agent:* Barthold Fles Literary Agency, 507 Fifth Ave., New York, N.Y. 10017. *Office:* 480-2184 West Broadway, Vancouver, British Columbia, Canada.

CAREER: Staedt Krankenhaus, Solingen, West Germany, junior intern, 1946; Kreis Krankenhaus, Bad Hersfeld, West Germany, surgical resident, 1947-50; Chemische Fabrik Tempelhof, Berlin, West Germany, pharmaceutical research assistant, 1950-51; Royal Alexander Hospital, Edmonton, Alberta, junior intern, 1952-53; Charles Camsell Indian Hospital, Edmonton, house physician, 1953; physician in family practice in Vancouver, British Columbia, 1960—. Member of active staff of St. Vincent's Hospital, 1960—; member of visiting staff at Vancouver General Hospital, Vancouver St. Paul's Hospital, and Grace Hospital, all 1960—. Member of board of directors of Westminster Foundation for Religion and Health, 1970—. *Military service:* German Army, 1938-45; became lieutenant. *Member:* Canadian Medical Association, College of Family Physicians of Canada, College of Physicians and Surgeons of British Columbia.

WRITINGS: (With Raymond Hull) *The Male Climacteric,* Hawthorn, 1975. Contributor of articles on spiritual healing to church publications.

WORK IN PROGRESS: *The Hypochondriac,* with Raymond Hull; *Your Body: How It Works,* a layman's book; a German translation of *The Male Climacteric.*

SIDELIGHTS: Ruebsaat writes that he is "particularly interested in the phenomenon of healing, including so-called spiritual (divine) healing." *Avocational interests:* Scuba-diving, sea-life, collecting shells and coral, folksinging, playing the guitar, linguistics.

* * *

RUNYON, Catherine 1947-

PERSONAL: Born April 2, 1947, in Reed City, Mich.; daughter of James Henry (a laborer) and Blanche Irene (a laborer; maiden name, Joslin) Hatfield; married Randall Ray Runyon (a piano technician), November 23, 1967; children: Nathan Randall. *Education:* Attended Moody Bible Institute, diploma, 1971. *Politics:* Independent. *Religion:* "Conservative evangelical." *Home:* 1101 Griggs S.E., Grand Rapids, Mich. 49507.

CAREER: Moody Bible Institute, Chicago, Ill., secretary, retail bookstore clerk, and editorial assistant, 1969-71; free-lance writer, and speaker for churh groups, 1971—.

WRITINGS—Juvenile: *All-Wrong Mrs. Bear,* Moody, 1972; *The Trouble with Jud,* Moody, 1973; *Mrs. Oodle's Noodles,* Moody, 1973; *The Missionary Mouse,* Moody, 1973; *A Trace of Blackmail,* Moody, 1974. Contributor to religious periodicals.

WORK IN PROGRESS: A youth adventure novel set in a summer camp.

SIDELIGHTS: Catherine Runyon writes: "I really believe that a person cannot attain his true potential as an artist until he is in a right relationship to God. Of course, my writing reflects that relationship. I believe that a writer cannot help but convey his own philosophy in his writing, and I don't try to conceal it. Jesus Christ is a motivating force in my life, and I try to create tasteful, beautiful writing that portrays Him as the Person He is."

RUSCH, Hermann G. 1907-

PERSONAL: Born September 26, 1907, in Appenzell, Switzerland; came to United States in 1939; son of Arnold J. (a charcutier) and Emilie (Faessler) Rusch; married Violet Loertscher, 1941; children: Gregory, Preston, Ronald (deceased), Christopher. Office: Greenbrier, White Sulphur Springs, W.Va. 24986.

CAREER: Has worked as chef at hotels in France, Switzerland, Egypt, Sweden, New York, N.Y., Charleston, S.C., and Miami Beach, Fla., 1924-55; Greenbrier, White Sulphur Springs, W.Va., executive chef steward, 1955-57, executive food director, 1957—. Supervising chef for U.S. Olympic Committee, 1956, 1959, 1960, 1963, 1964; has directed food and housing for Olympic games and Pan American Games since 1967; has served as chairman of judges for numerous culinary competitions, including International Food Festival, 1972, 1973. Organized American team to Culinary Olympic competition. Member of board of directors of Culinary Institute of America and member of its Order of the Golden Toque.

MEMBER: International Chef's Association of America, International Chef's Association (Frankfurt, honorary member), International Steward's and Caterers' Association, American Culinary Federation (member of board of governors), Chef de Cuisine Association of America (past chairman), American National Council on Hotel and Restaurant Education, Helvetia Association of America, Guild of Sommeliers and Society of Bacchus, Societe Culinaire Philanthropique (president, 1951-56; honorary president, 1974), Les Amis d'Escoffier (officer), Culinary Academy of France (corresponding member), Circle de Chef de Cuisine (Bern; honorary member), Confrerie de la Chaine Des Rotisseurs, Confrerie de Gastronomie Normande, British Culinary Association (honorary member), Oesterreichischer Kochverband (honorary member), Circle de Chef de Cuisine (Zurich; honorary member), Epicurean Club (London; honorary member), La Priperie d'Or, Chef's Association of Pittsburgh (honorary member), Vatel Club (New York, N.Y.; honorary member).

AWARDS, HONORS: Culinary awards include gold medal awards at Zurich International Exhibition, 1930, Exposition de Alberghieri, 1932, Societe Culinaire Philanthropique, Academie Culinaire de Paris, and U.S. Culinary Federation; five grand prizes and two prizes of honor from National Hotel Exposition; Silver Medal of the French Republic; DeBand Award, 1956; Partridge Award, 1957; named "Chef of the Golden Dozen," 1958; Otto Gentsch Gold Medal, 1959; Caesar Ritz Award from Society of Bacchus, 1966; August Escoffier's gold plaque; Eugene Lacroix Medaille of Frankfurt, Germany; Silver Plate Award from International Food Service Association, 1971; named honorary citizen of West Virginia, 1971; Medaille de Merit from Government of France, 1972; citation from U.S. Olympic Committee, 1973; diploma and medal from Societe des Cuisiniers de Paris, 1973; Educational Institute Award from American Culinary Federation, 1974.

WRITINGS: (With Martina Neely) The Hermann Rusch Greenbrier Cookbook, Regnery, 1975.

* * *

RUSE, Gary Alan 1946-

PERSONAL: Born August 24, 1946, in Miami, Fla.; son of Layton Newman (an electronics technician) and Virginia Mae (Singer) Ruse. Education: University of Miami, Coral Gables, Fla., B.A., 1968. Politics: "Registered Democrat; hopeful skeptic." Religion: Methodist. Residence and office: Miami, Fla.

CAREER: William Morrow & Co., New York, N.Y., book illustrator, 1968; free-lance writer and artist, 1971—. Military service: U.S. Army, Engineer Corps, 1969-70; served in Vietnam; received Commendation Medal with oak leaf cluster. Member: Science Fiction Writers of America.

WRITINGS: Houndstooth (novel), Prentice-Hall, 1975. Contributor to Analog.

WORK IN PROGRESS: A suspense novel.

SIDELIGHTS: Ruse told CA: "I became interested in writing out of a love for reading and daydreaming.... I write the kind of stories I like to read, and have always been most impressed by writers who are primarily good story-tellers.... my basic outlook has, and I hope will, remain the same: writing is often hard work, but it is simply too much fun to avoid."

* * *

RUSH, Anne Kent 1945-

PERSONAL: Born July 28, 1945, in Mobile, Ala.; daughter of George Legrand and Cynthia (Boyd Williams) Rush. Education: Wayne State University, B.A., 1967. Politics: Feminist.

CAREER: Little, Brown & Co. (publishers), Boston, Mass., trade copywriter, 1968; Esalen Institute, San Francisco, Calif., staff teacher, 1970-72; Bookworks (publishers), Berkeley, Calif., art editor, 1970-73; Alyssum: Center for Feminist Consciousness, San Francisco, member of organizing collective, 1973-75; Moon Books (publishers), San Francisco, partner, 1974—. Partner in feminist theatre company, Amazon Grace, San Francisco, 1974.

WRITINGS—All self-illustrated: (Editor) George Downing, The Massage Book, Bookworks/Random House, 1972; Getting Clear: Body Work for Women, Bookworks/n Books/Random House, 1976. Contributor to Issues in Radical Therapy.

WORK IN PROGRESS: Exploration into feminist politics and body therapy.

* * *

RUSH, Michael (David) 1937-

PERSONAL: Born October 29, 1937, in Kingston-upon-Thames, Surrey, England; son of Wilfred George (a wholesale manager for an educational publisher) and Elizabeth (maiden name, Gurney; an executive clerical worker) Rush; married Jean Margaret Telford (a teacher), July 25, 1964; children: Jonathan David, Anthony Michael. Education: University of Sheffield, B.A. (with honors), 1964, Ph.D., 1966. Home: 2 St. Loyes Rd., Heavitree, Exeter, Devonshire EX2 5HA, England. Office: Department of Politics, University of Exeter, Devonshire EX4 4RJ, England.

CAREER: University of Exeter, Exeter, England, lecturer in politics, 1964—. Visiting lecturer, University of Western Ontario, 1967-68; visiting professor, Carleton University, 1975. Military service: British Army, 1957-59; service corps. Member: Political Studies Association (England), Royal Institute of Public Administration, Study of Parliament Group (joint secretary, 1975—). Awards, honors: Campion Award from Hansard Society for Parliamentary Government, 1965-66, for doctoral thesis.

WRITINGS: The Selection of Parliamentary Candidates, Thomas Nelson, 1969; (with Anthony Barker) *The Member of Parliament and His Information,* Allen & Unwin, 1970, published as *The British Member of Parliament and His Information,* University of Toronto Press, 1970; (with Phillip Althoff) *An Introduction to Political Sociology,* Thomas Nelson, 1971, Bobbs-Merrill, 1972; (editor with Malcolm Shaw and contributor) *The House of Commons: Services and Facilities,* Allen & Unwin for Political and Economic Planning and the Study of Parliament Group, 1974, International Publishers, 1974; *Parliament and the Public,* Longman, in press. Contributor to journals in his field including *Parliamentary Affairs* and *Parliamentarian.*

WORK IN PROGRESS: A book on parliamentary government, publication expected in 1977 or 1978; compiling a biographical dictionary of British members of parliament elected between 1885 and the present; contributing a chapter to a book on legislative committees; research on Canadian parliament.

SIDELIGHTS: Rush told *CA* he is interested in comparative parliamentary politics and information problems in the social sciences. *Avocational interests:* Theatre, music (mainly classical), reading (mainly biography), squash, tennis, swimming, and watching rugby.

* * *

RUSSELL, D(iana) E(lizabeth) H(amilton) 1938-

PERSONAL: Born November 6, 1938, in Cape Town, South Africa; daughter of James Hamilton and Kathleen Mary Russell. *Education:* University of Cape Town, B.A., 1958; London School of Economics and Political Science, graduate study, 1960-61; Harvard University, M.A., 1967, Ph.D., 1970. *Politics:* "Feminist." *Religion:* Agnostic. *Residence:* Berkeley, Calif. *Office:* Division of Social Science, Mills College, Oakland, Calif. 94613.

CAREER: Mills College, Oakland, Calif., assistant professor, 1969-75, associate professor of sociology, 1975—. Member of coordinating committee of International Tribunal on Crimes Against Women. *Member:* American Sociological Association, Sociologists for Women in Society, Anti-Slavery Society.

WRITINGS: Rebellion, Revolution, and Armed Force, Academic Press, 1974; *The Politics of Rape: The Victim's Perspective,* Stein & Day, 1975.

WORK IN PROGRESS: Crimes Against Women.

SIDELIGHTS: Diana Russell writes: "The motivation behind my first book came from my being born and reared in South Africa, my coming to believe in the necessity of a social revolution there, but wishing to find out the possibilities for success. The book deals with South Africa—among other countries—at some length. The motivation behind my second book was a concern to raise public awareness about a widespread brutality against women in the U.S.A.—rape, in the hope that this will increase the struggle against it, as well as all other sexist practices."

* * *

RUSSELL, William H. 1911-

PERSONAL: Born August 6, 1911, in Washington, D.C.; son of William H. (an administrator) and Mary (Bresnahan) Russell; married Eunice Morgan Jones, June 2, 1937. *Education:* Haverford College, A.B., 1933; Harvard University, M.A., 1934. *Home and office:* 3 Cumberland Ct., Annapolis, Md. 21401.

CAREER: Teacher of history at private schools in Bethesda, Md., and Watertown, Conn., 1935-39; *Sussex Countian,* Georgetown, Del., business manager, 1939-42; U.S. Naval Academy, Annapolis, Md., instructor in history, 1946-73; Academic Fellowship, Inc., Annapolis, overseer and secretary, 1963—. Trustee, American Military Institute, 1957-72; director of Historic Annapolis, 1958-63, Westminster Foundation, 1964—, and Casyndekan Inc., 1968-71. *Military service:* U.S. Naval Reserve, 1942-46; became lieutenant commander. *Member:* Friends Historical Association, Marine Corps Association.

WRITINGS: (Contributor) E. B. Potter, editor, *The United States and World Sea Power,* Prentice-Hall, 1955; (contributor) E. B. Potter, editor, *Sea Power: A Naval History,* Prentice-Hall, 1960; (contributor) Werner Hahlweg, editor, *Klassiker der Kriegskunst,* Wehr & Wissen (Darmstadt), 1960; (editor with Winslow D. Shaw) *When Insurgency Begot Tyrants: First Book of the Maccabees,* U.S. Naval Academy, 1968. Contributor to military journals.

* * *

RUSSO, Anthony 1933-

PERSONAL: Born November 1, 1933, in Passaic, N.J.; son of Fausto (a factory worker) and Yolanda (De Capite) Russo. *Education:* Virginia Military Institute, B.S. in C.E., 1955; Mount St. Alphonsus Seminary, B.A., 1962, M.R.E., 1966, M.Div., 1967. *Home:* 174 West Diamond St., Philadelphia, Pa. 19122. *Office:* Catholic Apostolate to the Deaf, 174 West Diamond St., Philadelphia, Pa. 19122.

CAREER: Entered Congregation of the Most Holy Redeemer (Redemptorist Fathers), 1958, ordained Roman Catholic priest, 1965; Department of Sanitary Engineering, Washington, D.C., civil engineer, 1955; Pitometer Associates (consulting engineers), Philadelphia, Pa., civil engineer, 1957; Catholic Apostolate to the Deaf, Philadelphia, Pa., director, 1967—. *Military service:* U.S. Army Reserve, 1956-63; became first lieutenant. *Member:* International Catholic Deaf Association, Registry of Interpreters for the Deaf, Visual Literacy Association, Philadelphia Hearing Society.

WRITINGS: The God of the Deaf Adolescent, Paulist/Newman, 1975.

WORK IN PROGRESS: Religion Books for the Deaf (tentative title); a series of books utilizing a special approach to communicate abstract and religious concepts to the profoundly deaf.

SIDELIGHTS: Russo writes: "Deafness affects more than physical hearing, especially in someone who becomes deaf before the acquisition of language. Educationally, for example, the deaf person must grope for the meaning of the printed word. Indeed, not only the vocabulary and syntax of written English, but the entire process of conceptualization is thrown into disarray in the minds of the deaf. This is the motivation which led to my first book and to the research in progress."

* * *

RYALL, Edward W(illiam) 1902-

PERSONAL: Born June 21, 1902, in South Shoebury, Essex, England; son of George (a laborer) and Annie (Woodley) Ryall; married Winifred Elizabeth Grist, October 4, 1924; children: Nelson (deceased), Iris (Mrs. John Driver), Raymond, Colin, Anthony. *Education:* Educated in Essex, England. *Politics:* Conservative. *Religion:* Church of England.

CAREER: Negotiator and branch manager of estate agency in Leigh-on-Sea, Essex, England, 1918-67. *Military service:* Royal Corps of Signals, 1940-45; served in North Africa and Italy. *Member:* Association of Land and Property Agents (associate member), Friendly Society.

WRITINGS: Born Twice, Harper, 1975 (published in England as *Second Time Round,* Neville Spearman, 1975). Contributor to London *Daily Express.*

SIDELIGHTS: Edward Ryall's book, *Born Twice,* is a chronicle of his experiences of remembering vivid scenes, persons, places, and events which seemed to be unconnected with his present life. He told *CA* that as a child he spoke a dialect foreign to his surroundings and that "matters came to a head one night in 1910 when Halley's Comet was visible in England. My father thought he would show . . . me this spectacle in the heavens. Quite simply and naturally . . . I told him I had seen this same phenomenon before, a long while previously, and had indeed shown it to two sons of my own! Save to say that my father thoroughly convinced me that it would be far better for me never to say anything of such memories of the past again, lest I be shut away. . . ."

Ryall didn't speak of his experiences until 1970, when he answered a newspaper invitation to submit accounts of reincarnation experiences. His story was duly published in the paper and it came to the attention of an American psychiatrist who encouraged Ryall to write his book.

* * *

RYAN, Elizabeth (Anne) 1943-
(Betsy Ryan)

PERSONAL: Born November 13, 1943, in New York, N.Y.; daughter of William H. (a lawyer) and Dorothy (Devereaux) Ryan. *Education:* Maryville College, St. Louis, Mo., B.A., 1965; Fordham University, M.A., 1967. *Residence:* New York, N.Y. *Office:* Scholastic Magazines, Inc., 50 West 44th St., New York, N.Y. 10036.

CAREER: Howard Sanders Advertising, New York, N.Y., copy writer, 1966-68; Scholastic Magazines, Inc., New York, N.Y., book club editor, 1968—. Member of alumnae board of Convent of the Sacred Heart (New York, N.Y.). *Member:* Women's National Book Association.

WRITINGS—All under name Betsy Ryan: *Love,* Scholastic Book Service, 1971; *Sounds of Silence,* Scholastic Book Service, 1972; *Within You/Without You,* Scholastic Book Service, 1973; *Search the Silence,* Scholastic Book Service, 1974; *The Sexes,* Scholastic Book Service, 1975; *Loving, Dying, Living: Faces of America,* Scholastic Book Service, in press.

* * *

RYAN, Peter (Charles) 1939-

PERSONAL: Born November 18, 1939, in Harrogate, England; son of Charles Edmund (a brigadier general) and Joyce Mary (Dodgson) Ryan. *Education:* Trinity College, Dublin, B.A., 1963. *Home and office:* 11 Moore Park Rd., London S.W.6, England. *Agent:* Deborah Rogers, 29 Goodge St., London W.1, England.

CAREER: British Broadcasting Corp., Television Service, London, England, member of production staff in science and current affairs departments, 1963-68; free-lance journalist, photographer, translator, and broadcaster, 1968—. *Member:* British Interplanetary Society (fellow), Geological Society (London; fellow), National Union of Journalists, Naval and Military Club.

WRITINGS: Invasion of the Moon, Penguin, 1969, revised edition, 1971; *Journey to the Planets,* Penguin, 1972, revised edition, 1973; *Planet Earth,* Penguin, 1972, revised edition, 1973; *The Ocean World,* Penguin, 1973; *UFOs and Other Worlds,* Penguin, 1975. Project editor for *Sunday Times,* 1973-74, editor of "The Facts of Life" series, 1974; technical editor for Bureau de Recherches Geologiques et Minieres (Saudi Arabia), 1975—.

WORK IN PROGRESS: The Solar System, publication by Penguin expected in 1977; *The Penguin Dictionary of Space,* 1977.

* * *

RYAN, Sister Joseph Eleanor

PERSONAL: Born in Joliet, Ill.; daughter of Thomas J. and Nellie A. Ryan. *Education:* St. Mary-of-the-Woods College, A.B., 1936; Catholic University of America, M.A., 1940; also studied at Universite Laval, Indiana State University, and University of Besancon. *Residence:* St. Mary-of-the-Woods, Ind. 47876. *Office:* Providence High School, 1800 West Lincoln Highway, New Lenox, Ill. 60451.

CAREER: Roman Catholic nun of Sisters of Providence (S.P.), 1933—; principal, librarian, and teacher of English, French, and Latin in secondary schools in Indiana and Illinois, 1935-75. *Member:* American Association of Teachers of French, National Council of Teachers of English, Catholic Poetry Society of America.

WRITINGS: Call to Courage (biography), Dujarie Press, 1968.

Plays—All produced at St. Mary-of-the-Woods, except as indicated: "The Silver Bells," 1934; "Alabaster," Providence High School, Chicago, Ill., 1936; "Candle Beams," Hyattsville, Md., 1939; "Christmas Comes to the Cure," 1944; "Mavoumeen," 1946; "In This Sign," 1947; "The Flowering of Janey," 1950; "The Royal Road," 1952.

Translator from French to English. Contributor of articles and poems to magazines including *Spirit, St. Anthony Messenger* and *Young Catholic Messenger.*

WORK IN PROGRESS: No Second Best; Life Is Wonderful; research on religious life and on missionaries in the American West.

* * *

RYANS, John K(elley), Jr. 1932-

PERSONAL: Born August 12, 1932, in Cynthiana, Ky.; son of John Kelley (an editor) and Alta (Aldridge) Ryans; married Cynthia Collis (a library professor), January, 1957. *Education:* University of Kentucky, A.B., 1954; University of Tennessee, M.S., 1958; Indiana University, D.B.A., 1965. *Office:* Graduate School of Business, Kent State University, Kent, Ohio 44242.

CAREER: Memphis State University, Memphis, Tenn., assistant professor of marketing, 1959-61; University of Maryland, College Park, assistant professor, 1964-67, associate professor of marketing, 1967-68; University of Kentucky, Lexington, associate professor of marketing, 1968-69; Kent State University, Kent, Ohio, associate professor, 1969-70, professor of marketing, 1970—, assistant dean,

1969-70, associate dean, 1970—. *Military service:* U.S. Air Force, 1955-57. U.S. Air Force Reserve, 1957-59; became captain. *Member:* American Academy of Advertising (treasurer, 1970-71), Academy of International Business, American Marketing Association, Academy of Management, American Society of International Law, Southern Marketing Association. *Awards, honors:* Ayres fellow at Stonier Graduate School of Banking, Rutgers University, summer, 1971.

WRITINGS: (Editor with James Baker) *World Marketing: A Multinational Approach,* Wiley, 1967; (with James Donnelly and John Ivancevich) *New Dimensions in Retailing: A Decision-Oriented Approach,* Wadsworth, 1970; (editor) *The Multinational Business World of the 1980's: A Challenge to Colleges of Business,* College of Business, Kent State University Press, 1974; (editor with Baker and A. Negandhi) *China, the U.S.S.R., and Eastern Europe: A U.S. Trade Perspective,* Kent State University Press, 1974; (editor with Baker) *Multinational Marketing: Dimensions in Strategy,* Grid Press, 1975. Contributor of over forty articles to business and marketing journals. Member of editorial board of *Journal of the Academy of Marketing Science* and *Organization and Administrative Sciences.*

WORK IN PROGRESS: Co-authoring with Richard Hise an introductory marketing text; co-editing a book on regulation of the multinational corporation from the business/government perspective.

*   *   *

RYDER, Ron   1904-

PERSONAL: Born in 1904, in Boonville, N.Y.; married Jean Veitch, 1931; children: Richard. *Education:* Attended high school. *Politics:* Independent. *Religion:* "My own brand." *Home address:* Lansing Kill Rd., Boonville, N.Y. 13309.

CAREER: Owned and operated a hardware store in Booneville, N.Y.; writer.

WRITINGS: Black Cotton Stockings, Country Books, 1954; *The Way It Was: Saved by the Camera,* Country Books, 1974, enlarged edition, 1975. Contributor of articles and photographs to newspapers.

WORK IN PROGRESS: "Think tank stage."

SIDELIGHTS: Ryder writes that he is a "long time carnival and circus fan, saint and sinner. Small time director of hometown theatricals; country fair manager; promoter of historical observances. Used to watch the front gate like a hawk watching chickens to see how fast the crowd was coming in. Now run in opposite direction if I see a gathering of more than six folk.

"Have spent years at and now own a collection of several thousand plates, negatives, and photographs. Many date to the glass plate era and all depict small town life as it used to be.

"Me? An author? Questionable—sez me. But many seem to have enjoyed it. And anything I ever wrote can be shown to Aunt Emeretta or to your six-year-old granddaughter."

*   *   *

RYE, Bjoern Robinson   1942-

PERSONAL: First name is pronounced Burn; born July 28, 1942, in Los Angeles, Calif.; son of Bjoern Melvin (a lumberman) and Margaret (Robinson) Rye. *Education:*

Attended London School of Film Technique, 1967-69; Columbia University, B.A., 1971; City College of the City University of New York, M.A., 1972. *Politics:* "Contradictory." *Home:* 201 West 85th St., New York, N.Y. 10024. *Agent:* Russell & Volkening, Inc., 551 Fifth Ave., New York, N.Y. 10017.

CAREER: Free-lance film maker for United Artists, Metro-Goldwyn-Mayer, British Broadcasting Corp., and other companies, 1965-70; truckdriver in Kindt and Vernal, Utah, 1972; School of Visual Arts, New York, N.Y., instructor in creative writing, 1973—; Bernard M. Baruch School of Business and Public Administration of the City University of New York, New York, N.Y., instructor in composition, 1974—. *Member:* Phi Beta Kappa. *Awards, honors:* Barnard playwriting prize, 1972, for "Grand Guignol"; Mary Roberts Rinehart grant, 1973, for *The Expatriate;* Dejur Foundation award for fiction, 1974.

WRITINGS—Novels: *The Expatriate,* Bobbs-Merrill, 1975; *A Feast of Pikes,* Bobbs-Merrill, 1976. Author of filmscripts and off-off-Broadway plays.

WORK IN PROGRESS: A catastrophic novel; co-translating a book of modern Persian short stories; a biography of a famous American woman photographer.

AVOCATIONAL INTERESTS: Carpentry, horses, geology, skiing.

*   *   *

SABALIUNAS, Leonas   1934-

PERSONAL: Born January 25, 1934, in Kaunas, Lithuania; son of Lionginas and Jadvyga (Navickas) Sabaliunas; married Ona Eringis, June 3, 1967; children: Imsre, Medea (daughters). *Education:* University of Illinois, B.A., 1956; Columbia University, M.I.A., 1958, Ph.D., 1963. *Home:* 6593 Fleming Creek Dr., Ann Arbor, Mich. 48105. *Office:* Department of Political Science, Eastern Michigan University, Ypsilanti, Mich. 48197.

CAREER: St. John's University, New York, N.Y., instructor in political science, 1963-66; Eastern Michigan University, Ypsilanti, assistant professor, 1966-68, associate professor, 1968-73, professor of political science, 1973—. *Member:* American Association for the Advancement of Slavic Studies, Association for the Advancement of Baltic Studies, American Political Science Association, American Academy of Political and Social Science, Institute of Lithuanian Studies. *Awards, honors:* Summer stipend from National Endowment for the Humanities, 1968; research grant from Earhart Foundation, 1974.

WRITINGS: Lithuania in Crisis: Nationalism to Communism, 1939-1940, Indiana University Press, 1972; (editor with Vincas Rastenis) *Antanas Smetona: Kalbos ir pareiskimai, 1935-1940* (title means "Antanas Smetona: Speeches and Statements, 1935-1940"), Lithuanian Encyclopedia Press, 1974.

*   *   *

SABLOFF, Jeremy A(rac)   1944-

PERSONAL: Born April 16, 1944, in New York, N.Y.; son of Louis (a dentist) and Helen (Arac) Sabloff; married Paula Lynne Weinberg, May 26, 1968; children: Joshua Marc. *Education:* University of Pennsylvania, B.A., 1964; Harvard University, M.A., 1969, Ph.D., 1969. *Home:* 3017 East 4505 S., Salt Lake City, Utah 84117. *Office:* Department of Anthropology, Stewart Bldg., University of Utah, Salt Lake City, Utah 84112.

CAREER: Harvard University, Cambridge, Mass., assistant professor, 1969-74, associate professor of anthropology, 1974-76, Peabody Museum, assistant curator, 1970-74, associate curator of Middle American archaeology, 1974-76; University of Utah, Salt Lake City, associate professor of anthropology, 1976—. *Member:* American Anthropological Association (fellow), Society for American Archaeology, Royal Anthropological Institute (fellow), American Association for the Advancement of Science. *Awards, honors:* National Geographical Society grant to Cozumel, Mexico, 1972-73.

WRITINGS: (With G. R. Willey) *A History of American Archaeology,* Freeman, 1974; (editor with C. C. Lamberg-Karlovsky) *The Rise and Fall of Civilizations,* Cummings, 1974; (editor with Lamberg-Karlovsky) *Ancient Civilization and Trade,* University of New Mexico Press, 1975; *Excavations at Seibal: Ceramics,* Peabody Museum, Harvard University, 1975; (editor with W. L. Rathje) *Ancient Maya Commercial Systems,* Peabody Museum, Harvard University, 1975.

Contributor: J. Harte and R. Socolow, editors, *The Patient Earth,* Holt, 1971; R. Brill, editor, *Science and Archaeology,* M.I.T. Press, 1971; T. P. Culbert, editor, *The Classic Maya Collapse,* University of New Mexico Press, 1973; N. Hammond, editor, *Mesoamerican Archaeology: New Approaches,* University of Texas Press, 1974; E. Benson, editor, *The Cult of the Sea,* Dumbarton Oaks, 1975.

WORK IN PROGRESS: A book on the ancient civilizations of Mesoamerica and the Near East, with Lamberg-Karlovsky; recording the results of archaeological research on the island of Cozumel, Mexico, with publication expected to result.

* * *

SABRI-TABRIZI, Gholam-Reza 1934-

PERSONAL: Born March 21, 1934, in Tabriz, Iran; son of Muhammed-Ali and Fizeh (Sofiyani) Sabri-Tabrizi; married Jacqueline Marjorie Sparkes (a teacher), August 2, 1964; children: Sarah, Leila, Mina, Jamal. *Education:* University of Tabriz, B.A., 1956, Dip.Ed., 1958; University of Edinburgh, Ph.D., 1969. *Home:* 34 Liberton Dr., Edinburgh EH16 6NN, Scotland. *Office:* Department of Persian, University of Edinburgh, 8 Buccleuch Pl., Edinburgh EH8 9LW, Scotland.

CAREER: University of Edinburgh, Edinburgh, Scotland, assistant lecturer, 1965, lecturer in Persian, 1965—. *Member:* British Association of Orientalists (secretary-treasurer, 1975—), Scottish Association for Asian Studies.

WRITINGS: The Heaven and Hell of William Blake, Lawrence & Wishart, 1973. Contributor to proceedings and journals.

WORK IN PROGRESS: Research on modern Persian and Azarbaijani literature.

* * *

SACCIO, Peter (Churchill) 1941-

PERSONAL: Born May 28, 1941, in Brooklyn, N.Y.; son of Leonard J. and Churchill (Freshman) Saccio. *Education:* Yale University, B.A., 1962; Princeton University, Ph.D., 1968. *Home:* 6 Reservoir Rd., Hanover, N.H. *Office:* Department of English, Dartmouth College, Hanover, N.H. 03755.

CAREER: Princeton University, Princeton, N.J., instructor in English, 1965-66; Dartmouth College, Hanover, N.H., instructor, 1966-68, assistant professor, 1968-73, associate professor of English, 1973—. Faculty fellow, Dartmouth College, 1969-70. *Member:* Modern Language Association of America, Renaissance Society of America, Shakespeare Association of America.

WRITINGS: The Court Comedies of John Lyly: A Study in Allegorical Dramaturgy, Princeton University Press, 1969; (contributor) G. R. Hibbard, editor, *Elizabethan Theatre Five,* Macmillan, 1975; *Shakespeare's Plantagenets,* Oxford University Press, in press.

* * *

SACHAROFF, Shanta Nimbark 1945-

PERSONAL: Born March 23, 1945, in Bhoringada, India; daughter of Dharmadas Govindram (a temple keeper) and Nanbai (Deomurari) Nimbark; married Stanley Sacharoff (a day coordinator of food store), August 14, 1969; children: Reyaz Gautam. *Education:* Attended Russell Sage College, 1964-66; Adelphi Suffolk College, B.A., 1969; San Francisco State University, M.A., 1975. *Home:* 1135 Lincoln Way, San Francisco, Calif. 94122.

CAREER: Substitute day coordinator of Haight Community Food Store, 1974—; director of a child care center. Teacher at Dowling College, Oakdale, N.Y., summers, 1974, 1975. Member of board of Unbiased Non-Sexist Inter-Ethnic Training and Education Association, 1973—.

WRITINGS: Flavors of India (cookbook), 101 Productions, 1971. Contributor to *Fits, Rags,* and *Cauliflower.* Writer of television program on Indian cooking for KEMO-Television, San Francisco.

* * *

SACHS, Lewis Benjamen 1938-

PERSONAL: Born August 18, 1938, in New York, N.Y.; son of Jack Lewis (an optometrist) and Annetta (Shields) Sachs; married Lily Tsai, November 9, 1962; children: Lance B. *Education:* Grinnell College, B.A., 1960; Tulane University, M.S., 1962; Washington State University, Ph.D., 1966. *Home:* 1912 Edgewood Dr., Palo Alto, Calif. *Office:* Department of Psychology, Veterans Administration Hospital, San Francisco, Calif.

CAREER: Certified clinical psychologist in state of California. College of San Mateo, San Mateo, Calif., instructor in psychology, 1965-68; West Virginia University, Morgantown, assistant professor of psychology, 1968-71; Veterans Administration Hospital, San Francisco, Calif., assistant chief, 1972—. Instructor, Foothill College, 1966-68; lecturer, Stanford University, 1966-68, De Anza College, 1972-74. Consultant to hospitals and clinics, 1967—. *Member:* American Psychological Association, Sigma Xi, Psi Chi.

WRITINGS: (Editor with Alfred Jacobs) *The Psychology of Private Events,* Academic Press, 1971. Contributor to psychology journals.

* * *

SACKLER, Howard (Oliver) 1929-

PERSONAL: Born December 19, 1929, in New York, N.Y.; son of Martin and Ida Sackler; married Greta Lynn Lungren, December 15, 1963; children: Molly, Daniel. *Education:* Brooklyn College (now of the City University of New York), B.A., 1950. *Home:* Sta. Eulalia del Rio,

Ibiza, Spain. *Agent:* Milton Goldman and Ben Benjamin, International Creative Management, 40 West 57th St., New York, N.Y. 10019.

CAREER: Playwright and screenwriter. Director of Caedmon Records, New York, N.Y., and London, England, 1953-68. Theatre director in New York, London, Dublin, and Los Angeles of plays, including "The Family Reunion," 1954, "Women of Trachis," 1954, "Purgatory" and "The Words upon the Windowpane," 1955, "Hamlet," 1957, "Krapp's Last Tape," 1960, "Chin, Chin," 1960, "Suzanna Andler," 1973, "Duchess of Malfi," 1976; director of film, "A Midsummer Night's Dream," 1961, and of television program, "Shakespeare: Soul of an Age," broadcast by National Broadcasting Co., 1964. *Awards, honors:* Rockefeller Foundation grant, 1953; Littauer Foundation grant, 1954; Maxwell Anderson Award, 1954; Sergel Award, 1959; Pulitzer Prize for drama, New York Drama Critics Circle Award, and Antoinette Perry Award, all 1969, all for *The Great White Hope.*

WRITINGS—Plays: "Uriel Acosta," first produced in Berkeley, Calif., 1954; "Mr. Welk and Jersy Jim," first produced in New York at Actors Studio Theatre, 1960; "The Yellow Loves," first produced in Chicago, 1960; "A Few Enquiries," first produced in Boston by Theatre Company, 1965; "The Nine O'Clock Mail," first broadcast on television in Canada, 1965, produced in Boston at Charles Theatre, 1967; "The Pastime of Monsieur Robert," first produced in London at Hampsted Theatre, 1966; *The Great White Hope* (first produced in Washington, D.C. at Arena Stage, 1967, produced in New York at Alvin Theatre, 1968), Dial, 1968. Also author of "Semmelweiss," to be produced in 1976, and "Medea," not yet produced. Work included in anthology, *New Theatre in America,* edited by Edward Parone, Dell, 1974.

Collections: *A Few Inquiries* (includes "A FEW Inquiries," "Sarah," "The Nine O'Clock Mail," "Mr. Welk and Jersy Jim," and "Skippy"), Dial, 1970.

Screenplays: "Desert Padre," 1950; "Killer's Kiss," 1955; "Fear and Desire," 1953; "A Midsummer Night's Dream," 1961; "The Great White Hope," adapted from own play, 1970; "Bugsy," 1973; "Jaws II," 1976.

Poetry: *Want My Shepherd: Poems,* Caedmon, 1954.

WORK IN PROGRESS: "Goodbye to Fidel," a play, and "Mama's Angel Birdie," a screenplay.

SIDELIGHTS: "Mr. Sackler regards himself as a poet first of all," Kimmis Hendrick has surprisingly revealed. "As he turned 20, T. S. Eliot and William Butler Yeats were his mentors, and then he had the help and encouragement about that time of W. H. Auden."

Sackler's play, *The Great White Hope,* his first production on Broadway, had great impact on critics. "The play of the season was still Howard Sackler's remarkable drama, *The Great White Hope*—one which ... featured not only a large and excellent cast but the most excitingly staged scenes in recent Broadway history," wrote Cleveland Amory. Walter Kerr remarked, "The most striking, the most transparent, thing about Mr. Sackler is that he never writes a scene without throwing a hand grenade into it.... When the audience gets to its feet for the curtain calls (as it did at the preview I saw), it does so out of nothing so simple as respect. The fearlessness onstage has infected it, lifted it into wishing to share a kind of theatrical experience that it had almost forgotten was possible." *The Great White Hope* was the fifth play in history to receive all three

highest American theatre honors. Elizabeth Hardwick believes: "Sackler's unexpected success in making something newly living from the moribund materials of popular art is a challenge to dramatic criticism. . . . It had seemed that only the spare and the abstract of European art could yield up the fat essence. In this play I think the newness and truth comes from the conscious intelligence, writing not *for* us, but out of a saturation *in* us and in American life."

Besides his playwrighting and directing work, Sackler's contribution to the theatre includes his direction or production of nearly 200 spoken arts recordings for Caedmon with such artists as Paul Scofield in "Hamlet," Albert Finney and Claire Bloom in "Romeo and Juliet," and Rex Harrison in "Cyrano de Bergerac."

BIOGRAPHICAL/CRITICAL SOURCES: New York Review of Books, February 1, 1968; *Village Voice,* October 10, 1968; *New Republic,* October 26, 1968; *National Review,* December 17, 1968.

*   *   *

SAFFELL, David C(lyde)   1941-

PERSONAL: Born February 10, 1941, in Wheeling, W.Va.; son of Lloyd and Helen (Smith) Saffell; married Ainsley Brye, 1965; children: Paul, Heather. *Education:* Baldwin-Wallace College, B.A., 1963; University of Minnesota, M.A., 1965, Ph.D., 1969. *Religion:* Protestant. *Home:* 502 West North St., Ada, Ohio 45810. *Office:* Department of Political Science, Ohio Northern University, Ada, Ohio 45810.

CAREER: St. Cloud State University, St. Cloud, Minn., assistant professor of political science, 1966-70; Ashland College, Ashland, Ohio, assistant professor of political science, 1970-72; Ohio Northern State University, Ada, associate professor of political science, 1972—. *Member:* American Political Science Association, Midwest Political Science Association.

WRITINGS: Politics of American National Government, Winthrop Publishing, 1973, 2nd edition, 1975; *Watergate: Its Effects on the American Political System,* Winthrop Publishing, 1974; *American Government: Reform in the Post-Watergate Era,* Winthrop Publishing, 1976. Contributor of articles and reviews to *Dictionary of American History* and *Perspective.*

WORK IN PROGRESS: Introduction to State and Local Government, for Addison-Wesley.

*   *   *

SAGE, George Harvey   1929-

PERSONAL: Born December 27, 1929, in Rifle, Colo.; son of George Everett (a mechanic) and Maybell (Bonis) Sage; married Amalie Elizabeth Aguerre (a teacher), August 20, 1955; children: Michael George, Larry Allen. *Education:* University of Northern Colorado, A.B., 1955, M.A., 1957, postdoctoral study, 1969, 1971; University of California, Los Angeles, Ed.D., 1963; Colorado State University, postdoctoral study, 1973. *Home:* 1933 26th Ave., Greeley, Colo. 80631. *Office:* Department of Men's Physical Education, University of Northern Colorado, Greeley, Colo. 80639.

CAREER: High school physical education teacher in Greeley, Colo., 1955-57, and Chandler, Ariz., 1957-58 (athletic coach, 1957-58); Pomona College, Claremont, Calif., assistant professor of physical education and head basketball coach, 1959-63; University of Northern Colorado, Greeley, associate professor of physical education, 1963—. Visiting professor at Kansas State University, 1973, and Eastern Washington State College and University of Colorado, both 1974. *Military service:* U.S. Army, 1948-51.

MEMBER: International Society for Sport Psychology, North American Society for the Psychology of Sport and Physical Activity, American Association for the Advancement of Science, American Association for Health, Physical Education and Recreation (member of research council), National College Physical Education Association for Men, National Association of Basketball Coaches of the United States, American Sociological Association, Society for the History of Physical Education in the Asia and Pacific Area, Colorado Association for Health, Physical Education and Recreation (president-elect, 1971-72; president, 1972-73), Phi Delta Kappa.

WRITINGS: (Editor and contributor) *Sport and American Society,* Addison-Wesley, 1970, 2nd edition, 1974; *Introduction to Motor Behavior: A Neuropsychological Approach,* Addison-Wesley, 1971, 2nd edition, in press; (contributor) Michael G. Wade and Rainer Martens, editors, *Psychology of Motor Behavior and Sport,* Human Kinetics, 1974; (contributor) Donald Ball and John W. Loy, editors, *Sport and the Social Order,* Addison-Wesley, 1975. Contributor of articles and reviews to academic journals. Editor of "Kinesiology," a column in *Journal of Health, Physical Education and Recreation,* 1968-72.

WORK IN PROGRESS: Research on socialization of youth into sport and socialization via sport.

* * *

SAGE, Leland L(ivingston) 1899-

PERSONAL: Born April 23, 1899, in Magnolia, Ark.; son of Jesse Abner (a minister) and Mary (Livingston) Sage; married Margaret Pearson, December 30, 1929; children: Carolyn Elizabeth (Mrs. Richard R. Robinson). *Education:* Attended Mississippi A&M College (now Mississippi State University), 1916-17, and Henderson-Brown College, 1917-19; Vanderbilt University, B.A., 1922; University of Illinois, M.A., 1928, Ph.D., 1932. *Politics:* Independent. *Religion:* Methodist. *Home and office:* 2301 Clay St., Cedar Falls, Iowa 50613.

CAREER: DePauw University, Greencastle, Ind., instructor in history, 1928-30; University of Northern Iowa, Cedar Falls, instructor, 1932-34, assistant professor, 1934-37, associate professor, 1937-45, professor of history, 1945-67, professor emeritus, 1967—. *Member:* Organization of American Historians, Southern Historical Association.

WRITINGS: William Boyd Allison: A Study in Practical Politics, State Historical Society of Iowa, 1956; *A History of Iowa,* Iowa State University Press, 1974. Contributor to historical journals.

* * *

SAINT, Phil(ip) 1912-

PERSONAL: Born October 19, 1912, in Jenkintown, Pa.; son of Lawrence Bradford (an artist) and Catharine Wright (Proctor) Saint; married Ruth Brooker, October 18, 1941; children: Ruth Ellyn (deceased), Martha Joanne (Mrs. Samuel Berberian), David Lawrence, James Vreeland, Joseph Allen, Evelyn Gertrude. *Education:* Wheaton College, Wheaton, Ill., B.S. (high honors), 1941. *Politics:* "Traditionally Republican, but open." *Office:* Box 1002, Greensboro, N.C. 27402; and, Victor Manuel 333, Suc 9, Cordoba, Argentina 5009.

CAREER: President and director of Spanish Evangelistic Crusades, Inc., in Cordoba, Argentina, 1957—. Founder and director of Bible Conference Centers in Argentina, 1967, and Paraguay, 1973.

WRITINGS: Drawing Men to Christ, Christian Publications, 1935; *Amazing Saints,* Logos International, 1972; *Cataclismo,* Logos International, 1974. Contributor of articles and illustrations to *Christian Life* and *Logos Journal.* Writer and producer of films in English and Spanish.

WORK IN PROGRESS: Religious cartoons; conference building programs; periodical articles.

SIDELIGHTS: Saint "began preaching at the age of twenty-one, drawing before the audience with chalk. I conducted rallies and evangelistic campaigns in many parts of the United States and Canada. I worked in the army camps with the Pocket Testament League, then went to Japan for nine months with the same organization. While there I produced two films on Japan, then went to the Caribbean Islands with the Latin America Mission, where another sound film was produced. I then went with a team of the same mission to Uruguay and Argentina. . . . I am a brother of Nate Saint, one of the five martyrs in Ecuador, and of Rachel Saint, the translator to the Auca Indians, the tribe that killed our brother."

* * *

SAITO, Hiroyuki 1917-
(Fred Saito)

PERSONAL: Surname pronounced "sight-oh"; born July 16, 1917, in Ashikaga, Japan; son of Orinosuke and Hatsu Saito; married Yukiko Shiba, May 15, 1949; children: Junko (daughter), Tadashi (son). *Education:* Attended Sophia University, Tokyo, 1938; also studied music privately. *Office:* Japan Council of World Veterans Federation, 2-1-19 Mejirodai, Bunkyo-Ku, Tokyo, Japan 112.

CAREER: Japan Broadcasting Corp., Tokyo, Japan, news, script, and music writer, 1942-45; Associated Press, Tokyo, reporter, 1948-60, war correspondent in Korea, 1953; Japanese correspondent and contributing editor of *American Metal Market, Oil Daily,* and *Industrial World* (all American periodicals), 1961—. Executive secretary of Japan Council of World Veterans Federation, 1965—. *Member:* Iron and Steel Institute of Japan.

WRITINGS—Translations into Japanese: Hugo Leichtentritt, *Serge Koussevitzky,* Harvard University-Sogensha (Tokyo), 1949; Denis Warner, *Beiso no Setten Tonan Ajia* (title means "Southeast Asia Report"), Asahi Shimbun, 1951; *Dokoku no Michi o Yuku, Chosen Senso* (title means "Korean War Report"), Seikei Shoin, 1951; J. W. N. Sullivan, *Beethoven,* Sogensha, 1954.

Nonfiction; under name Fred Saito: (With Saburo Sakai and Martin Caidin) *Samurai!,* Dutton, 1957; (with Tameichi Hara and Roger Pineau) *Japanese Destroyer Captain,* Ballantine, 1961; (with Alexander Werth) *Der Tiger Indiens* (biography of Subhas Chandra Bose, Indian revolutionary), Bechtle (Munich), 1971.

Contributor of articles on numerous subjects to American, British, and Japanese periodicals.

WORK IN PROGRESS: Japanese Pirates and Catholics, a history of Japan, c. 1200-1650.

SIDELIGHTS: Saito reads Chinese, English, French, and German. He told *CA:* "A long time journalist for American and British periodicals, I consider it my act of faith to help foreigners understand more about the Japanese people. In the past 100 years, the Japanese kept themselves just too busy learning about occidental cultures. So the Japanese failed to delineate their own profile and quintessentials. Most books written about Japan by foreigners read to me biased, ill-informed or shallowly observed."

* * *

SALAMAN, Esther 1900-

PERSONAL: Born January 6, 1900, in Russia; daughter of Moses Nathan (a timber merchant) and Batia (Berry) Polianowsky; married Myer Head Salaman (a medical scientist), September 5, 1926; children: Nina Salaman Wedderburn, Thalia (Mrs. A. Polak), Ruth Salaman Barlow, David. *Education:* Attended University of Berlin, 1922-25, and Cavendish Laboratory, 1925-28. *Home:* 23 Bisham Gardens, Highgate, London N6 6DJ, England.

CAREER: Writer. *Member:* Society of Authors.

WRITINGS: Two Silver Roubles (novel), Macmillan, 1932; (translator with Frances Cornford) *Poems from the Russian,* Faber, 1943; *The Fertile Plain* (novel), Hogarth, 1956, Abelard, 1957; *A Collection of Moments: A Study of Involuntary Memories,* Longmans, Green, 1970, St. Martin's, 1971; *The Great Confession: From Aksakov and De Quincey to Tolstoy and Proust,* Penguin, 1973. Author of "A Talk with Einstein," British Broadcasting Corp., 1955. Contributor to *Listener.*

WORK IN PROGRESS: A long historical novel, covering life in Cambridge, England between 1925 and 1941.

* * *

SALOMON, Janet Lynn (Nowicki) 1953-
(Janet Lynn)

PERSONAL: Born April 6, 1953, in Chicago, Ill.; daughter of Florian Walter (a pharmacist) and Ethelyne (Gehrke) Nowicki; married Richard Salomon. *Education:* Attended Colorado College and Rockford College. *Religion:* Christian. *Residence:* Rockford, Ill.

CAREER: Ice skater. Guest star on "Ice Follies," 1973, 1975-76; appeared on special ABC-Television program with Julie Andrews; has made media commercials in Japan and worked as spokeswoman for Kodak. Active in civic affairs; has performed in benefits for crippled children. *Member:* American Guild of Variety Artists, American Federation of Television and Radio Artists. *Awards, honors:* Won U.S. Ladies' Figure Skating Championships annually, 1969-73; World Figure Skating Championship medalist, 1972, 1973; Olympic bronze medalist, 1972.

WRITINGS: (Under name Janet Lynn, with Dean Merrill) *Peace & Love,* Creation House, 1973.

* * *

SALTER, Paul Sanford 1926-

PERSONAL: Born May 21, 1926, in Springfield, Mass.; son of Leonard Austin, Sr. and Clara Ann (Weary) Salter; married Barbara Jean Kirby, September 9, 1950; children: Paul, Jr., Kim Ann, Nancy Eileen. *Education:* Massachusetts State College at Westfield, B.S.E., 1950; Indiana University, M.A., 1951; University of North Carolina at Chapel Hill, Ph.D., 1965. *Home:* 9710 Southwest 84th St., Miami, Fla. 33173. *Office:* Department of Geography, Box 8152, University of Miami, Coral Gables, Fla. 33124.

CAREER: Holyoke High School, Holyoke, Mass., teacher of history and geography, 1951-55; Springfield Trade High School, Springfield, Mass., teacher of English, 1955-56; Massachusetts State College at Westfield, instructor and critic-teacher in Department of Education Laboratory School, 1956-60; University of North Carolina at Chapel Hill, laboratory and staff instructor in geography, 1960-64; University of Miami, Coral Gables, Fla., assistant professor, 1964-68, associate professor, 1969-71, professor of geography, 1975—, director of Office for General Students, 1969-70, associate dean for undergraduate student academic affairs and coordinator of research for College of Arts and Sciences, 1969-75. Visiting assistant professor, Birmingham Southern College, summer, 1962, East Carolina University, summer, 1966; visiting associate professor, University of South Carolina, summer, 1969. *Military service:* U.S. Navy, 1944-46. *Member:* Association of American Geographers, American Association of University Professors, National Council of University Research Administrators, Florida Society of Geographers, Gamma Theta Upsilon. *Awards, honors:* Smith Fund grant from University of North Carolina, 1964; National Science Foundation institutional research grants, 1965, 1969, 1971; Humanities research grant from University of Miami, 1969; Shell Foundation grant, 1971, 1974.

WRITINGS: (Contributor) W.H.Johnson and W.C.Steere, editors, *Challenge for Survival,* Holt, 1974; *Conservation in an Urban Age,* Wiley, in press. Contributor to professional journals.

* * *

SAMOLIN, William 1911-

PERSONAL: Born October 29, 1911, in New York, N.Y.; married Ruth Mary Zwicker, 1944. *Education:* New York University, B.S., 1933; Columbia University, M.A., 1936, Ph.D., 1953. *Office:* Department of History, University of Hartford, West Hartford, Conn. 06117.

CAREER: Adelphi College (now University), Garden City, N.Y., lecturer in Asiatic history, 1952-53; Academy of Aeronautics, New York, N.Y., instructor in mathematics, 1954-55; Monmouth College, West Long Branch, N.J., instructor in mathematics and history, 1955-57; high school mathematics and science teacher at private school in Montclair, N.J., 1957-58; Columbia University, New York, N.Y., assistant professor of Uralic and Altaic languages, 1959-63, assistant professor of art history and archaeology, 1963-64, associate professor of art history and archaeology, 1964-66; University of Hartford, West Hartford, Conn., associate professor, 1966-69, professor of history, 1969—. Adjunct professor at Brooklyn College of Pharmacy, 1959-65; research associate at Columbia University, 1966-71. *Military service:* U.S. Army, 1941-47; served in European theater; became captain. U.S. Army Reserve, 1947-52; became major.

MEMBER: American Military Institute, American Oriental Society, American Historical Association, Archaeological Institute of America, Society for the History of Technology, American Association for the Advancement of Science. *Awards, honors:* Social Science Research Council faculty research fellowship, 1959; Guggenheim fellowship, 1964-65.

WRITINGS: Archaeological and Historical Background of the Altaic Peoples, American Council of Learned Societies, 1963; *East Turkistan to the Twelfth Century,* Mouton, 1964; (contributor) Noel Barnard and Douglas Fraser, editors, *Early Chinese Art and Its Possible Influence in the*

Pacific Basin, Intercultural Arts Press, 1972. Editor of films on the Germans in World War II for University of Hartford Archival Film Center. Contributor to professional journals.

WORK IN PROGRESS: A book on the Kimmerians, for publication in the United States and England; research on German armored operations in World War II.

* * *

SANDARS, N(ancy K(atharine) 1914-

PERSONAL: Born June 29, 1914, in Little Tew, Oxford, England; daughter of Edward Carew and Gertrude Annie (Phipps) Sandars. *Education:* Attended University of London, 1946-49; St. Hugh's College, Oxford, B.Litt., 1953. *Home:* Manor House, Little Tew, Oxford OX7 4JF, England. *Agent:* Curtis Brown Ltd., 7 Craven Hill, London, England.

CAREER: Archaeological research resident at British Schools of Archaeology in Athens (Greece), Ankara (Turkey), and Jerusalem (Israel), and British School of Persian Studies in Tehran (Iran), 1950—; free-lance writer, 1972—. *Military service:* Motorized Transport Corps, 1940-42; Women's Royal Naval Service (WRENS), 1943-44. *Member:* Society of Antiquaries of London (fellow), University Women's Club. *Awards, honors:* Thomas Eric Peet prize, 1957, 1958.

WRITINGS: Bronze Age Cultures in France, Cambridge University Press, 1957; *The Epic of Gilgamesh: An English Version,* Penguin, 1960, 3rd edition, 1972; *Prehistoric Art in Europe: Pelican History of Art,* Penguin, 1967; *Poems of Heaven and Hell from Ancient Mesopotamia,* Penguin, 1971. Contributor to archaeological and literary journals.

WORK IN PROGRESS: The Sea Peoples, for Thames & Hudson; *Ancient Peoples and Places.*

SIDELIGHTS: Nancy Sandars told *CA:* "From my childhood I have been deeply interested in the past, and more recently have been occupied with its many aspects more from the sense of scale and perspective that it gives to the present than from any nostalgia. My wish to make accessible the poetry of ancient Mesopotamia was encouraged by a conviction as to the continuity of the imagination over the centuries and across many frontiers."

* * *

SANDBERG, Margaret M(ay) 1919-

PERSONAL: Born December 29, 1919, in Tacoma, Wash.; daughter of William Wallace (a laborer) and Fern (a teacher; maiden name, Jones) Miner; married John R. Sandberg (a watchmaker and jeweler), April 10, 1943; children: Joan M. (Mrs. John C. McNichols, Jr.), Steven T., David W., Carol F. *Education:* Multnomah School of the Bible, Bible diploma, 1942. *Religion:* "Regular Baptist." *Home:* 2131 Northwest Cascade Ave., East Wenatchee, Wash. 98801.

CAREER: Stenographer and typist for U.S. government and private industry in Maryland and Washington, 1942-46. Writer, 1968—.

WRITINGS: The Mystery of the Man in the Tall Black Hat (juvenile), Moody, 1972. Author of church school material for Union Gospel Press. Contributor of short stories to church publications.

AVOCATIONAL INTERESTS: Oil painting, reading (especially C. S. Lewis).

SANDBERG, Peter Lars 1934-

PERSONAL: Born December 13, 1934, in Winchester, Mass.; son of Lars Josef (a management consultant) and Janice (Whittaker) Sandberg; married Nancy Bell (an English professor), September 8, 1956. *Education:* Florida Southern College, B.S., 1958; University of Colorado, M.A., 1959; graduate study at University of Iowa, 1959-61. *Residence:* Manchester, N.H. *Agent:* McIntosh & Otis, Inc., 475 Fifth Ave., New York, N.Y. 10017. *Office:* Department of English, Northeastern University, Boston, Mass. 02115.

CAREER: Phoenix College, Phoenix, Ariz., instructor in English, 1961-64; *Phoenix Point West,* Phoenix, editor, 1964-66; National Forge Co., Warren, Pa., writer and researcher, 1966-68; Northeastern University, Boston, Mass., lecturer in English, 1968—.

WRITINGS: (With Robert Parker) *Order and Diversity: The Craft of Prose,* Wiley, 1973; *Wolf Mountain* (novel), Playboy Press, 1975. Short stories anthologized in *Best Little Magazine Fiction,* edited by Curt Johnson, New York University Press, 1970; *Best American Short Stories,* edited by Martha Foley, Houghton, 1974; and *Playboy's Laughing Lovers,* Playboy Press, 1975. Contributor to *Playboy, McCall's* and literary journals.

WORK IN PROGRESS: A novel, *Checkmate Caribbean* (tentative title).

SIDELIGHTS: Sandberg told *CA:* "I have always been intrigued with the ways in which a man can define his courage and/or cowardice in a confrontation with nature. The first story I wrote had to do with a young man climbing a mountain, and I suspect the last one will have to do with an old man climbing a mountain—though I hasten to add I do write about other things."

* * *

SANDROW, Edward T. 1906-1975

December 23, 1906—December 16, 1975; American rabbi, theologian, educator, lecturer, and author of books on religious topics. Obituaries: *New York Times,* December 17, 1975.

* * *

SANGSTER, Ian 1934-

PERSONAL: Born April 6, 1934, in Scotland; son of Robert (an engineman) and Elizabeth (MacQueen) Sangster; married Esther Duffie, August 15, 1957 (divorced, 1967); married Sheila Joy Durrant (a food technologist), September 2, 1973; children: Fiona, Morag. *Education:* University of Edinburgh, B.Sc. (honors), 1963; University of Hamburg, Dr.Rer.Nat., 1966. *Politics:* Scottish Nationalist. *Religion:* Humanist. *Home:* World's End, Gordon Town, Jamaica. *Office address:* Sugar Industry Authority, P.O. Box 127, Kingston 10, Jamaica.

CAREER: Painter and decorator in Edinburgh, Scotland, 1949-54; played professional saxophone and clarinet in Scotland and Germany, 1952-54; production manager of paint factory in Edinburgh, Scotland, 1956-59; University of West Indies, Jamaica, research scientist, 1966-67; University of Glasgow, Glasgow, Scotland, research scientist, 1968; Sugar Industry Authority, Kingston, chief technologist, 1969—. *Military service:* First King's Dragoon Guards, 1954-56. *Member:* International Society of Sugar Cane Technologists.

WRITINGS: Jamaica: A Holiday Guide, Benn, 1974; *Sugar and Jamaica,* Nelson, 1974. Contributor to scientific journals.

SIDELIGHTS: Sangster described himself for *CA* as, "a perfervid Scot now married to a Jamaican and living in the blue mountains of Jamaica. I am engaged in scientific research, writing, establishing a family liqueur empire, growing coffee, meeting people, and growing graciously old."

*   *   *

SANKEY, Alice (Ann-Susan) 1910-

PERSONAL: Born February 2, 1910, in Waukegan, Ill.; daughter of Philip John (a musician) and Katherine (De-Young) Dahlberg; married Thomas Riddell Sankey, June 21, 1930 (died, 1968); children: Thomas, Enid (Mrs. Stephen Bartnicki), Brien. *Education:* Writing courses at University of Minnesota, University of Wisconsin, Racine, Indiana University, and Northwestern University. *Politics:* Republican. *Religion:* Protestant. *Home:* 1036 Lathrop Ave., Racine, Wis. 53405. *Office: Journal Times,* 212 Fourth St., Racine, Wis. 53403.

CAREER: Racine *Times-Call,* Racine, Wis., society editor, 1929-31; Whitman Publishing Co., Racine, staff writer, 1942-46; Racine *Journal Times,* Racine, telegraph and copy desk editor, 1943-45, part-time editor and reporter, 1952-66, women's editor and feature columnist, 1967-74. Member of board of directors, Help Establish Adequate Day Care (H.E.A.D.), 1976—. *Member:* National Federation of Press Women (member of executive board, 1970-74), Wisconsin Press Women (vice-president, 1970-72; president, 1972-74). *Awards, honors:* National Federation of Press Women awards for juvenile fiction and non-fiction writing, 1965; Wisconsin Press Women juvenile book award, 1968, for *Three-in-One Car,* and column award, 1970, 1971, 1972, 1973, for "People-Watching".

WRITINGS—Children's books; all published by Whitman Publishing (Racine, Wis.), except as indicated: *365 Bedtime Stories,* 1942; *Tuffy the Tugboat,* 1947; *Santa Claus and Jingle Bell,* 1947; *Little Hank,* 1948; *Petunia the Pelican,* 1949; *Marcus-Tale of a Monkey,* 1951; *Timmy and Tommy,* 1951; *Hide-Away Henry,* 1953; *Jack of Trades,* Bobbs-Merrill, 1953; *Roy Roger's Surprise for Donnie,* 1954; *Roy Rogers and the Desert Treasure,* 1954; *The Lone Ranger and the Ghost Horse,* 1955.

School texts; all published by Racine Board of Education in 1956: *Racine the Belle City; Racine Industries; Why Work Where?.*

Children's books; all published by Albert Whitman (Chicago, Ill.): *Basketballs for Breakfast,* 1963; *Three-in-One Car,* 1967; *Music by the Got-Rocks,* 1970; *Judo Yell,* 1972; *Hit the Bike Trail,* 1974.

Also author of one-act play, *Silver Wedding,* Row-Peterson, 1958; two radio plays, "Angel on Leash," and "Cupid Has Grey Hair." Ghost writer of more than thirty juvenile books and junior novels. Writer of column, "Windows on the World," in *Elementary English,* 1959-62. Former contributor of adult fiction to *Chicago Daily News.*

WORK IN PROGRESS: Juvenile book tentatively titled *Cruising with a Magic Duck* for Albert Whitman, publication expected in 1976.

SIDELIGHTS: Alice Sankey has traveled in Europe, the Orient, Mexico, and took a 92 day cruise around the world in 1974.

SANSWEET, Stephen Jay 1945-

PERSONAL: Born June 14, 1945, in Philadelphia, Pa.; son of Jack Morris (a salesman) and Fannie (Axelrod) Sansweet. *Education:* Temple University, B.S., 1966. *Home:* 14000 Old Harbor Lane #105, Marina Del Rey, Calif. 90291. *Office: Wall Street Journal,* 514 Shatto Pl., Los Angeles, Calif. 90020.

CAREER: Philadelphia Inquirer, Philadelphia, Pa., reporter and feature writer, 1966-68; *Wall Street Journal,* staff reporter in Philadelphia, 1969-71, Montreal, Quebec, 1971-73, and Los Angeles, Calif., 1973—. *Military service:* U.S. Air Force Reserve, 1966-72. *Member:* Society of Professional Journalists, Sigma Delta Chi. *Awards, honors:* Philadelphia Firefighters Association writing award, 1968.

WRITINGS: The Punishment Cure (nonfiction), Mason/Charter, 1975. Contributor to *Philadelphia Magazine, Changes in Higher Education,* and *Wanderlust.*

*   *   *

SARGENT, Pamela

PERSONAL: Born in Ithaca, N.Y. *Education:* State University of New York at Binghamton, B.A., 1968, M.A., 1970. *Residence:* Johnson City, N.Y.

CAREER: Honigsbaum's, Albany, N.Y., sales clerk and model, 1964-65; Endicott Coil Co., Inc., Binghamton, N.Y., solderer on assembly line, 1965; Towne Distributors, Binghamton, N.Y., sales clerk, 1965; State University of New York at Binghamton, typist in cataloging department of library, 1965-66, teaching assistant in philosophy, 1969-71; Webster Paper Co., Albany, N.Y., office worker, 1969; writer, 1969—. *Member:* Science Fiction Writers of America.

WRITINGS: (Editor and contributor) *Women of Wonder: Science Fiction Stories by Women About Women,* Vintage Books, 1975; *Cloned Lives* (science fiction novel), Fawcett, in press.

Stories for children have been anthologized in *The Missing World and Other Stories,* edited by Roger Elwood, Lerner, 1974; *The Killer Plants and Other Stories,* edited by Elwood, Lerner, 1974; *Night of the Sphinx and Other Stories,* Lerner, 1974.

Stories for adults have been anthologized in *Protostars,* edited by David Gerrold, Ballantine, 1971; *New Worlds Quarterly Three,* edited by Michael Moorcock, Berkley Books, 1972; *Universe Two,* edited by Terry Carr, Ace, 1972; *Wandering Stars* (Science Fiction Book Club selection), edited by Jack Dann, Harper, 1972; *Ten Tomorrows,* edited by Elwood, Fawcett, 1973; *And Walk Now Gently Through the Fire* (Science Fiction Book Club selection), edited by Elwood, Chilton, 1973; *Eros in Orbit,* edited by Joseph Elder, Trident, 1973; *Two Views of Wonder,* edited by Thomas N. Scortia and Chelsea Quinn Yarbro, Ballantine, 1973; *Universe Four* (Science Fiction Book Club selection), edited by Carr, Random House, 1974; *Continuum Three,* edited by Elwood, Putnam, 1974; *Fellowship of the Stars* (Science Fiction Book Club selection), edited by Carr, Simon & Schuster, 1974. Contributor to science fiction magazines.

WORK IN PROGRESS: Editing *Bio-Futures: Stories of Biological Change,* for Vintage Books; editing *More Women of Wonder: More Science Fiction Stories by Women About Women,* Vintage Books; a novel, for Fawcett; "Weapons," with George Zebrowski, a story to be included in an anthology, edited by Elwood, for Prentice-Hall.

SATZ, Paul 1932-

PERSONAL: Born September 12, 1932, in Ware, Mass.; son of Leo (a jeweler) and Milly (Hurst) Satz; married Gladys McLeod, September 5, 1957; children: George Scott, Mark Gregory, Julie Gavina. Education: Attended Boston University, 1953-54; University of Miami, Coral Gables, Fla., B.A., 1957, M.A., 1959; University of Kentucky, Ph.D., 1963; University of Florida, post-doctoral study, 1964. Office: Neuropsychology Laboratory, College of Health Related Professions, University of Florida, Gainesville, Fla. 32610.

CAREER: University of Kentucky, Speech Clinic, Lexington, research assistant, 1958-59; Veterans Administration Hospital, Coral Gables, Fla., psychology trainee, 1960; Veterans Administration Hospital, Lexington, Ky., psychology trainee, 1960-63; Veterans Administration Hospital, Cincinnati, Ohio, psychology trainee, 1963; University of Florida, Gainesville, assistant professor, 1964-67, associate professor, 1967-71, professor of psychology and clinical psychology, 1971—, director of Neuropsychology Laboratory, including Health Center, Life Sciences, and Mobile Laboratory Unit, member of Center for Neurobiological Sciences, 1965—. Research assistant at South Florida State Hospital, 1958-59.

MEMBER: International Neuropsychology Society (president, 1973-74), International Federation of Learning Disabilities, American Association for the Advancement of Science, Academy of Aphasia, American Psychological Association, Florida Psychological Association, Orton Society. Awards, honors: National Institute of Mental Health fellowship, 1963-64; National Institutes of Health grants, 1964-71, 1966-78, 1970-77, 1972-74, 1972; Florida Council on Training and Research in Mental Health grant, 1967-68; National Foundation of Birth Defects grant, 1968-71; Florida Mental Health grant, 1970-71; National Institute of Drug and Alcohol Abuse grant, 1973-75.

WRITINGS: (Editor with D. J. Bakker, and contributor) Specific Reading Disability: Advances in Theory and Method, University of Rotterdam Press, 1970; (editor with J. Ross, and contributor) The Disabled Learner: Early Detection and Intervention, University of Rotterdam Press, 1972; (contributor) D. Stein, J. Rosen, and N. Butters, editors, Plasticity and Recovery of Function in the Central Nervous System, Academic Press, 1974; Learning Disorders and Remediation of Learning Disorders (monograph), Research Task Force, National Institute of Mental Health, 1974; (contributor) J. T. Guthrie, editor, Aspects of Reading Acquisition, Johns Hopkins Press, in press. Also contributor to Brain and Language, 1974. Contributor of about fifty articles to professional journals. Consulting editor of Journal of Supplement Abstracts and Journal of the International Federation of Learning Disabilities.

* * *

SATZ, Ronald Norman 1944-

PERSONAL: Surname rhymes with "cats"; born February 8, 1944, in Chicago, Ill.; son of David Harold (a master locksmith and salesman) and Gertrude (Smith) Satz; married Christa Grete Ilgaudas, July 4, 1969; children: Ani Berta, Jakob Samuel. Education: Illinois Institute of Technology, B.S., 1965; Illinois State University, M.A., 1967; University of Maryland, Ph.D., 1972. Home: University Courts S., Apt. G17, Martin, Tenn. 38237. Office: Department of History, University of Tennessee, Martin, Tenn. 38238.

CAREER: University of Tennessee, Martin, assistant professor, 1971-75, associate professor of history, 1975—. Visiting assistant professor at University of Maryland, summer, 1973.

MEMBER: American Historical Association, Organization of American Historians, National Association of Interdisciplinary Studies for Native American, Black, Chicano, Puerto Rican, and Asian Americans, American Association of University Professors (president of Martin chapter, 1974-76), Southern Anthropological Association, Southwestern American Indian Society, Western History Association, Pi Gamma Mu, Delta Tau Kappa, Phi Alpha Theta, Phi Kappa Phi. Awards, honors: Ford Foundation fellowship, 1971; National Endowment for the Humanities fellowship, 1974.

WRITINGS: American Indian Policy in the Jacksonian Era, University of Nebraska Press, 1975; Tennessee's Indian Peoples: 1540 to 1840, University of Tennessee Press, 1976; (contributor) Wilcomb Washburn, editor, Handbook of North American Indians, Volume IV, Smithsonian Institution Press, in press. Contributor of articles and reviews to history journals. Member of editorial board of Maryland Historian, 1970-71, and of University of Tennessee Press, 1975—.

WORK IN PROGRESS: History of America: Change and Continuity, with Joan Gunderson, H. Vincent Nelson, Jr., and Gary Reichard, publication by Wiley expected in 1978; contributions to The Commissioners of Indian Affairs: From Thomas L. McKenney to John Collier, edited by Herman J. Viola and Robert M. Kvasnicka, University of Nebraska Press, 1978; research on American government and bureaucratic reform in the nineteenth century, on ethnic minorities in Tennessee, on ethnic minorities in America, and on the U.S. government and efforts to thwart native American self-government in the Trans-Mississippi West.

SIDELIGHTS: "I believe that a study of past events can provide helpful insights into some of today's problems," Satz wrote. "Hopefully, objective studies of the sources and results of ethnic conflicts in our nation's past will provide some clues ... [to] deal more effectively with such tensions in contemporary times."

BIOGRAPHICAL/CRITICAL SOURCES: American Indian Quarterly, autumn, 1974.

* * *

SAUER, Carl Ortwin 1889-1975

PERSONAL: Born December 24, 1889, in Warrenton, Mo.; married, 1913; children: two. Education: Central Wesleyan College, A.B., 1908; Northwestern University, graduate study, 1908-09; University of Chicago, Ph.D., 1915.

CAREER: University of Michigan, Ann Arbor, instructor, 1915-18, assistant professor, 1918-20, associate professor, 1920-22, professor of geography, 1922-23; University of California, Berkeley, professor of geography, 1923-57, chairman of department, 1923-56, acting chairman of department, 1956-57, professor emeritus, 1957-75. Agent, Office of Farm Management, U.S. Department of Agriculture, 1919-20; member of selection board, J. S. Guggenheim Memorial Foundation, 1936-55; member of board, Air University, 1949-52; senior consultant, Soil Conservation Service; founder, Michigan Land Economy Survey.

MEMBER: American Philosophical Society, American

Geographical Society, Association of American Geographers (president, 1940; honorary president, 1955), Austrian Geographical Society, Royal Scottish Geographical Society (honorary fellow), Royal Netherlands Geographical Society (honorary member), Finnish Geographical Society (honorary member), Mexican National Academy of Science (honorary member). *Awards, honors:* Guggenheim Memorial fellow, 1931; Charles P. Daly medal from American Geographical Society, 1940; Ph.D., from University of Heidelberg, 1956; Vega Medal from Swedish Society of Anthropology and Geology, 1957; Humboldt Medal from Berlin Geographical Society, 1959; LL.D. from Syracuse University, 1958, University of California, Berkeley, 1960, and University of Glasgow, 1965.

WRITINGS: Geography of the Upper Illinois Valley and History of Development, Illinois State Geological Survey, University of Illinois, 1916; (with Gilbert H. Cady and Henry C. Cowles) *Starved Rock State Park and Its Environs,* University of Chicago Press, 1918; *The Geography of the Ozark Highland of Missouri,* University of Chicago Press, 1920; *The Morphology of Landscape,* University of California Press, 1925, reprinted, Johnson Reprint, 1968; (with Pervil Meigs) *Site and Culture at San Fernando de Velicata,* University of California Press, 1927, reprinted, Johnson Reprint, 1968; (with John B. Leighly, Kenneth McMurray, and Clarence W. Newman) *Geography of the Pennroyal: A Study of the Influence of Geology and Physiography upon the Industry, Commerce and Life of the People,* Kentucky Geological Survey, 1927; *Land Forms in the Peninsular Range of California as Developed about Warner's Hot Springs and Mesa Grande,* University of California Press, 1929, reprinted, Johnson Reprint, 1968; *Basin and Range Forms in the Chiricahua Area,* University of California Press, 1930, reprinted, Johnson Reprint, 1968; (with Donald Brand) *Pueblo Sites in Southeastern Arizona,* University of California Press, 1930, reprinted, Johnson Reprint, 1968; (with Brand) *Prehistoric Settlements of Sonora, with Special Reference to Cerros de Trincheras,* University of California Press, 1931, reprinted, Johnson Reprint, 1968; (with Leo Baisden, Isabel Kelly, Margaret Warthin, and Aileen Corwin) *Man in Nature: America before the Days of the White Men,* Scribner, 1939.

Agricultural Origins and Dispersals, American Geographical Society, 1952, 2nd edition published as *Agricultural Origins and Dispersals: The Domestication of Animals and Foodstuffs,* M.I.T. Press, 1969, published as *Seeds, Spades, Hearths, and Herbs: The Domestication of Animals and Foodstuff,* 1974; *Land and Life: A Selection from the Writings of Carl Ortwin Sauer,* University of California Press, 1963; *The Early Spanish Main,* University of California Press, 1966; *Northern Mists,* University of California Press, 1968; *Sixteenth Century North America: The Land and the People as Seen by the Europeans,* University of California Press, 1971.

OBITUARIES: Time, August 4, 1975; *AB Bookman's Weekly,* August 25, 1975.*

(Died July 18, 1975, in Berkeley, Calif.)

*   *   *

SAUNDERS, Charles B(askerville), Jr.   1928-

PERSONAL: Born December 26, 1928, in Boston, Mass.; son of Charles Baskerville and Lucy (Carmichael) Saunders; married Margaret MacIntire Shafer, September 9, 1950; children: Charles Baskerville III, George Carlton, Margaret Keyser, Lucy C., John R. *Education:* Princeton

University, A.B., 1950. *Politics:* Republican. *Religion:* Presbyterian. *Home:* 7622 Winterberry Pl., Bethesda, Md. 20034. *Office:* 1 DuPont Cir., Washington, D.C. 20036.

CAREER: Ogdensburg Journal, Ogdensburg, N.Y., news reporter, political columnist, 1950-51; *Hartford Times,* Hartford, Conn., educational reporter, 1951-53; Trinity College, Hartford, assistant director of public relations, 1953-55; Princeton University, Princeton, N.J., assistant director of public information, 1955-57; legislative assistant to Senator H. Alexander Smith, 85th Congress, Washington, D.C., 1957-58; U.S. Department of Health, Education, and Welfare, Washington, D.C., assistant to assistant secretary for legislation, 1958-59, assistant to Secretary Arthur S. Flemming, 1959-61; Brookings Institution, Washington, D.C., assistant to president, 1961-69; U.S. Department of Health, Education, and Welfare, deputy assistant secretary for legislation, 1969-71, deputy commissioner of education for external affairs, 1971-73, deputy assistant secretary for education, 1973-74; American Council on Education, Washington, D.C., director of governmental relations, 1975—. Trustee, Montgomery College, 1969-70. Member, Montgomery County board of education, 1966-70.

WRITINGS: The Brookings Institution: A Fifty Year History, Brookings Institution, 1966; *Upgrading the American Police: Education and Training for Better Law Enforcement,* Brookings Institution, 1970.

*   *   *

SAUTEL, Maureen Ann   1951-
(Maureen Ann McGinn)

PERSONAL: Born February 25, 1951, in St. Louis, Mo.; daughter of James A. and Ilene (Lee) McGinn; married F. Timothy Sautel (a teacher), September 11, 1975. *Education:* University of Missouri, St. Louis, B.S., 1973. *Religion:* Roman Catholic. *Home:* 5675 East Golf Ridge Lane, St. Louis, Mo. 63128. *Office:* Special School District of St. Louis County, St. Louis, Mo.

CAREER: Special School District of St. Louis County, St. Louis, Mo., teacher of art for educable mentally retarded, 1973—.

WRITINGS—Under name Maureen Ann McGinn: *I Used to Be an Artichoke* (juvenile), Concordia, 1973.

WORK IN PROGRESS: Refining and revising a numbers book introducing counting by tens, tentatively titled, *Mr. Zero.*

*   *   *

SAWYER, Jack   1931-

PERSONAL: Born June 8, 1931, in Beatrice, Neb.; son of Proctor Herbert and Elisabeth Ann (Jack) Sawyer. *Education:* Iowa State University, B.S., 1952; Ohio State University, M.A., 1953; Purdue University, Ph.D., 1955. *Politics:* Democratic. *Religion:* Christian. *Home:* 3029 Benvenue Ave., Berkeley, Calif. 94705. *Office:* Wright Institute, 2728 Durant Ave., Berkeley, Calif. 94704.

CAREER: Department of the Army, Washington, D.C., research psychologist, 1955-58; University of Chicago, Chicago, Ill., lecturer, 1959-60, assistant professor of psychology, 1960-67; Northwestern University, Evanston, Ill., associate professor of psychology, 1967-72; Harvard University, Cambridge, Mass., special research fellow, 1971-72; Wright Institute, Berkeley, fellow, 1972—. Member of Chicago Board of Trade, 1962-64; national co-chairman of Psychologists for Social Action, 1968-69. *Military service:* U.S. Naval Reserve, 1949-57.

MEMBER: American Psychological Association (member of council of representatives, 1969-72), Association for Humanistic Psychology, American Sociological Association, American Association for the Advancement of Science (fellow), Society for the Psychological Study of Social Issues (council member, 1972-74). *Awards, honors:* Rockefeller Foundation fellowship, 1958-59; National Science Foundation fellowship, 1959-60; National Institute of Mental Health special research fellowship, 1971-73.

WRITINGS: (Editor with Joseph H. Pleck) *Men and Masculinity,* Prentice-Hall, 1974. Contributor of about fifty articles to journals in his field.

WORK IN PROGRESS: Research on human consciousness, on integration of body, mind, and spirit, and on social-political context.

*   *   *

SAXE, Thomas E., Jr.   1903-1975

1903—December 20, 1975; American entrepreneur, foundation director, and author. Obituaries: *New York Times,* December 21, 1975.

*   *   *

SAYCE, Richard Anthony   1917-

PERSONAL: Born January 11, 1917, in Bolton, England; son of James Arthur and Mary Ellen (Waddington) Sayce; married Olive Lenore Davison, 1948; children: Catharine Mary, Lucy Elizabeth. *Education:* Oxford University, B.A., 1937, M.A., 1945, D.Phil., 1950. *Office:* Worcester College, Oxford University, Oxford OX1 3BD, England.

CAREER: Oxford University, Oxford, England, lecturer at Worcester and Lincoln colleges and university lecturer in French, 1947-50, fellow of Worcester College, 1950—, university reader in French literature, 1966—. Librarian, Worcester College, 1958—. *Military service:* British Army, Intelligence Corps, 1940-46; became captain. *Member:* Bibliographical Society (council member, 1964—; vice-president, 1975—), Modern Humanities Research Association (secretary, 1954-60), Societa Universitaria per gli Studi di Lingua e Letteratura Francese (honorary member).

WRITINGS: (Editor) Pierre Corneille, *Polyeucte,* Basil Blackwell, 1949; (compiler with Reginald Charles Dennis Perman) *Twentieth-Century French Prose: Passages for Translation,* Basil Blackwell, 1950; *Style in French Prose: A Method of Analysis,* Clarendon Press, 1953, revised edition, 1958; *The French Biblical Epic in the Seventeenth Century,* Clarendon Press, 1955; *The Essays of Montaigne: A Critical Exploration,* Northwestern University Press, 1972.

Contributor of articles to *Bibliotheque d'Humanisme et Renaissance, Comparative Literature, French Studies, Library,* and *Modern Language Review.* Editor, *The Library,* 1965-70.

*   *   *

SAYLOR, Neville   1922-

PERSONAL: Born September 2, 1922, in Helena, Ark.; daughter of Neval Preston (an accountant) and Lou Eunice (Bennett) Swaim; married Earney Allen Saylor, December 27, 1951 (deceased); children: Cheryll, Anita, Jeanne (Mrs. Steve Coker), Allen, Jack. *Education:* Ouachita Baptist University, B.A., 1944; Henderson State University, M.S.E., 1969. *Home:* 1838 Center, Arkadelphia, Ark. 71923.

CAREER: Mid-South Milk Products Association, Memphis, Tenn., laboratory technician, 1944-47; University of California, Extension Service, Bakersfield, laboratory technician, 1947-49; public school English teacher in Morrilton, Ark., 1950-51, and Sparkman, Ark., 1970-73; Emmet School, Emmet, Ark., English teacher, 1974—. *Member:* National Education Association, National Poetry Society, Arkansas Education Association, Poets Round Table of Arkansas. *Awards, honors:* John D. Womack Award from Arkansas Poetry Day festival, 1972, for ballad poem. Certificate of merit from Centro Studi e Scambi Internationali, 1972; Choya Award from Arkansas Poetry Day festival, 1973.

WRITINGS: The New Genesis (poems), Burro Books, 1971. Poetry editor of *Southern Standard,* 1967-69, and *Daily Siftings Herald,* 1970—.

WORK IN PROGRESS: Saylor's Songs (tentative title), a book of poems.

AVOCATIONAL INTERESTS: Working with remedial students; collecting rocks and stamps.

BIOGRAPHICAL/CRITICAL SOURCES: Modern Images, autumn, 1970; *American Poetry League Bulletin,* April, 1975, July, 1975.

*   *   *

SAYRE, Anne   1923-

PERSONAL: Born April 10, 1923, in Milwaukee, Wis.; daughter of Edward (a banker) and Claudie (deVinny) Colquhoun; married David Sayre (a scientist), December 26, 1947. *Education:* Attended Middlebury College, 1940-42; Radcliffe College, B.A. (cum laude), 1943; New York University, graduate study, 1975—. *Religion:* Episcopalian. *Home and office:* Shore House, Harbor Rd., St. James, N.Y. 11780. *Agent:* John Schaffner, 425 East 51st St., New York, N.Y. 10022.

WRITINGS: Never Call Retreat (juvenile novel), Crowell, 1957; (contributor) Martha Foley and David Burnett, editors, *Best American Short Stories,* Houghton, 1959; *Rosalind Franklin and DNA,* (biography), Norton, 1975. Contributor of short stories to *Redbook, McCall's, Woman's Home Companion, Seventeen, Colorado Review,* and *Mademoiselle.*

WORK IN PROGRESS: A novel.

SIDELIGHTS: Anne Sayre told *CA:* "*Rosalind Franklin and DNA* was five years in the writing; and represents the effort of a short-story writer to put into perspective the significant work of a brilliant woman scientist whose personality has been much misunderstood and whose contributions much neglected."

*   *   *

SCALLY, Robert James   1937-

PERSONAL: Born August 3, 1937, in New York, N.Y.; son of Patrick Martin (a musician) and Anne (Regan) Scally; married Dena Wolfe (a nursery school teacher), June 29, 1963; children: Terence Paul. *Education:* Attended University of Michigan, 1957-58; Queens College of the City University of New York, A.B., 1961; Princeton University, Ph.D., 1966. *Home:* 39-91 48th St., Sunnyside, N.Y. 11104. *Office:* Department of History, New York University, 19 University Place, New York, N.Y. 10003.

CAREER: New York University, New York, N.Y., associate professor of history, 1965—. *Member:* American Historical Association, Conference on British Studies.

WRITINGS: Forces of Order and Movement in Europe Since 1815, Houghton, 1971; *Origins of the Lloyd George Coalition,* Princeton University Press, 1975.

WORK IN PROGRESS: (With David L. Hicks, Frank Bartholemew, and Robert Zaller) *European Society since 1500,* completion expected in 1976; *Children of the English Working Classes: Study in Culture of Childhood in 19th Century,* 1976.

* * *

SCAMMON, Richard M(ontgomery) 1915-

PERSONAL: Born July 17, 1915, in Minneapolis, Minn.; son of Richard Everingham (a university professor) and Julia (Simms) Scammon; married Mary Stark Allen, February 20, 1952; children: Anne Valerie. *Education:* University of Minnesota, A.B., 1935; London School of Economics and Political Science, L.S.E., 1936; University of Michigan, A.M., 1938. *Politics:* "Farmer-Labor." *Home:* 5508 Greystone St., Chevy Chase, Md. 20015. *Office:* Elections Research Center, 1619 Massachusetts Ave. N.W., Washington, D.C. 20036.

CAREER: University of Chicago, Radio Office, Chicago, Ill., research secretary for the program "University of Chicago-NBC Round Table of the Air," 1939-41; U.S. Office of Military Government for Germany, Civil Administrative Division, Berlin, Germany, chief of elections and political parties branch, 1946-48; U.S. Department of State, Washington, D.C., chief of division of research for Western Europe, 1948-55; Governmental Affairs Institute, Elections Research Center, Washington, D.C., director, 1955-61; U.S. Bureau of the Census, Washington, D.C., director, 1961-65; Elections Research Center, director, 1965—. Chairman, U.S. delegation to observe elections in Union of Soviet Socialist Republics, 1958; chairman, President's Commission on Registration and Voting Participation, 1963-64; member, Organization of American States electoral mission to Dominican Republic, 1966; chairman, U.S. Select Commission on Western Hemisphere Immigration, 1966-68; National Council on Public Polls, president, 1969-70, member of board of trustees, 1970—; member, President's Commission on Federal Statistics, 1970-71; member, U.S. delegation to United Nations General Assembly, 1973. *Military service:* U.S. Army, 1941-46; served in England, France, and Germany; became captain; deputy military governor of Kreis Mergentheim, Wuerttemberg, 1945, and political officer of Wuerttemberg-Baden, 1945-46. *Member:* American Political Science Association, Canadian Political Science Association, American Academy of Political and Social Sciences, Academy of Political Science, Cosmos Club (Washington). *Awards, honors:* Phi Beta Kappa visiting scholar, 1970-71.

WRITINGS: Governing Post-war Germany, Cornell University Press, 1953; (editor) *America Votes: A Handbook of Contemporary American Election Statistics,* eleven volumes, Macmillan, 1956-75; (with Dean B. Mahin) *Soviet Russia: A Guidebook for Tourists,* Governmental Affairs Institute, 1959; (compiler and editor) *America at the Polls: A Handbook of American Presidential Election Statistics, 1920-64,* University of Pittsburgh Press, 1965; (with Ben J. Wattenberg) *This U.S.A.,* Doubleday, 1965; (with Wattenberg) *The Real Majority: An Extraordinary Examination of the American Electorate,* Coward, 1970. Also author of pamphlets for Governmental Affairs Institute and U.S. Industrial College of the Armed Forces. Contributor of articles on political and social statistics to journals and magazines, including *American Weekly, Newsweek, New York Times Magazine, Business Week,* and *World Affairs.*

* * *

SCARGILL, (David) Ian 1935-

PERSONAL: Born March 22, 1935, in Batley, England; son of Arthur Firth (an electrical engineer) and Evelyn (Goodall) Scargill; married Mary Leslie Branch (a novelist), August 8, 1964; children: Katherine Eugenie. *Education:* St. Edmund Hall, Oxford, B.A. (first class honors), 1957, M.A. and D.Phil., both 1961. *Religion:* United Reformed Church. *Home:* 25 Portland Rd., Oxford, England. *Office:* School of Geography, Oxford University, Mansfield, Rd., Oxford, England.

CAREER: Oxford University, Oxford, England, departmental demonstrator, 1959-64, lecturer in geography, 1964—, fellow of St. Edmund Hall, 1962—. Trustee of Oxford Preservation Trust. *Member:* Royal Geographical Society (fellow), Geographical Association (member of executive committee), Institute of British Geographers.

WRITINGS: Economic Geography of France, Macmillan, 1968; *The Dordogne Region of France,* David & Charles, 1974. Editor of "Problem Regions of Europe" series, eighteen books, Oxford University Press, 1972—. Contributor to geography and town planning journals.

WORK IN PROGRESS: Geography of the British Isles, completion expected in 1977; *The Form of Cities,* 1977.

SIDELIGHTS: Scargill told *CA:* "My principal interests lie in the study of France, where I have a cottage, and in the contemporary problems of cities. Much of my spare time is devoted to church work, the operation of a community help scheme, and the conservation work of the Oxford Preservation Trust."

* * *

SCHACKNE, Stewart 1905-1975

July 15, 1905—December 12, 1975; American public relations director and author. Obituaries: *New York Times,* December 13, 1975; *AB Bookman's Weekly,* March 1, 1976.

* * *

SCHAEFFER, K(laus) H(eymann) 1921-

PERSONAL: Born February 28, 1921, in Germany; son of Ernst Johann Heymann (a historian) and Olga Elisabet Kurnik Schaeffer (an educator); married Eunice Barth (a school nurse), January 26, 1945; children: Mark H. (deceased), Frank H. *Education:* Oberlin College, B.A., 1943; Lutheran Theological Seminary, Gettysburg, Pa., B.D., 1946; University of Nebraska, M.A., 1947; also studied at Yale University, 1943-44, and University of Michigan, 1949-52. *Religion:* Lutheran. *Home:* 3 Acacia St., Cambridge, Mass. 02138. *Office:* U.S. Transportation Systems Center, Kendall Sq., Cambridge, Mass. 02142.

CAREER: College of William & Mary, Norfolk, Va., instructor in philosophy, 1947-48; Alma College, Alma, Mich., assistant professor of philosophy and psychology, 1948-51; University of Michigan, Ann Arbor, sampling statistician at Institute of Social Research, 1951-52, and operations research analyst at Willow Run Laboratory, 1952-58; Stanford Research Institute, Menlo Park, Calif.; operations research analyst, 1958-63; Mitre Corp., Bedford, Mass., operations research analyst, 1963-69; U.S. Transportation

Systems Center, Cambridge, Mass., operations research analyst, 1970—. *Member:* Operations Research Society of America, Philosophy of Science Association, Transportation Research Forum, Transportation Research Board.

WRITINGS: (With Elliott Sclar) *Access for All: Transportation and Urban Growth,* Penguin, 1975.

WORK IN PROGRESS: A History of the Family, with emphasis on the influence of urban structure and technology on the family structure.

*   *   *

SCHAFER, Charles (Louis) 1916-

PERSONAL: Born October 18, 1916, in Silverton, Colo.; son of Louis (a mining engineer) and Erma (Chill) Schafer; married Violet Smith (an executive editor and writer), January 31, 1948. *Education:* Stanford University, A.B., 1938; San Francisco State College (now University), M.A., 1961; also studied at Rudolph Schaeffer School of Design, 1959. *Residence:* Corte Madera, Calif.

CAREER: Pan American Airways, San Francisco, Calif., district sales manager in San Francisco and the Orient, 1939-47; G. E. Supply Corp., San Francisco, Calif., staff assistant, 1947; Crosley Distributing Corp., New York, N.Y., sales promotion manager, 1948-49; Brisacher-Wheeler & Staff, San Francisco, Calif., director of public relations, 1950; California Spray-Chemical Corp., Richmond, Calif., assistant advertising manager, 1950-59; conference coordinator and public relations consultant, 1959—. Co-chairman of International Conference on General Semantics, Mexico, 1958, Honolulu, 1960; regional chairman of International Design Conference at Aspen, 1961-64. *Military service:* U.S. Naval Reserve, 1943-53; became lieutenant junior grade.

MEMBER: Common Cause, Public Citizen, Sierra Club, Corte Madera Open Space Committee (vice-chairman), San Francisco Press Club. *Awards, honors:* Citation and certificate from Family Service Association of America, 1959.

WRITINGS: Ortho Dealer Promotional Plan Book: How to Plan Ortho Garden Clinics, California Spray-Chemical Corp., 1958, 2nd edition published as *Forty-Five Successful Dealer Promotions and What They Can Do to Make Your Open House and Garden Clinic Pay Off,* 1959; (editor with wife, Violet Schafer, and contributor) *New Directions in Western Family Service,* Western Workshop, Family Service Association of America, 1959; *WESCON Speaker's Handbook,* Western Electronic Show and Convention, 1968, 5th edition, 1975; (with Violet Schafer) *Wokcraft: A Stirring Compendium of Chinese Cookery,* Yerba Buena Press, 1972; (with Violet Schafer) *Breadcraft: A Connoisseur's Collection of Bread Recipes—What Bread Is, How You Make It and How You Can Create Your Own Bread Style,* Yerba Buena Press, 1973; (with Violet Schafer) *Teacraft: A Treasury of Romance, Rituals, and Recipes,* Yerba Buena Press, 1974.

Author of training manuals for Pan American Airways Pacific-Alaska Division and Crosley Distributing Corp. Writer of "The Old Pro" and "Meeting Planners' Workbook" columns in *Successful Meetings,* 1959—, of "Avoiding Meeting Hazards," in *Advertising and Sales Promotion,* 1963-67, and of "Conference Problems and Solutions," in *Association Management,* 1967-73. Contributor of nearly two-hundred-fifty articles to sales and advertising magazines. Consulting editor of *Successful Meetings,* 1966—.

WORK IN PROGRESS: A craft book and a book on entertainment, both with wife, Violet Schafer.

SIDELIGHTS: Schafer writes: "Prior to graduation from Stanford in 1938, I organized and for three years managed Stanford Speakers Bureau. . . . My experience living in China before and after World War II, my travels in Europe and South Seas provided many incidents recounted in *Wokcraft* and *Teacraft.*" *Avocational interests:* Gourmet cooking, collecting gavels, inventing games, making toys, oriental art and history, building a conference library.

*   *   *

SCHAFER, Violet (Christine) 1910-

PERSONAL: Born November 14, 1910, in Jamestown, N.D.; daughter of Henry Beaver (a railroad man) and Alice (Kirch) Smith; married Charles Louis Schafer (a writer and consulting editor), January 31, 1948; children: "None, though I have many former students who behave like mine." *Education:* Superior State Teachers College (now University of Wisconsin, Superior), B.E. (high honors), 1932; University of Minnesota, M.A., 1940; also attended Rudolph Schaeffer School of Design, two years. *Residence:* Corte Madera, Calif.

CAREER: University of Minnesota, Minneapolis, worked in publicity department of Little Gallery and art columnist and script writer for university radio station WLB, 1941; director of publicity for Waukesha (Wis.) public schools, 1941-43; William Woods College, Fulton, Mo., director of public relations, 1943-44; associate to editor of *Sunset,* 1947. Trustee of Family Service Agency of Marin County (Calif.), 1954-59; general chairman and architect for regional meeting of Family Service Association of America, 1959. *Member:* Future Farmers of America (honorary member), Sierra Club, Public Citizen, Common Cause, San Francisco Press Club, Friends of the Marin County Library, Station KQED Public Broadcasting (San Francisco, Calif.). *Awards, honors:* Citation from Family Service Association of America, 1959, for outstanding leadership.

WRITINGS: (Editor with husband, Charles Schafer) *New Directions in Western Family Service,* Western Workshop, Family Service Association of America, 1959; *Herbcraft,* Yerba Buena Press, 1971; (with Charles Schafer) *Wokcraft: A Stirring Compendium of Chinese Cookery,* Yerba Buena Press, 1972; (with Charles Schafer) *Breadcraft: A Connoisseur's Collection of Bread Recipes—What Bread Is, How You Make It, and How You Can Create Your Own Bread Style,* Yerba Buena Press, 1973; *Eggcraft,* Yerba Buena Press, 1973; (with Charles Schafer) *Teacraft: A Treasury of Romance, Rituals, and Recipes,* Yerba Buena Press, 1974. Editor of division publications of Pan American World Airways, 1945-47.

WORK IN PROGRESS: Researching and traveling to complete a sixth co-authored book in "craft" series.

SIDELIGHTS: Violet Schafer writes: "As a teacher . . . I emphasized the importance of steady effort rather than burst of energy for examinations (which I seldom gave). I wanted my young people to pass the tests of life, not simply qualify as test passers. As editor/writer, I care very much about sense and simplicity and warmth. If I must choose between correctness and communication, I choose communication. As a person I care about the world, the earth and all its peoples. . . . I like to explore the little things in the grass."

In addition to extensive travels across the United States

and Canada by car and train, Mrs. Schafer has toured Alaska, Hawaii, Mexico, France, and England. Her first book, *Herbcraft,* has appeared in Dutch and braille editions. *Avocational interests:* Herb gardening, international cooking and baking, "writing to friends on beautiful stationery," solving crossword puzzles.

* * *

SCHEMMER, Benjamin Franklin 1932-

PERSONAL: Born April 22, 1932, in Winner, S.D.; son of Clinton Henry (a cowboy) and Minna Mathilda (Heese) Schemmer; married Cynthia Blythe (an artist), February 14, 1955 (deceased); children: Clinton Howard. *Education:* U.S. Military Academy, B.S., 1954. *Religion:* Presbyterian. *Home:* 2130 P St. N.W., Washington, D.C. 20037. *Office: Armed Forces Journal,* 1414 22nd St. N.W., Washington, D.C. 20037.

CAREER: Volkswagen of America, sales manager in California, 1957-59; Boeing Co., Seattle, Wash., military aircraft sales manager, 1959-65; U.S. Department of Defense, Washington, D.C., consultant, 1965, director of Land Force Weapons Systems for Office of the Secretary of State, 1965-68; *Armed Forces Journal,* Washington, D.C., editor, 1968—. *Military service:* U.S. Army, Airborne, Ranger, 1954-57; became first lieutenant.

WRITINGS: Almanac of Liberty (nonfiction), Macmillan, 1974; *The Raid* (nonfiction), Harper, in press. Contributor to magazines and newspapers, including *Penthouse, Look,* and *New Republic.*

WORK IN PROGRESS: The Spook, a novel; non-fiction books, *The Howard Hughes Affair* and *Because It's There.*

AVOCATIONAL INTERESTS: Flying, sailing.

* * *

SCHEUB, Harold 1931-

PERSONAL: Born August 26, 1931, in Gary, Ind. *Education:* University of Michigan, B.A., 1958, M.A., 1960; University of Wisconsin, Madison, Ph.D., 1969. *Office:* Department of African Languages and Literature, University of Wisconsin, Madison, Wis. 53706.

CAREER: Valparaiso University, Valparaiso, Ind., instructor in English literature, 1960-61, 1964-65; secondary school teacher in Masindi, Uganda, 1961-63; University of Wisconsin, Madison, assistant professor, 1970-74, associate professor of African languages and literature, 1974—. *Member:* Modern Language Association of America, American Folklore Society, American Comparative Literature Association.

WRITINGS: African Images, McGraw, 1971; *The Xhosa Ntsomi,* Oxford University Press, 1975; *Tales from Southern Africa,* University of Chicago Press, in press. Author of scripts for a series on Africa, for Wisconsin Educational Television Network.

WORK IN PROGRESS: Research on oral narrative tradition, nature of narrative, nonverbal communication, and oral performance and the written word.

SIDELIGHTS: Scheub has made research trips to southern Africa in 1967-68, 1972-73, 1975-76, making tapes and films of oral narrative performance among Xhosa, Zulu, Swazi, and Ndebele peoples.

SCHEUER, Joseph F(rancis) 1918-1975

July 24, 1918—June 19, 1975; American sociologist, priest, educator, and author of books on religion. Obituaries: *New York Times,* June 23, 1975.

* * *

SCHINHAN, Jan Philip 1887-1975

October 17, 1887—March 26, 1975; Austrian-born American opera conductor, educator, composer, and author or editor of books on folk music. Obituaries: *Washington Post,* March 29, 1975. (*CAP*-2; earlier sketch in *CA*-23/24)

* * *

SCHIPF, Robert G(eorge) 1923-

PERSONAL: Surname is pronounced *Ship*-ff; born April 12, 1923, in Mount Vernon, N.Y.; son of Henry Joseph (a New York City fireman) and Anna Edith (Staker) Schipf; married Mary Ann Downs, August 18, 1952; children: Karen Elizabeth, John Andrew, James Robert. *Education:* Brooklyn College (now of the City University of New York), B.A., 1950; University of Nebraska, M.A., 1953, B.Sc., 1954; University of Oklahoma, M.L.S., 1961; further graduate study at University of Iowa, University of Southwestern Louisiana, and Florida State University. *Politics:* None. *Religion:* None. *Home:* 3100 Bancroft, Missoula, Mont. 59801. *Office:* University of Montana Library, Missoula, Mont. 59801.

CAREER: Ground-water geologist in North Carolina and Louisiana for U.S. Geological Survey, 1953-55; University of Southwestern Louisiana, Lafayette, assistant professor of geology, 1955-59; Humboldt State College (now University), Arcata, Calif., assistant professor of physical sciences, 1959-60; Southern Illinois University, Carbondale, assistant professor and science librarian, 1961-68; University of Montana, Missoula, associate professor and science librarian, 1968—. Member of board of directors of Carbondale Young Men's Christian Association, 1965-68. *Military service:* U.S. Naval Reserve, 1942—; lieutenant. *Member:* National Rifle Association, National Muzzle Loading Rifle Association, National Association of Primitive Riflemen, Sigma Xi.

WRITINGS: Automotive Repair and Maintenance, Libraries Unlimited, 1973; *Home Repair and Improvement,* Libraries Unlimited, 1974; *Outdoor Recreation,* Libraries Unlimited, 1975. Contributor of book reviews and articles to library and geology journals.

WORK IN PROGRESS: Researching a biography of Andrew Jackson Stone, arctic explorer.

AVOCATIONAL INTERESTS: Hunting, fishing, shooting, camping, travel, gourmet foods.

* * *

SCHLEGEL, Stuart A(llen) 1932-

PERSONAL: Born December 11, 1932, in Sewickley, Pa.; son of Glenn Marcus (an engineer) and Elizabeth (Wagner) Schlegel; married Audrey Stier, June 7, 1958; children: Leonard Bruce, William Fredrick. *Education:* University of California, Los Angeles, A.B., 1957; Church Divinity School of the Pacific, M.A., 1960; University of Chicago, M.A., 1965, Ph.D., 1969. *Politics:* Democrat. *Home:* 226 Fridley Dr., Santa Cruz, Calif. 95060. *Office:* Merrill College, University of California, Santa Cruz, Calif. 95064.

CAREER: University of California, Santa Cruz, assistant

professor, 1968-71, associate professor of anthropology, 1971—. Senior academic preceptor of Merrill College, University of Southern California, 1968—; member of board of directors of Volunteers in Asia, 1975—; consultant to Tiruray Cooperative Association and Dansalan Research Center. *Military service:* U.S. Navy, 1950-54. *Member:* American Anthropological Association (fellow), Association for Asian Studies, Philippine Sociological Society, Sumatra Research Council, Phi Beta Kappa.

WRITINGS: Tiruray Justice: Traditional Tiruray Law and Morality, University of California Press, 1970; (translator from the Tiruray) Jose Tenorio, *Customs of the Tiruray People,* Philippine Studies, 1970; *Tiruray-English Lexicon,* University of California Press, 1971. Contributor of articles and reviews to scholarly journals.

WORK IN PROGRESS: Tiruray Subsistence: The Transformation from Shifting Cultivation to Plow Agriculture; research on Maguindanaon Islam in the Philippines and Acehnese culture and society in Indonesia.

*　　*　　*

SCHLESINGER, Joseph A(braham) 1922-

PERSONAL: Born January 4, 1922, in Boston, Mass.; son of Monroe Jacob (a pathologist) and Millie (Romansky) Schlesinger; married Mildred Saks, September 6, 1951; children: Elizabeth, Jacob. *Education:* University of Chicago, A.B., 1942; Harvard University, A.M. (education), 1947; Yale University, A.M. (political science), 1950, Ph.D., 1955. *Religion:* Jewish. *Home:* 930 Roxburgh Rd., East Lansing, Mich. 48823. *Office:* Department of Political Science, Michigan State University, East Lansing, Mich. 48824.

CAREER: Boston University, Boston, Mass., instructor in social science, 1947-49; Wesleyan University, Middletown, Conn., teaching fellow, 1952-53; Michigan State University, East Lansing, instructor, 1953-56, assistant professor, 1956-58, associate professor, 1958-63, professor of political science, 1963—. Visiting professor, University of California, Berkeley, 1964-65. *Military service:* U.S. Army, 1943-45. *Member:* American Political Science Association, Midwest Conference of Political Scientists (vice-president, 1970-71), University Club. *Awards, honors:* Social Science Research Council grant, 1957-58; distinguished faculty award, Michigan State University, 1976.

WRITINGS: How They Became Governor, Governmental Research Bureau, Michigan State University, 1957; (contributor) J. G. March, editor, *Handbook of Organizations,* Rand McNally, 1965; (contributor) Herbert Jacob and K. Vines, *Politics in the American States,* Little, Brown, 1965, revised edition, 1971; *Ambition and Politics,* Rand McNally, 1966; (contributor) Lewis Edinger, editor, *Political Leadership in Industrialized Societies,* Wiley, 1967. Contributor of articles to journals in his field.

WORK IN PROGRESS: A manuscript on American political party organization.

*　　*　　*

SCHMID, Claus-Peter 1942-

PERSONAL: Born May 21, 1942, in Garmisch, Germany; son of Karl (an artist) and Gertrud (Rademacher) Schmid; married Bonny Burleson (a writer), November 25, 1968; children: Allan, Stefan. *Education:* Attended University of Exeter, 1963-64; University of Munich, M.A., 1968. *Home:* Steingaedele 8, 8924 Steingaden, Germany.

CAREER: College of Business Administration, Munich, Germany, lecturer, 1968-72; Center of Education, Murnau, Germany, lecturer, 1972—.

WRITINGS: Photography for Artists and Craftsmen, Van Nostrand, 1975. Contributor of photographs to periodicals and craft books.

WORK IN PROGRESS: Old Printing Techniques in Photography.

*　　*　　*

SCHMIDT, Hans 1938-

PERSONAL: Born August 20, 1938, in Yonkers, N.Y.; son of Hans Robert (a pharmacognocist) and Elizabeth (Teetz) Schmidt; married Joan McKee (a librarian), December 18, 1960; children: Julie, Jenny. *Education:* University of California, Berkeley, A.B., 1960; Rutgers University, M.A., 1965, Ph.D., 1968. *Home:* 5 Huguenot St., New Paltz, N.Y. 12561. *Office:* Department of History, State University of New York College, New Paltz, N.Y. 12561.

CAREER: State University of New York College at New Paltz, assistant professor, 1968-71, associate professor of history, 1971—. Lecturer, University of Hong Kong, 1971-73; part-time mentor, Empire State College, 1974—. *Military service:* U.S. Navy, 1960-63; became lieutenant junior grade.

WRITINGS: The United States Occupation of Haiti, 1915-34, Rutgers University Press, 1971.

WORK IN PROGRESS: A biography of Major General Smedley D. Butler.

AVOCATIONAL INTERESTS: Travel, photography, painting.

*　　*　　*

SCHMIDT, Lyle D(arrel) 1933-

PERSONAL: Born May 21, 1933, in St. Cloud, Minn.; son of Hilding E. (a mechanic) and Pearl (Olson) Schmidt; married Arma Haldorson, June 9, 1956; children: Mara Lanay, Lars John Frederick, Derick Lyle Russell. *Education:* St. Cloud State College, B.A., 1955; University of Missouri, A.M., 1957, Ph.D., 1959. *Home:* 927 Clayton Dr., Worthington, Ohio 43085. *Office:* Department of Psychology, Ohio State University, 1945 North High St., Columbus, Ohio 43210.

CAREER: University of Missouri, Columbia, psychometrist for university testing and counseling service, 1956-57; St. Cloud State College, St. Cloud, Minn., instructor in psychology and counselor at Psycho-Educational Clinic, 1957-58; University of Maryland, College Park, assistant professor of psychology and counseling psychologist, 1959-61; Ohio State University, Columbus, assistant professor, 1961-64, associate professor of psychology, 1964-67; University of Minnesota, Minneapolis, associate professor of educational psychology, 1967-69; Ohio State University, professor of psychology, 1969—. Visiting professor, University of Nebraska, summer, 1961, Ohio Wesleyan University, 1961-63, and Sacramento State College (now California State University), summer, 1964. Fulbright lecturer at University of Keele, 1970-71. *Member:* American Psychological Association (fellow), American Association for the Advancement of Science, Sigma Xi.

WRITINGS: (Editor with J. F. McGowan) *Counseling: Readings in Theory and Practice,* Holt, 1962; (with P. L.

Bandt and B. R. Fretz) *Practice in Effective Study,* privately printed, 1964, revised edition, 1966; (contributor) J. F. Adams, editor, *Counseling and Guidance: A Summary View,* Macmillan, 1965; (with Bandt and N. M. Meara) *A Time to Learn,* Holt, 1974. Contributor of about thirty articles and reviews to psychology and counseling journals. Consulting editor, *Journal of Counseling Psychology.*

WORK IN PROGRESS: Research on interpersonal influence in therapeutic relationships and on the social psychology of psychological counseling.

AVOCATIONAL INTERESTS: International travel, photography.

*   *   *

SCHMIDT, Stanley (Albert)   1944-

PERSONAL: Born March 7, 1944, in Cincinnati, Ohio; son of Otto E. W. (an electrical engineer) and Georgia (Metcalf) Schmidt. *Education:* University of Cincinnati, B.S. (with high honors), 1966; Case Western Reserve University, M.A., 1968, Ph.D., 1969. *Home:* 386½ South Washington St., Tiffin, Ohio 44883. *Agent:* Scott Meredith Literary Agency, Inc., 845 Third Ave., New York, N.Y. 10022. *Office:* Department of Physics, Heidelberg College, Tiffin, Ohio 44883.

CAREER: Heidelberg College, Tiffin, Ohio, assistant professor of physics, 1969—; free-lance writer, musician, and photographer. Teacher of courses in astronomy, science fiction, and biology at Heidelberg College. *Member:* American Association of Physics Teachers, Science Fiction Writers of America, Appalachian Trail Conference, Cleveland Philharmonic Orchestra, Phi Beta Kappa, Sigma Xi.

WRITINGS: Newton and the Quasi-Apple (science fiction novel), Doubleday, 1975; (contributor) Jack Williamson, editor, *Science Fiction: Education for Tomorrow,* Mirage Press, 1975; *The Sins of the Fathers* (science fiction novel; first serialized in *Analog,* 1973-74), Berkley Publishing, 1976; (contributor) Thomas D. Clareson, editor, *Many Futures, Many Worlds,* Kent State University Press, 1976. Work anthologized in *Anthropology Through Science Fiction,* edited by Martin H. Greenberg and others, St. Martin's, 1974; *Sociology Through Science Fiction,* edited by Greenberg and others, St. Martin's, 1974; *American Government Through Science Fiction,* edited by Joseph Olander and others, Rand McNally, 1974. Contributor to science fiction and physics journals.

WORK IN PROGRESS: A multi-part sequel to *The Sins of the Fathers;* another novel; short stories.

SIDELIGHTS: Schmidt reads Spanish, German, Russian, Portuguese, French, Italian, Dutch, and Swahili. *Avocational interests:* Music (Schmidt plays several instruments and composes music), travel (camping, hiking, backpacking), photography, flying, and linguistics.

BIOGRAPHICAL/CRITICAL SOURCES: Toledo Blade, January 31, 1975.

*   *   *

SCHNACKE, Richard N(ye)   1919-
    (Dick Schnacke)

PERSONAL: Born February 16, 1919, in Topeka, Kan.; son of Austin Davis (a civil engineer) and Esther (a nurse; maiden name, Nye) Schnacke; married Jeanne Perkins, May 18, 1943; children: Richard N., Jr., Gary R., Annette

J., Nancy J. *Education:* Attended Baker University, Baldwin City, Kan., 1937; Iowa State University, B.S., 1941. *Home and office address:* Route 1, Proctor, W.Va. 26055.

CAREER: Alcoa (aluminum manufacturing company), Massena, N.Y., engineer, 1941-46; Kaiser Aluminum, Spokane, Wash., engineer, 1946-49, engineer at Newark, Ohio, 1949-56; Olin Corp. (aluminum manufacturers), Hannibal, Ohio, engineer, 1956-72; Mountain Craft Shop, Proctor, W.Va., owner, 1972—. Has appeared on television programs, "The David Frost Show," 1971, "To Tell the Truth," 1971, and "The Today Show," 1973. *Member:* American Society of Mechanical Engineers, American Crafts Council, Southern Region School Boards Association (vice-president, 1975), West Virginia Artists and Craftsmens Guild (president, 1963-66), West Virginia School Boards Association (president, 1968-69), West Virginia 4-H Club Foundation (director, 1972—).

WRITINGS—Under name Dick Schnacke: *American Folk Toys,* Putnam, 1973, abridged edition, Penguin, 1974.

WORK IN PROGRESS: Two more toy-related books.

SIDELIGHTS: Schnacke was national Amateur Athletic Union high jump champion in 1945. He holds two patents for inventions in aluminum casting. He is a toymaker, at present, with exhibits at major arts and crafts fairs. Schnacke specializes in American folk toys distributed mainly by gift shops in museums.

BIOGRAPHICAL/CRITICAL SOURCES: Smithsonian, December, 1974.

*   *   *

SCHNEIDER, Daniel J(ohn)   1927-

PERSONAL: Born July 1, 1927, in Chicago, Ill.; son of Daniel Charles (a mechanical engineer) and Gertrude (Schwartzkopf) Schneider; married Jeanne E. Jones, August 10, 1950; children: James, Geoffrey, Alexandra. *Education:* Northwestern University, B.S., 1948, Ph.D., 1957; University of Chicago, A.M., 1949. *Religion:* Unitarian-Universalist. *Home address:* School St., Walpole, N.H. 03608. *Office:* Department of English, Windham College, Putney, Vt. 05346.

CAREER: Southern Illinois University, Carbondale, instructor in English, 1949-50, 1952-56; Brooklyn College of the City University of New York, Brooklyn, N.Y., instructor in English, 1958-65; Windham College, Putney, Vt., professor of English, 1965—. *Military service:* U.S. Navy, 1945-46. *Member:* Modern Language Association of America.

WRITINGS: Symbolism: The Manichean Vision, University of Nebraska Press, 1975.

Work is anthologized in *Hemingway: Five Decades of Criticism,* edited by Linda Wagner, Michigan State University Press, 1974. Contributor of stories and articles to literature journals, including *University Review, Ball State Forum, Minnesota Review, Discourse, Modern Fiction Stories, Criticism,* and *D. H. Lawrence Review.*

WORK IN PROGRESS: Adventures of the Imagination in the Fiction of Henry James; research on forms of psychic process in modern fiction.

*   *   *

SCHNEIDERMAN, Harry   1885-1975

January 23, 1885—September 1, 1975; Polish-born American journalist, editor, translator, and author of books on religion and history. Obituaries: *New York Times,* September 2, 1975.

* * *

SCHOB, David Eugene 1941-

PERSONAL: Born March 2, 1941, in Chicago, Ill.; son of Albert W. and Martha (Lund) Schob. *Education:* Attended Carthage College, 1959-60; University of Illinois, B.A., 1963, M.A., 1965, Ph.d., 1970. *Religion:* Lutheran. *Home:* 4302 College Main #207, Bryan, Tex. 77801. *Office:* Department of History, Texas A & M University, College Station, Tex. 77801.

CAREER: Texas A & M University, College Station, Tex.; assistant professor of history, 1970—. *Member:* Western History Association, Illinois State Historical Society, Phi Alpha Theta, Phi Kappa Phi, Phi Chi Eta. *Awards, honors:* Oliver Dickerson Award, 1975, for *Hired Hands and Plowboys: Farm Labor in the Midwest, 1815-1860.*

WRITINGS: Hired Hands and Plowboys: Farm Labor in the Midwest, 1815-1860, University of Illinois Press, 1975.

WORK IN PROGRESS: Editing of forty-niner Gold Rush diary; translation pre-Civil War immigrant guidebooks; research on fuel industry prior to Civil War; *American Agriculture,* for University of Chicago Press "History of American Civilization" series.

BIOGRAPHICAL/CRITICAL SOURCES: Illinois Alumni News, Volume 54, number 7, October, 1975.

* * *

SCHOONMAKER, Frank 1905-1976

1905—January 11, 1976; American enologist, importer, and author of books on wine and travel. Obituaries: *New York Times,* January 13, 1976; *Washington Post,* January 14, 1976; *Time,* January 26, 1976; *Publishers Weekly,* February 23, 1976.

* * *

SCHORB, E(dwin) M(arsh) 1940-
(Edwin Marsh; Doyle McGrath)

PERSONAL: Born September 12, 1940, in Plainfield, N.J.; son of Edwin Marsh (a stockbroker and salesman) and Mary Ann (McGrath) Schorb; married Patricia Hill (a writer), January 29, 1961; children: Selah Brett, Leslie Helene. *Education:* Attended University of Hawaii, New York University, Irwin Piscator's Dramatic Workshop, Neighborhood Playhouse School of the Theater, LaSalle Extension University, and Henry George School. *Politics:* "Necessarily Eclectic." *Religion:* "The Great Search." *Home:* 507 Second St., Brooklyn, N.Y. 11215. *Agent:* (prose) Alex Jackinson Agency, 50 West 42nd St., New York, N.Y. 10036; (poetry) Patricia Hill Agency, P.O. Box 482, Bowling Green Station, New York, N.Y. 10004.

CAREER: Free-lance writer, illustrator, painter, and cartoonist. Has given public readings of poems and appeared on television and radio programs. *Military service:* U.S. Marines, brig turnkey and rifle instructor, 1958-60. *Member:* International Poetry Society, World Poetry Society Intercontinental, Mystery Writers of America. *Awards, honors:* Second prize from International Keats Poetry Prize Competition, 1973, for poem "Poor Boy;" art grant from Change, Inc., 1975, for illustrations for *The Poor Boy and Other Poems.*

WRITINGS: The Poor Boy and Other Poems (self-illustrated), Dragon's Teeth Press, 1975.

Poems have been anthologized in *Keats Prize Poems,* edited by Geraldine Calca Cash, London Literary Editions, 1973. Contributor of poems, illustrations and stories, sometimes under pseudonyms Doyle McGrath and Edwin Marsh, to mystery and science fiction magazines, and to literary journals, including *Orbis, Poet Lore, Bitterroot, Poet, Epos, Poetry View,* and *Encore.*

WORK IN PROGRESS: A suspense novel, *Encounter with Evil;* revising the novel, *Walking the Edge;* a collection of poems, *The Morbid Album;* a long poem, tentatively titled "The Distraught Garden;" short stories; research on social conditions, with special regard to crime in New York, 1800-1840, for a novel, *Paradise Square.*

SIDELIGHTS: Schorb writes: "It's sad to think that an athlete, whose comparable talent may not be superior to that of a poet, is paid in thousands and hundreds of thousands of dollars, while all over the world a poet is paid, if not in derision, then most certainly in small change.... If the world were set right, poets would earn more than presidents. Their minds give the ultimate life to language and language as used by great poets gives the ultimate life to the mind, thence to the heart, a metaphor for all secrets.... The crime novel should deal with the causes of poverty—greed; moral, and thence, political corruption; greed's agencies: power, coercion, murder. It should be the contemporary morality play." *Avocational interests:* Painting and drawing (work has been shown in galleries and in Brooklyn area art shows), chess.

BIOGRAPHICAL/CRITICAL SOURCES: Brooklyn Phoenix, September 6, 1973.

* * *

SCHREIBER, Vernon R(oy) 1925-

PERSONAL: Born January 21, 1925, in Chicago, Ill.; son of Frank J. (in retail food business) and Margaret A. (a secretary; maiden name, Lord) Schreiber; married Jane Ingrid Swanson (a secretary), June 11, 1949; children: Margaret (Mrs. Lawrence Graff), David, Victoria. *Education:* Concordia College, Milwaukee, Wis., student, 1942-45; Concordia Seminary, St. Louis, Mo., B.A., 1946, M.Div., 1949, M.Sac.Theol., 1950; graduate study at Wayne State University, 1956, and General Seminary, New York City, 1960-62. *Home:* 28 Stewart Lane, Berkeley Heights, N.J. 07922. *Office:* New Jersey District-Lutheran Church, 1896 Morris Ave., Union, N.J. 07083.

CAREER: Ordained to Lutheran ministry, 1950; pastor of churches in Detroit, Mich., 1950-57, Paramus, N.J., 1957-69, and Arlington Heights, Ill., 1969-73; New Jersey District-Lutheran Church, Union, assistant to president, 1973—. *Awards, honors:* B'nai B'rith Brotherhood Award, 1965, for work in open housing.

WRITINGS: My Redeemer Lives, Augsburg, 1974; *My Servant Job,* Augsburg, 1975. Contributor of sermons to various religious magazines.

WORK IN PROGRESS: Studies on the life of Jacob.

SIDELIGHTS: Schreiber told *CA:* "The stories of the Bible, and in a unique way, especially the stories of the Old Testament are the stories of Everyman. They need to be translated into modern situations."

SCHUESSLER, Hermann E.   1929(?)-1975

1929(?)—August 14, 1975; German-born American historian, educator, lecturer, and author. Obituaries: *Washington Post,* August 22, 1975.

*   *   *

SCHUL, Bill D(ean)   1928-

PERSONAL: Born March 16, 1928, in Winfield, Kans.; son of Fred M. (a teacher and farmer) and Mildred (Miles) Schul; married Jeanne Duboise, August 3, 1952; children: Robert Dean, Deva Elizabeth (Mrs. Mark Randel). *Education:* Southwestern College, B.A., 1952; University of Denver, M.A., 1954. *Politics:* "Republican—but actually bipartisan." *Religion:* "Eclectic." *Address:* R.R. #3, Winfield, Kan. 67156.

CAREER: Augusta Daily Gazette, Augusta, Kan., reporter and editor, 1954-57; *St. Petersburg Independent,* St. Petersburg, Fla., reporter, 1957-58; *Wichita Eagle-Beacon,* Wichita, Kan., reporter and columnist, 1958-61; Attorney General's Office, Topeka, Kan., director of juvenile affairs, 1961-65; Seventh Step Foundation, Topeka, state director, 1965-66; Menninger Foundation, Topeka, editorial consultant, 1966-71; full-time writer, 1971—. President, Kansas Council for Children and Youth, 1965; executive director, Shawnee City Mental Health Corp., Topeka, 1966-67; founder, Kansas Youth Council, 1969; founder and first president, Association for Strengthening the Higher Realities and Aspirations of Man, 1970. *Military service:* U.S. Navy, 1945-46. *Member:* American Academy of Parapsychology and Medicine. *Awards, honors:* Editorial award, Freedoms Foundation, 1966; John H. McGinnis Memorial Award, Southern Methodist University, 1972, for the essay, "Exploration of Inner Space."

WRITINGS: Community Planning for Youth, State of Kansas, 1964; *Let Me Do This Thing* (a book-length poem), Rubert, 1969; (with Ed Pettit) *The Secret Powers of Pyramids,* Fawcett, 1975; *How To Be An Effective Group Leader,* Nelson-Hall, 1975; (with Pettit) *The Psychic Power of Pyramids,* Fawcett, 1976. Contributor of about two hundred articles to magazines, including *Intellectual Digest, Town and Country, 'Teen, Catholic Digest, Science of Mind, Psychic,* and *Probe the Unknown.* Writer of a weekly column, "Accent on Youth", that appeared in 116 Kansas newspapers, 1961-65.

WORK IN PROGRESS: New Frontiers of Medicine, a study of various non-traditional methods of healing, completion expected in late 1976; *The Psychic World of Animals,* for Fawcett; a novel, *The Eve of Spring.*

SIDELIGHTS: Bill Schul told *CA:* "I find myself involved from time to time in organic gardening, sports, and oil painting, but my current priorities have to do with methods or techniques—philosophies, if you will—of expanding human consciousness and the resulting social applications; this I am trying to do through my writing, lecturing, and my teaching of Raja Yoga and meditation, the latter of which I have done for many years. I have been deeply affected by the philosophy and life of Gandhi. Disenchanted by traditional methods of social control, I believe that change must come from the individual understanding of the inner life or inner awareness."

*   *   *

SCHULBERG, Herbert C(harles)   1934-

PERSONAL: Born February 10, 1934, in New York, N.Y.; married Phyllis Gitelman (a teacher), June 23, 1957; children: Mark Ira, Michelle Tobi. *Education:* Yeshiva College (now University), B.A., 1955; Columbia University, M.A., 1956, Ph.D., 1960; Harvard University, M.S.Hyg., 1963. *Home:* 28 Dunbar St., Sharon, Mass. 02067. *Office:* United Community Planning Corp., 14 Somerset St., Boston, Mass. 02067.

CAREER: Certified psychologist in Connecticut, 1961, and Massachusetts, 1964, licensed in Massachusetts, 1974. Veterans Administration Hospital, Lyons, N.J., psychology trainee, 1956-57; Veterans Administration Hospital, Brooklyn, N.Y., psychology trainee, 1957-58; Veterans Administration Mental Hygiene Clinic, Brooklyn, N.Y., psychology trainee, 1958-60; Fairfield State Hospital, Newtown, Conn., clinical psychologist, 1960-62; Massachusetts Mental Health Planning Project, Boston, director of research, 1963-65; South Shore Mental Health Center, Quincy, Mass., clinical psychologist, 1964; Professional Counseling Center, Quincy, Mass., clinical psychologist, 1964-66; Attleboro Area Mental Health Center, Attleboro, Mass., clinical psychologist, 1966-67; private practice of clinical psychology in Norwood, Mass., 1967—. Harvard University, research associate, 1964-66, associate, 1966-69, assistant clinical professor, 1969-73, associate clinical professor, 1973—, head of program research unit at community psychiatry laboratory, 1965-69. Lecturer at University of Bridgeport, 1960-61, Boston University, 1965-66, and University of Massachusetts, 1973-74; associate executive vice-president of United Community Planning Corp., 1969—.

MEMBER: American Psychological Association (fellow), Society for General Systems Research, Eastern Psychological Association, New England Psychological Association, New York State Psychological Association, Massachusetts Psychological Association, Massachusetts Public Health Association. *Awards, honors:* U.S. Public Health Service grant, 1962-63.

WRITINGS: (With Alexander Tolor) *An Evaluation of the Bender-Gestalt Test,* C. C Thomas, 1963; (with Frank Baker) *The Baker-Schulberg CMHI Scale,* Behavioral Publications, 1967; (editor with Baker and Alan Sheldon) *Program Evaluation in the Health Fields,* Behavioral Publications, 1970; (editor with Baker and Sheldon Roen and contributor) *Developments in Human Services,* Behavioral Publications, Volume I, 1973, Volume II, 1975; (with Baker) *The Mental Hospital and Human Services,* Behavioral Publications, 1975.

Contributor: Rox Penchansky, editor, *Health Services Administration: Policy Cases and the Case Method,* Harvard University Press, 1968; Henry Grunebaum, editor, *The Practice of Community Mental Health,* Little, Brown, 1970; Sheldon, Baker, and Curtis McLaughlin, editors, *Systems and Medical Care,* M.I.T. Press, 1970; Baker, editor, *Organizational Systems,* Irwin, 1973; Harold Demone and Dwight Harshbarger, editors, *A Handbook of Human Service Organizations,* Behavioral Publications, 1974; Jack Zusman and Elmer Bertsch, editors, *The Future Role of the State Hospital,* Heath, 1975; Clifford Attkisson, William Hargreaves, and Mardi Horowitz, editors, *Evaluation of Human Service Programs,* Academic Press, in press. Contributor to *Encyclopedia of Social Work* and of about forty articles and reviews to psychology and medical journals.

*   *   *

SCHULZINGER, Robert D(avid)   1945-

PERSONAL: Born November 24, 1945, in Cincinnati,

Ohio; son of Maurice (an architect) and Ann (Zusman) Schulzinger. *Education:* Columbia University, B.A. (magna cum laude), 1967; Yale University, M.Phil., 1969, Ph.D., 1971; also studied at London School of Economics and Political Science, 1965-66. *Home:* 2331 Ash St., Denver, Colo. 80207. *Office:* Graduate School of International Studies, University of Denver, Denver, Colo. 80210.

CAREER: Wesleyan University, Middletown, Conn., visiting lecturer in history, 1970-71; University of Denver, Denver, Colo., visiting assistant professor of international studies, 1971-72; University of Arizona, Tucson, assistant professor of history, 1972-73; University of Denver, assistant professor of international studies, 1973—. *Member:* American Historical Association, Organization of American Historians, International Studies Association, Phi Beta Kappa.

WRITINGS: The Making of the Diplomatic Mind: The Training Outlook and Style of United States Foreign Service Officers, 1908-1931, Wesleyan University Press, 1975; *Beyond the Water's Edge,* Dorsey, 1975. Editor of "Monograph Series in World Affairs." Contributor of articles and reviews to history and political science journals.

WORK IN PROGRESS: A comparative study of the organization ideas and influence of the Council on Foreign Relations and the Royal Institute of International Affairs.

* * *

SCHURFRANZ, Vivian 1925-

PERSONAL: Born July 12, 1925, in Mason City, Iowa; daughter of Michael Frank and Alma (Gjellefald) Zack; married Robert Schurfranz (divorced, 1965). *Education:* Iowa State Teachers College, two-year certificate, 1945; University of North Carolina, M.Ed., 1954; University of Arkansas, M.A., 1967. *Politics:* Democrat. *Home:* 1321 West Birchwood, Chicago, Ill. 60626. *Office:* Evanston Township High School, Evanston, Ill. 60204.

CAREER: Elementary school teacher in the public schools of Chapel Hill, N.C., 1954-57; junior high and high school teacher of history in the public schools of Fayetteville, Ark., 1957-65; high school teacher of history in the public schools of Evanston Township, Ill., 1967—. *Member:* National Council of Social Studies, National Education Association, Illinois Education Association, North Shore Writers Club, Art Institute of Chicago, Field Museum of Chicago, Chicago Council of Foreign Affairs.

WRITINGS: Roman Hostage (novel), Follett, 1975. Contributor of about fifty short stories to *Hi-Venture, Grade Teacher, Friends, Upward, Teen Time, Catholic Miss, Instructor, Educational Research Reading Laboratory, Twelve/Fifteen, Discovery, Venture,* and *Calling All Girls.* Author of puppet plays for primary grades.

WORK IN PROGRESS: Warrior to Charlemagne, a juvenile; *Simonetta,* a novel set in Renaissance Florence; a book for teenagers set in France in the eighth century.

AVOCATIONAL INTERESTS: Skeet shooting, entertaining at small dinner parties, cooking, visiting art museums, the theater, biking, reading.

* * *

SCHWARTZ, Arthur Nathaniel 1922-

PERSONAL: Born June 14, 1922, in Chicago, Ill.; son of Isadore (a clergyman) and Faye (Garfinkel) Schwartz; married Patricia Stratton (divorced); married Eileen Miller (divorced); married Betty Barsha, January 13, 1968; children: (first marriage) Andrew Christopher; (second marriage) Andrea Thompson, David Paul, Brian Jeremy, Cynthia Osborne; (third marriage) Jonathan Matthew. *Education:* Concordia Seminary, St. Louis, Mo., B.A., 1944; graduate study at University of Houston, 1950-51, and Eastern Washington State College, 1957; Washington University, St. Louis, Mo., Ph.D., 1962. *Home:* 3564 Summerfield Dr., Sherman Oaks, Calif. 91423. *Office:* Ethel Percy Andrus Gerontology Center, University of Southern California, Los Angeles, Calif. 90007.

CAREER: Veterans Administration Hospital, American Lake, Tacoma, Wash., staff clinical psychologist, 1962-65; Veterans Administration Center, Los Angeles, Calif., chief of clinical psychology section, 1965-72, clinical researcher on aging, 1967-72; University of Southern California, Los Angeles, lecturer on aging, 1970—, consultant to Ethel Percy Andrus Gerontology Center, 1968—, and adjunct professor of psychology, 1973—, director of long term care education, 1972—, director of adult counseling training program, 1973—. Elementary school teacher in Seymour, Ind., 1942-43. Instructor at University of Puget Sound, 1962-64, Pacific Lutheran University, 1963-65, and University of California, Los Angeles, 1967-70; associate professor at California State University, Los Angeles, 1969-73; member of faculty at California School of Professional Psychology, 1970-72. Private practice in clinical psychology in Tacoma, Wash. Therapist and director of gerontological training programs at Peterson-Guedel Family Center, 1969—. Chairman of Los Angeles County Affiliated Committee on Aging, 1969-71; member of board of directors of Los Angeles County Psychology Center, 1971—; member of California State White House Conference on Aging, 1971; member of board of examiners of nursing home administrators of California, 1972—. *Member:* American Psychological Association, Gerontological Society. *Awards, honors:* National Institute of Mental Health fellowship, 1972—; Jessie L. Terry Community Service award.

WRITINGS: (Editor with I. N. Mensh) *Professional Obligations and Approaches to the Aged,* C. C Thomas, 1964, revised edition, 1973; (contributor) P. Woodruff and J. Birren, editors, *Aging: Scientific Perspectives and Social Issues,* Van Nostrand, 1975. Contributor to professional journals.

* * *

SCOTT, Eleanor 1921-

PERSONAL: Born September 22, 1921, in Providence, R.I.; daughter of Houghton P. and Katharine (Herrick) Metcalf; married Winfield Townley Scott (died in April, 1968); children: Joel Townley, Susan, Jeannette, Douglas Herrick. *Education:* Bennington College, B.A., 1943. *Politics:* Democrat. *Religion:* None. *Home address:* Mountain Rd., North Spur, Santa Fe, N.M.

CAREER: Newspaper reporter for *P.M.,* 1941-42, *Commonsense,* 1942-43, and *Providence Journal,* 1943-45; review writer for *New York Herald Tribune, Saturday Review of Literature,* and *Rio Grande Sun,* 1946-75. Owner of f22 Photography Gallery (Santa Fe). Member of board of directors and executive committee of Albuquerque Symphony; member of board of directors of Santa Fe Preparatory School and Santa Fe Chamber Music Festival. One-woman photography show on South American archaeology at Brown University, 1975; photographs included in shows at Dallas Museum of Fine Arts, Museum of New Mexico, and Spectrum Gallery.

WRITINGS: Fin de Fiesta: A Journey to Yucatan (photographs and text), Sunstone Press, 1975.

WORK IN PROGRESS: The First Twenty Years: A History of the Santa Fe Opera.

*   *   *

SCOTT, Harold George   1925-

PERSONAL: Born August 20, 1925, in Williams, Ariz.; son of Milton Raymond (an accountant) and Lucile (Crosby) Scott; married Bettie Tabakin, August 8, 1948; children: Jasmine (Mrs. Rod Williams), Lorelei (Mrs. John Barber), Rodger, Clifford, Curtis, Conrad, Dolores. *Education:* Attended Montana State University, 1943, University of the Philippines, 1946, and Temple University, 1946-49; University of New Mexico, B.S., 1950, M.S., 1953, Ph.D., 1957. *Religion:* Jewish. *Home:* 8137 River Rd., Waggaman, La. 70094. *Office:* Medical Center, Tulane University, New Orleans, La. 70112.

CAREER: U.S. Army, served in preventive medicine in United States, Marshall Islands, Caroline Islands, and Philippine Islands, 1943-52; U.S. Air Force, Kirtland Air Force Base, N.M., civil engineer, 1952-55; U.S. Public Health Service, ecologist and entomologist with various agencies including Center for Disease Control, Consumer Protection and Environmental Health Service, and U.S. Environmental Protection Agency, 1955-72; Tulane University, New Orleans, La., professor of tropical medicine, 1971—. Director of environmental health for City of New Orleans, 1971-74. *Member:* Association of Military Surgeons of the United States, Commissioned Officers Association of the U.S. Public Health Service, Entomological Society of America, Society of Systematic Zoology, Sigma Xi, Delta Omega.

WRITINGS: Epithalamion (poetry), Foote & Davies, 1955; *Lelia: The Compleat Ballerina* (biography), Pelican, 1975. Contributor of nearly six hundred articles to scientific and popular journals.

WORK IN PROGRESS: "Lelia: A Bright Spark Passing," a theatrical motion picture based on his book for Associated Productions.

*   *   *

SCOTT, Margaret B(rodie)   ?-1976

?—January 6, 1976; Scottish-born Canadian librarian, educator, editor, and author of books in her field. Obituaries: *School Library Journal,* February, 1976.

*   *   *

SCOTT MONCRIEFF, Martha Christian   1897-

PERSONAL: Born May 3, 1897, in Chatham, Kent, England; daughter of Sir George K. (a major general in the British Army) and Helen M. (Moubray) Scott-Moncrieff. *Education:* Lady Margaret Hall, Oxford, B.A. (second class honours), 1923. *Politics:* "Middle of the road." *Religion:* Church of Scotland. *Home:* 20 Melbourne Pl., St. Andrews, Fife KY16 9EY, Scotland.

CAREER: Avery Hill College, London, England, 1923-29, lecturer, later senior lecturer in history, English and French; assistant teacher of history in secondary school for girls in Aberdeen, Scotland, 1934-40; worked in Moral Rearmament centers in Switzerland and England, during World War II, and until 1957; teacher in private school, 1957-61; retired, 1961—. *Member:* Writers' Club, St. Andrew's Club.

WRITINGS: Kings and Queens of England, Blandford, 1964, Macmillan, 1966, second edition, 1973.

For children: *Makers of Scotland,* Oxford University Press, 1931; *Kezia the Kitchenmaid,* Blandford, 1942; *The Lass from Lorraine,* Blandford, 1947; (editor with Dorothy Mildred Prescott) *The Christmas Stocking Book,* Blandford, 1950; *Founders of Europe,* two volumes, Blandford, 1964; *Brigid's Brooch,* privately printed, 1974.

WORK IN PROGRESS: Teacups in Tillydrum, a novel set in a small Scottish town.

SIDELIGHTS: Martha Scott Moncrieff writes: "I spent two of my childhood years in Ireland. In later years my most memorable travels were to the Baltic states and to Greece. I have spent months in Germany, have visited Sweden, Denmark, Belgium, and Holland, and been many times to Switzerland, but above all I regard France as my second 'patrie.'

Founders of Europe began when a group of teachers dissatisfied with the materialist outlook of the text-books they had to use, gave me ideas for narrating the lives of early European founders of Christian civilisation. My basic conviction is that in a dangerously materialistic age, the values of Christian civilisation must be upheld." *Avocational interests:* Music (violin music; choral singing), theater (especially local theater productions), gardening.

*   *   *

SEARS, Francis W.   1898-1975

October 1, 1898—November 12, 1975; American physicist, educator, author of books on science for laymen and the scientific community. Obituaries: *New York Times,* November 14, 1975.

*   *   *

SEARS, William P(aul), Jr.   1902-1976

1902—January 29, 1976; American educator, editor, and writer on industrial education. Obituaries: *New York Times,* January 31, 1976.

*   *   *

SECONDARI, John Hermes   1919-1975

PERSONAL: Born November 1, 1919, in Rome, Italy; came to the United States in 1924, naturalized citizen, 1929; son of Epaminonda (a physician) and Linda (Agostini) Secondari; married Rita Hume, October 2, 1948 (deceased); married Helen Jean Rogers (a film producer), July 1, 1961; children: (first marriage) John Gerry; (second marriage) Linda Helen. *Education:* Fordham University, B.A., 1939; Columbia University, M.S., 1940. *Residence:* New York, N.Y.

CAREER: Employed in radio section of United Press, 1939-40; reporter for Rome *Daily American* after military service; Columbia Broadcasting System (CBS), Rome, Italy, foreign correspondent, 1946-48; Economic Cooperation Administration (Marshall Plan), deputy chief of Information Division for Special Mission to Italy, based in Rome, 1948-51; free-lance writer, 1951-56; American Broadcasting Co. (ABC), New York, N.Y., chief of Washington, D.C., news bureau and moderator of "Open Hearing," 1956-59, executive producer (and sometimes writer and narrator) of special projects, including documentary series "Close-Up!" and "The Saga of Western Man", 1960-68; John H. Secondari Productions, New York City, founder, and president, 1968-75. *Military service:* U.S. Army, 1941-46; served in European theater; became captain.

MEMBER: National Academy of Television Arts and Sciences (past vice-president; past member of board of governors), Radio and Television News Directors Association, Overseas Writers Association, Radio-Television Correspondents Association, National Press Club. *Awards, honors:* Overseas Press Club award for best photographic reporting from abroad, 1962, for "Meet Comrade Student"; named television writer of the year by *Radio Television Daily,* 1963, for documentary television films "1492" and "1776"; Cine Golden Eagle Award from Council on International Non-theatrical Events, 1964, for "1492"; three George Foster Peabody Awards, including one in 1964, for series "The Saga of Western Man"; Guglielmo Marconi World Television Award, 1964, for contributions to the first "Telstar" live trans-Atlantic television program; more than twenty Emmy Awards from Academy of Television Arts and Sciences, including one in 1965, for "I, Leonardo da Vinci"; and over sixty other awards.

WRITINGS—Novels: *Coins in the Fountain,* Lippincott, 1952; *Temptation for a King,* Lippincott, 1954; *Spinner of the Dream,* Little, Brown, 1955. Author of television plays, including "The Commentator," 1956, and scripts for television series "Playhouse 90" and "The Alcoa Hour."

WORK IN PROGRESS: Secondari was working on a bicentennial series for television, "From Sea to Shining Sea."

SIDELIGHTS: Included in the over eighty documentary films produced by Secondari at American Broadcasting Co. are "Korea: No Parallel," "The Vatican," "Custer to the Little Big Horn," "The Pilgrim Adventure," "Beethoven: Ordeal and Triumph," "I Am a Soldier," "A Visit to Washington with Mrs. Lyndon B. Johnson," and "The Birth of Christ." His first book was adapted as "Three Coins in the Fountain," Twentieth Century Fox, 1954. Secondari was fluent in five languages. *Avocational interests:* Hunting.*

(Died February 8, 1975, in New York, N.Y.)

* * *

SEGRAVES, Kelly L(ee) 1942-

PERSONAL: Born November 24, 1942, in San Francisco, Calif.; son of Ardean Lee (a salesman) and Nell J. (Schamuel) Segraves; married Pauline Loretta Rasmussen, December 8, 1962; children: Kasey, Jason, Kevin, Kanda. *Education:* Biola College, B.A., 1965; Sequoia University, M.A., 1972, D.R.E., 1973. *Politics:* Republican. *Religion:* Protestant. *Residence:* San Diego, Calif. *Office:* Creation-Science Research Center, 6709 Convoy Court, San Diego, Calif. 92111.

CAREER: Self-employed salesman, in Orange, Calif., 1960-68; Bible-Science Radio, Orange, Calif., director, 1968-70; Creation-Science Research Center, San Diego, Calif., assistant director, 1970-72, director, 1973—. President and co-owner of Beta Books, 1975—. Host and producer of "And God Created" and "Creation Counseling," national radio series; host, producer, and director of "Creation Research," on local television, 1969-70. *Awards, honors:* D.Sc. from Christian University, 1972.

WRITINGS: (With Robert E. Kofahl) *This Wonderful World,* Creation-Science Research Center, 1970; *Evidence of a Worldwide Flood* (booklet), Creation-Science Research Center, 1972; *Importance of Creation* (booklet),

Creation-Science Research Center, 1972; *Jesus Christ Creator,* Zondervan, 1973; (editor) *And God Created* (science books for laymen), four volumes, Creation-Science Research Center, 1973; (with Kofahl) *Science and Creation: A Scripture Supplement,* Creation-Science Research Center, 1973; *The Great Dinosaur Mistake,* Beta Books, 1975; *Sons of God Return,* Pyramid Publications, 1975; *Whaling Through Jonah,* Pyramid Publications, 1975; *When You're Dead, You're Dead,* Beta Books, 1975; *The Great Flying Saucer Myth,* Beta Books, 1975; *Search for Noah's Ark,* Beta Books, 1975; *Double Minded Man,* Beta Books, 1975; (with Kofahl) *The Creation Explanation,* H. Shaw, 1975; *Everything You Always Wanted to Know About Dinosaurs, Flying Saucers, the Beginning, and the End,* Beta Books, in press; *There's an Aardvark in My Ark,* Beta Books, in press.

Children's books: *ABC's of the Flood,* Tri-Media, 1974; *ABC's of Creation,* Tri-Media, 1974; *The Aardvark in the Ark,* Tri-Media, 1974; *The Tale of a Whale,* Tri-Media, 1974; *The Elephant in Eden,* Tri-Media, 1974; *The Gift of Love,* Creation-Science Research Center, in press; *The Lion in the Den,* Creation-Science Research Center, in press; *Jackal at Jericho,* Creation-Science Research Center, in press; *Dinosaur No More,* Creation-Science Research Center, in press; *And Then There Were . . . Three,* Creation-Science Research Center, in press.

Author of script for tape recording "Jesus Christ Creator," Creation-Science Research Center, 1973, and filmstrip "Search for Noah's Ark," Creation-Science Research Center, 1973. Managing editor of "Science and Creation," a series of textbooks for schools. Author of columns on science in *Christian Youth Today,* 1973-74, and *Young Ambassador,* 1976-77. Contributor to religious magazines. Editor and publisher of *Science and Scripture.*

WORK IN PROGRESS: A trilogy on extraterrestrials and time; another book on flying saucers; a fantasy story of the game of life.

SIDELIGHTS: All Segraves' work is aimed at presenting "creation as a viable alternative to the theory of evolution." He narrated "And God Created" and "Creation Counseling," two series of tape recordings.

* * *

SELF, Jerry M(arvin) 1938-

PERSONAL: Born January 29, 1938, in Colorado Springs, Colo.; son of Calvin Fuller (a business manager) and Mildred Berniece (Trammell) Self; married Peggy Joyce Glazner (an accounting professor), June 11, 1960; children: Jay Mark, Angela Berniece. *Education:* Hardin-Simmons University, B.A., 1960; Southwestern Baptist Theological Seminary, B.D., 1964, M.Th., 1966, Th.D., 1970. *Home:* 4107 Tara Lane, Nacogdoches, Tex. 75961. *Office:* Austin Heights Baptist Church, 2806 Appleby Rd., Nacogdoches, Tex. 75961.

CAREER: Ordained to Baptist ministry, 1959; Austin Heights Baptist Church, Nacogdoches, Tex., pastor, 1968—. Visiting lecturer, Stephen F. Austin State University, 1972-75. Member of board, Deep East Texas Regional Mental Health/Mental Retardation Services. *Member:* Nacogdoches Mental Health Association (president, 1973; vice-president, 1975), Nacogdoches Ministerial Alliance (president, 1971-72).

WRITINGS: Men and Women in John's Gospel, Broadman, 1974.

SEMMENS, James P(ike) 1919-

PERSONAL: Born August 16, 1919, in Milwaukee, Wis.; son of Thomas Perry (a manufacturer) and Corrine (Pike) Semmens; married Florence Jane Henshaw (a sexual dysfunction therapist), September 5, 1942; children: James Alan, Michael Paul, Christine Ann, Gregory George, John Patrick. *Education:* Marquette University, B.S., 1941, M.D., 1943. *Politics:* Independent. *Home:* 3360 Seabrook Island Rd., Rt. #1, St. John's Island, S.C. 29455. *Office:* Department of Obstetrics and Gynecology, Medical University of South Carolina, 80 Barre St., Charleston, S.C. 29401.

CAREER: Certified by American Board of Obstetrics and Gynecology, 1960; Milwaukee Hospital, Milwaukee, Wis., intern, 1943-44; Milwaukee Children's Hospital, Milwaukee, Wis., assistant resident in pediatric surgery and pediatrics, 1944-45; U.S. Navy, medical officer, 1945-46; St. Joseph's Hospital, Beaver Dam, Wis., medical staff member, 1947-53; Lutheran Deaconess Hospital, Beaver Dam, Wis., staff member, 1947-53; Waupun Memorial Hospital, Waupun, Wis., staff member, 1948-53; U.S. Navy, senior medical officer in dispensery, Port Chicago, Calif., 1953-54, medical officer in naval hospitals in Portsmouth, Va., 1954-57, Charleston, S.C., 1957-61, Pensacola, Fla., 1961-63, Oakland, Calif., 1963-69, and Long Beach, Calif., 1969-70, retiring as captain, 1971; University of Southern California School of Medicine, Los Angeles, associate professor of obstetrics and gynecology, 1970-71; University of California, College of Medicine, Irvine, associate clinical professor of obstetrics and gynecology, 1970-71; Medical University of South Carolina, Charleston, associate professor of obstetrics and gynecology, 1971—. Medical University of South Carolina, visiting clinical instructor, 1958, and visiting professor, 1968; staff member of St. Anne's Maternity Hospital, Los Angeles, Calif., 1969, Los Angeles County-University of Southern California Medical Center, 1970, Medical University Hospital, Charleston, S.C., 1971, Charleston County Hospital, Charleston, S.C., 1973, and Veterans Administration Hospital, Charleston, S.C., 1973.

MEMBER: International Association of Psychosomatic Obstetrics and Gynecology, American College of Surgeons (fellow), American College of Obstetricians and Gynecologists (fellow; member of executive board, 1968-71), American Academy of Family Practice (charter fellow), American Fertility Society, American Academy of Family Physicians, American Medical Association, Association of Military Surgeons of the United States, American Association of Sex Educators and Counselors, Eastern Association of Sex Therapists (charter member), Pacific Coast Fertility Society, Wisconsin State Medical Society, South Carolina Obstetrical and Gynecological Society, Alameda County Gynecological Society, San Francisco Gynecological Society (courtesy member), Alpha Kappa Kappa. *Awards, honors:* W. Herbert Burwig Award from Deconess Hospital, Buffalo, N.Y., 1968.

WRITINGS: (With William M. Lamers) *Teenage Pregnancy: Including Management of Emotional and Constitutional Problems,* C. C Thomas, 1968; (editor with Kermit E. Krantz) *The Adolescent Experience: A Counseling Guide to Social and Sexual Behavior,* Macmillan, 1970. Contributor to medical journals.

WORK IN PROGRESS: Reviewing the results of a psychotherapeutic approach to the treatment of sexual dysfunction involving two hundred couples; a continuing evaluation of a teen sex counseling program involving three hundred and fifty sexually active adolescents.

AVOCATIONAL INTERESTS: Sailing.

*   *   *

SERENYI, Peter 1931-

PERSONAL: Born January 13, 1931, in Budapest, Hungary; came to United States in 1950, naturalized U.S. citizen; son of Count Nicholas (a landowner and member of Parliament) and Emma (Baroness Josika) Serenyi; married Agnes Kertesz (a translator and editor), August 28, 1969; children: Peter, Denis. *Education:* Dartmouth College, A.B. (cum laude), 1957; Yale University, M.A., 1958; Washington University, St. Louis, Mo., Ph.D., 1968. *Home:* 79 Greenough St., Brookline, Mass. 02146. *Office:* Department of Art, Northeastern University, Boston, Mass. 02115.

CAREER: U.S. Ordinance Center, Wels, Austria, clerk, 1949-50; Equity Corp., New York, N.Y., office boy, 1950-51; Larchmont Cleaners, Larchmont, N.Y., driver, 1951-52; City Bank Farmers Trust Co., New York, N.Y., bank clerk, 1952; Calvin Bullock Investment Co., New York, N.Y., clerk, 1952-53; Washington University, St. Louis, Mo., part-time instructor in art and archaeology, 1958-61; Amherst College, Amherst, Mass., instructor in fine arts, 1961-64; University of Pennsylvania, Philadelphia, visiting lecturer in art, 1964-66; Boston University, Boston, Mass., visiting lecturer in art, 1966-68; Northeastern University, Boston, assistant professor, 1968-73, associate professor of art, 1973—. Visiting lecturer at Smith College, 1962-63. *Military service:* U.S. Army, clerk in Medical Corps, 1953-55; served in France.

MEMBER: College Art Association of America, National Society of Literature and the Arts, Society of Architectural Historians, Victorian Society in America. *Awards, honors:* National Endowment for the Humanities summer grant, 1970; American Philosophical Society grant, 1970; grant from Graham Foundation for Advanced Studies in the Fine Arts, 1974-75; Fulbright senior research grant, 1974-75, to India.

WRITINGS: Le Corbusier in Perspective, Prentice-Hall, 1975. Contributor of articles and reviews to art and architecture journals.

WORK IN PROGRESS: Le Corbusier: Artist and Thinker; research on contemporary Indian architecture.

SIDELIGHTS: In 1970, Serenyi visited Le Corbusier's birthplace, La Chaux-de-Fonds, where he found unpublished drawings and manuscripts by Le Corbusier. He interviewed surviving artist friends and relatives of the architect, and studied at Centre Le Corbusier and Fondation Le Corbusier.

BIOGRAPHICAL/CRITICAL SOURCES: Humanities, February, 1974.

*   *   *

SERGIO, Lisa 1905-

PERSONAL: Born March 17, 1905, in Florence, Italy; naturalized U.S. citizen in 1944; daughter of the Baron Agostino (a landowner) and Marguerite (FitzGerald) Sergio. *Education:* Attended University of Florence. *Politics:* Democrat. *Religion:* Episcopalian. *Home:* 1531 34th St. N.W., Washington, D.C. 20007.

CAREER: Italian Mail (English-language literary weekly), Florence, Italy, assistant editor, 1920-22, editor, 1922-27, also translator in English, French, and Italian; free-lance writer in Florence, 1928-30; Association of Mediterranean Studies (for archaeological research and excavation), Rome, Italy, executive secretary and bibliographer, 1930-32; at invitation of Guglielmo Marconi became first woman broadcaster in Europe, from 2RO, Rome, broadcaster in English and French, and official interpreter of Benito Mussolini's speeches, 1932-37; National Broadcasting Co. (NBC), New York City, conducted "Let's Talk It Over with Lisa Sergio," "Tales of Great Rivers," and commentaries on opera and symphony concerts, 1937-39; WQXR-Radio, New York City, news commentator, 1940-47; Columbia University, New York City, instructor in department of sociology, 1947-50, also conducted European study tours; lecturer throughout United States and Canada, 1950-60; Worldaround Press (weekly news service), Woodstock, Vt., editor, 1955-58; Association of American Colleges, Washington, D.C., Danforth visiting lecturer in international affairs (at more than two hundred colleges and universities), 1960-71; writer, 1965—. News commentator for ABC-Radio, 1942-47; broadcast "Frontiers of Faith," on NBC-TV, "New Nations of Africa," on ABC-TV, 1960—, and "Prayers Through the Ages," on WMAL-Radio (Washington, D.C.), 1962—. Member of board of managers of Broadcasting and Film Commission of the National Council of Churches; director of Vermont Council on World Affairs; member of the President's Commission for the International Cooperation Year, 1965. Trustee of Helen Dwight Reid Foundation, and Washington Community Music School; member of board of directors of Bacon House (Washington, D.C.).

MEMBER: International Federation of Business and Professional Women (member of board of directors; trustee of Lena Madesin Phillips Fund), United Church Women (member of board of managers), Washington Opera Society (trustee). *Awards, honors:* American Woman's Association award; New Jersey Women's Press award, 1943, for news and commentary on WQXR; award from Women's National Radio Committee, 1946, for programs on ABC-Radio; named chevalier of French Legion of Honor, 1947; Billboard award, 1948, for commentaries on WOV (N.Y.); D.H.L. from Keuka College, 1963; LL.D. from St. Mary's College of the University of Notre Dame, 1966, and Valparaiso University, 1970; Timken Foundation grant, 1970, to be William McKinley scholar and lecturer at a consortium of Ohio colleges; named cavaliere of Order of the Star of Italian Solidarity, 1975.

WRITINGS: Shorter Italian (grammar), Hirschfeld Brothers, 1935; *Synoptical History of Fascism,* Government of Italy, 1936; (editor) *Prayers of Women,* Harper, 1965; *I Am My Beloved: The Life of Anita Garibaldi,* Weybright & Talley, 1969; *A Measure Filled* (biography of feminist Lena Madesin Phillips), Luce, 1972; *Jesus and Woman,* EPM Publications, 1975. Contributor of articles and stories to magazines in Italy and the United States, including *Reader's Digest* and *Rotarian.* Editor of *Widening Horizons,* of the International Federation of Business and Professional Women, 1947-60.

SIDELIGHTS: The daughter of a prominent Italian anti-Fascist during the Mussolini period, Lisa Sergio first worked for Mussolini, broadcasting on Italian radio in English and French. Her unauthorized changes in approved scripts led to a prison sentence, which she escaped by fleeing from Italy, to the United States, with the help of Guglielmo Marconi.

During the U.S. anti-war movement of the late 1960's, Lisa Sergio toured college campuses, urging students to continue in their efforts, but disapproving of their method of expression. She continues her career as a lecturer on international affairs.

* * *

SERNETT, Milton C(harles) 1942-

PERSONAL: Born July 21, 1942, in Hampton, Iowa; married Janet Mae Rosenwinkel (an elementary school teacher); children: two. *Education:* Student at Iowa State University, 1960-61, and Concordia College, St. Paul, Minn., 1961-62; Concordia College, Fort Wayne, Ind., B.A. (summa cum laude), 1964; Concordia Seminary, St. Louis, Mo., M.Div., 1968; University of Delaware, M.A., 1969, Ph.D., 1972. *Politics:* Democrat. *Home:* 200 Scott Ave., Syracuse, N.Y. 13224. *Office:* Department of Afro-American Studies, Syracuse University, 735 Ostrom, Syracuse, N.Y. 13210.

CAREER: "Worker-priest" with ministry in Rocky Mountain National Park, Colo., summer, 1966; intern-vicar in Lutheran church in Milwaukee, Wis., 1966-67; University of Delaware, Newark, instructor in black history, 1971-72; Concordia Seminary, Springfield, Ill., instructor, 1972-73, assistant professor of modern church history and Christian social ethics, 1973-75; Syracuse University, Syracuse, N.Y., assistant professor of Afro-American studies, 1975—. Instructor at Brandywine Junior College and Wilmington College, 1971-72.

MEMBER: American Historical Association, American Society of Church Historians, Evangelical Lutherans in Mission, Association for the Study of Afro-American Life and History, Institute of Society, Ethics, and the Life Sciences, Lutheran Historical Conference, Concordia Historical Institute, Organization of American Historians, American Association of University Professors.

WRITINGS: (Contributor) M. G. Quimby, editor, *Winterthur Portfolio VIII,* University Press of Virginia, 1973; *Black Religion and American Evangelicalism: White Protestants, Plantation Missions, and the Flowering of Negro Christianity, 1787-1865,* Scarecrow, 1975. Contributor to *Springfielder.*

WORK IN PROGRESS: Research on black and white religion during reconstruction in the South; research on the history of the British Methodist Episcopal Church in Canada, separated in 1854 from the African Methodist Episcopal Church; a book on Afro-Americans and U.S. Lutheranism, 1776-1976.

SIDELIGHTS: Sernett writes that he "resigned from Concordia Seminary, Springfield, Illinois, in August of 1975 in protest of the abuse of power and limitation of academic freedom and similar Lutheran Church—Missouri Synod policies toward Concordia Seminary—in Exile." He "came to study the black church because I realized my woeful ignorance of it even after having been trained in theology and church history at one of the best and largest Lutheran seminaries in the world . . . "

* * *

SEULING, Barbara 1937-

PERSONAL: Born July 22, 1937, in Brooklyn, N.Y.; daughter of Kaspar Joseph (a postman) and Helen Veronica (Gadie) Seuling. *Education:* Attended Columbia University, New School for Social Research, and School of Visual Arts. *Home and office:* 55 West 92nd St., New York, N.Y. 10025. *Agent:* Harriet Wasserman, Russell & Volkening, Inc., 551 Fifth Ave., New York, N.Y. 10017.

CAREER: Dell Publishing Co., New York, N.Y., editor, 1965-71; J. B. Lippincott Co., New York, N.Y., editor, 1971-73; free-lance children's book writer and illustrator, 1966—. Member: Society of Children's Book Writers, Media Educators Association (film society), School of Visual Arts Alumni Society.

WRITINGS—Self-illustrated children's books: The Last Legal Spitball and Other Little Known Facts About Sports, Doubleday, 1975; You Can't Eat Peanuts in Church and Other Little Known Laws, Doubleday, 1975; Abracadabra!, Messner, 1975; The Teeny Tiny Woman, Viking, 1976; The Loudest Screen Kiss and Other Little Known Movie Facts, Doubleday, 1976; (with Winnette Glasgow) Fun With Crafts, Xerox, 1976. Contributor to journals and books for and about children, including Cricket.

WORK IN PROGRESS: Picture books; a teenage book on the influence of rock music; a book on movie monsters; a novel; two humorous books for Doubleday.

SIDELIGHTS: Barbara Seuling mentions that she worked at the World's Fair in 1964, with the General Electric Progressland exhibit, "where I sat in an office directly over a nuclear fission exhibit, with a boom going off every four minutes precisely." She told CA: "I have always been an observer of the world around me, and I have usually seen the funny side of most situations. This inevitably appears in my work, whether in illustrations or in writing, although it is harder to put across in writing. I believe that most cases can be won and most moods changed with humor, and want to do my part to add some to the world."

AVOCATIONAL INTERESTS: Movies (silent to modern).

* * *

SHAIN, Merle 1935-

PERSONAL: Born October 14, 1935, in Toronto, Ontario, Canada; daughter of Jack Merton (a businessman) and Rose (Scholes) Shain; married Brian Grosman, May 22, 1957 (divorced December 16, 1964); children: John Shain Grosman. Education: University of Toronto, B.A., 1957, B.S.W., 1959. Home: 50 Chestnut Park Rd., Toronto, Ontario, Canada M4W 1W8. Agent: Steve Shepherd, Paul R. Reynolds, Inc., 12 East 41st St., New York, N.Y. 10017. Office: Paul Simmons Management, 125 Dupont St., Toronto, Ontario, Canada.

CAREER: Young Women's Christian Association (YWCA), Toronto, Ontario, group social worker, 1957-59; Children's Aid Society, Toronto, case worker, 1959-62; Humewood House (for unmarried mothers), Toronto, case worker, 1963; Canadian Broadcasting Corp., Toronto, writer, editor, and broadcaster of radio program "The Changing Role of Women" for "The Learning Stage," 1963; hostess of "W5," "Sweet City Woman," 1972, "The Summer of '75," 1975, and regular interviewer on "This Hour Has Seven Days," 1964-65, "Show on Shows," 1964, "The Observer," 1965, and "Generation," 1965. Critic at large for station CFTO, 1969—; frequent guest on Canadian and United States television programs; public speaker. Aide to Prime Minister Pierre Trudeau in 1968 political campaign.

WRITINGS: Some Men Are More Perfect Than Others, Charterhouse, 1973. Author of special programs for Canadian television programs "Seven Days," 1964-65, and "Take Thirty," 1965. Feature writer for Toronto Telegram, 1968-69; book critic for Globe and Mail, 1970—.

Contributor to popular magazines in the United States, Canada, and abroad, including McCall's, Cosmopolitan, New York Post, Viva, Reader's Digest, and New Woman. Associate editor of Chatelaine, 1970-71.

WORK IN PROGRESS: Two screenplays, "I've Loved You Since Monday" and "To Whomever It Might Concern."

BIOGRAPHICAL/CRITICAL SOURCES: "Take Thirty," Canadian Broadcasting Corp.-Television, June, 1965; Playgirl, February, 1973; Newsweek, March 11, 1973."

* * *

SHANNON, Doris 1924-

PERSONAL: Born August 7, 1924, in Elmira, N.Y.; daughter of Edwin (an engineer) and Elizabeth (a telephone operator; maiden name, Graham) Giroux; married Frank Shannon (a customs officer), August 1, 1947; children: Patricia Anne, Deborah Elizabeth. Education: Napanee Collegiate Institute, student, 1939-42. Home: 10580 154A St., Surrey, British Columbia, Canada. Agent: Kirby McCauley, 220 East 26th St., New York, N.Y. 10010.

CAREER: Royal Bank of Canada, teller in Napanee, Ontario, 1942-47, in Vancouver, British Columbia, 1948-49. Member: Science Fiction Writers of America. Awards, honors: Writer's Digest creative writing award, 1969, for short story, "And Then There Was the Youngest."

WRITINGS—Novels: The Whispering Runes, Lenox Hill, 1972; Twenty-two Hallowfield, Fawcett, 1974; The Seekers, Fawcett, 1975; Hawthorn Hill, St. Martin's, 1976; Northwest by Nemesis, Popular Library, 1976.

WORK IN PROGRESS: Research on the American Civil War for an historical epic, tentatively titled Jemmy Reb; a Canadian Gothic novel.

SIDELIGHTS: Doris Shannon writes that at the age of forty, "without quite realizing my own motivation I turned to writing. Much to my surprise . . . editors expressed . . . confidence in a talent I had never realized I possessed. . . . Writing appears to be a profession where gray hair and age are not signals that one's working life is over. I share with many writers the desire to write that special book, the fine one, and also eventually I should like to teach creative writing."

* * *

SHANNON, Lyle William 1920-

PERSONAL: Born September 19, 1920, in Storm Lake, Iowa; son of Bert Book and Amy I. (Sivits) Shannon; married Magdaline W. Eckes, 1943; children: Mary Louise, Robert William, John Thomas, Susan Michelle. Education: Cornell College, Mt. Vernon, Iowa, B.A., 1942; University of Washington, Seattle, M.A., 1947, Ph.D., 1951. Office: Urban Community Research Center, University of Iowa, Iowa City, Iowa 52240.

CAREER: University of Washington, Seattle, acting instructor in sociology, 1951-52; University of Wisconsin, Madison, instructor, 1952-54, assistant professor, 1954-58, associate professor of sociology, 1958-62; University of Iowa, Iowa City, professor of sociology, 1962—, chairman of department, 1962-70, director of Urban Community Research Center, 1970—. Visiting lecturer at Portland State College, summer, 1956, Wayne State University, 1956-57, University of Colorado, summers, 1960-61, and University of Wyoming, Director of National Science Foundation undergraduate research participation program on value assimilation, 1960-61. *Military service:* U.S. Naval Reserve, 1942-66, active duty, 1942-46; became lieutenant commander.

MEMBER: American Association for the Advancement of Science, American Sociological Association, Society for the Study of Social Problems, Society of Applied Anthropology, Society for International Development, Population Association of America, Midwest Sociological Association, Pacific Sociological Association, Phi Beta Kappa, Alpha Kappa Delta. *Awards, honors:* U.S. Public Health Service grants at University of Iowa, 1962-66, 1969-72; Office of Economic Opportunity juvenile delinquency grant, 1966-67; Fleischman Foundation grant, 1974-75; Law Enforcement Assistance Administration grant, 1975-76.

WRITINGS: (Editor) *Underdeveloped Areas: A Book of Readings and Research,* Harper, 1957; (contributor) David Manning White and Morris Rosenberg, editors, *Mass Culture,* Free Press, 1957; (contributor) Robert W. O'Brien, Walter Martin, and Clarence Schrag, editors, *Readings in General Sociology,* Houghton, 1957; *Social Factors in Economic Growth,* UNESCO, 1957; (contributor) *Goals and Values in Agricultural Policy,* Iowa State University Press, 1961; (contributor) *Labor Mobility and Population in Agriculture,* Iowa State University Press, 1961; (contributor) *Economic Development of Agriculture,* Iowa State University Press, 1965; (with others) *A Bilingual Community Self-Survey System,* Iowa Urban Community Research Center, University of Iowa, 1967; (with others) *A Community Self-Survey System,* Iowa Urban Community Research Center, University of Iowa, 1968; (contributor) Eugene B. Brody, editor, *Migration and Human Adaptation,* Sage Publications, 1970; (with wife, Magdaline Shannon) *Minority Migrants in the Urban Community: Mexican-American and Negro Adjustment to Industrial Society,* Sage Publications, 1973. Contributor to *American Peoples' Encyclopedia Yearbook;* contributor of articles and reviews to sociology journals.

* * *

SHANOR, Donald Read 1927-

PERSONAL: Born July 11, 1927, in Ann Arbor, Mich.; son of William Wilson (an engineer) and Katherine (Read) Shanor; married Constance Collier (administrative assistant for American Heart Association), 1951; children: Rebecca Read, Elizabeth Lynne. *Education:* Northwestern University, B.S., 1951; Columbia University, M.A., 1964. *Politics:* Liberal Democrat. *Home:* 285 Riverside Dr., New York, N.Y. 10025. *Agent:* A. L. Hart, Fox-Chase Agency, 419 East 57th St., New York, N.Y. 10022. *Office:* Graduate School of Journalism, Columbia University, New York, N.Y. 10027.

CAREER: During his early career was factory worker, railroad and construction worker, night cook and deck hand on a Lake Michigan passenger steamer, bartender, golf greens mower, bowling pins refinisher, apple and cherry picker, chicken raiser, painter and carpenter; American Forces Network, Frankfurt, Germany, editor/reporter, 1952-54; United Press International, editor/reporter in Frankfurt, Germany, London, England, New York, N.Y., and at the United Nations, 1954-65; Columbia University, New York, N.Y., lecturer in journalism, 1965-67; *Chicago Daily News,* Chicago, Ill., correspondent in Eastern and Western Europe and the Mideast, 1967-71; Columbia University, associate professor of journalism, 1971—. *Military service:*

U.S. Navy, 1945-46. *Member:* Society of Professional Journalists, Association for Education in Journalism, Academy of Political Science, American Academy of Political and Social Science.

WRITINGS: The New Voice of Radio Free Europe (monograph), Columbia University Press, 1967; *Soviet Europe,* Harper, 1975. Contributing editor, *Atlas World Press Review,* 1973—; advisory editor, *Columbia Journalism Review,* 1971—.

WORK IN PROGRESS: Portrait of a Communist Society, (tentative title).

SIDELIGHTS: Shanor says of *Soviet Europe:* "The book wrote itself, on long train rides through Poland, during interviews with Party leaders, dissidents, and collective farm chairmen, on lonely nights walking the silent old streets of Prague. For that reason, it isn't the political science analysis of the area.... It's journalism, because I am a journalist." *Avocational interests:* Carpentry, hiking.

* * *

SHARKEY, (Neil) Owen 1917-

PERSONAL: Born March 25, 1917, in Philadelphia, Pa.; son of Owen (an engineer) and Mary (Nevins) Sharkey. *Education:* Passionist Seminary, B.A., 1941, M.A., 1945; Catholic University of America, S.T.L., 1946, S.T.D., 1950; postdoctoral study, University of Tuebingen, 1965-66. *Home:* Passionist Seminary, 178th St., Jamaica, N.Y. 11431. *Office:* Department of Theology, St. John's University, Utopia Blvd., Jamaica, N.Y. 11439.

CAREER: Ordained Roman Catholic priest, May 5, 1945. Lector in theology at Eastern province Passionist seminaries, 1948-65; St. John's University, Jamaica, N.Y., associate professor of systematic theology, 1967—. *Member:* Society for the Scientific Study of Religion, Catholic Theological Society of America.

WRITINGS: (Under name Neil Sharkey) *St. Gregory's Concept of Papal Power,* Catholic University of America Press, 1950; *The Mystery of Man,* Franklin Publishing, 1975. Contributor to *New Catholic Encyclopedia,* McGraw, 1966.

WORK IN PROGRESS: A book, *Personal Existence and the Mystery of God.*

* * *

SHAW, Donald Lewis 1936-

PERSONAL: Born October 27, 1936, in Raleigh, N.C.; son of Luther (a professor) and Lowell (Lewis) Shaw; married Ilse Feichter (a teacher), September 3, 1960; children: Matthew, Dona, Lauren, David. *Education:* Mars Hill College, A.A., 1957; University of North Carolina, A.B., 1959, M.A., 1960; University of Wisconsin, Ph.D., 1966. *Religion:* Methodist. *Home:* 416 North Tinkerbell Rd., Chapel Hill, N.C. 27514. *Office:* School of Journalism, University of North Carolina, Chapel Hill, N.C. 27514.

CAREER: Reporter for *Burlington Times-News,* Burlington, N.C., 1959, *Asheville Citizen,* Asheville, N.C., 1960-61, and *Asheville Times,* 1961-62; University of Wisconsin Medical School, Madison, science writer, 1965-66; University of North Carolina, Chapel Hill, assistant professor, 1966-70, associate professor of journalism, 1970—. Visiting associate professor and senior associate at Newhouse School of Public Communications, Syracuse University, spring, 1974. *Military service:* North Carolina National

Guard, 1960—; publication information officer, 1972—; present rank, major. *Member:* Association for Education in Journalism (chairman of History Division, 1974—), Organization of American Historians, Phi Beta Kappa, Kappa Tau Alpha.

WRITINGS: (Contributor) Ronald T. Farrar and John D. Stevens, editors, *Mass Media and the National Experience,* Harper, 1971; (with M. C. McCombs and D. L. Grey) *Exploring Your Community: Applying Behavioral Science Techniques in Journalism,* Houghton, in press; (editor with Roy L. Moore, Richard R. Cole, and L. E. Mullins) *Gathering and Writing News: Selected Readings,* College & University Press, in press. Contributor of articles and reviews to *Journalism Quarterly* and other journals. Compiler of *Journalism Abstracts,* Volumes VII-VIII, Association for Education in Journalism, 1969-70; editor, *CLIO* (publication of History Division, Association for Education in Journalism), 1973.

WORK IN PROGRESS: A book about the role of mass media and American politics.

*   *   *

SHEBL, James M(ichael) 1942-

PERSONAL: Born July 1, 1942, in Tacoma, Wash.; son of Joseph J. (a physician) and Mary Ellen (Hurley) Shebl; married Patricia A. Pedroni, August 22, 1964; children: Bonnie Marie, Catherine Theresa. *Education:* Creighton University, B.A., 1965; University of Nebraska, M.A., 1969; University of the Pacific, Ph.D., 1974. *Politics:* "Left Conservative." *Religion:* Roman Catholic. *Home:* 6810 Wilderness Court, Stockton, Calif. 95207. *Office:* Pacific Center for Western Studies, University of the Pacific, Stockton, Calif. 95211.

CAREER: Worked as civilian instructor for U.S. Air Force in swimming and diving, 1964-65, as inspector of agricultural crops in California, 1969-70; University of the Pacific, Stockton, Calif., director of university townhouse, 1970-73; assistant to academic vice-president, 1972—, assistant professor of humanities, 1975—, associate director of Pacific Center for Western Historical Studies, 1975—. *Member:* Modern Language Associate of America, American Association of University Professors, American Association of University Administrators, Western Literature Association, Westerners, Western History Association, Southwestern American Literature Association, Phi Kappa Psi (past president), Phi Kappa Phi (president). *Awards, honors:* Nominated for gold medallion for western writing by Commonwealth Club of California, 1974, for *King, of the Mountains.*

WRITINGS: (Author of introduction) Clarence King, *Mountaineering in the Sierra Nevada,* University of Nebraska Press, 1969; *King, of the Mountains,* University of the Pacific Press, 1974.

WORK IN PROGRESS: In This Wild Water: The Biography of Some Unpublished Poems by Robinson Jeffers, 1887-1962, for Ward Richie; *Pike County West; California Basque,* for National Geographic Society; *Green Gold,* a historical novel of the Salinas Valley, completion expected in 1978; *Windmills and Watertowers,* a photographic essay.

SIDELIGHTS: Shebl writes: "I write to bring to our people a taste of what went before. Hopefully, there is a lesson to be learned, hope to be gained, pride to be restored. I suspect literary history and fictionalized history—which is not to say untrue accounts—shall always be

my way." *Avocational interests:* International travel (Spain, Italy, Mexico), reading, films, athletics, the Sierra Nevadas.

*   *   *

SHEEAN, (James) Vincent 1899-1975

PERSONAL: Born December 5, 1899, in Pana, Ill.; son of William Charles and Susan (MacDermot) Sheean; married Diana Forbes-Robertson, August 24, 1935; children: Linda Sheean Staniecki, Ellen. *Education:* Attended University of Chicago, 1916-20. *Politics:* Socialist. *Residence:* Arolo, Italy.

CAREER: Chicago Daily News, Chicago, Ill., reporter, briefly in 1920; *New York Daily News,* New York, N.Y., reporter, 1920-22; *Chicago Tribune,* correspondent in Europe, 1922-25; free-lance political journalist and foreign correspondent, contributing to North American Newspaper Alliance, New York *Herald Tribune* syndicate, and various newspapers and magazines, beginning in 1925; author, 1925-75. *Military service:* U.S. Army Air Corps, intelligence officer during World War II; served in North Africa, Italy, and the East.

WRITINGS: An American among the Riffi (nonfiction), Century, 1926; *The Anatomy of Virtue* (novel), Century, 1927; *The New Persia* (nonfiction), Century, 1927; *Gog and Magog* (novel), Harcourt, 1930; *The Tide* (novel), Doubleday, 1933; *Personal History* (autobiography; Literary Guild selection), Doubleday, 1935 (published in England as *In Search of History,* Hamish Hamilton, 1935), 2nd edition with new introduction by the author, Houghton, 1969; *Sanfelice* (novel), Doubleday, 1936; *The Pieces of a Fan* (short stories), Doubleday, 1937; *A Day of Battle* (novel), Doubleday, 1938; (translator) Eve Curie, *Madame Curie: A Biography,* Doubleday, 1938; *Not Peace But a Sword* (nonfiction; Book-of-the-Month Club selection), Doubleday, 1939 (published in England as *The Eleventh Hour,* Hamish Hamilton, 1939); *Bird of the Wilderness* (novel), Random House, 1941; *Between the Thunder and the Sun* (personal narratives), Random House, 1943; *This House Against This House* (personal narratives), Random House, 1946; *A Certain Rich Man* (novel), Random House, 1947; *Lead, Kindly Light* (tribute to Mahatma Gandhi), Random House, 1949; *The Indigo Bunting: A Memoir of Edna St. Vincent Millay,* Harper, 1951, reprinted, Schocken, 1973; *Rage of the Soul* (novel), Random House, 1952; *Thomas Jefferson, Father of Democracy* (juvenile biography), Random House, 1953; *Mahatma Gandhi: A Great Life in Brief* (biography), Knopf, 1954; *Lily* (novel), Random House, 1954; *Oscar Hammerstein I: The Life and Exploits of an Impresario* (biography), with preface by Oscar Hammerstein II, Simon & Schuster, 1956 (published in England as *The Amazing Oscar Hammerstein,* Weidenfeld & Nicolson, 1956); *First and Last Love* (nonfiction), Random House, 1956; *Orpheus At Eighty* (biography of Guiseppe Verdi), Random House, 1958; *Nehru: The Years of Power,* Random House, 1960; *Dorothy and Red* (biography of Dorothy Thompson and Sinclair Lewis), Houghton, 1963; *Beware of Caesar* (novel), Random House, 1965. Contributor of short stories to magazines.

WORK IN PROGRESS: Personal History II.

SIDELIGHTS: Vincent Sheean covered many of the important world events from the end of World War I to the Korean War. He had described his particular brand of commentary as "a sort of semi-autobiographical political journalism—the external world and its graver struggles seen from the point of view of an observer who is not indifferent to them." When the 1969 edition of *Personal History* appeared, William McWhirter said: "With the exception of Norman Mailer's *Armies of the Night,* there has never been a better book about what journalism is really like and what it should be when it is very, very good. And, naturally, like Mailer's book, it is not about journalism at all. . . . Sheean instead shows a good many of us not only how to report but how to live—to dare to be involved, vulnerable and exposed. It is impossible to turn away from the humanity of this book. Its pain, anger, passion and agony shine through all the ashes of its years. Were Sheean's facts, after all, ever so important as what he learned from them?"

OBITUARIES: New York Times, March 17, 1975; *Washington Post,* March 17, 1975; *Time,* March 31, 1975; *Newsweek,* March 31, 1975; *AB Bookman's Weekly,* April 28, 1975; *Current Biography,* May, 1975.*

(Died March 15, 1975, in Arolo, Italy)

* * *

SHEEHAN, Arthur 1910(?)-1975

1910(?)—August 5, 1975; American journal and film editor, and biographer. Obituaries: *New York Times,* August 10, 1975; *AB Bookman's Weekly,* September 8, 1975.

* * *

SHEEHAN, Ethna 1908-

PERSONAL: Born November 22, 1908, in Castletown Bearhaven (also known as Berehaven and Castletownbere), County Cork, Ireland; daughter of John Vincent (a businessman) and Christina (O'Dwyer) Sheehan. *Education:* Hunter College (now of the City University of New York), A.B., 1938; Columbia University, M.S. in L.S., 1945. *Politics:* "In general, Republican." *Religion:* Roman Catholic. *Home:* 179 Linden St., Rockville Centre, N.Y. 11570. *Office:* School of Education, St. John's University, Jamaica, N.Y. 11432.

CAREER: Queens Borough Public Library, Jamaica, N.Y., staff member, 1930-63, St. John's University, School of Education, Jamaica, N.Y., assistant professor of children's literature and secondary school literature, 1966—. Part-time instructor at various times between 1950-63 at Queens College of the City University of New York, at Library School of Pratt Institute, at School of Library Services, Columbia University, and at St. John's University. Consultant to publishers and distributors of literary materials for young people. *Member:* American Library Association, Catholic Library Association (honorary life member), American Association of University Professors, National Council of Teachers of English, North Shore Literary Guild (Long Island). *Awards, honors:* Named librarian of the year by Catholic Library Association, 1975.

WRITINGS: (Compiler) *A Treasury of Catholic Children's Stories,* M. Evans, 1963; (reviser and author of introduction) Kate Doublas Wiggin and N. A. Smith, original editors, *The Fairy Ring,* new edition, Doubleday, 1967; (compiler) *Folk and Fairy Tales from Around the World,* Dodd, 1970. Contributor to *Grolier's Encyclopedia, New Catholic Encyclopedia,* and professional and literary periodicals.

WORK IN PROGRESS: A selection of folktales and modern tales for storytelling; research into sources for a collection of Irish folktales.

SIDELIGHTS: "I was born in a little seaside town in the south of Ireland. My father and his father before him were businessmen, but they handed down their love for books and history to all the family. My mother's people (though also in business) had a tradition of adventure and romance. War-like O'Dwyers had been outlawed from the Irish midlands by Queen Elizabeth I. Three of their equally rebellious descendants made a dramatic escape from the exile to which the young Queen Victoria had had them sentenced. A late-19th century O'Dwyer sent his own trading vessel to Argentina and contracts were maintained with friends in that country for a long time afterward.

"As a child I loved not only to read all the books I could find but also to produce family newspapers and magazines. My friends and I loved to put on plays—many of which we made up ourselves. We explored the lovely Bantry Bay region with its historical associations and prehistoric remains. I longed to see over the surrounding mountains, and I had my wish when I went away to boarding school and ultimately crossed the ocean to live on Long Island. Since then I have traveled extensively through the U.S. and Canada. I have been to Iceland and North Africa as well as to the Continent of Europe and—many times—to England and Ireland. I now spend my summers on the shores of Bantry Bay, about a mile from the town in which I was born. From my house—called Harbour Lights—I can see a ruined castle which was the centre of a great battle in Elizabethan times, several lighthouses, and a mountainous island; and I can watch ships from far-away places coming and going.

"My interest in people and books led me into the library profession. Here I could introduce good books to young people, and could tell stories to children. Some of my happiest memories are of storytelling times at various libraries and schools. I find that the children of today enjoy stories as much as their parents did. It is a great thrill to have modern-day boys or girls tell me that they recognize a story from Grimm or Perrault as a variant of one they have heard at home as a tale from Lithuania or Puerto Rico. I have put many of the stories into collections for reading and storytelling. To do this I had to undertake considerable research in reference libraries to be sure I had the correct sources. I often have to re-work some of the material to make it enjoyable in style for modern readers and listeners.

"Writing is always hard work, whether one is composing a book review, or writing a literary or technical article, or even if a person is inventing an original story. It takes discipline and perserverance to work and re-work one's prose and to smooth out awkward or confusing passages. The preliminary research can be fun if one enjoys seeking out half-forgotten materials and comparing early versions of traditional tales. But it can be tiring and at times discouraging. And yet, isn't there a satisfaction in overcoming obstacles? And isn't there some drudgery in every worthwhile and enjoyable undertaking?"

* * *

SHEINWOLD, Alfred 1912-

PERSONAL: Born January 26, 1912, in London, England; came to United States in 1921; naturalized citizen, 1940; son of Nathan (a manufacturer) and Mary (Sugarman) Sheinwold; married Patricia Fox, December 18, 1963 (divorced, 1972); married Paula Jean, February 24, 1973. *Education:* City College of New York (now City College of the City University of New York), B.S.S., 1933. *Home:*

236 South Spalding Dr., Beverly Hills, Calif. 90212. *Office:* 9056 Santa Monica Blvd., Los Angeles, Calif. 90069.

CAREER: Autobridge, Salem, Mass., editor, 1936—. *Military service:* U.S. Army, Office of Strategic Services, chief of cryptographic section, 1942-45. *Member:* American Contract Bridge League (chairman of board of governors).

WRITINGS: The First Book of Bridge, Sterling, 1952, published as *Sheinwold's Bridge Guide for Beginners: The First Book of Bridge,* 1966; *The Second Book of Bridge: The Play of the Hand,* Sterling, 1953 (published in England as *Bridge Play for Beginners,* Faber, 1955); *The Third Book of Bridge: How to Bid and Play in Duplicate Tournaments,* Sterling, 1954, published as *Duplicate Bridge,* Dover, 1971; *Winning Calypso: Including the Official 1955 Laws of the Game,* Sterling, 1955; *The Fourth Book of Bridge: How to Improve Your Game,* Barnes & Noble, 1956, published as *The Bridge Players' Guide to Bidding,* 1958, and as *How to Improve Your Bridge: The Fourth Book of Bridge,* Sterling, 1963; *A Hundred One Card Games for Children,* Sterling, 1956; (with Edgar Kaplan) *How to Play Winning Bridge,* Fleet Press, 1958, revised edition published as *The Kaplan-Sheinwold System of Winning Bridge,* Collier Books, 1962, 2nd revised edition, Fleet Press, 1963; *Complete Bridge Course,* Sterling, 1959; *Five Weeks to Winning Bridge,* Permabooks, 1959; *A Short Cut to Winning Bridge: My One Hundred Most Interesting Bridge Hands,* Fleet Press, 1961; *Duplicate Bridge,* Sterling, 1961; (contributor) Terence Reese, editor, *Improve Your Bridge,* Jenkins, 1965; *The Pocket Book of Bridge Puzzles,* Numbers 1 to 6, Simon & Schuster, 1970.

Author of "Sheinwold on Bridge," a syndicated column in about two hundred newspapers, 1957—. Contributor to bridge magazines. Editor of *Bridge World,* 1936-37, and for Cambridge Book Co., 1945-50; public relations editor for American Contract Bridge League, 1951-58; contributing editor of *Bridge World, Popular Bridge,* and *American Contract Bridge League Bulletin.*

* * *

SHELDON, Aure 1917-

PERSONAL: Born October 12, 1917, in Peoria, Ill.; daughter of Irving Weir and Retha (Crumrine) Stevens; married George Andrew Sheldon, October 8, 1938 (died in January, 1956); children: Jeannine (Mrs. George V. Kallal), William George, James Allen. *Education:* Northern Illinois University, B.S.Ed., 1962. *Residence:* North Carolina.

CAREER: Elementary school teacher in Massachusetts, 1962-71; Pisgah Forest School, Pisgah Forest, N.C., elementary school teacher, 1971—. *Member:* National Education Association, National Wildlife Federation, Wilderness Society, Audubon Society, Sierra Club, North Carolina Association of Educators.

WRITINGS—For children: *Fit for a King,* Lerner, 1975; *Of Cobblers and Kings,* Parents' Magazine Press, in press. Contributor of articles to adult magazines and stories to children's magazines.

WORK IN PROGRESS: Long Trail Winding; Into the Stubborn Wind; other fiction books for young teen-agers.

SIDELIGHTS: Aure Sheldon actively participates in conservation, wildlife protection, and nature projects. She writes: "A long time interest in children's literature led to a writing career, primarily for children." *Avocational interests:* Wilderness vacations, hiking, canoeing, rafting, horseback trips, camping, needlework, painting.

SHENKIN, Elizabeth Shoemaker ?-1975

?—July 6, 1975; American advertising account executive and author of mystery novels. Obituaries: *New York Times,* July 7, 1975.

* * *

SHEPHERD, Donald (Lee) 1932-
(Barbara Kevern)

PERSONAL: Born May 26, 1932, in Jackson, Mich.; son of Hershell Nixon and Marianne (White) Shepherd; married Barbara Kevern (a literary agent), May 26, 1954; children: Trudy (Mrs. Gregory Humphrey), Linda, Michael. *Education:* Los Angeles Harbor College, A.A., 1960; California State Polytechnic University, Pomona, B.S., 1966. *Office:* Don Shepherd Agency, 1680 Vine St., Suite 1105, Hollywood, Calif. 90028.

CAREER: Worked as magazine and book editor; Don Shepherd Agency, Hollywood, Calif., owner, 1969—. Lecturer on writing, literary contracts, and the book market. *Military service:* U.S. Army, 1953-56. *Member:* Authors Guild, Authors League of America.

WRITINGS: (Editor and compiler) *Women in History,* Mankind, 1973.

Novels; under pseudonym Barbara Kevern: *Dark Eden,* Pocket Books, 1973; *Darkness Falling,* Pinnacle, 1974; *The Key,* Ballantine, 1974; *The Devil's Vineyard,* Pinnacle, 1975. Contributor of more than forty articles and short stories to magazines. Ghost writer of an autobiography.

WORK IN PROGRESS: Ghosting another autobiography; television and screen writing.

* * *

SHEPPARD, Barry 1937-

PERSONAL: Born October 16, 1937, in Morristown, N.J. *Education:* Massachusetts Institute of Technology, B.A., 1959. *Politics:* Marxist; Socialist Workers Party. *Address:* c/o Pathfinder Press, Inc., 410 West St., New York, N.Y.

CAREER: Political organizer.

WRITINGS: (With Jack Barnes, George Breitman, Derrick Morrison, and Mary-Alice Waters) *Towards an American Socialist Revolution,* Pathfinder, 1972. Contributor to *Militant.*

* * *

SHEPPARD, Joseph 1930-

PERSONAL: Born December 20, 1930, in Baltimore, Md.; son of Joseph E. and Edna (Marquiss) Sheppard; married wife Marlene; children: Jonathan, William, Joseph; stepchildren: David, Lisa. *Education:* Maryland Institute of Art, fine art certificate; studied privately with Jacques Maroger. *Home:* 222 Wendover Rd., Baltimore, Md. 21218.

CAREER: Artist. Artist-in-residence and instructor in oil painting, Dickinson College, 1955-57; instructor in oil painting, Maryland Institute of Art, 1963—. One-man shows at Butler Institute of American Art, 1964 and 1972, Westmoreland County Museum, 1966 and 1972, and Davenport Municipal Art Gallery, 1967. Work included in many public and private collections including Baltimore Museum of Art, Columbus Museum of Fine Arts, and University of Arizona Museum. *Member:* Allied Artists of America. *Awards, honors:* Emily Lowe Prize from Allied Artists exhibition, 1956; Guggenheim fellowship, 1957-58; John F. and Anna Lee Stacy award, 1958; first purchase prize, Butler Institute of American Art, 1967.

WRITINGS: Anatomy: A Complete Guide for Artists, Watson-Guptill, 1975; *Drawing The Female Figure,* Watson-Guptill, 1975; *Illustrations for Socrates,* Stemmer House, 1975. Also author of *Drawing the Male Figure,* 1976.

*　　*　　*

SHERIDAN, Thomas 1938-

PERSONAL: Born September 13, 1938, in Liverpool, England; son of Thomas (a toolmaker) and Catherine (Mitchell) Sheridan; married Kyoko Takahashi (a university lecturer), May 8, 1965; children: Adam Thomas. *Education:* University of Leeds, B.A., 1960; Australian National University, Ph.D., 1967. *Politics:* "Egalitarian." *Religion:* "Nil." *Office:* Department of Economics, University of Adelaide, Adelaide 5001, South Australia.

CAREER: University of Adelaide, Adelaide, South Australia, lecturer, 1968-72, senior lecturer in economic history, 1973—. *Member:* Society for the Study of Labor History, Industrial Relations Society, Economic Society of Australia and New Zealand, Economic History Society of Australia and New Zealand, North Adelaide Football Club.

WRITINGS: (Contributor) Robert Cooksey, editor, *The Great Depression in Australia,* Angus & Robertson, 1970; (contributor) John Iremonger and others, editors, *Strikes: Studies in Twentieth Century Australian Social History,* Angus & Robertson, 1973; *Mindful Militants,* Cambridge University Press, 1975. Contributor to economic journals.

WORK IN PROGRESS: Research on the relationship between industrial and political labor movements in Australia in the 1930's and 1940's.

SIDELIGHTS: Sheridan writes that a working class environment in Liverpool led to his early interest in labor politics. "Entry to middle class via university education took some getting used to—necessitated three years odd-jobbing after graduation." He moved to Australia because he was ". . . sick of U.K. social attitudes." *Avocational interests:* Talking, walking, drinking, watching football.

*　　*　　*

SHERRIFF, R(obert) C(edric) 1896-1975

June 6, 1896—November 13, 1975; British playwright, novelist, and scriptwriter for films, television, and radio. Obituaries: *New York Times,* November 18, 1975; *AB Bookman's Weekly,* January 5, 1976.

*　　*　　*

SHETH, Jagdish N(anchand) 1938-

PERSONAL: Born September 3, 1938, in Rangoon, Burma; son of Nanchand J. (a businessman) and Diwaliben (Mehta) Sheth; married Madhu Shah, December 22, 1962; children: Reshma J., Raju J. *Education:* Madras University, B.Com. (honors), 1960; University of Pittsburgh, M.B.A., 1962, Ph.D., 1966. *Home:* 414 Brookens Dr., Urbana, Ill. 61801. *Office:* Department of Business Administration, University of Illinois, 146 Commerce W., Urbana, Ill. 61801.

CAREER: Columbia University, New York, N.Y., research associate in business, 1963-65; Massachusetts Insti-

tute of Technology, Cambridge, assistant professor of business administration, 1965-66; Columbia University, assistant professor of business, 1966-69; University of Illinois, Urbana, associate professor, 1969-71, professor, 1971-73, Illinois Business Associates Distinguished Professor of Business and research professor of business, 1973—, member of executive committee of Office of West European Studies, 1973—, co-chairman of National Conference on Social Marketing, 1972. Visiting professor at Indian Institute of Management, spring, 1968, and Columbia University, summer, 1970; visiting lecturer at Harvard University, summer, 1969; Albert Frey Visiting Professor of Marketing at University of Pittsburgh, 1974. Consultant to General Motors, American Telephone & Telegraph, Bell Canada, and B. F. Goodrich.

MEMBER: Association of International Business, American Association of Public Opinion Research, American Academy of Advertising, Association for Consumer Research, American Institute for Decision Sciences, American Statistical Association, American Marketing Association (director of Central Illinois chapter, 1972-73), Psychometric Society, American Psychological Association (fellow), British Psychological Society.

WRITINGS: (With John A. Howard) *The Theory of Buyer Behavior,* Wiley, 1969; (editor with S. P. Sethi, and contributor) *Multinational Business Operations: Advanced Readings,* four volumes, Volume I: *Environmental Aspects of Operating Abroad,* Volume II: *Long-Range Planning, Organization, and Management,* Volume III: *Marketing Management,* Volume IV: *Financial Management,* Goodyear Publishing, 1973; (editor and contributor) *Models of Buyer Behavior: Conceptual, Quantitative, and Empirical,* Harper, 1974; (editor with Peter Wright, and contributor) *Marketing Analysis for Societal Problems,* Bureau of Economics and Business Research, University of Illinois, 1974; (editor) *Multivariate Methods in Marketing* (monograph), American Marketing Association, in press.

Contributor: Reed Moyer, editor, *Changing Marketing Systems,* American Marketing Association, 1967; J. B. Kernan and M. S. Sommers, editors, *Perspectives in Marketing Theory,* Appleton, 1968; Johan Arndt, editor, *Insights into Consumer Behavior,* Allyn & Bacon, 1968; P. R. McDonald, editor, *Marketing Involvement in Society and the Economy,* American Marketing Association, 1970; Paul Pellemans, editor, *Insights in Consumer and Market Behavior,* Namur University, 1971; *Segmentation and Typology,* European Society for Opinion Surveys and Market Research, 1972; M. Venkatesan, editor, *Proceedings of the Third Annual Conference of the Association for Consumer Research,* Association for Consumer Research, 1972; *Consumer Psychology and Motivation Research,* European Society for Opinion Surveys and Market Research, 1972; Richard Holton and S. P. Sethi, editors, *Management of the Multinationals,* Free Press, 1974; Robert Ferber, editor, *Handbook of Marketing Research,* McGraw, 1974. Contributor of more than fifty articles and reviews to business and advertising journals. Advisory editor of Harper, 1970—.

WORK IN PROGRESS: Behavioral Sciences in Marketing, publication by Wiley expected in 1977; *Consumer Behavior,* for Harper, 1977; *Applied Statistics,* two volumes, 1978; *Attitude Theory and Prediction,* 1978.

*　　*　　*

SHOOK, Robert L. 1938-

PERSONAL: Born April 7, 1938, in Pittsburgh, Pa.; son of

Herbert M. (an insurance executive) and Belle (Slutsky) Shook; married Roberta Gay Wolk, April 18, 1962; children: Faith Caroline, Robert James, Michael David. *Education:* Ohio State University, B.S., 1959. *Religion:* Jewish. *Home:* 291 South Drexel Ave., Columbus, Ohio 43209. *Office:* Shook Associates Corp., 1156 Alum Creek Dr., Columbus, Ohio 43209.

CAREER: Shook Associates Corp., Columbus, Ohio, chairman of board, 1961—, partner in Atlantic Division, 1964—; American Executive Corp., Columbus, chairman of board, 1973—; American Executive Life Insurance Co., Phoenix, Ariz., chairman of board, 1973—. Chairman of board of Shook Associates Corp. of New England, North Carolina, Alabama, Florida, California, Indiana, Georgia, Tennessee, and Ohio; member of Columbus United Jewish Appeal, 1967—; director, J. Ashburn Youth Center, 1974—. *Military service:* U.S. Army, 1960; U.S. Army Reserves, 1960-61. *Member:* B'nai B'rith.

WRITINGS: (With father, Herbert M. Shook) *How to Be the Complete Professional Salesman,* Fell, 1974; (with Ronald L. Bingaman) *Total Commitment,* Fell, 1975.

WORK IN PROGRESS: Total Commitment: Part II, Twenty Successful American Women.

* * *

SHOR, Ronald (Edwin) 1930-

PERSONAL: Born November 20, 1930, in Cambridge, Mass.; son of Louis and Sophia (Meltzer) Shor; married Marilyn Beatrice Perlmutter (a secretary), November 14, 1952; children: Steven John, Karen Jill. *Education:* Brandeis University, B.A., 1953, Ph.D., 1959; University of Kansas, M.A., 1955. *Home:* 5 Bartlett Rd., Durham, N.H. 03824. *Office:* Department of Psychology, University of New Hampshire, Durham, N.H. 03824.

CAREER: Harvard University, Cambridge, Mass., research associate in psychology at Massachusetts Mental Health Center, 1960-64; University of Pennsylvania, Philadelphia, assistant professor of psychology and associate director of experimental psychiatry unit, 1964-66; La Salle College, Philadelphia, Pa., associate professor of psychology, 1966-67; University of New Hampshire, Durham, associate professor, 1967-73, professor of psychology, 1973—, chairman of department, 1975—. *Member:* American Psychological Association, Society for Psychophysiological Research, Society for Clinical and Experimental Hypnosis, Psychonomic Society.

WRITINGS: (Editor with M. T. Orne) *The Nature of Hypnosis: Selected Basic Readings,* Holt, 1965; (editor with Erica Fromm) *Hypnosis: Research Developments and Perspectives,* Aldine-Atherton, 1972. Also co-author of booklet and short monograph on hypnosis. Contributor to psychology journals.

WORK IN PROGRESS: Research on hypnosis, the psychology of humor, and the cognitive control of emotion.

* * *

SHORT, Alison 1920-

PERSONAL: Born January 19, 1920, in Beirut, Lebanon; daughter of Arthur B. (a clergyman) and Katharine (Bronson) Fowler; married Lester Charles Short (an electrician), December 31, 1941; children: Lois (Mrs. David Huisman), Daniel, Mary (Mrs. Dan Gautier), Timothy. *Education:* Attended National Bible Institute, 1937; Wheaton College, Wheaton, Ill., A.B., 1941. *Politics:* Con-

servative. *Religion:* Evangelical Christian. *Home:* 14554 23rd N.E., Seattle, Wash. 98155.

CAREER: Pioneer Girls, Inc., Wheaton, Ill., member of writing staff, 1958-72, regional representative, 1973—. Member of board of directors of Oregon Camp Cherith, and Christian Camping International (Northwest section). *Member:* American Camping Association (past member of board of directors of Evergreen Section).

WRITINGS: Pearls and a Pilgrim (juvenile novel), Moody, 1959; *Cousin Red and Til* (juvenile novel), Moody, 1975. Contributor to camping magazines, religious publications, and newspapers.

* * *

SHORT, Howard E(lmo) 1907-

PERSONAL: Born November 27, 1907, in Salem, Ind.; son of Walter Hartford (a farmer) and Nettie May (Gilstrap) Short; married Margaret Duncan (a nursery school teacher), June 29, 1935; children: Charlotte May (Mrs. William H. Drummond, Jr.), Catherine Jean Moore. *Education:* Eureka College, A.B., 1929; Hartford Seminary Foundation, B.D., 1932, Ph.D., 1942; also studied at University of Marburg, 1932-33, Oberlin Graduate School of Theology, 1936-38, Graduate School of Ecumenical Studies, Geneva, Switzerland, 1952, and Union Theological Seminary, New York, N.Y., 1953. *Politics:* Republican. *Home:* 7364 Cornell Ave., St. Louis, Mo. 63130.

CAREER: Ordained minister of Christian Church (Disciples of Christ), 1929; pastor of Christian churches in Washington, Ill., 1927-29, Granville, Mass., 1930-33, Springfield, Mass., 1934-36, and Cuyahoga Falls, Ohio, 1936-41; Hiram College, Hiram, Ohio, assistant professor of philosophy and religion, 1942-46; Lexington Theological Seminary, Lexington, Ky., professor of church history, 1946-58; Christian Board of Publication, St. Louis, Mo., vice-president, 1958-73, editor of *Christian,* 1958-73, and editor, Bethany Press, 1968-73; writer, 1973—. Assistant professor at Lake Erie College for Women, 1943-44; and visiting professor, Chapman College's World Campus Afloat, 1974. Trustee of Cuyahoga Falls Welfare Department, 1939-41, and of Eureka College. Fraternal delegate to World Lutheran Federation Assembly, 1952; delegate to World Council of Churches; member of National Conference of Christians and Jews; member of world interfaith relations committee of World Convention of Churches of Christ. *Wartime service:* Civilian member of U.S. State Department's Strategic Bombing Survey (research chief in Morale Division) in Germany, 1945; served as captain.

MEMBER: Newcomen Society of North America, American Society of Church History, Disciples of Christ Historical Society (vice-chairman of board of trustees), Sigma Delta Chi, Pi Kappa Delta, Lions International, St. Louis Chamber of Commerce. *Awards, honors:* LL.D. from Eureka College, 1958; Litt.D. from Bethany College, Bethany, W.Va., 1972.

WRITINGS: Doctrine and Thought of the Disciples of Christ, Christian Board of Publication, 1951; *Christian Unity Is Our Business,* Bethany Press, 1953; (with Ronald E. Osborn and Robert Tobias) *A Response to Lund,* Council on Christian Unity, 1953; (with Osborn and Tobias) *A Response to Evanston,* Council on Christian Unity, 1955; *Reformation, Restoration, and Renewal,* Church of Christ Press, 1956; (with Osborne and Tobias) *A Response to Oberlin,* Council on Christian Unity, 1958; (with James M. Flanagan, Perry E. Gresham, Granville T. Walker, and others) *What We Believe*, Bethany Press, 1956, revised edition, 1960; (with Osborne, Samuel F. Pugh, A. T. De-Groot, William L. Reed, and others) *Primer for New Disciples*, Bethany Press, 1964; (with Edwin T. Dahlberg, Samuel McCrea Cavert, Billy Graham, Charles P. Taft, and others) *Herald of the Evangel*, Bethany Press, 1965; (with Osborne, George G. Beazley, Jr., Harold E. Fey, and others) *The Christian Church (Disciples of Christ): An Interpretive Examination in the Cultural Context*, Bethany Press, 1973. Writer of "Where the Scriptures Speak," weekly commentary on church school lessons, in *Christian-Evangelist, Front Rank, Christian,* and *Disciple,* all 1950-75. Contributor to church publications.

SIDELIGHTS: Short writes: "When Pope Paul VI . . . invited world bodies of Protestants to send delegated observers to the third session of the Second Vatican Council, in 1964, I was appointed by my denomination to represent us. Living with the bishops, archbishops and cardinals for several months and a private audience with His Holiness, was a great joy to one who once expected to spend the bulk of his career teaching church history." *Avocational interests:* International travel.

* * *

SHOSTECK, Robert 1910-

PERSONAL: Born April 25, 1910, in Newark, N.J.; married Dora G. Rabinovitz; married second wife, Ruth Okrent (a social worker), December 19, 1970; children: Herschel, Sara Shosteck Williams. *Education:* George Washington University, A.B., 1939, B.A., 1953. *Politics:* Democrat. *Religion:* Jewish. *Home:* 5100 Alta Vista Rd., Bethesda, Md. 20014.

CAREER: National Roster of Scientific and Specialized Personnel, Washington, D.C., assistant director of placement, 1940-45; B'nai B'rith Vocational Service, Washington, D.C., director of research, 1945-56; B'nai B'rith Museum, Washington, D.C., curator, 1957-75, curator-consultant, 1975—; National Park Service, Washington, D.C., consultant, 1975—. *Member:* Jewish Historical Society of Washington (president, 1961).

WRITINGS: Potomac Trail Book, Potomac Books, 1967; *Weekender's Guide,* Potomac Books, 1969; *Flowers and Plants: An International Lexicon,* Quadrangle, 1974; (with others) *Washington Guide,* Washingtonian Magazine, 1975; *Field Guide to Rock Creek Park: District of Columbia,* National Park Service, in press.

* * *

SHUCARD, Alan R(obert) 1935-

PERSONAL: Born December 2, 1935, in Brooklyn, N.Y.; son of Jack Donald and Dorothy (Weber) Shucard; married Maureen O'Higgins (a journal manager), June 23, 1962; children: Sarah Elizabeth. *Education:* Attended University of St. Andrews, 1955-56; Union College, Schenectady, N.Y., A.B., 1957; University of Connecticut, M.A., 1963; University of Arizona, Ph.D., 1971. *Politics:* "Less naive than formerly." *Religion:* "Corned beef and egg roll worship." *Home:* 741 South Newman Rd., Racine, Wis. 53406. *Office:* Department of English, University of Wisconsin—Parkside, Wood Rd., Kenosha, Wis. 53140.

CAREER: University of British Columbia, Vancouver, instructor in English, 1965-70; University of Wisconsin-Parkside, Kenosha, assistant professor, 1970-73, associate professor of English, 1973—. *Military service:* U.S. Army,

Security Agency, 1959-62. *Member:* Modern Language Association of America.

WRITINGS—Poetry: *The Gorgon Bag,* Ladysmith Press, 1970; *The Louse on the Head of a Yawning Lord,* Ladysmith Press, 1972. Contributor to English and poetry journals, including *Arizona Quarterly, Hawk and Whipoorwill Recalled,* and *Beloit Poetry Journal.*

WORK IN PROGRESS: Watcher in Shadows, new poems; *Countee Cullen,* for Twayne; *Countee Cullen, Langston Hughes, and Claude McKay,* an annotated secondary bibliography for G. K. Hall.

SIDELIGHTS: "I criticize to sustain life; I write poems and teach to make sense of it," Shucard wrote. "I have a nonsensical predilection for attacking manhole covers and find comfort in shadows because in them manhole covers escape my notice."

* * *

SHUMAN, James B(urrow) 1932-

PERSONAL: Born September 8, 1932, in New York, N.Y.; son of Ik (an editor) and Elizabeth (Davies) Shuman; married Victoria Grove, October 4, 1958 (divorced, 1975); children: James, Jr., Robert. *Education:* Wesleyan University, Middletown, Conn., B.A., 1954. *Religion:* Quaker. *Home:* 4706 Hunt Ave., Chevy Chase, Md. 20015. *Agent:* Phyllis Jackson, International Creative Management, 1300 Ave. of the Americas, New York, N.Y. 10019. *Office:* White House, Washington, D.C.

CAREER: Sharon Herald, Sharon, Pa., reporter, 1956-59; United Press International, Washington, D.C., member of staff, 1959-62; *Reader's Digest,* Pleasantville, N.Y., associate editor, 1962-71; consultant to John D. Rockefeller III in New York, N.Y., 1971-72; free-lance writer, 1972-75; White House, Washington, D.C., member of staff, 1975—. *Military service:* U.S. Navy, 1954-56; became lieutenant junior grade. *Member:* National Press Club, Players (New York, N.Y.).

WRITINGS: (With David Rosenau) *The Kondratieff Wave,* World Publishing, 1972; (with Peter Remick) *In Constant Fear,* Reader's Digest Press, 1975. Contributor to national periodicals.

WORK IN PROGRESS: And He Hath Made the Rivers . . ., on the construction of the Indus Waters Project in West Pakistan.

* * *

SHUY, Roger W(ellington) 1931-

PERSONAL: Born January 5, 1931, in Akron, Ohio; son of Reo W. and Gladys (Day) Shuy; married Mary Lou Werner, July 26, 1952; children: Timothy, Joel. *Education:* Wheaton College, Wheaton, Ill., A.B., 1952; Kent State University, M.A., 1954; Western Reserve University (now Case Western Reserve University), Ph.D., 1962. *Home:* 8119 Thoreau Dr., Bethesda, Md. 20034. *Office:* Sociolinguistics Program, Georgetown University, Washington, D.C. 20007.

CAREER: High school teacher of English in Akron, Ohio, 1956-58; Wheaton College, Wheaton, Ill., assistant professor of English and linguistics, 1958-64; Michigan State University, East Lansing, associate professor of English and linguistics, 1964-67, co-director, National Defense Education Act Institute for Linguistics, summer, 1965, director, Detroit Dialect Study, 1966-67; Center for Applied Linguistics, Washington, D.C., director of sociolinguistics program, 1967-71, associate director of center, 1974; Georgetown University, Washington, D.C., professor of linguistics and director of sociolinguistics program, 1970—. Member of Inter-American Program for Linguistics and Language Teaching, 1968-72, Northwest Regional Educational Laboratory, 1971-72, Social Science Research Council, 1972-76, and Bilingual Task Force of Teacher Corps, 1975-76; U.S. Office of Education, member of Bureau of Educational and Professional Development, Leadership Training Institute, 1970-75, and member of advisory board, Education Resources Information Center, 1974-76. Visiting faculty member, State University of New York at Buffalo, 1971, University of California, Santa Cruz, 1972, University of Michigan, summer, 1974. Consultant or advisor to government, public, and private organizations, including U.S. Department of Health, Education and Welfare, National Science Foundation, Canada Council, and Carnegie Corp., 1967—.

MEMBER: International Reading Association, Linguistic Society of America, American Dialect Society, American Association for the Advancement of Science, National Council of Teachers of English (chairman, committee on special dialects, 1967-70), American Educational Research Association, Modern Language Association of America, Lectological Association (president, 1972-75), American Anthropoligical Association, Teachers of English to Speakers of Other Languages, National Conference on Research in English, Linguistic Society of Great Britain, Australian Society of Teachers of English, Associacion de Linguistas y Filogos de la America Latina. *Awards, honors:* American Council of Learned Societies fellowship, summer, 1957, travel grant to Copenhagen, summer, 1972; University of Chicago research fellow, summer, 1963; U.S. Air Force research fellow, summer, 1964.

WRITINGS: The Northern-Midland Dialect Boundary in Illinois, University of Alabama Press, 1962; *Discovering American Dialects,* National Council of Teachers of English, 1967; (with Walter A Wolfram and William K. Riley) *Field Techniques in an Urban Language Study,* Center for Applied Linguistics, 1968; (with Irwin Feigenbaum and Allene Grognet) *Sociolinguistic Theory, Materials, and Training Programs: Three Related Studies,* U.S. Office of Education, 1970.

Editor: *Social Dialects and Language Learning,* National Council of Teachers of English, 1965; (with J. C. Baratz) *Teaching Black Children to Read,* Center for Applied Linguistics, 1969; (with R. W. A. Fasold, and contributor) *Teaching Standard English in the Inner City,* Center for Applied Linguistics, 1970; *Sociolinguistics: A Cross Disciplinary Perspective,* Center for Applied Linguistics, 1971; (with David M. Smith and contributor) *Sociolinguistics in Cross-Cultural Analysis,* Georgetown University Press, 1972; *Sociolinguistics: Current Trends and Prospects,* Georgetown University Press, 1973; *New Ways of Analyzing Variation in English,* Georgetown University Press, 1973; (with Jane Laffey, and contributor) *Language Differences: Do They Interfere?,* International Reading Association, 1973; *Some New Directions in Linguistics,* Georgetown University Press, 1973; (editor with Fasold, and contributor) *Language Attitudes: Current Trends and Prospects,* Georgetown University Press, 1973; (with Joan Rubin) *Language Planning: Current Issues and Research,* Georgetown University Press, 1973; (with C. J. N. Bailey) *Toward Tomorrow's Linguistics,* Georgetown University Press, 1974.

Contributor: Paul Garvin and Bernard Spolsky, editors, *Computation in Linguistics: A Casebook,* Indiana University Press, 1966; *New Directions in Reading,* Bantam, 1967; A. L. Davis, editor, *On the Dialects of Children,* National Council of Teachers of English, 1968; Kenneth Goodman and James Fleming, editors, *Psycholinguistics and Reading,* International Reading Association, 1969; James Walden, editor, *Oral Language and Reading,* National Council of Teachers of English, 1969; Frederick Williams, editor, *Langauge and Poverty,* Markham, 1970; Sanford Newell, editor, *Dimensions: Language 70,* Converse College, 1970; J. Allen Figurel, editor, *Reading Goals for the Disadvantaged,* International Reading Association, 1970.

William K. Riley and David M. Smith, editors, *Languages and Linguistics,* Georgetown University Press, 1972; R. E. Hodges and E. H. Rudorf, editors, *Language and Learning to Read: What Teachers Should Know About Language,* Houghton, 1972; John Irwin and Michael Marge, editors, *Principles of Childhood Language Disabilities,* Appleton, 1972; Howard Klein, editor, *The Quest for Competency in Teaching Reading,* International Reading Association, 1972; Martha King, Robert Emans, and P. Cianciolo, editors, *A Forum for Focus,* National Council of Teachers of English, 1973; W. W. Gage, editor, *Language in its Social Setting,* Anthropology Society of Washington, 1974; Harvey Sartain and Paul Stanton, editors, *Modular Preparation for Teaching Reading,* International Reading Association, 1974; F. P. Dinneen, editor, *Linguistics: Teaching and Interdisciplinary Relations,* Georgetown University Press, 1975; Stanley Wanat, editor, *Intelligence and Reading,* International Reading Association, in press; Wanat, Harry Singer, and Martin Kling, editors, *Extracting Meaning from Written Language,* International Reading Association, in press.

Contributor of articles to symposia, proceedings, and journals in his field. General editor, *Urban Language Series* of the Center for Applied Linguistics, 1967-74, and *Sociolinguistic Series* of Newbury House Publishers, 1975—; linguistic advisor, *Xerox Intermediate Dictionary,* 1972. Member of editorial board, *American Speech,* 1968-76, *Language and Society,* 1973-76, *International Journal of the Sociology of Language,* 1973-76, *Discourse Processes,* 1975-76, and *Reviews in Reading,* 1975-76.

* * *

SIBLEY, Agnes M(arie) 1914-

PERSONAL: Born October 20, 1914, in Marston, Mo.; daughter of William Austin (a physician) and Erna (Quickert) Sibley. *Education:* University of Oklahoma, B.A. and M.A., both 1936; Columbia University, Ph.D., 1947. *Home:* Upper Cranmore, Heyshott, Midhurst, Sussex, England.

CAREER: Columbia University, New York City, secretarial and research work, 1937-41; Cottey Junior College, Nevada, Mo., instructor in English, 1941-43; Lindenwood College, St. Charles, Mo., began as instructor, became professor of English, 1943-73. Exchange lecturer at Bishop Otter College, 1951-53. *Member:* American Association of University Professors. *Awards, honors:* Fulbright grant, 1951-52.

WRITINGS: Alexander Pope's Prestige in America, King's Crown Press (Columbia University), 1948; *Exchange Teacher,* Caxton, 1961; *May Sarton,* Twayne, 1972.

WORK IN PROGRESS: Charles Williams, for Twayne.

SIDDIQI, Akhtar Husain 1925-

PERSONAL: Born April 20, 1925, in Budaun, India; son of Rahat Husain (a teacher) and Miraj (Bano) Siddiqi; married Ismat Hamid (a counselor), December 16, 1966; children: Kausar, Tasnim, Yawar (all stepchildren). *Education:* Aligarh Muslim University, B.A. (honors), 1946; London School of Economics and Political Science, M.A., 1953; University of London, Ph.D., 1959. *Religion:* Islam. *Home:* 4415 Trudy's Drive, Terre Haute, Ind. 47802. *Office:* Department of Geography and Geology, Indiana State University, Terre Haute, Ind. 47809.

CAREER: University of Dacca, Ramna, East Pakistan, senior lecturer, 1959-61; Pakistan International Airlines, Karachi, chief planning officer, 1961-63; Indiana State University, Terre Haute, assistant professor, 1964-67, associate professor, 1967-72, professor of geography, 1972—. *Member:* Association of American Geographers. *Awards, honors:* Purdue University fellowship, 1963-64.

WRITINGS: Pakistan: A Selected Bibliography, Its Land, Resources, and Economic Development, Department of Geography and Geology, Indiana State University, 1971; *Socioeconomic Changes in Northeast Baluchistan, Pakistan,* Department of Geography and Geology, Indiana State University, 1972. Contributor to geography and economics journals.

WORK IN PROGRESS: The Role of Natural Resources in the Economic Development of Pakistan; Economic Growth and Development in Southern Indiana.

SIDELIGHTS: Siddiqi has traveled in Western Europe, throughout all of Asia, and in the Far East.

* * *

SIEGEL, Adrienne 1936-

PERSONAL: Born June 10, 1936, in New York, N.Y.; daughter of Nathan (a physician) and Jean (an attorney; maiden name, Mark) Spitzer; married Martin Siegel (a professor of history), May 7, 1972. *Education:* University of Pennsylvania, B.S., 1957; Columbia University, M.A., 1959; New York University, Ph.D., 1973. *Home:* 330 West Jersey St., Elizabeth, N.J. 07202. *Office:* James Madison High School, 3787 Bedford Ave., Brooklyn, N.Y. 11229.

CAREER: William Howard Taft High School, New York, N.Y., teacher of history, 1959-62; James Madison High School, New York, N.Y., teacher of history, 1962—. *Member:* American Historical Association, Columbia University Post Doctoral Seminars in Urban History. *Awards, honors:* Danforth Associate, 1972—.

WRITINGS: Philadelphia, Oceana, 1975. Contributor to *North Dakota Quarterly* and *Journal of Popular Culture.*

WORK IN PROGRESS: Mysteries, Miseries and Miracles: The Image of the American City in Popular Literature, 1820-1870, completion expected in 1976.

SIDELIGHTS: Adrienne Siegel told *CA:* "What people have thought of their cities is as much a reality as what has happened in them. The impact of the media in fashioning the perceptions of Americans to their urban communities has been the focus of my research for the last several years." *Avocational interests:* Travel, theater, ballet, music, gourmet cooking, sailing, motorcycling.

BIOGRAPHICAL/CRITICAL SOURCES: Publishers' Weekly, June 2, 1975; *Interact,* December, 1975.

SILBERG, Moshe 1900-1975

1900—August 16, 1975; Russian-born Israeli Supreme Court justice, educator, and author of books in his field. Obituaries: *New York Times,* August 18, 1975.

* * *

SIM, Myre 1915-

PERSONAL: Born October 2, 1915, in Edinburgh, Scotland; son of Julius (a shopkeeper) and Sarah (Hoffenberg) Sim; married Winifred Thomas, October 4, 1941. *Education:* University of Edinburgh, M.B.Ch.B., 1938, M.D., 1948. *Politics:* Conservative. *Religion:* Jewish. *Office:* Royal Ottawa Hospital, Carleton Ave., Ottawa, Ontario, Canada.

CAREER: Consulting psychiatrist in private practice in Birmingham, England, 1948-75; Midland Nerve Hospital, Birmingham, England, consulting psychiatrist, 1947-50; Queen Elizabeth Hospital, Birmingham, England, consulting psychiatrist, 1950-75; University of Ottawa, Ottawa, Ontario, professor of psychiatry, 1975—. Member of General Medical Council (England), 1970-75; member of advisory panel on neurosciences of World Health Organization, 1971—. *Military service:* British Army, 1942-46; became major. *Member:* Royal College of Physicians (England; fellow), Royal College of Psychiatrists (England; fellow); Royal College of Physicians (Canada; fellow).

WRITINGS: Guide to Psychiatry, Churchill-Livingstone, 1963, 3rd edition, 1974; *Tutors and Their Students,* Churchill-Livingstone, 1966, revised edition, 1970; (with E. B. Gordon) *Basic Psychiatry,* Churchill-Livingstone, 1968, 3rd edition, in press; *Forensic Psychiatry,* Saunders, in press. Contributor to medical and popular journals.

WORK IN PROGRESS: Research on instability in pregnancy, on pre-senile dementia, and on methodology of clinical trials.

SIDELIGHTS: Sim writes: "I am concerned at the over-enthusiasm of unbridled reformers who initiate costly and frequently useless or even dangerous schemes. Progress is not synonymous with radicalism."

* * *

SIMEON, Richard 1943-

PERSONAL: Born March 2, 1943, in England; son of John E. B. (a social worker) and Anne (a writer; maiden name, Dean) Simeon; married Joan Weld, August 6, 1966; children: Stephen, Rachel. *Education:* University of British Columbia, B.A. (honors), 1964; Yale University, M.A., 1966, Ph.D., 1968. *Home:* 95 Mack St., Kingston, Ontario, Canada. *Office:* Department of Political Studies, Queen's University, Kingston, Ontario, Canada.

CAREER: Queen's University, Kingston, Ontario, assistant professor, 1968-71, associate professor of political studies, 1971—. Visiting associate professor at University of British Columbia, 1972-73, and University of Essex, 1975-76. *Member:* Canadian Political Science Association (member of board of directors, 1973-75), Canadian Tax Foundation, American Political Science Association.

WRITINGS: Federal-Provincial Diplomacy: The Making of Recent Policy in Canada, University of Toronto Press, 1972. Contributor to political science journals. Associate editor of *Canadian Public Policy.*

WORK IN PROGRESS: Canadian Public Policy; research on political conflict, ideology, and policy-making.

SIMON, Eckehard 1939-

PERSONAL: Born January 5, 1939, in Schneidemuehl, Germany; naturalized U.S. citizen; son of Herbert (a lawyer) and Doris (Keiler) Simon; married Eileen Higginbottom (a scientific researcher), December 19, 1959; children: Anders, Conrad, Matthew. *Education:* Columbia University, A.B. (summa cum laude), 1960; Harvard University, A.M., 1961, Ph.D. (with distinction), 1964. *Politics:* Democrat. *Religion:* Lutheran. *Home:* 120 Highland Ave., Arlington, Mass. 02174. *Office:* Department of Germanic Languages and Literatures, Harvard University, 417 Boylston Hall, Cambridge, Mass. 02138.

CAREER: Harvard University, Cambridge, Mass., instructor, 1964-65, assistant professor, 1965-69, associate professor, 1969-71, professor of German, 1971—, head tutor, 1964-68, 1974—, coordinator of language instruction, 1969-73. *Member:* Mediaeval Academy of America, Modern Language Association of America, American Association of Teachers of German. *Awards, honors:* Woodrow Wilson fellowship, 1960-61; National Endowment for the Humanities younger scholar fellowship, 1969; Guggenheim fellowship, 1969.

WRITINGS: Neidhart von Reuental: Geschichte der Forschung und Bibliographie (title means "Neidhart von Reuental: Research Report and Bibliography"), Harvard University Press, 1968; *Neidhart von Reuental* (biography), Twayne, 1975. Contributor to literary and philological journals in the United States and Europe.

WORK IN PROGRESS: An edition of the fifteenth century German Shrovetide plays, consisting of several volumes with commentary, first volume completion expected in 1977; *A History of Medieval German Drama.*

* * *

SIMONT, Marc 1915-

PERSONAL: Born November 23, 1915, in Paris, France; came to United States, 1927, but later went back to Europe with parents, returning to America, 1935; naturalized citizen, 1936; son of Jose (a draftsman on staff of *L'Illustration*) and Dolores (Baste) Simont; married Sara Dalton (a teacher of handicapped children), April 7, 1945; children: Marc Dalton. *Education:* Studied art in Paris at Academie Ranson, Academie Julien, and with Andre Lhote, 1932-35, and in New York at National Academy of Design, 1935-37. *Home:* Town St., West Cornwall, Conn. 06706. *Office:* 31 West 11th St., New York, N.Y. 10011.

CAREER: Did portrait painting and advertising art in late 1930's; illustrator of children's books, 1939—. Also author and translator of books for children. *Military service:* U.S. Army, 1943-46; became sergeant. *Awards, honors:* Tiffany fellow, 1937; Caldecott Medal of American Library Association for best illustrated book for children, 1957, for *A Tree Is Nice.*

WRITINGS—Self-illustrated: Opera Souffle: 60 Pictures in Bravura, Schuman, 1950; *Polly's Oats,* Harper, 1951; (with Red Smith) *How to Get to First Base: A Picture Book of Baseball,* Schuman, 1952; *The Lovely Summer,* Harper, 1952; *Mimi,* Harper, 1954; *The Plumber Out of the Sea,* Harper, 1955; *The Contest at Paca,* Harper, 1959; *How Come Elephants?,* Harper, 1965; *Afternoon in Spain,* Morrow, 1965; (translator) Federico Lorca Garcia, *The Lieutenant Colonel and the Gypsy,* Doubleday, 1971; (with members of staff of Boston Children's Medical Center) *A Child's Eye View of the World,* Delacorte, 1972.

Illustrator: Emma G. Sterne, *The Pirate of Chatham Square: A Story of Old New York,* Dodd, 1939; Ruth Bryan Owens, *The Castle in the Silver Woods,* Dodd, 1939.

Albert Carr, *Men Of Power,* Viking, 1940; Mildred Cross, *Isabella, Young Queen of Spain,* Dodd, 1941; Charlotte Jackson, *Sarah Deborah's Day,* Dodd, 1941; Richard Hatch, *All Aboard the Whale,* Dodd, 1942; *Dougal's Wish,* Harper, 1942; Meindert DeJong, *Billy and the Unhappy Bull,* Harper, 1946; Margaret Wise Brown, *The First Story,* Harper, 1947; Iris Vinton, *Flying Ebony,* Dodd, 1947; Robbie Trent, *The First Christmas,* Harper, 1948; Andrew Lang, editor, *The Red Fairy Book,* new edition, Longmans, Green, 1948; Ruth Krauss, *The Happy Day,* Harper, 1949; Ruth Krauss, *The Big World and the Little House,* Schuman, 1949.

Meindert DeJong, *Good Luck Duck,* Harper, 1950; Ruth Krauss, *The Backward Day,* Harper, 1950; James Thurber, *The Thirteen Clocks,* Simon & Schuster, 1951; Marjorie B. Paradis, *Timmy and the Tiger,* Harper, 1952; Miriam Powell, *Jareb,* Crowell, 1952; *The American Riddle Book,* Schuman, 1954; Elizabeth H. Lansing, *Deer Mountain Hideaway,* Crowell, 1954; Jean Fritz, *Fish Head,* Coward, 1954; Elizabeth H. Lansing, *Deer River Raft,* Crowell, 1955; Fred Gipson, *The Trail-Driving Rooster,* Harper, 1955; Julius Schwartz, *Now I Know,* Whittlesey House, 1955; Janice May Udry, *A Tree Is Nice,* Harper, 1955; Julius Schwartz, *I Know a Magic House,* Whittlesey House, 1956; Thomas Liggett, *Pigeon Fly Home,* Holiday House, 1956; Chad Walsh, *Nellie and Her Flying Crocodile,* Harper, 1956; James Thurber, *The Wonderful "O",* Simon & Schuster, 1957; Maria Leach, *The Rainbow Book of American Folk Tales and Legends,* World Publishing, 1958; Alexis Ladas, *The Seal That Couldn't Swim,* Little, Brown, 1959.

James A. Kjelgaard, *The Duckfooted Hound,* Crowell, 1960; Ruth Krauss, *A Good Man and His Wife,* Harper, 1962; Julius Schwartz, *The Earth Is Your Spaceship,* Whittlesey House, 1963; David McCord, *Every Time I Climb a Tree,* Little, Brown, 1967; Janet Chenery, *Wolfie,* Harper, 1969; Janice May Udry, *Glenda,* Harper, 1969.

Marjorie Sharmat, *Nate the Great,* Coward, 1972; Marjorie Sharmat, *Nate Goes Undercover,* Coward, 1974.

AVOCATIONAL INTERESTS: Skiing and other sports.

BIOGRAPHICAL/CRITICAL SOURCES: Lee Bennett Hopkins, *Books Are by People,* Citation Press, 1969.

* * *

SIMPER, Robert 1937-

PERSONAL: Born December 12, 1937, in Blaxhall, Suffolk, England; son of Norman Edward (a farmer) and Lillian (Turner) Simper; married Pearl Bater (a potter), July 18, 1959; children: Caroline Sara, Joanna Eleanor, Jonathan Robert. *Education:* Attended Royal Agricultural College, 1957-58. *Politics:* "Middle of the road." *Home:* Sluice Cottage, Ramsholt, Woodbridge, Suffolk 1P12 3AD, England.

CAREER: Worker on family farm, 1953—; sailor and writer on agriculture, sailing, traditional vessels, and travel, 1962—; N. E. Simper & Son (farm management company), Suffolk, England, director, 1962—. *Member:* Society for Nautical Research.

WRITINGS: Over Snape Bridge, East Anglian Magazine, 1967; *Woodbridge and Beyond,* East Anglian Magazine, 1972; *East Coast Sail,* David & Charles, 1972; *Scottish*

Sail, David & Charles, 1974; *North East Sail,* David & Charles, 1976; *British Sail,* David & Charles, in press. Author of "Sail Review," a column in *Sea Breezes,* 1966—. Contributor to agricultural and sailing magazines, to *Lady,* and to newspapers.

WORK IN PROGRESS: International Sail; research on North American and European small working sailing craft.

SIDELIGHTS: Simper writes: "Began writing almost accidentally because of a back injury. Much of my writing is intended to encourage people to preserve traditional working sailing craft.... I have researched, so far, in western Europe and the West Indies.... I am a believer in the idea that Europe should be united economically and politically and deplore the current trends in Britain to try and split up ... the old countries which have been so successfully united under the monarchy and Parliament of Westminster."

AVOCATIONAL INTERESTS: Photography (has used several of own photographs to illustrate books), meeting people.

* * *

SIMPICH, Frederick, Jr. 1911-1975

PERSONAL: Born June 2, 1911, in New Franklin, Mo.; son of Frederick (an assistant editor of *National Geographic*) and Margaret (Edwards) Simpich; married Alice Louise Judd, September 30, 1955; children: Frederick III; (stepchildren) Michael Banfield, Louli Miller. *Education:* Attended University of Pennsylvania, 1928-30. *Residence:* Maui, Hawaii.

CAREER: National Recovery Act, deputy administrator in Hawaii, 1935; Institute of Pacific Relations, Hawaii, acting secretary, 1935-36; Castle & Cooke, Inc., Honolulu, Hawaii, served as vice-president, secretary, and director, 1936-61; Oceanic Properties, Inc., Honolulu, president and director, 1961-68; writer and consultant, 1968-75. Chairman of Hawaii Visitors Bureau, 1958-60. *Military service:* U.S. Army, 1942-45; became colonel; received Bronze Star, Croix de Guerre, Order of the British Empire.

WRITINGS: Anatomy of Hawaii, Coward, 1971; *Dynasty in the Pacific,* McGraw, 1974. Contributor to *National Geographic.**

(Died May 2, 1975, in Hawaii)

* * *

SINCLAIR, Olga 1923-

PERSONAL: Born January 23, 1923, in Watton, England; daughter of Daniel Robert and Betty (Sapey) Waters; married Stanley George Sinclair (a headmaster), April 1, 1945; children: Michael, Alistair, Jeremy. *Education:* Educated in Norfolk, England. *Politics:* "Left of centre." *Religion:* None. *Home and office:* The Beeches, Coltishall, Norwich, England.

CAREER: Writer. Bank clerk, 1940-42; justice of the peace in county of Norfolk, 1966; district councillor. *Wartime service:* Auxiliary Territorial Service, payclerk, 1942-45. *Member:* Society of Authors, Society of Women Writers and Journalists, Romantic Novelists Association. *Awards, honors:* Margaret Rhonda Award from Society of Authors, 1972, for research on Lithuanian immigrants.

WRITINGS—All novels, except as noted: *Gypsies* (children's nonfiction), Basil Blackwell, 1967; *Night of the Black Tower,* Lancer Books, 1968; *Dancing in Britain:* *Toys* (children's nonfiction) Basil Blackwell, 1970; *The Man at the Manor,* Dell, 1972; *Bitter Sweet Summer,* Simon & Schuster, 1972; *Wild Dreams,* R. Hale, 1973; *My Dear Fugitive,* R. Hale, 1976.

WORK IN PROGRESS: Re-writing a novel about Lithuanian immigrants to the Scottish coal mines at the turn of the century; research on the problems of gypsies in England, Europe, and the rest of the world.

SIDELIGHTS: Olga Sinclair writes: "This novel, *Bitter Sweet Summer,* was based on a camping holiday with my family in the summer of 1968, through East Germany to Czechoslovakia, that fateful summer when Czechoslovakia was invaded. Whilst in Prague the sound of machine gun fire in Wenceslas Square made us hasten for the Austrian border."

* * *

SINGER, Judith 1926-

PERSONAL: Born February 26, 1926, in New York, N.Y.; married Alexander Singer (a film director), September 10, 1950; children: Jethro. *Education:* Hunter College of the City University of New York, B.A., 1946. *Agent:* Warren Bayless, 156 East 52nd St., New York, N.Y. 10022.

CAREER: Writer. *Member:* Writers Guild of America East.

WRITINGS: Glass Houses, Bantam, 1971; *Threshold,* Bantam, 1975. Author of screenplay for *Glass Houses,* with husband, Alexander Singer, Columbia Pictures, 1971.

* * *

SINGER, Susan (Mahler) 1941-

PERSONAL: Born July 30, 1941, in Brooklyn, N.Y.; daughter of Ernest (a lawyer) and Pearl (Smith) Mahler; married Marshall R. Singer (a professor), January 1, 1960; children: Shepherd, Paul. *Education:* Studied at Brooklyn College, 1958-60 and Hunter College, 1961-62 (both now of the City University of New York), New School for Social Research, 1962-64, and University of Pittsburgh, at intervals, 1964—. *Religion:* Jewish. *Home:* 1520 Shady Ave., Pittsburgh, Pa. 15217. *Agent:* McIntosh & Otis, Inc., 18 East 41st St., New York, N.Y. 10021.

CAREER: Worked in former years as secretary and editorial assistant for professional journals and a publishing firm; free-lance writer and editor. *Awards, honors:* Bread Loaf Writers' Conference fellowship, 1972.

WRITINGS: Kenny's Monkey (juvenile), Scholastic Book Services, 1963.

WORK IN PROGRESS: The Magic Radio, a book about the adventures of children who find an old radio in a trash pile.

SIDELIGHTS: Susan Singer said: "I have always like to read and loved to write. In addition to my children's stories, I have written many stories for adults, as well as half a novel. I do believe that art imitates life, and my writing tends to follow closely behind my life experience—not too closely, of course. It takes several years for the full meaning of events to filter into my imagination....

"I've had the benefits of the academic life without being in it myself, and thus have had much opportunity for travel in Europe, Central America, and a two-year stay in Southeast Asia. Travel provides a new world view, new tastes, vivid memories. But the writer's work is done anywhere, anywhere his energies are taxed, anywhere his mind is stimulated.

"I write because it is my way of interpreting life."

* * *

SIVULICH, Sandra (Jeanne) Stroner 1941-

PERSONAL: Born April 8, 1941, in Berwyn, Ill.; daughter of Frank Joseph (a policeman) and Helen (Rench) Stroner; married Kenneth G. Sivulich (director of Erie Metropolitan Library), May 22, 1971. *Education:* Marygrove College, B.A., 1962; Rosary College, M.A.L.S., 1963. *Politics:* Democratic. *Religion:* Roman Catholic. *Home:* 1238 West Ninth, Erie, Pa. 16502.

CAREER: Chicago Public Library, Chicago, Ill., branch children's librarian, 1963-66; Skokie Public Library, Skokie, Ill., children's librarian, 1966-68; Evanston Public Library, Evanston, Ill., director of children's services, 1968-71; Mercyhurst College, Erie, Pa., lecturer in children's literature, 1971—. Lecturer and conductor of workshops on children's books; consultant to Encyclopaedia Britannica Educational Corp. *Member:* American Library Association, Catholic Library Association, Pennsylvania Library Association, League of Women Voters.

WRITINGS: I'm Going on a Bear Hunt, Dutton, 1973. Contributor to library journals.

WORK IN PROGRESS: A chapter for a National Council of Teachers of English book about literary experience for preschool children.

* * *

SKARDAL, Dorothy Burton 1922-

PERSONAL: Born July 24, 1922, in Omaha, Neb.; daughter of William Matthew (a lawyer) and Jennie (a high school teacher; maiden name Nuquist) Burton; married Olav Skardal (a university teacher), June 12, 1953; children: Ellen Tone, Randi Anne. *Education:* Middlebury College, A.B., 1944; Radcliffe College, M.A., 1945; Harvard University, Ph.D., 1963. *Home:* Soekedalsveien 229, Oslo 7, Norway. *Office:* American Institute, University of Oslo, P.O. Box 1002, Blindern, Oslo 3, Norway.

CAREER: University of Oslo, American Institute, Oslo, Norway, instructor, 1965-68, lecturer, 1968-73, senior lecturer in American Studies, 1973—. Member of board of directors, Fulbright Office, United States Educational Foundation in Norway, 1972—.

WRITINGS: Social Insurance in Norway, Norwegian Joint Committee on International Social Policy, 1955, 2nd edition, 1960; (editor and translator) Karl Evang, *Health Services in Norway,* Norwegian Joint Committee on International Social Policy, 1956, 3rd edition, 1970; *The Divided Heart: Scandinavian Immigrant Experience through Literary Sources,* University of Nebraska Press and Universitetsforlaget (Oslo), 1974.

WORK IN PROGRESS: An anthology on the history of Norwegian-American immigrant literature, in both Norwegian and English; a history of Norwegian-American literature in English; with Torbjoern Sirevaag, *American Society and Culture,* a textbook for Scandinavian universities.

* * *

SKEEL, Dorothy J(une)

PERSONAL: Born in Erie, Pa.; daughter of Kenneth Selby and Cora (Gidner) Skeel. *Education:* Edinboro State College, B.S.; Pennsylvania State University, M.Ed., 1961, D.Ed., 1966; post-doctoral study at University of Washington, Seattle, 1968-69. *Home:* 1600 East Hillside Dr., No. 32, Bloomington, Ind. 47401.

CAREER: Elementary and high school teacher at public schools in Pennsylvania; Kutztown State College, Kutztown, Pa., assistant professor of education, 1961-64; Pennsylvania State University, University Park, associate instructor in education, 1964-66; Indiana University, Bloomington, associate professor of education, 1966—, director of TEAM experimental program, and coordinator for social studies. Visiting professor at University of Southern Nevada, summer, 1968, and University of Washington, summer, 1969. Secretary of Indiana Sponsors' Coordinating Council of the State Education Agency, 1969. *Member:* National Council for the Social Studies, National Society for the Study of Education, Indiana Council for the Social Studies (member of board of directors, 1971-73), Pi Lambda Theta, Delta Kappa Gamma (vice-president, 1972-74), Beta Beta Beta, Pi Gamma Mu.

WRITINGS: (With Oscar A. Rogers) *Objectives and Evaluation* (monograph), Tri-University Project, University of Washington, 1969; (contributor) James L. Olivero and E. G. Buffie, editors, *Educational Manpower: From Aides to Differentiated Staff Patterns,* Indiana University Press, 1970; *The Challenge of Teaching Social Studies in the Elementary School,* Goodyear Publishing, 1970, 2nd edition, 1974; (with Owen A. Hagen) *Process of Curriculum Change,* Goodyear Publishing, 1971; *Children of the Street: Teaching in the Inner-City,* Goodyear Publishing, 1971; (contributor) D. W. Beggs and Buffie, editors, *Nongraded Schools in Action: Bold New Venture,* Indiana University Press, revised edition (Skeel was not associated with earlier edition), 1971; *The Challenge of Teaching Social Studies: A Book of Readings,* Goodyear Publishing, 1972; *The People of United States and Canada* (juvenile), Sadlier, 1972; *The People of Latin America* (juvenile), Sadlier, 1972. Contributor to education journals. Author of two records, "Developing Creative Ability," and "Developing Language Arts Skills," produced by H. W. Wilson.

WORK IN PROGRESS: The Social Sciences and You (juvenile); research on "Behavioral Objectives: Fact or Fantasy," and "How Do Children in Various Geographic Areas of the United States Rank Values?".

* * *

SKIDMORE, Ian 1929-

PERSONAL: Born May 16, 1929, in Manchester, England; son of Elijah Edward (a police constable) and Irene (a chorus girl; maiden name, Knowles) Skidmore; married Leah Chesstok, November 19, 1951 (divorced July 15, 1971); married Celia Lucas (an author), October 20, 1971; children: (first marriage) Gay Heather, Lynn Charmian (Mrs. Richard May), Nicholas. *Education:* Educated in England. *Politics:* "Practicing pragmatic." *Religion:* Agnostic. *Home:* 65B The Rows, Watergate St., Chester, England. *Agent:* Toby Eady, 313 Fulham Rd., Fulham, London, England. *Office:* Virgin and Child House, Brynsiencyn, Anglesey, Wales.

CAREER: Manchester City News, Manchester, England, reporter, 1949-50; *Yorkshire Evening News,* Yorkshire, England, reporter, 1950-52; *Yorkshire Evening Post,* Yorkshire, reporter, 1952-54; *Daily Dispatch,* Manchester, reporter, 1954-56; *Daily Mirror,* Manchester, reporter, 1956-59, night news editor, 1959-61; free-lance journalist, 1961-

74; *Sunday Mirror,* Manchester, night news editor, 1961-63; *People,* Manchester, night news editor, 1963-65; writer, 1974—. *Military service:* British Army, Black Watch Regiment, 1947-49; became sergeant. *Member:* Liverpool Press Club, Royal Scot Club, Black Watch Association, British Museum Reading Room, John Rylands Library, Confrerie de la Chaine de Rotisseurs.

WRITINGS: Escape from the Rising Sun, Leo Cooper, 1972; *Escape from Singapore: 1942,* Scribner, 1974; *Nestful of Chieftains* (biography of Owain Glyndwr), Leo Cooper, in press; *While Shepherds Watched,* Cassell, in press. Author of radio documentaries.

WORK IN PROGRESS: Forgive Us Our Press Passes and *Hold the Front Page I Have Got Nowhere to Put My Chips,* both newspaper reminiscences.

SIDELIGHTS: "I am motivated by the rising cost of beer," Skidmore told *CA,* "and an inability to stop writing which probably comes from years as a newspaperman. The incestuous aspect worries me. Owain Glyndwr was an ancestor, and *Escape from the Rising Sun* and *While Shepherds Watched* are both about close friends. . . . I worry that one day I will run out of commercially viable friends and worry more when I realize this is a problem shared by insurance salesmen."

BIOGRAPHICAL/CRITICAL SOURCES: Trevor Fishlock, *Wales and the Welsh,* Cassell, 1973; Ray Gosling, "Chester: Portrait of a City" (Granada prizewinning television documentary), 1974.

* * *

SKILLINGS, R(oger) D(eering)   1937-

PERSONAL: Born October 20, 1937, in Maine. *Education:* Attended Bowdoin College. *Office:* Fine Arts Work Center, Provincetown, Mass. 02657.

CAREER: Fine Arts Work Center, Provincetown, Mass., chairman pro-tempore of writers, 1973—.

WRITINGS: Alternative Lives (fiction), Ithaca House, 1974.

WORK IN PROGRESS: Two books, *In a Murderous Time* and *The Meatrack.*

* * *

SKINNER, Rulon Dean   1931-

PERSONAL: Born June 26, 1931, in Safford, Ariz.; son of Rulon Moroni (a farmer) and Violet (Whipple) Skinner; married Margaret Ruth Walters, February 23, 1956; children: Kumen Dean, Diane Hazel, Susan Violet, Maria Ruth. *Education:* Eastern Arizona Junior College, A.A., 1950; Brigham Young University, B.A., 1954, M.A., 1971. *Religion:* Church of Jesus Christ of the Latter-day Saints. *Home:* 1717 West 1460 North, Provo, Utah 84601. *Office:* Department of Youth Leadership, Brigham Young University, 221D Richards Bldg., Provo, Utah 84602.

CAREER: Boy Scouts of America, Provo, Utah, Utah National Parks Council district scout executive, 1954-62, assistant scout executive, 1962-69, national staff professional training executive, 1969—; Brigham Young University, Provo, instructor, 1969-72, assistant professor, 1972-75, associate professor of youth leadership, 1975—. Certified rifle instructor, 1965—. *Member:* American Camping Association (national director of instructor certification program, 1975—), National Rifle Association, Timpanogos Lions Club (Provo; president, 1970-71).

WRITINGS: That Scouting Spirit, Carlton Press, 1970; *Boy Scout Merit Badge Powwows Conducted in Selected Community Schools,* Brigham Young University Press, 1971; *Techniques of Outdoor Adventure* (camping workbook with answer booklet), Brigham Young University Publications, 1973, 2nd edition, 1974; *Community Relationships of Youth Agencies,* Brigham Young University Publications, 1973; *100 Youth Agencies and Organizations in the U.S.A.,* Brigham Young University Publications, 1974; *Cub Scouting Workbook,* Brigham Young Publications, 1974; *Youth Meetings, Activities, and Conferences,* Brigham Young University Publications, 1974; *Basic Canoeing Techniques,* Brigham Young University Publications, 1975.

WORK IN PROGRESS: Two books, *Utah Valley Trails* and *Youth Camp Administration and Program.*

* * *

SKVORECKY, Josef (Valcav)   1924-

PERSONAL: Surname pronounced *Shquor-et-skee;* born September 27, 1924, in Nachod, Czechoslovakia; son of Josef (a bank clerk) and Anna (Kurazova) Skvorecky; married Zdene Salivarova (a writer and publisher), March 31, 1958. *Education:* Charles University, Prague, Ph.D., 1951. *Politics:* Christian socialist. *Religion:* Roman Catholic. *Home:* 487 Sackville St., Toronto, Ontario, Canada M4X 1T6. *Office:* Erindale College, University of Toronto, 3599 Mississagua Rd., Clarkson, Ontario, Canada.

CAREER: Odeon Publishers, Prague, Czechoslovakia, editor, 1953-63; free-lance writer in Prague, 1963-69; University of Toronto, Erindale College, Clarkson, Ontario, special lecturer in English and Slavic drama, 1969-71, writer-in-residence, 1970-71, associate professor, 1971-75, professor of English, 1975—. *Military service:* Czechoslovak Army, 1951-53. *Member:* Authors Guild, PEN (acting chairman, Canadian Branch of PEN in Exile). *Awards, honors:* Literary Award of Czechoslovakian Writers Union, 1968.

WRITINGS: Zbabelci (novel), Ceskoslovensky spisovatel (Prague), 1958, 4th edition, Nase vojsko (Prague), 1968, translation by Jeanne Nemcova published as *The Cowards,* Grove, 1970; *Legenda Emoke* (novel; title means "The Legend of Emoke"), Ceskoslovensky spisovatel, 1963, 2nd edition, 1965; *Sedmiramenny svicen* (stories; title means "The Menorah"), Nase Vojsko, 1964, 2nd edition, 1965; *Napady ctenare detektivek* (essays; title means "Reading Detective Stories"), Ceskoslovensky spisovatel, 1965; *Ze zivota lepsi spolecnosti* (stories; title means "The Life of Better Society"), Mlada fronta (Prague), 1965; *Babylonsky pribeh* (stories; title means "A Babylonian Story"), Svovodne Slovo (Prague), 1965; *Smutek porucika Boruvka* (stories; title means "The Mournful Demeanor of Lieutenant Boruvka"), Mlada fronta, 1966; *Konec nylonoveho veku* (novel; title means "The End of the Nylon Age") Ceskoslovensky spisovatel, 1967; *O nich—o nas* (essays; title means "About Them Which is About Us") Kruh (Hradec Kralove), 1968; (with Evaldem Schormem) *Fararuv Konec* (novelization of filmscript by same title; title means "End of a Priest"), Kruh, 1969; *Lvice* (novel), Ceskoslovensky spisovatel, 1969, translation published as *Miss Silver's Past,* Grove, 1973; *Horkej svet; Povidky z let 1946-1967* (title means "The Bitter World: Selected Stories, 1947-1967), Odeon (Prague), 1969; *Tankovy Prapor* (novel; title means "The Tank Corps"), 68 Publishers (Toronto), 1971; *All the Bright Young Men and Women: A Personal History of the Czech Cinema,* translated from the original Czech by Michael Schonberg, Peter Martin Associates, 1971; *Mirakl* (novel; title means "The Miracle Play"), 68 Publishers, 1972; *Hrichy pro patery Knoxe* (novel; title means "Sins for Father Knox"), 68 Publishers, 1973; *Prima Sezona* (novel; title means "A Fine Season"), 68 Publishers, 1974; *Konec porucika Boruvka* (novel; title means "The End of Lieutenant Boruvka"), 68 Publishers, 1975.

Editor: *Selected Writings of Sinclair Lewis,* Odeon, 1964-69; *Collected Writings of Ernest Hemingway,* Odeon, 1965-69; *Three Times Hercule Poirot,* Odeon, 1965; (with P. L. Doruzka) *Tvar jazzu* (anthology; title means "The Face of Jazz"), Statni hudebni vydavatelstvi (Prague), Part 1, 1964, Part 2, 1966; (with Doruzka) *Jazzova inspirace* (poetry anthology; title means "The Jazz Inspiration"), Odeon, 1966; *Nachrichten aus der CSSR* (title means "News from Czechoslovakia"), translated from the original Czech by Vera Cerna and others, Suhrkamp Verlag (Frankfurt), 1968.

Films: "Zlocin v divci skole" (title means "Crime in a Girl's School"), 1966; "Zlocin v santanu" (title means "Crime in a Night Club"), 1968; "Konec farare" (title means "End of a Priest"), 1969; "Flirt se slecnou Stribrnou" (title means "Flirtations with Miss Silver"), 1969; "Sest cernych divek" (title means "Six Brunettes"), 1969. Also writer of scripts for television programs.

Translator of numerous books from English to Czech, including the works of Ray Bradbury, Henry James, Ernest Hemingway, William Faulkner, Raymond Chandler, and others. Writer of prefaces and introductions to Czech and Slovak editions of the works of Saul Bellow, Bernard Malamud, Stephen Crane, Rex Stout, Dorothy Sayers, Charles Dickens, Sinclair Lewis, and others.

WORK IN PROGRESS: Neuilly, a novella; *The Engineer of Human Souls,* a novel.

SIDELIGHTS: Skvorecky served as a member of the central committees of the Czeckoslovak Writers' Union and the Czechoslovak Film and Television Artists. In 1959, when his novel *The Cowards* was banned, he lost his post as editor of *Svetova Literatura.* He was also a disc jockey on Radio Prague with a show dedicated to swing music. Since immigrating to Canada, Skvorecky has been active as a book reviewer for the Czechoslovak Service of the Voice of America. *Avocational interests:* Film, jazz, American folklore.

* * *

SLACK, Charles W(illiam) 1929-

PERSONAL: Born January 2, 1929, in Orange, N.J.; son of Charles M. (a physicist) and Evelyn (Francis) Slack; married Josephine Ives, June, 1950 (divorced, 1969); married Eileen Newton (a superintendent of a training school), May 28, 1971; children: Frances T., Roma E., Gordon W. *Education:* Princeton University, B.A., 1950, M.A., 1952, Ph.D., 1954. *Home address:* P.O. Box 9486, Birmingham, Ala. 35215. *Office:* Office of Learning Resources, University of Alabama, Box 345, University Station, Birmingham, Ala. 35294.

CAREER: National Naval Medical Center, Bethesda, Md., visiting scientist at Naval Medical Research Institute, 1953-54; Princeton University, Princeton, N.J., instructor in experimental psychology, 1954-55; Harvard University, Cambridge, Mass., assistant professor of clinical psychology and research associate at Laboratory of Social

Relations, 1955-60; University of Alabama, Tuscaloosa, research associate at Behavior Research and Development Center, 1960-61; Brooklyn College (now of the City University of New York), Brooklyn, N.Y., research associate, 1962-64; consultant on educational technology, educational, and professional evaluation to industry and government, 1964-67; Columbia University, Teachers College, New York, N.Y., lecturer in education, 1967-70, research associate at Institute for Educational Technology, 1967-68; University of Alabama, Birmingham, professor of research in education, 1970—, associate director of Office of Learning Resources, 1970-71, director of computer assisted self-assessment in medicine program, 1971—. Research associate with Jefferson County, Ala. Mental Health Association, 1960-61; adjunct professor of psychology at New York University, 1969-70.

MEMBER: Association of Educational Data Systems, American Association for the Advancement of Science, National Society for Performance and Instruction. *Awards, honors:* Ford Foundation fellowship, 1962-64; grants from Office of Naval Research, 1964-66, Foundation for Medical Education, 1972, and Merck Foundation, 1974.

WRITINGS: Word Pacers (English grammar for fourth, fifth, and sixth grades), Random House, 1971; *Timothy Leary, the Madness of the Sixties, and Me,* Wyden-McKay, 1973. Contributor to professional journals and to *Psychology Today.* Contributing editor, *Eye* (magazine), 1968-69.

SIDELIGHTS: Slack writes: "I am really a drop-out psychologist. I got disgusted with the field of psychology. Am now doing popular writing, educational materials, writing for computing medicine and other scientific/educational technologies."

* * *

SLADE, Caroline (Beach) 1886-1975

1886—June 25, 1975; American social worker, welfare executive, and novelist. Obituaries: *New York Times,* June 29, 1975.

* * *

SLAVET, Joseph S. 1920-

PERSONAL: Born March 31, 1920, in Boston, Mass.; son of Daniel (a salesman) and Anna (Knatcher) Slavet; married Muriel Vigor (a secretary), June 11, 1947; children: Amy M. (Mrs. Edward Glaser), Beth S., Julie. *Education:* Boston University, S.B. (with distinction), 1941, M.A., 1942; Syracuse University, M.S., 1949. *Politics:* Democrat. *Religion:* Hebrew. *Home:* 41 Lyall St., West Roxbury, Mass. 02132. *Office:* University of Massachusetts, Boston Harbor Campus, Dorchester, Mass. 02125.

CAREER: Boston Municipal Research Bureau, Boston, Mass., executive director, 1952-62; Action for Boston Community Development, Inc., Boston, Mass., executive director, 1962-66; Boston University, Boston, Mass., member of urban affairs faculty at Metropolitan College, 1967-72, director of Boston Urban Observatory, 1969-72; University of Massachusetts, Boston Harbor Campus, Dorchester, director of Boston Urban Observatory, 1972—. *Military service:* U.S. Army, 1942-45; served in European theater; received five battle stars. *Member:* Phi Beta Kappa.

WRITINGS: (With Melvin Levin) *Continuing Education,* Lexington Books, 1970; (with Levin and Jerome Rose)

New Approaches to State Land-Use, Lexington Books, 1974; (with Katherine Bradbury and Philip Moss) State-Local Financing, Lexington Books, 1975.

* * *

SLOGGATT, Arthur H(astings) 1917(?)-1975

1917(?)—August 6, 1975; American editorial cartoonist. Obituaries: New York Times, August 12, 1975.

* * *

SLOSSON, Preston (William) 1892-

PERSONAL: Born September 2, 1892, in Laramie, Wyo.; son of Edwin Emory (a journalist and chemist) and May (Preston) Slosson; married Lucy Denny Wright, June 21, 1927 (died, 1974); children: Flora May (Mrs. Wilhelm Wuellner), Edith Denny (Mrs. Ivan Aron); (stepdaughters) Lucy Chase (Mrs. Jim Bob Stephenson), Mary Elizabeth (Mrs. George Fearnehough). Education: Columbia University, B.S., 1912, M.A., 1913, Ph.D., 1916. Religion: Congregationalist. Home: 1401 South State St., Ann Arbor, Mich. 48104.

CAREER: New York Independent, New York, N.Y., junior editor, 1917; U.S. Department of State, Washington, D.C., assistant in New York City, 1917-18; American Commission to Negotiate Peace, Paris, France, assistant librarian, 1918-19; New York Independent, literary editor, 1920-21; University of Michigan, Ann Arbor, instructor, 1921-23, assistant professor, 1923-27, associate professor, 1927-37, professor of history, 1937-62, professor emeritus, 1962—. Distinguished professor at Kansas State University, 1960; Carnegie Foundation visiting professor at Universities of Bristol, Manchester, and Glasgow, 1932-33, and Universities of Bristol, Sheffield, and Aberystwyth, 1938-39; also taught at Baldwin-Wallace College, Columbia University, University of Minnesota, University of Wyoming, University of North Carolina at Greensboro and University of South Carolina. Haynes fellow at Redlands University, 1954-55. Broadcaster on current events for WWJ-Radio, 1941-45. Democratic candidate for U.S. House of Representatives, 1948; member of Washtenaw County Committee.

MEMBER: American Historical Association, American Association of University Professors, American Civil Liberties Union, Atlantic Union, United World Federalists, Research Club (University of Michigan), Phi Beta Kappa. Awards, honors: LL.D. from Hillsdale College, 1944.

WRITINGS: Fated Or Free?: A Dialogue on Destiny, Sherman, French, 1914; Peace with Honor (pamphlet), New York Independent, 1915; The Decline of the Chartist Movement, Columbia University Press, 1916, International Scholastic Book Service, 1967; Twentieth Century Europe (edited by J. T. Shotwell), Houghton, 1927; The Problems of Austro-German Union, Carnegie Endowment for International Peace, 1929; America and the Anschluss Question (pamphlet), Braumiller, 1930; (editor and contributor) Edwin E. Slosson, A Number of Things, Harcourt, 1930; The Great Crusade and After, 1914-1928: A History of American Life, Macmillan, 1930, F. Watts, 1971; Europe Since 1870, Houghton, 1935; (with Arthur E. R. Boak and Albert Hyma) The Growth of European Civilization, Crofts, 1938.

War Returns to the World, 1938-41, F. S. Crofts & Co., 1941; Why We Are at War, Houghton, 1942; (with Boak and H. R. Anderson) World History, Houghton, 1942, revised edition (with Boak, Anderson, and Bartlett) published as The History of Our World, Houghton, 1959; (with Robert B. Mowat) History of the English-Speaking Peoples, Oxford University Press, 1943; After the War—What?, Houghton, 1943, revised edition, 1945; Swords of Peace: Problems of Disarmament, Foreign Policy Association, 1947; (with wife, Lucy Slosson) From Washington to Roosevelt, Ginn, 1949; Europe Since 1815, Scribner, 1954; A Teacher's Report Card, Wahr, 1975. Contributor of several hundred articles and reviews to history journals and newspapers.

WORK IN PROGRESS: Pitt and Fox, for Barron's; Bright and Cobden, also for Barron's.

AVOCATIONAL INTERESTS: International government.

* * *

SLOTE, Michael A(nthony) 1941-

PERSONAL: Born April 30, 1941, in New York, N.Y.; son of Edwin M. (an attorney) and Tisha (Kunst) Slote; married Jenny Reed (a school administrator), September 24, 1967; children: Cressida, Nathaniel. Education: Harvard University, A.B., 1961, Ph.D., 1965. Home: 55 East 76th St., New York, N.Y. 10021. Office: Department of Philosophy, State University of New York, Stony Brook, N.Y. 11790.

CAREER: Columbia University, New York, N.Y., assistant professor of philosophy, 1965-70; State University of New York at Stony Brook, associate professor of philosophy, 1970—. Member: American Philosophical Association (Eastern Division), Society for Philosophy and Public Affairs.

WRITINGS: Reason and Scepticism, Allen & Unwin, 1970; Metaphysics and Essence, Basil Blackwell, 1975. Contributor to philosophy journals.

WORK IN PROGRESS: Research on causality and law, ethics and rationality, the nature of thinghood, paradoxes of hope and fear.

* * *

SLOTE, Stanley J(ames) 1917-

PERSONAL: Born June 17, 1917, in New York, N.Y.; son of Benjamin William (a lawyer and builder) and Muriel (Lerner) Slote; married Margaret Larson (an executive assistant), June 21, 1946 (divorced, 1975); children: Audray (Mrs. Richard Tirendi), Patricia Ann, Jonathan Allan. Education: Cornell University, B.A., 1939; Rutgers University, M.L.S., 1964, Ph.D., 1969. Politics: Independent Republican. Religion: "Jewish-Christian." Home: 2 Old Mamaroneck Rd., Apt. 5A, White Plains, N.Y. 10605. Office: Community Facilities Building, Queens College of the City University of New York, Flushing, N.Y. 11368.

CAREER: Crossway Construction Co., Inc., White Plains, N.Y., president, 1946-63; consultant in business and librarianship, 1963–; Queens College of the City University of New York, Flushing, N.Y., assistant professor of library science, 1971—. Member of Westchester County Rent Guidelines Board; trustee of White Plains Public Library and Westchester County Library System. President of Crossway Motor Hotels, Inc., 1946-63; former president of Builders Institute of Westchester. Military service: U.S. Navy, 1942-46; became lieutenant senior grade. Member: American Library Association, Special Library Association, New York State Library Association, Beta Phi Mu.

WRITINGS: Weeding Library Collections: Research Studies in Library Science, Libraries Unlimited, 1975. Contributor to library journals. Editor of *De-Acquisition Librarian.*

WORK IN PROGRESS: Managing Libraries; research on a system of weeding libraries.

SIDELIGHTS: Slote writes: "I am an iconoclast in many ways. I believe that computers are a waste of time and money ninety-five percent of the time. I believe that government should be honest and efficient, and that more basic research should be done in education so that its goals can be established." *Avocational interests:* Tennis, reading, travel (Cuba, Mexico, South America, Europe, Africa, Far East).

*   *   *

SMALL, Dwight Hervey 1919-

PERSONAL: Born March 1, 1919, in Oakland, Calif.; son of Benjamin (an engineer and salesman) and Ragnhild (Ostrom) Small; married Ruth Ida Elizabeth Stone, June 13, 1942; children: Lynne Tahmisian, Sharon Cudworth. *Education:* University of California, Berkeley, B.A., 1940; San Francisco Theological Seminary, M.Div., 1943. *Home:* 142 La Vista Grande, Santa Barbara, Calif. 93108. *Office:* Department of Sociology, Westmont College, 955 La Paz Rd., Santa Barbara, Calif. 93108.

CAREER: Ordained Presbyterian minister, 1943; pastor of Presbyterian churches in Fresno, Calif., San Jose, Calif., Philadelphia, Pa., and Chicago, Ill., 1943-60; ordained minister of the Evangelical Covenant Church of the United States, 1960; pastor of Evangelical Covenant church in Redwood City, Calif., 1960-70; Westmont College, Santa Barbara, Calif., assistant professor, 1970-75, associate professor of sociology, 1975—.

WRITINGS: Design for Christian Marriage, Revell, 1958; *The Biblical Basis for Infant Baptism,* Revell, 1959; *The High Cost of Holy Living,* Revell, 1964; *After You've Said I Do,* Revell, 1968; *Christian, Celebrate Your Sexuality,* Revell, 1974; *The Right to Remarry,* Revell, 1975. Contributor to religious periodicals.

WORK IN PROGRESS: It's a Single's World; Sociology for Pastoral Counselors.

SIDELIGHTS: Small writes: "The majority of my writing over twenty-five years, has to do with the Christian perspective on marriage and sexuality. *Christian, Celebrate Your Sexuality* is recognized as one of the first attempts by an American writer to produce a theology of sexuality from the perspective of conservative Protestantism."

*   *   *

SMART, Mollie S(tevens) 1916-

PERSONAL: Born April 11, 1916, in Chatham, Ontario, Canada; came to United States in 1936, naturalized in 1942; daughter of Stanley Starr and Mildred (MacLean) Stevens; married Russell Cook Smart, August 9, 1939; children: Susan (Mrs. Jack Smith), Ellen, Laura. *Education:* University of Toronto, A.B., 1936; graduate study at Merrill-Palmer Institute, 1936-37; University of Michigan, M.A., 1941; University of Delhi, Ph.D., 1969. *Home:* 10 Bayberry Rd., Kingston, R.I. 02881.

CAREER: Merrill-Palmer Institute, Detroit, Mich., staff member in psychology department, 1937-41; Consultation Bureau, Detroit, Mich., clinical psychologist, 1941-42;

Cornell University, Ithaca, N.Y., lecturer in child development and family relations, 1945-50; University of Rhode Island, Kingston, associate professor, 1953-73, professor, 1973-74, adjunct professor of child development and family relations, 1974-75, professor emerita, 1976—. Fulbright research scholar at University of Delhi, 1966-67, and Massey University, 1971-72; visiting professor at University of Guelph, 1974-75. Consultant and director of teacher training courses for Head Start, U.S. Office of Economic Opportunity, 1965-66; co-ordinator of College-Year-In-India Program, University of Wisconsin, 1967-68. *Member:* American Psychological Association, Society for Research in Child Development (fellow), National Council on Family Relations, Groves Conference, Phi Kappa Phi.

WRITINGS: (With L. R. Schulz) *Understanding Your Baby,* Sun Dial, 1941; (with husband, R. C. Smart) *It's a Wise Parent,* Scribner, 1944; (with R. C. Smart) *Living and Learning with Children,* Houghton, 1949; *Babe in a House,* Scribner, 1950; (with R. C. Smart) *An Introduction to Family Relationships,* Saunders, 1953; (editor) *Mothers' Encyclopedia,* Parents' Institute, 1965; (with R. C. Smart) *Living in Families,* Houghton, 1958, 2nd edition, 1965; (with R. C. Smart) *Children: Development and Relationships,* Macmillan, 1967, 3rd edition, in press; *Readings in Child Development and Relationships,* Macmillan, 1972, 2nd edition, in press; (with R. C. Smart) *Infants: Development and Relationships,* Macmillan, 1973; (with R. C. Smart) *Preschool Children: Development and Relationships,* Macmillan, 1973; (with R. C. Smart) *School-Age Children: Development and Relationships,* Macmillan, 1973; (with R. C. Smart) *Adolescents: Development and Relationships,* Macmillan, 1973; (with daughter, Laura Smart Szwed) *Families: Developing Relationships,* Macmillan, 1976.

Author of discussion guides for *Parents' Magazine,* 1949-66, and of homemaker's bulletins for Cornell University, 1946-50, and University of Rhode Island, 1953-54. Contributor to *Baby Talk, Parents' Magazine, Childhood Education,* and to professional journals.

*   *   *

SMITH, Allen William 1938-

PERSONAL: Born March 2, 1938, in Tipton County, Ind.; son of Leon W. (a farmer) and Inez (Wiley) Smith; married Deanna Reynolds, June 12, 1965; children: Mark Allen, Michael William, Lisa Ann. *Education:* Ball State University, B.S., 1964; Indiana University, Bloomington, M.A., 1967, Ph.D., 1970. *Religion:* United Methodist. *Home:* R.R. #4, Charleston, Ill. 61920. *Office:* Department of Economics, Eastern Illinois University, Charleston, Ill. 61920.

CAREER: High school social science teacher in Blackford County, Ind., 1964-66; Eastern Illinois University, Charleston, assistant professor of economics, 1970—. *Member:* American Economic Association, American Association of University Professors.

WRITINGS: Indiana Public Schools: Unionism and Collective Negotiations, Graduate School of Business, Indiana University, 1971; *Understanding Inflation and Unemployment,* Nelson-Hall, 1976. Contributor to *Phi Delta Kappan* and *School and Community.*

*   *   *

SMITH, C(harles) W(illiam) 1940-

PERSONAL: Born March 28, 1940, in Corpus Christi,

Tex.; son of William L. (a gas engineer) and Helen (Gibson) Smith; married Gay Parrish (a television producer and reporter), January 28, 1962; children: Morgan and Holly (twins). *Education:* North Texas State University, B.A., 1964; Northern Illinois University, M.A., 1966. *Residence:* Indianapolis, Ind. *Agent:* Elaine Markson, 44 Greenwich Ave., New York, N.Y. 10011.

CAREER: Southwest Missouri State University, Springfield, instructor in English, 1965-68; writer, 1968-70; Drury College, Springfield, Mo., instructor in English, 1970; writer, 1971-74. *Awards, honors:* Award for "most enjoyable and significant work of fiction which contributed to an understanding of the Southwest" from Southwestern Library Association, and Jesse H. Jones Award from Texas Institute of Letters, both 1974, both for *Thin Men of Haddam;* Dobie-Paisano fellowship from Texas, 1974-75.

WRITINGS: Thin Men of Haddam (novel), Grossman, 1974; *Country Music* (novel), Farrar, Straus, 1975. Author of screenplay, "Country Music." Contributor of stories to *Mademoiselle* and *Focus: Media* and of articles to scholarly journals.

WORK IN PROGRESS: A third novel; *Letters from the Horse Latitudes,* a collection of stories.

SIDELIGHTS: Smith writes: "I enjoy hearing people tell their histories and watching them grow. Or change. Novels I enjoy reading are those which incorporate and crystallize that interest, and that notion forms the core of my own work. Of specific interest to me is the human capacity for self-deception, for living with illusions and finding ways to be oblivious to time." *Avocational interests:* Classical guitar, repairing furniture.

* * *

SMITH, Dennis 1940-

PERSONAL: Born September 9, 1940, in New York, N.Y.; son of John and Mary (Harrigan) Smith; married Patricia Kearney, August 24, 1963; children: Brendan Kearney, Dennis Emmet, Sean Patrick. *Education:* New York University, B.A., 1970, M.A., 1972. *Politics:* Democrat. *Religion:* Roman Catholic. *Residence:* Garrison, N.Y. *Address: Firehouse* Magazine, 4 West 57th St., New York, N.Y. 10019.

CAREER: New York City Fire Department, New York, N.Y., fireman, 1963—. Member of board of trustees of Kips Bay Boys Club, 1972—. *Military service:* U.S. Air Force, 1957-60.

WRITINGS: Report from Engine Co. 82 (Book-of-the-Month Club selection), Saturday Review Press, 1972; *The Final Fire,* (Book-of-the-Month Club selection), Saturday Review Press, 1975. Contributor to *True, Reader's Digest,* and other periodicals. Editor of *Firehouse,* 1975—.

SIDELIGHTS: Smith was assigned to Engine Co. 82, the busiest unit in the New York City Fire Department, by his own request. Statistically, he is in the most dangerous profession in the United States.

BIOGRAPHICAL/CRITICAL SOURCES: Time, February 28, 1972; *New York,* March 20, 1972.

* * *

SMITH, Elliott Dunlap 1890(?)-1976

1890(?)—January 26, 1976; American lawyer, educator, university official, and author of books on human relations and aging. Obituaries: *New York Times,* January 28, 1976.

SMITH, Hale G(illiam) 1918-

PERSONAL: Born July 24, 1918, in Jacksonville, Ill.; son of Sidney Lee and Nina (Hale) Smith; married Carolyn Jane Inman, February 14, 1952; children: Robin May, Kevin, Pamela. *Education:* Beloit College, B.A., 1940; University of Chicago, M.A., 1945; University of Michigan, Ph.D., 1951. *Home:* 120 White Dr., Tallahassee, Fla. 32306. *Office:* Department of Anthropology, G-24 Bellamy Bldg., Florida State University, Tallahassee, Fla. 32306.

CAREER: Assistant archaeologist for Florida Park Service, 1946-48; Florida State University, Tallahassee, professor of anthropology, 1949—, head of department, and director of University Museum, 1949-72. Has done archaeological excavations and research in Florida, Puerto Rico, Panama, and Canal Zone, 1958-67. Research consultant in Quito, Ecuador; Popayan, Colombia; and in Canal Zone and Panama.

MEMBER: American Anthropological Association (fellow), Society for American Archaeology, Grupo Guama de Cuba (honorary member), Museo Nacional de Cuba (honorary member), Southeastern Anthropological Society, Florida Anthropological Society, St. Augustine Historical Society, Sigma Xi. *Awards, honors:* National Park Service research grant, 1961, 1973-76.

WRITINGS: The Extension of History through Archaeology, Florida Park Service, 1947; *Two Archaeological Sites in Brevard County, Florida,* University of Florida for Florida Anthropological Society, 1949; *The Crable Site, Fulton County, Ill.: A Late Prehistoric Site in the Central Illinois Valley,* University of Michigan Press, 1951; (with others) *Here They Once Stood,* University of Florida Press, 1952; *Tallahassee,* [Tallahassee, Fla.], 1955; *The European and the Indian: European-Indian Contacts in Georgia and Florida,* Florida Anthropological Society, 1956; *Archaeological Excavation at El Morro, San Juan, Puerto Rico, with Historical Background Sections by Ricardo Torres Reyes,* Florida State University Department of Anthropology, 1962; *Archaeological Excavations at Santa Rosa, Pensacola,* Florida State University, 1965.

Contributor: *Contributions to the Archaeology of Florida,* Volume I, Florida Park Service, 1948; *Patrimonio Cultural, Preservacion de Monumentos* (title means "Cultural Properties, Preservation of Monuments"), Division de Relaciones Culturales, 1966; William Sturtevant, editor, *Handbook of North American Indians,* Smithsonian Institution Press, 1976. Also contributor to *Keeping Pace with Progress,* 1958, and to Eastern States Archaeological Federation bulletins.

Contributor of articles to *American Antiquity, Florida Historical Quarterly, Florida Anthropologist,* and other journals in his field. *Notes in Anthropology,* founder, 1949, editor, 1952-53, and contributor.

WORK IN PROGRESS: Research in Tallahassee for *Ethno-Botanical and Entomology-Archaeology in Prehistoric and Historic Sites.*

* * *

SMITH, Huston (Cummings) 1919-

PERSONAL: Born May 31, 1919, in Soochow, China; son of Wesley Moreland and Alice (Longden) Smith; married Eleanor Brunhilda Wieman, September 15, 1943; children: Karen, Gael, Robin, Kimberly. *Education:* Central Methodist College, A.B., 1940; graduate study at University of California, Berkeley, 1944-45; University of Chicago,

Ph.D., 1945. *Home:* 887 Salt Springs Rd., Syracuse, N.Y. 13224. *Office:* Department of Religion, Syracuse University, Syracuse, N.Y. 13210.

CAREER: University of Denver, Denver, Colo., assistant professor of philosophy, 1945-47; Washington University, St. Louis, Mo., associate professor of philosophy, 1947-58; Massachusetts Institute of Technology, Cambridge, professor of philosophy, 1958-73; Syracuse University, Syracuse, N.Y., professor of religion, 1973—. Visiting lecturer, University of Colorado, 1944, 1947; visiting professor, Iliff School of Theology, 1947; Charles Strong Lecturer on World Religions to universities in Australia, 1961.

MEMBER: World University Service (chairman of American committee, 1966-70), American Philosophical Association, Society for Religion in Higher Education (fellow), Phi Beta Kappa. *Awards, honors:* D.Hum., Central Methodist College, 1958; D.Let., Concord College, 1961; L.H.D., Franklin College of Indiana, 1964; Sc.D., Lake Forest College, 1965; LL.D., MacMurray College, 1967.

WRITINGS: The Purposes of Higher Education, Harper, 1955; *The Religions of Man,* Harper, 1958; *The Search for America,* Prentice-Hall, 1959; *Condemned to Meaning,* Harper, 1964; (with others) *Great Religions of the World,* National Geographic Society, 1971; *Forgotten Truth: The Primordial Tradition,* Harper, 1976.

*   *   *

SMITH, Joan 1935-

PERSONAL: Born May 6, 1935, in Chicago, Ill.; daughter of Hugh J. and Alice (Kelley) Heaney; children: Beth, Mary, Bill, John, Pancho. *Education:* Roosevelt University, B.A., 1967; Illinois Institute of Technology, M.S., 1969; New York University, Ph.D., 1970. *Politics:* Socialist. *Religion:* Roman Catholic. *Office:* Department of Sociology, Dartmouth College, Hanover, N.H. 03755.

CAREER: Researcher for International Business Machines (IBM), Armonk, N.Y.; former member of faculty at Queens College of the City University of New York, Queens, N.Y.; currently on the faculty of Dartmouth College, Hanover, N.H.

WRITINGS: (With William Fried) *Uses of the American Prison,* Heath, 1974.

WORK IN PROGRESS: Women and the Working Class.

*   *   *

SMITH, Julian 1937-

PERSONAL: Born December 14, 1937, in New Orleans, La.; son of Julian Henry, Jr. and Winifred (Riggs) Smith; married Monica Pontzen, March 16, 1964; children: Una, Christian, Joshua. *Education:* Tulane University, B.A., 1959; graduate study at Columbia University, 1959-60, and Tulane University, 1960-62. *Politics:* "Suitably confused." *Home:* Woodman Barn, Packers Falls Rd., Durham, N.H. 03824.

CAREER: Spring Hill College, Mobile, Ala., instructor in English, 1962-63; Georgetown University, Washington, D.C., instructor in American literature, 1963-65; University of New Hampshire, Durham, instructor in American literature, 1965-69; Ithaca College, Ithaca, N.Y., assistant professor of American literature, 1969-73; University of New Hampshire, honorary fellow, 1973-75; San Diego State University, San Diego, Calif., lecturer, 1975-76. *Member:* American Film Institute, Modern Language As-

sociation of America. *Awards, honors:* Woodrow Wilson fellow, 1959-60; National Endowment for the Humanities research grant, 1970.

WRITINGS: Looking Away: Hollywood and Vietnam, Scribner, 1975; *Nevil Shute,* Twayne, 1976. Contributor to journals in his field.

WORK IN PROGRESS: CL-TEN: The First Cousin, Once Removed, of the Man Who Shot Huey Long, a novel.

SIDELIGHTS: Smith writes that he "was to be a lawyer, but fell into bad company and started reading novels." *Avocational interests:* Building houses.

*   *   *

SMITH, Karl U(lrich) 1907-

PERSONAL: Born May 1, 1907, in Zanesville, Ohio; son of Harry Howard (a trainmaster) and Katherine (Hoobing) Smith; married Sarah Margaret Foltz, August 3, 1937; children: Thomas Jay, Eric Alan, Joanna Margaret, Sarah Louise, Nicholas Ulrich. *Education:* Attended Ohio University, 1926-27; Miami University, Oxford, Ohio, B.A., 1931; Brown University, M.A., 1933, Ph.D., 1936. *Politics:* Independent Democrat. *Home:* 1915 Arlington Pl., Madison, Wis. 53705. *Office:* Behavioral Cybernetics Laboratory, University of Wisconsin, 918 Conklin Ct., Madison, Wis. 53706.

CAREER: Brown University, Providence, R.I., instructor in psychology, 1935-36; University of Rochester, Rochester, N.Y., instructor, 1936-38, assistant professor of psychology, 1938-43; National Defense Research Council, Washington, D.C., assistant director of a research project at Camp Murphy, Fla., contracted by Yale University, 1943-44, director of a project at Orlando Army Air Forces Tactical Center, Orlando, Fla. and Research Division of Laredo Army Air Field, Laredo, Tex., contracted by University of Wisconsin, 1944, director of University of Wisconsin project at Laredo Army Air Field, 1945; University of Wisconsin, Madison, assistant professor, 1945-47, associate professor, 1947-49, professor of psychology, 1949—, director of Bureau of Industrial Psychology, 1945-47, director of Behavioral Cybernetics Laboratory, 1964—, director of Independent House Learning Center and Social Cybernetics Laboratory, 1967—. Ford Foundation Distinguished Professor of Business Administration at Indiana University, 1960, 1961; distinguished visiting professor at University of South Dakota, 1972, and University of Trondheim, 1974. Director of training programs for National Institute of Mental Health, 1959-75; consultant in cybernetics.

MEMBER: Society for Experimental Psychology, American Association for the Advancement of Science (fellow), American Physiological Society, Phi Beta Kappa. *Awards, honors:* Citation from U.S. Army and Navy, 1945, for National Defense Research Council work during World War II; National Institutes of Health grants, 1958-75; Ford Foundation grant, 1959-63; National Science Foundation grants, 1959—; research prize from Television, Inc., 1961.

WRITINGS: (With W. M. Smith) *The Behavior of Man,* with workbook (with William M. Smith and Janet Hansche), teacher's manual, and test manual, Holt, 1958; *Behavior Organization and Work: A New Approach to Industrial Behavioral Science,* College Printing & Typing, 1962, 3rd edition, 1975; (with W. M. Smith) *Perception and Motion: An Analysis of Space-Structured Behavior,* Saunders, 1962; *Delayed Sensory Feedback and Behavior,*

Saunders, 1962; *Work Theory and Economic Behavior* (monograph), Bureau of Business Research, Indiana University, 1962; (with M. F. Smith) *Cybernetic Principles of Learning and Educational Design,* with instructor's manual and student manual, Holt, 1966; *Review of Principles of Human Factors in Design of the Exoskeleton and Four-Legged Pedipulator,* Behavioral Cybernetics Laboratory, University of Wisconsin, Madison, 1966; *The Human Social Yoke: The Educational Bond Between Parent and Child,* Parker Pen Co., 1968; (with T. J. Smith) *Educational Feedback Designs,* George Rainey Harper College, 1968; *Outlook for Development and Application of Behavioral Cybernetics and Educational Feedback Designs in Instructional Technology* (pamphlet), Federal Commission on Instructional Technology, 1968; *New Horizons of Research in Physical Behavior Science and Rehabilitation: Dynamic Feedback Designs in Learning and Training* (pamphlet), National Association of Physical Education of College Women, 1968.

(with Charles Hagberg) *Self-Governed Behavioral Safety Codes for Industry: Management Feedback Control of Accident Prevention in the Work Place* (pamphlet), Department of Industry and Human Relations, Safety Division, State of Wisconsin, and Behavioral Cybernetics Laboratory, University of Wisconsin, Madison, 1970; *Real-Time Computer Analysis of Body Motions: Systems Feedback Analysis and Techniques in Rehabilitation,* Social and Rehabilitation Administration, 1971; (with Larry Schiamberg) *The Infraschool: A Positive Approach to Parent Education for Early Childhood Development,* Behavioral Cybernetics Laboratory, University of Wisconsin, Madison, 1973; *Lectures in Cybernetic Psychology,* Behavioral Cybernetics Laboratory, University of Wisconsin, Madison, 1973; *Ethnic Science: The Alternatives to Academic Racism and Jensenism* (monograph), Behavioral Cybernetics Laboratory, University of Wisconsin, Madison, 1973; *Civil Rights and Psychological Testing: The Psychometric Foundations of Academic Racism* (monograph), Behavioral Cybernetics Laboratory, University of Wisconsin, Madison, 1973; (with M. F. Smith) *Psychology: Introduction to Behavior Science,* with instructor's manual, Little, Brown, 1973; *Industrial Social Cybernetics,* Behavioral Cybernetics Laboratory, University of Wisconsin, Madison, 1975.

Contributor: Leon Arons and Mark May, editors, *Television and Human Behavior,* Appleton, 1962; Virgil Herrick, editor, *New Horizons of Handwriting Research,* University of Wisconsin Press, 1963; Edward A. Bilodeau, editor, *Acquisition of Skill,* Academic Press, 1966; E. A. Bilodeau and Ina Bilodeau, editors, *Principles of Skill Acquisition,* Academic Press, 1969.

Charles Wedemeyer, editor, *Report of the William Kellet Commission on Education and the Open School,* Governor's Commission on Education, 1970; Leon Smith, editor, *Motor Skill and Learning,* Athletic Institute, 1970; I. E. Asmussen, editor, *Psychological Aspects of Driver Behavior,* Volume I: *Driver Behavior: NATO Symposium on Psychological Aspects of Driver Behavior,* Institute of Road Safety Research (Voorburg, Netherlands), 1971; R. N. Singer, editor, *The Psychomotor Domain,* Lea & Febiger, 1972; Joanne T. Widner, editor, *Selected Readings in Safety,* Academy Press (Macon, Ga.), 1973; Jack Maser, editor, *Efferent Organization and the Integration of Behavior,* Academic Press, 1973; Henry Gemeinder, editor, *Conference on Defining and Developing a Model Worker*

Compensation Statistics Program, Department of Labor, Industry, and Human Relations, State of Wisconsin, 1974.

Gemeinder, editor, *Bureau of Research and Statistics Issue Reports on Industrial Safety and Worker Compensation,* Department of Labor, Industry, and Human Relations, State of Wisconsin, 1975; Gemeinder, editor, *Interservice Conference on New Systems Approaches to Risk Management of Worker's Compensation and Industrial Safety and Health Concepts and Practices,* Numbers 1-16, Bureau of Research and Statistics, Department of Labor, Industry, and Human Relations, State of Wisconsin, 1975.

Also writer of more than ten scientific films. Contributor to *McGraw Hill Encyclopedia of Science and Technology.* Contributor of more than two hundred articles to research journals in his field.

WORK IN PROGRESS: Research on behavioral cybernetics, feedback mechanisms of eye movement and vision, and other areas in his field.

* * *

SMITH, M(ahlon) Brewster   1919-

PERSONAL: Born June 26, 1919, in Syracuse, N.Y.; son of Mahlon Ellwood (an educator) and Blanche Alice (Hinman) Smith; married Deborah Anderson (a public health nurse), June 21, 1947; children: Joshua Hinman, Toby Daniel, Rebecca Motte, Jeremy Torquil. *Education:* Reed College, student, 1935-38; Stanford University, B.A., 1939, M.A., 1940; Harvard University, Ph.D., 1947. *Politics:* Independent Democrat. *Religion:* None. *Home:* 316 Escalona Dr., Santa Cruz, Calif. 95060. *Office:* Stevenson College, University of California, Santa Cruz, Calif. 95064.

CAREER: U.S. Government, Office of the Coordinator of Information, Cambridge, Mass., junior analyst, 1941; Harvard University, Cambridge, Mass., assistant professor of social psychology, 1947-49; Vassar College, Poughkeepsie, N.Y., professor of psychology and chairman of department, 1949-52; Social Science Research Council, New York City, staff associate, 1952-56; New York University, New York City, professor of psychology, and director of graduate training in psychology, 1956-59; University of California, Berkeley, professor of psychology, 1959-68, director of Institute of Human Development, 1965-68; University of Chicago, Chicago, Ill., professor of psychology and chairman of department, 1968-70; University of California, Santa Cruz, professor of psychology, 1970—, vice-chancellor of social sciences, 1970-75. Fellow of Center for Advanced Study in the Behavioral Sciences (Stanford, Calif.), 1964-65. Vice-president of Joint Commission on Mental Illness and Health, 1955-61. Member of advisory committee on social science of National Science Foundation, 1966-70, chairman, 1968-70; member of psychology training review committee of National Institute of Mental Health, 1967-71, chairman, 1969-70, member of social science research review committee, 1972-76, chairman, 1973-76; member of board of directors of Bureau of Social Science Research, 1969—; member of board of directors of Social Science Research Council, 1970-74; member of national advisory council of Hogg Foundation for Mental Health, 1972-75. *Military service:* U.S. Army, Adjutant General's Department, 1942-46, research officer in Information and Education Division of War Department, 1943-46; became major; received Bronze Star Medal.

MEMBER: American Association for the Advancement of Science (fellow), American Psychological Association (member of board of directors, 1960-63, 1967-70, 1972-75),

American Sociological Association, Society for Research in Child Development, Society for the Psychological Study of Social Issues (president, 1958-59), Society for Experimental Social Psychology (member of executive committee, 1965-69), Phi Beta Kappa, Sigma Xi, Cosmos Club (Washington, D.C.). *Awards, honors:* Social Science Research Council fellowship, Harvard University, 1946-47; National Institute of Mental Health senior research fellowship, 1964-65; National Endowment for the Humanities fellowship, 1975-76.

WRITINGS: (With S. A. Stouffer and others) *The American Soldier,* Volume II: *Combat and Its Aftermath* (Smith was not associated with Volume I), Princeton University Press, 1949; (senior author, with J. S. Bruner and R. W. White) *Opinions and Personality,* Wiley, 1956; *Social Psychology and Human Values: Selected Essays,* Aldine, 1969; *Humanizing Social Psychology,* Jossey Bass, 1974. Contributor of more than a hundred fifty articles to psychology and related journals. Editor of *Journal of Social Issues,* 1951-55, and *Journal of Abnormal and Social Psychology,* 1956-61; advisory editor of *Journal of Youth and Adolescence,* 1973—, and *Ethos,* 1974—; member of editorial board, *Journal of Personality and Social Psychology,* 1976—.

WORK IN PROGRESS: The Psychology of Self (tentative title), publication by McGraw expected in 1977.

SIDELIGHTS: Smith writes: "My current writing is an attempt to bridge the gulf between 'humanistic' and 'scientific' psychology, communicating to fellow social scientists and (I hope) a broader literate public, a view of historically emerging human nature, appropriate to our present predicaments, that is neither transcendental nor mechanistic but suitably 'anthropomorphic.'"

* * *

SMITH, M. Estellie 1935-

PERSONAL: Born December 1, 1935, in Buffalo, N.Y.; daughter of O. Roy (a businessman) and Marietta C. Perry (a businesswoman; maiden name, Pereira) Smith; married Charles A. Bishop (an anthropologist), September 16, 1968. *Education:* University of Buffalo, B.A. (magna cum laude), 1962; State University of New York, Buffalo, M.A. (with honors), 1964, Ph.D. (with highest honors), 1967. *Politics:* Republican. *Religion:* Episcopalian. *Home:* 51 East Main St., Ontario, N.Y. 14519. *Office:* Department of Anthropology, State University of New York, Brockport, N.Y. 14420.

CAREER: Florida State University, Tallahassee, assistant professor of anthropology, 1966-69; Eastern New Mexico University, Portales, assistant professor of anthropology, 1969-70; State University of New York, Brockport, associate professor of anthropology, 1970—. Visiting professor at Southern Methodist University, 1970; adjunct professor at Texas Tech University, 1970; visiting lecturer at Erie Community College, 1973. Permanent research associate at Fort Burgwyn Research Center, 1968—; permanent research professor at Eastern New Mexico University, 1972—.

MEMBER: American Ethnological Society, American Anthropological Association (fellow), Ethnologica European (associate), Linguistic Society of America, Society for American Archeology, American Association for the Advancement of Science, Royal Anthropological Institute (fellow), Society for Applied Anthropology (fellow), Society for American Ethnohistory, Current Anthropology (associate), Northeast Anthropological Association, Southern

Anthropological Society, Phi Beta Kappa, Sigma Xi. *Awards, honors:* American Philosophical Society research grant, 1968; National Foundation in the Humanities and Arts fellow, 1968; Sigma Xi research grant, 1969, and grant-in-aid of research, 1974; National Science Foundation research grants, 1970 (two), and travel grant to Rome, Italy, 1972.

WRITINGS: Governing at Taos Pueblo (monograph), Eastern New Mexico University Press, 1969; (editor) *Studies in Linguistics: Papers in Honor of George L. Trager,* Mouton & Co., 1972; (contributor) Roger Wescott, Gordon Hewes, and William Stokoe, editors, *Language Origins,* American International Press, in press. Contributor to proceedings; contributor to anthropology journals. Founder and first editor of *Abstracts in Anthropology,* 1969-72, senior advisory editor, 1969-73; book review editor for *Urban Anthropology,* 1972—, and *Studies in European Society,* 1972-75; associate editor of *Political Anthropology Newsletter,* 1974—; member of editorial board of "Collins' Archaeological Series," New World segment, 1974—.

WORK IN PROGRESS: A study of socioeconomic change at Isleta Pueblo; editing *Those Who Live from the Sea;* studies in cultural change and stability in immigrant enclaves; Portuguese ethnic studies.

* * *

SMITH, Rex Alan 1921-

PERSONAL: Born May 15, 1921, in Bend, S.D.; son of John Henry (a rancher) and Mabel (Howard) Smith; married Ahda Schlemmer, April 21, 1946 (divorced January, 1974); children: Mary Chantry. *Home and office address:* P.O. Box 538, Fayetteville, Ark. 72701.

CAREER: New York Life Insurance Co., worked as agent; producer and moderator of weekly one-hour talk show on KGTO-Television, 1969-73; writer, 1973—. Director of First Federal Savings & Loan Association (Fayetteville). *Military service:* U.S. Army, Corps of Engineers, 1942-45. *Member:* American Society of Chartered Life Underwriters, American MENSA, Western History Association, Northwest Arkansas Estate Planning Council (president), South Dakota State Historical Society, Rotary International (Fayetteville).

WRITINGS: Straight Talk About Life Insurance Dividends (consumer booklet), Farnsworth Publishing, 1972; *Moon of Popping Trees,* Reader's Digest Press, 1975. Contributor to *Reader's Digest* and *Life Association News.*

WORK IN PROGRESS: Flash Flood (tentative title), the story of the Rapid City flood disaster of 1972.

SIDELIGHTS: Smith writes that he "was born and raised on a ranch in western South Dakota, an area in which my grandparents (and even my parents, almost) were pioneers. Therefore, from childhood was steeped in the flavor of the last true frontier in the continental United States. My friends and playmates were both non-Indian and Indian, just as the story of that frontier is the story of both Indians and non-Indians. Out of this grew a deep interest in the history of the area, and in the life and cultures of both the non-Indian settlers and of the Sioux Indians whom they displaced."

* * *

SMITH, Robert Kimmel 1930-
(Peter Marks)

PERSONAL: Born July 31, 1930, in Brooklyn, N.Y.; son

of Theodore (in civil service) and Sally (Kimmel) Smith; married Claire Medney (a literary agent), September 4, 1954; children: Heidi, Roger. *Education:* Attended Brooklyn College (now of the City University of New York), 1947-48. *Residence:* Brooklyn, N.Y. *Agent:* (Literary) Harold Ober Associates, 40 E. 49th St., New York, N.Y. 11226 (Television/plays) Lois Berman, WB Agency, 156 E. 52 St. New York, N.Y.

CAREER: Doyle, Dane, Bernbach (advertising), New York City, copywriter, 1957-61; Grey Advertising, New York City, copy chief, 1963-65; Smith & Toback (advertising), New York City, partner and writer, 1967-70; full-time writer, 1970—. *Military service:* U.S. Army, 1951-53. *Member:* Writer's Guild, Dramatists Guild, Leukemia Society of America, Eugene O'Neill Theatre Center, Eugene O'Neill Playwrights (co-chairman, 1974-75), Kayoodle Club (president, 1969), Knickerbocker Field Club. *Awards, honors:* Named Eugene O'Neill Playwright, 1971, for "A Little Singing, A Little Dancing."

WRITINGS: Ransom (novel), McKay, 1971; "A Little Singing, A Little Dancing" (play; produced at O'Neill Memorial Theatre, July, 1971; published as "A Little Dancing," in *Best Short Plays of 1975,* edited by Stanley Richards, Chilton, 1975); *Chocolate Fever* (juvenile), Coward, 1972; *Sadie Shapiro's Knitting Book* (novel), Simon & Schuster, 1973.

Contributor of short fiction to periodicals, writing under pseudonym Peter Marks prior to 1970.

WORK IN PROGRESS: A comedy series for CBS; another novel for Simon & Schuster; two film scripts.

SIDELIGHTS: Smith told *CA:* "In 1970, at the age of forty, I decided to give full-time writing a shot and haven't looked back since. I have been pleased to discover a comic, human side of myself and I plan to keep writing in this vein. I feel that dialogue is my strength, and plan to concentrate on plays, film, and television scripts—with the occasional novel thrown in if I'm lucky enough to have a good idea."

* * *

SMITH, Russell F. W. 1915(?)-1975

1915(?)—August 29, 1975; American educator, university official, short story writer, and author. Obituaries: *New York Times,* August 30, 1975.

* * *

SMITH, Vivian (Brian) 1933-

PERSONAL: Born June 3, 1933, in Hobart, Tasmania, Australia; son of Vivian and Sibyl (Daniels) Smith; married Sybille Gottwald, February 15, 1960; children: Vanessa, Gabrielle, Nicholas. *Education:* University of Tasmania, M.A., 1956; University of Sydney, Ph.D., 1971. *Home:* 19 McLeod St., Mosman, New South Wales 2088, Australia.

CAREER: University of Tasmania, Hobart, lecturer in French, 1955-67; University of Sydney, Sydney, Australia, lecturer, 1967-74, senior lecturer in English, 1974—; poet. *Member:* Poetry Society of Australia, Australian Society of Authors.

WRITINGS: The Other Meaning (poems), Edwards & Shaw, 1956; *James McAuley,* Lansdowne Press, 1965; *An Island South,* Angus & Robertson, 1967; *Les Vige en Australie* (juvenile; title means "The Vige Family in Australia"), Longmans, Green (Melbourne), 1967; (editor) *Australian Poetry,* Angus & Robertson, 1969; *The Poetry of*

Robert Lowell, University of Sydney Press, 1974; *Vance and Nettie Palmer,* Twayne, 1975.

Poems anthologized in *Young Commonwealth Poets '65,* edited by Howard Sergeant, Heinemann, 1965; *Modern Australian Writing,* edited by G. P. Dutton, Fontana, 1966; *Commonwealth Poems of Today,* edited by Sergeant, John Murray, 1967; *Modern Australian Poetry,* edited by David Campbell, Sun Books, 1974; *A Map of Australian Verse,* edited by James McAuley, Oxford University Press, 1975. Contributor to Australian newspapers and literary journals.

WORK IN PROGRESS: An edition of the selected letters of Vance and Nettie Palmer.

AVOCATIONAL INTERESTS: Translating from French and German.

* * *

SMYSER, Jane Worthington 1914-1975

August 1, 1914—October 1, 1975; American educator, editor, and author of works on English literature. Obituaries: *New York Times,* October 2, 1975; *AB Bookman's Weekly,* December 1, 1975.

* * *

SMYTH, David 1929-

PERSONAL: Born February 7, 1929, in Buenos Aires, Argentina; son of Currell Hutchinson (a manager) and Jessie (Dodds) Smyth; married Elli Helene Dusterhoft (a nurse), November 9, 1968; children: Clifford Dieter. *Education:* Cambridge University, M.A., 1951. *Politics:* Independent. *Religion:* "Protestant agnostic." *Home:* 23 Lake Ave., Metuchen, N.J. *Agent:* Arthur Pine, 1780 Broadway, New York, N.Y. 10019. *Office:* Associated Press, 50 Rockefeller Center, New York, N.Y. 10020.

CAREER: Associated Press, New York, N.Y., Latin American news editor, 1963-72, financial editor, 1973—. *Military service:* Argentine Army, 1952. *Member:* New York Financial Writers Association.

WRITINGS: The Speculator's Handbook, Regnery, 1974. Contributor of articles to *Nation* and *Freeman.*

WORK IN PROGRESS: A book tentatively titled *Your Financial Survival,* for Regnery.

* * *

SMYTH, Howard McGaw 1901-1975

July 6, 1901—November 16, 1975; American historian, educator, editor, and author of books on foreign policy and related topics. Obituaries: *Washington Post,* November 17, 1975; *New York Times,* November 17, 1975.

* * *

SMYTH, John (George) 1893-

PERSONAL: Born October 24, 1893, in Teignmouth, England; son of W. J. Smyth (in Indian civil service); married Margaret Dundas, 1920; married Frances Read Chambers, 1940; children: (first marriage) three sons, one daughter. *Education:* Educated at Sandhurst Royal Military College. *Home:* 807 Nelson House, Dolphin Sq., London SW1V 3PA, England.

CAREER: British Army, regular officer, 1912-42, retiring as brigadier; newspaper correspondent, 1943-51; member of Parliament for Norwood Division of Lambeth, 1950-66; writer. Served in both World Wars and in seven Indian

Frontier campaigns, was instructor at Camberley Staff College, 1931-34, commander of infantry brigade in France and Belgium, 1940-41, commanded 17th Division in Burma at time of Japanese invasion. Parliamentary secretary in Ministry of Pensions, 1951-53, and in Ministry of Pensions and National Insurance, 1953-55. Governor, Queen Mary's Hospital, Roehampton, 1956-62; trustee of Far East Prisoners of War and Internee Fund, 1959-61; director, Creative Journals, 1957-63.

MEMBER: International Lawn Tennis Clubs of England, United States and France, Returned British Prisoners of War Association (honorary vice-president, 1960), Victoria Cross and George Cross Association (founder; first chairman, 1956-71; life president, 1966—), Not Forgotten Association (vice-president, 1956), Burma Star Association (president of South London branch, 1957—), Distinguished Conduct Medal League (vice-president, 1957; president, 1958-70), Freeman of City of London in Worshipful Company of Farriers, Dunkirk Veterans Association (vice-president, 1963—), Far Eastern Prisoners of War Federation (honorary vice-president, 1960), Old Reptonian Society (president, 1960-61), Queen's Club, All England Lawn Tennis Club, Carlton Club. *Awards, honors:* Victoria Cross, 1915; Russian Order of St. George; created first baronet, 1955; appointed privy councillor, 1962.

WRITINGS: Defence Is Our Business, Hutchinson, 1945; (editor and author of introduction) *The Western Defences,* Allan Wingate, 1951; *Lawn Tennis,* Batsford, 1953; *The Game's the Same: Lawn Tennis in the World of Sport,* Cassell, 1956, Philosophical Library, 1957; *Before the Dawn: A Story of Two Historic Retreats,* Cassell, 1957, 2nd edition, 1957; *Paradise Island* (juvenile), Max Parrish, 1958; *The Only Enemy: An Autobiography,* Hutchinson, 1959; *Trouble in Paradise: The Further Adventures of Ann Sheldon,* Max Parrish, 1959.

Ann Goes Hunting (juvenile), Max Parrish, 1960; *Sandhurst: The History of the Royal Military Academy, Woolwich, The Royal Military College, Sandhurst, and The Royal Military Academy, Sandhurst, 1741-1961,* Weidenfeld & Nicholson, 1961; *The Story of the Victoria Cross, 1856-1963,* Muller, 1962, abridged edition, 1965; *Beloved Cats,* Muller, 1963, Citadel, 1965; *Blue Magnolia,* Muller, 1964; (with Archibald Duncan Campbell Macauley) *Behind the Scenes at Wimbledon,* Collins, 1965, St. Martin's, 1966; *Ming: The Story of a Cat Family,* Muller, 1966; *The Rebellious Rani,* Muller, 1966; *Bolo Whistler: The Life of General Sir Lashmer Whistler,* Muller, 1967; *The Story of the George Cross,* Arthur Barker, 1968; *In This Sign Conquer: The Story of the Army Chaplains,* Mowbray, 1968.

The Valiant, Mowbray, 1970; *The Will to Live: The Story of Dame Margot Turner,* Cassell, 1970; *Percival and the Tragedy of Singapore,* Macdonald & Co., 1971; *Leadership in War, 1939-1945; The Generals in Victory and Defeat,* St. Martin's, 1974; *Jean Borotra, the Bounding Basque: His Life and Work and Play,* Stanley Paul, 1974; *Leadership in Battle, 1914-1918,* David & Charles, 1975.

Plays—With Ian Hays: "Burma Road," 1945; "Until Morning," 1950.

*   *   *

SMYTH, Paul 1944-

PERSONAL: Born January 31, 1944, in Boston, Mass.; son of Paul and Nona (Long) Smyth. *Education:* Harvard University, B.A., 1968. *Home address:* P.O. Box 489, Amherst, Mass. 01002. *Office:* Department of English, Mount Holyoke College, South Hadley, Mass. 01075.

CAREER: Mount Holyoke College, South Hadley, Mass., assistant professor of English, 1969—.

*WRITINGS—*Poetry: *Native Grass,* Windy Row Press, 1972; *Fifty Sonnets,* Windy Row Press, 1973; *Shadowed Leaves,* Press Porcepic, 1973; *Conversions,* University of Georgia Press, 1974.

*   *   *

SNADOWSKY, Alvin M. 1938-

PERSONAL: Born June 29, 1938, in New York, N.Y. *Education:* City College of the City University of New York, B.S. (cum laude), 1960, M.A., 1963, Ph.D., 1969. *Home address:* P.O. Box 182, Kensington Station, Brooklyn, N.Y. 11218. *Office:* Department of Psychology, Brooklyn College of the City University of New York, Brooklyn, N.Y. 11210.

CAREER: Research psychologist for U.S. Government at Rome Air Development Center, 1962-64; Brooklyn College of the City University of New York, Brooklyn, N.Y., research assistant, fellow, lecturer, 1965-69; York College of the City University of New York, Jamaica, N.Y., assistant professor of psychology, 1969-72; Brooklyn College of the City University of New York, assistant professor, 1972-74, associate professor of psychology, 1974—. President of Student Houses at City College of the City University of New York, 1971—.

MEMBER: American Psychological Association, American Sociological Association, Society for the Psychological Study of Social Issues, Association for Humanistic Psychology, American Association for the Advancement of Science, Eastern Psychological Association, New York State Psychological Association, New York Academy of Sciences, City College Alumni Association (member of board of directors, 1971—; member of executive committee, 1972—), Phi Beta Kappa, Sigma Xi, Psi Chi. *Awards, honors:* Alumni service award from City College Alumni Association, 1975.

WRITINGS: (Editor) *Social Psychology Research: Laboratory-Field Relationships,* Free Press, 1972; (editor) *Child and Adolescent Development: Laboratory-Field Relationships,* Free Press, 1973; (with B. Seidenberg) *Social Psychology: An Introduction,* Free Press, 1976. Contributor to professional journals.

WORK IN PROGRESS: The Intensive Group Experience, for Free Press.

*   *   *

SNOW, Davis W. 1913(?)-1975

1913(?)—December 5, 1975; American public relations executive, and playwright. Obituaries: *New York Times,* December 9, 1975.

*   *   *

SNYDER, Gerald S(eymour) 1933-

PERSONAL: Born June 4, 1933, in New York, N.Y.; son of David and Minnie (Beenstock) Snyder; married Arlette Amsellem, August 2, 1961; children: Michele, Daniel. *Education:* Missouri School of Journalism, B.J., 1958; Middlebury College, Graduate School of Spanish at University of Madrid, graduate study, 1961-62. *Home and office:* 11353 Columbia Pike, Silver Spring, Md. 20904.

CAREER: Religious News Service, New York, N.Y., writer, 1958-60, and free-lance writer in Europe and North

Africa, 1958-62; United Press International, New York, N.Y., reporter and writer, 1962-66; National Geographic Society, Washington, D.C., writer, 1966-71; free-lance writer, 1961—. *Military service:* U.S. Army, 1954-56. *Member:* Lewis & Clark Trail Heritage Foundation. *Awards, honors:* Feature writing award from Sigma Delta Chi, 1958.

WRITINGS: In the Footsteps of Lewis and Clark, National Geographic Society, 1970; *The Computer: How It's Changing Our Lives,* U.S. News & World Report, 1972; *The Religious Reawakening in America,* U.S. News & World Report, 1972; *Let's Talk About Computers,* Jonathan David, 1973; *Your Car: How to Buy It, Take Care of It, and Save Money,* U.S. News & World Report, 1973; *1994: The World of Tomorrow,* U.S. News & World Report, 1973; *The Right to Be Let Alone,* Messner, 1975; (editor) Wallace Stettinius, *Management Planning and Control: The Printers Path to Profitability,* Printing Industries of America, 1975; *The Right to Be Informed: Censorship in the United States,* Messner, in press. Contributor to national magazines, including *National Observer.*

WORK IN PROGRESS: A book on the Philippines resistance movement in World War II; a book on German submarine missions in World War II; research for a book on Palestine during World War II.

AVOCATIONAL INTERESTS: Raising children, collecting stamps, watching sports, reading.

*   *   *

SNYDER, Richard C(arlton)   1916-

PERSONAL: Born August 21, 1916, in Kingston, N.Y.; married Marjorie Lois Leibel, March 28, 1942. *Education:* Union College, Schenectady, N.Y., A.B.; Columbia University, M.A., 1939, Ph.D., 1945. *Home:* 3440 Olentangy River Rd., Columbus, Ohio 43202. *Office:* Mershon Center, Ohio State University, 199 West Tenth Ave., Columbus, Ohio 43201.

CAREER: American University, Washington, D.C., instructor in political science, 1941-42; Columbia University, New York, N.Y., instructor in government at Columbia College, 1942-46; Princeton University, Princeton, N.J., assistant professor, 1946-50, associate professor of politics, 1950-55, member of board of advisers, 1950-53, director of Foreign Policy Analysis Project, 1953-55; Northwestern University, Evanston, Ill., professor of political science, 1955-60, Benjamin Franklin Professor of Decision-Making, 1960-65, president's fellow, 1963-64, chairman of department of political science, 1957-65; University of California, Irvine, professor of administration and political science, 1965-70, dean of Graduate School of Administration, 1965-67; Ohio State University, Columbus, professor of Educational Development, professor of public administration, professor of political science, and director of Mershon Center, all 1970—. Lecturer at Foreign Service Institute, 1957-59, and Army War College, 1958-59. Fellow of Center for Advanced Study in the Behavioral Sciences, 1956-57; visiting fellow at Western Behavioral Sciences Institute, 1963-64; visiting scholar at Russell Sage Foundation, 1967-68. Chairman of advisory committee to Project Michelson at Naval Ordnance Test Station, 1960-65. Member of board of trustees of University of Denver's Social Science Foundation, 1960-73; senior associate of University of Michigan's Center for Conflict Research. Member of committee on undergraduate non-Western studies of American Council on Education, 1959-60; member of Social Science Research Council committee on international organization research, 1963-65; member of National Academy of Sciences study group, 1969-70; member of U.S. Office of Education Environmental Studies Panel, 1963-65; member of Education Professions Development Act panel on educational administration, 1969—. Member of executive council of Midwest Universities Consortium on the Social Sciences and the Secondary Schools, 1963-65.

MEMBER: American Political Science Association (member of executive council, 1960-62; member of executive committee, 1961-62; vice-president, 1966-68), International Studies Association (member of advisory committee, 1960-65; president, 1971-72), American Association for the Advancement of Science, Foreign Policy Association, Council on Foreign Relations.

WRITINGS: The Most Favored Nation Clause, King's Crown Press, 1948; (editor with L. H. Chamberlain) *American Foreign Policy,* Rinehart, 1948; (with H. H. Wilson) *Roots of Political Behavior,* American Book Club, 1949; (with R. K. Carr, Morison, and Bernstein) *American Democracy in Theory and Practice,* Holt, 1952, revised edition, 1955; (with B. M. Sapin) *The Role of the Military in American Foreign Policy,* Doubleday, 1954; (with E. S. Furniss, Jr.) *American Foreign Policy: Formulation, Principles, and Practices,* Holt, 1954; *Deterrence, Decision-Making, and Weapons Systems* (monograph), U.S. Naval Ordnance Test Station, China Lake, 1961; (with J. A. Robinson) *National and International Decision-Making* (monograph), Institute for International Order, 1961; (with H. W. Bruck and Sapin) *Foreign Policy Decision-Making,* Free Press of Glencoe, 1962; (with Dean Pruitt) *Theory and Research on the Causes of War,* Prentice-Hall, 1969.

Contributor: *Contemporary Civilization in the West,* Volume II, Columbia University Press, 1947; *Research Frontiers in Politics and Government,* Brookings Institution, 1955; R. Young, editor, *Approaches to the Study of Politics,* Northwestern University Press, 1958; A. Ranney, editor, *Essays on the Behavioral Study of Politics,* University of Illinois Press, 1962; J. C. Charlesworth, editor, *The Limits of Behavioralism in Political Science,* American Academy of Political and Social Science, (Philadelphia), 1962; Harold Guetzkow, editor, *Simulation in International Relations,* Prentice-Hall, 1963; *A Design for International Relations Research: Scope, Theory, Methods, and Relevance* (monograph), American Academy of Political and Social Science, 1970; Osborn T. Smallwood, editor, *Universities and Transnational Approaches to the Solution of World Problems,* University Publication Sales and Distributions (Columbus, Ohio), 1973.

Contributor of articles and reviews to political science journals. Editor of *Public Opinion Quarterly,* 1950-53; member of advisory board of *World Politics,* 1954-59, and *Current Thought on War and Peace,* 1960-65; member of editorial board of *Journal of Conflict Resolution,* 1957—, Ohio State University Press, 1970—, and *Teaching Political Science,* 1973—; member of editorial committee of *International Behavior,* 1965; member of editorial advisory board of *Law and Society,* 1966—.

*   *   *

SOBEL, Harold W(illiam)   1933-

PERSONAL: Born April 20, 1933, in Brooklyn, N.Y.; son of Larry (a salesman) and Helen (a travel agent; maiden name, Horowitz) Sobel; married Mildred Stein, September 3, 1961 (divorced January 19, 1966); children: David Alan,

Daniel Andrew. *Education:* University of Rochester, B.A., 1954; City College (now of the City University of New York), M.S., 1959; Columbia University, Ed.D., 1970. *Politics:* Democrat. *Religion:* Jewish. *Home:* 149-43 35th Ave., Flushing, N.Y. 11354. *Office:* Department of Elementary Education, Queens College of the City University of New York, Flushing, N.Y. 11367.

CAREER: High school social studies teacher in New York, N.Y., 1958-67, language arts teacher, 1959-67; Queens College of the City University of New York, Flushing, lecturer, 1967-70, assistant professor of education, 1970—. Vice-president of Open Education Consulting Service. *Military service:* U.S. Army, 1954-56.

MEMBER: United Federation of College Teachers (member of executive committee, 1969-72), Committee for a Sane Nuclear Policy, American Civil Liberties Union, Environmental Defense Fund, Phi Delta Kappa. *Awards, honors:* Planning grant from New York State Education Department in Albany, 1973.

WRITINGS: (Editor with Arthur E. Salz) *The Radical Papers: Readings in Education,* Harper, 1972. Contributor to education journals. Editor of *Open Education Newsletter,* 1972.

SIDELIGHTS: Sobel writes: "I entered teaching almost by accident and soon realized that the institution known as the school was just as archaic as our politico-economic institutions.... All of my professional writing is designed to promote the open classroom concept. Recently, I have come to realize that there is a significant relationship between radical schooling and radical politics. One can't hope to achieve the former without the latter. Hence, what we need now is a fusion between workers in each discipline—pedagogue and political scientist—so that reform can be achieved simultaneously in the two domains."

* * *

SOBOL, Harriet Langsam 1936-

PERSONAL: Born April 30, 1936, in New York, N.Y.; daughter of Morris (an investments broker) and Rose (a teacher; maiden name, Hirschtritt) Kaye; married Barry Langsam, June 15, 1958 (divorced, March, 1973); married Thomas Sobol (an education administrator), June 24, 1973; children: (first marriage) Gregory, Jennifer, Jeffrey. *Education:* Attended Skidmore College, 1953-55; Boston University, B.A., 1957; New York University, M.A., 1958. *Home:* 10 Claremont Rd., Scarsdale, N.Y. 10583.

CAREER: Sixth grade teacher in Cherry Hill, N.J., 1958-61, White Plains (N.Y.) Adult School, creative writing instructor, 1976—. *Member:* League of Women Voters (vice-president of local chapter, 1970-71).

WRITINGS: Jeff's Hospital Book (nonfiction), Walck, 1975.

WORK IN PROGRESS: A book for children about being the sibling of a retarded child.

SIDELIGHTS: Jeff's Hospital Book is about the author's youngest child's experience in a hospital. Her second book is concerned with the effect her oldest child's mental retardation has on his siblings.

* * *

SOLANO, Solita 1888-1975

1888—November 22, 1975; Drama editor and critic, novelist, and poet. Obituaries: *New York Times,* November 26, 1975; *Washington Post,* November 28, 1975; *AB Bookman's Weekly,* December 22-29, 1975.

* * *

SOLBERG, Carl Edward 1940-

PERSONAL: Born April 4, 1940, in St. Paul, Minn.; son of Walter O. (a railroad worker) and Helen (Worden) Solberg. *Education:* University of Minnesota, B.A., 1962; Stanford University, M.A., 1963, Ph.D., 1967. *Politics:* Democrat. *Office:* Department of History, DP-20, University of Washington, Seattle, Wash. 98195.

CAREER: University of Washington, Seattle, assistant professor of history, 1966-67; University of California, Los Angeles, assistant professor of history, 1967-68; University of Washington, assistant professor, 1968-70, associate professor of history, 1970—. Visiting professor at Simon Fraser University, 1974. *Member:* American Historical Association, Latin American Studies Association. *Awards, honors:* Annual prize of American Historical Association's Conference on Latin American History, 1972, for article "Rural Unrest and Agrarian Policy in Argentina: 1912-1930"; Social Science Research Council foreign area program fellowship, 1973-74.

WRITINGS: Immigration and Nationalism: Argentina and Chile, 1890-1914, University of Texas Press, 1970. Contributor to professional journals.

WORK IN PROGRESS: Oil and Politics in Argentina: 1907-1930, publication expected about 1977.

SIDELIGHTS: Solberg has traveled extensively in Latin America.

* * *

SOLIDAY, Gerald Lyman 1939-

PERSONAL: Born November 25, 1939, in Wooster, Ohio; son of Vaughn Gerald and Mary A. (Snell) Soliday; married Donna Warren, May 26, 1961; children: Elizabeth Anne, Karin Tamara. *Education:* Ohio State University, B.A., 1961, M.A., 1963; Harvard University, Ph.D., 1969. *Home:* 20 Branchaud Rd., Belmont, Mass. 02178. *Office:* Department of History, Brandeis University, Waltham, Mass. 02154.

CAREER: Brandeis University, Waltham, Mass., assistant professor of history, 1968—. *Member:* Bruno Walter Society. *Awards, honors:* American Council of Learned Societies grant, summer, 1969; Alexander von Humboldt Foundation fellowship, Germany, 1972-74.

WRITINGS: Community in Conflict: Frankfurt Society in the Seventeenth and Early Eighteenth Centuries, University Press of New England, 1974.

WORK IN PROGRESS: A Social History of Marburg, Germany: The Sixteenth through the Eighteenth Centuries; A Study of Marriage Patterns and Social Mobility in Frankfurt, Germany: The Seventeenth to the Early Eighteenth Century.

* * *

SOLOMON, Bernard S(imon) 1924-

PERSONAL: Born June 10, 1924, in New York, N.Y.; son of Israel and Rose (Stuchinski) Solomon. *Education:* City College (now of the City University of New York), B.S.S.S., 1946; Harvard University, M.A., 1949, Ph.D., 1952. *Religion:* Jewish. *Home:* 35 East Ninth St., New York, N.Y. 10003. *Office:* Department of Classical and

Oriental Languages, Queens College of the City University of New York, Flushing, N.Y. 11367.

CAREER: Harvard University, Cambridge, Mass., research assistant on Chinese-English dictionary project, 1952-58; State University of New York College, New Paltz, assistant professor of humanities, 1959-62; Queens College of the City University of New York, Flushing, N.Y., assistant professor, 1962-65, associate professor, 1966-70, professor of Chinese, 1970—. *Military service:* U.S. Army, 1943-45. *Awards, honors:* Fulbright fellowships to Italy, 1955-56, and Taiwan, summer, 1965; National Foundation for the Humanities senior fellowship, 1967-68.

WRITINGS: The Shun-tsung Shih-lu: The Veritable Record of the T'ang Emporor Shun-tsung, Harvard University Press, 1955.

Contributor to *Encyclopaedia Britannica* and to professional journals.

WORK IN PROGRESS: A book on Taoism.

* * *

SOLOMON, Charles J. 1906(?)-1975

1906(?)—May 1, 1975; American contract bridge player, association official, lecturer, editor, and author. Obituaries: *New York Times,* May 2, 1975.

* * *

SOROKIN, Elena 1894(?)-1975

1894(?)—September 2, 1975; Russian-born American botanist, translator, and editor. Obituaries: *New York Times,* September 5, 1975.

* * *

SORTOR, June Elizabeth 1939-
(Toni Sortor)

PERSONAL: Born June 4, 1939, in Utica, N.Y.; daughter of Ralph H. (a watchmaker) and Ada B. (an insurance clerk; maiden name, Lacey) Schneider; married John D. Blanchard, August 19, 1961 (died, October, 1962); married William G. Sortor (a fuel oil dealer), February 1, 1964; children: (second marriage) Laura Jean, James Henry, Steven Van Dyke. *Education:* Skidmore College, B.A., 1961. *Religion:* Episcopalian. *Home:* 50 Parkhill Rd., Harrington Park, N.J. 07640.

CAREER: High school teacher of English in public schools in Berne, N.Y., 1962-63. *Member:* Society of Childrens' Book Writers, Girl Scouts of the U.S.A. (chairman of Harrington Park chapter, 1973-75).

WRITINGS: (Under name Toni Sortor) *Adventures of B.J.: The Amateur Detective* (juvenile novel), Abingdon, 1975. Contributor of short stories and poems to periodicals.

WORK IN PROGRESS: A second adventure of B. J.; an adult mystery.

* * *

SPARKMAN, Brandon B(uster) 1929-

PERSONAL: Born August 2, 1929, in Hartselle, Ala.; son of George Olen and Mary Louise (Jones) Sparkman; married Wanda Phillips, September 13, 1952; children: Ricky Brandon, Rita Sharon, Robert Lee. *Education:* Florence State University, B.S., 1952; University of Alabama, M.A., 1958, Ed.S., 1961; Auburn University, Ed.D., 1970.

Religion: Methodist. *Home:* Apt. 3N., Spanish Trace, Hartselle, Ala. 35640. *Office:* Hartselle City Schools, 113 Sparkman St., Hartselle, Ala. 35640.

CAREER: High school teacher in Bear Creek, Ala., 1954-55, assistant principal, 1955-57; principal of public school in Tuscumbia, Ala., 1958-65, assistant superintendent, 1965-67; Auburn University, Auburn, Ala., part-time consultant at Auburn Center, 1969-70, assistant professor of school administration, 1970; assistant superintendent for staff personnel development in public schools in Jackson, Miss., 1970-71, superintendent of schools, 1971-73; Richland County School District One, Columbia, S.C., superintendent of schools, 1973-75; Hartselle City Schools, Hartselle, Ala., assistant superintendent for instruction, 1975—. Adjunct professor at University of South Carolina, 1974—. Member of board of directors of United Givers Fund, Jackson Teen Pregnancy Center, Sheffield-Tuscumbia Credit Union, and Colbert-Lauderdale Child Study Center; member of board of advisers of Southern Educators Life Insurance Co. and Jackson Mental Health Center; member of board of governors of Jackson Symphony Orchestra. *Military service:* Served, 1952-54.

MEMBER: American Association of School Administrators, Association for Supervision and Curriculum Development, Alabama Council for School Administration and Supervision, Phi Delta Kappa, Kappa Delta Pi, Civitan Club (past president).

WRITINGS: Blueprint for a Brighter Child, McGraw, 1973; *Program Management Through Computer Systems,* McGraw, 1975. Senior author of "STEPS" (System of Teacher Evaluation of Prereading Skills), revised edition, 1975. Contributor to education journals.

* * *

SPAULDING, Dayton M(athewson) 1922-

PERSONAL: Born March 25, 1922, in Prattsville, N.Y.; son of Harry Edward (a farmer) and Elsie (Barlow) Spaulding; married Concepcion Aguilera (a teacher), January 30, 1957; children: Christopher, Deborah, Michelle. *Education:* University of Oklahoma, B.S., 1949, Syracuse University, M.S., 1950; Boston University, Ed.D., 1974. *Office:* Department of Physical Education, Plymouth State College, Plymouth, N.H. 03264.

CAREER: Basketball coach and lecturer at private and public schools and military academies in New York, Connecticut, Louisiana, and New Jersey, 1950-65; Plymouth State College, Plymouth, N.H., assistant professor, 1965-72, associate professor of physical education, 1972—, head basketball coach, 1965—. Physical education specialist for U.S. State Department in Spain and Panama, 1956-57, and Brazil, 1958-59; basketball instructor in Spain, 1968, and Colombia, summer, 1974. *Military service:* U.S. Air Force, 1942-45; became captain. *Member:* National Basketball Coaches Association, American Alliance for Health, Physical Education and Recreation.

WRITINGS: Basketball's Destroyer Offense, Parker Publishing, 1972.

* * *

SPEIRS, John (Hastie) 1906-

PERSONAL: Born April 28, 1906, in Aberdeen, Scotland; son of Alexander (a teacher) and Elizabeth Logan (Hastie) Speirs; married Ruth Marga Tifentals (a translator of poetry), June 15, 1936; children: Logan. *Education:* University of Aberdeen, M.A., 1928; Emmanuel College, Cambridge, B.A., 1931. *Home:* 25 Grove Ter., Highgate Rd., London NW5 1PL, England.

CAREER: Writer and teacher in various schools, London, England, 1931-34; Heriot-Watt College, Edinburgh, Scotland, part-time lecturer, 1934-35; Institute of English, Riga, Latvia, lecturer in English literature, 1935-37; Fuad I University, Cairo, Egypt, lecturer in English literature, 1937-46; University of Exeter, Exeter, England, lecturer, 1946-60, senior lecturer, 1960-65, reader in English literature, 1965-71; writer, 1971—. *Member:* Cambridge Union.

WRITINGS: The Scots Literary Tradition, Chatto & Windus, 1940, enlarged edition, Faber, 1962; *Chaucer the Maker,* Faber, 1951, text edition, Hillary, 1962; *Medieval English Poetry,* Faber, 1957, text edition, Hillary, 1958; *Poetry Towards Novel,* New York University Press, 1971, text edition, 1972. Contributor to *Scrutiny: A Quarterly Review* and *Pelican Guide to English Literature.*

WORK IN PROGRESS: Two books.

*   *   *

SPEIRS, Russell   1901-1975

February 19, 1901—December 27, 1975; American educator, poet, and playwright. Obituaries: *New York Times,* December 29, 1975. (See index for previous *CA* sketch)

*   *   *

SPERBER, Murray A(rnold)   1940-

PERSONAL: Born November 30, 1940, in Montreal, Quebec, Canada; son of Lawrence L. (a retailer) and Gladys (Epstein) Sperber; married Aneta Wharry (a photographer), March 26, 1966. *Education:* Purdue University, B.A., 1961; University of California, Berkeley, M.A., 1963, Ph.D., 1974. *Politics:* "Left." *Religion:* Jewish. *Home address:* R.R. 11, Box 375, Bloomington, Ind. 47401. *Office:* Department of English, BH-442, Indiana University, Bloomington, Ind. 47401.

CAREER: College of the Holy Names, Oakland, Calif., instructor in English, 1964-65; University of California, Extension Divisions in San Francisco and Berkeley, instructor in English, 1966-68; Indiana University, Bloomington, lecturer, 1971-74, assistant professor of modern literature, film, and creative writing, 1974—. *Member:* American Federation of Teachers. *Awards, honors:* Canada Council fellow in England and France, 1969-71.

WRITINGS: (Editor) *And I Remember Spain: A Spanish Civil War Anthology,* Macmillan, 1974; *Politics and Literature: A Textbook,* Hayden, in press. Contributor to literature and film journals.

WORK IN PROGRESS: Arthur Koestler: A Collection of Critical Essays, publication by Prentice-Hall expected in 1977; *Orwell, Koestler, and Cold War Culture.*

SIDELIGHTS: Sperber writes: "In my writing and teaching, I attempt to persuade people that politics informs all of life, including literature and film, and that the serious question for the artist is not how to escape from politics (those who try to flee merely serve the regime in power) but how best to become aware of politics and how best to integrate this awareness into one's life and work. Colleagues tell me that politics and literature is no longer fashionable; I reply that I'm in it for the duration."

SPERO, Sterling D.   1896-1976

November 20, 1896—January 2, 1976; American educator, and author of books on labor relations. Obituaries: *New York Times,* January 4, 1976.

*   *   *

SPERRY, Len   1943-

PERSONAL: Born December 1, 1943, in Milwaukee, Wis.; son of Leonard V. (an engineer) and Wanda R. (a nurse; maiden name, Sadowski) Sperry. *Education:* St. Mary's College, Winona, Minn., A.B. (cum laude), 1966; Northwestern University, Ph.D., 1970; Alfred Adler Institute, postdoctoral certificate in psychotherapy; U.S. International University, Ph.D. (clinical psychology), 1976. *Politics:* Independent. *Religion:* Roman Catholic. *Home:* 268 Rancho Santa Fe Rd., Olivenhain, Calif. 92024. *Office:* 7755 Fay, La Jolla, Calif.

CAREER: St. Mary's College and Notre Dame University, South Bend, Ind., assistant professor of educational psychology, 1970-71; Marquette University, Milwaukee, Wis., associate professor of educational psychology, 1971-74; University of Wisconsin, Milwaukee, visiting associate professor of educational psychology, 1974-75; U.S. International University, San Diego, Calif., clinical supervisor in psychology, 1975—. Consultant with American Appraisal Associates, 1972—. *Member:* American Psychological Association, American Personnel and Guidance Association, Wisconsin Society of Adlerian Psychology (president, 1974-75).

WRITINGS: (Editor) *Learning Performance and Individual Differences,* Scott, Foresman, 1972; (with L. R. Hess) *Contact Counseling: Developing People in Organizations,* Addison-Wesley, 1974; *Developing Skills in Contact Counseling,* Addison-Wesley, 1975; (with D. J. Mickelson and P. H. Hunsaker) *You Can Make It Happen: A Guide to Self-Actualization and Organizational Change,* Addison-Wesley, in press. Contributor to psychology journals.

WORK IN PROGRESS: A book on marriage and family therapy, completion expected in 1977; a collection of his own essays on counseling, consulting, and psychotherapy; developing a multi-media counseling skills program.

*   *   *

SPIEGLER, Michael D(avid)   1943-

PERSONAL: Born March 27, 1943, in Brooklyn, N.Y. *Education:* University of Rochester, A.B., 1964; State University of New York at Albany, M.A., 1966; Vanderbilt University, Ph.D., 1969. *Office:* Department of Psychology, Providence College, Providence, R.I. 02918.

CAREER: Vanderbilt University, Nashville, Tenn., visiting instructor in psychology, 1967, 1968; Veterans Administration Hospital, Palo Alto, Calif., director of day treatment center, 1969-70; University of Texas, Austin, assistant professor of psychology, 1970-75; Providence College, Providence, R.I., associate professor of psychology, 1975—. Certified psychologist in Texas, 1973—. *Member:* American Psychological Association, Association for the Advancement of Behavior Therapy, Psi Chi.

WRITINGS: (With R. M. Liebert) *Personality: An Introduction to Theory and Research,* Dorsey, 1970; (contributor) Liebert and R. A. Baron, editors, *Human Social Behavior: A Contemporary View of Experimental Research,* Dorsey, 1971; (with Liebert) *Personality: Strate-*

gies for the Study of Man, Dorsey, 1974; (with Haig Agigian) The Community Training Center: The Educational, Behavioral, Social Systems Model for Social Rehabilitation, Brunner, in press; Contemporary Behavioral Therapy, Mayfield, in press. Contributor to psychology journals. Editorial consultant for Journal of Abnormal Psychology, 1971—, Journal Supplement Abstract Service, 1973, Social Science Quarterly, 1974, Random House, Prentice-Hall, and Mayfield.

WORK IN PROGRESS: Articles entitled "School Days: Creditable Treatment," "The Role of Observational Learning in Assertive Training," with G. J. Marshall, E. J. Cooley, and H. T. Prince II; "Saturday Night Blues: Should a Bright, Ambitious Woman Fear Success?," with L. S. Davis; "Modeling as a Treatment for Stubborn Avoidance Behavior," "The Use of Tape-Recorded Feedback in Supervision"; research on behavior modification, token economies, therapeutic and applied uses of modeling, basic theoretical issues of imitation, underlying processes of anxiety, social learning theory, and experimental teaching methods with college classes.

* * *

SPINK, Walter M(ilton) 1928-

PERSONAL: Born February 16, 1928, in Worcester, Mass.; son of Herbert E. (an engineer) and Amy Anne (a teacher; maiden name, Whitford) Spink; married Nesta F. Rubidge (a museum curator), June 20, 1952; children: David, Philip, Anne. Education: Amherst College, B.A. (summa cum laude), 1949; Harvard University, M.A., 1950, Ph.D., 1954. Religion: Unitarian-Universalist. Home: 2 Geddes Heights, Ann Arbor, Mich. 48104. Office: Department of the History of Art, Tappan Hall, University of Michigan, Ann Arbor, Mich. 48104.

CAREER: Brandeis University, Waltham, Mass., instructor, 1956-58, assistant professor of fine arts, 1958-61, acting chairman of department, 1959-60, curator of art collection, 1956-61; University of Michigan, Ann Arbor, associate professor, 1961-70, professor of the history of art, 1970—, member of executive committee of Center for South and Southeast Asian Studies, 1961-64, 1972, director of Asian art archives, 1962—, member of Indian historical atlas committee, 1964—, director of photographic expedition to India, 1964-65. Visiting lecturer at Brown University, 1960, and University of Chicago, summer, 1972. Organized photographic exhibition of Indian art for International Congress of Orientalists, 1967; member of board of directors of American Academy of Benares, 1965-71, acting director, summer, 1966; Birdwood memorial lecturer at Royal Society for the Arts, 1974. Military service: U.S. Army, Medical Corps, 1954-56.

MEMBER: Association for Asian Studies, Asia Society, American Committee for South Asian Art (president, 1972—), American Institute of Indian Studies (trustee, 1962-65, 1972-73), South Asia Regional Council (chairman of committee on fine arts, 1974—), Bharata Itihasa Samshodhaka Mandala (life member). Awards, honors: Fulbright grant, 1952-53, to study art in India; American Council of Learned Societies grants, summer, 1959, for research on Indian art in Europe, winter, 1963, to attend conference in India, 1972, to study Buddhist and Hindu cave temples of India; Bollingen Foundation research grant, 1964-65, to study Indian art; American Institute of Indian Studies senior fellowship, 1966, to study Indian cave temples; Smithsonian Institution travel grant, winter, 1971, to India.

WRITINGS: (Contributor) Joseph Campbell, editor, H. R. Zimmer, Art of Indian Asia, two volumes, Pantheon, 1955; (contributor) Milton Singer, editor, Introducing India in Liberal Education, University of Chicago Press, 1959; Ajanta to Ellora, Center for South and Southeast Asian Studies, University of Michigan, 1967; Krishnamandala, Center for South and Southeast Asian Studies, University of Michigan, 1971; (contributor) Pratapaditya Pal, editor, Aspects of Indian Art, E. J. Brill, 1972; The Axis of Eros, Schocken, 1973.

Author of booklet, The Quest for Krishna, 1972, and of exhibition catalogs, including one for Brandeis University. Contributor to Oxford American Encyclopedia. Contributor of more than twenty articles and reviews to symposia and professional journals.

WORK IN PROGRESS: A series of books on the cave temples of India; a book on ideas and images of the East and the West.

* * *

SPIRA, Ruth Rodale 1928-

PERSONAL: Born December 9, 1928, in New York, N.Y.; daughter of J. I. (a publisher) and Anna (Andrews) Rodale; married Joel S. Spira (president of Lutron Electronics), November 7, 1954; children: Susan, Lily, Juno. Education: Wellesley College, B.A., 1950; graduate study at China Institute, New York, N.Y., 1958. Home address: R.D. 1, Coopersburg, Pa. 18036. Office: Rodale Books, Inc., 33 East Minor St., Emmaus, Pa. 18049.

CAREER: Organic Gardening and Farming, Emmaus, Pa., associate editor, 1950, managing editor, 1951-52; Grolier Encyclopedia, New York, N.Y., consultant, 1954-55; free-lance writer, 1955—; Rodale Press, Emmaus, Pa., consultant, 1961—; Lutron Electronics, Coopersburg, Pa., co-founder and secretary, 1961—. Member: Lehigh Valley Wellesley Group.

WRITINGS: Naturally Chinese, Rodale Books, 1974. Contributor to House Beautiful, House and Garden, and Organic Gardening: Prevention.

* * *

SPITZER, Leo 1939-

PERSONAL: Born September 11, 1939, in La Paz, Bolivia; naturalized U.S. citizen; son of Eugene (a plumber) and Rose (Wolfinger) Spitzer; married Manon L. Settel (an editor), August 23, 1961; children: Alexander. Education: Brandeis University, B.A. (magna cum laude), 1961; University of Wisconsin, Madison, M.A., 1963, Ph.D., 1969. Home address: R.F.D., East Thetford, Vt. 05043. Office: Department of History, Dartmouth College, Hanover, N.H. 03755.

CAREER: Dartmouth College, Hanover, N.H., instructor, 1967-69, assistant professor, 1969-74, associate professor of history, 1974—. Member: American Historical Association, National Humanities Faculty, African Studies Association, New England Council of Latin American Studies, Phi Beta Kappa. Awards, honors: Woodrow Wilson fellowship, 1961-62, 1962-63; Ford Foundation Foreign Area Training Fellowship, 1963-65, for research in England and Sierra Leone; Social Science Research Council fellowship, 1972, for a comparative study of the intellectual reactions to Western culture of Afro-Brazilian freedmen and the Sierra Leone Creoles; research grant from comparative world history program of University of Wisconsin, 1974, for a book comparing African and New World ideas about race and racism, and 1975, for a comparative world history workshop.

WRITINGS: (Contributor) Philip D. Curtin, editor, *Africa and the West*, University of Wisconsin Press, 1972; *The Sierra Leone Creoles: Responses to Colonialism, 1870-1945*, University of Wisconsin Press, 1974; (editor with LaRay Denzer) *I.T.A. Wallace-Johnson: Selected Papers*, Frank Cass, 1975. Contributor to *World Book Encyclopedia* and to African studies journals.

WORK IN PROGRESS: A book on African resistance and revolution, with Allen Isaacman; a project focusing on a West African, Brazilian, and South African family comparing African and New World ideas about race and racism in the last century and a half.

SIDELIGHTS: Spitzer writes: "I am particularly concerned with Third World responses to colonialism and racism. My main focus of study has been West Africa and South Africa (although I have never been permitted to enter the Republic of South Africa for research purposes) and I have become increasingly interested in Brazil as an area for comparative analysis. My main effort has been to perceive the world and historical forces from the perspective of the people about whom I write. Empathy is what I strive for." Spitzer speaks Spanish, German, Portuguese, and Krio, and reads French and Xhosa.

* * *

SPITZER, Robert S(idney) 1926-

PERSONAL: Born September 16, 1926, in St. Louis, Mo; son of Harry H. (a manufacturer) and Ann (Weisstein) Spitzer; married Becky Brown, October 31, 1953; children: Ann, Dan, David. *Education:* Yale University, B.A., 1949; Harvard University, LL.B., 1952; Washington University, St. Louis, Mo., M.D., 1956. *Office:* Science and Behavior Books, 577 College Ave., Palo Alto, Calif. 94306.

CAREER: Harvard Student Health Service, Cambridge, Mass., psychiatrist, 1960-61; Mental Research Institute, Palo Alto, Calif., director of family training project, 1961-66; Science and Behavior Books, Palo Alto, Calif., president, 1968—; Multiple Psychotherapy Center, Sunnyvale, Calif., psychiatrist, 1974—. Certified by American Board of Psychiatry and Neurology. *Member:* American Psychiatric Association.

WRITINGS: *Tidings of Comfort and Joy*, Science & Behavior Books, 1975.

* * *

SPRING, Gerald M(ax) 1897-
(Richard Bodwell)

PERSONAL: Born March 30, 1897, in Dresden, Germany; son of William Arthur (a dentist) and Blanche (Powell) Spring; married Mildred Cecelia Hammill, December 17, 1932. *Education:* University of Vermont, B.S., 1916; Columbia University, M.A., 1917, Ph.D., 1932. *Home:* 2021 Newell Rd., Palo Alto, Calif. 94303.

CAREER: Goucher College, Baltimore, Md., instructor in French and Spanish, 1919-22; Williams College, Williamstown, Mass., instructor of Romance languages and French literature, 1926-28, 1929-31; University of California, Los Angeles, instructor, 1933-39, assistant professor of German and German literature, 1939-41. *Member:* Commonwealth Club (San Francisco), Sons in Retirement (Palo Alto, Calif.), University Club (Winter Park, Fla.).

WRITINGS: *The Vitalism of Count de Gobineau*, Institute of French Studies, 1932; *Nationalism on the Defensive* (monograph), Arthur Clark, 1937; *The Return from Babel*, Philosophical Library, 1951; (translator) Jules de Gaultier, *From Kant to Nietzsche*, Philosophical Library, 1961; *Man's Invincible Surmise: A Personal Interpretation of Bovarysm*, Philosophical Library, 1968; (translator) de Gaultier, *Bovarysm*, Philosophical Library, 1970; (translator) de Gaultier, *Official Philosophy and Philosophy*, Philosophical Library, 1974; (under pseudonym Richard Bodwell) *The Mystery of Fernridge Manor* (novel), Vantage, 1974; *The Ultimate Meaning of Jules de Gaultier*, Philosophical Library, 1975.

WORK IN PROGRESS: Research on the philosophy of Friedrich Nietzsche.

SIDELIGHTS: Spring writes: "Dresden, Germany (before the First World War) was a delightful cultured and cosmopolitan city with large American and English colonies. I grew up trilingual.... Except for several visits to Vermont ... I spent the first seventeen years of my life in Dresden. My father (who was born in Vermont) ... had an interesting clientele largely among the German aristocracy. Among his patients were the Arch-Duke Franz Ferdinand of Austria and his ... wife.... My parents and this couple became close friends."

* * *

SPRING, Norma 1917-

PERSONAL: Born March 28, 1917, in Orviston, Pa.; daughter of Norman Franklin (a clergyman) and Julia Irene (Pickett) Johnson; married Robert Walton Spring (a photographer), March 21, 1942; children: Terry Walton, Jacqueline Lee, Tracy Ann. *Education:* University of Washington, Seattle, B.A., 1940. *Religion:* Christian. *Home and office:* 18961 Marine View Circle S.W., Seattle, Wash. 98166.

CAREER: Music teacher and supervisor in public school in Shelton, Wash., 1940-45; Queens College of the City University of New York, New York, N.Y., secretary, 1946-47; Bob and Ira Spring (photographers), Seattle, Wash., writer, 1947—. *Member:* Society of American Travel Writers (member of national board of directors, 1972-75).

WRITINGS: (With Patricia Spring) *High Adventure*, Superior, 1952; (with P. Spring) *Adventuring on Mount Rainier*, Superior, 1954; *Alaska: Pioneer State*, Thomas Nelson, 1966; *Alaska: The Complete Travel Book*, Macmillan, 1970, revised edition, 1975; *Roaming Russia, Siberia, and Middle Asia*, Superior, 1973; *Exploring the Unspoiled West*, Volume I: *Alaska Chapter*, Ritchie, 1974. Contributor to magazines, including *Discovery, Outdoor Photographer's Digest, Today's Health*, and *Humble Way*, and to newspapers.

WORK IN PROGRESS: Research for a book of photographs with comprehensive text, on the contemporary scene in Alaska, publication expected in 1977; travel to Alaska, followed by a trip around the world, sponsored by U.S. Information Service and U.S. Travel Service, for the purpose of publicizing the U.S. Bicentennial.

SIDELIGHTS: Norma Spring began her writing and traveling career in earnest after losing a leg to cancer in 1960. She recovered and learned to walk again in the rough terrain of some of her favorite spots in Alaska. She writes: "We believe one of the best ways to achieve world peace and understanding is through encouraging travel exchange on people-to-people basis. We look forward to our up-coming world jaunt and opportunity to meet with foreign travel press counterparts . . ." *Avocational interests:* Camping, hiking, skiing, snowshoeing, foldboating, mountain climbing, international travel, "all outdoor delights in the Pacific Northwest and Alaska."

* * *

SQUIRES, Michael (George) 1941-

PERSONAL: Born July 18, 1941, in Alexandria, Va.; son of Fay Calvin (a statistician) and Arvilla (Windell) Squires; married Sylvia Nottingham (a learning disabilities teacher), August 15, 1964; children: Kelly Michael, Cameron Windell. *Education:* Bucknell University, B.A., 1963; University of Virginia, M.A., 1964; University of Maryland, Ph.D., 1969. *Home:* 1021 McBryde Lane, Blacksburg, Va. 24060. *Office:* Department of English, Virginia Polytechnic Institute and State University, Blacksburg, Va. 24061.

CAREER: Virginia Commonwealth University, Richmond, instructor in English, 1964-65; University of Maryland, College Park, instructor in English, 1967-69; Virginia Polytechnic Institute and State University, Blacksburg, assistant professor, 1969-75, associate professor of English, 1975—. *Member:* Modern Language Association of America, College English Association, Conference on College Composition and Communication.

WRITINGS: The Pastoral Novel: Studies in George Eliot, Thomas Hardy, and D. H. Lawrence, University Press of Virginia, 1974. Also author of *Handbook for Graduate Teaching Assistants,* for Virginia Polytechnic Institute and State University, 1970, 5th annual revision, 1975. Contributor to journals in his field.

WORK IN PROGRESS: The Composition of 'Lady Chatterley's Lover': A Study of the Manuscripts.

* * *

STACK, Frank H(untington) 1937-
(Foolbert Sturgeon)

PERSONAL: Born October 31, 1937, in Houston, Tex.; son of Maurice Z. (a sales manager) and Norma Rose (Huntington) Stack; married Mildred Roberta Powell (a teacher), June 12, 1959; children: Joan Elaine, Robert Huntington. *Education:* University of Texas, B.F.A., 1959; Art Institute of Chicago, graduate study, 1960-61; University of Wyoming, M.A., 1963. *Home:* 418 West Walnut, Columbia, Mo. 65201. *Office:* Department of Art, University of Missouri, A-126 Fine Arts Center, Columbia, Mo. 65201.

CAREER: Houston Chronicle, Houston, Tex., assistant fine arts editor, 1959; University of Missouri, Columbia, instructor, 1963-68, assistant professor, 1968-73, associate professor of art, 1973—. Artist with Lakeside Studio (etchings and lithographs), 1974—. Member of board of directors of Columbia Art League, 1975. *Military service:* U.S. Army, 1960, 1961-62. *Member:* College Art Association of America, Graphics Society, Columbia Art League.

WRITINGS: (Editor with Robert Bussabarger and Peter Morse) *A Selection of Etchings by John Sloan,* University of Missouri Press, 1968.

Cartoon books under pseudonym Foolbert Sturgeon: *New Adventures of Jesus,* three volumes, Rip Off Press, Volume I, 1968, Volume II, 1969, Volume III, 1974; *Feelgood Funnies,* Rip Off Press, 1971; *Amazon Comics,* Rip Off Press, 1972.

Author of "Between the Lines," an art news column in *Houston Chronicle.* Contributor to art magazines and literary journals, including *Rip Off Review, Sunday Clothes, Help!, Motive,* and *Liberation.*

WORK IN PROGRESS: A Book of Watercolors by Master Painters; American Newspaper Comic Strip Artists, especially V. T. Hamlin, Roy Crane, and Harold Gray; *Fine Book Illustration; Nineteenth- and Twentieth-Century Etchers and Lithographers; Art Teaching by Aphorism;* a study of Edward Hopper's development as an artist.

SIDELIGHTS: Stack writes: "I am primarily a painter and graphic artist and have pursued a career as an artist after some diversion as magazine designer, journalist, art critic, and writer of satirical pieces. I have always felt our society needed good satire on one hand balanced with serious sympathetic art—a reason I have made a book about John Sloan who was critical without being brutal, and have written and drawn underground comic books criticizing military and academic bureaucracies, cultural and ethical travesties, mechanistic intellectuals, and the appalling ugliness of our drive-in society."

BIOGRAPHICAL/CRITICAL SOURCES: Kansas City Star, July 29, 1973; *Missouri Historical Review,* October, 1973.

* * *

STAGG, James Martin 1900-1975

June 30, 1900—June 23, 1975; British meteorologist, weather consultant, and author of books in his field. Obituaries: *New York Times,* June 26, 1975.

* * *

STAMATY, Mark Alan 1947-

PERSONAL: Born August 1, 1947, in Brooklyn, N.Y.; son of Stanley (an artist) and Clara (an artist; maiden name, Kastner) Stamaty. *Education:* The Cooper Union, B.F.A., 1969. *Home:* 118 MacDougal St., Apt. 15, New York, N.Y. 10012. *Agent:* Sheldon Fogelman, 10 East 40th St., New York, N.Y.

CAREER: Formerly worked as a taxi driver, cabana boy at beach club, camp counselor, file clerk, and snack bar attendant. Author. Artist. *Awards, honors:* Citations from Brooklyn Museum and Brooklyn Public Library, 1973, for *Yellow, Yellow,* and 1975, for *Who Needs Donuts?;* gold medal from Society of Illustrators, 1974, for title page of *Who Needs Donuts?;* cover of *Small in the Saddle* was selected for American Institute of Graphic Arts exhibition, 1975; many fine art awards for etchings.

WRITINGS—All children's books: (Illustrator) Frank Asch, *Yellow, Yellow,* McGraw, 1971; *Who Needs Donuts?,* Dial, 1973; *Small in the Saddle,* Windmill Books, 1975.

WORK IN PROGRESS: Minnie Maloney and Macaroni, for Dial.

SIDELIGHTS: Stamaty told *CA:* "I believe in trying to save the earth from pollution and garbage . . . [and] in other things too numerous to name and difficult to explain. Then, of course, I believe in my art, in self-expression, and in creativity. I hope these things will always be at the center of my life, unless something better comes along. But what I'm doing now gives me considerable joy at times. My motivation is a deep desire to live and feel alive."

STANKE, Don E(dward) 1929-

PERSONAL: Born July 14, 1929, in Hastings, Minn.; son of Walter A. (an electrician) and Madolin (Franklin) Stanke. Education: Attended high school in St. Paul, Minn. Residence: Moraga, Calif. Office: CGR Medical Corp., San Leandro, Calif. 94577.

CAREER: San Francisco Examiner, San Francisco, Calif., want ad coordinator, 1952-67; employed briefly with World Wide Advertising Agency, 1967; CGR Medical Corp., San Leandro, Calif., operations manager, 1968—. Military service: U.S. Army, 1948-51; became sergeant.

WRITINGS—With James R. Parish: The Glamour Girls, Arlington House, 1975; The Debonairs, Arlington House, in press; The Swashbucklers, Arlington House, in press; The All-Americans, Arlington House, in press.

Contributor: Leonard Maltin, editor, The Real Stars #2, Curtis Books, 1973. Contributor to Films-in-Review, Film Fan Monthly, and Filmography.

WORK IN PROGRESS: With James R. Parish, The Indestructibles and The Forties Gals, both expected to be published by Arlington House in 1977.

* * *

STANTON, Graham N(orman) 1940-

PERSONAL: Born July 9, 1940, in Christchurch, New Zealand; son of Norman Scholfield (an editor) and Gladys (McGregor) Stanton; married Esther Douglas, July 24, 1965; children: Roger Graham, Michael Philip. Education: University of Otago, B.A., 1960, M.A. (honors), 1961, B.D., 1964; Cambridge University, Ph.D., 1968. Religion: United Reformed Church. Home: 45 Tubbenden Lane, Orpington, Kent BR6 9PW, England. Office: King's College, University of London, Strand, London W.C.2, England.

CAREER: Princeton Theological Seminary, Princeton, N.J., lecturer in New Testament studies, 1969; University of London, King's College, London, England, lecturer in New Testament studies, 1970—. Member: British Society for Old Testament Studies, British Association for Jewish Studies, Studiorum Novi Testamenti Societas. Awards, honors: Naden postdoctoral studentship at St. John's College, Cambridge, 1969-70; Alexander von Humboldt Stiftung research fellowship at University of Tuebingen, 1974.

WRITINGS: Jesus of Nazareth in New Testament Preaching, Cambridge University Press, 1974.

Contributor: S. W. Sykes and J. P. Clayton, editors, Christ, Faith, and History, Cambridge University Press, 1972; B. Lindars and S. Smalley, editors, Christ and Spirit in the New Testament, Cambridge University Press, 1973; M. Hooker and C. Hickling, editors, What About the New Testament?, SCM Press, 1975; I. H. Marshall, editor, New Testament Interpretation, Paternoster Press, 1976.

WORK IN PROGRESS: Matthew: Apologist and Theologian.

* * *

STANTON, Peggy Smeeton 1939-

PERSONAL: Born January 6, 1939, in Des Moines, Iowa; daughter of Cecil Brooks (a professor) and Florence (Rooney) Smeeton; married J. William Stanton (a U.S. Congressman), December 3, 1966; children: Kelly. Education: Marquette University, B.S., 1962. Home: 2260 48th St. N.W., Washington, D.C. 20007.

CAREER: WISN-TV, Milwaukee, Wis., news reporter, 1962-64, assignment editor, 1962-64, woman's editor, 1963-64; press secretary for U.S. Congressman Glenn Davis, in Washington, D.C., 1965; Metromedia Radio Bureau, Washington, D.C., news correspondent, covering the House of Representatives, the Senate, the State Department, and the White House, 1965-66; American Broadcasting Co. (ABC), Washington, D.C., news correspondent, covering Capitol Hill and the White House, 1966-67; author. Promotions manager of the National Institute of Dry-Cleaning, 1964. Member: Republican Congressional Wives (president, 1972-74).

WRITINGS: (Self-illustrated; with Antoinette Hatfield) Help! My Child Won't Eat Right, Acropolis Books, 1973.

WORK IN PROGRESS: A factual account of a political marriage.

AVOCATIONAL INTERESTS: Travel (Latin America, Far East, Africa, Europe), tennis, golf, painting.

* * *

STANYER, Jeffrey 1936-

PERSONAL: Born November 5, 1936, in Tarporley, Cheshire, England; son of Gordon (a local government officer) and Eleanor (Williamson) Stanyer; married Ann Hilda Radford (a polytechnic lecturer), September 3, 1962; children: Antony, Caroline. Education: Balliol College, Oxford, B.A., 1958, B.Phil., 1960. Politics: Labour. Religion: "Anti-clerical." Home: 1 Thornton Hill, Exeter EX4 4NJ, Devonshire, England. Agent: Curtis Brown Academic, 1 Craven Hill, London W2 3EP, England. Office: Department of Politics, University of Exeter, Rennes Dr., Exeter EX4 4RJ, England.

CAREER: Exeter University, Exeter, England, research fellow in local government, 1960-62, assistant lecturer in government, 1962-64, lecturer in politics, 1964—. Member: Royal Institute of Public Administration, Political Studies Association (member of executive committee), Exeter Cricket Club, Devon Dumplings Cricket Club.

WRITINGS: County Government in England and Wales, Humanities, 1967; (with B. C. Smith) Administering Britain, Collins, 1976; Understanding Local Government, Collins, 1976. Author of "Understanding Local Government," a series of programs for Westward Television, 1968. Contributor to political science, and public and social administration journals. Editor, Newsletter of the Political Studies Association.

AVOCATIONAL INTERESTS: Sport (once played soccer for local leagues; now plays cricket), reading, writing fiction (has plans for a detective story and a book on sporting behavior).

* * *

STAPLER, Harry 1919-

PERSONAL: Born March 10, 1919, in New York, N.Y.; son of Henry B. and Gertrude (Haupert) Stapler; married Catherine Haun, June 23, 1947 (divorced, 1960); married Kit Waggoner (an artist), May 16, 1961; children: (first marriage) Paul, Holly. Education: College of Wooster, B.A., 1950; Central Michigan University, graduate study, 1975—. Religion: Presbyterian. Home: 521 Fuller, Apt. 302-D, Big Rapids, Mich. 49307. Office: Department of Language and Literature, Ferris State College, Big Rapids, Mich. 49307.

CAREER: Associated Press, Detroit, Mich., reporter and

sports editor, 1950-53; *Detroit News,* Detroit, Mich., reporter, 1953-58; *Towne Courier,* East Lansing, Mich., editor and publisher, 1962-73; Ferris State College, Big Rapids, Mich., instructor in journalism, 1973—. Secretary-treasurer of University International Research Co., 1968-72; director of East Lansing Chamber of Commerce, 1971-73; director of East Lansing Young Men's Christian Association, 1969-71. *Military service:* U.S. Navy, chief photographer's mate, 1941-45. *Awards, honors:* John V. Field Award from Michigan Interscholastic Press Association, 1972, for contributions to journalism education.

WRITINGS: Student Journalist and Sports Editing, Richards Rosen, 1964; *Student Journalist and Sports Reporting,* Richards Rosen, 1964; *Student Journalist and Sports Writing,* Richards Rosen, 1974; *Your Future in Professional Sports,* Richards Rosen, in press. Author of "Harry Stapler" column in East Lansing *Towne Courier,* 1966-72.

WORK IN PROGRESS: Research on media coverage of the U.S. President; books on professional sports and on suburban journalism.

* * *

STASZ, Clarice
(Clarice Stasz Stoll)

PERSONAL: Daughter of Clarence (an engineer) and Mary (a publicist; maiden name, Zboray) Stasz; married Carl Stoll, 1962 (divorced, 1969); children: Kendra. *Education:* Rutgers University, A.B. (with honors), 1962, Ph.D., 1967; University of Wisconsin, Madison, M.A., 1964. *Residence:* Petaluma, Calif. *Office:* Department of Sociology, California State College–Sonoma, Rohnert Park, Calif. 94928.

CAREER: Johns Hopkins University, Baltimore, Md., research scientist in department of social relations, 1967-70, member of Center for the Social Organization of Schools, 1967-70; California State College–Sonoma, Rohnert Park, assistant professor, 1970-73, associate professor of sociology, 1973—. *Member:* Sociologists for Women in Society, Society for Photographic Education, Society for the Study of Social Problems, American Sociological Association. *Awards, honors:* National Endowment for the Humanities grant, summer, 1973.

WRITINGS—All under name Clarice Stasz Stoll: (With Michael Inbar) *Simulation and Gaming in Social Science,* Free Press, 1971; (with Samuel Livingston) *Simulation Games for the Social Studies Teacher,* Free Press, 1973; (editor) *Sexism: Scientific Debates,* Addison-Wesley, 1973; *Female and Male: Socialization, Social Roles, and Social Structure,* W. C. Brown, 1974.

Contributor: Jack D. Douglas, editor, *Situations and Structures,* Free Press, 1973; Marcello Truzzi, editor, *The Humanities as Sociology,* C. E. Merrill, 1973; Richard Hawkins and Ronald Akers, editors, *Law and Control in Society,* Prentice-Hall, 1974; Portele, editor, *Play in School,* Beltz Verlag, in press; Peter Manning, editor, *Social Control,* Free Press, in press. Contributor to *International Encyclopedia of the Social Sciences* and to behavioral sciences and literature journals, including *Modern Fiction Studies, Western American Literature, Media and Methods,* and *Society.*

WORK IN PROGRESS: A biography of Charmian Kittredge London, Jack London's second wife; a photo-essay on country fairs; research on the preparation and analysis of biography.

SIDELIGHTS: Clarice Stasz writes: "In 1971 I visited Jack London State Park, knowing nothing about the noted author, and caring to know little else. As I looked at a portrait of her [London's wife, Charmian] posed midst a South Seas tribe with a pistol on her hip—her spirit enchanted me. I tried for several years to exorcise it, by writing on other topics and exploring photography. I gave myself long lectures to the effect that (1) serious sociologists don't write such books, (2) there are many other women more in tune with my feminism who deserve to be written about. Charmian appeared in my dreams and had tea with me. One day I simply capitulated. . . . I could do nothing else and retain peace of mind. Since then I have been deep at work in over 10,000 letters and forty years of diaries."

* * *

STEAHLY, Vivian Eugenia Emrick   1915-

PERSONAL: Born July 10, 1915, in Wapakoneta, Ohio; daughter of Daniel and Catherine (Bush) Emrick; married Frank Lester Steahly (a chemist and business executive), October 17, 1936 (died May 19, 1967); children: Lance Preston. *Education:* Ohio State University, B.Sc. and B.A. (cum laude), both 1936; University of Cincinnati, M.A., 1941; University of Virginia, graduate study, 1941-42; Michigan State University, summer workshop, 1961. *Home:* 206 Stinebaugh Dr., Wapakoneta, Ohio 45895. *Office:* Department of English, Ohio State University, Lima Campus, Lima, Ohio 45804.

CAREER: High school teacher of Latin, French, English, and history in Georgetown, Ohio, 1936-39, and of English in Seaford, Del., 1942-43; free-lance writer, book reviewer, and monologuist, 1943-48; University of Tennessee, Knoxville, instructor in English at Extension Division in Oak Ridge, 1948; free-lance writer, book reviewer, and monologuist, 1948-55; high school teacher of Latin, French, and English in Winfield, W.Va., 1955-58; Morris Harvey College, Charleston, W.Va., assistant professor of English and French, 1958-66, assistant professor of education, 1964-65, head of department of modern languages, 1962-64; Ohio State University, Lima Campus, assistant professor of English, 1967—. Member of West Virginia state committees on teacher certification in English, 1961-63. Editorial consultant, West Virginia University, board of governors, 1966, West Virginia State Department of Education, 1966.

MEMBER: Modern Language Association of America, National Council of Teachers of English, American Association for the Advancement of Science, American Association for Higher Education, Ohio Academy of Science, Ohio State University Association, University of Cincinnati Alumni Association, Phi Beta Kappa (vice-president of Charleston association, 1964; president, 1965), Pi Lambda Theta, Eta Sigma Phi, Scholaris.

WRITINGS: Seven Steps to Sensible Structure and Style, Whitehall Co., 1970; *I Always Wanted to Live in the Chicken Yard* (juvenile), Yale Brothers, 1973; *The Gift and Other Tales* (juvenile), Yale Brothers, 1974. Contributor to Mott Basic Language Skills Program, Series 600B, published by Allied Education Council (Galien, Mich.), 1966. Author of television script, "What Chemistry Has Done for the Housewife," 1957. Feature writer for *Charleston Gazette,* 1954-55. Contributor to journals, including *NEA Journal, West Virginia School Journal,* and *Missouri English Bulletin.*

STEELE, Phillip W(ayne) 1934-

PERSONAL: Born July 20, 1934, in Fort Smith, Ark.; son of Joe M. (a food processor, industrialist, and banker) and Gretchen (an artist; maiden name, Gilliland) Steele; married Charlotte Smith, September 9, 1956; children: Meagan Elizabeth, Jason Ross. *Education:* Attended University of California, Los Angeles; University of Arkansas, B.S.B.A., 1956, graduate study, 1957. *Religion:* Methodist. *Home:* 1104 Ranch Dr., Springdale, Ark. 72764. *Office:* Forest Park Foods, P.O. Box 191, Springdale, Ark. 72764.

CAREER: Steele Canning Co., Springdale, Ark., executive vice-president, 1957-72; Ole South Foods Co., Springdale, Ark., senior vice-president, 1973-75; Forest Park Foods Co. (a food processing and marketing company), Springdale, Ark., president, 1975—. Member of board of directors of First State Bank (Springdale) and Ozark Art Center. Member of board of directors of local Chamber of Commerce. *Military service:* U.S. Army National Guard, 1957-64. *Member:* National Canners Association (past member of board of directors), Ozark Canners and Freezers Board, Ozark Artist and Writers Guild, Ozark Arts and Crafts Fair Association (vice-president), Washington County Historical Society (vice-president), Rotary International.

WRITINGS: The Butterfield Run: A History of the John Butterfield Stage Line, Springdale News Press, 1966, revised edition, 1974; *The Last Cherokee Warriors* (history and biography), Pelican, 1974; *Hearth Tales of the Ozarks* (legends and folklore), Phillips Litho Co., 1974; *Lost Treasures of the Ozarks,* Phillips Litho Co., 1974. Contributor to adventure magazines, to mountineering and history journals, and to newspapers.

WORK IN PROGRESS: Enlarged versions of *Hearth Tales of the Ozarks* and *Lost Treasures of the Ozarks;* a book on early Ozark farm life and customs; a movie script, based on *The Last Cherokee Warriors.*

SIDELIGHTS: Steele writes: "Having a trace of Cherokee ancestry my interest in the history and struggles of the early Cherokee and Indian nations resulted. Being a native of the Northwest Arkansas region my interest developed in the areas of Ozark folklore, folkmusic, lost treasure tales, Civil War history, and Arkansas border frontier and outlaw gang history.... My writings began as a release from business pressures, developed from newspaper articles to magazines, and finally to books."

*   *   *

STEELE, Thomas J(oseph) 1933-

PERSONAL: Born November 6, 1933, in St. Louis County, Mo.; son of Harry L. (a civil engineer) and Genevieve (Harder) Steele. *Education:* St. Louis University, A.B., 1957, Ph.L., 1958, M.A., 1959, S.T.L., 1965; University of New Mexico, Ph.D., 1968. *Politics:* "Christian Socialist." *Home and office:* Regis College, 5000 Lowell Blvd., Denver, Colo. 80221.

CAREER: Entered Society of Jesus (Jesuits), 1951, ordained Roman Catholic priest, 1964; high school teacher of English in Wichita, Kan., 1959-61; Regis College, Denver, Colo., assistant professor, 1968-74, associate professor of English, 1974—. *Member:* Rocky Mountain Modern Language Association.

WRITINGS: Santos and Saints: Essays and Handbook, Calvin Horn, 1974; *Holy Week in Tome: A New Mexico Passion Play,* Sunstone Press, in press.

STEEN, Marguerite 1894-1975

May 12, 1894—August 4, 1975; British novelist, playwright, and biographer. Obituaries: *New York Times,* August 6, 1975; *Publishers Weekly,* August 18, 1975; *AB Bookman's Weekly,* September 8, 1975; *Current Biography,* September, 1975.

*   *   *

STEIN, Harry 1938-

PERSONAL: Born July 9, 1938, in Pittsburgh, Pa.; married Ellen Claire Haney, October 12, 1968; children: Christopher. *Education:* University of Pittsburgh, B.A., 1960, M.Ed., 1963. *Home address:* R.D. 1, Box 234, Branchville, N.J. 07826. *Office:* New Jersey State Department of Education, 18 Church St., Newton, N.J.

CAREER: Government of Kenya, Rift Valley Province, education officer, 1963-66; African-American Institute, New York, N.Y., program director, 1966-73; New Jersey State Department of Education, Newton, N.J., program officer, 1973—. *Member:* International Reading Association, World Future Society, National Council for the Social Studies.

WRITINGS: (With E. J. Murphy) *Africa: A Curriculum Handbook for Teachers,* Citation, 1973; *A First Book of Southern Africa,* F. Watts, 1975. Contributor to educational journals.

WORK IN PROGRESS: Research for a book on Portuguese colonial empire; a book on learning in subject areas, for high school programs.

*   *   *

STEIN, Philip L(awrence) 1939-

PERSONAL: Born May 26, 1939, in Los Angeles, Calif.; married Carol Freed (a pianist and writer), July 4, 1965; children: Amy Jean, Rebecca Lynne. *Education:* University of California, Los Angeles, B.A., 1961, M.A., 1963. *Residence:* Woodland Hills, Calif. *Office:* Department of Life and Earth Sciences, Los Angeles Pierce College, 6201 Winnetka Ave., Woodland Hills, Calif. 91364.

CAREER: Los Angeles Pierce College, Woodland Hills, Calif., instructor, 1964-68, assistant professor, 1968-73, associate professor of anthropology, 1974—, chairman of department of life and earth sciences, 1975—. *Member:* American Anthropological Association (fellow), American Association for the Advancement of Science (fellow), American Association of Physical Anthropologists, Society for California Archaeology.

WRITINGS: (With B. M. Rowe) *Physical Anthropology,* with workbook, McGraw, 1974.

WORK IN PROGRESS: The Primates, with wife, Carol Stein, for McGraw; *Physical Anthropology and Archaeology,* with others, for McGraw.

*   *   *

STEINBERG, Aaron Zacharovich 1891-1975
(M. Avrelin)

June 12, 1891—August 17, 1975; Russian-born British religious society administrator, educator, editor, translator, and author. Obituaries: *New York Times,* August 18, 1975.

*   *   *

STEINBERG, Rafael (Mark) 1927-

PERSONAL: Born June 2, 1927, in Newark, N.J.; son of

Isador N. (an artist) and Polly N. (Rifkind) Steinberg; married Tamiko Okamoto (a teacher of Japanese), November 21, 1953; children: Summer Eve, Joy Nathania. *Education:* Harvard University, A.B. (cum laude), 1950. *Home:* 1391 Somerset Gate, Teaneck, N.J. 07666. *Agent:* Roberta Pryor, International Creative Management, 40 West 57th St., New York, N.Y. 10019.

CAREER: Fire Island Reporter, Long Island, N.Y., editor and publisher, summers, 1949-50; International News Service, New York, N.Y., war correspondent from Korea, 1951-52; *Time* (magazine), New York, war correspondent from Korea and Japan, 1952, and New York, 1953-55, member of London Bureau, 1955-58; *Newsweek* (magazine), New York, Far Eastern correspondent and Tokyo bureau chief, 1959-63; free-lance journalist in Tokyo, Japan, serving as correspondent for *Washington Post* and *Saturday Evening Post,* 1963-67, and the United States, 1968-70; *Newsweek,* general editor, 1970-72, senior editor, 1972-73, managing editor of international edition, 1973; free-lance writer, 1973-75; *Cue* magazine, New York, editor, 1975—. Executive director of Academic and Professional Alliance for a Responsible Congress, 1970. *Military service:* U.S. Naval Reserve, active duty, 1945-46. *Member:* Authors Guild of Authors League of America, Japan Society, Foreign Correspondents Club of Japan, Harvard Club (New York, N.Y.).

WRITINGS: Postscript from Hiroshima, Random House, 1966; *Japan,* Macmillan, 1969.

With the editors of Time-Life Books: *Cooking of Japan,* Time-Life, 1969; *Pacific and Southeast Asian Cooking,* Time-Life, 1970; *Man and the Organization,* Time-Life, 1975. Contributor of articles and stories to magazines, including *Playboy,* and newspapers.

* * *

STEPHENSON, John B(ell) 1937-

PERSONAL: Born September 26, 1937, in Staunton, Va.; son of Louis Bell (a banker) and Edna Mae (Moles) Stephenson; married Jane Ellen Baucom (a piano teacher), March 30, 1962; children: Jennifer Ann, Rebecca Jane, John David. *Education:* College of William and Mary, B.A., 1959; University of North Carolina, M.A., 1961, Ph.D., 1966. *Politics:* "Bumper-sticker liberal." *Religion:* Presbyterian. *Office:* Department of Undergraduate Studies, University of Kentucky, Lexington, Ky. 40506.

CAREER: Lees-McRae College, Banner Elk, N.C., instructor in social studies and chairman of Division, 1961-64; University of Kentucky, Lexington, assistant professor, 1966-69, associate professor of sociology, 1969—, dean of undergraduate studies, 1970—. *Member:* American Association for Higher Education, Association for General and Liberal Studies, Southern Sociological Society. *Awards, honors:* Fellowship from American Council on Education, 1973-74.

WRITINGS: Shiloh: A Mountain Community, University Press of Kentucky, 1968; (editor with David S. Walls) *Appalachia in the Sixties: Decade of Reawakening,* University Press of Kentucky, 1972; (contributor) Sidney Hook and other editors, *The Philosophy of the Curriculum,* Prometheus Books, 1975. Contributor to sociology journals.

WORK IN PROGRESS: Research on the impact of schools and problems in Appalachian development.

SIDELIGHTS: Stephenson writes: "Most of my writing is directed toward problem-solving of one kind or another,

whether it is a technical problem in social science research, a social problem or an educational problem.... Were I a professional writer, I would probably not find the university the most supportive setting in which to work. It is unbelievably distracting at times. For the most part, however, I find such distractions important, informing, and psychologically stimulating."

* * *

STERN, Jane 1946-

PERSONAL: Born October 24, 1946, in New York, N.Y.; daughter of Milton S. (a salesman) and Norma J. (a nurse; maiden name, Wexler) Grossman; married Michael Stern (a filmmaker), October 25, 1970. *Education:* Pratt Institute, B.F.A., 1968; Yale University, M.F.A., 1971. *Religion:* Jewish. *Home and office address:* P.O. Box 288, Guilford, Conn. 06437. *Agent:* Betty Anne Clarke, International Creative Management, 40 West 57th St., New York, N.Y. 10019.

CAREER: Writer, photographer, and screenwriter. Consultant on truckdrivers to Smithsonian Institution and CBS news program "60 Minutes." *Member:* Screenwriters Guild. *Awards, honors:* Pulitzer Prize nomination, 1975, for *Trucker.*

WRITINGS: Trucker: A Portrait of the Last American Cowboy, McGraw, 1975; *Road Food,* McGraw, in press. Writer of screenplays, "Strange Surroundings," 1971, "Apache Bill," 1974, "The Last American Cowboy," 1975. Writer of television script, "The Dirty Side," broadcast on WNBC-TV, January 17, 1976, and of television commercials for WNHT-TV.

SIDELIGHTS: Jane Stern told *CA:* "I was an artist before a writer ... [and] took to the road for three years traveling with the truckers to research my book. I was impressed by their romantic image of their job and their rich culture. I hope to continue writing screenplays and books focusing on individuals who lead lives of mystery and romance, often times overlooked by the general public. I have a lovely bulldog and a home on the seashore in Connecticut."

* * *

STERN, Karl 1906-1975

April 8, 1906—November 7, 1975; German-born Canadian psychiatrist, educator, and author of a novel and books on religion and psychiatry. Obituaries: *New York Times,* November 8, 1975. (See index for previous *CA* sketch)

* * *

STEVENS, Lucile Vernon 1899-

PERSONAL: Born March 7, 1899, in St. Paul, Minn.; daughter of J. L. (a salesman) and Mattie (Carter) Vernon; married Harry L. Stevens (a school administrator; deceased). *Education:* Wichita State University, A.B., 1919; University of Arkansas, graduate study, 1954. *Politics:* Democrat. *Religion:* Protestant. *Home:* 400 East Harrison St., Apt. 507, Tampa, Fla. 33602.

CAREER: High school teacher of English and social studies in Kansas, 1919 and 1922-27, Oklahoma, 1921, and Arkansas, 1943-59. *Member:* Pensters (Mobile, Ala.; vice-president, 1970).

WRITINGS—All published by Bouregy: Death Wore Gold Shoes, 1966; *Love-in-a-Mist,* 1967; *Dowry of Diamonds,* 1968; *Threads of Gold,* 1968; *The Red Tower,*

1968; *Crape Myrtle Tree*, 1970; *Search Through the Mist*, 1971; *Home to Cypresswood*, 1972; *Green Shadows*, 1973; *The Redbird Affair*, 1974; *Joni of Storm Hill*, in press.

WORK IN PROGRESS: A light mystery-romance novel.

SIDELIGHTS: Lucile Stevens writes: "I always wanted to be a writer but life interfered until after I was alone and without obligations. I have been writing steadily since and expect to continue as long as I live, because I like to write. I do not undertake profound work but I do try to go deeply into human motivation and to have some conflict of spirit, also to bring descriptions of Nature into our cement-and-brick world. I like today's young people—the decent majority. They are strong and wonderful, better than we were.

"My hobbies are many as I am interested in practically everything on earth. I do all my own sewing, do needle-point and knitting, have polished gems and worked silver to make jewelry, done ceramics from the clay up, and do beadwork, the French type of bead flowers from tiny beads on fine wire. . . . I enjoy politics, watch television, read mysteries and non-fiction. I am interested in the American West. . . . I have traveled over this country except for the Far West. . . ."

* * *

STEVENSON, Gloria 1945-

PERSONAL: Born May 19, 1945, in Cleveland, Ohio; daughter of Metro (a laborer) and Helen (Patrick) Berzonsky. *Education:* Pennsylvania State University, B.A., 1967. *Home:* 3850 Tunlaw Rd. N.W., Washington, D.C. 20007. *Office:* Manpower, U.S. Department of Labor, 601 D St. N.W., Washington, D.C. 20213.

CAREER: U.S. Department of Labor, Washington, D.C., writer in Information Office, 1967-71, writer and editor of *Occupational Outlook Quarterly* of Bureau of Labor Statistics, 1971-74, assistant editor of *Manpower* magazine, 1974—. Instructor at George Washington University, 1974—. *Member:* American Personnel and Guidance Association, National Vocational Guidance Association, National Organization for Women, Federal Editors Association.

WRITINGS: Your Future as a Working Woman, Richards Rosen, 1975.

SIDELIGHTS: Gloria Stevenson writes: "My own experience as a girl and working woman, plus my knowledge and interest in the field of career guidance, led me to write a book that would urge high school girls to try to find satisfaction and rewards in the work world. These rewards are there, but many people—especially women—need encouragement and help in finding them."

* * *

STEVENSON, T(homas) H(ulbert) 1919-

PERSONAL: Born September 7, 1919, in Cleveland, Ohio; son of Thomas (an attorney) and Mary E. (Hulbert) Stevenson; married Dorothy A. Ruggles, May 19, 1950; children: Mary A., James R. *Education:* Oberlin College, A.B., 1941; University of Chicago, A.M., 1945, Ph.D., 1964. *Politics:* Republican. *Home and office:* 902 Pearl St., Wayne, Neb. 68787.

CAREER: William Woods College, Fulton, Mo., instructor in history and government, 1947-48; Stanford University, Stanford, Calif., research assistant in behavioral sciences, 1955; University of Santa Clara, Santa Clara, Calif., lec-

turer in municipal government, 1955-56; Michigan Technological University, Houghton, Mich., instructor in history and government, 1958-59; Wayne State College, Wayne, Neb., assistant professor, 1965-66, associate professor of history, 1966-70, acting chairman of division of social sciences, 1968; research and writing, 1970—. Translations consultant, *American Behavioral Scientist*, 1959-60. *Military service:* U.S. Army Air Forces, 1942-43. *Member:* Mensa.

WRITINGS: (With George Bernard de Huszar) *Political Science*, Littlefield, 1951, 4th edition, 1965; (contributor) Huszar, editor, *Soviet Power and Policy*, Crowell, 1955; (editor) *Building Better Volunteer Programs: Eleven Accounts of Why and How Volunteers Are Employed in Active Welfare Work*, Foundation for Voluntary Welfare, 1958; (with Alfred De Grazia) *World Politics: A Study in International Relations*, Barnes & Noble, 1962, 2nd edition, 1966; *Politics and Government*, Littlefield, 1973. Also author or co-author of additional works. Contributor of articles and translations to encyclopedias and professional journals.

* * *

STEWART, Seumas 1919-

PERSONAL: Given name is pronounced *Shay*-mus; born November 7, 1919, in Aberdeen, Scotland; son of Seumas (a ship's plater) and Jeannie (an accountant; maiden name, Macpherson) Stewart; married Penelope Barron (an actress), November 14, 1947; children: Rachel Christina. *Education:* Educated in Aberdeen, Scotland. *Politics:* "Scottish Nationalist/Liberal." *Religion:* Society of Friends (Quakers). *Home and office:* Harrow House, Chipping Campden, Gloucestershire GL55 6DY, England.

CAREER: Thomson/Leng Publications, Dundee, Scotland, journalist, 1938-42; Byre Theatre, St. Andrews, Scotland, actor, 1942-43; Adelphi Guild Theatre, London, England, 1943-51, began as actor, became artistic director in London and Macclesfield; *Warrington Guardian*, Warrington, England, features editor, 1951-59; self-employed antiquarian bookseller in Chipping Campden, England, 1959—. *Member:* Robert Dover's Games Society (secretary).

WRITINGS: Book Collecting: A Beginner's Guide, Dutton, 1975; *A Book of Books*, David & Charles, in press.

Plays: "Alice in Wonderland," adapted from the book by Lewis Carroll; first performed on tour by Adelphi Guild Theatre, December, 1949; "Rumpelstiltskin," first produced in Altrincham, England, at Garrick Drama School, 1953; "A Smoke for the King" (one-act), first produced in Nantwich, England, at Nantwich Playwriting Festival, 1954.

Author of "Mr. Carr's Tragedy" (radio script, on the history of the theater in Lascashire), first broadcast by British Broadcasting Corp.'s Northern Region sound radio service. Ghost writer and "play doctor." Contributor of articles, poems, and reviews to magazines, including *New Theatre*, *Scots*, and *New Statesman*, and to newspapers.

WORK IN PROGRESS: Before the Oil, an autobiographical history of north-east Scotland.

SIDELIGHTS: Stewart explains that the "Robert Dover Games Society is of considerable local antiquarian interest. These yearly games were founded circa 1612 by Robert Dover, an attorney, and were given national significance in 1636 by the publication of a book of poems in praise of Dover and his games. The contributors included Michael

Drayton, the aging Ben Jonson, and other poets of note. With breaks, the Games have continued to the present day and are about two hundred years older than any other comparable games in Britain."

Of himself, Stewart writes: "Bibliomania is a hereditary disease in my family, so I have been a life-long collector of books—not the rare and fine, but the unusual and unexpected. For most of my life I have had a narcissistic love affair with my native area of Scotland and have delved into its history and literature."

* * *

STEWART, Suzanne

PERSONAL: Born in Fayetteville, N.C.; daughter of Pryor Franklin (a cotton broker) and Sue (Sappington) Johnson; married John Sydney Stewart, September 28, 1951; children: Sue (Mrs. Bryan Romig True), Sydney Hart (daughter), Huntington John. Education: Attended Brenau College; University of Georgia, B.F.A.; Emory University, M.Ed., 1964. Religion: Christian. Home: 6395 Vernon Woods Dr. N.E., Atlanta, Ga. 30328.

CAREER: Speech therapist in the public schools of Atlanta, Ga., 1963—. Speech therapist and lecturer, Atlanta Counseling Center, 1971.

WRITINGS: Divorced! I Wouldn't Have Given a Nickel for Your Chances, Zondervan, 1974.

WORK IN PROGRESS: The Endurable Emotion.

* * *

STIEHM, Judith 1935-

PERSONAL: Surname is pronounced "steam"; born October 4, 1935, in Madison, Wis.; daughter of Stratton E. (an engineer) and Eleanor (Kilbourn) Hicks; married E. Richard Stiehm (a physician), July 12, 1958; children: Jamie Elizabeth, Carrie Eleanor, Meredith Ellen. Education: University of Wisconsin, B.A., 1957; Temple University, M.A., 1961; Columbia University, Ph.D., 1969. Office: Department of Political Science, University of Southern California, Los Angeles, Calif. 90007.

CAREER: San Francisco State College (now University), San Francisco, Calif., lecturer in political science, 1964-65; University of Wisconsin, Madison, lecturer in political science, 1966-69; University of California, Los Angeles, lecturer in political science, 1969-70; University of Southern California, Los Angeles, assistant professor, 1970-74, associate professor of political science, 1974—. Member: American Political Science Association, American Association of University Professors, Western Political Science Association.

WRITINGS: Nonviolent Power, Heath, 1972.

WORK IN PROGRESS: Investigations into political participation, conflict, resolution, and the status of women.

* * *

STIGUM, Marcia (Lee) 1934-

PERSONAL: Born August 26, 1934, in Oyster Bay, N.Y.; daughter of Peter N. (an arborist) and Helen (a secretary; maiden name, Hill) Hanson; married Bernt Petter Stigum (a professor), August 4, 1956; children: Tove, Erik. Education: Middlebury College, B.A. (cum laude), 1956; Massachusetts Institute of Technology, Ph.D., 1961. Politics: Independent. Home: 1731 de l'Ogier Dr., Glenview, Ill. 60025. Office: Department of Economics, Loyola University of Chicago, Chicago, Ill.

CAREER: New England Mutual Life Insurance Co., Boston, Mass., member of economic research staff, 1961; Northeastern University, Boston, Mass., instructor in economics, 1961-62; Wellesley College, Wellesley, Mass., instructor in economics, 1962-63; Cornell University, Ithaca, N.Y., assistant professor of economics, 1963-66; Loyola University of Chicago, Chicago, Ill., assistant professor, 1970-73, associate professor of economics, 1974—. Member: American Economic Association, American Finance Association, Phi Beta Kappa.

WRITINGS: (With husband, Bernt P. Stigum) Economics, Addison-Wesley, 1968, study guide, 1969, 2nd edition, 1972; Problems in Microeconomics, Irwin, 1975; How to Turn Your Money into More Money, Dow Jones-Irwin, in press. Contributor to finance journals.

WORK IN PROGRESS: Portfolio Manager's Guide to Money Market Securities, publication by Dow Jones-Irwin expected in 1977.

AVOCATIONAL INTERESTS: International travel, skiing, tennis.

* * *

STILLEY, Frank 1918-

PERSONAL: Born April 18, 1918, in Wardville, Okla.; son of William Frank (a railroad agent) and Mabel (Watson) Stilley; married Joy Turner (a writer and editor for Associated Press), September 3, 1943; children: Brenn, Gay. Education: University of Oklahoma, A.B., 1942. Home: 254-13 75th Ave., Glen Oaks, N.Y. 11004.

CAREER: Shawnee News-Star, Shawnee, Okla., managing editor, 1942-43; Associated Press, New York, N.Y., reporter, writer, editor, 1943-65; media relations director for New York firms, Dudley-Anderson-Yutzy, 1965-69, Partners for Growth, Inc., 1969-71; independent public relations consultant in New York, 1971-72; media relations director for American Can Co., New York, 1972-74; writer, and independent public relations consultant, 1974—. Member: Society of Professional Journalists, New York Press Club.

WRITINGS: The $100,000 Rat, and Other Animal Heroes for Human Health, Putnam, 1975; Here Is Your Career: Veterinarian (for young people), Putnam, 1976. Contributor to popular magazines.

SIDELIGHTS: Stilley writes that he enjoys "writing for general public on complex subjects, such as new discoveries in atomic structure and astronomy, medicine, and research, in such a way that people can understand."

* * *

STILLMAN, Irwin M(axwell) 1895-1975

September 11, 1895—August 26, 1975; American physician, educator, and author of diet books. Obituaries: Washington Post, August 28, 1975; New York Times, August 28, 1975; Time, September 8, 1975. (See index for previous CA sketch)

* * *

STOCKING, George Ward 1892-1975

September 24, 1892—June 7, 1975; American economist, educator, and author of books in his field. Obituaries: AB Bookman's Weekly, September 22-29, 1975.

STOFFLE, Carla J(oy) 1943-

PERSONAL: Born June 19, 1943, in Pueblo, Colo.; daughter of Samuel B. (a steelworker) and Virginia (Berry) Hayden; married Richard William Stoffle (a professor of anthropology), June 12, 1964; children: Brent William, Kami Ann. *Education:* Southern Colorado State College, A.A., 1963; University of Colorado, B.A. (with distinction), 1965; University of Kentucky, M.S.L.S., 1969. *Home:* 455 Melvin, Racine, Wis. 53402. *Office:* Library, University of Wisconsin—Parkside, Kenosha, Wis. 53140.

CAREER: Peace Corps, Washington, D.C., volunteer high school teacher in Barbados, West Indies, 1965-67; University of Kentucky, Lexington, intern at Margaret I. King Library, 1967-69; Eastern Kentucky University, Richmond, head of government publications department of John G. Crabbe Library, 1969-72; University of Wisconsin—Parkside, Kenosha, reference librarian in charge of library instruction, 1972-73, head of reference department, 1973-74, head of Public Services Division, 1974—. *Member:* American Library Association, Wisconsin Library Association, Kenosha Library Association, Phi Beta Mu, Phi Theta Kappa.

WRITINGS: (With Rebekah Harleston) *Administration of Government Documents Collections,* Libraries Unlimited, 1974. Contributor to library journals. Editor of *Library Instruction News Communique,* 1973-75.

WORK IN PROGRESS: A *Library Directory,* for Wisconsin Library Association.

*   *   *

STOKER, H(oward) Stephen 1939-

PERSONAL: Born April 16, 1939, in Salt Lake City, Utah; son of Howard Seymour (an electrician) and Alice Maud (Child) Stoker; married Sharon Rosella Stevenson, June 16, 1964; children: Rebecca Elizabeth, Deborah Rosella, Howard Scott, Henry Stephen, Howard Spencer. *Education:* University of Utah, B.A., 1963, University of Wisconsin, Ph.D., 1968. *Religion:* Church of Jesus Christ of Latter Day Saints. *Home:* 765 Ben Lomond Dr., Ogden, Utah 84403. *Office:* Department of Chemistry, Weber State College, Ogden, Utah 84408.

CAREER: Weber State College, Ogden, Utah, professor of inorganic chemistry, 1968—. *Member:* American Chemical Society, Sigma Xi.

WRITINGS: (With Spencer L. Seager) *Environmental Chemistry: Air and Water Pollution,* Scott, Foresman, 1972, 2nd edition, 1976; (with Seager) *Chemistry: A Science for Today,* Scott, Foresman, 1973; (with Seager and R. L. Capener) *Energy: From Source to Use,* Scott, Foresman, 1975.

*   *   *

STONE, Frank A(ndrews) 1929-

PERSONAL: Born January 12, 1929, in Wilmington, Del.; son of Royal Amidon (a mechanical engineer) and Ruth Sherman (Andrews) Stone; married Barbara May Tinkham (an educator), June 14, 1957; children: David, Ruth, Beth, Priscilla. *Education:* Heidelberg College, A.B., 1949; Oberlin College, M.Div., 1952, D.Min., 1953; Western Michigan University, M.A., 1960; University of Ankara, graduate study, 1962-63; Boston University, Ed.D., 1968. *Politics:* Democrat. *Religion:* United Church of Christ. *Home:* 3 Westgate Lane, Storrs, Conn. 06268. *Office:* U-32, University of Connecticut, Storrs, Conn. 06268.

CAREER: American College, Tarsus, Turkey, teacher, associate director, and later director, 1953-66; University of Connecticut, Storrs, assistant professor, 1968-69, associate professor, 1970-75, professor of international education, 1975—, director of world education project, 1971—. Member, Turkey Schools Council, 1957-66; member of board of visitors, Near East School of Theology, 1958-70; visiting professor, Hacettepe University, 1969-70; president of Connecticut chapter, World Education Fellowship, 1974-76; member of Connecticut Partners of the Americas. *Member:* American Educational Studies Association, Comparative and International Education Society, History of Education Society, Middle East Institute (fellow), Middle East Studies Association (fellow), Philosophy of Education Society (fellow), Society for Educational Reconstruction.

WRITINGS: Translate: A Casebook of Texts and Projects for Learning to Translate Between Turkish and English, Tarsus College (Tarsus, Turkey), 1965; *Emphases in Modern Turkish Literature,* Redhouse Press (Istanbul), 1969; *The Impact of Culture on Education in Modern Turkey,* Redhouse Press, 1970; *Communities of Learning: People and Their Programs,* Redhouse Press, 1970; *Modern Turkish Educational Thought: A Bibliographic Introduction,* Hacettepe University Press (Ankara), 1971; *The Rub of Cultures in Modern Turkey: Literary Views of Education,* Indiana University, 1973; (editor) *The New World of Educational Thought,* Mss Information, 1973; *Armenian Studies for Secondary Students,* World Education Project, University of Connecticut, 1975; *The Irish: In Their Homeland, In America, In Connecticut,* World Education Project, University of Connecticut, 1975. Contributor of twenty-eight articles to journals. Editor, *Current Turkish Thought,* 1968-71, *Cutting Edge* (publication of the Society for Educational Reconstruction), 1974—.

WORK IN PROGRESS: Academies for Anatolia, a study of the American board schools in Turkey from 1820 until the 1970's, completion expected in 1976; *Modern Turkish Educational Thought,* completion expected, 1977; *The Scots: In Their Homeland, In America, In Connecticut,* 1977; *Patterns of Transformation: Philosophical Alternatives for Educators,* a graduate level textbook in educational philosophy, 1978.

*   *   *

STONE, I(sidor) F(einstein) 1907-

PERSONAL: Name originally Isidor Feinstein; legally changed, 1938; born December 24, 1907, in Philadelphia, Pa.; son of Bernard (a merchant) and Katherine (Novak) Feinstein; married Esther M. Roisman, July 7, 1929; children: Celia (Mrs. Walter Gilbert), Jeremy J., Christopher D. *Education:* Attended University of Pennsylvania, 1924-27, and American University, 1974—. *Home:* 4420 29th St. N.W., Washington, D.C. 20008. *Office:* c/o *New York Review of Books,* 250 West 57th St., New York, N.Y. 10019.

CAREER: Ran his own newspaper, *The Progress,* while still in high school, 1922; reporter for *Haddonfield Press,* Haddonfield, N.J., *Courier Post,* Camden, N.J., *Philadelphia Record,* and *Philadelphia Inquirer,* 1923-33; editorial writer for *Philadelphia Record,* 1933, and *New York Post,* 1933-39; *The Nation,* New York City, associate editor, 1938-40, Washington editor, 1940-46; reporter, columnist, and editorial writer for *PM, New York Star, New York Post,* and *New York Daily Compass,* all New York City, at various times, 1942-52; *I. F. Stone's Bi-Weekly* (titled *I. F.*

Stone's Weekly, 1953-67), Washington, D.C., publisher and editor, 1953-71; *New York Review of Books,* contributing editor, 1971—. Distinguished scholar in residence, American University, 1974. *Awards, honors:* George Polk Memorial Award, Long Island University, 1970; journalism award, Columbia University, 1971; A. J. Liebling Award, 1972; Eleanor Roosevelt Peace Award from National Committee for a Sane Nuclear Policy, 1975. Honorary degrees from Amherst College, 1970, Brown University, 1971, and University of Pennsylvania, 1975.

WRITINGS: The Court Disposes, Covici-Friede, 1937; *Business as Usual: The First Year of Defense,* Modern Age, 1941; *Underground to Palestine,* Boni & Gaer, 1946; *This Is Israel,* with photographs by Robert Capa and others, Boni & Gaer, 1948; *The Hidden History of the Korean War,* Monthly Review Press, 1952; *The Truman Era* (collected articles, 1945-53), Monthly Review Press, 1953, new edition, Random House, 1972; *The Haunted Fifties* (collected articles, 1953-63), Random House, 1963; *In a Time of Torment* (collected articles, 1957-67), Random House, 1967; *Polemics and Prophecies, 1967-70,* Random House, 1970; *The Killings at Kent State: How Murder Went Unpunished,* introduction by Senator Stephen Young, Vintage Books, 1971; *The I. F. Stone's Weekly Reader,* edited by Neil Middleton, Random House, 1973.

WORK IN PROGRESS: "I have resumed my scholarly studies and hope . . . to make a contribution in a fundamental study of freedom of thought and expression in human society."

SIDELIGHTS: I. F. Stone is best known for his "little fleabite paper," the *I. F. Stone Weekly* (after 1967, the *I. F. Stone Bi-Weekly*) that rose to a circulation of 70,000 before its end in 1971. Nicolas von Hoffman wrote in 1970: "Many of us news people venerate I. F. Stone as being that superb combination of guts, erudition, judgment and talent which we admire in the sad knowledge that equalling him is impossible. Yet I. F. Stone has no mass audience. He's a journalist's journalist, a man whose work never appears in the big, metropolitan dailies. To profit from what he had to tell us you must either read his books or subscribe to I. F. Stone's Bi-Weekly." As sole writer, editor, and publisher of the newspaper he appeared an anachronism in an age when newspapers had become large corporate institutions. Stone has said: "The important thing about the so-called communications industry in America is that it's basically concerned with merchandising. News is a kind of by-product. And if you want to sell things, you don't want to offend anybody. There is a tendency toward blandness." Bland is never a work used to describe Stone. "He may infuriate or inspire, but he never bores," wrote Ronald Steel. "'Izzy' had been spoiled," observed Sol Stern, "having always enjoyed the good fortune of writing for publishers who let him have his say." And when the *New York Compass* failed in 1953 all that changed. Rather than compromise his controversial opinions and style Stone began the weekly.

Stone's individual brand of journalism springs from his diligent reading and his unerring memory. As a young Washington correspondent, he was forced to read transcripts of press conferences because of a hearing problem that wasn't cured until 1965. In addition, the enterprising reporter regularly read a number of American, British, and French newspapers, the UP and AP wires, and numerous government releases, reports, and statements. This use of such open research material was also fostered by his being a political maverick without an influential corporate structure

behind him opening up otherwise guarded information sources. Stone became the minute examiner of significant facts other reporters had missed or passed over lightly. Stern believes: "This is Stone's great strength. The Washington press corps is virtually unable to distinguish the important from the trivial, although they are the ones who create our sense of political reality. But it is Stone, poring through the clippings, reports, congressional hearings and official briefings, who provides the interpretation and the corrective. Stone's weekly might be read as a primer for working Washington journalists, telling them where they went wrong each week."

Held in high esteem by fellow journalists, Stone's talents are considered to match those of the leading American muckrakers and the greatest of the Enlightenment pamphleteers. He has been compared to Tom Paine, Alexis de Tocqueville, Edmund Burke, Theodore Parker, Upton Sinclair, and Lincoln Steffens. In a review of his book, *In a Time of Torment,* the *Christian Science Monitor* praised Stone's own use of historical perspective: "Typically he will start off with an unusual historical comparison. He may lay side by side a pamphlet from the Secretary of Defense and a memo from Metternich. He may juxtapose Lyndon Johnson and Louis XIV as revealed in Saint-Simon's memoirs. In an appraisal of Malcolm X, he will cite Tertullian, William James, a pre-Socratic philosopher, an Italian sociologist.

"The cross-reference is more apt at some times than at others, but almost always it forces the reader out of the protection of the standard cliches, compelling him to see people and events from some fresh, oblique angle." Christopher Serpell asserted this excellence comes from his "style—a pellucid, unpretentious Defoe-like treatment of the English language which gets its message over with economy and deadly competence. Occasionally he will rise to an epigrammatic level, but he never falls into the trap of mere invective, which must surely be a temptation for the lone ranger in the fields of journalism." "But much of his style," adds Robert Sherrill, ". . . isn't a luxury with Stone; it is very much a necessity. Cramming his stuff into four pages a week, he has come to lean on the sharp, sassy phrase, the neo-slogan head to make his point quickly and unforgettably. . . ."

Stone told *CA:* "As I see myself: I tried to bring the instincts of a scholar to the service of journalism; to take nothing for granted; to turn journalism into literature; to provide radical analysis with a conscientious concern for accuracy, and in studying the current scene to do my very best to preserve human values and free institutions." After giving up his bi-weekly because of poor health, Stone returned to college and is studying Greek philosophy, history, society, and literature.

A special program on I. F. Stone's life and work appeared on the National Education Television network in 1971 and a one-hour movie, "I. F. Stone's Weekly," has been made by Gerry Bruck.

BIOGRAPHICAL/CRITICAL SOURCES: Christian Science Monitor, November 30, 1967; *Commonweal,* January 26, 1968; *Ramparts,* February, 1968; *Listener,* October 24, 1968, October 31, 1968; *New York Review of Books,* December 5, 1968; *Washington Post,* June 3, 1970; *Wall Street Journal,* July 14, 1970; *Time,* February 8, 1971; *Newsweek,* December 20, 1971; Thomas G. Paterson, editor, *Cold War Critics: Alternatives to American Foreign Policy in the Truman Years,* Quadrangle, 1971; *Life,* January 21, 1972.

STONE, L(awrence) Joseph 1912-1975

May 20, 1912—December 13, 1975; American educator, psychologist, educational film producer, editor, and author. Obituaries: *New York Times,* December 14, 1975.

* * *

STONE, Shelley C(lyde, Jr.) 1928-

PERSONAL: Born April 20, 1928, in Alliance, Ohio; son of Shelley Clyde (a businessman) and Mildred Anne (Watkins) Stone; married Charlene Fairchild Mullins, June 29, 1951; children: Shelley Clyde III, Shannon Carol, Lynn Ann, Joel Allen. *Education:* Mount Union College, B.S., 1950; University of Rochester, M.Ed., 1956; University of Chicago, Ph.D., 1960. *Home:* 212 East Navajo St., West Lafayette, Ind. 47906. *Office:* Department of Education, Purdue University, West Lafayette, Ind. 47907.

CAREER: High school teacher in Augusta, Ohio, 1950-51; National Security Agency, Washington, D.C., research analyst, 1953-54; Purdue University, West Lafayette, Ind., assistant professor, 1960-63, associate professor, 1963-67, professor of counseling and personnel services in education, 1967—, assistant head of department of education and chairperson of special education section, 1975—. Certified psychologist in Indiana; visiting professor at University of Hawaii, summer, 1968, and University of Reading, 1969. Member of board of directors of Tippecanoe Mental Health Center, 1965-71; Wabash Valley Comprehensive Mental Retardation Center, member of board, 1971-75, first vice-president, 1974-75; member of advisory committee to board of directors of Tippecanoe County Welfare Board, 1966-68; president of Tippecanoe Parents for Special Education, 1974-75. *Military service:* U.S. Air Force, 1951-53. U.S. Air Force Reserve, 1953-58; became first lieutenant.

MEMBER: American Psychological Association (fellow), American Personnel and Guidance Association, National Rehabilitation Association (professional member, 1965-68), Indiana Personnel and Guidance Association. *Awards, honors:* Grant from Vocational Rehabilitation Administration, 1965-68, for Crossroads Rehabilitation Center.

WRITINGS—With B. E. Shertzer: *Fundamentals of Guidance,* Houghton, 1966, 3rd edition, in press; *Fundamentals of Counseling,* Houghton, 1968, 2nd edition, 1974; *Introduction to Guidance,* Houghton, 1971; (editors) *Careers in Counseling and Guidance,* Houghton, 1972. Co-editor of ten sets in "Guidance Monograph Series," Houghton, 1968—. Contributor to education and counseling journals. Member of board of editors of *Student Personnel Association for Teacher Education Journal,* of American Personnel and Guidance Association, 1964-68.

WORK IN PROGRESS: Research on counseling and on counselor preparation.

* * *

STONE, Susan Berch 1944-
(Ann Whitefield, "M")

PERSONAL: Born August 23, 1944, in Massachusetts; daughter of Jack S. (a physician) and Dorothy (Robrish) Berch; married Errol M. Stone (an attorney), June 26, 1965. *Education:* Simmons College, B.A. (cum laude), 1966; University of Maryland, graduate study, 1967-69. *Home:* 20481 Royalstone Dr., Malibu, Calif. 90265. *Agent:* Arthur Pine, 1780 Broadway, New York, N.Y. 10019.

CAREER: High school teacher of British literature in Prince George's County, Md., 1966-71; writer, 1971—.

Member of board of directors of Tierra del Sol (school for mentally retarded adults); local courthouse docent; member of Pacific Palisades Coordinating Council. *Member:* National Association of Teachers of English, Lawyers Wives of Los Angeles, Pacific Palisades Junior Women's Club.

WRITINGS: Bisexuality: Some Case Studies, Carlyle, 1975; (under pseudonym Ann Whitefield) *The Joy of Swinging: A Gourmet's Guide to Group Sex,* Pinnacle Books, 1975; (under pseudonym "M") *The Happy Housewife,* Carlyle, 1975; *Honeymoon Sexual Patterns,* Carlyle, in press. Contributor to education and English journals.

WORK IN PROGRESS: Power Play, a novel dealing with the generation conflict between a mother and her four daughters; *Alicia,* with Nancy Sackett Handler, dealing with mother-daughter relations, to be issued both in novel and screenplay form.

AVOCATIONAL INTERESTS: Sailing, cooking, theater, good restaurants (especially French), travel.

* * *

STONG, Clair L. 1902(?)-1975
(Red Stong)

1902(?)—December 9, 1975; American electrical engineer, columnist, and science writer. Obituaries: *New York Times,* December 16, 1975.

* * *

STORM, Marian 1892(?)-1975

1892(?)—August 20, 1975; American journalist, naturalist, and author. Obituaries: *New York Times,* August 23, 1975.

* * *

STOTT, William (Merrell) 1940-

PERSONAL: Born June 2, 1940, in New York, N.Y.; son of William G. (a banker) and Jane (Merrell) Stott; married Jane Kielty, June 16, 1962; children: Molly, Gordon. *Education:* Yale University, B.A., 1962, M.Ph., 1970, Ph.D., 1972; attended Stanford University, 1963-64. *Politics:* Liberal. *Religion:* Catholic. *Home:* 1213 Red Bud Trail, Austin, Tex. 78746. *Office:* American Studies, University of Texas, Austin, Tex. 78712.

CAREER: U.S. Information Agency, Washington, D.C., foreign service officer in Senegal and Morocco, 1964-68; University of Texas, Austin, 1971—, began as assistant professor, now associate professor of American studies and English, and associate dean of Division of General and Comparative Studies. *Awards, honors:* Carnegie teaching fellow, 1962-63; Woodrow Wilson fellow, 1963-64; National Defense Education Act fellow, 1968-71.

WRITINGS: Documentary Expression and Thirties America, Oxford University Press, 1973. Contributor to *Afterimage, Artscanada, Bookletter,* and *Harper's.*

* * *

STOUCK, David (Hamilton) 1940-

PERSONAL: Surname sounds like "stowk"; born October 28, 1940, in Beamsville, Ontario, Canada; son of Henry J. W. (a farmer) and Winnifred (Hamilton) Stouck; married Mary-Ann Quick (a professor), August 22, 1964; children: Jordan Wardell (daughter). *Education:* McMaster University, B.A., 1963; University of Toronto, M.A., 1966. *Home:* 354 Moyne Dr., West Vancouver, British Columbia V7S 1J5, Canada. *Office:* Department of English, Simon Fraser University, Burnaby 2, British Columbia, Canada.

CAREER: Simon Fraser University, Burnaby, British Columbia, assistant professor, 1970-72, associate professor of American literature, 1972—.

WRITINGS: Willa Cather's Imagination, University of Nebraska Press, 1975. Contributor to Prairie Schooner, Mosaic, Centennial Review, University of Toronto Quarterly, and other journals.

* * *

STOUGHTON, Clarence Charles 1895-1975

February 8, 1895—August 31, 1975; American university president, religious organization administrator, educator, editor, and author. Obituaries: New York Times, September 1, 1975.

* * *

STOUT, Rex (Todhunter) 1886-1975

PERSONAL: Born December 1, 1886, in Noblesville, Ind.; son of John Wallace and Lucetta Elizabeth (Todhunter) Stout; married Fay Kennedy, December 16, 1916 (divorced); married Pola Hoffman (a textile designer), December 21, 1932; children: Barbara Stout Selleck, Rebecca Stout Bradbury. Education: Educated in public schools of Topeka, Kan.; attended University of Kansas for two weeks. Home: High Meadow, Brewster, N.Y. 10509.

CAREER: Author. Worked in numerous states at over thirty jobs, including cook, salesman, bookkeeper, pueblo guide, bellhop, hotel manager, architect, and cabinetmaker, 1908-12; free-lance magazine writer in New York City, 1912-16; created and managed Educational Thrift Service, a school banking system eventually enrolling over two million children, 1916-27; writer in Paris, 1927-29; novelist, 1927-75. Founder and former director of Vanguard Press. Radio broadcaster, "Speaking of Liberty," 1941, "Voice of Freedom," 1942, "Our Secret Weapon," 1942-43. Chairman, Writers War Board (later Writers Board), 1941-46, Writers Board for World Government, 1949-75; president, Friends of Democracy, 1941-51; treasurer, Freedom House, 1957-75. Military service: U.S. Navy, 1906-08. Member: Author's Guild (president, 1943-45), Authors League of America (president, 1951-55 and 1961-69; vice-president, 1956-61) Mystery Writers of America (president, 1958-75), Society for Prevention of World War Three (president, 1943-46), Society of Amateur Chefs. Awards, honors: Silver Dagger award from Crime Writers' Association (England), 1970, for The Father Hunt.

WRITINGS—Nero Wolfe mystery books; all published by Viking, except as indicated: Fer-de-Lance, Farrar & Rinehart, 1934; The League of Frightened Men, Farrar & Rinehart, 1935; The Rubber Band, Farrar & Rinehart, 1936, published as To Kill Again, Hillman Books, 1960; The Red Box, Farrar & Rinehart, 1937; Too Many Cooks, Farrar & Rinehart, 1938; Some Buried Caesar, Farrar & Rinehart, 1939, condensed edition published as The Red Bull, Dell, 1945.

Over My Dead Body, Farrar & Rinehart, 1940; Where There's a Will, Farrar & Rinehart, 1940; Black Orchids (two novellas, "Black Orchids" and "Cordially Invited to Meet Death"), Farrar & Rinehart, 1942, "Cordially Invited to Meet Death" published as Invitation to Murder, Avon, 1956 (also see below); Not Quite Dead Enough (two novellas, "Not Quite Dead Enough" and "Booby Trap"), Farrar & Rinehart, 1944; The Silent Speaker, 1946; Too Many Women, 1947; And Be a Villain, 1948 (published in England as More Deaths Than One, Collins, 1949); Trouble in Triplicate (three novellas, "Before I Die," "Help Wanted, Male," and "Instead of Evidence"), 1949; The Second Confession, 1949.

Three Doors to Death (three novellas, "Man Alive," "Omit Flowers," and "Door to Death"), 1950; In the Best Families, 1950 (published in England as Even in the Best Families, Collins, 1951); Murder by the Book, 1951; Curtains for Three (three novellas, "The Gun with Wings," "Bullet for One," and "Disguise for Murder"), 1951; Triple Jeopardy (three novellas, "Home to Roost," "The Cop Killer," and "The Squirt and the Monkey"), 1952; Prisoner's Base, 1952 (published in England as Out She Goes, Collins, 1955); The Golden Spiders, 1953; The Black Mountain, 1954; Three Men Out (three novellas, "Invitation to Murder," "The Zero Clue," and "This Won't Kill You"), 1954; Before Midnight, 1955; Three Witnesses (three novellas, "The Next Witness," "When a Man Murders," and "Die Like a Dog"), 1956; Might as Well Be Dead, 1956; Three for the Chair (three novellas, "A Window for Death," "Immune to Murder," and "Too Many Detectives"), 1957; If Death Ever Slept, 1957; Champagne for One, 1958; And Four to Go (four novellas, "Christmas Party," "Easter Parade," "Fourth of July Picnic," and "Murder Is No Joke"), 1958; Plot It Yourself, 1959; Crime and Again, Collins, 1959.

Murder in Style, Collins, 1960; Three at Wolfe's Door (three novellas, "Poison a la Carte," "Method Three for Murder," and "The Rodeo Murder"), 1960; Too Many Clients, 1960; The Final Deduction, 1961; Gambit, 1962; Homicide Trinity (three novellas, "Eeny Meeny Murder Mo," "Death of a Demon," and "Counterfeit for Murder"), 1962; The Mother Hunt, 1963; Trio for Blunt Instruments (three novellas, "Kill Now, Pay Later," "Murder Is Corny," and "Blood Will Tell"), 1964; A Right to Die, 1964; The Doorbell Rang, 1965; Death of a Doxy, 1966; The Father Hunt, 1968; Death of a Dude, 1969; Please Pass the Guilt, 1973; A Family Affair, 1975.

Omnibus volumes; all published by Viking: Full House (includes The League of Frightened Men, And Be a Villain, and Curtains for Three), 1955; All Aces (includes Some Buried Caesar, Too Many Women, and Trouble in Triplicate), 1958; Five of a Kind (includes The Rubber Band, In the Best Families, and Three Doors to Death), 1961; Royal Flush (includes Fer-de-Lance, Murder by the Book, and Three Witnesses), 1965; Kings Full of Aces (includes Too Many Cooks, Plot It Yourself, and Triple Jeopardy), 1969; Three Aces (includes Too Many Clients, Might as Well Be Dead, and The Final Deduction), 1971; Three Trumps (includes The Black Mountain, If Death Ever Slept, and Before Midnight), 1973; Triple Zeck (includes And Be a Villain, The Second Confession, and In the Best Families), 1974; The First Rex Stout Omnibus (includes The Doorbell Rang, The Second Confession, and More Deaths Than One), Penguin, in press.

Other: How Like a God (psychological novel), Vanguard, 1929; Seed on the Wind (psychological novel), Vanguard, 1930; Golden Remedy (psychological novel), Vanguard, 1931; Forest Fire (psychological novel), Farrar & Rinehart, 1933; O Careless Love! (novel), Farrar & Rinehart, 1935; The Hand in the Glove: A Dol Bonner Mystery, Farrar & Rinehart, 1937 (published in England as Crime on Her Hands, Collins, 1939); Mr. Cinderella (novel), Farrar & Rinehart, 1938; Double for Death: A Tecumseh Fox Mystery, Farrar & Rinehart, 1939; Mountain Cat: A Mystery Novel, Farrar & Rinehart, 1939; Red Threads (an

Inspector Cramer mystery), Farrar & Rinehart, 1939; *Bad for Business* (a Tecumseh Fox mystery), Farrar & Rinehart, 1940; *The Broken Vase: A Tecumseh Fox Mystery*, Farrar & Rinehart, 1941; *Alphabet Hicks: A Mystery*, Farrar & Rinehart, 1941, published as *The Sound of Murder*, Pyramid Publications, 1965; *The President Vanishes* (some sources report this book first published in the 1930's or '40's), Pyramid Publications, 1967; (with others) *The Nero Wolfe Cookbook*, Viking, 1973.

Editor: *The Illustrious Dunderheads*, Knopf, 1942; (with Louis Greenfield) *Rue Morgue No. 1* (short stories), Creative Age Press, 1946; (and author of introduction) *Eat, Drink, and Be Buried* (short stories), Viking, 1956; (and author of introduction) *For Tomorrow We Die*, Macdonald & Co., 1958.

Contributor of stories and articles to periodicals, including *American Magazine*. Founder and editor, *Rex Stout's Mystery Monthly*, beginning, 1945, *Nero Wolfe Mystery Magazine*, 1954; former editor, *Author's League of America Bulletin*.

SIDELIGHTS: Ian Fleming once called Rex Stout "one of the most civilized minds that has ever been applied to the art of the thriller." Stout was the creator of Nero Wolfe, the 286-pound genius detective who, with the legwork done by his sidekick Archie Goodwin, solved most cases without ever leaving his apartment. "If there is anybody in detective fiction remotely comparable to England's Sherlock Holmes," noted *Time* magazine, "it is Rex Stout's corpulent genius, Nero Wolfe." The Nero Wolfe books have sold between forty-five and sixty million copies in some twenty four languages. "They have been popular enough so that I didn't have any difficulty for 40 years making a nice living from it," Stout once told Israel Shenker. "That should be the fundamental concern of any healthy man."

Rex Stout claimed to have left Indiana with his family at the age of one because he was already "fed up with Indiana politics." Settling in Kansas, his parents discovered their son was a mathematical prodigy. He went on an exhibition tour at the age of nine, adding huge columns of numbers in seemingly impossible time. Returning home Stout stayed out of school in order to read his father's twelve hundred volume library; at age thirteen he was state spelling champion. These abilities would seem to have predicted a scholarly life, but he left the University of Kansas after only two weeks. Drifting to the East coast, he joined the Navy. "I was assigned to Teddy Roosevelt's yacht, *Mayflower*, as pay-yeoman. I saw a lot of the Caribbean and became a good whist player. I was promoted to warrant officer because there were seven commissioned officers on board and they needed an eighth for two tables of whist. I earned $26.20 a month in salary and made up to $400 a month playing whist." After two years Stout decided he wanted to see more of the United States, so with some of what he had won in whist he purchased his release. He drifted across the country working numerous odd jobs and storing away "11,000 impressions a minute." In 1912 he found himself in New York City and tried his hand at journalism. Stout wrote a magazine story on then-presidential candidate William Howard Taft's palm prints, and sold it for two-hundred dollars. For a few years he would spend himself penniless, "dash off 8,000 words and run up to *Argosy* for the check," and then do it all over again. Stout once wagered that he was "the only professional writer who hasn't got a single unpublished paragraph in a drawer anywhere." Stout wanted to take on more serious work, and in order to

finance himself he invented the school savings account system. Its success enabled Stout to retire to Paris in 1927. While there, he wrote five psychological suspense novels, but in spite of their good reception, he realized: "I was a good storyteller but would never make a great novelist, so I decided to write detective stories. You just tell stories and you don't have to worry about making new comments on life and human beings. That's when I started Nero Wolfe for *American Magazine*."

Stout once described his method of writing the Wolfe stories: "Most of my writing career, I've started my book on the tenth or twelfth of January and finished it in 39 or 40 days. The rest of the year, I read, argue, play chess and do any number of other things." Before beginning a book Stout spent little time on groundwork. "When I start at the typewriter I have a slip of paper with the names of the people, their ages and what they do, and that's all the outline I have," he once remarked. "You see, in my life I've done maybe a thousand interesting things, and I think that nine hundred and thirty-seven of them happened in my subconscious. I remember when I was writing *How Like a God* I had a scene where the hero's son comes into his office and talks to him for two or three pages. Suddenly I pushed back from the typewriter, jumped up and said, 'Jesus Christ! I didn't know he had a son!'" Stout once declared that he would rather dig ditches than write outlines or construct synopses before beginning a book. After a book was finished, Stout thought about it even less than he did in its preparation. He never revised, rewrote, or reread one of his books; he explained that "writing is a sort of explosion, when the explosion has taken place, there is no use going around looking at the debris."

However the books were written, they were and are popular. As readers probably find many reasons for liking the Wolfe books, critics find widely different qualities to admire. Frank Jellinek pointed out that "the puzzle [of each work] and its solution are impeccably fair, in the sense that the reader knows all that Archie does and can even make an informed guess at 'the specific thing that was strikingly suggestive' to Wolfe, but not to the others." J. J. McAleer said: "Paramount in our appreciation of what [Stout] has wrought in this tale [*Please Pass the Guilt*], and in the saga that it continues, is our awareness of his adherence to the ground rules Poe laid down for the detective story. First, there must be no extraneous matter—everything must converge on a single effect; and, second, it is not who committed the crime that is important, but how the detective arrives at his identity." Allen J. Hubin admired the variation of the Sherlock Holmes—Dr. Watson, brilliant detective—awestruck companion team: "Now and then the 'Watson' explodes out of this mold and becomes a vital character in his own right. I can think of no more impressive instance of this than Rex Stout's Archie Goodwin, who since 1934 (in *Fer-de-Lance*) has played an equally important and far more active role than Nero Wolfe, no mean slouch himself. . . . What a pleasure it is to watch this pair at work!" Stout commented on the success of his stories in his own inimitable way: "You know goddam well why, of all kinds of stories, the detective story is the most popular. It supports, more than any other kind of story, man's favorite myth, that he's Homo sapiens, the rational animal. And of course the poor son-of-a-bitch isn't a rational animal at all. I think the most important function of the brain is thinking up reasons for the decisions his emotions have made. Detective stories support that myth. That accounts for the fact that that fantastic bloodhound, Sherlock Holmes, is known to more people around the world than any other character created in fiction.''

Stout's books have been adapted for film and radio. Some of his early novels were published in condensed form and with different titles in *American Magazine.*

AVOCATIONAL INTERESTS: Stout had over three-hundred house plants, and maintained large outdoor flower, fruit, and vegetable gardens. He delighted in growing huge fruits and vegetables that were notorious in county fair exhibitions—he once grew a 210-pound pumpkin, force-fed on evaporated milk. Stout also enjoyed animals, and had trained owls, crows, and at one time, a jumping pig. Something of an experimenter, he is reported to have tried to duplicate the taste of some grouse he had eaten on a hunting trip by raising some chickens on nothing but blue-berries.

BIOGRAPHICAL/CRITICAL SOURCES: New Yorker (profile), July 16 and July 23, 1949; *New York Herald Tribune,* October 10, 1965; Jacques Barzun, *A Birthday Tribute to Rex Stout, December 1, 1965,* Viking, 1965; *New York Times Book Review,* June 30, 1968, July 14, 1968, November 11, 1973; W. S. Baring-Gould, *Nero Wolfe of West Thirty-Fourth Street,* Viking, 1969; *Time,* March 21, 1969; *Washington Post,* October 5, 1969; *Holiday,* November, 1969; *Newsweek,* March 22, 1971; *New York Times,* December 1, 1971; *Publishers Weekly,* October 29, 1973; *Best Sellers,* November 1, 1973; Carolyn Riley, editor, *Contemporary Literary Criticism,* Volume III, Gale, 1975.

OBITUARIES: Detroit Free Press, October 28, 1975; *New York Times,* October 28, 1975; *Washington Post,* October 29, 1975; *Publishers Weekly,* November 10, 1975; *Time,* November 10, 1975; *Newsweek,* November 10, 1975; *AB Bookman's Weekly,* December 22-29, 1975; *Current Biography,* January, 1976.*

(Died October 27, 1975, in Danbury, Conn.)

*   *   *

STRACHAN, Hew (Francis Anthony)   1949-

PERSONAL: Born September 1, 1949, in Edinburgh, Scotland; son of Michael Francis (a ship owner) and Iris (a landscape architect; maiden name, Hemingway) Strachan; married Catherine Margaret Blackburn, June 26, 1971; children: Emily. *Education:* Corpus Christi College, Cambridge, B.A., 1971, M.A., 1975. *Office:* Corpus Christi College, Cambridge University, Cambridge CB2 1RH, England.

CAREER: National Army Museum, Sandhurst, England, museum assistant, 1968; Ben Line Steamers, Edinburgh, Scotland, management trainee, 1972; Cambridge University, Corpus Christi College, Cambridge, England, research fellow, 1975—. *Member:* Society for Army Historical Research.

WRITINGS: British Military Uniforms, 1768-1796, Hippo-crene, 1975. Contributor to professional journals.

WORK IN PROGRESS: A history of Cambridge University Officers Training Corps; research on nineteenth-century British military history.

SIDELIGHTS: In 1968, Strachan worked his passage around the world as a merchant seaman. In 1971 he organized an India overland expedition, and in 1973, worked as a member of a survey on Sudanese Red Sea coast antiquities. *Avocational interests:* Rugby football, country pursuits.

STRATTON, Arthur M.   1910(?)-1975

1910(?)—September 3, 1975; American educator, and author of fiction and nonfiction. Obituaries: *New York Times,* September 3, 1975; *Washington Post,* September 3, 1975.

*   *   *

STRATTON, J(ohn) T(heodore)   1902-
(Ted Stratton)

PERSONAL: Born May 17, 1902, in Far Hills, N.J.; son of John Theodore (a contractor) and Sara (Howell) Stratton; married Alicia L. Hegarty, November 19, 1925; children: John, C. Theodore, Nancy Alicia Wayland; R. Wayne, Judith Ann James. *Education:* Colgate University, B.S., 1924. *Politics:* Independent Republican. *Religion:* None. *Home:* 969 New Galena Rd., R.D. 1, Doylestown, Pa. 18901. *Agent:* Lenninger Literary Agency, Inc., 437 5th Ave., New York, N.Y. 10016.

CAREER: Ridgewood High School, Ridgewood, N.J., teacher of English and public speaking, 1926-64. Taught briefly at Patterson State College, and at Rutgers University.

WRITINGS—Under name Ted Stratton: *Wild Breed,* Fawcett, 1954; *Tourist Trap,* Putnam, 1975. Work has been represented in anthologies. Contributor of more than two hundred stories and articles to pulp magazines, including *Doc Savage, Black Masks, All American Football,* and *Flynn's.*

WORK IN PROGRESS: Murders on the Ramapo Rampart; Shoot Arrows at the Sun.

SIDELIGHTS: Stratton told *CA,* "I have traveled in Europe, Central America, and two thirds of the U.S. I am an expert gardener, a specialist in Dutch bulb growing, an avid ornithologist, a former professional football player in the old N.F.L., a word researcher, a student of law and police procedure, crossword puzzle addict, and a local history buff. At my age, I am still eager to learn about any subject.''

*   *   *

STRAUSS, William Louis   1914-

PERSONAL: Born April 5, 1914, in Robinson, Tex.; son of John David and Bertha (Rau) Strauss; married Allene Edith Atkinson, September 2, 1941; children: Barbara Lee (Mrs. G. L. Kramer), Linda Karen (Mrs. J. Patrick Britt). *Education:* Baylor University, A.B. (summa cum laude), 1935; University of Texas, A.M., 1936; Harvard University, A.M., 1938, Ph.D., 1948. *Home:* 333 East David Dr., Flagstaff, Ariz. 86001. *Office:* Department of Political Science, Northern Arizona University, Box 6023, Flagstaff, Ariz. 86001.

CAREER: University of Texas, Austin, instructor in political science, 1939-40; Works Progress Administration, Texas Historical Records Project, assistant state supervisor in San Antonio and Fort Worth, 1940-42; University of Texas, Austin, instructor in political science, 1942-48; University of Redlands, Redlands, Calif., assistant professor of political science, 1948-49; San Diego State College (now University), San Diego, Calif., assistant professor of political science, 1949-50; Long Beach State College (now California State University, Long Beach), Long Beach, Calif., assistant professor of political science, 1950-53; California State Employment Service, Sacramento, research technician, 1953-56; Northern Arizona University, Flagstaff, associate professor of political science, 1956-62; Seoul

National University, Seoul, Korea, Fulbright lecturer in political science, 1962-63; U.S. Educational Commission, Seoul, Korea, executive director, 1963-66; Northern Arizona University, Flagstaff, professor of political science, 1967—. Member of Coconino County Central Democratic Committee, 1968—, and State Central Democratic Committee, 1968—.

MEMBER: International Political Science Association, American Political Science Association, American Association of University Professors (local chapter president, 1958-59; state president, 1959-61), Western Political Science Association, Southwestern Social Science Association, Harvard Club (Phoenix, Ariz.), Alpha Chi, Pi Gamma Mu, Pi Sigma Alpha. *Awards, honors:* Fulbright senior research grant, 1972-73, for study in Korea.

WRITINGS: Joseph Chamberlain and the Theory of Imperialism, Fertig, 1942, revised edition, 1971; (editor with H. Malcolm McDonald, Wilfred Webb, and Edward G. Lewis) *Readings in American Government,* Crowell, 1949, 5th edition, 1967; (editor with McDonald, Webb, and Lewis) *Readings in American National Government,* Crowell, 1963. Contributor to professional journals, including *Western Political Quarterly, Koreana Quarterly,* and *Journal of Korean Affairs.*

* * *

STRAX, Philip 1909-

PERSONAL: Born January 1, 1909, in New York, N.Y.; son of Jacob and Molly (Pelchow) Strax; married Bertha Goldberg, December 26, 1932 (marriage ended, 1948); married Gertrude Jacobson (a psychologist), January 25, 1949; children: (first marriage) Norman, Rita Strax Weil, Polly (Mrs. Mark Hammer), Marshall; (second marriage) Gayle, Richard. *Education:* New York University, B.S., 1928, M.D., 1931. *Home and office:* 1056 Fifth Ave., New York, N.Y. 10028. *Agent:* Patricia Berens, 660 Madison Ave., New York, N.Y. 10021.

CAREER: Bellevue Hospital, New York City, radiologist, 1936-53; City Hospital, New York City, director of radiology, 1953-63; LaGuardia Hospital, Forest Hills, N.Y., director of radiology, 1966—.

WRITINGS: (Contributor) C. L. Sharp and H. Keen, editors, *Preventive Medicine: Pre-Symptomatic Detection and Early Diagnosis,* Pitman Medical Publishing, 1968; (contributor) *Davis' Gynecology and Obstetrics,* Harper, 1971; *Early Detection: Breast Cancer Is Curable,* Harper, 1974. Contributor to medical journals and proceedings.

* * *

STREETER, James (Jr.)

PERSONAL: Born in Black Hawk, Miss.; son of James (a minister) and Tanna (Streeter) Streeter; married Bertha D. Dorch (a librarian), 1946; children: Tanna Ambush, Steven Ambush. *Education:* Attended Ohio Valley Business College, 1935-39, Massachusetts Institute of Technology and American Baptist Bible School, 1951, U.S. Air Force Institute, 1956-60, Boston University, 1966-69, and Harvard University. *Politics:* "Democrat-Republican." *Religion:* Kingdom of God. *Home and office:* 21 Barbara Rd., West Newton, Mass. 12065.

CAREER: Sharecropper with family in Mississippi until 1915; has worked as laborer on farms, in lumber camps, in steel mills, and in a brickyard, has been messenger for U.S. Civil Service, clerk for Works Progress Administration,

and door-to-door salesman; U.S. Army, 1942-62, became master sergeant, taught courses, and supervised information and educational programs, served as assistant chaplain for 82nd Airborne Division, and reporter for *Paraglide* (82nd Airborne publication); Myrtle Baptist Church, West Newton, Mass., associate minister, 1967-68; Universal Christian Association for the Improvement of Black People, Inc., West Newton, founder and president, 1969—. Conductor of international youth forums on minority youth job markets, 1970-74. *Member:* Veterans of Foreign Wars, National Association for the Advancement of Colored People, Armed Forces Writer's League (lifetime member), National Writer's Club, Black United Front, Urban League (Greater Boston). *Awards, honors:* National Writer's Club short story award, 1968; Interracial Books for Children contest, finalist, 1968, award, 1970, for *Home Is Over the Mountains.*

WRITINGS: Home Is Over the Mountains: The Journey of Five Black Children (juvenile), Garrard, 1972.

Plays: "Father Time" (two-act), produced in Knoxville, Tenn., at Veterans Hall, 1933; "The Road to Heaven" (three-act), first produced in New Orleans, La., at Veterans Hall, 1938, produced in Boston, Mass., at Veterans Hall, 1975. Also author of "Way Down in Mississippi," three-act play, as yet neither published nor produced.

WORK IN PROGRESS: 217 Corn Bread Eaters; When Eternal Peace Breaks Out; Better Hang Me High; Nigger Son Call Me Mister; Son Caged the Panther; Son and Sister the Traders; Son's Journey In the Forest; I Went to Freetown; Blood Hounds Chasing Me; She's a Lovely Girl; Dark Down Here; She Saw Death Running; Stand Upright on Feet; Aunt Mag, Parson and Devil; Run Nigger Run; Hold This Land; Big Nigger Fall Hard; Black Devil White Angel; Come Tonight Please; Panther Called Son II.

SIDELIGHTS: James Streeter feels there is a vast imbalance concerning white and black employees, and has organized the Universal Christian Association for the Improvement of Black People in an attempt to adjust the ratio of Blacks in skills and professional trades to twenty percent. He commented: "I teach Blacks that they must be the next chief of police, the next police commissioner, the next county sheriff, the next governor. They must be the next U.S. cabinet head. They must be the next secretary of state. They must be the next vice-president. They shall be the next U.S. president."

AVOCATIONAL INTERESTS: Singing.

BIOGRAPHICAL/CRITICAL SOURCES: Newton Graphic, March 22, 1973; *Newton Times,* April 9, 1975.

* * *

STRELKA, Joseph P(eter) 1927-

PERSONAL: Listed in some sources as Josef Strelka; born May 3, 1927, in Wiener Neustadt, Austria; came to United States, 1964; son of Josef and Maria (Lisetz) Strelka; married Lucy Zambal, 1951 (divorced, 1957); married Brigitte Vollmer, July 13, 1963; children: Alexandra. *Education:* University of Vienna, Ph.D., 1950. *Home:* 1188 Avon Rd., Schenectady, N.Y. 12308. *Office:* Department of German, State University of New York, 1400 Washington Ave., Albany, N.Y. 12222.

CAREER: Municipal Office of Cultural Activities, Wiener Neustadt, Austria, director, 1950-51; free-lance critic in Vienna, Austria, 1951-64; University of Southern California, Los Angeles, visiting associate professor, 1964, assistant director of program at University of Vienna, 1964-65, professor of German literature, 1965-66; Pennsylvania State University, University Park, professor of German, 1966-71; State University of New York, Albany, professor of German and comparative literature, 1971—. *Member:* International Robert Musil Society, International Association of Germanic Studies, P.E.N. (Austria), Modern Language Association of America, American Comparative Literature Association, Vienna Goethe Society. *Awards, honors:* Theodor Koerner Foundation award, 1955-57; City of Vienna award, 1958; Austrian Institute of Cultural Affairs research fellow in Paris, 1958-59.

WRITINGS: Georg Forsters literarhistorische Bedeutung (title means "Georg Forster's Literary-Historical Significance"), F. Berger, 1955; *Der burgundische Renaissancehof Margarethes von Oesterreich und seine literarhistorische Bedeutung* (title means "The Burgundian Renaissance Court of Margaret of Austria and Its Literary-Historical Significance"), A. Sexl, 1957; *Kafka, Musil, Broch und die Entwicklung des modernen Romans* (title means "Kafka, Musil, Broch, and the Development of the Modern Novel"), Forum Verlag, 1959.

Rilke, Benn, Schoenwiese und die Entwicklung der modernen Lyrik (title means "Rilke, Benn, Schoenwiese, and the Development of Modern Poetry"), Forum Verlag, 1960; *Brecht, Horvath, Duerrenmatt: Wege und Abwege des modernen Dramas* (title means "Brecht, Horvath, Durrenmatt: Paths and Deviations of Modern Drama"), Forum Verlag, 1962; *Bruecke zu vielen Ufern* (title means "Bridges to Many Shores"), Europa Verlag, 1966; (with Harold von Hofe) *Luegendichtung* (title means "Tall Tales"), Scribner, 1966; (with von Hofe) *Vorboten der Gegenwart: Marx, Nietzsche, Freud, Einstein* (title means "Precursers to the Present: Marx, Nietzsche, Freud, Einstein"), Holt, 1967.

Vergleichende Literaturkritik (title means "Comparative Literary Criticism"), Francke, 1970; *Die gelenkten Musen* (title means "The Bound Muses"), Europa Verlag, 1971.

Editor or compiler: *Gedichte Margarethe's von Oesterreich* (title means "Poems of Margaret of Austria"), A. Sexl, 1954; (and author of introduction) Alfred Kubin, *Dichtungen* (title means "Collected Works"), Bergland Verlag, 1961; (and author of introduction) *Das zeitlose Wort: Eine Anthologie oesterreichischer Lyrik von Peter Altenberg bis zur Gegenwart* (title means "The Timeless Word: An Anthology of Austrian Verse from Peter Attenberg Up to the Present"), Stiasny Verlag, 1964; (with Robert Stauffer and Paul Wimmer) *Aufruf zur Wende: Eine Anthologie neuer Dichtung, Ernst Schoenwiese zum 60* (title means "A Call to Change: An Anthology of Modern Literature"), Oesterreichische Verlagsanstalt, 1965; (and author of introduction) Gustav Meyrink, *Der Engel vom westlichen Fenster* (title means "Angel of the Western Window"), Stiasny Verlag, 1966; (with Walter Hinderer) *Moderne amerikanische Literaturtheorien* (title means "Modern American Theories of Literature"), S. Fischer Verlag, 1970.

Editor: "Yearbook of Comparative Criticism" series, Pennsylvania State University Press, Volume I: *Perspectives in Literary Symbolism,* 1968, Volume II: *Problems of Literary Evaluation,* 1969, Volume III: *Patterns of Literary Style,* 1971, Volume IV: *Anagogic Qualities of Literature,* 1971, Volume V: *Literary Criticism and Sociology,* 1973, Volume VI: *The Personality of the Critic,* 1973, Volume

VII: *Literary Criticism and Psychology,* 1976, Volume VIII: *Theories of Literary Genres,* in press; "Penn State Series in German Literature," Pennsylvania State University Press, Volume I, 1971, Volume II, 1971, Volume III, 1974, Volume IV, 1975.

Contributor of articles to journals in his field, including *Wort in Zeit* and *German Quarterly.* Co-editor, *Deutsche Exilliteratur,* 1976—; member of editorial board, *Colloquia Germanica,* 1971—, *North Carolina Studies in Comparative Literature,* 1972—, and *Michigan Germanic Studies,* 1975—.

WORK IN PROGRESS: Einfuehrung in die methodologie der Literaturwissenschaft, on literary theory, for Metzler Verlag, expected in 1977; *Auf der Suche nach dem verlorenen Selbst,* on twentieth-century German fiction.

* * *

STRONGMAN, K(enneth) T(homas) 1940-

PERSONAL: Born December 2, 1940, in Ware, Hertfordshire, England; son of Alfred Thomas (in building trade) and Grace (Dew) Strongman; married Thelma Madeline Francis, March 28, 1964; children: Lara Madeline, Luke. *Education:* University of London, B.Sc., 1962, Ph.D., 1964. *Politics:* Independent. *Religion:* None. *Home:* Middle Earth, Trusham, Newton Abbot, Devonshire, England. *Agent:* Curtis Brown, 1 Craven Hill, London W2 3EP, England. *Office:* Department of Psychology, University of Exeter, Exeter, Devonshire, England.

CAREER: University of Victoria, Victoria, British Columbia, visiting professor of psychology, 1962; University of Exeter, Exeter, England, lecturer, 1964-75, senior lecturer in psychology, 1975—. *Member:* British Psychological Society.

WRITINGS: The Psychology of Emotion, Wiley, 1972; (editor with others) *The Times Anthology of Detective Stories,* J. Cape, 1972; *Decent Exposure: Living with Your Emotions,* David & Charles, 1974, St. Martin's, 1975. Author of radio script "Listen," for the B.B.C., 1960. Contributor to psychology journals.

WORK IN PROGRESS: The Experience of Emotion; Sober Reflections, on alcoholism; *Fat: How to Live With It and Without It;* research on emotion.

SIDELIGHTS: Strongman writes that he "ideally would prefer to work as full-time writer, of fiction and popularized science, but the academic life is too good to give up. I am prejudiced against religion (can a person really be both intelligent and religious?) and loathe the thought of people acting as groups, clubs, etc., rather than as individuals." *Avocational interests:* Sport (squash, badminton, running, soccer).

* * *

STRUM, Philippa 1938-

PERSONAL: Born December 14, 1938, in New York, N.Y. *Education:* Brandeis University, B.A., 1959; Harvard University, Ed.M., 1960; New School for Social Research, Ph.D., 1964. *Office:* Department of Political Science, Brooklyn College of the City University of New York, Brooklyn, N.Y. 11210.

CAREER: Brooklyn College of the City University of New York, Brooklyn, N.Y., lecturer in political science, 1962-64; Rutgers University, Newark, N.J. instructor, 1964-65, assistant professor, 1965-72, associate professor of political science, 1972-73; Brooklyn College of the City University of New York, associate professor of political science, 1973—. Instructor at New School for Social Research, summers, 1962-64; visiting associate professor at Brooklyn College of the City University of New York, 1972-73. *Member:* American Political Science Association, American Association of University Professors, Caucus for a New Political Science, American Civil Liberties Union, New York Civil Liberties Union.

WRITINGS: (With Michael Shmidman) *On Studying Political Science,* Goodyear Publishing, 1969; *Presidential Power and American Democracy,* Goodyear Publishing, 1972; *The Supreme Court and "Political Questions",* University of Alabama Press, 1974. Contributor to professional journals and to *New Republic.*

WORK IN PROGRESS: The Supreme Court and Sexual Equality; a biography of Louis Dembitz Brandeis; research on the American presidency and foreign policy-making, and on adaptation of parliamentary forms within the presidential system.

*   *   *

STUNTZ, Laurance F(itzhugh) 1908-

PERSONAL: Surname is pronounced "stoontz"; born June 9, 1908, in Vienna, Va.; son of Stephen Conrad (a government botanist) and Lena (Fitzhugh) Stuntz; married Faris Beehler, July 30, 1942; children: Cita, Stephen Conrad. *Education:* Attended McKinley Manual Training School, Washington, D.C., 1921-29. *Religion:* Presbyterian. *Home:* 137 Manor Lane, Pelham Manor, N.Y. 10803. *Agent:* Arthur Pine Associates, Inc., 1780 Broadway, New York, N.Y. 10019.

CAREER: Washington Post, Washington, D.C., reporter, 1929-35; Associated Press, New York, N.Y., editor, 1935-41, Latin American foreign correspondent, 1941-55, chief of Rio de Janeiro bureau, 1955-57, editor in Latin American department, 1957-65, foreign financial editor, 1965-74. *Member:* New York Association of Financial Writers. *Awards, honors:* John Hancock Award for excellence in business and financial journalism, 1971, for series explaining the effect of the revaluation of the Deutsche Mark on the American man in the street.

WRITINGS: (With David Smyth) *The Speculator's Handbook,* Regnery, 1974. Contributor of regular weekly column to *Financial Times of London,* 1958-72.

*   *   *

SUENENS, Leon Joseph 1904-

PERSONAL: Born July 16, 1904, in Ixelles, Belgium; son of Jean (owner of a brewery) and Jeanne (Janssens) Suenens. *Education:* Gregorian University, Rome, Ph.D., 1924, B.C.L., 1927, S.T.D., 1927, additional study, 1927-29. *Home and office:* Aartsbisdom Wollemarkt 15, 2800 Malines, Belgium

CAREER: Ordained Roman Catholic priest, 1927, consecrated bishop, 1945, created cardinal, 1962. Teacher at St. Mary's High School, Brussels, Belgium, 1929; Seminary of Malines, Malines, Belgium, professor of philosophy, 1930-40; Catholic University of Louvain, Louvain, Belgium, vice-rector, 1940-45; Archdiocese of Malines, Malines, auxiliary bishop and vicar-general, 1945-61, Archbishop of Malines-Brussels and Primate of Belgium, 1961—. Served as private chamberlain to Pope Pius XII, 1941; clerical advisor to Pax Christi and Legion of Mary; moderator,

Vatican Council II, 1962-65; member of Pontifical Commission for Revision Code of Canon Law, 1962—; chairman, Belgian Bishop's Conference, 1966—. *Military service:* Belgian Army, chaplain for 9th artillery regiment, 1939. *Awards, honors:* Honorary doctorates from Catholic University of America, College of Mount St. Vincent, Harvard University, and Emory University; Templeton Foundation prize, 1976.

WRITINGS: Theology of the Apostolate of the Legion of Mary, Mercier Press, 1951; *Edel Quinn,* Concilium Legionis Mariae (Dublin), 1952; *The Right View on Moral Rearmament,* Burns & Oates, 1953; *The Gospel to Every Creature,* Burns & Oates, 1955; *Mary the Mother of God,* Hawthorn, 1957; *Love and Control,* Burns & Oates, 1959; *Christian Life Day by Day,* Burns & Oates, 1961; *The Nun in the World,* Burns & Oates, 1962; (contributor) Hans Kung and Yves Congor, editors, *Council Speeches of Vatican II,* Paulist Press, 1964; *Coresponsibility in the Church,* Herder & Herder, 1968; (with Michael Ramsey) *The Future of the Christian Church,* Morehouse, 1971; *A New Pentecost?,* Seabury, 1975.

*   *   *

SULLIVAN, D(ale) H(owill) 1936-

PERSONAL: Born August 2, 1936, in Los Angeles, Calif.; son of Keith E. (a clerk) and Dorothy (Wade) Sullivan; married Sheila Pratt, June 6, 1960 (divorced, 1973); married Donna Love, September 14, 1973; children: (first marriage) Karin, Kathleen; (second marriage) Molly. *Education:* California State University, Humboldt, B.A., 1962; University of Oregon, M.S. (with honors), 1964, M.F.A. (with honors), 1967. *Politics:* "Existential." *Religion:* None. *Residence:* White Rock, British Columbia, Canada. *Office:* Department of English, Simon Fraser University, Burnaby 2, British Columbia, Canada.

CAREER: Aerojet General Corp., Los Angeles, Calif., research engineer, 1959-61; Southern Oregon College, Ashland, instructor in English, 1964-65; Simon Fraser University, Burnaby, British Columbia, instructor, 1965-67, professor of English, 1967—, dean of Faculty of Arts, 1968-73. *Military service:* U.S. Army, 1955-58.

WRITING—Poems: *He: A Short Biography of Him,* University of Windsor Press, 1973; *The Pandora Sequence: Alice Among the Sisterpeople,* Cherry Tree Press, 1975. Contributor of short fiction, satire, criticism, and poetry to Canadian and American literature journals. Poetry editor, *West Coast Review,* 1966-67.

WORK IN PROGRESS: Molly and the Tractors and *Rose Marie I Love You,* both Canadian satires in verse.

AVOCATIONAL INTERESTS: Sullivan writes that he "photographs flowers, feeds a pet raven, and tends a big garden with his wife and three daughters."

*   *   *

SULLIVAN, Edmund V(incent) 1938-

PERSONAL: Born August 13, 1938, in Jersey City, N.J.; son of Patrick (a carpenter) and Nora (Buckley) Sullivan; married Patricia Kay Walters, February 4, 1970; children: Jeremy. *Education:* St. Peter's College, B.A., 1960; University of Geneva, graduate study, 1960-61; Syracuse University, M.A., 1965, Ph.D., 1966. *Residence:* Toronto, Ontario, Canada. *Office:* Ontario Institute for Studies in Education, University of Toronto, 252 Bloor St. W., Toronto, Ontario, Canada M5S 1V6.

CAREER: Syracuse University, Syracuse, N.Y., instructor in education, 1961-65; Mental Health Research Unit, Syracuse, N.Y., research psychologist, 1965; State University of New York, Upstate Medical Center, Syracuse, research psychologist in pediatrics, 1965-66; University of Toronto, Ontario Institute for Studies in Education, Toronto, Ontario, assistant professor, 1966-69, associate professor, 1969-75, professor of educational psychology, 1975—, associate chairman of applied psychology, 1974—. Has taught at Harvard University, summer, 1974, and York University, 1974.

MEMBER: American Psychological Association, American Educational Research Association, National Society for the Study of Education, American Association for the Advancement of Science, Society for the Study of Social Issues. *Awards, honors:* Swiss Government fellowship, University of Geneva, 1960-61.

WRITINGS: (With D. P. Ausubel) *Theories and Problems of Child Development,* Grune, 1957, 2nd edition, 1970; (editor with D. W. Brison and contributor) *Recent Research on the Acquisition of Conservation of Substance* (monograph), Ontario Institute for Studies in Education, University of Toronto, 1967; (contributor) Bruce Joyce, editor, *The Teacher-Innovator: A Program to Prepare Teachers,* U.S. Department of Health, Education and Welfare, 1968; (with Neil Byrne, Michael Daly, Peter Gazzola, and others) *Election 1969: The Toronto Municipal Elections* (teacher's guide), Metropolitan Separate School Boards of Toronto, 1969.

(Contributor) Lawrence Kohlberg and Elliot Turiel, editors, *Recent Research in Moral Development,* Holt, 1970; (contributor) Ellis Evans and Boyd McCandless, editors, *Adolescents: Readings in Behaviour and Development,* Dryden, 1970; (contributor) E. Burns and G. Brooks, editors, *Curriculum Design in Changing Society,* Educational Technology Publications, 1970; (contributor) Joyce, editor, *Teacher Education: Perspectives for Reformation,* Prentice-Hall, 1971; (contributor) Byrne and Jack Quarter, editors, *Issues in Education in Canada,* McClelland & Stewart, 1971; (editor with Clive Beck and Brian Crittenden, and contributor) *Moral Education: An Interdisciplinary Discussion of Selected Questions,* University of Toronto Press, 1971; (with David Hunt) *Psychological Analysis of the Educational Process,* Dryden, 1973; (with Hunt) *Between Psychology and Education,* Dryden, 1974; (with Beck, Maureen Joy, and Susan Pagliuso) *Moral Learning: Findings, Issues, and Questions,* Paulist/Newman, 1975.

Contributor to *German-Language Encyclopedia of Psychology.* Contributor of about twenty articles and reviews to professional journals. Associate editor of *Interchange: A Journal of Educational Studies.*

* * *

SULLIVAN, Frank 1912-1975

June 6, 1912—August 7, 1975; American educator and author of books on Sir Thomas More. Obituaries: *New York Times,* August 10, 1975; *AB Bookman's Weekly,* October 13, 1975.

* * *

SURKIN, Marvin 1938-

PERSONAL: Born October 27, 1938, in Philadelphia, Pa.; son of Abraham Jack (a shopkeeper) and Betty (Levin) Surkin; married Lourdes Beneria (a professor), July 8, 1963; children: Jordi, Marc. *Education:* University of Florida, B.A., 1960; New York University, M.A., 1965, Ph.D., 1972. *Religion:* Jewish. *Home:* 240 West 102nd St., New York, N.Y. 10025. *Office:* School of Contemporary Studies, Brooklyn College of the City University of New York, 96 Schermerhorn St., Brooklyn, N.Y. 11201.

CAREER: Brooklyn College of the City University of New York, Brooklyn, N.Y., assistant professor of political science, 1974—. *Member:* American Association of University Professors, Union of Radical Political Economists, Caucus for a New Political Science. *Awards, honors:* Louis Rabinowitz Foundation research grant, 1972-74.

WRITINGS: An End to Political Science, Basic Books, 1969; *Detroit: I Do Mind Dying,* St. Martin's, 1975; *The Politics of Everyday Life: An Analysis of American Society,* Random House, in press. Contributor to journals of the social sciences and to *Nation.*

* * *

SUTTON, William A(lfred) 1915-

PERSONAL: Born December 2, 1915, in Cleveland, Ohio; son of Leonard (a patternmaker) and Susan A. (Bayliss) Sutton; married Marion R. Weaver, December 26, 1939; children: Robert W. *Education:* Western Reserve University (now Case Western Reserve University), A.B., 1936; Ohio State University, M.A., 1937, Ph.D., 1943. *Home:* 3311 Torquay Rd., Muncie, Ind. 47304. *Office:* Department of English, Ball State University, Muncie, Ind. 47306.

CAREER: Muskingum College, New Concord, Ohio, instructor in English, 1939-41; University of Tennessee, Knoxville, assistant professor of English, 1946-47; Ball State University, Muncie, Ind., assistant professor, 1947-51, associate professor, 1951-56, professor of English, 1956—. Member of Muncie (Ind.) City Council, 1960-67. *Military service:* U. S. Army, 1943-46; became captain.

WRITINGS: The Road to Winesburg, Scarecrow, 1972; *Black Like It Is (Was),* Scarecrow, 1974; *Newdick's Season of Frost,* State University of New York Press, 1975; *Dear Bab,* Everett Edwards, 1975.

* * *

SVENSON, Andrew E. 1910-1975
(Jerry West)

May 8, 1910—August 21, 1975; American author of children's fiction, and partner in Stratemeyer Syndicate. Obituaries: *New York Times,* August 23, 1975; *Publishers Weekly,* September 29, 1975; *AB Bookman's Weekly,* October 13, 1975. (See index for previous *CA* sketch)

* * *

SWIDLER, Arlene (Anderson) 1929-

PERSONAL: Born March 6, 1929, in Milwaukee, Wis.; daughter of Perry H. (an engineer) and Marie (a teacher; maiden name, Wittman) Anderson; married Leonard J. Swidler (a teacher), May 11, 1957; children: Carmel, Eva-Maria. *Education:* Marquette University, A.B., 1950; University of Wisconsin, M.A., 1952. *Religion:* Roman Catholic. *Home:* 7501 Woodcrest Ave., Philadelphia, Pa. 19151.

CAREER: Valparaiso University, Valparaiso, Ind., instructor in English, 1953-55; University of Maryland, Munich, Germany, lecturer in English, 1958-60; Duquesne University, Pittsburgh, Pa., lecturer in English, 1960-64;

National Council of Catholic Women, Washington, D.C., director of Ecumenical and Liturgical Affairs, 1967-71, editor, 1970-71. *Awards, honors:* Institute for Ecumenical and Cultural Research resident fellow in Collegeville, Minn., 1968-69.

WRITINGS: (Translator from the German) Richard Gutzwiller, *The Parables of the Lord,* Herder & Herder, 1964; (translator from the German) Heinrich Kahlefeld, *Parables and Instructions in the Gospels,* Herder & Herder, 1966; (translator from the German) Bernard Haering, *This Time of Salvation,* Herder & Herder, 1966; (translator from the German) Haering, *Christian Maturity,* Herder & Herder, 1967; (translator from the German, and editor with husband, Leonard Swidler) *Bishops and People,* Westminster Press, 1970; *Concern: World Religions,* Silver Burdett, 1970; *Woman in a Man's Church,* Paulist/Newman, 1972; (translator from the German with L. Swidler) Haye van der Meer, *Woman Priests in the Catholic Church?,* Temple University, 1973; (editor) *Sistercelebrations* (collection of feminist liturgies), Fortress, 1974. Contributor of regular column to *National Catholic Reporter,* 1971-74. Contributor to *America, American Benedictine Review, Commonweal, Liturgy,* and *National Catholic Reporter.* Co-founder and managing editor of *Journal of Ecumenical Studies,* 1964-71, education editor, 1972—.

WORK IN PROGRESS: Research on American Catholic Church history.

AVOCATIONAL INTERESTS: Music, ballet, camping, traveling.

* * *

SWINBURNE, Laurence 1924-

PERSONAL: Born July 2, 1924, in New York, N.Y.; son of Laurence T. (an artist) and Marie-Louise (a teacher; maiden name, Floris) Swinburne; married Irene Kallini (collaborator on her husband's books), June 14, 1947; children: Virginia Louise (Mrs. Thomas Bowman), Susan Elizabeth. *Education:* Princeton University, A.B., 1949; Rutgers University, M.Ed., 1958. *Politics:* Independent. *Religion:* Roman Catholic. *Home:* 49 Cord Pl., East Norwich, N.Y. 11732. *Agent:* Bertha Klausner International Literary Agency, Inc., 71 Park Ave., New York, N.Y. 10016. *Office:* de Merlier Swinburne Associates, 49 Cord Pl., East Norwich, N.Y. 11732.

CAREER: Textbook salesman after finishing Princeton; American Educational Publications, Middletown, Conn., educational sales promotion manager, 1959-61; Doubleday & Co., Inc., Garden City, N.Y., educational sales promotion manager, 1961-64; Great Society Press (educational materials), East Norwich, N.Y., vice-president, 1964-65; McGraw-Hill Book Co., New York, N.Y., an editor, 1965-68; Educreative Systems, Inc., New York, N.Y., vice-president, 1968-72; de Merlier Swinburne Associates (educational materials), East Norwich, N.Y., vice-president, 1974—. Writer of juvenile books and textbooks, 1964—. Library trustee, Oyster Bay, N.Y., 1965-68. *Military service:* U.S. Marines, infantryman, 1943-45; served in Pacific theater.

MEMBER: Authors Guild. *Awards, honors: Detli* was among the thirty best books for children in grades four through eight on list for Dorothy Canfield Fisher Memorial Children's Book Award, 1970; Nice Book Fair Award for "Crossroads" series, 1970.

WRITINGS: Joe, the Salesman, McGraw, 1966; (editor and contributor) *Ramblers, Gamblers and Lovers* (poems), McGraw, 1968; (adapter) *Dark Sea Running,* McGraw, 1968; (adapter) *Art Arfons: Fastest Man on Wheels,* McGraw, 1968; (adapter) *Stories by Jesse Stuart,* McGraw, 1968; *Angelita Nobody* (junior high novel for slow readers), McGraw, 1968; *Chico* (junior high novel for slow readers), McGraw, 1968; (adapter) *Follow the Free Wind,* McGraw, 1969; (with Eric Broudy and Warren Halliburton) *They Had a Dream,* Pyramid Publications, 1969; *RFK: The Last Knight* (biography), Pyramid Publications, 1969; *Detli,* Bobbs-Merrill, 1970; *Robby on Ice,* Creative Educational Society, 1972.

Editor with James Olsen, "Crossroads" program (for inner city junior high students), published by Noble & Noble, 1969: *Love's Blues; Me, Myself and I; Dreamer of Dreams; He Who Does; Tomorrow Won't Wait; Breaking Loose; In Other's Eyes; Playing It Cool.*

In N.O.W. program (filmstrips and books), published by Simon & Schuster, 1970: *Timmy Tims, a Perfect Man; Timmy Tims and His Floating Bed; Timmy Timms and the Suction Shoes; Timmy Timms and the Forest Fire; Timmy Timms Builds a Kite; Johnny Hope and the Deserted Apartment House; Johnny Hope and Old Man Corrigan; Johnny Hope, the Campaign Manager; Johnny Hope and the Great Snowball Fight; Johnny Hope's Thanksgiving; Bernardo the Detective; Bernardo the Baseball Player; Bernardo's Halloween; Bernardo at the Amusement Park; Bernardo at the Beach; Saltine Keeps Cool; Saltine Goes Fishing; Saltine the Cowboy; Saltine's New House; Saltine and the Skiis.*

(With Sister Agnes A. Pastva) "Composing with Words," published by Cambridge Book Co., 1974: Unit I: *Slippery Words;* Unit 2: *Making a Difference;* Unit 3: *The Writer Sees.*

"Audobook" series (cassette and print for slow or unmotivated students), published by Swinburne Press, 1974: *Ragnar and the Winged Horses; The Ice Dragon; The Jungle of Evil; The High Poet of Ireland; Tin Lion on a Roof; The Tin Lion and His Friends; The Boy Who Had No Name and Other Stories; The Girl Who Took Care of Her Parents and Other Stories; 1-2-3! And Other Stories.*

In "Series R" (basal readers), published by Macmillan, 1975: *Pastimes; Birds and Beasts; Journeys.*

Filmstrips: "Career Education Planning," six filmstrips, Appalachia Research Laboratory, 1967; "American Folktales," five filmstrips, Audio-Visual, Inc., 1968; "Middle American Folktales," five filmstrips, Audio-Visual, Inc., 1968; "Black Leaders," six filmstrips, Audio-Visual, Inc., 1968; "City Streets," twelve filmstrips, McGraw, 1972; and others.

Other: Ninety short stories, articles, and poems for Educational Development Laboratories "Learning 100" (adult reading program), 1964-65; more than forty stories and articles for "Springboards" program, Great Society Press and Portal Press, 1965-67; sixty stories for "Mission Read," Random House, 1970; twenty-five stories for "Listen and Read" program, Heath, 1970-71; ten stories for "Urban Reading" program, Heath, 1970-71; twenty-five stories and articles for Reader's Digest Services, 1973-74; and other stories and articles in texts. Also contributor of stories and articles to popular magazines in 1940's and 1950's.

WORK IN PROGRESS: Cows and Cowboys, a book on the growth of the cattle industry, for Parents' Magazine Press; *The Horse Children,* about the first people to ride horses, circa 3000 B.C., for Parents' Magazine Press; short stories and articles.

SIDELIGHTS: Swinburne comments: "As long as I can remember, I wanted to write—even *before* I could write. I recall that before I went to school, my mother would write the poems and stories that I made up. The other day, I ran across one of these poems (it concerned looking at the moon as I lay in bed). It was fairly good and left me with the odd feeling that it might have been the best piece I have done in my life.

"I love writing for kids and believe with Isaac Singer that they are the most receptive reading audience in the country. How do I get my ideas? Why, usually by asking the kids themselves. Over the past four years, I have given talks to about 40,000 children here on Long Island. They ask a lot of good questions about the writing craft, and they also tell me what they would like to read.

"I collaborate with my wife in writing nowadays. She does a great deal of research and gives me invaluable criticism. I also ask kids for their reactions; their comments are most helpful. I believe that a great deal of problems in the school and library publishing field would be eliminated if publishers took the time to ask the children what they think.

"I don't exactly know where I got the yen for writing. My father and brother became artists. The poet Algernon Charles Swinburne is a very, very distant cousin, but I discount him as an influence. Perhaps it is primarily due to an aunt, who was a professional lecturer and gave fascinating talks on historical subjects."

*   *   *

SWINEFORD, Ada   1917-

PERSONAL: Born July 12, 1917, in Chicago, Ill.; daughter of Charles Roscoe (a professor) and Kate (Watson) Swineford. *Education:* University of Chicago, S.B., 1940, S.M., 1942; Pennsylvania State University, Ph.D., 1954. *Politics:* Democrat. *Religion:* Liberal Prostestant. *Home:* 904 Chuckanut Dr., Bellingham, Wash. 98225. *Office:* Department of Geology, Western Washington State College, Bellingham, Wash. 98225.

CAREER: Kansas Geological Survey, Lawrence, geologist, 1942-66; Western Washington State College, Bellingham, associate professor, 1966-69, professor of geology, 1969—. Assistant professor at University of Kansas, 1958-65, associate professor, 1965-66. Member of Whatcom County Land-Use Code Committee, 1973-75. *Member:* Societe Internationale pour l'Etude des Argiles, Geological Society of America (fellow), Mineralogical Society of America (fellow), Society of Economic Paleontologists and Mineralogists, Mineralogical Society (London).

WRITINGS: (With L. L. Tolsted) *Kansas Rocks and Minerals,* Kansas Geological Survey, 1948; (with Grace Mullenburg) *Land of the Post Rock,* University Press of Kansas, 1975. Contributor to technical journals.

WORK IN PROGRESS: Research on the Flint Hills of Kansas, with Grace Mullenburg, with a book expected to result.

SIDELIGHTS: Ada Swineford writes: "I have been involved with the study of Kansas geology for more than twenty-four years. I think it is important to relate geology to human activities and human history."

SWISHER, Robert K., Jr.   1947-

PERSONAL: Born May 8, 1947, in Logan, Utah; son of Robert K. and Billie Lee Swisher; married Vicki Saavedra; children: Monique, Dedra, Daphne. *Education:* Attended University of Texas; College of Santa Fe, B.A. *Politics:* "Not really." *Religion:* Roman Catholic. *Home:* 2023 Hopi Rd., Santa Fe, N.M. 87501.

CAREER: Writer. *Military service:* U.S. Army, Infantry, 1965-67; served in Vietnam.

WRITINGS: The Man from the Mountain (nonfiction), Echo Publishers, 1969; *The Weaver* (collected fables), Echo Publishers, 1974; *Touch Me If You Love Me,* Sunston Press, in press. Contributor to Santa Fe newspapers.

WORK IN PROGRESS: A novelette; three books of poems; a book about Vietnam.

*   *   *

SWYHART, Barbara Ann DeMartino   1942-

PERSONAL: Born September 24, 1942, in Brooklyn, N.Y.; daughter of Joseph John and Rose Regina (Arnao) DeMartino, Jr.; married Paul Richard Swyhart (a clinical psychologist), December 5, 1971. *Education:* Marquette University, B.A., 1967, M.A., 1968; Temple University, Ph.D., 1972. *Home:* 6250 Lake Arrowhead Dr., San Diego, Calif. 92119. *Office:* Department of Religion, San Diego State University, San Diego, Calif. 92115.

CAREER: San Diego State University, San Diego, Calif., associate professor of religion, 1972—. Harvard University, Divinity School, Cambridge, Mass., director of religion and public education, 1975-76. Consultant, California School of Professional Psychology, 1972-76. *Member:* American Association of University Professors (executive secretary, San Diego chapter, 1974-75), American Academy of Religion (co-chairman, 1975). *Awards, honors:* American Association of University Women fellow, 1971-72; Amita Achievement Award, 1975.

WRITINGS: Bioethical Decision-Making: Releasing Religion From the Spiritual, Fortress, 1975; *Narratives About Cosmic and Human Origins,* San Diego Unified School District, in press. Contributor to *Judaism.*

WORK IN PROGRESS: Developing a methodology for teaching religion and science, and religion and ethics in public schools; developing the philosophical rationale for the agent ethician in bioethics.

AVOCATIONAL INTERESTS: Travel.

*   *   *

SYLVESTER, Robert (McPhierson)   1907-1975

PERSONAL: Born February 7, 1907, in Newark, N.J.; son of Robert Franklin and Edna (Brown) Sylvester; married Raye Davis, September 9, 1932; married Bunty Pendleton, October 5, 1946; married Kay Norton, May 14, 1956; married Jane Meehan, July 31, 1965; children: (third marriage) Kathy Roberta, Karin Courtney. *Education:* Attended Yale University and Columbia University. *Residence:* Montauk, Long Island, N.Y.

CAREER: New Haven Evening Register, New Haven, Conn., editorial writer, prior to 1929; publicity agent for RKO Palace, New York City, and theatrical public relations consultant, c. 1929-32; rewrite man for *New York Evening World, New York American,* and *New York Post,* 1932-36; *New York Daily News,* New York City, drama and amusement writer, 1936-75, writing column "Dream

Street," 1951-75. Operated his own public relations consulting firm; commentator for WINS-Radio, 1962-63. *Military service:* U.S. Navy, World War II; served in Pacific theater. *Member:* National Arts Club (New York City). *Awards, honors:* Named Officer of the Order of Carlos Manolo Cespedes (Cuba).

WRITINGS—Novels: *Dream Street,* Dial, 1946; *Rough Sketch,* Dial, 1948, reissued as *We Were Strangers,* New American Library, 1949; *The Second Oldest Profession,* Dial, 1950; *Indian Summer,* Random House, 1952; *The Big Boodle,* Random House, 1954; *Tropical Paradise,* Random House, 1960.

Non-fiction: *No Cover Charge: A Backward Look at the Night Clubs,* Dial, 1956; *Notes of a Guilty Bystander,* Prentice-Hall, 1970.

Author of script for the film "The Joe Lewis Story" and of television scripts for the series "Naked City." Contributor of articles and stories to popular magazines, including *Saturday Evening Post, New Yorker, Holiday,* and *Esquire.*

SIDELIGHTS: The material for much of Sylvester's writing emerged from his newspaper reporting experiences covering the "night club scene" in New York City, particularly the Broadway area. Several of the books have been made into feature films, including "Dream Street," "Rough Sketch," "The Second Oldest Profession," and "The Big Boodle." Sylvester's "Dream Street" column was syndicated and carried by more than thirty newspapers.*

(Died February 9, 1975, in Montauk, N.Y.)

*   *   *

SYLVESTRE, (Joseph Jean) Guy 1918-
(Jean Bruneau, Blaise Orlier)

PERSONAL: Born May 17, 1918, in Sorel, Quebec, Canada; son of Maxime Arthur and Yvonne (Lapierre) Sylvestre; married Francoise Poitevin, February 27, 1943; children: Marie, Jean, Paul. *Education:* University of Ottawa, B.A., 1939, L.Ph., 1940, M.A., 1942. *Religion:* Roman Catholic. *Home:* 1870 Rideau Garden Dr., Ottawa, Ontario, Canada K1S 1G6. *Office:* National Library of Canada, 395 Wellington St., Ottawa, Ontario, Canada K1A 0N4.

CAREER: Canada Department of Resources and Development, Ottawa, Ontario, administration officer, 1950-53; Library of Parliament, Ottawa, Ontario, assistant parliamentary librarian, 1953-56, associate parliamentary librarian, 1956-68; National Library of Canada, Ottawa, Ontario, national librarian of Canada, 1968—. Canadian adviser to *Funk & Wagnall's Encyclopedia;* Canadian delegate to UNESCO Conference, 1949; chairman of Governor General's Literary Awards, 1960-62; chairman of Canada Council committee on aid-to-publication, 1960-68; chairman of World Poetry Conference, Expo '67.

MEMBER: Association canadienne des bibliothecaires de langue francaise, Academie canadienne-francaise, Canadian Library Association, Canadian Writers Foundation (president, 1960-61), Royal Society of Canada (president, 1973-74), Societe des scrivains canadiens, Alliance francaise d'Ottawa (president, 1960-62), Library Association of Ottawa, Le Cercle universitaire, Rivermead Golf Club. *Awards, honors:* D.L.S., University of Ottawa, 1969; D.Litt., Mt. Allison University, 1970; also received L.L.D., 1974.

WRITINGS: (Under pseudonym, Blaise Orlier) *Louis*

Francoeur, journaliste, Editions du Droit, 1941; *Situation de la poesie canadienne, regards et jeux dans l'espace, axe et parallaxes,* Editions du Droit, 1941; *Anthologie de la poesie canadienne d'expression francaise, precedee d'une introduction,* Valiquette, 1942, 6th edition, Beauchemin, 1971; *Poetes catholiques de la France contemporaine,* Fides, 1943; *La Poesie francaise au canada, guide du lecteur,* Services educatifs de la Legion canadienne, 1944; *Sondages,* Beauchemin, 1945; (under pseudonym Jean Bruneau) *Amours, delices et orgues,* Institut litteraire du Quebec, 1953; (contributor) R. L. McDougall, editor, *Our Living Tradition,* University of Toronto Press, 1959.

(Editor) James P. Manion, *A Canadian Errant: Twenty-Five Years in the Canadian Foreign Service,* Ryerson, 1960; (editor with George Stanley) *Canadian Universities Today,* University of Toronto Press, 1961; (editor with Brandon Conron and Carl F. Klink) *Canadian Writers: A Biographical Dictionary,* Ryerson, 1964, revised edition, 1966; *Panorama des lettres canadiennes-francaises,* Ministere des affaires culturelles (Quebec), 1964, translation published as *Literature in French Canada,* Department of Cultural Affairs (Quebec), 1967; (editor) *Structures sociales du Canada francais: Etudes de membres de la Section I de la Societe royale du Canada,* Laval University Press, 1966; (compiler with H. Gordon Green) *A Century of Canadian Literature,* Ryerson, 1967; (contributor) Louis Baudoin, editor, *La Recherche au Canada francais,* University of Montreal Press, 1968; (editor) *Report of the National Librarian for the Year 1968,* Information Canada, 1969; (contributor) Leopold Lamontagne, editor, *Visages de la civilisation au Canada francais,* University of Toronto Press, 1970.

Also author of *Impressions de theatre,* 1949. Contributor to *Encyclopaedia Britannica, Encyclopedie Grolier, Reader's Encyclopedia of American Literature,* and *Encyclopedia Canadiana.* Contributor of more than one hundred fifty articles to library journals and to popular and literary magazines, including *Revue dominicaine, Nouvelle revue canadienne, Canada francais, Dalhousie Review, Saturday Night, Notre temps, Queen's Quarterly, Cahiers, University of Toronto Quarterly, Top of the News, Gants du ciel,* and *Culture.* Editor of *Gants de ciel,* 1943, *Le Droit,* 1940-49, and *Nouvelle revue canadienne,* 1951-56.

WORK IN PROGRESS: A study of the administration of libraries and the improvement of research tools.

BIOGRAPHICAL/CRITICAL SOURCES: Le Droit, July 9, 1949, April 1, 1953, January 12, 1963, December 14, 1967, May 6, 1968; Pierre Daveault, *Presentation de M. Louis Philippe Robidaux, M. Guy Sylvestre,* Royal Society of Canada, 1952; *Ottawa Journal,* February 2, 1952, June 13, 1970; *Ottawa Citizen,* February 25, 1952, February 14, 1959, February 20, 1960, July 8, 1960, July 10, 1973; *La Tribune,* March 1, 1952; *Notre temps,* March 1, 1952; *Bulletin* of Association canadienne des bibliothecaires de langue francaise, March, 1957, March, 1970; *Canadian Library,* March, 1964; *La Presse,* February 12, 1966, February 15, 1966, February 7, 1967, November 25, 1967; *Le journal de Montreal,* February 15, 1966; *Le petit journal,* February 27, 1966; *Recherches sociographiques,* January-April, 1967; *Poetry-Australian,* June, 1967; *Poesie,* summer, 1967; *Le Soleil,* October 30, 1967, May 31, 1968; *La Frontiere,* December 27, 1967; *Le Devoir,* May 30, 1968; *Le nouvelliste,* May 30, 1968; *Library Journal,* July, 1968; *Information Bulletin* of U.S. Library of Congress, July 25, 1968.

SZANCER, Henryk ?-1976

?—January 25, 1976; Polish-born American pharmaceutical chemist, cosmetics executive, author of prose and verse in Polish, and of books in his field. Obituaries: *New York Times*, January 28, 1976.

* * *

TAGORE, Amitendranath 1922-
(Musafir)

PERSONAL: Born October 9, 1922, in Calcutta, India; son of Alokendranath (an industrialist) and Parul (Mukherjee) Tagore; married Arundhati Chakravarti (a library assistant), 1953; children: Ayanendranath (son). *Education:* University of Calcutta, B.Com., 1942; Visva-Bharati University, graduate study, 1943-46, Ph.D., 1962; Yale University, College of Chinese Studies in Peip'ing, China, further graduate study, 1947; National Peking University, M.A., 1950. *Politics:* None. *Religion:* Hindu. *Home:* 6884 Deerhill Dr., Clarkston, Mich. 48016. *Office:* Department of Modern Languages and Literature, Oakland University, Rochester, Mich. 48063.

CAREER: Visva-Bharati University, Santiniketan, West Bengal, India, lecturer in Chinese, 1950-63; Oakland University, Rochester, Mich., assistant professor, 1963-65, associate professor, 1965-68, professor of Chinese language and literature, 1968—, acting chairman of area studies program, 1969—. Lecturer at National Defense Academy (India), 1952-57; visiting lecturer at University of Pennsylvania, 1961-62; member of executive board, International Congress of Orientalists, 1963.

MEMBER: American Oriental Society, American Association for Asian Studies, American Council on the Teaching of Foreign Languages, Chinese Language Teachers Association of America, Michigan Academy of Science, Arts and Letters, Asia Society (New York, N.Y.). *Awards, honors:* Government of India scholar in China, 1947-50; Fulbright grants, 1961-62, and 1963-64.

WRITINGS: Tao-te-Ching (Bengali translation of Lao Tzu), Sahitya Akademi, 1960; *Cheena Mati* (title means "The Chinese Soil"; Bengali anthology of modern Chinese short stories), Rupa & Co., 1961; (editor of Chinese section) *Sapta Sindhu Dasha Diganta* (Bengali anthology of modern world poetry; title means "Seven Seas and Ten Horizons"), Notun Sahitya Bhavan (Calcutta), 1962; *Lun Yu* (Bengali translation of *Analects of Confucius*), Sahitya Akademi, 1964; *Literary Debates in Modern China: 1918-1937*, Centre for East Asian Cultural Studies (Tokyo), 1967; (translator) Mushinsha, *Moments of Rising Mist: Sung Dynasty Landscape Poetry*, Grossman, 1973; (contributor) C. Coppola, editor, *Marxist Influence and South Asian Literature*, Basic Books, 1974; (contributor) Renate Gerutaitis, editor, *Oakland Symposium on Socialist Realism in Literature*, Oakland University, 1975. Contributor to *Dictionary of Oriental Literatures*. Contributor of articles and translations from the Chinese to American and Indian journals, in English and Bengali. Contributor of reviews, sometimes under pseudonym Musafir, to professional journals including *Journal of South Asian Literature* and *Mahfil*.

WORK IN PROGRESS: Symbolic Poets of China in the Twenties; Ming Dynasty Poets of China.

SIDELIGHTS: Tagore writes that his major influences have been "... the Nobel Laureate poet of India, my great grandfather Rabindranath Tagore and my grandfather artist Abanindranath Tigore ... I have studied and traveled all over China, Japan, U.S.A., Canada, and European countries. ..."

* * *

TANENBAUM, Jan Karl 1936-

PERSONAL: Born December 21, 1936, in Chicago, Ill.; son of Lewis (a physician) and Gertrude (Lunder) Tanenbaum; married Joanne DeLove, August 10, 1958; children: Michelle, Stephanie, Nadine. *Education:* University of Michigan, B.A., 1958; University of California, Berkeley, M.A., 1960, Ph.D., 1969. *Office:* Department of History, Florida State University, Tallahassee, Fla. 32306.

CAREER: Florida State University, Tallahassee, instructor, 1966-67, assistant professor, 1967-74, associate professor of history, 1974—. *Member:* American Historical Association, Society for French Historical Studies, Society for French Colonial History, Societe D'Histoire Moderne.

WRITINGS: General Maurice Sarrail, 1856-1929: The French Army and Left-Wing Politics, University of North Carolina Press, 1974.

WORK IN PROGRESS: Research on the French mandate in Syria and Lebanon, 1914-1945.

* * *

TANNER, Helen Hornbeck 1916-

PERSONAL: Born July 5, 1916, in Northfield, Minn.; daughter of John Wesley (a professor of physics) and Frances (Wolfe) Hornbeck; married Wilson Pennell Tanner, Jr. (a professor of psychology), November 22, 1940; children: Frances, Margaret (Mrs. Timothy J. Tewson), Wilson III, Robert. *Education:* Swarthmore College, A.B. (with honors), 1937; University of Florida, M.A., 1949; University of Michigan, Ph.D., 1961. *Home and office:* 1319 Brooklyn Ave., Ann Arbor, Mich. 48104.

CAREER: Assistant to director of public relations for public schools of Kalamazoo, Mich., 1937-39; American Airlines, Inc., New York, N.Y., in sales department, 1940-43; worked as part-time secretary, 1943-48; University of Michigan, Ann Arbor, teaching fellow, 1949-53, assistant in Russian and Latin American history, 1957-61, lecturer in history for Extension Service, 1961—, assistant director of Center for Continuing Education for Women, 1964-68. Member of Michigan Commission on Indian Affairs, 1966-70; consultant to various Indian Tribes.

MEMBER: American Historical Association, Conference on Latin American History, American Society for Ethnohistory, Indian Historical Society, Society for the History of Discoveries, Florida Historical Society, Clements Library Associates, Women's Research Club (University of Michigan; president, 1967-68).

WRITINGS: Zespedes in East Florida, 1784-1790, University of Miami Press, 1963; *General Greene Visits St. Augustine,* Clements Library (Ann Arbor, Mich.), 1964; *Opportunities for Women Through Education,* Center for Continuing Education for Women, University of Michigan, 1965; *The Greenville Treaty, 1795,* Clearwater Publishing, 1973; *Historical Report on the Chippewa of Eastern Lower Michigan,* Clearwater Publishing, 1973; *The Location of Indian Tribes in Southeastern Michigan and Northern Ohio: A History,* Clearwater Publishing, 1973; *The Territory of the Caddo Tribe of Oklahoma: Rebuttal Statement,* Clearwater Publishing, 1973; *The Chippewa of Eastern Lower Michigan, 1785-1837,* Clearwater Publishing, 1974;

Ethnohistorical Report on the Sisseton and Wahpeton Tribes in North Dakota and South Dakota and the Treaty of 1867 and the Agreement of 1872, Clearwater Publishing, 1974, *The Territory of the Caddo Tribe of Oklahoma, 1541-1859,* Clearwater Publishing, 1974. Author of reports and contributor to history journals.

WORK IN PROGRESS: Research on ethnohistory and historical cartography of Michigan and Upper Great Lakes Indians.

SIDELIGHTS: Helen Tanner spent four years helping to found and launch the Center for Continuing Education of Women at the University of Michigan, which was almost fatal to her career as historian and ethnohistorian. She is currently active in presenting testimony regarding Indian fishing rights as guaranteed in nineteenth century Indian treaties. Helen Tanner represents various Indian tribes before the Indian Claims Commission in Washington, D.C.

BIOGRAPHICAL/CRITICAL SOURCES: Swarthmore College Alumni, autumn, 1971; *Latin American Research Review,* summer, 1972.

*   *   *

TANNER, Paul O(ra) W(arren) 1917-

PERSONAL: Born October 15, 1917, in Skunk Hollow, Ky.; son of Archibald E. and Janet (Daniel) Tanner; married Alma E. Smith (secretary of World Jazz Association), May 2, 1936. *Education:* University of California, Los Angeles, B.A., 1958, M.A., 1960; University of Southern California, graduate study, 1962. *Home:* 10966 Rochester Ave., Los Angeles, Calif. 90024. *Office:* Department of Music, University of California, Los Angeles, Calif. 90024.

CAREER: Worked as professional musician as member of Glenn Miller orchestra and other musical organizations, and as studio musician in Hollywood, beginning 1930; arranged numerous trombone works from large concertos to pieces for small groups. University of California, Los Angeles, professor of music, 1958—. Executive director of World Jazz Association, 1975—. *Military service:* Noncommissioned officer during World War II. *Member:* American Society of Composers, Authors and Publishers, National Academy of Recording Arts and Sciences, National Association of Jazz Educators (director of higher education, 1968). *Awards, honors:* Distinguished professor award from University of California, Los Angeles, 1972.

WRITINGS: A Study of Jazz, William C. Brown, 1964, revised edition (with Maurice Gerow), 1973; *The Complete Trombone Book,* Western International, 1970. Author of screenplay and music for *Discovering Jazz,* for Bailey-Film Associates. Writer of works for trombone.

SIDELIGHTS: Tanner writes: "Because I have been a professional performing musician since the age of thirteen, it is natural that I continue to write works for trombone performances. When I started teaching the history of jazz at UCLA, there was no complete book to use as a text—the William C. Brown Co. suggested that they publish my notes. It has become the most used text on the subject in the world."

*   *   *

TANOUS, Peter (Joseph) 1938-

PERSONAL: Born May 21, 1938, in New York, N.Y.; son of Joseph Carrington and Rose Marie (Mokarzel) Tanous; married Barbara Ann MacConnell, August 17, 1962; children: Christopher, Helene, William. *Education:* George-

town University, B.A., 1960. *Religion:* Roman Catholic. *Residence:* New York, N.Y. *Agent:* Theron Raines, 244 Madison Ave., New York, N.Y. 10016. *Office:* Smith, Barney & Co., 1345 Avenue of the Americas, New York, N.Y. 10019.

CAREER: Smith, Barney & Co. (investment bankers and stockbrokers), New York, N.Y., registered representative, 1963-67, second vice-president and manager of Paris office, 1967, vice-president, 1968—, resident European sales manager in Paris, 1969-71, international sales manager in New York, 1971—. Director of Union Bank of Beirut, Lebanon. *Military service:* U.S. Army, 1961-63; became first lieutenant. *Member:* Automobile Club de France (Paris), Georgetown University Alumni Association (governor, 1968-71), Georgetown Club France (president, 1968-71).

WRITINGS: (With Paul Rubinstein) *The Petrodollar Takeover,* Putnam, 1975.

*   *   *

TARG, William 1907-
    (Charles Yu)

PERSONAL: Original name, William Torgownik, legally changed, 1946; born March 4, 1907, in Chicago, Ill.; son of Max and Esther (Solomon) Torgownik; married Anne Jesselson, May 1, 1933 (died February, 1965); married Roslyn Siegel, July 30, 1965; children: (first marriage) Russell. *Education:* Attended public schools in Chicago. *Home:* 101 West 12th St., New York, N.Y. 10011. *Office:* G. P. Putnam's Sons, 200 Madison Ave., New York, N.Y. 10016.

CAREER: Black Archer Press, Chicago, Ill., publisher, 1928-42; World Publishing Co., Cleveland, Ohio, editor-in-chief and vice-president, 1942-64; G. P. Putnam's Sons, New York, N.Y., editor-in-chief and vice-president, 1964—. *Member:* International P.E.N., Grolier Club.

WRITINGS: Targ's American First Editions and Their Prices: A Checklist of the Foremost American Firsts, privately printed, 1930, published as *American First Editions and Their Prices: A Checklist of the Foremost American First Editions from 1640 to the Present Day,* Black Archer Press, 1930, revised edition, 1931, published as *American Books and Their Prices,* Black Archer Press, 1941; *Modern English First Editions and Their Prices, 1931: A Checklist of the Foremost English First Editions from 1860 to the Present Day,* Black Archer Press, 1932; *The Pauper's Guide to Book Collecting: Being a Series of Random Notes and Informal Jottings on a Noble Hobby,* Black Archer Press, 1933; (compiler) *Nine Hundred Ninety-Nine Books Worth Reading: A Checklist of the World's Best Books,* Black Archer Press, 1934; *Lafcadio Hearn: First Editions and Values—A Checklist for Collectors,* Black Archer Press, 1935; (editor) *Rare American Books, Valued from Fifty Dollars to Twenty-Five Thousand Dollars: A Checklist of the Scarcest and Most Valuable American First Editions,* Black Archer Press, 1935; (compiler with Harry F. Marks) *Ten Thousand Rare Books and Their Prices: A Handbook for Collectors, Dealers, and Librarians,* H. F. Marks, Inc., 1936.

Adventures in Good Reading, Black Archer Press, 1940; (editor) *The Western Story Omnibus: A Collection of Short Stories,* World Publishing, 1945; (editor and author of introduction) *The American West: A Treasury of Stories, Legends, Narratives, Songs, and Ballads of Western America,* World Publishing, 1946; (editor) *Carrousel for Bibliophiles: A Treasury of Tales, Narratives, Songs, Epigrams, and Sundry Curious Studies Relating to a Noble Theme,* P. C.

Duschnes, 1947, reprinted, Scarecrow, 1967; (editor) *Great Western Stories: A Western Story Omnibus,* Penguin, 1947.

(Editor) *A Reader for Writers,* Hermitage House, 1951; (editor and author of introduction) *Bouillabaisse for Bibliophiles: A Treasury of Bookish Lore, Wit and Wisdom, Tales, Poetry and Narrative, and Certain Curious Studies of Interest to Bookmen and Collectors,* World Publishing, 1955; (editor) *Bibliophile in the Nursery: A Bookman's Treasury of Collectors' Lore on Old and Rare Children's Books,* World Publishing, 1957.

(Editor) *Bookman's Progress: The Selected Writings of Lawrence Clark Powell,* Ritchie, 1968; *Indecent Pleasures: The Life and Colorful Times of William Targ* (memoirs), Macmillan, 1975.

Under pseudonym Charles Yu: *Poems of a Chinese Student,* Black Archer Press, 1941.

SIDELIGHTS: In *Indecent Pleasures,* Targ advises beginning writers: "Learn to light small fires so that you can burn your early drafts. Discipline yourself not to read stories aloud to friends. Develop a geiger counter for the detection of cliches and platitudes, tired and ineffectual words and phrases. . . . Most would-be writers will never be published because they haven't the necessary strength and patience. Authorship is a fantasy, a dream of most aspirants. It's a glittering notion, a mirage with one's name on the title page. Writing demands self-conspiracy, sweat and humility—a touch of madness, too. . . . Writing a first-rate book is no easier than climbing Mount Everest. I think Everest is easier." *Avocational interests:* Collecting rare books.

BIOGRAPHICAL/CRITICAL SOURCES: Publishers Weekly, November 10, 1975; *Berkshire Eagle,* November 11, 1975.

* * *

TARR, Yvonne Young 1929-

PERSONAL: Born December 10, 1929, in Covington, Ky.; daughter of Elwood Stinson (an architect) and Margaret (Linehan) Young; married William Tarr (a sculptor), March 7, 1952; children: Jonathon Young, Nicolas Joseph. *Politics:* None. *Religion:* None. *Residence:* Scarsdale, N.Y.

CAREER: Writer.

WRITINGS: The Ten-Minute Gourmet Cookbook, Lyle Stuart, 1965; *The Ten-Minute Gourmet Diet Cookbook,* Lyle Stuart, 1967; *A Hundred and One Desserts to Make You Famous,* Lyle Stuart, 1971; *The New York Times Bread and Soup Cookbook,* Quadrangle, 1972; *Love Portions,* Citadel, 1972; *The Complete Outdoor Cookbook,* Quadrangle, 1973; *The Farmhouse Cookbook,* 1973. Also author of "The Decameron" (a musical drama). Writer of syndicated column, "The Ten-Minute Gourmet Cook." Contributor to magazines.*

* * *

TARSHIS, Jerome 1936-

PERSONAL: Born June 27, 1936, in New York, N.Y.; son of Benjamin (a postal worker) and Freda (Wiener) Tarshis. *Education:* Columbia University, A.B., 1957. *Home:* 1315 Polk St., San Francisco, Calif. 94109.

CAREER: Dancer-Fitzgerald-Sample, Inc. (advertising agency), New York, N.Y., research analyst, 1957-59; Pageant Press, New York, N.Y., editorial assistant, 1959-60; *Television* (magazine), New York, N.Y., assistant editor, 1960; Physicians Publications, Inc., New York, N.Y., writer and editor, 1962-67; free-lance writer, 1967—; art critic, 1970—. *Awards, honors: Claude Bernard* was included in the Child Study Association of America's list of best books of 1968.

*WRITINGS—*For young adults: *Claude Bernard: Father of Experimental Medicine,* Dial, 1968; *Andreas Vesalius: Father of Modern Anatomy,* Dial, 1970. Contributor of reviews and articles to *Boys' Life, Evergreen Review, Village Voice, Art Forum, Art News, Studio International,* and other publications.

WORK IN PROGRESS: A book on art and literature of the 1960's.

SIDELIGHTS: Tarshis writes: "I came to write my biographies of Claude Bernard and Andreas Vesalius by what might be called a series of accidents. Taking them in no particular order, I can begin by saying that I spent the middle sixties working on a magazine published for doctors. This magazine tried to present the latest news of medicine—if possible, so late that it had not yet been published elsewhere—and often not even a recent event, but only a proposal for the future.

"Before long I despised the worship of the new. To do my job I had to suppress my understanding that many of the promising new lines of research I was writing about would come to nothing; I wished I could write about research that would still stand up 25 years later.

"By 1964 I had decided to move from New York to San Francisco, and I thought I should sell a high-priced magazine article to ease the transition period in which I would be looking for a new job. Bearing in mind my interest in medical research, I wrote an article for *Reader's Digest* about the 19th-century physiologist Claude Bernard. My article was rejected, whereupon I decided that someone had better pay me for my time. That article turned into my first book, and when the editor who bought it asked me what else I'd like to write for him, I suggested Andreas Vesalius, and he said yes.

"As for how I decided to write juveniles, that is another story. I had read a life of Louis Pasteur, by John Mann, and hadn't realized at the time that it was a book for young people. . . .I thought that if Mann could write a juvenile biography I had read with pleasure, then I myself could write a juvenile biography without compromising my standards as a writer. I spoke about this idea with Robert Silverberg, a college classmate of mine who has written many juveniles, and he encouraged me to go ahead. . . .

"For a variety of reasons, I stopped writing books in 1969, and have only recently started again. I've been an art critic since 1970, and I'm pleased to be able to turn my interests into books. As I write this, I don't have any clear vision of the future of book publishing, or of my own future, and I can't say whether I will someday write more books for young people."

* * *

TASHJIAN, Dickran (Levon) 1940-

PERSONAL: Born January 25, 1940, in Medford, Mass.; son of Martin H. Tashjian; married Ann Hulting, June 14, 1964; children: R. Lootfi. *Education:* Brown University, A.B., 1962, Ph.D., 1969; University of Minnesota, M.A., 1964. *Home:* 461 Shadow Lane, Laguna Beach, Calif. 92651. *Office:* Program in Comparative Culture, University of California, Irvine, Calif. 92664.

CAREER: Providence College, Providence, R.I., lecturer in American literature, 1967-68; University of California, Irvine, assistant professor, 1969-73, associate professor of comparative culture, 1973—, Humanities Institute summer fellow, 1972.

WRITINGS: (With wife, Ann Tashjian) *Memorials for Children of Change: The Art of Early New England Stonecarving,* Wesleyan University Press, 1974; *Skyscraper Primitives: Dada and the American Avant-Garde, 1910-1925,* Wesleyan University Press, 1975. Contributor to journals.

* * *

TASSIN, Myron Jude 1933-

PERSONAL: Surname is pronounced *Tah-*san; born February 6, 1933, in Longbridge, La.; son of Pliny (a farmer) and Emma (Ducote) Tassin; married Shirley Hill, December 26, 1953; children: Mike, Tim, Jay, Anne. *Education:* Louisiana State University, B.A., 1956. *Religion:* Roman Catholic. *Home:* 804 South Beach, Waveland, Miss. 39576. *Office:* 2609 Canal, New Orleans, La. 70119.

CAREER: United Fund of Baton Rouge, Baton Rouge, La., public relations director, 1955-58; self-employed in advertising, 1958-60; Louisiana Architects Association, Baton Rouge, executive director, 1960-67; Tassin-Ferachi, Inc. (publishers), Baton Rouge, La., president, 1968-72; Myron Tassin, Inc. (public relations firm), New Orleans, La., owner, 1972—. *Military service:* Louisiana National Guard, 1949-58; became master sergeant. *Member:* Cousteau Society, Louisiana Mental Health Society (past director), Baton Rouge Advertising Club (formerly first vice-president), East Baton Rouge Lions Club, Krewe of Triton.

WRITINGS—Historical nonfiction: (Editor) *Louisiana Antebellum Arthitecture,* Claitor, 1971; (editor) *The Last Line: A Streetcar Named St. Charles,* Pelican, 1972; (editor) *The Delta Queen: Last of the Paddlewheel Palaces,* Pelican, 1973; *Bacchus,* with introduction by Frances Parkinson Keyes, Pelican, 1974; (with Jerry Henderson) *Fifty Years at the Grand Ole Opry,* Pelican, 1975. Editor of *Entree,* 1960-66; founder and editor of *Louisiana Architect;* managing editor of *Louisiana Municipal Review,* 1968-72, *Louisiana Engineer,* 1968-72, *Savings and Loan Dividend,* 1968-72, *National Architectural Student,* 1969-72, and *Louisiana Realtor,* 1971-72.

* * *

TATUM, Billy Joe 1933-

PERSONAL: Born February 15, 1933, in Little Rock, Ark.; daughter of William O. (a Baptist minister) and Minnie (White) Taylor; married Harold Maury Tatum (a doctor), August 25, 1951; children: Angel (Mrs. Bob White), Lisa Suzanne, Lori Julianne, Maury White (daughter), Martin Bradley Tobias. *Education:* Attended Ouachita Baptist University. *Religion:* Baptist. *Home and office:* Wildflower, Melbourne, Ark. 72556.

CAREER: University of Arkansas, Medical School, Little Rock, librarian, 1951-53.

WRITINGS: Billy Joe Tatum's Wild Foods Cookbook, Workman Publishing, 1975. Writer of monthly column, "A Country Doctor's Wife," in *Ozarks Mountaineer.* Contributor of articles to *Organic Gardening, Ozark Digest,* and *Ozark Access Catalog.*

WORK IN PROGRESS: A book of collected pieces from her column, "A Country Doctor's Wife"; a photographic fieldguide, *Wildflowers of the Ozarks;* a fieldguide to medicinal herbs; a book on medicinal folklore; a book on flower folklore.

SIDELIGHTS: Billy Joe Tatum's interest in wild foods and herbs began when she discovered many of her husband's patients still used home remedies. Already interested in wildflowers and mushrooms of the Ozarks, she began botany studies while collecting these herbal remedies. She often lectures on these topics to garden, nature, and botany clubs.

* * *

TAUBE, Evert 1890-1976

March 12, 1890—January 31, 1976; Swedish poet, songwriter, novelist, and author of works for the stage. Obituaries: *Washington Post,* February 2, 1976; *AB Bookman's Weekly,* March 1, 1976.

* * *

TAYLOR, Alice L(ouise) 1911-

PERSONAL: Born August 4, 1911, in New York, N.Y.; daughter of Norman (a botanist) and Bertha (Fanning) Taylor; married Louis Lubrano, June, 1940 (divorced, 1945). *Education:* Ecole Alsacienne, Paris, France, baccalaureates, 1929 and 1930; attended University of Paris, 1931-32, and Ecole du Louvre and Ecole des Arts Decoratifs, both Paris, 1933-36; Columbia University, graduate study, 1942-44. *Home:* 120 East 36th St., New York, N.Y. 10016; and 1108 Fireplace Rd., East Hampton, N.Y. 11937. *Office:* American Geographical Society, Broadway at 156th St., New York, N.Y. 10032.

CAREER: Free-lance designer in New York, N.Y., 1937-40; American Geographical Society, New York, N.Y., secretary to director, 1941-49, editor of *Focus* (monthly magazine), 1950—. *Member:* Society for International Development, American Association for the Advancement of Science, Association of American Geographers, National Council for the Social Studies, Society of Woman Geographers, American Academy of Political and Social Science. *Awards, honors:* Publication award of the Geographic Society of Chicago, 1973.

WRITINGS—All published by Doubleday, except as otherwise indicated: *Egypt,* Holiday House, 1953; *South Africa,* Holiday House, 1954; *Iran,* Holiday House, 1955; *Switzerland,* 1955; *France,* 1956; *India,* Holiday House, 1957; *Boston,* 1957; *Philadelphia,* 1958; *New York City,* 1958; *Maryland and Delaware,* 1959; *Egypt and Syria,* 1960; *Gold Rush of '49,* 1960; *New York State,* 1962; *United Arab Republic,* 1964; *Syria,* 1965; *Taiwan,* 1967; *Republic of Ireland,* 1967; *England,* 1967; *Iraq,* 1968; *Iran,* 1970; *Western Europe,* Macmillan, 1972.

Editor: *Focus on the Middle East,* Praeger, 1971; *Focus on Southeast Asia,* Praeger, 1972; *Focus on South America,* Praeger, 1973. Editor of "Around the World Series," 1955-73, and of "Know Your America Series," 1956-74, both published by Doubleday.

AVOCATIONAL INTERESTS: Theatre, painting, fiction, history, golf, gardening, tennis, and canoeing.

* * *

TAYLOR, Irving A. 1925-

PERSONAL: Born August 23, 1925, in Pennsylvania; son of Peter and Eva (Coopersmith) Taylor; married Janet

Anderson, November 8, 1969. *Education:* University of Houston, B.A., 1950, M.A., 1951; New York University, Ph.D., 1954. *Home address:* R.R. 13, Lakeshore Dr., Thunder Bay, Ontario, Canada P7B 5E4. *Office:* Department of Psychology, Lakehead University, Thunder Bay, Ontario, Canada.

CAREER: New York State College for Teachers at Albany, assistant professor of psychology, 1953-54; Pratt Institute, Brooklyn, N.Y., assistant professor of psychology, 1954-59; Northeast Missouri State Teachers College (now University), Kirksville, professor of psychology and chairman of department, 1959-60; New York Medical College, New York, N.Y., senior research associate and project coordinator at Institute for Developmental Studies and associate in psychiatry, 1960-61; I. A. Taylor Associates, Los Angeles, Calif., self-employed consultant in psychology, 1961-68; Smith Richardson Foundation (now Center for Creative Leadership), Greensboro, N.C., director of creativity program, 1968-74; Lakehead University, Thunder Bay, Ontario, professor of psychology, 1974—. Certified psychologist in New York, 1958, California, 1962, North Carolina, 1969, and Ontario, 1974. Child counselor at Berkeley Institute, 1952; vocational counselor at Hunter College (now of the City University of New York), 1955; research director for Nowland & Co., 1961. Lecturer at Barnard College, 1954-56, Bronx Community College, 1960-61, University of California, Los Angeles, spring, 1963, and Tri-College Consortium (North Carolina), summer, 1970; associate professor at San Fernando Valley State Teachers College, 1961-63; visiting lecturer at Guilford College, 1969-72; University of North Carolina, visiting lecturer, 1969-70, adjunct professor, 1971—; visiting professor at North Carolina Agricultural and Technical State University, 1971-72; adjunct professor at Wake Forest University, autumn, 1972. Associate research director of Music Research Foundation, 1957-58; research director and member of board of directors for Richard J. Neutra Foundation, 1962-68; acting president, member of board of directors, and professor at Western Institute for Advanced Study, 1965-68; colleague and resource leader of Creative Education Foundation, 1970—; also employed by Foundation for Inter-Racial Study, National Project in Agricultural Communication, and National Science Foundation. Consultant to industry, 1956—. *Military service:* U.S. Army, Combat Engineers, 1942-44.

MEMBER: International Society for General Semantics (founder of Houston chapter, 1950-51; president and member of board of directors of Los Angeles chapter, 1962-63; member of international board of directors, 1963-67), American Psychological Association, Canadian Psychological Association, Southeastern Psychological Association, North Carolina Psychological Association, New York Academy of Science. *Awards, honors:* Psychosocial research award from American Association for the Advancement of Science, 1957.

WRITINGS: Theory of Creative Transactualization: A Systematic Approach to Creativity with Implications for Creative Leadership (monograph), Creative Education Foundation, 1973; (editor with Alton Barbour and contributor) *Creativity in Action,* New York University Press, 1975; (editor with Jacob Getzels and contributor) *Perspectives in Creativity,* Aldine, 1975.

Contributor: Paul Smith, editor, *Creativity: An Examination of the Creative Process,* Hastings House, 1959; Elwood Whitney, editor, *Symbology: The Use of Symbols in Visual Communication,* Hastings House, 1960; John Ball

and Francis C. Byrnes, editors, *Research, Principles, and Practices in Visual Communication,* Michigan State University Press, 1960; Edward Gottshall and Arthur Hawkins, editors, *Ad Directions: Trends in Visual Advertising,* Art Directions Book, 1960; J. L. Steinberg, W. S. Zimmerman, and J. G. Whelen, editors, *Implications of Creativity Research,* Los Angeles State College, 1962; Eric Pfeiffer, editor, *Successful Aging: A Conference Report,* Center for the Study of Aging and Human Development, Duke University, 1974.

Films: "The Nature of Creativity," Pratt Institute, 1958; "Creativity," Perceptual Development Laboratories, 1958; "Visual Communication," Art Directors Club of New York, 1959; "Richard Neutra and Architecture," Pratt Institute, 1962; "Creativity and Creative Leadership," Center for Creative Leadership, 1971; "A Psychology of Creativity," CCM Films, 1972. Contributor of articles and reviews to psychology, psychiatry, education, communication, and art journals. Editor of *Communication,* 1975.

SIDELIGHTS: Taylor mentions that he had early training in art and "contact with various highly creative individuals. I consider creativity to be the highest value and most important function of the human being. I continue to do research and develop theories on the nature of the creative process."

BIOGRAPHICAL/CRITICAL SOURCES: "Psychology of Creativity," film produced by Richard Evans, CCM Films, 1972.

* * *

TAYLOR, John (Alfred)   1931-
(Abiezer Coppe, August Dupont Dupin, Charles Dexter Ward)

PERSONAL: Born September 12, 1931, in Springfield, Mo.; son of John James (a clergyman) and Emma (Newmann) Taylor; married Rosemary Templeman (divorced, 1971); married Dorothy Vance, May 3, 1973; children: (second marriage) Warren J. Keller, Jr. (stepson). *Education:* Southwest Missouri State University, student, 1948-50; University of Missouri, B.A., 1952; University of Iowa, M.A., 1957, Ph.D., 1959. *Politics:* "Confused and bemused; vaguely 'liberal.'" *Religion:* "Taoist trying to be Christian at same time." *Residence:* Washington, Pa. *Office:* Department of English, Washington & Jefferson College, Washington, Pa. 15301.

CAREER: University of New Hampshire, Durham, instructor, 1959-61, assistant professor of English, 1961-62; Rice University, Houston, Tex., assistant professor of English, 1962-64; State University of New York College at Buffalo, assistant professor of English, 1964-66; Washington & Jefferson College, Washington, Pa., associate professor of English, 1966—. *Military service:* U.S. Army, 1952-55. *Member:* Modern Language Association of America, American Association of University Professors, American Civil Liberties Union, Wilderness Society. *Awards, honors:* Rockefeller Foundation grant, 1970.

WRITINGS: The Soap Duckets (poems), Verb Press, 1965; *Portfolio Three* (poems), Portfolio, 1971; *The London Poems,* Fort Necessity Press, 1975.

Poetry is included in anthologies: *Midland,* edited by Paul Engle, Random House, 1961; *Best Poems of 1968* (Borestone Mountain Awards), Pacific Books, 1968, as well as 1971 and 1972 editions; *The Now Voices,* edited by Angelo Carli and Theodore Kilman, Scribner, 1971.

Contributor to *Mandala,* under pseudonym August Dupont Dupin, and to *Washington and Jefferson Literary Journal* under pseudonyms Charles Dexter Ward and Abiezer Coppe; contributor to *Poetry Northwest, Colorado State Review, New York Quarterly,* and other journals.

WORK IN PROGRESS: Life As We Know It, a book of poems; another book of poems; *Ballad of G. E. Rasputin;* "Zizka," a play about the Hussite Wars; ghost stories and science fiction stories.

SIDELIGHTS: Taylor writes: "'All other men's worlds are the poet's chaos.' I read this in my early teens, and it has kept haunting me just as my desire to be a poet has. I believe a poet should be a man of wide (though unfortunately often shallow) knowledge; and when I don't have it, I believe there are honest ways of 'faking' it. . . .I like being alive, even when it hurts." *Avocational interests:* Science, archaeology, history, mythology, nature, foreign languages, cants and jargons, puns, paradoxes, Presocratics, Taoist books, dictionaries, ghost stories, "the unconscious humor of politicians and journalists."

*   *   *

TAYLOR, Philip Elbert   1908-1975

February 29, 1908—October 7, 1975; American economist, educator, fiscal advisor, and author. Obituaries: *New York Times,* October 9, 1975; *AB Bookman's Weekly,* December 1, 1975.

*   *   *

TAYLOR, Phoebe Atwood   1909-1976
(Alice Tilton)

1909—January 9, 1976; American mystery novelist. Obituaries: *New York Times,* January 12, 1976; *Washington Post,* January 17, 1976.

*   *   *

TAYLOR, Robert Brown   1936-

PERSONAL: Born May 31, 1936, in Elmira, N.Y.; son of Olaf C. (a book salesman) and Elizabeth (Brown) Taylor; married Anita Dopico (a real estate broker), July 30, 1959; children: Diana Marie, Sharon Jean. *Education:* Attended Bucknell University, 1957; Temple University, M.D., 1961. *Religion:* Protestant. *Home:* 48 North Oakwood Terrace, New Paltz, N.Y. 12561. *Address:* P.O. Box 562, 66 Forest Glen Rd., New Paltz, N.Y. 12561.

CAREER: In private practice of medicine in New Paltz, N.Y., 1964—. Kingston City Hospital, Kingston, N.Y., attending staff member, 1964—; Benedictine Hospital, Kingston, N.Y., staff physician, 1964—. Diplomate from American Board of Family Practice, 1971. Member of advisory committee of Dutchess Community College. *Wartime service:* U.S. Public Health Service, 1961-64. *Member:* American Academy of Family Physicians (charter fellow), Medical Society of State of New York.

WRITINGS: Common Problems in Office Practice, Harper, 1972; *The Practical Art of Medicine,* Harper, 1972; *A Primer of Clinical Symptoms,* Harper, 1972; *Feeling Alive after Sixty-five,* Arlington House, 1973; *Doctor Taylor's Guide to Healthy Skin for All Ages,* Arlington House, 1974; (editor) Jean Valnet, *Organic Garden Medicine,* Erbonia Books, 1975.

WORK IN PROGRESS: For ages nine to twelve, *A Shot in Time: The Story of Immunization; Making It in Middle*

Age: A Medical Guide for the Prime Years; a book of home therapy of common ailments with diet, exercise, natural remedies, and non-prescription medication, *Doctor Taylor's No Hassle, Money-Saving, Self-Help Medical Guide.*

SIDELIGHTS: Dr. Taylor writes about the medical problems faced by people of all ages in easy to understand language. His books stress the importance of exercise, diet, and good health habits. He believes that writing is a logical extension of the family physician's role as health counselor.

*   *   *

TAYLOR, Walter W(illard)   1913-

PERSONAL: Born October 17, 1913, in Chicago, Ill.; son of Walter N. (in oil business) and Marjorie (Wells) Taylor; married Lyda Averill, 1937 (died, 1960); married Nancy Thompson, 1962 (divorced, 1970); married Mary Henderson, November 1, 1970; children: (first marriage) Peter Wells, Ann Averill Taylor Cover, Gordon McAuliffe. *Education:* Yale University, A.B. (with honors), 1935, graduate study, 1935-36; University of New Mexico, further graduate study, 1937; Harvard University, Ph.D., 1943. *Home address:* P.O. Box 5334, Santa Fe, N.M. 87501.

CAREER: Arizona State Teachers College (now Northern Arizona University), Flagstaff, instructor in science, 1937-38; Harvard University, Cambridge, Mass., assistant instructor in anthropology, 1940-42; U.S. Marine Corps, career officer, 1942-55 (instructor in anthropology and geology at prisoner-of-war schools in Germany, 1944-45, also served in Algeria, Corsica, Italy, and France), leaving service as captain; Mexico City College, Mexico City, Mexico, professor of anthropology, 1955-57; Southern Illinois University, Carbondale, professor of anthropology, 1958-74, professor emeritus, 1974—, chairman of department, 1958-63. Instructor at University of Texas, 1942-43; visiting lecturer for Friends Service Committee, 1948-53; University of Washington, Seattle, visiting assistant professor, 1949, visiting professor, 1953; visiting professor at Escuela Nacional de Antropologia e Historia, 1955-58, University of Merida, 1956, and St. Michael's College (Santa Fe), 1965. Director of Smithsonian Institution's Northern Mexico Archaeological Fund, 1940-49, 1957—, director of Southwest Archaeological Fund, 1949-57; member of National Research Council's committee on archaeological identifications, 1955-57, director of Program in Cultural Ecology, 1959; member of board of directors of Human Relations Area Files, 1960-74, member of executive committee, 1970-74. President of Indian Arts Fund, 1948, and Foundation for Anthropological Research in Latin America, 1956-57; vice-president of Centro de Investigaciones Antropologicas de Mexico, 1955-56, and Illinois Archaeological Survey, 1958-60. Field foreman of University of New Mexico summer field school, 1938-40; conducted field work in Arizona, New Mexico, Georgia, Mexico, and Spain. Member of Santa Fe Little Theater, 1949-55, president, 1950; member of Mexico City Players, Inc., 1956-58, member of board of directors, 1957-58.

MEMBER: American Anthropological Association (fellow), American Association for the Advancement of Science (fellow), Society for American Archaeology, Prehistoric Society, Society of Antiquaries of Scotland (fellow), Societe Prehistorique Francaise, Sociedad Mexicana de Antropologia, Archaeological Society of New Mexico, Arizona Archaeological and Historical Society, Colorado Archaeological Society, Texas Archaeological Society,

Sigma Xi, Delta Kappa Epsilon. *Awards, honors*—Military: Purple Heart, Bronze Star with citation. Other: Rockefeller Foundation fellow in humanities, 1946; Guggenheim fellow, 1950-51; National Science Foundation grants for study in Mexico, 1964, Spain, 1967, and New Mexico, 1971-73; Wenner-Gren Foundation grant for research in New Mexico, 1969-70; Leo Kaplan research award from Sigma Xi, 1973.

WRITINGS: A Study of Archaeology, American Anthropological Association, 1948; (editor and contributor) *The Identification of Non-Artifactual Archaeological Materials,* National Academy of Sciences and National Research Council, 1957; (contributor) Edward Jelks and John A. Graham, editors, *Appraisal of the Archaeological Resources of Diablo Reservoir, Val Verde County, Texas,* Archaeological Salvage Program Field Office (Austin, Tex.), 1958; (contributor) Robert Wauchope and Gordon R. Willey, editors, *Handbook of Middle American Indians,* Volume IV, University of Texas Press, 1966; (editor with Carroll L. Riley, and contributor) *American Historical Anthropology: Essays in Honor of Leslie Spier,* Southern Illinois University Press, 1967; (contributor) Albert H. Schroeder, editor, *Collected Papers in Honor of Lyndon Lane Hargrave,* Archaeological Society of New Mexico, 1968; (editor with John L. Fischer and Evon Z. Vogt and contributor) *Culture and Life: Essays in Memory of Clyde Kluckhohn,* Southern Illinois University Press, 1973; (contributor) C. L. Redman, editor, *Research and Theory in Current Archeology,* Wiley, 1973. Contributor to anthropology and archaeology journals.

WORK IN PROGRESS: The Cave Cultures of Coahuila, Mexico, a report on field research over a period of thirty-nine years; *Excavations in Cueva Tetavejo, Sonora, Mexico,* a monograph.

SIDELIGHTS: Taylor writes: "My major viewpoint in my professional work has been that archaeology, as a subdiscipline of the discipline of anthropology, is a study of culture, not merely culture-history...." *Avocational interests:* Hunting, fishing, gardening (vegetables), photography, wines, reading.

BIOGRAPHICAL/CRITICAL SOURCES: R. F. Spencer, editor, *Method and Perspective in Anthropology,* University of Minnesota Press, 1954; G. R. Willey and Jeremy Sabloff, *A History of American Archaeology,* W. H. Freeman, 1973; *Yale Alumni Magazine,* December, 1973.

*   *   *

TEAL, Val(entine M.) 1903-

PERSONAL: Born February 14, 1903, in Bottineau, N.D.; daughter of August Anderson (an owner and operator of a flour mill) and Georgiana (Berntson) Moline; married Clarence William Teal (an engineering executive) September 4, 1926; children: John Moline, Peter Valentine, Thomas Augustus, Alison (daughter). *Education:* University of Minnesota, B.A., 1925. *Politics:* Independent. *Religion:* Episcopalian. *Home and office:* 5620 Western Ave., Omaha, Neb. 68132.

CAREER: Puzzle editor for *Rural American* and *Minneapolis Daily News,* both Minneapolis, Minn., 1922-24; legal secretary in Minneapolis Council of Social Agencies, 1925-27; tutor in humanities, University of Nebraska, Omaha, 1947-65. Writer, 1943—. Member of board of Omaha Junior Theater; member of local family and child welfare board.

MEMBER: P.E.O. Sisterhood, American Association of

University Women, Omaha Community Playhouse Guild (historian). *Awards, honors:* First prize in Omaha Junior Theater play writing contest, 1954, for "Grandmother's Magic Clock"; Omaha Community Playhouse Awards, for service, 1965, 1975.

WRITINGS: The Little Woman Wanted Noise (juvenile), Rand McNally, 1943; *Angel Child* (juvenile) Rand McNally, 1946, reissued, 1965; *It Was Not What I Expected,* Duell, Sloan & Pearce, 1948. Also author of play, "Grandmother's Magic Clock," first produced in Omaha, Neb., 1954.

Work is represented in about two dozen books, including: *Read Me More Stories,* Crowell, 1951; *The Years Between,* edited by Frances T. Humphreville, Scott, Foresman, 1953; *Youth, Youth, Youth,* edited by Albert B. Tibbets, F. Watts, 1955; *Adventures for You,* edited by Eva Pumphrey and Eric W. Johnson, Harcourt, 1968; *This Cool World,* edited by Nicholas J. Silvaroli and William D. Sheldon, Allyn & Bacon, 1969; *Reading Goals,* edited by Glenn McCracken and Charles C. Walcutt, Lippincott, 1970.

Contributor of short stories to popular magazines for adults and children, including *Saturday Evening Post, Ladies' Home Journal, Good Housekeeping, American, Woman's Day, Woman's Home Companion, Child Life,* and *Parents' Magazine.* Contributing editor, Omaha Community Playhouse *Promptor* (playbill).

SIDELIGHTS: Val Teal writes: "I am a zealous conservationist and environmentalist. I wash dishes by hand, wash clothes with a wringer-type washer to conserve water. I hang them out to dry to conserve energy. I even make my own laundry soap and my clothes are cleaner and whiter than those washed with detergents which are polluting our streams. I have no garbage disposal or dishwasher. I have always baked our bread.

"I make braided rugs—one room-size one and have even made braided carpeting for the front hall, stairs, and long upstairs hall. I am interested in early American antiques. Our early American house is completely furnished with them, many of them family heirlooms, all refurbished by us. I suppose we are among the few couples in the country who had a house built for themselves back in 1933 and have lived in it ever since. I also make quilts—right now crazy quilts of all silk or velvet pieces rich with embroidery. We have traveled almost all over the world."

*   *   *

TEGNER, Bruce 1928-

PERSONAL: Born October 28, 1928, in Chicago, Ill. *Education:* LaVerne College, B.A., 1975. *Address:* P.O. Box 1782, Ventura, Calif. 93001.

CAREER: Specialist in self-defense and sport forms of weaponless fighting; has trained actors and devised fight scenes for films and television. Operator of Bruce Tegner School, 1952-67; instructor in defense tactics at Moorpark College, 1970— . *Military service:* U.S. Army, 1950-52; trained instructors to teach weaponless fighting, taught military police tactics, and coached sport judo teams.

WRITINGS—All published by Thor Publishing, except as noted: *Karate,* Volume I: *The Open Hand and Foot Fighting,* 1959, 3rd edition, 1965, Volume II: *Traditional Forms for Sport,* 1959, 3rd edition, 1963.

Bruce Tegner Method of Self-Defense: The Best of Judo, Jiu-jitsu, Karate, Savate, Yawara, Aikido, Ate-waza, 1960,

3rd edition, 1971; *Savate: French Foot Fighting, Self-Defense, Sport,* 1960, 3rd edition, 1965; *Aikido Self-Defense: Holds and Locks for Modern Use,* 1961; *Judo for Fun: Sport Techniques Made Easy,* 1961; *Self-Defense for Women: A Simple Method,* 1961, 2nd edition (with Alice McGrath), 1969; *Stick Fighting for Self-Defense: Yawara, Police Club, Aikido, Cane, Quarter-Staff,* 1961, 3rd edition, 1972; *Teach Your Boy Self-Defense and Self-Confidence,* 1961; *Judo-Karate for Police Officers: Defense and Control, a Simple Method,* 1962; *Bruce Tegner's Complete Book of Self Defense,* Stein & Day, 1963; *Judo and Karate Belt Degrees: Requirements, Rules, Regulations,* 1963, revised edition, 1967; *Judo and Karate Exercises: Physical Conditioning for the Un-Armed Fighting Arts,* 1963; *Karate: Self Defense and Sport,* Dell, 1963; *Isometric Power Exercises,* Dell, 1964.

Instant Self-Defense, Grosset, 1965; *Bruce Tegner's Complete Book of Karate,* Bantam, 1966, 3rd edition, Thor Publishing, 1970; *Black Belt Judo, Karate, and Jukado: Advanced Techniques for Experts,* 1967, *Complete Book of Judo,* 1967; *Complete Book of Karate,* 1967, 3rd edition, 1970; (with McGrath) *Self-Defense for Girls: A Secondary School and College Manual,* 1967, revised edition, Grosset, 1969; *Complete Book of Jukado Self-Defense: Judo, Karate, Aikido (Jiu-jitsu Modernized),* 1968; *Kung Fu and Tai Chi: Chinese Karate and Classical Exercises,* 1968; *Self-Defense: Nerve Centers and Pressure Points for Atemiwaza, Jukado, and Karate,* 1968; *Self-Defense for Boys and Men: A Secondary School and College Manual,* 1968, revised edition, 1969; *Aikido and Jiu Jitsu Holds and Locks,* 1969.

Bruce Tegner's Complete Book of Aikido and Holds and Locks, Grosset, 1970; *Judo for Fun: Sport Techniques,* 1970; *Self-Defense You Can Teach Your Boy: A Confidence-Building Course,* 1970; *Defense Tactics for Law Enforcement,* Volume I: *Weaponless Defense and Control,* 1972.

WORK IN PROGRESS: Self-Defense for Your Child (to replace earlier publication, *Self-Defense You Can Teach Your Boy*).

SIDELIGHTS: Tegner, who holds black belts in judo and karate, was born to the teaching of unarmed fighting skills. Both his parents were professional teachers of judo and jiu-jitsu and began to train him when he was two years old. After the age of eight, Tegner was instructed by Oriental and European experts, receiving instruction in sword and stick fighting as well as the various forms of weaponless fighting.

Before he gave up competitive judo, Tegner became the California state judo champion. He has taught men, women, and children, exceptionally gifted students, and blind and disabled people.

*   *   *

TEMPLE, Ruth Z(abriskie) 1908-

PERSONAL: Born December 26, 1908, in Passaic, N.J.; daughter of Arthur Henry (a physician) and Ruth (Van Brunt) Temple. *Education:* Mount Holyoke College, A.B. (magna cum laude), 1929; Radcliffe College, A.M., 1930; Bryn Mawr College, further graduate study, 1932-33; Columbia University, Ph.D., 1947. *Politics:* Liberal. *Religion:* Episcopal. *Home address:* South St., Chesterfield, Mass. 01012. *Office:* Graduate Center, City University of New York, 33 West 42nd St., New York, N.Y. 10036.

CAREER: French teacher in preparatory school in Passaic, N.J., 1930-31; Mount Holyoke College, South Hadley, Mass., instructor in English literature, 1931-32; Columbia University, New York, N.Y., instructor in English, 1935-36; Barnard College, New York, N.Y., instructor in English, 1938-39; Queens College (now of the City University of New York), Flushing, N.Y., instructor in English, 1939-42; Wells College, Aurora, N.Y., instructor in English, 1942-43; Russell Sage College, Troy, N.Y., assistant professor of English, 1943-48; Brooklyn College (now of the City University of New York), Brooklyn, N.Y., assistant professor, 1948-58, associate professor, 1958-66, professor of English, 1966-73; City University of New York, Graduate Center, New York, N.Y., adjunct professor of comparative literature, 1973—. Fulbright professor at University of Strasbourg, 1963-64. Member of supervising committee of English Institute, 1958-61.

MEMBER: International Association of University Professors of English, American Association of University Professors (president of Russell Sage chapter, 1946-47; member of executive committee of Brooklyn College chapter, 1960-62), Modern Language Association of America, Comparative Literature Association, National Council of Teachers of English, Modern Humanities Research Association, New York Council of Teachers of English (member of executive board, 1949-55), English Graduate Union (Columbia University), Chesterfield Historical Society (past president; curator), Phi Beta Kappa. *Awards, honors:* New Jersey Fellowship from American Association of University Women, 1950-51.

WRITINGS: The Critic's Alchemy: A Study of the Introduction of French Symbolism into England, Twayne, 1953; (contributor) Richard Ellmann, editor, *Edwardians and Late Victorians,* Columbia University Press, 1960; (contributor) Lawrence E. Wikender and other editors, *The Hampshire History,* Hampshire County Commissioners, 1964; (contributor) Leon Edel, editor, *Literary History and Literary Criticism,* New York University Press, 1964; (editor with Martin Tucker) *A Library of Literary Criticism: Modern British Literature,* three volumes, Ungar, 1966; (editor) *Twentieth Century British Literature: A Reference Guide and Bibliography,* Ungar, 1968; *Nathalie Sarraute,* Columbia University Press, 1968; (editor with George B. Parks) *The Literatures of the World in English Translation: A Bibliography,* Ungar, Volume I: *The Greek and Latin Literatures,* 1968, Volume III (Temple was not associated with Volume II): *Romance Literatures,* Part I: *Catalan, Italian, Portuguese and Brazilian, Provencal, Rumanian, Spanish and Spanish American,* 1970, Part II: *French Literature, General, Sixteenth Century, Seventeenth Century, Eighteenth Century, Nineteenth Century, Twentieth Century,* 1970; (contributor) Claire Sprague, editor, *Virginia Woolf: A Collection of Critical Essays,* Prentice-Hall, 1971. Contributor of articles and reviews to literature journals. Member of editorial board of *English Literature in Transition,* 1960—.

WORK IN PROGRESS: A book on the theory of the novel.

SIDELIGHTS: Ruth Temple has traveled and studied in England, France, Italy, Greece, the Soviet Union, Austria, and Sicily.

*   *   *

TERHUNE, William Barclay 1893-

PERSONAL: Born November 2, 1893, in Senoia, Ga.;

married second wife, Caroline Phelps Hunter, December 26, 1961; children: Jane (Mrs. Eben Hall), William Barclay, Jr., Constance (Mrs. William Lancaster). *Education:* Tulane University, M.D., 1915. *Home:* River House, Valley Rd., New Canaan, Conn. *Office:* Silver Hill Foundation, P.O. Box 1177, New Canaan, Conn. 06840.

CAREER: Touro Infirmary, New Orleans, La., intern, 1915-16; Louisiana State Hospital, Jackson, resident, 1915-16; Louisiana Hospital for the Insane, staff physician, 1916-19; trainee at Queen's Square Hospital, London, England; Austen Riggs Foundation, Stockbridge, Mass., staff physician, 1922-29, associate medical director, 1929-34; Silver Hill Foundation, New Canaan, Conn., founder and medical director, 1934-65, senior consultant, 1965—. Diplomate of American Board of Psychiatry and Neurology. Lecturer at Yale University, 1919-27, associate clinical professor, 1938-60. *Military service:* U.S. Army, Neuropsychiatry Unit, 1917-19; became lieutenant.

MEMBER: American Psychological Association (vice-president, 1958), American College of Physicians, American Medical Association, American Psychopathological Association (president, 1950; vice-president, 1959), American Clinical and Climatological Association (first vice-president, 1951), Research Society for Nervous and Mental Disorders, American Psychosomatic Society, Eastern Psychological Association (member of council), New England Society for Neurology and Psychology, New York Academy of Medicine, Connecticut Society for Neurology and Psychiatry, Connecticut State Medical Society.

WRITINGS: (Editor) *Living Wisely and Well,* Dutton, 1949; *Integration of Psychiatry and Medicine,* Grune, 1951; *Emotional Problems and What You Can Do About Them,* Morrow, 1955; *Mastering Your Emotions: Mental Health Through the Reeducation of Self,* Morrow, 1970. Contributor to medical journals.*

* * *

THIMM, Alfred L. 1923-

PERSONAL: Born December 10, 1923; married; children: two. *Education:* New York University, B.A. (cum laude), 1948, M.A., 1949, Ph.D., 1959; summer post-doctoral study at University of Wyoming, 1959, and State University of Iowa, 1961. *Home address:* R.D. #1, Galway, N.Y. 12074. *Office:* Institute of Administration and Management, Union College, Schenectady, N.Y. 12308.

CAREER: Industrial engineer for American Can Co., 1951-52; St. Lawrence University, Canton, N.Y., assistant professor of economics, 1953-55; Clarkson College, Potsdam, N.Y., associate professor of business administration and mechanical engineering, 1956-59; Union College, Schenectady, N.Y., associate professor, 1960-62, professor of economics and industrial administration, 1968—, Institute of Administration and Management, director of graduate program, 1962-68, director of institute, 1968—. Visiting professor at University of Munich, 1972. Management consultant to New York State Bureau of the Budget, New York State Department of Transportation, and other public and private agencies; associate with Stochos, Inc. (management consulting firm), 1973. *Awards, honors:* National Science Foundation grants, 1959, 1961; Ford Foundation summer research grants, 1960, 1962; Fulbright research scholar at Technische Hochschule, Graz, Austria, 1967-68.

WRITINGS: (Contributor) L. R. Robinson and Adams, editors, *Introduction to Modern Economics,* Dryden, 1950; (contributor) John M. Champion and Francis J. Bridges,

editors, *Critical Incidents in Management,* Irwin, 1963; (with J. Finkelstein) *Economists and Society: From Aquinas to Keynes,* Harper, 1973; *The Dynamics of Project Management,* Administrative and Engineering Systems Monograph, Union College, 1974; *American Business Opinion,* University of Alabama Press, 1975; (with Eberhard Witte) *Neue Richtlinien in der Amerikanischen Management Theorie,* Westdeutscher Press, 1975. Contributor to journals in his field.

WORK IN PROGRESS: With J. Finkelstein, *The Political Economy of Planning and Control; The Foundations of Systems Analysis;* research on the dynamics of economic planning in the Soviet Union and Eastern Europe and the impact of administrative and political behavior on the planning-decision process.

* * *

THOBY-MARCELIN, Philippe 1904-1975

1904—August 13, 1975; Haitian-born American novelist, poet, translator, and author of nonfiction. Obituaries: *New York Times,* August 17, 1975; *AB Bookman's Weekly,* October 13, 1975.

* * *

THOM, Robert Anderson 1915-

PERSONAL: Born February 28, 1915, in Oudtshoorn, South Africa; came to the United States, 1952; son of Alexander and Maria (Moore) Thom; married Joyce Magdalene O'Connor, April 10, 1935 (died January 27, 1974); children: Drummond, Lionel, Roy, Elaine, Robert, David, Bernard, Leonard, Robyn. *Education:* South Africa Military College, National Commercial Certificate, 1948. *Home:* 504 Belgravia Ct., Louisville, Ky. 40208. *Office address:* Deeper Life Center, P.O. Box 351, Louisville, Ky. 40201.

CAREER: Traveling evangelist in Africa, Asia, Europe, Australia, South America and North America, 1952—. Has broadcast on radio and television. *Military service:* South African Army, 1940-51; served in South Africa, Egypt, and Italy; received seven medals and decorations.

WRITINGS: You and Your Ministry, Christ for the Nations, 1973; *The New Wine is Better,* Whitaker House, 1974. Also author of *Africa's Man of Faith,* 1960, and booklets in Afrikaans published in South Africa. Contributor to *Jessup Journal.*

WORK IN PROGRESS: Making Known His Deeds.

* * *

THOMAE, Betty Kennedy 1920-

PERSONAL: Born September 9, 1920, in Columbus, Ohio; daughter of Ralph D. and Pearle Althea (Bawden) Kennedy; married William Rudolph Meyer, 1939 (divorced, 1945); married Edwin Leroy Thomae, 1945 (divorced, 1946); children: (first marriage) Bonnie Sue (Mrs. Jack Stephen Horstman); (second marriage) William Lee. *Education:* Attended Franklin University. *Home:* 1008 Hardesty Pl. W., Columbus, Ohio 43204. *Office:* 330 South High St., Columbus, Ohio 43215.

CAREER: Kenneth P. Bessey (an attorney), Columbus, Ohio, legal secretary, 1958—. *Member:* International Clover Poetry Association, National Secretaries Association, National Association of Legal Secretaries, National Association of Legal Assistants, American Society of Composers, Authors, and Publishers. *Awards, honors:*

Diploma of merit and medal of honor from Centro Studi e Scambi Internazionali, both 1968.

WRITINGS: Stand Still, Summer (poems), Centro Studi e Scambi Internazionali, 1968; *Roses and Thorns* (poems), Mitre Press, 1969; *Legal Secretary's Desk Book—With Forms,* Parker Publishing, 1973. Contributor of one hundred and fifty poems to magazines and newspapers; contributor to secretarial magazines. Composer of songs, "My Honey" and "Only Ashes."

WORK IN PROGRESS: A collection of poems; editing and revising *Legal Secretary's Encyclopedic Dictionary* for Parker Publishing.

AVOCATIONAL INTERESTS: Travel, the stage, reading biographies.

* * *

THOMAS, Abraham V(azhayil) 1934-

PERSONAL: Born October 1, 1934, in Kerala, India; son of T. Abraham (a plantation owner) and Chachykutty (Lukose) Vazhayil; married Santhamma Punnoose (a teacher and sociologist), April 10, 1967; children: Anil, Paul. *Education:* University of Kerala, student; University of Madras, B.A. (with honors), 1956, M.A., 1959; University of Sydney, diploma in social work, 1959; Moore Theological College (Sydney), L.Th., 1959; Union Theological Seminary, New York, N.Y., S.T.M., 1962; Boston University, Th.D., 1968. *Home:* 540 Plymouth St., Bridgewater, Mass. 02324. *Office:* Department of Sociology, Bridgewater State College, Bridgewater, Mass. 02324.

CAREER: Catholicate College, Pathanamthitta, Kerala, India, instructor in English, 1959-61; Bridgewater State College, Bridgewater, Mass., instructor, 1967-69, assistant professor, 1969-72, associate professor of sociology, 1972—. Ordained priest of Syrian Orthodox Church of India, 1973; honorary pastor of Bridgewater-Boston Indian Orthodox Congregation, 1973—. *Member:* American Sociological Association, Massachusetts Sociological Association.

WRITINGS: (With others) *Indian Politics after Nehru,* Christian Institute for the Study of Religion and Society (Bangalore, India), 1967; *Christians in Secular India,* Fairleigh Dickinson University Press, 1974.

AVOCATIONAL INTERESTS: Playing tennis, photography.

* * *

THOMAS, Bill 1934-

PERSONAL: Born November 11, 1934, in Elizabethtown, Ky.; son of William Roy (a farmer) and Elizabeth (Crabtree) Thomas; married Joan McBroom, February 2, 1954 (divorced, 1965); married Phyllis Newkirk, 1965; children: (first marriage) David, Dianne, Lisa, Alan Lowell. *Education:* Western Kentucky State University, A.B., 1958. *Politics:* "May the best man win." *Religion:* Sometimes. *Home and office address:* Route 4, Box 411B, Nashville, Ind. 47448.

CAREER: Park City Daily News, Bowling Green, Ky., reporter, 1955-58; United Press International, Louisville, Ky., staff writer, 1959-62; *Cincinnati Enquirer,* Cincinnati, Ohio, bureau chief in Lebanon, Ohio, 1962-63, travel editor, 1964-66; free-lance magazine photojournalist, 1966—. *Military service:* U.S. Army, Intelligence, 1958-59; became captain. *Member:* Society of American Travel Writers,

Outdoor Writers of America, American Society of Magazine Photographers, International Platform Association, Hoosier Outdoor Writers. *Awards, honors: Writer's Digest* Award, 1967, for nonfiction magazine article; Ohio Governor's Award, 1972.

WRITINGS: Tripping in America: Off the Beaten Track, Chilton, 1974; *Eastern Trips and Trails,* Stackpole, 1975; *Mid-America Trips and Trails,* Stackpole, 1975; *The Swamp,* Norton, 1976. Contributor to popular magazines, including *Outdoor Life, Argosy, Field & Stream, Saga, Sports Afield, Popular Science, Good Housekeeping, Parent's* and *Redbook.* Editor of *Travel Writer,* 1964-66.

WORK IN PROGRESS: The Complete Book of Kites, for Lippincott; *Rivers of America* and *Canals of America,* both for Norton; *The Ohio River Catalog,* for Harper; *A Guide to Lakeside Recreation Areas,* for Stackpole.

SIDELIGHTS: Thomas' first book, on outdoor recreation in America, was written in 1972 under contract to the U.S. Information Agency. It was published in color and presented as a gift to the peoples of the Soviet Union as an educational and goodwill gesture. *Avocational interests:* Bicycling, jogging, swimming, mountain climbing, camping, boating, canoeing, fishing, backpacking.

* * *

THOMAS, D(onald) M(ichael) 1935-

PERSONAL: Born January 27, 1935, in Cornwall, England; son of Harold Redvers and Amy Thomas; children: Caitlin, Sean. *Education:* New College, Oxford, B.A. (first class honors), 1958, M.A., 1961. *Home:* 10 Greyfriars Ave., Hereford, England. *Office:* Hereford College of Education, Hereford, England.

CAREER: Grammar school English teacher in Teignmouth, Devonshire, England, 1960-64; Hereford College of Education, Hereford, England, lecturer, 1964-66, senior lecturer in English, 1966—. *Member:* Bard of the Cornish Gorseth. *Awards, honors:* Richard Hilary Award, 1960; Translators Award from British Arts Council, 1975, for translations of Anna Akhmatova.

WRITINGS: (With Peter Redgrove and D. M. Black) *Modern Poets II,* Penguin, 1968; *Two Voices* (poems), Grossman, 1968; *Logan Stone* (poems), Grossman, 1971; *Love and Other Deaths* (poems), Elek, 1975; *Poetry in Crosslight* (textbook), Longmans, Green, 1975; (translator) Anna Akhmatova, *Requiem and Poem without a Hero,* Elek, 1976.

Work is represented in anthologies, including: *Best SF: 1969,* edited by Harry Harrison and Brian W. Aldiss, Putnam, 1970; *Inside Outer Space,* edited by Robert Vas Dias, Anchor Books, 1970; *23 Modern British Poets,* edited by John Matthias, Swallow, 1971. Contributor to literature journals in England and the United States.

SIDELIGHTS: Thomas writes: "Yeats once said that there are only two subjects of conversation worth engaging an intelligent man: sex and the dead. As the title of my most recent collection implies, I go along with that.... Typically Cornish (my background is in tin-mining) I feel much closer to America than to the continent of Europe." *Avocational interests:* "Besides sex and death, I am interested in Russian literature, music, most sport, and my Celtic homeland, Cornwall."

* * *

THOMAS, Tony 1947-

PERSONAL: Born May 29, 1947, in Washington, D.C.

Education: Attended American University, 1968. *Politics:* Marxist. *Office:* c/o Pathfinder Press, Inc., 410 West St., New York, N.Y. 10014.

CAREER: Writer.

WRITINGS: (Editor and contributor) *Black Liberation and Socialism,* Pathfinder, 1974; (with Ernest Harsch) *Angola: The Hidden History of Washington's War,* Pathfinder, 1976. Contributor to *Black Scholar* and *Militant.*

AVOCATIONAL INTERESTS: Travel.

* * *

THOMPSON, A(rthur) L(eonard) B(ell)   1917-1975
(Francis Clifford)

December 1, 1917—August 25, 1975; British journalist and writer of suspense novels. Obituaries: *Washington Post,* August 30, 1975; *New York Times,* August 30, 1975; *Publishers Weekly,* September 15, 1975; *AB Bookman's Weekly,* December 8, 1975. (See index for previous *CA* sketch)

* * *

THOMPSON, Corrie   1887-

PERSONAL: Born August 21, 1887, in Rockport, Tex.; daughter of William (a ship's navigator) and Theodosia (Harlan) Evans; married John William Thompson, June 24, 1924 (deceased); children: Pearlyn (Mrs. Dave Stepp). *Education:* Attended Southwest Texas State Normal School (now Southwest Texas State College), 1914, University of Southern California, 1926, and Draughn's Business College, 1918; Sul Ross Teachers College (now Sul Ross State University), B.A., 1937, M.A., 1940. *Religion:* Episcopalian. *Home:* 3409 La Luz Ave., El Paso, Tex. 79903.

CAREER: Teacher in public schools in Rockport, Tex., 1905-16, and Olmita, Tex., 1916-17; U.S. Army in San Antonio, Tex., civilian accountant, 1918-20; Corona Oil Co., Tampico, Mexico, translator, 1920-24; El Paso Public Schools, El Paso, Tex., teacher of Spanish, 1926-48; freelance writer and artist, 1948—; Radford School for Girls, El Paso, teacher of Spanish, 1961.

MEMBER: El Paso Teachers Association (president, 1956), El Paso Writers League (president, 1942), El Paso Art Association (president, 1964-66), Eastern Star (matron, 1951-52; state representative, 1965-66). *Awards, honors:* National Press Women award, 1964, for play "Cinco Comedias"; Odessa Writers Contest awards for plays, 1966, 1967, and 1968; El Paso Writers League prize, 1968, for play "Aladdin's Lamp."

WRITINGS: Cinco Comedias (plays in Spanish), Banks Upshaw, 1946, new edition, National Textbook Corp., 1964; *Spike Lassos El Paso* (poems), Merchant's Press, 1967; *My Beach Buddies* (juvenile autobiography), Nortex, 1974. Author of "Amigos," a monthly column in *American Boy,* 1972-73. Contributor to regional periodicals.

WORK IN PROGRESS: Leyendas de Mexico, a book of plays in Spanish; another book of plays, in English, for use in schools.

BIOGRAPHICAL/CRITICAL SOURCES: El Paso Times, September 27, 1970.

* * *

THOMPSON, J(ohn) Eric S(idney)   1898-1975

December 31, 1898—September 9, 1975; British archaeolo-
gist, paleographer, museum curator, expert on Mayan civilization, and author of books in his field. Obituaries: *New York Times,* September 11, 1975; *Publishers Weekly,* October 13, 1975; *AB Bookman's Weekly,* December 1, 1975.

* * *

THOMPSON, Richard A(rlen)   1930-

PERSONAL: Born October 6, 1930, in Brazil, Ind.; son of Richard Arlen and Janet M. (Warken) Thompson; married Janet R. Redick, March 2, 1968; children: George, Kimberly, David, Timothy, Carol. *Education:* Indiana State University, B.S., 1957; Butler University, M.S., 1960; Ball State University, Ed.D., 1968. *Home:* 8608 Baylor Circle, Orlando, Fla. 32807. *Office:* Department of Elementary Education, Florida Technological University, Orlando, Fla. 32816.

CAREER: Elementary school teacher in Warren Township, Marion County, Ind., 1957-65, and Indianapolis, Ind., 1965-66; Ball State University, Muncie, Ind., instructor in reading, 1966-68, supervisor of student teachers, 1967-68; McNeese State University, Lake Charles, La., assistant professor of elementary education, 1968-69; Florida Technological University, Orlando, associate professor of elementary education, 1969—. Teacher of adult classes in Indianapolis public schools, 1962-67. *Military service:* U.S. Army, 1948-51. *Member:* International Reading Association, International Platform Association, National Council of Teachers of English, Organization of Teacher Educators of Reading (president).

WRITINGS: (Editor with B. Betty Anderson, and contributor) *Trends in Reading,* Simon & Schuster, 1971; *Energizers for Reading Instruction,* Parker Publishing, 1973; (editor with Anderson) *Trends in Reading Instruction,* MSS Information Corp., 1973; *Treasury of Teaching Activities for Elementary Language Arts,* Parker Publishing, 1975. Contributor to reading and education journals.

* * *

THOMPSON, Stith   1885-1976

March 7, 1885—January 10, 1976; American educator, folklore specialist, editor, and author. Obituaries: *New York Times,* January 12, 1976; *Publishers Weekly,* February 23, 1976. (See index for previous *CA* sketch)

* * *

THOMSON, George Paget   1892-1975

May 3, 1892—September 10, 1975; British nuclear physicist, educator, and author of works on science for laymen and scientists. Obituaries: *New York Times,* September 11, 1975; *Washington Post,* September 13, 1975; *Current Biography,* October, 1975. (See index for previous *CA* sketch)

* * *

THOMSON, James C(utting)   1909-
(Adam Chase)

PERSONAL: Born June 12, 1909, in Chicago, Ill.; son of James Clark (a banker) and Helen (Shaw) Thomson; married Frieda Fischl, January 2, 1934; married Selma Wertime (a college teacher), July 24, 1948; children: Ralph Gordon, Jean Ellen, Margaret Celia, Vivian Elizabeth. *Education:* Middlebury College, A.B., 1929; Hochschule fuer Musik, Berlin, Germany, Staatl. gepr., 1934; Baylor University, M.A. (German), 1940; Yale University, M.A. (musicology), 1948; New York University, Ph.D., 1959. *Politics:*

Republican. *Home:* 1638 Green Lane, R.D. #3, West Chester, Pa. 19380. *Office:* Department of Music, West Chester State College, West Chester, Pa. 19380.

CAREER: College of the Ozarks, Clarksville, Ark., assistant professor of violin, 1934-35; Baylor University, Waco, Tex., assistant professor of violin, 1935-42; U.S. Department of Defense, Washington, D.C., translator, 1951-52; Wilson College, Chambersburg, Pa., professor of music, 1952-63; University of Kansas, Lawrence, associate professor of musicology, 1963-68; West Chester State College, West Chester, Pa., professor of music history and literature and chairman of department, 1968—. *Military service:* U.S. Army, Signal Corps, 1942-45. *Member:* International Musicological Society, American Musicological Society, Music Educators National Conference, Pennsylvania Music Educators Association, Pi Kappa Lambda, Phi Mu Alpha Sinfonia. *Awards, honors:* American Council of Learned Societies scholarship, 1942; Kellogg Fugue prize, Yale University, 1949; Fulbright lecturer, Iran, 1962.

WRITINGS: (Under pseudonym Adam Chase) *The Golden Ape,* Bouregy, 1959; *An Introduction to Philippe Caron,* Institute of Medieval Music, 1964; *Music Through the Renaissance,* W. C. Brown, 1968. Also editor of *Complete Works of Caron,* Volume I, 1971.

Author of song texts and musical settings, "Four Laments," 1972. Contributor of articles to *Southwestern Musician,* 1937-38, and to *American Choral Review.*

WORK IN PROGRESS: Editing the second volume of *Complete Works of Caron.*

SIDELIGHTS: Thomson has knowledge of French and German. He has traveled extensively through England, Scotland, France, Belgium, Holland, Germany, and Iran.

* * *

THOMSON, S(amuel) Harrison 1895-1975

November 5, 1895—November 19, 1975; American medieval historian, educator, editor, and author of books in his field. Obituaries: *New York Times,* November 23, 1975; *AB Bookman's Weekly,* December 22-29, 1975. (See index for previous *CA* sketch)

* * *

THORNBER, Jean H(ewitt) 1919-

PERSONAL: Born June 10, 1919, in Tacoma, Wash.; daughter of Robert Ruthven (a pressman) and Beatrice (Robinson) Hewitt; married Fordyce S. Thornber (a supervisor for an aircraft company), September 7, 1949; children: Thomas Edward, Barbara Jean. *Education:* Attended Metropolitan Business College and Comptometer School, both in Seattle, Wash. *Religion:* Presbyterian. *Home:* 1841 South 124th, Seattle, Wash. 98168.

CAREER: Comptometer operator for firms in Seattle, Wash., 1939-41; Naval Air Station, Seattle, supervisor in supply department, 1941-52; Kent Park and Recreation Department, Kent, Wash., teacher of driftwood sculpture, 1968-73; Kent Senior Citizen Center, Kent, Wash., teacher of driftwood sculpture, 1973—. Teacher at Highline Community College, 1970-73, and Green River Community College, 1970-72. *Member:* Northwest Driftwood Artists, Washington Alpine Club.

WRITINGS: Driftwood Sculpture, Celestial Arts, 1975.

THORPE, Earl(ie) E(ndris) 1924-

PERSONAL: Born November 9, 1924, in Durham, N.C.; son of Eural E. (a laborer) and Vina C. (Dean) Thorpe; married Martha V. Branch (a teacher), August 24, 1946; children: Rita H., Gloria E. *Education:* North Carolina College at Durham (now North Carolina Central University), B.A., 1948, M.A., 1949; Ohio State University, Ph.D., 1953. *Politics:* Independent. *Religion:* Baptist. *Home:* 164 Oakmont Ave., Durham, N.C. *Office:* Department of History and Social Science, Box 19657, North Carolina Central University, Durham, N.C. 27707.

CAREER: Stowe Teachers College (now Harris Teachers College), St. Louis, Mo., instructor, 1951-52; Alabama Agricultural and Mechanical College (now University), Normal, assistant professor, 1952-55; Southern University, Baton Rouge, La., associate professor, 1955, professor of history, 1955-62; North Carolina Central University, Durham, professor of history, 1962—. *Military service:* U.S. Army, 1943-46; served in Infantry. *Member:* American Historical Association, Association for the Study of Negro Life and History, Association of Social Science Teachers, Organization of American Historians, Phi Alpha Theta, Pi Gamma Mu.

*WRITINGS—*All published by Harrington Publications, except as noted: *Negro Historians in the United States,* 1958, revised edition published as *Black Historians: A Critique,* Morrow, 1971; *The Desertion of Man: A Critique of Philosophy of History,* 1958; *The Mind of the Negro: An Intellectual History of Afro-Americans,* 1961; *Eros and Freedom in Southern Life and Thought,* 1967; *The Old South: A Psychohistory,* 1972.

WORK IN PROGRESS: A psychohistory of the new South.

* * *

THRASHER, Crystal (Faye) 1921-

PERSONAL: Born December 5, 1921, in Oolitic, Ind.; daughter of Virgil Leroy (a stonecutter) and Rozella (Bennett) Knight; married Joseph Martin Thrasher, April 22, 1939; children: Carol (Mrs. Rex Hatfield), Joseph, Jr., Janis. *Education:* Attended Indiana University, 1972-73. *Politics:* "Mixed emotions." *Religion:* "A little." *Home:* 18 Somerdale Park, Yoder, Ind. 46798. *Agent:* Marilyn Marlow, Curtis Brown Ltd., 60 East 56th St., New York, N.Y. 10022.

CAREER: Fort Wayne Country Club, Fort Wayne, Ind., waitress, 1957-75. Part-time office worker and model, Sears, Fort Wayne, 1960-61. *Member:* Zonta International, Greater Fort Wayne Writer's Club.

WRITINGS: The Dark Didn't Catch Me (juvenile), Atheneum, 1975.

WORK IN PROGRESS: Three books for young people, *The Prettiest Girl on the Ridge, The Daisy Patch,* and *Down the Dark Hollow;* short stories; poems.

AVOCATIONAL INTERESTS: Walking through the forest, travel, reading.

* * *

THURLEY, Geoffrey John 1936-

PERSONAL: Born March 9, 1936, in London, England; son of James (a bricklayer) and Amelia (Coles) Thurley; married Wendy Felton (a librarian), March 9, 1966; children: Djuna Esme, Lucy Jessamine. *Education:* Downing

College, Cambridge, B.A. (with honors), 1959; University College, London, M.A., 1962; Trinity College, Dublin, Ph.D., 1967. *Politics:* "Nil." *Religion:* "Nil." *Home:* 78 Terningham St., Adelaide, South Australia. *Agent:* Ursula Winant, 14 Cliffords Inn, London E.C. 4, England. *Office:* University of Adelaide, South Australia.

CAREER: Trinity College, Dublin, Ireland, junior lecturer, 1963-67; University of Lodz, Lodz, Poland, lecturer, 1967-68; University of Adelaide, Adelaide, Australia, lecturer, 1969-73, senior lecturer, 1973-75, reader, 1976—. *Military service:* British Army, Intelligence Corps, 1954-56.

WRITINGS: (Translator and author of introduction) S. Esenin, *Confessions of a Hooligan: 50 Poems,* Carcanet Press, 1973; *The Ironic Harvest: English Poetry in the Twentieth Century,* St. Martin's, 1974; *The Psychology of Hardy's Novels: The Nervous and the Statuesque,* Humanities, 1975; *Quiet Flowers: Poems,* Maximus Books, 1975; *The Dickens Myth,* Queensland University Press (St. Lucia, Australia), 1976; (translator) Akhamova, *White Flock: Poems,* Oasis Books, 1976; *The House in Astrakhan* (novel), Hodder & Stoughton, 1976; *The American Moment: U.S. Poetry Now,* Edward Arnold, 1976. Contributor of poems and articles to literary journals, including *Encounter, Southern Review,* and *Ariel.*

WORK IN PROGRESS: Zaradza: Poems, publication by Maximus Books expected in 1977; *Wythenshawe,* a novel, publication by Hodder & Stoughton expected in 1977; translating *The Terrible World: 50 Poems of A. Blok* from the Russian for Carcanet Press, expected in 1977; *The Heroic Tradition: Post-Symbolist Poetry,* for Edward Arnold, expected in 1977; *A Theory of the English Novel,* for Queensland University Press, expected in 1977 or 1978.

* * *

TIBBS, Ben 1907-

PERSONAL: Born January 2, 1907, in Martinsville, Ill.; son of James Daniel (a clerk) and Nina B. (Spear) Tibbs; married Myrna Mignon, October 29, 1928 (deceased); children: William R., Richard D., Robert B. *Education:* Attended high school in Martinsville, Ill. *Politics:* Independent. *Religion:* "Zen Christian." *Home:* 522 Cherokee, Apt. 108, Kalamazoo, Mich. 49007.

CAREER: Commercial lithographer, 1932—. Served apprenticeship in lithography in Paris, Ill. *Awards, honors:* Prizes for photography, drawings, paintings, and poems.

WRITINGS:—All books of poems, except as indicated: *lower case drawings* (cartoons), privately printed, 1962; *A Birdness Flown,* Hors Commerce, 1966; *Time and Against,* Hors Commerce, 1968; *Tattoos on the Enigma,* Humble Hills Press, 1969; *Anatomy of a Broad Based Apparition* (pamphlet), Pilot Press, 1973; *First Savings and Loan Association,* Pilot Press, 1973; *Poems A to Z, Etc.,* Pilot Press, 1973; *The Illustrious Maybes,* Free Press, 1974; *Thirty Poems,* Stove Pipe Press, 1974; *Bombs,* Pilot Press, 1975. Contributor to photography magazines, *Coronet,* and newspapers.

WORK IN PROGRESS: An autobiography; prose poems; short stories.

SIDELIGHTS: Tibbs writes: "My first medium was photography.... Next was painting.... Exhibited in Detroit Art Institute. Lost interest in color painting, gravitating to black and white graphics, drawings.... Became interested in writing in 1954. Kenneth Patchen's *Journal of Albion Moonlight* being the seminal point. Writing finally took over from the graphic thing and have been at it ever since, although I infrequently do drawings for poetry chapbooks.

"I once did a lithograph on stone and when I was inspecting the print, I noticed that the crescent moon in the drawing looked like a big wink. A cosmic wink, I said. I have come to believe that this wink in the Creation comes from the eye in which I view my writing. The left eye. I traveled in Europe for three weeks in 1972. A most expanding experience. No photographs, only a journal from which I sometimes squeeze a real drop of nectar." *Avocational interests:* Music (jazz and classical), reading, films.

* * *

TICE, George A(ndrew) 1938-

PERSONAL: Born October 13, 1938, in Newark, N.J.; son of William S. and Margaret T. (Robertson) Tice; divorced; children: Christopher, Loretta, Lisa, Lynn, Jennifer. *Education:* Attended high school in Newark, N.J. *Home:* 35 Wedgewood Dr., Apt. 21-A, Carteret, N.J. 07008.

CAREER: New School for Social Research, New York, N.Y., instructor in photography, 1970—. *Military service:* U.S. Navy, 1956-59. *Awards, honors:* Grand Prix du Festival d'Arles, 1973, for *Paterson.*

WRITINGS: (Illustrator) Millen Brand, *Fields of Peace,* Doubleday, 1970; (illustrator) George Mendoza, *Goodbye, River, Goodbye* (juvenile), Doubleday, 1971; *Paterson,* Rutgers University Press, 1972; (illustrator) Martin Dibner, *Seacoast Maine: The People and Places,* Doubleday, 1973; *George A. Tice: Photographs, 1953-1973,* Rutgers University Press, 1975; *Urban Landscapes: A New Jersey Portrait,* Rutgers University Press, 1976.

* * *

TILTON, Timothy Alan 1942-

PERSONAL: Born August 3, 1942; son of Robert Gillian (a farmer) and Ruth (Wilt) Tilton; married Mary Coffman (a music teacher), August 27, 1966; children: Andrew Robert, Anna Elizabeth. *Education:* College of Wooster, B.A., 1965; Oxford University, B.A., 1968; Harvard University, Ph.D., 1972. *Office:* Department of Political Science, Indiana University, Bloomington, Ind. 47401.

CAREER: Indiana University, Bloomington, lecturer, 1970-72, assistant professor, 1972-75, associate professor of political science, 1975—. *Member:* American Political Science Association, Society for the Advancement of Scandinavian Studies.

WRITINGS: Nazism, Neo-Nazism, and the Peasantry, Indiana University Press, 1975. Contributor to political science and social research journals.

WORK IN PROGRESS: The Welfare State and Its Critics.

* * *

TIMONEY, Francis 1938-

PERSONAL: Born November 3, 1938, in Scotland; son of Denis and Jean (a seamstress; maiden name, Brennan) Timoney. *Education:* Strathclyde University, B.S.; St. John's College, Waterford, Ireland, B.A. *Home:* 800 A St., Hawthorne, Nev. 89415. *Office address:* P.O. Box 857, Hawthorne, Nev. 89415.

CAREER: Ordained Roman Catholic priest; associate pastor in Las Vegas, Nev., 1969-72, and Reno, Nev., 1972-74; pastor in Hawthorne, Nev., 1974—. Consultant to Diocese of Reno, 1971-73; member of personnel board of Diocese of Reno, 1974—. *Member:* Nevada Priests Senate, Knights of Columbus (chaplain).

WRITINGS: Our Debt to the First Christians, Liguori, 1974; *The Three Talking Trees,* Our Sunday Visitor, 1975. Columnist for *Nevada Register.*

WORK IN PROGRESS: All You Ever Wanted to Know about Hell, But Were Afraid to Ask; Mungo (juvenile); *A Catholic Catechism for Simpletons.*

AVOCATIONAL INTERESTS: Travel, local lore.

* * *

TODD, Barbara K(eith) 1917-

PERSONAL: Born September 11, 1917, in Durango, Colo.; daughter of Keith Sunderland (a banker) and Doris (a secretary; maiden name, Dyer) Rucker; married John Edwin Todd (a station attendant), July 11, 1945; children: John Anthony, Stanley Keith, Richard Dwight. *Education:* Arizona State University, B.A., 1939. *Politics:* Republican. *Religion:* Episcopal. *Home:* 368 West 23rd St., Durango, Colo. 81301. *Office:* Florida Mesa Elementary School, Durango, Colo. 81301.

CAREER: Teacher of third grade in Prescott, Ariz., 1939-43; student nurse at Los Angeles General Hospital, 1943-44; Florida Mesa Elementary School, Durango, Colo., first-grade teacher, 1959—. *Member:* American Association of University Women, National League of American Pen Women, Delta Kappa Gamma. *Awards, honors:* First place in National League of American Pen Women Biennial Contest, 1974, for *Juan Patricio,* second place for unpublished fiction, 1975, for *Where Have All the Colors Gone?*

WRITINGS: Juan Patricio (juvenile), Putnam, 1972. Contributor to *Trails, Empire, Pacific Traveler,* and *Our Little Friend.*

WORK IN PROGRESS: Salamanders; How They Celebrated Admission.

SIDELIGHTS: Barbara Todd writes: "As a teacher of beginning readers, I was appalled at the material offered. I felt I could do better. So after attending a writers workshop I got busy and began writing. *Juan Patricio* was written especially for the many Chicano students that I have taught." *Avocational interests:* Reading (especially murder mysteries), sewing, gardening.

* * *

TODRIN, Boris 1915-

PERSONAL: Born May 1, 1915, in Brooklyn, N.Y.; son of Emanuel (a scholar) and Tina (Aronson) Todrin; married Regina Portnoy, June 10, 1937 (died, 1945); married Vivien Breslove Neider, July 11, 1952; children: (first marriage) Edwina Robin (Mrs. Allen Weltmann). *Education:* Columbia University, A.B. (with honors), 1937, M.A., 1938. *Religion:* Jewish. *Home:* Canter Hill Farm, R.D.1, Box 60, Malvern, Pa. 19355. *Office:* Mel Richman Inc., Marketing Communications, 15 North Presidential Blvd., Bala Cynwyd, Pa. 19004.

CAREER: Editor or associate editor in New York, N.Y., for *One-Act Play* (magazine), 1938-39, *Shipping Digest,* 1941-42; *PM* (newspaper), New York, N.Y., reporter, 1942-43, department editor, 1943-45, feature reporter, 1945-47; *New York Star,* New York, N.Y., correspondent during Arab-Israeli war, 1948; *Photography Workshop,* New York, N.Y., associate editor, 1950-51; *Time,* New

York, N.Y., special writer, 1951-53; Equitable Life Insurance Society of the United States, copy supervisor in advertising and public relations and member of president's staff, 1953-56; N. W. Ayer & Son, Inc. (advertising agency), Philadelphia, Pa., senior copywriter, 1956-64, copy supervisor, 1964-66, creative director, 1966-70, vice-president in creative services, 1970-73; Mel Richman Inc., Marketing Communications, Bala Cynwyd, Pa., senior vice-president and creative director, 1973—. Aide to former New York mayor Fiorello LaGuardia.

MEMBER: American Medical Writers Association, Pharmaceutical Advertising Club, MacDowell Colony Association (past vice-president). *Awards, honors:* Columbia University poetry prizes include Boar's Head Award, 1935, Van Rensselaer Prize, 1936, and Philolexian Prize, 1937; Manhattan College Award for Moral Tone in Advertising, 1964.

WRITINGS—Books of poems: *First Furrow,* Henry Harrison, 1932; *The Room by the River,* Black Cat Press, 1936; *Five Days,* Black Cat Press, 1936; *Seven Men,* Putnam, 1938; *At the Gates,* James A. Decker, 1944.

Novels: *Out of These Roots,* Caxton, 1944, Popular Library, 1973; *Paradise Walk,* Dutton, 1946; *The Plundered Heart,* Dutton, 1948.

Author of scripts and narrator for "Speaking of Books," on WQXR-Radio, 1943. Contributor of poems to popular magazines, including *Ladies' Home Journal, Poetry,* and *Parents' Magazine.* Founder and editor of *Read,* 1940—.

SIDELIGHTS: Todrin's books have been published in France, Italy, Belgium, and the Netherlands. *Avocational interests:* Horseback riding, swimming, farming.

BIOGRAPHICAL/CRITICAL SOURCES: Henry Wells, *New Poets from Old,* Columbia University Press, 1940; Harry Redcay Warfel, *American Novelists of Today,* American Book Co., 1951.

* * *

TOMKINS, Mary E(ileen) 1914-

PERSONAL: Born October 16, 1914, in Philadelphia, Pa.; daughter of William M. (a lawyer) and Mary F. (a social case worker; maiden name, O'Malley) Hussie; married Jack Q. Tomkins, 1942 (divorced, 1959); children: Monica (Mrs. L. A. Pamer), David, James. *Education:* University of Utah, B.A., 1959, Ph.D., 1964. *Home:* 1036 Chesterfield Parkway, East Lansing, Mich. 48823. *Office:* Department of American Thought and Language, Michigan State University, 229 Bessey Hall, East Lansing, Mich. 48824.

CAREER: Portland State University, Portland, Ore., instructor in English, 1963-65; Michigan State University, East Lansing, professor of American thought and language, 1965—. *Member:* Society for the Study of Mid-Western Literature, Midwest Modern Language Association, Michigan Women's Studies Association, Michigan State University American Studies Association, Phi Beta Kappa (president of Epsilon chapter, 1973-74).

WRITINGS: Ida M. Tarbell (biography), Twayne, 1974.

WORK IN PROGRESS: Research on Benjamin Thompson, Count Rumford, and on T. W. Higginson.

SIDELIGHTS: Mary Tomkins writes: "I am a comparatively early example of the movement of women, particularly mature women, into higher education, having graduated from college following the birth of my children. I am interested in following and expediting the slow, but hopefully steady progress of affirmative action in higher education as it affects both women and racial minorities. My study of Ida M. Tarbell happens to coincide with the rise of the women's studies movement, although its inception predates the movement by a couple of years."

* * *

TOPSFIELD, L(eslie) T(homas) 1920-

PERSONAL: Born January 6, 1920, in Westcliff-on-Sea, Essex, England; son of Frederick Thomas and Lilian Grace (Cross) Topsfield; married Valerie Green, April 20, 1943; children: David, Andrew. *Education:* St. Catharine's College, Cambridge, B.A., 1946, M.A., 1948, Ph.D., 1951. *Home:* 1 Silver St., Cambridge, England.

CAREER: Cambridge University, Cambridge, England, university lecturer in Provencal and French, 1950—, St. Catharine's College, fellow, 1953—, praelector, 1955-60, domestic bursar, 1960-65, tutor, 1966—. *Military service:* British Army, 1940-46; served in Far East, 1943-45; became major. *Member:* Modern Humanities Research Association (secretary, 1950-56), Society for the Study of Medieval Languages and Literature, Society for French Studies, International Arthurian Society.

WRITINGS: (Contributor) Anthony Thorlby, editor, *Penguin Companion to Literature: European Literature,* Penguin, 1969; *Les Poesies du troubadour Raimon de Miraval,* Nizet (Paris), 1971; *Troubadours and Love,* Cambridge University Press, 1975. Editor of the *Year's Work in Modern Language Studies,* three volumes, Cambridge University Press, 1957-59; member of executive committee of *Medium Aevum,* 1970—. Contributor of articles and reviews to journals in his field.

WORK IN PROGRESS: Research in Arthurian romance and troubadour poetry.

AVOCATIONAL INTERESTS: Archaeological sites of Greek and Roman antiquity.

* * *

TORCHIO, Menico 1932-

PERSONAL: Born November 12, 1932, in Turin, Italy; son of Severino (a geometer) and Annetta (Pironetti) Torchio; married Cecilia Roggero (a professor and painter), February 1, 1961. *Education:* University of Turin, Laureate (cum laude), 1957, Libera Docenza, 1971. *Religion:* Catholic. *Home:* via Martinengo 32, Milan, Italy 20139. *Office:* Hydrobiological Station, Viale Gadio 2, Milan, Italy 20121.

CAREER: University of Turin, Turin, Italy, assistant professor of anthropology, 1958-59; Museum of Natural History, Milan, Italy, 1960-64, vice-director, 1964-68; Hydrobiological Station, Milan, director, 1968—; University of Pavia, Pavia, Italy, associate professor of zoology, 1969-73, professor of marine biology, 1974—. *Military service:* Italian Air Force, 1969—; currently lieutenant in the reserves. *Member:* International Commission on the Scientific Study of the Mediterranean, Intercontinental Biographical Association (fellow), International Oceanographic Foundation, Italian Natural Science Society (member of board of directors), Italian Society of Marine Biology, Italian Malacological Society (member of board of directors), Italian Ecological Group (secretary). *Awards, honors:* Encomium of Mayor of Milan, 1964.

WRITINGS: Biologica marina (title means "Marine Biology"), Martello (Milan), 1964; *La vita nel mare,* De Agos-

tini (Novara), 1967, 3rd edition, 1975, translation published as *The Life Beneath the Sea,* World Publishing, 1972; *Animali s'acquario* (title means "Aquarium Animals"), Istituto Propaganda Internazionale (Milan), 1968; *Agnati e Pesci* (title means "Jawless Fishes and Fishes"), Mondadori (Verona), 1971. Contributor of articles to journals in his field.

* * *

TORMEY, John Connolly 1942-

PERSONAL: Born February 12, 1942, in Attleboro, Mass.; son of Patrick John (a police detective) and Marie (McManus) Tormey. *Education:* Our Lady of Providence College, B.A., 1963; St. Bernard's Seminary, B.D., 1967, M.Div., 1975. *Politics:* Democrat. *Home:* 21 Peace St., Providence, R.I. 02907. *Address:* P.O. Box 4168, East Providence, R.I. 02914.

CAREER: Ordained Roman Catholic priest, 1967; associate pastor in East Providence, R.I., 1967-73; House of Affirmation, Whitinsville, Mass., director of pastoral services, 1973-74; St. Xavier's Academy, Providence, R.I., chaplain and teacher of theology and psychology, 1974—. Chaplain, St. Joseph's Hospital, 1974—, East Providence Fire Department, 1968—, and East Providence Police Department, 1968—. *Awards, honors:* Citations from East Providence Police and Fire Departments, 1972, for dedicated service as chaplain; Citizen of the Year award from City of East Providence, 1972.

WRITINGS: Rocks Are for Lizards, Liguori Press, 1972; *Priests Are Only Human,* Alba, 1974; *Only You Can Make You Happy,* Liguori Press, 1975; *What's Cooking in the Priesthood,* Alba, 1975; *Hitch Your Wagon to a Star,* Shalom, 1975; *Time for TLC,* Shalom, 1975; *Death Our Destiny,* Shalom, 1975; *Tell Me Again You Love Me,* Alba, 1976. Contributor of more than eighty articles to periodicals. Associate editor of *Pastoral Life,* 1975—; guest editor of *My Daily Visitor,* 1974-75.

WORK IN PROGRESS: The Art of Seci, completion expected in 1976; *Loyalty and the Absolute,* 1976.

* * *

TOWNS, James Edward 1944-

PERSONAL: Born February 27, 1944, in Clovis, N.M.; son of Verney Edward (a businessman) and Mona (Hancock) Towns. *Education:* Hardin-Simmons University, B.A., 1965; Southern Illinois University, M.A., 1966, Ph.D., 1970. *Politics:* Democrat. *Religion:* Baptist. *Home address:* Box 6174, S.F.A. Station, Nacogdoches, Tex. 75961. *Office:* Department of Communication, Stephen F. Austin State University, Nacogdoches, Tex. 75961.

CAREER: Stephen F. Austin State University, Nacogdoches, Tex., instructor, 1966-68, assistant professor of communication, 1970—. Communications consultant for businesses and local churches. *Member:* Speech Communication Association of America, Southern Speech Communication Association, Texas Speech Communication Association, Phi Kappa Phi.

WRITINGS: Faith Stronger Than Death: How to Communicate with a Person in Sorrow, Warner Press, 1975; *The Social Conscience of W. A. Criswell,* Crescendo Book, 1976.

WORK IN PROGRESS: The Identity Crisis of the Single Adult; The Speaking of Buckner Fanning, completion expected in 1977.

SIDELIGHTS: Towns is deeply involved with campus and local church organizations. He speaks at religious conferences and retreats.

* * *

TOWNSEND, Richard E. 1897(?)-1975

1897(?)—October 1, 1975; American sales executive, expert on early American sheet music, and author. Obituaries: *AB Bookman's Weekly,* December 8, 1975.

* * *

TOYNBEE, Arnold J(oseph) 1889-1975

April 14, 1889—October 22, 1975; British historian, educator, editor, and author. Obituaries: *New York Times,* October 23, 1975; *Detroit News,* October 23, 1975; *Time,* November 3, 1975; *AB Bookman's Weekly,* December 22-29, 1975; *Current Biography,* January, 1976. (See index for previous *CA* sketch)

* * *

TRACY, Doris 1925-

PERSONAL: Born October 30, 1925, in Chicago, Ill.; daughter of Arvid N. (an electrical engineer) and Mabel (Johnson) Hanson; married Frank W. Tracy (a pediatrician), June 15, 1950; children: James F., Steven W., Paul R., Patrick J. *Education:* William Woods College, A.A., 1945; North Central College, B.A., 1948. *Religion:* United Church of Christ. *Residence:* Hinsdale, Ill. *Office address:* Tree Toys, P.O. Box 492, Hinsdale, Ill. 60521.

CAREER: Secretary and clerical worker, 1948-51; Tree Toys (quilling supplies and kit business), Hinsdale, Ill., co-owner, 1972—. Teacher of quilling in adult education classes. *Member:* Inland Craftsmen and Artists (treasurer, 1973).

WRITINGS: (With Betty Christy) *Quilling: Paper Art for Everyone,* Regnery, 1974. Also co-author of instruction booklets on quilling. Contributor to hobby trade magazine.

WORK IN PROGRESS: Research on women's role, on crafts, and on psychology and counseling.

AVOCATIONAL INTERESTS: Travel.

BIOGRAPHICAL/CRITICAL SOURCES: Turpen Times, December, 1972; *Chicago Sun-Times,* December 1, 1974.

* * *

TRACY, Honor (Lilbush Wingfield) 1913-

PERSONAL: Born October 19, 1913, in Bury St. Edmunds, East Anglia, England; daughter of Humphrey Wingfield (a surgeon) and Christabel May Clare (Miller) Tracy. *Education:* Educated privately in London, England. *Home:* Four Chimneys, Achill Sound, County Mayo, Ireland. *Agent:* Curtis Brown, 1 Craven Hill, London W2 3EW, England.

CAREER: Simpkin Marshall Ltd., publishers, London, England, general assistant, 1934-37; free-lance writer, 1937-39; Ministry of Information, London, England, Japanese specialist, 1941-45; *Observer,* London, England, special correspondent, 1946, 1947-48 (from Japan in 1947); *Sunday Times,* London, England, Dublin correspondent, 1950; British Broadcasting Corp., Third Programme, contributor of talks and features, 1950-68, roving correspondent, 1951-52; novelist, 1968—. *Military service:* British Women's Auxiliary Air Force, Intelligence, 1939-41; became ser-

geant. *Member:* Royal Irish Automobile Club. *Awards, honors:* Award from British Writers Guild, 1968, for radio feature script "Sorrows of Ireland."

WRITINGS: (Translator) B. de Ligt, *The Conquest of Violence,* Dutton, 1937; *Kakemono: A Sketch Book of Post-War Japan,* Methuen, 1950; *Mind You, I've Said Nothing!: Forays in the Irish Republic* (essays), Methuen, 1953, British Book Centre, 1958; *Silk Hats and No Breakfast: Notes on a Spanish Journey,* Methuen, 1957, Random House, 1958; *Spanish Leaves,* Random House, 1964.

Fiction: *The Deserters,* Methuen, 1954; *The Straight and Narrow Path,* Random House, 1956; *The Prospects Are Pleasing,* Random House, 1958; *A Number of Things,* Random House, 1960; *A Season of Mists,* Random House, 1961; *The First Day of Friday,* Random House, 1963; *Men at Work,* Methuen, 1966, Random House, 1967; *The Beauty of the World,* Methuen, 1967, published as *Settled in Chambers,* Random House, 1968; *The Butterflies of the Province,* Random House, 1970; *The Quiet End of Evening,* Random House, 1972; *In a Year of Grace,* Random House, 1974; *Winter in Castile,* Random House, 1975. Contributor to *Daily Telegraph* (London), 1973—.

WORK IN PROGRESS: The Man From Next Door, a novel.

SIDELIGHTS: A writer for the *Spectator* noted: "Miss Tracy is rightly regarded as one of the most rewarding contemporary practitioners of the humourous novel." However, of her novel, *Settled in Chambers,* some reviewers were less than enthusiastic. Walter Allen wrote, "If *Settled in Chambers* were . . . a first novel it would not, I think, create much stir. It is witty enough, and it has . . . some amusing sequences. There is nothing wrong with the basic situation. . . . But this novel, unlike Miss Tracy's others, did not induce me in that willing suspension of disbelief which, according to Coleridge, constitutes poetic faith."

Richard Boeth commented on the reviewers' hesitancy to fully endorse *Settled in Chambers.* He said, "they all seem to be saying the same things that all American reviews have said about all her books beginning with *The Prospects Are Pleasing*—which was the one after *The Straight and Narrow Path.* To wit: Yes, Miss Tracy is very funny, of course, but there is an ineffable something lacking . . . which adds up to general disappointment that Miss Tracy has once again failed to reissue *The Straight and Narrow Path.* What foolishness. It is true that *TSANP* seems in retrospect to have been unique, unrepeatable, unmatchable. But it was after all our wedding night with Miss Tracy. Whose fault is it that we can never recapture our sense of wonder, discovery, delight and sheer good luck. . . ."

He went on to say that "*Settled in Chambers* is, with no reservations whatever, a beautiful novel—continuously, peremptorily funny, flawlessly put together and peopled at every hand with characters drawn too perfectly to have been drawn from life. Miss Tracy's people are all Platonic ideals of satiric subjects, and we miserable sinners can hope to achieve no more than dim approximations of their asininity, their malice and their folly."

AVOCATIONAL INTERESTS: International travel, music, wildlife, gardening.

BIOGRAPHICAL/CRITICAL SOURCES: New York Times Book Review, March 10, 1968; *Time,* April 5, 1968; *Book World,* April 28, 1968; *National Observer,* August 12, 1968.

TREACY, William 1919-

PERSONAL: Born May 31, 1919, in Ireland; son of John (a farmer) and Mary (Delaney) Tracy. *Education:* Attended St. Patrick's Seminary, Maynooth, Ireland. *Home and office:* 1021 South Boundary, Olympia, Wash. 98507.

CAREER: Ordained Roman Catholic priest, 1944; parish curate in Ireland, 1944-45; priest in Roman Catholic churches in Seattle, Wash., 1945-65, pastor in Seattle, 1965-71; St. Michael's Parish, Olympia, Wash., pastor, 1971—. Assistant chancellor of Seattle Archdiocese, 1947-62, chairman of Diocesan Ecumenical Commission, 1965—. Member of panel on "Challenge" (inter-faith television program), 1960-74. Co-founder of Camp Brotherhood (interfaith communications center). Member of Seattle-King County Commission on Alcoholism; member of local Catholic Information Committee. *Member:* Knights of Columbus (chaplain), Rotary International (Seattle chapter). *Awards, honors:* Award from National Conference of Christians and Jews, 1962, for television program "Challenge," also named their "man of the year," 1975.

WRITINGS: (With Raphael Levine) *Wild Branch on the Olive Tree,* Binfords, 1974.

WORK IN PROGRESS: Scriptural reflections.

SIDELIGHTS: Treacy writes: "Rabbi Raphael Levine and I wrote *Wild Branch on the Olive Tree* because both of us are convinced that understandings and brotherhood will come about mainly through relationships. Our backgrounds and personalities are very different, yet our own friendship is close and this has been communicated to our TV audiences. In 1963 we led a two-month People-to-People tour of Europe and the Far East; in 1972 we led an ecumenical tour to the Holy Land during which we made four TV programs."

*   *   *

TREGER, Harvey 1924-

PERSONAL: Born July 5, 1924, in Chicago, Ill.; son of Sam (a tailor) and Lillian (Ertrachter) Treger; married Shirley Feldman (a vocational rehabilitation counselor), October 24, 1954. *Education:* Roosevelt University, B.S., 1948; University of Chicago, M.A., 1956; Chicago Institute for Psychoanalysis, further graduate study, 1960-63. *Religion:* Jewish. *Home:* 1501 Maple, #804, Evanston, Ill. 60201. *Office:* Jane Addams School of Social Work, University of Illinois at Chicago Circle, Box 4348, Chicago, Ill. 60680.

CAREER: U.S. Probation and Parole Service, Chicago, Ill., probation officer, 1957-65; University of Illinois at Chicago Circle, Jane Addams School of Social Work, assistant professor, 1965-70, associate professor, 1970-74, professor of social work and professor in department of criminal justice, 1974—. Instructor at University of Illinois at Chicago Circle, 1961-65, and University of Indiana, Gary Extension, autumn, 1971; private social work consulting service, 1965-66; oral examiner for Illinois Department of Personnel, 1969; director of police social service projects, 1970-75; member of Illinois Council Committee on Diagnosis and Treatment of the Offender, 1971. *Military service:* U.S. Army, 1943-45.

MEMBER: American Society of Criminology, National Council on Crime and Delinquency, American Correctional Association, American Orthopsychiatric Association (fellow), National Association of Social Workers (member of board of directors of Chicago chapter, 1965-67), Academy of Certified Social Workers, Council on Social Work Education, American Association of University Professors, Illinois Academy of Criminology (president, 1969-70). *Awards, honors:* Illinois Governor's Justice Award, 1972; John Howard Award, 1973; Morris J. Wexler Award from Illinois Academy of Criminology, 1974.

WRITINGS: (With wife, Shirley Treger, Ernest A. Rappaport, Rhoda Michaels, and others) *The Police-Social Work Team,* C. C Thomas, 1975. Contributor of articles and reviews to professional journals.

AVOCATIONAL INTERESTS: Playing the cello, photography, travel, art, collecting classical sound recordings.

*   *   *

TREGGIARI, Susan (Mary) 1940-

PERSONAL: Born March 11, 1940, in Moreton-in-Marsh, England; married Arnaldo Treggiari, 1964; children: Joanna, Silvia. *Education:* Oxford University, B.A., 1962, M.A., 1965, B.Litt., 1967. *Office:* Department of Classical Studies, University of Ottawa, Ottawa, Ontario, Canada K1N 6N5.

CAREER: North-Western Polytechnic, London, England, lecturer in classics, 1966-69; Sweet Briar College, Sweet Briar, Va., visiting professor of classics, 1969-70; University of Ottawa, Ottawa, Ontario, assistant professor, 1970-71, associate professor of classics, 1971—. *Member:* Classical Association of Canada, Joint Association of Classical Teachers, Society for the Promotion of Roman Studies, Association of Ancient Historians, Classical Association (England), American Philological Association, Kipling Society, Classical Association of the Middle West and South. *Awards, honors:* Grants from Canada Council, 1971-72, 1972-73, 1976-77.

WRITINGS: Roman Freedmen During the Late Republic, Clarendon Press, 1969; *Cicero's Cilician Letters,* London Association of Classical Teachers, 1973. Contributor to classical journals. *Classical News and Views,* acting editor, 1973-74, co-editor, 1974—; member of editorial board of *Phoenix,* 1972, 1975-78.

WORK IN PROGRESS: Research on Roman women from the first century B.C. to the second century A.D.

*   *   *

TRIGG, Harry Davis 1927-
(Parlin Clark)

PERSONAL: Born July 11, 1927, in Ottumwa, Iowa; son of Stuart Eugene (a business executive) and Goldie (McReynolds) Trigg; married Yolanda Fichera, July 5, 1952; children: Christopher Stuart. *Education:* Attended Iowa State College (now University), 1944; Art Institute of Chicago, B.F.A., 1949; Iowa Wesleyan College, graduate study, 1950. *Residence:* Evanston, Ill. *Agent:* Ellen Levine, Curtis Brown, Ltd., 60 East 56th St., New York, N.Y. 10022. *Office:* WGN-TV, 2501 West Bradley Pl., Chicago, Ill. 60618.

CAREER: WMAQ-TV, Chicago, Ill., program manager, 1957-74; WGN-TV, Chicago, Ill., program manager, 1974—. *Member:* National Association of Television Program Executives (president, 1974-75), Academy of Television Arts and Sciences (member of board of directors of Chicago chapter, 1959—).

WRITINGS: (With wife, Yolanda L. Trigg) *The Compleat Motion Picture Quiz Book: Or Sixty Thousand Points about Motion Pictures,* Doubleday, 1975. Author of television scripts for NBC, "Chicago Emmy Awards Shows," 1959, 1963, 1967, "Flowers Before Bread," 1966, and "A Nice Place to Visit?," 1967.

WORK IN PROGRESS: A sequel to *The Compleat Motion Picture Quiz Book;* a novel about television.

SIDELIGHTS: Trigg served as executive producer on five television programs which won Annual National Association of Television Program Executives Awards: "The New Performers," "Not Just Any Fire," "Three from Illinois," "Royko at Best," and "The Giants and the Common Man." He is considered an expert on motion picture lore and lectures extensively on the subject.

BIOGRAPHICAL/CRITICAL SOURCES: Broadcasting, February 18, 1974.

* * *

TRIGG, Yolanda Lillian 1926-

PERSONAL: Born December 9, 1926, in Chicago, Ill.; daughter of Carl G. (a barber) and Francis Carlotta Fichera; married Harry Davis Trigg (a television executive), July 5, 1952; children: Christopher Stuart. *Education:* Attended Ohio State College (now University), 1945; Art Institute of Chicago, B.F.A., 1949; DePaul University, graduate study, 1950. *Residence:* Evanston, Ill. *Agent:* Ellen Levine, Curtis Brown Ltd., 60 East 56th St., New York, N.Y. 10022.

CAREER: Writer.

WRITINGS: (With husband, Harry Davis Trigg) *The Compleat Motion Picture Quiz Book: Or Sixty Thousand Points about Motion Pictures,* Doubleday, 1975.

* * *

TRILLING, Lionel 1905-1975

July 4, 1905—November 5, 1975; American literary and social critic, educator, essayist, editor, and author. Obituaries: *Washington Post,* November 7, 1975; *New York Times,* November 7, 1975; *Publishers Weekly,* November 17, 1975; *Newsweek,* November 17, 1975; *Time,* November 17, 1975; *AB Bookman's Weekly,* December 8, 1975; *New York Times Book Review,* February 8, 1976. (See index for previous *CA* sketch)

* * *

TROLANDER, Judith Ann 1942-

PERSONAL: Born May 31, 1942, in Minneapolis, Minn.; daughter of Everett William (a telephone repairman) and Harriett (a teacher; maiden name, Woolery) Trolander. *Education:* University of Minnesota, B.A., 1964; Western Reserve University (now Case Western Reserve University), M.S.L.S., 1966, M.A., 1969, Ph.D., 1972. *Politics:* Democrat. *Religion:* Methodist. *Home:* 1380 Highland Village Dr., #22, Duluth, Minn. 55811. *Office:* Department of History, University of Minnesota, Duluth, Minn. 55812.

CAREER: St. Louis County Welfare Department, Virginia, Minn., caseworker, 1964-65; Los Angeles County Public Library, Los Angeles, Calif., librarian, 1966-67; Western Illinois University, Macomb, assistant professor of history, 1971-75; University of Minnesota, Duluth, associate professor of history, 1975—. Lecturer at Cleveland State University, spring, 1971; instructor at University of Akron, summer, 1971. *Member:* American Historical Association, Organization of American Historians, Social Welfare History Group.

WRITINGS: Settlement Houses and the Great Depression, Wayne State University Press, 1975. Contributor to *Dictionary of American Biography,* and to social work and history journals.

WORK IN PROGRESS: A history of settlement houses since 1939; research on Lillie Peck.

SIDELIGHTS: Judith Trolander writes: "My interest in social welfare history is an outgrowth of my previous experience as a caseworker, during which a number of incidents occurred that made real to me the fact that the welfare system is often run more in the interests of the taxpayers than the poor themselves. I find settlement houses worth studying, not only because they have provided needed services in low income areas, but also because they have a traditional commitment to act as an ally and advocate for the disadvantaged."

* * *

TROST, Lucille W(ood) 1938-

PERSONAL: Born November 4, 1938, in Candor, N.Y.; daughter of Stiles and Alice (Keim) Wood; married Charles H. Trost (a biologist and professor), June 18, 1960; children: Scott Anthony. *Education:* Pennsylvania State University, B.S., 1960; University of Florida, M.S., 1963. *Politics:* Democrat. *Religion:* "Unaffiliated Unitarian." *Agent:* Shirley Collier, Stradella Rd., Los Angeles, Calif. 90024.

CAREER: University of Florida, Gainesville, research associate in biology, 1962-64. *Member:* Phi Sigma.

WRITINGS: Coping with Crib-Sized Campers, Stackpole, 1968.

For children: *Biography of a Cottontail,* Putnam, 1971; *A Cycle of Seasons: The Little Brown Bat,* Addison-Wesley, 1971; *The Fence Lizard: A Cycle of Seasons,* Addison-Wesley, 1972; *Lives and Deaths of a Meadow,* Putnam, 1973.*

* * *

TRUBO, Richard 1946-

PERSONAL: Born April 2, 1946, in Los Angeles, Calif.; son of William and Ida (Singer) Trubo; married Donna Grodin (a teacher), June 24, 1973; children: Melissa Suzanne. *Education:* University of California at Los Angeles, B.A., 1967, M.A., 1968. *Home and office:* 10800 Rose Ave., Los Angeles, Calif. 90034.

CAREER: KOST Radio, Los Angeles, Calif., producer-writer, 1968-71; free-lance writer, 1971—. *Member:* American Society of Journalists and Authors, Authors Guild.

WRITINGS: An Act of Mercy, Nash Publishing, 1973; (with Richard Guarino) *The Great American Insurance Hoax,* Nash Publishing, 1974. Contributor to popular magazines, including *Holiday, True, Coronet, TV Guide, Parade,* and *Family Weekly;* contributor to newspapers, including *Detroit News, San Francisco Chronicle, Chicago Sun-Times, Chicago Tribune,* and *Los Angeles Times.*

WORK IN PROGRESS: A documentary motion picture about emotionally-disturbed teenage girls.

* * *

TUCKER, Ernest E(dward) 1916-1969

PERSONAL: Born November 18, 1916, in Chicago, Ill.; son of Irwin St. John (a clergyman) and Ellen Dorothy (O'Reilly) Tucker; married Margaret Humes (a librarian), March 9, 1941; children: Barbara Ellen (Mrs. Joseph Philipps), Margaret Leigh, Ernest Humes. *Education:* University of Illinois, B.A. (with high honors), 1938. *Religion:* Roman Catholic. *Agent:* Eleanor Langdon, 2930 North Sheridan Rd., Chicago, Ill.

CAREER: Chicago American Publishing Co. (now *Chicago Today*), Chicago, Ill., copy reader, 1938-41, 1945-48, feature writer, 1948-58, columnist, 1958-62, city editor, 1963-69, assistant managing editor, 1969. Member of faculty of Medill Campus of Northwestern University, 1950-60. Has appeared on television programs "Your Right to Say It" and "City Desk." *Military service:* U.S. Naval Reserve, 1942-66; became commander. *Member:* Phi Beta Kappa, Sigma Delta Chi.

WRITINGS: Dan Morgan: Rifleman, Wheeler, 1955; *Are Our Schools Flunking?,* Great Books Foundation, 1956; *The Story of Knights and Armor,* Lothrop, 1961; *The Story of Fighting Ships,* Lothrop, 1963; *Soldiers and Armies,* Lothrop, 1965.

(Died January 26, 1969)

* * *

TUCKER, Michael R(ay) 1941-

PERSONAL: Born April 3, 1941, in Dallas, Tex.; son of Raymond E. (an administrator) and Irene (an artist; maiden name, Wallace) Tucker; married Nancy E. Shull, August 26, 1961; children: Mark David, Haddon Criswell, Shannon Noel. *Education:* Western Baptist Bible College, B.A., 1963; Dallas Theological Seminary, Th.M., 1967. *Home:* 2873 Jon St., Colorado Springs, Colo. 80907. *Office:* Temple Church, 1311 East Columbine, Colorado Springs, Colo. 80907.

CAREER: Ordained Baptist minister, 1970; pastor of Baptist church in Birmingham, Ala., 1967-70; Southeastern Bible College, Birmingham, Ala., teacher, 1968-70; Colorado Springs Christian School, Colorado Springs, Colo., president of board of directors, 1971—. Chaplain for Civil Air Patrol, 1971-73. *Member:* National Association of Evangelicals, Conservative Baptist Association of America (board member, 1975—), Rocky Mountain Conservative Baptist Association (board member, 1973—).

WRITINGS: The Church That Dared to Change, Tyndale, 1975; *Live Confidently: How to Know God's Will,* Tyndale, 1976. Contributor to church periodicals.

SIDELIGHTS: Tucker writes: "I believe the evangelical church has gained a new place in American life. Presidents, well known athletes, movie stars, senators, and other spotlight people are publicly acknowledging their faith in Jesus Christ. People are looking for an anchor and a guide. Evangelical Christianity provides both, and Christian books are part of what God is doing in the last quarter of the twentieth century."

* * *

TUCKER, William R(ayburn) 1923-

PERSONAL: Born July 4, 1923, in Duncan, Okla.; son of William Asa and Allie (Johnson) Tucker; married Monica Garrity, September 6, 1957; children: Giselle, William Johnson. *Education:* University of Oklahoma, B.A., 1947, M.A., 1948; Graduate Institute of International Studies, Geneva, Switzerland, Docteur es Sciences Politiques, 1950. *Politics:* Independent. *Religion:* Methodist. *Home:* 2580 Gladys, Beaumont, Tex. 77702. *Office:* Department of Government, Lamar University, Box 10030, Beaumont, Tex. 77710.

CAREER: Oklahoma Baptist University, Shawnee, instructor in government, 1951-53; University of Louisville, Louisville, Ky., assistant professor of political science, 1953-54; University of Delaware, Newark, assistant professor of political science, 1954-55; Lamar University, Beaumont, Tex., assistant professor, 1956-59, associate professor, 1959-65, professor of government, 1965—, head of department, 1970-73. First vice-president of board of directors of Beaumont Symphony Orchestra, 1969-70. *Military service:* U.S. Naval Reserve, active duty, 1943-46. *Member:* American Political Science Association. *Awards, honors:* Research grant from American Philosophical Society, 1967.

WRITINGS: The Attitude of the British Labour Party towards European and Collective Security Problems 1920-1939, Institut Universitaire, 1950; *The Fascist Ego: A Political Biography of Robert Brasillach,* University of California Press, 1975. Contributor of articles and reviews to political science journals.

WORK IN PROGRESS: Research on Maurice Bardeche and literary fascism.

SIDELIGHTS: Tucker writes: "My interest in French right-wing politics developed during my stay in Paris, 1945-46, primarily through conversations about pre-war French politics with Madame Odette Marchegay (the former Madame Maurice Petsche)."

* * *

TUDOR, Dean 1943-

PERSONAL: Born May 26, 1943, in Toronto, Ontario, Canada; son of Frederick (a radio engineer) and Jean (Pasquantonio) Tudor; married Nancy Rice (a librarian), June 3, 1967. *Education:* University of Toronto, B.A., 1965; McGill University, M.L.S., 1967. *Politics:* Socialist (New Democratic Party). *Religion:* Humanist. *Home:* 300 Robert St., Toronto, Ontario, Canada M5S 2K8. *Office:* Ryerson Polytechnical Institute, 50 Gould St., Toronto, Ontario, Canada M5B 1E8.

CAREER: York University Libraries, Downsview, Ontario, reference librarian, 1967-68; Ontario Department of Revenue Library (now Ministry of Treasury, Economics and Intergovernmental Affairs Library), Toronto, Ontario, director of library branch, 1968-73; Ryerson Polytechnical Institute, Toronto, chairman of Library Arts Department, 1973—. Consultant to Treasury Board Survey of Ontario Government Libraries, 1969-72; director, Peter Martin Associates, 1973—; editorial manuscript consultant to Libraries Unlimited, R. R. Bowker, Special Libraries Association, and Canadian Library Association. *Member:* Canadian Association for Information Sciences, Canadian Library Association, Council of Planning Librarians, Special Library Association (treasurer of Toronto branch, 1969-71, executive director, 1971-72), Institute of Professional Librarians of Ontario (member of board of directors, 1971-73), Ontario Government Librarians Council (member of board of directors, 1970-72), Ontario Library Association, International Wine and Food Society.

WRITINGS: Regional Development and Regional Government in Ontario (annotated bibliography), Council of Planning Librarians, 1970; (compiler with wife, Nancy Tudor) *Popular Music Periodicals Index, 1973,* Scarecrow, 1974; *Wine, Beer and Spirits,* Libraries Unlimited, 1975; (editor) *The Compleat Library Guide to Toronto,* Canadian Library Association, 1975.

Compiler, with Andrew Armitage, *Annual Index to Popular Music Record Reviews*, Scarecrow, 1973—. Contributor of articles and reviews to *Ragtimer, Coda*, and library journals. Editor, *OGLE* (Ontario Government Librarians Exchange), 1969-72; contributing editor, *LJ/SLJ Previews*, 1972-73, *Blues Link*, 1973-74, *Blues Is*—, 1975; music editor, *Ontario Library Review*, 1972—, editorial consultant to *Canadian Essay and Literature Index*, University of Toronto Press, 1973—, *Canadian Serials Directory*, University of Toronto Press, 1974, *Canadian Historical Calendar and Day Book*, Peter Martin Associates, 1974—.

WORK IN PROGRESS: Canadian Record Catalogue; Popular Music Discography and Selection Today; Canadian Book Review Annual.

* * *

TUNIS, John R(oberts) 1889-1975

PERSONAL: Born December 7, 1889, in Boston, Mass.; married Lucy Rogers. *Education:* Harvard University, A.B., 1911. *Home:* Stanford Hill Rd., Essex, Conn.

CAREER: Sportswriter, *New York Evening Post*, 1925-32, Universal Service, 1932-35; broadcaster of tennis matches for National Broadcasting Co.; writer. *Military service:* Served in France during World War I. *Awards, honors:* New York *Herald Tribune* spring festival prize, 1938, for *The Iron Duke;* junior book award from Boys' Clubs of America, 1949, for *Highpockets.*

WRITINGS: $port$, Heroics, and Hysterics, John Day, 1928; *American Girl* (novel), Brewer & Warren, 1930; *Was College Worth While?*, Harcourt, 1936; *Choosing a College*, Harcourt, 1940; *Sport for the Fun of It*, A. S. Barnes, 1940, 2nd revised edition, Ronald, 1958; *Democracy and Sport*, A. S. Barnes, 1941; *This Writing Game: Selections from Twenty Years of Free-Lancing*, A. S. Barnes, 1941; *Lawn Games*, A. S. Barnes, 1943; *The American Way in Sport*, Duell, Sloan & Pearce, 1958; *A Measure of Independence* (autobiography), Atheneum, 1964.

Primarily for young readers: *The Iron Duke*, Harcourt, 1938; *The Duke Decides*, Harcourt, 1939; *Champion's Choice*, Harcourt, 1940; *The Kid from Tomkinsville*, Harcourt, 1940, reprint, Bantam, in press; *World Series*, Harcourt, 1941; *All-American*, Harcourt, 1942; *Million-Miler: The Story of an Air Pilot*, Messner, 1942; *Keystone Kids*, Harcourt, 1943; *Rookie of the Year*, Harcourt, 1944; *Yea! Wildcats!*, Harcourt, 1944; *A City for Lincoln*, Harcourt, 1945; *The Kid Comes Back*, Morrow, 1946, reprinted, 1967; *Highpockets*, Morrow, 1948 (also see below); *Son of the Valley*, Morrow, 1949; *Young Razzle*, Morrow, 1949.

The Other Side of the Fence, Morrow, 1953; *Go, Team, Go!*, Morrow, 1954 (also see below); *Buddy and the Old Pro*, Morrow, 1955; *Schoolboy Johnson*, Morrow, 1958; *Silence Over Dunkerque*, Morrow, 1962; *His Enemy, His Friend*, Morrow, 1967; *Two by Tunis: Highpockets* [*and*] *Go, Team, Go!*, Morrow, 1972; *Grand National*, Morrow, 1973.

Contributor of more than two thousand articles to magazines, including *Collier's, Esquire, Reader's Digest, New Yorker*, and *Saturday Evening Post.*

OBITUARIES: New York Times, February 5, 1975; *AB Bookman's Weekly*, February 24, 1975; *Publishers Weekly*, March 24, 1975.*

(Died February 4, 1975, in Essex, Conn.)

TUNNEY, John V(arick) 1934-

PERSONAL: Born June 26, 1934, in New York, N.Y.; son of James Joseph (world heavyweight champion boxer, Gene Tunney; later a businessman) and Mary Josephine (Lauder) Tunney; married Maria Sprengers (divorced); children: Edward Eugene, Mark Andrew, Arianne Sprengers. *Education:* Yale University, B.A., 1956; Academy of International Law, the Hague, Netherlands, graduate study, summer, 1957; University of Virginia, LL.B., 1959. *Religion:* Roman Catholic. *Agent:* Hal Ross, 21323 Pacific Coast Highway, Malibu, Calif. 90265. *Office:* U.S. Senate, 6221 Dirksen Senate Building, Washington, D.C. 20510.

CAREER: Admitted to New York bar, 1959, and California bar, 1963; Cahill, Gordon, Reindel & Ohl, New York, N.Y., lawyer, 1959-60; University of California, Riverside, lecturer in business law, 1961-62; law practice in Riverside, Calif., 1963-64; U.S. Congress, Washington, D.C., Democratic member of House of Representatives from California, 1965-71, senator, 1971—. Special adviser to the President's Commission on Juvenile Delinquency and Youth Crime, 1963-65; delegate to Democratic National Convention, 1972. Legal adviser to Riverside area Aiding Leukemic Stricken American Children (ALSAC), 1962; member of board of trustees of California Indian Legal Services; member of board of councilors of University of Southern California; member of University of Chicago's Center for Policy Study on Urban Environment. *Military service:* U.S. Air Force, 1963-65; became captain.

MEMBER: Academia Internationalis-Lex et Scientia, California Bar Association, Junior Chamber of Commerce, Lions, Delta Psi. *Awards, honors:* Chubb fellow of Yale University, 1967.

WRITINGS: The Changing Dream, Doubleday, 1975.

SIDELIGHTS: As a member of the Senate, Tunney's projects have included spearheading legislation to conserve energy and other vital resources, developing legislation to make auto engines more efficient and to label home appliances for energy costs. He also wrote the first anti-trust reform measures in twenty years, and has moved for legislation on noise control standards and water quality standards for lakes and rivers. Tunney is chairman of the Constitutional Rights Subcommittee of the Judiciary Committee, and the Subcommittee on Science, Technology and Commerce of the Commerce Committee. He also serves on the Joint Atomic Energy Committee, the National Commission on Supplies and Shortages, and the Special Committee on Aging.

AVOCATIONAL INTERESTS: Golf, tennis, skiing, swimming, sailing, scuba diving, mountain climbing.

BIOGRAPHICAL/CRITICAL SOURCES: New York Herald Tribune, November 22, 1964; *Washington Post*, January 5, 1965; *New York Post*, January 27, 1965; *Christian Science Monitor*, October 13, 1970; *U.S. News*, November 16, 1970; *Time*, November 16, 1970, February 1, 1971; *American Home*, July, 1971; *New York Times Magazine*, December 26, 1971; George Douth, *Leaders in Profile: The U.S. Senate*, Sperr & Douth, 1972.

* * *

TURNER, Dennis C(lair) 1948-

PERSONAL: Born August 3, 1948, in Pennsylvania; son of Clair Gilbert (a foreman) and Jane (Taylor) Turner; married Heidi Schmid, June 20, 1973; children: Christian Michael. *Education:* San Diego State College (now University),

B.S., 1970; Johns Hopkins University, Sc.D., 1974. *Politics:* Independent. *Religion:* Protestant. *Home:* Einsiedlerstrasse 292, 8810 Horgen, Switzerland. *Office:* Zoology Institute, University of Zurich, Zurich, Switzerland.

CAREER: University of Zurich, Zurich, Switzerland, lecturer in ethology and wildlife biology, 1974—. *Member:* American Society of Mammalogists, Animal Behavior Society, Phi Eta Sigma (chapter vice-president, 1970), Alpha Mu Gamma, Phi Kappa Phi.

WRITINGS: The Vampire Bat: A Field Study in Behavior and Ecology, Johns Hopkins Press, 1975. Contributor of articles to journals in his field.

WORK IN PROGRESS: Current research on the socio-ecology of Roe Deer in Switzerland and baboons in Ethiopia; a textbook, *Socio-Ecology: The Ecology of Social Systems in Animals and Man* (tentative title), completion expected in 1978.

SIDELIGHTS: Turner told *CA:* "I first became interested in natural history on camping trips with my parents, and my first interest in animal behavior was stimulated by the writings of Konrad Lorenz. I have participated on scientific expeditions in Central America and Africa, and enjoy travelling, especially to archaeological excavations with my family."

AVOCATIONAL INTERESTS: Singing, classical and folk music, model building.

* * *

TURNER, Henry Dicken 1919-

PERSONAL: Born December 30, 1919, in Sheffield, England; son of Alfred (a joiner) and Mary Elizabeth (Dicken) Turner; married Christina MacCorquodale, November 28, 1945; children: Mairi Fiona. *Education:* University of Sheffield, B.Sc. (honors), 1941, Ph.D., 1949. *Religion:* Church of England. *Home:* Old Forge Cottage, Coopers Green, St. Albans, Hertfordshire AL4 9HL, England. *Office:* Council for Education and Training of Health Visitors, Clifton House, Euston Rd., London, England.

CAREER: Unilever, Sheffield, England, senior executive and chief chemist, 1949-50; University of Sheffield, Sheffield, England, staff tutor in science, 1950-53, deputy to director of science, 1953-60, assistant registrar, 1960-65, senior assistant registrar, 1965-68; British Association for the Advancement of Science, London, England, secretary, 1968-71; University of Sierra Leone, Freetown, secretary, 1971-74; Council for the Education and Training of Health Visitors, London, England, principal administrative officer, 1975—. Commissioner of income tax of St. James Division, Westminster, 1968-72. *Military service:* British Army, Royal Electrical and Mechanical Engineers, 1941-46; became captain. *Member:* Athenaeum Club.

WRITINGS: (With G. K. T. Conn) *The Evolution of the Nuclear Atom,* Iliffe Books, 1965; (editor with Frederick R. Jevons) *What Kinds of Graduates Do We Need?,* Oxford University Press, 1972. Contributor to professional journals.

WORK IN PROGRESS: Biography of Robert Hooke; a companion book to *The Evolution of the Nuclear Atom, Evolution of the Chemical Bond.*

SIDELIGHTS: Turner has travelled and lectured in the United States, Canada, India, Africa, and Germany. *Avocational interests:* Collecting antiques and antique firearms, shooting, walking, music, theatre.

TUTTLE, Frank W(aldo) 1896-

PERSONAL: Born November 6, 1896, in State College, Pa.; son of Franklin Eliot and Clara R. (Palmer) Tuttle; married Vada Lee Nelson (a former teacher), September 1, 1929; children: Clara Frances (Mrs. William B. Weaver), Charles E. *Education:* University of Kentucky, A.B., 1920; University of Illinois, M.A., 1924; State University of Iowa, Ph.D., 1934. *Religion:* Episcopalian. *Home:* 1540 Northwest Sixth Ave., Gainesville, Fla. 32601.

CAREER: University of Illinois, Urbana, instructor in economics, 1922-29; Washington and Jefferson College, Washington, Pa., assistant professor of economics, 1929-33; Southwestern College, Winfield, Kan., professor of economics and head of department, 1934-35; University of Florida, Gainesville, assistant professor, 1935-47, associate professor, 1947-63, professor of economics, 1963-67, professor emeritus, 1967—. Associate economist for Fourth Regional War Labor Board (Atlanta, Ga.), 1943-46, and Wage Stabilization Board, 1946. *Member:* American Economic Association, Athenaeum, Pi Gamma Mu, Alpha Kappa Psi, Order of Artus (ODE).

WRITINGS: (With J. M. Perry) *An Economic History of the United States,* Southwestern Publishing, 1970. Contributor to social science journals. Associate editor of *Social Science,* 1937-73.

* * *

TYMIENIECKA, Anna-Teresa

PERSONAL: Surname pronounced "tim-yen-yets-ka"; born in Marianowo, Poland; naturalized U.S. citizen; daughter of Wladyslaw (a country squire) and Maria-Ludwika (de Lanval) Zaremba-Tymieniecka; married Hendrik Houthakker (a professor), 1955; children: Louis, Isabel, John-Nicholas. *Education:* University of Cracow, B.A., 1946; Sorbonne, University of Paris, M.A., 1951; University of Fribourg, Ph.D., 1952. *Home:* 348 Payson Rd., Belmont, Mass. *Office:* Philosophy Department, St. John's University, Jamaica, N.Y. 11432.

CAREER: University of California, Berkeley, teaching assistant in philosophy, 1954-55; Oregon State College (now University), Corvallis, instructor in mathematics, 1955-56; Pennsylvania State University, University Park, assistant professor, 1957; Bryn Mawr College, Bryn Mawr, Pa., lecturer, 1957-58; Radcliff College, Institute for Independent Study, Cambridge, Mass., associate scholar, 1961-66; St. John's University, Jamaica, N.Y., professor of philosophy, 1972-73. Visiting professor, Duquesne University, 1966-68, University of Waterloo, 1969-72. *Member:* American Philosophical Association, Society of Phenomenology and Existential Philosophy, International Husserl and Phenomenological Research Society (secretary-general, 1969—), Swiss Society for the Philosophy of Science, Societe Europeene de la Culture.

WRITINGS: Essence et existence: Etude a propos de la philosophie de Roman Ingarden et Nicolai Hartman, Aubier Montaigne (Paris, France), 1957; (with others), *For Roman Ingarden: Nine Essays in Phenomenology,* Nijhoff (The Hague, Netherlands), 1959; *Phenomenology and Science in Contemporary European Thought,* Farrar, Straus, 1962; *Leibniz' Cosmological Synthesis,* Van Gorcum (Assen, Netherlands), 1964; (editor with Charles Parsons, and contributor) *Contributions to Logic and Methodology in Honor of J. M. Bochenski,* North-Holland Publishing (Amsterdam), 1965; *Why Is There Something Rather Than Nothing? Prolegomena to the Phenomenology of Cosmic*

Creation, Van Gorcum, 1966; *Eros et Logos,* Nauwelearts (Louvain, Belgium), 1972. Also author of *Phenomenologie et Creation,* 1972. Editor of *Analecta Husserliana* (yearbook of phenomenological research), 1971—.

* * *

UFFENBECK, Lorin A(rthur) 1924-

PERSONAL: Born September 25, 1924, in Fond du Lac, Wis.; son of Carl W. (a jeweler) and Erna (Groenke) Uffenbeck. *Education:* University of Wisconsin, B.A., 1949, Ph.D., 1957; Universite de Grenoble, certificat, 1950; Middlebury College, M.A., 1952. *Home:* 2320 Kendall Ave., Madison, Wis. 53705. *Office:* Department of French and Italian, 618 Van Hise Hall, University of Wisconsin, Madison, Wis. 53706.

CAREER: U.S. Department of State, Washington, D.C., foreign staff officer, 1950-51; Hamilton College, Clinton, N.Y., assistant professor of French, 1957-64; University of Minnesota, Minneapolis, lecturer in French, 1964-65; University of Wisconsin, Madison, associate professor, 1965-69, professor of French, 1969—. Director, Hamilton College Junior Year in Paris, France, 1959-60, University of Michigan and University of Wisconsin Junior Year in Aix-en-Provence, France, 1970-71. *Military service:* U.S. Army, 1943-46. *Member:* Modern Language Association of America, American Association of Teachers of French, Society of 19th Century French Studies, Societe Chateaubriand, Groupe d'Etudes Balzaciennes, Societe Etudes Romantiques, Phi Beta Kappa.

WRITINGS: (Editor) Hortense Allart, *Nouvelles Lettres a Sainte-Beuve, 1832-1864,* Droz (Geneva), 1965; (with Rouben Cholakian) *A la recherche de Paris: A French Cultural Reader,* Oxford University Press, 1966; (editor) Charles Sainte-Beuve, *Chateaubriand et son groupe litteraire sous l'Empire: Index alphabetique et analytique,* University of North Carolina Press, 1973. Contributor of articles to French and English journals in his field.

WORK IN PROGRESS: Madame Honore de Balzac's correspondance with Champfleury; an editor of Sainte-Beuve's *Chateaubriand et son groupe,* Le Cours de Liege.

AVOCATIONAL INTERESTS: Foreign travel and book collecting.

* * *

ULAM, S(tanislaw) M(arcin) 1909-

PERSONAL: Born April 13, 1909, in Lwow, Poland; son of Jozef (a lawyer) and Anna (Auerbach) Ulam; married Francoise Aron (a free-lance writer), August 19, 1941; children: Claire Anne (Mrs. Steven Weiner). *Education:* Polytechnic Institute, Lwow, Poland, Dr.Sci., 1933. *Residence:* Santa Fe, N.M. *Office:* Department of Mathematics, University of Colorado, Boulder, Colo. 80304.

CAREER: Princeton University, Princeton, N.J., visiting scientist at Institute for Advanced Study, 1936; Harvard University, Cambridge, Mass., junior fellow, 1936-40; University of Wisconsin, assistant professor, 1940-41, professor of mathematics, 1941-43; Los Alamos Scientific Laboratory, Los Alamos, N.M., member of scientific staff, 1944—, research adviser, 1957-67; University of Colorado, Boulder, professor of mathematics, 1965—. Graduate research professor at University of Florida, 1973—; visiting professor at Harvard University, 1951, Massachusetts Institute of Technology, 1956, and University of California at San Diego, 1962. *Member:* American Academy of Arts and Sciences, National Academy of Sciences, American Philosophical Society, American Mathematical Society, American Physical Society, Royal Society of Arts.

WRITINGS: Collection of Mathematical Problems, Interscience, 1960; *Problems of Modern Mathematics,* Wiley, 1964; (with Mark Kac) *Mathematics and Logic,* Praeger, 1967; *Sets, Numbers, and Universes,* M.I.T. Press, 1974; *Adventures of a Mathematician,* Scribner, 1976. Contributor to mathematics and physics journals.

WORK IN PROGRESS: Research on mathematics, mathematical physics, astronomy, and biology.

AVOCATIONAL INTERESTS: Playing chess and tennis.

* * *

ULYATT, Kenneth 1920-

PERSONAL: Born March 16, 1920, in London, England; married Patricia Brealey, 1945; children: Susan, Keith. *Education:* Educated in England; attended art school. *Politics:* "Pretty middle-of-the-road." *Home and office:* 13 Market St., Poole, Dorsetshire, England.

CAREER: Has worked for advertising agencies and for publishers, as designer and writer; currently employed by Book Club Associates in England. *Military service:* Royal Air Force, 1940-45; served in North Africa. *Member:* English Westerners, Western History Association of America, Poole Museum Society.

WRITINGS—All juveniles: *North Against the Sioux,* Collins, 1965, Prentice-Hall, 1967; *The Longhorn Trail,* Collins, 1967, Prentice-Hall, 1968; *Custer's Gold,* Collins, 1971; *The Day of the Cowboy,* Penguin, 1973; *The Time of the Indian,* Penguin, 1975; *Badmen of the Old West,* Penguin, in press. Contributor of articles and stories to magazines.

WORK IN PROGRESS: A History of the West, for Longman; an anthology of Western themes, for Penguin.

SIDELIGHTS: Ulyatt lives in an old house in Poole, about five hundred yards up the street from the quay. He spends a lot of his time exploring the West Country of England, but it is a much bigger and wilder West which has interested him since he was a boy. The period of history which particularly interests him is the time of westward expansion in the second half of the nineteenth century. It is an exciting period of history to study, he thinks, because the Americans today are making great efforts to record the full story of those times before they recede too far from memory. He recently completed a trip to the California gold fields, collecting material for a new book.

* * *

UMLAND, Craig (Owen) 1947-

PERSONAL: Born July 2, 1947, in Lincoln, Neb.; son of Rudolph Ernest (a government employee) and Elsie Lillian (a teacher; maiden name, Rockenbach) Umland. *Education:* University of Chicago, B.A., 1969, M.A., 1970. *Politics:* None. *Religion:* None. *Home:* 105 Ward Parkway, Apt. 314, Kansas City, Mo. 64112. *Office:* Traders National Bank, 1125 Grand, Kansas City, Mo. 64106.

CAREER: Bank teller, Traders National Bank, Kansas City, Mo. *Military service:* U.S. Army, artillery meteorologist, 1970-71; served in Korea. *Awards, honors:* Kearney Wornall scholarship award from American Institute of Banking, 1975.

WRITINGS: (With Eric Umland) *Mystery of the Ancients: Early Spacemen and the Mayas,* Walker & Co., 1974.

WORK IN PROGRESS: World History at a Glance, completion expected in 1977.

SIDELIGHTS: Umland writes: "While our little book is obviously in the von Daniken tradition, it was specifically inspired by Robert Charroux's *Forgotten Worlds.*" He adds, "I am fluent in German—adequate in French, and have a reading knowledge of Spanish and Italian—my masters degree was in Akkadian (Babylonian) and Sumerian, but I haven't read a tablet for some years now—I am currently working on Russian and Japanese." *Avocational interests:* Travel (Germany and Luxembourg, Switzerland, France, Spain).

* * *

UNDERHILL, Miriam E.   1898(?)-1976

1898(?)—January 7, 1976; American mountain climber, editor, and author. Obituaries: *New York Times,* January 9, 1976.

* * *

UNDERWOOD, Jane H(ammons)   1931-

PERSONAL: Born October 30, 1931, in Fort Bliss, Tex.; daughter of Frank and Lydia (Williams) Hammons; married Van K. Hainline, October 20, 1947 (divorced April, 1966); married John W. Underwood, July 4, 1968; children: (first marriage) Michael K., Susan J. (Mrs. Wayne Sigleo); (second marriage) Anne K. *Education:* Imperial Valley Junior College, A.A., 1957; University of California, Riverside, B.A. (summa cum laude), 1960; University of California, Los Angeles, M.A., 1962, Ph.D., 1964; postdoctoral study at Cornell University, summer, 1971, Lawrence University, summer, 1975. *Home:* 2228 East Fourth St., Tucson, Ariz. 85719. *Office:* Department of Anthropology, University of Arizona, Tucson, Ariz. 85721.

CAREER: University of California, Riverside, assistant professor of anthropology, 1962-68; University of Arizona, Tucson, associate professor, 1968-73, professor of anthropology, 1973—. *Member:* American Association for the Advancement of Science (fellow), American Anthropological Association (fellow), American Association of Physical Anthropologists, Association for Anthropology in Micronesia, Association for Social Anthropology in Oceania, American Eugenics Society, Society for the Study of Human Biology, Sigma Xi. *Awards, honors:* Woodrow Wilson fellowship, 1960-61; Social Science Research Council grants, summer, 1964, and summer, 1969; National Science Foundation grant, 1965-66; Wenner-Gren Foundation grant.

WRITINGS: Biocultural Interactions and Human Variation, W. C. Brown, 1975. Contributor to anthropology journals.

WORK IN PROGRESS: Population History of Micronesia, completion expected in 1977; *Pacific Islands Ethnohistorical Atlas,* 1978.

* * *

UNGER, Jim   1937-

PERSONAL: Born January 21, 1937, in London, England; moved to Canada, 1968; son of Cecil James (an electronics engineer) and Lillian Maud Unger; married Patricia M. Smith, November, 1969 (divorced July, 1975). *Education:* Attended art schools, 1952-59. *Politics:* "A-political." *Religion:* None. *Home and office:* 1275 Richmond Rd., Ottawa, Ontario, Canada K2B 8E3. *Agent:* Universal Press Syndicate, 6700 Squibb Rd., Mission, Kan. 66202.

CAREER: Until 1968 worked as insurance clerk, policeman in England, driving instructor, taxicab driver, and office manager; Minto Construction Co., Ottawa, Ontario, graphic artist in advertising department, 1968-71; *Mississauga Times* (newspaper), Mississauga, Ontario, art director, 1971-74; Jim Unger, Inc., Ottawa, syndicated cartoonist appearing in more than fifty newspapers daily, 1974—. *Military service:* British Army, surveyor, 1955-57. *Awards, honors:* Named "cartoonist of the year" by Ontario Weekly Newspapers Association, 1972, 1973, 1974.

WRITINGS: Apart from a Little Dampness, Herman, How's Everything Else? (cartoons), Sheed, 1975. Editorial cartoonist for newspapers, including *Mississauga Times, Mississauga News,* and *Oakville Daily Journal.* Contributor of humorous articles to magazines and newspapers.

SIDELIGHTS: Unger writes: "I am an avid traveller now based in Canada. . . . I like French Canada immensely . . . I have a great love of humanity which I think is the strength of my humour. I rarely meet anyone I don't like! Grew up during the London Blitz. Survived enough near misses to take life less seriously than most people."

* * *

UNRAU, Ruth   1922-

PERSONAL: Second syllable of surname rhymes with "now"; born February 28, 1922, in Kouts, Ind.; daughter of A. E. (a farmer) and Martha (Zook) Baughman; married Walter D. Unrau (an accountant), August 1, 1953; children: Susan (Mrs. Greg Stucky), Paula. *Education:* Ball State University, B.S., 1943; Indiana University, M.C.S., 1945. *Religion:* General Conference Mennonite. *Home address:* Box 214, North Newton, Kan. 67117. *Office:* Department of Business, Bethel College, North Newton, Kan. 67117.

CAREER: Bethel College, North Newton, Kan., 1947—, now associate professor of business. Teacher of high school English and business courses at Woodstock School in northern India, 1965-66, 1970-73. *Member:* American Association of University Women (local chapter treasurer, 1974-75).

WRITINGS: Buckwheat Summer, Herald Press, 1962; *Who Needs an Oil Well?,* Abingdon, 1968.

WORK IN PROGRESS: A book about her experiences in India.

SIDELIGHTS: Ruth Unrau writes: "Writing is my avocation, since teaching takes almost full time. I started with children's stories, thinking after having read one hundred books to my older daughter that surely I could write stories like those, and I found I could. Then I told the story of my own growing up in *Buckwheat Summer,* and then my husband's story in *Who Needs an Oil Well?* Our family spent four years working in Woodstock School in northern India, and when I have stopped making speeches about the experience, I will start writing."

* * *

UNTERMAN, Issar Y(ehuda)   1886-1976

1886—January 25, 1976; Russian-born Israeli rabbi, religious official, and author. Obituaries: *New York Times,* January 27, 1976.

* * *

UPSON, Norma   1919-
   (Nancy Kimball)

PERSONAL: Born December 23, 1919, in New Britain,

Conn.; daughter of Orrin E. (a golf course architect) and Letty E. (Lewis) Smith; married Robert A. Upson (a territorial sales manager); children: William S., Daniel W. *Education:* Attended public schools in East Northfield, Mass., and New Britain, Conn. *Home address:* Route 1, Box 681, Portland, Ore. 97231. *Agent:* Maxwell Aley Associates, 145 East 35th St., New York, N.Y. 10016.

CAREER: Writer and public speaker; has appeared on television programs. Teacher of creative writing in department of continuing education at Portland State University. Established Haystack pilot program in writing, 1969; founder and director of Denver Young Writers Workshop; co-founder, director, and teacher for Braille Teens; director of Sun Country Writer's Roundup. Vice-president of Friends of Multnomah County Library. *Member:* Denver Women's Press Club, Willamette Writers.

WRITINGS: How to Survive as a Corporate Wife, Doubleday, 1974. Author, under pseudonym, of "Nancy Kimball's Column," in *American Salesman,* 1964-75. Contributor of articles and juvenile stories to national magazines. Contributing editor of *American Salesman.*

WORK IN PROGRESS: Boat Is a Four-Letter Word; Crayfish Cookbook; Crayfish Life-Cycle.

SIDELIGHTS: Norma Upson lives on a houseboat on the Willamette River. *Avocational interests:* Natural sciences, fishing, boating, collecting and polishing gemstones, early American history, music, biography, crafts, hiking, golf, camping.

*   *   *

UPTON, L(eslie) F(rancis) S(tokes)   1931-

PERSONAL: Born December 8, 1931, in Leigh-on-Sea, Essex, England; son of L. W. S. (a barrister) and F. A. (Jesson) Upton; married Marilyn A. Stearns, February 11, 1955; children: Elizabeth, Lynn, Leslie, Jr., Colin. *Education:* St. John's College, Oxford, B.A. (honors), 1954; University of Minnesota, Ph.D., 1957. *Home:* 3185 Benbow Rd., West Vancouver, British Columbia, Canada. *Office:* Department of History, University of British Columbia, Vancouver, British Columbia, Canada V6T 1W5.

CAREER: St. John's College, Winnipeg, Manitoba, assistant professor, 1957-58, associate professor of history, 1958-64; University of British Columbia, Vancouver, assistant professor, 1964-65, associate professor, 1965-71, professor of history, 1971—. Research fellow at Charles Warren Center of Harvard University, 1968-69. *Military service:* Royal Air Force, 1950-51; became sergeant. Royal Canadian Air Force Auxiliary, 1958-64; became flight lieutenant. *Member:* Canadian Historical Association. *Awards, honors:* Canada Council fellowship, 1968-69.

WRITINGS: (Editor) *Diary and Selected Papers of Chief Justice William Smith, 1784-1793,* Champlain Society, Volume I, 1963, Volume II, 1965; (editor) *United Empire Loyalists: Men and Myths,* Copp, 1967; *The Loyal Whig: Chief Justice William Smith of New York and Quebec,* University of Toronto Press, 1968; (editor) *Revolutionary Versus Loyalist: The First American Civil War, 1774-1784,* Blaisdell, 1968; (contributor) W. L. Morton, editor, *The Shield of Achilles,* McClelland & Stewart, 1968. Contributor to history journals.

WORK IN PROGRESS: Editing *Loyalist Pamphlets of the American Revolution* and *The John Anstey Mission, 1786-1788; The Indians of Atlantic Canada.*

URIS, Dorothy

PERSONAL: Born in Brooklyn, N.Y.; married Michael Uris (deceased); children: Joseph. *Education:* Attended Cornell University and Columbia University Teachers College. *Home:* 215 East 68th St., New York, N.Y. 10021. *Agent:* Curtis Brown Ltd., 60 East 56th St., New York, N.Y. 10022.

CAREER: Began career as stage and film actress; Manhattan School of Music, New York, N.Y., instructor in English diction, 1955—; Mannes College of Music, New York, N.Y., instructor in English diction. English diction coach with Metropolitan Opera Co. and Santa Fe Opera Co. *Member:* Speech Communication Association.

WRITINGS: Everybody's Book of Better Speaking, Boosey & Hawkes, 1960; *To Sing in English,* Boosey & Hawkes, 1971; *A Woman's Voice,* Stein & Day, 1975. Contributor to journals in her field.

*   *   *

URSINI, James   1947-

PERSONAL: Born May 10, 1947, in Pittsburgh, Pa.; son of Vincent (a tailor) and Marie (Riccardelli) Ursini. *Education:* University of California at Los Angeles, A.B., 1969, M.A., 1972. *Politics:* Radical left. *Religion:* Roman Catholic. *Residence:* Woodland Hills, Calif. *Office:* Department of Communications, El Camino College, 16007 South Crenshaw Blvd., Los Angeles County, Calif. 90506.

CAREER: El Camino College, Los Angeles, Calif., instructor in communications, 1972—. *Member:* American Film Institute, Association for Educational Communications and Technology, Common Cause, Center for the Study of Democratic Institutions.

WRITINGS: The Fabulous Life and Times of Preston Sturges: An American Dreamer, Curtis Books, 1973; (with Alain Silver) *The Films of David Lean,* Leslie Frewin, 1974; (with Silver) *The Vampire Film,* A. S. Barnes, 1975; (with Silver) *Supernatural Horror in Literature and Film,* Leslie Frewin, 1975.

AVOCATIONAL INTERESTS: Politics.

*   *   *

USEEM, Michael   1942-

PERSONAL: Born November 6, 1942, in Vermillion, S.D.; son of John H. (a professor of sociology) and Ruth (a sociologist; maiden name, Hill) Useem; married Elizabeth Livingston (a sociologist), June 15, 1968; children: Jerry Voorhis, Andrea Hill. *Education:* University of Michigan, B.S., 1964; Harvard University, M.A., 1966, Ph.D., 1970. *Home:* 33 Mosman St., Newton, Mass. 02165. *Office:* Department of Sociology, Boston University, Boston, Mass. 02215.

CAREER: Harvard University, Cambridge, Mass., instructor, 1969-70, assistant professor of sociology, 1970-74; Boston University, Boston, Mass., associate professor of sociology, 1974—. Member of research advisory committee for Office of Research of American Council on Education, 1972-73. *Member:* American Sociological Association, American Political Science Association, Society for the Study of Social Problems, American Association for the Advancement of Science, Conference on Peace Research in History, Phi Beta Kappa. *Awards, honors:* U.S. Office of Education research grant, Harvard University, 1971-73; Spencer Foundation research grant, 1973.

WRITINGS: Conscription, Protest, and Social Conflict: The Life and Death of a Draft Resistance Movement, Wiley, 1973; (editor with wife, Elizabeth Useem) *The Education Establishment,* Prentice-Hall, 1974; *Protest Movements in America,* Bobbs-Merrill, 1975. Contributor to sociology journals. Associate editor of *American Sociologist,* 1975—.

WORK IN PROGRESS: Research on the relationship between the academic social sciences and the federal government.

* * *

VAID, Krishna Baldev 1927-

PERSONAL: Born July 27, 1927, in Dinga, India; son of Ishar Dass (a civil servant) and Ramrakhi Vaid; married Champa Bali, December 12, 1952; children: Rachna, Jyotsna, Urvashi (all daughters). *Education:* Panjab University, B.A. (honors), 1946, M.A., 1949; Harvard University, Ph.D., 1961. *Home:* 3 Pierrepont Ave., Potsdam, N.Y. 13676. *Agent:* Gunther Stuhlmann, 65 Irving Pl., New York, N.Y. 10003. *Office:* Department of English, State University of New York College, Potsdam, N.Y. 13676.

CAREER: Delhi University, Delhi, India, lecturer in English, 1950-62; Panjab University, Chandigarh, India, reader in English, 1962-66; State University of New York College at Potsdam, professor of English, 1966—, acting chairman of department, 1971-72, director of Star Lake Writing Conference, summers, 1967-68. Member of Indian delegation, P.E.N. International Conference, 1966; visiting professor at Case Western Reserve University, summer, 1968, and Brandeis University, 1968-69; has lectured at University of Chicago, Harvard University, University of Iowa, University of Rochester, University of Mysore, Osmania University, and Jadavpur University; consultant to (Indian) National Academy of Letters and Indian Institute of American Studies. *Awards, honors:* Smith-Mundt Fulbright fellowship, 1958-61; Rockefeller Foundation fellowship, 1959-61.

WRITINGS: Steps in Darkness, Orion Press, 1962; *Technique in the Tales of Henry James,* Harvard University Press, 1964; *Silence and Other Stories,* Interculture Associates, 1972; *Bimal in Bog,* two volumes, Interculture Associates, 1972; (translator from Hindi) Nirmal Verma, *Days of Longing,* Interculture Associates, 1972; (translator from Hindi) Srikant Varma, *Bitter Sweet Longing,* Vikas, 1975.

Books in Hindi: *Us Ka Bachpan* (title means "His Childhood"), Saraswati, 1957; *Beech Ka Darvaza* (title means "The Connecting Door"), Neelabh, 1962; *Mera Dushman* (title means "My Enemy"), Rajkamal, 1966; *Doosre Kinare Se* (title means "From the Other Shore"), Radhakrishna, 1970; *Lapata* (title means "Incognito"), Sindhu, 1973; *Bimal,* Kalpana, 1974; *Us Ke Bayan* (title means "His Statements"), Rajpal, 1974; *Nasreen,* Sambhavna, 1975.

Translator into Hindi: Samuel Beckett, *Waiting for Godot,* Radhakrishna, 1970; Beckett, *Endgame,* Radhakrishna, 1971.

Work anthologized in *Span: An Anthology of Asian and Australian Writing,* Canberra Fellowship of Writers (Canberra, Australia), 1959; *A Death in Delhi,* edited by Gordon Roadermel, University of California Press, 1972. Contributor of stories, articles, and reviews to literary journals in the United States and abroad, including *Books Abroad, Botteghe Oscure,* and *TriQuarterly.*

WORK IN PROGRESS: A play; a trilogy of short novels.

SIDELIGHTS: Vaid writes: "I have spent the most formative years of my life in India where I was born. Transplantation to U.S.A. where I now live more or less permanently has had a tremendous influence on my writing. I take it as an intense experience of a self-imposed exile. This experience has given me an insight into alienation, marginal living, transience, void, pain, and one's capacity to transcend all this. I write primarily in Hindi and am my own translator into English. In India I am a controversial figure because of my style." His work has been translated into Italian, German, Spanish, Polish, Japanese, Gujarati, and Marathi.

BIOGRAPHICAL/CRITICAL SOURCES: Vagartha (New Delhi), October, 1973.

* * *

van BUREN, Paul (Matthews) 1924-

PERSONAL: Born April 20, 1924, in Norfolk, Va.; son of Harold Sheffield and Charlotte (Matthews) van Buren; married Anne Hagopian, February 7, 1948; children: Alice, Eleanor, Philip, Thomas. *Education:* Harvard University, B.A., 1948; Episcopal Theological School, B.D., 1951; University of Basel, Th.D., 1957. *Home:* 107 Garden St., Cambridge, Mass. 02138. *Office:* Department of Religion, Temple University, Philadelphia, Pa. 19122.

CAREER: Ordained to the ministry of the Episcopal Church, 1951; minister in Detroit, Mich., 1954-57; Episcopal Theological Seminary of the Southwest, Austin, Tex., assistant professor, 1957-60, associate professor of theology, 1960-64; Temple University, Philadelphia, Pa., associate professor, 1964-66, professor of religion, 1966—, chairman of department, 1974—. Consultant to Detroit Industrial Mission, 1956-66; Jeffrey lecturer, Goucher College, 1966; Fulbright senior lecturer, Oxford University, 1967-68. *Military service:* U.S. Coast Guard Reserve, 1943; U.S. Naval Reserve, 1943-45.

MEMBER: Society for Religion in Higher Education (fellow), American Academy of Religion, National Association for the Advancement of Colored People (NAACP), American Association of University Professors, American Civil Liberties Union. *Awards, honors:* American Association of Theological Schools fellowship, 1962-63; Guggenheim fellowship, 1967-69.

WRITINGS: Christ in Our Place: The Substitutionary Character of Calvin's Doctrine of Reconciliation, Oliver & Boyd, 1957; *The Secular Meaning of the Gospel: Based on an Analysis of Its Language,* Macmillan, 1963; *Theological Explorations,* Macmillan, 1968; (contributor) Peter Vorkink, compiler, *Bonhoeffer in a World Come of Age: Essays by Paul M. van Buren and Others,* Fortress, 1968; *The Edges of Language: An Essay in the Logic of a Religion,* Macmillan, 1972; *The Mystery of Freedom,* Seabury Press, in press. Contributor of articles to scholarly journals, including *Religion in Life* and *Religious Studies.*

* * *

VANCE, Rupert B(ayless) 1899-1975

1899—August 25, 1975; American sociologist, educator, and author of books in his field. Obituaries: *New York Times,* August 26, 1975; *AB Bookman's Weekly,* December 8, 1975.

VANDENBERG, Philipp   1941-

PERSONAL: Original name Klaus D. Hartel, name legally changed in 1972; born September 20, 1941, in Breslau, Germany; son of Josef (a gynecologist) and Dorothea Hartel; married Doris Priske, 1964; children: Sascha. *Education:* Attended University of Munich, 1963-64 *Politics:* None. *Religion:* Roman Catholic. *Home:* D 8151 Baiernrain, Villa Vandenberg, Germany.

CAREER: Passauer Neue Presse (newspaper), Passau, Bavaria, local editor, 1964-67; *Abendzeitung,* Munich, Germany, news editor, 1967-69; *Quick* (magazine), Munich, Germany, editor and writer, 1969-74; *Playboy*—Germany, Munich, non-fiction editor, 1974—.

WRITINGS: Der Fluch der Pharaonen, Scherz Verlag, 1973, translation by Thomas Weyr published as *The Curse of the Pharaohs,* Lippincott, 1975; *Nofretete* (title means "Nefertiti"; biography), Scherz Verlag, 1975.

WORK IN PROGRESS: Another archaeological book about the oracles of antiquity.

SIDELIGHTS: Vandenberg's books have been published in sixteen languages, and have been published in Japan, Turkey, Brazil, Spain, Finland, Sweden, and the Netherlands.

*   *   *

VANDENBOSCH, Amry   1894-

PERSONAL: Born December 14, 1894, in Zeeland, Mich.; son of Graddus (a farmer) and Mary (Van Ekelenburg) Vandenbosch; married Mary Belle Wilcox, March 22, 1926; children: Robert, Margaret Ann (Mrs. Duane A. Meeter). *Education:* Calvin College, student, 1915-17; University of Chicago, Ph.B., 1920, Ph.D., 1926. *Politics:* Democrat. *Religion:* Presbyterian. *Home:* 149 Edgemoor Dr., Lexington, Ky. 40503.

CAREER: Pullman Free School of Manual Training, Chicago, Ill., instructor in history, 1920-23; Iowa State College (now Iowa State University), Ames, instructor in government, 1924-26; University of Kentucky, Lexington, assistant professor, 1926-27, associate professor, 1927-28, professor of political science, 1928-65, head of department, 1934-58; writer, 1965—. Member of secretariat of San Francisco United Nations Conference, 1945. Visiting professor at University of Chicago, summer, 1939, also at University of North Carolina, Centre College, and University of Tennessee; lecturer at Columbia University, 1943; director of William Andrew Patterson School of Diplomacy and International Commerce; Fulbright lecturer at University of Leiden. Member of Brookhaven Nuclear Research Center Mission to Asian Colombo Plan Countries, 1956; president of Midwest Conference of Political Scientists, 1959-60. *Military service:* U.S. Army, American Expeditionary Forces, Machine Gun Battery, 1918-19; Office of Strategic Services, 1941-42, U.S. Department of State, Postwar Planning Section, 1942-44.

MEMBER: American Society for International Law, American Political Science Association (member of executive council, 1942-45), American Association of University Professors, American Council of the Institute of Pacific Relations, Southern Political Science Association (president, 1963), Midwest Political Science Association (president, 1961-62). *Awards, honors:* Social Science Research Council fellowship, 1929-30; LL.D. from University of Kentucky, 1965, and Centre College, 1973; distinguished alumnus award from Calvin College, 1966.

WRITINGS: The Dutch Communities of Chicago, Knickerbocker Society, 1927; *The Neutrality of the Netherlands during the World War,* Eerdmans, 1927; (editor with wife, Mary Belle Vandenbosch, and J. C. Jones) *Readings in Citizenship,* Macmillan, 1932; *The Dutch East Indies: Its Government, Problems, and Politics,* Eerdmans, 1933, 3rd edition, University of California Press, 1942.

The Dutch in the Far East, University of California Press, 1943; (with Samuel J. Eldersveld) *Government of the Netherlands,* Bureau of Government Research, Department of Political Science, University of Kentucky, 1947; (editor) Thomas D. Clark and others, *The Constitution of Kentucky: Suggestions for Revision,* Bureau of Government Research, Department of Political Science, University of Kentucky, 1948; (with Willard Newton Hogan) *The United Nations: Background, Organization, Functions, Activities,* McGraw, 1952; (with Richard Butwell) *Southeast Asia among the World Powers,* University Press of Kentucky, 1957; *Dutch Foreign Policy Since 1815: A Study in Small Power Politics,* Nijhoff, 1959.

(Editor) *Some Problems of World Politics Today,* Bureau of School Service, College of Education, University of Kentucky, 1962; (with Hogan) *Toward World Order,* McGraw, 1963; (with Edgar Harry Brookes) *The City of God and the City of Man in Africa,* University Press of Kentucky, 1964; (with Butwell) *The Changing Face of Southeast Asia,* University Press of Kentucky, 1966; (with wife, M. B. Vandenbosch) *Australia Faces Southeast Asia: The Emergence of a Foreign Policy,* University Press of Kentucky, 1967; *South Africa and the World: The Foreign Policy of Apartheid,* University Press of Kentucky, 1970. Contributor to encyclopedias and to scholarly journals.

WORK IN PROGRESS: Research on southern African politics and international relations, and on the political struggle between Flemings and Walloons.

*   *   *

VAN DEUSEN, L. Marshall   1922-

PERSONAL: Born June 14, 1922, in Hudson, N.Y.; son of Leslie Marshall and Helen (Doland) Van Deusen; married Jeanie Teresa McNally, October 15, 1946 (died March, 1973); children: Charles B., Marshall, Kathleen. *Education:* Williams College, A.B. (summa cum laude), 1943; graduate study at Carnegie Institute of Technology (now Carnegie-Mellon University), 1943-44, and University of Birmingham, 1945-46; University of Pennsylvania, M.A., 1948, Ph.D., 1953. *Home:* 3060 Panorama Rd., Riverside, Calif. 92506. *Office:* Department of English, University of California, Riverside, Calif. 92502.

CAREER: University of California, Los Angeles, lecturer in English, 1950-53; Stanford University, Stanford, Calif., instructor in English, 1953-54; University of California, Riverside, assistant professor, 1954-60, associate professor, 1960-67, professor of English, 1967—, chairman of American studies, 1972—, chairman of department of English, 1975—. Fulbright lecturer at University of Oslo, 1958-59; senior lecturer and chairman of Division of Humanities at University of the West Indies, 1964-65. *Military service:* U.S. Army, Combat Engineers, 1942-46. *Member:* Modern Language Association of America.

WRITINGS: A Metaphor for the History of American Criticism, A. B. Lundequistska Bokhandeln, 1961; (contributor) Thomas M. Davis, editor, *Fourteen by Emily,* Scott, Foresman, 1964; *J. E. Spingarn,* Twayne, 1971; (contributor) J. Donald Crowley, editor, *Nathaniel Haw-*

thorne: A Collection of Criticism, McGraw, 1975; (contributor) Marcus Cunliffe, editor, American Literature Since 1900, Sphere Books, 1975. Contributor to scholarly journals.

* * *

VAN de VATE, Dwight, Jr. 1928-

PERSONAL: Born February 25, 1928, in Rochester, N.Y.; son of Dwight and Helen (Hagood) Van de Vate; married Nancy Hayes (a composer), June 9, 1952; children: Katherine, Barbara, Dwight III. Education: Wesleyan University, B.A., 1952; Yale University, M.A., 1953, Ph.D., 1956. Home: 5610 Holstan Hills Rd., Knoxville, Tenn. 37914. Office: Department of Philosophy, University of Tennessee, Knoxville, Tenn. 37916.

CAREER: University of Mississippi, Oxford, assistant professor, 1955-60, associate professor of philosophy, 1960-63; Florida State University, Tallahassee, assistant professor of philosophy, 1963-64; Memphis State University, Memphis, Tenn., associate professor, 1964-65, professor of philosophy, 1965-66; University of Tennessee, Knoxville, professor of philosophy, 1966—. Military serivce: U.S. Navy, 1946-48. Member: American Philosophical Association, Southern Society for Philosophy and Psychology (member of council, 1968-70; president, 1970).

WRITINGS: (Editor and contributor) Persons, Privacy, and Feeling, Memphis State University Press, 1970. Contributor to philosophy journals.

* * *

VAN EERDE, Katherine S(ommerlatte) 1920-

PERSONAL: Born June 17, 1920, in Terre Haute, Ind.; daughter of Ewald (a minister) and Flora (Hoff) Sommerlatte; married John A. Van Eerde (a professor of Romance languages), July 23, 1946; children: Elizabeth. Education: College of Wooster, B.A. (with honors), 1941; Yale University, M.A., 1942, Ph.D., 1945. Politics: Democrat. Religion: United Church of Christ. Home: 2423 Washington St., Allentown, Pa. 18104. Office: Department of History, Muhlenberg College, Allentown, Pa. 18104.

CAREER: Instructor in history, Scripps College, Claremont, Calif., 1944-46, Smith College, Northampton, Mass., 1946-48, Johns Hopkins University, Baltimore, Md., 1948-50; U.S. Department of State, Office of Intelligence Research, Washington, D.C., editor and reviewing officer, 1951-55; University of Rhode Island, Kingston, assistant professor of history, 1955-61; Muhlenberg College, Allentown, Pa., associate professor, 1961-66, professor of history, 1966—. Member: American Historical Association, Renaissance Society of America, Conference on British Studies, American Association of University Professors, Phi Beta Kappa. Awards, honors: Lindback Foundation teaching award, Muhlenberg College, 1968; Guggenheim fellowship, 1971-72, for research on John Ogilby; American Philosophical Society grant, 1974.

WRITINGS: (Editor with Nelvin Vos, and contributor) Muhlenberg Essays, Muhlenberg College, 1968; Wenceslaus Hollar: Delineator of His Time (monograph), University Press of Virginia, 1970; John Ogilby and the Taste of His Times, Dawson & Sons, 1976. Contributor of articles and reviews to professional journals and newspapers, including Journal of Modern History and Social Research. Assistant editor, Journal of Economic History, 1950-51.

VAN EGMOND, Peter (George) 1937-

PERSONAL: Born October 25, 1937, in Montgomery, Ala.; son of George Peter (in sales) and Lois (Everett) Van Egmond; married Dorothy McKinnie (a food service supervisor), August 17, 1958; children: Katherine Diane, Stephen. Education: Mississippi College, B.A., 1959; University of Mississippi, M.A., 1961; University of North Carolina, Ph.D., 1966. Religion: American Transcendentalist. Home: 3106 Old Largo Rd., Upper Marlboro, Md. 20870. Office: Department of English, University of Maryland, College Park, Md. 20742.

CAREER: Davidson College, Davidson, N.C., instructor in English, 1964-66; University of Maryland, College Park, assistant professor of English, 1966—. Visiting summer professor at Vanderbilt University, 1966; Fulbright-Hays lecturer at University of Graz, Austria, 1968-69. Military service: U.S. Naval Reserve, 1955-63. Member: Modern Language Association of America.

WRITINGS: (Editor and author of introduction) The Memoirs of Thomas B. Harned: Walt Whitman's Friend and Literary Executor, Transcendental, 1972; The Critical Reception of Robert Frost, G. K. Hall, 1974. Contributor of poetry and stories to Shenandoah, Laurel Review, Per/Se, and other literary journals.

WORK IN PROGRESS: A study of the work of Conrad Aiken.

AVOCATIONAL INTERESTS: Horses, vegetables, wild flowers, roses.

* * *

VAN ESS, Dorothy 1885(?)-1975

1885(?)—September 1, 1975; American missionary and author. Obituaries: Washington Post, September 5, 1975.

* * *

VAN HUSS, Wayne D(aniel) 1917-

PERSONAL: Born September 5, 1917, in Pekin, Ill.; son of John Joseph (a steamfitter) and Nellie (Hodgsen) Van Huss; married Edna Goetzke (a registered nurse), November 10, 1942; children: Terry E. (Mrs. James Golden), Randie K. (Mrs. Tom Black), Trudy J. (Mrs. Stephen Stewart). Education: Illinois State University, B.Ed., 1939; University of Illinios, M.S., 1950, Ph.D., 1953. Religion: Protestant. Home: 1727 Woodside Dr., East Lansing, Mich. 48823. Office: 109 Women's I. M., Michigan State University, East Lansing, Mich. 48824.

CAREER: Ben Funk School, Shirley, Ill., teacher of biology, 1939-41; University of Illinois, Urbana, assistant professor of physical education, 1952-53; Michigan State University, East Lansing, assistant professor, 1953-55, associate professor, 1955-56, professor of physical education, 1956—. Military service: U.S. Army, Field Artillery, 1941-42. U.S. Army Air Forces, 1942-45; became captain. Member: International Association of Sports Information (member of executive committee, 1970-75), American Physiological Society, American Association of Anatomists, American College of Sports Medicine, American Association of Health, Physical Education and Recreation, American Academy of Physical Education, New York Academy of Science.

WRITINGS: (With Henry Montoye and Herbert Olson) Longevity and Morbidity of College Athletes, Phi Epsilon Kappa, 1957; (with Olson, Roy Niemeyer, and John Friedrich) *Fitness in Modern Living*, Prentice-Hall, 1960, 2nd edition, 1969; (contributor) Warren Johnson, editor, *Science and Medicine of Exercise and Sports*, Harper, 1962, 2nd edition, 1973; (contributor) Montoye, editor, *An Introduction to Measurement in Physical Education*, Phi Epsilon Kappa, 1970; (contributor) Alfred Hubbard, editor, *Research in Health, Physical Education and Recreation*, American Association of Health, Physical Education and Recreation, 1972. Contributor of seventy research articles to scientific journals.

WORK IN PROGRESS: A text on the physiology of exercise; research papers.

* * *

VARTAN, Vartanig Garabed 1923-

PERSONAL: Born June 28, 1923, in Pasadena, Calif.; son of Garabed S. and Yeranig (Saxenian) Vartan; married Cynthia Kirk Smith, November 18, 1961; children: Kirk Spencer. *Education:* Yale University, B.A., 1948. *Home:* 14 Sutton Place S., New York, N.Y. 10022. *Agent:* Ms. Roberta Pryor, International Creative Management, 40 West 57th St., New York, N.Y. 10019.

CAREER: Reporter in Mississippi for *Laurel Leader-Call*, 1948-49, and *Tupelo Journal*, 1949-52, and for United Press in New York City, 1952-55; *New York Herald-Tribune*, New York City, financial writer, 1955-62; *Christian Science Monitor*, Boston, Mass., Wall Street columnist, 1957-62; *New York Times*, New York City, financial writer, 1963—; free-lance writer. *Military service:* U.S. Army, 1943-45.

WRITINGS: 50 Wall Street (novel), McGraw, 1968; *The Dinosaur Fund*, McGraw, 1972.

SIDELIGHTS: "[Vartan] certainly writes with a flair for the character behind the action. There's as much melodrama . . . as you'll find in other theatres of the experimentally absurd. All in all this is the best Wall St. novel I've ever read," is how Charles Poore described Vartan's first book.

* * *

VASSI, Marco 1937-

PERSONAL: Born November 6, 1937, in New York, N.Y.; son of William (a painter) and Angelina Freda Vassi; divorced. *Education:* Brooklyn College of the City University of New York, B.A., 1963. *Politics:* "Authoritarian Anarchist." *Religion:* "Audience." *Home:* 105 Hudson St., New York, N.Y. 10013. *Office: Penthouse*, 909 Third Ave., New York, N.Y. 10022.

CAREER: Writer, teacher, and editor. Co-founder of Anthos (a growth center), Raindance, Inc. (a video cooperative), and Institute for Holistic Personality Research (a therapy center). *Military service:* U.S. Air Force, 1956-60.

WRITINGS: Mind Blower, Olympia, 1970; *The Gentle Degenerates*, Olympia, 1971; *The Saline Solution*, Olympia, 1972; *The Stoned Apocalypse*, Trident, 1972; *Contours of Darkness*, Olympia, 1973; *Metaself, Mirth, and Madness*, Penthouse Press, 1975; *In Touch*, Manor, 1975. Contributor to popular magazines, including *Penthouse, Forum, Evergreen Review, Oui, Screw, Gay*, and *Village Voice*.

WORK IN PROGRESS: A screenplay from the novel *Mind Blower*.

BIOGRAPHICAL/CRITICAL SOURCES: Michael Perkins, *A Critical Review of Modern Erotic Literature*, Morrow, in press.

* * *

VAUGHAN, Denis 1920-

PERSONAL: Born November 4, 1920, in Chicago, Ill.; son of Edward Perry (a physician) and Nancy (a nurse; maiden name, McGuire) Vaughan. *Education:* University of Virginia, B.A., 1948. *Politics:* Liberal. *Religion:* None. *Home and office address:* P.O. Box 696, Amagansett, N.Y. 11930. *Agent:* Arthur Pine Associates, Inc., 1780 Broadway, New York, N.Y. 10019.

CAREER: Theatrical director and writer. Co-owner of The Store in Amagansett. *Military service:* Served in U.S. Air Force.

WRITINGS: (With Bert Greene) *The Store Cookbook*, Regnery, 1974.

WORK IN PROGRESS: Another book.

* * *

VAUGHAN, John Edmund 1935-

PERSONAL: Born November 23, 1935, in King's Norton, Birmingham, England. *Education:* Attended University of Exeter and University of Birmingham; University of Bristol, M.A., 1960. *Office:* Library, School and Institute of Education, University of Liverpool, P.O. Box 147, Liverpool L69 3BX, England.

CAREER: University of Liverpool, Liverpool, England, assistant librarian in faculty of arts, 1960-62, assistant librarian, 1962-64, tutor librarian in Institute of Education, 1964-66, in Institute and School of Education, 1966—. *Member:* Librarians of Institutes and Schools of Education (chairman, 1975), Victorian Society (past vice-chairman of Liverpool regional group).

WRITINGS: The English Guide Book, circa 1780-1870: An Illustrated History, David & Charles, 1974.

WORK IN PROGRESS: Continuing research on the history of circulating libraries in England, 1800-1850.

* * *

VAUGHN, Robert (Francis) 1932-

PERSONAL: Born November 22, 1932, in New York, N.Y.; son of (Gerald) Walter (an actor) and Marcella Frances (an actress; maiden name, Gaudel) Vaughn. *Education:* Los Angeles State College of Applied Arts and Sciences (now California State University), B.S., 1956; University of Southern California, M.A., 1960, Ph.D., 1970. *Politics:* Democrat. *Religion:* Roman Catholic. *Address:* c/o Creative Management Associates, 8899 Beverly Blvd., Hollywood, Calif. 90048.

CAREER: Began as child actor on radio in the 1940's; *Minneapolis Star-Journal*, Minneapolis, Minn., sports reporter in the early 1950's; full-time actor on television, in motion pictures, and on stage since the late 1950's. *Military service:* U.S. Army, 1956-57. *Member:* American Academy of Political and Social Sciences. *Awards, honors:* Nominated for best supporting actor award, 1960, by the Academy of Motion Picture Arts and Sciences for his role in "The Young Philadelphians."

WRITINGS: Only Victims: A Study of Show Business Blacklisting, foreword by George McGovern, Putnam, 1972.

SIDELIGHTS: Vaughn gained national acclaim in the role of Napoleon Solo in the television series, "The Man from U.N.C.L.E.," in the mid-1960's. His motion pictures include "The Young Philadelphians," Warner Bros., 1959, "The Magnificent Seven," United Artists, 1960, and "Bullitt," Warner Bros., 1968, and stage performances include the title role of *Hamlet* at Pasadena Playhouse, Pasadena, Calif., 1964. Also politically active, Vaughn is a former chairman of registration and of the Speaker's Bureau of the Southern California Democratic Central Committee.

*　　*　　*

VECSEY, George 1939-

PERSONAL: Surname is pronounced Vessy; born July 4, 1939, in Jamaica, N.Y.; son of George (a copy editor with Associated Press) and May (a society editor; maiden name, Spencer) Vecsey; married Marianne Graham (an artist and teacher), October 1, 1960; children: Laura, Corinna, David. *Education:* Hofstra College (now Hofstra University), B.A., 1960. *Religion:* Christian. *Home:* 9 Chelsea Dr., Port Washington, Long Island, N.Y. 11050. *Agent:* Philip Spitzer, 111-25 76th Ave., Forest Hills, N.Y. 11375.

CAREER: Newsday, Garden City, Long Island, N.Y., sportswriter, 1956-68; *New York Times,* New York, N.Y., sportswriter, 1968-70, Appalachian correspondent, based in Louisville, Ky., 1970-72, Long Island correspondent, based in Port Washington, 1972—.

WRITINGS: Baseball's Most Valuable Players, Random House, 1966; (with John Biever) *Young Sports Photographer With the Green Bay Packers,* Norton, 1969; *The Baseball Life of Sandy Koufax,* Scholastic Book Services, 1969; *Joy in Mudville: Being a Complete Account of the Unparalled History of the New York Mets from Their Most Perturbed Beginnings to Their Amazing Rise to Glory and Renown,* McCall Publishing, 1970; *Pro Basketball Champions,* Scholastic Book Services, 1970; *The Harlem Globetrotters,* Scholastic Book Services, 1971; *Frazier/Ali,* Scholastic Book Services, 1972; *One Sunset a Week: The Story of a Coal Miner,* Saturday Review Press, 1974; (editor) *The Way It Was,* McGraw, 1974; (with wife, Marianne Vecsey) *The Bermuda Triangle: Fact or Fiction?,* Macmillan, 1975; (with Loretta Lynn) *Coal Miner's Daughter,* Geis, in press.

SIDELIGHTS: Vecsey writes: "From age 21 to 31, I travelled around the country, covering the New York Mets and Yankees, meeting interesting people like Casey Stengel and Bill Russell, seeing all the great cities I had dreamed about. In 1970, I decided I had seen enough games for a while—it was time to learn about other people. So I became a correspondent for *New York Times,* based in Louisville, Kentucky. I was privileged to meet coal miners, farmers, small-town people in Appalachia and the South. They were two of the best years in this city boy's life. . . ."

Vecsey continues to say that some of his best adventures have come while travelling—"chatting in an old country store in Tennessee, talking politics with an old soldier in Italy, poking around villages in New England. I hope to write about different parts of the world in my future books.

"My favorite writers are Thomas Wolfe, Charles Dickens and Joyce Carol Oates. My children *adore* the work of Louise Fitzhugh and Laura Ingalls Wilder."

AVOCATIONAL INTERESTS: Bicycling, fishing, swimming, travel.

VENTURI, Robert 1925-

PERSONAL: Born June 25, 1925, in Philadelphia, Pa.; son of Robert Charles and Vanna (Lanzetta) Venturi; married Denise Lakofski Scott Brown, July 23, 1967; children: James Charles. *Education:* Princeton University, A.B. (summa cum laude), 1947, M.F.A., 1950. *Religion:* Society of Friends. *Home:* 6904 Wissahickon Ave., Philadelphia, Pa. 19119. *Office:* 333 South 16th St., Philadelphia, Pa. 19102.

CAREER: Architect. Designer for Eero Saarinen & Associates, Bloomfield Hills, Mich., 1950-52, and Louis I. Kahn, Philadelphia, Pa., 1956-57; partner in architectural firms of Venturi, Cope and Lippincott, 1958-60, Venturi and Short, 1960-64, and Venturi and Rauch, 1964—, all Philadelphia, Pa. Instructor then associate professor of architecture at University of Pennsylvania, 1957-64; U.S. State Department visiting expert to the U.S.S.R., 1965; Charlotte Shepherd Davenport Professor, Yale University, 1965-69; visiting professor, Rice University, 1969; trustee of American Academy in Rome, 1967-72. *Member:* American Institute of Architects, Phi Beta Kappa. *Awards, honors:* American Academy in Rome fellowship, 1954-56; Graham Foundation research grant, 1962.

WRITINGS: Complexity and Contradiction in Architecture, Museum of Modern Art, 1966; (with others) *Learning from Las Vegas,* M.I.T. Press, 1972. Contributor of articles to professional journals.

WORK IN PROGRESS: Learning from Levittown, with Denise Scott Brown and Virginia Carol.

*　　*　　*

VERDUIN, Leonard 1897-

PERSONAL: Born March 9, 1897, in Cook County, Ill.; son of Cornelius (a farmer) and Aartje (Swets) Verduin; married Hattie Timmermans, March 5, 1918; children: Arthur, Thelma (Mrs. Wendell Grigsby), Calvin, Luella (Mrs. John Slagter), Ronald. *Education:* Calvin College, A.B., 1926; Calvin Seminary, Th.B., 1929; University of Michigan, A.M., 1945.

CAREER: Ordained minister of Christian Reformed Church, 1929; pastor of church in Corsica, S.D., 1929-41; Campus Chapel, Ann Arbor, Mich., director, 1941-62. Leader of exchange program between the United States and South Africa, 1966. *Awards, honors:* Fulbright grant for research in Holland and Belgium, 1950.

WRITINGS: Toward a Theistic Creationism, Baker Book, 1956; (translator) *The Complete Writing of Menno Simons,* Herald Press, 1956; (contributor) K. A. Strand, editor, *The Dawn of Modern Civilization* (festschrift), Edwards Letter Shop, 1962, 2nd edition, 1964; *The Reformers and Their Stepchildren,* Eerdmans, 1964; *Somewhat Less Than God,* Eerdmans, 1970; *The Anatomy of a Hybrid,* Eerdmans, 1976. Contributor to religious magazines.

SIDELIGHTS: Verduin speaks Dutch, German, Afrikaans, and has studied Latin, Greek, and French.

*　　*　　*

VERHOEVEN, Corn(elius) 1928-

PERSONAL: Born February 2, 1928, in Udenhout, Netherlands; son of Johannes (a farmer) and Johanna Verhoeven; married Janine Van de Kamp (a teacher), July 10, 1965. *Education:* University Nymegen, Ph.D., 1956. *Home:* Flaas 5, Den Dungen, Netherlands.

CAREER: Jeroen Bosch College, s.Hertogenbosch, Netherlands, teacher of Greek and Latin, 1955—. *Member:* Maatschappy der Nederlandse Letterkunde. *Awards, honors:* Anne Frank Prize from Dutch Government, 1964.

WRITINGS: Symboliek van de Voet (title means "The Symbolism of the Foot"), Van Gorcum, 1957; *Symboliek van de Sluier* (title means "The Symbolism of the Veil"), Standaard, 1961; *Rondom de Leegte* (title means "Around Emptiness"), Ambo, 1965; *Het grote gebeuren* (title means "The Great Event"), Ambo, 1966; *Tegen het geweld* (title means "Against Violence"), Ambo, 1967; *Inleiding tot de verwondering,* Ambo, 1967, translation by Mary Foran published as *The Philosophy of Wonder,* Macmillan, 1972; *Omzien naar het heden: De mythe van de vooruitgang* (title means "Look Back at the Present"), Ambo, 1968; *Afscheid van Brabant?* (title means "A Farewell to Brabant?"), Ambo, 1968; *Voor eigen gebruik* (title means "For the Use of Myself"), Ambo, 1969; (with Frederik Jacobus Johannes Buytendijk) *Taal en gezondheid* (title means "Language and Health"), Spectrum, 1969.

Bijna niets (title means "Hardly Anything"), Ambo, 1970; (with Cas Eijsbouts) *Zakelijkheid en ethiek* (title means "Facts and Ethics"), Ambo, 1971; *Het Leedwezen: Beschouwingen over troost en verdriet, leven en dood* (title means "Mourning: Essays About Consolation and Sorrow"), Ambo, 1971; *Het gewicht van de Buitenstaander* (title means "The Importance of the Outsider"), Ambo, 1972; *Het axioma van Geulincx* (title means "The Axiom of Geulincx"), Ambo, 1973; *Parafilosofen* (title means "Paraphilosophers"), Ambo, 1974; *De Resten van het vaderschap* (title means "The Rests of Fatherhood"), Ambo, 1975; *Een Vogeltje in myn buik* (title means "A Little Bird in My Belly"), Ambo, 1976.

Weekly columnist, 1966—; editor of *Raam* literary magazine.

* * *

VICKER, Ray 1917-

PERSONAL: Born August 27, 1917, in Amherst, Wis.; son of Joseph John and Mary (Young) Vicker; married Margaret Ella Leach (a writer and photographer), February 23, 1944. *Education:* Attended Wisconsin State University, Stevens Point, 1934, Los Angeles City College, 1940-41, and Northwestern University, 1947-49. *Religion:* Roman Catholic. *Home:* 22 Roebuck House, Palace St., London S.W.1, England. *Agent:* Paul R. Reynolds, Inc., 12 East 41st St., New York, N.Y. 10017. *Office: Wall Street Journal,* New Printing House Sq., Gray's Inn Rd., London WC1X 8EZ, England.

CAREER: Chicago Journal of Commerce, Chicago, Ill., automobile editor, 1946-50; *Wall Street Journal,* New York, N.Y., reporter and news editor in Chicago, 1950-59, European editor from London, 1960-75, senior international editor in London, 1975—. *Military service:* U.S. Merchant Marine, 1941-45. *Member:* Society of Automotive Engineers, Overseas Press Club, Adventurers Club, Sigma Delta Chi. *Awards, honors:* Outstanding reporting award from Chicago Newspaper Guild, 1959; E. W. Fairchild Award from Overseas Press Club, 1963 and 1967, for best business reporting abroad; honorable mention from Overseas Press Club, 1965.

WRITINGS: How an Election Was Won, Regnery, 1962; *Those Swiss Money Men,* Scribner, 1973; *Kingdom of Oil,* Scribner, 1974; *Realms of Oil,* Scribner, 1975; *This Hungry World,* Scribner, 1975. Contributor of more than two hundred articles and stories to popular magazines.

WORK IN PROGRESS: The Waterbake Affair, a novel.

AVOCATIONAL INTERESTS: Travel, fishing, opera (especially Puccini and Verdi), music (plays violin, amateur member of symphony), archaeology, work.

* * *

VILKITIS, James R(ichard) 1941-

PERSONAL: Born October 31, 1941, in Rush, Pa.; son of Joseph and Kathryn Ann (an office worker; maiden name, Fetchkowsky) Vilkitis. *Education:* Michigan State University, B.S., 1965; University of Idaho, M.S., 1968; University of Massachusetts, Ph.D., 1970, postdoctoral study, 1974. *Home address:* R.F.D. 2, West Pelham Rd., Amherst, Mass. 01002. *Office address:* Carlozzi, Sinton & Vilkitis, Inc., P.O. Box 831, Amherst, Mass. 01002.

CAREER: Research Planning and Design Associates, Amherst, Mass., consulting biostatistician, 1969-70; Department of Inland Fisheries and Game, Bangor, Maine, special big game project leader, 1970-71; University of Massachusetts, Amherst, lecturer in ecology and conservation, 1971—. Vice-president of Total Environment Group; principal of Carlozzi, Sinton & Vilkitis, Inc. (resource planners). Research associate of Institute for Man and the Environment, 1973-74. *Member:* Wildlife Society, Project Management Institute, Northeast Deer Study Group, Kung Fu Academy, Phi Sigma, Xi Sigma Pi.

WRITINGS: Fish Cookery, Stephen Greene Press, 1974; *Management Model for Terrestrial Wildlife Based on Energy Relationships* (booklet), Water Resources Research Center, University of Massachusetts, 1973. Contributor to *Northeast Handbook of Shrubs and Vines* and to professional journals.

WORK IN PROGRESS: Plants, Wildlife, and You (tentative title); *Vegetation of North America* (tentative title), for the layman; articles on fly fishing and big game poaching; developing new techniques for analyzing terrestrial ecosystems; conducting studies of soil dredging on the terrestrial ecosystem; research on the effects of dam construction on diversity of vegetative species; economic impact analyses of vegetation and wildlife.

SIDELIGHTS: Vilkitis feels that "proper planning and management of . . . natural resources . . . can mitigate most of the natural and social problems that exist in the living environments" despite the fact that natural resources are "as in the past, being overused and abused." He and his consulting firm work on the principle: "Nature can survive in harmony with man."

* * *

VINTON, Eleanor W(inthrop) 1899-

PERSONAL: Born July 25, 1899, in Stoneham, Mass.; daughter of Clarence D. and Annie M. (Downs) Vinton. *Education:* Attended Concord Business College, 1918. *Politics:* Republican. *Religion:* Episcopalian. *Home:* 8 Humphrey St., Concord, N.H. 03301.

CAREER: Clerk in Apple Tree Book Shop, 1929-52; practical nurse in private homes, 1955-65. *Member:* Western World Haiku Society, Massachusetts State Poetry Society (honorary member), Poetry Society of New Hampshire (charter member), Stratford Shakespeare Club (president, 1966-67). *Awards, honors:* New Hampshire Woman's Club poetry prizes, 1938, 1968, and 1969; Poetry Society of New Hampshire, Recchia Medal, 1965, prizes, 1966, 1971, and 1974; appointed Poet Laureate of New Hampshire by Governor Peterson, 1972; Massachusetts State Poetry Society prize, 1974; and other prizes.

WRITINGS: (Editor and contributor) *An Anthology of New Hampshire Poetry,* New Hampshire Federation of Women's Clubs, 1938; *Sounding Piquant Verses* (poems), Falmouth, 1940; *On the Contoocook* (poems), William Bauhan, 1974. Contributor of poems to numerous newspapers, magazines, and journals, including *Christian Science Monitor, Life, Town and Country, Ladies' Home Journal,* and *New Hampshire Troubadour.*

WORK IN PROGRESS: A collection of light verse.

SIDELIGHTS: Eleanor Vinton helped form a small group of writers in Concord, New Hampshire, in the late nineteen-twenties.

BIOGRAPHICAL/CRITICAL SOURCES: Concord Monitor, August 9, 1972; *Boston Globe,* August 10, 1972, November 25, 1973; *Manchester Union Leader,* October 23, 1972; *Norwalk Hour,* November 3, 1973; *New Hampshire Sunday News,* November 25, 1973.

* * *

VIOLA, Herman J(oseph) 1938-

PERSONAL: Born February 24, 1938, in Chicago, Ill.; son of Joseph (a carpenter) and Mary (Incollingo) Viola; married Susan Bennett (a librarian), June 13, 1964; children: Joseph, Paul, Peter. *Education:* Marquette University, B.A., 1960, M.A., 1964; Indiana University, Ph.D., 1970. *Office:* National Anthropological Archives, Smithsonian Institution, Washington, D.C. 20560.

CAREER: National Archives, Washington, D.C., archivist, 1966-68; *Prologue: Journal of the National Archives,* Washington, D.C., founding editor, 1968-72; Smithsonian Institution, National Anthropological Archives, Washington, D.C., director, 1972—. *Military service:* U.S. Navy, 1962-64. *Member:* Society of American Archivists, Ethnohistory Association, Organization of American Historians, American Historical Association, Western History Association.

WRITINGS: Thomas L. McKenney: Architect of America's Early Indian Policy, 1816-1830, Swallow Press, 1974; *The American Indian Portraits of Charles Bird King,* Smithsonian Institution, in press.

WORK IN PROGRESS: A History of Indian Visitors to Washington, completion expected in 1977.

* * *

VLOYANTES, John P. 1918-

PERSONAL: Born November 22, 1918, in Jersey City, N.J.; married Gloria Simmons (an executive secretary); children: Jane (Mrs. Miguel Ponce). *Education:* Western State College of Colorado, B.S., 1943; University of Utah, M.S., 1949, Ph.D., 1954. *Politics:* Liberal Democrat. *Religion:* Unitarian-Universalist. *Home:* 807 Whedbee St., Fort Collins, Colo. 80521. *Office:* Department of Political Science, Colorado State University, Fort Collins, Colo. 80521.

CAREER: Fulbright professor of political science in the Netherlands, 1950-51; Pacific University, Forest Grove, Ore., associate professor of political science, 1954-64; University of Wyoming, Laramie, associate professor of political science, 1964-65; Colorado State University, Fort Collins, associate professor of political science, 1965—. *Member:* International Studies Association (president of

Western Division, 1970-71), American Political Science Association, Western Political Science Association.

WRITINGS: Spheres of Influence: A Framework for Analysis (monograph), Institute of Government Research, University of Arizona, 1970; *Silk Glove Hegemony, Finnish-Soviet Relations, 1944-1974: A Case Study of the Theory of the Soft Sphere of Influence,* Kent State University Press, 1975. Contributor to political science journals.

WORK IN PROGRESS: Spheres of Influence and World War Two Diplomacy; research on inter-nation influence between the Soviet Union and Finland.

SIDELIGHTS: Vloyantes writes: "I hope to open the field of systematic and theoretical analysis of spheres of influence in international directions."

* * *

VOGEL, Linda Jane 1940-

PERSONAL: Born February 12, 1940, in Topeka, Kan.; daughter of Samuel P. and Gladys M. (Cornelius) Baker; married Dwight W. Vogel (a professor), June 14, 1959; children: Peter Jonathan, Kristin Deborah. *Education:* Boston University, B.S., 1962; Andover Newton Theological School, M.R.E. (cum laude), 1964; further study at University of Nebraska. *Religion:* United Methodist. *Office:* Department of Religion, Westmar College, LeMars, Iowa 51031.

CAREER: Westmar College, LeMars, Iowa, instructor in religion, 1965—. Director of Christian Education of United Methodist Church, Iowa Conference, 1971—. *Member:* League of Women Voters (president of LeMars chapter, 1967-71), Religious Education Association, Gerontological Society, College Theology Society. *Awards, honors:* Institute for Ecumenical and Cultural Research associate fellow at St. John's University, Collegeville, Minn., 1972-73.

WRITINGS: Helping a Child Understand Death, Fortress, 1975.

WORK IN PROGRESS: Research on marriage and on aging.

* * *

VOGET, Fred W. 1913-

PERSONAL: Born February 12, 1913, in Salem, Ore.; son of F. A. (a lumberman) and Faye (Isham) Voget; married Mary K. Mee (a teacher), May, 1942; children: Antoinette, Jane, Colleen. *Education:* Reed College, student, 1931-33; University of Oregon, B.A., 1936; Yale University, Ph.D., 1948. *Home:* 133 West Lake Dr., Edwardsville, Ill. 62025. *Office:* Department of Anthropology, Southern Illinois University, Edwardsville, Ill. 62025.

CAREER: University of Nebraska, Lincoln, instructor in anthropology, 1947-48; McGill University, Montreal, Quebec, assistant professor of anthropology, 1948-52; University of Arkansas, Fayetteville, associate professor, 1952-56, professor of anthropology, 1956-61; University of Toronto, professor of anthropology, 1961-64; Southern Illinois University, Edwardsville, professor of anthropology, 1965—. Visiting professor, University of Toronto, 1959. *Military service:* U.S. Army, 1942-46; served in Europe; became sergeant major. *Member:* American Anthropological Association (fellow), Society for Applied Anthropology (fellow; member of executive committee), Current Anthropology (fellow), Society for American Archaeology, American Ethnological Society. *Awards, honors:* Canada Council grant, 1964-65; Fulbright award, 1971.

WRITINGS: (Contributor) Bernard Siegel, editor, *Biennial Review of Anthropology,* Stanford University Press, 1963; (contributor) Ward Goodenough, editor, *Explorations in Cultural Anthropology,* McGraw, 1964; *Osage Indians: Osage Research Project,* Volume I, Garland Publishing, 1973; *A History of Ethnology,* Holt, 1975. Editor, "American Indians and Their Development," special issue of *Human* Organization, 1961-62. Contributor to anthropology journals.

WORK IN PROGRESS: Research on Shoshone and Crow cultures, and on Indian society and culture in general.

* * *

VOLLERT, Cyril (Oscar) 1901-

PERSONAL: Born June 15, 1901, in Milwaukee, Wis.; son of Oscar Joseph (a theatrical manager) and Amalia (Steinberg) Vollert. *Education:* Marquette University, B.A., 1924; St. Louis University, M.A., 1927; Gregorian University, Ph.D., 1929, S.T.D., 1939; St. Mary's College, St. Marys, Kan., S.T.L., 1936. *Politics:* Independent. *Home:* 1404 West Wisconsin Ave., Milwaukee, Wis. 53233. *Office:* Department of Theology, Marquette University, 1303 West Wisconsin Ave., Milwaukee, Wis. 53233.

CAREER: Entered Society of Jesus (Jesuits), 1924, ordained Roman Catholic priest, 1936; Marquette University, Milwaukee, Wis., instructor in classical antiquity, 1927-29; St. Louis University, St. Louis, Mo., instructor, 1939-43, assistant professor, 1943-48, associate professor, 1948-55, professor of theology, 1955-68, dean of School of Divinity, 1940-60; Marquette University, Milwaukee, professor of theology, 1968—. Guest lecturer at Gregorian University, 1948-49.

MEMBER: National Catholic Educational Association, Catholic Theological Society of America, Mariological Society of America (president, 1954-56), Jesuit Education Association. *Awards, honors:* Mariological Society of America award, 1956; Cardinal Spellman Award for Theology from Catholic Theological Society of America, 1961.

WRITINGS: The Doctrine of Hervaeus Natalis on Primitive Justice and Original Sin, Gregorian University Press, 1947; *Francis Suarez on the Various Kinds of Distinctions,* Marquette University Press, 1947; *Thomas Aquinas on the Eternity of the World,* Marquette University Press, 1964; *A Theology of Mary,* Herder & Herder, 1965.

Translator: Matthias Joseph Scheeben, *Mysteries of Christianity,* Herder Book Co., 1946; S. Thomas Aquinas, *Compendium of Theology,* Herder Book Co., 1947; Eugenio Zolli, *The Nazarene,* Herder Book Co., 1950; Emile Mersch, *The Theology of the Mystical Body,* Herder Book Co., 1951; Maurice de la Taille, *The Hypostatic Union and Created Actuation by Uncreated Grace,* West Baden College, 1952; Scheeben, *Nature and Grace,* Herder Book Co., 1954.

Contributor of more than seventy articles to theology journals.

WORK IN PROGRESS: Research on the sacerdotal character in tradition and on a new approach to economic theology.

SIDELIGHTS: Vollert reads classical Greek and Latin, German, French, Italian, Spanish, and Dutch.

* * *

WADDINGTON, C(onrad) H(al) 1905-1975

November 8, 1905—September 26, 1975; British geneticist and author. Obituaries: *New York Times,* September 29, 1975; *Current Biography,* November, 1975; *AB Bookman's Weekly,* December 1, 1975. (See index for previous *CA* sketch)

* * *

WADE, Rex A(rvin) 1936-

PERSONAL: Born October 9, 1936, in Piedmont, Kan.; son of Herman F. Wade (a factory foreman) and Vola (a teaching aide; maiden name, Johnson) Wade Hotvedt; married Beryl Schreiber, August 25, 1957; children: three. *Education:* Southwestern College, Winfield, Kan., B.A., 1958; University of Nebraska, M.A., 1960, Ph.D., 1963. *Home:* 285 Ilikaa Pl., Kailua, Hawaii 96734. *Office:* Department of History, University of Hawaii, Honolulu, Hawaii 96822.

CAREER: University of Nebraska, Lincoln, instructor in history, 1963; Wisconsin State University, La Crosse, assistant professor, 1963-65, associate professor, 1965-66, professor of history, 1966-68; University of Hawaii, Honolulu, professor of history, 1968—. Visiting professor at University of North Carolina, 1971. *Member:* American Historical Association, American Association for the Advancement of Slavic Studies. *Awards, honors:* National Endowment for the Humanities grant, summers, 1968 and 1972; American Philosophical Society grant, 1970; Fulbright grant to Finland, 1972; American Council of Learned Societies grant, 1974-75; International Research and Exchange Board (IREX) grant, 1975.

WRITINGS: The Russian Search for Peace, February to October, 1917, Stanford University Press, 1969. Contributor to professional journals.

WORK IN PROGRESS: A book on the Red Guard and spontaneity in the Russian Revolution.

SIDELIGHTS: Wade has conducted studies in the Soviet Union. *Avocational interests:* Potter.

* * *

WADEPUHL, Walter 1895-

PERSONAL: Born December 29, 1895, in Berlin, Germany; came to United States, 1910, naturalized citizen, 1916; son of Otto (an artist) and Wanda (Weiher) Wadepuhl; married Marguerite Mueller, 1922 (died, 1926); married Berniece A. Brown, April 16, 1930. *Education:* City College (now of the City University of New York), A.B., 1918; Columbia University, A.M., 1919; University of Wisconsin, Ph.D., 1921. *Politics:* "No political connections." *Religion:* Evangelical. *Home and office:* 3884 Carnation Circle N., Palm Beach Gardens, Fla. 33410.

CAREER: University of Pittsburgh, Pittsburgh, Pa., instructor in German, 1921-22; University of Illinois, Urbana, associate, 1922-26; West Virginia University, Morgantown, assistant professor, 1926-35, associate professor of German, 1935-38; Elmhurst College, Elmhurst, Ill., professor of German, 1946-65, professor emeritus, 1965—, head of department of languages and comparative literatures, 1946-65. Visiting professor, City College (now of the City University of New York), 1935-38; distinguished visiting professor, Florida Atlantic University, 1965-66. *Member:* Modern Language Association of America, American Association of Teachers of German, German Goethe Society (Weimar, Germany). *Awards, honors:* American Council of Learned Societies fellowships, 1930-31, 1933, 1935, and 1973.

WRITINGS: Goethes Stellung zur franzoesischen Romantik, [Berlin], 1924; (with B. Q. Morgan) *Minimum Standard German Vocabulary*, Crofts, 1934; *Goethe's Interest in the New World*, Frommann (Jena, Germany), 1934, reprinted, Haskell House, 1973; *Heine-Studien*, Arion-Verlag (Weimar, Germany), 1956; *The Ancient Maya and Their Culture*, Seeman-Verlag (Leipzig, Germany), 1964; *Basic German Grammar and Vocabulary*, Florida Atlantic University, 1965; *Heinrich Heine: Sein Leben und seine Werke*, Boehlau-Verlag (Cologne, Germany), 1974.

WORK IN PROGRESS: Two Books, *Aaron Burr in Weimar, Germany* and *The First Continental Criticism of American Literature, 1824-30;* research on the contemplated founding of a Prussian colony in Texas when it was a Mexican state.

* * *

WAGNER, Francis S(tephen) 1911-

PERSONAL: Born February 28, 1911, in Krupina, Austria-Hungary (now Czechoslovakia), came to United States, 1949, became U.S. citizen, 1956; son of Ferenc (a restaurateur) and Maria (Miko) Wagner; married Irene Trefny (a bank teller), February 2, 1947; children: Christina Maria Teresa. *Education:* University of Szeged, Hungary, high school teacher's diploma (summa cum laude), 1935, college teacher's diploma (summa cum laude), 1937, Ph.D. (summa cum laude), 1940. *Religion:* Roman Catholic. *Home:* 4610 Franklin St., Kensington, Md. 20795. *Office:* Library of Congress, Washington, D.C.

CAREER: Budapest State College, Budapest, Hungary, professor of history and of Hungarian and Slavic languages, 1938-45; Ministry of Foreign Affairs, Budapest, Hungary, head of Czechoslovak division, 1945-46; Hungarian Consulate General, Bratislava, Czechoslovakia, consul general, 1946-48; Library of Congress, Washington, D.C., staff member of East European accessions index project, 1953-61, of Cyrillic bibliography project, 1962-65, of subject cataloging division, 1965—. *Member:* International Platform Association, American Historical Association, American Studies Association, Helicon Society (Toronto, Ontario), Philosophy Club (Washington, D.C.), Civil War Round Table of the District of Columbia, Harry S. Truman Library Institute for National and International Affairs (honorary fellow).

WRITINGS: A csehszlovak nacionalizmus tortenetirasa (title means "Historiography of Czechoslovak Nationalism"), Tortenetiras, 1938; *Citanka* (title means "Primer"), Egyetemi Nyomda, 1939; *A szlovak nacionalizmus elso korszaka* (title means "First Period of Slovak Nationalism"), Ferenc Jozsef Tudomanyegyetem, 1940; *Cultural Revolution in East Europe*, Danubian Research Service, 1955; *A magyar tortenetiras uj utjai* (title means "New Ways of Hungarian Historiography"), privately printed, 1956; *Szechenyi and the Nationality Problem in the Hapsburg Empire*, privately printed, 1960; (editor and author of introduction) *The Hungarian Revolution in Perspective*, Freedom Fighters Memorial Foundation, 1967; (editor) *Toward a New Central Europe: A Symposium on the Problems of the Danubian Nations*, Danubian Press, 1970.

Contributor: *Guide to Historical Literature*, American Historical Association, 1961; Eric H. Boehm, editor, *Historical Periodicals: An Annotated World List of Historical and Related Serial Publications*, Clio Press, 1961; Boris V. Kit and Frederick I. Ordway, editors, *U.S.S.R. Space Program: Manpower, Training, and Research Developments,*

Department of Physics and Astronomy, University of Maryland, 1964; Thomas T. Taylor, editor, *Soviet Foreign Relations and World Communism: A Selected, Annotated Bibliography of 7,000 Books in Thirty Languages*, Princeton University Press, 1965; Eugene P. Wigner, editor, *Survival and the Bomb: Methods of Civil Defense*, Indiana University Press, 1969; Paul L. Horecky, editor, *East Central Europe: A Guide to Basic Publications*, University of California Press, 1969.

Contributor to *Collier's Encyclopedia*. Contributor of over 220 articles in six languages to professional journals and magazines. Editor of *Studies for a New Central Europe*, Volume 3, number 1, 1972; consulting editor, *Historical Abstracts*, 1955, *America: History and Life*, 1965—; member of editorial board, *Foreign Areas Survey*, 1965-72; member of advisory board, *Historical Abstracts*, 1971—.

WORK IN PROGRESS: Hungarian Contributions to American and World Culture, publication expected in late 1976; a world guide to nationality and racial problems including a bibliography; *U.S. Foreign Prestige, 1776—;* studies in ethnic minorities in the United States and the concept of the American nation, historical knowledge and dialectical materialism, the diplomatic history of World War II, and global analysis of the concept of nationalism.

SIDELIGHTS: Wagner knows, in order of proficiency, Hungarian, Slovak, Czech, German, Russian, Polish, Serbo-Croatian, Bulgarian, French, Slovenian, and Latin. *Avocational interests:* Research, publishing, lecturing, music, sports (chiefly walking and gymnastics).

* * *

WAHLOO, Per 1926-1975
(Peter Wahloo)

PERSONAL: Born August 5, 1926, in Gothenburg, Sweden; son of Waldemar and Karin Helena (Svensson) Wahloo; married Maj Sjoewall (a writer), 1962; children: Tetz, Jens. *Education:* Attended University of Lund, 1946. *Residence:* Malmoe, Sweden.

CAREER: Worked for several magazines and newspapers in Sweden, until becoming full-time novelist in 1961. *Awards, honors:* Edgar Allan Poe Award for best mystery novel from Mystery Writers of America, 1971, and Gran Giallo Citta di Cattolica, 1973, both for *The Laughing Policeman.*

WRITINGS—All novels, except as noted; all published by Norstedt in Stockholm, except as noted: *Himmelsgeten*, 1959, published as *Hoevdingen*, 1967; *Vinden och regnet*, 1961; *Lastbilen*, 1962, translation by Joan Tate published, under name Peter Wahloo, as *The Lorry*, M. Joseph, 1968, published as *A Necessary Action*, Pantheon, 1969; *Uppdraget*, 1963, translation by Joan Tate published, under name Peter Wahloo, as *The Assignment*, M. Joseph, 1965, Knopf, 1966; *Mord paa 31: A vaaningen*, 1964, translation by Joan Tate published, under name Peter Wahloo, as *Murder on the 31st Floor*, M. Joseph, 1966, published as *The Thirty-First Floor*, Knopf, 1967; *Det vaexer inga rosor paa Odenplan* (short stories, 1957-63), 1964; *Generalerna*, 1965, translation by Joan Tate published as *The Generals*, Pantheon, 1974; *Staalspraanget*, 1968, translation by Joan Tate published, under name Peter Wahloo, as *The Steel Spring*, Delacorte, 1970.

Martin Beck detective series; all with wife, Maj Sjoewall; all published by Norstedt, except as noted: *Roseanna*, 1965, translation by Lois Roth published under same title,

Pantheon, 1967; *Mannen som gick upp i roek,* 1966, translation by Joan Tate published as *The Man Who Went Up in Smoke,* Pantheon, 1969; *Mannen paa balkongen,* 1967, translation by Alan Blair published as *The Man on the Balcony,* Pantheon, 1968; *Den skrattande polisen,* 1968, translation by Alan Blair published as *The Laughing Policeman,* Pantheon, 1970; *Brandbilen som foersvann,* 1969, translation by Joan Tate published as *The Fire Engine that Disappeared,* Pantheon, 1970; *Polis, polis, potatismos!,* 1970, translation by Amy Knoespel and Ken Knoespel published as *Murder at the Savoy,* Pantheon, 1971; *Den Vedervaerdige mannen fraan Saeffle,* 1971, translation by Thomas Teal published as *The Abominable Man,* Pantheon, 1972; *Det slutna rummet,* 1972, translation by Paul Britten Austin published as *The Locked Room,* Pantheon, 1973; *Polismoerdaren,* 1974, translation by Thomas Teal published as *The Cop Killer,* Pantheon, 1975; *Terroristerna,* 1975.

WORK IN PROGRESS: Terroristerna, the tenth novel in the Martin Beck series was finished just before Wahloo's death; translation by Joan Tate to be published by Pantheon.

SIDELIGHTS: Alan Levensohn wrote in a review of the *Thirty-First Floor:* "Taking a genre (the detective novel) whose usual aim is to entertain and mildly stimulate the reader, Wahloo has used its conventions *a la nouvelle vague* to disturb and awaken—to create, in effect, an anti-detective novel.... At moments of taut suspense, when he knows the reader is bound to keep reading, he introduces exasperating passages of irrelevant detail, rendered in a tense, important tone. At moments of genuine revelation, on the other hand, the tone is likely to be somewhat monotonous and apologetic.... "Despite this nihilistic technique, Wahloo has not escaped from the genre. His book, while serious, remains an exceptionally intelligent detective novel."

When Wahloo met Maj Sjoewall, who became his wife and co-author, he had discovered another writer with the same wish to use the detective novel as something more than entertainment. In the Martin Beck series, they set out to show the personality changes in their detective mirror Sweden's political, economic, and social change over a period of ten years. The series was seen as one long novel of 300 chapters and plotted out in its entirety beforehand on that basis. The novels were done by each author writing an alternate chapter at the same desk at night after putting their children to sleep. The quiet hours between three and five A.M. were revealed as the most productive. "The mode of their collaboration is singular," explained McCandlish Phillips. "Out of their journalistic backgrounds they have devised a reportorial style—spare, disciplined and full of sharply observed detail—that allows them to write alternate chapters in seamless prose."

The success of their effort was described by Clifford A. Ridley: "The number of mystery writers who may also be called 'novelists'—that is, who traffic more than perfunctorily in such matters as character and social comment—may still, unhappily, be counted on the fingers of one hand. Ross Macdonald, Georges Simenon, and ...? And Maj Sjowall and Per Wahloo, that's who." Of the laconic character they created, a reviewer for *Book World* said, "it's not often in fiction that one not only identifies completely with the hero, but hopes fervently and protectively that he will cheer up."

Film rights to *The Man on the Balcony* were sold to Uni-

versal in 1969; *The Laughing Policeman* was filmed by Twentieth-Century Fox and released under the same title in 1974.

BIOGRAPHICAL/CRITICAL SOURCES: Christian Science Monitor, May 2, 1967; *Book World,* August 17, 1969; *Saturday Review,* February 27, 1971; *New York Times,* May 5, 1971.

OBITUARIES: New York Times, June 24, 1975; *Publishers Weekly,* August 4, 1975; *AB Bookman's Weekly,* August 25, 1975.

(Died June 22, 1975, in Malmoe, Sweden)

[Sketch verified by wife, Maj Sjoewall]

* * *

WAHTERA, John (Edward) 1929-

PERSONAL: Surname is pronounced Wah-*teer*-ah; born September 25, 1929, in Peabody, Mass.; son of John (a carpenter) and Aino (Lindgren) Wahtera; married Lilli Roos, October 3, 1954; children: Judith Lynne, David Victor. *Education:* Boston University, A.A., 1952, B.S., 1954. *Politics:* Democrat. *Religion:* Unitarian-Universalist. *Home:* 93 Perry St., Brookline, Mass. 02146. *Agent:* Paul R. Reynolds Inc., 12 East 41st St., New York, N.Y. 10017. *Office:* First National Bank of Boston, 100 Federal St., Boston, Mass. 02106.

CAREER: First National Bank of Boston, Boston, Mass., trust officer, 1956—. *Military service:* U.S. Army Artillery, 1954-56. *Member:* Authors Guild.

WRITINGS: The Happening (novel), Atlantic-Little, Brown, 1974; (contributor) L. Hillyer and C. Silitch, editors, *A Treasury of New England Short Stories,* Yankee, Inc., 1974. Contributor of short stories and nonfiction to *Audience, Redbook, American Girl, Yankee, Family Circle,* and *Writer.*

WORK IN PROGRESS: A novel, *A Prudent Man.*

AVOCATIONAL INTERESTS: Woodcarving, working with stained glass.

* * *

WALBERG, Herbert J(ohn) 1937-

PERSONAL: Born December 27, 1937, in Chicago, Ill.; son of Herbert J. (a steel plant foreman) and Helen (Bauer) Walberg; married Madoka Bessho, August 20, 1965; children: Herbert J. *Education:* Chicago State University, B.E., 1959; University of Illinois, M.E., 1960; University of Chicago, Ph.D., 1964. *Office:* College of Education, University of Illinois at Chicago Circle, Box 4348, Chicago, Ill. 60680.

CAREER: Substitute teacher in elementary schools in Chicago, Ill., 1960-62; Chicago State University, Chicago, Ill., instructor, 1962-63, assistant professor of psychology, 1964-65; Rutgers University, New Brunswick, N.J., lecturer in education, 1965-66; Harvard University, Cambridge, Mass., assistant professor of education, 1966-69; University of Illinois at Chicago Circle, associate professor of education, 1970-71, professor of human development and learning and research professor of urban education, 1971—, research associate at Office of Evaluation Research, 1970—. Chicago Testing Center of Educational Testing Service, supervisor, 1963-65, associate research psychologist at Princeton headquarters, 1965-66; research associate at Research and Development Center for Cognitive Learning of University of Wisconsin, 1969-70; consultant to

National Science Foundation, Canada Council, American Institute of Physics, Kettering Foundation, and to U.S. Government agencies.

MEMBER: American Association for the Advancement of Science, American Sociological Association, American Educational Research Association, American Psychological Association, National Society for the Study of Education, Royal Statistical Society (fellow), Australian Educational Research Association (visiting fellow), Phi Delta Kappa (trustee of Havighurst Fund).

WRITINGS: (With Louis Lowy and Leonard M. Blokesberg) *Integrative Teaching and Learning in Schools of Social Work: A Study of Organizational Development in Professional Education,* Association Press, 1971; (with Wayne W. Welch and Fletcher G. Watson) *Evaluation Strategies and Results: A Case Study of Project Physics,* Harvard University, 1971; (with Susan C. Thomas) *Open Education: Toward an Operational Definition,* Educational Development Center, 1971; (with Maurice J. Eash, Harriet Talmage, and Robert M. Rippey) *Consumer Educational Materials,* Educational Products Information Exchange, 1971; (editor with Andrew T. Kopan and contributor) *Rethinking Urban Education,* Jossey-Bass, 1972; (with Eash, Talmage, and Rippey) *Evaluating "Individualized" Materials,* Educational Products Information Exchange, 1972; (with Lowy and Blokesberg) *Teaching Records for Integrative Teaching and Learning,* Association Press, 1973; (editor and contributor) *Evaluating Educational Performance: A Sourcebook of Instruments, Methods, and Examples,* McCutchan, 1974; (editor with Kopan and contributor) *Rethinking Educational Equality,* McCutchan, 1974; (with Eash and Talmage) *Evaluating IPI, IGE, and PLAN,* Educational Products Information Exchange, 1974; (editor with Bernard Spodek and contributor) *Studies in Open Education,* Agathon, 1975; (editor with Daniel J. Amick and contributor) *Introductory Multivariate Analysis for Educational, Psychological, and Social Research,* McCutchan, 1975; (with Brian Berry and others) *Chicago: A Metropolis Transforms Itself,* University of Chicago Press, in press; (editor with Spodek) *Education in Early Childhood,* McCutchan, in press.

Contributor: James Counelis, editor, *The Educational Professoriate as Phoenix,* Phi Delta Kappa, 1970; A. V. Olsen, editor, *Accountability: Curricular Applications,* International Textbook Co., 1971; R. M. Rippey, editor, *Studies in Transactional Evaluation,* McCutchan, 1972; Jack Culbertson and others, editors, *Social Science Content for Preparing Educational Leaders,* C. E. Merrill, 1973; D. E. Edgar, editor, *The Competent Teacher: Studies in the Socialization of Teachers,* Angus & Robertson, 1973; E. F. Thibadeau, editor, *Foundations of Education,* Kendall-Hunt, 1973; Michael W. Apple and others, editors, *Educational Evaluation: Analysis and Responsibility,* McCutchan, 1974; Kevin Marjoribanks, editor, *Environments for Learning,* Humanities, 1974; John E. Bowers and others, editors, *Evaluation of the Automated Graphogestalt Technique for Identifying Children with Learning Disabilities,* American Institutes for Research, 1974; W. M. Cave, editor, *Social Issues in Education,* Macmillan, 1974; Marjoribanks, editor, *Environment and Learning,* National Foundation for Educational Research (London, England), 1974; Harriet Talmage, editor, *Systems of Individualization Education,* McCutchan, 1975; K. F. Riegel, editor, *The Developing Individual in a Changed World,* Mouton, 1975; H. J. Klausmeier, editor, *Learning and Human Abilities: Educa-*

tional Psychology, Harper, 1975; Lee S. Shulman, editor, *Review of Research in Education,* F. E. Peacock, in press.

Author of educational aids, "Learning Environment Inventory" and "Observation Scales on Open Education." Editor of behavioral science series for McCutchan, 1974—. Contributor of about eighty articles to academic journals. Member of editorial board of *American Educational Research Journal,* 1970-73; associate editor of *Educational Psychologist;* manuscript reviewer for *American Sociological Review, Canadian Journal of the Behavioral Sciences, Journal of Educational Psychology, Psychometrika, Psychological Bulletin, Review of Educational Research, School Review,* and *Sociology of Work and Occupations: An International Journal.*

WORK IN PROGRESS: Research on educational environments, resources, and attainments, on peer counseling, on population and environmental correlates of mental test scores, and on other topics in education and psychology.

SIDELIGHTS: Walberg supported himself in graduate school by performing as a guitarist in clubs and coffee houses in the Chicago area.

*   *   *

WALKER, C(larence) Eugene 1939-

PERSONAL: Born January 8, 1939, in Monangahela, Pa.; son of Lewis G. and Olga (Brioli) Walker; married Lois E. Strom, February 28, 1964; children: Chad Eugene, Kyle Lewis, Cass Emanuel. *Education:* Geneva College, B.S. (summa cum laude), 1960; Purdue University, M.S., 1963, Ph.D., 1965. *Politics:* Democrat. *Religion:* Methodist. *Home:* 10308 Cricket Canyon Rd., Oklahoma City, Okla. 73132. *Office:* Department of Pediatrics, Children's Memorial Hospital, P.O. Box 26901, Oklahoma City, Okla. 73190.

CAREER: Licensed psychologist in states of Oklahoma and Texas. Veterans Administration Neuropsychiatric Hospital, Marion, Ind., psychology trainee, 1961-62; Veterans Administration Regional Office, Mental Hygiene Clinic, Indianapolis, Ind., psychology trainee, 1962-63; West Tenth Street Veterans Administration Hospital, Indianapolis, Ind., psychology trainee, 1963, intern in clinical psychology, 1963-64; Westmont College, Santa Barbara, Calif., assistant professor of psychology, 1964-68, chairman of Division of Education and Psychology, 1966-68, director of institutional research, 1967-68; Baylor University, Waco, Tex., assistant professor, 1968-70, associate professor of psychology, 1970-74; University of Oklahoma, Medical School, Norman, associate professor of psychology and director of Outpatient Pediatric Psychology Clinic, 1974—. Clinical psychology intern at Riley Children's Hospital Child Guidance Clinic, 1963-64; staff psychologist at Camarillo State Hospital, 1965-68; private practice of clinical psychology in Santa Barbara, Calif., 1965-68, and Waco, Tex., 1970-74; member of executive council of National Council on Graduate Education in Psychology.

MEMBER: American Psychological Association, American Association for the Advancement of Science, American Society of Clinical Hypnosis, American Scientific Affiliation, Corresponding Committee of Fifty (chairman), Southwestern Psychological Association (president-elect), Oklahoma Psychological Association, Sigma Xi.

WRITINGS: (Contributor) O. R. Herron, editor, *New Dimensions in Student Personnel Administration,* International Textbook, 1970; (contributor) G. R. Collins, editor,

Our Society in Turmoil, Creation House, 1970; (contributor) Paul J. Woods, editor, *Source Book on the Teaching of Psychology,* Scholars' Press, 1973; (editor with Allan G. Hedberg, Donald K. Freedheim, and Logan Wright) *A Newsletter Editor's Handbook,* Division of State Psychological Association Affairs, American Psychological Association, 1974; *Learn to Relax,* Prentice-Hall, 1975.

Author of "The Sex Form," a test for assessing sexual functioning and adjustment. Contributor of about twenty-five articles to psychology journals. Editor of *Southwestern Psychological Association Newsletter;* contributing editor of *Professional Psychology* and *Journal of the American Scientific Affiliation;* book review editor of *Clinical Psychologist,* 1968-69; former editor of *Corresponding Committee of Fifty Newsletter.*

WORK IN PROGRESS: A drug education book for children; *Laboratory Manual for Psychological Testing and Measurements Course; Handbook of Behavior Therapy;* a marriage adjustment book.

*　　*　　*

WALKER, Jeanne 1924-

PERSONAL: Born November 2, 1924, in Brooklyn, N.Y.; daughter of I. V. (a minister) and Dona (Marshall) Johnson; married Thomas M. Walker (a professor), October 29, 1943; children: Karen (deceased). *Education:* University of Southern California, B.A., 1945; graduate study at Claremont Graduate School, 1962-63. *Residence:* Alta Loma, Calif. *Office:* Department of English, Chaffey College, Alta Loma, Calif. 91701.

CAREER: High school teacher of English in the public schools in Ontario, 1962-63; Alta Loma (Calif.) High School, teacher of English, 1963-69, chairman of department, 1965-69; Chaffey College, Alta Loma, Calif., assistant professor, 1970-74, associate professor of English, 1974—. *Member:* Southern California Society for Psychical Research.

WRITINGS: Always, Karen, Hawthorn, 1975.

WORK IN PROGRESS: Spiritual Enchantments (tentative title).

SIDELIGHTS: Jeanne Walker told *CA* that her second book uses " . . . the same medium (automatic writing)" as her first book. "It elaborates on the teachings in *Always, Karen* dictated from 'the other side'." Karen died in 1970 at the age of twenty-one.

*　　*　　*

WALKER, Nigel (David) 1917-

PERSONAL: Born August 6, 1917, in Tientsin, China; son of David B. and Violet (Johnson) Walker; married Sheila Margaret Johnston, December 5, 1939; children: Valerie. *Education:* Christ's Church, Oxford, B.A., 1939, M.A., 1961; University of Edinburgh, Ph.D., 1954. *Office:* Institute of Criminology, 7 West Rd., Cambridge, England.

CAREER: Scottish Office, Edinburgh, administrator, 1946-61; Oxford University, Oxford, England, professional fellow of Nuffield College and university reader in criminology, 1961-73; Cambridge University, Cambridge, England, Wolfson Professor of Criminology, 1973—, director of Institute of Criminology, 1973—, fellow of King's College, 1973—. Home Secretary's Advisory Council on Probation and After-Care, member, 1962—, chairman, 1972—; member of Home Secretary's Television Research Committee, 1963-69; member of Advisory Council on the Penal System, 1969—; vice-president of Howard League for Penal Reform, 1971—; member of Committee on Mentally Abnormal Offenders, 1972—; chairman of Study Group on Legal Training of Social Workers, 1973-74; member of Worker's Party on Judicial Training and Information, 1975—. *Military service:* British Army, Camerons and Lovat Scouts, 1940-46; became captain. *Member:* Royal Society of Medicine, British Society of Criminology. *Awards, honors:* Gwilym Gibbon fellow at Nuffield College, Oxford, 1958-59; D.Litt., Oxford University, 1970; Sellin-Glueck Medal from American Society of Criminology, 1975.

WRITINGS: Delphi (Latin verse), Basil Blackwell, 1936; *A Short History of Psychotherapy in Theory and Practice,* Routledge & Kegan Paul, 1957, Noonday Press, 1959; *Morale in the Civil Service: A Study of the Desk Worker,* Edinburgh University Press, 1961; *Crime and Punishment in Britain: An Analysis of the Penal System in Theory, Law, and Practice,* Edinburgh University Press, 1965, 2nd edition, 1968; *The Aims of a Penal System* (lecture), Edinburgh University Press, 1966; *Crime and Insanity in England,* Edinburgh University Press, Volume I: *The Historical Perspective,* 1967, Volume II: *New Solutions and New Problems* (with Sarah McCabe), 1973; *Sentencing in a Rational Society,* Allen Lane, 1969, Basic Books, 1971.

(With W. Hammond, D. Steer, and R. Carr-Hill) *The Violent Offender: Reality or Illusion?,* Basil Blackwell, 1970; *Crimes, Courts, and Figures: An Introduction to Criminal Statistics,* Penguin, 1971. Contributor of articles to *British Journal of Criminology, British Journal for the Philosophy of Science, Criminal Law Review,* and *Public Administration.*

SIDELIGHTS: A Short History of Psychotherapy has been translated into Italian, Spanish, and French; *Sentencing in a Rational Society* has been translated into Spanish. *Avocational interests:* Chess, hill climbing.

*　　*　　*

WALKER, Stella Archer 1907-

PERSONAL: Born March 29, 1907, in Leicester, England; daughter of James and Mary Elizabeth (Archer) Batten. *Education:* Educated privately in England and France. *Home:* Watermill Farm, Warbleton, Heathfield, Sussex, England.

CAREER: Worked on historical pageants in England, 1933-36; actress with Wilson Barret Theatre Company, 1937-42; author and farmer, 1945—. *Member:* National Book League, Arab Horse Society (council member), English Speaking Union.

WRITINGS: (Compiler) *In Praise of Kent,* Muller, 1952; (compiler) *In Praise of Horses,* Muller, 1953, revised edition, 1976; *Horses of Renown,* Country Life, 1954; (compiler) *Long Live the Horse!,* Country Life, 1954; (compiler) *In Praise of Spring,* Muller, 1958; (with R. S. Summerhays) *The Controversial Horse,* J. A. Allen, 1966; *Sporting Art: England 1700-1900,* Potter, 1972; (compiler) *Enamoured of an Ass,* Angus & Robertson, 1976. Art correspondent for *Horse and Hound* and *Chronicle of the Horse.* Editor of *Summerhays Encyclopedia for Horsemen,* 6th edition. Contributor of articles to art and equestrian periodicals in England, France, and the United States.

SIDELIGHTS: Stella Walker told *CA* she had ridden horses from childhood until an accident in 1958. After the accident her continued interests in horses led her to promote the Arabian breed and organize pony club activities. She also has become increasingly "given to the study of and writing about British sporting art."

*   *   *

WALLACE, Anthony F(rancis) C(larke)   1923-

PERSONAL: Born April 15, 1923, in Toronto, Ontario, Canada; son of Paul A. and Dorothy Eleanor (Clarke) Wallace; married Betty Louise Shillott, December 1, 1942; children: Anthony C. M., Daniel D. S., Elizabeth Sun Ai, Samuel Si Won. *Education:* University of Pennsylvania, B.A., 1948, M.A., 1949, Ph.D., 1950; graduate studies at Rorschach Institute, 1948-49, and Philadelphia Psychoanalytic Institute, 1950-53. *Office:* Department of Anthropology, University of Pennsylvania, 33rd and Spruce Sts., Philadelphia, Pa. 19104.

CAREER: Bryn Mawr College, Bryn Mawr, Pa., instructor in anthropology, 1948-50; University of Pennsylvania, Philadelphia, assistant instructor in anthropology, 1948-49, instructor in sociology, 1950-52, research assistant professor, 1952-55, visiting associate professor, 1955-61, professor of anthropology, 1961—, chairman of department of anthropology, 1961-71. Consultant to Philadelphia Housing Authority, 1951-52; Eastern Pennsylvania Psychiatric Institute, medical research scientist, 1955—, director of clinical research, 1960-61; National Research Council, consultant to the Committee on Disaster Studies, 1953-56, member of council, 1956-57, member of division of behavioral sciences, 1963-66; National Institute of Mental Health, member of the fellowship review panel of behavioral sciences, 1961-64, member of the behavioral sciences study section, 1964-68; member of the research advisory committee, Commonwealth Mental Health Research Foundation, 1957; consultant to the Veterans Administration, Perry Point, Md., 1958-60; member of the technical advisory committee, New Jersey Neuropsychiatric Institute, 1958-61; U.S. Office of Education, member of the environmental panel of the cooperative research program, 1962, member of the research advisory council, 1965-68; National Science Foundation, social science research advisory committee, member, 1968-69, chairman, 1971; member of the Surgeon General's Science Advisory Committee on Television and Social Behavior, 1969-71; member of the board of directors, Foundation Fund for Research in Psychiatry, 1969-71. *Military service:* U.S. Army, 1942-45.

MEMBER: National Academy of Sciences, American Philosophical Society, American Anthropological Association (president, 1971-72), American Academy of Arts and Sciences. *Awards, honors:* Social Science Research Council research fellow, 1951-54; National Science Foundation grant, 1972-74.

WRITINGS: King of the Delawares: Teedyuscung, 1700-1763, University of Pennsylvania Press, 1949, reprinted, Books for Libraries Press, 1970; *The Modal Personality Structure of the Tuscarora Indians as Revealed by the Rorschach Test,* U.S. Government Printing Office, 1952; *Human Behavior in Extreme Situations: A Study of the Literature and Suggestions for Further Research,* National Academy of Sciences, 1956; *Tornado in Worcester: An Exploratory Study of Individual and Community Behavior in an Extreme Situation,* National Academy of Sciences, 1956.

(Editor) *Men and Cultures: Selected Papers,* University of Pennsylvania Press, 1960; *Culture and Personality,* Random House, 1961, 2nd edition, 1970; *Religion: An Anthropological View,* Random House, 1966; (with Sheila C. Steen) *The Death and Rebirth of the Seneca,* Knopf, 1970. Contributor of articles to professional journals.

*   *   *

WALLACE, Helen M(argaret)   1913-

PERSONAL: Born February 18, 1913, in Hoosick Falls, N.Y.; daughter of Jonas and Ray (Schweizer) Wallace. *Education:* Wellesley College, A.B., 1933; Columbia University, M.D., 1937; Harvard University, M.P.H. (cum laude), 1943. *Home:* 1515 Oxford St., Berkeley, Calif. 94709. *Office:* School of Public Health, University of California, Berkeley, Calif. 94720.

CAREER: New York City Department of Health, New York, N.Y., began as junior health officer, became director of Bureau for Handicapped Children, 1943-55; New York Medical College, New York, N.Y., professor of preventive medicine and chairman of department, 1955-56; University of Minnesota, Minneapolis, professor of maternal and child health, 1956-59; U.S. Children's Bureau, Washington, D.C., chief of professional training, 1959-60, chief of child health research, 1961-62; University of California, Berkeley, professor of maternal, child, and family health, 1962—, chairman of program, 1962—, director of Makerere Medical School, 1968-73. Visiting professor of Makerere Medical School, 1969, 1971. Member of advisory committee to welfare commissioner of the U.S. Department of Health, Education and Welfare; member of advisory committee of California State Health Department; member of board of directors of Knudsen Corp.; consultant to World Health Organization, Ford Foundation, and UNICEF.

MEMBER: American Public Health Association (fellow; member of governing council), American Academy of Pediatrics (fellow), American Medical Association (fellow), American School Health Association (fellow), American College of Preventive Medicine (fellow), American Academy of Cerebral Palsy (fellow), National League for Nursing (member of board of directors), American College of Obstetricians and Gynecologists, Association of Teachers of Maternal and Child Health (president), Planned Parenthood (member of board of directors), World Population (member of board of directors), Alameda-Contra Costa County Medical Society. *Awards, honors:* Awards from United Cerebral Palsy of New York City, United Cerebral Palsy of Minnesota, New York Philanthropic League, and Muscular Dystrophy Association of New York City; World Health Organization traveling fellowship to South America, summer, 1957; National Institutes of Health and Ford Foundation grants to England and Sweden, 1973.

WRITINGS: The Child with Cardiac Limitations, Board of Education (New York, N.Y.), 1953; *The Child with Orthopedic Limitations,* Board of Education (New York, N.Y.), 1954; *Standards for General Convalescent Homes Caring for Cardiac Children,* Public Health Committee, New York Heart Association, 1954; *Standards and Recommendations for Hospital Care of New Born Infants,* Committee on Fetus and Newborn, American Academy of Pediatrics, 1954; *Health Supervision of Young Children,* Child Health Committee, American Public Health Association, 1955; *Services for Handicapped Children,* Committee on Child Health, American Public Health Association, 1955; *Services for Children with Cleft Lip and Cleft Palate,* Committee on Child Health, American Public Health Association, 1955; *Services for Children with Cerebral Palsy,* Committee on Child Health, American Public Health Association, 1955; *Services for Children with Dento-Facial Handicaps,* Committee on Child Health, American Public Health Association, 1955; (with C. Meinert and P. J. Englund) *A Study of Cerebral Palsy,* United Cerebral Palsy of Minnesota, 1962; (with others) *Services for Children with Orthopedic Handicaps,* American Public Health Association, 1962; *Health Services for Mothers and Children,* Saunders, 1962; (with others) *Maternal and Newborn Care in Fallout Shelters,* U.S. Children's Bureau, 1963; (with others) *The Care of Infants and Children in Community Fallout Shelters,* U.S. Children's Bureau, 1963; *Maternal and Child Health Practices,* C. C Thomas, 1973; *Health Care of Mothers and Children under National Health Services,* Ballenger Publishing, 1975; (editor) *Infant Mortality Around the World,* Ross Laboratories, 1975.

Contributor: Frampton and Gall, editors, *Special Education for the Exceptional,* Volume II, Sargent, 1955; H. Michal-Smith, editor, *Management of the Handicapped Child,* Grune, 1957; Fred Delli Quadri, editor, *Helping the Family in Urban Society,* Columbia University Press, 1963; *Rural Youth in Crisis,* U.S. Government Printing Office, 1965; Green and Hagerty, editors, *Textbook on Ambulatory Pediatrics,* Saunders, 1968; John G. Howells, editor, *Modern Perspectives in Psycho-Obstetrics,* Oliver & Boyd, 1972. Contributor to *Encyclopedia of Educational Research.* Contributor of about two hundred and thirty articles and reviews to medical journals. Guest editor of *Woman Physician,* October, 1971.

WORK IN PROGRESS: Research studies in maternal and child health.

* * *

WALLACE, Paul 1931-

PERSONAL: Born July 21, 1931, in Los Angeles, Calif.; son of Raymond (a businessman) and Goldie Wallace; divorced; children: Steven, Lisa. *Education:* University of California, Berkeley, A.B., 1953, M.A., 1957, Ph.D., 1966. *Home:* 400 Westwood, Columbia, Mo. 65201. *Office:* Department of Political Science, University of Missouri, Columbia, Mo. 65201.

CAREER: San Jose State College, San Jose, Calif., part-time instructor in government, spring, 1961; California State College, Hayward, part-time instructor in government, 1963; University of Missouri, Columbia, assistant professor, 1964-69, associate professor of political science, 1969—, coordinator of Peace Corps training for West Bengal, 1967, director of South Asia Language and Area Center, 1966-69, 1973—. Conducted "Press Reports from India," on KPFA-Radio, 1958-63. Member of Asia Foundation, 1957-60. *Military service:* U.S. Army, in personnel administration, 1953-55.

MEMBER: American Political Science Association, Association for Asian Studies, American Institute of Indian Studies (trustee), Research Committee on the Punjab (chairman, 1968-69), Midwest Conference of Asian Studies, Missouri Political Science Association. *Awards, honors:* Fulbright-Hays grant, 1972, for study in India.

WRITINGS: (Contributor) M. H. Jatri, E. K. Bauer, and N. R. Keddie, editors, *Economy of Pakistan* (monograph), Volume I, Human Relations Area File Press, 1956; (with N. G. Barrier) *Punjab Press: 1880-1905,* Asian Studies Center, Michigan State University, 1970; (contributor) Harbans Singh and N. G. Barrier, editors, *Punjab: Past*

and Present, Punjabi University Press, in press. Contributor of articles and reviews to academic journals.

WORK IN PROGRESS—Monographs: *Political Development in Northwest India; The Press in the Developing Bargaining Culture of India; The Punjab Press, 1905-1934.*

* * *

WALLECHINSKY, David 1948-

PERSONAL: Wallechinsky is original family surname: the surname Wallace was bestowed on the author's grandfather by a U.S. immigration agent at Ellis Island; born February 5, 1948, in Los Angeles, Calif.; son of Irving (a novelist) and Sylvia (a novelist; maiden name, Kahn) Wallace. *Education:* Attended University of California at Los Angeles, Santa Monica College, and San Francisco State College (now University). *Politics:* "Believe in federated neighborhood councils." *Agent:* Paul Gitlin, 7 West 51st St., New York, N.Y. 10019.

CAREER: Film-maker, 1968—; writer, 1970—. *Awards, honors:* The film "Gas" was selected as a U.S. entry to the Venice Film Festival in 1971.

WRITINGS: (With Frank "Chico" Bucaro) *Chico's Organic Gardening and Natural Living,* Lippincott, 1972; (editor with Michael Shedlin) *Laughing Gas,* And/Or Press, 1973; (with father, Irving Wallace) *The People's Almanac,* Doubleday, 1975.

Author and director of documentary feature film "Gas," 1969, and of short comedy films. Contributor of articles and poems to magazines.

WORK IN PROGRESS: The Best of Times, with Michael Medved, for Random House.

SIDELIGHTS: Wallechinsky's proposed book deals with graduates of the 1965 Pacific Palisades, California high school class, who were featured in a *Time* article in 1965.

He writes of one of his earliest lasting impressions: "During my senior year in high school the U.S. Government teachers decided to set up a mock government in class to help teach us the way democracy really works. I was elected to the legislature. Our first act as legislators was to vote that the teacher had to leave the room. He told us that wasn't allowed and stayed." He describes some of his current feeling in the following list of "favorites": "RELIGIOUS SECTS—Zen and Sufism/ ECONOMIC SYSTEM—Workers' self management/ ARTISTIC MOVEMENT—Surrealism and its cousins/ AUTHORS—Lewis Carroll, Poe, Wilde, Shaw/ DISC JOCKEY—Dr. Demento/ CONTEMPORARY MUSICAL PERFORMER—Janis Joplin/ DANGER TO THE WORLD—Obedience to authority."

AVOCATIONAL INTERESTS: Playing table tennis; rooting for University of California at Los Angeles basketball team; baking desserts; "pursuing the bizarre, unusual, and extreme"; collecting postcards, high school annuals, and letters from parents to their children.

* * *

WALLER, Charles T(homas) 1934-

PERSONAL: Born January 18, 1934, in Dublin, Ga.; son of Charles Thomas (an electrician) and Pearl (Camp) Waller. *Education:* Mars Hill College, A.A., 1954; Wake Forest College, A.B., 1956; Yale University, graduate study, 1956-57; University of Georgia, M.A., 1960; University of Pittsburgh, Ph.D., 1965. *Politics:* Democrat. *Home:*

215 Vista Dr., Athens, Ga. 30601. *Office:* Department of English, University of Georgia, Athens, Ga. 30601.

CAREER: University of Georgia, Athens, instructor, 1958-60, and 1964-65, assistant professor of eighteenth-century literature and folklore, 1966—. *Military service:* U.S. Army, 1959-61. *Member:* Modern Language Association of America, American Folklore Society, Southern Folklore Society, South Atlantic Modern Language Association.

WRITINGS: (With Ronald Killion) *A Treasury of Georgia Folklore,* Cherokee, 1972; *Slavery Times When I Wuz Chillun Down on Marster's Plantation,* Beehive Press, 1973; (with Killion) *Georgia and the Revolution,* Cherokee, 1975. Contributor to literature journals.

* * *

WALLER, J(ames) Irvin 1944-

PERSONAL: Born July 24, 1944, in England; naturalized Canadian citizen; married; children: two. *Education:* Cambridge University, B.A., 1965, diploma in criminology, 1966, Ph.D., 1973. *Office:* Ministry of the Solicitor General, 340 Laurier, Ottawa, Ontario, Canada K1A 0P8.

CAREER: University of Toronto, Toronto, Ontario, senior research assistant at Centre of Criminology, 1966-69, research associate, 1969; Cambridge University, Cambridge, England, Laidlaw Research Fellow at Institute of Criminology, 1969-70; University of Toronto, research associate at Centre of Criminology, 1970-73, senior research associate, 1973, assistant professor, 1972-73, associate professor of law, 1973; Ministry of the Solicitor General, Ottawa, Ontario, director of Research Division, 1974, director general, 1974—. Conducted research at University of Abidjan, 1973. *Member:* Ontario Association of Criminology and Corrections (director, 1971—), John Howard Society (Toronto; director, 1973—).

WRITINGS: (Contributor) D. J. West, editor, *The Future of Parole,* Duckworth, 1972; (contributor) Edward Sagarin and Donal E. J. McNamara, editors, *Corrections: Problems of Punishment and Rehabilitation,* Praeger, 1973; *Men Released from Prison* (monograph), University of Toronto Press, 1974; (with J. K. Hugessen, J. A. Phelps, and R. G. Gervais) *Report of the Task Force on Release of Inmates,* Information Canada, 1974. Contributor to professional journals.

WORK IN PROGRESS: Editing *Selected Readings for the National Conference on the Disposition of Offenders in Canada,* with John Edwards.

SIDELIGHTS: Waller's main concerns have been parole and release experiences, parole supervisor role studies, and research on burglary and the public. He has conducted study tours of prison and after-care systems in Czechoslovakia, Poland, Belgium, and the Netherlands, as well as in England and the United States.

* * *

WALLICH-CLIFFORD, Anton 1923-

PERSONAL: Born July 27, 1923, in London, England; son of Cyril and Monica M. (Buckwell) Wallich-Clifford; married Marie Therese McQuade, December 2, 1967; children: Luke Christian. *Education:* Attended St. Laurences College Seminary in Lancaster, England. *Politics:* Liberal. *Religion:* "Radical Catholic." *Home and office:* Simon Community Trust, 13 North St., St. Leonards, Sussex, England. *Agent:* John James & Associates, 118 Grove Green Rd., Leyton, London E.10, England.

CAREER: Employed in field of social work, 1948—; London Probation Service, London, England, probation officer, 1953-62; Simon Community Trust, St. Leonards, Sussex, England, founder and executive trustee, 1963—. Has appeared on television and radio programs. Active in local residents' associations. *Military service:* Royal Air Force, Volunteer Reserve, 1942-47.

WRITINGS: One Man's Answer, Golborne, 1962; *Simon Scene,* Housmans, 1968; *No Fixed Abode,* Macmillan, 1974; *Caring on Skidrow,* Veritas, 1976. Editor of *Simon Star,* 1963-66, and *Social Action,* 1969-70.

SIDELIGHTS: It was as a probation officer that Wallich-Clifford first dealt with rootless and socially handicapped people, "some of the thousands who fall yearly through the gaping holes in the welfare net." His involvement led him to create and run the Simon Community, an international movement dedicated to helping such people. He writes: "I am convinced that society needs protection from the outbursts of Red Kelly, the car-taking of Wally and the nicking activities of Paul. But that is just why I have fought, struggled, debated and argued that however much you protest about our work, you, who have rights I respect and support, need me and people like me, who are prepared to contain, to care for and to love society's misfits."

BIOGRAPHICAL/CRITICAL SOURCES: Catholic Herald, October 9, 1964; *Times,* December 24, 1964.

* * *

WALMSLEY, Lewis C(alvin) 1897-

PERSONAL: Born December 3, 1897, in Milford, Ontario, Canada; son of James Franklin (a farmer) and Sarah (Welbanks) Walmsley; married Constance Ellen Kilborn, August 9, 1921 (deceased); married Dorothy Brush, December 1, 1961 (died June, 1968); children: Glenn K., J. Omar, Enid E. (Mrs. Bruce G. Sills), Marion A. (Mrs. D. N. Anderson). *Education:* University of Toronto, B.A., 1919, specialist certificate in education, 1920, D.Paed., 1945. *Religion:* United Church of Canada. *Home:* 1 Massey Sq., Apt. 2807, Toronto, Ontario, Canada M4C 5L4.

CAREER: Regina College, Regina, Saskatchewan, member of faculty, 1920-21; Canadian School, Chengtui Sze, China, principal, 1923-43, 1947-48; Woodstock School, Mussoorie, India, principal, 1945-47; University of Toronto, Toronto, Ontario, associate professor of East Asiatic studies, 1948-63, chairman of department, 1948-52. Associate professor at West China Union University, 1931-34. *Military service:* Canadian Army, 1917-18.

WRITINGS: An Interpretation of China, Canadian Broadcasting Corp., 1959; (with My Chang Yin-nan) *Poems by Wang Wei,* Tuttle, 1959; (with wife, Dorothy B. Walmsley) *Wang Wei, the Painter-Poet,* Tuttle, 1968; *A Biography of Bishop William C. White,* University of Toronto Press, 1974; *A History of the West China Union University,* Mennonite Press, 1975.

* * *

WANG, C(hing) H(sien) 1940-
(Yang Mu, Yeh Shan)

PERSONAL: Born September 6, 1940, in Taiwan, China (now seat of Nationalist Chinese Government); son of Shui-sheng Yang (a printer) and Pao-hsiu Wang; married Nora Chen (an instructor), September 3, 1966. *Education:* Tunghai University, Taiwan, B.A., 1963; University of Iowa, M.F.A., 1966; University of California, Berkeley,

Ph.D., 1971. *Home:* 10655 Exeter Ave., N.E., Seattle, Wash. 98125. *Office:* Department of Asian Languages and Literature, University of Washington, Seattle, Wash. 98195.

CAREER: University of Massachusetts, Amherst, instructor, 1970-71, assistant professor of Chinese and comparative literature, 1971; University of Washington, Seattle, assistant professor, 1971-74, associate professor of Chinese and comparative literature, 1974—. *Military service:* Army of the Republic of China, 1963-64. *Member:* American Oriental Society, Association for Asian Studies. *Awards, honors:* Time-Life Award for poetry translation, 1965; first prize for lyrical essay from Republic of China, 1966; Mainstream Prize for poetry, 1971; Asia Society award for Chinese epic project, 1971; University of Washington research grants, summers, 1972-75; American Council of Learned Societies-Social Science Research Council grant, 1975-76.

WRITINGS: The Bell and the Drum: Shih Ching as Formulaic Poetry in an Oral Tradition, University of California Press, 1974.

Under pseudonym Yeh Shan: *Shui chih mei* (poems; title means "On the Water Margin"), Lan-hsing Poetry Association (Taipei), 1960; *Hua chi* (poems; title means "Flower Season"), Lan-hsing Poetry Association, 1963; *Yeh Shan san-wen chi* (title means "First Essays"), Wen-hsing Bookstore (Taipei), 1966; *Teng ch'uan* (poems; title means "Lantern Boat"), Wen-hsing Bookstore, 1966; (translator) Fredrico Garcia Lorca, *Hsi-pan-ya lang-jen yin* (translation of *Romancero Gitano*), Hsien-tai Wen-hsueh (Taipei), 1966; (translator with others) *Mei-kuo hsien-tai ch'i ta hsio-shuo-chia* (translation of *Seven Modern American Novelists,* edited by William Van O'Connor), Chin-jih Shih-chieh Press (Hong Kong), 1969; *Fei tu chi* (title means "Selected Poems, 1956-1960"), Hsien-jen-chang Press (Taipei), 1969; *Ch'uan shuo* (poems; title means "Legends"), Chih-wen Press (Taipei), 1971.

Under pseudonym Yang Mu: *Ch'uan-t'ung-ti yu hsien-tai-ti* (essays; title means "Traditional and Modern"), Chih-wen Press, 1974; *Yang Mu tsu-hsuan chi* (title means "Selected Essays, 1960-1975"), Li-ming Enterprise (Taipei), 1975; *P'ing Chung Kao* (poems; title means "Manuscripts Sealed in a Bottle"), Chin-wen Press, 1975.

Anthologies: *New Chinese Poetry,* edited and translated by Yu Kwang-chung, Heritage Press (Hong Kong), 1960; *New Voices 1961,* edited and translated by Nancy Chang, Heritage Press, 1961; *Modern Chinese Poetry: Twenty Poets from the Republic of China,* edited and translated by Wailim Yip, University of Iowa Press, 1970; *Modern Verse from Taiwan,* edited and translated by Angela Jung Palandri, University of California Press, 1972; *Anthology of Chinese Literature,* Volume II: *From the 14th Century to the Present Day,* edited by Cyril Birch, Grove Press, 1972; *An Anthology of Contemporary Chinese Literature,* Volume I (also includes essays and translations by Wang), edited by Ch'i Pang-yuan and others, National Office of Compilation and Translation (Taipei), 1975.

Contributor of articles, reviews, and poems to *The Chinese Pen, China Times Literary Supplement, Journal of the Oriental Society, TriQuarterly, Tamkang Review, Literature East and West, Metaphrasis, Tsing Hua Journal of Chinese Studies, Journal of Asian Studies,* and numerous other Chinese and American publications. Co-editor, *Hai-ou* (title means "Sea Gull Poetry Weekly"), 1957-59; contributing editor, *Ts'uang-shih-chi* (title means "Epoch Po-

etry Quarterly"), 1962-68, *Hsien-tai wen-hsueh* (title means "Modern Literature"), 1965-72, *Chung-wai wen-hsueh* (title means "Chung-wai Literary Monthly"), 1973—; editor, *Tung-feng* (title means "East Wind"), 1961-62, *Hsin-ch'ao ts'ung-shu* (title means "New Currents Series"), 1969—.

WORK IN PROGRESS: A volume on modern Chinese literary criticism; a sequel to *The Bell and the Drum,* on ancient Chinese verse as epic; a book in Chinese about American experience.

SIDELIGHTS: Although he is a permanent resident in the United States, Wang retains his Chinese citizenship and does his writing in both English and Chinese. He finds his bilingual writing in both scholarly and creative areas "a challenge, sometimes exciting and sometimes frustrating." Some of Wang's poems have been translated into Korean, French, and Japanese.

*   *   *

WANG, Yi Chu 1916-

PERSONAL: Born August 14, 1916, in Peiping, China; naturalized U.S. citizen, 1961. *Education:* London School of Economics and Political Science, University of London, B.Sc. (honors), 1939; University of Chicago, Ph.D., 1957. *Office:* Department of History, Queens College of the City University of New York, Flushing, N.Y. 11367.

CAREER: University of Chicago, Chicago, Ill., instructor in Oriental language and literature, 1954-55; Shippensburg State College, Shippensburg, Pa., associate professor of economics, 1957-59; Dickinson College, Carlisle, Pa., visiting professor of sociology and Far Eastern culture, 1959-60; University of Chicago, visiting assistant professor of Far Eastern history, 1960-62; University of Kansas, Lawrence, visiting associate professor of history, 1962; University of North Carolina, Chapel Hill, associate professor of history, 1962-65; Columbia University, New York, N.Y., visiting associate professor of history, 1966-67; Queens College of the City University of New York, Flushing, N.Y., professor of history, 1967—. Visiting associate professor at University of Texas, summer, 1961. *Awards, honors:* Grant from American Council of Learned Societies and Social Science Research Council, 1961-62; research award from Duke University-University of North Carolina humanities program, 1965.

WRITINGS: Chinese Intellectuals and the West, University of North Carolina Press, 1966; (editor) *Chinese Education,* International Arts and Science Press, 1970. Contributor to *Encyclopaedia Britannica* and to professional journals. Member of editorial advisory board of *Journal of Asian Studies,* 1969—.

*   *   *

WANLASS, Stanley G(len) 1941-

PERSONAL: Born April 3, 1941, in American Fork, Utah; son of L. Glen (geologist and service station owner) and Alta (a women's fashion buyer; maiden name, Butler) Wanlass; married Joy Erikson (a photo and fashion model), February 17, 1966; children: Lincoln Stanley. *Education:* Brigham Young University, B.F.A., 1966, M.A., 1968. *Religion:* Church of Jesus Christ of Latter Day Saints (Mormon). *Home:* 907 5th St., Astoria, Ore. 97103. *Office:* Department of Art, Clatsop College, 16th and Jerome, Astoria, Ore. 97103.

CAREER: Brigham Young University, Provo, Utah, instructor, 1965-68, assistant professor of art, 1968-70; Clatsop College, Astoria, Ore., associate professor of art, 1971—. Visiting lecturer at European Art Academy in London, Amsterdam, and Paris, summer, 1966; professor of art at University of Grenoble, winter-spring, 1970, and Medicine Hat College, summers, 1970, 1971. Organizer and art director of Artifacts Design, Inc. (manufacturer of interior decor), 1965-67; director of art programs for Study Guild International, Salt Lake City, Utah, 1970-71; director of Stanley Studios (new products and creative design), 1971-75. *Military service:* U.S. Army, 1959. *Awards, honors:* Winner in nationwide contest for bicentennial medal design for the State of Oregon.

WRITINGS: An Illustrated Compilation with Some Aesthetic Consideration of Major Radiator Emblems of Automobiles Manufactured in the United States During the Years 1900 to 1930, privately printed, 1967; (self-illustrated) *Dictionary of America's Early Automobiles and their Radiator Emblems,* Dover, 1975.

WORK IN PROGRESS: A basic design text and a drawing text; a novel, *The Pursuit of Excellence.*

SIDELIGHTS: Wanlass' paintings and sculpture are in galleries, museums, universities, and private collections throughout the country.

BIOGRAPHICAL/CRITICAL SOURCES: New Era, March, 1971; *Today,* May, 1973; *Daily Astorian,* September 26, 1974, December 26, 1974.

* * *

WARBURTON, Amber Arthun 1898(?)-1976

1898(?)—January 27, 1976; American economist, educational consultant, and author of books on rural education. Obituaries: *Washington Post,* January 31, 1976.

* * *

WARD, Justine Bayard Cutting 1879-1975

August 7, 1879—November 27, 1975; American musician, educator and innovator, and author. Obituaries: *New York Times,* November 29, 1975; *Washington Post,* December 2, 1975.

* * *

WARD, William R(eed) 1918-

PERSONAL: Born May 20, 1918, in Norton, Kan.; son of Joseph Aloysius and Maude (Jones) Ward; married Elizabeth Jane Adam, August 8, 1943; children: Claudia Christine (Mrs. William S. Bartosiewicz), Joseph Andrew, John David. *Education:* University of Kansas, Mus.B., Mus.Ed.B., 1941; Eastman School of Music, Mus.M., 1942, Ph.D., 1954. *Home:* 120 Occidental Ave., Burlingame, Calif. 94010. *Office:* Department of Music, San Francisco State University, San Francisco, Calif. 94132.

CAREER: Colorado State College (now University), Ft. Collins, instructor in music, 1942-44; Lawrence College (now University), Appleton, Wis., assistant professor of music, 1944-47; San Francisco State University, San Francisco, Calif., assistant professor, 1947-54, associate professor, 1954-59, professor of music, 1959—, chairman of department, 1954-69. Lecturer or panelist at schools and conferences, including Idyllwild Institute of the Arts, Music Educators National Conference, and University of California School of Medicine; church choir director in Ft. Collins, Colo., 1942-44, Appleton, Wis., 1944-47, and in

Burlingame, Calif., 1949—; advisor, California Youth Symphony. Compositions have been performed by Eastman-Rochester Symphony Orchestra, San Francisco Symphony Orchestra, Whittier College Choir, and other groups.

MEMBER: American Society of Composers, Authors, and Publishers, Music Teachers National Association, American Society of University Composers, American Association of University Professors, Music Educators National Conference, Choral Conductors Guild. *Awards, honors:* National Arrangers contest award, 1947, for "Lullaby for a Pinto Colt."

WRITINGS: Examples for the Study of Musical Styles, W. C. Brown, 1948, revised edition, 1970; *American Bicentennial Song Book,* Hansen, 1975.

Music: *Little Dance Suite* (for woodwind quintet), Mills Music, 1947; *Response in Ancient Style* (for mixed choir and organ), Carl Fischer, 1948; *Variations on a Western Tune* (for symphonic band), Rochester Music Publishers, 1954; *Father, We Praise Thee* (for mixed choir and brass) [and] *A Prayer for Christian Unity* (for a cappella choir), Edward B. Marks Music, 1957; *The World Itself Keeps Easter Day* (for mixed choir), Neil A. Kjos, 1958; *Be Thou My Vision* (for mixed choir), Carl Fischer, 1958; *Listen, Lord* (for a cappella choir), Lawson-Gould, 1958; *O For a Thousand Tongues to Sing* (for choir, congregation, and organ), Sacred Music Press, 1974; *O Come, O Come Emmanuel* (hymn prelude on tune "Veni Emmanuel" for organ), World Library Publications, 1974; *Lord Jesus, Think on Me* (hymn prelude on tune "Southwell" for organ), World Library Publications, 1975. Recorded music includes "A Vision of the World," Audiosonics Associates, 1955, and "Listen, Lord," Music Library Recordings, 1963.

WORK IN PROGRESS: A book on gospel music; a book on American Christmas songs.

SIDELIGHTS: Ward helped establish the DeBellis collection of Italian manuscripts, music, and books at San Francisco State University.

* * *

WARHAFT, Sidney 1921-

PERSONAL: Born December 8, 1921, in Winnipeg, Manitoba, Canada; son of Benjamin and Bertha (Glassman) Warhaft; married Marion Glassman, January 21, 1953; children: Mark Joel. *Education:* University of Manitoba, B.A. (honors), 1949; Northwestern University, M.A., 1952, Ph.D., 1954; also studied at University of Paris, 1949-52. *Home:* 312 Waverley St., Winnipeg, Manitoba, Canada. *Office:* Department of English, University of Manitoba, Winnipeg, Manitoba, Canada.

CAREER: University of Manitoba, Winnipeg, lecturer in English, 1954-55; University of Michigan, Ann Arbor, assistant professor of English, 1955-57; University of Southern California, Los Angeles, assistant professor of English, 1957-58; University of Manitoba, assistant professor, 1958-62, associate professor, 1962-66, professor of English, 1966—, head of department, 1966-71. Member of academic panel of Canada Council, 1969-71. *Military service:* Royal Canadian Air Force, 1942-45. *Member:* International Association of University Professors of English, Association of Canadian University Teachers of English (executive officer, 1970-71), Canadian Association of University Teachers, Modern Language Association of America, Shakespeare Association of America. *Awards, honors:* Canada Council fellowships, 1964-65, 1971-72.

WRITINGS: (Compiler with John Woodbury) *English Poems, 1250-1660*, Macmillan, 1961, 2nd edition (with Woodbury and Patrick O'Flaherty) published as *English Poems, 1250-1800*, St. Martin's, 1966; (editor) Francis Bacon, *A Selection of His Works*, Macmillan, 1966. Contributor to literature journals, and to *Personalist* and *Queen's Quarterly*.

*   *   *

WARK, Robert R(odger) 1924-

PERSONAL: Born October 7, 1924, in Edmonton, Alberta, Canada; came to United States, 1948, naturalized citizen, 1970; son of Joseph Henry (a grain inspector) and Louise (Rodger) Wark. *Education:* University of Alberta, B.A., 1944, M.A., 1946; Harvard University, A.M., 1949, Ph.D., 1952. *Religion:* Episcopalian. *Home:* 1330 Lombardy Rd., Pasadena, Calif. 91106. *Office:* Henry E. Huntington Library and Art Gallery, San Marino, Calif. 91108.

CAREER: Harvard University, Cambridge, Mass., instructor, 1952-54; Yale University, New Haven, Conn., instructor, 1954-56; Henry E. Huntington Library and Art Gallery, San Marino, Calif., curator of art, 1956—. Lecturer in art, California Institute of Technology, 1960—, University of California, Los Angeles, 1966—. *Military service:* Royal Canadian Air Force, 1944-45; Royal Canadian Naval Volunteer Reserve, 1945. *Member:* College Art Association, Association of Art Museum Directors, American Museum Association, American Society for Eighteenth Century Studies, Twilight Club.

WRITINGS—All published by Henry E. Huntington Library and Art Gallery, except as noted: (Editor) C. Collins Baker, *Catalogue of William Blake's Drawings and Paintings in the Huntington Library*, 2nd edition (Wark was not associated with earlier edition), 1957; (editor) Joshua Reynolds, *Discourses on Art*, 1959, Yale University Press, 1975; *Sculpture in the Huntington Collection*, 1959; *French Decorative Art in the Huntington Collection*, 1961, 2nd edition, 1968; (author of introduction and notes) Thomas Rowlandson, *Drawings for a Tour in a Post Chaise*, 1963; (author of introduction and notes) Rowlandson, *Drawings for the English Dance of Death*, 1966; (author of introduction and notes) Isaac Cruikshank, *Drawings for Drolls*, 1968; *Early British Drawings in the Huntington Collection, 1600-1750*, 1969; *Drawings by John Flaxman in the Huntington Collection*, 1970; *The Huntington Art Collection* (handbook), 1970; *Ten British Pictures, 1740-1840*, 1971; *Meet the Ladies: Personalities in Huntington Portraits*, 1972; *Drawings from the Turner Shakespeare*, 1973; *Drawings by Thomas Rowlandson in the Huntington Collection*, 1975. Also author of art history papers on English painting and catalogs of art exhibitions.

WORK IN PROGRESS: British Drawings of the Late Eighteenth Century.

*   *   *

WARNER, Sylvia Townsend 1893-

PERSONAL: Born December 6, 1893, in Harrow, Middlesex, England; daughter of George Townsend and Eleanor Mary (Hudleston) Warner. *Education:* Privately educated in England. *Office:* c/o Chatto & Windus, 40 William IV St., London W.C.2, England.

CAREER: Novelist, poet, short-story writer, biographer, translator, and editor, 1926—. *Member:* Royal Society of Literature (fellow), American Academy of Arts and Letters (honorary member), Rachel Carson Trust (sponsor).

WRITINGS—Novels: *Lolly Willowes; or, The Loving Huntsman* (Book of the Month Club selection; also see below), Viking, 1926; *Mr. Fortune's Maggot* (Literary Guild selection), Viking, 1927, published in *Lolly Willowes, and Mr. Fortune's Maggot*, Viking, 1966; *The True Heart*, Viking, 1929; *Summer Will Show*, Viking, 1936; *The Corner That Held Them*, Viking, 1948; *The Flint Anchor*, Viking, 1954.

Short story collections: *Some World Far From Ours, and Stay, Corydon, Thou Swain*, Mathews, 1929; *Elinor Barley*, Cresset Press, 1930; *A Moral Ending and Other Stories*, Joiner & Steele, 1931; *The Salutation*, Viking, 1932; *More Joy in Heaven and Other Stories*, Cresset Press, 1935; (with Graham Greene and James Laver) *Twenty-four Stories*, Cresset Press, 1939; *The Cat's Cradle Book*, Viking, 1940; *A Garland of Straw: Twenty-Eight Stories*, Viking, 1943 (published in England as *A Garland of Straw and Other Stories*, Chatto & Windus, 1943); *The Museum of Cheats: Stories*, Viking, 1947; *Winter in the Air and Other Stories*, Chatto & Windus, 1955, Viking, 1956; *A Spirit Rises: Short Stories*, Viking, 1962; *Swans on an Autumn River: Stories*, Viking, 1966 (published in England as *A Stranger With a Bag and Other Stories*, Chatto & Windus, 1966); *The Innocent and the Guilty*, Viking, 1971. Also author of *This Our Brother*, published by Lanston Monotype Corp.

Poetry: *The Espalier*, Viking, 1925; *Time Importuned*, Viking, 1928; *Opus 7: A Poem*, Viking, 1931; *Rainbow*, Knopf, 1932; (with Valentine Ackland) *Whether a Dove or Seagull*, Viking, 1933; (with Reynolds Stone) *Boxwood*, Monotype Corp., 1958, new enlarged edition, Chatto & Windus, 1960; *King Duffus and Other Poems*, Clare, 1968.

Biographical works: *The Portrait of a Tortoise: Extracted from the Journals of Gilbert White*, Chatto & Windus, 1946; *Somerset*, Elek, 1949; *Jane Austen: 1775-1817*, Longmans, Green, 1951, revised edition, 1957; *Sketches from Nature* (autobiographical reminiscences), Clare, 1963; *T. H. White: A Biography*, J. Cape, 1967, Viking, 1968.

Translator: Marcel Proust, *By Way of Saint-Beuve*, Chatto & Windus, 1958, published as *On Art and Literature: 1896-1917*, Dell, 1964; Jean Rene Huguenin, *A Place of Shipwreck*, Chatto & Windus, 1963.

Editor: (With others) *Tudor Church Music*, ten volumes, Oxford University Press, c.1925-30; *The Weekend Dickens*, MacLehose, 1932. Contributor of articles to *New Yorker*, 1935—.

WORK IN PROGRESS: A collection of stories from the *New Yorker*.

*   *   *

WARREN, Doug(las) 1935-

PERSONAL: Born January 28, 1935, in Oberlin, Ohio; son of Ralph Beal and Coressia (Beal) Rosecrans; divorced; children: Tim, Craig. *Education:* Attended Kent State University. *Home:* 3903 Fernwood Ave., Los Angeles, Calif. 90027. *Agent:* Don Shepherd, 1680 Vine St., Hollywood, Calif. 90028.

CAREER: Worked as television announcer for KPRC-TV, Houston, Tex.; and as television writer for Ralph Edwards Productions, 1959-64; *Akron Beacon Journal*, Akron, Ohio, Sunday magazine writer, 1964-65; *Albany Times Union*,

Albany, N.Y., Sunday magazine writer, 1965-67; United Press International, field reporter in Vietnam, 1967-71; Multimedia-Asia, Inc., Saigon, Vietnam, bureau chief; *Cleveland Plain Dealer,* Cleveland, Ohio, Sunday magazine writer, 1971-73; full-time writer, 1974—. Worked as a photographer for *Silver Screen* and *Screenland* in Hollywood, and as an actor in New York.

WRITINGS: Walking Tall, Pinnacle Books, 1974; *Demonic Possession,* Pyramid Publications, 1975; *A Case of Rape,* Pyramid Publications, 1975. Also author of fifty-six additional titles, 1959-73.

WORK IN PROGRESS: Researching astrology.

SIDELIGHTS: Doug Warren told *CA:* "I evolved into successful authorship because I am totally unemployable and have no mechanical (or other useful) talents—I wish I were a skilled plumber or undertaker or television repairman."

* * *

WARRICK, Patricia Scott 1925-

PERSONAL: Born February 6, 1925, in La Grange, Ind.; daughter of Ross B. (a beekeeper) and DeEtte (Ulman) Scott; married James E. Warrick, 1965; children: Scott McArt, David McArt, Kristin McArt. *Education:* Indiana University, B.S., 1946; Goshen College, B.A., 1964; Purdue University, M.A., 1965; University of Wisconsin—Milwaukee, doctoral candidate, 1975. *Home:* 1925 North McDonald St., Appleton, Wis. 54911. *Office:* Technology and Culture Program, University of Wisconsin—Fox Valley, Menasha, Wis. 54952.

CAREER: Long Island University, Brooklyn, N.Y., employed in Office of Development, 1946-48; St. Elizabeth's Hospital, Indianapolis, Ind., director of technicians-medical laboratory, 1948-52; Lawrence University, Appleton, Wis., instructor in English, 1965-66; University of Wisconsin—Fox Valley, Menasha, instructor, 1966-71, assistant professor, 1971-74, associate professor of English, 1974—, director of technology and culture program, 1975—. *Member:* Modern Language Association of America, National Council of Teachers of English, World Future Society, Science Fiction Research Association.

WRITINGS: (Editor with Carol Mason and Martin Greenberg) *Anthropology through Science Fiction,* St. Martin's, 1974; (editor with Greenberg and Joseph Olander) *American Government through Science Fiction,* Rand McNally, 1974; (editor with Greenberg and Harvey Katz) *Introductory Psychology through Science Fiction,* Rand McNally, 1974; (editor with Greenberg) *Political Science Fiction,* Prentice-Hall, 1974; (editor with Greenberg, Olander, and John Milstead) *Sociology through Science Fiction,* St. Martin's, 1974; (editor with Greenberg and Milstead) *Social Problems through Science Fiction,* St. Martin's, 1974; (editor with Greenberg and Olander) *School and Society through Science Fiction,* Rand McNally, 1974; (editor with Greenberg) *The New Awareness,* Dell, 1975; (contributor) Jack Williamson, editor, *Teaching the Future,* Mirage Press, in press; (contributor) Thomas Clareson, editor, *Themes in Science Fiction,* Kent State University Press, in press. Contributor to literature journals.

WORK IN PROGRESS: Senior editor, with Martin Greenberg and Joseph Olander, of *The Myths of Contemporary Man* (tentative title), for Harper; a book-length study of the social, aesthetic, and political implications of the development of computers and machine intelligence as these areas are explored by the literary imagination.

SIDELIGHTS: Patricia Warrick writes: "I am deeply involved in writing literary criticism about science fiction, and also involved in futurology: the study of innovation and change. My interest in studying change probably stems from the fact that my life has been so full of it. I have already experienced three different careers: as a medical technologist, a mother, and now a professor of English. I became intrigued with science fiction because it is one of the most creative and flexible devices available for modelling alternative futures—futures made possible or probable because of science and technology." *Avocational interests:* "Prowling through the Wisconsin woods on horseback."

* * *

WARSH, Lewis 1944-

PERSONAL: Born November 9, 1944, in New York, N.Y.; married Bernadette Mayer (poet), November, 1975; children: Marie Ray. *Education:* City College of the City University of New York, B.A., 1966, M.A., 1975. *Home:* Parish Rd., Worthington, Mass. 01098. *Office address:* Angel Hair Books, Box 257, Stuyvesant Station, New York, N.Y. 10009.

CAREER: Poet. Co-founder and co-editor, *Angel Hair* magazine, and Angel Hair Books, New York, N.Y., 1966—; co-editor, *The Boston Eagle,* Boston, Mass., 1973—. Teacher in St. Mark's in the Bowery Poetry Project, 1973-75. *Awards, honors:* Poet's Foundation Award, 1972.

WRITINGS—Poetry: The Suicide Rates, Toad Press, 1967; *Highjacking: Poems,* Boke Press, 1968; *Moving Through Air,* Angel Hair Books, 1968; (with Tom Clark) *Chicago,* Angel Hair Books, 1969; *Words, Staring,* Orange Bear Reader, 1971; *Dreaming as One: Poems,* Corinth Books, 1971; *Long Distance,* Ferry Press, 1971; *Part of My History,* Coach House Press, 1972; (translator) Robert Desnos, *Night of Loveless Nights,* The Ant's Forefoot, 1973; *Immediate Surrounding,* Others Books, 1974; *Today,* Adventures in Poetry, 1974. Contributor to *Poetry, Paris Review, Big Sky* and other publications.

SIDELIGHTS: A reviewer for *Poetry* wrote about Warsh's collection *Moving Through Air:* "Reading one of these poems is like being resistlessly drawn into somebody else's daydream, full of lingering tones and quaking alarms. Through it all the anxious, elegant voice of the poet intermittently insinuates itself in one's ear."

* * *

WASSERMAN, Jack 1921-

PERSONAL: Born April 27, 1921, in New York, N.Y.; son of William (a businessman) and Pearl (Bajcz) Wasserman; married Ambra Amati (a fashion designer), July 6, 1952; children: Shara (daughter), Talya (daughter). *Education:* New York University, B.A., 1949, M.A., 1953, Ph.D., 1961. *Home:* 8314 Fairview Rd., Elkins Park, Pa. 19126. *Office:* Tyler School of Art, Temple University, Elkins Park, Pa. 19126.

CAREER: New York University, New York, N.Y., instructor in art history, 1953-54; University of Connecticut, Storrs, instructor in art history, 1954-60; Indiana University, Bloomington, assistant professor of art history, 1960-62; University of Wisconsin, Milwaukee, professor of art history, 1962-75, head of department, 1962-75; Temple University, Elkins Park, Pa., professor of art history and dean of Tyler School of Art, 1975—. *Military service:* U.S. Army Air Forces, 1942-45. *Member:* College Art Association, Society of Architectural Historians (director, 1970-72), Royal Society of Arts, Phi Beta Kappa. *Awards, honors:* Grants from American Philsophical Society, 1970, from American Council of Learned Societies, 1971, and from Kress Foundation, 1975.

WRITINGS: Ottaviano Mascarino, Accademia di San Luca, 1966; *Leonardo da Vinci,* Abrams, 1975. Contributor to *Burlington Magazine, Art Bulletin* and art journals.

WORK IN PROGRESS: A multi-volume study of all the art and other activities of Leonardo da Vinci.

AVOCATIONAL INTERESTS: Travel.

*   *   *

WATERFIELD, Gordon 1903-

PERSONAL: Born May 24, 1903, in Canterbury, Kent, England; son of Aubrey William (a painter) and Caroline (a journalist and writer; maiden name, Duff Gordon) Waterfield; married Margaret Hornsby, August 10, 1929; children: Harriet (Mrs. Christopher Green), Michael. *Education:* Oxford University, B.A., 1923, M.A., 1924. *Home:* 83 North Rd., Hythe, Kent, England; and Castello della Brunella, Aulla, Massa Carrara, Italy.

CAREER: Assistant editor of *Egyptian Gazette,* 1926-30; acting correspondent in Egypt for London (England) national newspapers, 1928-30); Reuters News Agency, London, correspondent from Rome, Paris, and Lisbon, 1931-40, war correspondent from Chungking and India, 1942-43, and from Egypt, Turkey, Algeria, and Italy, 1943; Kemsley Newspapers, New York, N.Y., chief correspondent, 1946-47; British Broadcasting Corp. (BBC), London, diplomatic correspondent for External Services, 1947-48, head of Eastern Service, 1948-56, head of Arabic Service, 1956-63; writer, 1963—. *Military service:* British Army, Commandos (later in charge of radio station and newspapers under Ministry of Information in Ethiopia), 1940-42, 1943-45; served in Aden, Somalia, and Addis Ababa; became major. *Member:* Authors and Playwrights Society (London), Travellers Club (London). *Awards, honors:* Order of the British Empire, 1963.

WRITINGS: Lucie Duff Gordon in England, South Africa, and Egypt, Dutton, 1937 (published in England as *Lucie Duff Gordon,* J. Murray, 1937); *What Happened to France* (memoirs), J. Murray, 1940, Books for Libraries, 1972; *Morning Will Come* (memoirs), J. Murray, 1944; *Layard of Ninevah* (biography), J. Murray, 1963, Praeger, 1969; (editor) Richard Burton, *First Footsteps in East Africa,* Praeger, 1966; *Egypt,* Walker & Co., 1967; *Sultans of Aden* (biographies), International Publications Service, 1968; (editor) *Lady Duff Gordon's Letters from Egypt, 1862-1869,* Routledge & Kegan Paul, 1969; *Professional Diplomat* (biography of Sir Percy Loraine), J. Murray, 1973.

*   *   *

WATERS, Mary-Alice 1942-

PERSONAL: Born January 12, 1942, in the Philippine Islands. *Education:* Carleton College, B.A., 1963; graduate study at University of California, Berkeley, 1963-64. *Politics:* Marxist. *Religion:* Atheist. *Office: Militant,* 14 Charles Lane, New York, N.Y. 10014.

CAREER: Young Socialist, New York, N.Y., editor, 1966-67; Young Socialist Alliance, New York, N.Y., na-

tional chairwoman, 1968; *Militant,* New York, N.Y., managing editor, 1970-71, editor, 1971—. *Member:* Phi Beta Kappa.

WRITINGS: (Editor) *Rosa Luxemburg Speaks,* Pathfinder, 1970; (with Jack Barnes, George Breitman, Derrick Morrison, and Barry Sheppard) *Towards an American Socialist Revolution,* Pathfinder, 1972; *Feminism and Socialism* (pamphlet), Pathfinder, 1972.

WORK IN PROGRESS: A book on the history of the feminist movement and its relationship with the Marxist and radical movements.

*   *   *

WATSON, Charles S(t. Denis), Jr. 1934-

PERSONAL: Born August 14, 1934, in Cleveland, Ohio; son of Charles S. and Ruth C. (McAteer) Watson. *Education:* University of Nevada, B.S., 1960. *Politics:* Liberal Republican. *Religion:* Roman Catholic. *Home and office address:* P.O. Box 1245, Carson City, Nev. 89701.

CAREER: U.S. Government, cartographer in Bureau of Land Management, 1960-65, in Department of the Navy, 1965-67, with Defense Mapping Agency in St. Louis, Mo., 1967-72; Nevada Outdoor Recreation Association, Carson City, director, 1958-65, 1972—. Writer for National Parks and Conservation Society, 1965, 1967-68, for Sierra Club, 1973. Representative-at-large for National Public Lands Task Force, 1967—. *Military service:* U.S. Army. *Member:* American Forestry Association, Sierra Club, Alaska Geographic Society. *Awards, honors:* Edward Hobbs Hilliard, Jr. Memorial Award, from Rocky Mountain Center on Environment, 1974; first place award from Reno Gem and Mineral Exposition, 1975, for show "Jackpot of Gems."

WRITINGS: The Lands No One Knows, Sierra Club, 1975. Contributor to conservation magazines.

WORK IN PROGRESS: Compiling, with others, the *Nevada Outdoor Recreation Resources Index and Survey,* a study of public land wilderness and recreational resources.

AVOCATIONAL INTERESTS: Mineralogy.

BIOGRAPHICAL/CRITICAL SOURCES: Sierra Club Bulletin, September, 1973.

*   *   *

WATSON, Ian 1943-

PERSONAL: Born April 20, 1943, in North Shields, England; son of John William (a postmaster) and Ellen (Rowley) Watson; married Judith Jackson, September 1, 1962; children: Jessica Scott. *Education:* Balliol College, Oxford, B.A. (first class honors), 1963, B.Litt., 1965, M.A., 1966. *Home:* 37 St. John St., Oxford OX1 2LH, England.

CAREER: University of Dar es Salaam, Dar es Salaam, Tanzania, lecturer in literature, 1965-67; Tokyo University of Education, Tokyo, Japan, lecturer in English, 1967-70; Birmingham Polytechnic, Birmingham, England, lecturer, 1970-75, senior lecturer in complementary studies (science fiction and futures studies) for School of the History of Art in Art and Design Center, 1975—; writer, 1976—. *Member:* Science Fiction Writers of America, Science Fiction Foundation (London; member of governing council, 1974—). *Awards, honors: The Embedding* was named runner-up for John W. Campbell Memorial Award, 1974, and in French translation won Prix Apollo, 1975; guest of honor at Second French National Science Fiction Congress, 1975, and Leodicon (in Belgium), 1976.

WRITINGS: Japan: A Cat's Eye View, Bunken, 1970; *The Embedding* (science fiction novel), Gollancz, 1973, Scribner, 1975; *The Jonah Kit* (science fiction novel), Gollancz, 1975, Scribner, 1976; *Orgasmachine* (French translation of manuscript of science fiction novel), Editions Champ-Libre, 1976; *Japan Tomorrow,* Bunken, in press.

Work has been anthologized in *Best SF: 1974,* edited by H. Harrison and B. W. Aldiss, Bobbs-Merrill, 1975. Contributor of stories and articles to science fiction magazines and literary journals, including *Chicago Review, London Magazine, Ambit, Transition,* and *Transatlantic Review.* Features editor of *Foundation: The Review of Science Fiction,* 1975—.

WORK IN PROGRESS: The Martian Inca, a science fiction novel.

SIDELIGHTS: Watson writes: "I first started writing Science Fiction as the only sane response to the contemporary Japanese environment. The Science Fiction I am interested in should be scientific—in that it deals with the impact of scientific ideas and discoveries; and however farfetched these ideas or discoveries may be, they should be dealt with from a standpoint of realism, not fantasy or magic. But at the same time SF should be metaphorical—in that it functions as a tool for thinking about the world and its future, Man and the Universe, flexibly and boldly, but not along downright predictive lines. SF does not predict or forecast specific events or inventions. (If it happens to, this is purely by chance, a pleasant bonus, but this is not its function.) SF should be contradictory, in that it envisages a multiplicity of possible futures. SF should be rooted in a sense of Man (adequate characterization, not puppets; sense of real social milieu). Yet it should be this without being 'earthbound' (by refusing to consider the nature of Alien experience or the Universe at large.) Indeed, it must try to tackle ultimate questions: about the nature of Reality, about the origin and significance of the Universe, and of life within this Universe."

* * *

WATT, Kenneth E(dmund) F(erguson) 1929-

PERSONAL: Born July 13, 1929, in Toronto, Ontario, Canada; son of William B. Ferguson and Irene E. (Hubbard) Watt; married Genevieve Bernice Bendig (a painter), October 28, 1955; children: Tanis Jocelyn, Tara Alexis. *Education:* University of Toronto, B.A. (honors), 1951; University of Chicago, Ph.D., 1954. *Home:* 1116 Dartmouth Pl., Davis, Calif. 95616. *Office:* Department of Zoology, University of California, Davis, Calif. 95616.

CAREER: Ontario Department of Lands and Forests, Toronto, biometrician, 1954-57; Canadian Department of Agriculture, Ottawa, senior biometrician, 1957-60; Canadian Department of Forestry, Ottawa, head statistician in research service, 1960-63; University of California, Davis, associate professor, 1963-64, professor of zoology and environmental studies, 1965—. *Member:* Ecological Society of America, Society for General Systems Research, Society for Computer Simulation, Society for Population Ecology (Japan), Ecological Society of Australia, Sigma Xi. *Awards, honors:* Fisheries ecology and management award from Wildlife Society, 1961; gold medal from Entomological Society of Canada, 1969; LL.D. from Simon Fraser University, 1970.

WRITINGS: (Editor and contributor) *Systems Analysis in Ecology,* Academic Press, 1966; *Ecology and Resource Management,* McGraw, 1968; *Principles of Environmental Science,* McGraw, 1973; *The Titanic Effect,* Dutton, 1974; (with others) *The Unsteady State: Growth, Culture, and Environmental Problems,* University Press of Hawaii, in press; (with others) *Simulation of Socio-Economic Phenomena,* Academic Press, in press. Contributor of about a hundred articles to professional journals and popular magazines, including *Natural History* and *Saturday Review.* Associate editor of *Mathematical Biosciences,* 1968—; member of editorial board of *Oecologia,* 1968—; consulting editor for McGraw, 1965—.

SIDELIGHTS: Watt writes "to bring new understandings of problems of the world obtained through statistical analysis of national and international data, and computer simulation." *Avocational interests:* International travel (Switzerland, Trinidad, Guatemala, Venezuela, Mexico, Fiji, Netherlands, England, Scotland, Malta, Australia).

BIOGRAPHICAL/CRITICAL SOURCES: Anne Chisholm, *Philosophers of the Earth,* Dutton, 1972.

* * *

WAYMAN, Dorothy G. 1893-1975 (Theodate Geoffrey)

January 7, 1893—October 27, 1975; American journalist, librarian, and author. Obituaries: *New York Times,* October 30, 1975; *AB Bookman's Weekly,* December 22-29, 1975.

* * *

WEAL, Michele 1936-

PERSONAL: Born November 18, 1936, in Nyack, N.Y.; daughter of Edward Kaye (in real estate) and Florence (Karp) Kaye; married Roy M. Hendrickson; married second husband, Bertram Weal, Jr. (an investment broker), August 31, 1965; children: (first marriage) David A. Weal. *Education:* Sarah Lawrence College, B.A., 1957; also studied at Skowhegan School of Painting and Sculpture, 1957, and Wayne State University, 1958. *Home:* 11 Robinhood Rd., White Plains, N.Y. 10605.

CAREER: French teacher in elementary schools in Bloomfield Hills, Mich., 1958-59; elementary school teacher in Buffalo, N.Y., 1959-60, and Brooklyn, N.Y., 1963-65; needlepoint designer and artist, teacher, lecturer, author, working from own studio, 1969—. Paintings, drawings, pastels, and needlework have been exhibited in the United States and abroad. *Member:* American Crafts Council, Art Students League, Westchester Art Society. *Awards, honors:* Second prize from third annual textile design competition, sponsored by National Curtain Drapery and Allied Products Association, 1975.

WRITINGS: Texture and Color in Needlepoint, Harper, 1975.

WORK IN PROGRESS: Research and needlework, for another book.

SIDELIGHTS: Michele Weal writes: "As an artist, I believe I have found in needlework an exciting and versatile medium. My literary efforts are the products of my desire to communicate my designs and my point of view. I am attempting to move needlepoint into the art world."

WEATHERHEAD, Leslie D(ixon)   1893-1976

October 14, 1893—January 3, 1976; British theologian, minister, lecturer, and author of books on religious topics. Obituaries: *New York Times,* January 5, 1976. (See index for previous *CA* sketch)

*   *   *

WEAVER, Herbert   1905-

PERSONAL: Born July 28, 1905, in Brewton, Ala.; son of Levi P. and Anne (Holladay) Weaver; married Blanche Henry Clark, March 5, 1944. *Education:* Birmingham-Southern College, A.B., 1926, M.A., 1935; Vanderbilt University, Ph.D., 1941. *Home:* 3718 Brighton Rd., Nashville, Tenn. 37205. *Office:* Department of History, Vanderbilt University, Nashville, Tenn. 37203.

CAREER: Teacher in Alabama secondary schools, 1926-35; Georgia Teachers College (now Georgia Southern College), Statesboro, associate professor, 1940, professor of history and chairman of department, 1942-49; Vanderbilt University, Nashville, Tenn., associate professor, 1949-52, professor of history, 1952—, chairman of department, 1962-67. *Military service:* U.S. Army Air Forces, 1942-46; became major. *Member:* American Historical Association, Organization of American Historians, Tennessee Historical Society (president, 1961-63), Kappa Phi Kappa, Pi Gamma Mu, Old Oak Club, University Club.

WRITINGS: Mississippi Farmers, 1850-1860, Vanderbilt University Press, 1945; (editor with Paul H. Bergeron) *Correspondence of James K. Polk,* Vanderbilt University Press, Volume I: *1817-1832,* 1969, Volume II: *1833 and 1834,* 1972, Volume III: *1835-1836* (with Kermit L. Hall), 1975. Contributor to the *History of the United States Air Force in World War II,* University of Chicago, 1948-58. Member of editorial board, *Tennessee History Quarterly,* 1948-52, and *Journal of Southern History,* 1957-59.

*   *   *

WEAVER, Thomas   1929-

PERSONAL: Born May 1, 1929, in Grenville, N.M.; married, 1950; children: three. *Education:* University of New Mexico, B.A., 1955, M.A., 1960; University of California, Berkeley, Ph.D., 1965. *Office:* Bureau of Ethnic Research, University of Arizona, Tucson, Ariz. 85721.

CAREER: University of New Mexico, Albuquerque, field assistant in archaeology and ethnology for Indian land grant cases, 1955; National Institute of Mental Health, Rural Health Survey, Santa Fe, N.M., staff anthropologist, summers, 1959-61; research assistant on epidemiology of alcoholic beverage usage pattern project, California Department of Public Health, 1963; executive secretary and ex-officio chairman of advisory committee, California State Advisory Commission on Indian Affairs, 1964; University of Kentucky, Lexington, assistant professor of anthropology and behavioral science, 1964-67; University of Pittsburgh, Pittsburgh, Pa., assistant professor of anthropology and psychiatry and Maurice Falk Senior Faculty Fellow, 1967-69; University of Arizona, Tucson, associate professor, 1969-75, professor of anthropology, 1975—, director of Bureau of Ethnic Research, 1969—. Has conducted field work in New Mexico, California, Chile, Pittsburgh, Arizona, Nevada, and Mexico. Member of board of directors of Governors' Interstate Indian Council, 1964-65.

MEMBER: American Anthropological Association (fellow; committee chairman, 1970-74), Society for Applied Anthropology (fellow; secretary, 1971-74; president, 1976-77), Current Anthropology (associate), American Ethnological Society, American Association for the Advancement of Science (fellow), Latin American Anthropology Group, Southwestern Anthropological Association, Sigma Xi. *Awards, honors:* Research grant from California State Advisory Commission on Indian Affairs, 1965-66; urban anthropology conference grant from School of American Research, 1968; political organization and business management grant from Gila River Indian Community and U.S. Department of Housing and Urban Development, 1970-71; National Science Foundation grants, 1971, travel grant to Italy, 1972, research grant, 1974-76; U.S. Department of Health, Education and Welfare grant, 1972-73; U.S. Forest Service grant, 1972; grant from U.S. Department of Housing and Urban Development and from Arizona Division of Economic Development, 1973-74; grant from U.S. Department of the Interior, Bureau of Indian Affairs, and U.S. Department of Justice, 1974.

WRITINGS: Indians in Rural and Reservation Areas: Report for the California State Advisory Commission on Indian Affairs, State of California Printing Office, 1966; (with F.L.K. Hsu, D. J. Jones, Diane Lewis, Bee Medicine, and J. L. Gibbs) *The Minority Experience in Anthropology: Report of the Committee on Minorities and Anthropology,* American Anthropological Association, 1973; (with Theodore Downing and Sanford Newmark) *Summary of the Tribal Management Procedures Study,* Bureau of Ethnic Research, University of Arizona, 1974.

Editor: (And contributor) *Essays on Medical Anthropology,* University of Georgia Press, 1968; (with Alvin Magid and contributor) *Poverty: New Interdisciplinary Perspectives,* Chandler Publishing, 1969; (and contributor) *The Arizona Indian People and Their Relationship to the State's Total Structure,* Arizona Academy, 1971; (and contributor) *Political Organization and Business Management in the Gila River Indian Community,* Bureau of Ethnic Research, University of Arizona, 1971; (with Douglas White and contributor) *The Anthropology of Urban Environments* (monograph), Society for Applied Anthropology, 1972; Andrew Laurie and Carol Mudgett, *Enrollee Dissatisfaction in Youth Conservation Corp Attributable to Ethnic Background: Literature Abstracts,* Bureau of Ethnic Research, University of Arizona, 1972; (and contributor) *To See Ourselves: Anthropology and Modern Social Issues,* Scott, Foresman, 1973; (and contributor) *Indians of Arizona,* University of Arizona Press, 1974; *Tribal Management Procedures Study of Seven Reservations: Ak Chin, Camp Verde, Cocopah, Fort McDowell, Hayasupai, Hualapai, and Payson,* Bureau of Ethnic Research, University of Arizona, 1974; *Guidelines for Submission of Proposals to the Human Subjects Committee,* University of Arizona, 1974.

Contributor to academic journals. Associate editor of *Ethnology,* 1967-69, and of monographs of *Human Organization,* 1970-75.

*   *   *

WEBB, Pauline M(ary)   1927-

PERSONAL: Born June 28, 1927, in London, England; daughter of Leonard F. (a Methodist minister) and Daisy (Barnes) Webb. *Education:* King's College, London, B.A. (honors), 1948; London Institute of Education, teaching diploma, 1949; Union Theological Seminary, New York,

N.Y., S.T.M., 1965. *Office:* Methodist Missionary Society, Overseas Division, 25 Marylebone Rd., London NW1 5JR, England.

CAREER: Teacher and assistant mistress of grammar school in Twickenham, England, 1949-52; Methodist Missionary Society, London, England, youth officer, 1952-54, editor, 1954-64, director of lay training, 1967-73, executive secretary, 1973—. Became accredited local preacher of Methodist Church, 1953. Vice-president of Methodist Conference, 1965-66, member of World Methodist Executive Committee, 1966-74. Teacher at Adult Evening Institute of Westminster College of Commerce, 1952-54; member of Anglican-Methodist Negotiating Commission, 1965-68; vice-chairman of central committee of World Council of Churches, 1968-75.

WRITINGS: Women of Our Company, Cargate, 1958; *Women of Our Time,* Cargate, 1960; *Operation Healing: Stories of the Work of Medical Missions throughout the World, with Bible Links and Things to Do,* Edinburgh House Press, 1964; *All God's Children,* Oliphants, 1965; *Are We Yet Alive? Addresses on the Mission of the Church in the Modern World,* Epworth, 1966; *Agenda for the Churches,* S.C.M. Press, 1968; (contributor) Rupert E. Davies, editor, *We Believe in God,* Allen & Unwin, 1968; *Salvation Today,* S.C.M. Press, 1974.

Pageants: "Kingdoms Ablaze," 1958; "Set My People Free," 1960; "Bring Them to Me," 1964.

Film scripts: "Bright Diadem" (on southern India); "The Road to Dabou"; "New Life in Nigeria"; "Beauty for Ashes."

Television scripts: "Man on Fire"; "Let Loose in the World"; "A Woman's Place?" Editor of *Kingdom Overseas,* 1954-66.

SIDELIGHTS: Pauline Webb's emphasis is on "the mission and unity of the Church; the ministry of the laity; race relations; world poverty; the contribution of women in Church and community." She has traveled in Ceylon, India, Burma, Nigeria, Kenya, Zambia, the Caribbean, the United States, and most of western Europe.

* * *

WEBER, Hans H. 1935-

PERSONAL: Born May 22, 1935, in Manila, Philippines; son of Herman Eduard (a businessman) and Marie Louise Holzborn; married Georgia D. Allen, September 11, 1957; children: Diana, Brian, Darin. *Education:* University of Montana, B.A., 1958; University of Washington, Seattle, M.L.S., 1964. *Home:* 1920 West Alabama, Houston, Tex. 77006. *Office:* Main Library, University of Houston, Houston, Tex.

CAREER: U.S. Forest Service, Coeur d'Alene, Idaho, fire fighter, 1957; high school librarian in Lovelock, Nev., 1959-62; junior high school librarian in Lacey, Wash., 1962-64; University of Washington, Seattle, book order librarian, 1964-66; Oregon State University, Corvallis, head of library's business records department, 1966-71; University of California, Riverside, head of serials department in general library, 1971-75; University of Houston, Main Library, Houston, Tex., assistant director for technical services, 1975—. *Member:* American Library Association, California Library Association, Beta Phi Mu.

WRITINGS: (With Marty Bloomberg) *World War Two and Its Origins: A Select Annotated Bibliography of Books in English,* Libraries Unlimited, 1975; (with Bloomberg) *Introduction to Classification for Small and Medium Libraries,* Libraries Unlimited, 1976. Co-editor of "Foundations in Library and Information Science," a monograph series for Johnson Associates, 1976—.

WORK IN PROGRESS: The Arab-Israeli Conflict: A Select Annotated Bibliography.

SIDELIGHTS: Weber writes: "My interest in World War II had its inception with my experiences in the Philippines during this war. Subsequent reading, years later, served to heighten this interest. It is from the past that humanity draws upon for the future. Unfortunately, mankind consistently fails to pay much attention to history's lessons, thereby precipitating continual debilitating conflicts. By learning more about the origins and consequences of such conflicts one can hope to secure a better understanding of perhaps how they can and should be prevented in the future." *Avocational interests:* Philately (Philippines, United States).

* * *

WECHSLER, Herman J. 1904-1976

August 21, 1904—January 13, 1976; American art gallery owner, educator, editor, and author of biographies and works in his field. Obituaries: *New York Times,* January 14, 1976.

* * *

WEES, W(ilfred) R(usk) 1899-

PERSONAL: Born November 24, 1899, in Bracebridge, Ontario, Canada; son of Frederick Milton (a clergyman) and Josie (Rusk) Wees; married Frances Shelley (a novelist), September, 1924; children: Margarita (Mrs. Edgar Smith), Timothy John. *Education:* University of Alberta, B.A., 1923, M.A., 1925, M.Ed., 1928; Stanford University, further graduate study, 1931-32; University of Toronto, Ph.D., 1935. *Politics:* "Liberally inclined." *Religion:* "Gospel according to Wilf Wees!" *Home address:* R.R. 3, Stouffville, Ontario, Canada LOH 1LO. *Office:* Ontario Institute for Studies in Education, 252 Bloor St., Toronto, Ontario, Canada M5S 1V6.

CAREER: Teacher in rural schools in Saskatchewan, 1916-19; Alberta College, Edmonton, dean of residence, 1919-20; vice-principal of public schools in Edmonton, 1923-29; Camrose Teacher's College, Camrose, Alberta, instructor in psychology, 1929-33; University of Toronto, Toronto, Ontario, instructor in psychology, 1934-35; W. J. Gage Ltd. (stationery and publishing firm), Toronto, editor, 1935-41; Canadian Department of Veterans Affairs, Ottawa, Ontario, director of training, 1945-46; W. J. Gage Ltd., vice-president, 1946-68; Ontario Institute for Studies in Education, Toronto, associate professor of curriculum and field development, 1968—, head of regional Field Development Centre, 1971—. Diplomate of American Psychological Association, 1948; registered psychologist in Ontario, 1960. Annual Quance lecturer at University of Saskatchewan, 1967; visiting lecturer at University of Alberta, 1929, 1930, 1933. Member of board of directors of World Council for Curriculum and Instruction and for Overseas Book Centre; chairman of Committee on Statutory Registration of Psychologists in Ontario. *Military service:* Canadian Army, director of personnel selection, and Canadian Army Overseas, deputy adjutant general, 1941-45; became lieutenant colonel.

MEMBER: Canadian Education Association (life member), Canadian Psychological Association (life member), Canadian Association of University Teachers, Canadian Society for the Study of Education, Canadian Curriculum Association, Canadian Association of Professors of Education, National Society for the Study of Education, Commercial Traveller's Association (life member), Ontario Association for Continuing Education (honorary president), Ontario Association for Curriculum Development (president; life member), Ontario Education Association (life member), Ontario Psychological Association (life member), Ontario Teacher's Federation (fellow), Phi Delta Kappa. *Awards, honors:* LL.D. from University of Alberta, 1961; centennial medal from Canadian Government, 1967.

WRITINGS: Science in the Classroom, Gage, 1961; *Unto One of the Least of These* (monograph), Etobicoke Board of Education, 1964; (contributor) *New Dimensions in Curriculum Development,* Ontario Curriculum Institute, 1966; (contributor) *Values and the Curriculum,* National Education Association, 1970; *The Way Ahead: The Quance Lectures in Education,* Gage, 1967; *OISE and the Schools,* Ontario Institute for Studies in Education, 1970; *Nobody Can Teach Anyone Anything,* Doubleday, 1971. Writer of column, "The Second Reader," *Alberta Teacher's Association* magazine, 1924-28, and "Hodge Podge," in *Edmonton Journal,* 1927-28. Contributor of about sixty articles to education and psychology journals, and to *Monday Morning* and *Toronto Star Weekly.* Former editor of *Ontario Psychological Association Quarterly.*

SIDELIGHTS: Wees writes: "When I was at the robust age of twelve, selling papers on the streets of the frontier town of Moose Jaw, some recently imported Chinese gentlemen working in a restaurant asked me if I would spend my Wednesday evenings with them to teach them English. I said I would. The experience of teaching those quiet, earnest, responsive men was such a joy that I decided to become a teacher. The lure of education is the educator's never-ending involvement in and evolvement of human values. Unfortunately, and almost universally, values in education have been confined to obedience and the inculcation of knowledge. Child and youth in school have seldom been valued, either for their own sakes or for the sake of that society that our children will create tomorrow. The schools, always away behind the times, only now are beginning to twig the worthwhileness of the value concept in education—and only a few of them, spotted here and there." *Avocational interests:* "I like to nurture nature: plant the seed or seedlings, watch life greening and help it grow."

* * *

WEHMEYER, Lillian (Mabel) Biermann 1933-
(Lillian Biermann)

PERSONAL: Born October 29, 1933, in Milwaukee, Wis.; daughter of William Alfred (an electrical engineer) and Mabel (Knippel) Biermann; married Gerald C. Edson, August 29, 1953 (divorced, 1957); married Werner F. Wehmeyer (a real estate broker), August 28, 1962; children: (first marriage) Paula Nancy (Mrs. James Cory). *Education:* Wisconsin Conservatory of Music, piano teacher's diploma, 1951; Alverno College, further study, 1956-62; University of California, Berkeley, B.A. (with great distinction), 1965, M.L.S., 1969, doctoral study, 1969—. *Religion:* Lutheran. *Home:* 1333 37th Ave., San Francisco, Calif. 94122. *Office:* Lafayette School District, P.O. Box 714, Lafayette, Calif. 94549.

CAREER: Comptometer operator in Milwaukee, Wis., 1950-51; library aide at Milwaukee Public Library, 1951-54; Industrial Writers and Illustrators, Wauwatosa, Wis., typist, 1957-58; instrumental music teacher in Milwaukee public schools, 1958-59; junior high school librarian in Elm Grove, Wis., 1959-62; Lafayette School District, Lafayette, Calif., junior high school librarian, 1965-69, district librarian, 1969-73, administrative assistant for curriculum and library services, 1973-75, curriculum director, 1975—. Private music teacher, 1955-59, 1963-68; church choir director, 1957-60, 1963-64; piano accompanist for Damenchor Liederkranz Women's Chorus; vocal soloist. *Member:* American Library Association, National Council of Teachers of English, Association of California School Administrators, California Association for the Gifted, California Association of School Librarians, Phi Beta Kappa, Beta Phi Mu, Pi Lambda Theta, Phi Delta Kappa.

WRITINGS: (Under name Lillian Biermann) *Your Library: How to Use It,* Harper, 1962; (under name Lillian Biermann Wehmeyer) *The School Library Volunteer,* Libraries Unlimited, 1975. Contributor to juvenile, education, and library journals.

WORK IN PROGRESS: The School Librarian as Educator (tentative title); research on children's response to literature, on moral and religious values in children's literature, and on evaluation of education.

* * *

WEINGARTEN, Roger 1945-

PERSONAL: Born December 8, 1945, in Cleveland, Ohio. *Education:* Goddard College, B.A., 1968; University of Iowa, M.F.A., 1970.

CAREER: Western Michigan University, Kalamazoo, instructor in English, 1970-73; writer. *Awards, honors:* National Endowment for the Arts creative writing fellowship, 1973-74; Vermont Council on the Arts grant, 1975.

WRITINGS: Ethan Benjamin Boldt, Knopf, 1975; *What Are Birds Worth,* Cummington Press, 1975. Contributor of poems to *Pig Farmers Almanac, Antaeus, American Review, Chicago Review, Iowa Review,* and *Rune.*

WORK IN PROGRESS: With Bernard Kaplan, *Symbiosis;* a book length poem, *For the Dodge Street Nude.*

* * *

WEINSTEIN, Grace W(ohlner) 1935-

PERSONAL: Born November 19, 1935, in New York, N.Y.; daughter of David (chief of property department of New York State Insurance Bureau) and Esther (Lobel) Wohlner; married Stephen D. Weinstein (an architect), February 24, 1957; children: Lawrence, Janet. *Education:* Cornell University, B.A., 1957. *Home:* 283 Maitland Ave., Teaneck, N.J. 07666. *Agent:* Claire Smith, Harold Ober Associates, 40 East 49th St., New York, N.Y. 10017.

CAREER: Equitable Life Assurance Society, New York, N.Y., member of group annuity department, interpreting contract provisions, 1957-60; *Party Line* (weekly public relations newsletter), New York City, editorial associate, 1961—. Editorial researcher and ghostwriter, 1962-68; freelance writer, 1967—. Instructor at Bergen Community College, 1974-75. *Member:* Society of Magazine Writers, Authors Guild of Authors League of America, League of Women Voters (director of New York chapter, 1969-70; director of Teaneck chapter, 1971-73; second vice-president of Teaneck chapter, 1972-75), New Jersey Press Women.

Awards, honors: Honorable mention in National Media Awards, from American Psychological Foundation, 1975, for *Children and Money.*

WRITINGS: Children and Money: A Guide for Parents, Charterhouse, 1975; *An Introduction to Educational Psychology,* McGraw, 1976.

Author of column "You and Retirement," in *Elks Magazine,* 1975—; New Jersey correspondent for *New York Times.* Contributor to popular magazines, including *Parents' Magazine, Saturday Review/World, Money, House Beautiful, Family Weekly, Physician's World, True,* and *Scholastic Teacher.*

*   *   *

WEIS, Norman D(wight)   1923-

PERSONAL: Born January 9, 1923, in Des Moines, Iowa; son of Leroy Lewis (a Methodist minister) and Lenoir (Fausch) Weis; married Janet Marie Hanson (a secretary), June 22, 1952; children: Wade Allen. *Education:* Iowa Wesleyan College, B.S., 1944; University of Colorado, M.S., 1958. *Home:* 150 Buck Creek Rd., Casper, Wyo. 82601. *Office:* Department of Physical Science, Casper College, 125 College Dr., Casper, Wyo. 82601.

CAREER: Casper College, Casper, Wyo., member of faculty in department of physical sciences, 1959—. *Member:* American Association of University Professors, Experimental Aircraft Association. *Awards, honors:* First place award in photography from Garcia Corp., 1969; award from Wyoming Historical Society, 1972, for publications about Wyoming.

WRITINGS: All About Grizzly Bears, Denlinger's, 1966; *All About the White-Tailed Deer,* Denlinger's, 1969; *Ghost Towns of the Northwest,* Caxton, 1971; *Helldoradoes, Ghosts, and Camps of the Southwest,* Caxton, in press. Contributor of stories to publications of the U.S. State Department and to popular magazines, including *Field and Stream, Outdoor Life, Scientific American, In Wyoming, Road and Track,* and *Mechanix Illustrated.*

WORK IN PROGRESS: A backpacking text.

SIDELIGHTS: Weis has invented a device he calls an electron locator, designed to portray distribution of electrons in neutral atoms. He also built a single-place biplane from scratch, and test flew it successfully in 1975.

BIOGRAPHICAL/CRITICAL SOURCES: In Wyoming, summer, 1968.

*   *   *

WEISS, Elizabeth S(chwartz)   1944-

PERSONAL: Born January 14, 1944, in Rochester, N.Y.; daughter of Raymond (a lawyer) and Josephine (a guidance counselor) Schwartz; married Stanley E. Weiss (an internist and nephrologist), November 22, 1970; children: Mark William. *Education:* Skidmore College, B.A., 1965; Boston University, M.A., 1966. *Residence:* New York, N.Y.

CAREER: Scholastic Book Services, New York, N.Y., associate editor, 1967-68; Doubleday & Co., Inc., New York, N.Y., associate editor, 1968-71; writer, 1971—.

WRITINGS: (With Rita Wolfson) *The Gourmet's Low Cholesterol Cookbook,* Regnery, 1973; (with Wolfson) *The Cholesterol Counter,* Pyramid Publications, 1973; (with Joan Lasky) *Cookmates* (juvenile cookbook), Macrae, 1973; (with Wolfson) *Protein Planner,* Pyramid Publications, 1974; *The Female Breast,* Bantam, 1975. Contributor to *New Woman.*

SIDELIGHTS: Elizabeth Weiss reports that she wrote her first article at the age of seven, submitted it to a national magazine, and still remembers the disappointment when it was coldly rejected by form letter.

*   *   *

WELDING, Patsy Ruth   1924-

PERSONAL: Born December 5, 1924, in Denver, Colo.; daughter of James Edward and Jo Hannah (Koehler) Curley; married John Joseph Welding (a data processing supervisor), July 29, 1943; children: Michael David, Patrick John. *Education:* Attended Colorado State Teachers College, 1942-43, and University of Nevada, Las Vegas, 1958. *Home:* 2408 Isabelle Ave., Las Vegas, Nev. 89101. *Office:* Fremont Junior High School, Las Vegas, Nev.

CAREER: Presbyterian Junior College, Laurinberg, N.C., secretary, 1943-44; Dakota Wesleyan University, Mitchell, S.D., secretary, 1949; substitute teacher in public schools in Carlsbad, N.M., 1950-51; medical secretary in Carlsbad, N.M., 1953; *Las Vegas Review Journal,* Las Vegas, Nev., assistant society editor, 1954-55; Justice Court, Las Vegas, court clerk, 1955-59; Oceanside Municipal Court, San Diego County, Calif., deputy court clerk, 1960-63; Justice Court, Las Vegas, court clerk, 1963-65; Dorsey & Harrison, Las Vegas, legal secretary, 1966-67; Albright & Heaton, Las Vegas, legal secretary, 1967-68; junior high school secretary in North Las Vegas, Nev., 1968-72; Fremont Junior High School, Las Vegas, Nev., secretary, 1972—.

MEMBER: National League of American Pen Women, Nevada School Employees Association, Clark County Educational Secretaries Association, Beta Sigma Phi. *Awards, honors:* Commendation from the governor of Nevada, 1975, for contributions to the welfare of children and youth.

WRITINGS: Let E.S.P. Work for You!, Dial, 1976. Contributor to magazines.

WORK IN PROGRESS: An inspirational volume; an autobiography, for young people; a secretarial handbook.

SIDELIGHTS: Patsy Welding writes: "I take readings by appointment . . . to generate new thought patterns, uncover new paths to success, happiness, and peace of mind. There is never any charge for these readings, for I feel to put a 'price tag' on a special and extraordinary experience would be to lessen the impact, to place the experience with the ordinary and also might serve to diffuse the purity of the reading to a common place: payment for services rendered.

"I do not profess to know how ESP works . . . I only know that it does . . . it did for me yesterday, today, and I know it will tomorrow. It is my opinion that all persons have a contribution to make in the field of ESP research with a recording of their own personal experiences and/or research."

AVOCATIONAL INTERESTS: Music, needlepoint, art, antiques.

*   *   *

WELLINGTON, R(ichard) A(nthony)   1919-

PERSONAL: Born July 6, 1919, in Moseley, England; son of Alec Martin and Dorothy (Marshall) Wellington; married Irene Smallbones, February 15, 1944; children: Nicholas Anthony Peter, Sandra Inga. *Education:* Attended Harrow School, 1933-36. *Politics:* None. *Religion:* Church of England. *Home and office:* Rua Dias de Barros 51/S402, Santa Teresa, Rio de Janeiro, Brazil.

CAREER: Farmer in State of Sao Paulo, Brazil, 1936-40; British Diplomatic Service, first secretary in London (England), Berlin and Frankfurt (Germany), Madrid (Spain), Tehran (Iran), and Recife and Rio de Janeiro (Brazil), 1951-72; adviser to commercial manager of *Jornal do Brasil,* 1974; Cia Algimar Industria Quimica de Alginatos, Natal, Brazil, international and public relations manager, 1975; writer, 1976—. *Military service:* Royal Air Force Volunteer Reserve, pilot, 1940-46; air attache to British embassy, Lisbon, 1944-46; received Distinguished Flying Cross, Polish Medal, Polish Gold Emblem. *Member:* Pathfinder Club, Royal Air Force Club. *Awards, honors:* Distinguished Service Order, 1943; Order of Rio Branco, 1968; Order of the British Empire, 1972; honorable mention from the Foundation for Space Activities and Studies, Brazil.

WRITINGS: *The Brazilians: How They Live and Work,* David & Charles, 1974. Contributor of monthly column to *Money Manager,* 1974—.

WORK IN PROGRESS: A book on Kadiweu Indians of Mato Grosso, *Seek It Lovingly;* a book on war experiences in the Royal Air Force, *Press on Regardless;* editing memoirs of his uncle from World War I.

SIDELIGHTS: Wellington arrived in Brazil in 1919. Brazilian Indians have always fascinated him, and he has visited nearly a dozen tribes. His "main affection is for the Kadiweu Indians of Mato Grosso, who are descendents of the Brazilian Horsemen Indians, the only equestrian tribe of Brazil."

*   *   *

WELLMAN, William A(ugustus) 1896-1975

February 29, 1896—December 9, 1975; American film director, producer, scriptwriter, and author. Obituaries: *New York Times,* December 11, 1975; *Washington Post,* December 11, 1975; *Newsweek,* December 22, 1975; *Time,* December 22, 1975; *Current Biography,* February, 1976.

*   *   *

WELLS, (William) Dicky 1910-

PERSONAL: Born June 10, 1910, in Centersville, Tenn.; son of Wynn George and Florence (Sheldon) Wells; married wife Cherry, June 10, 1936. *Education:* Educated in public high school in Louisville, Ky. *Home:* 153 West 139th St., New York, N.Y. 10030. *Office:* A. E. Ames & Co., Inc., 2 Wall St., New York, N.Y.

CAREER: Jazz musician; has worked as trombonist and music arranger for entertainers including Count Basie, Ray Charles, Fletcher Henderson, Teddy Hill, and Charly Johnson. Presently messenger for A. E. Ames & Co. (stock brokers). *Member:* American Society of Composers, Authors and Publishers, Musicians Union #802, New Amsterdam Musical Association, Masons.

WRITINGS: *Night People: Reminiscences of a Jazzman* (edited by Stanley Dance), Crescendo, 1971.

SIDELIGHTS: Wells' musical performances have taken him to Paris, London, Switzerland, Germany, Denmark, the Netherlands, and Belgium.

*   *   *

WELLS, Linton 1893-1976

April 1, 1893—January 31, 1976; American journalist, foreign correspondent, and author. Obituaries: *New York Times,* February 1, 1976; *Washington Post,* February 2, 1976.

WELLS, William D(eWitt) 1926-

PERSONAL: Born June 22, 1926 in Easton, Pa.; married, 1951; children: one. *Education:* Lafayette College, A.B. (magna cum laude), 1950; Stanford University, A.M., 1952, Ph.D., 1954. *Home:* 5433 South Blackstone Ave., Chicago, Ill. 60615.

CAREER: Stanford Research Institute, Stanford, Calif., statistician for Bureau of Industrial Economics, 1951; Rutgers University, New Brunswick, N.J., instructor, 1953-55, assistant professor, 1955-60, professor of psychology, 1960-66; University of Chicago, Chicago, Ill., professor of psychology and marketing, 1966-74; Needham, Harper & Steers Advertising, Inc., vice-president and director of corporate research, 1974—. Certified psychologist in state of New York. Consultant to government and industry. *Military service:* U.S. Army, Infantry and Counter Intelligence Corps, 1944-47; served in Europe.

MEMBER: American Psychological Association (fellow; member of council of representatives, 1962-65), American Marketing Association (member of board of directors, 1972-74), Association for Consumer Research (member of board of directors, 1971-72; president, 1974), American Association for Public Opinion Research, Institute of Management Sciences, Phi Beta Kappa, Sigma Xi. *Awards, honors:* Grants from Bowles & Bowles, Inc., 1957-66, Ford Foundation, 1966-68, Leo Burnett Co., 1967-72, *Time, National Geographic, Better Homes,* and *Playboy* magazines, 1969-72, and from Committee for Research on Television and Children, 1969-71.

WRITINGS: (Author of instructor's manual with E. Hilgard, E. Jandron, and R. Teevan) *Introduction to Psychology,* Harcourt, 1954, 4th edition, 1962; *The Rutgers Social Attribute Inventory,* Psychometric Affiliates, 1959; *Key Concepts: A Guide to Active Study of Williams' "Psychology: A First Course",* Harcourt, 1970; *Life Style and Psychographics,* American Marketing Association, 1974.

Contributor: G. Williams, editor, *Psychology: A First Course,* Harcourt, 1960; J. Newman, editor, *On Knowing the Consumer,* Wiley, 1966; J. M. Brown and others, editors, *Applied Psychology,* Macmillan, 1966; S. H. Britt, editor, *Consumer Behavior and the Behavioral Sciences,* Wiley, 1966; R. Moyer, editor, *Changing Marketing Systems,* American Marketing Association, 1967; M. S. Moyer, editor, *Marketing for Tomorrow Today,* American Marketing Association, 1967; Johan Arndt, editor, *Insights into Consumer Behavior,* Allyn & Bacon, 1968; M. S. Moyer, editor, *Science in Marketing Management,* University of York, 1969; S. G. Lee and M. Herbert, editors, *Penguin Modern Psychology,* Penguin, 1969; O. Kleppner and I. Seitel, editors, *Exploring Advertising,* Prentice-Hall, 1970; D. T. Kollat, editor, *Research in Consumer Behavior,* Holt, 1970; Britt, editor, *Consumer Behavior in Theory and Action,* Wiley, 1971; D. Aaker, editor, *Multivariate Analysis in Marketing: Theory and Applications,* Wadsworth, 1971; H. F. Fiorillo, editor, *Market Segmentation: Concepts and Applications,* Holt, 1972; S. Ward and T. Robertson, editors, *Consumer Behavior: Theoretical Sources,* Prentice-Hall, 1973; John R. Thompson, editor, *Cases and Readings in Marketing Research,* Random House, 1973; R. Ferber, editor, *Handbook of Marketing Research,* McGraw, in press.

General editor of "Seven Perspectives in Marketing" series published by Harper. Contributor of about thirty-five articles and reviews to business and psychology journals. Member of editorial board of *Journal of Marketing Re-*

                                            597

search, 1968—; *Journal of Consumer Research,* member of editorial board, 1972-74, member of policy board, 1972—.

* * *

WELS, Byron G(erald) 1924-

PERSONAL: Born April 20, 1924, in New York, N.Y.; son of Joseph and Henrietta (Schreiber) Wels; divorced; children: Joshua, Deborah, Heather. *Education:* Attended Brooklyn College of City University of New York; also studied at Cleveland Institute of Electronics and various military radio and radar schools. *Home:* 32-L Riverview Gardens, North Arlington, N.J. 07032. *Office: Magic Magazine,* 381 Park Ave. S., New York, N.Y. 10016.

CAREER: Prior to 1963 worked as advanced research and developmental electronics technician for such firms as Potter Instruments, Amperex, and Fairchild Engine Division, and in publications departments of other firms, including Radio Engineering Laboratories, Westbury Electronics, and Eldico Electronics; *Popular Mechanics,* electronics editor based in New York, N.Y., and Chicago, Ill., 1963-66; Davis Publications, Inc., New York, N.Y., editor-in-chief of *Radio-TV Experimenter* and *Elementary Electronics* and also electronics editor of sister magazine, *Science and Mechanics,* 1964-66; *Popular Electronics,* New York, N.Y., feature editor, 1966-67; Conover-Mast, Inc., New York, N.Y., started as engineering editor for *Mill & Factory,* became managing editor of *Construction Equipment* 1967-69; *Data Products News,* New York, N.Y., editor-in-chief, 1969-70; writer or executive for public relations firms in New York, N.Y., and Princeton, N.J., 1970-72; Singer Communications Corp., Little Falls, N.J., public relations and advertising and writer of correspondence courses, 1972—; currently editor-in-chief of *Magic* magazine. Holds Federal Communications Commission second class radiotelephone license, amateur radio operator's license, and pilot certificate. *Military service:* U.S. Army Air Forces; received Air Medal. *Member:* Flying Engineers, New York Advertising Sportsmen's Club, Masons.

WRITINGS: Layman's Guide to Hi-Fi, American Electronics Co., 1959; *Getting the Most from Your Hi-Fi and Stereo System,* Editors and Engineers, 1966; *Here Is Your Hobby: Magic* (juvenile), Putnam, 1967; *Here Is Your Hobby: Amateur Radio* (juvenile), Putnam, 1968; *Transistor Circuit Guidebook,* TAB Books, 1968; *Electronics in Photography,* Sams, 1968; *Fell's Guide to Guns and How to Use Them Safely—Legally—Responsibly,* Fell, 1969; *Computer Circuits and How They Work,* TAB Books, 1970; *Fire and Theft Security Systems,* TAB Books, 1971; *How to Build Clocks and Watches,* Auerbach, 1971; *Science Fair Experiments* (juvenile), Auerbach, 1971; *Simple Wall Paneling,* Doubleday, 1971; *How to Repair Musical Instrument Amplifiers,* TAB Books, 1973.

Contributor to about eighty popular, technical, and trade magazines, including *Argosy, Popular Photography, Reader's Digest, Bachelor, Guns and Hunting, True, Holiday, National Wildlife, Skiing, Boys' Life, American Sportsman,* and *Civil Engineering.*

WORK IN PROGRESS: Revising *Fire and Theft Security Systems,* for TAB Books; a book on how to upholster furniture, also for TAB Books; a book on candle making, for Putnam; a book on hot air balloons, for Drake.

SIDELIGHTS: Wels commented: "Mort Persky, of *Family Weekly* calls me his 'man of perilous adventure,' and continually gives me assignments that his staffers won't

touch. It was Mort that got me to solo in a balloon for the first time, and has had me in race cars at Daytona, and Lord knows what he'll have for me in the future. I'm a licensed pilot, and love to use my writing skills to explore new and different areas that I might never have been able to expose myself to had I to depend on my own finances.

"Writing is not a suitable career for anybody, as there are so few who are howlingly successful. I've received royalty checks for as little as 68¢, and would actively discourage any who would pursue this as a full-time career. Once, I tried freelancing on a full-time basis, was writing a book, and my daughter was approached by a nosy neighbor who asked, 'Honey, what does your daddy do?' Debbie knew I was writing a book, so she said, 'He's a book-maker!' Try to live THAT down!

"But the *cacothes scrivendi* is a strong urge, and once you start, you can't stop. I simply stumble along, doing my best, and wishing I could do better. the *Magic* magazine certainly looks promising, and I'm working diligently at making it a success. If all it took was hard work, we'd be over the top now. Still, it IS my best shot, and I'm giving it my all."

* * *

WENDEL, Natalja Rose 1900-

PERSONAL: Born April 16, 1900, in Odessa, Russia; daughter of Theodore Michael (a wheat expert) and Isabelle (a translator of poetry; maiden name, Rochere) Hirschberg; married Eugenius Kudla deKudlevsky, June, 1917; married Rudolf Pierre Wendel (inventor of Wendelighting) May, 1928 (died, 1955); children: Alex R. Wendel, Natalja Wendel Loeb, Francesca M. Cancian, Christina M. Wendel, Vera A. Wendel Finnerty. *Education:* Attended nursing schools in Vienna; received R.N. diploma in Berlin, 1923. *Politics:* Democrat. *Religion:* Roman Catholic. *Home and office:* 3400 Guerneville Rd., Santa Rosa, Calif. 95401.

CAREER: Worked as nurse in hospitals, including Grinzing Hospital, and as welfare worker, in Vienna, Austria, 1915-22; welfare worker in Berlin, Germany, 1922-23; served as chief of Quaker-rehabilitated hospitals in Poland, established nursing school and taught nurses at St. Lazarus Hospital in Lvov, and worked in a clinic in Grudziadz, 1923-25; guide and lecturer on art treasures in Italy, especially Rome, 1925-28; worked in husband's lighting business, in New York and later in Santa Rosa, Calif., 1930-54; translator, writer, 1955—. Maintains a dairy herd of 240 cattle in Santa Rosa. *Member:* American Institute of Fine Arts (fellow). *Awards, honors:* Decoration for bravery beyond the call of duty from Empress Zita of Austria, 1918, for medical work under fire at the front.

WRITINGS: Sketchbook of a Wayfarer (poems), Book Craftsmen Associates, 1963; *Summer in Spoleto* (novel), Fell, 1967; *Born in April: The Story of Natascha and Pierre* (autobiography), Fell, 1975.

WORK IN PROGRESS: Friday Bus, a book of short stories and a novelette; *Homeless Angel,* a book of poems.

SIDELIGHTS: Natalja Wendel describes herself as "motivated since early childhood by interest and compassion for the short-changed in society. Pacifist since I can remember, with passionate concern for the sanctity of life and importance of the individual, my leitmotiv remains that life without friendship and love is a desert."

Born in April is based on Mrs. Wendel's journal writings

that she has been keeping since leaving Russia in 1915. *Summer in Spoleto* has been adapted as a screenplay, released by Dimitrios Films in 1969.

BIOGRAPHICAL/CRITICAL SOURCES: San Francisco Sunday Examiner and Chronicle, July 13, 1975.

*   *   *

WERLIN, Herbert Holland 1932-

PERSONAL: Born May 23, 1932, in Chicago, Ill.; son of Joseph Sidney (a professor) and Rosella (Horowitz) Werlin; married Mary Kathryn Hansman (an educational consultant), April 5, 1969; children: one daughter. *Education:* University of Chicago, A.B. (liberal arts), 1953; Exeter College, Oxford, B.A. and M.A. (in politics, philosophy, and economics), both 1955; Yale University, M.A. (political science), 1957; University of California, Berkeley, Ph.D., 1966. *Politics:* Democrat. *Religion:* Unitarian-Universalist. *Home:* 4002 Beechwood, Hyattsville, Md. 20782. *Office:* Montgomery County Office of Comprehensive Health Planning, Rockville, Md.

CAREER: Texas Technological College (now Texas Tech University), Lubbock, instructor in government, 1958-60; University of Nairobi, Nairobi, Kenya, lecturer in government, autumn, 1963; State University of New York at Stony Brook, instructor, 1965-66, assistant professor of government and politics, 1966-67; United Nations Institute for Training and Research, New York City, affiliate, 1967-68; Queens College of the City University of New York, Flushing, N.Y., visiting assistant professor of African politics, summer, 1968; University of Maryland, College Park, assistant professor of African studies and politics, 1968-74; Hofstra University, Hempstead, N.Y., adjunct associate professor of political science, 1974-75; Montgomery County Office of Comprehensive Health Planning, Rockville, Md., research analyst, 1976—. *Military service:* U.S. Army, 1957-58. U.S. Army Reserve, 1958-60.

MEMBER: African Studies Association, American Political Science Association, American Association of University Professors, American Society for Public Administration, Pi Sigma Alpha (president of Iota chapter, 1962-63). *Awards, honors:* Adlai Stevenson fellow at United Nations Institute for Training and Research, 1967-68.

WRITINGS: Governing an African City: A Study of Nairobi, Africana Publishing, 1974. Contributor to professional journals. Consultant to *Choice,* 1966—.

*   *   *

WERTSMAN, Vladimir 1929-

PERSONAL: Born April 6, 1929, in Secureni, Romania; came to the United States in 1967; naturalized U.S. citizen, 1972; son of Filip and Anna Wertsman. *Education:* University A.I. Cuza, diploma in legal sciences (LL.M.; summa cum laude), 1953; Columbia University, M.S.L.S., 1969. *Home:* 55 East 208th St., Bronx, N.Y. 10467. *Office:* Brooklyn Public Library, 1580 Rockaway Parkway, Brooklyn, N.Y. 11236.

CAREER: Lawyer with practice in criminal and civil law in Romania, 1953-67; First National City Bank, New York, N.Y., stock certificates examiner, 1967-68; Brooklyn Public Library, Brooklyn, N.Y., reference librarian in Science and Industry Division, 1969-74, senior librarian and assistant branch librarian at Canarsie Branch, 1974—, member of committee on African materials, 1974.

MEMBER: American Library Association, American Top-

ical Association (philatelic organization), National Travel Club, National Writers Club, Brooklyn Public Library Chess Club (president, 1974), Brooklyn Public Library Stamp Club (president, 1974), Brooklyn Public Library Canarsie Branch Chess Club (president, 1975), Delta Tau Kappa.

WRITINGS: The Romanians in America, 1748-1974, Oceana, 1975; *The Russians in America, 1727-1975,* Oceana, in press; *The Ukrainians in America, 1608-1975,* Oceana, in press. Poems have been anthologized in *The 1973 Collection,* Graphicopy, 1973. Contributor of about thirty articles to law, library, and philatelic periodicals.

SIDELIGHTS: "American history is in essence ethnic history," Wertsman wrote. "I view ethnicity as the spice of America." In addition to Romanian, Wertsman is fluent in Russian and Ukrainian, and has working knowledge of German, French, and Spanish. *Avocational interests:* Chess, stamp-collecting, music, travel (Europe, North, Central, and South America, and Asia).

BIOGRAPHICAL/CRITICAL SOURCES: Ethnic American News, October, 1975.

*   *   *

WESCHCKE, Carl L(ouis) 1930-
(Gnosticus)

PERSONAL: Born September 10, 1930, in St. Paul, Minn.; son of Carl (a horticulturist) and Magdalene (Tipple) Weschcke; married Sandra Kae Heggum (a publishing executive), December 21, 1972; children: Gabriel Llewellyn. *Education:* Babson Institute, B.Sc., 1951; University of Minnesota, graduate study. *Politics:* Independent. *Religion:* Wiccan. *Home:* 476 Summit Ave., St. Paul, Minn. 55102. *Office:* Llewellyn Publications, P.O. Box 3383, St. Paul, Minn. 55165.

CAREER: General manager, Chester-Kent, Inc., 1951-58; St. Paul Advertising Co., St. Paul, Minn., president, 1958—. President of Llewellyn Publications, 1960—, Gnostica Book Stores, 1970—, and Hazel Hills Corp., 1972—. Chairman of Council of American Witches, 1973—. *Military service:* U.S. Army. *Member:* American Federation of Astrologers, Gnostic-Aquarian Society (chairman, 1975).

WRITINGS: The Science of Feeling Fine, Chester-Kent, 1964; (with Louis Culling) *The Occult Renaissance,* Llewellyn, 1972; (with wife, Sandra Kae Weschcke) *A Wiccan Rite of Marriage,* Llewellyn, in press. Author of columns on the occult, under pseudonym Gnosticus, in *Gnostica,* 1973—. Editor of *Gnosis: Essays on the New Occultism.*

WORK IN PROGRESS: So You Want to Be a Witch.

SIDELIGHTS: Weschcke writes: "My personal interests are entirely involved with the Occult—as 'Ancient Wisdom,' as New Age Science, as religion, as a cultural phenomenon. I see the Occult as concerned with Man's evolution both individually and as race—and the technologies of Magick, WitchCraft, etc. are methods for accelerating personal growth."

BIOGRAPHICAL/CRITICAL SOURCES: Armand Biteau, *The New Consciousness,* Scribner, 1975.

*   *   *

WESENCRAFT, Charles Frederick 1928-

PERSONAL: Born January 17, 1928; son of Frederick Percival (a teacher) and Sally (Parker) Wesencraft; married Anne Urron Waister (a biology teacher), August 1, 1953;

children: Elizabeth Anne, John Douglas. *Education:* Attended School of Architecture, Newcastle, 1948-51. *Home:* 44 Pembroke Dr., Ponteland, Northumberland, England. *Office:* Museum Services, Higham Pl., Newcastle-on-Tyne, England.

CAREER: Museum Services, Newcastle-on-Tyne, England, senior administrative officer; lecturer. *Military service:* British Army, Royal Artillery, 1947-49; became lieutenant. *Member:* Morpeth Round Table, Morpeth Al Club.

WRITINGS: Practical Wargaming, Hippocrene Books, 1974.

WORK IN PROGRESS: With Pike and Musket; Seven Steps to Freedom.

* * *

WESTERBERG, Christine 1950-

PERSONAL: Born September 26, 1950, in Glen Cove, N.Y.; daughter of Arthur R. (a personnel manager) and Jane (an artist; maiden name, McCaffrey) Westerberg; married Richard J. DiMonda (a biomedical engineer), October 5, 1974. *Education:* Philadelphia College of Art, B.F.A., 1972; also studied at C. W. Post College of Long Island University. *Agent:* Kirchoff-Wohlberg, 331 East 50th St., New York, N.Y. 10022.

CAREER: American Institute of Physics, New York, N.Y., member of art staff, 1972; children's book illustrator, 1972—.

WRITINGS: A Little Lion (self-illustrated children's book), Prentice-Hall, 1975.

Illustrator of children's books: *Tom Thumb,* retold by Mercy Yates, Prentice-Hall, 1973; Eleanor J. Lapp, *Duane the Collector,* Addison Wesley, 1975; Mark Taylor, *The Hiding Place,* Allyn & Bacon, 1975.

SIDELIGHTS: Christine Westerberg writes: "My interest in illustrating children's stories and writing them is partly because I enjoy it, and partly because I feel a child's interest in reading must be stimulated early and be cultivated, as a basis for his whole attitude toward reading and learning as an adult."

* * *

WESTERVELT, Virginia Veeder 1914-

PERSONAL: Born September 19, 1914, in Schenectady, N.Y.; daughter of Eugene W. (a pharmacist) and Millicent (a writer and teacher; maiden name, Winton) Veeder; married Ralph V. Westervelt (a school superintendent), September 1, 1936; children: Dirck Eugene, Deidre Virginia (Mrs. David Hunt). *Education:* Attended Pomona College, 1931-33; Wellesley College, A.B., 1935; graduate study, summers, Central School of Speech and Drama, London, England, 1935, New York University, 1940, Columbia University, 1954; Syracuse University, M.A., 1960. *Religion:* Protestant. *Home:* 1050 Bermuda Dr., Redlands, Calif. 92372. *Agent:* McIntosh & Otis, 18 East 41st St., New York, N.Y. 10017.

CAREER: Jordan Marsh Co., Boston, Mass., executive trainee, 1935-36; high school teacher of English at public and private schools in Schenectady, N.Y., 1938-40, 1948-57, and in New Hartford, N.Y., 1958-66; University of Redlands, Redlands, Calif., instructor in English, 1969-73; Crafton Hills College, Yucaipa, Calif., instructor in English, 1973—. Teacher of extension courses, Ithaca College, 1960-66; visiting professor, Hong Kong Baptist Bible College, 1975; consultant to leadership conferences. *Member:* P.E.N. International, American Association of University Professors, American Association of University Women, National League of American Pen Women, Chaparral Poets, California Writers' Guild, Lutheran Church Women (president, 1971), Sierra Club, Friends of Smiley Library, Foothill Wellesley Club. *Awards, honors:* American Newspaper Publishers Association grant, 1960; Achievement Award, 1970, and state poetry and article prizes, 1969, 1970, 1972, and 1975, from National League of American Pen Women.

WRITINGS: Getting Along in the Teen-Age World, Putnam, 1957; *Choosing a Career in a Changing World,* Putnam, 1959; *The World Was His Laboratory,* Messner, 1964; *Incredible Man of Science: Irving Langmuir,* Messner, 1968. Writer of church school curriculum materials and pamphlets for Muhlenberg Press. Contributor of articles, reviews and stories to *American Girl, Christian Science Monitor, The Lutheran, Modern Maturity, Nature Magazine, Wilderness Camping,* and other periodicals.

WORK IN PROGRESS: A fictional account of the Battle of Saratoga for young people in collaboration with mother, Millicent Winton Veeder, tentatively titled *Guns on the Heights;* a biography of Pearl Buck for young people, completion expected in 1976.

* * *

WETHERILL, Peter Michael 1932-

PERSONAL: Born October 18, 1932, in Leeds, England; son of Sydney (an electrician) and Agnes (Sowden) Wetherill; married Francine Hatchuel (a university professor), January 25, 1958; children: Katherine Anne, Isabelle Jean. *Education:* University of Birmingham, B.A., 1954, M.A., 1956; University of Strasbourg, Docteur de l'Universite, 1962. *Home:* 14 Alma Rd., Stockport SK4 4PU, England. *Office:* Department of French, University of Manchester, Manchester M13 9PL, England.

CAREER: University of New England, Armidale, New South Wales, Australia, lecturer in French, 1958-60; University of Leeds, Leeds, England, lecturer in French, 1961-68; University of Manchester, Manchester, England, senior lecturer, 1968-75, reader in French, 1975—. *Military service:* British Army, Signal Corps, 1956-58; became second lieutenant. *Member:* Society for French Studies, Association of University Teachers.

WRITINGS: Baudelaire et la poesie d'E.A. Poe (title means "Baudelaire and the Poetry of E. A. Poe"), Nizet, 1962; *Flaubert et la creation litteraire* (title means "Flaubert and Literary Creation"), Nizet, 1964; *The Literary Text: An Examination of Critical Methods,* University of California Press, 1974. Contributor to language and literature journals.

WORK IN PROGRESS: Research on cliches in popular fiction, on the manuscript of Flaubert's *Salammbo,* on Flaubert and the growth of the modern novel, and on the novel and society.

AVOCATIONAL INTERESTS: Music, travel (Europe and Southeast Asia).

* * *

WEYL, Woldemar A. 1901(?)-1975

1901(?)—July 30, 1975; German-born American educator, expert on glass technology, and author of books in his field. Obituaries: *New York Times,* August 4, 1975; *AB Bookman's Weekly,* December 1, 1975.

WHEELER, Robert C(ordell) 1913-

PERSONAL: Born August 5, 1913, in Columbus, Ohio; son of Carl L. (a salesman) and Caroline (Cordell) Wheeler; married Ardis M. Hillman (a teacher), June 9, 1939; children: Kristi (Mrs. John Andrew Dickwall), Jonathan. *Education:* Ohio State University, B.S., 1938. *Home:* 2183 Payne Ave., St. Paul, Minn. 55117. *Office:* Minnesota Historical Society, 690 Cedar, St. Paul, Minn. 55101.

CAREER: Ohio Historical Society, Columbus, head of newspaper library, 1942-49, assistant director, Ohio Sesquicentennial Commission, 1949-54, field director, 1954-57; Minnesota Historical Society, St. Paul, assistant director, 1957-64, associate director, 1964—. Director of American phase, Quetico-Superior Underwater Archaeology Project, 1961—. *Military service:* U.S. Army, 1942-45; became sergeant. *Member:* Society for Historical Archaeology, Council on Underwater Archaeology (chairman of board, 1970-76).

WRITINGS: Ohio Newspapers: A Living Record, Ohio History Press, 1950; (contributor) George Bass, editor, *History of Seafaring Based on Underwater Archaeology,* Walker & Co., 1972; *Voices from the Rapids,* Minnesota Historical Society, 1975.

SIDELIGHTS: Wheeler is an authority on the history of the North American fur trade.

* * *

WHEELER-BENNETT, John 1902-1975

October 13, 1902—December 9, 1975; British historian, educator, authority on international affairs, and author of books in his field. Obituaries: *New York Times,* December 11, 1975; *Time,* December 22, 1975; *Publishers Weekly,* January 5, 1976; *AB Bookman's Weekly,* March 1, 1976.

* * *

WHEELOCK, (Kinch) Carter 1924-

PERSONAL: Born July 6, 1924, in Amarillo, Tex.; son of Howard E. and Fannie B. (Carter) Wheelock; married Ernestine S. Gibson (a journalist), August 15, 1945; children: Elizabeth Ann, David Carter. *Education:* Texas Technological College (now Texas Tech University), B.A., 1948, M.A., 1949; University of Texas, Ph.D., 1966. *Politics:* "Moderate conservative." *Home:* 4008 Greenhill Pl., Austin, Tex. 78759. *Office:* Department of Spanish and Portuguese, 112 Batts Hall, University of Texas, Austin, Tex. 78712.

CAREER: Good Neighborhood Commission of Texas (state agency), Austin, assistant director, 1951-52; Office of the Attorney General of Texas, Austin, public information officer, 1952-56; *Tipro Reporter* (oil industry trade publication), Austin, associate editor, 1956-59; University of Texas, Austin, instructor, 1959-65, assistant professor, 1966-69, associate professor of Spanish-American literature, 1969—, associate dean of humanities, 1974—. Head of department of modern languages at Universidad del Valle, 1962-64. *Military service:* U.S. Navy, 1943-46. *Member:* Modern Language Association of America, American Association of Teachers of Spanish and Portuguese, Alpha Chi, Phi Kappa Phi.

WRITINGS: The Mythmaker: A Study of Motif and Symbol in the Short Stories of Jorge Luis Borges, University of Texas Press, 1969. Contributor to literature journals.

WORK IN PROGRESS: Research on Spanish-American literature of the nineteenth and early twentieth centuries, especially the fantastic short story and realist short story and novel.

SIDELIGHTS: Wheelock has traveled extensively in South America and Europe.

* * *

WHETTEN, Lawrence L. 1932-

PERSONAL: Born June 12, 1932, in Provo, Utah. *Education:* Brigham Young University, B.A., 1954, M.A., 1955; Rutgers University, graduate study, 1955-56; New York University, Ph.D., 1963.

CAREER: U.S. Air Force, operations intelligence officer, 10th Tactical Reconnaisance Wing, Europe, 1960-63, senior political analyst, Headquarters USAF Europe, Wiesbaden, Germany, 1963-70; University of Oklahoma European Program, Munich, Germany, guest professor of political science, 1970-71; University of Southern California Graduate Program in International Relations, Munich, Germany, resident professor and director of program, 1971—. Part-time guest professor, University of Maryland European Programs, Heidelberg, various periods between 1963-71. Staff consultant, Foreign Policy Research Institute, Philadelphia, 1969-70, 1971-72. *Member:* American Academy of Political and Social Science, American Association for the Advancement of Soviet Studies, Royal Institute of International Affairs (London), International Institute for Strategic Studies.

WRITINGS: Germany's Ostpolitik: Relations Between the Federal Republic and the Warsaw Pact, Oxford University Press for Royal Institute of International Affairs, 1971; *The Soviet Presence in the Middle East* (monograph), National Strategy Information Agency, 1971; *Contemporary American Foreign Policy: Minimal Diplomacy, Defensive Strategy and Detente Management,* Heath, 1974; *The Canal War: Four Power Conflict in the Middle East,* M.I.T. Press, 1974; (editor) *Detente and Security Matters Within the Warsaw Pact,* M.I.T. Press, in press; (with Gerald Livingston) *Germany East and West,* Council on Foreign Relations, in press. Also author of *The Soviet-American Special Relationship: Case Studies and Observations.*

Contributor: Robert Pfaltzgraff, editor, *Alliance Problems in the 1970's,* Foreign Policy Research Institute for U.S. Department of Defense, 1972; Phillip A. Richardson, editor, *American Strategy at the Crossroads,* U.S. Government Printing Office, 1973; Robert Dean, editor, *East European Perspectives on European Security and Cooperation,* Praeger, 1974; Stephen Kirby, editor, *Sovereignty and International Law,* Macmillan, in press. Also contributor to *European Security for the 1970's,* edited by William Kinter, published by Foreign Policy Research Institute.

Contributor of about forty articles to international relations and military journals in United States, Switzerland, England, and Argentina.

* * *

WHIFFEN, Marcus 1916-

PERSONAL: Born March 4, 1916, near Ross, England; son of Harold Alfred and Joyce (Thomas) Whiffen; married Jean le Fleming Burrow (a physical therapist), March 1, 1941; children: Paul, Godfrey, Pamela. *Education:* Cambridge University, B.A., 1937, M.A., 1945. *Home:* 4703

East Exeter Blvd., Phoenix, Ariz. 85018. *Office:* College of Architecture, Arizona State University, Tempe, Ariz. 85281.

CAREER: Architect and Building News, London, England, editorial assistant, 1938-39; *Architectural Review,* London, England, assistant editor, 1946-52; Massachusetts Institute of Technology, Cambridge, lecturer in architectural history, 1952-53; University of Texas, Austin, visiting lecturer in architectural history, 1953-54; Colonial Williamsburg, Williamsburg, Va., architectural historian, 1954-59; Vassar College, Poughkeepsie, N.Y., lecturer in architectural history, 1959-60; Arizona State University, Tempe, associate professor, 1960-65, professor of architecture, 1966—. Visiting professor at University of British Columbia, 1971.

MEMBER: College Art Association of America, Society of Architectural Historians (director, 1967-69, 1975—), Architectural Association (England), Association of Collegiate Schools of Architecture (director, 1962-67). *Awards, honors:* Annual book award and Alice Hitchcock Medallion from Society of Architectural Historians, 1958, for *The Public Buildings of Williamsburg.*

WRITINGS: Stuart and Georgian Churches, Batsford, 1948; *Thomas Archer: Architect of the English Baroque,* Art and Technics, 1950, revised edition, Hennessey, 1973; *An Introduction to Elizabethan and Jacobean Architecture,* Art and Technics, 1952; *The Public Buildings of Williamsburg,* Colonial Williamsburg, 1958; *The Eighteenth-Century Houses of Williamsburg,* Holt for Colonial Williamsburg, 1960; (editor) *The Teaching of Architecture,* American Institute of Architects, 1964; (editor) *The History, Theory, and Criticism of Architecture,* M.I.T. Press, 1965; (editor) *The Architect and the City,* M.I.T. Press, 1966; *American Architecture since 1780: A Guide to the Styles,* M.I.T. Press, 1969.

Contributor to art, architecture, education, and literary journals, and to *Listener, Burlington, Times Literary Supplement, New Statesman,* and *Nation.* Editor of *Journal of Architectural Education,* 1962-68.

SIDELIGHTS: Whiffen writes: "That I should be a writer at all is due to my father, with his love of literature and respect for the profession of author.... He chose my first name to look well in print in combination with my surname—so skilfully that in London I used to meet people who would tell me that they had always assumed that Marcus Whiffen was a nom de plume."

* * *

WHINNEY, Margaret Dickens 1897-1975

February 4, 1897—September 5, 1975; British educator, art historian, author of books in her field. Obituaries: *AB Bookman's Weekly,* December 1, 1975.

* * *

WHITE, Alice Violet 1922-

PERSONAL: Born June 10, 1922, in England; daughter of Harold James and Sarah (Gittens) White. *Education:* F. L. Calder College, teacher's diploma, 1942; London Institute, teacher's certificate in dressmaking, 1942, home upholstery, 1950, and needlework, 1951; College of Handicraft, M. Coll. H., 1953. *Home:* 66 Liverpool Rd. S., Burscough, Lancashire, England. *Office:* St. Katharine's Training College, Taggart Ave., Liverpool, England.

CAREER: Shropshire College of Domestic Science and Dairywork, Shropshire, England, teacher of needlework, 1946-53; St. Katharine's Training College, Liverpool, England, senior lecturer in crafts, 1954—. Has also taught at University of Liverpool and for Lancashire Education Authority. Certified in dressmaking, hand embroidery, needlework, tailoring, and dress design by City and Guild of London Institute and by Union of Lancashire and Cheshire Institutes. Member of management committee for Children's Society Home. *Military service:* Women's Auxiliary Air Force (England), electrician, 1943-46.

MEMBER: Society of Authors, College of Handicraft Teachers, Embroiderers Guild (committee member of northwest England branch), Association of Teachers in Colleges and Departments of Education.

WRITINGS: Concise Manual of Sewing, E. J. Arnold, 1955; *Soft Furnishing and Home Embroidery,* Routledge & Kegan Paul, 1956; *Stage Costume for Amateurs,* Routledge & Kegan Paul, 1957; *Blackwork Embroidery of Today,* Taplinger, 1958; *Weaving Is Fun,* Taplinger, 1959; *Needlecraft for Juniors* (juvenile), Routledge & Kegan Paul, 1960; *Look and Stitch* (juvenile), E. J. Arnold, 1962; *Primary Embroidery,* Routledge & Kegan Paul, 1964; *Performing Toys* (juvenile), Taplinger, 1972; *More Performing Toys,* Taplinger, 1972; *Using Fabrics for Fun,* Drake, 1972; *Walter in Love* (juvenile), Lothrop, 1973.

* * *

WHITE, Edgar B. 1947-

PERSONAL: Born April 4, 1947, in Montserrat, West Indies; came to United States, 1952; son of Charles and Phyllis White. *Education:* Attended City College of the City University of New York, 1964-65, New York University, 1966-69, Yale University, 1971-73. *Politics:* "Rastafarian." *Religion:* "Rastafarian." *Home:* 230 East 4th St., New York, N.Y. 10009. *Agent:* Rosemary Stewart, 242 East Tenth St., New York, N.Y. 10009. *Office:* 24 Bond St., New York, N.Y. 10003.

CAREER: Musician, playwright, and novelist. Playwright-in-residence at Yale University Drama School, 1971-72, and currently at New York Shakespeare Festival Public Theatre. Artistic director of The Yardbird Players acting company, 1971—; currently member of Black Theatre Alliance. *Member:* Authors Guild. *Awards, honors:* O'Neill playwright award; grants from Rockefeller Foundation, Creative Artists Public Service, and state of New York.

WRITINGS—Plays: *Underground: Four Plays* (includes "The Burghers of Calais"; "Fun in Lethe; or, The Feast of Misrule"; "The Mummer's Play," first produced in New York at Shakespeare Festival Public Theatre, 1965; and "The Wonderful Yeare," first produced in New York at Other Stage Theatre, October 24, 1969), Morrow, 1970; *The Crucificado: Two Plays* (includes "The Crucificado"; and "The Life and Times of J. Walter Smintheus," first produced in New York at Shakespeare Festival Public Theatre, April 18, 1971), Morrow, 1973.

Other: *Sati, the Rastifarian* (novel), Lothrop, 1973; *Omar at Christmas* (novel), Lothrop, 1973; *The Yardbird Reader,* privately printed, 1973; *Children of Night* (novel), Lothrop, 1974.

WORK IN PROGRESS: The Pygmies and the Pyramid, a novel; *The Aromancy Tales; The Defense,* a play.

BIOGRAPHICAL/CRITICAL SOURCES: New York Post, September 22, 1974.

WHITEHEAD, G(eorge) Kenneth 1913-

PERSONAL: Born May 16, 1913, in Bury, Lancashire, England; son of Percy Kay (a dyer) and Dorothy Myrtle (Wike) Whitehead; married Nancy Bagot, 1965 (divorced, 1972). *Education:* Attended Uppingham School, 1927-31. *Religion:* Church of England. *Home:* Old House, Withnell Fold, Chorley, Lancashire, England.

CAREER: Withnell Fold Paper Mill, Chorley, Lancashire, England, manager, 1947-68, raw material buyer, 1968—. Former director of Liverpool Storage Co. Ltd. *Military service:* British Army, Royal Artillery, 1940-45; became major. *Member:* Fauna Preservation Society, British Deer Society, Zoological Society of London (fellow), Conseil International de la Chasse.

WRITINGS: Deer and Their Management, Country Life, 1950; *The Ancient White Cattle of Great Britain,* Faber, 1953; *The Deer-Stalking Grounds of Great Britain and Ireland,* Hollis & Carter, 1960; *Deerstalking in Scotland,* Percival Marshall & Co., 1964; *The Deer of Great Britain and Ireland,* Routledge & Kegan Paul, 1964; *Wild Goats of Great Britain and Ireland,* David & Charles, 1972; *Deer of the World,* Viking, 1972. Contributor to *Country Life, Field, Shooting Times,* and other outdoor magazines.

WORK IN PROGRESS: Hunting and Stalking Deer through the Ages.

SIDELIGHTS: Whitehead has studied ruminants and collected specimens in most European countries, Australasia, the United States, Canada, Morocco, and West Africa for a private museum. As an amateur, he played in all of England's Association Football (soccer) team matches, 1938-39, and he formerly played tennis for the Lancashire county team. *Avocational interests:* Nature filmmaking.

* * *

WHITFIELD, Stephen J(ack) 1942-

PERSONAL: Born December 3, 1942, in Houston, Tex.; son of Bert (a salesman) and Joan (Schwarz) Whitfield. *Education:* Tulane University, B.A., 1964; Yale University, M.A., 1966; Brandeis University, Ph.D., 1972. *Politics:* Social democratic. *Religion:* Judaism. *Office:* Department of American Studies, Brandeis University, Waltham, Mass. 02154.

CAREER: Southern University, New Orleans, La., instructor in history, 1966-68; high school teacher of history in the public schools of Jacksonville, Fla., 1968-69; Brandeis University, Waltham, Mass., assistant professor of American studies, 1972—. *Member:* American Studies Association, American Civil Liberties Union, Democratic Socialist Organizing Committee.

WRITINGS: Scott Nearing: Apostle of American Radicalism, Columbia University Press, 1974. Book reviewer for *New Leader,* 1971-75.

WORK IN PROGRESS: A study of the impact of totalitarianism on American thought.

* * *

WHITMAN, John 1944-

PERSONAL: Born November 26, 1944, in Norwalk, Conn.; son of Albert R. (in advertising) and Edith (Whitridge) Whitman. *Education:* Attended Princeton University, 1962-65; College of St. Thomas, M.A.T., 1970; also studied at University of Grenoble and University of Bordeaux. *Agent:* Sterling Lord Agency, 600 Madison Ave., New York, N.Y. 10021.

CAREER: Translator for newsmen during the Olympic Games at Grenoble, France; French teacher at Highcroft Country Day School, 1966-67; researcher for Simplified Travel, Inc., 1972. *Member:* American Society for Psychical Research, New York Horticultural Society, New York Botanical Gardens.

WRITINGS: The Special Guide to Europe, New American Library, 1972; *The Psychic Power of Plants,* New American Library, 1974; *Whitman's Off Season Travel Guide to Europe,* St. Martin's, 1975; *Starting from Scratch,* Quadrangle, 1976.

WORK IN PROGRESS: A travel series for St. Martin's, including *Whitman's Europe You Can Afford;* books on plant care and cultivation.

SIDELIGHTS: Whitman is competent in French, Italian, Spanish, Portuguese, and Swedish. He has traveled almost a million miles in the past ten years, and has traveled through Europe and North Africa on a motorcycle.

* * *

WIEMAN, Harold F(rancis) 1917-

PERSONAL: Born October 10, 1917, in Sacramento, Calif.; son of Drury Park and Edith L. (Tidball) Wieman; married Althea Bilsborrow, June 12, 1943; children: James Drury, Elizabeth Jane. *Education:* San Bernardino Junior College, A.A., 1937; Occidental College (Los Angeles), B.A., 1939. *Religion:* Methodist. *Home:* 550 Dunes, Morro Bay, Calif. 93442. *Agent:* Lachlan P. MacDonald, 2719 El Cerrito, San Luis Obispo, Calif. 93406.

CAREER: Recreation director for City of San Bernardino (Calif.), 1940-66; Paddlefleet Kayak and Canoe Rentals and Sales, Morro Bay, Calif., owner, 1967-73; school bus driver in Morro Bay, 1968-75. *Military service:* U.S. Air Force, 1941-45; became sergeant.

WRITINGS: Morro Bay Meanderings, Padre Productions, 1975. Author of a weekly newspaper column for the *Sun Bulletin* in Morro Bay, 1969—.

WORK IN PROGRESS: A novel, *The Spirit of Play.*

* * *

WIEMAN, Henry N(elson) 1884-1975

PERSONAL: Born August 19, 1884, in Richhill, Mo.; son of William Henry and Alma (Morgan) Wieman; married Anna M. Orr, January 15, 1912 (died, 1931); married Regina H. Westcott, 1932 (divorced); married Laura Matlack, September 11, 1948; children: (first marriage) Florence Margaret, Nelson Orr, Marion Isabelle, Robert Morgan, Eleanor Brunhilde. *Education:* Park College, B.A., 1907; attended San Francisco Theological Seminary, 1910, University of Jena and University of Heidelberg, both 1910-11; Harvard University, Ph.D., 1917. *Religion:* Unitarian-Universalist. *Residence:* Grinnell, Iowa.

CAREER: Occidental College, Los Angeles, Calif., professor of philosophy, 1917-27; University of Chicago, Divinity School, Chicago, Ill., professor of philosophy of religion, 1927-47, professor emeritus, 1947-75; University of Oregon, Eugene, professor of philosophy, 1949-51; University of Houston, Houston, Tex., professor of philosophy, 1951-53; Southern Illinois University, Carbondale, professor of philosophy, 1956-66, professor emeritus, 1966-75. Lecturer at McCormick Theological Seminary, 1926-27; Mendenhall Lecturer at DePauw University, 1930; Swander Lecturer at Theological Seminary of the Reformed Church, 1930; Earl Foundation Lecturer at Pacific School of Religion, 1932; Carew Lecturer at Hartford Seminary Foundation, 1938; Nathaniel William Taylor Lecturer at Yale University, 1939; Ayer Lecturer at Colgate-Rochester Seminary, 1947.

MEMBER: American Philosophical Association, American Theological Association (past president), American Association of University Professors, Phi Beta Kappa, Quadrangle Club. *Awards, honors:* D.D. from Park College, 1929; Litt.D. from Occidental College, 1930.

WRITINGS: The Wrestle of Religion with Truth, Macmillan, 1927; *Religious Experience and Scientific Method,* Macmillan, 1926, reprinted, Greenwood Press, 1970; *Methods of Private Religious Living,* Macmillan, 1929; *The Issues of Life,* Abingdon, 1930; (with Douglas Clyde Macintosh and Max Carl Otto) *Is There a God? A Conversation,* Willett, Clark, 1932; (with Regina Westcott-Wieman) *Normative Psychology of Religion,* Crowell, 1935, reprinted, Greenwood Press, 1971; (with Bernard Eugene Meland) *American Philosophies of Religion,* Willett, Clark, 1936; (with Walter Marshall Horton) *The Growth of Religion,* Willett, Clark, 1938; *Now We Must Choose,* Macmillan, 1941; *The Source of Human Good,* University of Chicago Press, 1946; (with others) *Religious Liberals Reply,* Beacon Press, 1947; *The Directive in History,* Beacon Press, 1949.

Man's Ultimate Commitment, Southern Illinois University Press, 1958; *The Intellectual Foundation of Faith,* Philosophical Library, 1961; *Religious Inquiry: Some Explorations,* Beacon Press, 1968; *Seeking Faith for a New Age,* edited by Cedric L. Hepler, Scarecrow, 1975. Contributor to *New National Encyclopedia* and *Encyclopedia of Religion.* Contributor to theology and philosophy journals, and to national magazines.*

(Died June 19, 1975, in Grinnell, Iowa)

*   *   *

WIIG, Howard (Calvert) 1940-

PERSONAL: Born November 7, 1940, in Honolulu, Hawaii; son of Howard Edgerton (an administrator and attorney) and Jean Carolyn (Calvert) Wiig. *Education:* Attended University of California, Santa Barbara, 1958-59, University of Hawaii, 1959-60, Harvard University, 1960, Mississippi State University, 1962, and University of Heidelberg, 1962; University of California, Berkeley, A.B., 1964; University of Hawaii, M.A., 1969, currently doctoral candidate. *Politics:* Democrat. *Religion:* Humanist. *Home:* 3593-A Alani Dr., Honolulu, Hawaii 96822. *Office:* 577 Pohukaina St., Honolulu, Hawaii 96813.

CAREER: International Planned Parenthood Federation, Singapore, researcher and fieldworker, 1964-65; *Berkeley Barb,* Berkeley, Calif., reporter, 1968; University of Hawaii, Honolulu, instructor in American studies, 1968-70; executive assistant for Hawaii State Senator Anson Chong in Honolulu, 1972-74; Charger Hawaii (distributor of electric motorcycles), Honolulu, Hawaii, partner, 1975—. Precinct delegate of Democratic party of Hawaii, 1971-73; member of board of directors of Hawaii Youth Congress, 1972, and Citizens for Hawaii, 1975—; vice-chairman of Humanists Hawaii, 1974—.

MEMBER: United Nations Association, Alan Guttmacher Society, American Humanist Association, Audubon Society, National Parks and Conservation Association, Cousteau Society, American Civil Liberties Union, Negative

Population Society, Zero Population Growth (president of Hawaiian chapter, 1972-73), Wilderness Society, Planned Parenthood (member of board of directors of Hawaii chapter, 1968-74), SANE, Population Crisis Committee, Environmental Action, Cooperative of Small Magazine Editors and Publishers, Hawaii Performing Arts Company, Honolulu Junior Chamber of Commerce. *Awards, honors:* Outstanding contribution award from International Planned Parenthood Federation, 1968, for contribution to build family planning riverboat to Bangladesh.

WRITINGS: Freedom or Jail for Imogene Cole, Clean Energy Press, 1975. Contributor to *Honolulu Star Bulletin, Honolulu Advertiser, San Francisco Chronicle, Reno Evening Gazette, Singapore Today,* and *Sunbums.* Contributor of pamphlets to Dan Ostrow and Associates, 1970-71, and Teddi Medina Associates, 1973. News editor of *Zero Population Growth,* 1970-72.

WORK IN PROGRESS: A History of American Societies for the Suppression of Vice; a biography of infamous San Francisco socialite, Joan Hitchcock; research on the environmental justification for widespread use of electrical vehicles.

SIDELIGHTS: Wiig told *CA:* "As far as travel goes, I hitch-hiked and bummed and odd-jobbed through sixty nations. I've had the dubious distinction of having gone broke in every continent of the world, Antarctica excepted. Malaria, stomach bugs, a strange accent, and an extremely international outlook have resulted from my travels. I'm a football (National Football League) freak to the point where I could possibly make a living off it if I knew the proper bookie. But my real passion is plants, composting, and landscaping. I'd love to spend four hours a day fussing with same, but I spend the whole day at our electric vehicle office.

"As seems to be the case with many writers; women, alcohol, good food, romantic sunsets, and other pleasures of the flesh occupy an inordinate portion of my time and energy. I write best in noisy, funky bars."

*   *   *

WILDER, Thornton (Niven) 1897-1975

April 17, 1897—December 7, 1975; American playwright and novelist. Obituaries: *New York Times,* December 8, 1975; *Washington Post,* December 8, 1975; *Detroit Free Press,* December 8, 1975; *Detroit News,* December 8, 1975; *Time,* December 22, 1975; *Newsweek,* December 22, 1975; *AB Bookman's Weekly,* January 5, 1976; *Current Biography,* February, 1976. (See index for previous *CA* sketch)

*   *   *

WILDMON, Donald E(llis) 1938-

PERSONAL: Born January 18, 1938, in Dumas, Miss.; son of Ellis C. and Berniece T. Wildmon; married Lynda Lou Bennett, June 18, 1961; children: Timothy, Angela, Donna, Mark. *Education:* Millsaps College, B.A., 1960; Emory University, M.Div., 1965. *Home:* 1411 Van Buren, Tupelo, Miss. 38801. *Office address:* P.O. Box 1368, Tupelo, Miss. 38801.

CAREER: Ordained United Methodist minister, 1964; pastor of United Methodist church in Tupelo, Miss., 1968—. *Military service:* U.S. Army, 1961-63.

WRITINGS—All published by Five Star Publishers, except as noted: *Thoughts Worth Thinking,* 1968; *A Gift for*

Living, 1969; *Nuggets of Gold*, 1970; *Leaves of Silver*, 1971; *Pebbles in the Sand*, 1971; *Practical Help for Daily Living*, 1972; *Treasured Thoughts*, 1973; *Stepping Stones*, 1973; *Windows to Life*, 1973; *Springs of Faith*, 1973; *Think on These Things*, 1973; *A Gift for the Graduate*, 1973; *Living Thoughts*, 1973; *The Book of Love*, 1974; *Stand Up to Life: A Man's Reflection on Living*, Abingdon, 1975.

* * *

WILENSKI, R(eginald) H(oward)   1887-1975

PERSONAL: Born in March, 1887, in London, England; married Marjorie Harland (a writer and businesswoman), 1914 (died, 1965). *Education:* Attended Balliol College, Oxford; further study at art schools in Munich and Paris. *Home:* Maldah, Marlow, Buckinghamshire, England.

CAREER: Free-lance artist in London, England until 1914; in government service in London during World War I; art critic for London newspapers, and London correspondent for *L'Amour de l'Art*, Paris, France, during 1920's; Bristol University, Bristol, England, special lecturer in art history, 1929-30; Victoria University of Manchester, Manchester, England, special lecturer in art history, 1933-46; employed in government service and in foreign service department of British Broadcasting Corp., during World War II; artist, writer, and art critic, 1927-75. Exhibitor, Paris Autumn Salon and others. *Member:* International Society of Sculptors, Painters, and Gravers (exhibiting member), Royal Society of Portrait Painters, Royal Institute of Oil Painters, Savile Club. *Awards, honors:* M.A. from University of Manchester, 1938; Chevalier, Legion of Honor, 1967.

WRITINGS: The Modern Movement in Art, Faber & Gwyer, 1927, 4th edition, T. Yoseloff, 1947; *An Introduction to Dutch Art*, Faber & Gwyer, 1929, 3rd revised and enlarged edition published as *Dutch Painting*, Beechurst Press, 1955; *A Miniature History of European Art*, Oxford University Press, 1930, American edition published as *A Miniature History of Art* (with chapter by Edward Alden Jewell), 1930; *French Painting*, Hale, Cushman & Flint, 1931, 3rd revised edition, Dover, 1973; *An Outline of French Painting*, Faber, 1932; *The Meaning of Modern Sculpture*, Faber, 1932, new edition, Beacon Press, 1961; *An Outline of English Painting from the Middle Ages to the Period of the Pre-Raphaelites*, Faber, 1933, revised edition published as *An Outline of English Painting*, 1969; *John Ruskin: An Introduction to Further Study of His Life and Work* (biography), Faber, 1934, reprinted, R. West, 1973; *The Study of Art*, Faber, 1934; *Masters of English Painting*, Hale, Cushman & Flint, 1934; *Modern French Painters*, Reynal & Hitchcock, 1940, 3rd edition in two volumes, Vintage, 1960, 4th edition, Harcourt, 1963; *English Painting*, Faber, 1943, 4th revised edition, 1964; *Flemish Painters: 1430-1830*, two volumes, Viking, 1960.

Monographs: *Stanley Spencer*, E. Benn, 1924; *Degas: 1834-1917*, Faber, 1946, published as *Degas*, Pitman, 1948; *Royal Portraits*, Faber, 1946, Pitman, 1949; *English Outdoor Paintings*, Faber, 1946, Pitman, 1949; *Mantegna and the Paduan School*, Faber, 1947; (with B. Denvir) *Renoir: 1841-1949*, two volumes (Volume I by Wilenski; Volume II by Denvir), Faber, 1948; *Seurat*, Faber, 1949, Pitman, 1951; *Bosch*, Faber, 1953; *Douanier Rousseau*, Faber, 1953; *Toulouse-Latrec*, Faber, 1955; *Poussin: 1594-1665*, Faber, 1958; *Picasso*, two volumes, Volume I: *Early Years*, Volume II: *Later Years*, Faber, 1961. General editor, Faber Gallery series.

AVOCATIONAL INTERESTS: Wilenski enjoyed travel in France, Italy, and Spain, and gardening.*

(Died April 19, 1975)

* * *

WILEY, David Sherman   1935-

PERSONAL: Born November 9, 1935, in Eldorado, Ill.; son of Kenneth L. (an auto dealer) and Martha Louise (Summers) Wiley; married Marylee Crofts (a curriculum consultant), June 20, 1959; children: Stephen B., Thomas M. C. *Education:* Wabash College, B.A., 1957; Yale University, B.D., 1961; Princeton Theological Seminary, Ph.D., 1971. *Religion:* Protestant. *Home:* 1720 Vilas Ave., Madison, Wis. 53711. *Office:* African Studies Program, University of Wisconsin, 1450 Van Hise, Madison, Wis. 53706.

CAREER: University of Zambia, instructor, 1966-67; University of Wisconsin, Madison, assistant professor of sociology, 1968—, chairman of African studies program, 1972—. Worked with the Madison Area Committee on Southern Africa, 1969. *Member:* American Sociological Association, Society for Scientific Study of Religion, African Studies Association.

WRITINGS: (With Marylee C. Wiley) *The Third World: Africa*, Pendulum Press, 1972; *Social Stratification in Africa*, Bobbs-Merrill, 1976. Guest editor and editorial advisor for *Issue*, 1973—.

WORK IN PROGRESS: A study of housing, health, education, and the labor force in Zambia; a book on urban society in Zambia, completion expected in 1976.

SIDELIGHTS: Wiley told *CA* that he is "deeply concerned with United States policy concerning Southern Africa and Africa in general; involved in extension of information and interest concerning Africa into schools and universities in the Midwest; working actively in policy-related research for the development of independent African nations."

* * *

WILEY, Jack   1936-

PERSONAL: Born December 4, 1936, in Fresno, Calif. *Education:* University of Illinois, Ph.D., 1968. *Residence:* San Diego, Calif.

CAREER: University of South Alabama, Mobile, assistant professor and director of Human Performance Laboratory, 1968-70; University of Illinois, Champaign-Urbana, assistant professor, 1970-71; University of California, Santa Barbara, assistant research physiologist at Institute of Environmental Research, 1971-72; writer, 1972—.

WRITINGS: The Unicycle Book, Stackpole, 1973; *Fiberglass Kit Boats*, International Marine Publishing, 1973; *Basic Circus Skills*, Stackpole, 1974; *Modifying Fiberglass Boats*, International Marine Publishing, 1975; *Living Aboard Boats*, International Marine Publishing, in press. Contributor to *Mechanix Illustrated, Popular Mechanics, Popular Science*, and other magazines.

BIOGRAPHICAL/CRITICAL SOURCES: Newsletter of Unicycling Society of America, Volume 2, number 3, July, 1975.

* * *

WILEY, Karla H(ummel)   1918-

PERSONAL: Born July 20, 1918, in Brooklyn, N.Y.;

daughter of August Karl (a businessman) and Elizabeth (Ammon) Hummel; married Joseph B. Wiley, Jr., October 31, 1941; children: Joseph B III. *Education:* Attended Duke University and Trap Hagen School of Fashion. *Politics:* Liberal Republican. *Religion:* Episcopalian. *Home address:* River Rd., Bedminster, N.J. *Agent:* Maurice Crain, Inc., 18 East 41st St., New York, N.Y. 10017.

CAREER: Fashion designer, 1936-59; non-governmental observer at United Nations, 1958-59; free-lance writer, 1959—. Director of public relations for Madison branch of Fairleigh Dickinson University, 1964. *Awards, honors:* Award from Association of English Teachers of New Jersey, 1965.

WRITINGS—For young people: *Styles by Suzy,* McKay, 1965; *Assignment Latin America: A Story of the Peace Corps,* McKay, 1968. Also author of *Passport to Adventure,* Vantage. Editor, and contributor of weekly column to *United Nations Listening Post,* 1959-65, and author of other columns.

* * *

WILHELM, Paul A(lexander) 1916-

PERSONAL: Born April 16, 1916, in Blytheville, Ark.; son of John Paul (a lumber merchant) and Atchie (Alexander) Wilhelm; married Jayne Tuttle (an art teacher), April 16, 1943; children: Mark T., Carolyn. *Education:* Little Rock Junior College, A.A., 1936; Washington University, St. Louis, Mo., B.Arch., 1939, M.Arch., 1940; University of Pennsylvania, certification in public administration, 1952. *Politics:* Democrat. *Religion:* Quaker. *Home and office:* 209 East Johnson St., Philadelphia, Pa. 19144.

CAREER: John Wanamaker Stores, Philadelphia, Pa., store architect and planner, 1946-51; City of Philadelphia, Department of Commerce, Philadelphia, Pa., 1951-1959, began as consultant, became assistant director; Philadelphia Industrial Development Corp., Philadelphia, Pa., plant development director, 1958-61; Greater Wilmington Development Council, Inc., Wilmington, Del., executive director, 1961-69; consultant to government and private land developers. *Wartime service:* Civilian public service as conscientious objector, 1941-45. *Member:* American Institute of Planners, Urban Land Institute (sustaining member), Lambda Alpha Land Economics Society.

WRITINGS: (With Robert Terrone) *Urban Growth,* Hayden, 1975. Contributor to journals in his field.

* * *

WILKINS, Beatrice (Brunson) 1928-

PERSONAL: Born November 19, 1928, in Pensacola, Fla.; daughter of E. Jesse (a physician) and Mary (Cutts) Brunson; married Russell E. Wilkins (an executive for Southern Bell), December 6, 1947; children: Robert E. *Education:* Educated in public schools in Pensacola, Fla. *Politics:* Democrat. *Religion:* Episcopalian. *Home:* 1800 South St. Lucie Blvd., Building 8, Apt. 304, Stuart, Fla. 33494.

CAREER: Writer.

WRITINGS: One Love Have I (novel), Crescent, 1974.

* * *

WILKINS, William R(ichard) 1933-

PERSONAL: Born December 3, 1933, in Knoblick, Mo.; son of Lawrence L. (in construction) and Margaret (Bates) Wilkins; married Jerilyn Struthers, 1950 (marriage ended,

1968); married Patricia Ardell Morgan, February 14, 1968; children: Georgia, Carolyn, William, Kim, Jacquelyn. *Education:* Attended University of Oklahoma, 1951; La Salle Extension University, diploma, 1954; Columbia Basin College, A.A., 1959. *Politics:* Democrat. *Home:* 312 West Bonneville, Pasco, Wash. 99301. *Office:* 408 South 9th, Walla Walla, Wash. 99352; 331 West Bonneville, Pasco, Wash. 99301.

CAREER: General Electric Co., Richland, Wash., payroll analyst, 1955-58; private business as an accountant and tax consultant, in Walla Walla, Pasco, Wash., 1959—. *Military service:* U.S. Air Force, 1951-55; became sergeant; received Republic of Korea Medal. *Member:* International Auto Biographical Association (fellow), International Platform Association, Veterans of Foreign Wars, Common Cause, American Association of Tax Consultants, Authors Guild, Academy of American Poets, Washington Association of Tax Consultants.

WRITINGS: A Whisper in the Wind, Goldermood Rainbow Press, 1962; *Something Personal,* Goldermood Rainbow Press, 1974; *Lookin' for the Pony,* Angst World Library, 1975. Poems anthologized in *Avant Garde Anthology, Best in Poetry, J. & C.'s Anthology,* and *Sunburst Anthology.* Contributor of poems to fifty literary magazines and poetry journals including *Bitterroot, Girl Talk,* and *Other Voice.* Editor of *Nitty-Gritty and Brass Tacks,* 1975.

WORK IN PROGRESS: Hard Knocks and Low Blows (poetry); *December 7, 1941* (novel); *Roughin' the Road* (novel); *Schizophrenium* (novel); *A Strange Thing Happened on the Way to the IRS* (novel), completion expected in 1977; two novels, *The Freeway Freak* and *Dear John,* 1978.

* * *

WILLIAMS, George M(ason, Jr.) 1940-

PERSONAL: Born April 21, 1940, in Bristol, Va.; son of George Mason (a clergyman) and Eureka (Carr) Williams; married Marcia Jane Roider, April 3, 1965; children: George, Elizabeth. *Education:* Grand Canyon College, B.A., 1962; Baptist Theological Seminary, Ruschlikon, Switzerland, graduate study, 1963-64; Southern Baptist Theological Seminary, B.D., 1966; University of Iowa, Ph.D., 1972. *Religion:* Unitarian-Universalist. *Home:* 1012 Bryant Ave., Chico, Calif. 95926. *Office:* Department of Religious Studies, California State University, Chico, Calif. 95929.

CAREER: Newton College of the Sacred Heart, Newton, Mass., assistant professor of the history of Eastern religions, 1971-72; California State University, Chico, assistant professor of the history of Eastern religions, 1972—. *Member:* American Academy of Religion, Association of Asian Studies, Mormon History Association, American Oriental Society, Chinese Historical Society.

WRITINGS: The Quest for Meaning of Svami Vivekananda, New Horizons Press, 1974. Contributor to theology journals.

WORK IN PROGRESS: Temples of Gold, a study of Chinese temples of California; *The Doubting Saint,* a second study of Vivekananda, using the "psychohistorical" method.

SIDELIGHTS: Williams writes: "The great personal reward came in writing *The Quest* when I recognized that Svami Vivekananda had changed dramatically in his spiritual pilgrimage. This violated the myth of the Spiritual Hero who, once having found enlightenment, cannot change fundamentally without violating the previous Truth which had been realized. That 'the saint' . . . could doubt and even change direction in his quest for meaning . . . constituted an insight which left the pursuit of truth open for discovery and growth.''

* * *

WILLIAMS, Gilbert M. 1917-
(Michael Wolfe)

PERSONAL: Born May 5, 1917, in Pittsburgh, Pa. *Education:* University of Arizona, B.F.A.; Yale University, M.F.A. *Home:* 16 Norman Pl., Tenafly, N.J. 07670. *Agent:* McIntosh & Otis, Inc., 18 East 41st St., New York, N.Y. 10017.

CAREER: Film director and writer of documentary, industrial, and training films. *Awards, honors:* Edgar Allen Poe Award nomination, 1974.

WRITINGS—Under pseudonym Michael Wolfe; ''Mike Keefe'' series, published by Harper: *Man on a String,* 1973; *Two Star Pigeon,* 1975; *Chinese Fire Drill,* 1976.

WORK IN PROGRESS: Research ''deals with serious aspects of Southeast Asia war, the situation in the Panama Canal Zone, etc.''

SIDELIGHTS: Gilbert Williams told *CA* that his topics and background material are drawn from his travels as a film director in the Far East, Europe, the Arctic, Panama, and elsewhere.

* * *

WILSON, A. Jeyaratnam 1928-

PERSONAL: Born October 4, 1928, in Colombo, Sri Lanka; son of Kanasasabai Rajaratnam (a businessman) and Elizabeth (Dutton) Wilson; married Susilavati Chelvanayakam (a librarian), April 10, 1953; children: Mallihai (daughter), Maithili (daughter), Kumanan (son). *Education:* University of Ceylon, B.A., 1950; London School of Economics and Political Science, Ph.D., 1956. *Politics:* ''Suffer from a social conscience.'' *Religion:* Methodist. *Home:* 79 Colonial Heights St., Fredericton, New Brunswick, Canada. *Office:* Department of Political Science, University of New Brunswick, Fredericton, New Brunswick, Canada.

CAREER: University of Ceylon, Peradeniya, professor of economics and political science and head of department of economics and political science, 1970-72; University of New Brunswick, Fredericton, professor of political science and chairman of department, 1972—. Research fellow in politics at University of Leicester, 1964-65; research associate at McGill University, 1970-71; Simon senior fellow at University of Manchester, 1971-72.

WRITINGS: Politics in Sri Lanka, 1947-1973, Macmillan (London), 1974; *Electoral Politics in an Emergent State: The Ceylon General Elections of May, 1970,* Cambridge University Press, 1975. Contributor to journals in his field. Member of editorial board of *Round Table, Journal of Commonwealth and Comparative Politics,* and *Ceylon Journal of Historical and Social Studies.*

WORK IN PROGRESS: South Asian Political Facts, for Macmillan (London); research on federalism and planning in India, Pakistan, and Malaysia.

AVOCATIONAL INTERESTS: ''Addicted to work, eccentric pleasure lover, despise exercise, excessively introvertish, though on occasion capable of communicating, widely traveled.''

WILSON, Alton H(orace) 1925-

PERSONAL: Born December 9, 1925, in Olden, Tex.; son of Hubert Ecil (a salesman) and Lue Priscilla (Henson) Wilson; married Janet Eilene Pritz, July 6, 1956; children: Martha Ellen, Melissa Anne. *Education:* Attended Hardin-Simmons University, 1946-47, and North Texas State University, 1947-48; Wayland Baptist College, B.A., 1952. *Religion:* Evangelical Protestant. *Home:* 1510 Parkridge Ter., Arlington, Tex. 76012. *Office:* Unilit, Inc., 2224 Commerce St., Arlington, Tex. 76011.

CAREER: Music and Christian education director in Baptist churches in Texas and New Mexico, 1952-69; Outreach, Inc., San Antonio, Tex., president, 1969-73; Unilit, Inc. (wholesale literature distributor), Arlington, Tex., manager, 1973—. Owner of Scripture Stall (bookstore), 1969—. *Military service:* U.S. Coast Guard, 1943-46; became petty officer second class. *Member:* American Choral Directors Association.

WRITINGS: So . . . Help Me, Lord, Doubleday, 1974; *Lord, It's Me Again,* Doubleday, 1975. Author of lyrics for about fifty songs, for Singspiration, Crescendo Publications, and Hope Publishing.

WORK IN PROGRESS: The Disciple; Mothers of the Bible; The Quiet Heart; Her Mother and I Do; Parallel Promises in the Bible; research for *Fathers and Sons in the Bible.*

SIDELIGHTS: Wilson has traveled in South America, Europe, and Hawaii. He sponsored a tour of young people to Europe in 1968. *Avocational interests:* Collecting carnival glass.

* * *

WILSON, Arthur M(cCandless) 1902-

PERSONAL: Born July 29, 1902, in Sherrard, Ill.; son of Arthur M. (a farmer) and Clara (Zollinger) Wilson; married Julia Mary Tolford, June 13, 1927. *Education:* Yankton College, A.B., 1922; Oxford University, B.A., 1926, B.Litt., 1927, M.A., 1931; Harvard University, M.A., 1930, Ph.D., 1933. *Politics:* Democrat. *Home:* 1 Brookside, Norwich, Vt. 05055.

CAREER: High school teacher in Canova, S.D., 1922-23, and Chippewa Falls, Wis., 1923-24; Dartmouth College, Hanover, N.H., instructor in biography, 1933-36, assistant professor, 1936-40, professor of biography, 1940-64, professor of government, 1944-64, Daniel Webster Professor, 1964-67, Daniel Webster Professor Emeritus, 1967—, chairman of department of biography, 1942-47 and 1951-55, director of great issues course, 1946-48. Visiting professor, University of Washington, Seattle, summer, 1931, University of Missouri, summer, 1937, State University of Iowa, summer, 1948, Columbia University Graduate Faculties, 1967-69, University Seminar Association, 1969—; Fulbright professor, University of London, 1956-57. Consultant to U.S. Air Force Academy, 1949; member of steering committee of Anglo-American History Conference, University of London, 1956-59.

MEMBER: American Academy of Arts and Sciences (fellow), American Historical Association, Modern Language Association of America, American Association of University Professors, Royal Historical Society (fellow), Modern Humanities Research Association (England), Society of French History Studies (vice-president, 1962-63), American Political Science Association, Association Internationale des Etudes Francaises, Societe Francaise Etude XVIII

Siecle, Phi Beta Kappa. *Awards, honors:* Rhodes scholar, Oxford University, 1924-27; Herbert Baxter Adams Prize from American Historical Association, 1938, for *French Foreign Policy under the Administration of Cardinal Fleury, 1726-1743,* and 1958, for *Diderot: The Testing Years, 1713-1759;* Guggenheim fellowships, 1939-40 and 1956-57; M.A. from Dartmouth College, 1940; Press Award from Modern Language Association of America and Oxford University, 1953, for *Diderot: The Testing Years, 1713-1759;* Chevalier de l'Ordre des Palmes Academiques, 1967; National Book Award in Arts and Letters, 1973, for *Diderot;* D.Litt. from Dartmouth College, 1973.

WRITINGS: French Foreign Policy under the Administration of Cardinal Fleury, 1726-1743: A Study in Diplomacy and Commercial Development, Harvard University Press, 1936, reprinted, Greenwood Press, 1972; *Diderot,* Oxford University Press, Part I: *The Testing Years, 1713-1759,* 1957, Part II: *The Appeal to Posterity, 1759-1784,* 1972. Member of editorial board, *Journal of Modern History,* 1962-65, *French Historical Studies,* 1969-72.

* * *

WILSON, Camilla Jeanne 1945-
(Cammy Wilson)

PERSONAL: Born June 25, 1945, in Somerset, Pa.; daughter of Kenneth and Carrie (Lee) Wilson. *Education:* Mississippi State University, B.S., 1966, M.S. (sociology), 1967; Columbia University, M.S. (journalism), 1971. *Home and office:* 3220 Valerie Arms Dr., #D, Dayton, Ohio 45405. *Agent:* Charles Neighbors, Inc., 240 Waverly Pl., New York, N.Y. 10014.

CAREER: Star, Inc., Holly Springs, Miss., job development coordinator, 1966-67; foreign correspondent for the Far East (especially military coverage from South Vietnam for southern daily newspapers, 1968-69; substitute teacher in public schools in New York, N.Y., 1970-71; English and history teacher in public schools in Memphis, Tenn., 1971-73; *Dayton Daily News,* Dayton, Ohio, reporter, 1973-75; author. *Member:* Sigma Delta Chi (vice-president of Columbia University chapter, 1970-71).

WRITINGS—All under name Cammy Wilson: *Caution: Reading May Be Dangerous to Your Children's Health,* Stein & Day, 1976. Contributor to literary journals, including *New Times, Mid South,* and *New South,* and to newspapers.

SIDELIGHTS: Camilla Wilson comments: "School textbooks are the least recognized but most successful inculcators of sexual stereotypes in the United States; television runs a close second, no doubt ..." *Avocational interests:* Photography, flying, horticulture, snorkeling.

BIOGRAPHICAL/CRITICAL SOURCES: Viva, September, 1974.

* * *

WILSON, Carlos 1941-

PERSONAL: Born July 9, 1941, in Guadalajara, Mexico. *Education:* Attended San Francisco Bay area universities, B.A., 1972, graduate study, 1971-73. *Politics:* Marxist. *Religion:* None. *Address:* P.O. Box 755, San Pablo, Calif. 94806.

CAREER: Revolutionary author and suspected Latin American guerrilla.

WRITINGS: The Tupamaros: The Unmentionables, Branden Press, 1974.

WORK IN PROGRESS: Urban Guerrilla Warfare: Methods and Tactics; Paraguay: Cries from the Wretched.

SIDELIGHTS: Kathy Lam told *CA:* "Background on Major Wilson remains a mystery. He seems to have appeared suddenly out of nowhere as one of the foremost authorities on an international scale on modern urban guerrilla warfare. Several reviewers of his works have placed his writings above those of Carlos Marighela and Che Guevara. The Major refuses any comments on himself stating only that to focus on him is in error as his struggles are small compared to the cries from earth's wretched, cries which will no longer remain unheard and unanswered. Although publicly unknown in the United States, his actions are carefully watched by the CIA, FBI, CIC, MI, NSA, and Secret Service as learned through the Freedom of Information Act. The Major refused to read these records stating that he has no time for science fiction and children's stories. He was also not surprised to learn that the FBI had contacted his publisher about the *Tupamaro* book prior to market release. Major Wilson has stated that in some lifetime he dreams that there will be no need or place for such agencies and for people such as himself."

* * *

WILSON, Don W(hitman) 1942-

PERSONAL: Born December 17, 1942, in Clay Center, Kan.; son of Donald J. (an owner of a printing company) and Lois (Sutton) Wilson; married Gayle L. Gibson, August 30, 1964; children: Todd Whitman, Jeffrey Scott. *Education:* Washburn University, A.B., 1964; University of Cincinnati, M.A., 1965, Ph.D., 1972. *Politics:* Republican. *Religion:* Protestant. *Home:* 615 Northwest Third St., Abilene, Kan. 67410. *Office:* Dwight D. Eisenhower Presidential Library, Abilene, Kan. 67410.

CAREER: Washburn University, Topeka, Kan., lecturer in history, 1967-69; Dwight D. Eisenhower Presidential Library, Abilene, Kan., historian, 1969-74, assistant director, 1974—. Lecturer at Marymount College (Salina, Kan.), 1974. Ambassador of Abilene Chamber of Commerce, 1973-75, chairman of education committee, 1974-75, member of board of directors, 1975-78; member of executive board of Abilene United Fund, 1973-76; member of Abilene Public Library Board, 1974-77; chairman of Abilene Public Television Board, 1975-77. *Military service:* U.S. Army Reserve, 1961-69.

MEMBER: American Association for State and Local History, American Society for Public Administration, Kansas Corral of the Westerners, Kansas State Historical Society (archivist, 1967-69), Kansas Museum Association, Kansas History Teachers Association (member of executive council), Nebraska State Historical Society, Dickinson County Historical Society (vice-president), Phi Alpha Theta.

WRITINGS: Governor Charles Robinson of Kansas, University Press of Kansas, 1975. Contributor to history journals.

WORK IN PROGRESS: Early Kansas Newspaper Editors, 1854-1900.

* * *

WILSON, E(dward) Raymond 1896-

PERSONAL: Born September 20, 1896, in Morning Sun, Iowa; son of Charles B. (a farmer) and Anna Jane (Willson) Wilson; married Miriam Davidson, August 4, 1932 (died December 16, 1965); children: Kent Raymond, Lee Roy.

Education: Iowa State College, B.S., 1921, M.S., 1923; Columbia University, M.A., 1925. *Politics:* Independent. *Religion:* Quaker. *Home:* 17320 Quaker Lane, B-17, Sandy Spring, Md. 20860. *Office:* Friends Committee on National Legislation, 245 Second St. N.E., Washington, D.C. 20002.

CAREER: American Friends Service Committee, Peace Section, Philadelphia, Pa., educational secretary, 1931-43; Friends Committee on National Legislation, Washington, D.C., executive secretary, 1943-62, executive secretary emeritus, 1962—. Member of governing board of National Council of Churches, 1963-75; member of peace education executive committee of American Friends Service Committee, 1974—. *Military service:* U.S. Navy, 1918. *Awards, honors:* L.L.D., Haverford College, 1958; Doctor of Human Reconstruction, Wilmington College, 1971; D.H.L., Swarthmore College, 1975.

WRITINGS: Uphill for Peace, Friends United Press, 1975; *Thus Far on My Journey* (autobiography), Friends United Press, 1976. Editor and contributor, *Friends Committee on National Legislation Washington Newsletter,* 1943-62; contributor to religious journals.

SIDELIGHTS: Wilson writes that he has "worked forty-seven years for international peace and social justice. Helped found the Friends Committee on National Legislation, the first full-time registered Protestant lobby in Washington." His personal papers are in the Swarthmore College Peace Collection. *Avocational interests:* Photography, raising flowers, collecting linens from foreign countries.

* * *

WILSON, Edward O(sborne) 1929-

PERSONAL: Born June 10, 1929, in Birmingham, Ala.; son of Edward O., Sr. (an accountant) and Inez (Freeman) Wilson; married Irene Kelley, October 30, 1955; children: Catherine. *Education:* University of Alabama, B.S., 1949, M.S., 1950; Harvard University, Ph.D., 1955. *Home:* 52 Harding Rd., Lexington, Mass. 02173. *Office:* Museum of Comparative Zoology, Harvard University, Cambridge, Mass. 02138.

CAREER: Harvard University, Cambridge, Mass., assistant professor of biology, 1956-58, associate professor of zoology, 1958-64, professor of zoology, 1964—, curator of entymology at Museum of Comparative Zoology, 1972—. Trustee of Marine Biological Laboratory (Woods Hole). *Member:* National Academy of Sciences, American Academy of Arts and Sciences (fellow). *Awards, honors:* Award from American Association for the Advancement of Science, 1969; Mercer Award from Ecological Society of America, 1971; Founders Memorial Award from Entomological Society of America, 1972.

WRITINGS: (With R. H. MacArthur) *The Theory of Island Biogeography,* Princeton University Press, 1967; *The Insect Societies,* Belknap Press, 1971; (with W. H. Bossert) *A Primer of Population Biology,* Sinauer Associates, 1971; (co-author) *Life on Earth,* Sinauer Associates, 1973; *Sociobiology: The New Synthesis,* Belknap Press, 1975. Contributor of about a hundred fifty articles to scientific and popular journals. Co-editor, *Theoretical Population Biology,* 1971-74, *Behavioral Ecology and Sociobiology,* 1975—.

WORK IN PROGRESS: A book on the biological basis of ethics; a book on the biology of caste and slavery in social insects and man.

WIMSATT, James I(rving) 1927-

PERSONAL: Born September 25, 1927, in Detroit, Mich.; son of James Irving (a businessman) and Margaret (Rodman) Wimsatt; married Mary Ann Coslow (a college professor), September 11, 1960; children: Andrew James, Alison Ross. *Education:* University of Michigan, A.B., 1950; Wayne State University, M.A., 1958; Duke University, Ph.D., 1964. *Politics:* Republican. *Home:* 3400 Kirby Drive, Greensboro, N.C. 27403. *Office:* Department of English, University of North Carolina, Greensboro, N.C. 27412.

CAREER: University of Tennessee, Knoxville, instructor in English, 1963-64; Texas Christian University, Fort Worth, assistant professor of English, 1964-66; University of North Carolina, Greensboro, assistant professor, 1966-68, associate professor, 1968-71, professor of English, 1971—. Consultant to Wimsatt Brothers, Inc., Louisville, 1970—. *Member:* International Arthurian Society, Modern Language Association of America, Mediaeval Academy of America, South Atlantic Modern Language Association. *Awards, honors:* Duke University of North Carolina Cooperative Program in Humanities fellow, 1969-70; Huntington Library summer fellow, 1973; American Council of Learned Societies fellow, 1974-75.

WRITINGS: Chaucer and the French Love Poets, University of North Carolina Press, 1968; *The Marguerite Poetry of Guillaume de Machaut,* University of North Carolina Press, 1970; *Allegory and Mirror: Tradition and Structure in Middle English Literature,* Pegasus, 1970. Contributor to professional journals.

WORK IN PROGRESS: Editing poems of Machaut for the Chaucer Library, for University of Georgia Press; editing Chaucer's *Book of the Duchess* for Chaucer Variorum, to be published by University of Oklahoma Press.

* * *

WIMSATT, W(illiam) K(urtz) 1907-1975

November 17, 1907—December 17, 1975; American educator, expert on eighteenth-century literature, author of books in his field. Obituaries: *New York Times,* December 18, 1975; *AB Bookman's Weekly,* January 5, 1976. (See index for previous *CA* sketch)

* * *

WINCHELL, Carol Ann 1936-

PERSONAL: Born July 16, 1936, in Columbus, Ohio; daughter of Homer S. (an engineer) and Mary (Stultz) French; married James F. Winchell (an attorney), 1963; children: Philip. *Education:* Ohio State University, B.M., 1958, M.A., 1960; Case Western Reserve University, M.S.L.S., 1964. *Religion:* Methodist. *Home:* 3840 Schirtzinger Rd., Columbus, Ohio 43220. *Office:* Library, Ohio State University, 1858 Neil Ave. Mall, Columbus, Ohio 43210.

CAREER: Ohio State University, Libraries, Columbus, reference librarian and assistant professor of library administration, 1964—. *Member:* American Association of University Professors, American Association of University Women, American Library Association, Ohio Library Association.

WRITINGS: (Editor) *Music: Twelve-Tone Row,* M.I.T. Press, 1974; *Richard Wright,* M.I.T. Press, 1974; *The Hyperkinetic Child: A Bibliography of Medical, Educational, and Behavioral Studies,* Greenwood Press, 1975.

WORK IN PROGRESS: The Hyperkinetic Child: A Five-Year Supplement, completion expected in 1979; editing bibliography series "Current Topics in Child Behavior," for Greenwood Press, 1977-80.

* * *

WINICK, Steven 1944-

PERSONAL: Born July 7, 1944, in Brooklyn, N.Y.; son of Gilbert (a dentist) and Regina (Kaps) Winick; married Sharon Smolensky, June 18, 1967; children: Suellen, Jeffrey Alan. *Education:* Attended Juilliard School of Music, 1960-62; Eastman School of Music, B.M. (with distinction), 1966, M.M., 1968, D.M.A., 1973. *Home:* 2877 St. Andrews Way, Marietta, Ga. 30062. *Office:* Department of Music, Georgia State University, Atlanta, Ga. 30303.

CAREER: Part-time music teacher in elementary schools in Rochester, N.Y., 1962-66, Penfield, N.Y., 1966-69, and Monroe and Woodbury, N.Y., 1969-72; Eastman School of Music, Rochester, N.Y., instructor, 1966-69; Georgia State University, Atlanta, assistant professor of music, 1972—, interim chairman of department, 1975—, musical conductor, 1972—. Has performed with orchestras, wind ensembles, chamber music groups, and popular music groups; trumpet clinician for DeKalb, Fulton, and Cobb county schools. *Military service:* U.S. Army, solo cornetist for U.S. Military Academy Band; conducted Lydian Chamber Players, 1969-72.

MEMBER: International Trumpet Guild, National Association of Schools of Music, Music Educators National Conference, College Music Society, American Association of University Professors, National Association of College Wind and Percussion Instructors (state chairman), American Federation of Musicians, Georgia Music Educators Association, Georgia Council for the Arts, Greater Atlanta Arts Council, Phi Mu Alpha, Pi Kappa Lambda.

WRITINGS: Rhythm: An Annotated Bibliography, Scarecrow, 1974.

Composer of "Confrontations," Autograph Editions, 1969; "Equinoctial Points," Autograph Editions, 1970. Editor and transcriber of musical compositions by Francois Joseph Gossec (for Carl Fischer, Inc.), and Oskar Boehme (for Autograph Editions). Contributor to music journals.

WORK IN PROGRESS: A textbook on conducting music.

SIDELIGHTS: Winick played solo cornet for recordings by the Eastman Wind Ensemble: "Fiesta!," Decca, 1966; "American Music for Symphonic Winds," Decca, 1967; "Music of Penderecki, Williams, Mayuzumi," Deutsche Grammophon, 1968.

* * *

WINNETT, Thomas 1921-

PERSONAL: Born July 30, 1921, in Los Angeles, Calif.; son of Earle L. (an attorney) and Grace (Rogers) Winnett; married Lucille Liddell, May 14, 1948; children: Jason, Caroline. *Education:* Attended University of Southern California, 1940-43, and Pomona College, 1943-44; University of California, Berkeley, A.B., 1948. *Home:* 975 Miller Ave., Berkeley, Calif. 94708. *Office:* 2440 Bancroft Way, Berkeley, Calif. 94704.

CAREER: Fybate Lecture Notes, Berkeley, Calif., president and editor-in-chief, 1950—. President and editor-in-chief of Wilderness Press, 1966—. President of California Federation of Young Democrats, 1954-56; vice-president of

California Democratic Council, 1957-61. *Military service:* U.S. Army, Signal Corps, 1943-46. *Member:* National Parks and Recreation Association, Wilderness Society, Sierra Club (life member), California Native Plant Association.

WRITINGS: (With Karl Schwenke) *Sierra North,* Wilderness Press, 1967, 2nd edition, 1971; (with Schwenke) *Sierra South,* Wilderness Press, 1968, 2nd edition, 1975; (with Don Denison) *The Tahoe-Yosemite Trail,* Wilderness Press, 1970; *Tuolumne Meadows,* Wilderness Press, 1970; *Mount Whitney,* Wilderness Press, 1971; *The Comstock Guide to California Backpacking,* Ballantine, 1972; *The Comstock Backpacking Guide to the Pacific Northwest,* Ballantine, 1972; (with Kurt Rademacher, Beverly Hartline, Norman Jensen, and Ed Roberts) *Backpacking in the Wilderness Rockies,* Ballantine, 1973; (with Jeffrey P. Schaffer, John W. Robinson, J. C. Jenkins, and Andy Husari) *The Pacific Crest Trail,* Volume I: *California,* Wilderness Press, 1973; *Backpacking for Fun,* Wilderness Press, 1973; *Mono Craters,* Wilderness Press, 1975.

WORK IN PROGRESS: A book about playing tennis; a book about making money by selling stock options; a third edition of *Sierra North.*

BIOGRAPHICAL/CRITICAL SOURCES: California Monthly, June, 1966.

* * *

WINTERS, Francis Xavier 1933-

PERSONAL: Born October 12, 1933, in Roaring Springs, Pa. *Education:* Fordham University, B.A., 1957, M.A.T., 1958, Ph.D., 1972; Woodstock College, Ph.L., 1958, S.T.B., 1962, S.T.L., 1965. *Office:* Institute for the Study of Ethics and International Affairs, Georgetown University, Washington, D.C. 20007.

CAREER: Entered Society of Jesus (Jesuits), 1951, ordained Roman Catholic priest, 1964; teacher of French and Latin in Roman Catholic high school in Baltimore, Md., 1958-61; Loyola College, Baltimore, Md., instructor in Christian ethics, 1966-67; Woodstock College, New York, N.Y., instructor, 1970-71, assistant professor of Christian ethics, 1971-72, dean of faculty, 1971-72; Georgetown University, Washington, D.C., assistant professor of theology, 1972—, director of Institute for the Study of Ethics and International Affairs, 1974—. Instructor at Immaculate Heart College, Hollywood, Calif., summer, 1970, winter, 1970. Member of board of trustees of Council on Religion and International Affairs, 1971—; member of board of directors of Wheeling College, 1972—, and Woodstock Theological Center. *Member:* American Teilhard de Chardin Society.

WRITINGS: Politics and Ethics, Paulist/Newman, 1975. Contributor of articles and reviews to political science and theology journals.

* * *

WIRTENBERG, Patricia Z(arrella) 1932-

PERSONAL: Born May 21, 1932, in Arlington, Mass.; daughter of Joseph S. and Lillian M. (Lepore) Zarrella; married Leon Wirtenberg (a writer), August 26, 1975. *Education:* Attended Mt. Holyoke College, 1949-50, and Jackson Von Ladau School, 1950-54. *Home:* 111 Perkins St., Jamaica Plain, Mass. 02130. *Office:* Folio Communications Service, 581 Boylston St., Boston, Mass. 02116.

CAREER: Artist and sculptor, 1949—; has exhibited work

at institutions and associations, including Columbus Museum, Children's Art Centre, Boston, Cambridge Art Association, and in Positano, Italy; work in many private and public collections, including Columbus Museum, Huntington Hartford Collection, and Stone Library, Boston. Children's Art Centre, Boston, Mass., assistant director, 1956-65; Folio Communications Service, Boston, vice-president, 1965—. Special writer for *Boston Globe Magazine,* 1965-66. *Awards, honors:* Copley Society annual prize, 1958; Huntington Hartford Foundation fellowships, 1960 and 1961.

WRITINGS: The All-Around-the-House Art Book, Houghton, 1968, paperback edition published as *The All-Around-the-House Art and Craft Book,* 1974.

WORK IN PROGRESS: "My second book—if I can get the time to write it!"

SIDELIGHTS: Mrs. Wirtenberg is the originator of the unique medium of vegetarian mosaics. She has appeared and shown her work on the national television shows, "Today," "To Tell the Truth," and "Mike Douglas."

*   *   *

WITTKOWSKI, Wolfgang 1925-

PERSONAL: Born August 15, 1925, in Halle, Germany; came to United States, 1963; son of Gerhard (an economist) and Margarete (Linckelmann) Wittkowski; married Maria Jokiel, August 13, 1954 (divorced, 1972); children: Mechtild, Ute, Isa, Albrecht. *Education:* Attended University of Goettingen, 1944-50; University of Frankfurt, staatsexamen, 1953, Ph.D., 1964. *Office:* Department of German, Ohio State University, Columbus, Ohio 43210.

CAREER: Assistant master of secondary school in Bad Nauheim, Germany, 1956-63; Ohio State University, Columbus, associate professor, 1963-66, professor of German, 1966—. *Military service:* German Army, 1943-45. *Member:* Modern Language Association of America, American Association of Teachers of German, Hebbel und Kleist Gesellschaft.

WRITINGS: (Contributor) H. Kreuzer, editor, *Hebbel in neuer Sicht,* Kohlhammer (Stuttgart), 1963; *Der Junge Hebbel,* De Gruyter (Berlin), 1969; (with Claude David and Lawrence Ryan) *Kleist und Frankreich,* E. Schmidt (Berlin), 1969; (contributor) Klaus Berghahn, editor, *Friedrich Schiller: Theorie und Praxis der Dramen,* Wege der Forschung (Darmstadt), 1972. Contributor to German literature journals.

WORK IN PROGRESS: Research on Nicolai Hartmann's philosophy of values, ethics, and social criticism, and on the elements of dialectical structure.

*   *   *

WOLD, Jo Anne 1938-

PERSONAL: Born April 20, 1938, in Fairbanks, Alaska; daughter of Arnold (a mechanic) and Eleanor (a cook; maiden name, Gatzck) Wold. *Education:* Attended University of Alaska, 1961-70. *Politics:* Republican. *Residence:* Fairbanks, Alaska.

CAREER: Conducted "The Magic Storybook" (broadcast for children), on KFAR-Radio, Fairbanks, Alaska, 1954-57; *Fairbanks Daily News-Miner,* Fairbanks, Alaska, stringer, 1958-60, editor of women's page, 1960-67; *Jessen's Daily,* Fairbanks, Alaska, editor of family page, 1967-69; reporter for *All Alaska Weekly,* and free-lance writer, 1969-

72; assistant to U.S. Senator Ted Stevens, 1972—. *Awards, honors:* Five awards from Alaska Press Club, 1965-69, for best women's page, and 1969, for best editorial; awards for excellence from National Federation of Press Women, 1967 and 1969.

WRITINGS: Fairbanks: The $200 Million Gold Rush Town, Wold Press, 1971; *Gold City Girl* (novel), Albert Whitman, 1972; *Well! Why Didn't You Say So?* (picture book), Albert Whitman, 1975; *This Old House* (biography), Alaska Northwest Publishing, in press.

WORK IN PROGRESS: An Eskimo folk tale; a sequel to *Gold City Girl.*

*   *   *

WOOD, June S(mallwood) 1931-

PERSONAL: Born August 6, 1931, in New Albany, Miss.; daughter of Mark Wiseman (a banker) and Lillie (Barkley) Smallwood; married J. W. Wood (an engineer), December 23, 1949 (marriage ended, November, 1966); children: James, Joe, Bob. *Education:* University of Mississippi, B.A., 1952. *Religion:* Presbyterian. *Home and office:* 309 Madison Ave., New Albany, Miss. 38652.

CAREER: Has worked as teacher of music and speech in public schools, 1953-54, and as part-time teacher of English; free-lance writer, 1954—; rehabilitation worker, 1975; currently proprietor of Treasures of Sheba (import business).

WRITINGS: A Workable Faith, Philosophical Library, 1975. Also editor of *Messianic Prophesy,* by Arron Aligerman, Zondervan.

WORK IN PROGRESS: Unbroken Promises.

*   *   *

WOOD, Marion N(ewman) 1909-

PERSONAL: Born December 11, 1909, in Canaan, Vt.; daughter of Richard Steven and Nellie Harriet (Bryan) Newman; married Hubert F. Wood (an insurance agent), August 1, 1934. *Education:* Lyndon State College, diploma, 1931; also studied at University of Vermont, summer, 1936, and Paul Revere School of Pottery, 1937-38. *Politics:* Republican. *Religion:* Presbyterian. *Home:* 410 South Fourth St., Globe, Ariz. 85501.

CAREER: Elementary school teacher in Vermont, 1931-37; Elizabeth Peabody House, Boston, Mass., group social worker, 1937-38; substitute teacher in elementary schools in Vermont, 1938-42; National Youth Administration, Phoenix, Ariz., youth personnel officer, 1943; National Red Cross, Phoenix, Ariz., home service worker, 1943-44; Arizona Welfare Office, Globe, Ariz., 1944-48, holding positions social worker, child welfare worker, and acting executive secretary. Teacher of pottery. *Member:* League of Women Voters (past president of local chapter), Manzanita Garden Club, Tuesday Book Club, Lioness Club (past president).

WRITINGS: Gourmet Food on a Wheat-Free Diet, C. C Thomas, 1967; *Delicious and Easy Rice Flour Recipes: A Sequel to Gourmet Food on a Wheat-Free Diet,* C. C Thomas, 1972; (contributor) Margaret B. Salmon and Althea E. Quigley, editors, *Enjoying Your Restricted Diet,* C. C Thomas, 1972.

WORK IN PROGRESS: Continuing research on wheat-free and gluten-free cookery, especially using rice flour as a substitute for wheat, rye, barley, and oats.

SIDELIGHTS: Marion Wood writes: "In 1959, my husband was put on a non-gluten diet, a diet which excluded wheat, rye, barley, oats, and their derivatives. I obtained an allergy cookbook and a few additional recipes using rice flour. The taste was unappealing, the texture against one's tongue unpleasant, and the gastronomical outlook on food grim. I became determined that somehow we would enjoy food that would be similar to that we had been accustomed to eating, not queer dishes concocted to remain alive, however unpalatable." *Avocational interests:* Pottery (holds a patent for one of her pieces).

* * *

WOOD, Paul W(inthrop) 1922-

PERSONAL: Born August 29, 1922, in Kingsville, Ontario, Canada; son of Albert G. (an architect) and Louise (Moyer) Wood; married Jacqueline Stark (a pianist), September 4, 1953; children: Stephen, Gregory, Mark, Paul M. *Education:* Attended Grand Central School of Art, 1938, New School for Social Research, 1939, and Art Students League, 1939-41, 1946-47. *Politics:* Independent. *Religion:* Roman Catholic. *Home:* 6 Glamford Ave., Port Washington, N.Y. 11050.

CAREER: Portrait painter, 1948; Paul W. Wood Studio, Port Washington, N.Y., owner, 1949-68. President of Pleasant Hill, Inc.; director of Albert Wood and Five Sons, Inc., and of Paul W. Wood School of Art. Member of art advisory council of Port Washington Public Library, 1960-68. *Military service:* U.S. Army, 1943-46; served in Asiatic-Pacific theater; became sergeant.

MEMBER: Professional Artists Guild of Long Island (member of board of directors, 1965). *Awards, honors:* Emily Lowe Award for Contemporary Art, 1960, and Audubon Artists Award, 1961, both from Audubon Artists, Inc.

WRITINGS: Starting with Stained Glass, Sterling, 1963; *Stained Glass Crafting,* Sterling, 1967, revised edition, 1971; *Painting Abstract Landscapes,* Sterling, 1969.

SIDELIGHTS: Wood writes: "My professional activities include stained glass and religious tapestry commissions for churches and synagogues in the U.S. and abroad, lectures and demonstrations on art and on stained glass, the teaching of private classes in painting, graphics, and specialized crafts such as mosaic and silk screen, portraiture, especially memorial portraits. My wife, my four sons, and myself designed and quite literally built our own modern ranch home, where our own string quartet can be heard practicing and performing."

BIOGRAPHICAL/CRITICAL SOURCES: Newsday, December 21, 1967.

* * *

WOOD, Raymund F(rancis) 1911-

PERSONAL: Born November 9, 1911, in London, England, son of George S. (an accountant) and Ida Agnes (Lawes) Wood; married Margaret Ann Peed (a teacher), February 26, 1943; children: Paul, Gregory, David. *Education:* St. Mary's University, Baltimore, Md., A.B., 1931; Gonzaga University, M.A., 1939; University of California, Los Angeles, Ph.D., 1949; University of Southern California, M.S.L.S., 1950. *Politics:* Democrat. *Religion:* Roman Catholic. *Home:* 18052 Rosita St., Encino, Calif. 91316. *Office:* Graduate School of Library and Information Science, University of California, Los Angeles, Calif. 90024.

CAREER: University of Santa Clara, Santa Clara, Calif., instructor in English, 1939-41; Veterans Administration Rehabilitation Program, Los Angeles, Calif., registration officer, 1946-48; Fresno State College (now California State University, Fresno), Fresno, Calif., principal reference librarian, 1950-66; University of California, Los Angeles, associate professor of library science, 1966—, assistant dean of Graduate School of Library and Information Science, 1967-70, associate dean, 1975—. Curator at Will Rogers State Park, 1948. *Military service:* U.S. Army, 1942-46; served in European theater; became warrant officer junior grade; received Bronze Star Medal.

MEMBER: American Library Association, E Clampus Vitus (Platrix chapter), Chesterton Society, Oral History Association, Westerners (Los Angeles corral), California Library Association, Southern California Historical Society, Fresno County Historical Society (life member; member of board of directors, 1954-66), Mariposa County Historical Society (life member). *Awards, honors:* Award of merit from Alliance Francaise de Fresno, 1966; research fellowship from Del Amo Foundation, 1974.

WRITINGS: California's Agua Fria: The Early History of Mariposa County, Academy Library Guild (Fresno, Calif.), 1954; *The Life and Death of Peter Lebec,* Academy Library Guild, 1954; *A Brief History of Mission San Jose,* Academy Library Guild, 1958; (editor) Francis F. McCarthy, *The History of Mission San Jose, California, 1797-1835,* Academy Library Guild, 1958; (editor) Lucy Nealy McLane, *A Piney Paradise by Monterey Bay,* Academy Library Guild, 2nd edition (Wood was not associated with original edition), 1960; (editor) Floyd L. Otter, *The Men of Mammoth Forest,* Edwards Brothers, 1963; *Mariana la Loca: Prophetess of the Cantua, and Alleged Spouse of Joaquin Murrieta,* Fresno County Historical Society, 1970; (with Josephine D. Rhodehamel) *Ina Coolbrith: Librarian and Laureate,* Brigham Young University Press, 1973.

Contributor to *Fresno County Almanac.* Contributor of about seventy articles and reviews to library and history journals. Editor of *Fresno Past and Present: The Quarterly Bulletin of the Fresno County Historical Society,* 1959-66, and *News Notes on California and Books About the West,* 1960-61. Book review editor of *Out West,* 1972.

WORK IN PROGRESS: A biographical director of all military personnel in California from 1769 to the end of the "Spanish period."

* * *

WOODMAN, Anthony John 1945-

PERSONAL: Born April 11, 1945, in Newcastle upon Tyne, England. *Education:* University of Newcastle upon Tyne, B.A., 1965; King's College, Cambridge, Ph.D., 1970. *Office:* Department of Classics, University of Newcastle upon Tyne, Newcastle upon Tyne NE1 7RU, England.

CAREER: University of Newcastle upon Tyne, Newcastle upon Tyne, England, lecturer in classics, 1968—. *Member:* Classical Association of England and Wales, Society for the Promotion of Roman Studies, Cambridge Philological Society.

WRITINGS: (Contributor) Jacqueline Bibauw, editor, *Hommages a Marcel Renard* (title means "Studies in Honor of Marcel Renard"), Latomus (Brussels), 1968; (editor with David West, and contributor) *Quality and Pleasure in Latin Poetry,* Cambridge University Press,

1975; (contributor) T. A. Dorey, editor, *Empire and Aftermath: Silver Latin II,* Routledge & Kegan Paul, 1975. Contributor to classical journals.

WORK IN PROGRESS: An edition of Velleius Paterculus, with commentary.

AVOCATIONAL INTERESTS: Football, mountains, poetry, table tennis.

* * *

WRIGGINS, W(illiam) Howard 1918-

PERSONAL: Born February 14, 1918, in Philadelphia, Pa.; son of Charles Cornelius and Evelyn (Walker) Wriggins; married Sarah Edith Hovey, December 22, 1947; children: Diana, Charles Christopher, Jennifer. *Education:* Ecole Libres des Sciences Politiques, Paris, certificat, 1939; Dartmouth College, B.A. (cum laude), 1940; University of Chicago, graduate study, 1940-41; Yale University, M.A., 1948, Ph.D., 1951. *Religion:* Society of Friends (Quaker). *Home:* 5249 Sycamore Ave., Riverdale, Bronx, New York, N.Y. 10471.

CAREER: American Friends Service Committee, wartime and postwar relief service administrator, 1942-49; Vassar College, Poughkeepsie, N.Y., began as assistant professor, became associate professor of political science, 1952-57; Library of Congress, Legislative Reference Service, chief of foreign affairs division, 1958-61; Department of State, Washington, D.C., member of policy planning council, 1961-65; Johns Hopkins University, School of Advanced International Studies, research associate of Washington Center for Foreign Policy Research, 1965-66; National Security Council, Washington, D.C., senior staff member, 1966-67; Columbia University, New York City, professor of government and director of Southern Asian Institute, 1967—. George Washington University, part-time member of graduate faculty, 1958-59, professorial lecturer, 1959-61; member of board of directors, Institute on Current World Affairs, 1971—; interim president, American Institute of Pakistan Studies, 1975-76; consultant to U.S. Department of State, 1967—, and to U.S. Agency for International Development, 1967—. Member of founding committee, Sandy Springs Friends School, 1959—; member of board of directors, American Friends Service Committee, 1959-61.

MEMBER: American Political Science Association, Council on Foreign Relations, Association for Asian Studies, Asia Society (director, 1972—; member of board of trustees, 1972—), American Association of University Professors. *Awards, honors:* Sterling fellowship, Yale University, 1951-52; Rockefeller Foundation research fellowship, 1955-57; Rhodes fellowship, Oxford University, 1973-74.

WRITINGS: Ceylon, Dilemmas of a New Nation, Princeton University Press, 1960; (co-editor) *Pakistan: The Long View,* Duke University Press, 1962; (with others) *Development of the Emerging Countries: An Agenda for Research,* Brookings Institution, 1962; *Ruler's Imperative: Strategies for Political Survival in Asia and Africa,* Columbia University Press, 1969; (editor with James Guyot) *Population, Politics, and the Future of Southern Asia,* Columbia University Press, 1973; (co-editor) *Ceylon, 25 Years of Independence,* Ceylon Journal of Historical and Social Studies, 1976. Research assistant to Gabriel Almond for *Appeals of Communism,* published by Princeton University Press, 1954, and editor of *Pakistan in Transition,* published by Southern Asia Institute. Contributor of articles to political science journals.

WORK IN PROGRESS: Research in diplomacy and economic policy of third and fourth world states.

AVOCATIONAL INTERESTS: Tennis, riding, sailing, and reading biography.

* * *

WRIGHT, Austin 1904-

PERSONAL: Born May 20, 1904, in Bedford, Pa.; son of Jacob Anson (a banker and state legislator) and Anna Julia (Colvin) Wright; married Gertrude Bertralle Colwell, June 18, 1935; children: Juliet Anne (Mrs. D. N. Leenher). *Education:* Haverford College, B.A., 1925; Harvard University, M.A., 1926, Ph.D., 1931. *Religion:* Presbyterian. *Home:* 118 East Watson, Bedford, Pa. 15522.

CAREER: Carnegie Institute of Technology (now Carnegie-Mellon University), Pittsburgh, Pa., instructor, 1927-29, 1930-33, assistant professor, 1933-43, associate professor, 1943-46, professor of English, 1946-72, professor emeritus, 1972—, assistant to university president, 1941-46, head of department, 1946-68, university historian, 1972-73; writer, 1973—. Instructor at Haverford College, 1931-32. *Member:* Modern Language Association of America, Historical Society of Western Pennsylvania, Pittsburgh Bibliophiles, Phi Beta Kappa, Phi Kappa Phi.

WRITINGS: (Editor with T. J. Gates) *College Prose,* Heath, 1942, 2nd edition, 1946; *Joseph Spence: A Critical Biography,* University of Chicago Press, 1950; (with James A. S. McPeek) *Handbook of English,* Ronald, 1956; (editor) *Bibliographies of Studies in Victorian Literature for the Years 1945-1954,* University of Illinois Press, 1956; (editor) *Victorian Literature: Modern Essays in Criticism,* Oxford University Press, 1961; *The Warner Administration at Carnegie Institute of Technology, 1950-1965,* Carnegie Press, 1973.

Contributor of a hundred articles and reviews to professional journals. Drama reviewer for *Carnegie* magazine, 1942-49.

* * *

WRIGHT, Barton A(llen) 1920-

PERSONAL: Born December 21, 1920, in Bisbee, Ariz.; son of Roy Joline and Anna (Harris) Wright; married Margaret Anna Nickelson, April 16, 1949; children: Frances Elena, Matthew Allen. *Education:* University of Arizona, B.A., 1952, M.A., 1954. *Home address:* P.O. Box 176, Flagstaff, Ariz. 86001. *Office:* Museum of Northern Arizona, Route 4, Box 720, Flagstaff, Ariz. 86001.

CAREER: Town Creek Indian Mound State Park, Mt. Gilead, N.C., state archaeological assistant, 1949-51; Arizona State Museum, Tucson, museum assistant, 1951-52; Amerind Foundation, Dragoon, Ariz., archaeologist, 1952-55; Museum of Northern Arizona, Flagstaff, curator of arts and exhibits, 1955-58, museum curator, 1958—. Artist and illustrator; commissioned for display at Wupatki National Monument, 1962; work exhibited throughout southwestern United States, 1967—. *Military service:* U.S. Army, 1943-45. *Member:* American Archaeological Society, American Association of Museums, Western Museum League, Southwestern Museums Association, Arizona Academy of Science.

WRITINGS: Kachinas: A Hopi Artist's Documentary, Northland Press, 1973; *The Unchanging Hopi,* Northland Press, 1975. Also author of *Pueblo Shields,* 1975, and of pamphlets, *This Is a Hopi Kachina,* with Evelyn Roat, and

Age of Dinosaurs in Northern Arizona, with William Breed. Contributor of articles to Southwestern periodicals and to *American Indian.*

* * *

WRIGHT, Charles H(oward) 1918-

PERSONAL: Born September 20, 1918, in Dothan, Ala.; son of William P. (a clergyman) and Laura (Florence) Wright; married Louise L. Lovett (a librarian), February 11, 1950; children: Stephanie Jeanne, Carla Louise. *Education:* Alabama State College (now University), B.S., 1939; Meharry Medical College, M.D., 1943. *Religion:* Protestant. *Home:* 1342 Nicolet, Detroit, Mich. 48207. *Office:* 50 Westminster, Detroit, Mich. 48202.

CAREER: Harlem Hospital, New York, N.Y., intern, 1943-44, assistant resident in pathology, 1944; Cleveland Hospital, Cleveland, Ohio, resident in pathology, 1945-46; physician in private practice in Detroit, Mich., 1946-50; Harlem Hospital, resident in obstetrics and gynecology, 1950-53; private practice in obstetrics and gynecology in Detroit, Mich., 1953—. Certified by American Board of Obstetrics and Gynecology, 1955. Assistant clinical professor at Wayne State University, 1965—; guest lecturer at Rutgers University, 1973. Member of staff of Grace Hospital, Sinai Hospital, and Highland Park General Hospital (chairman of department of obstetrics and gynecology); senior attending physician at Woman's Hospital; conducted medical surveys for U.S. Government in Nigeria, Liberia, and Sierra Leone, 1964, and Dahomey, 1965; worked on "S.S. Hope" in Colombia, 1967. Founder and president of African Medical Education Fund, and Afro-American Museum of Detroit; member of board of trustees of local public television station WTVS, 1968—, and University of Detroit, 1971-75.

MEMBER: American College of Surgeons (fellow), American College of Obstetrics and Gynecology (fellow), National Association for the Advancement of Colored People (life member), National Medical Association, Michigan Obstetrics-Gynecology Society. *Awards, honors:* Named "national man of the year" by Omega Psi Phi, 1965, and "doctor of the year" by Detroit Medical Society, 1966; citation of merit from Michigan State Medical Society, 1967.

WRITINGS: Robeson: Labor's Forgotten Champion, Balamp, 1975.

Plays: "Were You There?" (musical drama), first performed in Detroit, Mich., at Institute of Arts, March, 1963; "The Caracas Gang" (three-act), 1975. Author of program "Venereal Disease," on WTVS-Television, 1973. Executive producer of medical recruitment films "You Can Be a Doctor," 1968, and "The Bank Is Open to You," 1969. Contributor to medical journals.

WORK IN PROGRESS: A critical review of one of Detroit's newspaper's editorial positions on minorities.

SIDELIGHTS: Wright narrated radio documentary programs on Paul Robeson and Rosa Parks in Detroit, 1970, 1971. He was actively involved in civil rights movements in Selma, Ala. and Bogalusa, La. He writes: "My whole life has been a continuous quest for freedom. The practice of medicine, the plays and book are a part of that quest.

* * *

WRIGHT, Leonard M(arshall), Jr. 1923-

PERSONAL: Born January 2, 1923, in Boston, Mass.; son of Leonard Marshall (an investment banker) and Priscilla (May) Wright; married Shirley Anson (a teacher), October 3, 1954; children: Anson Elizabeth, Leonard Marshall III, Alexander Winslow. *Education:* Harvard University, A.B., 1947. *Home:* 320 West 11th St., New York, N.Y. 10014. *Agent:* Knox Burger, 39½ Washington Sq. S., New York, N.Y. 10012. *Office: New York Times,* 229 West 43rd St., New York, N.Y. 10036.

CAREER: Batten, Barton, Durstine & Osborn (advertising agency), New York, N.Y., creative group head, 1947-59; J. Walter Thompson (advertising agency), New York, creative group head, 1960-66; *Look* (magazine), New York, creative director of promotion, 1966-70; *New York Times,* New York, assistant promotion manager, 1971—. *Military service:* U.S. Army Air Forces, fighter pilot, 1942-46; served in European theater. *Member:* Anglers Club of New York, D.U. Club (Harvard University).

WRITINGS: Fishing the Dry Fly As a Living Insect, Dutton, 1972; *Fly-Fishing Heresies,* Winchester Press, 1975. Contributor to fishing magazines, and to *Esquire, New York Times Magazine, Sports Afield,* and *Signature.*

* * *

WRIGHT, Rosalind 1952-

PERSONAL: Born January 7, 1952, in Atlanta, Ga.; daughter of John Donald (a banker) and Dorothy (Peacock) Wright. *Education:* Attended Emory University, 1970-71; Sarah Lawrence College, B.A., 1974. *Residence:* Boston, Mass.

CAREER: Writer.

WRITINGS: Rocking (novel), Harper, 1975. Contributor to *Harper's Weekly,* and to Boston newspapers.

WORK IN PROGRESS: Blood Ties (tentative title), a novel about Americans in Mexico before the revolution there, completion expected in 1977.

BIOGRAPHICAL/CRITICAL SOURCES: Dallas Morning News, March 20, 1975; *Whiterocker News,* April 3, 1975.

* * *

WUCHERER, Ruth Marie 1948-

PERSONAL: Born June 17, 1948, in Milwaukee, Wis.; daughter of Frank Edward (a machinist) and Helen Antoinette (Wieczorek) Wucherer. *Education:* University of Wisconsin, Milwaukee, B.A., 1970. *Home:* 3045 South Ninth Pl., Milwaukee, Wis. 53215. *Office:* Gimbel's Department Store, 101 West Wisconsin Ave., Milwaukee, Wis. 53260.

CAREER: Gimbel's Department Store, Milwaukee, Wis., advertising copywriter, 1971—. *Member:* Associated Business Writers of America, American Medical Writers Association, Women in Communications (publicity chairman of Southeastern chapter, 1975-76), Wisconsin Regional Writers Association, Council for Wisconsin Writers.

WRITINGS: How to Sell Your Crafts, Drake, in press. Contributor of travel articles to magazines and newspapers.

WORK IN PROGRESS: Women in America: Past and Present; Super Sportswomen in America; travel articles; movie quizzes, possibly for syndication.

AVOCATIONAL INTERESTS: Travel, skiing, tennis, bicycling, sewing, reading, attending the theater and concerts.

WULFF, Lee 1905-

PERSONAL: Born February 10, 1905, in Valdez, Alaska; son of Charles Goddard and Lillie (Arneberg) Wulff; married Joan Salvato (a writer), September 7, 1967. *Education:* Stanford University, B.S., 1926. *Home and office:* Holly Farm, Surry, N.H. 03431.

CAREER: Free-lance writer and film producer, 1938—. Chairman of New Hampshire Fish and Game Commission, 1975-76. *Member:* International Atlantic Salmon Foundation (vice-president, 1974-76), Atlantic Salmon Association (vice-president, 1974-76), Restoration of Atlantic Salmon in America (vice-president, 1973—), Federation of Fly Fisherman. *Awards, honors:* National conservation award from Trout Unlimited, 1967; Winchester Outdoorsman of the Year, 1967.

WRITINGS: (Self-illustrated) *Sports Photography,* A. S. Barnes, 1942; (self-illustrated) *New Handbook of Freshwater Fishing,* Lippincott, 1951; (self-illustrated) *Let's Go Fishing* (juvenile nonfiction), Lippincott, 1955; *The Atlantic Salmon,* A. S. Barnes, 1958; (editor) *The Sportsman's Companion,* Harper, 1968; *Fishing with Lee Wulff,* edited by Edward C. Janes, Knopf, 1972. Contributor to *Field and Stream, Outdoor Life, Esquire, Flying,* and other sports journals. Contributing editor of *Sports Afield,* 1973—.

SIDELIGHTS: Wulff has accumulated more than five thousand hours of flying time in the Canadian bush.

* * *

WURMBRAND, Richard 1909-

PERSONAL: Born March 24, 1909, in Bucharest, Romania; son of Henry (a dentist) and Amalia Wurmbrand; married Sabine Oster (a writer), October 26, 1936; children: Mihai. *Education:* Attended a theological university in Cluj, Romania, 1956. *Address:* P.O. Box 11, Glendale, Calif. 91209.

CAREER: Ordained Lutheran minister. President of International Christian Mission to the Communist World, Geneva, Switzerland, and Jesus to the Communist World, Glendale, Calif.

WRITINGS: Tortured for Christ, Revell, 1968; *In God's Underground,* Coward, 1969; *If That Were Christ, Would You Give Him Your Blanket,* Word Publications, 1969; *If Prison Walls Could Speak,* Hodder & Stoughton, 1970; *Wurmbrand's Letters,* Diane Publishing, 1971; *Christ on the Jewish Road,* Diane Publishing, 1971; *Stronger than Prison Walls,* Logos International, 1973; *Victorious Faith,* Harper, 1975. Contributor to Christian magazines in the United States and abroad.

WORK IN PROGRESS: Answer to Moscow's Bible, for Hodder & Stoughton; *Answer to Half a Million Letters; Prison Meditations.*

SIDELIGHTS: Wurmbrand told *CA:* "I have lived under Communism, worked in the underground church in Romania under Nazism and Communism, have been in prison under both regimes (under the Communists, 14 years). I share with the readers my experiences in the underground church and in prison. I tell the activity of the underground church today, my whole life being dedicated now to helping the persecuted Christians in Communist countries."

BIOGRAPHICAL/CRITICAL SOURCES: Anutza Moise, *A Ransom for Wurmbrand,* Zondervan, 1973; Mary Drewer, *Richard Wurmbrand: The Man Who Came Back,* Hodder & Stoughton, 1974.

WYLIE, Max 1904-1975

May 12, 1904—September 21, 1975; American television and advertising executive, novelist, playwright, and author. Obituaries: *New York Times,* September 23, 1975; *Time,* October 5, 1975; *Newsweek,* October 5, 1975; *Current Biography,* November, 1975; *AB Bookman's Weekly,* December 1, 1975.

* * *

WYMAN, Mary Alice 1889(?)-1976

1889(?)—January 27, 1976; American educator and author. Obituaries: *New York Times,* February 3, 1976.

* * *

YARMOLINSKY, Avrahm (Abraham) 1890-1975

January 13, 1890—September 28, 1975; Russian-born American educator, librarian, Russian literature expert, translator, editor, and author of books in his field. Obituaries: *New York Times,* September 29, 1975; *AB Bookman's Weekly,* December 1, 1975. (See index for previous *CA* sketch)

* * *

YAUKEY, David (William) 1927-

PERSONAL: Born May 17, 1927, in Kobe, Japan; U.S. citizen; son of Jesse B. (a biostatistician) and Grace (Sydenstricker) Yaukey; married Barbara Behrns (an artist), July 4, 1957; children: Timothy John, Peter Hunt. *Education:* Oberlin College, B.A., 1949; State College of Washington (now Washington State University), M.A., 1950; University of Washington, Seattle, Ph.D., 1956. *Politics:* Democrat. *Office:* Department of Sociology, University of Massachusetts, Amherst, Mass. 01002.

CAREER: Psychological Corp., New York, N.Y., trainee in marketing and social research, 1950-51; U.S. Department of the Army, Adjutant General's Office, Washington, D.C., research psychologist, 1951-52; American University, Beirut, Lebanon, assistant professor of sociology, 1956-59; Princeton University, Princeton, N.J., research associate at Office of Population Research, 1959-61; Population Council, New York, N.Y., field associate in Bangladesh, 1961-63, staff associate, 1963-64; University of Massachusetts, Amherst, assistant professor, 1964-66, associate professor, 1966-71, professor of sociology, 1971—. Senior demographer with United Nations in Chile, 1968-69, and in Geneva, Switzerland, 1974. *Military service:* U.S. Navy, 1945-46.

MEMBER: International Union for the Scientific Study of Population, Population Association of America, American Sociological Association, National Council on Family Relations. *Awards, honors:* Research grants from Population Council, 1958-61, 1966-67; Beryl G. Roberts Memorial Award (corecipient), 1972, for research in public health.

WRITINGS: Fertility Differences in a Modernizing Country: A Survey of Lebanese Couples, Princeton University Press, 1961; (with Lawrence W. Green, H. C. Gustafson, and W. Griffiths) *The Dacca Family Planning Study,* School of Public Health, University of California, Berkeley, 1972; *Marriage Reduction and Fertility,* Heath, 1973. Contributor to professional journals.

SIDELIGHTS: Yaukey's parents were missionaries in China during his early childhood. He has lived in Lebanon, Bangladesh, Chile, and Switzerland.

YOHN, Rick 1937-

PERSONAL: Born April 16, 1937, in Fresno, Calif.; son of Henry M. (an engineer) and Ada A. Yohn; married Linda H. Anderson (a high school teacher), June 18, 1960; children: Ricky, Steven. *Education:* Franklin & Marshall College, student, 1955-56; Philadelphia College of Bible, B.S., 1960; Dallas Theological Seminary, Th.M., 1964. *Office:* Evangelical Free Church, Fresno, Calif. 93726.

CAREER: Christian education director of Presbyterian church in Minneapolis, Minn., 1964-67; pastor of Evangelical Free church in Winnipeg, Manitoba, 1967-71; Fresno Evangelical Free Church, Fresno, Calif., pastor, 1971—. President of Twin Cities Directors of Christian Education, 1969; soccer coach for young boys in Fresno, Calif., 1973, 1974.

WRITINGS: Discover Your Spiritual Gift and Use It, Tyndale, 1974.

WORK IN PROGRESS: Another book on spiritual character, with the premise that when spiritual character governs spiritual gifts, it will result in spiritual fruit.

*   *   *

YOUNG, Virginia Brady 1921-

PERSONAL: Born December 2, 1921, in New York, N.Y.; daughter of Joseph (an engineer) and Anna (Meagher) Brady; married Clarence Whitford Young (a professor), February 28, 1946; stepchildren: Mary E. Young, Robert M. Young. *Education:* Attended Columbia University, 1941-43. *Politics:* Democrat. *Religion:* Episcopalian. *Home:* 12 Chetelat Dr., Mansfield Center, Conn. 06250.

CAREER: Columbia University, New York, N.Y., private secretary, 1938-46; Colgate University, Hamilton, N.Y., private secretary, 1946-71. State Democratic committee woman from Madison County, N.Y., 1952-53. *Member:* Poetry Society of America, Haiku Society of America (president, 1974-75).

WRITINGS—All poetry: *The Clooney Beads,* Folder Editions, 1970; *Double Windows,* Folder Editions, 1970; *Circle of Thaw* (poetry), Barlenmir House, 1972; (editor) *The Haiku Anthology,* Doubleday, 1974; *Shedding the River* (poetry), Shelters Press, 1975.

WORK IN PROGRESS: Yard of Cedar Poles, a long narrative poem; a book of lyrics, *Sun Bouncing; The Yes Poems,* a book of "short short" poems.

AVOCATIONAL INTERESTS: Travel.

*   *   *

YOUNGQUIST, Walter 1921-

PERSONAL: Born May 5, 1921, in Minneapolis, Minn.; son of Walter Raymond and Selma (Knock) Youngquist; married Elizabeth Pearson, December 11, 1943; children: John, Karen, Louise, Robert. *Education:* Gustavus Adolphus College, B.A. (magna cum laude), 1942; University of Iowa, M.S., 1943, Ph.D., 1948. *Home:* 780 West 40th Ave., Eugene, Ore. 97405. *Address:* P.O. Box 5501, Eugene, Ore. 97405.

CAREER: Junior geologist with U.S. Geological Survey in Iowa, Virginia, and Louisiana, 1943-44; University of Idaho, Moscow, assistant professor of geology, 1948-51; International Petroleum Corp., Talara, Peru, geologist, 1951-52, senior geologist, 1952-53, chief of special studies section, 1953-54; University of Kansas, Lawrence, pro-

fessor of geology, 1954-57; University of Oregon, Eugene, associate professor, 1957-59, professor of geology, 1959-66; Humble Oil and Refinery Co., Houston, Tex., consultant to department of minerals, 1966-71; Mechanical Contractors, Inc., Eugene, Ore., chairman of board, 1970—. Director of Glen Lake State Bank, 1966-67, and International Kings Table, Inc., 1970—. Visiting professor, World Campus Afloat, fall, 1974. Lecturer at Brazilian National Nuclear Energy Commission, 1974, and University of Bogacici, 1974. *Military service:* U.S. Naval Reserve, 1944-45.

MEMBER: World Future Society, Geological Society of America (fellow), American Association for the Advancement of Science, American Association of Petroleum Geologists, American Institute of Professional Geologists, Geothermal Resources Council, National Planning Association, Paleontological Society.

WRITINGS: Over the Hill and Down the Creek (nonfiction), Caxton, 1966; *Our Natural Resources: How to Invest in Them,* Fell, 1966; *Investing in Natural Resources,* Dow Jones-Irwin, 1975. Contributor of more than fifty articles to journals.

WORK IN PROGRESS: A book on physical parameters of our natural resource base projected up into society to determine structure and changes in coming years, tentatively titled, *Framework of the Future; Energy Sources,* an elementary book on the subject.

SIDELIGHTS: Youngquist traveled over the Andes and down the Amazon River in 1954. He has visited thirty-three countries.

*   *   *

ZADEH, Norman 1950-

PERSONAL: Born April 17, 1950, in New York, N.Y.; son of Lotfi (a professor of computer science) and Fania (Sand) Zadeh. *Education:* University of California, Berkeley, B.A., 1970, Ph.D., 1972. *Agent:* Oscar Collier, 280 Madison Ave., New York, N.Y. *Office:* Department of Mathematical Methods and Operations Research, Columbia University, Seely W. Mudd Bldg., New York, N.Y. 10027.

CAREER: International Business Machines (IBM), Thomas J. Watson Research Center, Yorktown Heights, N.Y., research staff member, 1972-73; Columbia University, New York, N.Y., assistant professor of mathematical methods and operations research, 1975—. *Member:* Phi Beta Kappa. *Awards, honors:* National Science Foundation fellow, 1970-72.

WRITINGS: Winning Poker Systems, Prentice-Hall, 1974. Contributor to journals in his field.

*   *   *

ZARCONE, Vincent P(eter), Jr. 1937-

PERSONAL: Born July 10, 1937, in Decatur, Ill.; son of Vincent Peter (a physician) and Alice E. (a nurse; maiden name, Irving) Zarcone; married Joyce Ann Cale (a nurse), July 13, 1958; children: Julia Lynn, Laura Elizabeth. *Education:* University of Illinois, M.D., 1962. *Home:* 227 Verano Dr., Los Altos, Calif. 94022. *Office:* Veterans Administration Hospital, 3801 Miranda Ave., Palo Alto, Calif. 94034.

CAREER: University of California, Moffitt Hospital, San Francisco, intern, 1962-63; Stanford University, Stanford,

Calif., resident in psychiatry, 1963-67, instructor, 1967-69, assistant professor, 1969-71, associate professor of clinical psychiatry and senior attending physician, 1971—. Diplomate of American Board of Psychiatry and Neurology, 1973. Veterans Administration Hospital (Palo Alto), staff psychiatrist, 1963-71, physician chief grade, 1971—.

MEMBER: Association for the Psychophysiological Study of Sleep, Society for Psychophysiological Research, San Francisco Psychoanalytic Institute, Phi Sigma Eta, Alpha Omega Alpha. *Awards, honors:* Second prize in psychopharmacology from American Psychological Association, 1970; certificate of merit in psychiatry from American Medical Association, 1972; Rush Silver Medal Award from American Psychiatric Association, 1972; grants from National Institutes of Health, 1971-75, for sleep research, and from National Institute of Mental Health, 1972-75, for studies of alcohol and drug abuse.

WRITINGS: (Contributor) D. V. Siva Sankar, editor, *Schizophrenia: Current Concepts and Research,* PJD Publications, 1969; (contributor) David Hamburg, editor, *Perception and Its Disorders,* Williams & Wilkins, 1970; (contributor) L. Madow and L. Snow, editors, *The Psychodynamic Implications of the Physiological Studies on Dreams,* C. C Thomas, 1970; (contributor) J. D. Barchas and E. Usdin, editors, *Serotonin and Behavior,* Academic Press, 1973; (contributor) S. Garratini, E. Mussini, and L. O. Randall, editors, *The Benzodiazepines: Monographs of the Mario Negri Institute for Pharmacological Research,* Raven Press, 1973; (contributor) Milton Gross, editor, *Advances in Experimental Medicine and Biology,* Plenum, 1975; *Drug Addicts in a Therapeutic Community: The Satori Approach,* York Press, 1975; (contributor) H. J. Widroe, editor, *Human Behavior and Brain Function,* C. C Thomas, in press; (contributor) C. Guilleminault, P. Passouant, and W. C. Dement, editors, *Narcolepsy,* Spectrum, in press; (contributor) J. H. Masserman, editor, *Current Psychiatric Theory,* Grune, in press. Contributor to *Proceedings of First Canadian International Symposium on Sleep,* 1973. Contributor of nearly a hundred articles and reviews to medical journals.

WORK IN PROGRESS: A research study evaluating the effectiveness of four different drug dependence treatment units.

AVOCATIONAL INTERESTS: Philosophy and history of science (especially biology and behavioral science).

*   *   *

ZELENY, Lawrence   1904-

PERSONAL: Born April 30, 1904, in Minneapolis, Minn.; son of Anthony (a university professor) and Mattie L. (Day) Zeleny; married Olive M. Lowen, June 19, 1930; children: Nancy Jane (Mrs. Richard J. Kuhn), William Bardwell. *Education:* University of Minnesota, B.A., 1925, M.S., 1927, Ph.D., 1930. *Religion:* Protestant. *Home and office:* 4312 Van Buren St., University Park, Hyattsville, Md.

CAREER: Lake States Forest Experimental Station, St. Paul, Minn., agent, 1930-32; Visual Display, Inc., Le Sueur, Minn., chief chemist, 1933-35; U.S. Department of Agriculture, Grain Division, chemist in Washington, D.C., 1935-38, grain technologist in Beltsville, Md., 1938-43, chief of standardization and testing branch in Hyattsville, Md., 1943-66, consultant, 1967-69; writer and proponent of active bluebird conservation, 1969—. Guest fellow at University of Minnesota, 1932-33; member of U.S. Department of

Agriculture cultural and scientific exchange team to Soviet Union, 1960. *Member:* National Audubon Society, National Wildlife Federation, Defenders of Wildlife, Environmental Action Foundation, Inland Bird Banding Association, Mid-Atlantic Bird Banding Group, Audubon Naturalist Society of the Central Atlantic States (member of board of directors, 1974—), Maryland Ornithological Society (president, 1971-72; member of executive council, 1971—), Griggsville Wild Bird Society, Cornell Laboratory of Ornithology, Sigma Xi, Phi Lambda Upsilon, Gamma Alpha. *Awards, honors:* Certificate of merit from Agricultural Marketing Service, 1958; superior service award from U.S. Department of Agriculture, 1958.

WRITINGS: The Bluebird: How You Can Help Its Fight for Survival, Indiana University Press, 1976. Author of "The Bluebird Trail," a monthly column in *Purple Martin News,* 1969—. Contributor of nearly 150 articles to agricultural biochemistry journals and to wildlife conservation magazines.

WORK IN PROGRESS: Research on improved ways to protect nesting bluebirds from competitors and predators.

SIDELIGHTS: Zeleny writes that he "retired early from government service in order to devote full time to organizing and promoting a nation-wide effort to save the bluebird from probable extinction."

*   *   *

ZIMMER, Eric   1932-

PERSONAL: Born July 16, 1932, in Frankfurt on the Main, Germany; son of Henry (a businessman) and Lilli Zimmer; married Ora Dominitz, July 2, 1958; children: Gila, Rena, Aviva, Danny. *Education:* Yeshiva University, B.A., 1954, M.H.L., 1958, Ph.D., 1965. *Residence:* Jerusalem, Israel.

CAREER: Rabbi of Jewish congregation in New York, N.Y., 1959-71; Bar Ilan University, Ramat Gan, Israel, assistant professor of Jewish history, 1971—. Assistant professor at Yeshiva University, 1965-71. *Member:* Rabbinic Council of America, Religious Zionists of America.

WRITINGS: Harmony and Discord: An Analysis of the Decline of Jewish Self-Government in Fifteenth-Century Central Europe, Bloch Publishing, 1970; *Aspects of Jewish Life in the Principality of Ansbach,* Bar Ilan University, 1975. Contributor of articles to periodicals.

WORK IN PROGRESS: Jewish Synods in Germany during the Middle Ages; The Book of Customs of Jeseph Juspa, Shamash of Worms.

*   *   *

ZIMMERMAN, Eleanor (Goedeke)   1916-

PERSONAL: Born February 9, 1916, in Baltimore, Md.; daughter of Milton Thomas and Eva (Lindenberger) Goedeke; married Theo Herman Zimmerman (an engineer), March 3, 1943; children: Gale, Mark. *Education:* Maryland State Teachers College (now Towson State College), diploma, 1935; Johns Hopkins University, B.S., 1942. *Religion:* Lutheran. *Home:* 3015 Iona Ter., Baltimore, Md.

CAREER: Baltimore (Md.) public schools, elementary school teacher, 1935-40, junior high school English teacher, 1940-42, senior high school English teacher, 1964—.

WRITINGS: Now We Are Three (teacher's guide), Muhlenberg Press, 1960; *Our Own Winter Book,* Muhlenberg Press, 1960; *Our Own Summer Book,* Muhlenberg Press,

1960; *Bible and Doctrine for Threes to Fives,* Lutheran Church, 1963; *All Around Me,* Fortress, 1970; *When Jesus Came,* Fortress, 1970. Also author of "Fellow Workers for God," series of three readers with teacher's guide, Lutheran Church, 1964.

*   *   *

ZION, Eugene   1913(?)-1975
(Gene Zion)

1913(?)—December 5, 1975; American graphics designer, art director, and author of books for children. Obituaries: *New York Times,* December 9, 1975; *Publishers Weekly,* December 29, 1975.

*   *   *

ZWERLING, L. Steven   1938-

PERSONAL: Born October 2, 1938, in Brooklyn, N.Y.; son of David Louis (a construction supervisor) and Ray (a teacher; maiden name, Mooney) Zwerling; married Lisa Robinson (a painter), June 18, 1961. *Education:* Columbia University, A.B., 1960, M.A., 1961; Rutgers University, graduate study, 1961-64. *Home:* 1429 Avenue H, Brooklyn, N.Y. 11230. *Office:* Department of Experimenting and Special Programs, Staten Island Community College, Staten Island, N.Y. 10301.

CAREER: Queens College of the City University of New York, Flushing, N.Y., instructor in English, 1963-67, assistant director of SEEK program, 1967-69; Staten Island Community College, Staten Island, N.Y., dean of evening session, director of open admissions, and director of the Circle experimenting program, all 1969—. Producer and host of "Education on the Line" and "Metroscope," on WRVR-Radio, 1973—, and of "New York Voices," on WNYC-Television, 1974-75. *Member:* Authors Guild of Authors League of America, American Federation of Television and Radio Artists.

WRITINGS: Second Best: The Crises of the Community College, McGraw, 1976. Editor of *Niobe.*

*   *   *

CONTEMPORARY AUTHORS

INDEX (Volumes 1—64)

Including references to
Contemporary Authors Revised Volumes and Permanent Series*
Something About the Author, Volumes 1-8
Contemporary Literary Criticism, Volumes 1-5

---

* Authors transferred to *Contemporary Authors* Permanent Series are indexed according to the volume of that series in which they now appear, with the number of the original sketch following. CAP-1 is now in print; CAP-2 will be ready late in 1976.

Contemporary Authors Revised Volumes are indicated by the letter *R.*

CAP-2 refers to CONTEMPORARY AUTHORS Permanent Series, Volume 2, to be published late 1976